STO

ACPL ITEM
DISCARDED

ALLEN COUNTY PUBLIC LIBRARY
3 1833 03836 4409

 Y0-BWS-111

Not to leave the library

I·N·F·O·R·M·A·T·I·O·N,
F·I·N·A·N·C·E,
& S·E·R·V·I·C·E·S
USA

Industry Analyses,
Statistics, and Leading Organizations

ISSN 1531-0752

I·N·F·O·R·M·A·T·I·O·N,
F·I·N·A·N·C·E,
&S·E·R·V·I·C·E·S
USA

Industry Analyses,
Statistics, and Leading Organizations

- A comprehensive guide to economic activity in 320 industries engaged in the Information, Finance, and Services sectors.

- Covers 11 sectors, including Information, Finance, and Insurance, Real Estate, Professional and Technical Services, Management of Companies, Administration and Waste Management, Educational Services, Health Care and Social Assistance, Arts and Entertainment, Hotels and Restaurants, and other services.

- Provides data in the new NAICS format in a pre-analyzed format, with graphics, maps and ratios.

- Presents SIC data for bridging between the old and the new formats.

- Includes contact information on more than 7,000 companies and leading nonprofit organizations participating in the sectors.

Arsen J. Darnay, Editor

GALE GROUP

Detroit
New York
San Francisco
London
Boston
Woodbridge, CT

Arsen J. Darnay, *Editor*

Editorial Code & Data Inc. Staff

Sherae R. Carroll, *Data Entry*
Joyce Piwowarski, *Data Processing*

Gale Group Staff

Eric Hoss, *Editorial Coordinator*
Mary Beth Trimper, *Production Director*
Nekita McKee, *Buyer*
Kenn Zorn, *Product Design Manager*
Mike Logusz, *Graphic Artist*
Theresa Rocklin, *Technical Support Services Manager*
Richard Antonowicz, *Programmer*

While an extensive verification and proofing process preceded the printing of this directory, Gale Group makes no warranties or representation regarding its accuracy or completeness, and each subscriber or user of the directory understands that Gale Group disclaims any liability for any damages (even if Gale Group has been advised of such damages) in connection with its use.

This publication is a creative work fully protected by all applicable copyright laws, as well as by misappropriation, trade secret, unfair competition, and other applicable laws. The authors and editors of this work have added value to the underlying factual material herein through one or more of the following: unique and original selection, coordination, expression, arrangement, and classification of the information.

Gale Group will vigorously defend all of its rights in this publication.

Copyright © 2001 by Arsen J. Darnay

All rights reserved including the right of reproduction in whole or in part in any form.

This book is printed on acid-free paper that meets the minimum requirements of American National Standard for Information Sciences — Permanence Paper for Printed Library Materials, ANSI Z39.48-1984.

This book is printed on recycled paper that meets Environmental Protection Agency standards.

Gale Group
27500 Drake Road
Farmington Hills, MI 48331-3535

ISBN 0-7876-5058-7
ISSN 1531-0752

Printed in the United States of America

TABLE OF CONTENTS

Introduction

Information, Finance, and Services USA (IFS-USA presents information on 11 economic sectors as defined by the North American Industry Classifcation System (NAICS). Data are drawn from a variety of federal statistical sources and are combined with information on leading public and private corporations from the *Ward's Business Directory of U.S. Private and Public Companies* and representative nonprofit organizations drawn from *National Directory of Nonprofit Organizations*.

History

Gale's "USA" series grew out of a need to present federal statistical data, from different agencies, in a more "user friendly" format and, at the same time, combined with data on corporate participation in various industries. The series features preanalyzed data, ratios, and projections — in a standard format — so that all the data are handily available to the analyst or student in one place. This approach continues with *IFS-USA*.

IFS-USA contains information heretofore presented as follows:

- Information on the publishing industry (Part I, Information) was formerly a part of *Manufacturing USA*.

- The former *Finance, Insurance, and Real Estate USA* held information, in this volume, on those industries, now classified as Finance & Insurance (Part II) and Real Estate & Rental & Leasing (Part III).

- The former *Service Industries USA* held all information presented on services, in this volume. The service categories are now divided into seven separate parts, to be outlined below.

This first edition of *IFS-USA* is, in a way, a transitional presentation. The statistical world is making a transition between the old Standard Industrial Classification (SIC) coding to the new North American Industry Classification System (NAICS). *IFS-USA* contains data NAICS format. But a number of industries have remained unchanged in the transition. These are shown with multiple years of data, under NAICS codes. They are, of course, cross-referenced to the old SIC system. In most cases, NAICS tables also show data on their SIC "predecessors."

'The Most Current Data Available'

IFS-USA reports the most current data available at the time of the book's preparation. The objective is to present *hard* information — data based on actual survey by authoritative bodies — for all industries within these sectors, on a *comparable* basis. A few industries may collect more recent information through their industry associations or other bodies. Similarly, estimates are published on this or that industry based on the analyses and guesses of knowledgeable individuals. These data are rarely in the same format as the Federal data and are not available for a large cross section of industry. Therefore, the data in *IFS-USA* are, indeed, the most current at this level of detail and spanning the entirety of the activities profiled. The book is meant to serve as the foundation on which others can base their own projections.

In addition to presenting current survey data, the editors also provide projected data for most categories from 1997 to the year 2001.

Scope and Coverage

IFS-USA presents statistical data on 320 distinct industries. Of this total 47 are equivalent to the earlier SIC definitions. The rest represent newly defined industries. In most cases, old SIC industries have been divided into new industries. In other cases, a NAICS industry may contain all or parts of two or more NAICS industries. To get a flavor of the manner in which SIC industries have been transformed into NAICS industries, please examine the SIC index (p. 919). More information on content is presented in *Overview of Contents and Sources.*

NAICS Presentation. For the Majority of the industries data are presented for the year 1997 — the first NAICS Economic Census year. Those industries that have remained essentially unchanged feature a full time series, from 1982 or 1987 forward, with projections to 2001. Those industries that do not have SIC equivalents feature a table entitled *SIC Industries Related to NAICS 000000*, where the 0s stand for a NAICS code. The table presents, where available, data from 1990 to 1997. These tables enable the user to see which SIC industry or industries make up the NAICS account.

All presentation feature indices of change and selected, precalculated rations (for 1997). State level information, also for 1997, is also provided.

SIC and NAICS

The transition between SIC and NAICS was implemented for the 1997 Economic Census. An updating of the industrial classification system was long overdue. Relatively minor modifications had last taken place in 1987. The new NAICS coding — which is used by the U.S., Canada, and Mexico — represents a major revamping. Additional sectors have been created (e.g., Information) and the "services" categories have increased substantially.

In *IFS-USA*, looking to the future, the organization of data is based on the "new order," but as much help as possible is provided to die-hard SIC usersasthe Federal data sources allow — if for no other reason than to provide longer time series. But the SIC is dead, long live the NAICS! A new dispensation has arrived — at least so far as economic statistics are concerned. We hope that the Bureau of the Census will soon publish "retrospective" series on at least some of the new industries so that analysts everywhere can once more anchor their work in good data. Major changes in national coding inevitably mean some loss of information. Restatement of past years in NAICS terms will require some time — provided budgets for it are available. In some case, no data for years before 1997 will ever be available.Only time will correct the deficiency.

Under the NAICS coding, 6-digit industry codes replace the familiar 4-digit SIC codes. The first two digits indicate the sector, the last four specify the industry. The code 511110 - Newspaper Publishers, can be parsed as follows: 531 is the sector code used for Information; 511 is Publishing Industries, the industry group; 1110 is the actual industry designation. In normal practice, all six digits are used to designate the industry. In the NAICS manual, a trailing zero is suppressed. The zero appears in published data series, however, and is also used in *IFS-USA*.

Organization and Content

IFS-USA presents data on 11 economic sectors. Each sector is presented as a part. Parts are numbered in Roman format, as shown below. Information for each industry is also detailed, further, in a table. Data for some industries in the NAICS series were not always available. NAICS not included in this volume are shown behind bullets below.

Part I - Information - NAICS 511110 to 514210

Part II - Finance and Insurance - NAICS 521110 to 525930
   Part II excludes the following industries because no data on them have been provided by the Bureau of the Census:
   - 525120 - Health and Welfare Funds
   - 525910 - Open-End Investment Funds
   - 525920 - Trusts, Estates, and Agency Accounts
   - 525990 - Other Financial Vehicles

Part III - Real Estate & Rental & Leasing - NAICS 531110 to 533110

Part IV - Professional, Scientific, & Technical Services - NAICS 541110 to 541990
   Excluded for lack of data are:
   - 541320 - Landscape Architectural Services
   - 541940 - Veterinary Services

Part V - Management of Companies & Enterprises - NAICS 551111 to 551114

Part VI - Administrative Support and Waste Management/Remediation Services - NAICS 561110 to 562998
   Excluded for lack of data:
   - 561730 - Landscaping Services

Part VII - Education Services - NAICS 611410 to 611710
   Excluded for lack of data are:
   - 611110 - Elementary and Secondary Schools
   - 611210 - Junior Colleges
   - 611310 - Colleges, Universities, and Professional Schools

Part VIII - Health Care and Social Assistance - NAICS 621111 to 624410

Part IX - Arts, Entertainment & Recreation - NAICS 711110 to 713990

Part X - Accommodation & Food Services - NAICS 721110 to 722410

Part XI - Other Services - NAICS 811111 to 813990
    Excluded for lack of data:

- 812910 - Pet Care (except Veterinary) Services
- 813110 - Religious Organizations
- 813930 Labor Unions and Similar Labor Organizations
- 813940 Political Organizations

Each industry begins on a new page. The order of graphics and tables is invariable. In some instances, data may not be available in a category, e.g., company data or geographical data. The absence of data is indicated in each section. Data presented for each industry is shown in the table that follows:

Graphics and Tables for Each Industry

1	Trend Graphic	Provided when multiple years of data are available.
2	General Statistics	National statistics.
3	Indices of Change	National data in index format.
4	SIC Industries Related to NAICS	Provided when NAICS-SIC do not match exactly.
5	Selected Ratios	Precalculated ratios for the industry for 1997.
6	Leading Companyies	Up to 75 companies per industry when available.
7	Representative Nonprofit Organizations	Presented for selected NAICS codes only.
8	Maps	States and regions where the industry is active.
9	Industry Data by State	State-level statistics.

Four indexes are provided:

- **SIC Index**. Data are arranged, first, by SIC number and then in alphabetical order by SIC name.One or more NAICS industries in which the SIC is presented are shown as dashed items under each SIC. Page references are provided to the start of the relevant NAICS industry or industries.

- **NAICS Index**. The NAICS index is also in two parts — by NAICS code and by industry name arranged in alphabetical order. Page references are to the page on which the industry begins.

- **Subject Index**. Services, products, and references to occupations (e.g., professional athletes, medical specialties) are show in an alphabetical arrangement. One or more page references are provided to the first page of the industry concerned with the indexed topic.

- **Company Index**. The company index holds all corporations shown in *IFS-USA*'s *Leading Companies* table. Also included in this index are nonprofit organizations that appear in the *Representative Nonprofit Organizations* table. Company/organization names are labelled by the NAICS code where each is listed. References are to the pages where the tables that hold the organizations appear.

- In other editions of this series, an occupational index has been provided in the past. This time — and we hope only temporarily — the occupational index has been omitted because occupational data are not, as yet, available in NAICS formats.

- For more detailed information on *IFS-USA*'s industry profiles, please consult the *Overview of Contents and Sources*, which follows.

Comments and Suggestions are Welcome

Comments on this volume — or suggestions on how to improve it — are welcome. Every effort is made to maintain accuracy, but errors may occasionally occur. The editor will be grateful if these are called to his attention. Please contact the editor below with comments and suggestsion. To discuss technical matters, call the editor directly at Editorial Code & Data, Inc. at (248) 356-6990.

Editor
Information, Finance, and Services USA
Gale Group
27500 Drake Road
Farmington Hills, MI 48331-3535
248-699-GALE

Overview of Content and Sources

Industry Coding Structure

Data in *IFS-USA* are ordered in conformity with 1997 North American Industry Classification System (NAICS).

The NAICS coding system is new. Many industries have been reclassified so that they no longer resemble the SIC codes. However, a fairly large number of NAICS codes correspond directly — without change — to the older SIC codes. Of the 320 NAICS industries presented in *IFS-USA*, 47 have direct SIC equivalents. When the industries coincide, multiple years of data are provided. In each case, the data are presented under NAICS codes, but an asterisk is used to mark the industry, and the equivalent SIC code is supplied at the bottom of the page. New industries that have no SIC equivalent show only one year of data, for 1997 — but in most cases, data for the period 1990 to 1997 are presentedfor the SIC industries that make up the NAICS.

Naming Conventions

Industry and sector names are taken from *North American Industry Classification System*, Office of Management and Budget, 1997. In an attempt to be as descriptive as possible, the authors of this classification scheme sometimes use awkward-sounding or verbose titles, e.g., Real Estate and Rental and Leasing. Names of sectors and of industries have been generally left unchanged, with one exception. Industries that begin with the word "Other" or "All Other" have been modified using the old SIC designation of "nec," meaning "not elsewhere classified." NEC is well known to users of the *USA* series. Thus for instance, "Other Accounting Services" (NAICS 541219) is rendered in *IFS-USA* as "Accounting Services nec". In the information banner above the pages (the so-called "running head") names of industries have been shortened in order to ensure that they will fit on one line.

Industry Profiles

Each industry profile contains the tables and graphics listed in the *Introduction*. A detailed discussion of each graphic and table follows; the meaning of each data element is explained, and the sources from which the data were obtained are cited.

Trends Graphics

At the beginning of each industry profile, two graphs are presented showing (1) industry revenues and (2) employment plotted for the years 1982 to 2001 on logarithmic scale. The curves are provided primarily to give the user an at-a-glance assessment of important trends in the industry. The logarithmic scale ensures that the revenue and employment trends can be compared visually despite different magnitudes and denominations of the data (millions of dollars and thousands of employees); in this mode of presentation, if two curves have the same slope, the values are growing or declining at the same rate. If the values fit within a single cycle (1 to 9, 10 to 90, etc.), a single cycle is shown; if the values bridge two cycles, both are shown.

The data graphed are derived from the first table, *General Statistics*. All available years of data are plotted. If data gaps appear in the series, missing points are calculated using a least-squares curve fitting algorithm.

In the case of a few industries, data discontinuities are present in the general statistics; data for the 1982-1986 period are not strictly comparable to the data for 1987 and later. In such cases, the line of the graph is interrupted between 1986 and 1987 to show this discontinuity.

Those portions of curves based on projections by the editors are shown in a dotted-line format.

General Statistics

This table shows national statistics for the industry. If the industry is equivalent to an earlier SIC definition, data for 1982-2001 or 1987-2001 are shown. If the NAICS industry is new, only data for 1997 are presented. Four elements of data and three ratios are displayed. Data shown are Establishments (number), Employment (number), Payroll (in millions of dollars), and Revenues (in millions of dollars). The ratios shown are Employees per Establishment (number), Revenues per Establishment (in dollars), and Payroll per Employee (in dollars). Data for the period 1998-2001 are projected by the editors. A discussion of the methods of projection is presented below. Projected data are followed by the letter "p". Some data are extrapolations to fill gaps in the data series. These figures are marked with an "e".

Data for 1982, 1987, 1992, and 1997 are from Economic Census held in each of those years. Data for other years, through and including 1996, are from the *Annual Survey of Manufactures (ASM)*. Establishment counts in the *ASM* years are from the *County Business Patterns* for those years; exceptions are the years 1983 and 1984; establishment data for these years are extrapolations of data from the 1982 and 1985 values. New industries created in the 1987 SIC reclassification will not show data earlier than 1987. In all of these cases, the SIC data and the NAICS data are identical.

Indices of Change

The data presented in the *General Statistics* table are partially restated as indices for all industries where multiple years of data are available. The purpose of the table is to show the user rapidly how different categories of the industry have changed since 1997. Indices are shown for the census years (1982, 1987, 1992, and 1997) and for the years 1998 through 2001.

The year 1997 is used as the base and is therefore shown as 100 in every category. Other values are expressed in relation to the 1997 value.

Values of 100 indicate no change in relation to the base year; values above 100 mean "better" and values below 100 indicate "worse" performance — all relative to the 1997 base. Note, however, that these are *indices* rather than compounded annual rates of growth or decline.

Indexes based on projections by the editors are followed by a "p".

A table of Indices of Change is also provided for industries that have only one year of data. All values shown are 100. No other data being available, no "change" can be shown. These tables are shown, nevertheless, to ensure a consistent presentation, industry to industry.

SIC Industries Related to NAICS

This table is present only in those situations where the NAICS industry is new. The purpose of the table is to show where the NAICS industry "comes from." New industries are constructed from pieces of one or more of the old SIC industries. Where parts of an SIC have been incorporated, the SIC industry name is followed by the abbreviation "(pt)". In cases where the entire SIC industry is now embedded in the NAICS industry, only the name is shown. **Please note**: The statistics shown for each such SIC industry are the statistics for that industry *as a whole*, not just that portion which is now reported under the NAICS classification. It is possible to get some feel for how much of the SIC industry contributes to the NAICS by comparing items for 1997 from this table to the data in the General Statistics table.

This table shows, for each "participating" SIC, the SIC code, the industry name (with or without the "part" designation. Thereafter, statistics are shown for the period 1990 to 1997 for Establishments (number), Employment (in thousands), and Revenues (in millions of dollars). Where the precursor industry is a manufacturing enterprise, Value of Shipments is shown in place of Revenues.

This table is presented even in those instances where no SIC data are available. This is frequently the case in financial categories. In that sector, data in the *USA* series have usually been reported at a higher level (3-digit rather than 4-digit SIC) and are therefore not suitable for display in this context. In some instances, only partial data are available, e.g., for the year 1992.

Selected Ratios

To understand an industry, analysts calculate ratios of various kinds so that the absolute numbers can be placed in a more global perspective. Six important industrial ratios are precalculated for the user in the *Selected Ratios* table. Additionally, the same ratios are also provided for the average of each of the 11 sectors into which this volume is divided.

The ratios are calculated for the most recent complete year available, 1997.

The first column of values represents the **Average of All . . .** — that phrase being followed by the name of the sector. These ratios are calculated by (1) using reported totals for each sector and (2) calculating the ratios based on the totals.

The second column of values shows the ratios for the **Analyzed Industry**, i.e., the industry currently under consideration.

The third column is an **Index** comparing the Analyzed Industry to the Average of All . . . Industries. The index is useful for determining quickly and consistently how the Analyzed Industry stands in relation to its sector, e.g., Information or Accommodation & Food Services. Index values of 100 mean that the Analyzed Industry, within a given ratio, is identical to the average of all industries. An index value of 500 means that the Analyzed Industry is five times the average — for instance, that it has five times as many employees per establishment or pays five times as much. An index value of 50 would indicate that the Analyzed Industry is half of the average of all industries (50%). Similarly, an index of 105 means 5% above average and 95 indicates 5% below.

Leading Companies

The table of *Leading Companies* shows up to 75 companies that participate in the industry. The listings are sorted in descending order of sales and show the company name, address, name of the Chief Executive Officer (or person with a similar title), telephone, company type, sales (in millions of dollars) and employment (in thousands of employees). The number of companies shown, their total sales, and total employment are summed at the top of the table for the user's convenience.

The data are from the *Ward's Business Directory of U.S. Private and Public Companies* for 2000. Public and private corporations, divisions, subsidiaries, joint ventures, and corporate groups are shown. Thus a listing for an industry may show the parent company as well as important divisions and subsidiaries of the same company (usually in a different location).

While this method of presentation has the disadvantage of duplication (the sales of a parent corporation include the sales of any divisions listed separately), it has the advantage of providing the user with information on major components of an enterprise at different locations. In any event, the user should *not* assume that the sum of the sales (or employment) shown in the *Leading Companies* table represents the total sales (or employment) of an industry. The Revenues column of the *General Statistics* table is a better guide to industry sales.

The company's type (private, public, division, etc.) is shown under the column headed "Co Type," thus providing the user with a means of roughly determining the total "net" sales (or employment) represented in the table; this can be accomplished by adding the values and then deducting values corresponding to divisions and subsidiaries of parent organizations also shown in the table. The code used is as follows:

P	Public corporation
R	Private corporation
S	Subsidiary
D	Division
J	Joint venture
G	Corporate group

An asterisk (*) placed behind the sales volume indicates an estimate; the absence of an asterisk indicates that the sales value has been obtained from annual reports, other formal submissions to regulatory bodies, or from the corporation. The symbol "<" appears in front of some employment values to indicate that the actual value is "less than" the value shown. Thus the value of "<0.1" means that the company employs fewer than 100 people.

Company data were sometimes unavailable for a NAICS industry. In those cases, the absence of data is noted in the company profile with the phrase: *No company data available for this industry*. As databases are updated and old SIC coding is replaced with NAICS coding, more company data will become available in future editions.

Representative Nonprofit Organizations

When an industry has a nonprofit component, a table of Representative Nonprofit Organizations is presented. The data are drawn from the *National Directory of Non-profit Organizations*, 2000. The original source does not provide actual numbers for the income of organizations listed. Income data are provided in ranges, e.g., $1 to $9 million. This foreclosed the option of selecting the largest of these institutions for inclusion in *IFS-USA*. As an alternative data were sorted by income range before organizations were selected. Organizations are shown in alphabetical order. The name of the organization, its address, telephone number, and income range are shown.

Map Graphics

The geographical presentation of data begins with two maps titled *Location by State* and *Regional Concentration*.

In the first map, those states are shaded on the map where the industry's activity is proportionally *greater* than would be indicated by the state's share of total U.S. population. An example will illustrate the procedure used. If a state's share of industry revenues was 4.5 percent, and its share of the U.S. population was 2.3 percent, the state is shaded on the map. But if the state share of revenues was 5.0 percent, and its population share 7.5, the state on the map is left blank.

In the second map, the industry's concentration is shown by Census region. The two maps, together, tell the user at a glance where the industry is most active and which regions rank first, second, and third in revenues or in number of establishments; establishment counts are used for ranking in those industries where shipment data are withheld (the (D) symbol) for the majority of states. In the case of some industries, only one or two regions are shaded because the industry is concentrated in a few states. The data for ranking are taken from the table on *Industry Data by State* which immediately follows the maps.

The regional boundaries are those of the Census Regions and are named, from left to right and top to bottom as follows:

Pacific (includes Alaska and Hawaii)	East South Central
Mountain	New England
West North Central	Middle Atlantic
West South Central	South Atlantic
East North Central	

In the case of the Pacific region, all parts of the region are shaded (including Alaska and Hawaii), even if the basis for the ranking is the industry's predominance in California (the usual case).

Although regional data are only graphed and not reported in a separate table, the table of *Industry Data by State* provides all the necessary information for constructing a regional table.

Industry Data by State

The table on *Industry Data by State* provides ten data elements for each state in which the industry is active. The data come from the 1997 Economic Census, the most recently available data set on states. Even in this series, certain data elements are suppressed by the Bureau of the Census to prevent disclosure of competitive information. This may come about in instances where only a few operations are present in the state or they are operated by a small number of companies. The states are shown in descending order of revenues.

Elements provided are:

- Establishments — total number and as a percent of all establishments in this industry.

- Employment — total number, as a percent of industry employment, and employees per establishment.

- Payroll — total, in millions of dollars, and payroll per employee, in dollars.

- Revenues — total, in millions of dollars, as a percent of total industry revenues, and revenues per establishment, in dollars.

The symbol (D) is used when data are withheld to prevent disclosure of proprietary information. Dashes are used to indicate that the corresponding data element cannot be calculated because some part of the ratio is missing or withheld.

Where revenue and payroll data are withheld, the Bureau of the Census still provides two values: number of establishments and an employment range. *IFS-USA* shows the midpoint of a range when an employment range is used. The ranges, and their midpoints, are shown in the following table:

Range	Midpoint
0-19	10
20-99	60
100-249	175
250-499	375
500-999	750
1000-2499	1750
2500-4999	3750
5000-9999	7500
10000-24999	17500
25000-99999	37500
100000+	100000+

Projected Data Series

As a service to the busy user of this book, *IFS-USA* features trend projections of data — when a sufficient number of years of data is available.

Projections are based on a curve-fitting algorithm using the least-squares method. In essence, the algorithm calculates a trend line for the data using existing data points. Extensions of the trend line are used to predict future years of data.

The first four columns under General Statistics were projected. In those cases where a coherent series existed from 1982 to the present, the entire series was used. In those cases where the industry definition underwent a change in 1987, trends were calculated from 1987 forward.

Limitations of Projections

Projections are simply means of detecting trends. But extensions of a trend line into the future may not be legitimate — if conditions suddenly change. The projections in *IFS-USA*, therefore, are not as reliable as actual survey data. Most analysts trying to project the future routinely turn to trend projection. In *IFS-USA*, the work of doing the projections has been done for the user in advance.

Part I

INFORMATION

NAICS 511110 - NEWSPAPER PUBLISHERS*

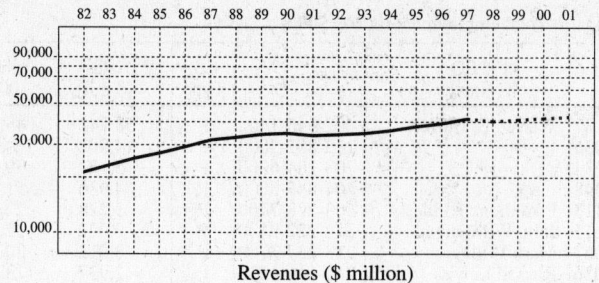

Revenues ($ million)

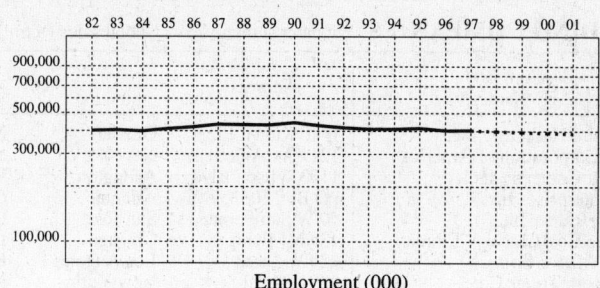

Employment (000)

GENERAL STATISTICS

Year	Establishments (number)	Employment (number)	Payroll ($ million)	Revenues ($ million)	Employees per Establishment (number)	Revenues per Establishment ($)	Payroll per Employee ($)
1982	8,846	401,500	6,555.0	21,276.0	45.4	2,405,155	16,326
1983	8,895 e	404,100	7,059.0	23,259.0	45.4 e	2,614,840 e	17,468
1984	8,944 e	398,600	7,367.0	25,302.0	44.6 e	2,828,936 e	18,482
1985	8,993 e	411,000	7,905.0	27,015.0	45.7 e	3,004,003 e	19,234
1986	9,042 e	420,000	8,380.0	29,206.0	46.4 e	3,230,038 e	19,952
1987	9,091	434,400	9,025.0	31,850.0	47.8	3,503,465	20,776
1988	8,848 e	432,400	9,349.0	32,927.0	48.9 e	3,721,406 e	21,621
1989	8,605	430,900	9,842.0	34,146.0	50.1	3,968,158	22,841
1990	8,630 e	443,400	10,407.0	34,642.0	51.4 e	4,014,137 e	23,471
1991	8,654 e	428,400	10,309.0	33,702.0	49.5 e	3,894,384 e	24,064
1992	8,679	417,000	10,506.0	34,124.0	48.0	3,931,789	25,194
1993	8,695 e	410,300	10,395.0	34,651.0	47.2 e	3,985,164 e	25,335
1994	8,711 e	410,100	10,585.0	35,837.0	47.1 e	4,113,994 e	25,811
1995	8,726 e	414,800	11,095.0	37,732.0	47.5 e	4,324,089 e	26,748
1996	8,742 e	403,300	11,199.0	39,171.0	46.1 e	4,480,782 e	27,768
1997	8,758	403,355	11,789.0	41,601.0	46.1	4,750,057	29,227
1998	8,657 p	398,689 p	11,796.0 p	40,280.0 p	46.1 p	4,652,882 p	29,587 p
1999	8,643 p	395,011 p	12,027.0 p	41,079.0 p	45.7 p	4,752,864 p	30,447 p
2000	8,629 p	391,332 p	12,258.0 p	41,877.0 p	45.4 p	4,853,054 p	31,324 p
2001	8,615 p	387,654 p	12,489.0 p	42,675.0 p	45.0 p	4,953,569 p	32,217 p

Sources: Economic Census of the United States, 1982, 1987, 1992, 1997. Establishment counts, employment, and payroll are from *County Business Patterns* for non-Census years. In non-Census years, industries in the Manufacturing range under SIC coding include data from the *Annual Survey of Manufactures* (*ASM*); those in the old Services range include data from the *Services Annual Survey* (*SAS*). Values followed by a 'p' are projections by the editors. Extrapolations are marked by 'e'. Data are the most recent available at this level of detail.

INDICES OF CHANGE

Year	Establishments (number)	Employment (number)	Payroll ($ million)	Revenues ($ million)	Employees per Establishment (number)	Revenues per Establishment ($)	Payroll per Employee ($)
1982	101.0	99.5	55.6	51.1	98.5	50.6	55.9
1987	103.8	107.7	76.6	76.6	103.8	73.8	71.1
1992	99.1	103.4	89.1	82.0	104.3	82.8	86.2
1993	99.3 e	101.7	88.2	83.3	102.5 e	83.9 e	86.7
1994	99.5 e	101.7	89.8	86.1	102.2 e	86.6 e	88.3
1995	99.6 e	102.8	94.1	90.7	103.2 e	91.0 e	91.5
1996	99.8 e	100.0	95.0	94.2	100.2 e	94.3 e	95.0
1997	100.0	100.0	100.0	100.0	100.0	100.0	100.0
1998	98.8 p	98.8 p	100.1 p	96.8 p	100.0 p	98.0 p	101.2 p
1999	98.7 p	97.9 p	102.0 p	98.7 p	99.2 p	100.1 p	104.2 p
2000	98.5 p	97.0 p	104.0 p	100.7 p	98.5 p	102.2 p	107.2 p
2001	98.4 p	96.1 p	105.9 p	102.6 p	97.7 p	104.3 p	110.2 p

Sources: Same as General Statistics. The values shown reflect change from the base year, 1997. Values above 100 mean greater than 1997, values below 100 mean less than 1997, and a value of 100 in the 1982-96 or 1998-2001 period means same as 1997. Values followed by a 'p' are projections by the editors; 'e' stands for extrapolation. Data are the most recent available at this level of detail.

SELECTED RATIOS

For 1997	Avg. of Information	Analyzed Industry	Index	For 1997	Avg. of Information	Analyzed Industry	Index
Employees per establishment	27	46	172	Payroll per establishment	1,131,090	1,346,084	119
Revenue per establishment	5,444,104	4,750,057	87	Payroll as % of revenue	21	28	136
Revenue per employee	203,255	103,137	51	Payroll per employee	42,229	29,227	69

Sources: Same as General Statistics. The 'Average' column represents the average for the industry sector, in 1997, where the currently shown industry is classified. The Index shows the relationship between the Average and the Analyzed Industry. For example, 100 means that they are equal; 500 that the Analyzed Industry is five times the average; 50 means that the Analyzed Industry is half the national average. The abbreviation 'na' is used to show that data are 'not available'.

*Equivalent to SIC 2711.

LEADING COMPANIES   Number shown: **75**   Total sales ($ mil): **139,613**   Total employment (000): **500.8**

Company Name	Address			CEO Name	Phone	Co. Type	Sales ($ mil)	Empl. (000)
Berkshire Hathaway Inc.	1440 Kiewit Plz	Omaha	NE 68131	Warren E. Buffett	402-346-1400	P	58,742*	45.0
News Corporation of America	1211 Av Americas	New York	NY 10036		212-852-7000	S	14,002	0.0
Gannett Company Inc.	1100 Wilson Blvd	Arlington	VA 22234		703-284-6000	P	5,121	39.4
Cox Enterprises Inc.	PO Box 105357	Atlanta	GA 30348		404-843-5000	R	4,936	51.0
Knight-Ridder Inc.	50 W San Fernando	San Jose	CA 95113	P Anthony Ridder	408-938-7700	P	3,228	22.0
Tribune Co. (Chicago, Illinois)	435 N Michigan Ave	Chicago	IL 60611	John W Madigan	312-222-9100	P	3,222	12.7
Times Mirror Co.	220 W 1st St	Los Angeles	CA 90053	Mark Willes	213-237-3700	P	3,012*	20.6
New York Times Co.	229 W 43rd St	New York	NY 10036	Russell Lewis	212-556-1234	P	2,937	13.2
Hearst Corp.	959 8th Ave	New York	NY 10019		212-649-2000	R	2,833*	15.0
Advance Publications Inc.	950 W Fingerboard	Staten Island	NY 10305		718-981-1234	R	2,750	20.0
News America Inc.	1211 Av Americas	New York	NY 10036	Anthea Disney	212-852-7000	S	2,571*	12.0
Washington Post Co.	1150 15th St NW	Washington	DC 20071	Donald Graham	202-334-6000	P	2,216	8.5
Dow Jones and Company Inc.	200 Liberty St	New York	NY 10281	Peter R Kann	212-416-2000	P	2,158	8.3
Hollinger International Inc.	401 N Wabash Ave	Chicago	IL 60611	Conrad Black	312-321-2299	P	2,147	3.3
Crepusculo Inc.	PO Box U	Taos	NM 87571	Robin Martin	505-758-2241	R	1,832	<0.1
E.W. Scripps Co.	PO Box 5380	Cincinnati	OH 45201	William Burleigh	513-977-3000	P	1,559	7.9
American City Business Journals	120 W Morehead St	Charlotte	NC 28202	Ray Shaw	704-973-1000	S	1,538*	1.8
A.H. Belo Corp.	PO Box 655237	Dallas	TX 75265	Robert W Decherd	214-977-6606	P	1,434	7.0
Gannett Inc. Newspaper Div.	1100 Wilson Blvd	Arlington	VA 22229	John Curley	703-284-6000	D	1,320*	32.4
Curry Coastal Pilot	PO Box 700	Brookings	OR 97415		541-469-3123	R	1,300	<0.1
McClatchy Newspapers Inc.	2100 Q St	Sacramento	CA 95816	Erwin Potts	916-321-1846	P	1,088	10.0
Paso Robles News Press	P O Box 427	Paso Robles	CA 93447		805-237-6060	S	850	<0.1
Harte-Hanks Inc.	PO Box 269	San Antonio	TX 78291	Larry Franklin	210-829-9000	P	830	7.1
Media General Inc.	PO Box 85333	Richmond	VA 23293	J Stewart Bryan III	804-649-6000	P	795	8.9
Central Newspapers Inc.	PO Box 1950	Phoenix	AZ 85001		602-444-1100	P	753	5.0
Journal Communications Inc.	PO Box 661	Milwaukee	WI 53201		414-224-2000	R	732	7.0
Freedom Communications Inc.	PO Box 19549	Irvine	CA 92623	James Rosse	949-553-9292	R	681	7.0
Hartz Group Inc.	667 Madison Ave	New York	NY 10021	Leonard Stern	212-308-3336	R	640	2.6
Press-Enterprise Co.	PO Box 792	Riverside	CA 92502	Marcia McQuern	909-684-1200	S	615*	1.0
Landmark Communications Inc.	PO Box 449	Norfolk	VA 23501		757-446-2000	R	575	4.5
Lee Enterprises Inc.	215 N Main St	Davenport	IA 52801	Richard Gottlieb	319-383-2100	P	536	6.1
Thomson Newspapers Inc.	1 Station Pl Ste 6	Stamford	CT 06902	W Brown	203-328-9400	S	512*	6.0
Copley Press Inc.	7776 Ivanhoe Ave	La Jolla	CA 92037	Helen Copley	619-454-0411	R	500	4.7
Thomson Information Inc.	1 Station Pl.	Stamford	CT 06902	Patrick J Tierney	203-969-8700	R	495*	2.8
Chronicle Publishing Co.	901 Mission St	San Francisco	CA 94103	John Sias	415-777-1111	R	490	3.0
CMP Media Inc.	600 Community Dr	Manhasset	NY 11030	Michael S Leeds	516-562-5000	P	478	1.8
Journal Register Co.	50 W State St	Trenton	NJ 08608	Robert Jelenic	609-396-2200	P	470	5.5
Garden State Newspapers Inc.	1560 Broadway	Denver	CO 80202		303-837-0886	S	467*	8.0
John Wiley and Sons Inc.	605 3rd Ave	New York	NY 10158	William J Pesce	212-850-6000	P	467	2.1
Morris Communications Corp.	PO Box 936	Augusta	GA 30903		706-724-0851	R	411*	5.6
Schurz Communications Inc.	225 W Colfax Ave	South Bend	IN 46626	Franklin D Schurz Jr	219-287-1001	R	410*	1.5
Southeastern Newspapers Corp.	PO Box 1928	Augusta	GA 30903		706-724-0851	S	400*	8.0
Booth Newspapers Inc.	PO Box 2168	Grand Rapids	MI 49501		616-222-5444	R	386*	4.5
Pulitzer Inc.	900 N Tucker Blvd	St. Louis	MO 63101	Michael E Pulitzer	314-340-8000	P	373	2.3
Trader Publishing Co.	PO Box 2576	Norfolk	VA 23501		757-640-4000	R	354*	5.1
Chicago Sun-Times Inc.	401 N Wabash Ave	Chicago	IL 60611		312-321-3000	S	333*	1.5
Seattle Times Co.	PO Box 70	Seattle	WA 98111	F Blethen	206-464-2111	R	319	2.6
Affiliated Newspapers	1560 Broadway	Denver	CO 80202		303-837-0886	R	303	6.7
Tribune Co. (Tampa, Florida)	PO Box 191	Tampa	FL 33601		813-259-7711	S	293*	3.5
Ottaway Newspapers Inc.	PO Box 401	Campbell Hall	NY 10916	J Ottaway	914-294-8181	S	287*	4.0
Abarta Inc.	1000 R I D C Plz	Pittsburgh	PA 15238	John F Bitzer III	412-963-6226	R	280*	1.2
Miami Herald Publishing Inc.	1 Herald Plz	Miami	FL 33132		305-350-2111	S	260	2.1
San Jose Mercury News Inc.	750 Ridder Park Dr	San Jose	CA 95190	Jay Harris	408-920-5000	S	260	1.6
San Francisco Newspaper Agency	925 Mission St	San Francisco	CA 94103	Steven Falk	415-777-5700	R	250	2.8
Macromedia Inc.	150 River St	Hackensack	NJ 07601		201-646-4000	R	240	1.6
Times Publishing Co.	PO Box 1121	Saint Petersburg	FL 33731		813-893-8111	R	240	3.7
Journal Sentinel Inc.	PO Box 661	Milwaukee	WI 53201		414-224-2000	S	236	1.4
Sentinel Communications Co.	633 N Orange Ave	Orlando	FL 32801		407-420-5000	S	231	1.4
Star-Telegram Newspaper Inc.	PO Box 1870	Fort Worth	TX 76101		817-390-7400	S	225	1.6
Denver Publishing Co.	PO Box 719	Denver	CO 80201	Larry Strutton	303-892-5000	P	215*	1.4
Donrey Media Group	PO Box 17017	Fort Smith	AR 72917	Emmett Jones	501-785-7810	R	201*	2.0
Detroit Free Press Inc.	615 W Lafayette	Detroit	MI 48226		313-222-6400	S	200*	0.3
Orange County Register	PO Box 11626	Santa Ana	CA 92711	Ron Redfern	714-835-1234	S	192*	2.0
Hartford Courant Co.	285 Broad St	Hartford	CT 06115	Marty Petty	860-241-6200	S	190*	1.1
Calkins Newspapers Inc.	8400 Route 13	Levittown	PA 19057		215-949-4011	R	180*	1.9
Baltimore Sun Co.	PO Box 1377	Baltimore	MD 21278		410-332-6000	S	172*	2.0
Houston Chronicle Publishing Co.	PO Box 4260	Houston	TX 77210	Jack Sweeney	713-220-7171	S	171*	2.0
Indianapolis Newspapers Inc.	PO Box 145	Indianapolis	IN 46206		317-633-1240	S	164*	1.5
Providence Journal Co.	75 Fountain St	Providence	RI 02902		401-277-7000	S	160*	1.3
Wick Communications Co.	333 W Wilcox Dr	Sierra Vista	AZ 85635	Walter Wick	520-458-0200	R	156*	1.7
Blade Communications Inc.	541 N Superior St	Toledo	OH 43660			R	140*	1.5
Hagadone Corp.	PO Box 6200	Coeur D Alene	ID 83816	Duane B Hagadone	208-667-3431	R	140*	1.5
Small Newspaper Group Inc.	PO Box 632	Kankakee	IL 60901		815-937-3300	R	139*	1.6
Paxton Media Group Inc.	PO Box 2300	Paducah	KY 42002		502-443-1771	R	136*	1.6
Guy Gannett Communications	P O Box 15277	Portland	ME 04101	James B Shaffer	207-828-8100	R	135	1.4

Source: Ward's Business Directory of U.S. Private and Public Companies, Volumes 1 and 2, 2000. The company type code used is as follows: P - Public, R - Private, S - Subsidiary, D - Division, J - Joint Venture, A - Affiliate, G - Group, N - Company type not reported. Sales are in millions of dollars, employees are in thousands. An asterisk (*) indicates an estimated sales volume. The symbol < stands for 'less than'. Company names and addresses are truncated, in some cases, to fit into the available space.

LOCATION BY STATE AND REGIONAL CONCENTRATION

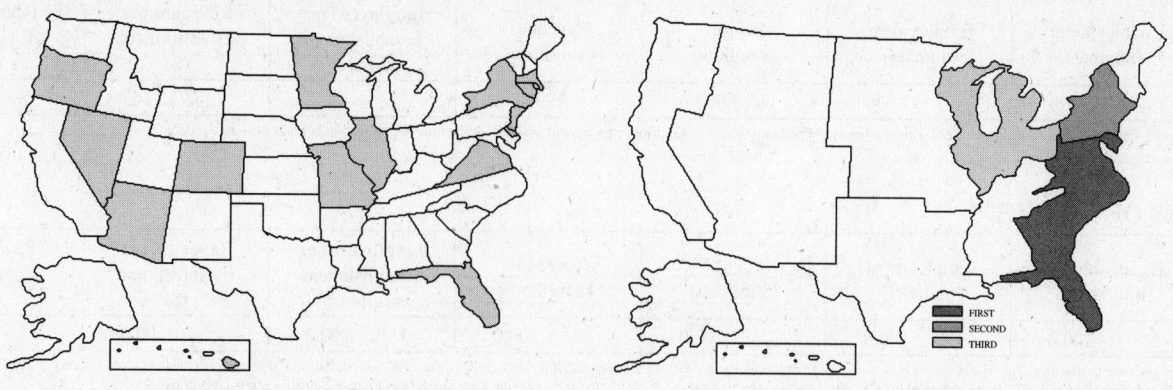

INDUSTRY DATA BY STATE

State	Establishments Total (number)	Establishments % of U.S.	Employment Total (number)	Employment % of U.S.	Employment Per Estab.	Payroll Total ($ mil.)	Payroll Per Empl. ($)	Revenues Total ($ mil.)	Revenues % of U.S.	Revenues Per Estab. ($)
California	663	7.6	44,763	11.1	68	1,463.0	32,683	5,000.7	12.0	7,542,517
New York	480	5.5	25,285	6.3	53	998.7	39,497	3,678.1	8.8	7,662,683
Florida	317	3.6	22,020	5.5	69	677.1	30,747	2,652.7	6.4	8,368,256
Texas	665	7.6	19,493	4.8	29	538.1	27,607	2,473.1	5.9	3,719,002
Illinois	417	4.8	19,413	4.8	47	585.6	30,166	2,196.8	5.3	5,268,000
Pennsylvania	282	3.2	20,727	5.1	73	610.3	29,443	1,962.9	4.7	6,960,592
Ohio	318	3.6	16,970	4.2	53	505.9	29,814	1,746.2	4.2	5,491,113
New Jersey	177	2.0	14,020	3.5	79	510.3	36,398	1,665.7	4.0	9,410,695
Massachusetts	178	2.0	14,076	3.5	79	503.5	35,767	1,462.1	3.5	8,214,079
Virginia	177	2.0	10,043	2.5	57	306.4	30,506	1,243.6	3.0	7,025,949
Michigan	237	2.7	13,082	3.2	55	363.8	27,811	1,230.0	3.0	5,189,954
Georgia	256	2.9	11,481	2.8	45	299.2	26,062	966.4	2.3	3,774,906
North Carolina	234	2.7	10,779	2.7	46	278.3	25,820	937.2	2.3	4,005,068
Missouri	268	3.1	9,047	2.2	34	228.1	25,207	856.8	2.1	3,196,881
Washington	187	2.1	10,024	2.5	54	273.8	27,313	841.8	2.0	4,501,786
Indiana	198	2.3	10,436	2.6	53	264.1	25,302	815.0	2.0	4,116,162
Minnesota	293	3.3	8,737	2.2	30	261.8	29,966	800.7	1.9	2,732,730
D.C.	33	0.4	3,425	0.8	104	186.6	54,490	767.4	1.8	23,253,667
Wisconsin	231	2.6	9,729	2.4	42	222.9	22,906	748.2	1.8	3,238,970
Colorado	189	2.2	7,250	1.8	38	212.3	29,289	724.6	1.7	3,833,778
Arizona	99	1.1	5,897	1.5	60	178.3	30,235	704.5	1.7	7,116,152
Tennessee	174	2.0	8,000	2.0	46	176.7	22,086	659.4	1.6	3,789,667
Connecticut	86	1.0	6,330	1.6	74	192.7	30,449	637.9	1.5	7,417,163
Maryland	93	1.1	4,716	1.2	51	116.5	24,703	587.9	1.4	6,321,667
Oregon	131	1.5	5,015	1.2	38	150.7	30,053	512.0	1.2	3,908,038
Iowa	238	2.7	5,943	1.5	25	120.4	20,258	441.9	1.1	1,856,828
Louisiana	116	1.3	4,610	1.1	40	127.2	27,592	435.8	1.0	3,756,560
South Carolina	116	1.3	5,186	1.3	45	114.1	21,993	410.4	1.0	3,537,552
Kentucky	164	1.9	4,811	1.2	29	117.2	24,352	409.9	1.0	2,499,177
Oklahoma	172	2.0	4,378	1.1	25	100.8	23,034	360.3	0.9	2,094,733
Alabama	117	1.3	4,317	1.1	37	112.9	26,152	323.7	0.8	2,766,299
Nevada	49	0.6	2,054	0.5	42	57.0	27,743	286.8	0.7	5,852,755
Kansas	200	2.3	4,290	1.1	21	93.3	21,744	280.4	0.7	1,401,940
Utah	57	0.7	2,668	0.7	47	62.7	23,490	254.7	0.6	4,468,965
Nebraska	137	1.6	3,188	0.8	23	65.5	20,533	243.6	0.6	1,777,942
Arkansas	119	1.4	3,534	0.9	30	74.1	20,961	231.2	0.6	1,942,706
Hawaii	24	0.3	1,551	0.4	65	62.4	40,221	214.3	0.5	8,929,958
Mississippi	107	1.2	2,689	0.7	25	58.3	21,663	198.9	0.5	1,858,822
West Virginia	81	0.9	2,828	0.7	35	53.7	18,987	187.9	0.5	2,319,210
New Mexico	64	0.7	2,460	0.6	38	54.2	22,014	184.0	0.4	2,875,109
Rhode Island	25	0.3	2,345	0.6	94	73.0	31,113	177.8	0.4	7,113,440
Maine	68	0.8	2,451	0.6	36	61.4	25,049	164.8	0.4	2,423,279
New Hampshire	63	0.7	2,189	0.5	35	54.2	24,761	144.1	0.3	2,287,317
Idaho	55	0.6	2,071	0.5	38	37.9	18,314	132.1	0.3	2,401,709
Montana	84	1.0	1,667	0.4	20	33.2	19,928	123.5	0.3	1,470,619
Delaware	22	0.3	992	0.2	45	30.8	31,039	114.4	0.3	5,200,045
South Dakota	94	1.1	1,639	0.4	17	28.4	17,326	99.2	0.2	1,055,362
North Dakota	65	0.7	1,471	0.4	23	27.9	18,940	93.0	0.2	1,430,938
Alaska	39	0.4	1,119	0.3	29	21.8	19,499	87.3	0.2	2,239,205
Vermont	53	0.6	1,124	0.3	21	24.7	22,016	80.1	0.2	1,510,547
Wyoming	46	0.5	1,022	0.3	22	17.6	17,242	49.5	0.1	1,076,804

Source: 1997 *Economic Census*. The states are in descending order of revenues or establishments (if revenue data are missing for the majority). The symbol (D) appears when data are withheld to prevent disclosure of competitive information. States marked with (D) are sorted by number of establishments. A dash (-) indicates that the data element cannot be calculated. * indicates the midpoint of a range; 175, for example is the range 100-249. Shaded *states* on the state map indicate those states which have proportionately greater representation in the industry than would be indicated by the state's population; the ratio is based on total revenues or number of establishments. Shaded *regions* indicate where the industry is regionally most concentrated.

NAICS 511120 - PERIODICAL PUBLISHERS

GENERAL STATISTICS

Year	Establishments (number)	Employment (number)	Payroll ($ million)	Revenues ($ million)	Employees per Establishment (number)	Revenues per Establishment ($)	Payroll per Employee ($)
1997	6,298	137,550	5,993.0	29,885.0	21.8	4,745,157	43,570

Source: Economic Census of the United States, 1997. This is a newly defined industry. Data for prior years were unavailable at the time of publication but may become available over time.

INDICES OF CHANGE

Year	Establishments (number)	Employment (number)	Payroll ($ million)	Revenues ($ million)	Employees per Establishment (number)	Revenues per Establishment ($)	Payroll per Employee ($)
1997	100.0	100.0	100.0	100.0	100.0	100.0	100.0

Sources: Same as General Statistics. The values shown reflect change from the base year, 1997. Values above 100 mean greater than 1997, values below 100 mean less than 1997, and a value of 100 in the 1982-96 or 1998-2001 period means same as 1997. Values followed by a 'p' are projections by the editors; 'e' stands for extrapolation. Data are the most recent available at this level of detail.

SIC INDUSTRIES RELATED TO NAICS 511120

Each new NAICS code represents an industry that used to be part of an SIC or a part of several SIC industries. Data in this table are shown to provide transitional information for these cases. All available data for the precursor SIC(s) are shown. Even if only a part of an SIC is included in the NAICS, *all* data for the SIC are reproduced. If the SIC industry is not marked as being a part (pt) of the NAICS, the entire industry is embedded in the NAICS data. The SIC composition of the new industry provides some hints of the relative importance of its "ancestors." Data marked with a 'p' are projected. Projections begin with 1982 data. Data earlier than 1990 are not shown but are reflected in the projections.

SIC	Industry	1990	1991	1992	1993	1994	1995	1996	1997
2721	**Periodicals**								
	Establishments (number)	-	-	4,699	-	-	-	-	-
	Employment (thousands)	115.2	110.6	116.2	117.1	116.4	123.1	120.5	126.5p
	Value of Shipments ($ million)	20,396.7	20,345.1	22,033.9	22,652.5	21,723.3	23,904.9	24,929.8	26,073.0p
2741	**Miscellaneous Publishing (pt)**								
	Establishments (number)	-	-	3,390	-	-	-	-	-
	Employment (thousands)	65.2	65.0	65.4	66.6	71.2	67.4	68.8	-
	Value of Shipments ($ million)	8,874.7	9,762.0	10,977.1	11,806.6	12,332.4	11,992.1	12,510.5	14,309.8p

Source: Economic Census of the United States, 1992, annual surveys of economic sectors conducted by the Bureau of the Census, and estimates or projections based on the 1982-1992 period; not all data are shown. 'e' marks estimates made by the editors; 'p' indicates projections based on time series. A dash (-) indicates that data for this SIC or year were not available. The abbreviation (pt) next to the industry name indicates that only a part of the industry is present within the NAICS data. If no (pt) is shown, the entire industry is contained within the NAICS data.

SELECTED RATIOS

For 1997	Avg. of Information	Analyzed Industry	Index	For 1997	Avg. of Information	Analyzed Industry	Index
Employees per establishment	27	22	82	Payroll per establishment	1,131,090	951,572	84
Revenue per establishment	5,444,104	4,745,157	87	Payroll as % of revenue	21	20	97
Revenue per employee	203,255	217,266	107	Payroll per employee	42,229	43,570	103

Sources: Same as General Statistics. The 'Average' column represents the average for the industry sector, in 1997, where the currently shown industry is classified. The Index shows the relationship between the Average and the Analyzed Industry. For example, 100 means that they are equal; 500 that the Analyzed Industry is five times the average; 50 means that the Analyzed Industry is half the national average. The abbreviation 'na' is used to show that data are 'not available'.

LEADING COMPANIES   Number shown: **75**   Total sales ($ mil): **121,006**   Total employment (000): **486.1**

Company Name	Address				CEO Name	Phone	Co. Type	Sales ($ mil)	Empl. (000)
American Express Company	AmEx Twr	New York	NY	10285	Ken Chenault	212-640-2000	S	15,428*	65.0
Sunset Publishing Corp.	2 Embarcadero Ctr	San Francisco	CA	94111	Gerald M Levin	650-321-3600	S	14,582	67.5
News Corporation of America	1211 Av Americas	New York	NY	10036		212-852-7000	S	14,002	0.0
Thomson Professional Publishing	1 Station Place	Stamford	CT	06902	Richard J Harrington	203-969-8700	S	13,236*	7.0
R.R. Donnelley and Sons Co.	77 W Wacker Dr	Chicago	IL	60601	William Davis	312-326-8000	P	5,183	36.3
Time Inc.	Time & Life Bldg	New York	NY	10020	Dawn Logan	212-522-1212	S	4,490	55.0
McGraw-Hill Inc.	1221 Av Americas	New York	NY	10020	Harold McGraw III	212-512-2000	P	3,992	15.9
New York Times Co.	229 W 43rd St	New York	NY	10036	Russell Lewis	212-556-1234	P	2,937	13.2
Hearst Corp.	959 8th Ave	New York	NY	10019		212-649-2000	R	2,833*	15.0
Advance Publications Inc.	950 W Fingerboard	Staten Island	NY	10305		718-981-1234	R	2,750	20.0
News America Inc.	1211 Av Americas	New York	NY	10036	Anthea Disney	212-852-7000	S	2,571*	12.0
Reader's Digest Association Inc.	Readers Digest Rd	Pleasantville	NY	10570	Thomas O Ryder	914-238-1000	P	2,532	4.8
Quebecor World (USA) Inc.	340 Pemberwick Rd	Greenwich	CT	06831	Robert Burton	203-532-4200	P	2,357	16.0
International Data Group Inc.	1 Exeter Plz	Boston	MA	02116	Kelly Conlin	617-534-1200	R	2,350	9.0
Washington Post Co.	1150 15th St NW	Washington	DC	20071	Donald Graham	202-334-6000	P	2,216	8.5
Dow Jones and Company Inc.	200 Liberty St	New York	NY	10281	Peter R Kann	212-416-2000	P	2,158	8.3
Hollinger International Inc.	401 N Wabash Ave	Chicago	IL	60611	Conrad Black	312-321-2299	P	2,147	3.3
Big Flower Press Holdings Inc.	3 East 54th St	New York	NY	10022	Edward T Reilly	212-521-1600	P	1,740	10.0
PRIMEDIA Inc.	745 5th Ave	New York	NY	10151	C McCurdy	212-745-0100	P	1,531	6.3
Bloomberg L.P.	499 Park Ave	New York	NY	10022	Michael Bloomberg	212-318-2000	R	1,500	4.0
Scholastic Corp.	555 Broadway	New York	NY	10012		212-343-6100	P	1,154	7.5
Ziff-Davis Inc.	28 East 28th St	New York	NY	10016	Eric Hippeau	212-503-3500	P	1,109	2.9
Meredith Corp.	1716 Locust St	Des Moines	IA	50309	William Kerr	515-284-3000	P	1,036	2.6
Wolters Kluwer U.S. Corp.	161 N Clark St	Chicago	IL	60601	Hugh Yarringron	312-425-7000	S	1,012*	4.0
Harcourt Brace and Co.	6277 Sea Harbor Dr	Orlando	FL	32821	Brian Knez	407-345-2000	S	998*	5.0
Cahners Business Information	275 Washington St	Newton	MA	02158	Bruce A Barnet	617-558-4249	S	875*	5.7
Standex International Corp.	6 Manor Pkwy	Salem	NH	03079	Thomas L King	603-893-9701	P	641	5.4
Gruner & Jahr USA Publishing Co	375 Lexington Ave	New York	NY	10017		212-499-2000	R	628*	3.6
American Color Graphics Inc.	100 Winners Cir	Brentwood	TN	37027	Jack Anderson	615-377-0377	S	505*	3.0
Rodale Inc.	33 E Minor St	Emmaus	PA	18098	Steve Murphy	610-967-5171	R	500*	1.3
United Advertising Publications	15400 Knoll Trail Dr	Dallas	TX	75248	Nigel A Donaldson	972-701-0244	S	498*	3.0
Thomson Information Inc.	1 Station Pl	Stamford	CT	06902	Patrick J Tierney	203-969-8700	R	495*	2.8
CMP Media Inc.	600 Community Dr	Manhasset	NY	11030	Michael S Leeds	516-562-5000	P	478	1.8
John Wiley and Sons Inc.	605 3rd Ave	New York	NY	10158	William J Pesce	212-850-6000	P	467	2.1
Cadmus Communications Corp.	PO Box 27367	Richmond	VA	23261	C Gillispie	804-287-5680	P	443	4.1
Morris Communications Corp.	PO Box 936	Augusta	GA	30903		706-724-0851	R	411*	5.6
Medical Economics Company Inc.	5 Paragon Dr	Montvale	NJ	07645	Curtis Allen	201-358-7500	S	400	2.1
CMP Media	600 Community Dr	Manhasset	NY	11030	Gary Marshall	516-562-5000	S	382*	1.5
Newsweek Inc.	251 W 57th St	New York	NY	10019	Harold Shain	212-445-4000	S	380	1.0
McGraw-Hill Inc	1221 Av Americas	New York	NY	10020	Stephen B Bonner	212-512-2000	D	373*	2.1
Trader Publishing Co.	PO Box 2576	Norfolk	VA	23501		757-640-4000	R	354*	5.1
Advanstar Communications Inc.	7500 Old Oak Blvd	Cleveland	OH	44130	Robert L Krakoff	440-243-8100	S	328	1.5
Playboy Enterprises Inc.	680 N Lake Shore	Chicago	IL	60611	Christie Hefner	312-751-8000	P	318	0.8
Penton Media Inc.	1100 Superior Ave	Cleveland	OH	44114	Thomas L Kemp	216-696-7000	P	301	1.5
Pleasant Co.	PO Box 620998	Middleton	WI	53562	Pleasant Rowland	608-836-4848	S	300	0.7
American Media Inc.	600 East Coast Ave	Lantana	FL	33464	David Pecker	561-540-1000	R	294	2.0
Standard and Poor's Corp.	25 Broadway	New York	NY	10004		212-208-8000	S	290*	1.9
Wenner Media Inc.	120 Av Americas	New York	NY	10104	Jann S Wenner	212-484-1616	R	270	0.3
Miller Freeman Inc.	600 Harrison St	San Francisco	CA	94107	Marshall Freeman	415-905-2200	S	264*	1.8
Bureau of National Affairs Inc.	1231 25th St NW	Washington	DC	20037	William Beltz	202-452-4200	R	259*	1.7
Intertec Publishing Corp.	PO Box 12901	Shaw Msn	KS	66282	Raymond Maloney	913-341-1300	S	250*	1.6
Johnson Publishing Company Inc.	820 S Michigan Ave	Chicago	IL	60605	John Johnson	312-322-9200	R	250*	1.5
Crain Communications Inc.	1400 Woodbridge St	Detroit	MI	48207		313-446-6000	R	242	1.0
Emmis Communications Corp.	40 Monument Circle	Indianapolis	IN	46204	Jeffrey H Smulyan	317-266-0100	P	233	1.6
Marvel Entertainment Group Inc.	387 Park Ave S	New York	NY	10016	Joseph Calamari	212-696-0808	S	232	1.6
Congressional Quarterly Inc.	1414 22nd St NW	Washington	DC	20037		202-887-8500	S	230	0.3
Topps Company Inc.	1 Whitehall St	New York	NY	10004		212-376-0300	P	229	0.5
Mosby Inc.	PO Box 28430	St. Louis	MO	63146	Patrick A Clifford	314-872-8370	S	212*	1.4
Stevens Graphics Inc.	713 Abernathy SW	Atlanta	GA	30310		404-752-0543	S	208	0.8
Advanstar Holdings Inc.	7500 Old Oak Blvd	Cleveland	OH	44130		440-243-8100	R	200	1.1
Bill Communications Inc.	355 Park Ave S	New York	NY	10010	John Wickersham	212-592-6200	S	200	0.7
BPI Communications L.P.	1515 Broadway	New York	NY	10036	Howard Lander	212-764-7300	R	200	0.9
Fairchild Publications Inc.	7 W 34th St	New York	NY	10001	Michael Coady	212-630-4000	S	200	0.8
TV Guide Magazine	4 Radnor Corporate	Radnor	PA	19087	Paul Carlucci	610-293-8500	S	199*	1.2
Ziff-Davis Publishing Co.	1 Park Ave	New York	NY	10016		212-503-3500	R	191*	1.1
BET Holdings Inc.	1900 W Pl NE	Washington	DC	20018	Robert Johnson	202-608-2000	P	178	0.6
Waverly Inc.	351 W Camden St	Baltimore	MD	21201		410-528-4000	S	172	1.0
Baltimore Sun Co.	PO Box 1377	Baltimore	MD	21278		410-332-6000	S	172*	2.0
Academic Press Inc.	525 B St	San Diego	CA	92101	Pieter Bolman	619-699-6826	D	150	0.3
Southern Progress Corp.	PO Box 2581	Birmingham	AL	35202	Tom Angelillo	205-877-6000	S	147*	0.9
Children's Television Workshop	1 Lincoln Plz	New York	NY	10023	David Britt	212-595-3456	R	138*	0.5
Publishers Printing Co.	PO Box 37500	Louisville	KY	40233		502-543-2251	R	127*	1.8
Imperial Printing Co.	PO Box 26	St. Joseph	MI	49085		616-983-7105	S	122*	0.6
McMullen & Argus Publishing Inc	2400 E Katella Ave	Anaheim	CA	92806	Bill Porter	714-939-2400	S	117*	0.4
MAC America Communications	5555 N 7th Ave	Phoenix	AZ	85013	Delbert R Lewis	602-207-3333	S	111*	0.4

Source: Ward's Business Directory of U.S. Private and Public Companies, Volumes 1 and 2, 2000. The company type code used is as follows: P - Public, R - Private, S - Subsidiary, D - Division, J - Joint Venture, A - Affiliate, G - Group, N - Company type not reported. Sales are in millions of dollars, employees are in thousands. An asterisk (*) indicates an estimated sales volume. The symbol < stands for 'less than'. Company names and addresses are truncated, in some cases, to fit into the available space.

LOCATION BY STATE AND REGIONAL CONCENTRATION

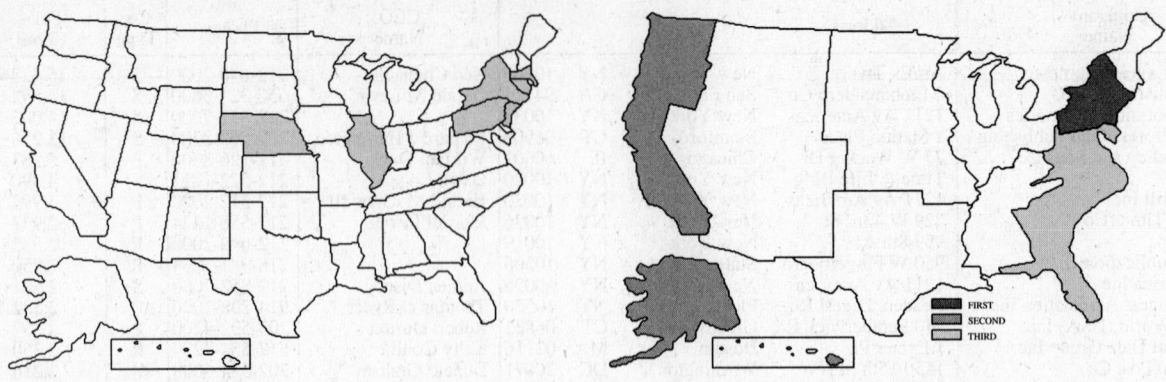

INDUSTRY DATA BY STATE

State	Establishments Total (number)	Establishments % of U.S.	Employment Total (number)	Employment % of U.S.	Employment Per Estab.	Payroll Total ($ mil.)	Payroll Per Empl. ($)	Revenues Total ($ mil.)	Revenues % of U.S.	Revenues Per Estab. ($)
New York	709	11.3	35,051	25.5	49	1,952.0	55,690	11,237.9	37.6	15,850,319
California	831	13.2	15,689	11.4	19	663.5	42,290	3,455.1	11.6	4,157,711
Illinois	298	4.7	7,942	5.8	27	331.4	41,730	1,524.8	5.1	5,116,762
Pennsylvania	203	3.2	6,877	5.0	34	248.0	36,067	1,460.6	4.9	7,195,251
New Jersey	263	4.2	5,821	4.2	22	278.7	47,883	1,166.7	3.9	4,436,141
D.C.	91	1.4	4,876	3.5	54	252.3	51,742	1,161.4	3.9	12,762,637
Massachusetts	261	4.1	5,066	3.7	19	243.1	47,984	927.3	3.1	3,552,686
Connecticut	136	2.2	3,690	2.7	27	179.3	48,585	763.0	2.6	5,610,654
Florida	416	6.6	4,925	3.6	12	166.2	33,750	757.9	2.5	1,821,966
Texas	306	4.9	4,029	2.9	13	133.3	33,090	603.8	2.0	1,973,157
Ohio	140	2.2	3,443	2.5	25	131.2	38,107	575.7	1.9	4,112,014
Georgia	167	2.7	3,904	2.8	23	122.2	31,302	551.5	1.8	3,302,515
Minnesota	132	2.1	1,950	1.4	15	67.1	34,430	403.0	1.3	3,052,697
Wisconsin	111	1.8	2,258	1.6	20	69.6	30,804	398.6	1.3	3,590,829
Virginia	188	3.0	2,674	1.9	14	103.5	38,718	392.3	1.3	2,086,798
Maryland	147	2.3	2,908	2.1	20	114.5	39,389	372.7	1.2	2,535,673
Alabama	71	1.1	1,503	1.1	21	53.3	35,457	358.4	1.2	5,048,352
Michigan	148	2.3	2,325	1.7	16	94.4	40,600	336.6	1.1	2,274,162
North Carolina	119	1.9	1,774	1.3	15	55.1	31,045	320.5	1.1	2,692,916
Colorado	139	2.2	1,984	1.4	14	75.1	37,860	314.0	1.1	2,258,971
Tennessee	105	1.7	2,930	2.1	28	113.7	38,814	310.3	1.0	2,955,267
Nebraska	25	0.4	1,250	0.9	50	49.2	39,334	215.1	0.7	8,605,160
Arizona	125	2.0	1,155	0.8	9	37.7	32,661	145.6	0.5	1,164,912
Washington	123	2.0	1,220	0.9	10	35.9	29,389	125.6	0.4	1,021,081
Oklahoma	46	0.7	488	0.4	11	14.8	30,357	120.9	0.4	2,627,935
Indiana	83	1.3	1,039	0.7	13	27.2	26,227	105.7	0.4	1,273,398
Oregon	85	1.3	936	0.7	11	24.8	26,465	103.0	0.3	1,212,176
New Hampshire	38	0.6	423	0.3	11	25.4	60,118	89.9	0.3	2,365,447
New Mexico	47	0.7	294	0.2	6	13.5	46,078	54.5	0.2	1,159,702
Kentucky	50	0.8	444	0.3	9	12.9	29,151	47.5	0.2	949,940
Vermont	34	0.5	349	0.3	10	10.4	29,885	44.3	0.1	1,303,265
Hawaii	35	0.6	349	0.3	10	11.1	31,739	41.6	0.1	1,187,886
Utah	38	0.6	339	0.2	9	9.6	28,339	38.8	0.1	1,020,632
Maine	37	0.6	268	0.2	7	9.2	34,384	37.6	0.1	1,015,459
Nevada	47	0.7	329	0.2	7	9.0	27,477	33.3	0.1	708,745
Rhode Island	18	0.3	287	0.2	16	7.5	26,073	30.8	0.1	1,708,722
South Carolina	51	0.8	263	0.2	5	7.3	27,852	29.0	0.1	568,647
Louisiana	55	0.9	295	0.2	5	8.0	27,047	27.8	0.1	504,618
Idaho	30	0.5	172	0.1	6	4.7	27,378	17.7	0.1	588,367
Alaska	9	0.1	60	0.0	7	1.7	28,267	10.4	0.0	1,153,222
West Virginia	13	0.2	63	0.0	5	1.3	20,317	4.5	0.0	344,615
Missouri	108	1.7	3,750*	-	-	(D)	-	(D)	-	-
Iowa	57	0.9	1,750*	-	-	(D)	-	(D)	-	-
Kansas	46	0.7	750*	-	-	(D)	-	(D)	-	-
Arkansas	29	0.5	175*	-	-	(D)	-	(D)	-	-
Montana	26	0.4	175*	-	-	(D)	-	(D)	-	-
Mississippi	19	0.3	175*	-	-	(D)	-	(D)	-	-
Delaware	12	0.2	60*	-	-	(D)	-	(D)	-	-
North Dakota	12	0.2	175*	-	-	(D)	-	(D)	-	-
South Dakota	12	0.2	60*	-	-	(D)	-	(D)	-	-
Wyoming	7	0.1	60*	-	-	(D)	-	(D)	-	-

Source: 1997 *Economic Census*. The states are in descending order of revenues or establishments (if revenue data are missing for the majority). The symbol (D) appears when data are withheld to prevent disclosure of competitive information. States marked with (D) are sorted by number of establishments. A dash (-) indicates that the data element cannot be calculated. * indicates the midpoint of a range; 175, for example is the range 100-249. Shaded *states* on the state map indicate those states which have proportionately greater representation in the industry than would be indicated by the state's population; the ratio is based on total revenues or number of establishments. Shaded *regions* indicate where the industry is regionally most concentrated.

NAICS 511130 - BOOK PUBLISHERS

GENERAL STATISTICS

Year	Establishments (number)	Employment (number)	Payroll ($ million)	Revenues ($ million)	Employees per Establishment (number)	Revenues per Establishment ($)	Payroll per Employee ($)
1997	2,684	89,898	3,643.0	22,648.0	33.5	8,438,152	40,524

Source: Economic Census of the United States, 1997. This is a newly defined industry. Data for prior years were unavailable at the time of publication but may become available over time.

INDICES OF CHANGE

Year	Establishments (number)	Employment (number)	Payroll ($ million)	Revenues ($ million)	Employees per Establishment (number)	Revenues per Establishment ($)	Payroll per Employee ($)
1997	100.0	100.0	100.0	100.0	100.0	100.0	100.0

Sources: Same as General Statistics. The values shown reflect change from the base year, 1997. Values above 100 mean greater than 1997, values below 100 mean less than 1997, and a value of 100 in the 1982-96 or 1998-2001 period means same as 1997. Values followed by a 'p' are projections by the editors; 'e' stands for extrapolation. Data are the most recent available at this level of detail.

SIC INDUSTRIES RELATED TO NAICS 511130

Each new NAICS code represents an industry that used to be part of an SIC or a part of several SIC industries. Data in this table are shown to provide transitional information for these cases. All available data for the precursor SIC(s) are shown. Even if only a part of an SIC is included in the NAICS, *all* data for the SIC are reproduced. If the SIC industry is not marked as being a part (pt) of the NAICS, the entire industry is embedded in the NAICS data. The SIC composition of the new industry provides some hints of the relative importance of its "ancestors." Data marked with a 'p' are projected. Projections begin with 1982 data. Data earlier than 1990 are not shown but are reflected in the projections.

SIC	Industry	1990	1991	1992	1993	1994	1995	1996	1997
2731	**Book Publishing (pt)**								
	Establishments (number)	2,144	2,284	2,644	2,699	2,756	2,904	2,781p	2,843p
	Employment (thousands)	74.4	77.3	79.6	83.2	87.1	83.6	85.4	86.8p
	Value of Shipments ($ million) . . .	15,317.9	16,596.1	16,731.1	18,615.9	19,418.9	20,603.6	21,362.7	22,352.7p
2741	**Miscellaneous Publishing (pt)**								
	Establishments (number)	-	-	3,390	-	-	-	-	-
	Employment (thousands)	65.2	65.0	65.4	66.6	71.2	67.4	68.8	-
	Value of Shipments ($ million) . . .	8,874.7	9,762.0	10,977.1	11,806.6	12,332.4	11,992.1	12,510.5	14,309.8p

Source: Economic Census of the United States, 1992, annual surveys of economic sectors conducted by the Bureau of the Census, and estimates or projections based on the 1982-1992 period; not all data are shown. 'e' marks estimates made by the editors; 'p' indicates projections based on time series. A dash (-) indicates that data for this SIC or year were not available. The abbreviation (pt) next to the industry name indicates that only a part of the industry is present within the NAICS data. If no (pt) is shown, the entire industry is contained within the NAICS data.

SELECTED RATIOS

For 1997	Avg. of Information	Analyzed Industry	Index	For 1997	Avg. of Information	Analyzed Industry	Index
Employees per establishment	27	33	125	Payroll per establishment	1,131,090	1,357,303	120
Revenue per establishment	5,444,104	8,438,152	155	Payroll as % of revenue	21	16	77
Revenue per employee	203,255	251,930	124	Payroll per employee	42,229	40,524	96

Sources: Same as General Statistics. The 'Average' column represents the average for the industry sector, in 1997, where the currently shown industry is classified. The Index shows the relationship between the Average and the Analyzed Industry. For example, 100 means that they are equal; 500 that the Analyzed Industry is five times the average; 50 means that the Analyzed Industry is half the national average. The abbreviation 'na' is used to show that data are 'not available'.

LEADING COMPANIES   Number shown: **75**   Total sales ($ mil): **140,340**   Total employment (000): **437.0**

Company Name	Address				CEO Name	Phone	Co. Type	Sales ($ mil)	Empl. (000)
Berkshire Hathaway Inc.	1440 Kiewit Plz	Omaha	NE	68131	Warren E. Buffett	402-346-1400	P	58,742*	45.0
Sunset Publishing Corp.	2 Embarcadero Ctr	San Francisco	CA	94111	Gerald M Levin	650-321-3600	S	14,582	67.5
Thomson Professional Publishing	1 Station Place	Stamford	CT	06902	Richard J Harrington	203-969-8700	S	13,236*	7.0
Viacom Inc.	1515 Broadway	New York	NY	10036	Sumner M Redstone	212-258-6000	P	12,096	116.7
McGraw-Hill Inc.	1221 Av Americas	New York	NY	10020	Harold McGraw III	212-512-2000	P	3,992	15.9
Times Mirror Co.	220 W 1st St	Los Angeles	CA	90053	Mark Willes	213-237-3700	P	3,012*	20.6
Reader's Digest Association Inc.	Readers Digest Rd	Pleasantville	NY	10570	Thomas O Ryder	914-238-1000	P	2,532	4.8
Harcourt General Inc.	27 Boylston St	Chestnut Hill	MA	02467	Brian J Knez	617-232-8200	P	2,143	13.6
THI Holdings Corp.	1 Station Pl	Stamford	CT	06902	Richard J Harrington	203-969-8700	S	1,939*	12.0
Paramount Publishing	1230 Av Americas	New York	NY	10020		212-698-7000	S	1,588*	9.0
McGraw-Hill Inc	1221 Av Americas	New York	NY	10020	Harold McGraw	212-512-2000	D	1,540*	2.0
Bloomberg L.P.	499 Park Ave	New York	NY	10022	Michael Bloomberg	212-318-2000	R	1,500	4.0
Scholastic Corp.	555 Broadway	New York	NY	10012		212-343-6100	P	1,154	7.5
Ziff Communications Co.	1 Park Ave	New York	NY	10016		212-503-3500	P	1,109	2.9
Meredith Corp.	1716 Locust St	Des Moines	IA	50309	William Kerr	515-284-3000	P	1,036	2.6
Wolters Kluwer U.S. Corp.	161 N Clark St	Chicago	IL	60601	Hugh Yarringron	312-425-7000	S	1,012*	4.0
Random House Inc.	201 E 50th St	New York	NY	10022	Peter Olson	212-751-2600	S	1,000*	1.5
Harcourt Brace and Co.	6277 Sea Harbor Dr	Orlando	FL	32821	Brian Knez	407-345-2000	S	998*	5.0
Addison Wesley Longman Inc.	1 Jacob Way	Reading	MA	01867	Peter Jovanovich	781-944-3700	S	954*	5.0
Houghton Mifflin Co.	222 Berkeley St	Boston	MA	02116	Nader Darehshari	617-351-5000	P	920	2.8
Intern. Thomson Publishing Inc.	10 Davis Dr	Belmont	CA	94002	Tim McEwen	650-595-2350	S	800*	5.0
HarperCollins Publishers Inc.	10 E 53rd St	New York	NY	10022	Therese Burke	212-207-7000	S	764	3.0
VNU USA Inc.	1515 Broadway	New York	NY	10036	Gerald Hobbs	212-536-6700	S	677	3.9
CCH Inc.	2700 Lake Cook Rd	Riverwoods	IL	60015	Rebecca K Hensley	847-267-7000	S	670	5.0
Pearson Inc.	1330 Av Americas	New York	NY	10019	Phil Hoffman	212-713-1919	S	647*	3.0
Simon and Schuster Inc.	1230 Av Americas	New York	NY	10020		212-698-7000	S	565	2.3
Insilco Holding Co.	PO Box 7196	Dublin	OH	43017	John Fort	614-792-0468	P	536	5.5
World Book Inc.	525 W Monroe St	Chicago	IL	60661		312-258-3700	S	515*	8.0
Justin Industries Inc.	PO Box 425	Fort Worth	TX	76101	J T Dickenson	817-336-5125	P	510	4.1
Rodale Inc.	33 E Minor St	Emmaus	PA	18098	Steve Murphy	610-967-5171	R	500*	1.3
Thomson Information Inc.	1 Station Pl	Stamford	CT	06902	Patrick J Tierney	203-969-8700	R	495*	2.8
John Wiley and Sons Inc.	605 3rd Ave	New York	NY	10158	William J Pesce	212-850-6000	P	467	2.1
Encyclopaedia Britannica Inc.	310 S Michigan Ave	Chicago	IL	60604		312-347-7000	R	460*	2.4
McGraw-Hill Higher Education	1333 Burr Ridge	Burr Ridge	IL	60521	Edward H Stanford	630-789-4000	S	385	1.0
Grolier Inc.	90 Old Sherman	Danbury	CT	06810		203-797-3500	R	380*	2.0
Penguin Putnam Inc.	375 Hudson St	New York	NY	10014		212-366-2000	S	377*	1.8
McGraw-Hill Inc	1221 Av Americas	New York	NY	10020	Stephen B Bonner	212-512-2000	D	373*	2.1
Thomson Financial Services	22 Thomas Pl 11F2	Boston	MA	02210	Patrick J Tierney	617-856-4636	S	354*	2.2
Franklin Covey Co.	2230 W Parkway	Salt Lake City	UT	84119	John H Rowberry	801-975-1776	P	319	3.5
Standard and Poor's Corp.	25 Broadway	New York	NY	10004		212-208-8000	S	290*	1.9
Deseret Management Corp.	60 E South Temple	Salt Lake City	UT	84111	Rodney H Brady	801-538-0651	R	281*	2.0
Thomas Nelson Inc.	PO Box 141000	Nashville	TN	37214		615-889-9000	P	262	1.1
Intertec Publishing Corp.	PO Box 12901	Shaw Msn	KS	66282	Raymond Maloney	913-341-1300	S	250*	1.6
Congressional Quarterly Inc.	1414 22nd St NW	Washington	DC	20037		202-887-8500	S	230	0.3
G.P. Putnam's Sons	375 Hudson St	New York	NY	10014		212-366-2000	S	214*	0.7
Mosby Inc.	PO Box 28430	St. Louis	MO	63146	Patrick A Clifford	314-872-8370	S	212*	1.4
BPI Communications L.P.	1515 Broadway	New York	NY	10036	Howard Lander	212-764-7300	R	200	0.9
Chronimed Inc.	10900 Red Circle Dr	Minnetonka	MN	55343	Henry F Blissenbach	612-979-3600	P	198	0.4
Golden Books Family	888 7th Ave	New York	NY	10106	Eric Ellenbogen	212-547-6700	P	194	1.0
Ziff-Davis Publishing Co.	1 Park Ave	New York	NY	10016		212-503-3500	R	191*	1.1
Rand McNally and Co.	8255 N Central Park	Skokie	IL	60076	Henry Feinberg	847-329-8100	R	179	0.9
Waverly Inc.	351 W Camden St	Baltimore	MD	21201		410-528-4000	S	172	1.0
R.R. Bowker	121 Chanlon Rd	New Providence	NJ	07974		908-464-6800	D	151*	0.9
Academic Press Inc.	525 B St	San Diego	CA	92101	Pieter Bolman	619-699-6826	D	150	0.3
Lexis Publishing	PO Box 7587	Charlottesville	VA	22906		804-972-7600	S	149*	0.8
Hazelden Publishing & Education	PO Box 176	Center City	MN	55012		651-257-4010	R	142*	0.8
IDG Books Worldwide Inc.	919 E Hillsdale Blvd	Foster City	CA	94404	Steven Berkowitz	650-655-3000	P	137	0.4
Little, Brown and Company Inc.	3 Center Plz	Boston	MA	02108	Larry Kirsbaum	617-227-0730	S	136	0.6
Southwestern/Great American Inc.	P O Box 305140	Nashville	TN	37230	Ralph W Mosley	615-391-2500	R	130*	0.6
Zondervan Corp.	5300 Patterson SE	Grand Rapids	MI	49512	Bruce Ryskamp	616-698-6900	S	125	0.3
Network Communications Inc.	PO Box 100001	Lawrenceville	GA	30046	K Hughes	770-962-7220	R	124*	0.7
W.B. Saunders Co.	Curtis Ctr	Philadelphia	PA	19106	Lewis Reines	215-238-7800	D	120*	0.6
EMAP Petersen Inc.	6420 Wilshire Blvd	Los Angeles	CA	90048	James Dunning	213-782-2000	R	109*	0.7
Cook Communications Ministries	4050 Lee Vance Vw	Co Springs	CO	80918	David Mehlis	719-535-2905	R	107*	1.0
J.J. Keller and Associates Inc.	PO Box 368	Neenah	WI	54957	John Keller	920-722-2848	R	100	0.8
Oxford University Press Inc.	198 Madison Ave	New York	NY	10016	Edward Barry	212-726-6000	R	100	0.3
Warner/Chappell Music Inc.	PO Box 4340	Hialeah	FL	33014		305-620-1500	S	100	0.3
World Book Educational Products	233 N Michigan	Chicago	IL	60601	Robert C Martin	312-258-3700	S	100	0.2
NTC/Contemporary Publishing	PO Box 73437	Chicago	IL	60673		847-679-5500	S	96*	0.4
Curtis Publishing Co.	1000 Waterway	Indianapolis	IN	46202	Burt Servaas	317-636-1000	R	92*	0.6
McDougal Littell Inc.	P O Box 1667	Evanston	IL	60204	Julie McGee	847-869-2300	D	86*	0.3
Brooks/Cole Publishing Co.	511 Forest	Pacific Grove	CA	93950	Geoffrey Burn	408-373-0728	S	85	0.1
United Methodist Publishing	PO Box 801	Nashville	TN	37202	Neil Alexander	615-749-6000	R	85*	0.3
Kumho U.S.A. Inc.	14605 Miller Ave	Fontana	CA	92336	Jong G Kahng	909-428-3999	N	83	<0.1
Delmar Publishers	3 Columbia Cir	Albany	NY	12203		518-464-3500	S	82	0.3

Source: Ward's Business Directory of U.S. Private and Public Companies, Volumes 1 and 2, 2000. The company type code used is as follows: P - Public, R - Private, S - Subsidiary, D - Division, J - Joint Venture, A - Affiliate, G - Group, N - Company type not reported. Sales are in millions of dollars, employees are in thousands. An asterisk (*) indicates an estimated sales volume. The symbol < stands for 'less than'. Company names and addresses are truncated, in some cases, to fit into the available space.

3 1833 03836 4409

LOCATION BY STATE AND REGIONAL CONCENTRATION

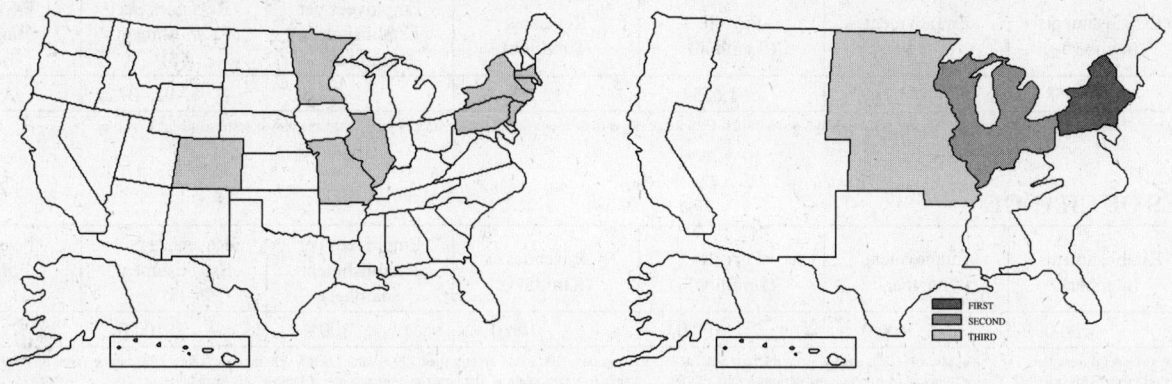

FIRST
SECOND
THIRD

INDUSTRY DATA BY STATE

State	Establishments		Employment			Payroll		Revenues		
	Total (number)	% of U.S.	Total (number)	% of U.S.	Per Estab.	Total ($ mil.)	Per Empl. ($)	Total ($ mil.)	% of U.S.	Per Estab. ($)
New York	329	12.3	18,992	21.1	58	969.1	51,029	7,348.0	32.4	22,334,401
California	380	14.2	7,500	8.3	20	306.4	40,851	1,769.4	7.8	4,656,205
Illinois	148	5.5	5,717	6.4	39	225.0	39,352	1,618.6	7.1	10,936,216
Missouri	47	1.8	4,833	5.4	103	136.7	28,283	1,378.8	6.1	29,335,702
Massachusetts	115	4.3	6,267	7.0	54	265.4	42,347	1,354.7	6.0	11,780,104
New Jersey	97	3.6	4,956	5.5	51	235.9	47,607	1,275.6	5.6	13,150,588
Minnesota	61	2.3	7,627	8.5	125	319.1	41,839	1,091.4	4.8	17,892,295
Pennsylvania	80	3.0	4,165	4.6	52	157.7	37,853	1,083.3	4.8	13,541,100
Texas	141	5.3	4,970	5.5	35	163.8	32,957	900.9	4.0	6,389,433
Ohio	68	2.5	3,184	3.5	47	127.9	40,177	579.7	2.6	8,525,618
Florida	102	3.8	1,937	2.2	19	75.5	39,003	463.0	2.0	4,538,902
Indiana	34	1.3	1,716	1.9	50	68.4	39,856	424.5	1.9	12,485,265
Colorado	69	2.6	2,346	2.6	34	80.8	34,461	345.2	1.5	5,002,638
Connecticut	72	2.7	1,233	1.4	17	50.4	40,895	323.8	1.4	4,497,569
Michigan	62	2.3	1,140	1.3	18	38.7	33,974	304.8	1.3	4,916,452
Wisconsin	41	1.5	1,039	1.2	25	32.3	31,076	246.1	1.1	6,001,780
Tennessee	43	1.6	1,206	1.3	28	34.4	28,551	245.0	1.1	5,698,767
North Carolina	70	2.6	1,058	1.2	15	32.8	30,995	187.7	0.8	2,681,986
Virginia	54	2.0	1,364	1.5	25	43.5	31,910	181.9	0.8	3,367,741
Iowa	22	0.8	1,069	1.2	49	37.0	34,628	153.5	0.7	6,979,136
Washington	81	3.0	578	0.6	7	19.0	32,810	107.5	0.5	1,327,630
Oregon	48	1.8	556	0.6	12	17.7	31,912	107.0	0.5	2,228,312
Georgia	39	1.5	495	0.6	13	14.2	28,598	91.9	0.4	2,357,615
Oklahoma	24	0.9	405	0.5	17	13.7	33,862	74.8	0.3	3,115,833
Kentucky	18	0.7	413	0.5	23	12.6	30,416	74.8	0.3	4,153,389
D.C.	18	0.7	168	0.2	9	6.2	36,976	46.0	0.2	2,555,278
Arizona	61	2.3	360	0.4	6	12.4	34,533	35.1	0.2	576,148
Idaho	10	0.4	363	0.4	36	11.9	32,747	33.6	0.1	3,358,800
Utah	34	1.3	182	0.2	5	5.6	30,648	31.0	0.1	910,588
New Hampshire	20	0.7	163	0.2	8	5.1	31,509	29.7	0.1	1,486,450
Nebraska	9	0.3	255	0.3	28	7.1	27,804	24.4	0.1	2,713,778
Vermont	20	0.7	135	0.2	7	4.4	32,948	20.7	0.1	1,033,900
New Mexico	24	0.9	158	0.2	7	4.9	30,791	17.2	0.1	716,917
Maine	25	0.9	135	0.2	5	3.7	27,185	17.0	0.1	680,520
Louisiana	13	0.5	189	0.2	15	3.3	17,704	16.8	0.1	1,294,615
Nevada	14	0.5	91	0.1	7	3.7	40,681	16.0	0.1	1,141,357
South Carolina	15	0.6	84	0.1	6	1.8	21,893	10.2	0.0	680,600
West Virginia	4	0.1	13	0.0	3	0.3	19,385	1.5	0.0	384,250
South Dakota	3	0.1	7	0.0	2	0.1	18,286	0.8	0.0	260,000
Maryland	54	2.0	1,750*	-	-	(D)	-	(D)	-	-
Kansas	25	0.9	175*	-	-	(D)	-	(D)	-	-
Alabama	22	0.8	375*	-	-	(D)	-	(D)	-	-
Arkansas	18	0.7	375*	-	-	(D)	-	(D)	-	-
Hawaii	10	0.4	60*	-	-	(D)	-	(D)	-	-
Montana	8	0.3	60*	-	-	(D)	-	(D)	-	-
Alaska	7	0.3	60*	-	-	(D)	-	(D)	-	-
Wyoming	7	0.3	60*	-	-	(D)	-	(D)	-	-
Mississippi	6	0.2	60*	-	-	(D)	-	(D)	-	-
Rhode Island	6	0.2	10*	-	-	(D)	-	(D)	-	-
Delaware	5	0.2	10*	-	-	(D)	-	(D)	-	-
North Dakota	1	-	10*	-	-	(D)	-	(D)	-	-

Source: 1997 Economic Census. The states are in descending order of revenues or establishments (if revenue data are missing for the majority). The symbol (D) appears when data are withheld to prevent disclosure of competitive information. States marked with (D) are sorted by number of establishments. A dash (-) indicates that the data element cannot be calculated. * indicates the midpoint of a range; 175, for example is the range 100-249. Shaded *states* on the state map indicate those states which have proportionately greater representation in the industry than would be indicated by the state's population; the ratio is based on total revenues or number of establishments. Shaded *regions* indicate where the industry is regionally most concentrated.

NAICS 511140 - DATABASE AND DIRECTORY PUBLISHERS

GENERAL STATISTICS

Year	Establishments (number)	Employment (number)	Payroll ($ million)	Revenues ($ million)	Employees per Establishment (number)	Revenues per Establishment ($)	Payroll per Employee ($)
1997	1,458	43,115	1,655.0	12,258.0	29.6	8,407,407	38,386

Source: *Economic Census of the United States*, 1997. This is a newly defined industry. Data for prior years were unavailable at the time of publication but may become available over time.

INDICES OF CHANGE

Year	Establishments (number)	Employment (number)	Payroll ($ million)	Revenues ($ million)	Employees per Establishment (number)	Revenues per Establishment ($)	Payroll per Employee ($)
1997	100.0	100.0	100.0	100.0	100.0	100.0	100.0

Sources: Same as General Statistics. The values shown reflect change from the base year, 1997. Values above 100 mean greater than 1997, values below 100 mean less than 1997, and a value of 100 in the 1982-96 or 1998-2001 period means same as 1997. Values followed by a 'p' are projections by the editors; 'e' stands for extrapolation. Data are the most recent available at this level of detail.

SIC INDUSTRIES RELATED TO NAICS 511140

Each new NAICS code represents an industry that used to be part of an SIC or a part of several SIC industries. Data in this table are shown to provide transitional information for these cases. All available data for the precursor SIC(s) are shown. Even if only a part of an SIC is included in the NAICS, *all* data for the SIC are reproduced. If the SIC industry is not marked as being a part (pt) of the NAICS, the entire industry is embedded in the NAICS data. The SIC composition of the new industry provides some hints of the relative importance of its "ancestors." Data marked with a 'p' are projected. Projections begin with 1982 data. Data earlier than 1990 are not shown but are reflected in the projections.

SIC	Industry	1990	1991	1992	1993	1994	1995	1996	1997
2741	**Miscellaneous Publishing (pt)**								
	Establishments (number)	-	-	3,390	-	-	-	-	-
	Employment (thousands)	65.2	65.0	65.4	66.6	71.2	67.4	68.8	-
	Value of Shipments ($ million)	8,874.7	9,762.0	10,977.1	11,806.6	12,332.4	11,992.1	12,510.5	14,309.8p
7331	**Direct Mail Advertising Services (pt)**								
	Establishments (number)	3,503	3,662	3,878	3,981	4,060	4,124	4,403p	4,543p
	Employment (thousands)	84.1	84.4	79.1	84.1	82.3	87.9	96.0p	98.9p
	Revenues ($ million)	6,956.0	6,546.0	6,805.0	7,346.0	7,312.0	7,532.0	8,198.0	8,550.4p

Source: *Economic Census of the United States*, 1992, annual surveys of economic sectors conducted by the Bureau of the Census, and estimates or projections based on the 1982-1992 period; not all data are shown. 'e' marks estimates made by the editors; 'p' indicates projections based on time series. A dash (-) indicates that data for this SIC or year were not available. The abbreviation (pt) next to the industry name indicates that only a part of the industry is present within the NAICS data. If no (pt) is shown, the entire industry is contained within the NAICS data.

SELECTED RATIOS

For 1997	Avg. of Information	Analyzed Industry	Index	For 1997	Avg. of Information	Analyzed Industry	Index
Employees per establishment	27	30	110	Payroll per establishment	1,131,090	1,135,117	100
Revenue per establishment	5,444,104	8,407,407	154	Payroll as % of revenue	21	14	65
Revenue per employee	203,255	284,309	140	Payroll per employee	42,229	38,386	91

Sources: Same as General Statistics. The 'Average' column represents the average for the industry sector, in 1997, where the currently shown industry is classified. The Index shows the relationship between the Average and the Analyzed Industry. For example, 100 means that they are equal; 500 that the Analyzed Industry is five times the average; 50 means that the Analyzed Industry is half the national average. The abbreviation 'na' is used to show that data are 'not available'.

LEADING COMPANIES   Number shown: **4**   Total sales ($ mil): **20**   Total employment (000): **0.1**

Company Name	Address				CEO Name	Phone	Co. Type	Sales ($ mil)	Empl. (000)
Promotional Products Assn Intl	3125 Skyway Cir N	Irving	TX	75038	G. Stephen Slagle	972-252-0404	R	12	<0.1
Ross, Norman Publishing Inc.	330 W 58th St	New York	NY	10019	Norman A Ross	212-765-8200	R	4*	<0.1
Offshore Data Services Inc.	PO Box 19909	Houston	TX	77224	Loran R Sheffer	713-781-2713	R	3	<0.1
The Rosenbaum Group Inc.	3107 Rolling Rd	Chevy Chase	MD	20815		301-654-1988	N	1	<0.1

Source: *Ward's Business Directory of U.S. Private and Public Companies*, Volumes 1 and 2, 2000. The company type code used is as follows: P - Public, R - Private, S - Subsidiary, D - Division, J - Joint Venture, A - Affiliate, G - Group, N - Company type not reported. Sales are in millions of dollars, employees are in thousands. An asterisk (*) indicates an estimated sales volume. The symbol < stands for 'less than'. Company names and addresses are truncated, in some cases, to fit into the available space.

LOCATION BY STATE AND REGIONAL CONCENTRATION

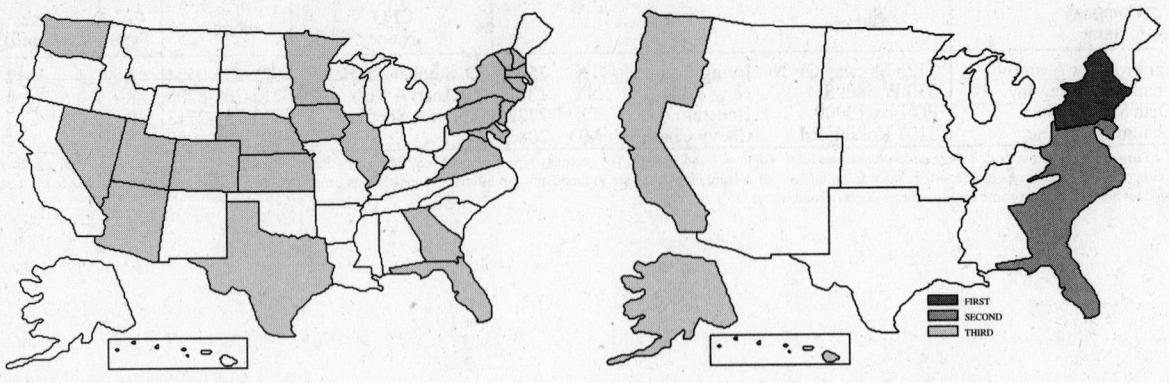

FIRST
SECOND
THIRD

INDUSTRY DATA BY STATE

State	Establishments Total (number)	% of U.S.	Employment Total (number)	% of U.S.	Per Estab.	Payroll Total ($ mil.)	Per Empl. ($)	Revenues Total ($ mil.)	% of U.S.	Per Estab. ($)
California	173	11.9	3,553	8.2	21	142.4	40,077	1,556.9	12.7	8,999,434
New York	140	9.6	3,712	8.6	27	162.3	43,734	909.8	7.4	6,498,507
Illinois	80	5.5	1,842	4.3	23	80.0	43,409	741.4	6.0	9,267,950
Ohio	51	3.5	4,717	10.9	92	179.2	37,995	726.8	5.9	14,250,569
New Jersey	71	4.9	3,175	7.4	45	135.5	42,681	585.6	4.8	8,247,746
Colorado	48	3.3	1,623	3.8	34	73.5	45,281	490.7	4.0	10,222,792
Nebraska	12	0.8	2,727	6.3	227	78.4	28,758	393.9	3.2	32,827,917
Washington	33	2.3	457	1.1	14	13.6	29,713	264.5	2.2	8,013,727
Pennsylvania	73	5.0	1,723	4.0	24	66.5	38,601	249.0	2.0	3,410,849
Texas	104	7.1	1,679	3.9	16	62.3	37,130	230.8	1.9	2,219,490
Maryland	38	2.6	1,112	2.6	29	51.1	45,952	193.8	1.6	5,100,000
Florida	96	6.6	1,392	3.2	15	44.0	31,612	190.7	1.6	1,986,510
Minnesota	32	2.2	492	1.1	15	20.4	41,510	187.1	1.5	5,845,438
Connecticut	37	2.5	752	1.7	20	26.3	34,910	162.6	1.3	4,393,514
Iowa	19	1.3	1,481	3.4	78	40.2	27,151	149.7	1.2	7,877,421
Georgia	39	2.7	556	1.3	14	15.8	28,385	77.6	0.6	1,988,667
Wisconsin	17	1.2	672	1.6	40	18.2	27,106	72.1	0.6	4,242,824
Utah	13	0.9	575	1.3	44	11.1	19,243	69.9	0.6	5,376,462
Vermont	6	0.4	817	1.9	136	20.3	24,878	66.3	0.5	11,051,667
Tennessee	16	1.1	416	1.0	26	13.8	33,243	39.9	0.3	2,492,750
Indiana	18	1.2	448	1.0	25	16.7	37,297	38.5	0.3	2,139,500
Louisiana	9	0.6	140	0.3	16	3.7	26,550	9.5	0.1	1,050,333
Maine	6	0.4	30	0.1	5	0.7	22,300	2.8	0.0	473,833
Alabama	8	0.5	32	0.1	4	0.7	20,906	2.0	0.0	253,000
Virginia	52	3.6	1,750*	-	-	(D)	-	(D)	-	-
Massachusetts	42	2.9	1,750*	-	-	(D)	-	(D)	-	-
Arizona	31	2.1	750*	-	-	(D)	-	(D)	-	-
Michigan	27	1.9	1,750*	-	-	(D)	-	(D)	-	-
Missouri	23	1.6	750*	-	-	(D)	-	(D)	-	-
Kansas	17	1.2	1,750*	-	-	(D)	-	(D)	-	-
North Carolina	17	1.2	175*	-	-	(D)	-	(D)	-	-
D.C.	14	1.0	175*	-	-	(D)	-	(D)	-	-
Oregon	13	0.9	375*	-	-	(D)	-	(D)	-	-
Nevada	12	0.8	60*	-	-	(D)	-	(D)	-	-
Kentucky	9	0.6	60*	-	-	(D)	-	(D)	-	-
New Hampshire	9	0.6	175*	-	-	(D)	-	(D)	-	-
South Carolina	9	0.6	60*	-	-	(D)	-	(D)	-	-
Arkansas	8	0.5	60*	-	-	(D)	-	(D)	-	-
Oklahoma	8	0.5	60*	-	-	(D)	-	(D)	-	-
New Mexico	5	0.3	10*	-	-	(D)	-	(D)	-	-
Mississippi	4	0.3	60*	-	-	(D)	-	(D)	-	-
West Virginia	4	0.3	60*	-	-	(D)	-	(D)	-	-
Idaho	3	0.2	60*	-	-	(D)	-	(D)	-	-
North Dakota	3	0.2	10*	-	-	(D)	-	(D)	-	-
South Dakota	3	0.2	10*	-	-	(D)	-	(D)	-	-
Montana	2	0.1	10*	-	-	(D)	-	(D)	-	-
Rhode Island	2	0.1	10*	-	-	(D)	-	(D)	-	-
Alaska	1	0.1	10*	-	-	(D)	-	(D)	-	-
Hawaii	1	0.1	10*	-	-	(D)	-	(D)	-	-

Source: 1997 *Economic Census*. The states are in descending order of revenues or establishments (if revenue data are missing for the majority). The symbol (D) appears when data are withheld to prevent disclosure of competitive information. States marked with (D) are sorted by number of establishments. A dash (-) indicates that the data element cannot be calculated. * indicates the midpoint of a range; 175, for example is the range 100-249. Shaded *states* on the state map indicate those states which have proportionately greater representation in the industry than would be indicated by the state's population; the ratio is based on total revenues or number of establishments. Shaded *regions* indicate where the industry is regionally most concentrated.

NAICS 511191 - GREETING CARD PUBLISHERS

GENERAL STATISTICS

Year	Establishments (number)	Employment (number)	Payroll ($ million)	Revenues ($ million)	Employees per Establishment (number)	Revenues per Establishment ($)	Payroll per Employee ($)
1997	106	20,518	628.0	5,339.0	193.6	50,367,925	30,607

Source: Economic Census of the United States, 1997. This is a newly defined industry. Data for prior years were unavailable at the time of publication but may become available over time.

INDICES OF CHANGE

Year	Establishments (number)	Employment (number)	Payroll ($ million)	Revenues ($ million)	Employees per Establishment (number)	Revenues per Establishment ($)	Payroll per Employee ($)
1997	100.0	100.0	100.0	100.0	100.0	100.0	100.0

Sources: Same as General Statistics. The values shown reflect change from the base year, 1997. Values above 100 mean greater than 1997, values below 100 mean less than 1997, and a value of 100 in the 1982-96 or 1998-2001 period means same as 1997. Values followed by a 'p' are projections by the editors; 'e' stands for extrapolation. Data are the most recent available at this level of detail.

SIC INDUSTRIES RELATED TO NAICS 511191

Each new NAICS code represents an industry that used to be part of an SIC or a part of several SIC industries. Data in this table are shown to provide transitional information for these cases. All available data for the precursor SIC(s) are shown. Even if only a part of an SIC is included in the NAICS, *all* data for the SIC are reproduced. If the SIC industry is not marked as being a part (pt) of the NAICS, the entire industry is embedded in the NAICS data. The SIC composition of the new industry provides some hints of the relative importance of its "ancestors." Data marked with a 'p' are projected. Projections begin with 1982 data. Data earlier than 1990 are not shown but are reflected in the projections.

SIC	Industry	1990	1991	1992	1993	1994	1995	1996	1997
2771	**Greeting Cards**								
	Establishments (number)	-	-	173	-	-	-	-	-
	Employment (thousands)	24.6	23.9	22.8	22.2	23.2	23.0	21.4	-
	Value of Shipments ($ million) . . .	3,720.7	3,809.9	4,195.6	4,274.5	4,507.2	4,726.4	5,010.9	5,174.4p

Source: Economic Census of the United States, 1992, annual surveys of economic sectors conducted by the Bureau of the Census, and estimates or projections based on the 1982-1992 period; not all data are shown. 'e' marks estimates made by the editors; 'p' indicates projections based on time series. A dash (-) indicates that data for this SIC or year were not available. The abbreviation (pt) next to the industry name indicates that only a part of the industry is present within the NAICS data. If no (pt) is shown, the entire industry is contained within the NAICS data.

SELECTED RATIOS

For 1997	Avg. of Information	Analyzed Industry	Index	For 1997	Avg. of Information	Analyzed Industry	Index
Employees per establishment	27	194	723	Payroll per establishment	1,131,090	5,924,528	524
Revenue per establishment	5,444,104	50,367,925	925	Payroll as % of revenue	21	12	57
Revenue per employee	203,255	260,211	128	Payroll per employee	42,229	30,607	72

Sources: Same as General Statistics. The 'Average' column represents the average for the industry sector, in 1997, where the currently shown industry is classified. The Index shows the relationship between the Average and the Analyzed Industry. For example, 100 means that they are equal; 500 that the Analyzed Industry is five times the average; 50 means that the Analyzed Industry is half the national average. The abbreviation 'na' is used to show that data are 'not available'.

LEADING COMPANIES
No company data available for this industry.

LOCATION BY STATE AND REGIONAL CONCENTRATION

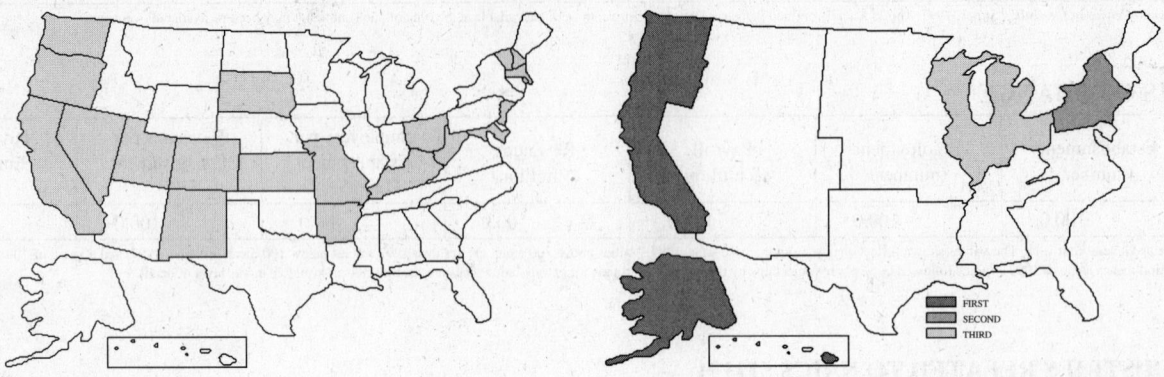

FIRST
SECOND
THIRD

INDUSTRY DATA BY STATE

State	Establishments		Employment			Payroll		Revenues		
	Total (number)	% of U.S.	Total (number)	% of U.S.	Per Estab.	Total ($ mil.)	Per Empl. ($)	Total ($ mil.)	% of U.S.	Per Estab. ($)
Illinois	3	2.8	676	3.3	225	28.2	41,765	118.1	2.2	39,356,333
Pennsylvania	4	3.8	627	3.1	157	12.9	20,646	88.8	1.7	22,204,250
California	13	12.3	231	1.1	18	8.6	37,325	55.7	1.0	4,282,462
New York	7	6.6	111	0.5	16	2.3	20,414	12.8	0.2	1,824,571
Oregon	6	5.7	12	0.1	2	0.3	23,417	1.6	0.0	273,833
Missouri	6	5.7	7,500*	-	-	(D)	-	(D)	-	-
Colorado	5	4.7	375*	-	-	(D)	-	(D)	-	-
Ohio	5	4.7	750*	-	-	(D)	-	(D)	-	-
Washington	5	4.7	10*	-	-	(D)	-	(D)	-	-
Arkansas	4	3.8	3,750*	-	-	(D)	-	(D)	-	-
Kentucky	4	3.8	3,750*	-	-	(D)	-	(D)	-	-
Maryland	4	3.8	175*	-	-	(D)	-	(D)	-	-
Massachusetts	4	3.8	60*	-	-	(D)	-	(D)	-	-
New Jersey	4	3.8	375*	-	-	(D)	-	(D)	-	-
Kansas	3	2.8	3,750*	-	-	(D)	-	(D)	-	-
Michigan	3	2.8	175*	-	-	(D)	-	(D)	-	-
New Hampshire	3	2.8	375*	-	-	(D)	-	(D)	-	-
Florida	2	1.9	60*	-	-	(D)	-	(D)	-	-
Indiana	2	1.9	750*	-	-	(D)	-	(D)	-	-
North Carolina	2	1.9	60*	-	-	(D)	-	(D)	-	-
Utah	2	1.9	60*	-	-	(D)	-	(D)	-	-
Vermont	2	1.9	10*	-	-	(D)	-	(D)	-	-
Georgia	1	0.9	375*	-	-	(D)	-	(D)	-	-
Minnesota	1	0.9	10*	-	-	(D)	-	(D)	-	-
Nevada	1	0.9	10*	-	-	(D)	-	(D)	-	-
New Mexico	1	0.9	10*	-	-	(D)	-	(D)	-	-
Oklahoma	1	0.9	10*	-	-	(D)	-	(D)	-	-
Rhode Island	1	0.9	375*	-	-	(D)	-	(D)	-	-
South Carolina	1	0.9	10*	-	-	(D)	-	(D)	-	-
South Dakota	1	0.9	10*	-	-	(D)	-	(D)	-	-
Tennessee	1	0.9	175*	-	-	(D)	-	(D)	-	-
Texas	1	0.9	175*	-	-	(D)	-	(D)	-	-
Virginia	1	0.9	10*	-	-	(D)	-	(D)	-	-
West Virginia	1	0.9	10*	-	-	(D)	-	(D)	-	-
Wisconsin	1	0.9	10*	-	-	(D)	-	(D)	-	-

Source: 1997 *Economic Census*. The states are in descending order of revenues or establishments (if revenue data are missing for the majority). The symbol (D) appears when data are withheld to prevent disclosure of competitive information. States marked with (D) are sorted by number of establishments. A dash (-) indicates that the data element cannot be calculated. * indicates the midpoint of a range; 175, for example is the range 100-249. Shaded *states* on the state map indicate those states which have proportionately greater representation in the industry than would be indicated by the state's population; the ratio is based on total revenues or number of establishments. Shaded *regions* indicate where the industry is regionally most concentrated.

NAICS 511199 - PUBLISHERS NEC

GENERAL STATISTICS

Year	Establishments (number)	Employment (number)	Payroll ($ million)	Revenues ($ million)	Employees per Establishment (number)	Revenues per Establishment ($)	Payroll per Employee ($)
1997	2,502	45,398	1,263.0	5,605.0	18.1	2,240,208	27,821

Source: Economic Census of the United States, 1997. This is a newly defined industry. Data for prior years were unavailable at the time of publication but may become available over time.

INDICES OF CHANGE

Year	Establishments (number)	Employment (number)	Payroll ($ million)	Revenues ($ million)	Employees per Establishment (number)	Revenues per Establishment ($)	Payroll per Employee ($)
1997	100.0	100.0	100.0	100.0	100.0	100.0	100.0

Sources: Same as General Statistics. The values shown reflect change from the base year, 1997. Values above 100 mean greater than 1997, values below 100 mean less than 1997, and a value of 100 in the 1982-96 or 1998-2001 period means same as 1997. Values followed by a 'p' are projections by the editors; 'e' stands for extrapolation. Data are the most recent available at this level of detail.

SIC INDUSTRIES RELATED TO NAICS 511199

Each new NAICS code represents an industry that used to be part of an SIC or a part of several SIC industries. Data in this table are shown to provide transitional information for these cases. All available data for the precursor SIC(s) are shown. Even if only a part of an SIC is included in the NAICS, *all* data for the SIC are reproduced. If the SIC industry is not marked as being a part (pt) of the NAICS, the entire industry is embedded in the NAICS data. The SIC composition of the new industry provides some hints of the relative importance of its "ancestors." Data marked with a 'p' are projected. Projections begin with 1982 data. Data earlier than 1990 are not shown but are reflected in the projections.

SIC	Industry	1990	1991	1992	1993	1994	1995	1996	1997
2741	**Miscellaneous Publishing (pt)**								
	Establishments (number)	-	-	3,390	-	-	-	-	-
	Employment (thousands)	65.2	65.0	65.4	66.6	71.2	67.4	68.8	-
	Value of Shipments ($ million)	8,874.7	9,762.0	10,977.1	11,806.6	12,332.4	11,992.1	12,510.5	14,309.8p

Source: Economic Census of the United States, 1992, annual surveys of economic sectors conducted by the Bureau of the Census, and estimates or projections based on the 1982-1992 period; not all data are shown. 'e' marks estimates made by the editors; 'p' indicates projections based on time series. A dash (-) indicates that data for this SIC or year were not available. The abbreviation (pt) next to the industry name indicates that only a part of the industry is present within the NAICS data. If no (pt) is shown, the entire industry is contained within the NAICS data.

SELECTED RATIOS

For 1997	Avg. of Information	Analyzed Industry	Index	For 1997	Avg. of Information	Analyzed Industry	Index
Employees per establishment	27	18	68	Payroll per establishment	1,131,090	504,796	45
Revenue per establishment	5,444,104	2,240,208	41	Payroll as % of revenue	21	23	108
Revenue per employee	203,255	123,464	61	Payroll per employee	42,229	27,821	66

Sources: Same as General Statistics. The 'Average' column represents the average for the industry sector, in 1997, where the currently shown industry is classified. The Index shows the relationship between the Average and the Analyzed Industry. For example, 100 means that they are equal; 500 that the Analyzed Industry is five times the average; 50 means that the Analyzed Industry is half the national average. The abbreviation 'na' is used to show that data are 'not available'.

LEADING COMPANIES Number shown: **75** Total sales ($ mil): **82,392** Total employment (000): **332.6**

Company Name	Address				CEO Name	Phone	Co. Type	Sales ($ mil)	Empl. (000)
SBC Communications Inc.	175 E Houston	San Antonio	TX	78205	Royce Caldell	210-821-4105	P	49,489	129.9
Pacific Bell	140 N Montgomery	San Francisco	CA	94105	Edward A Mueller	415-542-9000	S	9,406	46.4
R.R. Donnelley and Sons Co.	77 W Wacker Dr	Chicago	IL	60601	William Davis	312-326-8000	P	5,183	36.3
Quebecor World (USA) Inc.	340 Pemberwick Rd	Greenwich	CT	06831	Robert Burton	203-532-4200	P	2,357	16.0
THI Holdings Corp.	1 Station Pl	Stamford	CT	06902	Richard J Harrington	203-969-8700	S	1,939*	12.0
PRIMEDIA Inc.	745 5th Ave	New York	NY	10151	C McCurdy	212-745-0100	P	1,531	6.3
Ziff Communications Co.	1 Park Ave	New York	NY	10016		212-503-3500	P	1,109	2.9
Harcourt Brace and Co.	6277 Sea Harbor Dr	Orlando	FL	32821	Brian Knez	407-345-2000	S	998*	5.0
Cahners Business Information	275 Washington St	Newton	MA	02158	Bruce A Barnet	617-558-4249	S	875*	5.7
Jostens Inc.	5501 Norman Center	Minneapolis	MN	55437	Robert C Buhrmaster	612-830-3300	P	782	6.8
R.L. Polk and Co.	26955 Northwestern	Southfield	MI	48034	Arthur Olsen	248-728-7111	R	756*	6.0
Stream International Holdings Inc.	85 Dan Rd	Canton	MA	02021	Stephen DR Moore	781-575-6800	S	609*	6.0
EMI Music	1290 Av Americas	New York	NY	10104	Jim Fifield	212-261-3000	S	540	3.0
Merrill Corp.	1 Merrill Cir	Saint Paul	MN	55108	John W Castro	651-646-4501	R	510	3.4
Thomson Information Inc.	1 Station Pl	Stamford	CT	06902	Patrick J Tierney	203-969-8700	R	495*	2.8
Brooke Group Ltd.	100 SE 2nd St	Miami	FL	33131	Bennett LeBow	305-579-8000	P	446	2.1
Cadmus Communications Corp.	PO Box 27367	Richmond	VA	23261	C Gillispie	804-287-5680	P	443	4.1
Berlitz International Inc.	400 Alexander Park	Princeton	NJ	08540	Hiromasa Yokoi	609-514-9650	P	437	6.0
Moody's Investors Service Inc.	99 Church St	New York	NY	10007	John Rutherfurd	212-553-0300	S	430	1.5
McGraw-Hill Higher Education	1333 Burr Ridge	Burr Ridge	IL	60521	Edward H Stanford	630-789-4000	S	385	1.0
infoUSA Inc.	5711 S 86th Cir	Omaha	NE	68127	Vinod Gupta	402-593-4500	P	266	2.0
Devon Group Inc.	450 Park Ave	New York	NY	10022	Marne Obernauer Jr	203-964-1444	S	264	2.2
Stevens Graphics Inc.	713 Abernathy SW	Atlanta	GA	30310		404-752-0543	S	208	0.8
Ziff-Davis Publishing Co.	1 Park Ave	New York	NY	10016		212-503-3500	R	191*	1.1
Gray Communications Systems	PO Box 48	Albany	GA	31702	T Mack Robinson	404-504-9828	P	129	1.2
Zondervan Corp.	5300 Patterson SE	Grand Rapids	MI	49512	Bruce Ryskamp	616-698-6900	S	125	0.3
Research Institute of America	395 Hudson St	New York	NY	10014	Euan Menzies	212-367-6300	S	120*	1.0
Simplicity Holdings Inc.	2 Park Ave	New York	NY	10016	Louis R Morris	212-372-0500	R	120*	1.0
Butterick Company Inc.	161 6th Ave	New York	NY	10013		212-620-2500	R	113*	0.9
J.J. Keller and Associates Inc.	PO Box 368	Neenah	WI	54957	John Keller	920-722-2848	R	100	0.8
Taylor Publishing Co.	PO Box 597	Dallas	TX	75221		214-637-2800	S	100*	2.0
Thomas Publishing Co.	5 Penn Plz	New York	NY	10001		212-695-0500	R	100	0.5
Aegis Communications Group Inc.	7880 Bent Branch	Irving	TX	75063	Stephen A McNeely	972-830-1800	P	92	4.1
Elsevier Science Inc	655 of the Americas	New York	NY	10010	Russell White	212-633-3971	D	90*	0.5
Scott-Levin Associates Inc.	60 Blacksmith Rd	Newtown	PA	18940	Larry Levin	215-860-0440	S	81*	0.3
Add Inc.	PO Box 609	Waupaca	WI	54981	Steve Huhta	715-258-8450	S	80*	1.2
CYGNUS PUBLISHING	PO Box 803	Fort Atkinson	WI	53538		920-563-6388	S	80	0.5
Hal Leonard Corp.	7777 W Bluemound	Milwaukee	WI	53213	Keith Mardak	414-774-3630	R	80*	0.3
Provident Music Group	741 Cool Sprgs Blvd	Franklin	TN	37067	James Van Hook	615-261-6500	S	80	0.3
Illinois Consolidated Telephone	121 S 17th St	Mattoon	IL	61938	Dennis Erickson	217-235-3311	S	78*	0.4
Standard and Poor's	7400 S Alton Ct	Englewood	CO	80112		303-771-6510	D	78*	0.4
Riverside Publishing Co.	425 Spring Lake Dr	Itasca	IL	60143	Beverly Longfellow	630-467-7000	S	69	0.2
Andrews McMeel Universal	PO Box 419150	Kansas City	MO	64141		816-932-6700	R	58*	0.3
Bacon's Information Inc.	PO Box 98869	Chicago	IL	60693		312-922-2400	S	53*	0.4
Leisure Arts Inc.	PO Box 5595	Little Rock	AR	72215		501-868-8800	S	50*	0.4
Cold Spring Harbor Laboratory	P O Box 100	Cld Sprg Hrbr	NY	11724		516-367-8397	R	49	0.6
CRC Press L.L.C.	2000 NW Corporate	Boca Raton	FL	33431	Dennis Buda	561-994-0555	S	46	0.3
Dayton T. Brown Inc.	555 Church St	Bohemia	NY	11716	Dayton Brown	516-589-6300	R	42*	0.4
Cedco Publishing Co.	100 Pelican Way	San Rafael	CA	94901	Charles Ditlefsen	415-458-2000	R	41*	<0.1
Trade Service Corp.	PO Box 85007	San Diego	CA	92186	James Simpson	619-457-5920	R	41	0.4
DeLorme Publishing Inc.	2 Delorme Dr	Yarmouth	ME	04096	Dale Akeley	207-846-7000	R	40*	0.3
Logistic Services International Inc.	6200 Lake Gray	Jacksonville	FL	32244	James McKinney	904-771-2100	R	40	0.3
Business and Legal Reports Inc.	PO Box 1513	Madison	CT	06443	Robert Brady	203-245-7448	R	38	0.2
Wave Technologies Intern. Inc.	10845 Olive Street	St. Louis	MO	63141	Kenneth W Kousky	314-995-5767	P	37	0.2
Automated Graphic Systems Inc.	4590 Graphics Dr	White Plains	MD	20695			R	35	0.3
Map Quest.com Inc.	PO Box 601	Mountville	PA	17554	Michael J Mulligan	717-285-8500	P	34	0.3
PhotoDisc Inc.	2013 Fourth Ave	Seattle	WA	98121	Sally Von Bargen	206-441-9355	R	32*	0.2
Age Wave Communications Corp.	2000 Powell St	Emeryville	CA	94608	Mark Mullins	510-652-9099	R	30*	0.2
EBSCO Publishing	P O Box 692	Ipswich	MA	01938		978-356-6500	D	30*	0.3
MathSoft Inc.	101 Main St	Cambridge	MA	02142	Charles J Digate	617-577-1017	P	29	0.2
Fronteer Financial Holdings Ltd.	216 N 23rd St	Bismarck	ND	58501	Fai H Chan	308-860-1700	P	27	0.2
Philip Wood Inc.	PO Box 7123	Berkeley	CA	94707		510-559-1600	R	25*	<0.1
TV Host Inc.	PO Box 1665	Harrisburg	PA	17105		717-657-1700	R	25*	<0.1
National Underwriter Co.	505 Gest St	Cincinnati	OH	45203		513-721-2140	R	23*	0.2
Tarrant Dallas Printing Inc.	3200 W Euless Blvd	Euless	TX	76040		817-571-9966	R	22*	0.2
Thomson Financial Publishing	4709 W Golf Rd	Skokie	IL	60076	Thomas A Eder	847-677-8037	D	22*	0.2
National Journal Group Inc.	1501 M St N W	Washington	DC	20005	John F Sullivan	202-739-8400	S	21	0.2
American Web Inc.	PO Box 16472	Denver	CO	80216	Gary Hansen	303-321-2422	R	20	<0.1
Productivity Inc.	541 NE 20th Ave	Portland	OR	97232	Robert Shoemaker	503-235-0600	P	20	0.1
Grand Rapids Label Co.	2351 Oak Ind Dr NE	Grand Rapids	MI	49505		616-459-8134	R	19*	0.1
Gospel Light Publications	PO Box 3875	Ventura	CA	93006	Bill Greig	805-644-9721	R	18	0.2
Corbis Corp.	15395 S E 30th Pl	Bellevue	WA	98007		425-641-4505	R	17*	0.2
Pantone Inc.	590 Commerce Blvd	Carlstadt	NJ	07072	Lawrence Herbert	201-935-5500	R	17*	0.1
FDC Reports Inc.	5550 Friendship	Chevy Chase	MD	20815		301-657-9830	S	14	0.1
Consulting Psychologists Press	PO Box 10096	Palo Alto	CA	94303		650-969-8901	R	14*	0.1

Source: Ward's Business Directory of U.S. Private and Public Companies, Volumes 1 and 2, 2000. The company type code used is as follows: P - Public, R - Private, S - Subsidiary, D - Division, J - Joint Venture, A - Affiliate, G - Group, N - Company type not reported. Sales are in millions of dollars, employees are in thousands. An asterisk (*) indicates an estimated sales volume. The symbol < stands for 'less than'. Company names and addresses are truncated, in some cases, to fit into the available space.

LOCATION BY STATE AND REGIONAL CONCENTRATION

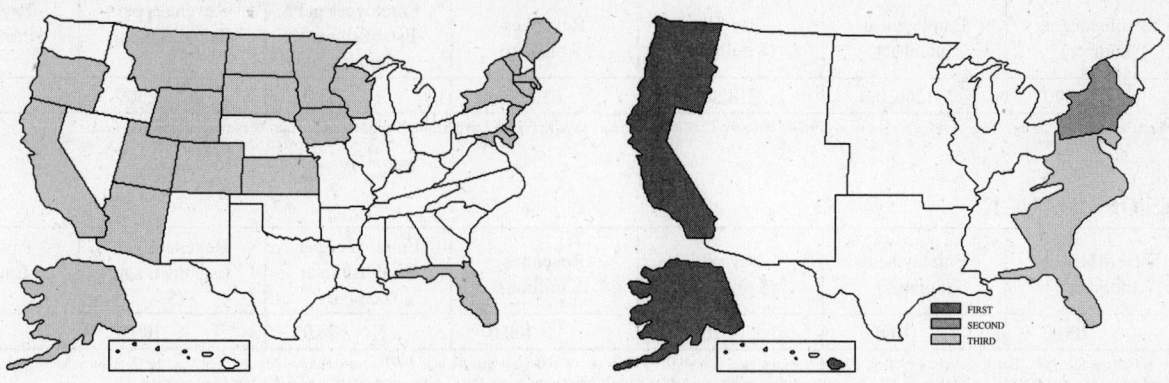

INDUSTRY DATA BY STATE

State	Establishments Total (number)	Establishments % of U.S.	Employment Total (number)	Employment % of U.S.	Employment Per Estab.	Payroll Total ($ mil.)	Payroll Per Empl. ($)	Revenues Total ($ mil.)	Revenues % of U.S.	Revenues Per Estab. ($)
California	350	14.0	5,824	12.8	17	179.6	30,838	729.6	13.0	2,084,503
Pennsylvania	89	3.6	2,901	6.4	33	78.8	27,146	652.8	11.6	7,335,281
New York	258	10.3	5,492	12.1	21	192.7	35,092	631.4	11.3	2,447,318
Illinois	96	3.8	1,530	3.4	16	45.2	29,531	178.0	3.2	1,854,385
Connecticut	40	1.6	812	1.8	20	25.9	31,890	101.9	1.8	2,548,450
Maine	13	0.5	304	0.7	23	10.8	35,454	47.1	0.8	3,623,846
North Carolina	41	1.6	426	0.9	10	11.3	26,423	40.0	0.7	974,415
South Carolina	29	1.2	281	0.6	10	7.7	27,416	33.4	0.6	1,153,241
Louisiana	12	0.5	230	0.5	19	6.3	27,270	20.4	0.4	1,698,667
New Hampshire	10	0.4	85	0.2	9	2.2	25,659	10.0	0.2	1,000,200
Nebraska	11	0.4	127	0.3	12	3.9	30,654	9.6	0.2	868,455
Florida	166	6.6	1,750*	-	-	(D)	-	(D)	-	-
Texas	149	6.0	3,750*	-	-	(D)	-	(D)	-	-
New Jersey	90	3.6	1,750*	-	-	(D)	-	(D)	-	-
Minnesota	77	3.1	750*	-	-	(D)	-	(D)	-	-
Michigan	74	3.0	3,750*	-	-	(D)	-	(D)	-	-
Massachusetts	67	2.7	750*	-	-	(D)	-	(D)	-	-
Wisconsin	67	2.7	1,750*	-	-	(D)	-	(D)	-	-
Colorado	65	2.6	1,750*	-	-	(D)	-	(D)	-	-
Ohio	61	2.4	750*	-	-	(D)	-	(D)	-	-
Virginia	59	2.4	750*	-	-	(D)	-	(D)	-	-
Maryland	52	2.1	1,750*	-	-	(D)	-	(D)	-	-
Washington	49	2.0	750*	-	-	(D)	-	(D)	-	-
Missouri	46	1.8	750*	-	-	(D)	-	(D)	-	-
Georgia	45	1.8	375*	-	-	(D)	-	(D)	-	-
Tennessee	43	1.7	375*	-	-	(D)	-	(D)	-	-
Iowa	42	1.7	750*	-	-	(D)	-	(D)	-	-
Oregon	42	1.7	175*	-	-	(D)	-	(D)	-	-
Arizona	41	1.6	375*	-	-	(D)	-	(D)	-	-
Indiana	39	1.6	375*	-	-	(D)	-	(D)	-	-
Kansas	26	1.0	1,750*	-	-	(D)	-	(D)	-	-
Alabama	24	1.0	750*	-	-	(D)	-	(D)	-	-
D.C.	21	0.8	375*	-	-	(D)	-	(D)	-	-
Kentucky	21	0.8	750*	-	-	(D)	-	(D)	-	-
Utah	20	0.8	375*	-	-	(D)	-	(D)	-	-
Montana	17	0.7	175*	-	-	(D)	-	(D)	-	-
Vermont	17	0.7	175*	-	-	(D)	-	(D)	-	-
New Mexico	15	0.6	175*	-	-	(D)	-	(D)	-	-
Arkansas	12	0.5	175*	-	-	(D)	-	(D)	-	-
Oklahoma	11	0.4	175*	-	-	(D)	-	(D)	-	-
Idaho	10	0.4	175*	-	-	(D)	-	(D)	-	-
Nevada	10	0.4	60*	-	-	(D)	-	(D)	-	-
Rhode Island	10	0.4	175*	-	-	(D)	-	(D)	-	-
South Dakota	10	0.4	175*	-	-	(D)	-	(D)	-	-
West Virginia	10	0.4	60*	-	-	(D)	-	(D)	-	-
Alaska	9	0.4	60*	-	-	(D)	-	(D)	-	-
Mississippi	9	0.4	175*	-	-	(D)	-	(D)	-	-
Delaware	7	0.3	175*	-	-	(D)	-	(D)	-	-
Hawaii	7	0.3	60*	-	-	(D)	-	(D)	-	-
North Dakota	7	0.3	60*	-	-	(D)	-	(D)	-	-
Wyoming	6	0.2	60*	-	-	(D)	-	(D)	-	-

Source: 1997 *Economic Census*. The states are in descending order of revenues or establishments (if revenue data are missing for the majority). The symbol (D) appears when data are withheld to prevent disclosure of competitive information. States marked with (D) are sorted by number of establishments. A dash (-) indicates that the data element cannot be calculated. * indicates the midpoint of a range; 175, for example is the range 100-249. Shaded *states* on the state map indicate those states which have proportionately greater representation in the industry than would be indicated by the state's population; the ratio is based on total revenues or number of establishments. Shaded *regions* indicate where the industry is regionally most concentrated.

NAICS 511210 - SOFTWARE PUBLISHERS

GENERAL STATISTICS

Year	Establishments (number)	Employment (number)	Payroll ($ million)	Revenues ($ million)	Employees per Establishment (number)	Revenues per Establishment ($)	Payroll per Employee ($)
1997	12,090	266,380	18,387.0	61,699.0	22.0	5,103,309	69,025

Source: Economic Census of the United States, 1997. This is a newly defined industry. Data for prior years were unavailable at the time of publication but may become available over time.

INDICES OF CHANGE

Year	Establishments (number)	Employment (number)	Payroll ($ million)	Revenues ($ million)	Employees per Establishment (number)	Revenues per Establishment ($)	Payroll per Employee ($)
1997	100.0	100.0	100.0	100.0	100.0	100.0	100.0

Sources: Same as General Statistics. The values shown reflect change from the base year, 1997. Values above 100 mean greater than 1997, values below 100 mean less than 1997, and a value of 100 in the 1982-96 or 1998-2001 period means same as 1997. Values followed by a 'p' are projections by the editors; 'e' stands for extrapolation. Data are the most recent available at this level of detail.

SIC INDUSTRIES RELATED TO NAICS 511210

Each new NAICS code represents an industry that used to be part of an SIC or a part of several SIC industries. Data in this table are shown to provide transitional information for these cases. All available data for the precursor SIC(s) are shown. Even if only a part of an SIC is included in the NAICS, *all* data for the SIC are reproduced. If the SIC industry is not marked as being a part (pt) of the NAICS, the entire industry is embedded in the NAICS data. The SIC composition of the new industry provides some hints of the relative importance of its "ancestors." Data marked with a 'p' are projected. Projections begin with 1982 data. Data earlier than 1990 are not shown but are reflected in the projections.

SIC	Industry	1990	1991	1992	1993	1994	1995	1996	1997
7372	**Prepackaged Software (pt)**								
	Establishments (number)	3,755	3,786	7,108	6,970	6,853	6,991	8,030p	8,622p
	Employment (thousands)	76.3	87.2	131.0	142.4	149.9	162.2	178.8p	193.9p
	Revenues ($ million)	16,523.0	18,306.0	21,236.0	25,188.0	28,864.0	33,249.0	39,325.0	41,230.1p

Source: Economic Census of the United States, 1992, annual surveys of economic sectors conducted by the Bureau of the Census, and estimates or projections based on the 1982-1992 period; not all data are shown. 'e' marks estimates made by the editors; 'p' indicates projections based on time series. A dash (-) indicates that data for this SIC or year were not available. The abbreviation (pt) next to the industry name indicates that only a part of the industry is present within the NAICS data. If no (pt) is shown, the entire industry is contained within the NAICS data.

SELECTED RATIOS

For 1997	Avg. of Information	Analyzed Industry	Index	For 1997	Avg. of Information	Analyzed Industry	Index
Employees per establishment	27	22	82	Payroll per establishment	1,131,090	1,520,844	134
Revenue per establishment	5,444,104	5,103,309	94	Payroll as % of revenue	21	30	143
Revenue per employee	203,255	231,620	114	Payroll per employee	42,229	69,025	163

Sources: Same as General Statistics. The 'Average' column represents the average for the industry sector, in 1997, where the currently shown industry is classified. The Index shows the relationship between the Average and the Analyzed Industry. For example, 100 means that they are equal; 500 that the Analyzed Industry is five times the average; 50 means that the Analyzed Industry is half the national average. The abbreviation 'na' is used to show that data are 'not available'.

LEADING COMPANIES

Number shown: **75**   Total sales ($ mil): **450,734**   Total employment (000): **1,433.1**

Company Name	Address				CEO Name	Phone	Co. Type	Sales ($ mil)	Empl. (000)
Intern. Business Machines Corp.	New Orchard Rd	Armonk	NY	10504	Louis V. Gerstner Jr.	914-499-1900	P	87,548	291.1
Hewlett-Packard Co.	3000 Hanover St	Palo Alto	CA	94304	Carleton S Fiorina	650-857-1501	P	42,370	84.4
Lucent Technologies Inc.	600 Mountain Ave	Murray Hill	NJ	07974	Richard A McGinn	908-582-8500	P	38,303	141.6
Sony USA Inc.	550 Madison Ave	New York	NY	10022		212-833-6800	R	20,000	32.0
Microsoft Corp.	1 Microsoft Way	Redmond	WA	98052	Steven A Ballmer	425-882-8080	P	19,747	31.4
Electronic Data Systems Corp.	5400 Legacy Dr	Plano	TX	75024	Richard H Brown	972-604-6000	P	18,534	121.0
Dell Computer Corp.	1 Dell Way	Round Rock	TX	78682	Michael S Dell	512-338-4400	P	18,243	24.0
Cisco Systems Inc.	170 W Tasman Dr	San Jose	CA	95134	John T Chambers	408-526-4000	P	12,154	21.0
Sun Microsystems Inc.	901 San Antonio Rd	Palo Alto	CA	94303	Scott G McNealy	650-960-1300	P	11,726	29.0
Oracle Corp.	500 Oracle Pkwy	Redwood City	CA	94065	Lawrence J Ellison	650-506-7000	P	8,827	43.8
Iris Graphics Inc.	3 Federal St	Billerica	MA	01821		781-275-8777	S	8,764*	0.3
Articulate Systems Inc.	600 W Cummings	Woburn	MA	01801	Ivan Mimica	781-935-5656	R	7,741*	<0.1
Computer Sciences Corp.	2100 E Grand Ave	El Segundo	CA	90245	Van B Honeycutt	310-615-0311	P	7,660	50.0
Unisys Corp.	Unisys Way	Blue Bell	PA	19424	L A Weinbach	215-986-4011	P	7,545	33.2
EMC Corp.	PO Box 9103	Hopkinton	MA	01748	Michael C Ruettgers	508-435-1000	P	6,916	9.7
SCI Systems Inc	PO Box 1000	Huntsville	AL	35807	Olin B King	256-882-4800	S	6,711	25.2
ALLTEL Corp.	1 Allied Dr	Little Rock	AR	72202	Joe T Ford	501-905-8000	P	6,302	21.5
CB Technologies Inc.	1487 Dunwoody Dr	West Chester	PA	19380	James L Ooyne	610-889-7300	R	6,242	2.0
Apple Computer Inc.	1 Infinite Loop	Cupertino	CA	95014	Steve Jobs	408-996-1010	P	6,134	9.7
Hughes Electronics Corp.	PO Box 956	El Segundo	CA	90245	Gareth Chang	310-364-6000	P	5,964	15.0
3Com Corp. Switching Div.	85 Rangeway Rd	North Billerica	MA	01862	Eric Benhamou	978-670-9009	D	5,600	13.5
Williams Energy Services	1 Williams Ctr	Tulsa	OK	74172	Steve Malcolm	918-573-2000	S	5,593	9.0
Computer Associates Intern. Inc.	1 Comp Assoc	Islandia	NY	11749	Charles B Wang	516-342-5224	P	5,253	14.7
Tel Tech International	39 Broadway	New York	NY	10006	Jonathan Gross	212-514-5600	R	5,217*	0.5
Personal Library Software Inc.	22000 AOL Way	Dulles	VA	20166	Paul Kagan	703-448-8700	P	4,777	12.1
Motorola Inc	5401 N Beach St	Fort Worth	TX	76137		817-245-2000	S	3,900*	19.5
Hasbro Inc.	1027 Newport Ave	Pawtucket	RI	02861	Alan Hassenfeld	401-431-8697	P	3,304	10.0
Insignia Solutions PLC.	41300 Christy St	Fremont	CA	94538	Richard M Noling	510-360-3700	P	3,160	<0.1
Lotus Development Corp.	55 Cambridge	Cambridge	MA	02142	Al Zollar	617-577-8500	S	3,000	8.5
Silicon Graphics Inc.	PO Box 7311	Mountain View	CA	94039	Edward R McCracken	650-960-1980	P	2,749	9.2
Infotec Development Inc.	7755 Center Ave	Huntington Bch	CA	92647	Michael B Alexander	714-549-0460	S	2,581*	11.0
Henry Schein Inc.	135 Duryea Rd	Melville	NY	11747	Stanley M Bergman	516-843-5500	P	2,286	6.5
Fidelity Investments	82 Devonshire St	Boston	MA	02109		617-563-7000	S	2,235*	14.9
Amdahl Corp.	PO Box 3470	Sunnyvale	CA	94088	David B Wright	408-746-6000	S	2,200	13.0
Baker Atlas	10205 Westheimer	Houston	TX	77042	Gary Jones	713-972-4000	S	2,000*	<0.1
Teradyne Inc.	321 Harrison Ave	Boston	MA	02118	George W Chamillard	617-482-2700	S	1,791	6.8
SABRE Group Inc.	4255 Amon Carter	Fort Worth	TX	76155	Michael J Durham	817-931-7300	S	1,783	7.9
GEMISYS Corp.	7103 S Revere Pkwy	Englewood	CO	80112	Darrall E Robbins	303-705-6000	R	1,734*	0.1
Compuware Corp.	31440 Northwestern	Farmington Hills	MI	48334	Peter Karmanos Jr	248-737-7300	P	1,638	10.9
Care Insite	1 Executive Dr	Somerset	NJ	08873	Sajid Khan	732-560-1000	R	1,618*	<0.1
Rearden Technology	1901 Shoreline Dr	Alameda	CA	94501	Brad Lowe	501-523-2267	R	1,600	5.0
Paramount Publishing	1230 Av Americas	New York	NY	10020		212-698-7000	S	1,588*	9.0
McGraw-Hill Inc	1221 Av Americas	New York	NY	10020	Harold McGraw	212-512-2000	D	1,540*	2.0
H and R Block Inc.	4400 Main St	Kansas City	MO	64111	Frank L Salizzoni	816-753-6900	P	1,522	86.5
PeopleSoft Inc.	4460 Hacienda Dr	Pleasanton	CA	94588	Craig A Conway	925-225-3000	P	1,475	6.0
Cabletron Systems Inc.	PO Box 5005	Rochester	NH	03866	Craig R Benson	603-332-9400	P	1,411	6.0
Standard Register Co.	PO Box 1167	Dayton	OH	45401		937-443-1000	P	1,397	8.7
SunGard Data Systems Inc.	1285 Drummers Ln	Wayne	PA	19087	James L Mann	610-341-8700	P	1,393	6.9
IBM	5600 Cottle Rd	San Jose	CA	95193		408-256-1600	S	1,361*	5.1
BMC Software Inc.	2101 CityWest Blvd	Houston	TX	77042	Max P Watson Jr	713-918-8800	P	1,304	4.9
Novell Inc.	122 E 1700 S	Provo	UT	84606	Eric Schmidt	801-861-7000	P	1,273	5.6
Electronic Arts Inc.	209 Redwood Shores	Redwood City	CA	94065	Lawrence F Probst III	650-628-1500	P	1,222	2.5
Sunsoft Inc.	901 San Antonio Rd	Palo Alto	CA	94303	Janpieter Scheerder	650-345-2412	S	1,212*	3.0
Ceridian Employer Services	5500 Wayzata Blvd	Minneapolis	MN	55416	Carl Keil	612-853-8100	P	1,200	4.7
Diebold Inc.	PO Box 3077	North Canton	OH	44720	Robert Mahoney	330-489-4000	P	1,186	6.5
ALLTEL Information Services Inc	4001 RParham	Little Rock	AR	72212	Jeffrey H Fox	501-220-5100	S	1,162	8.1
Scholastic Corp.	555 Broadway	New York	NY	10012		212-343-6100	P	1,154	7.5
Siscom Inc.	7464 Arapahoe Rd	Boulder	CO	80303	Michael J Ellis	303-449-0442	P	1,136	<0.1
Cadence Design Systems Inc.	San Jose	San Jose	CA	95134	Raymond Bugham	408-943-1234	P	1,093	4.2
Follett Corp.	2233 West St	River Grove	IL	60171	Kenneth J Hull	708-583-2000	R	1,073	7.5
Parametric Technologies Corp.	14 Crosby Dr	Bedford	MA	01730	Kathleen A Cote	781-398-5000	P	1,058	5.0
Adobe Systems Inc.	345 Park Ave	San Jose	CA	95110	Charles M Geschke	408-536-6000	P	1,015	2.8
Kaman Corp.	PO Box 1	Bloomfield	CT	06002	Charles Kaman	860-243-7100	P	1,006	4.3
Keane Inc	290 Broadhollow Rd	Melville	NY	11747	John Keane, Sr	516-351-7000	D	1,000	11.0
Spire Software	338 Church Rd	Milford	NJ	08848	Paul Zucker	908-995-7818	R	1,000	<0.1
Thomson Information Services Inc	22 Thompson Pl	Boston	MA	02210	David Flaschen	617-345-2700	R	1,000	7.0
Tivoli Systems Inc.	9442 Cap of TX	Austin	TX	78759	Jan Lindelow	512-436-8000	S	1,000*	3.0
Western Geophysical Co.	PO Box 2469	Houston	TX	77252	R White	713-789-9600	S	1,000*	6.0
Network Associates Inc.	3965 Freedom Cir	Santa Clara	CA	95054	Leslie G Denand	408-988-3832	P	990	2.7
J.D. Edwards and Co.	1 Technology Way	Denver	CO	80237	Douglas S Massingill	303-334-4000	P	944	5.7
Intergraph Corp.	Intergraph	Huntsville	AL	35894	James W Meadlock	256-730-2000	P	939	6.7
Telcordia Technologies	445 South St	Morristown	NJ	07960	Richard C Smith	973-829-2000	S	925*	5.3
Houghton Mifflin Co.	222 Berkeley St	Boston	MA	02116	Nader Dareh'shari	617-351-5000	P	920	2.8
Bell and Howell Co.	5215 Old Orchard	Skokie	IL	60077	James P Roemer	847-470-7100	P	900	6.2
Broadwing	PO Box 2301	Cincinnati	OH	45201	Richard G Ellenberger	513-397-9900	P	885	20.8

Source: Ward's Business Directory of U.S. Private and Public Companies, Volumes 1 and 2, 2000. The company type code used is as follows: P - Public, R - Private, S - Subsidiary, D - Division, J - Joint Venture, A - Affiliate, G - Group, N - Company type not reported. Sales are in millions of dollars, employees are in thousands. An asterisk (*) indicates an estimated sales volume. The symbol < stands for 'less than'. Company names and addresses are truncated, in some cases, to fit into the available space.

LOCATION BY STATE AND REGIONAL CONCENTRATION

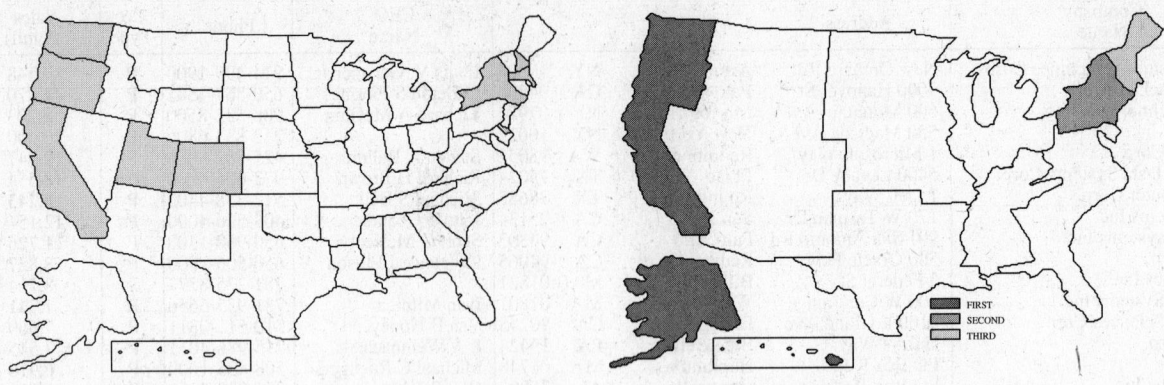

FIRST
SECOND
THIRD

INDUSTRY DATA BY STATE

State	Establishments		Employment			Payroll		Revenues		
	Total (number)	% of U.S.	Total (number)	% of U.S.	Per Estab.	Total ($ mil.)	Per Empl. ($)	Total ($ mil.)	% of U.S.	Per Estab. ($)
California	2,389	19.8	77,277	29.0	32	6,059.6	78,414	18,558.4	30.1	7,768,273
Washington	429	3.5	10,464	3.9	24	1,020.2	97,498	6,004.6	9.7	13,996,830
New York	658	5.4	11,249	4.2	17	877.1	77,970	5,578.2	9.0	8,477,457
Massachusetts	759	6.3	29,670	11.1	39	1,934.5	65,199	5,485.8	8.9	7,227,717
Texas	866	7.2	16,018	6.0	18	1,262.9	78,844	3,403.6	5.5	3,930,247
Illinois	531	4.4	13,176	4.9	25	841.6	63,876	2,733.8	4.4	5,148,341
Pennsylvania	396	3.3	7,595	2.9	19	612.7	80,670	2,172.3	3.5	5,485,659
New Jersey	458	3.8	8,199	3.1	18	571.8	69,737	1,717.5	2.8	3,749,900
Georgia	405	3.3	7,144	2.7	18	515.3	72,133	1,422.3	2.3	3,511,970
Virginia	364	3.0	6,970	2.6	19	446.3	64,025	1,310.7	2.1	3,600,714
Florida	529	4.4	7,544	2.8	14	419.4	55,589	1,207.6	2.0	2,282,730
Colorado	415	3.4	5,953	2.2	14	360.8	60,612	1,113.7	1.8	2,683,593
Oregon	259	2.1	6,220	2.3	24	319.6	51,389	1,069.5	1.7	4,129,452
Wisconsin	147	1.2	1,718	0.6	12	88.8	51,710	1,049.6	1.7	7,140,299
Ohio	327	2.7	6,453	2.4	20	303.1	46,974	1,022.8	1.7	3,127,804
Maryland	249	2.1	4,519	1.7	18	305.5	67,605	845.7	1.4	3,396,378
Michigan	278	2.3	5,009	1.9	18	283.2	56,535	802.8	1.3	2,887,705
Arizona	227	1.9	4,287	1.6	19	204.9	47,802	703.7	1.1	3,100,132
Connecticut	204	1.7	3,210	1.2	16	254.0	79,134	700.2	1.1	3,432,245
Minnesota	279	2.3	3,967	1.5	14	226.0	56,961	665.8	1.1	2,386,412
Utah	173	1.4	4,532	1.7	26	255.0	56,277	526.8	0.9	3,045,081
North Carolina	256	2.1	3,291	1.2	13	182.9	55,568	514.8	0.8	2,010,773
New Hampshire	128	1.1	2,606	1.0	20	165.3	63,416	411.9	0.7	3,217,828
Missouri	144	1.2	2,076	0.8	14	115.5	55,622	394.2	0.6	2,737,375
Indiana	121	1.0	1,750	0.7	14	100.5	57,456	317.3	0.5	2,622,603
D.C.	21	0.2	478	0.2	23	45.0	94,069	301.3	0.5	14,347,238
Alabama	81	0.7	2,100	0.8	26	78.6	37,439	194.5	0.3	2,401,691
Delaware	29	0.2	342	0.1	12	25.9	75,795	174.7	0.3	6,025,759
Iowa	80	0.7	2,550	1.0	32	94.1	36,900	171.2	0.3	2,139,700
South Carolina	66	0.5	1,371	0.5	21	54.6	39,840	144.9	0.2	2,195,955
Tennessee	106	0.9	1,060	0.4	10	48.7	45,976	132.2	0.2	1,246,726
Oklahoma	83	0.7	1,141	0.4	14	44.5	38,966	120.9	0.2	1,456,482
Kansas	78	0.6	948	0.4	12	49.8	52,504	108.8	0.2	1,394,795
New Mexico	57	0.5	718	0.3	13	23.5	32,762	90.0	0.1	1,579,667
North Dakota	12	0.1	976	0.4	81	36.8	37,669	77.2	0.1	6,429,833
Nebraska	54	0.4	552	0.2	10	22.7	41,053	68.8	0.1	1,274,111
Idaho	33	0.3	363	0.1	11	17.8	49,080	63.5	0.1	1,925,212
Rhode Island	42	0.3	421	0.2	10	23.0	54,558	62.6	0.1	1,491,548
Louisiana	56	0.5	412	0.2	7	15.6	37,883	59.9	0.1	1,070,518
Nevada	59	0.5	333	0.1	6	16.4	49,315	39.2	0.1	664,000
Kentucky	46	0.4	419	0.2	9	15.7	37,458	38.8	0.1	843,196
Maine	35	0.3	315	0.1	9	12.6	39,860	30.2	0.0	861,486
Vermont	27	0.2	229	0.1	8	8.4	36,572	21.4	0.0	793,630
Mississippi	27	0.2	203	0.1	8	7.6	37,463	17.8	0.0	660,778
Arkansas	30	0.2	158	0.1	5	5.8	36,785	14.6	0.0	485,167
South Dakota	16	0.1	125	0.0	8	3.8	30,296	9.0	0.0	565,250
Montana	21	0.2	90	0.0	4	2.3	25,000	6.9	0.0	328,048
Hawaii	16	0.1	61	0.0	4	2.2	35,984	6.3	0.0	390,813
West Virginia	13	0.1	71	0.0	5	1.8	24,803	4.6	0.0	356,538
Wyoming	6	-	34	0.0	6	1.2	35,971	3.3	0.0	550,667
Alaska	5	-	13	0.0	3	2.0	155,692	3.2	0.0	632,400

Source: 1997 *Economic Census*. The states are in descending order of revenues or establishments (if revenue data are missing for the majority). The symbol (D) appears when data are withheld to prevent disclosure of competitive information. States marked with (D) are sorted by number of establishments. A dash (-) indicates that the data element cannot be calculated. * indicates the midpoint of a range; 175, for example is the range 100-249. Shaded *states* on the state map indicate those states which have proportionately greater representation in the industry than would be indicated by the state's population; the ratio is based on total revenues or number of establishments. Shaded *regions* indicate where the industry is regionally most concentrated.

NAICS 512110 - MOTION PICTURE AND VIDEO PRODUCTION*

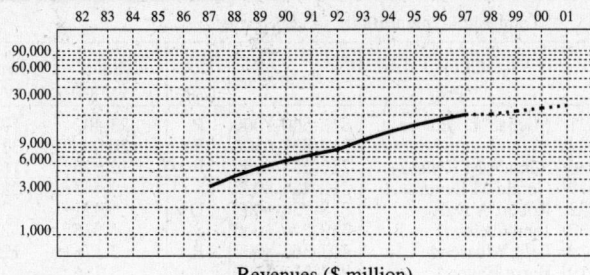

Revenues ($ million)

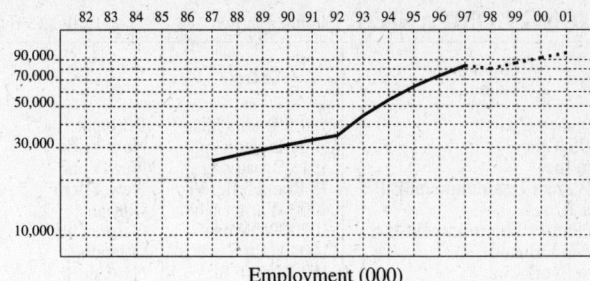

Employment (000)

GENERAL STATISTICS

Year	Establishments (number)	Employment (number)	Payroll ($ million)	Revenues ($ million)	Employees per Establishment (number)	Revenues per Establishment ($)	Payroll per Employee ($)
1982	-	-	-	-	-	-	-
1983	-	-	-	-	-	-	-
1984	-	-	-	-	-	-	-
1985	-	-	-	-	-	-	-
1986	-	-	-	-	-	-	-
1987	3,086	25,371	820.0	3,353.0	8.2	1,086,520	32,320
1988	3,277 e	27,266 e	1,057.0 e	4,370.0 e	8.3 e	1,333,537 e	38,766 e
1989	3,468 e	29,161 e	1,295.0 e	5,386.0 e	8.4 e	1,553,057 e	44,409 e
1990	3,660 e	31,055 e	1,532.0 e	6,402.0 e	8.5 e	1,749,180 e	49,332 e
1991	3,851 e	32,950 e	1,769.0 e	7,418.0 e	8.6 e	1,926,253 e	53,687 e
1992	4,042	34,845	2,007.0	8,434.0	8.6	2,086,591	57,598
1993	4,989 e	44,588 e	2,594.0 e	10,778.0 e	8.9 e	2,160,353 e	58,177 e
1994	5,936 e	54,330 e	3,182.0 e	13,121.0 e	9.2 e	2,210,411 e	58,568 e
1995	6,883 e	64,073 e	3,769.0 e	15,465.0 e	9.3 e	2,246,840 e	58,824 e
1996	7,830 e	73,815 e	4,357.0 e	17,808.0 e	9.4 e	2,274,330 e	59,026 e
1997	8,777	83,558	4,945.0	20,152.0	9.5	2,296,001	59,180
1998	8,487 p	80,459 p	4,959.0 p	20,324.0 p	9.5 p	2,394,721 p	61,634 p
1999	9,056 p	86,277 p	5,372.0 p	22,003.0 p	9.5 p	2,429,660 p	62,265 p
2000	9,626 p	92,096 p	5,784.0 p	23,683.0 p	9.6 p	2,460,316 p	62,804 p
2001	10,195 p	97,915 p	6,197.0 p	25,363.0 p	9.6 p	2,487,788 p	63,290 p

Sources: Economic Census of the United States, 1982, 1987, 1992, 1997. Establishment counts, employment, and payroll are from *County Business Patterns* for non-Census years. In non-Census years, industries in the Manufacturing range under SIC coding include data from the *Annual Survey of Manufactures* (*ASM*); those in the old Services range include data from the *Services Annual Survey* (*SAS*). Values followed by a 'p' are projections by the editors. Extrapolations are marked by 'e'. Data are the most recent available at this level of detail.

INDICES OF CHANGE

Year	Establishments (number)	Employment (number)	Payroll ($ million)	Revenues ($ million)	Employees per Establishment (number)	Revenues per Establishment ($)	Payroll per Employee ($)
1982	-	-	-	-	-	-	-
1987	35.2	30.4	16.6	16.6	86.4	47.3	54.6
1992	46.1	41.7	40.6	41.9	90.6	90.9	97.3
1993	56.8 e	53.4 e	52.5 e	53.5 e	93.9 e	94.1 e	98.3 e
1994	67.6 e	65.0 e	64.3 e	65.1 e	96.1 e	96.3 e	99.0 e
1995	78.4 e	76.7 e	76.2 e	76.7 e	97.8 e	97.9 e	99.4 e
1996	89.2 e	88.3 e	88.1 e	88.4 e	99.0 e	99.1 e	99.7 e
1997	100.0	100.0	100.0	100.0	100.0	100.0	100.0
1998	96.7 p	96.3 p	100.3 p	100.9 p	99.6 p	104.3 p	104.1 p
1999	103.2 p	103.3 p	108.6 p	109.2 p	100.1 p	105.8 p	105.2 p
2000	109.7 p	110.2 p	117.0 p	117.5 p	100.5 p	107.2 p	106.1 p
2001	116.2 p	117.2 p	125.3 p	125.9 p	100.9 p	108.4 p	106.9 p

Sources: Same as General Statistics. The values shown reflect change from the base year, 1997. Values above 100 mean greater than 1997, values below 100 mean less than 1997, and a value of 100 in the 1982-96 or 1998-2001 period means same as 1997. Values followed by a 'p' are projections by the editors; 'e' stands for extrapolation. Data are the most recent available at this level of detail.

SELECTED RATIOS

For 1997	Avg. of Information	Analyzed Industry	Index	For 1997	Avg. of Information	Analyzed Industry	Index
Employees per establishment	27	10	36	Payroll per establishment	1,131,090	563,404	50
Revenue per establishment	5,444,104	2,296,001	42	Payroll as % of revenue	21	25	118
Revenue per employee	203,255	241,174	119	Payroll per employee	42,229	59,180	140

Sources: Same as General Statistics. The 'Average' column represents the average for the industry sector, in 1997, where the currently shown industry is classified. The Index shows the relationship between the Average and the Analyzed Industry. For example, 100 means that they are equal; 500 that the Analyzed Industry is five times the average; 50 means that the Analyzed Industry is half the national average. The abbreviation 'na' is used to show that data are 'not available'.

*Equivalent to SIC 7812.

LEADING COMPANIES   Number shown: **75**   Total sales ($ mil): **110,683**   Total employment (000): **433.0**

Company Name	Address				CEO Name	Phone	Co. Type	Sales ($ mil)	Empl. (000)
Walt Disney Co.	500 S Buena Vista	Burbank	CA	91521	Michael D. Eisner	818-560-1000	P	23,402	117.0
Sony USA Inc.	550 Madison Ave	New York	NY	10022		212-833-6800	R	20,000	32.0
Viacom Inc.	1515 Broadway	New York	NY	10036	Sumner M Redstone	212-258-6000	P	12,096	116.7
Time Warner Entertainment L.P.	75 Rockefeller Plz	New York	NY	10019	Gerald M Levin	212-484-8000	S	9,453*	29.5
Warner Bros.	4000 Warner Blvd	Burbank	CA	91522	Robert A Daly	818-954-6000	D	6,971*	7.9
Sony Pictures Entertainment Inc.	10202 W Wash	Culver City	CA	90232	John Calley	310-244-4000	S	4,535	2.5
Universal Orlando	1000 Univ Studios	Orlando	FL	32819	Felix Mussenden	407-363-8000	S	3,376*	12.0
USA Networks Inc.	152 W 57th St	New York	NY	10019	Barry Baker	212-314-7300	P	3,236	9.2
Reebok International Ltd.	100 Tech Ctr	Stoughton	MA	02072	Paul Fireman	781-401-5000	P	2,900	6.6
Lefrak Organization Inc.	97-77 Queens Blvd	Rego Park	NY	11374	Samuel J LeFrak	718-459-9021	R	2,750	16.0
Viacom International Inc.	1515 Broadway	New York	NY	10036	Sumner Redstone	212-258-6000	S	1,900*	5.0
Universal Studios Inc.	100 Universal City	Universal City	CA	91608	Ron Meyer	818-777-1000	S	1,794*	13.0
Home Box Office	1100 Av Americas	New York	NY	10036	Jeff Bewkes	212-512-1000	D	1,591*	2.0
Paramount Publishing	1230 Av Americas	New York	NY	10020		212-698-7000	S	1,588*	9.0
Fox Inc.	P O Box 900	Beverly Hills	CA	90213	Rupert Murdoch	310-369-1000	S	1,344*	4.0
Twentieth Century Fox Film Corp.	10201 W Pico Blvd	Los Angeles	CA	90064	Rupert Murdoch	310-369-1000	S	1,200*	3.6
International Management Group	1360 E 9th St	Cleveland	OH	44114	Mark H McCormack	216-522-1200	R	1,150*	2.1
Metro-Goldwyn-Mayer Inc.	2500 Broadway St	Santa Monica	CA	90404	Alex Yemenidjian	310-449-3000	P	1,142	0.9
PolyGram Filmed Entertainment	9333 Wilshire Blvd	Beverly Hills	CA	90210	Peter Graves	310-777-7700	S	900	12.4
COMSAT Corp.	6560 Rock Spring	Bethesda	MD	20817	Betty C Alewine	301-214-3200	P	617	2.7
Dreamworks SKG	100 Universal Plz	Universal City	CA	91608		818-733-7500	R	606*	2.0
Spelling Entertainment Group Inc.	5700 Wilshire Blvd	Los Angeles	CA	90036	Peter H Bachmann	323-965-5700	P	586	0.4
Twentieth Century-Fox Film Corp	PO Box 900	Beverly Hills	CA	90213	William Mechanic	310-369-1000	S	551*	1.8
Paramount Pictures Corp.	5555 Melrose Ave	Los Angeles	CA	90038	Jonathan Dolgen	213-956-5000	S	526*	3.8
Fox Kids Worldwide Inc.	10960 Wilshire Blvd	Los Angeles	CA	90024	Mel Woods	310-235-5100	S	368*	1.2
Ascent Entertainment Group Inc.	1225 17th St	Denver	CO	80202	Charles Neinas	303-308-7000	P	344	1.0
Industrial Light and Magic Div.	PO Box 2459	San Rafael	CA	94912	Jim Morris	415-258-2000	D	336*	1.1
DreamWorks Interactive	100 Universal City	Universal City	CA	91608		818-777-4600	R	283*	1.3
Spelling Entertainment Inc.	5700 Wilshire Blvd	Los Angeles	CA	90036	Aaron Spelling	323-965-5888	S	272*	0.5
Saban Entertainment	10960 Wilshire Blvd	Los Angeles	CA	90024	Haim Saban	310-235-5100	D	253*	0.8
MGM-UA Inc.	2500 Broadway St	Santa Monica	CA	90404	Alex Yemenidjian	310-449-3000	D	245*	0.8
UST Enterprises Inc.	100 W Putnam Ave	Greenwich	CT	06830	Garry Smith	203-863-5200	S	244*	0.4
RYSHER TPE Inc.	2401 Colorado Ave	Santa Monica	CA	90404	Tim Helfet	310-309-5200	S	243*	0.1
Metromedia Intern. Group Inc.	1 Meadowlands	East Rutherford	NJ	07073	John W Kluge	201-531-8000	P	240	1.0
Saban Productions	10960 Wilshire Blvd	Los Angeles	CA	90024	Haim Saban	310-235-5100	R	212*	0.4
Bonneville International Corp.	P O Box 1160	Salt Lake City	UT	84110	Bruce T Reese	801-575-7500	R	197*	1.3
Artisan Entertainment	2700 Colorado	Santa Monica	CA	90404	Mark Curcio	310-449-9200	P	179*	0.2
New Line Cinema Corp.	888 7th Ave	New York	NY	10106	Robert Shaye	212-649-4900	S	159*	0.5
Deluxe Laboratories Inc.	1377 N Serrano Ave	Hollywood	CA	90027	Cyril Drabinsky	323-462-6171	S	150*	0.5
Children's Television Workshop	1 Lincoln Plz	New York	NY	10023	David Britt	212-595-3456	N	138*	0.5
Buena Vista Home Entertainment	350 S Buena Vista	Burbank	CA	91521	Michael Johnson	818-295-5200	S	133*	0.8
Rentrak Corp.	7700 NE Ambass	Portland	OR	97220	Ron Berger	503-284-7581	P	124	0.3
Pacific Data Images Inc.	3101 Park Blvd	Palo Alto	CA	94306	James DeRose Jr	650-846-8100	R	119*	0.4
Chambers Communications Corp.	P O Box 7009	Eugene	OR	97401	Scott D Chambers	541-485-5611	R	117*	0.4
Propaganda Films	940 N Mansfield	Hollywood	CA	90038	Rick Hess	323-462-6400	S	106	0.1
Crawford Communications Inc.	535 Plasamour Dr	Atlanta	GA	30324	Jesse Crawford	404-876-7149	R	101*	0.3
Chicago Story	401 W Superior St	Chicago	IL	60610	Mark Androw	312-642-3173	R	100*	0.3
H-B Cartoons Inc.	15303 Ventura	Sherman Oaks	CA	91403	Jean MacCurdy	818-977-7500	S	100	0.5
Lucasfilm Ltd.	P O Box 2009	San Rafael	CA	94912	Gordon Radley	415-662-1800	R	100*	0.3
Coastal Training Technologies	3083 Brickhouse Ct	Virginia Beach	VA	23452	Paul Michaels	757-498-9014	R	92*	0.3
Concrete Productions Inc.	302 N Market St	Dallas	TX	75202	Lisa Cobb	214-747-2400	R	92*	0.3
Vinton Studios Inc.	1400 NW 22nd Ave	Portland	OR	97210	David Altschul	503-225-1130	R	92*	0.3
Cinesite Inc.	1017 N Las Palmas	Hollywood	CA	90038	Aidan Foley	213-468-4400	S	81*	0.3
Post Group Inc.	6335 Homewood	Los Angeles	CA	90028	Frederic Rheinstein	213-462-2300	R	79*	0.3
Image Entertainment Inc.	9333 Oso Ave	Chatsworth	CA	91311	Martin W Greenwald	818-407-9100	P	77	0.1
Playboy Entertainment Group Inc.	9242 Beverly Blvd	Beverly Hills	CA	90210	Tony Lynn	310-246-4000	S	73*	0.2
Dick Clark Productions Inc.	3003 W Olive Ave	Burbank	CA	91510	Richard W Clark	818-841-3003	P	72	0.8
Jim Henson Co.	117 E 69th St	New York	NY	10021	Brian Henson	212-794-2400	R	67*	0.2
Harmony Holdings Inc.	5501 Excelsior Blvd	Minneapolis	MN	55416	Christopher T Dahl	612-925-8840	P	66	<0.1
Spelling Entertainment Group Inc	5700 Wilshire Blvd	Los Angeles	CA	90036	Aaron Spelling	323-965-5888	S	61*	0.2
Broadcast Video Inc.	20377 NE 15th Ct	Miami	FL	33179	Rick Legow	305-653-7440	R	58	0.2
CNET Inc.	150 Chestnut St	San Francisco	CA	94111	Richard Marino	415-395-7800	P	56	0.5
Hite Co.	PO Box 1754	Altoona	PA	16603	R Lee Hite	814-944-6121	R	56*	0.2
Galjour Video	P O Box 640355	Kenner	LA	70064	Mark Galjour	504-466-5805	R	55*	<0.1
Unitel Video Inc.	555 W 57th St	New York	NY	10019	Barry Knepper	212-265-3600	P	52	0.2
Beyond Films Ltd.	1875 Century Park E	Los Angeles	CA	90067		310-785-2255	S	50	0.3
Consolidated Film Industries	959 Seward St	Hollywood	CA	90038	Bob Boitcher	323-960-7444	D	50*	0.4
Miramax Films	375 Greenwich St	New York	NY	10013	Harvey Weinstein	212-941-3800	S	50*	0.2
White Hawk Pictures Inc.	567 Bishopgate Ln	Jacksonville	FL	32204	Charlie U Barth	904-634-0500	R	50*	<0.1
Kushner-Locke Co.	11601 Wilshire	Los Angeles	CA	90025	Donald Kushner	310-481-2000	P	50	0.3
Hollywood Digital	6690 Sunset Blvd	Hollywood	CA	90028	Salah Hassanein	213-465-0101	R	46*	0.2
Manhattan Transfer/Edit Inc.	545 5th Ave	New York	NY	10017	Daniel Rosen	212-687-4000	S	46*	0.2
Resolution Inc.	19 Gregory Dr	S. Burlington	VT	05403	Karen Makowski	802-862-8881	R	46*	0.2
EUE/Screen Gems Ltd.	222 E 44th St	New York	NY	10017	George Cooney	212-867-4030	R	45*	0.3
NBA Entertainment	450 Harmon	Secaucus	NJ	07094		201-865-1500	S	45*	0.2

Source: Ward's Business Directory of U.S. Private and Public Companies, Volumes 1 and 2, 2000. The company type code used is as follows: P - Public, R - Private, S - Subsidiary, D - Division, J - Joint Venture, A - Affiliate, G - Group, N - Company type not reported. Sales are in millions of dollars, employees are in thousands. An asterisk (*) indicates an estimated sales volume. The symbol < stands for 'less than'. Company names and addresses are truncated, in some cases, to fit into the available space.

LOCATION BY STATE AND REGIONAL CONCENTRATION

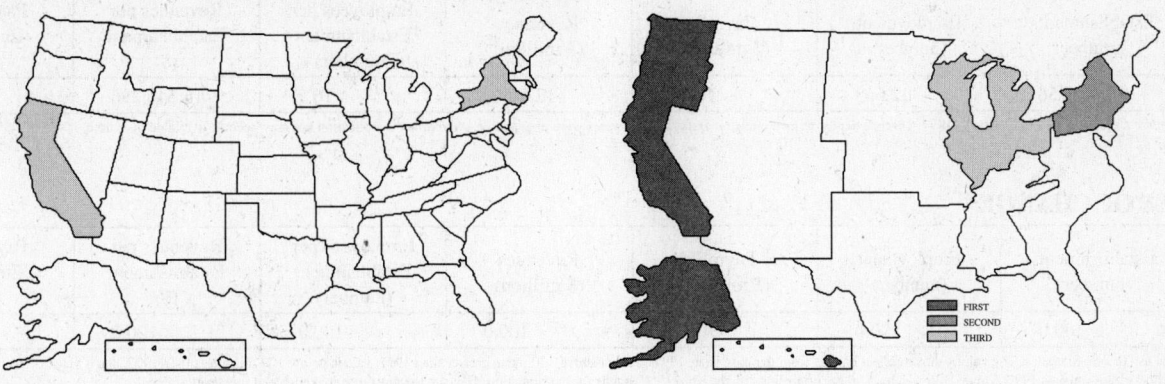

FIRST
SECOND
THIRD

INDUSTRY DATA BY STATE

State	Establishments Total (number)	Establishments % of U.S.	Employment Total (number)	Employment % of U.S.	Employment Per Estab.	Payroll Total ($ mil.)	Payroll Per Empl. ($)	Revenues Total ($ mil.)	Revenues % of U.S.	Revenues Per Estab. ($)
California	3,321	37.8	49,762	59.6	15	3,408.9	68,504	14,256.2	70.7	4,292,753
New York	1,232	14.0	7,372	8.8	6	442.7	60,051	1,960.3	9.7	1,591,148
Illinois	348	4.0	2,169	2.6	6	194.1	89,479	619.5	3.1	1,780,060
Florida	405	4.6	2,428	2.9	6	91.0	37,500	385.8	1.9	952,472
Texas	305	3.5	2,996	3.6	10	115.2	38,443	359.4	1.8	1,178,370
New Jersey	214	2.4	1,639	2.0	8	74.1	45,235	263.6	1.3	1,231,701
Ohio	129	1.5	2,638	3.2	20	76.4	28,955	230.3	1.1	1,785,388
Pennsylvania	169	1.9	1,428	1.7	8	55.7	39,034	217.2	1.1	1,285,243
Georgia	164	1.9	653	0.8	4	30.3	46,335	166.4	0.8	1,014,939
Virginia	151	1.7	1,023	1.2	7	42.5	41,518	143.2	0.7	948,298
Massachusetts	180	2.1	1,208	1.4	7	35.9	29,748	129.6	0.6	719,828
Michigan	176	2.0	768	0.9	4	26.5	34,555	126.7	0.6	719,892
Tennessee	109	1.2	1,055	1.3	10	33.7	31,938	111.4	0.6	1,022,055
Colorado	158	1.8	563	0.7	4	18.6	33,027	106.4	0.5	673,639
Washington	141	1.6	634	0.8	4	31.5	49,615	89.8	0.4	636,865
Utah	68	0.8	396	0.5	6	12.4	31,354	89.1	0.4	1,310,265
Minnesota	122	1.4	577	0.7	5	23.0	39,873	88.4	0.4	724,279
North Carolina	109	1.2	502	0.6	5	15.8	31,432	84.0	0.4	770,431
D.C.	77	0.9	497	0.6	6	29.2	58,795	82.4	0.4	1,069,909
Maryland	150	1.7	498	0.6	3	20.7	41,631	76.4	0.4	509,020
Connecticut	108	1.2	351	0.4	3	23.8	67,892	70.8	0.4	655,241
Arizona	99	1.1	358	0.4	4	13.9	38,858	68.0	0.3	686,424
Oregon	74	0.8	570	0.7	8	20.8	36,411	48.7	0.2	658,162
Missouri	78	0.9	432	0.5	6	12.9	29,801	41.7	0.2	534,731
Wisconsin	80	0.9	402	0.5	5	10.9	27,015	40.7	0.2	508,150
Nevada	48	0.5	285	0.3	6	10.7	37,460	31.8	0.2	662,271
Louisiana	44	0.5	230	0.3	5	5.8	25,357	31.1	0.2	706,636
Indiana	64	0.7	268	0.3	4	9.4	35,090	31.1	0.2	486,031
Hawaii	47	0.5	205	0.2	4	8.5	41,312	25.7	0.1	546,681
South Carolina	31	0.4	188	0.2	6	3.8	20,319	20.0	0.1	646,000
Oklahoma	31	0.4	167	0.2	5	3.5	20,940	15.2	0.1	489,871
Alabama	34	0.4	154	0.2	5	4.2	27,448	13.8	0.1	404,676
Arkansas	25	0.3	132	0.2	5	3.6	26,977	13.5	0.1	539,200
New Mexico	32	0.4	125	0.1	4	3.6	28,968	12.7	0.1	397,719
Iowa	23	0.3	126	0.2	5	4.6	36,508	12.6	0.1	546,261
Montana	11	0.1	87	0.1	8	3.3	37,759	10.5	0.1	951,182
Kansas	26	0.3	83	0.1	3	2.3	27,494	9.5	0.0	365,346
Maine	20	0.2	50	0.1	3	1.7	33,500	8.3	0.0	413,350
Vermont	21	0.2	89	0.1	4	2.4	27,404	6.9	0.0	328,476
Nebraska	13	0.1	38	0.0	3	0.8	20,895	4.4	0.0	338,846
South Dakota	11	0.1	40	0.0	4	0.9	22,625	4.1	0.0	368,818
Alaska	12	0.1	30	0.0	3	0.8	27,167	3.9	0.0	321,250
Delaware	18	0.2	28	0.0	2	0.8	29,250	3.2	0.0	178,111
Mississippi	8	0.1	29	0.0	4	0.8	27,690	2.8	0.0	352,750
West Virginia	13	0.1	27	0.0	2	0.6	22,889	2.2	0.0	165,615
North Dakota	4	-	10	0.0	3	0.1	10,100	0.3	0.0	79,000
Kentucky	22	0.3	60*	-	-	(D)	-	(D)	-	-
New Hampshire	21	0.2	60*	-	-	(D)	-	(D)	-	-
Rhode Island	13	0.1	60*	-	-	(D)	-	(D)	-	-
Idaho	9	0.1	60*	-	-	(D)	-	(D)	-	-
Wyoming	9	0.1	60*	-	-	(D)	-	(D)	-	-

Source: 1997 *Economic Census*. The states are in descending order of revenues or establishments (if revenue data are missing for the majority). The symbol (D) appears when data are withheld to prevent disclosure of competitive information. States marked with (D) are sorted by number of establishments. A dash (-) indicates that the data element cannot be calculated. * indicates the midpoint of a range; 175, for example is the range 100-249. Shaded *states* on the state map indicate those states which have proportionately greater representation in the industry than would be indicated by the state's population; the ratio is based on total revenues or number of establishments. Shaded *regions* indicate where the industry is regionally most concentrated.

NAICS 512120 - MOTION PICTURE AND VIDEO DISTRIBUTION

GENERAL STATISTICS

Year	Establishments (number)	Employment (number)	Payroll ($ million)	Revenues ($ million)	Employees per Establishment (number)	Revenues per Establishment ($)	Payroll per Employee ($)
1997	756	12,663	767.0	12,509.0	16.7	16,546,296	60,570

Source: *Economic Census of the United States*, 1997. This is a newly defined industry. Data for prior years were unavailable at the time of publication but may become available over time.

INDICES OF CHANGE

Year	Establishments (number)	Employment (number)	Payroll ($ million)	Revenues ($ million)	Employees per Establishment (number)	Revenues per Establishment ($)	Payroll per Employee ($)
1997	100.0	100.0	100.0	100.0	100.0	100.0	100.0

Sources: Same as General Statistics. The values shown reflect change from the base year, 1997. Values above 100 mean greater than 1997, values below 100 mean less than 1997, and a value of 100 in the 1982-96 or 1998-2001 period means same as 1997. Values followed by a 'p' are projections by the editors; 'e' stands for extrapolation. Data are the most recent available at this level of detail.

SIC INDUSTRIES RELATED TO NAICS 512120

Each new NAICS code represents an industry that used to be part of an SIC or a part of several SIC industries. Data in this table are shown to provide transitional information for these cases. All available data for the precursor SIC(s) are shown. Even if only a part of an SIC is included in the NAICS, *all* data for the SIC are reproduced. If the SIC industry is not marked as being a part (pt) of the NAICS, the entire industry is embedded in the NAICS data. The SIC composition of the new industry provides some hints of the relative importance of its "ancestors." Data marked with a 'p' are projected. Projections begin with 1982 data. Data earlier than 1990 are not shown but are reflected in the projections.

SIC	Industry	1990	1991	1992	1993	1994	1995	1996	1997
7822	**Motion Picture & Tape Distribution (pt)**								
	Establishments (number)	-	-	1,070	-	-	-	-	-
	Employment (thousands)	-	-	15.5	-	-	-	-	-
	Revenues ($ million)	-	-	9,354.6	-	-	-	-	-
7829	**Motion Picture Distribution Services (pt)**								
	Establishments (number)	164	169	210	202	188	199	200p	203p
	Employment (thousands)	1.3	1.1	0.9	1.1	1.1	1.3	1.1p	1.1p
	Revenues ($ million)	-	-	104.2	-	-	-	-	-

Source: *Economic Census of the United States*, 1992, annual surveys of economic sectors conducted by the Bureau of the Census, and estimates or projections based on the 1982-1992 period; not all data are shown. 'e' marks estimates made by the editors; 'p' indicates projections based on time series. A dash (-) indicates that data for this SIC or year were not available. The abbreviation (pt) next to the industry name indicates that only a part of the industry is present within the NAICS data. If no (pt) is shown, the entire industry is contained within the NAICS data.

SELECTED RATIOS

For 1997	Avg. of Information	Analyzed Industry	Index	For 1997	Avg. of Information	Analyzed Industry	Index
Employees per establishment	27	17	63	Payroll per establishment	1,131,090	1,014,550	90
Revenue per establishment	5,444,104	16,546,296	304	Payroll as % of revenue	21	6	30
Revenue per employee	203,255	987,839	486	Payroll per employee	42,229	60,570	143

Sources: Same as General Statistics. The 'Average' column represents the average for the industry sector, in 1997, where the currently shown industry is classified. The Index shows the relationship between the Average and the Analyzed Industry. For example, 100 means that they are equal; 500 that the Analyzed Industry is five times the average; 50 means that the Analyzed Industry is half the national average. The abbreviation 'na' is used to show that data are 'not available'.

LEADING COMPANIES   Number shown: **75**   Total sales ($ mil): **37,846**   Total employment (000): **65.2**

Company Name	Address			CEO Name	Phone	Co. Type	Sales ($ mil)	Empl. (000)
Warner-Elektra-Atlantic Corp.	111 N Hollywood	Burbank	CA 91505	David Mount	818-843-6311	S	10,000*	1.2
Time Warner Entertainment L.P.	75 Rockefeller Plz	New York	NY 10019	Gerald M Levin	212-484-8000	S	9,453*	29.5
Warner Bros.	4000 Warner Blvd	Burbank	CA 91522	Robert A Daly	818-954-6000	D	6,971*	7.9
Turner Home Entertainment Intern	1888 Century Park E	Los Angeles	CA 90067		310-788-6800	D	2,333*	5.0
Ingram Entertainment Inc.	2 Ingram Blvd	La Vergne	TN 37089	David B Ingram	615-287-4000	R	1,179	1.0
Handleman Co.	PO Box 7045	Troy	MI 48084	Stephen Strome	248-362-4400	P	1,059	2.3
Baker and Taylor Books	2709 Water Ridge	Charlotte	NC 28217	Craig M Richards	704-357-3500	S	981*	2.5
MGM/UA	2500 Broadway St	Santa Monica	CA 90404	Alex Yemenidjian	310-449-3000	S	904*	0.9
Lacy Diversified Industries	54 Monument Cir	Indianapolis	IN 46204	Andre Lacy	317-237-2251	R	866	3.0
King World Productions Inc.	12400 Wilshire	Los Angeles	CA 90025	Michael King	310-826-1108	P	684	0.4
Technicolor Video Services Inc.	3233 E Miss Oaks	Camarillo	CA 93012	Orlando Raimondo	805-445-1122	S	500*	5.0
Time Life Inc.	2000 Duke St	Alexandria	VA 22314		703-838-7000	S	500*	1.5
GoodTimes Entertainment Co.	16 E 40th St	New York	NY 10016	Joseph Cayre	212-951-3100	R	475	0.5
RYSHER TPE Inc.	2401 Colorado Ave	Santa Monica	CA 90404	Tim Helfet	310-309-5200	S	243*	0.1
Odyssey Corp.	12700 Ventura Blvd	Studio City	CA 91604	Margaret Loesch	818-755-2400	D	240*	0.5
Video Products Distributors Inc.	P O Box 293030	Sacramento	CA 95829	Tim Shanahan	916-386-2220	R	170	0.2
New Line Cinema Corp.	888 7th Ave	New York	NY 10106	Robert Shaye	212-649-4900	S	159*	0.5
Buena Vista International Inc.	350 S Buena Vista	Burbank	CA 91521	Mark Zoradi	818-972-3565	S	120*	0.2
VDI Multimedia	6920 Sunset Blvd	Hollywood	CA 90038	R Luke Stefanko	323-957-5500	P	99*	0.6
BBC Worldwide America Inc.	747 3rd Ave	New York	NY 10017	Peter Phippen	212-705-9300	R	96*	0.2
Trimark Holdings Inc.	2644 30th St	Santa Monica	CA 90401	M Mark Amin	310-314-2000	P	92	<0.1
Beyond Films Ltd.	1875 Century Park E	Los Angeles	CA 90067		310-785-2255	S	50	0.3
Miramax Films	375 Greenwich St	New York	NY 10013	Harvey Weinstein	212-941-3800	R	50*	0.2
Jack of All Games Inc.	2909 Crescentville	West Chester	OH 45069	Dave Rosenbaum	513-326-3020	S	41*	<0.1
Unapix Entertainment Inc.	200 Madison Ave	New York	NY 10016	Herbert M Pearlman	212-252-7600	P	37	<0.1
Films for the Humanities	PO Box 2053	Princeton	NJ 08543	Betsy Sherer	609-275-1400	S	33*	<0.1
AIMS Media	9710 De Soto Ave	Chatsworth	CA 91311	Wynn A Sherman	818-773-4300	R	27*	<0.1
Venture Group International Inc.	250 W 57th St	New York	NY 10107	John O'Donnell	212-977-7456	R	27*	<0.1
Overseas Filmgroup Inc.	8800 Sunset Blvd	Los Angeles	CA 90069	Ellen Dinerman Little	310-855-1199	P	26	<0.1
Eyemark Entertainment	10877 Wilshire	Los Angeles	CA 90024	Ed Wilson	310-446-6000	D	24*	<0.1
Fox-Lorber Associates Inc.	419 Park Ave S	New York	NY 10016	Richard Lorber	212-686-6777	R	24*	<0.1
Kingsland Entertainment Agency	PO Box 4360	Pineville	LA 71361		318-640-5555	R	24*	<0.1
Metro Global Media Inc.	1060 Park Ave	Cranston	RI 02910	Kenneth Guarino	401-942-7876	P	23	0.1
Facets Multimedia Inc.	1517 W Fullerton	Chicago	IL 60614	Milos Stehlik	773-281-9075	R	22*	<0.1
Maljack Productions Inc.	16101 South 108th	Orland Park	IL 60462	Waleed B Ali	708-460-0555	R	20*	<0.1
Metro Inc.	1 Metro Park Dr	Cranston	RI 02910	Dennis Nicholas	401-461-2200	D	18	<0.1
Public Media/Films Inc.	4411 N Ravenswood	Chicago	IL 60640	Adrianne Furniss	773-878-7300	R	17*	<0.1
MCA Music Entertainment Group	70 Universal City	Universal City	CA 91608		818-777-4000	S	15*	0.1
4Kids Entertainment Inc.	1414 Av Americas	New York	NY 10019	Sheldon Hirsch	212-758-7666	P	15	<0.1
Home Vision	5547 N Ravenswood	Chicago	IL 60640		773-878-2600	R	14*	<0.1
Central Park Media Corp.	250 W 57th St	New York	NY 10107		212-977-7456	S	13*	<0.1
Unicorn Video Inc.	21119 Osborne St	Canoga Park	CA 91304	Joanne Goldstein	818-407-1333	R	13*	<0.1
Celebrity Home Entertainment Inc	PO Box 549	Woodland Hills	CA 91365	Noel Bloom	818-595-0666	R	12*	<0.1
Devillier-Donegan Enterprises Inc.	4401 Conn N W	Washington	DC 20008	Ron Devillier	202-686-3980	R	12*	<0.1
Library Video Co.	P O Box 580	Wynnewood	PA 19096	Andrew Schlessinger	610-645-4000	R	12*	0.1
Modern Mass Media Inc.	P O Box 950	Chatham	NJ 07928	Chip Del Coro	973-635-6000	R	12	<0.1
NYC Liquidators Inc.	158 W 27th St	New York	NY 10001	Norman Brill	212-675-7400	R	11	<0.1
Quality Books Inc.	1003 W Pines Rd	Oregon	IL 61061		815-732-4450	S	10	<0.1
Video Music Inc.	PO Box 1128	Norristown	PA 19404	Tom Seaman	610-666-6080	R	10*	<0.1
Brentwood Communications Inc.	31344 Via Colinas	Westlake Village	CA 91362	Davis Catun	818-879-9090	R	9	<0.1
Questar Inc.	680 N Lake Shore	Chicago	IL 60611	Albert Nader	312-266-9400	R	8*	<0.1
V.I.E.W. Video Inc.	34 E 23rd St	New York	NY 10010	Bob Karcy	212-674-5550	R	8*	<0.1
Ambrose Video Publishing Inc.	28 W 44th St	New York	NY 10036	William Ambrose	212-265-7272	R	7*	<0.1
Search by Video Inc.	211 N 13th St	Philadelphia	PA 19107	Shelly Spiegel	215-564-6443	R	7*	<0.1
West Glen Communications Inc.	1430 Broadway	New York	NY 10018	Stanley S Zeitlin	212-921-2800	R	7*	<0.1
Great Plains National	P O Box 80669	Lincoln	NE 68501		402-472-2007	S	6	<0.1
American Education Corp.	7506 N Broadway	Oklahoma City	OK 73116	Jeffrey E Butler	405-840-6031	P	6	<0.1
Omega Entertainment Ltd.	8760 Shoreham Dr	Los Angeles	CA 90069	Nico Mastorakis	310-855-0516	R	5	<0.1
Video Buyers Group Inc.	199 NW Coon Rap	Minneapolis	MN 55433	Ted Engen	612-780-6012	R	5*	<0.1
Wishing Well Distributing Co.	P O Box 7040	Santa Rosa	CA 95407	Debra Giusti	707-525-9355	R	5*	<0.1
Hollywood Edge	7080 Hollywood	Hollywood	CA 90028		323-603-3252	S	4	<0.1
IVN Communications Inc.	1390 Willow Pass	Concord	CA 94520	Bob Brownell	925-688-0833	R	4*	<0.1
Acorn Media Publishing	7910 Woodmont	Bethesda	MD 20814		301-907-0030	R	3*	<0.1
Media Funding Corp.	8430 Terminal Rd	Newington	VA 22122	Donald Evans	703-550-1500	R	3*	<0.1
Media Studio Group Inc.	7024 Central Ave	St. Petersburg	FL 33707	Tony Little	727-347-8774	R	3*	<0.1
Mystic Fire Video Inc.	P O Box 422	New York	NY 10012	Sheldon Rochlin	212-941-0999	R	3	<0.1
First Entertainment Holding Corp.	7887 East Bellview	Englewood	CO 80111	Douglas Olson	303-228-1650	P	2	<0.1
All-Star Music Corp.	9655 S Dixie Hwy	Miami	FL 33156	Richard N Friedman	305-666-2747	R	2	<0.1
Blair and Associates Ltd.	11333 East 60th Pl	Tulsa	OK 74146	Robert Blair	918-254-6337	R	2*	<0.1
DW Diversified	7471 Melrose Ave	Los Angeles	CA 90046	Douglas Witkins	323-852-1396	R	2*	<0.1
Million Dollar Video Corp.	5420 McConnell	Los Angeles	CA 90066	Miguel Kahan	310-301-7474	R	2*	<0.1
Pyramid Film and Video Inc.	2801 Colorado	Santa Monica	CA 90404	Randolph Wright	310-828-7577	R	2*	<0.1
Sellthrough Entertainment	4531 Oak Fair Blvd	Tampa	FL 33610		813-621-6087	S	2*	<0.1
Video Department Set-Ups	P O Box 650219	Newton	MA 02165	Barry Glovsky	617-965-0357	R	2*	<0.1
First National Entertainment Corp.	477 E Butterfield Rd	Oak Brook	IL 60148	Kenneth E Scripta	630-971-9924	P	2	<0.1

Source: Ward's Business Directory of U.S. Private and Public Companies, Volumes 1 and 2, 2000. The company type code used is as follows: P - Public, R - Private, S - Subsidiary, D - Division, J - Joint Venture, A - Affiliate, G - Group, N - Company type not reported. Sales are in millions of dollars, employees are in thousands. An asterisk (*) indicates an estimated sales volume. The symbol < stands for 'less than'. Company names and addresses are truncated, in some cases, to fit into the available space.

LOCATION BY STATE AND REGIONAL CONCENTRATION

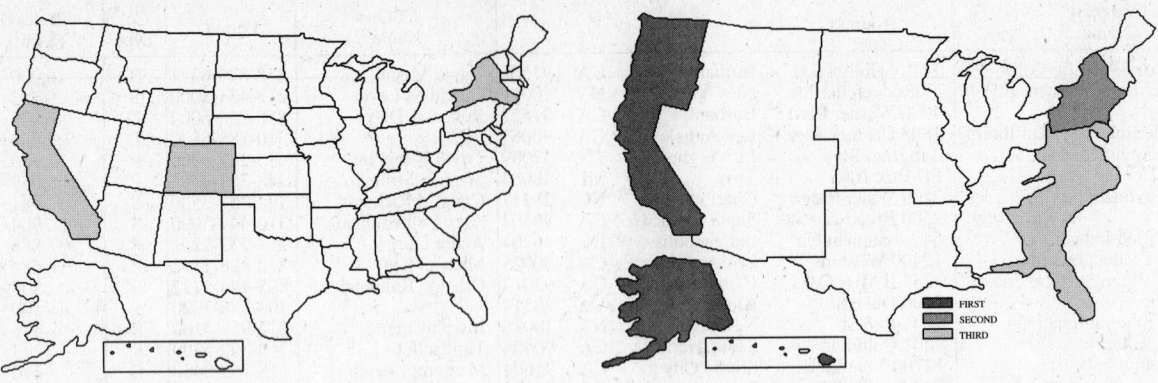

INDUSTRY DATA BY STATE

State	Establishments Total (number)	% of U.S.	Employment Total (number)	% of U.S.	Per Estab.	Payroll Total ($ mil.)	Per Empl. ($)	Revenues Total ($ mil.)	% of U.S.	Per Estab. ($)
California	317	41.9	6,934	54.8	22	454.9	65,604	8,171.3	65.3	25,777,050
New York	146	19.3	2,350	18.6	16	178.5	75,946	2,612.5	20.9	17,893,815
Texas	32	4.2	552	4.4	17	16.8	30,395	698.1	5.6	21,814,281
Illinois	32	4.2	443	3.5	14	16.0	36,205	314.4	2.5	9,825,531
Massachusetts	12	1.6	82	0.6	7	4.3	53,024	107.6	0.9	8,969,750
Colorado	11	1.5	247	2.0	22	7.5	30,401	50.1	0.4	4,558,727
New Jersey	13	1.7	144	1.1	11	7.2	49,951	47.9	0.4	3,681,385
Pennsylvania	14	1.9	197	1.6	14	11.0	55,868	39.8	0.3	2,844,786
Virginia	12	1.6	315	2.5	26	8.1	25,587	37.6	0.3	3,135,667
Missouri	9	1.2	154	1.2	17	5.5	35,974	27.5	0.2	3,057,222
Florida	28	3.7	152	1.2	5	6.9	45,691	26.7	0.2	952,714
Arizona	6	0.8	90	0.7	15	1.5	17,167	14.0	0.1	2,329,167
North Carolina	7	0.9	34	0.3	5	1.3	38,500	8.1	0.1	1,154,143
D.C.	5	0.7	94	0.7	19	4.0	42,745	7.9	0.1	1,576,000
Nevada	3	0.4	24	0.2	8	0.9	38,250	5.3	0.0	1,781,333
Indiana	5	0.7	32	0.3	6	0.9	27,250	2.7	0.0	539,800
Ohio	4	0.5	9	0.1	2	0.4	48,667	2.1	0.0	520,750
Tennessee	5	0.7	12	0.1	2	0.7	57,750	1.5	0.0	292,800
New Mexico	4	0.5	21	0.2	5	0.7	31,524	1.2	0.0	302,750
Georgia	15	2.0	175*	-	-	(D)	-	(D)	-	-
Maryland	13	1.7	175*	-	-	(D)	-	(D)	-	-
Minnesota	11	1.5	60*	-	-	(D)	-	(D)	-	-
Connecticut	9	1.2	60*	-	-	(D)	-	(D)	-	-
Oregon	8	1.1	60*	-	-	(D)	-	(D)	-	-
Washington	6	0.8	60*	-	-	(D)	-	(D)	-	-
Iowa	4	0.5	175*	-	-	(D)	-	(D)	-	-
Kentucky	3	0.4	10*	-	-	(D)	-	(D)	-	-
Kansas	2	0.3	10*	-	-	(D)	-	(D)	-	-
Louisiana	2	0.3	10*	-	-	(D)	-	(D)	-	-
Nebraska	2	0.3	10*	-	-	(D)	-	(D)	-	-
New Hampshire	2	0.3	10*	-	-	(D)	-	(D)	-	-
Oklahoma	2	0.3	10*	-	-	(D)	-	(D)	-	-
Wisconsin	2	0.3	60*	-	-	(D)	-	(D)	-	-
Alaska	1	0.1	10*	-	-	(D)	-	(D)	-	-
Arkansas	1	0.1	10*	-	-	(D)	-	(D)	-	-
Hawaii	1	0.1	10*	-	-	(D)	-	(D)	-	-
Idaho	1	0.1	10*	-	-	(D)	-	(D)	-	-
Maine	1	0.1	10*	-	-	(D)	-	(D)	-	-
Michigan	1	0.1	10*	-	-	(D)	-	(D)	-	-
Montana	1	0.1	10*	-	-	(D)	-	(D)	-	-
Rhode Island	1	0.1	10*	-	-	(D)	-	(D)	-	-
South Carolina	1	0.1	60*	-	-	(D)	-	(D)	-	-
Utah	1	0.1	10*	-	-	(D)	-	(D)	-	-

Source: 1997 *Economic Census*. The states are in descending order of revenues or establishments (if revenue data are missing for the majority). The symbol (D) appears when data are withheld to prevent disclosure of competitive information. States marked with (D) are sorted by number of establishments. A dash (-) indicates that the data element cannot be calculated. * indicates the midpoint of a range; 175, for example is the range 100-249. Shaded *states* on the state map indicate those states which have proportionately greater representation in the industry than would be indicated by the state's population; the ratio is based on total revenues or number of establishments. Shaded *regions* indicate where the industry is regionally most concentrated.

NAICS 512131 - MOTION PICTURE THEATERS (EXCEPT DRIVE-INS)*

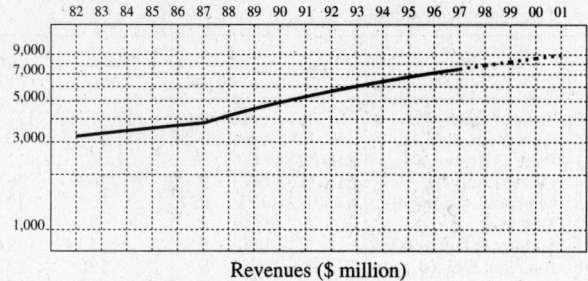

Revenues ($ million)

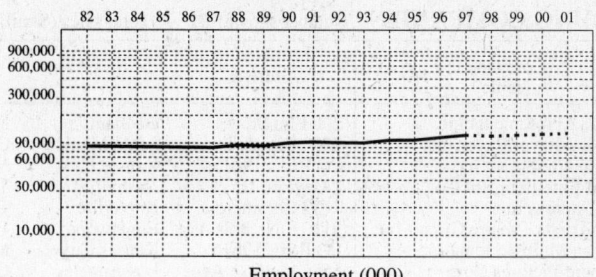

Employment (000)

GENERAL STATISTICS

Year	Establishments (number)	Employment (number)	Payroll ($ million)	Revenues ($ million)	Employees per Establishment (number)	Revenues per Establishment ($)	Payroll per Employee ($)
1982	7,738	92,203	497.0	3,224.0	11.9	416,645	5,390
1983	7,546 e	91,685 e	508.0 e	3,341.0 e	12.2 e	442,751 e	5,541 e
1984	7,354 e	91,167 e	519.0 e	3,458.0 e	12.4 e	470,220 e	5,693 e
1985	7,161 e	90,649 e	529.0 e	3,575.0 e	12.7 e	499,232 e	5,836 e
1986	6,969 e	90,131 e	540.0 e	3,692.0 e	12.9 e	529,775 e	5,991 e
1987	6,777	89,613	551.0	3,809.0	13.2	562,048	6,149
1988	6,364	95,445	597.0	4,180.0 e	15.0	656,820	6,255
1989	6,140	93,604	642.0	4,552.0 e	15.2	741,368	6,859
1990	6,150	101,356	721.0	4,923.0 e	16.5	800,488	7,114
1991	6,055	103,435	763.0	5,294.0 e	17.1	874,319	7,377
1992	6,358	101,863	761.0	5,665.0	16.0	891,003	7,471
1993	6,278	101,256	784.0	6,029.0 e	16.1	960,338	7,743
1994	6,155	108,358	806.0	6,394.0 e	17.6	1,038,830	7,438
1995	6,085	108,975	838.0	6,758.0 e	17.9	1,110,600	7,690
1996	6,041 e	116,010 e	881.0 e	7,123.0 e	19.2 e	1,179,109 e	7,594 e
1997	5,998	123,045	924.0	7,487.0	20.5	1,248,249	7,509
1998	5,939 p	120,670 p	958.0 p	7,862.0 p	20.3 p	1,323,792 p	7,939 p
1999	5,893 p	123,465 p	992.0 p	8,230.0 p	21.0 p	1,396,572 p	8,035 p
2000	5,846 p	126,259 p	1,026.0 p	8,598.0 p	21.6 p	1,470,749 p	8,126 p
2001	5,799 p	129,053 p	1,060.0 p	8,966.0 p	22.3 p	1,546,129 p	8,214 p

Sources: *Economic Census of the United States*, 1982, 1987, 1992, 1997. Establishment counts, employment, and payroll are from *County Business Patterns* for non-Census years. In non-Census years, industries in the Manufacturing range under SIC coding include data from the *Annual Survey of Manufactures* (*ASM*); those in the old Services range include data from the *Services Annual Survey* (*SAS*). Values followed by a 'p' are projections by the editors. Extrapolations are marked by an 'e'. Data are the most recent available at this level of detail.

INDICES OF CHANGE

Year	Establishments (number)	Employment (number)	Payroll ($ million)	Revenues ($ million)	Employees per Establishment (number)	Revenues per Establishment ($)	Payroll per Employee ($)
1982	129.0	74.9	53.8	43.1	58.1	33.4	71.8
1987	113.0	72.8	59.6	50.9	64.5	45.0	81.9
1992	106.0	82.8	82.4	75.7	78.1	71.4	99.5
1993	104.7	82.3	84.8	80.5 e	78.6	76.9	103.1
1994	102.6	88.1	87.2	85.4 e	85.8	83.2	99.1
1995	101.5	88.6	90.7	90.3 e	87.3	89.0	102.4
1996	100.7 e	94.3 e	95.3	95.1 e	93.6 e	94.5 e	101.1 e
1997	100.0	100.0	100.0	100.0	100.0	100.0	100.0
1998	99.0 p	98.1 p	103.7 p	105.0 p	99.0 p	106.1 p	105.7 p
1999	98.2 p	100.3 p	107.4 p	109.9 p	102.1 p	111.9 p	107.0 p
2000	97.5 p	102.6 p	111.0 p	114.8 p	105.3 p	117.8 p	108.2 p
2001	96.7 p	104.9 p	114.7 p	119.8 p	108.5 p	123.9 p	109.4 p

Sources: Same as General Statistics. The values shown reflect change from the base year, 1997. Values above 100 mean greater than 1997, values below 100 mean less than 1997, and a value of 100 in the 1982-96 or 1998-2001 period means same as 1997. Values followed by a 'p' are projections by the editors; 'e' stands for extrapolation. Data are the most recent available at this level of detail.

SELECTED RATIOS

For 1997	Avg. of Information	Analyzed Industry	Index	For 1997	Avg. of Information	Analyzed Industry	Index
Employees per establishment	27	21	77	Payroll per establishment	1,131,090	154,051	14
Revenue per establishment	5,444,104	1,248,249	23	Payroll as % of revenue	21	12	59
Revenue per employee	203,255	60,848	30	Payroll per employee	42,229	7,509	18

Sources: Same as General Statistics. The 'Average' column represents the average for the industry sector, in 1997, where the currently shown industry is classified. The Index shows the relationship between the Average and the Analyzed Industry. For example, 100 means that they are equal; 500 that the Analyzed Industry is five times the average; 50 means that the Analyzed Industry is half the national average. The abbreviation 'na' is used to show that data are 'not available'.

*Equivalent to SIC 7832.

LEADING COMPANIES　　Number shown: **32**　　Total sales ($ mil): **26,722**　　Total employment (000): **232.4**

Company Name	Address				CEO Name	Phone	Co. Type	Sales ($ mil)	Empl. (000)
National Amusements Inc.	200 Elm St	Dedham	MA	02026	Sumner Redstone	781-461-1600	R	17,412*	121.7
Metro-Goldwyn-Mayer Inc.	2500 Broadway St	Santa Monica	CA	90404	Alex Yemenidjian	310-449-3000	P	1,142	0.9
AMC Entertainment Inc.	PO Box 219615	Kansas City	MO	64121	Peter C Brown	816-221-4000	P	1,027	12.3
Gaylord Entertainment Co	1 Gaylord Dr	Nashville	TN	37214	Carrie London	615-316-6000	R	768*	6.0
Regal Cinemas Inc.	7132 Commercial	Knoxville	TN	37918	Michael L Campbell	423-922-1123	P	707	12.0
United Artists Theatre Circuit Inc.	9110 E Nichols Ave	Englewood	CO	80112	Kurt Hall	303-792-3600	R	686	11.0
American Multi-Cinema Inc.	PO Box 219615	Kansas City	MO	64121	Stanley H Durwood	816-221-4000	R	658*	9.5
Paramount Pictures Corp.	5555 Melrose Ave	Los Angeles	CA	90038	Jonathan Dolgen	213-956-5000	S	526*	3.8
Carmike Cinemas Inc.	1301 1st Ave	Columbus	GA	31901	CL Patrick	706-576-3400	P	482	10.2
General Cinema Theaters	1280 Boylston St	Chestnut Hill	MA	02467	Paul R Del Rossi	617-278-5600	S	446*	7.4
GC Companies Inc.	27 Boylston St	Chestnut Hill	MA	02167	Richard Smith	617-277-4320	P	386	6.1
Whiteco Industries Inc.	1000 E 80th Pl	Merrillville	IN	46410		219-769-6601	R	380*	3.9
Marcus Corp.	250 E Wisconsin	Milwaukee	WI	53202	Stephen H Marcus	414-905-1000	P	333	7.3
Cinemark USA Inc.	3900 Dallas Pky	Plano	TX	75093	Lee Roy Mitchell	972-665-1000	R	330*	7.0
Pacific Theatres Corp.	120 N Robertson	Los Angeles	CA	90048	Jerome Forman	310-657-8420	R	280*	3.5
Reading Entertainment Inc.	1 Penn Sq	Philadelphia	PA	19102	Robert F Smerling	215-569-3344	P	172	0.3
Century Theaters	150 Pelican Wy	San Rafael	CA	94901	Raymond W Syufy	415-448-8400	R	170*	2.1
Malco Theatres Inc.	5851 Ridgeway	Memphis	TN	38120	Steve Lightman	901-761-3480	R	110*	0.6
Loeks-Star Theatres	3020 Charlevoix S E	Grand Rapids	MI	49546	Barrie L Loeks	616-940-0866	R	104*	0.6
Eastern Federal Corp.	901 East Blvd	Charlotte	NC	28203	Ira S Meiselman	704-377-3495	R	101*	0.6
Metropolitan Theaters Corp.	8727 W 3rd St	Los Angeles	CA	90048	Bruce Corwin	310-858-2800	R	82	1.0
Harkins Amusement Enterprises	7511 McDonald	Scottsdale	AZ	85250	Dan Harkins	480-627-7777	R	79*	1.2
Jack Loeks Theaters Inc.	1400 28th St S W	Grand Rapids	MI	49509	John D Loeks	616-532-6302	R	76*	0.4
Trans-Lux Corp.	PO Box 5090	Norwalk	CT	06856	Richard Brandt	203-853-4321	P	64	0.5
Cinema Grill Systems Inc.	PO Box 28467	Atlanta	GA	30358	James T Duffy	404-250-9536	R	50*	<0.1
Mann Theaters Inc.	711 Hennepin Ave	Minneapolis	MN	55403	Stephen Mann	612-332-3303	R	45*	0.6
Iwerks Entertainment Inc.	4540 W Valerio St	Burbank	CA	91505	Charles Goldwater	818-841-7766	P	35	0.1
CinemaStar Luxury Theaters Inc.	12230 Cam Real	San Diego	CA	92130	Frank Moreno	858-509-2777	P	28	0.5
Clearview Cinema Group Inc.	7 Waverly Pl	Madison	NJ	07940	A Dale Mayo	973-377-4646	P	17	0.8
Chakeres Theatres Inc.	222 N Murray St	Springfield	OH	45503	Michael H Chakeres	937-323-6447	R	12	0.5
City Cinemas	1001 3rd Ave	New York	NY	10022	Robert Smerling	212-758-5600	S	10*	<0.1
International Tourist	3562 Shep ot Hls	Branson	MO	65616	Paul E Rasmussen	417-335-3533	P	5	0.1

Source: Ward's Business Directory of U.S. Private and Public Companies, Volumes 1 and 2, 2000. The company type code used is as follows: P - Public, R - Private, S - Subsidiary, D - Division, J - Joint Venture, A - Affiliate, G - Group, N - Company type not reported. Sales are in millions of dollars, employees are in thousands. An asterisk (*) indicates an estimated sales volume. The symbol < stands for 'less than'. Company names and addresses are truncated, in some cases, to fit into the available space.

LOCATION BY STATE AND REGIONAL CONCENTRATION

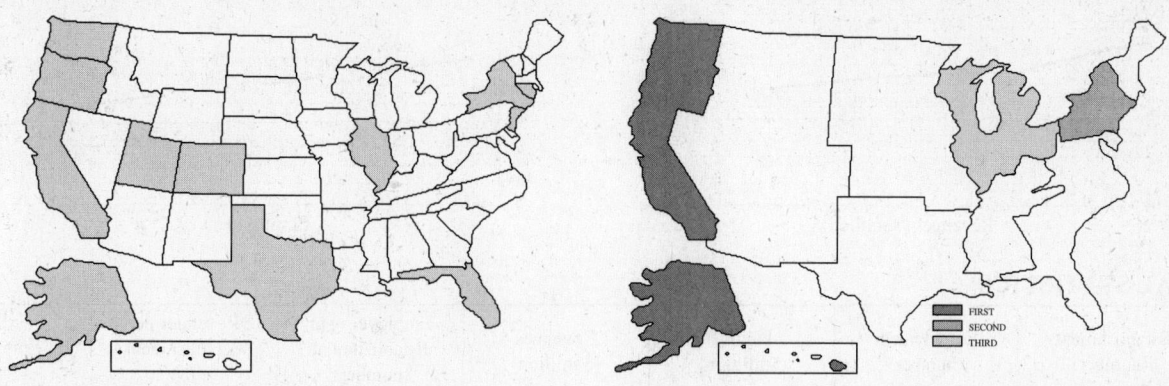

FIRST
SECOND
THIRD

INDUSTRY DATA BY STATE

State	Establishments Total (number)	Establishments % of U.S.	Employment Total (number)	Employment % of U.S.	Employment Per Estab.	Payroll Total ($ mil.)	Payroll Per Empl. ($)	Revenues Total ($ mil.)	Revenues % of U.S.	Revenues Per Estab. ($)
California	728	12.1	18,639	15.1	26	146.5	7,862	1,262.5	16.9	1,734,174
New York	383	6.4	7,255	5.9	19	78.7	10,846	630.1	8.4	1,645,230
Texas	391	6.5	10,562	8.6	27	73.6	6,967	604.0	8.1	1,544,854
Florida	283	4.7	6,325	5.1	22	45.3	7,157	433.6	5.8	1,532,134
Illinois	254	4.2	5,522	4.5	22	50.1	9,077	357.9	4.8	1,408,953
Michigan	193	3.2	4,581	3.7	24	35.5	7,743	262.3	3.5	1,358,979
New Jersey	152	2.5	3,449	2.8	23	30.3	8,778	249.0	3.3	1,638,125
Pennsylvania	212	3.5	4,125	3.4	19	27.4	6,632	243.7	3.3	1,149,354
Ohio	191	3.2	4,699	3.8	25	31.0	6,605	241.7	3.2	1,265,366
Washington	146	2.4	2,974	2.4	20	21.1	7,108	180.8	2.4	1,238,678
Virginia	128	2.1	2,586	2.1	20	19.7	7,632	174.7	2.3	1,365,227
Georgia	137	2.3	2,625	2.1	19	19.7	7,490	167.9	2.2	1,225,854
North Carolina	169	2.8	3,050	2.5	18	20.5	6,724	150.2	2.0	888,982
Colorado	131	2.2	2,345	1.9	18	15.5	6,629	139.5	1.9	1,064,779
Missouri	137	2.3	3,038	2.5	22	19.1	6,295	138.4	1.8	1,010,270
Indiana	134	2.2	2,655	2.2	20	18.0	6,789	137.0	1.8	1,022,373
Wisconsin	128	2.1	2,329	1.9	18	15.6	6,690	111.8	1.5	873,570
Tennessee	104	1.7	1,772	1.4	17	13.7	7,755	108.7	1.5	1,045,394
Oregon	104	1.7	1,749	1.4	17	11.3	6,484	107.2	1.4	1,030,654
Connecticut	72	1.2	1,330	1.1	18	11.1	8,354	97.3	1.3	1,351,917
Utah	78	1.3	1,515	1.2	19	9.8	6,462	69.1	0.9	885,615
Kentucky	70	1.2	1,516	1.2	22	8.9	5,900	66.7	0.9	952,871
South Carolina	73	1.2	1,198	1.0	16	8.5	7,068	65.9	0.9	902,329
Oklahoma	88	1.5	1,330	1.1	15	8.6	6,498	63.6	0.8	722,534
Kansas	102	1.7	1,457	1.2	14	9.2	6,342	58.5	0.8	573,382
Idaho	61	1.0	649	0.5	11	4.2	6,394	29.3	0.4	480,770
Alaska	20	0.3	306	0.2	15	2.3	7,497	25.1	0.3	1,253,250
New Hampshire	28	0.5	475	0.4	17	4.7	9,819	24.3	0.3	867,321
D.C.	16	0.3	287	0.2	18	3.7	12,941	23.2	0.3	1,449,125
West Virginia	31	0.5	436	0.4	14	3.5	8,112	22.6	0.3	728,258
Maine	34	0.6	335	0.3	10	2.3	6,722	22.1	0.3	648,882
Montana	50	0.8	574	0.5	11	2.8	4,869	21.6	0.3	432,780
Delaware	15	0.3	263	0.2	18	1.7	6,441	17.1	0.2	1,142,067
Vermont	25	0.4	236	0.2	9	1.7	7,144	15.4	0.2	615,640
Minnesota	136	2.3	3,750*	-	-	(D)	-	(D)	-	-
Massachusetts	128	2.1	3,750*	-	-	(D)	-	(D)	-	-
Iowa	107	1.8	1,750*	-	-	(D)	-	(D)	-	-
Arizona	97	1.6	3,750*	-	-	(D)	-	(D)	-	-
Maryland	91	1.5	1,750*	-	-	(D)	-	(D)	-	-
Louisiana	77	1.3	1,750*	-	-	(D)	-	(D)	-	-
Nebraska	71	1.2	750*	-	-	(D)	-	(D)	-	-
Arkansas	70	1.2	750*	-	-	(D)	-	(D)	-	-
Alabama	68	1.1	750*	-	-	(D)	-	(D)	-	-
New Mexico	65	1.1	1,750*	-	-	(D)	-	(D)	-	-
Mississippi	44	0.7	750*	-	-	(D)	-	(D)	-	-
Hawaii	35	0.6	1,750*	-	-	(D)	-	(D)	-	-
Nevada	33	0.6	750*	-	-	(D)	-	(D)	-	-
Wyoming	33	0.6	375*	-	-	(D)	-	(D)	-	-
South Dakota	28	0.5	375*	-	-	(D)	-	(D)	-	-
North Dakota	26	0.4	375*	-	-	(D)	-	(D)	-	-
Rhode Island	21	0.4	375*	-	-	(D)	-	(D)	-	-

Source: 1997 *Economic Census*. The states are in descending order of revenues or establishments (if revenue data are missing for the majority). The symbol (D) appears when data are withheld to prevent disclosure of competitive information. States marked with (D) are sorted by number of establishments. A dash (-) indicates that the data element cannot be calculated. * indicates the midpoint of a range; 175, for example is the range 100-249. Shaded *states* on the state map indicate those states which have proportionately greater representation in the industry than would be indicated by the state's population; the ratio is based on total revenues or number of establishments. Shaded *regions* indicate where the industry is regionally most concentrated.

NAICS 512132 - DRIVE-IN MOTION PICTURE THEATERS*

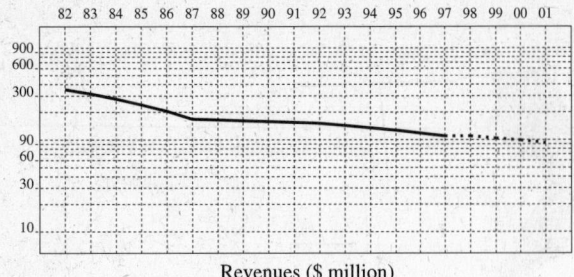

Revenues ($ million)

Employment (000)

GENERAL STATISTICS

Year	Establishments (number)	Employment (number)	Payroll ($ million)	Revenues ($ million)	Employees per Establishment (number)	Revenues per Establishment ($)	Payroll per Employee ($)
1982	2,282	11,258	70.0	351.0	4.9	153,812	6,218
1983	2,025 e	9,901 e	62.0 e	315.0 e	4.9 e	155,556 e	6,262 e
1984	1,769 e	8,544 e	55.0 e	278.0 e	4.8 e	157,151 e	6,437 e
1985	1,512 e	7,187 e	48.0 e	241.0 e	4.8 e	159,392 e	6,679 e
1986	1,256 e	5,830 e	41.0 e	205.0 e	4.6 e	163,217 e	7,033 e
1987	999	4,473	33.0	168.0	4.5	168,168	7,378
1988	798	5,634	38.0	165.0 e	7.1	206,767	6,745
1989	689	4,727	35.0	161.0 e	6.9	233,672	7,404
1990	629	4,313	33.0	158.0 e	6.9	251,192	7,651
1991	648	4,407	36.0	155.0 e	6.8	239,198	8,169
1992	534	3,325	27.0	151.0	6.2	282,772	8,120
1993	453	3,096	27.0	143.0 e	6.8	315,673	8,721
1994	435	3,195	25.0	135.0 e	7.3	310,345	7,825
1995	412	2,450	25.0	127.0 e	5.9	308,252	10,204
1996	386 e	2,223 e	23.0 e	118.0 e	5.8 e	305,699 e	10,346 e
1997	360	1,996	21.0	110.0	5.5	305,556	10,521
1998	235 p	1,636 p	20.0 p	110.0 p	7.0 p	468,085 p	12,225 p
1999	178 p	1,305 p	18.0 p	104.0 p	7.3 p	584,270 p	13,793 p
2000	122 p	974 p	16.0 p	99.0 p	8.0 p	811,475 p	16,427 p
2001	65 p	643 p	15.0 p	93.0 p	9.9 p	1,430,769 p	23,328 p

Sources: Economic Census of the United States, 1982, 1987, 1992, 1997. Establishment counts, employment, and payroll are from *County Business Patterns* for non-Census years. In non-Census years, industries in the Manufacturing range under SIC coding include data from the *Annual Survey of Manufactures* (ASM); those in the old Services range include data from the *Services Annual Survey* (SAS). Values followed by a 'p' are projections by the editors. Extrapolations are marked by 'e'. Data are the most recent available at this level of detail.

INDICES OF CHANGE

Year	Establishments (number)	Employment (number)	Payroll ($ million)	Revenues ($ million)	Employees per Establishment (number)	Revenues per Establishment ($)	Payroll per Employee ($)
1982	633.9	564.0	333.3	319.1	89.0	50.3	59.1
1987	277.5	224.1	157.1	152.7	80.8	55.0	70.1
1992	148.3	166.6	128.6	137.3	112.3	92.5	77.2
1993	125.8	155.1	128.6	130.0 e	123.3	103.3	82.9
1994	120.8	160.1	119.0	122.7 e	132.5	101.6	74.4
1995	114.4	122.7	119.0	115.5 e	107.3	100.9	97.0
1996	107.2 e	111.4 e	109.5 e	107.3 e	103.9 e	100.0 e	98.3 e
1997	100.0	100.0	100.0	100.0	100.0	100.0	100.0
1998	65.3 p	82.0 p	95.2 p	100.0 p	125.6 p	153.2 p	116.2 p
1999	49.4 p	65.4 p	85.7 p	94.5 p	132.2 p	191.2 p	131.1 p
2000	33.9 p	48.8 p	76.2 p	90.0 p	144.0 p	265.6 p	156.1 p
2001	18.1 p	32.2 p	71.4 p	84.5 p	178.4 p	468.3 p	221.7 p

Sources: Same as General Statistics. The values shown reflect change from the base year, 1997. Values above 100 mean greater than 1997, values below 100 mean less than 1997, and a value of 100 in the 1982-96 or 1998-2001 period means same as 1997. Values followed by a 'p' are projections by the editors; 'e' stands for extrapolation. Data are the most recent available at this level of detail.

SELECTED RATIOS

For 1997	Avg. of Information	Analyzed Industry	Index	For 1997	Avg. of Information	Analyzed Industry	Index
Employees per establishment	27	6	21	Payroll per establishment	1,131,090	58,333	5
Revenue per establishment	5,444,104	305,556	6	Payroll as % of revenue	21	19	92
Revenue per employee	203,255	55,110	27	Payroll per employee	42,229	10,521	25

Sources: Same as General Statistics. The 'Average' column represents the average for the industry sector, in 1997, where the currently shown industry is classified. The Index shows the relationship between the Average and the Analyzed Industry. For example, 100 means that they are equal; 500 that the Analyzed Industry is five times the average; 50 means that the Analyzed Industry is half the national average. The abbreviation 'na' is used to show that data are 'not available'.

*Equivalent to SIC 7833.

LEADING COMPANIES   Number shown: **2**   Total sales ($ mil): **117**   Total employment (000): **0.9**

Company Name	Address				CEO Name	Phone	Co. Type	Sales ($ mil)	Empl. (000)
Jack Loeks Theaters Inc.	1400 28th St S W	Grand Rapids	MI	49509	John D. Loeks	616-532-6302	R	76*	0.4
De Anza Land and Leisure Corp.	1615 Cordova St	Los Angeles	CA	90007	William Oldknow	213-734-9951	R	41*	0.5

Source: Ward's Business Directory of U.S. Private and Public Companies, Volumes 1 and 2, 2000. The company type code used is as follows: P - Public, R - Private, S - Subsidiary, D - Division, J - Joint Venture, A - Affiliate, G - Group, N - Company type not reported. Sales are in millions of dollars, employees are in thousands. An asterisk (*) indicates an estimated sales volume. The symbol < stands for 'less than'. Company names and addresses are truncated, in some cases, to fit into the available space.

LOCATION BY STATE AND REGIONAL CONCENTRATION

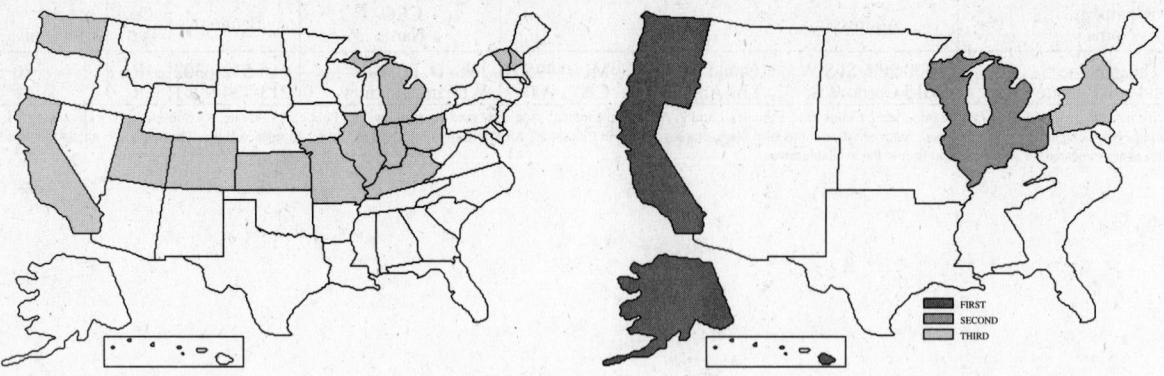

FIRST
SECOND
THIRD

INDUSTRY DATA BY STATE

State	Establishments Total (number)	Establishments % of U.S.	Employment Total (number)	Employment % of U.S.	Employment Per Estab.	Payroll Total ($ mil.)	Payroll Per Empl. ($)	Revenues Total ($ mil.)	Revenues % of U.S.	Revenues Per Estab. ($)
California	42	11.7	915	45.8	22	7.2	7,879	35.0	31.7	833,214
Texas	8	2.2	52	2.6	7	0.9	16,558	5.9	5.3	736,250
Ohio	37	10.3	27	1.4	1	1.0	37,889	5.9	5.4	160,703
Illinois	16	4.4	127	6.4	8	1.4	11,000	5.9	5.4	369,375
Florida	9	2.5	107	5.4	12	0.8	7,523	4.8	4.3	529,889
Pennsylvania	29	8.1	30	1.5	1	0.6	20,000	4.7	4.3	163,241
New York	21	5.8	13	0.7	1	0.6	44,385	4.5	4.0	212,714
Michigan	9	2.5	24	1.2	3	1.1	46,875	4.2	3.8	465,889
Indiana	19	5.3	18	0.9	1	0.4	22,944	3.0	2.7	159,000
Utah	6	1.7	63	3.2	10	0.4	6,825	3.0	2.7	499,167
Washington	10	2.8	35	1.8	4	0.5	14,086	2.7	2.5	270,500
Kentucky	15	4.2	35	1.8	2	0.6	16,657	2.6	2.4	173,133
Missouri	10	2.8	33	1.7	3	0.4	12,242	2.5	2.2	245,700
Georgia	6	1.7	69	3.5	11	0.4	5,188	2.2	2.0	359,667
Tennessee	9	2.5	49	2.5	5	0.3	6,224	2.1	1.9	235,000
Colorado	6	1.7	32	1.6	5	0.2	6,969	1.5	1.4	250,833
Oregon	7	1.9	39	2.0	6	0.2	4,231	1.2	1.1	174,286
Kansas	6	1.7	22	1.1	4	0.2	9,909	1.2	1.1	196,000
Connecticut	3	0.8	3	0.2	1	0.3	90,333	1.2	1.0	385,333
New Hampshire	6	1.7	17	0.9	3	0.3	16,000	1.1	1.0	176,333
Wisconsin	7	1.9	19	1.0	3	0.2	9,632	1.1	1.0	159,000
Virginia	5	1.4	4	0.2	1	0.1	20,750	0.7	0.6	141,400
Oklahoma	5	1.4	3	0.2	1	0.1	43,000	0.7	0.7	146,400
Vermont	3	0.8	4	0.2	1	0.1	35,250	0.7	0.7	240,000
North Carolina	5	1.4	15	0.8	3	0.1	8,000	0.6	0.5	116,400
West Virginia	7	1.9	3	0.2	-	0.1	21,333	0.4	0.4	59,286
Maine	4	1.1	3	0.2	1	0.1	17,333	0.4	0.3	89,500
Montana	5	1.4	-	-	-	-	-	0.3	0.2	50,200
Idaho	3	0.8	-	-	-	-	-	0.2	0.2	65,667
South Dakota	6	1.7	10*	-	-	(D)	-	(D)	-	-
Arizona	4	1.1	60*	-	-	(D)	-	(D)	-	-
Iowa	4	1.1	10*	-	-	(D)	-	(D)	-	-
Massachusetts	4	1.1	10*	-	-	(D)	-	(D)	-	-
Minnesota	4	1.1	10*	-	-	(D)	-	(D)	-	-
Nevada	3	0.8	60*	-	-	(D)	-	(D)	-	-
Alabama	2	0.6	10*	-	-	(D)	-	(D)	-	-
Arkansas	2	0.6	10*	-	-	(D)	-	(D)	-	-
Nebraska	2	0.6	10*	-	-	(D)	-	(D)	-	-
New Mexico	2	0.6	10*	-	-	(D)	-	(D)	-	-
Rhode Island	2	0.6	10*	-	-	(D)	-	(D)	-	-
Wyoming	2	0.6	10*	-	-	(D)	-	(D)	-	-
Hawaii	1	0.3	60*	-	-	(D)	-	(D)	-	-
Louisiana	1	0.3	10*	-	-	(D)	-	(D)	-	-
Maryland	1	0.3	10*	-	-	(D)	-	(D)	-	-
Mississippi	1	0.3	10*	-	-	(D)	-	(D)	-	-
North Dakota	1	0.3	10*	-	-	(D)	-	(D)	-	-

Source: 1997 *Economic Census*. The states are in descending order of revenues or establishments (if revenue data are missing for the majority). The symbol (D) appears when data are withheld to prevent disclosure of competitive information. States marked with (D) are sorted by number of establishments. A dash (-) indicates that the data element cannot be calculated. * indicates the midpoint of a range; 175, for example is the range 100-249. Shaded *states* on the state map indicate those states which have proportionately greater representation in the industry than would be indicated by the state's population; the ratio is based on total revenues or number of establishments. Shaded *regions* indicate where the industry is regionally most concentrated.

NAICS 512191 - TELEPRODUCTION AND OTHER POSTPRODUCTION SERVICES

GENERAL STATISTICS

Year	Establishments (number)	Employment (number)	Payroll ($ million)	Revenues ($ million)	Employees per Establishment (number)	Revenues per Establishment ($)	Payroll per Employee ($)
1997	3,001	29,114	1,437.0	3,684.0	9.7	1,227,591	49,358

Source: Economic Census of the United States, 1997. This is a newly defined industry. Data for prior years were unavailable at the time of publication but may become available over time.

INDICES OF CHANGE

Year	Establishments (number)	Employment (number)	Payroll ($ million)	Revenues ($ million)	Employees per Establishment (number)	Revenues per Establishment ($)	Payroll per Employee ($)
1997	100.0	100.0	100.0	100.0	100.0	100.0	100.0

Sources: Same as General Statistics. The values shown reflect change from the base year, 1997. Values above 100 mean greater than 1997, values below 100 mean less than 1997, and a value of 100 in the 1982-96 or 1998-2001 period means same as 1997. Values followed by a 'p' are projections by the editors; 'e' stands for extrapolation. Data are the most recent available at this level of detail.

SIC INDUSTRIES RELATED TO NAICS 512191

Each new NAICS code represents an industry that used to be part of an SIC or a part of several SIC industries. Data in this table are shown to provide transitional information for these cases. All available data for the precursor SIC(s) are shown. Even if only a part of an SIC is included in the NAICS, *all* data for the SIC are reproduced. If the SIC industry is not marked as being a part (pt) of the NAICS, the entire industry is embedded in the NAICS data. The SIC composition of the new industry provides some hints of the relative importance of its "ancestors." Data marked with a 'p' are projected. Projections begin with 1982 data. Data earlier than 1990 are not shown but are reflected in the projections.

SIC	Industry	1990	1991	1992	1993	1994	1995	1996	1997
7819	**Services Allied to Motion Pictures (pt)**								
	Establishments (number)	2,984	2,955	3,895	3,799	3,691	3,289	3,584p	3,622p
	Employment (thousands)	113.1	102.4	162.2	158.8	130.9	136.7	160.9p	169.5p
	Revenues ($ million)	-	-	7,514.7	-	-	-	-	-

Source: Economic Census of the United States, 1992, annual surveys of economic sectors conducted by the Bureau of the Census, and estimates or projections based on the 1982-1992 period; not all data are shown. 'e' marks estimates made by the editors; 'p' indicates projections based on time series. A dash (-) indicates that data for this SIC or year were not available. The abbreviation (pt) next to the industry name indicates that only a part of the industry is present within the NAICS data. If no (pt) is shown, the entire industry is contained within the NAICS data.

SELECTED RATIOS

For 1997	Avg. of Information	Analyzed Industry	Index	For 1997	Avg. of Information	Analyzed Industry	Index
Employees per establishment	27	10	36	Payroll per establishment	1,131,090	478,840	42
Revenue per establishment	5,444,104	1,227,591	23	Payroll as % of revenue	21	39	188
Revenue per employee	203,255	126,537	62	Payroll per employee	42,229	49,358	117

Sources: Same as General Statistics. The 'Average' column represents the average for the industry sector, in 1997, where the currently shown industry is classified. The Index shows the relationship between the Average and the Analyzed Industry. For example, 100 means that they are equal; 500 that the Analyzed Industry is five times the average; 50 means that the Analyzed Industry is half the national average. The abbreviation 'na' is used to show that data are 'not available'.

LEADING COMPANIES Number shown: **75** Total sales ($ mil): **4,630** Total employment (000): **31.8**

Company Name	Address				CEO Name	Phone	Co. Type	Sales ($ mil)	Empl. (000)
Universal Studios Inc.	100 Universal City	Universal City	CA	91608	Ron Meyer	818-777-1000	S	1,794*	13.0
Technicolor Video Services Inc.	3233 E Miss Oaks	Camarillo	CA	93012	Orlando Raimondo	805-445-1122	S	500*	5.0
Lucas Digital Limited L.L.C.	PO Box 2459	San Rafael	CA	94912	Jim Morris	415-448-9000	D	243*	1.0
Four Media Co.	2813 W Alameda	Burbank	CA	91505	Jeffrey J Marcketta	818-840-7000	P	197	1.5
Video Monitoring Service	330 W 42nd St	New York	NY	10036	Bob Cohen	212-736-2010	R	195*	0.8
Deluxe Laboratories Inc.	1377 N Serrano Ave	Hollywood	CA	90027	Cyril Drabinsky	323-462-6171	S	150*	0.5
Todd-AO Corp.	900 N Seward St	Hollywood	CA	90038	Salah M Hassanein	323-962-5304	P	118	0.9
VDI Multimedia	6920 Sunset Blvd	Hollywood	CA	90038	R Luke Stefanko	323-957-5500	P	99*	0.6
Cinram Inc.	1600 Rich Rd	Richmond	IN	47374		765-962-9511	R	97*	0.8
Cine Magnetics Inc.	100 Business	Armonk	NY	10504	JJ Barber Jr	914-273-7500	R	79*	0.3
Media Copy	1739 Doolittle Dr	San Leandro	CA	94577	Herb Fischer	510-618-2400	R	75*	0.6
Allied-Vaughn Div.	7951 Computer S	Bloomington	MN	55435	E David Willette		D	74	0.8
Digital Domain Inc.	300 Rose Ave	Venice	CA	90291	Scott Ross	310-314-2800	R	73*	0.3
Modern Videofilm Inc.	4411 W Olive Ave	Burbank	CA	91505	Moshe Barkat	818-840-1700	R	61*	0.3
Consolidated Film Industries	959 Seward St	Hollywood	CA	90038	Bob Boitcher	323-960-7444	D	50*	0.4
Soundelux Entertainment Group	7080 Hollywood	Hollywood	CA	90028	Jeff Edell	323-603-3200	R	49*	0.2
Henninger Media Services Inc.	2601-A Wilson Blvd	Arlington	VA	22201	Robert Henninger	703-243-3444	R	48*	0.2
New York Media Group	220 E 42nd St 2nd Fl	New York	NY	10017	Jean Winkler	212-972-3400	R	48*	0.2
Complete Post Inc.	6087 W Sunset Blvd	Hollywood	CA	90028	Bob Brian	323-467-1244	S	41*	0.2
Pioneer Video Manufacturing Inc.	PO Box 4368	Carson	CA	90749	Shinichi Suzuki	310-518-0710	S	41*	0.3
Todd-AO Studios	900 N Seward St	Los Angeles	CA	90039	Christopher D Jenkins	213-962-4000	S	40*	0.3
Laser-Pacific Media Corp.	809 N Cahuenga	Hollywood	CA	90038	Emory M Cohen	323-462-6266	P	31	0.2
Universal Studios Home Video	10 Universal City	Universal City	CA	91608	Craig Kronblay	818-777-4300	D	30*	0.1
Dream Quest Images	2635 Park Center Dr	Simi Valley	CA	93065		805-581-2671	S	28*	0.2
Tape House Editorial Co.	216 East 45th St	New York	NY	10017	Mark Polyocan	212-557-4949	R	28	0.0
WRS Motion Picture & Video	1000 Napor Blvd	Pittsburgh	PA	15205	FJ Napor	412-937-7700	R	26*	0.3
Broadway Video Inc.	1619 Broadway	New York	NY	10019	Peter Rudoy	212-265-7600	R	25*	0.3
Raleigh TV and Film Studios	5300 Melrose Ave	Hollywood	CA	90038	Micahel Moore	323-466-3111	R	25*	0.1
Duplication Factory Inc.	4275 Norex Dr	Chaska	MN	55318	Barry Johnson	612-448-9912	R	23*	0.1
Hollywood Rental Company Inc.	3111 Kenwood St	Burbank	CA	91505	Carly Barber	818-525-5250	S	21	0.1
Digital Lab Inc.	321 Hampton Dr	Venice	CA	90291	Alan Barnett	310-399-5670	R	20	<0.1
American Production Services	2247 15th Ave W	Seattle	WA	98119	Conrad W Denke	206-282-1776	R	16*	<0.1
Digital Image	100 Universal City	Universal City	CA	91608		818-777-7999	D	16*	0.3
Avenue Edit Inc.	625 N Michigan Ave	Chicago	IL	60611	Richard Ledyard	312-943-7100	R	13*	<0.1
C.I.S. Hollywood	1144 N Las Palmas	Hollywood	CA	90038	Marie Davis	213-463-8811	D	12	<0.1
Digital Magic Co.	3000 W Olympic	Santa Monica	CA	90404	Mark Miller	310-315-9505	D	12*	<0.1
Las Palmas Productions Inc.	1144 N Las Palmas	Los Angeles	CA	90038	Marie Davis	323-463-8811	R	12	<0.1
Chapman/Leonard Studio	12950 Raymer St	N. Hollywood	CA	91605	Leonard Chapman		R	11*	<0.1
Roland House Inc.	2020 N 14th St	Arlington	VA	22201	Fritz Roland	703-525-7000	R	11*	<0.1
Audio Plus Video Intern. Inc.	235 Pegasus Ave	Northvale	NJ	07647	Donald Buck	201-767-3800	S	10	<0.1
Fayette Products Inc.	400 W Erie St	Chicago	IL	60610	Mike Fayette	312-944-1690	R	10*	<0.1
Filmworkers Club	232 E Ohio St	Chicago	IL	60611	Alan Kubicka	312-664-9333	R	10*	<0.1
Manhattan Transfer Miami	1111 Lincoln Rd	Miami	FL	33139		305-674-0700	S	9*	<0.1
Motion Picture Laboratories Inc.	781 S Main St	Memphis	TN	38106	David Powers	901-774-4944	R	9*	<0.1
Todd-AO Video Services	1135 N Mansfield	Hollywood	CA	90038	Richard O'Hare	213-465-1231	D	9	<0.1
Cutters Inc.	515 State St	Chicago	IL	60610	Tim McGuire	312-644-2500	R	8*	<0.1
Video Post and Transfer Inc.	2727 Inwood Rd	Dallas	TX	75235	Neil Feldman	214-350-2676	R	8*	<0.1
Camera Service Center Inc.	619 W 54th St	New York	NY	10019	Volker Bahnemann	212-757-0906	S	7*	<0.1
Chicago Scenic Studios Inc.	1315 N N Branch	Chicago	IL	60622	Robert F Doepel	312-274-9900	R	7*	<0.1
Interface Video Systems Inc.	1233 20th St N W	Washington	DC	20036	Tom Angell	202-861-0500	R	7	<0.1
Recorded Publications	1100 State St	Camden	NJ	08105	John Oliano	856-963-3000	R	7*	<0.1
Century Park Pictures Corp.	4701 IDS Ctr	Minneapolis	MN	55402	Thomas K Scallen	612-333-5100	P	7	0.3
Crew Connection Inc.	P O Box 2101	Evergreen	CO	80437	Heidi McLean	303-670-0303	R	7	<0.1
Archive Films/Archive Photos	530 W 25th St	New York	NY	10001	Patrick Montgomery	212-822-7800	S	6*	0.1
TPFV Group Inc.	501 N IH 35	Austin	TX	78702	Richard Kooris	512-476-3876	R	6*	<0.1
Western Images	600 Townsend St	San Francisco	CA	94103	Michael Cunningham	415-252-6000	D	6*	<0.1
Cabana Corp.	535 5th Ave	New York	NY	10017	David E Cooper	212-450-9200	S	5*	<0.1
Crew Cuts Film and Tape Inc.	28 W 44th St	New York	NY	10036	Clayton Hemmert	212-302-2828	R	5*	<0.1
Media City Teleproduction Center	2525 N Naomi St	Burbank	CA	91504	Marty Giller	818-848-5800	R	5	<0.1
Video Post Productions Inc.	4600 Madison Ave	Kansas City	MO	64112	Michael Wunsch	816-531-1225	R	5*	<0.1
Banner Media Services	6215 S 107 E Ave	Tulsa	OK	74133	Mike Loomis	918-254-2540	R	4*	<0.1
Hollywood Film and Video Inc.	6060 Sunset Blvd	Hollywood	CA	90028	Alex A Moradian	213-464-2181	R	4*	<0.1
SMA Video Inc.	100 Av Americas	New York	NY	10013	Michael J Morrissey	212-226-7474	R	4*	<0.1
501 Group Inc.	501 N Interregional	Austin	TX	78702	Mark Welch	512-476-3876	S	4	<0.1
City Post Film Co.	510 Marquette	Minneapolis	MN	55402	Charles Lach	612-338-6577	R	4	<0.1
EFILM	1146 N Las Palmas	Hollywood	CA	90038		213-463-7041	R	4	<0.1
Avenue Entertainment Group Inc.	11755 Wilshire Blvd	Los Angeles	CA	90025	Cary Brokaw	310-996-6800	P	3*	<0.1
CitiCam Video Productions Inc.	630 9th Ave	New York	NY	10036	Gary Nardilla	212-315-4855	R	3*	<0.1
Edit Sweet Inc.	515 N State St	Chicago	IL	60610	Jeanne Bonansinga	312-755-0155	R	3	<0.1
Media Funding Corp.	8430 Terminal Rd	Newington	VA	22122	Donald Evans	703-550-1500	R	3*	<0.1
Video Communications Inc.	11333 E 60th Pl	Tulsa	OK	74146	Robert Blair	918-254-6337	R	3*	<0.1
Chace Productions Inc.	201 S Victory Blvd	Burbank	CA	91502	Robert J Heiber	818-842-8346	R	2	<0.1
Jeff Meltzer Editorial Inc.	729 7th Ave	New York	NY	10019	Jeff Meltzer	212-302-5423	R	2	<0.1
Lost Planet Inc.	113 Spring St	New York	NY	10012	Hank Corwin	212-226-5678	R	2	<0.1
Pi Edit	23 E 22nd 2nd Fl	New York	NY	10010	Rob Cauicchio	212-254-0202	D	2*	<0.1

Source: Ward's Business Directory of U.S. Private and Public Companies, Volumes 1 and 2, 2000. The company type code used is as follows: P - Public, R - Private, S - Subsidiary, D - Division, J - Joint Venture, A - Affiliate, G - Group, N - Company type not reported. Sales are in millions of dollars, employees are in thousands. An asterisk (*) indicates an estimated sales volume. The symbol < stands for 'less than'. Company names and addresses are truncated, in some cases, to fit into the available space.

LOCATION BY STATE AND REGIONAL CONCENTRATION

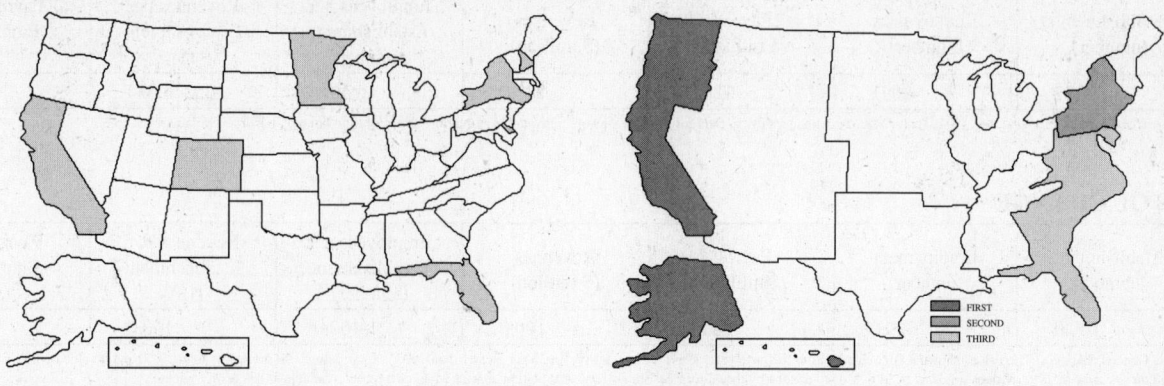

FIRST
SECOND
THIRD

INDUSTRY DATA BY STATE

State	Establishments Total (number)	% of U.S.	Employment Total (number)	% of U.S.	Per Estab.	Payroll Total ($ mil.)	Per Empl. ($)	Revenues Total ($ mil.)	% of U.S.	Per Estab. ($)
California	997	33.2	13,195	45.3	13	752.5	57,031	1,716.3	46.6	1,721,509
New York	403	13.4	4,113	14.1	10	252.7	61,429	647.4	17.6	1,606,514
Illinois	120	4.0	1,070	3.7	9	51.1	47,719	153.9	4.2	1,282,775
Florida	159	5.3	1,000	3.4	6	35.7	35,699	117.4	3.2	738,094
Texas	109	3.6	775	2.7	7	28.0	36,169	96.4	2.6	884,844
Georgia	65	2.2	839	2.9	13	37.8	45,018	88.0	2.4	1,353,215
Pennsylvania	66	2.2	478	1.6	7	21.2	44,347	84.0	2.3	1,272,833
Michigan	57	1.9	622	2.1	11	25.6	41,082	70.9	1.9	1,243,947
Colorado	42	1.4	480	1.6	11	17.1	35,669	60.2	1.6	1,433,095
New Jersey	74	2.5	461	1.6	6	14.1	30,544	50.2	1.4	678,230
Massachusetts	45	1.5	345	1.2	8	14.2	41,301	40.0	1.1	888,111
D.C.	29	1.0	344	1.2	12	15.8	45,965	39.7	1.1	1,369,069
Tennessee	33	1.1	316	1.1	10	8.4	26,503	35.9	1.0	1,087,667
Wisconsin	35	1.2	291	1.0	8	9.5	32,660	28.5	0.8	813,000
Washington	44	1.5	317	1.1	7	10.3	32,615	27.4	0.7	621,750
Missouri	35	1.2	234	0.8	7	8.7	37,051	24.2	0.7	690,600
North Carolina	43	1.4	173	0.6	4	5.1	29,526	18.2	0.5	423,000
New Hampshire	14	0.5	63	0.2	5	3.2	50,794	16.5	0.4	1,180,857
Kentucky	22	0.7	129	0.4	6	3.4	26,659	13.8	0.4	626,318
Utah	19	0.6	144	0.5	8	5.0	34,715	11.7	0.3	613,316
Louisiana	24	0.8	133	0.5	6	3.4	25,880	10.0	0.3	414,750
Oklahoma	16	0.5	93	0.3	6	2.7	28,527	8.6	0.2	539,875
Vermont	5	0.2	14	0.0	3	0.4	25,429	1.2	0.0	248,600
West Virginia	4	0.1	11	0.0	3	0.2	17,182	0.8	0.0	196,500
Virginia	74	2.5	750*	-	-	(D)	-	(D)	-	-
Minnesota	71	2.4	750*	-	-	(D)	-	(D)	-	-
Ohio	66	2.2	750*	-	-	(D)	-	(D)	-	-
Maryland	41	1.4	375*	-	-	(D)	-	(D)	-	-
Connecticut	36	1.2	175*	-	-	(D)	-	(D)	-	-
Indiana	31	1.0	175*	-	-	(D)	-	(D)	-	-
Arizona	29	1.0	175*	-	-	(D)	-	(D)	-	-
Oregon	24	0.8	175*	-	-	(D)	-	(D)	-	-
Alabama	20	0.7	60*	-	-	(D)	-	(D)	-	-
Iowa	17	0.6	60*	-	-	(D)	-	(D)	-	-
South Carolina	15	0.5	60*	-	-	(D)	-	(D)	-	-
Nevada	14	0.5	60*	-	-	(D)	-	(D)	-	-
Kansas	13	0.4	175*	-	-	(D)	-	(D)	-	-
Nebraska	12	0.4	60*	-	-	(D)	-	(D)	-	-
Delaware	11	0.4	60*	-	-	(D)	-	(D)	-	-
Hawaii	11	0.4	60*	-	-	(D)	-	(D)	-	-
New Mexico	11	0.4	60*	-	-	(D)	-	(D)	-	-
Arkansas	10	0.3	60*	-	-	(D)	-	(D)	-	-
South Dakota	6	0.2	10*	-	-	(D)	-	(D)	-	-
Maine	5	0.2	60*	-	-	(D)	-	(D)	-	-
Mississippi	5	0.2	10*	-	-	(D)	-	(D)	-	-
Rhode Island	5	0.2	10*	-	-	(D)	-	(D)	-	-
Alaska	4	0.1	10*	-	-	(D)	-	(D)	-	-
North Dakota	4	0.1	60*	-	-	(D)	-	(D)	-	-
Idaho	3	0.1	10*	-	-	(D)	-	(D)	-	-
Montana	3	0.1	10*	-	-	(D)	-	(D)	-	-

Source: 1997 *Economic Census*. The states are in descending order of revenues or establishments (if revenue data are missing for the majority). The symbol (D) appears when data are withheld to prevent disclosure of competitive information. States marked with (D) are sorted by number of establishments. A dash (-) indicates that the data element cannot be calculated. * indicates the midpoint of a range; 175, for example is the range 100-249. Shaded *states* on the state map indicate those states which have proportionately greater representation in the industry than would be indicated by the state's population; the ratio is based on total revenues or number of establishments. Shaded *regions* indicate where the industry is regionally most concentrated.

NAICS 512199 - MOTION PICTURE AND VIDEO INDUSTRIES NEC

GENERAL STATISTICS

Year	Establishments (number)	Employment (number)	Payroll ($ million)	Revenues ($ million)	Employees per Establishment (number)	Revenues per Establishment ($)	Payroll per Employee ($)
1997	377	4,091	188.0	843.0	10.9	2,236,074	45,955

Source: Economic Census of the United States, 1997. This is a newly defined industry. Data for prior years were unavailable at the time of publication but may become available over time.

INDICES OF CHANGE

Year	Establishments (number)	Employment (number)	Payroll ($ million)	Revenues ($ million)	Employees per Establishment (number)	Revenues per Establishment ($)	Payroll per Employee ($)
1997	100.0	100.0	100.0	100.0	100.0	100.0	100.0

Sources: Same as General Statistics. The values shown reflect change from the base year, 1997. Values above 100 mean greater than 1997, values below 100 mean less than 1997, and a value of 100 in the 1982-96 or 1998-2001 period means same as 1997. Values followed by a 'p' are projections by the editors; 'e' stands for extrapolation. Data are the most recent available at this level of detail.

SIC INDUSTRIES RELATED TO NAICS 512199

Each new NAICS code represents an industry that used to be part of an SIC or a part of several SIC industries. Data in this table are shown to provide transitional information for these cases. All available data for the precursor SIC(s) are shown. Even if only a part of an SIC is included in the NAICS, *all* data for the SIC are reproduced. If the SIC industry is not marked as being a part (pt) of the NAICS, the entire industry is embedded in the NAICS data. The SIC composition of the new industry provides some hints of the relative importance of its "ancestors." Data marked with a 'p' are projected. Projections begin with 1982 data. Data earlier than 1990 are not shown but are reflected in the projections.

SIC	Industry	1990	1991	1992	1993	1994	1995	1996	1997
7819	**Services Allied to Motion Pictures (pt)**								
	Establishments (number)	2,984	2,955	3,895	3,799	3,691	3,289	3,584p	3,622p
	Employment (thousands)	113.1	102.4	162.2	158.8	130.9	136.7	160.9p	169.5p
	Revenues ($ million)	-	-	7,514.7	-	-	-	-	-
7829	**Motion Picture Distribution Services (pt)**								
	Establishments (number)	164	169	210	202	188	199	200p	203p
	Employment (thousands)	1.3	1.1	0.9	1.1	1.1	1.3	1.1p	1.1p
	Revenues ($ million)	-	-	104.2	-	-	-	-	-

Source: Economic Census of the United States, 1992, annual surveys of economic sectors conducted by the Bureau of the Census, and estimates or projections based on the 1982-1992 period; not all data are shown. 'e' marks estimates made by the editors; 'p' indicates projections based on time series. A dash (-) indicates that data for this SIC or year were not available. The abbreviation (pt) next to the industry name indicates that only a part of the industry is present within the NAICS data. If no (pt) is shown, the entire industry is contained within the NAICS data.

SELECTED RATIOS

For 1997	Avg. of Information	Analyzed Industry	Index	For 1997	Avg. of Information	Analyzed Industry	Index
Employees per establishment	27	11	41	Payroll per establishment	1,131,090	498,674	44
Revenue per establishment	5,444,104	2,236,074	41	Payroll as % of revenue	21	22	107
Revenue per employee	203,255	206,062	101	Payroll per employee	42,229	45,955	109

Sources: Same as General Statistics. The 'Average' column represents the average for the industry sector, in 1997, where the currently shown industry is classified. The Index shows the relationship between the Average and the Analyzed Industry. For example, 100 means that they are equal; 500 that the Analyzed Industry is five times the average; 50 means that the Analyzed Industry is half the national average. The abbreviation 'na' is used to show that data are 'not available'.

LEADING COMPANIES   Number shown: **3**   Total sales ($ mil): **63**   Total employment (000): **0.3**

Company Name	Address				CEO Name	Phone	Co. Type	Sales ($ mil)	Empl. (000)
Beyond Films Ltd.	1875 Century Park E	Los Angeles	CA	90067		310-785-2255	S	50	0.3
EastCoast Entertainment Inc.	PO Box 11283	Richmond	VA	23230	Lee Moore	804-355-2178	R	11*	<0.1
Concepts Video Productions Inc.	170 Changebridge	Montville	NJ	07045	Collette Liantonio	973-808-5646	R	2*	<0.1

Source: Ward's Business Directory of U.S. Private and Public Companies, Volumes 1 and 2, 2000. The company type code used is as follows: P - Public, R - Private, S - Subsidiary, D - Division, J - Joint Venture, A - Affiliate, G - Group, N - Company type not reported. Sales are in millions of dollars, employees are in thousands. An asterisk (*) indicates an estimated sales volume. The symbol < stands for 'less than'. Company names and addresses are truncated, in some cases, to fit into the available space.

LOCATION BY STATE AND REGIONAL CONCENTRATION

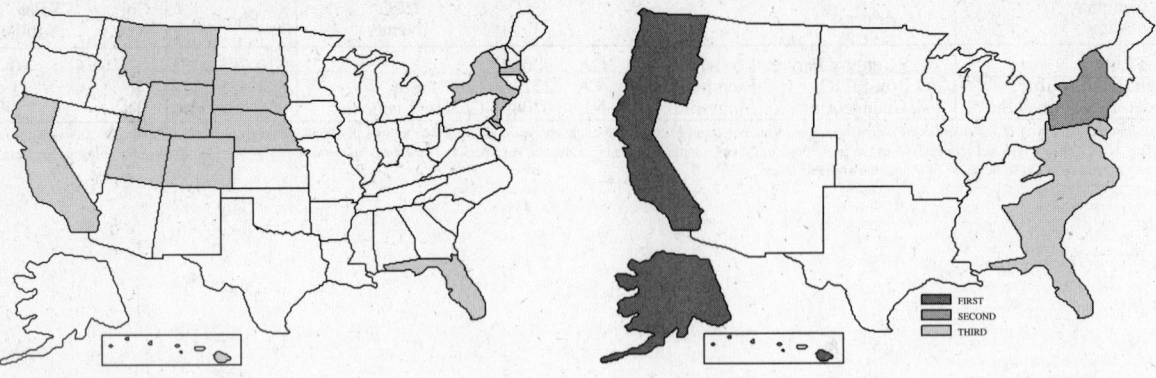

INDUSTRY DATA BY STATE

State	Establishments Total (number)	% of U.S.	Employment Total (number)	% of U.S.	Per Estab.	Payroll Total ($ mil.)	Per Empl. ($)	Revenues Total ($ mil.)	% of U.S.	Per Estab. ($)
California	135	35.8	2,160	52.8	16	130.9	60,584	654.3	77.6	4,846,696
New York	57	15.1	356	8.7	6	17.0	47,854	53.9	6.4	945,789
Illinois	16	4.2	249	6.1	16	7.8	31,289	28.8	3.4	1,799,312
Florida	21	5.6	104	2.5	5	2.7	26,029	11.3	1.3	538,810
Missouri	7	1.9	29	0.7	4	1.0	33,241	4.0	0.5	578,000
Massachusetts	11	2.9	49	1.2	4	1.1	22,041	3.8	0.4	342,273
Pennsylvania	10	2.7	19	0.5	2	1.0	51,211	3.8	0.4	376,100
Colorado	8	2.1	44	1.1	6	1.1	24,455	3.3	0.4	409,375
Tennessee	5	1.3	39	1.0	8	1.3	34,256	3.0	0.4	594,600
Texas	6	1.6	21	0.5	4	0.9	42,857	2.8	0.3	462,833
Hawaii	4	1.1	13	0.3	3	0.3	22,769	1.0	0.1	261,250
North Carolina	4	1.1	6	0.1	2	0.1	22,833	0.5	0.1	132,000
New Jersey	12	3.2	175*	-	-	(D)	-	(D)	-	-
Michigan	8	2.1	60*	-	-	(D)	-	(D)	-	-
Ohio	8	2.1	175*	-	-	(D)	-	(D)	-	-
Georgia	7	1.9	60*	-	-	(D)	-	(D)	-	-
Washington	7	1.9	60*	-	-	(D)	-	(D)	-	-
Maryland	5	1.3	175*	-	-	(D)	-	(D)	-	-
Wisconsin	5	1.3	10*	-	-	(D)	-	(D)	-	-
Minnesota	4	1.1	10*	-	-	(D)	-	(D)	-	-
Montana	3	0.8	10*	-	-	(D)	-	(D)	-	-
Nebraska	3	0.8	10*	-	-	(D)	-	(D)	-	-
Utah	3	0.8	60*	-	-	(D)	-	(D)	-	-
Alabama	2	0.5	10*	-	-	(D)	-	(D)	-	-
Arizona	2	0.5	10*	-	-	(D)	-	(D)	-	-
Connecticut	2	0.5	10*	-	-	(D)	-	(D)	-	-
Indiana	2	0.5	60*	-	-	(D)	-	(D)	-	-
Kansas	2	0.5	175*	-	-	(D)	-	(D)	-	-
Louisiana	2	0.5	10*	-	-	(D)	-	(D)	-	-
Nevada	2	0.5	10*	-	-	(D)	-	(D)	-	-
Oklahoma	2	0.5	10*	-	-	(D)	-	(D)	-	-
Oregon	2	0.5	10*	-	-	(D)	-	(D)	-	-
Virginia	2	0.5	10*	-	-	(D)	-	(D)	-	-
Delaware	1	0.3	10*	-	-	(D)	-	(D)	-	-
Iowa	1	0.3	10*	-	-	(D)	-	(D)	-	-
Maine	1	0.3	10*	-	-	(D)	-	(D)	-	-
Mississippi	1	0.3	10*	-	-	(D)	-	(D)	-	-
New Mexico	1	0.3	10*	-	-	(D)	-	(D)	-	-
South Carolina	1	0.3	10*	-	-	(D)	-	(D)	-	-
South Dakota	1	0.3	10*	-	-	(D)	-	(D)	-	-
Wyoming	1	0.3	10*	-	-	(D)	-	(D)	-	-

Source: 1997 *Economic Census*. The states are in descending order of revenues or establishments (if revenue data are missing for the majority). The symbol (D) appears when data are withheld to prevent disclosure of competitive information. States marked with (D) are sorted by number of establishments. A dash (-) indicates that the data element cannot be calculated. * indicates the midpoint of a range; 175, for example is the range 100-249. Shaded *states* on the state map indicate those states which have proportionately greater representation in the industry than would be indicated by the state's population; the ratio is based on total revenues or number of establishments. Shaded *regions* indicate where the industry is regionally most concentrated.

NAICS 512210 - RECORD PRODUCTION

GENERAL STATISTICS

Year	Establishments (number)	Employment (number)	Payroll ($ million)	Revenues ($ million)	Employees per Establishment (number)	Revenues per Establishment ($)	Payroll per Employee ($)
1997	283	998	47.0	182.0	3.5	643,110	47,094

Source: Economic Census of the United States, 1997. This is a newly defined industry. Data for prior years were unavailable at the time of publication but may become available over time.

INDICES OF CHANGE

Year	Establishments (number)	Employment (number)	Payroll ($ million)	Revenues ($ million)	Employees per Establishment (number)	Revenues per Establishment ($)	Payroll per Employee ($)
1997	100.0	100.0	100.0	100.0	100.0	100.0	100.0

Sources: Same as General Statistics. The values shown reflect change from the base year, 1997. Values above 100 mean greater than 1997, values below 100 mean less than 1997, and a value of 100 in the 1982-96 or 1998-2001 period means same as 1997. Values followed by a 'p' are projections by the editors; 'e' stands for extrapolation. Data are the most recent available at this level of detail.

SIC INDUSTRIES RELATED TO NAICS 512210

Each new NAICS code represents an industry that used to be part of an SIC or a part of several SIC industries. Data in this table are shown to provide transitional information for these cases. All available data for the precursor SIC(s) are shown. Even if only a part of an SIC is included in the NAICS, *all* data for the SIC are reproduced. If the SIC industry is not marked as being a part (pt) of the NAICS, the entire industry is embedded in the NAICS data. The SIC composition of the new industry provides some hints of the relative importance of its "ancestors." Data marked with a 'p' are projected. Projections begin with 1982 data. Data earlier than 1990 are not shown but are reflected in the projections.

SIC	Industry	1990	1991	1992	1993	1994	1995	1996	1997
8999	**Services, nec (pt)**								
	Establishments (number)	-	-	14,587	-	-	-	-	-
	Employment (thousands)	-	-	81.1	-	-	-	-	-
	Revenues ($ million)	-	-	7,966.2	-	-	-	-	-

Source: Economic Census of the United States, 1992, annual surveys of economic sectors conducted by the Bureau of the Census, and estimates or projections based on the 1982-1992 period; not all data are shown. 'e' marks estimates made by the editors; 'p' indicates projections based on time series. A dash (-) indicates that data for this SIC or year were not available. The abbreviation (pt) next to the industry name indicates that only a part of the industry is present within the NAICS data. If no (pt) is shown, the entire industry is contained within the NAICS data.

SELECTED RATIOS

For 1997	Avg. of Information	Analyzed Industry	Index	For 1997	Avg. of Information	Analyzed Industry	Index
Employees per establishment	27	4	13	Payroll per establishment	1,131,090	166,078	15
Revenue per establishment	5,444,104	643,110	12	Payroll as % of revenue	21	26	124
Revenue per employee	203,255	182,365	90	Payroll per employee	42,229	47,094	112

Sources: Same as General Statistics. The 'Average' column represents the average for the industry sector, in 1997, where the currently shown industry is classified. The Index shows the relationship between the Average and the Analyzed Industry. For example, 100 means that they are equal; 500 that the Analyzed Industry is five times the average; 50 means that the Analyzed Industry is half the national average. The abbreviation 'na' is used to show that data are 'not available'.

LEADING COMPANIES
No company data available for this industry.

LOCATION BY STATE AND REGIONAL CONCENTRATION

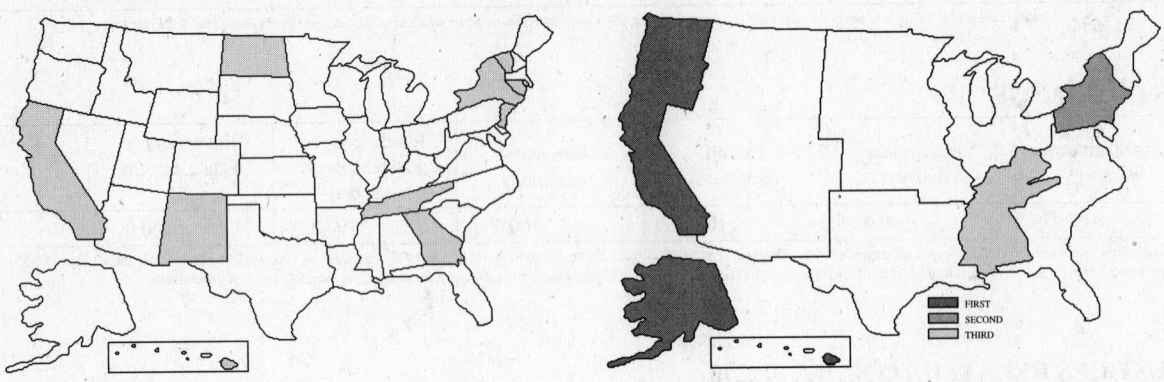

FIRST
SECOND
THIRD

INDUSTRY DATA BY STATE

State	Establishments Total (number)	Establishments % of U.S.	Employment Total (number)	Employment % of U.S.	Employment Per Estab.	Payroll Total ($ mil.)	Payroll Per Empl. ($)	Revenues Total ($ mil.)	Revenues % of U.S.	Revenues Per Estab. ($)
New York	65	23.0	275	27.6	4	14.5	52,662	63.7	34.9	979,523
California	78	27.6	341	34.2	4	15.5	45,554	56.4	31.0	723,654
Tennessee	31	11.0	97	9.7	3	4.0	41,237	17.8	9.8	575,516
Georgia	8	2.8	35	3.5	4	1.8	50,771	4.5	2.5	562,625
Texas	10	3.5	21	2.1	2	1.0	47,238	4.2	2.3	423,200
New Jersey	14	4.9	18	1.8	1	1.2	67,167	3.5	1.9	247,214
Florida	12	4.2	10	1.0	1	0.4	39,200	3.3	1.8	273,500
Colorado	3	1.1	5	0.5	2	0.7	135,800	1.9	1.0	621,333
Louisiana	4	1.4	8	0.8	2	0.2	20,000	1.0	0.5	244,500
Massachusetts	3	1.1	16	1.6	5	0.2	10,375	0.7	0.4	217,667
Illinois	7	2.5	60*	-	-	(D)	-	(D)	-	-
Pennsylvania	5	1.8	10*	-	-	(D)	-	(D)	-	-
Connecticut	4	1.4	10*	-	-	(D)	-	(D)	-	-
Virginia	4	1.4	10*	-	-	(D)	-	(D)	-	-
Ohio	3	1.1	10*	-	-	(D)	-	(D)	-	-
Washington	3	1.1	10*	-	-	(D)	-	(D)	-	-
Arizona	2	0.7	10*	-	-	(D)	-	(D)	-	-
D.C.	2	0.7	10*	-	-	(D)	-	(D)	-	-
Hawaii	2	0.7	10*	-	-	(D)	-	(D)	-	-
Michigan	2	0.7	10*	-	-	(D)	-	(D)	-	-
New Mexico	2	0.7	10*	-	-	(D)	-	(D)	-	-
North Carolina	2	0.7	10*	-	-	(D)	-	(D)	-	-
North Dakota	2	0.7	10*	-	-	(D)	-	(D)	-	-
Alabama	1	0.4	10*	-	-	(D)	-	(D)	-	-
Arkansas	1	0.4	10*	-	-	(D)	-	(D)	-	-
Indiana	1	0.4	10*	-	-	(D)	-	(D)	-	-
Kentucky	1	0.4	10*	-	-	(D)	-	(D)	-	-
Maine	1	0.4	10*	-	-	(D)	-	(D)	-	-
Maryland	1	0.4	10*	-	-	(D)	-	(D)	-	-
Missouri	1	0.4	10*	-	-	(D)	-	(D)	-	-
Nevada	1	0.4	10*	-	-	(D)	-	(D)	-	-
Oklahoma	1	0.4	10*	-	-	(D)	-	(D)	-	-
Oregon	1	0.4	10*	-	-	(D)	-	(D)	-	-
Rhode Island	1	0.4	10*	-	-	(D)	-	(D)	-	-
South Carolina	1	0.4	10*	-	-	(D)	-	(D)	-	-
Utah	1	0.4	10*	-	-	(D)	-	(D)	-	-
Vermont	1	0.4	10*	-	-	(D)	-	(D)	-	-
Wisconsin	1	0.4	60*	-	-	(D)	-	(D)	-	-

Source: 1997 *Economic Census*. The states are in descending order of revenues or establishments (if revenue data are missing for the majority). The symbol (D) appears when data are withheld to prevent disclosure of competitive information. States marked with (D) are sorted by number of establishments. A dash (-) indicates that the data element cannot be calculated. * indicates the midpoint of a range; 175, for example is the range 100-249. Shaded *states* on the state map indicate those states which have proportionately greater representation in the industry than would be indicated by the state's population; the ratio is based on total revenues or number of establishments. Shaded *regions* indicate where the industry is regionally most concentrated.

NAICS 512220 - INTEGRATED RECORD PRODUCTION/DISTRIBUTION

GENERAL STATISTICS

Year	Establishments (number)	Employment (number)	Payroll ($ million)	Revenues ($ million)	Employees per Establishment (number)	Revenues per Establishment ($)	Payroll per Employee ($)
1997	285	7,879	598.0	8,736.0	27.6	30,652,632	75,898

Source: Economic Census of the United States, 1997. This is a newly defined industry. Data for prior years were unavailable at the time of publication but may become available over time.

INDICES OF CHANGE

Year	Establishments (number)	Employment (number)	Payroll ($ million)	Revenues ($ million)	Employees per Establishment (number)	Revenues per Establishment ($)	Payroll per Employee ($)
1997	100.0	100.0	100.0	100.0	100.0	100.0	100.0

Sources: Same as General Statistics. The values shown reflect change from the base year, 1997. Values above 100 mean greater than 1997, values below 100 mean less than 1997, and a value of 100 in the 1982-96 or 1998-2001 period means same as 1997. Values followed by a 'p' are projections by the editors; 'e' stands for extrapolation. Data are the most recent available at this level of detail.

SIC INDUSTRIES RELATED TO NAICS 512220

Each new NAICS code represents an industry that used to be part of an SIC or a part of several SIC industries. Data in this table are shown to provide transitional information for these cases. All available data for the precursor SIC(s) are shown. Even if only a part of an SIC is included in the NAICS, *all* data for the SIC are reproduced. If the SIC industry is not marked as being a part (pt) of the NAICS, the entire industry is embedded in the NAICS data. The SIC composition of the new industry provides some hints of the relative importance of its "ancestors." Data marked with a 'p' are projected. Projections begin with 1982 data. Data earlier than 1990 are not shown but are reflected in the projections.

SIC	Industry	1990	1991	1992	1993	1994	1995	1996	1997
3652	**Prerecorded Records & Tapes (pt)**								
	Establishments (number)	423	415	419	424	414	280	336p	320p
	Employment (thousands)	16.3	13.5	15.7	16.2	17.0	17.8	17.7	18.2p
	Value of Shipments ($ million)	1,856.1	1,829.0	1,808.2	1,966.3	2,342.5	2,434.0	2,277.4	2,310.4p

Source: Economic Census of the United States, 1992, annual surveys of economic sectors conducted by the Bureau of the Census, and estimates or projections based on the 1982-1992 period; not all data are shown. 'e' marks estimates made by the editors; 'p' indicates projections based on time series. A dash (-) indicates that data for this SIC or year were not available. The abbreviation (pt) next to the industry name indicates that only a part of the industry is present within the NAICS data. If no (pt) is shown, the entire industry is contained within the NAICS data.

SELECTED RATIOS

For 1997	Avg. of Information	Analyzed Industry	Index	For 1997	Avg. of Information	Analyzed Industry	Index
Employees per establishment	27	28	103	Payroll per establishment	1,131,090	2,098,246	186
Revenue per establishment	5,444,104	30,652,632	563	Payroll as % of revenue	21	7	33
Revenue per employee	203,255	1,108,770	546	Payroll per employee	42,229	75,898	180

Sources: Same as General Statistics. The 'Average' column represents the average for the industry sector, in 1997, where the currently shown industry is classified. The Index shows the relationship between the Average and the Analyzed Industry. For example, 100 means that they are equal; 500 that the Analyzed Industry is five times the average; 50 means that the Analyzed Industry is half the national average. The abbreviation 'na' is used to show that data are 'not available'.

LEADING COMPANIES
No company data available for this industry.

LOCATION BY STATE AND REGIONAL CONCENTRATION

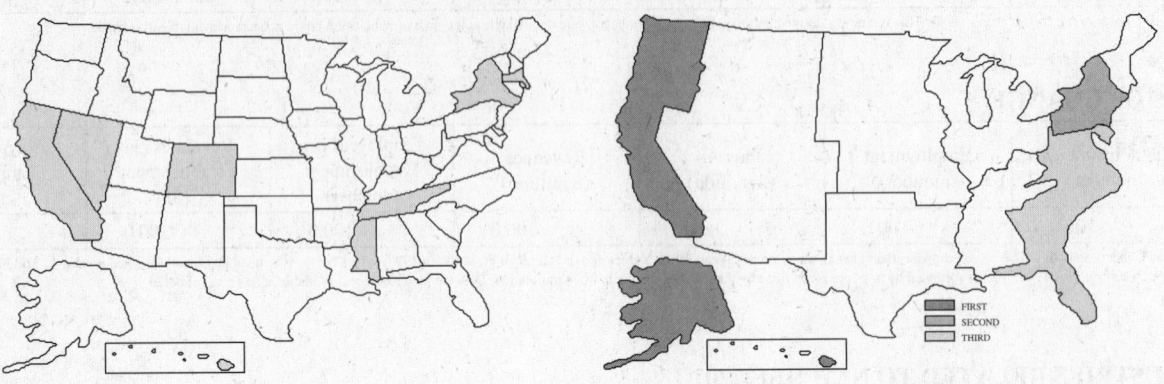

FIRST
SECOND
THIRD

INDUSTRY DATA BY STATE

State	Establishments		Employment			Payroll		Revenues		
	Total (number)	% of U.S.	Total (number)	% of U.S.	Per Estab.	Total ($ mil.)	Per Empl. ($)	Total ($ mil.)	% of U.S.	Per Estab. ($)
New York	64	22.5	3,604	45.7	56	293.8	81,527	4,323.9	49.5	67,561,703
California	91	31.9	3,409	43.3	37	258.3	75,757	3,928.7	45.0	43,172,637
Tennessee	21	7.4	285	3.6	14	21.1	74,105	365.7	4.2	17,413,095
North Carolina	7	2.5	104	1.3	15	5.1	49,500	34.7	0.4	4,962,571
Texas	9	3.2	132	1.7	15	5.0	37,591	10.6	0.1	1,172,778
Florida	12	4.2	40	0.5	3	1.3	32,675	5.0	0.1	416,333
Michigan	4	1.4	11	0.1	3	1.5	136,636	4.6	0.1	1,152,500
Massachusetts	7	2.5	23	0.3	3	0.6	26,913	4.2	0.0	598,714
Illinois	8	2.8	16	0.2	2	0.6	36,312	3.6	0.0	449,500
Colorado	5	1.8	15	0.2	3	0.4	29,467	0.8	0.0	163,600
New Jersey	8	2.8	60*	-	-	(D)	-	(D)	-	-
Georgia	4	1.4	60*	-	-	(D)	-	(D)	-	-
Mississippi	4	1.4	10*	-	-	(D)	-	(D)	-	-
Pennsylvania	4	1.4	10*	-	-	(D)	-	(D)	-	-
Virginia	4	1.4	10*	-	-	(D)	-	(D)	-	-
Hawaii	3	1.1	10*	-	-	(D)	-	(D)	-	-
Ohio	3	1.1	10*	-	-	(D)	-	(D)	-	-
South Carolina	3	1.1	10*	-	-	(D)	-	(D)	-	-
Washington	3	1.1	10*	-	-	(D)	-	(D)	-	-
Arizona	2	0.7	10*	-	-	(D)	-	(D)	-	-
Connecticut	2	0.7	10*	-	-	(D)	-	(D)	-	-
D.C.	2	0.7	10*	-	-	(D)	-	(D)	-	-
Indiana	2	0.7	10*	-	-	(D)	-	(D)	-	-
Nevada	2	0.7	10*	-	-	(D)	-	(D)	-	-
Alabama	1	0.4	10*	-	-	(D)	-	(D)	-	-
Kansas	1	0.4	10*	-	-	(D)	-	(D)	-	-
Louisiana	1	0.4	10*	-	-	(D)	-	(D)	-	-
Maine	1	0.4	10*	-	-	(D)	-	(D)	-	-
Maryland	1	0.4	10*	-	-	(D)	-	(D)	-	-
Minnesota	1	0.4	10*	-	-	(D)	-	(D)	-	-
New Mexico	1	0.4	10*	-	-	(D)	-	(D)	-	-
Oregon	1	0.4	10*	-	-	(D)	-	(D)	-	-
Rhode Island	1	0.4	10*	-	-	(D)	-	(D)	-	-
Utah	1	0.4	10*	-	-	(D)	-	(D)	-	-
West Virginia	1	0.4	10*	-	-	(D)	-	(D)	-	-

Source: 1997 *Economic Census.* The states are in descending order of revenues or establishments (if revenue data are missing for the majority). The symbol (D) appears when data are withheld to prevent disclosure of competitive information. States marked with (D) are sorted by number of establishments. A dash (-) indicates that the data element cannot be calculated. * indicates the midpoint of a range; 175, for example is the range 100-249. Shaded *states* on the state map indicate those states which have proportionately greater representation in the industry than would be indicated by the state's population; the ratio is based on total revenues or number of establishments. Shaded *regions* indicate where the industry is regionally most concentrated.

NAICS 512230 - MUSIC PUBLISHERS

GENERAL STATISTICS

Year	Establishments (number)	Employment (number)	Payroll ($ million)	Revenues ($ million)	Employees per Establishment (number)	Revenues per Establishment ($)	Payroll per Employee ($)
1997	721	4,335	215.0	1,368.0	6.0	1,897,365	49,596

Source: Economic Census of the United States, 1997. This is a newly defined industry. Data for prior years were unavailable at the time of publication but may become available over time.

INDICES OF CHANGE

Year	Establishments (number)	Employment (number)	Payroll ($ million)	Revenues ($ million)	Employees per Establishment (number)	Revenues per Establishment ($)	Payroll per Employee ($)
1997	100.0	100.0	100.0	100.0	100.0	100.0	100.0

Sources: Same as General Statistics. The values shown reflect change from the base year, 1997. Values above 100 mean greater than 1997, values below 100 mean less than 1997, and a value of 100 in the 1982-96 or 1998-2001 period means same as 1997. Values followed by a 'p' are projections by the editors; 'e' stands for extrapolation. Data are the most recent available at this level of detail.

SIC INDUSTRIES RELATED TO NAICS 512230

Each new NAICS code represents an industry that used to be part of an SIC or a part of several SIC industries. Data in this table are shown to provide transitional information for these cases. All available data for the precursor SIC(s) are shown. Even if only a part of an SIC is included in the NAICS, *all* data for the SIC are reproduced. If the SIC industry is not marked as being a part (pt) of the NAICS, the entire industry is embedded in the NAICS data. The SIC composition of the new industry provides some hints of the relative importance of its "ancestors." Data marked with a 'p' are projected. Projections begin with 1982 data. Data earlier than 1990 are not shown but are reflected in the projections.

SIC	Industry	1990	1991	1992	1993	1994	1995	1996	1997
2731	**Book Publishing (pt)**								
	Establishments (number)	2,144	2,284	2,644	2,699	2,756	2,904	2,781p	2,843p
	Employment (thousands)	74.4	77.3	79.6	83.2	87.1	83.6	85.4	86.8p
	Value of Shipments ($ million)	15,317.9	16,596.1	16,731.1	18,615.9	19,418.9	20,603.6	21,362.7	22,352.7p
2741	**Miscellaneous Publishing (pt)**								
	Establishments (number)	-	-	3,390	-	-	-	-	-
	Employment (thousands)	65.2	65.0	65.4	66.6	71.2	67.4	68.8	-
	Value of Shipments ($ million)	8,874.7	9,762.0	10,977.1	11,806.6	12,332.4	11,992.1	12,510.5	14,309.8p
8999	**Services, nec (pt)**								
	Establishments (number)	-	-	14,587	-	-	-	-	-
	Employment (thousands)	-	-	81.1	-	-	-	-	-
	Revenues ($ million)	-	-	7,966.2	-	-	-	-	-

Source: Economic Census of the United States, 1992, annual surveys of economic sectors conducted by the Bureau of the Census, and estimates or projections based on the 1982-1992 period; not all data are shown. 'e' marks estimates made by the editors; 'p' indicates projections based on time series. A dash (-) indicates that data for this SIC or year were not available. The abbreviation (pt) next to the industry name indicates that only a part of the industry is present within the NAICS data. If no (pt) is shown, the entire industry is contained within the NAICS data.

SELECTED RATIOS

For 1997	Avg. of Information	Analyzed Industry	Index	For 1997	Avg. of Information	Analyzed Industry	Index
Employees per establishment	27	6	22	Payroll per establishment	1,131,090	298,197	26
Revenue per establishment	5,444,104	1,897,365	35	Payroll as % of revenue	21	16	76
Revenue per employee	203,255	315,571	155	Payroll per employee	42,229	49,596	117

Sources: Same as General Statistics. The 'Average' column represents the average for the industry sector, in 1997, where the currently shown industry is classified. The Index shows the relationship between the Average and the Analyzed Industry. For example, 100 means that they are equal; 500 that the Analyzed Industry is five times the average; 50 means that the Analyzed Industry is half the national average. The abbreviation 'na' is used to show that data are 'not available'.

45

LEADING COMPANIES
No company data available for this industry.

LOCATION BY STATE AND REGIONAL CONCENTRATION

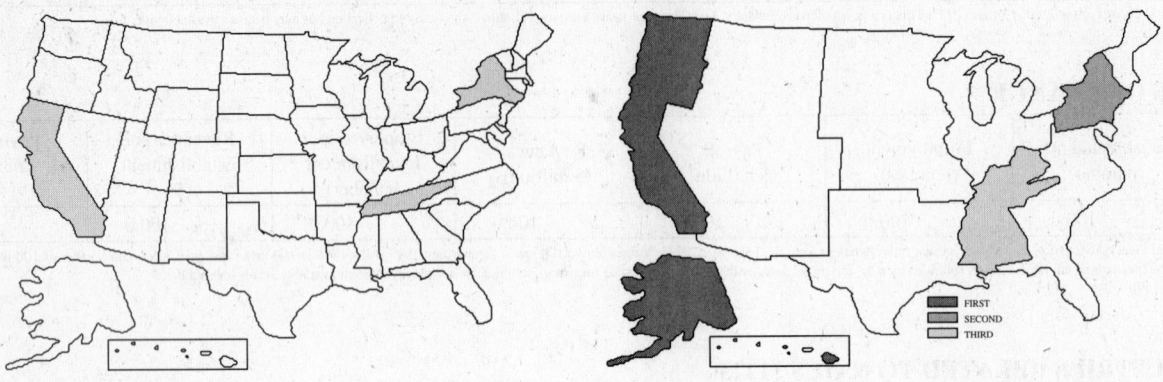

FIRST
SECOND
THIRD

INDUSTRY DATA BY STATE

State	Establishments Total (number)	% of U.S.	Employment Total (number)	% of U.S.	Per Estab.	Payroll Total ($ mil.)	Per Empl. ($)	Revenues Total ($ mil.)	% of U.S.	Per Estab. ($)
California	140	19.4	920	21.2	7	66.1	71,820	496.8	36.3	3,548,321
New York	161	22.3	1,360	31.4	8	84.7	62,268	471.9	34.5	2,931,280
Tennessee	125	17.3	434	10.0	3	17.2	39,714	154.7	11.3	1,237,752
Texas	33	4.6	184	4.2	6	5.9	31,918	28.1	2.1	851,394
Florida	29	4.0	331	7.6	11	11.1	33,571	23.6	1.7	815,483
Illinois	19	2.6	67	1.5	4	2.9	43,433	10.6	0.8	558,789
Ohio	7	1.0	101	2.3	14	3.0	29,574	10.3	0.8	1,477,429
Maryland	10	1.4	43	1.0	4	1.1	24,674	5.8	0.4	582,300
Massachusetts	11	1.5	38	0.9	3	1.6	40,842	5.5	0.4	498,636
Indiana	7	1.0	23	0.5	3	0.8	35,609	5.4	0.4	774,143
Colorado	8	1.1	24	0.6	3	1.1	45,458	4.7	0.3	582,625
Georgia	8	1.1	30	0.7	4	1.0	33,600	4.2	0.3	525,500
North Carolina	9	1.2	33	0.8	4	0.8	23,545	3.1	0.2	343,333
Iowa	5	0.7	25	0.6	5	0.7	26,640	2.9	0.2	576,200
Louisiana	4	0.6	14	0.3	4	0.5	35,643	2.0	0.1	502,750
Arizona	10	1.4	18	0.4	2	0.5	26,889	2.0	0.1	197,200
Nevada	7	1.0	5	0.1	1	0.2	48,200	2.0	0.1	279,857
Connecticut	7	1.0	11	0.3	2	0.7	62,455	1.9	0.1	276,571
Virginia	10	1.4	32	0.7	3	0.4	13,219	1.4	0.1	138,600
Alabama	5	0.7	10	0.2	2	0.3	29,000	1.2	0.1	247,200
Kentucky	3	0.4	15	0.3	5	0.3	21,200	1.1	0.1	355,000
New Mexico	4	0.6	15	0.3	4	0.2	10,200	0.7	0.1	174,000
New Jersey	13	1.8	10*	-	-	(D)	-	(D)	-	-
Minnesota	12	1.7	175*	-	-	(D)	-	(D)	-	-
Washington	9	1.2	60*	-	-	(D)	-	(D)	-	-
Missouri	8	1.1	60*	-	-	(D)	-	(D)	-	-
Oregon	8	1.1	60*	-	-	(D)	-	(D)	-	-
Pennsylvania	8	1.1	60*	-	-	(D)	-	(D)	-	-
Kansas	5	0.7	10*	-	-	(D)	-	(D)	-	-
Michigan	5	0.7	60*	-	-	(D)	-	(D)	-	-
Utah	5	0.7	60*	-	-	(D)	-	(D)	-	-
D.C.	4	0.6	60*	-	-	(D)	-	(D)	-	-
Oklahoma	4	0.6	60*	-	-	(D)	-	(D)	-	-
Arkansas	3	0.4	60*	-	-	(D)	-	(D)	-	-
Idaho	2	0.3	10*	-	-	(D)	-	(D)	-	-
Mississippi	2	0.3	10*	-	-	(D)	-	(D)	-	-
New Hampshire	2	0.3	10*	-	-	(D)	-	(D)	-	-
Vermont	2	0.3	10*	-	-	(D)	-	(D)	-	-
Wisconsin	2	0.3	60*	-	-	(D)	-	(D)	-	-
Hawaii	1	0.1	10*	-	-	(D)	-	(D)	-	-
Maine	1	0.1	10*	-	-	(D)	-	(D)	-	-
Montana	1	0.1	10*	-	-	(D)	-	(D)	-	-
South Carolina	1	0.1	10*	-	-	(D)	-	(D)	-	-
West Virginia	1	0.1	10*	-	-	(D)	-	(D)	-	-

Source: 1997 *Economic Census*. The states are in descending order of revenues or establishments (if revenue data are missing for the majority). The symbol (D) appears when data are withheld to prevent disclosure of competitive information. States marked with (D) are sorted by number of establishments. A dash (-) indicates that the data element cannot be calculated. * indicates the midpoint of a range; 175, for example is the range 100-249. Shaded *states* on the state map indicate those states which have proportionately greater representation in the industry than would be indicated by the state's population; the ratio is based on total revenues or number of establishments. Shaded *regions* indicate where the industry is regionally most concentrated.

NAICS 512240 - SOUND RECORDING STUDIOS

GENERAL STATISTICS

Year	Establishments (number)	Employment (number)	Payroll ($ million)	Revenues ($ million)	Employees per Establishment (number)	Revenues per Establishment ($)	Payroll per Employee ($)
1997	1,269	5,528	163.0	541.0	4.4	426,320	29,486

Source: Economic Census of the United States, 1997. This is a newly defined industry. Data for prior years were unavailable at the time of publication but may become available over time.

INDICES OF CHANGE

Year	Establishments (number)	Employment (number)	Payroll ($ million)	Revenues ($ million)	Employees per Establishment (number)	Revenues per Establishment ($)	Payroll per Employee ($)
1997	100.0	100.0	100.0	100.0	100.0	100.0	100.0

Sources: Same as General Statistics. The values shown reflect change from the base year, 1997. Values above 100 mean greater than 1997, values below 100 mean less than 1997, and a value of 100 in the 1982-96 or 1998-2001 period means same as 1997. Values followed by a 'p' are projections by the editors; 'e' stands for extrapolation. Data are the most recent available at this level of detail.

SIC INDUSTRIES RELATED TO NAICS 512240

Each new NAICS code represents an industry that used to be part of an SIC or a part of several SIC industries. Data in this table are shown to provide transitional information for these cases. All available data for the precursor SIC(s) are shown. Even if only a part of an SIC is included in the NAICS, *all* data for the SIC are reproduced. If the SIC industry is not marked as being a part (pt) of the NAICS, the entire industry is embedded in the NAICS data. The SIC composition of the new industry provides some hints of the relative importance of its "ancestors." Data marked with a 'p' are projected. Projections begin with 1982 data. Data earlier than 1990 are not shown but are reflected in the projections.

SIC	Industry	1990	1991	1992	1993	1994	1995	1996	1997
7389	**Business Services, nec (pt)**								
	Establishments (number)	44,079	50,252	52,375	56,829	60,725	53,596	60,893p	63,269p
	Employment (thousands)	489.6	550.4	523.6	607.9	648.7	623.0	680.2p	710.9p
	Revenues ($ million)	-	-	32,885.9	-	-	-	-	-

Source: Economic Census of the United States, 1992, annual surveys of economic sectors conducted by the Bureau of the Census, and estimates or projections based on the 1982-1992 period; not all data are shown. 'e' marks estimates made by the editors; 'p' indicates projections based on time series. A dash (-) indicates that data for this SIC or year were not available. The abbreviation (pt) next to the industry name indicates that only a part of the industry is present within the NAICS data. If no (pt) is shown, the entire industry is contained within the NAICS data.

SELECTED RATIOS

For 1997	Avg. of Information	Analyzed Industry	Index	For 1997	Avg. of Information	Analyzed Industry	Index
Employees per establishment	27	4	16	Payroll per establishment	1,131,090	128,448	11
Revenue per establishment	5,444,104	426,320	8	Payroll as % of revenue	21	30	145
Revenue per employee	203,255	97,865	48	Payroll per employee	42,229	29,486	70

Sources: Same as General Statistics. The 'Average' column represents the average for the industry sector, in 1997, where the currently shown industry is classified. The Index shows the relationship between the Average and the Analyzed Industry. For example, 100 means that they are equal; 500 that the Analyzed Industry is five times the average; 50 means that the Analyzed Industry is half the national average. The abbreviation 'na' is used to show that data are 'not available'.

LEADING COMPANIES
No company data available for this industry.

LOCATION BY STATE AND REGIONAL CONCENTRATION

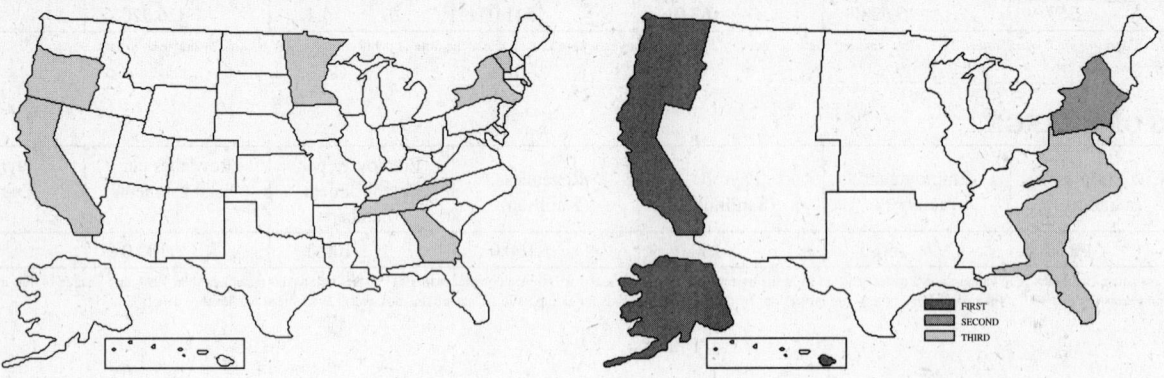

FIRST
SECOND
THIRD

INDUSTRY DATA BY STATE

State	Establishments Total (number)	Establishments % of U.S.	Employment Total (number)	Employment % of U.S.	Employment Per Estab.	Payroll Total ($ mil.)	Payroll Per Empl. ($)	Revenues Total ($ mil.)	Revenues % of U.S.	Revenues Per Estab. ($)
California	242	19.1	1,328	24.0	5	49.2	37,031	162.3	30.0	670,682
New York	203	16.0	976	17.7	5	37.2	38,155	115.2	21.3	567,315
Texas	86	6.8	424	7.7	5	10.0	23,585	32.7	6.1	380,640
Tennessee	83	6.5	247	4.5	3	6.8	27,360	24.5	4.5	294,675
Florida	63	5.0	373	6.7	6	6.8	18,298	21.0	3.9	332,619
Illinois	52	4.1	218	3.9	4	5.8	26,665	19.1	3.5	367,077
Georgia	41	3.2	142	2.6	3	4.5	31,373	13.3	2.5	324,902
North Carolina	33	2.6	191	3.5	6	3.2	16,518	12.1	2.2	366,273
Missouri	25	2.0	93	1.7	4	2.7	28,817	10.5	1.9	418,120
Massachusetts	21	1.7	138	2.5	7	3.1	22,370	9.2	1.7	439,810
Colorado	16	1.3	76	1.4	5	2.0	26,211	8.9	1.7	558,125
Pennsylvania	28	2.2	75	1.4	3	2.1	28,533	7.4	1.4	265,071
Indiana	25	2.0	81	1.5	3	1.9	23,198	6.9	1.3	275,000
Ohio	33	2.6	116	2.1	4	1.9	16,422	6.8	1.3	206,970
Michigan	26	2.0	66	1.2	3	1.8	26,727	6.7	1.2	258,462
New Jersey	29	2.3	71	1.3	2	1.8	25,746	5.7	1.1	197,345
Connecticut	13	1.0	35	0.6	3	1.8	52,686	5.1	0.9	393,538
Virginia	23	1.8	61	1.1	3	1.4	22,541	4.0	0.7	173,565
Kansas	9	0.7	37	0.7	4	1.2	31,216	4.0	0.7	439,889
Arizona	14	1.1	45	0.8	3	0.9	19,489	2.8	0.5	202,929
Oregon	15	1.2	31	0.6	2	1.0	30,677	2.7	0.5	179,400
Louisiana	10	0.8	27	0.5	3	0.6	21,037	2.0	0.4	200,400
Iowa	8	0.6	18	0.3	2	0.4	20,889	1.6	0.3	195,750
D.C.	4	0.3	9	0.2	2	0.2	22,556	0.9	0.2	213,500
Washington	24	1.9	175*	-	-	(D)	-	(D)	-	-
Minnesota	23	1.8	175*	-	-	(D)	-	(D)	-	-
Maryland	22	1.7	60*	-	-	(D)	-	(D)	-	-
Kentucky	12	0.9	60*	-	-	(D)	-	(D)	-	-
Alabama	9	0.7	60*	-	-	(D)	-	(D)	-	-
Wisconsin	9	0.7	60*	-	-	(D)	-	(D)	-	-
Vermont	8	0.6	10*	-	-	(D)	-	(D)	-	-
New Mexico	7	0.6	60*	-	-	(D)	-	(D)	-	-
Oklahoma	6	0.5	10*	-	-	(D)	-	(D)	-	-
South Carolina	6	0.5	60*	-	-	(D)	-	(D)	-	-
Arkansas	5	0.4	60*	-	-	(D)	-	(D)	-	-
Rhode Island	5	0.4	10*	-	-	(D)	-	(D)	-	-
Utah	5	0.4	10*	-	-	(D)	-	(D)	-	-
Montana	4	0.3	10*	-	-	(D)	-	(D)	-	-
Nebraska	4	0.3	10*	-	-	(D)	-	(D)	-	-
Maine	3	0.2	10*	-	-	(D)	-	(D)	-	-
Nevada	3	0.2	10*	-	-	(D)	-	(D)	-	-
Delaware	2	0.2	10*	-	-	(D)	-	(D)	-	-
Hawaii	2	0.2	10*	-	-	(D)	-	(D)	-	-
Idaho	2	0.2	10*	-	-	(D)	-	(D)	-	-
West Virginia	2	0.2	10*	-	-	(D)	-	(D)	-	-
Alaska	1	0.1	10*	-	-	(D)	-	(D)	-	-
Mississippi	1	0.1	10*	-	-	(D)	-	(D)	-	-
New Hampshire	1	0.1	10*	-	-	(D)	-	(D)	-	-
South Dakota	1	0.1	10*	-	-	(D)	-	(D)	-	-

Source: 1997 *Economic Census*. The states are in descending order of revenues or establishments (if revenue data are missing for the majority). The symbol (D) appears when data are withheld to prevent disclosure of competitive information. States marked with (D) are sorted by number of establishments. A dash (-) indicates that the data element cannot be calculated. * indicates the midpoint of a range; 175, for example is the range 100-249. Shaded *states* on the state map indicate those states which have proportionately greater representation in the industry than would be indicated by the state's population; the ratio is based on total revenues or number of establishments. Shaded *regions* indicate where the industry is regionally most concentrated.

NAICS 512290 - SOUND RECORDING INDUSTRIES NEC

GENERAL STATISTICS

Year	Establishments (number)	Employment (number)	Payroll ($ million)	Revenues ($ million)	Employees per Establishment (number)	Revenues per Establishment ($)	Payroll per Employee ($)
1997	377	2,774	89.0	313.0	7.4	830,239	32,084

Source: Economic Census of the United States, 1997. This is a newly defined industry. Data for prior years were unavailable at the time of publication but may become available over time.

INDICES OF CHANGE

Year	Establishments (number)	Employment (number)	Payroll ($ million)	Revenues ($ million)	Employees per Establishment (number)	Revenues per Establishment ($)	Payroll per Employee ($)
1997	100.0	100.0	100.0	100.0	100.0	100.0	100.0

Sources: Same as General Statistics. The values shown reflect change from the base year, 1997. Values above 100 mean greater than 1997, values below 100 mean less than 1997, and a value of 100 in the 1982-96 or 1998-2001 period means same as 1997. Values followed by a 'p' are projections by the editors; 'e' stands for extrapolation. Data are the most recent available at this level of detail.

SIC INDUSTRIES RELATED TO NAICS 512290

Each new NAICS code represents an industry that used to be part of an SIC or a part of several SIC industries. Data in this table are shown to provide transitional information for these cases. All available data for the precursor SIC(s) are shown. Even if only a part of an SIC is included in the NAICS, *all* data for the SIC are reproduced. If the SIC industry is not marked as being a part (pt) of the NAICS, the entire industry is embedded in the NAICS data. The SIC composition of the new industry provides some hints of the relative importance of its "ancestors." Data marked with a 'p' are projected. Projections begin with 1982 data. Data earlier than 1990 are not shown but are reflected in the projections.

SIC	Industry	1990	1991	1992	1993	1994	1995	1996	1997
7389	**Business Services, nec (pt)**								
	Establishments (number)	44,079	50,252	52,375	56,829	60,725	53,596	60,893p	63,269p
	Employment (thousands)	489.6	550.4	523.6	607.9	648.7	623.0	680.2p	710.9p
	Revenues ($ million)	-	-	32,885.9	-	-	-	-	-
7922	**Theatrical Producers & Services (pt)**								
	Establishments (number)	4,470	4,992	5,924	6,229	6,323	6,428	6,542p	6,792p
	Employment (thousands)	63.9	63.1	69.5	88.8	77.8	79.3	87.3p	91.2p
	Revenues ($ million)	-	-	5,730.5	4,396.6p	4,647.8p	4,899.0p	5,150.2p	5,401.4p

Source: Economic Census of the United States, 1992, annual surveys of economic sectors conducted by the Bureau of the Census, and estimates or projections based on the 1982-1992 period; not all data are shown. 'e' marks estimates made by the editors; 'p' indicates projections based on time series. A dash (-) indicates that data for this SIC or year were not available. The abbreviation (pt) next to the industry name indicates that only a part of the industry is present within the NAICS data. If no (pt) is shown, the entire industry is contained within the NAICS data.

SELECTED RATIOS

For 1997	Avg. of Information	Analyzed Industry	Index	For 1997	Avg. of Information	Analyzed Industry	Index
Employees per establishment	27	7	27	Payroll per establishment	1,131,090	236,074	21
Revenue per establishment	5,444,104	830,239	15	Payroll as % of revenue	21	28	137
Revenue per employee	203,255	112,833	56	Payroll per employee	42,229	32,084	76

Sources: Same as General Statistics. The 'Average' column represents the average for the industry sector, in 1997, where the currently shown industry is classified. The Index shows the relationship between the Average and the Analyzed Industry. For example, 100 means that they are equal; 500 that the Analyzed Industry is five times the average; 50 means that the Analyzed Industry is half the national average. The abbreviation 'na' is used to show that data are 'not available'.

LEADING COMPANIES
No company data available for this industry.

LOCATION BY STATE AND REGIONAL CONCENTRATION

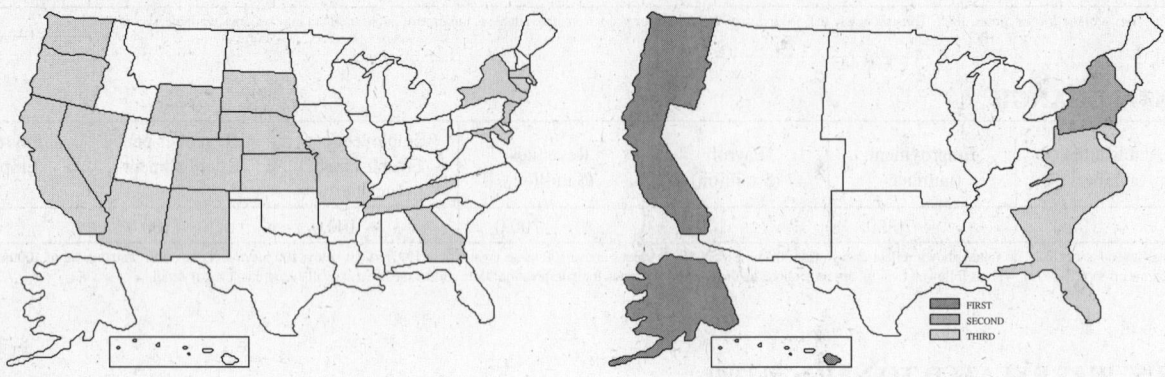

FIRST
SECOND
THIRD

INDUSTRY DATA BY STATE

State	Establishments Total (number)	Establishments % of U.S.	Employment Total (number)	Employment % of U.S.	Employment Per Estab.	Payroll Total ($ mil.)	Payroll Per Empl. ($)	Revenues Total ($ mil.)	Revenues % of U.S.	Revenues Per Estab. ($)
California	66	17.5	548	19.8	8	27.0	49,254	97.0	31.0	1,469,576
New York	42	11.1	217	7.8	5	7.1	32,696	34.0	10.9	809,929
Ohio	10	2.7	71	2.6	7	1.7	23,972	14.0	4.5	1,402,400
Pennsylvania	12	3.2	31	1.1	3	3.8	121,677	8.8	2.8	736,167
D.C.	5	1.3	96	3.5	19	2.5	26,417	6.7	2.1	1,338,400
Massachusetts	11	2.9	52	1.9	5	1.8	33,654	6.5	2.1	594,909
Texas	20	5.3	72	2.6	4	1.6	22,167	4.7	1.5	236,600
Tennessee	12	3.2	60	2.2	5	1.4	23,117	4.6	1.5	386,083
Florida	19	5.0	82	3.0	4	2.0	24,207	4.6	1.5	241,579
Michigan	10	2.7	40	1.4	4	0.8	20,200	2.3	0.7	231,500
Colorado	7	1.9	50	1.8	7	0.7	14,820	1.9	0.6	277,143
Virginia	8	2.1	18	0.6	2	0.3	17,833	1.2	0.4	152,875
Arizona	6	1.6	23	0.8	4	0.7	31,696	1.2	0.4	201,833
New Mexico	4	1.1	15	0.5	4	0.2	13,800	0.7	0.2	185,500
Kentucky	4	1.1	7	0.3	2	0.2	33,143	0.4	0.1	92,750
Alabama	3	0.8	4	0.1	1	0.1	13,250	0.3	0.1	90,667
South Dakota	3	0.8	7	0.3	2	0.1	9,429	0.3	0.1	87,667
Georgia	17	4.5	60*	-	-	(D)	-	(D)	-	-
Illinois	14	3.7	175*	-	-	(D)	-	(D)	-	-
New Jersey	14	3.7	375*	-	-	(D)	-	(D)	-	-
Maryland	10	2.7	60*	-	-	(D)	-	(D)	-	-
Washington	10	2.7	375*	-	-	(D)	-	(D)	-	-
Connecticut	8	2.1	60*	-	-	(D)	-	(D)	-	-
Missouri	8	2.1	60*	-	-	(D)	-	(D)	-	-
Oregon	7	1.9	60*	-	-	(D)	-	(D)	-	-
Wisconsin	7	1.9	60*	-	-	(D)	-	(D)	-	-
Indiana	5	1.3	10*	-	-	(D)	-	(D)	-	-
Minnesota	5	1.3	60*	-	-	(D)	-	(D)	-	-
Kansas	4	1.1	60*	-	-	(D)	-	(D)	-	-
Nebraska	4	1.1	175*	-	-	(D)	-	(D)	-	-
Oklahoma	4	1.1	60*	-	-	(D)	-	(D)	-	-
Arkansas	3	0.8	10*	-	-	(D)	-	(D)	-	-
Nevada	3	0.8	10*	-	-	(D)	-	(D)	-	-
North Carolina	3	0.8	10*	-	-	(D)	-	(D)	-	-
Louisiana	2	0.5	10*	-	-	(D)	-	(D)	-	-
West Virginia	2	0.5	10*	-	-	(D)	-	(D)	-	-
Hawaii	1	0.3	10*	-	-	(D)	-	(D)	-	-
Maine	1	0.3	10*	-	-	(D)	-	(D)	-	-
Montana	1	0.3	10*	-	-	(D)	-	(D)	-	-
South Carolina	1	0.3	10*	-	-	(D)	-	(D)	-	-
Wyoming	1	0.3	10*	-	-	(D)	-	(D)	-	-

Source: 1997 *Economic Census*. The states are in descending order of revenues or establishments (if revenue data are missing for the majority). The symbol (D) appears when data are withheld to prevent disclosure of competitive information. States marked with (D) are sorted by number of establishments. A dash (-) indicates that the data element cannot be calculated. * indicates the midpoint of a range; 175, for example is the range 100-249. Shaded *states* on the state map indicate those states which have proportionately greater representation in the industry than would be indicated by the state's population; the ratio is based on total revenues or number of establishments. Shaded *regions* indicate where the industry is regionally most concentrated.

NAICS 513111 - RADIO NETWORKS

GENERAL STATISTICS

Year	Establishments (number)	Employment (number)	Payroll ($ million)	Revenues ($ million)	Employees per Establishment (number)	Revenues per Establishment ($)	Payroll per Employee ($)
1997	303	5,648	217.0	851.0	18.6	2,808,581	38,421

Source: Economic Census of the United States, 1997. This is a newly defined industry. Data for prior years were unavailable at the time of publication but may become available over time.

INDICES OF CHANGE

Year	Establishments (number)	Employment (number)	Payroll ($ million)	Revenues ($ million)	Employees per Establishment (number)	Revenues per Establishment ($)	Payroll per Employee ($)
1997	100.0	100.0	100.0	100.0	100.0	100.0	100.0

Sources: Same as General Statistics. The values shown reflect change from the base year, 1997. Values above 100 mean greater than 1997, values below 100 mean less than 1997, and a value of 100 in the 1982-96 or 1998-2001 period means same as 1997. Values followed by a 'p' are projections by the editors; 'e' stands for extrapolation. Data are the most recent available at this level of detail.

SIC INDUSTRIES RELATED TO NAICS 513111

Each new NAICS code represents an industry that used to be part of an SIC or a part of several SIC industries. Data in this table are shown to provide transitional information for these cases. All available data for the precursor SIC(s) are shown. Even if only a part of an SIC is included in the NAICS, *all* data for the SIC are reproduced. If the SIC industry is not marked as being a part (pt) of the NAICS, the entire industry is embedded in the NAICS data. The SIC composition of the new industry provides some hints of the relative importance of its "ancestors." Data marked with a 'p' are projected. Projections begin with 1982 data. Data earlier than 1990 are not shown but are reflected in the projections.

SIC	Industry	1990	1991	1992	1993	1994	1995	1996	1997
4832	**Radio Broadcasting Stations (pt)**								
	Establishments (number)	-	-	6,956	-	-	-	-	-
	Employment (thousands)	-	-	112.4	-	-	-	-	-
	Revenues ($ million)	7,173.0	6,890.0	6,865.4	7,402.0	8,089.0	8,795.0	9,631.0	10,533.0

Source: Economic Census of the United States, 1992, annual surveys of economic sectors conducted by the Bureau of the Census, and estimates or projections based on the 1982-1992 period; not all data are shown. 'e' marks estimates made by the editors; 'p' indicates projections based on time series. A dash (-) indicates that data for this SIC or year were not available. The abbreviation (pt) next to the industry name indicates that only a part of the industry is present within the NAICS data. If no (pt) is shown, the entire industry is contained within the NAICS data.

SELECTED RATIOS

For 1997	Avg. of Information	Analyzed Industry	Index	For 1997	Avg. of Information	Analyzed Industry	Index
Employees per establishment	27	19	70	Payroll per establishment	1,131,090	716,172	63
Revenue per establishment	5,444,104	2,808,581	52	Payroll as % of revenue	21	25	123
Revenue per employee	203,255	150,673	74	Payroll per employee	42,229	38,421	91

Sources: Same as General Statistics. The 'Average' column represents the average for the industry sector, in 1997, where the currently shown industry is classified. The Index shows the relationship between the Average and the Analyzed Industry. For example, 100 means that they are equal; 500 that the Analyzed Industry is five times the average; 50 means that the Analyzed Industry is half the national average. The abbreviation 'na' is used to show that data are 'not available'.

LEADING COMPANIES   Number shown: **75**   Total sales ($ mil): **47,262**   Total employment (000): **219.4**

Company Name	Address				CEO Name	Phone	Co. Type	Sales ($ mil)	Empl. (000)
CBS Broadcasting Inc.	51 West 52nd St	New York	NY	10019	Laurence A. Tisch	212-975-4321	S	6,805	6.4
National Broadcasting Inc.	30 Rockefeller Plz	New York	NY	10112	Robert C Wright	212-664-4444	S	5,269	6.5
Gannett Company Inc.	1100 Wilson Blvd	Arlington	VA	22234		703-284-6000	P	5,121	39.4
Gannett Broadcasting Group	1100 Wilson Blvd	Arlington	VA	22234	Cecil Walker	703-284-6760	D	5,100	45.2
Tribune Co. (Chicago, Illinois)	435 N Michigan Ave	Chicago	IL	60611	John W Madigan	312-222-9100	P	3,222	12.7
Infinity Broadcasting Corp.	40 W 57th St	New York	NY	10019	Mel Karmazin	212-314-9200	P	2,449	8.3
Viacom International Inc.	1515 Broadway	New York	NY	10036	Sumner Redstone	212-258-6000	S	1,900*	5.0
Scripps Howard Broadcasting Co.	PO Box 5380	Cincinnati	OH	45201		513-977-3000	P	1,804*	10.2
Bloomberg L.P.	499 Park Ave	New York	NY	10022	Michael Bloomberg	212-318-2000	R	1,500	4.0
Clear Channel Communications	PO Box 659512	San Antonio	TX	78265	L Lowry Mays	210-822-2828	P	1,351	7.0
AMFM Inc.	1845 W Rogers	Dallas	TX	75201	Thomas O Hicks	214-922-8700	P	1,274	6.7
Susquehanna Pfaltzgraff Co.	PO Box 2026	York	PA	17405	William Simpson	717-848-5500	R	1,064*	7.0
SFX Entertainment Inc.	650 Madison Ave	New York	NY	10022	Michael G Ferrel	212-838-3100	P	884	1.3
Cox Broadcasting Inc.	P O Box 105357	Atlanta	GA	30348	Nichlos Trigony	404-843-5000	S	791*	5.0
Opryland USA Inc.	2808 Opryland Dr	Nashville	TN	37214	Terry London	615-889-1000	P	609*	4.8
Hubbard Broadcasting Inc.	3415 University Ave	St. Paul	MN	55114	Stanley Hubbard	612-646-5555	R	600	1.5
Landmark Communications Inc.	PO Box 449	Norfolk	VA	23501		757-446-2000	R	575	4.5
Century Communications Corp.	50 Locust Ave	New Canaan	CT	06840	Bernard P Gallagher	203-972-2000	P	520	2.9
Jones Intercable Inc.	P O Box 3309	Englewood	CO	80155	Glenn R Jones	303-792-3111	P	461	3.1
Schurz Communications Inc.	225 W Colfax Ave	South Bend	IN	46626	Franklin D Schurz Jr	219-287-1001	R	410*	1.5
Pulitzer Inc.	900 N Tucker Blvd	St. Louis	MO	63101	Michael E Pulitzer	314-340-8000	P	373	2.3
New Gaylord Entertainment Co.	PO Box 25125	Oklahoma City	OK	73125		405-475-3311	S	340	4.6
Cox Radio Inc.	PO Box 105357	Atlanta	GA	30348	Robert F Neil	404-843-5000	P	261	1.5
Westwood One Inc.	9540 Washington	Culver City	CA	90232	Joel Hollander	310-204-5000	P	259	0.8
Fisher Companies Inc.	600 University St	Seattle	WA	98101	W W Krippaehne Jr	206-624-2752	P	252	1.0
Metromedia Intern. Group Inc.	1 Meadowlands	East Rutherford	NJ	07073	John W Kluge	201-531-8000	P	240	1.0
Emmis Communications Corp.	40 Monument Circle	Indianapolis	IN	46204	Jeffrey H Smulyan	317-266-0100	P	233	1.6
Jefferson-Pilot Communications	1 Julian Price Pl	Charlotte	NC	28208	Terry Stone	704-374-3500	S	229	1.0
Katz Radio Group	125 W 55th St	New York	NY	10019	Jim Beloyranis	212-424-6000	D	213*	1.4
Guardian Corp.	P O Box 7397	Rocky Mount	NC	27804	Leon A Dunn Jr	252-443-4101	R	205*	1.5
Journal Broadcast Group	720 E Capitol Dr	Milwaukee	WI	53212	Jim Prather	414-332-9611	S	204*	1.3
Bonneville International Corp.	P O Box 1160	Salt Lake City	UT	84110	Bruce T Reese	801-575-7500	R	197*	1.3
Entercom Communications Corp.	401 City Ave	Bala Cynwyd	PA	19004	Joseph M Field	610-660-5610	R	170	1.2
Fisher Broadcasting Inc.	2001 6th Ave	Seattle	WA	98109	Patrick Scott	206-770-3815	S	170	0.7
Hispanic Broadcasting Corp.	3102 Oak Lawn	Dallas	TX	75219	M T Tichenor Jr	214-525-7700	P	164	0.7
Midstates Development Inc.	P O Box 338	Fergus Falls	MN	56538	Lauras N Molbert	218-736-4712	S	160*	0.8
Paxson Communications Corp.	601 Clearwater	W. Palm Beach	FL	33401	James B Bocock	561-659-4122	P	134	1.3
Premiere Radio Networks Inc.	15260 Ventura Blvd	Sherman Oaks	CA	91403	Kraig T Kitchin	818-377-5300	P	130	0.3
Capitol Broadcasting Inc.	PO Box 12800	Raleigh	NC	27605	James F Goodmon	919-890-6000	R	120	0.6
MAC America Communications	5555 N 7th Ave	Phoenix	AZ	85013	Delbert R Lewis	602-207-3333	S	111*	0.4
Spanish Broadcasting System Inc.	3191 Coral Way	Miami	FL	33145	Raul Alarcon Jr	305-446-5148	P	97	0.4
Spartan Communications Inc.	P O Box 1717	Spartanburg	SC	29304	Nick Evans	843-576-7777	R	86	1.0
Max Media Inc.	900 Laskin Rd	Virginia Beach	VA	23451	Gene Loving	757-437-9800	R	83*	0.3
Noble Broadcast Group Inc.	4891 Pacific Hwy	San Diego	CA	92110	John T Lynch	619-291-8510	S	79*	0.5
Jacor Broadcasting Corp.	50 E River Center	Covington	KY	41011	Randy Michaels	606-655-2267	S	76*	0.5
National Public Radio	635 Mass N W	Washington	DC	20001	Kevin Klose	202-414-2000	R	76	0.6
Saga Communications Inc.	73 Kerchaeval Ave	GrPointe Fms	MI	48236	Edward Christian	313-886-7070	P	76	0.8
Midcontinent Media Inc.	7900 Xerxes Ave S	Minneapolis	MN	55431	Nathan L Bentson	612-844-2600	R	71	0.5
iNTELEFILM Corp.	5501 Exelsior Blvd	Minneapolis	MN	55416	Christopher T Dahl	612-925-8840	P	67	<0.1
Alexander Broadcasting Co.	PO Box 3010	Bellevue	WA	98009		425-455-0923	R	61*	0.4
Barden Companies Inc.	400 RenCen	Detroit	MI	48243	Don Barden	313-259-0050	R	47*	0.3
Journal Broadcasting Group	4200 N O Lwrnc	Wichita	KS	67219	FF Mike Lynch	316-838-9141	R	39*	0.3
Trinity Broadcasting Network Inc.	P O Box A	Santa Ana	CA	92711	Paul Crouch	714-832-2950	R	39*	0.2
Professional Impressions Media	PO Box 677	Champaign	IL	61824		217-351-5252	R	39*	0.4
Buckley Broadcasting Corp.	166 W Putnam Ave	Greenwich	CT	06830	Richard Buckley	203-661-4307	R	38*	0.3
News-Gazette	PO Box 677	Champaign	IL	61824		217-351-5252	S	33*	0.4
Associated Group Inc.	200 Gateway Towers	Pittsburgh	PA	15222	Miles Berkman	412-281-1907	P	33	2.2
Superior Distributing Co.	P O Box 107	Fostoria	OH	44830	Kris Klepper	419-435-1938	R	32*	<0.1
Radio 1 Inc.	2994 E Grand Blvd	Detroit	MI	48202		313-871-0590	R	31*	0.2
Bloomington Broadcasting Corp.	236 Greenwood Ave	Bloomington	IL	61704	Ken Maness	309-829-1221	R	25	0.3
Am/Fm Transfer Media	840 N Central Ave	Phoenix	AZ	85004	Marv Nylan	602-258-8181	R	24*	0.2
Free Lance-Star Publishing Co.	616 Amelia St	Fredericksburg	VA	22401	Josiah Rowe	540-374-5000	R	22*	0.3
Pacific Star Communications Inc.	1066 E Shaw Ave	Fresno	CA	93710	Dex Allen	209-243-4300	R	22*	0.1
Liggett Broadcast Inc.	3420 Pinetree Rd	Lansing	MI	48911	James Jensen		R	21*	0.1
CRN International	1 Circular Ave	Hamden	CT	06514	Barry Berman	203-288-2002	R	20*	<0.1
Bliss Communications Inc.	PO Box 5001	Janesville	WI	53547		608-754-3311	R	18	0.2
Mercury Radio Communications	464 Franklin St	Buffalo	NY	14202	Charles W Banta	716-881-4555	S	17	0.1
Evergreen Media/Pyramid Corp.	P O Box 128	Medford	MA	02155		781-396-1430	S	16*	0.1
WDIA	112 Union Ave	Memphis	TN	38103		901-529-4300	S	16*	0.1
WSM Inc.	2644 McGavock	Nashville	TN	37214	Brian Payne	615-889-6595	S	16*	0.2
Michiana Telecasting Corp.	P O Box 1616	South Bend	IN	46634	James P Behling	219-631-1616	R	15*	0.2
Sconnix Broadcasting Co.	1921 Gallows Rd	Vienna	VA	22182		703-356-6000	R	15	0.1
G.H. Buck Broadcasting Inc.	7176 Briarcliff N E	Atlanta	GA	30306	George H Buck	404-875-1110	R	14*	<0.1
Green Bay Broadcasting Inc.	P O Box 310	Green Bay	WI	54305	William Laird	920-468-4100	R	12*	<0.1
Good News Broadcasting	P O Box 82808	Lincoln	NE	68501	Woodrow Kroll	402-474-4567	R	11	0.1

Source: Ward's Business Directory of U.S. Private and Public Companies, Volumes 1 and 2, 2000. The company type code used is as follows: P - Public, R - Private, S - Subsidiary, D - Division, J - Joint Venture, A - Affiliate, G - Group, N - Company type not reported. Sales are in millions of dollars, employees are in thousands. An asterisk (*) indicates an estimated sales volume. The symbol < stands for 'less than'. Company names and addresses are truncated, in some cases, to fit into the available space.

LOCATION BY STATE AND REGIONAL CONCENTRATION

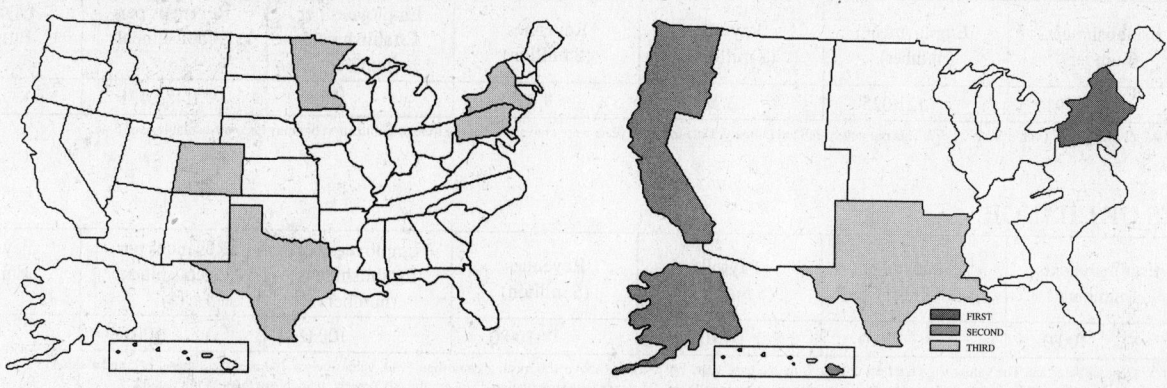

INDUSTRY DATA BY STATE

State	Establishments Total (number)	% of U.S.	Employment Total (number)	% of U.S.	Per Estab.	Payroll Total ($ mil.)	Per Empl. ($)	Revenues Total ($ mil.)	% of U.S.	Per Estab. ($)
New York	19	6.3	416	7.4	22	19.0	45,594	201.0	23.6	10,578,316
California	42	13.9	558	9.9	13	24.0	43,007	79.0	9.3	1,882,095
Texas	31	10.2	691	12.2	22	27.7	40,104	72.4	8.5	2,334,677
Pennsylvania	13	4.3	343	6.1	26	18.4	53,630	68.1	8.0	5,238,385
Minnesota	10	3.3	164	2.9	16	5.8	35,067	26.5	3.1	2,650,500
Colorado	9	3.0	245	4.3	27	6.0	24,384	25.4	3.0	2,825,778
Illinois	10	3.3	158	2.8	16	6.7	42,089	14.6	1.7	1,457,800
Alabama	6	2.0	127	2.2	21	2.6	20,252	13.3	1.6	2,223,000
Tennessee	15	5.0	207	3.7	14	3.7	18,063	13.3	1.6	886,333
Arizona	12	4.0	148	2.6	12	4.0	27,162	12.6	1.5	1,047,083
Georgia	9	3.0	110	1.9	12	4.0	36,355	12.2	1.4	1,359,778
New Jersey	5	1.7	93	1.6	19	2.9	30,817	10.9	1.3	2,179,800
Wisconsin	4	1.3	78	1.4	20	1.3	16,500	5.7	0.7	1,425,000
Michigan	9	3.0	55	1.0	6	1.9	35,418	5.6	0.7	620,222
Massachusetts	4	1.3	53	0.9	13	1.3	25,264	4.5	0.5	1,113,500
Florida	15	5.0	59	1.0	4	1.5	25,339	3.8	0.4	253,200
Kentucky	4	1.3	35	0.6	9	0.8	22,257	2.2	0.3	545,000
Nevada	3	1.0	42	0.7	14	1.0	23,429	1.9	0.2	642,333
Oregon	8	2.6	45	0.8	6	0.8	17,911	1.9	0.2	231,250
Oklahoma	4	1.3	44	0.8	11	1.1	24,773	1.7	0.2	416,000
Arkansas	3	1.0	20	0.4	7	0.6	27,500	1.6	0.2	545,000
Ohio	6	2.0	69	1.2	11	0.6	9,246	1.5	0.2	245,000
Mississippi	3	1.0	30	0.5	10	0.4	13,633	1.1	0.1	377,667
Indiana	4	1.3	34	0.6	9	0.3	9,176	0.9	0.1	217,750
South Carolina	3	1.0	33	0.6	11	0.2	7,394	0.8	0.1	259,333
Utah	3	1.0	30	0.5	10	0.3	8,433	0.7	0.1	246,000
Louisiana	4	1.3	10	0.2	3	0.1	5,800	0.2	0.0	57,000
North Carolina	6	2.0	175*	-	-	(D)	-	(D)	-	-
Missouri	5	1.7	175*	-	-	(D)	-	(D)	-	-
Washington	5	1.7	175*	-	-	(D)	-	(D)	-	-
Maryland	4	1.3	10*	-	-	(D)	-	(D)	-	-
D.C.	3	1.0	750*	-	-	(D)	-	(D)	-	-
Nebraska	3	1.0	60*	-	-	(D)	-	(D)	-	-
Virginia	3	1.0	175*	-	-	(D)	-	(D)	-	-
Idaho	2	0.7	60*	-	-	(D)	-	(D)	-	-
New Mexico	2	0.7	60*	-	-	(D)	-	(D)	-	-
Vermont	2	0.7	10*	-	-	(D)	-	(D)	-	-
West Virginia	2	0.7	10*	-	-	(D)	-	(D)	-	-
Alaska	1	0.3	10*	-	-	(D)	-	(D)	-	-
Hawaii	1	0.3	60*	-	-	(D)	-	(D)	-	-
Iowa	1	0.3	10*	-	-	(D)	-	(D)	-	-
Kansas	1	0.3	10*	-	-	(D)	-	(D)	-	-
Montana	1	0.3	10*	-	-	(D)	-	(D)	-	-
North Dakota	1	0.3	10*	-	-	(D)	-	(D)	-	-
South Dakota	1	0.3	10*	-	-	(D)	-	(D)	-	-
Wyoming	1	0.3	10*	-	-	(D)	-	(D)	-	-

Source: 1997 *Economic Census*. The states are in descending order of revenues or establishments (if revenue data are missing for the majority). The symbol (D) appears when data are withheld to prevent disclosure of competitive information. States marked with (D) are sorted by number of **establishments**. A dash (-) indicates that the data element cannot be calculated. * indicates the midpoint of a range; 175, for example is the range 100-249. Shaded *states* on the state map indicate those states which have proportionately greater representation in the industry than would be indicated by the state's population; the ratio is based on total revenues or number of establishments. Shaded *regions* indicate where the industry is regionally most concentrated.

NAICS 513112 - RADIO STATIONS

GENERAL STATISTICS

Year	Establishments (number)	Employment (number)	Payroll ($ million)	Revenues ($ million)	Employees per Establishment (number)	Revenues per Establishment ($)	Payroll per Employee ($)
1997	6,591	121,025	3,388.0	9,797.0	18.4	1,486,421	27,994

Source: Economic Census of the United States, 1997. This is a newly defined industry. Data for prior years were unavailable at the time of publication but may become available over time.

INDICES OF CHANGE

Year	Establishments (number)	Employment (number)	Payroll ($ million)	Revenues ($ million)	Employees per Establishment (number)	Revenues per Establishment ($)	Payroll per Employee ($)
1997	100.0	100.0	100.0	100.0	100.0	100.0	100.0

Sources: Same as General Statistics. The values shown reflect change from the base year, 1997. Values above 100 mean greater than 1997, values below 100 mean less than 1997, and a value of 100 in the 1982-96 or 1998-2001 period means same as 1997. Values followed by a 'p' are projections by the editors; 'e' stands for extrapolation. Data are the most recent available at this level of detail.

SIC INDUSTRIES RELATED TO NAICS 513112

Each new NAICS code represents an industry that used to be part of an SIC or a part of several SIC industries. Data in this table are shown to provide transitional information for these cases. All available data for the precursor SIC(s) are shown. Even if only a part of an SIC is included in the NAICS, *all* data for the SIC are reproduced. If the SIC industry is not marked as being a part (pt) of the NAICS, the entire industry is embedded in the NAICS data. The SIC composition of the new industry provides some hints of the relative importance of its "ancestors." Data marked with a 'p' are projected. Projections begin with 1982 data. Data earlier than 1990 are not shown but are reflected in the projections.

SIC	Industry	1990	1991	1992	1993	1994	1995	1996	1997
4832	**Radio Broadcasting Stations (pt)**								
	Establishments (number)	-	-	6,956	-	-	-	-	-
	Employment (thousands)	-	-	112.4	-	-	-	-	-
	Revenues ($ million)	7,173.0	6,890.0	6,865.4	7,402.0	8,089.0	8,795.0	9,631.0	10,533.0

Source: Economic Census of the United States, 1992, annual surveys of economic sectors conducted by the Bureau of the Census, and estimates or projections based on the 1982-1992 period; not all data are shown. 'e' marks estimates made by the editors; 'p' indicates projections based on time series. A dash (-) indicates that data for this SIC or year were not available. The abbreviation (pt) next to the industry name indicates that only a part of the industry is present within the NAICS data. If no (pt) is shown, the entire industry is contained within the NAICS data.

SELECTED RATIOS

For 1997	Avg. of Information	Analyzed Industry	Index	For 1997	Avg. of Information	Analyzed Industry	Index
Employees per establishment	27	18	69	Payroll per establishment	1,131,090	514,034	45
Revenue per establishment	5,444,104	1,486,421	27	Payroll as % of revenue	21	35	166
Revenue per employee	203,255	80,950	40	Payroll per employee	42,229	27,994	66

Sources: Same as General Statistics. The 'Average' column represents the average for the industry sector, in 1997, where the currently shown industry is classified. The Index shows the relationship between the Average and the Analyzed Industry. For example, 100 means that they are equal; 500 that the Analyzed Industry is five times the average; 50 means that the Analyzed Industry is half the national average. The abbreviation 'na' is used to show that data are 'not available'.

LEADING COMPANIES   Number shown: **1**   Total sales ($ mil): **286**   Total employment (000): **1.8**

Company Name	Address				CEO Name	Phone	Co. Type	Sales ($ mil)	Empl. (000)
Raycom Media Inc.	201 Monroe St	Montgomery	AL	36104	John Hayes	334-206-1400	R	286*	1.8

Source: Ward's Business Directory of U.S. Private and Public Companies, Volumes 1 and 2, 2000. The company type code used is as follows: P - Public, R - Private, S - Subsidiary, D - Division, J - Joint Venture, A - Affiliate, G - Group, N - Company type not reported. Sales are in millions of dollars, employees are in thousands. An asterisk (*) indicates an estimated sales volume. The symbol < stands for 'less than'. Company names and addresses are truncated, in some cases, to fit into the available space.

LOCATION BY STATE AND REGIONAL CONCENTRATION

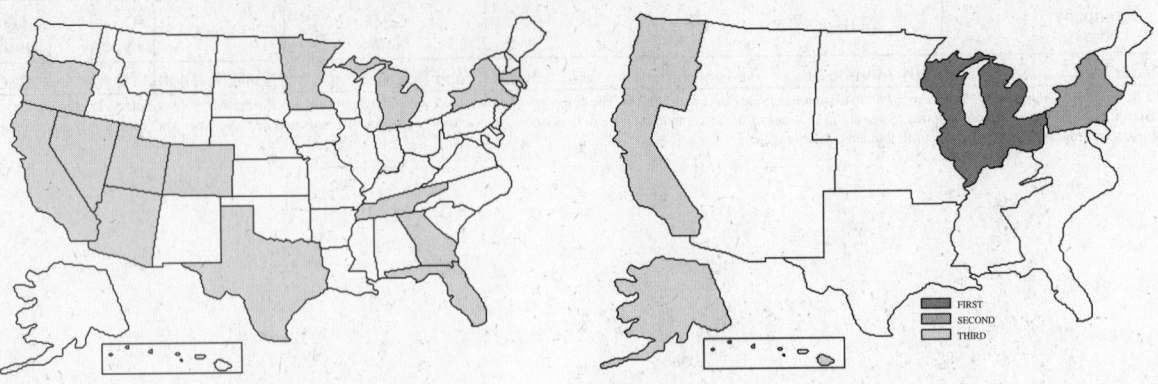

FIRST
SECOND
THIRD

INDUSTRY DATA BY STATE

State	Establishments		Employment			Payroll		Revenues		
	Total (number)	% of U.S.	Total (number)	% of U.S.	Per Estab.	Total ($ mil.)	Per Empl. ($)	Total ($ mil.)	% of U.S.	Per Estab. ($)
California	474	7.2	10,452	8.6	22	407.6	38,997	1,262.0	12.9	2,662,525
Texas	455	6.9	9,369	7.7	21	281.0	29,991	800.4	8.2	1,759,114
New York	309	4.7	6,753	5.6	22	218.9	32,411	791.9	8.1	2,562,854
Florida	343	5.2	6,259	5.2	18	193.4	30,899	598.1	6.1	1,743,685
Illinois	221	3.4	4,378	3.6	20	149.5	34,137	438.8	4.5	1,985,380
Pennsylvania	238	3.6	4,934	4.1	21	150.4	30,476	433.1	4.4	1,819,765
Michigan	187	2.8	4,337	3.6	23	132.8	30,614	431.1	4.4	2,305,091
Ohio	226	3.4	4,905	4.1	22	142.6	29,067	416.5	4.3	1,842,752
Georgia	222	3.4	3,059	2.5	14	87.4	28,578	300.3	3.1	1,352,532
Massachusetts	107	1.6	2,208	1.8	21	95.9	43,432	259.7	2.7	2,427,271
Tennessee	190	2.9	4,772	3.9	25	118.5	24,840	252.4	2.6	1,328,642
Minnesota	158	2.4	3,367	2.8	21	80.0	23,749	220.8	2.3	1,397,481
New Jersey	79	1.2	1,753	1.4	22	46.7	26,647	180.0	1.8	2,278,709
Arizona	101	1.5	1,950	1.6	19	64.1	32,882	173.0	1.8	1,712,812
Indiana	154	2.3	2,698	2.2	18	64.8	24,014	171.4	1.7	1,112,779
Colorado	110	1.7	2,421	2.0	22	56.8	23,473	165.9	1.7	1,508,027
Oregon	105	1.6	1,691	1.4	16	45.8	27,079	132.7	1.4	1,263,400
Louisiana	131	2.0	2,010	1.7	15	45.8	22,780	132.5	1.4	1,011,618
Wisconsin	136	2.1	2,525	2.1	19	53.6	21,244	132.4	1.4	973,360
Kentucky	162	2.5	2,173	1.8	13	43.6	20,085	111.8	1.1	690,340
Alabama	173	2.6	2,178	1.8	13	43.3	19,863	108.2	1.1	625,549
South Carolina	120	1.8	1,810	1.5	15	37.6	20,799	99.4	1.0	828,233
Connecticut	59	0.9	1,207	1.0	20	36.2	30,017	95.5	1.0	1,617,915
Utah	55	0.8	1,455	1.2	26	33.9	23,303	90.4	0.9	1,643,491
Oklahoma	96	1.5	1,445	1.2	15	35.0	24,197	85.0	0.9	885,302
Nevada	38	0.6	881	0.7	23	23.1	26,187	62.4	0.6	1,642,158
Mississippi	118	1.8	1,125	0.9	10	18.6	16,566	52.7	0.5	446,568
Arkansas	113	1.7	1,299	1.1	11	21.2	16,299	48.1	0.5	425,593
Maine	45	0.7	577	0.5	13	11.4	19,841	27.3	0.3	605,600
North Carolina	232	3.5	3,750*	-	-	(D)	-	(D)	-	-
Virginia	189	2.9	3,750*	-	-	(D)	-	(D)	-	-
Missouri	159	2.4	1,750*	-	-	(D)	-	(D)	-	-
Washington	123	1.9	1,750*	-	-	(D)	-	(D)	-	-
Iowa	120	1.8	1,750*	-	-	(D)	-	(D)	-	-
Maryland	100	1.5	1,750*	-	-	(D)	-	(D)	-	-
Kansas	86	1.3	1,750*	-	-	(D)	-	(D)	-	-
Nebraska	71	1.1	1,750*	-	-	(D)	-	(D)	-	-
West Virginia	69	1.0	750*	-	-	(D)	-	(D)	-	-
New Mexico	65	1.0	750*	-	-	(D)	-	(D)	-	-
South Dakota	52	0.8	750*	-	-	(D)	-	(D)	-	-
Montana	49	0.7	750*	-	-	(D)	-	(D)	-	-
Idaho	46	0.7	750*	-	-	(D)	-	(D)	-	-
North Dakota	46	0.7	750*	-	-	(D)	-	(D)	-	-
New Hampshire	42	0.6	750*	-	-	(D)	-	(D)	-	-
Wyoming	42	0.6	750*	-	-	(D)	-	(D)	-	-
Vermont	39	0.6	375*	-	-	(D)	-	(D)	-	-
Alaska	38	0.6	375*	-	-	(D)	-	(D)	-	-
Hawaii	32	0.5	750*	-	-	(D)	-	(D)	-	-
D.C.	25	0.4	750*	-	-	(D)	-	(D)	-	-
Rhode Island	24	0.4	375*	-	-	(D)	-	(D)	-	-
Delaware	17	0.3	375*	-	-	(D)	-	(D)	-	-

Source: 1997 Economic Census. The states are in descending order of revenues or establishments (if revenue data are missing for the majority). The symbol (D) appears when data are withheld to prevent disclosure of competitive information. States marked with (D) are sorted by number of establishments. A dash (-) indicates that the data element cannot be calculated. * indicates the midpoint of a range; 175, for example is the range 100-249. Shaded *states* on the state map indicate those states which have proportionately greater representation in the industry than would be indicated by the state's population; the ratio is based on total revenues or number of establishments. Shaded *regions* indicate where the industry is regionally most concentrated.

NAICS 513120 - TELEVISION BROADCASTING*

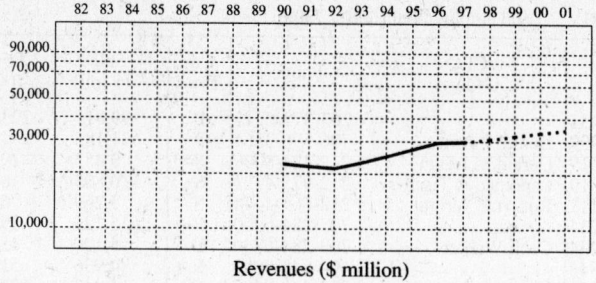

Revenues ($ million)

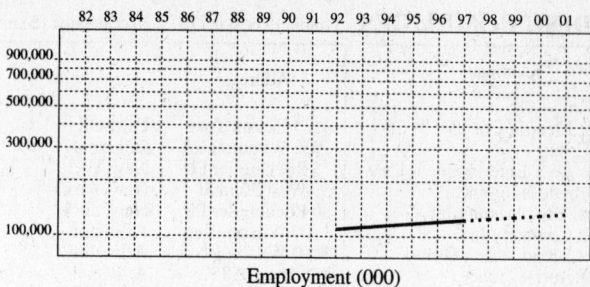

Employment (000)

GENERAL STATISTICS

Year	Establishments (number)	Employment (number)	Payroll ($ million)	Revenues ($ million)	Employees per Establishment (number)	Revenues per Establishment ($)	Payroll per Employee ($)
1982	-	-	-	-	-	-	-
1983	-	-	-	-	-	-	-
1984	-	-	-	-	-	-	-
1985	-	-	-	-	-	-	-
1986	-	-	-	-	-	-	-
1987	-	-	-	-	-	-	-
1988	-	-	-	-	-	-	-
1989	-	-	-	-	-	-	-
1990	-	-	4,179.0	22,534.0	-	-	-
1991	-	-	4,168.0	21,851.0	-	-	-
1992	1,593	109,370	4,429.0	21,364.0	68.7	13,411,174	40,496
1993	1,653 e	112,104 e	4,449.0	22,876.0	67.8 e	13,839,080 e	39,686 e
1994	1,714 e	114,839 e	4,860.0	24,843.0	67.0 e	14,494,166 e	42,320 e
1995	1,774 e	117,573 e	5,365.0	27,112.0	66.3 e	15,282,976 e	45,631 e
1996	1,835 e	120,308 e	5,737.0	29,551.0	65.6 e	16,104,087 e	47,686 e
1997	1,895	123,042	6,264.0	29,777.0	64.9	15,713,456	50,909
1998	1,956 p	125,777 p	6,306.0 p	30,796.0 p	64.3 p	15,744,376 p	50,136 p
1999	2,016 p	128,511 p	6,612.0 p	32,087.0 p	63.7 p	15,916,171 p	51,451 p
2000	2,077 p	131,246 p	6,917.0 p	33,378.0 p	63.2 p	16,070,294 p	52,703 p
2001	2,137 p	133,980 p	7,223.0 p	34,668.0 p	62.7 p	16,222,742 p	53,911 p

Sources: Economic Census of the United States, 1982, 1987, 1992, 1997. Establishment counts, employment, and payroll are from County Business Patterns for non-Census years. In non-Census years, industries in the Manufacturing range under SIC coding include data from the Annual Survey of Manufactures (ASM); those in the old Services range include data from the Services Annual Survey (SAS). Values followed by a 'p' are projections by the editors. Extrapolations are marked by 'e'. Data are the most recent available at this level of detail.

INDICES OF CHANGE

Year	Establishments (number)	Employment (number)	Payroll ($ million)	Revenues ($ million)	Employees per Establishment (number)	Revenues per Establishment ($)	Payroll per Employee ($)
1982	-	-	-	-	-	-	-
1987	-	-	-	-	-	-	-
1992	84.1	88.9	70.7	71.7	105.7	85.3	79.5
1993	87.2 e	91.1 e	71.0	76.8	104.4 e	88.1 e	78.0 e
1994	90.4 e	93.3 e	77.6	83.4	103.2 e	92.2 e	83.1 e
1995	93.6 e	95.6 e	85.6	91.1	102.1 e	97.3 e	89.6 e
1996	96.8 e	97.8 e	91.6	99.2	101.0 e	102.5 e	93.7 e
1997	100.0	100.0	100.0	100.0	100.0	100.0	100.0
1998	103.2 p	102.2 p	100.7 p	103.4 p	99.0 p	100.2 p	98.5 p
1999	106.4 p	104.4 p	105.6 p	107.8 p	98.2 p	101.3 p	101.1 p
2000	109.6 p	106.7 p	110.4 p	112.1 p	97.3 p	102.3 p	103.5 p
2001	112.8 p	108.9 p	115.3 p	116.4 p	96.6 p	103.2 p	105.9 p

Sources: Same as General Statistics. The values shown reflect change from the base year, 1997. Values above 100 mean greater than 1997, values below 100 mean less than 1997, and a value of 100 in the 1982-96 or 1998-2001 period means same as 1997. Values followed by a 'p' are projections by the editors; 'e' stands for extrapolation. Data are the most recent available at this level of detail.

SELECTED RATIOS

For 1997	Avg. of Information	Analyzed Industry	Index	For 1997	Avg. of Information	Analyzed Industry	Index
Employees per establishment	27	65	242	Payroll per establishment	1,131,090	3,305,541	292
Revenue per establishment	5,444,104	15,713,456	289	Payroll as % of revenue	21	21	101
Revenue per employee	203,255	242,007	119	Payroll per employee	42,229	50,909	121

Sources: Same as General Statistics. The 'Average' column represents the average for the industry sector, in 1997, where the currently shown industry is classified. The Index shows the relationship between the Average and the Analyzed Industry. For example, 100 means that they are equal; 500 that the Analyzed Industry is five times the average; 50 means that the Analyzed Industry is half the national average. The abbreviation 'na' is used to show that data are 'not available'.

*Equivalent to SIC 4833.

57

LEADING COMPANIES   Number shown: 75   Total sales ($ mil): 221,381   Total employment (000): 730.0

Company Name	Address				CEO Name	Phone	Co. Type	Sales ($ mil)	Empl. (000)
General Electric Co.	3135 Easton Tpke	Fairfield	CT	06431		203-373-2211	P	99,817	293.0
AFLAC Inc.	1932 Wynnton Rd	Columbus	GA	31999	Daniel P Amos	706-596-3264	P	31,183	4.0
Time Warner Entertainment L.P.	75 Rockefeller Plz	New York	NY	10019	Gerald M Levin	212-484-8000	S	9,453*	29.5
CBS Broadcasting Inc.	51 West 52nd St	New York	NY	10019	Laurence A Tisch	212-975-4321	S	6,805	6.4
National Broadcasting Inc.	30 Rockefeller Plz	New York	NY	10112	Robert C Wright	212-664-4444	S	5,269	6.5
Gannett Company Inc.	1100 Wilson Blvd	Arlington	VA	22234		703-284-6000	P	5,121	39.4
Gannett Broadcasting Group	1100 Wilson Blvd	Arlington	VA	22234	Cecil Walker	703-284-6760	D	5,100	45.2
Cox Enterprises Inc.	PO Box 105357	Atlanta	GA	30348		404-843-5000	R	4,936	51.0
Time Warner Cable	290 Harbor Dr	Stamford	CT	06902	Joseph J Collins	203-328-0600	D	4,243	25.0
McGraw-Hill Inc.	1221 Av Americas	New York	NY	10020	Harold McGraw III	212-512-2000	P	3,992	15.9
USA Networks Inc.	152 W 57th St	New York	NY	10019	Barry Baker	212-314-7300	P	3,236	9.2
Tribune Co. (Chicago, Illinois)	435 N Michigan Ave	Chicago	IL	60611	John W Madigan	312-222-9100	P	3,222	12.7
New York Times Co.	229 W 43rd St	New York	NY	10036	Russell Lewis	212-556-1234	P	2,937	13.2
Hearst Corp.	959 8th Ave	New York	NY	10019		212-649-2000	R	2,833*	15.0
News America Inc.	1211 Av Americas	New York	NY	10036	Anthea Disney	212-852-7000	S	2,571*	12.0
Washington Post Co.	1150 15th St NW	Washington	DC	20071	Donald Graham	202-334-6000	P	2,216	8.5
Viacom International Inc.	1515 Broadway	New York	NY	10036	Sumner Redstone	212-258-6000	S	1,900*	5.0
E.W. Scripps Co.	PO Box 5380	Cincinnati	OH	45201	William Burleigh	513-977-3000	P	1,559	7.9
Bloomberg L.P.	499 Park Ave	New York	NY	10022	Michael Bloomberg	212-318-2000	R	1,500	4.0
PRIMESTAR Inc.	8085 S Chester St	Englewood	CO	80112	Dan O'Brien	303-712-4600	R	1,500	3.8
A.H. Belo Corp.	PO Box 655237	Dallas	TX	75265	Robert W Decherd	214-977-6606	P	1,434	7.0
Clear Channel Communications	PO Box 659512	San Antonio	TX	78265	L Lowry Mays	210-822-2828	P	1,351	7.0
Meredith Corp.	1716 Locust St	Des Moines	IA	50309	William Kerr	515-284-3000	P	1,036	2.6
Tribune Broadcasting Co.	435 N Michigan Ave	Chicago	IL	60611	Dennis FitzSimons	312-222-3333	S	1,031*	3.0
Harte-Hanks Inc.	PO Box 269	San Antonio	TX	78291	Larry Franklin	210-829-9000	P	830	7.1
Media General Inc.	PO Box 85333	Richmond	VA	23293	J Stewart Bryan III	804-649-6000	P	795	8.9
Cox Broadcasting Inc.	P O Box 105357	Atlanta	GA	30348	Nichlos Trigony	404-843-5000	S	791*	5.0
Sinclair Broadcast Group Inc.	10706 Beaver Dam	Hunt Valley	MD	21030	David D Smith	410-568-1500	P	737	2.3
Journal Communications Inc.	PO Box 661	Milwaukee	WI	53201		414-224-2000	R	732	7.0
Univision Communications Inc.	1999 Av of the Stars	Los Angeles	CA	90067	Henry Cisneros	310-556-7676	P	693	1.7
Freedom Communications Inc.	PO Box 19549	Irvine	CA	92623	James Rosse	949-553-9292	R	681	7.0
Hubbard Broadcasting Inc.	3415 University Ave	St. Paul	MN	55114	Stanley Hubbard	612-646-5555	R	600	1.5
Landmark Communications Inc.	PO Box 449	Norfolk	VA	23501		757-446-2000	R	575	4.5
Liberty Corp.	P O Box 789	Greenville	SC	29602	W Hayne Hipp	864-609-8111	P	556	1.3
Lee Enterprises Inc.	215 N Main St	Davenport	IA	52801	Richard Gottlieb	319-383-2100	P	536	6.1
Gaylord Entertainment Co.	1 Gaylord Dr	Nashville	TN	37214	Ek Gaylord II	615-316-6000	P	525	6.2
Lynch Corp.	401 Theodore Fremd	Rye	NY	10580	Mario J Gabelli	914-921-7601	P	468	1.9
BHC Communications Inc.	767 5th Ave Ste 46th	New York	NY	10153	Herbert J Siegel	212-421-0200	P	446	1.1
Schurz Communications Inc.	225 W Colfax Ave	South Bend	IN	46626	Franklin D Schurz Jr	219-287-1001	R	410*	1.5
Hearst-Argyle Television Inc.	888 Seventh Ave	New York	NY	10106	Bob Marbut	212-887-6800	P	407	1.6
Pulitzer Inc.	900 N Tucker Blvd	St. Louis	MO	63101	Michael E Pulitzer	314-340-8000	P	373	2.3
A and E Television Networks	235 East 45th St	New York	NY	10017	Nickolas Davatzes	212-210-1400	J	349	0.4
Entertainment Inc.	1 Commercial Plz	Hartford	CT	06103	Robert E Fowler III	860-549-1674	P	348	1.4
New Gaylord Entertainment Co.	PO Box 25125	Oklahoma City	OK	73125		405-475-3311	S	340	4.6
LIN Television Corp.	4 Richmond Sq	Providence	RI	02906	Gary R Chapman	401-454-2880	P	294	1.3
Ackerley Group Inc.	1301 5th Ave	Seattle	WA	98101	Barry Ackerley	206-624-2888	P	278	1.3
Young Broadcasting Inc.	599 Lexington Ave	New York	NY	10022	Ronald J Kwasnick	212-754-7070	P	277	1.4
Corporation for Public	901 E St N W	Washington	DC	20004	Robert T Coonrod	202-879-9600	R	275	0.1
KING Broadcasting Co.	PO Box 24525	Seattle	WA	98124		206-448-5555	S	270*	1.0
Univision Network L.P.	9405 N W 41st St	Miami	FL	33178	Ray Rodriguez	305-471-3900	S	248*	0.7
D.T. Chase Enterprises	1 Commercial Plz	Hartford	CT	06103	David T Chase	203-549-1674	R	247*	0.8
Macromedia Inc.	150 River St	Hackensack	NJ	07601		201-646-4000	R	240	1.6
Jefferson-Pilot Communications	1 Julian Price Pl	Charlotte	NC	28208	Terry Stone	704-374-3500	S	229	1.0
Perpetual Corp.	808 17th St N W	Washington	DC	20006	Joe L Allbritton	202-789-2130	R	212*	0.9
Journal Broadcast Group	720 E Capitol Dr	Milwaukee	WI	53212	Jim Prather	414-332-9611	S	204*	1.3
ValueVision International Inc.	6740 Shady Oak Rd	Minneapolis	MN	55401	Gene McCaffrey	612-947-5200	P	204	1.0
Intern. Family Entertainment Inc.	P O Box 2050	Virginia Beach	VA	23450	Timothy B Robertson	757-459-6000	P	200*	0.5
Telemundo Group Inc.	2290 W 8th Ave	Hialeah	FL	33010	Peter Tortorici	305-884-8200	S	198	1.2
Bonneville International Corp.	P O Box 1160	Salt Lake City	UT	84110	Bruce T Reese	801-575-7500	R	197*	1.3
Pegasus Communications Corp.	225 City Line Ave	Bala Cynwyd	PA	19004	Marshall W Pagon	610-934-7000	P	195	0.9
United Television Inc.	132 S Rodeo Dr	Beverly Hills	CA	90212	Evan C Thompson	310-281-4844	P	183	0.6
Allbritton Communications Co.	808 17th St	Washington	DC	20006	Lawrence I Hebert	202-789-2130	S	173*	0.8
Fisher Broadcasting Inc.	2001 6th Ave	Seattle	WA	98109	Patrick Scott	206-770-3815	S	170	0.7
Granite Broadcasting Corp.	767 3rd Ave	New York	NY	10017	W Don Cornwell	212-826-2530	P	161	1.0
Post-Newsweek Stations Inc.	3 Constitution Plz	Hartford	CT	06103	G William Ryan	860-493-6530	S	160	0.7
Shop at Home Inc.	PO Box 305249	Nashville	TN	37230	Kent E Lillie	615-263-8000	P	152	0.5
Williams Vyvx Services	111 E 1st St	Tulsa	OK	74103	Laura Kenny	918-573-5760	S	150*	0.5
Blade Communications Inc.	541 N Superior St	Toledo	OH	43660			R	140*	1.5
Guy Gannett Communications	P O Box 15277	Portland	ME	04101	James B Shaffer	207-828-8100	R	135	1.4
Paxson Communications Corp.	601 Clearwater	W. Palm Beach	FL	33401	James B Bocock	561-659-4122	P	134	1.3
Cosmos Broadcasting Corp.	PO Box 19023	Greenville	SC	29602	James M Keelor	864-609-4370	S	129*	1.2
Gray Communications Systems	PO Box 48	Albany	GA	31702	T Mack Robinson	404-504-9828	P	129	1.2
Capitol Broadcasting Inc.	PO Box 12800	Raleigh	NC	27605	James F Goodmon	919-890-6000	R	120	0.6
Morris Newspaper Corp.	PO Box 8167	Savannah	GA	31412	Charles Morris	912-233-1281	P	120	1.3
National Broadcasting Inc	925 Wood Ridge	Charlotte	NC	28217	Robert Horner	704-329-8700	S	120*	0.2

Source: Ward's Business Directory of U.S. Private and Public Companies, Volumes 1 and 2, 2000. The company type code used is as follows: P - Public, R - Private, S - Subsidiary, D - Division, J - Joint Venture, A - Affiliate, G - Group, N - Company type not reported. Sales are in millions of dollars, employees are in thousands. An asterisk (*) indicates an estimated sales volume. The symbol < stands for 'less than'. Company names and addresses are truncated, in some cases, to fit into the available space.

LOCATION BY STATE AND REGIONAL CONCENTRATION

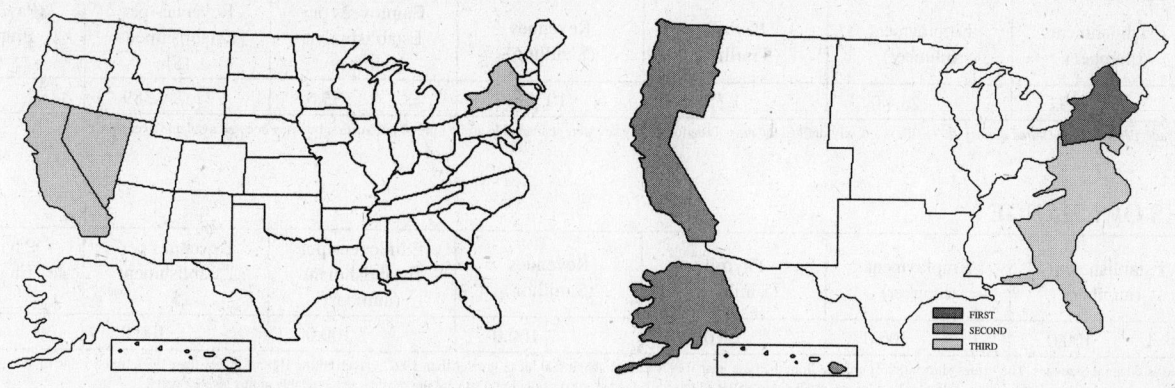

FIRST
SECOND
THIRD

INDUSTRY DATA BY STATE

State	Establishments Total (number)	Establishments % of U.S.	Employment Total (number)	Employment % of U.S.	Employment Per Estab.	Payroll Total ($ mil.)	Payroll Per Empl. ($)	Revenues Total ($ mil.)	Revenues % of U.S.	Revenues Per Estab. ($)
New York	117	6.2	18,100	14.7	155	1,734.0	95,800	10,503.2	35.3	89,770,709
California	201	10.6	15,976	13.0	79	932.0	58,337	4,293.6	14.4	21,361,090
Florida	129	6.8	7,880	6.4	61	323.0	40,993	1,473.9	4.9	11,425,961
Texas	139	7.3	9,107	7.4	66	318.7	34,997	1,377.3	4.6	9,908,288
Illinois	59	3.1	4,058	3.3	69	217.3	53,558	1,064.1	3.6	18,034,814
Ohio	70	3.7	4,466	3.6	64	187.1	41,889	801.5	2.7	11,450,114
Pennsylvania	56	3.0	3,769	3.1	67	160.9	42,690	787.7	2.6	14,066,696
Virginia	60	3.2	4,080	3.3	68	140.7	34,495	716.0	2.4	11,932,667
Massachusetts	36	1.9	2,830	2.3	79	145.3	51,349	630.3	2.1	17,509,639
Michigan	51	2.7	2,879	2.3	56	120.1	41,732	577.8	1.9	11,329,765
D.C.	14	0.7	1,635	1.3	117	146.4	89,527	564.3	1.9	40,304,643
North Carolina	53	2.8	3,081	2.5	58	120.2	39,030	521.8	1.8	9,845,736
Georgia	50	2.6	2,087	1.7	42	91.9	44,034	424.2	1.4	8,484,860
Arizona	29	1.5	2,016	1.6	70	86.5	42,898	387.7	1.3	13,369,310
Minnesota	33	1.7	2,089	1.7	63	81.9	39,213	374.2	1.3	11,337,909
Tennessee	44	2.3	2,355	1.9	54	85.1	36,150	370.3	1.2	8,415,091
Missouri	38	2.0	2,232	1.8	59	96.1	43,056	365.4	1.2	9,616,605
Washington	36	1.9	1,974	1.6	55	100.4	50,837	350.5	1.2	9,735,306
Colorado	41	2.2	1,621	1.3	40	78.1	48,203	316.9	1.1	7,729,415
Alabama	50	2.6	2,441	2.0	49	79.9	32,753	283.2	1.0	5,664,400
Louisiana	37	2.0	2,078	1.7	56	76.7	36,915	268.7	0.9	7,263,378
Indiana	39	2.1	2,292	1.9	59	79.9	34,839	265.6	0.9	6,810,154
Wisconsin	30	1.6	1,851	1.5	62	74.9	40,481	253.9	0.9	8,461,733
New Jersey	17	0.9	692	0.6	41	35.5	51,309	225.8	0.8	13,284,353
Oregon	35	1.8	1,667	1.4	48	70.6	42,349	225.3	0.8	6,437,086
Connecticut	25	1.3	1,159	0.9	46	49.1	42,403	211.4	0.7	8,457,080
Oklahoma	21	1.1	1,371	1.1	65	48.5	35,380	209.4	0.7	9,971,381
South Carolina	24	1.3	1,334	1.1	56	44.8	33,548	179.5	0.6	7,479,375
Maryland	19	1.0	920	0.7	48	41.2	44,741	174.0	0.6	9,155,895
Nevada	24	1.3	1,189	1.0	50	45.3	38,135	166.1	0.6	6,919,083
Kentucky	23	1.2	1,437	1.2	62	50.6	35,211	164.1	0.6	7,136,522
Mississippi	29	1.5	1,215	1.0	42	37.1	30,552	120.7	0.4	4,161,897
Arkansas	22	1.2	910	0.7	41	27.5	30,182	100.5	0.3	4,570,045
Kansas	23	1.2	950	0.8	41	31.8	33,511	97.4	0.3	4,234,957
Iowa	19	1.0	967	0.8	51	29.6	30,612	97.2	0.3	5,118,053
Hawaii	17	0.9	683	0.6	40	31.0	45,448	97.0	0.3	5,703,353
Utah	9	0.5	531	0.4	59	24.6	46,418	92.8	0.3	10,307,444
New Mexico	17	0.9	694	0.6	41	23.4	33,705	82.6	0.3	4,860,529
Nebraska	11	0.6	697	0.6	63	24.4	34,947	73.5	0.2	6,679,909
West Virginia	14	0.7	746	0.6	53	20.1	27,004	72.9	0.2	5,208,214
Maine	15	0.8	782	0.6	52	26.0	33,233	70.6	0.2	4,705,600
North Dakota	19	1.0	733	0.6	39	17.9	24,389	51.3	0.2	2,697,421
Idaho	14	0.7	637	0.5	46	16.6	26,116	40.8	0.1	2,912,714
Montana	22	1.2	588	0.5	27	12.6	21,398	34.0	0.1	1,545,545
Alaska	15	0.8	482	0.4	32	16.4	34,089	34.0	0.1	2,265,333
South Dakota	8	0.4	369	0.3	46	10.0	27,141	31.0	0.1	3,873,875
Vermont	14	0.7	175*	-	-	(D)	-	(D)	-	-
Wyoming	10	0.5	175*	-	-	(D)	-	(D)	-	-
Rhode Island	8	0.4	750*	-	-	(D)	-	(D)	-	-
New Hampshire	7	0.4	175*	-	-	(D)	-	(D)	-	-
Delaware	2	0.1	60*	-	-	(D)	-	(D)	-	-

Source: 1997 *Economic Census*. The states are in descending order of revenues or establishments (if revenue data are missing for the majority). The symbol (D) appears when data are withheld to prevent disclosure of competitive information. States marked with (D) are sorted by number of establishments. A dash (-) indicates that the data element cannot be calculated. * indicates the midpoint of a range; 175, for example is the range 100-249. Shaded *states* on the state map indicate those states which have proportionately greater representation in the industry than would be indicated by the state's population; the ratio is based on total revenues or number of establishments. Shaded *regions* indicate where the industry is regionally most concentrated.

59

NAICS 513210 - CABLE NETWORKS

GENERAL STATISTICS

Year	Establishments (number)	Employment (number)	Payroll ($ million)	Revenues ($ million)	Employees per Establishment (number)	Revenues per Establishment ($)	Payroll per Employee ($)
1997	494	26,488	1,358.0	10,390.0	53.6	21,032,389	51,268

Source: *Economic Census of the United States*, 1997. This is a newly defined industry. Data for prior years were unavailable at the time of publication but may become available over time.

INDICES OF CHANGE

Year	Establishments (number)	Employment (number)	Payroll ($ million)	Revenues ($ million)	Employees per Establishment (number)	Revenues per Establishment ($)	Payroll per Employee ($)
1997	100.0	100.0	100.0	100.0	100.0	100.0	100.0

Sources: Same as General Statistics. The values shown reflect change from the base year, 1997. Values above 100 mean greater than 1997, values below 100 mean less than 1997, and a value of 100 in the 1982-96 or 1998-2001 period means same as 1997. Values followed by a 'p' are projections by the editors; 'e' stands for extrapolation. Data are the most recent available at this level of detail.

SIC INDUSTRIES RELATED TO NAICS 513210

Each new NAICS code represents an industry that used to be part of an SIC or a part of several SIC industries. Data in this table are shown to provide transitional information for these cases. All available data for the precursor SIC(s) are shown. Even if only a part of an SIC is included in the NAICS, *all* data for the SIC are reproduced. If the SIC industry is not marked as being a part (pt) of the NAICS, the entire industry is embedded in the NAICS data. The SIC composition of the new industry provides some hints of the relative importance of its "ancestors." Data marked with a 'p' are projected. Projections begin with 1982 data. Data earlier than 1990 are not shown but are reflected in the projections.

SIC	Industry	1990	1991	1992	1993	1994	1995	1996	1997
4841	**Cable and Other Pay TV (pt)**								
	Establishments (number)	3,478	4,157	4,468	4,475	4,545	4,750	4,786	5,111p
	Employment (thousands)	120.2	123.8	129.0	135.5	134.3	149.1	170.3	165.5p
	Revenues ($ million)	23,192.0	24,954.0	27,512.1	29,639.0	30,289.0	33,890.0	38,488.0	43,412.0

Source: *Economic Census of the United States*, 1992, annual surveys of economic sectors conducted by the Bureau of the Census, and estimates or projections based on the 1982-1992 period; not all data are shown. 'e' marks estimates made by the editors; 'p' indicates projections based on time series. A dash (-) indicates that data for this SIC or year were not available. The abbreviation (pt) next to the industry name indicates that only a part of the industry is present within the NAICS data. If no (pt) is shown, the entire industry is contained within the NAICS data.

SELECTED RATIOS

For 1997	Avg. of Information	Analyzed Industry	Index	For 1997	Avg. of Information	Analyzed Industry	Index
Employees per establishment	27	54	200	Payroll per establishment	1,131,090	2,748,988	243
Revenue per establishment	5,444,104	21,032,389	386	Payroll as % of revenue	21	13	63
Revenue per employee	203,255	392,253	193	Payroll per employee	42,229	51,268	121

Sources: Same as General Statistics. The 'Average' column represents the average for the industry sector, in 1997, where the currently shown industry is classified. The Index shows the relationship between the Average and the Analyzed Industry. For example, 100 means that they are equal; 500 that the Analyzed Industry is five times the average; 50 means that the Analyzed Industry is half the national average. The abbreviation 'na' is used to show that data are 'not available'.

LEADING COMPANIES

Number shown: **75**   Total sales ($ mil): **131,427**   Total employment (000): **543.0**

Company Name	Address				CEO Name	Phone	Co. Type	Sales ($ mil)	Empl. (000)
Reliant Energy Inc.	PO Box 4567	Houston	TX	77210	Steve Letbetter	713-207-3000	P	22,000	12.9
Viacom Inc.	1515 Broadway	New York	NY	10036	Sumner M Redstone	212-258-6000	P	12,096	116.7
Discovery Communications Inc.	7700 Wisconsin Ave	Bethesda	MD	20814	John S Hendricks	301-986-0444	R	10,954*	43.3
Time Warner Entertainment L.P.	75 Rockefeller Plz	New York	NY	10019	Gerald M Levin	212-484-8000	S	9,453*	29.5
AT & T Broadband & Internet	9197 S Peoria Ave	Englewood	CO	80112	Leo J Hindery Jr	720-875-5500	D	7,351	37.0
Hughes Electronics Corp.	PO Box 956	El Segundo	CA	90245	Gareth Chang	310-364-6000	P	5,964	15.0
Turner Broadcasting System Inc.	1 CNN Ctr	Atlanta	GA	30348	Terence McGuirk	404-827-1700	S	5,401*	11.0
Comcast Corp.	1500 Market St	Philadelphia	PA	19102	Brian L Roberts	215-665-1700	P	5,146	17.4
Cox Enterprises Inc.	PO Box 105357	Atlanta	GA	30348		404-843-5000	R	4,936	51.0
Time Warner Cable	290 Harbor Dr	Stamford	CT	06902	Joseph J Collins	203-328-0600	D	4,243	25.0
Cablevision Systems Corp.	1111 Stewart Ave	Bethpage	NY	11714	James L Dolan	516-803-2300	P	3,943	15.8
Liberty Media Corp.	8101 E Prentice	Englewood	CO	80111	Peter R Barton	303-721-5400	P	2,946	5.8
MediaOne Group Inc.	188 Inverness West	Englewood	CO	80112	Charles M Lillis	303-858-3000	P	2,882	16.8
Washington Post Co.	1150 15th St NW	Washington	DC	20071	Donald Graham	202-334-6000	P	2,216	8.5
MediaOne	188 Inverness Dr	Englewood	CO	80112	Janice Peters	303-754-5400	S	2,091*	11.5
Viacom International Inc.	1515 Broadway	New York	NY	10036	Sumner Redstone	212-258-6000	S	1,900*	5.0
DIRECTV Inc.	2230 E Imperial	El Segundo	CA	90245	Eddie Hartenstein	310-535-5000	S	1,816	1.4
Cox Communications Inc.	PO Box 105357	Atlanta	GA	30348		404-843-5000	P	1,717	9.8
Home Box Office	1100 Av Americas	New York	NY	10036	Jeff Bewkes	212-512-1000	D	1,591*	2.0
E.W. Scripps Co.	PO Box 5380	Cincinnati	OH	45201	William Burleigh	513-977-3000	P	1,559	7.9
Sunstates Corp.	4600 Marriott Dr	Raleigh	NC	27612	Clyde W Engle	919-781-5611	P	1,550*	2.3
Arvig Enterprises Inc.	160 2nd Ave S W	Perham	MN	56573	Allen Arvig	218-346-4200	R	1,254*	0.1
Ameritech Indiana	240 N Meridian St	Indianapolis	IN	46204	Kent A Lebherz	317-265-2266	S	1,105*	5.8
Meredith Corp.	1716 Locust St	Des Moines	IA	50309	William Kerr	515-284-3000	P	1,036	2.6
MTV Networks Inc.	1515 Broadway	New York	NY	10036	Tom Freston	212-258-8000	S	1,030*	1.1
Citizens Communications Inc.	3 High Ridge Park	Stamford	CT	06905	O Lee Jobe	203-614-5600	S	860*	3.5
Media General Inc.	PO Box 85333	Richmond	VA	23293	J Stewart Bryan III	804-649-6000	P	795	8.9
NTL Inc.	110 East 59th St	New York	NY	10022	George S Blumenthal	212-906-8440	P	747	9.1
PRIMEDIA Workplace Learning	1303 Marsh Ln	Carrollton	TX	75006	Jack L Farnsworth	972-716-5100	S	713	1.0
United Video Inc.	7140 S Lewis Ave	Tulsa	OK	74136	Barry Knepper	918-488-4000	S	688*	3.5
Charter Communications Inc.	12444 Powerscourt	St. Louis	MO	63131	Jerald L Kent	314-965-0555	R	594	4.7
Time Warner Cable	1266 Dublin Rd	Delaware	OH	43015	Petty O'Connell	614-481-5050	S	556*	0.5
Adelphia Communications Corp.	P O Box 472	Coudersport	PA	16915	John J Rigas	814-274-9830	P	528	3.9
Gaylord Entertainment Co.	1 Gaylord Dr	Nashville	TN	37214	Ek Gaylord II	615-316-6000	P	525	6.2
Century Communications Corp.	50 Locust Ave	New Canaan	CT	06840	Bernard P Gallagher	203-972-2000	P	520	2.9
Newhouse Broadcasting Corp.	P O Box 4739	Syracuse	NY	13221	Robert Miron	315-463-7675	R	499*	2.0
Rainbow Media Holdings Inc.	150 Crossways Pk	Woodbury	NY	11797	Josh Sapan	516-396-3000	S	499*	2.0
Lenfest Communications Inc.	PO Box 8985	Wilmington	DE	19899	HF Lenfest	302-427-8602	R	470	2.0
Jones Intercable Inc.	P O Box 3309	Englewood	CO	80155	Glenn R Jones	303-792-3111	P	461	3.1
Jones Interdigital Inc.	P O Box 3309	Englewood	CO	80112	Glenn R Jones	303-792-3111	R	450*	3.5
Prime Cable	600 Congress Ave	Austin	TX	78701	Robert Hughes	512-476-7888	R	424	0.8
Ascent Entertainment Group Inc.	1225 17th St	Denver	CO	80202	Charles Neinas	303-308-7000	P	344	1.0
Adelphia Communications	PO Box 472	Coudersport	PA	16915	John J Rigas	814-274-9830	R	330*	1.3
Multimedia Cablevision Inc.	701 E Douglas St	Wichita	KS	67202	Mike Burrus	316-262-4270	P	321	1.7
Playboy Enterprises Inc.	680 N Lake Shore	Chicago	IL	60611	Christie Hefner	312-751-8000	P	318	0.8
KING Broadcasting Co.	PO Box 24525	Seattle	WA	98124		206-448-5555	S	270*	1.0
UnitedGlobalCom Inc.	4643 S Ulster St	Denver	CO	80237	Michael T Fries	303-770-4001	P	254	2.5
On Command Corp.	6331 San Ignacio	San Jose	CA	95119	Brian A Steel	408-360-4500	P	239	0.8
Jefferson-Pilot Communications	1 Julian Price Pl	Charlotte	NC	28208	Terry Stone	704-374-3500	S	229	1.0
Commonwealth Telephone	100 CTE Dr	Dallas	PA	18612	Michael I Gottdenker	570-674-2700	P	226	1.3
Vision Cable Communications	2300 Yorkmont Rd	Charlotte	NC	28217	V Mitch Roberts	704-357-6900	S	212*	0.9
RCN Corp.	105 Carnegie Ctr	Princeton	NJ	08540	Michael A Adams	609-734-3700	P	211	2.2
Pegasus Communications Corp.	225 City Line Ave	Bala Cynwyd	PA	19004	Marshall W Pagon	610-934-7000	P	195	0.9
Showtime Networks Inc.	1633 Broadway	New York	NY	10019	Matthew Blank	212-708-1600	S	186*	0.8
Pacific Telesis Video Services	2410 Camino Ramon	San Ramon	CA	94583		925-806-5818	R	184*	0.7
LodgeNet Entertainment Corp.	3900 W Innovation	Sioux Falls	SD	57107	Scott C Petersen	605-988-1000	P	181	0.7
BET Holdings Inc.	1900 W Pl NE	Washington	DC	20018	Robert Johnson	202-608-2000	P	178	0.6
Shop at Home Inc.	PO Box 305249	Nashville	TN	37230	Kent E Lillie	615-263-8000	P	152	0.5
E! Entertainment Television Inc.	5670 Wilshire Blvd	Los Angeles	CA	90036	Fran Shea	323-954-2400	R	145*	0.8
Blade Communications Inc.	541 N Superior St	Toledo	OH	43660			R	140*	1.5
Cable TV Montgomery	20 W Gude Dr	Rockville	MD	20850	Robert J Gordon	301-294-7600	S	134*	0.6
ESPN Inc.	935 Middle St	Bristol	CT	06010	Steven Bornstein	860-585-2242	S	129	1.5
Black Entertainment Television	One BET	Washington	DC	20018	Robert L Johnson	202-608-2000	S	116*	0.4
Insight Communications Inc.	126 E 56th St	New York	NY	10022	Michael S Willner	212-371-2266	P	113	1.1
Pioneer Electric Cooperative Inc.	PO Box 468	Greenville	AL	36037		334-382-6636	R	112*	<0.1
Triax Communications Corp.	100 Fillmore St	Denver	CO	80206	Jim DeSorrento	303-333-2424	R	112*	0.7
Oceanic Cablevision Inc.	200 Akimainui St	Mililani	HI	96789	Don E Carroll	808-625-2100	S	110	0.4
Data Broadcasting Corp.	3490 Clubhouse Dr	Jackson	WY	83001	Stuart Clark	307-733-9742	P	108	0.6
International FiberCom Inc.	3410 E University	Phoenix	AZ	85034	Joseph P Kealy	602-941-1900	P	105	0.9
On Command Video Corp.	6331 San Ignacio	San Jose	CA	95119	Robert M Kavner	408-360-4500	P	102*	0.4
Suburban Cablevision	800 Rahway Ave	Union	NJ	07083		973-736-7444	R	100*	0.4
Cox Cable of San Diego Inc.	5159 Federal Blvd	San Diego	CA	92105	Scott Hatfield	404-843-5000	S	98*	0.6
Harron Communications Corp.	70 E Lancaster Ave	Frazer	PA	19355	Paul H Harron	610-644-7500	R	90*	0.5
Video Services Corp.	240 Pegasus Ave	Northvale	NJ	07647	Terrence Elkes	201-767-1000	P	89	0.5
GE American Communications	4 Research Way	Princeton	NJ	08540	John F Connelly	609-987-4000	D	85*	0.5

Source: Ward's Business Directory of U.S. Private and Public Companies, Volumes 1 and 2, 2000. The company type code used is as follows: P - Public, R - Private, S - Subsidiary, D - Division, J - Joint Venture, A - Affiliate, G - Group, N - Company type not reported. Sales are in millions of dollars, employees are in thousands. An asterisk (*) indicates an estimated sales volume. The symbol < stands for 'less than'. Company names and addresses are truncated, in some cases, to fit into the available space.

LOCATION BY STATE AND REGIONAL CONCENTRATION

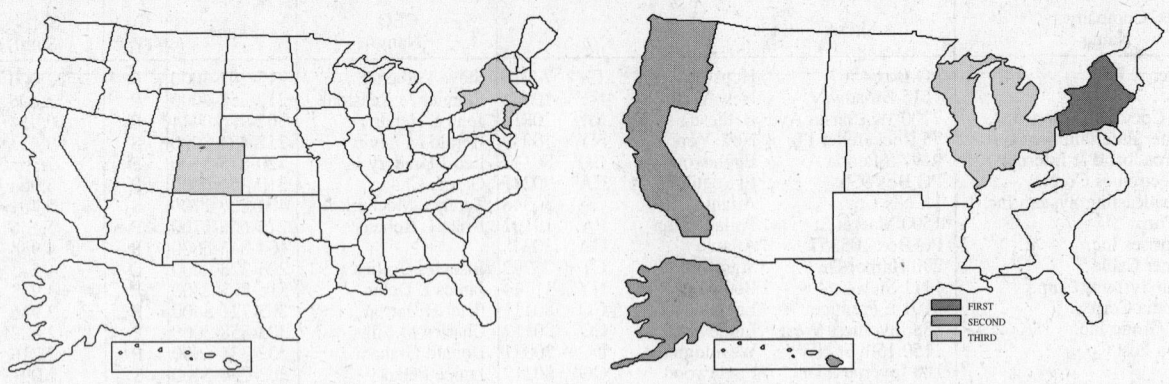

FIRST
SECOND
THIRD

INDUSTRY DATA BY STATE

State	Establishments Total (number)	Establishments % of U.S.	Employment Total (number)	Employment % of U.S.	Employment Per Estab.	Payroll Total ($ mil.)	Payroll Per Empl. ($)	Revenues Total ($ mil.)	Revenues % of U.S.	Revenues Per Estab. ($)
New York	58	11.7	5,604	21.2	97	432.2	77,126	3,520.0	33.9	60,690,052
California	79	16.0	4,082	15.4	52	173.8	42,568	1,048.8	10.1	13,276,076
New Jersey	12	2.4	1,364	5.1	114	66.0	48,371	330.0	3.2	27,503,333
Florida	22	4.5	963	3.6	44	53.5	55,558	192.5	1.9	8,748,955
Illinois	26	5.3	481	1.8	19	20.1	41,711	173.3	1.7	6,665,038
Texas	21	4.3	736	2.8	35	24.7	33,522	159.1	1.5	7,577,095
Colorado	21	4.3	424	1.6	20	22.2	52,427	140.4	1.4	6,687,000
Pennsylvania	15	3.0	314	1.2	21	9.6	30,525	72.8	0.7	4,850,400
Massachusetts	18	3.6	382	1.4	21	13.7	35,864	69.3	0.7	3,851,111
North Carolina	8	1.6	170	0.6	21	8.0	47,276	66.4	0.6	8,297,875
Ohio	19	3.8	301	1.1	16	7.5	25,003	59.5	0.6	3,130,947
Michigan	17	3.4	86	0.3	5	3.9	45,221	54.3	0.5	3,196,235
Minnesota	9	1.8	97	0.4	11	4.4	45,608	47.0	0.5	5,219,444
Missouri	4	0.8	63	0.2	16	2.5	39,460	25.7	0.2	6,418,750
Washington	6	1.2	113	0.4	19	4.1	36,398	9.3	0.1	1,554,500
Maine	5	1.0	58	0.2	12	1.2	20,000	4.7	0.0	932,600
Oregon	6	1.2	36	0.1	6	1.0	26,694	4.5	0.0	752,500
Alaska	6	1.2	33	0.1	6	1.5	45,667	4.1	0.0	684,833
Alabama	6	1.2	41	0.2	7	0.7	16,732	3.0	0.0	499,833
Mississippi	4	0.8	10	0.0	3	0.4	39,400	2.4	0.0	592,250
Arkansas	6	1.2	17	0.1	3	0.4	25,765	2.2	0.0	370,500
Indiana	3	0.6	32	0.1	11	0.5	15,750	1.4	0.0	479,667
Wisconsin	5	1.0	25	0.1	5	0.3	12,720	1.3	0.0	258,000
Montana	3	0.6	3	0.0	1	-	10,667	0.3	0.0	114,667
Kansas	4	0.8	5	0.0	1	0.1	11,200	0.3	0.0	71,750
Georgia	28	5.7	7,500*	-	-	(D)	-	(D)	-	-
Virginia	16	3.2	750*	-	-	(D)	-	(D)	-	-
Tennessee	10	2.0	750*	-	-	(D)	-	(D)	-	-
Connecticut	9	1.8	1,750*	-	-	(D)	-	(D)	-	-
Maryland	7	1.4	175*	-	-	(D)	-	(D)	-	-
D.C.	6	1.2	375*	-	-	(D)	-	(D)	-	-
Louisiana	4	0.8	1,750*	-	-	(D)	-	(D)	-	-
Oklahoma	4	0.8	375*	-	-	(D)	-	(D)	-	-
West Virginia	4	0.8	10*	-	-	(D)	-	(D)	-	-
Arizona	3	0.6	60*	-	-	(D)	-	(D)	-	-
Idaho	3	0.6	60*	-	-	(D)	-	(D)	-	-
Kentucky	3	0.6	10*	-	-	(D)	-	(D)	-	-
Iowa	2	0.4	10*	-	-	(D)	-	(D)	-	-
Nebraska	2	0.4	10*	-	-	(D)	-	(D)	-	-
New Hampshire	2	0.4	10*	-	-	(D)	-	(D)	-	-
South Carolina	2	0.4	60*	-	-	(D)	-	(D)	-	-
Vermont	2	0.4	10*	-	-	(D)	-	(D)	-	-
Nevada	1	0.2	10*	-	-	(D)	-	(D)	-	-
North Dakota	1	0.2	10*	-	-	(D)	-	(D)	-	-
South Dakota	1	0.2	10*	-	-	(D)	-	(D)	-	-
Utah	1	0.2	60*	-	-	(D)	-	(D)	-	-

Source: 1997 *Economic Census*. The states are in descending order of revenues or establishments (if revenue data are missing for the majority). The symbol (D) appears when data are withheld to prevent disclosure of competitive information. States marked with (D) are sorted by number of establishments. A dash (-) indicates that the data element cannot be calculated. * indicates the midpoint of a range; 175, for example is the range 100-249. Shaded *states* on the state map indicate those states which have proportionately greater representation in the industry than would be indicated by the state's population; the ratio is based on total revenues or number of establishments. Shaded *regions* indicate where the industry is regionally most concentrated.

NAICS 513220 - CABLE AND OTHER PROGRAM DISTRIBUTION

GENERAL STATISTICS

Year	Establishments (number)	Employment (number)	Payroll ($ million)	Revenues ($ million)	Employees per Establishment (number)	Revenues per Establishment ($)	Payroll per Employee ($)
1997	4,185	147,863	4,793.0	35,000.0	35.3	8,363,202	32,415

Source: Economic Census of the United States, 1997. This is a newly defined industry. Data for prior years were unavailable at the time of publication but may become available over time.

INDICES OF CHANGE

Year	Establishments (number)	Employment (number)	Payroll ($ million)	Revenues ($ million)	Employees per Establishment (number)	Revenues per Establishment ($)	Payroll per Employee ($)
1997	100.0	100.0	100.0	100.0	100.0	100.0	100.0

Sources: Same as General Statistics. The values shown reflect change from the base year, 1997. Values above 100 mean greater than 1997, values below 100 mean less than 1997, and a value of 100 in the 1982-96 or 1998-2001 period means same as 1997. Values followed by a 'p' are projections by the editors; 'e' stands for extrapolation. Data are the most recent available at this level of detail.

SIC INDUSTRIES RELATED TO NAICS 513220

Each new NAICS code represents an industry that used to be part of an SIC or a part of several SIC industries. Data in this table are shown to provide transitional information for these cases. All available data for the precursor SIC(s) are shown. Even if only a part of an SIC is included in the NAICS, *all* data for the SIC are reproduced. If the SIC industry is not marked as being a part (pt) of the NAICS, the entire industry is embedded in the NAICS data. The SIC composition of the new industry provides some hints of the relative importance of its "ancestors." Data marked with a 'p' are projected. Projections begin with 1982 data. Data earlier than 1990 are not shown but are reflected in the projections.

SIC	Industry	1990	1991	1992	1993	1994	1995	1996	1997
4841	**Cable and Other Pay TV (pt)**								
	Establishments (number)	3,478	4,157	4,468	4,475	4,545	4,750	4,786	5,111*p*
	Employment (thousands)	120.2	123.8	129.0	135.5	134.3	149.1	170.3	165.5*p*
	Revenues ($ million)	23,192.0	24,954.0	27,512.1	29,639.0	30,289.0	33,890.0	38,488.0	43,412.0

Source: Economic Census of the United States, 1992, annual surveys of economic sectors conducted by the Bureau of the Census, and estimates or projections based on the 1982-1992 period; not all data are shown. 'e' marks estimates made by the editors; 'p' indicates projections based on time series. A dash (-) indicates that data for this SIC or year were not available. The abbreviation (pt) next to the industry name indicates that only a part of the industry is present within the NAICS data. If no (pt) is shown, the entire industry is contained within the NAICS data.

SELECTED RATIOS

For 1997	Avg. of Information	Analyzed Industry	Index	For 1997	Avg. of Information	Analyzed Industry	Index
Employees per establishment	27	35	132	Payroll per establishment	1,131,090	1,145,281	101
Revenue per establishment	5,444,104	8,363,202	154	Payroll as % of revenue	21	14	66
Revenue per employee	203,255	236,706	116	Payroll per employee	42,229	32,415	77

Sources: Same as General Statistics. The 'Average' column represents the average for the industry sector, in 1997, where the currently shown industry is classified. The Index shows the relationship between the Average and the Analyzed Industry. For example, 100 means that they are equal; 500 that the Analyzed Industry is five times the average; 50 means that the Analyzed Industry is half the national average. The abbreviation 'na' is used to show that data are 'not available'.

LEADING COMPANIES   Number shown: **3**   Total sales ($ mil): **491**   Total employment (000): **0.7**

Company Name	Address				CEO Name	Phone	Co. Type	Sales ($ mil)	Empl. (000)
Lifetime Entertainment Services	309 W 49th St	New York	NY	10019	Carol Black	212-957-4610	R	400*	0.3
Helicon Corp.	630 E Palisade Ave	Englewd Clfs	NJ	07632	Theodore Baum	201-568-7720	R	90	0.4
Chequemate International Inc.	330 Washington	Marina del Rey	CA	90292	J Michael Heil	310-823-4957	P	1	<0.1

Source: *Ward's Business Directory of U.S. Private and Public Companies*, Volumes 1 and 2, 2000. The company type code used is as follows: P - Public, R - Private, S - Subsidiary, D - Division, J - Joint Venture, A - Affiliate, G - Group, N - Company type not reported. Sales are in millions of dollars, employees are in thousands. An asterisk (*) indicates an estimated sales volume. The symbol < stands for 'less than'. Company names and addresses are truncated, in some cases, to fit into the available space.

LOCATION BY STATE AND REGIONAL CONCENTRATION

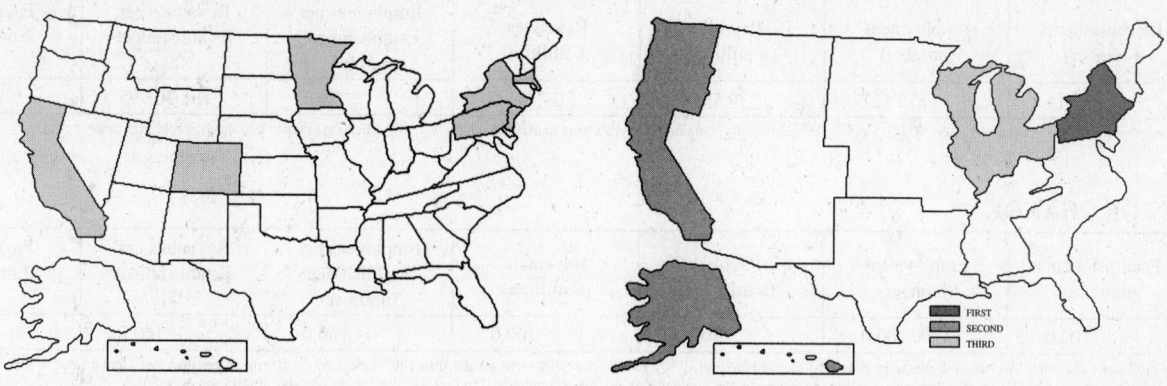

INDUSTRY DATA BY STATE

State	Establishments Total (number)	% of U.S.	Employment Total (number)	% of U.S.	Per Estab.	Payroll Total ($ mil.)	Per Empl. ($)	Revenues Total ($ mil.)	% of U.S.	Per Estab. ($)
California	326	7.8	16,161	10.9	50	619.1	38,306	4,982.7	14.2	15,284,405
New York	217	5.2	11,385	7.7	52	452.8	39,768	3,576.1	10.2	16,479,899
Pennsylvania	179	4.3	6,939	4.7	39	228.6	32,949	2,169.3	6.2	12,119,240
Texas	294	7.0	9,782	6.6	33	283.8	29,013	1,790.1	5.1	6,088,888
Florida	227	5.4	8,665	5.9	38	263.9	30,456	1,732.7	5.0	7,633,035
Ohio	151	3.6	6,294	4.3	42	193.2	30,698	1,394.7	4.0	9,236,523
Illinois	151	3.6	6,254	4.2	41	202.8	32,427	1,361.4	3.9	9,015,801
New Jersey	78	1.9	4,857	3.3	62	157.7	32,460	1,218.1	3.5	15,616,128
Colorado	116	2.8	5,721	3.9	49	177.8	31,083	1,177.8	3.4	10,153,198
Michigan	147	3.5	4,412	3.0	30	130.8	29,637	1,006.6	2.9	6,847,476
Massachusetts	77	1.8	4,840	3.3	63	163.0	33,681	972.9	2.8	12,634,584
Minnesota	83	2.0	1,882	1.3	23	61.3	32,596	818.9	2.3	9,866,301
North Carolina	127	3.0	3,138	2.1	25	98.7	31,445	720.3	2.1	5,671,843
Washington	85	2.0	2,616	1.8	31	87.0	33,270	552.4	1.6	6,498,871
Missouri	98	2.3	2,691	1.8	27	71.2	26,446	534.1	1.5	5,450,245
Indiana	86	2.1	2,387	1.6	28	64.1	26,850	481.5	1.4	5,599,000
Alabama	92	2.2	2,042	1.4	22	53.3	26,102	424.1	1.2	4,609,272
Wisconsin	82	2.0	1,560	1.1	19	43.6	27,967	347.6	1.0	4,239,512
Oregon	79	1.9	1,438	1.0	18	51.5	35,818	312.9	0.9	3,961,380
Mississippi	69	1.6	1,390	0.9	20	39.1	28,140	282.5	0.8	4,094,072
Kansas	78	1.9	1,119	0.8	14	28.1	25,098	214.0	0.6	2,744,192
Arkansas	59	1.4	848	0.6	14	21.2	24,998	170.4	0.5	2,887,373
Hawaii	18	0.4	618	0.4	34	29.5	47,715	153.3	0.4	8,518,722
New Mexico	44	1.1	786	0.5	18	22.7	28,927	153.0	0.4	3,477,886
Maine	25	0.6	602	0.4	24	17.2	28,630	120.4	0.3	4,816,960
Montana	27	0.6	431	0.3	16	12.0	27,752	78.5	0.2	2,905,778
Alaska	15	0.4	243	0.2	16	8.4	34,753	51.5	0.1	3,430,000
Georgia	139	3.3	3,750*	-	-	(D)	-	(D)	-	-
Virginia	116	2.8	3,750*	-	-	(D)	-	(D)	-	-
Kentucky	88	2.1	1,750*	-	-	(D)	-	(D)	-	-
Oklahoma	88	2.1	1,750*	-	-	(D)	-	(D)	-	-
Tennessee	86	2.1	3,750*	-	-	(D)	-	(D)	-	-
Louisiana	76	1.8	1,750*	-	-	(D)	-	(D)	-	-
Iowa	52	1.2	1,750*	-	-	(D)	-	(D)	-	-
South Carolina	51	1.2	1,750*	-	-	(D)	-	(D)	-	-
Arizona	49	1.2	1,750*	-	-	(D)	-	(D)	-	-
Maryland	48	1.1	3,750*	-	-	(D)	-	(D)	-	-
West Virginia	47	1.1	750*	-	-	(D)	-	(D)	-	-
Connecticut	42	1.0	3,750*	-	-	(D)	-	(D)	-	-
Nebraska	38	0.9	1,750*	-	-	(D)	-	(D)	-	-
Vermont	33	0.8	375*	-	-	(D)	-	(D)	-	-
South Dakota	31	0.7	750*	-	-	(D)	-	(D)	-	-
Idaho	29	0.7	750*	-	-	(D)	-	(D)	-	-
North Dakota	28	0.7	375*	-	-	(D)	-	(D)	-	-
Nevada	26	0.6	750*	-	-	(D)	-	(D)	-	-
Utah	25	0.6	750*	-	-	(D)	-	(D)	-	-
Wyoming	18	0.4	175*	-	-	(D)	-	(D)	-	-
New Hampshire	17	0.4	375*	-	-	(D)	-	(D)	-	-
D.C.	11	0.3	750*	-	-	(D)	-	(D)	-	-
Delaware	9	0.2	3,750*	-	-	(D)	-	(D)	-	-
Rhode Island	8	0.2	750*	-	-	(D)	-	(D)	-	-

Source: 1997 *Economic Census*. The states are in descending order of revenues or establishments (if revenue data are missing for the majority). The symbol (D) appears when data are withheld to prevent disclosure of competitive information. States marked with (D) are sorted by number of establishments. A dash (-) indicates that the data element cannot be calculated. * indicates the midpoint of a range; 175, for example is the range 100-249. Shaded *states* on the state map indicate those states which have proportionately greater representation in the industry than would be indicated by the state's population; the ratio is based on total revenues or number of establishments. Shaded *regions* indicate where the industry is regionally most concentrated.

NAICS 513310 - WIRED TELECOMMUNICATIONS CARRIERS

GENERAL STATISTICS

Year	Establishments (number)	Employment (number)	Payroll ($ million)	Revenues ($ million)	Employees per Establishment (number)	Revenues per Establishment ($)	Payroll per Employee ($)
1997	20,815	815,427	39,565.0	208,791.0	39.2	10,030,795	48,521

Source: *Economic Census of the United States*, 1997. This is a newly defined industry. Data for prior years were unavailable at the time of publication but may become available over time.

INDICES OF CHANGE

Year	Establishments (number)	Employment (number)	Payroll ($ million)	Revenues ($ million)	Employees per Establishment (number)	Revenues per Establishment ($)	Payroll per Employee ($)
1997	100.0	100.0	100.0	100.0	100.0	100.0	100.0

Sources: Same as General Statistics. The values shown reflect change from the base year, 1997. Values above 100 mean greater than 1997, values below 100 mean less than 1997, and a value of 100 in the 1982-96 or 1998-2001 period means same as 1997. Values followed by a 'p' are projections by the editors; 'e' stands for extrapolation. Data are the most recent available at this level of detail.

SIC INDUSTRIES RELATED TO NAICS 513310

Each new NAICS code represents an industry that used to be part of an SIC or a part of several SIC industries. Data in this table are shown to provide transitional information for these cases. All available data for the precursor SIC(s) are shown. Even if only a part of an SIC is included in the NAICS, *all* data for the SIC are reproduced. If the SIC industry is not marked as being a part (pt) of the NAICS, the entire industry is embedded in the NAICS data. The SIC composition of the new industry provides some hints of the relative importance of its "ancestors." Data marked with a 'p' are projected. Projections begin with 1982 data. Data earlier than 1990 are not shown but are reflected in the projections.

SIC	Industry	1990	1991	1992	1993	1994	1995	1996	1997
4813	**Telephone Communications, Except Radio (pt)**								
	Establishments (number)	16,576	21,198	21,667	21,520	22,273	22,258	22,062	24,560p
	Employment (thousands)	819.3	908.6	867.2	842.0	824.3	820.9	808.5	833.3p
	Revenues ($ million)	-	-	159,310.4	170,255.9e	181,201.5e	192,147.0	208,064.0	220,876.0
4822	**Telegraph and Other Communications**								
	Establishments (number)	576	512	489	526	564	470	466	304p
	Employment (thousands)	12.8	8.9	5.5	5.7	5.8	4.7	5.8	2.4p
	Revenues ($ million)	-	-	988.1	-	-	-	-	-

Source: *Economic Census of the United States*, 1992, annual surveys of economic sectors conducted by the Bureau of the Census, and estimates or projections based on the 1982-1992 period; not all data are shown. 'e' marks estimates made by the editors; 'p' indicates projections based on time series. A dash (-) indicates that data for this SIC or year were not available. The abbreviation (pt) next to the industry name indicates that only a part of the industry is present within the NAICS data. If no (pt) is shown, the entire industry is contained within the NAICS data.

SELECTED RATIOS

For 1997	Avg. of Information	Analyzed Industry	Index	For 1997	Avg. of Information	Analyzed Industry	Index
Employees per establishment	27	39	146	Payroll per establishment	1,131,090	1,900,793	168
Revenue per establishment	5,444,104	10,030,795	184	Payroll as % of revenue	21	19	91
Revenue per employee	203,255	256,051	126	Payroll per employee	42,229	48,521	115

Sources: Same as General Statistics. The 'Average' column represents the average for the industry sector, in 1997, where the currently shown industry is classified. The Index shows the relationship between the Average and the Analyzed Industry. For example, 100 means that they are equal; 500 that the Analyzed Industry is five times the average; 50 means that the Analyzed Industry is half the national average. The abbreviation 'na' is used to show that data are 'not available'.

LEADING COMPANIES Number shown: **75** Total sales ($ mil): **680,142** Total employment (000): **1,352.5**

Company Name	Address				CEO Name	Phone	Co. Type	Sales ($ mil)	Empl. (000)
GTE North Inc.	PO Box 407	Westfield	IN	46074	John G. Appel	317-896-6464	S	188,671*	17.8
AT and T Corp.	32 Av Americas	New York	NY	10013	C Michael Armstrong	212-387-5400	P	62,391	107.8
SBC Communications Inc.	175 E Houston	San Antonio	TX	78205	Royce Caldell	210-821-4105	P	49,489	129.9
MCI WorldCom Inc.	500 Clinton Center	Clinton	MS	39056	Bernard J Ebbers	601-460-8608	P	37,120	77.0
Bell Atlantic Corp.	1095 Av Americas	New York	NY	10036	james Cullen	212-395-2121	P	33,174	140.0
MCI/WORLDCOM	2 International Dr	Rye Brook	NY	10573	Bernie Ebbers	914-881-6100	P	30,000	70.0
GTE Corp.	PO Box 152257	Irving	TX	75015	Kent Foster	972-507-5000	P	25,336	12.0
BellSouth Corp.	1155 Peachtree	Atlanta	GA	30309	F Duane Ackerman	404-249-2000	P	25,224	96.2
Sprint Corp.	PO Box 11315	Kansas City	MO	64112	William T Esrey	913-624-3000	P	20,000	77.6
Ameritech Corp.	30 S Wacker Dr	Chicago	IL	60606	Richard C Notebaert	312-750-5000	P	17,154	75.0
GST Telecom Inc.	4001 Main St	Vancouver	WA	98662	Thomas M Malone	360-356-4700	S	14,393*	1.4
U S WEST Inc.	1801 California St	Denver	CO	80202	Solomon D Trujillo	303-793-6500	P	13,182	58.3
PacifiCorp	700 N E Multnomah	Portland	OR	97232	Alan Richardson	503-731-2000	S	12,989	9.1
Southwestern Bell Telephone Co.	175 E Houston St	San Antonio	TX	78205		210-821-4105	S	10,752	50.7
Pacific Bell	140 N Montgomery	San Francisco	CA	94105	Edward A Mueller	415-542-9000	S	9,406	46.4
New York Telephone Co.	1095 Av Americas	New York	NY	10036		212-395-2121	S	7,957	38.6
ALLTEL Corp.	1 Allied Dr	Little Rock	AR	72202	Joe T Ford	501-905-8000	P	6,302	21.5
Citizens Utilities Co.	PO Box 3801	Stamford	CT	06905	Rudy J Graf	203-614-5600	P	5,293	6.7
Operator Service Co.	5302 Ave #Q	Lubbock	TX	79412	Mike Smith	806-747-2474	R	4,718*	0.5
New England Telephone	125 High St	Boston	MA	02110	Ivan G Seidenberg	617-743-9800	S	4,566	18.5
Vitelco	PO Box 6100	Char Amalie	VI	00803	Samuel Ebbesen	340-776-5555	S	4,547*	0.4
Gulf Telephone Company Inc.	19812 Counter 24	Foley	AL	36536	Ken Amburn	334-952-5100	R	4,109*	0.4
Qwest Communications Intern	555 17th St	Denver	CO	80202	Joseph P Nacchio	303-992-1400	P	3,928	8.7
Illinois Bell Telephone Co.	225 W Randolph St	Chicago	IL	60606	Douglas L Whitley	312-727-9411	S	3,808	14.9
Bell Atlantic - New Jersey Inc.	540 Broad St	Newark	NJ	07101	Len J Lauer	973-649-9900	S	3,754*	12.5
Michigan Bell Telephone Co.	444 Michigan Ave	Detroit	MI	48226	Robert N Cooper	313-223-9900	S	3,385	12.2
Bell Atlantic - Pennsylvania Inc.	1717 Arch St	Philadelphia	PA	19103	Ivan Seidenberg	212-395-2121	S	3,320*	12.5
Alltel Communications Co.	PO Box 400	Cornelia	GA	30531	Jim Johnson	706-778-2201	S	3,150*	0.3
North Pittsburgh Telephone Co.	4008 Gibsonia Rd	Gibsonia	PA	15044		724-443-9600	S	3,147*	0.3
Schlumberger Omnes	5599 San Felipe	Houston	TX	77056	Xavier Slinolis	713-963-9863	P	3,135*	0.3
Farmers Telephone Cooperative	P O Box 588	Kingstree	SC	29556	John MdDaniels	843-382-2333	R	2,989*	0.3
MediaOne Group Inc.	188 Inverness West	Englewood	CO	80112	Charles M Lillis	303-858-3000	P	2,882	16.8
Matanuska Telephone Association	1740 S Chugach St	Palmer	AK	99645	Scott Smith	907-745-3211	R	2,798*	0.3
Frontier Corp.	180 S Clinton Ave	Rochester	NY	14646		716-777-1000	P	2,594	8.2
STAR Telecommunications Inc.	223 E De La Guerra	Santa Barbara	CA	93101	C E Edgecomb	805-899-1962	P	2,090*	0.2
Williams Communications	5 Greentree Ctr	Marlton	NJ	08053	Garry McGuire	856-988-5600	J	2,090*	0.2
Bell Atlantic - Virginia Inc.	600 E Main St	Richmond	VA	23219	Hugh R Stallard	804-225-6300	S	2,071*	6.5
Bell Atlantic - Maryland Inc.	1 E Pratt St	Baltimore	MD	21202	Sherry F Bellamy	410-539-9900	S	2,048*	7.0
Southern New England	310 Orange St	New Haven	CT	06510	Tom Morgan	203-771-5200	P	2,022	9.8
Ohio Bell Telephone Co.	45 Erieview Plz	Cleveland	OH	44114	Jacqueline F Woods	216-822-9700	S	1,971*	10.0
Telephone and Data Systems Inc.	30 N LaSalle St	Chicago	IL	60602	LeRoy T Carlson Jr	312-630-1900	P	1,963	9.9
Metromedia Co.	1 Meadowlands Plz	East Rutherford	NJ	07073	John W Kluge	201-531-8000	R	1,950	63.0
EXCEL Communications Inc.	8750 N Cen Expwy	Dallas	TX	75231	Kenny A Troutt	214-863-8000	P	1,881	3.8
Shenandoah Telecommunications	P O Box 459	Edinburg	VA	22824	Christopher French	703-984-4141	R	1,859*	0.2
GTE Florida Inc.	1 Tampa City Ctr	Tampa	FL	33602	Peter A Daks	813-224-4011	S	1,617	8.2
Northwestern Indiana Telephone	P O Box 67	Hebron	IN	46341	Robert Mussman	219-996-2981	R	1,581*	0.2
CenturyTel Inc	100 Century Park Dr	Monroe	LA	71203	Glen F Post III	318-388-9000	P	1,577	5.8
Coalfield Telephone Inc.	P O Box 160	Harold	KY	41635	Paul Gearheart	606-478-9401	R	1,572*	0.2
LDDS Metromedia	1111 North Loop W	Houston	TX	77008		713-850-1003	P	1,568*	0.2
Southern New England Telephone	227 Church St	New Haven	CT	06510	Daniel J Miglio	203-771-5200	P	1,508	8.2
CenturyTel Inc.	100 Century Park Dr	Monroe	LA	71203	Glen F Post III	318-388-9000	P	1,499	5.8
GTE South Inc.	P O Box 407	Westfield	IN	46074	John C Appel	972-718-5600	S	1,494	4.9
Panhandle Telephone Cooperative	P O Box 1188	Guymon	OK	73942	Ron Strecker	580-338-2556	R	1,381*	0.1
Nemont Telephone Cooperative	PO Box 600	Scobey	MT	59263		406-783-5654	R	1,291*	0.1
Arvig Enterprises Inc.	160 2nd Ave S W	Perham	MN	56573	Allen Arvig	218-346-4200	R	1,254*	0.1
Iowa Network Services Inc.	4201 Corporate Dr	W. Des Moines	IA	50266	William P Bagley	515-830-0110	R	1,158*	0.1
GTE Northwest Inc.	1800 41st St	Everett	WA	98201	Eileen O'Neill Odum	425-261-5321	P	1,143	3.6
Ameritech Indiana	240 N Meridian St	Indianapolis	IN	46204	Kent A Lebherz	317-265-2266	S	1,105*	5.8
Cameron Telephone Company Inc.	P O Box 167	Sulphur	LA	70664	George Mack	318-583-2111	S	1,080*	<0.1
ALLTEL Missouri Inc.	1705 S Lillian Ave	Bolivar	MO	65613		417-326-8000	S	1,068*	0.1
McCloud USA	3600 109th St	Urbandale	IA	50322	Clark McCloud	515-251-3320	D	1,046*	0.1
McLeodUSA Inc.	P O Box 3177	Cedar Rapids	IA	52406	Stephen C Gray	319-364-0000	P	909	5.6
ALLTEK Missouri Inc.	P O Box 180	Bolivar	MO	65613		417-326-8000	S	907*	<0.1
Intermedia Communications Inc.	3625 Queen Palm Dr	Tampa	FL	33619	David C Ruberg	813-829-0011	P	906	5.1
RSL Communications Ltd.	767 Fifth Ave	New York	NY	10153	Itzhak Fisher	212-317-1800	P	886	2.5
Broadwing	PO Box 2301	Cincinnati	OH	45201	Richard G Ellenberger	513-397-9900	P	885	20.8
Citizens Communications Inc.	3 High Ridge Park	Stamford	CT	06905	O Lee Jobe	203-614-5600	S	860*	3.5
Ace Telephone Association	PO Box 360	Houston	MN	55943		507-896-3111	R	858*	<0.1
Frontier Communications	PO Box 37	Atmore	AL	36504	Joseph Clayton	334-368-0717	S	850*	<0.1
CommuniGroup Inc.	P O Box 940	Jackson	MS	39205	Jospeh Fail	601-353-9118	S	789*	<0.1
Furst Group	459 Oakshade Rd	Shamong	NJ	08088		609-268-8000	R	787*	<0.1
NTL Inc.	110 East 59th St	New York	NY	10022	George S Blumenthal	212-906-8440	P	747	9.1
Bishop Communications	9938 State 55 N W	Annandale	MN	55302	JM Bishop	320-274-8201	R	742*	<0.1
IDT Corp.	190 Main St	Hackensack	NJ	07601	Howard S Jonas	201-928-1000	P	732	1.3
Journal Communications Inc.	PO Box 661	Milwaukee	WI	53201		414-224-2000	R	732	7.0

Source: Ward's Business Directory of U.S. Private and Public Companies, Volumes 1 and 2, 2000. The company type code used is as follows: P - Public, R - Private, S - Subsidiary, D - Division, J - Joint Venture, A - Affiliate, G - Group, N - Company type not reported. Sales are in millions of dollars, employees are in thousands. An asterisk (*) indicates an estimated sales volume. The symbol < stands for 'less than'. Company names and addresses are truncated, in some cases, to fit into the available space.

LOCATION BY STATE AND REGIONAL CONCENTRATION

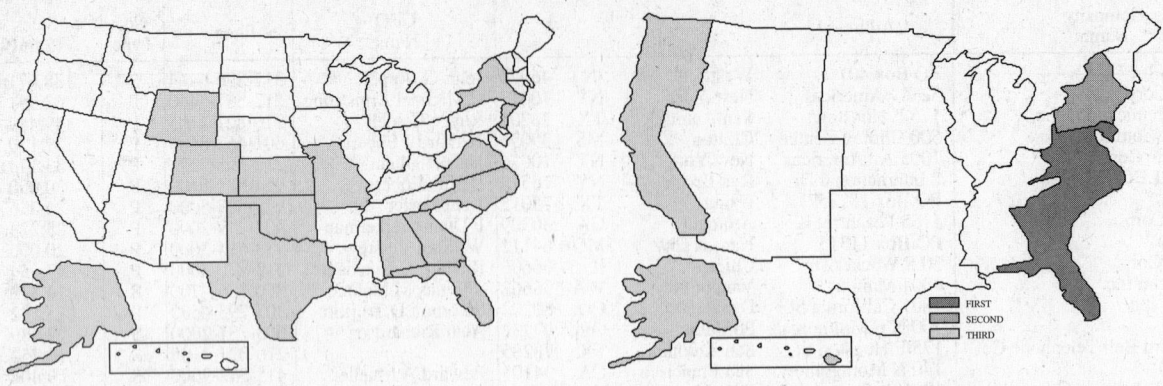

FIRST
SECOND
THIRD

INDUSTRY DATA BY STATE

State	Establishments Total (number)	% of U.S.	Employment Total (number)	% of U.S.	Per Estab.	Payroll Total ($ mil.)	Per Empl. ($)	Revenues Total ($ mil.)	% of U.S.	Per Estab. ($)
California	1,429	6.9	91,100	11.2	64	4,089.4	44,889	24,270.7	11.6	16,984,361
New York	1,223	5.9	68,664	8.4	56	3,945.4	57,459	18,170.8	8.7	14,857,590
Texas	1,588	7.6	61,566	7.6	39	2,935.7	47,684	17,328.7	8.3	10,912,304
Florida	1,076	5.2	42,925	5.3	40	1,966.7	45,817	12,202.7	5.8	11,340,777
Illinois	1,021	4.9	34,203	4.2	33	1,710.4	50,008	8,861.2	4.2	8,678,914
Virginia	550	2.6	28,847	3.5	52	1,491.9	51,716	8,325.6	4.0	15,137,396
New Jersey	674	3.2	61,174	7.5	91	3,813.6	62,341	7,695.5	3.7	11,417,607
Georgia	585	2.8	36,320	4.5	62	1,756.5	48,362	7,300.8	3.5	12,480,024
Pennsylvania	812	3.9	30,841	3.8	38	1,180.1	38,265	7,288.0	3.5	8,975,335
Ohio	770	3.7	24,109	3.0	31	1,127.8	46,778	7,224.1	3.5	9,381,896
Michigan	741	3.6	18,861	2.3	25	890.5	47,216	6,803.5	3.3	9,181,463
North Carolina	566	2.7	21,030	2.6	37	928.6	44,154	5,936.7	2.8	10,488,841
Colorado	438	2.1	26,698	3.3	61	1,430.8	53,592	5,522.1	2.6	12,607,507
Missouri	519	2.5	27,644	3.4	53	1,267.1	45,836	5,031.7	2.4	9,695,077
Massachusetts	466	2.2	19,923	2.4	43	976.3	49,005	4,449.9	2.1	9,549,155
Indiana	550	2.6	8,856	1.1	16	413.1	46,645	3,963.2	1.9	7,205,884
Washington	471	2.3	14,357	1.8	30	675.6	47,054	3,818.5	1.8	8,107,276
Kansas	353	1.7	11,872	1.5	34	641.3	54,015	3,696.5	1.8	10,471,788
Alabama	389	1.9	13,365	1.6	34	701.7	52,499	3,681.5	1.8	9,464,131
Maryland	334	1.6	15,612	1.9	47	642.4	41,147	3,519.3	1.7	10,536,958
Minnesota	459	2.2	11,660	1.4	25	521.9	44,759	2,925.3	1.4	6,373,257
Arizona	320	1.5	13,185	1.6	41	540.0	40,956	2,924.6	1.4	9,139,241
Tennessee	393	1.9	10,068	1.2	26	460.1	45,696	2,914.4	1.4	7,415,863
Wisconsin	531	2.6	9,238	1.1	17	402.4	43,559	2,883.4	1.4	5,430,183
South Carolina	294	1.4	7,472	0.9	25	341.9	45,762	2,708.4	1.3	9,212,167
Oklahoma	354	1.7	10,109	1.2	29	394.8	39,059	2,646.8	1.3	7,476,918
Oregon	295	1.4	6,797	0.8	23	318.1	46,807	2,221.1	1.1	7,529,125
Louisiana	324	1.6	8,796	1.1	27	420.5	47,808	2,046.6	1.0	6,316,571
Iowa	441	2.1	6,506	0.8	15	239.7	36,850	1,958.6	0.9	4,441,186
D.C.	84	0.4	5,105	0.6	61	327.9	64,238	1,936.6	0.9	23,054,381
Connecticut	151	0.7	12,193	1.5	81	598.8	49,113	1,856.3	0.9	12,293,152
Kentucky	275	1.3	5,825	0.7	21	249.2	42,782	1,768.8	0.8	6,431,935
Mississippi	259	1.2	4,832	0.6	19	239.9	49,650	1,414.1	0.7	5,459,676
Utah	147	0.7	6,268	0.8	43	233.4	37,238	1,352.8	0.6	9,202,599
Arkansas	221	1.1	4,714	0.6	21	206.7	43,847	1,338.2	0.6	6,055,271
Nebraska	199	1.0	5,742	0.7	29	241.3	42,019	1,310.0	0.6	6,582,693
New Mexico	151	0.7	2,720	0.3	18	112.7	41,451	966.6	0.5	6,401,503
West Virginia	194	0.9	3,968	0.5	20	139.8	35,230	943.4	0.5	4,862,789
New Hampshire	98	0.5	2,507	0.3	26	121.9	48,627	691.7	0.3	7,058,061
Idaho	118	0.6	2,052	0.3	17	95.9	46,746	651.2	0.3	5,518,881
Nevada	94	0.5	1,726	0.2	18	84.7	49,044	649.6	0.3	6,911,064
Montana	127	0.6	1,575	0.2	12	61.4	38,976	572.3	0.3	4,505,984
Maine	113	0.5	2,302	0.3	20	96.6	41,943	540.6	0.3	4,783,664
Alaska	86	0.4	1,486	0.2	17	91.0	61,260	525.2	0.3	6,107,047
North Dakota	89	0.4	1,439	0.2	16	57.8	40,152	440.0	0.2	4,943,876
South Dakota	111	0.5	1,204	0.1	11	45.6	37,853	394.4	0.2	3,553,036
Wyoming	74	0.4	690	0.1	9	31.0	44,904	337.2	0.2	4,557,405
Hawaii	82	0.4	3,750*	-	-	(D)	-	(D)	-	-
Rhode Island	65	0.3	1,750*	-	-	(D)	-	(D)	-	-
Delaware	59	0.3	1,750*	-	-	(D)	-	(D)	-	-
Vermont	52	0.2	1,750*	-	-	(D)	-	(D)	-	-

Source: 1997 *Economic Census*. The states are in descending order of revenues or establishments (if revenue data are missing for the majority). The symbol (D) appears when data are withheld to prevent disclosure of competitive information. States marked with (D) are sorted by number of establishments. A dash (-) indicates that the data element cannot be calculated. * indicates the midpoint of a range; 175, for example is the range 100-249. Shaded *states* on the state map indicate those states which have proportionately greater representation in the industry than would be indicated by the state's population; the ratio is based on total revenues or number of establishments. Shaded *regions* Tedicate where the industry is regionally most concentrated.

NAICS 513321 - PAGING

GENERAL STATISTICS

Year	Establishments (number)	Employment (number)	Payroll ($ million)	Revenues ($ million)	Employees per Establishment (number)	Revenues per Establishment ($)	Payroll per Employee ($)
1997	3,427	70,445	2,584.0	16,970.0	20.6	4,951,853	36,681

Source: Economic Census of the United States, 1997. This is a newly defined industry. Data for prior years were unavailable at the time of publication but may become available over time.

INDICES OF CHANGE

Year	Establishments (number)	Employment (number)	Payroll ($ million)	Revenues ($ million)	Employees per Establishment (number)	Revenues per Establishment ($)	Payroll per Employee ($)
1997	100.0	100.0	100.0	100.0	100.0	100.0	100.0

Sources: Same as General Statistics. The values shown reflect change from the base year, 1997. Values above 100 mean greater than 1997, values below 100 mean less than 1997, and a value of 100 in the 1982-96 or 1998-2001 period means same as 1997. Values followed by a 'p' are projections by the editors; 'e' stands for extrapolation. Data are the most recent available at this level of detail.

SIC INDUSTRIES RELATED TO NAICS 513321

Each new NAICS code represents an industry that used to be part of an SIC or a part of several SIC industries. Data in this table are shown to provide transitional information for these cases. All available data for the precursor SIC(s) are shown. Even if only a part of an SIC is included in the NAICS, *all* data for the SIC are reproduced. If the SIC industry is not marked as being a part (pt) of the NAICS, the entire industry is embedded in the NAICS data. The SIC composition of the new industry provides some hints of the relative importance of its "ancestors." Data marked with a 'p' are projected. Projections begin with 1982 data. Data earlier than 1990 are not shown but are reflected in the projections.

SIC	Industry	1990	1991	1992	1993	1994	1995	1996	1997
4812	**Radiotelephone Communications (pt)**								
	Establishments (number)	1,583	2,464	3,063	3,462	3,810	4,344	5,191	5,478p
	Employment (thousands)	37.1	49.0	61.1	70.4	83.7	91.4	119.3	119.8p
	Revenues ($ million)	-	-	12,269.7	16,229.5e	20,189.2e	24,149.0	29,999.0	35,240.0

Source: Economic Census of the United States, 1992, annual surveys of economic sectors conducted by the Bureau of the Census, and estimates or projections based on the 1982-1992 period; not all data are shown. 'e' marks estimates made by the editors; 'p' indicates projections based on time series. A dash (-) indicates that data for this SIC or year were not available. The abbreviation (pt) next to the industry name indicates that only a part of the industry is present within the NAICS data. If no (pt) is shown, the entire industry is contained within the NAICS data.

SELECTED RATIOS

For 1997	Avg. of Information	Analyzed Industry	Index	For 1997	Avg. of Information	Analyzed Industry	Index
Employees per establishment	27	21	77	Payroll per establishment	1,131,090	754,012	67
Revenue per establishment	5,444,104	4,951,853	91	Payroll as % of revenue	21	15	73
Revenue per employee	203,255	240,897	119	Payroll per employee	42,229	36,681	87

Sources: Same as General Statistics. The 'Average' column represents the average for the industry sector, in 1997, where the currently shown industry is classified. The Index shows the relationship between the Average and the Analyzed Industry. For example, 100 means that they are equal; 500 that the Analyzed Industry is five times the average; 50 means that the Analyzed Industry is half the national average. The abbreviation 'na' is used to show that data are 'not available'.

LEADING COMPANIES   Number shown: **75**   Total sales ($ mil): **199,003**   Total employment (000): **629.6**

Company Name	Address				CEO Name	Phone	Co. Type	Sales ($ mil)	Empl. (000)
SBC Communications Inc.	175 E Houston	San Antonio	TX	78205	Royce Caldell	210-821-4105	P	49,489	129.9
Bell Atlantic Corp.	1095 Av Americas	New York	NY	10036	james Cullen	212-395-2121	P	33,174	140.0
GTE Corp.	PO Box 152257	Irving	TX	75015	Kent Foster	972-507-5000	P	25,336	12.0
Ameritech Corp.	30 S Wacker Dr	Chicago	IL	60606	Richard C Notebaert	312-750-5000	P	17,154	75.0
U S WEST Inc.	1801 California St	Denver	CO	80202	Solomon D Trujillo	303-793-6500	P	13,182	58.3
At and T Wireless	PO Box 6028	Artesia	CA	90702	Dan Hesse	562-924-0000	J	6,760*	13.0
ALLTEL Corp.	1 Allied Dr	Little Rock	AR	72202	Joe T Ford	501-905-8000	P	6,302	21.5
AirTouch Communications Inc.	One California St	San Francisco	CA	94111	Sam Ginn	415-658-2000	P	5,181	13.0
Comcast Corp.	1500 Market St	Philadelphia	PA	19102	Brian L Roberts	215-665-1700	P	5,146	17.4
QUALCOMM Inc.	3775 Morehouse Dr	San Diego	CA	92121	Irwin Jacobs	858-587-1121	P	3,937	9.7
Matanuska Telephone Association	1740 S Chugach St	Palmer	AK	99645	Scott Smith	907-745-3211	R	2,798*	0.3
Frontier Corp.	180 S Clinton Ave	Rochester	NY	14646		716-777-1000	P	2,594	8.2
Southern New England	310 Orange St	New Haven	CT	06510	Tom Morgan	203-771-5200	P	2,022	9.8
Telephone and Data Systems Inc.	30 N LaSalle St	Chicago	IL	60602	LeRoy T Carlson Jr	312-630-1900	P	1,963	9.9
Nextel Communications Inc.	2001 Edmund Halley	Reston	VA	20191	Daniel Akerson	703-433-4000	P	1,847	9.7
Loral Space & Communications	600 3rd Ave	New York	NY	10016	Gregory J Clark	212-697-1105	P	1,458	3.9
AirTouch Cellular	P O Box 19707	Irvine	CA	92614	Arun Sarin	949-223-1500	D	1,425*	3.5
Contel Cellular Inc.	245 Perimeter Center	Atlanta	GA	30346	Mark Fiethner	770-804-3400	S	1,415*	6.0
Nemont Telephone Cooperative	PO Box 600	Scobey	MT	59263		406-783-5654	R	1,291*	0.1
Southwestern Bell Mobile	17330 Preston Rd	Dallas	TX	75252	Stan Sigman	972-733-2000	S	1,200*	3.0
United States Cellular Corp.	8410 W Bryn Mawr	Chicago	IL	60631	LeRoy T Carlson Jr	773-399-8900	P	1,163	4.8
Ameritech Indiana	240 N Meridian St	Indianapolis	IN	46204	Kent A Lebherz	317-265-2266	S	1,105*	5.8
DukeNet Communications Inc.	P O Box 1244	Charlotte	NC	28201	Marian H Smith	704-382-7111	S	881*	<0.1
Paging Network Inc.	14911 Quorum Dr	Dallas	TX	75240	Jack Frazee	972-801-8000	P	880*	6.0
Citizens Communications Inc.	3 High Ridge Park	Stamford	CT	06905	O Lee Jobe	203-614-5600	S	860*	3.5
Pacific Telecom Inc.	P O Box 9901	Vancouver	WA	98668	Charles E Robinson	360-905-5800	S	620*	2.1
COMSAT Corp.	6560 Rock Spring	Bethesda	MD	20817	Betty C Alewine	301-214-3200	P	617	2.7
Western Wireless Corp.	3650 131st Ave	Bellevue	WA	98006	John W Stanton	425-586-8700	P	585	4.0
Cellone	651 Gateway Blvd	S. San Francisco	CA	94080	Mike Donnell	650-871-9500	R	550*	1.0
Century Communications Corp.	50 Locust Ave	New Canaan	CT	06840	Bernard P Gallagher	203-972-2000	P	520	2.9
SkyTel Communications Inc.	200 S Lamar St	Jackson	MS	39201	John N Palmer	601-944-1300	S	518	3.6
Metrocall Inc.	6677 Richmond	Alexandria	VA	22306	William L Collins III	703-660-6677	P	465	3.8
SkyTel Corp.	200 S Lamar St	Jackson	MS	39201	John T Stupka	601-944-1300	P	408*	3.0
Arch Communications Group Inc.	1800 W Park Dr	Westborough	MA	01581	C Edward Baker Jr	508-870-6700	P	384	2.6
ICG Communications Inc.	161 Inverness Dr W	Englewood	CO	80112	Bill Beans	303-414-5000	P	350*	3.0
Aliant Communications Inc.	PO Box 81309	Lincoln	NE	68501	Frank H Hilsabeck	402-436-3737	P	338	1.7
PageMart Wireless Inc.	546 Milton STE 100	Dallas	TX	75206	John D Beletic	214-765-4000	P	325	2.4
GTE Wireless Inc.	100 Glenborough Dr	Houston	TX	77067	Charles R Lee	281-876-5000	S	298*	1.7
Comcast Cellular	480 E Swedesford	Wayne	PA	19087	David Watson	610-975-5000	S	287*	1.6
Mobile Communications	1800 E County Line	Ridgeland	MS	39157	Stephen E Pazian	601-977-0888	S	269*	3.5
Cellular One of Chicago	930 National Pkwy	Schaumburg	IL	60173	Robert Nelson	847-762-2000	S	263*	1.3
Metromedia Intern. Group Inc.	1 Meadowlands	East Rutherford	NJ	07073	John W Kluge	201-531-8000	P	240	1.0
Centennial Cellular Corp.	50 Locust Ave	New Canaan	CT	06840	Bernard P Gallagher	203-972-2000	P	236	1.5
ICG Holdings Inc.	161 Inverness	Englewood	CO	80112	J Shelby Bryan	303-572-5960	S	217*	1.7
CommNet Cellular Inc.	8350 E Crescent	Englewood	CO	80111	Daniel P Dwyer	303-694-3234	P	211	0.6
Price Communications Corp.	45 Rockefeller Plz	New York	NY	10020	Robert Price	212-757-5600	P	197	0.6
Powertel Inc.	1233 O G Skinner	West Point	GA	31833	Allen E Smith	706-645-2000	P	175	1.8
Omnipoint Corp.	3 Bethesda Metro	Bethesda	MD	20814	Douglas Smith	301-951-2500	P	173	1.9
Aerial Communications Inc.	8410 W Bryn Mawr	Chicago	IL	60631	Donald W Warkentin	773-399-4200	P	155	1.9
BellSouth Mobility Inc.	1100 Peachtree St	Atlanta	GA	30309	Mark C Feidler	404-249-5000	S	150*	1.2
AirTouch Paging	12221 Merit Dr	Dallas	TX	75251	Gary Cuccio	972-860-3200	S	140*	0.7
Working Assets Funding Service	101 Market St #700	San Francisco	CA	94105	Laura Scher	415-788-0777	R	117	<0.1
GTE Airfone Inc.	2809 Butterfield Rd	Oak Brook	IL	60522	Kathy Harless	630-572-1800	S	115*	0.3
InfoNXX	3864 Courtney St	Bethlehem	PA	18017	Robert A Pines	610-997-1000	R	105*	0.6
Comverse Network Systems Div.	100 Quannapowitt	Wakefield	MA	01880	Francis E Girard	781-246-9000	S	105*	2.0
Rural Cellular Corp.	P O Box 1027	Alexandria	MN	56308	Richard Ekstrand	320-762-2000	P	98	0.5
Cox Cable of San Diego Inc.	5159 Federal Blvd	San Diego	CA	92105	Scott Hatfield	404-843-5000	S	98*	0.6
Ameritech MBL Communications	500 N Kingshighway	Cape Girardeau	MO	63701	Linda Wokoun	573-334-4444	S	97*	0.3
Cellular One Inc.	100 Lawder Brook	Westwood	MA	02090	Paul Roth	617-462-4000	S	96	0.7
American Mobile Satellite Corp.	10802 Parkridge	Reston	VA	20191	Gary M Parsons	703-758-6000	P	91	0.2
Midwest Wireless	P O Box 4069	Mankato	MN	56002	Dennis Miller	507-345-2440	R	78*	0.2
BellSouth Wireless Data L.P.	10 Woodbridge Ctr	Woodbridge	NJ	07095	William Lenahan	732-602-5500	S	74*	0.4
National Dispatch Center Inc.	8911 Balboa Ave	San Diego	CA	92123	John B MacLeod	619-654-9000	R	70*	0.4
Geotek Communications Inc.	102 Chestnut Ridge	Montvale	NJ	07645	Anne Eilse	201-930-9305	P	65	0.7
HighwayMaster Communications	1155 Kas Dr	Richardson	TX	75081	Jana A Bell	972-301-2000	P	63	0.2
Conestoga Enterprises Inc.	202 E 1st St	Birdsboro	PA	19508	Albert H Kramer	610-582-8711	P	63	0.1
Nebraska Cellular Telephone Corp	P O Box 5075	Grand Island	NE	68803		402-720-9000	D	57*	0.2
Teletouch Communications Inc.	110 N College	Tyler	TX	75702	J Richard Carlson	903-595-8800	P	51	0.4
Cincinnati Bell Long Distance Inc.	36 E 7th St	Cincinnati	OH	45202	Barry L Nelson	513-369-2100	S	50	0.2
Honolulu Cellular	500 Kahelu Ave	Mililani	HI	96789		808-623-2355	R	50	0.3
CenturyTel Telecommunications	P O Box 846	San Marcos	TX	78667		512-754-1414	S	49*	0.3
Positive Communications Inc.	P O Box 9003	Pleasanton	CA	94588	Rick Martin	925-416-2300	R	48	0.3
Preferred Networks Inc.	850 Center Way	Norcross	GA	30071	Mark H Dunaway	770-582-3500	P	39	0.3
ARCH Communications	5901 S W Macadan	Portland	OR	97201		503-228-2255	R	38*	0.1
Associated Group Inc.	200 Gateway Towers	Pittsburgh	PA	15222	Miles Berkman	412-281-1907	P	33	2.2

Source: Ward's Business Directory of U.S. Private and Public Companies, Volumes 1 and 2, 2000. The company type code used is as follows: P - Public, R - Private, S - Subsidiary, D - Division, J - Joint Venture, A - Affiliate, G - Group, N - Company type not reported. Sales are in millions of dollars, employees are in thousands. An asterisk (*) indicates an estimated sales volume. The symbol < stands for 'less than'. Company names and addresses are truncated, in some cases, to fit into the available space.

LOCATION BY STATE AND REGIONAL CONCENTRATION

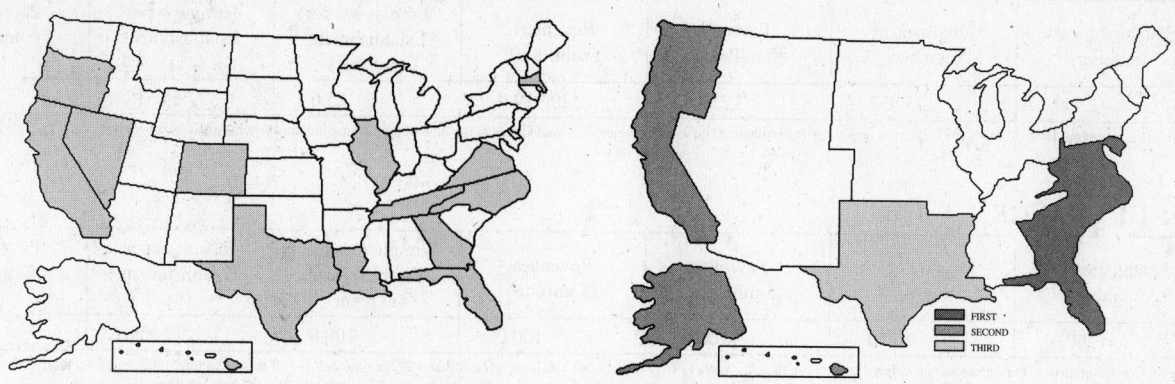

FIRST
SECOND
THIRD

INDUSTRY DATA BY STATE

State	Establishments Total (number)	Establishments % of U.S.	Employment Total (number)	Employment % of U.S.	Employment Per Estab.	Payroll Total ($ mil.)	Payroll Per Empl. ($)	Revenues Total ($ mil.)	Revenues % of U.S.	Revenues Per Estab. ($)
California	428	12.5	11,530	16.4	27	441.8	38,321	2,427.5	14.3	5,671,787
Texas	284	8.3	10,264	14.6	36	367.3	35,788	1,894.5	11.2	6,670,673
Georgia	181	5.3	4,292	6.1	24	200.4	46,684	1,823.7	10.7	10,075,751
Florida	276	8.1	4,935	7.0	18	174.4	35,342	1,213.4	7.2	4,396,460
New York	241	7.0	4,750	6.7	20	171.1	36,016	1,113.3	6.6	4,619,444
Illinois	132	3.9	2,575	3.7	20	97.8	37,966	821.1	4.8	6,220,485
Massachusetts	88	2.6	3,625	5.1	41	162.6	44,864	738.6	4.4	8,392,795
Tennessee	90	2.6	1,916	2.7	21	69.7	36,390	609.4	3.6	6,770,633
North Carolina	88	2.6	1,940	2.8	22	65.9	33,947	501.1	3.0	5,693,852
Louisiana	72	2.1	1,022	1.5	14	41.9	40,994	479.5	2.8	6,659,625
Pennsylvania	148	4.3	1,886	2.7	13	65.2	34,547	450.9	2.7	3,046,703
Ohio	125	3.6	1,932	2.7	15	62.4	32,307	448.3	2.6	3,586,552
Virginia	89	2.6	2,255	3.2	25	90.3	40,036	439.9	2.6	4,943,258
Indiana	65	1.9	1,344	1.9	21	39.6	29,489	369.6	2.2	5,685,831
Minnesota	49	1.4	1,811	2.6	37	55.6	30,685	272.7	1.6	5,565,980
Colorado	59	1.7	773	1.1	13	26.5	34,320	264.6	1.6	4,484,051
Alabama	54	1.6	855	1.2	16	24.1	28,130	255.7	1.5	4,734,574
Wisconsin	41	1.2	759	1.1	19	28.1	36,978	253.8	1.5	6,189,146
Oregon	33	1.0	547	0.8	17	21.7	39,665	229.0	1.3	6,939,364
Nevada	33	1.0	458	0.7	14	22.2	48,535	208.5	1.2	6,318,242
New Jersey	84	2.5	1,731	2.5	21	52.6	30,363	194.2	1.1	2,312,429
Kentucky	57	1.7	717	1.0	13	25.9	36,160	180.9	1.1	3,173,544
Mississippi	36	1.1	535	0.8	15	18.5	34,563	152.1	0.9	4,226,000
Michigan	74	2.2	770	1.1	10	23.1	29,962	120.5	0.7	1,628,405
Maryland	51	1.5	918	1.3	18	28.6	31,105	111.4	0.7	2,185,137
Oklahoma	39	1.1	454	0.6	12	17.1	37,661	106.7	0.6	2,736,179
Arizona	49	1.4	625	0.9	13	16.8	26,950	94.6	0.6	1,931,551
Hawaii	24	0.7	322	0.5	13	12.4	38,522	83.4	0.5	3,475,583
Washington	37	1.1	430	0.6	12	12.4	28,923	71.4	0.4	1,929,595
West Virginia	26	0.8	311	0.4	12	8.5	27,299	66.5	0.4	2,556,346
Maine	17	0.5	185	0.3	11	8.4	45,557	56.8	0.3	3,339,118
Missouri	56	1.6	501	0.7	9	13.0	25,994	56.1	0.3	1,002,429
Utah	15	0.4	177	0.3	12	5.7	32,000	32.1	0.2	2,137,467
Idaho	8	0.2	156	0.2	20	5.1	32,622	8.6	0.1	1,076,250
Montana	5	0.1	17	0.0	3	0.3	16,882	0.7	0.0	144,200
Kansas	40	1.2	750*	-	-	(D)	-	(D)	-	-
South Carolina	40	1.2	750*	-	-	(D)	-	(D)	-	-
New Mexico	37	1.1	175*	-	-	(D)	-	(D)	-	-
South Dakota	27	0.8	60*	-	-	(D)	-	(D)	-	-
Iowa	22	0.6	375*	-	-	(D)	-	(D)	-	-
Arkansas	20	0.6	175*	-	-	(D)	-	(D)	-	-
Connecticut	19	0.6	375*	-	-	(D)	-	(D)	-	-
New Hampshire	16	0.5	175*	-	-	(D)	-	(D)	-	-
Nebraska	13	0.4	175*	-	-	(D)	-	(D)	-	-
Vermont	11	0.3	175*	-	-	(D)	-	(D)	-	-
Rhode Island	7	0.2	60*	-	-	(D)	-	(D)	-	-
D.C.	6	0.2	175*	-	-	(D)	-	(D)	-	-
Alaska	5	0.1	60*	-	-	(D)	-	(D)	-	-
Delaware	4	0.1	60*	-	-	(D)	-	(D)	-	-
North Dakota	4	0.1	10*	-	-	(D)	-	(D)	-	-
Wyoming	2	0.1	10*	-	-	(D)	-	(D)	-	-

Source: 1997 *Economic Census*. The states are in descending order of revenues or establishments (if revenue data are missing for the majority). The symbol (D) appears when data are withheld to prevent disclosure of competitive information. States marked with (D) are sorted by number of establishments. A dash (-) indicates that the data element cannot be calculated. * indicates the midpoint of a range; 175, for example is the range 100-249. Shaded *states* on the state map indicate those states which have proportionately greater representation in the industry than would be indicated by the state's population; the ratio is based on total revenues or number of establishments. Shaded *regions* indicate where the industry is regionally most concentrated.

NAICS 513322 - CELLULAR AND OTHER WIRELESS TELECOMMUNICATIONS

GENERAL STATISTICS

Year	Establishments (number)	Employment (number)	Payroll ($ million)	Revenues ($ million)	Employees per Establishment (number)	Revenues per Establishment ($)	Payroll per Employee ($)
1997	2,959	75,857	3,256.0	20,919.0	25.6	7,069,618	42,923

Source: *Economic Census of the United States*, 1997. This is a newly defined industry. Data for prior years were unavailable at the time of publication but may become available over time.

INDICES OF CHANGE

Year	Establishments (number)	Employment (number)	Payroll ($ million)	Revenues ($ million)	Employees per Establishment (number)	Revenues per Establishment ($)	Payroll per Employee ($)
1997	100.0	100.0	100.0	100.0	100.0	100.0	100.0

Sources: Same as General Statistics. The values shown reflect change from the base year, 1997. Values above 100 mean greater than 1997, values below 100 mean less than 1997, and a value of 100 in the 1982-96 or 1998-2001 period means same as 1997. Values followed by a 'p' are projections by the editors; 'e' stands for extrapolation. Data are the most recent available at this level of detail.

SIC INDUSTRIES RELATED TO NAICS 513322

Each new NAICS code represents an industry that used to be part of an SIC or a part of several SIC industries. Data in this table are shown to provide transitional information for these cases. All available data for the precursor SIC(s) are shown. Even if only a part of an SIC is included in the NAICS, *all* data for the SIC are reproduced. If the SIC industry is not marked as being a part (pt) of the NAICS, the entire industry is embedded in the NAICS data. The SIC composition of the new industry provides some hints of the relative importance of its "ancestors." Data marked with a 'p' are projected. Projections begin with 1982 data. Data earlier than 1990 are not shown but are reflected in the projections.

SIC	Industry	1990	1991	1992	1993	1994	1995	1996	1997
4812	**Radiotelephone Communications (pt)**								
	Establishments (number)	1,583	2,464	3,063	3,462	3,810	4,344	5,191	5,478p
	Employment (thousands)	37.1	49.0	61.1	70.4	83.7	91.4	119.3	119.8p
	Revenues ($ million)	-	-	12,269.7	16,229.5e	20,189.2e	24,149.0	29,999.0	35,240.0
4899	**Communications Services, nec (pt)**								
	Establishments (number)	1,201	1,320	1,008	1,105	1,034	1,305	1,488	468p
	Employment (thousands)	34.6	25.0	9.7	15.3	13.1	20.0	22.4	-
	Revenues ($ million)	-	-	2,357.9	-	-	-	-	-

Source: *Economic Census of the United States*, 1992, annual surveys of economic sectors conducted by the Bureau of the Census, and estimates or projections based on the 1982-1992 period; not all data are shown. 'e' marks estimates made by the editors; 'p' indicates projections based on time series. A dash (-) indicates that data for this SIC or year were not available. The abbreviation (pt) next to the industry name indicates that only a part of the industry is present within the NAICS data. If no (pt) is shown, the entire industry is contained within the NAICS data.

SELECTED RATIOS

For 1997	Avg. of Information	Analyzed Industry	Index	For 1997	Avg. of Information	Analyzed Industry	Index
Employees per establishment	27	26	96	Payroll per establishment	1,131,090	1,100,372	97
Revenue per establishment	5,444,104	7,069,618	130	Payroll as % of revenue	21	16	75
Revenue per employee	203,255	275,769	136	Payroll per employee	42,229	42,923	102

Sources: Same as General Statistics. The 'Average' column represents the average for the industry sector, in 1997, where the currently shown industry is classified. The Index shows the relationship between the Average and the Analyzed Industry. For example, 100 means that they are equal; 500 that the Analyzed Industry is five times the average; 50 means that the Analyzed Industry is half the national average. The abbreviation 'na' is used to show that data are 'not available'.

LEADING COMPANIES   Number shown: **10**   Total sales ($ mil): **1,236**   Total employment (000): **5.3**

Company Name	Address				CEO Name	Phone	Co. Type	Sales ($ mil)	Empl. (000)
COMSAT Corp.	6560 Rock Spring	Bethesda	MD	20817	Betty C. Alewine	301-214-3200	P	617	2.7
PBS Enterprises Inc.	1320 Braddock Pl	Alexandria	VA	22314	Jacqueline Weiss	703-739-5400	R	352*	0.5
PhoneTel Technologies Inc.	1001 Lakeside	Cleveland	OH	44114	John D Chichester	216-241-2555	P	91	0.4
ERIM International Inc.	PO Box 134001	Ann Arbor	MI	48113	Dr Peter Banks	734-994-1200	S	70	0.6
Intek Global Corp.	99 Park Ave	New York	NY	10016	Robert J Shiver	212-949-4490	P	36	0.4
Titan Linkabit	3033 Science	San Diego	CA	92121	Frederick L Judge	858-552-9500	D	33*	0.2
Teletrac Inc.	7391 Lincoln Way	Garden Grove	CA	92841	John F Santo	714-897-0877	D	25*	0.4
National Wireless Holdings Inc.	249 Royal Palm	Palm Beach	FL	33480	Terrence S Cassidy	561-822-9933	P	5	<0.1
PHONEWORKS Inc.	146 2nd St N	St. Petersburg	FL	33701	Brad Wendkos	727-823-7144	R	5*	<0.1
PATHCOR Design Consultants	8390 E Via Ventu	Scottsdale	AZ	85258	Sidney Swanson	602-905-9100	R	2	<0.1

Source: *Ward's Business Directory of U.S. Private and Public Companies*, Volumes 1 and 2, 2000. The company type code used is as follows: P - Public, R - Private, S - Subsidiary, D - Division, J - Joint Venture, A - Affiliate, G - Group, N - Company type not reported. Sales are in millions of dollars, employees are in thousands. An asterisk (*) indicates an estimated sales volume. The symbol < stands for 'less than'. Company names and addresses are truncated, in some cases, to fit into the available space.

LOCATION BY STATE AND REGIONAL CONCENTRATION

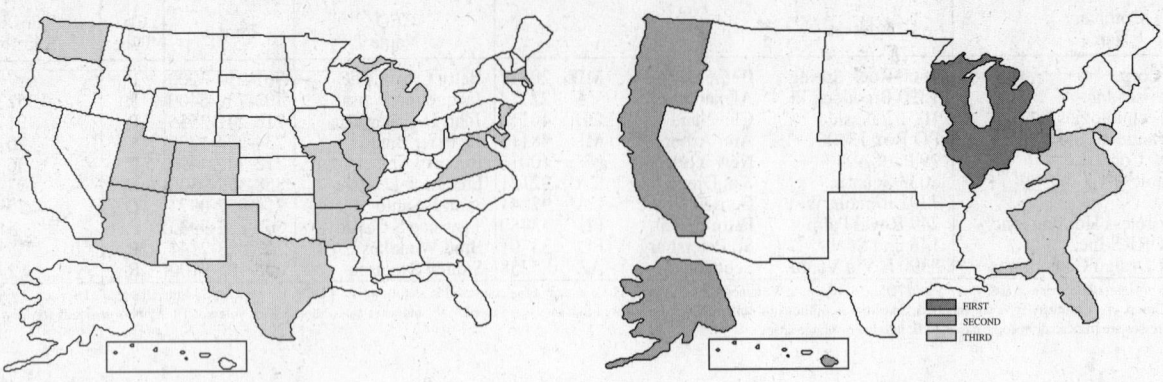

FIRST
SECOND
THIRD

INDUSTRY DATA BY STATE

State	Establishments Total (number)	Establishments % of U.S.	Employment Total (number)	Employment % of U.S.	Employment Per Estab.	Payroll Total ($ mil.)	Payroll Per Empl. ($)	Revenues Total ($ mil.)	Revenues % of U.S.	Revenues Per Estab. ($)
California	210	7.1	7,485	9.9	36	358.2	47,860	2,064.0	9.9	9,828,576
Texas	233	7.9	6,935	9.1	30	280.1	40,383	1,891.0	9.0	8,116,013
New Jersey	94	3.2	4,760	6.3	51	233.3	49,006	1,728.0	8.3	18,382,628
Illinois	195	6.6	4,869	6.4	25	193.5	39,736	1,455.1	7.0	7,461,974
Michigan	107	3.6	2,820	3.7	26	114.4	40,574	1,122.8	5.4	10,493,374
Washington	100	3.4	7,024	9.3	70	470.2	66,945	1,104.5	5.3	11,045,150
Florida	142	4.8	3,822	5.0	27	159.8	41,799	1,082.0	5.2	7,619,859
Ohio	154	5.2	2,939	3.9	19	138.2	47,038	830.9	4.0	5,395,227
Pennsylvania	100	3.4	2,947	3.9	29	106.7	36,210	830.1	4.0	8,301,210
Maryland	85	2.9	2,349	3.1	28	117.6	50,043	706.6	3.4	8,313,294
New York	151	5.1	1,916	2.5	13	72.7	37,948	647.4	3.1	4,287,139
Virginia	63	2.1	1,727	2.3	27	125.8	72,826	630.6	3.0	10,009,032
Missouri	81	2.7	1,672	2.2	21	54.8	32,783	624.1	3.0	7,704,951
Massachusetts	63	2.1	2,493	3.3	40	98.9	39,661	599.3	2.9	9,513,444
Georgia	75	2.5	4,123	5.4	55	148.0	35,901	538.6	2.6	7,180,773
Arizona	62	2.1	1,573	2.1	25	46.7	29,709	471.6	2.3	7,606,726
North Carolina	71	2.4	1,325	1.7	19	43.8	33,063	408.2	2.0	5,748,831
Minnesota	44	1.5	2,328	3.1	53	47.4	20,358	348.2	1.7	7,913,614
Colorado	79	2.7	1,064	1.4	13	52.4	49,212	324.9	1.6	4,113,076
Arkansas	36	1.2	1,353	1.8	38	46.1	34,106	307.2	1.5	8,533,278
Oklahoma	42	1.4	913	1.2	22	30.6	33,473	259.3	1.2	6,173,952
Oregon	44	1.5	923	1.2	21	27.9	30,213	226.7	1.1	5,151,659
Utah	40	1.4	326	0.4	8	17.2	52,761	207.9	1.0	5,197,875
Wisconsin	39	1.3	711	0.9	18	23.9	33,582	204.5	1.0	5,244,744
Iowa	60	2.0	433	0.6	7	13.2	30,540	198.6	0.9	3,310,633
Louisiana	40	1.4	808	1.1	20	22.6	27,916	191.1	0.9	4,778,025
Indiana	58	2.0	860	1.1	15	25.5	29,600	140.2	0.7	2,416,879
Idaho	31	1.0	116	0.2	4	4.3	37,474	89.2	0.4	2,876,065
Mississippi	31	1.0	513	0.7	17	13.8	26,986	88.2	0.4	2,846,548
Tennessee	28	0.9	309	0.4	11	10.3	33,298	80.7	0.4	2,882,857
Alabama	32	1.1	315	0.4	10	11.8	37,530	80.5	0.4	2,514,875
Maine	15	0.5	202	0.3	13	7.4	36,698	59.3	0.3	3,954,133
Nevada	11	0.4	93	0.1	8	3.6	38,462	4.9	0.0	443,455
Connecticut	45	1.5	750*	-	-	(D)	-	(D)	-	-
Kansas	42	1.4	375*	-	-	(D)	-	(D)	-	-
Montana	32	1.1	175*	-	-	(D)	-	(D)	-	-
South Carolina	29	1.0	375*	-	-	(D)	-	(D)	-	-
Kentucky	23	0.8	375*	-	-	(D)	-	(D)	-	-
North Dakota	23	0.8	60*	-	-	(D)	-	(D)	-	-
Wyoming	22	0.7	60*	-	-	(D)	-	(D)	-	-
New Mexico	20	0.7	175*	-	-	(D)	-	(D)	-	-
Nebraska	18	0.6	175*	-	-	(D)	-	(D)	-	-
New Hampshire	18	0.6	175*	-	-	(D)	-	(D)	-	-
Alaska	15	0.5	175*	-	-	(D)	-	(D)	-	-
Hawaii	14	0.5	175*	-	-	(D)	-	(D)	-	-
Delaware	9	0.3	60*	-	-	(D)	-	(D)	-	-
Rhode Island	9	0.3	60*	-	-	(D)	-	(D)	-	-
D.C.	8	0.3	175*	-	-	(D)	-	(D)	-	-
West Virginia	8	0.3	175*	-	-	(D)	-	(D)	-	-
South Dakota	6	0.2	60*	-	-	(D)	-	(D)	-	-
Vermont	2	0.1	10*	-	-	(D)	-	(D)	-	-

Source: 1997 *Economic Census*. The states are in descending order of revenues or establishments (if revenue data are missing for the majority). The symbol (D) appears when data are withheld to prevent disclosure of competitive information. States marked with (D) are sorted by number of establishments. A dash (-) indicates that the data element cannot be calculated. * indicates the midpoint of a range; 175, for example is the range 100-249. Shaded *states* on the state map indicate those states which have proportionately greater representation in the industry than would be indicated by the state's population; the ratio is based on total revenues or number of establishments. Shaded *regions* indicate where the industry is regionally most concentrated.

NAICS 513330 - TELECOMMUNICATIONS RESELLERS

GENERAL STATISTICS

Year	Establishments (number)	Employment (number)	Payroll ($ million)	Revenues ($ million)	Employees per Establishment (number)	Revenues per Establishment ($)	Payroll per Employee ($)
1997	1,656	30,028	1,185.0	7,592.0	18.1	4,584,541	39,463

Source: Economic Census of the United States, 1997. This is a newly defined industry. Data for prior years were unavailable at the time of publication but may become available over time.

INDICES OF CHANGE

Year	Establishments (number)	Employment (number)	Payroll ($ million)	Revenues ($ million)	Employees per Establishment (number)	Revenues per Establishment ($)	Payroll per Employee ($)
1997	100.0	100.0	100.0	100.0	100.0	100.0	100.0

Sources: Same as General Statistics. The values shown reflect change from the base year, 1997. Values above 100 mean greater than 1997, values below 100 mean less than 1997, and a value of 100 in the 1982-96 or 1998-2001 period means same as 1997. Values followed by a 'p' are projections by the editors; 'e' stands for extrapolation. Data are the most recent available at this level of detail.

SIC INDUSTRIES RELATED TO NAICS 513330

Each new NAICS code represents an industry that used to be part of an SIC or a part of several SIC industries. Data in this table are shown to provide transitional information for these cases. All available data for the precursor SIC(s) are shown. Even if only a part of an SIC is included in the NAICS, *all* data for the SIC are reproduced. If the SIC industry is not marked as being a part (pt) of the NAICS, the entire industry is embedded in the NAICS data. The SIC composition of the new industry provides some hints of the relative importance of its "ancestors." Data marked with a 'p' are projected. Projections begin with 1982 data. Data earlier than 1990 are not shown but are reflected in the projections.

SIC	Industry	1990	1991	1992	1993	1994	1995	1996	1997
4812	**Radiotelephone Communications (pt)**								
	Establishments (number)	1,583	2,464	3,063	3,462	3,810	4,344	5,191	5,478p
	Employment (thousands)	37.1	49.0	61.1	70.4	83.7	91.4	119.3	119.8p
	Revenues ($ million)	-	-	12,269.7	16,229.5e	20,189.2e	24,149.0	29,999.0	35,240.0
4813	**Telephone Communications, Except Radio (pt)**								
	Establishments (number)	16,576	21,198	21,667	21,520	22,273	22,258	22,062	24,560p
	Employment (thousands)	819.3	908.6	867.2	842.0	824.3	820.9	808.5	833.3p
	Revenues ($ million)	-	-	159,310.4	170,255.9e	181,201.5e	192,147.0	208,064.0	220,876.0

Source: Economic Census of the United States, 1992, annual surveys of economic sectors conducted by the Bureau of the Census, and estimates or projections based on the 1982-1992 period; not all data are shown. 'e' marks estimates made by the editors; 'p' indicates projections based on time series. A dash (-) indicates that data for this SIC or year were not available. The abbreviation (pt) next to the industry name indicates that only a part of the industry is present within the NAICS data. If no (pt) is shown, the entire industry is contained within the NAICS data.

SELECTED RATIOS

For 1997	Avg. of Information	Analyzed Industry	Index	For 1997	Avg. of Information	Analyzed Industry	Index
Employees per establishment	27	18	68	Payroll per establishment	1,131,090	715,580	63
Revenue per establishment	5,444,104	4,584,541	84	Payroll as % of revenue	21	16	75
Revenue per employee	203,255	252,831	124	Payroll per employee	42,229	39,463	93

Sources: Same as General Statistics. The 'Average' column represents the average for the industry sector, in 1997, where the currently shown industry is classified. The Index shows the relationship between the Average and the Analyzed Industry. For example, 100 means that they are equal; 500 that the Analyzed Industry is five times the average; 50 means that the Analyzed Industry is half the national average. The abbreviation 'na' is used to show that data are 'not available'.

LEADING COMPANIES

No company data available for this industry.

LOCATION BY STATE AND REGIONAL CONCENTRATION

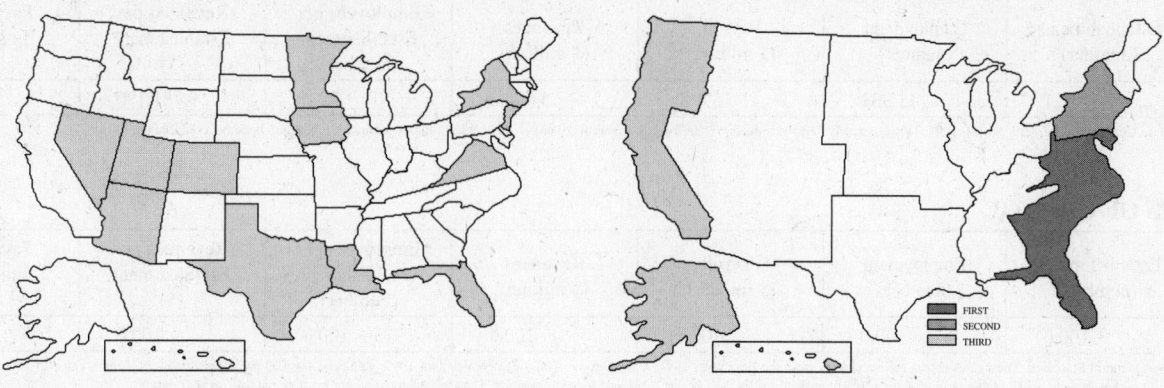

INDUSTRY DATA BY STATE

State	Establishments		Employment			Payroll		Revenues		
	Total (number)	% of U.S.	Total (number)	% of U.S.	Per Estab.	Total ($ mil.)	Per Empl. ($)	Total ($ mil.)	% of U.S.	Per Estab. ($)
California	200	12.1	3,532	11.8	18	126.3	35,771	832.3	11.0	4,161,655
New York	141	8.5	1,548	5.2	11	70.7	45,697	747.8	9.8	5,303,780
Texas	154	9.3	3,146	10.5	20	93.3	29,670	656.9	8.7	4,265,312
Florida	174	10.5	1,695	5.6	10	61.0	35,996	545.1	7.2	3,132,966
Iowa	23	1.4	1,015	3.4	44	44.8	44,125	439.6	5.8	19,114,522
New Jersey	60	3.6	1,331	4.4	22	40.0	30,032	406.8	5.4	6,779,183
Colorado	55	3.3	3,653	12.2	66	192.9	52,803	391.7	5.2	7,121,164
Virginia	41	2.5	1,969	6.6	48	86.4	43,886	372.7	4.9	9,090,927
Illinois	49	3.0	557	1.9	11	22.7	40,811	289.5	3.8	5,907,449
Louisiana	22	1.3	470	1.6	21	18.9	40,162	231.4	3.0	10,518,818
Nevada	21	1.3	746	2.5	36	31.7	42,441	166.3	2.2	7,920,333
Minnesota	35	2.1	467	1.6	13	21.9	46,957	156.1	2.1	4,460,057
Georgia	54	3.3	446	1.5	8	17.9	40,078	139.5	1.8	2,583,130
Arizona	33	2.0	767	2.6	23	29.0	37,764	138.0	1.8	4,182,909
Indiana	27	1.6	750	2.5	28	21.6	28,825	137.7	1.8	5,101,704
Washington	35	2.1	624	2.1	18	32.7	52,351	136.7	1.8	3,905,229
Michigan	42	2.5	434	1.4	10	16.1	37,051	111.7	1.5	2,660,286
Wisconsin	20	1.2	265	0.9	13	9.9	37,430	90.5	1.2	4,525,600
Tennessee	26	1.6	285	0.9	11	10.7	37,674	75.3	1.0	2,896,885
Ohio	35	2.1	405	1.3	12	20.6	50,889	74.0	1.0	2,115,629
Massachusetts	34	2.1	341	1.1	10	12.1	35,449	72.5	1.0	2,132,235
Utah	14	0.8	255	0.8	18	8.6	33,667	60.6	0.8	4,331,357
Kansas	19	1.1	209	0.7	11	6.6	31,799	60.6	0.8	3,187,526
North Carolina	27	1.6	176	0.6	7	8.6	48,983	36.3	0.5	1,344,407
Maryland	33	2.0	398	1.3	12	11.6	29,063	33.3	0.4	1,010,364
South Carolina	16	1.0	138	0.5	9	7.0	50,913	31.0	0.4	1,937,625
South Dakota	6	0.4	121	0.4	20	3.7	30,884	18.4	0.2	3,067,000
Montana	5	0.3	70	0.2	14	1.9	27,471	6.8	0.1	1,367,000
Pennsylvania	52	3.1	750*	-	-	(D)	-	(D)	-	-
Oregon	25	1.5	375*	-	-	(D)	-	(D)	-	-
Kentucky	24	1.4	375*	-	-	(D)	-	(D)	-	-
Oklahoma	23	1.4	175*	-	-	(D)	-	(D)	-	-
Connecticut	22	1.3	375*	-	-	(D)	-	(D)	-	-
Missouri	18	1.1	375*	-	-	(D)	-	(D)	-	-
Alaska	17	1.0	750*	-	-	(D)	-	(D)	-	-
Alabama	12	0.7	750*	-	-	(D)	-	(D)	-	-
Arkansas	8	0.5	60*	-	-	(D)	-	(D)	-	-
New Hampshire	8	0.5	175*	-	-	(D)	-	(D)	-	-
D.C.	6	0.4	175*	-	-	(D)	-	(D)	-	-
Nebraska	6	0.4	10*	-	-	(D)	-	(D)	-	-
Idaho	5	0.3	10*	-	-	(D)	-	(D)	-	-
New Mexico	5	0.3	60*	-	-	(D)	-	(D)	-	-
Vermont	5	0.3	10*	-	-	(D)	-	(D)	-	-
Wyoming	4	0.2	10*	-	-	(D)	-	(D)	-	-
Hawaii	3	0.2	10*	-	-	(D)	-	(D)	-	-
Maine	3	0.2	60*	-	-	(D)	-	(D)	-	-
Delaware	2	0.1	60*	-	-	(D)	-	(D)	-	-
North Dakota	2	0.1	10*	-	-	(D)	-	(D)	-	-
Rhode Island	2	0.1	10*	-	-	(D)	-	(D)	-	-
West Virginia	2	0.1	60*	-	-	(D)	-	(D)	-	-
Mississippi	1	0.1	10*	-	-	(D)	-	(D)	-	-

Source: 1997 *Economic Census.* The states are in descending order of revenues or establishments (if revenue data are missing for the majority). The symbol (D) appears when data are withheld to prevent disclosure of competitive information. States marked with (D) are sorted by number of establishments. A dash (-) indicates that the data element cannot be calculated. * indicates the midpoint of a range; 175, for example is the range 100-249. Shaded *states* on the state map indicate those states which have proportionately greater representation in the industry than would be indicated by the state's population; the ratio is based on total revenues or number of establishments. Shaded *regions* indicate where the industry is regionally most concentrated.

NAICS 513340 - SATELLITE TELECOMMUNICATIONS

GENERAL STATISTICS

Year	Establishments (number)	Employment (number)	Payroll ($ million)	Revenues ($ million)	Employees per Establishment (number)	Revenues per Establishment ($)	Payroll per Employee ($)
1997	521	11,931	599.0	5,096.0	22.9	9,781,190	50,205

Source: *Economic Census of the United States*, 1997. This is a newly defined industry. Data for prior years were unavailable at the time of publication but may become available over time.

INDICES OF CHANGE

Year	Establishments (number)	Employment (number)	Payroll ($ million)	Revenues ($ million)	Employees per Establishment (number)	Revenues per Establishment ($)	Payroll per Employee ($)
1997	100.0	100.0	100.0	100.0	100.0	100.0	100.0

Sources: Same as General Statistics. The values shown reflect change from the base year, 1997. Values above 100 mean greater than 1997, values below 100 mean less than 1997, and a value of 100 in the 1982-96 or 1998-2001 period means same as 1997. Values followed by a 'p' are projections by the editors; 'e' stands for extrapolation. Data are the most recent available at this level of detail.

SIC INDUSTRIES RELATED TO NAICS 513340

Each new NAICS code represents an industry that used to be part of an SIC or a part of several SIC industries. Data in this table are shown to provide transitional information for these cases. All available data for the precursor SIC(s) are shown. Even if only a part of an SIC is included in the NAICS, *all* data for the SIC are reproduced. If the SIC industry is not marked as being a part (pt) of the NAICS, the entire industry is embedded in the NAICS data. The SIC composition of the new industry provides some hints of the relative importance of its "ancestors." Data marked with a 'p' are projected. Projections begin with 1982 data. Data earlier than 1990 are not shown but are reflected in the projections.

SIC	Industry	1990	1991	1992	1993	1994	1995	1996	1997
4813	**Telephone Communications, Except Radio (pt)**								
	Establishments (number)	16,576	21,198	21,667	21,520	22,273	22,258	22,062	24,560p
	Employment (thousands)	819.3	908.6	867.2	842.0	824.3	820.9	808.5	833.3p
	Revenues ($ million)	-	-	159,310.4	170,255.9e	181,201.5e	192,147.0	208,064.0	220,876.0
4899	**Communications Services, nec (pt)**								
	Establishments (number)	1,201	1,320	1,008	1,105	1,034	1,305	1,488	468p
	Employment (thousands)	34.6	25.0	9.7	15.3	13.1	20.0	22.4	-
	Revenues ($ million)	-	-	2,357.9	-	-	-	-	-

Source: *Economic Census of the United States*, 1992, annual surveys of economic sectors conducted by the Bureau of the Census, and estimates or projections based on the 1982-1992 period; not all data are shown. 'e' marks estimates made by the editors; 'p' indicates projections based on time series. A dash (-) indicates that data for this SIC or year were not available. The abbreviation (pt) next to the industry name indicates that only a part of the industry is present within the NAICS data. If no (pt) is shown, the entire industry is contained within the NAICS data.

SELECTED RATIOS

For 1997	Avg. of Information	Analyzed Industry	Index	For 1997	Avg. of Information	Analyzed Industry	Index
Employees per establishment	27	23	85	Payroll per establishment	1,131,090	1,149,712	102
Revenue per establishment	5,444,104	9,781,190	180	Payroll as % of revenue	21	12	57
Revenue per employee	203,255	427,123	210	Payroll per employee	42,229	50,205	119

Sources: Same as General Statistics. The 'Average' column represents the average for the industry sector, in 1997, where the currently shown industry is classified. The Index shows the relationship between the Average and the Analyzed Industry. For example, 100 means that they are equal; 500 that the Analyzed Industry is five times the average; 50 means that the Analyzed Industry is half the national average. The abbreviation 'na' is used to show that data are 'not available'.

LEADING COMPANIES
No company data available for this industry.

LOCATION BY STATE AND REGIONAL CONCENTRATION

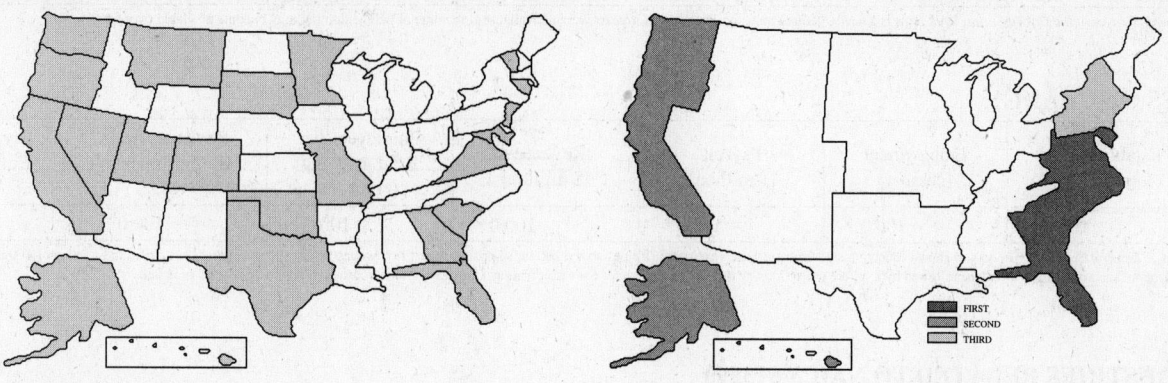

FIRST
SECOND
THIRD

INDUSTRY DATA BY STATE

State	Establishments Total (number)	% of U.S.	Employment Total (number)	% of U.S.	Per Estab.	Payroll Total ($ mil.)	Per Empl. ($)	Revenues Total ($ mil.)	% of U.S.	Per Estab. ($)
California	76	14.6	2,062	17.3	27	102.1	49,508	942.6	18.5	12,402,303
Virginia	25	4.8	646	5.4	26	40.5	62,653	442.0	8.7	17,680,880
Connecticut	9	1.7	340	2.8	38	35.1	103,338	423.6	8.3	47,064,000
Texas	39	7.5	686	5.7	18	29.1	42,468	347.9	6.8	8,919,308
Georgia	15	2.9	1,141	9.6	76	48.4	42,407	315.8	6.2	21,050,333
New Jersey	19	3.6	568	4.8	30	34.1	59,993	277.4	5.4	14,600,474
Florida	44	8.4	750	6.3	17	27.5	36,603	255.6	5.0	5,809,614
Illinois	23	4.4	834	7.0	36	37.4	44,827	160.4	3.1	6,973,870
D.C.	13	2.5	174	1.5	13	43.1	247,753	113.9	2.2	8,760,000
Massachusetts	7	1.3	66	0.6	9	2.9	44,015	50.8	1.0	7,256,714
Minnesota	11	2.1	269	2.3	24	12.1	45,100	43.8	0.9	3,978,000
Arizona	8	1.5	65	0.5	8	4.3	65,492	29.0	0.6	3,629,250
North Carolina	10	1.9	58	0.5	6	2.3	40,190	21.1	0.4	2,114,500
Colorado	12	2.3	134	1.1	11	5.5	40,709	14.4	0.3	1,199,750
Ohio	7	1.3	82	0.7	12	2.1	25,390	13.3	0.3	1,898,429
Tennessee	7	1.3	112	0.9	16	5.6	50,259	8.3	0.2	1,188,143
Michigan	12	2.3	45	0.4	4	1.3	28,689	7.0	0.1	582,000
South Carolina	8	1.5	73	0.6	9	1.0	13,808	4.3	0.1	534,625
New York	34	6.5	375*	-	-	(D)	-	(D)	-	-
Maryland	19	3.6	1,750*	-	-	(D)	-	(D)	-	-
Washington	15	2.9	175*	-	-	(D)	-	(D)	-	-
Missouri	12	2.3	375*	-	-	(D)	-	(D)	-	-
Pennsylvania	11	2.1	375*	-	-	(D)	-	(D)	-	-
Oklahoma	9	1.7	175*	-	-	(D)	-	(D)	-	-
Oregon	7	1.3	175*	-	-	(D)	-	(D)	-	-
Utah	7	1.3	175*	-	-	(D)	-	(D)	-	-
Wisconsin	7	1.3	60*	-	-	(D)	-	(D)	-	-
Alabama	5	1.0	10*	-	-	(D)	-	(D)	-	-
Hawaii	5	1.0	10*	-	-	(D)	-	(D)	-	-
Indiana	4	0.8	10*	-	-	(D)	-	(D)	-	-
Kansas	4	0.8	60*	-	-	(D)	-	(D)	-	-
Mississippi	4	0.8	60*	-	-	(D)	-	(D)	-	-
Nevada	4	0.8	10*	-	-	(D)	-	(D)	-	-
Vermont	4	0.8	10*	-	-	(D)	-	(D)	-	-
Alaska	3	0.6	10*	-	-	(D)	-	(D)	-	-
Kentucky	3	0.6	10*	-	-	(D)	-	(D)	-	-
Arkansas	2	0.4	10*	-	-	(D)	-	(D)	-	-
Iowa	2	0.4	10*	-	-	(D)	-	(D)	-	-
Maine	2	0.4	10*	-	-	(D)	-	(D)	-	-
Montana	2	0.4	60*	-	-	(D)	-	(D)	-	-
Nebraska	2	0.4	10*	-	-	(D)	-	(D)	-	-
New Hampshire	2	0.4	60*	-	-	(D)	-	(D)	-	-
South Dakota	2	0.4	175*	-	-	(D)	-	(D)	-	-
Idaho	1	0.2	10*	-	-	(D)	-	(D)	-	-
Louisiana	1	0.2	10*	-	-	(D)	-	(D)	-	-
New Mexico	1	0.2	10*	-	-	(D)	-	(D)	-	-
North Dakota	1	0.2	10*	-	-	(D)	-	(D)	-	-
West Virginia	1	0.2	375*	-	-	(D)	-	(D)	-	-

Source: 1997 *Economic Census*. The states are in descending order of revenues or establishments (if revenue data are missing for the majority). The symbol (D) appears when data are withheld to prevent disclosure of competitive information. States marked with (D) are sorted by number of establishments. A dash (-) indicates that the data element cannot be calculated. * indicates the midpoint of a range; 175, for example is the range 100-249. Shaded *states* on the state map indicate those states which have proportionately greater representation in the industry than would be indicated by the state's population; the ratio is based on total revenues or number of establishments. Shaded *regions* indicate where the industry is regionally most concentrated.

NAICS 513390 - TELECOMMUNICATIONS NEC

GENERAL STATISTICS

Year	Establishments (number)	Employment (number)	Payroll ($ million)	Revenues ($ million)	Employees per Establishment (number)	Revenues per Establishment ($)	Payroll per Employee ($)
1997	634	6,701	271.0	1,133.0	10.6	1,787,066	40,442

Source: Economic Census of the United States, 1997. This is a newly defined industry. Data for prior years were unavailable at the time of publication but may become available over time.

INDICES OF CHANGE

Year	Establishments (number)	Employment (number)	Payroll ($ million)	Revenues ($ million)	Employees per Establishment (number)	Revenues per Establishment ($)	Payroll per Employee ($)
1997	100.0	100.0	100.0	100.0	100.0	100.0	100.0

Sources: Same as General Statistics. The values shown reflect change from the base year, 1997. Values above 100 mean greater than 1997, values below 100 mean less than 1997, and a value of 100 in the 1982-96 or 1998-2001 period means same as 1997. Values followed by a 'p' are projections by the editors; 'e' stands for extrapolation. Data are the most recent available at this level of detail.

SIC INDUSTRIES RELATED TO NAICS 513390

Each new NAICS code represents an industry that used to be part of an SIC or a part of several SIC industries. Data in this table are shown to provide transitional information for these cases. All available data for the precursor SIC(s) are shown. Even if only a part of an SIC is included in the NAICS, *all* data for the SIC are reproduced. If the SIC industry is not marked as being a part (pt) of the NAICS, the entire industry is embedded in the NAICS data. The SIC composition of the new industry provides some hints of the relative importance of its "ancestors." Data marked with a 'p' are projected. Projections begin with 1982 data. Data earlier than 1990 are not shown but are reflected in the projections.

SIC	Industry	1990	1991	1992	1993	1994	1995	1996	1997
4899	**Communications Services, nec (pt)**								
	Establishments (number)	1,201	1,320	1,008	1,105	1,034	1,305	1,488	468p
	Employment (thousands)	34.6	25.0	9.7	15.3	13.1	20.0	22.4	-
	Revenues ($ million)	-	-	2,357.9	-	-	-	-	-

Source: Economic Census of the United States, 1992, annual surveys of economic sectors conducted by the Bureau of the Census, and estimates or projections based on the 1982-1992 period; not all data are shown. 'e' marks estimates made by the editors; 'p' indicates projections based on time series. A dash (-) indicates that data for this SIC or year were not available. The abbreviation (pt) next to the industry name indicates that only a part of the industry is present within the NAICS data. If no (pt) is shown, the entire industry is contained within the NAICS data.

SELECTED RATIOS

For 1997	Avg. of Information	Analyzed Industry	Index	For 1997	Avg. of Information	Analyzed Industry	Index
Employees per establishment	27	11	39	Payroll per establishment	1,131,090	427,445	38
Revenue per establishment	5,444,104	1,787,066	33	Payroll as % of revenue	21	24	115
Revenue per employee	203,255	169,079	83	Payroll per employee	42,229	40,442	96

Sources: Same as General Statistics. The 'Average' column represents the average for the industry sector, in 1997, where the currently shown industry is classified. The Index shows the relationship between the Average and the Analyzed Industry. For example, 100 means that they are equal; 500 that the Analyzed Industry is five times the average; 50 means that the Analyzed Industry is half the national average. The abbreviation 'na' is used to show that data are 'not available'.

LEADING COMPANIES
No company data available for this industry.

LOCATION BY STATE AND REGIONAL CONCENTRATION

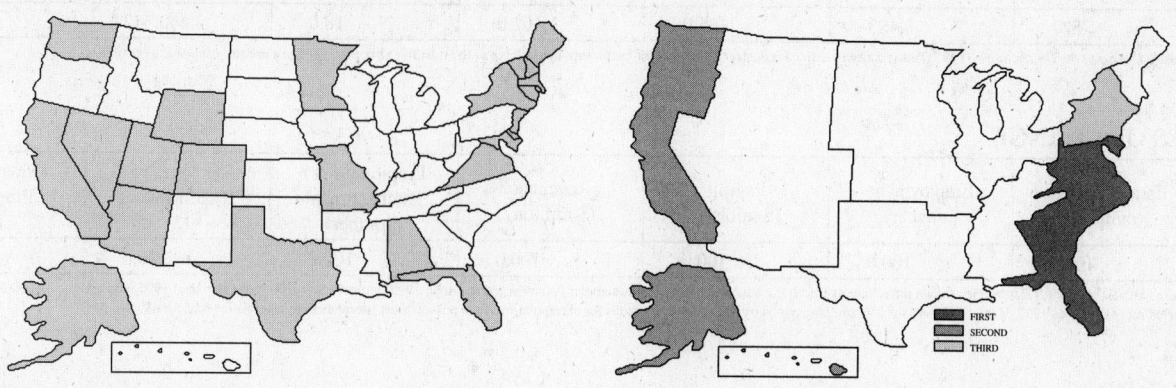

FIRST
SECOND
THIRD

INDUSTRY DATA BY STATE

State	Establishments Total (number)	% of U.S.	Employment Total (number)	% of U.S.	Per Estab.	Payroll Total ($ mil.)	Per Empl. ($)	Revenues Total ($ mil.)	% of U.S.	Per Estab. ($)
Texas	49	7.7	2,079	31.0	42	77.0	37,028	434.9	38.4	8,875,694
California	80	12.6	544	8.1	7	28.2	51,770	118.2	10.4	1,477,200
Florida	58	9.1	234	3.5	4	7.0	29,910	57.2	5.0	985,397
Colorado	20	3.2	385	5.7	19	13.4	34,714	48.7	4.3	2,433,950
Georgia	14	2.2	159	2.4	11	6.6	41,686	44.2	3.9	3,155,500
Virginia	26	4.1	348	5.2	13	5.5	15,664	20.8	1.8	799,154
North Carolina	15	2.4	95	1.4	6	2.8	30,000	14.7	1.3	983,200
New Jersey	29	4.6	79	1.2	3	4.7	59,861	14.3	1.3	494,034
Ohio	15	2.4	93	1.4	6	2.3	24,570	13.2	1.2	883,000
Illinois	27	4.3	69	1.0	3	2.1	31,043	10.7	0.9	394,630
Massachusetts	17	2.7	54	0.8	3	3.0	56,222	9.7	0.9	573,235
South Carolina	7	1.1	50	0.7	7	1.1	22,380	7.6	0.7	1,082,714
Minnesota	14	2.2	51	0.8	4	1.2	23,804	5.4	0.5	385,357
Arizona	11	1.7	61	0.9	6	1.6	26,656	5.2	0.5	468,818
Missouri	13	2.1	47	0.7	4	0.9	19,681	3.4	0.3	262,231
Tennessee	6	0.9	14	0.2	2	0.6	41,000	3.4	0.3	566,667
Michigan	21	3.3	89	1.3	4	1.0	11,034	2.9	0.3	136,429
Rhode Island	3	0.5	9	0.1	3	0.3	35,556	1.3	0.1	439,333
Oklahoma	5	0.8	6	0.1	1	0.1	11,667	0.2	0.0	43,200
New York	48	7.6	175*	-	-	(D)	-	(D)	-	-
Maryland	21	3.3	750*	-	-	(D)	-	(D)	-	-
Pennsylvania	19	3.0	60*	-	-	(D)	-	(D)	-	-
Washington	14	2.2	175*	-	-	(D)	-	(D)	-	-
Alabama	11	1.7	375*	-	-	(D)	-	(D)	-	-
Indiana	11	1.7	60*	-	-	(D)	-	(D)	-	-
Connecticut	9	1.4	60*	-	-	(D)	-	(D)	-	-
Utah	7	1.1	175*	-	-	(D)	-	(D)	-	-
Kentucky	6	0.9	10*	-	-	(D)	-	(D)	-	-
Nevada	6	0.9	175*	-	-	(D)	-	(D)	-	-
Wisconsin	6	0.9	175*	-	-	(D)	-	(D)	-	-
New Hampshire	5	0.8	10*	-	-	(D)	-	(D)	-	-
Louisiana	4	0.6	10*	-	-	(D)	-	(D)	-	-
Oregon	4	0.6	10*	-	-	(D)	-	(D)	-	-
Arkansas	3	0.5	10*	-	-	(D)	-	(D)	-	-
D.C.	3	0.5	10*	-	-	(D)	-	(D)	-	-
Kansas	3	0.5	10*	-	-	(D)	-	(D)	-	-
Maine	3	0.5	10*	-	-	(D)	-	(D)	-	-
Mississippi	3	0.5	10*	-	-	(D)	-	(D)	-	-
Alaska	2	0.3	10*	-	-	(D)	-	(D)	-	-
Delaware	2	0.3	10*	-	-	(D)	-	(D)	-	-
Montana	2	0.3	10*	-	-	(D)	-	(D)	-	-
Nebraska	2	0.3	10*	-	-	(D)	-	(D)	-	-
New Mexico	2	0.3	10*	-	-	(D)	-	(D)	-	-
Vermont	2	0.3	10*	-	-	(D)	-	(D)	-	-
West Virginia	2	0.3	10*	-	-	(D)	-	(D)	-	-
Hawaii	1	0.2	60*	-	-	(D)	-	(D)	-	-
Idaho	1	0.2	10*	-	-	(D)	-	(D)	-	-
North Dakota	1	0.2	10*	-	-	(D)	-	(D)	-	-
Wyoming	1	0.2	60*	-	-	(D)	-	(D)	-	-

Source: 1997 *Economic Census*. The states are in descending order of revenues or establishments (if revenue data are missing for the majority). The symbol (D) appears when data are withheld to prevent disclosure of competitive information. States marked with (D) are sorted by number of establishments. A dash (-) indicates that the data element cannot be calculated. * indicates the midpoint of a range; 175, for example is the range 100-249. Shaded *states* on the state map indicate those states which have proportionately greater representation in the industry than would be indicated by the state's population; the ratio is based on total revenues or number of establishments. Shaded *regions* indicate where the industry is regionally most concentrated.

NAICS 514110 - NEWS SYNDICATES

GENERAL STATISTICS

Year	Establishments (number)	Employment (number)	Payroll ($ million)	Revenues ($ million)	Employees per Establishment (number)	Revenues per Establishment ($)	Payroll per Employee ($)
1997	527	9,483	465.0	1,402.0	18.0	2,660,342	49,035

Source: *Economic Census of the United States*, 1997. This is a newly defined industry. Data for prior years were unavailable at the time of publication but may become available over time.

INDICES OF CHANGE

Year	Establishments (number)	Employment (number)	Payroll ($ million)	Revenues ($ million)	Employees per Establishment (number)	Revenues per Establishment ($)	Payroll per Employee ($)
1997	100.0	100.0	100.0	100.0	100.0	100.0	100.0

Sources: Same as General Statistics. The values shown reflect change from the base year, 1997. Values above 100 mean greater than 1997, values below 100 mean less than 1997, and a value of 100 in the 1982-96 or 1998-2001 period means same as 1997. Values followed by a 'p' are projections by the editors; 'e' stands for extrapolation. Data are the most recent available at this level of detail.

SIC INDUSTRIES RELATED TO NAICS 514110

Each new NAICS code represents an industry that used to be part of an SIC or a part of several SIC industries. Data in this table are shown to provide transitional information for these cases. All available data for the precursor SIC(s) are shown. Even if only a part of an SIC is included in the NAICS, *all* data for the SIC are reproduced. If the SIC industry is not marked as being a part (pt) of the NAICS, the entire industry is embedded in the NAICS data. The SIC composition of the new industry provides some hints of the relative importance of its "ancestors." Data marked with a 'p' are projected. Projections begin with 1982 data. Data earlier than 1990 are not shown but are reflected in the projections.

SIC	Industry	1990	1991	1992	1993	1994	1995	1996	1997
7383	**News Syndicates (pt)**								
	Establishments (number)	576	642	598	532	511	512	512p	500p
	Employment (thousands)	10.0	9.5	8.2	8.4	8.5	9.3	8.9p	9.0p
	Revenues ($ million)	-	-	1,020.8	-	-	-		

Source: *Economic Census of the United States*, 1992, annual surveys of economic sectors conducted by the Bureau of the Census, and estimates or projections based on the 1982-1992 period; not all data are shown. 'e' marks estimates made by the editors; 'p' indicates projections based on time series. A dash (-) indicates that data for this SIC or year were not available. The abbreviation (pt) next to the industry name indicates that only a part of the industry is present within the NAICS data. If no (pt) is shown, the entire industry is contained within the NAICS data.

SELECTED RATIOS

For 1997	Avg. of Information	Analyzed Industry	Index	For 1997	Avg. of Information	Analyzed Industry	Index
Employees per establishment	27	18	67	Payroll per establishment	1,131,090	882,353	78
Revenue per establishment	5,444,104	2,660,342	49	Payroll as % of revenue	21	33	160
Revenue per employee	203,255	147,844	73	Payroll per employee	42,229	49,035	116

Sources: Same as General Statistics. The 'Average' column represents the average for the industry sector, in 1997, where the currently shown industry is classified. The Index shows the relationship between the Average and the Analyzed Industry. For example, 100 means that they are equal; 500 that the Analyzed Industry is five times the average; 50 means that the Analyzed Industry is half the national average. The abbreviation 'na' is used to show that data are 'not available'.

LEADING COMPANIES   Number shown: **18**   Total sales ($ mil): **6,403**   Total employment (000): **30.5**

Company Name	Address				CEO Name	Phone	Co. Type	Sales ($ mil)	Empl. (000)
New York Times Co.	229 W 43rd St	New York	NY	10036	Russell Lewis	212-556-1234	P	2,937	13.2
Dow Jones and Company Inc.	200 Liberty St	New York	NY	10281	Peter R Kann	212-416-2000	P	2,158	8.3
Reuters America Inc.	1700 Broadway	New York	NY	10019	Thomas Glocer	212-603-3300	S	524*	2.8
Associated Press	50 Rockefeller Plz	New York	NY	10020	Louis D Boccardi	212-621-1500	R	485*	3.5
PR Newswire Association Inc.	810 7th Ave	New York	NY	10019	Ian Capps	212-596-1500	S	77*	0.7
Andrews McMeel Universal	PO Box 419150	Kansas City	MO	64141		816-932-6700	R	58*	0.3
Universal Press Syndicate	PO Box 419150	Kansas City	MO	64141		816-932-6700	S	38*	0.4
CONUS Communications	3415 University Ave	Minneapolis	MN	55414	Chuck Dutcher	612-642-4645	S	33*	0.3
Business Wire	44 Montgomery St	San Francisco	CA	94104	Lorry I Lokey	415-986-4422	R	25*	0.3
Burrelle's Information Services	75 E Northfield Rd	Livingston	NJ	07039	Robert Waggoner	973-992-6600	S	19*	0.3
United Feature Syndicate Inc.	200 Madison Ave	New York	NY	10016	Douglas R Stern	212-293-8500	S	18*	0.2
New York Times Syndication	122 E 42nd St	New York	NY	10168	G Brown Anderson	212-499-3300	S	15*	<0.1
Tribune Media Services Inc.	435 N Michigan	Chicago	IL	60611	David D Williams	312-222-4444	S	6*	0.2
Comtex Scientific Corp.	4900 Seminary Rd	Alexandria	VA	22311	CW Gilluly	703-820-2000	P	5	<0.1
Knight-Ridder-Tribune News	790 Nat Press Bldg	Washington	DC	20045		202-383-6080	S	3*	<0.1
Arizona News Service Inc.	PO Box 2260	Phoenix	AZ	85002		602-258-7026	R	2	<0.1
Empire Information Services Inc.	P O Box 742	Schenectady	NY	12301	Peter G Pollak	518-372-0785	R	1	<0.1
Wordservice International	400 E 89th St	New York	NY	10128	Martha Palubniak	212-360-6541	R	0	<0.1

Source: *Ward's Business Directory of U.S. Private and Public Companies*, Volumes 1 and 2, 2000. The company type code used is as follows: P - Public, R - Private, S - Subsidiary, D - Division, J - Joint Venture, A - Affiliate, G - Group, N - Company type not reported. Sales are in millions of dollars, employees are in thousands. An asterisk (*) indicates an estimated sales volume. The symbol < stands for 'less than'. Company names and addresses are truncated, in some cases, to fit into the available space.

LOCATION BY STATE AND REGIONAL CONCENTRATION

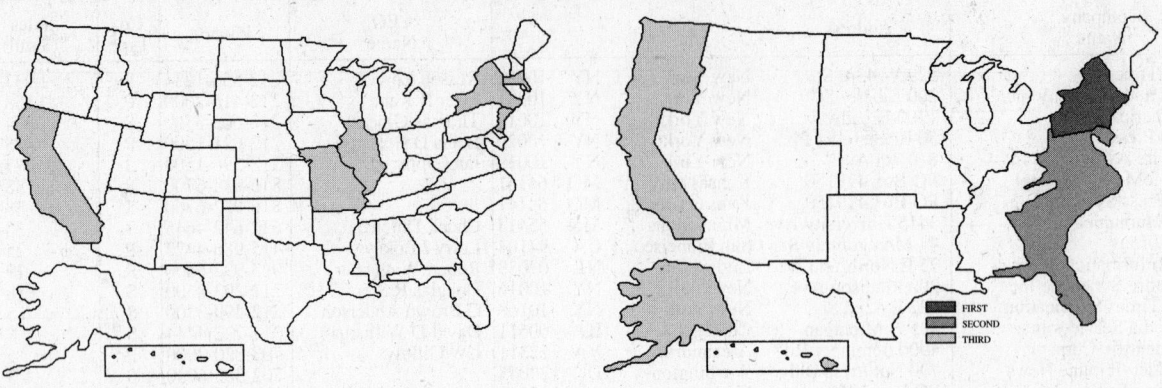

INDUSTRY DATA BY STATE

State	Establishments Total (number)	Establishments % of U.S.	Employment Total (number)	Employment % of U.S.	Employment Per Estab.	Payroll Total ($ mil.)	Payroll Per Empl. ($)	Revenues Total ($ mil.)	Revenues % of U.S.	Revenues Per Estab. ($)
New York	80	15.2	2,270	23.9	28	130.9	57,679	307.0	21.9	3,837,537
New Jersey	12	2.3	741	7.8	62	35.5	47,892	189.5	13.5	15,789,250
California	85	16.1	1,069	11.3	13	67.5	63,138	171.7	12.2	2,020,153
D.C.	46	8.7	1,350	14.2	29	71.7	53,088	156.2	11.1	3,395,196
Illinois	19	3.6	532	5.6	28	26.9	50,504	99.2	7.1	5,218,842
Pennsylvania	22	4.2	298	3.1	14	11.3	38,081	45.1	3.2	2,050,409
Missouri	10	1.9	213	2.2	21	12.6	59,178	40.7	2.9	4,073,700
Texas	15	2.8	311	3.3	21	10.9	34,913	38.6	2.8	2,574,267
Florida	32	6.1	291	3.1	9	10.3	35,395	38.6	2.8	1,206,406
Massachusetts	14	2.7	284	3.0	20	9.7	34,306	37.5	2.7	2,681,071
Virginia	11	2.1	157	1.7	14	6.8	43,554	26.3	1.9	2,393,636
Georgia	14	2.7	95	1.0	7	4.7	49,537	19.2	1.4	1,374,571
Michigan	10	1.9	111	1.2	11	4.3	38,694	18.2	1.3	1,818,700
Colorado	9	1.7	95	1.0	11	5.8	61,021	15.1	1.1	1,679,222
Minnesota	10	1.9	114	1.2	11	3.7	32,711	14.3	1.0	1,427,900
Washington	7	1.3	89	0.9	13	3.7	41,798	13.4	1.0	1,916,571
North Carolina	9	1.7	98	1.0	11	3.0	30,571	13.3	0.9	1,473,333
Arizona	7	1.3	59	0.6	8	3.5	59,102	12.0	0.9	1,718,143
Indiana	5	0.9	222	2.3	44	2.8	12,599	9.5	0.7	1,905,800
Tennessee	7	1.3	78	0.8	11	2.7	34,154	9.2	0.7	1,316,429
Alabama	4	0.8	35	0.4	9	1.4	40,143	5.5	0.4	1,371,250
Kentucky	3	0.6	42	0.4	14	1.4	33,738	5.1	0.4	1,686,333
Utah	3	0.6	33	0.3	11	1.2	36,242	4.0	0.3	1,322,667
Nevada	4	0.8	27	0.3	7	1.5	55,852	3.5	0.2	870,750
New Mexico	4	0.8	30	0.3	8	1.2	41,333	3.5	0.3	883,750
Montana	3	0.6	57	0.6	19	1.2	20,860	3.2	0.2	1,067,667
Hawaii	5	0.9	15	0.2	3	0.6	42,200	3.2	0.2	639,600
Ohio	12	2.3	175*	-	-	(D)	-	(D)	-	-
Maryland	11	2.1	175*	-	-	(D)	-	(D)	-	-
Oklahoma	7	1.3	60*	-	-	(D)	-	(D)	-	-
South Carolina	6	1.1	60*	-	-	(D)	-	(D)	-	-
Wisconsin	5	0.9	60*	-	-	(D)	-	(D)	-	-
Oregon	4	0.8	60*	-	-	(D)	-	(D)	-	-
Connecticut	3	0.6	60*	-	-	(D)	-	(D)	-	-
Idaho	3	0.6	10*	-	-	(D)	-	(D)	-	-
Arkansas	2	0.4	10*	-	-	(D)	-	(D)	-	-
Delaware	2	0.4	10*	-	-	(D)	-	(D)	-	-
Kansas	2	0.4	60*	-	-	(D)	-	(D)	-	-
Louisiana	2	0.4	60*	-	-	(D)	-	(D)	-	-
Maine	2	0.4	10*	-	-	(D)	-	(D)	-	-
Nebraska	2	0.4	10*	-	-	(D)	-	(D)	-	-
New Hampshire	2	0.4	10*	-	-	(D)	-	(D)	-	-
Rhode Island	2	0.4	60*	-	-	(D)	-	(D)	-	-
South Dakota	2	0.4	10*	-	-	(D)	-	(D)	-	-
Vermont	2	0.4	10*	-	-	(D)	-	(D)	-	-
Alaska	1	0.2	10*	-	-	(D)	-	(D)	-	-
Iowa	1	0.2	10*	-	-	(D)	-	(D)	-	-
Mississippi	1	0.2	10*	-	-	(D)	-	(D)	-	-
North Dakota	1	0.2	10*	-	-	(D)	-	(D)	-	-
West Virginia	1	0.2	10*	-	-	(D)	-	(D)	-	-
Wyoming	1	0.2	10*	-	-	(D)	-	(D)	-	-

Source: 1997 *Economic Census*. The states are in descending order of revenues or establishments (if revenue data are missing for the majority). The symbol (D) appears when data are withheld to prevent disclosure of competitive information. States marked with (D) are sorted by number of establishments. A dash (-) indicates that the data element cannot be calculated. * indicates the midpoint of a range; 175, for example is the range 100-249. Shaded *states* on the state map indicate those states which have proportionately greater representation in the industry than would be indicated by the state's population; the ratio is based on total revenues or number of establishments. Shaded *regions* indicate where the industry is regionally most concentrated.

NAICS 514120 - LIBRARIES AND ARCHIVES

GENERAL STATISTICS

Year	Establishments (number)	Employment (number)	Payroll ($ million)	Revenues ($ million)	Employees per Establishment (number)	Revenues per Establishment ($)	Payroll per Employee ($)
1997	2,298	22,044	373.0	861.0	9.6	374,674	16,921

Source: Economic Census of the United States, 1997. This is a newly defined industry. Data for prior years were unavailable at the time of publication but may become available over time.

INDICES OF CHANGE

Year	Establishments (number)	Employment (number)	Payroll ($ million)	Revenues ($ million)	Employees per Establishment (number)	Revenues per Establishment ($)	Payroll per Employee ($)
1997	100.0	100.0	100.0	100.0	100.0	100.0	100.0

Sources: Same as General Statistics. The values shown reflect change from the base year, 1997. Values above 100 mean greater than 1997, values below 100 mean less than 1997, and a value of 100 in the 1982-96 or 1998-2001 period means same as 1997. Values followed by a 'p' are projections by the editors; 'e' stands for extrapolation. Data are the most recent available at this level of detail.

SIC INDUSTRIES RELATED TO NAICS 514120

Each new NAICS code represents an industry that used to be part of an SIC or a part of several SIC industries. Data in this table are shown to provide transitional information for these cases. All available data for the precursor SIC(s) are shown. Even if only a part of an SIC is included in the NAICS, *all* data for the SIC are reproduced. If the SIC industry is not marked as being a part (pt) of the NAICS, the entire industry is embedded in the NAICS data. The SIC composition of the new industry provides some hints of the relative importance of its "ancestors." Data marked with a 'p' are projected. Projections begin with 1982 data. Data earlier than 1990 are not shown but are reflected in the projections.

SIC	Industry	1990	1991	1992	1993	1994	1995	1996	1997
7829	**Motion Picture Distribution Services (pt)**								
	Establishments (number)	164	169	210	202	188	199	200p	203p
	Employment (thousands)	1.3	1.1	0.9	1.1	1.1	1.3	1.1p	1.1p
	Revenues ($ million)	-	-	104.2	-	-	-	-	-
8231	**Libraries**								
	Establishments (number)	-	-	1,804	2,264	2,432	2,601	2,770p	2,939p
	Employment (thousands)	-	-	17.0	22.2	23.9	25.7	27.4p	29.2p
	Revenues ($ million)	476.0	481.0	527.0	606.0	655.0	730.0	754.0	812.7p

Source: Economic Census of the United States, 1992, annual surveys of economic sectors conducted by the Bureau of the Census, and estimates or projections based on the 1982-1992 period; not all data are shown. 'e' marks estimates made by the editors; 'p' indicates projections based on time series. A dash (-) indicates that data for this SIC or year were not available. The abbreviation (pt) next to the industry name indicates that only a part of the industry is present within the NAICS data. If no (pt) is shown, the entire industry is contained within the NAICS data.

SELECTED RATIOS

For 1997	Avg. of Information	Analyzed Industry	Index	For 1997	Avg. of Information	Analyzed Industry	Index
Employees per establishment	27	10	36	Payroll per establishment	1,131,090	162,315	14
Revenue per establishment	5,444,104	374,674	7	Payroll as % of revenue	21	43	209
Revenue per employee	203,255	39,058	19	Payroll per employee	42,229	16,921	40

Sources: Same as General Statistics. The 'Average' column represents the average for the industry sector, in 1997, where the currently shown industry is classified. The Index shows the relationship between the Average and the Analyzed Industry. For example, 100 means that they are equal; 500 that the Analyzed Industry is five times the average; 50 means that the Analyzed Industry is half the national average. The abbreviation 'na' is used to show that data are 'not available'.

LEADING COMPANIES

No company data available for this industry.

LOCATION BY STATE AND REGIONAL CONCENTRATION

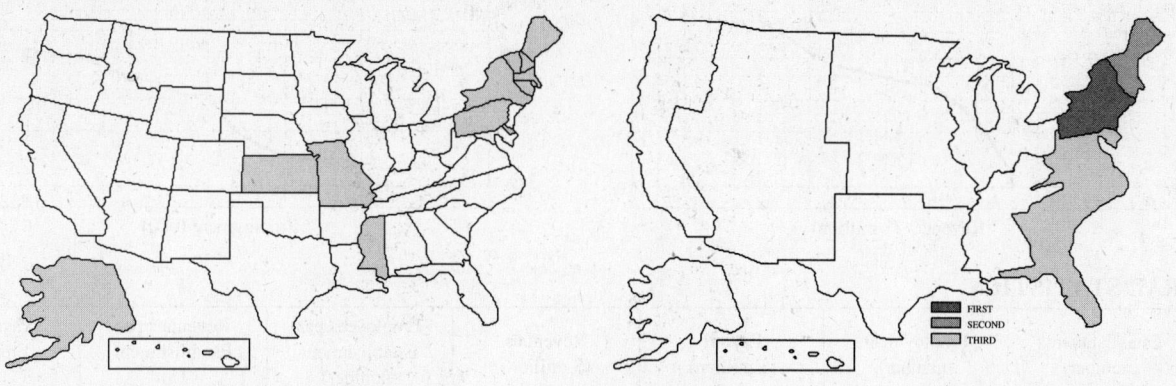

INDUSTRY DATA BY STATE

State	Establishments Total (number)	Establishments % of U.S.	Employment Total (number)	Employment % of U.S.	Employment Per Estab.	Payroll Total ($ mil.)	Payroll Per Empl. ($)	Revenues Total ($ mil.)	Revenues % of U.S.	Revenues Per Estab. ($)
New York	532	23.2	7,370	33.4	14	145.2	19,701	278.0	32.3	522,538
Pennsylvania	385	16.8	3,901	17.7	10	52.8	13,524	129.4	15.0	336,205
California	84	3.7	912	4.1	11	24.6	26,950	75.7	8.8	901,357
Connecticut	92	4.0	1,391	6.3	15	20.9	15,002	40.8	4.7	443,304
Massachusetts	76	3.3	622	2.8	8	13.0	20,924	28.3	3.3	372,961
Colorado	30	1.3	357	1.6	12	8.9	24,810	27.1	3.1	901,967
Georgia	34	1.5	487	2.2	14	6.8	13,916	21.2	2.5	624,765
Florida	42	1.8	306	1.4	7	5.2	17,124	19.8	2.3	471,643
Missouri	56	2.4	625	2.8	11	10.7	17,178	19.7	2.3	351,536
Maryland	29	1.3	460	2.1	16	7.3	15,891	16.2	1.9	557,276
Texas	117	5.1	350	1.6	3	4.5	12,734	13.5	1.6	115,222
Michigan	51	2.2	298	1.4	6	3.7	12,379	12.6	1.5	247,333
Minnesota	13	0.6	104	0.5	8	2.3	22,019	9.0	1.0	692,615
Maine	79	3.4	305	1.4	4	3.6	11,793	8.9	1.0	112,785
North Carolina	23	1.0	218	1.0	9	3.3	15,174	7.9	0.9	343,391
Indiana	21	0.9	277	1.3	13	4.0	14,448	7.8	0.9	369,857
Alabama	20	0.9	259	1.2	13	3.9	14,927	7.4	0.9	369,550
Vermont	65	2.8	227	1.0	3	2.0	8,921	6.1	0.7	93,738
Oklahoma	8	0.3	212	1.0	27	2.7	12,717	4.4	0.5	544,500
Kentucky	13	0.6	128	0.6	10	1.8	14,203	4.3	0.5	331,538
Kansas	39	1.7	187	0.8	5	1.8	9,620	3.8	0.4	98,128
Washington	16	0.7	94	0.4	6	1.2	13,085	2.3	0.3	146,313
Louisiana	15	0.7	59	0.3	4	1.0	16,661	2.2	0.3	148,267
New Hampshire	31	1.3	94	0.4	3	0.8	8,777	2.0	0.2	62,935
South Dakota	4	0.2	3	0.0	1	-	11,000	0.1	0.0	27,750
Illinois	63	2.7	750*	-	-	(D)	-	(D)	-	-
New Jersey	53	2.3	375*	-	-	(D)	-	(D)	-	-
Virginia	44	1.9	375*	-	-	(D)	-	(D)	-	-
Mississippi	36	1.6	175*	-	-	(D)	-	(D)	-	-
Ohio	32	1.4	175*	-	-	(D)	-	(D)	-	-
Rhode Island	28	1.2	175*	-	-	(D)	-	(D)	-	-
Tennessee	18	0.8	60*	-	-	(D)	-	(D)	-	-
Arizona	17	0.7	60*	-	-	(D)	-	(D)	-	-
Iowa	15	0.7	60*	-	-	(D)	-	(D)	-	-
Delaware	13	0.6	175*	-	-	(D)	-	(D)	-	-
West Virginia	12	0.5	60*	-	-	(D)	-	(D)	-	-
Wisconsin	12	0.5	60*	-	-	(D)	-	(D)	-	-
Idaho	10	0.4	60*	-	-	(D)	-	(D)	-	-
Oregon	10	0.4	60*	-	-	(D)	-	(D)	-	-
South Carolina	9	0.4	60*	-	-	(D)	-	(D)	-	-
Alaska	8	0.3	60*	-	-	(D)	-	(D)	-	-
Utah	8	0.3	60*	-	-	(D)	-	(D)	-	-
Nebraska	7	0.3	10*	-	-	(D)	-	(D)	-	-
New Mexico	6	0.3	10*	-	-	(D)	-	(D)	-	-
Hawaii	5	0.2	60*	-	-	(D)	-	(D)	-	-
Nevada	4	0.2	10*	-	-	(D)	-	(D)	-	-
North Dakota	4	0.2	10*	-	-	(D)	-	(D)	-	-
D.C.	3	0.1	175*	-	-	(D)	-	(D)	-	-
Arkansas	2	0.1	10*	-	-	(D)	-	(D)	-	-
Montana	2	0.1	10*	-	-	(D)	-	(D)	-	-
Wyoming	2	0.1	10*	-	-	(D)	-	(D)	-	-

Source: 1997 *Economic Census*. The states are in descending order of revenues or establishments (if revenue data are missing for the majority). The symbol (D) appears when data are withheld to prevent disclosure of competitive information. States marked with (D) are sorted by number of establishments. A dash (-) indicates that the data element cannot be calculated. * indicates the midpoint of a range; 175, for example is the range 100-249. Shaded *states* on the state map indicate those states which have proportionately greater representation in the industry than would be indicated by the state's population; the ratio is based on total revenues or number of establishments. Shaded *regions* indicate where the industry is regionally most concentrated.

NAICS 514191 - ON-LINE INFORMATION SERVICES*

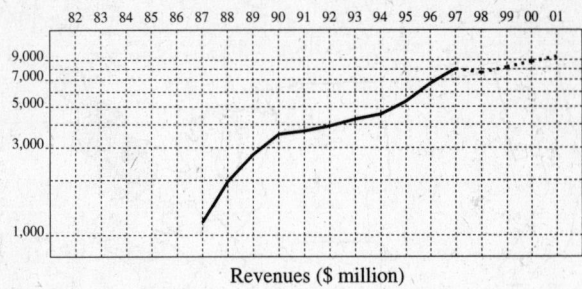

Revenues ($ million)

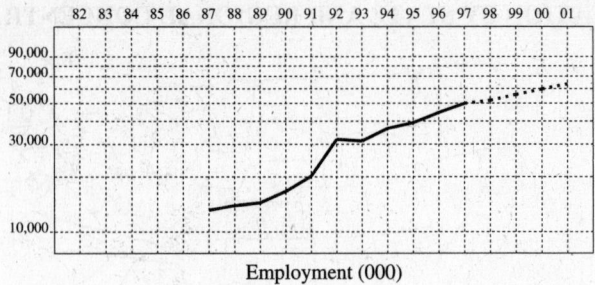

Employment (000)

GENERAL STATISTICS

Year	Establishments (number)	Employment (number)	Payroll ($ million)	Revenues ($ million)	Employees per Establishment (number)	Revenues per Establishment ($)	Payroll per Employee ($)
1982	-	-	-	-	-	-	-
1983	-	-	-	-	-	-	-
1984	-	-	-	-	-	-	-
1985	-	-	-	-	-	-	-
1986	-	-	-	-	-	-	-
1987	463	13,121	355.0	1,176.0	28.3	2,539,957	27,056
1988	494	13,944	396.0	1,966.0 e	28.2	3,979,757	28,399
1989	446	14,453	436.0	2,757.0 e	32.4	6,181,614	30,167
1990	508	16,654	516.0	3,547.0	32.8	6,982,283	30,984
1991	690	20,172	630.0	3,691.0	29.2	5,349,275	31,231
1992	1,090	31,869	1,098.0	3,931.0	29.2	3,606,422	34,454
1993	1,128	31,234	1,107.0	4,277.0	27.7	3,791,667	35,442
1994	1,245	36,529	1,388.0	4,559.0	29.3	3,661,847	37,997
1995	1,694	39,222	1,660.0	5,343.0	23.2	3,154,073	42,323
1996	2,929 e	44,578 e	2,008.0 e	6,693.0 e	15.2 e	2,285,080 e	45,045 e
1997	4,165	49,935	2,356.0	8,043.0	12.0	1,931,092	47,181
1998	3,200 p	51,886 p	2,305.0 p	7,650.0 p	16.2 p	2,390,625 p	44,424 p
1999	3,508 p	55,811 p	2,508.0 p	8,228.0 p	15.9 p	2,345,496 p	44,937 p
2000	3,816 p	59,736 p	2,712.0 p	8,806.0 p	15.7 p	2,307,652 p	45,400 p
2001	4,124 p	63,660 p	2,915.0 p	9,385.0 p	15.4 p	2,275,703 p	45,790 p

Sources: Economic Census of the United States, 1982, 1987, 1992, 1997. Establishment counts, employment, and payroll are from *County Business Patterns* for non-Census years. In non-Census years, industries in the Manufacturing range under SIC coding include data from the *Annual Survey of Manufactures* (*ASM*); those in the old Services range include data from the *Services Annual Survey* (*SAS*). Values followed by a 'p' are projections by the editors. Extrapolations are marked by 'e'. Data are the most recent available at this level of detail.

INDICES OF CHANGE

Year	Establishments (number)	Employment (number)	Payroll ($ million)	Revenues ($ million)	Employees per Establishment (number)	Revenues per Establishment ($)	Payroll per Employee ($)
1982	-	-	-	-	-	-	-
1987	11.1	26.3	15.1	14.6	236.4	131.5	57.3
1992	26.2	63.8	46.6	48.9	243.9	186.8	73.0
1993	27.1	62.5	47.0	53.2	231.0	196.3	75.1
1994	29.9	73.2	58.9	56.7	244.7	189.6	80.5
1995	40.7	78.5	70.5	66.4	193.1	163.3	89.7
1996	70.3 e	89.3 e	85.2 e	83.2 e	126.9 e	118.3 e	95.5 e
1997	100.0	100.0	100.0	100.0	100.0	100.0	100.0
1998	76.8 p	103.9 p	97.8 p	95.1 p	135.2 p	123.8 p	94.2 p
1999	84.2 p	111.8 p	106.5 p	102.3 p	132.7 p	121.5 p	95.2 p
2000	91.6 p	119.6 p	115.1 p	109.5 p	130.6 p	119.5 p	96.2 p
2001	99.0 p	127.5 p	123.7 p	116.7 p	128.8 p	117.8 p	97.1 p

Sources: Same as General Statistics. The values shown reflect change from the base year, 1997. Values above 100 mean greater than 1997, values below 100 mean less than 1997, and a value of 100 in the 1982-96 or 1998-2001 period means same as 1997. Values followed by a 'p' are projections by the editors; 'e' stands for extrapolation. Data are the most recent available at this level of detail.

SELECTED RATIOS

For 1997	Avg. of Information	Analyzed Industry	Index	For 1997	Avg. of Information	Analyzed Industry	Index
Employees per establishment	27	12	45	Payroll per establishment	1,131,090	565,666	50
Revenue per establishment	5,444,104	1,931,092	35	Payroll as % of revenue	21	29	141
Revenue per employee	203,255	161,069	79	Payroll per employee	42,229	47,181	112

Sources: Same as General Statistics. The 'Average' column represents the average for the industry sector, in 1997, where the currently shown industry is classified. The Index shows the relationship between the Average and the Analyzed Industry. For example, 100 means that they are equal; 500 that the Analyzed Industry is five times the average; 50 means that the Analyzed Industry is half the national average. The abbreviation 'na' is used to show that data are 'not available'.

*Equivalent to SIC 7375.

LEADING COMPANIES   Number shown: **75**   Total sales ($ mil): **86,750**   Total employment (000): **436.6**

Company Name	Address				CEO Name	Phone	Co. Type	Sales ($ mil)	Empl. (000)
Microsoft Corp.	1 Microsoft Way	Redmond	WA	98052	Steven A. Ballmer	425-882-8080	P	19,747	31.4
Ameritech Corp.	30 S Wacker Dr	Chicago	IL	60606	Richard C Notebaert	312-750-5000	P	17,154	75.0
McGraw-Hill Inc.	1221 Av Americas	New York	NY	10020	Harold McGraw III	212-512-2000	P	3,992	15.9
Quest Communications	700 Qwest Tower	Denver	CO	80202	Afshin Mohebbi	303-992-1400	P	3,928	8.7
Moore USA Inc.	275 N Field Dr	Lake Forest	IL	60045	Reto Braun	847-615-6000	S	2,718	19.0
SABRE Group Holdings Inc.	4255 Amon Carter	Fort Worth	TX	76155	Michael J Durham	817-963-6400	P	2,306	10.8
American Greetings Corp.	1 American Rd	Cleveland	OH	44144	E Fruchtenbaum	216-252-7300	P	2,205	35.5
Dow Jones and Company Inc.	200 Liberty St	New York	NY	10281	Peter R Kann	212-416-2000	P	2,158	8.3
Dow Jones News Wires	800 Plaza 2	Jersey City	NJ	07311	Paul Ingrassia		D	2,016	1.2
THI Holdings Corp.	1 Station Pl	Stamford	CT	06902	Richard J Harrington	203-969-8700	S	1,939*	12.0
SABRE Group Inc.	4255 Amon Carter	Fort Worth	TX	76155	Michael J Durham	817-931-7300	S	1,783	7.9
Galileo International Inc.	9700 W Higgins Rd	Rosemont	IL	60018	James E Barlett	847-518-4000	P	1,526	3.0
H and R Block Inc.	4400 Main St	Kansas City	MO	64111	Frank L Salizzoni	816-753-6900	P	1,522	86.5
Bloomberg L.P.	499 Park Ave	New York	NY	10022	Michael Bloomberg	212-318-2000	R	1,500	4.0
Fiserv Inc.	PO Box 979	Brookfield	WI	53008	George Dalton	262-879-5000	P	1,407	12.5
Bridge Information Systems Inc.	3 W Financial Ctr	New York	NY	10281	Thomas M Wendel	212-372-7100	R	1,330	4.5
LEXIS-NEXIS	PO Box 933	Dayton	OH	45401	Hans Gieskes	937-865-6800	S	1,230	7.8
Thomson Financial	22 Thomson Place	Boston	MA	02210	Patrick Tierney	617-856-2000	S	924*	5.0
CompuServe Interactive Services	PO Box 20212	Columbus	OH	43220	Mayo Stuntz Jr	614-457-8600	S	842	3.0
Libraries Online Inc.	123 Broad St	Middletown	CT	06457		860-347-1704	R	790	<0.1
Renaissance Worldwide Inc.	189 Wells Ave	Newton	MA	02159	G Drew Conway	781-290-3000	P	776	6.0
R.L. Polk and Co.	26955 Northwestern	Southfield	MI	48034	Arthur Olsen	248-728-7111	R	756*	6.0
IDT Corp.	190 Main St	Hackensack	NJ	07601	Howard S Jonas	201-928-1000	P	732	1.3
Press-Enterprise Co.	PO Box 792	Riverside	CA	92502	Marcia McQuern	909-684-1200	S	615*	1.0
Yahoo! Inc.	3420 Central Expwy	Santa Clara	CA	95050	Timothy Koogle	408-731-3300	P	589	0.8
PSINet Inc.	510 Huntmar	Herndon	VA	20170	William L Schrader	703-904-4100	P	555	1.8
Information Resources Inc.	150 N Clinton St	Chicago	IL	60661	Joe Durrett	312-726-1221	P	546	4.4
CMP Media Inc.	600 Community Dr	Manhasset	NY	11030	Michael S Leeds	516-562-5000	P	478	1.8
BBN Corp.	150 Cambridgepark	Cambridge	MA	02140		617-873-2000	S	468*	4.0
Netscape Communications Corp.	501 E Middlefield	Mountain View	CA	94043	James L Barksdale	650-254-1900	P	448	2.9
Primark Corp.	1000 Winter St	Waltham	MA	02451	Joseph Kasputys	781-466-6611	P	435	2.9
UUNet	3060 Williams Dr	Fairfax	VA	22031	John W Sidgmore III	703-206-5600	S	432*	1.4
Catalina Information Resources	150 N Clinton St	Chicago	IL	60661	Joe Duriett	312-726-1221	D	428*	2.0
Nielson Media Research Inc.	299 Park Ave	New York	NY	10171	John A Dimling	212-708-7500	P	402	3.1
Complete Business Solutions, Inc.	32605 W 12 Mile	Farmington Hills	MI	48334	Charles W Costello	248-488-2088	R	377	4.3
Thomson Financial Services	22 Thomas Pl 11F2	Boston	MA	02210	Patrick J Tierney	617-856-4636	S	354*	2.2
ICG Communications Inc.	161 Inverness Dr W	Englewood	CO	80112	Bill Beans	303-414-5000	P	350*	3.0
Excite@Home Inc.	555 Broadway	Redwood City	CA	94063	Thomas A Jermoluk	650-568-6000	P	337	2.3
BTG Inc. (Fairfax, Virginia)	3877 Fairfax Ridge	Fairfax	VA	22030	Edward H Bersoff	703-383-8000	P	316	1.3
Infonet Services Corp.	2160 E Grand Ave	El Segundo	CA	90245	Jose Collazo	310-335-2600	P	303	1.5
Dialog Corp.	1100 Regency	Cary	NC	27511		919-462-8600	S	283	0.9
infoUSA Inc.	5711 S 86th Cir	Omaha	NE	68127	Vinod Gupta	402-593-4500	P	266	2.0
Cerner Corp.	2800 Rockcreek	Kansas City	MO	64117	Neal L Patterson	816-221-1024	P	251	2.5
Faxon, RoweCom's Academic	15 Southwest Pk	Westwood	MA	02090	Dan Tonkery	781-329-3350	D	250*	0.5
Logix Development Corp.	473 E Post St	Camarillo	CA	93010	David K Howington	805-384-1460	R	250*	1.0
Exodus Communications Inc.	2831 Miss Coll	Santa Clara	CA	95051	Ellen Hancock	408-346-2200	P	242	0.5
Congressional Quarterly Inc.	1414 22nd St NW	Washington	DC	20037		202-887-8500	S	230	0.3
eBay Inc.	2005 Hamilton Ave	San Jose	CA	95125	Margaret C Whitman	408-558-7400	P	225	0.1
Mosby Inc.	PO Box 28430	St. Louis	MO	63146	Patrick A Clifford	314-872-8370	S	212*	1.4
RCN Corp.	105 Carnegie Ctr	Princeton	NJ	08540	Michael A Adams	609-734-3700	P	211	2.2
CCC Information Services Group	444 Merch Mart	Chicago	IL	60654	David M Phillips	312-222-4636	P	208	1.5
ONSALE Inc.	1350 Willow Rd	Menlo Park	CA	94025	S Jerrold Kaplan	650-470-2400	P	208	0.2
Powerhouse Technologies Inc.	2311 S 7th Ave	Bozeman	MT	59715	Michael Eide	406-585-6600	P	201	1.4
Prodigy Communications Corp.	44 S Broadway	White Plains	NY	10601	Samer F Salameh	914-448-8000	P	189	0.4
EarthLink Network Inc.	1430 W Peachtree	Atlanta	GA	30309	Charles Brewer	404-815-0770	P	176	1.3
Data Transmission Network Corp.	9110 W Dodge Rd	Omaha	NE	68114	Roger R Brodersen	402-390-2328	P	167	0.9
4Front Technologies Inc.	6300 S Syracuse	Englewood	CO	80111	Anil Doshi	303-721-7341	P	149	1.3
BAE Systems	6500 Tracor Ln	Austin	TX	78725		512-929-2053	D	148*	0.8
Concentric Network Corp.	1400 Parkmoor Ave	San Jose	CA	95126	Henry R Nothhaft	408-342-2800	P	148	0.6
OCLC Online Computer Library	6565 Frantz Rd	Dublin	OH	43017	Jay Jordan	614-764-6000	R	146	1.1
Seitel Inc.	50 Briar Hollow Ln	Houston	TX	77027	Paul A Frame	713-881-8900	P	145	0.1
Go.com	1399 Moffett	Sunnyvale	CA	94089	Harry Motro	408-543-6000	P	137	0.3
Inter Voice-Brite Inc.	250 International	Heathrow	FL	32746	David Berger	972-454-8000	R	137	0.7
Lycos Inc.	400-2 Totten Pond	Waltham	MA	02451	Robert J Davis	781-320-2700	P	135	0.8
Physician Computer Network Inc.	1200 The American	Morris Plains	NJ	07950	Carter Evans	973-490-3100	P	133	0.4
J.J. Kenny Company Inc.	65 Broadway	New York	NY	10006	Robert Hunter	212-770-4000	S	132*	0.6
Interactive Data Corp.	22 Crosby Dr	Bedford	MA	01730	Stuart Clark	781-687-8800	S	126*	0.5
QuickResponse Services Inc.	1400 Marina Way, S	Richmond	CA	94804	Shawn M O'Connor	510-215-5000	P	125	0.3
Network Communications Inc.	PO Box 100001	Lawrenceville	GA	30046	K Hughes	770-962-7220	R	124*	0.7
Amadeus Global Travel	9250 N W 36th St	Miami	FL	33178	Jim Davidson		S	121*	0.7
Verio Inc.	8005 S Chester St	Englewood	CO	80112	Herbert R Hribar	303-645-1900	P	121	1.4
Mindspring Inc.	1430 W Peach Tree	Atlanta	GA	30309	Charles Brewer	404-287-0770	P	115	1.6
RealSelect Inc.	225 Hillcrest Dr	Thousand Oaks	CA	91360	Mike Buckman	805-557-2300	R	110*	0.5
Yellow Services Inc.	10990 Roe Ave	Overland Park	KS	66211	Thomas L Smith	913-491-6363	S	109*	0.5
Data Broadcasting Corp.	3490 Clubhouse Dr	Jackson	WY	83001	Stuart Clark	307-733-9742	P	108	0.6

Source: Ward's Business Directory of U.S. Private and Public Companies, Volumes 1 and 2, 2000. The company type code used is as follows: P - Public, R - Private, S - Subsidiary, D - Division, J - Joint Venture, A - Affiliate, G - Group, N - Company type not reported. Sales are in millions of dollars, employees are in thousands. An asterisk (*) indicates an estimated sales volume. The symbol < stands for 'less than'. Company names and addresses are truncated, in some cases, to fit into the available space.

LOCATION BY STATE AND REGIONAL CONCENTRATION

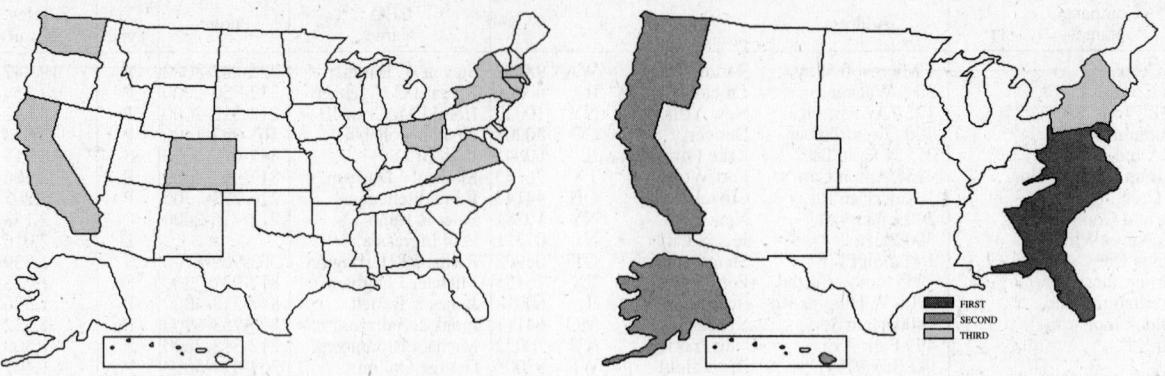

INDUSTRY DATA BY STATE

State	Establishments Total (number)	% of U.S.	Employment Total (number)	% of U.S.	Per Estab.	Payroll Total ($ mil.)	Per Empl. ($)	Revenues Total ($ mil.)	% of U.S.	Per Estab. ($)
Virginia	150	3.6	6,772	13.6	45	684.2	101,040	2,497.3	31.1	16,648,613
California	722	17.3	9,822	19.7	14	454.4	46,265	1,404.6	17.5	1,945,443
New York	266	6.4	6,401	12.8	24	192.6	30,081	761.3	9.5	2,862,015
Massachusetts	159	3.8	2,738	5.5	17	156.8	57,278	427.2	5.3	2,686,673
Ohio	125	3.0	1,609	3.2	13	64.3	39,981	383.9	4.8	3,071,248
Texas	274	6.6	2,378	4.8	9	80.0	33,624	258.6	3.2	943,796
Illinois	152	3.6	1,311	2.6	9	52.5	40,013	217.6	2.7	1,431,493
Colorado	122	2.9	1,783	3.6	15	79.7	44,700	211.3	2.6	1,731,910
Florida	235	5.6	1,866	3.7	8	58.0	31,072	198.0	2.5	842,762
Pennsylvania	140	3.4	1,658	3.3	12	58.3	35,145	191.2	2.4	1,365,400
Washington	142	3.4	1,607	3.2	11	71.0	44,199	168.9	2.1	1,189,549
New Jersey	119	2.9	910	1.8	8	39.4	43,254	139.1	1.7	1,169,319
Connecticut	59	1.4	551	1.1	9	24.5	44,461	106.0	1.3	1,796,576
Michigan	95	2.3	997	2.0	10	35.5	35,645	105.9	1.3	1,114,326
Maryland	86	2.1	1,008	2.0	12	42.1	41,732	104.5	1.3	1,214,965
Georgia	97	2.3	881	1.8	9	38.1	43,238	93.0	1.2	958,897
Minnesota	80	1.9	566	1.1	7	18.5	32,751	81.9	1.0	1,024,125
Oklahoma	46	1.1	512	1.0	11	16.1	31,514	62.2	0.8	1,351,609
North Carolina	90	2.2	403	0.8	4	13.1	32,427	47.4	0.6	526,633
Wisconsin	66	1.6	454	0.9	7	11.9	26,251	41.5	0.5	629,348
Missouri	77	1.8	368	0.7	5	10.0	27,277	39.6	0.5	514,636
Indiana	59	1.4	314	0.6	5	7.1	22,462	39.6	0.5	670,932
Oregon	75	1.8	433	0.9	6	12.2	28,199	36.6	0.5	487,493
Arizona	48	1.2	322	0.6	7	9.8	30,339	36.1	0.4	751,729
Nevada	50	1.2	226	0.5	5	8.8	39,137	33.7	0.4	674,300
Iowa	46	1.1	437	0.9	10	17.4	39,815	32.3	0.4	702,196
Tennessee	57	1.4	374	0.7	7	11.6	31,142	31.0	0.4	543,614
Kansas	38	0.9	228	0.5	6	8.3	36,219	30.9	0.4	814,237
Utah	45	1.1	336	0.7	7	7.4	22,173	23.7	0.3	527,000
New Hampshire	29	0.7	180	0.4	6	7.0	38,639	22.7	0.3	783,724
New Mexico	33	0.8	148	0.3	4	5.5	37,155	17.7	0.2	535,182
Kentucky	34	0.8	222	0.4	7	5.9	26,369	17.6	0.2	517,029
Louisiana	36	0.9	237	0.5	7	4.2	17,527	15.6	0.2	433,389
Nebraska	22	0.5	115	0.2	5	2.8	24,070	15.5	0.2	704,136
Mississippi	21	0.5	157	0.3	7	3.0	18,987	12.5	0.2	597,286
Arkansas	24	0.6	131	0.3	5	2.5	18,947	11.1	0.1	461,917
Alabama	34	0.8	113	0.2	3	2.3	20,062	9.5	0.1	279,912
Alaska	15	0.4	91	0.2	6	2.9	32,352	9.1	0.1	608,933
South Carolina	32	0.8	175*	-	-	(D)	-	(D)	-	-
Maine	27	0.6	375*	-	-	(D)	-	(D)	-	-
Hawaii	19	0.5	60*	-	-	(D)	-	(D)	-	-
Montana	18	0.4	175*	-	-	(D)	-	(D)	-	-
D.C.	17	0.4	375*	-	-	(D)	-	(D)	-	-
Idaho	14	0.3	60*	-	-	(D)	-	(D)	-	-
Vermont	13	0.3	60*	-	-	(D)	-	(D)	-	-
Rhode Island	11	0.3	60*	-	-	(D)	-	(D)	-	-
South Dakota	11	0.3	60*	-	-	(D)	-	(D)	-	-
West Virginia	11	0.3	60*	-	-	(D)	-	(D)	-	-
Wyoming	10	0.2	60*	-	-	(D)	-	(D)	-	-
Delaware	7	0.2	60*	-	-	(D)	-	(D)	-	-
North Dakota	7	0.2	60*	-	-	(D)	-	(D)	-	-

Source: 1997 *Economic Census*. The states are in descending order of revenues or establishments (if revenue data are missing for the majority). The symbol (D) appears when data are withheld to prevent disclosure of competitive information. States marked with (D) are sorted by number of establishments. A dash (-) indicates that the data element cannot be calculated. * indicates the midpoint of a range; 175, for example is the range 100-249. Shaded *states* on the state map indicate those states which have proportionately greater representation in the industry than would be indicated by the state's population; the ratio is based on total revenues or number of establishments. Shaded *regions* indicate where the industry is regionally most concentrated.

NAICS 514199 - INFORMATION SERVICES NEC

GENERAL STATISTICS

Year	Establishments (number)	Employment (number)	Payroll ($ million)	Revenues ($ million)	Employees per Establishment (number)	Revenues per Establishment ($)	Payroll per Employee ($)
1997	317	5,805	283.0	795.0	18.3	2,507,886	48,751

Source: Economic Census of the United States, 1997. This is a newly defined industry. Data for prior years were unavailable at the time of publication but may become available over time.

INDICES OF CHANGE

Year	Establishments (number)	Employment (number)	Payroll ($ million)	Revenues ($ million)	Employees per Establishment (number)	Revenues per Establishment ($)	Payroll per Employee ($)
1997	100.0	100.0	100.0	100.0	100.0	100.0	100.0

Sources: Same as General Statistics. The values shown reflect change from the base year, 1997. Values above 100 mean greater than 1997, values below 100 mean less than 1997, and a value of 100 in the 1982-96 or 1998-2001 period means same as 1997. Values followed by a 'p' are projections by the editors; 'e' stands for extrapolation. Data are the most recent available at this level of detail.

SIC INDUSTRIES RELATED TO NAICS 514199

Each new NAICS code represents an industry that used to be part of an SIC or a part of several SIC industries. Data in this table are shown to provide transitional information for these cases. All available data for the precursor SIC(s) are shown. Even if only a part of an SIC is included in the NAICS, *all* data for the SIC are reproduced. If the SIC industry is not marked as being a part (pt) of the NAICS, the entire industry is embedded in the NAICS data. The SIC composition of the new industry provides some hints of the relative importance of its "ancestors." Data marked with a 'p' are projected. Projections begin with 1982 data. Data earlier than 1990 are not shown but are reflected in the projections.

SIC	Industry	1990	1991	1992	1993	1994	1995	1996	1997
7389	**Business Services, nec (pt)**								
	Establishments (number)	44,079	50,252	52,375	56,829	60,725	53,596	60,893p	63,269p
	Employment (thousands)	489.6	550.4	523.6	607.9	648.7	623.0	680.2p	710.9p
	Revenues ($ million)	-	-	32,885.9	-	-	-	-	-
8999	**Services, nec (pt)**								
	Establishments (number)	-	-	14,587	-	-	-	-	-
	Employment (thousands)	-	-	81.1	-	-	-	-	-
	Revenues ($ million)	-	-	7,966.2	-	-	-	-	-

Source: Economic Census of the United States, 1992, annual surveys of economic sectors conducted by the Bureau of the Census, and estimates or projections based on the 1982-1992 period; not all data are shown. 'e' marks estimates made by the editors; 'p' indicates projections based on time series. A dash (-) indicates that data for this SIC or year were not available. The abbreviation (pt) next to the industry name indicates that only a part of the industry is present within the NAICS data. If no (pt) is shown, the entire industry is contained within the NAICS data.

SELECTED RATIOS

For 1997	Avg. of Information	Analyzed Industry	Index	For 1997	Avg. of Information	Analyzed Industry	Index
Employees per establishment	27	18	68	Payroll per establishment	1,131,090	892,744	79
Revenue per establishment	5,444,104	2,507,886	46	Payroll as % of revenue	21	36	171
Revenue per employee	203,255	136,951	67	Payroll per employee	42,229	48,751	115

Sources: Same as General Statistics. The 'Average' column represents the average for the industry sector, in 1997, where the currently shown industry is classified. The Index shows the relationship between the Average and the Analyzed Industry. For example, 100 means that they are equal; 500 that the Analyzed Industry is five times the average; 50 means that the Analyzed Industry is half the national average. The abbreviation 'na' is used to show that data are 'not available'.

LEADING COMPANIES

No company data available for this industry.

LOCATION BY STATE AND REGIONAL CONCENTRATION

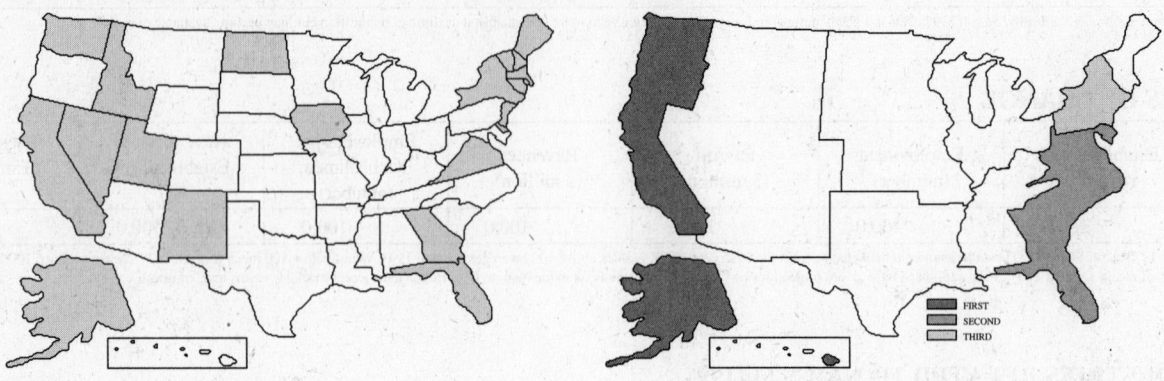

FIRST
SECOND
THIRD

INDUSTRY DATA BY STATE

State	Establishments Total (number)	% of U.S.	Employment Total (number)	% of U.S.	Per Estab.	Payroll Total ($ mil.)	Per Empl. ($)	Revenues Total ($ mil.)	% of U.S.	Per Estab. ($)
California	50	15.8	1,559	26.9	31	103.6	66,449	289.1	36.4	5,782,700
Texas	19	6.0	426	7.3	22	23.6	55,437	87.7	11.0	4,615,632
New York	33	10.4	541	9.3	16	24.4	45,098	76.8	9.7	2,327,364
Florida	19	6.0	199	3.4	10	4.4	22,055	13.8	1.7	728,526
Washington	10	3.2	60	1.0	6	3.5	58,167	11.0	1.4	1,101,100
Georgia	10	3.2	62	1.1	6	2.7	42,968	9.9	1.2	991,900
Pennsylvania	9	2.8	81	1.4	9	3.9	47,642	9.4	1.2	1,042,000
Massachusetts	11	3.5	95	1.6	9	3.4	35,768	7.3	0.9	662,182
Kentucky	4	1.3	62	1.1	15	2.2	35,145	4.2	0.5	1,059,000
North Carolina	6	1.9	24	0.4	4	0.4	16,958	1.4	0.2	240,333
Minnesota	5	1.6	17	0.3	3	0.4	23,118	1.1	0.1	222,400
Michigan	6	1.9	11	0.2	2	0.3	29,455	1.0	0.1	174,500
Colorado	4	1.3	12	0.2	3	0.3	28,583	1.0	0.1	247,500
Missouri	4	1.3	16	0.3	4	0.2	13,875	0.7	0.1	172,500
Rhode Island	3	0.9	2	0.0	1	-	17,000	0.1	0.0	48,000
Virginia	13	4.1	375*	-	-	(D)	-	(D)	-	-
New Jersey	12	3.8	60*	-	-	(D)	-	(D)	-	-
Illinois	11	3.5	60*	-	-	(D)	-	(D)	-	-
Alaska	10	3.2	60*	-	-	(D)	-	(D)	-	-
D.C.	8	2.5	60*	-	-	(D)	-	(D)	-	-
Connecticut	6	1.9	375*	-	-	(D)	-	(D)	-	-
Ohio	6	1.9	1,750*	-	-	(D)	-	(D)	-	-
Louisiana	5	1.6	60*	-	-	(D)	-	(D)	-	-
Maryland	5	1.6	60*	-	-	(D)	-	(D)	-	-
Arizona	4	1.3	60*	-	-	(D)	-	(D)	-	-
Iowa	4	1.3	60*	-	-	(D)	-	(D)	-	-
New Mexico	4	1.3	10*	-	-	(D)	-	(D)	-	-
Utah	4	1.3	60*	-	-	(D)	-	(D)	-	-
Delaware	3	0.9	60*	-	-	(D)	-	(D)	-	-
Idaho	3	0.9	60*	-	-	(D)	-	(D)	-	-
Maine	3	0.9	10*	-	-	(D)	-	(D)	-	-
New Hampshire	3	0.9	10*	-	-	(D)	-	(D)	-	-
Tennessee	3	0.9	10*	-	-	(D)	-	(D)	-	-
Arkansas	2	0.6	10*	-	-	(D)	-	(D)	-	-
Kansas	2	0.6	10*	-	-	(D)	-	(D)	-	-
Nevada	2	0.6	10*	-	-	(D)	-	(D)	-	-
Oklahoma	2	0.6	10*	-	-	(D)	-	(D)	-	-
West Virginia	2	0.6	10*	-	-	(D)	-	(D)	-	-
Hawaii	1	0.3	10*	-	-	(D)	-	(D)	-	-
Mississippi	1	0.3	10*	-	-	(D)	-	(D)	-	-
Nebraska	1	0.3	10*	-	-	(D)	-	(D)	-	-
North Dakota	1	0.3	60*	-	-	(D)	-	(D)	-	-
South Carolina	1	0.3	10*	-	-	(D)	-	(D)	-	-
Vermont	1	0.3	10*	-	-	(D)	-	(D)	-	-
Wisconsin	1	0.3	10*	-	-	(D)	-	(D)	-	-

Source: 1997 *Economic Census*. The states are in descending order of revenues or establishments (if revenue data are missing for the majority). The symbol (D) appears when data are withheld to prevent disclosure of competitive information. States marked with (D) are sorted by number of establishments. A dash (-) indicates that the data element cannot be calculated. * indicates the midpoint of a range; 175, for example is the range 100-249. Shaded *states* on the state map indicate those states which have proportionately greater representation in the industry than would be indicated by the state's population; the ratio is based on total revenues or number of establishments. Shaded *regions* indicate where the industry is regionally most concentrated.

NAICS 514210 - DATA PROCESSING SERVICES

GENERAL STATISTICS

Year	Establishments (number)	Employment (number)	Payroll ($ million)	Revenues ($ million)	Employees per Establishment (number)	Revenues per Establishment ($)	Payroll per Employee ($)
1997	7,588	262,250	9,774.0	30,837.0	34.6	4,063,917	37,270

Source: *Economic Census of the United States*, 1997. This is a newly defined industry. Data for prior years were unavailable at the time of publication but may become available over time.

INDICES OF CHANGE

Year	Establishments (number)	Employment (number)	Payroll ($ million)	Revenues ($ million)	Employees per Establishment (number)	Revenues per Establishment ($)	Payroll per Employee ($)
1997	100.0	100.0	100.0	100.0	100.0	100.0	100.0

Sources: Same as General Statistics. The values shown reflect change from the base year, 1997. Values above 100 mean greater than 1997, values below 100 mean less than 1997, and a value of 100 in the 1982-96 or 1998-2001 period means same as 1997. Values followed by a 'p' are projections by the editors; 'e' stands for extrapolation. Data are the most recent available at this level of detail.

SIC INDUSTRIES RELATED TO NAICS 514210

Each new NAICS code represents an industry that used to be part of an SIC or a part of several SIC industries. Data in this table are shown to provide transitional information for these cases. All available data for the precursor SIC(s) are shown. Even if only a part of an SIC is included in the NAICS, *all* data for the SIC are reproduced. If the SIC industry is not marked as being a part (pt) of the NAICS, the entire industry is embedded in the NAICS data. The SIC composition of the new industry provides some hints of the relative importance of its "ancestors." Data marked with a 'p' are projected. Projections begin with 1982 data. Data earlier than 1990 are not shown but are reflected in the projections.

SIC	Industry	1990	1991	1992	1993	1994	1995	1996	1997
7374	**Data Processing Services**								
	Establishments (number)	6,773	6,821	7,286	7,093	7,093	7,914	7,460*p*	7,532*p*
	Employment (thousands)	228.9	225.2	230.3	235.7	236.8	270.1	259.5*p*	265.4*p*
	Revenues ($ million)	17,820.0	18,824.0	20,477.0	23,716.0	29,177.0	35,607.0	41,036.0	34,478.4*p*
7379	**Computer Related Services, nec (pt)**								
	Establishments (number)	6,823	8,133	8,722	11,174	13,820	17,688	16,728*p*	18,269*p*
	Employment (thousands)	51.2	59.0	57.7	76.4	87.7	115.0	107.4*p*	116.3*p*
	Revenues ($ million)	4,537.0	4,894.0	6,234.0	7,845.0	10,285.0	13,176.0	16,504.0	11,341.1*p*
7389	**Business Services, nec (pt)**								
	Establishments (number)	44,079	50,252	52,375	56,829	60,725	53,596	60,893*p*	63,269*p*
	Employment (thousands)	489.6	550.4	523.6	607.9	648.7	623.0	680.2*p*	710.9*p*
	Revenues ($ million)	-	-	32,885.9	-	-	-	-	-

Source: *Economic Census of the United States*, 1992, annual surveys of economic sectors conducted by the Bureau of the Census, and estimates or projections based on the 1982-1992 period; not all data are shown. 'e' marks estimates made by the editors; 'p' indicates projections based on time series. A dash (-) indicates that data for this SIC or year were not available. The abbreviation (pt) next to the industry name indicates that only a part of the industry is present within the NAICS data. If no (pt) is shown, the entire industry is contained within the NAICS data.

SELECTED RATIOS

For 1997	Avg. of Information	Analyzed Industry	Index	For 1997	Avg. of Information	Analyzed Industry	Index
Employees per establishment	27	35	129	Payroll per establishment	1,131,090	1,288,086	114
Revenue per establishment	5,444,104	4,063,917	75	Payroll as % of revenue	21	32	153
Revenue per employee	203,255	117,586	58	Payroll per employee	42,229	37,270	88

Sources: Same as General Statistics. The 'Average' column represents the average for the industry sector, in 1997, where the currently shown industry is classified. The Index shows the relationship between the Average and the Analyzed Industry. For example, 100 means that they are equal; 500 that the Analyzed Industry is five times the average; 50 means that the Analyzed Industry is half the national average. The abbreviation 'na' is used to show that data are 'not available'.

LEADING COMPANIES   Number shown: **75**   Total sales ($ mil): **681,406**   Total employment (000): **1,303.1**

Company Name	Address				CEO Name	Phone	Co. Type	Sales ($ mil)	Empl. (000)
Bank One Corp.	1 First National Plz	Chicago	IL	60670	James Dimon	312-732-4000	P	398,241*	86.2
General Motors Corp.	100 Renaissance Ctr	Detroit	MI	48243	John F Smith Jr	313-556-5000	P	176,558	594.0
American Express Co.	W Fin Ctr	New York	NY	10285	Kenneth I Chenault	212-640-2000	P	19,483	85.0
Electronic Data Systems Corp.	5400 Legacy Dr	Plano	TX	75024	Richard H Brown	972-604-6000	P	18,534	121.0
TRW Inc.	1900 Richmond Rd	Cleveland	OH	44124	Joseph Gorman	216-291-7000	P	16,969	78.0
ALLTEL Corp.	1 Allied Dr	Little Rock	AR	72202	Joe T Ford	501-905-8000	P	6,302	21.5
Automatic Data Processing Inc.	1 ADP Blvd	Roseland	NJ	07068	Gary C Butler	973-994-5000	P	5,540	37.0
First Data Corp.	5660 New Northside	Atlanta	GA	30328	Henry C Duques	770-857-7001	P	5,540	32.0
Pershing and Co.	1 Pershing Plz	Jersey City	NJ	07399		201-413-2000	D	3,460	2.8
Express Scripts Inc.	13900 Riverport Dr	Maryland H.	MO	63043	Barrett A Toan	314-770-1666	P	2,825	3.4
Telephone and Data Systems Inc.	30 N LaSalle St	Chicago	IL	60602	LeRoy T Carlson Jr	312-630-1900	P	1,963	9.9
Affiliated Computer Services Inc.	2828 N Haskell	Dallas	TX	75204	Darwin Deason	214-841-6111	P	1,642	16.0
Ceridian Corp.	8100 34th Ave S	Minneapolis	MN	55425	Lawrence Perlman	612-853-8100	S	1,342	9.6
Kansas City Southern Industries	114 W 11th St	Kansas City	MO	64105	Landon H Rowland	816-983-1303	P	1,248	4.5
American Management Systems	4050 Legato Rd	Fairfax	VA	22033	Paul A Brands	703-267-8000	P	1,240	9.0
DST Systems Inc.	333 W 11th St	Kansas City	MO	64105	Thomas McDonnell	816-435-1000	P	1,203	8.6
ALLIED Group Inc.	701 5th Ave	Des Moines	IA	50391	Douglas L Andeson	515-280-4211	S	1,201	2.4
ALLTEL Information Services Inc	4001 RParham	Little Rock	AR	72212	Jeffrey H Fox	501-220-5100	S	1,162	8.1
Western Geophysical Co.	PO Box 2469	Houston	TX	77252	R White	713-789-9600	S	1,000*	6.0
Shared Medical Systems Corp.	51 Valley Stream	Malvern	PA	19355	Marvin S Cadwell	610-219-6300	P	915	7.6
Broadwing	PO Box 2301	Cincinnati	OH	45201	Richard G Ellenberger	513-397-9900	P	885	20.8
National Data Corp.	2 Nat Data	Atlanta	GA	30329	Robert A Yellowlees	404-728-2000	P	785	6.0
Lockheed Martin IMS	300 Frank Burr Blvd	Teaneck	NJ	07666	John Brophy	201-692-2900	S	750*	4.0
GE Information Services	11555 Darnestown	Gaithersburg	MD	20877	Harvey F Seegers	301-340-4000	D	700*	2.6
Alltel Information Services	1 Allied Dr	Little Rock	AR	72202	Joe Ford	501-661-8000	R	663*	4.0
National Computer Systems Inc.	PO Box 9365	Eden Prairie	MN	55344	Russell A Gullotti	612-829-3000	P	629	3.7
Rurban Financial Corp.	P O Box 467	Defiance	OH	43512	Thomas C Williams	419-782-8950	P	537	0.1
Computer Horizons Corp.	49 Old Bloomfield	Mountain Lakes	NJ	07046	John J Cassese	973-299-4000	P	535	4.1
GTE Data Services Inc.	P O Box 290152	Temple Terrace	FL	33687	Don A Hayes	813-978-4000	S	520	4.0
National Processing Inc.	1231 Durrett Ln	Louisville	KY	40285	Robert E Showalter	502-315-2000	P	483	10.8
SunTrust Service Corp.	250 Piedmont Ave	Atlanta	GA	30308	Robert Long	404-588-7711	S	476*	3.3
BISYS Group Inc.	150 Clove Rd	Little Falls	NJ	07424	Lynn J Mangum	973-812-8600	P	473	3.1
First Decatur Bancshares Inc.	130 N Water St	Decatur	IL	62525	Phillip C Wise	217-424-1111	P	442	0.3
M and I Data Services Div.	P O Box 23528	Milwaukee	WI	53223	Joe L Delgadillo	414-357-2560	D	431	3.8
National Processing Co.	101 Bullit Ln	Louisville	KY	40222	Bob Showalter	502-326-7000	S	406	10.6
Total System Services Inc.	PO Box 1755	Columbus	GA	31902	Phillip W Tomlinson	706-649-2204	P	396	3.9
Veritas DGC Inc.	3701 Kirby Dr	Houston	TX	77098	Stephen J Ludlow	713-512-8300	P	389	2.8
Habersham Bancorp.	P O Box 1980	Cornelia	GA	30531	Davide D Stovall	706-778-1000	P	384	0.3
SPS Transaction Services Inc.	2500 Lake Cook Rd	Riverwoods	IL	60015	Thomas C Schneider	847-405-3700	P	347	3.7
Boston Financial Data Services	2 Heritage Dr	North Quincy	MA	02171	Joseph Hooley	617-328-5000	J	330*	2.0
Electronic Data Systems Corp	5400 Legacy Dr	Plano	TX	75024	Jeff Kelly	972-605-6000	D	282*	3.0
NDCE Commerce	Four Corporate Sq	Atlanta	GA	30329	Paul Garcia	404-235-4400	S	279*	1.6
MedQuist Inc.	5 Greentree Centre	Marlton	NJ	08053	David Cohen	856-596-8877	P	272	2.4
First Data Resources Inc.	7373 Scottsdale Rd	Scottsdale	AZ	85253	Aldo Tesi	602-331-2800	S	240*	35.0
ADP Claims Solutions Group Inc.	2010 Crow Canyon	San Ramon	CA	94583	John Barfitt	925-866-1100	D	206*	1.5
JM Smith Corp.	P O Box 1779	Spartanburg	SC	29304	Bill Cobb	864-582-1216	R	200	0.4
Vital Processing Services L.L.C.	PO Box 64084	Phoenix	AZ	85082	Johnathan J Palmer	602-333-7500	J	200*	0.8
Dynamics Research Corp.	60 Frontage Rd	Andover	MA	01810	John Anderegg Jr	978-475-9090	P	192	1.6
BA Merchant Services Inc.	1 S Van Ness Ave	San Francisco	CA	94103	Sharif M Bayyari	415-241-3390	S	188	1.0
ENVOY Corp.	15 Century Blvd	Nashville	TN	37214	Fred C Goad Jr	615-885-3700	S	185	0.6
Chesapeake Utilities Corp.	909 Silver Lake	Dover	DE	19904	Ralph J Adkins	302-734-6799	P	184	0.5
CAD MUS	P O Box 27481	Richmond	VA	23261	Steve Gillispie	804-264-2711	D	132*	0.8
Bowne Business Services Inc.	161 N Clark	New York	NY	10014	Robert M Johnson	312-418-7600	S	129	1.9
Securities Industry Automation	2 Metro Tech Ctr	Brooklyn	NY	11201	Charles B McQuade	212-383-4800	S	128*	1.4
APEX Data Services Inc.	198 Van Buren St	Herndon	VA	20170	Shashikant Gupta	703-709-3000	R	115*	2.1
Health Management Systems Inc.	401 Park Ave S	New York	NY	10016	Paul J Kerz	212-685-4545	P	115	1.0
Vestcom International Inc.	1100 Valley Brook	Lyndhurst	NJ	07071	Joel Cartun	201-935-7666	P	109	1.1
Jones International Inc.	9697 E Mineral Ave	Englewood	CO	80112	Glenn Jones	303-792-3111	S	105*	0.6
BRC Holdings Inc.	1111 W Mockngbrd	Dallas	TX	75247	Perry E Esping	214-688-1800	P	104	1.0
Federated Systems Group	5985 State Bridge	Duluth	GA	30097	Jim Amann	678-474-2000	S	101*	1.1
Hickory Tech Corp.	P O Box 3248	Mankato	MN	56002	Robert D Alton Jr	507-387-3355	P	97	0.5
TSYS Total Solutions Inc.	7101 Stone Mill	Columbus	GA	31990	Clifford Mason	706-649-6800	S	90*	0.9
Multimedia Games Inc.	8900 Schoal Creek	Austin	TX	78759	Gordon T Graves	512-371-7100	P	89	0.2
BISYS Inc.	11 Greenway Plz	Houston	TX	77046	Paul H Bourke	713-622-8911	S	80*	0.5
ProBusiness Services Inc.	4125 Hopyard Rd	Pleasanton	CA	94588	Thomas H Sinton	925-737-3500	P	70	0.8
ImageMax	1100 E Hector	Conshohocken	PA	19428	Dave Model	610-832-2111	R	70	1.0
Litton Industries Inc	5490 Canoga Ave	Woodland Hills	CA	91367	Henry Bodurka	818-715-5200	D	69*	0.3
Systems Management Specialists	3 Hutton Center Dr	Santa Ana	CA	92707	Patrick Dolan	714-850-6600	R	67*	0.6
Muller Data Corp.	395 Hudson St	New York	NY	10014	Stuart Clark	212-807-3800	S	66*	0.4
Gelco Information Network Inc.	10700 Prairie Lakes	Eden Prairie	MN	55344	Neil Zill	612-947-1500	R	59*	0.4
Computer Services Inc.	3901 Technology Dr	Paducah	KY	42001	Steven A Powless	270-442-7361	P	54	0.5
Sunrise Intern. Leasing Corp.	5500 Wayzata Blvd	Golden Valley	MN	55416	Peter J King	612-593-1904	P	52	<0.1
Kinney Service Corp.	3543 Simpson Ferry	Camp Hill	PA	17011	Roger Farah	717-763-5200	S	50*	0.5
Midwest Payment Systems Co.	38 Fountain Suare	Cincinnati	OH	45263	George Landery	513-579-5447	S	50*	0.4
CenturyTel Telecommunications	P O Box 846	San Marcos	TX	78667		512-754-1414	S	49*	0.3

Source: Ward's Business Directory of U.S. Private and Public Companies, Volumes 1 and 2, 2000. The company type code used is as follows: P - Public, R - Private, S - Subsidiary, D - Division, J - Joint Venture, A - Affiliate, G - Group, N - Company type not reported. Sales are in millions of dollars, employees are in thousands. An asterisk (*) indicates an estimated sales volume. The symbol < stands for 'less than'. Company names and addresses are truncated, in some cases, to fit into the available space.

LOCATION BY STATE AND REGIONAL CONCENTRATION

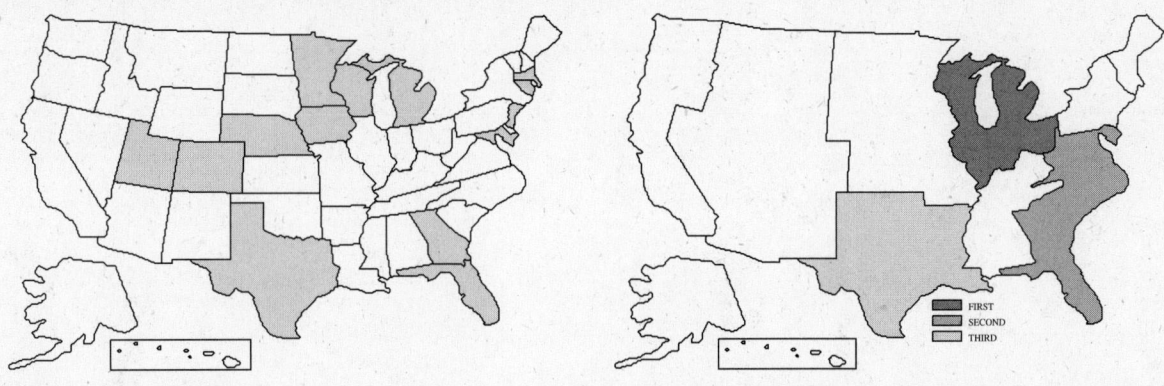

INDUSTRY DATA BY STATE

State	Establishments Total (number)	% of U.S.	Employment Total (number)	% of U.S.	Per Estab.	Payroll Total ($ mil.)	Per Empl. ($)	Revenues Total ($ mil.)	% of U.S.	Per Estab. ($)
Texas	567	7.5	27,088	10.3	48	1,275.0	47,071	3,484.4	11.3	6,145,386
Michigan	383	5.0	21,436	8.2	56	872.6	40,708	3,469.0	11.2	9,057,339
California	860	11.3	20,679	7.9	24	775.9	37,521	2,493.9	8.1	2,899,891
New York	627	8.3	23,011	8.8	37	642.9	27,940	1,901.5	6.2	3,032,662
Florida	381	5.0	13,210	5.0	35	572.3	43,322	1,670.1	5.4	4,383,591
Nebraska	85	1.1	10,165	3.9	120	400.6	39,407	1,405.3	4.6	16,532,647
Georgia	212	2.8	8,947	3.4	42	322.9	36,095	1,351.5	4.4	6,375,071
Massachusetts	246	3.2	10,322	3.9	42	389.7	37,752	1,242.9	4.0	5,052,553
Maryland	192	2.5	7,013	2.7	37	263.4	37,556	1,080.4	3.5	5,627,010
New Jersey	334	4.4	7,137	2.7	21	325.8	45,644	1,019.5	3.3	3,052,467
Connecticut	172	2.3	6,882	2.6	40	290.6	42,224	879.5	2.9	5,113,401
Illinois	376	5.0	7,959	3.0	21	264.5	33,236	852.6	2.8	2,267,585
Ohio	304	4.0	8,753	3.3	29	314.8	35,965	840.9	2.7	2,766,043
Pennsylvania	285	3.8	8,274	3.2	29	278.3	33,639	761.6	2.5	2,672,168
Wisconsin	133	1.8	5,530	2.1	42	206.5	37,337	692.5	2.2	5,206,526
Minnesota	153	2.0	5,909	2.3	39	205.3	34,748	685.3	2.2	4,479,314
Missouri	144	1.9	6,527	2.5	45	224.9	34,459	600.9	1.9	4,172,993
Virginia	233	3.1	6,947	2.6	30	277.0	39,877	582.4	1.9	2,499,451
Iowa	67	0.9	5,925	2.3	88	154.4	26,061	533.7	1.7	7,966,418
North Carolina	123	1.6	3,489	1.3	28	130.6	37,434	513.3	1.7	4,172,984
Indiana	156	2.1	3,925	1.5	25	134.9	34,367	478.9	1.6	3,070,179
Colorado	203	2.7	5,648	2.2	28	216.7	38,375	467.8	1.5	2,304,537
Kentucky	75	1.0	4,569	1.7	61	111.0	24,290	337.9	1.1	4,504,760
Utah	64	0.8	2,743	1.0	43	54.9	20,021	327.5	1.1	5,116,875
Arizona	123	1.6	3,236	1.2	26	108.6	33,569	280.2	0.9	2,277,935
Tennessee	96	1.3	2,394	0.9	25	93.0	38,837	274.8	0.9	2,862,302
Oklahoma	86	1.1	2,323	0.9	27	72.3	31,128	234.7	0.8	2,729,535
Arkansas	41	0.5	2,075	0.8	51	84.7	40,842	214.6	0.7	5,233,732
Alabama	74	1.0	2,376	0.9	32	76.5	32,213	208.5	0.7	2,817,514
Washington	134	1.8	1,982	0.8	15	71.2	35,936	194.3	0.6	1,449,739
D.C.	37	0.5	1,267	0.5	34	48.9	38,599	189.1	0.6	5,110,865
Kansas	58	0.8	1,303	0.5	22	41.5	31,843	144.5	0.5	2,492,241
Oregon	66	0.9	1,057	0.4	16	35.6	33,677	122.9	0.4	1,861,379
Louisiana	80	1.1	1,028	0.4	13	27.4	26,613	118.4	0.4	1,479,675
Montana	33	0.4	573	0.2	17	19.8	34,468	78.7	0.3	2,383,697
Maine	37	0.5	384	0.1	10	13.5	35,216	55.9	0.2	1,511,622
Mississippi	26	0.3	342	0.1	13	9.2	26,848	50.8	0.2	1,954,885
West Virginia	23	0.3	464	0.2	20	13.8	29,804	49.9	0.2	2,170,435
New Mexico	30	0.4	257	0.1	9	7.2	27,930	36.6	0.1	1,218,700
New Hampshire	44	0.6	439	0.2	10	13.9	31,667	31.6	0.1	717,659
Idaho	16	0.2	361	0.1	23	8.5	23,416	22.7	0.1	1,418,813
Nevada	28	0.4	102	0.0	4	4.2	40,784	22.2	0.1	793,036
Vermont	12	0.2	418	0.2	35	9.0	21,457	20.1	0.1	1,672,000
Hawaii	30	0.4	187	0.1	6	6.7	35,930	17.9	0.1	598,300
Alaska	8	0.1	23	0.0	3	0.7	32,261	2.2	0.0	280,375
South Carolina	37	0.5	3,750*	-	-	(D)	-	(D)	-	-
Rhode Island	36	0.5	1,750*	-	-	(D)	-	(D)	-	-
Delaware	24	0.3	1,750*	-	-	(D)	-	(D)	-	-
North Dakota	17	0.2	1,750*	-	-	(D)	-	(D)	-	-
South Dakota	9	0.1	60*	-	-	(D)	-	(D)	-	-
Wyoming	8	0.1	60*	-	-	(D)	-	(D)	-	-

Source: 1997 *Economic Census*. The states are in descending order of revenues or establishments (if revenue data are missing for the majority). The symbol (D) appears when data are withheld to prevent disclosure of competitive information. States marked with (D) are sorted by number of establishments. A dash (-) indicates that the data element cannot be calculated. * indicates the midpoint of a range; 175, for example is the range 100-249. Shaded *states* on the state map indicate those states which have proportionately greater representation in the industry than would be indicated by the state's population; the ratio is based on total revenues or number of establishments. Shaded *regions* indicate where the industry is regionally most concentrated.

Part II

FINANCE AND INSURANCE

Part II
FINANCE AND INSURANCE

NAICS 521110 - MONETARY AUTHORITIES - CENTRAL BANK

GENERAL STATISTICS

Year	Establishments (number)	Employment (number)	Payroll ($ million)	Revenues ($ million)	Employees per Establishment (number)	Revenues per Establishment ($)	Payroll per Employee ($)
1997	42	21,674	903.0	24,582.0	516.0	585,285,714	41,663

Source: Economic Census of the United States, 1997. This is a newly defined industry. Data for prior years were unavailable at the time of publication but may become available over time.

INDICES OF CHANGE

Year	Establishments (number)	Employment (number)	Payroll ($ million)	Revenues ($ million)	Employees per Establishment (number)	Revenues per Establishment ($)	Payroll per Employee ($)
1997	100.0	100.0	100.0	100.0	100.0	100.0	100.0

Sources: Same as General Statistics. The values shown reflect change from the base year, 1997. Values above 100 mean greater than 1997, values below 100 mean less than 1997, and a value of 100 in the 1982-96 or 1998-2001 period means same as 1997. Values followed by a 'p' are projections by the editors; 'e' stands for extrapolation. Data are the most recent available at this level of detail.

SIC INDUSTRIES RELATED TO NAICS 521110

Each new NAICS code represents an industry that used to be part of an SIC or a part of several SIC industries. Data in this table are shown to provide transitional information for these cases. All available data for the precursor SIC(s) are shown. Even if only a part of an SIC is included in the NAICS, *all* data for the SIC are reproduced. If the SIC industry is not marked as being a part (pt) of the NAICS, the entire industry is embedded in the NAICS data. The SIC composition of the new industry provides some hints of the relative importance of its "ancestors." Data marked with a 'p' are projected. Projections begin with 1982 data. Data earlier than 1990 are not shown but are reflected in the projections.

SIC	Industry	1990	1991	1992	1993	1994	1995	1996	1997
6011	**Federal Reserve Banks (pt)**	-	-	-	-	-	-	-	-

Source: Economic Census of the United States, 1992, annual surveys of economic sectors conducted by the Bureau of the Census, and estimates or projections based on the 1982-1992 period; not all data are shown. 'e' marks estimates made by the editors; 'p' indicates projections based on time series. A dash (-) indicates that data for this SIC or year were not available. The abbreviation (pt) next to the industry name indicates that only a part of the industry is present within the NAICS data. If no (pt) is shown, the entire industry is contained within the NAICS data.

SELECTED RATIOS

For 1997	Avg. of Information	Analyzed Industry	Index	For 1997	Avg. of Information	Analyzed Industry	Index
Employees per establishment	15	516	3,494	Payroll per establishment	669,406	21,500,000	3,212
Revenue per establishment	5,561,120	585,285,714	10,525	Payroll as % of revenue	12	4	31
Revenue per employee	376,639	1,134,170	301	Payroll per employee	45,337	41,663	92

Sources: Same as General Statistics. The 'Average' column represents the average for the industry sector, in 1997, where the currently shown industry is classified. The Index shows the relationship between the Average and the Analyzed Industry. For example, 100 means that they are equal; 500 that the Analyzed Industry is five times the average; 50 means that the Analyzed Industry is half the national average. The abbreviation 'na' is used to show that data are 'not available'.

LEADING COMPANIES   Number shown: **9**   Total sales ($ mil): **428,675**   Total employment (000): **37.5**

Company Name	Address				CEO Name	Phone	Co. Type	Sales ($ mil)	Empl. (000)
Federal Reserve Bank of New	33 Liberty St	New York	NY	10045	William J. McDonough	212-720-5000	R	197,870*	22.7
Federal Reserve Bank of San	PO Box 7702	San Francisco	CA	94120	Robert T Parry	415-974-2000	R	65,733	2.5
Federal Reserve Bank of Chicago	PO Box 834	Chicago	IL	60690	Michael H Moskow	312-322-5322	R	51,757*	1.7
Federal Reserve Bank of Atlanta	104 Marietta St N W	Atlanta	GA	30303	Jack Guynn	404-521-8020	R	36,711	2.4
Federal Reserve Bank	P O Box 6387	Cleveland	OH	44101	Jerry L Jordan	216-579-2000	R	33,200	1.4
Federal Reserve Bank of St. Louis	P O Box 442	St. Louis	MO	63166	William Poole	314-444-8444	R	18,786	1.2
Federal Reserve Bank of Kansas	925 Grand Blvd	Kansas City	MO	64198	Thomas M Hoenig	816-881-2000	R	14,276*	1.7
Federal Reserve Bank	90 Hennepin Ave	Minneapolis	MN	55401	Gary H Stern	612-204-5000	R	7,672	1.4
Federal Reserve Bank	P O Box 27622	Richmond	VA	23261	J Alfred Broaddus Jr	804-697-8000	R	2,670	2.6

Source: Ward's Business Directory of U.S. Private and Public Companies, Volumes 1 and 2, 2000. The company type code used is as follows: P - Public, R - Private, S - Subsidiary, D - Division, J - Joint Venture, A - Affiliate, G - Group, N - Company type not reported. Sales are in millions of dollars, employees are in thousands. An asterisk (*) indicates an estimated sales volume. The symbol < stands for 'less than'. Company names and addresses are truncated, in some cases, to fit into the available space.

LOCATION BY STATE AND REGIONAL CONCENTRATION

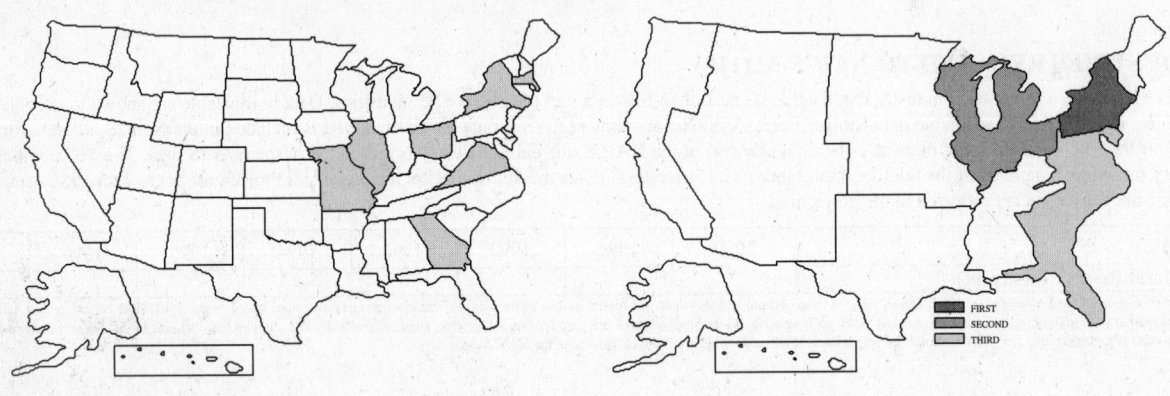

FIRST
SECOND
THIRD

INDUSTRY DATA BY STATE

State	Establishments Total (number)	% of U.S.	Employment Total (number)	% of U.S.	Per Estab.	Payroll Total ($ mil.)	Per Empl. ($)	Revenues Total ($ mil.)	% of U.S.	Per Estab. ($)
New York	2	4.8	3,337	15.4	1,668	169.8	50,895	8,690.0	35.4	4,345,000,000
California	2	4.8	1,971	9.1	985	94.3	47,844	2,192.0	8.9	1,096,000,000
Illinois	1	2.4	1,560	7.2	1,560	71.4	45,754	2,150.0	8.7	2,150,000,000
Georgia	1	2.4	1,041	4.8	1,041	45.1	43,340	1,467.3	6.0	1,467,305,000
Virginia	1	2.4	1,234	5.7	1,234	49.0	39,704	1,428.0	5.8	1,428,000,000
Massachusetts	1	2.4	1,143	5.3	1,143	52.8	46,215	1,403.0	5.7	1,403,000,000
Ohio	3	7.1	1,084	5.0	361	40.6	37,485	1,262.0	5.1	420,666,667
Missouri	2	4.8	1,739	8.0	869	69.2	39,804	1,212.4	4.9	606,224,000
Pennsylvania	2	4.8	1,664	7.7	832	61.4	36,918	1,151.0	4.7	575,500,000
Texas	4	9.5	1,504	6.9	376	60.4	40,161	848.4	3.5	212,093,250
Michigan	1	2.4	344	1.6	344	13.5	39,154	406.0	1.7	406,000,000
Maryland	1	2.4	380	1.8	380	12.7	33,511	371.0	1.5	371,000,000
Minnesota	1	2.4	1,133	5.2	1,133	47.9	42,236	367.6	1.5	367,635,000
North Carolina	1	2.4	364	1.7	364	11.9	32,574	346.0	1.4	346,000,000
Colorado	1	2.4	359	1.7	359	13.0	36,150	158.7	0.6	158,736,000
Washington	1	2.4	178	0.8	178	6.3	35,213	146.0	0.6	146,000,000
Utah	1	2.4	134	0.6	134	5.4	40,134	125.0	0.5	125,000,000
Tennessee	2	4.8	340	1.6	170	10.0	29,556	106.7	0.4	53,334,000
Kentucky	1	2.4	143	0.7	143	4.4	30,524	101.9	0.4	101,857,000
Oregon	1	2.4	140	0.6	140	4.3	30,850	100.0	0.4	100,000,000
Connecticut	1	2.4	127	0.6	127	3.4	27,024	91.0	0.4	91,000,000
Arkansas	1	2.4	128	0.6	128	3.8	29,445	87.9	0.4	87,950,000
Oklahoma	1	2.4	198	0.9	198	6.0	30,343	73.5	0.3	73,485,000
Florida	2	4.8	575	2.7	288	20.1	34,941	63.1	0.3	31,535,000
South Carolina	1	2.4	62	0.3	62	2.0	31,774	57.0	0.2	57,000,000
Nebraska	1	2.4	148	0.7	148	4.3	28,959	52.4	0.2	52,423,000
West Virginia	1	2.4	50	0.2	50	1.5	30,760	45.0	0.2	45,000,000
Maine	1	2.4	21	0.1	21	1.1	51,667	29.0	0.1	29,000,000
Louisiana	1	2.4	224	1.0	224	7.2	32,161	22.0	0.1	21,995,000
Alabama	1	2.4	212	1.0	212	6.5	30,467	20.4	0.1	20,405,000
Montana	1	2.4	137	0.6	137	4.1	30,058	7.2	0.2	7,209,000

Source: 1997 *Economic Census*. The states are in descending order of revenues or establishments (if revenue data are missing for the majority). The symbol (D) appears when data are withheld to prevent disclosure of competitive information. States marked with (D) are sorted by number of establishments. A dash (-) indicates that the data element cannot be calculated. * indicates the midpoint of a range; 175, for example is the range 100-249. Shaded *states* on the state map indicate those states which have proportionately greater representation in the industry than would be indicated by the state's population; the ratio is based on total revenues or number of establishments. Shaded *regions* indicate where the industry is regionally most concentrated.

NAICS 522110 - COMMERCIAL BANKING

GENERAL STATISTICS

Year	Establishments (number)	Employment (number)	Payroll ($ million)	Revenues ($ million)	Employees per Establishment (number)	Revenues per Establishment ($)	Payroll per Employee ($)
1997	70,860	1,575,399	57,247.0	421,759.0	22.2	5,952,004	36,338

Source: *Economic Census of the United States*, 1997. This is a newly defined industry. Data for prior years were unavailable at the time of publication but may become available over time.

INDICES OF CHANGE

Year	Establishments (number)	Employment (number)	Payroll ($ million)	Revenues ($ million)	Employees per Establishment (number)	Revenues per Establishment ($)	Payroll per Employee ($)
1997	100.0	100.0	100.0	100.0	100.0	100.0	100.0

Sources: Same as General Statistics. The values shown reflect change from the base year, 1997. Values above 100 mean greater than 1997, values below 100 mean less than 1997, and a value of 100 in the 1982-96 or 1998-2001 period means same as 1997. Values followed by a 'p' are projections by the editors; 'e' stands for extrapolation. Data are the most recent available at this level of detail.

SIC INDUSTRIES RELATED TO NAICS 522110

Each new NAICS code represents an industry that used to be part of an SIC or a part of several SIC industries. Data in this table are shown to provide transitional information for these cases. All available data for the precursor SIC(s) are shown. Even if only a part of an SIC is included in the NAICS, *all* data for the SIC are reproduced. If the SIC industry is not marked as being a part (pt) of the NAICS, the entire industry is embedded in the NAICS data. The SIC composition of the new industry provides some hints of the relative importance of its "ancestors." Data marked with a 'p' are projected. Projections begin with 1982 data. Data earlier than 1990 are not shown but are reflected in the projections.

SIC	Industry	1990	1991	1992	1993	1994	1995	1996	1997
6021	**National Commercial Banks (pt)**	-	-	-	-	-	-	-	-
6022	**State Commercial Banks (pt)**	-	-	-	-	-	-	-	-
6029	**Commercial Banks, nec**	-	-	-	-	-	-	-	-
6081	**Foreign Bank & Branches & Agencies (pt)**	-	-	-	-	-	-	-	-

Source: *Economic Census of the United States*, 1992, annual surveys of economic sectors conducted by the Bureau of the Census, and estimates or projections based on the 1982-1992 period; not all data are shown. 'e' marks estimates made by the editors; 'p' indicates projections based on time series. A dash (-) indicates that data for this SIC or year were not available. The abbreviation (pt) next to the industry name indicates that only a part of the industry is present within the NAICS data. If no (pt) is shown, the entire industry is contained within the NAICS data.

SELECTED RATIOS

For 1997	Avg. of Information	Analyzed Industry	Index	For 1997	Avg. of Information	Analyzed Industry	Index
Employees per establishment	15	22	151	Payroll per establishment	669,406	807,889	121
Revenue per establishment	5,561,120	5,952,004	107	Payroll as % of revenue	12	14	113
Revenue per employee	376,639	267,716	71	Payroll per employee	45,337	36,338	80

Sources: Same as General Statistics. The 'Average' column represents the average for the industry sector, in 1997, where the currently shown industry is classified. The Index shows the relationship between the Average and the Analyzed Industry. For example, 100 means that they are equal; 500 that the Analyzed Industry is five times the average; 50 means that the Analyzed Industry is half the national average. The abbreviation 'na' is used to show that data are 'not available'.

LEADING COMPANIES   Number shown: **75**   Total sales ($ mil): **11,618,894**   Total employment (000): **1,582.0**

Company Name	Address				CEO Name	Phone	Co. Type	Sales ($ mil)	Empl. (000)
Bank of America Arizona	P O Box 16290	Phoenix	AZ	85011	Steven J. Silvestri	602-597-5000	S	5,165,000	6.7
Bank of America Corp.	100 N Tryon St	Charlotte	NC	28255	Kenneth D Lewis	704-386-5000	P	617,679	171.0
Bank of America Texas N.A.	901 Main St	Dallas	TX	75202	Hugh McColl	214-209-0537	S	486,451*	180.0
Bank One Corp.	1 First National Plz	Chicago	IL	60670	James Dimon	312-732-4000	P	398,241*	86.2
Chase Manhattan Corp.	270 Park Ave	New York	NY	10017	William B Harrison Jr	212-270-6000	P	365,875	72.7
Citibank N.A.	399 Park Ave	New York	NY	10043	John S Reed	212-559-1000	S	262,500	74.3
J.P. Morgan and Company Inc.	60 Wall St	New York	NY	10260	Douglas A Warner III	212-483-2323	P	261,067	15.7
First Union Corp.	1 First Union Ctr	Charlotte	NC	28288	Edward E Crutchfield	704-374-6565	P	253,000	71.5
Bank of America National Trust	P O Box 37000	San Francisco	CA	94137	Hugh McColl	415-622-3456	S	236,982	67.7
Chase Manhattan Bank N.A.	270 Park Ave	New York	NY	10017	William B Harrison Jr	212-270-6000	S	216,032*	33.0
Morgan Guaranty Trust of New	60 Wall St	New York	NY	10005	Douglas A Warner III	212-483-2323	S	196,000	12.0
Norwest Bank Wisconsin N.A.	P O Box 2057	Milwaukee	WI	53201	J Lanier Little	414-224-4668	S	175,596*	1.4
Sanwa Bank California	601 S Figueroa St	Los Angeles	CA	90017	Tom Takakura	213-896-7000	S	155,556*	3.0
Bankers Trust Co.	130 Liberty St	New York	NY	10006	Frank N Newman	212-250-2500	D	140,010	17.0
MNB Bancshares Inc.	800 Poyntz Ave	Manhattan	KS	66505	Patrick L Alexander	785-565-2000	P	135,830	<0.1
First Cherokee Bancshares Inc.	P O Box 1238	Woodstock	GA	30188	R O Kononen, Jr	770-591-9000	P	110,230	<0.1
Crestar Financial Corp.	P O Box 26665	Richmond	VA	23261	Richard G Tilghman	804-782-5000	P	93,170	30.5
SunTrust Banks Inc.	P O Box 4418	Atlanta	GA	30302	L Phillip Humann	404-588-7711	P	93,170	30.5
HSBC USA INC.	One HSBC Center	Buffalo	NY	14203		716-841-2424	S	90,240	14.4
Wells Fargo Bank N.A.	420 Montgomery St	San Francisco	CA	94163	Paul Hazen	415-477-1000	S	89,529	44.3
Norwest Bank Minnesota N.A.	6th & Marquette	Minneapolis	MN	55479	R M Kovacevich	612-667-1234	S	88,500	5.4
Norwest Bank Colorado N.A.	1740 Broadway	Denver	CO	80274	David Bailey	303-861-8811	S	85,000	3.0
U.S. Bancorp	PO Box 522	Minneapolis	MN	55480	John F Grundhofer	612-973-1111	P	81,530	33.0
BankBoston Corp.	PO Box 1987	Boston	MA	02105	Henrique Meirelles	617-349-7450	P	75,700	25.0
PNC Bank Corp.	1 PNC Plz 249 5th	Pittsburgh	PA	15222	Thomas H O'Brien	412-762-1553	P	75,464	25.5
Bank of Eureka Springs	P O Box 309	Eureka Springs	AR	72632	John F Cross	501-253-8241	R	74,956	<0.1
Firstar Corp.	777 E Wisconsin	Milwaukee	WI	53202	Jerry A Grundhofer	414-765-4321	P	72,800	8.0
KeyBank N.A.	127 Public Sq	Cleveland	OH	44114	Gary R Allen		S	69,708	20.8
Wachovia Bank N.A.	100 N Main St	Winston-Salem	NC	27150	LM Baker Jr	336-770-5000	S	65,400	22.0
Bank of New York Company Inc.	1 Wall St	New York	NY	10286	Thomas A Renyi	212-495-1784	P	63,141*	17.2
Bank One N.A. (Chicago, Illinois)	1 Bank One Plz	Chicago	IL	60670	John B McCoy	312-732-4000	S	58,000	92.0
Bank of New York	48 Wall St	New York	NY	10286	Thomas A Renyi	212-530-1784	S	56,154	15.1
Republic New York Corp.	452 5th Ave	New York	NY	10018	Dov C Schlein	212-525-6100	P	50,424	5.8
Mellon Bank Corp.	1 Mellon Bank Ctr	Pittsburgh	PA	15258	C M Condron	412-234-5000	P	48,071	28.5
State Street Corp.	PO Box 351	Boston	MA	02101	Marshall N Carter	617-786-3000	P	47,082	16.3
SunTrust Bank	P O Box 3303	Tampa	FL	33601	Daniel W Mahurin	813-224-2121	S	45,162	0.7
Regions Financial Corp.	PO Box 10247	Birmingham	AL	35202	Carl E Jones, Jr	205-326-7100	P	42,700	14.7
Charter State Bank	P O Box 2000	Beebe	AR	72012		501-882-6406	R	36,168*	13.0
Comerica Inc.	500 Woodward Ave	Detroit	MI	48226	Eugene A Miller	313-222-4000	P	33,900	10.7
SouthTrust Bank	P O Box 327	Concord	NC	28026	Wallace Malone	704-788-3193	P	33,374*	12.0
Union Planters Banc	7130 Goodlett Farms	Cordova	TN	38018	Jackson W Moore	901-580-6000	P	33,300	1.5
Summit Bancorp.	PO Box 2066	Princeton	NJ	08543	Robert G Cox	609-987-3200	P	33,101	8.6
HSBC Bank USA	One HSBC Center	Buffalo	NY	14203	Malcom Burnett	716-841-2424	S	33,000	9.5
SouthTrust Bank N.A.	PO Box 2554	Birmingham	AL	35290	Julian W Banton	205-254-5000	S	33,000	10.0
Chase Manhattan Bank (USA)	802 Delaware Ave	Wilmington	DE	19801	Michael S Barrett	302-575-5000	S	31,846	1.2
Union Bank of California N.A.	400 California St	San Francisco	CA	94104	Kanetaka Yoshida	415-765-0400	S	30,800	9.8
Mellon Bank N.A.	1 Mellon Bank Ctr	Pittsburgh	PA	15258	Frank V Cahouet	412-234-4100	S	30,001	27.5
Comerica Bank	500 Woodward Ave	Detroit	MI	48226	Eugene A Miller	313-222-3300	S	28,936	6.6
Fifth Third Bancorp.	38 Fountain Sq Plz	Cincinnati	OH	45263	George A Schaefer Jr	513-579-5300	P	28,900	8.8
Fifth Third Bank of Western Ohio	P O Box 1117	Piqua	OH	45356	George Schaefer	937-773-1212	S	28,870*	10.0
Northern Trust Corp.	50 S La Salle St	Chicago	IL	60675	Barry G Hastings	312-630-6000	P	28,708	8.2
SunTrust Bank, Nature Coast	P O Box 156	Brooksville	FL	34605	James H Kimbrough	352-796-5151	S	28,333	0.5
Huntington Bancshares Inc.	41 S High St	Columbus	OH	43287	P Geier	614-480-8300	P	28,296	10.2
SunTrust Banks of Florida Inc.	P O Box 3833	Orlando	FL	32802	George W Koehn	407-237-4141	S	27,585	7.9
Huntington National Bank	41 S High St	Columbus	OH	43215	Frank Wobst	614-480-8300	S	27,014*	10.0
Popular Inc.	P O Box 362708	San Juan	PR	00936	Richard L Carrion	787-765-9800	P	24,760	10.5
First Security Corp.	79 S Main St	Salt Lake City	UT	84130	Spencer F Eccles	801-246-5706	P	23,000	9.4
Regions Bank	P O Box 10247	Birmingham	AL	35202	Carl E Jones	205-326-7100	S	23,000	9.2
MBNA Corp.	1100 N King St	Wilmington	DE	19801	Alfred Lerner	302-453-9930	P	22,982	19.0
Branch Banking and Trust Co.	P O Box 1260	Winston-Salem	NC	27102	John A Allison	336-733-2000	S	22,530	7.8
M and T Bancorp.	PO Box 223	Buffalo	NY	14240	Robert G Wilmers	716-842-5138	P	22,400	6.5
Bank One, Michigan	P O Box 116	Detroit	MI	48226	Walter C Watkins, Jr	313-225-1000	S	22,363	9.2
Harris Bankcorp Inc.	111 W Monroe St	Chicago	IL	60603	Alan G McNally	312-461-2121	S	22,200	6.6
LaSalle National Bank	135 S LaSalle St	Chicago	IL	60603	Norman R Bobins	312-443-2000	S	22,000	1.2
Marshall and Ilsley Corp.	770 N Water St	Milwaukee	WI	53202	DJ Kuester	414-765-7801	P	21,566	10.8
Bank One, Texas N.A.	PO Box 655415	Dallas	TX	75265	Terry Kelley	214-290-2000	S	21,500	8.0
SunTrust Banks of Georgia Inc.	P O Box 4418	Atlanta	GA	30302	Robert Long	404-827-6554	S	21,275	4.5
Northern Trust Co.	50 S La Salle St	Chicago	IL	60675	Barry G Hastings	312-630-6000	S	21,185*	5.0
M and T Bank	1 M&T Plaza, 5th Fl	Buffalo	NY	14203	Robert G Wilmers	716-842-5445	S	20,583	6.5
AmSouth Bancorp.	PO Box 11007	Birmingham	AL	35288	C Dowd Ritter	205-320-7151	P	19,900	6.7
Old Kent Bank	111 Lion St NW	Grand Rapids	MI	49503	David Wagner	616-771-5000	S	19,238*	9.0
First Tennessee National Corp.	PO Box 84	Memphis	TN	38101	Ralph Horn	901-523-5630	P	18,400	10.2
Union Planters Bank of Florida	1221 Brickell Ave	Miami	FL	33131	Adolfo Enriquez	305-536-1500	S	18,105*	0.7
Frost Bank	P O Box 160	San Antonio	TX	78205	Tom Frost	210-420-5200	P	17,526*	6.3
Citizens Financial Group Inc.	1 Citizens Plz	Providence	RI	02903	Lawrence K Fish	401-456-7000	S	17,300	4.1

Source: Ward's Business Directory of U.S. Private and Public Companies, Volumes 1 and 2, 2000. The company type code used is as follows: P - Public, R - Private, S - Subsidiary, D - Division, J - Joint Venture, A - Affiliate, G - Group, N - Company type not reported. Sales are in millions of dollars, employees are in thousands. An asterisk (*) indicates an estimated sales volume. The symbol < stands for 'less than'. Company names and addresses are truncated, in some cases, to fit into the available space.

LOCATION BY STATE AND REGIONAL CONCENTRATION

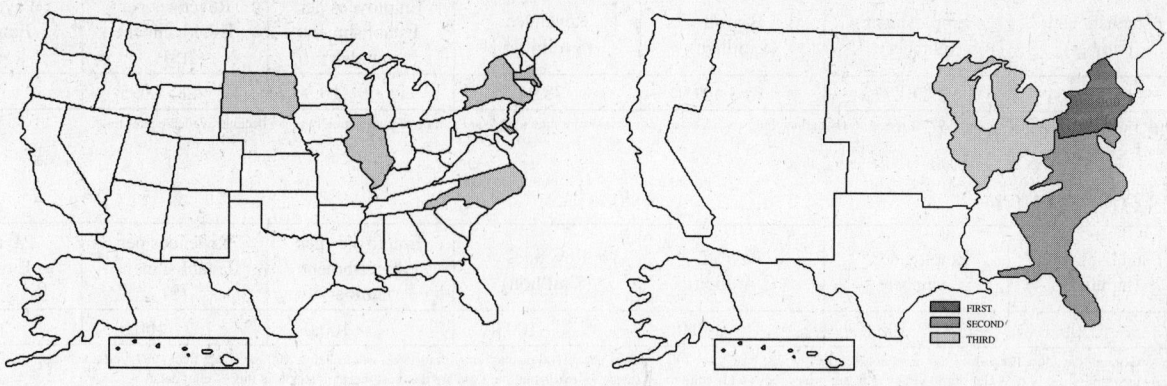

FIRST
SECOND
THIRD

INDUSTRY DATA BY STATE

State	Establishments Total (number)	% of U.S.	Employment Total (number)	% of U.S.	Per Estab.	Payroll Total ($ mil.)	Per Empl. ($)	Revenues Total ($ mil.)	% of U.S.	Per Estab. ($)
New York	3,877	5.5	155,519	9.9	40	11,222.1	72,159	109,419.0	25.9	28,222,593
California	5,740	8.1	162,522	10.3	28	6,083.8	37,434	36,583.1	8.7	6,373,358
Illinois	3,053	4.3	85,223	5.4	28	3,258.6	38,237	24,861.1	5.9	8,143,184
Florida	4,005	5.7	84,356	5.4	21	2,586.8	30,665	19,728.3	4.7	4,925,907
Texas	3,711	5.2	93,329	5.9	25	2,910.6	31,186	18,197.3	4.3	4,903,608
Pennsylvania	3,758	5.3	79,678	5.1	21	2,459.5	30,868	17,945.2	4.3	4,775,197
Ohio	3,355	4.7	70,187	4.5	21	2,192.0	31,231	14,125.1	3.3	4,210,153
North Carolina	2,458	3.5	53,223	3.4	22	1,907.5	35,840	12,828.4	3.0	5,219,058
Massachusetts	1,266	1.8	33,971	2.2	27	1,655.0	48,717	11,616.7	2.8	9,175,926
Michigan	2,793	3.9	65,214	4.1	23	1,942.7	29,789	11,203.6	2.7	4,011,311
Georgia	2,066	2.9	44,512	2.8	22	1,380.6	31,017	10,076.8	2.4	4,877,465
Delaware	224	0.3	17,107	1.1	76	915.0	53,488	8,847.1	2.1	39,496,134
New Jersey	1,970	2.8	36,180	2.3	18	1,210.2	33,450	7,743.2	1.8	3,930,542
Tennessee	1,893	2.7	31,871	2.0	17	970.9	30,463	7,316.8	1.7	3,865,167
Virginia	2,101	3.0	44,001	2.8	21	1,248.6	28,376	7,093.2	1.7	3,376,085
Indiana	2,034	2.9	32,070	2.0	16	883.3	27,544	6,966.0	1.7	3,424,797
Missouri	1,720	2.4	36,270	2.3	21	1,074.2	29,618	6,806.5	1.6	3,957,247
Minnesota	1,352	1.9	29,548	1.9	22	978.2	33,104	6,276.4	1.5	4,642,271
Alabama	1,192	1.7	31,744	2.0	27	893.7	28,154	6,119.2	1.5	5,133,564
Wisconsin	1,405	2.0	30,840	2.0	22	917.8	29,759	6,076.1	1.4	4,324,653
Kentucky	1,380	1.9	21,974	1.4	16	621.0	28,259	5,934.4	1.4	4,300,296
Washington	1,351	1.9	21,382	1.4	16	738.5	34,537	5,504.1	1.3	4,074,118
Arizona	1,164	1.6	23,141	1.5	20	674.8	29,161	4,709.3	1.1	4,045,828
Louisiana	1,344	1.9	23,988	1.5	18	723.3	30,151	4,343.9	1.0	3,232,045
Maryland	1,351	1.9	22,406	1.4	17	764.1	34,101	3,912.8	0.9	2,896,211
Iowa	1,110	1.6	18,062	1.1	16	524.3	29,027	3,797.6	0.9	3,421,242
Colorado	835	1.2	17,851	1.1	21	549.2	30,765	3,412.2	0.8	4,086,411
Oklahoma	901	1.3	18,514	1.2	21	529.0	28,572	3,305.5	0.8	3,668,720
Oregon	938	1.3	18,207	1.2	19	533.1	29,279	3,178.7	0.8	3,388,787
Kansas	1,040	1.5	17,031	1.1	16	501.5	29,445	3,123.1	0.7	3,003,015
Mississippi	1,047	1.5	15,101	1.0	14	413.6	27,390	2,701.5	0.6	2,580,275
Arkansas	963	1.4	14,417	0.9	15	376.2	26,094	2,571.1	0.6	2,669,904
South Carolina	1,018	1.4	13,621	0.9	13	369.3	27,112	2,523.5	0.6	2,478,924
Connecticut	672	0.9	9,914	0.6	15	343.6	34,653	2,497.7	0.6	3,716,796
Rhode Island	223	0.3	6,109	0.4	27	180.3	29,513	1,987.5	0.5	8,912,709
Nevada	450	0.6	10,939	0.7	24	281.9	25,770	1,967.9	0.5	4,373,044
West Virginia	562	0.8	10,560	0.7	19	237.6	22,497	1,923.4	0.5	3,422,482
Utah	522	0.7	9,493	0.6	18	291.7	30,728	1,757.9	0.4	3,367,680
Nebraska	726	1.0	10,975	0.7	15	301.4	27,459	1,724.3	0.4	2,375,110
Hawaii	300	0.4	8,157	0.5	27	264.1	32,375	1,691.5	0.4	5,638,303
New Mexico	489	0.7	7,866	0.5	16	203.5	25,872	1,206.3	0.3	2,466,857
Idaho	361	0.5	5,337	0.3	15	159.2	29,835	1,106.6	0.3	3,065,321
South Dakota	349	0.5	5,229	0.3	15	151.5	28,982	1,076.9	0.3	3,085,665
New Hampshire	308	0.4	3,977	0.3	13	108.3	27,232	954.1	0.2	3,097,656
North Dakota	297	0.4	4,888	0.3	16	138.5	28,344	918.5	0.2	3,092,747
Maine	304	0.4	3,321	0.2	11	91.8	27,650	760.9	0.2	2,502,872
Montana	215	0.3	4,752	0.3	22	133.7	28,138	740.7	0.2	3,444,995
Vermont	207	0.3	2,912	0.2	14	83.0	28,492	730.3	0.2	3,528,174
D.C.	193	0.3	2,798	0.2	14	118.8	42,458	695.1	0.2	3,601,461
Wyoming	129	0.2	2,462	0.2	19	66.7	27,097	598.3	0.1	4,638,240
Alaska	138	0.2	2,650	0.2	19	82.5	31,148	574.3	0.1	4,161,732

Source: 1997 *Economic Census.* The states are in descending order of revenues or establishments (if revenue data are missing for the majority). The symbol (D) appears when data are withheld to prevent disclosure of competitive information. States marked with (D) are sorted by number of establishments. A dash (-) indicates that the data element cannot be calculated. * indicates the midpoint of a range; 175, for example is the range 100-249. Shaded *states* on the state map indicate those states which have proportionately greater representation in the industry than would be indicated by the state's population; the ratio is based on total revenues or number of establishments. Shaded *regions* indicate where the industry is regionally most concentrated.

NAICS 522120 - SAVINGS INSTITUTIONS

GENERAL STATISTICS

Year	Establishments (number)	Employment (number)	Payroll ($ million)	Revenues ($ million)	Employees per Establishment (number)	Revenues per Establishment ($)	Payroll per Employee ($)
1997	16,264	264,775	8,409.0	78,947.0	16.3	4,854,095	31,759

Source: *Economic Census of the United States*, 1997. This is a newly defined industry. Data for prior years were unavailable at the time of publication but may become available over time.

INDICES OF CHANGE

Year	Establishments (number)	Employment (number)	Payroll ($ million)	Revenues ($ million)	Employees per Establishment (number)	Revenues per Establishment ($)	Payroll per Employee ($)
1997	100.0	100.0	100.0	100.0	100.0	100.0	100.0

Sources: Same as General Statistics. The values shown reflect change from the base year, 1997. Values above 100 mean greater than 1997, values below 100 mean less than 1997, and a value of 100 in the 1982-96 or 1998-2001 period means same as 1997. Values followed by a 'p' are projections by the editors; 'e' stands for extrapolation. Data are the most recent available at this level of detail.

SIC INDUSTRIES RELATED TO NAICS 522120

Each new NAICS code represents an industry that used to be part of an SIC or a part of several SIC industries. Data in this table are shown to provide transitional information for these cases. All available data for the precursor SIC(s) are shown. Even if only a part of an SIC is included in the NAICS, *all* data for the SIC are reproduced. If the SIC industry is not marked as being a part (pt) of the NAICS, the entire industry is embedded in the NAICS data. The SIC composition of the new industry provides some hints of the relative importance of its "ancestors." Data marked with a 'p' are projected. Projections begin with 1982 data. Data earlier than 1990 are not shown but are reflected in the projections.

SIC	Industry	1990	1991	1992	1993	1994	1995	1996	1997
6035	Federal Savings Institutions	-	-	-	-	-	-	-	-
6036	Savings Institutions, Except Federal	-	-	-	-	-	-	-	-

Source: *Economic Census of the United States*, 1992, annual surveys of economic sectors conducted by the Bureau of the Census, and estimates or projections based on the 1982-1992 period; not all data are shown. 'e' marks estimates made by the editors; 'p' indicates projections based on time series. A dash (-) indicates that data for this SIC or year were not available. The abbreviation (pt) next to the industry name indicates that only a part of the industry is present within the NAICS data. If no (pt) is shown, the entire industry is contained within the NAICS data.

SELECTED RATIOS

For 1997	Avg. of Information	Analyzed Industry	Index	For 1997	Avg. of Information	Analyzed Industry	Index
Employees per establishment	15	16	110	Payroll per establishment	669,406	517,031	77
Revenue per establishment	5,561,120	4,854,095	87	Payroll as % of revenue	12	11	88
Revenue per employee	376,639	298,166	79	Payroll per employee	45,337	31,759	70

Sources: Same as General Statistics. The 'Average' column represents the average for the industry sector, in 1997, where the currently shown industry is classified. The Index shows the relationship between the Average and the Analyzed Industry. For example, 100 means that they are equal; 500 that the Analyzed Industry is five times the average; 50 means that the Analyzed Industry is half the national average. The abbreviation 'na' is used to show that data are 'not available'.

LEADING COMPANIES

Number shown: **75**   Total sales ($ mil): **4,847,209**   Total employment (000): **329.8**

Company Name	Address				CEO Name	Phone	Co. Type	Sales ($ mil)	Empl. (000)
First Federal Bank of California	401 Wilshire Blvd	Santa Monica	CA	90401	Babette Heimbuch	310-319-6000	S	3,857,000	0.5
BankBoston Corp.	PO Box 1987	Boston	MA	02105	Henrique Meirelles	617-349-7450	P	75,700	25.0
Household International Inc.	2700 Sanders Rd	Prospect Heights	IL	60070	William F Aldinger	847-564-5000	P	52,893	23.5
Home Savings of America F.S.B.	4900 Rivergrade Rd	Irwindale	CA	91706	Bruce Willison	626-960-6311	S	49,902	9.5
First Savings Bank of Washington	PO Box 907	Walla Walla	WA	99362	Gary L Sirmon	509-527-3636	S	45,756	0.3
Regions Financial Corp.	PO Box 10247	Birmingham	AL	35202	Carl E Jones, Jr	205-326-7100	P	42,700	14.7
ALBANK F.S.B.	P O Box 70	Albany	NY	12201	Herbert G Chorbajian	518-445-2100	S	41,000	1.4
Golden West Financial Corp.	1901 Harrison St	Oakland	CA	94612	Herbert M Sandler	510-466-3420	P	38,469	4.4
Charter One Financial Inc.	1215 Superior Ave	Cleveland	OH	44114	Charles J Koch	216-566-5300	P	31,819	5.7
Huntington Bancshares Inc.	41 S High St	Columbus	OH	43287	P Geier	614-480-8300	P	28,296	10.2
Sovereign Bancorp Inc.	PO Box 12646	Reading	PA	19612	Jay S Sidhu	610-320-8400	P	26,587	4.4
Popular Inc.	P O Box 362708	San Juan	PR	00936	Richard L Carrion	787-765-9800	P	24,760	10.5
Washington Mutual Bank	1201 Third Ave	Seattle	WA	98101	Kerry K Killinger	206-461-2000	S	24,129	5.5
Astoria Financial Corp.	1 Astoria Federal Plz	Lake Success	NY	11042	George L Engelke Jr	516-327-3000	P	23,000	1.8
Dime Bancorp Inc.	589 5th Ave	New York	NY	10017	Lawrence J Toal	212-326-6170	P	22,321	7.4
Dime Savings Bank of New York	589 Fifth Ave	New York	NY	10017	Richard D Parsons	212-326-6006	S	21,792	6.0
Citizens Financial Group Inc.	1 Citizens Plz	Providence	RI	02903	Lawrence K Fish	401-456-7000	S	17,300	4.1
ABN AMRO North America Inc.	135 S La Salle St	Chicago	IL	60603	Harrison F Tempest	312-443-2000	D	17,150*	5.5
Harris Bank (Matteson, Illinois)	4749 Lincoln Mall	Matteson	IL	60443	Alan G McNally	708-747-7300	D	17,045*	5.0
First Star	200 E Main St	Richmond	KY	40475	Tony D Whitaker	606-623-2548	S	16,896*	5.0
Standard Federal Bank	P O Box 3703	Troy	MI	48007	Scott Heitzmann	248-643-9600	S	16,100	4.0
Pacific Century Financial Corp.	PO Box 2900	Honolulu	HI	96846	Richard J Dahl	808-643-3888	P	14,400	5.1
Charter One Bank F.S.B.	1215 Superior Ave	Cleveland	OH	44114	Charles J Koch	216-566-5300	S	13,905*	2.6
Peoples Heritage Financial Group	P O Box 9540	Portland	ME	04112	William J Ryan	207-761-8500	P	13,900	3.3
Commercial Federal Bank F.S.B.	2120 S 72nd St	Omaha	NE	68124	William A Fitzgerald	402-554-9200	S	13,877*	3.0
Washington Mutual Inc.	PO Box 834	Seattle	WA	98111	Kerry K Killinger	206-461-2000	P	13,571	27.3
GreenPoint Bank	807 Manhattan Ave	Brooklyn	NY	11222	Thomas S Johnson	718-670-7600	S	13,077	1.8
Commercial Federal Corp.	2120 S 72nd St	Omaha	NE	68124	William A Fitzgerald	402-554-9200	P	12,800	3.6
Bank United (Houston, Texas)	PO Box 13786	Kansas City	MO	64199	Barry C Burkholder	713-543-6958	S	11,941	1.5
Astoria Federal Savings & Loan	1 Astoria Federal Plz	Lake Success	NY	11042	George L Engelke Jr	516-327-3000	S	10,896	1.4
Midland Financial Co.	501W I-44 Service	Oklahoma City	OK	73118	Robert Dilg	405-840-7600	R	10,600*	1.5
TCF Financial Corp.	801 Marquette Ave	Minneapolis	MN	55402	William A Cooper	612-661-6500	P	10,293	7.0
Guaranty Federal Bank F.S.B.	8333 Douglas Ave	Dallas	TX	75225	Ken Dubuque	214-360-3360	S	10,000*	1.5
Michigan National Corp.	P O Box 9065	Farmington Hills	MI	48333	Douglas E Ebert	248-473-3000	S	9,329	4.0
FirstMerit Corp.	3 Cascade Plz	Akron	OH	44308	Sid A Bostic	330-996-6300	P	9,100	2.7
Webster Financial Corp.	Webster Plz	Waterbury	CT	06702	James C Smith	203-753-2921	P	8,893	1.9
National City Corp.	1900 E 9th St	Cleveland	OH	44114	David A Daberko	216-575-2000	P	8,293	38.1
Webster Bank	Webster Plz	Waterbury	CT	06702	James C Smith	203-578-2230	S	7,413*	2.0
CNB Bancshares Inc.	P O Box 778	Evansville	IN	47705	James J Giancola	812-464-3400	P	7,142	2.8
Telebanc	PO Box 1537	Arlington	VA	22210	David Smilow	703-524-6880	S	6,818*	2.0
Emigrant Savings Bank	5 E 42nd St	New York	NY	10017	Philip L Milstein	212-850-4000	R	6,261	1.3
Chevy Chase Bank F.S.B.	8401 Connecticut	Chevy Chase	MD	20815	B Francis Saul II	301-986-7000	R	6,160	2.9
Fulton Financial Corp.	PO Box 4887	Lancaster	PA	17604	Rufus A Fulton Jr	717-291-2411	P	6,100	2.7
St. Paul Bancorp Inc.	6700 W North Ave	Elmwood Park	IL	60707	Joseph C Scully	773-622-5000	P	6,005	1.1
American Savings Bank F.S.B.	915 Fort Street Mall	Honolulu	HI	96813	Wayne K Minami	808-627-6900	S	5,929*	1.4
Downey Savings & Loan	PO Box 6000	Newport Beach	CA	92658	James W Lokey	949-854-0300	S	5,853	1.1
Washington Federal Savings	425 Pike St	Seattle	WA	98101	Guy C Pinkerton	206-624-7930	S	5,637	0.6
Bay View Capital Corp.	1840 Gateway Dr	San Mateo	CA	94404	John R McKean	650-312-7200	P	5,596	0.9
Third Federal Savings & Loan	7007 Broadway Ave	Cleveland	OH	44105	Marc A Stefanski	216-441-6000	R	5,443	0.6
Long Island Bancorp Inc.	201 Old Country Rd	Melville	NY	11747	John J Conefry Jr	516-547-2000	P	5,330*	1.4
Citizens Bank of Massachusetts	28 State St	Boston	MA	02110	Robert M Mahoney	617-482-2600	S	5,147	0.9
Westcorp	P O Box 19733	Irvine	CA	92623	Ernest S Rady	949-727-1000	P	5,000	2.3
St. Paul Federal Bank for Savings	6700 W North Ave	Chicago	IL	60707	Patrick J Agnew	773-622-5000	S	4,557	1.1
MAF Bancorp Inc.	55th St & Holmes	Clarendon Hills	IL	60514	Allen H Koranda	630-325-7300	P	4,283	0.9
First Federal Savings Bank	401 Wilshire Blvd	Santa Monica	CA	90401	B Heimbuch	310-319-6000	S	4,100*	0.4
Ohio Savings Bank	1801 East 9th St	Cleveland	OH	44114	Robert Goldberg	216-622-4100	S	4,060*	0.9
Capital One Financial Corp.	2980 Fairview	Falls Church	VA	22042	Richard D Fairbank	703-205-1000	P	3,966	10.4
Temple-Inland Inc.	303 S Temple Dr	Diboll	TX	75941	Kenneth M Jastrow II	409-829-5111	N	3,915*	15.7
FirstFed Financial Corp.	401 Wilshire Blvd	Santa Monica	CA	90401	Babette E Heimbuch	310-319-6000	P	3,857	0.5
MidFirst Bank	P O Box 26750	Oklahoma City	OK	73126	Robert Dilg Jr	405-840-7600	S	3,800	0.3
Western Financial Savings Bank F	15750 Alton Pkwy	Irvine	CA	92618	Ernest S Rady	949-727-1000	S	3,729*	1.7
Peoples Heritage	PO Box 9540	Portland	ME	04112	William J Ryan	207-761-8500	S	3,689*	2.0
TCF National Bank Minnesota	801 Marquette Ave	Minneapolis	MN	55402	Lynn A Nagorske	612-661-6500	S	3,687	2.2
First Republic Bank	111 Pine St	San Francisco	CA	94111	James H Herbert	415-392-1400	P	3,599	0.3
Wilshire Financial Services Group	1776 S W Madison	Portland	OR	97205	Steven Glennon	503-223-5600	P	3,587*	0.6
Union Planters	PO Box 1858	Hattiesburg	MS	39403	Kenneth Plunk	601-545-4700	S	3,410*	1.0
Sterling Financial Corp.	111 N Wall St	Spokane	WA	99201	Harold B Gilkey	509-458-2711	P	3,220*	0.7
Fidelity Federal Bank F.S.B.	600 N Brand Blvd	Glendale	CA	91203	R M Greenwood	818-549-3621	S	3,206*	0.9
Bay View Bank	1840 Gateway Dr	San Mateo	CA	94404	Edward H Sondker	650-573-7300	S	3,203	0.4
Ocwen Federal Bank F.S.B.	1675 Palm Beach	W. Palm Beach	FL	33401	William C Erbey	561-681-8000	S	3,069	1.2
BankAtlantic F.S.B.	P O Box 8608	Fort Lauderdale	FL	33310	Alan B Levan	954-760-5000	S	3,064	1.1
PFF Bank and Trust	P O Box 1520	Pomona	CA	91769	Larry M Rinehart	909-623-2323	P	3,000	0.6
Republic Security Financial Corp.	P O Box 4298	W. Palm Beach	FL	33402	Rudy E Schupp	561-650-2500	P	3,000	0.9
Coastal Bancorp Inc.	5718 Westheimer	Houston	TX	77057	Manuel J Mehos	713-435-5000	P	2,947	0.7
St. Francis Bank	13400 Bishops Ln	Brookfield	WI	53005	Thomas Perz	416-744-8600	R	2,938*	0.5

Source: Ward's Business Directory of U.S. Private and Public Companies, Volumes 1 and 2, 2000. The company type code used is as follows: P - Public, R - Private, S - Subsidiary, D - Division, J - Joint Venture, A - Affiliate, G - Group, N - Company type not reported. Sales are in millions of dollars, employees are in thousands. An asterisk (*) indicates an estimated sales volume. The symbol < stands for 'less than'. Company names and addresses are truncated, in some cases, to fit into the available space.

LOCATION BY STATE AND REGIONAL CONCENTRATION

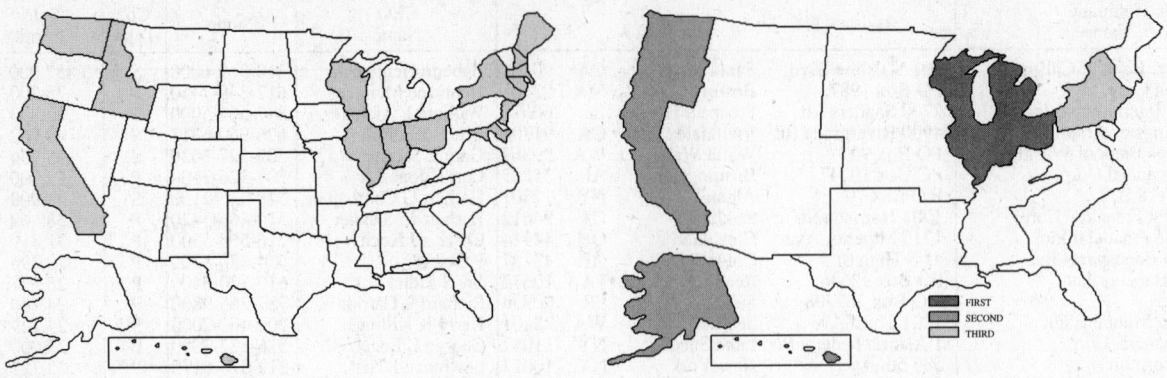

FIRST
SECOND
THIRD

INDUSTRY DATA BY STATE

State	Establishments Total (number)	% of U.S.	Employment Total (number)	% of U.S.	Per Estab.	Payroll Total ($ mil.)	Per Empl. ($)	Revenues Total ($ mil.)	% of U.S.	Per Estab. ($)
California	2,626	16.1	41,822	15.8	16	1,537.2	36,755	12,723.5	16.1	4,845,216
New York	1,121	6.9	25,285	9.5	23	890.6	35,222	8,606.8	10.9	7,677,812
Illinois	844	5.2	21,797	8.2	26	669.4	30,713	6,806.5	8.6	8,064,532
Massachusetts	954	5.9	17,244	6.5	18	541.8	31,422	4,693.9	5.9	4,920,181
Ohio	838	5.2	12,354	4.7	15	344.0	27,846	4,430.7	5.6	5,287,285
New Jersey	873	5.4	11,440	4.3	13	394.2	34,461	4,266.4	5.4	4,887,008
Texas	603	3.7	11,381	4.3	19	387.3	34,028	4,222.1	5.3	7,001,833
Connecticut	627	3.9	11,795	4.5	19	398.7	33,806	3,239.3	4.1	5,166,421
Pennsylvania	881	5.4	11,388	4.3	13	312.8	27,464	3,129.2	4.0	3,551,879
Washington	510	3.1	6,613	2.5	13	238.1	35,999	2,789.3	3.5	5,469,137
Florida	747	4.6	10,706	4.0	14	330.9	30,903	2,442.7	3.1	3,270,047
Michigan	493	3.0	8,144	3.1	17	217.0	26,647	2,215.6	2.8	4,494,166
Maryland	361	2.2	8,404	3.2	23	260.1	30,955	2,191.1	2.8	6,069,665
Indiana	325	2.0	5,596	2.1	17	158.1	28,261	1,804.8	2.3	5,553,332
Wisconsin	530	3.3	7,605	2.9	14	211.1	27,754	1,598.7	2.0	3,016,425
Virginia	274	1.7	3,927	1.5	14	112.9	28,759	1,202.9	1.5	4,390,252
North Carolina	241	1.5	3,374	1.3	14	93.1	27,607	1,078.5	1.4	4,475,207
Georgia	153	0.9	4,269	1.6	28	117.7	27,567	1,061.9	1.3	6,940,405
Kansas	180	1.1	2,168	0.8	12	66.3	30,579	749.2	0.9	4,162,244
Missouri	238	1.5	3,851	1.5	16	96.7	25,113	713.1	0.9	2,996,025
South Carolina	203	1.2	2,982	1.1	15	86.5	29,004	707.1	0.9	3,483,227
Maine	202	1.2	3,508	1.3	17	116.6	33,241	694.6	0.9	3,438,550
Hawaii	156	1.0	2,238	0.8	14	60.4	26,967	627.3	0.8	4,021,064
Oklahoma	134	0.8	1,578	0.6	12	41.9	26,575	514.9	0.7	3,842,261
Idaho	53	0.3	459	0.2	9	14.9	32,420	509.5	0.6	9,612,717
Iowa	182	1.1	1,837	0.7	10	49.5	26,947	461.5	0.6	2,535,489
Kentucky	148	0.9	1,531	0.6	10	47.2	30,803	445.6	0.6	3,011,000
Minnesota	103	0.6	1,156	0.4	11	40.1	34,698	428.0	0.5	4,155,049
Nebraska	129	0.8	1,466	0.6	11	41.7	28,432	426.1	0.5	3,303,341
Colorado	220	1.4	1,726	0.7	8	42.3	24,532	424.2	0.5	1,928,364
New Hampshire	116	0.7	1,925	0.7	17	63.2	32,814	366.0	0.5	3,155,388
Tennessee	102	0.6	1,868	0.7	18	45.7	24,480	341.2	0.4	3,345,314
Louisiana	103	0.6	1,354	0.5	13	34.7	25,662	288.6	0.4	2,802,243
Arkansas	106	0.7	1,444	0.5	14	31.0	21,456	272.4	0.3	2,569,358
Rhode Island	48	0.3	744	0.3	15	18.0	24,199	252.6	0.3	5,262,729
Alabama	41	0.3	747	0.3	18	23.4	31,347	178.6	0.2	4,355,927
Vermont	36	0.2	548	0.2	15	14.7	26,768	160.3	0.2	4,453,083
Arizona	73	0.4	506	0.2	7	14.6	28,929	154.2	0.2	2,111,781
Montana	73	0.4	820	0.3	11	20.5	25,056	151.3	0.2	2,072,260
D.C.	36	0.2	464	0.2	13	16.8	36,211	137.5	0.2	3,820,333
New Mexico	33	0.2	707	0.3	21	22.8	32,198	126.6	0.2	3,837,485
West Virginia	48	0.3	618	0.2	13	11.2	18,073	100.8	0.1	2,100,083
South Dakota	35	0.2	370	0.1	11	12.0	32,376	77.4	0.1	2,210,943
Nevada	19	0.1	137	0.1	7	4.1	29,978	69.6	0.1	3,661,000
Mississippi	25	0.2	247	0.1	10	7.3	29,364	60.3	0.1	2,413,760
Oregon	252	1.5	1,750*	-	-	(D)	-	(D)	-	-
Utah	61	0.4	750*	-	-	(D)	-	(D)	-	-
North Dakota	47	0.3	375*	-	-	(D)	-	(D)	-	-
Delaware	43	0.3	750*	-	-	(D)	-	(D)	-	-
Wyoming	10	0.1	175*	-	-	(D)	-	(D)	-	-
Alaska	8	-	60*	-	-	(D)	-	(D)	-	-

Source: 1997 *Economic Census*. The states are in descending order of revenues or establishments (if revenue data are missing for the majority). The symbol (D) appears when data are withheld to prevent disclosure of competitive information. States marked with (D) are sorted by number of establishments. A dash (-) indicates that the data element cannot be calculated. * indicates the midpoint of a range; 175, for example is the range 100-249. Shaded *states* on the state map indicate those states which have proportionately greater representation in the industry than would be indicated by the state's population; the ratio is based on total revenues or number of establishments. Shaded *regions* indicate where the industry is regionally most concentrated.

NAICS 522130 - CREDIT UNIONS

GENERAL STATISTICS

Year	Establishments (number)	Employment (number)	Payroll ($ million)	Revenues ($ million)	Employees per Establishment (number)	Revenues per Establishment ($)	Payroll per Employee ($)
1997	15,640	172,114	4,308.0	29,694.0	11.0	1,898,593	25,030

Source: *Economic Census of the United States*, 1997. This is a newly defined industry. Data for prior years were unavailable at the time of publication but may become available over time.

INDICES OF CHANGE

Year	Establishments (number)	Employment (number)	Payroll ($ million)	Revenues ($ million)	Employees per Establishment (number)	Revenues per Establishment ($)	Payroll per Employee ($)
1997	100.0	100.0	100.0	100.0	100.0	100.0	100.0

Sources: Same as General Statistics. The values shown reflect change from the base year, 1997. Values above 100 mean greater than 1997, values below 100 mean less than 1997, and a value of 100 in the 1982-96 or 1998-2001 period means same as 1997. Values followed by a 'p' are projections by the editors; 'e' stands for extrapolation. Data are the most recent available at this level of detail.

SIC INDUSTRIES RELATED TO NAICS 522130

Each new NAICS code represents an industry that used to be part of an SIC or a part of several SIC industries. Data in this table are shown to provide transitional information for these cases. All available data for the precursor SIC(s) are shown. Even if only a part of an SIC is included in the NAICS, *all* data for the SIC are reproduced. If the SIC industry is not marked as being a part (pt) of the NAICS, the entire industry is embedded in the NAICS data. The SIC composition of the new industry provides some hints of the relative importance of its "ancestors." Data marked with a 'p' are projected. Projections begin with 1982 data. Data earlier than 1990 are not shown but are reflected in the projections.

SIC	Industry	1990	1991	1992	1993	1994	1995	1996	1997
6061	**Federal Credit Unions**	-	-	-	-	-	-	-	-
6062	**State Credit Unions**	-	-	-	-	-	-	-	-

Source: *Economic Census of the United States*, 1992, annual surveys of economic sectors conducted by the Bureau of the Census, and estimates or projections based on the 1982-1992 period; not all data are shown. 'e' marks estimates made by the editors; 'p' indicates projections based on time series. A dash (-) indicates that data for this SIC or year were not available. The abbreviation (pt) next to the industry name indicates that only a part of the industry is present within the NAICS data. If no (pt) is shown, the entire industry is contained within the NAICS data.

SELECTED RATIOS

For 1997	Avg. of Information	Analyzed Industry	Index	For 1997	Avg. of Information	Analyzed Industry	Index
Employees per establishment	15	11	75	Payroll per establishment	669,406	275,448	41
Revenue per establishment	5,561,120	1,898,593	34	Payroll as % of revenue	12	15	120
Revenue per employee	376,639	172,525	46	Payroll per employee	45,337	25,030	55

Sources: Same as General Statistics. The 'Average' column represents the average for the industry sector, in 1997, where the currently shown industry is classified. The Index shows the relationship between the Average and the Analyzed Industry. For example, 100 means that they are equal; 500 that the Analyzed Industry is five times the average; 50 means that the Analyzed Industry is half the national average. The abbreviation 'na' is used to show that data are 'not available'.

LEADING COMPANIES   Number shown: **75**   Total sales ($ mil): **79,919**   Total employment (000): **19.1**

Company Name	Address				CEO Name	Phone	Co. Type	Sales ($ mil)	Empl. (000)
Food Lion Credit Association	P O Box 278	Salisbury	NC	28145		704-636-0643	R	15,712	<0.1
North Carolina State Employees'	P O Box 27665	Raleigh	NC	27611	Jim Blaine	919-839-5000	R	12,340*	2.0
State Employee's Credit Union	900 Wade Ave	Raleigh	NC	27605	Jim Blaine	919-839-5003	R	4,609	1.9
Pentagon Federal Credit Union	P O Box 1432	Alexandria	VA	22313	Ronald L Snellings	703-838-1000	R	2,800*	1.0
Suncoast Schools Federal Credit	P O Box 11904	Tampa	FL	33680	Tom R Dorety	813-621-7511	R	2,566*	0.8
Patelco Credit Union	156 2nd St	San Francisco	CA	94105	Ed Callahan	415-442-6200	R	2,044*	0.3
American Airlines Employees	PO Box 619001	Dallas	TX	75261	John M Tippets	817-963-6000	R	2,000	0.3
Golden 1 Credit Union	P O Box 15966	Sacramento	CA	95852	Stan Hollen	916-732-2900	R	2,000*	0.9
Credit Union ONE	400 E 9 Mile Rd	Ferndale	MI	48220	Armando R Cavazos	248-398-1210	R	1,899*	0.3
Orange County Teachers Federal	PO Box 11547	Santa Ana	CA	92711	Rudy Hanley	714-258-4000	R	1,442*	0.5
Granite State Credit Union	P O Box 6420	Manchester	NH	03108	Denise Caristi	603-668-2221	R	1,305*	<0.1
Wisconsin Corporate Central	P O Box 469	Hales Corners	WI	53130	Mark Schroeder	414-425-5555	R	1,251	<0.1
Jeanne D'Arc Credit Union	658 Merrimack St	Lowell	MA	01854	Paul Mayotte	978-452-5001	R	1,230*	0.2
Hughes Credit Union	1440 Rosecrans Ave	Manhattan Bch	CA	90266	Tom Graham	310-643-5400	S	1,218*	0.5
Delta Employees Credit Union	P O Box 20541	Atlanta	GA	30320	W Joe Williams	404-715-4725	R	1,213	0.2
San Antonio Federal Credit Union	P O Box 1356	San Antonio	TX	78295	Jeffrey H Farver	210-258-1414	R	1,100*	0.5
U.S. Central Credit Union	7300 College Blvd	Overland Park	KS	66210	Dan Kampen	913-661-3800	R	1,071*	0.2
Educational Community Credit	PO Box 2600	Jacksonville	FL	32232	John Hirabayasha	904-354-8537	R	994*	0.2
Portland Teachers Credit Union	P O Box 3750	Portland	OR	97208	Cliff Diaf	503-228-8255	R	936	0.3
State Employees Credit Union	8501 LaSalle Rd	Towson	MD	21286	Teresa A Halleck	410-296-7328	R	900	0.5
Mission Federal Credit Union	P O Box 919023	San Diego	CA	92191	Ron Martin	619-546-2000	R	820	0.3
Coast Central Credit Union	2650 Harrison Ave	Eureka	CA	95501	Dean Christensen	707-445-8801	R	795*	0.1
Florida Telco Credit Union	101 Bell Tel Way	Jacksonville	FL	32216	W R Braddock Jr	904-723-6300	R	763*	0.1
AT & T Family Federal Credit	P O Box 26000	Winston-Salem	NC	27114	Marcus Schaefer	336-659-1955	R	635	0.3
Meriwest Credit Union	PO Box 530953	San Jose	CA	95153	Christopher Owen		R	620	0.3
SEFCU	PO Box 12189	Albany	NY	12212	Patrick G Calhoun	518-452-8183	R	606	0.2
Indiana Members Credit Union	P O Box 47769	Indianapolis	IN	46247	Edward Lechner	317-788-0366	R	599*	0.2
OmniAmerican Federal Credit	PO Box 150099	Fort Worth	TX	76108	Larry E Duckworth	817-246-0111	R	570	0.3
N.W.A. Federal Credit Union	4 Appletree Sq	Bloomington	MN	55425	Paul V Parish	612-726-2073	R	567	0.2
Rhode Island State Employees	160 Francis St	Providence	RI	02903	Paul Filippone	401-751-7440	R	565*	<0.1
First Community Credit Union	15715 Manchester	Ellisville	MO	63011	Donald C Berra	314-256-9292	R	550	0.2
USAlliance Federal Credit Union	600 Midland Ave	Rye	NY	10580	Kevin Foster-Keddie	914-921-0500	R	525	0.1
MacDill Federal Credit Union	PO Box 19100	Tampa	FL	33686	Robert L Fisher	813-837-2451	R	522*	0.3
Premier America Federal Credit	19867 Prairie St	Chatsworth	CA	91311	John M Merlo	818-772-4000	R	488*	0.2
American Electronic Association	505 N Mathilda Ave	Sunnyvale	CA	94086	Tim Kramer	408-731-4100	R	460	0.2
Brockton Credit Union	P O Box 720	Brockton	MA	02403	James W Blake	508-586-2080	R	460	0.2
Pacific Service Federal Credit	2850 Shadelands Dr	Walnut Creek	CA	94598	Thomas S Smigielski	925-296-6200	R	450	<0.1
Keesler Federal Credit Union	P O Box 7001	Biloxi	MS	39534	D Scott Broome	228-385-5500	R	447*	0.2
Finance Center Federal	PO Box 26501	Indianapolis	IN	46226	Roger Youngs	317-543-5800	R	437*	0.2
Government Employees Credit	P O Box 20998	El Paso	TX	79998	Harriet May	915-778-9221	R	427*	0.4
Oregon Telco Credit Union	2121 S W 4th Ave	Portland	OR	97201	Wayne Gaylin	503-227-5571	R	427	<0.1
Baxter Credit Union	1425 Lake Cook Rd	Deerfield	IL	60015	Mike Valentine	847-522-8600	R	422	0.2
S.A.F.E. Credit Union	P O Box 1057	North Highlands	CA	95660	Henry W Wirz	916-979-7233	R	421*	0.3
Excel Federal Credit Union	5070 Peachtree-Ind	Atlanta	GA	30371	Gary R Nalley	770-441-9235	R	420	<0.1
Fort Worth Federal Credit Union	819 Taylor St	Fort Worth	TX	76102	Richard Howdeshell	817-335-2525	R	420	<0.1
Anheuser-Busch Employees	1001 Lynch St	St. Louis	MO	63118	J David Osborn	314-771-7700	R	386	0.2
Landmark Credit Union	2400 N Grandview	Waukesha	WI	53188	Ron Kase	262-574-4900	R	377*	0.2
La Capitol Federal Credit Union	PO Box 3398	Baton Rouge	LA	70821	Betsy Hooper	504-342-5055	R	371*	0.1
United Cooperative Bank	P O Box 9020	West Springfield	MA	01090	Raymond J Labbe	413-787-1700	R	370	0.1
Kitsap Community Federal Credit	1025 Burwell St	Bremerton	WA	98337	Elliot Gregg	360-478-2200	R	365	0.2
Fibre Federal Credit Union	P O Box 1234	Longview	WA	98632	Dennis Curtin	360-423-8750	R	350	0.1
Los Angeles Police Federal Credit	P O Box 10188	Van Nuys	CA	91410	Stephen M Endaya	818-787-6520	R	325*	<0.1
T and C Federal Credit Union	2525 Telegraph Rd	Bloomfield Hills	MI	48302	Dianne Addington	248-858-2323	R	316	0.1
Energy First Credit Union	1155 Corp Center	Monterey Park	CA	91754	Lynn Bowers	323-981-4000	R	308	<0.1
St. Louis Telephone Employees	4650 Hampton Ave	St. Louis	MO	63109	Charles Waalkes	314-832-8500	R	286*	<0.1
Kraft Foods Federal Credit Union	777 Westchester	White Plains	NY	10604	Holly E Herman	914-641-3700	R	285	0.1
Detroit Teachers Credit Union	7700 Puritan	Detroit	MI	48238	Ernest Holland	313-345-7200	R	285	0.1
Educators Credit Union	1400 N Newman Rd	Racine	WI	53406	Eugene Szymczak	414-886-5900	R	278*	0.2
NWC Community Federal Credit	P O Box 1209	Ridgecrest	CA	93556	Robert M Boland	760-371-7000	R	260*	0.1
First City Savings Federal Credit	PO Box 2007	Glendale	CA	91209	Stephen R Punch	818-546-2489	R	245	0.1
Merrimack Valley Federal Credit	1475 Osgood St	North Andover	MA	01845	Duncan M MacLeod	978-975-4095	R	241	<0.1
Dupaco Community Credit Union	PO Box 179	Dubuque	IA	52004	Robert Hoefer	319-557-7600	R	240	0.1
Rockland Federal Credit Union	241 Union St	Rockland	MA	02370	Thomas White	781-878-0232	R	225	0.1
Dade County Federal Credit Union	1500 N W 107th	Miami	FL	33172	John Muncey	305-471-5080	R	218	0.1
Health Services Credit Union	9790 Touchton Rd	Jacksonville	FL	32246	Maurice Pilver	904-296-1292	R	213*	<0.1
Rainier Pacific	P O Box 11628	Tacoma	WA	98411	John A Hall	253-926-4000	R	209	0.2
Associated Credit Union	PO Box 756	Deer Park	TX	77536	Jack Click	281-479-3441	R	204*	<0.1
Co-op Services Credit Union	29550 Five Mile Rd	Livonia	MI	48154	Robert L Huston	734-522-3700	R	200	0.1
Fort Knox Federal Credit Union	PO Box 100	Fort Wayne	IN	46801	William J Rissel	502-942-0254	R	200	0.1
First South Credit Union	6th & F St	Millington	TN	38053	W Craig Esrael	901-873-2300	R	194	0.1
Credit Union of Denver	P O Box 261420	Lakewood	CO	80226	Wayne Harubin	303-234-1700	R	187	<0.1
Georgia Federal Credit Union	2301 Parklake Drive	Atlanta	GA	30345	Mack D Ivey	770-493-4328	R	187	0.1
Heritage Trust Federal Credit	PO Box 118000	Charleston	SC	29423	Quince E Cody	843-552-4040	R	185*	0.1
Unit Number 1 Federal Credit	PO Box 830	Lockport	NY	14095	Ann M Brittin	716-434-2290	R	183*	<0.1
Valley Credit Union	2635 Zanker Rd	San Jose	CA	95134	Anthony Jones	408-955-1300	R	180	0.1

Source: Ward's Business Directory of U.S. Private and Public Companies, Volumes 1 and 2, 2000. The company type code used is as follows: P - Public, R - Private, S - Subsidiary, D - Division, J - Joint Venture, A - Affiliate, G - Group, N - Company type not reported. Sales are in millions of dollars, employees are in thousands. An asterisk (*) indicates an estimated sales volume. The symbol < stands for 'less than'. Company names and addresses are truncated, in some cases, to fit into the available space.

LOCATION BY STATE AND REGIONAL CONCENTRATION

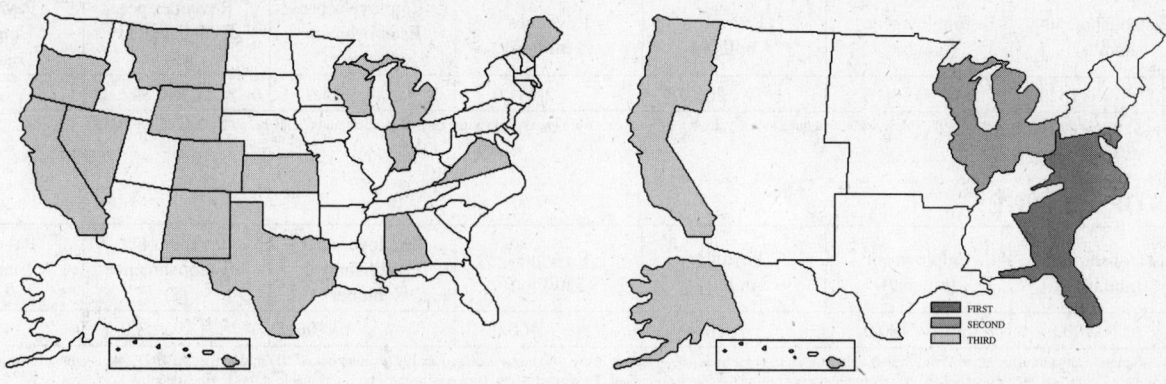

INDUSTRY DATA BY STATE

State	Establishments Total (number)	Establishments % of U.S.	Employment Total (number)	Employment % of U.S.	Employment Per Estab.	Payroll Total ($ mil.)	Payroll Per Empl. ($)	Revenues Total ($ mil.)	Revenues % of U.S.	Revenues Per Estab. ($)
California	1,306	8.4	18,393	10.7	14	552.5	30,037	3,648.7	12.3	2,793,810
Texas	1,074	6.9	13,517	7.9	13	328.5	24,304	2,204.3	7.4	2,052,433
Michigan	754	4.8	9,800	5.7	13	244.2	24,916	1,616.1	5.4	2,143,350
Florida	591	3.8	9,052	5.3	15	219.2	24,210	1,525.3	5.1	2,580,941
Virginia	393	2.5	7,286	4.2	19	207.2	28,436	1,437.9	4.8	3,658,654
Kansas	185	1.2	1,412	0.8	8	35.2	24,958	1,313.8	4.4	7,101,768
Illinois	691	4.4	5,399	3.1	8	129.5	23,988	888.4	3.0	1,285,645
Ohio	771	4.9	6,161	3.6	8	137.2	22,263	838.6	2.8	1,087,690
Indiana	469	3.0	4,938	2.9	11	115.4	23,364	735.8	2.5	1,568,953
North Carolina	349	2.2	4,260	2.5	12	92.4	21,694	701.8	2.4	2,010,777
Wisconsin	490	3.1	5,216	3.0	11	109.4	20,973	639.9	2.2	1,305,829
Maryland	215	1.4	3,221	1.9	15	85.6	26,588	568.9	1.9	2,645,833
Colorado	265	1.7	3,568	2.1	13	85.7	24,013	568.6	1.9	2,145,479
Georgia	329	2.1	3,241	1.9	10	84.6	26,111	543.9	1.8	1,653,131
Alabama	329	2.1	3,199	1.9	10	72.9	22,799	515.0	1.7	1,565,258
Tennessee	391	2.5	3,478	2.0	9	78.4	22,532	513.7	1.7	1,313,767
Oregon	213	1.4	2,917	1.7	14	80.1	27,469	473.1	1.6	2,221,042
Minnesota	284	1.8	2,751	1.6	10	68.2	24,786	451.3	1.5	1,588,937
Arizona	188	1.2	2,463	1.4	13	64.1	26,005	370.6	1.2	1,971,213
Connecticut	277	1.8	1,993	1.2	7	55.1	27,662	366.4	1.2	1,322,632
Missouri	229	1.5	2,401	1.4	10	57.0	23,751	364.9	1.2	1,593,533
Louisiana	339	2.2	2,498	1.5	7	54.0	21,604	333.2	1.1	982,752
Oklahoma	152	1.0	2,647	1.5	17	52.1	19,697	328.6	1.1	2,161,730
South Carolina	200	1.3	2,120	1.2	11	50.9	23,990	314.9	1.1	1,574,255
Hawaii	136	0.9	1,353	0.8	10	37.9	28,015	277.2	0.9	2,038,051
Iowa	263	1.7	2,051	1.2	8	42.2	20,599	276.2	0.9	1,050,103
New Mexico	96	0.6	1,501	0.9	16	38.6	25,721	228.6	0.8	2,381,063
Maine	134	0.9	1,619	0.9	12	37.4	23,111	225.7	0.8	1,684,604
Kentucky	172	1.1	1,532	0.9	9	34.4	22,444	217.6	0.7	1,265,366
D.C.	97	0.6	907	0.5	9	28.9	31,891	214.0	0.7	2,206,134
Nevada	76	0.5	1,144	0.7	15	31.2	27,237	206.7	0.7	2,719,447
Nebraska	117	0.7	1,056	0.6	9	24.3	22,968	161.6	0.5	1,381,274
Rhode Island	67	0.4	825	0.5	12	20.0	24,192	147.7	0.5	2,204,776
Mississippi	149	1.0	908	0.5	6	19.3	21,211	125.7	0.4	843,691
New Hampshire	53	0.3	858	0.5	16	22.2	25,819	124.8	0.4	2,353,830
Montana	102	0.7	817	0.5	8	16.2	19,803	116.0	0.4	1,137,275
Idaho	128	0.8	934	0.5	7	19.9	21,346	114.5	0.4	894,602
West Virginia	139	0.9	732	0.4	5	14.9	20,363	110.9	0.4	797,806
Arkansas	84	0.5	485	0.3	6	10.9	22,546	80.1	0.3	953,036
South Dakota	80	0.5	579	0.3	7	12.3	21,185	67.3	0.2	841,800
Vermont	56	0.4	389	0.2	7	9.2	23,620	57.9	0.2	1,034,482
Wyoming	44	0.3	388	0.2	9	8.1	20,827	52.3	0.2	1,188,409
Pennsylvania	836	5.3	7,500*	-	-	(D)	-	(D)	-	-
New York	745	4.8	7,500*	-	-	(D)	-	(D)	-	-
Massachusetts	404	2.6	3,750*	-	-	(D)	-	(D)	-	-
Washington	358	2.3	7,500*	-	-	(D)	-	(D)	-	-
New Jersey	347	2.2	1,750*	-	-	(D)	-	(D)	-	-
Utah	261	1.7	3,750*	-	-	(D)	-	(D)	-	-
North Dakota	91	0.6	750*	-	-	(D)	-	(D)	-	-
Alaska	61	0.4	1,750*	-	-	(D)	-	(D)	-	-
Delaware	60	0.4	375*	-	-	(D)	-	(D)	-	-

Source: 1997 *Economic Census*. The states are in descending order of revenues or establishments (if revenue data are missing for the majority). The symbol (D) appears when data are withheld to prevent disclosure of competitive information. States marked with (D) are sorted by number of establishments. A dash (-) indicates that the data element cannot be calculated. * indicates the midpoint of a range; 175, for example is the range 100-249. Shaded *states* on the state map indicate those states which have proportionately greater representation in the industry than would be indicated by the state's population; the ratio is based on total revenues or number of establishments. Shaded *regions* indicate where the industry is regionally most concentrated.

NAICS 522190 - DEPOSITORY CREDIT INTERMEDIATION NEC

GENERAL STATISTICS

Year	Establishments (number)	Employment (number)	Payroll ($ million)	Revenues ($ million)	Employees per Establishment (number)	Revenues per Establishment ($)	Payroll per Employee ($)
1997	152	5,416	266.0	2,734.0	35.6	17,986,842	49,114

Source: *Economic Census of the United States*, 1997. This is a newly defined industry. Data for prior years were unavailable at the time of publication but may become available over time.

INDICES OF CHANGE

Year	Establishments (number)	Employment (number)	Payroll ($ million)	Revenues ($ million)	Employees per Establishment (number)	Revenues per Establishment ($)	Payroll per Employee ($)
1997	100.0	100.0	100.0	100.0	100.0	100.0	100.0

Sources: Same as General Statistics. The values shown reflect change from the base year, 1997. Values above 100 mean greater than 1997, values below 100 mean less than 1997, and a value of 100 in the 1982-96 or 1998-2001 period means same as 1997. Values followed by a 'p' are projections by the editors; 'e' stands for extrapolation. Data are the most recent available at this level of detail.

SIC INDUSTRIES RELATED TO NAICS 522190

Each new NAICS code represents an industry that used to be part of an SIC or a part of several SIC industries. Data in this table are shown to provide transitional information for these cases. All available data for the precursor SIC(s) are shown. Even if only a part of an SIC is included in the NAICS, *all* data for the SIC are reproduced. If the SIC industry is not marked as being a part (pt) of the NAICS, the entire industry is embedded in the NAICS data. The SIC composition of the new industry provides some hints of the relative importance of its "ancestors." Data marked with a 'p' are projected. Projections begin with 1982 data. Data earlier than 1990 are not shown but are reflected in the projections.

SIC	Industry	1990	1991	1992	1993	1994	1995	1996	1997
6022	**State Commercial Banks (pt)**	-	-	-	-	-	-	-	-

Source: *Economic Census of the United States*, 1992, annual surveys of economic sectors conducted by the Bureau of the Census, and estimates or projections based on the 1982-1992 period; not all data are shown. 'e' marks estimates made by the editors; 'p' indicates projections based on time series. A dash (-) indicates that data for this SIC or year were not available. The abbreviation (pt) next to the industry name indicates that only a part of the industry is present within the NAICS data. If no (pt) is shown, the entire industry is contained within the NAICS data.

SELECTED RATIOS

For 1997	Avg. of Information	Analyzed Industry	Index	For 1997	Avg. of Information	Analyzed Industry	Index
Employees per establishment	15	36	241	Payroll per establishment	669,406	1,750,000	261
Revenue per establishment	5,561,120	17,986,842	323	Payroll as % of revenue	12	10	81
Revenue per employee	376,639	504,801	134	Payroll per employee	45,337	49,114	108

Sources: Same as General Statistics. The 'Average' column represents the average for the industry sector, in 1997, where the currently shown industry is classified. The Index shows the relationship between the Average and the Analyzed Industry. For example, 100 means that they are equal; 500 that the Analyzed Industry is five times the average; 50 means that the Analyzed Industry is half the national average. The abbreviation 'na' is used to show that data are 'not available'.

LEADING COMPANIES

No company data available for this industry.

LOCATION BY STATE AND REGIONAL CONCENTRATION

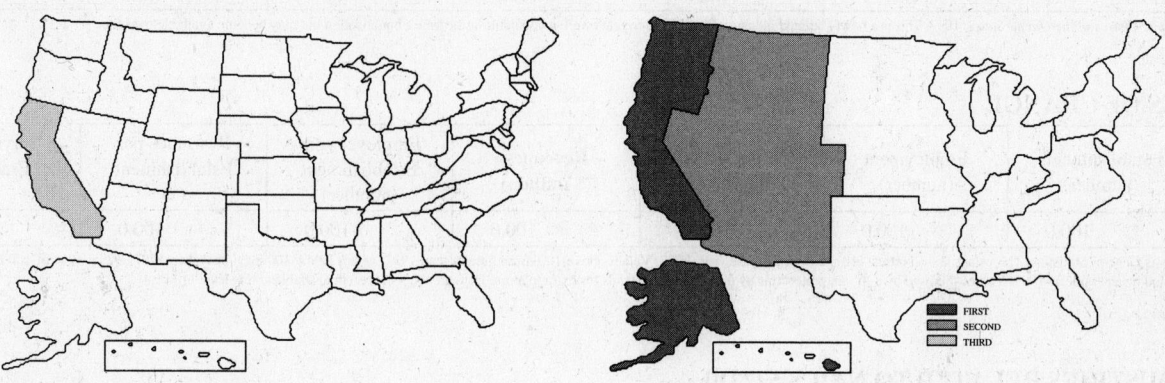

FIRST
SECOND
THIRD

INDUSTRY DATA BY STATE

State	Establishments		Employment			Payroll		Revenues		
	Total (number)	% of U.S.	Total (number)	% of U.S.	Per Estab.	Total ($ mil.)	Per Empl. ($)	Total ($ mil.)	% of U.S.	Per Estab. ($)
California	124	81.6	2,285	42.2	18	100.2	43,842	857.5	31.4	6,915,637
Colorado	12	7.9	117	2.2	10	3.7	31,547	20.4	0.7	1,702,417
Utah	10	6.6	750*	-	-	(D)	-	(D)	-	-

Source: 1997 *Economic Census*. The states are in descending order of revenues or establishments (if revenue data are missing for the majority). The symbol (D) appears when data are withheld to prevent disclosure of competitive information. States marked with (D) are sorted by number of establishments. A dash (-) indicates that the data element cannot be calculated. * indicates the midpoint of a range; 175, for example is the range 100-249. Shaded *states* on the state map indicate those states which have proportionately greater representation in the industry than would be indicated by the state's population; the ratio is based on total revenues or number of establishments. Shaded *regions* indicate where the industry is regionally most concentrated.

NAICS 522210 - CREDIT CARD ISSUING

GENERAL STATISTICS

Year	Establishments (number)	Employment (number)	Payroll ($ million)	Revenues ($ million)	Employees per Establishment (number)	Revenues per Establishment ($)	Payroll per Employee ($)
1997	588	58,773	1,783.0	24,503.0	100.0	41,671,769	30,337

Source: *Economic Census of the United States*, 1997. This is a newly defined industry. Data for prior years were unavailable at the time of publication but may become available over time.

INDICES OF CHANGE

Year	Establishments (number)	Employment (number)	Payroll ($ million)	Revenues ($ million)	Employees per Establishment (number)	Revenues per Establishment ($)	Payroll per Employee ($)
1997	100.0	100.0	100.0	100.0	100.0	100.0	100.0

Sources: Same as General Statistics. The values shown reflect change from the base year, 1997. Values above 100 mean greater than 1997, values below 100 mean less than 1997, and a value of 100 in the 1982-96 or 1998-2001 period means same as 1997. Values followed by a 'p' are projections by the editors; 'e' stands for extrapolation. Data are the most recent available at this level of detail.

SIC INDUSTRIES RELATED TO NAICS 522210

Each new NAICS code represents an industry that used to be part of an SIC or a part of several SIC industries. Data in this table are shown to provide transitional information for these cases. All available data for the precursor SIC(s) are shown. Even if only a part of an SIC is included in the NAICS, *all* data for the SIC are reproduced. If the SIC industry is not marked as being a part (pt) of the NAICS, the entire industry is embedded in the NAICS data. The SIC composition of the new industry provides some hints of the relative importance of its "ancestors." Data marked with a 'p' are projected. Projections begin with 1982 data. Data earlier than 1990 are not shown but are reflected in the projections.

SIC	Industry	1990	1991	1992	1993	1994	1995	1996	1997
6021	**National Commercial Banks (pt)**	-	-	-	-	-	-	-	-
6022	**State Commercial Banks (pt)**	-	-	-	-	-	-	-	-
6141	**Personal Credit Institutions (pt)**								
	Establishments (number)	-	-	16,900	-	-	-	-	-
	Employment (thousands)	-	-	158.8	-	-	-	-	-
	Revenues ($ million)	-	-	47,668.4	-	-	-	-	-
6153	**Short-Term Business Credit (pt)**	-	-	-	-	-	-	-	-

Source: *Economic Census of the United States*, 1992, annual surveys of economic sectors conducted by the Bureau of the Census, and estimates or projections based on the 1982-1992 period; not all data are shown. 'e' marks estimates made by the editors; 'p' indicates projections based on time series. A dash (-) indicates that data for this SIC or year were not available. The abbreviation (pt) next to the industry name indicates that only a part of the industry is present within the NAICS data. If no (pt) is shown, the entire industry is contained within the NAICS data.

SELECTED RATIOS

For 1997	Avg. of Information	Analyzed Industry	Index	For 1997	Avg. of Information	Analyzed Industry	Index
Employees per establishment	15	100	677	Payroll per establishment	669,406	3,032,313	453
Revenue per establishment	5,561,120	41,671,769	749	Payroll as % of revenue	12	7	60
Revenue per employee	376,639	416,909	111	Payroll per employee	45,337	30,337	67

Sources: Same as General Statistics. The 'Average' column represents the average for the industry sector, in 1997, where the currently shown industry is classified. The Index shows the relationship between the Average and the Analyzed Industry. For example, 100 means that they are equal; 500 that the Analyzed Industry is five times the average; 50 means that the Analyzed Industry is half the national average. The abbreviation 'na' is used to show that data are 'not available'.

LEADING COMPANIES

No company data available for this industry.

LOCATION BY STATE AND REGIONAL CONCENTRATION

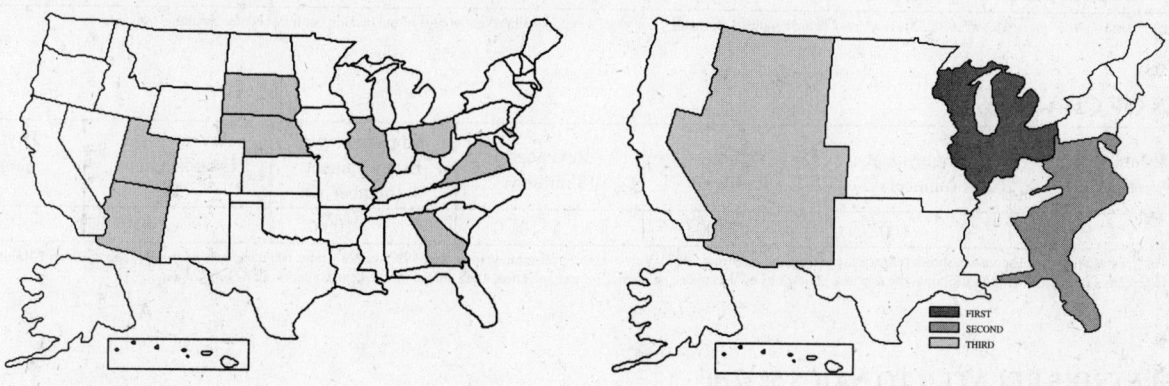

INDUSTRY DATA BY STATE

State	Establishments		Employment			Payroll		Revenues		
	Total (number)	% of U.S.	Total (number)	% of U.S.	Per Estab.	Total ($ mil.)	Per Empl. ($)	Total ($ mil.)	% of U.S.	Per Estab. ($)
Delaware	56	9.5	8,036	13.7	143	227.7	28,331	6,418.0	26.2	114,607,321
South Dakota	20	3.4	4,784	8.1	239	105.5	22,049	3,918.3	16.0	195,913,500
Ohio	60	10.2	17,721	30.2	295	538.2	30,371	3,209.2	13.1	53,487,400
Illinois	147	25.0	1,958	3.3	13	126.0	64,345	668.6	2.7	4,548,497
Arizona	37	6.3	4,896	8.3	132	107.7	21,999	473.2	1.9	12,790,432
Texas	10	1.7	775	1.3	78	28.5	36,726	194.0	0.8	19,398,500
Florida	15	2.6	750*	-	-	27.0	-	193.2	0.8	12,880,867
Pennsylvania	6	1.0	375*	-	-	5.8	-	15.0	0.1	2,506,167
Utah	47	8.0	3,750*	-	-	(D)	-	(D)	-	-
California	29	4.9	1,750*	-	-	(D)	-	(D)	-	-
New York	24	4.1	1,750*	-	-	(D)	-	(D)	-	-
Virginia	22	3.7	7,500*	-	-	(D)	-	(D)	-	-
Georgia	17	2.9	1,750*	-	-	(D)	-	(D)	-	-
Nebraska	11	1.9	3,750*	-	-	(D)	-	(D)	-	-
Louisiana	8	1.4	175*	-	-	(D)	-	(D)	-	-
New Jersey	8	1.4	175*	-	-	(D)	-	(D)	-	-
Massachusetts	7	1.2	60*	-	-	(D)	-	(D)	-	-

Source: 1997 *Economic Census*. The states are in descending order of revenues or establishments (if revenue data are missing for the majority). The symbol (D) appears when data are withheld to prevent disclosure of competitive information. States marked with (D) are sorted by number of establishments. A dash (-) indicates that the data element cannot be calculated. * indicates the midpoint of a range; 175, for example is the range 100-249. Shaded *states* on the state map indicate those states which have proportionately greater representation in the industry than would be indicated by the state's population; the ratio is based on total revenues or number of establishments. Shaded *regions* indicate where the industry is regionally most concentrated.

NAICS 522220 - SALES FINANCING

GENERAL STATISTICS

Year	Establishments (number)	Employment (number)	Payroll ($ million)	Revenues ($ million)	Employees per Establishment (number)	Revenues per Establishment ($)	Payroll per Employee ($)
1997	8,143	127,832	6,163.0	78,133.0	15.7	9,595,112	48,212

Source: Economic Census of the United States, 1997. This is a newly defined industry. Data for prior years were unavailable at the time of publication but may become available over time.

INDICES OF CHANGE

Year	Establishments (number)	Employment (number)	Payroll ($ million)	Revenues ($ million)	Employees per Establishment (number)	Revenues per Establishment ($)	Payroll per Employee ($)
1997	100.0	100.0	100.0	100.0	100.0	100.0	100.0

Sources: Same as General Statistics. The values shown reflect change from the base year, 1997. Values above 100 mean greater than 1997, values below 100 mean less than 1997, and a value of 100 in the 1982-96 or 1998-2001 period means same as 1997. Values followed by a 'p' are projections by the editors; 'e' stands for extrapolation. Data are the most recent available at this level of detail.

SIC INDUSTRIES RELATED TO NAICS 522220

Each new NAICS code represents an industry that used to be part of an SIC or a part of several SIC industries. Data in this table are shown to provide transitional information for these cases. All available data for the precursor SIC(s) are shown. Even if only a part of an SIC is included in the NAICS, *all* data for the SIC are reproduced. If the SIC industry is not marked as being a part (pt) of the NAICS, the entire industry is embedded in the NAICS data. The SIC composition of the new industry provides some hints of the relative importance of its "ancestors." Data marked with a 'p' are projected. Projections begin with 1982 data. Data earlier than 1990 are not shown but are reflected in the projections.

SIC	Industry	1990	1991	1992	1993	1994	1995	1996	1997
6141	**Personal Credit Institutions (pt)**								
	Establishments (number)	-	-	16,900	-	-	-	-	-
	Employment (thousands)	-	-	158.8	-	-	-	-	-
	Revenues ($ million)	-	-	47,668.4	-	-	-	-	-
6153	**Short-Term Business Credit (pt)**	-	-	-	-	-	-	-	-
6159	**Misc. Business Credit Institutions (pt)**	-	-	-	-	-	-	-	-

Source: Economic Census of the United States, 1992, annual surveys of economic sectors conducted by the Bureau of the Census, and estimates or projections based on the 1982-1992 period; not all data are shown. 'e' marks estimates made by the editors; 'p' indicates projections based on time series. A dash (-) indicates that data for this SIC or year were not available. The abbreviation (pt) next to the industry name indicates that only a part of the industry is present within the NAICS data. If no (pt) is shown, the entire industry is contained within the NAICS data.

SELECTED RATIOS

For 1997	Avg. of Information	Analyzed Industry	Index	For 1997	Avg. of Information	Analyzed Industry	Index
Employees per establishment	15	16	106	Payroll per establishment	669,406	756,846	113
Revenue per establishment	5,561,120	9,595,112	173	Payroll as % of revenue	12	8	66
Revenue per employee	376,639	611,216	162	Payroll per employee	45,337	48,212	106

Sources: Same as General Statistics. The 'Average' column represents the average for the industry sector, in 1997, where the currently shown industry is classified. The Index shows the relationship between the Average and the Analyzed Industry. For example, 100 means that they are equal; 500 that the Analyzed Industry is five times the average; 50 means that the Analyzed Industry is half the national average. The abbreviation 'na' is used to show that data are 'not available'.

LEADING COMPANIES

No company data available for this industry.

LOCATION BY STATE AND REGIONAL CONCENTRATION

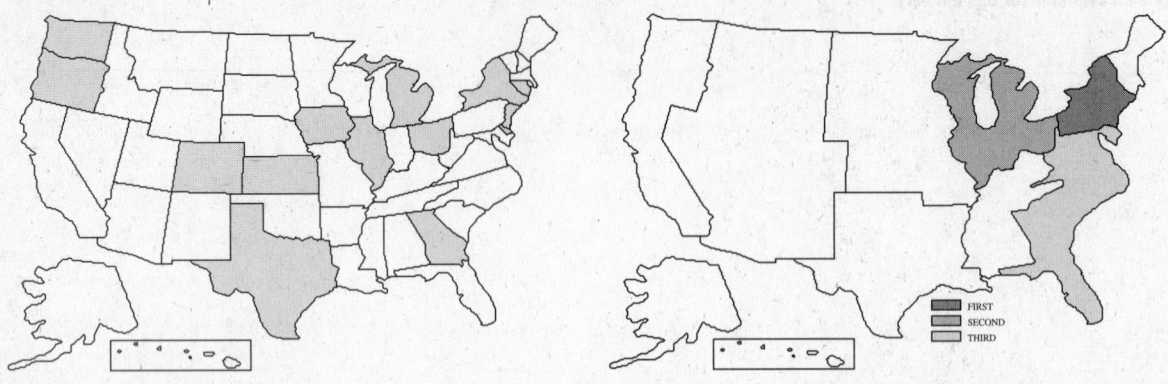

INDUSTRY DATA BY STATE

State	Establishments Total (number)	Establishments % of U.S.	Employment Total (number)	Employment % of U.S.	Employment Per Estab.	Payroll Total ($ mil.)	Payroll Per Empl. ($)	Revenues Total ($ mil.)	Revenues % of U.S.	Revenues Per Estab. ($)
New York	419	5.1	9,450	7.4	23	639.2	67,638	9,751.1	12.5	23,272,234
California	783	9.6	15,483	12.1	20	807.7	52,166	9,024.2	11.5	11,525,180
Texas	614	7.5	14,075	11.0	23	648.6	46,080	6,479.6	8.3	10,553,046
Illinois	402	4.9	7,995	6.3	20	448.0	56,038	5,775.4	7.4	14,366,619
Connecticut	104	1.3	4,704	3.7	45	337.9	71,827	4,000.1	5.1	38,462,760
Georgia	458	5.6	5,988	4.7	13	272.1	45,439	3,717.2	4.8	8,116,175
Michigan	200	2.5	4,933	3.9	25	248.8	50,442	3,657.8	4.7	18,288,825
Florida	642	7.9	7,777	6.1	12	284.9	36,628	3,484.8	4.5	5,428,055
Ohio	275	3.4	5,336	4.2	19	183.7	34,430	3,444.5	4.4	12,525,284
New Jersey	223	2.7	4,895	3.8	22	313.7	64,094	2,768.8	3.5	12,416,184
Pennsylvania	248	3.0	4,617	3.6	19	203.7	44,112	2,046.8	2.6	8,253,040
Washington	172	2.1	1,969	1.5	11	102.7	52,180	1,692.0	2.2	9,837,157
North Carolina	346	4.2	3,240	2.5	9	122.8	37,909	1,592.7	2.0	4,603,234
Tennessee	230	2.8	3,669	2.9	16	135.0	36,790	1,398.1	1.8	6,078,522
Colorado	159	2.0	2,226	1.7	14	100.1	44,966	1,342.6	1.7	8,444,050
Maryland	162	2.0	2,944	2.3	18	137.9	46,838	1,252.4	1.6	7,730,611
Iowa	57	0.7	1,378	1.1	24	43.4	31,495	1,124.6	1.4	19,729,263
Minnesota	154	1.9	1,941	1.5	13	97.0	49,952	1,122.2	1.4	7,287,299
Missouri	145	1.8	2,316	1.8	16	97.2	41,948	1,011.1	1.3	6,973,097
Oregon	101	1.2	1,636	1.3	16	74.4	45,483	1,007.4	1.3	9,974,693
Kansas	96	1.2	1,033	0.8	11	43.4	42,040	945.9	1.2	9,853,531
Wisconsin	103	1.3	1,185	0.9	12	44.5	37,552	822.7	1.1	7,987,369
Virginia	177	2.2	1,329	1.0	8	51.9	39,065	778.4	1.0	4,397,695
Delaware	57	0.7	739	0.6	13	37.7	50,982	750.8	1.0	13,172,228
Indiana	151	1.9	1,900	1.5	13	66.1	34,809	724.6	0.9	4,798,901
Louisiana	184	2.3	1,121	0.9	6	37.9	33,809	585.0	0.7	3,179,418
Alabama	177	2.2	1,008	0.8	6	33.1	32,813	522.4	0.7	2,951,158
South Carolina	239	2.9	1,270	1.0	5	42.2	33,191	489.3	0.6	2,047,448
Oklahoma	88	1.1	824	0.6	9	31.5	38,204	367.2	0.5	4,172,648
Mississippi	134	1.6	633	0.5	5	18.2	28,724	218.9	0.3	1,633,500
Utah	62	0.8	461	0.4	7	19.6	42,547	216.5	0.3	3,492,726
Kentucky	82	1.0	581	0.5	7	20.3	34,935	207.5	0.3	2,530,537
Arkansas	26	0.3	259	0.2	10	9.5	36,792	193.1	0.2	7,427,154
Vermont	7	0.1	375*	-	-	21.5	-	162.5	0.2	23,220,857
New Mexico	39	0.5	1,014	0.8	26	20.3	20,047	151.5	0.2	3,884,667
Nebraska	29	0.4	177	0.1	6	6.0	33,887	141.3	0.2	4,871,414
Hawaii	41	0.5	250	0.2	6	9.9	39,752	113.5	0.1	2,768,049
West Virginia	30	0.4	197	0.2	7	6.7	33,858	104.3	0.1	3,477,933
Idaho	28	0.3	157	0.1	6	8.1	51,414	102.3	0.1	3,653,679
North Dakota	6	0.1	72	0.1	12	2.2	30,806	72.1	0.1	12,014,833
Maine	11	0.1	60*	-	-	2.5	-	61.1	0.1	5,551,727
Montana	18	0.2	98	0.1	5	3.1	32,051	52.7	0.1	2,928,667
South Dakota	17	0.2	143	0.1	8	4.4	30,706	51.6	0.1	3,037,294
Wyoming	8	0.1	43	0.0	5	1.1	26,628	38.3	0.0	4,783,625
Alaska	8	0.1	48	0.0	6	2.4	49,208	16.4	0.0	2,051,875
Arizona	155	1.9	1,750*	-	-	(D)	-	(D)	-	-
Massachusetts	146	1.8	1,750*	-	-	(D)	-	(D)	-	-
Nevada	69	0.8	1,750*	-	-	(D)	-	(D)	-	-
New Hampshire	29	0.4	175*	-	-	(D)	-	(D)	-	-
Rhode Island	19	0.2	375*	-	-	(D)	-	(D)	-	-
D.C.	13	0.2	60*	-	-	(D)	-	(D)	-	-

Source: 1997 *Economic Census.* The states are in descending order of revenues or establishments (if revenue data are missing for the majority). The symbol (D) appears when data are withheld to prevent disclosure of competitive information. States marked with (D) are sorted by number of establishments. A dash (-) indicates that the data element cannot be calculated. * indicates the midpoint of a range; 175, for example is the range 100-249. Shaded *states* on the state map indicate those states which have proportionately greater representation in the industry than would be indicated by the state's population; the ratio is based on total revenues or number of establishments. Shaded *regions* indicate where the industry is regionally most concentrated.

NAICS 522291 - CONSUMER LENDING

GENERAL STATISTICS

Year	Establishments (number)	Employment (number)	Payroll ($ million)	Revenues ($ million)	Employees per Establishment (number)	Revenues per Establishment ($)	Payroll per Employee ($)
1997	13,123	90,961	2,688.0	20,721.0	6.9	1,578,983	29,551

Source: Economic Census of the United States, 1997. This is a newly defined industry. Data for prior years were unavailable at the time of publication but may become available over time.

INDICES OF CHANGE

Year	Establishments (number)	Employment (number)	Payroll ($ million)	Revenues ($ million)	Employees per Establishment (number)	Revenues per Establishment ($)	Payroll per Employee ($)
1997	100.0	100.0	100.0	100.0	100.0	100.0	100.0

Sources: Same as General Statistics. The values shown reflect change from the base year, 1997. Values above 100 mean greater than 1997, values below 100 mean less than 1997, and a value of 100 in the 1982-96 or 1998-2001 period means same as 1997. Values followed by a 'p' are projections by the editors; 'e' stands for extrapolation. Data are the most recent available at this level of detail.

SIC INDUSTRIES RELATED TO NAICS 522291

Each new NAICS code represents an industry that used to be part of an SIC or a part of several SIC industries. Data in this table are shown to provide transitional information for these cases. All available data for the precursor SIC(s) are shown. Even if only a part of an SIC is included in the NAICS, *all* data for the SIC are reproduced. If the SIC industry is not marked as being a part (pt) of the NAICS, the entire industry is embedded in the NAICS data. The SIC composition of the new industry provides some hints of the relative importance of its "ancestors." Data marked with a 'p' are projected. Projections begin with 1982 data. Data earlier than 1990 are not shown but are reflected in the projections.

SIC	Industry	1990	1991	1992	1993	1994	1995	1996	1997
6141	**Personal Credit Institutions (pt)**								
	Establishments (number)	-	-	16,900	-	-	-	-	-
	Employment (thousands)	-	-	158.8	-	-	-	-	-
	Revenues ($ million)	-	-	47,668.4	-	-	-	-	-

Source: Economic Census of the United States, 1992, annual surveys of economic sectors conducted by the Bureau of the Census, and estimates or projections based on the 1982-1992 period; not all data are shown. 'e' marks estimates made by the editors; 'p' indicates projections based on time series. A dash (-) indicates that data for this SIC or year were not available. The abbreviation (pt) next to the industry name indicates that only a part of the industry is present within the NAICS data. If no (pt) is shown, the entire industry is contained within the NAICS data.

SELECTED RATIOS

For 1997	Avg. of Information	Analyzed Industry	Index	For 1997	Avg. of Information	Analyzed Industry	Index
Employees per establishment	15	7	47	Payroll per establishment	669,406	204,831	31
Revenue per establishment	5,561,120	1,578,983	28	Payroll as % of revenue	12	13	108
Revenue per employee	376,639	227,801	60	Payroll per employee	45,337	29,551	65

Sources: Same as General Statistics. The 'Average' column represents the average for the industry sector, in 1997, where the currently shown industry is classified. The Index shows the relationship between the Average and the Analyzed Industry. For example, 100 means that they are equal; 500 that the Analyzed Industry is five times the average; 50 means that the Analyzed Industry is half the national average. The abbreviation 'na' is used to show that data are 'not available'.

LEADING COMPANIES   Number shown: **66**   Total sales ($ mil): **764,942**   Total employment (000): **261.8**

Company Name	Address				CEO Name	Phone	Co. Type	Sales ($ mil)	Empl. (000)
General Electric Capital Corp.	260 Long Ridge Rd	Stamford	CT	06927	Gary C. Wendt	203-357-4000	S	228,777	51.0
General Motors Acceptance Corp.	3044 W Grand Blvd	Detroit	MI	48202	JM Losh	313-556-5000	S	131,417	23.6
Ford Motor Credit Co.	P O Box 1732	Dearborn	MI	48121	Phillip Paillart	313-322-3000	S	119,608*	15.0
American General Finance Inc.	P O Box 59	Evansville	IN	47701	F R Geissinger	812-424-8031	S	67,000	16.1
Household International Inc.	2700 Sanders Rd	Prospect Heights	IL	60070	William F Aldinger	847-564-5000	P	52,893	23.5
Morgan Stanley Dean Witter	1585 Broadway	New York	NY	10036	John J Mack	212-761-4000	P	33,928	55.3
Citicorp Diners Club Inc.	8430 W Bryn Mawr	Chicago	IL	60631	William Frisell	773-380-5100	S	25,000	3.5
Toyota Motor Credit Corp.	19001 S Western	Torrance	CA	90509	Shingi Sakai	310-787-1310	S	19,830	2.4
HSBC Inc.	1 HSBC Ctr	Buffalo	NY	14203	Malcolm Burnett	716-841-2424	D	16,564*	10.0
Avco Financial Services Inc.	PO Box 5011	Costa Mesa	CA	92628	Warren R Lyons	714-435-1200	D	8,898	8.0
Commercial Credit Co.	300 St Paul Pl	Baltimore	MD	21202	Marjorie Magner	410-332-3000	S	8,635*	5.0
Student Loan Corp.	P O Box 22944	Rochester	NY	14692	Bill Beckman	716-248-7187	P	7,873	0.8
NOVUS Services Inc.	2500 Lake Cook Rd	Riverwoods	IL	60015	Thomas Butler	847-405-0900	S	5,100*	4.0
Transamerica Financial Services	1150 S Olive St	Los Angeles	CA	90015	Thomas J Cusach	213-742-4411	S	4,600	2.5
Banc One Financial Services Inc.	8604 Alisonville Rd	Indianapolis	IN	46250	Dave Freeman	317-595-8100	S	3,952*	1.6
World Omni Financial Corp.	P O Box 8544	Deerfield Beach	FL	33443	Louis R Feagles	954-429-2200	S	3,798	0.9
Advanta Corp.	PO Box 844	Spring House	PA	19477	Dennis Alter	215-657-4000	P	3,796	2.6
First Family Financial Services	4362 Peachtree NE	Atlanta	GA	30319	Ron Mables	404-266-5400	S	3,295*	2.0
Household Retail Services	2700 Sanders Rd	Prospect Heights	IL	60070		847-564-5000	S	2,270*	1.1
Norwest Financial Inc.	206 8th St	Des Moines	IA	50309	David C Wood	515-243-2131	S	2,184	8.5
Providian Financial Corp.	201 Mission St	San Francisco	CA	94105	Shailesh J Mehta	415-543-0404	P	2,109	6.8
WFS Financial Inc.	23 Pasteur	Irvine	CA	92618	Joy Schaefer	949-727-1000	P	1,444	1.8
Credit Acceptance Corp.	25505 W 12 Mile	Southfield	MI	48076	Richard E Beckman	248-353-2700	P	1,421	0.7
CIT Group/Consumer Finance Inc.	650 CIT Dr	Livingston	NJ	07039		973-740-5000	S	1,160*	0.7
Nissan Motor Acceptance Corp.	P O Box 2870	Torrance	CA	90509	Yoichiro Nagashima	310-719-8000	S	1,135	1.0
AmeriCredit Corp.	801 Cherry St	Fort Worth	TX	76102		817-302-7000	P	1,064	1.4
Foothill Capital Corp.	11111 Santa Monica	Los Angeles	CA	90025	Peter E Schwab	310-996-7000	S	1,000*	0.2
Charter One Mortgage Corp.	2812 Emerywood	Richmond	VA	23233	Richard D Powers	804-756-6800	S	981*	0.5
Fidelity National Corp.	PO Box 105075	Atlanta	GA	30348	James B Miller Jr	404-639-6500	P	784	0.4
American General Finance Corp.	PO Box 59	Evansville	IN	47701	F R Geissinger	812-424-8031	P	588*	0.5
American Investment Bank	PO Box 68929	Indianapolis	IN	46278		317-872-6000	R	579*	0.4
AmeriCredit Financial Services	200 Bailey Ave	Fort Worth	TX	76107	Edward H Esstman	817-332-7000	S	493	1.3
Bank of America Speciality Group	PO Box 87024	Yorba Linda	CA	92885	Don Kaczor	714-921-3400	S	391*	0.2
Litchfield Financial Corp.	430 Main Rd	Williamstown	MA	01267	Richard A Stratton	413-458-1000	P	341	0.1
HomeGold Financial Inc.	3901 Pelham Rd	Greenville	SC	29615	Keith B Giddens	864-289-5000	P	257	0.5
MFN Financial Corp.	100 Field Dr	Lake Forest	IL	60045	Edward G Harshfield	847-295-8600	P	194	1.4
Eaglemark Financial Services Inc.	150 S Wacker Dr	Chicago	IL	60606	Steven F Deli	312-368-9501	S	160	0.2
Mego Financial Corp.	4310 Paradise Rd	Las Vegas	NV	89109	Robert Nederlander	702-737-3700	P	154	1.3
Central Financial Acceptance	5480 E Ferguson Dr	Los Angeles	CA	90022	Gary M Cypres	323-720-8600	P	129	0.5
First Investors Financial Services	675 Bering Dr	Houston	TX	77057	Tommy A Moore Jr	713-977-2600	S	100*	<0.1
Union Acceptance Corp.	PO Box 1083	Indianapolis	IN	46206	John M Stainbrook	317-231-6400	P	99	0.6
Transmedia Network Inc.	11900 Biscayne	Miami	FL	33181	Gene M Henderson	305-892-3300	P	94	0.2
World Acceptance Corp.	PO Box 6429	Greenville	SC	29606	R Harold Owens	864-298-9800	P	92	1.3
CDC Small Business Finance	925 Fort Stockton Dr	San Diego	CA	92103	Arthur Goodman	619-291-3594	R	81*	<0.1
Safeline Leasing Inc.	10915 Willows N E	Redmond	WA	98052		206-545-3000	S	78*	<0.1
First Virginia Credit Services Inc.	6402 Arlington Blvd	Falls Church	VA	22042	John F Chimento	703-241-3500	S	74*	<0.1
Linc Capital	303 E Wacker Dr	Chicago	IL	60601	Martin E Zimmerman	312-946-1000	P	73	0.2
Shelter Financial Bank	1905 W Ash	Columbia	MO	65203	Dan Scotten	573-445-8441	R	55*	<0.1
Aegis Consumer Funding Group	525 Washington	Jersey City	NJ	07310	Matthew B Burns	201-418-7300	P	49	0.5
Pacific Crest Capital Inc.	30343 Canwood St	Agoura Hills	CA	91301	Gary L Wehrle	818-865-3300	P	48	<0.1
1st Franklin Corp.	PO Box 880	Toccoa	GA	30577	Ben F Cheek III	706-886-7571	R	47	0.6
Standard Funding Corp.	335 Crossways	Woodbury	NY	11797	Alan J Karp	516-364-0200	P	43	<0.1
TFC Enterprises Inc.	5425 Robin Hood	Norfolk	VA	23513	Robert S Raley Jr	757-858-4054	P	40	0.4
First Investors Financial Services	675 Bering Dr	Houston	TX	77057	Tommy A Moore Jr	713-977-2600	P	34	0.1
Susquebanc Lease Co.	P O Box 8	Manheim	PA	17545	Richard Cloney	717-665-6665	S	23*	<0.1
Westar Financial Services Inc.	PO Box 919	Olympia	WA	98507	R W Christensen Jr	360-754-6227	P	20	<0.1
KBK Capital Corp.	2200 City Center II	Fort Worth	TX	76102	Robert J McGee	817-258-6000	P	18	<0.1
K and C Investment Co.	16291 Const Cir	Irvine	CA	92606	Bob Cuttler	949-551-6655	R	17*	<0.1
Jayhawk Acceptance Corp.	P O Box 803505	Dallas	TX	75380	Richard B Hoffmann	214-754-1000	P	15	<0.1
Nicholas Financial Inc.	2454 McMullen	Clearwater	FL	33759	Peter L Vosotas	727-726-0763	P	10	<0.1
AutoInfo Inc.	PO Box 4383	Stamford	CT	06907	Tom Scott Robertson		P	7	<0.1
Freedom Finance Inc.	1307 Assembly St	Columbia	SC	29201	Billy Covington	803-779-0667	S	7*	<0.1
Susquehanna Bancshares Leasing	P O Box 1000	Lititz	PA	17543	Gregory A Duncan	717-626-4721	S	5	<0.1
Point West Capital Corp.	1700 Montgomery	San Francisco	CA	94111	Alan B Perper	415-394-9469	P	5	<0.1
National Auto Finance Inc.	10302 Deerwood	Jacksonville	FL	32256	William G Magro	904-996-2500	P	4	0.2
Royal Premium Budget Inc.	PO Box 257	Southfield	MI	48037	Herbert W Kaufman	248-932-9020	S	2*	<0.1

Source: Ward's Business Directory of U.S. Private and Public Companies, Volumes 1 and 2, 2000. The company type code used is as follows: P - Public, R - Private, S - Subsidiary, D - Division, J - Joint Venture, A - Affiliate, G - Group, N - Company type not reported. Sales are in millions of dollars, employees are in thousands. An asterisk (*) indicates an estimated sales volume. The symbol < stands for 'less than'. Company names and addresses are truncated, in some cases, to fit into the available space.

LOCATION BY STATE AND REGIONAL CONCENTRATION

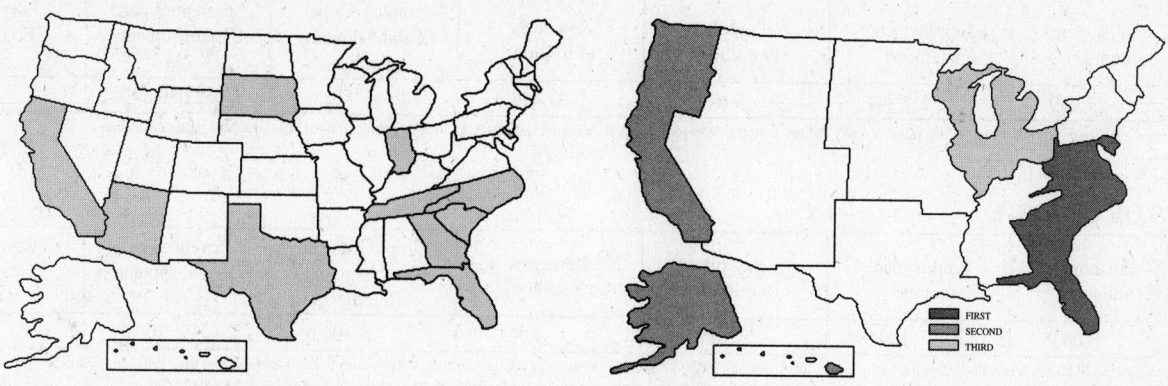

FIRST
SECOND
THIRD

INDUSTRY DATA BY STATE

State	Establishments Total (number)	% of U.S.	Employment Total (number)	% of U.S.	Per Estab.	Payroll Total ($ mil.)	Per Empl. ($)	Revenues Total ($ mil.)	% of U.S.	Per Estab. ($)
California	826	6.3	8,167	9.0	10	265.9	32,557	4,059.4	19.6	4,914,472
Florida	562	4.3	7,413	8.1	13	224.8	30,321	1,861.6	9.0	3,312,541
Texas	1,534	11.7	9,759	10.7	6	253.2	25,947	1,593.7	7.7	1,038,904
North Carolina	564	4.3	5,704	6.3	10	149.2	26,158	1,324.1	6.4	2,347,606
New York	269	2.0	2,726	3.0	10	82.4	30,219	1,025.0	4.9	3,810,431
Arizona	121	0.9	5,445	6.0	45	163.3	29,990	1,023.0	4.9	8,454,727
Pennsylvania	490	3.7	2,449	2.7	5	105.9	43,227	864.4	4.2	1,764,104
Indiana	289	2.2	4,353	4.8	15	142.7	32,774	832.3	4.0	2,880,066
Illinois	519	4.0	3,109	3.4	6	98.9	31,823	818.2	3.9	1,576,461
Georgia	833	6.3	4,399	4.8	5	129.0	29,328	693.5	3.3	832,486
Ohio	375	2.9	2,061	2.3	5	61.8	29,998	528.5	2.6	1,409,328
South Carolina	812	6.2	3,200	3.5	4	77.9	24,344	474.7	2.3	584,608
Tennessee	524	4.0	3,313	3.6	6	126.1	38,054	414.4	2.0	790,836
Louisiana	860	6.6	3,103	3.4	4	70.8	22,815	331.1	1.6	385,052
Delaware	94	0.7	3,416	3.8	36	102.6	30,038	314.2	1.5	3,342,830
New Jersey	151	1.2	766	0.8	5	31.3	40,863	309.5	1.5	2,049,530
Alabama	407	3.1	1,907	2.1	5	43.2	22,650	277.4	1.3	681,555
Kentucky	374	2.8	1,686	1.9	5	42.3	25,080	263.6	1.3	704,829
Colorado	129	1.0	1,774	2.0	14	48.7	27,475	251.0	1.2	1,945,426
Missouri	280	2.1	1,044	1.1	4	29.9	28,650	247.3	1.2	883,196
Massachusetts	74	0.6	827	0.9	11	39.0	47,162	243.2	1.2	3,286,811
Virginia	257	2.0	1,189	1.3	5	36.0	30,318	238.0	1.1	925,899
Mississippi	464	3.5	1,853	2.0	4	43.0	23,227	209.4	1.0	451,300
Oklahoma	592	4.5	1,899	2.1	3	35.7	18,775	195.8	0.9	330,696
Wisconsin	176	1.3	774	0.9	4	20.7	26,729	157.5	0.8	894,636
New Mexico	214	1.6	894	1.0	4	21.1	23,616	133.7	0.6	624,565
Minnesota	88	0.7	528	0.6	6	16.4	31,134	111.7	0.5	1,269,784
South Dakota	42	0.3	395	0.4	9	11.3	28,537	111.3	0.5	2,650,048
Washington	125	1.0	551	0.6	4	17.9	32,561	100.4	0.5	803,256
Kansas	98	0.7	484	0.5	5	14.6	30,225	85.1	0.4	868,265
Nevada	124	0.9	359	0.4	3	10.4	28,944	83.4	0.4	672,968
Iowa	83	0.6	957	1.1	12	32.3	33,773	83.1	0.4	1,001,470
Oregon	77	0.6	291	0.3	4	9.0	31,048	77.9	0.4	1,012,091
Michigan	63	0.5	558	0.6	9	15.5	27,841	60.6	0.3	962,000
West Virginia	65	0.5	295	0.3	5	7.1	24,037	53.7	0.3	826,877
Montana	30	0.2	154	0.2	5	3.9	25,513	50.2	0.2	1,674,233
Idaho	54	0.4	192	0.2	4	5.0	25,901	42.9	0.2	794,037
Nebraska	48	0.4	208	0.2	4	5.5	26,553	38.4	0.2	800,896
Connecticut	37	0.3	185	0.2	5	7.9	42,832	31.5	0.2	850,541
Hawaii	51	0.4	151	0.2	3	4.2	27,656	31.2	0.2	612,588
North Dakota	16	0.1	60*	-	-	1.4	-	10.6	0.1	662,812
Wyoming	16	0.1	47	0.1	3	1.3	26,660	8.5	0.0	532,063
Maryland	133	1.0	750*	-	-	(D)	-	(D)	-	-
Utah	90	0.7	375*	-	-	(D)	-	(D)	-	-
New Hampshire	24	0.2	60*	-	-	(D)	-	(D)	-	-
Rhode Island	20	0.2	60*	-	-	(D)	-	(D)	-	-
Arkansas	18	0.1	750*	-	-	(D)	-	(D)	-	-
Alaska	12	0.1	60*	-	-	(D)	-	(D)	-	-
D.C.	12	0.1	175*	-	-	(D)	-	(D)	-	-

Source: 1997 *Economic Census*. The states are in descending order of revenues or establishments (if revenue data are missing for the majority). The symbol (D) appears when data are withheld to prevent disclosure of competitive information. States marked with (D) are sorted by number of establishments. A dash (-) indicates that the data element cannot be calculated. * indicates the midpoint of a range; 175, for example is the range 100-249. Shaded *states* on the state map indicate those states which have proportionately greater representation in the industry than would be indicated by the state's population; the ratio is based on total revenues or number of establishments. Shaded *regions* indicate where the industry is regionally most concentrated.

NAICS 522292 - REAL ESTATE CREDIT

GENERAL STATISTICS

Year	Establishments (number)	Employment (number)	Payroll ($ million)	Revenues ($ million)	Employees per Establishment (number)	Revenues per Establishment ($)	Payroll per Employee ($)
1997	17,959	215,849	9,070.0	37,477.0	12.0	2,086,809	42,020

Source: Economic Census of the United States, 1997. This is a newly defined industry. Data for prior years were unavailable at the time of publication but may become available over time.

INDICES OF CHANGE

Year	Establishments (number)	Employment (number)	Payroll ($ million)	Revenues ($ million)	Employees per Establishment (number)	Revenues per Establishment ($)	Payroll per Employee ($)
1997	100.0	100.0	100.0	100.0	100.0	100.0	100.0

Sources: Same as General Statistics. The values shown reflect change from the base year, 1997. Values above 100 mean greater than 1997, values below 100 mean less than 1997, and a value of 100 in the 1982-96 or 1998-2001 period means same as 1997. Values followed by a 'p' are projections by the editors; 'e' stands for extrapolation. Data are the most recent available at this level of detail.

SIC INDUSTRIES RELATED TO NAICS 522292

Each new NAICS code represents an industry that used to be part of an SIC or a part of several SIC industries. Data in this table are shown to provide transitional information for these cases. All available data for the precursor SIC(s) are shown. Even if only a part of an SIC is included in the NAICS, *all* data for the SIC are reproduced. If the SIC industry is not marked as being a part (pt) of the NAICS, the entire industry is embedded in the NAICS data. The SIC composition of the new industry provides some hints of the relative importance of its "ancestors." Data marked with a 'p' are projected. Projections begin with 1982 data. Data earlier than 1990 are not shown but are reflected in the projections.

SIC	Industry	1990	1991	1992	1993	1994	1995	1996	1997
6111	**Federal & Federally Sponsored Credit (pt)**								
	Establishments (number)	-	-	1,349	-	-	-	-	-
	Employment (thousands)	-	-	21.3	-	-	-	-	-
	Revenues ($ million)	-	-	28,092.0	-	-	-	-	-
6159	**Misc. Business Credit Institutions (pt)**	-	-	-				-	-
6162	**Mortgage Bankers & Correspondents (pt)**	-	-	-			-	-	-

Source: Economic Census of the United States, 1992, annual surveys of economic sectors conducted by the Bureau of the Census, and estimates or projections based on the 1982-1992 period; not all data are shown. 'e' marks estimates made by the editors; 'p' indicates projections based on time series. A dash (-) indicates that data for this SIC or year were not available. The abbreviation (pt) next to the industry name indicates that only a part of the industry is present within the NAICS data. If no (pt) is shown, the entire industry is contained within the NAICS data.

SELECTED RATIOS

For 1997	Avg. of Information	Analyzed Industry	Index	For 1997	Avg. of Information	Analyzed Industry	Index
Employees per establishment	15	12	81	Payroll per establishment	669,406	505,039	75
Revenue per establishment	5,561,120	2,086,809	38	Payroll as % of revenue	12	24	201
Revenue per employee	376,639	173,626	46	Payroll per employee	45,337	42,020	93

Sources: Same as General Statistics. The 'Average' column represents the average for the industry sector, in 1997, where the currently shown industry is classified. The Index shows the relationship between the Average and the Analyzed Industry. For example, 100 means that they are equal; 500 that the Analyzed Industry is five times the average; 50 means that the Analyzed Industry is half the national average. The abbreviation 'na' is used to show that data are 'not available'.

LEADING COMPANIES   Number shown: **75**   Total sales ($ mil): **631,742**   Total employment (000): **228.6**

Company Name	Address				CEO Name	Phone	Co. Type	Sales ($ mil)	Empl. (000)
General Motors Acceptance Corp.	3044 W Grand Blvd	Detroit	MI	48202	J.M. Losh	313-556-5000	S	131,417	23.6
Crestar Financial Corp.	P O Box 26665	Richmond	VA	23261	Richard G Tilghman	804-782-5000	P	93,170	30.5
Associates First Capital Corp.	250 Carpenter Pkwy	Irving	TX	75062	Keith W Hughes	972-652-4000	P	80,900	28.0
Firstar Corp.	777 E Wisconsin	Milwaukee	WI	53202	Jerry A Grundhofer	414-765-4321	P	72,800	8.0
Associates Corporation	PO Box 660237	Dallas	TX	75266	Keith W Hughes	972-652-4000	S	56,777	18.3
Norwest Mortgage Inc.	405 S W 5th St	Des Moines	IA	50309		515-237-7900	S	24,255*	15.7
Dominion Resources Inc.	PO Box 26532	Richmond	VA	23261	Thomas E Capps	804-819-2000	P	17,517	11.0
SouthTrust Mortgage Corp.	210 Wildwood Pkwy	Birmingham	AL	35209	Wade O King	205-667-8100	S	13,841	0.7
Fleet Real Estate Mortgage	PO Box 11988	Columbia	SC	29211	Mike Torke	803-253-7900	S	13,003*	0.9
Temple-Inland Mortgage Corp.	1300 S MoPac	Austin	TX	78746	Joe Far	512-434-8000	S	11,548*	0.8
Capstead Mortgage Corp.	One Lincoln Park	Dallas	TX	75225	Ronn K Lytle	214-874-2323	P	7,100	<0.1
Fleet Mortgage Group Inc.	1333 Main St	Columbia	SC	29201	A William Schenck	803-929-7900	S	4,614*	3.1
ComNet Mortgage Services Inc.	PO Box 2101	Valley Forge	PA	19482	Charles Meecham	610-313-1600	D	4,292*	0.3
Saxon Mortgage Inc.	4880 Cox Rd	Glen Allen	VA	23060	Mike Sawyer	804-967-7400	S	4,292*	0.3
Pulte Corp.	33 Bloomfield Hills	Bloomfield Hills	MI	48304	Robert K Burgess	248-647-2750	P	3,830	4.3
SunTrust Mortgage Inc.	P O Box 100100	Atlanta	GA	30348	Ralph Carrigain	770-352-5600	S	3,668*	0.4
Seattle Mortgage Co.	229 Queen Anne N	Seattle	WA	98109	Robert Story	206-281-1500	R	3,584*	0.3
Money Store Inc.	707 Third St	W. Sacramento	CA	95605	James Maynor	916-617-2000	S	3,137	4.4
Countrywide Credit Industries Inc.	4500 Park Granada	Calabasas	CA	91302	Angelo R Mozilo	818-225-3000	P	2,963	11.4
HomeBanc Mortgage Corp.	5555 Glenridge N E	Atlanta	GA	30342	Patrick S Flood	404-303-4280	S	2,800	0.7
ContiFinancial Corp.	277 Park Ave	New York	NY	10172	James J Bigham	212-207-2800	P	2,775	3.3
Source One Mortgage Corp.	27555 Farmington	Farmington Hills	MI	48334	James A Conrad	248-488-7000	P	2,650*	1.7
CRIIMI MAE Inc.	11200 Rockville	Rockville	MD	20852	William B Dockser	301-816-2300	P	2,438	0.2
First Eastern Mortgage Corp.	100 Brickstone Sq	Andover	MA	01810	Richard F Kalagher	978-749-3100	S	2,217*	0.1
Republic Bancorp Inc.	PO Box 70	Owosso	MI	48867	Jerry D Campbell	517-725-7337	P	2,196	2.1
Meritech Mortgage Services Inc.	4708 Mercantile Dr	Fort Worth	TX	76137	Dennis Stowe	817-665-7200	S	2,154*	0.2
Household Commercial Financial	2700 Sanders Rd	Prospect Heights	IL	60070	William Aldinger	847-564-5000	S	2,064*	1.0
White Mountains Insurance Group	80 S Main St	Hanover	NH	03755	John J Byrne	603-643-1567	P	2,049	2.8
Ryland Group Inc.	11000 Broken Land	Columbia	MD	21044	R Chad Dreier	410-715-7000	P	2,009	2.1
JRMK Company Inc.	7935 E Prentice Ave	Englewood	CO	80111	Milton Karavites	303-771-5008	R	2,000	0.1
HomeAmerican Mortgage Corp.	3600 S Yosemite St	Denver	CO	80237	Stew Larsen	303-773-1155	S	1,950*	0.1
NVR Inc.	7601 Lewinsville	McLean	VA	22102	Dwight C Schar	703-761-2000	P	1,943	3.1
Flagstar Bank F.S.B.	2600 Telegraph Rd	Bloomfield Hills	MI	48302		248-338-7700	S	1,901*	1.2
United Companies Financial Corp.	PO Box 1591	Baton Rouge	LA	70821	James J Bailey III	225-987-0000	P	1,850	3.5
Spectrum Home Mortgage	2929 Walden Ave	Depew	NY	14043	Robert E Roth	716-633-6255	S	1,848*	0.7
Commerce Group Inc.	211 Main St	Webster	MA	01570	Arthur J Remillard Jr	508-943-9000	P	1,756	1.5
Prudential Fox and Roach	1409 Kings North	Cherry Hill	NJ	08034	G William Fox	609-429-7227	R	1,736*	0.5
Merrill Lynch Credit Corp.	4802 Deer Lake E	Jacksonville	FL	32246	Kevin O'Hanlon	904-928-6000	S	1,722	0.8
Phh Mortgage Corp.	6000 Atrium Way	Mount Laurel	NJ	08054	Terry Edwards	609-439-6000	S	1,600*	2.5
M.D.C. Holdings Inc.	3600 S Yosemite St	Denver	CO	80237	Larry A Mizel	303-773-1100	P	1,568	1.4
Metropolitan Mortgage	601 W 1st Ave	Spokane	WA	99201	C Paul Sandifur Jr	509-838-3111	R	1,538*	0.5
U.S. Home Corp.	PO Box 2863	Houston	TX	77252	Isaac Heimbinder	713-877-2311	P	1,498	2.0
Charles F. Curry Inc.	P O Box 419888	Kansas City	MO	64141	Bill Curry	816-471-8300	R	1,434*	0.1
Harry Mortgage Co.	5929 N May Ave	Oklahoma City	OK	73112	Robert Harry	405-840-2501	R	1,432*	0.1
Preferred Mortgage Associates Ltd	3030 Finley Rd	Downers Grove	IL	60515		630-241-1266	R	1,431*	0.1
City Bank	PO Box 3709	Honolulu	HI	96811	Ronald K Migita	808-546-2411	P	1,428*	0.5
Green Tree Financial Corp.	1100 Landmark Twr	St. Paul	MN	55102	Bruce A Crittenden	651-293-3400	P	1,390	6.5
Regional Investment Co.	9221 Ward Pkwy	Kansas City	MO	64114	Brad Ives	816-363-5444	R	1,366*	<0.1
York Financial Corp.	101 S George St	York	PA	17401	Robert W Pullo	717-846-8777	P	1,365	0.4
GFC Mortgage Bankers Inc.	50 Broadway	New York	NY	10004	Allan Gross	212-668-1444	R	1,289*	<0.1
American Western Mortgage Co.	9350 E Arapahoe Rd	Englewood	CO	80112	Joe B Fortson	303-790-1800	R	1,255*	<0.1
GreenPoint Mortgage Corp.	50332 Parkway	Charlotte	NC	28217		704-329-6400	S	1,219*	<0.1
Atlantic Coast Mortgage Co.	12700 Fair Lakes	Fairfax	VA	22033	Larry Rice	703-631-0098	S	1,150*	<0.1
Continental Homes Holding Corp.	7001 N Scottsdale	Scottsdale	AZ	85253	W Thomas Hickcox	602-483-0006	P	1,124	1.0
Sterling Financial Corp.	PO Box 10608	Lancaster	PA	17605	John E Stefan	717-581-6030	P	1,059	0.5
CB Richard Ellis Services Inc.	333 S Beaudry Ave	Los Angeles	CA	90071	James J Didion	213-613-3123	P	1,034	9.4
Legg Mason Real Estate Service	1735 Market St	Philadelphia	PA	19103	Walter D'Alessil	215-496-3000	S	1,019*	<0.1
Delmar Financial Co.	1030 Woodcrest Ter	St. Louis	MO	63141	Carl Mirowitz	314-434-7000	R	1,001*	<0.1
Foothill Group Inc.	11111 Santa Monica	Los Angeles	CA	90025	John Nikoll	310-478-8383	S	1,000	0.2
CB Richard Ellis Inc.	533 S Fremont Ave	Los Angeles	CA	90071	Barry White	213-613-3242	S	936*	8.0
Option One Mortgage Corp.	2020 E 1st St	Santa Ana	CA	92705	Bob Durbish		S	900*	0.9
Action Mortgage Co.	120 N 111 St	Spokane	WA	99201		509-458-2894	S	870*	0.8
Coldwell Banker Burnet	7550 France Ave S	Edina	MN	55435	Mary Baymler	612-844-6800	D	864*	<0.1
Prime Lending Inc.	17950 Preston Rd	Dallas	TX	75252	Rosenna Mc Gill	972-248-7866	R	863*	<0.1
Jupiter Mortgage Corp.	1070 E Indiantown	Jupiter	FL	33477	Michael Boneo	561-744-5626	R	859*	<0.1
AMI Capital Inc.	7200 Wisconsin	Bethesda	MD	20814	Michael Sullivan	301-654-0033	S	789*	<0.1
PNC Mortgage Corporation	75 N Fairway Dr	Vernon Hills	IL	60061	Saiyid T Naqvi	847-549-6500	S	784*	0.7
Castle BancGroup Inc.	121 W Lincoln Hwy	Dekalb	IL	60115	John W Castle	815-758-7007	R	759*	0.2
Fireside Thrift Co.	PO Box 9010	Pleasanton	CA	94566		510-490-6511	S	660	0.6
Mission Mortgage Inc.	901 S Mopac Bldg 5	Austin	TX	78746	Leigh Ann McCoy	512-328-0400	R	659*	<0.1
Weyerhaeuser Mortgage Co.	6320 Canoga Ave	Woodland Hills	CA	91367	Scott McAfee	831-422-2307	S	600*	0.6
AccuBanc Mortgage Corp.	12377 Merit Dr	Dallas	TX	75251	William R Starkey Sr	972-458-9200	R	595*	1.5
Bank One (Deerfield, Illinois)	745 Deerfield Rd	Deerfield	IL	60015		847-945-2550	P	572*	<0.1
Arbor National Commercial	333 Earle Ovington	Uniondale	NY	11553	Ivan Kaufman	716-557-0100	R	533*	<0.1
CrossLand Mortgage Corp.	3902 S State St	Salt Lake City	UT	84107	Christopher Sumner	801-269-7600	S	533*	1.6

Source: Ward's Business Directory of U.S. Private and Public Companies, Volumes 1 and 2, 2000. The company type code used is as follows: P - Public, R - Private, S - Subsidiary, D - Division, J - Joint Venture, A - Affiliate, G - Group, N - Company type not reported. Sales are in millions of dollars, employees are in thousands. An asterisk (*) indicates an estimated sales volume. The symbol < stands for 'less than'. Company names and addresses are truncated, in some cases, to fit into the available space.

LOCATION BY STATE AND REGIONAL CONCENTRATION

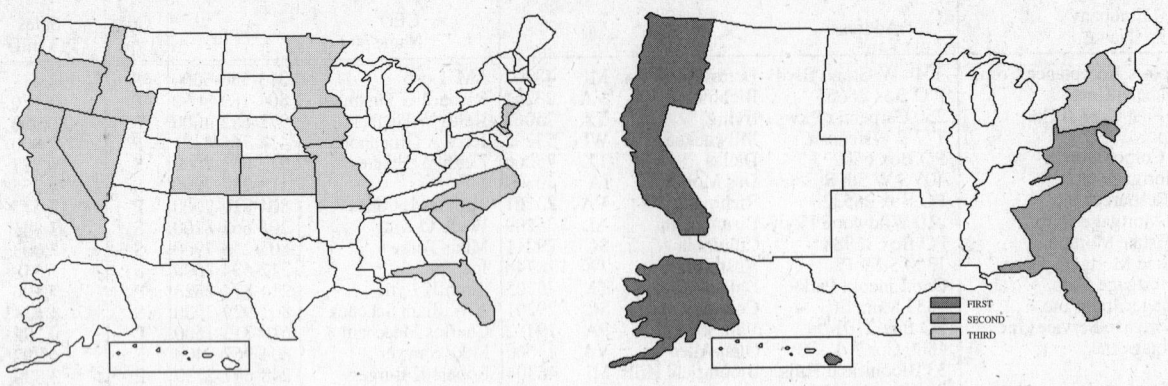

INDUSTRY DATA BY STATE

State	Establishments Total (number)	Establishments % of U.S.	Employment Total (number)	Employment % of U.S.	Employment Per Estab.	Payroll Total ($ mil.)	Payroll Per Empl. ($)	Revenues Total ($ mil.)	Revenues % of U.S.	Revenues Per Estab. ($)
California	2,692	15.0	34,880	16.2	13	1,667.9	47,819	6,172.2	16.5	2,292,794
Florida	1,468	8.2	13,475	6.2	9	526.0	39,039	2,965.5	7.9	2,020,093
New York	632	3.5	10,657	4.9	17	559.5	52,504	2,512.1	6.7	3,974,880
New Jersey	485	2.7	9,518	4.4	20	451.7	47,461	1,851.5	4.9	3,817,478
Texas	930	5.2	11,585	5.4	12	466.9	40,302	1,811.6	4.8	1,947,968
Illinois	724	4.0	9,662	4.5	13	401.7	41,577	1,661.3	4.4	2,294,680
Ohio	734	4.1	10,198	4.7	14	379.4	37,199	1,397.1	3.7	1,903,392
Minnesota	317	1.8	5,541	2.6	17	251.5	45,390	1,395.6	3.7	4,402,555
North Carolina	622	3.5	9,030	4.2	15	282.6	31,291	1,327.5	3.5	2,134,246
Michigan	506	2.8	7,578	3.5	15	326.8	43,124	1,115.8	3.0	2,205,225
South Carolina	266	1.5	4,300	2.0	16	177.8	41,352	1,048.8	2.8	3,942,891
Iowa	148	0.8	3,231	1.5	22	116.1	35,936	999.8	2.7	6,755,216
Georgia	645	3.6	6,591	3.1	10	269.2	40,843	989.0	2.6	1,533,389
Pennsylvania	582	3.2	6,218	2.9	11	287.6	46,256	981.8	2.6	1,686,995
Virginia	545	3.0	5,438	2.5	10	232.1	42,690	822.4	2.2	1,509,028
Missouri	339	1.9	3,992	1.8	12	149.8	37,522	772.1	2.1	2,277,584
Indiana	394	2.2	4,688	2.2	12	177.9	37,956	712.9	1.9	1,809,381
Colorado	497	2.8	4,717	2.2	9	205.6	43,597	698.4	1.9	1,405,169
Kansas	150	0.8	1,416	0.7	9	65.1	45,992	633.9	1.7	4,226,020
Washington	523	2.9	3,920	1.8	7	175.9	44,879	617.8	1.6	1,181,306
Arizona	430	2.4	4,096	1.9	10	163.7	39,962	549.6	1.5	1,278,253
Oregon	294	1.6	3,127	1.4	11	124.7	39,891	527.7	1.4	1,794,820
Massachusetts	290	1.6	3,378	1.6	12	164.2	48,607	506.5	1.4	1,746,510
Tennessee	402	2.2	3,557	1.6	9	122.5	34,444	486.0	1.3	1,209,022
Wisconsin	206	1.1	2,959	1.4	14	108.2	36,581	392.0	1.0	1,902,947
Kentucky	188	1.0	2,331	1.1	12	71.5	30,665	370.2	1.0	1,969,213
Alabama	231	1.3	2,836	1.3	12	101.1	35,645	367.4	1.0	1,590,628
Connecticut	188	1.0	1,621	0.8	9	92.3	56,919	290.3	0.8	1,543,936
Nevada	221	1.2	1,907	0.9	9	91.5	47,994	280.1	0.7	1,267,543
Utah	241	1.3	2,438	1.1	10	95.1	39,022	279.9	0.7	1,161,402
Idaho	122	0.7	810	0.4	7	28.5	35,205	228.0	0.6	1,869,123
Louisiana	224	1.2	2,442	1.1	11	67.0	27,428	218.2	0.6	974,040
Oklahoma	153	0.9	1,498	0.7	10	48.3	32,254	191.9	0.5	1,254,046
Nebraska	87	0.5	1,518	0.7	17	39.9	26,270	186.7	0.5	2,146,310
Hawaii	81	0.5	705	0.3	9	27.2	38,559	134.7	0.4	1,662,963
Delaware	69	0.4	732	0.3	11	27.2	37,143	125.2	0.3	1,814,565
Mississippi	171	1.0	911	0.4	5	27.7	30,370	124.1	0.3	725,678
New Mexico	134	0.7	740	0.3	6	27.6	37,235	108.2	0.3	807,119
West Virginia	50	0.3	266	0.1	5	9.0	33,868	91.8	0.2	1,835,700
New Hampshire	53	0.3	566	0.3	11	24.1	42,574	73.5	0.2	1,386,283
Arkansas	101	0.6	681	0.3	7	20.3	29,739	73.3	0.2	725,901
Montana	63	0.4	390	0.2	6	13.6	34,877	63.4	0.2	1,006,444
South Dakota	36	0.2	259	0.1	7	8.1	31,313	60.0	0.2	1,667,806
Alaska	22	0.1	246	0.1	11	13.0	53,004	29.3	0.1	1,332,091
Vermont	23	0.1	224	0.1	10	5.9	26,219	23.6	0.1	1,027,739
Wyoming	32	0.2	107	0.0	3	4.0	37,140	19.4	0.1	606,937
Maryland	521	2.9	7,500*	-	-	(D)	-	(D)	-	-
Rhode Island	65	0.4	1,750*	-	-	(D)	-	(D)	-	-
Maine	32	0.2	175*	-	-	(D)	-	(D)	-	-
D.C.	17	0.1	175*	-	-	(D)	-	(D)	-	-
North Dakota	13	0.1	60*	-	-	(D)	-	(D)	-	-

Source: 1997 *Economic Census*. The states are in descending order of revenues or establishments (if revenue data are missing for the majority). The symbol (D) appears when data are withheld to prevent disclosure of competitive information. States marked with (D) are sorted by number of establishments. A dash (-) indicates that the data element cannot be calculated. * indicates the midpoint of a range; 175, for example is the range 100-249. Shaded *states* on the state map indicate those states which have proportionately greater representation in the industry than would be indicated by the state's population; the ratio is based on total revenues or number of establishments. Shaded *regions* indicate where the industry is regionally most concentrated.

NAICS 522293 - INTERNATIONAL TRADE FINANCING

GENERAL STATISTICS

Year	Establishments (number)	Employment (number)	Payroll ($ million)	Revenues ($ million)	Employees per Establishment (number)	Revenues per Establishment ($)	Payroll per Employee ($)
1997	194	4,577	341.0	3,109.0	23.6	16,025,773	74,503

Source: Economic Census of the United States, 1997. This is a newly defined industry. Data for prior years were unavailable at the time of publication but may become available over time.

INDICES OF CHANGE

Year	Establishments (number)	Employment (number)	Payroll ($ million)	Revenues ($ million)	Employees per Establishment (number)	Revenues per Establishment ($)	Payroll per Employee ($)
1997	100.0	100.0	100.0	100.0	100.0	100.0	100.0

Sources: Same as General Statistics. The values shown reflect change from the base year, 1997. Values above 100 mean greater than 1997, values below 100 mean less than 1997, and a value of 100 in the 1982-96 or 1998-2001 period means same as 1997. Values followed by a 'p' are projections by the editors; 'e' stands for extrapolation. Data are the most recent available at this level of detail.

SIC INDUSTRIES RELATED TO NAICS 522293

Each new NAICS code represents an industry that used to be part of an SIC or a part of several SIC industries. Data in this table are shown to provide transitional information for these cases. All available data for the precursor SIC(s) are shown. Even if only a part of an SIC is included in the NAICS, *all* data for the SIC are reproduced. If the SIC industry is not marked as being a part (pt) of the NAICS, the entire industry is embedded in the NAICS data. The SIC composition of the new industry provides some hints of the relative importance of its "ancestors." Data marked with a 'p' are projected. Projections begin with 1982 data. Data earlier than 1990 are not shown but are reflected in the projections.

SIC	Industry	1990	1991	1992	1993	1994	1995	1996	1997
6081	**Foreign Bank & Branches & Agencies (pt)**	-	-	-	-	-	-		-
6082	**Foreign Trade & International Banks (pt)**	-	-	-	-	-	-		
6111	**Federal & Federally Sponsored Credit (pt)**								
	Establishments (number)	-	-	1,349	-	-	-	-	-
	Employment (thousands)	-	-	21.3	-	-	-	-	-
	Revenues ($ million)	-	-	28,092.0	-	-	-	-	-
6159	**Misc. Business Credit Institutions (pt)**	-	-	-	-	-	-	-	-

Source: Economic Census of the United States, 1992, annual surveys of economic sectors conducted by the Bureau of the Census, and estimates or projections based on the 1982-1992 period; not all data are shown. 'e' marks estimates made by the editors; 'p' indicates projections based on time series. A dash (-) indicates that data for this SIC or year were not available. The abbreviation (pt) next to the industry name indicates that only a part of the industry is present within the NAICS data. If no (pt) is shown, the entire industry is contained within the NAICS data.

SELECTED RATIOS

For 1997	Avg. of Information	Analyzed Industry	Index	For 1997	Avg. of Information	Analyzed Industry	Index
Employees per establishment	15	24	160	Payroll per establishment	669,406	1,757,732	263
Revenue per establishment	5,561,120	16,025,773	288	Payroll as % of revenue	12	11	91
Revenue per employee	376,639	679,266	180	Payroll per employee	45,337	74,503	164

Sources: Same as General Statistics. The 'Average' column represents the average for the industry sector, in 1997, where the currently shown industry is classified. The Index shows the relationship between the Average and the Analyzed Industry. For example, 100 means that they are equal; 500 that the Analyzed Industry is five times the average; 50 means that the Analyzed Industry is half the national average. The abbreviation 'na' is used to show that data are 'not available'.

LEADING COMPANIES   Number shown: **3**   Total sales ($ mil): **41,152**   Total employment (000): **90.6**

Company Name	Address				CEO Name	Phone	Co. Type	Sales ($ mil)	Empl. (000)
American Express Co.	W Fin Ctr	New York	NY	10285	Kenneth I. Chenault	212-640-2000	P	19,483	85.0
American Express Bank Ltd.	#3 World Financial	New York	NY	10285	Harvey Golub	212-640-2000	S	12,324*	4.0
Inter-American Development	1300 NY N W	Washington	DC	20577	Enrique V Iglesias	202-623-1000	R	9,345*	1.6

Source: *Ward's Business Directory of U.S. Private and Public Companies*, Volumes 1 and 2, 2000. The company type code used is as follows: P - Public, R - Private, S - Subsidiary, D - Division, J - Joint Venture, A - Affiliate, G - Group, N - Company type not reported. Sales are in millions of dollars, employees are in thousands. An asterisk (*) indicates an estimated sales volume. The symbol < stands for 'less than'. Company names and addresses are truncated, in some cases, to fit into the available space.

LOCATION BY STATE AND REGIONAL CONCENTRATION

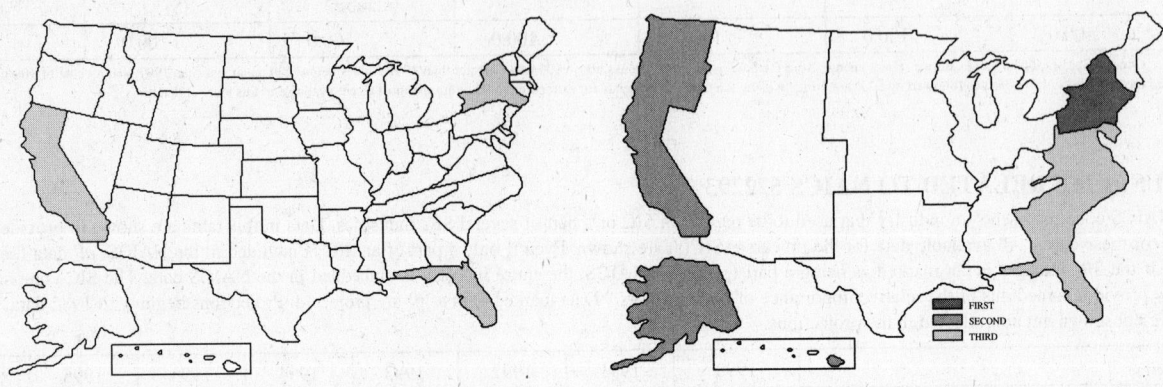

INDUSTRY DATA BY STATE

State	Establishments		Employment			Payroll		Revenues		
	Total (number)	% of U.S.	Total (number)	% of U.S.	Per Estab.	Total ($ mil.)	Per Empl. ($)	Total ($ mil.)	% of U.S.	Per Estab. ($)
New York	62	32.0	2,221	48.5	36	202.3	91,089	1,571.9	50.6	25,353,500
California	37	19.1	698	15.3	19	41.6	59,576	449.7	14.5	12,153,054
Florida	26	13.4	753	16.5	29	48.1	63,825	405.0	13.0	15,578,577
Illinois	16	8.2	258	5.6	16	13.8	53,306	76.4	2.5	4,774,187
Texas	12	6.2	151	3.3	13	8.6	56,954	61.8	2.0	5,146,833
Georgia	7	3.6	175*	-	-	(D)	-	(D)	-	-
New Jersey	6	3.1	175*	-	-	(D)	-	(D)	-	-

Source: 1997 *Economic Census*. The states are in descending order of revenues or establishments (if revenue data are missing for the majority). The symbol (D) appears when data are withheld to prevent disclosure of competitive information. States marked with (D) are sorted by number of establishments. A dash (-) indicates that the data element cannot be calculated. * indicates the midpoint of a range; 175, for example is the range 100-249. Shaded *states* on the state map indicate those states which have proportionately greater representation in the industry than would be indicated by the state's population; the ratio is based on total revenues or number of establishments. Shaded *regions* indicate where the industry is regionally most concentrated.

NAICS 522294 - SECONDARY MARKET FINANCING

GENERAL STATISTICS

Year	Establishments (number)	Employment (number)	Payroll ($ million)	Revenues ($ million)	Employees per Establishment (number)	Revenues per Establishment ($)	Payroll per Employee ($)
1997	210	13,692	1,000.0	48,948.0	65.2	233,085,714	73,035

Source: *Economic Census of the United States*, 1997. This is a newly defined industry. Data for prior years were unavailable at the time of publication but may become available over time.

INDICES OF CHANGE

Year	Establishments (number)	Employment (number)	Payroll ($ million)	Revenues ($ million)	Employees per Establishment (number)	Revenues per Establishment ($)	Payroll per Employee ($)
1997	100.0	100.0	100.0	100.0	100.0	100.0	100.0

Sources: Same as General Statistics. The values shown reflect change from the base year, 1997. Values above 100 mean greater than 1997, values below 100 mean less than 1997, and a value of 100 in the 1982-96 or 1998-2001 period means same as 1997. Values followed by a 'p' are projections by the editors; 'e' stands for extrapolation. Data are the most recent available at this level of detail.

SIC INDUSTRIES RELATED TO NAICS 522294

Each new NAICS code represents an industry that used to be part of an SIC or a part of several SIC industries. Data in this table are shown to provide transitional information for these cases. All available data for the precursor SIC(s) are shown. Even if only a part of an SIC is included in the NAICS, *all* data for the SIC are reproduced. If the SIC industry is not marked as being a part (pt) of the NAICS, the entire industry is embedded in the NAICS data. The SIC composition of the new industry provides some hints of the relative importance of its "ancestors." Data marked with a 'p' are projected. Projections begin with 1982 data. Data earlier than 1990 are not shown but are reflected in the projections.

SIC	Industry	1990	1991	1992	1993	1994	1995	1996	1997
6111	**Federal & Federally Sponsored Credit (pt)**								
	Establishments (number)	-	-	1,349	-	-	-	-	-
	Employment (thousands)	-	-	21.3	-	-	-	-	-
	Revenues ($ million)	-	-	28,092.0	-	-	-	-	-
6159	**Misc. Business Credit Institutions (pt)**	-	-	-	-	-	-	-	-

Source: *Economic Census of the United States*, 1992, annual surveys of economic sectors conducted by the Bureau of the Census, and estimates or projections based on the 1982-1992 period; not all data are shown. 'e' marks estimates made by the editors; 'p' indicates projections based on time series. A dash (-) indicates that data for this SIC or year were not available. The abbreviation (pt) next to the industry name indicates that only a part of the industry is present within the NAICS data. If no (pt) is shown, the entire industry is contained within the NAICS data.

SELECTED RATIOS

For 1997	Avg. of Information	Analyzed Industry	Index	For 1997	Avg. of Information	Analyzed Industry	Index
Employees per establishment	15	65	441	Payroll per establishment	669,406	4,761,905	711
Revenue per establishment	5,561,120	233,085,714	4,191	Payroll as % of revenue	12	2	17
Revenue per employee	376,639	3,574,934	949	Payroll per employee	45,337	73,035	161

Sources: Same as General Statistics. The 'Average' column represents the average for the industry sector, in 1997, where the currently shown industry is classified. The Index shows the relationship between the Average and the Analyzed Industry. For example, 100 means that they are equal; 500 that the Analyzed Industry is five times the average; 50 means that the Analyzed Industry is half the national average. The abbreviation 'na' is used to show that data are 'not available'.

LEADING COMPANIES
No company data available for this industry.

LOCATION BY STATE AND REGIONAL CONCENTRATION

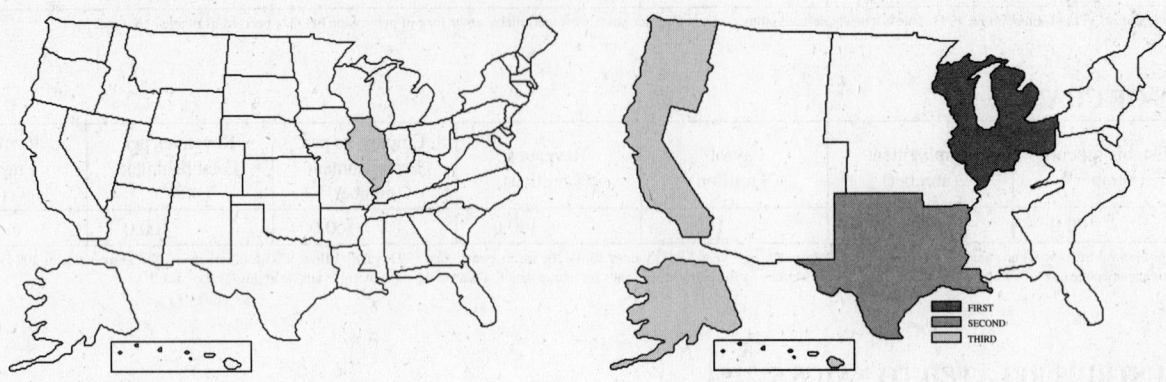

FIRST
SECOND
THIRD

INDUSTRY DATA BY STATE

State	Establishments		Employment			Payroll		Revenues		
	Total (number)	% of U.S.	Total (number)	% of U.S.	Per Estab.	Total ($ mil.)	Per Empl. ($)	Total ($ mil.)	% of U.S.	Per Estab. ($)
Illinois	12	5.7	464	3.4	39	51.2	110,409	3,590.0	7.3	299,168,167
Texas	22	10.5	1,634	11.9	74	75.8	46,417	2,788.2	5.7	126,736,409
California	28	13.3	581	4.2	21	51.4	88,482	2,063.4	4.2	73,692,607
Florida	15	7.1	1,038	7.6	69	24.6	23,704	308.4	0.6	20,558,267
Georgia	6	2.9	65	0.5	11	4.7	71,662	258.3	0.5	43,043,333
New York	7	3.3	140	1.0	20	5.5	39,371	117.4	0.2	16,777,286
Washington	6	2.9	146	1.1	24	3.6	24,884	45.9	0.1	7,652,833
Colorado	7	3.3	33	0.2	5	0.9	26,394	5.7	0.0	813,571
Ohio	6	2.9	25	0.2	4	1.7	69,720	3.7	0.0	615,167
Virginia	16	7.6	3,750*	-	-	(D)	-	(D)	-	-
New Jersey	7	3.3	60*	-	-	(D)	-	(D)	-	-
Pennsylvania	6	2.9	750*	-	-	(D)	-	(D)	-	-

Source: 1997 *Economic Census*. The states are in descending order of revenues or establishments (if revenue data are missing for the majority). The symbol (D) appears when data are withheld to prevent disclosure of competitive information. States marked with (D) are sorted by number of establishments. A dash (-) indicates that the data element cannot be calculated. * indicates the midpoint of a range; 175, for example is the range 100-249. Shaded *states* on the state map indicate those states which have proportionately greater representation in the industry than would be indicated by the state's population; the ratio is based on total revenues or number of establishments. Shaded *regions* indicate where the industry is regionally most concentrated.

NAICS 522298 - NONDEPOSITORY CREDIT INTERMEDIATION NEC

GENERAL STATISTICS

Year	Establishments (number)	Employment (number)	Payroll ($ million)	Revenues ($ million)	Employees per Establishment (number)	Revenues per Establishment ($)	Payroll per Employee ($)
1997	7,339	45,059	1,616.0	16,323.0	6.1	2,224,145	35,864

Source: *Economic Census of the United States*, 1997. This is a newly defined industry. Data for prior years were unavailable at the time of publication but may become available over time.

INDICES OF CHANGE

Year	Establishments (number)	Employment (number)	Payroll ($ million)	Revenues ($ million)	Employees per Establishment (number)	Revenues per Establishment ($)	Payroll per Employee ($)
1997	100.0	100.0	100.0	100.0	100.0	100.0	100.0

Sources: Same as General Statistics. The values shown reflect change from the base year, 1997. Values above 100 mean greater than 1997, values below 100 mean less than 1997, and a value of 100 in the 1982-96 or 1998-2001 period means same as 1997. Values followed by a 'p' are projections by the editors; 'e' stands for extrapolation. Data are the most recent available at this level of detail.

SIC INDUSTRIES RELATED TO NAICS 522298

Each new NAICS code represents an industry that used to be part of an SIC or a part of several SIC industries. Data in this table are shown to provide transitional information for these cases. All available data for the precursor SIC(s) are shown. Even if only a part of an SIC is included in the NAICS, *all* data for the SIC are reproduced. If the SIC industry is not marked as being a part (pt) of the NAICS, the entire industry is embedded in the NAICS data. The SIC composition of the new industry provides some hints of the relative importance of its "ancestors." Data marked with a 'p' are projected. Projections begin with 1982 data. Data earlier than 1990 are not shown but are reflected in the projections.

SIC	Industry	1990	1991	1992	1993	1994	1995	1996	1997
6019	**Central Reserve Depository, nec**	-	-	-	-	-	-	-	-
6081	**Foreign Bank & Branches & Agencies (pt)**	-	-	-	-	-	-	-	-
6082	**Foreign Trade & International Banks (pt)**	-	-	-	-	-	-	-	-
6111	**Federal & Federally Sponsored Credit (pt)**								
	Establishments (number)	-	-	1,349	-	-	-	-	-
	Employment (thousands)	-	-	21.3	-	-	-	-	-
	Revenues ($ million)	-	-	28,092.0	-	-	-	-	-
6141	**Personal Credit Institutions (pt)**								
	Establishments (number)	-	-	16,900	-	-	-	-	-
	Employment (thousands)	-	-	158.8	-	-	-	-	-
	Revenues ($ million)	-	-	47,668.4	-	-	-	-	-
6153	**Short-Term Business Credit (pt)**	-	-	-	-	-	-	-	-
6159	**Misc. Business Credit Institutions (pt)**	-	-	-	-	-	-	-	-

Source: *Economic Census of the United States*, 1992, annual surveys of economic sectors conducted by the Bureau of the Census, and estimates or projections based on the 1982-1992 period; not all data are shown. 'e' marks estimates made by the editors; 'p' indicates projections based on time series. A dash (-) indicates that data for this SIC or year were not available. The abbreviation (pt) next to the industry name indicates that only a part of the industry is present within the NAICS data. If no (pt) is shown, the entire industry is contained within the NAICS data.

SELECTED RATIOS

For 1997	Avg. of Information	Analyzed Industry	Index	For 1997	Avg. of Information	Analyzed Industry	Index
Employees per establishment	15	6	42	Payroll per establishment	669,406	220,193	33
Revenue per establishment	5,561,120	2,224,145	40	Payroll as % of revenue	12	10	82
Revenue per employee	376,639	362,258	96	Payroll per employee	45,337	35,864	79

Sources: Same as General Statistics. The 'Average' column represents the average for the industry sector, in 1997, where the currently shown industry is classified. The Index shows the relationship between the Average and the Analyzed Industry. For example, 100 means that they are equal; 500 that the Analyzed Industry is five times the average; 50 means that the Analyzed Industry is half the national average. The abbreviation 'na' is used to show that data are 'not available'.

LEADING COMPANIES   Number shown: **2**   Total sales ($ mil): **90**   Total employment (000): **0.9**

Company Name	Address				CEO Name	Phone	Co. Type	Sales ($ mil)	Empl. (000)
American Business Financial	111 Presidential	Bala Cynwyd	PA	19004	Anthony J. Santilli, Jr.	610-668-2440	P	86	0.9
Chicago Deferred Exchange	401 B St	San Diego	CA	92101	BW Pattishall Jr	619-239-3091	S	4	<0.1

Source: *Ward's Business Directory of U.S. Private and Public Companies*, Volumes 1 and 2, 2000. The company type code used is as follows: P - Public, R - Private, S - Subsidiary, D - Division, J - Joint Venture, A - Affiliate, G - Group, N - Company type not reported. Sales are in millions of dollars, employees are in thousands. An asterisk (*) indicates an estimated sales volume. The symbol < stands for 'less than'. Company names and addresses are truncated, in some cases, to fit into the available space.

LOCATION BY STATE AND REGIONAL CONCENTRATION

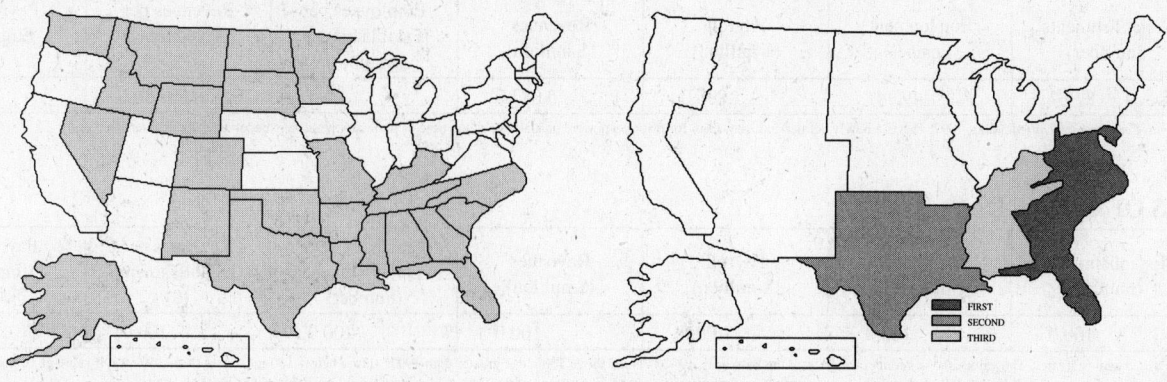

INDUSTRY DATA BY STATE

State	Establishments		Employment			Payroll		Revenues		
	Total (number)	% of U.S.	Total (number)	% of U.S.	Per Estab.	Total ($ mil.)	Per Empl. ($)	Total ($ mil.)	% of U.S.	Per Estab. ($)
Texas	1,195	16.3	7,576	16.8	6	216.7	28,601	1,918.6	11.8	1,605,493
Georgia	509	6.9	2,003	4.4	4	66.5	33,189	636.2	3.9	1,249,910
Florida	687	9.4	3,267	7.3	5	107.1	32,788	446.9	2.7	650,566
North Carolina	341	4.6	1,866	4.1	5	53.4	28,613	383.1	2.3	1,123,358
Illinois	153	2.1	788	1.7	5	38.0	48,199	332.7	2.0	2,174,327
Missouri	162	2.2	638	1.4	4	16.8	26,292	190.2	1.2	1,174,296
Indiana	116	1.6	556	1.2	5	11.6	20,879	82.2	0.5	708,233
Alabama	222	3.0	949	2.1	4	17.6	18,554	78.9	0.5	355,441
West Virginia	41	0.6	127	0.3	3	2.9	22,827	18.0	0.1	439,854
South Dakota	31	0.4	161	0.4	5	3.0	18,745	16.3	0.1	526,452
Montana	51	0.7	190	0.4	4	3.2	16,742	16.3	0.1	318,863
California	493	6.7	7,500*	-	-	(D)	-	(D)	-	-
Tennessee	284	3.9	1,750*	-	-	(D)	-	(D)	-	-
Oklahoma	231	3.1	1,750*	-	-	(D)	-	(D)	-	-
Colorado	191	2.6	1,750*	-	-	(D)	-	(D)	-	-
Mississippi	177	2.4	750*	-	-	(D)	-	(D)	-	-
New York	165	2.2	3,750*	-	-	(D)	-	(D)	-	-
Louisiana	164	2.2	750*	-	-	(D)	-	(D)	-	-
South Carolina	161	2.2	750*	-	-	(D)	-	(D)	-	-
Washington	159	2.2	750*	-	-	(D)	-	(D)	-	-
Virginia	140	1.9	750*	-	-	(D)	-	(D)	-	-
Arkansas	135	1.8	750*	-	-	(D)	-	(D)	-	-
Kentucky	133	1.8	750*	-	-	(D)	-	(D)	-	-
Ohio	130	1.8	1,750*	-	-	(D)	-	(D)	-	-
Minnesota	129	1.8	1,750*	-	-	(D)	-	(D)	-	-
Maryland	106	1.4	750*	-	-	(D)	-	(D)	-	-
Arizona	85	1.2	375*	-	-	(D)	-	(D)	-	-
Michigan	84	1.1	375*	-	-	(D)	-	(D)	-	-
Nevada	79	1.1	750*	-	-	(D)	-	(D)	-	-
Pennsylvania	79	1.1	375*	-	-	(D)	-	(D)	-	-
New Mexico	75	1.0	375*	-	-	(D)	-	(D)	-	-
Kansas	67	0.9	375*	-	-	(D)	-	(D)	-	-
Iowa	58	0.8	375*	-	-	(D)	-	(D)	-	-
Utah	55	0.7	175*	-	-	(D)	-	(D)	-	-
Wisconsin	55	0.7	750*	-	-	(D)	-	(D)	-	-
Idaho	48	0.7	175*	-	-	(D)	-	(D)	-	-
New Jersey	42	0.6	375*	-	-	(D)	-	(D)	-	-
Massachusetts	41	0.6	750*	-	-	(D)	-	(D)	-	-
North Dakota	38	0.5	175*	-	-	(D)	-	(D)	-	-
Nebraska	35	0.5	175*	-	-	(D)	-	(D)	-	-
Connecticut	32	0.4	175*	-	-	(D)	-	(D)	-	-
Oregon	30	0.4	375*	-	-	(D)	-	(D)	-	-
Alaska	23	0.3	60*	-	-	(D)	-	(D)	-	-
Wyoming	22	0.3	60*	-	-	(D)	-	(D)	-	-
Delaware	18	0.2	175*	-	-	(D)	-	(D)	-	-
Hawaii	15	0.2	60*	-	-	(D)	-	(D)	-	-
Maine	15	0.2	60*	-	-	(D)	-	(D)	-	-
New Hampshire	12	0.2	60*	-	-	(D)	-	(D)	-	-
D.C.	10	0.1	175*	-	-	(D)	-	(D)	-	-
Rhode Island	8	0.1	10*	-	-	(D)	-	(D)	-	-
Vermont	7	0.1	60*	-	-	(D)	-	(D)	-	-

Source: 1997 *Economic Census*. The states are in descending order of revenues or establishments (if revenue data are missing for the majority). The symbol (D) appears when data are withheld to prevent disclosure of competitive information. States marked with (D) are sorted by number of establishments. A dash (-) indicates that the data element cannot be calculated. * indicates the midpoint of a range; 175, for example is the range 100-249. Shaded *states* on the state map indicate those states which have proportionately greater representation in the industry than would be indicated by the state's population; the ratio is based on total revenues or number of establishments. Shaded *regions* indicate where the industry is regionally most concentrated.

NAICS 522310 - MORTGAGE AND NON-MORTGAGE LOAN BROKERS

GENERAL STATISTICS

Year	Establishments (number)	Employment (number)	Payroll ($ million)	Revenues ($ million)	Employees per Establishment (number)	Revenues per Establishment ($)	Payroll per Employee ($)
1997	8,967	49,341	1,896.0	5,087.0	5.5	567,302	38,426

Source: *Economic Census of the United States*, 1997. This is a newly defined industry. Data for prior years were unavailable at the time of publication but may become available over time.

INDICES OF CHANGE

Year	Establishments (number)	Employment (number)	Payroll ($ million)	Revenues ($ million)	Employees per Establishment (number)	Revenues per Establishment ($)	Payroll per Employee ($)
1997	100.0	100.0	100.0	100.0	100.0	100.0	100.0

Sources: Same as General Statistics. The values shown reflect change from the base year, 1997. Values above 100 mean greater than 1997, values below 100 mean less than 1997, and a value of 100 in the 1982-96 or 1998-2001 period means same as 1997. Values followed by a 'p' are projections by the editors; 'e' stands for extrapolation. Data are the most recent available at this level of detail.

SIC INDUSTRIES RELATED TO NAICS 522310

Each new NAICS code represents an industry that used to be part of an SIC or a part of several SIC industries. Data in this table are shown to provide transitional information for these cases. All available data for the precursor SIC(s) are shown. Even if only a part of an SIC is included in the NAICS, *all* data for the SIC are reproduced. If the SIC industry is not marked as being a part (pt) of the NAICS, the entire industry is embedded in the NAICS data. The SIC composition of the new industry provides some hints of the relative importance of its "ancestors." Data marked with a 'p' are projected. Projections begin with 1982 data. Data earlier than 1990 are not shown but are reflected in the projections.

SIC	Industry	1990	1991	1992	1993	1994	1995	1996	1997
6163	Loan Brokers (pt)	-	-	-	-	-	-	-	-

Source: *Economic Census of the United States*, 1992, annual surveys of economic sectors conducted by the Bureau of the Census, and estimates or projections based on the 1982-1992 period; not all data are shown. 'e' marks estimates made by the editors; 'p' indicates projections based on time series. A dash (-) indicates that data for this SIC or year were not available. The abbreviation (pt) next to the industry name indicates that only a part of the industry is present within the NAICS data. If no (pt) is shown, the entire industry is contained within the NAICS data.

SELECTED RATIOS

For 1997	Avg. of Information	Analyzed Industry	Index	For 1997	Avg. of Information	Analyzed Industry	Index
Employees per establishment	15	6	37	Payroll per establishment	669,406	211,442	32
Revenue per establishment	5,561,120	567,302	10	Payroll as % of revenue	12	37	310
Revenue per employee	376,639	103,099	27	Payroll per employee	45,337	38,426	85

Sources: Same as General Statistics. The 'Average' column represents the average for the industry sector, in 1997, where the currently shown industry is classified. The Index shows the relationship between the Average and the Analyzed Industry. For example, 100 means that they are equal; 500 that the Analyzed Industry is five times the average; 50 means that the Analyzed Industry is half the national average. The abbreviation 'na' is used to show that data are 'not available'.

LEADING COMPANIES   Number shown: 21   Total sales ($ mil): 1,933   Total employment (000): 8.7

Company Name	Address				CEO Name	Phone	Co. Type	Sales ($ mil)	Empl. (000)
Jones Lang/LaSalle Partners Inc.	200 E Randolph Dr	Chicago	IL	60601	Christopher Peacock	312-782-5800	P	755	2.2
Trendwest Resorts Inc.	9805 Willows Rd	Redmond	WA	98052	William F Peare	425-498-2500	P	274	1.5
Delta Funding Corp.	1000 Woodbury Rd	Woodbury	NY	11797	Hugh I Miller	516-364-8500	S	210*	0.5
Resort Funding Inc.	2 Clinton Sq	Syracuse	NY	13202	Richard C Breeden	315-422-9088	S	147*	<0.1
Delta Financial Corp.	1000 Woodbury Rd	Woodbury	NY	11797	Hugh I Miller	516-364-8500	P	140	1.1
DeWolfe Companies Inc.	80 Hayden Ave	Lexington	MA	02421	Richard B DeWolfe	781-863-5858	P	137	2.0
Nationwide Capital Inc.	1859 N Pine Island	Fort Lauderdale	FL	33322	Howard Kaye	954-748-7700	R	74	<0.1
Equivest Finance Inc.	2 Clinton Sq	Syracuse	NY	13202	Richard C Breeden	315-422-9088	P	30	<0.1
Home Gold Financial Inc.	3901 Pelham Rd	Greenville	SC	29615	John M Sterling, Jr	864-289-5000	P	29	0.4
Mortgage Resource Inc.	14430 S Outer 40	Chesterfield	MO	63017	Steven Carrico	314-576-5577	R	25*	<0.1
Mid America Bancorp	PO Box 1101	Louisville	KY	40201	Bertram Klein	502-589-3351	R	20	0.6
Randall Mortgage	1033 Semoran Blvd	Casselberry	FL	32707	Al Feldman	407-830-9551	R	19*	<0.1
Ashford Financial Corp.	14180 Dallas Pkwy	Dallas	TX	75240	David Kimichik	972-490-9600	R	16*	<0.1
Western Foothill Mortgage Inc.	6060 Enterprise Dr	Diamond Sprgs	CA	95619	Steven Cockerell	530-621-0222	R	14	<0.1
P/R Mortgage & Investment Corp.	320 N Meridian St	Indianapolis	IN	46204	Mike Petrie	317-263-0250	R	12*	<0.1
Specialty Group	3205 E McKnight Dr	Pittsburgh	PA	15237	Ned Sokoloff	412-369-1555	R	9*	<0.1
Gallatin Mortgage Co.	409 S Division	Ann Arbor	MI	48104	Richard H Hedlund	734-994-1202	R	7*	<0.1
Schwartz and Co.	P O Box 10072	Phoenix	AZ	85065	Ethan Schwartz	602-840-4977	R	7	<0.1
TRI Commercial Real Estate	100 Pine St	San Francisco	CA	94111	Edward J Welch	415-268-2200	R	5*	0.1
Michael V	502 Laguardia Pl	New York	NY	10012	Michael V Coratolo	212-254-9800	R	2	<0.1
Mutual Mortgage Corp.	9200 Glenwood	Overland Park	KS	66212	Thomas J Rosberg	913-341-3800	R	1*	<0.1

Source: Ward's Business Directory of U.S. Private and Public Companies, Volumes 1 and 2, 2000. The company type code used is as follows: P - Public, R - Private, S - Subsidiary, D - Division, J - Joint Venture, A - Affiliate, G - Group, N - Company type not reported. Sales are in millions of dollars, employees are in thousands. An asterisk (*) indicates an estimated sales volume. The symbol < stands for 'less than'. Company names and addresses are truncated, in some cases, to fit into the available space.

LOCATION BY STATE AND REGIONAL CONCENTRATION

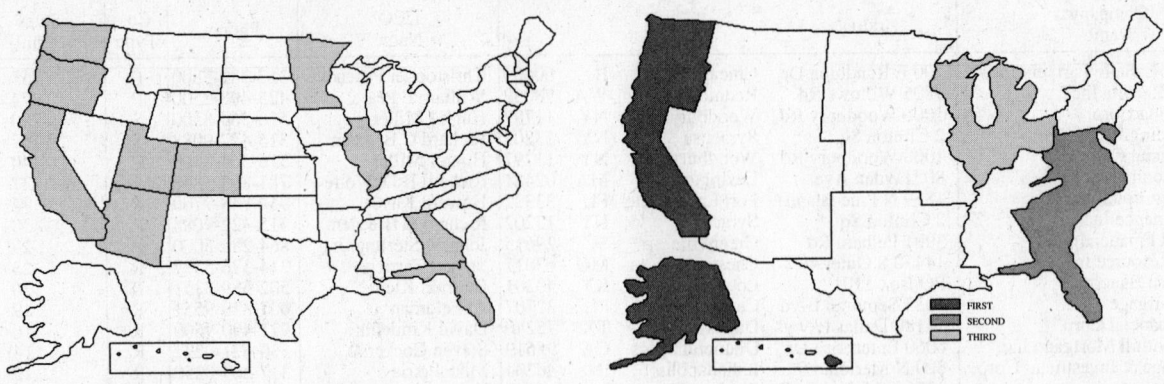

INDUSTRY DATA BY STATE

State	Establishments Total (number)	% of U.S.	Employment Total (number)	% of U.S.	Per Estab.	Payroll Total ($ mil.)	Per Empl. ($)	Revenues Total ($ mil.)	% of U.S.	Per Estab. ($)
California	1,680	18.7	8,931	18.1	5	372.4	41,694	1,300.3	25.6	774,010
Florida	826	9.2	3,135	6.4	4	102.2	32,590	313.0	6.2	378,892
New York	418	4.7	2,104	4.3	5	94.9	45,081	312.2	6.1	746,849
Illinois	393	4.4	3,391	6.9	9	127.7	37,661	278.6	5.5	708,959
Georgia	340	3.8	1,955	4.0	6	82.4	42,159	199.8	3.9	587,603
Washington	304	3.4	1,726	3.5	6	75.3	43,612	184.0	3.6	605,299
Colorado	397	4.4	1,903	3.9	5	72.6	38,163	180.6	3.5	454,806
Texas	367	4.1	1,693	3.4	5	71.2	42,069	178.0	3.5	485,038
Ohio	290	3.2	2,604	5.3	9	88.7	34,080	175.1	3.4	603,728
Arizona	237	2.6	1,607	3.3	7	55.5	34,545	148.9	2.9	628,325
Pennsylvania	280	3.1	1,562	3.2	6	51.3	32,828	142.0	2.8	507,296
New Jersey	139	1.6	806	1.6	6	38.9	48,288	131.8	2.6	948,173
Michigan	204	2.3	1,313	2.7	6	50.1	38,155	115.8	2.3	567,887
Massachusetts	135	1.5	842	1.7	6	47.8	56,727	113.8	2.2	843,000
Oregon	228	2.5	1,061	2.2	5	45.3	42,668	102.8	2.0	450,759
North Carolina	224	2.5	1,497	3.0	7	48.9	32,647	98.3	1.9	438,897
Minnesota	171	1.9	1,012	2.1	6	43.2	42,692	95.8	1.9	559,977
Virginia	206	2.3	1,241	2.5	6	46.9	37,814	95.5	1.9	463,728
Indiana	212	2.4	1,491	3.0	7	44.0	29,491	92.8	1.8	437,844
Missouri	110	1.2	577	1.2	5	29.1	50,369	82.5	1.6	749,827
Utah	144	1.6	638	1.3	4	18.8	29,509	66.6	1.3	462,354
Wisconsin	120	1.3	682	1.4	6	32.4	47,562	59.5	1.2	495,933
Tennessee	131	1.5	704	1.4	5	23.5	33,389	49.4	1.0	376,939
Connecticut	82	0.9	331	0.7	4	18.5	55,843	45.7	0.9	557,463
South Carolina	141	1.6	569	1.2	4	18.4	32,281	44.4	0.9	314,851
Kentucky	93	1.0	523	1.1	6	14.8	28,256	32.2	0.6	346,355
Rhode Island	44	0.5	397	0.8	9	10.4	26,098	25.7	0.5	583,477
Alabama	92	1.0	332	0.7	4	9.4	28,190	25.3	0.5	275,239
Kansas	50	0.6	232	0.5	5	9.2	39,668	20.9	0.4	417,300
Oklahoma	64	0.7	181	0.4	3	6.2	33,983	17.0	0.3	265,609
Hawaii	52	0.6	242	0.5	5	7.3	29,959	16.6	0.3	318,635
Idaho	53	0.6	176	0.4	3	6.3	35,511	15.5	0.3	291,830
Mississippi	52	0.6	177	0.4	3	5.8	32,599	13.5	0.3	259,558
New Mexico	46	0.5	165	0.3	4	5.4	32,933	12.9	0.3	281,348
Arkansas	32	0.4	111	0.2	3	3.9	35,396	9.3	0.2	291,375
Vermont	11	0.1	82	0.2	7	3.0	36,573	6.2	0.1	565,909
Nebraska	16	0.2	48	0.1	3	1.5	31,292	3.2	0.1	197,688
Maine	8	0.1	15	0.0	2	0.8	51,133	2.1	0.0	259,500
Maryland	254	2.8	1,750*	-	-	(D)	-	(D)	-	-
Louisiana	106	1.2	375*	-	-	(D)	-	(D)	-	-
Nevada	96	1.1	375*	-	-	(D)	-	(D)	-	-
Delaware	36	0.4	175*	-	-	(D)	-	(D)	-	-
Iowa	16	0.2	60*	-	-	(D)	-	(D)	-	-
Montana	16	0.2	60*	-	-	(D)	-	(D)	-	-
New Hampshire	16	0.2	60*	-	-	(D)	-	(D)	-	-
West Virginia	11	0.1	60*	-	-	(D)	-	(D)	-	-
Alaska	8	0.1	60*	-	-	(D)	-	(D)	-	-

Source: 1997 *Economic Census.* The states are in descending order of revenues or establishments (if revenue data are missing for the majority). The symbol (D) appears when data are withheld to prevent disclosure of competitive information. States marked with (D) are sorted by number of establishments. A dash (-) indicates that the data element cannot be calculated. * indicates the midpoint of a range; 175, for example is the range 100-249. Shaded *states* on the state map indicate those states which have proportionately greater representation in the industry than would be indicated by the state's population; the ratio is based on total revenues or number of establishments. Shaded *regions* indicate where the industry is regionally most concentrated.

NAICS 522320 - FINANCIAL TRANSACTIONS PROCESSING, RESERVE, AND CLEARINGHOUSE ACTIVITIES

GENERAL STATISTICS

Year	Establishments (number)	Employment (number)	Payroll ($ million)	Revenues ($ million)	Employees per Establishment (number)	Revenues per Establishment ($)	Payroll per Employee ($)
1997	1,239	63,727	2,257.0	34,780.0	51.4	28,071,025	35,417

Source: Economic Census of the United States, 1997. This is a newly defined industry. Data for prior years were unavailable at the time of publication but may become available over time.

INDICES OF CHANGE

Year	Establishments (number)	Employment (number)	Payroll ($ million)	Revenues ($ million)	Employees per Establishment (number)	Revenues per Establishment ($)	Payroll per Employee ($)
1997	100.0	100.0	100.0	100.0	100.0	100.0	100.0

Sources: Same as General Statistics. The values shown reflect change from the base year, 1997. Values above 100 mean greater than 1997, values below 100 mean less than 1997, and a value of 100 in the 1982-96 or 1998-2001 period means same as 1997. Values followed by a 'p' are projections by the editors; 'e' stands for extrapolation. Data are the most recent available at this level of detail.

SIC INDUSTRIES RELATED TO NAICS 522320

Each new NAICS code represents an industry that used to be part of an SIC or a part of several SIC industries. Data in this table are shown to provide transitional information for these cases. All available data for the precursor SIC(s) are shown. Even if only a part of an SIC is included in the NAICS, *all* data for the SIC are reproduced. If the SIC industry is not marked as being a part (pt) of the NAICS, the entire industry is embedded in the NAICS data. The SIC composition of the new industry provides some hints of the relative importance of its "ancestors." Data marked with a 'p' are projected. Projections begin with 1982 data. Data earlier than 1990 are not shown but are reflected in the projections.

SIC	Industry	1990	1991	1992	1993	1994	1995	1996	1997
6099	**Functions Related to Deposit Banking (pt)**	-	-	-	-	-	-	-	-
6153	**Short-Term Business Credit (pt)**	-	-	-	-	-	-	-	-
7389	**Business Services, nec (pt)**								
	Establishments (number)	44,079	50,252	52,375	56,829	60,725	53,596	60,893*p*	63,269*p*
	Employment (thousands)	489.6	550.4	523.6	607.9	648.7	623.0	680.2*p*	710.9*p*
	Revenues ($ million)	-	-	32,885.9	-	-	-	-	-

Source: Economic Census of the United States, 1992, annual surveys of economic sectors conducted by the Bureau of the Census, and estimates or projections based on the 1982-1992 period; not all data are shown. 'e' marks estimates made by the editors; 'p' indicates projections based on time series. A dash (-) indicates that data for this SIC or year were not available. The abbreviation (pt) next to the industry name indicates that only a part of the industry is present within the NAICS data. If no (pt) is shown, the entire industry is contained within the NAICS data.

SELECTED RATIOS

For 1997	Avg. of Information	Analyzed Industry	Index	For 1997	Avg. of Information	Analyzed Industry	Index
Employees per establishment	15	51	348	Payroll per establishment	669,406	1,821,630	272
Revenue per establishment	5,561,120	28,071,025	505	Payroll as % of revenue	12	6	54
Revenue per employee	376,639	545,766	145	Payroll per employee	45,337	35,417	78

Sources: Same as General Statistics. The 'Average' column represents the average for the industry sector, in 1997, where the currently shown industry is classified. The Index shows the relationship between the Average and the Analyzed Industry. For example, 100 means that they are equal; 500 that the Analyzed Industry is five times the average; 50 means that the Analyzed Industry is half the national average. The abbreviation 'na' is used to show that data are 'not available'.

LEADING COMPANIES   Number shown: **47**   Total sales ($ mil): **897,360**   Total employment (000): **91.7**

Company Name	Address				CEO Name	Phone	Co. Type	Sales ($ mil)	Empl. (000)
Federal Home Loan Bank of Des	907 Walnut St	Des Moines	IA	50309	Thurmond C. Connell	515-243-4211	R	260,000*	0.1
Federal Home Loan Bank	P O Box 105565	Atlanta	GA	30348	R R Christman	404-888-8000	R	221,000	0.2
CIT Group/Factoring	650 CIT Dr	Livingston	NJ	07039	Al Gamper	973-740-5000	S	60,763*	3.0
Federal Home Loan Bank	111 E Wacker Dr	Chicago	IL	60601	Alex J Pollock	312-565-5700	R	33,846*	0.2
Federal Home Loan Bank	PO Box 619026	Dallas	TX	75261	George M Barclay	214-944-8500	R	32,183*	0.1
Federal Home Loan Bank	P O Box 598	Cincinnati	OH	45201	Charles L Thiemann	513-852-7500	R	32,000	0.1
Federal Home Loan Bank of New	7 World Trade Ctr	New York	NY	10048	Alfred A Dellibovi	212-441-6600	R	28,513*	0.2
Federal Home Loan Bank	1501 4th Ave	Seattle	WA	98101	Norman B Rice	206-340-2300	R	28,084*	<0.1
Federal Home Loan Bank of San	P O Box 7948	San Francisco	CA	94120	Dean Schultz	415-616-1000	R	25,971*	0.2
CIT Group Inc.	1211 Av Americas	New York	NY	10036	Albert R Gamper Jr	212-536-1390	P	24,303	3.2
Federal Home Loan Bank	P O Box 60	Indianapolis	IN	46206	Martin L Heger	317-465-0200	R	23,491	0.2
Federal Home Loan Bank	P O Box 9106	Boston	MA	02111	Michael A Jessee	617-542-0150	R	19,529*	0.1
CIT Group	650 CIT Dr	Livingston	NJ	07039	Albert R Gamper Jr	973-740-5000	S	19,300	3.0
Federal Home Loan Bank	P O Box 176	Topeka	KS	66601	Frank A Lowman	785-233-0507	R	19,000	0.1
American Express Company	AmEx Twr	New York	NY	10285	Ken Chenault	212-640-2000	S	15,428*	65.0
NationsBank Card Services	P O Box 7029	Dover	DE	19903	Eileen Friars	302-741-1000	D	11,000	3.0
Heller International Inc.	500 W Monroe St	Chicago	IL	60661	Richard J Almeida	312-441-7000	S	10,000*	1.5
American Express Credit Corp.	301 N Walnut St	Wilmington	DE	19801	Vincent P Lisanke	302-594-3350	S	6,945*	<0.1
US Trust Co.	4380 SW Macadam	Portland	OR	97201	Marshall Schwarz	503-228-2300	S	6,097*	0.3
Sears Roebuck Acceptance Corp.	3711 Kennett Pike	Greenville	DE	19807	Keith E Trost	302-888-3100	S	5,273*	<0.1
CIT Commercial Services	1211 Av Americas	New York	NY	10036	John F Daly	212-382-7000	S	4,527*	0.9
Rosenthal and Rosenthal Inc.	1370 Broadway	New York	NY	10018	Stephen J Rosenthal	212-356-1400	R	2,000*	0.2
Heller Financial Inc.	500 W Monroe St	Chicago	IL	60661	Richard J Almeida	312-441-7000	P	1,407	2.7
Foothill Group Inc.	11111 Santa Monica	Los Angeles	CA	90025	John Nikoll	310-478-8383	S	1,000	0.2
Arcadia Financial Ltd.	7825 Washinton S	Minneapolis	MN	55439	Richard A Greenawalt	612-942-9880	P	846*	1.4
ABN AMRO Inc.	208 S La Salle St	Chicago	IL	60604	Timothy O'Gorman	312-855-5880	D	813*	<0.1
Capital Factors Holding Inc.	120 E Palmetto	Boca Raton	FL	33432	John W Kiefer	561-368-5011	P	766	0.3
Fremont Financial Corp.	2020 Santa Monica	Santa Monica	CA	90404	Steven C Bierman	310-315-5550	S	600*	0.2
Merchant Factors Corp.	1430 Broadway	New York	NY	10018	Walter Kaye	212-840-7575	R	511*	<0.1
Premium Financing Specialists Inc	P O Box 13367	Kansas City	MO	64199	Tom Charbonneau	816-391-2350	R	490*	0.2
First Union Energy Group	1001 Fannin St	Houston	TX	77002		713-346-2700	S	330*	<0.1
Tokai Financial Services Inc.	1055 Westlakes Dr	Berwyn	PA	19312	Don Campbell	610-651-5000	R	273*	0.6
GK Financing L.L.C.	2 Embarcadero	San Francisco	CA	94111	Ernest Bates	415-788-5300	S	202*	<0.1
PACCAR Financial Corp.	P O Box 1518	Bellevue	WA	98004	A J Wold	425-468-7100	S	180	0.3
Bay Area Development Co.	1801 Oakland Blvd	Walnut Creek	CA	94596	James Baird	925-926-1020	R	162*	<0.1
Fidelity Funding Inc.	12770 Merit Dr	Dallas	TX	75251	Michael Haddad	972-687-8000	R	110	0.2
MTB Bank. Trading Alliance Div.	90 Broad St	New York	NY	10004		212-858-3450	D	103*	<0.1
Consumer Portfolio Services Inc.	16355 Laguna	Irvine	CA	92618	Charles E Bradley Jr	949-753-6800	P	84	3.5
Allstate Financial Corp.	2700 S Quincy St	Arlington	VA	22206	Charles G Johnson	703-931-2274	P	47	<0.1
AMGRO Inc.	100 North Pkwy	Worcester	MA	01605	Dennis Howard	508-757-1628	S	45*	<0.1
Frost Capital Group	1010 Lamar St	Houston	TX	77002	Peter J Levy	713-652-7530	D	42*	<0.1
Metro Financial Services	P O Box 38604	Dallas	TX	75238	Richard Worthy	214-363-4557	R	42*	<0.1
Xerox Financial Services Inc.	100 1st Stamford Pl	Stamford	CT	06902	Stuart B Ross	203-325-6600	S	20*	<0.1
Mazon Associates Inc.	600 W Arpt Fwy	Irving	TX	75062	John Mazon	972-554-6967	R	12	<0.1
Global Assurance L.L.C.	2020 Hogback Rd	Ann Arbor	MI	48105	Gary Crispin	734-971-1570	R	12	<0.1
Nissan Capital of America Inc.	399 Park Ave	New York	NY	10022	Tadaoki Terasawa	212-572-9100	S	7	<0.1
Caribou Capital Corp.	5350 S Roslyn St	Englewood	CO	80111	Vicki Barone	303-694-6956	R	3	<0.1

Source: *Ward's Business Directory of U.S. Private and Public Companies*, Volumes 1 and 2, 2000. The company type code used is as follows: P - Public, R - Private, S - Subsidiary, D - Division, J - Joint Venture, A - Affiliate, G - Group, N - Company type not reported. Sales are in millions of dollars, employees are in thousands. An asterisk (*) indicates an estimated sales volume. The symbol < stands for 'less than'. Company names and addresses are truncated, in some cases, to fit into the available space.

LOCATION BY STATE AND REGIONAL CONCENTRATION

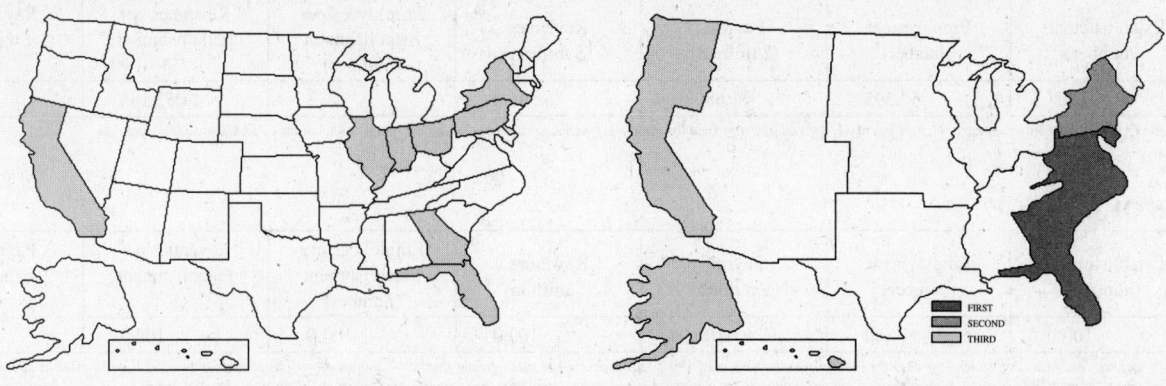

FIRST
SECOND
THIRD

INDUSTRY DATA BY STATE

State	Establishments Total (number)	Establishments % of U.S.	Employment Total (number)	Employment % of U.S.	Employment Per Estab.	Payroll Total ($ mil.)	Payroll Per Empl. ($)	Revenues Total ($ mil.)	Revenues % of U.S.	Revenues Per Estab. ($)
California	203	16.4	5,413	8.5	27	323.8	59,811	4,925.6	14.2	24,264,207
Georgia	38	3.1	4,151	6.5	109	124.9	30,084	3,619.5	10.4	95,250,816
New York	130	10.5	4,431	7.0	34	265.2	59,852	3,393.4	9.8	26,103,162
Florida	98	7.9	7,927	12.4	81	275.2	34,722	2,256.2	6.5	23,022,816
Ohio	12	1.0	1,156	1.8	96	34.8	30,072	1,767.4	5.1	147,280,667
Pennsylvania	30	2.4	1,609	2.5	54	70.9	44,037	1,712.2	4.9	57,074,467
Illinois	145	11.7	2,166	3.4	15	91.6	42,277	1,657.7	4.8	11,432,228
Texas	81	6.5	1,561	2.4	19	78.6	50,340	1,619.6	4.7	19,994,531
Indiana	7	0.6	420	0.7	60	12.7	30,250	1,163.3	3.3	166,186,571
Tennessee	31	2.5	4,248	6.7	137	93.6	22,035	494.0	1.4	15,936,323
Virginia	24	1.9	915	1.4	38	50.6	55,340	450.4	1.3	18,768,500
Maryland	21	1.7	3,442	5.4	164	110.0	31,946	309.3	0.9	14,726,905
New Jersey	48	3.9	1,524	2.4	32	91.1	59,804	239.7	0.7	4,993,042
Nebraska	11	0.9	750*	-	-	29.3	-	145.2	0.4	13,197,182
Colorado	23	1.9	1,125	1.8	49	38.3	34,016	129.0	0.4	5,607,870
Utah	16	1.3	1,769	2.8	111	34.7	19,636	124.0	0.4	7,750,688
Missouri	17	1.4	2,772	4.3	163	53.5	19,310	104.8	0.3	6,166,294
Wisconsin	7	0.6	466	0.7	67	18.5	39,727	95.2	0.3	13,602,286
Minnesota	16	1.3	870	1.4	54	27.5	31,569	90.2	0.3	5,636,937
Michigan	37	3.0	476	0.7	13	14.4	30,345	57.5	0.2	1,554,405
Alabama	7	0.6	27	0.0	4	1.1	39,667	11.3	0.0	1,618,714
Oklahoma	15	1.2	132	0.2	9	2.7	20,470	10.6	0.0	708,000
Hawaii	8	0.6	23	0.0	3	0.7	28,696	4.7	0.0	589,875
Massachusetts	36	2.9	1,750*	-	-	(D)	-	(D)	-	-
Kentucky	21	1.7	3,750*	-	-	(D)	-	(D)	-	-
North Carolina	17	1.4	750*	-	-	(D)	-	(D)	-	-
Connecticut	13	1.0	175*	-	-	(D)	-	(D)	-	-
Kansas	12	1.0	750*	-	-	(D)	-	(D)	-	-
Nevada	12	1.0	375*	-	-	(D)	-	(D)	-	-
Arizona	11	0.9	60*	-	-	(D)	-	(D)	-	-
Louisiana	11	0.9	1,750*	-	-	(D)	-	(D)	-	-
South Carolina	10	0.8	175*	-	-	(D)	-	(D)	-	-
South Dakota	10	0.8	1,750*	-	-	(D)	-	(D)	-	-
Washington	10	0.8	375*	-	-	(D)	-	(D)	-	-
Delaware	9	0.7	1,750*	-	-	(D)	-	(D)	-	-
Iowa	8	0.6	1,750*	-	-	(D)	-	(D)	-	-

Source: 1997 *Economic Census*. The states are in descending order of revenues or establishments (if revenue data are missing for the majority). The symbol (D) appears when data are withheld to prevent disclosure of competitive information. States marked with (D) are sorted by number of establishments. A dash (-) indicates that the data element cannot be calculated. * indicates the midpoint of a range; 175, for example is the range 100-249. Shaded *states* on the state map indicate those states which have proportionately greater representation in the industry than would be indicated by the state's population; the ratio is based on total revenues or number of establishments. Shaded *regions* indicate where the industry is regionally most concentrated.

NAICS 522390 - ACTIVITIES RELATED TO CREDIT INTERMEDIATION NEC

GENERAL STATISTICS

Year	Establishments (number)	Employment (number)	Payroll ($ million)	Revenues ($ million)	Employees per Establishment (number)	Revenues per Establishment ($)	Payroll per Employee ($)
1997	6,204	57,395	1,680.0	6,596.0	9.3	1,063,185	29,271

Source: *Economic Census of the United States*, 1997. This is a newly defined industry. Data for prior years were unavailable at the time of publication but may become available over time.

INDICES OF CHANGE

Year	Establishments (number)	Employment (number)	Payroll ($ million)	Revenues ($ million)	Employees per Establishment (number)	Revenues per Establishment ($)	Payroll per Employee ($)
1997	100.0	100.0	100.0	100.0	100.0	100.0	100.0

Sources: Same as General Statistics. The values shown reflect change from the base year, 1997. Values above 100 mean greater than 1997, values below 100 mean less than 1997, and a value of 100 in the 1982-96 or 1998-2001 period means same as 1997. Values followed by a 'p' are projections by the editors; 'e' stands for extrapolation. Data are the most recent available at this level of detail.

SIC INDUSTRIES RELATED TO NAICS 522390

Each new NAICS code represents an industry that used to be part of an SIC or a part of several SIC industries. Data in this table are shown to provide transitional information for these cases. All available data for the precursor SIC(s) are shown. Even if only a part of an SIC is included in the NAICS, *all* data for the SIC are reproduced. If the SIC industry is not marked as being a part (pt) of the NAICS, the entire industry is embedded in the NAICS data. The SIC composition of the new industry provides some hints of the relative importance of its "ancestors." Data marked with a 'p' are projected. Projections begin with 1982 data. Data earlier than 1990 are not shown but are reflected in the projections.

SIC	Industry	1990	1991	1992	1993	1994	1995	1996	1997
6099	**Functions Related to Deposit Banking (pt)**	-	-	-	-	-	-	-	-
6162	**Mortgage Bankers & Correspondents (pt)**	-	-	-	-	-	-	-	-

Source: *Economic Census of the United States*, 1992, annual surveys of economic sectors conducted by the Bureau of the Census, and estimates or projections based on the 1982-1992 period; not all data are shown. 'e' marks estimates made by the editors; 'p' indicates projections based on time series. A dash (-) indicates that data for this SIC or year were not available. The abbreviation (pt) next to the industry name indicates that only a part of the industry is present within the NAICS data. If no (pt) is shown, the entire industry is contained within the NAICS data.

SELECTED RATIOS

For 1997	Avg. of Information	Analyzed Industry	Index	For 1997	Avg. of Information	Analyzed Industry	Index
Employees per establishment	15	9	63	Payroll per establishment	669,406	270,793	40
Revenue per establishment	5,561,120	1,063,185	19	Payroll as % of revenue	12	25	212
Revenue per employee	376,639	114,923	31	Payroll per employee	45,337	29,271	65

Sources: Same as General Statistics. The 'Average' column represents the average for the industry sector, in 1997, where the currently shown industry is classified. The Index shows the relationship between the Average and the Analyzed Industry. For example, 100 means that they are equal; 500 that the Analyzed Industry is five times the average; 50 means that the Analyzed Industry is half the national average. The abbreviation 'na' is used to show that data are 'not available'.

LEADING COMPANIES   Number shown: **7**   Total sales ($ mil): **207,901**   Total employment (000): **3.0**

Company Name	Address				CEO Name	Phone	Co. Type	Sales ($ mil)	Empl. (000)
Rock Financial Corp.	30600 Telegraph Rd	Bingham Farms	MI	48025	Daniel Gilbert	248-540-8000	P	204,437	0.8
Doral Financial Corp.	1159 FD Roosevelt	San Juan	PR	00920	Salomon Levis	787-749-7100	P	2,918	1.4
MuniMae	218 N Charles St	Baltimore	MD	21201	Michael L Falcone	410-962-8044	P	359*	<0.1
NovaStar Financial Inc.	1901 W 47th Place	Westwood	KS	66205	W Lance Anderson	913-362-1090	P	101	0.3
WMF Group Ltd.	1593 Spring Hill Rd	Vienna	VA	22182	Shekar Narasimhan	703-610-1400	P	73	0.3
Anchor Mortgage Corp.	520 W Erie St	Chicago	IL	60610	John MC Munson		R	9	0.2
Thornburg Mortage Asset Corp.	119 E Marcy St	Santa Fe	NM	87501	Larry A Goldstone	505-989-1900	P	4	<0.1

Source: Ward's Business Directory of U.S. Private and Public Companies, Volumes 1 and 2, 2000. The company type code used is as follows: P - Public, R - Private, S - Subsidiary, D - Division, J - Joint Venture, A - Affiliate, G - Group, N - Company type not reported. Sales are in millions of dollars, employees are in thousands. An asterisk (*) indicates an estimated sales volume. The symbol < stands for 'less than'. Company names and addresses are truncated, in some cases, to fit into the available space.

LOCATION BY STATE AND REGIONAL CONCENTRATION

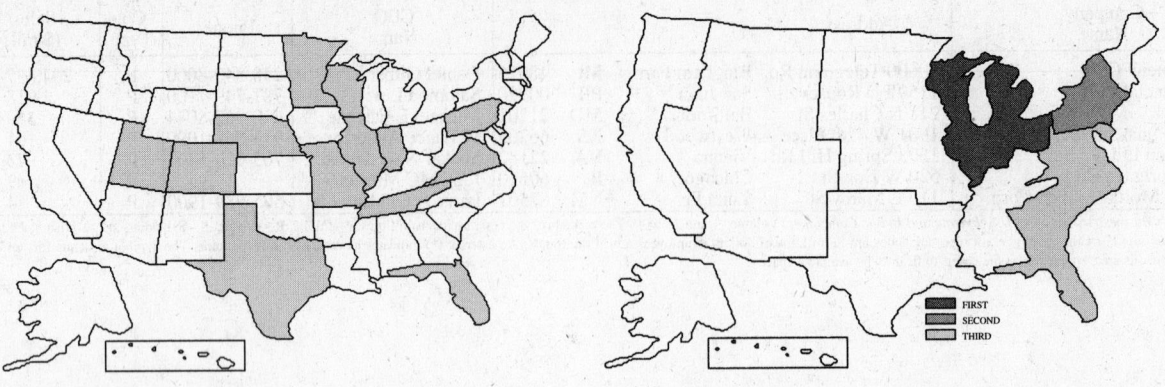

INDUSTRY DATA BY STATE

State	Establishments Total (number)	% of U.S.	Employment Total (number)	% of U.S.	Per Estab.	Payroll Total ($ mil.)	Per Empl. ($)	Revenues Total ($ mil.)	% of U.S.	Per Estab. ($)
California	908	14.6	5,572	9.7	6	168.7	30,281	587.7	8.9	647,301
Texas	656	10.6	3,321	5.8	5	95.4	28,735	472.3	7.2	719,989
New York	432	7.0	4,990	8.7	12	182.1	36,487	470.4	7.1	1,088,861
Illinois	508	8.2	4,510	7.9	9	141.5	31,370	452.8	6.9	891,341
Florida	373	6.0	3,406	5.9	9	97.6	28,657	412.2	6.2	1,105,086
Pennsylvania	220	3.5	3,271	5.7	15	99.9	30,546	335.5	5.1	1,524,859
Wisconsin	71	1.1	1,482	2.6	21	39.1	26,372	262.9	4.0	3,703,183
Tennessee	271	4.4	1,864	3.2	7	45.2	24,267	236.2	3.6	871,513
Colorado	133	2.1	2,901	5.1	22	102.7	35,409	226.1	3.4	1,700,331
Minnesota	57	0.9	1,490	2.6	26	50.4	33,822	217.8	3.3	3,821,088
Missouri	94	1.5	2,065	3.6	22	49.1	23,798	197.4	3.0	2,100,117
Virginia	99	1.6	1,681	2.9	17	39.6	23,539	168.4	2.6	1,701,253
Indiana	156	2.5	1,730	3.0	11	70.4	40,683	159.9	2.4	1,024,718
New Jersey	178	2.9	1,309	2.3	7	43.7	33,357	137.4	2.1	771,629
Georgia	179	2.9	1,451	2.5	8	39.8	27,432	130.0	2.0	726,089
Ohio	231	3.7	1,307	2.3	6	31.8	24,303	129.4	2.0	559,983
Arizona	138	2.2	902	1.6	7	21.2	23,558	88.0	1.3	637,928
Utah	51	0.8	1,439	2.5	28	21.3	14,834	64.5	1.0	1,264,314
Oklahoma	90	1.5	758	1.3	8	16.0	21,103	52.3	0.8	581,611
Nebraska	40	0.6	495	0.9	12	10.4	20,976	46.3	0.7	1,156,975
Michigan	66	1.1	526	0.9	8	15.7	29,804	43.9	0.7	664,576
Alabama	60	1.0	199	0.3	3	4.5	22,643	25.7	0.4	428,933
D.C.	33	0.5	102	0.2	3	2.8	27,912	15.7	0.2	476,424
Idaho	24	0.4	91	0.2	4	3.0	32,681	13.7	0.2	569,792
Hawaii	18	0.3	81	0.1	5	2.3	28,481	9.8	0.1	546,056
Maryland	123	2.0	1,750*	-	-	(D)	-	(D)	-	-
Washington	119	1.9	750*	-	-	(D)	-	(D)	-	-
Kentucky	112	1.8	375*	-	-	(D)	-	(D)	-	-
Mississippi	106	1.7	750*	-	-	(D)	-	(D)	-	-
North Carolina	97	1.6	1,750*	-	-	(D)	-	(D)	-	-
South Carolina	82	1.3	750*	-	-	(D)	-	(D)	-	-
Louisiana	74	1.2	750*	-	-	(D)	-	(D)	-	-
Massachusetts	57	0.9	175*	-	-	(D)	-	(D)	-	-
Oregon	57	0.9	375*	-	-	(D)	-	(D)	-	-
Kansas	51	0.8	1,750*	-	-	(D)	-	(D)	-	-
Arkansas	48	0.8	750*	-	-	(D)	-	(D)	-	-
Connecticut	48	0.8	175*	-	-	(D)	-	(D)	-	-
Nevada	42	0.7	750*	-	-	(D)	-	(D)	-	-
New Mexico	36	0.6	175*	-	-	(D)	-	(D)	-	-
Iowa	16	0.3	1,750*	-	-	(D)	-	(D)	-	-
Delaware	12	0.2	60*	-	-	(D)	-	(D)	-	-
Montana	7	0.1	60*	-	-	(D)	-	(D)	-	-
Rhode Island	6	0.1	10*	-	-	(D)	-	(D)	-	-

Source: 1997 *Economic Census*. The states are in descending order of revenues or establishments (if revenue data are missing for the majority). The symbol (D) appears when data are withheld to prevent disclosure of competitive information. States marked with (D) are sorted by number of establishments. A dash (-) indicates that the data element cannot be calculated. * indicates the midpoint of a range; 175, for example is the range 100-249. Shaded *states* on the state map indicate those states which have proportionately greater representation in the industry than would be indicated by the state's population; the ratio is based on total revenues or number of establishments. Shaded *regions* indicate where the industry is regionally most concentrated.

NAICS 523110 - INVESTMENT BANKING AND SECURITIES DEALING

GENERAL STATISTICS

Year	Establishments (number)	Employment (number)	Payroll ($ million)	Revenues ($ million)	Employees per Establishment (number)	Revenues per Establishment ($)	Payroll per Employee ($)
1997	4,136	140,782	22,330.0	118,386.0	34.0	28,623,308	158,614

Source: Economic Census of the United States, 1997. This is a newly defined industry. Data for prior years were unavailable at the time of publication but may become available over time.

INDICES OF CHANGE

Year	Establishments (number)	Employment (number)	Payroll ($ million)	Revenues ($ million)	Employees per Establishment (number)	Revenues per Establishment ($)	Payroll per Employee ($)
1997	100.0	100.0	100.0	100.0	100.0	100.0	100.0

Sources: Same as General Statistics. The values shown reflect change from the base year, 1997. Values above 100 mean greater than 1997, values below 100 mean less than 1997, and a value of 100 in the 1982-96 or 1998-2001 period means same as 1997. Values followed by a 'p' are projections by the editors; 'e' stands for extrapolation. Data are the most recent available at this level of detail.

SIC INDUSTRIES RELATED TO NAICS 523110

Each new NAICS code represents an industry that used to be part of an SIC or a part of several SIC industries. Data in this table are shown to provide transitional information for these cases. All available data for the precursor SIC(s) are shown. Even if only a part of an SIC is included in the NAICS, *all* data for the SIC are reproduced. If the SIC industry is not marked as being a part (pt) of the NAICS, the entire industry is embedded in the NAICS data. The SIC composition of the new industry provides some hints of the relative importance of its "ancestors." Data marked with a 'p' are projected. Projections begin with 1982 data. Data earlier than 1990 are not shown but are reflected in the projections.

SIC	Industry	1990	1991	1992	1993	1994	1995	1996	1997
6211	**Security Brokers and Dealers (pt)**								
	Establishments (number)	-	-	17,787	-	-	-	-	-
	Employment (thousands)	-	-	300.0	-	-	-	-	-
	Revenues ($ million)	-	-	88,171.4	-	-	-	-	-

Source: Economic Census of the United States, 1992, annual surveys of economic sectors conducted by the Bureau of the Census, and estimates or projections based on the 1982-1992 period; not all data are shown. 'e' marks estimates made by the editors; 'p' indicates projections based on time series. A dash (-) indicates that data for this SIC or year were not available. The abbreviation (pt) next to the industry name indicates that only a part of the industry is present within the NAICS data. If no (pt) is shown, the entire industry is contained within the NAICS data.

SELECTED RATIOS

For 1997	Avg. of Information	Analyzed Industry	Index	For 1997	Avg. of Information	Analyzed Industry	Index
Employees per establishment	15	34	230	Payroll per establishment	669,406	5,398,936	807
Revenue per establishment	5,561,120	28,623,308	515	Payroll as % of revenue	12	19	157
Revenue per employee	376,639	840,917	223	Payroll per employee	45,337	158,614	350

Sources: Same as General Statistics. The 'Average' column represents the average for the industry sector, in 1997, where the currently shown industry is classified. The Index shows the relationship between the Average and the Analyzed Industry. For example, 100 means that they are equal; 500 that the Analyzed Industry is five times the average; 50 means that the Analyzed Industry is half the national average. The abbreviation 'na' is used to show that data are 'not available'.

LEADING COMPANIES

No company data available for this industry.

LOCATION BY STATE AND REGIONAL CONCENTRATION

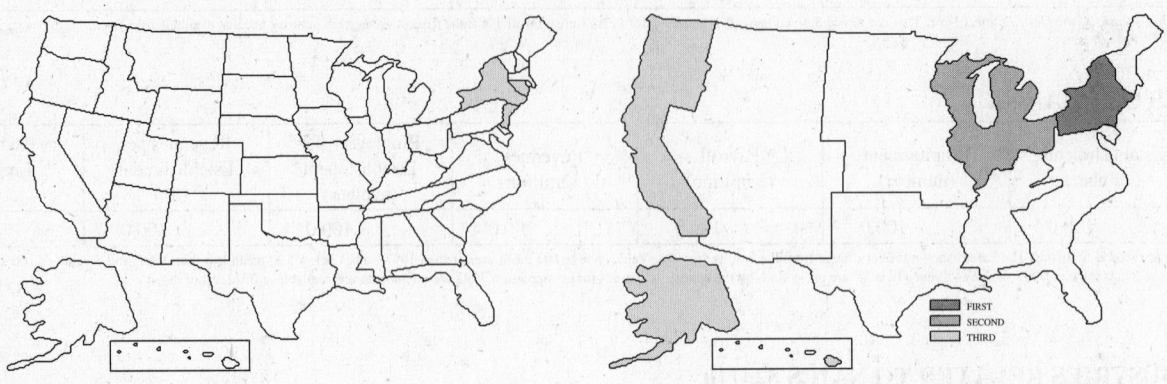

FIRST
SECOND
THIRD

INDUSTRY DATA BY STATE

State	Establishments Total (number)	Establishments % of U.S.	Employment Total (number)	Employment % of U.S.	Employment Per Estab.	Payroll Total ($ mil.)	Payroll Per Empl. ($)	Revenues Total ($ mil.)	Revenues % of U.S.	Revenues Per Estab. ($)
New York	823	19.9	71,918	51.1	87	15,469.1	215,093	95,740.8	80.9	116,331,428
New Jersey	192	4.6	14,789	10.5	77	1,262.2	85,348	4,424.4	3.7	23,043,964
California	476	11.5	8,697	6.2	18	1,090.8	125,419	3,609.4	3.0	7,582,845
Illinois	438	10.6	6,585	4.7	15	826.4	125,491	3,194.0	2.7	7,292,210
Connecticut	105	2.5	1,730	1.2	16	433.4	250,499	2,210.5	1.9	21,052,857
Texas	230	5.6	3,574	2.5	16	398.2	111,410	1,339.4	1.1	5,823,491
Minnesota	104	2.5	3,461	2.5	33	339.9	98,214	1,262.1	1.1	12,135,567
Florida	273	6.6	4,552	3.2	17	312.3	68,612	1,099.8	0.9	4,028,590
Ohio	85	2.1	2,862	2.0	34	236.9	82,764	720.1	0.6	8,471,918
Missouri	59	1.4	4,204	3.0	71	284.3	67,626	633.1	0.5	10,730,237
Tennessee	42	1.0	1,208	0.9	29	101.3	83,866	494.0	0.4	11,761,810
D.C.	33	0.8	577	0.4	17	176.0	305,075	330.6	0.3	10,018,152
Washington	74	1.8	1,455	1.0	20	112.0	76,959	307.6	0.3	4,157,270
Georgia	75	1.8	708	0.5	9	74.3	104,997	295.7	0.2	3,942,333
North Carolina	40	1.0	613	0.4	15	76.0	123,953	282.9	0.2	7,073,625
Arizona	53	1.3	1,800	1.3	34	85.7	47,620	241.7	0.2	4,560,811
Colorado	113	2.7	1,179	0.8	10	98.2	83,304	221.6	0.2	1,960,823
Nebraska	17	0.4	232	0.2	14	10.4	44,759	104.0	0.1	6,117,059
Virginia	64	1.5	349	0.2	5	35.1	100,573	103.6	0.1	1,618,594
Michigan	51	1.2	645	0.5	13	38.6	59,784	99.6	0.1	1,952,078
Indiana	49	1.2	682	0.5	14	45.6	66,924	89.0	0.1	1,815,959
South Carolina	24	0.6	168	0.1	7	9.3	55,595	67.0	0.1	2,790,792
Oregon	35	0.8	314	0.2	9	19.9	63,525	62.2	0.1	1,778,171
Kansas	35	0.8	189	0.1	5	11.4	60,571	49.6	0.0	1,417,657
Arkansas	13	0.3	240	0.2	18	15.4	64,096	37.9	0.0	2,915,692
Alabama	23	0.6	192	0.1	8	17.2	89,745	35.9	0.0	1,561,435
Utah	15	0.4	159	0.1	11	12.4	77,931	31.7	0.0	2,116,533
Iowa	20	0.5	66	0.0	3	6.0	90,848	30.8	0.0	1,541,250
Wisconsin	33	0.8	114	0.1	3	7.6	66,351	28.8	0.0	871,788
Oklahoma	45	1.1	177	0.1	4	5.8	32,876	28.4	0.0	630,556
Nevada	31	0.7	73	0.1	2	3.4	46,616	16.6	0.0	536,355
Louisiana	26	0.6	90	0.1	3	8.8	98,222	13.0	0.0	500,385
Kentucky	17	0.4	51	0.0	3	1.9	36,941	9.3	0.0	547,412
Idaho	9	0.2	26	0.0	3	2.0	78,615	8.3	0.0	918,111
West Virginia	7	0.2	23	0.0	3	0.6	25,435	2.8	0.0	406,000
Pennsylvania	154	3.7	1,750*	-	-	(D)	-	(D)	-	-
Massachusetts	110	2.7	3,750*	-	-	(D)	-	(D)	-	-
Maryland	42	1.0	175*	-	-	(D)	-	(D)	-	-
Delaware	18	0.4	60*	-	-	(D)	-	(D)	-	-
New Mexico	17	0.4	60*	-	-	(D)	-	(D)	-	-
Mississippi	11	0.3	60*	-	-	(D)	-	(D)	-	-
Rhode Island	11	0.3	60*	-	-	(D)	-	(D)	-	-
New Hampshire	9	0.2	60*	-	-	(D)	-	(D)	-	-
Maine	6	0.1	10*	-	-	(D)	-	(D)	-	-
Montana	6	0.1	60*	-	-	(D)	-	(D)	-	-

Source: 1997 Economic Census. The states are in descending order of revenues or establishments (if revenue data are missing for the majority). The symbol (D) appears when data are withheld to prevent disclosure of competitive information. States marked with (D) are sorted by number of establishments. A dash (-) indicates that the data element cannot be calculated. * indicates the midpoint of a range; 175, for example is the range 100-249. Shaded states on the state map indicate those states which have proportionately greater representation in the industry than would be indicated by the state's population; the ratio is based on total revenues or number of establishments. Shaded regions indicate where the industry is regionally most concentrated.

NAICS 523120 - SECURITIES BROKERAGE

GENERAL STATISTICS

Year	Establishments (number)	Employment (number)	Payroll ($ million)	Revenues ($ million)	Employees per Establishment (number)	Revenues per Establishment ($)	Payroll per Employee ($)
1997	19,869	290,656	26,520.0	72,756.0	14.6	3,661,785	91,242

Source: Economic Census of the United States, 1997. This is a newly defined industry. Data for prior years were unavailable at the time of publication but may become available over time.

INDICES OF CHANGE

Year	Establishments (number)	Employment (number)	Payroll ($ million)	Revenues ($ million)	Employees per Establishment (number)	Revenues per Establishment ($)	Payroll per Employee ($)
1997	100.0	100.0	100.0	100.0	100.0	100.0	100.0

Sources: Same as General Statistics. The values shown reflect change from the base year, 1997. Values above 100 mean greater than 1997, values below 100 mean less than 1997, and a value of 100 in the 1982-96 or 1998-2001 period means same as 1997. Values followed by a 'p' are projections by the editors; 'e' stands for extrapolation. Data are the most recent available at this level of detail.

SIC INDUSTRIES RELATED TO NAICS 523120

Each new NAICS code represents an industry that used to be part of an SIC or a part of several SIC industries. Data in this table are shown to provide transitional information for these cases. All available data for the precursor SIC(s) are shown. Even if only a part of an SIC is included in the NAICS, *all* data for the SIC are reproduced. If the SIC industry is not marked as being a part (pt) of the NAICS, the entire industry is embedded in the NAICS data. The SIC composition of the new industry provides some hints of the relative importance of its "ancestors." Data marked with a 'p' are projected. Projections begin with 1982 data. Data earlier than 1990 are not shown but are reflected in the projections.

SIC	Industry	1990	1991	1992	1993	1994	1995	1996	1997
6211	**Security Brokers and Dealers (pt)**								
	Establishments (number)	-	-	17,787	-	-	-	-	-
	Employment (thousands)	-	-	300.0	-	-	-	-	-
	Revenues ($ million)	-	-	88,171.4	-	-	-	-	-

Source: Economic Census of the United States, 1992, annual surveys of economic sectors conducted by the Bureau of the Census, and estimates or projections based on the 1982-1992 period; not all data are shown. 'e' marks estimates made by the editors; 'p' indicates projections based on time series. A dash (-) indicates that data for this SIC or year were not available. The abbreviation (pt) next to the industry name indicates that only a part of the industry is present within the NAICS data. If no (pt) is shown, the entire industry is contained within the NAICS data.

SELECTED RATIOS

For 1997	Avg. of Information	Analyzed Industry	Index	For 1997	Avg. of Information	Analyzed Industry	Index
Employees per establishment	15	15	99	Payroll per establishment	669,406	1,334,743	199
Revenue per establishment	5,561,120	3,661,785	66	Payroll as % of revenue	12	36	303
Revenue per employee	376,639	250,317	66	Payroll per employee	45,337	91,242	201

Sources: Same as General Statistics. The 'Average' column represents the average for the industry sector, in 1997, where the currently shown industry is classified. The Index shows the relationship between the Average and the Analyzed Industry. For example, 100 means that they are equal; 500 that the Analyzed Industry is five times the average; 50 means that the Analyzed Industry is half the national average. The abbreviation 'na' is used to show that data are 'not available'.

LEADING COMPANIES   Number shown: **75**   Total sales ($ mil): **446,704**   Total employment (000): **550.2**

Company Name	Address				CEO Name	Phone	Co. Type	Sales ($ mil)	Empl. (000)
Bessemer Group Inc.	100 Woodbridge Ctr	Woodbridge	NJ	07095	Donald J. Herrera	732-855-0800	R	151,000	0.3
Morgan Stanley International Inc.	1585 Broadway	New York	NY	10036	Phillip Purcell	212-761-4000	S	63,583*	50.0
Goldman Sachs and Co.	85 Broad St	New York	NY	10004	Henry M Paulson	212-902-1000	P	25,363	14.2
Merrill Lynch and Company Inc.	World Financial Ctr	New York	NY	10281	Herbert M Allison Jr	212-449-1000	P	21,869	63.8
Salomon Smith Barney Holdings	388 Greenwich St	New York	NY	10013	Michael A Carpenter	212-816-6000	S	20,673	36.3
American Express Co.	W Fin Ctr	New York	NY	10285	Kenneth I Chenault	212-640-2000	P	19,483	85.0
J.P. Morgan Securities Inc.	60 Wall St	New York	NY	10260	Douglas A Warner III	212-483-2323	P	18,110	15.7
Warburg Dillon Read	299 Park Ave	New York	NY	10171	Richard C Capone	212-906-7000	D	14,243*	15.0
Weiss, Peck and Greer L.L.C.	1 New York Plz	New York	NY	10004		212-908-9500	R	12,567*	0.3
Lehman Brothers Holdings Inc.	3 World Financial	New York	NY	10285	Richard S Fuld Jr	212-526-7000	P	11,300	8.9
Bear Stearns Companies Inc.	245 Park Ave	New York	NY	10167	James E Cayne	212-272-2000	P	7,882	9.5
Credit Suisse First Boston	11 Madison Ave	New York	NY	10010	Rainer E Gut	212-325-2000	S	6,713	14.1
PaineWebber Inc.	1285 Av Americas	New York	NY	10019	Donald B Marron	212-713-2000	S	5,976*	17.9
Donaldson, Lufkin & Jenrette Inc.	277 Park Ave	New York	NY	10172	Joe L Roby	212-892-3000	P	5,407	8.5
PaineWebber Group Inc.	1285 Av Americas	New York	NY	10019	Donald B Marron	212-713-2000	P	5,300	19.6
IMATEL Holdings Inc.	74900 Hwy 111	Indian Wells	CA	92210	Riccardo Mortara	714-836-2400	P	4,443	<0.1
Charles Schwab Corp.	101 Montgomery St	San Francisco	CA	94104	Charles R Schwab	415-627-7000	P	3,945	13.3
Prudential Securities Inc.	199 Water St	New York	NY	10292	Hardwick Simmons	212-214-1000	S	3,400*	17.0
Dean Witter Reynolds Inc.	2 World Trade Ctr	New York	NY	10048	Philip J Purcell	212-392-2222	S	3,100	25.0
Charles Schwab Inc.	101 Montgomery St	San Francisco	CA	94104	Charles Schwab	415-398-1000	S	2,736	11.6
A.G. Edwards Inc.	1 N Jefferson Ave	St. Louis	MO	63103	B F Edwards III	314-955-3000	P	2,240	14.0
Robinson-Humphrey L.L.C.	3333 Peachtree N E	Atlanta	GA	30326	Thomas K Tracy	404-266-6000	S	2,087*	2.2
Spear Leeds and Kellogg	120 Broadway	New York	NY	10271	Peter R Kellogg	212-433-7000	R	2,015*	2.4
Edward Jones	201 Progress Pkwy	Maryland H.	MO	63043	John W Bachmann	314-515-2000	R	1,450	15.8
Donaldson, Lufkin & Jenrette	277 Park Ave	New York	NY	10172	Joe L Roby	212-892-3000	P	1,287	8.5
Raymond James Financial Inc.	880 Carillon Pkwy	St. Petersburg	FL	33716	Thomas A James	727-573-3800	P	1,232	4.5
Bridge Trading Co.	717 Office Pkwy	St. Louis	MO	63141	Tom Wendel	314-567-8100	R	1,208*	1.0
Kohlberg, Kravis, Roberts L.P.	9 W 57th St	New York	NY	10019	Henry Kravis	212-750-8300	R	1,200	<0.1
Legg Mason Inc.	PO Box 1476	Baltimore	MD	21202	James W Brinkley	410-539-0000	P	1,046	4.3
Murphey Favre Inc.	17875 V Karman	Irvine	CA	92614	Pamala Dawson		S	980	1.0
Legg Mason Wood Walker Inc.	P O Box 1476	Baltimore	MD	21203	JW Brinkley	410-539-0000	S	899*	3.2
PNC Mortgage Securities Corp.	75 N Fairway Dr	Vernon Hills	IL	60061	Sy Naqvi	847-549-6500	S	890*	0.7
Bear, Stearns and Company Inc.	245 Park Ave	New York	NY	10167	James Cayne	212-272-2000	P	825*	6.4
Dain Rauscher Corp.	Dain Rauscher Plz	Minneapolis	MN	55402	Irving Weiser	612-371-7750	P	820	3.6
Quick & Reilly/Fleet Securities	26 Broadway	New York	NY	10004	Thomas C Quick	212-747-1200	S	800*	2.1
John Nuveen and Company Inc.	333 W Wacker Dr	Chicago	IL	60606	Timothy Schwertfeger	312-917-7700	S	764*	0.6
National Financial Services Corp.	200 Liberty St	New York	NY	10281		212-335-5000	S	763*	0.6
Capital Institutional Services Inc.	750 N St Paul St	Dallas	TX	75201	Don C Potts	214-720-0055	R	735	<0.1
Cantor Fitzgerald and Co.	1 World Trade Ctr	New York	NY	10048	Howard Lutnick	212-938-5000	R	727*	2.5
NationsBanc Montgomery	600 Montgomery St	San Francisco	CA	94111	Lewis Coleman	415-627-2000	S	705	1.5
AIM Management Group Inc.	11 Greenway Plz	Houston	TX	77046	Charles T Bauer	713-626-1919	R	681*	2.5
Churchill Capital Inc.	3100 Lincoln Center	Minneapolis	MN	55402	John Fauth	612-673-6700	R	673*	1.9
E*TRADE Group Inc.	4500 Bohannon Dr	Menlo Park	CA	94025	Christos M Cotsakos	650-331-6000	P	662	1.7
Jefferies Group Inc.	11100 Santa Monica	Los Angeles	CA	90025	Frank E Baxter	310-445-1199	P	640	1.0
Whale Securities Company L.P.	650 5th Ave	New York	NY	10019	Billy Walters	212-484-2000	R	637*	0.5
DA Davidson and Co.	15350 S W Sequoia	Portland	OR	97224	Ian Davidson	503-603-3000	R	636*	0.5
TD Waterhouse Group Inc.	100 Wall St	New York	NY	10005	A Charles Baillies	212-806-3500	P	614	5.1
Cantor Fitzgerald L.P.	1 World Trade Ctr	New York	NY	10048	Howard Lutnick	212-938-5000	S	610*	2.2
U.S. Bancorp Piper Jaffray Inc.	222 S 9th St	Minneapolis	MN	55402	Andrew S Duff	612-342-6000	S	605*	3.2
Wheat First Union	901 E Byrd St	Richmond	VA	23219	Marshall B Wishnack	804-649-2311	P	593	3.2
Rauscher Pierce Refsnes Inc.	2711 N Haskell Ave	Dallas	TX	75204	Ervin Rauscher	214-989-1000	S	586*	3.0
J.C. Bradford and Co.	330 Commerce St	Nashville	TN	37201		615-748-9000	R	578*	2.5
Greenwich Capital Markets Inc.	600 Steamboat Rd	Greenwich	CT	06830	Edwin Knetzger	203-625-2700	R	570*	0.6
Huntington Holdings Inc.	633 W 5th St	Los Angeles	CA	90071	Jack Corwin	213-617-1500	R	554*	0.6
M and H Brokerage Inc.	155 White Plains Rd	Tarrytown	NY	10591	Robert Huson	914-524-9100	R	552*	0.4
Quick and Reilly Inc.	26 Broadway	New York	NY	10004	Leslie C Quick Jr	212-747-1200	S	550	2.1
Meridian Investments	10220 River Rd	Potomac	MD	20854		301-983-5000	R	510*	<0.1
AIM Distributors Inc.	11 Greenway Plz	Houston	TX	77046	Charles T Bauer	713-626-1919	S	504*	0.6
D.E. Shaw and Company L.P.	120 W 45th St	New York	NY	10036	David E Shaw	212-478-0000	R	486*	0.5
John Hancock Funds Inc.	101 Huntington Ave	Boston	MA	02199	Edward J Boudreau Jr	617-375-1500	S	474*	0.5
Nikko Securities International Inc.	200 Liberty St	New York	NY	10281	Timothy Cronin	212-416-5400	S	466*	0.3
John Hsu Capital Group Inc.	767 3rd Ave	New York	NY	10017	John Hsu	212-223-7515	R	457	<0.1
Gruntal and Company L.L.C.	14 Wall St	New York	NY	10005	Lee Fensterstock	212-267-8800	S	441	2.0
BankBoston Robertson Stephens	555 California St	San Francisco	CA	94104	Mike McCaffery	415-781-9700	R	400	0.9
Cowen and Co.	Financial Sq	New York	NY	10005	Joseph Cohen	212-495-6000	R	400	1.6
Furman Selz L.L.C.	230 Park Ave	New York	NY	10169	Edmund A Hajim	212-309-8200	S	400	0.8
Southwest Securities Group Inc.	1201 Elm St	Dallas	TX	75270	David Glatstein	214-859-1800	P	337	0.8
AmeriTrade Holding Corp.	POB 3288	Omaha	NE	68103	JJoe Ricketts	402-331-7856	P	315	2.4
Dain Bosworth Inc.	60 S 6th St	Minneapolis	MN	55402	John C Appel	612-371-2711	R	302	2.1
Hambrecht and Quist L.L.C.	1 Bush St	San Francisco	CA	94104	Daniel H Case III	415-576-3300	S	298*	0.8
Westamerica Bancorporation	P O Box 40	Dewey	OK	74029	David L Payne	415-257-8000	P	298	1.1
Nomura Securities Intern. Inc.	2 World Financial	New York	NY	10281	Atsushi Yoshikawa	212-667-9300	P	280	1.0
Schroder Wertheim Inc.	787 7th Ave	New York	NY	10019	Steven Kotler	212-492-6000	R	280*	1.0
First Southwest Co.	1700 Pacific Ave	Dallas	TX	75201	Hill A Feinberg	214-953-4000	R	277*	0.2
Advest Inc.	90 State House Sq	Hartford	CT	06103	Allen Weintraub	860-509-1000	S	270	1.6

Source: Ward's Business Directory of U.S. Private and Public Companies, Volumes 1 and 2, 2000. The company type code used is as follows: P - Public, R - Private, S - Subsidiary, D - Division, J - Joint Venture, A - Affiliate, G - Group, N - Company type not reported. Sales are in millions of dollars, employees are in thousands. An asterisk (*) indicates an estimated sales volume. The symbol < stands for 'less than'. Company names and addresses are truncated, in some cases, to fit into the available space.

LOCATION BY STATE AND REGIONAL CONCENTRATION

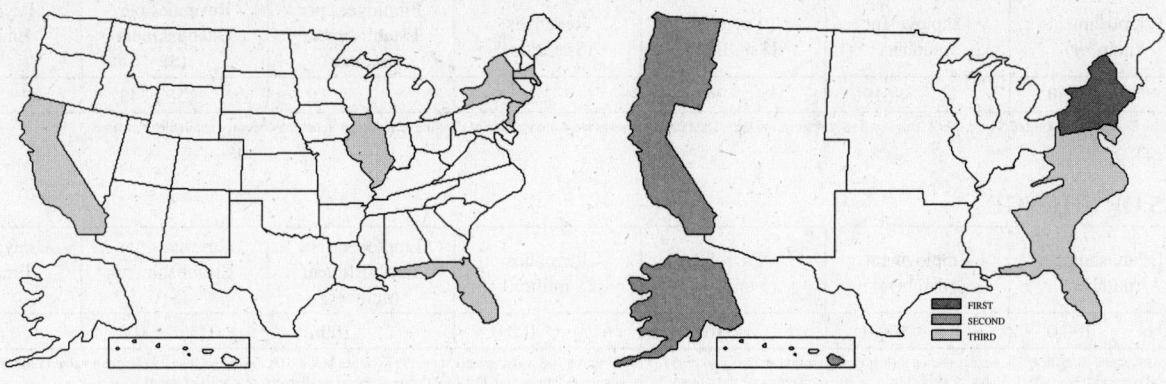

INDUSTRY DATA BY STATE

State	Establishments Total (number)	% of U.S.	Employment Total (number)	% of U.S.	Per Estab.	Payroll Total ($ mil.)	Per Empl. ($)	Revenues Total ($ mil.)	% of U.S.	Per Estab. ($)
New York	1,969	9.9	70,169	24.1	36	7,954.5	113,361	22,104.9	30.4	11,226,460
California	2,401	12.1	34,297	11.8	14	3,268.0	95,286	9,083.1	12.5	3,783,032
Massachusetts	450	2.3	17,452	6.0	39	1,646.9	94,367	4,590.4	6.3	10,200,911
Florida	1,314	6.6	17,786	6.1	14	1,353.7	76,108	3,822.8	5.3	2,909,294
Illinois	1,007	5.1	12,702	4.4	13	1,251.0	98,490	3,608.4	5.0	3,583,297
New Jersey	656	3.3	17,107	5.9	26	1,245.4	72,799	3,293.4	4.5	5,020,457
Texas	1,350	6.8	12,476	4.3	9	1,068.4	85,640	3,043.7	4.2	2,254,609
Pennsylvania	787	4.0	9,371	3.2	12	825.9	88,129	2,307.0	3.2	2,931,367
Ohio	656	3.3	7,105	2.4	11	554.0	77,967	1,553.4	2.1	2,368,056
Georgia	424	2.1	5,035	1.7	12	494.9	98,296	1,337.0	1.8	3,153,415
Minnesota	443	2.2	4,982	1.7	11	375.0	75,266	1,133.3	1.6	2,558,205
Michigan	650	3.3	5,478	1.9	8	437.9	79,931	1,119.1	1.5	1,721,762
Missouri	511	2.6	6,535	2.2	13	423.8	64,856	1,068.0	1.5	2,089,953
Maryland	239	1.2	3,703	1.3	15	460.6	124,386	1,034.9	1.4	4,330,071
North Carolina	442	2.2	4,713	1.6	11	408.5	86,679	1,016.4	1.4	2,299,649
Wisconsin	456	2.3	4,672	1.6	10	347.5	74,380	978.7	1.3	2,146,373
Virginia	365	1.8	5,208	1.8	14	411.1	78,943	948.7	1.3	2,599,170
Tennessee	301	1.5	3,354	1.2	11	298.5	88,992	848.7	1.2	2,819,721
Washington	485	2.4	3,653	1.3	8	290.7	79,569	830.8	1.1	1,713,021
Colorado	432	2.2	5,770	2.0	13	354.3	61,407	828.9	1.1	1,918,769
Arizona	294	1.5	3,004	1.0	10	226.7	75,469	620.0	0.9	2,108,769
Indiana	393	2.0	2,772	1.0	7	216.3	78,025	598.1	0.8	1,522,008
Oregon	277	1.4	2,432	0.8	9	187.8	77,209	498.0	0.7	1,797,866
D.C.	65	0.3	1,810	0.6	28	179.6	99,250	474.3	0.7	7,297,108
Arkansas	176	0.9	1,994	0.7	11	135.1	67,773	443.8	0.6	2,521,824
Alabama	160	0.8	1,870	0.6	12	156.5	83,684	403.7	0.6	2,523,319
Louisiana	238	1.2	1,735	0.6	7	146.4	84,373	362.6	0.5	1,523,525
South Carolina	226	1.1	1,645	0.6	7	123.4	75,027	310.4	0.4	1,373,243
Iowa	305	1.5	1,759	0.6	6	102.1	58,045	304.0	0.4	996,610
Nebraska	171	0.9	1,388	0.5	8	88.9	64,050	295.3	0.4	1,726,801
Kentucky	194	1.0	1,755	0.6	9	130.2	74,177	256.6	0.4	1,322,778
Oklahoma	227	1.1	1,383	0.5	6	99.6	72,033	251.5	0.3	1,108,035
Kansas	242	1.2	1,258	0.4	5	78.4	62,320	244.0	0.3	1,008,202
Nevada	104	0.5	1,071	0.4	10	84.8	79,177	234.4	0.3	2,253,423
Utah	106	0.5	992	0.3	9	71.8	72,352	190.0	0.3	1,792,151
Rhode Island	59	0.3	757	0.3	13	60.8	80,258	148.5	0.2	2,516,492
New Mexico	104	0.5	686	0.2	7	48.6	70,876	136.1	0.2	1,309,038
Hawaii	64	0.3	612	0.2	10	45.7	74,632	136.1	0.2	2,126,187
Mississippi	113	0.6	702	0.2	6	51.7	73,647	126.2	0.2	1,117,204
New Hampshire	87	0.4	672	0.2	8	49.8	74,155	115.9	0.2	1,332,391
Montana	101	0.5	698	0.2	7	44.9	64,338	111.6	0.2	1,104,832
Idaho	77	0.4	573	0.2	7	35.4	61,728	96.6	0.1	1,254,883
West Virginia	63	0.3	478	0.2	8	39.1	81,810	93.6	0.1	1,485,333
Maine	61	0.3	540	0.2	9	40.7	75,324	85.6	0.1	1,402,984
Vermont	38	0.2	333	0.1	9	25.6	76,835	84.3	0.1	2,218,132
South Dakota	81	0.4	549	0.2	7	27.5	50,100	64.1	0.1	791,568
North Dakota	69	0.3	379	0.1	5	21.6	56,984	54.0	0.1	783,304
Alaska	33	0.2	247	0.1	7	18.6	75,490	54.0	0.1	1,636,091
Connecticut	296	1.5	3,750*	-	-	(D)	-	(D)	-	-
Delaware	58	0.3	750*	-	-	(D)	-	(D)	-	-
Wyoming	49	0.2	175*	-	-	(D)	-	(D)	-	-

Source: 1997 *Economic Census*. The states are in descending order of revenues or establishments (if revenue data are missing for the majority). The symbol (D) appears when data are withheld to prevent disclosure of competitive information. States marked with (D) are sorted by number of establishments. A dash (-) indicates that the data element cannot be calculated. * indicates the midpoint of a range; 175, for example is the range 100-249. Shaded *states* on the state map indicate those states which have proportionately greater representation in the industry than would be indicated by the state's population; the ratio is based on total revenues or number of establishments. Shaded *regions* indicate where the industry is regionally most concentrated.

NAICS 523130 - COMMODITY CONTRACTS DEALING

GENERAL STATISTICS

Year	Establishments (number)	Employment (number)	Payroll ($ million)	Revenues ($ million)	Employees per Establishment (number)	Revenues per Establishment ($)	Payroll per Employee ($)
1997	630	4,519	341.0	2,241.0	7.2	3,557,143	75,459

Source: *Economic Census of the United States*, 1997. This is a newly defined industry. Data for prior years were unavailable at the time of publication but may become available over time.

INDICES OF CHANGE

Year	Establishments (number)	Employment (number)	Payroll ($ million)	Revenues ($ million)	Employees per Establishment (number)	Revenues per Establishment ($)	Payroll per Employee ($)
1997	100.0	100.0	100.0	100.0	100.0	100.0	100.0

Sources: Same as General Statistics. The values shown reflect change from the base year, 1997. Values above 100 mean greater than 1997, values below 100 mean less than 1997, and a value of 100 in the 1982-96 or 1998-2001 period means same as 1997. Values followed by a 'p' are projections by the editors; 'e' stands for extrapolation. Data are the most recent available at this level of detail.

SIC INDUSTRIES RELATED TO NAICS 523130

Each new NAICS code represents an industry that used to be part of an SIC or a part of several SIC industries. Data in this table are shown to provide transitional information for these cases. All available data for the precursor SIC(s) are shown. Even if only a part of an SIC is included in the NAICS, *all* data for the SIC are reproduced. If the SIC industry is not marked as being a part (pt) of the NAICS, the entire industry is embedded in the NAICS data. The SIC composition of the new industry provides some hints of the relative importance of its "ancestors." Data marked with a 'p' are projected. Projections begin with 1982 data. Data earlier than 1990 are not shown but are reflected in the projections.

SIC	Industry	1990	1991	1992	1993	1994	1995	1996	1997
6099	**Functions Related to Deposit Banking (pt)**	-	-	-	-	-	-	-	-
6221	**Commodity Contracts Brokers, Dealers (pt)**								
	Establishments (number)	-	-	1,450	-	-	-	-	-
	Employment (thousands)	-	-	12.9	-	-	-	-	-
	Revenues ($ million)	-	-	2,558.2	-	-	-	-	-
6799	**Investors, nec (pt)**								
	Establishments (number)	-	-	6,202	-	-	-	-	-
	Employment (thousands)	-	-	24.4	-	-	-	-	-
	Revenues ($ million)	-	-	9,750.1	-	-	-	-	-

Source: *Economic Census of the United States*, 1992, annual surveys of economic sectors conducted by the Bureau of the Census, and estimates or projections based on the 1982-1992 period; not all data are shown. 'e' marks estimates made by the editors; 'p' indicates projections based on time series. A dash (-) indicates that data for this SIC or year were not available. The abbreviation (pt) next to the industry name indicates that only a part of the industry is present within the NAICS data. If no (pt) is shown, the entire industry is contained within the NAICS data.

SELECTED RATIOS

For 1997	Avg. of Information	Analyzed Industry	Index	For 1997	Avg. of Information	Analyzed Industry	Index
Employees per establishment	15	7	49	Payroll per establishment	669,406	541,270	81
Revenue per establishment	5,561,120	3,557,143	64	Payroll as % of revenue	12	15	126
Revenue per employee	376,639	495,906	132	Payroll per employee	45,337	75,459	166

Sources: Same as General Statistics. The 'Average' column represents the average for the industry sector, in 1997, where the currently shown industry is classified. The Index shows the relationship between the Average and the Analyzed Industry. For example, 100 means that they are equal; 500 that the Analyzed Industry is five times the average; 50 means that the Analyzed Industry is half the national average. The abbreviation 'na' is used to show that data are 'not available'.

LEADING COMPANIES
No company data available for this industry.

LOCATION BY STATE AND REGIONAL CONCENTRATION

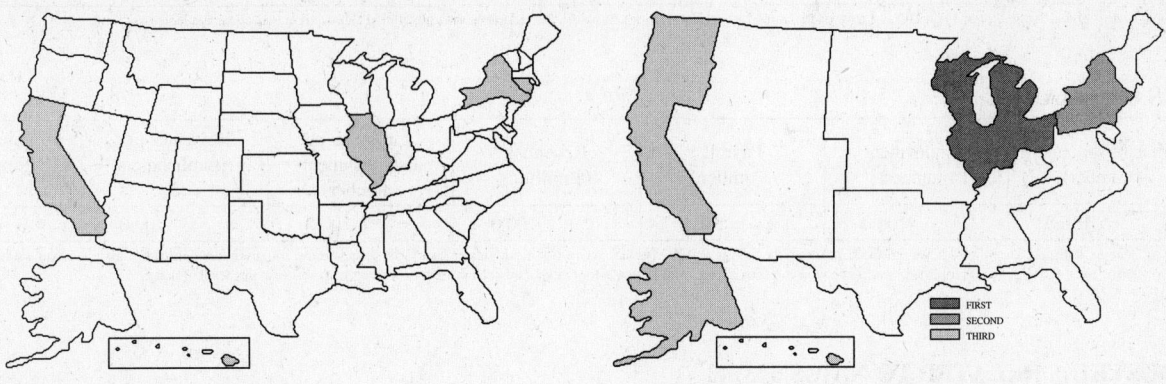

FIRST
SECOND
THIRD

INDUSTRY DATA BY STATE

State	Establishments Total (number)	% of U.S.	Employment Total (number)	% of U.S.	Per Estab.	Payroll Total ($ mil.)	Per Empl. ($)	Revenues Total ($ mil.)	% of U.S.	Per Estab. ($)
Illinois	187	29.7	1,298	28.7	7	110.5	85,147	447.9	20.0	2,395,150
California	101	16.0	558	12.3	6	23.4	41,968	115.5	5.2	1,143,743
Texas	32	5.1	123	2.7	4	3.0	24,073	69.5	3.1	2,172,813
Florida	27	4.3	153	3.4	6	12.9	84,444	38.0	1.7	1,405,778
Colorado	8	1.3	28	0.6	4	2.3	81,786	15.1	0.7	1,889,750
North Carolina	6	1.0	10*	-	-	0.3	-	8.1	0.4	1,355,000
Minnesota	8	1.3	81	1.8	10	1.7	20,395	5.5	0.2	687,500
Missouri	8	1.3	32	0.7	4	1.8	54,875	3.1	0.1	383,750
New York	111	17.6	1,750*	-	-	(D)	-	(D)	-	-
New Jersey	18	2.9	60*	-	-	(D)	-	(D)	-	-
Connecticut	9	1.4	60*	-	-	(D)	-	(D)	-	-
Maryland	7	1.1	60*	-	-	(D)	-	(D)	-	-
Ohio	7	1.1	60*	-	-	(D)	-	(D)	-	-
Hawaii	6	1.0	60*	-	-	(D)	-	(D)	-	-
Massachusetts	6	1.0	175*	-	-	(D)	-	(D)	-	-
Virginia	6	1.0	60*	-	-	(D)	-	(D)	-	-
Washington	6	1.0	60*	-	-	(D)	-	(D)	-	-

Source: 1997 *Economic Census.* The states are in descending order of revenues or establishments (if revenue data are missing for the majority). The symbol (D) appears when data are withheld to prevent disclosure of competitive information. States marked with (D) are sorted by number of establishments. A dash (-) indicates that the data element cannot be calculated. * indicates the midpoint of a range; 175, for example is the range 100-249. Shaded *states* on the state map indicate those states which have proportionately greater representation in the industry than would be indicated by the state's population; the ratio is based on total revenues or number of establishments. Shaded *regions* indicate where the industry is regionally most concentrated.

NAICS 523140 - COMMODITY CONTRACTS BROKERAGE

GENERAL STATISTICS

Year	Establishments (number)	Employment (number)	Payroll ($ million)	Revenues ($ million)	Employees per Establishment (number)	Revenues per Establishment ($)	Payroll per Employee ($)
1997	1,414	13,244	792.0	3,034.0	9.4	2,145,686	59,801

Source: Economic Census of the United States, 1997. This is a newly defined industry. Data for prior years were unavailable at the time of publication but may become available over time.

INDICES OF CHANGE

Year	Establishments (number)	Employment (number)	Payroll ($ million)	Revenues ($ million)	Employees per Establishment (number)	Revenues per Establishment ($)	Payroll per Employee ($)
1997	100.0	100.0	100.0	100.0	100.0	100.0	100.0

Sources: Same as General Statistics. The values shown reflect change from the base year, 1997. Values above 100 mean greater than 1997, values below 100 mean less than 1997, and a value of 100 in the 1982-96 or 1998-2001 period means same as 1997. Values followed by a 'p' are projections by the editors; 'e' stands for extrapolation. Data are the most recent available at this level of detail.

SIC INDUSTRIES RELATED TO NAICS 523140

Each new NAICS code represents an industry that used to be part of an SIC or a part of several SIC industries. Data in this table are shown to provide transitional information for these cases. All available data for the precursor SIC(s) are shown. Even if only a part of an SIC is included in the NAICS, *all* data for the SIC are reproduced. If the SIC industry is not marked as being a part (pt) of the NAICS, the entire industry is embedded in the NAICS data. The SIC composition of the new industry provides some hints of the relative importance of its "ancestors." Data marked with a 'p' are projected. Projections begin with 1982 data. Data earlier than 1990 are not shown but are reflected in the projections.

SIC	Industry	1990	1991	1992	1993	1994	1995	1996	1997
6221	**Commodity Contracts Brokers, Dealers (pt)**								
	Establishments (number)	-	-	1,450	-	-	-	-	-
	Employment (thousands)	-	-	12.9	-	-	-	-	-
	Revenues ($ million)	-	-	2,558.2	-	-	-	-	-

Source: Economic Census of the United States, 1992, annual surveys of economic sectors conducted by the Bureau of the Census, and estimates or projections based on the 1982-1992 period; not all data are shown. 'e' marks estimates made by the editors; 'p' indicates projections based on time series. A dash (-) indicates that data for this SIC or year were not available. The abbreviation (pt) next to the industry name indicates that only a part of the industry is present within the NAICS data. If no (pt) is shown, the entire industry is contained within the NAICS data.

SELECTED RATIOS

For 1997	Avg. of Information	Analyzed Industry	Index	For 1997	Avg. of Information	Analyzed Industry	Index
Employees per establishment	15	9	63	Payroll per establishment	669,406	560,113	84
Revenue per establishment	5,561,120	2,145,686	39	Payroll as % of revenue	12	26	217
Revenue per employee	376,639	229,085	61	Payroll per employee	45,337	59,801	132

Sources: Same as General Statistics. The 'Average' column represents the average for the industry sector, in 1997, where the currently shown industry is classified. The Index shows the relationship between the Average and the Analyzed Industry. For example, 100 means that they are equal; 500 that the Analyzed Industry is five times the average; 50 means that the Analyzed Industry is half the national average. The abbreviation 'na' is used to show that data are 'not available'.

LEADING COMPANIES   Number shown: **31**   Total sales ($ mil): **5,423**   Total employment (000): **5.3**

Company Name	Address				CEO Name	Phone	Co. Type	Sales ($ mil)	Empl. (000)
Metropolitan Mortgage	601 W 1st Ave	Spokane	WA	99201	C. Paul Sandifur Jr.	509-838-3111	R	1,538*	0.5
First Options of Chicago Inc.	440 S La Salle St	Chicago	IL	60605	Tim Mullins	312-362-3000	S	984*	0.8
Gerald Metals Inc.	P O Box 10134	Stamford	CT	06904	Gerald L Lennard	203-609-8300	R	800*	0.6
Geldermann Inc.	440 S La Salle St	Chicago	IL	60605	James Curley	312-663-7500	R	527*	0.4
Refco Group Ltd.	200 Liberty St	New York	NY	10281	Tone Grant	212-693-7000	R	390*	0.5
Rosenthal Collins Group L.P.	216 W Jackson Blvd	Chicago	IL	60606		312-984-5900	R	262*	0.7
Glendore Ltd.	301 Tresser Blvd	Stamford	CT	06901	Willy R Strothotte	203-328-4900	S	208*	0.2
Southeastern Thrift & Bank Fund	PO Box 8200	Boston	MA	02266	Franklin C Golden		P	96	0.0
McVean Trading & Investments	850 Ridge Lake	Memphis	TN	38120	Charles McVean	901-761-8400	R	94*	<0.1
Sakura Dellsher Inc.	10 S Wacker Dr	Chicago	IL	60606	Leo Melamed	312-930-0001	R	78*	0.1
KBC Trading and Processing Co.	PO Box 609	Stockton	CA	95201	S Vincent O'Brien	209-955-0100	S	64*	0.5
EBCO U.S.A. Inc.	6613 N Meridian	Oklahoma City	OK	73116	Paul Smart	405-720-0313	R	52*	<0.1
Siegel Trading Company Inc.	118 N Clinton Ave	Chicago	IL	60661	Frank Mazza	312-879-1000	R	43*	<0.1
ADM Investors Services Inc.	141 W Jackson	Chicago	IL	60604	Paul Krug	312-435-7000	S	41*	0.3
Barex World Trade Corp.	777 W Putnam Ave	Greenwich	CT	06830		203-531-1059	R	40	<0.1
Brody White and Company Inc.	4 World Trade Ctr	New York	NY	10048	Steve Bergan	212-984-1450	R	39*	<0.1
Farmers Commodities Corp.	P O Box 4887	Des Moines	IA	50306	Paul Anderson	515-223-3788	R	37*	0.2
Rand Financial Services Inc.	141 West Jackson	Chicago	IL	60604	Jeff Ouinto	312-559-8800	S	26	0.1
Allied Deals Inc.	180 Centennial Ave	Piscataway	NJ	08854		212-532-7644	R	16*	<0.1
Intern. Marketing Group Inc.	1900 Elm Hill Pike	Nashville	TN	37210	Moe Lytle	615-889-8000	R	15*	<0.1
Alaron Trading Corp.	822 W Washington	Chicago	IL	60607	Steven Greenberg	312-563-8000	R	13	0.1
Vincent Commodities Corp.	PO Box 620481	Middleton	WI	53562	Ronald M Vincent	608-831-4447	R	13	<0.1
Colorado Commodities	1050 Walnut St	Boulder	CO	80302	Tenny Lode	303-444-8200	R	9*	<0.1
DKB Financial Futures Corp.	10 S Wacker #1835	Chicago	IL	60606	Akira Watanabe	312-466-1700	S	8*	<0.1
FSI Future Inc.	675 Berkmar Ct	Charlottesville	VA	22901	Robin Rodriguez	804-975-5959	S	8*	<0.1
FCT Group Inc.	10255 S Ridgeland	Chicago Ridge	IL	60415		708-636-1175	R	6*	<0.1
GK Capital Management Inc.	102 S East St	Bloomington	IL	61701	Gary Klopfenstein	309-827-5550	R	6	<0.1
Ingredient Quality Consultants Inc	1800 2nd St	Sarasota	FL	34236	Wayne Whittaker	941-365-7079	R	3	<0.1
Commodities Resource Corp.	P O Box 8700	Incline Village	NV	89452	George Kleinman	775-833-2700	R	3*	<0.1
I.J. Cohen Company Inc.	5200 W 94th Ter	Shaw Msn	KS	66207	Phillip L Gershon	913-648-6668	R	3*	<0.1
Simonds-Shields-Theis Grain Co.	4800 Main St	Kansas City	MO	64112	Steven O Theis	816-561-4155	R	1*	<0.1

Source: Ward's Business Directory of U.S. Private and Public Companies, Volumes 1 and 2, 2000. The company type code used is as follows: P - Public, R - Private, S - Subsidiary, D - Division, J - Joint Venture, A - Affiliate, G - Group, N - Company type not reported. Sales are in millions of dollars, employees are in thousands. An asterisk (*) indicates an estimated sales volume. The symbol < stands for 'less than'. Company names and addresses are truncated, in some cases, to fit into the available space.

LOCATION BY STATE AND REGIONAL CONCENTRATION

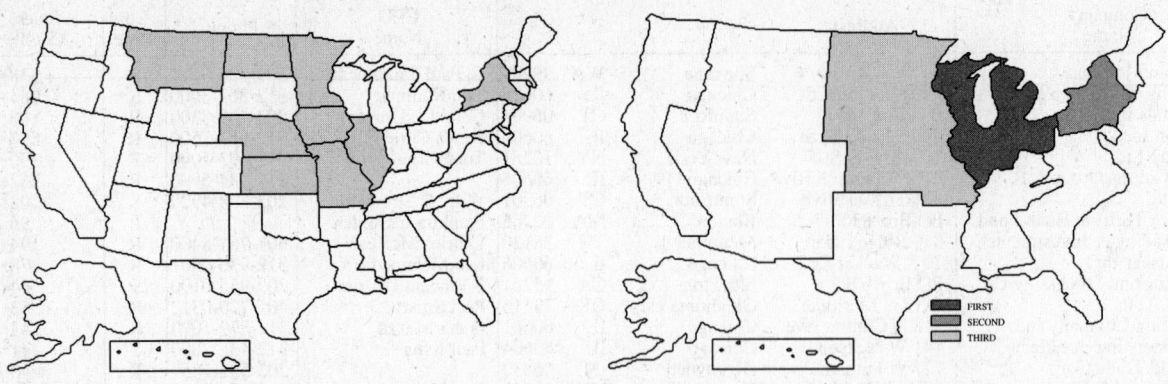

INDUSTRY DATA BY STATE

State	Establishments Total (number)	% of U.S.	Employment Total (number)	% of U.S.	Per Estab.	Payroll Total ($ mil.)	Per Empl. ($)	Revenues Total ($ mil.)	% of U.S.	Per Estab. ($)
Illinois	478	33.8	7,908	59.7	17	419.0	52,986	1,588.1	52.3	3,322,387
Florida	58	4.1	562	4.2	10	34.9	62,110	95.1	3.1	1,639,293
California	64	4.5	435	3.3	7	25.2	57,989	88.9	2.9	1,388,531
Texas	61	4.3	200	1.5	3	22.6	112,870	58.4	1.9	958,148
Missouri	33	2.3	143	1.1	4	8.1	56,336	42.4	1.4	1,285,424
Iowa	59	4.2	301	2.3	5	13.9	46,033	38.0	1.3	643,983
Minnesota	38	2.7	121	0.9	3	6.2	51,347	24.9	0.8	655,974
Georgia	16	1.1	61	0.5	4	3.2	52,164	17.1	0.6	1,068,250
Colorado	18	1.3	64	0.5	4	4.3	67,828	16.9	0.6	938,333
Oklahoma	17	1.2	62	0.5	4	2.9	46,855	11.8	0.4	695,824
Kansas	30	2.1	80	0.6	3	3.3	41,263	8.6	0.3	285,133
North Carolina	9	0.6	18	0.1	2	0.5	28,722	3.0	0.1	335,667
New York	268	19.0	1,750*	-	-	(D)	-	(D)	-	-
New Jersey	30	2.1	60*	-	-	(D)	-	(D)	-	-
Nebraska	29	2.1	60*	-	-	(D)	-	(D)	-	-
Tennessee	21	1.5	60*	-	-	(D)	-	(D)	-	-
Connecticut	16	1.1	175*	-	-	(D)	-	(D)	-	-
Indiana	16	1.1	60*	-	-	(D)	-	(D)	-	-
Ohio	15	1.1	60*	-	-	(D)	-	(D)	-	-
Wisconsin	12	0.8	60*	-	-	(D)	-	(D)	-	-
Oregon	9	0.6	60*	-	-	(D)	-	(D)	-	-
Virginia	9	0.6	10*	-	-	(D)	-	(D)	-	-
Washington	9	0.6	10*	-	-	(D)	-	(D)	-	-
Arizona	8	0.6	60*	-	-	(D)	-	(D)	-	-
Massachusetts	8	0.6	60*	-	-	(D)	-	(D)	-	-
Michigan	8	0.6	60*	-	-	(D)	-	(D)	-	-
Maryland	7	0.5	10*	-	-	(D)	-	(D)	-	-
Montana	7	0.5	10*	-	-	(D)	-	(D)	-	-
Idaho	6	0.4	10*	-	-	(D)	-	(D)	-	-
North Dakota	6	0.4	10*	-	-	(D)	-	(D)	-	-
Pennsylvania	6	0.4	10*	-	-	(D)	-	(D)	-	-

Source: 1997 *Economic Census*. The states are in descending order of revenues or establishments (if revenue data are missing for the majority). The symbol (D) appears when data are withheld to prevent disclosure of competitive information. States marked with (D) are sorted by number of establishments. A dash (-) indicates that the data element cannot be calculated. * indicates the midpoint of a range; 175, for example is the range 100-249. Shaded *states* on the state map indicate those states which have proportionately greater representation in the industry than would be indicated by the state's population; the ratio is based on total revenues or number of establishments. Shaded *regions* indicate where the industry is regionally most concentrated.

NAICS 523210 - SECURITIES AND COMMODITY EXCHANGES

GENERAL STATISTICS

Year	Establishments (number)	Employment (number)	Payroll ($ million)	Revenues ($ million)	Employees per Establishment (number)	Revenues per Establishment ($)	Payroll per Employee ($)
1997	30	6,716	442.0	1,900.0	223.9	63,333,333	65,813

Source: *Economic Census of the United States*, 1997. This is a newly defined industry. Data for prior years were unavailable at the time of publication but may become available over time.

INDICES OF CHANGE

Year	Establishments (number)	Employment (number)	Payroll ($ million)	Revenues ($ million)	Employees per Establishment (number)	Revenues per Establishment ($)	Payroll per Employee ($)
1997	100.0	100.0	100.0	100.0	100.0	100.0	100.0

Sources: Same as General Statistics. The values shown reflect change from the base year, 1997. Values above 100 mean greater than 1997, values below 100 mean less than 1997, and a value of 100 in the 1982-96 or 1998-2001 period means same as 1997. Values followed by a 'p' are projections by the editors; 'e' stands for extrapolation. Data are the most recent available at this level of detail.

SIC INDUSTRIES RELATED TO NAICS 523210

Each new NAICS code represents an industry that used to be part of an SIC or a part of several SIC industries. Data in this table are shown to provide transitional information for these cases. All available data for the precursor SIC(s) are shown. Even if only a part of an SIC is included in the NAICS, *all* data for the SIC are reproduced. If the SIC industry is not marked as being a part (pt) of the NAICS, the entire industry is embedded in the NAICS data. The SIC composition of the new industry provides some hints of the relative importance of its "ancestors." Data marked with a 'p' are projected. Projections begin with 1982 data. Data earlier than 1990 are not shown but are reflected in the projections.

SIC	Industry	1990	1991	1992	1993	1994	1995	1996	1997
6231	**Security and Commodity Exchanges (pt)**								
	Establishments (number)	-	-	35	-	-	-	-	-
	Employment (thousands)	-	-	6.7	-	-	-	-	-
	Revenues ($ million)	-	-	993.5	-	-	-	-	-

Source: *Economic Census of the United States*, 1992, annual surveys of economic sectors conducted by the Bureau of the Census, and estimates or projections based on the 1982-1992 period; not all data are shown. 'e' marks estimates made by the editors; 'p' indicates projections based on time series. A dash (-) indicates that data for this SIC or year were not available. The abbreviation (pt) next to the industry name indicates that only a part of the industry is present within the NAICS data. If no (pt) is shown, the entire industry is contained within the NAICS data.

SELECTED RATIOS

For 1997	Avg. of Information	Analyzed Industry	Index	For 1997	Avg. of Information	Analyzed Industry	Index
Employees per establishment	15	224	1,516	Payroll per establishment	669,406	14,733,333	2,201
Revenue per establishment	5,561,120	63,333,333	1,139	Payroll as % of revenue	12	23	193
Revenue per employee	376,639	282,906	75	Payroll per employee	45,337	65,813	145

Sources: Same as General Statistics. The 'Average' column represents the average for the industry sector, in 1997, where the currently shown industry is classified. The Index shows the relationship between the Average and the Analyzed Industry. For example, 100 means that they are equal; 500 that the Analyzed Industry is five times the average; 50 means that the Analyzed Industry is half the national average. The abbreviation 'na' is used to show that data are 'not available'.

LEADING COMPANIES   Number shown: **15**   Total sales ($ mil): **1,985**   Total employment (000): **11.1**

Company Name	Address				CEO Name	Phone	Co. Type	Sales ($ mil)	Empl. (000)
National Association of Securities	1735 K St N W	Washington	DC	20006	Frank Zarb	202-728-8000	R	634	3.5
Nasdaq Stock Market Inc.	1735 K St N W	Washington	DC	20006	Alfred R Berkeley	202-496-2500	S	634*	3.5
Chicago Board Options Exchange	400 S LaSalle St	Chicago	IL	60605	William J Brodsky	312-786-5600	R	145	0.0
Chicago Board of Trade	141 W Jackson Blvd	Chicago	IL	60604	Thomas R Donovan	312-435-3500	R	139*	0.8
Chicago Mercantile Exchange	30 S Wacker Dr	Chicago	IL	60606		312-930-1000	R	103*	1.0
American Stock Exchange Inc.	86 Trinity Pl	New York	NY	10006	Sal Sadono	212-306-1000	R	89*	0.4
Pacific Exchange Inc.	301 Pine St	San Francisco	CA	94104	Phillip DeFeo	415-393-4000	R	71*	0.5
Philadelphia Stock Exchange Inc.	1900 Market St	Philadelphia	PA	19103	Sandy Frucher	215-496-5000	R	50	0.6
Chicago Stock Exchange Inc.	440 S LaSalle St	Chicago	IL	60605	Robert J Forney	312-663-2222	P	45*	0.2
New York Board of Trade	4 World Trade Ctr	New York	NY	10048	James J Bowe	212-742-6000	R	33*	0.2
Boston Stock Exchange Inc.	100 Franklin St	Boston	MA	02110	James B Crofwell	617-235-2000	R	18	0.1
Cincinnati Stock Exchange	440 S LaSalle St	Chicago	IL	60605	David Colker	312-786-8803	R	8	<0.1
Exchange Inc.	2305 Camino Ramon	San Ramon	CA	94583	Richard Wilkes	925-983-2000	R	7*	<0.1
Minneapolis Grain Exchange	400 S 4th St	Minneapolis	MN	55415	James H Lindau	612-338-6212	R	6*	<0.1
MidAmerica Commodity	141 W Jackson Blvd	Chicago	IL	60604	Thomas R Donovan	312-341-3000	R	3*	<0.1

Source: *Ward's Business Directory of U.S. Private and Public Companies*, Volumes 1 and 2, 2000. The company type code used is as follows: P - Public, R - Private, S - Subsidiary, D - Division, J - Joint Venture, A - Affiliate, G - Group, N - Company type not reported. Sales are in millions of dollars, employees are in thousands. An asterisk (*) indicates an estimated sales volume. The symbol < stands for 'less than'. Company names and addresses are truncated, in some cases, to fit into the available space.

LOCATION BY STATE AND REGIONAL CONCENTRATION

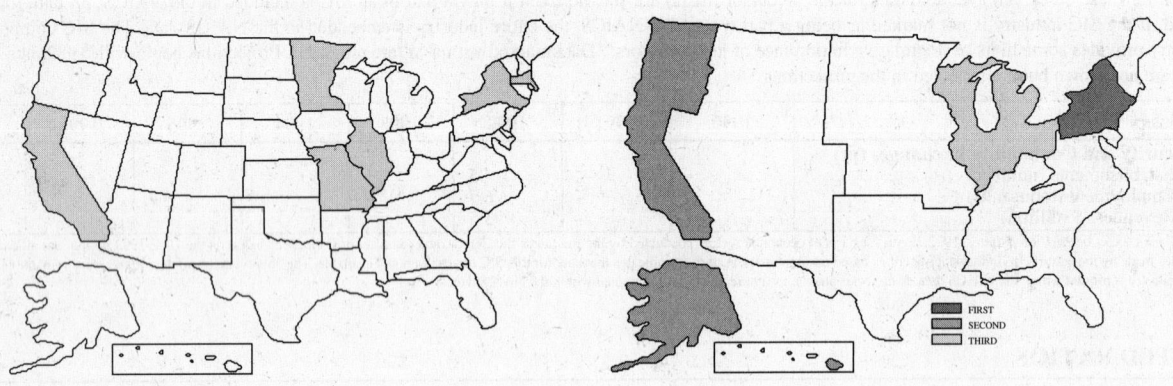

FIRST
SECOND
THIRD

INDUSTRY DATA BY STATE

State	Establishments		Employment			Payroll		Revenues		
	Total (number)	% of U.S.	Total (number)	% of U.S.	Per Estab.	Total ($ mil.)	Per Empl. ($)	Total ($ mil.)	% of U.S.	Per Estab. ($)
New York	12	40.0	3,077	45.8	256	233.5	75,889	1,004.5	52.9	83,711,417
Illinois	4	13.3	2,564	38.2	641	134.6	52,514	420.4	22.1	105,089,750
California	5	16.7	375*	-	-	(D)	-	(D)	-	-
D.C.	4	13.3	375*	-	-	(D)	-	(D)	-	-
Missouri	2	6.7	60*	-	-	(D)	-	(D)	-	-
Massachusetts	1	3.3	60*	-	-	(D)	-	(D)	-	-
Minnesota	1	3.3	60*	-	-	(D)	-	(D)	-	-
Pennsylvania	1	3.3	375*	-	-	(D)	-	(D)	-	-

Source: 1997 *Economic Census*. The states are in descending order of revenues or establishments (if revenue data are missing for the majority). The symbol (D) appears when data are withheld to prevent disclosure of competitive information. States marked with (D) are sorted by number of establishments. A dash (-) indicates that the data element cannot be calculated. * indicates the midpoint of a range; 175, for example is the range 100-249. Shaded *states* on the state map indicate those states which have proportionately greater representation in the industry than would be indicated by the state's population; the ratio is based on total revenues or number of establishments. Shaded *regions* indicate where the industry is regionally most concentrated.

NAICS 523910 - MISCELLANEOUS INTERMEDIATION

GENERAL STATISTICS

Year	Establishments (number)	Employment (number)	Payroll ($ million)	Revenues ($ million)	Employees per Establishment (number)	Revenues per Establishment ($)	Payroll per Employee ($)
1997	7,190	30,381	1,592.0	15,346.0	4.2	2,134,353	52,401

Source: Economic Census of the United States, 1997. This is a newly defined industry. Data for prior years were unavailable at the time of publication but may become available over time.

INDICES OF CHANGE

Year	Establishments (number)	Employment (number)	Payroll ($ million)	Revenues ($ million)	Employees per Establishment (number)	Revenues per Establishment ($)	Payroll per Employee ($)
1997	100.0	100.0	100.0	100.0	100.0	100.0	100.0

Sources: Same as General Statistics. The values shown reflect change from the base year, 1997. Values above 100 mean greater than 1997, values below 100 mean less than 1997, and a value of 100 in the 1982-96 or 1998-2001 period means same as 1997. Values followed by a 'p' are projections by the editors; 'e' stands for extrapolation. Data are the most recent available at this level of detail.

SIC INDUSTRIES RELATED TO NAICS 523910

Each new NAICS code represents an industry that used to be part of an SIC or a part of several SIC industries. Data in this table are shown to provide transitional information for these cases. All available data for the precursor SIC(s) are shown. Even if only a part of an SIC is included in the NAICS, *all* data for the SIC are reproduced. If the SIC industry is not marked as being a part (pt) of the NAICS, the entire industry is embedded in the NAICS data. The SIC composition of the new industry provides some hints of the relative importance of its "ancestors." Data marked with a 'p' are projected. Projections begin with 1982 data. Data earlier than 1990 are not shown but are reflected in the projections.

SIC	Industry	1990	1991	1992	1993	1994	1995	1996	1997
6153	**Short-Term Business Credit (pt)**	-	-	-	-	-	-	-	-
6211	**Security Brokers and Dealers (pt)**								
	Establishments (number)	-	-	17,787	-	-	-	-	-
	Employment (thousands)	-	-	300.0	-	-	-	-	-
	Revenues ($ million)	-	-	88,171.4	-	-	-	-	-
6792	**Oil Royalty Traders (pt)**								
	Establishments (number)	-	-	746	-	-	-	-	-
	Employment (thousands)	-	-	2.2	-	-	-	-	-
	Revenues ($ million)	-	-	686.7	-	-	-	-	-
6799	**Investors, nec (pt)**								
	Establishments (number)	-	-	6,202	-	-	-	-	-
	Employment (thousands)	-	-	24.4	-	-	-	-	-
	Revenues ($ million)	-	-	9,750.1	-	-	-	-	-

Source: Economic Census of the United States, 1992, annual surveys of economic sectors conducted by the Bureau of the Census, and estimates or projections based on the 1982-1992 period; not all data are shown. 'e' marks estimates made by the editors; 'p' indicates projections based on time series. A dash (-) indicates that data for this SIC or year were not available. The abbreviation (pt) next to the industry name indicates that only a part of the industry is present within the NAICS data. If no (pt) is shown, the entire industry is contained within the NAICS data.

SELECTED RATIOS

For 1997	Avg. of Information	Analyzed Industry	Index	For 1997	Avg. of Information	Analyzed Industry	Index
Employees per establishment	15	4	29	Payroll per establishment	669,406	221,419	33
Revenue per establishment	5,561,120	2,134,353	38	Payroll as % of revenue	12	10	86
Revenue per employee	376,639	505,118	134	Payroll per employee	45,337	52,401	116

Sources: Same as General Statistics. The 'Average' column represents the average for the industry sector, in 1997, where the currently shown industry is classified. The Index shows the relationship between the Average and the Analyzed Industry. For example, 100 means that they are equal; 500 that the Analyzed Industry is five times the average; 50 means that the Analyzed Industry is half the national average. The abbreviation 'na' is used to show that data are 'not available'.

LEADING COMPANIES

No company data available for this industry.

LOCATION BY STATE AND REGIONAL CONCENTRATION

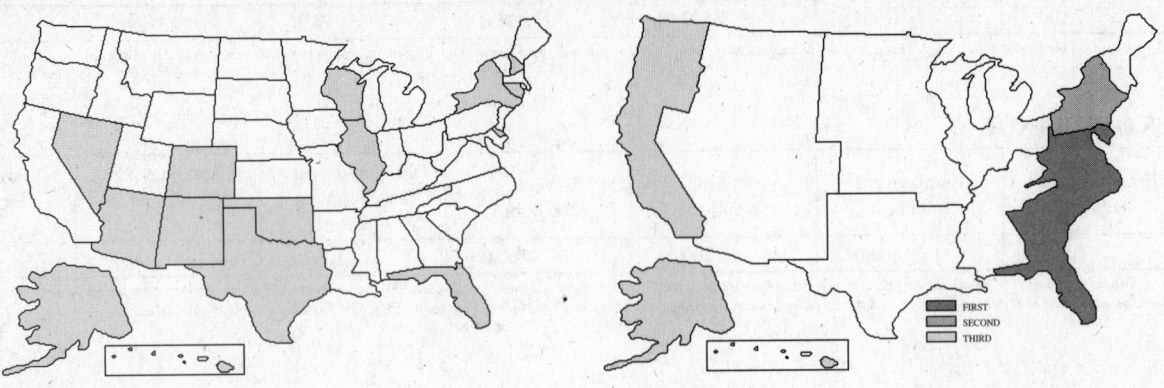

FIRST
SECOND
THIRD

INDUSTRY DATA BY STATE

State	Establishments		Employment			Payroll		Revenues		
	Total (number)	% of U.S.	Total (number)	% of U.S.	Per Estab.	Total ($ mil.)	Per Empl. ($)	Total ($ mil.)	% of U.S.	Per Estab. ($)
New York	599	8.3	2,714	8.9	5	235.4	86,739	2,234.6	14.6	3,730,516
California	879	12.2	4,341	14.3	5	225.9	52,030	1,689.5	11.0	1,922,121
Texas	1,131	15.7	3,967	13.1	4	175.3	44,200	1,558.8	10.2	1,378,291
Delaware	292	4.1	838	2.8	3	44.3	52,895	1,410.2	9.2	4,829,401
Florida	454	6.3	1,773	5.8	4	64.9	36,619	859.5	5.6	1,893,178
Illinois	324	4.5	1,635	5.4	5	101.6	62,138	812.0	5.3	2,506,139
Connecticut	105	1.5	520	1.7	5	37.4	71,950	693.8	4.5	6,607,210
Wisconsin	75	1.0	175*	-	-	12.7	-	565.2	3.7	7,536,560
Nevada	197	2.7	563	1.9	3	31.5	55,975	341.5	2.2	1,733,421
Colorado	183	2.5	600	2.0	3	35.3	58,752	331.7	2.2	1,812,699
Michigan	144	2.0	900	3.0	6	38.7	43,031	311.8	2.0	2,165,104
Arizona	116	1.6	746	2.5	6	25.7	34,386	263.5	1.7	2,271,259
Virginia	100	1.4	665	2.2	7	40.6	61,000	231.7	1.5	2,316,500
Oklahoma	197	2.7	1,084	3.6	6	44.8	41,323	225.1	1.5	1,142,741
Washington	143	2.0	635	2.1	4	27.1	42,655	203.5	1.3	1,422,867
Louisiana	146	2.0	456	1.5	3	18.3	40,202	196.3	1.3	1,344,555
Georgia	142	2.0	517	1.7	4	24.3	47,060	185.4	1.2	1,305,894
Pennsylvania	119	1.7	427	1.4	4	24.4	57,026	174.6	1.1	1,466,832
New Hampshire	13	0.2	45	0.1	3	5.6	124,978	170.0	1.1	13,075,538
North Carolina	106	1.5	311	1.0	3	19.5	62,559	151.1	1.0	1,425,632
New Mexico	55	0.8	272	0.9	5	14.2	52,070	150.4	1.0	2,734,127
Hawaii	38	0.5	257	0.8	7	16.0	62,335	133.6	0.9	3,516,947
Utah	57	0.8	191	0.6	3	7.0	36,414	99.5	0.6	1,745,439
West Virginia	53	0.7	162	0.5	3	6.1	37,778	91.8	0.6	1,731,943
Kansas	66	0.9	187	0.6	3	7.6	40,840	90.1	0.6	1,365,091
Kentucky	54	0.8	260	0.9	5	11.3	43,292	88.0	0.6	1,629,278
Alabama	69	1.0	221	0.7	3	9.3	42,104	79.0	0.5	1,145,000
Tennessee	76	1.1	770	2.5	10	17.6	22,861	73.6	0.5	968,618
Oregon	71	1.0	220	0.7	3	10.4	47,150	54.9	0.4	773,732
South Carolina	46	0.6	223	0.7	5	5.5	24,816	53.3	0.3	1,158,283
Alaska	22	0.3	171	0.6	8	6.6	38,696	52.8	0.3	2,400,318
Arkansas	45	0.6	108	0.4	2	2.4	22,611	46.3	0.3	1,029,822
Iowa	58	0.8	214	0.7	4	6.3	29,229	29.8	0.2	513,017
Mississippi	50	0.7	170	0.6	3	4.1	24,200	29.4	0.2	588,560
Montana	20	0.3	51	0.2	3	1.3	25,804	22.6	0.1	1,131,350
Idaho	32	0.4	57	0.2	2	2.6	46,211	18.4	0.1	574,031
Nebraska	23	0.3	68	0.2	3	1.4	19,985	13.7	0.1	595,261
South Dakota	24	0.3	58	0.2	2	1.0	16,517	6.4	0.0	265,792
Massachusetts	148	2.1	750*	-	-	(D)	-	(D)	-	-
Missouri	134	1.9	375*	-	-	(D)	-	(D)	-	-
New Jersey	124	1.7	750*	-	-	(D)	-	(D)	-	-
Ohio	115	1.6	375*	-	-	(D)	-	(D)	-	-
Maryland	99	1.4	750*	-	-	(D)	-	(D)	-	-
Minnesota	95	1.3	375*	-	-	(D)	-	(D)	-	-
Indiana	51	0.7	175*	-	-	(D)	-	(D)	-	-
D.C.	28	0.4	175*	-	-	(D)	-	(D)	-	-
Wyoming	28	0.4	175*	-	-	(D)	-	(D)	-	-
Maine	17	0.2	60*	-	-	(D)	-	(D)	-	-
Rhode Island	16	0.2	60*	-	-	(D)	-	(D)	-	-
Vermont	6	0.1	60*	-	-	(D)	-	(D)	-	-

Source: 1997 Economic Census. The states are in descending order of revenues or establishments (if revenue data are missing for the majority). The symbol (D) appears when data are withheld to prevent disclosure of competitive information. States marked with (D) are sorted by number of establishments. A dash (-) indicates that the data element cannot be calculated. * indicates the midpoint of a range; 175, for example is the range 100-249. Shaded states on the state map indicate those states which have proportionately greater representation in the industry than would be indicated by the state's population; the ratio is based on total revenues or number of establishments. Shaded regions indicate where the industry is regionally most concentrated.

NAICS 523920 - PORTFOLIO MANAGEMENT

GENERAL STATISTICS

Year	Establishments (number)	Employment (number)	Payroll ($ million)	Revenues ($ million)	Employees per Establishment (number)	Revenues per Establishment ($)	Payroll per Employee ($)
1997	10,888	123,971	13,533.0	43,643.0	11.4	4,008,358	109,163

Source: Economic Census of the United States, 1997. This is a newly defined industry. Data for prior years were unavailable at the time of publication but may become available over time.

INDICES OF CHANGE

Year	Establishments (number)	Employment (number)	Payroll ($ million)	Revenues ($ million)	Employees per Establishment (number)	Revenues per Establishment ($)	Payroll per Employee ($)
1997	100.0	100.0	100.0	100.0	100.0	100.0	100.0

Sources: Same as General Statistics. The values shown reflect change from the base year, 1997. Values above 100 mean greater than 1997, values below 100 mean less than 1997, and a value of 100 in the 1982-96 or 1998-2001 period means same as 1997. Values followed by a 'p' are projections by the editors; 'e' stands for extrapolation. Data are the most recent available at this level of detail.

SIC INDUSTRIES RELATED TO NAICS 523920

Each new NAICS code represents an industry that used to be part of an SIC or a part of several SIC industries. Data in this table are shown to provide transitional information for these cases. All available data for the precursor SIC(s) are shown. Even if only a part of an SIC is included in the NAICS, *all* data for the SIC are reproduced. If the SIC industry is not marked as being a part (pt) of the NAICS, the entire industry is embedded in the NAICS data. The SIC composition of the new industry provides some hints of the relative importance of its "ancestors." Data marked with a 'p' are projected. Projections begin with 1982 data. Data earlier than 1990 are not shown but are reflected in the projections.

SIC	Industry	1990	1991	1992	1993	1994	1995	1996	1997
6282	**Investment Advice (pt)**	-		-	-	-	-	-	-
6371	**Pension, Health, and Welfare Funds (pt)**								
	Establishments (number)	-	-	1,491	-	-	-	-	-
	Employment (thousands)	-	-	20.4	-	-	-	-	-
	Revenues ($ million)	-	-	1,379.4	-	-	-	-	-
6733	**Trusts, nec (pt)**	-	-	-	-	-	-	-	-
6799	**Investors, nec (pt)**								
	Establishments (number)	-	-	6,202	-	-	-	-	-
	Employment (thousands)	-	-	24.4	-	-	-	-	-
	Revenues ($ million)	-	-	9,750.1	-	-	-	-	-

Source: Economic Census of the United States, 1992, annual surveys of economic sectors conducted by the Bureau of the Census, and estimates or projections based on the 1982-1992 period; not all data are shown. 'e' marks estimates made by the editors; 'p' indicates projections based on time series. A dash (-) indicates that data for this SIC or year were not available. The abbreviation (pt) next to the industry name indicates that only a part of the industry is present within the NAICS data. If no (pt) is shown, the entire industry is contained within the NAICS data.

SELECTED RATIOS

For 1997	Avg. of Information	Analyzed Industry	Index	For 1997	Avg. of Information	Analyzed Industry	Index
Employees per establishment	15	11	77	Payroll per establishment	669,406	1,242,928	186
Revenue per establishment	5,561,120	4,008,358	72	Payroll as % of revenue	12	31	258
Revenue per employee	376,639	352,042	93	Payroll per employee	45,337	109,163	241

Sources: Same as General Statistics. The 'Average' column represents the average for the industry sector, in 1997, where the currently shown industry is classified. The Index shows the relationship between the Average and the Analyzed Industry. For example, 100 means that they are equal; 500 that the Analyzed Industry is five times the average; 50 means that the Analyzed Industry is half the national average. The abbreviation 'na' is used to show that data are 'not available'.

LEADING COMPANIES
No company data available for this industry.

LOCATION BY STATE AND REGIONAL CONCENTRATION

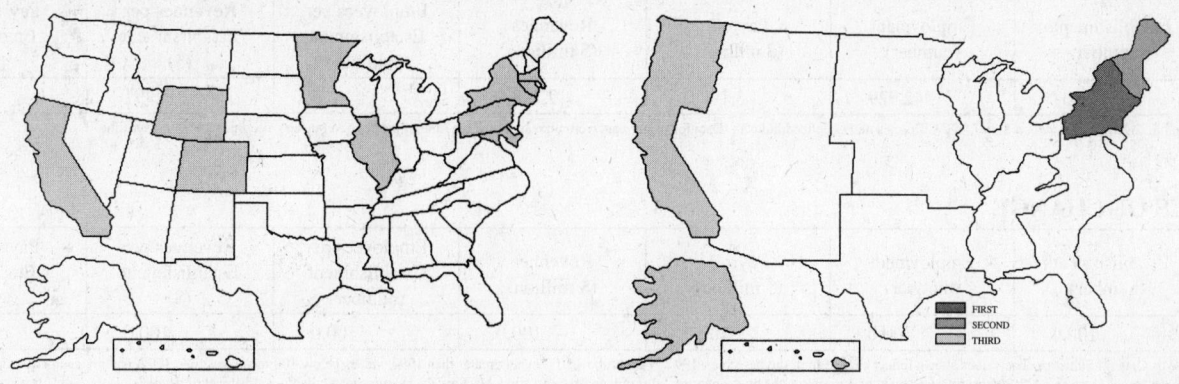

INDUSTRY DATA BY STATE

State	Establishments Total (number)	% of U.S.	Employment Total (number)	% of U.S.	Per Estab.	Payroll Total ($ mil.)	Per Empl. ($)	Revenues Total ($ mil.)	% of U.S.	Per Estab. ($)
New York	1,399	12.8	21,070	17.0	15	3,459.1	164,170	11,013.5	25.2	7,872,402
Massachusetts	531	4.9	19,370	15.6	36	2,018.7	104,219	7,326.1	16.8	13,796,815
California	1,600	14.7	14,148	11.4	9	1,826.2	129,076	5,423.0	12.4	3,389,381
Pennsylvania	436	4.0	11,445	9.2	26	803.5	70,206	2,407.2	5.5	5,521,071
Minnesota	220	2.0	6,574	5.3	30	523.0	79,553	2,222.8	5.1	10,103,836
Texas	736	6.8	6,469	5.2	9	645.4	99,771	2,127.4	4.9	2,890,541
Illinois	578	5.3	6,206	5.0	11	687.9	110,844	1,992.4	4.6	3,447,000
Connecticut	356	3.3	3,926	3.2	11	633.3	161,302	1,859.3	4.3	5,222,722
Florida	581	5.3	4,707	3.8	8	344.9	73,264	1,166.9	2.7	2,008,432
New Jersey	381	3.5	2,428	2.0	6	288.9	118,967	973.6	2.2	2,555,320
Maryland	209	1.9	3,108	2.5	15	264.2	85,003	939.9	2.2	4,497,110
Colorado	315	2.9	2,122	1.7	7	205.7	96,929	880.0	2.0	2,793,495
Georgia	274	2.5	2,382	1.9	9	201.4	84,539	692.3	1.6	2,526,653
Ohio	320	2.9	2,376	1.9	7	190.6	80,214	501.2	1.1	1,566,325
Wisconsin	144	1.3	1,711	1.4	12	164.9	96,370	438.0	1.0	3,041,701
Virginia	241	2.2	1,324	1.1	5	134.0	101,239	373.6	0.9	1,550,178
Washington	239	2.2	1,645	1.3	7	104.4	63,460	272.7	0.6	1,141,013
Missouri	145	1.3	1,155	0.9	8	85.7	74,165	255.1	0.6	1,759,338
Michigan	227	2.1	1,238	1.0	5	86.1	69,531	253.3	0.6	1,116,075
Tennessee	140	1.3	678	0.5	5	120.7	177,987	220.5	0.5	1,574,993
Oregon	106	1.0	1,107	0.9	10	88.4	79,818	200.6	0.5	1,892,019
Iowa	62	0.6	267	0.2	4	26.9	100,685	196.0	0.4	3,162,000
Wyoming	16	0.1	79	0.1	5	13.9	175,468	189.3	0.4	11,833,438
Indiana	124	1.1	757	0.6	6	63.6	84,055	169.5	0.4	1,366,976
North Carolina	168	1.5	817	0.7	5	61.4	75,160	153.7	0.4	915,060
Kansas	81	0.7	521	0.4	6	43.8	84,075	144.1	0.3	1,778,580
New Mexico	39	0.4	332	0.3	9	25.0	75,304	117.6	0.3	3,015,359
Kentucky	57	0.5	473	0.4	8	43.3	91,474	103.9	0.2	1,823,579
Arizona	162	1.5	654	0.5	4	28.6	43,685	88.8	0.2	548,401
Nevada	114	1.0	250	0.2	2	18.1	72,536	67.2	0.2	589,044
North Dakota	9	0.1	175*	-	-	9.2	-	47.0	0.1	5,223,778
Maine	40	0.4	281	0.2	7	20.2	71,754	42.6	0.1	1,065,800
Louisiana	78	0.7	437	0.4	6	18.7	42,719	41.9	0.1	537,179
Rhode Island	41	0.4	216	0.2	5	13.1	60,477	40.2	0.1	980,683
Nebraska	56	0.5	237	0.2	4	13.6	57,329	35.6	0.1	636,214
Alabama	62	0.6	248	0.2	4	15.2	61,371	34.9	0.1	562,758
New Hampshire	67	0.6	191	0.2	3	18.5	97,084	34.7	0.1	518,119
Oklahoma	68	0.6	190	0.2	3	10.3	54,253	33.9	0.1	499,015
South Carolina	49	0.5	159	0.1	3	10.1	63,314	33.5	0.1	684,265
Utah	63	0.6	224	0.2	4	14.9	66,679	30.4	0.1	481,984
Hawaii	31	0.3	98	0.1	3	6.9	70,714	23.5	0.1	757,677
Mississippi	37	0.3	123	0.1	3	5.9	48,057	19.3	0.0	521,189
Vermont	28	0.3	128	0.1	5	8.0	62,703	17.7	0.0	632,857
Alaska	12	0.1	69	0.1	6	6.7	97,377	15.8	0.0	1,314,333
Arkansas	40	0.4	121	0.1	3	5.6	46,289	15.8	0.0	394,800
Idaho	29	0.3	84	0.1	3	3.9	46,036	10.8	0.0	372,172
Delaware	78	0.7	1,750*	-	-	(D)	-	(D)	-	-
D.C.	59	0.5	375*	-	-	(D)	-	(D)	-	-
Montana	15	0.1	60*	-	-	(D)	-	(D)	-	-
West Virginia	14	0.1	60*	-	-	(D)	-	(D)	-	-
South Dakota	11	0.1	10*	-	-	(D)	-	(D)	-	-

Source: 1997 *Economic Census*. The states are in descending order of revenues or establishments (if revenue data are missing for the majority). The symbol (D) appears when data are withheld to prevent disclosure of competitive information. States marked with (D) are sorted by number of establishments. A dash (-) indicates that the data element cannot be calculated. * indicates the midpoint of a range; 175, for example is the range 100-249. Shaded *states* on the state map indicate those states which have proportionately greater representation in the industry than would be indicated by the state's population; the ratio is based on total revenues or number of establishments. Shaded *regions* indicate where the industry is regionally most concentrated.

NAICS 523930 - INVESTMENT ADVICE

GENERAL STATISTICS

Year	Establishments (number)	Employment (number)	Payroll ($ million)	Revenues ($ million)	Employees per Establishment (number)	Revenues per Establishment ($)	Payroll per Employee ($)
1997	7,807	42,929	3,197.0	9,398.0	5.5	1,203,791	74,472

Source: *Economic Census of the United States*, 1997. This is a newly defined industry. Data for prior years were unavailable at the time of publication but may become available over time.

INDICES OF CHANGE

Year	Establishments (number)	Employment (number)	Payroll ($ million)	Revenues ($ million)	Employees per Establishment (number)	Revenues per Establishment ($)	Payroll per Employee ($)
1997	100.0	100.0	100.0	100.0	100.0	100.0	100.0

Sources: Same as General Statistics. The values shown reflect change from the base year, 1997. Values above 100 mean greater than 1997, values below 100 mean less than 1997, and a value of 100 in the 1982-96 or 1998-2001 period means same as 1997. Values followed by a 'p' are projections by the editors; 'e' stands for extrapolation. Data are the most recent available at this level of detail.

SIC INDUSTRIES RELATED TO NAICS 523930

Each new NAICS code represents an industry that used to be part of an SIC or a part of several SIC industries. Data in this table are shown to provide transitional information for these cases. All available data for the precursor SIC(s) are shown. Even if only a part of an SIC is included in the NAICS, *all* data for the SIC are reproduced. If the SIC industry is not marked as being a part (pt) of the NAICS, the entire industry is embedded in the NAICS data. The SIC composition of the new industry provides some hints of the relative importance of its "ancestors." Data marked with a 'p' are projected. Projections begin with 1982 data. Data earlier than 1990 are not shown but are reflected in the projections.

SIC	Industry	1990	1991	1992	1993	1994	1995	1996	1997
6282	Investment Advice (pt)	-	-	-	-	-	-	-	-

Source: *Economic Census of the United States*, 1992, annual surveys of economic sectors conducted by the Bureau of the Census, and estimates or projections based on the 1982-1992 period; not all data are shown. 'e' marks estimates made by the editors; 'p' indicates projections based on time series. A dash (-) indicates that data for this SIC or year were not available. The abbreviation (pt) next to the industry name indicates that only a part of the industry is present within the NAICS data. If no (pt) is shown, the entire industry is contained within the NAICS data.

SELECTED RATIOS

For 1997	Avg. of Information	Analyzed Industry	Index	For 1997	Avg. of Information	Analyzed Industry	Index
Employees per establishment	15	5	37	Payroll per establishment	669,406	409,504	61
Revenue per establishment	5,561,120	1,203,791	22	Payroll as % of revenue	12	34	283
Revenue per employee	376,639	218,920	58	Payroll per employee	45,337	74,472	164

Sources: Same as General Statistics. The 'Average' column represents the average for the industry sector, in 1997, where the currently shown industry is classified. The Index shows the relationship between the Average and the Analyzed Industry. For example, 100 means that they are equal; 500 that the Analyzed Industry is five times the average; 50 means that the Analyzed Industry is half the national average. The abbreviation 'na' is used to show that data are 'not available'.

LEADING COMPANIES

Number shown: **75**   Total sales ($ mil): **1,253,563**   Total employment (000): **662.4**

Company Name	Address				CEO Name	Phone	Co. Type	Sales ($ mil)	Empl. (000)
J.P. Morgan and Company Inc.	60 Wall St	New York	NY	10260	Douglas A. Warner III	212-483-2323	P	261,067	15.7
AXA Financial Inc.	1290 Av Americas	New York	NY	10104	Edward D Miller	212-554-1234	P	109,185	14.7
Teachers Insurance & Annuity	730 3rd Ave	New York	NY	10017	John H Biggs	212-490-9000	R	100,000	4.3
Aetna Services Inc.	151 Farmington Ave	Hartford	CT	06156	Richard L Huber	860-273-0123	S	96,053*	27.2
Equitable Life Assurance Society	1290 Av Americas	New York	NY	10104	Edward P Miller	212-554-1234	S	71,494*	16.0
United Services Automobile	9800 Fredricksburg	San Antonio	TX	78288	Robert Herres	210-498-2211	R	52,000*	17.0
INVESCO Capital Management	1360 Peachtree	Atlanta	GA	30309	Frank Bishop	404-892-0896	P	50,000	0.2
State Street Corp.	PO Box 351	Boston	MA	02101	Marshall N Carter	617-786-3000	P	47,082	16.3
St. Paul Companies Inc.	385 Washington St	St. Paul	MN	55102	James E Gustafson	612-310-7911	P	38,300	14.0
Morgan Stanley Dean Witter	1585 Broadway	New York	NY	10036	John J Mack	212-761-4000	P	33,928	55.3
Prudential Insurance of America	751 Broad St	Newark	NJ	07102	Arthur F Ryan	973-802-6000	R	27,087	50.0
Lincoln National Life Insurance	1300 S Clinton St	Fort Wayne	IN	46802	Gabriel Shaheen	219-455-2000	S	25,000	3.7
USAA Group Inc.	9800 Fredricksburg	San Antonio	TX	78288	Robert T Herres	210-498-2211	R	24,474*	18.0
ReliaStar Financial Corp.	20 Washington S	Minneapolis	MN	55401	John H Flittie	612-372-5432	P	22,609	3.5
Merrill Lynch and Company Inc.	World Financial Ctr	New York	NY	10281	Herbert M Allison Jr	212-449-1000	P	21,869	63.8
Principal Financial Advisors Inc.	711 High St	Des Moines	IA	50392	Ralph Eucher	515-247-5111	S	21,719*	15.3
Aetna Inc.	151 Farmington Ave	Hartford	CT	06156	Richard L Huber	860-273-0123	P	20,604	33.5
AEGON USA Inc.	1111 N Charles St	Baltimore	MD	21201	Donald J Shepard	410-576-4571	S	20,330*	11.3
Liberty Financial Companies Inc.	600 Atlantic Ave	Boston	MA	02210	Kenneth R Leibler	617-722-6000	P	16,519	2.1
Fortis Inc.	1 Chase Man Plz	New York	NY	10005	Allen R Freedman	212-859-7000	J	14,578	0.0
First of America Investment Corp.	1900 E 9th St	Cleveland	OH	44114	Richard A Wolf	616-385-0200	S	12,901*	<0.1
Mutual Life Insurance of New	1740 Broadway	New York	NY	10019	Samuel J Foti	212-708-2000	P	12,110	4.7
Lehman Brothers Holdings Inc.	3 World Financial	New York	NY	10285	Richard S Fuld Jr	212-526-7000	P	11,300	8.9
Westwood Group Inc.	190 VFW Pkwy	Revere	MA	02151	Charles F Sarkis	781-284-2600	P	10,903*	2.3
New England Financial	501 Boylston St	Boston	MA	02116	James M Benson	617-578-2000	S	10,569*	4.4
Boston Company Inc.	1 Boston Pl	Boston	MA	02108	W Keith Smith	617-722-7000	S	9,200*	4.5
Marsh & McLennan Companies	1166 Av Americas	New York	NY	10036	AJC Smith	212-345-5000	P	9,157	54.3
FMR Corp.	82 Devonshire St	Boston	MA	02109	Edward C Johnson III	617-563-7000	R	6,800	28.0
PanAgora Asset Management Inc.	260 Franklin St	Boston	MA	02110	William Poutsiaka	617-439-6300	R	6,000	<0.1
PaineWebber Inc.	1285 Av Americas	New York	NY	10019	Donald B Marron	212-713-2000	S	5,976*	17.9
American Express Financial	80 S 8th St	Minneapolis	MN	55402	David R Hubers	612-671-3131	S	5,514*	11.2
Donaldson, Lufkin & Jenrette Inc.	277 Park Ave	New York	NY	10172	Joe L Roby	212-892-3000	P	5,407	8.5
PaineWebber Group Inc.	1285 Av Americas	New York	NY	10019	Donald B Marron	212-713-2000	P	5,300	19.6
Federated Investors Inc.	1001 Liberty Ave	Pittsburgh	PA	15222	JC Donahue	412-288-1900	P	4,700	1.9
Nationwide Financial Services Inc.	P O Box 1492	Columbus	OH	43216	Joseph J Gasper	614-249-7111	P	4,619	4.1
Anthem Insurance Company Inc.	120 Monument Cir	Indianapolis	IN	46204	L Ben Lytle	317-488-6000	R	4,589	15.0
Franklin Management Inc.	951 Mariners Island	San Mateo	CA	94404	Howard McEldowney	650-312-2000	S	4,254*	3.0
Charles Schwab Corp.	101 Montgomery St	San Francisco	CA	94104	Charles R Schwab	415-627-7000	P	3,945	13.3
Royce and Associates	1414 Av Americas	New York	NY	10019	Charles M Royce	212-355-7311	R	3,000	<0.1
Fortis Inc.(Woodbury, Minnesota)	500 Bielenberg Dr	Woodbury	MN	55125	Dean Kopperud	651-738-4000	S	2,841*	2.0
Brandes Investment Partners Inc.	12750 High Bluff Dr	San Diego	CA	92130		619-755-0239	R	2,500	0.3
Franklin Resources Inc.	PO Box 7777	San Mateo	CA	94404	Charles B Johnson	650-312-2000	P	2,263	6.7
Oxford Realty Services Corp.	7200 Wisconsin	Bethesda	MD	20814	Leo Zickler	301-654-3100	R	2,255*	1.6
White Mountains Insurance Group	80 S Main St	Hanover	NH	03755	John J Byrne	603-643-1567	P	2,049	2.8
M.D.C. Holdings Inc.	3600 S Yosemite St	Denver	CO	80237	Larry A Mizel	303-773-1100	P	1,568	1.4
Providian Corp.	P O Box 32830	Louisville	KY	40232	Don Shepherd	502-560-2000	S	1,559*	0.5
Colonial Management Associates	1 Financial Ctr	Boston	MA	02111	Harold W Cogger	617-426-3750	S	1,489*	1.0
Sanford C. Bernstein Inc.	767 5th Ave	New York	NY	10153	Lewis A Sanders	212-486-5800	R	1,487*	1.2
Capital Group Companies Inc.	333 S Hope St	Los Angeles	CA	90071	Larry Clemmensen	213-486-9000	R	1,434*	4.7
SunGard Data Systems Inc.	1285 Drummers Ln	Wayne	PA	19087	James L Mann	610-341-8700	P	1,393	6.9
Alliance Capital Management L.P.	1345 Av Americas	New York	NY	10105	John D Carifa	212-969-1000	P	1,324	1.7
Barclays Global Investments	45 Fremont St	San Francisco	CA	94105	Patricia Dunn	415-597-2000	J	1,278*	0.9
Kansas City Southern Industries	114 W 11th St	Kansas City	MO	64105	Landon H Rowland	816-983-1303	P	1,248	4.5
Raymond James Financial Inc.	880 Carillon Pkwy	St. Petersburg	FL	33716	Thomas A James	727-573-3800	P	1,232	4.5
Peninsula Asset Management Inc.	1111 3rd Ave W	Bradenton	FL	34205	W E Middlebrooks, Jr	941-748-8680	R	1,065	<0.1
Legg Mason Inc.	PO Box 1476	Baltimore	MD	21202	James W Brinkley	410-539-0000	P	1,046	4.3
T. Rowe Price Associates Inc.	100 E Pratt St	Baltimore	MD	21202	George A Roche	410-345-2000	P	1,036	3.5
Composite Research	1201 3rd Ave	Seattle	WA	98101	William Papesh	206-461-3800	R	1,000	<0.1
Foothill Group Inc.	11111 Santa Monica	Los Angeles	CA	90025	John Nikoll	310-478-8383	S	1,000	0.2
Franklin Advisers Inc.	P O Box 7777	San Mateo	CA	94403	Rupert H Johnson Jr	650-312-3200	S	1,000*	5.0
Wellington Management Co.	75 State St	Boston	MA	02109	Duncan M McFarland	617-951-5000	R	982*	0.8
PIMCO Advisors L.P.	800 Newport Center	Newport Beach	CA	92660		949-717-7022	P	961	1.1
United Asset Management Corp.	1 International Pl	Boston	MA	02110	Charles E Haldeman	617-330-8900	P	882	2.3
Business Men's Assurance	PO Box 419458	Kansas City	MO	64141	Robert T Rakich	816-753-8000	S	805	0.6
Magten Asset Management Corp.	35 E 21st St	New York	NY	10010	Talton M Embry	212-529-6600	R	800	<0.1
Topa Equities Ltd.	1800 Av of the Stars	Los Angeles	CA	90067	John E Anderson	310-203-9199	R	760*	1.2
Jones Lang/LaSalle Partners Inc.	200 E Randolph Dr	Chicago	IL	60601	Christopher Peacock	312-782-5800	P	755	2.2
IJL Wachovia	201 N Tryon	Charlotte	NC	28202	James Morgan	704-379-9000	S	710*	0.5
NationsBanc Montgomery	600 Montgomery St	San Francisco	CA	94111	Lewis Coleman	415-627-2000	S	705	1.5
Boston Financial Group Inc.	101 Arch St	Boston	MA	02110	Fred N Pratt	617-439-3911	R	690*	2.3
AIM Management Group Inc.	11 Greenway Plz	Houston	TX	77046	Charles T Bauer	713-626-1919	R	681*	2.5
Nvest L.P.	399 Boylston St	Boston	MA	02116	Peter S Voss	617-578-3500	P	670	1.5
Putnam Investments Inc.	1 Post Office Sq	Boston	MA	02109	Lawrence J Lasser	617-292-1000	S	665	6.0
Liberty Financial Company Inc.	600 Atlantic Ave	Boston	MA	02210	Kenneth R Leibler	617-722-6000	S	655*	2.1
Van Kampen American Capital	1 Parkview Plz	Oakbrk Ter	IL	60181	Don G Powell	708-684-6000	S	633*	0.5

Source: Ward's Business Directory of U.S. Private and Public Companies, Volumes 1 and 2, 2000. The company type code used is as follows: P - Public, R - Private, S - Subsidiary, D - Division, J - Joint Venture, A - Affiliate, G - Group, N - Company type not reported. Sales are in millions of dollars, employees are in thousands. An asterisk (*) indicates an estimated sales volume. The symbol < stands for 'less than'. Company names and addresses are truncated, in some cases, to fit into the available space.

LOCATION BY STATE AND REGIONAL CONCENTRATION

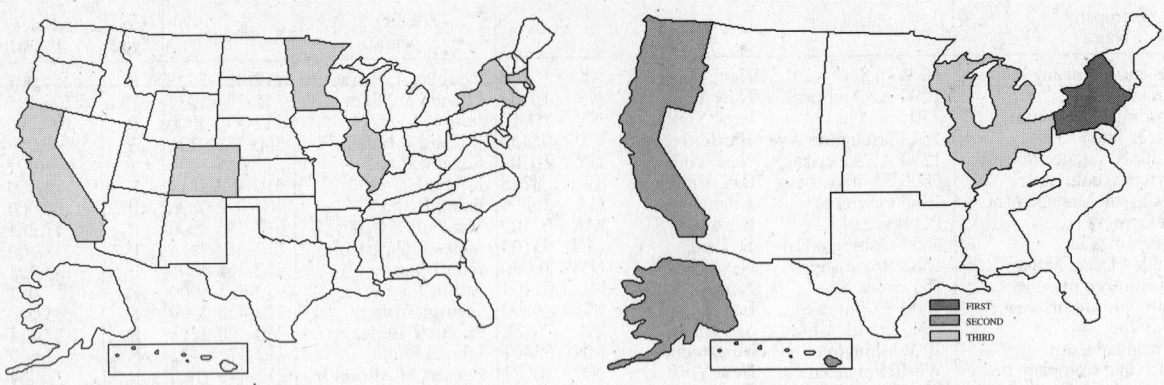

INDUSTRY DATA BY STATE

State	Establishments Total (number)	Establishments % of U.S.	Employment Total (number)	Employment % of U.S.	Employment Per Estab.	Payroll Total ($ mil.)	Payroll Per Empl. ($)	Revenues Total ($ mil.)	Revenues % of U.S.	Revenues Per Estab. ($)
New York	953	12.2	7,385	17.2	8	980.5	132,766	2,625.9	27.9	2,755,413
California	1,028	13.2	6,134	14.3	6	410.0	66,840	1,231.6	13.1	1,198,076
Illinois	418	5.4	3,150	7.3	8	254.8	80,877	809.0	8.6	1,935,435
Massachusetts	283	3.6	3,481	8.1	12	234.1	67,261	763.8	8.1	2,698,890
Texas	449	5.8	2,215	5.2	5	129.9	58,661	406.8	4.3	906,080
Pennsylvania	293	3.8	1,493	3.5	5	95.4	63,879	290.9	3.1	992,884
Florida	550	7.0	1,719	4.0	3	99.9	58,087	263.9	2.8	479,789
New Jersey	324	4.2	1,318	3.1	4	95.5	72,452	258.0	2.7	796,250
Minnesota	172	2.2	1,347	3.1	8	78.6	58,388	252.8	2.7	1,470,006
Ohio	252	3.2	1,125	2.6	4	55.1	48,934	216.0	2.3	857,274
Georgia	211	2.7	1,099	2.6	5	58.9	53,594	181.8	1.9	861,483
Michigan	201	2.6	986	2.3	5	36.0	36,542	146.6	1.6	729,229
Maryland	145	1.9	519	1.2	4	30.7	59,206	140.8	1.5	970,897
Colorado	183	2.3	1,100	2.6	6	51.5	46,785	138.5	1.5	756,874
Virginia	166	2.1	793	1.8	5	61.3	77,272	135.3	1.4	815,120
Washington	156	2.0	1,302	3.0	8	85.1	65,364	118.1	1.3	757,071
North Carolina	181	2.3	511	1.2	3	23.8	46,519	112.6	1.2	622,326
D.C.	65	0.8	299	0.7	5	34.4	115,154	105.0	1.1	1,615,415
Tennessee	90	1.2	496	1.2	6	19.4	39,123	88.4	0.9	981,911
Wisconsin	96	1.2	343	0.8	4	19.0	55,335	70.4	0.7	733,479
Arizona	143	1.8	407	0.9	3	14.3	35,091	64.7	0.7	452,427
Oregon	80	1.0	347	0.8	4	20.7	59,692	58.1	0.6	726,075
Iowa	71	0.9	323	0.8	5	15.3	47,220	54.1	0.6	761,620
Indiana	90	1.2	357	0.8	4	15.2	42,482	51.7	0.6	574,744
Missouri	114	1.5	330	0.8	3	16.8	50,979	47.0	0.5	411,886
Kansas	73	0.9	252	0.6	3	10.1	39,952	37.9	0.4	518,589
Oklahoma	65	0.8	215	0.5	3	9.7	45,047	31.2	0.3	480,415
Rhode Island	26	0.3	122	0.3	5	10.2	84,008	31.1	0.3	1,196,577
South Carolina	83	1.1	256	0.6	3	9.1	35,703	31.1	0.3	374,795
Louisiana	51	0.7	252	0.6	5	6.5	25,698	29.3	0.3	573,961
Nevada	65	0.8	134	0.3	2	7.6	57,045	25.6	0.3	393,523
New Mexico	37	0.5	91	0.2	2	5.7	63,099	24.9	0.3	671,973
Kentucky	39	0.5	101	0.2	3	4.7	46,188	21.5	0.2	552,487
Utah	53	0.7	170	0.4	3	4.5	26,229	19.7	0.2	372,264
Nebraska	32	0.4	93	0.2	3	5.3	56,581	18.3	0.2	571,000
Alabama	41	0.5	144	0.3	4	4.3	30,104	17.6	0.2	429,512
Maine	34	0.4	74	0.2	2	3.8	51,419	14.6	0.2	429,029
Arkansas	24	0.3	91	0.2	4	1.4	15,330	10.0	0.1	416,833
Idaho	27	0.3	72	0.2	3	1.7	23,917	9.7	0.1	359,704
Vermont	19	0.2	70	0.2	4	4.4	63,529	9.7	0.1	509,947
Montana	24	0.3	60	0.1	3	1.9	32,383	7.7	0.1	321,708
Mississippi	26	0.3	83	0.2	3	1.8	21,928	7.0	0.1	268,115
Alaska	14	0.2	36	0.1	3	0.8	21,000	3.0	0.0	214,143
Connecticut	232	3.0	1,750*	-	-	(D)	-	(D)	-	-
New Hampshire	46	0.6	175*	-	-	(D)	-	(D)	-	-
Delaware	24	0.3	60*	-	-	(D)	-	(D)	-	-
South Dakota	18	0.2	60*	-	-	(D)	-	(D)	-	-
Hawaii	16	0.2	175*	-	-	(D)	-	(D)	-	-
Wyoming	9	0.1	60*	-	-	(D)	-	(D)	-	-
West Virginia	8	0.1	10*	-	-	(D)	-	(D)	-	-
North Dakota	7	0.1	60*	-	-	(D)	-	(D)	-	-

Source: 1997 *Economic Census.* The states are in descending order of revenues or establishments (if revenue data are missing for the majority). The symbol (D) appears when data are withheld to prevent disclosure of competitive information. States marked with (D) are sorted by number of establishments. A dash (-) indicates that the data element cannot be calculated. * indicates the midpoint of a range; 175, for example is the range 100-249. Shaded *states* on the state map indicate those states which have proportionately greater representation in the industry than would be indicated by the state's population; the ratio is based on total revenues or number of establishments. Shaded *regions* indicate where the industry is regionally most concentrated.

NAICS 523991 - TRUST, FIDUCIARY, AND CUSTODY ACTIVITIES

GENERAL STATISTICS

Year	Establishments (number)	Employment (number)	Payroll ($ million)	Revenues ($ million)	Employees per Establishment (number)	Revenues per Establishment ($)	Payroll per Employee ($)
1997	2,286	47,843	2,180.0	6,935.0	20.9	3,033,683	45,566

Source: Economic Census of the United States, 1997. This is a newly defined industry. Data for prior years were unavailable at the time of publication but may become available over time.

INDICES OF CHANGE

Year	Establishments (number)	Employment (number)	Payroll ($ million)	Revenues ($ million)	Employees per Establishment (number)	Revenues per Establishment ($)	Payroll per Employee ($)
1997	100.0	100.0	100.0	100.0	100.0	100.0	100.0

Sources: Same as General Statistics. The values shown reflect change from the base year, 1997. Values above 100 mean greater than 1997, values below 100 mean less than 1997, and a value of 100 in the 1982-96 or 1998-2001 period means same as 1997. Values followed by a 'p' are projections by the editors; 'e' stands for extrapolation. Data are the most recent available at this level of detail.

SIC INDUSTRIES RELATED TO NAICS 523991

Each new NAICS code represents an industry that used to be part of an SIC or a part of several SIC industries. Data in this table are shown to provide transitional information for these cases. All available data for the precursor SIC(s) are shown. Even if only a part of an SIC is included in the NAICS, *all* data for the SIC are reproduced. If the SIC industry is not marked as being a part (pt) of the NAICS, the entire industry is embedded in the NAICS data. The SIC composition of the new industry provides some hints of the relative importance of its "ancestors." Data marked with a 'p' are projected. Projections begin with 1982 data. Data earlier than 1990 are not shown but are reflected in the projections.

SIC	Industry	1990	1991	1992	1993	1994	1995	1996	1997
6091	Nondeposit Trust Facilities	-	-	-	-	-	-	-	-
6099	Functions Related to Deposit Banking (pt)	-	-	-	-	-	-	-	-
6289	Services for Security Exchanges, nec (pt)	-	-	-	-	-	-	-	-
6733	Trusts, nec (pt)	-	-	-	-	-	-	-	-

Source: Economic Census of the United States, 1992, annual surveys of economic sectors conducted by the Bureau of the Census, and estimates or projections based on the 1982-1992 period; not all data are shown. 'e' marks estimates made by the editors; 'p' indicates projections based on time series. A dash (-) indicates that data for this SIC or year were not available. The abbreviation (pt) next to the industry name indicates that only a part of the industry is present within the NAICS data. If no (pt) is shown, the entire industry is contained within the NAICS data.

SELECTED RATIOS

For 1997	Avg. of Information	Analyzed Industry	Index	For 1997	Avg. of Information	Analyzed Industry	Index
Employees per establishment	15	21	142	Payroll per establishment	669,406	953,631	142
Revenue per establishment	5,561,120	3,033,683	55	Payroll as % of revenue	12	31	261
Revenue per employee	376,639	144,953	38	Payroll per employee	45,337	45,566	101

Sources: Same as General Statistics. The 'Average' column represents the average for the industry sector, in 1997, where the currently shown industry is classified. The Index shows the relationship between the Average and the Analyzed Industry. For example, 100 means that they are equal; 500 that the Analyzed Industry is five times the average; 50 means that the Analyzed Industry is half the national average. The abbreviation 'na' is used to show that data are 'not available'.

LEADING COMPANIES Number shown: **31** Total sales ($ mil): **562,035** Total employment (000): **59.6**

Company Name	Address				CEO Name	Phone	Co. Type	Sales ($ mil)	Empl. (000)
Key Trust Co.	3777 Tamiami Tr N	Naples	FL	34103	Tom Becker	941-261-0990	S	403,138*	28.5
PNC Bank Corp.	1 PNC Plz 249 5th	Pittsburgh	PA	15222	Thomas H O'Brien	412-762-1553	P	75,464	25.5
Mercantile Trust Company N.A.	P O Box 387	St. Louis	MO	63166	Edward D Higgins	314-425-2600	S	28,702	0.2
First of America Trust Co.	301 S W Adams St	Peoria	IL	61602		309-655-5895	S	14,351*	1.0
Imperial Trust Co.	201 N Figueroa St	Los Angeles	CA	90012		213-627-5600	S	9,300	<0.1
AmalgaTrust Company Inc.	1 W Monroe St	Chicago	IL	60603	Robert Wrobel	312-822-3296	S	6,100*	<0.1
U.S. Trust Corp.	114 W 47th St	New York	NY	10036	Jeffrey S Maurer	212-852-1000	P	4,143	1.5
Huntington Trust Company N.A.	41 S High St	Columbus	OH	43287		480-463-4225	S	4,002*	0.3
North American Trust Co.	P O Box 84419	San Diego	CA	92138	Michael Mayer	619-237-5528	R	4,000	0.2
Glenmede Trust Co.	1650 Market St	Philadelphia	PA	19103	James Kermes	215-419-6000	R	2,858*	0.2
Fleet Trust Co.	1 East Ave	Rochester	NY	14604		716-546-9085	S	2,320*	0.2
Custodial Trust Co.	101 Carnegie Ctr	Princeton	NJ	08540	Ronald D Watson	609-951-2300	S	1,955*	<0.1
GEMISYS Corp.	7103 S Revere Pkwy	Englewood	CO	80112	Darrall E Robbins	303-705-6000	R	1,734*	0.1
Harris Trust of California	601 S Figueroa St	Los Angeles	CA	90017	Steven R Rothbloom	213-239-0600	S	1,400*	<0.1
Pennsylvania Trust Co.	5 Radnor Corporate	Radnor	PA	19087	R T Merriman	610-975-4300	S	938*	<0.1
Capital Guardian Trust Co.	333 S Hope St	Los Angeles	CA	90071	Robert Ronus	213-486-9200	S	700*	0.3
Participants Trust Co.	1 World Financial	New York	NY	10281	John J Robinson	212-786-1526	R	300	0.1
Firstar Trust Co.	P O Box 2077	Milwaukee	WI	53201	Sun Hoffer	414-276-3737	S	202*	0.4
Columbian Trust Co.	4701 W 110th St	Overland Park	KS	66211	Carl McCaffree	913-491-1061	D	147*	<0.1
American Stock Transfer & Trust	40 Wall St	New York	NY	10005	Michael Karfunkel	212-936-5100	R	66*	0.2
Capital Crossing Bank	101 Summer St	Boston	MA	02110	Nicholas W Lazares	617-880-1000	P	61	0.1
Marshall and Ilsley Trust Co.	1000 N Water St	Milwaukee	WI	53202	Morry O Birnbaum	414-765-8200	S	47*	0.3
Key Assets Management	101 W Benson Blvd	Anchorage	AK	99503		907-564-0400	S	25*	<0.1
Wayne Savings Bancshares Inc.	PO Box 858	Wooster	OH	44691	Charles Finn	330-264-5767	P	20	<0.1
IAA Trust Co.	PO Box 2901	Bloomington	IL	61702	Robert Rush	309-557-3222	S	19*	<0.1
Resource Asset Investment Trust	1845 Walnut	Philadelphia	PA	19103	Betsy Z Cohen	215-861-7900	P	17	<0.1
InnSuites Hospitality Trust	1625 E Northern	Phoenix	AZ	85020	James F Wirth	602-944-1500	P	10	<0.1
M & I Marshall & Ilsley Trust	7702 E Doubletree	Scottsdale	AZ	85258	George H Isbell		P	7*	<0.1
Chicago Trust of California	401 B St	San Diego	CA	92101		619-239-3091	S	5	<0.1
Austin Trust Co.	100 Congress Ave	Austin	TX	78701	William J Hudspeth Jr	512-478-2121	R	2	<0.1
First Midwest Trust N.A.	121 N Chicago St	Joliet	IL	60432	Robert P O'Meara	815-740-7700	S	2	<0.1

Source: Ward's Business Directory of U.S. Private and Public Companies, Volumes 1 and 2, 2000. The company type code used is as follows: P - Public, R - Private, S - Subsidiary, D - Division, J - Joint Venture, A - Affiliate, G - Group, N - Company type not reported. Sales are in millions of dollars, employees are in thousands. An asterisk (*) indicates an estimated sales volume. The symbol < stands for 'less than'. Company names and addresses are truncated, in some cases, to fit into the available space.

LOCATION BY STATE AND REGIONAL CONCENTRATION

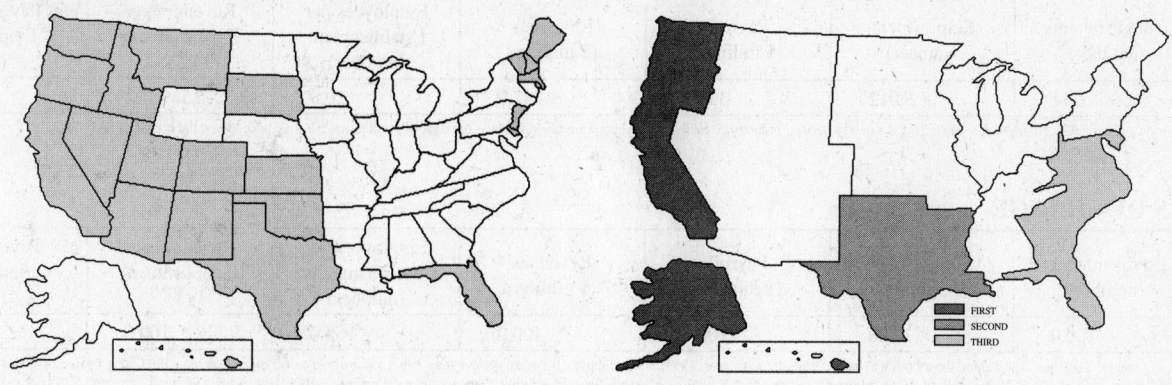

INDUSTRY DATA BY STATE

State	Establishments Total (number)	Establishments % of U.S.	Employment Total (number)	Employment % of U.S.	Employment Per Estab.	Payroll Total ($ mil.)	Payroll Per Empl. ($)	Revenues Total ($ mil.)	Revenues % of U.S.	Revenues Per Estab. ($)
Massachusetts	80	3.5	8,163	17.1	102	387.0	47,413	1,402.3	20.2	17,528,488
California	448	19.6	5,454	11.4	12	351.8	64,502	872.7	12.6	1,947,958
Missouri	33	1.4	4,878	10.2	148	230.8	47,306	561.8	8.1	17,024,273
Illinois	96	4.2	1,438	3.0	15	70.3	48,856	307.8	4.4	3,206,687
Ohio	46	2.0	1,020	2.1	22	48.0	47,103	232.1	3.3	5,046,239
Texas	224	9.8	1,712	3.6	8	60.3	35,227	174.8	2.5	780,406
Minnesota	23	1.0	1,176	2.5	51	46.1	39,241	141.4	2.0	6,145,696
Colorado	46	2.0	1,229	2.6	27	46.3	37,648	136.8	2.0	2,973,261
Washington	75	3.3	537	1.1	7	24.3	45,298	99.4	1.4	1,325,013
Kansas	23	1.0	375*	-	-	16.3	-	93.4	1.3	4,062,478
New Hampshire	14	0.6	351	0.7	25	13.2	37,604	85.9	1.2	6,135,571
Indiana	36	1.6	670	1.4	19	22.0	32,852	70.3	1.0	1,954,111
Virginia	44	1.9	608	1.3	14	21.6	35,569	54.4	0.8	1,235,318
Oklahoma	56	2.4	385	0.8	7	12.7	32,995	52.7	0.8	940,661
Georgia	37	1.6	393	0.8	11	15.5	39,394	33.3	0.5	899,541
Louisiana	30	1.3	287	0.6	10	9.9	34,491	31.4	0.5	1,046,600
North Carolina	33	1.4	257	0.5	8	10.0	39,097	27.9	0.4	845,303
Alabama	17	0.7	156	0.3	9	5.3	33,974	11.0	0.2	647,529
Maine	18	0.8	126	0.3	7	4.7	37,492	10.3	0.1	571,056
Montana	13	0.6	88	0.2	7	2.4	26,966	10.0	0.1	769,462
Michigan	31	1.4	161	0.3	5	3.5	21,882	8.6	0.1	277,419
Oregon	28	1.2	111	0.2	4	3.1	27,982	7.3	0.1	259,536
South Carolina	13	0.6	29	0.1	2	1.0	33,172	1.8	0.0	141,077
New York	159	7.0	7,500*	-	-	(D)	-	(D)	-	-
Florida	138	6.0	1,750*	-	-	(D)	-	(D)	-	-
New Jersey	73	3.2	3,750*	-	-	(D)	-	(D)	-	-
Pennsylvania	66	2.9	1,750*	-	-	(D)	-	(D)	-	-
Arizona	51	2.2	375*	-	-	(D)	-	(D)	-	-
Wisconsin	37	1.6	750*	-	-	(D)	-	(D)	-	-
Nevada	33	1.4	175*	-	-	(D)	-	(D)	-	-
Tennessee	28	1.2	375*	-	-	(D)	-	(D)	-	-
Connecticut	23	1.0	175*	-	-	(D)	-	(D)	-	-
Maryland	23	1.0	750*	-	-	(D)	-	(D)	-	-
Rhode Island	22	1.0	750*	-	-	(D)	-	(D)	-	-
Arkansas	20	0.9	175*	-	-	(D)	-	(D)	-	-
Utah	20	0.9	175*	-	-	(D)	-	(D)	-	-
New Mexico	16	0.7	60*	-	-	(D)	-	(D)	-	-
Delaware	13	0.6	750*	-	-	(D)	-	(D)	-	-
Hawaii	11	0.5	375*	-	-	(D)	-	(D)	-	-
Idaho	11	0.5	60*	-	-	(D)	-	(D)	-	-
Iowa	10	0.4	60*	-	-	(D)	-	(D)	-	-
Kentucky	9	0.4	60*	-	-	(D)	-	(D)	-	-
Mississippi	9	0.4	60*	-	-	(D)	-	(D)	-	-
West Virginia	8	0.3	60*	-	-	(D)	-	(D)	-	-
D.C.	7	0.3	60*	-	-	(D)	-	(D)	-	-
South Dakota	7	0.3	10*	-	-	(D)	-	(D)	-	-
Vermont	7	0.3	60*	-	-	(D)	-	(D)	-	-
Nebraska	6	0.3	60*	-	-	(D)	-	(D)	-	-

Source: 1997 *Economic Census*. The states are in descending order of revenues or establishments (if revenue data are missing for the majority). The symbol (D) appears when data are withheld to prevent disclosure of competitive information. States marked with (D) are sorted by number of establishments. A dash (-) indicates that the data element cannot be calculated. * indicates the midpoint of a range; 175, for example is the range 100-249. Shaded *states* on the state map indicate those states which have proportionately greater representation in the industry than would be indicated by the state's population; the ratio is based on total revenues or number of establishments. Shaded *regions* indicate where the industry is regionally most concentrated.

NAICS 523999 - MISCELLANEOUS FINANCIAL INVESTMENT ACTIVITIES

GENERAL STATISTICS

Year	Establishments (number)	Employment (number)	Payroll ($ million)	Revenues ($ million)	Employees per Establishment (number)	Revenues per Establishment ($)	Payroll per Employee ($)
1997	241	5,012	354.0	1,347.0	20.8	5,589,212	70,630

Source: Economic Census of the United States, 1997. This is a newly defined industry. Data for prior years were unavailable at the time of publication but may become available over time.

INDICES OF CHANGE

Year	Establishments (number)	Employment (number)	Payroll ($ million)	Revenues ($ million)	Employees per Establishment (number)	Revenues per Establishment ($)	Payroll per Employee ($)
1997	100.0	100.0	100.0	100.0	100.0	100.0	100.0

Sources: Same as General Statistics. The values shown reflect change from the base year, 1997. Values above 100 mean greater than 1997, values below 100 mean less than 1997, and a value of 100 in the 1982-96 or 1998-2001 period means same as 1997. Values followed by a 'p' are projections by the editors; 'e' stands for extrapolation. Data are the most recent available at this level of detail.

SIC INDUSTRIES RELATED TO NAICS 523999

Each new NAICS code represents an industry that used to be part of an SIC or a part of several SIC industries. Data in this table are shown to provide transitional information for these cases. All available data for the precursor SIC(s) are shown. Even if only a part of an SIC is included in the NAICS, *all* data for the SIC are reproduced. If the SIC industry is not marked as being a part (pt) of the NAICS, the entire industry is embedded in the NAICS data. The SIC composition of the new industry provides some hints of the relative importance of its "ancestors." Data marked with a 'p' are projected. Projections begin with 1982 data. Data earlier than 1990 are not shown but are reflected in the projections.

SIC	Industry	1990	1991	1992	1993	1994	1995	1996	1997
6211	**Security Brokers and Dealers (pt)**								
	Establishments (number)	-	-	17,787	-	-	-	-	-
	Employment (thousands)	-	-	300.0	-	-	-	-	-
	Revenues ($ million)	-	-	88,171.4	-	-	-	-	-
6289	**Services for Security Exchanges, nec (pt)**								

Source: Economic Census of the United States, 1992, annual surveys of economic sectors conducted by the Bureau of the Census, and estimates or projections based on the 1982-1992 period; not all data are shown. 'e' marks estimates made by the editors; 'p' indicates projections based on time series. A dash (-) indicates that data for this SIC or year were not available. The abbreviation (pt) next to the industry name indicates that only a part of the industry is present within the NAICS data. If no (pt) is shown, the entire industry is contained within the NAICS data.

SELECTED RATIOS

For 1997	Avg. of Information	Analyzed Industry	Index	For 1997	Avg. of Information	Analyzed Industry	Index
Employees per establishment	15	21	141	Payroll per establishment	669,406	1,468,880	219
Revenue per establishment	5,561,120	5,589,212	101	Payroll as % of revenue	12	26	218
Revenue per employee	376,639	268,755	71	Payroll per employee	45,337	70,630	156

Sources: Same as General Statistics. The 'Average' column represents the average for the industry sector, in 1997, where the currently shown industry is classified. The Index shows the relationship between the Average and the Analyzed Industry. For example, 100 means that they are equal; 500 that the Analyzed Industry is five times the average; 50 means that the Analyzed Industry is half the national average. The abbreviation 'na' is used to show that data are 'not available'.

LEADING COMPANIES   Number shown: **75**   Total sales ($ mil): **72,991**   Total employment (000): **88.2**

Company Name	Address			CEO Name	Phone	Co. Type	Sales ($ mil)	Empl. (000)
MCN Investment Corp.	150 W Jefferson Ave	Detroit	MI 48226	Steven Ewing	313-256-5886	S	11,830*	2.8
Chase Capital Partners	380 Madison Ave	New York	NY 10017	Jeffrey C Walker	212-622-3100	S	6,000*	0.1
First Data Corp.	5660 New Northside	Atlanta	GA 30328	Henry C Duques	770-857-7001	P	5,540	32.0
Midwest Capital Group Inc.	370 W Anchor Dr	Dakota Dunes	SD 57049	Gregory E Abel	605-232-5900	S	4,862*	1.1
Pershing and Co.	1 Pershing Plz	Jersey City	NJ 07399		201-413-2000	D	3,460	2.8
Nelson Communications Inc.	41 Madison Ave	New York	NY 10010	Thomas Moore	212-684-9400	R	3,133*	0.7
Telecheck (Atlanta, Georgia)	5660 Northside Blvd	Atlanta	GA 30328	Steve Shapes	404-250-6170	S	2,508*	2.2
American Beverage Corp.	1 Daily Way	Verona	PA 15147	David Bober	412-828-9020	R	2,237*	0.5
Prebon Yamane Inc.	101 Hudson St	Jersey City	NJ 07302	Harry Fry	201-557-5000	R	2,025*	0.5
American Industrial Partners	1 Maritime Plz	San Francisco	CA 94111	W Richard Bingham	415-788-7354	R	1,480*	0.6
Centre Capital Investors L.P.	30 Rockefeller Plz	New York	NY 10020	Lester Pollack	212-332-5800	R	1,480*	<0.1
Thomas H. Lee Co.	75 State St	Boston	MA 02109	Thomas H Lee	617-227-1050	R	1,250*	<0.1
Golder, Thoma, Cressey, Rauner	233 S Wacker Dr	Chicago	IL 60606		312-382-2200	R	1,200	<0.1
Wingate Partners L.P.	750 N St Paul St	Dallas	TX 75201		214-720-1313	R	1,200*	<0.1
FirstCity Financial Corp.	6400 Imperial Dr	Waco	TX 76712	James R Hawkins	254-751-1750	P	1,110	1.9
Safeguard Scientifics Inc.	800 Safeguard Bldg	Wayne	PA 19087	Warren V Musser	610-293-0600	P	1,069	5.1
Cal Fed Bancorp Inc.	5670 Wilshire Blvd	Los Angeles	CA 90036	E Harshfield	323-932-4200	R	1,050	2.1
Mayfield Fund	2800 Sand Hill Rd	Menlo Park	CA 94025		650-854-5560	R	1,000	<0.1
Hissong Group Inc.	PO Box 495	Bath	OH 44210	Robert E Hissong	330-659-3770	R	895*	0.2
Intuition Inc.	6420 S Point Pkwy	Jacksonville	FL 32216	David Graham	904-281-7132	R	840*	0.5
Star System Inc.	401 W A St	San Diego	CA 92101	Ronald V Congemi	619-234-4774	R	833*	0.5
Concord EFS Inc.	2525 Horizon Lake	Memphis	TN 38133	Edward A Labry III	901-371-8000	P	830	2.0
Knight/Trimark Group Inc.	525 Washington	Jersey City	NJ 07310	Kenneth D Pastemak	201-222-9400	P	801	0.4
Concord Computing Corp.	2525 Horizon Lake	Memphis	TN 38133	Dan M Palmer	901-371-8000	R	753*	0.7
Austin Ventures L.P.	114 W 7th St	Austin	TX 78701		512-479-0055	R	750	<0.1
Specialty Foods Corp.	520 Lake Cook Rd	Deerfield	IL 60015	Larry Benjamin	847-405-5300	R	740	8.3
Churchill Capital	333 S 7th St	Minneapolis	MN 55402	Mike Hahn	612-673-6633	R	638	<0.1
InterWest Partners	3000 Sand Hill Rd	Menlo Park	CA 94025		650-854-8585	R	615*	<0.1
TL Ventures	435 Devon Park Dr	Wayne	PA 19087	Robert E Keith Jr	610-975-9770	R	602*	<0.1
Rauscher Pierce Refsnes Inc.	2711 N Haskell Ave	Dallas	TX 75204	Ervin Rauscher	214-989-1000	S	586*	3.0
Fenway Partners Inc.	152 W 57th St	New York	NY 10019	Peter Lamm	212-698-9400	R	527	<0.1
Sevin Rosen Funds	13455 Noel Rd	Dallas	TX 75240	Jon Bayless	972-702-1100	R	500	<0.1
Westar Capital L.L.C.	949 S Coast Dr	Costa Mesa	CA 92626		714-481-5160	R	500	<0.1
Advent International Corp.	101 Federal St	Boston	MA 02110	Douglas R Brown	617-951-9400	R	493*	0.2
CMG Direct Corp.	187 Ballardvale St	Wilmington	MA 01887	Jeremy Barbera	978-657-7000	S	450*	0.1
Equity Group	2 N Riverside Plz	Chicago	IL 60606		312-454-0100	R	447*	0.1
Galen Associates	610 5th Ave	New York	NY 10020	Bruce F Wesson	212-218-4990	R	400	<0.1
Kirtland Capital Corp.	2550 SOM Center	Willghby Hls	OH 44094	John F Turben	440-585-9010	R	400*	<0.1
Domain Associates	28202 Cabot Rd	Laguna Niguel	CA 92677		714-434-6227	R	380*	<0.1
Boston Financial Data Services	2 Heritage Dr	North Quincy	MA 02171	Joseph Hooley	617-328-5000	J	330*	2.0
Game Financial Corp.	PO Box 26008	Minneapolis	MN 55426	Gary A Dachis	612-476-8500	P	328	0.3
Capital Southwest Corp.	12900 Preston Rd	Dallas	TX 75230	William R Thomas	972-233-8242	P	311	<0.1
Litton Loan Servicing Inc.	5373 W Alabama St	Houston	TX 77056	Larry Litton Sr	713-960-9676	S	288*	0.3
Comdata Corp.	5301 Maryland Way	Brentwood	TN 37027	Tony Holcombe	615-370-7000	S	286*	1.9
Healthcare Financial Partners Inc.	2 Wisconsin Cir	Chevy Chase	MD 20815	John K Delaney		S	272	<0.1
Grotech Capital Group Inc.	9690 Deereco Rd	Lutherville	MD 21093	Frank A Adams	410-560-2000	R	250*	<0.1
Madison Capital Partners Corp.	500 W Madison	Chicago	IL 60661	Larry W Gies, Jr	312-277-0156	R	250	1.2
Pioneer Group Inc.	60 State St	Boston	MA 02109	John F Cogan Jr	617-742-7825	P	250	3.4
Code, Hennessy and Simmons Inc.	10 S Wacker Dr	Chicago	IL 60606		312-876-1840	R	237	6.0
Harbour Group	7701 Forsyth Blvd	St. Louis	MO 63105		314-727-5550	N	225*	<0.1
PAS Financial Group Inc.	6301 Campus Cir	Irving	TX 75063	Jerry Beck	972-756-0212	S	225*	<0.1
Magnet Industrial Group Inc.	25 High St	Milford	CT 06460	John Soto	203-877-2034	R	224*	<0.1
W.M. Sprinkman Corp.	PO Box 390	Franksville	WI 53126	Robert Sprinkman	414-835-2390	R	224*	<0.1
Florida Capital Partners	601 Ashley Drive	Tampa	FL 33602		813-222-8000	R	216*	<0.1
Arvida Realty Services	300 S Park Pl 19 N	Clearwater	FL 33759	Richard W Cope	727-723-8887	R	211	0.7
Lombard Inc.	600 Montgomery St	San Francisco	CA 94111	Joseph Chulick	415-397-5900	R	210*	<0.1
Instinet Corp.	850 3rd Ave Fl 6	New York	NY 10022	Michael Sanderson	212-310-9500	S	209*	0.8
Investment Technology Group Inc.	380 Madison Ave	New York	NY 10022	Raymond L Killian Jr	212-755-6800	P	205	0.3
Ross Marine L.L.C.	2676 Swygert Blvd	Johns Island	SC 29455	AR Swygert	843-559-0346	R	201*	<0.1
Hummer Winblad Venture	2 South Park 2nd Fl	San Francisco	CA 94107		415-979-9600	R	200	<0.1
Lee Capital Holdings L.L.C.	1 International Pl	Boston	MA 02110		617-345-0477	R	190*	1.1
Saugatuck Capital Company L.P.	1 Canterbury Green	Stamford	CT 06901		203-348-6669	R	190*	<0.1
ABB Energy Ventures	202 Carnegie Ctr	Princeton	NJ 08540	Peter Giller	609-243-7575	S	180*	<0.1
KSCI Holding Inc.	1990 S Bundy #850	Los Angeles	CA 90025	Ray Beindors	310-478-1818	R	179*	<0.1
Clayton, Dubilier and Rice Inc.	375 Park Ave	New York	NY 10152	Joseph L Rice III	212-355-0740	R	177*	<0.1
Linsco/Private Ledger Corp.	9785 Town Centre	San Diego	CA 92121	Todd Robinson	619-450-9240	R	165*	0.3
Sierra Ventures	3000 Sandhill Rd	Menlo Park	CA 94025		650-854-1000	R	160*	<0.1
EnCompass Group Inc.	4040 Lake Wash	Kirkland	WA 98033	Yasuki Matsumoto	425-828-1030	R	159*	<0.1
Apex Investment Partners	233 S Wacker Dr	Chicago	IL 60606		312-258-0320	R	154*	<0.1
Battery Ventures	20 William St	Wellesley	MA 02481		781-996-1000	R	153*	<0.1
Ampersand Ventures Management	55 William St	Wellesley	MA 02481	Richard Charpie	781-239-0700	R	150	<0.1
Cordova Ventures	2500 Northwinds	Alpharetta	GA 30004	Gerald F Schmidt	678-942-0300	R	150	<0.1
Resource America Inc.	1521 Locust St	Philadelphia	PA 19102	Daniel G Cohen	215-546-5005	P	142	0.4
Triumph Capital L.P.	237 Park Ave	New York	NY 10017		212-551-3636	R	140	<0.1
ITG Inc.	380 Madison Ave	New York	NY 10017	Scott P Mason	212-588-4000	S	137	0.2

Source: *Ward's Business Directory of U.S. Private and Public Companies*, Volumes 1 and 2, 2000. The company type code used is as follows: P - Public, R - Private, S - Subsidiary, D - Division, J - Joint Venture, A - Affiliate, G - Group, N - Company type not reported. Sales are in millions of dollars, employees are in thousands. An asterisk (*) indicates an estimated sales volume. The symbol < stands for 'less than'. Company names and addresses are truncated, in some cases, to fit into the available space.

LOCATION BY STATE AND REGIONAL CONCENTRATION

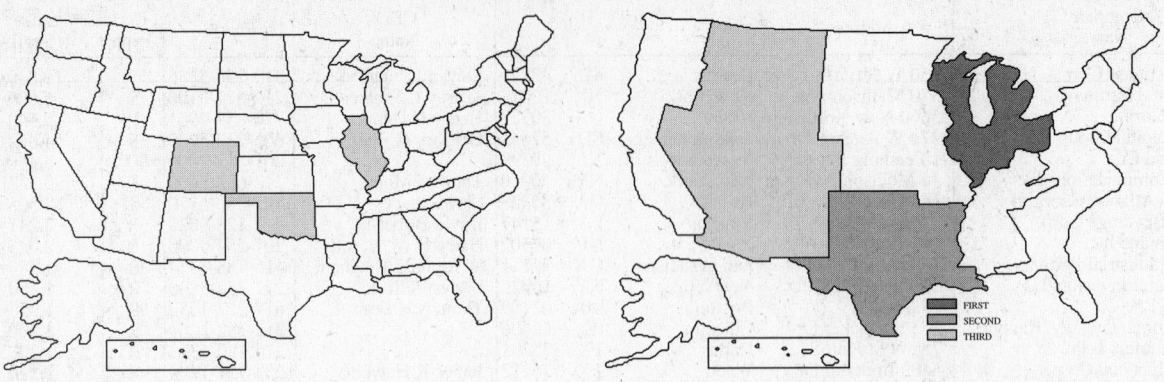

INDUSTRY DATA BY STATE

State	Establishments Total (number)	Establishments % of U.S.	Employment Total (number)	Employment % of U.S.	Employment Per Estab.	Payroll Total ($ mil.)	Payroll Per Empl. ($)	Revenues Total ($ mil.)	Revenues % of U.S.	Revenues Per Estab. ($)
Illinois	9	3.7	686	13.7	76	51.9	75,608	147.8	11.0	16,425,889
Texas	38	15.8	241	4.8	6	18.2	75,614	62.1	4.6	1,634,421
Colorado	12	5.0	172	3.4	14	8.6	50,151	41.0	3.0	3,413,667
Oklahoma	34	14.1	127	2.5	4	3.8	29,535	21.2	1.6	623,059
Louisiana	15	6.2	38	0.8	3	3.0	80,211	9.3	0.7	617,600
Michigan	6	2.5	18	0.4	3	0.5	27,000	3.0	0.2	507,333
New York	37	15.4	1,750*	-	-	(D)	-	(D)	-	-
California	15	6.2	175*	-	-	(D)	-	(D)	-	-
North Dakota	8	3.3	60*	-	-	(D)	-	(D)	-	-
Florida	6	2.5	175*	-	-	(D)	-	(D)	-	-
Massachusetts	6	2.5	750*	-	-	(D)	-	(D)	-	-
Montana	6	2.5	10*	-	-	(D)	-	(D)	-	-

Source: 1997 Economic Census. The states are in descending order of revenues or establishments (if revenue data are missing for the majority). The symbol (D) appears when data are withheld to prevent disclosure of competitive information. States marked with (D) are sorted by number of establishments. A dash (-) indicates that the data element cannot be calculated. * indicates the midpoint of a range; 175, for example is the range 100-249. Shaded states on the state map indicate those states which have proportionately greater representation in the industry than would be indicated by the state's population; the ratio is based on total revenues or number of establishments. Shaded regions indicate where the industry is regionally most concentrated.

NAICS 524113 - DIRECT LIFE INSURANCE CARRIERS

GENERAL STATISTICS

Year	Establishments (number)	Employment (number)	Payroll ($ million)	Revenues ($ million)	Employees per Establishment (number)	Revenues per Establishment ($)	Payroll per Employee ($)
1997	11,406	561,385	21,852.0	463,376.0	49.2	40,625,636	38,925

Source: Economic Census of the United States, 1997. This is a newly defined industry. Data for prior years were unavailable at the time of publication but may become available over time.

INDICES OF CHANGE

Year	Establishments (number)	Employment (number)	Payroll ($ million)	Revenues ($ million)	Employees per Establishment (number)	Revenues per Establishment ($)	Payroll per Employee ($)
1997	100.0	100.0	100.0	100.0	100.0	100.0	100.0

Sources: Same as General Statistics. The values shown reflect change from the base year, 1997. Values above 100 mean greater than 1997, values below 100 mean less than 1997, and a value of 100 in the 1982-96 or 1998-2001 period means same as 1997. Values followed by a 'p' are projections by the editors; 'e' stands for extrapolation. Data are the most recent available at this level of detail.

SIC INDUSTRIES RELATED TO NAICS 524113

Each new NAICS code represents an industry that used to be part of an SIC or a part of several SIC industries. Data in this table are shown to provide transitional information for these cases. All available data for the precursor SIC(s) are shown. Even if only a part of an SIC is included in the NAICS, *all* data for the SIC are reproduced. If the SIC industry is not marked as being a part (pt) of the NAICS, the entire industry is embedded in the NAICS data. The SIC composition of the new industry provides some hints of the relative importance of its "ancestors." Data marked with a 'p' are projected. Projections begin with 1982 data. Data earlier than 1990 are not shown but are reflected in the projections.

SIC	Industry	1990	1991	1992	1993	1994	1995	1996	1997
6311	**Life Insurance (pt)**								
	Establishments (number)	-	-	13,424	-	-	-	-	-
	Employment (thousands)	-	-	609.2	-	-	-	-	-
	Revenues ($ million)	-	-	378,401.7	-	-	-	-	-
6321	**Accident and Health Insurance (pt)**								
	Establishments (number)	-	-	1,100	-	-	-	-	-
	Employment (thousands)	-	-	53.6	-	-	-	-	-
	Revenues ($ million)	-	-	23,446.3	-	-	-	-	-

Source: Economic Census of the United States, 1992, annual surveys of economic sectors conducted by the Bureau of the Census, and estimates or projections based on the 1982-1992 period; not all data are shown. 'e' marks estimates made by the editors; 'p' indicates projections based on time series. A dash (-) indicates that data for this SIC or year were not available. The abbreviation (pt) next to the industry name indicates that only a part of the industry is present within the NAICS data. If no (pt) is shown, the entire industry is contained within the NAICS data.

SELECTED RATIOS

For 1997	Avg. of Information	Analyzed Industry	Index	For 1997	Avg. of Information	Analyzed Industry	Index
Employees per establishment	15	49	333	Payroll per establishment	669,406	1,915,834	286
Revenue per establishment	5,561,120	40,625,636	731	Payroll as % of revenue	12	5	39
Revenue per employee	376,639	825,416	219	Payroll per employee	45,337	38,925	86

Sources: Same as General Statistics. The 'Average' column represents the average for the industry sector, in 1997, where the currently shown industry is classified. The Index shows the relationship between the Average and the Analyzed Industry. For example, 100 means that they are equal; 500 that the Analyzed Industry is five times the average; 50 means that the Analyzed Industry is half the national average. The abbreviation 'na' is used to show that data are 'not available'.

LEADING COMPANIES   Number shown: **75**   Total sales ($ mil): **4,511,652**   Total employment (000): **1,233.2**

Company Name	Address				CEO Name	Phone	Co. Type	Sales ($ mil)	Empl. (000)
Citigroup Inc.	399 Park Ave	New York	NY	10043	John S. Reed	212-559-1000	P	668,641	173.7
Transamerica Asset MGT Group	1150 S Olive St	Los Angeles	CA	90015	Thomas J Cusack	213-742-3111	S	361,626*	0.7
Metropolitan Life Insurance Co.	1 Madison Ave	New York	NY	10010	Robert H Benmosche	212-578-2211	P	358,000	45.1
American International Group Inc.	70 Pine St	New York	NY	10270	Maurice R Greenberg	212-770-7000	P	267,000	40.0
Hartford Financial Services Group	690 Asylum Ave	Hartford	CT	06115	Ramani Ayer	860-547-5000	P	135,000	25.0
Hartford Life Inc.	200 Hopmeadow St	Simsbury	CT	06089	Lowndes A Smith	860-525-8555	P	122,022	4.5
CIGNA Corp.	PO Box 7716	Philadelphia	PA	19192	H Edward Hanway	215-761-1000	P	114,612	49.9
AXA Financial Inc.	1290 Av Americas	New York	NY	10104	Edward D Miller	212-554-1234	P	109,185	14.7
American General Corp.	PO Box 3247	Houston	TX	77253	Robert M Devlin	713-522-1111	P	105,000	16.1
Teachers Insurance & Annuity	730 3rd Ave	New York	NY	10017	John H Biggs	212-490-9000	R	100,000	4.3
Aetna Services Inc.	151 Farmington Ave	Hartford	CT	06156	Richard L Huber	860-273-0123	S	96,053*	27.2
Lincoln National Corp.	PO Box 1110	Fort Wayne	IN	46802	Jon A Boscia	219-455-2000	P	93,836	8.0
John Hancock Mutual Life	P O Box 111	Boston	MA	02117	Stephen L Brown	617-572-6000	R	89,122	18.0
Nationwide Life Insurance Co.	One Nationwide Plz	Columbus	OH	43216	Dimon McFerson	614-249-7111	P	83,214	33.4
Principal National Life Insurance	711 High St	Des Moines	IA	50392	Barry Griswell	515-247-5111	S	81,457*	17.0
Northwestern Mutual Life	720 E Wisconsin	Milwaukee	WI	53202	James D Ericson	414-271-1444	R	78,000	3.8
Allstate Insurance Co.	2775 Sanders Rd	Northbrook	IL	60062	Jerry D Choate	847-402-5000	S	77,291*	50.0
State Farm Mutual Automobile	1 State Farm Plz	Bloomington	IL	61710	Edward B Rust Jr	309-766-2311	R	75,579	76.3
Loews Corp.	667 Madison Ave	New York	NY	10021	James S Tisch	212-521-2000	P	73,300	34.3
Canada Life Assurance Co.	PO Box 105087	Atlanta	GA	30348	David A Nield	770-953-1959	R	72,826*	0.7
Equitable Life Assurance Society	1290 Av Americas	New York	NY	10104	Edward P Miller	212-554-1234	R	71,494*	16.0
New York Life Insurance Co.	51 Madison Ave	New York	NY	10010	Seymour Sternberg	212-576-7000	R	68,851	12.6
CNA Financial Corp.	CNA Plz	Chicago	IL	60685	Philip L Engel	312-822-5000	P	62,359	23.6
Massachusetts Mutual Life	1295 State St	Springfield	MA	01111	Thomas Wheeler	413-788-8411	R	59,695*	7.8
Transamerica Corp.	600 Montgomery St	San Francisco	CA	94111	Frank C Herringer	415-983-4000	S	58,503	9.2
Household International Inc.	2700 Sanders Rd	Prospect Heights	IL	60070	William F Aldinger	847-564-5000	P	52,893	23.5
United Services Automobile	9800 Fredricksburg	San Antonio	TX	78288	Robert Herres	210-498-2211	R	52,000*	17.0
Principal Mutual Life Insurance	711 High St	Des Moines	IA	50392	David J Drury	515-247-5111	R	51,268	14.8
Liberty Mutual Insurance Co.	175 Berkeley St	Boston	MA	02117	Edmund F Kelly	617-357-9500	R	50,192	23.0
Travelers Insurance Co.	1 Tower Sq	Hartford	CT	06183	John E Daniels	860-277-0111	S	41,243	0.0
IDS Life Insurance Co.	IDS Tower 10	Minneapolis	MN	55440	James A Mitchell	612-671-3131	S	39,410*	0.3
Nationwide Corp.	1 Nationwide Plz	Columbus	OH	43216	Diamond McFerson	614-249-7111	R	38,108*	8.0
Aetna Life Insurance Co.	151 Farmington Ave	Hartford	CT	06156	Richard Huber	860-273-0123	S	36,516*	27.5
Prudential Insurance of America	751 Broad St	Newark	NJ	07102	Arthur F Ryan	973-802-6000	R	27,087	50.0
Guardian Life Insurance	201 Park Ave S	New York	NY	10004	Joseph D Sargent	212-598-8000	R	25,860	4.8
Lincoln National Life Insurance	1300 S Clinton St	Fort Wayne	IN	46802	Gabriel Shaheen	219-455-2000	S	25,000	3.7
USAA Group Inc.	9800 Fredricksburg	San Antonio	TX	78288	Robert T Herres	210-498-2211	R	24,474*	18.0
Jefferson-Pilot Corp.	PO Box 21008	Greensboro	NC	27420	David A Stonecipher	336-691-3000	P	24,338	2.2
CNA	333 S Wabash Ave	Chicago	IL	60685	Bernie Hengesbough	312-822-5000	S	23,730*	5.0
Provident Companies Inc.	1 Fountain Sq	Chattanooga	TN	37402	J Harold Chandler	423-755-1011	P	23,088	3.7
ReliaStar Financial Corp.	20 Washington S	Minneapolis	MN	55401	John H Flittie	612-372-5432	P	22,609	3.5
Merrill Lynch and Company Inc.	World Financial Ctr	New York	NY	10281	Herbert M Allison Jr	212-449-1000	P	21,869	63.8
State Farm Life Insurance Co.	1 State Farm Plz	Bloomington	IL	61710	Edward B Rust Jr	309-766-2311	S	21,071	2.2
Aetna Inc.	151 Farmington Ave	Hartford	CT	06156	Richard L Huber	860-273-0123	P	20,604	33.5
AEGON USA Inc.	1111 N Charles St	Baltimore	MD	21201	Donald J Shepard	410-576-4571	S	20,330*	11.3
Aon Corp.	123 N Wacker Dr	Chicago	IL	60606	Patrick G Ryan	312-701-3000	P	19,688	33.0
American Family Life Assurance	1932 Wynnton Rd	Columbus	GA	31999	Daniel P Amos	706-323-3431	S	19,001	3.0
Transamerica Occidental Life	1150 S Olive St	Los Angeles	CA	90015	Thomas J Cusack	213-742-2111	S	17,652	2.7
ING North America Insurance	5780 Powers Ferry	Atlanta	GA	30327	R Glenn Hilliard	770-980-3300	S	17,178*	3.8
Zurich American Insurance Co.	1400 American Ln	Schaumburg	IL	60196	Constantine Fordanou	847-605-6000	S	16,770*	3.5
Liberty Financial Companies Inc.	600 Atlantic Ave	Boston	MA	02210	Kenneth R Leibler	617-722-6000	P	16,519	2.1
Minnesota Mutual Life Insurance	400 N Robert St	St. Paul	MN	55101	Robert Senkler	651-665-3500	R	16,433	2.5
American Financial Corp.	1 E 4th St	Cincinnati	OH	45202	Carl H Lindner	513-579-2121	S	15,700	9.0
Great-West Life & Annuity	8515 E Orchard Rd	Englewood	CO	80111	William T McCallum	303-689-3000	S	15,000	1.9
Fortis Inc.	1 Chase Man Plz	New York	NY	10005	Allen R Freedman	212-859-7000	J	14,578	0.0
MBL Life Assurance Corp.	520 Broad St	Newark	NJ	07102	Alan J Bowers	973-481-8000	R	14,400	0.6
Great-West Life Assurance Co.	8515 E Orchard Rd	Englewood	CO	80111	William McCallum	303-689-3000	S	12,581	2.4
Anchor National Life Insurance	1 SunAmerica Ctr	Los Angeles	CA	90067	Eli Broad	310-445-7862	S	12,571	2.0
Western & Southern Life	400 Broadway	Cincinnati	OH	45202	John F Barrett	513-629-1800	R	12,252	4.9
Mutual Life Insurance of New	1740 Broadway	New York	NY	10019	Samuel J Foti	212-708-2000	P	12,110	4.7
Conseco Inc.	P O Box 1911	Carmel	IN	46032	Stephen C Hilbert	317-817-6100	P	12,004	14.0
Protective Life Corp.	PO Box 2606	Birmingham	AL	35202	John D Johns	205-879-9230	P	11,989	1.6
Textron Inc.	PO Box 878	Providence	RI	02901	Lewis Campbell	401-421-2800	P	11,579	64.0
Pacific Life Insurance Co.	700 Newport Center	Newport Beach	CA	92660	Glenn S Schafer	949-640-3011	R	11,547*	2.5
Torchmark Corp.	2001 3rd Ave S	Birmingham	AL	35233	CB Hudson	205-325-4200	P	11,249	4.1
Cincinnati Financial Corp.	PO Box 145496	Cincinnati	OH	45250	John J Schliff	513-870-2000	P	11,087	2.8
Sun Life Assurance of Canada	1 Sun Life Executive	Wellesley Hills	MA	02481		781-237-6030	S	10,965	1.5
Unum Providence Corp.	1 Fountain Sq	Chattanooga	TN	37402	J Harold Chandler	423-755-1011	S	10,862*	4.2
New England Financial	501 Boylston St	Boston	MA	02116	James M Benson	617-578-2000	S	10,569*	4.4
Penn Mutual Life Insurance Co.	600 Dresher Rd	Horsham	PA	19044	Robert E Chappell	215-956-8000	R	10,100	0.8
Mutual of America Life Insurance	320 Park Ave	New York	NY	10022	Thomas Moran	212-224-1600	R	9,500*	1.0
American Capitol Insurance Co.	10555 Richmond	Houston	TX	77042	John D Cornett	713-974-2242	S	8,942	0.1
American General Life	American General	Nashville	TN	37250	Joe Kelley	615-749-1000	S	8,744	0.0
Liberty Mutual Insurance	175 Berkeley St	Boston	MA	02117	E F 'Ted' Kelly	617-357-9500	R	7,904*	24.0
Monumental Life Insurance Co.	2 E Chase St	Baltimore	MD	21202	Henry G Hagan	410-685-2900	S	7,824*	4.5

Source: Ward's Business Directory of U.S. Private and Public Companies, Volumes 1 and 2, 2000. The company type code used is as follows: P - Public, R - Private, S - Subsidiary, D - Division, J - Joint Venture, A - Affiliate, G - Group, N - Company type not reported. Sales are in millions of dollars, employees are in thousands. An asterisk (*) indicates an estimated sales volume. The symbol < stands for 'less than'. Company names and addresses are truncated, in some cases, to fit into the available space.

LOCATION BY STATE AND REGIONAL CONCENTRATION

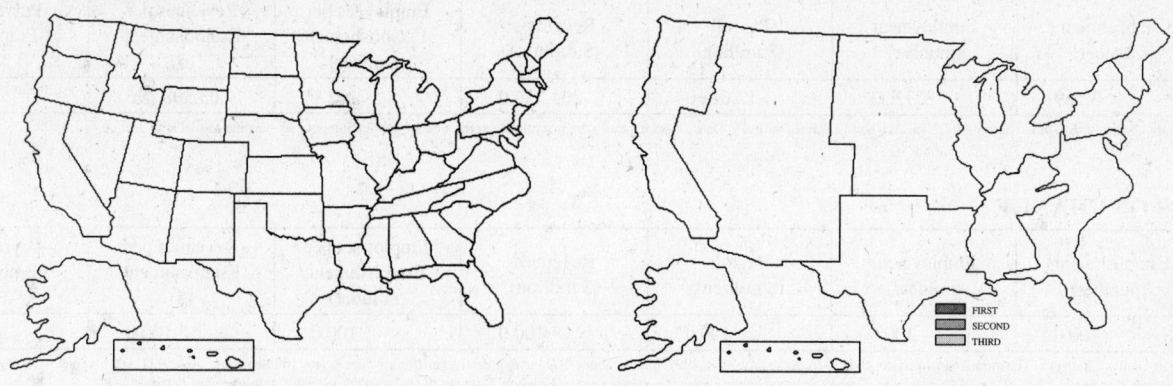

FIRST
SECOND
THIRD

INDUSTRY DATA BY STATE

State	Establishments Total (number)	% of U.S.	Employment Total (number)	% of U.S.	Per Estab.	Payroll Total ($ mil.)	Per Empl. ($)	Revenues Total ($ mil.)	% of U.S.	Per Estab. ($)
Kansas	158	1.4	3,030	0.5	19	105.0	34,656	-	-	-
Utah	71	0.6	1,795	0.3	25	63.6	35,435	-	-	-
Connecticut	166	1.5	22,053	3.9	133	853.1	38,685	-	-	-
Mississippi	139	1.2	2,661	0.5	19	82.4	30,963	-	-	-
Minnesota	218	1.9	16,845	3.0	77	740.2	43,942	-	-	-
Vermont	31	0.3	1,750*	-	-	(D)	-	-	-	-
Nevada	42	0.4	369	0.1	9	13.5	36,485	-	-	-
California	862	7.6	26,615	4.7	31	1,098.7	41,281	-	-	-
Missouri	242	2.1	9,877	1.8	41	364.2	36,870	-	-	-
Virginia	269	2.4	8,481	1.5	32	313.1	36,920	-	-	-
Michigan	302	2.6	10,857	1.9	36	376.7	34,699	-	-	-
Arkansas	90	0.8	2,091	0.4	23	61.8	29,549	-	-	-
Rhode Island	44	0.4	3,750*	-	-	(D)	-	-	-	-
Colorado	177	1.6	8,314	1.5	47	388.1	46,681	-	-	-
Texas	823	7.2	28,614	5.1	35	1,109.5	38,773	-	-	-
D.C.	23	0.2	757	0.1	33	42.0	55,476	-	-	-
New York	727	6.4	59,267	10.6	82	2,449.3	41,326	-	-	-
Kentucky	157	1.4	3,462	0.6	22	117.9	34,065	-	-	-
Pennsylvania	638	5.6	38,419	6.8	60	1,255.7	32,685	-	-	-
Oregon	93	0.8	3,639	0.6	39	117.9	32,399	-	-	-
Oklahoma	141	1.2	4,624	0.8	33	138.5	29,951	-	-	-
Iowa	132	1.2	16,828	3.0	127	725.6	43,121	-	-	-
Indiana	273	2.4	8,521	1.5	31	340.1	39,915	-	-	-
Wyoming	12	0.1	180	0.0	15	6.4	35,394	-	-	-
North Carolina	368	3.2	10,627	1.9	29	365.0	34,350	-	-	-
Georgia	408	3.6	16,984	3.0	42	617.0	36,325	-	-	-
New Jersey	422	3.7	38,652	6.9	92	1,781.3	46,085	-	-	-
Montana	32	0.3	356	0.1	11	10.0	28,194	-	-	-
Florida	707	6.2	28,252	5.0	40	1,022.3	36,184	-	-	-
North Dakota	29	0.3	750*	-	-	(D)	-	-	-	-
Tennessee	279	2.4	9,059	1.6	32	304.0	33,563	-	-	-
Massachusetts	274	2.4	36,167	6.4	132	1,482.3	40,985	-	-	-
Delaware	47	0.4	1,959	0.3	42	93.3	47,628	-	-	-
South Dakota	39	0.3	750*	-	-	(D)	-	-	-	-
Ohio	508	4.5	25,249	4.5	50	866.3	34,311	-	-	-
Hawaii	44	0.4	965	0.2	22	39.3	40,758	-	-	-
Idaho	33	0.3	375*	-	-	(D)	-	-	-	-
South Carolina	195	1.7	7,053	1.3	36	226.8	32,157	-	-	-
New Mexico	51	0.4	1,179	0.2	23	28.3	23,990	-	-	-
Wisconsin	210	1.8	25,946	4.6	124	1,215.3	46,839	-	-	-
Maine	47	0.4	3,976	0.7	85	209.6	52,710	-	-	-
West Virginia	73	0.6	1,228	0.2	17	32.0	26,061	-	-	-
Washington	178	1.6	6,083	1.1	34	227.1	37,333	-	-	-
Nebraska	101	0.9	12,323	2.2	122	420.3	34,110	-	-	-
Alaska	8	0.1	60*	-	-	(D)	-	-	-	-
Alabama	227	2.0	5,808	1.0	26	198.0	34,099	-	-	-
Maryland	222	1.9	5,432	1.0	24	218.5	40,230	-	-	-
Illinois	561	4.9	28,379	5.1	51	1,136.6	40,052	-	-	-
Louisiana	285	2.5	5,847	1.0	21	200.5	34,296	-	-	-
New Hampshire	64	0.6	2,983	0.5	47	105.6	35,400	-	-	-
Arizona	164	1.4	3,387	0.6	21	112.2	33,132	-	-	-

Source: 1997 *Economic Census*. The states are in descending order of revenues or establishments (if revenue data are missing for the majority). The symbol (D) appears when data are withheld to prevent disclosure of competitive information. States marked with (D) are sorted by number of establishments. A dash (-) indicates that the data element cannot be calculated. * indicates the midpoint of a range; 175, for example is the range 100-249. Shaded *states* on the state map indicate those states which have proportionately greater representation in the industry than would be indicated by the state's population; the ratio is based on total revenues or number of establishments. Shaded *regions* indicate where the industry is regionally most concentrated.

NAICS 524114 - DIRECT HEALTH AND MEDICAL INSURANCE CARRIERS

GENERAL STATISTICS

Year	Establishments (number)	Employment (number)	Payroll ($ million)	Revenues ($ million)	Employees per Establishment (number)	Revenues per Establishment ($)	Payroll per Employee ($)
1997	3,209	327,633	12,622.0	203,156.0	102.1	63,308,196	38,525

Source: *Economic Census of the United States*, 1997. This is a newly defined industry. Data for prior years were unavailable at the time of publication but may become available over time.

INDICES OF CHANGE

Year	Establishments (number)	Employment (number)	Payroll ($ million)	Revenues ($ million)	Employees per Establishment (number)	Revenues per Establishment ($)	Payroll per Employee ($)
1997	100.0	100.0	100.0	100.0	100.0	100.0	100.0

Sources: Same as General Statistics. The values shown reflect change from the base year, 1997. Values above 100 mean greater than 1997, values below 100 mean less than 1997, and a value of 100 in the 1982-96 or 1998-2001 period means same as 1997. Values followed by a 'p' are projections by the editors; 'e' stands for extrapolation. Data are the most recent available at this level of detail.

SIC INDUSTRIES RELATED TO NAICS 524114

Each new NAICS code represents an industry that used to be part of an SIC or a part of several SIC industries. Data in this table are shown to provide transitional information for these cases. All available data for the precursor SIC(s) are shown. Even if only a part of an SIC is included in the NAICS, *all* data for the SIC are reproduced. If the SIC industry is not marked as being a part (pt) of the NAICS, the entire industry is embedded in the NAICS data. The SIC composition of the new industry provides some hints of the relative importance of its "ancestors." Data marked with a 'p' are projected. Projections begin with 1982 data. Data earlier than 1990 are not shown but are reflected in the projections.

SIC	Industry	1990	1991	1992	1993	1994	1995	1996	1997
6321	**Accident and Health Insurance (pt)**								
	Establishments (number)	-	-	1,100	-	-	-	-	-
	Employment (thousands)	-	-	53.6	-	-	-	-	-
	Revenues ($ million)	-	-	23,446.3	-	-	-	-	-
6324	**Hospital and Medical Service Plans (pt)**								
	Establishments (number)	-	-	1,746	-	-	-	-	-
	Employment (thousands)	-	-	196.6	-	-	-	-	-
	Revenues ($ million)	-	-	124,813.2	-	-	-	-	-

Source: *Economic Census of the United States*, 1992, annual surveys of economic sectors conducted by the Bureau of the Census, and estimates or projections based on the 1982-1992 period; not all data are shown. 'e' marks estimates made by the editors; 'p' indicates projections based on time series. A dash (-) indicates that data for this SIC or year were not available. The abbreviation (pt) next to the industry name indicates that only a part of the industry is present within the NAICS data. If no (pt) is shown, the entire industry is contained within the NAICS data.

SELECTED RATIOS

For 1997	Avg. of Information	Analyzed Industry	Index	For 1997	Avg. of Information	Analyzed Industry	Index
Employees per establishment	15	102	691	Payroll per establishment	669,406	3,933,313	588
Revenue per establishment	5,561,120	63,308,196	1,138	Payroll as % of revenue	12	6	52
Revenue per employee	376,639	620,072	165	Payroll per employee	45,337	38,525	85

Sources: Same as General Statistics. The 'Average' column represents the average for the industry sector, in 1997, where the currently shown industry is classified. The Index shows the relationship between the Average and the Analyzed Industry. For example, 100 means that they are equal; 500 that the Analyzed Industry is five times the average; 50 means that the Analyzed Industry is half the national average. The abbreviation 'na' is used to show that data are 'not available'.

LEADING COMPANIES   Number shown: **75**   Total sales ($ mil): **1,449,885**   Total employment (000): **572.2**

Company Name	Address				CEO Name	Phone	Co. Type	Sales ($ mil)	Empl. (000)
Hartford Life Inc.	200 Hopmeadow St	Simsbury	CT	06089	Lowndes A. Smith	860-525-8555	P	122,022	4.5
CIGNA Corp.	PO Box 7716	Philadelphia	PA	19192	H Edward Hanway	215-761-1000	P	114,612	49.9
Aetna Services Inc.	151 Farmington Ave	Hartford	CT	06156	Richard L Huber	860-273-0123	S	96,053*	27.2
Lincoln National Corp.	PO Box 1110	Fort Wayne	IN	46802	Jon A Boscia	219-455-2000	P	93,836	8.0
Northwestern Mutual Life	720 E Wisconsin	Milwaukee	WI	53202	James D Ericson	414-271-1444	R	78,000	3.8
Canada Life Assurance Co.	PO Box 105087	Atlanta	GA	30348	David A Nield	770-953-1959	R	72,826*	0.7
Delta Dental Plan of Minnesota	P O Box 330	Minneapolis	MN	55440	Michael F Walsh	651-406-5900	R	69,255	0.2
Massachusetts Mutual Life	1295 State St	Springfield	MA	01111	Thomas Wheeler	413-788-8411	R	59,695*	7.8
Principal Mutual Life Insurance	711 High St	Des Moines	IA	50392	David J Drury	515-247-5111	R	51,268	14.8
Liberty Mutual Insurance Co.	175 Berkeley St	Boston	MA	02117	Edmund F Kelly	617-357-9500	R	50,192	23.0
Travelers Insurance Co.	1 Tower Sq	Hartford	CT	06183	John E Daniels	860-277-0111	S	41,243	0.0
Aetna Life Insurance Co.	151 Farmington Ave	Hartford	CT	06156	Richard Huber	860-273-0123	S	36,516*	27.5
Medica Choice Self-Insured Co.	P O Box 9310	Minneapolis	MN	55440	David Strand	612-992-2000	S	34,878*	15.0
AFLAC Inc.	1932 Wynnton Rd	Columbus	GA	31999	Daniel P Amos	706-596-3264	P	31,183	4.0
Prudential Insurance of America	751 Broad St	Newark	NJ	07102	Arthur F Ryan	973-802-6000	R	27,087	50.0
Guardian Life Insurance	201 Park Ave S	New York	NY	10004	Joseph D Sargent	212-598-8000	R	25,860	4.8
Jefferson-Pilot Corp.	PO Box 21008	Greensboro	NC	27420	David A Stonecipher	336-691-3000	P	24,338	2.2
Provident Companies Inc.	1 Fountain Sq	Chattanooga	TN	37402	J Harold Chandler	423-755-1011	P	23,088	3.7
ReliaStar Financial Corp.	20 Washington S	Minneapolis	MN	55401	John H Flittie	612-372-5432	P	22,609	3.5
Aetna Inc.	151 Farmington Ave	Hartford	CT	06156	Richard L Huber	860-273-0123	P	20,604	33.5
Aon Corp.	123 N Wacker Dr	Chicago	IL	60606	Patrick G Ryan	312-701-3000	P	19,688	33.0
Transamerica Occidental Life	1150 S Olive St	Los Angeles	CA	90015	Thomas J Cusack	213-742-2111	S	17,652	2.7
Minnesota Mutual Life Insurance	400 N Robert St	St. Paul	MN	55101	Robert Senkler	651-665-3500	R	16,433	2.5
UNUM Holding Co.	2211 Congress St	Portland	ME	04122	Harold Chandler	207-770-2211	S	16,034*	7.0
Empire Blue Cross & Blue Shield	1 World Tr Ctr	New York	NY	10048	Michael A Stockers	212-476-1000	R	13,743*	6.0
Independence Blue Cross	1901 Market St	Philadelphia	PA	19103	G Fred DiBona Jr	215-241-2400	R	13,558*	7.0
Great-West Life Assurance Co.	8515 E Orchard Rd	Englewood	CO	80111	William McCallum	303-689-3000	S	12,581	2.4
Western & Southern Life	400 Broadway	Cincinnati	OH	45202	John F Barrett	513-629-1800	R	12,252	4.9
Protective Life Corp.	PO Box 2606	Birmingham	AL	35202	John D Johns	205-879-9230	P	11,989	1.6
Torchmark Corp.	2001 3rd Ave S	Birmingham	AL	35233	CB Hudson	205-325-4200	P	11,249	4.1
Cincinnati Financial Corp.	PO Box 145496	Cincinnati	OH	45250	John J Schliff	513-870-2000	P	11,087	2.8
Unum Providence Corp.	1 Fountain Sq	Chattanooga	TN	37402	J Harold Chandler	423-755-1011	S	10,862*	4.2
Humana Inc.	PO Box 1438	Louisville	KY	40201	David A Jones	502-580-1000	P	10,100	16.3
PacifiCare Health Systems Inc.	3120 Lake Center Dr	Santa Ana	CA	92704	Jeffrey M Folick	714-825-5200	P	9,989	8.9
Wisconsin Physician Service	P O Box 8190	Madison	WI	53708	James Riordan	608-221-4711	R	8,763*	2.8
American General Life	American General	Nashville	TN	37250	Joe Kelley	615-749-1000	S	8,744	0.0
UNUM Life Insurance of America	2211 Congress St	Portland	ME	04122	James F Orr	207-770-2211	S	7,640*	4.7
Wellpoint Health Networks Inc.	One WellPoint Way	Thousand Oaks	CA	91362	Leonard D Schaeffer	818-703-4000	P	7,485	10.6
Protective Life Insurance Co.	P O Box 2606	Birmingham	AL	35202	John D Johns	205-879-9230	S	7,231*	1.2
Medical Mutual of Ohio	2060 E 9th St	Cleveland	OH	44115	Kent Clapp	216-687-7000	R	7,181*	3.0
SAFECO Corp.	SAFECO Plz	Seattle	WA	98185	Boh A Dickey	206-545-5000	P	6,866	11.0
Fortis Benefits Insurance Co.	2323 Grand Blvd	Kansas City	MO	64108	Robert Pollock	816-474-2345	S	6,330	1.6
Group Health Cooperative	521 Wall St	Seattle	WA	98121	Cheryl Scott	206-326-3000	R	5,850*	8.6
Standard Insurance Co.	P O Box 711	Portland	OR	97207	Ronald E Timpe	503-321-7000	S	5,279	1.8
Anthem Inc.	120 Monument Cir	Indianapolis	IN	46204	Ben Lytle	317-488-6000	R	5,242*	0.4
Oxford Health Plans Inc.	800 Connecticut Ave	Norwalk	CT	06854	Norman C Payson	203-852-1442	P	4,719	5.0
Anthem Insurance Company Inc.	120 Monument Cir	Indianapolis	IN	46204	L Ben Lytle	317-488-6000	R	4,589	15.0
American Bankers Insurance	11222 Quail Roost	Miami	FL	33157	Gerald N Gaston	305-253-2244	P	4,368	3.3
Life Reassurance Corporation	969 High Ridge Rd	Stamford	CT	06905	Jaques E Dubois	203-321-3000	S	4,276	0.1
Leucadia National Corp.	315 Park Ave S	New York	NY	10010	Ian M Cumming	212-460-1900	P	3,959	1.4
CareFirst Blue Cross Blue Shield	10455 Mill Run Cir	Owings Mills	MD	21117	William L Jews	410-581-3000	R	3,900	5.7
Blue Cross & Blue Shield	600 Lafayette E	Detroit	MI	48226	Charles L Burkett	313-225-9000	R	3,839	8.8
Blue Cross & Blue Shield	P O Box 995	Birmingham	AL	35298	Horace L Jones	205-988-2100	R	3,800	3.1
Health Net	21600 Oxnard St	Woodland Hills	CA	91302	Cora M Tellez	818-676-6775	S	3,800	3.5
American Family Mutual	P O Box 7430	Madison	WI	53783	Dale F Mathwich	608-249-2111	R	3,602	6.8
Cuna Mutual Insurance Society	P O Box 391	Madison	WI	53701	Michael Kitchen	608-238-5851	R	3,585	5.0
Life Re Corp.	969 High Ridge Rd	Stamford	CT	06905	Jacques E Dubois	203-321-3000	R	3,469	0.1
Blue Cross & Blue Shield	PO Box 1040	New York	NY	10276	Richard J Hale	601-932-3704	R	3,441*	1.0
Mutual of Omaha Insurance Co.	Mutual of Omaha	Omaha	NE	68175	John Sturgeon	402-342-7600	R	3,253	7.1
Blue Cross & Blue Shield	PO Box 1795	Orleans	MA	02653	Ed Cullinan	904-791-6111	R	3,000	6.8
Horizon Blue Cross & Blue Shield	PO Box 200145	Newark	NJ	07102		973-466-4000	P	3,000	3.6
Bankers Life and Casualty Co.	222 Merch Mart	Chicago	IL	60654	Stephen Hilbert	312-396-6000	S	2,619*	1.5
Mercy Health Services	34605 12 Mile Rd	Farmington Hills	MI	48331	Judy Pelham	248-489-6000	R	2,534	26.4
Family & Business Insurance	P O Box 1138	Baltimore	MD	21203	Douglas Leatherdale	410-547-3000	S	2,389*	1.0
Delta Dental Plan of California	P O Box 7736	San Francisco	CA	94120	William T Ward	415-972-8300	R	2,278*	2.0
Blue Shield of California	P O Box 7168	San Francisco	CA	94120	Wayne R Moon	415-229-5000	R	2,250*	3.5
Trigon Healthcare Inc.	P O Box 27401	Richmond	VA	23279	Norwood H Davis	804-354-7000	P	2,236	3.7
Amalgamated Life Insurance Co.	730 Broadway	New York	NY	10003	Ronald L Minikes	212-539-5000	R	2,228*	0.5
Blue Cross & Blue Shield	10455 Mill Run Cir	Owings Mills	MD	21117	William L Jews	410-581-3000	R	2,111*	5.0
UICI	4001 McEwen Dr	Dallas	TX	75244	Gregory T Mutz	972-392-6700	P	2,088	4.0
New Hampshire-Vermont Health	3000 Goffs Falls Rd	Manchester	NH	03111	David Jensen	603-695-7000	R	2,063*	0.9
Regence Group	P O Box 1271	Portland	OR	97207	Richard L Woolworth	503-225-5221	R	2,049*	6.8
Blue Cross & Blue Shield	P O Box 1991	Wilmington	DE	19899	Paul King Jr	302-421-3000	R	1,853*	0.8
Fortis Insurance Co.	P O Box 3050	Milwaukee	WI	53201	Ben Cutler	414-271-3011	S	1,841*	2.0
American National Insurance Co.	1 Moody Plz	Galveston	TX	77550	Robert L Moody	409-763-4661	P	1,753	4.4

Source: Ward's Business Directory of U.S. Private and Public Companies, Volumes 1 and 2, 2000. The company type code used is as follows: P - Public, R - Private, S - Subsidiary, D - Division, J - Joint Venture, A - Affiliate, G - Group, N - Company type not reported. Sales are in millions of dollars, employees are in thousands. An asterisk (*) indicates an estimated sales volume. The symbol < stands for 'less than'. Company names and addresses are truncated, in some cases, to fit into the available space.

LOCATION BY STATE AND REGIONAL CONCENTRATION

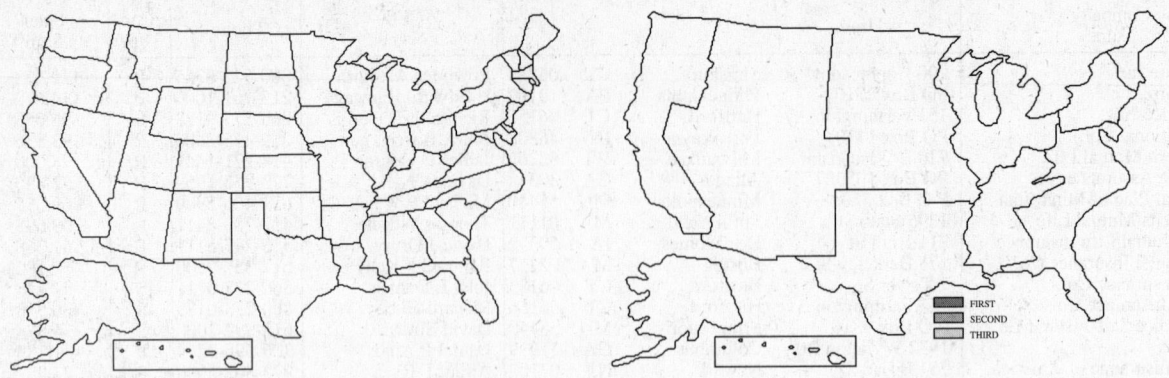

FIRST
SECOND
THIRD

INDUSTRY DATA BY STATE

State	Establishments Total (number)	% of U.S.	Employment Total (number)	% of U.S.	Per Estab.	Payroll Total ($ mil.)	Per Empl. ($)	Revenues Total ($ mil.)	% of U.S.	Per Estab. ($)
New Hampshire	16	0.5	2,454	0.7	153	86.8	35,374	-	-	-
Hawaii	28	0.9	1,907	0.6	68	69.9	36,677	-	-	-
Georgia	78	2.4	4,575	1.4	59	188.7	41,243	-	-	-
New Mexico	19	0.6	1,133	0.3	60	35.7	31,531	-	-	-
Michigan	95	3.0	12,884	3.9	136	547.2	42,474	-	-	-
Texas	212	6.6	14,143	4.3	67	519.2	36,713	-	-	-
Delaware	14	0.4	1,419	0.4	101	56.4	39,729	-	-	-
Virginia	52	1.6	5,595	1.7	108	213.9	38,227	-	-	-
Wisconsin	100	3.1	10,901	3.3	109	323.6	29,685	-	-	-
Arkansas	28	0.9	1,877	0.6	67	67.6	35,992	-	-	-
Ohio	124	3.9	8,065	2.5	65	316.6	39,252	-	-	-
Minnesota	58	1.8	8,945	2.7	154	331.3	37,042	-	-	-
Wyoming	15	0.5	175*	-	-	(D)	-	-	-	-
California	315	9.8	43,575	13.3	138	1,843.3	42,302	-	-	-
Pennsylvania	132	4.1	25,996	7.9	197	1,005.6	38,681	-	-	-
New Jersey	77	2.4	8,710	2.7	113	379.3	43,544	-	-	-
Idaho	18	0.6	750*	-	-	(D)	-	-	-	-
Utah	20	0.6	2,133	0.7	107	70.3	32,977	-	-	-
Arizona	93	2.9	5,084	1.6	55	207.4	40,788	-	-	-
Kentucky	69	2.2	5,040	1.5	73	166.5	33,039	-	-	-
South Carolina	29	0.9	7,129	2.2	246	180.6	25,331	-	-	-
South Dakota	16	0.5	375*	-	-	(D)	-	-	-	-
North Carolina	64	2.0	5,624	1.7	88	223.3	39,713	-	-	-
Tennessee	72	2.2	8,190	2.5	114	294.7	35,989	-	-	-
Maryland	61	1.9	6,051	1.8	99	214.6	35,465	-	-	-
Nebraska	23	0.7	2,523	0.8	110	71.2	28,239	-	-	-
Oregon	47	1.5	4,665	1.4	99	178.4	38,241	-	-	-
Montana	11	0.3	750*	-	-	(D)	-	-	-	-
Maine	13	0.4	1,750*	-	-	59.3	-	-	-	-
Massachusetts	68	2.1	10,711	3.3	158	458.1	42,769	-	-	-
Connecticut	36	1.1	7,766	2.4	216	381.7	49,144	-	-	-
Indiana	45	1.4	2,982	0.9	66	116.5	39,058	-	-	-
Louisiana	41	1.3	2,490	0.8	61	84.7	34,034	-	-	-
Florida	317	9.9	20,873	6.4	66	788.4	37,770	-	-	-
Washington	58	1.8	6,930	2.1	119	254.3	36,690	-	-	-
Colorado	55	1.7	3,937	1.2	72	150.2	38,162	-	-	-
North Dakota	13	0.4	1,750*	-	-	(D)	-	-	-	-
Mississippi	30	0.9	1,029	0.3	34	34.9	33,934	-	-	-
Illinois	170	5.3	13,496	4.1	79	584.3	43,292	-	-	-
Oklahoma	23	0.7	2,114	0.6	92	71.0	33,571	-	-	-
Nevada	35	1.1	1,213	0.4	35	36.6	30,165	-	-	-
New York	164	5.1	26,036	7.9	159	986.2	37,878	-	-	-
Iowa	41	1.3	3,161	1.0	77	98.8	31,240	-	-	-
Vermont	7	0.2	375*	-	-	(D)	-	-	-	-
West Virginia	14	0.4	1,349	0.4	96	35.5	26,281	-	-	-
Rhode Island	8	0.2	2,078	0.6	260	80.1	38,571	-	-	-
Alabama	51	1.6	3,750*	-	-	163.0	-	-	-	-
Missouri	94	2.9	8,418	2.6	90	330.9	39,306	-	-	-
Kansas	24	0.7	3,750*	-	-	(D)	-	-	-	-
D.C.	15	0.5	1,911	0.6	127	93.2	48,761	-	-	-

Source: 1997 *Economic Census*. The states are in descending order of revenues or establishments (if revenue data are missing for the majority). The symbol (D) appears when data are withheld to prevent disclosure of competitive information. States marked with (D) are sorted by number of establishments. A dash (-) indicates that the data element cannot be calculated. * indicates the midpoint of a range; 175, for example is the range 100-249. Shaded *states* on the state map indicate those states which have proportionately greater representation in the industry than would be indicated by the state's population; the ratio is based on total revenues or number of establishments. Shaded *regions* indicate where the industry is regionally most concentrated.

NAICS 524126 - DIRECT PROPERTY AND CASUALTY INSURANCE CARRIERS

GENERAL STATISTICS

Year	Establishments (number)	Employment (number)	Payroll ($ million)	Revenues ($ million)	Employees per Establishment (number)	Revenues per Establishment ($)	Payroll per Employee ($)
1997	20,903	639,751	28,655.0	299,236.0	30.6	14,315,457	44,791

Source: Economic Census of the United States, 1997. This is a newly defined industry. Data for prior years were unavailable at the time of publication but may become available over time.

INDICES OF CHANGE

Year	Establishments (number)	Employment (number)	Payroll ($ million)	Revenues ($ million)	Employees per Establishment (number)	Revenues per Establishment ($)	Payroll per Employee ($)
1997	100.0	100.0	100.0	100.0	100.0	100.0	100.0

Sources: Same as General Statistics. The values shown reflect change from the base year, 1997. Values above 100 mean greater than 1997, values below 100 mean less than 1997, and a value of 100 in the 1982-96 or 1998-2001 period means same as 1997. Values followed by a 'p' are projections by the editors; 'e' stands for extrapolation. Data are the most recent available at this level of detail.

SIC INDUSTRIES RELATED TO NAICS 524126

Each new NAICS code represents an industry that used to be part of an SIC or a part of several SIC industries. Data in this table are shown to provide transitional information for these cases. All available data for the precursor SIC(s) are shown. Even if only a part of an SIC is included in the NAICS, *all* data for the SIC are reproduced. If the SIC industry is not marked as being a part (pt) of the NAICS, the entire industry is embedded in the NAICS data. The SIC composition of the new industry provides some hints of the relative importance of its "ancestors." Data marked with a 'p' are projected. Projections begin with 1982 data. Data earlier than 1990 are not shown but are reflected in the projections.

SIC	Industry	1990	1991	1992	1993	1994	1995	1996	1997
6331	**Fire, Marine, and Casualty Insurance (pt)**								
	Establishments (number)	-	-	19,002	-	-	-	-	-
	Employment (thousands)	-	-	588.3	-	-	-	-	-
	Revenues ($ million)	-	-	258,394.7	-	-	-	-	-
6351	**Surety Insurance (pt)**								
	Establishments (number)	-	-	548	-	-	-	-	-
	Employment (thousands)	-	-	11.2	-	-	-	-	-
	Revenues ($ million)	-	-	4,005.4	-	-	-	-	-

Source: Economic Census of the United States, 1992, annual surveys of economic sectors conducted by the Bureau of the Census, and estimates or projections based on the 1982-1992 period; not all data are shown. 'e' marks estimates made by the editors; 'p' indicates projections based on time series. A dash (-) indicates that data for this SIC or year were not available. The abbreviation (pt) next to the industry name indicates that only a part of the industry is present within the NAICS data. If no (pt) is shown, the entire industry is contained within the NAICS data.

SELECTED RATIOS

For 1997	Avg. of Information	Analyzed Industry	Index	For 1997	Avg. of Information	Analyzed Industry	Index
Employees per establishment	15	31	207	Payroll per establishment	669,406	1,370,856	205
Revenue per establishment	5,561,120	14,315,457	257	Payroll as % of revenue	12	10	80
Revenue per employee	376,639	467,738	124	Payroll per employee	45,337	44,791	99

Sources: Same as General Statistics. The 'Average' column represents the average for the industry sector, in 1997, where the currently shown industry is classified. The Index shows the relationship between the Average and the Analyzed Industry. For example, 100 means that they are equal; 500 that the Analyzed Industry is five times the average; 50 means that the Analyzed Industry is half the national average. The abbreviation 'na' is used to show that data are 'not available'.

LEADING COMPANIES   Number shown: **75**   Total sales ($ mil): **14,417,462**   Total employment (000): **1,479.9**

Company Name	Address				CEO Name	Phone	Co. Type	Sales ($ mil)	Empl. (000)
Gates, McDonald and Co.	3455 MIll Run Dr	Hilliard	OH	43026	Danny M. Fullerton	614-777-3000	S	11,082,900	1.5
Citigroup Inc.	399 Park Ave	New York	NY	10043	John S Reed	212-559-1000	P	668,641	173.7
General Electric Capital Services	260 Long Ridge Rd	Stamford	CT	06927	D D Dammerman	203-357-6978	S	303,980	83.0
American International Group Inc.	70 Pine St	New York	NY	10270	Maurice R Greenberg	212-770-7000	P	267,000	40.0
General Electric Capital Corp.	260 Long Ridge Rd	Stamford	CT	06927	Gary C Wendt	203-357-4000	S	228,777	51.0
Hartford Financial Services Group	690 Asylum Ave	Hartford	CT	06115	Ramani Ayer	860-547-5000	P	135,000	25.0
General Motors Acceptance Corp.	3044 W Grand Blvd	Detroit	MI	48202	JM Losh	313-556-5000	S	131,417	23.6
American General Corp.	PO Box 3247	Houston	TX	77253	Robert M Devlin	713-522-1111	P	105,000	16.1
Lincoln National Corp.	PO Box 1110	Fort Wayne	IN	46802	Jon A Boscia	219-455-2000	P	93,836	8.0
Allstate Insurance Co.	2775 Sanders Rd	Northbrook	IL	60062	Jerry D Choate	847-402-5000	S	77,291*	50.0
State Farm Mutual Automobile	1 State Farm Plz	Bloomington	IL	61710	Edward B Rust Jr	309-766-2311	R	75,579	76.3
Loews Corp.	667 Madison Ave	New York	NY	10021	James S Tisch	212-521-2000	P	73,300	34.3
CNA Financial Corp.	CNA Plz	Chicago	IL	60685	Philip L Engel	312-822-5000	P	62,359	23.6
Berkshire Hathaway Inc.	1440 Kiewit Plz	Omaha	NE	68131	Warren E Buffett	402-346-1400	P	58,742*	45.0
Transamerica Corp.	600 Montgomery St	San Francisco	CA	94111	Frank C Herringer	415-983-4000	S	58,503	9.2
Employers Reinsurance Corp.	P O Box 2991	Shaw Msn	KS	66201	Kaj Ahlmann	913-676-5200	S	57,817*	4.2
Hartford Fire Insurance Co.	690 Asylum Ave	Hartford	CT	06115	Ramani Ayer	860-547-5000	S	53,128*	22.0
United Services Automobile	9800 Fredricksburg	San Antonio	TX	78288	Robert Herres	210-498-2211	R	52,000*	17.0
Liberty Mutual Insurance Co.	175 Berkeley St	Boston	MA	02117	Edmund F Kelly	617-357-9500	R	50,192	23.0
General Reinsurance Corp.	P O Box 10351	Stamford	CT	06904	James Gustafson	203-328-5000	S	41,459	3.9
Travelers Insurance Co.	1 Tower Sq	Hartford	CT	06183	John E Daniels	860-277-0111	S	41,243	0.0
St. Paul Companies Inc.	385 Washington St	St. Paul	MN	55102	James E Gustafson	612-310-7911	P	38,300	14.0
Nationwide Corp.	1 Nationwide Plz	Columbus	OH	43216	Diamond McFerson	614-249-7111	S	38,108*	8.0
National Indemnity Co.	3024 Harney St	Omaha	NE	68131	Donald F Wurster	402-536-3000	S	28,034*	0.3
Cincinnati Insurance Co.	P O Box 145496	Cincinnati	OH	45250	Robert B Morgan	513-870-2000	S	28,000	2.5
Travelers Casualty and Surety Co.	1 Tower Sq	Hartford	CT	06153	Jay S Fishman	860-277-0111	P	27,000*	200.0
Fireman's Fund Insurance Co.	777 San Marin Dr	Novato	CA	94998	Herbert Hanemeyer	415-899-3600	S	26,732*	9.8
Nationwide Mutual Insurance Co.	1 Nationwide Plz	Columbus	OH	43216	D Richard McFerson	614-249-7111	R	25,301	32.8
Hanover Insurance Co.	100 North Pkwy	Worcester	MA	01605	John F O'Brien	508-853-7200	S	24,500	5.0
Jefferson-Pilot Corp.	PO Box 21008	Greensboro	NC	27420	David A Stonecipher	336-691-3000	P	24,338	2.2
Alistar Insurance Co.	616 P St	Fresno	CA	93721	Howard Lamb	559-495-3200	R	22,000*	<0.1
Chubb Executive Risk Inc.	PO Box 1615	Plainfield	NJ	07061	Dean R O'Hare	908-903-2000	P	20,746	9.5
AEGON USA Inc.	1111 N Charles St	Baltimore	MD	21201	Donald J Shepard	410-576-4571	S	20,330*	11.3
Continental Casualty Co.	CNA Plz	Chicago	IL	60685	Phillip L Engel	312-822-5000	D	19,512	0.0
Xerox Corp.	800 Long Ridge Rd	Stamford	CT	06904	Paul A Allaire	203-968-3000	P	19,220	94.6
ING North America Insurance	5780 Powers Ferry	Atlanta	GA	30327	R Glenn Hilliard	770-980-3300	S	17,178*	3.8
Lawley Service Insurance	120 Delaware Ave	Buffalo	NY	14202	William J Lawley Sr	716-849-8618	R	16,000*	0.2
American Financial Corp.	1 E 4th St	Cincinnati	OH	45202	Carl H Lindner	513-579-2121	P	15,700	9.0
Halliburton Co.	3600 Lincoln Plaza	Dallas	TX	75201	Williams Bradford	214-978-2600	P	14,898	107.8
State Farm Fire and Casualty Co.	1 State Farm Plz	Bloomington	IL	61710	Edward B Rust Jr	309-766-1972	S	14,317*	13.4
Reliance Insurance Co.	4 Penn Center Plz	Philadelphia	PA	19103	Robert M Steinberg	215-864-4000	S	13,565*	5.5
MBIA	113 King St	Armonk	NY	10504	Gary Dunton	914-273-4545	S	12,340*	<0.1
Market Agency Markets	P O Box 507	Keene	NH	03431		603-352-3221	R	12,309*	5.0
MBIA Inc.	113 King St	Armonk	NY	10504	Joseph W Brown, Jr	914-273-4545	P	11,797	0.9
Deere and Co.	1 John Deere Pl	Moline	IL	61265	Hans W Becherer	309-765-8000	P	11,522	38.7
Torchmark Corp.	2001 3rd Ave S	Birmingham	AL	35233	CB Hudson	205-325-4200	P	11,249	4.1
Cincinnati Financial Corp.	PO Box 145496	Cincinnati	OH	45250	John J Schliff	513-870-2000	P	11,087	2.8
MBIA Insurance Corp.	113 King St	Armonk	NY	10504	David H Elliott	914-273-4545	S	9,810	0.4
American Re-Insurance Co.	555 College Rd E	Princeton	NJ	08543	Edward J Noonan	609-243-4200	S	8,622	1.5
Ohio Casualty Group Corp.	9450 Seaward Rd	Fairfield	OH	45014	Coy Leonard	513-867-3000	S	8,447*	3.5
Government Employees Insurance	1 Geico Plz	Washington	DC	20076	Olza M Nicely	202-986-3000	S	7,700	11.5
Fremont General Corp.	2020 Santa Monica	Santa Monica	CA	90404	James A McIntyre	310-315-5500	P	7,370	3.2
GEICO Corp.	1 GEICO Plz	Washington	DC	20076	Olza M Nicely	202-986-3000	S	7,351*	10.5
Farmers Insurance Exchange	P O Box 2478	Los Angeles	CA	90051	Martin D Feinstein	213-932-3200	S	7,205*	17.5
State Compensation Insurance	P O Box 420807	San Francisco	CA	94142	Kenneth C Bollier	415-565-1234	R	7,175*	6.5
Old Republic International Corp.	307 N Michigan Ave	Chicago	IL	60601	AC Zucaro	312-346-8100	P	7,020	6.6
Ingram Industries Inc.	P O Box 23049	Nashville	TN	37202	Martha Ingram	615-298-8200	R	6,930*	6.3
SAFECO Corp.	SAFECO Plz	Seattle	WA	98185	Boh A Dickey	206-545-5000	P	6,866	11.0
Chubb Corp.	15 Mountainview Rd	Warren	NJ	07059	John J Degnan	908-903-2000	P	6,350	10.7
Anthem Insurance Companies Inc.	120 Monument Cir	Indianapolis	IN	46204	L Ben Lytle	317-488-6000	R	6,299	15.0
Harleysville Mutual Insurance Co.	355 Maple Ave	Harleysville	PA	19438	Walter R Bateman II	215-256-5000	R	6,164*	2.5
Unitrin Inc.	1 E Wacker Dr	Chicago	IL	60601	Richard C Vie	312-661-4600	P	6,099	7.8
Fremont Compensation Insurance	PO Box 7928	San Francisco	CA	94120	James Little	415-362-3333	S	6,091	2.8
Employers General Insurance	1601 Elm St	Dallas	TX	75201	Robert Ramsower	214-665-6100	S	6,042*	2.5
Royal and SunAlliance USA	P O Box 1000	Charlotte	NC	28201	Robert V Mendelsohn	704-522-2000	S	5,320*	3.8
Mutual Savings Life Insurance Co.	P O Box 2222	Decatur	AL	35609	Don A Johnson	256-552-7011	P	5,298*	1.1
The Progressive Corp.	6300 Wilson Mills	Mayfield Village	OH	44143	Peter B Lewis	440-461-5000	P	5,292	15.7
Transatlantic Reinsurance Co.	80 Pine St	New York	NY	10005	Robert F Orlich	212-770-2000	S	5,111*	0.4
Allianz Insurance Co.	P O Box 7780	Burbank	CA	91510	Wolfgang Schlink	818-972-8000	S	5,100	0.4
GMAC Insurance Holdings Inc.	3044 W Grand Blvd	Detroit	MI	48202	William B Noll	313-556-5000	S	5,100	4.2
PennCorp Financial Group Inc.	717 N Harwood St	Dallas	TX	75201	Keith A Maib	214-954-7111	P	4,724	1.4
Employers Insurance of Wausau A	PO Box 8017	Wausau	WI	54402	Dwight Davis	715-845-5211	R	4,700*	5.0
Lumbermens Mutual Casualty Co.	1 Kemper Dr	Long Grove	IL	60049	William D Smith	847-320-2000	R	4,400	9.5
Horace Mann Educators Corp.	1 Horace Mann Plz	Springfield	IL	62715	Louis G Lower II	217-789-2500	P	4,395	2.8
Orion Capital Corp.	9 Farm Sprgs Rd	Farmington	CT	06032	W Marston Becker	860-674-6600	P	4,164	4.1

Source: Ward's Business Directory of U.S. Private and Public Companies, Volumes 1 and 2, 2000. The company type code used is as follows: P - Public, R - Private, S - Subsidiary, D - Division, J - Joint Venture, A - Affiliate, G - Group, N - Company type not reported. Sales are in millions of dollars, employees are in thousands. An asterisk (*) indicates an estimated sales volume. The symbol < stands for 'less than'. Company names and addresses are truncated, in some cases, to fit into the available space.

LOCATION BY STATE AND REGIONAL CONCENTRATION

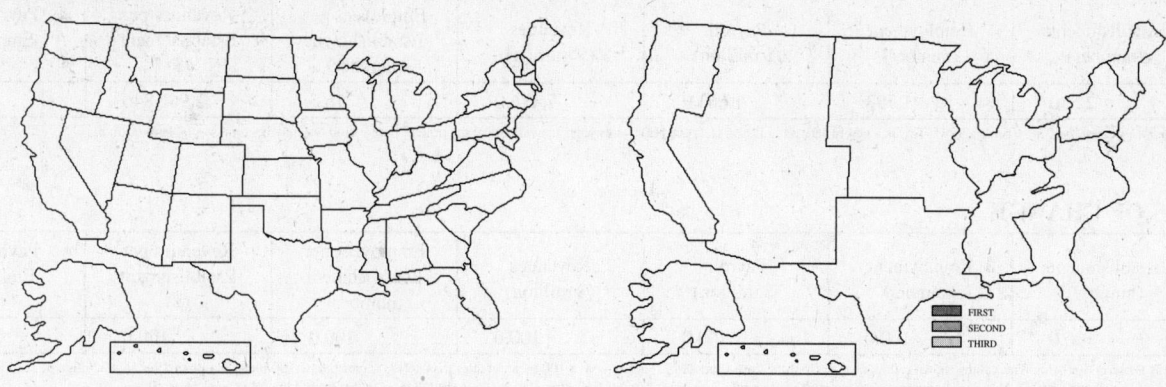

INDUSTRY DATA BY STATE

| State | Establishments | | Employment | | | Payroll | | Revenues | | |
	Total (number)	% of U.S.	Total (number)	% of U.S.	Per Estab.	Total ($ mil.)	Per Empl. ($)	Total ($ mil.)	% of U.S.	Per Estab. ($)
Hawaii	57	0.3	1,084	0.2	19	53.3	49,129	-	-	-
Maryland	463	2.2	17,500*	-	-	(D)	-	-	-	-
Utah	168	0.8	2,345	0.4	14	85.7	36,566	-	-	-
Rhode Island	73	0.3	3,750*	-	-	(D)	-	-	-	-
Kansas	234	1.1	7,319	1.1	31	303.1	41,410	-	-	-
New Jersey	430	2.1	25,228	3.9	59	1,283.3	50,870	-	-	-
Mississippi	136	0.7	2,648	0.4	19	95.2	35,964	-	-	-
Maine	96	0.5	1,750*	-	-	(D)	-	-	-	-
Wyoming	26	0.1	175*	-	-	(D)	-	-	-	-
Louisiana	354	1.7	5,442	0.9	15	234.5	43,087	-	-	-
Arkansas	159	0.8	1,267	0.2	8	49.2	38,870	-	-	-
South Carolina	206	1.0	3,750*	-	-	(D)	-	-	-	-
Kentucky	267	1.3	2,792	0.4	10	109.6	39,271	-	-	-
New Mexico	114	0.5	750*	-	-	(D)	-	-	-	-
Ohio	975	4.7	36,322	5.7	37	1,515.3	41,719	-	-	-
Delaware	53	0.3	1,750*	-	-	(D)	-	-	-	-
Colorado	351	1.7	9,561	1.5	27	402.6	42,114	-	-	-
North Carolina	560	2.7	15,684	2.5	28	669.7	42,703	-	-	-
New Hampshire	116	0.6	3,750*	-	-	(D)	-	-	-	-
Oregon	316	1.5	8,181	1.3	26	329.8	40,315	-	-	-
Missouri	432	2.1	11,466	1.8	27	435.1	37,950	-	-	-
Pennsylvania	951	4.5	37,565	5.9	40	1,522.3	40,523	-	-	-
New York	1,522	7.3	43,762	6.8	29	2,287.4	52,270	-	-	-
Oklahoma	260	1.2	5,277	0.8	20	201.1	38,114	-	-	-
Idaho	127	0.6	1,266	0.2	10	44.9	35,431	-	-	-
Minnesota	390	1.9	15,099	2.4	39	630.3	41,747	-	-	-
Alabama	586	2.8	5,936	0.9	10	252.7	42,566	-	-	-
North Dakota	64	0.3	1,750*	-	-	(D)	-	-	-	-
Nebraska	134	0.6	7,064	1.1	53	260.1	36,814	-	-	-
Florida	1,381	6.6	27,622	4.3	20	1,093.1	39,574	-	-	-
Illinois	1,179	5.6	50,667	7.9	43	2,659.4	52,488	-	-	-
Vermont	59	0.3	750*	-	-	(D)	-	-	-	-
Texas	1,689	8.1	43,416	6.8	26	1,903.5	43,843	-	-	-
Washington	506	2.4	10,176	1.6	20	464.8	45,677	-	-	-
Virginia	593	2.8	15,339	2.4	26	587.9	38,329	-	-	-
Indiana	476	2.3	17,500*	-	-	(D)	-	-	-	-
Alaska	48	0.2	375*	-	-	(D)	-	-	-	-
Michigan	816	3.9	21,820	3.4	27	1,002.1	45,926	-	-	-
Iowa	262	1.3	7,500*	-	-	(D)	-	-	-	-
California	1,412	6.8	65,203	10.2	46	3,102.7	47,586	-	-	-
Massachusetts	207	1.0	18,174	2.8	88	804.9	44,287	-	-	-
Nevada	155	0.7	757	0.1	5	40.6	53,571	-	-	-
Arizona	377	1.8	8,494	1.3	23	353.7	41,645	-	-	-
Montana	76	0.4	375*	-	-	(D)	-	-	-	-
Wisconsin	415	2.0	17,561	2.7	42	682.2	38,848	-	-	-
D.C.	33	0.2	375*	-	-	(D)	-	-	-	-
Tennessee	413	2.0	8,328	1.3	20	339.6	40,773	-	-	-
West Virginia	104	0.5	1,175	0.2	11	49.8	42,345	-	-	-
Connecticut	391	1.9	32,248	5.0	82	1,695.3	52,570	-	-	-
South Dakota	68	0.3	1,075	0.2	16	34.0	31,609	-	-	-
Georgia	623	3.0	18,325	2.9	29	817.8	44,626	-	-	-

Source: 1997 *Economic Census*. The states are in descending order of revenues or establishments (if revenue data are missing for the majority). The symbol (D) appears when data are withheld to prevent disclosure of competitive information. States marked with (D) are sorted by number of establishments. A dash (-) indicates that the data element cannot be calculated. * indicates the midpoint of a range; 175, for example is the range 100-249. Shaded *states* on the state map indicate those states which have proportionately greater representation in the industry than would be indicated by the state's population; the ratio is based on total revenues or number of establishments. Shaded *regions* indicate where the industry is regionally most concentrated.

NAICS 524127 - DIRECT TITLE INSURANCE CARRIERS

GENERAL STATISTICS

Year	Establishments (number)	Employment (number)	Payroll ($ million)	Revenues ($ million)	Employees per Establishment (number)	Revenues per Establishment ($)	Payroll per Employee ($)
1997	2,530	41,793	1,663.0	7,496.0	16.5	2,962,846	39,791

Source: Economic Census of the United States, 1997. This is a newly defined industry. Data for prior years were unavailable at the time of publication but may become available over time.

INDICES OF CHANGE

Year	Establishments (number)	Employment (number)	Payroll ($ million)	Revenues ($ million)	Employees per Establishment (number)	Revenues per Establishment ($)	Payroll per Employee ($)
1997	100.0	100.0	100.0	100.0	100.0	100.0	100.0

Sources: Same as General Statistics. The values shown reflect change from the base year, 1997. Values above 100 mean greater than 1997, values below 100 mean less than 1997, and a value of 100 in the 1982-96 or 1998-2001 period means same as 1997. Values followed by a 'p' are projections by the editors; 'e' stands for extrapolation. Data are the most recent available at this level of detail.

SIC INDUSTRIES RELATED TO NAICS 524127

Each new NAICS code represents an industry that used to be part of an SIC or a part of several SIC industries. Data in this table are shown to provide transitional information for these cases. All available data for the precursor SIC(s) are shown. Even if only a part of an SIC is included in the NAICS, *all* data for the SIC are reproduced. If the SIC industry is not marked as being a part (pt) of the NAICS, the entire industry is embedded in the NAICS data. The SIC composition of the new industry provides some hints of the relative importance of its "ancestors." Data marked with a 'p' are projected. Projections begin with 1982 data. Data earlier than 1990 are not shown but are reflected in the projections.

SIC	Industry	1990	1991	1992	1993	1994	1995	1996	1997
6361	**Title Insurance (pt)**								
	Establishments (number)	-	-	1,532	-	-	-	-	-
	Employment (thousands)	-	-	34.5	-	-	-	-	-
	Revenues ($ million)	-	-	4,883.6	-	-	-	-	-

Source: Economic Census of the United States, 1992, annual surveys of economic sectors conducted by the Bureau of the Census, and estimates or projections based on the 1982-1992 period; not all data are shown. 'e' marks estimates made by the editors; 'p' indicates projections based on time series. A dash (-) indicates that data for this SIC or year were not available. The abbreviation (pt) next to the industry name indicates that only a part of the industry is present within the NAICS data. If no (pt) is shown, the entire industry is contained within the NAICS data.

SELECTED RATIOS

For 1997	Avg. of Information	Analyzed Industry	Index	For 1997	Avg. of Information	Analyzed Industry	Index
Employees per establishment	15	17	112	Payroll per establishment	669,406	657,312	98
Revenue per establishment	5,561,120	2,962,846	53	Payroll as % of revenue	12	22	184
Revenue per employee	376,639	179,360	48	Payroll per employee	45,337	39,791	88

Sources: Same as General Statistics. The 'Average' column represents the average for the industry sector, in 1997, where the currently shown industry is classified. The Index shows the relationship between the Average and the Analyzed Industry. For example, 100 means that they are equal; 500 that the Analyzed Industry is five times the average; 50 means that the Analyzed Industry is half the national average. The abbreviation 'na' is used to show that data are 'not available'.

LEADING COMPANIES   Number shown: **49**   Total sales ($ mil): **32,721**   Total employment (000): **116.1**

Company Name	Address				CEO Name	Phone	Co. Type	Sales ($ mil)	Empl. (000)
Old Republic International Corp.	307 N Michigan Ave	Chicago	IL	60601	A.C. Zucaro	312-346-8100	P	7,020	6.6
Unitrin Inc.	1 E Wacker Dr	Chicago	IL	60601	Richard C Vie	312-661-4600	P	6,099	7.8
Reliance Group Holdings Inc.	55 E 52nd St	New York	NY	10055	Robert M Steinberg	212-909-1100	P	3,391	6.6
Lennar Corp.	700 NW 107th Ave	Miami	FL	33172	Leonard Miller	305-559-4000	P	3,119	4.1
First American Title Insurance Co.	114 E 5th St	Santa Ana	CA	92701	Gary L Kermott	714-558-3211	S	2,063	14.3
Chicago Title and Trust Co.	171 N Clark St	Chicago	IL	60601	John Rau	312-630-2000	P	2,059	10.6
LandAmerica Financial Group Inc.	101 Gateway Centre	Richmond	VA	23235	Charles H Foster Jr	804-267-8000	P	1,692	10.3
Fidelity National Financial Inc.	3916 State St	Santa Barbara	CA	93105	William P Foley II	805-563-1566	P	1,289	7.4
Stewart Title Guaranty Co.	1980 Post Oak Blvd	Houston	TX	77056	Malcolm Morris	713-625-8136	S	969	4.8
Lennar Title Services Inc.	700 N W 107th Ave	Miami	FL	33172	Stuart A Miller	305-559-4000	S	938*	3.0
Alleghany Corp.	375 Park Ave	New York	NY	10152	John J Burns Jr	212-752-1356	P	919	2.9
Lawyers Title Insurance Corp.	P O Box 27567	Richmond	VA	23261	Charles H Foster Jr	804-281-6700	S	555	3.8
Stewart Information Services Corp	PO Box 2029	Houston	TX	77252	Carloss Morris	713-625-8100	P	499	5.6
Republic Financial Services Inc.	PO Box 660560	Dallas	TX	75266	Bruce Milligan	214-559-1222	R	458*	0.5
Chicago Title Insurance Co.	171 N Clark St	Chicago	IL	60601	John Rou	312-630-2000	S	312*	1.0
Old Republic National Title	400 2nd Ave S	Minneapolis	MN	55401	Dick Cecchettini	612-371-1111	S	300*	1.2
Old Republic Title Co.	350 California Street	San Francisco	CA	94104	Michael Trudeau	415-421-3500	S	190*	1.2
Futura Corp. (Boise, Idaho)	P O Box 7968	Boise	ID	83707	Brent S Lloyd	208-336-0150	R	120*	0.6
Gateway Title Co.	1450 NS Fernando	Burbank	CA	91504	Norman Burlingame	818-953-2300	R	82	0.3
Alliance Title Co.	901 Campisi Way	Campbell	CA	95008		408-288-7800	R	78*	0.3
First American Title Insurance	200 SW Market	Portland	OR	97201	Chuck O'Rourke	503-222-3651	S	53*	0.2
Lawyers Title of Arizona Inc.	40 E Mitchell Dr	Phoenix	AZ	85012	Dan Robledo	602-248-0882	S	50*	0.2
Investors Title Co.	PO Drawer 2687	Chapel Hill	NC	27515	J Allen Fine	919-968-2200	P	48	0.2
South Coast Title Co.	4401 N Atlantic	Long Beach	CA	90807	Donald J Daly	562-422-0045	S	47*	0.2
Investors Title Insurance Co.	121 N Columbia St	Chapel Hill	NC	27514	J Allen Fine	919-968-2200	S	39*	0.2
Southwest Land Title Co.	500 N Akard St	Dallas	TX	75201	William G Moize	214-720-1020	R	38*	0.1
North Star Title Inc.	5075 Wayzata Blvd	Minneapolis	MN	55416	David Carnes	612-545-1041	S	37*	0.1
Southland Title Corp.	7530 N Glenoaks	Burbank	CA	91504	David Cronenbold	818-841-0666	R	36*	0.2
Beach Abstract and Guaranty Co.	P O Box 2580	Little Rock	AR	72203	George Pitts Jr	501-376-3301	R	29*	<0.1
Attorneys Title Insurance Fund	P O Box 628600	Orlando	FL	32862	Charles J Kovaleski	407-240-3863	R	27*	0.7
Financial Title Co.	701 Miller St	San Jose	CA	95110		408-288-7800	R	25*	<0.1
Monroe Title Insurance Corp.	47 W Main St	Rochester	NY	14614	Thomas P Moonan	716-232-2070	R	20	0.2
Northern Counties Title Insurance	4401 N Atlantic	Long Beach	CA	90807	Roy E Hearrean	562-422-7425	S	18	0.3
Fidelity National Title Insurance	2 Park Ave	New York	NY	10016		212-481-5858	S	14*	0.1
Commerce Land Title Inc.	114 W Glenview Dr	San Antonio	TX	78228	Greg Lyssy	210-736-1700	R	14*	<0.1
Ticor Title Agency of San Antonio	10010 San Pedro St	San Antonio	TX	78216	Jack Rogers	210-340-2921	R	14*	<0.1
Fidelity National Title	3500 188th St S W	Lynnwood	WA	98037	Chet Hodgson	425-771-3031	S	12*	0.1
Bay Title and Abstract Inc.	P O Box 173	Green Bay	WI	54305	John May	920-431-6100	R	11*	<0.1
Security Union Title Insurance Co.	535 N Brand Blvd	Glendale	CA	91203		626-821-1100	S	9*	<0.1
Old Republic Title of Texas	150 N Main St	Conroe	TX	77301	Linda Hawthornem	409-441-3121	R	6*	<0.1
Fidelity Title Co.	3115 W Parker Rd	Plano	TX	75023	John T Edwards	972-596-5000	R	4*	<0.1
Texas State Title	10000 Mem Dr	Houston	TX	77024	Steve Vallone	713-680-1155	D	4*	<0.1
Lawyers Title of North Carolina	201 S College	Charlotte	NC	28244	David A Baum	704-377-0093	S	3*	<0.1
Safeco Land Title Co.	777 Main St	Fort Worth	TX	76102	Jeff Davis	817-877-1481	R	3*	<0.1
First American Title of Utah	330 E 400 South	Salt Lake City	UT	84111	Gary Kermott	801-363-5841	S	3	20.0
Commerce Land Title	700 Highlander	Arlington	TX	76015	Karren P Bates	817-784-0101	S	2*	<0.1
Fort Bend Title Co.	600 Morton St	Richmond	TX	77469	Stanley Speer Jr	281-342-4657	S	2*	<0.1
Title Company Inc.	PO Box 578	La Crosse	WI	54602	Michael F Wille	608-791-2000	R	2*	<0.1
TITLETRUST Incorporated	PO Box 2228	Tampa	FL	33601	Carolyn Faulkner	813-933-8433	R	1	<0.1

Source: Ward's Business Directory of U.S. Private and Public Companies, Volumes 1 and 2, 2000. The company type code used is as follows: P - Public, R - Private, S - Subsidiary, D - Division, J - Joint Venture, A - Affiliate, G - Group, N - Company type not reported. Sales are in millions of dollars, employees are in thousands. An asterisk (*) indicates an estimated sales volume. The symbol < stands for 'less than'. Company names and addresses are truncated, in some cases, to fit into the available space.

LOCATION BY STATE AND REGIONAL CONCENTRATION

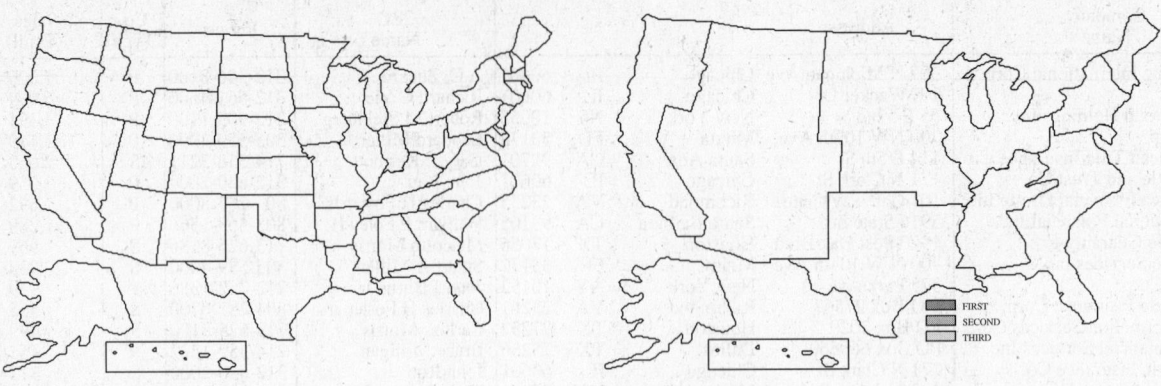

INDUSTRY DATA BY STATE

State	Establishments		Employment			Payroll		Revenues		
	Total (number)	% of U.S.	Total (number)	% of U.S.	Per Estab.	Total ($ mil.)	Per Empl. ($)	Total ($ mil.)	% of U.S.	Per Estab. ($)
Nebraska	8	0.3	60*	-	-	(D)	-	-	-	-
Idaho	13	0.5	175*	-	-	(D)	-	-	-	-
Hawaii	19	0.8	175*	-	-	(D)	-	-	-	-
Nevada	31	1.2	750*	-	-	(D)	-	-	-	-
Washington	55	2.2	1,750*	-	-	(D)	-	-	-	-
Kansas	16	0.6	133	0.3	8	3.9	29,406	-	-	-
South Carolina	13	0.5	60*	-	-	(D)	-	-	-	-
Florida	287	11.3	3,084	7.4	11	110.0	35,666	-	-	-
Georgia	16	0.6	189	0.5	12	8.0	42,360	-	-	-
California	524	20.7	13,526	32.4	26	577.1	42,668	-	-	-
Indiana	53	2.1	750*	-	-	(D)	-	-	-	-
Illinois	111	4.4	1,750*	-	-	(D)	-	-	-	-
Missouri	52	2.1	750*	-	-	(D)	-	-	-	-
New York	78	3.1	1,750*	-	-	(D)	-	-	-	-
Oklahoma	9	0.4	60*	-	-	2.8	-	-	-	-
Tennessee	25	1.0	175*	-	-	(D)	-	-	-	-
Wisconsin	10	0.4	175*	-	-	(D)	-	-	-	-
Louisiana	15	0.6	175*	-	-	(D)	-	-	-	-
Montana	10	0.4	60	0.1	6	1.2	19,483	-	-	-
Alabama	9	0.4	67	0.2	7	2.1	31,701	-	-	-
Iowa	7	0.3	375*	-	-	(D)	-	-	-	-
Oregon	84	3.3	1,750*	-	-	(D)	-	-	-	-
Colorado	62	2.5	1,750*	-	-	(D)	-	-	-	-
Utah	22	0.9	375*	-	-	(D)	-	-	-	-
Connecticut	15	0.6	175*	-	-	(D)	-	-	-	-
New Jersey	44	1.7	375*	-	-	(D)	-	-	-	-
North Carolina	62	2.5	375*	-	-	(D)	-	-	-	-
Wyoming	20	0.8	175*	-	-	(D)	-	-	-	-
New Mexico	17	0.7	175*	-	-	(D)	-	-	-	-
Virginia	103	4.1	750*	-	-	(D)	-	-	-	-
Minnesota	42	1.7	1,750*	-	-	(D)	-	-	-	-
Massachusetts	13	0.5	175*	-	-	(D)	-	-	-	-
Michigan	72	2.8	1,750*	-	-	(D)	-	-	-	-
Pennsylvania	85	3.4	1,050	2.5	12	41.8	39,836	-	-	-
Texas	218	8.6	3,750*	-	-	(D)	-	-	-	-
Mississippi	9	0.4	60*	-	-	(D)	-	-	-	-
Arizona	129	5.1	1,750*	-	-	(D)	-	-	-	-
Maryland	29	1.1	375*	-	-	(D)	-	-	-	-
Ohio	94	3.7	1,371	3.3	15	45.1	32,891	-	-	-
Arkansas	7	0.3	60*	-	-	(D)	-	-	-	-

Source: 1997 *Economic Census*. The states are in descending order of revenues or establishments (if revenue data are missing for the majority). The symbol (D) appears when data are withheld to prevent disclosure of competitive information. States marked with (D) are sorted by number of establishments. A dash (-) indicates that the data element cannot be calculated. * indicates the midpoint of a range; 175, for example is the range 100-249. Shaded *states* on the state map indicate those states which have proportionately greater representation in the industry than would be indicated by the state's population; the ratio is based on total revenues or number of establishments. Shaded *regions* indicate where the industry is regionally most concentrated.

NAICS 524128 - DIRECT INSURANCE CARRIERS (EXCEPT LIFE, HEALTH, AND MEDICAL)

GENERAL STATISTICS

Year	Establishments (number)	Employment (number)	Payroll ($ million)	Revenues ($ million)	Employees per Establishment (number)	Revenues per Establishment ($)	Payroll per Employee ($)
1997	128	1,575	56.0	963.0	12.3	7,523,438	35,556

Source: Economic Census of the United States, 1997. This is a newly defined industry. Data for prior years were unavailable at the time of publication but may become available over time.

INDICES OF CHANGE

Year	Establishments (number)	Employment (number)	Payroll ($ million)	Revenues ($ million)	Employees per Establishment (number)	Revenues per Establishment ($)	Payroll per Employee ($)
1997	100.0	100.0	100.0	100.0	100.0	100.0	100.0

Sources: Same as General Statistics. The values shown reflect change from the base year, 1997. Values above 100 mean greater than 1997, values below 100 mean less than 1997, and a value of 100 in the 1982-96 or 1998-2001 period means same as 1997. Values followed by a 'p' are projections by the editors; 'e' stands for extrapolation. Data are the most recent available at this level of detail.

SIC INDUSTRIES RELATED TO NAICS 524128

Each new NAICS code represents an industry that used to be part of an SIC or a part of several SIC industries. Data in this table are shown to provide transitional information for these cases. All available data for the precursor SIC(s) are shown. Even if only a part of an SIC is included in the NAICS, *all* data for the SIC are reproduced. If the SIC industry is not marked as being a part (pt) of the NAICS, the entire industry is embedded in the NAICS data. The SIC composition of the new industry provides some hints of the relative importance of its "ancestors." Data marked with a 'p' are projected. Projections begin with 1982 data. Data earlier than 1990 are not shown but are reflected in the projections.

SIC	Industry	1990	1991	1992	1993	1994	1995	1996	1997
6331	**Fire, Marine, and Casualty Insurance (pt)**								
	Establishments (number)	-	-	19,002	-	-	-	-	-
	Employment (thousands)	-	-	588.3	-	-	-	-	-
	Revenues ($ million)	-	-	258,394.7	-	-	-	-	-
6399	**Insurance Carriers, nec**								
	Establishments (number)	-	-	134	-	-	-	-	-
	Employment (thousands)	-	-	2.8	-	-	-	-	-
	Revenues ($ million)	-	-	700.7	-	-	-	-	-

Source: Economic Census of the United States, 1992, annual surveys of economic sectors conducted by the Bureau of the Census, and estimates or projections based on the 1982-1992 period; not all data are shown. 'e' marks estimates made by the editors; 'p' indicates projections based on time series. A dash (-) indicates that data for this SIC or year were not available. The abbreviation (pt) next to the industry name indicates that only a part of the industry is present within the NAICS data. If no (pt) is shown, the entire industry is contained within the NAICS data.

SELECTED RATIOS

For 1997	Avg. of Information	Analyzed Industry	Index	For 1997	Avg. of Information	Analyzed Industry	Index
Employees per establishment	15	12	83	Payroll per establishment	669,406	437,500	65
Revenue per establishment	5,561,120	7,523,438	135	Payroll as % of revenue	12	6	48
Revenue per employee	376,639	611,429	162	Payroll per employee	45,337	35,556	78

Sources: Same as General Statistics. The 'Average' column represents the average for the industry sector, in 1997, where the currently shown industry is classified. The Index shows the relationship between the Average and the Analyzed Industry. For example, 100 means that they are equal; 500 that the Analyzed Industry is five times the average; 50 means that the Analyzed Industry is half the national average. The abbreviation 'na' is used to show that data are 'not available'.

LEADING COMPANIES   Number shown: **21**   Total sales ($ mil): **61,825**   Total employment (000): **26.0**

Company Name	Address				CEO Name	Phone	Co. Type	Sales ($ mil)	Empl. (000)
Federal Deposit Insurance Corp.	550 17th St NW	Washington	DC	20429		202-898-6993	R	37,700*	9.0
Foundation Health Systems Inc.	21650 Oxnard St	Woodland Hills	CA	91367	Jay M Gellert	818-676-6000	P	8,797	14.0
Pension Benefit Guaranty Corp.	1200 K St NW	Washington	DC	20005	David M Strauss	202-326-4000	R	7,074*	0.8
New England Reinsurance Corp.	150 Federal St	Boston	MA	02110		617-526-8500	D	2,330*	0.5
Fidelity & Guaranty Life	100 E Pratt St	Baltimore	MD	21202	Harry N Stout	410-895-0100	S	1,401	0.2
St. Paul Reinsurance Corp.	195 Broadway	New York	NY	10007	James F Duffy	212-238-9200	S	1,165*	0.3
Securities Investor Protection	805 15th St N W	Washington	DC	20005	Michael E Don	202-371-8300	R	1,024*	<0.1
Western National Warranty Corp.	P O Box 2840	Scottsdale	AZ	85252	Tripp Marshall	602-941-1626	S	846*	0.2
Mutual Insurance of Arizona	2602 E Thomas Ave	Phoenix	AZ	85016	James F Carland, MD	602-956-5276	R	580	0.1
K and K Insurance Group Inc.	PO Box 2338	Fort Wayne	IN	46801	Stephen Lunsford	219-459-5000	S	290*	0.3
Danielson Holding Corp.	767 3rd Ave	New York	NY	10017	David M Barse	212-888-0347	P	181	0.2
Automobile Protection Corp.	15 Dunwood	Atlanta	GA	30338	Larry I Dorfman	770-394-7070	S	120	0.2
Veterinary Pet Insurance Co.	4175 E La Palma	Anaheim	CA	92807	Jack Stephens	714-996-2311	R	85*	0.1
Kansas Bankers Surety Co.	1220 Executive Dr	Topeka	KS	66615	Don Towel	785-228-0000	S	80	<0.1
California Veterinary Services Inc.	4175 E La Palma	Anaheim	CA	92807	Jack Stephens	714-996-2311	R	60	<0.1
Bancinsurance Corp.	20 E Broad St	Columbus	OH	43215	Si Sokol	614-228-2800	P	36	<0.1
Media/Professional Insurance	2300 Main St	Kansas City	MO	64108	John Pfannenstiel	816-471-6118	S	28*	0.1
Market Street Underwriters	1760 Market St	Philadelphia	PA	19103	Francis Reilly	215-563-3800	S	17*	<0.1
Preferred Warranties Inc.	PO Box 278	Orwigsburg	PA	17961	Wayne Herring		R	8	<0.1
Kirk Horse Insurance Inc.	129 Walton Ave	Lexington	KY	40508	Ronald K Kirk	606-231-0838	R	2	<0.1
First Risk Management Legal	The Plaza	Jenkintown	PA	19046		215-885-1125	N	1	<0.1

Source: *Ward's Business Directory of U.S. Private and Public Companies*, Volumes 1 and 2, 2000. The company type code used is as follows: P - Public, R - Private, S - Subsidiary, D - Division, J - Joint Venture, A - Affiliate, G - Group, N - Company type not reported. Sales are in millions of dollars, employees are in thousands. An asterisk (*) indicates an estimated sales volume. The symbol < stands for 'less than'. Company names and addresses are truncated, in some cases, to fit into the available space.

LOCATION BY STATE AND REGIONAL CONCENTRATION

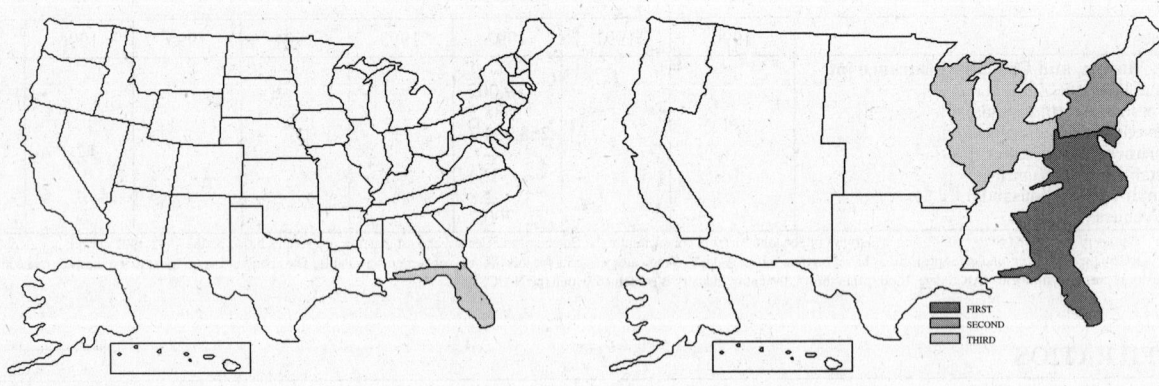

INDUSTRY DATA BY STATE

State	Establishments		Employment			Payroll		Revenues		
	Total (number)	% of U.S.	Total (number)	% of U.S.	Per Estab.	Total ($ mil.)	Per Empl. ($)	Total ($ mil.)	% of U.S.	Per Estab. ($)
Florida	9	7.0	175*	-	-	5.9	-	429.1	44.6	47,681,222
Pennsylvania	13	10.2	219	13.9	17	6.6	30,123	30.6	3.2	2,355,077
Ohio	6	4.7	40	2.5	7	2.4	59,275	7.9	0.8	1,318,167
California	7	5.5	39	2.5	6	1.7	42,436	3.4	0.4	481,857
Texas	7	5.5	60*	-	-	(D)	-	(D)	-	-
Virginia	7	5.5	175*	-	-	(D)	-	(D)	-	-
Alabama	6	4.7	175*	-	-	(D)	-	(D)	-	-

Source: 1997 *Economic Census*. The states are in descending order of revenues or establishments (if revenue data are missing for the majority). The symbol (D) appears when data are withheld to prevent disclosure of competitive information. States marked with (D) are sorted by number of establishments. A dash (-) indicates that the data element cannot be calculated. * indicates the midpoint of a range; 175, for example is the range 100-249. Shaded *states* on the state map indicate those states which have proportionately greater representation in the industry than would be indicated by the state's population; the ratio is based on total revenues or number of establishments. Shaded *regions* indicate where the industry is regionally most concentrated.

NAICS 524130 - REINSURANCE CARRIERS

GENERAL STATISTICS

Year	Establishments (number)	Employment (number)	Payroll ($ million)	Revenues ($ million)	Employees per Establishment (number)	Revenues per Establishment ($)	Payroll per Employee ($)
1997	563	15,878	1,010.0	21,285.0	28.2	37,806,394	63,610

Source: Economic Census of the United States, 1997. This is a newly defined industry. Data for prior years were unavailable at the time of publication but may become available over time.

INDICES OF CHANGE

Year	Establishments (number)	Employment (number)	Payroll ($ million)	Revenues ($ million)	Employees per Establishment (number)	Revenues per Establishment ($)	Payroll per Employee ($)
1997	100.0	100.0	100.0	100.0	100.0	100.0	100.0

Sources: Same as General Statistics. The values shown reflect change from the base year, 1997. Values above 100 mean greater than 1997, values below 100 mean less than 1997, and a value of 100 in the 1982-96 or 1998-2001 period means same as 1997. Values followed by a 'p' are projections by the editors; 'e' stands for extrapolation. Data are the most recent available at this level of detail.

SIC INDUSTRIES RELATED TO NAICS 524130

Each new NAICS code represents an industry that used to be part of an SIC or a part of several SIC industries. Data in this table are shown to provide transitional information for these cases. All available data for the precursor SIC(s) are shown. Even if only a part of an SIC is included in the NAICS, *all* data for the SIC are reproduced. If the SIC industry is not marked as being a part (pt) of the NAICS, the entire industry is embedded in the NAICS data. The SIC composition of the new industry provides some hints of the relative importance of its "ancestors." Data marked with a 'p' are projected. Projections begin with 1982 data. Data earlier than 1990 are not shown but are reflected in the projections.

SIC	Industry	1990	1991	1992	1993	1994	1995	1996	1997
6311	**Life Insurance (pt)**								
	Establishments (number)	-	-	13,424	-	-	-	-	-
	Employment (thousands)	-	-	609.2	-	-	-	-	-
	Revenues ($ million)	-	-	378,401.7	-	-	-	-	-
6321	**Accident and Health Insurance (pt)**								
	Establishments (number)	-	-	1,100	-	-	-	-	-
	Employment (thousands)	-	-	53.6	-	-	-	-	-
	Revenues ($ million)	-	-	23,446.3	-	-	-	-	-
6324	**Hospital and Medical Service Plans (pt)**								
	Establishments (number)	-	-	1,746	-	-	-	-	-
	Employment (thousands)	-	-	196.6	-	-	-	-	-
	Revenues ($ million)	-	-	124,813.2	-	-	-	-	-
6331	**Fire, Marine, and Casualty Insurance (pt)**								
	Establishments (number)	-	-	19,002	-	-	-	-	-
	Employment (thousands)	-	-	588.3	-	-	-	-	-
	Revenues ($ million)	-	-	258,394.7	-	-	-	-	-
6351	**Surety Insurance (pt)**								
	Establishments (number)	-	-	548	-	-	-	-	-
	Employment (thousands)	-	-	11.2	-	-	-	-	-
	Revenues ($ million)	-	-	4,005.4	-	-	-	-	-
6361	**Title Insurance (pt)**								
	Establishments (number)	-	-	1,532	-	-	-	-	-
	Employment (thousands)	-	-	34.5	-	-	-	-	-
	Revenues ($ million)	-	-	4,883.6	-	-	-	-	-

Source: Economic Census of the United States, 1992, annual surveys of economic sectors conducted by the Bureau of the Census, and estimates or projections based on the 1982-1992 period; not all data are shown. 'e' marks estimates made by the editors; 'p' indicates projections based on time series. A dash (-) indicates that data for this SIC or year were not available. The abbreviation (pt) next to the industry name indicates that only a part of the industry is present within the NAICS data. If no (pt) is shown, the entire industry is contained within the NAICS data.

SELECTED RATIOS

For 1997	Avg. of Information	Analyzed Industry	Index	For 1997	Avg. of Information	Analyzed Industry	Index
Employees per establishment	15	28	191	Payroll per establishment	669,406	1,793,961	268
Revenue per establishment	5,561,120	37,806,394	680	Payroll as % of revenue	12	5	39
Revenue per employee	376,639	1,340,534	356	Payroll per employee	45,337	63,610	140

Sources: Same as General Statistics. The 'Average' column represents the average for the industry sector, in 1997, where the currently shown industry is classified. The Index shows the relationship between the Average and the Analyzed Industry. For example, 100 means that they are equal; 500 that the Analyzed Industry is five times the average; 50 means that the Analyzed Industry is half the national average. The abbreviation 'na' is used to show that data are 'not available'.

LEADING COMPANIES

No company data available for this industry.

LOCATION BY STATE AND REGIONAL CONCENTRATION

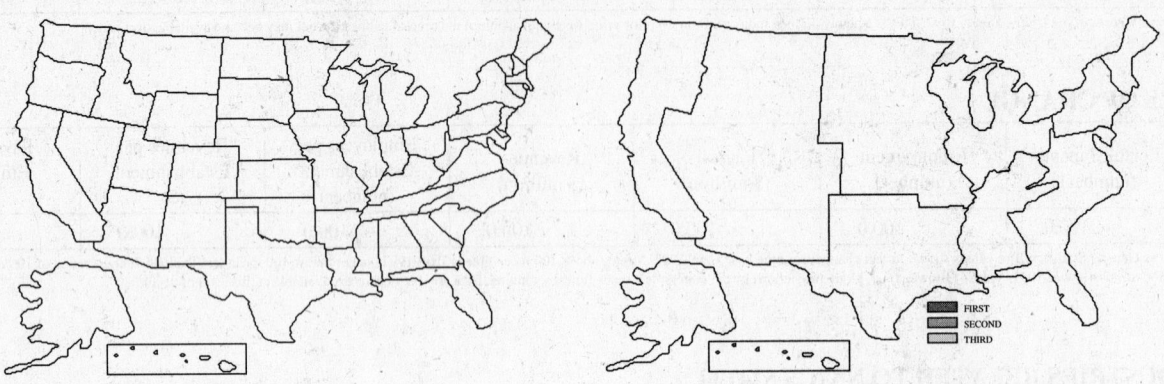

FIRST
SECOND
THIRD

INDUSTRY DATA BY STATE

State	Establishments Total (number)	% of U.S.	Employment Total (number)	% of U.S.	Per Estab.	Payroll Total ($ mil.)	Per Empl. ($)	Revenues Total ($ mil.)	% of U.S.	Per Estab. ($)
Florida	38	6.7	249	1.6	7	14.3	57,474	-	-	-
Maryland	11	2.0	109	0.7	10	5.9	54,422	-	-	-
Michigan	7	1.2	249	1.6	36	10.8	43,293	-	-	-
Indiana	8	1.4	3,750*	-	-	(D)	-	-	-	-
Virginia	21	3.7	175*	-	-	(D)	-	-	-	-
Minnesota	14	2.5	216	1.4	15	10.5	48,620	-	-	-
New York	45	8.0	2,128	13.4	47	237.0	111,354	-	-	-
Georgia	19	3.4	428	2.7	23	21.0	49,171	-	-	-
Texas	54	9.6	614	3.9	11	30.5	49,754	-	-	-
Arizona	12	2.1	234	1.5	20	9.0	38,598	-	-	-
Massachusetts	14	2.5	266	1.7	19	13.8	51,786	-	-	-
Pennsylvania	30	5.3	666	4.2	22	40.1	60,276	-	-	-
New Jersey	22	3.9	609	3.8	28	43.0	70,594	-	-	-
Kansas	14	2.5	750*	-	-	(D)	-	-	-	-
North Carolina	18	3.2	750*	-	-	(D)	-	-	-	-
Washington	7	1.2	51	0.3	7	1.7	32,804	-	-	-
Tennessee	9	1.6	60*	-	-	3.4	-	-	-	-
South Carolina	6	1.1	175*	-	-	(D)	-	-	-	-
Ohio	22	3.9	126	0.8	6	6.2	49,063	-	-	-
Connecticut	22	3.9	767	4.8	35	80.8	105,383	-	-	-
Missouri	15	2.7	937	5.9	62	47.6	50,848	-	-	-
California	56	9.9	2,184	13.8	39	148.4	67,937	-	-	-
Illinois	28	5.0	557	3.5	20	32.5	58,424	-	-	-

Source: 1997 *Economic Census*. The states are in descending order of revenues or establishments (if revenue data are missing for the majority). The symbol (D) appears when data are withheld to prevent disclosure of competitive information. States marked with (D) are sorted by number of establishments. A dash (-) indicates that the data element cannot be calculated. * indicates the midpoint of a range; 175, for example is the range 100-249. Shaded *states* on the state map indicate those states which have proportionately greater representation in the industry than would be indicated by the state's population; the ratio is based on total revenues or number of establishments. Shaded *regions* indicate where the industry is regionally most concentrated.

NAICS 524210 - INSURANCE AGENCIES AND BROKERAGES

GENERAL STATISTICS

Year	Establishments (number)	Employment (number)	Payroll ($ million)	Revenues ($ million)	Employees per Establishment (number)	Revenues per Establishment ($)	Payroll per Employee ($)
1997	120,392	557,670	19,533.0	59,174.0	4.6	491,511	35,026

Source: *Economic Census of the United States*, 1997. This is a newly defined industry. Data for prior years were unavailable at the time of publication but may become available over time.

INDICES OF CHANGE

Year	Establishments (number)	Employment (number)	Payroll ($ million)	Revenues ($ million)	Employees per Establishment (number)	Revenues per Establishment ($)	Payroll per Employee ($)
1997	100.0	100.0	100.0	100.0	100.0	100.0	100.0

Sources: Same as General Statistics. The values shown reflect change from the base year, 1997. Values above 100 mean greater than 1997, values below 100 mean less than 1997, and a value of 100 in the 1982-96 or 1998-2001 period means same as 1997. Values followed by a 'p' are projections by the editors; 'e' stands for extrapolation. Data are the most recent available at this level of detail.

SIC INDUSTRIES RELATED TO NAICS 524210

Each new NAICS code represents an industry that used to be part of an SIC or a part of several SIC industries. Data in this table are shown to provide transitional information for these cases. All available data for the precursor SIC(s) are shown. Even if only a part of an SIC is included in the NAICS, *all* data for the SIC are reproduced. If the SIC industry is not marked as being a part (pt) of the NAICS, the entire industry is embedded in the NAICS data. The SIC composition of the new industry provides some hints of the relative importance of its "ancestors." Data marked with a 'p' are projected. Projections begin with 1982 data. Data earlier than 1990 are not shown but are reflected in the projections.

SIC	Industry	1990	1991	1992	1993	1994	1995	1996	1997
6411	**Insurance Agents, Brokers, & Service (pt)**								
	Establishments (number)	-	-	121,662	-	-	-	-	-
	Employment (thousands)	-	-	635.5	-	-	-	-	-
	Revenues ($ million)	-	-	51,705.1	-	-	-	-	-

Source: *Economic Census of the United States*, 1992, annual surveys of economic sectors conducted by the Bureau of the Census, and estimates or projections based on the 1982-1992 period; not all data are shown. 'e' marks estimates made by the editors; 'p' indicates projections based on time series. A dash (-) indicates that data for this SIC or year were not available. The abbreviation (pt) next to the industry name indicates that only a part of the industry is present within the NAICS data. If no (pt) is shown, the entire industry is contained within the NAICS data.

SELECTED RATIOS

For 1997	Avg. of Information	Analyzed Industry	Index	For 1997	Avg. of Information	Analyzed Industry	Index
Employees per establishment	15	5	31	Payroll per establishment	669,406	162,245	24
Revenue per establishment	5,561,120	491,511	9	Payroll as % of revenue	12	33	274
Revenue per employee	376,639	106,109	28	Payroll per employee	45,337	35,026	77

Sources: Same as General Statistics. The 'Average' column represents the average for the industry sector, in 1997, where the currently shown industry is classified. The Index shows the relationship between the Average and the Analyzed Industry. For example, 100 means that they are equal; 500 that the Analyzed Industry is five times the average; 50 means that the Analyzed Industry is half the national average. The abbreviation 'na' is used to show that data are 'not available'.

LEADING COMPANIES　　Number shown: **75**　　Total sales ($ mil): **71,762**　　Total employment (000): **171.6**

Company Name	Address				CEO Name	Phone	Co. Type	Sales ($ mil)	Empl. (000)
Aon Risk Services Companies Inc.	123 N Wacker Dr	Chicago	IL	60606	Alan Diamond	312-701-3000	S	18,214*	15.0
Aon Group Inc.	125 Wacker Dr	Chicago	IL	60606	Michael D O'Halleran	312-701-4800	D	17,000	14.0
Marsh & McLennan Companies	1166 Av Americas	New York	NY	10036	AJC Smith	212-345-5000	P	9,157	54.3
Progressive Corp.	6300 Wilson Mills	Mayfield Village	OH	44143	Peter B Lewis		P	5,292	15.7
Arizona All Claims Inc.	11801 N Tatum	Phoenix	AZ	85028	Mark Tansey	602-997-5877	S	3,299*	6.0
GE Financial Assurance Holdings	6604 W Broad St	Richmond	VA	23230	Mike Fraizer		S	2,853*	4.0
F M Global	1151 B-Prov Tpk	Norwood	MA	02062	Paul M Fitzgerald	781-255-4200	R	1,968*	4.0
Scottsdale Insurance Co.	P O Box 4110	Scottsdale	AZ	85261	R Max Williamson	602-948-0505	S	954*	1.2
Horace Mann Service Corp.	1 Horace Mann Plz	Springfield	IL	62701	Paul J Kardos	217-789-2500	S	771	2.7
Crawford and Co.	5620 Glenridge NE	Atlanta	GA	30342	Grover L Davis	404-256-0830	P	667	7.7
Sedgwick James of Oregon Inc.	111 S W Columbia	Portland	OR	97201	Tom Elliott	503-248-6400	S	661	0.3
Superior National Insurance Co.	26541 Agoura Rd	Calabasas	CA	91302	Chris Seaman	818-880-1600	R	660*	1.2
Arthur J. Gallagher and Co.	2 Pierce Pl	Itasca	IL	60143	J Patrick Gallagher Jr	630-773-3800	P	606	4.3
ChoicePoint Inc.	1000 Alderman Dr	Alpharetta	GA	30005	Derek V Smith	770-752-6000	P	541*	4.8
Guy Carpenter and Company Inc.	2 World Trade Ctr	New York	NY	10048	Sal Zaffino	212-323-1000	P	502	1.5
MIM Corp.	100 Clearbrook Rd	Elmsford	NY	10523	Richard H Friedman	914-460-1600	P	451	0.3
American Medical Security Inc.	PO Box 19032	Green Bay	WI	54307	Sam Miller	920-661-2402	S	390*	2.0
Acordia Southeast Inc.	P O Box 31666	Tampa	FL	33631	James R Harper	727-796-6666	S	350	0.3
Acordia Inc.	111 Monument Cir	Indianapolis	IN	46204	Frank C Witthun	317-488-2500	R	340	3.6
Insurance Services Office Inc.	7 World Trade Ctr	New York	NY	10048	Frank J Coyne	212-898-6000	R	307	2.2
CIGNA RE Corp.	900 Cottage Grove	Hartford	CT	06152	Francine W Newman	215-761-1398	S	300*	0.1
McGriff, Seibels & Williams Inc.	PO Box 10265	Birmingham	AL	35202	Bruce C Dunbar Jr	205-252-9871	R	300*	0.3
HealthPlan Services Corp.	P O Box 30098	Tampa	FL	33630	James K Murray Jr	813-289-1000	P	289	3.3
Burns and Wilcox Ltd.	PO Box 707	Southfield	MI	48037	Herbert W Kaufman	248-932-9000	S	282	0.6
Great Northern Financial Services	PO Box 23100	Green Bay	WI	54305	Mike Meeuwsen	920-437-7101	S	249*	0.2
E.W. Blanch Holdings Inc.	500 N Akard	San Antonio	TX	78228	Edgar W Blanch Jr	214-756-7000	P	244	1.2
Near North Insurance Brokerage	875 N Michigan #19	Chicago	IL	60611	Michael Segal	312-280-5600	R	220*	0.4
Old Republic International Inc.	307 N Michigan Ave	Chicago	IL	60601	Aldo Zucaro	312-346-6130	S	219*	0.4
AON Re Inc.	123 N Wacker Dr	Chicago	IL	60606	Michael G Bungert	312-781-7900	S	218*	0.4
Kaye Insurance Associates Inc.	122 E 42nd St	New York	NY	10168	Bruce D Guthart	212-210-9200	R	214*	0.4
AON Re Worldwide	123 N Wacker Dr	Chicago	IL	60606	Rocker Charnell	312-781-7900	S	197*	0.4
National Loss Control Service	1 Kemper Dr	Long Grove	IL	60049	C David Sullivan		S	193*	0.4
ESIS Inc.	1601 Chestnut St	Philadelphia	PA	19192	Ray Hafner	215-761-8500	S	182	2.7
General Bank	4128 Temple City	Rosemead	CA	91770	Peter Wu	626-582-7243	S	181*	0.3
Hilb, Rogal and Hamilton Co.	P O Box 1220	Glen Allen	VA	23060	Martin L Vaughn	804-747-6500	P	181	1.6
Seabury and Smith Inc.	1166 Av Americas	New York	NY	10036	Claude Y Mercier	212-345-4000	S	180*	1.5
Poe and Brown Inc.	P O Box 2412	Daytona Beach	FL	32115	J Hyatt Brown	904-252-9601	P	176	1.4
Aon Services Group	123 N Wacker Dr	Chicago	IL	60606	Michael D Rice	312-701-4538	S	156*	0.6
GENEX Services Inc.	440 E Swedesford	Wayne	PA	19087	Peter Madeja	610-964-5100	S	151*	1.3
John L. Wortham L.L.P.	PO Box 1388	Houston	TX	77251		713-526-3366	R	138*	0.3
Holmes Murphy & Associates Inc.	3001 Westown Pky	W. Des Moines	IA	50266	J Douglas Reichardt	515-286-4400	R	124*	0.2
Medical Professional Liability	2 Depot Plz	Bedford Hills	NY	10507	Thomas J Dietz	914-666-0555	S	110	<0.1
The Epoch Group	10795 Watson Rd	St. Louis	MO	63127	L E Thurmond	314-821-3957	S	110*	0.2
HealthPlan Services Inc.	3501 Frontage Rd	Tampa	FL	33607	James K Murray Jr	813-289-1000	S	107	0.8
Kemper Risk Management	1 Kemper Dr	Long Grove	IL	60049	EM Lindner	708-320-2400	S	107*	0.3
Andreini and Co.	220 W 20th Ave	San Mateo	CA	94403	Michael Colzani	650-573-1111	R	102*	0.2
Riggs, Counselman, Michaels	555 Fairmount Ave	Baltimore	MD	21286	Albert R Counselman	410-339-7263	R	94*	0.2
Tri-City Insurance Brokers Inc.	110 William St	New York	NY	10038	John G Hahn	212-732-1360	R	93*	0.2
U.S. Risk Insurance Group Inc.	10210 N Central	Dallas	TX	75231	Randall G Goss	214-265-7090	R	86*	0.2
Brakke-Schafnitz Insurance	28202 Cabot Rd	Laguna Niguel	CA	92677	Jim Brakke	949-365-5100	R	85*	<0.1
National Electronics Warranty	44873 Falcon Pl	Sterling	VA	20166	Fred Schaufeld	703-318-7700	R	83*	0.2
Acordia Small Business Benefits	3760 Guion Rd	Indianapolis	IN	46222		317-921-7000	S	77*	0.1
Clarke, Bardes Holdings Inc.	212 San Jacinto	Dallas	TX	75201	WT Wambergv	214-871-8717	P	75	0.2
Ceridian Benefits Services	34125 U S 19 N	Palm Harbor	FL	34684	Jim O'Drobinak	727-785-2819	S	75	1.4
Ringler Associates Inc.	5000 Birch St	Newport Beach	CA	92660	Paul Hoffman	949-833-1821	R	74*	0.2
Aon Risk Services of Central	611 Anton Blvd	Costa Mesa	CA	92626		714-957-6005	S	72*	0.2
Southern Health Services Inc.	P O Box 85603	Richmond	VA	23285	Stewart Lavelle	804-747-3700	S	67*	0.1
Aon Risk Services of Michigan	500 Renaissance Ctr	Detroit	MI	48243	James W Webb	313-259-0200	S	66*	0.1
Haas and Wilkerson Inc.	P O Box 2946	Shaw Msn	KS	66201	J Philip Coulson	913-432-4400	R	66	<0.1
Kaye Group Inc.	122 E 42nd St	New York	NY	10168	Bruce D Guthart	212-338-2100	P	65	0.4
HCIA Inc.	300 E Lombard St	Baltimore	MD	21202	Donald S Good Jr	410-576-9600	P	63	0.5
Benova Inc.	1220 SW Morrison	Portland	OR	97205	Colleen Cain	503-228-2567	R	60*	0.6
Roger Bouchard Insurance Inc.	101 Starcrest Dr	Clearwater	FL	33765	Richard Bouchard	727-447-6481	R	60	<0.1
Gem Group	1200 Three Gateway	Pittsburgh	PA	15222	Leonard Spencer	412-471-2893	R	58*	0.1
First Chicago Insurance Services	400 Central Ave	Northfield	IL	60093	Kathy Wilcox	847-441-1730	S	57*	0.1
Brown and Brown	PO Box 33619	Phoenix	AZ	85067	Kenneth Kirk	602-277-6672	R	55*	0.1
Schmidt Insurance Agency Inc.	7410 Lagrange Rd	Louisville	KY	40222	Leonard Schmidt	502-429-0477	R	55*	0.1
Transcend Services Inc.	3353 Peachtree N E	Atlanta	GA	30326	Larry G Gerdes	404-836-8000	P	53	0.9
MetLife Brokerage	PO Box 6895	Bridgewater	NJ	08807	Robert W Powell	609-243-7100	S	50	0.1
Arthur A. Watson Inc.	225 Spring St	Weathersfield	CT	06109	Tom Willsey	860-563-8111	R	47*	<0.1
Financial Pacific Insurance Group	P O Box 29220	Sacramento	CA	95829	Robert C Goodell	916-630-5000	R	47	0.1
Aon Risk Services	1 Market St	San Francisco	CA	94105	Ed Kiessling	415-543-9360	S	45	0.4
Polar Rampart Intern	369 Lexington Ave	New York	NY	10017		212-867-7575	D	41*	<0.1
Aon Risk Services Incorporated	250 E 5th St	Cincinnati	OH	45202		513-621-0130	P	40*	<0.1
American Southern Insurance Co.	PO Box 723030	Atlanta	GA	31139	Calvin L Wall	404-266-9599	S	39	<0.1

Source: Ward's Business Directory of U.S. Private and Public Companies, Volumes 1 and 2, 2000. The company type code used is as follows: P - Public, R - Private, S - Subsidiary, D - Division, J - Joint Venture, A - Affiliate, G - Group, N - Company type not reported. Sales are in millions of dollars, employees are in thousands. An asterisk (*) indicates an estimated sales volume. The symbol < stands for 'less than'. Company names and addresses are truncated, in some cases, to fit into the available space.

LOCATION BY STATE AND REGIONAL CONCENTRATION

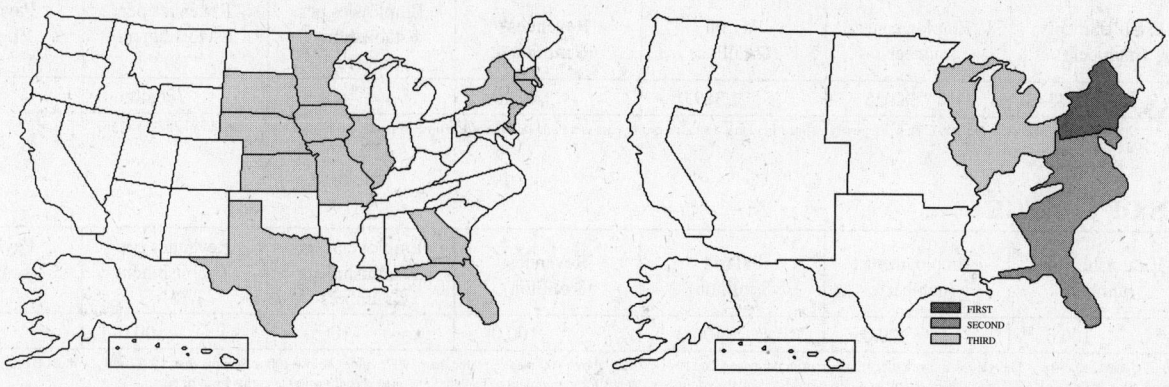

FIRST
SECOND
THIRD

INDUSTRY DATA BY STATE

State	Establishments Total (number)	% of U.S.	Employment Total (number)	% of U.S.	Per Estab.	Payroll Total ($ mil.)	Per Empl. ($)	Revenues Total ($ mil.)	% of U.S.	Per Estab. ($)
California	11,198	9.3	55,911	10.0	5	2,263.4	40,483	6,600.2	11.2	589,410
New York	6,553	5.4	42,273	7.6	6	1,929.0	45,633	5,835.9	9.9	890,574
Texas	8,828	7.3	42,445	7.6	5	1,361.8	32,083	4,550.0	7.7	515,402
Florida	7,515	6.2	34,994	6.3	5	1,166.7	33,341	3,800.2	6.4	505,677
Illinois	6,329	5.3	30,397	5.5	5	1,125.8	37,036	3,228.5	5.5	510,112
Pennsylvania	4,801	4.0	25,440	4.6	5	962.3	37,827	2,805.8	4.7	584,410
Ohio	5,434	4.5	23,042	4.1	4	732.7	31,798	2,173.8	3.7	400,044
New Jersey	2,750	2.3	17,696	3.2	6	796.3	45,002	2,009.4	3.4	730,685
Massachusetts	2,818	2.3	16,442	2.9	6	677.2	41,188	1,974.3	3.3	700,591
Michigan	4,042	3.4	19,447	3.5	5	656.0	33,731	1,817.6	3.1	449,667
Georgia	3,230	2.7	14,742	2.6	5	525.9	35,671	1,811.1	3.1	560,717
North Carolina	3,128	2.6	13,050	2.3	4	410.3	31,442	1,312.6	2.2	419,637
Virginia	2,914	2.4	11,746	2.1	4	385.1	32,787	1,254.7	2.1	430,587
Minnesota	3,158	2.6	11,980	2.1	4	399.8	33,369	1,234.3	2.1	390,849
Missouri	3,238	2.7	12,463	2.2	4	385.7	30,948	1,233.6	2.1	380,987
Indiana	2,898	2.4	12,279	2.2	4	368.6	30,022	1,138.2	1.9	392,736
Maryland	1,940	1.6	10,082	1.8	5	378.2	37,515	1,074.9	1.8	554,064
Tennessee	2,312	1.9	9,640	1.7	4	322.5	33,452	1,050.3	1.8	454,285
Washington	2,400	2.0	10,473	1.9	4	371.8	35,505	979.1	1.7	407,953
Wisconsin	3,067	2.5	11,402	2.0	4	332.1	29,123	973.3	1.6	317,362
Connecticut	1,461	1.2	8,474	1.5	6	370.4	43,716	963.9	1.6	659,735
Louisiana	1,964	1.6	8,952	1.6	5	258.7	28,902	859.9	1.5	437,809
Iowa	2,145	1.8	8,253	1.5	4	237.2	28,737	809.0	1.4	377,148
Arizona	2,050	1.7	8,615	1.5	4	260.9	30,279	803.8	1.4	392,117
Colorado	2,345	1.9	8,076	1.4	3	257.7	31,905	759.6	1.3	323,923
Kansas	1,883	1.6	7,121	1.3	4	199.1	27,958	747.2	1.3	396,805
Oregon	1,605	1.3	7,046	1.3	4	226.0	32,077	676.3	1.1	421,367
Alabama	1,463	1.2	6,487	1.2	4	209.1	32,236	637.3	1.1	435,613
Kentucky	1,628	1.4	7,058	1.3	4	208.1	29,489	633.2	1.1	388,921
Oklahoma	1,815	1.5	5,824	1.0	3	144.1	24,750	529.2	0.9	291,592
South Carolina	1,393	1.2	5,864	1.1	4	183.8	31,338	525.4	0.9	377,162
Nebraska	1,413	1.2	4,917	0.9	3	126.5	25,728	504.6	0.9	357,086
Utah	915	0.8	4,573	0.8	5	120.0	26,240	367.5	0.6	401,669
Arkansas	1,238	1.0	4,028	0.7	3	106.6	26,471	337.0	0.6	272,179
Mississippi	1,044	0.9	3,831	0.7	4	106.9	27,912	328.0	0.6	314,178
Nevada	664	0.6	3,082	0.6	5	98.8	32,045	308.8	0.5	465,069
New Mexico	720	0.6	4,181	0.7	6	96.8	23,149	284.3	0.5	394,863
Maine	512	0.4	2,614	0.5	5	81.4	31,146	219.0	0.4	427,779
Hawaii	315	0.3	2,045	0.4	6	73.0	35,702	207.6	0.4	659,206
West Virginia	759	0.6	2,551	0.5	3	68.4	26,830	198.1	0.3	261,005
New Hampshire	490	0.4	2,327	0.4	5	82.7	35,528	194.1	0.3	396,222
Rhode Island	377	0.3	1,796	0.3	5	63.8	35,545	182.8	0.3	484,950
D.C.	102	0.1	1,084	0.2	11	50.6	46,649	170.4	0.3	1,670,657
Delaware	285	0.2	1,770	0.3	6	60.9	34,429	169.9	0.3	596,056
Idaho	614	0.5	2,291	0.4	4	54.9	23,961	165.1	0.3	268,893
South Dakota	663	0.6	1,861	0.3	3	46.1	24,795	162.8	0.3	245,478
Montana	600	0.5	2,026	0.4	3	48.3	23,842	155.8	0.3	259,598
North Dakota	596	0.5	1,557	0.3	3	34.4	22,071	122.0	0.2	204,711
Vermont	288	0.2	1,366	0.2	5	44.2	32,339	117.1	0.2	406,535
Wyoming	295	0.2	1,750*	-	-	(D)	-	(D)	-	-
Alaska	197	0.2	750*	-	-	(D)	-	(D)	-	-

Source: 1997 *Economic Census*. The states are in descending order of revenues or establishments (if revenue data are missing for the majority). The symbol (D) appears when data are withheld to prevent disclosure of competitive information. States marked with (D) are sorted by number of establishments. A dash (-) indicates that the data element cannot be calculated. * indicates the midpoint of a range; 175, for example is the range 100-249. Shaded *states* on the state map indicate those states which have proportionately greater representation in the industry than would be indicated by the state's population; the ratio is based on total revenues or number of establishments. Shaded *regions* indicate where the industry is regionally most concentrated.

NAICS 524291 - CLAIMS ADJUSTING

GENERAL STATISTICS

Year	Establishments (number)	Employment (number)	Payroll ($ million)	Revenues ($ million)	Employees per Establishment (number)	Revenues per Establishment ($)	Payroll per Employee ($)
1997	4,443	38,055	1,389.0	3,494.0	8.6	786,406	36,500

Source: Economic Census of the United States, 1997. This is a newly defined industry. Data for prior years were unavailable at the time of publication but may become available over time.

INDICES OF CHANGE

Year	Establishments (number)	Employment (number)	Payroll ($ million)	Revenues ($ million)	Employees per Establishment (number)	Revenues per Establishment ($)	Payroll per Employee ($)
1997	100.0	100.0	100.0	100.0	100.0	100.0	100.0

Sources: Same as General Statistics. The values shown reflect change from the base year, 1997. Values above 100 mean greater than 1997, values below 100 mean less than 1997, and a value of 100 in the 1982-96 or 1998-2001 period means same as 1997. Values followed by a 'p' are projections by the editors; 'e' stands for extrapolation. Data are the most recent available at this level of detail.

SIC INDUSTRIES RELATED TO NAICS 524291

Each new NAICS code represents an industry that used to be part of an SIC or a part of several SIC industries. Data in this table are shown to provide transitional information for these cases. All available data for the precursor SIC(s) are shown. Even if only a part of an SIC is included in the NAICS, *all* data for the SIC are reproduced. If the SIC industry is not marked as being a part (pt) of the NAICS, the entire industry is embedded in the NAICS data. The SIC composition of the new industry provides some hints of the relative importance of its "ancestors." Data marked with a 'p' are projected. Projections begin with 1982 data. Data earlier than 1990 are not shown but are reflected in the projections.

SIC	Industry	1990	1991	1992	1993	1994	1995	1996	1997
6411	**Insurance Agents, Brokers, & Service (pt)**								
	Establishments (number)	-	-	121,662	-	-	-	-	-
	Employment (thousands)	-	-	635.5	-	-	-	-	-
	Revenues ($ million)	-	-	51,705.1	-	-	-	-	-

Source: Economic Census of the United States, 1992, annual surveys of economic sectors conducted by the Bureau of the Census, and estimates or projections based on the 1982-1992 period; not all data are shown. 'e' marks estimates made by the editors; 'p' indicates projections based on time series. A dash (-) indicates that data for this SIC or year were not available. The abbreviation (pt) next to the industry name indicates that only a part of the industry is present within the NAICS data. If no (pt) is shown, the entire industry is contained within the NAICS data.

SELECTED RATIOS

For 1997	Avg. of Information	Analyzed Industry	Index	For 1997	Avg. of Information	Analyzed Industry	Index
Employees per establishment	15	9	58	Payroll per establishment	669,406	312,627	47
Revenue per establishment	5,561,120	786,406	14	Payroll as % of revenue	12	40	330
Revenue per employee	376,639	91,814	24	Payroll per employee	45,337	36,500	81

Sources: Same as General Statistics. The 'Average' column represents the average for the industry sector, in 1997, where the currently shown industry is classified. The Index shows the relationship between the Average and the Analyzed Industry. For example, 100 means that they are equal; 500 that the Analyzed Industry is five times the average; 50 means that the Analyzed Industry is half the national average. The abbreviation 'na' is used to show that data are 'not available'.

LEADING COMPANIES

No company data available for this industry.

LOCATION BY STATE AND REGIONAL CONCENTRATION

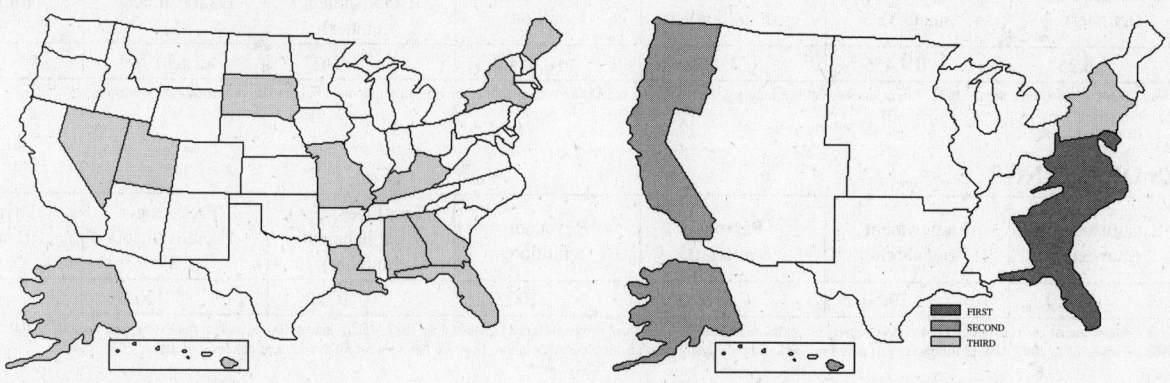

FIRST
SECOND
THIRD

INDUSTRY DATA BY STATE

State	Establishments Total (number)	Establishments % of U.S.	Employment Total (number)	Employment % of U.S.	Employment Per Estab.	Payroll Total ($ mil.)	Payroll Per Empl. ($)	Revenues Total ($ mil.)	Revenues % of U.S.	Revenues Per Estab. ($)
California	403	9.1	3,984	10.5	10	156.6	39,298	387.8	11.1	962,199
Florida	344	7.7	2,812	7.4	8	94.4	33,568	370.3	10.6	1,076,448
New York	277	6.2	3,550	9.3	13	150.0	42,244	328.2	9.4	1,184,715
Texas	390	8.8	2,771	7.3	7	95.9	34,605	242.5	6.9	621,779
Georgia	158	3.6	2,114	5.6	13	86.2	40,796	150.3	4.3	951,070
Pennsylvania	198	4.5	1,492	3.9	8	49.7	33,332	147.3	4.2	743,793
Illinois	163	3.7	1,488	3.9	9	63.5	42,694	133.8	3.8	821,092
Alabama	77	1.7	772	2.0	10	35.1	45,491	126.6	3.6	1,644,701
Missouri	94	2.1	694	1.8	7	23.1	33,346	99.7	2.9	1,060,521
Kentucky	58	1.3	969	2.5	17	32.1	33,119	73.9	2.1	1,273,759
Indiana	83	1.9	1,178	3.1	14	37.1	31,499	70.7	2.0	852,012
Michigan	98	2.2	877	2.3	9	28.2	32,145	70.1	2.0	715,408
Louisiana	110	2.5	823	2.2	7	30.5	36,999	64.7	1.9	588,245
Tennessee	83	1.9	832	2.2	10	27.7	33,234	62.7	1.8	755,060
Washington	93	2.1	811	2.1	9	26.1	32,232	60.4	1.7	649,634
Virginia	86	1.9	1,088	2.9	13	27.3	25,048	60.2	1.7	700,035
Ohio	115	2.6	674	1.8	6	22.7	33,632	60.2	1.7	523,591
North Carolina	126	2.8	643	1.7	5	21.0	32,712	57.7	1.7	457,730
Maryland	80	1.8	682	1.8	9	23.8	34,909	50.1	1.4	626,775
Connecticut	60	1.4	432	1.1	7	16.6	38,424	42.1	1.2	701,083
Colorado	56	1.3	261	0.7	5	16.3	62,625	35.7	1.0	636,893
Arizona	71	1.6	491	1.3	7	15.8	32,169	34.8	1.0	490,423
Minnesota	86	1.9	428	1.1	5	13.3	31,175	31.7	0.9	369,070
Utah	26	0.6	265	0.7	10	7.6	28,562	29.8	0.9	1,147,154
Wisconsin	67	1.5	443	1.2	7	13.8	31,090	27.3	0.8	408,045
Nevada	40	0.9	236	0.6	6	7.6	32,017	27.0	0.8	674,900
Oklahoma	63	1.4	359	0.9	6	9.9	27,694	24.4	0.7	387,698
Mississippi	48	1.1	301	0.8	6	9.3	30,824	20.7	0.6	431,583
Kansas	47	1.1	274	0.7	6	9.3	34,000	20.3	0.6	431,915
South Carolina	70	1.6	332	0.9	5	9.2	27,825	20.2	0.6	287,971
Hawaii	27	0.6	267	0.7	10	10.4	38,925	20.1	0.6	743,185
Iowa	36	0.8	307	0.8	9	8.3	27,104	19.1	0.5	531,583
Arkansas	33	0.7	233	0.6	7	6.3	26,863	17.4	0.5	527,273
Maine	31	0.7	185	0.5	6	5.9	31,962	17.2	0.5	553,516
West Virginia	16	0.4	138	0.4	9	3.8	27,341	13.7	0.4	858,188
New Mexico	42	0.9	183	0.5	4	5.9	32,038	13.5	0.4	320,667
Nebraska	28	0.6	177	0.5	6	5.5	30,921	12.5	0.4	444,893
Alaska	18	0.4	136	0.4	8	5.3	39,176	10.9	0.3	603,611
Montana	23	0.5	159	0.4	7	4.5	28,560	9.8	0.3	427,348
South Dakota	15	0.3	103	0.3	7	3.1	30,524	8.8	0.3	588,933
Idaho	16	0.4	81	0.2	5	3.0	36,728	6.5	0.2	405,625
New Jersey	155	3.5	1,750*	-	-	(D)	-	(D)	-	-
Massachusetts	150	3.4	1,750*	-	-	(D)	-	(D)	-	-
Oregon	62	1.4	375*	-	-	(D)	-	(D)	-	-
New Hampshire	33	0.7	175*	-	-	(D)	-	(D)	-	-
Rhode Island	27	0.6	175*	-	-	(D)	-	(D)	-	-
Vermont	18	0.4	60*	-	-	(D)	-	(D)	-	-
Wyoming	16	0.4	60*	-	-	(D)	-	(D)	-	-
North Dakota	13	0.3	60*	-	-	(D)	-	(D)	-	-
Delaware	10	0.2	175*	-	-	(D)	-	(D)	-	-

Source: 1997 *Economic Census*. The states are in descending order of revenues or establishments (if revenue data are missing for the majority). The symbol (D) appears when data are withheld to prevent disclosure of competitive information. States marked with (D) are sorted by number of establishments. A dash (-) indicates that the data element cannot be calculated. * indicates the midpoint of a range; 175, for example is the range 100-249. Shaded *states* on the state map indicate those states which have proportionately greater representation in the industry than would be indicated by the state's population; the ratio is based on total revenues or number of establishments. Shaded *regions* indicate where the industry is regionally most concentrated.

NAICS 524292 - THIRD PARTY ADMINISTRATION OF INSURANCE AND PENSION FUNDS

GENERAL STATISTICS

Year	Establishments (number)	Employment (number)	Payroll ($ million)	Revenues ($ million)	Employees per Establishment (number)	Revenues per Establishment ($)	Payroll per Employee ($)
1997	6,257	104,456	3,907.0	10,454.0	16.7	1,670,769	37,403

Source: Economic Census of the United States, 1997. This is a newly defined industry. Data for prior years were unavailable at the time of publication but may become available over time.

INDICES OF CHANGE

Year	Establishments (number)	Employment (number)	Payroll ($ million)	Revenues ($ million)	Employees per Establishment (number)	Revenues per Establishment ($)	Payroll per Employee ($)
1997	100.0	100.0	100.0	100.0	100.0	100.0	100.0

Sources: Same as General Statistics. The values shown reflect change from the base year, 1997. Values above 100 mean greater than 1997, values below 100 mean less than 1997, and a value of 100 in the 1982-96 or 1998-2001 period means same as 1997. Values followed by a 'p' are projections by the editors; 'e' stands for extrapolation. Data are the most recent available at this level of detail.

SIC INDUSTRIES RELATED TO NAICS 524292

Each new NAICS code represents an industry that used to be part of an SIC or a part of several SIC industries. Data in this table are shown to provide transitional information for these cases. All available data for the precursor SIC(s) are shown. Even if only a part of an SIC is included in the NAICS, *all* data for the SIC are reproduced. If the SIC industry is not marked as being a part (pt) of the NAICS, the entire industry is embedded in the NAICS data. The SIC composition of the new industry provides some hints of the relative importance of its "ancestors." Data marked with a 'p' are projected. Projections begin with 1982 data. Data earlier than 1990 are not shown but are reflected in the projections.

SIC	Industry	1990	1991	1992	1993	1994	1995	1996	1997
6371	**Pension, Health, and Welfare Funds (pt)**								
	Establishments (number)	-	-	1,491	-	-	-	-	-
	Employment (thousands)	-	-	20.4	-	-	-	-	-
	Revenues ($ million)	-	-	1,379.4	-	-	-	-	-
6411	**Insurance Agents, Brokers, & Service (pt)**								
	Establishments (number)	-	-	121,662	-	-	-	-	-
	Employment (thousands)	-	-	635.5	-	-	-	-	-
	Revenues ($ million)	-	-	51,705.1	-	-	-	-	-

Source: Economic Census of the United States, 1992, annual surveys of economic sectors conducted by the Bureau of the Census, and estimates or projections based on the 1982-1992 period; not all data are shown. 'e' marks estimates made by the editors; 'p' indicates projections based on time series. A dash (-) indicates that data for this SIC or year were not available. The abbreviation (pt) next to the industry name indicates that only a part of the industry is present within the NAICS data. If no (pt) is shown, the entire industry is contained within the NAICS data.

SELECTED RATIOS

For 1997	Avg. of Information	Analyzed Industry	Index	For 1997	Avg. of Information	Analyzed Industry	Index
Employees per establishment	15	17	113	Payroll per establishment	669,406	624,421	93
Revenue per establishment	5,561,120	1,670,769	30	Payroll as % of revenue	12	37	310
Revenue per employee	376,639	100,080	27	Payroll per employee	45,337	37,403	83

Sources: Same as General Statistics. The 'Average' column represents the average for the industry sector, in 1997, where the currently shown industry is classified. The Index shows the relationship between the Average and the Analyzed Industry. For example, 100 means that they are equal; 500 that the Analyzed Industry is five times the average; 50 means that the Analyzed Industry is half the national average. The abbreviation 'na' is used to show that data are 'not available'.

LEADING COMPANIES
No company data available for this industry.

LOCATION BY STATE AND REGIONAL CONCENTRATION

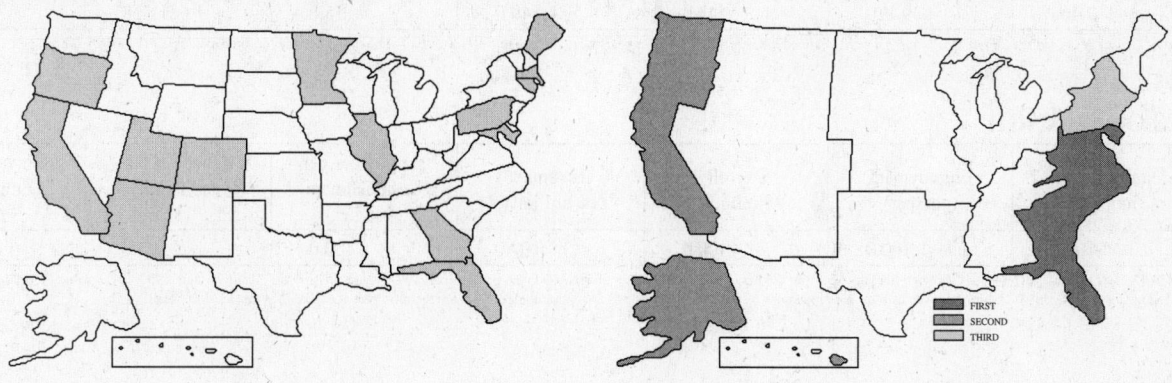

FIRST
SECOND
THIRD

INDUSTRY DATA BY STATE

State	Establishments Total (number)	Establishments % of U.S.	Employment Total (number)	Employment % of U.S.	Employment Per Estab.	Payroll Total ($ mil.)	Payroll Per Empl. ($)	Revenues Total ($ mil.)	Revenues % of U.S.	Revenues Per Estab. ($)
California	785	12.5	12,713	12.2	16	466.2	36,672	1,287.3	12.3	1,639,901
Florida	400	6.4	6,883	6.6	17	293.5	42,636	840.8	8.0	2,102,080
New York	438	7.0	7,032	6.7	16	308.4	43,858	731.0	7.0	1,668,963
Pennsylvania	314	5.0	5,645	5.4	18	199.4	35,330	704.3	6.7	2,243,057
Texas	449	7.2	8,029	7.7	18	280.2	34,893	688.2	6.6	1,532,659
Illinois	295	4.7	5,141	4.9	17	183.9	35,766	542.6	5.2	1,839,292
Arizona	127	2.0	2,933	2.8	23	161.2	54,959	442.6	4.2	3,485,047
Georgia	191	3.1	2,979	2.9	16	125.8	42,220	421.2	4.0	2,205,204
Ohio	235	3.8	4,880	4.7	21	168.5	34,525	393.2	3.8	1,673,315
Massachusetts	171	2.7	2,478	2.4	14	110.7	44,692	314.0	3.0	1,836,380
New Jersey	231	3.7	3,173	3.0	14	157.6	49,658	308.6	3.0	1,336,030
Oregon	103	1.6	1,643	1.6	16	58.8	35,771	307.8	2.9	2,988,272
Michigan	192	3.1	3,328	3.2	17	123.1	36,980	293.6	2.8	1,528,969
Maryland	125	2.0	3,655	3.5	29	141.7	38,774	287.5	2.8	2,300,160
Minnesota	138	2.2	3,331	3.2	24	110.9	33,301	263.8	2.5	1,911,746
Virginia	148	2.4	2,472	2.4	17	84.2	34,066	254.9	2.4	1,722,459
Tennessee	109	1.7	1,796	1.7	16	70.3	39,122	195.9	1.9	1,797,220
Wisconsin	107	1.7	2,013	1.9	19	64.5	32,021	189.1	1.8	1,767,598
North Carolina	125	2.0	1,997	1.9	16	65.2	32,647	186.9	1.8	1,495,440
Colorado	104	1.7	1,689	1.6	16	62.0	36,703	172.1	1.6	1,654,962
Indiana	125	2.0	2,064	2.0	17	62.6	30,334	172.1	1.6	1,376,440
Connecticut	92	1.5	1,542	1.5	17	60.2	39,058	137.3	1.3	1,491,870
Washington	114	1.8	1,746	1.7	15	60.9	34,878	132.2	1.3	1,159,386
Kentucky	65	1.0	1,417	1.4	22	44.2	31,169	117.8	1.1	1,812,431
Missouri	116	1.9	1,236	1.2	11	47.3	38,244	115.1	1.1	992,371
Utah	41	0.7	1,104	1.1	27	37.6	34,096	90.8	0.9	2,215,195
Oklahoma	94	1.5	1,141	1.1	12	31.3	27,396	84.4	0.8	897,777
Louisiana	131	2.1	1,082	1.0	8	33.5	31,006	82.2	0.8	627,435
Alabama	54	0.9	708	0.7	13	24.7	34,860	77.4	0.7	1,432,907
South Carolina	47	0.8	871	0.8	19	27.2	31,183	68.5	0.7	1,456,957
Kansas	59	0.9	749	0.7	13	29.7	39,709	66.6	0.6	1,128,220
Iowa	58	0.9	986	0.9	17	26.3	26,654	59.8	0.6	1,031,672
Maine	32	0.5	920	0.9	29	24.8	26,960	59.7	0.6	1,864,531
Arkansas	53	0.8	609	0.6	11	20.0	32,880	47.0	0.4	886,585
West Virginia	30	0.5	770	0.7	26	17.8	23,094	45.4	0.4	1,512,933
Nebraska	44	0.7	599	0.6	14	18.5	30,908	43.9	0.4	997,886
Nevada	47	0.8	467	0.4	10	14.5	31,139	40.0	0.4	851,596
Mississippi	49	0.8	363	0.3	7	12.9	35,548	28.9	0.3	589,918
New Hampshire	34	0.5	427	0.4	13	15.7	36,848	27.9	0.3	820,882
Hawaii	27	0.4	324	0.3	12	9.5	29,441	18.4	0.2	682,185
Montana	20	0.3	254	0.2	13	6.7	26,291	14.9	0.1	746,800
New Mexico	26	0.4	245	0.2	9	6.1	24,906	13.6	0.1	524,462
South Dakota	16	0.3	157	0.2	10	5.1	32,331	12.7	0.1	792,062
D.C.	11	0.2	102	0.1	9	3.3	32,500	8.0	0.1	725,545
Idaho	16	0.3	129	0.1	8	3.6	28,016	7.5	0.1	470,563
Vermont	18	0.3	94	0.1	5	3.6	38,691	6.9	0.1	383,667
Rhode Island	23	0.4	375*	-	-	(D)	-	(D)	-	-
Delaware	13	0.2	175*	-	-	(D)	-	(D)	-	-
North Dakota	6	0.1	60*	-	-	(D)	-	(D)	-	-

Source: 1997 *Economic Census.* The states are in descending order of revenues or establishments (if revenue data are missing for the majority). The symbol (D) appears when data are withheld to prevent disclosure of competitive information. States marked with (D) are sorted by number of establishments. A dash (-) indicates that the data element cannot be calculated. * indicates the midpoint of a range; 175, for example is the range 100-249. Shaded *states* on the state map indicate those states which have proportionately greater representation in the industry than would be indicated by the state's population; the ratio is based on total revenues or number of establishments. Shaded *regions* indicate where the industry is regionally most concentrated.

NAICS 524298 - INSURANCE RELATED ACTIVITIES NEC

GENERAL STATISTICS

Year	Establishments (number)	Employment (number)	Payroll ($ million)	Revenues ($ million)	Employees per Establishment (number)	Revenues per Establishment ($)	Payroll per Employee ($)
1997	2,468	39,110	1,543.0	4,149.0	15.8	1,681,118	39,453

Source: *Economic Census of the United States*, 1997. This is a newly defined industry. Data for prior years were unavailable at the time of publication but may become available over time.

INDICES OF CHANGE

Year	Establishments (number)	Employment (number)	Payroll ($ million)	Revenues ($ million)	Employees per Establishment (number)	Revenues per Establishment ($)	Payroll per Employee ($)
1997	100.0	100.0	100.0	100.0	100.0	100.0	100.0

Sources: Same as General Statistics. The values shown reflect change from the base year, 1997. Values above 100 mean greater than 1997, values below 100 mean less than 1997, and a value of 100 in the 1982-96 or 1998-2001 period means same as 1997. Values followed by a 'p' are projections by the editors; 'e' stands for extrapolation. Data are the most recent available at this level of detail.

SIC INDUSTRIES RELATED TO NAICS 524298

Each new NAICS code represents an industry that used to be part of an SIC or a part of several SIC industries. Data in this table are shown to provide transitional information for these cases. All available data for the precursor SIC(s) are shown. Even if only a part of an SIC is included in the NAICS, *all* data for the SIC are reproduced. If the SIC industry is not marked as being a part (pt) of the NAICS, the entire industry is embedded in the NAICS data. The SIC composition of the new industry provides some hints of the relative importance of its "ancestors." Data marked with a 'p' are projected. Projections begin with 1982 data. Data earlier than 1990 are not shown but are reflected in the projections.

SIC	Industry	1990	1991	1992	1993	1994	1995	1996	1997
6411	**Insurance Agents, Brokers, & Service (pt)**								
	Establishments (number)	-	-	121,662	-	-	-	-	-
	Employment (thousands)	-	-	635.5	-	-	-	-	-
	Revenues ($ million)	-	-	51,705.1	-	-	-	-	-

Source: *Economic Census of the United States*, 1992, annual surveys of economic sectors conducted by the Bureau of the Census, and estimates or projections based on the 1982-1992 period; not all data are shown. 'e' marks estimates made by the editors; 'p' indicates projections based on time series. A dash (-) indicates that data for this SIC or year were not available. The abbreviation (pt) next to the industry name indicates that only a part of the industry is present within the NAICS data. If no (pt) is shown, the entire industry is contained within the NAICS data.

SELECTED RATIOS

For 1997	Avg. of Information	Analyzed Industry	Index	For 1997	Avg. of Information	Analyzed Industry	Index
Employees per establishment	15	16	107	Payroll per establishment	669,406	625,203	93
Revenue per establishment	5,561,120	1,681,118	30	Payroll as % of revenue	12	37	309
Revenue per employee	376,639	106,085	28	Payroll per employee	45,337	39,453	87

Sources: Same as General Statistics. The 'Average' column represents the average for the industry sector, in 1997, where the currently shown industry is classified. The Index shows the relationship between the Average and the Analyzed Industry. For example, 100 means that they are equal; 500 that the Analyzed Industry is five times the average; 50 means that the Analyzed Industry is half the national average. The abbreviation 'na' is used to show that data are 'not available'.

LEADING COMPANIES
No company data available for this industry.

LOCATION BY STATE AND REGIONAL CONCENTRATION

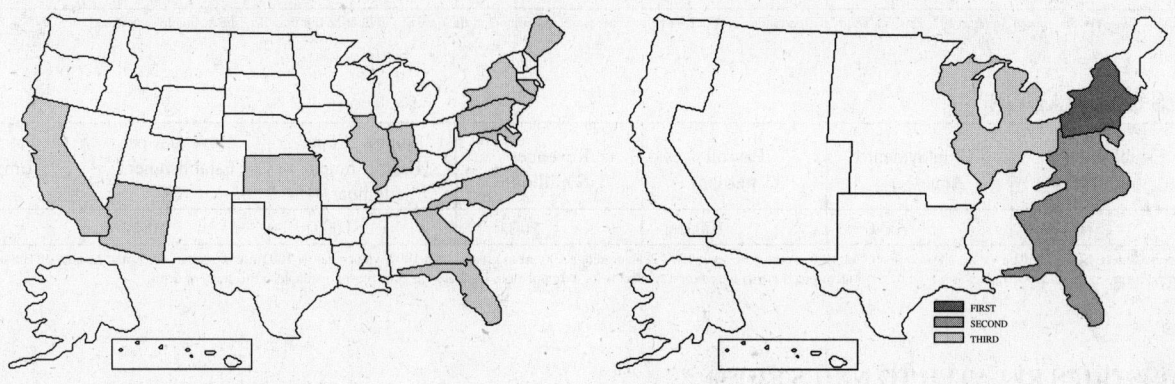

FIRST
SECOND
THIRD

INDUSTRY DATA BY STATE

State	Establishments Total (number)	Establishments % of U.S.	Employment Total (number)	Employment % of U.S.	Employment Per Estab.	Payroll Total ($ mil.)	Payroll Per Empl. ($)	Revenues Total ($ mil.)	Revenues % of U.S.	Revenues Per Estab. ($)
New York	186	7.5	3,587	9.2	19	184.5	51,449	695.7	16.8	3,740,527
California	288	11.7	4,549	11.6	16	185.0	40,665	525.2	12.7	1,823,622
Florida	192	7.8	3,856	9.9	20	134.8	34,964	334.4	8.1	1,741,740
Illinois	131	5.3	3,976	10.2	30	150.0	37,727	333.3	8.0	2,544,252
Texas	167	6.8	2,924	7.5	18	110.3	37,729	239.0	5.8	1,431,365
Pennsylvania	113	4.6	1,882	4.8	17	114.8	60,974	233.5	5.6	2,066,133
Ohio	78	3.2	1,590	4.1	20	52.7	33,132	152.8	3.7	1,959,526
Indiana	45	1.8	1,480	3.8	33	61.1	41,263	147.8	3.6	3,285,089
Georgia	84	3.4	1,189	3.0	14	53.1	44,675	133.0	3.2	1,582,917
North Carolina	44	1.8	648	1.7	15	36.0	55,506	115.3	2.8	2,621,182
Maryland	42	1.7	770	2.0	18	32.1	41,649	115.3	2.8	2,746,000
Arizona	46	1.9	416	1.1	9	17.5	42,188	88.6	2.1	1,925,609
Michigan	70	2.8	791	2.0	11	28.9	36,475	75.4	1.8	1,077,371
Minnesota	67	2.7	951	2.4	14	27.8	29,279	70.9	1.7	1,058,567
Wisconsin	51	2.1	1,005	2.6	20	28.1	27,983	61.7	1.5	1,210,176
Connecticut	51	2.1	561	1.4	11	28.4	50,540	60.8	1.5	1,192,373
Missouri	49	2.0	677	1.7	14	22.5	33,162	59.8	1.4	1,220,735
Kansas	31	1.3	415	1.1	13	16.3	39,364	53.0	1.3	1,709,516
Virginia	35	1.4	894	2.3	26	29.1	32,567	47.5	1.1	1,358,400
Oklahoma	28	1.1	347	0.9	12	12.8	36,767	32.6	0.8	1,163,429
Louisiana	37	1.5	288	0.7	8	7.7	26,844	28.2	0.7	762,919
Tennessee	40	1.6	427	1.1	11	11.2	26,218	26.9	0.6	673,725
Maine	16	0.6	233	0.6	15	8.4	35,841	26.0	0.6	1,626,813
West Virginia	10	0.4	375*	-	-	8.2	-	25.2	0.6	2,515,200
Kentucky	32	1.3	476	1.2	15	11.3	23,735	24.9	0.6	778,094
Nevada	21	0.9	210	0.5	10	7.0	33,471	21.9	0.5	1,044,524
Colorado	42	1.7	479	1.2	11	9.6	19,983	20.9	0.5	496,690
Washington	45	1.8	193	0.5	4	6.6	34,316	18.0	0.4	399,311
Alabama	23	0.9	249	0.6	11	5.2	21,076	17.2	0.4	748,174
Arkansas	13	0.5	133	0.3	10	4.1	31,180	11.7	0.3	899,308
South Carolina	16	0.6	107	0.3	7	3.4	32,206	10.7	0.3	670,812
Nebraska	15	0.6	360	0.9	24	5.3	14,839	8.3	0.2	555,867
Hawaii	13	0.5	94	0.2	7	3.1	33,011	7.9	0.2	607,308
Utah	18	0.7	78	0.2	4	2.1	27,090	7.5	0.2	418,778
Mississippi	10	0.4	100	0.3	10	2.4	24,350	7.4	0.2	735,300
New Mexico	14	0.6	61	0.2	4	1.3	20,787	6.9	0.2	491,500
Iowa	12	0.5	94	0.2	8	2.9	30,362	6.3	0.2	527,167
Idaho	7	0.3	26	0.1	4	0.6	21,846	4.8	0.1	681,143
South Dakota	8	0.3	22	0.1	3	0.7	30,636	2.4	0.1	295,000
Montana	7	0.3	45	0.1	6	0.8	17,778	2.0	0.0	287,429
New Jersey	113	4.6	1,750*	-	-	(D)	-	(D)	-	-
Massachusetts	61	2.5	750*	-	-	(D)	-	(D)	-	-
Oregon	34	1.4	175*	-	-	(D)	-	(D)	-	-
New Hampshire	16	0.6	60*	-	-	(D)	-	(D)	-	-
Delaware	11	0.4	175*	-	-	(D)	-	(D)	-	-
Vermont	10	0.4	60*	-	-	(D)	-	(D)	-	-
Rhode Island	7	0.3	10*	-	-	(D)	-	(D)	-	-
Alaska	6	0.2	60*	-	-	(D)	-	(D)	-	-

Source: 1997 *Economic Census*. The states are in descending order of revenues or establishments (if revenue data are missing for the majority). The symbol (D) appears when data are withheld to prevent disclosure of competitive information. States marked with (D) are sorted by number of establishments. A dash (-) indicates that the data element cannot be calculated. * indicates the midpoint of a range; 175, for example is the range 100-249. Shaded *states* on the state map indicate those states which have proportionately greater representation in the industry than would be indicated by the state's population; the ratio is based on total revenues or number of establishments. Shaded *regions* indicate where the industry is regionally most concentrated.

NAICS 525930 - REAL ESTATE INVESTMENT TRUSTS (REITS)

GENERAL STATISTICS

Year	Establishments (number)	Employment (number)	Payroll ($ million)	Revenues ($ million)	Employees per Establishment (number)	Revenues per Establishment ($)	Payroll per Employee ($)
1997	1,489	35,271	1,414.0	16,608.0	23.7	11,153,794	40,090

Source: *Economic Census of the United States*, 1997. This is a newly defined industry. Data for prior years were unavailable at the time of publication but may become available over time.

INDICES OF CHANGE

Year	Establishments (number)	Employment (number)	Payroll ($ million)	Revenues ($ million)	Employees per Establishment (number)	Revenues per Establishment ($)	Payroll per Employee ($)
1997	100.0	100.0	100.0	100.0	100.0	100.0	100.0

Sources: Same as General Statistics. The values shown reflect change from the base year, 1997. Values above 100 mean greater than 1997, values below 100 mean less than 1997, and a value of 100 in the 1982-96 or 1998-2001 period means same as 1997. Values followed by a 'p' are projections by the editors; 'e' stands for extrapolation. Data are the most recent available at this level of detail.

SIC INDUSTRIES RELATED TO NAICS 525930

Each new NAICS code represents an industry that used to be part of an SIC or a part of several SIC industries. Data in this table are shown to provide transitional information for these cases. All available data for the precursor SIC(s) are shown. Even if only a part of an SIC is included in the NAICS, *all* data for the SIC are reproduced. If the SIC industry is not marked as being a part (pt) of the NAICS, the entire industry is embedded in the NAICS data. The SIC composition of the new industry provides some hints of the relative importance of its "ancestors." Data marked with a 'p' are projected. Projections begin with 1982 data. Data earlier than 1990 are not shown but are reflected in the projections.

SIC	Industry	1990	1991	1992	1993	1994	1995	1996	1997
6798	**Real Estate Investment Trusts (pt)**								
	Establishments (number)	-	-	655	-	-	-	-	-
	Employment (thousands)	-	-	4.8	-	-	-	-	-
	Revenues ($ million)	-	-	2,507.5	-	-	-	-	-

Source: *Economic Census of the United States*, 1992, annual surveys of economic sectors conducted by the Bureau of the Census, and estimates or projections based on the 1982-1992 period; not all data are shown. 'e' marks estimates made by the editors; 'p' indicates projections based on time series. A dash (-) indicates that data for this SIC or year were not available. The abbreviation (pt) next to the industry name indicates that only a part of the industry is present within the NAICS data. If no (pt) is shown, the entire industry is contained within the NAICS data.

SELECTED RATIOS

For 1997	Avg. of Information	Analyzed Industry	Index	For 1997	Avg. of Information	Analyzed Industry	Index
Employees per establishment	15	24	160	Payroll per establishment	669,406	949,631	142
Revenue per establishment	5,561,120	11,153,794	201	Payroll as % of revenue	12	9	71
Revenue per employee	376,639	470,868	125	Payroll per employee	45,337	40,090	88

Sources: Same as General Statistics. The 'Average' column represents the average for the industry sector, in 1997, where the currently shown industry is classified. The Index shows the relationship between the Average and the Analyzed Industry. For example, 100 means that they are equal; 500 that the Analyzed Industry is five times the average; 50 means that the Analyzed Industry is half the national average. The abbreviation 'na' is used to show that data are 'not available'.

LEADING COMPANIES   Number shown: **74**   Total sales ($ mil): **2,596,441**   Total employment (000): **81.7**

Company Name	Address				CEO Name	Phone	Co. Type	Sales ($ mil)	Empl. (000)
DeBartolo Realty Corp.	7655 Market St	Youngstown	OH	44513	David Simon	330-758-7292	S	2,484,614*	7.0
Crocker Realty Trust	433 Plaza Real, #335	Boca Raton	FL	33432	Tom Crocker	561-395-9666	R	49,629*	0.1
Dynex Capital Inc.	10900 Nuckols Rd	Glen Allen	VA	23060	Thomas H Potts	804-217-5800	P	5,378	0.2
Boston Properties Inc.	Pru Ctr	Boston	MA	02199	Edward H Linde	617-236-3300	P	5,235	0.5
Security Capital Group Inc.	125 Lincoln Ave	Santa Fe	NM	87501	William D Sanders	505-982-9292	P	4,508	0.6
Thornburg Mortgage Asset Corp.	119 E Marcy St	Santa Fe	NM	87501	Larry A Goldstone	505-989-1900	P	4,345	<0.1
United Dominion Relty Trust	10 S 6th St	Richmond	VA	23219	John McCann	804-780-2691	P	3,755	2.7
Mack-Cali Realty Corp.	11 Commerce Dr	Cranford	NJ	07016	Mitchell E Hersh	908-272-8000	P	3,452	0.5
ROC Communities Inc.	6160 S Syracuse	Englewood	CO	80111	Gary P McDaniel	303-741-3707	S	2,129*	3.0
Developers Diversified Realty	3300 Enterprise	Beachwood	OH	44122	Scott A Wolstein	216-755-5500	P	2,126	0.2
Wyndham International Inc.	1950 Stemmons	Dallas	TX	75207	James D Carreker	214-863-1000	P	1,952	<0.1
Brandywine Realty Trust	14 Campus Blvd	Newtown Square	PA	19073	Anthony Nichols Sr	610-325-5600	P	1,912	0.2
Bradley Real Estate Inc.	40 Skokie Blvd	Northbrook	IL	60062	Thomas P D'Arcy	847-272-9800	P	1,901*	0.2
Prentiss Properties Trust	3890 W Northwest	Dallas	TX	75220	Thomas F August	214-654-0886	P	1,871	0.7
Equity Office Properties Trust	2 N Riverside Plz	Chicago	IL	60606	Timothy H Callahan	312-466-3300	P	1,703	1.7
BRE Properties Inc.	44 Montgomery St	San Francisco	CA	94104	Frank C McDowell	415-445-6530	P	1,631	1.0
Mid-America Apartment	6584 Poplar Ave	Memphis	TN	38138	H Eric Bolton	901-682-6600	P	1,456	0.5
Burnham Pacific Properties Inc.	PO Box 121551	San Diego	CA	92112	J David Martin	619-652-4700	P	1,114	0.2
Alexander Haagen Properties Inc.	PO Box 10010	Manhattan Bch	CA	90267	Edward D Fox, Jr	310-546-4520	P	987	0.1
Chateau Communities Inc.	6160 S Syracuse	Greenwood Vill.	CO	80111	C G Kellog	303-741-3707	P	959	1.2
Apex Mortgage Capital Inc.	865 S Figueroa St	Los Angeles	CA	90017	Philip A Barach	213-244-0460	P	865	0.0
Associated Estates Realty Corp.	5025 Swetland Ct	Richmond H.	OH	44143	Jeffrey I Friedman	216-261-5000	P	841	0.9
Koger Equity Inc.	PO Box 58120	Jacksonville	FL	32241	Victor A Hughes Jr	904-732-1000	P	834	0.2
Security Capital Atlantic Inc.	6 Piedmont Ctr	Atlanta	GA	30305		404-237-9292	D	792	0.6
American Health Properties Inc.	6400 S Fid's Grn	Englewood	CO	80111	Joseph P Sullivan	303-796-9793	P	754	<0.1
Crescent Real Estate Equities Inc.	777 Main St	Ft. Worth	TX	76102	John Goss	817-321-2100	P	738	0.5
Blue Gem Inc.	PO Box 29346	Greensboro	NC	27429	Alan W Cone	336-275-0756	R	710*	<0.1
Meditrust Corp.	197 First Ave	Needham H.	MA	02494	David F Benson	781-433-6000	P	639	8.0
Meditrust Inc.	197 1st Ave	Needham H.	MA	02194	Abraham D Gosman	781-433-6000	P	639	<0.1
National Golf Properties Inc.	2951 28th St	Santa Monica	CA	90405	James M Stenich	310-664-4100	3	597	<0.1
Duke-Weeks Realty Corp.	8888 Keystone	Indianapolis	IN	46240	Thomas L Hefner	317-808-6000	P	590	0.7
Kranzco Realty Trust	128 Fayette St	Conshohocken	PA	19428	Norman M Kranzdorf	610-941-9292	P	546*	0.1
MeriStar Hospitality Corp.	1010 Wisconsin Ave	Washington	DC	20007	Paul W Whetsell	202-295-1000	P	525	30.0
Highwoods Properties Inc.	3100 Smoketree Ct	Raleigh	NC	27604	Ronald P Gibson	919-872-4924	P	514	0.7
Crescent Operating Inc.	306 W 7th St	Fort Worth	TX	76102	Gerald W Haddock	817-339-2200	P	493	1.7
HRPT Properties Trust	400 Centre St	Newton	MA	02458	David J Hegarty	617-322-3990	P	367	0.2
Cornerstone Properties Inc.	126 E 56th St	New York	NY	10022	John S Moody	212-605-7100	P	360	0.3
AMB Property Corp.	505 Montgomery St	San Francisco	CA	94111	T Robert Burke	415-394-9000	P	359	0.1
First Industrial Realty Trust Inc.	311 S Wacker Dr	Chicago	IL	60606	Michael W Brennan	312-344-4300	P	347	0.3
Post Properties Inc.	One Riverside	Atlanta	GA	30327	John T Glover	404-846-5000	P	346	1.9
Macerich Co.	P O Box 2172	Santa Monica	CA	90407	Mace Siegel		P	298	1.4
IRET	12 S Main St	Minot	ND	58701	Roger R Odell	701-837-4738	P	292	0.0
Sizeler Property Investors Inc.	2542 Williams Blvd	Kenner	LA	70062	Sidney W Lassen	504-471-6200	P	286	<0.1
Colonial Properties Trust	2101 6th Ave N	Birmingham	AL	35203	Thomas H Lowder	205-250-9700	P	283	0.9
Charles E. Smith Residential	2345 Crystal Dr	Arlington	VA	22202	Ernest A Geradi Jr	703-920-8500	P	260	1.8
Storage USA	165 Madinson Ave	Memphis	TN	38103	Dean Jernigan	901-252-2000	P	223	1.7
PIMCO Commercial Mortgage	840 Newport Center	Newport Beach	CA	92660	R Wesley Burns	949-760-4743	R	211	1.1
Healthcare Realty Trust Inc.	3310 West End Ave	Nashville	TN	37203	David R Emery	615-269-8175	P	192	0.2
Glimcher Realty Trust	20 S 3rd St	Columbus	OH	43215	Herbert Glimcher	614-621-9000	P	186	0.5
Tri Net Corportate Reality Trust	1 Embarcad Ctr	San Francisco	CA	94111	Robert W Holman, Jr	415-391-4300	P	163	<0.1
Home Properties of New York Inc.	850 Clinton Sq	Rochester	NY	14604	Norman P Leenhouts	716-546-4900	P	149	1.6
Pacific Gulf Properties Inc.	4220 Von Karman	Newport Beach	CA	92660	Glenn L Carpenter	949-223-5000	P	148	0.2
Nationwide Health Properties Inc.	610 Newport Center	Newport Beach	CA	92660	R Bruce Andrews	949-718-4400	P	145	<0.1
Amli Residential Properties Trust	125 S Wacker Dr	Chicago	IL	60606	Allan J Sweet	312-443-1477	P	121	0.8
Belz Enterprises	P O Box 3661	Memphis	TN	38173	Jack A Belz		R	100*	3.0
Healthcare Reality Trust	3310 West End Ave	Nashville	TN	37203	David R Emery	615-269-8175	R	93	0.2
Pennsylvania Real Estate	200 S Broad St	Philadelphia	PA	19102	Ronald Rubin	215-875-0700	R	90	0.8
Transcontinental Realty Investors	10670 N Cen Expwy	Dallas	TX	75231	Randall Paulson	214-692-4700	P	84	<0.1
JDN Realty Corp.	359 E Paces Ferry	Atlanta	GA	30305	J Donald Nichols	404-262-3252	P	81	<0.1
Commercial Net Lease Realty Inc.	455 S Orange Ave	Orlando	FL	32801	Gary M Ralston	407-265-7348	P	77	<0.1
First Washington Realty Trust Inc.	4350 East-West	Bethesda	MD	20814	Stuart Halpert	301-907-7800	P	77	<0.1
Prison Realty Trust	10 Burton Hills	Nashville	TN	37215	Thomas Beasley	615-460-1220	P	71	<0.1
Continental Mortgage & Equity	10670 N Cen Expwy	Dallas	TX	75231	Randall M Paulson	214-692-4700	P	71	<0.1
Saul Centers Inc.	8401 Connecticut	Chevy Chase	MD	20815	Phillip D Caraci	301-986-6207	P	71	<0.1
HEI Investment Corp.	P O Box 730	Honolulu	HI	96808	Robert F Mougeot	808-543-5662	S	67	<0.1
Boddie-Noell Properties, Inc.	3850 1st Union	Charlotte	NC	28202	D Scott Wilkerson	704-944-0100	R	27	0.1
EastGroup-LNH Corp.	P O Box 22728	Jackson	MS	39225	David H Hoster II	601-354-3555	S	26	<0.1
Stratford American Corp.	2400 E AZ Biltmr	Phoenix	AZ	85016	David H Eaton	602-956-7809	P	11	<0.1
C.E.C. Industries Corp.	23 Cactus Garden	Henderson	NV	89014	Gerald H Levine	702-893-4747	P	8	0.0
J.T. Holding Co.	3400 Peachtree N E	Atlanta	GA	30326	Anthony H Harwood	404-240-0139	R	6*	<0.1
USP Real Estate Investment Trust	4333 Edgewood Rd	Cedar Rapids	IA	52499	David L Blankenship	319-398-8895	P	6	0.0
DVL Inc.	P O Box 408	Bogota	NJ	07603	Alan Casnoff	212-350-9900	P	3	<0.1
Cedar Income Fund Ltd.	44 S Byles Ave	Port Washington	NY	11050	Leo S Ullman	516-767-6492	P	3	<0.1
Gyrodyne of America Inc.	7 Flowerfield, Ste 28	St. James	NY	11780	Paul L Lamb	516-584-5400	P	2	<0.1

Source: Ward's Business Directory of U.S. Private and Public Companies, Volumes 1 and 2, 2000. The company type code used is as follows: P - Public, R - Private, S - Subsidiary, D - Division, J - Joint Venture, A - Affiliate, G - Group, N - Company type not reported. Sales are in millions of dollars, employees are in thousands. An asterisk (*) indicates an estimated sales volume. The symbol < stands for 'less than'. Company names and addresses are truncated, in some cases, to fit into the available space.

LOCATION BY STATE AND REGIONAL CONCENTRATION

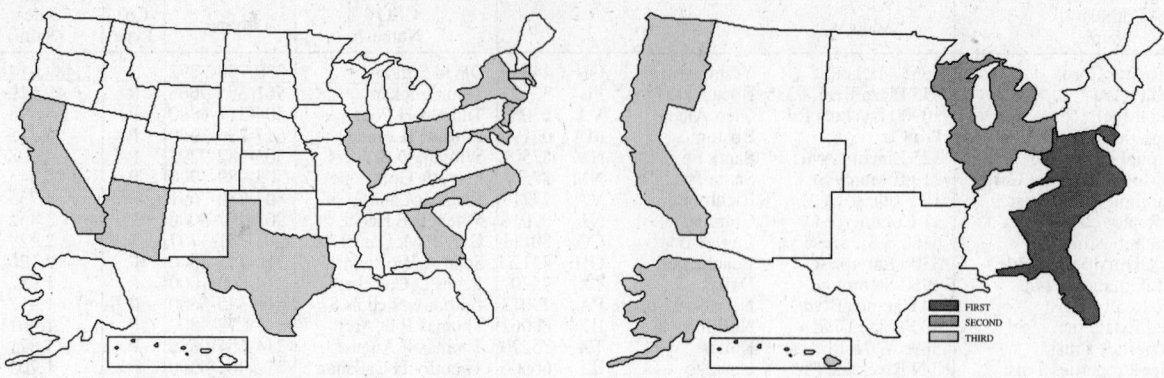

INDUSTRY DATA BY STATE

	Establishments		Employment			Payroll		Revenues		
State	Total (number)	% of U.S.	Total (number)	% of U.S.	Per Estab.	Total ($ mil.)	Per Empl. ($)	Total ($ mil.)	% of U.S.	Per Estab. ($)
Maryland	60	4.0	1,327	3.8	22	82.6	62,223	2,329.6	14.0	38,827,383
California	159	10.7	2,787	7.9	18	125.7	45,118	2,312.8	13.9	14,546,113
Texas	173	11.6	2,654	7.5	15	115.4	43,478	1,843.3	11.1	10,655,202
Illinois	76	5.1	5,684	16.1	75	401.6	70,653	1,732.5	10.4	22,795,776
New York	63	4.2	1,435	4.1	23	58.3	40,647	1,286.1	7.7	20,414,429
Ohio	37	2.5	3,900	11.1	105	93.5	23,986	1,190.5	7.2	32,174,865
Georgia	92	6.2	1,115	3.2	12	36.9	33,122	796.3	4.8	8,654,967
New Jersey	38	2.6	972	2.8	26	83.0	85,424	639.4	3.9	16,826,553
Massachusetts	54	3.6	2,826	8.0	52	48.7	17,216	551.4	3.3	10,210,944
North Carolina	85	5.7	1,194	3.4	14	43.2	36,186	495.8	3.0	5,832,918
Pennsylvania	37	2.5	1,147	3.3	31	34.8	30,328	484.6	2.9	13,098,432
Michigan	27	1.8	1,420	4.0	53	37.1	26,161	390.5	2.4	14,462,037
D.C.	14	0.9	375*	-	-	22.2	-	354.6	2.1	25,329,214
Florida	137	9.2	1,563	4.4	11	29.1	18,592	341.3	2.1	2,491,277
Arizona	24	1.6	925	2.6	39	31.4	33,948	259.6	1.6	10,817,208
Virginia	65	4.4	1,350	3.8	21	32.3	23,896	251.4	1.5	3,867,523
Washington	43	2.9	389	1.1	9	10.2	26,172	128.7	0.8	2,992,256
Colorado	17	1.1	60*	-	-	3.4	-	109.3	0.7	6,430,000
Louisiana	13	0.9	169	0.5	13	4.0	23,822	86.7	0.5	6,666,385
South Carolina	38	2.6	252	0.7	7	6.8	27,071	72.3	0.4	1,902,447
Missouri	14	0.9	324	0.9	23	8.3	25,694	66.6	0.4	4,754,714
Kansas	10	0.7	175*	-	-	2.9	-	61.2	0.4	6,119,700
Minnesota	10	0.7	195	0.6	20	6.0	30,826	54.4	0.3	5,440,300
Tennessee	29	1.9	189	0.5	7	6.8	35,730	49.2	0.3	1,696,862
Hawaii	6	0.4	60*	-	-	3.1	-	37.9	0.2	6,320,667
Connecticut	22	1.5	140	0.4	6	6.3	45,350	37.7	0.2	1,714,091
Arkansas	8	0.5	94	0.3	12	1.3	13,638	18.6	0.1	2,322,000
New Mexico	10	0.7	178	0.5	18	6.0	33,725	17.2	0.1	1,721,700
Oklahoma	9	0.6	89	0.3	10	1.6	17,865	17.2	0.1	1,905,667
Nebraska	12	0.8	48	0.1	4	0.7	14,333	13.1	0.1	1,088,583
Oregon	10	0.7	59	0.2	6	1.2	20,864	9.3	0.1	930,700
Indiana	21	1.4	750*	-	-	(D)	-	(D)	-	-
Nevada	10	0.7	60*	-	-	(D)	-	(D)	-	-
Delaware	7	0.5	60*	-	-	(D)	-	(D)	-	-
Maine	7	0.5	60*	-	-	(D)	-	(D)	-	-
Mississippi	7	0.5	60*	-	-	(D)	-	(D)	-	-
Idaho	6	0.4	60*	-	-	(D)	-	(D)	-	-
New Hampshire	6	0.4	60*	-	-	(D)	-	(D)	-	-

Source: 1997 *Economic Census*. The states are in descending order of revenues or establishments (if revenue data are missing for the majority). The symbol (D) appears when data are withheld to prevent disclosure of competitive information. States marked with (D) are sorted by number of establishments. A dash (-) indicates that the data element cannot be calculated. * indicates the midpoint of a range; 175, for example is the range 100-249. Shaded *states* on the state map indicate those states which have proportionately greater representation in the industry than would be indicated by the state's population; the ratio is based on total revenues or number of establishments. Shaded *regions* indicate where the industry is regionally most concentrated.

Part II

REAL ESTATE, RENTAL, AND LEASING

NAICS 531110 - LESSORS OF RESIDENTIAL BUILDINGS AND DWELLINGS

GENERAL STATISTICS

Year	Establishments (number)	Employment (number)	Payroll ($ million)	Revenues ($ million)	Employees per Establishment (number)	Revenues per Establishment ($)	Payroll per Employee ($)
1997	59,718	267,784	4,674.0	39,621.0	4.5	663,468	17,454

Source: Economic Census of the United States, 1997. This is a newly defined industry. Data for prior years were unavailable at the time of publication but may become available over time.

INDICES OF CHANGE

Year	Establishments (number)	Employment (number)	Payroll ($ million)	Revenues ($ million)	Employees per Establishment (number)	Revenues per Establishment ($)	Payroll per Employee ($)
1997	100.0	100.0	100.0	100.0	100.0	100.0	100.0

Sources: Same as General Statistics. The values shown reflect change from the base year, 1997. Values above 100 mean greater than 1997, values below 100 mean less than 1997, and a value of 100 in the 1982-96 or 1998-2001 period means same as 1997. Values followed by a 'p' are projections by the editors; 'e' stands for extrapolation. Data are the most recent available at this level of detail.

SIC INDUSTRIES RELATED TO NAICS 531110

Each new NAICS code represents an industry that used to be part of an SIC or a part of several SIC industries. Data in this table are shown to provide transitional information for these cases. All available data for the precursor SIC(s) are shown. Even if only a part of an SIC is included in the NAICS, *all* data for the SIC are reproduced. If the SIC industry is not marked as being a part (pt) of the NAICS, the entire industry is embedded in the NAICS data. The SIC composition of the new industry provides some hints of the relative importance of its "ancestors." Data marked with a 'p' are projected. Projections begin with 1982 data. Data earlier than 1990 are not shown but are reflected in the projections.

SIC	Industry	1990	1991	1992	1993	1994	1995	1996	1997
6513	**Apartment Building Operators**	-	-	-	-	-	-	-	-
6514	**Dwelling Operators Except Apartments**	-	-	-	-	-	-	-	-

Source: Economic Census of the United States, 1992, annual surveys of economic sectors conducted by the Bureau of the Census, and estimates or projections based on the 1982-1992 period; not all data are shown. 'e' marks estimates made by the editors; 'p' indicates projections based on time series. A dash (-) indicates that data for this SIC or year were not available. The abbreviation (pt) next to the industry name indicates that only a part of the industry is present within the NAICS data. If no (pt) is shown, the entire industry is contained within the NAICS data.

SELECTED RATIOS

For 1997	Avg. of Information	Analyzed Industry	Index	For 1997	Avg. of Information	Analyzed Industry	Index
Employees per establishment	6	4	76	Payroll per establishment	144,276	78,268	54
Revenue per establishment	835,727	663,468	79	Payroll as % of revenue	17	12	68
Revenue per employee	141,515	147,959	105	Payroll per employee	24,430	17,454	71

Sources: Same as General Statistics. The 'Average' column represents the average for the industry sector, in 1997, where the currently shown industry is classified. The Index shows the relationship between the Average and the Analyzed Industry. For example, 100 means that they are equal; 500 that the Analyzed Industry is five times the average; 50 means that the Analyzed Industry is half the national average. The abbreviation 'na' is used to show that data are 'not available'.

LEADING COMPANIES   Number shown: **50**   Total sales ($ mil): **15,842**   Total employment (000): **65.2**

Company Name	Address				CEO Name	Phone	Co. Type	Sales ($ mil)	Empl. (000)
Lefrak Organization Inc.	97-77 Queens Blvd	Rego Park	NY	11374	Samuel J. LeFrak	718-459-9021	R	2,750	16.0
Trammell Crow Residential	2859 Paces Ferry	Atlanta	GA	30339	J Ronald Terwilliger	770-801-1600	R	1,982*	3.0
Senior Campus Living	701 Maiden Choice	Catonsville	MD	21228	John Erickson	410-242-2880	R	1,562*	1.8
Wilmac Corp.	P O Box 5047	York	PA	17405	Karen McCormack	717-854-7857	R	1,241*	1.5
A.G. Spanos Construction Inc.	P O Box 7126	Stockton	CA	95267	Dean Spanos	209-478-7954	R	1,175	0.6
Helmsley Enterprises Inc.	230 Park Ave	New York	NY	10169	Abe Wolf	212-679-3600	S	1,000	7.9
Forest City Enterprises Inc.	1100 Terminal Twr	Cleveland	OH	44113	Charles A Ratner	216-621-6060	P	697	3.6
John Knox Village Inc.	400 N W Murray Rd	Lees Summit	MO	64081	Herman C Spahr	816-524-8400	R	689*	0.8
Inland Group Inc.	2901 Butterfield Rd	Oak Brook	IL	60523	Daniel L Goodwin	630-218-8000	R	645	0.8
Archstone Communities Trust	7670 S Chester St	Englewood	CO	80112	R Scott Sellers	303-708-5959	P	579	2.1
Erb Lumber Co.	PO Box 3013	Birmingham	MI	48012		313-644-6518	R	453*	2.0
Goodale and Barbieri Cos.	W 201 N River Dr	Spokane	WA	99201		509-459-6100	R	321*	2.5
Shilo Corp. Management Offices	11600 S W Shilo Ln	Portland	OR	97225	Mark S Hemstreet	503-641-6565	R	283*	2.5
Forest City Commercial Group Inc	1100 Terminal Twr	Cleveland	OH	44113	James Ratner	216-267-1200	S	270	1.7
Gertrude Gardner Inc.	3332 N Woodlawn	Metairie	LA	70006	Glenn M Gardner	504-887-7588	R	222*	<0.1
Fetterolf Group Inc.	227 New Centerville	Somerset	PA	15501	Donald L Fetterolf	814-443-4688	R	206*	0.3
JPI Investments Inc.	600 E Colinas	Irving	TX	75039	Robert D Page	972-556-1700	R	200	1.0
Highland Management Group Inc.	5290 Villa Way	Edina	MN	55436	Mark Z Jones II	612-925-1020	R	187*	0.2
American Retirement Corp.	111 Westwood Place	Brentwood	TN	37027	WE Sheriff	615-221-2250	P	142	5.2
Classic Residence by Hyatt	200 W Madison Ave	Chicago	IL	60606	Penny Pritzker	312-750-1234	S	133*	0.2
University City Housing Co.	3418 Sansom St	Philadelphia	PA	19104	Michael Karp	215-382-2986	R	117*	0.1
American Baptist Homes	6120 Stoneridge	Pleasanton	CA	94588	David B Ferguson	925-635-7600	R	100*	2.0
Bixby Ranch Co.	3010 Old Ranch	Seal Beach	CA	90740	Chase Morgan	562-493-1475	R	82*	0.2
Brookdale Living Communities	77 W Wacker Dr	Chicago	IL	60601	Michael W Reschke	312-977-3700	P	78	1.7
Gene B. Glick Company Inc.	PO Box 40177	Indianapolis	IN	46240	Eugene B Glick	317-469-0400	R	74*	0.7
Atria Communities Inc.	501 S 4th Ave	Louisville	KY	40202	W Patrick Mulloy II	502-596-7540	P	69	2.7
Benchmark Group Inc.	4043 Maple Rd	Amherst	NY	14226	George Gellman	716-833-4986	R	65*	0.3
Patterson-Erie Corp.	1250 Tower Ln	Erie	PA	16505	W L Patterson Jr	814-455-8031	R	62	1.7
Allen and O'Hara Inc.	530 Oak Court Dr	Memphis	TN	38117	Paul O'Bower	901-345-7620	R	48*	<0.1
Koller Enterprises Inc.	1400 S Hwy 141	Fenton	MO	63026	AJ Koller	314-343-9220	R	36	0.2
Bresler and Reiner Inc.	401 M St S W	Washington	DC	20024	Charles S Bresler	202-488-8800	P	33	0.1
Westminster Capital Inc.	9665 Wilshire Blvd	Beverly Hills	CA	90212	William Belzberg	310-278-1930	P	31	<0.1
Jonas Equities Inc.	725 Church Ave	Brooklyn	NY	11218		718-871-4840	R	30*	<0.1
Time Equities Inc.	55 5th Ave	New York	NY	10003	Francis Greenburger	212-206-6000	R	28*	<0.1
Milestone Properties Inc.	150 E Palmetto Park	Boca Raton	FL	33432	Leonard S Mandor	561-394-9533	P	25	<0.1
Ito Ham U.S.A. Inc.	3190 Corporate Pl	Hayward	CA	94545	Jack Mori	510-887-1612	R	25	0.1
Stoltz Management of Delaware	261 Old York Rd	Jenkintown	PA	19046		215-886-7260	R	23*	<0.1
Panorama City Corp.	150 Circle Dr	Lacey	WA	98503	Joseph J Di Santo	425-456-0111	R	22	0.3
D.C.G. Development Co.	1-A Lakeview Dr	Clifton Park	NY	12065	Donald Greene	518-383-0059	R	21	0.1
Crown Pointe Div.	2820 S 80th St	Omaha	NE	68124		402-391-7555	D	20*	<0.1
Village Homes Corp.	6 W Dry Creek Cir	Littleton	CO	80120	John Osborn	303-795-1976	R	20	0.3
New England Realty Associates L	39 Brighton Ave	Allston	MA	02134	Ronald Brown	617-783-0039	P	19	<0.1
Landar Corp.	515 Post Oak Blvd	Houston	TX	77027	Cecil Holley	713-622-0500	R	15	<0.1
William Lyon Property	4490 Von Karmen	Newport Beach	CA	92660	Frank T Suryan Jr	949-252-9101	R	13*	0.2
Eaton & Lauth Real Estate	9777 N College Ave	Indiannapolis	IN	46201	Robert L Lautl	317-848-6500	R	12*	<0.1
Focus Group Inc.	3565 Piedmont Rd	Atlanta	GA	30305	Michael Blonder	404-816-6300	R	12*	<0.1
Marriott Senior Living Services	1 Marriot Dr	Washington	DC	20001		301-380-4940	S	11*	0.3
Ralph Williams and Associates	1800 N Wabash Rd	Marion	IN	46952	Ralph Williams	765-668-7561	R	10*	<0.1
MBK Northwest	4949 SW Meadows	Lake Oswego	OR	97035	Mason Frank	503-636-2800	D	3*	<0.1
J.D. Industries Inc.	227 Harrison Ave	Panama City	FL	32401	John W Darrah	850-784-3900	R	2*	<0.1

Source: Ward's Business Directory of U.S. Private and Public Companies, Volumes 1 and 2, 2000. The company type code used is as follows: P - Public, R - Private, S - Subsidiary, D - Division, J - Joint Venture, A - Affiliate, G - Group, N - Company type not reported. Sales are in millions of dollars, employees are in thousands. An asterisk (*) indicates an estimated sales volume. The symbol < stands for 'less than'. Company names and addresses are truncated, in some cases, to fit into the available space.

LOCATION BY STATE AND REGIONAL CONCENTRATION

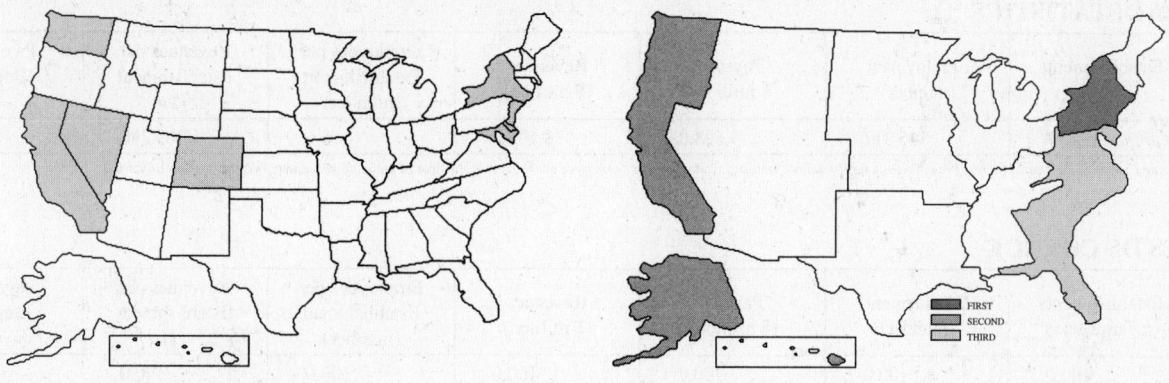

INDUSTRY DATA BY STATE

State	Establishments		Employment			Payroll		Revenues		
	Total (number)	% of U.S.	Total (number)	% of U.S.	Per Estab.	Total ($ mil.)	Per Empl. ($)	Total ($ mil.)	% of U.S.	Per Estab. ($)
New York	10,868	18.2	39,615	14.8	4	926.7	23,393	8,494.4	21.4	781,602
California	8,466	14.2	36,446	13.6	4	574.8	15,772	5,512.6	13.9	651,148
Texas	3,809	6.4	17,023	6.4	4	282.8	16,610	2,231.5	5.6	585,840
New Jersey	2,093	3.5	9,977	3.7	5	199.5	19,995	2,031.6	5.1	970,643
Florida	2,808	4.7	14,317	5.3	5	241.7	16,885	1,886.1	4.8	671,677
Illinois	2,059	3.4	10,756	4.0	5	210.6	19,581	1,695.7	4.3	823,560
Pennsylvania	1,555	2.6	8,562	3.2	6	151.3	17,673	1,286.9	3.2	827,558
Michigan	1,432	2.4	8,524	3.2	6	139.9	16,416	1,113.8	2.8	777,814
Ohio	1,952	3.3	8,520	3.2	4	134.3	15,761	1,074.1	2.7	550,262
Maryland	911	1.5	6,670	2.5	7	131.7	19,752	1,016.7	2.6	1,116,024
Virginia	1,056	1.8	6,287	2.3	6	115.0	18,287	939.2	2.4	889,406
Washington	1,950	3.3	7,913	3.0	4	109.4	13,823	917.2	2.3	470,365
Massachusetts	869	1.5	5,858	2.2	7	132.9	22,695	867.8	2.2	998,666
Georgia	1,155	1.9	5,471	2.0	5	107.5	19,645	803.2	2.0	695,388
Minnesota	1,139	1.9	5,293	2.0	5	70.0	13,219	685.3	1.7	601,651
Colorado	1,071	1.8	5,058	1.9	5	78.8	15,579	657.9	1.7	614,330
Indiana	910	1.5	4,413	1.6	5	70.1	15,876	624.2	1.6	685,919
Wisconsin	1,064	1.8	4,847	1.8	5	67.2	13,866	582.2	1.5	547,207
Tennessee	904	1.5	4,132	1.5	5	62.4	15,113	533.3	1.3	589,980
Missouri	1,083	1.8	4,716	1.8	4	74.8	15,858	500.1	1.3	461,741
Connecticut	609	1.0	3,032	1.1	5	56.9	18,764	476.5	1.2	782,361
North Carolina	966	1.6	3,738	1.4	4	62.7	16,775	467.1	1.2	483,567
Oregon	984	1.6	4,380	1.6	4	52.0	11,871	444.1	1.1	451,309
Nevada	512	0.9	2,703	1.0	5	44.2	16,357	438.2	1.1	855,822
Arizona	744	1.2	3,683	1.4	5	53.4	14,488	412.3	1.0	554,175
Louisiana	821	1.4	3,232	1.2	4	45.6	14,105	354.8	0.9	432,113
D.C.	351	0.6	1,983	0.7	6	36.8	18,541	329.3	0.8	938,151
Kentucky	660	1.1	2,756	1.0	4	40.9	14,851	304.7	0.8	461,602
Alabama	689	1.2	2,749	1.0	4	36.3	13,206	282.1	0.7	409,466
Kansas	485	0.8	2,161	0.8	4	33.3	15,387	260.4	0.7	536,821
Oklahoma	603	1.0	2,487	0.9	4	35.0	14,084	245.2	0.6	406,609
Iowa	537	0.9	1,944	0.7	4	25.2	12,962	205.1	0.5	381,873
South Carolina	385	0.6	1,479	0.6	4	21.5	14,552	169.9	0.4	441,387
Nebraska	347	0.6	1,676	0.6	5	23.1	13,758	166.0	0.4	478,305
Arkansas	445	0.7	1,510	0.6	3	19.9	13,158	162.7	0.4	365,596
Hawaii	313	0.5	1,105	0.4	4	23.0	20,859	157.0	0.4	501,476
Mississippi	453	0.8	1,362	0.5	3	16.5	12,095	151.0	0.4	333,342
New Mexico	312	0.5	1,461	0.5	5	19.7	13,472	143.1	0.4	458,788
Utah	269	0.5	1,392	0.5	5	18.3	13,149	136.3	0.3	506,658
Delaware	145	0.2	1,113	0.4	8	19.8	17,830	127.1	0.3	876,462
West Virginia	323	0.5	1,166	0.4	4	14.5	12,403	107.6	0.3	333,003
Rhode Island	140	0.2	858	0.3	6	18.6	21,711	106.2	0.3	758,621
New Hampshire	183	0.3	763	0.3	4	14.5	18,950	103.2	0.3	564,175
Maine	208	0.3	645	0.2	3	9.3	14,479	81.7	0.2	392,587
South Dakota	191	0.3	728	0.3	4	9.6	13,173	61.7	0.2	323,188
Alaska	105	0.2	461	0.2	4	9.6	20,822	60.2	0.2	573,133
North Dakota	198	0.3	607	0.2	3	6.9	11,300	58.0	0.1	292,732
Montana	235	0.4	908	0.3	4	10.9	11,980	58.0	0.1	246,685
Idaho	150	0.3	780	0.3	5	7.9	10,091	50.5	0.1	336,647
Wyoming	133	0.2	376	0.1	3	3.8	10,056	27.2	0.1	204,278
Vermont	68	0.1	148	0.1	2	3.0	20,081	20.6	0.1	302,574

Source: 1997 *Economic Census*. The states are in descending order of revenues or establishments (if revenue data are missing for the majority). The symbol (D) appears when data are withheld to prevent disclosure of competitive information. States marked with (D) are sorted by number of establishments. A dash (-) indicates that the data element cannot be calculated. * indicates the midpoint of a range; 175, for example is the range 100-249. Shaded *states* on the state map indicate those states which have proportionately greater representation in the industry than would be indicated by the state's population; the ratio is based on total revenues or number of establishments. Shaded *regions* indicate where the industry is regionally most concentrated.

NAICS 531120 - LESSORS OF NONRESIDENTIAL BUILDINGS (EXCEPT MINIWAREHOUSES)

GENERAL STATISTICS

Year	Establishments (number)	Employment (number)	Payroll ($ million)	Revenues ($ million)	Employees per Establishment (number)	Revenues per Establishment ($)	Payroll per Employee ($)
1997	31,497	145,317	3,828.0	38,105.0	4.6	1,209,798	26,342

Source: *Economic Census of the United States*, 1997. This is a newly defined industry. Data for prior years were unavailable at the time of publication but may become available over time.

INDICES OF CHANGE

Year	Establishments (number)	Employment (number)	Payroll ($ million)	Revenues ($ million)	Employees per Establishment (number)	Revenues per Establishment ($)	Payroll per Employee ($)
1997	100.0	100.0	100.0	100.0	100.0	100.0	100.0

Sources: Same as General Statistics. The values shown reflect change from the base year, 1997. Values above 100 mean greater than 1997, values below 100 mean less than 1997, and a value of 100 in the 1982-96 or 1998-2001 period means same as 1997. Values followed by a 'p' are projections by the editors; 'e' stands for extrapolation. Data are the most recent available at this level of detail.

SIC INDUSTRIES RELATED TO NAICS 531120

Each new NAICS code represents an industry that used to be part of an SIC or a part of several SIC industries. Data in this table are shown to provide transitional information for these cases. All available data for the precursor SIC(s) are shown. Even if only a part of an SIC is included in the NAICS, *all* data for the SIC are reproduced. If the SIC industry is not marked as being a part (pt) of the NAICS, the entire industry is embedded in the NAICS data. The SIC composition of the new industry provides some hints of the relative importance of its "ancestors." Data marked with a 'p' are projected. Projections begin with 1982 data. Data earlier than 1990 are not shown but are reflected in the projections.

SIC	Industry	1990	1991	1992	1993	1994	1995	1996	1997
6512	**Nonresidential Building Operators (pt)**	-	-	-	-	-	-	-	-

Source: *Economic Census of the United States*, 1992, annual surveys of economic sectors conducted by the Bureau of the Census, and estimates or projections based on the 1982-1992 period; not all data are shown. 'e' marks estimates made by the editors; 'p' indicates projections based on time series. A dash (-) indicates that data for this SIC or year were not available. The abbreviation (pt) next to the industry name indicates that only a part of the industry is present within the NAICS data. If no (pt) is shown, the entire industry is contained within the NAICS data.

SELECTED RATIOS

For 1997	Avg. of Information	Analyzed Industry	Index	For 1997	Avg. of Information	Analyzed Industry	Index
Employees per establishment	6	5	78	Payroll per establishment	144,276	121,535	84
Revenue per establishment	835,727	1,209,798	145	Payroll as % of revenue	17	10	58
Revenue per employee	141,515	262,220	185	Payroll per employee	24,430	26,342	108

Sources: Same as General Statistics. The 'Average' column represents the average for the industry sector, in 1997, where the currently shown industry is classified. The Index shows the relationship between the Average and the Analyzed Industry. For example, 100 means that they are equal; 500 that the Analyzed Industry is five times the average; 50 means that the Analyzed Industry is half the national average. The abbreviation 'na' is used to show that data are 'not available'.

LEADING COMPANIES　Number shown: **75**　　Total sales ($ mil): **25,034**　　Total employment (000): **97.7**

Company Name	Address				CEO Name	Phone	Co. Type	Sales ($ mil)	Empl. (000)
U.S. Steel Group	600 Grant St	Pittsburgh	PA	15219	Thomas J. Usher	412-433-1121	S	5,314	19.3
Jones, Lang and Lasalle Inc.	200 E Randolph Dr	Chicago	IL	60601		312-782-5800	S	3,102*	8.0
Ingles Markets Inc.	P O Box 6676	Asheville	NC	28816	Vaughn C Fisher	828-669-2941	P	1,805	13.0
Equity Office Properties Trust	2 N Riverside Plz	Chicago	IL	60606	Timothy H Callahan	312-466-3300	P	1,703	1.7
Charles Dunn Co.	800 W 6th St	Los Angeles	CA	90017	Tom McAndrews	213-683-0500	R	1,198*	0.4
A.G. Spanos Construction Inc.	P O Box 7126	Stockton	CA	95267	Dean Spanos	209-478-7954	R	1,175	0.6
Helmsley Enterprises Inc.	230 Park Ave	New York	NY	10169	Abe Wolf	212-679-3600	S	1,000	7.9
Rouse Co.	10275 L Patuxent	Columbia	MD	21044	Anothy W Deering	410-992-6000	P	977	4.1
Forest City Enterprises Inc.	1100 Terminal Twr	Cleveland	OH	44113	Charles A Ratner	216-621-6060	P	697	3.6
Inland Group Inc.	2901 Butterfield Rd	Oak Brook	IL	60523	Daniel L Goodwin	630-218-8000	R	645	0.8
Franklin Development Corp.	2200 W Parkway	Salt Lake City	UT	84119	Hyrum Smith	801-977-1834	S	547	3.5
TrizecHahn Centers Inc.	4350 La Jolla	San Diego	CA	92122	Lee Wagman	619-546-1001	D	529	2.4
Madison Square Garden L.P.	2 Penn Plz	New York	NY	10121	David Checketts	212-465-6000	S	375*	1.0
Central Management Inc.	5444 Westheimer	Houston	TX	77056	Vic Vacek	713-961-9777	R	333*	0.1
Goodale and Barbieri Cos.	W 201 N River Dr	Spokane	WA	99201		509-459-6100	R	321*	2.5
Taubman Realty Group L.P.	P O Box 200	Bloomfield Hills	MI	48303	Robert S Taubman	248-258-6800	R	313	0.4
Fairmount Copley Plaza	138 St James Ave	Boston	MA	02116		617-267-5300	R	281*	0.6
Shubert Organization Inc.	225 W 44th St	New York	NY	10036	Gerald Schoenfeld	212-944-3700	R	280*	2.0
Forest City Management Inc.	1200 Terminal Twr	Cleveland	OH	44113	Ron Ratner	216-621-6060	S	277*	0.6
Forest City Commercial Group Inc	1100 Terminal Twr	Cleveland	OH	44113	James Ratner	216-267-1200	S	270	1.7
Kemmons Wilson Inc.	1629 Winchester Rd	Memphis	TN	38116	Spence Wilson	901-346-8800	R	225	3.0
Konover and Associates Inc.	2410 Albany Ave	West Hartford	CT	06117	R Michael Goman	860-232-4545	R	211*	0.5
Sypris Solutions Inc.	455 S 4th Ave	Louisville	KY	40202	Jeffrey T Gill	502-585-5544	P	202	1.5
Charles E. Smith Management Inc.	2345 Crystal Dr	Arlington	VA	22202	Robert P Kogod	703-920-8500	R	202*	1.4
Renaissance Center Venture	400 Renaissance Ctr	Detroit	MI	48243	Steve Horn	313-568-5600	R	168*	0.4
Benderson Development Inc.	570 Delaware Ave	Buffalo	NY	14202	Randall Benderson	716-886-0211	R	164*	0.4
Portman Holdings L.P.	303 Peachtree St	Atlanta	GA	30308	John C Portman Jr	404-614-5555	R	150*	0.2
Catellus Development Corp.	201 Mission St	San Francisco	CA	94105	Nelson C Rising	415-974-4500	P	149*	0.4
Rockefeller Group Inc.	1221 Av Americas	New York	NY	10020	Lorian Marlantes	212-698-8500	R	145*	1.0
Chelsea GCA Realty Inc.	103 Eisenhower Pky	Roseland	NJ	07068	David C Bloom	973-228-6111	P	139	0.5
Palace Sports and Entertainment	2 Championship Dr	Auburn Hills	MI	48326	Tom Wilson	248-377-8200	S	137*	0.3
Amresco Inc	700 N Pear St	Dallas	TX	75201	Robert L Adair III	214-953-7700	P	131	3.7
Williard Inc.	PO Box 9002	Jenkintown	PA	19046	Joseph Doody	215-885-5000	R	130*	0.8
H.G. Hill Co.	P O Box 41503	Nashville	TN	37204	W Caldwell Jr	615-244-4520	R	103*	1.1
Gannett Fleming Affiliates Inc.	PO Box 67100	Harrisburg	PA	17106	Ronald Drnevich	717-763-7211	R	103*	1.6
First Republic Corporation	302 5th Ave	New York	NY	10001	Norman A Halper	212-279-6100	P	97	0.4
Horizon/Glen Outlet Centers L.P.	500 Hakes Dr	Norton Shores	MI	49441	James Wassel	616-798-9100	S	94*	0.5
Kimco Development Corp.	3333 New Hyde	New Hyde Park	NY	11042	Milton Cooper	516-484-5858	R	91*	0.1
Bixby Ranch Co.	3010 Old Ranch	Seal Beach	CA	90740	Chase Morgan	562-493-1475	R	82*	0.2
Pan Pacific Retail Properties Inc.	1631B S Melrose Dr	Vista	CA	92083	Stuart A Tanz	760-727-1002	P	79	<0.1
Ned West Inc.	6233 Hollywood	Los Angeles	CA	90028	James Nederlander	323-468-1700	R	69*	0.2
Gibraltar Trade Center Inc.	15525 Racho Rd	Taylor	MI	48180	James Koester	734-287-2000	R	65*	0.1
R.H. White Companies Inc.	PO Box 404	Auburn	MA	01501		508-832-3295	R	56*	0.3
Oppenheimer Companies Inc.	877 W Main St	Boise	ID	83702	A F Oppenheimer	208-343-2602	R	54	0.3
Selig Enterprises Inc.	1100 Spring St NW	Atlanta	GA	30309	SS Selig III	404-876-5511	R	54	0.7
Ford Motor Land Development	1 Park Lane 1500 E	Dearborn	MI	48126	Wayne S Doran	313-323-3100	S	52*	0.3
PIER 39 L.P.	P O Box 193730	San Francisco	CA	94119	Fritz Arko	415-705-5500	S	45*	0.1
Province Healthcare	105 Westwood Pl	Brentwood	TN	37027	Dave Woodland	615-309-6053	P	45*	0.1
Blue Ridge Real Estate Co.	PO Box 707	Blakeslee	PA	18610	Michael J Flynn		P	40*	0.1
Alexander's Inc.	Park 80 W	Saddle Brook	NJ	07663	Michael Fascitelli	201-587-8541	P	37	<0.1
Podolsky and Associates L.P.	1 Westbrook Corp	Westchester	IL	60154	Randy Podolsky	708-531-8200	R	35*	<0.1
Sunriver Resorts	P O Box 3609	Sunriver	OR	97707		541-593-1000	R	33*	0.6
Bresler and Reiner Inc.	401 M St S W	Washington	DC	20024	Charles S Bresler	202-488-8800	P	33	0.1
Mayfair Properties Inc.	2500 N Mayfair Rd	Wauwatosa	WI	53226	John Bucksbaum	414-771-1300	R	28*	<0.1
Time Equities Inc.	55 5th Ave	New York	NY	10003	Francis Greenburger	212-206-6000	R	28*	<0.1
Westfield Corp.	11601 Wilshire Blvd	Los Angeles	CA	90025	Richard E Green	310-478-4456	R	28*	0.2
Miller Industries Inc.	16295 NW 13th Ave	Miami	FL	33169	Angelo Napolitano	305-621-0501	P	27*	<0.1
Combined Properties Inc.	1899 L St N W	Washington	DC	20036	Ronald Haft	202-293-4500	R	26*	<0.1
Shuwa Investments Corp.	515 S Flower St	Los Angeles	CA	90071	Takaji Kobayashi	213-489-2757	R	26*	<0.1
Gardner Inc.	1150 Chesapeake	Columbus	OH	43212	JF Finn	614-488-7951	R	25	<0.1
TrizecHahn Office Properties Inc.	15760 Ventura Blvd	Encino	CA	91436	Kevin Benson	818-783-0660	S	25	<0.1
Bromberg Holdings Inc.	123 N 20th St	Birmingham	AL	35203	Paul M Byrne	205-252-0221	R	24*	0.2
Bazaar Del Mundo Inc.	2754 Calhoun St	San Diego	CA	92110	Diane Powers	619-296-6301	R	23	0.7
Stoltz Management of Delaware	261 Old York Rd	Jenkintown	PA	19046		215-886-7260	R	23*	<0.1
D.C.G. Development Co.	1-A Lakeview Dr	Clifton Park	NY	12065	Donald Greene	518-383-0059	R	21	0.1
Underground Atlanta Inc.	50 Upper Alabama	Atlanta	GA	30303	William Cicaglione	404-523-2311	R	21	<0.1
COMPASS-Retail Div.	5775 Peachtree	Atlanta	GA	30342		404-303-6100	D	20*	0.1
Michael Swerdlow Cos.	200 S Park Rd	Hollywood	FL	33021	Frank Zohn	954-981-1000	R	19*	0.1
Weitzman Group	3102 Maple Ave	Dallas	TX	75201	Herbert D Weitzman	214-954-0600	R	19*	<0.1
New England Realty Associates L	39 Brighton Ave	Allston	MA	02134	Ronald Brown	617-783-0039	P	19	<0.1
Watkins Associated Developers	PO Box 1738	Atlanta	GA	30301	Neal Freeman	404-872-8666	R	17*	<0.1
Consumer Cooperative Oil Co.	P O Box 668	Sauk City	WI	53583		608-643-3301	R	14*	<0.1
Transamerica Realty Services Inc.	600 Montgomery St	San Francisco	CA	94111	Richard Latzer	415-983-5420	S	13*	<0.1
Landau and Heyman Inc.	120 S Riverside Plz	Chicago	IL	60606	Patrick O'Leary	312-780-1933	R	12	0.4
INFOMART-Dallas L.P.	1950 Stemmons	Dallas	TX	75207	Tom Jones	214-800-8000	R	11	0.1

Source: Ward's Business Directory of U.S. Private and Public Companies, Volumes 1 and 2, 2000. The company type code used is as follows: P - Public, R - Private, S - Subsidiary, D - Division, J - Joint Venture, A - Affiliate, G - Group, N - Company type not reported. Sales are in millions of dollars, employees are in thousands. An asterisk (*) indicates an estimated sales volume. The symbol < stands for 'less than'. Company names and addresses are truncated, in some cases, to fit into the available space.

LOCATION BY STATE AND REGIONAL CONCENTRATION

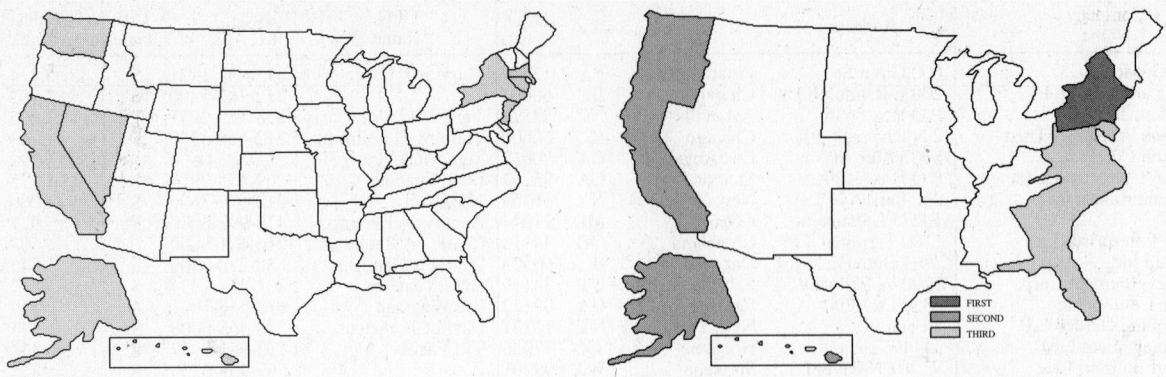

FIRST
SECOND
THIRD

INDUSTRY DATA BY STATE

State	Establishments Total (number)	Establishments % of U.S.	Employment Total (number)	Employment % of U.S.	Employment Per Estab.	Payroll Total ($ mil.)	Payroll Per Empl. ($)	Revenues Total ($ mil.)	Revenues % of U.S.	Revenues Per Estab. ($)
New York	4,055	12.9	21,579	14.8	5	697.0	32,299	8,543.4	22.4	2,106,892
California	3,993	12.7	20,544	14.1	5	604.0	29,398	6,321.9	16.6	1,583,258
Texas	2,377	7.5	10,733	7.4	5	288.4	26,870	2,272.0	6.0	955,806
Florida	2,177	6.9	9,160	6.3	4	195.6	21,354	1,894.5	5.0	870,212
Illinois	1,138	3.6	6,492	4.5	6	177.2	27,293	1,476.9	3.9	1,297,846
Pennsylvania	1,072	3.4	5,636	3.9	5	128.2	22,741	1,396.6	3.7	1,302,831
New Jersey	1,116	3.5	4,620	3.2	4	134.0	29,002	1,190.5	3.1	1,066,719
Michigan	779	2.5	3,225	2.2	4	88.0	27,285	1,072.5	2.8	1,376,805
Massachusetts	722	2.3	3,436	2.4	5	100.5	29,241	1,009.9	2.7	1,398,784
Washington	696	2.2	3,549	2.4	5	92.7	26,118	953.1	2.5	1,369,368
Georgia	707	2.2	3,216	2.2	5	92.3	28,713	801.4	2.1	1,133,485
Ohio	1,058	3.4	4,789	3.3	5	102.6	21,420	793.7	2.1	750,144
North Carolina	738	2.3	3,589	2.5	5	84.0	23,392	772.4	2.0	1,046,595
Missouri	643	2.0	2,859	2.0	4	70.5	24,659	717.6	1.9	1,116,050
Virginia	670	2.1	2,635	1.8	4	60.0	22,764	706.0	1.9	1,053,727
Maryland	467	1.5	2,379	1.6	5	72.8	30,586	677.9	1.8	1,451,574
Hawaii	308	1.0	1,712	1.2	6	61.3	35,798	653.3	1.7	2,121,179
Connecticut	516	1.6	1,846	1.3	4	53.0	28,736	589.8	1.5	1,143,103
Minnesota	403	1.3	1,967	1.4	5	47.9	24,358	560.8	1.5	1,391,511
D.C.	154	0.5	1,262	0.9	8	54.0	42,796	530.2	1.4	3,443,000
Tennessee	486	1.5	2,549	1.8	5	60.6	23,756	393.0	1.0	808,733
Colorado	447	1.4	2,033	1.4	5	44.4	21,828	358.7	0.9	802,468
Oregon	348	1.1	1,287	0.9	4	35.4	27,503	344.4	0.9	989,661
Arizona	393	1.2	1,915	1.3	5	37.8	19,758	296.1	0.8	753,499
Louisiana	483	1.5	2,008	1.4	4	35.2	17,541	295.7	0.8	612,133
Wisconsin	421	1.3	1,642	1.1	4	31.7	19,297	284.3	0.7	675,226
Alabama	377	1.2	1,446	1.0	4	28.0	19,368	279.0	0.7	739,944
Indiana	501	1.6	1,720	1.2	3	33.1	19,270	266.3	0.7	531,565
Iowa	271	0.9	1,268	0.9	5	32.4	25,540	230.9	0.6	851,893
Nevada	214	0.7	806	0.6	4	21.4	26,531	221.7	0.6	1,035,874
Kentucky	355	1.1	1,419	1.0	4	26.2	18,436	205.4	0.5	578,499
South Carolina	293	0.9	1,025	0.7	3	23.3	22,764	204.9	0.5	699,270
Oklahoma	392	1.2	1,469	1.0	4	30.6	20,820	203.1	0.5	518,191
Utah	208	0.7	888	0.6	4	19.8	22,320	161.9	0.4	778,452
Alaska	104	0.3	691	0.5	7	18.4	26,576	133.7	0.4	1,285,346
Arkansas	198	0.6	730	0.5	4	13.5	18,470	125.5	0.3	633,828
West Virginia	255	0.8	840	0.6	3	14.7	17,461	107.6	0.3	421,929
Rhode Island	142	0.5	658	0.5	5	12.3	18,710	95.7	0.3	673,887
Mississippi	218	0.7	737	0.5	3	10.2	13,813	92.5	0.2	424,454
New Mexico	220	0.7	706	0.5	3	11.6	16,499	92.5	0.2	420,536
Maine	145	0.5	417	0.3	3	9.5	22,811	89.7	0.2	618,572
Nebraska	176	0.6	502	0.3	3	11.0	21,876	78.8	0.2	447,824
New Hampshire	141	0.4	456	0.3	3	9.7	21,252	65.1	0.2	461,553
Montana	138	0.4	451	0.3	3	6.5	14,446	50.6	0.1	366,659
Idaho	100	0.3	354	0.2	4	7.6	21,568	49.6	0.1	495,820
Vermont	74	0.2	272	0.2	4	5.4	19,904	40.6	0.1	548,581
North Dakota	66	0.2	219	0.2	3	3.0	13,886	34.9	0.1	528,697
South Dakota	77	0.2	190	0.1	2	2.1	10,800	18.1	0.0	235,481
Wyoming	67	0.2	140	0.1	2	1.6	11,314	10.3	0.0	153,209
Kansas	285	0.9	750*	-	-	(D)	-	(D)	-	-
Delaware	113	0.4	375*	-	-	(D)	-	(D)	-	-

Source: 1997 Economic Census. The states are in descending order of revenues or establishments (if revenue data are missing for the majority). The symbol (D) appears when data are withheld to prevent disclosure of competitive information. States marked with (D) are sorted by number of establishments. A dash (-) indicates that the data element cannot be calculated. * indicates the midpoint of a range; 175, for example is the range 100-249. Shaded states on the state map indicate those states which have proportionately greater representation in the industry than would be indicated by the state's population; the ratio is based on total revenues or number of establishments. Shaded regions indicate where the industry is regionally most concentrated.

NAICS 531130 - LESSORS OF MINIWAREHOUSES AND SELF STORAGE UNITS

GENERAL STATISTICS

Year	Establishments (number)	Employment (number)	Payroll ($ million)	Revenues ($ million)	Employees per Establishment (number)	Revenues per Establishment ($)	Payroll per Employee ($)
1997	6,994	18,673	296.0	2,526.0	2.7	361,167	15,852

Source: Economic Census of the United States, 1997. This is a newly defined industry. Data for prior years were unavailable at the time of publication but may become available over time.

INDICES OF CHANGE

Year	Establishments (number)	Employment (number)	Payroll ($ million)	Revenues ($ million)	Employees per Establishment (number)	Revenues per Establishment ($)	Payroll per Employee ($)
1997	100.0	100.0	100.0	100.0	100.0	100.0	100.0

Sources: Same as General Statistics. The values shown reflect change from the base year, 1997. Values above 100 mean greater than 1997, values below 100 mean less than 1997, and a value of 100 in the 1982-96 or 1998-2001 period means same as 1997. Values followed by a 'p' are projections by the editors; 'e' stands for extrapolation. Data are the most recent available at this level of detail.

SIC INDUSTRIES RELATED TO NAICS 531130

Each new NAICS code represents an industry that used to be part of an SIC or a part of several SIC industries. Data in this table are shown to provide transitional information for these cases. All available data for the precursor SIC(s) are shown. Even if only a part of an SIC is included in the NAICS, *all* data for the SIC are reproduced. If the SIC industry is not marked as being a part (pt) of the NAICS, the entire industry is embedded in the NAICS data. The SIC composition of the new industry provides some hints of the relative importance of its "ancestors." Data marked with a 'p' are projected. Projections begin with 1982 data. Data earlier than 1990 are not shown but are reflected in the projections.

SIC	Industry	1990	1991	1992	1993	1994	1995	1996	1997
4225	**General Warehousing and Storage (pt)**								
	Establishments (number)	4,495	5,921	6,753	6,825	7,171	7,338	8,588	8,754p
	Employment (thousands)	45.1	47.6	49.1	51.7	57.2	61.3	66.8	66.8p
	Revenues ($ million)	3,257.0	3,568.0	3,919.2	4,633.0	5,294.0	6,143.0	6,522.0	7,457.0

Source: Economic Census of the United States, 1992, annual surveys of economic sectors conducted by the Bureau of the Census, and estimates or projections based on the 1982-1992 period; not all data are shown. 'e' marks estimates made by the editors; 'p' indicates projections based on time series. A dash (-) indicates that data for this SIC or year were not available. The abbreviation (pt) next to the industry name indicates that only a part of the industry is present within the NAICS data. If no (pt) is shown, the entire industry is contained within the NAICS data.

SELECTED RATIOS

For 1997	Avg. of Information	Analyzed Industry	Index	For 1997	Avg. of Information	Analyzed Industry	Index
Employees per establishment	6	3	45	Payroll per establishment	144,276	42,322	29
Revenue per establishment	835,727	361,167	43	Payroll as % of revenue	17	12	68
Revenue per employee	141,515	135,276	96	Payroll per employee	24,430	15,852	65

Sources: Same as General Statistics. The 'Average' column represents the average for the industry sector, in 1997, where the currently shown industry is classified. The Index shows the relationship between the Average and the Analyzed Industry. For example, 100 means that they are equal; 500 that the Analyzed Industry is five times the average; 50 means that the Analyzed Industry is half the national average. The abbreviation 'na' is used to show that data are 'not available'.

LEADING COMPANIES

No company data available for this industry.

LOCATION BY STATE AND REGIONAL CONCENTRATION

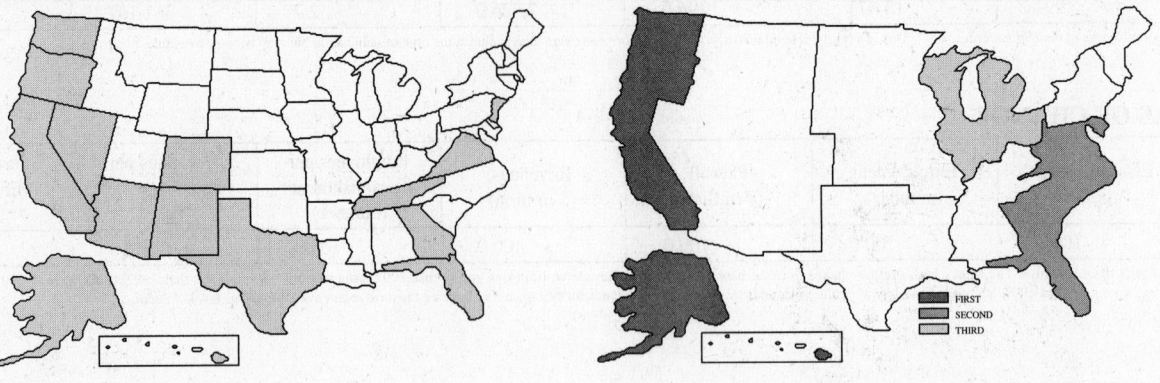

FIRST
SECOND
THIRD

INDUSTRY DATA BY STATE

State	Establishments Total (number)	% of U.S.	Employment Total (number)	% of U.S.	Per Estab.	Payroll Total ($ mil.)	Per Empl. ($)	Revenues Total ($ mil.)	% of U.S.	Per Estab. ($)
California	1,217	17.4	3,663	19.6	3	59.7	16,309	563.0	22.3	462,616
Florida	567	8.1	1,640	8.8	3	26.6	16,244	221.6	8.8	390,854
Texas	704	10.1	1,458	7.8	2	22.2	15,260	190.8	7.6	271,036
Washington	287	4.1	805	4.3	3	12.6	15,651	113.1	4.5	394,129
Georgia	240	3.4	568	3.0	2	8.3	14,692	94.9	3.8	395,342
Illinois	201	2.9	572	3.1	3	9.2	16,121	91.9	3.6	457,378
New Jersey	152	2.2	586	3.1	4	12.7	21,724	88.4	3.5	581,724
Virginia	204	2.9	591	3.2	3	9.2	15,494	79.3	3.1	388,632
North Carolina	230	3.3	586	3.1	3	9.9	16,940	61.9	2.5	269,174
Ohio	195	2.8	573	3.1	3	8.5	14,820	60.5	2.4	310,503
Michigan	166	2.4	399	2.1	2	6.0	15,088	59.0	2.3	355,711
Arizona	192	2.7	507	2.7	3	5.8	11,469	58.1	2.3	302,438
Tennessee	168	2.4	330	1.8	2	5.4	16,373	57.6	2.3	343,107
Colorado	158	2.3	367	2.0	2	4.9	13,324	56.5	2.2	357,658
Pennsylvania	149	2.1	344	1.8	2	5.7	16,692	49.7	2.0	333,617
Nevada	114	1.6	317	1.7	3	4.7	14,760	43.5	1.7	381,518
Massachusetts	90	1.3	249	1.3	3	5.8	23,297	39.9	1.6	443,467
Oregon	154	2.2	306	1.6	2	4.1	13,304	38.9	1.5	252,831
Missouri	124	1.8	310	1.7	3	4.7	15,223	36.0	1.4	290,258
Indiana	149	2.1	394	2.1	3	3.8	9,657	30.3	1.2	203,409
Louisiana	101	1.4	286	1.5	3	3.5	12,136	24.9	1.0	246,327
South Carolina	117	1.7	275	1.5	2	3.0	10,855	24.5	1.0	209,462
Connecticut	60	0.9	154	0.8	3	3.0	19,351	22.8	0.9	379,633
Minnesota	53	0.8	128	0.7	2	2.0	15,766	21.5	0.9	406,189
Oklahoma	87	1.2	168	0.9	2	2.2	12,893	20.5	0.8	236,184
Alabama	101	1.4	196	1.0	2	2.4	12,102	19.0	0.8	187,762
New Mexico	92	1.3	183	1.0	2	2.3	12,426	17.4	0.7	188,652
Hawaii	25	0.4	151	0.8	6	2.4	15,570	16.9	0.7	677,960
Utah	60	0.9	134	0.7	2	1.8	13,172	15.1	0.6	250,967
Wisconsin	43	0.6	118	0.6	3	1.9	15,856	13.9	0.5	322,488
Kentucky	63	0.9	159	0.9	3	1.7	10,975	12.5	0.5	197,841
Mississippi	68	1.0	120	0.6	2	1.5	12,533	12.2	0.5	179,147
New Hampshire	26	0.4	82	0.4	3	1.6	19,415	8.7	0.3	332,962
Idaho	34	0.5	114	0.6	3	1.3	11,693	8.5	0.3	248,588
Arkansas	60	0.9	104	0.6	2	1.1	10,327	8.1	0.3	135,733
Alaska	25	0.4	71	0.4	3	1.0	13,817	7.6	0.3	303,480
Maine	20	0.3	34	0.2	2	0.5	15,235	5.1	0.2	255,750
Nebraska	22	0.3	68	0.4	3	0.6	8,912	3.5	0.1	161,000
Montana	23	0.3	57	0.3	2	0.6	10,702	3.5	0.1	150,739
West Virginia	20	0.3	28	0.1	1	0.4	12,964	2.7	0.1	135,850
Iowa	14	0.2	29	0.2	2	0.3	12,034	2.7	0.1	195,500
South Dakota	6	0.1	32	0.2	5	0.6	17,375	2.4	0.1	400,833
Wyoming	18	0.3	29	0.2	2	0.3	11,586	2.3	0.1	126,111
Vermont	14	0.2	22	0.1	2	0.3	15,045	2.2	0.1	156,714
North Dakota	6	0.1	8	0.0	1	0.1	10,125	1.0	0.0	158,333
New York	176	2.5	750*	-	-	(D)	-	(D)	-	-
Maryland	98	1.4	375*	-	-	(D)	-	(D)	-	-
Kansas	70	1.0	175*	-	-	(D)	-	(D)	-	-
Delaware	14	0.2	60*	-	-	(D)	-	(D)	-	-
Rhode Island	12	0.2	60*	-	-	(D)	-	(D)	-	-

Source: 1997 *Economic Census.* The states are in descending order of revenues or establishments (if revenue data are missing for the majority). The symbol (D) appears when data are withheld to prevent disclosure of competitive information. States marked with (D) are sorted by number of establishments. A dash (-) indicates that the data element cannot be calculated. * indicates the midpoint of a range; 175, for example is the range 100-249. Shaded *states* on the state map indicate those states which have proportionately greater representation in the industry than would be indicated by the state's population; the ratio is based on total revenues or number of establishments. Shaded *regions* indicate where the industry is regionally most concentrated.

NAICS 531190 - LESSORS OF OTHER REAL ESTATE PROPERTY

GENERAL STATISTICS

Year	Establishments (number)	Employment (number)	Payroll ($ million)	Revenues ($ million)	Employees per Establishment (number)	Revenues per Establishment ($)	Payroll per Employee ($)
1997	12,017	37,623	686.0	5,539.0	3.1	460,930	18,234

Source: Economic Census of the United States, 1997. This is a newly defined industry. Data for prior years were unavailable at the time of publication but may become available over time.

INDICES OF CHANGE

Year	Establishments (number)	Employment (number)	Payroll ($ million)	Revenues ($ million)	Employees per Establishment (number)	Revenues per Establishment ($)	Payroll per Employee ($)
1997	100.0	100.0	100.0	100.0	100.0	100.0	100.0

Sources: Same as General Statistics. The values shown reflect change from the base year, 1997. Values above 100 mean greater than 1997, values below 100 mean less than 1997, and a value of 100 in the 1982-96 or 1998-2001 period means same as 1997. Values followed by a 'p' are projections by the editors; 'e' stands for extrapolation. Data are the most recent available at this level of detail.

SIC INDUSTRIES RELATED TO NAICS 531190

Each new NAICS code represents an industry that used to be part of an SIC or a part of several SIC industries. Data in this table are shown to provide transitional information for these cases. All available data for the precursor SIC(s) are shown. Even if only a part of an SIC is included in the NAICS, *all* data for the SIC are reproduced. If the SIC industry is not marked as being a part (pt) of the NAICS, the entire industry is embedded in the NAICS data. The SIC composition of the new industry provides some hints of the relative importance of its "ancestors." Data marked with a 'p' are projected. Projections begin with 1982 data. Data earlier than 1990 are not shown but are reflected in the projections.

SIC	Industry	1990	1991	1992	1993	1994	1995	1996	1997
6515	**Mobile Home Site Operators**	-	-	-	-	-	-	-	-
6517	**Railroad Property Lessors**	-	-	-	-	-	-	-	-
6519	**Real Property Lessors, nec**	-	-	-	-	-	-	-	-

Source: Economic Census of the United States, 1992, annual surveys of economic sectors conducted by the Bureau of the Census, and estimates or projections based on the 1982-1992 period; not all data are shown. 'e' marks estimates made by the editors; 'p' indicates projections based on time series. A dash (-) indicates that data for this SIC or year were not available. The abbreviation (pt) next to the industry name indicates that only a part of the industry is present within the NAICS data. If no (pt) is shown, the entire industry is contained within the NAICS data.

SELECTED RATIOS

For 1997	Avg. of Information	Analyzed Industry	Index	For 1997	Avg. of Information	Analyzed Industry	Index
Employees per establishment	6	3	53	Payroll per establishment	144,276	57,086	40
Revenue per establishment	835,727	460,930	55	Payroll as % of revenue	17	12	72
Revenue per employee	141,515	147,224	104	Payroll per employee	24,430	18,234	75

Sources: Same as General Statistics. The 'Average' column represents the average for the industry sector, in 1997, where the currently shown industry is classified. The Index shows the relationship between the Average and the Analyzed Industry. For example, 100 means that they are equal; 500 that the Analyzed Industry is five times the average; 50 means that the Analyzed Industry is half the national average. The abbreviation 'na' is used to show that data are 'not available'.

LEADING COMPANIES   Number shown: 26   Total sales ($ mil): 16,739   Total employment (000): 76.9

Company Name	Address				CEO Name	Phone	Co. Type	Sales ($ mil)	Empl. (000)
Carlson Hospitality Worldwide	P O Box 59159	Minneapolis	MN	55459	Curtis Nelson	612-212-1000	S	8,354*	71.0
Astrodome USA	PO Box 288	Houston	TX	77001	Mike Puryear	713-799-9500	D	5,355*	1.4
Center Trust Retail Properties Inc.	3500 Sepulveda	Manhattan Bch	CA	90266	Edward D Fox	310-546-4520	P	987	0.4
Corrigan Real Estate Services	3500 Oak Lawn Ave	Dallas	TX	75219	David Corrigan	214-520-1150	R	642*	0.2
Miller-Valentine Group	P O Box 744	Dayton	OH	45401	G Miller	937-293-0900	R	397*	0.1
CaliforniaMart	110 E 9th St	Los Angeles	CA	90079	Susan Scheimann	213-225-6278	R	297*	0.1
Airport Group International Inc.	330 N Brand Blvd	Glendale	CA	91214	George Casey	818-409-7500	S	250*	2.5
Boyle Investment Co.	5900 Poplar Ave	Memphis	TN	38119	Henry Morgan	901-767-0100	R	66*	0.1
Getty Realty Corp.	125 Jericho Tpke	Jericho	NY	11753	Leo Liebowitz	516-338-6000	P	61	<0.1
US Restaurant Properties Inc.	5310 Harvest Hl	Dallas	TX	75230	Robert J Stetson	972-387-1487	P	59	<0.1
Alico Inc.	P O Box 338	LaBelle	FL	33975	Ben H Griffin III	863-675-2966	P	43	<0.1
HQ International Inc.	1825 I St	Washington	DC	20006	Dede Bittenbring	202-429-2000	S	36*	<0.1
Strategic Capital Resources Inc.	2500 Mil Trl N	Boca Raton	FL	33431	David Miller	561-995-0043	R	32*	<0.1
Pocahontas Land Corp.	800 Princeton Ave	Bluefield	WV	24701	Daniel D Smith	304-327-5571	S	28*	<0.1
Stoltz Management of Delaware	261 Old York Rd	Jenkintown	PA	19046		215-886-7260	R	23*	<0.1
New Mexico & Arizona Land Co.	3033 N 44th St	Phoenix	AZ	85018	Stephen E Renneckai	602-952-8836	P	22	<0.1
Smithey Recycling Co.	PO Box 19050	Phoenix	AZ	85005	Sarah E Smithey	602-252-8125	S	16*	<0.1
Outdoor Resorts of America Inc.	2400 Crestmoor Rd	Nashville	TN	37215	Randall Henderson	615-244-5237	R	15*	0.1
Tulsa Metal Processing Co.	PO Box 19050	Phoenix	AZ	85005	Sarah E Smithey	602-252-8125	R	15*	<0.1
Great Northern Iron Ore Properties	332 Minnesota St	St. Paul	MN	55101	Joseph S Metcalf	651-224-2385	P	11	<0.1
Dahlem Company Inc.	6200 Dutchman	Louisville	KY	40205	Bernard Dahlem	502-479-0200	R	10	<0.1
United Park City Mines Co.	PO Box 1450	Park City	UT	84060	William H Rothwell	435-649-8011	P	7	<0.1
Justice Corp.	1150 Cleveland St	Clearwater	FL	33764	Albert N Justice	813-531-4600	R	5*	<0.1
Rancho Carlsbad	5200 Cam Real	Carlsbad	CA	92008		760-438-0332	R	3*	<0.1
Big Boulder Corp.	PO Box 707	Blakeslee	PA	18610	Gary A Smith		S	3	0.6
Central Coal and Coke Corp.	127 W 10th St	Kansas City	MO	64105	Beekman Winthrop	816-842-2430	P	2	<0.1

Source: Ward's Business Directory of U.S. Private and Public Companies, Volumes 1 and 2, 2000. The company type code used is as follows: P - Public, R - Private, S - Subsidiary, D - Division, J - Joint Venture, A - Affiliate, G - Group, N - Company type not reported. Sales are in millions of dollars, employees are in thousands. An asterisk (*) indicates an estimated sales volume. The symbol < stands for 'less than'. Company names and addresses are truncated, in some cases, to fit into the available space.

LOCATION BY STATE AND REGIONAL CONCENTRATION

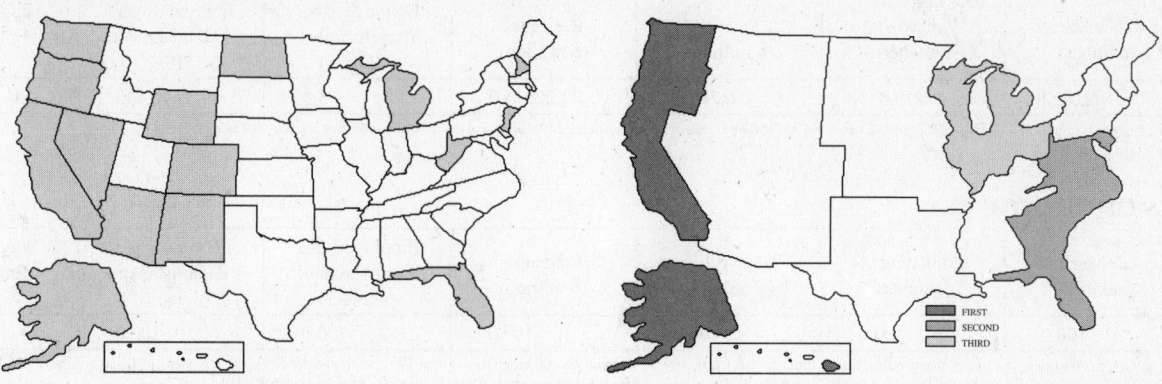

FIRST
SECOND
THIRD

INDUSTRY DATA BY STATE

State	Establishments Total (number)	Establishments % of U.S.	Employment Total (number)	Employment % of U.S.	Employment Per Estab.	Payroll Total ($ mil.)	Payroll Per Empl. ($)	Revenues Total ($ mil.)	Revenues % of U.S.	Revenues Per Estab. ($)
California	2,060	17.1	7,686	20.4	4	125.6	16,345	1,240.8	22.4	602,315
Florida	1,217	10.1	4,592	12.2	4	78.7	17,139	662.5	12.0	544,373
Michigan	440	3.7	1,446	3.8	3	25.4	17,574	272.2	4.9	618,700
Texas	735	6.1	2,038	5.4	3	37.0	18,141	241.0	4.4	327,869
Arizona	400	3.3	1,577	4.2	4	20.8	13,176	183.8	3.3	459,447
Illinois	350	2.9	1,165	3.1	3	33.3	28,571	181.2	3.3	517,783
New Jersey	248	2.1	910	2.4	4	22.2	24,381	175.8	3.2	708,827
Ohio	388	3.2	1,166	3.1	3	18.5	15,889	143.6	2.6	370,059
Pennsylvania	291	2.4	855	2.3	3	19.5	22,764	141.3	2.6	485,457
Washington	333	2.8	1,146	3.0	3	20.4	17,781	126.3	2.3	379,399
Colorado	229	1.9	768	2.0	3	11.6	15,044	104.4	1.9	456,017
Oregon	293	2.4	731	1.9	2	8.4	11,535	89.7	1.6	306,263
Georgia	271	2.3	705	1.9	3	11.9	16,940	84.1	1.5	310,358
Minnesota	191	1.6	449	1.2	2	8.1	18,091	82.1	1.5	429,848
Indiana	247	2.1	618	1.6	3	10.8	17,508	81.8	1.5	331,053
Virginia	208	1.7	501	1.3	2	10.2	20,289	81.3	1.5	390,630
Kentucky	136	1.1	365	1.0	3	7.8	21,452	77.0	1.4	566,485
Nevada	152	1.3	513	1.4	3	6.8	13,251	76.6	1.4	503,993
Louisiana	188	1.6	633	1.7	3	10.9	17,152	76.4	1.4	406,309
North Carolina	263	2.2	613	1.6	2	8.7	14,165	66.5	1.2	252,734
Wisconsin	176	1.5	423	1.1	2	8.6	20,239	63.2	1.1	359,085
West Virginia	89	0.7	226	0.6	3	5.4	24,066	55.6	1.0	624,236
Iowa	158	1.3	390	1.0	2	8.0	20,538	53.5	1.0	338,544
New Mexico	124	1.0	349	0.9	3	4.5	12,980	49.1	0.9	395,669
Massachusetts	110	0.9	338	0.9	3	8.2	24,115	48.6	0.9	441,882
Tennessee	132	1.1	352	0.9	3	6.2	17,699	46.2	0.8	349,735
Alaska	39	0.3	199	0.5	5	8.9	44,497	45.2	0.8	1,157,923
Missouri	204	1.7	432	1.1	2	7.9	18,280	44.8	0.8	219,578
South Carolina	148	1.2	367	1.0	2	6.4	17,379	44.6	0.8	301,682
New Hampshire	85	0.7	229	0.6	3	6.3	27,358	35.8	0.6	420,776
Oklahoma	152	1.3	323	0.9	2	5.9	18,180	32.8	0.6	215,500
Alabama	112	0.9	321	0.9	3	4.1	12,872	32.6	0.6	290,955
Connecticut	65	0.5	195	0.5	3	5.1	26,174	31.4	0.6	482,462
Utah	75	0.6	205	0.5	3	3.0	14,722	29.1	0.5	388,573
Arkansas	79	0.7	238	0.6	3	4.7	19,803	27.0	0.5	341,582
Mississippi	86	0.7	234	0.6	3	3.2	13,667	22.7	0.4	264,488
Nebraska	90	0.7	197	0.5	2	3.0	15,036	22.6	0.4	251,489
North Dakota	38	0.3	111	0.3	3	1.4	12,613	14.3	0.3	377,526
Montana	64	0.5	150	0.4	2	1.9	12,640	14.3	0.3	223,891
Maine	33	0.3	87	0.2	3	2.5	28,345	13.8	0.2	418,333
Wyoming	52	0.4	127	0.3	2	2.3	18,000	11.8	0.2	227,654
Idaho	45	0.4	101	0.3	2	1.2	12,257	11.2	0.2	248,133
South Dakota	52	0.4	107	0.3	2	1.5	14,187	10.5	0.2	201,923
Hawaii	26	0.2	55	0.1	2	1.1	20,873	7.9	0.1	304,692
Vermont	22	0.2	37	0.1	2	0.6	17,216	5.7	0.1	260,364
New York	824	6.9	1,750*	-	-	(D)	-	(D)	-	-
Maryland	106	0.9	375*	-	-	(D)	-	(D)	-	-
Kansas	105	0.9	375*	-	-	(D)	-	(D)	-	-
Delaware	54	0.4	375*	-	-	(D)	-	(D)	-	-
Rhode Island	26	0.2	60*	-	-	(D)	-	(D)	-	-
D.C.	6	-	175*	-	-	(D)	-	(D)	-	-

Source: 1997 *Economic Census*. The states are in descending order of revenues or establishments (if revenue data are missing for the majority). The symbol (D) appears when data are withheld to prevent disclosure of competitive information. States marked with (D) are sorted by number of establishments. A dash (-) indicates that the data element cannot be calculated. * indicates the midpoint of a range; 175, for example is the range 100-249. Shaded *states* on the state map indicate those states which have proportionately greater representation in the industry than would be indicated by the state's population; the ratio is based on total revenues or number of establishments. Shaded *regions* indicate where the industry is regionally most concentrated.

NAICS 531210 - OFFICES OF REAL ESTATE AGENTS AND BROKERS

GENERAL STATISTICS

Year	Establishments (number)	Employment (number)	Payroll ($ million)	Revenues ($ million)	Employees per Establishment (number)	Revenues per Establishment ($)	Payroll per Employee ($)
1997	60,620	219,633	6,792.0	38,945.0	3.6	642,445	30,924

Source: Economic Census of the United States, 1997. This is a newly defined industry. Data for prior years were unavailable at the time of publication but may become available over time.

INDICES OF CHANGE

Year	Establishments (number)	Employment (number)	Payroll ($ million)	Revenues ($ million)	Employees per Establishment (number)	Revenues per Establishment ($)	Payroll per Employee ($)
1997	100.0	100.0	100.0	100.0	100.0	100.0	100.0

Sources: Same as General Statistics. The values shown reflect change from the base year, 1997. Values above 100 mean greater than 1997, values below 100 mean less than 1997, and a value of 100 in the 1982-96 or 1998-2001 period means same as 1997. Values followed by a 'p' are projections by the editors; 'e' stands for extrapolation. Data are the most recent available at this level of detail.

SIC INDUSTRIES RELATED TO NAICS 531210

Each new NAICS code represents an industry that used to be part of an SIC or a part of several SIC industries. Data in this table are shown to provide transitional information for these cases. All available data for the precursor SIC(s) are shown. Even if only a part of an SIC is included in the NAICS, *all* data for the SIC are reproduced. If the SIC industry is not marked as being a part (pt) of the NAICS, the entire industry is embedded in the NAICS data. The SIC composition of the new industry provides some hints of the relative importance of its "ancestors." Data marked with a 'p' are projected. Projections begin with 1982 data. Data earlier than 1990 are not shown but are reflected in the projections.

SIC	Industry	1990	1991	1992	1993	1994	1995	1996	1997
6531	**Real Estate Agents and Managers (pt)**								
	Establishments (number)	-	-	106,552	-	-	-	-	-
	Employment (thousands)	-	-	646.6	-	-	-	-	-
	Revenues ($ million)	-	-	53,747.0	-	-	-	-	-

Source: Economic Census of the United States, 1992, annual surveys of economic sectors conducted by the Bureau of the Census, and estimates or projections based on the 1982-1992 period; not all data are shown. 'e' marks estimates made by the editors; 'p' indicates projections based on time series. A dash (-) indicates that data for this SIC or year were not available. The abbreviation (pt) next to the industry name indicates that only a part of the industry is present within the NAICS data. If no (pt) is shown, the entire industry is contained within the NAICS data.

SELECTED RATIOS

For 1997	Avg. of Information	Analyzed Industry	Index	For 1997	Avg. of Information	Analyzed Industry	Index
Employees per establishment	6	4	61	Payroll per establishment	144,276	112,042	78
Revenue per establishment	835,727	642,445	77	Payroll as % of revenue	17	17	101
Revenue per employee	141,515	177,319	125	Payroll per employee	24,430	30,924	127

Sources: Same as General Statistics. The 'Average' column represents the average for the industry sector, in 1997, where the currently shown industry is classified. The Index shows the relationship between the Average and the Analyzed Industry. For example, 100 means that they are equal; 500 that the Analyzed Industry is five times the average; 50 means that the Analyzed Industry is half the national average. The abbreviation 'na' is used to show that data are 'not available'.

LEADING COMPANIES

Number shown: **75**   Total sales ($ mil): **125,775**   Total employment (000): **82.4**

Company Name	Address				CEO Name	Phone	Co. Type	Sales ($ mil)	Empl. (000)
Weichert Realtors Inc.	1625 Route10 E	Morristown	NJ	07960	James Weichert	973-267-7777	R	24,384*	7.1
Realty One Inc.	6000 Rocksd Wds	Independence	OH	44131	Joseph T Aveni	216-328-2500	R	6,915*	2.0
N.D.C. Inc.	150 W Holt Ave	Milwaukee	WI	53207	Gary Pryda	414-481-0506	R	6,775*	2.0
Hunneman Real Estate Corp.	70-80 Lincoln St	Boston	MA	02111	Douglas Potter	617-426-4260	S	5,178*	1.5
J.D. Reece Realtors	7127 W 110th St	Overland Park	KS	66210	Jerry D Reece	913-491-1001	R	4,507*	1.3
Real Estate One Inc.	29630 Orchard Lake	Farmington Hills	MI	48334	R Elsea	248-851-2600	R	4,453*	1.3
TRI Realtors	1 California St	San Francisco	CA	94111	Ed Welch	415-268-2200	S	3,768*	1.1
Prudential Connecticut Realty	520 Cromwell Ave	Rocky Hill	CT	06067	Peter Helie	860-571-7000	R	3,338*	1.0
Long and Foster Real Estate Inc.	11351 Random Hills	Fairfax	VA	22030	P Wesley Foster Jr	703-359-1500	R	3,104*	0.9
LEDIC Management Group	5855 Ridge Bend Rd	Memphis	TN	38120	David L Shores	901-761-9300	R	2,703*	0.8
Jon Douglas Co.	11900 Olympic Blvd	Los Angeles	CA	90064		310-442-8002	R	2,702*	0.8
Polinger Shannon and Luchs Inc.	5530 Wisconsin Ave	Chevy Chase	MD	20815		301-657-3600	R	2,441*	0.7
Coldwell Banker Residential	27271 Las Rambles	Mission Viejo	CA	92691	Bob Becker	949-367-1800	R	2,394*	0.7
Merit Realty Inc.	9202 N Meridian	Indianapolis	IN	46260		317-571-2208	D	2,326*	0.7
Cohen-Esrey Real Estate Services	4435 Main St	Kansas City	MO	64111	Robert E Esrey	816-531-8100	R	2,240*	0.7
Jack Conway and Company Inc.	137 Washington St	Norwell	MA	02061	Richard F Cahill	781-871-0080	R	2,072*	0.6
Hayman Co.	5700 Crooks Rd	Troy	MI	48098	Stephen Hayman	248-879-7777	R	1,775	0.5
Prudential Fox and Roach	1409 Kings North	Cherry Hill	NJ	08034	G William Fox	609-429-7227	R	1,736*	0.5
HER Realtors Inc.	4656 Executive Dr	Columbus	OH	43220	Harley E Ruda	614-459-7400	R	1,622	0.6
Glimcher Properties L.P.	20 S 3rd St	Columbus	OH	43215	Herbert Glimcher	614-621-9000	S	1,569*	0.4
Peoples First Properties Inc.	PO Box 2950	Panama City	FL	32402	Raymond Powell	850-769-5261	R	1,523*	0.5
Capital Senior Living Corp.	14160 Dallas Pkwy	Dallas	TX	75240	Lawrence A Cohen	972-770-5600	P	1,464*	0.4
Fred Sands Realtors Corp.	11611 San Vicente	Los Angeles	CA	90049	Fred Sands	310-820-6811	R	1,450*	0.4
Metropolitan Properties	175 Federal St	Boston	MA	02110	Jeffrey J Cohen	617-422-0600	R	1,421*	0.4
Tri-City Rentals	2 Tower Pl	Albany	NY	12203	Morris Massry	518-458-8500	R	1,415*	0.4
Simon Property Group L.P.	P O Box 7033	Indianapolis	IN	46207	David Simon	317-636-1600	S	1,406	6.3
Ruffin Cos.	PO Box 17087	Wichita	KS	67217	Phillip Ruffin	316-942-7940	R	1,339*	0.4
Prudential New Jersey Realty	336 Hwy 18	East Brunswick	NJ	08816	William Kelaces	732-390-8000	R	1,332*	0.4
Stiles Realty Co.	6400 N Andrews	Fort Lauderdale	FL	33309	Terry Stiles	954-771-4900	R	1,329*	0.4
Charles Dunn Co.	800 W 6th St	Los Angeles	CA	90017	Tom McAndrews	213-683-0500	R	1,198*	0.4
Tarantino Properties Inc.	7887 San Felipe	Houston	TX	77063	Anthony Tarantino	713-974-4292	R	1,068*	0.3
CTL Management Inc.	9498 S W Barbur	Portland	OR	97219		503-245-1255	R	1,064*	0.3
Harry Reed and Co.	777 Post Oak Rd	Houston	TX	77056	Harry Reed	713-961-0110	R	1,064*	0.3
Mall of America Co.	60 E Broadway	Minneapolis	MN	55425		612-883-8800	S	1,052	2.0
CB Richard Ellis Services Inc.	333 S Beaudry Ave	Los Angeles	CA	90071	James J Didion	213-613-3123	P	1,034	9.4
CB Richard Ellis Inc.	533 S Fremont Ave	Los Angeles	CA	90071	Barry White	213-613-3242	S	936*	8.0
Re/Max North Realtors	870 High St	Worthington	OH	43085	Gail Linger	614-770-5531	R	894*	0.3
Jones Lang/LaSalle Partners Inc.	200 E Randolph Dr	Chicago	IL	60601	Christopher Peacock	312-782-5800	P	755	2.2
Insignia - ESS	601 13th St NW	Washington	DC	20005	Andrew Farkas	212-984-8075	D	746*	0.2
Ferland Corp.	30 Monticello Rd	Pawtucket	RI	02861	A Austin Ferland	401-728-4000	R	708*	0.2
Cushman and Wakefield Inc.	51 W 52nd St	New York	NY	10019	Arthur Mirante II	212-841-7500	S	700	7.7
Crescent Real Estate Equities Co.	777 Main St	Fort Worth	TX	76102	John C Goff	817-321-2100	S	698	0.6
Collier Enterprises	3003 Tamiami	Naples	FL	34101		941-261-4455	R	684*	0.2
CarrAmerica Realty Corp.	1850 K St NW	Washington	DC	20006	Tomas Carr	202-729-7500	P	652	1.9
Corrigan Real Estate Services	3500 Oak Lawn Ave	Dallas	TX	75219	David Corrigan	214-520-1150	R	642*	0.2
Gundaker Realtors/Better Homes	2458 Old Dorsett Rd	Maryland H.	MO	63043	G A Gundaker Jr	314-298-5000	R	603*	0.2
J.I. Sopher and Company Inc.	2100 Linwood Ave	Fort Lee	NJ	07024	Jacob I Sopher	201-461-8200	R	599*	0.2
Towne Realty Inc.	710 N Plankinton	Milwaukee	WI	53203	Arthur Wigchers	414-273-2200	R	565*	0.2
First Realty Management Corp.	151 Tremont St	Boston	MA	02111	William Kargman	617-423-7000	R	558*	0.2
Reeder Management Inc.	10520 Gravelly	Lakewood	WA	98499	Paul Reeder	253-584-6732	R	552*	0.2
Michael Stevens Interests Inc.	1160 Dairy Ashford	Houston	TX	77079		281-496-4141	R	529*	0.2
Insignia Financial Group Inc.	200 Park Ave	New York	NY	10166	Andrew L Farkas	212-984-8000	P	511	3.7
James R. Gary and Company Ltd.	21747 Erwin St	Woodland Hills	CA	91367	Linda Gary	818-703-6100	R	502*	0.1
Mack-Cali Realty L.P.	11 Commerce Dr	Cranford	NJ	07016	Mitchell E Hersh	908-272-8000	P	493	0.4
Shorenstein Co.	555 California St	San Francisco	CA	94104	Douglas Shorenstein	415-772-7000	R	486*	0.6
Cornish and Carey Commercial	2804 Miss Coll	Santa Clara	CA	95054	Bill Walsh	408-970-9990	R	474*	0.1
Trammell Crow Co.	2001 Ross Ave	Dallas	TX	75201	George L Lippe	214-863-3000	P	460	5.1
Arlington Properties Inc.	2117 2nd Ave N	Birmingham	AL	35203	William Hulsey	205-328-9600	R	444*	0.1
Metro-Prop Realty Inc.	10875 Indeco Dr	Cincinnati	OH	45241	Bruce Hellman	513-891-8801	R	440*	0.1
J.B. McLoughlin and Co.	2001st Ave W	Seattle	WA	98119	Brad Forrester	206-281-1188	R	432*	0.1
Presidential-Carruthers Realtors	10300 Eaton Pl	Fairfax	VA	22030	JT Carruthers Jr	703-934-1400	R	428*	0.1
Trans Western Carey Winston	6700 Rockledge Dr	Bethesda	MD	20817	Thomas Nordinger	301-571-0900	R	427*	0.1
Island One Resorts Management	2345 Sand Lake Rd	Orlando	FL	32809	Deb Linden	407-856-7190	R	417*	0.1
Colliers International	1100 Superior Ave	Cleveland	OH	44114	William M West	216-861-7200	R	410*	0.1
Morton G. Thalhimer Inc.	PO Box 702	Richmond	VA	23218	Paul F Silver	804-648-5881	R	403	0.1
ProLogis	14100 E 35th Pl	Aurora	CO	80011	KDane Brooksher	303-375-9292	P	378	0.5
Otis Warren Real Estate Services	7034 Liberty Rd	Baltimore	MD	21207	Otis Warren	410-484-6700	R	358*	0.1
Murdoch, Coll and Lillibridge Inc.	222 N LaSalle St	Chicago	IL	60601	Todd Lillibridge	312-362-0990	R	356*	0.1
Beeler Property Inc.	7500 San Felipe St	Houston	TX	77063	Richard Beeler	713-785-8200	R	351*	0.1
Rouse Milwaukee Inc.	275 W Wisconsin	Milwaukee	WI	53203		414-224-0384	R	347*	0.1
Planned Residential Communities	60 Monmouth Pkwy	W. Long Branch	NJ	07764	Robert M Kaye	732-222-5062	R	341*	0.1
C.B. Richard Ellis	600 Grant St	Pittsburgh	PA	15222		412-471-4455	R	334*	0.1
Harry Macklowe Real Estate Co.	142 W 57th St	New York	NY	10019	Harry Macklowe	212-265-5900	R	334*	0.1
Central Management Inc.	5444 Westheimer	Houston	TX	77056	Vic Vacek	713-961-9777	R	333*	0.1
Nitze-Stagen and Company Inc.	2401 Utah Ave S	Seattle	WA	98134	Kevin Daniels	206-467-0420	R	333*	0.1

Source: Ward's Business Directory of U.S. Private and Public Companies, Volumes 1 and 2, 2000. The company type code used is as follows: P - Public, R - Private, S - Subsidiary, D - Division, J - Joint Venture, A - Affiliate, G - Group, N - Company type not reported. Sales are in millions of dollars, employees are in thousands. An asterisk (*) indicates an estimated sales volume. The symbol < stands for 'less than'. Company names and addresses are truncated, in some cases, to fit into the available space.

LOCATION BY STATE AND REGIONAL CONCENTRATION

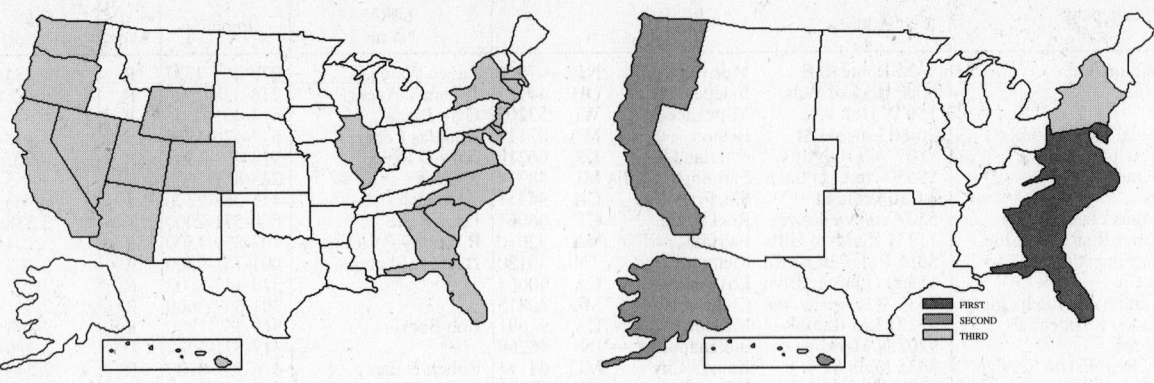

INDUSTRY DATA BY STATE

State	Establishments Total (number)	% of U.S.	Employment Total (number)	% of U.S.	Per Estab.	Payroll Total ($ mil.)	Per Empl. ($)	Revenues Total ($ mil.)	% of U.S.	Per Estab. ($)
California	6,828	11.3	29,140	13.3	4	1,113.3	38,205	6,141.2	15.8	899,413
Florida	5,561	9.2	18,678	8.5	3	517.4	27,699	3,283.9	8.4	590,522
New York	3,720	6.1	15,937	7.3	4	680.6	42,705	3,022.1	7.8	812,406
Texas	3,756	6.2	12,176	5.5	3	394.5	32,404	2,051.4	5.3	546,162
Illinois	2,597	4.3	10,103	4.6	4	326.9	32,359	1,849.4	4.7	712,119
New Jersey	1,685	2.8	6,010	2.7	4	228.2	37,964	1,370.2	3.5	813,147
Georgia	1,940	3.2	6,704	3.1	3	232.5	34,680	1,313.3	3.4	676,978
Washington	1,525	2.5	6,564	3.0	4	189.3	28,844	1,259.3	3.2	825,792
Pennsylvania	1,792	3.0	7,340	3.3	4	202.4	27,569	1,197.7	3.1	668,335
North Carolina	1,860	3.1	7,127	3.2	4	191.4	26,856	1,105.4	2.8	594,326
Virginia	1,645	2.7	7,207	3.3	4	205.1	28,461	1,090.5	2.8	662,919
Colorado	2,054	3.4	6,726	3.1	3	188.5	28,027	1,076.8	2.8	524,264
Massachusetts	1,333	2.2	4,846	2.2	4	191.6	39,542	1,053.3	2.7	790,194
Ohio	1,774	2.9	6,838	3.1	4	181.1	26,483	1,022.6	2.6	576,429
Michigan	1,830	3.0	5,640	2.6	3	141.4	25,068	987.9	2.5	539,825
Arizona	1,553	2.6	4,870	2.2	3	175.5	36,037	952.0	2.4	613,023
Maryland	1,130	1.9	5,235	2.4	5	152.3	29,088	794.6	2.0	703,171
Oregon	1,106	1.8	3,581	1.6	3	93.2	26,037	642.8	1.7	581,180
Missouri	1,195	2.0	4,541	2.1	4	124.9	27,505	642.1	1.6	537,290
Minnesota	1,309	2.2	3,886	1.8	3	96.2	24,768	639.0	1.6	488,169
Tennessee	991	1.6	3,609	1.6	4	92.9	25,735	626.3	1.6	632,014
South Carolina	927	1.5	3,810	1.7	4	103.6	27,181	605.6	1.6	653,250
Indiana	1,156	1.9	3,587	1.6	3	79.1	22,057	584.8	1.5	505,849
Connecticut	747	1.2	2,531	1.2	3	96.3	38,047	578.5	1.5	774,431
Wisconsin	1,093	1.8	3,360	1.5	3	79.7	23,714	548.7	1.4	502,053
Alabama	714	1.2	2,320	1.1	3	54.8	23,616	372.9	1.0	522,259
Nevada	496	0.8	2,550	1.2	5	74.2	29,088	339.9	0.9	685,321
Utah	650	1.1	1,798	0.8	3	45.5	25,321	325.6	0.8	500,966
Kentucky	599	1.0	1,489	0.7	2	31.7	21,269	284.4	0.7	474,855
Iowa	519	0.9	1,458	0.7	3	34.1	23,364	281.0	0.7	541,341
Kansas	558	0.9	1,892	0.9	3	40.5	21,385	274.5	0.7	491,851
Louisiana	574	0.9	1,882	0.9	3	38.6	20,505	274.2	0.7	477,720
Hawaii	369	0.6	1,882	0.9	5	53.7	28,515	251.5	0.6	681,699
Oklahoma	612	1.0	1,625	0.7	3	34.5	21,225	225.4	0.6	368,351
New Mexico	440	0.7	1,397	0.6	3	30.2	21,644	192.0	0.5	436,345
Nebraska	325	0.5	1,261	0.6	4	31.6	25,048	181.1	0.5	557,169
D.C.	121	0.2	937	0.4	8	61.9	66,012	178.9	0.5	1,478,306
Arkansas	457	0.8	1,269	0.6	3	23.6	18,600	163.9	0.4	358,626
New Hampshire	366	0.6	918	0.4	3	22.2	24,196	154.1	0.4	421,096
Idaho	386	0.6	879	0.4	2	16.0	18,215	146.6	0.4	379,917
Maine	297	0.5	725	0.3	2	16.2	22,324	115.6	0.3	389,215
Delaware	186	0.3	810	0.4	4	21.8	26,863	114.8	0.3	617,145
Rhode Island	223	0.4	529	0.2	2	13.4	25,346	106.1	0.3	475,713
Mississippi	361	0.6	750	0.3	2	14.1	18,823	101.9	0.3	282,324
Montana	306	0.5	645	0.3	2	10.1	15,614	79.3	0.2	259,072
Alaska	130	0.2	394	0.2	3	8.9	22,637	69.2	0.2	531,992
West Virginia	228	0.4	551	0.3	2	10.1	18,263	68.2	0.2	298,904
Wyoming	173	0.3	376	0.2	2	5.2	13,910	58.6	0.2	338,821
Vermont	193	0.3	460	0.2	2	8.4	18,361	57.3	0.1	297,114
South Dakota	133	0.2	385	0.2	3	7.0	18,265	49.1	0.1	369,481
North Dakota	97	0.2	405	0.2	4	5.7	14,007	39.9	0.1	410,979

Source: 1997 Economic Census. The states are in descending order of revenues or establishments (if revenue data are missing for the majority). The symbol (D) appears when data are withheld to prevent disclosure of competitive information. States marked with (D) are sorted by number of establishments. A dash (-) indicates that the data element cannot be calculated. * indicates the midpoint of a range; 175, for example is the range 100-249. Shaded *states* on the state map indicate those states which have proportionately greater representation in the industry than would be indicated by the state's population; the ratio is based on total revenues or number of establishments. Shaded *regions* indicate where the industry is regionally most concentrated.

NAICS 531311 - RESIDENTIAL PROPERTY MANAGERS

GENERAL STATISTICS

Year	Establishments (number)	Employment (number)	Payroll ($ million)	Revenues ($ million)	Employees per Establishment (number)	Revenues per Establishment ($)	Payroll per Employee ($)
1997	22,128	235,670	5,162.0	12,600.0	10.7	569,414	21,904

Source: *Economic Census of the United States*, 1997. This is a newly defined industry. Data for prior years were unavailable at the time of publication but may become available over time.

INDICES OF CHANGE

Year	Establishments (number)	Employment (number)	Payroll ($ million)	Revenues ($ million)	Employees per Establishment (number)	Revenues per Establishment ($)	Payroll per Employee ($)
1997	100.0	100.0	100.0	100.0	100.0	100.0	100.0

Sources: Same as General Statistics. The values shown reflect change from the base year, 1997. Values above 100 mean greater than 1997, values below 100 mean less than 1997, and a value of 100 in the 1982-96 or 1998-2001 period means same as 1997. Values followed by a 'p' are projections by the editors; 'e' stands for extrapolation. Data are the most recent available at this level of detail.

SIC INDUSTRIES RELATED TO NAICS 531311

Each new NAICS code represents an industry that used to be part of an SIC or a part of several SIC industries. Data in this table are shown to provide transitional information for these cases. All available data for the precursor SIC(s) are shown. Even if only a part of an SIC is included in the NAICS, *all* data for the SIC are reproduced. If the SIC industry is not marked as being a part (pt) of the NAICS, the entire industry is embedded in the NAICS data. The SIC composition of the new industry provides some hints of the relative importance of its "ancestors." Data marked with a 'p' are projected. Projections begin with 1982 data. Data earlier than 1990 are not shown but are reflected in the projections.

SIC	Industry	1990	1991	1992	1993	1994	1995	1996	1997
6531	**Real Estate Agents and Managers (pt)**								
	Establishments (number)	-	-	106,552	-	-	-	-	-
	Employment (thousands)	-	-	646.6	-	-	-	-	-
	Revenues ($ million)	-	-	53,747.0	-	-	-	-	-

Source: *Economic Census of the United States*, 1992, annual surveys of economic sectors conducted by the Bureau of the Census, and estimates or projections based on the 1982-1992 period; not all data are shown. 'e' marks estimates made by the editors; 'p' indicates projections based on time series. A dash (-) indicates that data for this SIC or year were not available. The abbreviation (pt) next to the industry name indicates that only a part of the industry is present within the NAICS data. If no (pt) is shown, the entire industry is contained within the NAICS data.

SELECTED RATIOS

For 1997	Avg. of Information	Analyzed Industry	Index	For 1997	Avg. of Information	Analyzed Industry	Index
Employees per establishment	6	11	180	Payroll per establishment	144,276	233,279	162
Revenue per establishment	835,727	569,414	68	Payroll as % of revenue	17	41	237
Revenue per employee	141,515	53,465	38	Payroll per employee	24,430	21,904	90

Sources: Same as General Statistics. The 'Average' column represents the average for the industry sector, in 1997, where the currently shown industry is classified. The Index shows the relationship between the Average and the Analyzed Industry. For example, 100 means that they are equal; 500 that the Analyzed Industry is five times the average; 50 means that the Analyzed Industry is half the national average. The abbreviation 'na' is used to show that data are 'not available'.

LEADING COMPANIES

No company data available for this industry.

LOCATION BY STATE AND REGIONAL CONCENTRATION

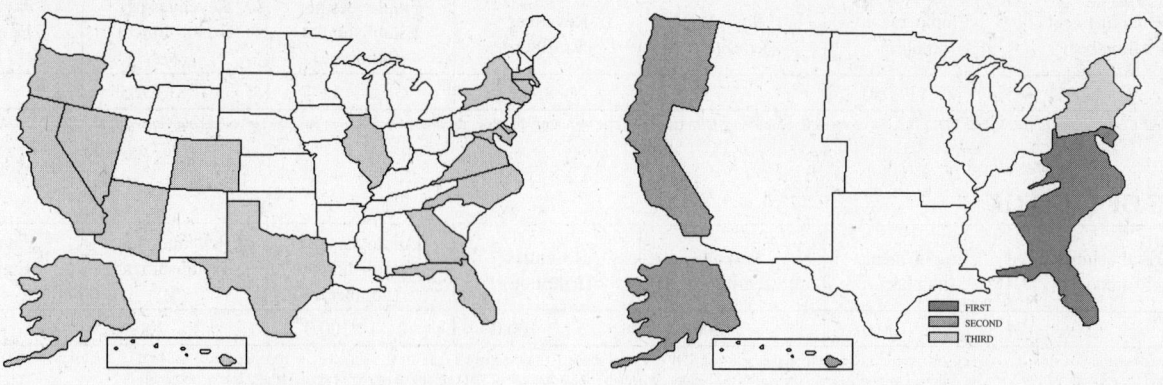

INDUSTRY DATA BY STATE

State	Establishments		Employment			Payroll		Revenues		
	Total (number)	% of U.S.	Total (number)	% of U.S.	Per Estab.	Total ($ mil.)	Per Empl. ($)	Total ($ mil.)	% of U.S.	Per Estab. ($)
California	3,261	14.7	35,507	15.1	11	778.0	21,912	1,716.9	13.6	526,482
New York	2,154	9.7	18,279	7.8	8	575.0	31,455	1,457.5	11.6	676,661
Texas	1,713	7.7	21,340	9.1	12	428.6	20,082	1,047.8	8.3	611,698
Florida	1,637	7.4	16,931	7.2	10	346.4	20,457	868.9	6.9	530,768
Illinois	910	4.1	9,416	4.0	10	254.6	27,043	633.5	5.0	696,176
Massachusetts	573	2.6	7,699	3.3	13	193.8	25,168	436.0	3.5	760,871
Maryland	521	2.4	7,941	3.4	15	177.6	22,364	433.0	3.4	831,102
Georgia	590	2.7	6,887	2.9	12	157.9	22,931	413.8	3.3	701,356
Virginia	565	2.6	6,883	2.9	12	162.7	23,645	413.6	3.3	732,016
Michigan	582	2.6	9,280	3.9	16	173.3	18,673	401.4	3.2	689,754
North Carolina	721	3.3	5,715	2.4	8	126.7	22,174	381.7	3.0	529,359
Pennsylvania	577	2.6	5,719	2.4	10	143.3	25,062	353.4	2.8	612,447
New Jersey	538	2.4	4,089	1.7	8	113.9	27,857	302.2	2.4	561,717
Ohio	645	2.9	6,530	2.8	10	126.1	19,315	290.9	2.3	450,946
Colorado	605	2.7	5,888	2.5	10	108.3	18,396	279.3	2.2	461,617
Tennessee	346	1.6	3,795	1.6	11	83.9	22,119	226.7	1.8	655,188
Arizona	402	1.8	4,512	1.9	11	90.4	20,040	220.8	1.8	549,162
Indiana	348	1.6	4,216	1.8	12	86.3	20,459	203.2	1.6	584,017
Washington	452	2.0	5,015	2.1	11	91.0	18,148	184.2	1.5	407,460
Minnesota	322	1.5	4,412	1.9	14	79.2	17,962	182.2	1.4	565,873
Missouri	354	1.6	4,615	2.0	13	85.6	18,549	182.1	1.4	514,362
South Carolina	342	1.5	3,632	1.5	11	64.8	17,835	167.7	1.3	490,322
Connecticut	262	1.2	2,723	1.2	10	62.9	23,105	158.6	1.3	605,408
Oregon	324	1.5	3,874	1.6	12	67.6	17,457	148.9	1.2	459,488
Wisconsin	315	1.4	3,062	1.3	10	60.9	19,902	139.9	1.1	444,019
Nevada	170	0.8	2,013	0.9	12	43.2	21,474	134.4	1.1	790,853
Alabama	228	1.0	3,202	1.4	14	61.0	19,049	122.5	1.0	537,443
Louisiana	223	1.0	2,680	1.1	12	48.0	17,894	106.6	0.8	478,036
Kansas	237	1.1	2,315	1.0	10	44.0	19,003	94.5	0.8	398,857
Hawaii	151	0.7	1,630	0.7	11	38.0	23,309	92.8	0.7	614,470
Utah	160	0.7	1,757	0.7	11	33.1	18,822	90.2	0.7	563,456
Oklahoma	259	1.2	2,070	0.9	8	34.6	16,731	76.5	0.6	295,282
D.C.	95	0.4	795	0.3	8	24.9	31,326	65.5	0.5	689,211
Mississippi	128	0.6	1,034	0.4	8	16.2	15,691	64.5	0.5	503,883
Kentucky	142	0.6	957	0.4	7	17.1	17,894	48.6	0.4	342,338
Iowa	141	0.6	1,264	0.5	9	19.5	15,398	48.1	0.4	341,220
New Hampshire	102	0.5	929	0.4	9	19.7	21,182	46.3	0.4	453,892
Rhode Island	73	0.3	628	0.3	9	16.0	25,428	41.2	0.3	564,247
Arkansas	122	0.6	761	0.3	6	11.8	15,456	40.5	0.3	331,861
Nebraska	84	0.4	914	0.4	11	15.9	17,386	36.0	0.3	428,786
Alaska	29	0.1	326	0.1	11	7.8	23,807	35.9	0.3	1,238,690
New Mexico	107	0.5	700	0.3	7	12.2	17,416	35.6	0.3	332,897
Delaware	55	0.2	389	0.2	7	10.1	25,949	33.5	0.3	608,945
Maine	152	0.7	695	0.3	5	10.7	15,328	30.6	0.2	201,000
Idaho	88	0.4	501	0.2	6	7.1	14,108	23.2	0.2	263,500
North Dakota	61	0.3	724	0.3	12	8.9	12,356	22.2	0.2	364,443
Vermont	60	0.3	285	0.1	5	5.5	19,179	16.7	0.1	278,900
South Dakota	55	0.2	387	0.2	7	6.0	15,406	16.5	0.1	300,018
Wyoming	41	0.2	292	0.1	7	5.0	17,058	13.2	0.1	321,732
Montana	54	0.2	217	0.1	4	3.6	16,576	12.8	0.1	237,481
West Virginia	52	0.2	245	0.1	5	2.9	11,931	7.6	0.1	145,788

Source: 1997 *Economic Census*. The states are in descending order of revenues or establishments (if revenue data are missing for the majority). The symbol (D) appears when data are withheld to prevent disclosure of competitive information. States marked with (D) are sorted by number of establishments. A dash (-) indicates that the data element cannot be calculated. * indicates the midpoint of a range; 175, for example is the range 100-249. Shaded *states* on the state map indicate those states which have proportionately greater representation in the industry than would be indicated by the state's population; the ratio is based on total revenues or number of establishments. Shaded *regions* indicate where the industry is regionally most concentrated.

NAICS 531312 - NONRESIDENTIAL PROPERTY MANAGERS

GENERAL STATISTICS

Year	Establishments (number)	Employment (number)	Payroll ($ million)	Revenues ($ million)	Employees per Establishment (number)	Revenues per Establishment ($)	Payroll per Employee ($)
1997	10,011	117,050	3,739.0	8,146.0	11.7	813,705	31,944

Source: *Economic Census of the United States*, 1997. This is a newly defined industry. Data for prior years were unavailable at the time of publication but may become available over time.

INDICES OF CHANGE

Year	Establishments (number)	Employment (number)	Payroll ($ million)	Revenues ($ million)	Employees per Establishment (number)	Revenues per Establishment ($)	Payroll per Employee ($)
1997	100.0	100.0	100.0	100.0	100.0	100.0	100.0

Sources: Same as General Statistics. The values shown reflect change from the base year, 1997. Values above 100 mean greater than 1997, values below 100 mean less than 1997, and a value of 100 in the 1982-96 or 1998-2001 period means same as 1997. Values followed by a 'p' are projections by the editors; 'e' stands for extrapolation. Data are the most recent available at this level of detail.

SIC INDUSTRIES RELATED TO NAICS 531312

Each new NAICS code represents an industry that used to be part of an SIC or a part of several SIC industries. Data in this table are shown to provide transitional information for these cases. All available data for the precursor SIC(s) are shown. Even if only a part of an SIC is included in the NAICS, *all* data for the SIC are reproduced. If the SIC industry is not marked as being a part (pt) of the NAICS, the entire industry is embedded in the NAICS data. The SIC composition of the new industry provides some hints of the relative importance of its "ancestors." Data marked with a 'p' are projected. Projections begin with 1982 data. Data earlier than 1990 are not shown but are reflected in the projections.

SIC	Industry	1990	1991	1992	1993	1994	1995	1996	1997
6531	**Real Estate Agents and Managers (pt)**								
	Establishments (number)	-	-	106,552	-	-	-	-	-
	Employment (thousands)	-	-	646.6	-	-	-	-	-
	Revenues ($ million)	-	-	53,747.0	-	-	-	-	-

Source: *Economic Census of the United States*, 1992, annual surveys of economic sectors conducted by the Bureau of the Census, and estimates or projections based on the 1982-1992 period; not all data are shown. 'e' marks estimates made by the editors; 'p' indicates projections based on time series. A dash (-) indicates that data for this SIC or year were not available. The abbreviation (pt) next to the industry name indicates that only a part of the industry is present within the NAICS data. If no (pt) is shown, the entire industry is contained within the NAICS data.

SELECTED RATIOS

For 1997	Avg. of Information	Analyzed Industry	Index	For 1997	Avg. of Information	Analyzed Industry	Index
Employees per establishment	6	12	198	Payroll per establishment	144,276	373,489	259
Revenue per establishment	835,727	813,705	97	Payroll as % of revenue	17	46	266
Revenue per employee	141,515	69,594	49	Payroll per employee	24,430	31,944	131

Sources: Same as General Statistics. The 'Average' column represents the average for the industry sector, in 1997, where the currently shown industry is classified. The Index shows the relationship between the Average and the Analyzed Industry. For example, 100 means that they are equal; 500 that the Analyzed Industry is five times the average; 50 means that the Analyzed Industry is half the national average. The abbreviation 'na' is used to show that data are 'not available'.

LEADING COMPANIES

No company data available for this industry.

LOCATION BY STATE AND REGIONAL CONCENTRATION

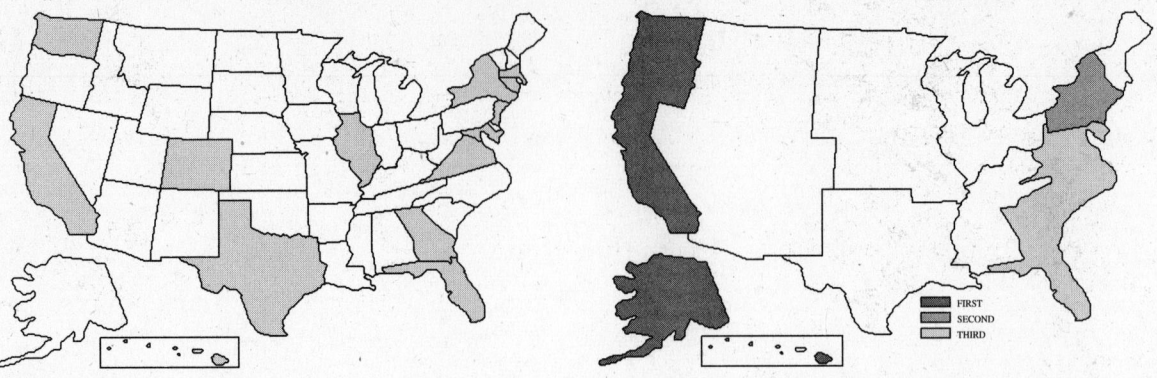

INDUSTRY DATA BY STATE

State	Establishments Total (number)	Establishments % of U.S.	Employment Total (number)	Employment % of U.S.	Employment Per Estab.	Payroll Total ($ mil.)	Payroll Per Empl. ($)	Revenues Total ($ mil.)	Revenues % of U.S.	Revenues Per Estab. ($)
California	1,765	17.6	17,744	15.2	10	639.6	36,045	1,452.1	17.8	822,699
New York	858	8.6	13,345	11.4	16	522.0	39,119	1,021.2	12.5	1,190,245
Texas	812	8.1	9,703	8.3	12	281.0	28,959	636.2	7.8	783,509
Florida	792	7.9	8,866	7.6	11	229.1	25,838	519.9	6.4	656,442
Illinois	454	4.5	5,087	4.3	11	225.2	44,269	460.9	5.7	1,015,123
Pennsylvania	273	2.7	4,619	3.9	17	133.3	28,849	299.7	3.7	1,097,637
Massachusetts	312	3.1	3,891	3.3	12	136.2	34,994	280.8	3.4	899,872
New Jersey	335	3.3	2,387	2.0	7	83.0	34,769	278.9	3.4	832,579
Georgia	266	2.7	4,227	3.6	16	143.6	33,972	265.9	3.3	999,504
Ohio	318	3.2	4,764	4.1	15	130.0	27,293	261.5	3.2	822,377
Michigan	268	2.7	3,283	2.8	12	113.0	34,407	241.8	3.0	902,410
Maryland	262	2.6	3,411	2.9	13	98.0	28,725	223.5	2.7	853,092
Virginia	252	2.5	3,599	3.1	14	94.7	26,320	212.5	2.6	843,421
Washington	227	2.3	2,554	2.2	11	72.6	28,436	177.8	2.2	783,220
Colorado	252	2.5	3,106	2.7	12	83.7	26,954	160.0	2.0	635,099
North Carolina	172	1.7	1,688	1.4	10	69.0	40,863	135.9	1.7	789,971
Minnesota	198	2.0	2,084	1.8	11	72.9	34,980	130.9	1.6	660,889
D.C.	74	0.7	1,436	1.2	19	58.7	40,866	111.3	1.4	1,504,622
Connecticut	131	1.3	1,349	1.2	10	48.9	36,236	105.1	1.3	802,076
Missouri	158	1.6	1,326	1.1	8	44.1	33,251	97.8	1.2	618,861
Kentucky	70	0.7	945	0.8	14	24.3	25,704	97.6	1.2	1,394,500
Arizona	211	2.1	1,681	1.4	8	43.0	25,577	92.9	1.1	440,152
Indiana	114	1.1	1,129	1.0	10	29.6	26,176	87.6	1.1	768,000
Tennessee	109	1.1	1,493	1.3	14	41.8	27,975	81.1	1.0	743,771
Hawaii	84	0.8	1,146	1.0	14	34.2	29,869	71.5	0.9	851,060
Alabama	81	0.8	1,380	1.2	17	34.8	25,225	64.3	0.8	793,951
Wisconsin	104	1.0	1,178	1.0	11	32.7	27,775	62.3	0.8	598,625
Oregon	93	0.9	514	0.4	6	14.0	27,208	60.7	0.7	652,473
Louisiana	103	1.0	1,454	1.2	14	29.0	19,949	53.2	0.7	516,029
Utah	64	0.6	1,356	1.2	21	23.0	16,943	45.9	0.6	717,625
Nebraska	55	0.5	652	0.6	12	18.8	28,764	42.1	0.5	765,109
South Carolina	77	0.8	665	0.6	9	15.8	23,716	37.9	0.5	492,506
Kansas	66	0.7	680	0.6	10	14.5	21,382	34.8	0.4	527,288
Iowa	64	0.6	599	0.5	9	14.5	24,212	29.6	0.4	462,719
Nevada	68	0.7	442	0.4	7	13.2	29,785	29.3	0.4	430,574
Oklahoma	89	0.9	516	0.4	6	13.1	25,446	27.6	0.3	310,011
New Mexico	54	0.5	429	0.4	8	6.6	15,392	26.2	0.3	485,352
New Hampshire	43	0.4	327	0.3	8	8.3	25,327	19.3	0.2	449,488
Maine	39	0.4	334	0.3	9	8.2	24,659	18.2	0.2	465,410
Alaska	19	0.2	360	0.3	19	9.2	25,578	16.1	0.2	849,000
Rhode Island	28	0.3	285	0.2	10	7.6	26,544	15.3	0.2	547,357
Arkansas	33	0.3	279	0.2	8	8.1	29,154	15.0	0.2	455,879
Mississippi	35	0.3	196	0.2	6	3.7	19,087	12.7	0.2	364,171
Idaho	22	0.2	81	0.1	4	1.5	19,012	6.1	0.1	278,545
West Virginia	21	0.2	108	0.1	5	3.0	28,083	6.0	0.1	284,000
Vermont	25	0.2	90	0.1	4	2.4	26,822	6.0	0.1	240,240
South Dakota	12	0.1	89	0.1	7	1.9	21,629	4.1	0.1	344,417
Montana	15	0.1	85	0.1	6	1.6	19,388	3.7	0.0	248,867
Delaware	19	0.2	55	0.0	3	1.3	23,818	3.2	0.0	170,000
Wyoming	8	0.1	21	0.0	3	0.3	16,238	1.3	0.0	160,875
North Dakota	7	0.1	12	0.0	2	0.2	13,750	0.9	0.0	132,571

Source: 1997 *Economic Census*. The states are in descending order of revenues or establishments (if revenue data are missing for the majority). The symbol (D) appears when data are withheld to prevent disclosure of competitive information. States marked with (D) are sorted by number of establishments. A dash (-) indicates that the data element cannot be calculated. * indicates the midpoint of a range; 175, for example is the range 100-249. Shaded *states* on the state map indicate those states which have proportionately greater representation in the industry than would be indicated by the state's population; the ratio is based on total revenues or number of establishments. Shaded *regions* indicate where the industry is regionally most concentrated.

NAICS 531320 - OFFICES OF REAL ESTATE APPRAISERS

GENERAL STATISTICS

Year	Establishments (number)	Employment (number)	Payroll ($ million)	Revenues ($ million)	Employees per Establishment (number)	Revenues per Establishment ($)	Payroll per Employee ($)
1997	11,387	34,399	1,055.0	2,966.0	3.0	260,472	30,669

Source: Economic Census of the United States, 1997. This is a newly defined industry. Data for prior years were unavailable at the time of publication but may become available over time.

INDICES OF CHANGE

Year	Establishments (number)	Employment (number)	Payroll ($ million)	Revenues ($ million)	Employees per Establishment (number)	Revenues per Establishment ($)	Payroll per Employee ($)
1997	100.0	100.0	100.0	100.0	100.0	100.0	100.0

Sources: Same as General Statistics. The values shown reflect change from the base year, 1997. Values above 100 mean greater than 1997, values below 100 mean less than 1997, and a value of 100 in the 1982-96 or 1998-2001 period means same as 1997. Values followed by a 'p' are projections by the editors; 'e' stands for extrapolation. Data are the most recent available at this level of detail.

SIC INDUSTRIES RELATED TO NAICS 531320

Each new NAICS code represents an industry that used to be part of an SIC or a part of several SIC industries. Data in this table are shown to provide transitional information for these cases. All available data for the precursor SIC(s) are shown. Even if only a part of an SIC is included in the NAICS, *all* data for the SIC are reproduced. If the SIC industry is not marked as being a part (pt) of the NAICS, the entire industry is embedded in the NAICS data. The SIC composition of the new industry provides some hints of the relative importance of its "ancestors." Data marked with a 'p' are projected. Projections begin with 1982 data. Data earlier than 1990 are not shown but are reflected in the projections.

SIC	Industry	1990	1991	1992	1993	1994	1995	1996	1997
6531	**Real Estate Agents and Managers (pt)**								
	Establishments (number)	-	-	106,552	-	-	-	-	-
	Employment (thousands)	-	-	646.6	-	-	-	-	-
	Revenues ($ million)	-	-	53,747.0	-	-	-	-	-

Source: Economic Census of the United States, 1992, annual surveys of economic sectors conducted by the Bureau of the Census, and estimates or projections based on the 1982-1992 period; not all data are shown. 'e' marks estimates made by the editors; 'p' indicates projections based on time series. A dash (-) indicates that data for this SIC or year were not available. The abbreviation (pt) next to the industry name indicates that only a part of the industry is present within the NAICS data. If no (pt) is shown, the entire industry is contained within the NAICS data.

SELECTED RATIOS

For 1997	Avg. of Information	Analyzed Industry	Index	For 1997	Avg. of Information	Analyzed Industry	Index
Employees per establishment	6	3	51	Payroll per establishment	144,276	92,650	64
Revenue per establishment	835,727	260,472	31	Payroll as % of revenue	17	36	206
Revenue per employee	141,515	86,223	61	Payroll per employee	24,430	30,669	126

Sources: Same as General Statistics. The 'Average' column represents the average for the industry sector, in 1997, where the currently shown industry is classified. The Index shows the relationship between the Average and the Analyzed Industry. For example, 100 means that they are equal; 500 that the Analyzed Industry is five times the average; 50 means that the Analyzed Industry is half the national average. The abbreviation 'na' is used to show that data are 'not available'.

LEADING COMPANIES

No company data available for this industry.

LOCATION BY STATE AND REGIONAL CONCENTRATION

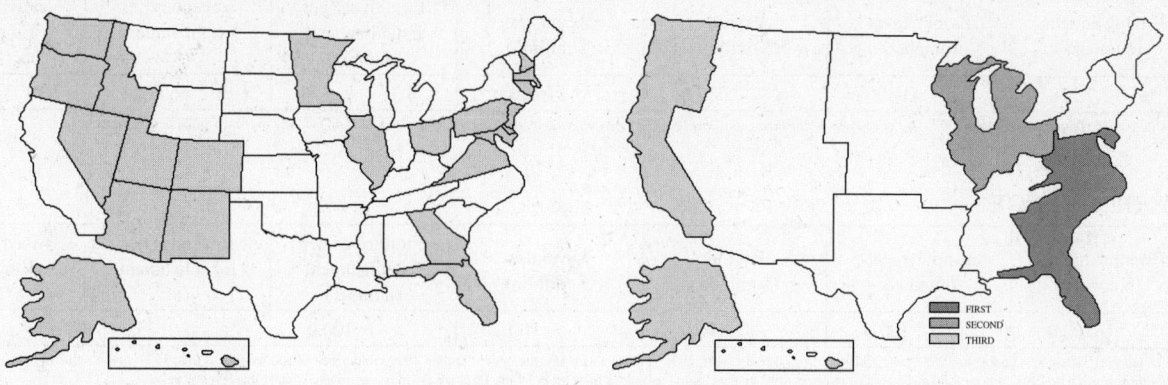

INDUSTRY DATA BY STATE

State	Establishments		Employment			Payroll		Revenues		
	Total (number)	% of U.S.	Total (number)	% of U.S.	Per Estab.	Total ($ mil.)	Per Empl. ($)	Total ($ mil.)	% of U.S.	Per Estab. ($)
California	939	8.2	3,049	8.9	3	102.3	33,554	303.8	10.2	323,550
Florida	923	8.1	2,436	7.1	3	81.0	33,246	231.5	7.8	250,766
New York	577	5.1	2,061	6.0	4	76.3	37,038	211.2	7.1	366,097
Texas	654	5.7	1,913	5.6	3	63.6	33,242	162.1	5.5	247,801
Pennsylvania	361	3.2	1,675	4.9	5	42.6	25,416	148.3	5.0	410,814
Illinois	522	4.6	1,527	4.4	3	52.7	34,480	143.3	4.8	274,603
Ohio	427	3.7	1,822	5.3	4	52.3	28,678	139.0	4.7	325,623
Michigan	387	3.4	931	2.7	2	28.4	30,467	92.8	3.1	239,742
New Jersey	303	2.7	1,054	3.1	3	35.8	33,923	92.0	3.1	303,752
Georgia	364	3.2	919	2.7	3	28.9	31,424	87.8	3.0	241,110
Minnesota	234	2.1	1,016	3.0	4	37.1	36,524	83.7	2.8	357,675
Massachusetts	217	1.9	821	2.4	4	26.9	32,767	80.8	2.7	372,230
Virginia	326	2.9	1,011	2.9	3	29.1	28,756	80.5	2.7	246,831
North Carolina	364	3.2	818	2.4	2	24.7	30,196	76.7	2.6	210,819
Washington	337	3.0	928	2.7	3	28.5	30,679	74.3	2.5	220,469
Maryland	268	2.4	855	2.5	3	23.8	27,785	70.8	2.4	264,187
Colorado	335	2.9	806	2.3	2	26.4	32,761	69.1	2.3	206,122
Arizona	256	2.2	880	2.6	3	25.3	28,775	66.0	2.2	257,844
Indiana	303	2.7	827	2.4	3	21.4	25,866	57.3	1.9	189,218
Tennessee	209	1.8	625	1.8	3	19.6	31,306	56.3	1.9	269,172
Wisconsin	269	2.4	820	2.4	3	22.0	26,830	54.3	1.8	201,725
Oregon	233	2.0	600	1.7	3	19.6	32,747	52.6	1.8	225,953
Missouri	228	2.0	722	2.1	3	23.0	31,906	50.5	1.7	221,605
Connecticut	132	1.2	425	1.2	3	13.1	30,833	40.3	1.4	305,205
Louisiana	172	1.5	469	1.4	3	8.8	18,714	37.4	1.3	217,279
South Carolina	179	1.6	502	1.5	3	10.7	21,221	37.1	1.2	207,123
Nevada	97	0.9	294	0.9	3	7.6	25,748	29.1	1.0	300,237
Alabama	170	1.5	363	1.1	2	9.0	24,741	27.6	0.9	162,629
Utah	132	1.2	384	1.1	3	10.1	26,372	27.2	0.9	205,780
Kentucky	134	1.2	285	0.8	2	6.0	21,119	23.8	0.8	177,552
Iowa	122	1.1	366	1.1	3	10.6	29,005	23.3	0.8	191,172
Kansas	120	1.1	251	0.7	2	7.8	31,064	23.1	0.8	192,817
New Mexico	90	0.8	234	0.7	3	7.9	33,923	20.6	0.7	228,333
Hawaii	63	0.6	211	0.6	3	8.4	39,697	18.3	0.6	291,206
Oklahoma	118	1.0	248	0.7	2	5.7	23,024	17.8	0.6	150,619
Arkansas	109	1.0	286	0.8	3	5.8	20,406	17.7	0.6	162,624
New Hampshire	61	0.5	206	0.6	3	6.9	33,583	17.3	0.6	284,180
Idaho	90	0.8	176	0.5	2	4.5	25,398	14.8	0.5	164,733
D.C.	14	0.1	337	1.0	24	8.5	25,136	13.9	0.5	995,000
Maine	71	0.6	217	0.6	3	5.2	24,037	13.2	0.4	186,592
Mississippi	70	0.6	158	0.5	2	3.5	22,468	13.1	0.4	186,971
Nebraska	68	0.6	162	0.5	2	4.5	28,080	12.0	0.4	175,838
Rhode Island	50	0.4	83	0.2	2	2.9	34,602	10.3	0.3	205,260
Delaware	40	0.4	111	0.3	3	3.7	33,577	8.4	0.3	209,550
Alaska	36	0.3	73	0.2	2	2.5	33,603	8.1	0.3	226,056
West Virginia	41	0.4	113	0.3	3	2.2	19,867	6.6	0.2	160,244
Montana	59	0.5	105	0.3	2	1.9	18,171	6.1	0.2	102,542
Vermont	39	0.3	83	0.2	2	2.3	27,711	5.2	0.2	132,154
Wyoming	33	0.3	54	0.2	2	1.2	22,074	3.7	0.1	111,152
North Dakota	23	0.2	48	0.1	2	1.2	24,917	3.0	0.1	130,261
South Dakota	18	0.2	39	0.1	2	0.9	22,410	2.7	0.1	149,389

Source: 1997 *Economic Census*. The states are in descending order of revenues or establishments (if revenue data are missing for the majority). The symbol (D) appears when data are withheld to prevent disclosure of competitive information. States marked with (D) are sorted by number of establishments. A dash (-) indicates that the data element cannot be calculated. * indicates the midpoint of a range; 175, for example is the range 100-249. Shaded *states* on the state map indicate those states which have proportionately greater representation in the industry than would be indicated by the state's population; the ratio is based on total revenues or number of establishments. Shaded *regions* indicate where the industry is regionally most concentrated.

NAICS 531390 - ACTIVITIES RELATED TO REAL ESTATE NEC

GENERAL STATISTICS

Year	Establishments (number)	Employment (number)	Payroll ($ million)	Revenues ($ million)	Employees per Establishment (number)	Revenues per Establishment ($)	Payroll per Employee ($)
1997	7,278	41,100	1,717.0	4,826.0	5.6	663,094	41,776

Source: *Economic Census of the United States*, 1997. This is a newly defined industry. Data for prior years were unavailable at the time of publication but may become available over time.

INDICES OF CHANGE

Year	Establishments (number)	Employment (number)	Payroll ($ million)	Revenues ($ million)	Employees per Establishment (number)	Revenues per Establishment ($)	Payroll per Employee ($)
1997	100.0	100.0	100.0	100.0	100.0	100.0	100.0

Sources: Same as General Statistics. The values shown reflect change from the base year, 1997. Values above 100 mean greater than 1997, values below 100 mean less than 1997, and a value of 100 in the 1982-96 or 1998-2001 period means same as 1997. Values followed by a 'p' are projections by the editors; 'e' stands for extrapolation. Data are the most recent available at this level of detail.

SIC INDUSTRIES RELATED TO NAICS 531390

Each new NAICS code represents an industry that used to be part of an SIC or a part of several SIC industries. Data in this table are shown to provide transitional information for these cases. All available data for the precursor SIC(s) are shown. Even if only a part of an SIC is included in the NAICS, *all* data for the SIC are reproduced. If the SIC industry is not marked as being a part (pt) of the NAICS, the entire industry is embedded in the NAICS data. The SIC composition of the new industry provides some hints of the relative importance of its "ancestors." Data marked with a 'p' are projected. Projections begin with 1982 data. Data earlier than 1990 are not shown but are reflected in the projections.

SIC	Industry	1990	1991	1992	1993	1994	1995	1996	1997
6531	**Real Estate Agents and Managers (pt)**								
	Establishments (number)	-	-	106,552	-	-	-	-	-
	Employment (thousands)	-	-	646.6	-	-	-	-	-
	Revenues ($ million)	-	-	53,747.0	-	-	-	-	-

Source: *Economic Census of the United States*, 1992, annual surveys of economic sectors conducted by the Bureau of the Census, and estimates or projections based on the 1982-1992 period; not all data are shown. 'e' marks estimates made by the editors; 'p' indicates projections based on time series. A dash (-) indicates that data for this SIC or year were not available. The abbreviation (pt) next to the industry name indicates that only a part of the industry is present within the NAICS data. If no (pt) is shown, the entire industry is contained within the NAICS data.

SELECTED RATIOS

For 1997	Avg. of Information	Analyzed Industry	Index	For 1997	Avg. of Information	Analyzed Industry	Index
Employees per establishment	6	6	96	Payroll per establishment	144,276	235,916	164
Revenue per establishment	835,727	663,094	79	Payroll as % of revenue	17	36	206
Revenue per employee	141,515	117,421	83	Payroll per employee	24,430	41,776	171

Sources: Same as General Statistics. The 'Average' column represents the average for the industry sector, in 1997, where the currently shown industry is classified. The Index shows the relationship between the Average and the Analyzed Industry. For example, 100 means that they are equal; 500 that the Analyzed Industry is five times the average; 50 means that the Analyzed Industry is half the national average. The abbreviation 'na' is used to show that data are 'not available'.

LEADING COMPANIES
No company data available for this industry.

LOCATION BY STATE AND REGIONAL CONCENTRATION

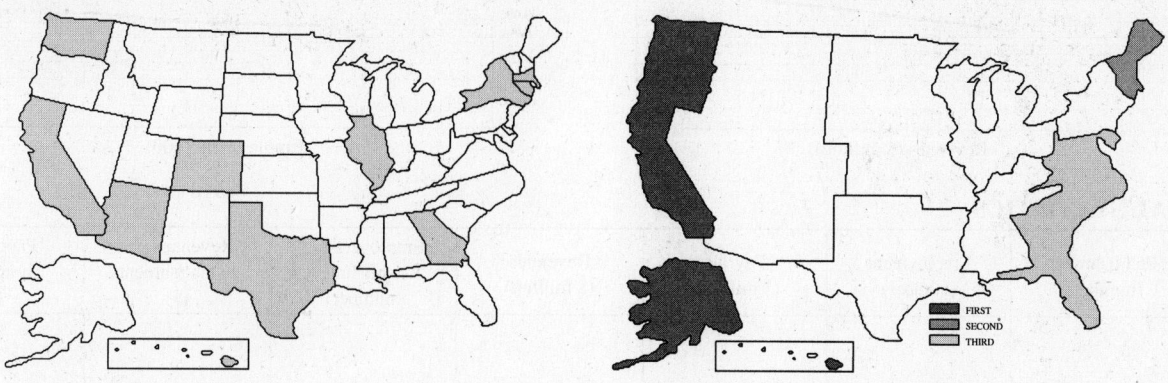

FIRST
SECOND
THIRD

INDUSTRY DATA BY STATE

State	Establishments Total (number)	Establishments % of U.S.	Employment Total (number)	Employment % of U.S.	Employment Per Estab.	Payroll Total ($ mil.)	Payroll Per Empl. ($)	Revenues Total ($ mil.)	Revenues % of U.S.	Revenues Per Estab. ($)
California	1,499	20.6	10,214	24.9	7	424.8	41,589	1,012.3	21.0	675,329
Connecticut	91	1.3	2,383	5.8	26	110.7	46,463	629.2	13.0	6,914,242
Texas	485	6.7	3,186	7.8	7	153.8	48,260	465.6	9.6	959,897
New York	572	7.9	3,030	7.4	5	170.9	56,417	398.3	8.3	696,413
Illinois	310	4.3	2,569	6.3	8	122.0	47,486	332.9	6.9	1,073,890
Florida	522	7.2	2,757	6.7	5	90.3	32,754	231.9	4.8	444,312
Georgia	210	2.9	1,249	3.0	6	59.1	47,344	197.2	4.1	938,910
Massachusetts	181	2.5	1,085	2.6	6	67.5	62,197	164.8	3.4	910,696
Pennsylvania	179	2.5	1,079	2.6	6	47.9	44,352	137.6	2.9	768,939
Washington	316	4.3	1,218	3.0	4	42.8	35,141	111.9	2.3	354,247
Colorado	201	2.8	988	2.4	5	39.5	39,980	96.6	2.0	480,552
Virginia	170	2.3	1,118	2.7	7	48.2	43,132	96.6	2.0	568,041
New Jersey	154	2.1	764	1.9	5	41.2	53,865	95.6	2.0	620,922
Arizona	186	2.6	759	1.8	4	29.8	39,211	89.4	1.9	480,441
Maryland	186	2.6	886	2.2	5	36.0	40,641	76.0	1.6	408,699
Ohio	156	2.1	614	1.5	4	20.3	33,007	64.0	1.3	410,224
Michigan	138	1.9	848	2.1	6	35.7	42,125	58.1	1.2	421,029
Oregon	109	1.5	713	1.7	7	15.8	22,191	52.3	1.1	480,083
Minnesota	118	1.6	518	1.3	4	16.4	31,614	47.0	1.0	398,398
Tennessee	98	1.3	418	1.0	4	12.3	29,390	42.3	0.9	431,500
North Carolina	143	2.0	328	0.8	2	9.8	29,939	40.3	0.8	281,671
Missouri	125	1.7	463	1.1	4	13.0	28,076	35.7	0.7	285,448
Indiana	91	1.3	270	0.7	3	7.4	27,244	29.3	0.6	321,593
D.C.	38	0.5	226	0.5	6	13.1	57,920	27.7	0.6	729,342
Kansas	63	0.9	253	0.6	4	8.9	35,261	26.1	0.5	413,667
Louisiana	78	1.1	284	0.7	4	6.4	22,370	23.0	0.5	295,077
Hawaii	60	0.8	276	0.7	5	9.3	33,725	22.7	0.5	377,700
South Carolina	78	1.1	330	0.8	4	7.4	22,530	21.8	0.5	278,987
Oklahoma	69	0.9	287	0.7	4	6.3	21,951	21.5	0.4	311,696
Wisconsin	77	1.1	200	0.5	3	4.6	23,160	19.9	0.4	258,065
Alabama	59	0.8	173	0.4	3	5.7	32,983	19.1	0.4	324,339
Nevada	63	0.9	149	0.4	2	4.7	31,416	14.8	0.3	235,111
Arkansas	46	0.6	135	0.3	3	2.8	20,459	14.0	0.3	303,978
Utah	41	0.6	159	0.4	4	2.9	18,403	13.5	0.3	329,683
Kentucky	46	0.6	131	0.3	3	2.9	21,840	12.3	0.3	268,043
Maine	37	0.5	107	0.3	3	3.5	32,822	11.5	0.2	309,892
New Hampshire	27	0.4	129	0.3	5	3.6	27,868	10.0	0.2	369,593
Iowa	38	0.5	148	0.4	4	3.4	22,743	9.9	0.2	260,842
New Mexico	44	0.6	119	0.3	3	3.4	28,672	8.5	0.2	193,045
West Virginia	14	0.2	94	0.2	7	2.6	27,479	8.0	0.2	574,000
Nebraska	31	0.4	79	0.2	3	1.3	16,620	5.4	0.1	174,065
Rhode Island	17	0.2	53	0.1	3	1.6	30,792	5.3	0.1	311,941
Idaho	20	0.3	42	0.1	2	1.0	24,167	5.1	0.1	255,650
Delaware	10	0.1	31	0.1	3	2.0	64,000	4.3	0.1	432,500
Mississippi	20	0.3	60	0.1	3	1.3	21,233	3.7	0.1	184,250
South Dakota	13	0.2	52	0.1	4	0.8	14,558	3.2	0.1	243,077
Montana	19	0.3	47	0.1	2	0.8	17,085	2.8	0.1	149,474
Alaska	7	0.1	16	0.0	2	0.3	20,000	2.5	0.1	353,000
Vermont	12	0.2	20	0.0	2	0.4	19,850	2.1	0.0	173,250
Wyoming	7	0.1	21	0.1	3	0.2	11,286	0.7	0.0	101,143

Source: 1997 *Economic Census*. The states are in descending order of revenues or establishments (if revenue data are missing for the majority). The symbol (D) appears when data are withheld to prevent disclosure of competitive information. States marked with (D) are sorted by number of establishments. A dash (-) indicates that the data element cannot be calculated. * indicates the midpoint of a range; 175, for example is the range 100-249. Shaded *states* on the state map indicate those states which have proportionately greater representation in the industry than would be indicated by the state's population; the ratio is based on total revenues or number of establishments. Shaded *regions* indicate where the industry is regionally most concentrated.

NAICS 532111 - PASSENGER CAR RENTAL*

	82 83 84 85 86 87 88 89 90 91 92 93 94 95 96 97 98 99 00 01
Revenues ($ million)	Employment (000)

GENERAL STATISTICS

Year	Establishments (number)	Employment (number)	Payroll ($ million)	Revenues ($ million)	Employees per Establishment (number)	Revenues per Establishment ($)	Payroll per Employee ($)
1982	-	-	-	-	-	-	-
1983	-	-	-	-	-	-	-
1984	-	-	-	-	-	-	-
1985	-	-	-	-	-	-	-
1986	-	-	-	-	-	-	-
1987	4,647	68,918	1,019.0	6,908.0	14.8	1,486,550	14,786
1988	5,099	76,917	1,227.0	7,602.0 e	15.1	1,490,881	15,952
1989	4,628	75,320	1,199.0	8,296.0 e	16.3	1,792,567	15,919
1990	4,463	78,301	1,315.0	8,990.0	17.5	2,014,340	16,794
1991	4,540	79,377	1,386.0	9,464.0	17.5	2,084,581	17,461
1992	4,894	81,170	1,475.0	10,370.0	16.6	2,118,921	18,172
1993	4,789	82,671	1,550.0	11,387.0	17.3	2,377,741	18,749
1994	4,631	86,018	1,715.0	12,172.0	18.6	2,628,374	19,938
1995	4,339	92,367	1,867.0	12,886.0	21.3	2,969,809	20,213
1996	4,353 e	97,495 e	1,998.0 e	13,835.0 e	22.4 e	3,178,268 e	20,493 e
1997	4,367	102,623	2,130.0	14,784.0	23.5	3,385,390	20,756
1998	4,359 p	101,236 p	2,168.0 p	15,319.0 p	23.2 p	3,514,338 p	21,415 p
1999	4,317 p	104,152 p	2,273.0 p	16,105.0 p	24.1 p	3,730,600 p	21,824 p
2000	4,274 p	107,067 p	2,379.0 p	16,890.0 p	25.1 p	3,951,802 p	22,220 p
2001	4,232 p	109,983 p	2,484.0 p	17,675.0 p	26.0 p	4,176,512 p	22,585 p

Sources: *Economic Census of the United States*, 1982, 1987, 1992, 1997. Establishment counts, employment, and payroll are from *County Business Patterns* for non-Census years. In non-Census years, industries in the Manufacturing range under SIC coding include data from the *Annual Survey of Manufactures* (ASM); those in the old Services range include data from the *Services Annual Survey* (SAS). Values followed by a 'p' are projections by the editors. Extrapolations are marked by 'e'. Data are the most recent available at this level of detail.

INDICES OF CHANGE

Year	Establishments (number)	Employment (number)	Payroll ($ million)	Revenues ($ million)	Employees per Establishment (number)	Revenues per Establishment ($)	Payroll per Employee ($)
1982	-	-	-	-	-	-	-
1987	106.4	67.2	47.8	46.7	63.1	43.9	71.2
1992	112.1	79.1	69.2	70.1	70.6	62.6	87.6
1993	109.7	80.6	72.8	77.0	73.5	70.2	90.3
1994	106.0	83.8	80.5	82.3	79.0	77.6	96.1
1995	99.4	90.0	87.7	87.2	90.6	87.7	97.4
1996	99.7 e	95.0 e	93.8 e	93.6 e	95.3 e	93.9 e	98.7 e
1997	100.0	100.0	100.0	100.0	100.0	100.0	100.0
1998	99.8 p	98.6 p	101.8 p	103.6 p	98.8 p	103.8 p	103.2 p
1999	98.9 p	101.5 p	106.7 p	108.9 p	102.7 p	110.2 p	105.1 p
2000	97.9 p	104.3 p	111.7 p	114.2 p	106.6 p	116.7 p	107.1 p
2001	96.9 p	107.2 p	116.6 p	119.6 p	110.6 p	123.4 p	108.8 p

Sources: Same as General Statistics. The values shown reflect change from the base year, 1997. Values above 100 mean greater than 1997, values below 100 mean less than 1997, and a value of 100 in the 1982-96 or 1998-2001 period means same as 1997. Values followed by a 'p' are projections by the editors; 'e' stands for extrapolation. Data are the most recent available at this level of detail.

SELECTED RATIOS

For 1997	Avg. of Information	Analyzed Industry	Index	For 1997	Avg. of Information	Analyzed Industry	Index
Employees per establishment	6	23	398	Payroll per establishment	144,276	487,749	338
Revenue per establishment	835,727	3,385,390	405	Payroll as % of revenue	17	14	83
Revenue per employee	141,515	144,061	102	Payroll per employee	24,430	20,756	85

Sources: Same as General Statistics. The 'Average' column represents the average for the industry sector, in 1997, where the currently shown industry is classified. The Index shows the relationship between the Average and the Analyzed Industry. For example, 100 means that they are equal; 500 that the Analyzed Industry is five times the average; 50 means that the Analyzed Industry is half the national average. The abbreviation 'na' is used to show that data are 'not available'.

*Equivalent to SIC 7514.

LEADING COMPANIES   Number shown: **33**   Total sales ($ mil): **43,117**   Total employment (000): **182.4**

Company Name	Address				CEO Name	Phone	Co. Type	Sales ($ mil)	Empl. (000)
AutoNation Inc.	110 SE 6th St	Fort Lauderdale	FL	33301	John Costello	954-769-6000	P	20,112	42.0
Hertz Corp.	225 Brae Blvd	Park Ridge	NJ	07656	Craig R Koch	201-307-2000	P	4,238	24.8
Enterprise Rent-A-Car Co.	600 Corporate	St. Louis	MO	63105	Andrew Taylor	314-512-5000	R	4,180	37.0
Budget Group Inc.	125 Basin St	Daytona Beach	FL	32114	Jean-Claude Ghiotti	904-238-7035	P	2,616	12.0
Avis Rent A Car Inc.	900 Old Country Rd	Garden City	NY	11530	R Craig Hoenshell	516-222-3000	P	2,298	19.0
Holman Enterprises	P O Box 1400	Pennsauken	NJ	08109	Joseph S Holman	609-663-5200	R	1,870	2.7
Budget Rent A Car Corp.	4225 Naperville Rd	Lisle	IL	60532	Sanford Miller	630-955-1900	S	1,600*	12.0
Alamo Rent A Car Inc.	110 Tower	Fort Lauderdale	FL	33301	George Gremge	954-522-0000	S	1,517*	8.5
National Car Rental System Inc.	7700 France Ave S	Minneapolis	MN	55435	Robert L Briggs	612-830-2121	S	1,300*	11.0
Dollar Thrifty Automotive Group	PO Box 35985	Tulsa	OK	74135	Joseph E Cappy	918-660-7700	P	999	4.9
Thrifty Rent-A-Car System Inc.	PO Box 35265	Tulsa	OK	74153	Ralph Mays	918-665-3930	S	680	5.2
Galpin Motors Inc.	15505 Roscoe Blvd	North Hills	CA	91343	Bert Boeckmann	818-787-3800	R	616	0.7
Geo. Byers Sons Inc.	P O Box 16513	Columbus	OH	43216	George W Byers III	614-228-5111	R	315*	0.6
Wade Ford Inc.	3860 S Cobb Dr	Smyrna	GA	30080	Alan K Arnold	770-436-1200	R	140	0.1
Heisler's Inc.	PO Box 1516	Mansfield	OH	44901	Rod Rafael	740-922-7239	R	107*	0.2
Dave Sinclair Ford Inc.	7466 S Lindbergh	St. Louis	MO	63125	D Sinclair	314-892-2600	R	78*	0.2
Auto Europe Inc.	P O Box 7006	Portland	ME	04112	Imad Khalidi	207-828-2525	R	71*	0.3
Beaudry Ford Inc.	141 NE Piedmont	Atlanta	GA	30303	Harmon M Born	404-659-3673	R	62	0.2
Hub Chrysler Plymouth Jeep Inc	PO Box 27226	West Allis	WI	53227	Jim Lecher	414-327-2400	S	47	0.1
Hoskins Chevrolet Inc.	P O Box 175	Elk Grove Vill.	IL	60007	Richard C Hoskins Jr	847-439-0900	R	40*	0.1
Brach Inc.	5301 Beethoven St	Los Angeles	CA	90066	Gary Pehota	310-822-1700	S	35*	0.1
Simpson Buick Co.	8400 E Firestone	Downey	CA	90241	David Simpson	562-861-1261	R	35*	<0.1
Jones Chevrolet Company Inc.	P O Box 458	Sumter	SC	29151	John T Jones Jr	803-469-2515	R	32	<0.1
Newins Bay Shore Ford Inc.	219 W Main St	Bay Shore	NY	11706	Charles Stickney	516-665-1300	R	27*	<0.1
U-Save Auto Rental of America	4780 I-55 N	Jackson	MS	39211	Tom McDonnell	601-713-4333	R	23	<0.1
Hayes Leasing Co.	P O Box 569650	Dallas	TX	75356	Cynthia Vlazajewski	972-869-2400	R	23*	<0.1
Thrifty Car and Truck Rental	3902 Crittenden Dr	Louisville	KY	40209	Steve Sternberg	502-367-0231	R	20*	<0.1
Auto Rental Inc.	P O Box 10097	St. Louis	MO	63145	J Farrell Browne Jr	314-426-6272	R	18	0.2
Wheelchair Getaways Inc.	P O Box 605	Versailles	KY	40383	Richard Gatewood	606-873-4973	R	6	<0.1
Barrett Capital Corp.	930 Mamaroneck	Mamaroneck	NY	10543	Barry P Korn	914-381-4600	R	5*	<0.1
Car Temps U.S.A.	4174 Mayfield Rd	South Euclid	OH	44121	Wayne Haisinger	216-321-3500	D	3*	<0.1
New Country Pontiac, GMC	PO Box 552	Mechanicville	NY	12118	Michael Cantanucci	518-664-9851	R	3	<0.1
Hub Leasing Inc.	PO Box 27226	West Allis	WI	53227	James Lecher	414-327-2400	R	1*	<0.1

Source: Ward's Business Directory of U.S. Private and Public Companies, Volumes 1 and 2, 2000. The company type code used is as follows: P - Public, R - Private, S - Subsidiary, D - Division, J - Joint Venture, A - Affiliate, G - Group, N - Company type not reported. Sales are in millions of dollars, employees are in thousands. An asterisk (*) indicates an estimated sales volume. The symbol < stands for 'less than'. Company names and addresses are truncated, in some cases, to fit into the available space.

LOCATION BY STATE AND REGIONAL CONCENTRATION

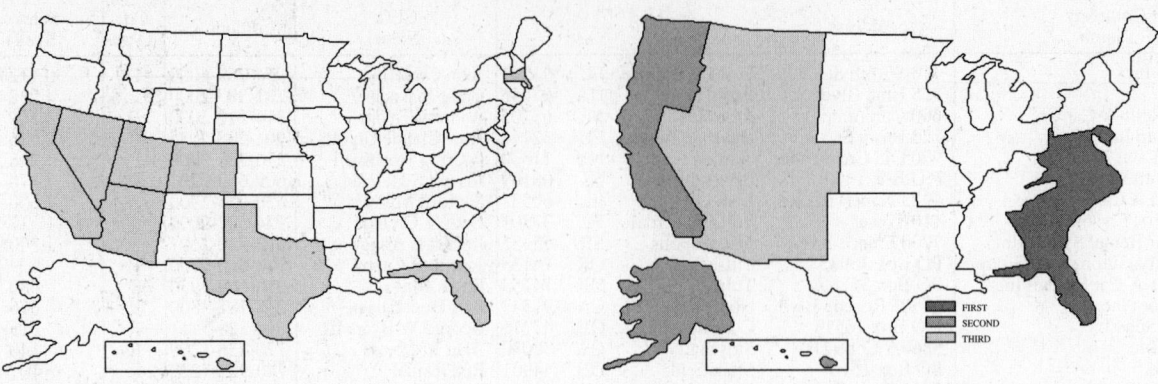

FIRST
SECOND
THIRD

INDUSTRY DATA BY STATE

State	Establishments Total (number)	% of U.S.	Employment Total (number)	% of U.S.	Per Estab.	Payroll Total ($ mil.)	Per Empl. ($)	Revenues Total ($ mil.)	% of U.S.	Per Estab. ($)
California	490	11.2	13,414	13.1	27	335.1	24,984	2,403.4	16.3	4,904,904
Florida	357	8.2	12,337	12.0	35	229.7	18,617	1,902.7	12.9	5,329,714
Texas	394	9.0	7,512	7.3	19	162.7	21,663	1,086.4	7.3	2,757,332
New York	212	4.9	4,811	4.7	23	89.1	18,515	599.3	4.1	2,827,000
Arizona	100	2.3	3,521	3.4	35	68.0	19,306	538.3	3.6	5,383,330
Illinois	133	3.0	3,970	3.9	30	83.7	21,083	507.5	3.4	3,815,857
Pennsylvania	173	4.0	3,662	3.6	21	82.7	22,590	490.8	3.3	2,837,168
Nevada	53	1.2	3,072	3.0	58	62.4	20,308	387.1	2.6	7,303,302
Georgia	162	3.7	2,964	2.9	18	59.6	20,103	382.0	2.6	2,358,327
Colorado	93	2.1	2,600	2.5	28	52.1	20,033	377.8	2.6	4,062,452
Virginia	123	2.8	2,620	2.6	21	53.6	20,458	376.1	2.5	3,058,122
North Carolina	128	2.9	2,790	2.7	22	55.4	19,859	374.8	2.5	2,927,992
Massachusetts	118	2.7	2,023	2.0	17	57.1	28,209	357.4	2.4	3,028,915
Hawaii	56	1.3	2,006	2.0	36	41.7	20,810	344.5	2.3	6,151,982
Michigan	123	2.8	2,597	2.5	21	55.3	21,298	343.1	2.3	2,789,203
Ohio	144	3.3	2,759	2.7	19	54.0	19,589	322.0	2.2	2,236,042
Washington	80	1.8	2,047	2.0	26	40.6	19,846	295.0	2.0	3,687,800
Maryland	84	1.9	2,298	2.2	27	49.7	21,645	275.4	1.9	3,278,857
Tennessee	85	1.9	1,770	1.7	21	35.6	20,087	237.8	1.6	2,797,929
Missouri	55	1.3	1,348	1.3	25	24.9	18,455	206.4	1.4	3,753,382
Kentucky	54	1.2	1,238	1.2	23	25.1	20,272	187.7	1.3	3,476,185
Louisiana	55	1.3	1,372	1.3	25	26.7	19,472	182.8	1.2	3,323,073
Alabama	50	1.1	1,472	1.4	29	28.2	19,175	181.6	1.2	3,632,300
Indiana	92	2.1	1,477	1.4	16	26.6	18,029	162.8	1.1	1,769,402
South Carolina	67	1.5	1,290	1.3	19	20.1	15,564	156.6	1.1	2,337,821
Minnesota	45	1.0	1,120	1.1	25	21.7	19,381	148.6	1.0	3,302,133
Utah	37	0.8	876	0.9	24	16.4	18,707	140.8	1.0	3,804,568
Connecticut	47	1.1	785	0.8	17	18.4	23,389	110.1	0.7	2,343,340
Wisconsin	60	1.4	984	1.0	16	16.7	16,962	106.5	0.7	1,775,383
New Mexico	26	0.6	692	0.7	27	10.1	14,582	92.3	0.6	3,548,308
Nebraska	25	0.6	359	0.3	14	5.0	13,964	43.5	0.3	1,740,920
Maine	12	0.3	584	0.6	49	10.8	18,408	42.7	0.3	3,561,750
Arkansas	37	0.8	387	0.4	10	4.5	11,674	35.5	0.2	958,459
North Dakota	15	0.3	254	0.2	17	3.0	11,898	19.6	0.1	1,309,667
Wyoming	24	0.5	124	0.1	5	2.0	16,169	15.4	0.1	640,375
New Jersey	134	3.1	3,750*	-	-	(D)	-	(D)	-	-
Oregon	52	1.2	1,750*	-	-	(D)	-	(D)	-	-
Oklahoma	51	1.2	1,750*	-	-	(D)	-	(D)	-	-
Alaska	39	0.9	375*	-	-	(D)	-	(D)	-	-
Montana	36	0.8	375*	-	-	(D)	-	(D)	-	-
Mississippi	33	0.8	375*	-	-	(D)	-	(D)	-	-
West Virginia	33	0.8	375*	-	-	(D)	-	(D)	-	-
Iowa	32	0.7	750*	-	-	(D)	-	(D)	-	-
Rhode Island	32	0.7	375*	-	-	(D)	-	(D)	-	-
Idaho	29	0.7	375*	-	-	(D)	-	(D)	-	-
Kansas	26	0.6	375*	-	-	(D)	-	(D)	-	-
New Hampshire	25	0.6	175*	-	-	(D)	-	(D)	-	-
South Dakota	14	0.3	175*	-	-	(D)	-	(D)	-	-
Delaware	9	0.2	60*	-	-	(D)	-	(D)	-	-
Vermont	9	0.2	175*	-	-	(D)	-	(D)	-	-

Source: 1997 *Economic Census*. The states are in descending order of revenues or establishments (if revenue data are missing for the majority). The symbol (D) appears when data are withheld to prevent disclosure of competitive information. States marked with (D) are sorted by number of establishments. A dash (-) indicates that the data element cannot be calculated. * indicates the midpoint of a range; 175, for example is the range 100-249. Shaded *states* on the state map indicate those states which have proportionately greater representation in the industry than would be indicated by the state's population; the ratio is based on total revenues or number of establishments. Shaded *regions* indicate where the industry is regionally most concentrated.

NAICS 532112 - PASSENGER CAR LEASING*

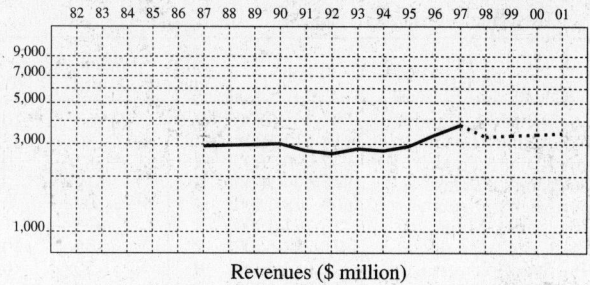

Revenues ($ million)

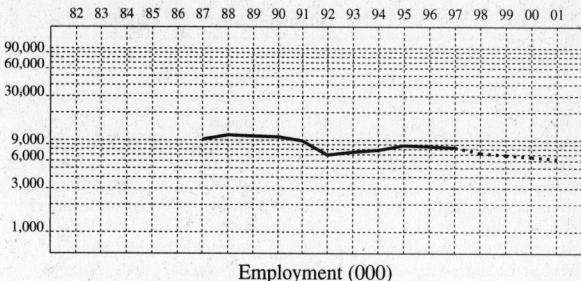

Employment (000)

GENERAL STATISTICS

Year	Establishments (number)	Employment (number)	Payroll ($ million)	Revenues ($ million)	Employees per Establishment (number)	Revenues per Establishment ($)	Payroll per Employee ($)
1982	-	-	-	-	-	-	-
1983	-	-	-	-	-	-	-
1984	-	-	-	-	-	-	-
1985	-	-	-	-	-	-	-
1986	-	-	-	-	-	-	-
1987	1,538	10,205	221.0	2,928.0	6.6	1,903,771	21,656
1988	1,341	11,395	281.0	2,955.0 e	8.5	2,203,579	24,660
1989	1,188	11,098	276.0	2,982.0 e	9.3	2,510,101	24,869
1990	1,144	10,848	279.0	3,010.0	9.5	2,631,119	25,719
1991	1,126	9,865	263.0	2,762.0	8.8	2,452,931	26,660
1992	919	6,936	208.0	2,657.0	7.5	2,891,186	29,988
1993	862	7,461	228.0	2,823.0	8.7	3,274,942	30,559
1994	882	7,829	243.0	2,755.0	8.9	3,123,583	31,038
1995	875	8,772	265.0	2,917.0	10.0	3,333,714	30,210
1996	877 e	8,549 e	291.0 e	3,359.0 e	9.7 e	3,830,103 e	34,039 e
1997	879	8,325	316.0	3,800.0	9.5	4,323,094	37,958
1998	682 p	7,233 p	281.0 p	3,286.0 p	10.6 p	4,818,182 p	38,850 p
1999	620 p	6,904 p	285.0 p	3,335.0 p	11.1 p	5,379,032 p	41,280 p
2000	557 p	6,575 p	288.0 p	3,383.0 p	11.8 p	6,073,609 p	43,802 p
2001	495 p	6,245 p	292.0 p	3,432.0 p	12.6 p	6,933,333 p	46,757 p

Sources: Economic Census of the United States, 1982, 1987, 1992, 1997. Establishment counts, employment, and payroll are from *County Business Patterns* for non-Census years. In non-Census years, industries in the Manufacturing range under SIC coding include data from the *Annual Survey of Manufactures (ASM)*; those in the old Services range include data from the *Services Annual Survey (SAS)*. Values followed by a 'p' are projections by the editors. Extrapolations are marked by 'e'. Data are the most recent available at this level of detail.

INDICES OF CHANGE

Year	Establishments (number)	Employment (number)	Payroll ($ million)	Revenues ($ million)	Employees per Establishment (number)	Revenues per Establishment ($)	Payroll per Employee ($)
1982	-	-	-	-	-	-	-
1987	175.0	122.6	69.9	77.1	70.1	44.0	57.1
1992	104.6	83.3	65.8	69.9	79.7	66.9	79.0
1993	98.1	89.6	72.2	74.3	91.4	75.8	80.5
1994	100.3	94.0	76.9	72.5	93.7	72.3	81.8
1995	99.5	105.4	83.9	76.8	105.9	77.1	79.6
1996	99.8 e	102.7 e	92.1 e	88.4 e	102.9 e	88.6 e	89.7 e
1997	100.0	100.0	100.0	100.0	100.0	100.0	100.0
1998	77.6 p	86.9 p	88.9 p	86.5 p	112.0 p	111.5 p	102.3 p
1999	70.5 p	82.9 p	90.2 p	87.8 p	117.6 p	124.4 p	108.8 p
2000	63.4 p	79.0 p	91.1 p	89.0 p	124.6 p	140.5 p	115.4 p
2001	56.3 p	75.0 p	92.4 p	90.3 p	133.2 p	160.4 p	123.2 p

Sources: Same as General Statistics. The values shown reflect change from the base year, 1997. Values above 100 mean greater than 1997, values below 100 mean less than 1997, and a value of 100 in the 1982-96 or 1998-2001 period means same as 1997. Values followed by a 'p' are projections by the editors; 'e' stands for extrapolation. Data are the most recent available at this level of detail.

SELECTED RATIOS

For 1997	Avg. of Information	Analyzed Industry	Index	For 1997	Avg. of Information	Analyzed Industry	Index
Employees per establishment	6	9	160	Payroll per establishment	144,276	359,499	249
Revenue per establishment	835,727	4,323,094	517	Payroll as % of revenue	17	8	48
Revenue per employee	141,515	456,456	323	Payroll per employee	24,430	37,958	155

Sources: Same as General Statistics. The 'Average' column represents the average for the industry sector, in 1997, where the currently shown industry is classified. The Index shows the relationship between the Average and the Analyzed Industry. For example, 100 means that they are equal; 500 that the Analyzed Industry is five times the average; 50 means that the Analyzed Industry is half the national average. The abbreviation 'na' is used to show that data are 'not available'.

*Equivalent to SIC 7515.

LEADING COMPANIES Number shown: **29** Total sales ($ mil): **32,890** Total employment (000): **53.1**

Company Name	Address				CEO Name	Phone	Co. Type	Sales ($ mil)	Empl. (000)
Popular Inc.	P O Box 362708	San Juan	PR	00936	Richard L. Carrion	787-765-9800	P	24,760	10.5
Enterprise Rent-A-Car Co.	600 Corporate	St. Louis	MO	63105	Andrew Taylor	314-512-5000	R	4,180	37.0
Frank Consolidated Enterprises	666 Garland Pl	Des Plaines	IL	60016	Elaine S Frank	847-699-7000	R	1,181	0.6
Wheels Inc.	666 Garland Pl	Des Plaines	IL	60016	James S Frank	847-699-7000	S	612*	0.6
Automotive Rentals Inc.	P O Box 5039	Mount Laurel	NJ	08054	Michael Laporta	609-778-1500	S	500*	0.6
PHH Vehicle Management	307 International Cir	Hunt Valley	MD	21030	Mark E Miller	410-771-1900	S	325*	1.0
Ewald Automotive Group Inc.	2201 N Mayfair Rd	Milwaukee	WI	53226	Craig A Ewald	414-258-5000	R	165	0.5
Executive Car Leasing Co.	7807 Santa Monica	Los Angeles	CA	90046	Sam Goldman	323-654-5000	R	150*	0.2
John Eagle Lincoln, Mercury	6200 Lemmon Ave	Dallas	TX	75209	RM Eagle	214-357-0700	R	140*	0.3
Wade Ford Inc.	3860 S Cobb Dr	Smyrna	GA	30080	Alan K Arnold	770-436-1200	R	140	0.1
Fette Ford Inc.	PO Box 1237	Clifton	NJ	07012	H Fette	973-779-7000	R	70*	0.2
Rothrock Motor Sales Inc.	Rte 22	Allentown	PA	18104	BL Rothrock	610-439-8485	R	60	0.2
Allstate Leasing Inc.	9428 Reistertown Rd	Owings Mills	MD	21117	LA Cohen	410-363-6500	S	55*	0.1
Hamilton Chevrolet Inc.	5800 14 Mile Rd	Warren	MI	48092	Donald Hamilton	810-264-1400	R	55*	<0.1
Normandin Chrysler-Plymouth	900 Auto Mall	San Jose	CA	95136	Louis O Normandin	408-266-9500	R	55	0.1
Hub Chrysler Plymouth Jeep Inc	PO Box 27226	West Allis	WI	53227	Jim Lecher	414-327-2400	S	47	0.1
Leasing Associates Inc.	PO Box 243	Houston	TX	77001	F Michael Nachman	713-522-9771	R	47*	<0.1
Dewey Ford Inc.	444 E 4th St	Des Moines	IA	50309	Mark Vukovich	515-282-2828	R	45*	<0.1
Gene Hamon Ford-Chrysler Inc.	2600 Palmer Hwy	Texas City	TX	77590	Tomy Hamon	409-948-2541	R	42*	<0.1
Childress Buick Co.	2223 W Camelback	Phoenix	AZ	85015	George Childress	602-249-1133	R	40*	<0.1
Futliff Capital Ford Inc.	1000 Paxton St	Harrisburg	PA	17105	Glenn Martin	717-233-4521	R	34*	<0.1
American Honda Finance Corp.	21041 S Western	Torrance	CA	90501	Koichi Amemiya	310-212-6619	S	33*	<0.1
Langhorne Leasing & Messenger	PO Box 3004	Langhorne	PA	19047	Stanley E Reedman Sr	215-757-4961	S	33*	<0.1
Salex Holding Corp.	PO Box 18929	Hauppauge	NY	11788	Angelo Crimi	516-436-5000	P	23	<0.1
Bauer Buick Company Inc.	555 E 162nd St	South Holland	IL	60473	Gordon Walker	708-331-4800	R	23	<0.1
Nabors Inc.	PO Box 1058	Clarksdale	MS	38614	Grady L Nabors	601-624-2585	R	21*	<0.1
Thrifty Car and Truck Rental	3902 Crittenden Dr	Louisville	KY	40209	Steve Sternberg	502-367-0231	R	20*	<0.1
Tunmore Oldsmobile Inc.	2677 Delaware Ave	Buffalo	NY	14216	Edward R Tunmore	716-877-1500	R	19*	<0.1
Jake Sweeney Auto Leasing Inc.	8755 Fieldertel Rd	Cincinnati	OH	45249	David Loper	513-489-5253	R	16*	<0.1

Source: Ward's Business Directory of U.S. Private and Public Companies, Volumes 1 and 2, 2000. The company type code used is as follows: P - Public, R - Private, S - Subsidiary, D - Division, J - Joint Venture, A - Affiliate, G - Group, N - Company type not reported. Sales are in millions of dollars, employees are in thousands. An asterisk (*) indicates an estimated sales volume. The symbol < stands for 'less than'. Company names and addresses are truncated, in some cases, to fit into the available space.

LOCATION BY STATE AND REGIONAL CONCENTRATION

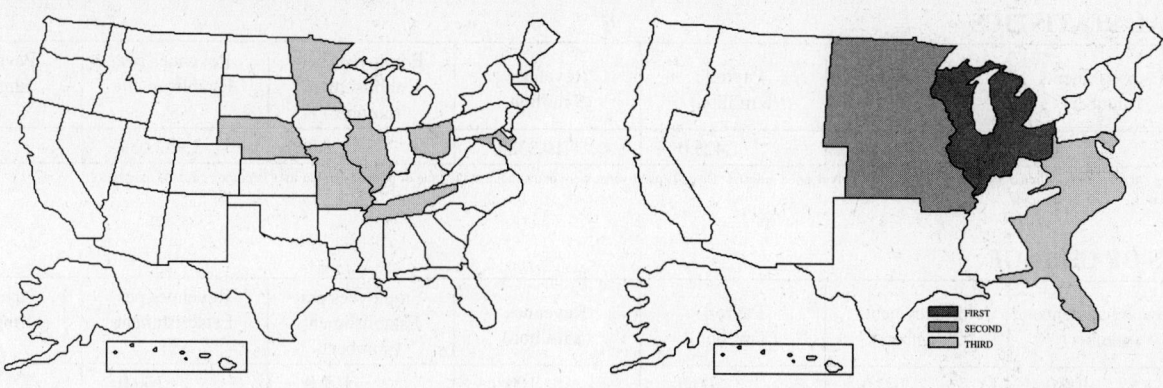

INDUSTRY DATA BY STATE

State	Establishments		Employment			Payroll		Revenues		
	Total (number)	% of U.S.	Total (number)	% of U.S.	Per Estab.	Total ($ mil.)	Per Empl. ($)	Total ($ mil.)	% of U.S.	Per Estab. ($)
Illinois	52	5.9	919	11.0	18	34.6	37,651	896.1	23.6	17,232,885
Minnesota	19	2.2	1,040	12.5	55	53.3	51,241	352.9	9.3	18,575,737
Ohio	83	9.4	726	8.7	9	25.0	34,464	298.0	7.8	3,590,831
New York	104	11.8	575	6.9	6	19.5	33,864	211.9	5.6	2,037,269
Florida	42	4.8	308	3.7	7	12.8	41,409	172.1	4.5	4,098,381
California	71	8.1	431	5.2	6	17.7	41,088	170.5	4.5	2,401,085
Missouri	16	1.8	719	8.6	45	20.9	29,075	144.6	3.8	9,036,875
Tennessee	17	1.9	129	1.5	8	5.1	39,667	121.3	3.2	7,133,118
Texas	63	7.2	291	3.5	5	12.4	42,536	96.4	2.5	1,530,714
Maryland	19	2.2	231	2.8	12	7.7	33,126	78.9	2.1	4,154,842
Georgia	25	2.8	216	2.6	9	14.5	67,361	72.6	1.9	2,903,600
Pennsylvania	34	3.9	193	2.3	6	6.5	33,912	69.4	1.8	2,040,147
Indiana	26	3.0	161	1.9	6	4.1	25,224	59.9	1.6	2,304,923
Michigan	30	3.4	147	1.8	5	5.3	35,776	59.6	1.6	1,986,433
Wisconsin	16	1.8	165	2.0	10	4.3	25,897	59.5	1.6	3,715,750
North Carolina	23	2.6	114	1.4	5	4.6	40,009	42.9	1.1	1,863,957
Massachusetts	20	2.3	132	1.6	7	4.2	32,152	36.4	1.0	1,822,000
Kentucky	8	0.9	49	0.6	6	1.4	29,327	29.9	0.8	3,735,750
Nebraska	11	1.3	53	0.6	5	1.4	26,679	28.2	0.7	2,562,091
Utah	7	0.8	22	0.3	3	1.0	43,364	25.4	0.7	3,633,857
Connecticut	13	1.5	65	0.8	5	1.9	29,215	23.7	0.6	1,820,154
Alabama	14	1.6	43	0.5	3	1.4	33,070	18.1	0.5	1,291,357
Washington	13	1.5	46	0.6	4	1.5	32,326	16.6	0.4	1,279,231
Colorado	15	1.7	56	0.7	4	1.8	31,393	13.0	0.3	868,667
South Carolina	8	0.9	21	0.3	3	0.5	24,143	5.0	0.1	622,000
Arizona	11	1.3	41	0.5	4	1.0	23,171	4.3	0.1	388,273
Hawaii	7	0.8	13	0.2	2	0.3	19,769	3.1	0.1	444,714
Louisiana	6	0.7	26	0.3	4	0.2	7,385	2.3	0.1	383,500
New Jersey	34	3.9	750*	-	-	(D)	-	(D)	-	-
Kansas	11	1.3	60*	-	-	(D)	-	(D)	-	-
Oregon	9	1.0	60*	-	-	(D)	-	(D)	-	-
Iowa	7	0.8	60*	-	-	(D)	-	(D)	-	-

Source: 1997 *Economic Census*. The states are in descending order of revenues or establishments (if revenue data are missing for the majority). The symbol (D) appears when data are withheld to prevent disclosure of competitive information. States marked with (D) are sorted by number of establishments. A dash (-) indicates that the data element cannot be calculated. * indicates the midpoint of a range; 175, for example is the range 100-249. Shaded *states* on the state map indicate those states which have proportionately greater representation in the industry than would be indicated by the state's population; the ratio is based on total revenues or number of establishments. Shaded *regions* indicate where the industry is regionally most concentrated.

NAICS 532120 - TRUCK, UTILITY TRAILER, AND RV (RECREATIONAL VEHICLE) RENTAL AND LEASING

GENERAL STATISTICS

Year	Establishments (number)	Employment (number)	Payroll ($ million)	Revenues ($ million)	Employees per Establishment (number)	Revenues per Establishment ($)	Payroll per Employee ($)
1997	5,296	47,114	1,425.0	10,338.0	8.9	1,952,039	30,246

Source: Economic Census of the United States, 1997. This is a newly defined industry. Data for prior years were unavailable at the time of publication but may become available over time.

INDICES OF CHANGE

Year	Establishments (number)	Employment (number)	Payroll ($ million)	Revenues ($ million)	Employees per Establishment (number)	Revenues per Establishment ($)	Payroll per Employee ($)
1997	100.0	100.0	100.0	100.0	100.0	100.0	100.0

Sources: Same as General Statistics. The values shown reflect change from the base year, 1997. Values above 100 mean greater than 1997, values below 100 mean less than 1997, and a value of 100 in the 1982-96 or 1998-2001 period means same as 1997. Values followed by a 'p' are projections by the editors; 'e' stands for extrapolation. Data are the most recent available at this level of detail.

SIC INDUSTRIES RELATED TO NAICS 532120

Each new NAICS code represents an industry that used to be part of an SIC or a part of several SIC industries. Data in this table are shown to provide transitional information for these cases. All available data for the precursor SIC(s) are shown. Even if only a part of an SIC is included in the NAICS, *all* data for the SIC are reproduced. If the SIC industry is not marked as being a part (pt) of the NAICS, the entire industry is embedded in the NAICS data. The SIC composition of the new industry provides some hints of the relative importance of its "ancestors." Data marked with a 'p' are projected. Projections begin with 1982 data. Data earlier than 1990 are not shown but are reflected in the projections.

SIC	Industry	1990	1991	1992	1993	1994	1995	1996	1997
7513	**Truck Rental & Leasing**								
	Establishments (number)	4,008	3,995	4,313	4,130	4,577	4,761	4,451p	4,478p
	Employment (thousands)	51.4	47.3	42.2	47.0	37.4	37.6	35.7p	33.4p
	Revenues ($ million)	8,529.0	7,854.0	7,568.0	8,120.0	8,964.0	10,113.0	11,172.0	10,748.6p
7519	**Utility Trailer Rental**								
	Establishments (number)	537	586	440	477	479	518	477p	470p
	Employment (thousands)	3.7	3.3	2.1	2.1	2.0	2.5	1.9p	1.7p
	Revenues ($ million)	-	-	294.4	-	-	-		

Source: Economic Census of the United States, 1992, annual surveys of economic sectors conducted by the Bureau of the Census, and estimates or projections based on the 1982-1992 period; not all data are shown. 'e' marks estimates made by the editors; 'p' indicates projections based on time series. A dash (-) indicates that data for this SIC or year were not available. The abbreviation (pt) next to the industry name indicates that only a part of the industry is present within the NAICS data. If no (pt) is shown, the entire industry is contained within the NAICS data.

SELECTED RATIOS

For 1997	Avg. of Information	Analyzed Industry	Index	For 1997	Avg. of Information	Analyzed Industry	Index
Employees per establishment	6	9	151	Payroll per establishment	144,276	269,071	186
Revenue per establishment	835,727	1,952,039	234	Payroll as % of revenue	17	14	80
Revenue per employee	141,515	219,425	155	Payroll per employee	24,430	30,246	124

Sources: Same as General Statistics. The 'Average' column represents the average for the industry sector, in 1997, where the currently shown industry is classified. The Index shows the relationship between the Average and the Analyzed Industry. For example, 100 means that they are equal; 500 that the Analyzed Industry is five times the average; 50 means that the Analyzed Industry is half the national average. The abbreviation 'na' is used to show that data are 'not available'.

LEADING COMPANIES   Number shown: **46**   Total sales ($ mil): **29,399**   Total employment (000): **159.8**

Company Name	Address				CEO Name	Phone	Co. Type	Sales ($ mil)	Empl. (000)
Penske Corp.	13400 Outer Dr W	Detroit	MI	48239	Roger S. Penske	313-592-5000	R	10,000	34.0
Ryder System Inc.	3600 N W 82nd Ave	Miami	FL	33166	M Anthony Burns	305-500-3726	P	4,952	45.4
Budget Group Inc.	125 Basin St	Daytona Beach	FL	32114	Jean-Claude Ghiotti	904-238-7035	P	2,616	12.0
Penske Truck Leasing L.P.	P O Box 563	Reading	PA	19603	Brian Hard	610-775-6000	S	1,900	14.0
Budget Rent A Car Corp.	4225 Naperville Rd	Lisle	IL	60532	Sanford Miller	630-955-1900	S	1,600*	12.0
AMERCO	1325 Airmotive Way	Reno	NV	89502	Edward J Shoen	775-688-6300	P	1,552	14.4
U-Haul International Inc.	2727 N Central Ave	Phoenix	AZ	85004	Edward J Shoen	602-263-6811	S	1,000*	10.0
Transamerica Leasing Inc.	505 Sansome St	San Francisco	CA	94111	Charles E Tingley	914-251-9000	S	734*	1.0
Rollins Leasing Corp.	PO Box 1791	Wilmington	DE	19899	Larry Brown	302-426-2700	S	667*	4.0
Rollins Truck Leasing Corp.	PO Box 1791	Wilmington	DE	19899	John W Rollins	302-426-2700	P	627	4.0
Wheels Inc.	666 Garland Pl	Des Plaines	IL	60016	James S Frank	847-699-7000	S	612*	0.6
XTRA Corp.	60 State St	Boston	MA	02109	Lewis Rubin	617-367-5000	P	461	0.9
PHH Vehicle Management	307 International Cir	Hunt Valley	MD	21030	Mark E Miller	410-771-1900	S	325*	1.0
XTRA Lease Inc.	1801 Park 270 Dr	St. Louis	MO	63146	William H Franz	314-579-9300	S	300	0.6
Salem National Corp.	PO Box 24788	Winston-Salem	NC	27114	Thomas L Teague	336-768-6800	R	195*	0.6
Aim National Lease	1500 Trumbull Ave	Girard	OH	44420	Thomas Fleming	330-759-0438	R	193*	0.6
Bobby Murray Chevrolet Geo Inc.	P O Box 40639	Raleigh	NC	27629	Bobby L Murray	919-834-6441	R	162*	0.1
Waters Truck and Tractor Inc.	P O Box 831	Columbus	MS	39701	Michael Waters	662-328-1575	R	160*	0.2
Executive Car Leasing Co.	7807 Santa Monica	Los Angeles	CA	90046	Sam Goldman	323-654-5000	R	150*	0.2
Modern Group Ltd.	P O Box 710	Bristol	PA	19007	David E Griffith	215-943-9100	R	145	0.6
R.L. French Corp.	4111 Delaware Ave	Des Moines	IA	50313	Rod L French	515-265-8111	R	110*	0.2
Cruise America Inc.	11 W Hampton Ave	Mesa	AZ	85210	Randall S Smalley	602-464-7300	S	96	0.4
Mendon Leasing Corp.	362 Kingsland Ave	Brooklyn	NY	11222	Don Resnicoff	718-391-5300	R	82*	0.3
Salem Leasing Corp.	P O Box 24788	Winston-Salem	NC	27114	Thomas L Teague	336-768-6800	S	81*	0.3
Interstate NationaLease Inc.	2700 Palmyra Rd	Albany	GA	31707	Jack Zolomy	912-883-7250	S	66*	0.2
Beaudry Ford Inc.	141 NE Piedmont	Atlanta	GA	30303	Harmon M Born	404-659-3673	R	62	0.2
Allstate Leasing Inc.	9428 Reisterstown Rd	Owings Mills	MD	21117	LA Cohen	410-363-6500	S	55*	0.1
Star Truck Rentals Inc.	3940 Eastern S E	Grand Rapids	MI	49508	Thomas Bylenga	616-243-7033	R	49*	0.2
Leasing Associates Inc.	PO Box 243	Houston	TX	77001	F Michael Nachman	713-522-9771	R	47*	<0.1
Nelson Leasing Inc.	PO Box 993	Willmar	MN	56201	Dale Nelson	320-235-2770	R	37*	0.1
Catawba Rental Company Inc.	PO Box 339	Claremont	NC	28610	TA Pope	828-459-3200	S	34*	0.4
A-P-A Truck Leasing	1207 Tonnelle Ave	North Bergen	NJ	07047	Armand Pohan	201-868-2533	S	33*	0.1
F.B. Hart Company Inc.	1441 Richards Blvd	Sacramento	CA	95814	Jim Coles	916-441-6151	R	33*	0.1
Chancellor Corp.	210 South St	Boston	MA	02111	Brian M Adley	617-368-2700	P	30	0.2
Toyota Material Handling	21053 Alexander Ct	Hayward	CA	94545	Rich Andres	510-887-0500	R	29*	0.2
Brody Transportation Inc.	621 S Bentalou St	Baltimore	MD	21223	Edward J Brody	410-947-5800	R	26*	<0.1
PACCAR Leasing Corp.	PO Box 1518	Bellevue	WA	98009		425-455-7400	S	24*	0.2
Thomas Truck Lease Inc.	PO Box 9040	Columbus	MS	39705	R Thomas	601-327-1372	R	24*	<0.1
Art's-Way Manufacturing Inc.	PO Box 288	Armstrong	IA	50514	David Pitt	712-864-3131	P	24	0.2
Hayes Leasing Co.	P O Box 569650	Dallas	TX	75356	Cynthia Vlazajewski	972-869-2400	R	23*	<0.1
Thrifty Car and Truck Rental	3902 Crittenden Dr	Louisville	KY	40209	Steve Sternberg	502-367-0231	R	20*	<0.1
Edart Truck Rental Corp.	185 W Service Rd	Hartford	CT	06120	EM Siegal	860-527-8274	R	17	0.1
De Carolis Truck Rental Inc.	333 Colfax St	Rochester	NY	14606	Paul De Carolis	716-254-1169	R	15*	0.2
Jersey Shore Peterbilt Inc.	PO Box 729	Clarksburg	NJ	08510	William Demidowitz	609-259-5950	R	14*	<0.1
U.S. and Gentges Inc.	P O Box 125	Jefferson City	MO	65102	James V Rau	573-635-6171	R	11*	<0.1
Idealease Services Inc.	28 W 144 Indust'l	Barrington	IL	60010	WW Kennedy	847-304-6000	R	7*	<0.1

Source: Ward's Business Directory of U.S. Private and Public Companies, Volumes 1 and 2, 2000. The company type code used is as follows: P - Public, R - Private, S - Subsidiary, D - Division, J - Joint Venture, A - Affiliate, G - Group, N - Company type not reported. Sales are in millions of dollars, employees are in thousands. An asterisk (*) indicates an estimated sales volume. The symbol < stands for 'less than'. Company names and addresses are truncated, in some cases, to fit into the available space.

LOCATION BY STATE AND REGIONAL CONCENTRATION

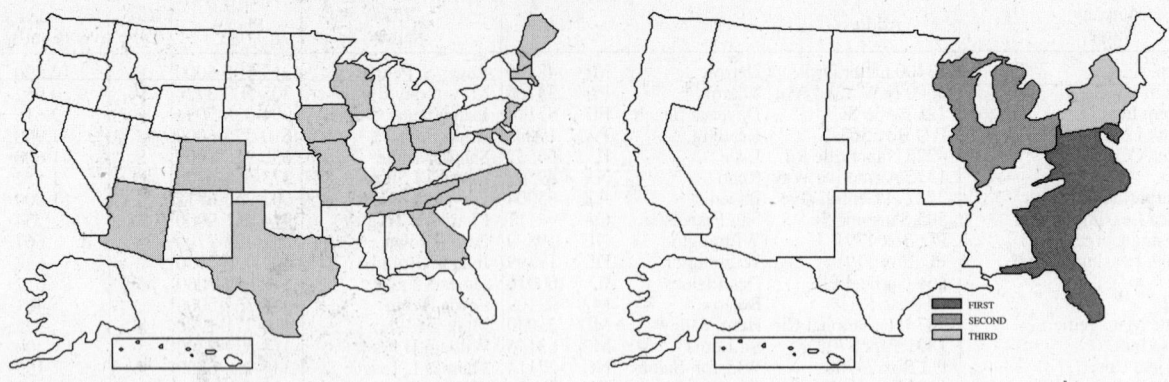

INDUSTRY DATA BY STATE

State	Establishments		Employment			Payroll		Revenues		
	Total (number)	% of U.S.	Total (number)	% of U.S.	Per Estab.	Total ($ mil.)	Per Empl. ($)	Total ($ mil.)	% of U.S.	Per Estab. ($)
California	499	9.4	4,764	10.1	10	151.2	31,731	964.9	9.3	1,933,599
Texas	398	7.5	3,355	7.1	8	94.7	28,218	762.0	7.4	1,914,683
Colorado	89	1.7	1,334	2.8	15	45.1	33,825	677.0	6.5	7,607,225
Ohio	254	4.8	2,546	5.4	10	78.6	30,860	558.2	5.4	2,197,602
Florida	300	5.7	2,391	5.1	8	74.8	31,300	510.4	4.9	1,701,293
New York	284	5.4	2,665	5.7	9	81.3	30,523	477.4	4.6	1,680,852
Pennsylvania	230	4.3	2,556	5.4	11	70.9	27,729	448.9	4.3	1,951,557
Illinois	238	4.5	1,832	3.9	8	64.0	34,927	421.1	4.1	1,769,235
North Carolina	185	3.5	1,755	3.7	9	54.2	30,906	414.8	4.0	2,242,011
New Jersey	168	3.2	1,767	3.8	11	63.3	35,844	408.4	4.0	2,430,786
Georgia	187	3.5	1,694	3.6	9	53.3	31,489	381.8	3.7	2,041,487
Michigan	174	3.3	1,542	3.3	9	48.8	31,663	362.9	3.5	2,085,563
Tennessee	154	2.9	1,359	2.9	9	41.3	30,355	336.5	3.3	2,185,318
Arizona	109	2.1	905	1.9	8	22.9	25,355	292.5	2.8	2,683,220
Indiana	159	3.0	1,350	2.9	8	38.4	28,410	285.5	2.8	1,795,748
Massachusetts	108	2.0	1,360	2.9	13	43.9	32,298	281.7	2.7	2,608,296
Wisconsin	126	2.4	1,039	2.2	8	32.5	31,251	224.7	2.2	1,783,389
Missouri	114	2.2	1,157	2.5	10	32.7	28,227	220.8	2.1	1,936,561
Maryland	85	1.6	991	2.1	12	34.9	35,179	218.0	2.1	2,565,259
Virginia	130	2.5	931	2.0	7	24.7	26,481	194.5	1.9	1,496,146
Washington	90	1.7	800	1.7	9	24.6	30,791	172.2	1.7	1,913,700
Iowa	83	1.6	960	2.0	12	24.7	25,678	148.8	1.4	1,792,675
Alabama	87	1.6	666	1.4	8	17.0	25,517	135.3	1.3	1,554,920
Minnesota	85	1.6	517	1.1	6	16.5	31,830	135.2	1.3	1,590,906
South Carolina	86	1.6	589	1.3	7	17.1	29,044	129.5	1.3	1,505,709
Connecticut	56	1.1	622	1.3	11	19.9	32,043	111.6	1.1	1,992,000
Kentucky	53	1.0	449	1.0	8	13.8	30,780	108.2	1.0	2,040,736
Louisiana	71	1.3	525	1.1	7	12.4	23,659	96.6	0.9	1,360,423
Oklahoma	68	1.3	461	1.0	7	12.1	26,341	93.7	0.9	1,378,603
Arkansas	59	1.1	441	0.9	7	11.3	25,544	93.3	0.9	1,580,797
Mississippi	60	1.1	360	0.8	6	10.4	28,831	81.4	0.8	1,357,383
Oregon	72	1.4	368	0.8	5	9.0	24,554	70.7	0.7	982,111
Kansas	53	1.0	356	0.8	7	9.4	26,472	69.1	0.7	1,303,981
Maine	31	0.6	426	0.9	14	11.6	27,148	63.5	0.6	2,049,065
New Hampshire	31	0.6	399	0.8	13	17.0	42,639	57.7	0.6	1,861,968
Nebraska	38	0.7	233	0.5	6	7.6	32,747	48.7	0.5	1,280,842
New Mexico	26	0.5	213	0.5	8	6.4	30,103	44.9	0.4	1,725,846
Utah	38	0.7	207	0.4	5	4.8	23,179	36.4	0.4	956,632
Nevada	40	0.8	174	0.4	4	3.8	21,649	28.7	0.3	717,050
Alaska	19	0.4	100	0.2	5	3.3	33,200	18.4	0.2	966,842
Idaho	20	0.4	125	0.3	6	2.6	20,672	17.9	0.2	892,850
North Dakota	17	0.3	101	0.2	6	1.9	18,980	14.9	0.1	876,647
West Virginia	25	0.5	108	0.2	4	2.1	19,519	14.8	0.1	590,560
Montana	16	0.3	81	0.2	5	1.3	15,494	12.0	0.1	750,000
Vermont	10	0.2	48	0.1	5	1.2	24,146	9.9	0.1	986,200
South Dakota	14	0.3	59	0.1	4	1.2	20,508	7.2	0.1	515,286
Hawaii	10	0.2	43	0.1	4	1.1	25,163	6.7	0.1	672,700
Wyoming	9	0.2	15	0.0	2	0.3	22,467	2.3	0.0	260,222
Delaware	18	0.3	175*	-	-	(D)	-	(D)	-	-
Rhode Island	16	0.3	175*	-	-	(D)	-	(D)	-	-

Source: 1997 *Economic Census*. The states are in descending order of revenues or establishments (if revenue data are missing for the majority). The symbol (D) appears when data are withheld to prevent disclosure of competitive information. States marked with (D) are sorted by number of establishments. A dash (-) indicates that the data element cannot be calculated. * indicates the midpoint of a range; 175, for example is the range 100-249. Shaded *states* on the state map indicate those states which have proportionately greater representation in the industry than would be indicated by the state's population; the ratio is based on total revenues or number of establishments. Shaded *regions* indicate where the industry is regionally most concentrated.

NAICS 532210 - CONSUMER ELECTRONICS AND APPLIANCES RENTAL

GENERAL STATISTICS

Year	Establishments (number)	Employment (number)	Payroll ($ million)	Revenues ($ million)	Employees per Establishment (number)	Revenues per Establishment ($)	Payroll per Employee ($)
1997	3,011	17,491	395.0	1,791.0	5.8	594,819	22,583

Source: Economic Census of the United States, 1997. This is a newly defined industry. Data for prior years were unavailable at the time of publication but may become available over time.

INDICES OF CHANGE

Year	Establishments (number)	Employment (number)	Payroll ($ million)	Revenues ($ million)	Employees per Establishment (number)	Revenues per Establishment ($)	Payroll per Employee ($)
1997	100.0	100.0	100.0	100.0	100.0	100.0	100.0

Sources: Same as General Statistics. The values shown reflect change from the base year, 1997. Values above 100 mean greater than 1997, values below 100 mean less than 1997, and a value of 100 in the 1982-96 or 1998-2001 period means same as 1997. Values followed by a 'p' are projections by the editors; 'e' stands for extrapolation. Data are the most recent available at this level of detail.

SIC INDUSTRIES RELATED TO NAICS 532210

Each new NAICS code represents an industry that used to be part of an SIC or a part of several SIC industries. Data in this table are shown to provide transitional information for these cases. All available data for the precursor SIC(s) are shown. Even if only a part of an SIC is included in the NAICS, *all* data for the SIC are reproduced. If the SIC industry is not marked as being a part (pt) of the NAICS, the entire industry is embedded in the NAICS data. The SIC composition of the new industry provides some hints of the relative importance of its "ancestors." Data marked with a 'p' are projected. Projections begin with 1982 data. Data earlier than 1990 are not shown but are reflected in the projections.

SIC	Industry	1990	1991	1992	1993	1994	1995	1996	1997
7359	**Equipment Rental & Leasing, nec (pt)**								
	Establishments (number)	16,213	16,430	17,687	17,439	17,564	17,607	17,431p	17,486p
	Employment (thousands)	145.6	143.2	134.1	139.9	143.8	151.3	148.8p	150.4p
	Revenues ($ million)	15,481.0	15,265.0	15,482.0	16,816.0	18,607.0	20,677.0	20,949.0	21,947.1p

Source: Economic Census of the United States, 1992, annual surveys of economic sectors conducted by the Bureau of the Census, and estimates or projections based on the 1982-1992 period; not all data are shown. 'e' marks estimates made by the editors; 'p' indicates projections based on time series. A dash (-) indicates that data for this SIC or year were not available. The abbreviation (pt) next to the industry name indicates that only a part of the industry is present within the NAICS data. If no (pt) is shown, the entire industry is contained within the NAICS data.

SELECTED RATIOS

For 1997	Avg. of Information	Analyzed Industry	Index	For 1997	Avg. of Information	Analyzed Industry	Index
Employees per establishment	6	6	98	Payroll per establishment	144,276	131,186	91
Revenue per establishment	835,727	594,819	71	Payroll as % of revenue	17	22	128
Revenue per employee	141,515	102,396	72	Payroll per employee	24,430	22,583	92

Sources: Same as General Statistics. The 'Average' column represents the average for the industry sector, in 1997, where the currently shown industry is classified. The Index shows the relationship between the Average and the Analyzed Industry. For example, 100 means that they are equal; 500 that the Analyzed Industry is five times the average; 50 means that the Analyzed Industry is half the national average. The abbreviation 'na' is used to show that data are 'not available'.

LEADING COMPANIES

No company data available for this industry.

LOCATION BY STATE AND REGIONAL CONCENTRATION

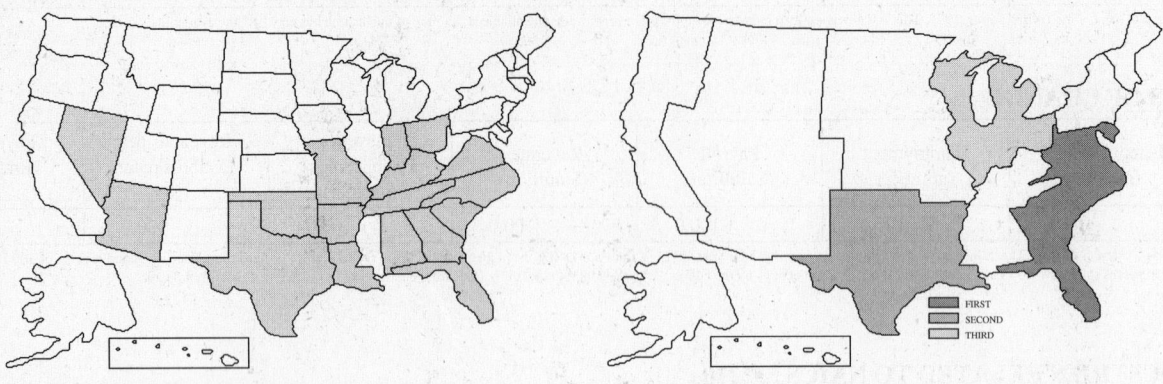

FIRST
SECOND
THIRD

INDUSTRY DATA BY STATE

State	Establishments Total (number)	% of U.S.	Employment Total (number)	% of U.S.	Per Estab.	Payroll Total ($ mil.)	Per Empl. ($)	Revenues Total ($ mil.)	% of U.S.	Per Estab. ($)
Texas	340	11.3	2,252	12.9	7	52.5	23,327	214.9	12.0	632,059
California	222	7.4	1,327	7.6	6	34.1	25,664	139.7	7.8	629,405
North Carolina	82	2.7	558	3.2	7	15.8	28,344	137.0	7.7	1,670,854
Florida	192	6.4	1,211	6.9	6	26.1	21,526	121.0	6.8	629,953
Ohio	175	5.8	954	5.5	5	21.8	22,898	98.9	5.5	565,029
Georgia	124	4.1	664	3.8	5	17.0	25,658	87.4	4.9	704,532
Indiana	144	4.8	790	4.5	5	16.3	20,603	70.7	3.9	490,896
Louisiana	98	3.3	553	3.2	6	12.8	23,174	64.2	3.6	654,816
Virginia	98	3.3	673	3.8	7	15.0	22,327	63.1	3.5	644,265
New York	82	2.7	469	2.7	6	12.0	25,650	53.6	3.0	653,268
New Jersey	45	1.5	459	2.6	10	12.4	27,111	52.1	2.9	1,156,711
Illinois	125	4.2	700	4.0	6	12.2	17,497	50.3	2.8	402,192
Missouri	82	2.7	484	2.8	6	10.7	22,145	44.7	2.5	545,220
Michigan	82	2.7	371	2.1	5	8.7	23,520	41.7	2.3	508,854
Pennsylvania	92	3.1	533	3.0	6	11.1	20,916	41.3	2.3	448,848
Tennessee	96	3.2	416	2.4	4	9.6	22,983	39.9	2.2	416,083
Arkansas	72	2.4	369	2.1	5	8.1	22,000	37.5	2.1	521,417
Kentucky	75	2.5	395	2.3	5	7.2	18,165	36.6	2.0	487,667
Alabama	65	2.2	397	2.3	6	7.4	18,695	33.1	1.8	509,615
Arizona	54	1.8	264	1.5	5	6.5	24,644	29.3	1.6	542,074
South Carolina	64	2.1	325	1.9	5	6.2	19,034	26.7	1.5	417,078
Massachusetts	36	1.2	210	1.2	6	5.7	27,200	25.9	1.4	720,389
Oklahoma	68	2.3	315	1.8	5	5.8	18,406	24.8	1.4	364,324
Maryland	30	1.0	307	1.8	10	5.6	18,309	19.0	1.1	631,867
Wisconsin	28	0.9	117	0.7	4	3.1	26,444	15.8	0.9	562,786
Colorado	35	1.2	176	1.0	5	3.9	22,062	15.2	0.9	435,629
Mississippi	46	1.5	230	1.3	5	3.7	16,104	14.8	0.8	322,609
Connecticut	16	0.5	104	0.6	7	3.4	32,904	13.7	0.8	853,750
Washington	25	0.8	123	0.7	5	3.1	25,285	13.7	0.8	549,400
West Virginia	29	1.0	143	0.8	5	2.7	18,706	12.8	0.7	440,483
Nevada	15	0.5	77	0.4	5	1.9	24,221	10.8	0.6	720,867
Minnesota	22	0.7	113	0.6	5	2.5	22,177	9.4	0.5	426,409
New Mexico	19	0.6	126	0.7	7	2.3	18,349	9.2	0.5	483,947
Nebraska	21	0.7	171	1.0	8	3.2	18,591	9.0	0.5	430,571
Oregon	18	0.6	101	0.6	6	2.1	20,436	7.9	0.4	436,222
Idaho	9	0.3	85	0.5	9	1.7	20,176	7.8	0.4	866,000
Iowa	22	0.7	123	0.7	6	1.7	14,195	7.4	0.4	334,955
New Hampshire	13	0.4	43	0.2	3	1.6	36,674	5.9	0.3	456,462
Vermont	12	0.4	59	0.3	5	1.0	16,780	4.2	0.2	346,333
South Dakota	11	0.4	44	0.3	4	0.9	20,250	3.1	0.2	277,909
Kansas	53	1.8	375*	-	-	(D)	-	(D)	-	-
Maine	30	1.0	175*	-	-	(D)	-	(D)	-	-
Rhode Island	10	0.3	60*	-	-	(D)	-	(D)	-	-
Delaware	9	0.3	60*	-	-	(D)	-	(D)	-	-

Source: 1997 *Economic Census*. The states are in descending order of revenues or establishments (if revenue data are missing for the majority). The symbol (D) appears when data are withheld to prevent disclosure of competitive information. States marked with (D) are sorted by number of establishments. A dash (-) indicates that the data element cannot be calculated. * indicates the midpoint of a range; 175, for example is the range 100-249. Shaded *states* on the state map indicate those states which have proportionately greater representation in the industry than would be indicated by the state's population; the ratio is based on total revenues or number of establishments. Shaded *regions* indicate where the industry is regionally most concentrated.

NAICS 532220 - FORMAL WEAR AND COSTUME RENTAL

GENERAL STATISTICS

Year	Establishments (number)	Employment (number)	Payroll ($ million)	Revenues ($ million)	Employees per Establishment (number)	Revenues per Establishment ($)	Payroll per Employee ($)
1997	2,683	14,036	204.0	781.0	5.2	291,092	14,534

Source: *Economic Census of the United States*, 1997. This is a newly defined industry. Data for prior years were unavailable at the time of publication but may become available over time.

INDICES OF CHANGE

Year	Establishments (number)	Employment (number)	Payroll ($ million)	Revenues ($ million)	Employees per Establishment (number)	Revenues per Establishment ($)	Payroll per Employee ($)
1997	100.0	100.0	100.0	100.0	100.0	100.0	100.0

Sources: Same as General Statistics. The values shown reflect change from the base year, 1997. Values above 100 mean greater than 1997, values below 100 mean less than 1997, and a value of 100 in the 1982-96 or 1998-2001 period means same as 1997. Values followed by a 'p' are projections by the editors; 'e' stands for extrapolation. Data are the most recent available at this level of detail.

SIC INDUSTRIES RELATED TO NAICS 532220

Each new NAICS code represents an industry that used to be part of an SIC or a part of several SIC industries. Data in this table are shown to provide transitional information for these cases. All available data for the precursor SIC(s) are shown. Even if only a part of an SIC is included in the NAICS, *all* data for the SIC are reproduced. If the SIC industry is not marked as being a part (pt) of the NAICS, the entire industry is embedded in the NAICS data. The SIC composition of the new industry provides some hints of the relative importance of its "ancestors." Data marked with a 'p' are projected. Projections begin with 1982 data. Data earlier than 1990 are not shown but are reflected in the projections.

SIC	Industry	1990	1991	1992	1993	1994	1995	1996	1997
7299	**Miscellaneous Personal Services, nec (pt)**								
	Establishments (number)	15,086	15,775	16,017	16,862	17,296	17,740	18,650p	19,294p
	Employment (thousands)	116.4	114.7	105.6	99.6	97.2	99.4	106.1p	106.9p
	Revenues ($ million)	-	-	3,885.0	-	-	-	-	-
7819	**Services Allied to Motion Pictures (pt)**								
	Establishments (number)	2,984	2,955	3,895	3,799	3,691	3,289	3,584p	3,622p
	Employment (thousands)	113.1	102.4	162.2	158.8	130.9	136.7	160.9p	169.5p
	Revenues ($ million)	-	-	7,514.7	-	-	-	-	-

Source: *Economic Census of the United States*, 1992, annual surveys of economic sectors conducted by the Bureau of the Census, and estimates or projections based on the 1982-1992 period; not all data are shown. 'e' marks estimates made by the editors; 'p' indicates projections based on time series. A dash (-) indicates that data for this SIC or year were not available. The abbreviation (pt) next to the industry name indicates that only a part of the industry is present within the NAICS data. If no (pt) is shown, the entire industry is contained within the NAICS data.

SELECTED RATIOS

For 1997	Avg. of Information	Analyzed Industry	Index	For 1997	Avg. of Information	Analyzed Industry	Index
Employees per establishment	6	5	89	Payroll per establishment	144,276	76,034	53
Revenue per establishment	835,727	291,092	35	Payroll as % of revenue	17	26	151
Revenue per employee	141,515	55,643	39	Payroll per employee	24,430	14,534	59

Sources: Same as General Statistics. The 'Average' column represents the average for the industry sector, in 1997, where the currently shown industry is classified. The Index shows the relationship between the Average and the Analyzed Industry. For example, 100 means that they are equal; 500 that the Analyzed Industry is five times the average; 50 means that the Analyzed Industry is half the national average. The abbreviation 'na' is used to show that data are 'not available'.

LEADING COMPANIES
No company data available for this industry.

LOCATION BY STATE AND REGIONAL CONCENTRATION

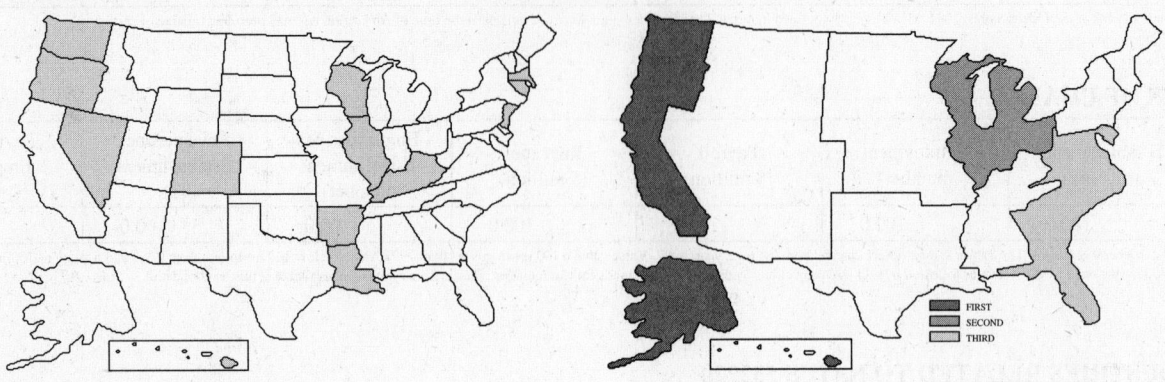

FIRST
SECOND
THIRD

INDUSTRY DATA BY STATE

State	Establishments Total (number)	% of U.S.	Employment Total (number)	% of U.S.	Per Estab.	Payroll Total ($ mil.)	Per Empl. ($)	Revenues Total ($ mil.)	% of U.S.	Per Estab. ($)
California	377	14.1	1,686	12.0	4	24.1	14,279	91.9	11.8	243,753
Hawaii	19	0.7	332	2.4	17	7.8	23,422	56.6	7.2	2,978,842
Texas	186	6.9	879	6.3	5	12.5	14,170	54.1	6.9	290,747
Illinois	125	4.7	799	5.7	6	13.3	16,645	47.2	6.0	377,320
New York	172	6.4	677	4.8	4	13.2	19,533	45.3	5.8	263,256
Florida	136	5.1	717	5.1	5	10.0	13,982	39.0	5.0	286,625
Pennsylvania	119	4.4	627	4.5	5	7.6	12,062	32.2	4.1	270,697
Michigan	120	4.5	505	3.6	4	7.5	14,766	28.4	3.6	236,675
Ohio	144	5.4	664	4.7	5	7.6	11,404	27.3	3.5	189,826
New Jersey	71	2.6	490	3.5	7	7.7	15,745	25.7	3.3	361,789
Massachusetts	63	2.3	349	2.5	6	6.2	17,802	21.8	2.8	345,603
Georgia	53	2.0	335	2.4	6	5.7	16,872	20.1	2.6	380,189
Washington	96	3.6	378	2.7	4	4.9	13,048	19.3	2.5	200,542
Virginia	68	2.5	314	2.2	5	3.9	12,411	18.9	2.4	277,265
Wisconsin	47	1.8	495	3.5	11	7.7	15,608	18.0	2.3	383,489
Indiana	53	2.0	319	2.3	6	4.4	13,765	15.6	2.0	294,962
Louisiana	63	2.3	273	1.9	4	4.0	14,476	14.5	1.9	230,460
Colorado	40	1.5	245	1.7	6	3.5	14,310	13.8	1.8	345,350
Minnesota	42	1.6	256	1.8	6	3.5	13,480	13.6	1.7	323,762
Kentucky	37	1.4	337	2.4	9	5.7	16,881	12.7	1.6	343,459
Tennessee	59	2.2	240	1.7	4	3.0	12,483	12.6	1.6	214,186
Maryland	39	1.5	209	1.5	5	2.7	12,885	12.3	1.6	316,256
Missouri	51	1.9	229	1.6	4	3.6	15,524	12.3	1.6	241,392
Connecticut	43	1.6	207	1.5	5	3.4	16,348	12.2	1.6	283,814
Alabama	51	1.9	227	1.6	4	3.4	15,066	11.6	1.5	226,608
North Carolina	44	1.6	259	1.8	6	3.1	12,023	11.3	1.4	256,273
Oregon	46	1.7	273	1.9	6	2.6	9,476	9.9	1.3	215,891
Arkansas	12	0.4	101	0.7	8	1.9	18,406	9.8	1.2	813,417
Arizona	37	1.4	159	1.1	4	1.7	10,428	8.1	1.0	219,135
Iowa	17	0.6	156	1.1	9	2.1	13,282	7.0	0.9	414,412
South Carolina	23	0.9	141	1.0	6	1.7	11,865	6.5	0.8	282,609
Nevada	21	0.8	144	1.0	7	1.8	12,458	5.9	0.8	280,190
Oklahoma	25	0.9	121	0.9	5	1.3	10,835	5.3	0.7	210,040
Utah	25	0.9	120	0.9	5	1.2	10,300	4.3	0.6	172,680
Mississippi	24	0.9	102	0.7	4	1.1	11,265	3.9	0.5	162,667
Nebraska	16	0.6	84	0.6	5	1.0	11,762	3.5	0.4	217,500
West Virginia	16	0.6	50	0.4	3	0.7	14,920	2.3	0.3	141,250
Maine	8	0.3	26	0.2	3	0.6	21,923	2.0	0.3	245,125
New Hampshire	7	0.3	20	0.1	3	0.4	20,250	1.7	0.2	238,000
New Mexico	10	0.4	40	0.3	4	0.4	11,225	1.4	0.2	141,200
Idaho	9	0.3	35	0.2	4	0.3	8,457	1.2	0.1	128,000
Montana	6	0.2	24	0.2	4	0.2	7,042	0.8	0.1	133,833
Vermont	6	0.2	11	0.1	2	0.1	11,182	0.6	0.1	102,667
Rhode Island	18	0.7	60*	-	-	(D)	-	(D)	-	-
Kansas	12	0.4	175*	-	-	(D)	-	(D)	-	-
Delaware	9	0.3	175*	-	-	(D)	-	(D)	-	-

Source: 1997 *Economic Census*. The states are in descending order of revenues or establishments (if revenue data are missing for the majority). The symbol (D) appears when data are withheld to prevent disclosure of competitive information. States marked with (D) are sorted by number of establishments. A dash (-) indicates that the data element cannot be calculated. * indicates the midpoint of a range; 175, for example is the range 100-249. Shaded *states* on the state map indicate those states which have proportionately greater representation in the industry than would be indicated by the state's population; the ratio is based on total revenues or number of establishments. Shaded *regions* indicate where the industry is regionally most concentrated.

NAICS 532230 - VIDEO TAPE AND DISK RENTAL*

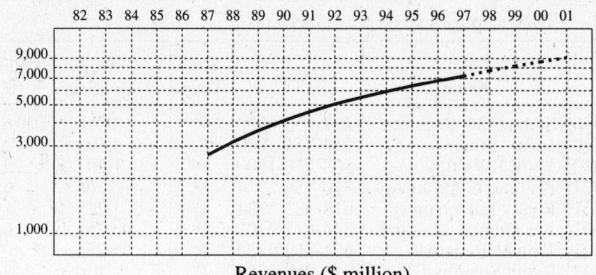

Revenues ($ million)

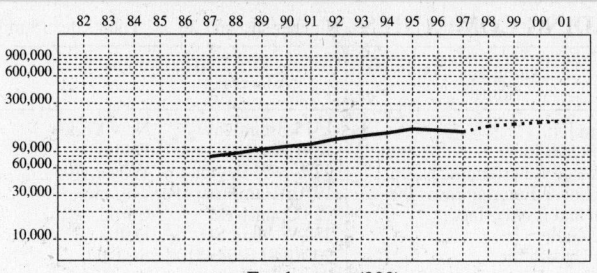

Employment (000)

GENERAL STATISTICS

Year	Establishments (number)	Employment (number)	Payroll ($ million)	Revenues ($ million)	Employees per Establishment (number)	Revenues per Establishment ($)	Payroll per Employee ($)
1982	-	-	-	-	-	-	-
1983	-	-	-	-	-	-	-
1984	-	-	-	-	-	-	-
1985	-	-	-	-	-	-	-
1986	-	-	-	-	-	-	-
1987	16,824	79,559	581.0	2,687.0	4.7	159,712	7,303
1988	15,515	86,550	645.0	3,165.0 e	5.6	203,996	7,452
1989	17,159	95,751	730.0	3,642.0 e	5.6	212,250	7,624
1990	16,442	102,673	767.0	4,120.0 e	6.2	250,578	7,470
1991	17,459	108,929	816.0	4,598.0 e	6.2	263,360	7,491
1992	21,998	123,671	944.0	5,075.0	5.6	230,703	7,633
1993	21,971	134,274	1,040.0	5,506.0 e	6.1	250,603	7,745
1994	21,562	144,644	1,103.0	5,937.0 e	6.7	275,346	7,626
1995	21,167	159,800	1,150.0	6,368.0 e	7.5	300,846	7,196
1996	22,101 e	154,827 e	1,220.0 e	6,799.0 e	7.0 e	307,633 e	7,880 e
1997	23,036	149,854	1,289.0	7,230.0	6.5	313,857	8,602
1998	24,158 p	172,377 p	1,371.0 p	7,737.0 p	7.1 p	320,267 p	7,953 p
1999	24,924 p	180,795 p	1,444.0 p	8,191.0 p	7.3 p	328,639 p	7,987 p
2000	25,689 p	189,213 p	1,517.0 p	8,646.0 p	7.4 p	336,564 p	8,017 p
2001	26,454 p	197,632 p	1,589.0 p	9,100.0 p	7.5 p	343,993 p	8,040 p

Sources: Economic Census of the United States, 1982, 1987, 1992, 1997. Establishment counts, employment, and payroll are from County Business Patterns for non-Census years. In non-Census years, industries in the Manufacturing range under SIC coding include data from the Annual Survey of Manufactures (ASM); those in the old Services range include data from the Services Annual Survey (SAS). Values followed by a 'p' are projections by the editors. Extrapolations are marked by 'e'. Data are the most recent available at this level of detail.

INDICES OF CHANGE

Year	Establishments (number)	Employment (number)	Payroll ($ million)	Revenues ($ million)	Employees per Establishment (number)	Revenues per Establishment ($)	Payroll per Employee ($)
1982	-	-	-	-	-	-	-
1987	73.0	53.1	45.1	37.2	72.7	50.9	84.9
1992	95.5	82.5	73.2	70.2	86.4	73.5	88.7
1993	95.4	89.6	80.7	76.2 e	93.9	79.8	90.0
1994	93.6	96.5	85.6	82.1 e	103.1	87.7	88.7
1995	91.9	106.6	89.2	88.1 e	116.1	95.9	83.7
1996	95.9 e	103.3 e	94.6 e	94.0 e	107.7 e	98.0 e	91.6 e
1997	100.0	100.0	100.0	100.0	100.0	100.0	100.0
1998	104.9 p	115.0 p	106.4 p	107.0 p	109.7 p	102.0 p	92.5 p
1999	108.2 p	120.6 p	112.0 p	113.3 p	111.5 p	104.7 p	92.9 p
2000	111.5 p	126.3 p	117.7 p	119.6 p	113.2 p	107.2 p	93.2 p
2001	114.8 p	131.9 p	123.3 p	125.9 p	114.8 p	109.6 p	93.5 p

Sources: Same as General Statistics. The values shown reflect change from the base year, 1997. Values above 100 mean greater than 1997, values below 100 mean less than 1997, and a value of 100 in the 1982-96 or 1998-2001 period means same as 1997. Values followed by a 'p' are projections by the editors; 'e' stands for extrapolation. Data are the most recent available at this level of detail.

SELECTED RATIOS

For 1997	Avg. of Information	Analyzed Industry	Index	For 1997	Avg. of Information	Analyzed Industry	Index
Employees per establishment	6	7	110	Payroll per establishment	144,276	55,956	39
Revenue per establishment	835,727	313,857	38	Payroll as % of revenue	17	18	103
Revenue per employee	141,515	48,247	34	Payroll per employee	24,430	8,602	35

Sources: Same as General Statistics. The 'Average' column represents the average for the industry sector, in 1997, where the currently shown industry is classified. The Index shows the relationship between the Average and the Analyzed Industry. For example, 100 means that they are equal; 500 that the Analyzed Industry is five times the average; 50 means that the Analyzed Industry is half the national average. The abbreviation 'na' is used to show that data are 'not available'.

*Equivalent to SIC 7841.

233

LEADING COMPANIES   Number shown: **20**   Total sales ($ mil): **18,508**   Total employment (000): **238.9**

Company Name	Address				CEO Name	Phone	Co. Type	Sales ($ mil)	Empl. (000)
Viacom Inc.	1515 Broadway	New York	NY	10036	Sumner M. Redstone	212-258-6000	P	12,096	116.7
Blockbuster Inc.	1201 Elm St	Dallas	TX	75270	John Antioco	214-854-3000	S	3,893	82.4
Hollywood Entertainment Corp.	9275 S W Peyton Ln	Wilsonville	OR	97070	Mark J Wattles	503-570-1600	P	1,097	22.2
Wherehouse Entertainment Inc.	19701 Hamilton Ave	Torrance	CA	90502	Antonio C Alvarez II	310-538-2314	R	366*	6.0
Martin and Bayley Inc.	928 County Rd	Carmi	IL	62821	Randy Fulkerson	618-382-2334	R	270*	1.5
Movie Gallery Inc.	739 W Main St	Dothan	AL	36301	Joe Thomas Malugen	334-677-2108	P	268	6.1
Video Update Inc.	30 7th St E Ste 3100	St. Paul	MN	55101	John M Bedard	651-312-2222	P	254	<0.1
West Coast Entertainment Corp.	Rte 413	Langhorne	PA	19047	Ralph Standby III	215-968-4318	P	120	2.3
Movies Unlimited Inc.	3015 Darnell Rd	Philadelphia	PA	19154	Jerry Frebowitz	215-637-4444	R	41*	0.1
Blowout Entertainment Inc.	7700 NE Ambass	Portland	OR	97220	Steve Berns	503-331-2729	P	32	0.7
West Coast Entertainment	1767 Morris Ave	Union	NJ	07083	Kyle Stanley	908-686-3030	S	26*	0.2
Video City Inc.	370 Amatola Ave	Torrance	CA	90501	Richard Gibson	310-533-3900	R	17*	0.4
Movie Exchange Inc.	PO Box 394	Oaks	PA	19456	Shellie Tibbitts	610-631-9180	R	10*	<0.1
Oregon Entertainment Corp.	P O Box 6354	Portland	OR	97228		503-239-6505	R	8*	<0.1
Family Video Superstores Inc.	7612 N Hills Blvd	N. Little Rock	AR	72116	Vincent Insalaco	501-834-0034	R	5*	<0.1
Video World	10 Sherman Hill Rd	Woodbury	CT	06798	Ed Kaczynski	203-266-0120	R	3*	<0.1
Hartford Rexall Drug & Video Inc	52 S Main St	Hartford	WI	53027	Jack Reinholz	414-673-2590	R	1*	<0.1
Intern. Film & Video Center Inc.	989 1st Ave	New York	NY	10022	B Maghsoudlou	212-826-8848	R	1*	<0.1
Evergreen Video	37 Carmine St	New York	NY	10014	Steve Feltes	212-691-7362	R	0	<0.1
Hood's	P O Box 636	New London	MN	56273	Holman Hood	320-354-2228	R	0*	<0.1

Source: Ward's Business Directory of U.S. Private and Public Companies, Volumes 1 and 2, 2000. The company type code used is as follows: P - Public, R - Private, S - Subsidiary, D - Division, J - Joint Venture, A - Affiliate, G - Group, N - Company type not reported. Sales are in millions of dollars, employees are in thousands. An asterisk (*) indicates an estimated sales volume. The symbol < stands for 'less than'. Company names and addresses are truncated, in some cases, to fit into the available space.

LOCATION BY STATE AND REGIONAL CONCENTRATION

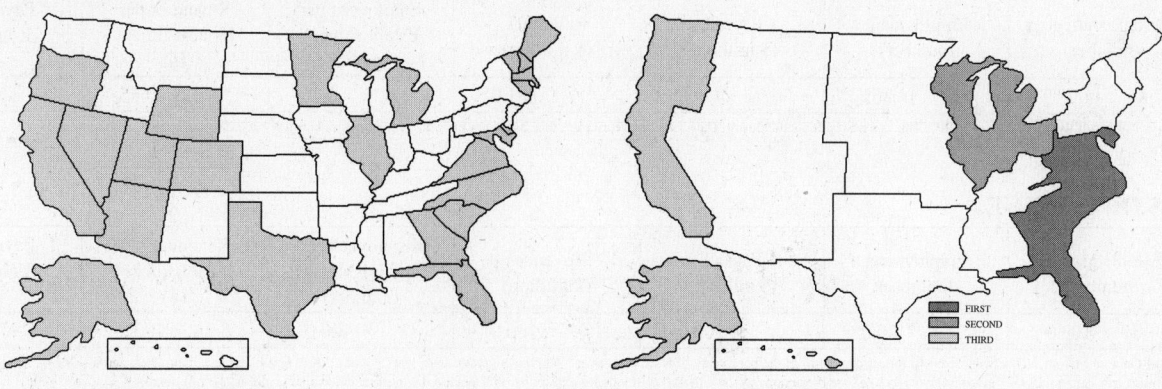

INDUSTRY DATA BY STATE

State	Establishments Total (number)	% of U.S.	Employment Total (number)	% of U.S.	Per Estab.	Payroll Total ($ mil.)	Per Empl. ($)	Revenues Total ($ mil.)	% of U.S.	Per Estab. ($)
California	2,405	10.4	15,174	10.1	6	152.3	10,037	916.7	12.7	381,169
Texas	1,834	8.0	12,494	8.3	7	111.6	8,935	655.5	9.1	357,396
Florida	1,116	4.8	6,788	4.5	6	64.4	9,482	393.5	5.4	352,582
New York	1,128	4.9	6,839	4.6	6	69.3	10,136	370.4	5.1	328,356
Illinois	1,107	4.8	7,631	5.1	7	65.2	8,542	355.6	4.9	321,188
Michigan	896	3.9	6,428	4.3	7	53.8	8,365	305.3	4.2	340,770
Ohio	968	4.2	6,464	4.3	7	52.1	8,064	291.9	4.0	301,541
Pennsylvania	849	3.7	6,280	4.2	7	48.0	7,648	262.1	3.6	308,749
Georgia	684	3.0	4,298	2.9	6	40.6	9,452	230.7	3.2	337,212
North Carolina	789	3.4	4,938	3.3	6	39.5	8,003	208.3	2.9	264,024
Virginia	589	2.6	4,442	3.0	8	36.7	8,260	195.3	2.7	331,640
New Jersey	530	2.3	3,318	2.2	6	30.1	9,057	185.9	2.6	350,794
Massachusetts	526	2.3	3,966	2.6	8	34.5	8,695	184.4	2.6	350,567
Indiana	591	2.6	3,894	2.6	7	30.3	7,773	157.0	2.2	265,601
Maryland	410	1.8	3,099	2.1	8	26.7	8,623	152.5	2.1	371,966
Missouri	488	2.1	3,091	2.1	6	25.3	8,179	145.1	2.0	297,361
Washington	533	2.3	3,196	2.1	6	26.1	8,161	142.0	2.0	266,471
Tennessee	546	2.4	3,240	2.2	6	24.8	7,643	130.4	1.8	238,870
Minnesota	478	2.1	3,712	2.5	8	23.8	6,410	126.7	1.8	264,992
Arizona	302	1.3	2,366	1.6	8	20.9	8,817	122.8	1.7	406,550
Wisconsin	416	1.8	3,259	2.2	8	24.2	7,435	120.1	1.7	288,599
Colorado	369	1.6	2,204	1.5	6	20.8	9,419	111.7	1.5	302,810
South Carolina	393	1.7	2,222	1.5	6	20.7	9,297	111.5	1.5	283,621
Alabama	440	1.9	2,552	1.7	6	18.9	7,409	108.0	1.5	245,539
Oregon	353	1.5	2,194	1.5	6	18.4	8,365	107.8	1.5	305,388
Connecticut	287	1.2	2,081	1.4	7	19.1	9,189	102.6	1.4	357,488
Kentucky	421	1.8	2,566	1.7	6	19.8	7,733	95.2	1.3	226,017
Louisiana	368	1.6	1,972	1.3	5	16.7	8,472	92.6	1.3	251,514
Oklahoma	326	1.4	1,861	1.2	6	14.2	7,608	80.4	1.1	246,534
Iowa	258	1.1	1,614	1.1	6	13.7	8,501	66.6	0.9	258,302
Utah	160	0.7	1,352	0.9	8	10.5	7,779	64.2	0.9	401,469
Nevada	137	0.6	1,056	0.7	8	10.2	9,634	60.6	0.8	442,642
Kansas	204	0.9	1,233	0.8	6	10.4	8,470	60.5	0.8	296,804
Arkansas	260	1.1	1,360	0.9	5	10.5	7,685	58.9	0.8	226,504
Mississippi	297	1.3	1,469	1.0	5	11.1	7,586	57.8	0.8	194,603
New Hampshire	160	0.7	1,054	0.7	7	9.6	9,127	45.9	0.6	286,869
Nebraska	143	0.6	896	0.6	6	6.2	6,919	37.3	0.5	261,049
Maine	163	0.7	836	0.6	5	6.3	7,594	37.2	0.5	228,466
West Virginia	158	0.7	728	0.5	5	5.7	7,816	33.8	0.5	213,715
New Mexico	122	0.5	780	0.5	6	5.6	7,167	28.1	0.4	230,279
Idaho	117	0.5	585	0.4	5	4.7	8,118	25.9	0.4	221,009
Alaska	79	0.3	505	0.3	6	4.8	9,600	24.4	0.3	308,975
Hawaii	81	0.4	451	0.3	6	4.3	9,636	23.9	0.3	294,593
Montana	108	0.5	616	0.4	6	4.7	7,594	23.9	0.3	220,935
Rhode Island	69	0.3	438	0.3	6	4.4	9,970	21.6	0.3	313,275
Delaware	83	0.4	461	0.3	6	4.0	8,614	21.1	0.3	254,699
Vermont	105	0.5	500	0.3	5	4.0	8,024	20.0	0.3	190,276
D.C.	30	0.1	309	0.2	10	2.6	8,330	16.8	0.2	561,533
South Dakota	58	0.3	357	0.2	6	2.8	7,731	13.8	0.2	237,190
North Dakota	49	0.2	366	0.2	7	2.5	6,850	13.5	0.2	274,939
Wyoming	53	0.2	319	0.2	6	1.9	6,094	12.0	0.2	225,604

Source: 1997 *Economic Census*. The states are in descending order of revenues or establishments (if revenue data are missing for the majority). The symbol (D) appears when data are withheld to prevent disclosure of competitive information. States marked with (D) are sorted by number of establishments. A dash (-) indicates that the data element cannot be calculated. * indicates the midpoint of a range; 175, for example is the range 100-249. Shaded *states* on the state map indicate those states which have proportionately greater representation in the industry than would be indicated by the state's population; the ratio is based on total revenues or number of establishments. Shaded *regions* indicate where the industry is regionally most concentrated.

NAICS 532291 - HOME HEALTH EQUIPMENT RENTAL

GENERAL STATISTICS

Year	Establishments (number)	Employment (number)	Payroll ($ million)	Revenues ($ million)	Employees per Establishment (number)	Revenues per Establishment ($)	Payroll per Employee ($)
1997	1,731	14,365	449.0	1,881.0	8.3	1,086,655	31,257

Source: Economic Census of the United States, 1997. This is a newly defined industry. Data for prior years were unavailable at the time of publication but may become available over time.

INDICES OF CHANGE

Year	Establishments (number)	Employment (number)	Payroll ($ million)	Revenues ($ million)	Employees per Establishment (number)	Revenues per Establishment ($)	Payroll per Employee ($)
1997	100.0	100.0	100.0	100.0	100.0	100.0	100.0

Sources: Same as General Statistics. The values shown reflect change from the base year, 1997. Values above 100 mean greater than 1997, values below 100 mean less than 1997, and a value of 100 in the 1982-96 or 1998-2001 period means same as 1997. Values followed by a 'p' are projections by the editors; 'e' stands for extrapolation. Data are the most recent available at this level of detail.

SIC INDUSTRIES RELATED TO NAICS 532291

Each new NAICS code represents an industry that used to be part of an SIC or a part of several SIC industries. Data in this table are shown to provide transitional information for these cases. All available data for the precursor SIC(s) are shown. Even if only a part of an SIC is included in the NAICS, *all* data for the SIC are reproduced. If the SIC industry is not marked as being a part (pt) of the NAICS, the entire industry is embedded in the NAICS data. The SIC composition of the new industry provides some hints of the relative importance of its "ancestors." Data marked with a 'p' are projected. Projections begin with 1982 data. Data earlier than 1990 are not shown but are reflected in the projections.

SIC	Industry	1990	1991	1992	1993	1994	1995	1996	1997
7352	**Medical Equipment Rental & Leasing (pt)**								
	Establishments (number)	1,959	2,270	3,276	3,248	3,292	3,220	3,531p	3,708p
	Employment (thousands)	20.8	23.7	31.1	31.1	33.3	33.2	36.8p	39.0p
	Revenues ($ million)	2,511.0	2,783.0	3,210.0	3,344.0	2,997.0	3,088.0	3,679.0	3,867.5p

Source: Economic Census of the United States, 1992, annual surveys of economic sectors conducted by the Bureau of the Census, and estimates or projections based on the 1982-1992 period; not all data are shown. 'e' marks estimates made by the editors; 'p' indicates projections based on time series. A dash (-) indicates that data for this SIC or year were not available. The abbreviation (pt) next to the industry name indicates that only a part of the industry is present within the NAICS data. If no (pt) is shown, the entire industry is contained within the NAICS data.

SELECTED RATIOS

For 1997	Avg. of Information	Analyzed Industry	Index	For 1997	Avg. of Information	Analyzed Industry	Index
Employees per establishment	6	8	141	Payroll per establishment	144,276	259,388	180
Revenue per establishment	835,727	1,086,655	130	Payroll as % of revenue	17	24	138
Revenue per employee	141,515	130,943	93	Payroll per employee	24,430	31,257	128

Sources: Same as General Statistics. The 'Average' column represents the average for the industry sector, in 1997, where the currently shown industry is classified. The Index shows the relationship between the Average and the Analyzed Industry. For example, 100 means that they are equal; 500 that the Analyzed Industry is five times the average; 50 means that the Analyzed Industry is half the national average. The abbreviation 'na' is used to show that data are 'not available'.

LEADING COMPANIES   Number shown: **1**   Total sales ($ mil): **5**   Total employment (000): **0.0**

Company Name	Address				CEO Name	Phone	Co. Type	Sales ($ mil)	Empl. (000)
TMC Orthopedic Supplies Inc.	4747 Bellaire Blvd	Bellaire	TX	77401	Joe Sansone	713-669-1800	R	5	<0.1

Source: Ward's Business Directory of U.S. Private and Public Companies, Volumes 1 and 2, 2000. The company type code used is as follows: P - Public, R - Private, S - Subsidiary, D - Division, J - Joint Venture, A - Affiliate, G - Group, N - Company type not reported. Sales are in millions of dollars, employees are in thousands. An asterisk (*) indicates an estimated sales volume. The symbol < stands for 'less than'. Company names and addresses are truncated, in some cases, to fit into the available space.

LOCATION BY STATE AND REGIONAL CONCENTRATION

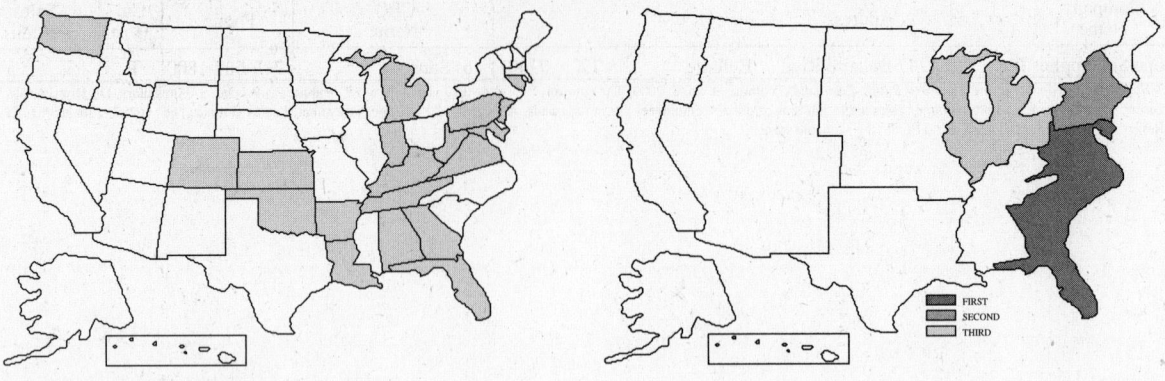

INDUSTRY DATA BY STATE

State	Establishments Total (number)	Establishments % of U.S.	Employment Total (number)	Employment % of U.S.	Employment Per Estab.	Payroll Total ($ mil.)	Payroll Per Empl. ($)	Revenues Total ($ mil.)	Revenues % of U.S.	Revenues Per Estab. ($)
California	118	6.8	1,058	7.4	9	34.9	32,945	161.0	8.6	1,364,415
Florida	185	10.7	1,262	8.8	7	35.2	27,929	145.8	7.8	788,184
Pennsylvania	102	5.9	1,101	7.7	11	37.6	34,148	132.8	7.1	1,301,539
Texas	128	7.4	882	6.1	7	36.4	41,240	120.2	6.4	938,805
New York	69	4.0	715	5.0	10	24.9	34,862	114.8	6.1	1,663,217
Ohio	48	2.8	545	3.8	11	14.9	27,257	75.8	4.0	1,579,396
Michigan	61	3.5	621	4.3	10	20.7	33,325	71.9	3.8	1,178,246
Georgia	72	4.2	533	3.7	7	15.7	29,473	66.6	3.5	924,889
Tennessee	69	4.0	537	3.7	8	15.7	29,250	63.1	3.4	914,507
Virginia	64	3.7	510	3.6	8	14.5	28,425	61.2	3.3	957,016
New Jersey	36	2.1	410	2.9	11	18.2	44,363	57.4	3.1	1,594,417
Illinois	55	3.2	509	3.5	9	14.1	27,640	57.4	3.1	1,043,455
Indiana	29	1.7	356	2.5	12	9.9	27,787	57.2	3.0	1,971,276
Maryland	28	1.6	454	3.2	16	15.2	33,414	56.4	3.0	2,013,214
Kentucky	65	3.8	442	3.1	7	11.4	25,903	50.2	2.7	771,985
Washington	25	1.4	322	2.2	13	7.1	22,034	48.3	2.6	1,930,400
North Carolina	51	2.9	259	1.8	5	8.8	33,954	45.6	2.4	893,569
Connecticut	24	1.4	261	1.8	11	8.9	33,992	36.8	2.0	1,532,042
Louisiana	29	1.7	284	2.0	10	7.2	25,482	34.8	1.9	1,199,793
Colorado	24	1.4	250	1.7	10	7.3	29,024	33.5	1.8	1,394,875
Alabama	62	3.6	367	2.6	6	8.9	24,338	31.7	1.7	512,016
Massachusetts	21	1.2	167	1.2	8	5.3	31,784	27.3	1.5	1,301,000
Oklahoma	30	1.7	168	1.2	6	5.2	30,804	26.9	1.4	897,233
South Carolina	30	1.7	165	1.1	6	5.7	34,533	25.1	1.3	835,267
Arkansas	26	1.5	128	0.9	5	5.2	40,898	25.0	1.3	961,423
Wisconsin	29	1.7	231	1.6	8	6.3	27,277	24.7	1.3	851,897
Minnesota	11	0.6	206	1.4	19	6.4	31,165	23.4	1.2	2,128,909
West Virginia	21	1.2	223	1.6	11	4.5	20,179	20.9	1.1	996,476
Kansas	14	0.8	127	0.9	9	3.6	28,134	20.5	1.1	1,460,857
Iowa	15	0.9	110	0.8	7	3.2	29,455	19.9	1.1	1,328,067
Missouri	33	1.9	189	1.3	6	8.1	42,683	19.6	1.0	593,879
Arizona	22	1.3	169	1.2	8	4.3	25,391	15.0	0.8	682,000
New Mexico	18	1.0	74	0.5	4	3.5	47,824	9.5	0.5	529,889
New Hampshire	7	0.4	45	0.3	6	1.5	33,089	7.6	0.4	1,080,000
Maine	7	0.4	73	0.5	10	2.1	28,548	6.8	0.4	965,857
Mississippi	13	0.8	59	0.4	5	1.6	26,983	6.7	0.4	518,692
Nebraska	11	0.6	57	0.4	5	1.1	19,088	6.5	0.3	595,091
Utah	9	0.5	40	0.3	4	1.2	30,575	6.5	0.3	724,333
Oregon	16	0.9	175*	-	-	(D)	-	(D)	-	-
Wyoming	15	0.9	60*	-	-	(D)	-	(D)	-	-
Nevada	14	0.8	60*	-	-	(D)	-	(D)	-	-
Delaware	6	0.3	10*	-	-	(D)	-	(D)	-	-

Source: 1997 *Economic Census*. The states are in descending order of revenues or establishments (if revenue data are missing for the majority). The symbol (D) appears when data are withheld to prevent disclosure of competitive information. States marked with (D) are sorted by number of establishments. A dash (-) indicates that the data element cannot be calculated. * indicates the midpoint of a range; 175, for example is the range 100-249. Shaded *states* on the state map indicate those states which have proportionately greater representation in the industry than would be indicated by the state's population; the ratio is based on total revenues or number of establishments. Shaded *regions* indicate where the industry is regionally most concentrated.

NAICS 532292 - RECREATIONAL GOODS RENTAL

GENERAL STATISTICS

Year	Establishments (number)	Employment (number)	Payroll ($ million)	Revenues ($ million)	Employees per Establishment (number)	Revenues per Establishment ($)	Payroll per Employee ($)
1997	1,812	7,948	124.0	560.0	4.4	309,051	15,601

Source: *Economic Census of the United States*, 1997. This is a newly defined industry. Data for prior years were unavailable at the time of publication but may become available over time.

INDICES OF CHANGE

Year	Establishments (number)	Employment (number)	Payroll ($ million)	Revenues ($ million)	Employees per Establishment (number)	Revenues per Establishment ($)	Payroll per Employee ($)
1997	100.0	100.0	100.0	100.0	100.0	100.0	100.0

Sources: Same as General Statistics. The values shown reflect change from the base year, 1997. Values above 100 mean greater than 1997, values below 100 mean less than 1997, and a value of 100 in the 1982-96 or 1998-2001 period means same as 1997. Values followed by a 'p' are projections by the editors; 'e' stands for extrapolation. Data are the most recent available at this level of detail.

SIC INDUSTRIES RELATED TO NAICS 532292

Each new NAICS code represents an industry that used to be part of an SIC or a part of several SIC industries. Data in this table are shown to provide transitional information for these cases. All available data for the precursor SIC(s) are shown. Even if only a part of an SIC is included in the NAICS, *all* data for the SIC are reproduced. If the SIC industry is not marked as being a part (pt) of the NAICS, the entire industry is embedded in the NAICS data. The SIC composition of the new industry provides some hints of the relative importance of its "ancestors." Data marked with a 'p' are projected. Projections begin with 1982 data. Data earlier than 1990 are not shown but are reflected in the projections.

SIC	Industry	1990	1991	1992	1993	1994	1995	1996	1997
7999	**Amusement & Recreation nec (pt)**								
	Establishments (number)	-	-	21,717	-	-	-	-	-
	Employment (thousands)	-	-	215.8	-	-	-	-	-
	Revenues ($ million)	-	-	10,430.3	-	-	-	-	-

Source: *Economic Census of the United States*, 1992, annual surveys of economic sectors conducted by the Bureau of the Census, and estimates or projections based on the 1982-1992 period; not all data are shown. 'e' marks estimates made by the editors; 'p' indicates projections based on time series. A dash (-) indicates that data for this SIC or year were not available. The abbreviation (pt) next to the industry name indicates that only a part of the industry is present within the NAICS data. If no (pt) is shown, the entire industry is contained within the NAICS data.

SELECTED RATIOS

For 1997	Avg. of Information	Analyzed Industry	Index	For 1997	Avg. of Information	Analyzed Industry	Index
Employees per establishment	6	4	74	Payroll per establishment	144,276	68,433	47
Revenue per establishment	835,727	309,051	37	Payroll as % of revenue	17	22	128
Revenue per employee	141,515	70,458	50	Payroll per employee	24,430	15,601	64

Sources: Same as General Statistics. The 'Average' column represents the average for the industry sector, in 1997, where the currently shown industry is classified. The Index shows the relationship between the Average and the Analyzed Industry. For example, 100 means that they are equal; 500 that the Analyzed Industry is five times the average; 50 means that the Analyzed Industry is half the national average. The abbreviation 'na' is used to show that data are 'not available'.

LEADING COMPANIES
No company data available for this industry.

LOCATION BY STATE AND REGIONAL CONCENTRATION

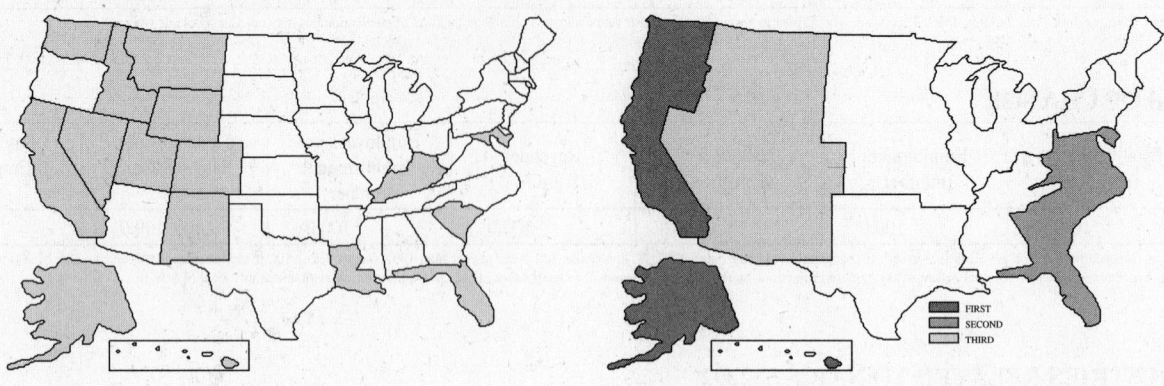

FIRST
SECOND
THIRD

INDUSTRY DATA BY STATE

State	Establishments Total (number)	% of U.S.	Employment Total (number)	% of U.S.	Per Estab.	Payroll Total ($ mil.)	Per Empl. ($)	Revenues Total ($ mil.)	% of U.S.	Per Estab. ($)
California	181	10.0	1,688	21.2	9	25.2	14,930	92.6	16.5	511,354
Florida	261	14.4	1,037	13.0	4	13.8	13,261	56.1	10.0	214,851
Colorado	122	6.7	956	12.0	8	8.0	8,333	40.9	7.3	335,148
Nevada	21	1.2	139	1.7	7	3.8	27,367	34.0	6.1	1,618,190
Texas	86	4.7	454	5.7	5	4.8	10,485	24.1	4.3	280,523
Hawaii	47	2.6	386	4.9	8	5.0	13,078	19.0	3.4	404,468
Kentucky	19	1.0	130	1.6	7	2.7	20,692	18.0	3.2	946,105
Pennsylvania	42	2.3	163	2.1	4	3.7	22,417	16.7	3.0	396,738
South Carolina	42	2.3	150	1.9	4	3.4	22,633	16.5	2.9	391,738
Louisiana	27	1.5	203	2.6	8	4.2	20,631	16.3	2.9	603,593
New York	75	4.1	193	2.4	3	3.6	18,435	16.1	2.9	214,267
Georgia	31	1.7	113	1.4	4	1.9	16,717	13.3	2.4	430,129
Michigan	75	4.1	124	1.6	2	3.2	25,903	13.1	2.3	174,707
Maryland	33	1.8	56	0.7	2	1.3	23,536	12.9	2.3	391,242
Washington	41	2.3	152	1.9	4	2.5	16,526	12.4	2.2	303,512
Illinois	42	2.3	257	3.2	6	4.2	16,233	12.3	2.2	292,429
Ohio	40	2.2	112	1.4	3	2.5	22,723	11.9	2.1	297,025
Massachusetts	38	2.1	62	0.8	2	2.5	39,984	9.6	1.7	252,579
Utah	36	2.0	239	3.0	7	2.1	8,757	9.5	1.7	264,361
Wisconsin	41	2.3	72	0.9	2	2.9	40,194	9.2	1.6	225,073
North Carolina	44	2.4	87	1.1	2	1.7	19,759	9.2	1.6	210,159
Minnesota	36	2.0	100	1.3	3	1.8	17,910	8.9	1.6	246,250
Arizona	21	1.2	93	1.2	4	1.8	18,935	8.1	1.5	388,048
Missouri	40	2.2	67	0.8	2	1.9	27,821	7.7	1.4	192,675
New Jersey	54	3.0	38	0.5	1	2.0	53,711	6.5	1.2	120,389
Idaho	18	1.0	64	0.8	4	0.9	14,031	6.4	1.1	356,556
Virginia	35	1.9	52	0.7	1	1.2	22,327	6.3	1.1	178,800
Indiana	22	1.2	54	0.7	2	1.4	26,315	6.1	1.1	276,455
Oregon	30	1.7	48	0.6	2	0.9	18,792	6.0	1.1	199,800
Tennessee	24	1.3	107	1.3	4	1.4	13,486	5.1	0.9	211,583
New Mexico	19	1.0	108	1.4	6	0.8	6,972	3.7	0.7	194,316
Montana	11	0.6	54	0.7	5	0.5	9,315	2.9	0.5	264,909
Iowa	11	0.6	24	0.3	2	0.7	28,750	2.9	0.5	262,000
Connecticut	9	0.5	33	0.4	4	0.7	20,909	2.8	0.5	311,556
Arkansas	17	0.9	31	0.4	2	0.5	15,516	2.3	0.4	135,882
Alabama	12	0.7	39	0.5	3	0.6	15,462	2.3	0.4	190,167
Oklahoma	15	0.8	36	0.5	2	0.4	9,944	1.7	0.3	113,067
Alaska	11	0.6	3	0.0	-	0.3	91,333	1.6	0.3	144,545
Rhode Island	8	0.4	8	0.1	1	0.3	32,125	1.2	0.2	144,250
Wyoming	7	0.4	7	0.1	1	0.2	22,000	1.0	0.2	139,714
New Hampshire	14	0.8	18	0.2	1	0.4	20,778	1.0	0.2	71,786
Maine	12	0.7	43	0.5	4	0.2	5,465	0.9	0.2	74,250
West Virginia	7	0.4	60*	-	-	(D)	-	(D)	-	-
Delaware	6	0.3	10*	-	-	(D)	-	(D)	-	-

Source: 1997 *Economic Census*. The states are in descending order of revenues or establishments (if revenue data are missing for the majority). The symbol (D) appears when data are withheld to prevent disclosure of competitive information. States marked with (D) are sorted by number of establishments. A dash (-) indicates that the data element cannot be calculated. * indicates the midpoint of a range; 175, for example is the range 100-249. Shaded *states* on the state map indicate those states which have proportionately greater representation in the industry than would be indicated by the state's population; the ratio is based on total revenues or number of establishments. Shaded *regions* indicate where the industry is regionally most concentrated.

NAICS 532299 - CONSUMER GOODS RENTAL NEC

GENERAL STATISTICS

Year	Establishments (number)	Employment (number)	Payroll ($ million)	Revenues ($ million)	Employees per Establishment (number)	Revenues per Establishment ($)	Payroll per Employee ($)
1997	3,150	26,298	636.0	2,154.0	8.3	683,810	24,184

Source: *Economic Census of the United States*, 1997. This is a newly defined industry. Data for prior years were unavailable at the time of publication but may become available over time.

INDICES OF CHANGE

Year	Establishments (number)	Employment (number)	Payroll ($ million)	Revenues ($ million)	Employees per Establishment (number)	Revenues per Establishment ($)	Payroll per Employee ($)
1997	100.0	100.0	100.0	100.0	100.0	100.0	100.0

Sources: Same as General Statistics. The values shown reflect change from the base year, 1997. Values above 100 mean greater than 1997, values below 100 mean less than 1997, and a value of 100 in the 1982-96 or 1998-2001 period means same as 1997. Values followed by a 'p' are projections by the editors; 'e' stands for extrapolation. Data are the most recent available at this level of detail.

SIC INDUSTRIES RELATED TO NAICS 532299

Each new NAICS code represents an industry that used to be part of an SIC or a part of several SIC industries. Data in this table are shown to provide transitional information for these cases. All available data for the precursor SIC(s) are shown. Even if only a part of an SIC is included in the NAICS, *all* data for the SIC are reproduced. If the SIC industry is not marked as being a part (pt) of the NAICS, the entire industry is embedded in the NAICS data. The SIC composition of the new industry provides some hints of the relative importance of its "ancestors." Data marked with a 'p' are projected. Projections begin with 1982 data. Data earlier than 1990 are not shown but are reflected in the projections.

SIC	Industry	1990	1991	1992	1993	1994	1995	1996	1997
7359	**Equipment Rental & Leasing, nec (pt)**								
	Establishments (number)	16,213	16,430	17,687	17,439	17,564	17,607	17,431*p*	17,486*p*
	Employment (thousands)	145.6	143.2	134.1	139.9	143.8	151.3	148.8*p*	150.4*p*
	Revenues ($ million)	15,481.0	15,265.0	15,482.0	16,816.0	18,607.0	20,677.0	20,949.0	21,947.1*p*

Source: *Economic Census of the United States*, 1992, annual surveys of economic sectors conducted by the Bureau of the Census, and estimates or projections based on the 1982-1992 period; not all data are shown. 'e' marks estimates made by the editors; 'p' indicates projections based on time series. A dash (-) indicates that data for this SIC or year were not available. The abbreviation (pt) next to the industry name indicates that only a part of the industry is present within the NAICS data. If no (pt) is shown, the entire industry is contained within the NAICS data.

SELECTED RATIOS

For 1997	Avg. of Information	Analyzed Industry	Index	For 1997	Avg. of Information	Analyzed Industry	Index
Employees per establishment	6	8	141	Payroll per establishment	144,276	201,905	140
Revenue per establishment	835,727	683,810	82	Payroll as % of revenue	17	30	171
Revenue per employee	141,515	81,907	58	Payroll per employee	24,430	24,184	99

Sources: Same as General Statistics. The 'Average' column represents the average for the industry sector, in 1997, where the currently shown industry is classified. The Index shows the relationship between the Average and the Analyzed Industry. For example, 100 means that they are equal; 500 that the Analyzed Industry is five times the average; 50 means that the Analyzed Industry is half the national average. The abbreviation 'na' is used to show that data are 'not available'.

LEADING COMPANIES

No company data available for this industry.

LOCATION BY STATE AND REGIONAL CONCENTRATION

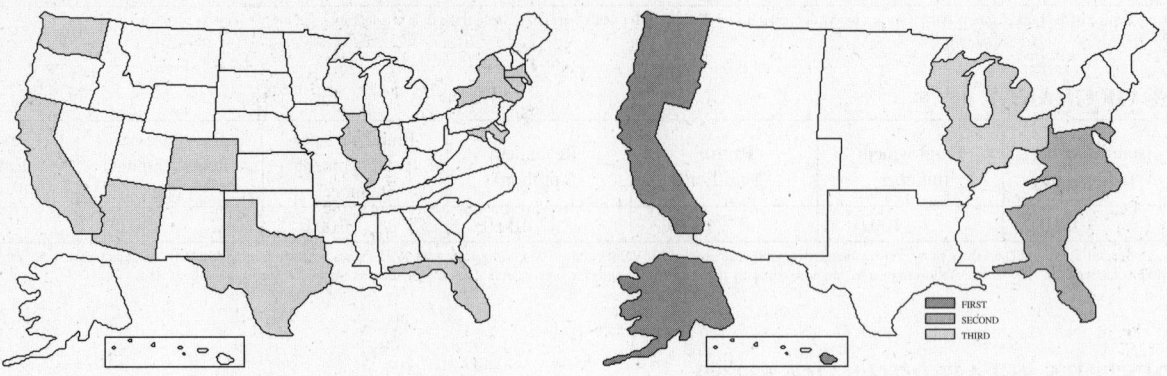

FIRST
SECOND
THIRD

INDUSTRY DATA BY STATE

State	Establishments Total (number)	Establishments % of U.S.	Employment Total (number)	Employment % of U.S.	Employment Per Estab.	Payroll Total ($ mil.)	Payroll Per Empl. ($)	Revenues Total ($ mil.)	Revenues % of U.S.	Revenues Per Estab. ($)
California	374	11.9	4,260	16.2	11	102.5	24,067	347.2	16.1	928,358
Texas	256	8.1	2,170	8.3	8	52.5	24,184	189.8	8.8	741,277
New York	238	7.6	2,233	8.5	9	52.0	23,270	178.1	8.3	748,109
Florida	173	5.5	1,372	5.2	8	32.3	23,519	114.2	5.3	659,896
Illinois	127	4.0	1,150	4.4	9	30.5	26,483	113.2	5.3	891,669
Ohio	124	3.9	1,143	4.3	9	29.0	25,416	85.1	4.0	686,065
Maryland	64	2.0	1,003	3.8	16	29.0	28,893	81.9	3.8	1,279,313
Massachusetts	87	2.8	729	2.8	8	20.3	27,879	77.9	3.6	895,966
Pennsylvania	143	4.5	989	3.8	7	23.3	23,566	73.9	3.4	516,566
Michigan	98	3.1	695	2.6	7	15.5	22,341	58.9	2.7	601,439
New Jersey	93	3.0	761	2.9	8	22.4	29,464	57.7	2.7	620,086
Georgia	82	2.6	642	2.4	8	14.3	22,243	51.1	2.4	623,037
Arizona	65	2.1	585	2.2	9	13.6	23,256	49.1	2.3	755,400
Colorado	62	2.0	579	2.2	9	13.7	23,596	47.4	2.2	763,887
Washington	53	1.7	583	2.2	11	14.0	24,003	44.4	2.1	837,038
Missouri	77	2.4	519	2.0	7	12.5	24,148	44.0	2.0	570,818
Virginia	66	2.1	599	2.3	9	17.7	29,506	43.9	2.0	665,697
Connecticut	57	1.8	356	1.4	6	11.6	32,469	36.6	1.7	642,930
Tennessee	56	1.8	468	1.8	8	10.9	23,293	36.6	1.7	653,179
Indiana	64	2.0	402	1.5	6	9.5	23,731	34.8	1.6	544,000
North Carolina	60	1.9	414	1.6	7	9.6	23,171	32.0	1.5	532,700
Minnesota	42	1.3	367	1.4	9	10.0	27,251	27.5	1.3	653,976
Wisconsin	45	1.4	342	1.3	8	7.5	21,825	26.3	1.2	584,133
Alabama	51	1.6	339	1.3	7	5.5	16,274	19.5	0.9	382,176
Mississippi	46	1.5	232	0.9	5	4.5	19,591	18.7	0.9	407,457
Kentucky	32	1.0	213	0.8	7	5.1	23,901	16.6	0.8	517,313
Oklahoma	42	1.3	253	1.0	6	4.4	17,561	14.3	0.7	339,905
Arkansas	39	1.2	190	0.7	5	2.9	15,468	11.8	0.5	302,385
South Carolina	39	1.2	184	0.7	5	3.1	16,967	10.7	0.5	273,590
Iowa	27	0.9	122	0.5	5	2.5	20,213	9.6	0.4	356,815
Utah	14	0.4	97	0.4	7	2.5	25,557	9.2	0.4	656,500
New Mexico	20	0.6	96	0.4	5	2.2	23,115	8.8	0.4	439,850
New Hampshire	14	0.4	76	0.3	5	1.9	25,539	5.7	0.3	409,571
Vermont	8	0.3	39	0.1	5	1.1	28,872	3.8	0.2	469,375
Alaska	6	0.2	25	0.1	4	0.7	26,520	2.7	0.1	455,333
South Dakota	10	0.3	50	0.2	5	0.5	9,280	2.6	0.1	264,100
Louisiana	77	2.4	750*	-	-	(D)	-	(D)	-	-
Oregon	47	1.5	375*	-	-	(D)	-	(D)	-	-
Nevada	34	1.1	175*	-	-	(D)	-	(D)	-	-
Kansas	25	0.8	175*	-	-	(D)	-	(D)	-	-
Nebraska	19	0.6	60*	-	-	(D)	-	(D)	-	-
Hawaii	16	0.5	60*	-	-	(D)	-	(D)	-	-
Delaware	13	0.4	175*	-	-	(D)	-	(D)	-	-
Maine	13	0.4	60*	-	-	(D)	-	(D)	-	-
Idaho	12	0.4	60*	-	-	(D)	-	(D)	-	-
Rhode Island	12	0.4	60*	-	-	(D)	-	(D)	-	-
North Dakota	10	0.3	60*	-	-	(D)	-	(D)	-	-

Source: 1997 *Economic Census*. The states are in descending order of revenues or establishments (if revenue data are missing for the majority). The symbol (D) appears when data are withheld to prevent disclosure of competitive information. States marked with (D) are sorted by number of establishments. A dash (-) indicates that the data element cannot be calculated. * indicates the midpoint of a range; 175, for example is the range 100-249. Shaded *states* on the state map indicate those states which have proportionately greater representation in the industry than would be indicated by the state's population; the ratio is based on total revenues or number of establishments. Shaded *regions* indicate where the industry is regionally most concentrated.

NAICS 532310 - GENERAL RENTAL CENTERS

GENERAL STATISTICS

Year	Establishments (number)	Employment (number)	Payroll ($ million)	Revenues ($ million)	Employees per Establishment (number)	Revenues per Establishment ($)	Payroll per Employee ($)
1997	6,509	40,284	941.0	3,911.0	6.2	600,860	23,359

Source: *Economic Census of the United States*, 1997. This is a newly defined industry. Data for prior years were unavailable at the time of publication but may become available over time.

INDICES OF CHANGE

Year	Establishments (number)	Employment (number)	Payroll ($ million)	Revenues ($ million)	Employees per Establishment (number)	Revenues per Establishment ($)	Payroll per Employee ($)
1997	100.0	100.0	100.0	100.0	100.0	100.0	100.0

Sources: Same as General Statistics. The values shown reflect change from the base year, 1997. Values above 100 mean greater than 1997, values below 100 mean less than 1997, and a value of 100 in the 1982-96 or 1998-2001 period means same as 1997. Values followed by a 'p' are projections by the editors; 'e' stands for extrapolation. Data are the most recent available at this level of detail.

SIC INDUSTRIES RELATED TO NAICS 532310

Each new NAICS code represents an industry that used to be part of an SIC or a part of several SIC industries. Data in this table are shown to provide transitional information for these cases. All available data for the precursor SIC(s) are shown. Even if only a part of an SIC is included in the NAICS, *all* data for the SIC are reproduced. If the SIC industry is not marked as being a part (pt) of the NAICS, the entire industry is embedded in the NAICS data. The SIC composition of the new industry provides some hints of the relative importance of its "ancestors." Data marked with a 'p' are projected. Projections begin with 1982 data. Data earlier than 1990 are not shown but are reflected in the projections.

SIC	Industry	1990	1991	1992	1993	1994	1995	1996	1997
7359	**Equipment Rental & Leasing, nec (pt)**								
	Establishments (number)	16,213	16,430	17,687	17,439	17,564	17,607	17,431*p*	17,486*p*
	Employment (thousands)	145.6	143.2	134.1	139.9	143.8	151.3	148.8*p*	150.4*p*
	Revenues ($ million)	15,481.0	15,265.0	15,482.0	16,816.0	18,607.0	20,677.0	20,949.0	21,947.1*p*

Source: *Economic Census of the United States*, 1992, annual surveys of economic sectors conducted by the Bureau of the Census, and estimates or projections based on the 1982-1992 period; not all data are shown. 'e' marks estimates made by the editors; 'p' indicates projections based on time series. A dash (-) indicates that data for this SIC or year were not available. The abbreviation (pt) next to the industry name indicates that only a part of the industry is present within the NAICS data. If no (pt) is shown, the entire industry is contained within the NAICS data.

SELECTED RATIOS

For 1997	Avg. of Information	Analyzed Industry	Index	For 1997	Avg. of Information	Analyzed Industry	Index
Employees per establishment	6	6	105	Payroll per establishment	144,276	144,569	100
Revenue per establishment	835,727	600,860	72	Payroll as % of revenue	17	24	139
Revenue per employee	141,515	97,086	69	Payroll per employee	24,430	23,359	96

Sources: Same as General Statistics. The 'Average' column represents the average for the industry sector, in 1997, where the currently shown industry is classified. The Index shows the relationship between the Average and the Analyzed Industry. For example, 100 means that they are equal; 500 that the Analyzed Industry is five times the average; 50 means that the Analyzed Industry is half the national average. The abbreviation 'na' is used to show that data are 'not available'.

LEADING COMPANIES   Number shown: **63**   Total sales ($ mil): **28,841**   Total employment (000): **56.4**

Company Name	Address				CEO Name	Phone	Co. Type	Sales ($ mil)	Empl. (000)
Danka Corp.	11201 Danka Circle	St. Petersburg	FL	33716	Larry K. Switzer	727-576-6003	D	22,287*	20.0
Rent-A-Center Inc. (Plano, Texas)	5700 Tennyson	Plano	TX	75024	J Ernest Talley	972-801-1100	P	810	10.6
Rental Service Corp.	6929 E Greenway	Scottsdale	AZ	85254	D A Waugaman	480-905-3300	S	578	3.5
Rent-Way Inc.	1 RentWay Pl	Erie	PA	16505	W E Morgenstern	814-455-5378	P	494	5.6
International Lease Finance Corp.	1999 Av of the Stars	Los Angeles	CA	90067	Steven Udvar-Hazy	310-788-1999	S	386*	<0.1
Brambles USA Inc.	400 N Michigan	Chicago	IL	60611	Robert J Anderson	312-836-0200	S	380*	2.0
CORT Furniture Rental Corp.	11250 Waples Milll	Fairfax	VA	22033	Paul N Arnold	703-968-8500	S	350	2.8
Inter-Tel Leasing Inc.	7300 W Boston	Chandler	AZ	85226	Kurt Kenip	480-961-9000	S	333*	0.3
CORT Business Services Corp.	4401 Fair Lks	Fairfax	VA	22033	Paul N Arnold	703-968-8500	P	319	2.7
Capital Associates Inc.	7175 W Jefferson	Lakewood	CO	80235	James D Walker	303-980-1000	P	243	0.2
GE Capital Container Finance	1111 Broadway	Oakland	CA	94607	Robert W Forth	510-891-9444	S	230	<0.1
Star Industries Inc.	130 Lakeside Ave	Seattle	WA	98122	L W Rabel	206-328-1600	R	186*	0.2
Interpool Inc.	211 College Rd E	Princeton	NJ	08540	Martin Tuchman	609-452-8900	P	182	0.1
Globe Business Resources Inc.	11260 Chester Rd	Cincinnati	OH	45246	David D Hoguet	513-771-8287	P	148	0.8
Aaron's Rental Purchase Div.	309 E Paces Ferry	Atlanta	GA	30305	William K Butler Jr	404-237-4016	D	147*	1.3
McGrath RentCorp	5700 Las Positas Rd	Livermore	CA	94550	Dennis C Kakures	925-606-9200	P	135	0.4
PLM Financial Services Inc.	1 Market Steu Twr	San Francisco	CA	94105	Doug Goodrich	415-974-1399	S	128*	<0.1
LINC Group Inc.	303 E Wacker Dr	Chicago	IL	60601	RE Lang	312-946-1000	R	120*	0.2
USA Capital L.L.C.	88 Steele St	Denver	CO	80206	Jeffery G Jones	303-321-0400	R	100	<0.1
Chep USA	8517 S Park Cir	Orlando	FL	32819	Bob Moore	407-422-4510	R	94*	0.5
Flexi-Van Corp.	251 Monroe Ave	Kenilworth	NJ	07033	George Elkas	908-276-8000	R	92	0.2
Oceaneering Production Systems	PO Box 40494	Houston	TX	77240		713-329-4500	S	90	0.4
Admiral Party and Tent Rentals	10665 Baur Blvd	St. Louis	MO	63132	Paul Belmont	314-993-3600	R	83*	<0.1
Rainbow Rentals Inc.	P O Box 9006	Boardman	OH	44513	Waylan Russell	330-533-5363	P	81	0.8
United Coin Machine Inc.	600 Pilot Rd	Las Vegas	NV	89119	Robert L Miodunski	702-270-7500	S	75	0.4
GES Exposition Services Inc.	950 Grier Dr	Las Vegas	NV	89119	Paul Mullen	702-263-1500	S	60*	0.3
A-1 Coast Rentals Inc.	24000 Crenshaw	Torrance	CA	90505	Allan C Billings	310-326-1910	R	59*	<0.1
PLM International Inc.	1 Market	San Francisco	CA	94105	Robert N Tidball	415-974-1399	P	59	0.2
Galjour Video	P O Box 640355	Kenner	LA	70064	Mark Galjour	504-466-5805	R	55*	<0.1
A and A Tool Rental and Sales	2911 E Fremont St	Stockton	CA	95205		209-948-9500	S	49*	<0.1
Brook Furniture Rental Inc.	2301 E Oakton St	Arlington H.	IL	60005	Robert Crawford	847-595-7775	R	48*	0.4
Sound Chek Music	P O Box 8085	Metairie	LA	70011	Chris Brown	504-454-6331	R	44*	<0.1
Rug Doctor L.P.	4701 Old Shepard Pl	Plano	TX	75093	Roger Kent	972-673-1400	R	32*	0.3
PS Group Holdings Inc.	4370 La Jolla	San Diego	CA	92122	C E Rickershauser Jr	619-642-2999	P	31	<0.1
Bestway Inc. (Dallas, Texas)	7800 Stemmons Fwy	Dallas	TX	75247	R Brooks Reed	214-630-6655	P	29	0.3
Keystone Leasing	433 New Park Ave	West Hartford	CT	06110	Edward W Lee	860-233-3663	R	29*	<0.1
Toyota Material Handling	21053 Alexander Ct	Hayward	CA	94545	Rich Andres	510-887-0500	R	29*	0.2
Ponder Industries Inc.	5005 Riverway Dr	Houston	TX	77056	Eugene L Butler	713-965-0653	P	21	0.2
Hy-Tek Material Handling Inc.	2222 Post Rd	Columbus	OH	43217	William J Miller	614-497-2500	R	20	0.1
L.B. Industries Inc.	PO Box 2797	Boise	ID	83701	Lawrence B Barnes	208-345-7515	R	20	<0.1
Powr-Lift Corp.	1400 S Loop 12	Irving	TX	75060	Mel Robinson	972-438-3613	R	20*	0.1
Franks Supply Company Inc.	3311 Stanford N E	Albuquerque	NM	87107	M Deaver-Rivera	505-884-0000	R	18*	0.1
Marr Scaffolding Company Inc.	1 D St	Boston	MA	02127	Robert L Marr	617-269-7200	R	18	0.1
Walnut Equipment Leasing Inc.	1 Belmont Ave	Bala Cynwyd	PA	19004	William Shapiro	610-668-0700	S	17	<0.1
Display Group	1701 W Lafayette	Detroit	MI	48216	Richard Portwood	313-965-3344	R	17*	<0.1
O'Brien Energy Services Co.	PO Box 2345	Wilmington	DE	19899	Dan Padgett	302-658-7100	S	11	<0.1
Creative Presentations Inc.	4400 Trenton St	Metairie	LA	70006	Barry Edwards	504-454-2749	R	11*	<0.1
PLM Transportation Equipment	1 Market Plz	San Francisco	CA	94105	Douglas P Goodrich	415-974-1399	S	8*	<0.1
Airlease Ltd.	P O Box 193985	San Francisco	CA	94104	David B Gebler	415-765-1814	P	8	<0.1
Andy Gump Inc.	26954 Ruether Ave	Canyon Country	CA	91351	Barry Gump	661-251-7721	R	7*	0.1
Sea Containers West Inc.	201 Spear St #1350	San Francisco	CA	94105	Robin Lynen	415-227-4600	S	7	<0.1
Audio Visual Mart Inc.	P O Box 23020	New Orleans	LA	70183	Rick Peyton	504-733-1500	R	6*	<0.1
Business Aircraft Leasing Inc.	PO Box 17056	Nashville	TN	37217	Charles Mulle	615-361-3781	R	6*	<0.1
SIMSCommunications Inc.	3333 S Congress	Delray Beach	FL	33445	Mark Bennett	949-724-9094	P	6	<0.1
Barrett Capital Corp.	930 Mamaroneck	Mamaroneck	NY	10543	Barry P Korn	914-381-4600	R	5*	<0.1
Commercial Finance Corp.	14595 Avion Pkwy	Chantilly	VA	20151	Jed Fochtman	703-222-9600	R	4*	<0.1
Crescent Sound and Light Inc.	237 N Peters St	New Orleans	LA	70130	Michael Cottage	504-828-5617	R	3*	<0.1
Energy Equipment Resources Inc.	8411 Preston Rd	Dallas	TX	75225	Mike Mullen	214-692-6690	R	3*	<0.1
Equipment Leasing Corporation	PO Box 1050	Bala Cynwyd	PA	19004	William Shapiro	610-668-0707	P	3	<0.1
Latin American Casinos Inc.	2000 NE 164th St	N. Miami Beach	FL	33162	Lloyd Lyons	305-945-9300	P	2	<0.1
US Airways Leasing & Sales Inc.	2345 Crystal Dr	Arlington	VA	22227	Stuart A Peebles	703-872-7500	S	2*	<0.1
Protocol Telecommunications Inc.	15635 Saticoy St	Van Nuys	CA	91406	Stefan Jovanovich	818-782-5705	R	2	<0.1
Andrew A	150 W 114th St	Cut Off	LA	70345		504-632-5584	R	1	<0.1

Source: Ward's Business Directory of U.S. Private and Public Companies, Volumes 1 and 2, 2000. The company type code used is as follows: P - Public, R - Private, S - Subsidiary, D - Division, J - Joint Venture, A - Affiliate, G - Group, N - Company type not reported. Sales are in millions of dollars, employees are in thousands. An asterisk (*) indicates an estimated sales volume. The symbol < stands for 'less than'. Company names and addresses are truncated, in some cases, to fit into the available space.

LOCATION BY STATE AND REGIONAL CONCENTRATION

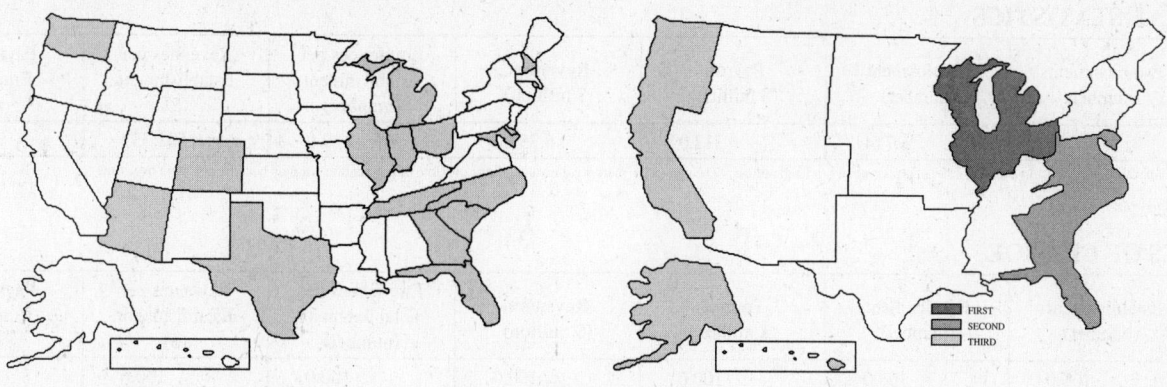

FIRST
SECOND
THIRD

INDUSTRY DATA BY STATE

State	Establishments Total (number)	Establishments % of U.S.	Employment Total (number)	Employment % of U.S.	Employment Per Estab.	Payroll Total ($ mil.)	Payroll Per Empl. ($)	Revenues Total ($ mil.)	Revenues % of U.S.	Revenues Per Estab. ($)
California	565	8.7	3,928	9.8	7	99.7	25,390	382.1	9.8	676,308
Texas	564	8.7	3,361	8.3	6	77.3	22,987	335.1	8.6	594,074
Florida	440	6.8	2,570	6.4	6	53.1	20,644	241.0	6.2	547,798
Ohio	362	5.6	2,491	6.2	7	57.2	22,962	240.4	6.1	664,204
New York	309	4.7	1,911	4.7	6	55.4	28,993	227.1	5.8	734,864
Illinois	270	4.1	1,755	4.4	7	46.9	26,721	198.9	5.1	736,793
Michigan	229	3.5	1,348	3.3	6	33.8	25,093	149.0	3.8	650,585
Georgia	238	3.7	1,342	3.3	6	33.0	24,580	146.4	3.7	615,101
Pennsylvania	222	3.4	1,298	3.2	6	33.3	25,669	139.0	3.6	626,131
Indiana	221	3.4	1,393	3.5	6	29.3	21,051	124.1	3.2	561,321
Washington	163	2.5	1,231	3.1	8	32.4	26,319	118.5	3.0	727,037
Tennessee	189	2.9	1,190	3.0	6	28.2	23,673	117.7	3.0	622,582
New Jersey	140	2.2	1,191	3.0	9	30.6	25,725	111.5	2.9	796,407
North Carolina	211	3.2	1,153	2.9	5	24.1	20,880	104.0	2.7	492,810
Colorado	142	2.2	1,102	2.7	8	25.5	23,100	101.5	2.6	714,592
Massachusetts	132	2.0	928	2.3	7	24.2	26,108	90.7	2.3	687,129
Maryland	125	1.9	793	2.0	6	20.0	25,158	82.4	2.1	659,576
Arizona	104	1.6	606	1.5	6	12.9	21,289	66.4	1.7	638,769
Virginia	125	1.9	649	1.6	5	14.7	22,670	62.2	1.6	497,392
Alabama	115	1.8	783	1.9	7	14.6	18,593	61.7	1.6	536,330
South Carolina	117	1.8	646	1.6	6	14.2	22,029	60.8	1.6	519,863
Minnesota	107	1.6	566	1.4	5	13.0	22,959	49.2	1.3	459,561
Kentucky	91	1.4	526	1.3	6	10.1	19,200	45.1	1.2	495,945
Oregon	76	1.2	534	1.3	7	11.4	21,326	43.6	1.1	573,224
Connecticut	72	1.1	356	0.9	5	9.0	25,390	38.0	1.0	528,417
Oklahoma	92	1.4	446	1.1	5	8.6	19,361	36.5	0.9	396,554
Wisconsin	78	1.2	454	1.1	6	8.6	18,932	35.1	0.9	450,500
Mississippi	67	1.0	355	0.9	5	6.9	19,532	29.1	0.7	434,716
Iowa	66	1.0	385	1.0	6	7.0	18,236	28.9	0.7	438,439
Arkansas	56	0.9	240	0.6	4	5.0	20,767	23.7	0.6	422,339
Utah	48	0.7	313	0.8	7	5.2	16,553	23.0	0.6	479,458
New Hampshire	46	0.7	222	0.6	5	6.6	29,703	22.0	0.6	478,543
New Mexico	53	0.8	256	0.6	5	4.8	18,836	21.8	0.6	411,170
Nevada	38	0.6	250	0.6	7	4.5	17,868	21.0	0.5	552,737
Idaho	33	0.5	219	0.5	7	4.3	19,616	16.3	0.4	495,424
Delaware	24	0.4	146	0.4	6	3.5	23,630	15.4	0.4	642,250
Rhode Island	22	0.3	156	0.4	7	3.7	24,000	14.2	0.4	647,091
Hawaii	27	0.4	140	0.3	5	3.7	26,214	13.9	0.4	515,111
Maine	26	0.4	134	0.3	5	2.8	20,925	11.2	0.3	430,500
Nebraska	25	0.4	173	0.4	7	3.3	18,821	10.1	0.3	403,960
Montana	28	0.4	155	0.4	6	2.5	15,910	9.9	0.3	355,036
Vermont	20	0.3	95	0.2	5	2.0	20,747	7.4	0.2	370,250
South Dakota	12	0.2	65	0.2	5	1.6	25,246	6.3	0.2	527,583
Alaska	10	0.2	43	0.1	4	1.1	26,186	5.8	0.1	577,800
Wyoming	12	0.2	70	0.2	6	1.2	17,700	4.8	0.1	397,083
North Dakota	8	0.1	52	0.1	7	0.8	14,808	3.0	0.1	372,875
Missouri	161	2.5	750*	-	-	(D)	-	(D)	-	-
Louisiana	115	1.8	750*	-	-	(D)	-	(D)	-	-
Kansas	78	1.2	375*	-	-	(D)	-	(D)	-	-
West Virginia	30	0.5	175*	-	-	(D)	-	(D)	-	-

Source: 1997 *Economic Census*. The states are in descending order of revenues or establishments (if revenue data are missing for the majority). The symbol (D) appears when data are withheld to prevent disclosure of competitive information. States marked with (D) are sorted by number of establishments. A dash (-) indicates that the data element cannot be calculated. * indicates the midpoint of a range; 175, for example is the range 100-249. Shaded *states* on the state map indicate those states which have proportionately greater representation in the industry than would be indicated by the state's population; the ratio is based on total revenues or number of establishments. Shaded *regions* indicate where the industry is regionally most concentrated.

NAICS 532411 - COMMERCIAL AIR, RAIL, AND WATER TRANSPORTATION EQUIPMENT RENTAL AND LEASING

GENERAL STATISTICS

Year	Establishments (number)	Employment (number)	Payroll ($ million)	Revenues ($ million)	Employees per Establishment (number)	Revenues per Establishment ($)	Payroll per Employee ($)
1997	748	6,714	312.0	6,359.0	9.0	8,501,337	46,470

Source: Economic Census of the United States, 1997. This is a newly defined industry. Data for prior years were unavailable at the time of publication but may become available over time.

INDICES OF CHANGE

Year	Establishments (number)	Employment (number)	Payroll ($ million)	Revenues ($ million)	Employees per Establishment (number)	Revenues per Establishment ($)	Payroll per Employee ($)
1997	100.0	100.0	100.0	100.0	100.0	100.0	100.0

Sources: Same as General Statistics. The values shown reflect change from the base year, 1997. Values above 100 mean greater than 1997, values below 100 mean less than 1997, and a value of 100 in the 1982-96 or 1998-2001 period means same as 1997. Values followed by a 'p' are projections by the editors; 'e' stands for extrapolation. Data are the most recent available at this level of detail.

SIC INDUSTRIES RELATED TO NAICS 532411

Each new NAICS code represents an industry that used to be part of an SIC or a part of several SIC industries. Data in this table are shown to provide transitional information for these cases. All available data for the precursor SIC(s) are shown. Even if only a part of an SIC is included in the NAICS, *all* data for the SIC are reproduced. If the SIC industry is not marked as being a part (pt) of the NAICS, the entire industry is embedded in the NAICS data. The SIC composition of the new industry provides some hints of the relative importance of its "ancestors." Data marked with a 'p' are projected. Projections begin with 1982 data. Data earlier than 1990 are not shown but are reflected in the projections.

SIC	Industry	1990	1991	1992	1993	1994	1995	1996	1997
4499	**Water Transportation Services, nec (pt)**								
	Establishments (number)	1,111	1,187	1,118	1,180	1,209	1,244	1,394	1,261p
	Employment (thousands)	10.6	13.1	9.4	8.7	8.6	9.4	9.7	9.1p
	Revenues ($ million)	1,151.3e	1,060.9e	970.6	880.3p	789.9p	699.6p	609.3p	519.0p
4741	**Rental of Railroad Cars (pt)**								
	Establishments (number)	148	147	125	123	113	111	116	111p
	Employment (thousands)	2.6	2.3	1.9	2.0	1.9	2.1	2.3	2.0p
	Revenues ($ million)	1,829.5e	1,855.3e	1,881.1	1,906.9p	1,932.7p	1,958.5p	1,984.3p	2,010.1p
7359	**Equipment Rental & Leasing, nec (pt)**								
	Establishments (number)	16,213	16,430	17,687	17,439	17,564	17,607	17,431p	17,486p
	Employment (thousands)	145.6	143.2	134.1	139.9	143.8	151.3	148.8p	150.4p
	Revenues ($ million)	15,481.0	15,265.0	15,482.0	16,816.0	18,607.0	20,677.0	20,949.0	21,947.1p

Source: Economic Census of the United States, 1992, annual surveys of economic sectors conducted by the Bureau of the Census, and estimates or projections based on the 1982-1992 period; not all data are shown. 'e' marks estimates made by the editors; 'p' indicates projections based on time series. A dash (-) indicates that data for this SIC or year were not available. The abbreviation (pt) next to the industry name indicates that only a part of the industry is present within the NAICS data. If no (pt) is shown, the entire industry is contained within the NAICS data.

SELECTED RATIOS

For 1997	Avg. of Information	Analyzed Industry	Index	For 1997	Avg. of Information	Analyzed Industry	Index
Employees per establishment	6	9	152	Payroll per establishment	144,276	417,112	289
Revenue per establishment	835,727	8,501,337	1,017	Payroll as % of revenue	17	5	28
Revenue per employee	141,515	947,125	669	Payroll per employee	24,430	46,470	190

Sources: Same as General Statistics. The 'Average' column represents the average for the industry sector, in 1997, where the currently shown industry is classified. The Index shows the relationship between the Average and the Analyzed Industry. For example, 100 means that they are equal; 500 that the Analyzed Industry is five times the average; 50 means that the Analyzed Industry is half the national average. The abbreviation 'na' is used to show that data are 'not available'.

LEADING COMPANIES   Number shown: **3**   Total sales ($ mil): **3,494**   Total employment (000): **7.4**

Company Name	Address				CEO Name	Phone	Co. Type	Sales ($ mil)	Empl. (000)
GATX Corp.	500 W Monroe St	Chicago	IL	60661	Ronald H. Zech	312-621-6200	P	1,859	6.0
Connell Co.	45 Cardinal Dr	Westfield	NJ	07090	Grover Connell	908-233-0700	R	1,275*	0.1
Greenbrier Leasing Corp.	6806 SE 35th Ave	Portland	OR	97202	William A Furman	503-774-4340	S	360	1.3

Source: Ward's Business Directory of U.S. Private and Public Companies, Volumes 1 and 2, 2000. The company type code used is as follows: P - Public, R - Private, S - Subsidiary, D - Division, J - Joint Venture, A - Affiliate, G - Group, N - Company type not reported. Sales are in millions of dollars, employees are in thousands. An asterisk (*) indicates an estimated sales volume. The symbol < stands for 'less than'. Company names and addresses are truncated, in some cases, to fit into the available space.

LOCATION BY STATE AND REGIONAL CONCENTRATION

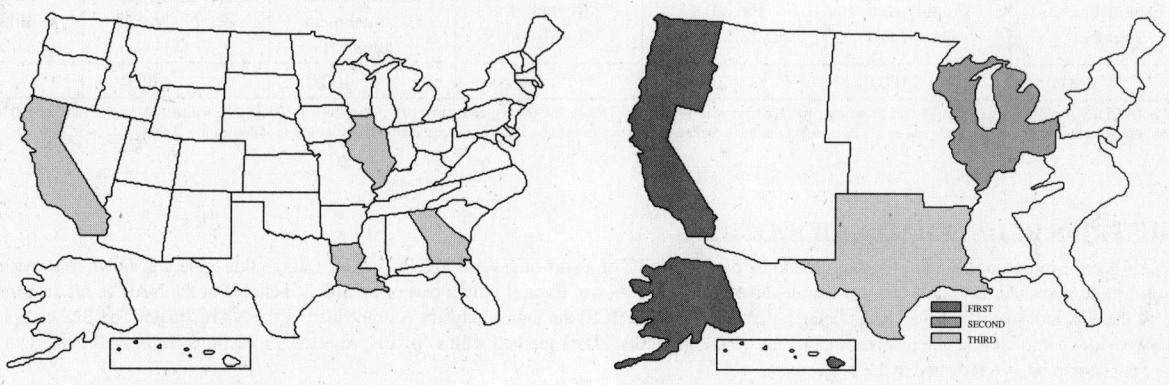

FIRST
SECOND
THIRD

INDUSTRY DATA BY STATE

State	Establishments Total (number)	% of U.S.	Employment Total (number)	% of U.S.	Per Estab.	Payroll Total ($ mil.)	Per Empl. ($)	Revenues Total ($ mil.)	% of U.S.	Per Estab. ($)
California	104	13.9	743	11.1	7	38.1	51,287	2,224.1	35.0	21,385,933
Illinois	45	6.0	1,465	21.8	33	80.7	55,106	1,655.5	26.0	36,789,933
Texas	83	11.1	639	9.5	8	30.1	47,136	437.9	6.9	5,275,843
Louisiana	60	8.0	1,372	20.4	23	49.7	36,220	291.5	4.6	4,858,567
Georgia	18	2.4	112	1.7	6	7.2	64,018	184.7	2.9	10,260,944
Pennsylvania	18	2.4	126	1.9	7	7.3	58,325	157.2	2.5	8,731,222
New York	30	4.0	107	1.6	4	7.7	71,822	141.7	2.2	4,723,233
Florida	43	5.7	274	4.1	6	12.0	43,741	129.3	2.0	3,006,116
New Jersey	20	2.7	148	2.2	7	11.3	76,108	101.8	1.6	5,088,600
Washington	16	2.1	146	2.2	9	8.6	59,116	48.2	0.8	3,009,438
Connecticut	12	1.6	38	0.6	3	2.6	67,921	46.7	0.7	3,892,500
Ohio	18	2.4	81	1.2	5	3.4	42,383	24.1	0.4	1,336,389
Iowa	10	1.3	103	1.5	10	4.4	42,864	20.9	0.3	2,094,200
Colorado	10	1.3	57	0.8	6	1.9	33,404	20.1	0.3	2,007,000
Nevada	14	1.9	65	1.0	5	2.3	35,985	15.1	0.2	1,078,929
Minnesota	8	1.1	74	1.1	9	2.0	26,770	13.3	0.2	1,668,375
Arizona	11	1.5	65	1.0	6	2.4	36,769	11.5	0.2	1,045,091
Kentucky	12	1.6	56	0.8	5	1.7	30,696	10.6	0.2	887,417
North Carolina	11	1.5	33	0.5	3	0.9	27,273	10.0	0.2	908,455
Utah	8	1.1	16	0.2	2	0.3	17,500	5.1	0.1	638,750
Oklahoma	11	1.5	20	0.3	2	0.5	26,600	4.7	0.1	425,273
Indiana	11	1.5	43	0.6	4	1.0	22,907	3.3	0.1	301,636
Arkansas	10	1.3	17	0.3	2	0.4	25,706	3.2	0.1	319,600
Alabama	12	1.6	27	0.4	2	0.7	26,667	3.2	0.1	269,667
Massachusetts	12	1.6	21	0.3	2	0.8	37,810	3.0	0.0	251,417
Mississippi	7	0.9	38	0.6	5	0.5	13,763	2.1	0.0	293,000
Hawaii	8	1.1	12	0.2	2	0.2	18,667	1.7	0.0	216,125
Tennessee	9	1.2	19	0.3	2	0.5	24,105	1.6	0.0	181,444
Virginia	18	2.4	175*	-	-	(D)	-	(D)	-	-
Missouri	17	2.3	375*	-	-	(D)	-	(D)	-	-
Michigan	13	1.7	10*	-	-	(D)	-	(D)	-	-
Oregon	11	1.5	175*	-	-	(D)	-	(D)	-	-
Maryland	8	1.1	60*	-	-	(D)	-	(D)	-	-
Kansas	7	0.9	10*	-	-	(D)	-	(D)	-	-

Source: 1997 Economic Census. The states are in descending order of revenues or establishments (if revenue data are missing for the majority). The symbol (D) appears when data are withheld to prevent disclosure of competitive information. States marked with (D) are sorted by number of establishments. A dash (-) indicates that the data element cannot be calculated. * indicates the midpoint of a range; 175, for example is the range 100-249. Shaded states on the state map indicate those states which have proportionately greater representation in the industry than would be indicated by the state's population; the ratio is based on total revenues or number of establishments. Shaded regions indicate where the industry is regionally most concentrated.

NAICS 532412 - CONSTRUCTION, MINING, AND FORESTRY MACHINERY AND EQUIPMENT RENTAL AND LEASING

GENERAL STATISTICS

Year	Establishments (number)	Employment (number)	Payroll ($ million)	Revenues ($ million)	Employees per Establishment (number)	Revenues per Establishment ($)	Payroll per Employee ($)
1997	3,957	41,545	1,448.0	6,894.0	10.5	1,742,229	34,854

Source: *Economic Census of the United States*, 1997. This is a newly defined industry. Data for prior years were unavailable at the time of publication but may become available over time.

INDICES OF CHANGE

Year	Establishments (number)	Employment (number)	Payroll ($ million)	Revenues ($ million)	Employees per Establishment (number)	Revenues per Establishment ($)	Payroll per Employee ($)
1997	100.0	100.0	100.0	100.0	100.0	100.0	100.0

Sources: Same as General Statistics. The values shown reflect change from the base year, 1997. Values above 100 mean greater than 1997, values below 100 mean less than 1997, and a value of 100 in the 1982-96 or 1998-2001 period means same as 1997. Values followed by a 'p' are projections by the editors; 'e' stands for extrapolation. Data are the most recent available at this level of detail.

SIC INDUSTRIES RELATED TO NAICS 532412

Each new NAICS code represents an industry that used to be part of an SIC or a part of several SIC industries. Data in this table are shown to provide transitional information for these cases. All available data for the precursor SIC(s) are shown. Even if only a part of an SIC is included in the NAICS, *all* data for the SIC are reproduced. If the SIC industry is not marked as being a part (pt) of the NAICS, the entire industry is embedded in the NAICS data. The SIC composition of the new industry provides some hints of the relative importance of its "ancestors." Data marked with a 'p' are projected. Projections begin with 1982 data. Data earlier than 1990 are not shown but are reflected in the projections.

SIC	Industry	1990	1991	1992	1993	1994	1995	1996	1997
7353	**Heavy Construction Equipment Rental (pt)**								
	Establishments (number)	3,764	3,634	3,853	3,796	3,661	3,624	3,394p	3,290p
	Employment (thousands)	39.6	36.1	34.7	36.8	37.3	39.7	37.0p	36.8p
	Revenues ($ million)	5,091.0	4,537.0	4,090.0	4,393.0	4,836.0	5,740.0	6,076.0	5,838.6p
7359	**Equipment Rental & Leasing, nec (pt)**								
	Establishments (number)	16,213	16,430	17,687	17,439	17,564	17,607	17,431p	17,486p
	Employment (thousands)	145.6	143.2	134.1	134.1	139.9	143.8	148.8p	150.4p
	Revenues ($ million)	15,481.0	15,265.0	15,482.0	16,816.0	18,607.0	20,677.0	20,949.0	21,947.1p

Source: *Economic Census of the United States*, 1992, annual surveys of economic sectors conducted by the Bureau of the Census, and estimates or projections based on the 1982-1992 period; not all data are shown. 'e' marks estimates made by the editors; 'p' indicates projections based on time series. A dash (-) indicates that data for this SIC or year were not available. The abbreviation (pt) next to the industry name indicates that only a part of the industry is present within the NAICS data. If no (pt) is shown, the entire industry is contained within the NAICS data.

SELECTED RATIOS

For 1997	Avg. of Information	Analyzed Industry	Index	For 1997	Avg. of Information	Analyzed Industry	Index
Employees per establishment	6	10	178	Payroll per establishment	144,276	365,934	254
Revenue per establishment	835,727	1,742,229	208	Payroll as % of revenue	17	21	122
Revenue per employee	141,515	165,941	117	Payroll per employee	24,430	34,854	143

Sources: Same as General Statistics. The 'Average' column represents the average for the industry sector, in 1997, where the currently shown industry is classified. The Index shows the relationship between the Average and the Analyzed Industry. For example, 100 means that they are equal; 500 that the Analyzed Industry is five times the average; 50 means that the Analyzed Industry is half the national average. The abbreviation 'na' is used to show that data are 'not available'.

LEADING COMPANIES   Number shown: **50**   Total sales ($ mil): **7,697**   Total employment (000): **29.2**

Company Name	Address				CEO Name	Phone	Co. Type	Sales ($ mil)	Empl. (000)
Patent Construction Systems	1 Mack Centre Dr	Paramus	NJ	07652	Derek C. Hathaway	201-261-5600	P	1,735	15.3
Connell Co.	45 Cardinal Dr	Westfield	NJ	07090	Grover Connell	908-233-0700	R	1,275*	0.1
Bat Rentals Inc.	2771 S Industrial Rd	Las Vegas	NV	89109	Kevin Rodgers	702-731-1122	R	1,043*	1.9
Sunbelt Rentals Inc.	611 Templeton Ave	Charlotte	NC	28203	Bruce Dressel	704-969-2700	S	545*	1.0
Weeks Marine Inc.	216 N Ave E	Cranford	NJ	07016	Richard S Weeks	908-272-4010	R	300	1.0
American Equipment Inc.	2106 Anderson Dr	Greenville	SC	29602	Charles Snyder	864-295-7800	S	293*	2.5
Holt of California	PO Box X	Sacramento	CA	95813	Ken Munroe	916-991-8200	R	288*	0.5
L.B. Foster Co.	415 Holiday Dr	Pittsburgh	PA	15220	Lee B Foster II	412-928-3400	P	242	0.8
Aggregate Equipment and Supply	1601 N Main St	East Peoria	IL	61611	Steve Micheletti	309-694-6644	R	220	0.6
ADCO Equipment Inc.	3455 S Gabriel	Pico Rivera	CA	90660	Lonnie E Duncan	562-695-0748	R	173*	0.2
American United Global Inc.	11634 Patton Rd	Downey	CA	90241	Robert M Rubin	425-803-5400	P	164	0.5
Western Power & Equipment	4601 N E 7th Ave	Vancouver	WA	98662	Dean McLain	360-253-2346	P	164	0.5
Terteling Company Inc.	3823 N 36th St	Boise	ID	83703	Joseph L Terteling	208-338-5200	R	121*	0.3
Morrow Equipment L.L.C.	P O Box 3306	Salem	OR	97302	Christian Chalupny	503-585-5721	R	65	0.2
D and D Equipment Rental Inc.	1101 E Spring St	Long Beach	CA	90807	Leslie Farrow	562-595-4555	S	60*	0.1
McCann Industries Inc.	543 S Rowting Rd	Addison	IL	60101	D Kruepke	630-627-8700	R	60	0.2
Strawn Rentals	10966 Harry Hines	Dallas	TX	75220	Bob E Brothers	214-357-4301	R	54*	0.1
George J. Igel and Company Inc.	2040 Alum Creek Dr	Columbus	OH	43207	John B Igel	614-445-8421	R	50	0.3
Victor L. Phillips Co.	P O Box 4915	Kansas City	MO	64120	James W Foreman	816-241-9290	S	50	0.1
Yezbak Enterprises	108 N Beeson Blvd	Uniontown	PA	15401		724-438-5543	R	50*	<0.1
S and R Equipment Company Inc.	P O Box 240	Perrysburg	OH	43552	Bill Rogers	419-872-8720	S	43	0.2
Brown Rental Equipment Inc.	621 South Fwy	Fort Worth	TX	76104	Gary T Brown	817-332-4191	R	42*	<0.1
Beco Construction Power Co.	5555 Dahlia St	Commerce City	CO	80022	KF Wilhelm	303-288-2613	R	41	<0.1
Raymond Equipment Inc.	PO Box 35096	Louisville	KY	40232		502-966-2118	R	40*	<0.1
G.W. Van Keppel Co.	P O Box 2923	Kansas City	KS	66110	TE Walker	913-281-4800	R	37*	0.1
AME Inc.	PO Box 909	Fort Mill	SC	29716	Frank Campbell	803-548-7766	R	35	0.2
E.F. Craven Co.	P O Box 20807	Greensboro	NC	27420	CC Carson	336-292-6921	R	35*	<0.1
C.J. Hughes Construction Co.	P O Box 7305	Huntington	WV	25776	James D Hughes	304-522-3868	R	33*	0.2
Herc-U-Lift Inc.	5655 Hwy 12 W	Maple Plain	MN	55359	Les Nielsen	612-479-2501	R	33	0.1
White Star Machinery & Supply	P O Box 1180	Wichita	KS	67201	J Engels	316-838-3321	S	32*	<0.1
E.A. Martin Machinery Co.	PO Box 988	Springfield	MO	65801	Don Martin, Jr	417-866-6651	R	30*	0.2
Maness Industries Inc.	P O Box 90939	Long Beach	CA	90809	Kenneth P Maness	562-595-4555	R	30*	0.2
Toyota Material Handling	21053 Alexander Ct	Hayward	CA	94545	Rich Andres	510-887-0500	R	29*	0.2
McAllister Equipment Co.	12500 S Cicero Ave	Alsip	IL	60803	Craig Harris	708-389-7700	R	26	0.1
OCT Equipment Inc.	7100 S W 3rd Ave	Oklahoma City	OK	73128	Robert H Vaughn	405-789-6812	R	23*	<0.1
Williams Crane and Rigging Inc.	938 E 4th St	Richmond	VA	23224	John D Williams Jr	804-233-9221	S	22*	<0.1
Albany Ladder Company Inc.	1586 Central Ave	Albany	NY	12205	Anthony Groat	518-869-5335	P	20*	0.2
Perry Engineering Company Inc.	1945 Millwood Pike	Winchester	VA	22602	RW Werner	540-667-4310	R	20*	0.3
Hoffman International Inc.	300 S Randolphville	Piscataway	NJ	08855	WA Hoffman Jr	732-752-3600	R	19*	<0.1
Rasmussen Equipment Co.	3333 W 2100 S	Salt Lake City	UT	84119	Richard F Rasmussen	801-972-5588	R	19*	<0.1
Pacific American Commercial Co.	PO Box 3742	Seattle	WA	98124	Ted Obermeite	206-762-3550	R	17*	<0.1
S.E.S. Inc.	1400 Powis Rd	West Chicago	IL	60185	SL Martines	630-231-4840	R	17	<0.1
Higgins Erectors and Haulers Inc.	PO Box 1008	Buffalo	NY	14240	Jeffrey Higgins	716-821-8000	R	15*	0.1
Interstate Equipment Co.	1604 Salisbury Rd	Statesville	NC	28677	Franklin H Eller	704-873-9048	R	15*	<0.1
Wales Industrial Service Inc.	P O Box 2298	Waco	TX	76703		254-772-3310	R	14*	<0.1
United Crane & Shovel Service	PO Box 8	Kenilworth	NJ	07033	Timothy H Shinn	908-245-6260	R	13*	<0.1
Washington Corporations	P O Box 16630	Missoula	MT	59808	Mike Haizht	406-523-1300	R	12*	0.1
N.E. Finch Co.	PO Box 5187	Peoria	IL	61601	Thomas E Finch	309-671-1433	R	12	<0.1
Reco Crane Inc.	PO Box 10296	New Orleans	LA	70181	Walter Crory	504-733-6881	R	11	<0.1
U.S. and Gentges Inc.	P O Box 125	Jefferson City	MO	65102	James V Rau	573-635-6171	R	11*	<0.1

Source: Ward's Business Directory of U.S. Private and Public Companies, Volumes 1 and 2, 2000. The company type code used is as follows: P - Public, R - Private, S - Subsidiary, D - Division, J - Joint Venture, A - Affiliate, G - Group, N - Company type not reported. Sales are in millions of dollars, employees are in thousands. An asterisk (*) indicates an estimated sales volume. The symbol < stands for 'less than'. Company names and addresses are truncated, in some cases, to fit into the available space.

LOCATION BY STATE AND REGIONAL CONCENTRATION

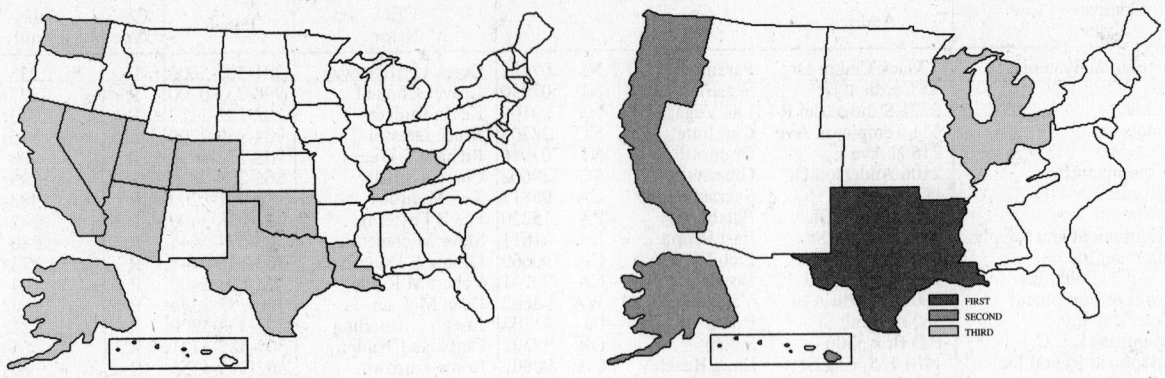

FIRST
SECOND
THIRD

INDUSTRY DATA BY STATE

State	Establishments Total (number)	Establishments % of U.S.	Employment Total (number)	Employment % of U.S.	Employment Per Estab.	Payroll Total ($ mil.)	Payroll Per Empl. ($)	Revenues Total ($ mil.)	Revenues % of U.S.	Revenues Per Estab. ($)
Texas	486	12.3	6,277	15.1	13	217.8	34,703	1,133.9	16.4	2,333,039
California	557	14.1	6,153	14.8	11	211.2	34,331	964.3	14.0	1,731,162
Louisiana	256	6.5	4,365	10.5	17	149.2	34,174	758.9	11.0	2,964,375
Florida	235	5.9	1,588	3.8	7	52.7	33,176	234.2	3.4	996,804
Ohio	117	3.0	1,278	3.1	11	45.8	35,867	220.1	3.2	1,881,231
New York	144	3.6	1,235	3.0	9	45.1	36,513	217.9	3.2	1,513,375
New Jersey	74	1.9	798	1.9	11	31.6	39,539	201.1	2.9	2,717,189
Nevada	58	1.5	945	2.3	16	37.1	39,292	186.0	2.7	3,206,069
Illinois	131	3.3	846	2.0	6	33.0	39,044	176.0	2.6	1,343,221
Georgia	120	3.0	1,214	2.9	10	37.7	31,025	175.8	2.5	1,464,667
Arizona	86	2.2	1,281	3.1	15	38.9	30,334	169.7	2.5	1,973,721
Kentucky	62	1.6	813	2.0	13	34.3	42,246	164.8	2.4	2,657,452
North Carolina	103	2.6	1,144	2.8	11	33.8	29,584	163.4	2.4	1,586,117
Washington	90	2.3	961	2.3	11	34.8	36,252	147.4	2.1	1,638,278
Colorado	83	2.1	783	1.9	9	29.1	37,217	143.1	2.1	1,723,518
Pennsylvania	93	2.4	1,048	2.5	11	34.0	32,445	133.1	1.9	1,431,108
Oklahoma	84	2.1	735	1.8	9	25.9	35,264	121.9	1.8	1,450,667
Michigan	100	2.5	699	1.7	7	24.9	35,688	120.7	1.8	1,206,640
Indiana	57	1.4	573	1.4	10	19.7	34,421	105.8	1.5	1,855,404
Alabama	63	1.6	773	1.9	12	23.0	29,713	105.6	1.5	1,676,365
Tennessee	68	1.7	667	1.6	10	21.5	32,231	94.0	1.4	1,382,324
Wisconsin	37	0.9	402	1.0	11	17.4	43,199	92.6	1.3	2,503,432
Utah	44	1.1	378	0.9	9	12.7	33,548	64.0	0.9	1,453,818
Massachusetts	52	1.3	323	0.8	6	13.8	42,746	59.3	0.9	1,141,288
South Carolina	43	1.1	340	0.8	8	11.1	32,668	56.9	0.8	1,322,744
West Virginia	34	0.9	236	0.6	7	8.2	34,780	43.8	0.6	1,287,147
Mississippi	35	0.9	350	0.8	10	10.7	30,500	42.7	0.6	1,221,286
Iowa	30	0.8	233	0.6	8	8.6	36,867	40.6	0.6	1,351,867
Arkansas	45	1.1	293	0.7	7	8.2	28,065	33.7	0.5	749,400
Alaska	23	0.6	111	0.3	5	5.5	49,541	30.1	0.4	1,310,130
Connecticut	8	0.2	115	0.3	14	8.6	74,904	28.3	0.4	3,537,000
Minnesota	24	0.6	99	0.2	4	4.2	42,162	18.5	0.3	772,708
Hawaii	20	0.5	67	0.2	3	2.2	33,000	7.3	0.1	362,950
Virginia	91	2.3	750*	-	-	(D)	-	(D)	-	-
Oregon	64	1.6	750*	-	-	(D)	-	(D)	-	-
Maryland	59	1.5	750*	-	-	(D)	-	(D)	-	-
Missouri	56	1.4	375*	-	-	(D)	-	(D)	-	-
New Mexico	46	1.2	750*	-	-	(D)	-	(D)	-	-
Kansas	37	0.9	375*	-	-	(D)	-	(D)	-	-
Wyoming	37	0.9	375*	-	-	(D)	-	(D)	-	-
Nebraska	17	0.4	60*	-	-	(D)	-	(D)	-	-
North Dakota	16	0.4	60*	-	-	(D)	-	(D)	-	-
Idaho	14	0.4	60*	-	-	(D)	-	(D)	-	-
New Hampshire	12	0.3	60*	-	-	(D)	-	(D)	-	-
Delaware	11	0.3	60*	-	-	(D)	-	(D)	-	-
Maine	11	0.3	175*	-	-	(D)	-	(D)	-	-
Montana	11	0.3	60*	-	-	(D)	-	(D)	-	-

Source: 1997 *Economic Census*. The states are in descending order of revenues or establishments (if revenue data are missing for the majority). The symbol (D) appears when data are withheld to prevent disclosure of competitive information. States marked with (D) are sorted by number of establishments. A dash (-) indicates that the data element cannot be calculated. * indicates the midpoint of a range; 175, for example is the range 100-249. Shaded *states* on the state map indicate those states which have proportionately greater representation in the industry than would be indicated by the state's population; the ratio is based on total revenues or number of establishments. Shaded *regions* indicate where the industry is regionally most concentrated.

NAICS 532420 - OFFICE MACHINERY AND EQUIPMENT RENTAL AND LEASING

GENERAL STATISTICS

Year	Establishments (number)	Employment (number)	Payroll ($ million)	Revenues ($ million)	Employees per Establishment (number)	Revenues per Establishment ($)	Payroll per Employee ($)
1997	1,346	12,007	671.0	6,181.0	8.9	4,592,125	55,884

Source: *Economic Census of the United States*, 1997. This is a newly defined industry. Data for prior years were unavailable at the time of publication but may become available over time.

INDICES OF CHANGE

Year	Establishments (number)	Employment (number)	Payroll ($ million)	Revenues ($ million)	Employees per Establishment (number)	Revenues per Establishment ($)	Payroll per Employee ($)
1997	100.0	100.0	100.0	100.0	100.0	100.0	100.0

Sources: Same as General Statistics. The values shown reflect change from the base year, 1997. Values above 100 mean greater than 1997, values below 100 mean less than 1997, and a value of 100 in the 1982-96 or 1998-2001 period means same as 1997. Values followed by a 'p' are projections by the editors; 'e' stands for extrapolation. Data are the most recent available at this level of detail.

SIC INDUSTRIES RELATED TO NAICS 532420

Each new NAICS code represents an industry that used to be part of an SIC or a part of several SIC industries. Data in this table are shown to provide transitional information for these cases. All available data for the precursor SIC(s) are shown. Even if only a part of an SIC is included in the NAICS, *all* data for the SIC are reproduced. If the SIC industry is not marked as being a part (pt) of the NAICS, the entire industry is embedded in the NAICS data. The SIC composition of the new industry provides some hints of the relative importance of its "ancestors." Data marked with a 'p' are projected. Projections begin with 1982 data. Data earlier than 1990 are not shown but are reflected in the projections.

SIC	Industry	1990	1991	1992	1993	1994	1995	1996	1997
7359	**Equipment Rental & Leasing, nec (pt)**								
	Establishments (number)	16,213	16,430	17,687	17,439	17,564	17,607	17,431p	17,486p
	Employment (thousands)	145.6	143.2	134.1	139.9	143.8	151.3	148.8p	150.4p
	Revenues ($ million)	15,481.0	15,265.0	15,482.0	16,816.0	18,607.0	20,677.0	20,949.0	21,947.1p
7377	**Computer Rental & Leasing**								
	Establishments (number)	808	875	854	766	812	821	740p	715p
	Employment (thousands)	15.2	13.1	8.1	7.8	7.8	10.2	9.2p	9.0p
	Revenues ($ million)	2,644.0	2,396.0	2,385.0	2,482.0	2,658.0	2,937.0	3,295.0	3,157.9p

Source: *Economic Census of the United States*, 1992, annual surveys of economic sectors conducted by the Bureau of the Census, and estimates or projections based on the 1982-1992 period; not all data are shown. 'e' marks estimates made by the editors; 'p' indicates projections based on time series. A dash (-) indicates that data for this SIC or year were not available. The abbreviation (pt) next to the industry name indicates that only a part of the industry is present within the NAICS data. If no (pt) is shown, the entire industry is contained within the NAICS data.

SELECTED RATIOS

For 1997	Avg. of Information	Analyzed Industry	Index	For 1997	Avg. of Information	Analyzed Industry	Index
Employees per establishment	6	9	151	Payroll per establishment	144,276	498,514	346
Revenue per establishment	835,727	4,592,125	549	Payroll as % of revenue	17	11	63
Revenue per employee	141,515	514,783	364	Payroll per employee	24,430	55,884	229

Sources: Same as General Statistics. The 'Average' column represents the average for the industry sector, in 1997, where the currently shown industry is classified. The Index shows the relationship between the Average and the Analyzed Industry. For example, 100 means that they are equal; 500 that the Analyzed Industry is five times the average; 50 means that the Analyzed Industry is half the national average. The abbreviation 'na' is used to show that data are 'not available'.

LEADING COMPANIES   Number shown: **35**   Total sales ($ mil): **7,403**   Total employment (000): **10.0**

Company Name	Address				CEO Name	Phone	Co. Type	Sales ($ mil)	Empl. (000)
Comdisco Inc.	6111 N River Rd	Rosemont	IL	60018	Nicholas K. Pontikes	847-698-3000	P	4,159	3.6
El Camino Resources Intern. Inc.	21051 Warner	Woodland Hills	CA	91367	David Harmon	818-226-6600	R	650	1.0
GENICOM Corp.	14800 Conf Ctr	Chantilly	VA	20151	Paul T Winn	703-802-9200	P	453	1.5
Copelco Capital Inc.	700 Eastgate Dr	Mount Laurel	NJ	08054	Robert Lemenze	609-231-9600	S	400*	0.6
Leasing Solutions Inc.	10 Almaden Blvd	San Jose	CA	95113	Louis Adimare	408-995-6565	P	300	0.3
Electro Rent Corp.	6060 Sepulveda	Van Nuys	CA	91411	Daniel Greenberg	818-786-2525	P	270	0.7
Capital Associates Inc.	7175 W Jefferson	Lakewood	CO	80235	James D Walker	303-980-1000	P	243	0.2
LINC Group Inc.	303 E Wacker Dr	Chicago	IL	60601	RE Lang	312-946-1000	R	120*	0.2
Winthrop Resources Corp.	1015 Opus Center	Minnetonka	MN	55343	Ronald Palmer	612-936-0226	S	109	0.1
USA Capital L.L.C.	88 Steele St	Denver	CO	80206	Jeffery G Jones	303-321-0400	R	100	<0.1
BancBoston Leasing Inc.	100 Federal St	Boston	MA	02110	James Westly	617-434-0131	S	85*	0.1
CRA Inc.	11011 N 23rd Ave	Phoenix	AZ	85029		602-944-1548	S	79*	<0.1
Amplicon Inc.	5 Hutton Centre Dr	Santa Ana	CA	92707		714-751-7551	P	69	0.2
Balboa Capital Corp.	2010 Main St	Irvine	CA	92614		949-756-0800	R	61*	0.1
InaCom Information Systems Inc.	393 Inverness Dr S	Englewood	CO	80112		303-754-5004	D	45*	0.2
CLG Inc.	3001 Spring Forest	Raleigh	NC	27604	Dean Painter	919-872-7920	S	40*	<0.1
Paramount Financial Corp.	One Jericho Plz	Jericho	NY	11753	Glenn Nortman	516-938-3400	P	38	0.6
Technical & Scientific Application	2040 W S Houst	Houston	TX	77043	William C Smith	713-935-1500	R	26*	<0.1
Alliance Corporate Resources Inc.	425 Metro Pl N	Dublin	OH	43017	David M Ciolek	614-792-4200	S	25	<0.1
InaCom Computer Rentals	10810 Farnam Dr	Omaha	NE	68154	Bill L Fairfield	402-392-3900	D	17*	<0.1
Electro Rent Corporation Data	6060 Sepulveda	Van Nuys	CA	91411		818-787-2100	D	16*	<0.1
Rent-A-PC Inc.	265 Oser Ave	Hauppauge	NY	11788	Julian Sandler	516-273-8888	R	15	<0.1
Continental Information Systems	45 Broadway Atrium	New York	NY	10006	Michael L Rosen	212-771-1000	P	14	<0.1
Rent-A-Bit Inc.	1247 W 3rd St	Osceola	IN	46561	Tom LaFree	219-674-5973	R	14*	<0.1
Chesterfield Financial Corp.	16100 N Outer Forty	Chesterfield	MO	63017	Alex Nowicki	636-532-2827	R	11*	<0.1
Cadshare Resources Inc.	P O Box 11859	Charlotte	NC	28220	Paul Pazzaglini	704-845-2845	R	10	<0.1
Rent-A-Computer Inc.	4853 Cordell Ave	Bethesda	MD	20814	Steve Bradley	301-951-0811	R	8*	<0.1
VeriFone Finance Inc.	16100 S W 72nd	Portland	OR	97224		503-684-6328	S	6*	<0.1
Cameron Computers Inc.	28 State St	Pittsford	NY	14534	Joseph Cameron	716-427-8190	R	5	<0.1
Phoenix Computer Associates Inc.	10 Sasco Hill Rd	Fairfield	CT	06430	Lawrence Erdmann	203-226-7545	R	5*	<0.1
C.W. Leasing Inc.	2554 Lincoln Blvd	Venice	CA	90291	Cynthia Walker	310-839-1775	R	3*	<0.1
Custom Computer Service Inc.	P O Box 689	New Castle	DE	19720	Robert Oratorio	302-325-5511	R	2	<0.1
Silicon Composers Inc.	256 Ferne Ave	Palo Alto	CA	94306	George A Nicol	650-493-6427	R	2*	<0.1
Sun Atlantic Corp.	3720 Vineland Rd	Orlando	FL	32811	Russell I Kacir	407-843-0721	R	2	<0.1
BRS Leasing Inc.	3401 E McDowell	Phoenix	AZ	85008	Virgil Bland	602-277-3282	R	1	<0.1

Source: *Ward's Business Directory of U.S. Private and Public Companies*, Volumes 1 and 2, 2000. The company type code used is as follows: P - Public, R - Private, S - Subsidiary, D - Division, J - Joint Venture, A - Affiliate, G - Group, N - Company type not reported. Sales are in millions of dollars, employees are in thousands. An asterisk (*) indicates an estimated sales volume. The symbol < stands for 'less than'. Company names and addresses are truncated, in some cases, to fit into the available space.

LOCATION BY STATE AND REGIONAL CONCENTRATION

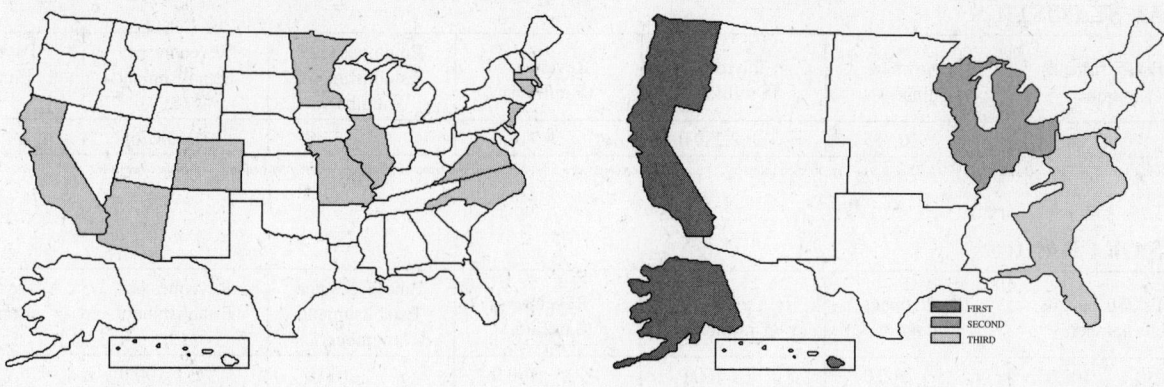

FIRST
SECOND
THIRD

INDUSTRY DATA BY STATE

State	Establishments Total (number)	Establishments % of U.S.	Employment Total (number)	Employment % of U.S.	Employment Per Estab.	Payroll Total ($ mil.)	Payroll Per Empl. ($)	Revenues Total ($ mil.)	Revenues % of U.S.	Revenues Per Estab. ($)
California	184	13.7	2,493	20.8	14	141.8	56,881	1,341.6	21.7	7,291,418
Illinois	103	7.7	1,038	8.6	10	75.9	73,131	689.5	11.2	6,694,184
Florida	82	6.1	651	5.4	8	30.7	47,204	305.0	4.9	3,719,988
New Jersey	73	5.4	906	7.5	12	45.0	49,643	283.3	4.6	3,880,986
Missouri	22	1.6	322	2.7	15	19.1	59,441	252.6	4.1	11,481,818
Massachusetts	48	3.6	714	5.9	15	34.4	48,185	249.3	4.0	5,193,354
Ohio	49	3.6	414	3.4	8	23.7	57,215	246.2	4.0	5,024,367
Arizona	33	2.5	339	2.8	10	17.3	50,994	229.8	3.7	6,962,606
Connecticut	38	2.8	498	4.1	13	32.1	64,442	227.5	3.7	5,987,211
Minnesota	29	2.2	288	2.4	10	19.9	69,038	219.5	3.6	7,569,069
Pennsylvania	43	3.2	286	2.4	7	19.8	69,245	212.9	3.4	4,952,209
Texas	91	6.8	369	3.1	4	24.2	65,645	210.3	3.4	2,311,066
Virginia	33	2.5	248	2.1	8	13.7	55,137	205.0	3.3	6,212,758
North Carolina	22	1.6	209	1.7	10	13.1	62,746	165.1	2.7	7,505,455
Georgia	41	3.0	237	2.0	6	14.5	61,219	162.5	2.6	3,962,561
Michigan	39	2.9	227	1.9	6	15.5	68,150	149.4	2.4	3,829,564
New York	96	7.1	624	5.2	7	28.6	45,785	148.5	2.4	1,547,177
Washington	40	3.0	417	3.5	10	17.0	40,878	126.4	2.0	3,159,975
Colorado	38	2.8	344	2.9	9	17.7	51,494	123.2	2.0	3,242,474
Indiana	19	1.4	143	1.2	8	7.7	53,860	98.6	1.6	5,187,579
Nevada	17	1.3	96	0.8	6	3.8	39,813	23.7	0.4	1,393,882
Louisiana	15	1.1	181	1.5	12	6.5	35,663	19.9	0.3	1,325,533
Oregon	17	1.3	67	0.6	4	3.2	47,657	11.3	0.2	667,118
Tennessee	21	1.6	50	0.4	2	1.7	34,940	7.6	0.1	359,619
Wisconsin	7	0.5	37	0.3	5	1.6	43,135	5.6	0.1	798,571
South Carolina	10	0.7	42	0.3	4	1.2	27,595	4.8	0.1	475,100
Oklahoma	7	0.5	17	0.1	2	0.3	16,000	2.5	0.0	362,286
Montana	8	0.6	16	0.1	2	0.3	21,688	1.1	0.0	142,375
New Mexico	7	0.5	13	0.1	2	0.3	22,154	1.0	0.0	144,857
Maryland	25	1.9	375*	-	-	(D)	-	(D)	-	-
Alabama	14	1.0	60*	-	-	(D)	-	(D)	-	-
Kansas	12	0.9	60*	-	-	(D)	-	(D)	-	-
Nebraska	9	0.7	60*	-	-	(D)	-	(D)	-	-
Utah	8	0.6	60*	-	-	(D)	-	(D)	-	-
Kentucky	7	0.5	10*	-	-	(D)	-	(D)	-	-

Source: 1997 *Economic Census*. The states are in descending order of revenues or establishments (if revenue data are missing for the majority). The symbol (D) appears when data are withheld to prevent disclosure of competitive information. States marked with (D) are sorted by number of establishments. A dash (-) indicates that the data element cannot be calculated. * indicates the midpoint of a range; 175, for example is the range 100-249. Shaded *states* on the state map indicate those states which have proportionately greater representation in the industry than would be indicated by the state's population; the ratio is based on total revenues or number of establishments. Shaded *regions* indicate where the industry is regionally most concentrated.

NAICS 532490 - COMMERCIAL AND INDUSTRIAL MACHINERY AND EQUIPMENT RENTAL AND LEASING NEC

GENERAL STATISTICS

Year	Establishments (number)	Employment (number)	Payroll ($ million)	Revenues ($ million)	Employees per Establishment (number)	Revenues per Establishment ($)	Payroll per Employee ($)
1997	5,947	70,775	2,230.0	9,716.0	11.9	1,633,765	31,508

Source: Economic Census of the United States, 1997. This is a newly defined industry. Data for prior years were unavailable at the time of publication but may become available over time.

INDICES OF CHANGE

Year	Establishments (number)	Employment (number)	Payroll ($ million)	Revenues ($ million)	Employees per Establishment (number)	Revenues per Establishment ($)	Payroll per Employee ($)
1997	100.0	100.0	100.0	100.0	100.0	100.0	100.0

Sources: Same as General Statistics. The values shown reflect change from the base year, 1997. Values above 100 mean greater than 1997, values below 100 mean less than 1997, and a value of 100 in the 1982-96 or 1998-2001 period means same as 1997. Values followed by a 'p' are projections by the editors; 'e' stands for extrapolation. Data are the most recent available at this level of detail.

SIC INDUSTRIES RELATED TO NAICS 532490

Each new NAICS code represents an industry that used to be part of an SIC or a part of several SIC industries. Data in this table are shown to provide transitional information for these cases. All available data for the precursor SIC(s) are shown. Even if only a part of an SIC is included in the NAICS, *all* data for the SIC are reproduced. If the SIC industry is not marked as being a part (pt) of the NAICS, the entire industry is embedded in the NAICS data. The SIC composition of the new industry provides some hints of the relative importance of its "ancestors." Data marked with a 'p' are projected. Projections begin with 1982 data. Data earlier than 1990 are not shown but are reflected in the projections.

SIC	Industry	1990	1991	1992	1993	1994	1995	1996	1997
7352	**Medical Equipment Rental & Leasing (pt)**								
	Establishments (number)	1,959	2,270	3,276	3,248	3,292	3,220	3,531p	3,708p
	Employment (thousands)	20.8	23.7	31.1	31.1	33.3	33.2	36.8p	39.0p
	Revenues ($ million)	2,511.0	2,783.0	3,210.0	3,344.0	2,997.0	3,088.0	3,679.0	3,867.5p
7359	**Equipment Rental & Leasing, nec (pt)**								
	Establishments (number)	16,213	16,430	17,687	17,439	17,564	17,607	17,431p	17,486p
	Employment (thousands)	145.6	143.2	134.1	139.9	143.8	151.3	148.8p	150.4p
	Revenues ($ million)	15,481.0	15,265.0	15,482.0	16,816.0	18,607.0	20,677.0	20,949.0	21,947.1p
7819	**Services Allied to Motion Pictures (pt)**								
	Establishments (number)	2,984	2,955	3,895	3,799	3,691	3,289	3,584p	3,622p
	Employment (thousands)	113.1	102.4	162.2	158.8	130.9	136.7	160.9p	169.5p
	Revenues ($ million)	-	-	7,514.7					
7922	**Theatrical Producers & Services (pt)**								
	Establishments (number)	4,470	4,992	5,924	6,229	6,323	6,428	6,542p	6,792p
	Employment (thousands)	63.9	63.1	69.5	88.8	77.8	79.3	87.3p	91.2p
	Revenues ($ million)	-	-	5,730.5	4,396.6p	4,647.8p	4,899.0p	5,150.2p	5,401.4p

Source: Economic Census of the United States, 1992, annual surveys of economic sectors conducted by the Bureau of the Census, and estimates or projections based on the 1982-1992 period; not all data are shown. 'e' marks estimates made by the editors; 'p' indicates projections based on time series. A dash (-) indicates that data for this SIC or year were not available. The abbreviation (pt) next to the industry name indicates that only a part of the industry is present within the NAICS data. If no (pt) is shown, the entire industry is contained within the NAICS data.

SELECTED RATIOS

For 1997	Avg. of Information	Analyzed Industry	Index	For 1997	Avg. of Information	Analyzed Industry	Index
Employees per establishment	6	12	202	Payroll per establishment	144,276	374,979	260
Revenue per establishment	835,727	1,633,765	195	Payroll as % of revenue	17	23	133
Revenue per employee	141,515	137,280	97	Payroll per employee	24,430	31,508	129

Sources: Same as General Statistics. The 'Average' column represents the average for the industry sector, in 1997, where the currently shown industry is classified. The Index shows the relationship between the Average and the Analyzed Industry. For example, 100 means that they are equal; 500 that the Analyzed Industry is five times the average; 50 means that the Analyzed Industry is half the national average. The abbreviation 'na' is used to show that data are 'not available'.

LEADING COMPANIES   Number shown: **13**   Total sales ($ mil): **2,566**   Total employment (000): **15.0**

Company Name	Address				CEO Name	Phone	Co. Type	Sales ($ mil)	Empl. (000)
Apria Healthcare Group Inc.	3560 Hyland Ave	Costa Mesa	CA	92626	Ralph V. Whitworth	714-427-2000	P	934	8.2
RoTech Medical Corp.	PO Box 536576	Orlando	FL	32853	Stephen P Griggs	407-841-2115	P	423	0.8
Copelco Capital Inc.	700 Eastgate Dr	Mount Laurel	NJ	08054	Robert Lemenze	609-231-9600	S	400*	0.6
Kinetic Concepts Inc.	PO Box 659508	San Antonio	TX	78265		210-524-9000	R	331	2.1
MEDIQ Inc.	1 MEDIQ Plz	Pennsauken	NJ	08110	Thomas E Carroll	609-665-9300	P	181	1.3
Ziegler Companies Inc.	PO Box 118	West Bend	WI	53095	Peter D Ziegler	262-334-5521	P	97	0.7
Universal Hospital Services Inc.	1250 Northland Plz	Bloomington	MN	55431	David E Dovenberg	612-893-3200	R	60	0.5
A-1 Coast Rentals Inc.	24000 Crenshaw	Torrance	CA	90505	Allan C Billings	310-326-1910	R	59*	<0.1
MediQuip International	1865 Summit Ave	Plano	TX	75074	Ralph Armstrong	972-423-1600	R	30*	<0.1
Home-Bound Medical Care Inc.	2165 Spicer Cr #1	Memphis	TN	38134	Kyle Altman	901-386-5061	S	20	0.6
King's Medical Co.	1920 Georgetown	Hudson	OH	44236	Samuel C Parris	330-653-3968	R	20	0.1
Chesterfield Financial Corp.	16100 N Outer Forty	Chesterfield	MO	63017	Alex Nowicki	636-532-2827	R	11*	<0.1
Continental Choice Care Inc.	P O Box 99	Florham Park	NJ	07932	Alvin S Trenk	973-898-9666	P	1	<0.1

Source: Ward's Business Directory of U.S. Private and Public Companies, Volumes 1 and 2, 2000. The company type code used is as follows: P - Public, R - Private, S - Subsidiary, D - Division, J - Joint Venture, A - Affiliate, G - Group, N - Company type not reported. Sales are in millions of dollars, employees are in thousands. An asterisk (*) indicates an estimated sales volume. The symbol < stands for 'less than'. Company names and addresses are truncated, in some cases, to fit into the available space.

LOCATION BY STATE AND REGIONAL CONCENTRATION

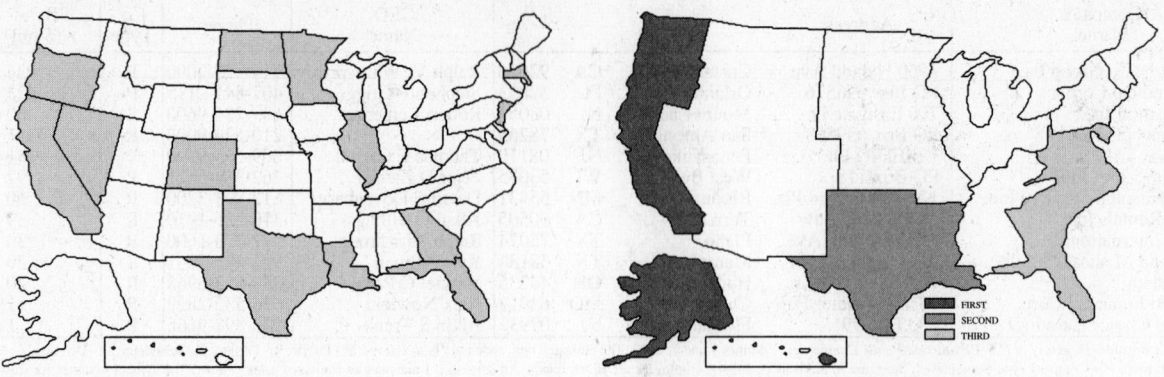

INDUSTRY DATA BY STATE

State	Establishments Total (number)	% of U.S.	Employment Total (number)	% of U.S.	Per Estab.	Payroll Total ($ mil.)	Per Empl. ($)	Revenues Total ($ mil.)	% of U.S.	Per Estab. ($)
California	819	13.8	18,838	26.6	23	587.3	31,178	2,027.3	20.9	2,475,284
Texas	551	9.3	6,622	9.4	12	198.3	29,941	882.5	9.1	1,601,566
Florida	508	8.5	4,990	7.1	10	145.6	29,185	700.1	7.2	1,378,132
New York	329	5.5	2,855	4.0	9	102.4	35,854	596.1	6.1	1,811,781
Illinois	252	4.2	2,705	3.8	11	105.0	38,807	546.0	5.6	2,166,575
New Jersey	146	2.5	1,831	2.6	13	72.7	39,723	437.2	4.5	2,994,397
Louisiana	140	2.4	2,889	4.1	21	89.3	30,924	373.4	3.8	2,667,371
Pennsylvania	219	3.7	2,044	2.9	9	67.5	33,019	310.4	3.2	1,417,288
Massachusetts	134	2.3	1,074	1.5	8	42.9	39,909	293.7	3.0	2,191,993
Georgia	148	2.5	2,237	3.2	15	55.8	24,941	275.9	2.8	1,863,946
Ohio	189	3.2	1,490	2.1	8	50.7	34,006	214.1	2.2	1,132,772
Minnesota	93	1.6	1,303	1.8	14	51.0	39,173	213.4	2.2	2,294,914
Virginia	142	2.4	1,814	2.6	13	52.4	28,863	188.9	1.9	1,330,592
Washington	121	2.0	1,478	2.1	12	48.1	32,524	187.0	1.9	1,545,215
Colorado	132	2.2	1,281	1.8	10	36.7	28,649	179.2	1.8	1,357,803
North Carolina	110	1.8	1,235	1.7	11	41.5	33,585	155.5	1.6	1,413,364
Arizona	128	2.2	1,467	2.1	11	43.0	29,301	150.3	1.5	1,173,937
Tennessee	119	2.0	1,054	1.5	9	36.2	34,338	147.2	1.5	1,237,143
Oregon	85	1.4	872	1.2	10	32.3	36,994	145.4	1.5	1,710,624
Indiana	100	1.7	650	0.9	7	25.7	39,500	105.8	1.1	1,057,860
Oklahoma	83	1.4	480	0.7	6	13.5	28,031	90.3	0.9	1,087,639
Arkansas	73	1.2	857	1.2	12	12.7	14,803	87.4	0.9	1,197,260
South Carolina	60	1.0	517	0.7	9	13.7	26,476	80.6	0.8	1,342,517
Wisconsin	76	1.3	511	0.7	7	16.9	33,123	76.3	0.8	1,003,513
Nevada	61	1.0	633	0.9	10	15.6	24,566	66.3	0.7	1,086,541
Connecticut	42	0.7	341	0.5	8	13.9	40,686	60.4	0.6	1,439,286
Iowa	53	0.9	348	0.5	7	10.3	29,474	48.7	0.5	918,038
Hawaii	47	0.8	638	0.9	14	9.9	15,470	37.3	0.4	794,000
North Dakota	24	0.4	231	0.3	10	5.8	25,126	32.0	0.3	1,334,375
Mississippi	44	0.7	158	0.2	4	5.7	35,759	29.0	0.3	659,159
Alaska	19	0.3	226	0.3	12	6.7	29,686	22.7	0.2	1,197,263
New Mexico	31	0.5	214	0.3	7	4.4	20,687	16.0	0.2	517,742
South Dakota	17	0.3	121	0.2	7	3.5	28,579	14.4	0.1	846,941
D.C.	13	0.2	99	0.1	8	4.0	39,970	14.4	0.1	1,109,154
Montana	29	0.5	147	0.2	5	3.0	20,313	13.5	0.1	465,793
Idaho	24	0.4	124	0.2	5	2.7	21,887	11.8	0.1	490,292
Wyoming	11	0.2	35	0.0	3	0.6	18,400	3.1	0.0	279,000
Michigan	163	2.7	1,750*	-	-	(D)	-	(D)	-	-
Missouri	130	2.2	1,750*	-	-	(D)	-	(D)	-	-
Alabama	80	1.3	750*	-	-	(D)	-	(D)	-	-
Maryland	76	1.3	750*	-	-	(D)	-	(D)	-	-
Kentucky	74	1.2	375*	-	-	(D)	-	(D)	-	-
Utah	57	1.0	375*	-	-	(D)	-	(D)	-	-
Kansas	49	0.8	375*	-	-	(D)	-	(D)	-	-
Nebraska	39	0.7	375*	-	-	(D)	-	(D)	-	-
West Virginia	32	0.5	375*	-	-	(D)	-	(D)	-	-
New Hampshire	24	0.4	175*	-	-	(D)	-	(D)	-	-
Maine	20	0.3	175*	-	-	(D)	-	(D)	-	-
Delaware	17	0.3	60*	-	-	(D)	-	(D)	-	-
Rhode Island	11	0.2	60*	-	-	(D)	-	(D)	-	-

Source: 1997 *Economic Census*. The states are in descending order of revenues or establishments (if revenue data are missing for the majority). The symbol (D) appears when data are withheld to prevent disclosure of competitive information. States marked with (D) are sorted by number of establishments. A dash (-) indicates that the data element cannot be calculated. * indicates the midpoint of a range; 175, for example is the range 100-249. Shaded *states* on the state map indicate those states which have proportionately greater representation in the industry than would be indicated by the state's population; the ratio is based on total revenues or number of establishments. Shaded *regions* indicate where the industry is regionally most concentrated.

NAICS 533110 - LESSORS OF INTANGIBLE ASSETS, EXCEPT COPYRIGHTED WORKS

GENERAL STATISTICS

Year	Establishments (number)	Employment (number)	Payroll ($ million)	Revenues ($ million)	Employees per Establishment (number)	Revenues per Establishment ($)	Payroll per Employee ($)
1997	2,151	25,792	1,075.0	11,264.0	12.0	5,236,634	41,680

Source: *Economic Census of the United States*, 1997. This is a newly defined industry. Data for prior years were unavailable at the time of publication but may become available over time.

INDICES OF CHANGE

Year	Establishments (number)	Employment (number)	Payroll ($ million)	Revenues ($ million)	Employees per Establishment (number)	Revenues per Establishment ($)	Payroll per Employee ($)
1997	100.0	100.0	100.0	100.0	100.0	100.0	100.0

Sources: Same as General Statistics. The values shown reflect change from the base year, 1997. Values above 100 mean greater than 1997, values below 100 mean less than 1997, and a value of 100 in the 1982-96 or 1998-2001 period means same as 1997. Values followed by a 'p' are projections by the editors; 'e' stands for extrapolation. Data are the most recent available at this level of detail.

SIC INDUSTRIES RELATED TO NAICS 533110

Each new NAICS code represents an industry that used to be part of an SIC or a part of several SIC industries. Data in this table are shown to provide transitional information for these cases. All available data for the precursor SIC(s) are shown. Even if only a part of an SIC is included in the NAICS, *all* data for the SIC are reproduced. If the SIC industry is not marked as being a part (pt) of the NAICS, the entire industry is embedded in the NAICS data. The SIC composition of the new industry provides some hints of the relative importance of its "ancestors." Data marked with a 'p' are projected. Projections begin with 1982 data. Data earlier than 1990 are not shown but are reflected in the projections.

SIC	Industry	1990	1991	1992	1993	1994	1995	1996	1997
6792	**Oil Royalty Traders (pt)**								
	Establishments (number)	-	-	746	-	-	-	-	-
	Employment (thousands)	-	-	2.2	-	-	-	-	-
	Revenues ($ million)	-	-	686.7	-	-	-	-	-
6794	**Patent Owners and Lessors**								
	Establishments (number)	-	-	1,514	-	-	-	-	-
	Employment (thousands)	-	-	17.4	-	-	-	-	-
	Revenues ($ million)	-	-	5,412.5	-	-	-	-	-

Source: *Economic Census of the United States*, 1992, annual surveys of economic sectors conducted by the Bureau of the Census, and estimates or projections based on the 1982-1992 period; not all data are shown. 'e' marks estimates made by the editors; 'p' indicates projections based on time series. A dash (-) indicates that data for this SIC or year were not available. The abbreviation (pt) next to the industry name indicates that only a part of the industry is present within the NAICS data. If no (pt) is shown, the entire industry is contained within the NAICS data.

SELECTED RATIOS

For 1997	Avg. of Information	Analyzed Industry	Index	For 1997	Avg. of Information	Analyzed Industry	Index
Employees per establishment	6	12	203	Payroll per establishment	144,276	499,768	346
Revenue per establishment	835,727	5,236,634	627	Payroll as % of revenue	17	10	55
Revenue per employee	141,515	436,725	309	Payroll per employee	24,430	41,680	171

Sources: Same as General Statistics. The 'Average' column represents the average for the industry sector, in 1997, where the currently shown industry is classified. The Index shows the relationship between the Average and the Analyzed Industry. For example, 100 means that they are equal; 500 that the Analyzed Industry is five times the average; 50 means that the Analyzed Industry is half the national average. The abbreviation 'na' is used to show that data are 'not available'.

LEADING COMPANIES   Number shown: **75**   Total sales ($ mil): **346,740**   Total employment (000): **3,533.1**

Company Name	Address				CEO Name	Phone	Co. Type	Sales ($ mil)	Empl. (000)
GNC Franchising Inc.	300 6th Ave	Pittsburgh	PA	15222	William Watts	412-288-4600	S	140,000	0.6
Carlson Holdings Inc.	PO Box 59159	Minneapolis	MN	55459	Marilyn C Nelson	612-449-1000	R	22,000	165.0
Sony USA Inc.	550 Madison Ave	New York	NY	10022		212-833-6800	R	20,000	32.0
Intern. Center Entrepreneurial	PO Box 777	Cypress	TX	77410		281-256-4100	R	17,100	0.1
McDonald's Corp.	McDonald's Plz	Oak Brook	IL	60523	Jack M Greenberg	630-623-3000	P	13,259	284.0
Manpower Inc.	PO Box 2053	Milwaukee	WI	53201	Jeffrey A Joerres	414-961-1000	P	8,814	15.0
Tricon Global Restaurants Inc.	1441 Gardiner Ln	Louisville	KY	40213	David C Novak	502-874-8300	P	8,468	260.0
7-Eleven Inc.	P O Box 711	Dallas	TX	75221	Clark J Matthews II	214-828-7587	S	7,350	32.4
MicroAge Inc.	2400 S MicroAge	Tempe	AZ	85282	Jeffrey D McKeever	480-366-2000	P	6,150	4.5
Turner Broadcasting System Inc.	1 CNN Ctr	Atlanta	GA	30348	Terence McGuirk	404-827-1700	S	5,401*	11.0
Cendant Corp.	6 Sylvan Way	Parsippany	NJ	07054	Henry Silverman	212-413-1800	P	5,284	35.0
Taco Bell Corp.	17901 Von Karman	Irvine	CA	92614	Peter C Waller	949-863-4500	S	5,000*	120.0
Pizza Hut Inc.	14841 Dallas Pkwy	Dallas	TX	75240	Michael S Rawlings	972-338-7700	D	4,800	135.0
Tandy Corp.	PO Box 17180	Fort Worth	TX	76102	Leonard H Roberts	817-390-3700	P	4,788	38.2
CFC Franchising Co.	3355 Michaelson Dr	Irvine	CA	92612	Craig Bushey	949-251-5700	S	4,643*	<0.1
Olsten Corp.	175 Broad Hollow	Melville	NY	11747	E H Blechschmidt	516-844-7800	P	4,603*	700.8
InaCom Corp.	10810 Farnam Dr	Omaha	NE	68154	G A Gagliardi	402-392-3900	P	4,258	12.0
Blockbuster Inc.	1201 Elm St	Dallas	TX	75270	John Antioco	214-854-3000	S	3,893	82.4
Tandy-Radio Shack	100 Thorockmorton	Fort Worth	TX	76102	Len Roberts	817-415-3011	D	3,260*	35.0
Domino's Pizza Inc.	P O Box 997	Ann Arbor	MI	48106	Thomas Monaghan	734-930-3030	R	3,200	120.0
Burger King Corp.	PO Box 020783	Miami	FL	33102	Dennis Malamatinas	305-378-7011	S	2,158	17.1
Robert Half International Inc.	2884 Sand Hill Rd	Menlo Park	CA	94025	Harold M Messmer Jr	650-234-6000	P	2,081	185.2
Wendy's International Inc.	PO Box 256	Dublin	OH	43016		614-764-3100	P	1,948	39.0
CKE Restaurants Inc.	401 W Carl Karcher	Anaheim	CA	92803	William P Foley II	714-774-5796	P	1,892	67.0
Brinker International Inc.	6820 LBJ Fwy	Dallas	TX	75240	Norman E Brinker	972-980-9917	P	1,871	62.3
Hilton Hotels Corp.	9336 Civic Center	Beverly Hills	CA	90210	Stephen F Bollenbach	310-278-4321	P	1,769	38.0
Advantica Restaurant Group Inc.	203 E Main St	Spartanburg	SC	29319	James B Adamson	864-597-8000	P	1,720	54.0
CDI Corp.	1717 Arch St	Philadelphia	PA	19103	Walter Garrison	215-569-2200	P	1,540	31.0
H and R Block Inc.	4400 Main St	Kansas City	MO	64111	Frank L Salizzoni	816-753-6900	P	1,522	86.5
Valenti Mid South Management	1845 Moriah Woods	Memphis	TN	38117	Peter Grant	901-684-1211	R	1,503*	2.0
Jack in the Box Inc.	PO Box 783	San Diego	CA	92112	Robert J Nugent	619-571-2121	P	1,456	37.8
General Nutrition Companies Inc.	300 6th Ave	Pittsburgh	PA	15222	William E Watts	412-288-4600	P	1,420	16.8
Norrell Corp.	3535 Piedmont N E	Atlanta	GA	30305	C Douglas Miller	404-240-3000	P	1,410	236.5
Outback Steakhouse Inc.	550 N Reo	Tampa	FL	33609	Robert D Basham	813-282-1225	P	1,359	36.5
Carlson Restaurants Worldwide	PO Box 809062	Dallas	TX	75380	Wallace B Doolin	972-450-5400	S	1,317	42.5
Casey's General Stores Inc.	1 Convenience Blvd	Ankeny	IA	50021	Ronald M Lamb	515-965-6100	P	1,251	11.4
Little Caesar Enterprises Inc.	2211 Woodward	Detroit	MI	48201	Michael Ilitch	313-983-6000	R	1,160	86.0
Denny's Inc.	203 E Main St	Spartanburg	SC	29319	John Romandetti	864-597-8000	S	1,148*	38.5
LCA Entertainment	4000 Warner Blvd	Burbank	CA	91522		818-954-6000	R	1,127*	1.5
TGI Friday's Inc.	PO Box 809062	Dallas	TX	75380	Wallace B Doolin	972-450-5400	S	1,043*	17.0
Watsco Inc.	2665 S Bayshore Dr	Coconut Grove	FL	33133	Albert Nahmad	305-858-0828	P	1,009	2.9
Shoney's Inc.	PO Box 1260	Nashville	TN	37202	J Michael Bodnar	615-391-5201	P	999	26.0
Dollar Thrifty Automotive Group	PO Box 35985	Tulsa	OK	74135	Joseph E Cappy	918-660-7700	P	999	4.9
Jack in the Box Div.	9330 Balboa Ave	San Diego	CA	92123	Robert J Nugent	619-571-2121	D	987	27.0
Personnel Group of America Inc.	6302 Fairview Rd	Charlotte	NC	28210	Edward P Drudge Jr	704-442-5100	P	918	5.4
Ground Round Inc.	P O Box 9078	Braintree	MA	02184	Thomas Russo	781-380-3100	S	879*	8.0
Buffets Inc.	10260 Viking Dr	Eden Prairie	MN	55344	Roe H Hatlen	612-942-9760	P	869	24.4
Avado Brands Inc.	Hancock at Wash	Madison	GA	30650	Thomas E DuPree Jr	706-342-4552	P	863	20.3
Drug Emporium Inc.	155 Hidden Ravines	Powell	OH	43065	David L Kriegel	740-548-7080	P	839	5.8
Papa John's International Inc.	PO Box 99900	Louisville	KY	40269	Blaine Hurst	502-266-5200	P	805	14.3
Just for Feet Inc.	7400 Cahaba Valley	Birmingham	AL	35242	Harold Ruttenberg	205-408-3000	P	775	15.0
UOP L.L.C.	PO Box 5017	Des Plaines	IL	60017	Mike Winfield	847-391-2000	R	770*	4.0
Triarc Companies Inc.	280 Park Ave	New York	NY	10017	Peter W May	212-451-3000	P	735	1.8
Ruby Tuesday Inc.	150 W Church Ave	Maryville	TN	37801	Samuel E Beall III	865-379-5700	P	722	27.2
Long John Silver's Restaurants	P O Box 11988	Lexington	KY	40579	John M Cranor III	606-388-6000	S	675	18.0
Ryan's Family Steak Houses Inc.	PO Box 100	Greer	SC	29652	Charles D Way	864-879-1000	P	665	19.0
Flooring America Inc.	210 TownPark Dr	Kennesaw	GA	30144	Ron McSwain	678-355-4000	P	664	2.7
Applebee's International Inc.	4551 W 107th St	Overland Park	KS	66207	Lloyd L Hill	913-967-4000	P	648	20.3
AFC Enterprises Inc.	6 Concourse N E	Atlanta	GA	30328	Frank Belatti	770-391-9500	R	609	18.1
Red Robin International Inc.	5575 DTC Pkwy	Englewood	CO	80111	Mike Snyder	303-846-6000	R	606*	4.5
Global Licensing Co.	430 Park Ave	New York	NY	10022	Tom Fandler	212-307-8100	D	604*	0.8
Fred's Inc.	4300 New Getwell	Memphis	TN	38118	Michael J Hayes	901-365-8880	P	601	6.0
Nautica Apparel Inc.	40 W 57th St	New York	NY	10019	David Chu	212-541-5990	S	580	0.5
Nautica Enterprises Inc.	40 West 57th St	New York	NY	10019	Harvey Sanders	212-541-5757	P	553	2.3
Immunex Corp.	51 University St	Seattle	WA	98101	Edward V Fritzky	206-587-0430	P	542	1.0
RTM Restaurant Group	5995 Barfield Rd	Atlanta	GA	30328	R V Umphenour Jr	404-256-4900	R	535	23.0
Sybra Inc.	9404 Genesee Ave	La Jolla	CA	92037	James R Arabia	858-587-8533	S	534*	3.9
Midas International Corp.	1300 N Arl Hght	Itasca	IL	60143		312-565-7500	R	519	1.5
Dairy Mart Convenience Stores	One Dairy Mart Way	Hudson	OH	44236	Robert B Stein Jr	330-342-6600	P	508	3.6
Westaff Inc.	P O Box 9280	Walnut Creek	CA	94598	Michael K Phippen	925-930-5300	P	482*	1.0
Eateries Inc.	3240 W Britton Rd	Oklahoma City	OK	73120	Vincent F Orza Jr	405-755-3607	P	468*	3.5
Boston Chicken Inc.	PO Box 4086	Golden	CO	80401	J Michael Jenkins	303-278-9500	P	462	12.5
Gymboree Corp.	700 Arpt Blvd	Burlingame	CA	94010	Stuart G Moldaw	650-579-0600	P	458	6.5
W.S. Badcock Corp.	PO Box 497	Mulberry	FL	33860	Ben Badcock	941-425-4921	R	450	1.5
Sylvan Learning Systems Inc.	1000 Lancaster St	Baltimore	MD	21202	Douglas Becker	410-843-8000	P	440	6.3

Source: *Ward's Business Directory of U.S. Private and Public Companies*, Volumes 1 and 2, 2000. The company type code used is as follows: P - Public, R - Private, S - Subsidiary, D - Division, J - Joint Venture, A - Affiliate, G - Group, N - Company type not reported. Sales are in millions of dollars, employees are in thousands. An asterisk (*) indicates an estimated sales volume. The symbol < stands for 'less than'. Company names and addresses are truncated, in some cases, to fit into the available space.

LOCATION BY STATE AND REGIONAL CONCENTRATION

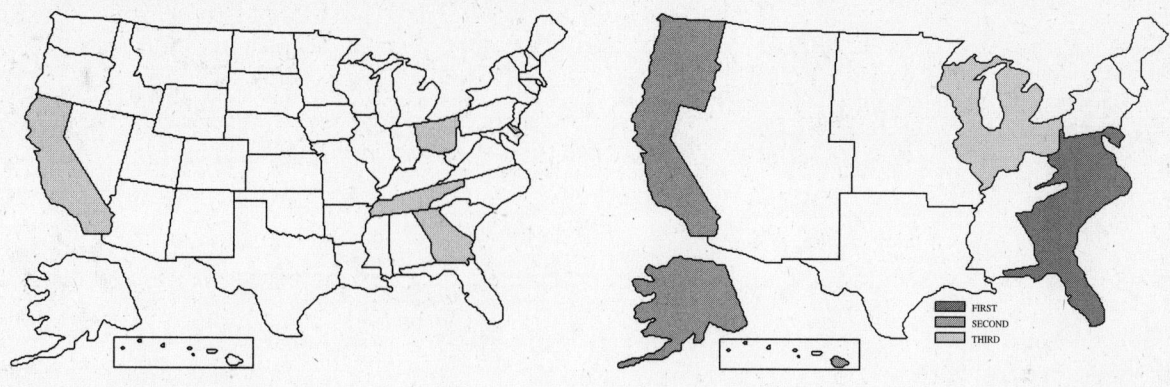

FIRST
SECOND
THIRD

INDUSTRY DATA BY STATE

State	Establishments		Employment			Payroll		Revenues		
	Total (number)	% of U.S.	Total (number)	% of U.S.	Per Estab.	Total ($ mil.)	Per Empl. ($)	Total ($ mil.)	% of U.S.	Per Estab. ($)
Delaware	248	11.5	751	2.9	3	18.1	24,153	4,442.2	39.4	17,911,923
California	249	11.6	3,218	12.5	13	186.4	57,929	1,445.6	12.8	5,805,618
Ohio	64	3.0	5,345	20.7	84	94.5	17,682	679.8	6.0	10,621,797
New York	138	6.4	2,466	9.6	18	121.2	49,148	678.3	6.0	4,915,428
Georgia	66	3.1	1,122	4.4	17	95.9	85,449	600.7	5.3	9,101,697
Florida	114	5.3	1,213	4.7	11	52.3	43,114	495.3	4.4	4,345,079
Texas	248	11.5	1,788	6.9	7	79.6	44,545	456.2	4.0	1,839,331
Tennessee	44	2.0	1,077	4.2	24	46.9	43,504	317.7	2.8	7,221,159
Michigan	77	3.6	528	2.0	7	30.4	57,542	275.3	2.4	3,575,026
Illinois	65	3.0	556	2.2	9	26.4	47,559	237.7	2.1	3,656,323
Massachusetts	32	1.5	952	3.7	30	55.0	57,730	224.8	2.0	7,025,500
New Jersey	50	2.3	843	3.3	17	32.5	38,571	191.0	1.7	3,819,420
Pennsylvania	56	2.6	784	3.0	14	33.0	42,128	136.9	1.2	2,444,500
Colorado	57	2.6	517	2.0	9	30.9	59,691	96.7	0.9	1,695,965
Minnesota	43	2.0	658	2.6	15	27.9	42,327	93.8	0.8	2,181,628
Iowa	18	0.8	183	0.7	10	7.8	42,732	87.9	0.8	4,884,000
Missouri	44	2.0	471	1.8	11	13.9	29,616	84.2	0.7	1,912,614
Virginia	34	1.6	301	1.2	9	13.2	43,887	73.8	0.7	2,170,441
Nevada	47	2.2	125	0.5	3	4.8	38,456	55.4	0.5	1,178,660
Wisconsin	25	1.2	142	0.6	6	5.0	34,972	53.2	0.5	2,128,800
Maryland	31	1.4	343	1.3	11	14.0	40,936	47.8	0.4	1,540,742
Oklahoma	56	2.6	207	0.8	4	5.8	28,232	45.2	0.4	806,982
North Carolina	26	1.2	199	0.8	8	7.6	38,015	44.4	0.4	1,707,000
Washington	35	1.6	327	1.3	9	10.6	32,407	44.0	0.4	1,258,486
Arizona	30	1.4	284	1.1	9	10.6	37,292	43.7	0.4	1,455,000
Connecticut	35	1.6	135	0.5	4	6.0	44,185	39.6	0.4	1,132,743
Kentucky	12	0.6	79	0.3	7	2.2	28,443	28.4	0.3	2,370,250
Oregon	16	0.7	204	0.8	13	7.0	34,417	26.7	0.2	1,666,563
Utah	15	0.7	141	0.5	9	5.1	35,851	26.0	0.2	1,736,467
Indiana	20	0.9	169	0.7	8	6.9	40,651	17.3	0.2	866,850
Louisiana	28	1.3	135	0.5	5	4.1	30,363	16.4	0.1	585,464
Nebraska	8	0.4	62	0.2	8	1.9	30,016	14.5	0.1	1,818,250
Alabama	17	0.8	59	0.2	3	2.5	41,746	14.3	0.1	839,059
South Carolina	9	0.4	37	0.1	4	1.9	51,946	7.3	0.1	810,333
Hawaii	6	0.3	19	0.1	3	0.3	17,789	4.7	0.0	776,500
Arkansas	7	0.3	25	0.1	4	0.6	24,440	4.2	0.0	600,143
South Dakota	8	0.4	23	0.1	3	0.9	38,696	4.2	0.0	522,125
Kansas	27	1.3	175*	-	-	(D)	-	(D)	-	-
West Virginia	8	0.4	60*	-	-	(D)	-	(D)	-	-

Source: 1997 *Economic Census*. The states are in descending order of revenues or establishments (if revenue data are missing for the majority). The symbol (D) appears when data are withheld to prevent disclosure of competitive information. States marked with (D) are sorted by number of establishments. A dash (-) indicates that the data element cannot be calculated. * indicates the midpoint of a range; 175, for example is the range 100-249. Shaded *states* on the state map indicate those states which have proportionately greater representation in the industry than would be indicated by the state's population; the ratio is based on total revenues or number of establishments. Shaded *regions* indicate where the industry is regionally most concentrated.

Part IV

PROFESSIONAL, SCIENTIFIC, AND TECHNICAL SERVICES

NAICS 541110 - OFFICES OF LAWYERS*

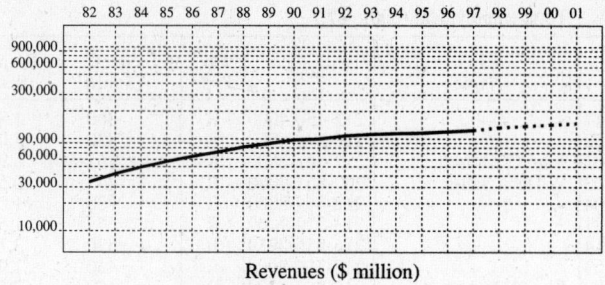

Revenues ($ million)

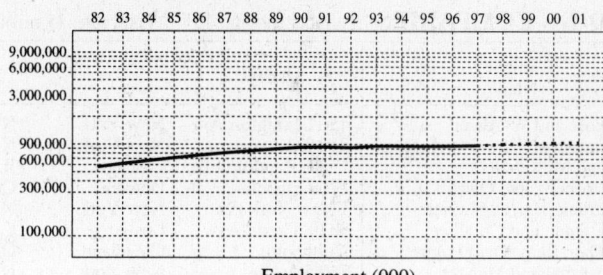

Employment (000)

GENERAL STATISTICS

Year	Establishments (number)	Employment (number)	Payroll ($ million)	Revenues ($ million)	Employees per Establishment (number)	Revenues per Establishment ($)	Payroll per Employee ($)
1982	122,671	569,359	12,555.0	34,325.0	4.6	279,813	22,051
1983	125,781 e	617,007 e	15,259.0 e	41,883.0 e	4.9 e	332,984 e	24,731 e
1984	128,891 e	664,655 e	17,964.0 e	49,441.0 e	5.2 e	383,588 e	27,028 e
1985	132,002 e	712,303 e	20,668.0 e	56,999.0 e	5.4 e	431,804 e	29,016 e
1986	135,112 e	759,951 e	23,373.0 e	64,557.0 e	5.6 e	477,804 e	30,756 e
1987	138,222	807,599	26,078.0	72,115.0	5.8	521,733	32,291
1988	135,709	848,507	30,270.0	81,636.0	6.3	601,552	35,674
1989	137,346	892,143	32,909.0	89,144.0	6.5	649,047	36,888
1990	142,436	931,807	36,020.0	97,640.0	6.5	685,501	38,656
1991	145,919	940,976	37,337.0	100,027.0	6.4	685,497	39,679
1992	151,737	923,617	39,328.0	108,443.0	6.1	714,677	42,580
1993	158,335	962,374	40,659.0	112,145.0	6.1	708,277	42,249
1994	161,622	962,908	41,690.0	114,603.0	6.0	709,080	43,296
1995	163,554	960,693	43,196.0	116,000.0	5.9	709,246	44,963
1996	165,921 e	970,041 e	45,701.0 e	120,057.0 e	5.8 e	723,579 e	47,112 e
1997	168,289	979,390	48,206.0	124,114.0	5.8	737,505	49,220
1998	173,586 p	1,014,605 p	50,193.0 p	132,736.0 p	5.8 p	764,670 p	49,470 p
1999	177,228 p	1,029,463 p	52,174.0 p	137,648.0 p	5.8 p	776,672 p	50,681 p
2000	180,870 p	1,044,321 p	54,155.0 p	142,560.0 p	5.8 p	788,190 p	51,857 p
2001	184,511 p	1,059,178 p	56,136.0 p	147,471.0 p	5.7 p	799,253 p	53,000 p

Sources: Economic Census of the United States, 1982, 1987, 1992, 1997. Establishment counts, employment, and payroll are from *County Business Patterns* for non-Census years. In non-Census years, industries in the Manufacturing range under SIC coding include data from the *Annual Survey of Manufactures* (*ASM*); those in the old Services range include data from the *Services Annual Survey* (*SAS*). Values followed by a 'p' are projections by the editors. Extrapolations are marked by 'e'. Data are the most recent available at this level of detail.

INDICES OF CHANGE

Year	Establishments (number)	Employment (number)	Payroll ($ million)	Revenues ($ million)	Employees per Establishment (number)	Revenues per Establishment ($)	Payroll per Employee ($)
1982	72.9	58.1	26.0	27.7	79.8	37.9	44.8
1987	82.1	82.5	54.1	58.1	100.4	70.7	65.6
1992	90.2	94.3	81.6	87.4	104.6	96.9	86.5
1993	94.1	98.3	84.3	90.4	104.4	96.0	85.8
1994	96.0	98.3	86.5	92.3	102.4	96.1	88.0
1995	97.2	98.1	89.6	93.5	100.9	96.2	91.4
1996	98.6 e	99.0 e	94.8 e	96.7 e	100.5 e	98.1 e	95.7 e
1997	100.0	100.0	100.0	100.0	100.0	100.0	100.0
1998	103.1 p	103.6 p	104.1 p	106.9 p	100.4 p	103.7 p	100.5 p
1999	105.3 p	105.1 p	108.2 p	110.9 p	99.8 p	105.3 p	103.0 p
2000	107.5 p	106.6 p	112.3 p	114.9 p	99.2 p	106.9 p	105.4 p
2001	109.6 p	108.1 p	116.5 p	118.8 p	98.6 p	108.4 p	107.7 p

Sources: Same as General Statistics. The values shown reflect change from the base year, 1997. Values above 100 mean greater than 1997, values below 100 mean less than 1997, and a value of 100 in the 1982-96 or 1998-2001 period means same as 1997. Values followed by a 'p' are projections by the editors; 'e' stands for extrapolation. Data are the most recent available at this level of detail.

SELECTED RATIOS

For 1997	Avg. of Information	Analyzed Industry	Index	For 1997	Avg. of Information	Analyzed Industry	Index
Employees per establishment	9	6	67	Payroll per establishment	372,545	286,448	77
Revenue per establishment	958,337	737,505	77	Payroll as % of revenue	39	39	100
Revenue per employee	111,029	126,726	114	Payroll per employee	43,162	49,220	114

Sources: Same as General Statistics. The 'Average' column represents the average for the industry sector, in 1997, where the currently shown industry is classified. The Index shows the relationship between the Average and the Analyzed Industry. For example, 100 means that they are equal; 500 that the Analyzed Industry is five times the average; 50 means that the Analyzed Industry is half the national average. The abbreviation 'na' is used to show that data are 'not available'.

*Equivalent to SIC 8111.

LEADING COMPANIES   Number shown: **75**   Total sales ($ mil): **19,519**   Total employment (000): **87.7**

Company Name	Address				CEO Name	Phone	Co. Type	Sales ($ mil)	Empl. (000)
Davis Polk and Wardwell	450 Lexington Ave	New York	NY	10017		212-450-4000	R	860*	1.3
Skadden, Arps, Slate, Meagher	919 3rd Ave	New York	NY	10022		212-371-6000	R	830	3.0
Baker and McKenzie	130 E Randolph Dr	Chicago	IL	60601	John C Klotsche	312-861-8800	R	751*	6.9
Holme Roberts and Owen L.L.P.	1700 Lincoln	Denver	CO	80203	W Dean Salter	303-861-7000	R	747*	0.5
Fried, Frank, Harris, Shriver	1 New York Plz	New York	NY	10004		212-859-8000	R	730*	1.5
Gibson, Dunn and Crutcher	333 S Grand Ave	Los Angeles	CA	90071		213-229-7000	R	679*	1.5
Jones, Day, Reavis and Pogue	Northpoint	Cleveland	OH	44114		216-586-3939	R	530	3.1
Weil, Gotshal and Manges	767 5th Ave	New York	NY	10153		212-310-8000	R	430	1.9
Morgan, Lewis & Bockius L.L.P.	1701 Market Street	Philadelphia	PA	19103	Francis M Milone	215-963-5000	R	400*	2.5
Latham and Watkins	520 S Grand Ave	Los Angeles	CA	90071		213-891-1200	R	363	2.0
Hunton and Williams	951 E Byrd St	Richmond	VA	23219		804-788-8200	R	334*	2.0
O'Melveny and Myers L.L.P.	400 S Hope St	Los Angeles	CA	90071	Charles Bender	213-430-6000	R	327	1.9
Cleary, Gottlieb, Steen	1 Liberty Plz	New York	NY	10006		212-225-2000	R	320*	1.2
Sidley and Austin	Bank 1 Plz	Chicago	IL	60603	Charles Douglas	312-853-7000	R	316*	2.0
Mayer, Brown and Platt	190 S La Salle St	Chicago	IL	60603		312-782-0600	R	309*	2.0
CCH Legal Information Services	1633 Broadway	New York	NY	10019	Nancy McKinsky	212-664-1666	D	298*	1.2
Fulbright and Jaworski L.L.P.	1301 McKinney St	Houston	TX	77010	AT Blackshear	713-651-5151	R	283	1.7
Thompson Hine and Flory L.L.P.	3900 Key Ctr	Cleveland	OH	44114		216-566-5500	R	276*	1.0
Morrison and Foerster L.L.P.	425 Market St	San Francisco	CA	94105	Stephen S Dunham	415-268-7000	R	274	1.6
Vinson and Elkins L.L.P.	2300 First City Twr	Houston	TX	77002		713-758-2222	R	255	1.5
Wilson, Elser, Moskowitz	150 E 42nd St	New York	NY	10017	Hal Stewart	212-490-3000	R	251*	0.9
Arter and Hadden	1100 Huntington	Cleveland	OH	44115		216-696-1100	R	239*	0.9
Cadwalader, Wickersham and Taft	100 Maiden Ln	New York	NY	10038		212-504-6000	R	230	1.0
Baker and Botts L.L.P.	1 Shell Plz	Houston	TX	77002		713-229-1234	R	226*	1.4
Cravath, Swaine and Moore	825 8th Ave	New York	NY	10019		212-474-1000	R	225*	1.4
Troutman and Sanders	600 Peachtree St	Atlanta	GA	30308	William R Ramsey	404-885-3000	R	225*	0.8
Jenner and Block	330 N Wabash	Chicago	IL	60611		312-222-9350	R	224*	0.8
Pillsbury Madison & Sutro L.L.P.	P O Box 7880	San Francisco	CA	94120	Mary B Cranston	415-983-1000	R	224	1.3
Schnader, Harrison, Segal	1600 Market St	Philadelphia	PA	19103	Dennis R Suplee	215-751-2000	R	223*	0.8
Baer Marks and Upham	805 3rd Ave	New York	NY	10022		212-702-5700	R	222*	0.8
Quarles and Brady	411 E Wisconsin	Milwaukee	WI	53202		414-277-5000	R	222*	0.8
Proskauer Rose L.L.P.	1585 Broadway	New York	NY	10036		212-969-3000	R	218*	1.2
Wilson, Sonsini, Goodrich	650 Page Mill Rd	Palo Alto	CA	94304	Larry Sonsini	650-493-9300	R	216	1.4
Kilpatrick Stockton L.L.P.	1100 Peachtree St	Atlanta	GA	30309		404-815-6500	R	212*	1.1
Bryan Cave L.L.P.	211 N Broadway	St. Louis	MO	63102	Walter L Metalfe Jr	314-259-2000	R	210	1.4
Sewell and Riggs	333 Clay Ave	Houston	TX	77002		713-652-8700	R	210*	0.8
Shearman and Sterling	599 Lexington Ave	New York	NY	10022		212-848-4000	R	210*	1.3
Dickstein, Shapiro, Morin	2101 L St NW	Washington	DC	20037		202-785-9700	R	208*	0.8
Simpson Thacher and Bartlett	425 Lexington Ave	New York	NY	10017	Richard I Beattie	212-455-2000	R	208*	1.3
Piper and Marbury L.L.P.	36 S Charles St	Baltimore	MD	21201	Jeffrey F Liss	410-539-2530	R	200*	0.8
Thompson Coburn L.L.P.	One Mercantile Ctr	St. Louis	MO	63101		314-552-6000	R	198*	0.7
Baker and Hostetler LLR	1900 E 9th St	Cleveland	OH	44114	Gary Bryenton	216-621-0200	R	197*	1.2
McCarter and English	100 Mulberry St	Newark	NJ	07102		973-622-4444	R	197*	0.7
Wilmer, Cutler and Pickering	2445 M St NW	Washington	DC	20037		202-663-6000	R	195*	0.7
Stoel Rives L.L.P.	900 SW 5th Ave	Portland	OR	97204		503-224-3380	R	190	1.0
Drinker Biddle and Reath L.L.P.	1 Logan Sq	Philadelphia	PA	19103	Morgan R Jones, Esq	215-988-2700	R	183*	0.6
Katten Muchin and Zavis	525 W Monroe	Chicago	IL	60661	Allan Muchin	312-902-5200	R	177	1.1
Dorsey and Whitney L.L.P.	220 S 6th St	Minneapolis	MN	55402		612-340-2600	R	177	1.4
Dewey Ballantine L.L.P.	1301 Av Americas	New York	NY	10019	Everett Jassy	212-259-8000	R	170*	1.0
Finnegan, Henderson, Farabow	1300 I St N W	Washington	DC	20005		202-408-4000	R	170*	0.6
Kirkpatrick and Lockhart L.L.P.	535 Smithfield	Pittsburgh	PA	15222		412-355-6500	R	170*	1.0
Dechert Price and Rhoads	4000 Bell Atl	Philadelphia	PA	19103	Barton J Winokur	215-994-4000	R	169*	1.1
Shaw, Pittman	2300 N St N W	Washington	DC	20037		202-663-8000	R	168*	0.6
Arent Fox Kintner Plotkin & Kahn	1050 Conn N W	Washington	DC	20036		202-857-6000	R	167*	0.6
Chapman and Cutler	111 W Monroe St	Chicago	IL	60603	John Dixon	312-845-3000	R	167*	0.6
Nelson, Mullins, Riley	P O Box 11070	Columbia	SC	29211	Robert J Heffron	803-799-2000	R	167*	0.6
Steptoe and Johnson L.L.P.	1330 Connecticut	Washington	DC	20036	JA Bouknight Jr	202-429-3000	R	167*	0.6
Sutherland, Asbill and Brennan	1275 Penn N W	Washington	DC	20004		202-383-0100	R	167*	0.6
Baker, Donelson, Bearman	165 Madison Ave	Memphis	TN	38103		901-526-2000	R	163*	0.6
Gray Cary Ware and Freidenrich	401 B St	San Diego	CA	92101	J Terence O'Malley	619-699-2700	R	162*	0.8
Miller, Canfield, Paddock & Stone	29201 Telegraph	Southfield	MI	48034		313-963-6420	R	162*	0.6
Locke, Liddell and Sapp L.L.P.	3400 Chase Tower	Houston	TX	77002		713-226-1200	R	160	0.8
Greenberg and Traurig P.A.	1221 Brickell Ave	Miami	FL	33131	Caesar Alvarez	305-579-0500	R	157*	0.6
Blank, Rome, Comisky	1 Logan Sq	Philadelphia	PA	19103		215-569-5500	R	156*	0.6
Bracewell and Patterson L.L.P.	711 Louisiana	Houston	TX	77002		713-223-2900	R	156*	0.6
Heller Ehrman White	333 Bush St	San Francisco	CA	94104		415-772-6000	R	156*	1.1
Chadbourne and Parke	30 Rockefeller Plz	New York	NY	10112	Neil Bianco	212-408-5100	R	154*	0.9
Porter, Wright, Morris & Arthur L	41 S High St	Columbus	OH	43215		614-227-2000	R	152*	0.5
Covington and Burling	PO Box 7566	Washington	DC	20004		202-662-6000	R	150*	0.9
Ice Miller Donadio and Ryan	Box 82001	Indianapolis	IN	46282		317-236-2159	D	150*	0.5
Loeb and Loeb LLP	1000 Wilshire #1800	Los Angeles	CA	90017		213-688-3400	R	149*	0.5
Honigman Miller Schwartz	2290 1st Nat	Detroit	MI	48226	Joel S Adelman	313-465-7000	R	146*	0.5
Perkins Coie L.L.P.	1201 3rd Ave	Seattle	WA	98101		206-583-8888	R	146*	1.3
Reed Smith Shaw and McClay	PO Box 2009	Pittsburgh	PA	15230		412-288-4232	R	146*	1.0
Hale and Dorr L.L.P.	60 State St	Boston	MA	02109		617-526-6000	R	143*	0.9

Source: Ward's Business Directory of U.S. Private and Public Companies, Volumes 1 and 2, 2000. The company type code used is as follows: P - Public, R - Private, S - Subsidiary, D - Division, J - Joint Venture, A - Affiliate, G - Group, N - Company type not reported. Sales are in millions of dollars, employees are in thousands. An asterisk (*) indicates an estimated sales volume. The symbol < stands for 'less than'. Company names and addresses are truncated, in some cases, to fit into the available space.

REPRESENTATIVE NONPROFIT ORGANIZATIONS

Organization Name	Address				Phone	Income Range ($ mil)
Acadiana Legal Service Corporation	PO Box 4823	Lafayette	LA	70502	337-237-4320	1-5
Alliance Defense Fund Inc	7819 E Greenway Rd	Scottsdale	AZ	85260	480-953-1200	1-5
American Center for Law and Justice Inc	PO Box 64429	Virginia BCH	VA	23467		5-9
Appalachian Research & Defense Fund of KY Inc	120 N Front St	Prestonsburg	KY	41653	606-886-3876	1-5
Bronx Legal Services	350 Broadway	New York	NY	10013		1-5
Center for Legal Advocacy	455 Sherman	Denver	CO	80203	303-722-0300	1-5
Central Florida Legal Services Inc	128 A Orange Avenue	Daytona Beach	FL	32114	904-255-6573	1-5
Central Mississippi Legal Services Corporation	414 S State St	Jackson	MS	39201		1-5
Connecticut Legal Rights Project Inc	PO Box 351	Middletown	CT	06457		1-5
Dakota Plains Legal Services Inc	PO Box 727	Mission	SD	57555	605-856-4444	1-5
Disability Law Center	455 E 400 S Ste 410	Salt Lake Cty	UT	84111	801-363-1347	1-5
Earthjustice Legal Defense Fund	180 Montgomery St	San Francisco	CA	94104	415-627-6700	10-19
Federal Defender Program Inc	100 Peachtree St NW	Atlanta	GA	30303	404-688-7530	1-5
Federal Defender Services of Eastern Tennessee	530 S Gay Ste 900	Knoxville	TN	37902	865-637-7979	1-5
Federal Defenders of Montana Inc	104 2nd St S 301	Great Falls	MT	59401	406-727-5328	1-5
Idaho Legal Aid Services Inc	PO Box 913	Boise	ID	83701	208-345-0106	1-5
Insurance Fraud Bureau of Massachusetts	101 Arch St	Boston	MA	02110	617-439-0439	5-9
Kansas Legal Services Inc	712 S Kansas	Topeka	KS	66603	785-233-2068	5-9
Lakeshore Legal Aid	21885 Dunham Rd Ste 4	Clinton Township	MI	48036		1-5
Landmark Legal Foundation	3100 Broadway Ste 515	Kansas City	MO	64111	816-931-5559	1-5
Lawyers Trust Fund of Illinois	55 E Monroe St	Chicago	IL	60603	312-357-3425	10-19
Legal Aid Services of Oregon	700 SW Taylor Ste 310	Portland	OR	97205	503-224-4094	5-9
Legal Aid Society of Cincinnati	901 Elm St	Cincinnati	OH	45202	513-241-9400	1-5
Legal Aid of Western Oklahoma Inc	2901 Classen Blvd	Oklahoma City	OK	73106	405-521-1302	1-5
Legal Foundation of Washington	500 Union St Bldg Ste 545	Seattle	WA	98101	206-624-2536	10-19
Legal Services Agency of Western Carolina Inc	PO Box 10706 F S	Greenville	SC	29603	864-467-3232	1-5
Legal Services Corporation of Alabama Inc	500 Bell Bldg	Montgomery	AL	36104	334-832-4570	1-5
Legal Services Corporation of Iowa	1111 9th St Ste 230	Des Moines	IA	50314	515-243-2151	1-5
Legal Services Corporation	750 First St NE Ste 10th F	Washington	DC	20002	202-336-8800	50+
Legal Services of NC Inc	PO Box 26087	Raleigh	NC	27611		5-9
Legal Services of New Jersey Inc	PO Box 1357	Edison	NJ	08818	732-572-9100	10-19
Maine Bar Foundation	72 Winthrop St	Augusta	ME	04330		1-5
Mid-Minnesota Legal Assistance Incorporated	430 First Ave N Ste 300	Minneapolis	MN	55401		5-9
National Senior Citizens Law Center	8737 Colesville Rd 4th Flr	Silver Spring	MD	20910		1-5
Native Hawaiian Legal Corporation	1164 Bishop St Ste 1205	Honolulu	HI	96813	808-521-2302	1-5
Nevada Legal Services Inc	701 E Bridger St Ste 101	Las Vegas	NV	89101	702-386-1070	1-5
Pennsylvania Legal Services	118 Locust St	Harrisburg	PA	17101		10-19
Public Defender Corporation for 13th Judicial Circuit	723 Kanawha Blvd E	Charleston	WV	25301	304-558-3905	1-5
Puerto Rico Legal Services Incorporated	PO Box 9134	San Juan	PR	00908		10-19
Rhode Island Legal Services Inc	200 Midway Rd Ste 169	Cranston	RI	02920		1-5
Southern New Mexico Legal Services Inc	300 N Downtown Mall	Las Cruces	NM	88001	505-522-8328	1-5
Texas Rural Legal Aid Inc	300 S Texas Blvd	Weslaco	TX	78596	956-968-9574	5-9
Wisconsin Judicare Incorporated	300 Third St Ste 210	Wausau	WI	54403	715-842-1681	1-5

Source: *National Directory of Nonprofit Organizations*, 2000, Volumes 1 and 2, The Taft Group. The table shows a selection of organizations for illustration and does not constitute a complete selection from the source. The organizations are arranged in alphabetical order.

LOCATION BY STATE AND REGIONAL CONCENTRATION

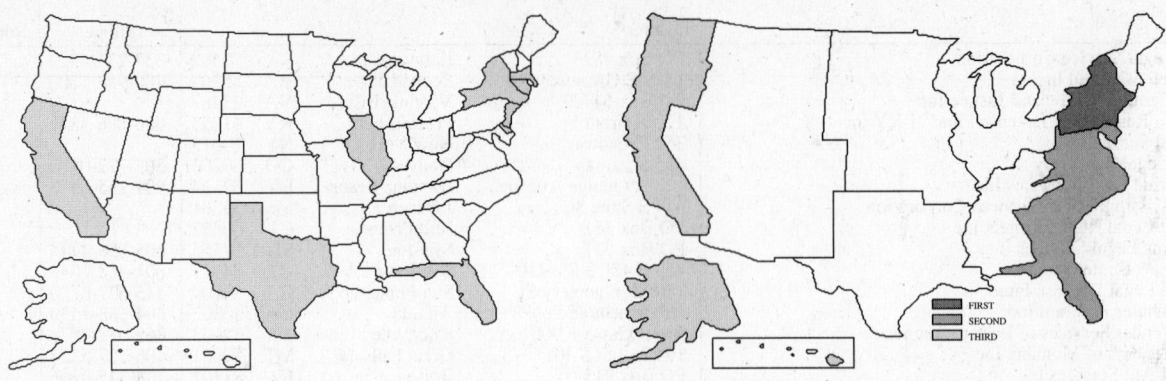

FIRST
SECOND
THIRD

INDUSTRY DATA BY STATE

State	Establishments Total (number)	% of U.S.	Employment Total (number)	% of U.S.	Per Estab.	Payroll Total ($ mil.)	Per Empl. ($)	Revenues Total ($ mil.)	% of U.S.	Per Estab. ($)
California	21,285	12.6	123,069	12.6	6	6,925.6	56,274	18,336.0	14.8	861,451
New York	13,250	7.9	108,946	11.1	8	6,100.2	55,993	18,128.9	14.6	1,368,215
Texas	12,468	7.4	66,635	6.8	5	3,488.7	52,356	8,880.2	7.2	712,237
Florida	12,769	7.6	65,507	6.7	5	3,391.9	51,780	7,101.4	5.7	556,142
Illinois	7,553	4.5	50,089	5.1	7	2,784.9	55,599	7,076.9	5.7	936,967
D.C.	1,622	1.0	29,100	3.0	18	2,110.1	72,511	5,893.2	4.7	3,633,277
Pennsylvania	6,608	3.9	45,078	4.6	7	2,195.6	48,707	5,441.7	4.4	823,497
New Jersey	6,277	3.7	38,147	3.9	6	1,865.7	48,909	4,330.5	3.5	689,899
Massachusetts	4,986	3.0	29,058	3.0	6	1,422.3	48,948	3,878.6	3.1	777,907
Ohio	5,657	3.4	32,047	3.3	6	1,293.4	40,360	3,397.3	2.7	600,547
Michigan	5,056	3.0	27,147	2.8	5	1,356.9	49,984	2,958.7	2.4	585,194
Georgia	4,387	2.6	23,089	2.4	5	1,018.9	44,129	2,916.9	2.4	664,906
Washington	3,362	2.0	18,684	1.9	6	865.0	46,298	2,079.8	1.7	618,619
Virginia	3,632	2.2	20,330	2.1	6	889.6	43,759	2,030.3	1.6	559,009
Missouri	2,807	1.7	17,047	1.7	6	744.3	43,662	1,924.2	1.6	685,501
Minnesota	2,394	1.4	16,829	1.7	7	826.7	49,124	1,857.2	1.5	775,783
North Carolina	3,408	2.0	17,699	1.8	5	678.0	38,308	1,834.3	1.5	538,237
Connecticut	2,682	1.6	14,906	1.5	6	667.5	44,782	1,741.8	1.4	649,426
Maryland	3,092	1.8	16,101	1.6	5	715.6	44,444	1,739.0	1.4	562,421
Colorado	3,113	1.8	14,280	1.5	5	706.7	49,490	1,619.3	1.3	520,180
Arizona	2,491	1.5	13,215	1.3	5	681.0	51,535	1,427.7	1.2	573,134
Alabama	2,339	1.4	12,511	1.3	5	517.1	41,331	1,388.1	1.1	593,462
Wisconsin	2,235	1.3	13,670	1.4	6	601.5	44,000	1,345.8	1.1	602,132
Indiana	2,588	1.5	12,736	1.3	5	411.3	32,296	1,293.8	1.0	499,931
Tennessee	2,480	1.5	12,120	1.2	5	434.3	35,832	1,271.1	1.0	512,544
Oregon	2,024	1.2	9,888	1.0	5	399.0	40,352	1,050.9	0.8	519,196
Kentucky	2,144	1.3	10,114	1.0	5	305.6	30,214	973.5	0.8	454,040
Oklahoma	2,344	1.4	9,540	1.0	4	399.9	41,923	946.8	0.8	403,935
Nevada	1,109	0.7	5,754	0.6	5	299.2	52,005	634.7	0.5	572,346
Iowa	1,508	0.9	6,702	0.7	4	217.6	32,472	588.8	0.5	390,460
West Virginia	993	0.6	4,979	0.5	5	143.6	28,842	523.5	0.4	527,149
Kansas	1,431	0.9	6,215	0.6	4	190.0	30,579	521.3	0.4	364,287
Hawaii	789	0.5	4,028	0.4	5	203.8	50,596	511.7	0.4	648,535
Utah	796	0.5	5,114	0.5	6	240.4	47,002	492.7	0.4	619,018
Arkansas	1,359	0.8	4,817	0.5	4	159.7	33,147	451.6	0.4	332,303
New Mexico	1,140	0.7	5,026	0.5	4	205.0	40,781	441.3	0.4	387,109
Delaware	327	0.2	3,811	0.4	12	190.3	49,947	436.8	0.4	1,335,664
Nebraska	884	0.5	4,094	0.4	5	148.7	36,327	392.0	0.3	443,493
Rhode Island	742	0.4	3,451	0.4	5	141.8	41,093	387.2	0.3	521,842
New Hampshire	788	0.5	4,336	0.4	6	176.4	40,683	365.6	0.3	463,956
Maine	727	0.4	3,847	0.4	5	147.8	38,426	364.9	0.3	501,928
Alaska	471	0.3	2,014	0.2	4	108.8	54,000	248.0	0.2	526,597
Idaho	639	0.4	2,737	0.3	4	90.7	33,122	238.7	0.2	373,584
Montana	625	0.4	2,529	0.3	4	82.7	32,720	225.5	0.2	360,770
Vermont	448	0.3	1,982	0.2	4	78.0	39,366	169.6	0.1	378,536
South Dakota	436	0.3	1,536	0.2	4	39.1	25,448	136.5	0.1	313,186
Wyoming	398	0.2	1,258	0.1	3	38.5	30,591	114.7	0.1	288,123
North Dakota	348	0.2	1,477	0.2	4	49.7	33,628	108.8	0.1	312,721

Source: 1997 *Economic Census*. The states are in descending order of revenues or establishments (if revenue data are missing for the majority). The symbol (D) appears when data are withheld to prevent disclosure of competitive information. States marked with (D) are sorted by number of establishments. A dash (-) indicates that the data element cannot be calculated. * indicates the midpoint of a range; 175, for example is the range 100-249. Shaded *states* on the state map indicate those states which have proportionately greater representation in the industry than would be indicated by the state's population; the ratio is based on total revenues or number of establishments. Shaded *regions* indicate where the industry is regionally most concentrated.

NAICS 541191 - TITLE ABSTRACT AND SETTLEMENT OFFICES

GENERAL STATISTICS

Year	Establishments (number)	Employment (number)	Payroll ($ million)	Revenues ($ million)	Employees per Establishment (number)	Revenues per Establishment ($)	Payroll per Employee ($)
1997	6,391	46,711	1,386.0	3,489.0	7.3	545,924	29,672

Source: *Economic Census of the United States*, 1997. This is a newly defined industry. Data for prior years were unavailable at the time of publication but may become available over time.

INDICES OF CHANGE

Year	Establishments (number)	Employment (number)	Payroll ($ million)	Revenues ($ million)	Employees per Establishment (number)	Revenues per Establishment ($)	Payroll per Employee ($)
1997	100.0	100.0	100.0	100.0	100.0	100.0	100.0

Sources: Same as General Statistics. The values shown reflect change from the base year, 1997. Values above 100 mean greater than 1997, values below 100 mean less than 1997, and a value of 100 in the 1982-96 or 1998-2001 period means same as 1997. Values followed by a 'p' are projections by the editors; 'e' stands for extrapolation. Data are the most recent available at this level of detail.

SIC INDUSTRIES RELATED TO NAICS 541191

Each new NAICS code represents an industry that used to be part of an SIC or a part of several SIC industries. Data in this table are shown to provide transitional information for these cases. All available data for the precursor SIC(s) are shown. Even if only a part of an SIC is included in the NAICS, *all* data for the SIC are reproduced. If the SIC industry is not marked as being a part (pt) of the NAICS, the entire industry is embedded in the NAICS data. The SIC composition of the new industry provides some hints of the relative importance of its "ancestors." Data marked with a 'p' are projected. Projections begin with 1982 data. Data earlier than 1990 are not shown but are reflected in the projections.

SIC	Industry	1990	1991	1992	1993	1994	1995	1996	1997
6541	**Title Abstract Offices (pt)**								
	Establishments (number)	-	-	4,716	-	-	-	-	-
	Employment (thousands)	-	-	33.7	-	-	-	-	-
	Revenues ($ million)	-	-	2,337.3	-	-	-	-	-

Source: *Economic Census of the United States*, 1992, annual surveys of economic sectors conducted by the Bureau of the Census, and estimates or projections based on the 1982-1992 period; not all data are shown. 'e' marks estimates made by the editors; 'p' indicates projections based on time series. A dash (-) indicates that data for this SIC or year were not available. The abbreviation (pt) next to the industry name indicates that only a part of the industry is present within the NAICS data. If no (pt) is shown, the entire industry is contained within the NAICS data.

SELECTED RATIOS

For 1997	Avg. of Information	Analyzed Industry	Index	For 1997	Avg. of Information	Analyzed Industry	Index
Employees per establishment	9	7	85	Payroll per establishment	372,545	216,867	58
Revenue per establishment	958,337	545,924	57	Payroll as % of revenue	39	40	102
Revenue per employee	111,029	74,693	67	Payroll per employee	43,162	29,672	69

Sources: Same as General Statistics. The 'Average' column represents the average for the industry sector, in 1997, where the currently shown industry is classified. The Index shows the relationship between the Average and the Analyzed Industry. For example, 100 means that they are equal; 500 that the Analyzed Industry is five times the average; 50 means that the Analyzed Industry is half the national average. The abbreviation 'na' is used to show that data are 'not available'.

LEADING COMPANIES   Number shown: **19**   Total sales ($ mil): **5,303**   Total employment (000): **30.1**

Company Name	Address				CEO Name	Phone	Co. Type	Sales ($ mil)	Empl. (000)
Lennar Corp.	700 NW 107th Ave	Miami	FL	33172	Leonard Miller	305-559-4000	P	3,119	4.1
Lennar Title Services Inc.	700 N W 107th Ave	Miami	FL	33172	Stuart A Miller	305-559-4000	S	938*	3.0
North American Title Co.	2185 N California	Walnut Creek	CA	94596	Gary B Beeny	925-935-5599	S	585*	1.2
First American Title of Alaska Inc.	3035 C St	Anchorage	AK	99503	Terry Bryan	907-562-0510	R	171*	<0.1
Old Republic Title	101 E Glenoaks	Glendale	CA	91202	Michael Trudeau	818-247-2917	S	140*	0.3
American Title Co.	17911 Von Karman	Irvine	CA	92614	Wayne Diaz	949-257-6300	S	100*	0.6
Fountainhead Title Group Corp.	6310 Stevens Forest	Columbia	MD	21046	Ed Brush	410-381-5300	R	56*	0.1
Houston Title Co.	777 Post Oak Blvd	Houston	TX	77056	Mary Chapman Cantu	713-626-9220	S	42*	<0.1
Old Republic Title of St. Louis	7730 Forsyth Blvd	Clayton	MO	63105	James Davis	314-863-0022	S	33*	<0.1
Beach Abstract and Guaranty Co.	P O Box 2580	Little Rock	AR	72203	George Pitts Jr	501-376-3301	R	29*	<0.1
Key Title	201 St Charles Ave	New Orleans	LA	70170	Eddie Koonce	504-523-4600	R	29*	<0.1
Monroe Title Insurance Corp.	47 W Main St	Rochester	NY	14614	Thomas P Moonan	716-232-2070	R	20	0.2
Commerce Land Title Inc.	114 W Glenview Dr	San Antonio	TX	78228	Greg Lyssy	210-736-1700	R	14*	<0.1
Bay Title and Abstract Inc.	P O Box 173	Green Bay	WI	54305	John May	920-431-6100	R	11*	<0.1
Stewart Title of Pinellas Inc.	4134 Central Ave	St. Petersburg	FL	33711	Kevin Hussey	727-327-5775	S	5*	<0.1
Fidelity Title Co.	3115 W Parker Rd	Plano	TX	75023	John T Edwards	972-596-5000	R	4*	<0.1
TownSquare Title Services Corp.	999 18th St	Denver	CO	80202		303-291-1010	R	3*	<0.1
First American Title of Utah	330 E 400 South	Salt Lake City	UT	84111	Gary Kermott	801-363-5841	S	3	20.0
Land Records of Texas Inc.	1945 Walnut Hill Ln	Irving	TX	75038	Jay Jacobs	972-580-8575	S	2*	<0.1

Source: Ward's Business Directory of U.S. Private and Public Companies, Volumes 1 and 2, 2000. The company type code used is as follows: P - Public, R - Private, S - Subsidiary, D - Division, J - Joint Venture, A - Affiliate, G - Group, N - Company type not reported. Sales are in millions of dollars, employees are in thousands. An asterisk (*) indicates an estimated sales volume. The symbol < stands for 'less than'. Company names and addresses are truncated, in some cases, to fit into the available space.

LOCATION BY STATE AND REGIONAL CONCENTRATION

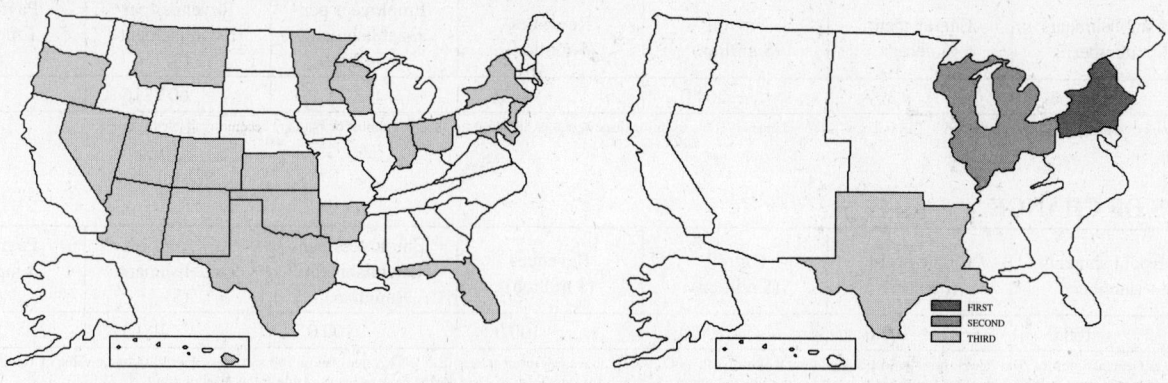

FIRST
SECOND
THIRD

INDUSTRY DATA BY STATE

State	Establishments Total (number)	Establishments % of U.S.	Employment Total (number)	Employment % of U.S.	Employment Per Estab.	Payroll Total ($ mil.)	Payroll Per Empl. ($)	Revenues Total ($ mil.)	Revenues % of U.S.	Revenues Per Estab. ($)
New York	445	7.0	3,234	6.9	7	124.3	38,429	356.3	10.2	800,780
Texas	548	8.6	4,006	8.6	7	111.8	27,915	306.1	8.8	558,622
California	265	4.1	2,913	6.2	11	106.6	36,598	246.4	7.1	929,713
Florida	467	7.3	2,853	6.1	6	85.0	29,787	234.2	6.7	501,394
Ohio	311	4.9	2,617	5.6	8	76.4	29,201	194.2	5.6	624,556
Pennsylvania	391	6.1	2,210	4.7	6	58.9	26,663	158.4	4.5	405,171
Illinois	276	4.3	2,059	4.4	7	58.6	28,480	151.9	4.4	550,272
Minnesota	212	3.3	1,915	4.1	9	54.8	28,607	141.8	4.1	668,854
Maryland	308	4.8	1,627	3.5	5	53.1	32,608	141.7	4.1	459,925
New Jersey	228	3.6	1,461	3.1	6	54.7	37,439	141.5	4.1	620,500
Oklahoma	166	2.6	1,578	3.4	10	42.9	27,212	98.5	2.8	593,169
Indiana	233	3.6	1,641	3.5	7	40.7	24,776	96.4	2.8	413,747
Colorado	131	2.0	1,266	2.7	10	40.9	32,335	93.2	2.7	711,412
Michigan	144	2.3	1,352	2.9	9	38.2	28,278	86.3	2.5	599,139
Wisconsin	182	2.8	1,347	2.9	7	34.2	25,401	81.3	2.3	446,516
Arizona	32	0.5	940	2.0	29	24.4	25,986	66.2	1.9	2,067,813
Oregon	72	1.1	895	1.9	12	25.0	27,965	58.3	1.7	809,264
Utah	74	1.2	808	1.7	11	23.8	29,407	56.4	1.6	761,959
Virginia	167	2.6	675	1.4	4	20.0	29,604	52.3	1.5	313,341
Tennessee	120	1.9	645	1.4	5	19.6	30,428	50.2	1.4	418,633
Arkansas	143	2.2	890	1.9	6	21.5	24,115	50.1	1.4	350,399
Nevada	47	0.7	669	1.4	14	25.5	38,111	49.9	1.4	1,061,979
Washington	62	1.0	719	1.5	12	20.1	28,021	47.0	1.3	757,694
Kansas	139	2.2	717	1.5	5	20.2	28,160	41.9	1.2	301,317
Louisiana	109	1.7	610	1.3	6	16.2	26,608	37.9	1.1	347,972
Massachusetts	65	1.0	262	0.6	4	10.3	39,321	33.0	0.9	508,077
Iowa	127	2.0	714	1.5	6	14.8	20,731	32.1	0.9	252,480
New Mexico	58	0.9	540	1.2	9	15.5	28,678	31.5	0.9	542,690
Hawaii	15	0.2	403	0.9	27	13.5	33,499	25.6	0.7	1,703,600
Georgia	85	1.3	326	0.7	4	9.5	29,141	25.2	0.7	296,282
Alabama	72	1.1	470	1.0	7	11.9	25,249	25.0	0.7	347,736
Montana	32	0.5	213	0.5	7	5.1	23,784	14.1	0.4	440,125
South Carolina	52	0.8	159	0.3	3	3.5	21,811	12.1	0.3	232,308
Kentucky	34	0.5	155	0.3	5	5.2	33,277	12.0	0.3	352,588
North Carolina	37	0.6	127	0.3	3	4.4	34,890	11.9	0.3	320,784
Maine	23	0.4	136	0.3	6	4.3	31,272	8.4	0.2	365,043
North Dakota	51	0.8	178	0.4	3	3.3	18,478	8.2	0.2	161,608
D.C.	13	0.2	80	0.2	6	2.4	30,050	6.7	0.2	512,385
Connecticut	26	0.4	67	0.1	3	2.0	30,507	5.9	0.2	227,577
Wyoming	14	0.2	69	0.1	5	1.6	22,623	3.5	0.1	246,429
West Virginia	9	0.1	32	0.1	4	0.8	23,531	2.0	0.1	223,444
Missouri	167	2.6	1,750*	-	-	(D)	-	(D)	-	-
Idaho	60	0.9	750*	-	-	(D)	-	(D)	-	-
Nebraska	60	0.9	375*	-	-	(D)	-	(D)	-	-
South Dakota	49	0.8	175*	-	-	(D)	-	(D)	-	-
New Hampshire	30	0.5	375*	-	-	(D)	-	(D)	-	-
Rhode Island	14	0.2	175*	-	-	(D)	-	(D)	-	-
Mississippi	11	0.2	60*	-	-	(D)	-	(D)	-	-
Delaware	7	0.1	60*	-	-	(D)	-	(D)	-	-
Alaska	5	0.1	60*	-	-	(D)	-	(D)	-	-
Vermont	3	-	10*	-	-	(D)	-	(D)	-	-

Source: 1997 *Economic Census*. The states are in descending order of revenues or establishments (if revenue data are missing for the majority). The symbol (D) appears when data are withheld to prevent disclosure of competitive information. States marked with (D) are sorted by number of establishments. A dash (-) indicates that the data element cannot be calculated. * indicates the midpoint of a range; 175, for example is the range 100-249. Shaded *states* on the state map indicate those states which have proportionately greater representation in the industry than would be indicated by the state's population; the ratio is based on total revenues or number of establishments. Shaded *regions* indicate where the industry is regionally most concentrated.

NAICS 541199 - LEGAL SERVICES NEC

GENERAL STATISTICS

Year	Establishments (number)	Employment (number)	Payroll ($ million)	Revenues ($ million)	Employees per Establishment (number)	Revenues per Establishment ($)	Payroll per Employee ($)
1997	1,568	9,307	264.0	946.0	5.9	603,316	28,366

Source: Economic Census of the United States, 1997. This is a newly defined industry. Data for prior years were unavailable at the time of publication but may become available over time.

INDICES OF CHANGE

Year	Establishments (number)	Employment (number)	Payroll ($ million)	Revenues ($ million)	Employees per Establishment (number)	Revenues per Establishment ($)	Payroll per Employee ($)
1997	100.0	100.0	100.0	100.0	100.0	100.0	100.0

Sources: Same as General Statistics. The values shown reflect change from the base year, 1997. Values above 100 mean greater than 1997, values below 100 mean less than 1997, and a value of 100 in the 1982-96 or 1998-2001 period means same as 1997. Values followed by a 'p' are projections by the editors; 'e' stands for extrapolation. Data are the most recent available at this level of detail.

SIC INDUSTRIES RELATED TO NAICS 541199

Each new NAICS code represents an industry that used to be part of an SIC or a part of several SIC industries. Data in this table are shown to provide transitional information for these cases. All available data for the precursor SIC(s) are shown. Even if only a part of an SIC is included in the NAICS, *all* data for the SIC are reproduced. If the SIC industry is not marked as being a part (pt) of the NAICS, the entire industry is embedded in the NAICS data. The SIC composition of the new industry provides some hints of the relative importance of its "ancestors." Data marked with a 'p' are projected. Projections begin with 1982 data. Data earlier than 1990 are not shown but are reflected in the projections.

SIC	Industry	1990	1991	1992	1993	1994	1995	1996	1997
7389	**Business Services, nec (pt)**								
	Establishments (number)	44,079	50,252	52,375	56,829	60,725	53,596	60,893p	63,269p
	Employment (thousands)	489.6	550.4	523.6	607.9	648.7	623.0	680.2p	710.9p
	Revenues ($ million)	-	-	32,885.9	-	-	-	-	-

Source: Economic Census of the United States, 1992, annual surveys of economic sectors conducted by the Bureau of the Census, and estimates or projections based on the 1982-1992 period; not all data are shown. 'e' marks estimates made by the editors; 'p' indicates projections based on time series. A dash (-) indicates that data for this SIC or year were not available. The abbreviation (pt) next to the industry name indicates that only a part of the industry is present within the NAICS data. If no (pt) is shown, the entire industry is contained within the NAICS data.

SELECTED RATIOS

For 1997	Avg. of Information	Analyzed Industry	Index	For 1997	Avg. of Information	Analyzed Industry	Index
Employees per establishment	9	6	69	Payroll per establishment	372,545	168,367	45
Revenue per establishment	958,337	603,316	63	Payroll as % of revenue	39	28	72
Revenue per employee	111,029	101,644	92	Payroll per employee	43,162	28,366	66

Sources: Same as General Statistics. The 'Average' column represents the average for the industry sector, in 1997, where the currently shown industry is classified. The Index shows the relationship between the Average and the Analyzed Industry. For example, 100 means that they are equal; 500 that the Analyzed Industry is five times the average; 50 means that the Analyzed Industry is half the national average. The abbreviation 'na' is used to show that data are 'not available'.

LEADING COMPANIES

No company data available for this industry.

LOCATION BY STATE AND REGIONAL CONCENTRATION

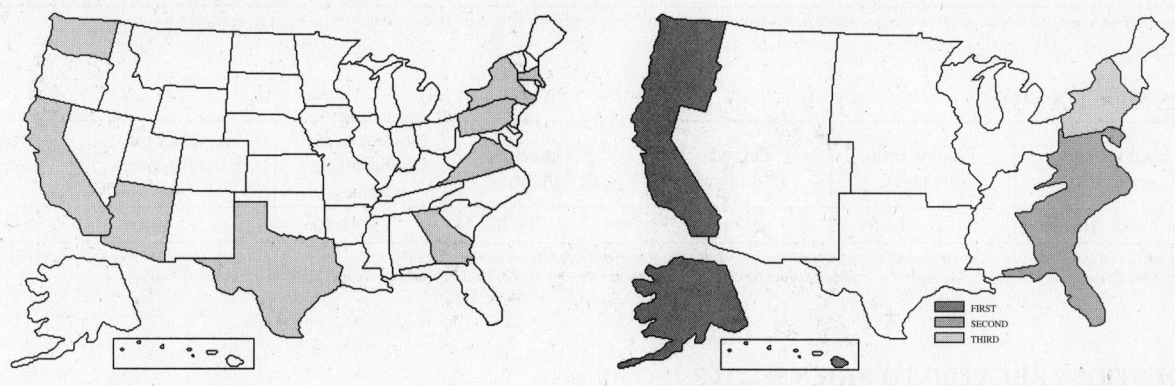

FIRST
SECOND
THIRD

INDUSTRY DATA BY STATE

State	Establishments Total (number)	Establishments % of U.S.	Employment Total (number)	Employment % of U.S.	Employment Per Estab.	Payroll Total ($ mil.)	Payroll Per Empl. ($)	Revenues Total ($ mil.)	Revenues % of U.S.	Revenues Per Estab. ($)
California	279	17.8	2,032	21.8	7	54.9	27,025	185.9	19.6	666,165
New York	159	10.1	1,106	11.9	7	35.6	32,204	122.7	13.0	771,491
Texas	102	6.5	697	7.5	7	21.1	30,313	121.4	12.8	1,189,843
Virginia	89	5.7	616	6.6	7	18.7	30,367	85.9	9.1	964,876
Pennsylvania	93	5.9	507	5.4	5	15.6	30,797	52.7	5.6	566,462
Florida	146	9.3	462	5.0	3	12.5	27,002	45.4	4.8	310,925
Georgia	29	1.8	249	2.7	9	7.6	30,610	29.7	3.1	1,025,379
Massachusetts	23	1.5	230	2.5	10	9.5	41,330	27.3	2.9	1,187,348
Washington	40	2.6	398	4.3	10	16.3	40,874	26.3	2.8	657,500
Ohio	31	2.0	182	2.0	6	5.7	31,187	26.3	2.8	848,903
D.C.	7	0.4	146	1.6	21	3.2	21,623	16.3	1.7	2,324,429
Arizona	39	2.5	247	2.7	6	5.3	21,462	15.3	1.6	391,872
Michigan	39	2.5	178	1.9	5	4.6	25,944	15.0	1.6	383,410
Illinois	54	3.4	195	2.1	4	5.5	28,123	14.7	1.6	272,481
New Jersey	37	2.4	101	1.1	3	3.6	35,475	13.0	1.4	351,703
Minnesota	25	1.6	178	1.9	7	4.9	27,809	12.7	1.3	506,600
Colorado	36	2.3	127	1.4	4	3.4	26,850	11.9	1.3	331,278
Louisiana	22	1.4	93	1.0	4	2.0	21,355	11.1	1.2	503,227
Maryland	27	1.7	149	1.6	6	2.7	17,852	8.0	0.8	295,407
North Carolina	40	2.6	103	1.1	3	2.9	27,689	7.0	0.7	175,650
Wisconsin	22	1.4	80	0.9	4	1.4	17,938	6.7	0.7	303,136
Tennessee	16	1.0	54	0.6	3	1.5	28,278	5.5	0.6	346,812
Nevada	22	1.4	82	0.9	4	2.0	24,390	5.2	0.5	235,955
Utah	7	0.4	123	1.3	18	1.4	11,325	4.6	0.5	659,857
Oregon	20	1.3	105	1.1	5	1.4	13,229	3.9	0.4	193,100
Iowa	9	0.6	43	0.5	5	1.7	38,512	3.5	0.4	388,889
Kentucky	13	0.8	38	0.4	3	0.8	20,711	2.9	0.3	226,615
Connecticut	14	0.9	22	0.2	2	0.5	23,909	2.4	0.3	172,929
South Carolina	18	1.1	37	0.4	2	0.8	20,649	2.1	0.2	116,889
New Mexico	7	0.4	24	0.3	3	0.9	36,250	2.0	0.2	284,857
Oklahoma	12	0.8	33	0.4	3	0.5	16,394	1.5	0.2	126,250
Alabama	5	0.3	19	0.2	4	0.5	24,211	1.1	0.1	219,200
Indiana	9	0.6	25	0.3	3	0.5	19,640	1.1	0.1	121,000
Montana	6	0.4	22	0.2	4	0.3	12,955	0.9	0.1	152,500
Kansas	4	0.3	16	0.2	4	0.3	19,375	0.9	0.1	222,500
West Virginia	6	0.4	12	0.1	2	0.1	9,667	0.5	0.1	79,333
Maine	5	0.3	8	0.1	2	0.2	22,250	0.3	0.0	52,800
Arkansas	4	0.3	8	0.1	2	0.1	9,750	0.2	0.0	49,000
Missouri	20	1.3	175*	-	-	(D)	-	(D)	-	-
Delaware	10	0.6	60*	-	-	(D)	-	(D)	-	-
Alaska	7	0.4	10*	-	-	(D)	-	(D)	-	-
Mississippi	6	0.4	375*	-	-	(D)	-	(D)	-	-
Idaho	2	0.1	10*	-	-	(D)	-	(D)	-	-
Rhode Island	2	0.1	10*	-	-	(D)	-	(D)	-	-
South Dakota	2	0.1	10*	-	-	(D)	-	(D)	-	-
Nebraska	1	0.1	10*	-	-	(D)	-	(D)	-	-
New Hampshire	1	0.1	10*	-	-	(D)	-	(D)	-	-
Vermont	1	0.1	10*	-	-	(D)	-	(D)	-	-

Source: 1997 *Economic Census*. The states are in descending order of revenues or establishments (if revenue data are missing for the majority). The symbol (D) appears when data are withheld to prevent disclosure of competitive information. States marked with (D) are sorted by number of establishments. A dash (-) indicates that the data element cannot be calculated. * indicates the midpoint of a range; 175, for example is the range 100-249. Shaded *states* on the state map indicate those states which have proportionately greater representation in the industry than would be indicated by the state's population; the ratio is based on total revenues or number of establishments. Shaded *regions* indicate where the industry is regionally most concentrated.

NAICS 541211 - OFFICES OF CERTIFIED PUBLIC ACCOUNTANTS

GENERAL STATISTICS

Year	Establishments (number)	Employment (number)	Payroll ($ million)	Revenues ($ million)	Employees per Establishment (number)	Revenues per Establishment ($)	Payroll per Employee ($)
1997	53,651	389,340	15,167.0	38,601.0	7.3	719,483	38,956

Source: *Economic Census of the United States*, 1997. This is a newly defined industry. Data for prior years were unavailable at the time of publication but may become available over time.

INDICES OF CHANGE

Year	Establishments (number)	Employment (number)	Payroll ($ million)	Revenues ($ million)	Employees per Establishment (number)	Revenues per Establishment ($)	Payroll per Employee ($)
1997	100.0	100.0	100.0	100.0	100.0	100.0	100.0

Sources: Same as General Statistics. The values shown reflect change from the base year, 1997. Values above 100 mean greater than 1997, values below 100 mean less than 1997, and a value of 100 in the 1982-96 or 1998-2001 period means same as 1997. Values followed by a 'p' are projections by the editors; 'e' stands for extrapolation. Data are the most recent available at this level of detail.

SIC INDUSTRIES RELATED TO NAICS 541211

Each new NAICS code represents an industry that used to be part of an SIC or a part of several SIC industries. Data in this table are shown to provide transitional information for these cases. All available data for the precursor SIC(s) are shown. Even if only a part of an SIC is included in the NAICS, *all* data for the SIC are reproduced. If the SIC industry is not marked as being a part (pt) of the NAICS, the entire industry is embedded in the NAICS data. The SIC composition of the new industry provides some hints of the relative importance of its "ancestors." Data marked with a 'p' are projected. Projections begin with 1982 data. Data earlier than 1990 are not shown but are reflected in the projections.

SIC	Industry	1990	1991	1992	1993	1994	1995	1996	1997
8721	**Accounting, Auditing & Bookkeeping (pt)**								
	Establishments (number)	67,905	71,277	79,097	81,439	83,033	84,851	85,397p	87,507p
	Employment (thousands)	523.7	559.3	520.6	543.2	547.5	587.5	616.8p	635.9p
	Revenues ($ million)	32,593.0	33,738.0	37,191.0	39,807.0	42,633.0	48,769.0	54,484.0	53,214.7p

Source: *Economic Census of the United States*, 1992, annual surveys of economic sectors conducted by the Bureau of the Census, and estimates or projections based on the 1982-1992 period; not all data are shown. 'e' marks estimates made by the editors; 'p' indicates projections based on time series. A dash (-) indicates that data for this SIC or year were not available. The abbreviation (pt) next to the industry name indicates that only a part of the industry is present within the NAICS data. If no (pt) is shown, the entire industry is contained within the NAICS data.

SELECTED RATIOS

For 1997	Avg. of Information	Analyzed Industry	Index	For 1997	Avg. of Information	Analyzed Industry	Index
Employees per establishment	9	7	84	Payroll per establishment	372,545	282,697	76
Revenue per establishment	958,337	719,483	75	Payroll as % of revenue	39	39	101
Revenue per employee	111,029	99,145	89	Payroll per employee	43,162	38,956	90

Sources: Same as General Statistics. The 'Average' column represents the average for the industry sector, in 1997, where the currently shown industry is classified. The Index shows the relationship between the Average and the Analyzed Industry. For example, 100 means that they are equal; 500 that the Analyzed Industry is five times the average; 50 means that the Analyzed Industry is half the national average. The abbreviation 'na' is used to show that data are 'not available'.

LEADING COMPANIES Number shown: **6** Total sales ($ mil): **80** Total employment (000): **0.7**

Company Name	Address				CEO Name	Phone	Co. Type	Sales ($ mil)	Empl. (000)
Geo. S. Olive and Co.	201 N Illinois St	Indianapolis	IN	46204		317-383-4008	N	60	0.5
Clark Schaefer Hackett and Co.	105 E Fourth St	Cincinnati	OH	45202		513-241-3111	N	15	0.2
Kaufman, Davis, Ruebelmann	7475 Wisconsin	Bethesda	MD	20814		301-951-3636	N	3	<0.1
Indian Development Corp.	PO Box 15613	Oklahoma City	OK	73155		405-670-1551	N	1	<0.1
Complete Business & Tax	4550 McKnight Rd	Pittsburgh	PA	15237		412-931-1617	N	0	<0.1
Perry L. Smith Consulting	800 Bellevue NE	Bellevue	WA	98004		425-462-2072	N	0	<0.1

Source: *Ward's Business Directory of U.S. Private and Public Companies*, Volumes 1 and 2, 2000. The company type code used is as follows: P - Public, R - Private, S - Subsidiary, D - Division, J - Joint Venture, A - Affiliate, G - Group, N - Company type not reported. Sales are in millions of dollars, employees are in thousands. An asterisk (*) indicates an estimated sales volume. The symbol < stands for 'less than'. Company names and addresses are truncated, in some cases, to fit into the available space.

LOCATION BY STATE AND REGIONAL CONCENTRATION

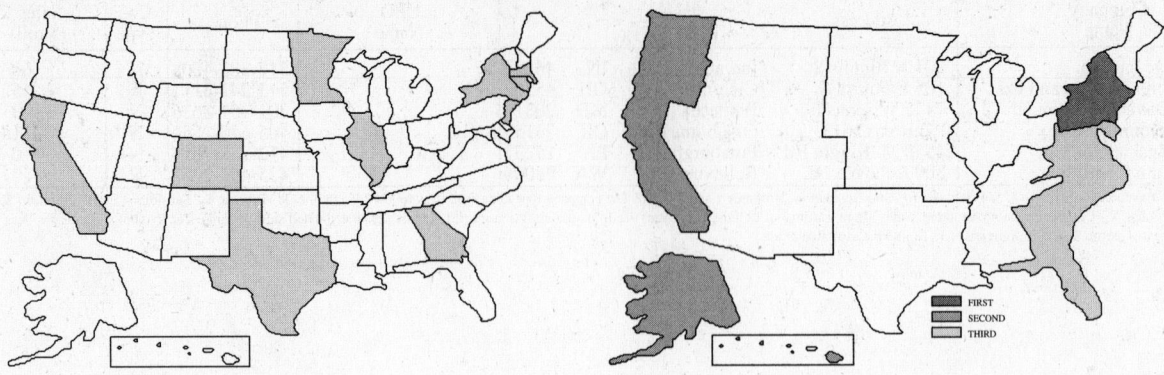

FIRST
SECOND
THIRD

INDUSTRY DATA BY STATE

State	Establishments Total (number)	% of U.S.	Employment Total (number)	% of U.S.	Per Estab.	Payroll Total ($ mil.)	Per Empl. ($)	Revenues Total ($ mil.)	% of U.S.	Per Estab. ($)
California	7,045	13.1	47,900	12.3	7	2,034.0	42,463	5,502.2	14.3	781,014
New York	3,821	7.1	37,923	9.7	10	1,712.8	45,165	5,027.5	13.0	1,315,744
Texas	4,272	8.0	26,744	6.9	6	1,052.7	39,361	2,720.4	7.0	636,809
Illinois	2,333	4.3	22,681	5.8	10	996.8	43,947	2,522.5	6.5	1,081,207
Florida	3,638	6.8	23,983	6.2	7	781.4	32,580	1,831.2	4.7	503,344
Pennsylvania	1,962	3.7	17,519	4.5	9	696.9	39,781	1,797.2	4.7	915,986
Ohio	2,008	3.7	15,181	3.9	8	555.5	36,591	1,412.5	3.7	703,417
New Jersey	1,876	3.5	12,545	3.2	7	554.7	44,215	1,410.7	3.7	751,979
Massachusetts	1,265	2.4	12,331	3.2	10	533.0	43,222	1,388.1	3.6	1,097,330
Georgia	1,476	2.8	11,519	3.0	8	493.0	42,800	1,148.2	3.0	777,898
Michigan	1,582	2.9	12,698	3.3	8	512.7	40,380	1,133.8	2.9	716,700
Virginia	1,156	2.2	9,116	2.3	8	367.0	40,258	889.0	2.3	768,988
North Carolina	1,289	2.4	8,546	2.2	7	288.8	33,797	748.7	1.9	580,839
Missouri	920	1.7	8,028	2.1	9	282.3	35,170	737.5	1.9	801,652
Minnesota	853	1.6	7,600	2.0	9	294.9	38,807	730.9	1.9	856,824
Connecticut	777	1.4	6,221	1.6	8	277.5	44,612	729.3	1.9	938,647
Maryland	1,225	2.3	7,864	2.0	6	327.2	41,608	722.2	1.9	589,548
Washington	1,116	2.1	6,898	1.8	6	269.3	39,036	671.2	1.7	601,430
Indiana	871	1.6	7,601	2.0	9	243.8	32,071	615.5	1.6	706,704
Wisconsin	808	1.5	7,596	2.0	9	252.2	33,207	597.7	1.5	739,686
D.C.	98	0.2	4,488	1.2	46	247.2	55,088	556.4	1.4	5,677,367
Colorado	1,207	2.2	5,922	1.5	5	229.7	38,789	526.2	1.4	435,936
Tennessee	876	1.6	5,427	1.4	6	188.0	34,634	457.6	1.2	522,418
Arizona	930	1.7	4,783	1.2	5	164.4	34,380	383.2	1.0	411,989
Oregon	860	1.6	4,686	1.2	5	145.3	31,002	366.1	0.9	425,660
Louisiana	902	1.7	4,461	1.1	5	140.0	31,382	364.7	0.9	404,279
Alabama	637	1.2	4,443	1.1	7	152.5	34,331	326.1	0.8	511,989
Oklahoma	902	1.7	4,196	1.1	5	115.8	27,588	298.8	0.8	331,299
Kentucky	565	1.1	3,650	0.9	6	113.1	30,974	273.8	0.7	484,536
Iowa	451	0.8	3,373	0.9	7	105.2	31,179	268.0	0.7	594,177
Kansas	514	1.0	3,320	0.9	6	103.7	31,246	227.8	0.6	443,284
South Carolina	575	1.1	3,043	0.8	5	92.4	30,369	222.5	0.6	386,950
Nebraska	320	0.6	2,520	0.6	8	77.8	30,860	185.1	0.5	578,406
Utah	386	0.7	2,248	0.6	6	69.3	30,807	169.4	0.4	438,935
Hawaii	275	0.5	1,878	0.5	7	62.9	33,504	163.9	0.4	596,153
Arkansas	522	1.0	2,338	0.6	4	66.0	28,209	163.6	0.4	313,389
Mississippi	376	0.7	2,128	0.5	6	66.6	31,276	150.3	0.4	399,848
Nevada	297	0.6	1,613	0.4	5	58.8	36,458	143.2	0.4	482,077
New Mexico	366	0.7	1,915	0.5	5	56.0	29,256	128.4	0.3	350,697
Rhode Island	240	0.4	1,338	0.3	6	42.8	32,021	113.0	0.3	470,796
West Virginia	276	0.5	1,498	0.4	5	40.2	26,845	106.6	0.3	386,395
Maine	199	0.4	1,302	0.3	7	48.7	37,396	100.3	0.3	503,889
Idaho	293	0.5	1,392	0.4	5	38.9	27,930	92.2	0.2	314,703
New Hampshire	264	0.5	1,154	0.3	4	43.7	37,893	89.2	0.2	337,848
Montana	272	0.5	1,413	0.4	5	38.0	26,912	83.8	0.2	307,930
Delaware	132	0.2	832	0.2	6	30.3	36,393	62.7	0.2	474,871
Alaska	130	0.2	606	0.2	5	24.6	40,561	58.3	0.2	448,362
South Dakota	124	0.2	831	0.2	7	19.5	23,484	53.0	0.1	427,645
North Dakota	121	0.2	845	0.2	7	23.9	28,228	50.1	0.1	414,298
Vermont	131	0.2	598	0.2	5	19.6	32,729	41.3	0.1	314,885
Wyoming	117	0.2	605	0.2	5	16.1	26,537	39.6	0.1	338,265

Source: 1997 *Economic Census*. The states are in descending order of revenues or establishments (if revenue data are missing for the majority). The symbol (D) appears when data are withheld to prevent disclosure of competitive information. States marked with (D) are sorted by number of establishments. A dash (-) indicates that the data element cannot be calculated. * indicates the midpoint of a range; 175, for example is the range 100-249. Shaded *states* on the state map indicate those states which have proportionately greater representation in the industry than would be indicated by the state's population; the ratio is based on total revenues or number of establishments. Shaded *regions* indicate where the industry is regionally most concentrated.

NAICS 541213 - TAX RETURN PREPARATION SERVICES*

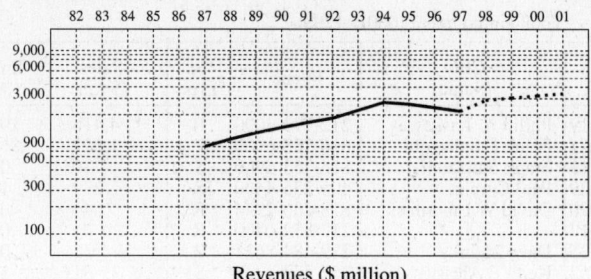

Revenues ($ million)

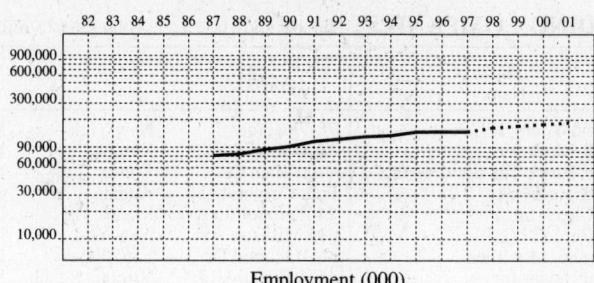

Employment (000)

GENERAL STATISTICS

Year	Establishments (number)	Employment (number)	Payroll ($ million)	Revenues ($ million)	Employees per Establishment (number)	Revenues per Establishment ($)	Payroll per Employee ($)
1982	-	-	-	-	-	-	-
1983	-	-	-	-	-	-	-
1984	-	-	-	-	-	-	-
1985	-	-	-	-	-	-	-
1986	-	-	-	-	-	-	-
1987	7,297	81,083	343.0	905.0	11.1	124,024	4,230
1988	6,978	84,325	373.0	1,088.0 e	12.1	155,919	4,423
1989	6,397	95,220	367.0	1,272.0 e	14.9	198,843	3,854
1990	6,323	102,268	404.0	1,455.0	16.2	230,112	3,950
1991	6,931	116,379	483.0	1,643.0	16.8	237,051	4,150
1992	7,924	122,954	522.0	1,838.0	15.5	231,954	4,245
1993	8,327	130,761	542.0	2,239.0	15.7	268,884	4,145
1994	8,526	134,574	559.0	2,732.0	15.8	320,432	4,154
1995	8,616	147,028	591.0	2,608.0	17.1	302,693	4,020
1996	10,723 e	147,363 e	676.0 e	2,396.0 e	13.7 e	223,445 e	4,587 e
1997	12,830	147,698	760.0	2,184.0	11.5	170,226	5,146
1998	11,267 p	163,767 p	747.0 p	2,876.0 p	14.5 p	255,259 p	4,561 p
1999	11,768 p	171,219 p	786.0 p	3,046.0 p	14.5 p	258,838 p	4,591 p
2000	12,269 p	178,670 p	826.0 p	3,217.0 p	14.6 p	262,206 p	4,623 p
2001	12,770 p	186,121 p	865.0 p	3,388.0 p	14.6 p	265,309 p	4,648 p

Sources: Economic Census of the United States, 1982, 1987, 1992, 1997. Establishment counts, employment, and payroll are from County Business Patterns for non-Census years. In non-Census years, industries in the Manufacturing range under SIC coding include data from the Annual Survey of Manufactures (ASM); those in the old Services range include data from the Services Annual Survey (SAS). Values followed by a 'p' are projections by the editors. Extrapolations are marked by 'e'. Data are the most recent available at this level of detail.

INDICES OF CHANGE

Year	Establishments (number)	Employment (number)	Payroll ($ million)	Revenues ($ million)	Employees per Establishment (number)	Revenues per Establishment ($)	Payroll per Employee ($)
1982	-	-	-	-	-	-	-
1987	56.9	54.9	45.1	41.4	96.5	72.9	82.2
1992	61.8	83.2	68.7	84.2	134.8	136.3	82.5
1993	64.9	88.5	71.3	102.5	136.4	158.0	80.6
1994	66.5	91.1	73.6	125.1	137.1	188.2	80.7
1995	67.2	99.5	77.8	119.4	148.2	177.8	78.1
1996	83.6 e	99.8 e	88.9 e	109.7 e	119.4 e	131.3 e	89.1 e
1997	100.0	100.0	100.0	100.0	100.0	100.0	100.0
1998	87.8 p	110.9 p	98.3 p	131.7 p	126.3 p	150.0 p	88.6 p
1999	91.7 p	115.9 p	103.4 p	139.5 p	126.4 p	152.1 p	89.2 p
2000	95.6 p	121.0 p	108.7 p	147.3 p	126.5 p	154.0 p	89.8 p
2001	99.5 p	126.0 p	113.8 p	155.1 p	126.6 p	155.9 p	90.3 p

Sources: Same as General Statistics. The values shown reflect change from the base year, 1997. Values above 100 mean greater than 1997, values below 100 mean less than 1997, and a value of 100 in the 1982-96 or 1998-2001 period means same as 1997. Values followed by a 'p' are projections by the editors; 'e' stands for extrapolation. Data are the most recent available at this level of detail.

SELECTED RATIOS

For 1997	Avg. of Information	Analyzed Industry	Index	For 1997	Avg. of Information	Analyzed Industry	Index
Employees per establishment	9	12	133	Payroll per establishment	372,545	59,236	16
Revenue per establishment	958,337	170,226	18	Payroll as % of revenue	39	35	90
Revenue per employee	111,029	14,787	13	Payroll per employee	43,162	5,146	12

Sources: Same as General Statistics. The 'Average' column represents the average for the industry sector, in 1997, where the currently shown industry is classified. The Index shows the relationship between the Average and the Analyzed Industry. For example, 100 means that they are equal; 500 that the Analyzed Industry is five times the average; 50 means that the Analyzed Industry is half the national average. The abbreviation 'na' is used to show that data are 'not available'.

*Equivalent to SIC 7291.

LEADING COMPANIES   Number shown: **15**   Total sales ($ mil): **7,150**   Total employment (000): **120.0**

Company Name	Address				CEO Name	Phone	Co. Type	Sales ($ mil)	Empl. (000)
Ernst and Young L.L.P.	787 7th Ave	New York	NY	10019	Philip A. Laskaway	212-773-3000	R	4,416*	29.0
H and R Block Inc.	4400 Main St	Kansas City	MO	64111	Frank L Salizzoni	816-753-6900	P	1,522	86.5
H and R Block Tax Services Inc.	4400 Main St	Kansas City	MO	64111	Frank Salizzoni	816-753-6900	S	730*	0.9
NDCE Commerce	Four Corporate Sq	Atlanta	GA	30329	Paul Garcia	404-235-4400	S	279*	1.6
Triple Check Inc.	2441 Honolulu Ave	Montrose	CA	91020	David W Liberman	818-236-2944	R	46*	<0.1
David Berdon L.L.P.	415 Madison Ave	New York	NY	10017		212-832-0400	R	41	0.3
DuCharme, McMillen	6610 Mutual Dr	Fort Wayne	IN	46825	Dave Meinka	219-484-8631	R	32	0.3
Jackson Hewitt Inc.	4575 Bonney Rd	Virginia Beach	VA	23462	Keith E Alessi	757-473-3300	S	31*	1.2
Burr, Wolff and Associates	3355 W Alabama	Houston	TX	77098	Kirk Burr	713-986-5000	R	24*	<0.1
Meridian VAT Reclaim Inc.	125 W 55th St N W	New York	NY	10019		212-554-6700	R	12*	<0.1
LedgerPlus Inc.	401 St Francis St	Tallahassee	FL	32301	John Harrison	850-681-1941	R	7	<0.1
GRA, Thompson, White and Co.	4600 Madison	Kansas City	KS	64112	George D Thompson	816-753-0030	R	5*	<0.1
Niessen Dunlap and Pritchard P.C.	590 Bethlehem Pike	Colmar	PA	18915	Albert W Pritchard	215-997-7200	R	4*	<0.1
Labbe, Morton & Associates Ltd.	P O Box 142	Glendale	AZ	85311	Michael Monton	623-939-8299	R	1*	<0.1
T and W Tax Service	4717 W Orgwd	Glendale	AZ	85301	Ron Tobes	623-931-2177	R	1*	<0.1

Source: *Ward's Business Directory of U.S. Private and Public Companies*, Volumes 1 and 2, 2000. The company type code used is as follows: P - Public, R - Private, S - Subsidiary, D - Division, J - Joint Venture, A - Affiliate, G - Group, N - Company type not reported. Sales are in millions of dollars, employees are in thousands. An asterisk (*) indicates an estimated sales volume. The symbol < stands for 'less than'. Company names and addresses are truncated, in some cases, to fit into the available space.

LOCATION BY STATE AND REGIONAL CONCENTRATION

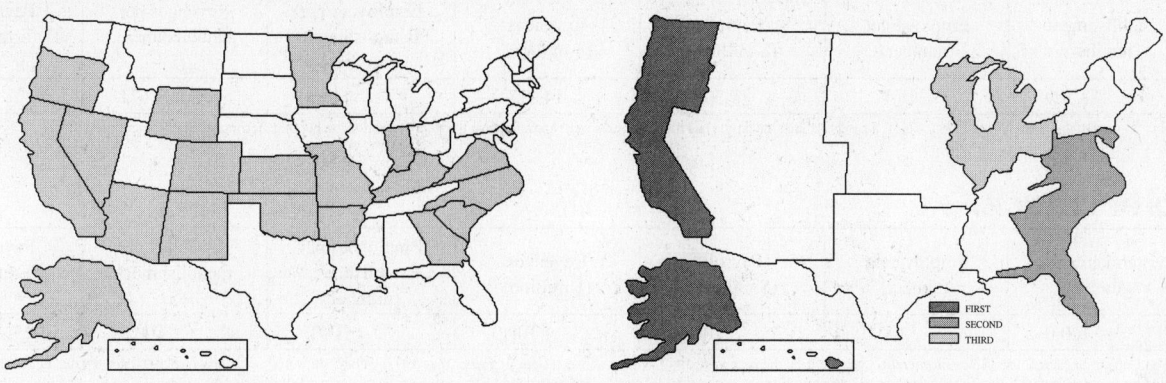

FIRST
SECOND
THIRD

INDUSTRY DATA BY STATE

State	Establishments Total (number)	% of U.S.	Employment Total (number)	% of U.S.	Per Estab.	Payroll Total ($ mil.)	Per Empl. ($)	Revenues Total ($ mil.)	% of U.S.	Per Estab. ($)
California	1,849	14.4	13,636	9.2	7	105.4	7,726	326.0	14.9	176,294
New York	679	5.3	8,410	5.7	12	47.6	5,661	132.6	6.1	195,352
Texas	815	6.4	8,048	5.4	10	42.2	5,238	125.4	5.7	153,842
Florida	522	4.1	8,503	5.8	16	40.4	4,747	107.2	4.9	205,406
Ohio	474	3.7	7,647	5.2	16	34.4	4,492	94.0	4.3	198,405
Illinois	484	3.8	7,282	4.9	15	33.2	4,561	90.1	4.1	186,169
Pennsylvania	440	3.4	8,145	5.5	19	29.6	3,638	82.6	3.8	187,839
North Carolina	394	3.1	5,319	3.6	14	24.9	4,672	75.0	3.4	190,434
Michigan	405	3.2	5,494	3.7	14	30.5	5,544	75.0	3.4	185,212
Georgia	332	2.6	4,840	3.3	15	23.2	4,788	68.9	3.2	207,611
Virginia	339	2.6	5,081	3.4	15	22.7	4,461	60.7	2.8	179,094
Indiana	307	2.4	4,409	3.0	14	19.7	4,469	55.1	2.5	179,625
Missouri	337	2.6	4,029	2.7	12	18.4	4,568	54.0	2.5	160,154
New Jersey	250	1.9	3,952	2.7	16	21.1	5,351	51.0	2.3	203,968
Massachusetts	228	1.8	3,520	2.4	15	18.1	5,149	45.3	2.1	198,737
Wisconsin	303	2.4	3,048	2.1	10	15.6	5,103	42.4	1.9	139,809
Minnesota	317	2.5	2,224	1.5	7	14.4	6,477	42.0	1.9	132,587
Tennessee	209	1.6	3,375	2.3	16	13.9	4,124	41.9	1.9	200,316
Oregon	296	2.3	1,649	1.1	6	13.3	8,041	37.9	1.7	128,122
Maryland	220	1.7	2,999	2.0	14	14.3	4,763	37.5	1.7	170,623
Arizona	223	1.7	2,748	1.9	12	13.4	4,864	37.4	1.7	167,583
South Carolina	258	2.0	2,626	1.8	10	11.1	4,214	36.3	1.7	140,682
Washington	243	1.9	1,901	1.3	8	11.6	6,126	35.8	1.6	147,296
Oklahoma	242	1.9	1,405	1.0	6	11.3	8,046	34.2	1.6	141,136
Louisiana	175	1.4	3,551	2.4	20	11.6	3,280	33.6	1.5	192,269
Kentucky	259	2.0	2,438	1.7	9	10.1	4,149	33.1	1.5	127,645
Colorado	194	1.5	2,221	1.5	11	12.1	5,451	32.9	1.5	169,696
Kansas	183	1.4	1,932	1.3	11	10.3	5,321	28.6	1.3	156,180
Alabama	218	1.7	1,993	1.3	9	8.3	4,174	26.1	1.2	119,642
Connecticut	120	0.9	1,760	1.2	15	8.7	4,947	24.1	1.1	200,917
Arkansas	174	1.4	1,264	0.9	7	6.2	4,887	22.8	1.0	131,190
Iowa	175	1.4	1,399	0.9	8	7.7	5,523	22.8	1.0	130,069
New Mexico	82	0.6	845	0.6	10	4.6	5,449	17.3	0.8	210,598
Mississippi	134	1.0	1,438	1.0	11	4.9	3,424	16.9	0.8	126,463
West Virginia	83	0.6	1,063	0.7	13	4.6	4,288	14.9	0.7	179,988
Nevada	109	0.8	899	0.6	8	4.9	5,440	14.5	0.7	133,119
Nebraska	101	0.8	814	0.6	8	4.2	5,147	13.3	0.6	131,792
Utah	65	0.5	761	0.5	12	3.4	4,488	11.1	0.5	171,492
Hawaii	42	0.3	670	0.5	16	4.2	6,310	9.4	0.4	224,095
New Hampshire	68	0.5	700	0.5	10	3.5	4,937	9.4	0.4	137,750
Maine	72	0.6	463	0.3	6	2.8	6,058	8.8	0.4	122,583
Idaho	57	0.4	416	0.3	7	2.4	5,853	7.7	0.4	135,754
Alaska	44	0.3	237	0.2	5	2.2	9,173	7.5	0.3	171,364
Montana	58	0.5	356	0.2	6	2.2	6,067	6.6	0.3	113,862
Delaware	46	0.4	494	0.3	11	2.5	5,154	6.2	0.3	134,500
North Dakota	49	0.4	287	0.2	6	1.5	5,143	5.1	0.2	103,469
Rhode Island	29	0.2	425	0.3	15	2.0	4,595	5.1	0.2	174,759
D.C.	12	0.1	305	0.2	25	1.6	5,331	5.1	0.2	421,917
South Dakota	46	0.4	259	0.2	6	1.4	5,544	4.9	0.2	105,522
Vermont	38	0.3	189	0.1	5	1.1	6,048	4.3	0.2	112,868
Wyoming	31	0.2	229	0.2	7	1.1	4,729	3.6	0.2	117,097

Source: 1997 *Economic Census*. The states are in descending order of revenues or establishments (if revenue data are missing for the majority). The symbol (D) appears when data are withheld to prevent disclosure of competitive information. States marked with (D) are sorted by number of establishments. A dash (-) indicates that the data element cannot be calculated. * indicates the midpoint of a range; 175, for example is the range 100-249. Shaded *states* on the state map indicate those states which have proportionately greater representation in the industry than would be indicated by the state's population; the ratio is based on total revenues or number of establishments. Shaded *regions* indicate where the industry is regionally most concentrated.

NAICS 541214 - PAYROLL SERVICES

GENERAL STATISTICS

Year	Establishments (number)	Employment (number)	Payroll ($ million)	Revenues ($ million)	Employees per Establishment (number)	Revenues per Establishment ($)	Payroll per Employee ($)
1997	2,709	316,425	7,598.0	14,113.0	116.8	5,209,671	24,012

Source: *Economic Census of the United States*, 1997. This is a newly defined industry. Data for prior years were unavailable at the time of publication but may become available over time.

INDICES OF CHANGE

Year	Establishments (number)	Employment (number)	Payroll ($ million)	Revenues ($ million)	Employees per Establishment (number)	Revenues per Establishment ($)	Payroll per Employee ($)
1997	100.0	100.0	100.0	100.0	100.0	100.0	100.0

Sources: Same as General Statistics. The values shown reflect change from the base year, 1997. Values above 100 mean greater than 1997, values below 100 mean less than 1997, and a value of 100 in the 1982-96 or 1998-2001 period means same as 1997. Values followed by a 'p' are projections by the editors; 'e' stands for extrapolation. Data are the most recent available at this level of detail.

SIC INDUSTRIES RELATED TO NAICS 541214

Each new NAICS code represents an industry that used to be part of an SIC or a part of several SIC industries. Data in this table are shown to provide transitional information for these cases. All available data for the precursor SIC(s) are shown. Even if only a part of an SIC is included in the NAICS, *all* data for the SIC are reproduced. If the SIC industry is not marked as being a part (pt) of the NAICS, the entire industry is embedded in the NAICS data. The SIC composition of the new industry provides some hints of the relative importance of its "ancestors." Data marked with a 'p' are projected. Projections begin with 1982 data. Data earlier than 1990 are not shown but are reflected in the projections.

SIC	Industry	1990	1991	1992	1993	1994	1995	1996	1997
7819	**Services Allied to Motion Pictures (pt)**								
	Establishments (number)	2,984	2,955	3,895	3,799	3,691	3,289	3,584p	3,622p
	Employment (thousands)	113.1	102.4	162.2	158.8	130.9	136.7	160.9p	169.5p
	Revenues ($ million)	-	-	7,514.7	-	-	-	-	-
8721	**Accounting, Auditing & Bookkeeping (pt)**								
	Establishments (number)	67,905	71,277	79,097	81,439	83,033	84,851	85,397p	87,507p
	Employment (thousands)	523.7	559.3	520.6	543.2	547.5	587.5	616.8p	635.9p
	Revenues ($ million)	32,593.0	33,738.0	37,191.0	39,807.0	42,633.0	48,769.0	54,484.0	53,214.7p

Source: *Economic Census of the United States*, 1992, annual surveys of economic sectors conducted by the Bureau of the Census, and estimates or projections based on the 1982-1992 period; not all data are shown. 'e' marks estimates made by the editors; 'p' indicates projections based on time series. A dash (-) indicates that data for this SIC or year were not available. The abbreviation (pt) next to the industry name indicates that only a part of the industry is present within the NAICS data. If no (pt) is shown, the entire industry is contained within the NAICS data.

SELECTED RATIOS

For 1997	Avg. of Information	Analyzed Industry	Index	For 1997	Avg. of Information	Analyzed Industry	Index
Employees per establishment	9	117	1,353	Payroll per establishment	372,545	2,804,725	753
Revenue per establishment	958,337	5,209,671	544	Payroll as % of revenue	39	54	138
Revenue per employee	111,029	44,601	40	Payroll per employee	43,162	24,012	56

Sources: Same as General Statistics. The 'Average' column represents the average for the industry sector, in 1997, where the currently shown industry is classified. The Index shows the relationship between the Average and the Analyzed Industry. For example, 100 means that they are equal; 500 that the Analyzed Industry is five times the average; 50 means that the Analyzed Industry is half the national average. The abbreviation 'na' is used to show that data are 'not available'.

LEADING COMPANIES
No company data available for this industry.

LOCATION BY STATE AND REGIONAL CONCENTRATION

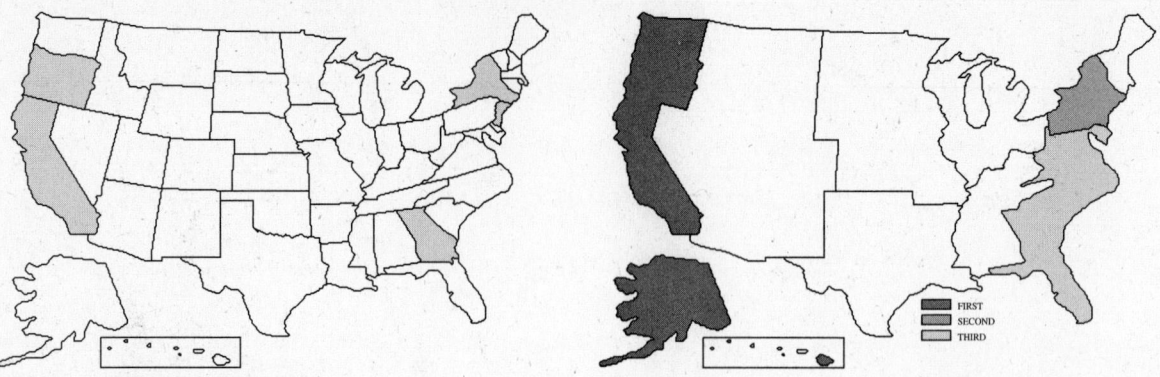

INDUSTRY DATA BY STATE

State	Establishments Total (number)	% of U.S.	Employment Total (number)	% of U.S.	Per Estab.	Payroll Total ($ mil.)	Per Empl. ($)	Revenues Total ($ mil.)	% of U.S.	Per Estab. ($)
California	350	12.9	165,300	52.2	472	3,520.8	21,300	6,468.1	45.8	18,480,411
New York	234	8.6	23,984	7.6	102	826.9	34,476	1,276.2	9.0	5,453,744
New Jersey	111	4.1	17,269	5.5	156	463.9	26,864	1,067.2	7.6	9,614,748
Florida	143	5.3	14,077	4.4	98	391.3	27,795	643.4	4.6	4,499,490
Illinois	130	4.8	9,342	3.0	72	274.6	29,399	545.2	3.9	4,193,838
Texas	174	6.4	10,397	3.3	60	273.8	26,332	457.2	3.2	2,627,420
Georgia	76	2.8	7,909	2.5	104	165.4	20,916	444.4	3.1	5,847,974
Michigan	105	3.9	5,729	1.8	55	193.2	33,716	333.1	2.4	3,172,705
Maryland	78	2.9	4,045	1.3	52	102.9	25,444	236.8	1.7	3,036,000
Pennsylvania	110	4.1	3,413	1.1	31	100.4	29,427	204.0	1.4	1,854,273
Massachusetts	69	2.5	3,125	1.0	45	106.0	33,917	202.7	1.4	2,937,217
Ohio	93	3.4	2,653	0.8	29	83.2	31,343	180.7	1.3	1,943,409
Oregon	40	1.5	2,844	0.9	71	66.6	23,407	164.9	1.2	4,123,300
Connecticut	33	1.2	1,743	0.6	53	81.7	46,873	159.4	1.1	4,829,636
Minnesota	40	1.5	2,408	0.8	60	59.2	24,604	155.3	1.1	3,883,400
Arizona	47	1.7	6,506	2.1	138	89.5	13,763	139.6	1.0	2,969,340
Missouri	49	1.8	1,916	0.6	39	69.0	35,991	138.8	1.0	2,833,388
Washington	47	1.7	3,617	1.1	77	79.0	21,836	134.1	1.0	2,854,128
Virginia	60	2.2	2,988	0.9	50	84.3	28,220	123.9	0.9	2,065,400
Colorado	54	2.0	1,969	0.6	36	52.9	26,850	110.7	0.8	2,050,537
Utah	38	1.4	2,621	0.8	69	55.2	21,070	105.3	0.7	2,770,026
Louisiana	52	1.9	3,583	1.1	69	71.3	19,902	91.1	0.6	1,752,000
North Carolina	46	1.7	2,174	0.7	47	47.3	21,760	89.9	0.6	1,953,761
Kansas	32	1.2	1,412	0.4	44	38.1	26,974	80.0	0.6	2,498,938
Kentucky	30	1.1	1,072	0.3	36	32.4	30,197	72.3	0.5	2,410,567
Indiana	47	1.7	960	0.3	20	29.8	31,019	58.7	0.4	1,249,191
Tennessee	41	1.5	1,397	0.4	34	32.5	23,288	56.8	0.4	1,386,585
Wisconsin	36	1.3	1,988	0.6	55	22.0	11,085	47.0	0.3	1,304,361
Alabama	24	0.9	422	0.1	18	13.2	31,244	36.1	0.3	1,502,292
New Hampshire	18	0.7	1,648	0.5	92	15.6	9,478	28.5	0.2	1,580,833
Arkansas	25	0.9	873	0.3	35	17.5	20,050	28.2	0.2	1,128,920
Nevada	26	1.0	836	0.3	32	14.0	16,804	26.8	0.2	1,031,192
South Carolina	35	1.3	845	0.3	24	13.6	16,093	21.7	0.2	620,286
Hawaii	12	0.4	201	0.1	17	7.1	35,542	19.7	0.1	1,644,833
Oklahoma	27	1.0	774	0.2	29	10.6	13,704	18.2	0.1	675,037
Iowa	18	0.7	333	0.1	19	12.3	36,871	15.9	0.1	881,667
Nebraska	17	0.6	581	0.2	34	10.5	18,133	14.3	0.1	838,412
Mississippi	16	0.6	484	0.2	30	9.5	19,643	13.3	0.1	828,375
D.C.	16	0.6	553	0.2	35	7.4	13,420	10.1	0.1	632,937
New Mexico	8	0.3	230	0.1	29	3.5	15,261	10.1	0.1	1,262,875
Maine	27	1.0	186	0.1	7	4.7	25,129	9.0	0.1	331,593
Montana	8	0.3	82	0.0	10	2.1	25,988	3.5	0.0	436,125
West Virginia	10	0.4	135	0.0	14	1.7	12,904	3.1	0.0	310,700
North Dakota	6	0.2	87	0.0	15	1.3	14,816	2.4	0.0	400,667
Vermont	4	0.1	41	0.0	10	1.0	24,293	2.1	0.0	524,500
Idaho	9	0.3	46	0.0	5	0.7	15,652	1.6	0.0	173,556
South Dakota	5	0.2	27	0.0	5	0.6	23,000	1.0	0.0	204,000
Rhode Island	14	0.5	1,750*	-	-	(D)	-	(D)	-	-
Delaware	12	0.4	60*	-	-	(D)	-	(D)	-	-
Wyoming	4	0.1	375*	-	-	(D)	-	(D)	-	-
Alaska	3	0.1	10*	-	-	(D)	-	(D)	-	-

Source: 1997 *Economic Census*. The states are in descending order of revenues or establishments (if revenue data are missing for the majority). The symbol (D) appears when data are withheld to prevent disclosure of competitive information. States marked with (D) are sorted by number of establishments. A dash (-) indicates that the data element cannot be calculated. * indicates the midpoint of a range; 175, for example is the range 100-249. Shaded *states* on the state map indicate those states which have proportionately greater representation in the industry than would be indicated by the state's population; the ratio is based on total revenues or number of establishments. Shaded *regions* indicate where the industry is regionally most concentrated.

NAICS 541219 - ACCOUNTING SERVICES NEC

GENERAL STATISTICS

Year	Establishments (number)	Employment (number)	Payroll ($ million)	Revenues ($ million)	Employees per Establishment (number)	Revenues per Establishment ($)	Payroll per Employee ($)
1997	28,322	113,070	2,578.0	6,219.0	4.0	219,582	22,800

Source: *Economic Census of the United States*, 1997. This is a newly defined industry. Data for prior years were unavailable at the time of publication but may become available over time.

INDICES OF CHANGE

Year	Establishments (number)	Employment (number)	Payroll ($ million)	Revenues ($ million)	Employees per Establishment (number)	Revenues per Establishment ($)	Payroll per Employee ($)
1997	100.0	100.0	100.0	100.0	100.0	100.0	100.0

Sources: Same as General Statistics. The values shown reflect change from the base year, 1997. Values above 100 mean greater than 1997, values below 100 mean less than 1997, and a value of 100 in the 1982-96 or 1998-2001 period means same as 1997. Values followed by a 'p' are projections by the editors; 'e' stands for extrapolation. Data are the most recent available at this level of detail.

SIC INDUSTRIES RELATED TO NAICS 541219

Each new NAICS code represents an industry that used to be part of an SIC or a part of several SIC industries. Data in this table are shown to provide transitional information for these cases. All available data for the precursor SIC(s) are shown. Even if only a part of an SIC is included in the NAICS, *all* data for the SIC are reproduced. If the SIC industry is not marked as being a part (pt) of the NAICS, the entire industry is embedded in the NAICS data. The SIC composition of the new industry provides some hints of the relative importance of its "ancestors." Data marked with a 'p' are projected. Projections begin with 1982 data. Data earlier than 1990 are not shown but are reflected in the projections.

SIC	Industry	1990	1991	1992	1993	1994	1995	1996	1997
8721	**Accounting, Auditing & Bookkeeping (pt)**								
	Establishments (number)	67,905	71,277	79,097	81,439	83,033	84,851	85,397*p*	87,507*p*
	Employment (thousands)	523.7	559.3	520.6	543.2	547.5	587.5	616.8*p*	635.9*p*
	Revenues ($ million)	32,593.0	33,738.0	37,191.0	39,807.0	42,633.0	48,769.0	54,484.0	53,214.7*p*

Source: *Economic Census of the United States*, 1992, annual surveys of economic sectors conducted by the Bureau of the Census, and estimates or projections based on the 1982-1992 period; not all data are shown. 'e' marks estimates made by the editors; 'p' indicates projections based on time series. A dash (-) indicates that data for this SIC or year were not available. The abbreviation (pt) next to the industry name indicates that only a part of the industry is present within the NAICS data. If no (pt) is shown, the entire industry is contained within the NAICS data.

SELECTED RATIOS

For 1997	Avg. of Information	Analyzed Industry	Index	For 1997	Avg. of Information	Analyzed Industry	Index
Employees per establishment	9	4	46	Payroll per establishment	372,545	91,025	24
Revenue per establishment	958,337	219,582	23	Payroll as % of revenue	39	41	107
Revenue per employee	111,029	55,001	50	Payroll per employee	43,162	22,800	53

Sources: Same as General Statistics. The 'Average' column represents the average for the industry sector, in 1997, where the currently shown industry is classified. The Index shows the relationship between the Average and the Analyzed Industry. For example, 100 means that they are equal; 500 that the Analyzed Industry is five times the average; 50 means that the Analyzed Industry is half the national average. The abbreviation 'na' is used to show that data are 'not available'.

LEADING COMPANIES

No company data available for this industry.

LOCATION BY STATE AND REGIONAL CONCENTRATION

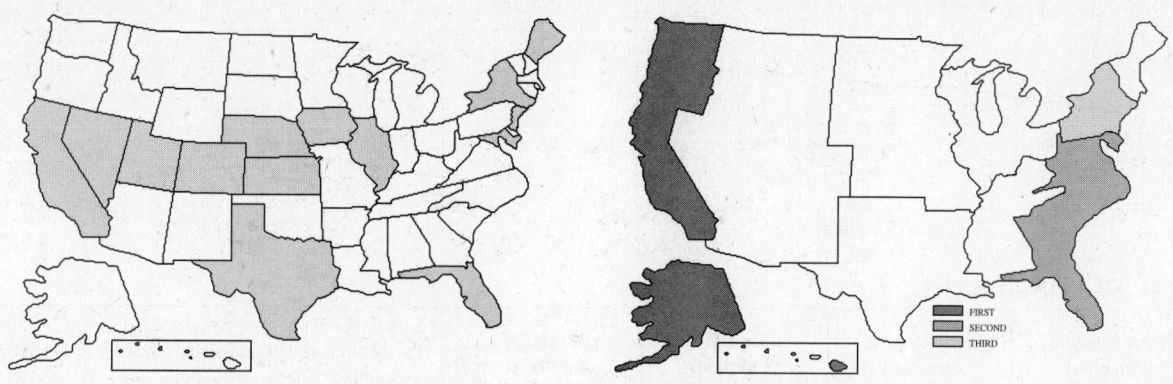

INDUSTRY DATA BY STATE

State	Establishments Total (number)	% of U.S.	Employment Total (number)	% of U.S.	Per Estab.	Payroll Total ($ mil.)	Per Empl. ($)	Revenues Total ($ mil.)	% of U.S.	Per Estab. ($)
California	3,522	12.4	16,021	14.2	5	423.4	26,431	981.6	15.8	278,715
Texas	1,858	6.6	7,954	7.0	4	182.9	22,996	553.5	8.9	297,902
New York	1,597	5.6	7,704	6.8	5	200.9	26,074	539.3	8.7	337,674
Florida	2,568	9.1	8,318	7.4	3	181.9	21,870	404.8	6.5	157,624
Illinois	1,310	4.6	5,395	4.8	4	137.2	25,437	311.6	5.0	237,866
Colorado	738	2.6	2,386	2.1	3	82.2	34,454	248.8	4.0	337,118
Pennsylvania	919	3.2	4,304	3.8	5	90.4	20,998	213.1	3.4	231,850
Michigan	1,066	3.8	4,523	4.0	4	100.4	22,189	208.5	3.4	195,609
Ohio	789	2.8	4,339	3.8	5	96.7	22,285	195.7	3.1	248,065
New Jersey	820	2.9	3,166	2.8	4	80.2	25,317	192.5	3.1	234,773
Massachusetts	582	2.1	2,751	2.4	5	65.4	23,786	142.4	2.3	244,698
Maryland	605	2.1	2,584	2.3	4	62.3	24,114	136.2	2.2	225,119
Virginia	775	2.7	2,711	2.4	3	56.8	20,958	131.2	2.1	169,312
Georgia	808	2.9	2,436	2.2	3	53.1	21,799	128.5	2.1	159,051
Indiana	454	1.6	2,694	2.4	6	58.5	21,701	113.4	1.8	249,780
Washington	753	2.7	2,381	2.1	3	46.8	19,649	110.4	1.8	146,552
Missouri	638	2.3	2,520	2.2	4	48.8	19,348	110.2	1.8	172,779
Wisconsin	510	1.8	2,244	2.0	4	42.5	18,935	102.1	1.6	200,278
North Carolina	773	2.7	2,276	2.0	3	41.7	18,309	99.1	1.6	128,141
Tennessee	380	1.3	1,631	1.4	4	41.1	25,217	98.4	1.6	259,034
Arizona	583	2.1	1,955	1.7	3	36.9	18,856	88.0	1.4	150,889
Nebraska	159	0.6	852	0.8	5	35.5	41,661	85.7	1.4	538,830
Louisiana	435	1.5	1,567	1.4	4	34.8	22,181	78.0	1.3	179,359
Iowa	310	1.1	1,242	1.1	4	22.7	18,261	77.6	1.2	250,448
Minnesota	504	1.8	1,458	1.3	3	30.9	21,200	76.1	1.2	151,056
Oregon	421	1.5	1,483	1.3	4	29.9	20,158	66.3	1.1	157,499
Kansas	338	1.2	1,422	1.3	4	26.7	18,793	64.6	1.0	191,136
Connecticut	244	0.9	813	0.7	3	24.1	29,598	60.8	1.0	249,111
Oklahoma	405	1.4	1,267	1.1	3	22.4	17,640	54.7	0.9	135,054
Kentucky	321	1.1	1,285	1.1	4	21.2	16,528	53.3	0.9	165,972
South Carolina	312	1.1	1,787	1.6	6	24.0	13,450	52.9	0.9	169,692
Alabama	386	1.4	1,239	1.1	3	18.2	14,660	49.9	0.8	129,233
Utah	220	0.8	881	0.8	4	18.5	21,001	48.1	0.8	218,445
Nevada	188	0.7	716	0.6	4	15.2	21,232	39.8	0.6	211,505
Maine	165	0.6	682	0.6	4	15.2	22,267	37.1	0.6	224,879
Arkansas	225	0.8	690	0.6	3	10.7	15,555	27.2	0.4	120,822
New Hampshire	129	0.5	506	0.4	4	12.4	24,589	25.6	0.4	198,147
Mississippi	207	0.7	652	0.6	3	9.4	14,446	25.5	0.4	123,338
West Virginia	143	0.5	657	0.6	5	10.3	15,618	22.8	0.4	159,294
New Mexico	202	0.7	487	0.4	2	7.4	15,181	21.6	0.3	107,010
Idaho	127	0.4	454	0.4	4	8.2	18,081	19.7	0.3	155,213
Hawaii	138	0.5	406	0.4	3	7.7	19,064	19.3	0.3	139,768
Vermont	92	0.3	223	0.2	2	5.7	25,637	13.2	0.2	143,554
South Dakota	73	0.3	302	0.3	4	4.9	16,315	11.2	0.2	153,096
Montana	100	0.4	224	0.2	2	2.9	13,152	8.9	0.1	89,000
North Dakota	55	0.2	130	0.1	2	1.8	13,908	5.5	0.1	100,418
D.C.	25	0.1	84	0.1	3	1.6	18,798	3.8	0.1	151,960
Rhode Island	95	0.3	375*	-	-	(D)	-	(D)	-	-
Delaware	90	0.3	375*	-	-	(D)	-	(D)	-	-
Wyoming	83	0.3	175*	-	-	(D)	-	(D)	-	-
Alaska	82	0.3	375*	-	-	(D)	-	(D)	-	-

Source: 1997 Economic Census. The states are in descending order of revenues or establishments (if revenue data are missing for the majority). The symbol (D) appears when data are withheld to prevent disclosure of competitive information. States marked with (D) are sorted by number of establishments. A dash (-) indicates that the data element cannot be calculated. * indicates the midpoint of a range; 175, for example is the range 100-249. Shaded *states* on the state map indicate those states which have proportionately greater representation in the industry than would be indicated by the state's population; the ratio is based on total revenues or number of establishments. Shaded *regions* indicate where the industry is regionally most concentrated.

NAICS 541310 - ARCHITECTURAL SERVICES*

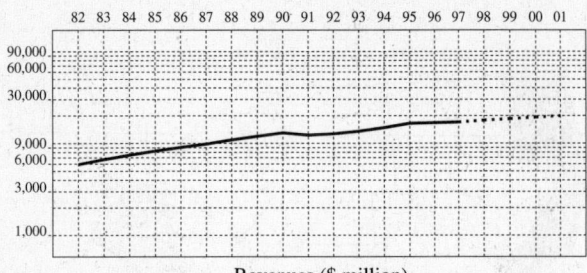

Revenues ($ million)

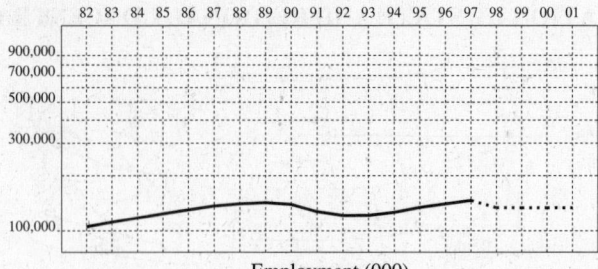

Employment (000)

GENERAL STATISTICS

Year	Establishments (number)	Employment (number)	Payroll ($ million)	Revenues ($ million)	Employees per Establishment (number)	Revenues per Establishment ($)	Payroll per Employee ($)
1982	14,089	105,270	2,404.0	5,914.0	7.5	419,760	22,837
1983	14,827 e	111,578 e	2,714.0 e	6,702.0 e	7.5 e	452,013 e	24,324 e
1984	15,564 e	117,886 e	3,024.0 e	7,491.0 e	7.6 e	481,303 e	25,652 e
1985	16,302 e	124,193 e	3,333.0 e	8,279.0 e	7.6 e	507,852 e	26,837 e
1986	17,039 e	130,501 e	3,643.0 e	9,067.0 e	7.7 e	532,132 e	27,915 e
1987	17,777	136,809	3,953.0	9,855.0	7.7	554,368	28,894
1988	17,094	140,685	4,542.0	10,910.0 e	8.2	638,236	32,285
1989	15,957	142,823	4,733.0	11,966.0 e	9.0	749,890	33,139
1990	15,742	139,557	4,788.0	13,021.0	8.9	827,150	34,309
1991	15,811	127,623	4,421.0	12,279.0	8.1	776,611	34,641
1992	17,875	121,675	4,408.0	12,682.0	6.8	709,483	36,228
1993	17,772	121,749	4,530.0	13,534.0	6.9	761,535	37,208
1994	18,295	126,421	4,993.0	14,779.0	6.9	807,816	39,495
1995	18,551	134,448	5,535.0	16,487.0	7.2	888,739	41,168
1996	19,577 e	140,575 e	6,002.0 e	16,738.0 e	7.2 e	854,983 e	42,696 e
1997	20,602	146,702	6,469.0	16,988.0	7.1	824,580	44,096
1998	19,854 p	134,011 p	6,107.0 p	17,784.0 p	6.7 p	895,739 p	45,571 p
1999	20,208 p	133,936 p	6,301.0 p	18,487.0 p	6.6 p	914,836 p	47,045 p
2000	20,562 p	133,861 p	6,495.0 p	19,190.0 p	6.5 p	933,275 p	48,520 p
2001	20,915 p	133,786 p	6,689.0 p	19,893.0 p	6.4 p	951,136 p	49,998 p

Sources: Economic Census of the United States, 1982, 1987, 1992, 1997. Establishment counts, employment, and payroll are from County Business Patterns for non-Census years. In non-Census years, industries in the Manufacturing range under SIC coding include data from the Annual Survey of Manufactures (ASM); those in the old Services range include data from the Services Annual Survey (SAS). Values followed by a 'p' are projections by the editors. Extrapolations are marked by 'e'. Data are the most recent available at this level of detail.

INDICES OF CHANGE

Year	Establishments (number)	Employment (number)	Payroll ($ million)	Revenues ($ million)	Employees per Establishment (number)	Revenues per Establishment ($)	Payroll per Employee ($)
1982	68.4	71.8	37.2	34.8	104.9	50.9	51.8
1987	86.3	93.3	61.1	58.0	108.1	67.2	65.5
1992	86.8	82.9	68.1	74.7	95.6	86.0	82.2
1993	86.3	83.0	70.0	79.7	96.2	92.4	84.4
1994	88.8	86.2	77.2	87.0	97.0	98.0	89.6
1995	90.0	91.6	85.6	97.1	101.8	107.8	93.4
1996	95.0 e	95.8 e	92.8 e	98.5 e	100.8 e	103.7 e	96.8 e
1997	100.0	100.0	100.0	100.0	100.0	100.0	100.0
1998	96.4 p	91.3 p	94.4 p	104.7 p	94.8 p	108.6 p	103.3 p
1999	98.1 p	91.3 p	97.4 p	108.8 p	93.1 p	110.9 p	106.7 p
2000	99.8 p	91.2 p	100.4 p	113.0 p	91.4 p	113.2 p	110.0 p
2001	101.5 p	91.2 p	103.4 p	117.1 p	89.8 p	115.3 p	113.4 p

Sources: Same as General Statistics. The values shown reflect change from the base year, 1997. Values above 100 mean greater than 1997, values below 100 mean less than 1997, and a value of 100 in the 1982-96 or 1998-2001 period means same as 1997. Values followed by a 'p' are projections by the editors; 'e' stands for extrapolation. Data are the most recent available at this level of detail.

SELECTED RATIOS

For 1997	Avg. of Information	Analyzed Industry	Index	For 1997	Avg. of Information	Analyzed Industry	Index
Employees per establishment	9	7	82	Payroll per establishment	372,545	313,999	84
Revenue per establishment	958,337	824,580	86	Payroll as % of revenue	39	38	98
Revenue per employee	111,029	115,799	104	Payroll per employee	43,162	44,096	102

Sources: Same as General Statistics. The 'Average' column represents the average for the industry sector, in 1997, where the currently shown industry is classified. The Index shows the relationship between the Average and the Analyzed Industry. For example, 100 means that they are equal; 500 that the Analyzed Industry is five times the average; 50 means that the Analyzed Industry is half the national average. The abbreviation 'na' is used to show that data are 'not available'.

*Equivalent to SIC 8712.

LEADING COMPANIES   Number shown: **75**   Total sales ($ mil): **15,074**   Total employment (000): **97.6**

Company Name	Address				CEO Name	Phone	Co. Type	Sales ($ mil)	Empl. (000)
Raytheon Engineers	1 Broadway	Cambridge	MA	02142	Shay Assad	617-494-7000	S	2,100	8.6
URS Corp.	100 California St	San Francisco	CA	94111	Martin M Koffel	415-774-2700	P	1,418	6.6
Day and Zimmermann Inc.	1818 Market St	Philadelphia	PA	19103		215-299-8000	R	1,080	16.5
AECOM Technology Corp.	3250 Wilshire Blvd	Los Angeles	CA	90010	Richard G Newman	213-381-3612	R	900	6.1
ABB Lummus Global	1515 Broad St	Bloomfield	NJ	07003	Stephen M Solomon	973-893-1515	S	800*	4.0
Austin Co.	3650 Mayfield Rd	Cleveland	OH	44121	J William Melsop	864-291-6625	R	700*	1.2
Anderson DeBartolo Pan	2480 N Arcadia Ave	Tucson	AZ	85712	Dale Harman	520-795-4500	S	470*	0.5
Carlson Group Inc.	959 Concord St	Framingham	MA	01701		508-370-0100	R	444*	0.5
HNTB Corp.	1201 Walnut, #700	Kansas City	MO	64106	H K Hammond Jr	816-472-1201	R	392	2.3
Lockwood Greene Engineers Inc.	P O Box 491	Spartanburg	SC	29304	Don R Luger	864-578-2000	S	327*	3.2
Willbros Energy Services Co.	2431 E 61st St	Tulsa	OK	74136	Larry J Bump	918-748-7000	P	282	2.3
HDR Inc.	8404 Indian Hills Dr	Omaha	NE	68114	Dick Bell	402-399-1000	R	277*	2.4
Facility Group Inc.	2233 Lake Park Dr	Smyrna	GA	30080	Robert L Moultrie	770-437-2700	R	220	0.3
Marshall Erdman & Associates	5117 University Ave	Madison	WI	53705	Timmothy B Erdman	608-238-0211	R	220*	0.9
Rudolph/Libbe Companies Inc.	6494 Latcha Rd	Walbridge	OH	43465	Frederick Rudolph	419-241-5000	R	220	0.8
Burns and Roe Enterprises Inc.	800 Kinderkamack	Oradell	NJ	07649	K Keith Roe	201-265-2000	R	204*	0.8
Hellmuth, Obata & Kassabaum	211 N Broadway	St. Louis	MO	63102	Jerry Sincoff	314-421-2000	R	197*	2.0
Heery International Inc.	999 Peachtree St	Atlanta	GA	30367	James Moynihan	404-881-9880	S	150*	0.8
STV Group Inc.	205 W Welsh Dr	Douglassville	PA	19518	Michael Haratunian	610-385-8200	P	139	1.1
American Architectural Products	755 B Canfield Rd	Youngstown	OH	44512	Frank Amedia	330-965-9910	P	132	2.8
Foster Wheeler USA Corp.	Perryville Corporate	Clinton	NJ	08809	Richard Swift	908-730-4000	S	132*	1.1
Ellerbe Becket Co.	800 LaSalle Ave	Minneapolis	MN	55402	Robert A Degenhardt	612-376-2000	R	128	0.8
Ellerbe Becket Inc.	800 LaSalle Ave	Minneapolis	MN	55402	Bob A Degenhardt	612-376-2000	S	122	0.7
NBBJ	111 S Jackson St	Seattle	WA	98104	Scott W Wyatt	206-223-5555	R	122	0.9
Pacific Architects & Engineers Inc	888 S Figuora St	Los Angeles	CA	90017	Allen Shay	213-481-2311	R	120*	5.0
L.J. Gonzer Associates	1225 Raymond Blvd	Newark	NJ	07102	Lawrence J Gonzer	973-624-5600	R	111*	0.4
SSOE Inc.	1001 Madison Ave	Toledo	OH	43624	Gary L McCreery	419-255-3830	R	108*	0.6
RTKL Associates Inc.	1 South St	Baltimore	MD	21202	Harold L Adams	410-528-8600	R	105	0.8
PACE Resources Inc.	P O Box 15055	York	PA	17405	RE Horn Sr	717-852-1300	R	104*	0.7
Tonn and Blank Construction	1623 Greenwood	Michigan City	IN	46360	WS Mueller	219-879-7321	R	103*	0.3
Carter and Burgess Inc.	P O Box 985006	Fort Worth	TX	76185	Jerry Allen	817-735-6000	R	100*	1.2
Stanley Consultants Inc.	225 Iowa Ave	Muscatine	IA	52761	Gregs Thomopulos	319-264-6600	S	97*	0.6
Henderson Corp.	575 State Hwy 28	Raritan	NJ	08869	Edward McMahon	908-685-1300	R	95*	<0.1
HLW International L.L.P.	115 5th Ave	New York	NY	10003		212-353-4600	R	94*	0.4
Daniel, Mann, Johnson	3250 Wilshire Blvd	Los Angeles	CA	90010	R W Holdsworth	213-381-3663	S	91*	1.6
Einhorn Yaffee Prescott	P O Box 617	Albany	NY	12201	Steven L Einhorn	518-431-3300	R	91*	0.5
RTKL International Ltd.	1 South St	Baltimore	MD	21202	Harold L Adams	410-528-8600	S	91	0.7
Campbell/Manix Inc.	21520 Bridge St	Southfield	MI	48034	Douglas Manix	248-354-5100	R	90	<0.1
Haines Lundberg Waehler	115 5th Ave	New York	NY	10003		212-353-4600	R	90*	0.4
Ibberson Co.	828 5th St S	Hopkins	MN	55343	Walter D Hanson	612-938-7007	R	89*	0.3
KBJ Architects Inc.	510 Julia St	Jacksonville	FL	32202	Walter Q Taylor	904-356-9491	R	89	<0.1
Wilbur Smith Associates	P O Box 92	Columbia	SC	29202	Robert J Zuelsdorf	803-758-4500	R	87	0.8
3D-International Inc.	1900 W Loop S	Houston	TX	77027	John Murph	713-871-7000	R	85*	0.5
Leo A. Daly Co.	8600 Indian Hills Dr	Omaha	NE	68114	Leo A Daly III	402-391-8111	R	83	0.8
Randers Killam Group Inc.	27 Bleeker St	Millburn	NJ	07041	Emil C Hekert		P	81	0.7
L. Robert Kimball and Associates	PO Box 1000	Ebensburg	PA	15931	L Robert Kimball	814-472-7700	R	80*	0.5
SHG Inc.	150 W Jefferson	Detroit	MI	48226		313-983-3600	N	80	0.7
TAMS Consultants Inc.	655 3rd Ave	New York	NY	10017	A R Dolcimascolo	212-867-1777	R	80*	0.5
Greenhorne and O'Mara Inc.	9001 Edmonston Rd	Greenbelt	MD	20770	A James O'Mara	301-982-2800	R	78*	0.7
DSAtlantic Corp.	801 Jones Franklin	Raleigh	NC	27606	Elmo Richardson	919-851-6866	R	76*	0.4
Hillier Group Inc.	500 Alexander Park	Princeton	NJ	08543	J Robert Hillier	609-452-8888	R	74	0.4
Kling-Lindquist Partnership Inc.	2301 Chestnut St	Philadelphia	PA	19103	Melvyn J Sotnick	215-569-2900	R	73*	0.4
McClier	401 E Illinois, #625	Chicago	IL	60611	Grant McCullagh	312-836-7700	R	73*	0.4
Waldemar S. Nelson Inc.	1200 St Charles Ave	New Orleans	LA	70130	Charles W Nelson	504-523-5281	R	73*	0.5
HarleyEllis	26913 N Western	Southfield	MI	48034	Dennis M King	248-262-1500	R	71*	0.3
Mid States Engineering L.L.C.	350 E New York St	Indianapolis	IN	46204	Sid Corder	317-624-6434	R	71*	0.3
SHG Associates Inc.	500 Griswald	Detroit	MI	48226	Arnold Mikon	313-983-3600	S	71*	0.4
Vincent, Hlavaty Architects Inc.	2505 Turtle Creek	Dallas	TX	75219	Martti J Benson	214-521-8500	R	71*	0.3
Zimmer Gunsul Frasca Partnership	320 S W Oak St	Portland	OR	97204		503-224-3860	R	66*	0.4
SC Companies Inc.	225 Iowa Ave	Muscatine	IA	52761	Richard H Stanley	319-264-6600	R	65	0.5
Woolpert L.L.P.	409 E Monument	Dayton	OH	45402		937-461-5660	R	65*	0.7
Reynolds, Smith, and Hills Inc.	PO Box 4850	Jacksonville	FL	32201	Leerie Jenkins Jr	904-296-2000	R	64*	0.4
Giffels Associates Inc.	7150 E Camelback	Scottsdale	AZ	85251	Richard A Bither	602-990-9715	R	62*	0.3
Maguire Group Inc.	1 Court St	New Britain	CT	06051	Richard J Repeta	860-224-9141	R	58*	0.4
Burgess and Niple Ltd.	5085 Reed Rd	Columbus	OH	43220	Francis C Smith	614-459-2050	R	55	0.6
Boyle Engineering Corp.	PO Box 7350	Newport Beach	CA	92660	Dan Boyd	949-476-3300	R	54	0.5
Arcadis-Geaghty and Miller	PO Box 1717	Greenville	SC	29602	Steve BlackeHastey	303-294-1200	S	51*	1.7
L.B. Knight and Associates Inc.	549 W Randolph St	Chicago	IL	60661	Stephen Mitchell	312-346-2300	S	50*	0.5
Ghafari Associates Inc.	17101 Michigan Ave	Dearborn	MI	48126	Yousif B Ghafari	313-441-3000	R	49	0.6
Callison Architecture Inc.	1420 5th Ave	Seattle	WA	98101	William Karst	206-623-4646	R	48*	0.4
Spillis Candela DMGM	800 Douglas	Coral Gables	FL	33134	P Spillis	305-444-4691	R	48*	0.2
Graef, Anhalt, Schloemer	125 S 84th St	Milwaukee	WI	53214	Rich Bub	414-259-1500	R	47*	0.3
Integrated Building Arts	200 Airport	N Cumbrlnd	PA	17070	James Scheiner	717-901-7055	R	47*	0.2
Sheladia Associates Inc.	15825 Shady Grove	Rockville	MD	20850	Manish Kothari	301-590-3939	R	47*	0.2
Middough Associates Inc.	1901 E 13th St	Cleveland	OH	44114	Ronald R Ledin	216-771-2060	R	46*	0.7

Source: Ward's Business Directory of U.S. Private and Public Companies, Volumes 1 and 2, 2000. The company type code used is as follows: P - Public, R - Private, S - Subsidiary, D - Division, J - Joint Venture, A - Affiliate, G - Group, N - Company type not reported. Sales are in millions of dollars, employees are in thousands. An asterisk (*) indicates an estimated sales volume. The symbol < stands for 'less than'. Company names and addresses are truncated, in some cases, to fit into the available space.

LOCATION BY STATE AND REGIONAL CONCENTRATION

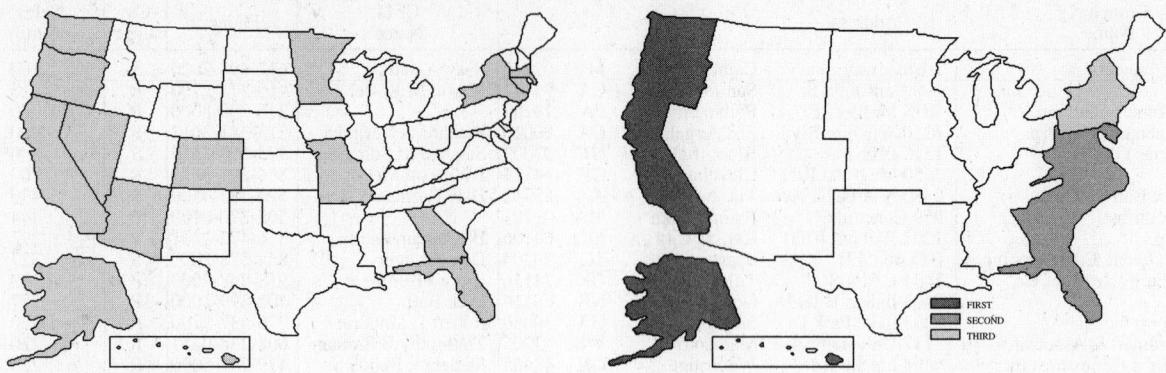

INDUSTRY DATA BY STATE

State	Establishments Total (number)	% of U.S.	Employment Total (number)	% of U.S.	Per Estab.	Payroll Total ($ mil.)	Per Empl. ($)	Revenues Total ($ mil.)	% of U.S.	Per Estab. ($)
California	2,789	13.5	18,911	12.9	7	909.1	48,071	2,482.3	14.6	890,016
New York	1,614	7.8	11,890	8.1	7	548.0	46,092	1,455.4	8.6	901,727
Texas	1,306	6.3	9,746	6.6	7	444.4	45,593	1,160.3	6.8	888,416
Massachusetts	699	3.4	8,005	5.5	11	393.7	49,183	1,147.2	6.8	1,641,270
Florida	1,472	7.1	7,826	5.3	5	307.2	39,251	937.6	5.5	636,945
Illinois	1,023	5.0	7,015	4.8	7	326.3	46,517	772.2	4.5	754,806
Pennsylvania	693	3.4	6,284	4.3	9	263.1	41,868	655.1	3.9	945,268
Ohio	665	3.2	5,212	3.6	8	216.8	41,589	520.8	3.1	783,179
Georgia	538	2.6	4,222	2.9	8	200.9	47,581	506.9	3.0	942,247
Washington	661	3.2	4,363	3.0	7	181.1	41,519	494.0	2.9	747,392
Missouri	400	1.9	3,767	2.6	9	177.9	47,216	427.8	2.5	1,069,615
Michigan	559	2.7	4,137	2.8	7	184.4	44,578	416.1	2.4	744,367
New Jersey	610	3.0	3,381	2.3	6	143.0	42,303	387.9	2.3	635,964
Colorado	596	2.9	3,389	2.3	6	143.6	42,363	382.5	2.3	641,730
Minnesota	378	1.8	3,701	2.5	10	165.9	44,817	377.1	2.2	997,690
Virginia	514	2.5	3,521	2.4	7	147.8	41,982	369.2	2.2	718,276
North Carolina	513	2.5	3,375	2.3	7	148.5	43,998	355.2	2.1	692,345
Arizona	474	2.3	2,910	2.0	6	116.5	40,034	323.7	1.9	683,017
Tennessee	296	1.4	2,623	1.8	9	116.8	44,517	292.1	1.7	986,703
Maryland	378	1.8	2,372	1.6	6	109.4	46,123	281.8	1.7	745,590
Oregon	308	1.5	2,215	1.5	7	91.2	41,176	247.6	1.5	803,782
D.C.	122	0.6	1,901	1.3	16	91.4	48,067	244.0	1.4	1,999,877
Connecticut	324	1.6	1,727	1.2	5	85.1	49,256	238.1	1.4	734,756
Wisconsin	286	1.4	2,125	1.4	7	86.6	40,750	217.0	1.3	758,769
Indiana	287	1.4	2,114	1.4	7	86.3	40,838	206.9	1.2	720,889
Oklahoma	168	0.8	1,685	1.1	10	63.2	37,526	170.2	1.0	1,013,065
Alabama	229	1.1	1,352	0.9	6	55.8	41,300	154.2	0.9	673,397
Nevada	131	0.6	1,069	0.7	8	49.8	46,577	144.8	0.9	1,105,084
Louisiana	262	1.3	1,428	1.0	5	52.9	37,014	143.0	0.8	545,962
Hawaii	165	0.8	1,013	0.7	6	45.8	45,180	141.7	0.8	858,715
South Carolina	229	1.1	1,337	0.9	6	61.2	45,781	141.4	0.8	617,441
Kansas	160	0.8	1,282	0.9	8	48.6	37,943	122.7	0.7	766,594
Kentucky	161	0.8	1,098	0.7	7	42.4	38,607	115.1	0.7	715,155
Utah	168	0.8	1,133	0.8	7	41.4	36,515	110.7	0.7	658,946
Nebraska	116	0.6	1,115	0.8	10	45.5	40,822	108.0	0.6	931,190
Iowa	130	0.6	840	0.6	6	33.1	39,433	86.3	0.5	663,623
New Mexico	161	0.8	962	0.7	6	30.2	31,345	85.8	0.5	532,739
Arkansas	147	0.7	811	0.6	6	29.6	36,506	80.1	0.5	545,027
Mississippi	112	0.5	679	0.5	6	27.3	40,270	68.2	0.4	608,705
Idaho	119	0.6	678	0.5	6	25.5	37,676	66.8	0.4	561,017
Maine	83	0.4	529	0.4	6	21.3	40,208	49.6	0.3	597,217
Alaska	47	0.2	337	0.2	7	16.4	48,715	45.4	0.3	965,298
Montana	82	0.4	519	0.4	6	16.5	31,765	43.1	0.3	526,024
Rhode Island	75	0.4	341	0.2	5	12.6	36,915	32.2	0.2	429,680
New Hampshire	66	0.3	313	0.2	5	12.7	40,633	32.2	0.2	487,758
Delaware	38	0.2	227	0.2	6	9.9	43,692	30.8	0.2	810,263
Vermont	84	0.4	328	0.2	4	10.3	31,375	28.8	0.2	342,345
North Dakota	36	0.2	251	0.2	7	8.5	33,725	24.4	0.1	678,944
West Virginia	45	0.2	222	0.2	5	9.4	42,468	22.7	0.1	504,489
South Dakota	40	0.2	239	0.2	6	8.4	35,218	20.9	0.1	522,875
Wyoming	43	0.2	182	0.1	4	5.3	29,077	20.6	0.1	478,419

Source: 1997 *Economic Census*. The states are in descending order of revenues or establishments (if revenue data are missing for the majority). The symbol (D) appears when data are withheld to prevent disclosure of competitive information. States marked with (D) are sorted by number of establishments. A dash (-) indicates that the data element cannot be calculated. * indicates the midpoint of a range; 175, for example is the range 100-249. Shaded *states* on the state map indicate those states which have proportionately greater representation in the industry than would be indicated by the state's population; the ratio is based on total revenues or number of establishments. Shaded *regions* indicate where the industry is regionally most concentrated.

NAICS 541330 - ENGINEERING SERVICES

GENERAL STATISTICS

Year	Establishments (number)	Employment (number)	Payroll ($ million)	Revenues ($ million)	Employees per Establishment (number)	Revenues per Establishment ($)	Payroll per Employee ($)
1997	52,526	730,048	35,338.0	88,181.0	13.9	1,678,807	48,405

Source: Economic Census of the United States, 1997. This is a newly defined industry. Data for prior years were unavailable at the time of publication but may become available over time.

INDICES OF CHANGE

Year	Establishments (number)	Employment (number)	Payroll ($ million)	Revenues ($ million)	Employees per Establishment (number)	Revenues per Establishment ($)	Payroll per Employee ($)
1997	100.0	100.0	100.0	100.0	100.0	100.0	100.0

Sources: Same as General Statistics. The values shown reflect change from the base year, 1997. Values above 100 mean greater than 1997, values below 100 mean less than 1997, and a value of 100 in the 1982-96 or 1998-2001 period means same as 1997. Values followed by a 'p' are projections by the editors; 'e' stands for extrapolation. Data are the most recent available at this level of detail.

SIC INDUSTRIES RELATED TO NAICS 541330

Each new NAICS code represents an industry that used to be part of an SIC or a part of several SIC industries. Data in this table are shown to provide transitional information for these cases. All available data for the precursor SIC(s) are shown. Even if only a part of an SIC is included in the NAICS, *all* data for the SIC are reproduced. If the SIC industry is not marked as being a part (pt) of the NAICS, the entire industry is embedded in the NAICS data. The SIC composition of the new industry provides some hints of the relative importance of its "ancestors." Data marked with a 'p' are projected. Projections begin with 1982 data. Data earlier than 1990 are not shown but are reflected in the projections.

SIC	Industry	1990	1991	1992	1993	1994	1995	1996	1997
8711	**Engineering Services**								
	Establishments (number)	33,089	33,974	41,834	41,529	42,614	43,778	44,064p	45,247p
	Employment (thousands)	651.6	652.1	657.6	655.7	663.0	687.6	729.7p	749.1p
	Revenues ($ million)	64,791.0	65,788.0	67,716.0	67,067.0	68,099.0	73,878.0	80,264.0	78,655.0p
8748	**Business Consulting Services, nec (pt)**								
	Establishments (number)	8,819	11,146	13,322	15,561	16,966	18,772	19,284p	20,712p
	Employment (thousands)	70.8	77.9	62.1	72.6	78.6	92.8	87.5p	90.8p
	Revenues ($ million)	6,278.0	6,714.0	7,710.0	8,832.0	9,843.0	12,016.0	13,997.0	14,469.1p

Source: Economic Census of the United States, 1992, annual surveys of economic sectors conducted by the Bureau of the Census, and estimates or projections based on the 1982-1992 period; not all data are shown. 'e' marks estimates made by the editors; 'p' indicates projections based on time series. A dash (-) indicates that data for this SIC or year were not available. The abbreviation (pt) next to the industry name indicates that only a part of the industry is present within the NAICS data. If no (pt) is shown, the entire industry is contained within the NAICS data.

SELECTED RATIOS

For 1997	Avg. of Information	Analyzed Industry	Index	For 1997	Avg. of Information	Analyzed Industry	Index
Employees per establishment	9	14	161	Payroll per establishment	372,545	672,772	181
Revenue per establishment	958,337	1,678,807	175	Payroll as % of revenue	39	40	103
Revenue per employee	111,029	120,788	109	Payroll per employee	43,162	48,405	112

Sources: Same as General Statistics. The 'Average' column represents the average for the industry sector, in 1997, where the currently shown industry is classified. The Index shows the relationship between the Average and the Analyzed Industry. For example, 100 means that they are equal; 500 that the Analyzed Industry is five times the average; 50 means that the Analyzed Industry is half the national average. The abbreviation 'na' is used to show that data are 'not available'.

LEADING COMPANIES Number shown: **75** Total sales ($ mil): **197,089** Total employment (000): **1,029.8**

Company Name	Address				CEO Name	Phone	Co. Type	Sales ($ mil)	Empl. (000)
ABB Pastech	6100 W by NW	Houston	TX	77040		713-460-9541	D	56,681*	300.0
Halliburton Co.	3600 Lincoln Plaza	Dallas	TX	75201	Williams Bradford	214-978-2600	P	14,898	107.8
Fluor Corp.	1 Enterprise Dr	Aliso Viejo	CA	92656	Philip J Carroll Jr	949-349-2000	P	12,417	53.6
Bechtel Group Inc.	50 Beale St	San Francisco	CA	94105	Riley Bechtel	415-768-1234	R	11,329	30.0
Fluor Daniel Inc.	3353 Michelson Dr	Irvine	CA	92698	Alan Boeckmann	949-975-2000	D	8,400*	17.1
Bechtel Corp.	50 Beale St	San Francisco	CA	94105	RP Bechtel	415-768-1234	R	8,250*	30.0
Computer Sciences Corp.	2100 E Grand Ave	El Segundo	CA	90245	Van B Honeycutt	310-615-0311	P	7,660	50.0
U.S. Steel Group	600 Grant St	Pittsburgh	PA	15219	Thomas J Usher	412-433-1121	S	5,314	19.3
Science Applications Intern. Corp.	10260 Campus Point	San Diego	CA	92121	J Robert Beyster	619-546-6000	R	4,200*	35.0
Foster Wheeler Corp.	Perryville Corporate	Clinton	NJ	08809	Richard J Swift	908-730-4000	P	3,944	11.1
Brown and Root Inc.	PO Box 3	Houston	TX	77001		713-676-3011	S	3,062	30.0
Jacobs Engineering Group Inc.	PO Box 7084	Pasadena	CA	91109	Joseph Jacobs	626-578-3500	P	2,875	15.9
ENSERCH Corp.	Energy Plz	Dallas	TX	75201	David W Biegler	214-651-8700	S	2,790*	3.0
Raytheon Engineers	1 Broadway	Cambridge	MA	02142	Shay Assad	617-494-7000	S	2,700	16.0
Allegheny Power Service Corp.	10435 Downsville	Hagerstown	MD	21740	Alan J Noia	301-790-3400	S	2,576	4.8
Thyssen Incorporated N.A.	400 Renaissance Ctr	Detroit	MI	48243		313-567-5600	S	2,500	4.5
Foster Wheeler International Corp.	Perryville Corp Park	Clinton	NJ	08809	John C Blythe	908-730-4030	S	2,381*	7.2
United Dominion Industries Inc.	301 S College St	Charlotte	NC	28202	William Holland	704-347-6800	P	2,148	12.0
HSB Group Inc.	PO Box 5024	Hartford	CT	06102	Gordon W Kreh	860-722-1866	P	2,144*	2.4
Volt Information Sciences Inc.	1221 Av Americas	New York	NY	10036	William Shaw	212-704-2400	P	2,141	38.7
Raytheon Engineers	1 Broadway	Cambridge	MA	02142	Shay Assad	617-494-7000	S	2,100	8.6
Telephone and Data Systems Inc.	30 N LaSalle St	Chicago	IL	60602	LeRoy T Carlson Jr	312-630-1900	P	1,963	9.9
Black and Veatch L.L.P.	P O Box 8405	Kansas City	MO	64114	PJ Adam	913-458-2000	R	1,800	8.0
Parsons Corp.	100 W Walnut St	Pasadena	CA	91124	James F McNulty	626-440-2000	R	1,710*	11.4
URS Corp.	100 California St	San Francisco	CA	94111	Martin M Koffel	415-774-2700	P	1,418	6.6
CILCORP Inc.	300 Hamilton Blvd	Peoria	IL	61602	Robert O Viets	309-675-8810	P	1,313	1.3
Stone and Webster Inc.	245 Summer St	Boston	MA	02210		617-589-5111	P	1,249	5.5
Stone & Webster Engineering	245 Summer St	Boston	MA	02210	H Kerner Smith	617-589-5111	S	1,248	6.9
Kaiser Engineers	9300 Lee Hwy	Fairfax	VA	22031	James O Maiwurm	703-934-3600	P	1,210	4.8
Day and Zimmermann Inc.	1818 Market St	Philadelphia	PA	19103		215-299-8000	R	1,080	16.5
Dames and Moore Group	911 Wilshire Blvd	Los Angeles	CA	90017	Arthur C Darrow	213-996-2200	S	1,030	7.7
Westinghouse Electric Co	P O Box 355	Pittsburgh	PA	15230	Charles W Pryor Jr	412-374-6500	S	970*	6.9
Tracor Applied Sciences Inc.	1601 Research Blvd	Rockville	MD	20850	K Bruce Hamilton	301-838-6000	S	946*	5.0
CH2M Hill Ltd.	6060 S Willow Dr	Greenwood Vill.	CO	80111	Ralph Peterson	303-771-0900	R	932	7.0
AECOM Technology Corp.	3250 Wilshire Blvd	Los Angeles	CA	90010	Richard G Newman	213-381-3612	R	900	6.1
Parsons Brinckerhoff Inc.	1 Penn Plz	New York	NY	10119	Thomas J O'Neill	212-465-5000	R	760	8.0
Austin Co.	3650 Mayfield Rd	Cleveland	OH	44121	J William Melsop	864-291-6625	R	700*	1.2
Halliburton/Brown and Root Inc.	400 Clinton Dr	Houston	TX	77020		713-676-3011	S	675*	1.5
Veridian Corp.	2001 N Beauregard	Alexandria	VA	22311	David N Langstaff	703-575-3100	R	613	5.0
AlliedSignal Technical Services	1 Bendix Rd	Columbia	MD	21045	Ivan Stern	410-964-7000	S	600	5.5
OSP Consultants Inc.	21400 Ridgetop Cir	Sterling	VA	20166	Sid Smith	703-444-1400	R	591*	2.0
Bechtel National Inc.	P O Box 193965	San Francisco	CA	94119	Riley P Bechtel	415-768-1234	S	568*	3.0
Continental Can Company Inc.	301 Merritt 7	Norwalk	CT	06856	Donald J Bainton	203-750-5900	S	546	3.4
Kvaerner Process	P O Box 720421	Houston	TX	77272	Thomas Chiles	713-988-2002	D	531	3.0
Michael Baker Corp.	PO Box 12259	Pittsburgh	PA	15231	Richard L Shaw	412-269-6300	P	521	3.7
Michael Baker Jr. Inc.	PO Box 12259	Pittsburgh	PA	15231	Charles I Homan	412-269-6300	S	521	3.8
Ralph M. Parsons Co.	100 W Walnut St	Pasadena	CA	91124	James S McNulty	626-440-2000	S	514*	4.0
Solectron Technology Inc.	PO Box 562148	Charlotte	NC	28256	Massued Behrouzi	704-598-3300	S	500	1.3
Aerospace Corp.	PO Box 92957	Los Angeles	CA	90009	E Aldridge	310-336-5000	R	487	3.1
ABB Lummus Global Inc.	1515 Broad St	Bloomfield	NJ	07003	Stephen M Solomon	973-893-1515	S	480*	4.0
Logicon Inc.	3701 Skypark Dr	Torrance	CA	90505	JR Woodhull	310-373-0220	S	478*	5.0
Earth Tech Inc.	100 W Broadway	Long Beach	CA	90802	Diane C Creel	562-951-2000	S	468*	7.0
Boldt Group Inc.	P O Box 373	Appleton	WI	54912	Oscar C Boldt	920-739-7800	R	450*	2.3
Henkels and McCoy Inc.	985 Jolly Rd	Blue Bell	PA	19422	Kenneth L Rose	215-283-7600	R	450*	5.0
Montgomery Watson Inc.	300 N Lake Ave	Pasadena	CA	91101	Murli Tolaney	626-796-9141	R	448*	3.6
Aqua Alliance	30 Harvard Mill Squ	Wakefield	MA	01880	Thierry M Mallet	781-246-5200	P	445	2.5
Carlson Group Inc.	959 Concord St	Framingham	MA	01701		508-370-0100	R	444*	0.5
Structural Dynamics Research	2000 Eastman Dr	Milford	OH	45150	William J Weyand	513-576-2400	P	442	2.5
TASC Inc.	55 Walkers Brook	Reading	MA	01867	James H Frey	781-942-2000	S	440	2.8
Exxon Research & Engineering	180 Park Ave	Florham Park	NJ	07932	WRK Inness	973-765-0100	S	438*	2.4
Tetra Tech Inc.	670 N Rosemead	Pasadena	CA	91107	Li-San Hwang	626-351-4664	P	432	5.4
Butler Service Group Inc.	110 Summit Ave	Montvale	NJ	07645	Edward M Kopko	201-573-8000	S	425	6.2
Fru-Con Construction Corp	15933 Clayton Rd	Ballwin	MO	63022		314-391-6700	N	420	2.0
Rapid Design Service Inc.	2905 Wilson Ave	Grand Rapids	MI	49504	Richard Tschirhart	616-532-5555	R	412*	1.5
Belcan Engineering Group Inc.	10200 Anderson	Cincinnati	OH	45242	Ralph G Anderson	513-891-0972	S	400	4.0
HNTB Corp.	1201 Walnut, #700	Kansas City	MO	64106	H K Hammond Jr	816-472-1201	R	392	2.3
Comsearch	2002 Edmund Halley	Reston	VA	20191	Douglas Hall	703-620-6300	S	388	0.1
Eichleay Engineers Inc.	6585 Penn Ave	Pittsburgh	PA	15206	Theodore W Nelson	412-363-9000	R	380*	2.0
Parsons Infrastructure	100 W Walnut St	Pasadena	CA	91124	James McNulty	626-440-2000	R	379*	2.0
Camp Dresser and McKee Inc.	1 Cambridge Ctr	Cambridge	MA	02142	Thomas Furman	617-621-8181	R	376	2.5
Mestek Inc.	260 N Elm St	Westfield	MA	01085	John E Reed	413-568-9571	P	375	2.8
URS Greiner Inc. Pacific	7901 Stoneridge Dr	Pleasanton	CA	94588		510-463-2000	N	340	3.0
Watkins Engineers & Constructors	P O Box 2194	Tallahassee	FL	32316	Eddie Aaron	850-576-7181	S	330	4.0
Lockwood Greene Engineers Inc.	P O Box 491	Spartanburg	SC	29304	Don R Luger	864-578-2000	S	327*	3.2
Golder Associates Inc.	3730 Ch Tucker	Atlanta	GA	30341	Hal Hamilton	770-496-1893	R	321*	2.0

Source: Ward's Business Directory of U.S. Private and Public Companies, Volumes 1 and 2, 2000. The company type code used is as follows: P - Public, R - Private, S - Subsidiary, D - Division, J - Joint Venture, A - Affiliate, G - Group, N - Company type not reported. Sales are in millions of dollars, employees are in thousands. An asterisk (*) indicates an estimated sales volume. The symbol < stands for 'less than'. Company names and addresses are truncated, in some cases, to fit into the available space.

LOCATION BY STATE AND REGIONAL CONCENTRATION

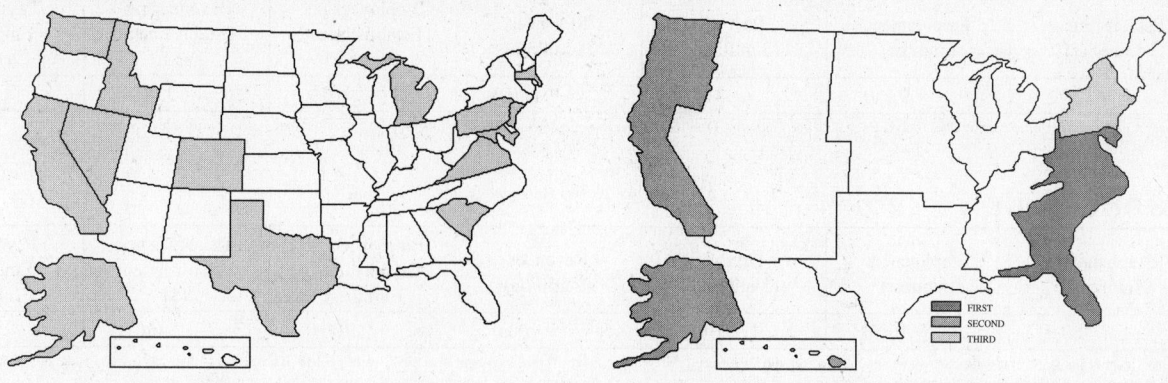

FIRST
SECOND
THIRD

INDUSTRY DATA BY STATE

State	Establishments		Employment			Payroll		Revenues		
	Total (number)	% of U.S.	Total (number)	% of U.S.	Per Estab.	Total ($ mil.)	Per Empl. ($)	Total ($ mil.)	% of U.S.	Per Estab. ($)
California	7,389	14.1	93,595	12.8	13	5,036.0	53,807	12,449.4	14.1	1,684,860
Texas	4,013	7.6	61,475	8.4	15	3,236.8	52,652	9,077.8	10.3	2,262,101
Pennsylvania	2,093	4.0	45,337	6.2	22	2,314.3	51,048	5,312.7	6.0	2,538,333
Virginia	1,803	3.4	44,907	6.2	25	2,160.2	48,105	4,957.0	5.6	2,749,304
South Carolina	577	1.1	13,255	1.8	23	697.5	52,625	3,909.1	4.4	6,774,924
Maryland	1,375	2.6	30,901	4.2	22	1,453.1	47,024	3,634.6	4.1	2,643,332
Massachusetts	1,582	3.0	26,618	3.6	17	1,340.7	50,370	3,618.3	4.1	2,287,170
Florida	3,270	6.2	34,323	4.7	10	1,446.2	42,136	3,565.7	4.0	1,090,414
New York	2,176	4.1	27,975	3.8	13	1,400.2	50,052	3,445.7	3.9	1,583,521
Illinois	1,960	3.7	27,077	3.7	14	1,330.3	49,131	3,381.0	3.8	1,724,980
Michigan	2,189	4.2	31,617	4.3	14	1,572.0	49,719	3,374.0	3.8	1,541,344
New Jersey	1,921	3.7	23,221	3.2	12	1,178.4	50,748	3,072.9	3.5	1,599,613
Ohio	1,925	3.7	24,990	3.4	13	1,072.0	42,897	2,522.3	2.9	1,310,276
Washington	1,382	2.6	18,335	2.5	13	926.0	50,503	2,072.9	2.4	1,499,944
Georgia	1,332	2.5	16,625	2.3	12	823.4	49,528	2,041.7	2.3	1,532,818
Colorado	1,592	3.0	17,049	2.3	11	816.1	47,866	1,927.0	2.2	1,210,397
Missouri	763	1.5	11,764	1.6	15	543.6	46,207	1,413.2	1.6	1,852,105
North Carolina	1,123	2.1	12,715	1.7	11	592.5	46,600	1,400.6	1.6	1,247,218
Louisiana	819	1.6	11,785	1.6	14	568.7	48,252	1,307.4	1.5	1,596,309
Tennessee	791	1.5	12,281	1.7	16	580.6	47,279	1,280.2	1.5	1,618,413
Idaho	233	0.4	9,046	1.2	39	447.3	49,453	1,209.9	1.4	5,192,742
Arizona	997	1.9	11,788	1.6	12	497.4	42,192	1,068.5	1.2	1,071,672
Wisconsin	903	1.7	9,747	1.3	11	421.5	43,246	1,003.6	1.1	1,111,437
Alabama	716	1.4	10,422	1.4	15	437.8	42,011	995.3	1.1	1,390,067
Minnesota	956	1.8	9,469	1.3	10	430.1	45,420	946.0	1.1	989,543
Indiana	931	1.8	9,129	1.3	10	374.3	41,003	865.7	1.0	929,857
Kansas	431	0.8	7,769	1.1	18	387.2	49,840	817.9	0.9	1,897,682
Connecticut	715	1.4	7,282	1.0	10	345.5	47,440	748.1	0.8	1,046,277
Nevada	399	0.8	6,279	0.9	16	298.5	47,534	710.5	0.8	1,780,812
Oregon	710	1.4	6,936	1.0	10	312.6	45,070	696.6	0.8	981,182
Oklahoma	561	1.1	5,290	0.7	9	223.3	42,213	590.4	0.7	1,052,401
Utah	483	0.9	5,686	0.8	12	225.2	39,598	538.3	0.6	1,114,406
Kentucky	542	1.0	6,155	0.8	11	232.8	37,829	505.4	0.6	932,391
New Mexico	374	0.7	4,938	0.7	13	214.9	43,519	503.3	0.6	1,345,615
Alaska	201	0.4	2,152	0.3	11	118.4	55,025	312.9	0.4	1,556,856
Mississippi	292	0.6	3,760	0.5	13	126.7	33,706	291.4	0.3	997,884
Hawaii	276	0.5	2,447	0.3	9	112.6	46,028	262.9	0.3	952,507
Rhode Island	204	0.4	2,518	0.3	12	104.4	41,458	258.3	0.3	1,266,078
D.C.	134	0.3	1,856	0.3	14	92.5	49,821	253.9	0.3	1,895,090
Iowa	285	0.5	2,791	0.4	10	111.5	39,942	239.5	0.3	840,502
New Hampshire	354	0.7	2,282	0.3	6	104.1	45,597	238.0	0.3	672,427
Maine	259	0.5	2,497	0.3	10	100.5	40,268	229.3	0.3	885,467
Delaware	178	0.3	1,931	0.3	11	87.4	45,281	193.4	0.2	1,086,270
Nebraska	190	0.4	2,515	0.3	13	102.2	40,619	191.9	0.2	1,009,884
Arkansas	254	0.5	2,293	0.3	9	82.1	35,783	174.9	0.2	688,728
Montana	198	0.4	1,776	0.2	9	65.8	37,070	159.6	0.2	806,268
West Virginia	214	0.4	2,149	0.3	10	66.6	30,971	147.0	0.2	686,780
Vermont	154	0.3	963	0.1	6	39.1	40,560	81.8	0.1	531,390
North Dakota	74	0.1	861	0.1	12	35.7	41,498	68.7	0.1	928,730
Wyoming	151	0.3	865	0.1	6	30.0	34,729	65.8	0.1	435,907
South Dakota	82	0.2	611	0.1	7	21.2	34,643	48.4	0.1	589,805

Source: 1997 *Economic Census*. The states are in descending order of revenues or establishments (if revenue data are missing for the majority). The symbol (D) appears when data are withheld to prevent disclosure of competitive information. States marked with (D) are sorted by number of establishments. A dash (-) indicates that the data element cannot be calculated. * indicates the midpoint of a range; 175, for example is the range 100-249. Shaded *states* on the state map indicate those states which have proportionately greater representation in the industry than would be indicated by the state's population; the ratio is based on total revenues or number of establishments. Shaded *regions* indicate where the industry is regionally most concentrated.

NAICS 541340 - DRAFTING SERVICES

GENERAL STATISTICS

Year	Establishments (number)	Employment (number)	Payroll ($ million)	Revenues ($ million)	Employees per Establishment (number)	Revenues per Establishment ($)	Payroll per Employee ($)
1997	1,872	9,150	310.0	605.0	4.9	323,184	33,880

Source: *Economic Census of the United States*, 1997. This is a newly defined industry. Data for prior years were unavailable at the time of publication but may become available over time.

INDICES OF CHANGE

Year	Establishments (number)	Employment (number)	Payroll ($ million)	Revenues ($ million)	Employees per Establishment (number)	Revenues per Establishment ($)	Payroll per Employee ($)
1997	100.0	100.0	100.0	100.0	100.0	100.0	100.0

Sources: Same as General Statistics. The values shown reflect change from the base year, 1997. Values above 100 mean greater than 1997, values below 100 mean less than 1997, and a value of 100 in the 1982-96 or 1998-2001 period means same as 1997. Values followed by a 'p' are projections by the editors; 'e' stands for extrapolation. Data are the most recent available at this level of detail.

SIC INDUSTRIES RELATED TO NAICS 541340

Each new NAICS code represents an industry that used to be part of an SIC or a part of several SIC industries. Data in this table are shown to provide transitional information for these cases. All available data for the precursor SIC(s) are shown. Even if only a part of an SIC is included in the NAICS, *all* data for the SIC are reproduced. If the SIC industry is not marked as being a part (pt) of the NAICS, the entire industry is embedded in the NAICS data. The SIC composition of the new industry provides some hints of the relative importance of its "ancestors." Data marked with a 'p' are projected. Projections begin with 1982 data. Data earlier than 1990 are not shown but are reflected in the projections.

SIC	Industry	1990	1991	1992	1993	1994	1995	1996	1997
7389	**Business Services, nec (pt)**								
	Establishments (number)	44,079	50,252	52,375	56,829	60,725	53,596	60,893*p*	63,269*p*
	Employment (thousands)	489.6	550.4	523.6	607.9	648.7	623.0	680.2*p*	710.9*p*
	Revenues ($ million)	-	-	32,885.9	-	-	-	-	-

Source: *Economic Census of the United States*, 1992, annual surveys of economic sectors conducted by the Bureau of the Census, and estimates or projections based on the 1982-1992 period; not all data are shown. 'e' marks estimates made by the editors; 'p' indicates projections based on time series. A dash (-) indicates that data for this SIC or year were not available. The abbreviation (pt) next to the industry name indicates that only a part of the industry is present within the NAICS data. If no (pt) is shown, the entire industry is contained within the NAICS data.

SELECTED RATIOS

For 1997	Avg. of Information	Analyzed Industry	Index	For 1997	Avg. of Information	Analyzed Industry	Index
Employees per establishment	9	5	57	Payroll per establishment	372,545	165,598	44
Revenue per establishment	958,337	323,184	34	Payroll as % of revenue	39	51	132
Revenue per employee	111,029	66,120	60	Payroll per employee	43,162	33,880	78

Sources: Same as General Statistics. The 'Average' column represents the average for the industry sector, in 1997, where the currently shown industry is classified. The Index shows the relationship between the Average and the Analyzed Industry. For example, 100 means that they are equal; 500 that the Analyzed Industry is five times the average; 50 means that the Analyzed Industry is half the national average. The abbreviation 'na' is used to show that data are 'not available'.

LEADING COMPANIES

No company data available for this industry.

LOCATION BY STATE AND REGIONAL CONCENTRATION

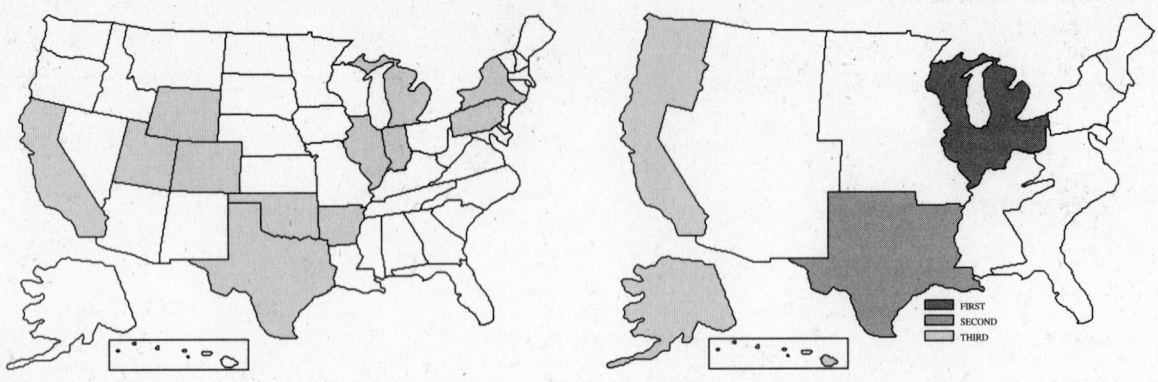

INDUSTRY DATA BY STATE

State	Establishments Total (number)	Establishments % of U.S.	Employment Total (number)	Employment % of U.S.	Employment Per Estab.	Payroll Total ($ mil.)	Payroll Per Empl. ($)	Revenues Total ($ mil.)	Revenues % of U.S.	Revenues Per Estab. ($)
California	193	10.3	1,249	13.7	6	38.3	30,631	85.3	14.1	441,788
Michigan	73	3.9	1,085	11.9	15	46.8	43,177	75.8	12.5	1,038,205
Texas	158	8.4	937	10.2	6	35.4	37,764	69.7	11.5	441,019
New York	94	5.0	651	7.1	7	28.6	43,935	48.5	8.0	515,798
Pennsylvania	71	3.8	537	5.9	8	19.8	36,946	32.9	5.4	462,972
Florida	177	9.5	393	4.3	2	11.3	28,830	31.0	5.1	175,051
Illinois	92	4.9	444	4.9	5	15.0	33,854	29.9	4.9	324,815
Ohio	63	3.4	337	3.7	5	10.5	31,300	21.0	3.5	333,889
Georgia	53	2.8	174	1.9	3	5.9	33,966	15.4	2.5	290,094
Indiana	46	2.5	270	3.0	6	8.3	30,833	14.4	2.4	313,087
Utah	33	1.8	164	1.8	5	6.4	38,756	13.7	2.3	416,030
Oklahoma	23	1.2	203	2.2	9	7.3	35,946	10.0	1.7	436,609
North Carolina	59	3.2	174	1.9	3	4.6	26,282	9.8	1.6	166,475
Alabama	44	2.4	162	1.8	4	4.7	28,716	9.8	1.6	222,955
Colorado	53	2.8	167	1.8	3	4.1	24,437	9.2	1.5	173,962
Arizona	47	2.5	143	1.6	3	3.7	26,196	8.5	1.4	180,809
Louisiana	30	1.6	152	1.7	5	4.3	28,441	8.1	1.3	269,300
Washington	49	2.6	127	1.4	3	3.7	29,307	7.9	1.3	160,918
Minnesota	37	2.0	119	1.3	3	3.4	28,303	7.1	1.2	192,351
Arkansas	15	0.8	151	1.7	10	4.7	31,073	6.8	1.1	454,400
Tennessee	23	1.2	105	1.1	5	3.0	29,019	6.6	1.1	287,522
Massachusetts	18	1.0	76	0.8	4	3.2	41,908	5.8	1.0	321,444
Kansas	14	0.7	65	0.7	5	1.4	21,538	3.3	0.5	234,714
Mississippi	16	0.9	59	0.6	4	1.5	25,102	3.0	0.5	185,438
Nevada	15	0.8	49	0.5	3	0.8	15,959	2.5	0.4	169,133
West Virginia	9	0.5	38	0.4	4	1.0	25,000	2.2	0.4	249,778
Idaho	12	0.6	32	0.3	3	0.7	22,906	1.8	0.3	149,333
Maine	13	0.7	30	0.3	2	0.7	21,867	1.6	0.3	119,769
Iowa	11	0.6	50	0.5	5	0.8	16,540	1.5	0.2	134,000
Nebraska	7	0.4	29	0.3	4	0.7	23,448	1.5	0.2	209,143
New Mexico	8	0.4	20	0.2	3	0.5	27,300	1.4	0.2	178,125
Delaware	5	0.3	18	0.2	4	0.6	33,056	1.3	0.2	258,200
Wyoming	8	0.4	18	0.2	2	0.4	21,778	1.1	0.2	143,375
New Hampshire	6	0.3	15	0.2	3	0.3	23,067	0.7	0.1	114,667
Hawaii	5	0.3	14	0.2	3	0.3	20,143	0.6	0.1	117,000
Montana	4	0.2	13	0.1	3	0.2	12,385	0.3	0.0	75,250
Alaska	3	0.2	4	0.0	1	0.1	13,250	0.2	0.0	72,000
Missouri	52	2.8	175*	-	-	(D)	-	(D)	-	-
New Jersey	46	2.5	60*	-	-	(D)	-	(D)	-	-
Virginia	43	2.3	175*	-	-	(D)	-	(D)	-	-
Oregon	32	1.7	60*	-	-	(D)	-	(D)	-	-
Wisconsin	30	1.6	175*	-	-	(D)	-	(D)	-	-
Maryland	28	1.5	60*	-	-	(D)	-	(D)	-	-
South Carolina	19	1.0	60*	-	-	(D)	-	(D)	-	-
Connecticut	12	0.6	10*	-	-	(D)	-	(D)	-	-
Kentucky	9	0.5	60*	-	-	(D)	-	(D)	-	-
Rhode Island	6	0.3	10*	-	-	(D)	-	(D)	-	-
South Dakota	3	0.2	10*	-	-	(D)	-	(D)	-	-
D.C.	2	0.1	60*	-	-	(D)	-	(D)	-	-
Vermont	2	0.1	10*	-	-	(D)	-	(D)	-	-
North Dakota	1	0.1	10*	-	-	(D)	-	(D)	-	-

Source: 1997 *Economic Census*. The states are in descending order of revenues or establishments (if revenue data are missing for the majority). The symbol (D) appears when data are withheld to prevent disclosure of competitive information. States marked with (D) are sorted by number of establishments. A dash (-) indicates that the data element cannot be calculated. * indicates the midpoint of a range; 175, for example is the range 100-249. Shaded *states* on the state map indicate those states which have proportionately greater representation in the industry than would be indicated by the state's population; the ratio is based on total revenues or number of establishments. Shaded *regions* indicate where the industry is regionally most concentrated.

NAICS 541350 - BUILDING INSPECTION SERVICES

GENERAL STATISTICS

Year	Establishments (number)	Employment (number)	Payroll ($ million)	Revenues ($ million)	Employees per Establishment (number)	Revenues per Establishment ($)	Payroll per Employee ($)
1997	2,771	8,674	240.0	639.0	3.1	230,603	27,669

Source: *Economic Census of the United States*, 1997. This is a newly defined industry. Data for prior years were unavailable at the time of publication but may become available over time.

INDICES OF CHANGE

Year	Establishments (number)	Employment (number)	Payroll ($ million)	Revenues ($ million)	Employees per Establishment (number)	Revenues per Establishment ($)	Payroll per Employee ($)
1997	100.0	100.0	100.0	100.0	100.0	100.0	100.0

Sources: Same as General Statistics. The values shown reflect change from the base year, 1997. Values above 100 mean greater than 1997, values below 100 mean less than 1997, and a value of 100 in the 1982-96 or 1998-2001 period means same as 1997. Values followed by a 'p' are projections by the editors; 'e' stands for extrapolation. Data are the most recent available at this level of detail.

SIC INDUSTRIES RELATED TO NAICS 541350

Each new NAICS code represents an industry that used to be part of an SIC or a part of several SIC industries. Data in this table are shown to provide transitional information for these cases. All available data for the precursor SIC(s) are shown. Even if only a part of an SIC is included in the NAICS, *all* data for the SIC are reproduced. If the SIC industry is not marked as being a part (pt) of the NAICS, the entire industry is embedded in the NAICS data. The SIC composition of the new industry provides some hints of the relative importance of its "ancestors." Data marked with a 'p' are projected. Projections begin with 1982 data. Data earlier than 1990 are not shown but are reflected in the projections.

SIC	Industry	1990	1991	1992	1993	1994	1995	1996	1997
7389	**Business Services, nec (pt)**								
	Establishments (number)	44,079	50,252	52,375	56,829	60,725	53,596	60,893*p*	63,269*p*
	Employment (thousands)	489.6	550.4	523.6	607.9	648.7	623.0	680.2*p*	710.9*p*
	Revenues ($ million)	-	-	32,885.9	-	-	-		

Source: *Economic Census of the United States*, 1992, annual surveys of economic sectors conducted by the Bureau of the Census, and estimates or projections based on the 1982-1992 period; not all data are shown. 'e' marks estimates made by the editors; 'p' indicates projections based on time series. A dash (-) indicates that data for this SIC or year were not available. The abbreviation (pt) next to the industry name indicates that only a part of the industry is present within the NAICS data. If no (pt) is shown, the entire industry is contained within the NAICS data.

SELECTED RATIOS

For 1997	Avg. of Information	Analyzed Industry	Index	For 1997	Avg. of Information	Analyzed Industry	Index
Employees per establishment	9	3	36	Payroll per establishment	372,545	86,611	23
Revenue per establishment	958,337	230,603	24	Payroll as % of revenue	39	38	97
Revenue per employee	111,029	73,668	66	Payroll per employee	43,162	27,669	64

Sources: Same as General Statistics. The 'Average' column represents the average for the industry sector, in 1997, where the currently shown industry is classified. The Index shows the relationship between the Average and the Analyzed Industry. For example, 100 means that they are equal; 500 that the Analyzed Industry is five times the average; 50 means that the Analyzed Industry is half the national average. The abbreviation 'na' is used to show that data are 'not available'.

LEADING COMPANIES

No company data available for this industry.

LOCATION BY STATE AND REGIONAL CONCENTRATION

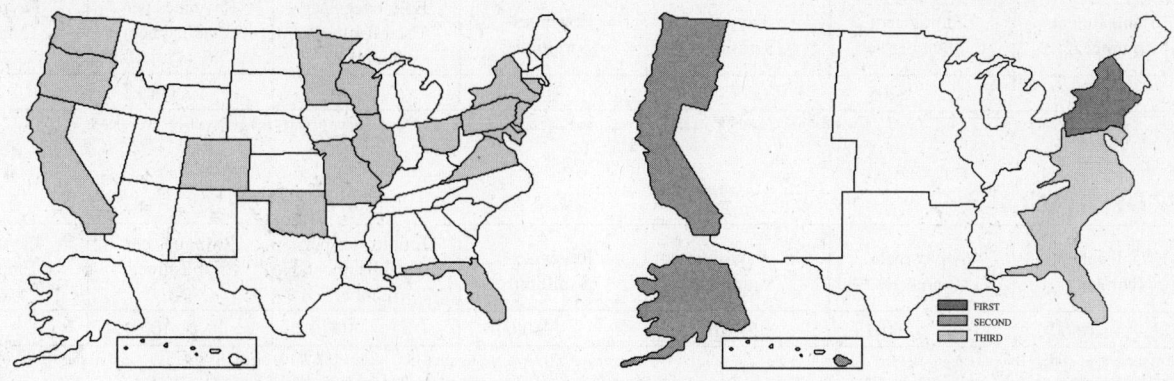

INDUSTRY DATA BY STATE

State	Establishments Total (number)	% of U.S.	Employment Total (number)	% of U.S.	Per Estab.	Payroll Total ($ mil.)	Per Empl. ($)	Revenues Total ($ mil.)	% of U.S.	Per Estab. ($)
California	271	9.8	1,124	13.0	4	37.1	32,999	90.9	14.2	335,362
New York	167	6.0	699	8.1	4	23.8	33,987	63.2	9.9	378,222
Florida	243	8.8	617	7.1	3	12.7	20,596	46.9	7.3	193,210
Pennsylvania	123	4.4	693	8.0	6	16.7	24,048	39.4	6.2	320,024
Ohio	104	3.8	362	4.2	3	8.3	22,798	39.0	6.1	374,894
Texas	160	5.8	437	5.0	3	13.0	29,751	37.8	5.9	236,012
Illinois	130	4.7	374	4.3	3	11.4	30,388	30.3	4.7	233,154
New Jersey	134	4.8	357	4.1	3	10.7	29,938	26.3	4.1	196,127
Maryland	90	3.2	305	3.5	3	8.6	28,079	23.6	3.7	262,622
Virginia	113	4.1	253	2.9	2	8.9	35,202	19.5	3.1	172,805
Wisconsin	68	2.5	321	3.7	5	8.9	27,632	17.5	2.7	257,147
Washington	79	2.9	255	2.9	3	7.0	27,427	16.7	2.6	210,949
Michigan	106	3.8	268	3.1	3	6.1	22,646	14.7	2.3	138,208
Missouri	44	1.6	262	3.0	6	6.9	26,519	14.6	2.3	332,886
Minnesota	61	2.2	232	2.7	4	5.3	22,832	14.0	2.2	229,164
Oregon	52	1.9	174	2.0	3	6.4	36,989	13.3	2.1	255,692
Colorado	73	2.6	186	2.1	3	4.4	23,489	12.9	2.0	176,685
Massachusetts	62	2.2	141	1.6	2	5.2	36,972	12.5	2.0	202,048
Connecticut	47	1.7	153	1.8	3	4.6	30,379	12.0	1.9	255,638
Georgia	79	2.9	150	1.7	2	4.4	29,320	11.0	1.7	138,899
Indiana	58	2.1	142	1.6	2	4.3	30,176	10.6	1.7	182,155
North Carolina	70	2.5	114	1.3	2	2.5	22,009	8.6	1.4	123,357
Oklahoma	29	1.0	156	1.8	5	3.2	20,378	8.0	1.3	275,552
Arizona	49	1.8	81	0.9	2	2.2	27,321	5.6	0.9	115,245
New Mexico	12	0.4	55	0.6	5	1.2	22,055	3.6	0.6	299,333
Louisiana	33	1.2	54	0.6	2	1.3	23,407	3.5	0.5	104,727
Tennessee	26	0.9	55	0.6	2	1.1	19,927	3.3	0.5	126,846
Utah	19	0.7	60	0.7	3	1.2	19,433	3.3	0.5	173,368
Kentucky	27	1.0	50	0.6	2	0.9	18,000	3.0	0.5	109,259
South Carolina	23	0.8	48	0.6	2	1.2	24,708	2.9	0.5	125,957
Delaware	13	0.5	43	0.5	3	1.2	28,442	2.4	0.4	188,000
Kansas	30	1.1	36	0.4	1	0.8	21,306	2.3	0.4	76,167
New Hampshire	19	0.7	25	0.3	1	0.8	30,320	2.0	0.3	105,895
Idaho	13	0.5	34	0.4	3	0.8	24,088	1.9	0.3	148,923
Iowa	10	0.4	25	0.3	3	0.5	19,360	1.8	0.3	177,500
Mississippi	9	0.3	28	0.3	3	0.4	15,393	1.7	0.3	189,778
West Virginia	11	0.4	36	0.4	3	0.6	16,944	1.7	0.3	150,091
Hawaii	8	0.3	16	0.2	2	0.7	44,187	1.6	0.3	203,625
Nevada	12	0.4	29	0.3	2	0.7	23,724	1.4	0.2	118,083
Alaska	11	0.4	17	0.2	2	0.6	35,706	1.4	0.2	126,636
Montana	10	0.4	24	0.3	2	0.3	11,583	1.1	0.2	111,600
Vermont	5	0.2	14	0.2	3	0.3	23,000	0.9	0.1	171,200
Nebraska	7	0.3	9	0.1	1	0.2	23,667	0.6	0.1	81,429
Wyoming	4	0.1	7	0.1	2	0.1	12,857	0.5	0.1	131,250
South Dakota	3	0.1	9	0.1	3	-	3,556	0.2	0.0	73,667
Alabama	22	0.8	60*	-	-	(D)	-	(D)	-	-
Arkansas	14	0.5	60*	-	-	(D)	-	(D)	-	-
Maine	8	0.3	10*	-	-	(D)	-	(D)	-	-
Rhode Island	8	0.3	60*	-	-	(D)	-	(D)	-	-
D.C.	1	-	10*	-	-	(D)	-	(D)	-	-
North Dakota	1	-	10*	-	-	(D)	-	(D)	-	-

Source: 1997 *Economic Census*. The states are in descending order of revenues or establishments (if revenue data are missing for the majority). The symbol (D) appears when data are withheld to prevent disclosure of competitive information. States marked with (D) are sorted by number of establishments. A dash (-) indicates that the data element cannot be calculated. * indicates the midpoint of a range; 175, for example is the range 100-249. Shaded *states* on the state map indicate those states which have proportionately greater representation in the industry than would be indicated by the state's population; the ratio is based on total revenues or number of establishments. Shaded *regions* indicate where the industry is regionally most concentrated.

NAICS 541360 - GEOPHYSICAL SURVEYING AND MAPPING SERVICES

GENERAL STATISTICS

Year	Establishments (number)	Employment (number)	Payroll ($ million)	Revenues ($ million)	Employees per Establishment (number)	Revenues per Establishment ($)	Payroll per Employee ($)
1997	587	9,905	446.0	1,088.0	16.9	1,853,492	45,028

Source: *Economic Census of the United States*, 1997. This is a newly defined industry. Data for prior years were unavailable at the time of publication but may become available over time.

INDICES OF CHANGE

Year	Establishments (number)	Employment (number)	Payroll ($ million)	Revenues ($ million)	Employees per Establishment (number)	Revenues per Establishment ($)	Payroll per Employee ($)
1997	100.0	100.0	100.0	100.0	100.0	100.0	100.0

Sources: Same as General Statistics. The values shown reflect change from the base year, 1997. Values above 100 mean greater than 1997, values below 100 mean less than 1997, and a value of 100 in the 1982-96 or 1998-2001 period means same as 1997. Values followed by a 'p' are projections by the editors; 'e' stands for extrapolation. Data are the most recent available at this level of detail.

SIC INDUSTRIES RELATED TO NAICS 541360

Each new NAICS code represents an industry that used to be part of an SIC or a part of several SIC industries. Data in this table are shown to provide transitional information for these cases. All available data for the precursor SIC(s) are shown. Even if only a part of an SIC is included in the NAICS, *all* data for the SIC are reproduced. If the SIC industry is not marked as being a part (pt) of the NAICS, the entire industry is embedded in the NAICS data. The SIC composition of the new industry provides some hints of the relative importance of its "ancestors." Data marked with a 'p' are projected. Projections begin with 1982 data. Data earlier than 1990 are not shown but are reflected in the projections.

SIC	Industry	1990	1991	1992	1993	1994	1995	1996	1997
1081	**Metal Mining Services**								
	Establishments (number)	218	224	266	210	193	193	264e	264e
	Employment (thousands)	3.4	3.6	3.3	2.3	2.7	2.7	3.8e	3.9e
	Revenues ($ million)	306.8e	327.9e	350.4	374.5e	400.2e	427.7e	457.2e	488.6e
1382	**Oil and Gas Exploration Services**								
	Establishments (number)	1,401	1,541	1,490	1,487	1,420	1,004	1,218e	1,158e
	Employment (thousands)	13.6	16.4	13.7	12.3	12.0	10.9	11.6e	11.1e
	Revenues ($ million)	1,015.2e	989.6e	964.6	940.2e	916.5e	893.4e	870.8e	848.8e
1481	**Nonmetallic Minerals Services**								
	Establishments (number)	161	160	178	138	143	106	179e	179e
	Employment (thousands)	1.8	1.9	2.0	1.5	1.6	1.3	2.2e	2.2e
	Revenues ($ million)	179.1e	183.9e	188.9	194.0e	199.2e	204.6e	210.1e	215.7e
8713	**Surveying Services (pt)**								
	Establishments (number)	7,704	7,715	8,418	8,664	8,870	9,003	8,878p	8,986p
	Employment (thousands)	49.0	43.7	45.3	46.7	49.8	51.5	52.2p	53.0p
	Revenues ($ million)	2,707.0	2,649.0	2,635.0	2,775.0	2,927.0	3,103.0	3,529.0	3,427.3p

Source: *Economic Census of the United States*, 1992, annual surveys of economic sectors conducted by the Bureau of the Census, and estimates or projections based on the 1982-1992 period; not all data are shown. 'e' marks estimates made by the editors; 'p' indicates projections based on time series. A dash (-) indicates that data for this SIC or year were not available. The abbreviation (pt) next to the industry name indicates that only a part of the industry is present within the NAICS data. If no (pt) is shown, the entire industry is contained within the NAICS data.

SELECTED RATIOS

For 1997	Avg. of Information	Analyzed Industry	Index	For 1997	Avg. of Information	Analyzed Industry	Index
Employees per establishment	9	17	195	Payroll per establishment	372,545	759,796	204
Revenue per establishment	958,337	1,853,492	193	Payroll as % of revenue	39	41	105
Revenue per employee	111,029	109,844	99	Payroll per employee	43,162	45,028	104

Sources: Same as General Statistics. The 'Average' column represents the average for the industry sector, in 1997, where the currently shown industry is classified. The Index shows the relationship between the Average and the Analyzed Industry. For example, 100 means that they are equal; 500 that the Analyzed Industry is five times the average; 50 means that the Analyzed Industry is half the national average. The abbreviation 'na' is used to show that data are 'not available'.

LEADING COMPANIES

No company data available for this industry.

LOCATION BY STATE AND REGIONAL CONCENTRATION

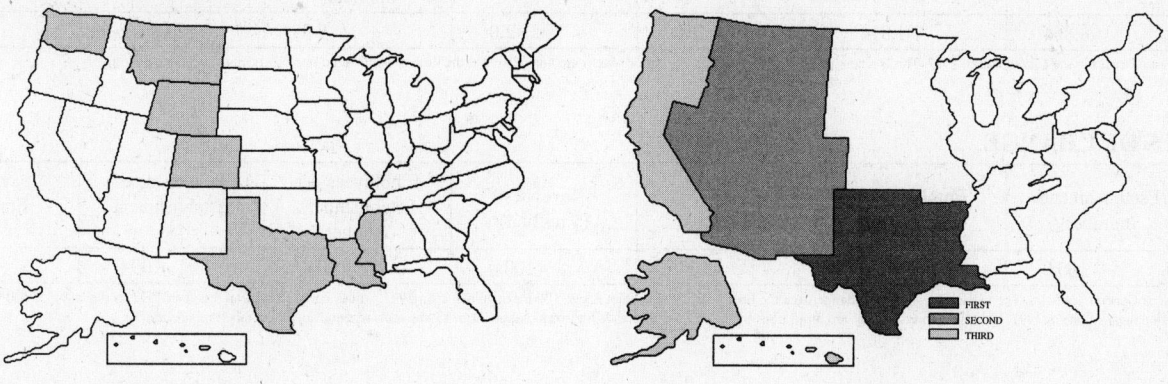

FIRST
SECOND
THIRD

INDUSTRY DATA BY STATE

State	Establishments Total (number)	% of U.S.	Employment Total (number)	% of U.S.	Per Estab.	Payroll Total ($ mil.)	Per Empl. ($)	Revenues Total ($ mil.)	% of U.S.	Per Estab. ($)
Texas	185	31.5	6,290	63.5	34	331.3	52,676	706.1	64.9	3,816,935
Louisiana	33	5.6	1,161	11.7	35	35.8	30,801	167.0	15.4	5,062,030
Colorado	49	8.3	283	2.9	6	12.8	45,194	37.7	3.5	769,367
Washington	9	1.5	387	3.9	43	12.4	32,165	32.9	3.0	3,660,556
Ohio	13	2.2	324	3.3	25	5.6	17,349	16.1	1.5	1,239,385
California	41	7.0	164	1.7	4	4.8	29,195	14.3	1.3	348,293
Mississippi	17	2.9	99	1.0	6	3.5	34,869	13.3	1.2	781,824
Oklahoma	35	6.0	155	1.6	4	4.1	26,245	12.3	1.1	350,771
Michigan	14	2.4	63	0.6	5	3.2	50,222	9.0	0.8	641,214
Montana	10	1.7	69	0.7	7	1.8	26,638	8.9	0.8	894,000
Pennsylvania	16	2.7	38	0.4	2	2.2	57,184	5.6	0.5	350,250
Utah	12	2.0	34	0.3	3	1.4	42,324	4.6	0.4	383,250
Nevada	8	1.4	45	0.5	6	2.0	45,133	4.1	0.4	515,750
Arizona	11	1.9	43	0.4	4	1.5	35,186	4.0	0.4	361,182
Indiana	6	1.0	35	0.4	6	1.8	51,714	3.5	0.3	581,000
Massachusetts	12	2.0	37	0.4	3	1.1	30,865	2.8	0.3	234,583
West Virginia	5	0.9	39	0.4	8	1.8	45,615	2.8	0.3	559,400
New York	5	0.9	15	0.2	3	1.2	80,333	2.6	0.2	528,400
Florida	13	2.2	18	0.2	1	0.5	29,444	2.0	0.2	152,308
New Mexico	6	1.0	25	0.3	4	0.9	35,720	2.0	0.2	326,833
Wyoming	6	1.0	28	0.3	5	0.6	20,643	1.8	0.2	293,500
Illinois	9	1.5	38	0.4	4	0.5	13,684	1.6	0.1	178,556
Georgia	8	1.4	29	0.3	4	0.7	25,172	1.5	0.1	181,625
Kansas	7	1.2	19	0.2	3	0.4	22,421	1.0	0.1	150,000
North Carolina	7	1.2	15	0.2	2	0.4	23,933	0.9	0.1	121,857
Minnesota	4	0.7	19	0.2	5	0.2	8,579	0.7	0.1	177,000
Idaho	4	0.7	11	0.1	3	0.1	11,273	0.6	0.1	143,000
Alaska	4	0.7	2	0.0	1	0.2	93,500	0.5	0.0	116,750
Tennessee	5	0.9	9	0.1	2	0.2	19,778	0.4	0.0	75,000
Alabama	4	0.7	60*	-	-	(D)	-	(D)	-	-
Missouri	4	0.7	60*	-	-	(D)		(D)	-	-
Arkansas	3	0.5	60*	-	-	(D)		(D)	-	-
Connecticut	3	0.5	60*	-	-	(D)	-	(D)	-	-
Maryland	3	0.5	10*	-	-	(D)	-	(D)	-	-
New Jersey	3	0.5	10*	-	-	(D)	-	(D)	-	-
Kentucky	2	0.3	10*	-	-	(D)	-	(D)	-	-
Maine	2	0.3	10*	-	-	(D)	-	(D)	-	-
North Dakota	2	0.3	10*	-	-	(D)	-	(D)	-	-
Oregon	2	0.3	10*	-	-	(D)	-	(D)	-	-
South Carolina	1	0.2	60*	-	-	(D)	-	(D)	-	-
South Dakota	1	0.2	10*	-	-	(D)	-	(D)	-	-
Vermont	1	0.2	10*	-	-	(D)	-	(D)	-	-
Virginia	1	0.2	10*	-	-	(D)	-	(D)	-	-
Wisconsin	1	0.2	10*	-	-	(D)		(D)		

Source: 1997 *Economic Census*. The states are in descending order of revenues or establishments (if revenue data are missing for the majority). The symbol (D) appears when data are withheld to prevent disclosure of competitive information. States marked with (D) are sorted by number of establishments. A dash (-) indicates that the data element cannot be calculated. * indicates the midpoint of a range; 175, for example is the range 100-249. Shaded *states* on the state map indicate those states which have proportionately greater representation in the industry than would be indicated by the state's population; the ratio is based on total revenues or number of establishments. Shaded *regions* indicate where the industry is regionally most concentrated.

NAICS 541370 - SURVEYING AND MAPPING (EXCEPT GEOPHYSICAL) SERVICES

GENERAL STATISTICS

Year	Establishments (number)	Employment (number)	Payroll ($ million)	Revenues ($ million)	Employees per Establishment (number)	Revenues per Establishment ($)	Payroll per Employee ($)
1997	8,864	51,814	1,432.0	3,042.0	5.8	343,186	27,637

Source: Economic Census of the United States, 1997. This is a newly defined industry. Data for prior years were unavailable at the time of publication but may become available over time.

INDICES OF CHANGE

Year	Establishments (number)	Employment (number)	Payroll ($ million)	Revenues ($ million)	Employees per Establishment (number)	Revenues per Establishment ($)	Payroll per Employee ($)
1997	100.0	100.0	100.0	100.0	100.0	100.0	100.0

Sources: Same as General Statistics. The values shown reflect change from the base year, 1997. Values above 100 mean greater than 1997, values below 100 mean less than 1997, and a value of 100 in the 1982-96 or 1998-2001 period means same as 1997. Values followed by a 'p' are projections by the editors; 'e' stands for extrapolation. Data are the most recent available at this level of detail.

SIC INDUSTRIES RELATED TO NAICS 541370

Each new NAICS code represents an industry that used to be part of an SIC or a part of several SIC industries. Data in this table are shown to provide transitional information for these cases. All available data for the precursor SIC(s) are shown. Even if only a part of an SIC is included in the NAICS, *all* data for the SIC are reproduced. If the SIC industry is not marked as being a part (pt) of the NAICS, the entire industry is embedded in the NAICS data. The SIC composition of the new industry provides some hints of the relative importance of its "ancestors." Data marked with a 'p' are projected. Projections begin with 1982 data. Data earlier than 1990 are not shown but are reflected in the projections.

SIC	Industry	1990	1991	1992	1993	1994	1995	1996	1997
7389	**Business Services, nec (pt)**								
	Establishments (number)	44,079	50,252	52,375	56,829	60,725	53,596	60,893*p*	63,269*p*
	Employment (thousands)	489.6	550.4	523.6	607.9	648.7	623.0	680.2*p*	710.9*p*
	Revenues ($ million)	-	-	32,885.9	-	-	-	-	-
8713	**Surveying Services (pt)**								
	Establishments (number)	7,704	7,715	8,418	8,664	8,870	9,003	8,878*p*	8,986*p*
	Employment (thousands)	49.0	43.7	45.3	46.7	49.8	51.5	52.2*p*	53.0*p*
	Revenues ($ million)	2,707.0	2,649.0	2,635.0	2,775.0	2,927.0	3,103.0	3,529.0	3,427.3*p*

Source: Economic Census of the United States, 1992, annual surveys of economic sectors conducted by the Bureau of the Census, and estimates or projections based on the 1982-1992 period; not all data are shown. 'e' marks estimates made by the editors; 'p' indicates projections based on time series. A dash (-) indicates that data for this SIC or year were not available. The abbreviation (pt) next to the industry name indicates that only a part of the industry is present within the NAICS data. If no (pt) is shown, the entire industry is contained within the NAICS data.

SELECTED RATIOS

For 1997	Avg. of Information	Analyzed Industry	Index	For 1997	Avg. of Information	Analyzed Industry	Index
Employees per establishment	9	6	68	Payroll per establishment	372,545	161,552	43
Revenue per establishment	958,337	343,186	36	Payroll as % of revenue	39	47	121
Revenue per employee	111,029	58,710	53	Payroll per employee	43,162	27,637	64

Sources: Same as General Statistics. The 'Average' column represents the average for the industry sector, in 1997, where the currently shown industry is classified. The Index shows the relationship between the Average and the Analyzed Industry. For example, 100 means that they are equal; 500 that the Analyzed Industry is five times the average; 50 means that the Analyzed Industry is half the national average. The abbreviation 'na' is used to show that data are 'not available'.

LEADING COMPANIES   Number shown: **5**   Total sales ($ mil): **1,031**   Total employment (000): **6.4**

Company Name	Address				CEO Name	Phone	Co. Type	Sales ($ mil)	Empl. (000)
Western Geophysical Co.	PO Box 2469	Houston	TX	77252	R. White	713-789-9600	S	1,000*	6.0
McLarens Toplis North America	233 S Wacker Dr	Chicago	IL	60606	Joseph A Dotoli	312-648-1300	R	27*	0.3
Environmental Resolutions Inc.	124 Gaither Dr	Mount Laurel	NJ	08054		609-235-7170	N	3	<0.1
CZR Inc.	140 Intarcoastal	Jupiter	FL	33477		407-747-7455	N	1	<0.1
Cornerstone Seminars	613 W 10th St	Yankton	SD	57078		605-665-4151	N	0	<0.1

Source: *Ward's Business Directory of U.S. Private and Public Companies*, Volumes 1 and 2, 2000. The company type code used is as follows: P - Public, R - Private, S - Subsidiary, D - Division, J - Joint Venture, A - Affiliate, G - Group, N - Company type not reported. Sales are in millions of dollars, employees are in thousands. An asterisk (*) indicates an estimated sales volume. The symbol < stands for 'less than'. Company names and addresses are truncated, in some cases, to fit into the available space.

LOCATION BY STATE AND REGIONAL CONCENTRATION

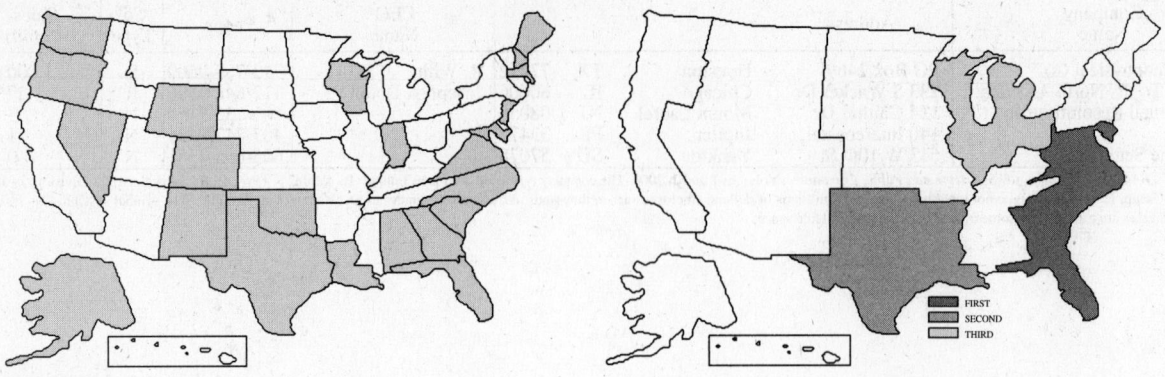

FIRST
SECOND
THIRD

INDUSTRY DATA BY STATE

State	Establishments Total (number)	Establishments % of U.S.	Employment Total (number)	Employment % of U.S.	Employment Per Estab.	Payroll Total ($ mil.)	Payroll Per Empl. ($)	Revenues Total ($ mil.)	Revenues % of U.S.	Revenues Per Estab. ($)
Texas	664	7.5	5,170	10.0	8	140.5	27,167	312.7	10.3	470,931
Florida	674	7.6	5,543	10.7	8	142.4	25,694	274.8	9.0	407,672
California	504	5.7	2,802	5.4	6	99.7	35,584	223.6	7.4	443,659
North Carolina	589	6.6	3,123	6.0	5	72.1	23,086	152.9	5.0	259,604
Louisiana	140	1.6	1,446	2.8	10	48.3	33,405	135.0	4.4	963,993
Virginia	290	3.3	2,017	3.9	7	55.5	27,504	114.2	3.8	393,793
Colorado	225	2.5	1,377	2.7	6	49.4	35,893	110.4	3.6	490,542
Georgia	359	4.1	2,107	4.1	6	50.7	24,082	102.5	3.4	285,379
New Jersey	285	3.2	1,454	2.8	5	49.2	33,803	100.0	3.3	350,818
New York	405	4.6	1,643	3.2	4	47.0	28,614	99.7	3.3	246,178
Indiana	171	1.9	1,502	2.9	9	44.0	29,292	90.9	3.0	531,608
Ohio	300	3.4	1,643	3.2	5	41.5	25,278	85.6	2.8	285,427
Massachusetts	200	2.3	1,320	2.5	7	47.0	35,574	84.2	2.8	421,230
Illinois	212	2.4	1,404	2.7	7	45.9	32,687	83.2	2.7	392,382
Michigan	197	2.2	1,396	2.7	7	38.9	27,852	75.7	2.5	384,046
Pennsylvania	324	3.7	1,213	2.3	4	28.3	23,369	66.8	2.2	206,244
Washington	221	2.5	1,076	2.1	5	31.8	29,572	65.9	2.2	298,290
Maryland	146	1.6	979	1.9	7	28.9	29,567	62.8	2.1	430,171
Wisconsin	169	1.9	1,132	2.2	7	28.1	24,860	62.2	2.0	368,148
Alabama	192	2.2	1,185	2.3	6	26.7	22,543	56.5	1.9	294,073
Missouri	148	1.7	1,046	2.0	7	29.5	28,209	55.7	1.8	376,601
Tennessee	237	2.7	1,088	2.1	5	23.0	21,120	53.2	1.7	224,456
Oklahoma	113	1.3	713	1.4	6	20.2	28,276	50.0	1.6	442,903
South Carolina	230	2.6	1,060	2.0	5	21.5	20,324	44.7	1.5	194,257
Oregon	141	1.6	658	1.3	5	20.6	31,337	40.7	1.3	288,738
Arizona	136	1.5	621	1.2	5	17.6	28,380	36.2	1.2	266,125
Connecticut	107	1.2	449	0.9	4	15.3	34,098	36.0	1.2	336,785
New Mexico	107	1.2	555	1.1	5	15.5	27,894	32.9	1.1	307,299
Kentucky	148	1.7	678	1.3	5	13.1	19,382	32.9	1.1	222,507
Nevada	76	0.9	398	0.8	5	15.0	37,754	32.8	1.1	431,263
Minnesota	106	1.2	507	1.0	5	16.2	31,907	31.6	1.0	298,019
Mississippi	95	1.1	525	1.0	6	11.3	21,547	24.8	0.8	261,000
Maine	101	1.1	428	0.8	4	10.1	23,533	21.8	0.7	216,287
Alaska	68	0.8	285	0.6	4	9.8	34,228	21.3	0.7	313,206
Utah	57	0.6	340	0.7	6	9.5	28,053	20.6	0.7	361,351
New Hampshire	87	1.0	337	0.7	4	9.0	26,644	17.0	0.6	195,103
Arkansas	106	1.2	399	0.8	4	7.5	18,797	16.9	0.6	159,840
West Virginia	92	1.0	371	0.7	4	5.5	14,817	12.9	0.4	140,065
Hawaii	27	0.3	150	0.3	6	5.2	34,960	10.2	0.3	377,704
Wyoming	40	0.5	189	0.4	5	4.3	22,566	9.7	0.3	242,875
Idaho	47	0.5	173	0.3	4	4.5	25,803	9.4	0.3	200,426
Iowa	46	0.5	176	0.3	4	4.3	24,682	9.3	0.3	202,370
Montana	50	0.6	144	0.3	3	2.9	20,028	7.5	0.2	149,180
Rhode Island	29	0.3	118	0.2	4	3.1	26,059	6.8	0.2	233,759
Delaware	24	0.3	108	0.2	5	2.7	25,037	5.6	0.2	232,417
Vermont	51	0.6	102	0.2	2	1.9	18,216	5.3	0.2	103,255
Nebraska	29	0.3	97	0.2	3	1.9	19,887	4.9	0.2	169,379
South Dakota	20	0.2	70	0.1	4	1.3	18,814	2.7	0.1	134,500
North Dakota	12	0.1	28	0.1	2	0.4	14,071	1.2	0.0	96,083
Kansas	66	0.7	375*	-	-	(D)	-	(D)	-	-
D.C.	1	-	10*	-	-	(D)	-	(D)	-	-

Source: 1997 *Economic Census*. The states are in descending order of revenues or establishments (if revenue data are missing for the majority). The symbol (D) appears when data are withheld to prevent disclosure of competitive information. States marked with (D) are sorted by number of establishments. A dash (-) indicates that the data element cannot be calculated. * indicates the midpoint of a range; 175, for example is the range 100-249. Shaded *states* on the state map indicate those states which have proportionately greater representation in the industry than would be indicated by the state's population; the ratio is based on total revenues or number of establishments. Shaded *regions* indicate where the industry is regionally most concentrated.

NAICS 541380 - TESTING LABORATORIES

GENERAL STATISTICS

Year	Establishments (number)	Employment (number)	Payroll ($ million)	Revenues ($ million)	Employees per Establishment (number)	Revenues per Establishment ($)	Payroll per Employee ($)
1997	5,488	82,024	2,709.0	6,443.0	14.9	1,174,016	33,027

Source: *Economic Census of the United States*, 1997. This is a newly defined industry. Data for prior years were unavailable at the time of publication but may become available over time.

INDICES OF CHANGE

Year	Establishments (number)	Employment (number)	Payroll ($ million)	Revenues ($ million)	Employees per Establishment (number)	Revenues per Establishment ($)	Payroll per Employee ($)
1997	100.0	100.0	100.0	100.0	100.0	100.0	100.0

Sources: Same as General Statistics. The values shown reflect change from the base year, 1997. Values above 100 mean greater than 1997, values below 100 mean less than 1997, and a value of 100 in the 1982-96 or 1998-2001 period means same as 1997. Values followed by a 'p' are projections by the editors; 'e' stands for extrapolation. Data are the most recent available at this level of detail.

SIC INDUSTRIES RELATED TO NAICS 541380

Each new NAICS code represents an industry that used to be part of an SIC or a part of several SIC industries. Data in this table are shown to provide transitional information for these cases. All available data for the precursor SIC(s) are shown. Even if only a part of an SIC is included in the NAICS, *all* data for the SIC are reproduced. If the SIC industry is not marked as being a part (pt) of the NAICS, the entire industry is embedded in the NAICS data. The SIC composition of the new industry provides some hints of the relative importance of its "ancestors." Data marked with a 'p' are projected. Projections begin with 1982 data. Data earlier than 1990 are not shown but are reflected in the projections.

SIC	Industry	1990	1991	1992	1993	1994	1995	1996	1997
8734	**Testing Laboratories (pt)**								
	Establishments (number)	3,616	3,895	4,704	4,947	5,077	5,342	6,010p	6,382p
	Employment (thousands)	59.3	64.0	76.7	77.4	77.3	82.2	94.7p	100.6p
	Revenues ($ million)	4,176.0	4,447.0	4,810.0	4,990.0	5,193.0	5,540.0	5,833.0	6,448.9p

Source: *Economic Census of the United States*, 1992, annual surveys of economic sectors conducted by the Bureau of the Census, and estimates or projections based on the 1982-1992 period; not all data are shown. 'e' marks estimates made by the editors; 'p' indicates projections based on time series. A dash (-) indicates that data for this SIC or year were not available. The abbreviation (pt) next to the industry name indicates that only a part of the industry is present within the NAICS data. If no (pt) is shown, the entire industry is contained within the NAICS data.

SELECTED RATIOS

For 1997	Avg. of Information	Analyzed Industry	Index	For 1997	Avg. of Information	Analyzed Industry	Index
Employees per establishment	9	15	173	Payroll per establishment	372,545	493,622	132
Revenue per establishment	958,337	1,174,016	123	Payroll as % of revenue	39	42	108
Revenue per employee	111,029	78,550	71	Payroll per employee	43,162	33,027	77

Sources: Same as General Statistics. The 'Average' column represents the average for the industry sector, in 1997, where the currently shown industry is classified. The Index shows the relationship between the Average and the Analyzed Industry. For example, 100 means that they are equal; 500 that the Analyzed Industry is five times the average; 50 means that the Analyzed Industry is half the national average. The abbreviation 'na' is used to show that data are 'not available'.

LEADING COMPANIES　Number shown: **75**　Total sales ($ mil): **9,578**　Total employment (000): **68.0**

Company Name	Address				CEO Name	Phone	Co. Type	Sales ($ mil)	Empl. (000)
Thermo Electron Corp.	81 Wyman St	Waltham	MA	02454	John N. Hatsopoulos	781-622-1000	P	4,261*	26.0
GAB Robin	9 Campus Dr Linden	Parsippany	NJ	07054	Richard A Simon	973-993-3803	S	489*	3.5
Thermo TerraTech Inc.	P O Box 9046	Waltham	MA	02254	John P Appleton	781-370-1500	P	300*	2.7
Core Laboratories Inc.	5295 Hollister St	Houston	TX	77040	David Demshur	713-460-9600	P	286	3.6
Veterinary Centers of America Inc	3420 Ocean Park	Santa Monica	CA	90405	Robert L Antin	310-392-9599	P	281	3.0
Bionetics Corp.	11833 Canon Blvd	Newport News	VA	23606	Charles Stern	757-873-0900	R	208*	1.3
Echlin Automotive	1900 Opdyke Ct	Auburn Hills	MI	48326	Allan Cameron	248-377-0700	S	180	1.9
Maxwell Technologies Inc.	9275 Sky Park Ct	San Diego	CA	92123	Carlton J Eibl	858-279-5100	P	180	1.1
Wyle Laboratories Inc.	128 Maryland St	El Segundo	CA	90245	Robert Rieth	310-322-1763	R	175*	1.0
Heritage Environmental Services	7901 W Morris St	Indianapolis	IN	46231	Kenneth Price	317-243-0811	R	150	0.9
Clinimetrics Research Assoc. Inc.	1732 N First St	San Jose	CA	95112		408-452-8215	N	149	0.1
Clean Harbors Inc.	PO Box 850327	Braintree	MA	02185		781-849-1800	P	146	1.2
Tyree Organization Inc.	208 Rte 109	Farmingdale	NY	11735	William Tyree	516-249-3150	R	142*	0.6
Artesian Resources Corp.	664 Churchmans Rd	Newark	DE	19702	Dian C Taylor	302-453-6900	P	137*	0.2
MNP Corp.	PO Box 189002	Utica	MI	48318	Larry Berman	810-254-1320	R	115	0.8
LabOne Inc.	10101 Renner Blvd	Lenexa	KS	66219	W Thomas Grant II	913-888-1770	P	102	0.9
Terracon	16000 College Blvd	Lenexa	KS	66219	Larry Davidson	913-599-6886	R	100	1.1
Groundwater Technology Inc.	100 River Ridge Dr	Norwood	MA	02062		781-769-7600	N	100	1.5
National Technical Systems Inc.	24040 Ventura Blvd	Calabasas	CA	91302	Jack Lin	818-591-0776	P	90	0.8
Defiance Inc.	28271 Cedar Park	Perrysburg	OH	43551	Ralph Passino	419-661-1333	S	89	0.7
UniHolding Corp.	96 Spring St	New York	NY	10012	Edgard Zwirn	212-219-9496	P	84	0.7
Viromed Biosafety Laboratories	1667 Davis St	Camden	NJ	08104	Anita Baskin	856-966-1305	S	78*	0.3
Marine Pollution Control Corp.	8631 W Jefferson	Detroit	MI	48209	David Usher	313-849-2333	R	75	<0.1
Cortez III Service Corp.	4841 Tramway	Albuquerque	NM	87111	Craig Wilson	505-296-4883	R	70*	0.5
EarthTech	2233 Tomlynn St	Richmond	VA	23230	Brian Redd	804-358-5858	S	70*	0.3
Quanterra Inc.	4955 Yarrow St	Arvada	CO	80002		303-421-6611	S	70	0.7
Surface Science Laboratories	625 B Clyde Ave	Mountain View	CA	94043	Charles Evans Jr	650-962-8767	D	67*	<0.1
Ecology and Environment Inc.	Buffalo Corporate	Lancaster	NY	14086	Gerhard J Neumaier	716-684-8060	P	63	0.8
TestAmerica Inc.	122 Lyman St	Asheville	NC	28801	Thomas Barr	828-258-3746	R	62	0.7
Clayton Group Services Inc.	41650 Gardenbrook	Novi	MI	48375	Tom P Kowalski	248-344-8550	R	57	0.5
Commercial Testing	1919 S Highland	Lombard	IL	60148	Scott Morrison	630-953-9300	S	54*	0.6
Ardaman and Associates Inc.	P O Box 593003	Orlando	FL	32859	Anwar Wissa	407-855-3860	R	48*	0.3
PEI Electronics Inc.	PO Box 1929	Huntsville	AL	35807	Thomas Keenan	256-895-2000	R	48	0.4
Stellex Aerospace	21550 Oxnard St	Woodland Hills	CA	91367	Bradley C Call	818-710-7707	R	46*	0.4
Tanknology-NDE Intern. Inc.	8900 Shoal Creek	Austin	TX	78757	A Daniel Sharplin	512-451-6334	P	46*	0.5
Bell Technologies Inc.	6120 Hanging Moss	Orlando	FL	32807		407-671-3600	S	45*	0.4
McNamee Porter and Seeley Inc.	3131 S State Rd	Ann Arbor	MI	48108	Glen Burkhardt	734-665-6000	S	44*	0.4
Landauer Inc.	2 Science Rd	Glenwood	IL	60425	Brent Latta	708-755-7000	P	44	0.3
PharmChem Laboratories Inc.	1505-A O'Brien Dr	Menlo Park	CA	94025	Joseph W Halligan	650-328-6200	P	43	0.3
Dayton T. Brown Inc.	555 Church St	Bohemia	NY	11716	Dayton Brown	516-589-6300	R	42*	0.4
Froehling and Robertson Inc.	PO Box 27524	Richmond	VA	23261	Samuel H Kirby	804-264-2701	R	42*	0.3
Qore Inc.	11420 Johns Creek	Duluth	GA	30097	Dave Albin	770-476-3555	R	38	0.5
Osborn Group	14901 West 117th St	Olathe	KS	66062	Derek Smith	913-764-5555	S	37*	0.4
ETL Testing Laboratories Inc.	8431 Murphy Dr	Middleton	WI	53562	Jag Sisodia	607-753-6711	S	33*	0.3
Aero Systems Engineering Inc.	358 E Fillmore Ave	St. Paul	MN	55107	Leon Ring	651-227-7515	P	27	0.2
Central Engineering Co.	2930 Anthony Ln	Minneapolis	MN	55418		612-781-6557	S	26	0.2
Hauser Inc.	5555 Arpt Blvd	Boulder	CO	80301		303-443-4662	P	25	0.3
SIMCO Electronics	382 Martin Ave	Santa Clara	CA	95050	L Kenna	408-727-3611	R	25	0.3
Universal Engineering Sciences	3532 Maggie Blvd	Orlando	FL	32811	Seymour Israel	407-423-0504	R	25	0.3
Environment One Corp.	2773 Balltown Rd	Schenectady	NY	12309	Stephen Vardia	518-346-6161	P	24	0.1
PED Manufacturing Ltd.	PO Box 1990	Oregon City	OR	97045	Richard Day	503-656-9653	S	23	0.2
Siegel Oil Co.	PO Box 40567	Denver	CO	80204		303-893-3211	S	22*	<0.1
Southern Petroleum Laboratory	PO Box 20807	Houston	TX	77225	Herb Brown	713-660-0901	R	22*	0.3
Scott Laboratories Inc.	PO Box 4559	Petaluma	CA	94955	Bruce Scott	707-765-6666	R	21	<0.1
Scott-Sims and Associates Inc.	4019 E Fowler Ave	Tampa	FL	33617	David D Scott	813-972-8722	R	21*	0.1
Barringer Technologies Inc.	30 Technology Dr	Warren	NJ	07059	Stanley S Binder	908-222-9100	P	20	0.1
Accutest Laboratories	2235 Rte 130	Dayton	NJ	08810	VJ Pugliese	732-329-0200	R	20	0.2
MQS Inspection Inc.	9910 Jordan Cir	Santa Fe Springs	CA	90670		562-944-8511	S	20	<0.1
Kemron Environmental Services	8150 Leesburg Pike	Vienna	VA	22182	Juan Gutierrez	703-636-0928	R	19	0.2
Oneida Research Services Inc.	1 Halsey Rd	Whitesboro	NY	13492	Thomas J Rossiter	315-736-5480	R	19*	0.1
InfraCorps Inc.	7400 Beaufont Sprgs	Richmond	VA	23225	James B Quarles	804-272-6600	P	19	0.2
National Environmental Service	12331 East 60th St	Tulsa	OK	74146	James Howell	918-250-2227	P	18	0.1
NEC Research Institute Inc.	4 Independence Way	Princeton	NJ	08540	C William Gear	609-520-1555	S	18*	0.1
Northview Laboratories Inc.	1880 Holste Rd	Northbrook	IL	60062	Martin Spalding	847-564-8181	S	17*	0.1
Biospherics Inc.	12051 Indian Creek	Beltsville	MD	20705	Gilbert V Levin	301-419-3900	P	16*	0.3
ABC Laboratories Inc.	7200 E ABC Ln	Columbia	MO	65202	Jake Halliday	573-474-8579	R	15	0.2
ABC Labs	7200 E ABC Ln	Columbia	MO	65205		573-474-8579	N	15	0.3
GA Environmental Services Inc.	15 W State St	Trenton	NJ	08608		609-393-4089	N	15	0.1
Magnetic Analysis Corp.	535 S 4th Ave	Mount Vernon	NY	10550	William S Gould III	914-699-9450	R	15	0.1
Western Technologies Inc.	PO Box 21387	Phoenix	AZ	85036	J Warne	602-437-3737	S	14*	0.3
DataChem Laboratories	960 Levoy Dr	Salt Lake City	UT	84123	James Sorenson	801-266-7700	R	14*	0.1
Lifecodes Corp.	550 West Ave	Stamford	CT	06902	Walter Fredericks	203-328-9500	R	14	0.1
Research Testing Laboratories Inc.	255 Great Neck Rd	Great Neck	NY	11021	Arthur Simon	516-773-7788	R	14*	0.1
ViroGroup Inc.	5217 Linbar Dr	Nashville	TN	37211	Charles S Higgens Jr	615-832-0081	P	14*	<0.1
QualMark Corp.	1329 W 121st Ave	Denver	CO	80234	H Robert Gill	303-254-8800	P	14	<0.1

Source: Ward's Business Directory of U.S. Private and Public Companies, Volumes 1 and 2, 2000. The company type code used is as follows: P - Public, R - Private, S - Subsidiary, D - Division, J - Joint Venture, A - Affiliate, G - Group, N - Company type not reported. Sales are in millions of dollars, employees are in thousands. An asterisk (*) indicates an estimated sales volume. The symbol < stands for 'less than'. Company names and addresses are truncated, in some cases, to fit into the available space.

LOCATION BY STATE AND REGIONAL CONCENTRATION

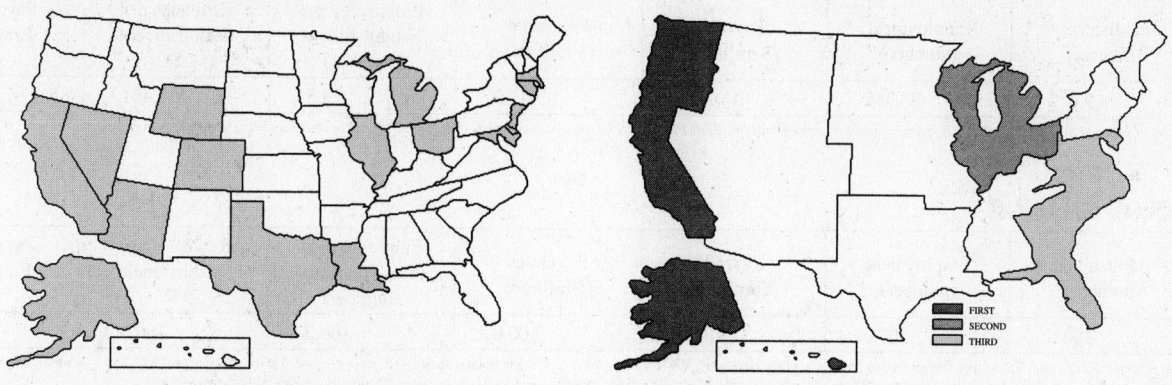

FIRST
SECOND
THIRD

INDUSTRY DATA BY STATE

State	Establishments		Employment			Payroll		Revenues		
	Total (number)	% of U.S.	Total (number)	% of U.S.	Per Estab.	Total ($ mil.)	Per Empl. ($)	Total ($ mil.)	% of U.S.	Per Estab. ($)
California	670	12.2	11,981	14.6	18	428.8	35,786	1,061.8	16.5	1,584,763
Texas	518	9.4	8,394	10.2	16	262.4	31,263	623.9	9.7	1,204,502
Illinois	208	3.8	4,318	5.3	21	170.5	39,496	370.4	5.7	1,780,904
New York	231	4.2	4,566	5.6	20	163.7	35,842	361.5	5.6	1,565,048
Ohio	242	4.4	4,430	5.4	18	135.5	30,595	328.0	5.1	1,355,310
Michigan	189	3.4	3,519	4.3	19	124.2	35,290	327.6	5.1	1,733,201
Pennsylvania	263	4.8	4,064	5.0	15	126.8	31,211	302.4	4.7	1,149,916
Florida	276	5.0	3,695	4.5	13	111.0	30,040	294.4	4.6	1,066,764
New Jersey	173	3.2	2,681	3.3	15	99.9	37,246	224.6	3.5	1,298,121
Louisiana	169	3.1	2,511	3.1	15	75.7	30,133	170.3	2.6	1,007,479
Massachusetts	121	2.2	1,828	2.2	15	69.6	38,091	158.3	2.5	1,308,380
Maryland	100	1.8	1,973	2.4	20	63.2	32,026	146.0	2.3	1,459,820
Arizona	104	1.9	1,957	2.4	19	59.1	30,177	144.2	2.2	1,386,587
North Carolina	121	2.2	1,864	2.3	15	63.1	33,830	138.2	2.1	1,141,769
Virginia	135	2.5	1,958	2.4	15	59.4	30,339	136.5	2.1	1,011,385
Connecticut	84	1.5	1,264	1.5	15	47.3	37,452	116.2	1.8	1,383,107
Georgia	121	2.2	1,411	1.7	12	45.3	32,112	114.5	1.8	946,545
Washington	116	2.1	1,594	1.9	14	54.0	33,888	112.8	1.8	972,819
Colorado	119	2.2	1,488	1.8	13	49.0	32,931	107.9	1.7	906,849
Indiana	108	2.0	1,217	1.5	11	36.6	30,101	93.9	1.5	869,204
Alabama	71	1.3	1,091	1.3	15	33.4	30,633	87.1	1.4	1,227,113
Tennessee	85	1.5	1,013	1.2	12	34.3	33,892	85.7	1.3	1,008,612
Wisconsin	93	1.7	1,174	1.4	13	32.4	27,637	84.7	1.3	910,269
Missouri	88	1.6	949	1.2	11	31.9	33,642	75.0	1.2	852,830
Minnesota	89	1.6	994	1.2	11	29.2	29,397	73.3	1.1	823,079
Oregon	80	1.5	740	0.9	9	23.4	31,668	57.9	0.9	724,325
South Carolina	60	1.1	728	0.9	12	24.7	33,890	56.0	0.9	933,850
Oklahoma	68	1.2	756	0.9	11	22.0	29,073	49.7	0.8	730,985
Utah	53	1.0	794	1.0	15	22.5	28,291	48.0	0.7	905,717
Kentucky	77	1.4	693	0.8	9	16.5	23,869	45.0	0.7	584,779
Nevada	40	0.7	526	0.6	13	16.0	30,471	41.4	0.6	1,035,700
New Mexico	37	0.7	592	0.7	16	20.0	33,718	40.1	0.6	1,083,568
Arkansas	51	0.9	524	0.6	10	15.7	29,937	38.9	0.6	762,431
Nebraska	29	0.5	553	0.7	19	17.5	31,709	37.2	0.6	1,283,379
West Virginia	63	1.1	677	0.8	11	16.0	23,682	36.7	0.6	581,762
Iowa	37	0.7	338	0.4	9	9.5	28,228	24.3	0.4	657,514
Alaska	27	0.5	230	0.3	9	10.6	45,900	22.9	0.4	849,370
Wyoming	42	0.8	349	0.4	8	10.4	29,831	22.0	0.3	524,762
New Hampshire	40	0.7	242	0.3	6	8.5	35,207	21.2	0.3	529,650
Idaho	33	0.6	251	0.3	8	7.1	28,271	17.1	0.3	518,242
Delaware	25	0.5	221	0.3	9	6.3	28,407	16.7	0.3	667,960
Vermont	15	0.3	185	0.2	12	6.1	32,832	15.6	0.2	1,036,733
Mississippi	39	0.7	294	0.4	8	6.7	22,656	14.6	0.2	374,436
Maine	22	0.4	151	0.2	7	5.3	34,768	11.8	0.2	536,591
Rhode Island	23	0.4	141	0.2	6	5.0	35,170	11.6	0.2	504,087
North Dakota	26	0.5	197	0.2	8	4.5	22,685	10.7	0.2	411,308
Montana	25	0.5	165	0.2	7	4.1	25,109	9.1	0.1	362,720
Hawaii	17	0.3	95	0.1	6	3.5	37,179	9.0	0.1	531,294
South Dakota	14	0.3	112	0.1	8	3.0	26,875	6.9	0.1	490,857
Kansas	50	0.9	750*	-	-	(D)	-	(D)	-	-
D.C.	1	-	10*	-	-	(D)	-	(D)	-	-

Source: 1997 *Economic Census*. The states are in descending order of revenues or establishments (if revenue data are missing for the majority). The symbol (D) appears when data are withheld to prevent disclosure of competitive information. States marked with (D) are sorted by number of establishments. A dash (-) indicates that the data element cannot be calculated. * indicates the midpoint of a range; 175, for example is the range 100-249. Shaded *states* on the state map indicate those states which have proportionately greater representation in the industry than would be indicated by the state's population; the ratio is based on total revenues or number of establishments. Shaded *regions* indicate where the industry is regionally most concentrated.

NAICS 541410 - INTERIOR DESIGN SERVICES

GENERAL STATISTICS

Year	Establishments (number)	Employment (number)	Payroll ($ million)	Revenues ($ million)	Employees per Establishment (number)	Revenues per Establishment ($)	Payroll per Employee ($)
1997	9,612	33,915	1,022.0	4,945.0	3.5	514,461	30,134

Source: Economic Census of the United States, 1997. This is a newly defined industry. Data for prior years were unavailable at the time of publication but may become available over time.

INDICES OF CHANGE

Year	Establishments (number)	Employment (number)	Payroll ($ million)	Revenues ($ million)	Employees per Establishment (number)	Revenues per Establishment ($)	Payroll per Employee ($)
1997	100.0	100.0	100.0	100.0	100.0	100.0	100.0

Sources: Same as General Statistics. The values shown reflect change from the base year, 1997. Values above 100 mean greater than 1997, values below 100 mean less than 1997, and a value of 100 in the 1982-96 or 1998-2001 period means same as 1997. Values followed by a 'p' are projections by the editors; 'e' stands for extrapolation. Data are the most recent available at this level of detail.

SIC INDUSTRIES RELATED TO NAICS 541410

Each new NAICS code represents an industry that used to be part of an SIC or a part of several SIC industries. Data in this table are shown to provide transitional information for these cases. All available data for the precursor SIC(s) are shown. Even if only a part of an SIC is included in the NAICS, *all* data for the SIC are reproduced. If the SIC industry is not marked as being a part (pt) of the NAICS, the entire industry is embedded in the NAICS data. The SIC composition of the new industry provides some hints of the relative importance of its "ancestors." Data marked with a 'p' are projected. Projections begin with 1982 data. Data earlier than 1990 are not shown but are reflected in the projections.

SIC	Industry	1990	1991	1992	1993	1994	1995	1996	1997
7389	**Business Services, nec (pt)**								
	Establishments (number)	44,079	50,252	52,375	56,829	60,725	53,596	60,893p	63,269p
	Employment (thousands)	489.6	550.4	523.6	607.9	648.7	623.0	680.2p	710.9p
	Revenues ($ million)	-	-	32,885.9	-	-	-	-	-

Source: Economic Census of the United States, 1992, annual surveys of economic sectors conducted by the Bureau of the Census, and estimates or projections based on the 1982-1992 period; not all data are shown. 'e' marks estimates made by the editors; 'p' indicates projections based on time series. A dash (-) indicates that data for this SIC or year were not available. The abbreviation (pt) next to the industry name indicates that only a part of the industry is present within the NAICS data. If no (pt) is shown, the entire industry is contained within the NAICS data.

SELECTED RATIOS

For 1997	Avg. of Information	Analyzed Industry	Index	For 1997	Avg. of Information	Analyzed Industry	Index
Employees per establishment	9	4	41	Payroll per establishment	372,545	106,325	29
Revenue per establishment	958,337	514,461	54	Payroll as % of revenue	39	21	53
Revenue per employee	111,029	145,806	131	Payroll per employee	43,162	30,134	70

Sources: Same as General Statistics. The 'Average' column represents the average for the industry sector, in 1997, where the currently shown industry is classified. The Index shows the relationship between the Average and the Analyzed Industry. For example, 100 means that they are equal; 500 that the Analyzed Industry is five times the average; 50 means that the Analyzed Industry is half the national average. The abbreviation 'na' is used to show that data are 'not available'.

LEADING COMPANIES

No company data available for this industry.

LOCATION BY STATE AND REGIONAL CONCENTRATION

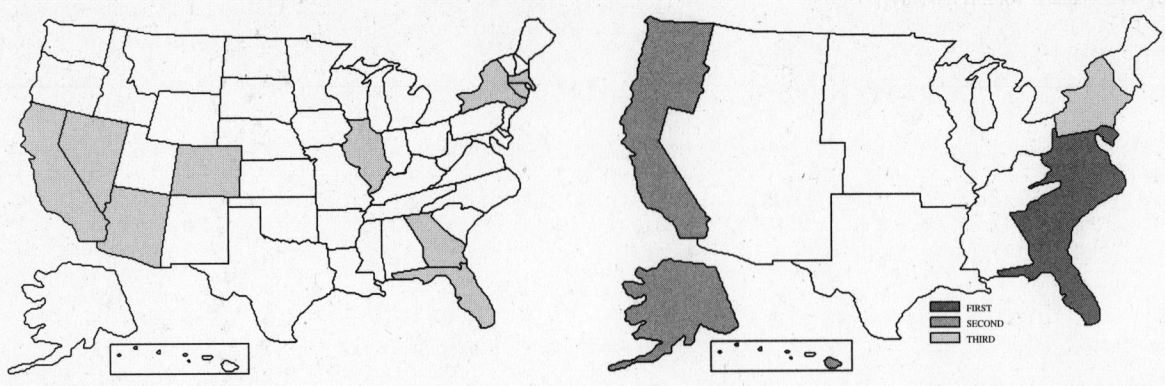

INDUSTRY DATA BY STATE

State	Establishments Total (number)	% of U.S.	Employment Total (number)	% of U.S.	Per Estab.	Payroll Total ($ mil.)	Per Empl. ($)	Revenues Total ($ mil.)	% of U.S.	Per Estab. ($)
California	1,122	11.7	5,169	15.2	5	171.1	33,096	791.7	16.0	705,575
New York	878	9.1	3,328	9.8	4	144.2	43,338	638.2	12.9	726,893
Florida	1,096	11.4	3,363	9.9	3	88.8	26,403	566.9	11.5	517,259
Texas	649	6.8	2,464	7.3	4	70.3	28,541	323.7	6.5	498,698
Illinois	533	5.5	1,978	5.8	4	68.9	34,839	266.8	5.4	500,499
Georgia	349	3.6	1,380	4.1	4	48.6	35,206	210.6	4.3	603,447
Ohio	337	3.5	1,306	3.9	4	34.8	26,665	162.6	3.3	482,599
Pennsylvania	281	2.9	1,132	3.3	4	33.2	29,322	141.4	2.9	503,295
Massachusetts	213	2.2	812	2.4	4	29.4	36,197	122.2	2.5	573,634
North Carolina	307	3.2	807	2.4	3	19.0	23,590	118.0	2.4	384,423
New Jersey	276	2.9	715	2.1	3	21.1	29,566	117.9	2.4	427,322
Colorado	228	2.4	729	2.1	3	20.6	28,199	112.8	2.3	494,768
Michigan	287	3.0	841	2.5	3	20.0	23,744	107.3	2.2	373,833
Arizona	169	1.8	465	1.4	3	14.3	30,695	88.7	1.8	525,041
Maryland	199	2.1	591	1.7	3	17.6	29,766	82.9	1.7	416,673
Minnesota	178	1.9	562	1.7	3	16.6	29,569	82.5	1.7	463,382
Virginia	250	2.6	812	2.4	3	20.2	24,906	79.2	1.6	316,988
Connecticut	132	1.4	479	1.4	4	18.2	37,956	78.7	1.6	596,508
Tennessee	136	1.4	458	1.4	3	12.4	27,055	68.3	1.4	502,375
Missouri	183	1.9	573	1.7	3	14.2	24,855	64.6	1.3	352,847
D.C.	51	0.5	377	1.1	7	20.5	54,483	62.0	1.3	1,216,431
Washington	151	1.6	465	1.4	3	12.1	25,968	60.9	1.2	403,298
Indiana	170	1.8	520	1.5	3	10.7	20,660	55.9	1.1	328,847
Wisconsin	121	1.3	459	1.4	4	9.2	20,050	48.2	1.0	398,355
Nevada	87	0.9	326	1.0	4	9.6	29,555	46.7	0.9	536,483
Oregon	107	1.1	310	0.9	3	7.1	22,903	43.1	0.9	402,467
South Carolina	105	1.1	317	0.9	3	6.2	19,401	42.2	0.9	401,829
Alabama	126	1.3	338	1.0	3	5.7	16,849	41.9	0.8	332,548
Louisiana	93	1.0	325	1.0	3	6.1	18,852	33.2	0.7	356,484
Utah	65	0.7	222	0.7	3	4.4	19,977	30.1	0.6	463,046
Oklahoma	94	1.0	240	0.7	3	5.3	22,025	28.9	0.6	307,766
Kentucky	90	0.9	259	0.8	3	5.0	19,116	28.2	0.6	313,622
Idaho	31	0.3	118	0.3	4	2.0	17,144	18.9	0.4	608,387
Nebraska	43	0.4	225	0.7	5	3.7	16,533	18.8	0.4	438,233
Iowa	55	0.6	117	0.3	2	2.3	19,667	16.0	0.3	290,455
Rhode Island	36	0.4	173	0.5	5	4.8	27,486	15.4	0.3	427,444
Mississippi	49	0.5	126	0.4	3	1.4	11,230	12.7	0.3	258,204
New Hampshire	27	0.3	58	0.2	2	1.7	29,086	9.2	0.2	341,259
New Mexico	31	0.3	69	0.2	2	1.5	21,072	8.4	0.2	271,806
West Virginia	21	0.2	84	0.2	4	1.4	16,167	6.6	0.1	312,762
Vermont	18	0.2	63	0.2	4	1.9	29,587	5.4	0.1	298,500
Alaska	9	0.1	40	0.1	4	1.1	28,275	5.2	0.1	583,222
North Dakota	14	0.1	49	0.1	4	0.6	11,837	3.7	0.1	266,857
South Dakota	12	0.1	22	0.1	2	0.3	12,773	2.2	0.0	184,917
Wyoming	8	0.1	10	0.0	1	0.2	16,400	1.2	0.0	146,625
Kansas	66	0.7	175*	-	-	(D)	-	(D)	-	-
Arkansas	35	0.4	175*	-	-	(D)	-	(D)	-	-
Hawaii	28	0.3	60*	-	-	(D)	-	(D)	-	-
Delaware	24	0.2	60*	-	-	(D)	-	(D)	-	-
Maine	24	0.2	60*	-	-	(D)	-	(D)	-	-
Montana	18	0.2	60*	-	-	(D)	-	(D)	-	-

Source: 1997 *Economic Census*. The states are in descending order of revenues or establishments (if revenue data are missing for the majority). The symbol (D) appears when data are withheld to prevent disclosure of competitive information. States marked with (D) are sorted by number of establishments. A dash (-) indicates that the data element cannot be calculated. * indicates the midpoint of a range; 175, for example is the range 100-249. Shaded *states* on the state map indicate those states which have proportionately greater representation in the industry than would be indicated by the state's population; the ratio is based on total revenues or number of establishments. Shaded *regions* indicate where the industry is regionally most concentrated.

NAICS 541420 - INDUSTRIAL DESIGN SERVICES

GENERAL STATISTICS

Year	Establishments (number)	Employment (number)	Payroll ($ million)	Revenues ($ million)	Employees per Establishment (number)	Revenues per Establishment ($)	Payroll per Employee ($)
1997	1,322	13,607	583.0	1,363.0	10.3	1,031,014	42,846

Source: *Economic Census of the United States*, 1997. This is a newly defined industry. Data for prior years were unavailable at the time of publication but may become available over time.

INDICES OF CHANGE

Year	Establishments (number)	Employment (number)	Payroll ($ million)	Revenues ($ million)	Employees per Establishment (number)	Revenues per Establishment ($)	Payroll per Employee ($)
1997	100.0	100.0	100.0	100.0	100.0	100.0	100.0

Sources: Same as General Statistics. The values shown reflect change from the base year, 1997. Values above 100 mean greater than 1997, values below 100 mean less than 1997, and a value of 100 in the 1982-96 or 1998-2001 period means same as 1997. Values followed by a 'p' are projections by the editors; 'e' stands for extrapolation. Data are the most recent available at this level of detail.

SIC INDUSTRIES RELATED TO NAICS 541420

Each new NAICS code represents an industry that used to be part of an SIC or a part of several SIC industries. Data in this table are shown to provide transitional information for these cases. All available data for the precursor SIC(s) are shown. Even if only a part of an SIC is included in the NAICS, *all* data for the SIC are reproduced. If the SIC industry is not marked as being a part (pt) of the NAICS, the entire industry is embedded in the NAICS data. The SIC composition of the new industry provides some hints of the relative importance of its "ancestors." Data marked with a 'p' are projected. Projections begin with 1982 data. Data earlier than 1990 are not shown but are reflected in the projections.

SIC	Industry	1990	1991	1992	1993	1994	1995	1996	1997
7389	**Business Services, nec (pt)**								
	Establishments (number)	44,079	50,252	52,375	56,829	60,725	53,596	60,893p	63,269p
	Employment (thousands)	489.6	550.4	523.6	607.9	648.7	623.0	680.2p	710.9p
	Revenues ($ million)	-	-	32,885.9	-	-	-	-	-

Source: *Economic Census of the United States*, 1992, annual surveys of economic sectors conducted by the Bureau of the Census, and estimates or projections based on the 1982-1992 period; not all data are shown. 'e' marks estimates made by the editors; 'p' indicates projections based on time series. A dash (-) indicates that data for this SIC or year were not available. The abbreviation (pt) next to the industry name indicates that only a part of the industry is present within the NAICS data. If no (pt) is shown, the entire industry is contained within the NAICS data.

SELECTED RATIOS

For 1997	Avg. of Information	Analyzed Industry	Index	For 1997	Avg. of Information	Analyzed Industry	Index
Employees per establishment	9	10	119	Payroll per establishment	372,545	440,998	118
Revenue per establishment	958,337	1,031,014	108	Payroll as % of revenue	39	43	110
Revenue per employee	111,029	100,169	90	Payroll per employee	43,162	42,846	99

Sources: Same as General Statistics. The 'Average' column represents the average for the industry sector, in 1997, where the currently shown industry is classified. The Index shows the relationship between the Average and the Analyzed Industry. For example, 100 means that they are equal; 500 that the Analyzed Industry is five times the average; 50 means that the Analyzed Industry is half the national average. The abbreviation 'na' is used to show that data are 'not available'.

LEADING COMPANIES

No company data available for this industry.

LOCATION BY STATE AND REGIONAL CONCENTRATION

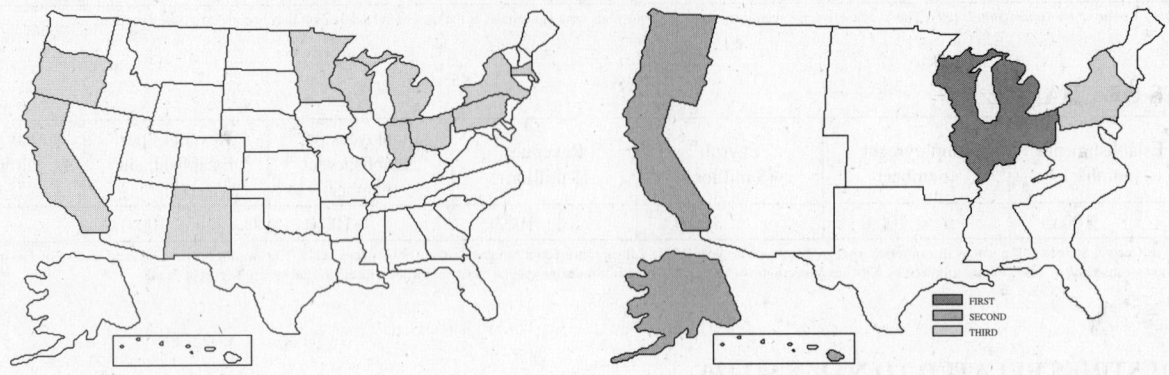

FIRST
SECOND
THIRD

INDUSTRY DATA BY STATE

State	Establishments Total (number)	Establishments % of U.S.	Employment Total (number)	Employment % of U.S.	Employment Per Estab.	Payroll Total ($ mil.)	Payroll Per Empl. ($)	Revenues Total ($ mil.)	Revenues % of U.S.	Revenues Per Estab. ($)
California	232	17.5	1,846	13.6	8	85.5	46,341	237.5	17.4	1,023,595
Michigan	104	7.9	2,066	15.2	20	86.7	41,988	166.5	12.2	1,601,394
Ohio	74	5.6	1,622	11.9	22	59.6	36,758	120.0	8.8	1,622,027
New York	122	9.2	836	6.1	7	41.5	49,696	114.3	8.4	937,197
Oregon	20	1.5	916	6.7	46	51.8	56,579	107.3	7.9	5,367,200
Pennsylvania	48	3.6	1,343	9.9	28	50.2	37,357	81.1	5.9	1,689,083
Wisconsin	26	2.0	448	3.3	17	26.3	58,712	69.7	5.1	2,679,154
Texas	66	5.0	643	4.7	10	30.6	47,549	62.8	4.6	951,182
Illinois	77	5.8	279	2.1	4	13.9	49,763	43.8	3.2	569,247
Massachusetts	33	2.5	292	2.1	9	12.3	42,099	39.2	2.9	1,187,455
Indiana	21	1.6	508	3.7	24	18.3	35,927	32.0	2.3	1,524,238
New Jersey	58	4.4	223	1.6	4	10.7	48,152	29.9	2.2	515,914
Georgia	36	2.7	183	1.3	5	5.5	30,137	27.7	2.0	768,778
Minnesota	34	2.6	237	1.7	7	9.0	37,966	24.9	1.8	731,029
Tennessee	17	1.3	261	1.9	15	9.4	36,176	22.9	1.7	1,347,235
Florida	54	4.1	178	1.3	3	4.1	23,281	16.5	1.2	304,815
North Carolina	38	2.9	119	0.9	3	5.1	43,059	15.5	1.1	408,105
Missouri	20	1.5	147	1.1	7	3.8	26,136	15.5	1.1	776,650
Colorado	31	2.3	157	1.2	5	4.7	30,032	15.4	1.1	495,258
Connecticut	24	1.8	137	1.0	6	7.2	52,234	15.3	1.1	635,458
Washington	18	1.4	139	1.0	8	5.9	42,108	14.9	1.1	826,333
Arizona	16	1.2	114	0.8	7	5.3	46,842	11.0	0.8	689,312
Virginia	17	1.3	106	0.8	6	4.2	39,415	10.7	0.8	629,059
New Mexico	9	0.7	161	1.2	18	6.6	40,876	9.5	0.7	1,055,667
South Carolina	7	0.5	57	0.4	8	3.6	63,491	5.4	0.4	773,286
Kansas	10	0.8	24	0.2	2	0.7	27,792	3.5	0.3	348,900
Nevada	5	0.4	8	0.1	2	0.5	61,000	2.9	0.2	579,800
Rhode Island	8	0.6	10	0.1	1	0.5	45,100	2.9	0.2	363,375
Kentucky	6	0.5	12	0.1	2	0.3	24,167	1.0	0.1	174,667
Louisiana	6	0.5	8	0.1	1	0.2	30,250	0.8	0.1	127,667
Mississippi	4	0.3	5	0.0	1	0.1	15,800	0.2	0.0	49,500
Utah	3	0.2	3	0.0	1	0.1	19,000	0.2	0.0	55,333
Maryland	20	1.5	60*	-	-	(D)	-	(D)	-	-
Idaho	12	0.9	60*	-	-	(D)	-	(D)	-	-
New Hampshire	9	0.7	60*	-	-	(D)	-	(D)	-	-
Alabama	8	0.6	60*	-	-	(D)	-	(D)	-	-
Oklahoma	8	0.6	60*	-	-	(D)	-	(D)	-	-
Arkansas	5	0.4	60*	-	-	(D)	-	(D)	-	-
Delaware	3	0.2	175*	-	-	(D)	-	(D)	-	-
Nebraska	3	0.2	10*	-	-	(D)	-	(D)	-	-
South Dakota	3	0.2	10*	-	-	(D)	-	(D)	-	-
Maine	2	0.2	10*	-	-	(D)	-	(D)	-	-
West Virginia	2	0.2	60*	-	-	(D)	-	(D)	-	-
D.C.	1	0.1	10*	-	-	(D)	-	(D)	-	-
Montana	1	0.1	10*	-	-	(D)	-	(D)	-	-
Vermont	1	0.1	60*	-	-	(D)	-	(D)	-	-

Source: 1997 *Economic Census.* The states are in descending order of revenues or establishments (if revenue data are missing for the majority). The symbol (D) appears when data are withheld to prevent disclosure of competitive information. States marked with (D) are sorted by number of establishments. A dash (-) indicates that the data element cannot be calculated. * indicates the midpoint of a range; 175, for example is the range 100-249. Shaded *states* on the state map indicate those states which have proportionately greater representation in the industry than would be indicated by the state's population; the ratio is based on total revenues or number of establishments. Shaded *regions* indicate where the industry is regionally most concentrated.

NAICS 541430 - GRAPHIC DESIGN SERVICES

GENERAL STATISTICS

Year	Establishments (number)	Employment (number)	Payroll ($ million)	Revenues ($ million)	Employees per Establishment (number)	Revenues per Establishment ($)	Payroll per Employee ($)
1997	14,631	61,622	2,355.0	7,555.0	4.2	516,369	38,217

Source: *Economic Census of the United States*, 1997. This is a newly defined industry. Data for prior years were unavailable at the time of publication but may become available over time.

INDICES OF CHANGE

Year	Establishments (number)	Employment (number)	Payroll ($ million)	Revenues ($ million)	Employees per Establishment (number)	Revenues per Establishment ($)	Payroll per Employee ($)
1997	100.0	100.0	100.0	100.0	100.0	100.0	100.0

Sources: Same as General Statistics. The values shown reflect change from the base year, 1997. Values above 100 mean greater than 1997, values below 100 mean less than 1997, and a value of 100 in the 1982-96 or 1998-2001 period means same as 1997. Values followed by a 'p' are projections by the editors; 'e' stands for extrapolation. Data are the most recent available at this level of detail.

SIC INDUSTRIES RELATED TO NAICS 541430

Each new NAICS code represents an industry that used to be part of an SIC or a part of several SIC industries. Data in this table are shown to provide transitional information for these cases. All available data for the precursor SIC(s) are shown. Even if only a part of an SIC is included in the NAICS, *all* data for the SIC are reproduced. If the SIC industry is not marked as being a part (pt) of the NAICS, the entire industry is embedded in the NAICS data. The SIC composition of the new industry provides some hints of the relative importance of its "ancestors." Data marked with a 'p' are projected. Projections begin with 1982 data. Data earlier than 1990 are not shown but are reflected in the projections.

SIC	Industry	1990	1991	1992	1993	1994	1995	1996	1997
7336	**Commercial Art & Graphic Design**								
	Establishments (number)	9,009	9,702	12,300	12,282	12,401	12,933	13,383*p*	13,920*p*
	Employment (thousands)	51.7	52.9	50.9	52.1	53.0	58.9	55.2*p*	55.7*p*
	Revenues ($ million)	6,069.0	6,129.0	6,168.0	6,018.0	6,277.0	6,795.0	7,254.0	7,100.9*p*
8099	**Health & Allied Services, nec (pt)**								
	Establishments (number)	-	-	5,011	-	-	-	-	-
	Employment (thousands)	-	-	71.9	-	-	-	-	-
	Revenues ($ million)	-	-	5,022.6	-	-	-	-	-

Source: *Economic Census of the United States*, 1992, annual surveys of economic sectors conducted by the Bureau of the Census, and estimates or projections based on the 1982-1992 period; not all data are shown. 'e' marks estimates made by the editors; 'p' indicates projections based on time series. A dash (-) indicates that data for this SIC or year were not available. The abbreviation (pt) next to the industry name indicates that only a part of the industry is present within the NAICS data. If no (pt) is shown, the entire industry is contained within the NAICS data.

SELECTED RATIOS

For 1997	Avg. of Information	Analyzed Industry	Index	For 1997	Avg. of Information	Analyzed Industry	Index
Employees per establishment	9	4	49	Payroll per establishment	372,545	160,960	43
Revenue per establishment	958,337	516,369	54	Payroll as % of revenue	39	31	80
Revenue per employee	111,029	122,602	110	Payroll per employee	43,162	38,217	89

Sources: Same as General Statistics. The 'Average' column represents the average for the industry sector, in 1997, where the currently shown industry is classified. The Index shows the relationship between the Average and the Analyzed Industry. For example, 100 means that they are equal; 500 that the Analyzed Industry is five times the average; 50 means that the Analyzed Industry is half the national average. The abbreviation 'na' is used to show that data are 'not available'.

LEADING COMPANIES Number shown: **75** Total sales ($ mil): **2,152** Total employment (000): **15.5**

Company Name	Address				CEO Name	Phone	Co. Type	Sales ($ mil)	Empl. (000)
Applied Graphics Technologies	450 W 33rd St	New York	NY	10001	Fred Drasner	212-716-6600	P	622	5.2
Continental Graphics Holdings Inc	4525 Wilshire Blvd	Los Angeles	CA	90010	Curtis F Bourland	213-930-2281	R	330*	2.8
Continental Graphics Corp.	4525 Wilshire Blvd	Los Angeles	CA	90010	Curt Bourland	323-930-2281	S	330*	2.8
L.J. Gonzer Associates	1225 Raymond Blvd	Newark	NJ	07102	Lawrence J Gonzer	973-624-5600	R	111*	0.4
Landor Associates	1001 Front St	San Francisco	CA	94111	Clay Timon	415-955-1400	S	66*	0.6
Balmar Printing and Graphics Inc.	PO Box 3330	Merrifield	VA	22116	James A O'Hare	703-289-9000	R	58	0.5
Callison Architecture Inc.	1420 5th Ave	Seattle	WA	98101	William Karst	206-623-4646	R	48*	0.4
Lehman Millet Inc.	60 Canal St	Boston	MA	02114	Bruce Lehman	617-722-0019	R	43	0.4
Ruder Finn Inc.	301 E 57th St	New York	NY	10022	Michael Cannata	212-593-6400	R	42	0.4
Ambrosi and Associates Inc.	1100 W Washington	Chicago	IL	60607	Nicholas S Ambrosi	312-666-9200	S	31*	0.3
FRCH Design Worldwide	860 Broadway	New York	NY	10003	James T Fitzgerald	212-254-1229	S	31*	0.1
Ground Zero	4235 Redwood Ave	Los Angeles	CA	90066		310-656-0050	R	30	<0.1
Wolf Blumberg Krody Inc.	537 E Pete Rose	Cincinnati	OH	45202	Steve Klein	513-784-0066	R	30	<0.1
Curran and Connors Inc.	333 Marcus Blvd	Hauppauge	NY	11788	Scott L Greenberg	516-435-0400	R	28*	<0.1
Prom Krog Altstiel Inc.	11053 N Towne Squ	Mequon	WI	53092		414-241-9414	R	20*	<0.1
Frch. Design Worldwide Inc.	311 Elm St	Cincinnati	OH	45202	James T Fitzgerald	513-241-3000	R	18	0.2
Entegee Engineering Technical	5309 Victoria Ave	Davenport	IA	52807	Derek Dewan	319-359-7042	S	16	<0.1
HT Medical Systems Inc.	55 W Watkins Mills	Rockville	MD	20847	Gregory L Merril	301-984-3706	R	16*	<0.1
Kenyon Press Inc.	PO Box 1850	Hawthorne	CA	90251	Neill Taylor	310-331-4500	R	14*	<0.1
7.30 Creative	100 N 6th St	Minneapolis	MN	55403		612-333-2322	R	11	<0.1
Esherick Homsey Dodge & Davis	500 Treat Ave	San Francisco	CA	94110		415-285-9193	R	11*	<0.1
Graphic Design Services Inc.	1801 E Lambert Rd	La Habra	CA	90631	Jan D Noller	562-905-3600	R	11*	<0.1
SA Communications Services	10801 Electron Dr	Louisville	KY	40222	Jerry DeWeese	502-267-0999	R	11*	<0.1
VirtualColor	1530 Morse Ave	Elk Grove Vill.	IL	60007	Steve Farkos	847-357-9500	D	10	0.1
Vivid Studios Inc.	510 3rd St	San Francisco	CA	94107	Craig Wingate	415-512-7200	R	10*	<0.1
Interbrand, Gerstman and Meyers	130 5th Ave	New York	NY	10011	Richard Gerstman	212-798-7600	R	9	<0.1
Manhattan Transfer Miami	1111 Lincoln Rd	Miami	FL	33139		305-674-0700	S	9*	<0.1
Metro Creative Graphics Inc.	33 W 34th St	New York	NY	10001	Robert S Zimmerman	212-947-5100	R	9*	<0.1
Mobium Corp.	200 World Trade Ctr	Chicago	IL	60654	Dennis Dunlap	312-527-0500	S	9*	<0.1
Kurtz and Friends	2312 W Olive Ave	Burbank	CA	91506	Bob Kurtz	818-841-8188	R	8*	<0.1
Mentus Inc.	8910 U Ctr	San Diego	CA	92122	Guy Iannuzzi	619-455-5500	R	8*	<0.1
Morris Advertising & Design Inc.	1601 Dove St	Newport Beach	CA	92660	Anne Morris	949-833-2142	R	8*	<0.1
Nicosia Creative Expresso Ltd.	355 W 52nd St	New York	NY	10019	Davide Nicosia	212-489-6423	R	7*	<0.1
ART and SIGN Inc.	615 Vermont St	Lawrence	KS	66044	Bob Treanor	785-842-4930	R	6*	<0.1
Byrne Johnson Inc.	3010 LBJ Freeway	Dallas	TX	75234	Kathleen Johnson	972-481-1946	R	6	<0.1
Guzofsky Communications Inc.	7535 E Hampden	Denver	CO	80231	Michael Guzofsky	303-337-7770	R	6	<0.1
Light and Power Productions Ltd.	26 N Broadway	Schenectady	NY	12305	Paul Madelone	518-381-6788	R	6*	<0.1
McNabb Kelley and Barre	P O Box 9000	Jonesboro	AR	72403		870-935-9544	R	6	<0.1
watersdesign.com	22 Cortlandt St	New York	NY	10007	John Waters	212-720-0700	R	5	<0.1
Avionics Research Corp.	706 E Colonial Dr	Orlando	FL	32803	Joseph Sicinski	407-841-1070	D	5	0.1
Microsearch Corp.	999 Broadway	Saugus	MA	01906	Charles Kelly	781-231-9991	R	5	<0.1
Pegasus Design Inc.	13831 Northwest	Houston	TX	77040	Larry Dunham	713-690-7878	R	5*	<0.1
Universal Promotions Inc.	3561 Valley Dr	Pittsburgh	PA	15234	Harry J Guidotti	412-831-8423	R	5	<0.1
Banner Media Services	6215 S 107 E Ave	Tulsa	OK	74133	Mike Loomis	918-254-2540	R	4*	<0.1
Grey Design and Promotion	777 3rd Ave	New York	NY	10017	Kurt Haiman	212-546-1300	S	4*	<0.1
The Chambers Group	1537 Pontius	Los Angeles	CA	90025	Keith Chambers	310-473-0010	R	4*	<0.1
West Creative Inc.	4144 Pennsylvania	Kansas City	MO	64111	Stan Chrzanowski	816-561-2022	R	4*	<0.1
Oswego Co.	2701 N W Vaughn	Portland	OR	97210	Ric Kimbell	503-274-9338	R	4	<0.1
VanDerKloot Film & Television	750 Ralph McGill	Atlanta	GA	30312	William VanDerKloot	404-221-0236	R	4	<0.1
CompuDraft Inc.	436 Creamery Way	Exton	PA	19341	James Kulp	610-524-1357	R	3	<0.1
Rowland Associates Inc.	701 E New York St	Indianapolis	IN	46202	Robert H Frist	317-636-3980	R	3	<0.1
Advertising Technologies Inc.	2880 Dr esden Dr	Chamblee	GA	30341	Stephen C Eigel	770-216-2800	R	3*	<0.1
Catapult Communications Inc.	3276 Haleakala Hwy	Makawao	HI	96768	Hillary Palmer	808-572-5151	R	3	<0.1
Mauk Design	39 Stillman St	San Francisco	CA	94107	Mitchell Mauk	415-243-9277	R	3*	<0.1
Metal Studio	1210 W Clay	Houston	TX	77019	Peat Jariya	713-523-5177	R	3*	<0.1
Tandem Design Inc.	1846 W Sequoia	Orange	CA	92868		714-978-7272	R	3	<0.1
Ready Industries Inc.	750 W 10th Pl	Los Angeles	CA	90015		213-749-2041	R	3	<0.1
Aplin Uno and Chibana Inc.	2685 Marine Way	Mountain View	CA	94043	Paul Aplin	650-966-8000	R	2*	<0.1
Barnet and Levinson Design	3120 Southwest	Houston	TX	77098	Barnet Levinson	713-528-3330	R	2*	<0.1
Creative Associates Inc.	1 Snoopy Pl	Santa Rosa	CA	95403	Charles Schulz	707-546-7121	R	2*	<0.1
Cummings 'N' Good	3 N Main St	Chester	CT	06412	Janet Cummings	860-526-9597	R	2*	<0.1
Deneen Powell Atelier Inc.	8989 Rio San Diego	San Diego	CA	92108	Jeri Deneen	619-294-9042	R	2*	<0.1
Howell Martin Co.	P O Box 1145	Brattleboro	VT	05302		802-257-7174	R	2*	<0.1
Intermedia Print Communications	PO Box 247	Hartford	VT	05047	Jonathan Sciadah	802-295-5327	R	2*	<0.1
Interphase (Oakland, California)	8470 Enterprise Way	Oakland	CA	94621	Richard Aston	510-569-4133	R	2	<0.1
Lenweaver Advertising & Design	108 W Jefferson St	Syracuse	NY	13202	Joanne Lenweaver	315-422-8729	R	2*	<0.1
MAGELLAN Geographix Inc.	6464 Hollister Ave	Goleta	CA	93117	Chris Baker	805-685-3100	R	2*	<0.1
Mallen & Friends Advertising	8522 Cherokee Ln	Leawood	KS	66206	Gary P Mallen	913-341-7300	R	2*	<0.1
Martin Communications Inc.	4016 Williamsburg	Fairfax	VA	22032	George R Martin	703-359-8900	R	2*	<0.1
Southern Exposure Advertising	424 E 6th St	Little Rock	AR	72202	Bob Wood	501-375-0300	R	2*	<0.1
Balsmeyer and Everett Inc.	230 W 17th St	New York	NY	10011	Mimi Everett	212-627-3430	R	2	<0.1
Welch Inc.	80 Grove St	Ridgefield	CT	06877	C William Welch	203-431-3400	R	2	<0.1
Glyphix Studio	21280 Erwin St	Woodland Hills	CA	91367	Larry Cohen	818-704-3994	R	2	<0.1
Sturges & Word Communications	104 W 9th St	Kansas City	MO	64105	Linda Word	816-221-7500	R	1	<0.1
AZTEK Inc.	15 Marconi	Irvine	CA	92618	Phillip Lippincott	949-770-8406	R	1*	<0.1

Source: Ward's Business Directory of U.S. Private and Public Companies, Volumes 1 and 2, 2000. The company type code used is as follows: P - Public, R - Private, S - Subsidiary, D - Division, J - Joint Venture, A - Affiliate, G - Group, N - Company type not reported. Sales are in millions of dollars, employees are in thousands. An asterisk (*) indicates an estimated sales volume. The symbol < stands for 'less than'. Company names and addresses are truncated, in some cases, to fit into the available space.

LOCATION BY STATE AND REGIONAL CONCENTRATION

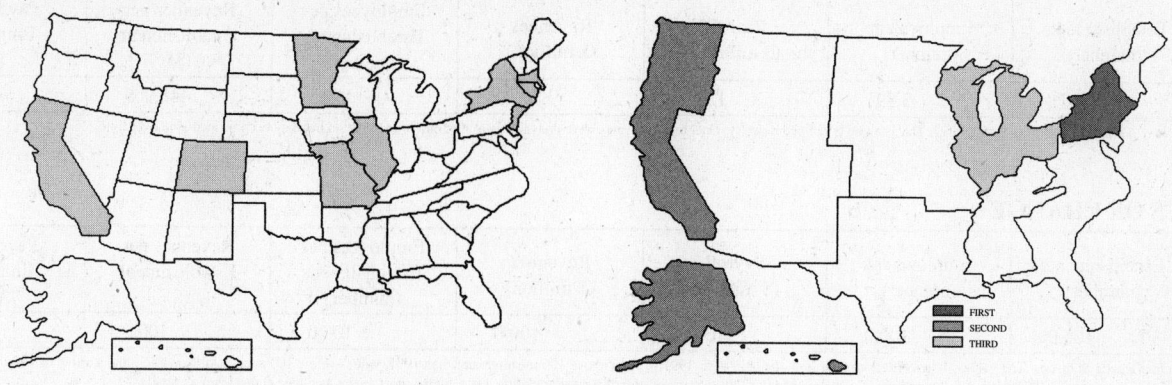

INDUSTRY DATA BY STATE

State	Establishments		Employment			Payroll		Revenues		
	Total (number)	% of U.S.	Total (number)	% of U.S.	Per Estab.	Total ($ mil.)	Per Empl. ($)	Total ($ mil.)	% of U.S.	Per Estab. ($)
California	2,069	14.1	10,754	17.5	5	447.0	41,563	1,443.3	19.1	697,606
New York	1,709	11.7	8,429	13.7	5	400.5	47,514	1,273.5	16.9	745,190
Illinois	1,071	7.3	5,282	8.6	5	220.1	41,675	674.1	8.9	629,445
Texas	681	4.7	2,875	4.7	4	105.7	36,758	374.6	5.0	550,141
New Jersey	625	4.3	2,154	3.5	3	84.9	39,405	281.3	3.7	450,045
Ohio	540	3.7	2,631	4.3	5	93.4	35,513	272.3	3.6	504,169
Massachusetts	428	2.9	1,831	3.0	4	78.6	42,915	245.0	3.2	572,449
Florida	848	5.8	2,479	4.0	3	65.5	26,437	240.2	3.2	283,297
Minnesota	463	3.2	2,020	3.3	4	81.9	40,527	236.8	3.1	511,363
Pennsylvania	474	3.2	1,801	2.9	4	64.4	35,785	219.5	2.9	463,148
Georgia	449	3.1	1,590	2.6	4	59.8	37,592	195.2	2.6	434,635
Michigan	435	3.0	1,839	3.0	4	65.4	35,566	187.0	2.5	429,984
Connecticut	306	2.1	1,208	2.0	4	57.6	47,719	171.6	2.3	560,820
Missouri	252	1.7	1,390	2.3	6	52.4	37,719	158.2	2.1	627,937
Maryland	379	2.6	1,345	2.2	4	41.9	31,116	134.5	1.8	354,868
Washington	332	2.3	1,208	2.0	4	41.9	34,715	120.1	1.6	361,608
Wisconsin	246	1.7	1,190	1.9	5	39.6	33,289	113.2	1.5	460,110
Colorado	333	2.3	975	1.6	3	31.7	32,475	112.1	1.5	336,541
Virginia	325	2.2	1,053	1.7	3	33.3	31,600	108.5	1.4	333,942
North Carolina	288	2.0	1,007	1.6	3	30.2	29,993	100.9	1.3	350,233
Tennessee	200	1.4	825	1.3	4	25.8	31,303	100.7	1.3	503,300
Indiana	206	1.4	983	1.6	5	32.1	32,623	99.7	1.3	483,767
Arizona	230	1.6	855	1.4	4	26.8	31,291	95.5	1.3	415,013
Oregon	216	1.5	833	1.4	4	25.5	30,653	81.1	1.1	375,310
Kentucky	101	0.7	552	0.9	5	17.1	30,949	60.7	0.8	601,099
Iowa	104	0.7	376	0.6	4	10.6	28,082	38.1	0.5	366,519
Kansas	104	0.7	333	0.5	3	10.0	30,138	37.1	0.5	356,644
Utah	106	0.7	346	0.6	3	7.7	22,214	30.2	0.4	285,349
Nevada	57	0.4	203	0.3	4	6.8	33,271	27.9	0.4	488,912
Louisiana	83	0.6	273	0.4	3	6.8	24,766	23.9	0.3	287,759
New Mexico	62	0.4	194	0.3	3	5.0	25,773	23.2	0.3	374,484
New Hampshire	72	0.5	211	0.3	3	6.7	31,896	23.2	0.3	321,958
Rhode Island	80	0.5	218	0.4	3	7.4	33,835	21.7	0.3	271,075
Nebraska	57	0.4	229	0.4	4	6.0	26,210	20.8	0.3	364,842
Oklahoma	111	0.8	263	0.4	2	6.6	25,000	19.7	0.3	177,225
Hawaii	58	0.4	173	0.3	3	4.6	26,474	18.8	0.2	323,362
South Carolina	78	0.5	167	0.3	2	4.3	25,802	16.7	0.2	214,026
Arkansas	49	0.3	164	0.3	3	3.8	23,250	14.6	0.2	297,082
Vermont	47	0.3	152	0.2	3	4.7	30,987	13.5	0.2	286,532
Delaware	46	0.3	142	0.2	3	5.0	35,275	13.4	0.2	290,413
Alabama	50	0.3	123	0.2	2	3.7	29,878	12.0	0.2	240,000
Maine	28	0.2	119	0.2	4	3.8	32,134	10.7	0.1	382,679
Idaho	39	0.3	91	0.1	2	2.7	29,297	9.7	0.1	247,846
Montana	32	0.2	87	0.1	3	1.3	15,310	5.3	0.1	165,031
Mississippi	20	0.1	74	0.1	4	1.5	19,595	3.8	0.1	189,450
South Dakota	13	0.1	44	0.1	3	0.8	18,432	3.2	0.0	245,615
Wyoming	7	-	14	0.0	2	0.3	19,857	1.4	0.0	204,571
North Dakota	11	0.1	22	0.0	2	0.3	15,318	1.2	0.0	109,909
Alaska	5	-	6	0.0	1	0.1	12,333	1.0	0.0	196,400
D.C.	91	0.6	375*	-	-	(D)	-	(D)	-	-
West Virginia	15	0.1	60*	-	-	(D)	-	(D)	-	-

Source: 1997 *Economic Census*. The states are in descending order of revenues or establishments (if revenue data are missing for the majority). The symbol (D) appears when data are withheld to prevent disclosure of competitive information. States marked with (D) are sorted by number of establishments. A dash (-) indicates that the data element cannot be calculated. * indicates the midpoint of a range; 175, for example is the range 100-249. Shaded *states* on the state map indicate those states which have proportionately greater representation in the industry than would be indicated by the state's population; the ratio is based on total revenues or number of establishments. Shaded *regions* indicate where the industry is regionally most concentrated.

NAICS 541490 - SPECIALIZED DESIGN SERVICES NEC

GENERAL STATISTICS

Year	Establishments (number)	Employment (number)	Payroll ($ million)	Revenues ($ million)	Employees per Establishment (number)	Revenues per Establishment ($)	Payroll per Employee ($)
1997	871	3,891	129.0	391.0	4.5	448,909	33,153

Source: Economic Census of the United States, 1997. This is a newly defined industry. Data for prior years were unavailable at the time of publication but may become available over time.

INDICES OF CHANGE

Year	Establishments (number)	Employment (number)	Payroll ($ million)	Revenues ($ million)	Employees per Establishment (number)	Revenues per Establishment ($)	Payroll per Employee ($)
1997	100.0	100.0	100.0	100.0	100.0	100.0	100.0

Sources: Same as General Statistics. The values shown reflect change from the base year, 1997. Values above 100 mean greater than 1997, values below 100 mean less than 1997, and a value of 100 in the 1982-96 or 1998-2001 period means same as 1997. Values followed by a 'p' are projections by the editors; 'e' stands for extrapolation. Data are the most recent available at this level of detail.

SIC INDUSTRIES RELATED TO NAICS 541490

Each new NAICS code represents an industry that used to be part of an SIC or a part of several SIC industries. Data in this table are shown to provide transitional information for these cases. All available data for the precursor SIC(s) are shown. Even if only a part of an SIC is included in the NAICS, *all* data for the SIC are reproduced. If the SIC industry is not marked as being a part (pt) of the NAICS, the entire industry is embedded in the NAICS data. The SIC composition of the new industry provides some hints of the relative importance of its "ancestors." Data marked with a 'p' are projected. Projections begin with 1982 data. Data earlier than 1990 are not shown but are reflected in the projections.

SIC	Industry	1990	1991	1992	1993	1994	1995	1996	1997
7389	**Business Services, nec (pt)**								
	Establishments (number)	44,079	50,252	52,375	56,829	60,725	53,596	60,893p	63,269p
	Employment (thousands)	489.6	550.4	523.6	607.9	648.7	623.0	680.2p	710.9p
	Revenues ($ million)	-	-	32,885.9	-	-	-	-	-

Source: Economic Census of the United States, 1992, annual surveys of economic sectors conducted by the Bureau of the Census, and estimates or projections based on the 1982-1992 period; not all data are shown. 'e' marks estimates made by the editors; 'p' indicates projections based on time series. A dash (-) indicates that data for this SIC or year were not available. The abbreviation (pt) next to the industry name indicates that only a part of the industry is present within the NAICS data. If no (pt) is shown, the entire industry is contained within the NAICS data.

SELECTED RATIOS

For 1997	Avg. of Information	Analyzed Industry	Index	For 1997	Avg. of Information	Analyzed Industry	Index
Employees per establishment	9	4	52	Payroll per establishment	372,545	148,106	40
Revenue per establishment	958,337	448,909	47	Payroll as % of revenue	39	33	85
Revenue per employee	111,029	100,488	91	Payroll per employee	43,162	33,153	77

Sources: Same as General Statistics. The 'Average' column represents the average for the industry sector, in 1997, where the currently shown industry is classified. The Index shows the relationship between the Average and the Analyzed Industry. For example, 100 means that they are equal; 500 that the Analyzed Industry is five times the average; 50 means that the Analyzed Industry is half the national average. The abbreviation 'na' is used to show that data are 'not available'.

LEADING COMPANIES

No company data available for this industry.

LOCATION BY STATE AND REGIONAL CONCENTRATION

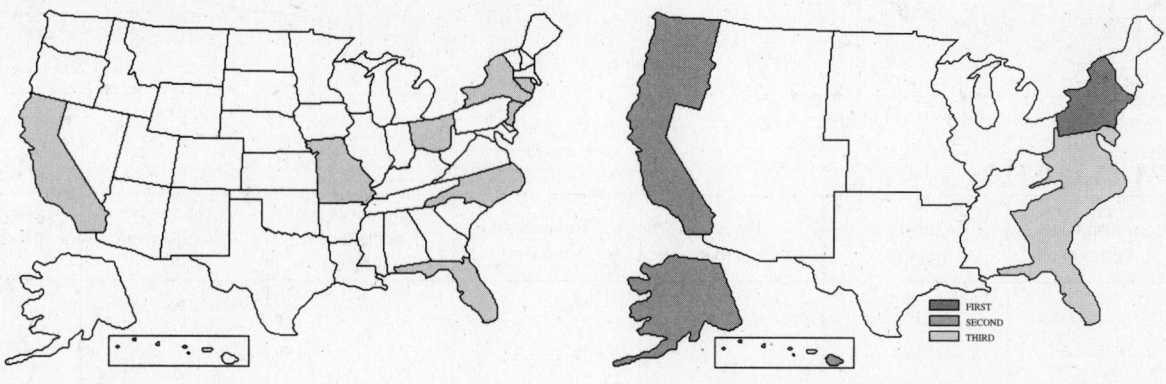

FIRST
SECOND
THIRD

INDUSTRY DATA BY STATE

State	Establishments Total (number)	% of U.S.	Employment Total (number)	% of U.S.	Per Estab.	Payroll Total ($ mil.)	Per Empl. ($)	Revenues Total ($ mil.)	% of U.S.	Per Estab. ($)
New York	249	28.6	982	25.2	4	41.0	41,765	129.7	33.2	520,984
California	163	18.7	891	22.9	5	18.5	20,799	64.8	16.6	397,337
Florida	53	6.1	479	12.3	9	16.2	33,912	36.4	9.3	686,906
Ohio	19	2.2	190	4.9	10	10.1	53,347	18.7	4.8	984,421
New Jersey	53	6.1	118	3.0	2	5.4	46,110	14.8	3.8	278,887
North Carolina	40	4.6	106	2.7	3	4.7	44,698	11.5	3.0	288,500
Missouri	10	1.1	50	1.3	5	1.6	32,180	11.0	2.8	1,101,900
Pennsylvania	20	2.3	90	2.3	5	3.8	42,711	9.0	2.3	451,700
Illinois	28	3.2	117	3.0	4	2.3	19,231	8.6	2.2	307,107
Texas	31	3.6	101	2.6	3	2.3	22,832	7.3	1.9	233,871
Connecticut	11	1.3	24	0.6	2	1.5	62,875	6.6	1.7	598,636
Georgia	16	1.8	62	1.6	4	1.9	31,274	6.3	1.6	393,875
Michigan	10	1.1	68	1.7	7	3.2	47,471	6.2	1.6	620,200
Massachusetts	15	1.7	77	2.0	5	1.8	23,494	5.1	1.3	338,533
Washington	15	1.7	62	1.6	4	1.5	23,597	4.7	1.2	315,133
Indiana	10	1.1	47	1.2	5	1.1	22,426	2.8	0.7	285,000
Wisconsin	11	1.3	30	0.8	3	0.6	20,800	2.8	0.7	252,182
Arizona	8	0.9	29	0.7	4	0.7	24,724	1.9	0.5	239,000
Virginia	10	1.1	23	0.6	2	0.5	21,870	1.6	0.4	163,700
Colorado	11	1.3	18	0.5	2	0.6	31,278	1.6	0.4	146,091
Nevada	4	0.5	18	0.5	5	0.4	20,611	1.2	0.3	292,000
Utah	4	0.5	26	0.7	7	0.4	13,808	1.2	0.3	310,250
Minnesota	4	0.5	10	0.3	3	0.6	64,400	1.1	0.3	275,500
Louisiana	6	0.7	15	0.4	3	0.2	11,600	1.1	0.3	181,333
Mississippi	7	0.8	22	0.6	3	0.3	12,227	0.8	0.2	117,000
Oregon	5	0.6	15	0.4	3	0.2	14,933	0.8	0.2	160,200
Tennessee	4	0.5	12	0.3	3	0.1	9,750	0.7	0.2	165,000
Rhode Island	6	0.7	12	0.3	2	0.2	14,750	0.6	0.2	101,000
New Mexico	3	0.3	5	0.1	2	0.1	18,600	0.4	0.1	138,000
South Carolina	4	0.5	8	0.2	2	0.1	9,375	0.4	0.1	98,500
Maine	3	0.3	3	0.1	1	-	6,333	0.1	0.0	31,333
Maryland	15	1.7	175*	-	-	(D)	-	(D)	-	-
Kansas	6	0.7	60*	-	-	(D)	-	(D)	-	-
New Hampshire	3	0.3	10*	-	-	(D)	-	(D)	-	-
Vermont	3	0.3	10*	-	-	(D)	-	(D)	-	-
Arkansas	2	0.2	10*	-	-	(D)	-	(D)	-	-
Hawaii	2	0.2	10*	-	-	(D)	-	(D)	-	-
South Dakota	2	0.2	10*	-	-	(D)	-	(D)	-	-
Alabama	1	0.1	10*	-	-	(D)	-	(D)	-	-
Idaho	1	0.1	10*	-	-	(D)	-	(D)	-	-
Montana	1	0.1	10*	-	-	(D)	-	(D)	-	-
Nebraska	1	0.1	10*	-	-	(D)	-	(D)	-	-
Oklahoma	1	0.1	10*	-	-	(D)	-	(D)	-	-

Source: 1997 Economic Census. The states are in descending order of revenues or establishments (if revenue data are missing for the majority). The symbol (D) appears when data are withheld to prevent disclosure of competitive information. States marked with (D) are sorted by number of establishments. A dash (-) indicates that the data element cannot be calculated. * indicates the midpoint of a range; 175, for example is the range 100-249. Shaded *states* on the state map indicate those states which have proportionately greater representation in the industry than would be indicated by the state's population; the ratio is based on total revenues or number of establishments. Shaded *regions* indicate where the industry is regionally most concentrated.

NAICS 541511 - CUSTOM COMPUTER PROGRAMMING SERVICES*

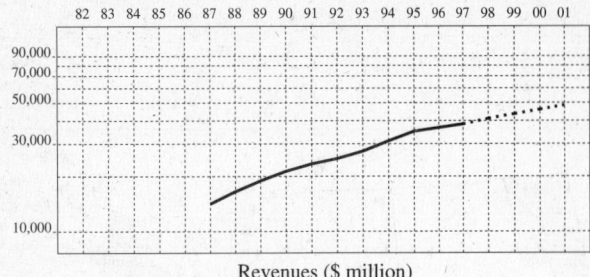

82 83 84 85 86 87 88 89 90 91 92 93 94 95 96 97 98 99 00 01

Revenues ($ million)

82 83 84 85 86 87 88 89 90 91 92 93 94 95 96 97 98 99 00 01

Employment (000)

GENERAL STATISTICS

Year	Establishments (number)	Employment (number)	Payroll ($ million)	Revenues ($ million)	Employees per Establishment (number)	Revenues per Establishment ($)	Payroll per Employee ($)
1982	-	-	-	-	-	-	-
1983	-	-	-	-	-	-	-
1984	-	-	-	-	-	-	-
1985	-	-	-	-	-	-	-
1986	-	-	-	-	-	-	-
1987	14,687	184,222	6,287.0	14,170.0	12.5	964,799	34,127
1988	13,182	202,539	7,781.0	16,553.0 e	15.4	1,255,728	38,417
1989	12,057	208,424	8,086.0	18,935.0 e	17.3	1,570,457	38,796
1990	12,443	217,239	8,907.0	21,318.0	17.5	1,713,252	41,001
1991	13,225	220,528	9,484.0	23,376.0	16.7	1,767,561	43,006
1992	23,265	242,707	10,890.0	24,973.0	10.4	1,073,415	44,869
1993	23,225	262,086	12,067.0	27,352.0	11.3	1,177,696	46,042
1994	23,957	272,365	13,417.0	31,069.0	11.4	1,296,865	49,261
1995	25,519	310,885	16,291.0	35,053.0	12.2	1,373,604	52,402
1996	28,571 e	314,541 e	17,354.0 e	36,677.0 e	11.0 e	1,283,714 e	55,172 e
1997	31,624	318,198	18,417.0	38,301.0	10.1	1,211,137	57,879
1998	32,141 p	336,362 p	19,098.0 p	41,051.0 p	10.5 p	1,277,216 p	56,778 p
1999	34,138 p	350,699 p	20,327.0 p	43,533.0 p	10.3 p	1,275,207 p	57,961 p
2000	36,134 p	365,036 p	21,556.0 p	46,014.0 p	10.1 p	1,273,427 p	59,052 p
2001	38,131 p	379,373 p	22,784.0 p	48,496.0 p	9.9 p	1,271,826 p	60,057 p

Sources: Economic Census of the United States, 1982, 1987, 1992, 1997. Establishment counts, employment, and payroll are from *County Business Patterns* for non-Census years. In non-Census years, industries in the Manufacturing range under SIC coding include data from the *Annual Survey of Manufactures* (ASM); those in the old Services range include data from the *Services Annual Survey* (SAS). Values followed by a 'p' are projections by the editors. Extrapolations are marked by 'e'. Data are the most recent available at this level of detail.

INDICES OF CHANGE

Year	Establishments (number)	Employment (number)	Payroll ($ million)	Revenues ($ million)	Employees per Establishment (number)	Revenues per Establishment ($)	Payroll per Employee ($)
1982	-	-	-	-	-	-	-
1987	46.4	57.9	34.1	37.0	124.7	79.7	59.0
1992	73.6	76.3	59.1	65.2	103.7	88.6	77.5
1993	73.4	82.4	65.5	71.4	112.2	97.2	79.5
1994	75.8	85.6	72.9	81.1	113.0	107.1	85.1
1995	80.7	97.7	88.5	91.5	121.1	113.4	90.5
1996	90.3 e	98.9 e	94.2 e	95.8 e	109.4 e	106.0 e	95.3 e
1997	100.0	100.0	100.0	100.0	100.0	100.0	100.0
1998	101.6 p	105.7 p	103.7 p	107.2 p	104.0 p	105.5 p	98.1 p
1999	107.9 p	110.2 p	110.4 p	113.7 p	102.1 p	105.3 p	100.1 p
2000	114.3 p	114.7 p	117.0 p	120.1 p	100.4 p	105.1 p	102.0 p
2001	120.6 p	119.2 p	123.7 p	126.6 p	98.9 p	105.0 p	103.8 p

Sources: Same as General Statistics. The values shown reflect change from the base year, 1997. Values above 100 mean greater than 1997, values below 100 mean less than 1997, and a value of 100 in the 1982-96 or 1998-2001 period means same as 1997. Values followed by a 'p' are projections by the editors; 'e' stands for extrapolation. Data are the most recent available at this level of detail.

SELECTED RATIOS

For 1997	Avg. of Information	Analyzed Industry	Index	For 1997	Avg. of Information	Analyzed Industry	Index
Employees per establishment	9	10	117	Payroll per establishment	372,545	582,374	156
Revenue per establishment	958,337	1,211,137	126	Payroll as % of revenue	39	48	124
Revenue per employee	111,029	120,368	108	Payroll per employee	43,162	57,879	134

Sources: Same as General Statistics. The 'Average' column represents the average for the industry sector, in 1997, where the currently shown industry is classified. The Index shows the relationship between the Average and the Analyzed Industry. For example, 100 means that they are equal; 500 that the Analyzed Industry is five times the average; 50 means that the Analyzed Industry is half the national average. The abbreviation 'na' is used to show that data are 'not available'.

*Equivalent to SIC 7371.

LEADING COMPANIES   Number shown: **75**   Total sales ($ mil): **45,459**   Total employment (000): **264.4**

Company Name	Address				CEO Name	Phone	Co. Type	Sales ($ mil)	Empl. (000)
EMC Corp.	PO Box 9103	Hopkinton	MA	01748	Michael C. Ruettgers	508-435-1000	P	6,916	9.7
IKON Office Solutions Inc.	PO Box 834	Valley Forge	PA	19482	James Forese	610-296-8000	P	5,522	39.4
Computer Science Corporation	3170 Fairview	Falls Church	VA	22042	Milt Cooper	703-876-1000	D	4,286*	30.0
Monotype Systems Inc.	2100 Golf Rd	Roll Meadows	IL	60008	Dennis E Nierman	847-427-8800	S	1,501*	<0.1
IBM	5600 Cottle Rd	San Jose	CA	95193		408-256-1600	S	1,361*	5.1
Western Atlas International Inc.	PO Box 1407	Houston	TX	77251	John R Russell	713-972-4000	S	1,180*	10.0
Keane Inc.	10 City Sq	Boston	MA	02129	John F Keane Jr	617-241-9200	P	1,076	10.5
Parametric Technology Corp.	128 Technology Dr	Waltham	MA	02154	Steven C Walske	781-398-5000	P	1,058	5.0
Keane Inc	290 Broadhollow Rd	Melville	NY	11747	John Keane, Sr	516-351-7000	D	1,000	11.0
GTECH Holdings Corp.	55 Technology Way	West Greenwich	RI	02817	William Y O'Connor	401-392-1000	P	973	4.8
Bell and Howell Co.	5215 Old Orchard	Skokie	IL	60077	James P Roemer	847-470-7100	P	900	6.2
Sybase Inc.	6475 Christie Ave	Emeryville	CA	94608	John S Chen	510-922-3500	P	872	4.2
SAP America Inc.	3999 Westchester	Newtown Square	PA	19073	Kevin McKay	610-661-1000	S	849*	1.0
Computer Sciences Corp	3190 Fairview	Falls Church	VA	22042	Jerome B Hilmes	703-876-1000	D	743*	5.5
CIBER Inc.	5251 DTC Pkwy	Englewood	CO	80111	Mac J Slingerlend	303-220-0100	P	720	6.5
CCH Inc.	2700 Lake Cook Rd	Riverwoods	IL	60015	Rebecca K Hensley	847-267-7000	P	670	5.0
National Computer Systems Inc.	PO Box 9365	Eden Prairie	MN	55344	Russell A Gullotti	612-829-3000	P	629	3.7
Analysts International Corp.	3601 W 76th St	Minneapolis	MN	55435	Victor C Benda	612-835-5900	P	620	4.9
Computer Sciences Corp	1100 West St	Laurel	MD	20707	George Meyerson	301-470-2500	D	571*	4.0
Data Reduction Inc.	302 Meacham St	Charlotte	NC	28203		704-332-3799	R	520*	13.0
USWeb/CKS	410 Townsend St	San Francisco	CA	94107	Robert Shaw	415-369-6700	P	511	2.0
Bull HN Information Systems Inc.	300 Concord Rd	Billerica	MA	01821	George McNeil	978-294-6000	R	500	1.3
IMI Systems Inc.	290 Broadhollow Rd	Melville	NY	11747	Carlton P Schowe	516-425-8487	S	500	5.0
Whittman-Hart Inc.	311 S Wacker Dr	Chicago	IL	60606	Robert F Bernard	312-922-9200	P	481	3.5
Logicon Inc.	3701 Skypark Dr	Torrance	CA	90505	JR Woodhull	310-373-0220	S	478*	5.0
Bisys Document Solution	121 Greenway Blvd	Carrollton	GA	30117	Tedd Wilson	770-834-0090	D	472	0.2
Computer Task Group Inc.	800 Delaware Ave	Buffalo	NY	14209	Gale Fitzgerald	716-882-8000	P	468	5.8
JBA International	3701 Algonquin Rd	Roll Meadows	IL	60008	Ken Briddon	847-590-0299	D	460	1.2
CACI International Inc.	1100 N Glebe Rd	Arlington	VA	22201	J P London	703-841-7800	P	442	4.2
Comsearch	2002 Edmund Halley	Reston	VA	20191	Douglas Hall	703-620-6300	S	388	0.1
S3 Inc.	PO Box 58058	Santa Clara	CA	95052	Kenneth F Potashner	408-588-8000	P	353	0.4
Structural Dynamics Research	7851 Metro Pkwy	Minneapolis	MN	55425	Robert J Majteles	612-854-5300	D	341*	1.6
Cotelligent Group Inc.	101 California St	San Francisco	CA	94111	Michael L Evans	415-439-6400	P	327	3.3
BTG Inc. (Fairfax, Virginia)	3877 Fairfax Ridge	Fairfax	VA	22030	Edward H Bersoff	703-383-8000	P	316	1.3
GenRad Inc.	7 Technology	Westford	MA	01886	James F Lyons	978-589-7000	P	302	1.3
Design Automation	905 W Eisenhower	Ann Arbor	MI	48108		734-761-1686	N	300	<0.1
Servantis Systems Inc.	25 Crossroads Dr	Owings Mills	MD	21117	Pete Kight	410-581-2900	D	296*	2.0
Analogic Data Conversion	360 Audubon Rd	Wakefield	MA	01880	Bruce R Rusch	978-977-3000	P	279	1.7
Stratus Computer Inc.	55 Fairbanks Blvd	Marlborough	MA	01752	Steve Keily	978-461-7000	R	277*	1.0
Sapient Corp.	1 Mem Dr	Cambridge	MA	02142	J Stuart Moore	617-621-0200	P	277	1.5
Wang Federal Inc.	7900 Westpark Dr	McLean	VA	22102	James Hogan	703-827-3000	S	260	1.0
Cerner Corp.	2800 Rockcreek	Kansas City	MO	64117	Neal L Patterson	816-221-1024	P	251	2.5
Interim Technology	630 Third Ave	New York	NY	10017		212-986-7600	N	250	2.0
Logix Development Corp.	473 E Post St	Camarillo	CA	93010	David K Howington	805-384-1460	R	250*	1.0
Modem Media . Poppe Tyson	230 East Ave	Norwalk	CT	06855	Bob Allen	203-299-7000	S	250*	0.4
Marconi Integrated Systems Inc.	PO Box 509009	San Diego	CA	92150		619-675-2600	S	240	2.2
First Consulting Group Inc.	111 W Ocean Blvd	Long Beach	CA	90802	Steven Heck	562-624-5200	P	238	1.5
Chevron Industries	PO Box 7753	San Francisco	CA	94120		415-894-7700	S	227*	0.3
Interim Technology Inc.	823 Commerce Dr	Oak Brook	IL	60523	Stewart Emanuel	630-574-3030	S	199*	2.5
Evans & Sutherland Computer	PO Box 58700	Salt Lake City	UT	84158	James R Oyler	801-588-1000	P	192	0.9
Mitek Industries Inc.	PO Box 7359	St. Louis	MO	63177		314-434-1200	S	180*	0.9
Analysis and Technology Inc.	P O Box 220	N. Stonington	CT	06359	Gary P Bennett	860-599-3910	R	170	1.6
Syntel Inc.	2800 Livernois Rd	Troy	MI	48083	Bharat Desai	248-619-2800	P	168	2.2
IRI Software	1601 Trapelo Rd	Waltham	MA	02154		781-890-1100	D	161*	1.2
IMRglobal Corp.	26750 VS 19 North	Clearwater	FL	33761	John Hindman	727-797-7080	P	158	2.5
Allstates Design & Development	1 Neshaminy Iplex	Trevose	PA	19053	Regis C Novak	215-633-3500	S	152*	0.8
Chemical Abstracts Service	PO Box 3012	Columbus	OH	43210	Robert J Massie	614-447-3600	D	150	1.2
4Front Technologies Inc.	6300 S Syracuse	Englewood	CO	80111	Anil Doshi	303-721-7341	P	149	1.3
Enterprise Consulting Group	4000 Town Ctr	Southfield	MI	48075	Richard D Helppie Jr	248-386-8300	S	147*	1.1
Intelligroup Inc.	499 Thornall St	Edison	NJ	08837	Stephen Carnes	732-750-1600	P	145	1.3
Kenan Systems Corp.	One Main St	Cambridge	MA	02142	Kenan Sahin	617-225-2200	R	144*	1.2
Inter Voice-Brite Inc.	250 International	Heathrow	FL	32746	David Berger	972-454-8000	R	137	0.7
Aura CAD/CAM Inc.	2335 Alaska Ave	El Segundo	CA	90245	Harry Kurtzman	310-536-9207	S	137	0.5
Lockheed Martin Mission Systems	9970 Federal Dr	Co Springs	CO	80921	Terry Drabant	719-594-1393	S	134*	1.0
Volt Directory Systems	1 Sentry Pkwy E	Blue Bell	PA	19422		610-825-7720	S	125	0.9
RWD Technologies Inc.	10480 Patuxent	Columbia	MD	21044	John H Beakes	410-730-4377	P	124	1.0
Scientech Inc. (Idaho Falls, Idaho)	1690 International	Idaho Falls	ID	83402	Nicholas Kaufman	208-523-2077	R	124	0.9
PAR Technology Corp.	8383 Seneca Tpke	New Hartford	NY	13413	DJW Sammon	315-738-0600	P	122	0.9
APEX Data Services Inc.	198 Van Buren St	Herndon	VA	20170	Shashikant Gupta	703-709-3000	R	115*	2.1
OAO Technology Solutions Inc.	7500 Greenway	Greenbelt	MD	20770	Jerry L Johnson	301-486-0400	P	113	2.0
RCG Information Technology	1900 N Loop W	Houston	TX	77092		713-548-1200	N	110	1.2
Union Pacific Technologies Inc.	7930 Clayton Rd	Richmond H.	MO	63117	L Merill Bryan Jr	314-768-6800	R	104*	0.5
Keithley Instruments Inc.	28775 Aurora Rd	Cleveland	OH	44139	Joseph P Keithley	440-248-0400	D	100	0.1
Lucas Assembly and Test Systems	12841 Stark Rd	Livonia	MI	48150		734-522-9680	S	100	0.7
Computer Dynamics Inc.	7640 Pelham Rd	Greenville	SC	29615	Earle Foster	864-627-8800	R	99	0.4

Source: Ward's Business Directory of U.S. Private and Public Companies, Volumes 1 and 2, 2000. The company type code used is as follows: P - Public, R - Private, S - Subsidiary, D - Division, J - Joint Venture, A - Affiliate, G - Group, N - Company type not reported. Sales are in millions of dollars, employees are in thousands. An asterisk (*) indicates an estimated sales volume. The symbol < stands for 'less than'. Company names and addresses are truncated, in some cases, to fit into the available space.

LOCATION BY STATE AND REGIONAL CONCENTRATION

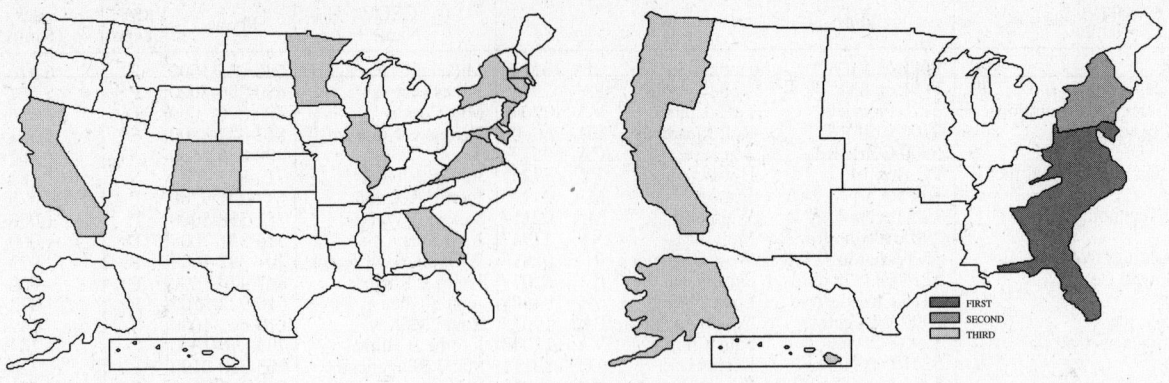

FIRST
SECOND
THIRD

INDUSTRY DATA BY STATE

State	Establishments Total (number)	% of U.S.	Employment Total (number)	% of U.S.	Per Estab.	Payroll Total ($ mil.)	Per Empl. ($)	Revenues Total ($ mil.)	% of U.S.	Per Estab. ($)
California	4,545	14.4	46,199	14.5	10	2,918.0	63,161	5,972.0	15.6	1,313,961
Virginia	1,253	4.0	26,476	8.3	21	1,485.5	56,108	3,518.9	9.2	2,808,406
New York	2,370	7.5	19,909	6.3	8	1,296.7	65,130	2,793.4	7.3	1,178,638
New Jersey	2,549	8.1	21,291	6.7	8	1,352.9	63,543	2,703.7	7.1	1,060,708
Texas	1,960	6.2	20,441	6.4	10	1,219.6	59,663	2,659.8	6.9	1,357,016
Illinois	1,895	6.0	18,345	5.8	10	1,087.4	59,277	2,129.4	5.6	1,123,699
Massachusetts	1,258	4.0	13,265	4.2	11	896.3	67,568	1,738.4	4.5	1,381,899
Colorado	883	2.8	10,648	3.3	12	623.3	58,540	1,560.6	4.1	1,767,360
Georgia	1,248	3.9	13,833	4.3	11	775.2	56,042	1,479.4	3.9	1,185,443
Maryland	921	2.9	12,980	4.1	14	730.6	56,286	1,461.8	3.8	1,587,199
Pennsylvania	988	3.1	12,866	4.0	13	718.6	55,852	1,461.0	3.8	1,478,766
Ohio	944	3.0	12,075	3.8	13	654.1	54,171	1,221.8	3.2	1,294,239
Florida	1,581	5.0	10,763	3.4	7	534.2	49,630	1,142.7	3.0	722,767
Minnesota	1,030	3.3	7,846	2.5	8	417.0	53,148	848.3	2.2	823,607
Missouri	459	1.5	5,475	1.7	12	303.6	55,455	750.5	2.0	1,635,124
North Carolina	689	2.2	6,690	2.1	10	356.8	53,327	746.3	1.9	1,083,177
Michigan	758	2.4	7,294	2.3	10	355.9	48,799	693.2	1.8	914,454
Connecticut	523	1.7	5,353	1.7	10	349.3	65,256	638.7	1.7	1,221,191
Washington	694	2.2	5,381	1.7	8	300.1	55,770	553.6	1.4	797,745
Arizona	428	1.4	3,792	1.2	9	191.2	50,413	353.2	0.9	825,171
Tennessee	268	0.8	3,078	1.0	11	168.9	54,871	348.2	0.9	1,299,086
Alabama	237	0.7	3,103	1.0	13	153.9	49,595	342.5	0.9	1,445,236
Wisconsin	364	1.2	3,162	1.0	9	172.6	54,576	329.9	0.9	906,223
Kansas	187	0.6	1,963	0.6	10	113.2	57,692	258.0	0.7	1,379,722
Indiana	362	1.1	2,837	0.9	8	128.4	45,271	257.8	0.7	712,033
Utah	266	0.8	2,415	0.8	9	115.9	47,983	255.3	0.7	959,677
Oregon	346	1.1	2,643	0.8	8	135.6	51,302	254.6	0.7	735,913
South Carolina	198	0.6	1,634	0.5	8	95.2	58,240	203.9	0.5	1,030,051
Iowa	149	0.5	1,589	0.5	11	74.8	47,093	182.5	0.5	1,224,846
D.C.	123	0.4	1,622	0.5	13	80.8	49,787	177.7	0.5	1,444,715
New Hampshire	282	0.9	1,089	0.3	4	66.0	60,601	132.8	0.3	470,996
Oklahoma	188	0.6	1,409	0.4	7	58.0	41,183	120.3	0.3	639,941
New Mexico	114	0.4	822	0.3	7	39.5	48,077	72.7	0.2	637,825
Nevada	162	0.5	564	0.2	3	27.8	49,227	65.4	0.2	403,580
Mississippi	82	0.3	517	0.2	6	27.1	52,456	55.0	0.1	671,293
Hawaii	57	0.2	460	0.1	8	19.3	41,950	44.1	0.1	774,333
Idaho	79	0.2	443	0.1	6	18.3	41,264	32.9	0.1	416,582
Rhode Island	103	0.3	342	0.1	3	15.5	45,175	32.4	0.1	314,456
Vermont	82	0.3	368	0.1	4	11.5	31,128	31.6	0.1	384,878
Alaska	27	0.1	300	0.1	11	15.6	52,163	29.1	0.1	1,077,963
West Virginia	41	0.1	298	0.1	7	8.8	29,550	20.8	0.1	506,805
Maine	88	0.3	233	0.1	3	8.5	36,691	18.9	0.0	214,216
South Dakota	37	0.1	316	0.1	9	8.6	27,282	15.6	0.0	420,757
Montana	53	0.2	187	0.1	4	5.0	26,770	12.2	0.0	230,528
Wyoming	25	0.1	120	0.0	5	4.7	39,292	10.4	0.0	414,840
Kentucky	167	0.5	1,750*	-	-	(D)	-	(D)	-	-
Louisiana	165	0.5	750*	-	-	(D)	-	(D)	-	-
Nebraska	143	0.5	1,750*	-	-	(D)	-	(D)	-	-
Arkansas	113	0.4	750*	-	-	(D)	-	(D)	-	-
Delaware	113	0.4	750*	-	-	(D)	-	(D)	-	-
North Dakota	27	0.1	175*	-	-	(D)	-	(D)	-	-

Source: 1997 *Economic Census*. The states are in descending order of revenues or establishments (if revenue data are missing for the majority). The symbol (D) appears when data are withheld to prevent disclosure of competitive information. States marked with (D) are sorted by number of establishments. A dash (-) indicates that the data element cannot be calculated. * indicates the midpoint of a range; 175, for example is the range 100-249. Shaded *states* on the state map indicate those states which have proportionately greater representation in the industry than would be indicated by the state's population; the ratio is based on total revenues or number of establishments. Shaded *regions* indicate where the industry is regionally most concentrated.

NAICS 541512 - COMPUTER SYSTEMS DESIGN SERVICES

GENERAL STATISTICS

Year	Establishments (number)	Employment (number)	Payroll ($ million)	Revenues ($ million)	Employees per Establishment (number)	Revenues per Establishment ($)	Payroll per Employee ($)
1997	30,804	337,526	18,460.0	51,213.0	11.0	1,662,544	54,692

Source: *Economic Census of the United States*, 1997. This is a newly defined industry. Data for prior years were unavailable at the time of publication but may become available over time.

INDICES OF CHANGE

Year	Establishments (number)	Employment (number)	Payroll ($ million)	Revenues ($ million)	Employees per Establishment (number)	Revenues per Establishment ($)	Payroll per Employee ($)
1997	100.0	100.0	100.0	100.0	100.0	100.0	100.0

Sources: Same as General Statistics. The values shown reflect change from the base year, 1997. Values above 100 mean greater than 1997, values below 100 mean less than 1997, and a value of 100 in the 1982-96 or 1998-2001 period means same as 1997. Values followed by a 'p' are projections by the editors; 'e' stands for extrapolation. Data are the most recent available at this level of detail.

SIC INDUSTRIES RELATED TO NAICS 541512

Each new NAICS code represents an industry that used to be part of an SIC or a part of several SIC industries. Data in this table are shown to provide transitional information for these cases. All available data for the precursor SIC(s) are shown. Even if only a part of an SIC is included in the NAICS, *all* data for the SIC are reproduced. If the SIC industry is not marked as being a part (pt) of the NAICS, the entire industry is embedded in the NAICS data. The SIC composition of the new industry provides some hints of the relative importance of its "ancestors." Data marked with a 'p' are projected. Projections begin with 1982 data. Data earlier than 1990 are not shown but are reflected in the projections.

SIC	Industry	1990	1991	1992	1993	1994	1995	1996	1997
7373	**Computer Integrated Systems Design**								
	Establishments (number)	3,273	3,510	5,011	5,179	5,402	5,781	5,970p	6,312p
	Employment (thousands)	81.6	85.5	97.6	115.2	103.4	110.9	121.7p	128.3p
	Revenues ($ million)	12,916.0	13,751.0	15,177.0	16,212.0	17,037.0	17,485.0	20,202.0	20,566.6p
7379	**Computer Related Services, nec (pt)**								
	Establishments (number)	6,823	8,133	8,722	11,174	13,820	17,688	16,728p	18,269p
	Employment (thousands)	51.2	59.0	57.7	76.4	87.7	115.0	107.4p	116.3p
	Revenues ($ million)	4,537.0	4,894.0	6,234.0	7,845.0	10,285.0	13,176.0	16,504.0	11,341.1p

Source: *Economic Census of the United States*, 1992, annual surveys of economic sectors conducted by the Bureau of the Census, and estimates or projections based on the 1982-1992 period; not all data are shown. 'e' marks estimates made by the editors; 'p' indicates projections based on time series. A dash (-) indicates that data for this SIC or year were not available. The abbreviation (pt) next to the industry name indicates that only a part of the industry is present within the NAICS data. If no (pt) is shown, the entire industry is contained within the NAICS data.

SELECTED RATIOS

For 1997	Avg. of Information	Analyzed Industry	Index	For 1997	Avg. of Information	Analyzed Industry	Index
Employees per establishment	9	11	127	Payroll per establishment	372,545	599,273	161
Revenue per establishment	958,337	1,662,544	173	Payroll as % of revenue	39	36	93
Revenue per employee	111,029	151,731	137	Payroll per employee	43,162	54,692	127

Sources: Same as General Statistics. The 'Average' column represents the average for the industry sector, in 1997, where the currently shown industry is classified. The Index shows the relationship between the Average and the Analyzed Industry. For example, 100 means that they are equal; 500 that the Analyzed Industry is five times the average; 50 means that the Analyzed Industry is half the national average. The abbreviation 'na' is used to show that data are 'not available'.

LEADING COMPANIES   Number shown: **75**   Total sales ($ mil): **190,269**   Total employment (000): **694.6**

Company Name	Address				CEO Name	Phone	Co. Type	Sales ($ mil)	Empl. (000)
Healtheon Web MD	4600 Patrick Henry	Santa Clara	CA	95054	Jeffrey T. Arnold	408-876-5000	P	45,477	0.6
Electronic Data Systems Corp.	5400 Legacy Dr	Plano	TX	75024	Richard H Brown	972-604-6000	P	18,534	121.0
ATS Money Systems Inc.	25 Rockwood Pl	Englewood	NJ	07631	Gerard F Murphy	201-894-1700	P	14,447	<0.1
Acotec Worldwide	3 Harbor Dr	Sausalito	CA	94965		415-332-5900	R	12,400	0.0
Computer Sciences Corp.	2100 E Grand Ave	El Segundo	CA	90245	Van B Honeycutt	310-615-0311	P	7,660	50.0
Unisys Corp.	Unisys Way	Blue Bell	PA	19424	L A Weinbach	215-986-4011	P	7,545	33.2
MicroAge Inc.	2400 S MicroAge	Tempe	AZ	85282	Jeffrey D McKeever	480-366-2000	P	6,150	4.5
IKON Office Solutions Inc.	PO Box 834	Valley Forge	PA	19482	James Forese	610-296-8000	P	5,522	39.4
Getronics Wang	Concord Rd	Billerica	MA	01821	Cees Van Luijk	978-625-5000	R	5,000	34.0
Litton Industries Inc.	21240 Burbank Blvd	Woodland Hills	CA	91367	Michael R Brown	818-598-5000	P	4,827	34.8
Computer Science Corporation	3170 Fairview	Falls Church	VA	22042	Milt Cooper	703-876-1000	D	4,286*	30.0
Science Applications Intern. Corp.	10260 Campus Point	San Diego	CA	92121	J Robert Beyster	619-546-6000	P	4,200*	35.0
Quest Communications	700 Qwest Tower	Denver	CO	80202	Afshin Mohebbi	303-992-1400	P	3,928	8.7
Lotus Development Corp.	55 Cambridge	Cambridge	MA	02142	Al Zollar	617-577-8500	S	3,000	8.5
Lockheed Martin Federal Systems	9500 Godwin Dr	Manassas	VA	20110	Gerald Ebker	703-367-0777	S	2,838*	2.5
Entex Information Services Inc.	6 International Dr	Port Chester	NY	10573		914-935-3600	R	2,456	8.2
CompuCom Systems Inc.	7171 Forest Ln	Dallas	TX	75230	Edward Coleman	972-856-3600	P	2,254	4.8
Volt Information Sciences Inc.	1221 Av Americas	New York	NY	10036	William Shaw	212-704-2400	P	2,141	38.7
Harris Corp.	1025 W NASA Blvd	Melbourne	FL	32919	Phillip W Farmer	407-727-9100	P	1,744	10.5
Modis Professional Services Inc.	1 Independent Dr	Jacksonville	FL	32202	Derek E Dewan	904-360-2000	P	1,702	19.5
Reynolds and Reynolds Co.	115 S Ludlow St	Dayton	OH	45402	David Holmes	937-485-2000	P	1,563	9.1
PeopleSoft Inc.	4460 Hacienda Dr	Pleasanton	CA	94588	Craig A Conway	925-225-3000	P	1,475	6.0
Logicon Northrop Grumman Co.	2411 Dulles Corner	Herndon	VA	20171	Herbert W Anderson	703-713-4000	D	1,362*	10.0
Ceridian Corp.	8100 34th Ave S	Minneapolis	MN	55425	Lawrence Perlman	612-853-8100	P	1,342	9.6
American Management Systems	4050 Legato Rd	Fairfax	VA	22033	Paul A Brands	703-267-8000	P	1,240	9.0
MasTec Inc.	3155 NW 77th Ave	Miami	FL	33122	Joel-Tomas Citron	305-599-1800	P	1,059	9.9
Western Geophysical Co.	PO Box 2469	Houston	TX	77252	R White	713-789-9600	S	1,000*	6.0
Perot Systems Corp.	12404 Park Central	Dallas	TX	75251	Ross Perot Sr	972-340-5000	R	994	6.0
Harris Government	P O Box 8100	Melbourne	FL	32902	Robert Henry	407-727-5612	D	960	4.0
Tracor Applied Sciences Inc.	1601 Research Blvd	Rockville	MD	20850	K Bruce Hamilton	301-838-6000	S	946*	5.0
Telcordia Technologies	445 South St	Morristown	NJ	07960	Richard C Smith	973-829-2000	S	925*	5.3
Shared Medical Systems Corp.	51 Valley Stream	Malvern	PA	19355	Marvin S Cadwell	610-219-6300	P	915	7.6
McLeodUSA Inc.	P O Box 3177	Cedar Rapids	IA	52406	Stephen C Gray	319-364-0000	P	909	5.6
Metamor Worldwide Inc.	4400 Post Oak	Houston	TX	77027	Peter T Dameris	713-548-3400	P	850	9.0
CompuServe Interactive Services	PO Box 20212	Columbus	OH	43220	Mayo Stuntz Jr	614-457-8600	S	842	3.0
VisiCom	10052 Mesa Ridge	San Diego	CA	92121	Michael Mollin	858-457-2111	S	725	0.3
PRC Inc.	1500 PRC Dr	McLean	VA	22102	Leonard M Pomata	703-556-1000	S	720*	5.6
Pomeroy Computer Resources Inc.	1020 Peterburg Rd	Hebron	KY	41048	David B Pomeroy II	606-586-0600	P	628	1.7
Litton Industries Inc	PO Box 338	Woodland Hills	CA	91365	Darwim Beckel	818-715-4040	S	620	2.6
Franklin Covey Co.	2200 W Parkway	Salt Lake City	UT	84119	Robert Guindon	801-975-1776	P	555	4.2
Computer Horizons Corp.	49 Old Bloomfield	Mountain Lakes	NJ	07046	John J Cassese	973-299-4000	P	535	4.1
GTE Data Services Inc.	P O Box 290152	Temple Terrace	FL	33687	Don A Hayes	813-978-4000	S	520	4.0
Computer Horizons Corp.	4555 Lake Forest	Cincinnati	OH	45242		513-769-3355	N	514	4.0
Mentor Graphics Corp.	8005 S W Boeckman	Wilsonville	OR	97070	Walden C Rhines	503-685-7000	P	511	2.6
Bechtel Software Inc.	50 Beale St	San Francisco	CA	94119	George Belonogoff	415-768-8947	R	500*	0.3
Bull Worldwide Information	300 Concord Rd	Billerica	MA	01821		978-294-6000	R	500*	0.9
Norstan Inc.	5101 Shady Oak Rd	Minnetonka	MN	55343	Paul Baszucki	612-352-4000	P	483	2.7
Whittman-Hart Inc.	311 S Wacker Dr	Chicago	IL	60606	Robert F Bernard	312-922-9200	P	481	3.5
Bisys Document Solution	121 Greenway Blvd	Carrollton	GA	30117	Tedd Wilson	770-834-0090	D	472	0.2
Sykes Enterprises Inc.	100 N Tampa St	Tampa	FL	33602	David L Grimes	813-274-1000	P	469	10.8
Computer Task Group Inc.	800 Delaware Ave	Buffalo	NY	14209	Gale Fitzgerald	716-882-8000	P	468	5.8
PrimeSource Corp.	4350 Haddonfield	Pennsauken	NJ	08109	Richard E Engebrecht	609-488-4888	P	453	0.9
CACI International Inc.	1100 N Glebe Rd	Arlington	VA	22201	J P London	703-841-7800	P	442	4.2
TASC Inc.	55 Walkers Brook	Reading	MA	01867	James H Frey	781-942-2000	S	440	2.8
Baseline Financial Services	2 W Trade Ctr	New York	NY	10048			R	435*	2.9
Primark Corp.	1000 Winter St	Waltham	MA	02451	Joseph Kasputys	781-466-6611	P	435	2.9
BOLData Technology Inc.	48363 Fremont Blvd	Fremont	CA		Eugene Kiang	510-490-8296	R	433*	0.1
CIC Systems Inc.	15720 Delaney	Charlotte	NC	28277	Frank Slovenec	704-714-4000	S	418	0.4
Belcan Engineering Group Inc.	10200 Anderson	Cincinnati	OH	45242	Ralph G Anderson	513-891-0972	S	400	4.0
CSC Healthcare Group	26711 Northwestern	Southfield	MI	48034	Art Spiegel	248-372-3000	D	400*	1.4
Unigraphics Solutions	13736 Riverport Dr	Maryland H.	MO	63043	John Mazzola	314-344-5900	S	400	2.2
Level 3 Communications Inc.	1025 Eldorado Blvd	Broomfield	CO	80021	James Q Crowe	402-536-3677	P	392	8.0
Telxon Corp.	PO Box 5582	Akron	OH	44334	Kenneth Cassady	330-664-1000	P	388	1.5
Complete Business Solutions Inc.	32605 W 12 Mile Rd	Farmington Hills	MI	48334	Rajendra B Vattikuti	248-488-2088	P	377	4.6
Achieve Global Inc.	8875 Hidden River	Tampa	FL	33637	Horst Bergman	813-971-1990	S	366*	0.9
Milgo Solutions Inc.	1601 N Harrison	Sunrise	FL	33323		954-846-1601	S	358*	1.2
Forsythe Technology Inc.	7500 Frontage Rd	Skokie	IL	60077	Rick Forsythe	847-675-8000	R	357*	0.3
Rockwell Autmomation Allen	1 Allen Bradley Dr	Mayfield H.	OH	44124			D	356*	2.0
GeoQuest Systems Inc.	5599 San Felipe St	Houston	TX	77056	Thierry Pilenko	713-513-2000	R	342*	2.7
MCMS Inc.	16399 Franklin Rd	Nampa	ID	83687	Richard Downing	208-898-2600	R	334	2.2
Sutherland Group Ltd.	1160 Pitts-Victor	Port Gibson	NY	14534		716-586-5757	R	324*	1.8
BTG Inc. (Fairfax, Virginia)	3877 Fairfax Ridge	Fairfax	VA	22030	Edward H Bersoff	703-383-8000	P	316	1.3
Litton Data Systems	PO Box 6008	Agoura Hills	CA	91376	Alan Powers	818-991-9660	S	309*	1.5
GenRad Inc.	7 Technology	Westford	MA	01886	James F Lyons	978-589-7000	P	302	1.3
First Image Management Co.	3951 Pender Dr	Fairfax	VA	22030		703-273-2001	N	300	1.0

Source: Ward's Business Directory of U.S. Private and Public Companies, Volumes 1 and 2, 2000. The company type code used is as follows: P - Public, R - Private, S - Subsidiary, D - Division, J - Joint Venture, A - Affiliate, G - Group, N - Company type not reported. Sales are in millions of dollars, employees are in thousands. An asterisk (*) indicates an estimated sales volume. The symbol < stands for 'less than'. Company names and addresses are truncated, in some cases, to fit into the available space.

LOCATION BY STATE AND REGIONAL CONCENTRATION

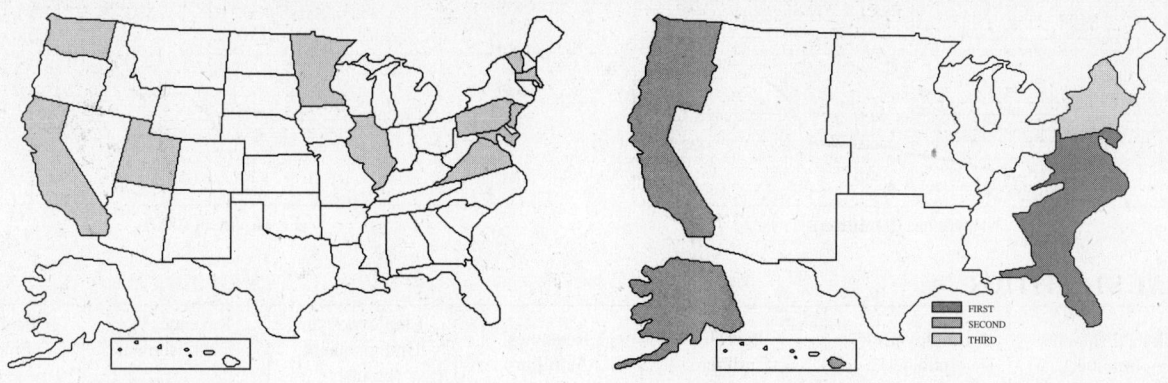

FIRST
SECOND
THIRD

INDUSTRY DATA BY STATE

State	Establishments Total (number)	% of U.S.	Employment Total (number)	% of U.S.	Per Estab.	Payroll Total ($ mil.)	Per Empl. ($)	Revenues Total ($ mil.)	% of U.S.	Per Estab. ($)
California	3,985	12.9	43,270	12.8	11	2,753.2	63,628	7,767.9	15.2	1,949,276
Virginia	1,405	4.6	33,825	10.0	24	1,807.3	53,432	5,549.4	10.8	3,949,779
Texas	1,917	6.2	21,809	6.5	11	1,209.9	55,476	3,462.5	6.8	1,806,206
New Jersey	2,445	7.9	22,969	6.8	9	1,421.3	61,879	3,201.3	6.3	1,309,336
Pennsylvania	1,084	3.5	18,943	5.6	17	1,025.2	54,122	2,871.1	5.6	2,648,643
Maryland	1,066	3.5	18,141	5.4	17	1,029.6	56,757	2,782.9	5.4	2,610,564
New York	2,417	7.8	17,027	5.0	7	940.0	55,204	2,649.0	5.2	1,095,982
Illinois	1,853	6.0	15,831	4.7	9	942.5	59,536	2,605.8	5.1	1,406,257
Massachusetts	1,173	3.8	16,877	5.0	14	1,009.3	59,802	2,304.3	4.5	1,964,461
Florida	1,564	5.1	12,543	3.7	8	630.1	50,234	1,741.2	3.4	1,113,311
Ohio	980	3.2	10,255	3.0	10	500.8	48,838	1,617.4	3.2	1,650,453
Minnesota	943	3.1	9,422	2.8	10	478.8	50,821	1,327.2	2.6	1,407,446
Georgia	1,053	3.4	8,905	2.6	8	488.4	54,849	1,324.5	2.6	1,257,840
Michigan	717	2.3	10,023	3.0	14	511.8	51,060	1,213.4	2.4	1,692,382
Washington	586	1.9	6,624	2.0	11	345.1	52,092	1,096.1	2.1	1,870,515
Missouri	439	1.4	6,702	2.0	15	328.9	49,069	980.1	1.9	2,232,636
Connecticut	510	1.7	3,190	0.9	6	192.6	60,388	634.4	1.2	1,243,925
North Carolina	707	2.3	4,808	1.4	7	233.0	48,459	604.8	1.2	855,437
Alabama	270	0.9	4,395	1.3	16	209.2	47,606	552.0	1.1	2,044,444
Arizona	410	1.3	4,509	1.3	11	194.8	43,198	509.5	1.0	1,242,588
Utah	204	0.7	3,784	1.1	19	167.1	44,157	494.8	1.0	2,425,490
Indiana	427	1.4	3,991	1.2	9	181.8	45,553	481.1	0.9	1,126,705
Wisconsin	395	1.3	3,724	1.1	9	167.1	44,864	449.6	0.9	1,138,175
Oregon	345	1.1	3,025	0.9	9	153.3	50,685	365.3	0.7	1,058,977
Kansas	204	0.7	2,318	0.7	11	111.3	48,003	332.5	0.6	1,629,672
Oklahoma	199	0.6	1,490	0.4	7	59.6	40,008	265.7	0.5	1,335,166
D.C.	118	0.4	1,705	0.5	14	89.6	52,558	259.9	0.5	2,202,958
Tennessee	295	1.0	2,113	0.6	7	85.8	40,604	241.1	0.5	817,176
New Hampshire	261	0.8	1,292	0.4	5	80.0	61,921	205.9	0.4	788,954
South Carolina	222	0.7	1,729	0.5	8	79.4	45,936	195.9	0.4	882,455
Kentucky	192	0.6	1,275	0.4	7	49.7	39,000	169.8	0.3	884,172
Iowa	147	0.5	1,214	0.4	8	44.5	36,658	156.9	0.3	1,067,490
Vermont	57	0.2	848	0.3	15	45.5	53,650	148.5	0.3	2,605,298
Rhode Island	112	0.4	766	0.2	7	39.3	51,272	101.2	0.2	903,518
Delaware	128	0.4	732	0.2	6	31.9	43,637	93.8	0.2	732,789
Nevada	153	0.5	800	0.2	5	33.4	41,704	90.2	0.2	589,268
New Mexico	122	0.4	780	0.2	6	36.3	46,474	73.3	0.1	600,566
Arkansas	97	0.3	447	0.1	5	17.5	39,040	67.3	0.1	693,928
Idaho	48	0.2	388	0.1	8	16.2	41,753	64.3	0.1	1,340,229
Mississippi	67	0.2	300	0.1	4	12.3	41,043	57.0	0.1	851,075
Maine	96	0.3	406	0.1	4	17.1	42,076	52.0	0.1	541,979
West Virginia	42	0.1	403	0.1	10	17.2	42,588	49.8	0.1	1,186,143
South Dakota	34	0.1	555	0.2	16	20.5	36,978	48.3	0.1	1,419,735
Hawaii	56	0.2	291	0.1	5	13.3	45,694	41.6	0.1	742,339
Montana	43	0.1	570	0.2	13	14.4	25,316	36.2	0.1	842,860
North Dakota	21	0.1	139	0.0	7	3.9	28,295	13.7	0.0	654,238
Alaska	19	0.1	94	0.0	5	4.4	46,670	12.1	0.0	636,632
Wyoming	15	-	44	0.0	3	1.9	43,159	4.2	0.0	279,933
Colorado	857	2.8	7,500*	-	-	(D)	-	(D)	-	-
Louisiana	175	0.6	1,750*	-	-	(D)	-	(D)	-	-
Nebraska	129	0.4	1,750*	-	-	(D)	-	(D)	-	-

Source: 1997 Economic Census. The states are in descending order of revenues or establishments (if revenue data are missing for the majority). The symbol (D) appears when data are withheld to prevent disclosure of competitive information. States marked with (D) are sorted by number of establishments. A dash (-) indicates that the data element cannot be calculated. * indicates the midpoint of a range; 175, for example is the range 100-249. Shaded *states* on the state map indicate those states which have proportionately greater representation in the industry than would be indicated by the state's population; the ratio is based on total revenues or number of establishments. Shaded *regions* indicate where the industry is regionally most concentrated.

NAICS 541513 - COMPUTER FACILITIES MANAGEMENT SERVICES*

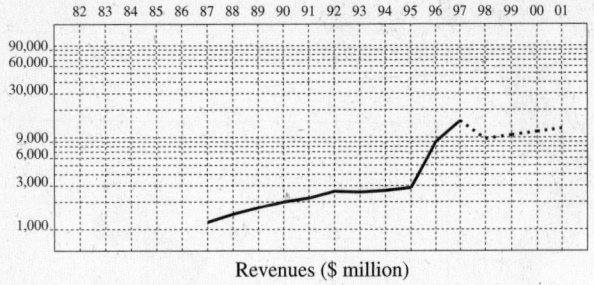

Revenues ($ million)

Employment (000)

GENERAL STATISTICS

Year	Establishments (number)	Employment (number)	Payroll ($ million)	Revenues ($ million)	Employees per Establishment (number)	Revenues per Establishment ($)	Payroll per Employee ($)
1982	-	-	-	-	-	-	-
1983	-	-	-	-	-	-	-
1984	-	-	-	-	-	-	-
1985	-	-	-	-	-	-	-
1986	-	-	-	-	-	-	-
1987	738	18,528	505.0	1,198.0	25.1	1,623,306	27,256
1988	731	22,167	606.0	1,463.0 e	30.3	2,001,368	27,338
1989	640	22,721	645.0	1,729.0 e	35.5	2,701,562	28,388
1990	639	24,310	753.0	1,994.0	38.0	3,120,501	30,975
1991	627	24,850	797.0	2,206.0	39.6	3,518,341	32,072
1992	675	23,356	934.0	2,608.0	34.6	3,863,704	39,990
1993	697	31,088	1,169.0	2,557.0	44.6	3,668,580	37,603
1994	728	29,808	1,171.0	2,652.0	40.9	3,642,857	39,285
1995	792	30,878	1,301.0	2,856.0	39.0	3,606,061	42,134
1996	1,119 e	51,349 e	2,345.0 e	8,985.0 e	45.9 e	8,029,491 e	45,668 e
1997	1,445	71,821	3,390.0	15,114.0	49.7	10,459,516	47,201
1998	1,119 p	55,074 p	2,577.0 p	9,654.0 p	49.2 p	8,627,346 p	46,792 p
1999	1,171 p	58,937 p	2,801.0 p	10,606.0 p	50.3 p	9,057,216 p	47,525 p
2000	1,224 p	62,799 p	3,024.0 p	11,558.0 p	51.3 p	9,442,810 p	48,154 p
2001	1,277 p	66,662 p	3,247.0 p	12,510.0 p	52.2 p	9,796,398 p	48,708 p

Sources: *Economic Census of the United States*, 1982, 1987, 1992, 1997. Establishment counts, employment, and payroll are from *County Business Patterns* for non-Census years. In non-Census years, industries in the Manufacturing range under SIC coding include data from the *Annual Survey of Manufactures* (*ASM*); those in the old Services range include data from the *Services Annual Survey* (*SAS*). Values followed by a 'p' are projections by the editors. Extrapolations are marked by 'e'. Data are the most recent available at this level of detail.

INDICES OF CHANGE

Year	Establishments (number)	Employment (number)	Payroll ($ million)	Revenues ($ million)	Employees per Establishment (number)	Revenues per Establishment ($)	Payroll per Employee ($)
1982	-	-	-	-	-	-	-
1987	51.1	25.8	14.9	7.9	50.5	15.5	57.7
1992	46.7	32.5	27.6	17.3	69.6	36.9	84.7
1993	48.2	43.3	34.5	16.9	89.7	35.1	79.7
1994	50.4	41.5	34.5	17.5	82.4	34.8	83.2
1995	54.8	43.0	38.4	18.9	78.4	34.5	89.3
1996	77.4 e	71.5 e	69.2 e	59.4 e	92.3 e	76.8 e	96.8 e
1997	100.0	100.0	100.0	100.0	100.0	100.0	100.0
1998	77.4 p	76.7 p	76.0 p	63.9 p	99.0 p	82.5 p	99.1 p
1999	81.0 p	82.1 p	82.6 p	70.2 p	101.3 p	86.6 p	100.7 p
2000	84.7 p	87.4 p	89.2 p	76.5 p	103.2 p	90.3 p	102.0 p
2001	88.4 p	92.8 p	95.8 p	82.8 p	105.0 p	93.7 p	103.2 p

Sources: Same as General Statistics. The values shown reflect change from the base year, 1997. Values above 100 mean greater than 1997, values below 100 mean less than 1997, and a value of 100 in the 1982-96 or 1998-2001 period means same as 1997. Values followed by a 'p' are projections by the editors; 'e' stands for extrapolation. Data are the most recent available at this level of detail.

SELECTED RATIOS

For 1997	Avg. of Information	Analyzed Industry	Index	For 1997	Avg. of Information	Analyzed Industry	Index
Employees per establishment	9	50	576	Payroll per establishment	372,545	2,346,021	630
Revenue per establishment	958,337	10,459,516	1,091	Payroll as % of revenue	39	22	58
Revenue per employee	111,029	210,440	190	Payroll per employee	43,162	47,201	109

Sources: Same as General Statistics. The 'Average' column represents the average for the industry sector, in 1997, where the currently shown industry is classified. The Index shows the relationship between the Average and the Analyzed Industry. For example, 100 means that they are equal; 500 that the Analyzed Industry is five times the average; 50 means that the Analyzed Industry is half the national average. The abbreviation 'na' is used to show that data are 'not available'.

*Equivalent to SIC 7376.

LEADING COMPANIES   Number shown: **22**   Total sales ($ mil): **30,884**   Total employment (000): **211.9**

Company Name	Address				CEO Name	Phone	Co. Type	Sales ($ mil)	Empl. (000)
Electronic Data Systems Corp.	5400 Legacy Dr	Plano	TX	75024	Richard H. Brown	972-604-6000	P	18,534	121.0
Computer Sciences Corp.	2100 E Grand Ave	El Segundo	CA	90245	Van B Honeycutt	310-615-0311	P	7,660	50.0
DynCorp.	2000 Edmund Halley	Reston	VA	20191	Dan Bannister	703-264-0330	R	1,527	16.0
Sales Technologies Inc.	3445 Peachtree N E	Atlanta	GA	30326	Ronald D Brown	404-841-4000	P	1,185	8.0
PRC Inc.	1500 PRC Dr	McLean	VA	22102	Leonard M Pomata	703-556-1000	S	720*	5.6
F. Dohmen Co.	P O Box 9	Germantown	WI	53022	John Dohmen	414-255-0022	R	340*	0.3
Vinnell Corp.	12150 E Monument	Fairfax	VA	22033		703-385-4544	S	300	5.5
Bowne Business Solutions Inc.	161 N Clark St	Chicago	IL	60601		312-419-7600	S	168*	1.8
SCB Computer Technology Inc.	1365 W Brierbrook	Memphis	TN	38138	Ben C Bryant Jr	901-754-6577	P	157	1.4
Maxima Corp.	4200 Parliament Pl	Lanham	MD	20706	Joshua Smith	301-459-2000	R	93*	0.7
Scientific & Commercial Systems	7600 Leesburg Pike	Falls Church	VA	22043	Vernon Stansbury	703-917-9171	R	81*	0.4
Collegis Inc.	2300 Maitland	Maitland	FL	32751	Robert Lund	407-660-1199	R	47*	0.6
Computers Unlimited Inc.	2407 Montana Ave	Billings	MT	59101	Michael Schaer	406-255-9500	R	20	0.2
KRA Corp.	1010 Wayne Ave	Silver Spring	MD	20910	K R Atterbeary	301-495-1591	R	14*	0.2
Intern. Software Solutions Inc.	198 Van Buren St	Herndon	VA	20170	Hari N Chembukave	703-709-1247	R	8	0.1
Telehouse Intern	7 Teleport Dr	Staten Island	NY	10311	Yasuhiro Shintani	718-355-2500	R	7	<0.1
Electronic Environments Corp.	60 Shawmut Rd	Canton	MA	02021	Ken Rapoport	781-828-9199	R	6*	<0.1
Explore Reasoning Systems Inc.	8229 Boone Blvd	Vienna	VA	22182	Karl Keller	703-748-2810	R	5	0.0
G. A. Sullivan Inc.	55 W Port Plz	St. Louis	MO	63146	Gregory A Sullivan	314-213-5600	R	5*	0.1
Visual Information Inc.	1009 Grant St	Denver	CO	80203	Joseph Burke	303-864-0490	R	3	<0.1
ConQwest Inc.	84 October Hill Rd	Holliston	MA	01746	Michelle Drolet	508-893-0111	R	2*	<0.1
Online Computers	638 Springfield St	Feeding Hills	MA	01030	Paul Byrne	413-789-1030	R	2*	<0.1

Source: *Ward's Business Directory of U.S. Private and Public Companies*, Volumes 1 and 2, 2000. The company type code used is as follows: P - Public, R - Private, S - Subsidiary, D - Division, J - Joint Venture, A - Affiliate, G - Group, N - Company type not reported. Sales are in millions of dollars, employees are in thousands. An asterisk (*) indicates an estimated sales volume. The symbol < stands for 'less than'. Company names and addresses are truncated, in some cases, to fit into the available space.

LOCATION BY STATE AND REGIONAL CONCENTRATION

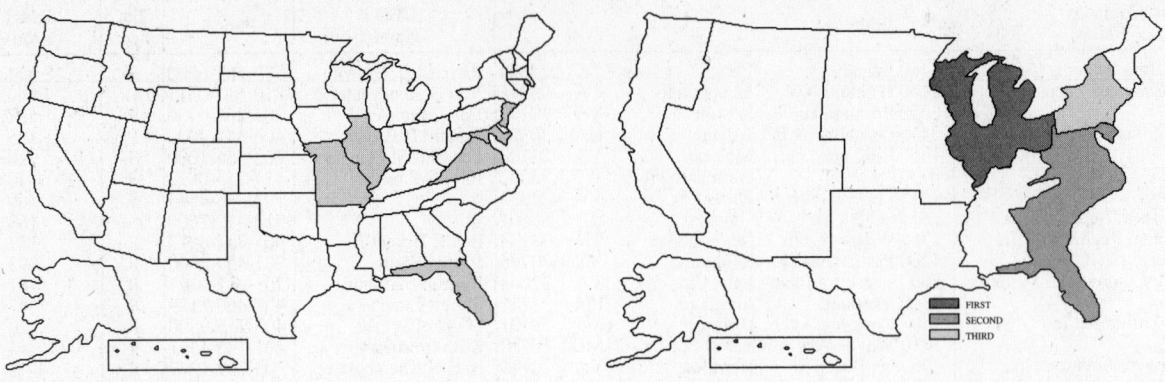

INDUSTRY DATA BY STATE

State	Establishments Total (number)	% of U.S.	Employment Total (number)	% of U.S.	Per Estab.	Payroll Total ($ mil.)	Per Empl. ($)	Revenues Total ($ mil.)	% of U.S.	Per Estab. ($)
Illinois	70	4.8	5,876	8.2	84	300.8	51,188	1,710.3	11.3	24,433,129
Florida	65	4.5	6,294	8.8	97	289.4	45,976	1,455.6	9.6	22,393,800
California	185	12.8	7,108	9.9	38	301.4	42,406	1,343.1	8.9	7,260,097
Texas	116	8.0	5,163	7.2	45	254.0	49,187	1,044.3	6.9	9,002,371
New Jersey	87	6.0	3,304	4.6	38	159.4	48,253	828.8	5.5	9,526,805
Missouri	19	1.3	2,562	3.6	135	127.8	49,867	655.5	4.3	34,501,211
Ohio	55	3.8	2,832	3.9	51	123.2	43,488	551.5	3.6	10,027,982
New York	86	6.0	2,505	3.5	29	125.0	49,915	445.9	3.0	5,184,779
Maryland	63	4.4	4,262	5.9	68	177.5	41,656	410.1	2.7	6,509,444
Virginia	102	7.1	3,210	4.5	31	163.5	50,920	399.2	2.6	3,914,049
Pennsylvania	60	4.2	1,960	2.7	33	117.5	59,951	280.6	1.9	4,677,000
Michigan	31	2.1	1,190	1.7	38	49.9	41,923	273.9	1.8	8,833,903
Indiana	28	1.9	1,029	1.4	37	43.8	42,563	182.2	1.2	6,506,786
Massachusetts	28	1.9	1,236	1.7	44	58.6	47,427	141.1	0.9	5,039,786
Washington	24	1.7	612	0.9	25	21.5	35,059	91.6	0.6	3,818,125
Connecticut	19	1.3	444	0.6	23	20.5	46,108	89.9	0.6	4,728,947
Arizona	17	1.2	501	0.7	29	29.7	59,196	82.8	0.5	4,872,412
Oklahoma	16	1.1	604	0.8	38	23.4	38,813	74.1	0.5	4,628,312
Rhode Island	9	0.6	478	0.7	53	15.1	31,540	70.5	0.5	7,830,333
D.C.	37	2.6	787	1.1	21	32.5	41,351	62.3	0.4	1,683,027
Louisiana	16	1.1	295	0.4	18	17.3	58,627	45.2	0.3	2,827,625
Alabama	12	0.8	161	0.2	13	6.4	39,826	15.4	0.1	1,280,417
Mississippi	8	0.6	197	0.3	25	5.6	28,675	15.0	0.1	1,874,500
Hawaii	3	0.2	141	0.2	47	5.2	37,021	10.8	0.1	3,613,000
South Carolina	8	0.6	94	0.1	12	3.7	39,394	9.8	0.1	1,219,875
New Mexico	7	0.5	114	0.2	16	5.1	44,386	9.3	0.1	1,328,571
West Virginia	9	0.6	82	0.1	9	3.3	40,744	7.4	0.0	826,889
Kansas	8	0.6	66	0.1	8	2.3	34,273	6.4	0.0	801,125
Utah	14	1.0	112	0.2	8	3.8	33,946	5.7	0.0	407,929
Oregon	12	0.8	231	0.3	19	4.1	17,913	5.7	0.0	476,833
Idaho	4	0.3	22	0.0	6	1.0	45,182	2.1	0.0	529,250
Georgia	47	3.3	3,750*	-	-	(D)	-	(D)	-	-
Colorado	40	2.8	7,500*	-	-	(D)	-	(D)	-	-
North Carolina	25	1.7	1,750*	-	-	(D)	-	(D)	-	-
Tennessee	25	1.7	1,750*	-	-	(D)	-	(D)	-	-
Minnesota	19	1.3	1,750*	-	-	(D)	-	(D)	-	-
Delaware	14	1.0	175*	-	-	(D)	-	(D)	-	-
Arkansas	12	0.8	1,750*	-	-	(D)	-	(D)	-	-
Kentucky	11	0.8	1,750*	-	-	(D)	-	(D)	-	-
Wisconsin	9	0.6	175*	-	-	(D)	-	(D)	-	-
Vermont	7	0.5	60*	-	-	(D)	-	(D)	-	-
Nevada	5	0.3	175*	-	-	(D)	-	(D)	-	-
Maine	3	0.2	60*	-	-	(D)	-	(D)	-	-
Nebraska	3	0.2	60*	-	-	(D)	-	(D)	-	-
Iowa	2	0.1	60*	-	-	(D)	-	(D)	-	-
New Hampshire	2	0.1	175*	-	-	(D)	-	(D)	-	-
Alaska	1	0.1	10*	-	-	(D)	-	(D)	-	-
Montana	1	0.1	10*	-	-	(D)	-	(D)	-	-
Wyoming	1	0.1	10*	-	-	(D)	-	(D)	-	-

Source: 1997 *Economic Census*. The states are in descending order of revenues or establishments (if revenue data are missing for the majority). The symbol (D) appears when data are withheld to prevent disclosure of competitive information. States marked with (D) are sorted by number of establishments. A dash (-) indicates that the data element cannot be calculated. * indicates the midpoint of a range; 175, for example is the range 100-249. Shaded *states* on the state map indicate those states which have proportionately greater representation in the industry than would be indicated by the state's population; the ratio is based on total revenues or number of establishments. Shaded *regions* indicate where the industry is regionally most concentrated.

NAICS 541519 - COMPUTER RELATED SERVICES NEC

GENERAL STATISTICS

Year	Establishments (number)	Employment (number)	Payroll ($ million)	Revenues ($ million)	Employees per Establishment (number)	Revenues per Establishment ($)	Payroll per Employee ($)
1997	8,405	37,114	1,884.0	4,340.0	4.4	516,359	50,763

Source: *Economic Census of the United States*, 1997. This is a newly defined industry. Data for prior years were unavailable at the time of publication but may become available over time.

INDICES OF CHANGE

Year	Establishments (number)	Employment (number)	Payroll ($ million)	Revenues ($ million)	Employees per Establishment (number)	Revenues per Establishment ($)	Payroll per Employee ($)
1997	100.0	100.0	100.0	100.0	100.0	100.0	100.0

Sources: Same as General Statistics. The values shown reflect change from the base year, 1997. Values above 100 mean greater than 1997, values below 100 mean less than 1997, and a value of 100 in the 1982-96 or 1998-2001 period means same as 1997. Values followed by a 'p' are projections by the editors; 'e' stands for extrapolation. Data are the most recent available at this level of detail.

SIC INDUSTRIES RELATED TO NAICS 541519

Each new NAICS code represents an industry that used to be part of an SIC or a part of several SIC industries. Data in this table are shown to provide transitional information for these cases. All available data for the precursor SIC(s) are shown. Even if only a part of an SIC is included in the NAICS, *all* data for the SIC are reproduced. If the SIC industry is not marked as being a part (pt) of the NAICS, the entire industry is embedded in the NAICS data. The SIC composition of the new industry provides some hints of the relative importance of its "ancestors." Data marked with a 'p' are projected. Projections begin with 1982 data. Data earlier than 1990 are not shown but are reflected in the projections.

SIC	Industry	1990	1991	1992	1993	1994	1995	1996	1997
7379	**Computer Related Services, nec (pt)**								
	Establishments (number)	6,823	8,133	8,722	11,174	13,820	17,688	16,728p	18,269p
	Employment (thousands)	51.2	59.0	57.7	76.4	87.7	115.0	107.4p	116.3p
	Revenues ($ million)	4,537.0	4,894.0	6,234.0	7,845.0	10,285.0	13,176.0	16,504.0	11,341.1p

Source: *Economic Census of the United States*, 1992, annual surveys of economic sectors conducted by the Bureau of the Census, and estimates or projections based on the 1982-1992 period; not all data are shown. 'e' marks estimates made by the editors; 'p' indicates projections based on time series. A dash (-) indicates that data for this SIC or year were not available. The abbreviation (pt) next to the industry name indicates that only a part of the industry is present within the NAICS data. If no (pt) is shown, the entire industry is contained within the NAICS data.

SELECTED RATIOS

For 1997	Avg. of Information	Analyzed Industry	Index	For 1997	Avg. of Information	Analyzed Industry	Index
Employees per establishment	9	4	51	Payroll per establishment	372,545	224,152	60
Revenue per establishment	958,337	516,359	54	Payroll as % of revenue	39	43	112
Revenue per employee	111,029	116,937	105	Payroll per employee	43,162	50,763	118

Sources: Same as General Statistics. The 'Average' column represents the average for the industry sector, in 1997, where the currently shown industry is classified. The Index shows the relationship between the Average and the Analyzed Industry. For example, 100 means that they are equal; 500 that the Analyzed Industry is five times the average; 50 means that the Analyzed Industry is half the national average. The abbreviation 'na' is used to show that data are 'not available'.

LEADING COMPANIES

No company data available for this industry.

LOCATION BY STATE AND REGIONAL CONCENTRATION

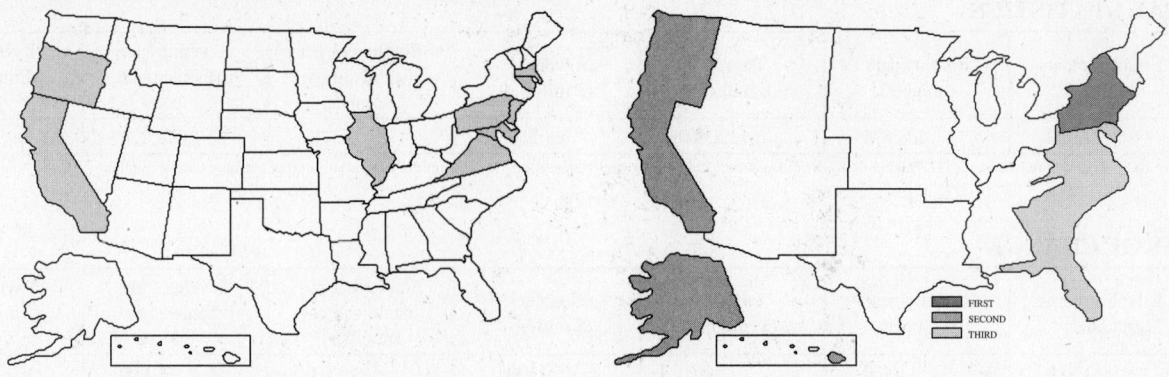

FIRST
SECOND
THIRD

INDUSTRY DATA BY STATE

State	Establishments Total (number)	Establishments % of U.S.	Employment Total (number)	Employment % of U.S.	Employment Per Estab.	Payroll Total ($ mil.)	Payroll Per Empl. ($)	Revenues Total ($ mil.)	Revenues % of U.S.	Revenues Per Estab. ($)
California	1,005	12.0	4,917	13.2	5	265.6	54,009	701.6	16.2	698,094
New Jersey	756	9.0	3,038	8.2	4	231.5	76,185	484.2	11.2	640,493
New York	799	9.5	2,437	6.6	3	148.7	61,023	309.7	7.1	387,641
Virginia	322	3.8	2,554	6.9	8	136.2	53,312	279.3	6.4	867,438
Texas	498	5.9	2,658	7.2	5	123.1	46,301	270.1	6.2	542,444
Pennsylvania	294	3.5	1,260	3.4	4	69.9	55,508	245.3	5.7	834,514
Illinois	537	6.4	1,947	5.2	4	98.1	50,408	240.2	5.5	447,387
Florida	510	6.1	1,672	4.5	3	79.9	47,773	185.7	4.3	364,133
Massachusetts	300	3.6	1,217	3.3	4	72.5	59,582	167.7	3.9	558,890
Maryland	252	3.0	1,257	3.4	5	66.8	53,174	140.9	3.2	559,266
Ohio	234	2.8	972	2.6	4	43.5	44,760	98.7	2.3	421,816
Michigan	187	2.2	789	2.1	4	40.8	51,712	94.1	2.2	502,947
Washington	165	2.0	615	1.7	4	39.0	63,418	87.1	2.0	528,176
Oregon	98	1.2	962	2.6	10	33.2	34,560	72.2	1.7	737,204
Connecticut	119	1.4	390	1.1	3	23.1	59,354	55.6	1.3	466,874
Arizona	126	1.5	393	1.1	3	15.9	40,519	49.3	1.1	390,873
Missouri	121	1.4	568	1.5	5	23.8	41,917	47.0	1.1	388,132
Kansas	68	0.8	389	1.0	6	14.9	38,337	34.5	0.8	507,750
Indiana	99	1.2	359	1.0	4	12.5	34,783	28.9	0.7	291,889
Oklahoma	53	0.6	664	1.8	13	10.7	16,166	23.7	0.5	447,396
Utah	45	0.5	419	1.1	9	8.5	20,289	22.6	0.5	501,222
Alabama	71	0.8	245	0.7	3	9.9	40,408	21.2	0.5	298,859
New Mexico	27	0.3	362	1.0	13	11.9	32,796	18.1	0.4	669,111
Idaho	24	0.3	156	0.4	7	7.7	49,571	17.4	0.4	723,542
Rhode Island	21	0.2	47	0.1	2	3.6	76,468	12.1	0.3	576,714
Louisiana	31	0.4	150	0.4	5	6.4	42,587	11.1	0.3	359,387
Kentucky	41	0.5	151	0.4	4	4.0	26,371	9.2	0.2	224,073
Nebraska	35	0.4	89	0.2	3	3.4	38,056	8.1	0.2	232,800
Delaware	33	0.4	50	0.1	2	2.1	41,780	5.3	0.1	161,727
D.C.	17	0.2	74	0.2	4	2.5	34,405	5.1	0.1	299,647
South Carolina	31	0.4	60	0.2	2	2.0	33,983	4.2	0.1	134,129
Arkansas	19	0.2	41	0.1	2	1.2	28,610	3.5	0.1	181,789
Mississippi	16	0.2	32	0.1	2	0.6	19,937	2.4	0.1	149,250
South Dakota	8	0.1	7	0.0	1	0.3	46,571	1.4	0.0	175,375
Hawaii	8	0.1	14	0.0	2	0.6	39,500	1.4	0.0	173,500
West Virginia	8	0.1	16	0.0	2	0.4	23,875	1.0	0.0	121,500
Georgia	354	4.2	1,750*	-	-	(D)	-	(D)	-	-
Minnesota	316	3.8	1,750*	-	-	(D)	-	(D)	-	-
Colorado	239	2.8	750*	-	-	(D)	-	(D)	-	-
North Carolina	196	2.3	1,750*	-	-	(D)	-	(D)	-	-
Wisconsin	85	1.0	175*	-	-	(D)	-	(D)	-	-
Tennessee	66	0.8	375*	-	-	(D)	-	(D)	-	-
New Hampshire	52	0.6	175*	-	-	(D)	-	(D)	-	-
Nevada	41	0.5	60*	-	-	(D)	-	(D)	-	-
Iowa	28	0.3	60*	-	-	(D)	-	(D)	-	-
Maine	15	0.2	60*	-	-	(D)	-	(D)	-	-
Vermont	10	0.1	10*	-	-	(D)	-	(D)	-	-
Alaska	9	0.1	60*	-	-	(D)	-	(D)	-	-
Montana	8	0.1	10*	-	-	(D)	-	(D)	-	-
North Dakota	4	-	1,750*	-	-	(D)	-	(D)	-	-
Wyoming	4	-	10*	-	-	(D)	-	(D)	-	-

Source: 1997 *Economic Census*. The states are in descending order of revenues or establishments (if revenue data are missing for the majority). The symbol (D) appears when data are withheld to prevent disclosure of competitive information. States marked with (D) are sorted by number of establishments. A dash (-) indicates that the data element cannot be calculated. * indicates the midpoint of a range; 175, for example is the range 100-249. Shaded *states* on the state map indicate those states which have proportionately greater representation in the industry than would be indicated by the state's population; the ratio is based on total revenues or number of establishments. Shaded *regions* indicate where the industry is regionally most concentrated.

NAICS 541611 - ADMINISTRATIVE MANAGEMENT AND GENERAL MANAGEMENT CONSULTING SERVICES

GENERAL STATISTICS

Year	Establishments (number)	Employment (number)	Payroll ($ million)	Revenues ($ million)	Employees per Establishment (number)	Revenues per Establishment ($)	Payroll per Employee ($)
1997	27,399	208,674	12,739.0	28,556.0	7.6	1,042,228	61,047

Source: *Economic Census of the United States*, 1997. This is a newly defined industry. Data for prior years were unavailable at the time of publication but may become available over time.

INDICES OF CHANGE

Year	Establishments (number)	Employment (number)	Payroll ($ million)	Revenues ($ million)	Employees per Establishment (number)	Revenues per Establishment ($)	Payroll per Employee ($)
1997	100.0	100.0	100.0	100.0	100.0	100.0	100.0

Sources: Same as General Statistics. The values shown reflect change from the base year, 1997. Values above 100 mean greater than 1997, values below 100 mean less than 1997, and a value of 100 in the 1982-96 or 1998-2001 period means same as 1997. Values followed by a 'p' are projections by the editors; 'e' stands for extrapolation. Data are the most recent available at this level of detail.

SIC INDUSTRIES RELATED TO NAICS 541611

Each new NAICS code represents an industry that used to be part of an SIC or a part of several SIC industries. Data in this table are shown to provide transitional information for these cases. All available data for the precursor SIC(s) are shown. Even if only a part of an SIC is included in the NAICS, *all* data for the SIC are reproduced. If the SIC industry is not marked as being a part (pt) of the NAICS, the entire industry is embedded in the NAICS data. The SIC composition of the new industry provides some hints of the relative importance of its "ancestors." Data marked with a 'p' are projected. Projections begin with 1982 data. Data earlier than 1990 are not shown but are reflected in the projections.

SIC	Industry	1990	1991	1992	1993	1994	1995	1996	1997
8742	**Management Consulting Services (pt)**								
	Establishments (number)	24,512	27,162	34,104	35,829	37,517	41,315	40,920p	42,928p
	Employment (thousands)	226.0	243.8	215.4	252.9	294.9	351.7	323.9p	339.6p
	Revenues ($ million)	28,931.0	29,839.0	31,913.0	34,516.0	38,506.0	46,430.0	53,716.0	53,997.3p

Source: *Economic Census of the United States*, 1992, annual surveys of economic sectors conducted by the Bureau of the Census, and estimates or projections based on the 1982-1992 period; not all data are shown. 'e' marks estimates made by the editors; 'p' indicates projections based on time series. A dash (-) indicates that data for this SIC or year were not available. The abbreviation (pt) next to the industry name indicates that only a part of the industry is present within the NAICS data. If no (pt) is shown, the entire industry is contained within the NAICS data.

SELECTED RATIOS

For 1997	Avg. of Information	Analyzed Industry	Index	For 1997	Avg. of Information	Analyzed Industry	Index
Employees per establishment	9	8	88	Payroll per establishment	372,545	464,944	125
Revenue per establishment	958,337	1,042,228	109	Payroll as % of revenue	39	45	115
Revenue per employee	111,029	136,845	123	Payroll per employee	43,162	61,047	141

Sources: Same as General Statistics. The 'Average' column represents the average for the industry sector, in 1997, where the currently shown industry is classified. The Index shows the relationship between the Average and the Analyzed Industry. For example, 100 means that they are equal; 500 that the Analyzed Industry is five times the average; 50 means that the Analyzed Industry is half the national average. The abbreviation 'na' is used to show that data are 'not available'.

LEADING COMPANIES   Number shown: **75**   Total sales ($ mil): **4,823**   Total employment (000): **219.7**

Company Name	Address				CEO Name	Phone	Co. Type	Sales ($ mil)	Empl. (000)
Knowledge Universe Inc.	150 Shoreline	Redwood City	CA	94065	Thomas Kalinske	650-628-3000	R	1,200	8.0
The Contact Group Inc.	1029 Plaxton Dr	Bethel Park	PA	15102		412-831-1978	N	600	<0.1
International Technology Corp.	23456 Hawthorne	Torrance	CA	90505		310-378-8833	N	421	2.8
The Wyatt Co.	6707 Democracy	Bethesda	MD	20817		301-581-4600	N	412	3.5
Korn/Ferry International	200 Park Ave	New York	NY	10166		212-687-1834	N	300	1.4
Proudfoot Co.	1700 Palm Beach	W. Palm Beach	FL	33401		561-697-9600	N	200	0.8
Calle' and Co.	132 Round Hill Rd	Greenwich	CT	06831		203-661-4889	N	105	0.1
Erskine Stone and James	300 E Washington	Effingham	IL	62401		217-347-7171	N	100	<0.1
Marks Management Services Inc.	31000 Telegraph Rd	Bingham Farms	MI	48025		248-646-1007	N	90	<0.1
MCRB Service Bureau	9171 Oso Ave	Chatsworth	CA	91311	Dick Yung	818-407-4300	R	89*	0.3
Economics Research Associates	10990 Wilshire	Los Angeles	CA	90024		310-477-9585	N	86	0.1
ABL Transportation	3746 Mt Diablo	Lafayette	CA	94549		510-284-7145	N	76	<0.1
Aon Consulting, Human	400 RenCen	Detroit	MI	48243		313-259-0116	N	70	0.5
Thomas Group Interactive	5215 N O'Connor	Irving	TX	75039	J Thomas Williams	972-869-3400	P	68	0.3
NCS International Inc.	9910 N 48th St	Omaha	NE	68152		402-453-9292	N	65	<0.1
AON Consulting	123 N Wacker Dr	Chicago	IL	60606		312-701-4055	N	58	40.0
CSP Associates Inc.	55 Cambridge Pky	Cambridge	MA	02142		617-225-2828	N	53	<0.1
Soza and Co.	8550 Arlington Blvd	Fairfax	VA	22031	William Soza	703-560-9477	R	48	0.4
Horton International Inc.	10 Tower Ln	Avon	CT	06001	Franklin Brown	860-674-8701	N	40	0.2
Craig Corp.	550 S Hope St	Los Angeles	CA	90071	James J Cotter	213-239-0555	P	34	0.4
W.C. Richey	5147 S Angela Rd	Memphis	TN	38117		901-368-3333	N	28	<0.1
M2Direct Inc.	4830 W Kennedy	Tampa	FL	33609	John P Kelly	813-289-5411	R	26	0.3
Employ America	6950 Squibb Rd	Shaw Msn	KS	66202		913-831-0300	N	25	<0.1
Henry Gill Inc.	1225 17th St	Denver	CO	80202		303-296-4100	N	25	<0.1
Pyramid Consulting Group	590 Howard St	San Francisco	CA	94105	Jim Burns	415-365-8800	S	21*	<0.1
Howard/Marquis Group	360 N Sepulveda	El Segundo	CA	90245		310-364-0224	N	20	<0.1
TVG Inc.	520 Virginia Dr	Fort Washington	PA	19034		215-646-7200	N	20	0.1
Weatherby Health Care	25 Van Zant St	Norwalk	CT	06855		203-866-1144	N	20	0.2
Menlo Logistics Inc.	1 Lagoon Dr	Redwood City	CA	94065	John Williford	650-596-4000	S	20	1.8
Chemtech Ltd.	781 Pearson St	Des Plaines	IL	60016		847-699-8800	N	18	<0.1
Cortex Communications Inc.	5313 Johns Rd	Tampa	FL	33634	Steve Huber	813-261-0062	S	18*	<0.1
Quadel Consulting Corporation	1250 Eye St NW	Washington	DC	20005		202-789-2500	N	18	<0.1
Linkage Inc.	One Forbes Rd	Lexington	MA	02421		781-862-3157	R	16	0.1
PricewaterhouseCoopers	1301 Av Americas	New York	NY	10019	Nicholas G Moore	212-596-7000	R	15	155.0
American Management Services	245 Winter St 400	Waltham	MA	02154		781-487-0400	N	15	0.1
Corporate Branding L.L.C.	470 west Ave	Stamford	CT	06902		203-327-6333	N	15	<0.1
Management Consulting	2000 Corp Ridge	McLean	VA	22102		703-506-4600	N	15	<0.1
Meritus Consulting Services	400 Park Ave	New York	NY	10022		212-745-9100	N	15	<0.1
Netscape Communications	4017 Washington Rd	McMurray	PA	15317		412-818-7656	N	15	0.3
TeamWorks International	56 Forest Rd	Randolph	NJ	07869		973-328-0020	N	15	<0.1
The Consulting Team Inc	1601 Forum Pl	W. Palm Beach	FL	33401		561-478-0022	N	14	0.1
Directech Corp.	10200 Linn Station	Louisville	KY	40223	Barry Silverstein	502-394-7600	R	13	<0.1
American Payroll Association	30 E 33rd St	New York	NY	10016		212-686-2030	N	13	<0.1
Consulting Partners Inc.	12700 Hillcrest Dr	Dallas	TX	75230		972-386-7858	N	13	0.1
Carnes Communications Inc.	1140 Welsh Rd	North Wales	PA	19454	Douglas Carnes	215-412-3900	S	12*	<0.1
Corporate Personnel Consultants	3700 Latrobe Dr	Charlotte	NC	28222		704-366-1800	N	12	<0.1
Donald L. Sheppard Inc.	130 N Brand Blvd	Glendale	CA	91203		818-247-9877	N	12	<0.1
MACI	2800 Shirlington Rd	Arlington	VA	22206		703-379-7080	N	11	0.4
Fairfaxx Corp.	17 High St	Norwalk	CT	06851		203-838-8300	N	11	<0.1
Network Direct Inc.	5643 Lighthouse Ln	Friday Harbor	WA	98250		360-378-3123	N	11	<0.1
Performance Strategies Inc.	PO Box 160	Upland	CA	91785		909-985-3000	N	11	<0.1
Access Management Corp.	PO Box 12059	Charlotte	NC	28220		704-554-9000	N	10	<0.1
Alamo Learning Systems	3160 Crow Canyon	San Ramon	CA	94583		925-277-1818	N	10	<0.1
Decision Point Marketing Inc.	4410-99 Providence	Winston-Salem	NC	27106		910-759-3038	N	10	<0.1
Information Resource Group	35200 Dequindre	Sterling Heights	MI	48310		810-978-3000	N	10	0.1
Robert E. Nolan Company Inc.	90 Hopmeadow St	Simsbury	CT	06070		860-658-1941	N	10	<0.1
The Atlanta Consulting Group	1600 Parkwood Cir	Atlanta	GA	30339		770-952-8000	N	10	<0.1
The Chasm Group	411 Borel Ave	San Mateo	CA	94402		650-312-1940	N	10	<0.1
Cheskin and Masten/Image Net	255 Shoreline Dr	Redwood City	CA	94065		415-802-2100	N	9	<0.1
Atlantic Resources Corp.	PO Box 3322	Reston	VA	20195		703-392-0918	N	9	<0.1
Charles Abbott Associates Inc.	371 Van Ness Way	Torrance	CA	90501		310-212-5778	N	9	<0.1
Quantum Computer Consultants	21415 Civic Center	Southfield	MI	48076		248-353-7030	N	8	<0.1
Automotive Service Consultants	2131 Data Office Dr	Birmingham	AL	35244		205-987-9222	N	8	0.1
International Technomic	500 Skokie Blvd	Northbrook	IL	60062		847-291-1212	N	8	0.1
PM Solutions Inc.	5114 Bond Ave	Drexel Hill	PA	19026		610-853-3679	N	8	<0.1
Princeton Economic Research Inc.	1700 Rockville Pike	Rockville	MD	20852		301-881-0650	N	8	<0.1
Great Lakes Strategies	2100 E Maple Rd	Birmingham	MI	48009		248-614-4600	N	7	<0.1
Paramount Inc.	31811 Vine St	Willowick	OH	44095		216-585-2560	N	7	0.2
Rue and Associates Inc.	PO Box 640	Mechanicsville	VA	23111		804-730-7455	N	7	<0.1
NTL Institute for Applied	300 N Lee, Ste 300	Alexandria	VA	22314		703-548-1500	N	7	<0.1
Suhr and Associates Inc.	2712 NE 31st Ct	Lighthouse Point	FL	33064		954-946-9062	N	6	<0.1
Meridian Resource Corp.	10 E Doty St	Madison	WI	53703		608-258-3350	N	6	0.1
Moneco Group	73 E Hanover Ave	Morristown	NJ	07962		201-267-1953	N	6	<0.1
Project Management Services Inc.	100 Hannover	Atlanta	GA	30350		770-641-1000	N	6	<0.1
Managed Business Solutions	PO Box 2281	Fort Collins	CO	80522	Jim Franzen	970-224-1016	R	5	<0.1

Source: Ward's Business Directory of U.S. Private and Public Companies, Volumes 1 and 2, 2000. The company type code used is as follows: P - Public, R - Private, S - Subsidiary, D - Division, J - Joint Venture, A - Affiliate, G - Group, N - Company type not reported. Sales are in millions of dollars, employees are in thousands. An asterisk (*) indicates an estimated sales volume. The symbol < stands for 'less than'. Company names and addresses are truncated, in some cases, to fit into the available space.

LOCATION BY STATE AND REGIONAL CONCENTRATION

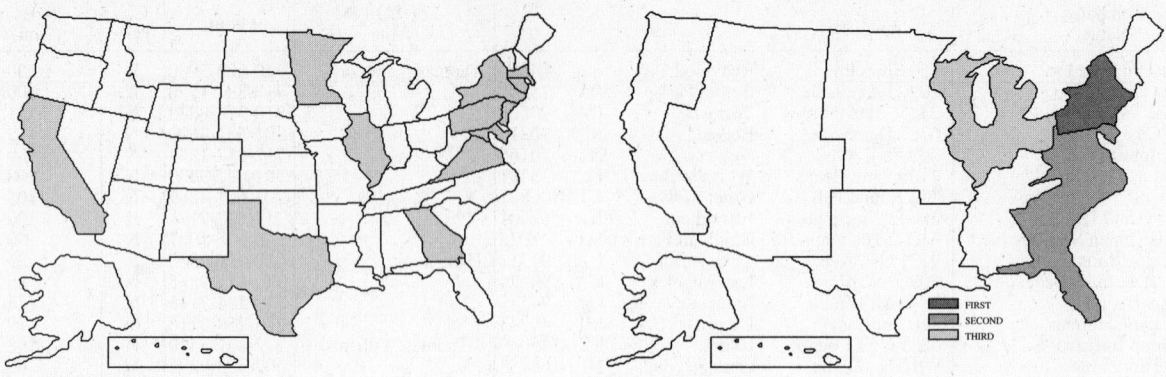

INDUSTRY DATA BY STATE

State	Establishments Total (number)	% of U.S.	Employment Total (number)	% of U.S.	Per Estab.	Payroll Total ($ mil.)	Per Empl. ($)	Revenues Total ($ mil.)	% of U.S.	Per Estab. ($)
California	3,252	11.9	25,557	12.2	8	1,601.7	62,671	3,781.5	13.2	1,162,818
New York	1,953	7.1	18,228	8.7	9	1,536.4	84,285	3,319.3	11.6	1,699,615
Illinois	1,591	5.8	20,079	9.6	13	1,362.4	67,851	2,539.7	8.9	1,596,285
Texas	1,739	6.3	15,067	7.2	9	912.2	60,542	2,020.9	7.1	1,162,123
Massachusetts	1,021	3.7	11,113	5.3	11	977.1	87,928	1,861.9	6.5	1,823,646
Pennsylvania	1,101	4.0	11,240	5.4	10	617.6	54,944	1,569.8	5.5	1,425,797
New Jersey	1,124	4.1	8,018	3.8	7	536.9	66,961	1,357.6	4.8	1,207,829
Florida	2,247	8.2	10,423	5.0	5	565.2	54,223	1,282.3	4.5	570,660
Virginia	1,030	3.8	12,571	6.0	12	624.1	49,642	1,243.3	4.4	1,207,098
D.C.	291	1.1	6,871	3.3	24	400.5	58,291	1,071.4	3.8	3,681,656
Ohio	859	3.1	7,113	3.4	8	429.4	60,374	1,055.5	3.7	1,228,761
Georgia	874	3.2	7,837	3.8	9	482.5	61,565	1,036.3	3.6	1,185,737
Michigan	860	3.1	5,122	2.5	6	257.3	50,241	662.2	2.3	770,003
Connecticut	479	1.7	3,434	1.6	7	303.1	88,270	620.9	2.2	1,296,159
Maryland	731	2.7	5,001	2.4	7	248.3	49,644	558.5	2.0	764,066
Minnesota	602	2.2	4,023	1.9	7	225.7	56,090	522.2	1.8	867,495
Missouri	446	1.6	3,058	1.5	7	149.6	48,923	385.3	1.3	863,942
North Carolina	579	2.1	2,678	1.3	5	128.8	48,090	365.5	1.3	631,195
Colorado	673	2.5	3,046	1.5	5	163.8	53,787	345.7	1.2	513,603
Washington	606	2.2	2,378	1.1	4	137.4	57,765	339.0	1.2	559,363
Tennessee	382	1.4	2,937	1.4	8	146.8	49,992	325.3	1.1	851,466
Arizona	564	2.1	3,513	1.7	6	135.7	38,627	301.8	1.1	535,176
Wisconsin	360	1.3	1,975	0.9	5	96.5	48,872	248.9	0.9	691,422
Kansas	199	0.7	1,011	0.5	5	47.8	47,230	177.5	0.6	892,136
Indiana	363	1.3	1,176	0.6	3	51.7	43,946	149.4	0.5	411,556
Nevada	304	1.1	1,132	0.5	4	54.9	48,454	148.3	0.5	487,707
Oregon	304	1.1	964	0.5	3	47.0	48,728	129.9	0.5	427,355
Utah	206	0.8	1,359	0.7	7	65.1	47,875	128.3	0.4	622,990
South Carolina	225	0.8	1,214	0.6	5	59.2	48,773	127.1	0.4	565,022
Louisiana	279	1.0	1,543	0.7	6	41.4	26,810	108.3	0.4	388,323
Oklahoma	225	0.8	1,152	0.6	5	41.7	36,210	94.7	0.3	420,853
Arkansas	109	0.4	733	0.4	7	31.0	42,291	90.1	0.3	826,945
Alabama	190	0.7	1,045	0.5	6	40.7	38,911	76.3	0.3	401,495
Kentucky	198	0.7	688	0.3	3	31.2	45,372	66.4	0.2	335,444
New Hampshire	161	0.6	433	0.2	3	29.2	67,379	63.7	0.2	395,503
Mississippi	98	0.4	672	0.3	7	23.5	34,914	49.9	0.2	508,837
New Mexico	113	0.4	556	0.3	5	18.9	34,065	42.5	0.1	376,106
Iowa	145	0.5	621	0.3	4	13.5	21,786	40.3	0.1	278,034
Nebraska	104	0.4	521	0.2	5	14.6	27,996	33.7	0.1	323,962
West Virginia	65	0.2	487	0.2	7	14.5	29,723	30.4	0.1	468,246
Maine	107	0.4	256	0.1	2	11.3	44,125	26.8	0.1	250,019
Idaho	75	0.3	302	0.1	4	9.6	31,781	26.4	0.1	351,413
Rhode Island	80	0.3	218	0.1	3	11.3	51,890	25.7	0.1	321,100
Hawaii	77	0.3	219	0.1	3	8.4	38,511	22.9	0.1	298,000
Delaware	98	0.4	231	0.1	2	8.7	37,584	16.8	0.1	171,663
Montana	78	0.3	202	0.1	3	6.4	31,767	16.4	0.1	210,667
Alaska	39	0.1	103	0.0	3	4.2	41,068	16.2	0.1	416,333
Vermont	69	0.3	133	0.1	2	4.4	33,263	11.0	0.0	159,812
North Dakota	33	0.1	249	0.1	8	4.3	17,430	9.3	0.0	282,727
South Dakota	50	0.2	117	0.1	2	3.5	30,205	7.8	0.0	155,840
Wyoming	41	0.1	55	0.0	1	2.0	37,036	5.3	0.0	128,268

Source: 1997 *Economic Census*. The states are in descending order of revenues or establishments (if revenue data are missing for the majority). The symbol (D) appears when data are withheld to prevent disclosure of competitive information. States marked with (D) are sorted by number of establishments. A dash (-) indicates that the data element cannot be calculated. * indicates the midpoint of a range; 175, for example is the range 100-249. Shaded *states* on the state map indicate those states which have proportionately greater representation in the industry than would be indicated by the state's population; the ratio is based on total revenues or number of establishments. Shaded *regions* indicate where the industry is regionally most concentrated.

NAICS 541612 - HUMAN RESOURCES AND EXECUTIVE SEARCH CONSULTING SERVICES

GENERAL STATISTICS

Year	Establishments (number)	Employment (number)	Payroll ($ million)	Revenues ($ million)	Employees per Establishment (number)	Revenues per Establishment ($)	Payroll per Employee ($)
1997	14,788	99,719	5,160.0	10,713.0	6.7	724,439	51,745

Source: Economic Census of the United States, 1997. This is a newly defined industry. Data for prior years were unavailable at the time of publication but may become available over time.

INDICES OF CHANGE

Year	Establishments (number)	Employment (number)	Payroll ($ million)	Revenues ($ million)	Employees per Establishment (number)	Revenues per Establishment ($)	Payroll per Employee ($)
1997	100.0	100.0	100.0	100.0	100.0	100.0	100.0

Sources: Same as General Statistics. The values shown reflect change from the base year, 1997. Values above 100 mean greater than 1997, values below 100 mean less than 1997, and a value of 100 in the 1982-96 or 1998-2001 period means same as 1997. Values followed by a 'p' are projections by the editors; 'e' stands for extrapolation. Data are the most recent available at this level of detail.

SIC INDUSTRIES RELATED TO NAICS 541612

Each new NAICS code represents an industry that used to be part of an SIC or a part of several SIC industries. Data in this table are shown to provide transitional information for these cases. All available data for the precursor SIC(s) are shown. Even if only a part of an SIC is included in the NAICS, *all* data for the SIC are reproduced. If the SIC industry is not marked as being a part (pt) of the NAICS, the entire industry is embedded in the NAICS data. The SIC composition of the new industry provides some hints of the relative importance of its "ancestors." Data marked with a 'p' are projected. Projections begin with 1982 data. Data earlier than 1990 are not shown but are reflected in the projections.

SIC	Industry	1990	1991	1992	1993	1994	1995	1996	1997
7361	**Employment Agencies (pt)**								
	Establishments (number)	12,846	12,750	12,146	12,423	12,474	13,150	13,167p	13,330p
	Employment (thousands)	246.9	261.2	132.8	174.5	199.6	249.3	244.3p	254.7p
	Revenues ($ million)	6,160.0	5,153.0	4,981.0	5,624.0	6,541.0	7,730.0	8,945.0	8,171.2p
8742	**Management Consulting Services (pt)**								
	Establishments (number)	24,512	27,162	34,104	35,829	37,517	41,315	40,920p	42,928p
	Employment (thousands)	226.0	243.8	215.4	252.9	294.9	351.7	323.9p	339.6p
	Revenues ($ million)	28,931.0	29,839.0	31,913.0	34,516.0	38,506.0	46,430.0	53,716.0	53,997.3p
8999	**Services, nec (pt)**								
	Establishments (number)	-	-	14,587	-	-	-	-	-
	Employment (thousands)	-	-	81.1	-	-	-	-	-
	Revenues ($ million)	-	-	7,966.2	-	-	-	-	-

Source: Economic Census of the United States, 1992, annual surveys of economic sectors conducted by the Bureau of the Census, and estimates or projections based on the 1982-1992 period; not all data are shown. 'e' marks estimates made by the editors; 'p' indicates projections based on time series. A dash (-) indicates that data for this SIC or year were not available. The abbreviation (pt) next to the industry name indicates that only a part of the industry is present within the NAICS data. If no (pt) is shown, the entire industry is contained within the NAICS data.

SELECTED RATIOS

For 1997	Avg. of Information	Analyzed Industry	Index	For 1997	Avg. of Information	Analyzed Industry	Index
Employees per establishment	9	7	78	Payroll per establishment	372,545	348,932	94
Revenue per establishment	958,337	724,439	76	Payroll as % of revenue	39	48	124
Revenue per employee	111,029	107,432	97	Payroll per employee	43,162	51,745	120

Sources: Same as General Statistics. The 'Average' column represents the average for the industry sector, in 1997, where the currently shown industry is classified. The Index shows the relationship between the Average and the Analyzed Industry. For example, 100 means that they are equal; 500 that the Analyzed Industry is five times the average; 50 means that the Analyzed Industry is half the national average. The abbreviation 'na' is used to show that data are 'not available'.

LEADING COMPANIES

No company data available for this industry.

LOCATION BY STATE AND REGIONAL CONCENTRATION

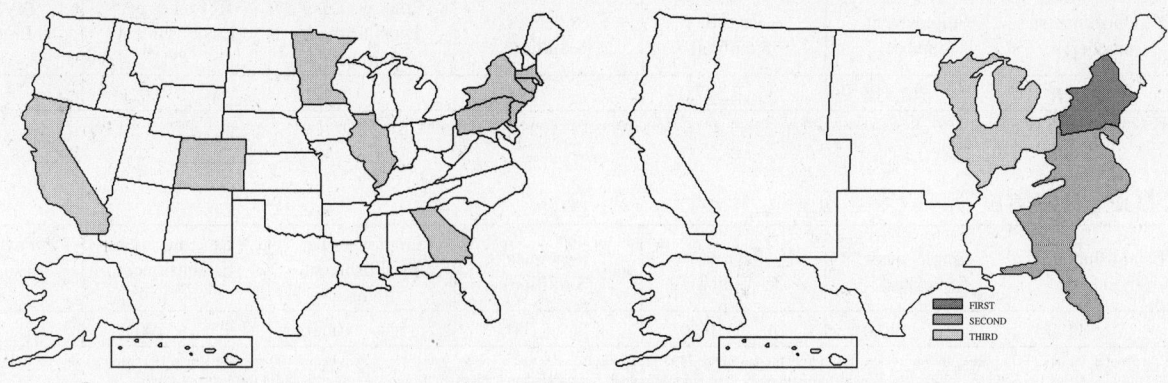

INDUSTRY DATA BY STATE

State	Establishments Total (number)	% of U.S.	Employment Total (number)	% of U.S.	Per Estab.	Payroll Total ($ mil.)	Per Empl. ($)	Revenues Total ($ mil.)	% of U.S.	Per Estab. ($)
New York	1,413	9.6	10,288	10.3	7	726.0	70,566	1,490.3	13.9	1,054,680
California	1,802	12.2	13,151	13.2	7	666.1	50,649	1,381.4	12.9	766,619
Illinois	1,061	7.2	8,378	8.4	8	481.4	57,465	936.9	8.7	883,020
Texas	961	6.5	6,392	6.4	7	338.7	52,992	699.9	6.5	728,332
New Jersey	729	4.9	4,793	4.8	7	248.1	51,764	538.6	5.0	738,781
Pennsylvania	635	4.3	5,003	5.0	8	249.4	49,842	521.3	4.9	820,898
Georgia	559	3.8	3,807	3.8	7	233.5	61,328	499.3	4.7	893,161
Massachusetts	518	3.5	3,471	3.5	7	242.8	69,963	496.1	4.6	957,774
Florida	852	5.8	4,785	4.8	6	214.8	44,901	467.0	4.4	548,082
Ohio	554	3.7	5,711	5.7	10	206.4	36,142	423.6	4.0	764,569
Connecticut	343	2.3	2,359	2.4	7	178.1	75,488	327.4	3.1	954,644
Minnesota	374	2.5	2,064	2.1	6	103.1	49,939	226.7	2.1	606,021
Virginia	414	2.8	1,970	2.0	5	108.0	54,820	226.0	2.1	546,005
Michigan	413	2.8	2,670	2.7	6	109.9	41,166	218.1	2.0	528,148
North Carolina	413	2.8	2,375	2.4	6	107.2	45,131	217.5	2.0	526,557
Missouri	258	1.7	2,620	2.6	10	102.0	38,915	207.9	1.9	805,922
D.C.	80	0.5	1,170	1.2	15	89.0	76,071	205.1	1.9	2,563,600
Washington	293	2.0	1,983	2.0	7	91.5	46,134	198.3	1.9	676,771
Maryland	320	2.2	1,640	1.6	5	81.4	49,612	172.1	1.6	537,675
Colorado	323	2.2	1,619	1.6	5	75.8	46,822	165.9	1.5	513,613
Arizona	238	1.6	1,438	1.4	6	58.4	40,606	132.5	1.2	556,592
Wisconsin	240	1.6	1,024	1.0	4	49.5	48,352	114.4	1.1	476,742
Tennessee	173	1.2	1,289	1.3	7	46.1	35,726	97.2	0.9	562,098
Indiana	217	1.5	1,450	1.5	7	46.9	32,326	92.9	0.9	427,991
Kansas	112	0.8	1,141	1.1	10	49.0	42,979	91.1	0.9	813,143
Oregon	153	1.0	694	0.7	5	30.1	43,369	68.0	0.6	444,529
Kentucky	97	0.7	733	0.7	8	31.2	42,548	59.3	0.6	610,959
South Carolina	164	1.1	717	0.7	4	26.0	36,294	54.0	0.5	329,244
Utah	74	0.5	366	0.4	5	15.7	42,822	41.9	0.4	566,838
Rhode Island	59	0.4	545	0.5	9	19.1	35,088	35.0	0.3	594,051
Alabama	98	0.7	654	0.7	7	18.3	28,005	34.7	0.3	354,561
Nebraska	74	0.5	351	0.4	5	14.9	42,322	33.8	0.3	456,797
New Hampshire	88	0.6	289	0.3	3	15.8	54,782	29.6	0.3	335,989
Oklahoma	85	0.6	438	0.4	5	12.4	28,253	28.2	0.3	331,776
Louisiana	78	0.5	288	0.3	4	9.8	34,142	26.2	0.2	335,821
Iowa	85	0.6	271	0.3	3	9.2	33,878	20.9	0.2	246,412
New Mexico	41	0.3	160	0.2	4	6.9	42,850	19.9	0.2	486,366
Nevada	66	0.4	357	0.4	5	7.7	21,560	18.8	0.2	284,424
Maine	44	0.3	184	0.2	4	6.5	35,109	15.0	0.1	341,455
Mississippi	38	0.3	143	0.1	4	5.4	38,091	14.1	0.1	371,947
Idaho	40	0.3	218	0.2	5	5.2	23,940	12.5	0.1	313,025
Hawaii	28	0.2	103	0.1	4	4.3	41,476	11.6	0.1	412,857
West Virginia	25	0.2	174	0.2	7	4.0	23,172	7.8	0.1	311,400
Vermont	38	0.3	69	0.1	2	3.4	49,435	7.6	0.1	201,289
Arkansas	39	0.3	122	0.1	3	4.0	32,451	7.5	0.1	192,256
Montana	21	0.1	107	0.1	5	2.9	26,832	6.5	0.1	310,714
Delaware	24	0.2	54	0.1	2	2.4	44,667	5.2	0.0	218,042
South Dakota	11	0.1	42	0.0	4	1.5	35,905	3.7	0.0	334,455
Alaska	6	-	11	0.0	2	0.1	13,364	2.2	0.0	360,500
North Dakota	11	0.1	26	0.0	2	0.4	13,692	0.9	0.0	84,182
Wyoming	6	-	12	0.0	2	0.2	15,417	0.6	0.0	100,833

Source: 1997 *Economic Census*. The states are in descending order of revenues or establishments (if revenue data are missing for the majority). The symbol (D) appears when data are withheld to prevent disclosure of competitive information. States marked with (D) are sorted by number of establishments. A dash (-) indicates that the data element cannot be calculated. * indicates the midpoint of a range; 175, for example is the range 100-249. Shaded *states* on the state map indicate those states which have proportionately greater representation in the industry than would be indicated by the state's population; the ratio is based on total revenues or number of establishments. Shaded *regions* indicate where the industry is regionally most concentrated.

NAICS 541613 - MARKETING CONSULTING SERVICES

GENERAL STATISTICS

Year	Establishments (number)	Employment (number)	Payroll ($ million)	Revenues ($ million)	Employees per Establishment (number)	Revenues per Establishment ($)	Payroll per Employee ($)
1997	12,498	61,418	2,547.0	7,874.0	4.9	630,021	41,470

Source: *Economic Census of the United States*, 1997. This is a newly defined industry. Data for prior years were unavailable at the time of publication but may become available over time.

INDICES OF CHANGE

Year	Establishments (number)	Employment (number)	Payroll ($ million)	Revenues ($ million)	Employees per Establishment (number)	Revenues per Establishment ($)	Payroll per Employee ($)
1997	100.0	100.0	100.0	100.0	100.0	100.0	100.0

Sources: Same as General Statistics. The values shown reflect change from the base year, 1997. Values above 100 mean greater than 1997, values below 100 mean less than 1997, and a value of 100 in the 1982-96 or 1998-2001 period means same as 1997. Values followed by a 'p' are projections by the editors; 'e' stands for extrapolation. Data are the most recent available at this level of detail.

SIC INDUSTRIES RELATED TO NAICS 541613

Each new NAICS code represents an industry that used to be part of an SIC or a part of several SIC industries. Data in this table are shown to provide transitional information for these cases. All available data for the precursor SIC(s) are shown. Even if only a part of an SIC is included in the NAICS, *all* data for the SIC are reproduced. If the SIC industry is not marked as being a part (pt) of the NAICS, the entire industry is embedded in the NAICS data. The SIC composition of the new industry provides some hints of the relative importance of its "ancestors." Data marked with a 'p' are projected. Projections begin with 1982 data. Data earlier than 1990 are not shown but are reflected in the projections.

SIC	Industry	1990	1991	1992	1993	1994	1995	1996	1997
8742	**Management Consulting Services (pt)**								
	Establishments (number)	24,512	27,162	34,104	35,829	37,517	41,315	40,920p	42,928p
	Employment (thousands)	226.0	243.8	215.4	252.9	294.9	351.7	323.9p	339.6p
	Revenues ($ million)	28,931.0	29,839.0	31,913.0	34,516.0	38,506.0	46,430.0	53,716.0	53,997.3p

Source: *Economic Census of the United States*, 1992, annual surveys of economic sectors conducted by the Bureau of the Census, and estimates or projections based on the 1982-1992 period; not all data are shown. 'e' marks estimates made by the editors; 'p' indicates projections based on time series. A dash (-) indicates that data for this SIC or year were not available. The abbreviation (pt) next to the industry name indicates that only a part of the industry is present within the NAICS data. If no (pt) is shown, the entire industry is contained within the NAICS data.

SELECTED RATIOS

For 1997	Avg. of Information	Analyzed Industry	Index	For 1997	Avg. of Information	Analyzed Industry	Index
Employees per establishment	9	5	57	Payroll per establishment	372,545	203,793	55
Revenue per establishment	958,337	630,021	66	Payroll as % of revenue	39	32	83
Revenue per employee	111,029	128,203	115	Payroll per employee	43,162	41,470	96

Sources: Same as General Statistics. The 'Average' column represents the average for the industry sector, in 1997, where the currently shown industry is classified. The Index shows the relationship between the Average and the Analyzed Industry. For example, 100 means that they are equal; 500 that the Analyzed Industry is five times the average; 50 means that the Analyzed Industry is half the national average. The abbreviation 'na' is used to show that data are 'not available'.

LEADING COMPANIES

No company data available for this industry.

LOCATION BY STATE AND REGIONAL CONCENTRATION

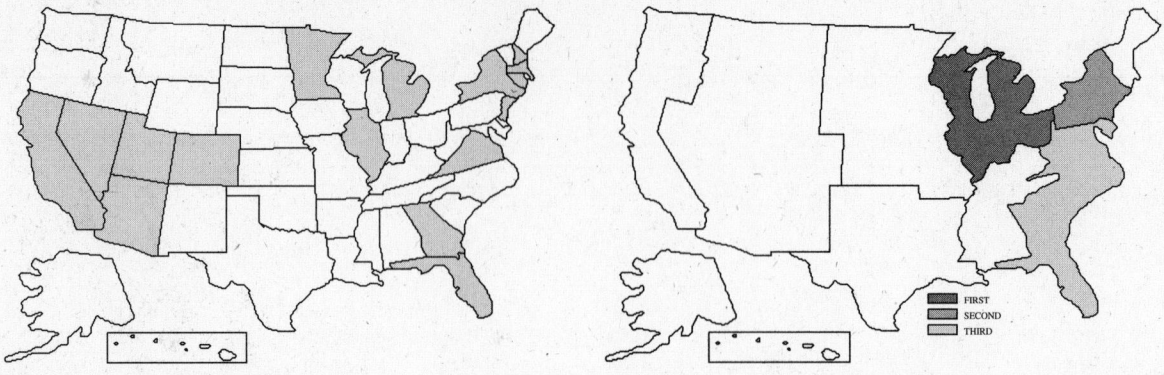

FIRST
SECOND
THIRD

INDUSTRY DATA BY STATE

State	Establishments Total (number)	% of U.S.	Employment Total (number)	% of U.S.	Per Estab.	Payroll Total ($ mil.)	Per Empl. ($)	Revenues Total ($ mil.)	% of U.S.	Per Estab. ($)
California	1,624	13.0	6,416	10.4	4	275.1	42,877	975.5	12.4	600,667
Illinois	870	7.0	8,059	13.1	9	270.7	33,592	802.0	10.2	921,792
New York	1,000	8.0	3,862	6.3	4	212.7	55,075	683.5	8.7	683,548
Florida	1,058	8.5	4,993	8.1	5	188.6	37,771	527.2	6.7	498,256
Minnesota	358	2.9	2,125	3.5	6	96.8	45,559	452.1	5.7	1,262,740
Massachusetts	446	3.6	2,868	4.7	6	138.9	48,448	423.3	5.4	949,016
New Jersey	570	4.6	4,330	7.1	8	143.7	33,188	408.0	5.2	715,868
Michigan	336	2.7	4,260	6.9	13	125.8	29,530	398.5	5.1	1,185,955
Connecticut	336	2.7	2,009	3.3	6	160.6	79,916	397.0	5.0	1,181,530
Texas	585	4.7	3,007	4.9	5	145.4	48,368	362.6	4.6	619,752
Pennsylvania	429	3.4	1,863	3.0	4	99.9	53,623	271.2	3.4	632,145
Georgia	443	3.5	1,295	2.1	3	60.9	47,054	213.8	2.7	482,528
Virginia	469	3.8	1,715	2.8	4	76.3	44,483	201.3	2.6	429,179
Ohio	388	3.1	1,253	2.0	3	52.4	41,785	151.7	1.9	390,948
Colorado	301	2.4	1,135	1.8	4	51.2	45,068	139.2	1.8	462,359
Arizona	244	2.0	1,038	1.7	4	37.2	35,858	128.2	1.6	525,287
Indiana	170	1.4	940	1.5	6	35.7	37,970	108.8	1.4	640,206
Maryland	279	2.2	800	1.3	3	33.4	41,791	107.9	1.4	386,878
Wisconsin	150	1.2	825	1.3	6	31.0	37,581	99.0	1.3	659,760
North Carolina	274	2.2	927	1.5	3	30.1	32,488	97.2	1.2	354,901
Nevada	127	1.0	694	1.1	5	24.8	35,674	89.2	1.1	702,598
Missouri	215	1.7	831	1.4	4	26.7	32,111	85.1	1.1	395,726
Washington	259	2.1	613	1.0	2	25.8	42,031	82.8	1.1	319,653
Tennessee	146	1.2	957	1.6	7	23.4	24,422	79.1	1.0	542,096
D.C.	99	0.8	382	0.6	4	25.0	65,359	70.8	0.9	715,626
Utah	99	0.8	509	0.8	5	19.6	38,424	66.9	0.9	676,253
South Carolina	100	0.8	405	0.7	4	17.0	41,899	52.5	0.7	525,460
New Hampshire	73	0.6	269	0.4	4	15.7	58,327	44.8	0.6	613,041
Kansas	109	0.9	440	0.7	4	12.5	28,418	42.7	0.5	392,128
Kentucky	90	0.7	223	0.4	2	7.9	35,489	36.2	0.5	402,267
Oregon	122	1.0	376	0.6	3	12.3	32,702	33.9	0.4	278,213
Alabama	64	0.5	154	0.3	2	6.2	40,201	27.7	0.4	433,172
Hawaii	48	0.4	184	0.3	4	6.2	33,522	25.9	0.3	540,208
Oklahoma	48	0.4	124	0.2	3	5.0	40,137	19.4	0.2	403,896
Iowa	52	0.4	203	0.3	4	6.1	29,897	19.4	0.2	372,442
Mississippi	26	0.2	85	0.1	3	3.3	38,741	16.9	0.2	651,808
Nebraska	48	0.4	103	0.2	2	5.0	48,990	14.4	0.2	299,521
Arkansas	50	0.4	88	0.1	2	3.2	36,273	13.9	0.2	277,380
New Mexico	41	0.3	70	0.1	2	3.3	46,443	12.0	0.2	291,780
Idaho	27	0.2	66	0.1	2	4.6	70,106	11.3	0.1	419,778
Rhode Island	40	0.3	103	0.2	3	4.0	39,126	11.3	0.1	282,575
Delaware	37	0.3	131	0.2	4	6.3	48,275	11.3	0.1	304,676
Maine	41	0.3	94	0.2	2	3.1	32,585	9.7	0.1	235,610
Wyoming	9	0.1	43	0.1	5	1.4	32,395	5.5	0.1	608,889
Montana	33	0.3	67	0.1	2	1.5	22,910	5.4	0.1	163,333
Vermont	29	0.2	56	0.1	2	1.8	31,643	5.3	0.1	184,241
West Virginia	29	0.2	203	0.3	7	2.4	11,611	5.3	0.1	181,586
South Dakota	17	0.1	39	0.1	2	0.8	19,667	2.8	0.0	162,412
Louisiana	67	0.5	175*	-	-	(D)	-	(D)	-	-
Alaska	12	0.1	10*	-	-	(D)	-	(D)	-	-
North Dakota	11	0.1	60*	-	-	(D)	-	(D)	-	-

Source: 1997 *Economic Census*. The states are in descending order of revenues or establishments (if revenue data are missing for the majority). The symbol (D) appears when data are withheld to prevent disclosure of competitive information. States marked with (D) are sorted by number of establishments. A dash (-) indicates that the data element cannot be calculated. * indicates the midpoint of a range; 175, for example is the range 100-249. Shaded *states* on the state map indicate those states which have proportionately greater representation in the industry than would be indicated by the state's population; the ratio is based on total revenues or number of establishments. Shaded *regions* indicate where the industry is regionally most concentrated.

NAICS 541614 - PROCESS, PHYSICAL DISTRIBUTION, AND LOGISTICS CONSULTING SERVICES

GENERAL STATISTICS

Year	Establishments (number)	Employment (number)	Payroll ($ million)	Revenues ($ million)	Employees per Establishment (number)	Revenues per Establishment ($)	Payroll per Employee ($)
1997	3,078	25,366	1,196.0	3,259.0	8.2	1,058,804	47,150

Source: *Economic Census of the United States*, 1997. This is a newly defined industry. Data for prior years were unavailable at the time of publication but may become available over time.

INDICES OF CHANGE

Year	Establishments (number)	Employment (number)	Payroll ($ million)	Revenues ($ million)	Employees per Establishment (number)	Revenues per Establishment ($)	Payroll per Employee ($)
1997	100.0	100.0	100.0	100.0	100.0	100.0	100.0

Sources: Same as General Statistics. The values shown reflect change from the base year, 1997. Values above 100 mean greater than 1997, values below 100 mean less than 1997, and a value of 100 in the 1982-96 or 1998-2001 period means same as 1997. Values followed by a 'p' are projections by the editors; 'e' stands for extrapolation. Data are the most recent available at this level of detail.

SIC INDUSTRIES RELATED TO NAICS 541614

Each new NAICS code represents an industry that used to be part of an SIC or a part of several SIC industries. Data in this table are shown to provide transitional information for these cases. All available data for the precursor SIC(s) are shown. Even if only a part of an SIC is included in the NAICS, *all* data for the SIC are reproduced. If the SIC industry is not marked as being a part (pt) of the NAICS, the entire industry is embedded in the NAICS data. The SIC composition of the new industry provides some hints of the relative importance of its "ancestors." Data marked with a 'p' are projected. Projections begin with 1982 data. Data earlier than 1990 are not shown but are reflected in the projections.

SIC	Industry	1990	1991	1992	1993	1994	1995	1996	1997
4731	**Freight Transportation Arrangement**								
	Establishments (number)	8,905	9,584	12,553	12,995	13,388	13,778	14,771	15,292p
	Employment (thousands)	116.0	112.7	107.0	111.5	117.8	130.1	137.5	132.8p
	Revenues ($ million)	8,125.9e	8,642.3e	9,158.6	9,675.0p	10,191.3p	10,707.6p	11,224.0p	11,740.3p
8742	**Management Consulting Services (pt)**								
	Establishments (number)	24,512	27,162	34,104	35,829	37,517	41,315	40,920p	42,928p
	Employment (thousands)	226.0	243.8	215.4	252.9	294.9	351.7	323.9p	339.6p
	Revenues ($ million)	28,931.0	29,839.0	31,913.0	34,516.0	38,506.0	46,430.0	53,716.0	53,997.3p

Source: *Economic Census of the United States*, 1992, annual surveys of economic sectors conducted by the Bureau of the Census, and estimates or projections based on the 1982-1992 period; not all data are shown. 'e' marks estimates made by the editors; 'p' indicates projections based on time series. A dash (-) indicates that data for this SIC or year were not available. The abbreviation (pt) next to the industry name indicates that only a part of the industry is present within the NAICS data. If no (pt) is shown, the entire industry is contained within the NAICS data.

SELECTED RATIOS

For 1997	Avg. of Information	Analyzed Industry	Index	For 1997	Avg. of Information	Analyzed Industry	Index
Employees per establishment	9	8	95	Payroll per establishment	372,545	388,564	104
Revenue per establishment	958,337	1,058,804	110	Payroll as % of revenue	39	37	94
Revenue per employee	111,029	128,479	116	Payroll per employee	43,162	47,150	109

Sources: Same as General Statistics. The 'Average' column represents the average for the industry sector, in 1997, where the currently shown industry is classified. The Index shows the relationship between the Average and the Analyzed Industry. For example, 100 means that they are equal; 500 that the Analyzed Industry is five times the average; 50 means that the Analyzed Industry is half the national average. The abbreviation 'na' is used to show that data are 'not available'.

LEADING COMPANIES

No company data available for this industry.

LOCATION BY STATE AND REGIONAL CONCENTRATION

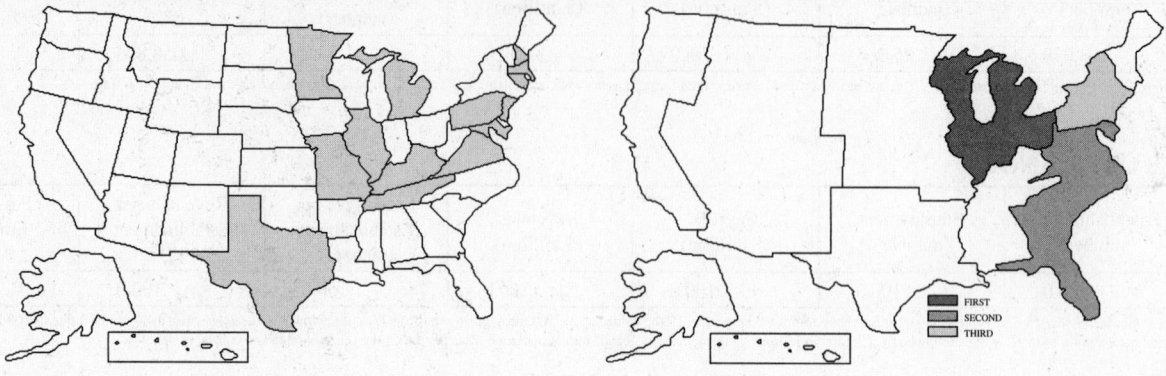

FIRST
SECOND
THIRD

INDUSTRY DATA BY STATE

State	Establishments Total (number)	% of U.S.	Employment Total (number)	% of U.S.	Per Estab.	Payroll Total ($ mil.)	Per Empl. ($)	Revenues Total ($ mil.)	% of U.S.	Per Estab. ($)
Illinois	204	6.6	2,415	9.5	12	156.4	64,749	362.2	11.1	1,775,260
California	294	9.6	2,455	9.7	8	123.7	50,404	336.6	10.3	1,144,803
Texas	201	6.5	1,937	7.6	10	94.9	48,994	260.2	8.0	1,294,622
Michigan	135	4.4	2,040	8.0	15	93.3	45,722	257.0	7.9	1,903,815
Pennsylvania	145	4.7	1,847	7.3	13	84.8	45,919	226.6	7.0	1,562,621
New Jersey	164	5.3	1,397	5.5	9	59.2	42,399	186.7	5.7	1,138,171
Massachusetts	112	3.6	825	3.3	7	68.1	82,530	144.3	4.4	1,288,232
Florida	192	6.2	1,582	6.2	8	44.5	28,117	142.0	4.4	739,682
Maryland	62	2.0	1,074	4.2	17	60.5	56,319	127.6	3.9	2,057,452
New York	177	5.8	767	3.0	4	40.1	52,327	116.5	3.6	658,384
Virginia	94	3.1	889	3.5	9	36.3	40,784	98.5	3.0	1,048,213
Ohio	139	4.5	953	3.8	7	31.0	32,563	88.8	2.7	638,993
Tennessee	53	1.7	715	2.8	13	28.5	39,920	80.5	2.5	1,518,868
Georgia	114	3.7	791	3.1	7	28.1	35,483	78.4	2.4	687,430
Missouri	58	1.9	511	2.0	9	14.0	27,487	74.2	2.3	1,278,828
North Carolina	85	2.8	649	2.6	8	26.6	40,978	70.2	2.2	825,341
Connecticut	49	1.6	246	1.0	5	17.3	70,467	63.9	2.0	1,303,735
Minnesota	75	2.4	476	1.9	6	21.8	45,847	59.2	1.8	788,693
Kentucky	35	1.1	190	0.7	5	12.7	66,953	57.9	1.8	1,655,457
Washington	67	2.2	348	1.4	5	17.2	49,563	48.4	1.5	722,179
Wisconsin	53	1.7	390	1.5	7	16.2	41,454	38.9	1.2	734,811
Indiana	57	1.9	313	1.2	5	10.6	33,824	38.9	1.2	682,632
Colorado	65	2.1	327	1.3	5	13.0	39,798	35.5	1.1	545,538
Oregon	47	1.5	293	1.2	6	13.5	45,928	34.3	1.1	729,660
Arizona	45	1.5	211	0.8	5	8.2	39,076	33.0	1.0	734,067
Iowa	25	0.8	131	0.5	5	6.9	52,901	27.5	0.8	1,098,200
South Carolina	38	1.2	220	0.9	6	11.5	52,359	24.6	0.8	647,395
New Hampshire	23	0.7	125	0.5	5	6.2	49,248	17.4	0.5	756,783
Oklahoma	24	0.8	69	0.3	3	4.7	68,812	17.4	0.5	725,708
D.C.	8	0.3	48	0.2	6	5.8	121,854	9.7	0.3	1,209,500
Alabama	28	0.9	79	0.3	3	4.2	52,949	9.1	0.3	324,214
Nevada	22	0.7	87	0.3	4	2.2	24,713	7.7	0.2	348,455
Arkansas	16	0.5	106	0.4	7	4.1	38,745	7.3	0.2	456,875
Utah	22	0.7	54	0.2	2	1.5	27,426	5.9	0.2	266,545
Delaware	13	0.4	42	0.2	3	2.1	49,048	5.1	0.2	390,769
Idaho	9	0.3	66	0.3	7	1.5	22,121	4.9	0.2	546,333
Montana	8	0.3	21	0.1	3	1.2	58,952	4.3	0.1	539,000
New Mexico	9	0.3	49	0.2	5	1.1	22,408	3.5	0.1	387,222
Hawaii	9	0.3	61	0.2	7	1.3	20,656	2.9	0.1	320,111
Mississippi	9	0.3	175	0.7	19	2.1	11,914	2.7	0.1	299,111
Wyoming	7	0.2	10	0.0	1	0.3	27,500	2.6	0.1	377,000
Vermont	6	0.2	22	0.1	4	0.7	30,727	2.2	0.1	364,333
Nebraska	8	0.3	19	0.1	2	0.4	21,737	1.5	0.0	183,000
Maine	8	0.3	6	0.0	1	0.2	41,167	0.6	0.0	74,875
West Virginia	6	0.2	10	0.0	2	0.3	26,500	0.6	0.0	93,000
South Dakota	7	0.2	3	0.0	-	0.1	47,000	0.2	0.0	34,143
Kansas	20	0.6	60*	-	-	(D)	-	(D)	-	-
Louisiana	14	0.5	60*	-	-	(D)	-	(D)	-	-
Rhode Island	10	0.3	60*	-	-	(D)	-	(D)	-	-
Alaska	7	0.2	175*	-	-	(D)	-	(D)	-	-

Source: 1997 *Economic Census.* The states are in descending order of revenues or establishments (if revenue data are missing for the majority). The symbol (D) appears when data are withheld to prevent disclosure of competitive information. States marked with (D) are sorted by number of establishments. A dash (-) indicates that the data element cannot be calculated. * indicates the midpoint of a range; 175, for example is the range 100-249. Shaded *states* on the state map indicate those states which have proportionately greater representation in the industry than would be indicated by the state's population; the ratio is based on total revenues or number of establishments. Shaded *regions* indicate where the industry is regionally most concentrated.

336

NAICS 541618 - MANAGEMENT CONSULTING SERVICES NEC

GENERAL STATISTICS

Year	Establishments (number)	Employment (number)	Payroll ($ million)	Revenues ($ million)	Employees per Establishment (number)	Revenues per Establishment ($)	Payroll per Employee ($)
1997	3,031	15,867	655.0	1,822.0	5.2	601,122	41,281

Source: Economic Census of the United States, 1997. This is a newly defined industry. Data for prior years were unavailable at the time of publication but may become available over time.

INDICES OF CHANGE

Year	Establishments (number)	Employment (number)	Payroll ($ million)	Revenues ($ million)	Employees per Establishment (number)	Revenues per Establishment ($)	Payroll per Employee ($)
1997	100.0	100.0	100.0	100.0	100.0	100.0	100.0

Sources: Same as General Statistics. The values shown reflect change from the base year, 1997. Values above 100 mean greater than 1997, values below 100 mean less than 1997, and a value of 100 in the 1982-96 or 1998-2001 period means same as 1997. Values followed by a 'p' are projections by the editors; 'e' stands for extrapolation. Data are the most recent available at this level of detail.

SIC INDUSTRIES RELATED TO NAICS 541618

Each new NAICS code represents an industry that used to be part of an SIC or a part of several SIC industries. Data in this table are shown to provide transitional information for these cases. All available data for the precursor SIC(s) are shown. Even if only a part of an SIC is included in the NAICS, *all* data for the SIC are reproduced. If the SIC industry is not marked as being a part (pt) of the NAICS, the entire industry is embedded in the NAICS data. The SIC composition of the new industry provides some hints of the relative importance of its "ancestors." Data marked with a 'p' are projected. Projections begin with 1982 data. Data earlier than 1990 are not shown but are reflected in the projections.

SIC	Industry	1990	1991	1992	1993	1994	1995	1996	1997
8748	**Business Consulting Services, nec (pt)**								
	Establishments (number)	8,819	11,146	13,322	15,561	16,966	18,772	19,284p	20,712p
	Employment (thousands)	70.8	77.9	62.1	72.6	78.6	92.8	87.5p	90.8p
	Revenues ($ million)	6,278.0	6,714.0	7,710.0	8,832.0	9,843.0	12,016.0	13,997.0	14,469.1p

Source: Economic Census of the United States, 1992, annual surveys of economic sectors conducted by the Bureau of the Census, and estimates or projections based on the 1982-1992 period; not all data are shown. 'e' marks estimates made by the editors; 'p' indicates projections based on time series. A dash (-) indicates that data for this SIC or year were not available. The abbreviation (pt) next to the industry name indicates that only a part of the industry is present within the NAICS data. If no (pt) is shown, the entire industry is contained within the NAICS data.

SELECTED RATIOS

For 1997	Avg. of Information	Analyzed Industry	Index	For 1997	Avg. of Information	Analyzed Industry	Index
Employees per establishment	9	5	61	Payroll per establishment	372,545	216,100	58
Revenue per establishment	958,337	601,122	63	Payroll as % of revenue	39	36	92
Revenue per employee	111,029	114,830	103	Payroll per employee	43,162	41,281	96

Sources: Same as General Statistics. The 'Average' column represents the average for the industry sector, in 1997, where the currently shown industry is classified. The Index shows the relationship between the Average and the Analyzed Industry. For example, 100 means that they are equal; 500 that the Analyzed Industry is five times the average; 50 means that the Analyzed Industry is half the national average. The abbreviation 'na' is used to show that data are 'not available'.

LEADING COMPANIES Number shown: **75** Total sales ($ mil): **10,359** Total employment (000): **81.2**

Company Name	Address				CEO Name	Phone	Co. Type	Sales ($ mil)	Empl. (000)
Prudential Real Estate Re-location	200 Summit Lake Dr	Valhalla	NY	10595	Steve Ozonian	914-741-6111	S	900*	2.2
National Shopping Service	P O Box 91312	Los Angeles	CA	90009	Susan Meyer	310-645-1927	R	698*	16.0
Corporate Development Group Inc	707 17th St	Denver	CO	80202	William E Schneider	303-295-6170	N	650	<0.1
Interim Technology Professionals	823 Commerce Dr	Oak Brook	IL	60523	Stuwart Emanuel	630-645-8800	D	528*	2.5
Post, Buckley, Schuh & Jernigan	2001 N W 107th	Miami	FL	33172	H Michael Dye	305-592-7275	R	463*	2.2
Rapid Design Service Inc.	2905 Wilson Ave	Grand Rapids	MI	49504	Richard Tschirhart	616-532-5555	R	412*	1.5
Buck Consultants Inc.	1 Penn Plz	New York	NY	10119	Joseph A Locicero	212-330-1000	P	332	3.0
DynCorp/Information	12750 Fair Lakes Cir	Fairfax	VA	22033	Mark Filtelu	703-222-1500	D	315*	1.5
Environmental Resources	855 Springdale Dr	Exton	PA	19341	Paul Woodruff	610-524-3500	R	300	2.4
SABRE Technology Solutions	4255 Amon Carter	Fort Worth	TX	76155		817-967-1000	N	300	3.0
National Utility Service Inc.	1 Maynard Dr	Park Ridge	NJ	07656	Gary Soultanian	201-391-4300	R	299	0.9
ENSR	35 Nagog Park	Acton	MA	01720	Robert Petersen	978-635-9500	S	259*	1.8
Environmental Resources Mgmt.	855 Springdale Dr	Exton	PA	19341	PH Woodruff	610-524-3500	R	250*	2.4
E.W. Blanch Company Inc.	500 N Akard	Dallas	TX	75201	Edgar W Blanch Jr	972-756-7000	P	244	1.2
First Consulting Group Inc.	111 W Ocean Blvd	Long Beach	CA	90802	Steven Heck	562-624-5200	P	238	1.5
ENSR Corp.	35 Nagog Park	Acton	MA	01720	Robert C Petersen	978-635-9500	S	200	1.5
Foster Wheeler Environmental	8 Peach Tree Hill Rd	Livingston	NJ	07039	Sam W Box	973-597-7000	R	200*	1.8
Kenneth Leventhal and Co.	2049 Century Park E	Los Angeles	CA	90067		310-277-0880	N	200	1.0
Mitre Corp.	202 Burlington Rd	Bedford	MA	01730	Victor DeMarines	781-271-2000	R	181*	4.2
ATC Vancom Inc.	1 Mid America Plz	Oakbrk Ter	IL	60181	Terry VanDerAA	708-571-7070	R	176*	4.0
Roy F. Weston Inc.	1440 Weston Way	West Chester	PA	19380	Patrick McCann	610-701-3000	P	148	1.6
Abt Associates Inc.	55 Wheeler St	Cambridge	MA	02138	Wendell J Knox	617-492-7100	R	147*	1.0
Eder Associates	480 Forest Ave	Locust Valley	NY	11560	Ronald Drnevich	516-763-7211	R	144*	0.7
Taurus Exploration U.S.A. Inc.	605 21st St N	Birmingham	AL	35203	James T McManus II	205-326-2710	S	130	0.2
ATC Group Services Inc.	104 E 25th St	New York	NY	10010	Ron H Danenberg	212-353-8280	R	119	2.0
Dynamac Corp.	2275 Research Blvd	Rockville	MD	20850	Diana T MacArthur	301-417-9800	R	111*	0.4
Bechtel Nevada Corp.	PO Box 98521	Las Vegas	NV	89193	John Mitchell	702-295-0577	S	100*	2.4
Development Dimensions Intern	1225 Washington	Bridgeville	PA	15017	William Byham	412-257-0600	R	100	1.1
Born Information Services Inc.	294 E Grove Ln	Wayzata	MN	55391		612-404-4000	N	92	1.0
F.A. Bartlett Tree Expert Co.	P O Box 3067	Stamford	CT	06905	RA Bartlett	203-323-1131	R	90	2.0
BETA Systems	350 N Sunny Slope	Brookfield	WI	53005		262-789-9000	D	87*	0.4
Exponent Environmental Group	15375 SE 30th Pl	Bellevue	WA	98007	D Paustenbach	425-643-9803	P	86	0.2
Diamond Technology Partners Inc.	875 N Michigan	Chicago	IL	60611	Mel Bergstein	312-255-5000	P	83	0.3
Arctic Slope Consulting Group	301 Artic Slope Ave	Anchorage	AK	99518	John McClellan	907-267-6314	R	82*	0.3
Hygienetics Enviromental	180 Portland St	Boston	MA	02114	Scott Feldman	617-723-4664	R	82*	0.4
Customer Development Corp.	8600 N Industrial Rd	Peoria	IL	61615	Derek Smith	309-689-1000	R	81*	0.4
ChemTreat Inc.	4301 Dominion Blvd	Glen Allen	VA	23060		804-935-2000	N	70	0.4
Ecology and Environment Inc.	Buffalo Corporate	Lancaster	NY	14086	Gerhard J Neumaier	716-684-8060	P	63	0.8
Jacobs Constructors Inc.	2 Ash Street	Conshohocken	PA	19428	Werner Poelck	610-238-1000	S	63*	1.2
SBA Inc.	1 Town Center Rd	Boca Raton	FL	33486	Steven Bernstein	561-995-7670	R	60	0.5
Osprey Systems Inc.	9401 Arrowpoint	Charlotte	NC	28273	David P Rizzo	704-522-0880	S	58*	0.3
SPEC Group Holdings Inc.	The Landings	Pittsburgh	PA	15238	JP Sakey	412-517-7700	R	51*	0.7
Betac Corp.	2001 N Beauregard	Alexandria	VA	22311	Frank Cardile	703-824-3100	P	50	0.5
GTS Transportation Services Inc.	2021 Las Posites Ct	Livermore	CA	94550		510-455-9050	N	50	<0.1
Xenergy Inc.	3 Burlington Woods	Burlington	MA	01803	Kello Warner	781-273-5700	S	50	0.3
Illinois Farm Bureau	1701 Towanda Ave	Bloomington	IL	61701	Ronald Warfield	309-557-2111	R	48*	0.2
SCS Engineers	3711 Long Beach	Long Beach	CA	90807	Robert P Stearns	562-426-9544	R	46	0.4
Development Alternatives Inc.	7250 Woodmont	Bethesda	MD	20814	Albert H Barclay Jr	301-718-8699	R	45*	0.3
Lancaster Laboratories	PO Box 12425	Lancaster	PA	17605		717-656-2300	S	44	0.7
Conferon Inc.	2500 Enterprise E	Twinsburg	OH	44087		330-425-8333	R	43*	0.2
Analysis Group Inc.	1 Brattle Sq	Cambridge	MA	02138	Bruce E Stangle	617-349-2100	R	42*	0.2
Indiana Energy Services Inc.	1630 N Meridian St	Indianapolis	IN	46202	Lawrence A Ferger	317-321-0512	S	41*	0.2
Charles River Associates Inc.	200 Clarendon St	Boston	MA	02116	James C Burrows	617-425-3000	R	40	0.2
DeWolff, Boberg & Associates	PO Box 21989	Charleston	SC	29413		803-686-4666	N	40	0.2
Miller Heiman Inc.	1595 Meadow Wood	Reno	NV	89502	Tom Martin	702-827-4411	R	40*	<0.1
Siegel and Gale Inc.	10 Rockerfeller Plz	New York	NY	10020	Alan Siegel	212-707-4000	R	40	0.3
LFR Levine Fricke	1920 Main St	Irvine	CA	92614	Charles R Henry	949-955-1390	R	39	0.5
STS Consultants Ltd.	750 Corp Woods	Vernon Hills	IL	60061	Thomas W Wolf	847-279-2500	R	37	0.4
Datatel Inc.	4375 Fair Lakes Ct	Fairfax	VA	22033		703-968-9000	R	35	0.3
Segal Co.	1 Park Ave	New York	NY	10016	Howard Fluhr	212-251-5000	R	35*	0.8
Carreker-Antinori Inc.	4055 Valley View	Dallas	TX	75244	JD Carreker	972-458-1981	R	34*	0.3
Clayton Environmental	41650 Gardenbrook	Novi	MI	48375	Thomas Kowalski	248-344-8550	R	32*	0.5
DuCharme, McMillen	6610 Mutual Dr	Fort Wayne	IN	46825	Dave Meinka	219-484-8631	R	32	0.3
ERM EnviroClean	1777 Botelho Dr	Walnut Creek	CA	94596	Richard A Stone	925-946-0455	R	30*	0.1
Walker Parking Consultants	2121 Hudson Ave	Kalamazoo	MI	49008		616-381-6080	N	30	0.2
EnecoTech Inc.	1580 Lincoln St	Denver	CO	80203	Barry L Stewart	303-861-2200	R	29	0.1
Combustion Unlimited Inc.	PO Box 8856	Elkins Park	PA	19027		215-537-0871	N	28	<0.1
S. Cohen and Associates Inc.	1355 Beverly Rd	McLean	VA	22101	Sanford Cohen	703-893-6600	R	27*	0.1
SandS Public Relations Inc.	400 Skokie Blvd	Northbrook	IL	60062		847-291-1616	N	25	<0.1
Value Options	PO Box 12438	RTP	NC	27709	David Dozoretz	919-941-5512	R	25*	<0.1
Belt Collins Intern. Design Group	680 Ala Moana	Honolulu	HI	96813		808-521-5361	N	24	0.2
The Linick Group Inc.	7 Putter Ln	Middle Island	NY	11953		516-924-3888	N	23	0.6
EMA Services Inc.	1970 Oakcrest Ave	St. Paul	MN	55113	Alan Manning	651-639-5600	R	21	0.2
Perkins and Company P.C.	1211 SW 5th Ave	Portland	OR	97204	James Jeddeloh	503-221-0336	R	21*	<0.1
Jones and Stokes Associates	2600 V St	Sacramento	CA	95818	Albert I Herson	916-737-3000	R	20	0.2

Source: *Ward's Business Directory of U.S. Private and Public Companies*, Volumes 1 and 2, 2000. The company type code used is as follows: P - Public, R - Private, S - Subsidiary, D - Division, J - Joint Venture, A - Affiliate, G - Group, N - Company type not reported. Sales are in millions of dollars, employees are in thousands. An asterisk (*) indicates an estimated sales volume. The symbol < stands for 'less than'. Company names and addresses are truncated, in some cases, to fit into the available space.

LOCATION BY STATE AND REGIONAL CONCENTRATION

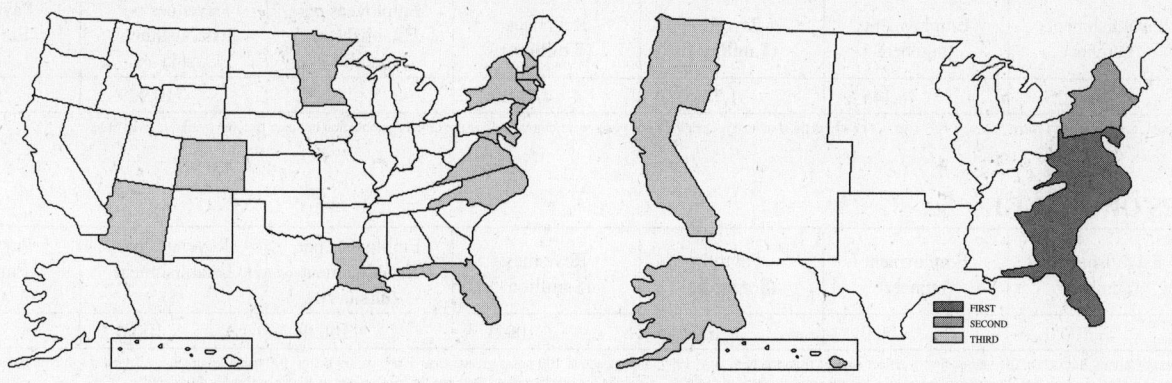

INDUSTRY DATA BY STATE

State	Establishments Total (number)	% of U.S.	Employment Total (number)	% of U.S.	Per Estab.	Payroll Total ($ mil.)	Per Empl. ($)	Revenues Total ($ mil.)	% of U.S.	Per Estab. ($)
California	317	10.5	1,895	11.9	6	71.8	37,893	190.5	10.5	600,830
New York	212	7.0	1,380	8.7	7	70.2	50,862	186.4	10.2	879,099
North Carolina	66	2.2	482	3.0	7	27.5	56,950	141.8	7.8	2,149,121
D.C.	40	1.3	688	4.3	17	56.6	82,337	134.8	7.4	3,369,825
New Jersey	133	4.4	1,070	6.7	8	39.3	36,729	128.6	7.1	967,090
Florida	221	7.3	748	4.7	3	31.3	41,783	108.2	5.9	489,638
Texas	243	8.0	1,105	7.0	5	38.7	34,996	96.1	5.3	395,412
Maryland	70	2.3	573	3.6	8	28.1	49,072	67.2	3.7	959,643
Massachusetts	73	2.4	638	4.0	9	26.9	42,158	64.3	3.5	880,616
Minnesota	84	2.8	403	2.5	5	19.3	47,963	62.7	3.4	747,000
Pennsylvania	106	3.5	511	3.2	5	20.5	40,063	59.3	3.3	559,575
Virginia	116	3.8	769	4.8	7	24.9	32,337	56.1	3.1	483,776
Louisiana	73	2.4	457	2.9	6	15.6	34,230	51.9	2.9	711,164
Georgia	91	3.0	314	2.0	3	17.4	55,347	43.3	2.4	476,231
Arizona	67	2.2	341	2.1	5	10.8	31,663	42.1	2.3	628,836
Illinois	126	4.2	444	2.8	4	16.0	36,029	41.5	2.3	329,278
Ohio	137	4.5	570	3.6	4	16.5	29,005	39.2	2.2	286,124
Colorado	64	2.1	369	2.3	6	13.0	35,127	30.5	1.7	476,078
Washington	62	2.0	261	1.6	4	9.5	36,222	26.9	1.5	434,677
Connecticut	35	1.2	229	1.4	7	11.9	51,956	25.7	1.4	733,000
Tennessee	49	1.6	268	1.7	5	10.6	39,545	21.8	1.2	445,735
Missouri	55	1.8	234	1.5	4	7.3	31,244	19.6	1.1	356,927
Oregon	53	1.7	213	1.3	4	6.5	30,737	17.6	1.0	331,528
Indiana	44	1.5	209	1.3	5	7.8	37,512	17.6	1.0	399,273
Michigan	56	1.8	154	1.0	3	5.2	33,623	14.4	0.8	257,250
New Hampshire	23	0.8	141	0.9	6	5.0	35,695	13.1	0.7	569,261
Wisconsin	40	1.3	115	0.7	3	5.4	47,357	12.7	0.7	317,900
Kentucky	32	1.1	148	0.9	5	5.7	38,845	10.9	0.6	339,063
Iowa	24	0.8	141	0.9	6	4.3	30,163	9.5	0.5	394,583
Utah	20	0.7	53	0.3	3	2.0	38,132	8.4	0.5	420,550
New Mexico	17	0.6	201	1.3	12	4.0	19,667	7.6	0.4	447,882
South Carolina	37	1.2	68	0.4	2	2.5	37,294	6.2	0.3	168,865
Alabama	32	1.1	76	0.5	2	2.4	31,395	5.6	0.3	175,531
Nevada	18	0.6	22	0.1	1	1.9	84,545	5.3	0.3	296,000
Oklahoma	26	0.9	54	0.3	2	1.9	35,500	5.3	0.3	204,615
Hawaii	11	0.4	38	0.2	3	1.2	32,842	5.2	0.3	475,545
Mississippi	10	0.3	41	0.3	4	1.3	31,146	4.4	0.2	442,700
Arkansas	17	0.6	33	0.2	2	0.9	26,788	3.6	0.2	210,941
Delaware	12	0.4	25	0.2	2	1.5	61,880	3.5	0.2	293,417
Nebraska	13	0.4	38	0.2	3	1.0	27,289	3.0	0.2	227,462
Maine	17	0.6	40	0.3	2	1.2	30,600	2.8	0.2	165,882
Alaska	7	0.2	17	0.1	2	1.1	66,471	2.3	0.1	328,143
West Virginia	14	0.5	53	0.3	4	0.7	14,000	2.1	0.1	146,857
Vermont	14	0.5	30	0.2	2	0.7	23,900	1.9	0.1	133,500
Montana	8	0.3	19	0.1	2	0.3	14,421	1.2	0.1	151,500
Wyoming	7	0.2	17	0.1	2	0.3	16,588	1.0	0.1	142,429
Idaho	6	0.2	7	0.0	1	0.2	27,571	0.7	0.0	110,167
South Dakota	5	0.2	7	0.0	1	0.2	29,286	0.4	0.0	81,600
Kansas	23	0.8	175*	-	-	(D)	-	(D)	-	-
Rhode Island	4	0.1	10*	-	-	(D)	-	(D)	-	-
North Dakota	1	-	10*	-	-	(D)	-	(D)	-	-

Source: 1997 *Economic Census*. The states are in descending order of revenues or establishments (if revenue data are missing for the majority). The symbol (D) appears when data are withheld to prevent disclosure of competitive information. States marked with (D) are sorted by number of establishments. A dash (-) indicates that the data element cannot be calculated. * indicates the midpoint of a range; 175, for example is the range 100-249. Shaded *states* on the state map indicate those states which have proportionately greater representation in the industry than would be indicated by the state's population; the ratio is based on total revenues or number of establishments. Shaded *regions* indicate where the industry is regionally most concentrated.

339

NAICS 541620 - ENVIRONMENTAL CONSULTING SERVICES

GENERAL STATISTICS

Year	Establishments (number)	Employment (number)	Payroll ($ million)	Revenues ($ million)	Employees per Establishment (number)	Revenues per Establishment ($)	Payroll per Employee ($)
1997	6,725	46,145	1,778.0	4,781.0	6.9	710,929	38,531

Source: Economic Census of the United States, 1997. This is a newly defined industry. Data for prior years were unavailable at the time of publication but may become available over time.

INDICES OF CHANGE

Year	Establishments (number)	Employment (number)	Payroll ($ million)	Revenues ($ million)	Employees per Establishment (number)	Revenues per Establishment ($)	Payroll per Employee ($)
1997	100.0	100.0	100.0	100.0	100.0	100.0	100.0

Sources: Same as General Statistics. The values shown reflect change from the base year, 1997. Values above 100 mean greater than 1997, values below 100 mean less than 1997, and a value of 100 in the 1982-96 or 1998-2001 period means same as 1997. Values followed by a 'p' are projections by the editors; 'e' stands for extrapolation. Data are the most recent available at this level of detail.

SIC INDUSTRIES RELATED TO NAICS 541620

Each new NAICS code represents an industry that used to be part of an SIC or a part of several SIC industries. Data in this table are shown to provide transitional information for these cases. All available data for the precursor SIC(s) are shown. Even if only a part of an SIC is included in the NAICS, *all* data for the SIC are reproduced. If the SIC industry is not marked as being a part (pt) of the NAICS, the entire industry is embedded in the NAICS data. The SIC composition of the new industry provides some hints of the relative importance of its "ancestors." Data marked with a 'p' are projected. Projections begin with 1982 data. Data earlier than 1990 are not shown but are reflected in the projections.

SIC	Industry	1990	1991	1992	1993	1994	1995	1996	1997
8999	**Services, nec (pt)**								
	Establishments (number)	-	-	14,587	-	-	-	-	-
	Employment (thousands)	-	-	81.1	-	-	-	-	-
	Revenues ($ million)	-	-	7,966.2	-	-	-	-	-

Source: Economic Census of the United States, 1992, annual surveys of economic sectors conducted by the Bureau of the Census, and estimates or projections based on the 1982-1992 period; not all data are shown. 'e' marks estimates made by the editors; 'p' indicates projections based on time series. A dash (-) indicates that data for this SIC or year were not available. The abbreviation (pt) next to the industry name indicates that only a part of the industry is present within the NAICS data. If no (pt) is shown, the entire industry is contained within the NAICS data.

SELECTED RATIOS

For 1997	Avg. of Information	Analyzed Industry	Index	For 1997	Avg. of Information	Analyzed Industry	Index
Employees per establishment	9	7	79	Payroll per establishment	372,545	264,387	71
Revenue per establishment	958,337	710,929	74	Payroll as % of revenue	39	37	96
Revenue per employee	111,029	103,608	93	Payroll per employee	43,162	38,531	89

Sources: Same as General Statistics. The 'Average' column represents the average for the industry sector, in 1997, where the currently shown industry is classified. The Index shows the relationship between the Average and the Analyzed Industry. For example, 100 means that they are equal; 500 that the Analyzed Industry is five times the average; 50 means that the Analyzed Industry is half the national average. The abbreviation 'na' is used to show that data are 'not available'.

LEADING COMPANIES

No company data available for this industry.

LOCATION BY STATE AND REGIONAL CONCENTRATION

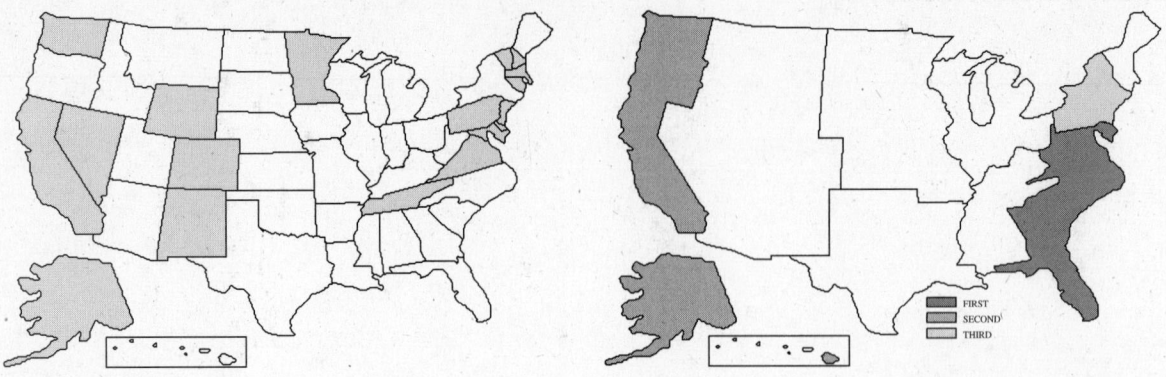

INDUSTRY DATA BY STATE

State	Establishments Total (number)	% of U.S.	Employment Total (number)	% of U.S.	Per Estab.	Payroll Total ($ mil.)	Per Empl. ($)	Revenues Total ($ mil.)	% of U.S.	Per Estab. ($)
California	798	11.9	6,221	13.5	8	253.4	40,740	682.4	14.3	855,180
New York	323	4.8	2,546	5.5	8	103.0	40,448	296.8	6.2	918,892
Texas	453	6.7	2,844	6.2	6	110.5	38,855	293.7	6.1	648,386
Pennsylvania	333	5.0	2,714	5.9	8	106.0	39,059	293.6	6.1	881,679
New Jersey	285	4.2	2,368	5.1	8	88.2	37,240	241.0	5.0	845,772
Virginia	223	3.3	2,537	5.5	11	108.2	42,665	238.0	5.0	1,067,152
Colorado	242	3.6	1,825	4.0	8	85.1	46,614	237.6	5.0	981,760
Ohio	241	3.6	1,584	3.4	7	55.5	35,028	206.4	4.3	856,523
Florida	414	6.2	2,355	5.1	6	77.0	32,703	199.4	4.2	481,614
Maryland	178	2.6	1,709	3.7	10	75.3	44,041	174.9	3.7	982,376
Massachusetts	214	3.2	1,534	3.3	7	65.5	42,726	155.4	3.2	726,033
Illinois	257	3.8	1,388	3.0	5	50.8	36,587	146.8	3.1	571,093
Washington	223	3.3	1,193	2.6	5	45.2	37,883	110.4	2.3	495,220
North Carolina	185	2.8	969	2.1	5	40.1	41,421	110.3	2.3	596,054
Tennessee	111	1.7	898	1.9	8	34.3	38,248	99.6	2.1	896,937
Georgia	162	2.4	937	2.0	6	36.7	39,180	97.0	2.0	598,938
Michigan	179	2.7	1,115	2.4	6	38.7	34,750	92.6	1.9	517,190
Minnesota	98	1.5	776	1.7	8	27.8	35,814	84.6	1.8	863,163
Louisiana	135	2.0	825	1.8	6	25.2	30,541	72.6	1.5	537,770
Indiana	136	2.0	621	1.3	5	21.7	34,882	64.7	1.4	475,750
Connecticut	76	1.1	577	1.3	8	26.1	45,270	61.9	1.3	814,632
Alabama	48	0.7	519	1.1	11	21.1	40,686	61.6	1.3	1,284,292
New Mexico	85	1.3	556	1.2	7	26.4	47,484	59.9	1.3	704,518
Arizona	111	1.7	583	1.3	5	22.5	38,612	54.0	1.1	486,865
Oregon	118	1.8	529	1.1	4	17.7	33,450	50.2	1.1	425,695
Wisconsin	98	1.5	564	1.2	6	18.4	32,585	45.6	1.0	465,173
Oklahoma	82	1.2	359	0.8	4	12.2	34,111	42.3	0.9	516,073
D.C.	40	0.6	300	0.7	8	18.0	60,157	41.2	0.9	1,030,550
Nevada	39	0.6	414	0.9	11	8.0	19,261	38.8	0.8	993,846
Missouri	77	1.1	410	0.9	5	13.5	32,929	36.7	0.8	476,117
South Carolina	72	1.1	369	0.8	5	11.0	29,772	35.0	0.7	485,903
Kentucky	61	0.9	277	0.6	5	8.7	31,516	28.2	0.6	462,000
New Hampshire	40	0.6	296	0.6	7	12.5	42,135	27.3	0.6	682,900
Arkansas	45	0.7	432	0.9	10	9.9	22,863	26.8	0.6	596,467
Alaska	35	0.5	187	0.4	5	9.5	50,813	26.7	0.6	762,200
Utah	59	0.9	320	0.7	5	9.5	29,575	25.4	0.5	430,593
Delaware	32	0.5	215	0.5	7	7.7	35,758	23.2	0.5	724,250
Hawaii	28	0.4	219	0.5	8	5.9	26,863	18.6	0.4	664,071
Iowa	48	0.7	198	0.4	4	6.7	33,732	17.9	0.4	372,500
Maine	52	0.8	185	0.4	4	6.4	34,865	15.8	0.3	303,692
Montana	47	0.7	179	0.4	4	5.4	30,056	15.3	0.3	325,362
Vermont	37	0.6	185	0.4	5	5.9	31,714	15.3	0.3	413,568
West Virginia	21	0.3	201	0.4	10	6.0	29,915	15.2	0.3	723,667
Wyoming	25	0.4	140	0.3	6	5.9	42,007	13.1	0.3	523,280
Idaho	39	0.6	128	0.3	3	5.2	40,430	12.6	0.3	323,769
Mississippi	19	0.3	96	0.2	5	3.0	30,854	10.9	0.2	575,316
Nebraska	13	0.2	90	0.2	7	3.5	38,333	8.2	0.2	633,692
South Dakota	6	0.1	61	0.1	10	2.0	32,262	4.1	0.1	679,667
North Dakota	6	0.1	41	0.1	7	0.5	11,927	1.4	0.0	229,167
Kansas	57	0.8	375*	-	-	(D)	-	(D)	-	-
Rhode Island	19	0.3	175*	-	-	(D)	-	(D)	-	-

Source: 1997 *Economic Census*. The states are in descending order of revenues or establishments (if revenue data are missing for the majority). The symbol (D) appears when data are withheld to prevent disclosure of competitive information. States marked with (D) are sorted by number of establishments. A dash (-) indicates that the data element cannot be calculated. * indicates the midpoint of a range; 175, for example is the range 100-249. Shaded *states* on the state map indicate those states which have proportionately greater representation in the industry than would be indicated by the state's population; the ratio is based on total revenues or number of establishments. Shaded *regions* indicate where the industry is regionally most concentrated.

NAICS 541690 - SCIENTIFIC AND TECHNICAL CONSULTING SERVICES NEC

GENERAL STATISTICS

Year	Establishments (number)	Employment (number)	Payroll ($ million)	Revenues ($ million)	Employees per Establishment (number)	Revenues per Establishment ($)	Payroll per Employee ($)
1997	12,907	54,063	2,507.0	6,423.0	4.2	497,637	46,372

Source: Economic Census of the United States, 1997. This is a newly defined industry. Data for prior years were unavailable at the time of publication but may become available over time.

INDICES OF CHANGE

Year	Establishments (number)	Employment (number)	Payroll ($ million)	Revenues ($ million)	Employees per Establishment (number)	Revenues per Establishment ($)	Payroll per Employee ($)
1997	100.0	100.0	100.0	100.0	100.0	100.0	100.0

Sources: Same as General Statistics. The values shown reflect change from the base year, 1997. Values above 100 mean greater than 1997, values below 100 mean less than 1997, and a value of 100 in the 1982-96 or 1998-2001 period means same as 1997. Values followed by a 'p' are projections by the editors; 'e' stands for extrapolation. Data are the most recent available at this level of detail.

SIC INDUSTRIES RELATED TO NAICS 541690

Each new NAICS code represents an industry that used to be part of an SIC or a part of several SIC industries. Data in this table are shown to provide transitional information for these cases. All available data for the precursor SIC(s) are shown. Even if only a part of an SIC is included in the NAICS, *all* data for the SIC are reproduced. If the SIC industry is not marked as being a part (pt) of the NAICS, the entire industry is embedded in the NAICS data. The SIC composition of the new industry provides some hints of the relative importance of its "ancestors." Data marked with a 'p' are projected. Projections begin with 1982 data. Data earlier than 1990 are not shown but are reflected in the projections.

SIC	Industry	1990	1991	1992	1993	1994	1995	1996	1997
0781	**Landscape Counseling and Planning (pt)**	-	-	-	-	-	-	-	-
8748	**Business Consulting Services, nec (pt)**								
	Establishments (number)	8,819	11,146	13,322	15,561	16,966	18,772	19,284p	20,712p
	Employment (thousands)	70.8	77.9	62.1	72.6	78.6	92.8	87.5p	90.8p
	Revenues ($ million)	6,278.0	6,714.0	7,710.0	8,832.0	9,843.0	12,016.0	13,997.0	14,469.1p
8999	**Services, nec (pt)**								
	Establishments (number)	-	-	14,587	-	-	-	-	-
	Employment (thousands)	-	-	81.1	-	-	-	-	-
	Revenues ($ million)	-	-	7,966.2	-	-	-	-	-

Source: Economic Census of the United States, 1992, annual surveys of economic sectors conducted by the Bureau of the Census, and estimates or projections based on the 1982-1992 period; not all data are shown. 'e' marks estimates made by the editors; 'p' indicates projections based on time series. A dash (-) indicates that data for this SIC or year were not available. The abbreviation (pt) next to the industry name indicates that only a part of the industry is present within the NAICS data. If no (pt) is shown, the entire industry is contained within the NAICS data.

SELECTED RATIOS

For 1997	Avg. of Information	Analyzed Industry	Index	For 1997	Avg. of Information	Analyzed Industry	Index
Employees per establishment	9	4	49	Payroll per establishment	372,545	194,236	52
Revenue per establishment	958,337	497,637	52	Payroll as % of revenue	39	39	100
Revenue per employee	111,029	118,806	107	Payroll per employee	43,162	46,372	107

Sources: Same as General Statistics. The 'Average' column represents the average for the industry sector, in 1997, where the currently shown industry is classified. The Index shows the relationship between the Average and the Analyzed Industry. For example, 100 means that they are equal; 500 that the Analyzed Industry is five times the average; 50 means that the Analyzed Industry is half the national average. The abbreviation 'na' is used to show that data are 'not available'.

LEADING COMPANIES   Number shown: **75**   Total sales ($ mil): **8,086**   Total employment (000): **65.8**

Company Name	Address				CEO Name	Phone	Co. Type	Sales ($ mil)	Empl. (000)
Constellation Energy Group	39 West Lexington	Baltimore	MD	21201	Edward A. Crooke	410-234-5678	P	3,786	9.4
Key Corporation	127 Public Squ	Cleveland	OH	44114	Robert W Gillespie	216-689-6300	R	996	25.9
Rare Hospitality International Inc.	8215 Roswell Rd	Atlanta	GA	30350	Philip J Hickey, Jr	770-399-9595	P	319	8.4
LawGIBB Group	112 Townpark Dr	Kennesaw	GA	30144		770-360-0600	N	317	4.3
Intern. Communications	1925 Century Park E	Los Angeles	CA	90067		310-557-2585	N	307	0.1
URS Greiner Inc.	100 California St	San Francisco	CA	94111		415-774-2700	N	306	3.0
Mandel Airplane Funding	PO Box 294	Wainscott	NY	11975		212-737-8917	N	200	<0.1
Invention Companies	217 9th St	Pittsburgh	PA	15222	Martin Burger	412-288-1300	R	185*	0.2
Billing Concepts Corp.	7411 John Smith Dr	San Antonio	TX	78229	Parris H Holmes Jr	210-949-7000	P	181	0.8
Metro Networks Inc.	2800 Post Oak Blvd	Houston	TX	77056	David I Saperstein	713-407-6000	S	172	2.2
Gateway Learning Group	665 3rd St	San Francisco	CA	94107	Byron Adams	415-512-7323	R	150	0.5
Smith Technology Corp.	Bayview Ctr	Newport Beach	CA	92660		714-725-9276	N	150	1.0
Metro Traffic Control Inc.	2800 Post Oak Blvd	Houston	TX	77056	Charles Bortnick	713-407-6000	S	109	1.9
United Payors & United Providers	2275 Research Blvd	Rockville	MD	20850	Thomas L Blair	301-548-1000	P	109	0.5
ATC Associates Inc.	5150 East Sixty Fifth	Indianapolis	IN	46220		317-849-5260	N	102	1.2
Law Companies Intern. Group	3 Ravinia Dr	Atlanta	GA	30346		770-396-8000	N	90	1.5
Inteq Group Inc.	5445 La Sierra Dr	Dallas	TX	75231	Andrew Fisk	214-739-9494	R	45	<0.1
GeoEngineers Inc.	8410 154th Ave N E	Redmond	WA	98052	James A Miller	425-861-6000	R	44*	0.2
KCS Energy Management	379 Thornall St	Edison	NJ	08837	James Christmas	732-632-1770	D	43	0.1
Earth Engineering & Sciences Inc.	3401 Carlins Park Dr	Baltimore	MD	21215		410-466-1400	N	35	0.1
Envirogen Inc.	480 Neponset St	Canton	MA	02021		781-821-5560	N	33	0.3
Maxim Technologies Inc	96 S Zuni	Denver	CO	80223		303-744-7105	N	30	0.4
MovieFone Inc.	333 Westchester	White Plains	NY	10604	Andrew R Jarecki	914-872-0333	P	25	0.1
Site-Blauvelt Engineers Inc.	200 E Park Dr	Mount Laurel	NJ	08054		609-273-1224	N	21	0.3
Groundwater & Environmental	1340 Campus	Wall	NJ	07719		908-919-0100	N	19	0.2
Management Systems Intern. Inc.	600 Water St SW	Washington	DC	20024	Lawrence Cooley	202-484-7170	N	16	<0.1
Leighton and Associates Inc.	17781 Cowan	Irvine	CA	92614		714-250-1421	N	15	0.2
TAL International Marketing Inc.	65 Madison Ave	Morristown	NJ	07960	Barbara Bochese	973-540-8333	R	14	0.2
DCM Group	1320 Old Ch Bridge	McLean	VA	22101		703-883-1355	N	13	<0.1
Better Management Corp. of Ohio	755 B Canfield Rd	Youngstown	OH	44512		330-758-5757	N	13	<0.1
ERD Environmental	6205 Easton Rd	Pipersville	PA	18947		215-766-7230	N	12	0.1
Haztrain Inc.	PO Box 2206	La Plata	MD	20646		301-932-0994	N	12	<0.1
R. Brooks Associates Inc.	6546 Pound Rd	Williamson	NY	14589		315-589-4006	R	12	<0.1
Allee King Rosen & Fleming Inc.	117 E 29th St	New York	NY	10016		212-696-0670	N	11	<0.1
Aguirre Engineers Inc.	PO Box 3814	Englewood	CO	80155		303-799-8378	N	10	<0.1
Quixx Corp.	4701 Parkside Dr	Amarillo	TX	79109	Henry Hamilton	806-342-2100	S	9*	0.1
BERGER/ABAM Engineers Inc.	33301 9th Ave S	Federal Way	WA	98003		253-431-2300	N	8	<0.1
Jellinek, Schwartz & Connolly Inc	1525 Wilson Blvd	Arlington	VA	22209		703-527-1670	N	8	<0.1
WeatherBank Inc.	1015 Waterwood	Edmond	OK	73034	Steven A Root	405-359-0773	R	8*	<0.1
Applied Geosciences Inc.	29 B Technology Dr	Irvine	CA	92618		714-453-8545	N	8	<0.1
Planning & Development	1012 N St NW	Washington	DC	20001		202-789-1140	N	7	<0.1
Bruce Liesch and Associates Inc.	13400 15th Ave N	Minneapolis	MN	55441		612-559-1423	N	6	<0.1
ET Technologies Inc.	6800 S Dawson Cir	Englewood	CO	80112		303-680-9414	N	6	<0.1
National Ground Water	601 Dempsey Rd	Westerville	OH	43081		614-898-7791	N	6	<0.1
Westin William and Penn	555 Grant St	Pittsburgh	PA	15219	Mark Dunbar	412-642-9040	R	6*	<0.1
ATC Environmental Inc.	600 W Cummings	Woburn	MA	01801		617-932-9400	N	5	0.7
EETCO Inc.	17117 W 9 Mile Rd	Southfield	MI	48075		248-569-8604	N	5	<0.1
IHI Environmental	4015 N 44th St	Phoenix	AZ	85018		602-840-9446	N	5	<0.1
Industrial Health Inc.	640 E Wilmington	Salt Lake City	UT	84106		801-466-2223	N	5	<0.1
S.M. Stoller Corp.	5665 Flatiron Pky	Boulder	CO	80301	Nicholas Lombardo	303-546-4300	N	5	<0.1
Tracor Technology Resources Inc.	1601 Research Blvd	Rockville	MD	20850		301-251-4941	N	5	<0.1
Midwest Environmental	1800 Indian Wood	Maumee	OH	43537		419-891-1800	N	5	<0.1
Simons, Li and Associates Inc.	3150 Bristol St	Costa Mesa	CA	92626		714-513-1280	N	5	<0.1
Admusic Inc.	1615 16th St	Santa Monica	CA	90404		310-399-6900	R	4*	<0.1
Engineering Design & Testing	PO Box 8027	Columbia	SC	29202		803-791-8800	N	4	<0.1
Evergreen Group Inc.	7416 Hwy 329	Crestwood	KY	40014		502-241-4171	N	4	<0.1
Greystone	5231 S Quebec St	Englewood	CO	80111		303-850-0930	N	4	<0.1
Olivia Cruises and Resorts	4400 Market St	Oakland	CA	94608	Judith Dlugacz	510-655-0364	R	4	<0.1
Relucent Exploration	P O Box 1357	Burleson	TX	76097	Sam Reaves	817-447-8056	R	4*	<0.1
Bregman and Company Inc.	4827 Rugby Ave	Bethesda	MD	20814		301-652-4818	N	4	<0.1
Galanty and Co.	1640 5th St	Santa Monica	CA	90401		310-451-2525	N	4	<0.1
Baldwin and Gregg Ltd.	221 W Bute St	Norfolk	VA	23510		757-623-7300	N	4	<0.1
Environmental Quality	PO Box 11458	San Juan	PR	00910		787-725-5333	N	4	<0.1
GTG Geotechnical/Environmental	4765 Independence	Wheat Ridge	CO	80033		303-424-5578	N	4	<0.1
Separation Systems Consultants	17041 Cam Real	Houston	TX	77058	Helen I Hodges	281-486-1943	N	4	<0.1
Cerrell Associates Inc.	1320 N Larchmont	Los Angeles	CA	90004		213-466-3445	N	3	<0.1
Metallurgical Services Co.	4102 Bishop Ln	Louisville	KY	40218	Richard Hallman	502-968-5000	N	3	<0.1
R & B Falcon Deepwater	P O Box 79627	Houston	TX	77279	David C Toalson	281-496-5000	S	3*	<0.1
Ross Gordon and Associates Inc.	2033 N Main St	Walnut Creek	CA	94596	Ross Gordon	925-943-7575	R	3*	<0.1
The Raring Corp.	12117 NE 99th St	Vancouver	WA	98682		360-892-1659	N	3	<0.1
Airtek Environmental Corp.	39 W 38th St	New York	NY	10018		212-768-0516	N	3	<0.1
TRC Garrow Associates Inc.	3772 Pleasantdale	Atlanta	GA	30340		770-270-1192	N	3	<0.1
National Environmental	PO Box 5131	River Forest	IL	60305		708-771-7350	N	3	<0.1
Squier Associates Inc.	PO Box 1317	Lake Oswego	OR	97035		503-635-4419	N	3	<0.1
Applied Science & Technology	7879 Jackson Rd	Ann Arbor	MI	48106		313-426-1200	N	3	<0.1

Source: Ward's Business Directory of U.S. Private and Public Companies, Volumes 1 and 2, 2000. The company type code used is as follows: P - Public, R - Private, S - Subsidiary, D - Division, J - Joint Venture, A - Affiliate, G - Group, N - Company type not reported. Sales are in millions of dollars, employees are in thousands. An asterisk (*) indicates an estimated sales volume. The symbol < stands for 'less than'. Company names and addresses are truncated, in some cases, to fit into the available space.

LOCATION BY STATE AND REGIONAL CONCENTRATION

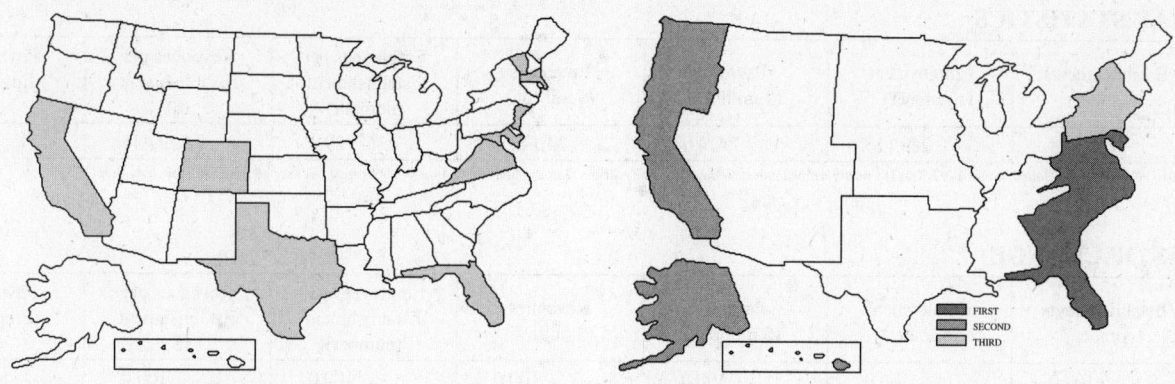

INDUSTRY DATA BY STATE

State	Establishments Total (number)	% of U.S.	Employment Total (number)	% of U.S.	Per Estab.	Payroll Total ($ mil.)	Per Empl. ($)	Revenues Total ($ mil.)	% of U.S.	Per Estab. ($)
California	1,509	11.7	6,279	11.6	4	338.9	53,977	871.5	13.6	577,539
Texas	1,046	8.1	4,771	8.8	5	227.0	47,576	709.2	11.0	677,972
Massachusetts	335	2.6	2,977	5.5	9	176.9	59,423	476.5	7.4	1,422,519
Virginia	501	3.9	4,349	8.0	9	185.1	42,564	438.1	6.8	874,407
New York	879	6.8	3,141	5.8	4	160.0	50,935	408.8	6.4	465,119
Florida	924	7.2	3,345	6.2	4	143.1	42,776	376.7	5.9	407,671
D.C.	209	1.6	1,970	3.6	9	148.2	75,215	318.8	5.0	1,525,440
Maryland	401	3.1	2,814	5.2	7	125.7	44,670	297.6	4.6	742,190
New Jersey	587	4.5	2,202	4.1	4	116.8	53,024	281.9	4.4	480,249
Illinois	591	4.6	1,727	3.2	3	92.7	53,696	261.6	4.1	442,653
Pennsylvania	423	3.3	2,158	4.0	5	89.0	41,242	215.7	3.4	509,898
Colorado	419	3.2	1,358	2.5	3	63.8	46,991	149.9	2.3	357,699
North Carolina	267	2.1	1,673	3.1	6	68.1	40,683	140.7	2.2	527,064
Georgia	390	3.0	1,245	2.3	3	55.9	44,903	131.1	2.0	336,159
Ohio	354	2.7	1,229	2.3	3	44.4	36,142	111.6	1.7	315,186
Washington	310	2.4	1,196	2.2	4	54.3	45,411	111.3	1.7	359,165
Arizona	280	2.2	814	1.5	3	30.2	37,053	98.6	1.5	352,239
Michigan	338	2.6	848	1.6	3	41.6	49,000	92.7	1.4	274,198
Connecticut	163	1.3	593	1.1	4	25.5	42,933	77.4	1.2	474,583
Louisiana	247	1.9	711	1.3	3	23.2	32,674	69.4	1.1	281,008
Indiana	163	1.3	738	1.4	5	23.9	32,398	67.0	1.0	411,135
Minnesota	249	1.9	686	1.3	3	26.6	38,815	64.5	1.0	258,863
Missouri	153	1.2	677	1.3	4	26.5	39,210	59.6	0.9	389,693
Oklahoma	165	1.3	799	1.5	5	17.5	21,892	47.8	0.7	290,000
Oregon	164	1.3	517	1.0	3	20.5	39,650	45.6	0.7	278,165
Wisconsin	163	1.3	525	1.0	3	16.0	30,505	41.8	0.7	256,577
Tennessee	134	1.0	383	0.7	3	14.6	38,021	38.9	0.6	290,328
Nevada	102	0.8	248	0.5	2	10.5	42,149	33.5	0.5	328,892
Utah	114	0.9	380	0.7	3	11.5	30,187	32.2	0.5	282,702
Vermont	29	0.2	160	0.3	6	9.0	55,963	31.2	0.5	1,076,655
New Mexico	88	0.7	315	0.6	4	11.8	37,549	28.5	0.4	323,852
South Carolina	114	0.9	252	0.5	2	11.0	43,603	27.5	0.4	241,149
New Hampshire	68	0.5	238	0.4	4	10.4	43,710	23.8	0.4	350,118
Alabama	94	0.7	237	0.4	3	7.8	32,810	21.2	0.3	225,904
Kentucky	97	0.8	230	0.4	2	7.3	31,870	19.6	0.3	201,918
Maine	61	0.5	149	0.3	2	5.9	39,443	15.6	0.2	254,984
Iowa	75	0.6	171	0.3	2	4.7	27,585	14.1	0.2	187,493
Mississippi	66	0.5	105	0.2	2	3.4	32,724	11.3	0.2	171,439
Montana	47	0.4	130	0.2	3	2.6	20,362	10.8	0.2	229,915
Hawaii	39	0.3	156	0.3	4	4.9	31,103	10.6	0.2	271,410
Nebraska	70	0.5	130	0.2	2	3.3	25,531	10.3	0.2	147,414
Alaska	37	0.3	90	0.2	2	3.2	35,711	10.2	0.2	276,730
Delaware	54	0.4	103	0.2	2	3.1	30,194	9.9	0.2	182,648
Arkansas	63	0.5	113	0.2	2	4.0	35,451	9.1	0.1	143,889
West Virginia	32	0.2	70	0.1	2	1.8	25,929	8.9	0.1	277,531
Wyoming	41	0.3	56	0.1	1	2.5	44,607	8.7	0.1	212,244
North Dakota	24	0.2	76	0.1	3	1.9	24,842	8.0	0.1	333,125
Idaho	44	0.3	93	0.2	2	2.1	23,043	6.3	0.1	142,045
South Dakota	15	0.1	25	0.0	2	0.7	29,720	2.1	0.0	140,600
Kansas	139	1.1	750*	-	-	(D)	-	(D)	-	-
Rhode Island	30	0.2	60*	-	-	(D)	-	(D)	-	-

Source: 1997 *Economic Census*. The states are in descending order of revenues or establishments (if revenue data are missing for the majority). The symbol (D) appears when data are withheld to prevent disclosure of competitive information. States marked with (D) are sorted by number of establishments. A dash (-) indicates that the data element cannot be calculated. * indicates the midpoint of a range; 175, for example is the range 100-249. Shaded *states* on the state map indicate those states which have proportionately greater representation in the industry than would be indicated by the state's population; the ratio is based on total revenues or number of establishments. Shaded *regions* indicate where the industry is regionally most concentrated.

345

NAICS 541710 - RESEARCH AND DEVELOPMENT IN THE PHYSICAL, ENGINEERING, AND LIFE SCIENCES

GENERAL STATISTICS

Year	Establishments (number)	Employment (number)	Payroll ($ million)	Revenues ($ million)	Employees per Establishment (number)	Revenues per Establishment ($)	Payroll per Employee ($)
1997	9,173	269,116	13,414.0	34,146.0	29.3	3,722,446	49,845

Source: Economic Census of the United States, 1997. This is a newly defined industry. Data for prior years were unavailable at the time of publication but may become available over time.

INDICES OF CHANGE

Year	Establishments (number)	Employment (number)	Payroll ($ million)	Revenues ($ million)	Employees per Establishment (number)	Revenues per Establishment ($)	Payroll per Employee ($)
1997	100.0	100.0	100.0	100.0	100.0	100.0	100.0

Sources: Same as General Statistics. The values shown reflect change from the base year, 1997. Values above 100 mean greater than 1997, values below 100 mean less than 1997, and a value of 100 in the 1982-96 or 1998-2001 period means same as 1997. Values followed by a 'p' are projections by the editors; 'e' stands for extrapolation. Data are the most recent available at this level of detail.

SIC INDUSTRIES RELATED TO NAICS 541710

Each new NAICS code represents an industry that used to be part of an SIC or a part of several SIC industries. Data in this table are shown to provide transitional information for these cases. All available data for the precursor SIC(s) are shown. Even if only a part of an SIC is included in the NAICS, *all* data for the SIC are reproduced. If the SIC industry is not marked as being a part (pt) of the NAICS, the entire industry is embedded in the NAICS data. The SIC composition of the new industry provides some hints of the relative importance of its "ancestors." Data marked with a 'p' are projected. Projections begin with 1982 data. Data earlier than 1990 are not shown but are reflected in the projections.

SIC	Industry	1990	1991	1992	1993	1994	1995	1996	1997
3721	**Aircraft (pt)**								
	Establishments (number)	181	198	182	260	204	224	222p	227p
	Employment (thousands)	300.0	258.3	264.9	241.2	217.9	201.4	188.3	223.4p
	Value of Shipments ($ million) . .	51,369.6	58,090.2	62,980.8	55,119.8	50,944.0	49,504.1	47,312.6	60,077.3p
3724	**Aircraft Engines & Engine Parts (pt)**								
	Establishments (number)	442	437	442	423	410	395	455p	462p
	Employment (thousands)	133.6	122.3	116.7	102.9	86.9	76.3	75.1	89.8p
	Value of Shipments ($ million) . .	22,812.8	22,746.2	21,968.5	18,946.1	16,663.7	17,519.4	18,769.2	21,399.3p
3728	**Aircraft Equipment, nec (pt)**								
	Establishments (number)	1,016	1,045	1,121	1,064	1,026	992	1,068p	1,079p
	Employment (thousands)	190.1	187.3	165.3	139.4	119.5	116.3	113.4	137.4p
	Value of Shipments ($ million) . .	20,457.9	21,544.4	19,834.6	18,264.3	16,679.4	16,841.3	17,311.8	20,087.0p
3761	**Guided Missiles & Space Vehicles (pt)**								
	Establishments (number)	46	44	38	35	33	33	40p	41p
	Employment (thousands)	157.0	135.8	100.1	86.6	76.8	60.8	55.7	82.7p
	Value of Shipments ($ million) . .	25,082.6	23,399.3	19,675.1	15,799.6	15,396.9	14,315.2	13,777.3	19,233.1p
3764	**Space Propulsion Units & Parts (pt)**								
	Establishments (number)	40	37	42	39	37	34	42p	43p
	Employment (thousands)	34.0	27.7	32.3	29.2	22.8	19.6	17.2	24.7p
	Value of Shipments ($ million) . .	3,755.8	3,657.9	5,328.1	6,201.0	3,373.6	2,953.6	2,715.0	4,322.7p
3769	**Space Vehicle Equipment, nec (pt)**								
	Establishments (number)	57	53	60	63	60	49	61p	61p
	Employment (thousands)	10.1	14.2	17.2	12.3	11.1	8.8	8.1	6.5p
	Value of Shipments ($ million) . .	1,715.6	1,907.3	2,070.7	2,014.9	1,944.4	1,397.9	1,435.9	1,425.5p
8731	**Commercial Physical Research**								
	Establishments (number)	3,670	4,075	4,170	4,563	4,953	5,281	5,808p	6,143p
	Employment (thousands)	164.8	166.7	159.1	164.3	175.2	176.5	208.9p	219.2p
	Revenues ($ million)	10,629.0	10,705.0	11,850.0	13,132.0	13,798.0	14,421.0	16,737.0	17,090.3p
8733	**Noncommercial Research Organizations (pt)**								
	Establishments (number)	2,639	2,834	2,769	2,863	3,024	3,148	3,222p	3,325p
	Employment (thousands)	67.2	73.1	66.9	74.7	76.7	79.6	82.9p	85.9p
	Revenues ($ million)	-	-	-	-	-	7,688.0	8,293.0	

Source: Economic Census of the United States, 1992, annual surveys of economic sectors conducted by the Bureau of the Census, and estimates or projections based on the 1982-1992 period; not all data are shown. 'e' marks estimates made by the editors; 'p' indicates projections based on time series. A dash (-) indicates that data for this SIC or year were not available. The abbreviation (pt) next to the industry name indicates that only a part of the industry is present within the NAICS data. If no (pt) is shown, the entire industry is contained within the NAICS data.

SELECTED RATIOS

For 1997	Avg. of Information	Analyzed Industry	Index	For 1997	Avg. of Information	Analyzed Industry	Index
Employees per establishment	9	29	340	Payroll per establishment	372,545	1,462,335	393
Revenue per establishment	958,337	3,722,446	388	Payroll as % of revenue	39	39	101
Revenue per employee	111,029	126,882	114	Payroll per employee	43,162	49,845	115

Sources: Same as General Statistics. The 'Average' column represents the average for the industry sector, in 1997, where the currently shown industry is classified. The Index shows the relationship between the Average and the Analyzed Industry. For example, 100 means that they are equal; 500 that the Analyzed Industry is five times the average; 50 means that the Analyzed Industry is half the national average. The abbreviation 'na' is used to show that data are 'not available'.

LEADING COMPANIES Number shown: 75   Total sales ($ mil): 149,406   Total employment (000): 333.3

Company Name	Address				CEO Name	Phone	Co. Type	Sales ($ mil)	Empl. (000)
Antech Ltd.	1 Triangle Ln	Export	PA	15632	David Miller	724-733-1161	S	74,495	<0.1
Abbott Laboratories	100 Abbott Park Rd	Abbott Park	IL	60064	Robert Parkinson	847-937-6100	P	13,178	56.2
Akzo Nobel Chemicals Inc.	5 Livingstone Ave	Dobbs Ferry	NY	10522		914-674-5000	P	13,000	68.0
CuraGen Corp.	555 Long Wharf Dr	New Haven	CT	06511	J M Rothberg,PhD	203-401-3330	P	9,257	0.3
Science Applications Intern. Corp.	10260 Campus Point	San Diego	CA	92121	J Robert Beyster	619-546-6000	R	4,200*	35.0
AMDL Inc.	14272 Franklin Ave	Tustin	CA	92780	Gary L Dreher	714-505-4460	P	3,943	29.7
Pharmacyclics Inc.	995 E Arques Ave	Sunnyvale	CA	94086	Richard Miller	408-774-0330	P	3,531	<0.1
DBS Industries Inc.	100 Shoreline	Mill Valley	CA	94941	Fred W Thompson	415-380-8055	P	3,513	<0.1
Silicon Graphics Inc	1600 Amphitheatre	Mountain View	CA	94043	Robert R Bishop	650-960-1980	P	2,749	9.2
Timken Co	PO Box 6930	Canton	OH	44706	WR Timken Jr	330-438-3000	R	2,495	21.0
Neogen Corp.	620 Lesher Pl	Lansing	MI	48912		517-372-9200	P	2,248	0.2
American Biogenetic Sciences Inc.	1375 Akron St	Copiague	NY	11726	John S North	516-789-2600	P	1,197	<0.1
Quintiles Transnational Corp.	4709 Creekstone Dr	Durham	NC	27703	Santo J Costa	919-998-2000	P	1,188	15.5
Covance Inc.	210 Carnegie Ctr	Princeton	NJ	08540	Christopher Kuebler	609-452-4440	P	829	7.2
Quintiles Inc.	P O Box 13979	RTP	NC	27709	Jim Ogle	919-998-2000	S	814*	1.1
Schering-Plough Research	2000 Galloping Hill	Kenilworth	NJ	07033	Dr J Spicehandler	908-298-4000	D	760*	3.0
Chiron Corp.	4560 Horton St	Emeryville	CA	94608	Sean Lane	510-655-8730	P	737	3.2
Sandia National Laboratories	PO Box 5800	Albuquerque	NM	87185	Paul Robinson	505-845-0011	R	720*	8.0
Battelle Memorial Institute	505 King Ave	Columbus	OH	43201	Douglas Olesen	614-424-6424	R	710	7.3
Trico Products Corp.	3255 W Hamlin Rd	Rochester Hills	MI	48309		248-371-1700	P	500	6.0
Agouron Pharmaceuticals Inc.	10350 N Torrey	La Jolla	CA	92037		619-622-3000	S	467	1.0
Jackson Laboratory	600 Main St	Bar Harbor	ME	04609		207-288-6000	R	464*	1.0
Battelle Pacific Northwest	PO Box 999	Richland	WA	99352		509-375-2121	S	454*	3.5
Exxon Research & Engineering	180 Park Ave	Florham Park	NJ	07932	WRK Inness	973-765-0100	S	438*	2.4
Nichols Research Corp.	PO Box 400002	Huntsville	AL	35815		256-883-1140	P	427	3.0
IDC Government Inc.	5 Speen St	Framingham	MA	01701	Kirk Campbell	508-872-8200	D	394*	0.8
PAREXEL International Corp.	195 West St	Waltham	MA	02154	J H von Rickenbach	781-487-9900	P	349	4.4
SRI International	333 Ravenswood	Menlo Park	CA	94025	Samuel Armacost	650-859-2000	R	329	2.7
Radian Intern	10389 Placerville	Sacramento	CA	95827		916-362-5332	N	300	2.2
Southwest Research Institute	PO Box 28510	San Antonio	TX	78228	J Bates	210-522-2122	R	270	2.5
Bionova Holding Corp.	6710 San Pablo Ave	Oakland	CA	94608	Bernardo Jimenez	510-547-2395	P	262	0.6
CALSTART	3360 E Foothill Blvd	Pasadena	CA	91107	Michael J Gage	818-565-5600	R	247*	0.1
Colsa Corp.	6726 Odyssey Dr	Huntsville	AL	35806	George Tidwell	256-922-1512	R	245*	0.5
PPD Pharmaco Inc.	3151 S 17th St	Wilmington	NC	28412	Thomas D'Alonzo	910-251-0081	P	235	3.0
ACT Inc.	PO Box 168	Iowa City	IA	52243	Richard L Ferguson	319-337-1000	R	228*	1.4
Janssen Pharmaceutica Inc.	PO Box 200	Titusville	NJ	08560	David Norton	609-730-2000	S	206	1.6
MedImmune Inc.	35 W Watkins Mill	Gaithersburg	MD	20878	Melvin D Booth	301-417-0770	P	201	0.4
MIT Lincoln Laboratory	244 Wood St	Lexington	MA	02173		781-981-5500	R	190*	2.2
Millennium Pharmaceuticals Inc.	640 Mem Dr	Cambridge	MA	02139	Mark J Levin	617-679-7000	P	184	0.7
Educational Testing Service	Rosedale Rd	Princeton	NJ	08541	Janet Bowker	609-921-9000	R	177*	2.3
Coleman Research Corp.	201 S Orange Ave	Orlando	FL	32801	James Morrison	407-244-3700	S	165	1.1
GRC International Inc.	1900 Gallows Rd	Vienna	VA	22182	Gary Denman	703-506-5000	P	165	1.2
Protein Genetics Inc.	PO Box 459	De Forest	WI	53532	M Van't Noordende	608-846-3721	R	147*	0.3
Kaman Sciences Corp.	PO Box 7463	Co Springs	CO	80933		719-599-1500	S	125	1.2
SyStemix Inc.	3155 Porter Dr	Palo Alto	CA	94304		650-856-4901	S	125*	0.3
IBAH Inc.	4 Valley Sq	Blue Bell	PA	19422	Geraldine A Henwood	215-283-0770	S	123	1.4
Premier Research Worldwide	30 S 17th, St	Philadelphia	PA	19103	Joel Morganroth	215-972-0420	S	122*	0.3
ICOS Corp.	22021 20th Ave SE	Bothell	WA	98021	Paul Clark	425-485-1900	P	111	0.3
General Atomics	PO Box 85608	San Diego	CA	92186	Neil Blue	619-455-3000	R	110	1.3
Pharmacopeia Inc.	101 College Rd East	Princeton	NJ	08540	Joseph A Mollica	609-452-3600	P	104	0.5
BTG Pharmaceuticals Corp.	70 Wood Ave S	Iselin	NJ	08830		732-632-8800	P	100	0.3
Roche Bioscience	PO Box 10850	Palo Alto	CA	94304	James Woody	650-855-5050	S	99*	1.1
Roper Starch Worldwide Inc.	500 Mamaroneck	Harrison	NY	10528	Jay Wilson	914-698-0800	R	97*	0.2
IDEC Pharmaceuticals Corp.	11011 Torreyana Rd	San Diego	CA	92121	William Rastetter	858-550-8500	P	93	0.4
Chiron Technologies	4560 Horton St	Emeryville	CA	94608	Lewis T Williams	510-655-8729	S	91*	0.5
Milliken Research Corp.	PO Box 1926	Spartanburg	SC	29304		864-503-2020	S	90*	1.0
ClinTrials Research Inc.	11000 Weston Pkwy	Cary	NC	27513	Jerry R Mitchell	919-460-9005	P	90	1.3
Kendle International Inc.	700 Carew Tower	Cincinnati	OH	45202	Candace Kendle	513-381-5550	P	90	1.1
Medical Manager Research	15151 N W 99th St	Alachua	FL	32615	Michael A Singer	904-462-2148	S	88*	0.2
Logicon R and D Associates	PO Box 92500	Los Angeles	CA	90009	James Dalton	310-645-1122	S	86*	0.9
Research Foundation for Mental	44 Holland Ave	Albany	NY	12229		518-474-5661	R	84*	0.5
Applied Analytical Industries Inc.	5051 New Centre Dr	Wilmington	NC	28403	Frederick D Sancilio	910-392-1606	P	80	1.0
Sharp Microelectronics	5700 NW Pac Rim	Camas	WA	98607	John M Manning	360-834-8700	S	80	0.4
OrthoLogic Corp.	1275 W Washington	Tempe	AZ	85281		602-286-5520	P	75	0.5
Scios Inc.	820 West Maude	Sunnyvale	CA	94086	Richard B Brewer	408-616-8200	P	74	0.3
Analex Corp.	3001 Aerospace	Brook Park	OH	44142	Lee Ann Kodger	216-977-0000	R	73*	0.2
Dynetics Inc.	PO Box 5500	Huntsville	AL	35814	Tom Baumbach	256-922-9230	R	72	0.5
Chevron Research & Technology	PO Box 1272	Richmond	CA	94802	Bruce Frolich	510-242-3000	S	70*	0.6
Medtronic	7000 Central N E	Minneapolis	MN	55432	Arthur Collins	612-514-2700	S	69*	5.0
Thermo Cardiosystems Inc.	PO Box 2697	Woburn	MA	01888	Victor L Poirier	781-932-8668	P	67	0.5
Midwest Research Institute	425 Volker Blvd	Kansas City	MO	64110	James Spigarelli	816-753-7600	R	64*	0.5
TKL Research Inc.	4 Forest Ave	Paramus	NJ	07652	Jon C Anderson	201-587-0500	R	64*	0.1
Genzyme Transgenics Corp.	PO Box 9322	Framingham	MA	01701	James A Geraghty	508-620-9700	P	62	0.5
Education Development Center	55 Chapel St	Newton	MA	02458	Janet Whitla	617-969-7100	R	62	0.4
PathoGenesis Corp.	201 Elliott Ave W	Seattle	WA	98119	Wilbur Gantz	206-467-8100	P	61	0.3

Source: Ward's Business Directory of U.S. Private and Public Companies, Volumes 1 and 2, 2000. The company type code used is as follows: P - Public, R - Private, S - Subsidiary, D - Division, J - Joint Venture, A - Affiliate, G - Group, N - Company type not reported. Sales are in millions of dollars, employees are in thousands. An asterisk (*) indicates an estimated sales volume. The symbol < stands for 'less than'. Company names and addresses are truncated, in some cases, to fit into the available space.

REPRESENTATIVE NONPROFIT ORGANIZATIONS

Organization Name	Address				Phone	Income Range ($ mil)
A Charitable Foundation Corporation	2657 Windmill Pkwy	Henderson	NV	89014		1-5
AARP Foundation	601 E St NW	Washington	DC	20049		50+
Aerospace Corporation	PO Box 92957 M5-655	Los Angeles	CA	90009		50+
Alfred P Sloan Foundation	630 Fifth Ave	New York	NY	10111	212-649-1649	50+
Alzheimers Disease & Related Disorders Association	919 N Michigan Ave 1000	Chicago	IL	60611	312-335-8700	50+
American Association of Petroleum Geologists Foundation	PO Box 979	Tulsa	OK	74101	918-584-2555	5-9
American Cancer Society Divisions Inc	1599 Clifton Rd NE	Atlanta	GA	30329	404-329-7980	50+
American Diabetes Association Inc	1701 N Beauregard St	Alexandria	VA	22311	703-549-1500	50+
American Society for Testing and Materials	100 Bar Harbor Dr	W Conshohocken	PA	19428	610-832-9500	50+
American Society of Radiologic Technologists	15000 Central SE	Albuquerque	NM	87123	505-298-4500	10-19
Aurora Foundation Inc	PO Box 343910	Milwaukee	WI	53234		50+
Barrow Neurological Foundation	350 W Thomas	Phoenix	AZ	85013	602-406-3000	50+
Bayfront Medical Center Inc	701 Sixth St S	St Petersburg	FL	33701	727-823-1234	50+
Biomedical Research Foundation of Northwest Louisiana	1505 Kings Hwy	Shreveport	LA	71103	318-675-4100	10-19
Burroughs Wellcome Fund	PO Box 13901	RTP	NC	27709		50+
Central Arkansas Radiation Therapy Institute Inc	PO Box 55050	Little Rock	AR	72215		20-29
Charles Stark Draper Laboratory Inc	555 Technology SQ # 69P	Cambridge	MA	02139	617-258-3555	50+
Cystic Fibrosis Foundation	6931 Arlington Rd	Bethesda	MD	20814	301-951-4422	50+
Dairy Herd Improvement Associations of Vermont Inc	Gilman Office Ctr Bldg 3	White River JCT	VT	05001		1-5
Donald Danforth Plant Science Center	7425 Forsyth Campus	Saint Louis	MO	63105		50+
Ducks Unlimited Inc	One Waterfowl Way	Memphis	TN	38120	901-758-3825	50+
Educational Testing Service	Rosedale Rd	Princeton	NJ	08541		50+
Fisher-Titus Medical Center	272 Benedict Ave	Norwalk	OH	44857	419-668-8101	50+
Fraunhofer Center for Research in Computer Graphics Inc	321 S Main St	Providence	RI	02903	401-453-6363	1-5
Fred Hutchinson Cancer Research Center	1100 Fairview	Seattle	WA	98109	206-667-5113	50+
French & American AIDS Foundation	1209 Orange St	Wilmington	DE	19801		5-9
George S Eccles and Delores Dore Eccles Foundation	79 S Main St 1201	Salt Lake City	UT	84111		20-29
Health Science Foundation of the Medical University of SC	PO Box 250450	Charleston	SC	29425	843-792-2677	50+
Henry Ford Health System	1 Ford PL 5E	Detroit	MI	48202		50+
Hitchcock Foundation	DH Medical Center	Lebanon	NH	03756		5-9
International Sematech Inc	2706 Montopolis Dr	Austin	TX	78741	512-356-3500	50+
Jackson Laboratory	PO Box 9741	Bar Harbor	ME	04609	207-288-6000	50+
Marshall University Research Corporation	400 Hal Greer Blvd	Huntington	WV	25755	304-696-3170	20-29
Mid-America Commercialization Corporation	1500 Hayes Drive	Manhattan	KS	66502		20-29
Minnesota Medical Foundation 1342	200 Oak St SE	Minneapolis	MN	55455	612-625-1440	50+
Mississippi Action for Progress Inc	1751 Morson Rd	Jackson	MS	39209	601-923-4100	20-29
Montana State University Foundation	1501 S 11th Ave	Bozeman	MT	59717		20-29
Mountain States Tumor Institute Inc	150 E Idaho	Boise	ID	83712		10-19
National Pork Producers Council	PO Box 10383	Des Moines	IA	50306	515-223-2600	50+
Neuropsychiatric Research Institute	PO Box 1415	Fargo	ND	58107		20-29
Northwest Regional Educational Laboratory	101 SW Main St 500	Portland	OR	97204		10-19
Norwalk Hospital Association	24 Stevens St	Norwalk	CT	06850	203-852-2292	50+
Oceanic Institute	41 202 Kalanianaole Hwy	Waimanalo	HI	96795		5-9
Purdue Research Foundation	3000 Kent Ave	W Lafayette	IN	47906		50+
Ryder Memorial Hospital Inc	Call Box 859	Humacao	PR	00791		40-49
South Dakota Community Foundation	207 E Capitol Box 296	Pierre	SD	57501	605-224-8241	20-29
Southern Research Institute	2000 9th Ave S	Birmingham	AL	35205	205-581-2000	50+
Southern Southeast Regional Aquaculture Association	2721 Tngass Ave	Ketchikan	AK	99901		5-9
University Corp Atmo	PO Box 3000	Boulder	CO	80307	303-497-1000	50+
University of Kentucky Research Foundation	369 Peterson Service Bldg	Lexington	KY	40506		50+
University of Nebraska Foundation	PO Box 82555	Lincoln	NE	68501		50+
University of Wyoming Research Corporation	365 N Ninth	Laramie	WY	82072		5-9

Source: National Directory of Nonprofit Organizations, 2000, Volumes 1 and 2, The Taft Group. The table shows a selection of organizations for illustration and does not constitute a complete selection from the source. The organizations are arranged in alphabetical order.

LOCATION BY STATE AND REGIONAL CONCENTRATION

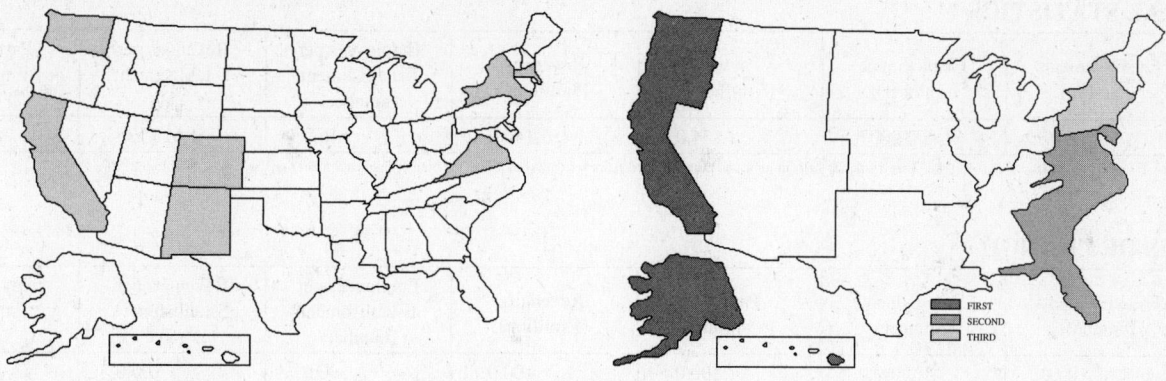

FIRST
SECOND
THIRD

INDUSTRY DATA BY STATE

State	Establishments Total (number)	Establishments % of U.S.	Employment Total (number)	Employment % of U.S.	Employment Per Estab.	Payroll Total ($ mil.)	Payroll Per Empl. ($)	Revenues Total ($ mil.)	Revenues % of U.S.	Revenues Per Estab. ($)
California	1,874	20.4	51,967	19.3	28	3,053.8	58,764	7,346.3	21.5	3,920,097
New York	552	6.0	29,694	11.0	54	1,107.6	37,301	2,854.4	8.4	5,171,024
Massachusetts	571	6.2	17,818	6.6	31	1,065.9	59,820	2,595.3	7.6	4,545,158
Virginia	402	4.4	19,314	7.2	48	1,061.1	54,938	2,435.3	7.1	6,058,042
New Mexico	132	1.4	10,705	4.0	81	565.7	52,840	1,509.0	4.4	11,431,447
Texas	454	4.9	12,627	4.7	28	582.6	46,141	1,472.6	4.3	3,243,531
Pennsylvania	331	3.6	10,484	3.9	32	517.7	49,384	1,446.5	4.2	4,370,021
Illinois	229	2.5	11,019	4.1	48	488.8	44,361	1,331.6	3.9	5,814,655
Washington	257	2.8	8,703	3.2	34	405.3	46,576	1,106.9	3.2	4,306,899
Ohio	284	3.1	7,752	2.9	27	373.7	48,204	1,078.0	3.2	3,795,789
Colorado	303	3.3	6,913	2.6	23	360.7	52,176	892.4	2.6	2,945,231
North Carolina	232	2.5	6,630	2.5	29	314.9	47,502	838.7	2.5	3,615,047
D.C.	116	1.3	3,383	1.3	29	166.5	49,230	656.3	1.9	5,657,905
Michigan	182	2.0	4,842	1.8	27	213.2	44,030	614.9	1.8	3,378,473
Florida	423	4.6	4,697	1.7	11	181.1	38,547	459.7	1.3	1,086,745
Arizona	140	1.5	2,098	0.8	15	90.7	43,215	275.8	0.8	1,969,679
Georgia	161	1.8	2,369	0.9	15	125.7	53,042	272.4	0.8	1,692,025
Connecticut	125	1.4	1,296	0.5	10	81.2	62,622	191.2	0.6	1,529,224
Missouri	113	1.2	1,370	0.5	12	54.8	39,965	177.3	0.5	1,569,345
Wisconsin	95	1.0	1,816	0.7	19	69.8	38,421	175.0	0.5	1,841,895
Nevada	55	0.6	1,925	0.7	35	92.5	48,077	164.9	0.5	2,997,655
Minnesota	136	1.5	1,349	0.5	10	55.5	41,133	163.4	0.5	1,201,728
Oregon	128	1.4	1,574	0.6	12	61.7	39,226	140.3	0.4	1,096,000
Utah	106	1.2	1,380	0.5	13	63.1	45,714	137.4	0.4	1,296,679
Indiana	52	0.6	1,137	0.4	22	40.4	35,571	135.6	0.4	2,607,212
New Hampshire	68	0.7	663	0.2	10	32.5	49,042	71.6	0.2	1,053,441
Oklahoma	40	0.4	449	0.2	11	18.3	40,735	66.7	0.2	1,666,250
Louisiana	63	0.7	573	0.2	9	20.7	36,197	62.9	0.2	997,667
Rhode Island	34	0.4	580	0.2	17	27.8	47,872	52.9	0.2	1,555,294
Montana	45	0.5	574	0.2	13	21.6	37,617	51.2	0.1	1,137,956
Mississippi	27	0.3	299	0.1	11	13.1	43,910	35.0	0.1	1,297,704
Vermont	22	0.2	208	0.1	9	6.9	33,034	24.5	0.1	1,112,091
Iowa	38	0.4	244	0.1	6	8.7	35,791	23.1	0.1	606,737
Arkansas	13	0.1	166	0.1	13	5.6	33,711	11.7	0.0	902,462
Wyoming	9	0.1	100	0.0	11	4.5	45,250	10.6	0.0	1,183,333
Delaware	17	0.2	91	0.0	5	2.8	31,000	7.8	0.0	456,706

Source: 1997 Economic Census. The states are in descending order of revenues or establishments (if revenue data are missing for the majority). The symbol (D) appears when data are withheld to prevent disclosure of competitive information. States marked with (D) are sorted by number of establishments. A dash (-) indicates that the data element cannot be calculated. * indicates the midpoint of a range; 175, for example is the range 100-249. Shaded states on the state map indicate those states which have proportionally greater representation in the industry than would be indicated by the state's population; the ratio is based on total revenues or number of establishments. Shaded regions indicate where the industry is regionally most concentrated.

NAICS 541720 - RESEARCH AND DEVELOPMENT IN THE SOCIAL SCIENCES AND HUMANITIES

GENERAL STATISTICS

Year	Establishments (number)	Employment (number)	Payroll ($ million)	Revenues ($ million)	Employees per Establishment (number)	Revenues per Establishment ($)	Payroll per Employee ($)
1997	1,949	33,007	1,134.0	3,144.0	16.9	1,613,135	34,356

Source: Economic Census of the United States, 1997. This is a newly defined industry. Data for prior years were unavailable at the time of publication but may become available over time.

INDICES OF CHANGE

Year	Establishments (number)	Employment (number)	Payroll ($ million)	Revenues ($ million)	Employees per Establishment (number)	Revenues per Establishment ($)	Payroll per Employee ($)
1997	100.0	100.0	100.0	100.0	100.0	100.0	100.0

Sources: Same as General Statistics. The values shown reflect change from the base year, 1997. Values above 100 mean greater than 1997, values below 100 mean less than 1997, and a value of 100 in the 1982-96 or 1998-2001 period means same as 1997. Values followed by a 'p' are projections by the editors; 'e' stands for extrapolation. Data are the most recent available at this level of detail.

SIC INDUSTRIES RELATED TO NAICS 541720

Each new NAICS code represents an industry that used to be part of an SIC or a part of several SIC industries. Data in this table are shown to provide transitional information for these cases. All available data for the precursor SIC(s) are shown. Even if only a part of an SIC is included in the NAICS, *all* data for the SIC are reproduced. If the SIC industry is not marked as being a part (pt) of the NAICS, the entire industry is embedded in the NAICS data. The SIC composition of the new industry provides some hints of the relative importance of its "ancestors." Data marked with a 'p' are projected. Projections begin with 1982 data. Data earlier than 1990 are not shown but are reflected in the projections.

SIC	Industry	1990	1991	1992	1993	1994	1995	1996	1997
8732	**Commercial Nonphysical Research (pt)**								
	Establishments (number)	4,821	4,804	5,701	5,688	5,579	5,611	5,532p	5,563p
	Employment (thousands)	100.7	98.7	105.4	112.9	116.2	123.1	124.8p	129.0p
	Revenues ($ million)	5,629.0	5,734.0	6,250.0	6,522.0	6,579.0	6,850.0	8,187.0	8,011.0p
8733	**Noncommercial Research Organizations (pt)**								
	Establishments (number)	2,639	2,834	2,769	2,863	3,024	3,148	3,222p	3,325p
	Employment (thousands)	67.2	73.1	66.9	74.7	76.7	79.6	82.9p	85.9p
	Revenues ($ million)						7,688.0	8,293.0	

Source: Economic Census of the United States, 1992, annual surveys of economic sectors conducted by the Bureau of the Census, and estimates or projections based on the 1982-1992 period; not all data are shown. 'e' marks estimates made by the editors; 'p' indicates projections based on time series. A dash (-) indicates that data for this SIC or year were not available. The abbreviation (pt) next to the industry name indicates that only a part of the industry is present within the NAICS data. If no (pt) is shown, the entire industry is contained within the NAICS data.

SELECTED RATIOS

For 1997	Avg. of Information	Analyzed Industry	Index	For 1997	Avg. of Information	Analyzed Industry	Index
Employees per establishment	9	17	196	Payroll per establishment	372,545	581,837	156
Revenue per establishment	958,337	1,613,135	168	Payroll as % of revenue	39	36	93
Revenue per employee	111,029	95,253	86	Payroll per employee	43,162	34,356	80

Sources: Same as General Statistics. The 'Average' column represents the average for the industry sector, in 1997, where the currently shown industry is classified. The Index shows the relationship between the Average and the Analyzed Industry. For example, 100 means that they are equal; 500 that the Analyzed Industry is five times the average; 50 means that the Analyzed Industry is half the national average. The abbreviation 'na' is used to show that data are 'not available'.

LEADING COMPANIES

No company data available for this industry.

REPRESENTATIVE NONPROFIT ORGANIZATIONS

Organization Name	Address				Phone	Income Range ($ mil)
AIDS Taskforce of Greater Cleveland Inc	2728 Euclid Ave Ste 400	Cleveland	OH	44115	216-621-0766	1-5
Academy of Producer Insurance Studies Inc	3630 C N Hills Dr	Austin	TX	78731	512-346-7050	1-5
Agile Manufacturing Enterprise Forum	2178 Industrial Dr Ste 914	Bethlehem	PA	18017		1-5
Associated Marine Institutes Inc	5915 Benjamin Center Dr	Tampa	FL	33634	813-887-3300	40-49
Bair Ranch Foundation	1601 Lewis Ave Ste 105	Billings	MT	59102		1-5
Bank Administration Institute	1 N Franklin St Ste 1000	Chicago	IL	60606	312-553-4600	20-29
Barry Goldwater Institute for Public Policy Research	201 N Central Ave	Phoenix	AZ	85073	602-256-7018	1-5
Center for Christian Studies Inc	107 S Greenlawn Ave	South Bend	IN	46617		5-9
Center for Healthcare Strategies Supporting Organization Inc	353 Nassau St	Princeton	NJ	08540		10-19
Center for Strategic and International Studies Inc	1800 K Street NW	Washington	DC	20006	202-887-0200	20-29
Citizens United	PO Box 1850	Milton	WA	98354		1-5
Concerns of Police Survivors	PO Box 3199	Camdenton	MO	65020	573-346-4911	1-5
Connecticut Assn for Comm Action	555 Windsor St	Hartford	CT	06120		20-29
Erickson Foundation Inc	701 Maiden Choice Lane	Baltimore	MD	21228		5-9
Freedom Forum First Amendment Center Inc	1207 15th Ave S	Nashville	TN	37212	615-321-9588	1-5
Georgia State University Research Foundation Inc	GA State Univ G76	Atlanta	GA	30303		1-5
Hawaii Carpenters Market Recovery Program Fund	1199 Dillingham Blvd 200	Honolulu	HI	96817		5-9
Institute for Global Ethics	11 13 Main St	Camden	ME	04843	207-236-6658	1-5
Institute of Professional Practice	PO Box 1249	Montpelier	VT	05601	802-229-9515	20-29
Lansing Regional Development Foundation	PO Box 14030	Lansing	MI	48901		1-5
Maharishi Spiritual Center of America	639 Whispering Hills	Boone	NC	28607		20-29
McRel Institute	2550 So Parker Rd	Aurora	CO	80014		1-5
Metropolitan New York Coordinating Council on Jewish Poverty	80 Maiden LN FL 21	New York	NY	10038		20-29
Midwest Assistance Program Inc	PO Box 81	New Prague	MN	56071		1-5
National Bureau of Economic Research Inc	1050 Massachusetts Ave	Cambridge	MA	02138	617-441-3895	20-29
North Louisiana Area Health Education Center Foundation	6007 Financial Plaza	Shreveport	LA	71129		1-5
Northwest Portland Area Indian Health Board	520 SW Harrison 335	Portland	OR	97201		1-5
Packard Humanities Institute	300 Second St Ste 201	Los Altos	CA	94022	650-948-0150	30-39
Printing Industries of America Inc	100 Daingerfield Rd	Alexandria	VA	22314	703-519-8100	30-39
Rhode Island Economic Policy	15 Westminster St	Providence	RI	02903		1-5
Salt Lake Legal Defender Association	1935 S Main 522	Salt Lake City	UT	84115	801-487-5619	5-9
Wisconsin Early Childhood Association Inc	2040 Sherman Ave	Madison	WI	53704	608-240-9880	5-9
Wyobraska Natural History Museum	PO Box 623	Gering	NE	69341	308-436-7104	1-5

Source: National Directory of Nonprofit Organizations, 2000, Volumes 1 and 2, The Taft Group. The table shows a selection of organizations for illustration and does not constitute a complete selection from the source. The organizations are arranged in alphabetical order.

LOCATION BY STATE AND REGIONAL CONCENTRATION

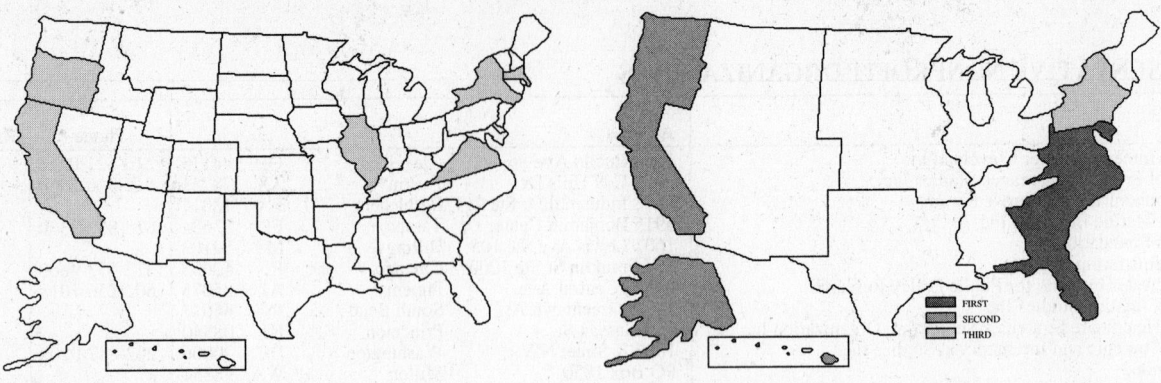

INDUSTRY DATA BY STATE

State	Establishments		Employment			Payroll		Revenues		
	Total (number)	% of U.S.	Total (number)	% of U.S.	Per Estab.	Total ($ mil.)	Per Empl. ($)	Total ($ mil.)	% of U.S.	Per Estab. ($)
D.C.	186	9.5	4,353	13.2	23	201.3	46,241	614.0	19.5	3,301,323
California	275	14.1	4,418	13.4	16	196.2	44,408	479.8	15.3	1,744,745
Massachusetts	114	5.8	4,671	14.2	41	131.2	28,094	360.7	11.5	3,164,298
New York	178	9.1	2,647	8.0	15	118.7	44,827	320.8	10.2	1,802,096
Illinois	75	3.8	2,525	7.6	34	59.5	23,560	153.6	4.9	2,047,360
Texas	85	4.4	739	2.2	9	19.7	26,641	144.9	4.6	1,704,565
Virginia	73	3.7	991	3.0	14	32.7	32,947	82.0	2.6	1,123,178
Pennsylvania	78	4.0	787	2.4	10	28.1	35,652	75.4	2.4	966,654
Florida	60	3.1	684	2.1	11	18.9	27,640	46.8	1.5	780,450
North Carolina	49	2.5	455	1.4	9	14.5	31,826	43.0	1.4	877,857
Oregon	36	1.8	630	1.9	18	16.8	26,738	37.7	1.2	1,046,556
Colorado	46	2.4	413	1.3	9	15.2	36,705	36.4	1.2	792,283
Ohio	45	2.3	353	1.1	8	10.3	29,040	28.8	0.9	639,844
Michigan	34	1.7	326	1.0	10	9.6	29,390	27.7	0.9	815,235
Minnesota	39	2.0	248	0.8	6	9.1	36,577	26.5	0.8	679,615
Connecticut	26	1.3	328	1.0	13	9.7	29,616	25.7	0.8	987,885
Arizona	41	2.1	360	1.1	9	8.4	23,456	24.6	0.8	600,488
Washington	40	2.1	184	0.6	5	6.7	36,451	16.2	0.5	406,050
Wisconsin	19	1.0	250	0.8	13	9.2	36,672	16.2	0.5	854,684
Kansas	16	0.8	101	0.3	6	4.6	46,030	11.1	0.4	694,062
New Mexico	18	0.9	93	0.3	5	2.8	30,495	7.6	0.2	419,889
Missouri	20	1.0	146	0.4	7	3.1	20,904	7.0	0.2	348,000
Rhode Island	11	0.6	82	0.2	7	2.9	34,976	6.1	0.2	557,545
Montana	10	0.5	56	0.2	6	2.0	35,679	5.6	0.2	557,300
Arkansas	7	0.4	157	0.5	22	3.9	24,994	5.6	0.2	801,286
Georgia	20	1.0	157	0.5	8	2.1	13,325	5.3	0.2	265,000
Kentucky	4	0.2	28	0.1	7	1.0	36,750	3.7	0.1	918,500
Iowa	13	0.7	50	0.2	4	1.3	26,600	3.6	0.1	280,000
Utah	18	0.9	44	0.1	2	1.3	29,250	3.4	0.1	187,000
Nevada	12	0.6	29	0.1	2	1.1	37,793	2.6	0.1	216,250
New Hampshire	9	0.5	69	0.2	8	1.3	18,565	2.6	0.1	283,778
Hawaii	8	0.4	21	0.1	3	0.8	37,476	2.4	0.1	294,250
Idaho	4	0.2	82	0.2	20	1.3	16,122	1.4	0.0	355,500
Delaware	5	0.3	11	0.0	2	0.1	12,455	0.5	0.0	93,600
Louisiana	5	0.3	23	0.1	5	0.2	8,652	0.4	0.0	81,800
Oklahoma	6	0.3	15	0.0	3	0.2	14,200	0.4	0.0	72,667

Source: 1997 Economic Census. The states are in descending order of revenues or establishments (if revenue data are missing for the majority). The symbol (D) appears when data are withheld to prevent disclosure of competitive information. States marked with (D) are sorted by number of establishments. A dash (-) indicates that the data element cannot be calculated. * indicates the midpoint of a range; 175, for example is the range 100-249. Shaded *states* on the state map indicate those states which have proportionately greater representation in the industry than would be indicated by the state's population; the ratio is based on total revenues or number of establishments. Shaded *regions* indicate where the industry is regionally most concentrated.

NAICS 541810 - ADVERTISING AGENCIES*

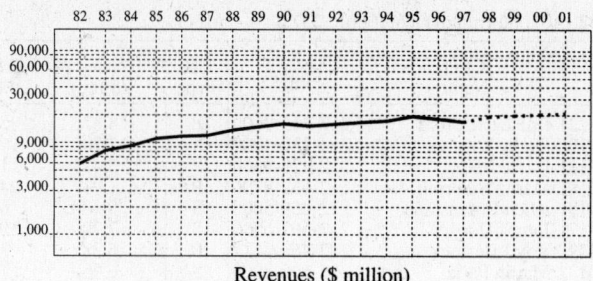

Revenues ($ million)

Employment (000)

GENERAL STATISTICS

Year	Establishments (number)	Employment (number)	Payroll ($ million)	Revenues ($ million)	Employees per Establishment (number)	Revenues per Establishment ($)	Payroll per Employee ($)
1982	10,225	106,777	2,655.0	5,920.0	10.4	578,973	24,865
1983	10,647 e	112,213 e	3,004.0 e	8,196.0	10.5 e	769,794 e	26,771 e
1984	11,069 e	117,649 e	3,353.0 e	9,248.0	10.6 e	835,486 e	28,500 e
1985	11,491 e	123,085 e	3,701.0 e	11,100.0	10.7 e	965,973 e	30,069 e
1986	11,913 e	128,521 e	4,050.0 e	11,748.0	10.8 e	986,150 e	31,512 e
1987	12,335	133,957	4,399.0	12,007.0	10.9	973,409	32,839
1988	12,048	135,712	4,906.0	13,695.0	11.3	1,136,703	36,150
1989	11,005	138,503	5,128.0	14,849.0	12.6	1,349,296	37,024
1990	11,068	137,373	5,352.0	16,089.0	12.4	1,453,650	38,960
1991	11,044	132,085	5,307.0	15,200.0	12.0	1,376,313	40,179
1992	13,879	132,042	5,649.0	15,956.0	9.5	1,149,651	42,782
1993	13,578	133,299	5,785.0	16,711.0	9.8	1,230,741	43,399
1994	13,690	136,399	6,229.0	17,259.0	10.0	1,260,701	45,667
1995	13,672	142,180	6,851.0	19,347.0	10.4	1,415,082	48,185
1996	13,531 e	140,833 e	7,204.0 e	18,109.0 e	10.4 e	1,338,334 e	51,153 e
1997	13,390	139,486	7,557.0	16,871.0	10.4	1,259,970	54,177
1998	14,130 p	139,720 p	7,618.0 p	19,244.0 p	9.9 p	1,361,925 p	54,523 p
1999	14,375 p	140,252 p	7,912.0 p	19,784.0 p	9.8 p	1,376,278 p	56,413 p
2000	14,621 p	140,783 p	8,206.0 p	20,323.0 p	9.6 p	1,389,987 p	58,288 p
2001	14,866 p	141,314 p	8,501.0 p	20,862.0 p	9.5 p	1,403,336 p	60,157 p

Sources: Economic Census of the United States, 1982, 1987, 1992, 1997. Establishment counts, employment, and payroll are from County Business Patterns for non-Census years. In non-Census years, industries in the Manufacturing range under SIC coding include data from the Annual Survey of Manufactures (ASM); those in the old Services range include data from the Services Annual Survey (SAS). Values followed by a 'p' are projections by the editors. Extrapolations are marked by 'e'. Data are the most recent available at this level of detail.

INDICES OF CHANGE

Year	Establishments (number)	Employment (number)	Payroll ($ million)	Revenues ($ million)	Employees per Establishment (number)	Revenues per Establishment ($)	Payroll per Employee ($)
1982	76.4	76.6	35.1	35.1	100.2	46.0	45.9
1987	92.1	96.0	58.2	71.2	104.3	77.3	60.6
1992	103.7	94.7	74.8	94.6	91.3	91.2	79.0
1993	101.4	95.6	76.6	99.1	94.2	97.7	80.1
1994	102.2	97.8	82.4	102.3	95.6	100.1	84.3
1995	102.1	101.9	90.7	114.7	99.8	112.3	88.9
1996	101.1 e	101.0 e	95.3 e	107.3 e	99.9 e	106.2 e	94.4 e
1997	100.0	100.0	100.0	100.0	100.0	100.0	100.0
1998	105.5 p	100.2 p	100.8 p	114.1 p	94.9 p	108.1 p	100.6 p
1999	107.4 p	100.5 p	104.7 p	117.3 p	93.7 p	109.2 p	104.1 p
2000	109.2 p	100.9 p	108.6 p	120.5 p	92.4 p	110.3 p	107.6 p
2001	111.0 p	101.3 p	112.5 p	123.7 p	91.3 p	111.4 p	111.0 p

Sources: Same as General Statistics. The values shown reflect change from the base year, 1997. Values above 100 mean greater than 1997, values below 100 mean less than 1997, and a value of 100 in the 1982-96 or 1998-2001 period means same as 1997. Values followed by a 'p' are projections by the editors; 'e' stands for extrapolation. Data are the most recent available at this level of detail.

SELECTED RATIOS

For 1997	Avg. of Information	Analyzed Industry	Index	For 1997	Avg. of Information	Analyzed Industry	Index
Employees per establishment	9	10	121	Payroll per establishment	372,545	564,376	151
Revenue per establishment	958,337	1,259,970	131	Payroll as % of revenue	39	45	115
Revenue per employee	111,029	120,951	109	Payroll per employee	43,162	54,177	126

Sources: Same as General Statistics. The 'Average' column represents the average for the industry sector, in 1997, where the currently shown industry is classified. The Index shows the relationship between the Average and the Analyzed Industry. For example, 100 means that they are equal; 500 that the Analyzed Industry is five times the average; 50 means that the Analyzed Industry is half the national average. The abbreviation 'na' is used to show that data are 'not available'.

*Equivalent to SIC 7311.

LEADING COMPANIES   Number shown: **75**   Total sales ($ mil): **168,232**   Total employment (000): **237.3**

Company Name	Address				CEO Name	Phone	Co. Type	Sales ($ mil)	Empl. (000)
Omnicom Group Inc.	437 Madison Ave	New York	NY	10022	Bruce Crawford	212-415-3600	P	28,876	35.6
Ogilvy & Mather Worldwide Inc.	309 W 49th St	New York	NY	10019	Shelly Lazarus	212-237-4000	S	12,700	10.5
True North Communications Inc.	101 E Erie St	Chicago	IL	60611	David Bell	312-425-6500	P	12,423	11.4
WPP Group USA Inc.	309 W 49th St	New York	NY	10019	Martin S Sorrell	212-632-2200	P	11,937	24.0
BBDO Worldwide Inc.	1285 Av Americas	New York	NY	10019	Allen Rosenshine	212-459-5000	S	8,400*	6.0
McCann-Erickson Worldwide Inc.	750 3rd Ave	New York	NY	10017	John J Dooner Jr	212-697-6000	S	7,200*	10.0
MacManus Group	1675 Broadway	New York	NY	10019	Roy J Bostock	212-468-3622	R	6,387*	7.6
Ammirati Puris Lintas Inc.	1 Hammarskjold	New York	NY	10017	Martin Puris	212-605-8000	S	6,000	7.4
J. Walter Thompson Co.	466 Lexington Ave	New York	NY	10017	Chris Jones	212-210-7000	R	6,000*	9.2
Foote, Cone and Belding	150 E 42nd St	New York	NY	10017	Brendan Ryan	212-885-3000	S	5,906	4.8
Leo Burnett Company Inc.	35 W Wacker Dr	Chicago	IL	60601	Richard B Fizdale	312-220-5959	R	5,548*	8.1
DDB Needham Worldwide	437 Madison Ave	New York	NY	10022	Keith L Reinhard	212-415-2000	P	5,513*	8.0
Western International Media Corp.	8544 Sunset Blvd	Los Angeles	CA	90069	Dennis F Holt	310-659-5711	S	4,132*	1.8
Bozell Worldwide	40 W 23rd St	New York	NY	10010	L Kelmenson	212-727-5000	S	3,060	3.1
Interpublic Group of Companies	1271 Av Americas	New York	NY	10020	Philip H Geier Jr	212-399-8000	P	2,990*	23.0
Visions USA Inc.	57 Forsyth St	Atlanta	GA	30303	Cyrus W Daniels Jr	404-880-0002	R	2,587*	<0.1
Petry Media Corp.	1290 Av Americas	New York	NY	10019	Thomas F Burchill	212-230-5800	R	2,000	1.1
McCann-Erickson USA Inc.	750 3rd Ave	New York	NY	10017	Don Dillon	212-697-6000	S	1,800*	1.8
Young and Rubicam Inc.	285 Madison Ave	New York	NY	10017	Thomas D Bell Jr	212-210-3000	P	1,522	13.0
BBDO New York	1285 Av Americas	New York	NY	10019	Bill Katz	212-459-5000	D	1,500*	0.8
DraftWorldwide Inc.	633 N St Clair St	Chicago	IL	60611	Howard Draft	312-944-3500	S	1,300	1.4
Carat North America	3 Park Ave	New York	NY	10016	David Verklin	212-252-0050	S	1,200*	0.5
TBWA Chiat/Day Inc.	180 Maiden Ln	New York	NY	10038	William G Tragos	212-804-1000	S	993*	1.0
Grey Advertising Inc.	777 3rd Ave	New York	NY	10017	Edward H Meyer	212-546-2000	P	935	10.7
Varon and Associates Inc.	31255 Southfield Rd	Beverly Hills	MI	48025	Shaaron Varon	248-645-9730	R	915*	<0.1
Campbell Mithun Esty L.L.C.	222 S 9th St	Minneapolis	MN	55402	Howard P Liszt	612-347-1000	S	904	0.6
Ketchum Communications Inc.	6 PPG Pl	Pittsburgh	PA	15222	Paul H Alvarez	412-456-3500	S	895*	0.9
Campbell-Ewald Co.	30400 Van Dyke	Warren	MI	48093	Frank Hoag	810-574-3400	S	860*	1.3
BBDO Chicago Inc.	410 N Michigan Ave	Chicago	IL	60611	Alan Rosenshine	312-337-7860	S	857*	0.8
CommonHealth	30 Lanidex Pl W	Parsippany	NJ	07054	Gilbert G Bash	973-884-2200	D	813	0.8
Visitor Marketing	610 S Peters St	New Orleans	LA	70130	Warren Reuther	504-528-9994	D	757*	1.0
Saatchi and Saatchi Los Angeles	3501 Sepulveda	Torrance	CA	90505	Scott Gilbert	310-214-6000	D	750	0.3
Bernard Hodes Advertising Inc.	555 Madison Ave	New York	NY	10022	Bernard Hodes	212-758-2600	S	730*	0.9
Lowe and Partners SMS Inc.	1114 Av Americas	New York	NY	10036	Lee Garfink	212-403-7000	S	718*	0.4
GSD and M	828 W 6th St	Austin	TX	78703	Steve Gurasich	512-427-4736	S	716*	0.6
Carat Freeman	2 Wells Ave	Newton	MA	02459	Don Byrnes	617-303-3000	S	700	0.1
Newspapers First Inc.	711 3rd Ave	New York	NY	10017	Jay Zitz	212-692-7100	R	700*	<0.1
Medicus Group International	1675 Broadway	New York	NY	10019	Glenn J De Jimone	212-468-3100	S	669*	0.6
Saatchi and Saatchi	375 Hudson St	New York	NY	10014	Jennifer Lang	212-463-2000	S	641*	0.9
McCann-Erickson-New York	750 3rd Ave	New York	NY	10017	Philip Geier	212-697-6000	S	640*	1.0
Harte-Hanks DiMark	2050 Cabot Blvd W	Langhorne	PA	19047	Wayne Rosenberger	215-750-6600	S	603	0.2
BBDO Minneapolis	625 4th Ave S	Minneapolis	MN	55415	Allen Rosenshane	612-338-8401	D	583*	0.5
Advanswers Media/Programming	10 S Broadway Ave	St. Louis	MO	63102	Donald A Stork	314-444-2100	S	565*	<0.1
Ross Roy Communications Inc.	100 Bloomfield Hills	Bloomfield Hills	MI	48304	Timothy Copacia	248-433-6000	R	563	0.8
Leo Burnett Worldwide Inc.	35 Wacker Dr	Chicago	IL	60601	Richard Fizdale	312-220-5959	S	554	6.7
Temerlin McClain	201 E Carpntr	Irving	TX	75062	Dennis McClain	972-556-1100	S	540*	0.6
Fallon McElligott	901 Marquette Ave	Minneapolis	MN	55402	Patrick Fallon	612-321-2345	R	500	0.5
Martin Agency Inc.	1 Shockoe Plz	Richmond	VA	23219	John Adams	804-698-8000	S	500	0.4
Messner, Vetere, Berger	350 Hudson St	New York	NY	10014	Louise McNamee	212-886-4100	R	500*	0.8
Arnold Communications Inc.	101 Huntington Ave	Boston	MA	02110	Ed Eskandarian	617-587-8000	S	479*	0.7
Richards Group Inc.	8750 N Cen Expwy	Dallas	TX	75231		214-891-5700	R	476*	0.5
Bates Worldwide	498 7th Ave	New York	NY	10018	Michael Bungey	212-297-7000	S	470	0.7
Baublitz Advertising	20 W Market St	York	PA	17401	Cindy Hoffman	717-854-3040	R	455*	0.6
Hill, Holliday, Connors	200 Clarendon St	Boston	MA	02116	Fred Bertino	617-437-1600	R	454*	0.6
William Douglas McAdams Inc.	1740 Broadway	New York	NY	10019	John R Puglisi	212-698-4000	P	452	0.4
EURO RSCG Tatham	980 N Michigan Ave	Chicago	IL	60611	Gary C Epstein	312-337-4400	R	448*	0.3
Rubin Postaer and Associates	1333 2nd St	Santa Monica	CA	90401	Gerrold R Rubin	310-394-4000	R	426*	0.4
Klemtner Advertising Inc.	375 Hudson St	New York	NY	10014	Gavin A Scotti	212-463-3400	S	419*	0.3
DDB Dallas Inc.	350 Maple Ave	Dallas	TX	75219	J Schropfer	214-599-5500	S	412*	0.6
TMP Worldwide Inc.	1633 Broadway	New York	NY	10019	Andrew J McKelvey	212-977-4200	P	407	5.2
Carat USA	1925 Ctry Park	Los Angeles	CA	90067	Bruce D Milner	310-557-2585	D	386*	0.2
W.B. Doner and Co.	25900 Northwestern	Southfield	MI	48075	Allan Kalter	248-354-9700	R	385*	0.6
Wunderman Cato Johnson	675 Av Americas	New York	NY	10010	Mitch Kuiz	212-941-3000	S	380*	0.5
Corporate Express	1400 N Price Rd	St. Louis	MO	63132	Michael Risso	314-432-1800	R	379*	0.5
BBDO (Sub)	2 Alhambra Plaza	Coral Gables	FL	33134	Bill Katz	212-459-6818	S	377*	0.8
Gotham Inc.	100 5th Ave	New York	NY	10011	Sheri Baron	212-414-7000	D	370	0.2
Nationwide Advertising Service	1228 Euclid Ave	Cleveland	OH	44115	John Graham	216-579-0300	R	360	0.4
Cramer-Krasselt Co.	733 N Van Buren St	Milwaukee	WI	53202	Peter Krivkobich	414-227-3500	R	356*	0.5
Petry Television Inc.	3 E 54th St	New York	NY	10022	John Heise	212-688-0200	S	353*	0.5
BBDO South	3414 Peachtree Rd	Atlanta	GA	30326	Chris Hall	404-231-1700	S	333	0.1
Cline, Davis and Mann Inc.	450 Lexington	New York	NY	10017	Morgan E Cline	212-907-4300	R	328*	0.2
Corinthian Communications Inc.	214 W 29th St	New York	NY	10001	Lawrence Miller	212-279-5700	R	320*	<0.1
Long Haymes Carr Inc.	140 Charlois Blvd	Winston-Salem	NC	27103	Steve Zades	336-765-3630	S	320	0.3
Bernstein-Rein Advertising Inc.	4600 Madison Ave	Kansas City	MO	64112	Robert A Bernstein	816-756-0640	R	304*	0.4
Avrett, Free & Ginsberg	800 3rd Ave	New York	NY	10022	Frank Ginsberg	212-832-3800	S	300	0.1

Source: Ward's Business Directory of U.S. Private and Public Companies, Volumes 1 and 2, 2000. The company type code used is as follows: P - Public, R - Private, S - Subsidiary, D - Division, J - Joint Venture, A - Affiliate, G - Group, N - Company type not reported. Sales are in millions of dollars, employees are in thousands. An asterisk (*) indicates an estimated sales volume. The symbol < stands for 'less than'. Company names and addresses are truncated, in some cases, to fit into the available space.

LOCATION BY STATE AND REGIONAL CONCENTRATION

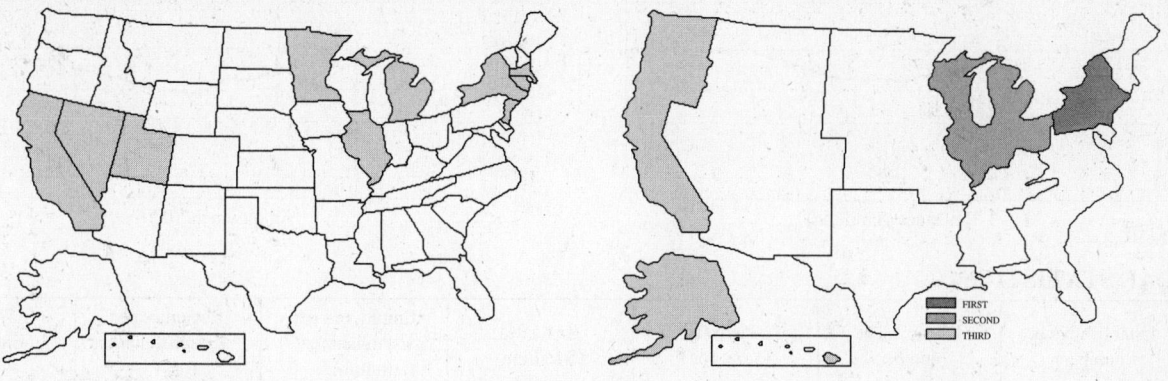

INDUSTRY DATA BY STATE

State	Establishments Total (number)	% of U.S.	Employment Total (number)	% of U.S.	Per Estab.	Payroll Total ($ mil.)	Per Empl. ($)	Revenues Total ($ mil.)	% of U.S.	Per Estab. ($)
New York	1,395	10.4	30,878	22.1	22	2,190.9	70,955	4,408.9	26.1	3,160,497
California	1,531	11.4	16,681	12.0	11	979.1	58,696	2,204.3	13.1	1,439,805
Illinois	789	5.9	10,904	7.8	14	689.8	63,260	1,546.3	9.2	1,959,842
Michigan	404	3.0	6,863	4.9	17	358.4	52,229	854.0	5.1	2,113,946
Texas	794	5.9	7,872	5.6	10	367.9	46,735	799.2	4.7	1,006,520
Massachusetts	353	2.6	4,462	3.2	13	227.0	50,883	567.5	3.4	1,607,558
New Jersey	536	4.0	4,560	3.3	9	234.7	51,472	519.8	3.1	969,748
Florida	955	7.1	5,273	3.8	6	218.5	41,432	503.8	3.0	527,557
Pennsylvania	570	4.3	4,601	3.3	8	204.7	44,495	477.2	2.8	837,179
Minnesota	315	2.4	3,745	2.7	12	196.2	52,402	457.7	2.7	1,452,952
Ohio	531	4.0	4,680	3.4	9	192.8	41,186	422.0	2.5	794,669
Georgia	367	2.7	3,059	2.2	8	142.3	46,519	334.6	2.0	911,777
Missouri	253	1.9	2,956	2.1	12	138.0	46,679	297.8	1.8	1,177,229
North Carolina	318	2.4	2,309	1.7	7	110.4	47,808	260.3	1.5	818,645
Connecticut	242	1.8	1,875	1.3	8	115.4	61,557	257.0	1.5	1,062,062
Virginia	299	2.2	2,215	1.6	7	109.6	49,464	235.9	1.4	788,890
Wisconsin	277	2.1	2,479	1.8	9	101.6	40,972	227.8	1.4	822,401
Utah	110	0.8	934	0.7	8	42.0	44,991	199.7	1.2	1,815,309
Maryland	238	1.8	2,083	1.5	9	87.6	42,055	192.8	1.1	810,046
Oregon	201	1.5	1,644	1.2	8	77.7	47,249	191.4	1.1	952,174
Tennessee	215	1.6	1,711	1.2	8	78.2	45,691	185.0	1.1	860,340
Washington	219	1.6	1,638	1.2	7	75.9	46,329	165.6	1.0	756,132
Arizona	200	1.5	1,117	0.8	6	38.6	34,538	145.0	0.9	724,785
Indiana	216	1.6	1,365	1.0	6	50.5	36,986	127.7	0.8	591,051
Alabama	147	1.1	1,065	0.8	7	42.6	40,020	109.6	0.6	745,429
Colorado	234	1.7	1,147	0.8	5	46.6	40,634	109.1	0.6	466,419
Kentucky	128	1.0	1,245	0.9	10	46.1	37,022	105.6	0.6	824,641
Nevada	111	0.8	727	0.5	7	28.3	38,884	99.9	0.6	900,324
Iowa	91	0.7	988	0.7	11	38.3	38,784	84.9	0.5	932,923
South Carolina	133	1.0	872	0.6	7	33.6	38,509	76.4	0.5	574,068
Oklahoma	112	0.8	729	0.5	7	29.7	40,678	71.6	0.4	639,643
Louisiana	169	1.3	868	0.6	5	28.4	32,726	64.6	0.4	382,349
Arkansas	85	0.6	585	0.4	7	22.8	38,944	52.4	0.3	616,247
Nebraska	78	0.6	717	0.5	9	26.5	36,900	51.3	0.3	657,436
Hawaii	67	0.5	475	0.3	7	19.6	41,202	51.1	0.3	762,328
D.C.	31	0.2	344	0.2	11	22.8	66,198	44.8	0.3	1,444,935
Rhode Island	52	0.4	329	0.2	6	14.7	44,772	41.0	0.2	788,308
New Mexico	69	0.5	288	0.2	4	8.6	29,826	36.6	0.2	530,855
Maine	60	0.4	315	0.2	5	13.3	42,175	33.9	0.2	564,550
New Hampshire	63	0.5	270	0.2	4	11.3	41,674	31.3	0.2	496,952
Mississippi	50	0.4	305	0.2	6	11.0	36,072	23.7	0.1	473,720
Idaho	33	0.2	201	0.1	6	6.5	32,408	21.8	0.1	661,970
Alaska	20	0.1	144	0.1	7	6.9	47,944	21.3	0.1	1,066,100
South Dakota	32	0.2	172	0.1	5	6.7	38,727	16.6	0.1	518,437
West Virginia	29	0.2	206	0.1	7	6.2	30,228	15.4	0.1	529,966
Vermont	31	0.2	174	0.1	6	5.8	33,460	14.5	0.1	466,387
North Dakota	21	0.2	174	0.1	8	4.9	28,201	9.1	0.1	435,619
Montana	32	0.2	158	0.1	5	3.9	24,500	8.8	0.1	275,312
Wyoming	18	0.1	44	0.0	2	1.3	30,114	4.1	0.0	228,000
Kansas	134	1.0	750*	-	-	(D)	-	(D)	-	-
Delaware	32	0.2	375*	-	-	(D)	-	(D)	-	-

Source: 1997 *Economic Census*. The states are in descending order of revenues or establishments (if revenue data are missing for the majority). The symbol (D) appears when data are withheld to prevent disclosure of competitive information. States marked with (D) are sorted by number of establishments. A dash (-) indicates that the data element cannot be calculated. * indicates the midpoint of a range; 175, for example is the range 100-249. Shaded *states* on the state map indicate those states which have proportionately greater representation in the industry than would be indicated by the state's population; the ratio is based on total revenues or number of establishments. Shaded *regions* indicate where the industry is regionally most concentrated.

NAICS 541820 - PUBLIC RELATIONS AGENCIES*

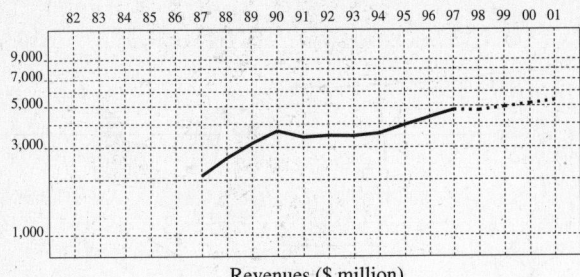

Revenues ($ million)

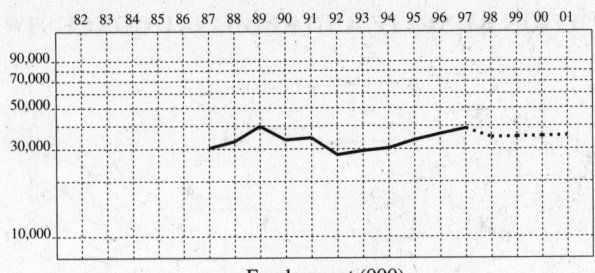

Employment (000)

GENERAL STATISTICS

Year	Establishments (number)	Employment (number)	Payroll ($ million)	Revenues ($ million)	Employees per Establishment (number)	Revenues per Establishment ($)	Payroll per Employee ($)
1982	-	-	-	-	-	-	-
1983	-	-	-	-	-	-	-
1984	-	-	-	-	-	-	-
1985	-	-	-	-	-	-	-
1986	-	-	-	-	-	-	-
1987	5,149	30,356	804.0	2,102.0	5.9	408,235	26,486
1988	4,705	32,958	978.0	2,627.0 e	7.0	558,342	29,674
1989	4,111	39,805	1,203.0	3,152.0 e	9.7	766,723	30,222
1990	4,288	33,535	1,116.0	3,677.0	7.8	857,509	33,279
1991	4,396	34,496	1,162.0	3,398.0	7.8	772,975	33,685
1992	5,308	27,835	1,107.0	3,468.0	5.2	653,353	39,770
1993	5,346	29,258	1,226.0	3,454.0	5.5	646,091	41,903
1994	5,404	30,305	1,316.0	3,571.0	5.6	660,807	43,425
1995	5,526	33,571	1,512.0	3,972.0	6.1	718,784	45,039
1996	6,020 e	36,153 e	1,732.0 e	4,372.0 e	6.0 e	726,246 e	47,908 e
1997	6,513	38,735	1,952.0	4,772.0	5.9	732,688	50,394
1998	6,225 p	34,688 p	1,836.0 p	4,740.0 p	5.6 p	761,446 p	52,929 p
1999	6,402 p	34,909 p	1,928.0 p	4,946.0 p	5.5 p	772,571 p	55,229 p
2000	6,579 p	35,130 p	2,021.0 p	5,152.0 p	5.3 p	783,098 p	57,529 p
2001	6,757 p	35,350 p	2,113.0 p	5,358.0 p	5.2 p	792,955 p	59,774 p

Sources: Economic Census of the United States, 1982, 1987, 1992, 1997. Establishment counts, employment, and payroll are from County Business Patterns for non-Census years. In non-Census years, industries in the Manufacturing range under SIC coding include data from the Annual Survey of Manufactures (ASM); those in the old Services range include data from the Services Annual Survey (SAS). Values followed by a 'p' are projections by the editors. Extrapolations are marked by 'e'. Data are the most recent available at this level of detail.

INDICES OF CHANGE

Year	Establishments (number)	Employment (number)	Payroll ($ million)	Revenues ($ million)	Employees per Establishment (number)	Revenues per Establishment ($)	Payroll per Employee ($)
1982	-	-	-	-	-	-	-
1987	79.1	78.4	41.2	44.0	99.1	55.7	52.6
1992	81.5	71.9	56.7	72.7	88.2	89.2	78.9
1993	82.1	75.5	62.8	72.4	92.0	88.2	83.2
1994	83.0	78.2	67.4	74.8	94.3	90.2	86.2
1995	84.8	86.7	77.5	83.2	102.1	98.1	89.4
1996	92.4 e	93.3 e	88.7 e	91.6 e	101.0 e	99.1 e	95.1 e
1997	100.0	100.0	100.0	100.0	100.0	100.0	100.0
1998	95.6 p	89.6 p	94.1 p	99.3 p	93.7 p	103.9 p	105.0 p
1999	98.3 p	90.1 p	98.8 p	103.6 p	91.7 p	105.4 p	109.6 p
2000	101.0 p	90.7 p	103.5 p	108.0 p	89.8 p	106.9 p	114.2 p
2001	103.7 p	91.3 p	108.2 p	112.3 p	88.0 p	108.2 p	118.6 p

Sources: Same as General Statistics. The values shown reflect change from the base year, 1997. Values above 100 mean greater than 1997, values below 100 mean less than 1997, and a value of 100 in the 1982-96 or 1998-2001 period means same as 1997. Values followed by a 'p' are projections by the editors; 'e' stands for extrapolation. Data are the most recent available at this level of detail.

SELECTED RATIOS

For 1997	Avg. of Information	Analyzed Industry	Index	For 1997	Avg. of Information	Analyzed Industry	Index
Employees per establishment	9	6	69	Payroll per establishment	372,545	299,708	80
Revenue per establishment	958,337	732,688	76	Payroll as % of revenue	39	41	105
Revenue per employee	111,029	123,196	111	Payroll per employee	43,162	50,394	117

Sources: Same as General Statistics. The 'Average' column represents the average for the industry sector, in 1997, where the currently shown industry is classified. The Index shows the relationship between the Average and the Analyzed Industry. For example, 100 means that they are equal; 500 that the Analyzed Industry is five times the average; 50 means that the Analyzed Industry is half the national average. The abbreviation 'na' is used to show that data are 'not available'.

*Equivalent to SIC 8743.

LEADING COMPANIES   Number shown: **75**   Total sales ($ mil): **23,320**   Total employment (000): **46.0**

Company Name	Address				CEO Name	Phone	Co. Type	Sales ($ mil)	Empl. (000)
Ogilvy & Mather Worldwide Inc.	309 W 49th St	New York	NY	10019	Shelly Lazarus	212-237-4000	S	12,700	10.5
Bozell Worldwide	40 W 23rd St	New York	NY	10010	L Kelmenson	212-727-5000	S	3,060	3.1
Ketchum Communications Inc.	6 PPG Pl	Pittsburgh	PA	15222	Paul H Alvarez	412-456-3500	S	895*	0.9
Burson-Marsteller	230 Park Ave S	New York	NY	10003	C Komisarjevsky	212-614-4000	S	687*	2.2
Martin Agency Inc.	1 Shockoe Plz	Richmond	VA	23219	John Adams	804-698-8000	S	500	0.4
Financial Relations Board Inc.	875 N Michigan	Chicago	IL	60611	Theodore Pincus	312-266-7800	R	395	12.0
Health & Medical	220 E 42nd St	New York	NY	10017	John J Fisher	212-771-3600	S	240*	0.2
Grey Healthcare Group Inc.	114 5th Ave	New York	NY	10011	Lynn O Vos	212-886-3000	S	210*	0.3
Miller/Shandwick International	387 Park Ave S	New York	NY	10016	Scott Meyer	212-686-6111	S	197*	0.9
HMS Partners	250 Civic Center Dr	Columbus	OH	43215	David Milenthal	614-221-7667	R	185*	0.3
Fleishman-Hillard Inc.	200 N Broadway	St. Louis	MO	63102	John D Graham	314-982-1700	S	148*	1.4
Daniel J	200 E Randolph Dr	Chicago	IL	60601	Richard W Edelman	312-240-3000	R	147*	1.4
TCI Group	777 3rd Ave	New York	NY	10017	Bob Feldman	212-546-2200	S	128*	0.4
Cohn and Wolfe	303 Peachtree St	Atlanta	GA	30308	Tony DeMartino	404-688-5900	S	125*	0.4
BSMG Worldwide	640 5th Ave	New York	NY	10019	Harris Diamond	212-445-8000	S	120	0.9
Carson Group	156 W 56th St	New York	NY	10019	Scott Ganeles	212-581-4000	R	118*	0.4
Eric Mower and Associates Inc.	500 Plum St	Syracuse	NY	13204	Eric Mower	315-466-1000	R	118	0.2
Burrell Communications Group	20 N Michigan Ave	Chicago	IL	60602	Thomas J Burrell	312-443-8600	R	115*	0.1
Ketchum	292 Madison Ave	New York	NY	10017	David Drobis	212-448-4200	S	111	1.2
Keller-Crescent Company Inc.	PO Box 3	Evansville	IN	47701		812-464-2461	R	109*	0.6
Bader Rutter and Associates Inc.	13555 Bishops Ct	Brookfield	WI	53005	Ronald L Bader	414-784-7200	R	104	0.2
Holland Communications Inc.	21125 Superior St	Chatsworth	CA	91311		818-341-4777	R	102	<0.1
Golin/Harris Communications Inc.	111 E Wacker Dr	Chicago	IL	60601	Richard Jernstedt	312-729-4000	S	96*	0.3
Creswell, Munsell, Fultz & Zirbel	PO Box 2879	Cedar Rapids	IA	52406	Frank C Baker Jr	319-395-6500	R	94	0.2
Doe-Anderson Advertising	620 W Main St	Louisville	KY	40202	David G Wilkins	502-589-1700	R	86	0.1
Laughlin/Constable Inc.	207 E Michigan St	Milwaukee	WI	53202		414-272-2400	R	85*	0.2
Middleberg and Associates	130 E 59th St	New York	NY	10022	Don Middleberg	212-888-6610	R	83*	0.1
Weber Public Relations	101 Main St	Cambridge	MA	02142	Lawrence Weber	617-661-7900	D	83	0.7
Ogilvy Public Relations	708 3rd Ave	New York	NY	10017	Bob Seltzer	212-880-5200	P	79	0.7
Rives Carlberg	2800 Post Oak Blvd	Houston	TX	77056	Charles Carlsberg	713-965-0764	R	76*	0.1
Dudnyk Advertising & Public	100 Tournament Dr	Horsham	PA	19044	Edward Dudnyk	215-443-9406	R	75*	0.1
Lewis Communications Inc.	PO Box 6829	Mobile	AL	36660	John H Lewis Jr	334-476-2507	R	73*	<0.1
Hill and Knowlton Inc.	466 Lexington Ave	New York	NY	10017	Howard Taster	212-885-0300	S	71*	0.7
St. John & Partners Advertising	5220 Belfort Rd	Jacksonville	FL	32256	Bruce Broder	904-281-2500	R	68*	<0.1
Fricks/Firestone Advertising	6 Concourse N E	Atlanta	GA	30328	John Fricks	770-396-6206	R	66*	<0.1
Lord, Sullivan & Yoder Marketing	250 O Wilson Br	Columbus	OH	43085	Bob Bender	614-846-8500	R	66	0.1
Shanwick International	8400 Normandale	Minneapolis	MN	55437		612-832-5000	S	66*	0.2
Brouillard Communications	420 Lexington Ave	New York	NY	10017	Bill Lyddan	212-867-8300	D	65	<0.1
Morgen-Walke Associates Inc.	380 Lexington Ave	New York	NY	10168		212-850-5600	R	63*	0.2
Basso and Associates Inc.	17780 Fitch, #175	Irvine	CA	92614	Joseph J Basso	949-252-1700	R	60*	<0.1
E.B. Lane and Associates Inc.	733 W McDowell	Phoenix	AZ	85007	Beau Lane	602-258-5263	R	58	<0.1
Henderson Advertising Inc.	60 Pointe Cir	Greenville	SC	29615	Ralph W Callahan Jr	864-271-6000	R	57*	<0.1
Barkley Evergreen & Partners Inc	423 W 8th St	Kansas City	MO	64105		816-432-2600	D	56*	0.2
Weightman Group	2129 Chestnut St	Philadelphia	PA	19103	John Goodchild	215-977-1700	R	55*	<0.1
Bacon's Information Inc.	PO Box 98869	Chicago	IL	60693		312-922-2400	S	53*	0.4
Marketing.Comm	10551 Barkley St	Overland Park	KS	66212	Frank G Weyforth Jr	913-648-8333	R	51	0.1
Advanced Electronic Computer	1977 O'Toole Ave	San Jose	CA	95131	Frank Yang	408-955-9268	R	50	<0.1
GCI Group Inc.	777 3rd Ave	New York	NY	10017	Robert Feldman	212-546-2200	S	50*	0.7
Mason and Madison Inc.	23 Amity Rd	New Haven	CT	06524	Charlie Mason	203-393-1101	R	50	<0.1
Rubenstein Associates Inc.	1345 Av Americas	New York	NY	10105	Howard Rubenstein	212-489-6900	R	48*	0.2
Thompson and Company Inc.	50 Peabody, 5th Fl	Memphis	TN	38103	Michael Thompson	901-527-8000	R	47*	<0.1
Cassidy Companies Inc.	700 13th St	Washington	DC	20005	Gerald SJ Cassidy	202-347-0787	P	44*	0.2
DDB Seattle	1008 Western Ave	Seattle	WA	98104	Ron Elgin	206-442-9900	S	44*	0.1
Lehman Millet Inc.	60 Canal St	Boston	MA	02114	Bruce Lehman	617-722-0019	R	43	<0.1
Thomas and Perkins Inc.	1451 Larimer Sq	Denver	CO	80202	Bryan Thomas	303-573-4911	R	43*	<0.1
Hensley Segal Rentschler Inc.	11590 Century Blvd	Cincinnati	OH	45246	Richard Segal Jr	513-671-3811	R	42*	<0.1
Phelps and Associates Inc.	901 Wilshire Blvd	Santa Monica	CA	90401	Joe Phelps	310-752-4400	R	42	<0.1
Ruder Finn Inc.	301 E 57th St	New York	NY	10022	Michael Cannata	212-593-6400	R	42	0.4
Ericson Marketing	1130 8th Ave S	Nashville	TN	37203	Gary Haynes	615-242-1050	R	42*	<0.1
Gilbert, Whitney and Johns	110 S Jefferson Rd	Whippany	NJ	07981	John Daltner	973-386-1776	R	42	<0.1
Manning, Selvage and Lee Inc.	79 Madison Ave	New York	NY	10016	Lou Capozzi	212-213-0909	S	40	0.4
Sive/Young and Rubicam	36 E 7th St	Cincinnati	OH	45202	Dale P Brown	513-345-3400	P	39	<0.1
Archer/Malmo Advertising Inc.	65 Union Ave	Memphis	TN	38103	Ward Archer	901-523-2000	R	39*	<0.1
Eisner and Associates Inc.	509 S Exeter St	Baltimore	MD	21202	Steven C Eisner	410-685-3390	R	34*	<0.1
Siddall, Matus and Coughter Inc.	830 E Main St	Richmond	VA	23219	John Martin	804-788-8011	R	34*	<0.1
Alexander Marketing Services Inc.	277 Crahen Ave	Grand Rapids	MI	49525	Robert C Milroy	616-957-2000	R	33*	<0.1
Harris Marketing Group Inc.	617 E Huron St	Ann Arbor	MI	48104	J Shukle-Rosenhaus	734-662-3442	R	33	<0.1
Regian & Wilson/Grey	219 S Main St	Fort Worth	TX	76104	Julie H Wilson	817-870-1128	P	32	<0.1
Black, Rogers, Sullivan	1900 St James Pl	Houston	TX	77056	Scott Black	713-781-6666	R	31*	<0.1
Stephan and Brady Inc.	1850 Hoffman St	Madison	WI	53704	Frank Fueger	608-241-4141	R	31*	<0.1
Cronin and Co.	50 Nye Rd #3	Glastonbury	CT	06033	William J Cronin Jr	860-659-0514	R	30	<0.1
Blue Horse Inc.	839 N Jefferson St	Milwaukee	WI	53202	Kit Vernon	414-291-7620	R	30	<0.1
FG*I Image Works Inc.	206 W Franklin St	Chapel Hill	NC	27516	Steve Lerner	919-929-7759	R	30*	0.2
Ground Zero	4235 Redwood Ave	Los Angeles	CA	90066		310-656-0050	R	30	<0.1
Brownstein Group	215 S Broad St	Philadelphia	PA	19107	Berny Brownstein	215-735-3470	R	28	<0.1

Source: Ward's Business Directory of U.S. Private and Public Companies, Volumes 1 and 2, 2000. The company type code used is as follows: P - Public, R - Private, S - Subsidiary, D - Division, J - Joint Venture, A - Affiliate, G - Group, N - Company type not reported. Sales are in millions of dollars, employees are in thousands. An asterisk (*) indicates an estimated sales volume. The symbol < stands for 'less than'. Company names and addresses are truncated, in some cases, to fit into the available space.

LOCATION BY STATE AND REGIONAL CONCENTRATION

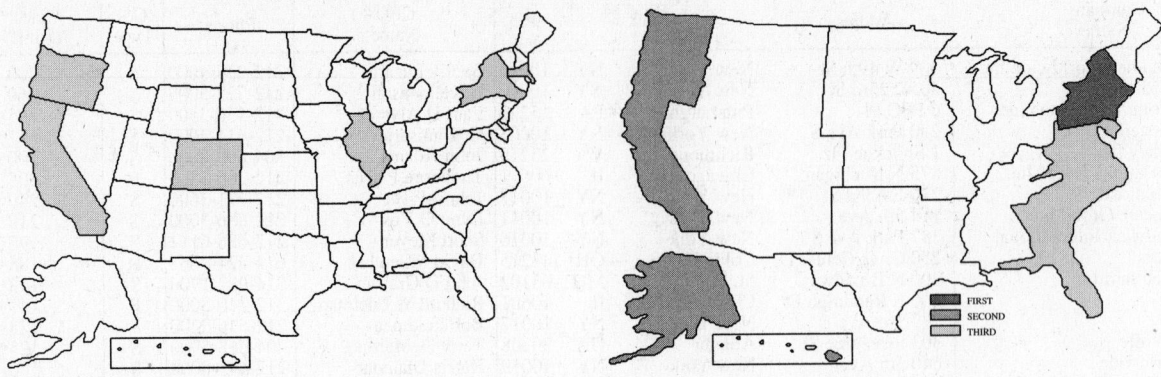

INDUSTRY DATA BY STATE

State	Establishments Total (number)	Establishments % of U.S.	Employment Total (number)	Employment % of U.S.	Employment Per Estab.	Payroll Total ($ mil.)	Payroll Per Empl. ($)	Revenues Total ($ mil.)	Revenues % of U.S.	Revenues Per Estab. ($)
New York	941	14.4	7,969	20.6	8	493.0	61,859	1,134.7	23.8	1,205,798
California	1,074	16.5	6,821	17.6	6	333.4	48,881	816.7	17.1	760,431
D.C.	312	4.8	3,192	8.2	10	230.6	72,252	493.9	10.4	1,583,093
Illinois	339	5.2	2,155	5.6	6	115.2	53,469	321.9	6.7	949,563
Massachusetts	195	3.0	2,018	5.2	10	93.8	46,477	224.5	4.7	1,151,185
Texas	333	5.1	1,411	3.6	4	59.9	42,449	165.4	3.5	496,628
New Jersey	246	3.8	1,069	2.8	4	51.6	48,234	142.1	3.0	577,667
Florida	385	5.9	1,441	3.7	4	48.0	33,299	135.7	2.8	352,545
Virginia	207	3.2	773	2.0	4	42.3	54,724	114.5	2.4	552,971
Pennsylvania	169	2.6	1,061	2.7	6	41.9	39,495	103.9	2.2	614,586
Ohio	185	2.8	807	2.1	4	34.2	42,382	92.6	1.9	500,714
Georgia	171	2.6	800	2.1	5	34.2	42,809	88.7	1.9	518,503
Michigan	141	2.2	820	2.1	6	37.4	45,635	86.7	1.8	614,965
Oregon	97	1.5	893	2.3	9	44.5	49,852	85.7	1.8	883,907
Missouri	104	1.6	805	2.1	8	41.0	50,876	82.2	1.7	790,125
Minnesota	123	1.9	749	1.9	6	35.3	47,115	80.9	1.7	657,390
Colorado	134	2.1	565	1.5	4	23.3	41,234	72.4	1.5	540,015
North Carolina	120	1.8	581	1.5	5	21.3	36,676	66.0	1.4	550,092
Washington	145	2.2	559	1.4	4	25.3	45,254	60.1	1.3	414,690
Connecticut	87	1.3	306	0.8	4	17.6	57,673	53.5	1.1	615,299
Tennessee	84	1.3	529	1.4	6	19.2	36,314	52.3	1.1	622,179
Wisconsin	86	1.3	401	1.0	5	15.4	38,484	38.8	0.8	450,826
Maryland	121	1.9	320	0.8	3	10.5	32,719	29.1	0.6	240,488
Indiana	49	0.8	215	0.6	4	6.6	30,753	23.6	0.5	481,592
Arizona	73	1.1	230	0.6	3	8.3	36,248	23.6	0.5	323,068
Alabama	42	0.6	148	0.4	4	5.6	38,020	18.7	0.4	444,738
Louisiana	66	1.0	190	0.5	3	5.3	27,637	16.9	0.4	256,000
Nevada	39	0.6	157	0.4	4	6.3	40,331	16.5	0.3	423,410
Utah	36	0.6	128	0.3	4	4.1	31,984	12.0	0.3	334,389
South Carolina	41	0.6	108	0.3	3	5.2	48,185	12.0	0.3	292,951
Kentucky	26	0.4	124	0.3	5	4.1	32,726	9.4	0.2	360,615
Oklahoma	41	0.6	147	0.4	4	3.5	23,925	8.8	0.2	213,805
West Virginia	19	0.3	97	0.3	5	3.9	39,845	8.6	0.2	451,368
Hawaii	14	0.2	88	0.2	6	3.7	42,375	7.9	0.2	564,714
New Hampshire	16	0.2	77	0.2	5	3.0	38,701	7.7	0.2	480,500
Maine	27	0.4	132	0.3	5	3.4	25,636	7.3	0.2	269,667
Iowa	32	0.5	64	0.2	2	2.0	31,000	6.2	0.1	192,750
Mississippi	11	0.2	92	0.2	8	1.8	19,272	6.0	0.1	549,364
Arkansas	19	0.3	56	0.1	3	1.4	25,036	4.9	0.1	258,211
Rhode Island	19	0.3	46	0.1	2	1.4	30,043	4.6	0.1	239,526
Idaho	16	0.2	73	0.2	5	1.7	23,493	4.3	0.1	268,813
Alaska	12	0.2	14	0.0	1	0.9	62,143	4.1	0.1	339,417
Vermont	9	0.1	22	0.1	2	0.7	32,136	3.3	0.1	362,556
Nebraska	16	0.2	38	0.1	2	1.1	29,816	3.3	0.1	203,188
New Mexico	24	0.4	33	0.1	1	1.2	37,818	3.0	0.1	124,250
Montana	10	0.2	251	0.6	25	2.1	8,490	2.8	0.1	275,400
South Dakota	5	0.1	8	0.0	2	0.3	39,625	1.2	0.0	236,200
Wyoming	6	0.1	19	0.0	3	0.3	17,421	1.1	0.0	190,500
Kansas	35	0.5	175*	-	-	(D)	-	(D)	-	-
Delaware	9	0.1	10*	-	-	(D)	-	(D)	-	-
North Dakota	2	-	10*	-	-	(D)	-	(D)	-	-

Source: 1997 *Economic Census.* The states are in descending order of revenues or establishments (if revenue data are missing for the majority). The symbol (D) appears when data are withheld to prevent disclosure of competitive information. States marked with (D) are sorted by number of establishments. A dash (-) indicates that the data element cannot be calculated. * indicates the midpoint of a range; 175, for example is the range 100-249. Shaded *states* on the state map indicate those states which have proportionately greater representation in the industry than would be indicated by the state's population; the ratio is based on total revenues or number of establishments. Shaded *regions* indicate where the industry is regionally most concentrated.

NAICS 541830 - MEDIA BUYING SERVICES

GENERAL STATISTICS

Year	Establishments (number)	Employment (number)	Payroll ($ million)	Revenues ($ million)	Employees per Establishment (number)	Revenues per Establishment ($)	Payroll per Employee ($)
1997	882	8,534	422.0	1,057.0	9.7	1,198,413	49,449

Source: Economic Census of the United States, 1997. This is a newly defined industry. Data for prior years were unavailable at the time of publication but may become available over time.

INDICES OF CHANGE

Year	Establishments (number)	Employment (number)	Payroll ($ million)	Revenues ($ million)	Employees per Establishment (number)	Revenues per Establishment ($)	Payroll per Employee ($)
1997	100.0	100.0	100.0	100.0	100.0	100.0	100.0

Sources: Same as General Statistics. The values shown reflect change from the base year, 1997. Values above 100 mean greater than 1997, values below 100 mean less than 1997, and a value of 100 in the 1982-96 or 1998-2001 period means same as 1997. Values followed by a 'p' are projections by the editors; 'e' stands for extrapolation. Data are the most recent available at this level of detail.

SIC INDUSTRIES RELATED TO NAICS 541830

Each new NAICS code represents an industry that used to be part of an SIC or a part of several SIC industries. Data in this table are shown to provide transitional information for these cases. All available data for the precursor SIC(s) are shown. Even if only a part of an SIC is included in the NAICS, *all* data for the SIC are reproduced. If the SIC industry is not marked as being a part (pt) of the NAICS, the entire industry is embedded in the NAICS data. The SIC composition of the new industry provides some hints of the relative importance of its "ancestors." Data marked with a 'p' are projected. Projections begin with 1982 data. Data earlier than 1990 are not shown but are reflected in the projections.

SIC	Industry	1990	1991	1992	1993	1994	1995	1996	1997
7319	**Advertising, nec (pt)**								
	Establishments (number)	1,535	1,567	1,931	1,985	2,025	2,194	2,126*p*	2,186*p*
	Employment (thousands)	19.7	19.4	32.2	39.0	38.8	46.5	40.8*p*	43.1*p*
	Revenues ($ million)	-	-	2,147.8	2,270.8*p*	2,428.0*p*	2,585.2*p*	2,742.4*p*	2,899.7*p*

Source: Economic Census of the United States, 1992, annual surveys of economic sectors conducted by the Bureau of the Census, and estimates or projections based on the 1982-1992 period; not all data are shown. 'e' marks estimates made by the editors; 'p' indicates projections based on time series. A dash (-) indicates that data for this SIC or year were not available. The abbreviation (pt) next to the industry name indicates that only a part of the industry is present within the NAICS data. If no (pt) is shown, the entire industry is contained within the NAICS data.

SELECTED RATIOS

For 1997	Avg. of Information	Analyzed Industry	Index	For 1997	Avg. of Information	Analyzed Industry	Index
Employees per establishment	9	10	112	Payroll per establishment	372,545	478,458	128
Revenue per establishment	958,337	1,198,413	125	Payroll as % of revenue	39	40	103
Revenue per employee	111,029	123,858	112	Payroll per employee	43,162	49,449	115

Sources: Same as General Statistics. The 'Average' column represents the average for the industry sector, in 1997, where the currently shown industry is classified. The Index shows the relationship between the Average and the Analyzed Industry. For example, 100 means that they are equal; 500 that the Analyzed Industry is five times the average; 50 means that the Analyzed Industry is half the national average. The abbreviation 'na' is used to show that data are 'not available'.

LEADING COMPANIES

No company data available for this industry.

LOCATION BY STATE AND REGIONAL CONCENTRATION

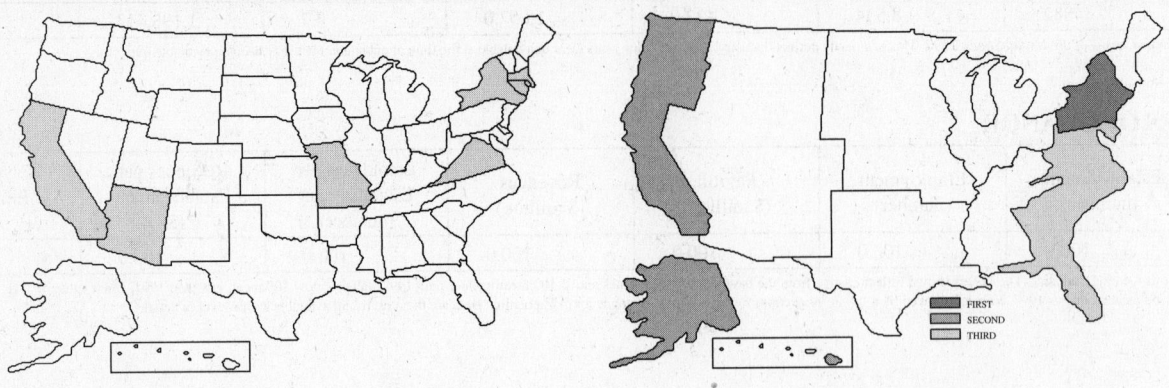

FIRST
SECOND
THIRD

INDUSTRY DATA BY STATE

State	Establishments Total (number)	Establishments % of U.S.	Employment Total (number)	Employment % of U.S.	Employment Per Estab.	Payroll Total ($ mil.)	Payroll Per Empl. ($)	Revenues Total ($ mil.)	Revenues % of U.S.	Revenues Per Estab. ($)
New York	115	13.0	1,899	22.3	17	143.8	75,749	340.0	32.2	2,956,296
California	130	14.7	2,351	27.5	18	104.2	44,310	230.8	21.8	1,775,462
Arizona	19	2.2	294	3.4	15	9.6	32,514	66.5	6.3	3,501,263
Texas	61	6.9	449	5.3	7	17.7	39,352	44.6	4.2	731,443
Illinois	47	5.3	443	5.2	9	17.1	38,679	38.5	3.6	819,766
Massachusetts	21	2.4	253	3.0	12	15.9	62,810	31.2	3.0	1,487,952
Florida	69	7.8	272	3.2	4	9.2	33,842	30.0	2.8	435,072
Missouri	26	2.9	229	2.7	9	10.9	47,782	27.6	2.6	1,062,462
Virginia	24	2.7	185	2.2	8	9.1	49,292	27.3	2.6	1,136,500
Pennsylvania	37	4.2	468	5.5	13	11.8	25,128	25.7	2.4	695,108
Ohio	20	2.3	217	2.5	11	9.4	43,364	25.0	2.4	1,248,250
New Jersey	27	3.1	153	1.8	6	7.8	50,974	20.4	1.9	756,889
Georgia	28	3.2	263	3.1	9	9.1	34,608	19.2	1.8	685,679
Connecticut	17	1.9	95	1.1	6	5.2	54,537	18.6	1.8	1,094,471
Minnesota	18	2.0	117	1.4	7	4.1	35,077	15.0	1.4	834,000
Washington	17	1.9	81	0.9	5	4.0	49,728	14.3	1.4	840,412
Tennessee	24	2.7	117	1.4	5	6.5	55,889	10.8	1.0	448,750
Colorado	21	2.4	95	1.1	5	4.4	46,137	9.6	0.9	456,286
Michigan	12	1.4	67	0.8	6	3.3	48,940	7.0	0.7	586,083
North Carolina	13	1.5	49	0.6	4	1.8	36,204	5.4	0.5	416,385
Indiana	11	1.2	36	0.4	3	1.6	43,833	4.7	0.4	428,000
Rhode Island	4	0.5	23	0.3	6	1.2	50,261	4.7	0.4	1,167,500
D.C.	4	0.5	27	0.3	7	1.7	61,852	3.2	0.3	804,000
Oregon	6	0.7	42	0.5	7	1.2	27,762	2.8	0.3	473,833
South Carolina	5	0.6	30	0.4	6	1.3	43,933	2.5	0.2	500,400
Utah	8	0.9	13	0.2	2	0.7	50,538	2.2	0.2	271,875
Wisconsin	7	0.8	15	0.2	2	0.6	36,733	2.1	0.2	298,286
Kansas	9	1.0	23	0.3	3	0.8	33,478	2.0	0.2	219,667
Louisiana	5	0.6	17	0.2	3	0.5	30,882	1.8	0.2	358,400
Nevada	7	0.8	8	0.1	1	0.4	44,375	1.7	0.2	246,000
Mississippi	6	0.7	20	0.2	3	0.5	26,750	1.4	0.1	232,000
Alabama	5	0.6	17	0.2	3	0.5	27,059	1.4	0.1	275,800
New Mexico	4	0.5	8	0.1	2	0.2	24,875	1.0	0.1	240,000
Montana	3	0.3	4	0.0	1	0.1	32,250	0.3	0.0	101,000
Maryland	14	1.6	60*	-	-	(D)	-	(D)	-	-
Oklahoma	6	0.7	60*	-	-	(D)	-	(D)	-	-
Iowa	4	0.5	10*	-	-	(D)	-	(D)	-	-
Nebraska	4	0.5	10*	-	-	(D)	-	(D)	-	-
Arkansas	3	0.3	10*	-	-	(D)	-	(D)	-	-
Idaho	3	0.3	10*	-	-	(D)	-	(D)	-	-
Kentucky	3	0.3	10*	-	-	(D)	-	(D)	-	-
Maine	3	0.3	10*	-	-	(D)	-	(D)	-	-
Hawaii	2	0.2	10*	-	-	(D)	-	(D)	-	-
New Hampshire	2	0.2	10*	-	-	(D)	-	(D)	-	-
North Dakota	2	0.2	10*	-	-	(D)	-	(D)	-	-
West Virginia	2	0.2	10*	-	-	(D)	-	(D)	-	-
Alaska	1	0.1	10*	-	-	(D)	-	(D)	-	-
Delaware	1	0.1	10*	-	-	(D)	-	(D)	-	-
South Dakota	1	0.1	10*	-	-	(D)	-	(D)	-	-
Vermont	1	0.1	10*	-	-	(D)	-	(D)	-	-

Source: 1997 *Economic Census*. The states are in descending order of revenues or establishments (if revenue data are missing for the majority). The symbol (D) appears when data are withheld to prevent disclosure of competitive information. States marked with (D) are sorted by number of establishments. A dash (-) indicates that the data element cannot be calculated. * indicates the midpoint of a range; 175, for example is the range 100-249. Shaded *states* on the state map indicate those states which have proportionately greater representation in the industry than would be indicated by the state's population; the ratio is based on total revenues or number of establishments. Shaded *regions* indicate where the industry is regionally most concentrated.

NAICS 541840 - MEDIA REPRESENTATIVES*

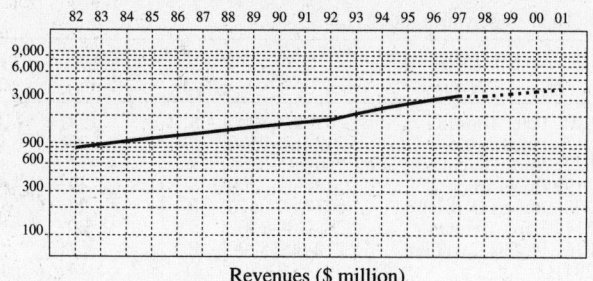

Revenues ($ million)

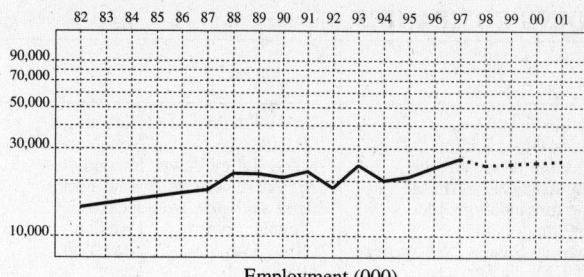

Employment (000)

GENERAL STATISTICS

Year	Establishments (number)	Employment (number)	Payroll ($ million)	Revenues ($ million)	Employees per Establishment (number)	Revenues per Establishment ($)	Payroll per Employee ($)
1982	1,308	14,416	344.0	889.0	11.0	679,664	23,862
1983	1,410 e	15,117 e	370.0 e	970.0 e	10.7 e	687,943 e	24,476 e
1984	1,511 e	15,818 e	396.0 e	1,051.0 e	10.5 e	695,566 e	25,035 e
1985	1,613 e	16,519 e	421.0 e	1,133.0 e	10.2 e	702,418 e	25,486 e
1986	1,714 e	17,220 e	447.0 e	1,214.0 e	10.0 e	708,285 e	25,958 e
1987	1,816	17,921	473.0	1,295.0	9.9	713,106	26,394
1988	1,806	21,975	687.0	1,398.0 e	12.2	774,086	31,263
1989	1,678	21,834	666.0	1,502.0 e	13.0	895,113	30,503
1990	1,611	20,910	696.0	1,605.0 e	13.0	996,276	33,286
1991	1,694	22,536	737.0	1,709.0 e	13.3	1,008,855	32,703
1992	1,905	18,336	639.0	1,812.0	9.6	951,181	34,849
1993	1,899	24,367	843.0	2,111.0 e	12.8	1,111,638	34,596
1994	1,820	20,088	763.0	2,411.0 e	11.0	1,324,725	37,983
1995	1,843	21,084	852.0	2,710.0 e	11.4	1,470,429	40,410
1996	2,265 e	23,760 e	956.0 e	3,009.0 e	10.5 e	1,328,477 e	40,236 e
1997	2,686	26,437	1,060.0	3,309.0	9.8	1,231,943	40,095
1998	2,310 p	24,349 p	1,024.0 p	3,287.0 p	10.5 p	1,422,944 p	42,055 p
1999	2,376 p	24,783 p	1,067.0 p	3,489.0 p	10.4 p	1,468,434 p	43,054 p
2000	2,442 p	25,216 p	1,111.0 p	3,690.0 p	10.3 p	1,511,057 p	44,059 p
2001	2,509 p	25,649 p	1,155.0 p	3,891.0 p	10.2 p	1,550,817 p	45,031 p

Sources: Economic Census of the United States, 1982, 1987, 1992, 1997. Establishment counts, employment, and payroll are from County Business Patterns for non-Census years. In non-Census years, industries in the Manufacturing range under SIC coding include data from the Annual Survey of Manufactures (ASM); those in the old Services range include data from the Services Annual Survey (SAS). Values followed by a 'p' are projections by the editors. Extrapolations are marked by 'e'. Data are the most recent available at this level of detail.

INDICES OF CHANGE

Year	Establishments (number)	Employment (number)	Payroll ($ million)	Revenues ($ million)	Employees per Establishment (number)	Revenues per Establishment ($)	Payroll per Employee ($)
1982	48.7	54.5	32.5	26.9	112.0	55.2	59.5
1987	67.6	67.8	44.6	39.1	100.3	57.9	65.8
1992	70.9	69.4	60.3	54.8	97.8	77.2	86.9
1993	70.7	92.2	79.5	63.8 e	130.4	90.2	86.3
1994	67.8	76.0	72.0	72.9 e	112.1	107.5	94.7
1995	68.6	79.8	80.4	81.9 e	116.2	119.4	100.8
1996	84.3 e	89.9 e	90.2 e	90.9 e	106.6 e	107.8 e	100.4 e
1997	100.0	100.0	100.0	100.0	100.0	100.0	100.0
1998	86.0 p	92.1 p	96.6 p	99.3 p	107.1 p	115.5 p	104.9 p
1999	88.5 p	93.7 p	100.7 p	105.4 p	106.0 p	119.2 p	107.4 p
2000	90.9 p	95.4 p	104.8 p	111.5 p	104.9 p	122.7 p	109.9 p
2001	93.4 p	97.0 p	109.0 p	117.6 p	103.9 p	125.9 p	112.3 p

Sources: Same as General Statistics. The values shown reflect change from the base year, 1997. Values above 100 mean greater than 1997, values below 100 mean less than 1997, and a value of 100 in the 1982-96 or 1998-2001 period means same as 1997. Values followed by a 'p' are projections by the editors; 'e' stands for extrapolation. Data are the most recent available at this level of detail.

SELECTED RATIOS

For 1997	Avg. of Information	Analyzed Industry	Index	For 1997	Avg. of Information	Analyzed Industry	Index
Employees per establishment	9	10	114	Payroll per establishment	372,545	394,639	106
Revenue per establishment	958,337	1,231,943	129	Payroll as % of revenue	39	32	82
Revenue per employee	111,029	125,165	113	Payroll per employee	43,162	40,095	93

Sources: Same as General Statistics. The 'Average' column represents the average for the industry sector, in 1997, where the currently shown industry is classified. The Index shows the relationship between the Average and the Analyzed Industry. For example, 100 means that they are equal; 500 that the Analyzed Industry is five times the average; 50 means that the Analyzed Industry is half the national average. The abbreviation 'na' is used to show that data are 'not available'.

*Equivalent to SIC 7313.

LEADING COMPANIES   Number shown: 13   Total sales ($ mil): 502   Total employment (000): 1.8

Company Name	Address				CEO Name	Phone	Co. Type	Sales ($ mil)	Empl. (000)
Telemundo Group Inc.	2290 W 8th Ave	Hialeah	FL	33010	Peter Tortorici	305-884-8200	S	198	1.2
McGavren Guild Radio	100 Park Ave	New York	NY	10017	Peter Doyle	212-916-0500	S	95*	0.1
Hutchins and Associates Inc.	1865 E Valley Pkwy	Escondido	CA	92027	Mick Hutchins	760-745-0685	R	77	<0.1
All American Television Inc.	1325 Av Americas	New York	NY	10019	Bob Turner	212-541-2800	S	30*	0.1
Love Communications Inc.	3010 Lakeland Cove	Jackson	MS	39208	Robert O'Brien	601-939-0420	R	25*	<0.1
CRN International	1 Circular Ave	Hamden	CT	06514	Barry Berman	203-288-2002	R	20*	<0.1
Metropolitan Sunday Newspapers	10 East 38th St	New York	NY	10016	Phyllis Cavaliere	212-689-8200	R	17*	<0.1
AT and T Media Services	2505 W 16th Ave	Denver	CO	80204		303-603-6100	D	14*	<0.1
Oregon Newspaper Inc.	7150 SW Hampton	Portland	OR	97223		503-624-6397	R	11	<0.1
Cable Advertising Network	3660 S Geyer Rd	St. Louis	MO	63127		314-984-8900	S	8*	<0.1
Rivendell Marketing Co.	P O Box 518	Westfield	NJ	07091	Todd Evans	908-232-2021	R	4*	<0.1
Mid-Atlantic Media Sales Inc.	1320 18th St N W	Washington	DC	20036	Nina Benton	202-775-9015	R	3	<0.1
Markham Media Inc.	850 7th Ave	New York	NY	10019	Beverly Weinstein	212-397-6067	R	1	<0.1

Source: *Ward's Business Directory of U.S. Private and Public Companies*, Volumes 1 and 2, 2000. The company type code used is as follows: P - Public, R - Private, S - Subsidiary, D - Division, J - Joint Venture, A - Affiliate, G - Group, N - Company type not reported. Sales are in millions of dollars, employees are in thousands. An asterisk (*) indicates an estimated sales volume. The symbol < stands for 'less than'. Company names and addresses are truncated, in some cases, to fit into the available space.

LOCATION BY STATE AND REGIONAL CONCENTRATION

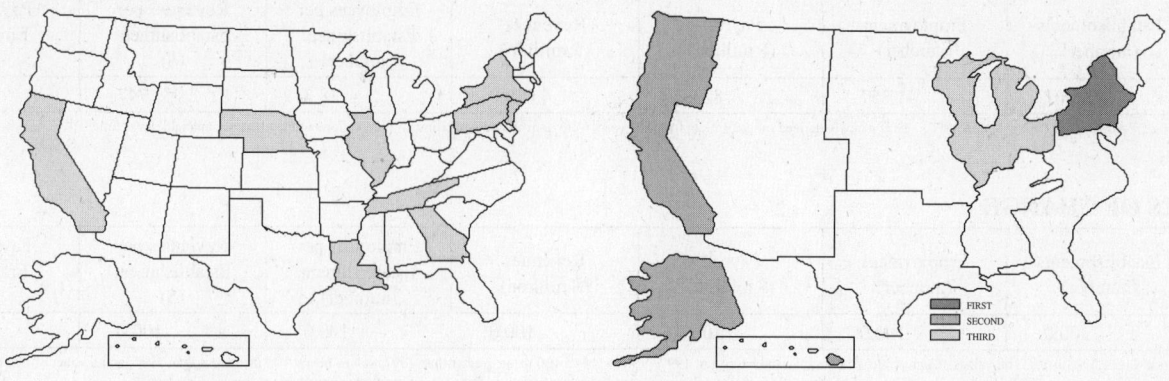

INDUSTRY DATA BY STATE

State	Establishments		Employment			Payroll		Revenues		
	Total (number)	% of U.S.	Total (number)	% of U.S.	Per Estab.	Total ($ mil.)	Per Empl. ($)	Total ($ mil.)	% of U.S.	Per Estab. ($)
New York	291	10.8	4,689	17.7	16	291.2	62,099	831.1	25.1	2,856,082
California	359	13.4	3,281	12.4	9	137.1	41,785	492.1	14.9	1,370,830
Illinois	199	7.4	2,262	8.6	11	88.6	39,159	268.8	8.1	1,350,975
Pennsylvania	102	3.8	1,165	4.4	11	49.7	42,697	161.8	4.9	1,585,902
Florida	214	8.0	1,469	5.6	7	48.0	32,673	157.6	4.8	736,388
Texas	182	6.8	1,410	5.3	8	46.3	32,803	146.2	4.4	803,170
Ohio	83	3.1	1,072	4.1	13	30.6	28,515	117.1	3.5	1,410,289
New Jersey	120	4.5	898	3.4	7	42.0	46,804	113.0	3.4	941,942
Georgia	117	4.4	1,236	4.7	11	43.5	35,214	103.0	3.1	879,966
Louisiana	27	1.0	532	2.0	20	14.2	26,603	84.8	2.6	3,140,111
Tennessee	31	1.2	691	2.6	22	28.0	40,590	80.6	2.4	2,600,968
Michigan	98	3.6	548	2.1	6	24.8	45,336	65.7	2.0	670,102
Massachusetts	72	2.7	394	1.5	5	16.2	41,236	55.4	1.7	769,694
Minnesota	60	2.2	552	2.1	9	15.6	28,297	46.2	1.4	769,717
Missouri	46	1.7	460	1.7	10	13.6	29,543	45.5	1.4	988,348
Alabama	34	1.3	544	2.1	16	16.9	31,077	44.3	1.3	1,302,882
Nebraska	17	0.6	180	0.7	11	4.6	25,383	42.8	1.3	2,519,529
Connecticut	27	1.0	306	1.2	11	14.2	46,451	40.0	1.2	1,482,778
Washington	49	1.8	513	1.9	10	13.6	26,550	38.1	1.2	777,082
North Carolina	58	2.2	440	1.7	8	12.1	27,568	36.1	1.1	621,741
Kansas	19	0.7	307	1.2	16	11.9	38,847	28.3	0.9	1,490,263
Indiana	29	1.1	283	1.1	10	9.2	32,495	27.0	0.8	931,690
Virginia	48	1.8	327	1.2	7	9.7	29,636	26.1	0.8	543,625
Oregon	33	1.2	247	0.9	7	7.5	30,470	24.8	0.8	752,788
Kentucky	28	1.0	284	1.1	10	10.2	35,764	24.0	0.7	858,536
Wisconsin	26	1.0	187	0.7	7	5.6	30,139	22.6	0.7	870,192
Colorado	44	1.6	212	0.8	5	6.4	30,316	17.8	0.5	404,568
Maryland	26	1.0	138	0.5	5	4.7	34,355	16.6	0.5	637,615
Iowa	20	0.7	242	0.9	12	5.8	24,161	15.2	0.5	759,850
Nevada	19	0.7	86	0.3	5	3.0	34,872	14.7	0.4	773,053
Arizona	27	1.0	150	0.6	6	3.1	20,473	12.4	0.4	458,519
Oklahoma	30	1.1	209	0.8	7	3.7	17,727	10.2	0.3	340,667
Mississippi	13	0.5	141	0.5	11	2.5	17,404	7.7	0.2	593,308
Arkansas	13	0.5	181	0.7	14	2.7	14,718	6.8	0.2	525,000
Hawaii	13	0.5	38	0.1	3	1.6	42,684	6.4	0.2	492,000
South Carolina	16	0.6	77	0.3	5	2.2	29,104	5.9	0.2	367,500
Idaho	9	0.3	60	0.2	7	1.4	23,067	5.3	0.2	588,889
West Virginia	12	0.4	92	0.3	8	1.7	18,207	4.8	0.1	398,917
Utah	12	0.4	58	0.2	5	1.4	24,741	4.1	0.1	342,750
North Dakota	6	0.2	20	0.1	3	1.6	78,850	3.6	0.1	599,333
New Mexico	12	0.4	56	0.2	5	1.0	17,821	3.1	0.1	256,750
Rhode Island	7	0.3	28	0.1	4	0.7	26,714	2.2	0.1	316,571
Wyoming	5	0.2	51	0.2	10	0.6	12,647	1.3	0.0	266,200
New Hampshire	4	0.1	28	0.1	7	0.5	16,071	0.9	0.0	220,750
Montana	4	0.1	29	0.1	7	0.2	6,517	0.4	0.0	110,250
Vermont	4	0.1	17	0.1	4	0.1	4,765	0.2	0.0	59,500
Maine	9	0.3	60*	-	-	(D)	-	(D)	-	-
D.C.	4	0.1	60*	-	-	(D)	-	(D)	-	-
Alaska	3	0.1	60*	-	-	(D)	-	(D)	-	-
South Dakota	3	0.1	10*	-	-	(D)	-	(D)	-	-
Delaware	2	0.1	60*	-	-	(D)	-	(D)	-	-

Source: 1997 *Economic Census*. The states are in descending order of revenues or establishments (if revenue data are missing for the majority). The symbol (D) appears when data are withheld to prevent disclosure of competitive information. States marked with (D) are sorted by number of establishments. A dash (-) indicates that the data element cannot be calculated. * indicates the midpoint of a range; 175, for example is the range 100-249. Shaded *states* on the state map indicate those states which have proportionately greater representation in the industry than would be indicated by the state's population; the ratio is based on total revenues or number of establishments. Shaded *regions* indicate where the industry is regionally most concentrated.

NAICS 541850 - DISPLAY ADVERTISING

GENERAL STATISTICS

Year	Establishments (number)	Employment (number)	Payroll ($ million)	Revenues ($ million)	Employees per Establishment (number)	Revenues per Establishment ($)	Payroll per Employee ($)
1997	2,261	41,357	823.0	4,639.0	18.3	2,051,747	19,900

Source: Economic Census of the United States, 1997. This is a newly defined industry. Data for prior years were unavailable at the time of publication but may become available over time.

INDICES OF CHANGE

Year	Establishments (number)	Employment (number)	Payroll ($ million)	Revenues ($ million)	Employees per Establishment (number)	Revenues per Establishment ($)	Payroll per Employee ($)
1997	100.0	100.0	100.0	100.0	100.0	100.0	100.0

Sources: Same as General Statistics. The values shown reflect change from the base year, 1997. Values above 100 mean greater than 1997, values below 100 mean less than 1997, and a value of 100 in the 1982-96 or 1998-2001 period means same as 1997. Values followed by a 'p' are projections by the editors; 'e' stands for extrapolation. Data are the most recent available at this level of detail.

SIC INDUSTRIES RELATED TO NAICS 541850

Each new NAICS code represents an industry that used to be part of an SIC or a part of several SIC industries. Data in this table are shown to provide transitional information for these cases. All available data for the precursor SIC(s) are shown. Even if only a part of an SIC is included in the NAICS, *all* data for the SIC are reproduced. If the SIC industry is not marked as being a part (pt) of the NAICS, the entire industry is embedded in the NAICS data. The SIC composition of the new industry provides some hints of the relative importance of its "ancestors." Data marked with a 'p' are projected. Projections begin with 1982 data. Data earlier than 1990 are not shown but are reflected in the projections.

SIC	Industry	1990	1991	1992	1993	1994	1995	1996	1997
7312	**Outdoor Advertising Services**								
	Establishments (number)	1,047	1,063	1,308	1,241	1,251	1,264	1,252p	1,267p
	Employment (thousands)	12.9	13.0	13.2	13.3	12.6	13.1	13.5p	13.6p
	Revenues ($ million)	-	-	-	-	-	2,377.0	2,679.0	-
7319	**Advertising, nec (pt)**								
	Establishments (number)	1,535	1,567	1,931	1,985	2,025	2,194	2,126p	2,186p
	Employment (thousands)	19.7	19.4	32.2	39.0	38.8	46.5	40.8p	43.1p
	Revenues ($ million)	-	-	2,147.8	2,270.8p	2,428.0p	2,585.2p	2,742.4p	2,899.7p

Source: Economic Census of the United States, 1992, annual surveys of economic sectors conducted by the Bureau of the Census, and estimates or projections based on the 1982-1992 period; not all data are shown. 'e' marks estimates made by the editors; 'p' indicates projections based on time series. A dash (-) indicates that data for this SIC or year were not available. The abbreviation (pt) next to the industry name indicates that only a part of the industry is present within the NAICS data. If no (pt) is shown, the entire industry is contained within the NAICS data.

SELECTED RATIOS

For 1997	Avg. of Information	Analyzed Industry	Index	For 1997	Avg. of Information	Analyzed Industry	Index
Employees per establishment	9	18	212	Payroll per establishment	372,545	363,998	98
Revenue per establishment	958,337	2,051,747	214	Payroll as % of revenue	39	18	46
Revenue per employee	111,029	112,170	101	Payroll per employee	43,162	19,900	46

Sources: Same as General Statistics. The 'Average' column represents the average for the industry sector, in 1997, where the currently shown industry is classified. The Index shows the relationship between the Average and the Analyzed Industry. For example, 100 means that they are equal; 500 that the Analyzed Industry is five times the average; 50 means that the Analyzed Industry is half the national average. The abbreviation 'na' is used to show that data are 'not available'.

LEADING COMPANIES   Number shown: **23**   Total sales ($ mil): **10,528**   Total employment (000): **92.8**

Company Name	Address				CEO Name	Phone	Co. Type	Sales ($ mil)	Empl. (000)
Gannett Company Inc.	1100 Wilson Blvd	Arlington	VA	22234		703-284-6000	P	5,121	39.4
Clear Channel Communications	PO Box 659512	San Antonio	TX	78265	L Lowry Mays	210-822-2828	P	1,351	7.0
Gannett Inc. Newspaper Div.	1100 Wilson Blvd	Arlington	VA	22229	John Curley	703-284-6000	D	1,320*	32.4
Outdoor Systems Inc.	2502 N Blk Can	Phoenix	AZ	85009	Arthur Moreno	602-246-9569	P	706	2.5
Lamar Advertising Co.	PO Box 66338	Baton Rouge	LA	70896		225-926-1000	P	444	1.7
Whiteco Industries Inc.	1000 E 80th Pl	Merrillville	IN	46410		219-769-6601	R	380*	3.9
Eller Media Co.	2850 E Camelback	Phoenix	AZ	85016	Carl Eller	602-957-8116	S	350*	1.0
Ackerley Group Inc.	1301 5th Ave	Seattle	WA	98101	Barry Ackerley	206-624-2888	P	278	1.3
Donrey Media Group	PO Box 17017	Fort Smith	AR	72917	Emmett Jones	501-785-7810	R	201*	2.0
Transportation Displays Inc.	275 Madison Ave	New York	NY	10016	W M Apfelbaum	212-599-1100	R	128	0.6
Adams Outdoor Advertising L.P.	1380 W Paces Fer	Atlanta	GA	30327	J Kevin Gleason	404-233-1366	R	43*	0.2
Drury Displays Inc.	8315 Dr ury Ind	St. John	MO	63114		314-423-5040	R	32*	<0.1
Lamar Corp.	PO Box 66338	Baton Rouge	LA	70896	Kevin Reilly	504-926-1000	S	31*	0.1
BOWLIN Outdoor Advertising	150 Louisiana NE	Albuquerque	NM	87108	Michael Bowlin	505-266-5985	P	30	0.3
Heard Communications Inc.	31 Rte 46	Hackettstown	NJ	07840	Craig P Heard	908-684-8122	R	29*	0.1
Vista Media Group	14400 Firestone	La Mirada	CA	90638	Glenn Emanuel	714-739-6900	R	22*	<0.1
ALA Acquisition L.L.C.	P O Box 2523	Birmingham	AL	35202	John Andrews	205-599-2700	D	18	0.1
Martin Media Inc.	P O Box 7003	Paso Robles	CA	93447	Tom Martin	805-239-1640	R	17*	<0.1
OCI Corporation of Michigan	3639 Cass Rd	Traverse City	MI	49684	Kevin Reilly	225-926-1000	R	17*	0.1
Egger Marketing Inc.	6632 Raytown Rd	Raytown	MO	64133	Janeil Egger	816-356-4130	R	3*	<0.1
Highway Displays Inc.	10 Winnikee Ave	Poughkeepsie	NY	12601	Jules Schwartz	914-452-2121	R	3*	<0.1
Rolling Billboards Inc.	P O Box 691073	Houston	TX	77269	J Michael Ordener	713-868-2821	R	2*	<0.1
Vollman Advertising	PO Box 855	Collinsville	IL	62234		618-345-5712	R	1	<0.1

Source: *Ward's Business Directory of U.S. Private and Public Companies*, Volumes 1 and 2, 2000. The company type code used is as follows: P - Public, R - Private, S - Subsidiary, D - Division, J - Joint Venture, A - Affiliate, G - Group, N - Company type not reported. Sales are in millions of dollars, employees are in thousands. An asterisk (*) indicates an estimated sales volume. The symbol < stands for 'less than'. Company names and addresses are truncated, in some cases, to fit into the available space.

LOCATION BY STATE AND REGIONAL CONCENTRATION

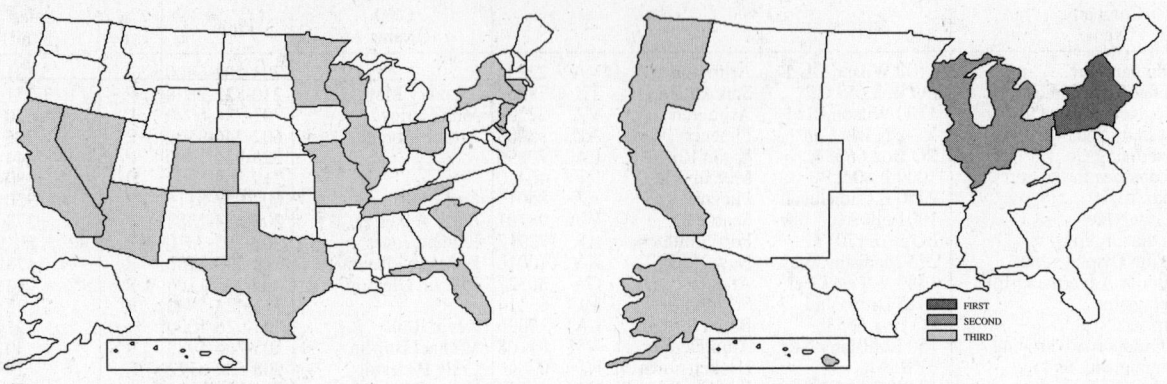

FIRST
SECOND
THIRD

INDUSTRY DATA BY STATE

State	Establishments Total (number)	% of U.S.	Employment Total (number)	% of U.S.	Per Estab.	Payroll Total ($ mil.)	Per Empl. ($)	Revenues Total ($ mil.)	% of U.S.	Per Estab. ($)
California	212	9.4	5,382	13.0	25	113.9	21,157	683.9	14.7	3,225,962
New York	151	6.7	2,527	6.1	17	78.3	30,985	563.9	12.2	3,734,603
Texas	173	7.7	2,992	7.2	17	55.4	18,526	334.4	7.2	1,932,942
Florida	166	7.3	3,425	8.3	21	48.7	14,210	308.4	6.6	1,857,681
Illinois	128	5.7	2,276	5.5	18	48.3	21,201	295.8	6.4	2,310,680
Ohio	80	3.5	2,110	5.1	26	29.7	14,064	212.6	4.6	2,658,050
New Jersey	78	3.4	1,303	3.2	17	33.5	25,730	184.5	4.0	2,365,410
Michigan	69	3.1	1,151	2.8	17	27.8	24,172	171.3	3.7	2,482,899
Pennsylvania	79	3.5	807	2.0	10	32.6	40,431	147.9	3.2	1,872,089
Arizona	46	2.0	1,026	2.5	22	19.0	18,528	126.7	2.7	2,753,370
Missouri	76	3.4	1,065	2.6	14	28.2	26,488	105.8	2.3	1,391,737
North Carolina	68	3.0	1,857	4.5	27	25.8	13,909	95.8	2.1	1,408,176
Tennessee	61	2.7	1,066	2.6	17	18.2	17,061	93.5	2.0	1,532,934
Georgia	78	3.4	1,211	2.9	16	20.9	17,221	93.3	2.0	1,196,103
Wisconsin	45	2.0	928	2.2	21	16.8	18,143	91.3	2.0	2,028,978
Minnesota	66	2.9	699	1.7	11	17.8	25,401	90.7	2.0	1,374,939
Massachusetts	30	1.3	599	1.4	20	12.9	21,503	84.6	1.8	2,818,400
Connecticut	22	1.0	2,535	6.1	115	37.8	14,918	81.4	1.8	3,698,500
Maryland	38	1.7	812	2.0	21	9.8	12,121	77.9	1.7	2,049,763
Washington	29	1.3	402	1.0	14	15.0	37,291	75.9	1.6	2,618,241
Indiana	59	2.6	494	1.2	8	17.3	35,030	74.1	1.6	1,255,508
Louisiana	45	2.0	719	1.7	16	10.7	14,917	71.8	1.5	1,595,600
Colorado	35	1.5	810	2.0	23	5.9	7,341	70.6	1.5	2,015,800
South Carolina	44	1.9	687	1.7	16	11.0	15,943	69.7	1.5	1,583,568
Nevada	27	1.2	233	0.6	9	8.0	34,185	48.7	1.0	1,803,148
Kentucky	23	1.0	501	1.2	22	5.7	11,327	48.1	1.0	2,089,565
Virginia	38	1.7	1,078	2.6	28	10.7	9,924	40.3	0.9	1,060,158
Alabama	34	1.5	249	0.6	7	8.0	32,213	37.4	0.8	1,101,059
Oklahoma	23	1.0	229	0.6	10	5.2	22,825	30.0	0.6	1,302,652
Oregon	21	0.9	429	1.0	20	7.7	17,860	29.0	0.6	1,383,286
Mississippi	19	0.8	293	0.7	15	6.8	23,174	27.5	0.6	1,448,632
Kansas	30	1.3	240	0.6	8	3.6	15,017	26.0	0.6	867,367
Utah	18	0.8	206	0.5	11	5.5	26,621	23.3	0.5	1,295,778
Iowa	18	0.8	268	0.6	15	6.0	22,541	19.8	0.4	1,100,722
Arkansas	27	1.2	131	0.3	5	3.3	24,840	15.4	0.3	570,148
Delaware	8	0.4	73	0.2	9	3.1	42,301	14.6	0.3	1,818,875
Nebraska	14	0.6	92	0.2	7	2.9	31,728	14.0	0.3	998,071
New Mexico	9	0.4	74	0.2	8	1.9	25,973	10.3	0.2	1,141,111
West Virginia	15	0.7	109	0.3	7	1.9	17,339	8.7	0.2	577,600
South Dakota	11	0.5	63	0.2	6	2.0	32,476	7.6	0.2	692,000
Idaho	7	0.3	38	0.1	5	1.0	27,026	5.8	0.1	827,000
Wyoming	4	0.2	22	0.1	6	0.8	34,545	3.6	0.1	909,500
Montana	8	0.4	32	0.1	4	0.6	18,906	3.4	0.1	428,000
North Dakota	4	0.2	21	0.1	5	0.4	20,810	2.3	0.0	572,250
Hawaii	6	0.3	17	0.0	3	0.3	16,412	1.7	0.0	289,667
New Hampshire	4	0.2	2	0.0	1	0.1	33,500	0.4	0.0	96,000
Rhode Island	7	0.3	60*	-	-	(D)	-	(D)	-	-
Vermont	3	0.1	10*	-	-	(D)	-	(D)	-	-
D.C.	2	0.1	10*	-	-	(D)	-	(D)	-	-
Maine	2	0.1	10*	-	-	(D)	-	(D)	-	-
Alaska	1	-	10*	-	-	(D)	-	(D)	-	-

Source: 1997 *Economic Census*. The states are in descending order of revenues or establishments (if revenue data are missing for the majority). The symbol (D) appears when data are withheld to prevent disclosure of competitive information. States marked with (D) are sorted by number of establishments. A dash (-) indicates that the data element cannot be calculated. * indicates the midpoint of a range; 175, for example is the range 100-249. Shaded *states* on the state map indicate those states which have proportionately greater representation in the industry than would be indicated by the state's population; the ratio is based on total revenues or number of establishments. Shaded *regions* indicate where the industry is regionally most concentrated.

NAICS 541860 - DIRECT MAIL ADVERTISING

GENERAL STATISTICS

Year	Establishments (number)	Employment (number)	Payroll ($ million)	Revenues ($ million)	Employees per Establishment (number)	Revenues per Establishment ($)	Payroll per Employee ($)
1997	3,454	85,669	2,427.0	8,672.0	24.8	2,510,712	28,330

Source: *Economic Census of the United States*, 1997. This is a newly defined industry. Data for prior years were unavailable at the time of publication but may become available over time.

INDICES OF CHANGE

Year	Establishments (number)	Employment (number)	Payroll ($ million)	Revenues ($ million)	Employees per Establishment (number)	Revenues per Establishment ($)	Payroll per Employee ($)
1997	100.0	100.0	100.0	100.0	100.0	100.0	100.0

Sources: Same as General Statistics. The values shown reflect change from the base year, 1997. Values above 100 mean greater than 1997, values below 100 mean less than 1997, and a value of 100 in the 1982-96 or 1998-2001 period means same as 1997. Values followed by a 'p' are projections by the editors; 'e' stands for extrapolation. Data are the most recent available at this level of detail.

SIC INDUSTRIES RELATED TO NAICS 541860

Each new NAICS code represents an industry that used to be part of an SIC or a part of several SIC industries. Data in this table are shown to provide transitional information for these cases. All available data for the precursor SIC(s) are shown. Even if only a part of an SIC is included in the NAICS, *all* data for the SIC are reproduced. If the SIC industry is not marked as being a part (pt) of the NAICS, the entire industry is embedded in the NAICS data. The SIC composition of the new industry provides some hints of the relative importance of its "ancestors." Data marked with a 'p' are projected. Projections begin with 1982 data. Data earlier than 1990 are not shown but are reflected in the projections.

SIC	Industry	1990	1991	1992	1993	1994	1995	1996	1997
7331	**Direct Mail Advertising Services (pt)**								
	Establishments (number)	3,503	3,662	3,878	3,981	4,060	4,124	4,403*p*	4,543*p*
	Employment (thousands)	84.1	84.4	79.1	84.1	82.3	87.9	96.0*p*	98.9*p*
	Revenues ($ million)	6,956.0	6,546.0	6,805.0	7,346.0	7,312.0	7,532.0	8,198.0	8,550.4*p*

Source: *Economic Census of the United States*, 1992, annual surveys of economic sectors conducted by the Bureau of the Census, and estimates or projections based on the 1982-1992 period; not all data are shown. 'e' marks estimates made by the editors; 'p' indicates projections based on time series. A dash (-) indicates that data for this SIC or year were not available. The abbreviation (pt) next to the industry name indicates that only a part of the industry is present within the NAICS data. If no (pt) is shown, the entire industry is contained within the NAICS data.

SELECTED RATIOS

For 1997	Avg. of Information	Analyzed Industry	Index	For 1997	Avg. of Information	Analyzed Industry	Index
Employees per establishment	9	25	287	Payroll per establishment	372,545	702,664	189
Revenue per establishment	958,337	2,510,712	262	Payroll as % of revenue	39	28	72
Revenue per employee	111,029	101,227	91	Payroll per employee	43,162	28,330	66

Sources: Same as General Statistics. The 'Average' column represents the average for the industry sector, in 1997, where the currently shown industry is classified. The Index shows the relationship between the Average and the Analyzed Industry. For example, 100 means that they are equal; 500 that the Analyzed Industry is five times the average; 50 means that the Analyzed Industry is half the national average. The abbreviation 'na' is used to show that data are 'not available'.

LEADING COMPANIES   Number shown: **75**   Total sales ($ mil): **42,090**   Total employment (000): **165.0**

Company Name	Address				CEO Name	Phone	Co. Type	Sales ($ mil)	Empl. (000)
American Express Company	AmEx Twr	New York	NY	10285	Ken Chenault	212-640-2000	S	15,428*	65.0
Ogilvy & Mather Worldwide Inc.	309 W 49th St	New York	NY	10019	Shelly Lazarus	212-237-4000	S	12,700	10.5
Centrobe	833 W S Boulder	Louisville	CO	80027	Mike Littell	303-666-7000	S	2,024*	10.0
Rapp Collins Worldwide Inc.	11 Madison Ave	New York	NY	10010	G Steven Dapper	212-590-7443	S	1,789	2.4
ADVO Inc.	PO Box 755	Windsor	CT	06095	Gary M Mulloy	860-285-6100	P	1,040	4.3
OgilvyOne Worldwide	309 W 49th St	New York	NY	10019	Reimer Thedens	212-237-6000	S	1,000*	1.9
Harte-Hanks Inc.	PO Box 269	San Antonio	TX	78291	Larry Franklin	210-829-9000	P	830	7.1
Snyder Communications Inc.	6903 Rockledge Dr	Bethesda	MD	20817	Daniel Snyder	301-468-1010	P	815	9.4
Acxiom Corp.	PO Box 2000	Conway	AR	72033	Charles D Morgan Jr	501-336-1000	P	730	5.3
Output Technologies Inc.	2519 Madison Ave	Kansas City	MO	64108	Charles Schellhorn	816-221-1234	S	521*	2.5
Cadmus Communications Corp.	PO Box 27367	Richmond	VA	23261	C Gillispie	804-287-5680	P	443	4.1
Ameridial Inc.	4535 Strausser	North Canton	OH	44720	Jim McGeorge	330-497-4888	R	380*	1.0
Neodata Services Inc.	833 W S Boulder	Louisville	CO	80027	Robert McCashin	303-666-7000	R	265*	4.7
DIMAC DIRECT Inc.	1 Corporate Woods	Bridgeton	MO	63044		314-344-8000	S	200	2.6
Hermann Companies Inc.	1400 N Price Rd	St. Louis	MO	63132	Robert R Hermann Sr	314-432-2800	R	200*	1.0
Kirshenbaum Bond and Partners	145 6th Ave	New York	NY	10013	Jonathan Bond	212-633-0080	R	190*	0.2
GLS Direct Inc.	2000 Market St	Philadelphia	PA	19103	Ross L Housley	215-568-1100	R	184*	0.7
CMGI Inc	100 Brickstone Sq	Andover	MA	01810	David S Weatherell	978-684-3600	P	176	1.6
Hickory Farms Inc.	PO Box 219	Maumee	OH	43537		419-893-7611	R	160	2.3
Val-Pak Direct Marketing Systems	8605 Largo Lakes	Largo	FL	33773	Joe Bourdow	813-393-1270	R	134	1.2
Southwestern/Great American Inc.	P O Box 305140	Nashville	TN	37230	Ralph W Mosley	615-391-2500	R	130*	0.6
S.A.W. Inc.	1275 Lakeside E	Cleveland	OH	44114	Dave Visocky	216-861-0250	R	120*	2.9
Bronner Co.	800 Boylston St	Boston	MA	02199	David Kenny	617-867-1000	R	116*	0.9
Rapp Collins Worldwide	901 Marquette S	Minneapolis	MN	55402		612-373-3000	D	109*	<0.1
Federal Direct	95 Main Ave	Clifton	NJ	07014	Larry Merse	973-667-9800	R	103*	0.5
North American Communications	1330 30th St	San Diego	CA	92154	Robert Herman	814-696-1647	R	102*	0.5
Jetson Direct Services Inc.	100 Industrial Dr	Hamburg	PA	19526	Vincent Carosella	610-562-1800	R	100*	0.5
Aegis Communications Group Inc.	7880 Bent Branch	Irving	TX		Stephen A McNeely	972-830-1800	P	92	4.1
CMGI Inc.	100 Brickstone Sq	Andover	MA	01810	David S Wetherell	978-684-3600	R	91	1.0
TSYS Total Solutions Inc.	7101 Stone Mill	Columbus	GA	31909	Clifford Mason	706-649-6800	S	90*	0.9
K/P Corp.	12647 Alcosta Blvd	San Ramon	CA	94583	James Knapp	925-543-5200	R	81*	0.7
Lee Marketing Service	8801 Autobahn	Dallas	TX	75237	Joe Ewers	972-293-5000	R	79*	0.4
Direct Mail Systems Inc.	12450 Automobile	Clearwater	FL	33762	Rocky Penington	813-573-1985	R	71*	0.1
Didlake Inc.	PO Box 161	Manassas	VA	20108		703-361-4195	R	69*	0.6
Outlook Group Corp.	PO Box 748	Neenah	WI	54957	Richard C Fischer	920-722-2333	P	67	0.6
DCI Marketing Inc.	PO Box 92910	Milwaukee	WI	53202	Peter Marshall	414-228-7000	S	65*	0.3
American Direct Mail Inc.	350 Hudson St	New York	NY	10014	Richard C Manfredi	212-924-5400	R	62*	0.3
Innotrac Corp.	6655 Sugarloaf	Duluth	GA	30097	Scott Dorfman	678-717-2000	R	62*	0.5
PRIDE Industries Inc.	1 Sierra Gate Plz	Roseville	CA	95678		916-783-5266	R	60	2.9
Balmar Printing and Graphics Inc.	PO Box 3330	Merrifield	VA	22116	James A O'Hare	703-289-9000	R	58	0.5
Marketing.Comm	10551 Barkley St	Overland Park	KS	66212	Frank G Weyforth Jr	913-648-8333	R	51	0.1
FALA Direct Marketing Inc.	70 Marcus Dr	Melville	NY	11747	Jeffrey Jurick	516-694-1919	R	47	0.6
FOCUS Direct Inc.	PO Box 17568	San Antonio	TX	78217	Fred Lederman	210-805-9185	R	47	0.5
Calmark Inc.	1400 W 44th St	Chicago	IL	60609	Jim Fitzgerald	773-247-7200	R	46*	0.4
G.B.F. Grafics Inc.	PO Box 457	Skokie	IL	60076	Richard Kuntz	708-677-1700	R	45	0.4
Gilbert, Whitney and Johns	110 S Jefferson Rd	Whippany	NJ	07981	John Daltner	973-386-1776	R	42	<0.1
Intern. Masters Publishers Inc.	300 1st Stamford Pl	Stamford	CT	06902	Hakan Lindskog	203-351-3000	R	41*	0.2
BEI Graphics Inc.	PO Box 9005	Boulder	CO	80301	Morgan O'Brien	303-449-8010	R	40*	0.2
Communication Concepts Inc.	1044 Pulinski Rd	Ivyland	PA	18974	Louis Teffeau	215-672-6900	R	40*	0.4
Archer/Malmo Advertising Inc.	65 Union Ave	Memphis	TN	38103	Ward Archer	901-523-2000	R	39*	<0.1
Professional Impressions Media	PO Box 677	Champaign	IL	61824		217-351-5252	R	39*	0.4
Hammer Graphics Inc.	PO Box 640	Piqua	OH	45356	James Troxell	937-773-1861	R	36	0.4
Ross-Martin Co.	PO Box 2450	Tulsa	OK	74101	Geoff Cole	918-627-4460	S	34*	0.3
Donnelley Marketing	470 Chestnut Ridge	Woodcliff Lake	NJ	07675	Al Ambrosino	203-552-6388	R	33*	0.3
New England Newspapers Inc.	PO Box 1171	Pittsfield	MA	01202		413-447-7311	S	33	0.7
News-Gazette	PO Box 677	Champaign	IL	61824		217-351-5252	R	33*	0.4
American List Counsel Inc.	88 Orchard Rd	Princeton	NJ	08543	Donn Rappaport	908-874-4300	R	32	<0.1
Berenson Isham and Partners Inc.	420 Boylston St	Boston	MA	02116	Paul S Berenson	617-423-1120	R	32	<0.1
W.A. Wilde Co.	200 Summer St	Holliston	MA	01746	Thomas H Wilde	508-429-5515	R	32*	0.5
Cronin and Co.	50 Nye Rd #3	Glastonbury	CT	06033	William J Cronin Jr	860-659-0514	R	30	<0.1
FG*I Image Works Inc.	206 W Franklin St	Chapel Hill	NC	27516	Steve Lerner	919-929-7759	R	30*	0.2
Dickinson Advertising	120 Campanelli Dr	Braintree	MA	02184	Donald Dickinson	781-849-3700	R	29	0.3
CAS Inc. (Omaha, Nebraska)	10303 Crown Point	Omaha	NE	68134	Mike Garrean	402-393-0313	R	27*	<0.1
AKA Direct Inc.	PO Box 2990	Tualatin	OR	97062		503-452-1094	R	26*	0.1
Brian Unlimited Distribution Co.	13131 Lyndon St	Detroit	MI	48227	William Brian	313-933-5100	R	26*	0.5
Merkle Computer Systems Inc.	800 Corporate Way	Hyattsville	MD	20785	David Williams	301-459-9700	R	26*	0.3
Money Mailer Inc.	14271 Corporate Dr	Garden Grove	CA	92843	Godfred Otuteye	714-265-4100	R	26*	0.3
SunMedia Corp.	5510 Cloverleaf	Cleveland	OH	44125	Gerald H Gordon	216-642-5516	S	26	0.3
Frank Mayer and Associates Inc.	PO Box 105	Grafton	WI	53024	Mike Mayer	414-377-4700	R	25	0.1
Mail Marketing Systems Inc.	8318 Sherwick Ct	Jessup	MD	20794	Norman Schultz	301-953-7202	R	25*	0.1
PrimeNet Marketing Services Inc.	2250 Pilot Knob Rd	St. Paul	MN	55120	Mark Keefe	651-405-4000	S	25*	<0.1
SCICOM Data Services Ltd.	10101 Bren Rd E	Hopkins	MN	55343	Richard Walter	612-933-4200	R	24*	0.2
Comac Inc.	565 Sinclair	Milpitas	CA	95035	Michael Smith	408-945-1600	D	23*	0.1
International Business List Inc.	162 N Franklin St	Chicago	IL	60606	Gary E Walter	312-236-0350	R	23	<0.1
Opportunities Inc.	925 Jefferson St	Fort Atkinson	WI	53538		920-563-2437	R	22*	0.2

Source: Ward's Business Directory of U.S. Private and Public Companies, Volumes 1 and 2, 2000. The company type code used is as follows: P - Public, R - Private, S - Subsidiary, D - Division, J - Joint Venture, A - Affiliate, G - Group, N - Company type not reported. Sales are in millions of dollars, employees are in thousands. An asterisk (*) indicates an estimated sales volume. The symbol < stands for 'less than'. Company names and addresses are truncated, in some cases, to fit into the available space.

LOCATION BY STATE AND REGIONAL CONCENTRATION

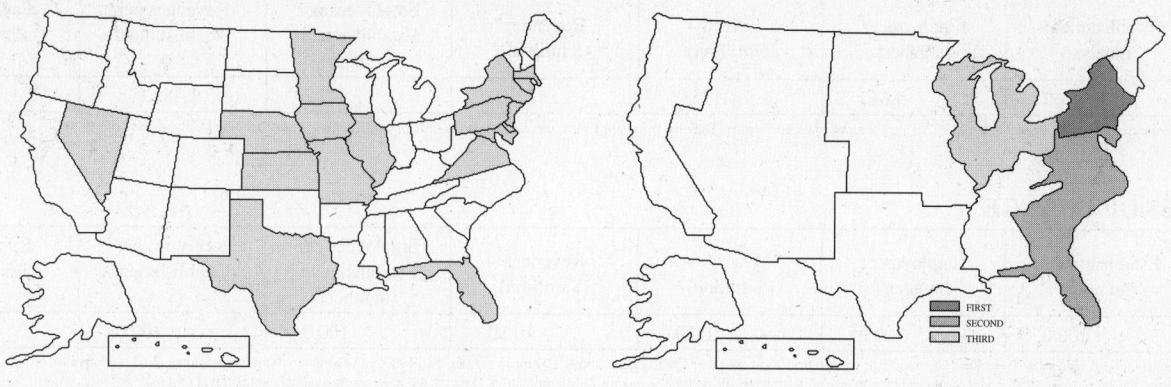

INDUSTRY DATA BY STATE

State	Establishments Total (number)	% of U.S.	Employment Total (number)	% of U.S.	Per Estab.	Payroll Total ($ mil.)	Per Empl. ($)	Revenues Total ($ mil.)	% of U.S.	Per Estab. ($)
California	432	12.5	10,464	12.2	24	268.8	25,684	1,019.1	11.8	2,358,951
New York	281	8.1	7,147	8.3	25	285.8	39,983	833.2	9.6	2,965,093
Illinois	248	7.2	6,167	7.2	25	177.6	28,804	668.5	7.7	2,695,673
Texas	211	6.1	6,166	7.2	29	168.1	27,263	621.9	7.2	2,947,213
Florida	208	6.0	3,914	4.6	19	109.7	28,017	538.5	6.2	2,589,034
Pennsylvania	171	5.0	5,598	6.5	33	175.1	31,274	538.3	6.2	3,148,064
New Jersey	169	4.9	4,967	5.8	29	130.9	26,359	467.5	5.4	2,766,533
Connecticut	96	2.8	2,728	3.2	28	104.2	38,209	426.4	4.9	4,442,083
Massachusetts	115	3.3	3,910	4.6	34	154.3	39,453	390.3	4.5	3,394,270
Virginia	149	4.3	3,859	4.5	26	97.7	25,320	303.9	3.5	2,039,732
Maryland	106	3.1	3,386	4.0	32	87.4	25,818	277.5	3.2	2,618,292
Minnesota	77	2.2	2,188	2.6	28	70.3	32,122	259.2	3.0	3,365,714
Ohio	110	3.2	2,358	2.8	21	58.8	24,954	207.0	2.4	1,881,436
Missouri	67	1.9	2,021	2.4	30	61.1	30,239	205.6	2.4	3,069,209
Michigan	95	2.8	1,895	2.2	20	51.4	27,116	204.3	2.4	2,150,253
Georgia	91	2.6	1,577	1.8	17	43.2	27,380	186.5	2.2	2,049,495
Wisconsin	50	1.4	1,072	1.3	21	30.2	28,143	137.8	1.6	2,756,220
Kansas	35	1.0	1,404	1.6	40	32.0	22,764	118.9	1.4	3,397,543
Iowa	22	0.6	3,212	3.7	146	49.1	15,288	108.2	1.2	4,916,000
Kentucky	17	0.5	869	1.0	51	20.1	23,163	103.9	1.2	6,109,294
Arizona	59	1.7	830	1.0	14	21.4	25,793	97.2	1.1	1,647,390
North Carolina	80	2.3	1,788	2.1	22	35.3	19,738	96.5	1.1	1,206,588
Washington	64	1.9	777	0.9	12	21.8	28,093	92.2	1.1	1,441,297
Nebraska	26	0.8	556	0.6	21	16.1	28,948	91.6	1.1	3,523,154
Delaware	16	0.5	488	0.6	30	11.8	24,252	82.9	1.0	5,184,313
Tennessee	51	1.5	769	0.9	15	17.9	23,294	70.1	0.8	1,373,824
Colorado	57	1.7	464	0.5	8	12.7	27,474	64.3	0.7	1,127,877
Nevada	22	0.6	495	0.6	23	10.8	21,832	63.6	0.7	2,890,909
Indiana	37	1.1	762	0.9	21	15.9	20,807	56.6	0.7	1,529,757
Oregon	42	1.2	544	0.6	13	12.9	23,789	48.0	0.6	1,142,024
Utah	24	0.7	373	0.4	16	8.6	23,088	43.2	0.5	1,801,083
Arkansas	19	0.6	378	0.4	20	9.9	26,320	40.2	0.5	2,115,947
D.C.	11	0.3	248	0.3	23	13.2	53,371	34.6	0.4	3,142,091
South Carolina	32	0.9	333	0.4	10	6.4	19,123	28.6	0.3	894,375
Oklahoma	22	0.6	451	0.5	20	6.1	13,545	27.9	0.3	1,266,409
Alabama	26	0.8	246	0.3	9	5.0	20,488	23.0	0.3	885,808
New Hampshire	20	0.6	235	0.3	12	4.8	20,630	18.9	0.2	942,600
Mississippi	10	0.3	213	0.2	21	4.7	21,869	18.1	0.2	1,811,500
West Virginia	7	0.2	132	0.2	19	4.2	31,735	12.8	0.1	1,826,429
Louisiana	19	0.6	107	0.1	6	2.0	18,673	10.3	0.1	540,000
Vermont	8	0.2	94	0.1	12	1.9	20,383	7.5	0.1	941,250
North Dakota	7	0.2	120	0.1	17	1.2	10,075	7.0	0.1	997,000
Maine	9	0.3	117	0.1	13	2.5	21,744	6.2	0.1	689,333
Hawaii	5	0.1	58	0.1	12	0.8	13,534	2.2	0.0	438,200
Wyoming	3	0.1	23	0.0	8	0.2	9,870	0.6	0.0	212,667
Idaho	7	0.2	60*	-	-	(D)	-	(D)	-	-
New Mexico	6	0.2	60*	-	-	(D)	-	(D)	-	-
Rhode Island	6	0.2	60*	-	-	(D)	-	(D)	-	-
Alaska	4	0.1	60*	-	-	(D)	-	(D)	-	-
Montana	4	0.1	60*	-	-	(D)	-	(D)	-	-
South Dakota	1	-	10*	-	-	(D)	-	(D)	-	-

Source: 1997 *Economic Census*. The states are in descending order of revenues or establishments (if revenue data are missing for the majority). The symbol (D) appears when data are withheld to prevent disclosure of competitive information. States marked with (D) are sorted by number of establishments. A dash (-) indicates that the data element cannot be calculated. * indicates the midpoint of a range; 175, for example is the range 100-249. Shaded *states* on the state map indicate those states which have proportionately greater representation in the industry than would be indicated by the state's population; the ratio is based on total revenues or number of establishments. Shaded *regions* indicate where the industry is regionally most concentrated.

NAICS 541870 - ADVERTISING MATERIAL DISTRIBUTION SERVICES

GENERAL STATISTICS

Year	Establishments (number)	Employment (number)	Payroll ($ million)	Revenues ($ million)	Employees per Establishment (number)	Revenues per Establishment ($)	Payroll per Employee ($)
1997	560	9,642	175.0	830.0	17.2	1,482,143	18,150

Source: Economic Census of the United States, 1997. This is a newly defined industry. Data for prior years were unavailable at the time of publication but may become available over time.

INDICES OF CHANGE

Year	Establishments (number)	Employment (number)	Payroll ($ million)	Revenues ($ million)	Employees per Establishment (number)	Revenues per Establishment ($)	Payroll per Employee ($)
1997	100.0	100.0	100.0	100.0	100.0	100.0	100.0

Sources: Same as General Statistics. The values shown reflect change from the base year, 1997. Values above 100 mean greater than 1997, values below 100 mean less than 1997, and a value of 100 in the 1982-96 or 1998-2001 period means same as 1997. Values followed by a 'p' are projections by the editors; 'e' stands for extrapolation. Data are the most recent available at this level of detail.

SIC INDUSTRIES RELATED TO NAICS 541870

Each new NAICS code represents an industry that used to be part of an SIC or a part of several SIC industries. Data in this table are shown to provide transitional information for these cases. All available data for the precursor SIC(s) are shown. Even if only a part of an SIC is included in the NAICS, *all* data for the SIC are reproduced. If the SIC industry is not marked as being a part (pt) of the NAICS, the entire industry is embedded in the NAICS data. The SIC composition of the new industry provides some hints of the relative importance of its "ancestors." Data marked with a 'p' are projected. Projections begin with 1982 data. Data earlier than 1990 are not shown but are reflected in the projections.

SIC	Industry	1990	1991	1992	1993	1994	1995	1996	1997
7319	**Advertising, nec (pt)**								
	Establishments (number)	1,535	1,567	1,931	1,985	2,025	2,194	2,126p	2,186p
	Employment (thousands)	19.7	19.4	32.2	39.0	38.8	46.5	40.8p	43.1p
	Revenues ($ million)	-	-	2,147.8	2,270.8p	2,428.0p	2,585.2p	2,742.4p	2,899.7p
7389	**Business Services, nec (pt)**								
	Establishments (number)	44,079	50,252	52,375	56,829	60,725	53,596	60,893p	63,269p
	Employment (thousands)	489.6	550.4	523.6	607.9	648.7	623.0	680.2p	710.9p
	Revenues ($ million)	-	-	32,885.9	-	-	-	-	-

Source: Economic Census of the United States, 1992, annual surveys of economic sectors conducted by the Bureau of the Census, and estimates or projections based on the 1982-1992 period; not all data are shown. 'e' marks estimates made by the editors; 'p' indicates projections based on time series. A dash (-) indicates that data for this SIC or year were not available. The abbreviation (pt) next to the industry name indicates that only a part of the industry is present within the NAICS data. If no (pt) is shown, the entire industry is contained within the NAICS data.

SELECTED RATIOS

For 1997	Avg. of Information	Analyzed Industry	Index	For 1997	Avg. of Information	Analyzed Industry	Index
Employees per establishment	9	17	199	Payroll per establishment	372,545	312,500	84
Revenue per establishment	958,337	1,482,143	155	Payroll as % of revenue	39	21	54
Revenue per employee	111,029	86,082	78	Payroll per employee	43,162	18,150	42

Sources: Same as General Statistics. The 'Average' column represents the average for the industry sector, in 1997, where the currently shown industry is classified. The Index shows the relationship between the Average and the Analyzed Industry. For example, 100 means that they are equal; 500 that the Analyzed Industry is five times the average; 50 means that the Analyzed Industry is half the national average. The abbreviation 'na' is used to show that data are 'not available'.

LEADING COMPANIES   Number shown: **35**   Total sales ($ mil): **4,010**   Total employment (000): **7.7**

Company Name	Address				CEO Name	Phone	Co. Type	Sales ($ mil)	Empl. (000)
L.M. Berry and Co.	PO Box 6000	Dayton	OH	45401	E.L. Smith	937-296-2121	S	1,023*	2.3
SFM Media Corp.	1180 Av Americas	New York	NY	10036	Robert Frank	212-790-4800	R	950*	0.2
TMP Worldwide	1633 Broadway	New York	NY	10019	Bart Catalane	212-977-4200	S	505*	0.3
News America Marketing	1211 Av Americas	New York	NY	10036	Paul Carlucci	212-782-8000	S	480*	1.2
Welcome Wagon Intern. Inc.	7 Cambridge Dr	Trumbull	CT	06611	Tom Vazzano	203-365-2000	D	390*	2.5
Camelot Communications Inc.	8140 Walnut Hill	Dallas	TX	75231	Tom Kalahar	214-373-6999	R	125*	<0.1
Grey Directory Marketing Inc.	350 W Hubbard	Chicago	IL	60610	Daniel Moricoli	312-222-0025	S	84*	<0.1
Telformation Inc.	1515 Poydras St	New Orleans	LA	70112	Ray Reggie	504-568-1600	R	51	<0.1
Robinson and Maites Inc.	35 E Wacker Dr	Chicago	IL	60601	Allan Maites	312-372-9333	R	50*	<0.1
Abex Display Systems Inc.	7101 Fair Ave	N. Hollywood	CA	91605	Robbie Blumenfeld	818-764-5126	R	48*	0.2
RDR Associates Inc.	888 7th Ave	New York	NY	10106	Frank Muratore	212-765-7710	R	48*	0.1
Kolon, Bittker and Desmond Inc.	18161 E 8 Mile Rd	Eastpointe	MI	48021	John Kolon	248-524-2500	R	45*	<0.1
CPM Inc. (Chicago, Illinois)	515 N State St	Chicago	IL	60610	Marge Navoloio	312-527-2100	R	29*	<0.1
Good Catalog Co.	5456 S E Intern	Portland	OR	97222	Barbara Todd	503-654-7464	R	23	<0.1
Ketchum Directory Advertising	225 N Michigan	Chicago	IL	60606	John Joseph	312-946-8111	S	18*	0.2
Williams and Helde Inc.	711 6th Ave N	Seattle	WA	98109	Jim Williams	206-285-1940	R	18*	<0.1
Alternate Marketing Networks Inc.	1 Ionia Ave SW	Grand Rapids	MI	49503	Ruth Ann Carroll	616-235-0698	P	16*	<0.1
Ernst Van Praag Inc.	10211 W Sample	Coral Springs	FL	33065	Raymond Van Praag	954-341-6130	R	16*	<0.1
Independent Television Network	747 3rd Ave	New York	NY	10017	Timothy J Connors Jr	212-572-9200	R	15	<0.1
Spectra Products Inc.	139 Grand Ave	Johnson City	NY	13790	David T Hamblett	607-770-1985	R	12	<0.1
Paradise Music & Entertainment	420 W 45th St	New York	NY	10036	M Jay Walkingshaw	212-242-0101	P	10	<0.1
Hawk Media Inc.	731 Sansome St	San Francisco	CA	94111	Kenneth Slater	415-777-4645	R	9*	<0.1
Barclay Communications Inc.	3550 N Central Ave	Phoenix	AZ	85012	Mary O'Hanlon	602-277-3550	R	8*	<0.1
SalesTalk Inc.	1225 Pear Ave	Mountain View	CA	94043	Jeffrey Wise	650-964-2000	R	8*	<0.1
The Lightship Group	5728 Major Blvd	Orlando	FL	32819	Chuck Ehrler	407-363-7777	R	7*	<0.1
American Ad Management Inc.	27710 Jefferson	Temecula	CA	92590	Donald Taylor	909-695-7700	R	7	<0.1
Commotion Promotions Ltd.	4638 E Shea Blvd	Phoenix	AZ	85028	Karen Kravitz	602-996-0006	R	4*	<0.1
Colsky Media Inc.	2740 Van Ness Ave	San Francisco	CA	94109	Richard Colsky	415-673-5400	R	3*	<0.1
Denver Transit Advertising	621 17th St	Denver	CO	80293	Beth Stewart	303-292-4242	R	3*	<0.1
National Communications Inc.	5999 Biscayne Blvd	Miami	FL	33137	Robert J Rodriguez	305-756-8600	R	2*	<0.1
Princeton Video Image Inc.	15 Princess Rd	Lawrenceville	NJ	08648	Douglas J Greenlaw	609-912-9400	P	1	<0.1
Beach Banners Inc.	855-4 St John's	Jacksonville	FL	32225	Joel Weaner	904-642-0721	R	1*	<0.1
Daymark Inc.	2010 Madison Rd	Cincinnati	OH	45208	Kerry Didday	513-979-2000	R	1*	<0.1
Smith, Dorian and Burman Inc.	1100 New Britain	West Hartford	CT	06110	Jerome H Levinson	860-522-3101	R	1	<0.1
Convention Channel Inc.	624 W Main St	Louisville	KY	40202	Neil Kuvin	502-568-2500	R	0*	<0.1

Source: Ward's Business Directory of U.S. Private and Public Companies, Volumes 1 and 2, 2000. The company type code used is as follows: P - Public, R - Private, S - Subsidiary, D - Division, J - Joint Venture, A - Affiliate, G - Group, N - Company type not reported. Sales are in millions of dollars, employees are in thousands. An asterisk (*) indicates an estimated sales volume. The symbol < stands for 'less than'. Company names and addresses are truncated, in some cases, to fit into the available space.

LOCATION BY STATE AND REGIONAL CONCENTRATION

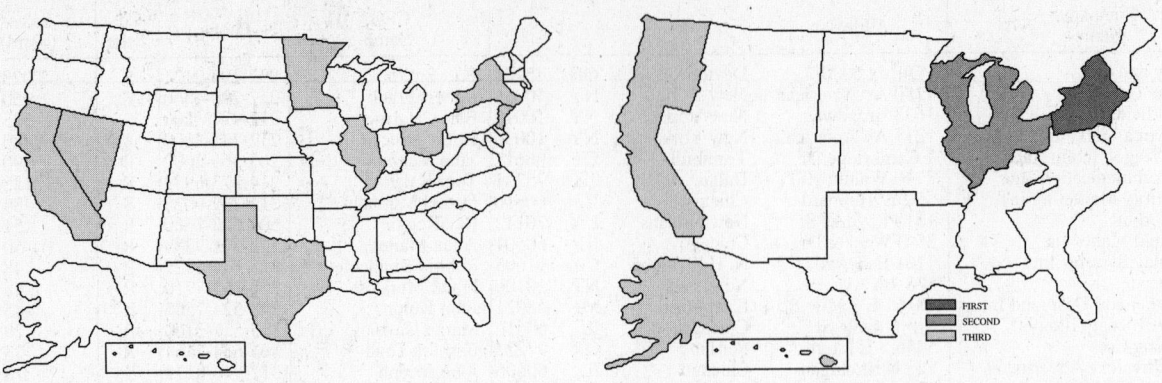

INDUSTRY DATA BY STATE

State	Establishments Total (number)	Establishments % of U.S.	Employment Total (number)	Employment % of U.S.	Employment Per Estab.	Payroll Total ($ mil.)	Payroll Per Empl. ($)	Revenues Total ($ mil.)	Revenues % of U.S.	Revenues Per Estab. ($)
New York	45	8.0	1,212	12.6	27	33.1	27,304	159.1	19.2	3,535,111
California	76	13.6	3,240	33.6	43	23.2	7,160	138.0	16.6	1,816,105
Illinois	32	5.7	472	4.9	15	13.8	29,269	87.7	10.6	2,741,625
Texas	43	7.7	322	3.3	7	10.2	31,696	62.3	7.5	1,448,581
New Jersey	27	4.8	803	8.3	30	20.3	25,245	58.6	7.1	2,171,481
Ohio	28	5.0	328	3.4	12	8.1	24,710	44.9	5.4	1,603,679
Minnesota	13	2.3	385	4.0	30	6.6	17,055	30.1	3.6	2,311,923
Michigan	24	4.3	371	3.8	15	4.9	13,272	28.2	3.4	1,173,542
Pennsylvania	22	3.9	242	2.5	11	4.1	16,996	16.5	2.0	750,318
Florida	32	5.7	132	1.4	4	3.3	24,689	16.5	2.0	514,938
North Carolina	11	2.0	175	1.8	16	6.9	39,171	15.7	1.9	1,423,091
Missouri	16	2.9	220	2.3	14	2.5	11,214	13.1	1.6	817,750
Georgia	17	3.0	146	1.5	9	3.4	23,329	11.3	1.4	666,588
Connecticut	6	1.1	130	1.3	22	3.7	28,769	9.0	1.1	1,504,500
Colorado	14	2.5	93	1.0	7	2.3	25,065	8.7	1.1	622,286
Massachusetts	10	1.8	37	0.4	4	1.0	28,162	7.7	0.9	770,600
Alabama	4	0.7	25	0.3	6	0.9	35,360	7.6	0.9	1,890,750
Wisconsin	8	1.4	252	2.6	32	2.3	9,202	7.5	0.9	934,750
Oregon	5	0.9	125	1.3	25	3.2	25,816	7.4	0.9	1,489,600
Arizona	11	2.0	172	1.8	16	2.3	13,244	7.2	0.9	651,636
Tennessee	10	1.8	96	1.0	10	2.2	22,813	6.8	0.8	679,100
Louisiana	7	1.3	54	0.6	8	0.6	11,722	6.0	0.7	859,857
Washington	11	2.0	56	0.6	5	1.4	24,304	5.2	0.6	476,818
Nevada	9	1.6	94	1.0	10	1.2	13,266	5.1	0.6	568,556
Indiana	10	1.8	34	0.4	3	1.0	29,500	3.7	0.4	367,000
New Hampshire	4	0.7	36	0.4	9	0.7	18,472	3.1	0.4	771,000
Virginia	10	1.8	32	0.3	3	0.4	13,344	2.1	0.3	209,200
Utah	6	1.1	8	0.1	1	0.3	37,625	1.6	0.2	270,500
South Carolina	4	0.7	8	0.1	2	0.1	16,375	0.7	0.1	175,750
South Dakota	4	0.7	6	0.1	2	-	6,833	0.5	0.1	130,750
Maryland	9	1.6	60*	-	-	(D)	-	(D)	-	-
Kentucky	5	0.9	60*	-	-	(D)	-	(D)	-	-
Nebraska	5	0.9	60*	-	-	(D)	-	(D)	-	-
Kansas	4	0.7	60*	-	-	(D)	-	(D)	-	-
Hawaii	2	0.4	60*	-	-	(D)	-	(D)	-	-
Idaho	2	0.4	60*	-	-	(D)	-	(D)	-	-
Iowa	2	0.4	60*	-	-	(D)	-	(D)	-	-
Maine	2	0.4	10*	-	-	(D)	-	(D)	-	-
Montana	2	0.4	10*	-	-	(D)	-	(D)	-	-
West Virginia	2	0.4	10*	-	-	(D)	-	(D)	-	-
Alaska	1	0.2	10*	-	-	(D)	-	(D)	-	-
Arkansas	1	0.2	10*	-	-	(D)	-	(D)	-	-
New Mexico	1	0.2	10*	-	-	(D)	-	(D)	-	-
North Dakota	1	0.2	10*	-	-	(D)	-	(D)	-	-
Oklahoma	1	0.2	10*	-	-	(D)	-	(D)	-	-
Vermont	1	0.2	10*	-	-	(D)	-	(D)	-	-

Source: 1997 *Economic Census*. The states are in descending order of revenues or establishments (if revenue data are missing for the majority). The symbol (D) appears when data are withheld to prevent disclosure of competitive information. States marked with (D) are sorted by number of establishments. A dash (-) indicates that the data element cannot be calculated. * indicates the midpoint of a range; 175, for example is the range 100-249. Shaded *states* on the state map indicate those states which have proportionately greater representation in the industry than would be indicated by the state's population; the ratio is based on total revenues or number of establishments. Shaded *regions* indicate where the industry is regionally most concentrated.

NAICS 541890 - SERVICES RELATED TO ADVERTISING NEC

GENERAL STATISTICS

Year	Establishments (number)	Employment (number)	Payroll ($ million)	Revenues ($ million)	Employees per Establishment (number)	Revenues per Establishment ($)	Payroll per Employee ($)
1997	9,086	67,354	1,596.0	9,140.0	7.4	1,005,943	23,696

Source: Economic Census of the United States, 1997. This is a newly defined industry. Data for prior years were unavailable at the time of publication but may become available over time.

INDICES OF CHANGE

Year	Establishments (number)	Employment (number)	Payroll ($ million)	Revenues ($ million)	Employees per Establishment (number)	Revenues per Establishment ($)	Payroll per Employee ($)
1997	100.0	100.0	100.0	100.0	100.0	100.0	100.0

Sources: Same as General Statistics. The values shown reflect change from the base year, 1997. Values above 100 mean greater than 1997, values below 100 mean less than 1997, and a value of 100 in the 1982-96 or 1998-2001 period means same as 1997. Values followed by a 'p' are projections by the editors; 'e' stands for extrapolation. Data are the most recent available at this level of detail.

SIC INDUSTRIES RELATED TO NAICS 541890

Each new NAICS code represents an industry that used to be part of an SIC or a part of several SIC industries. Data in this table are shown to provide transitional information for these cases. All available data for the precursor SIC(s) are shown. Even if only a part of an SIC is included in the NAICS, *all* data for the SIC are reproduced. If the SIC industry is not marked as being a part (pt) of the NAICS, the entire industry is embedded in the NAICS data. The SIC composition of the new industry provides some hints of the relative importance of its "ancestors." Data marked with a 'p' are projected. Projections begin with 1982 data. Data earlier than 1990 are not shown but are reflected in the projections.

SIC	Industry	1990	1991	1992	1993	1994	1995	1996	1997
5199	**Nondurable goods, nec (pt)**								
	Establishments (number)	12,796	13,131	15,535	18,293	17,778	18,822	19,717p	20,734p
	Employment (thousands)	116.0	111.5	101.1	129.1	117.1	130.4	130.2p	133.9p
	Revenues ($ million)	48,152.9e	48,561.2e	48,969.6	49,377.9p	49,786.2p	50,194.6p	50,602.9p	51,011.2p
7319	**Advertising, nec (pt)**								
	Establishments (number)	1,535	1,567	1,931	1,985	2,025	2,194	2,126p	2,186p
	Employment (thousands)	19.7	19.4	32.2	39.0	38.8	46.5	40.8p	43.1p
	Revenues ($ million)	-	-	2,147.8	2,270.8p	2,428.0p	2,585.2p	2,742.4p	2,899.7p
7389	**Business Services, nec (pt)**								
	Establishments (number)	44,079	50,252	52,375	56,829	60,725	53,596	60,893p	63,269p
	Employment (thousands)	489.6	550.4	523.6	607.9	648.7	623.0	680.2p	710.9p
	Revenues ($ million)	-	-	32,885.9	-	-	-	-	-

Source: Economic Census of the United States, 1992, annual surveys of economic sectors conducted by the Bureau of the Census, and estimates or projections based on the 1982-1992 period; not all data are shown. 'e' marks estimates made by the editors; 'p' indicates projections based on time series. A dash (-) indicates that data for this SIC or year were not available. The abbreviation (pt) next to the industry name indicates that only a part of the industry is present within the NAICS data. If no (pt) is shown, the entire industry is contained within the NAICS data.

SELECTED RATIOS

For 1997	Avg. of Information	Analyzed Industry	Index	For 1997	Avg. of Information	Analyzed Industry	Index
Employees per establishment	9	7	86	Payroll per establishment	372,545	175,655	47
Revenue per establishment	958,337	1,005,943	105	Payroll as % of revenue	39	17	45
Revenue per employee	111,029	135,701	122	Payroll per employee	43,162	23,696	55

Sources: Same as General Statistics. The 'Average' column represents the average for the industry sector, in 1997, where the currently shown industry is classified. The Index shows the relationship between the Average and the Analyzed Industry. For example, 100 means that they are equal; 500 that the Analyzed Industry is five times the average; 50 means that the Analyzed Industry is half the national average. The abbreviation 'na' is used to show that data are 'not available'.

LEADING COMPANIES

No company data available for this industry.

LOCATION BY STATE AND REGIONAL CONCENTRATION

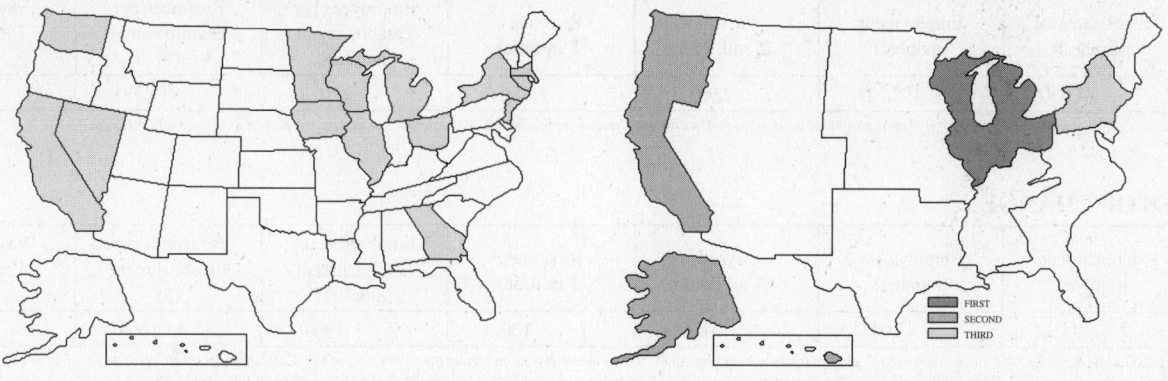

FIRST
SECOND
THIRD

INDUSTRY DATA BY STATE

State	Establishments Total (number)	Establishments % of U.S.	Employment Total (number)	Employment % of U.S.	Employment Per Estab.	Payroll Total ($ mil.)	Payroll Per Empl. ($)	Revenues Total ($ mil.)	Revenues % of U.S.	Revenues Per Estab. ($)
California	941	10.4	13,525	20.1	14	257.9	19,069	1,449.0	15.9	1,539,886
Illinois	519	5.7	3,493	5.2	7	115.4	33,033	1,024.4	11.2	1,973,742
New York	618	6.8	5,523	8.2	9	138.5	25,082	712.1	7.8	1,152,341
Texas	546	6.0	2,996	4.4	5	81.5	27,203	550.3	6.0	1,007,965
Florida	666	7.3	3,108	4.6	5	79.8	25,670	433.6	4.7	651,018
Ohio	392	4.3	2,569	3.8	7	73.3	28,544	426.6	4.7	1,088,288
New Jersey	316	3.5	1,773	2.6	6	60.1	33,908	389.7	4.3	1,233,313
Michigan	292	3.2	1,961	2.9	7	73.7	37,597	382.3	4.2	1,309,373
Massachusetts	193	2.1	1,294	1.9	7	47.5	36,682	281.2	3.1	1,457,119
Georgia	296	3.3	1,726	2.6	6	49.2	28,527	249.2	2.7	841,807
Wisconsin	212	2.3	1,230	1.8	6	34.9	28,354	239.3	2.6	1,128,632
Pennsylvania	349	3.8	1,797	2.7	5	42.4	23,611	233.6	2.6	669,481
Minnesota	231	2.5	2,010	3.0	9	46.6	23,185	232.9	2.5	1,008,169
North Carolina	262	2.9	1,174	1.7	4	33.3	28,339	217.7	2.4	830,737
Washington	189	2.1	4,832	7.2	26	63.6	13,166	214.6	2.3	1,135,228
Missouri	228	2.5	1,971	2.9	9	43.1	21,878	176.5	1.9	774,035
Connecticut	120	1.3	1,098	1.6	9	47.4	43,170	151.3	1.7	1,260,708
Iowa	86	0.9	761	1.1	9	15.7	20,653	149.5	1.6	1,737,849
Indiana	221	2.4	1,071	1.6	5	24.3	22,676	138.2	1.5	625,511
Virginia	212	2.3	819	1.2	4	20.6	25,154	111.9	1.2	527,660
Tennessee	188	2.1	910	1.4	5	21.3	23,375	110.6	1.2	588,096
Colorado	162	1.8	1,428	2.1	9	19.2	13,437	97.3	1.1	600,778
Arizona	148	1.6	970	1.4	7	16.2	16,668	77.3	0.8	522,095
Arkansas	66	0.7	312	0.5	5	9.0	28,737	71.3	0.8	1,079,758
Kentucky	121	1.3	602	0.9	5	13.2	21,895	71.0	0.8	586,438
Oklahoma	98	1.1	832	1.2	8	13.6	16,371	67.1	0.7	684,980
Louisiana	113	1.2	909	1.3	8	10.0	11,035	58.0	0.6	513,248
Nevada	74	0.8	458	0.7	6	12.4	27,024	51.6	0.6	697,541
Utah	68	0.7	358	0.5	5	8.9	24,927	51.4	0.6	756,088
Alabama	108	1.2	458	0.7	4	8.8	19,297	50.7	0.6	469,056
South Carolina	110	1.2	515	0.8	5	9.5	18,363	49.2	0.5	447,464
Oregon	103	1.1	619	0.9	6	7.5	12,191	37.2	0.4	361,039
Mississippi	62	0.7	211	0.3	3	4.8	22,569	30.2	0.3	486,919
Nebraska	44	0.5	269	0.4	6	5.1	18,781	26.9	0.3	611,500
D.C.	9	0.1	56	0.1	6	2.5	45,107	15.8	0.2	1,753,556
Delaware	26	0.3	78	0.1	3	2.3	29,423	14.1	0.2	541,077
New Mexico	39	0.4	179	0.3	5	2.5	13,916	12.2	0.1	311,692
South Dakota	26	0.3	102	0.2	4	1.9	18,814	9.8	0.1	375,846
West Virginia	34	0.4	127	0.2	4	3.0	23,898	9.6	0.1	282,676
Montana	43	0.5	390	0.6	9	2.7	6,956	9.4	0.1	218,837
North Dakota	17	0.2	101	0.1	6	1.5	15,257	9.1	0.1	538,235
Hawaii	26	0.3	106	0.2	4	1.6	15,368	8.2	0.1	316,885
Alaska	24	0.3	93	0.1	4	1.6	16,699	7.9	0.1	331,250
Vermont	19	0.2	51	0.1	3	1.6	30,647	7.6	0.1	398,053
Wyoming	28	0.3	52	0.1	2	0.9	16,769	4.2	0.0	150,964
Maryland	198	2.2	750*	-	-	(D)	-	(D)	-	-
Kansas	106	1.2	750*	-	-	(D)	-	(D)	-	-
Maine	38	0.4	750*	-	-	(D)	-	(D)	-	-
Rhode Island	37	0.4	175*	-	-	(D)	-	(D)	-	-
New Hampshire	33	0.4	60*	-	-	(D)	-	(D)	-	-
Idaho	29	0.3	175*	-	-	(D)	-	(D)	-	-

Source: 1997 Economic Census. The states are in descending order of revenues or establishments (if revenue data are missing for the majority). The symbol (D) appears when data are withheld to prevent disclosure of competitive information. States marked with (D) are sorted by number of establishments. A dash (-) indicates that the data element cannot be calculated. * indicates the midpoint of a range; 175, for example is the range 100-249. Shaded *states* on the state map indicate those states which have proportionately greater representation in the industry than would be indicated by the state's population; the ratio is based on total revenues or number of establishments. Shaded *regions* indicate where the industry is regionally most concentrated.

NAICS 541910 - MARKETING RESEARCH AND PUBLIC OPINION POLLING

GENERAL STATISTICS

Year	Establishments (number)	Employment (number)	Payroll ($ million)	Revenues ($ million)	Employees per Establishment (number)	Revenues per Establishment ($)	Payroll per Employee ($)
1997	4,030	107,552	2,963.0	7,880.0	26.7	1,955,335	27,549

Source: Economic Census of the United States, 1997. This is a newly defined industry. Data for prior years were unavailable at the time of publication but may become available over time.

INDICES OF CHANGE

Year	Establishments (number)	Employment (number)	Payroll ($ million)	Revenues ($ million)	Employees per Establishment (number)	Revenues per Establishment ($)	Payroll per Employee ($)
1997	100.0	100.0	100.0	100.0	100.0	100.0	100.0

Sources: Same as General Statistics. The values shown reflect change from the base year, 1997. Values above 100 mean greater than 1997, values below 100 mean less than 1997, and a value of 100 in the 1982-96 or 1998-2001 period means same as 1997. Values followed by a 'p' are projections by the editors; 'e' stands for extrapolation. Data are the most recent available at this level of detail.

SIC INDUSTRIES RELATED TO NAICS 541910

Each new NAICS code represents an industry that used to be part of an SIC or a part of several SIC industries. Data in this table are shown to provide transitional information for these cases. All available data for the precursor SIC(s) are shown. Even if only a part of an SIC is included in the NAICS, *all* data for the SIC are reproduced. If the SIC industry is not marked as being a part (pt) of the NAICS, the entire industry is embedded in the NAICS data. The SIC composition of the new industry provides some hints of the relative importance of its "ancestors." Data marked with a 'p' are projected. Projections begin with 1982 data. Data earlier than 1990 are not shown but are reflected in the projections.

SIC	Industry	1990	1991	1992	1993	1994	1995	1996	1997
8732	**Commercial Nonphysical Research (pt)**								
	Establishments (number)	4,821	4,804	5,701	5,688	5,579	5,611	5,532p	5,563p
	Employment (thousands)	100.7	98.7	105.4	112.9	116.2	123.1	124.8p	129.0p
	Revenues ($ million)	5,629.0	5,734.0	6,250.0	6,522.0	6,579.0	6,850.0	8,187.0	8,011.0p

Source: Economic Census of the United States, 1992, annual surveys of economic sectors conducted by the Bureau of the Census, and estimates or projections based on the 1982-1992 period; not all data are shown. 'e' marks estimates made by the editors; 'p' indicates projections based on time series. A dash (-) indicates that data for this SIC or year were not available. The abbreviation (pt) next to the industry name indicates that only a part of the industry is present within the NAICS data. If no (pt) is shown, the entire industry is contained within the NAICS data.

SELECTED RATIOS

For 1997	Avg. of Information	Analyzed Industry	Index	For 1997	Avg. of Information	Analyzed Industry	Index
Employees per establishment	9	27	309	Payroll per establishment	372,545	735,236	197
Revenue per establishment	958,337	1,955,335	204	Payroll as % of revenue	39	38	97
Revenue per employee	111,029	73,267	66	Payroll per employee	43,162	27,549	64

Sources: Same as General Statistics. The 'Average' column represents the average for the industry sector, in 1997, where the currently shown industry is classified. The Index shows the relationship between the Average and the Analyzed Industry. For example, 100 means that they are equal; 500 that the Analyzed Industry is five times the average; 50 means that the Analyzed Industry is half the national average. The abbreviation 'na' is used to show that data are 'not available'.

LEADING COMPANIES   Number shown: **75**   Total sales ($ mil): **14,153**   Total employment (000): **145.9**

Company Name	Address				CEO Name	Phone	Co. Type	Sales ($ mil)	Empl. (000)
Equifax Inc.	P O Box 4081	Atlanta	GA	30302	Thomas F. Chapman	404-885-8000	P	1,773	13.0
ACNielsen Corp.	177 Broad Street	Stamford	CT	06901	Robert J Lievense	203-961-3000	P	1,525	21.0
IMS Health Inc.	200 Nyala Farms	Westport	CT	06880	Victoria R Fash	203-222-4200	P	1,398	9.0
Quintiles Transnational Corp.	4709 Creekstone Dr	Durham	NC	27703	Santo J Costa	919-998-2000	P	1,188	15.5
Experian Information Solutions	505 City Pkwy W	Orange	CA	92863	John Peace	714-385-7000	S	1,000	7.5
GartnerGroup Inc.	PO Box 10212	Stamford	CT	06904	Manuel A Fernandez	203-316-1111	P	734	3.4
Moody's Investors Service Inc.	99 Church St	New York	NY	10007	John Rutherfurd	212-553-0300	R	430	1.5
Cal-Growers Corp.	1302 N Fourth St	San Jose	CA	95112	Clem Perrucci	408-573-1000	R	417*	0.1
Nielson Media Research Inc.	299 Park Ave	New York	NY	10171	John A Dimling	212-708-7500	P	402	3.1
Ameridial Inc.	4535 Strausser	North Canton	OH	44720	Jim McGeorge	330-497-4888	R	380*	1.0
Nielsen Media Research Inc.	299 Park Ave	New York	NY	10171	John A Dimling	212-708-7500	R	337*	2.0
NFO Worldwide Inc.	2 Pickwick Plz	Greenwich	CT	06830	Mark E Berry	203-629-8888	P	275	5.4
Audits & Surveys Worldwide Inc.	650 Av Americas	New York	NY	10011	Elaine Riddell	212-627-9700	S	240*	2.0
Arbitron Co.	142 W 57th St	New York	NY	10019	Stephen B Morris	212-887-1300	D	215	0.9
Sparta Inc.	4901 Corporate Dr	Huntsville	AL	35805	W Winton	256-837-5200	R	187*	0.6
Westat Inc.	1650 Research Blvd	Rockville	MD	20850	Joseph A Hunt	301-251-1500	R	182	1.3
Gallup Inc.	301 S 68th St	Lincoln	NE	68510	James K Clifton	402-489-9000	R	180*	30.0
Maritz Marketing Research Inc.	1297 N Hwy Dr	Fenton	MO	63099	Tom Rogers	314-827-1610	S	169	0.7
J.D. Power and Associates	30401 Agoura Rd	Agoura Hills	CA	91301	Steve Goodall	818-889-6330	R	161*	0.5
Abt Associates Inc.	55 Wheeler St	Cambridge	MA	02138	Wendell J Knox	617-492-7100	R	147*	1.0
ICT Group Inc.	800 Town Center Dr	Langhorne	PA	19047	John J Brennan	215-757-0200	P	121	5.3
Research Institute of America	395 Hudson St	New York	NY	10014	Euan Menzies	212-367-6300	S	120*	1.0
Nordhaus Research Inc.	20300 W 12 Mile Rd	Southfield	MI	48076	John King	248-827-2400	R	116*	0.4
Forrester Research Inc.	400 Technology Sq	Cambridge	MA	02139	George F Colony	617-497-7090	P	116	0.4
META Group Inc.	208 Harbor Dr	Stamford	CT	06912	Dale Kutnick	203-973-6700	P	100	0.4
Roper Starch Worldwide Inc.	500 Mamaroneck	Harrison	NY	10528	Jay Wilson	914-698-0800	R	97*	0.2
Intern. Research & Evaluation	21098 IRE Control	Eagan	MN	55121	Randall Voight	612-888-9635	R	94	0.1
RAND Corp.	PO Box 2138	Santa Monica	CA	90407	James A Thomson	310-393-0411	R	90*	1.0
M/A/R/C Group	7850 N Belt Line Rd	Irving	TX	75063	Sharon M Munger	972-506-3400	P	89	1.1
Logicon R and D Associates	PO Box 92500	Los Angeles	CA	90009	James Dalton	310-645-1122	S	86*	0.9
NPD Group Inc.	900 W Shore Rd	Port Washington	NY	11050	Tod Johnson	516-625-0700	R	81*	1.0
WEFA Inc.	800 Baldwin Twr	Eddystone	PA	19022	Patrick Richmond	610-490-4000	S	81*	0.3
AC Nielson Bases	50 E River Center	Covington	KY	41011	Jack E Brown	606-655-6000	R	78*	0.3
Opinion Research Corp.	PO Box 183	Princeton	NJ	08542	John F Short	908-281-5100	P	73	2.0
National Economic Research	50 Main St	White Plains	NY	10606	Richard T Rapp	914-448-4000	S	70*	0.4
VNU Marketing Information	11 W 42nd St	New York	NY	10036	Martin R Freely	212-789-3680	S	67	4.0
Midwest Research Institute	425 Volker Blvd	Kansas City	MO	64110	James Spigarelli	816-753-7600	R	64*	0.5
RMC Research Corp.	1000 Market St	Portsmouth	NH	03801	Everett Barnes	603-422-8888	R	64*	0.2
Shop 'n Chek Inc.	7616 Perimeter Ctr E	Atlanta	GA	30346	Carol Cherry	770-393-1072	R	62*	0.2
MACRO International	100 Av Americas	New York	NY	10013	Frank Quirk	212-941-5555	S	62	0.5
Knowledge Systems & Research	500 S Salina St	Syracuse	NY	13202	Ann Michel	315-470-1350	R	59*	0.2
Forum Corp.	1 Exchange Pl	Boston	MA	02109	John Humphrey	617-523-7300	R	56*	0.4
Migliara/Kaplan Associates	9 Park Center Ct	Owings Mills	MD	21117	Cheryl Olitzky	410-581-8188	R	56*	0.2
Griggs-Anderson GartnerGroup	308 SW 1st Ave	Portland	OR	97204		503-241-8036	S	48*	0.2
Abacus Direct Corp.	11101 W 120th Ave	Broomfield	CO	80021	Daniel C Snyder	303-657-2800	P	47	0.2
MORPACE International Inc.	31700 Middlebelt	Farmington Hills	MI	48334	Frank J Ward	248-737-5300	R	42	0.2
Charles River Associates Inc.	200 Clarendon St	Boston	MA	02116	James C Burrows	617-425-3000	R	40	0.2
Montgomery, Zukerman, Davis	1800 N Meridian St	Indianapolis	IN	46202	Allan B Zukerman	317-924-6271	R	40	<0.1
Decima Research Corp.	1363 Beverly Rd	McLean	VA	22101	James J Granger	703-556-0001	R	39	0.2
Standard and Poor's DRI	24 Hartwell Ave	Lexington	MA	02421		781-863-5100	S	39*	0.3
Creative & Response Research	500 N Michigan	Chicago	IL	60611		312-828-9200	R	38	0.2
Ask America Market Research	PO Box 1	Gold Beach	OR	97444	Michael K Pettengill	541-452-3300	R	36*	0.1
Walker Information Inc.	P O Box 40972	Indianapolis	IN	46240	Steven Walker	317-843-3939	R	35	0.4
Management Science Associates	6565 Penn & 5th	Pittsburgh	PA	15206		412-362-2000	R	34*	0.7
Alexander Marketing Services Inc.	277 Crahen Ave	Grand Rapids	MI	49525	Robert C Milroy	616-957-2000	R	33*	<0.1
Mediamap	215 1st St	Cambridge	MA	02142	Kirke Curtis	617-374-9300	R	31*	0.1
Elrick and Lavidge Inc.	1990 Lakeside	Tucker	GA	30084	Tom Flynn	770-621-7600	S	29*	<0.1
Claritas Inc.	1525 Wilson Blvd	Arlington	VA	22209	Bob Nuscenzi	703-812-2700	S	28*	0.4
Research Data Analysis Inc.	450 Enterprise Ct	Bloomfield Hills	MI	48302	Anthony Pietrowski	248-332-5000	R	26	0.2
Lieberman Research Worldwide	1900 Av of the Stars	Los Angeles	CA	90067	David Sackman	310-553-0550	R	25	0.1
Market Strategies Inc.	20255 Victor Pky	Livonia	MI	48152	Andrew Morrison	734-542-7600	R	25	0.4
O'Neal and Prelle Inc.	P O Box 1139	Hartford	CT	06143	William Ervin	860-527-3233	R	24*	<0.1
RSC The Quality Measurement	110 Walnut St	Evansville	IN	47708	Meg Blair	812-425-4562	R	24*	0.3
Brady Co.	N 80 W	Menomonee Fls	WI	53051	John B Liebenstein	262-255-0100	R	23	<0.1
CORSEARCH Inc.	28 W 23rd St	New York	NY	10010	Hal Espo	212-627-0330	S	23*	<0.1
Sanchez and Levitan Inc.	3191 Coral Way	Miami	FL	33145	Fausto Sanchez	305-442-1586	R	22*	<0.1
Source Information Management	11644 Lilburn	Saint Louis	MO	63146	S Leslie Flegel	314-995-9040	P	21	0.5
REIS Reports Inc.	5 W 37th St	New York	NY	10018	Lloyd Lynford	212-921-1122	R	21*	<0.1
Institute for International Research	708 3rd Ave	New York	NY	10017		212-661-3500	R	20	0.3
Kelliher/Samets/Volk Marketing	212 Battery St	Burlington	VT	05401		802-862-8261	R	18*	<0.1
Systems Applications Intern. Inc.	101 Lucas Valley Rd	San Rafael	CA	94903	C Shepherd Burton	415-507-7100	S	17*	<0.1
Chesapeake Surveys	4 Park Center Ct	Owings Mills	MD	21117	Bruce Schulman	410-356-3566	R	16*	<0.1
Cohners Instat Group	7418 E Helm Dr	Scottsdale	AZ	85260	Robert Calcagni	602-483-4440	R	16*	<0.1
FMJ Adcomm	340 Main St	Venice	CA	90291	Steve Johnson	310-581-7100	P	16	<0.1
International Strategy	717 5th Ave	New York	NY	10022	Edward Hyman	212-446-5600	R	15*	<0.1

Source: Ward's Business Directory of U.S. Private and Public Companies, Volumes 1 and 2, 2000. The company type code used is as follows: P - Public, R - Private, S - Subsidiary, D - Division, J - Joint Venture, A - Affiliate, G - Group, N - Company type not reported. Sales are in millions of dollars, employees are in thousands. An asterisk (*) indicates an estimated sales volume. The symbol < stands for 'less than'. Company names and addresses are truncated, in some cases, to fit into the available space.

LOCATION BY STATE AND REGIONAL CONCENTRATION

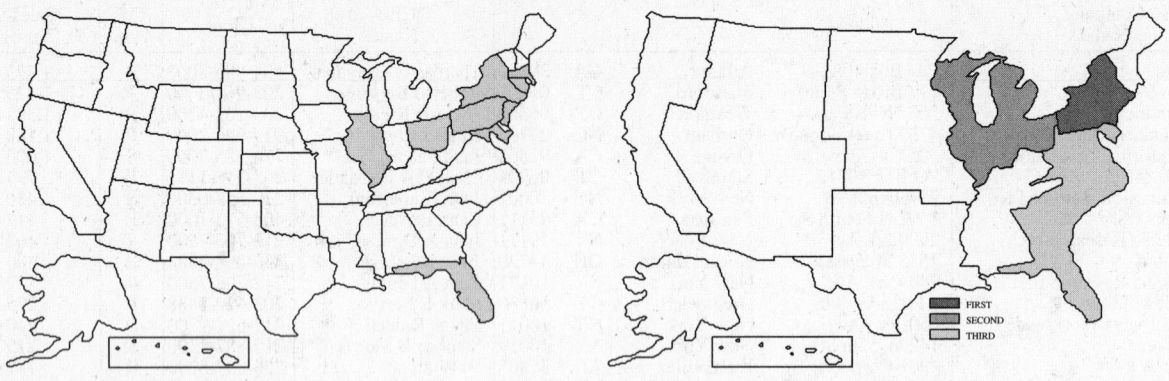

INDUSTRY DATA BY STATE

State	Establishments		Employment			Payroll		Revenues		
	Total (number)	% of U.S.	Total (number)	% of U.S.	Per Estab.	Total ($ mil.)	Per Empl. ($)	Total ($ mil.)	% of U.S.	Per Estab. ($)
New York	445	11.0	9,528	8.9	21	370.2	38,856	1,027.8	13.0	2,309,647
California	524	13.0	12,362	11.5	24	335.9	27,171	933.8	11.9	1,782,040
New Jersey	235	5.8	5,562	5.2	24	210.7	37,887	758.6	9.6	3,228,060
Connecticut	143	3.5	3,277	3.0	23	323.7	98,782	722.9	9.2	5,055,399
Illinois	301	7.5	9,238	8.6	31	258.6	27,998	643.3	8.2	2,137,322
Pennsylvania	150	3.7	5,626	5.2	38	181.3	32,229	437.4	5.6	2,916,273
Florida	208	5.2	7,023	6.5	34	132.5	18,860	424.3	5.4	2,039,769
Ohio	160	4.0	5,826	5.4	36	132.5	22,743	397.8	5.0	2,486,194
Texas	209	5.2	5,802	5.4	28	107.5	18,523	301.2	3.8	1,440,914
Maryland	90	2.2	2,576	2.4	29	93.3	36,219	244.1	3.1	2,712,233
Massachusetts	139	3.4	2,395	2.2	17	100.5	41,944	227.7	2.9	1,637,964
Michigan	99	2.5	3,555	3.3	36	75.4	21,206	203.4	2.6	2,054,687
Georgia	124	3.1	3,031	2.8	24	64.6	21,311	159.0	2.0	1,282,444
D.C.	47	1.2	1,357	1.3	29	62.1	45,795	135.5	1.7	2,883,404
Minnesota	102	2.5	1,829	1.7	18	46.8	25,610	133.6	1.7	1,310,000
Virginia	107	2.7	2,311	2.1	22	46.8	20,241	109.1	1.4	1,019,486
Missouri	74	1.8	1,579	1.5	21	32.2	20,399	98.0	1.2	1,324,068
North Carolina	70	1.7	1,441	1.3	21	30.5	21,167	86.1	1.1	1,230,543
Arizona	62	1.5	1,735	1.6	28	28.4	16,378	82.9	1.1	1,337,226
Indiana	56	1.4	2,161	2.0	39	30.2	13,985	79.9	1.0	1,427,268
Washington	72	1.8	1,729	1.6	24	36.6	21,164	78.8	1.0	1,093,931
Colorado	76	1.9	1,314	1.2	17	19.5	14,805	55.2	0.7	726,474
Kentucky	33	0.8	1,263	1.2	38	23.1	18,272	55.1	0.7	1,669,788
Oregon	49	1.2	1,472	1.4	30	19.9	13,520	43.1	0.5	879,673
Tennessee	54	1.3	870	0.8	16	22.5	25,834	39.4	0.5	729,389
Wisconsin	51	1.3	1,171	1.1	23	14.6	12,452	37.1	0.5	727,137
Iowa	31	0.8	1,148	1.1	37	17.6	15,327	34.5	0.4	1,113,935
Utah	23	0.6	1,164	1.1	51	12.8	11,034	24.0	0.3	1,042,043
Kansas	33	0.8	666	0.6	20	7.7	11,581	20.0	0.3	605,424
South Carolina	30	0.7	370	0.3	12	5.7	15,284	19.0	0.2	634,833
Arkansas	12	0.3	508	0.5	42	4.1	8,049	15.4	0.2	1,281,833
Louisiana	28	0.7	317	0.3	11	5.3	16,593	14.0	0.2	498,786
Oklahoma	21	0.5	504	0.5	24	4.9	9,762	12.0	0.2	573,429
Rhode Island	11	0.3	69	0.1	6	2.2	31,986	9.0	0.1	820,636
New Hampshire	10	0.2	72	0.1	7	3.0	42,333	8.9	0.1	885,400
West Virginia	6	0.1	363	0.3	61	2.4	6,581	7.6	0.1	1,266,833
Maine	16	0.4	155	0.1	10	2.6	17,039	6.9	0.1	432,625
Alabama	16	0.4	380	0.4	24	2.8	7,482	6.2	0.1	388,375
Vermont	9	0.2	228	0.2	25	3.2	13,899	6.2	0.1	690,556
Hawaii	6	0.1	304	0.3	51	2.8	9,046	6.0	0.1	997,167
New Mexico	16	0.4	192	0.2	12	2.0	10,193	5.2	0.1	321,875
Idaho	11	0.3	151	0.1	14	1.2	8,265	4.8	0.1	439,273
Nevada	12	0.3	92	0.1	8	1.2	13,022	3.3	0.0	274,917
South Dakota	4	0.1	150	0.1	38	1.6	10,887	3.3	0.0	814,750
North Dakota	4	0.1	168	0.2	42	1.5	9,125	2.8	0.0	705,750
Wyoming	6	0.1	50	0.0	8	0.8	16,560	2.4	0.0	403,500
Mississippi	8	0.2	51	0.0	6	0.7	14,000	2.0	0.0	249,500
Alaska	6	0.1	94	0.1	16	0.9	9,894	1.9	0.0	321,333
Nebraska	19	0.5	3,750*	-	-	(D)	-	(D)	-	-
Montana	7	0.2	60*	-	-	(D)	-	(D)	-	-
Delaware	5	0.1	60*	-	-	(D)	-	(D)	-	-

Source: 1997 *Economic Census.* The states are in descending order of revenues or establishments (if revenue data are missing for the majority). The symbol (D) appears when data are withheld to prevent disclosure of competitive information. States marked with (D) are sorted by number of establishments. A dash (-) indicates that the data element cannot be calculated. * indicates the midpoint of a range; 175, for example is the range 100-249. Shaded *states* on the state map indicate those states which have proportionately greater representation in the industry than would be indicated by the state's population; the ratio is based on total revenues or number of establishments. Shaded *regions* indicate where the industry is regionally most concentrated.

NAICS 541921 - PHOTOGRAPHIC STUDIOS, PORTRAIT*

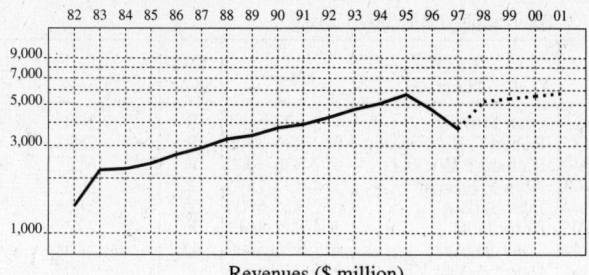

Revenues ($ million)

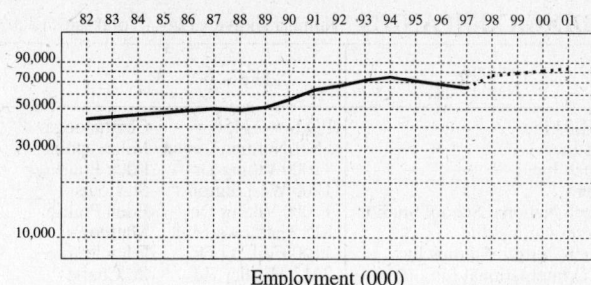

Employment (000)

GENERAL STATISTICS

Year	Establishments (number)	Employment (number)	Payroll ($ million)	Revenues ($ million)	Employees per Establishment (number)	Revenues per Establishment ($)	Payroll per Employee ($)
1982	7,415	44,036	358.0	1,409.0	5.9	190,020	8,130
1983	7,829 e	45,256 e	389.0 e	2,215.0	5.8 e	282,922 e	8,596 e
1984	8,243 e	46,476 e	420.0 e	2,249.0	5.6 e	272,838 e	9,037 e
1985	8,657 e	47,697 e	451.0 e	2,403.0	5.5 e	277,579 e	9,456 e
1986	9,071 e	48,917 e	483.0 e	2,688.0	5.4 e	296,329 e	9,874 e
1987	9,485	50,137	514.0	2,929.0	5.3	308,803	10,252
1988	8,854	49,200	561.0	3,261.0	5.6	368,308	11,402
1989	9,525	51,099	614.0	3,412.0	5.4	358,215	12,016
1990	9,747	56,257	691.0	3,749.0	5.8	384,631	12,283
1991	11,135	63,436	771.0	3,922.0	5.7	352,223	12,154
1992	11,381	66,822	853.0	4,280.0	5.9	376,065	12,765
1993	12,237	71,868	951.0	4,734.0	5.9	386,860	13,233
1994	12,436	74,990	1,003.0	5,093.0	6.0	409,537	13,375
1995	12,498	71,246	1,038.0	5,692.0	5.7	455,433	14,569
1996	12,872 e	68,321 e	1,014.0 e	4,699.0 e	5.3 e	365,056 e	14,842 e
1997	13,245	65,395	991.0	3,705.0	4.9	279,728	15,154
1998	13,962 p	76,749 p	1,160.0 p	5,223.0 p	5.5 p	374,087 p	15,114 p
1999	14,419 p	79,105 p	1,217.0 p	5,405.0 p	5.5 p	374,853 p	15,385 p
2000	14,876 p	81,460 p	1,274.0 p	5,587.0 p	5.5 p	375,571 p	15,640 p
2001	15,333 p	83,816 p	1,331.0 p	5,768.0 p	5.5 p	376,182 p	15,880 p

Sources: Economic Census of the United States, 1982, 1987, 1992, 1997. Establishment counts, employment, and payroll are from County Business Patterns for non-Census years. In non-Census years, industries in the Manufacturing range under SIC coding include data from the Annual Survey of Manufactures (ASM); those in the old Services range include data from the Services Annual Survey (SAS). Values followed by a 'p' are projections by the editors. Extrapolations are marked by 'e'. Data are the most recent available at this level of detail.

INDICES OF CHANGE

Year	Establishments (number)	Employment (number)	Payroll ($ million)	Revenues ($ million)	Employees per Establishment (number)	Revenues per Establishment ($)	Payroll per Employee ($)
1982	56.0	67.3	36.1	38.0	120.3	67.9	53.6
1987	71.6	76.7	51.9	79.1	107.1	110.4	67.7
1992	85.9	102.2	86.1	115.5	118.9	134.4	84.2
1993	92.4	109.9	96.0	127.8	119.0	138.3	87.3
1994	93.9	114.7	101.2	137.5	122.1	146.4	88.3
1995	94.4	108.9	104.7	153.6	115.5	162.8	96.1
1996	97.2 e	104.5 e	102.3 e	126.8 e	107.5 e	130.5 e	97.9 e
1997	100.0	100.0	100.0	100.0	100.0	100.0	100.0
1998	105.4 p	117.4 p	117.1 p	141.0 p	111.3 p	133.7 p	99.7 p
1999	108.9 p	121.0 p	122.8 p	145.9 p	111.1 p	134.0 p	101.5 p
2000	112.3 p	124.6 p	128.6 p	150.8 p	110.9 p	134.3 p	103.2 p
2001	115.8 p	128.2 p	134.3 p	155.7 p	110.7 p	134.5 p	104.8 p

Sources: Same as General Statistics. The values shown reflect change from the base year, 1997. Values above 100 mean greater than 1997, values below 100 mean less than 1997, and a value of 100 in the 1982-96 or 1998-2001 period means same as 1997. Values followed by a 'p' are projections by the editors; 'e' stands for extrapolation. Data are the most recent available at this level of detail.

SELECTED RATIOS

For 1997	Avg. of Information	Analyzed Industry	Index	For 1997	Avg. of Information	Analyzed Industry	Index
Employees per establishment	9	5	57	Payroll per establishment	372,545	74,821	20
Revenue per establishment	958,337	279,728	29	Payroll as % of revenue	39	27	69
Revenue per employee	111,029	56,656	51	Payroll per employee	43,162	15,154	35

Sources: Same as General Statistics. The 'Average' column represents the average for the industry sector, in 1997, where the currently shown industry is classified. The Index shows the relationship between the Average and the Analyzed Industry. For example, 100 means that they are equal; 500 that the Analyzed Industry is five times the average; 50 means that the Analyzed Industry is half the national average. The abbreviation 'na' is used to show that data are 'not available'.

*Equivalent to SIC 7221.

LEADING COMPANIES   Number shown: **12**   Total sales ($ mil): **9,941**   Total employment (000): **210.9**

Company Name	Address				CEO Name	Phone	Co. Type	Sales ($ mil)	Empl. (000)
Olan Mills Inc.	PO Box 23456	Chattanooga	TN	37422	Olan Mills II	423-622-5141	R	7,200*	160.0
Jostens Inc.	5501 Norman Center	Minneapolis	MN	55437	Robert C Buhrmaster	612-830-3300	P	782	6.8
Lifetouch Inc.	11000 Viking Dr	Eden Prairie	MN	55344	Richard P Erickson	612-826-4000	R	612	17.0
CPI Corp.	1706 Washington	St. Louis	MO	63103	Alyn V Essman	314-231-1575	P	390	8.2
Lifetouch National School Studios	11000 Viking Dr	Eden Prairie	MN	55344	Jake Barker	612-826-5500	D	362*	7.0
PCA International Inc.	815 Matthews-Mint	Matthews	NC	28105	Barry Feld	704-847-8011	P	227	5.6
Lifetouch Portrait Studios Inc.	11000 Viking Dr	Eden Prairie	MN	55344	Tony Sagol	612-826-5000	D	180*	3.5
HASCO International Inc.	3613 Mueller Rd	St. Charles	MO	63301	David A Van Vliet	636-946-5115	R	60	1.4
Olan Mills Incorporated of Ohio	1710 Valley Loop	Springfield	OH	45503	Jane Glass	937-322-9912	S	47*	0.6
Ambrosi and Associates Inc.	1100 W Washington	Chicago	IL	60607	Nicholas S Ambrosi	312-666-9200	S	31*	0.3
Multi-Image Network	312 Otterson Dr	Chico	CA	95928	Kathy Schifferle	530-345-4211	R	26*	<0.1
Jostens Photography Inc.	5501 Norman Center	Minneapolis	MN	55437		612-830-3300	S	24	0.5

Source: Ward's Business Directory of U.S. Private and Public Companies, Volumes 1 and 2, 2000. The company type code used is as follows: P - Public, R - Private, S - Subsidiary, D - Division, J - Joint Venture, A - Affiliate, G - Group, N - Company type not reported. Sales are in millions of dollars, employees are in thousands. An asterisk (*) indicates an estimated sales volume. The symbol < stands for 'less than'. Company names and addresses are truncated, in some cases, to fit into the available space.

LOCATION BY STATE AND REGIONAL CONCENTRATION

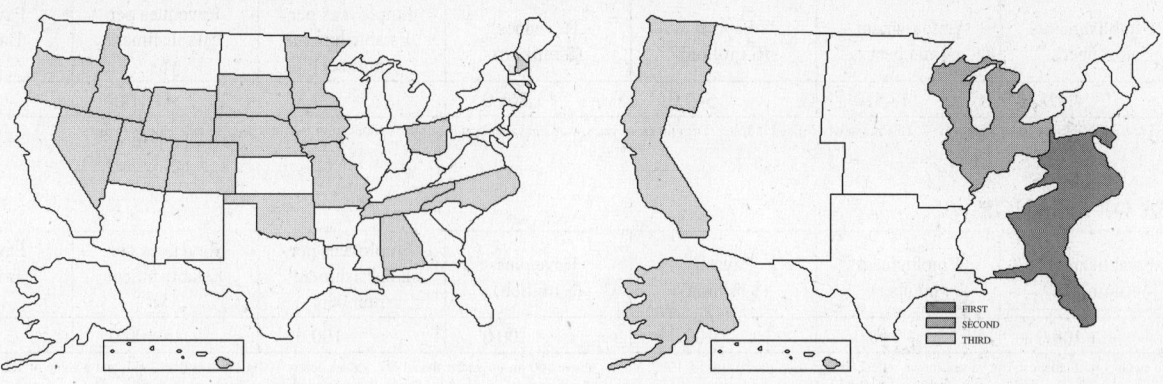

FIRST
SECOND
THIRD

INDUSTRY DATA BY STATE

State	Establishments Total (number)	% of U.S.	Employment Total (number)	% of U.S.	Per Estab.	Payroll Total ($ mil.)	Per Empl. ($)	Revenues Total ($ mil.)	% of U.S.	Per Estab. ($)
California	1,519	11.5	7,732	11.8	5	121.0	15,653	431.9	11.7	284,341
New York	738	5.6	3,126	4.8	4	66.6	21,305	254.6	6.9	344,981
Texas	847	6.4	4,739	7.2	6	67.1	14,161	224.0	6.0	264,481
North Carolina	374	2.8	3,862	5.9	10	43.0	11,141	188.1	5.1	502,933
Ohio	648	4.9	3,289	5.0	5	48.9	14,859	169.0	4.6	260,772
Florida	652	4.9	2,856	4.4	4	41.7	14,614	167.3	4.5	256,520
Illinois	634	4.8	2,763	4.2	4	47.4	17,152	166.1	4.5	262,002
Missouri	291	2.2	2,448	3.7	8	36.4	14,873	149.2	4.0	512,639
Pennsylvania	544	4.1	2,721	4.2	5	36.8	13,513	148.0	4.0	272,079
Michigan	530	4.0	2,225	3.4	4	32.3	14,538	126.5	3.4	238,658
Minnesota	303	2.3	2,201	3.4	7	44.5	20,215	126.2	3.4	416,429
Tennessee	308	2.3	2,018	3.1	7	41.1	20,390	118.5	3.2	384,799
New Jersey	327	2.5	1,562	2.4	5	27.6	17,641	94.6	2.6	289,287
Georgia	348	2.6	1,459	2.2	4	25.2	17,267	93.6	2.5	268,954
Indiana	348	2.6	1,354	2.1	4	18.2	13,468	78.1	2.1	224,411
Alabama	242	1.8	1,169	1.8	5	17.2	14,712	76.7	2.1	316,950
Washington	303	2.3	1,488	2.3	5	22.8	15,290	75.4	2.0	248,799
Virginia	297	2.2	1,292	2.0	4	19.0	14,726	70.5	1.9	237,414
Wisconsin	308	2.3	1,166	1.8	4	17.2	14,785	68.1	1.8	221,071
Massachusetts	257	1.9	1,035	1.6	4	16.9	16,312	65.4	1.8	254,409
Iowa	216	1.6	887	1.4	4	14.7	16,604	57.9	1.6	268,060
Louisiana	177	1.3	915	1.4	5	11.5	12,517	53.6	1.4	302,712
Maryland	227	1.7	994	1.5	4	14.2	14,314	53.2	1.4	234,436
Colorado	257	1.9	1,089	1.7	4	14.3	13,144	52.1	1.4	202,911
Oklahoma	152	1.1	1,110	1.7	7	13.7	12,314	48.1	1.3	316,474
Oregon	188	1.4	820	1.3	4	12.1	14,757	46.3	1.2	246,176
Arizona	201	1.5	992	1.5	5	13.7	13,859	44.0	1.2	218,682
Kentucky	193	1.5	808	1.2	4	10.0	12,423	42.9	1.2	222,098
Nevada	89	0.7	490	0.7	6	7.5	15,292	37.9	1.0	426,236
Connecticut	139	1.0	504	0.8	4	8.2	16,192	34.4	0.9	247,676
South Carolina	172	1.3	629	1.0	4	7.7	12,213	32.4	0.9	188,349
Utah	121	0.9	734	1.1	6	8.8	12,046	30.7	0.8	253,570
Nebraska	149	1.1	616	0.9	4	6.2	10,122	28.9	0.8	193,705
Hawaii	70	0.5	407	0.6	6	6.3	15,600	25.8	0.7	368,800
Mississippi	102	0.8	438	0.7	4	5.2	11,877	24.1	0.6	236,010
Arkansas	123	0.9	418	0.6	3	4.8	11,426	22.7	0.6	184,439
Idaho	75	0.6	347	0.5	5	3.9	11,354	17.2	0.5	228,787
New Hampshire	65	0.5	265	0.4	4	4.3	16,325	16.8	0.5	258,338
Rhode Island	57	0.4	286	0.4	5	4.7	16,360	16.8	0.5	294,158
New Mexico	65	0.5	220	0.3	3	2.8	12,591	12.1	0.3	186,554
South Dakota	61	0.5	175	0.3	3	2.1	11,726	11.4	0.3	186,426
Maine	53	0.4	170	0.3	3	2.0	12,000	9.2	0.2	174,208
Montana	46	0.3	117	0.2	3	1.2	10,222	7.1	0.2	154,152
Alaska	27	0.2	88	0.1	3	1.3	14,216	6.9	0.2	257,185
Delaware	35	0.3	114	0.2	3	1.9	16,982	6.1	0.2	175,371
Wyoming	36	0.3	79	0.1	2	1.3	16,190	5.7	0.2	159,306
Vermont	24	0.2	80	0.1	3	1.0	12,738	4.1	0.1	170,167
D.C.	11	0.1	27	0.0	2	0.5	18,778	2.2	0.1	201,364
Kansas	147	1.1	375*	-	-	(D)	-	(D)	-	-
West Virginia	95	0.7	375*	-	-	(D)	-	(D)	-	-
North Dakota	54	0.4	175*	-	-	(D)	-	(D)	-	-

Source: 1997 *Economic Census*. The states are in descending order of revenues or establishments (if revenue data are missing for the majority). The symbol (D) appears when data are withheld to prevent disclosure of competitive information. States marked with (D) are sorted by number of establishments. A dash (-) indicates that the data element cannot be calculated. * indicates the midpoint of a range; 175, for example is the range 100-249. Shaded *states* on the state map indicate those states which have proportionately greater representation in the industry than would be indicated by the state's population; the ratio is based on total revenues or number of establishments. Shaded *regions* indicate where the industry is regionally most concentrated.

NAICS 541922 - COMMERCIAL PHOTOGRAPHY

GENERAL STATISTICS

Year	Establishments (number)	Employment (number)	Payroll ($ million)	Revenues ($ million)	Employees per Establishment (number)	Revenues per Establishment ($)	Payroll per Employee ($)
1997	4,328	18,510	549.0	1,866.0	4.3	431,146	29,660

Source: *Economic Census of the United States*, 1997. This is a newly defined industry. Data for prior years were unavailable at the time of publication but may become available over time.

INDICES OF CHANGE

Year	Establishments (number)	Employment (number)	Payroll ($ million)	Revenues ($ million)	Employees per Establishment (number)	Revenues per Establishment ($)	Payroll per Employee ($)
1997	100.0	100.0	100.0	100.0	100.0	100.0	100.0

Sources: Same as General Statistics. The values shown reflect change from the base year, 1997. Values above 100 mean greater than 1997, values below 100 mean less than 1997, and a value of 100 in the 1982-96 or 1998-2001 period means same as 1997. Values followed by a 'p' are projections by the editors; 'e' stands for extrapolation. Data are the most recent available at this level of detail.

SIC INDUSTRIES RELATED TO NAICS 541922

Each new NAICS code represents an industry that used to be part of an SIC or a part of several SIC industries. Data in this table are shown to provide transitional information for these cases. All available data for the precursor SIC(s) are shown. Even if only a part of an SIC is included in the NAICS, *all* data for the SIC are reproduced. If the SIC industry is not marked as being a part (pt) of the NAICS, the entire industry is embedded in the NAICS data. The SIC composition of the new industry provides some hints of the relative importance of its "ancestors." Data marked with a 'p' are projected. Projections begin with 1982 data. Data earlier than 1990 are not shown but are reflected in the projections.

SIC	Industry	1990	1991	1992	1993	1994	1995	1996	1997
7335	**Commercial Photography**								
	Establishments (number)	3,328	3,439	4,213	4,054	3,964	3,982	4,142p	4,231p
	Employment (thousands)	16.8	16.1	16.2	17.2	16.3	16.8	16.3p	16.2p
	Revenues ($ million)	-	-	-	-	-	1,967.0	2,061.0	-
8099	**Health & Allied Services, nec (pt)**								
	Establishments (number)	-	-	5,011	-	-	-	-	-
	Employment (thousands)	-	-	71.9	-	-	-	-	-
	Revenues ($ million)	-	-	5,022.6	-	-	-	-	-

Source: *Economic Census of the United States*, 1992, annual surveys of economic sectors conducted by the Bureau of the Census, and estimates or projections based on the 1982-1992 period; not all data are shown. 'e' marks estimates made by the editors; 'p' indicates projections based on time series. A dash (-) indicates that data for this SIC or year were not available. The abbreviation (pt) next to the industry name indicates that only a part of the industry is present within the NAICS data. If no (pt) is shown, the entire industry is contained within the NAICS data.

SELECTED RATIOS

For 1997	Avg. of Information	Analyzed Industry	Index	For 1997	Avg. of Information	Analyzed Industry	Index
Employees per establishment	9	4	50	Payroll per establishment	372,545	126,848	34
Revenue per establishment	958,337	431,146	45	Payroll as % of revenue	39	29	76
Revenue per employee	111,029	100,810	91	Payroll per employee	43,162	29,660	69

Sources: Same as General Statistics. The 'Average' column represents the average for the industry sector, in 1997, where the currently shown industry is classified. The Index shows the relationship between the Average and the Analyzed Industry. For example, 100 means that they are equal; 500 that the Analyzed Industry is five times the average; 50 means that the Analyzed Industry is half the national average. The abbreviation 'na' is used to show that data are 'not available'.

LEADING COMPANIES   Number shown: **8**   Total sales ($ mil): **313**   Total employment (000): **2.5**

Company Name	Address				CEO Name	Phone	Co. Type	Sales ($ mil)	Empl. (000)
Devon Group Inc.	450 Park Ave	New York	NY	10022	Marne Obernauer Jr.	203-964-1444	S	264	2.2
M.J. Harden Associates Inc.	1019 Admiral Blvd	Kansas City	MO	64106	Ron Domsch	816-842-0141	R	35*	0.1
Paul Schultz Cos.	501 E Broadway	Louisville	KY	40202	Richard Schultz	502-587-8700	R	4*	<0.1
Colorvision International Inc.	8250 Exchange Dr	Orlando	FL	32809	Richard Simmons	407-851-0103	R	3*	<0.1
Kinetic Corp.	200 Dist Cmns	Louisville	KY	40206	GR Schuhmann	502-719-9500	R	3	<0.1
Black Star Publishing Inc.	116 E 27th St	New York	NY	10016	Benjamin Chapnick	212-679-3288	R	2*	<0.1
Ferderbar Studios Inc.	2356 S 102nd St	Milwaukee	WI	53227	Sara Straub	414-545-7770	R	1*	<0.1
Terry Heffernan Films	352 6th St	San Francisco	CA	94103	Terry Heffernan	415-626-1999	R	1*	<0.1

Source: *Ward's Business Directory of U.S. Private and Public Companies*, Volumes 1 and 2, 2000. The company type code used is as follows: P - Public, R - Private, S - Subsidiary, D - Division, J - Joint Venture, A - Affiliate, G - Group, N - Company type not reported. Sales are in millions of dollars, employees are in thousands. An asterisk (*) indicates an estimated sales volume. The symbol < stands for 'less than'. Company names and addresses are truncated, in some cases, to fit into the available space.

LOCATION BY STATE AND REGIONAL CONCENTRATION

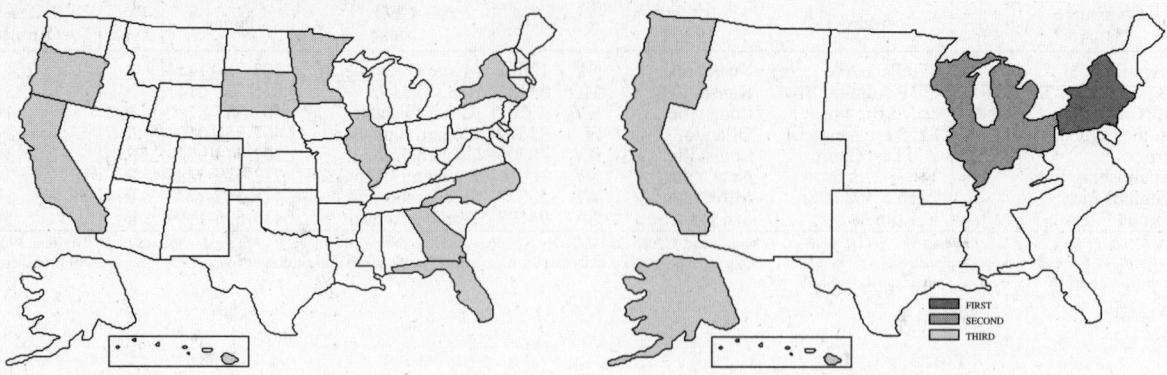

FIRST
SECOND
THIRD

INDUSTRY DATA BY STATE

State	Establishments Total (number)	% of U.S.	Employment Total (number)	% of U.S.	Per Estab.	Payroll Total ($ mil.)	Per Empl. ($)	Revenues Total ($ mil.)	% of U.S.	Per Estab. ($)
New York	663	15.3	2,941	15.9	4	128.3	43,614	427.2	22.9	644,315
California	539	12.5	2,116	11.4	4	70.3	33,233	251.8	13.5	467,083
Illinois	291	6.7	1,475	8.0	5	49.5	33,532	178.8	9.6	614,515
Florida	269	6.2	1,392	7.5	5	33.4	24,009	104.5	5.6	388,387
Texas	208	4.8	810	4.4	4	25.6	31,620	82.1	4.4	394,923
Minnesota	123	2.8	953	5.1	8	23.1	24,237	76.2	4.1	619,309
Ohio	148	3.4	746	4.0	5	20.5	27,539	63.0	3.4	425,392
North Carolina	105	2.4	869	4.7	8	21.6	24,883	60.5	3.2	576,038
Georgia	122	2.8	468	2.5	4	13.9	29,797	50.3	2.7	411,885
New Jersey	146	3.4	496	2.7	3	14.3	28,855	44.6	2.4	305,603
Michigan	124	2.9	320	1.7	3	10.3	32,231	43.0	2.3	347,113
Pennsylvania	134	3.1	431	2.3	3	10.8	25,030	38.7	2.1	288,993
Massachusetts	119	2.7	310	1.7	3	9.8	31,690	37.3	2.0	313,454
Washington	99	2.3	335	1.8	3	8.5	25,382	32.5	1.7	328,596
Missouri	94	2.2	277	1.5	3	9.7	34,957	29.9	1.6	318,298
Virginia	100	2.3	343	1.9	3	8.1	23,671	29.8	1.6	298,350
Wisconsin	78	1.8	348	1.9	4	8.6	24,569	27.6	1.5	354,218
Colorado	93	2.1	264	1.4	3	5.7	21,648	23.1	1.2	247,849
Oregon	68	1.6	220	1.2	3	6.6	29,991	22.1	1.2	324,985
Connecticut	63	1.5	206	1.1	3	6.0	29,291	20.1	1.1	319,619
Maryland	69	1.6	238	1.3	3	6.1	25,794	19.6	1.1	284,174
Indiana	72	1.7	254	1.4	4	5.7	22,354	18.4	1.0	255,764
Arizona	59	1.4	204	1.1	3	5.5	26,804	17.9	1.0	303,153
Hawaii	32	0.7	522	2.8	16	4.8	9,174	17.2	0.9	537,938
Tennessee	46	1.1	145	0.8	3	3.9	26,993	12.6	0.7	274,217
South Carolina	32	0.7	267	1.4	8	3.4	12,813	12.5	0.7	391,375
Utah	38	0.9	113	0.6	3	2.3	20,150	11.5	0.6	301,395
Louisiana	35	0.8	131	0.7	4	3.1	23,649	9.9	0.5	282,971
Iowa	32	0.7	165	0.9	5	3.4	20,709	9.5	0.5	296,844
Nevada	26	0.6	123	0.7	5	2.3	18,504	8.7	0.5	332,885
South Dakota	9	0.2	68	0.4	8	2.0	28,809	6.8	0.4	753,000
Alabama	29	0.7	91	0.5	3	1.8	19,670	6.6	0.4	225,966
Oklahoma	24	0.6	66	0.4	3	1.3	20,318	6.2	0.3	257,167
Maine	23	0.5	59	0.3	3	2.1	35,475	5.5	0.3	239,348
Rhode Island	22	0.5	39	0.2	2	1.2	31,513	5.1	0.3	229,773
D.C.	18	0.4	72	0.4	4	1.6	22,583	5.1	0.3	285,333
New Mexico	16	0.4	43	0.2	3	1.0	23,953	5.0	0.3	313,937
New Hampshire	17	0.4	39	0.2	2	1.3	33,641	4.7	0.3	274,706
Idaho	14	0.3	52	0.3	4	0.9	16,865	4.1	0.2	296,214
Kentucky	23	0.5	57	0.3	2	1.1	18,456	3.4	0.2	149,217
Arkansas	12	0.3	43	0.2	4	1.0	22,535	3.0	0.2	251,167
Delaware	10	0.2	29	0.2	3	0.9	32,034	2.8	0.1	275,400
Montana	19	0.4	31	0.2	2	0.5	17,581	2.7	0.1	143,737
Vermont	8	0.2	45	0.2	6	0.7	15,467	2.2	0.1	273,875
Nebraska	9	0.2	21	0.1	2	0.7	34,429	2.0	0.1	217,444
Mississippi	8	0.2	18	0.1	2	0.4	22,611	1.9	0.1	231,375
Alaska	6	0.1	22	0.1	4	0.2	11,136	1.7	0.1	282,167
Wyoming	3	0.1	9	0.0	3	0.1	10,778	0.6	0.0	212,667
Kansas	27	0.6	175*	-	-	(D)	-	(D)	-	-
West Virginia	3	0.1	60*	-	-	(D)	-	(D)	-	-
North Dakota	1	-	10*	-	-	(D)	-	(D)	-	-

Source: 1997 *Economic Census*. The states are in descending order of revenues or establishments (if revenue data are missing for the majority). The symbol (D) appears when data are withheld to prevent disclosure of competitive information. States marked with (D) are sorted by number of establishments. A dash (-) indicates that the data element cannot be calculated. * indicates the midpoint of a range; 175, for example is the range 100-249. Shaded *states* on the state map indicate those states which have proportionately greater representation in the industry than would be indicated by the state's population; the ratio is based on total revenues or number of establishments. Shaded *regions* indicate where photography is regionally most concentrated.

NAICS 541930 - TRANSLATION AND INTERPRETATION SERVICES

GENERAL STATISTICS

Year	Establishments (number)	Employment (number)	Payroll ($ million)	Revenues ($ million)	Employees per Establishment (number)	Revenues per Establishment ($)	Payroll per Employee ($)
1997	904	4,863	142.0	415.0	5.4	459,071	29,200

Source: *Economic Census of the United States*, 1997. This is a newly defined industry. Data for prior years were unavailable at the time of publication but may become available over time.

INDICES OF CHANGE

Year	Establishments (number)	Employment (number)	Payroll ($ million)	Revenues ($ million)	Employees per Establishment (number)	Revenues per Establishment ($)	Payroll per Employee ($)
1997	100.0	100.0	100.0	100.0	100.0	100.0	100.0

Sources: Same as General Statistics. The values shown reflect change from the base year, 1997. Values above 100 mean greater than 1997, values below 100 mean less than 1997, and a value of 100 in the 1982-96 or 1998-2001 period means same as 1997. Values followed by a 'p' are projections by the editors; 'e' stands for extrapolation. Data are the most recent available at this level of detail.

SIC INDUSTRIES RELATED TO NAICS 541930

Each new NAICS code represents an industry that used to be part of an SIC or a part of several SIC industries. Data in this table are shown to provide transitional information for these cases. All available data for the precursor SIC(s) are shown. Even if only a part of an SIC is included in the NAICS, *all* data for the SIC are reproduced. If the SIC industry is not marked as being a part (pt) of the NAICS, the entire industry is embedded in the NAICS data. The SIC composition of the new industry provides some hints of the relative importance of its "ancestors." Data marked with a 'p' are projected. Projections begin with 1982 data. Data earlier than 1990 are not shown but are reflected in the projections.

SIC	Industry	1990	1991	1992	1993	1994	1995	1996	1997
7389	**Business Services, nec (pt)**								
	Establishments (number)	44,079	50,252	52,375	56,829	60,725	53,596	60,893*p*	63,269*p*
	Employment (thousands)	489.6	550.4	523.6	607.9	648.7	623.0	680.2*p*	710.9*p*
	Revenues ($ million)	-	-	32,885.9	-	-	-		

Source: *Economic Census of the United States*, 1992, annual surveys of economic sectors conducted by the Bureau of the Census, and estimates or projections based on the 1982-1992 period; not all data are shown. 'e' marks estimates made by the editors; 'p' indicates projections based on time series. A dash (-) indicates that data for this SIC or year were not available. The abbreviation (pt) next to the industry name indicates that only a part of the industry is present within the NAICS data. If no (pt) is shown, the entire industry is contained within the NAICS data.

SELECTED RATIOS

For 1997	Avg. of Information	Analyzed Industry	Index	For 1997	Avg. of Information	Analyzed Industry	Index
Employees per establishment	9	5	62	Payroll per establishment	372,545	157,080	42
Revenue per establishment	958,337	459,071	48	Payroll as % of revenue	39	34	88
Revenue per employee	111,029	85,338	77	Payroll per employee	43,162	29,200	68

Sources: Same as General Statistics. The 'Average' column represents the average for the industry sector, in 1997, where the currently shown industry is classified. The Index shows the relationship between the Average and the Analyzed Industry. For example, 100 means that they are equal; 500 that the Analyzed Industry is five times the average; 50 means that the Analyzed Industry is half the national average. The abbreviation 'na' is used to show that data are 'not available'.

LEADING COMPANIES

No company data available for this industry.

LOCATION BY STATE AND REGIONAL CONCENTRATION

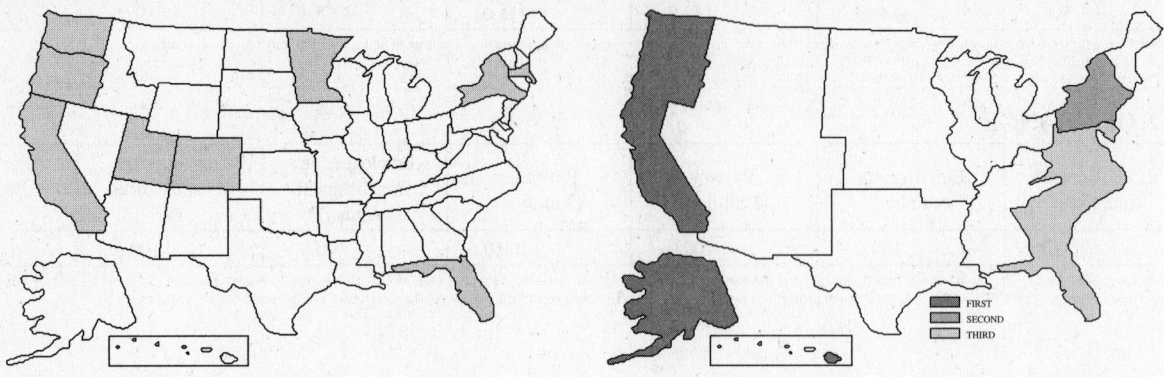

FIRST
SECOND
THIRD

INDUSTRY DATA BY STATE

State	Establishments Total (number)	Establishments % of U.S.	Employment Total (number)	Employment % of U.S.	Employment Per Estab.	Payroll Total ($ mil.)	Payroll Per Empl. ($)	Revenues Total ($ mil.)	Revenues % of U.S.	Revenues Per Estab. ($)
California	187	20.7	917	18.9	5	26.7	29,162	85.8	20.7	459,091
New York	89	9.8	690	14.2	8	25.8	37,390	66.8	16.1	750,247
Massachusetts	32	3.5	551	11.3	17	12.2	22,200	29.6	7.1	925,375
Texas	50	5.5	253	5.2	5	10.2	40,356	28.4	6.9	568,260
Florida	80	8.8	221	4.5	3	7.0	31,462	26.2	6.3	326,975
Colorado	20	2.2	283	5.8	14	9.2	32,431	24.5	5.9	1,226,550
Washington	37	4.1	192	3.9	5	3.7	19,094	12.7	3.1	342,270
Illinois	42	4.6	171	3.5	4	4.0	23,503	12.5	3.0	298,167
Minnesota	17	1.9	125	2.6	7	3.4	26,896	11.7	2.8	686,471
Oregon	26	2.9	119	2.4	5	3.0	25,353	10.8	2.6	415,231
Virginia	36	4.0	85	1.7	2	2.6	31,165	10.4	2.5	290,139
Utah	11	1.2	123	2.5	11	3.2	26,415	10.2	2.4	923,273
Michigan	26	2.9	99	2.0	4	3.6	36,343	9.7	2.3	374,538
New Jersey	25	2.8	86	1.8	3	2.5	29,163	8.3	2.0	332,760
Ohio	21	2.3	66	1.4	3	1.8	26,864	5.2	1.3	249,238
Pennsylvania	19	2.1	55	1.1	3	1.2	22,418	5.2	1.3	273,526
North Carolina	20	2.2	110	2.3	6	2.3	21,109	4.9	1.2	242,800
Georgia	23	2.5	49	1.0	2	1.3	26,510	3.9	1.0	171,652
Connecticut	6	0.7	28	0.6	5	1.3	45,607	3.6	0.9	602,500
Wisconsin	10	1.1	36	0.7	4	0.9	25,861	2.9	0.7	291,300
Indiana	12	1.3	66	1.4	6	0.7	11,091	2.9	0.7	239,750
D.C.	4	0.4	11	0.2	3	0.5	43,909	2.4	0.6	595,500
Kansas	7	0.8	32	0.7	5	0.8	24,719	2.1	0.5	298,714
Idaho	5	0.6	14	0.3	3	0.2	13,714	1.1	0.3	215,800
Hawaii	6	0.7	15	0.3	3	0.5	34,467	1.0	0.3	172,833
Louisiana	4	0.4	15	0.3	4	0.2	15,467	0.8	0.2	195,250
Arizona	8	0.9	14	0.3	2	0.3	19,429	0.6	0.1	77,125
Kentucky	4	0.4	19	0.4	5	0.2	7,947	0.5	0.1	116,250
Vermont	3	0.3	4	0.1	1	0.1	27,250	0.3	0.1	93,667
Nevada	3	0.3	5	0.1	2	0.1	21,000	0.2	0.1	76,000
Alaska	3	0.3	4	0.1	1	-	8,250	0.1	0.0	23,000
Maryland	20	2.2	175*	-	-	(D)	-	(D)	-	-
Missouri	10	1.1	60*	-	-	(D)	-	(D)	-	-
Tennessee	7	0.8	60*	-	-	(D)	-	(D)	-	-
Iowa	5	0.6	60*	-	-	(D)	-	(D)	-	-
Oklahoma	3	0.3	10*	-	-	(D)	-	(D)	-	-
Alabama	2	0.2	60*	-	-	(D)	-	(D)	-	-
Arkansas	2	0.2	10*	-	-	(D)	-	(D)	-	-
Delaware	2	0.2	10*	-	-	(D)	-	(D)	-	-
Maine	2	0.2	10*	-	-	(D)	-	(D)	-	-
Mississippi	2	0.2	10*	-	-	(D)	-	(D)	-	-
Nebraska	2	0.2	10*	-	-	(D)	-	(D)	-	-
Rhode Island	2	0.2	10*	-	-	(D)	-	(D)	-	-
South Carolina	2	0.2	10*	-	-	(D)	-	(D)	-	-
West Virginia	2	0.2	10*	-	-	(D)	-	(D)	-	-
Montana	1	0.1	10*	-	-	(D)	-	(D)	-	-
New Hampshire	1	0.1	10*	-	-	(D)	-	(D)	-	-
New Mexico	1	0.1	10*	-	-	(D)	-	(D)	-	-
South Dakota	1	0.1	10*	-	-	(D)	-	(D)	-	-
Wyoming	1	0.1	10*	-	-	(D)	-	(D)	-	-

Source: 1997 Economic Census. The states are in descending order of revenues or establishments (if revenue data are missing for the majority). The symbol (D) appears when data are withheld to prevent disclosure of competitive information. States marked with (D) are sorted by number of establishments. A dash (-) indicates that the data element cannot be calculated. * indicates the midpoint of a range; 175, for example is the range 100-249. Shaded *states* on the state map indicate those states which have proportionately greater representation in the industry than would be indicated by the state's population; the ratio is based on total revenues or number of establishments. Shaded *regions* indicate where the industry is regionally most concentrated.

NAICS 541990 - PROFESSIONAL, SCIENTIFIC, AND TECHNICAL SERVICES NEC

GENERAL STATISTICS

Year	Establishments (number)	Employment (number)	Payroll ($ million)	Revenues ($ million)	Employees per Establishment (number)	Revenues per Establishment ($)	Payroll per Employee ($)
1997	3,058	16,349	469.0	1,502.0	5.3	491,171	28,687

Source: *Economic Census of the United States*, 1997. This is a newly defined industry. Data for prior years were unavailable at the time of publication but may become available over time.

INDICES OF CHANGE

Year	Establishments (number)	Employment (number)	Payroll ($ million)	Revenues ($ million)	Employees per Establishment (number)	Revenues per Establishment ($)	Payroll per Employee ($)
1997	100.0	100.0	100.0	100.0	100.0	100.0	100.0

Sources: Same as General Statistics. The values shown reflect change from the base year, 1997. Values above 100 mean greater than 1997, values below 100 mean less than 1997, and a value of 100 in the 1982-96 or 1998-2001 period means same as 1997. Values followed by a 'p' are projections by the editors; 'e' stands for extrapolation. Data are the most recent available at this level of detail.

SIC INDUSTRIES RELATED TO NAICS 541990

Each new NAICS code represents an industry that used to be part of an SIC or a part of several SIC industries. Data in this table are shown to provide transitional information for these cases. All available data for the precursor SIC(s) are shown. Even if only a part of an SIC is included in the NAICS, *all* data for the SIC are reproduced. If the SIC industry is not marked as being a part (pt) of the NAICS, the entire industry is embedded in the NAICS data. The SIC composition of the new industry provides some hints of the relative importance of its "ancestors." Data marked with a 'p' are projected. Projections begin with 1982 data. Data earlier than 1990 are not shown but are reflected in the projections.

SIC	Industry	1990	1991	1992	1993	1994	1995	1996	1997
4499	**Water Transportation Services, nec (pt)**								
	Establishments (number)	1,111	1,187	1,118	1,180	1,209	1,244	1,394	1,261p
	Employment (thousands)	10.6	13.1	9.4	8.7	8.6	9.4	9.7	9.1p
	Revenues ($ million)	1,151.3e	1,060.9e	970.6	880.3p	789.9p	699.6p	609.3p	519.0p
7389	**Business Services, nec (pt)**								
	Establishments (number)	44,079	50,252	52,375	56,829	60,725	53,596	60,893p	63,269p
	Employment (thousands)	489.6	550.4	523.6	607.9	648.7	623.0	680.2p	710.9p
	Revenues ($ million)	-	-	32,885.9	-	-	-	-	-
8999	**Services, nec (pt)**								
	Establishments (number)	-	-	14,587	-	-	-	-	-
	Employment (thousands)	-	-	81.1	-	-	-	-	-
	Revenues ($ million)	-	-	7,966.2	-	-	-	-	-

Source: *Economic Census of the United States*, 1992, annual surveys of economic sectors conducted by the Bureau of the Census, and estimates or projections based on the 1982-1992 period; not all data are shown. 'e' marks estimates made by the editors; 'p' indicates projections based on time series. A dash (-) indicates that data for this SIC or year were not available. The abbreviation (pt) next to the industry name indicates that only a part of the industry is present within the NAICS data. If no (pt) is shown, the entire industry is contained within the NAICS data.

SELECTED RATIOS

For 1997	Avg. of Information	Analyzed Industry	Index	For 1997	Avg. of Information	Analyzed Industry	Index
Employees per establishment	9	5	62	Payroll per establishment	372,545	153,368	41
Revenue per establishment	958,337	491,171	51	Payroll as % of revenue	39	31	80
Revenue per employee	111,029	91,871	83	Payroll per employee	43,162	28,687	66

Sources: Same as General Statistics. The 'Average' column represents the average for the industry sector, in 1997, where the currently shown industry is classified. The Index shows the relationship between the Average and the Analyzed Industry. For example, 100 means that they are equal; 500 that the Analyzed Industry is five times the average; 50 means that the Analyzed Industry is half the national average. The abbreviation 'na' is used to show that data are 'not available'.

LEADING COMPANIES   Number shown: **75**   Total sales ($ mil): **44,201**   Total employment (000): **413.8**

Company Name	Address				CEO Name	Phone	Co. Type	Sales ($ mil)	Empl. (000)
Williams Energy Services	1 Williams Ctr	Tulsa	OK	74172	Steve Malcolm	918-573-2000	S	5,593	9.0
AmeriNet Inc.	2060 Craigshire Rd	St. Louis	MO	63146	Robert P Bowen	314-878-2525	R	4,100	<0.1
West Interactive Corp.	9910 Maple St	Omaha	NE	68134	Nancee R Berger	402-571-7700	S	2,772*	14.0
Belk Stores Services Inc.	2801 W Tyvola Rd	Charlotte	NC	28217	HW McKay Belk	704-357-1064	R	2,000	23.0
Convergys Corp. (Odgen, Utah)	1400 W 4400 South	Ogden	UT	84405	James F Orr	801-629-6423	S	1,800	35.0
Convergys Corp.	201 E 4th St	Cincinnati	OH	45202	Charles Mechem Jr	513-723-7000	P	1,763	42.5
EBSCO Industries Inc.	PO Box 1943	Birmingham	AL	35201		205-991-6600	R	1,530*	4.0
Pinkerton Consulting Services	39825 Paseo Padre	Fremont	CA	94538		510-445-3507	N	1,000	47.0
Software Spectrum/Technology	2140 Merritt Dr	Garland	TX	75041		972-850-6600	N	1,000	2.0
Celestica Asia Inc.	2071 Concourse Dr	San Jose	CA	95131	Robert Behlman	408-922-2727	R	950*	2.5
Snyder Communications Inc.	6903 Rockledge Dr	Bethesda	MD	20817	Daniel Snyder	301-468-1010	P	815	9.4
Sotheby's Inc.	1334 York Ave	New York	NY	10021	Diana D Brooks	212-606-7000	S	795*	1.9
George P. Reintjes Company Inc.	3800 Summit	Kansas City	MO	64111	Robert J Reintjes Sr	816-756-2150	R	789*	3.0
Dakotah Direct Inc.	9317 E Sinto	Spokane	WA	99206	Michael J Kuhn	509-789-4500	S	760*	2.0
A.H.L. Services	3465 N Desert Dr	Atlanta	GA	30344	Tom Marano	404-766-1212	S	747*	2.8
Caribiner International Inc.	16 W 61st St	New York	NY	10023	Raymond S Ingleby	212-541-5300	P	697	4.1
Freeman Cos.	PO Box 650036	Dallas	TX	75265	Don Freeman	214-670-9000	R	691	3.0
Ha-Lo Industries Inc.	5980 Touchy Ave	Niles	IL	60714	John Kelly	847-647-2300	P	590	4.5
SITEL Corp.	111 S Calvert, #1910	Baltimore	MD	21202	Phillip Clough	410-246-1505	P	586	19.0
West TeleServices Corp.	11808 Miracle Hls	Omaha	NE	68154	Thomas B Barker	402-693-1200	P	562	16.9
Data Reduction Inc.	302 Meacham St	Charlotte	NC	28203		704-332-3799	R	520*	13.0
Bob Rohrman Auto Group	701 Sagamore S	Lafayette	IN	47905	Bob Rohrman	765-448-1000	R	511	0.9
Technical Management Services	3250 Wilshire Blvd	Los Angeles	CA	90010	R W Holdsworth	213-383-5000	S	500	0.5
Telecheck Services Inc.	PO Box 4514	Houston	TX	77210	Jeff Baer	713-599-7600	S	490*	1.3
Lason Inc.	1305 Stephenson	Troy	MI	48083	John R Messinger	248-597-5800	P	480	10.3
Freeman Decorating Co.	8801 Ambassador	Dallas	TX	75247	Donald S Freeman Jr	214-634-1463	S	447*	2.0
Anacomp Inc.	12365 Crosthwaite	Poway	CA	92064	Ralph W Koehrer	619-679-9797	P	442	25.0
Carrols Corp.	968 James St	Syracuse	NY	13203	Daniel T Accordino	315-424-0513	R	417	12.7
The Raymond Corp.	South Canal St	Greene	NY	13778		607-656-2311	N	400	1.7
Visa U.S.A. Inc.	P O Box 8999	San Francisco	CA	94128	Carl Pascarella	650-432-3200	D	395	1.5
Ameridial Inc.	4535 Strausser	North Canton	OH	44720	Jim McGeorge	330-497-4888	R	380*	1.0
IQI Inc.	1645 N Vine St	Los Angeles	CA	90068	Stephen Mcneely		S	380*	4.0
Marathon Cheese Corp.	304 East St	Marathon	WI	54448	LaVern Stencil	715-443-2211	R	380*	1.0
Washington Inventory Service Inc.	9265 Sky Park Ct	San Diego	CA	92123		619-565-8111	S	371*	1.0
TeleTech Holdings Inc.	1700 Lincoln St	Denver	CO	80203	Scott Thompson	303-894-4000	P	369	10.0
InfoCision Management Corp.	325 Sprgside Dr	Akron	OH	44333	Gary Taylor	330-668-1400	R	368*	1.4
Century Business Services Inc.	6480 Rcksd Wds S	Cleveland	OH	44131	Michael G DeGroote	216-447-9000	P	352	4.2
HydroChem Industrial Services	6210 Rothway, #150	Houston	TX	77040	Tom Carter	713-462-2130	R	309*	1.3
CCH Legal Information Services	1633 Broadway	New York	NY	10019	Nancy McKinsky	212-664-1666	D	298*	1.2
CCL Custom Manufacturing Inc.	6133 N River Rd	Rosemont	IL	60018	Paul Cummings	847-823-0060	S	295*	3.8
PMT Services Inc.	3841 Green Hls	Nashville	TN	37215	Richardson M Roberts	615-254-1539	P	284	0.9
Hanover Compressor Co.	12001 N H-Rosslyn	Houston	TX	77086		281-447-8787	P	282	1.1
TeleTech Teleservices Inc.	1700 Lincoln St	Denver	CO	80203	Kenneth D Tuchman	303-894-4000	S	264	9.0
Anasazi Inc.	7500 N Dreamy Dr	Phoenix	AZ	85020	C Joseph Atteridge	602-870-3330	S	260*	0.7
TCI Marketing Inc.	1011 Centre Rd	Wilmington	DE	19805	Linda C Drake	302-633-3000	R	257*	1.0
PCI Services Inc.	3001 Red Lion Rd	Philadelphia	PA	19114	Daniel F Gerner	215-637-8100	D	250	2.9
RCG Information Technology	379 Thornall St	Edison	NJ	08837	George E Bello	732-744-3500	R	250	2.5
Precision Response Corp.	1505 NW167th St	Miami	FL	33169	David L Epstein	305-626-4600	P	216	5.2
Paymentech Inc.	1601 Elm St	Dallas	TX	75201	Pamela H Patsley	214-849-4770	P	213	1.3
ONSALE Inc.	1350 Willow Rd	Menlo Park	CA	94025	S Jerrold Kaplan	650-470-2400	P	208	0.2
HMS Partners Ltd.	10 W Broad St	Columbus	OH	43215		614-222-2555	N	200	0.2
Matrix Marketing Inc.	2121 N 117th Ave	Omaha	NE	68164	Basil Benett	402-498-4070	S	195*	2.2
Argenbright Inc.	3465 N Desert Dr	Atlanta	GA	30326	Thomas J Marano	404-766-1212	S	193	12.0
San Diego Convention Center	111 W Harbor Dr	San Diego	CA	92101	Carol Wallace	619-525-5000	P	193*	0.7
Equifax Payment Services Inc.	11601 N Roosevelt	St. Petersburg	FL	33716		813-556-9000	S	190	1.8
GLS Direct Inc.	2000 Market St	Philadelphia	PA	19103	Ross L Housley	215-568-1100	R	184*	0.7
R and B Inc.	PO Box 1800	Colmar	PA	18915	Richard Berman	215-997-1800	P	178	1.2
AmeriPath Inc.	7289 Garden Rd	Riviera Beach	FL	33404	James C New	561-845-1850	P	177	1.3
ChexSystems Inc.	1550 E 79th St	Minneapolis	MN	55425	Philip J Meyer	612-854-3422	P	173*	0.7
PSCU Service Centers Inc.	560 Carillon Pkwy	St. Petersburg	FL	33716	David J Serlo	727-572-8822	S	173*	0.7
Pre-Paid Legal Services Inc.	PO Box 145	Ada	OK	74820	Wilburn L Smith	580-436-1234	P	160	0.5
Island Deaf Sam Music Group	825 8th Ave	New York	NY	10019	Jim Caparro	212-333-8000	S	160*	0.6
I.T.I. Marketing Services Inc.	902 North 91st Plz	Omaha	NE	68114	Raymond Hipp	402-393-8000	R	153*	10.0
Time-Life Customer Service Inc.	1450 E Parham Rd	Richmond	VA	23228		804-261-1300	D	153*	0.4
Power Packaging Inc.	525 Dunham Rd	St. Charles	IL	60174		630-377-3838	R	153	2.4
Ferolie Group	PO Box 409	Montvale	NJ	07645	LJ Ferolie	201-307-9100	R	150*	0.6
Frankfurt Balkind Partners	244 East 58th St	New York	NY	10022	Aubrey Balkind	212-421-5888	R	150*	0.1
PIA Merchandising Company Inc.	19900 MacArthur	Irvine	CA	92623	Clinton E Owens	949-476-2200	S	150*	2.1
Boron, LePore and Associates Inc.	17-17 Rt 208, N	Fair Lawn	NJ	07410	Patrick G LePore	201-791-7272	P	149	1.1
Weston, Roy F Inc.	PO Box 2653	West Chester	PA	19380	William Robertson	610-701-3000	P	148	1.6
Payment Systems for Credit	560 Carillon Pkwy	St. Petersburg	FL	33716	David J Serlo	727-572-8822	R	142*	0.6
Copart Inc.	5500 E 2nd St	Benicia	CA	94510	A Jayson Adair	707-748-5000	P	142	1.4
StarTek Inc.	111 Havana St	Aurora	CO	80010	Michael W Morgan	303-361-6000	P	141	2.2
AMSEC L.L.C.	2829 Guardian Ln	Virginia Beach	VA	23452	Carl Albero	757-463-6666	S	134*	0.4
Icon International Inc.	281 Tresser Blvd	Stamford	CT	06901	Lance Lundberg	203-328-2300	R	130	0.1

Source: Ward's Business Directory of U.S. Private and Public Companies, Volumes 1 and 2, 2000. The company type code used is as follows: P - Public, R - Private, S - Subsidiary, D - Division, J - Joint Venture, A - Affiliate, G - Group, N - Company type not reported. Sales are in millions of dollars, employees are in thousands. An asterisk (*) indicates an estimated sales volume. The symbol < stands for 'less than'. Company names and addresses are truncated, in some cases, to fit into the available space.

LOCATION BY STATE AND REGIONAL CONCENTRATION

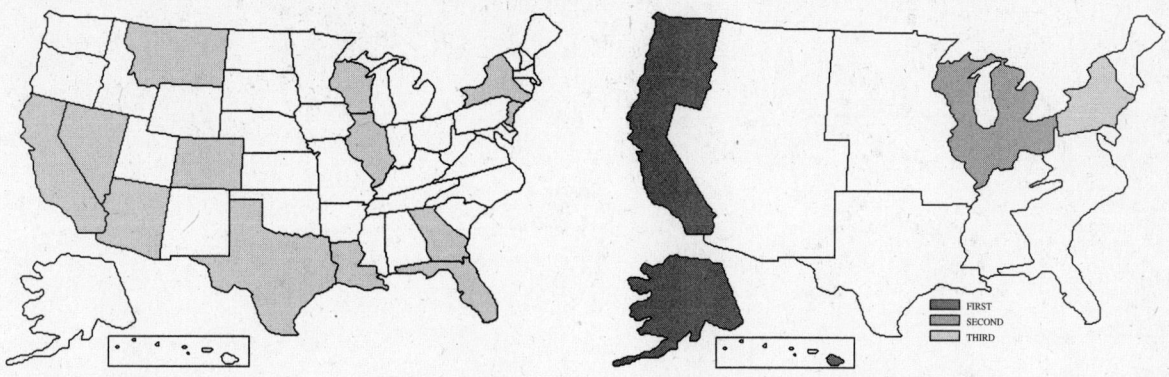

INDUSTRY DATA BY STATE

State	Establishments Total (number)	Establishments % of U.S.	Employment Total (number)	Employment % of U.S.	Employment Per Estab.	Payroll Total ($ mil.)	Payroll Per Empl. ($)	Revenues Total ($ mil.)	Revenues % of U.S.	Revenues Per Estab. ($)
California	400	13.1	2,150	13.2	5	68.2	31,740	240.5	16.0	601,247
Texas	223	7.3	1,597	9.8	7	47.5	29,730	146.3	9.7	655,973
New York	207	6.8	1,176	7.2	6	38.4	32,679	123.4	8.2	596,304
Illinois	161	5.3	1,044	6.4	6	37.5	35,919	111.7	7.4	693,783
Florida	217	7.1	878	5.4	4	22.3	25,425	81.2	5.4	374,415
New Jersey	111	3.6	559	3.4	5	25.1	44,853	66.1	4.4	595,108
Georgia	84	2.7	513	3.1	6	16.8	32,803	57.2	3.8	681,310
Michigan	96	3.1	559	3.4	6	13.2	23,551	48.2	3.2	501,677
Wisconsin	64	2.1	430	2.6	7	16.2	37,623	42.1	2.8	658,359
Pennsylvania	125	4.1	699	4.3	6	16.1	23,062	42.1	2.8	336,856
Louisiana	74	2.4	619	3.8	8	13.8	22,294	37.9	2.5	511,595
Arizona	46	1.5	349	2.1	8	8.2	23,630	33.5	2.2	728,848
Virginia	82	2.7	337	2.1	4	10.7	31,635	32.8	2.2	399,598
Colorado	65	2.1	285	1.7	4	7.2	25,256	31.8	2.1	489,092
Ohio	87	2.8	504	3.1	6	10.2	20,167	29.4	2.0	338,356
Massachusetts	71	2.3	247	1.5	3	9.1	36,972	25.6	1.7	359,972
Washington	72	2.4	184	1.1	3	4.5	24,582	23.3	1.6	324,167
Minnesota	70	2.3	249	1.5	4	5.6	22,313	20.0	1.3	285,786
Indiana	58	1.9	184	1.1	3	6.7	36,647	17.6	1.2	303,966
North Carolina	85	2.8	332	2.0	4	6.4	19,169	17.5	1.2	205,671
Kentucky	30	1.0	503	3.1	17	7.8	15,449	16.3	1.1	543,033
D.C.	9	0.3	54	0.3	6	4.5	83,722	12.1	0.8	1,344,667
Oregon	40	1.3	132	0.8	3	3.9	29,295	12.1	0.8	302,525
Nevada	20	0.7	141	0.9	7	2.6	18,348	9.9	0.7	496,400
Connecticut	28	0.9	80	0.5	3	2.4	29,625	6.6	0.4	236,607
Montana	14	0.5	76	0.5	5	2.3	30,789	5.7	0.4	407,429
Utah	14	0.5	78	0.5	6	1.5	19,692	5.7	0.4	410,429
Kansas	30	1.0	99	0.6	3	1.7	17,273	5.5	0.4	183,567
Hawaii	10	0.3	46	0.3	5	1.0	21,652	2.8	0.2	281,000
North Dakota	12	0.4	41	0.3	3	0.5	11,000	1.9	0.1	158,083
Idaho	11	0.4	18	0.1	2	0.4	23,167	1.6	0.1	146,364
Alaska	6	0.2	18	0.1	3	0.3	18,722	1.0	0.1	171,500
Vermont	5	0.2	21	0.1	4	0.2	7,905	0.4	0.0	74,800
Maryland	53	1.7	375*	-	-	(D)	-	(D)	-	-
Missouri	52	1.7	175*	-	-	(D)	-	(D)	-	-
Oklahoma	41	1.3	750*	-	-	(D)	-	(D)	-	-
Tennessee	39	1.3	175*	-	-	(D)	-	(D)	-	-
Iowa	36	1.2	175*	-	-	(D)	-	(D)	-	-
Alabama	34	1.1	175*	-	-	(D)	-	(D)	-	-
South Carolina	32	1.0	175*	-	-	(D)	-	(D)	-	-
Arkansas	25	0.8	175*	-	-	(D)	-	(D)	-	-
Nebraska	21	0.7	175*	-	-	(D)	-	(D)	-	-
West Virginia	15	0.5	60*	-	-	(D)	-	(D)	-	-
Maine	14	0.5	60*	-	-	(D)	-	(D)	-	-
New Mexico	14	0.5	60*	-	-	(D)	-	(D)	-	-
Mississippi	13	0.4	60*	-	-	(D)	-	(D)	-	-
Delaware	11	0.4	60*	-	-	(D)	-	(D)	-	-
Rhode Island	10	0.3	60*	-	-	(D)	-	(D)	-	-
New Hampshire	8	0.3	10*	-	-	(D)	-	(D)	-	-
South Dakota	7	0.2	10*	-	-	(D)	-	(D)	-	-
Wyoming	6	0.2	10*	-	-	(D)	-	(D)	-	-

Source: 1997 *Economic Census*. The states are in descending order of revenues or establishments (if revenue data are missing for the majority). The symbol (D) appears when data are withheld to prevent disclosure of competitive information. States marked with (D) are sorted by number of establishments. A dash (-) indicates that the data element cannot be calculated. * indicates the midpoint of a range; 175, for example is the range 100-249. Shaded *states* on the state map indicate those states which have proportionately greater representation in the industry than would be indicated by the state's population; the ratio is based on total revenues or number of establishments. Shaded *regions* indicate where the industry is regionally most concentrated.

Part V

MANAGEMENT OF COMPANIES AND ENTERPRISES

NAICS 551111 - OFFICES OF BANK HOLDING COMPANIES

GENERAL STATISTICS

Year	Establishments (number)	Employment (number)	Payroll ($ million)	Revenues ($ million)	Employees per Establishment (number)	Revenues per Establishment ($)	Payroll per Employee ($)
1997	2,390	26,921	1,608.0	21,306.0	11.3	8,914,644	59,730

Source: Economic Census of the United States, 1997. This is a newly defined industry. Data for prior years were unavailable at the time of publication but may become available over time.

INDICES OF CHANGE

Year	Establishments (number)	Employment (number)	Payroll ($ million)	Revenues ($ million)	Employees per Establishment (number)	Revenues per Establishment ($)	Payroll per Employee ($)
1997	100.0	100.0	100.0	100.0	100.0	100.0	100.0

Sources: Same as General Statistics. The values shown reflect change from the base year, 1997. Values above 100 mean greater than 1997, values below 100 mean less than 1997, and a value of 100 in the 1982-96 or 1998-2001 period means same as 1997. Values followed by a 'p' are projections by the editors; 'e' stands for extrapolation. Data are the most recent available at this level of detail.

SIC INDUSTRIES RELATED TO NAICS 551111

Each new NAICS code represents an industry that used to be part of an SIC or a part of several SIC industries. Data in this table are shown to provide transitional information for these cases. All available data for the precursor SIC(s) are shown. Even if only a part of an SIC is included in the NAICS, *all* data for the SIC are reproduced. If the SIC industry is not marked as being a part (pt) of the NAICS, the entire industry is embedded in the NAICS data. The SIC composition of the new industry provides some hints of the relative importance of its "ancestors." Data marked with a 'p' are projected. Projections begin with 1982 data. Data earlier than 1990 are not shown but are reflected in the projections.

SIC	Industry	1990	1991	1992	1993	1994	1995	1996	1997
6712	**Bank Holding Companies (pt)**	-	-	-	-	-	-	-	-

Source: Economic Census of the United States, 1992, annual surveys of economic sectors conducted by the Bureau of the Census, and estimates or projections based on the 1982-1992 period; not all data are shown. 'e' marks estimates made by the editors; 'p' indicates projections based on time series. A dash (-) indicates that data for this SIC or year were not available. The abbreviation (pt) next to the industry name indicates that only a part of the industry is present within the NAICS data. If no (pt) is shown, the entire industry is contained within the NAICS data.

SELECTED RATIOS

For 1997	Avg. of Information	Analyzed Industry	Index	For 1997	Avg. of Information	Analyzed Industry	Index
Employees per establishment	55	11	20	Payroll per establishment	3,258,261	672,803	21
Revenue per establishment	1,954,248	8,914,644	456	Payroll as % of revenue	167	8	5
Revenue per employee	35,328	791,427	2,240	Payroll per employee	58,902	59,730	101

Sources: Same as General Statistics. The 'Average' column represents the average for the industry sector, in 1997, where the currently shown industry is classified. The Index shows the relationship between the Average and the Analyzed Industry. For example, 100 means that they are equal; 500 that the Analyzed Industry is five times the average; 50 means that the Analyzed Industry is half the national average. The abbreviation 'na' is used to show that data are 'not available'.

LEADING COMPANIES   Number shown: **75**   Total sales ($ mil): **4,034,136**   Total employment (000): **1,078.1**

Company Name	Address				CEO Name	Phone	Co. Type	Sales ($ mil)	Empl. (000)
Bank of America Corp.	100 N Tryon St	Charlotte	NC	28255	Kenneth D. Lewis	704-386-5000	P	617,679	171.0
Bank One Corp.	1 First National Plz	Chicago	IL	60670	James Dimon	312-732-4000	P	398,241*	86.2
Chase Manhattan Corp.	270 Park Ave	New York	NY	10017	William B Harrison Jr	212-270-6000	P	365,875	72.7
J.P. Morgan and Company Inc.	60 Wall St	New York	NY	10260	Douglas A Warner III	212-483-2323	P	261,067	15.7
First Union Corp.	1 First Union Ctr	Charlotte	NC	28288	Edward E Crutchfield	704-374-6565	P	253,000	71.5
MNB Bancshares Inc.	800 Poyntz Ave	Manhattan	KS	66505	Patrick L Alexander	785-565-2000	P	135,830	<0.1
First Cherokee Bancshares Inc.	P O Box 1238	Woodstock	GA	30188	R O Kononen, Jr	770-591-9000	P	110,230	<0.1
Crestar Financial Corp.	P O Box 26665	Richmond	VA	23261	Richard G Tilghman	804-782-5000	P	93,170	30.5
SunTrust Banks Inc.	P O Box 4418	Atlanta	GA	30302	L Phillip Humann	404-588-7711	P	93,170	30.5
HSBC USA INC.	One HSBC Center	Buffalo	NY	14203		716-841-2424	S	90,240	14.4
U.S. Bancorp	PO Box 522	Minneapolis	MN	55480	John F Grundhofer	612-973-1111	P	81,530	33.0
BankBoston Corp.	PO Box 1987	Boston	MA	02105	Henrique Meirelles	617-349-7450	P	75,700	25.0
PNC Bank Corp.	1 PNC Plz 249 5th	Pittsburgh	PA	15222	Thomas H O'Brien	412-762-1553	P	75,464	25.5
Firstar Corp.	777 E Wisconsin	Milwaukee	WI	53202	Jerry A Grundhofer	414-765-4321	P	72,800	8.0
Wachovia Corp.	100 N Main St	Winston-Salem	NC	27150	LM Baker Jr	336-770-5000	P	66,982	21.0
Bank of New York Company Inc.	1 Wall St	New York	NY	10286	Thomas A Renyi	212-495-1784	P	63,141*	17.2
Golden State Bancorp Inc.	135 Main St	San Francisco	CA	94105	Gerald Ford	415-904-1100	P	54,869	3.0
Republic New York Corp.	452 5th Ave	New York	NY	10018	Dov C Schlein	212-525-6100	P	50,424	5.8
Mellon Bank Corp.	1 Mellon Bank Ctr	Pittsburgh	PA	15258	C M Condron	412-234-5000	P	48,071	28.5
State Street Corp.	PO Box 351	Boston	MA	02101	Marshall N Carter	617-786-3000	P	47,082	16.3
Regions Financial Corp.	PO Box 10247	Birmingham	AL	35202	Carl E Jones, Jr	205-326-7100	P	42,700	14.7
Golden West Financial Corp.	1901 Harrison St	Oakland	CA	94612	Herbert M Sandler	510-466-3420	P	38,469	4.4
Comerica Inc.	500 Woodward Ave	Detroit	MI	48226	Eugene A Miller	313-222-4000	P	33,900	10.7
Union Planters Banc	7130 Goodlett Farms	Cordova	TN	38018	Jackson W Moore	901-580-6000	P	33,300	1.5
Summit Bancorp.	PO Box 2066	Princeton	NJ	08543	Robert G Cox	609-987-3200	P	33,101	8.6
Charter One Financial Inc.	1215 Superior Ave	Cleveland	OH	44114	Charles J Koch	216-566-5300	P	31,819	5.7
Fifth Third Bancorp.	38 Fountain Sq Plz	Cincinnati	OH	45263	George A Schaefer Jr	513-579-5300	P	28,900	8.8
Northern Trust Corp.	50 S La Salle St	Chicago	IL	60675	Barry G Hastings	312-630-6000	P	28,708	8.2
Huntington Bancshares Inc.	41 S High St	Columbus	OH	43287	P Geier	614-480-8300	P	28,296	10.2
SunTrust Banks of Florida Inc.	P O Box 3833	Orlando	FL	32802	George W Koehn	407-237-4141	S	27,585	7.9
Sovereign Bancorp Inc.	PO Box 12646	Reading	PA	19612	Jay S Sidhu	610-320-8400	P	26,587	4.4
Popular Inc.	P O Box 362708	San Juan	PR	00936	Richard L Carrion	787-765-9800	P	24,760	10.5
Astoria Financial Corp.	1 Astoria Federal Plz	Lake Success	NY	11042	George L Engelke Jr	516-327-3000	P	23,000	1.8
First Security Corp.	79 S Main St	Salt Lake City	UT	84130	Spencer F Eccles	801-246-5706	P	23,000	9.4
MBNA Corp.	1100 N King St	Wilmington	DE	19801	Alfred Lerner	302-453-9930	P	22,982	19.0
M and T Bancorp.	PO Box 223	Buffalo	NY	14240	Robert G Wilmers	716-842-5138	P	22,400	6.5
Dime Bancorp Inc.	589 5th Ave	New York	NY	10017	Lawrence J Toal	212-326-6170	P	22,321	7.4
Harris Bankcorp Inc.	111 W Monroe St	Chicago	IL	60603	Alan G McNally	312-461-2121	S	22,200	6.6
Marshall and Ilsley Corp.	770 N Water St	Milwaukee	WI	53202	DJ Kuester	414-765-7801	P	21,566	10.8
SunTrust Banks of Georgia Inc.	P O Box 4418	Atlanta	GA	30302	Robert Long	404-827-6554	S	21,275	4.5
AmSouth Bancorp.	PO Box 11007	Birmingham	AL	35288	C Dowd Ritter	205-320-7151	P	19,900	6.7
First Tennessee National Corp.	PO Box 84	Memphis	TN	38101	Ralph Horn	901-523-5630	P	18,400	10.2
Citizens Financial Group Inc.	1 Citizens Plz	Providence	RI	02903	Lawrence K Fish	401-456-7000	S	17,300	4.1
Compass Bancshares Inc.	15 S 20th St	Birmingham	AL	35233	D Paul Jones, Jr	205-933-3000	P	17,289*	5.9
ABN AMRO North America Inc.	135 S La Salle St	Chicago	IL	60603	Harrison F Tempest	312-443-2000	D	17,150*	5.5
First Maryland Bancorp.	25 S Charles St	Baltimore	MD	21201	Frank P Bramble	410-244-4000	P	17,073	6.1
First Star	200 E Main St	Richmond	KY	40475	Tony D Whitaker	606-623-2548	S	16,896*	5.0
Zions Bancorp.	One Main St	Salt Lake City	UT	84111	Harris H Simmons	801-524-4787	P	16,649	4.9
Old Kent Financial Corp.	111 Lyon St N W	Grand Rapids	MI	49503	David J Wagner	616-771-5000	P	16,589	7.5
Hibernia Corp.	PO Box 61540	New Orleans	LA	70161	Stephen A Hansel	504-533-3332	P	15,300	5.0
BancWest Bancorp Inc.	999 Bishop St	Honolulu	HI	96813	Walter A Dods, Jr	808-525-7000	R	15,050	4.9
Pacific Century Financial Corp.	PO Box 2900	Honolulu	HI	96846	Richard J Dahl	808-643-3888	P	14,400	5.1
Peoples Heritage Financial Group	P O Box 9540	Portland	ME	04112	William J Ryan	207-761-8500	P	13,900	3.3
Washington Mutual Inc.	PO Box 834	Seattle	WA	98111	Kerry K Killinger	206-461-2000	P	13,571	27.3
Commercial Federal Corp.	2120 S 72nd St	Omaha	NE	68124	William A Fitzgerald	402-554-9200	P	12,800	3.6
Associated Banc-Corp.	PO Box 13307	Green Bay	WI	54307	Harry B Conlon	920-491-7000	P	12,109*	4.0
Midland Financial Co.	501 W I-44 Service	Oklahoma City	OK	73118	Robert Dilg	405-840-7600	R	10,600*	1.5
Commerce Bancshares Inc.	PO Box 13686	Kansas City	MO	64199	David W Kemper	816-234-2000	P	10,470	6.1
Colonial BancGroup Inc.	P O Box 1108	Montgomery	AL	36101	Robert E Lowder	334-240-5000	P	10,456	3.7
TCF Financial Corp.	801 Marquette Ave	Minneapolis	MN	55402	William A Cooper	612-661-6500	P	10,293	7.0
Synovus Financial Corp.	PO Box 120	Columbus	GA	31902	James H Blanchard	706-649-2387	P	9,944*	8.6
First Citizens BancShares Inc.	PO Box 151	Raleigh	NC	27602	Lewis R Holding	919-716-7000	P	9,720	5.0
First Virginia Banks Inc.	6400 Arlington Blvd	Falls Church	VA	22042	Barry J Fitzpatrick	703-241-4000	P	9,565	5.2
Michigan National Corp.	P O Box 9065	Farmington Hills	MI	48333	Douglas E Ebert	248-473-3000	S	9,329	4.0
FirstMerit Corp.	3 Cascade Plz	Akron	OH	44308	Sid A Bostic	330-996-6300	P	9,100	2.7
Centura Banks Inc.	PO Box 1220	Rocky Mount	NC	27802	Cecil W Sewell Jr	252-454-4400	P	9,001*	2.9
Webster Financial Corp.	Webster Plz	Waterbury	CT	06702	James C Smith	203-753-2921	P	8,893	1.9
National City Corp.	1900 E 9th St	Cleveland	OH	44114	David A Daberko	216-575-2000	P	8,293	38.1
First National of Nebraska Inc.	PO Box 3128	Omaha	NE	68103	Bruce Lauritzen	402-341-0500	P	8,000	5.0
KeyCorp.	127 Public Sq	Cleveland	OH	44114	Robert Gillespie	216-689-6300	P	7,989	25.9
Bank of Ireland	875 Elm St	Manchester	NH	03101	Kim Meader	603-668-5000	S	7,979*	2.4
CCB Financial Corp.	PO Box 931	Durham	NC	27702	Ernest C Roessler	919-683-7777	P	7,740	2.7
CNB Bancshares Inc.	P O Box 778	Evansville	IN	47705	James J Giancola	812-464-3400	P	7,142	2.8
Deposit Guaranty Corp.	P O Box 1200	Jackson	MS	39215	HL Hembree IV	601-354-8564	S	6,940	3.5
Keystone Financial Inc.	P O Box 3660	Harrisburg	PA	17105	Carl L Campbell	717-233-1555	P	6,874	3.1

Source: Ward's Business Directory of U.S. Private and Public Companies, Volumes 1 and 2, 2000. The company type code used is as follows: P - Public, R - Private, S - Subsidiary, D - Division, J - Joint Venture, A - Affiliate, G - Group, N - Company type not reported. Sales are in millions of dollars, employees are in thousands. An asterisk (*) indicates an estimated sales volume. The symbol < stands for 'less than'. Company names and addresses are truncated, in some cases, to fit into the available space.

LOCATION BY STATE AND REGIONAL CONCENTRATION

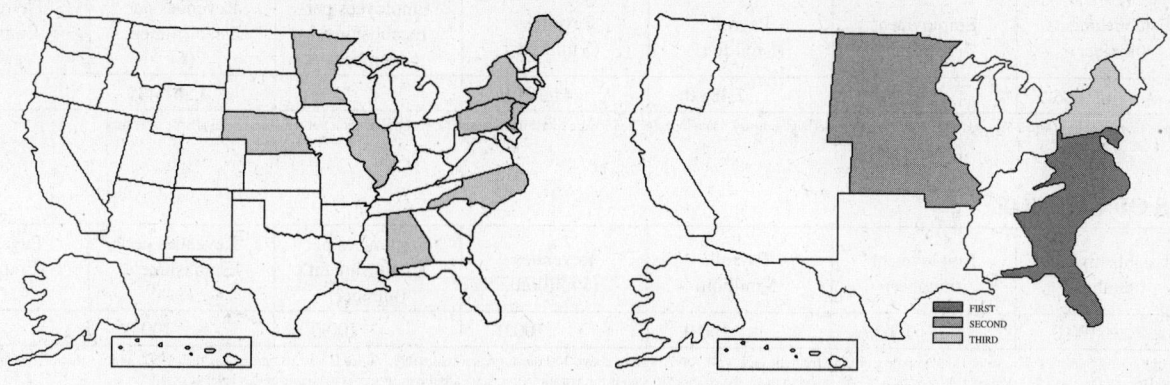

INDUSTRY DATA BY STATE

State	Establishments Total (number)	% of U.S.	Employment Total (number)	% of U.S.	Per Estab.	Payroll Total ($ mil.)	Per Empl. ($)	Revenues Total ($ mil.)	% of U.S.	Per Estab. ($)
North Carolina	31	1.3	388	1.4	13	261.1	672,933	4,175.9	19.6	134,706,742
Minnesota	84	3.5	1,945	7.2	23	159.8	82,148	3,124.2	14.7	37,193,167
New York	88	3.7	1,199	4.5	14	77.0	64,261	1,557.2	7.3	17,695,648
Pennsylvania	77	3.2	2,255	8.4	29	144.6	64,138	1,435.7	6.7	18,645,104
Illinois	207	8.7	2,232	8.3	11	119.4	53,485	1,114.9	5.2	5,386,155
New Jersey	26	1.1	410	1.5	16	20.8	50,688	865.3	4.1	33,280,231
Ohio	69	2.9	652	2.4	9	28.2	43,206	826.0	3.9	11,970,768
Florida	86	3.6	272	1.0	3	15.9	58,386	646.5	3.0	7,516,942
Delaware	79	3.3	102	0.4	1	1.8	17,451	588.6	2.8	7,451,063
Tennessee	52	2.2	955	3.5	18	43.3	45,371	400.7	1.9	7,705,423
Missouri	88	3.7	1,034	3.8	12	42.4	40,974	387.1	1.8	4,399,239
Alabama	38	1.6	522	1.9	14	35.9	68,843	385.0	1.8	10,132,500
Texas	166	6.9	686	2.5	4	28.7	41,840	372.7	1.7	2,245,458
Georgia	89	3.7	986	3.7	11	48.1	48,831	308.6	1.4	3,467,213
Michigan	65	2.7	1,054	3.9	16	46.8	44,407	295.7	1.4	4,549,138
Wisconsin	76	3.2	1,901	7.1	25	56.4	29,676	288.4	1.4	3,795,132
California	116	4.9	1,311	4.9	11	79.5	60,630	278.5	1.3	2,400,664
Nebraska	62	2.6	404	1.5	7	17.8	44,121	214.7	1.0	3,463,306
Indiana	48	2.0	761	2.8	16	30.6	40,187	180.6	0.8	3,761,521
Arkansas	58	2.4	318	1.2	5	11.8	37,104	177.2	0.8	3,055,672
Louisiana	41	1.7	111	0.4	3	1.9	17,216	170.8	0.8	4,166,659
Washington	35	1.5	2,090	7.8	60	23.0	10,981	150.2	0.7	4,290,029
Kentucky	57	2.4	385	1.4	7	16.2	42,008	122.9	0.6	2,155,474
West Virginia	21	0.9	368	1.4	18	11.1	30,266	117.3	0.6	5,586,619
Iowa	93	3.9	260	1.0	3	11.6	44,731	116.2	0.5	1,249,183
Colorado	50	2.1	194	0.7	4	11.0	56,876	114.3	0.5	2,285,140
Maine	9	0.4	56	0.2	6	7.9	141,429	102.9	0.5	11,438,667
Kansas	77	3.2	226	0.8	3	12.7	56,088	83.9	0.4	1,090,234
Hawaii	8	0.3	71	0.3	9	2.5	35,380	82.5	0.4	10,310,625
Mississippi	28	1.2	359	1.3	13	18.3	50,939	66.5	0.3	2,373,286
Oklahoma	40	1.7	82	0.3	2	5.9	71,695	64.3	0.3	1,607,425
Nevada	55	2.3	117	0.4	2	3.9	32,974	56.6	0.3	1,029,073
New Hampshire	10	0.4	454	1.7	45	19.4	42,802	52.9	0.2	5,286,000
Virginia	28	1.2	353	1.3	13	16.2	46,003	51.6	0.2	1,843,429
Connecticut	11	0.5	64	0.2	6	3.8	60,109	33.8	0.2	3,074,273
South Dakota	22	0.9	40	0.1	2	2.0	51,050	32.6	0.2	1,480,909
South Carolina	26	1.1	108	0.4	4	5.7	52,417	23.9	0.1	919,808
Montana	16	0.7	104	0.4	7	1.2	11,692	23.0	0.1	1,436,813
New Mexico	14	0.6	131	0.5	9	4.0	30,168	22.3	0.1	1,590,286
North Dakota	21	0.9	5	0.0	-	0.1	14,800	20.0	0.1	951,238
Maryland	18	0.8	44	0.2	2	3.0	68,455	17.5	0.1	971,667
Arizona	15	0.6	19	0.1	1	1.6	84,684	17.0	0.1	1,136,200
Utah	14	0.6	93	0.3	7	6.8	73,333	15.0	0.1	1,071,714
Massachusetts	30	1.3	60*	-	-	(D)	-	(D)	-	-
Massachusetts	30	1.3	60*	-	-	(D)	-	(D)	-	-
Oregon	16	0.7	750*	-	-	(D)	-	(D)	-	-
Oregon	16	0.7	750*	-	-	(D)	-	(D)	-	-
Vermont	11	0.5	375*	-	-	(D)	-	(D)	-	-
Vermont	11	0.5	375*	-	-	(D)	-	(D)	-	-
Wyoming	9	0.4	375*	-	-	(D)	-	(D)	-	-

Source: 1997 *Economic Census*. The states are in descending order of revenues or establishments (if revenue data are missing for the majority). The symbol (D) appears when data are withheld to prevent disclosure of competitive information. States marked with (D) are sorted by number of establishments. A dash (-) indicates that the data element cannot be calculated. * indicates the midpoint of a range; 175, for example is the range 100-249. Shaded *states* on the state map indicate those states which have proportionately greater representation in the industry than would be indicated by the state's population; the ratio is based on total revenues or number of establishments. Shaded *regions* indicate where the industry is regionally most concentrated.

NAICS 551112 - OFFICES OF HOLDING COMPANIES NEC

GENERAL STATISTICS

Year	Establishments (number)	Employment (number)	Payroll ($ million)	Revenues ($ million)	Employees per Establishment (number)	Revenues per Establishment ($)	Payroll per Employee ($)
1997	9,666	98,908	7,483.0	41,191.0	10.2	4,261,432	75,656

Source: *Economic Census of the United States*, 1997. This is a newly defined industry. Data for prior years were unavailable at the time of publication but may become available over time.

INDICES OF CHANGE

Year	Establishments (number)	Employment (number)	Payroll ($ million)	Revenues ($ million)	Employees per Establishment (number)	Revenues per Establishment ($)	Payroll per Employee ($)
1997	100.0	100.0	100.0	100.0	100.0	100.0	100.0

Sources: Same as General Statistics. The values shown reflect change from the base year, 1997. Values above 100 mean greater than 1997, values below 100 mean less than 1997, and a value of 100 in the 1982-96 or 1998-2001 period means same as 1997. Values followed by a 'p' are projections by the editors; 'e' stands for extrapolation. Data are the most recent available at this level of detail.

SIC INDUSTRIES RELATED TO NAICS 551112

Each new NAICS code represents an industry that used to be part of an SIC or a part of several SIC industries. Data in this table are shown to provide transitional information for these cases. All available data for the precursor SIC(s) are shown. Even if only a part of an SIC is included in the NAICS, *all* data for the SIC are reproduced. If the SIC industry is not marked as being a part (pt) of the NAICS, the entire industry is embedded in the NAICS data. The SIC composition of the new industry provides some hints of the relative importance of its "ancestors." Data marked with a 'p' are projected. Projections begin with 1982 data. Data earlier than 1990 are not shown but are reflected in the projections.

SIC	Industry	1990	1991	1992	1993	1994	1995	1996	1997
6719	Holding Companies, nec (pt)	-	-	-	-	-	-	-	-

Source: *Economic Census of the United States*, 1992, annual surveys of economic sectors conducted by the Bureau of the Census, and estimates or projections based on the 1982-1992 period; not all data are shown. 'e' marks estimates made by the editors; 'p' indicates projections based on time series. A dash (-) indicates that data for this SIC or year were not available. The abbreviation (pt) next to the industry name indicates that only a part of the industry is present within the NAICS data. If no (pt) is shown, the entire industry is contained within the NAICS data.

SELECTED RATIOS

For 1997	Avg. of Information	Analyzed Industry	Index	For 1997	Avg. of Information	Analyzed Industry	Index
Employees per establishment	55	10	18	Payroll per establishment	3,258,261	774,157	24
Revenue per establishment	1,954,248	4,261,432	218	Payroll as % of revenue	167	18	11
Revenue per employee	35,328	416,458	1,179	Payroll per employee	58,902	75,656	128

Sources: Same as General Statistics. The 'Average' column represents the average for the industry sector, in 1997, where the currently shown industry is classified. The Index shows the relationship between the Average and the Analyzed Industry. For example, 100 means that they are equal; 500 that the Analyzed Industry is five times the average; 50 means that the Analyzed Industry is half the national average. The abbreviation 'na' is used to show that data are 'not available'.

LEADING COMPANIES   Number shown: **75**   Total sales ($ mil): **8,109,361**   Total employment (000): **3,582.1**

Company Name	Address				CEO Name	Phone	Co. Type	Sales ($ mil)	Empl. (000)
Niagara Mohawk Holdings Inc.	300 Erie Blvd W	Syracuse	NY	13202	William E. Davis	315-474-1511	P	4,084,186	8.4
Citigroup Inc.	399 Park Ave	New York	NY	10043	John S Reed	212-559-1000	P	668,641	173.7
General Electric Capital Services	260 Long Ridge Rd	Stamford	CT	06927	D D Dammerman	203-357-6978	S	303,980	83.0
Akzo Nobel Inc.	300 S Riverside Plz	Chicago	IL	60606	Piet Provo Kluit	312-906-7500	S	300,000	9.0
American International Group Inc.	70 Pine St	New York	NY	10270	Maurice R Greenberg	212-770-7000	P	267,000	40.0
Wisconsin Energy Corp.	PO Box 2949	Milwaukee	WI	53201	Richard A Abdoo	414-221-2345	P	208,989	5.3
Bessemer Group Inc.	100 Woodbridge Ctr	Woodbridge	NJ	07095	Donald J Herrera	732-855-0800	R	151,000	0.3
Hartford Financial Services Group	690 Asylum Ave	Hartford	CT	06115	Ramani Ayer	860-547-5000	P	135,000	25.0
Hartford Life Inc.	200 Hopmeadow St	Simsbury	CT	06089	Lowndes A Smith	860-525-8555	P	122,022	4.5
AXA Financial Inc.	1290 Av Americas	New York	NY	10104	Edward D Miller	212-554-1234	P	109,185	14.7
Lincoln National Corp.	PO Box 1110	Fort Wayne	IN	46802	Jon A Boscia	219-455-2000	P	93,836	8.0
Associates First Capital Corp.	250 Carpenter Pkwy	Irving	TX	75062	Keith W Hughes	972-652-4000	P	80,900	28.0
Philip Morris Companies Inc.	120 Park Ave	New York	NY	10017	Geoffrey C Bible	917-663-5000	P	78,596	144.0
Loews Corp.	667 Madison Ave	New York	NY	10021	James S Tisch	212-521-2000	P	73,300	34.3
American General Finance Inc.	P O Box 59	Evansville	IN	47701	F R Geissinger	812-424-8031	S	67,000	16.1
Berkshire Hathaway Inc.	1440 Kiewit Plz	Omaha	NE	68131	Warren E Buffett	402-346-1400	P	58,742*	45.0
Xebec Corp.	5612 Brighton Ter	Kansas City	MO	64130	FL Thompson	816-444-9700	A	56,009*	0.4
SBC Communications Inc.	175 E Houston	San Antonio	TX	78205	Royce Caldell	210-821-4105	P	49,489	129.9
TXU	1601 Bryan St	Dallas	TX	75201		214-812-4600	P	39,514	22.1
Nationwide Corp.	1 Nationwide Plz	Columbus	OH	43216	Diamond McFerson	614-249-7111	S	38,108*	8.0
BP Amoco Chemicals	200 E Randolph St	Chicago	IL	60601		312-856-3200	S	36,287*	43.5
PG and E Corp.	1 Market	San Francisco	CA	94105	Robert D Glynn Jr	415-973-7000	P	33,234	23.3
Bell Atlantic Corp.	1095 Av Americas	New York	NY	10036	james Cullen	212-395-2121	P	33,174	140.0
AFLAC Inc.	1932 Wynnton Rd	Columbus	GA	31999	Daniel P Amos	706-596-3264	P	31,183	4.0
Omnicom Group Inc.	437 Madison Ave	New York	NY	10022	Bruce Crawford	212-415-3600	P	28,876	35.6
Photonics Management Corp.	360 Foothill Rd	Bridgewater	NJ	08807	T Hiruma	908-231-1116	R	28,268*	0.2
United Parcel Service of America	55 Glenlake Pkwy	Atlanta	GA	30328	James P Kelly	404-828-6000	P	27,052	331.6
Lockheed Martin Corp.	6801 Rockledge Dr	Bethesda	MD	20817	Vance Coffman	301-897-6000	P	25,530	149.0
GTE Corp.	PO Box 152257	Irving	TX	75015	Kent Foster	972-507-5000	P	25,336	12.0
BellSouth Corp.	1155 Peachtree	Atlanta	GA	30309	F Duane Ackerman	404-249-2000	P	25,224	96.2
Amoco Co.	200 E Randolph St	Chicago	IL	60601	Frederick S Addy	312-856-3200	S	25,042*	39.0
Cardinal Health Inc.	7000 Cardinal Place	Dublin	OH	43017	John C Kane	614-757-5000	P	25,034	36.0
Edison International	PO Box 400	Rosemead	CA	91770	John E Bryson	626-302-1212	P	24,698	13.2
Jefferson-Pilot Corp.	PO Box 21008	Greensboro	NC	27420	David A Stonecipher	336-691-3000	P	24,338	2.2
CIT Group Inc.	1211 Av Americas	New York	NY	10036	Albert R Gamper Jr	212-536-1390	P	24,303	3.2
Provident Companies Inc.	1 Fountain Sq	Chattanooga	TN	37402	J Harold Chandler	423-755-1011	P	23,088	3.7
Entergy Corp.	PO Box 61000	New Orleans	LA	70161	Donald C Hintz	504-529-5262	P	22,848	12.8
ReliaStar Financial Corp.	20 Washington S	Minneapolis	MN	55401	John H Flittie	612-372-5432	P	22,609	3.5
Carlson Holdings Inc.	PO Box 59159	Minneapolis	MN	55459	Marilyn C Nelson	612-449-1000	R	22,000	165.0
Reliant Energy Inc.	PO Box 4567	Houston	TX	77210	Steve Letbetter	713-207-3000	P	22,000	12.9
Merrill Lynch and Company Inc.	World Financial Ctr	New York	NY	10281	Herbert M Allison Jr	212-449-1000	P	21,869	63.8
Chrysler Financial L.L.C.	27777 Franklin Rd	Southfield	MI	48034	Darrell L Davis	248-948-3058	S	21,132*	3.5
Chubb Executive Risk Inc.	PO Box 1615	Plainfield	NJ	07061	Dean R O'Hare	908-903-2000	P	20,746	9.5
Salomon Smith Barney Holdings	388 Greenwich St	New York	NY	10013	Michael A Carpenter	212-816-6000	S	20,673	36.3
Aetna Inc.	151 Farmington Ave	Hartford	CT	06156	Richard L Huber	860-273-0123	P	20,604	33.5
AEGON USA Inc.	1111 N Charles St	Baltimore	MD	21201	Donald J Shepard	410-576-4571	S	20,330*	11.3
Sony USA Inc.	550 Madison Ave	New York	NY	10022		212-833-6800	R	20,000	32.0
Sprint Corp.	PO Box 11315	Kansas City	MO	64112	William T Esrey	913-624-3000	P	20,000	77.6
American Stores Co.	299 S Main St	Salt Lake City	UT	84111	Victor L Lund	801-539-0112	P	19,867	121.0
Aon Corp.	123 N Wacker Dr	Chicago	IL	60606	Patrick G Ryan	312-701-3000	P	19,688	33.0
Columbia/HCA Healthcare Corp.	1 Park Plaza	Nashville	TN	37203	Jack O Bovender Jr	615-344-9551	P	18,618	260.0
Aon Risk Services Companies Inc.	123 N Wacker Dr	Chicago	IL	60606	Alan Diamond	312-701-3000	S	18,214*	15.0
Public Service Enterprise Group	P O Box 1171	Newark	NJ	07101	Lawrence R Codey	973-430-7000	P	18,100	10.6
UAL Corp.	PO Box 66919	Chicago	IL	60666	Rono J Dutta	847-700-4000	P	18,027	95.0
Dominion Resources Inc.	PO Box 26532	Richmond	VA	23261	Thomas E Capps	804-819-2000	P	17,517	11.0
National Amusements Inc.	200 Elm St	Dedham	MA	02026	Sumner Redstone	781-461-1600	R	17,412*	121.7
Ameritech Corp.	30 S Wacker Dr	Chicago	IL	60606	Richard C Notebaert	312-750-5000	P	17,154	75.0
Aon Group Inc.	125 Wacker Dr	Chicago	IL	60606	Michael D O'Halleran	312-701-4800	D	17,000	14.0
American Electric Power Inc.	PO Box 16631	Columbus	OH	43216	E Linn Draper	614-223-1000	P	16,916	17.9
FedEx Corp.	6075 Poplar Ave	Memphis	TN	38119	Fredrick W Smith	901-369-3600	P	16,774	141.0
Liberty Financial Companies Inc.	600 Atlantic Ave	Boston	MA	02210	Kenneth R Leibler	617-722-6000	P	16,519	2.1
Ahold USA Inc.	950 E Paces Ferry	Atlanta	GA	30326	Allan Noddle	404-262-6050	S	16,174	116.8
UNUM Holding Co.	2211 Congress St	Portland	ME	04122	Harold Chandler	207-770-2211	S	16,034*	7.0
Federated Department Stores Inc.	7 West 7th St	Cincinnati	OH	45202	Terry J Lundgren	513-579-7000	P	15,883	118.0
American Financial Corp.	1 E 4th St	Cincinnati	OH	45202	Carl H Lindner	513-579-2121	P	15,700	9.0
Dynegy Inc.	PO Box 4777	Houston	TX	77210	Stephen W Bergstrom	713-507-6400	P	15,430	2.4
AMR Corp.	PO Box 619616	Dallas	TX	75261	Donald J Carty	817-963-1234	P	15,192*	92.0
Fortis Inc.	1 Chase Man Plz	New York	NY	10005	Allen R Freedman	212-859-7000	J	14,578	0.0
Central and South West Corp.	PO Box 660614	Dallas	TX	75266	ER Brooks	214-777-1000	P	13,744	11.0
U S WEST Inc.	1801 California St	Denver	CO	80202	Solomon D Trujillo	303-793-6500	P	13,182	58.3
True North Communications Inc.	101 E Erie St	Chicago	IL	60611	David Bell	312-425-6500	P	12,423	11.4
Market Agency Markets	P O Box 507	Keene	NH	03431		603-352-3221	R	12,309*	5.0
Conseco Inc.	P O Box 1911	Carmel	IN	46032	Stephen C Hilbert	317-817-6100	P	12,004	14.0
Protective Life Corp.	PO Box 2606	Birmingham	AL	35202	John D Johns	205-879-9230	P	11,989	1.6
WPP Group USA Inc.	309 W 49th St	New York	NY	10019	Martin S Sorrell	212-632-2200	P	11,937	24.0

Source: Ward's Business Directory of U.S. Private and Public Companies, Volumes 1 and 2, 2000. The company type code used is as follows: P - Public, R - Private, S - Subsidiary, D - Division, J - Joint Venture, A - Affiliate, G - Group, N - Company type not reported. Sales are in millions of dollars, employees are in thousands. An asterisk (*) indicates an estimated sales volume. The symbol < stands for 'less than'. Company names and addresses are truncated, in some cases, to fit into the available space.

LOCATION BY STATE AND REGIONAL CONCENTRATION

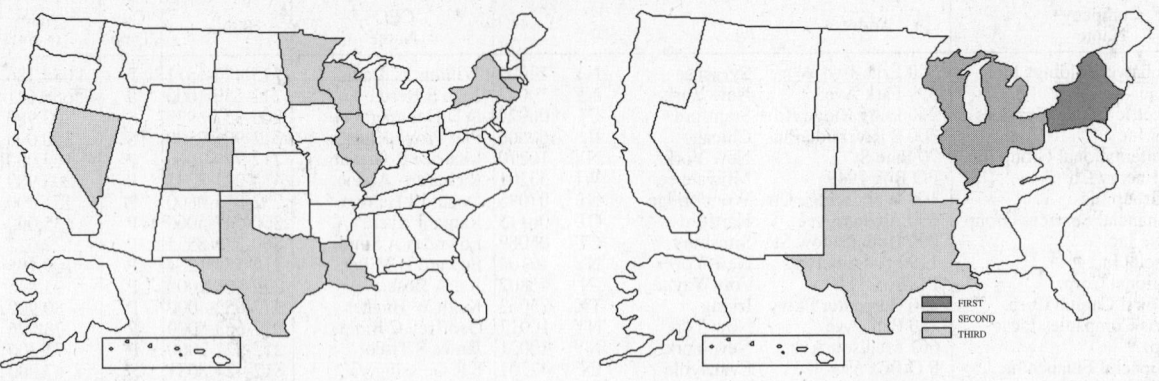

FIRST
SECOND
THIRD

INDUSTRY DATA BY STATE

State	Establishments Total (number)	% of U.S.	Employment Total (number)	% of U.S.	Per Estab.	Payroll Total ($ mil.)	Per Empl. ($)	Revenues Total ($ mil.)	% of U.S.	Per Estab. ($)
New York	818	8.5	9,241	9.3	11	1,160.9	125,625	8,848.0	21.5	10,816,660
Texas	682	7.1	6,652	6.7	10	684.0	102,831	3,782.6	9.2	5,546,327
California	769	8.0	11,138	11.3	14	807.2	72,472	2,320.0	5.6	3,016,899
Illinois	486	5.0	6,025	6.1	12	442.6	73,456	2,187.3	5.3	4,500,529
Connecticut	189	2.0	2,101	2.1	11	224.3	106,740	1,214.8	2.9	6,427,661
Florida	477	4.9	6,983	7.1	15	335.6	48,060	1,037.4	2.5	2,174,916
Virginia	184	1.9	1,782	1.8	10	202.3	113,503	1,034.3	2.5	5,621,397
Ohio	318	3.3	2,359	2.4	7	128.2	54,324	969.3	2.4	3,047,978
Pennsylvania	326	3.4	4,508	4.6	14	299.7	66,474	915.2	2.2	2,807,448
Massachusetts	223	2.3	3,304	3.3	15	278.3	84,225	883.7	2.1	3,962,879
Wisconsin	174	1.8	2,162	2.2	12	143.1	66,191	844.5	2.1	4,853,713
Colorado	157	1.6	1,979	2.0	13	161.2	81,446	822.9	2.0	5,241,134
Louisiana	89	0.9	948	1.0	11	67.1	70,747	785.5	1.9	8,825,674
New Jersey	252	2.6	3,767	3.8	15	284.8	75,613	772.3	1.9	3,064,790
Minnesota	155	1.6	1,962	2.0	13	122.9	62,628	728.0	1.8	4,696,677
Georgia	244	2.5	3,490	3.5	14	223.6	64,063	638.6	1.6	2,617,201
Michigan	241	2.5	2,764	2.8	11	280.2	101,366	598.1	1.5	2,481,643
Indiana	140	1.4	1,515	1.5	11	102.5	67,628	548.2	1.3	3,915,614
Missouri	195	2.0	2,335	2.4	12	129.6	55,520	539.6	1.3	2,767,190
Washington	137	1.4	1,160	1.2	8	90.7	78,163	534.6	1.3	3,901,891
Nevada	224	2.3	982	1.0	4	61.0	62,101	505.5	1.2	2,256,701
Kentucky	91	0.9	1,250	1.3	14	78.5	62,838	482.0	1.2	5,296,780
North Carolina	143	1.5	816	0.8	6	60.7	74,350	422.0	1.0	2,950,888
Tennessee	118	1.2	2,092	2.1	18	106.3	50,794	310.9	0.8	2,635,085
Arizona	99	1.0	757	0.8	8	46.1	60,859	299.5	0.7	3,025,566
Nebraska	61	0.6	872	0.9	14	60.0	68,787	198.5	0.5	3,254,475
Kansas	91	0.9	770	0.8	8	55.4	71,987	196.4	0.5	2,158,132
Iowa	102	1.1	1,102	1.1	11	53.3	48,347	151.9	0.4	1,489,578
Utah	52	0.5	552	0.6	11	43.7	79,225	135.8	0.3	2,610,962
Maryland	118	1.2	2,636	2.7	22	156.1	59,204	135.4	0.3	1,147,271
Oregon	92	1.0	1,216	1.2	13	78.7	64,715	130.4	0.3	1,417,554
Alabama	71	0.7	984	1.0	14	64.6	65,628	126.7	0.3	1,784,549
Arkansas	50	0.5	573	0.6	11	33.1	57,740	125.7	0.3	2,513,180
Oklahoma	102	1.1	1,014	1.0	10	59.0	58,206	121.8	0.3	1,193,716
South Carolina	73	0.8	632	0.6	9	38.4	60,742	80.7	0.2	1,105,178
Rhode Island	28	0.3	187	0.2	7	23.5	125,775	59.5	0.1	2,124,643
Mississippi	35	0.4	646	0.7	18	26.6	41,138	55.9	0.1	1,597,257
D.C.	41	0.4	175	0.2	4	18.8	107,280	45.9	0.1	1,119,268
New Hampshire	33	0.3	266	0.3	8	20.2	75,808	41.5	0.1	1,257,727
Maine	29	0.3	283	0.3	10	15.0	52,841	41.2	0.1	1,422,103
Hawaii	51	0.5	211	0.2	4	13.4	63,526	38.7	0.1	758,157
South Dakota	17	0.2	36	0.0	2	1.1	30,861	19.6	0.0	1,152,294
Montana	11	0.1	180	0.2	16	6.7	37,061	18.7	0.0	1,698,000
West Virginia	34	0.4	125	0.1	4	15.3	122,464	15.8	0.0	466,147
North Dakota	11	0.1	81	0.1	7	3.0	36,963	9.7	0.0	883,818
Wyoming	7	0.1	7	0.0	1	0.1	17,714	7.4	0.0	1,052,143
New Mexico	17	0.2	74	0.1	4	13.2	178,905	3.5	0.0	206,118
Delaware	1,543	16.0	3,750*	-	-	(D)	-	(D)	-	-
Vermont	23	0.2	60*	-	-	(D)	-	(D)	-	-
Idaho	22	0.2	175*	-	-	(D)	-	(D)	-	-
Alaska	21	0.2	375*	-	-	(D)	-	(D)	-	-

Source: 1997 *Economic Census*. The states are in descending order of revenues or establishments (if revenue data are missing for the majority). The symbol (D) appears when data are withheld to prevent disclosure of competitive information. States marked with (D) are sorted by number of establishments. A dash (-) indicates that the data element cannot be calculated. * indicates the midpoint of a range; 175, for example is the range 100-249. Shaded *states* on the state map indicate those states which have proportionately greater representation in the industry than would be indicated by the state's population; the ratio is based on total revenues or number of establishments. Shaded *regions* indicate where the industry is regionally most concentrated.

NAICS 551114 - CORPORATE, SUBSIDIARY, AND REGIONAL MANAGING OFFICES

GENERAL STATISTICS

Year	Establishments (number)	Employment (number)	Payroll ($ million)	Revenues ($ million)	Employees per Establishment (number)	Revenues per Establishment ($)	Payroll per Employee ($)
1997	35,263	2,491,698	145,086.0	29,976.0	70.7	850,069	58,228

Source: Economic Census of the United States, 1997. This is a newly defined industry. Data for prior years were unavailable at the time of publication but may become available over time.

INDICES OF CHANGE

Year	Establishments (number)	Employment (number)	Payroll ($ million)	Revenues ($ million)	Employees per Establishment (number)	Revenues per Establishment ($)	Payroll per Employee ($)
1997	100.0	100.0	100.0	100.0	100.0	100.0	100.0

Sources: Same as General Statistics. The values shown reflect change from the base year, 1997. Values above 100 mean greater than 1997, values below 100 mean less than 1997, and a value of 100 in the 1982-96 or 1998-2001 period means same as 1997. Values followed by a 'p' are projections by the editors; 'e' stands for extrapolation. Data are the most recent available at this level of detail.

SELECTED RATIOS

For 1997	Avg. of Information	Analyzed Industry	Index	For 1997	Avg. of Information	Analyzed Industry	Index
Employees per establishment	55	71	128	Payroll per establishment	3,258,261	4,114,398	126
Revenue per establishment	1,954,248	850,069	43	Payroll as % of revenue	167	484	290
Revenue per employee	35,328	12,030	34	Payroll per employee	58,902	58,228	99

Sources: Same as General Statistics. The 'Average' column represents the average for the industry sector, in 1997, where the currently shown industry is classified. The Index shows the relationship between the Average and the Analyzed Industry. For example, 100 means that they are equal; 500 that the Analyzed Industry is five times the average; 50 means that the Analyzed Industry is half the national average. The abbreviation 'na' is used to show that data are 'not available'.

LEADING COMPANIES

No company data available for this industry.

LOCATION BY STATE AND REGIONAL CONCENTRATION

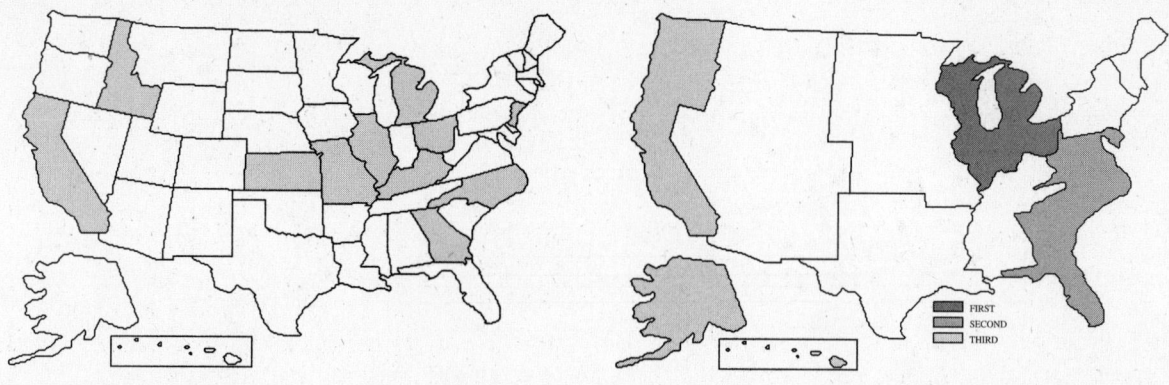

FIRST
SECOND
THIRD

INDUSTRY DATA BY STATE

State	Establishments		Employment			Payroll		Revenues		
	Total (number)	% of U.S.	Total (number)	% of U.S.	Per Estab.	Total ($ mil.)	Per Empl. ($)	Total ($ mil.)	% of U.S.	Per Estab. ($)
California	3,996	11.3	261,421	10.5	65	16,313.4	62,403	3,791.0	12.6	948,692
Illinois	1,706	4.8	147,273	5.9	86	9,288.3	63,069	3,410.1	11.4	1,998,899
Missouri	737	2.1	56,401	2.3	77	3,319.2	58,850	2,430.6	8.1	3,297,915
Texas	3,051	8.7	216,941	8.7	71	12,397.6	57,147	1,916.6	6.4	628,199
North Carolina	972	2.8	69,356	2.8	71	3,843.2	55,412	1,726.9	5.8	1,776,693
Michigan	1,159	3.3	120,156	4.8	104	7,733.5	64,362	1,700.5	5.7	1,467,202
New Jersey	1,207	3.4	131,109	5.3	109	8,654.7	66,011	1,656.6	5.5	1,372,498
Ohio	1,540	4.4	140,896	5.7	91	7,632.0	54,168	1,526.8	5.1	991,455
Georgia	1,179	3.3	88,005	3.5	75	4,645.7	52,789	1,396.0	4.7	1,184,085
Idaho	137	0.4	5,781	0.2	42	318.3	55,062	1,363.0	4.5	9,949,248
Kentucky	624	1.8	26,763	1.1	43	1,346.4	50,308	1,043.7	3.5	1,672,617
Pennsylvania	1,647	4.7	119,427	4.8	73	6,793.0	56,880	856.4	2.9	520,004
New York	2,096	5.9	168,029	6.7	80	12,062.2	71,787	788.5	2.6	376,169
Kansas	416	1.2	19,633	0.8	47	1,005.7	51,225	598.1	2.0	1,437,805
Virginia	1,016	2.9	51,767	2.1	51	2,625.9	50,726	558.9	1.9	550,147
Wisconsin	595	1.7	45,165	1.8	76	2,355.8	52,161	548.3	1.8	921,450
Massachusetts	914	2.6	69,053	2.8	76	4,336.7	62,802	535.7	1.8	586,079
Minnesota	716	2.0	82,847	3.3	116	4,669.5	56,362	408.0	1.4	569,818
Florida	1,645	4.7	92,729	3.7	56	4,236.0	45,681	396.0	1.3	240,740
Maryland	634	1.8	39,105	1.6	62	2,125.1	54,342	391.4	1.3	617,279
Tennessee	935	2.7	73,089	2.9	78	3,305.8	45,230	387.2	1.3	414,080
Connecticut	517	1.5	46,607	1.9	90	3,757.8	80,627	341.5	1.1	660,542
Oregon	429	1.2	36,003	1.4	84	2,096.8	58,240	274.0	0.9	638,760
Washington	720	2.0	53,960	2.2	75	4,035.3	74,782	189.2	0.6	262,807
Colorado	683	1.9	32,734	1.3	48	1,416.5	43,272	181.8	0.6	266,127
South Carolina	375	1.1	22,598	0.9	60	1,097.8	48,579	180.7	0.6	481,987
Louisiana	454	1.3	14,912	0.6	33	750.3	50,316	164.9	0.5	363,130
Arizona	710	2.0	33,703	1.4	47	1,700.0	50,442	128.6	0.4	181,154
Indiana	690	2.0	36,824	1.5	53	2,082.0	56,540	111.9	0.4	162,126
Iowa	305	0.9	11,571	0.5	38	672.2	58,097	101.1	0.3	331,548
Alabama	393	1.1	24,951	1.0	63	1,010.7	40,506	88.4	0.3	224,997
Nevada	184	0.5	4,686	0.2	25	277.2	59,152	80.9	0.3	439,685
D.C.	200	0.6	7,055	0.3	35	292.6	41,469	51.5	0.2	257,530
Oklahoma	345	1.0	24,470	1.0	71	1,250.6	51,106	48.3	0.2	139,959
Arkansas	251	0.7	16,862	0.7	67	702.6	41,668	45.3	0.2	180,410
Nebraska	193	0.5	10,618	0.4	55	443.3	41,746	35.8	0.1	185,254
Delaware	121	0.3	18,422	0.7	152	1,178.5	63,970	35.6	0.1	294,529
Mississippi	219	0.6	9,267	0.4	42	340.1	36,700	25.1	0.1	114,790
New Hampshire	137	0.4	7,615	0.3	56	486.2	63,851	23.7	0.1	173,350
Hawaii	214	0.6	5,687	0.2	27	255.0	44,846	21.1	0.1	98,743
Maine	136	0.4	4,404	0.2	32	187.2	42,510	20.0	0.1	147,316
South Dakota	72	0.2	1,312	0.1	18	55.3	42,113	18.0	0.1	249,667
Montana	85	0.2	1,624	0.1	19	61.1	37,623	16.9	0.1	199,035
New Mexico	175	0.5	6,792	0.3	39	355.7	52,370	9.9	0.0	56,583
West Virginia	161	0.5	4,227	0.2	26	199.9	47,284	8.8	0.0	54,783
Wyoming	60	0.2	1,634	0.1	27	69.5	42,538	7.7	0.0	127,567
Alaska	63	0.2	2,011	0.1	32	141.6	70,421	6.8	0.0	108,635
Utah	248	0.7	16,026	0.6	65	691.0	43,117	(D)	-	-
Rhode Island	81	0.2	7,038	0.3	87	353.9	50,278	(D)	-	-
North Dakota	66	0.2	1,740	0.1	26	66.3	38,095	(D)	-	-
Vermont	54	0.2	1,399	0.1	26	51.5	36,816	(D)	-	-

Source: 1997 Economic Census. The states are in descending order of revenues or establishments (if revenue data are missing for the majority). The symbol (D) appears when data are withheld to prevent disclosure of competitive information. States marked with (D) are sorted by number of establishments. A dash (-) indicates that the data element cannot be calculated. * indicates the midpoint of a range; 175, for example is the range 100-249. Shaded states on the state map indicate those states which have proportionately greater representation in the industry than would be indicated by the state's population; the ratio is based on total revenues or number of establishments. Shaded regions indicate where the industry is regionally most concentrated.

Part VI

ADMINISTRATIVE AND WASTE MANAGEMENT SERVICES

NAICS 561110 - OFFICE ADMINISTRATIVE SERVICES

GENERAL STATISTICS

Year	Establishments (number)	Employment (number)	Payroll ($ million)	Revenues ($ million)	Employees per Establishment (number)	Revenues per Establishment ($)	Payroll per Employee ($)
1997	24,537	338,386	11,971.0	28,054.0	13.8	1,143,335	35,377

Source: *Economic Census of the United States*, 1997. This is a newly defined industry. Data for prior years were unavailable at the time of publication but may become available over time.

INDICES OF CHANGE

Year	Establishments (number)	Employment (number)	Payroll ($ million)	Revenues ($ million)	Employees per Establishment (number)	Revenues per Establishment ($)	Payroll per Employee ($)
1997	100.0	100.0	100.0	100.0	100.0	100.0	100.0

Sources: Same as General Statistics. The values shown reflect change from the base year, 1997. Values above 100 mean greater than 1997, values below 100 mean less than 1997, and a value of 100 in the 1982-96 or 1998-2001 period means same as 1997. Values followed by a 'p' are projections by the editors; 'e' stands for extrapolation. Data are the most recent available at this level of detail.

SIC INDUSTRIES RELATED TO NAICS 561110

Each new NAICS code represents an industry that used to be part of an SIC or a part of several SIC industries. Data in this table are shown to provide transitional information for these cases. All available data for the precursor SIC(s) are shown. Even if only a part of an SIC is included in the NAICS, *all* data for the SIC are reproduced. If the SIC industry is not marked as being a part (pt) of the NAICS, the entire industry is embedded in the NAICS data. The SIC composition of the new industry provides some hints of the relative importance of its "ancestors." Data marked with a 'p' are projected. Projections begin with 1982 data. Data earlier than 1990 are not shown but are reflected in the projections.

SIC	Industry	1990	1991	1992	1993	1994	1995	1996	1997
8741	**Management Services (pt)**								
	Establishments (number)	15,267	16,556	20,186	21,920	23,803	21,674	23,348*p*	24,255*p*
	Employment (thousands)	285.2	306.6	285.1	357.7	386.3	312.7	368.9*p*	381.9*p*
	Revenues ($ million)	20,627.0	21,788.0	23,774.0	23,373.0	24,328.0	27,611.0	27,569.0	28,870.9*p*

Source: *Economic Census of the United States*, 1992, annual surveys of economic sectors conducted by the Bureau of the Census, and estimates or projections based on the 1982-1992 period; not all data are shown. 'e' marks estimates made by the editors; 'p' indicates projections based on time series. A dash (-) indicates that data for this SIC or year were not available. The abbreviation (pt) next to the industry name indicates that only a part of the industry is present within the NAICS data. If no (pt) is shown, the entire industry is contained within the NAICS data.

SELECTED RATIOS

For 1997	Avg. of Information	Analyzed Industry	Index	For 1997	Avg. of Information	Analyzed Industry	Index
Employees per establishment	27	14	52	Payroll per establishment	496,890	487,875	98
Revenue per establishment	1,070,709	1,143,335	107	Payroll as % of revenue	46	43	92
Revenue per employee	40,278	82,905	206	Payroll per employee	18,692	35,377	189

Sources: Same as General Statistics. The 'Average' column represents the average for the industry sector, in 1997, where the currently shown industry is classified. The Index shows the relationship between the Average and the Analyzed Industry. For example, 100 means that they are equal; 500 that the Analyzed Industry is five times the average; 50 means that the Analyzed Industry is half the national average. The abbreviation 'na' is used to show that data are 'not available'.

LEADING COMPANIES   Number shown: **75**   Total sales ($ mil): **442,299**   Total employment (000): **963.6**

Company Name	Address				CEO Name	Phone	Co. Type	Sales ($ mil)	Empl. (000)
J.P. Morgan and Company Inc.	60 Wall St	New York	NY	10260	Douglas A. Warner III	212-483-2323	P	261,067	15.7
EmCare Inc.	1717 Main St	Dallas	TX	75201	John Gringer	905-712-2000	S	37,847*	95.0
ING North America Insurance	5780 Powers Ferry	Atlanta	GA	30327	R Glenn Hilliard	770-980-3300	S	17,178*	3.8
Bechtel Group Inc.	50 Beale St	San Francisco	CA	94105	Riley Bechtel	415-768-1234	R	11,329	30.0
Eli Lilly and Co.	Lilly Corporate Ctr	Indianapolis	IN	46285	Sidney Taurel	317-276-2000	P	10,003	29.8
Solectron Corp.	847 Gibraltar Dr	Milpitas	CA	95035	Koichi Nishimura	408-957-8500	P	8,391	43.0
Marriott International Inc.	10400 Fernwood Rd	Bethesda	MD	20817	JW Marriott Jr	301-380-3000	P	7,968	133.0
Marmon Group Inc.	225 W Washington	Chicago	IL	60606		312-372-9500	R	6,132	35.0
ServiceMaster Co.	1 ServiceMaster	Downers Grove	IL	60515	C William Pollard	630-271-1300	P	5,704	51.7
Ohio Health	3555 Olentangy	Columbus	OH	43214	William W Wilkins	614-566-5424	R	5,700*	60.0
Allegiance Corp.	1430 Waukegan Rd	Mc Gaw Park	IL	60085	Lester B Knight	847-689-8410	P	4,719	25.0
Pitney Bowes Inc.	1 Elmcroft Rd	Stamford	CT	06926	Marc C Breslawsky	203-356-5000	P	4,221	29.9
Concentra Managed Care Inc.	312 Union Wharf	Boston	MA	02109	John Carlyle	617-367-2163	P	3,484*	8.8
Interpublic Group of Companies	1271 Av Americas	New York	NY	10020	Philip H Geier Jr	212-399-8000	P	2,990*	23.0
Sutter Health	1 Capitol Mall	Sacramento	CA	95816	Van Johnson	916-733-8800	R	2,881	35.0
Jacobs Engineering Group Inc.	PO Box 7084	Pasadena	CA	91109	Joseph Jacobs	626-578-3500	P	2,875	15.9
Mid-Atlantic Cars Inc.	10287 Lee Hwy	Fairfax	VA	22030	Charles Stringfellow	703-352-5555	R	2,640	4.8
Caremark Rx Inc.	3000 Galleria Tower	Birmingham	AL	35244	Edwin Crawford	205-733-8996	P	2,634	19.6
Allegheny Power Service Corp.	10435 Downsville	Hagerstown	MD	21740	Alan J Noia	301-790-3400	S	2,576	4.8
Life Care Centers of America Inc.	PO Box 3480	Cleveland	TN	37320	Michael Waddell	423-472-9585	R	2,375*	25.0
Gilbane Building Co.	7 Jackson Walkway	Providence	RI	02903	Paul J Choquette Jr	401-456-5800	R	2,100	1.2
J.A. Jones Inc.	J A Jones Dr	Charlotte	NC	28287	Charles T Davidson	704-553-6000	S	1,792	6.0
Stone & Webster Engineering	245 Summer St	Boston	MA	02210	H Kerner Smith	617-589-5111	S	1,248	6.9
American Management Systems	4050 Legato Rd	Fairfax	VA	22033	Paul A Brands	703-267-8000	P	1,240	9.0
Owen Healthcare Inc.	P O Box 4936	Houston	TX	77210	Dwight Winstead	281-749-4000	S	1,200*	3.0
Mullikin Medical Centers Inc.	5000 Arpt Plaza Dr	Long Beach	CA	90815	Bradley Karro	562-497-4800	S	1,189*	3.0
Dillingham Construction Corp.	5960 Inglewood Dr	Pleasanton	CA	94588	DE Sundgren	925-463-3300	S	1,175	8.0
FPA Medical Management Inc.	3636 Nobel Dr	San Diego	CA	92122	Stephen J Dresnick	619-453-1000	P	1,166	4.7
Day and Zimmermann Inc.	1818 Market St	Philadelphia	PA	19103		215-299-8000	R	1,080	16.5
Flowserve Corp.	PO Box 1145	Dayton	OH	45401	Bernard Rethore	972-443-6500	P	1,061	7.0
Huber, Hunt and Nichols Inc.	2450 S Tibbs Ave	Indianapolis	IN	46241	Robert G Hunt	317-227-7800	S	1,032	0.6
Dames and Moore Group	911 Wilshire Blvd	Los Angeles	CA	90017	Arthur C Darrow	213-996-2200	S	1,030	7.7
Dillingham Construction Holdings	5960 Inglewood Dr	Pleasanton	CA	94588	Donald Sumden	925-463-3300	R	1,023*	8.0
Archer Management Services Inc.	855 Av Americas	New York	NY	10001	Stanley Katz	212-502-2100	D	1,000	4.5
Hunt Corp. (Indianapolis, Indiana)	250 E 96th St	Indianapolis	IN	46240	Robert G Hunt	317-575-6301	R	1,000	0.5
Elderwood Affiliates Inc.	7 Limestone Dr	Buffalo	NY	14221	Robert Chur	716-633-3900	R	954*	2.4
Davidson Hotel Co.	1755 Lynnfield Rd	Memphis	TN	38119	Wilton D Hill	901-761-4664	S	950*	2.4
AECOM Technology Corp.	3250 Wilshire Blvd	Los Angeles	CA	90010	Richard G Newman	213-381-3612	R	900	6.1
Platinum Equity Holdings	2049 Century Park E	Los Angeles	CA	90067	Tom Gores	310-712-1850	R	900	10.0
Barton Malow Enterprises Inc.	27777 Franklin Rd	Southfield	MI	48034	Ben C Maibach III	248-351-4500	R	850	1.5
ScrippsHealth	4275 Campus Point	San Diego	CA	92121	Ed Danenhauer	619-678-7000	D	850*	7.5
Legacy Health System	1919 N W Lovejoy	Portland	OR	97209	Robert Pallari	503-415-5600	R	750	5.5
Barton Malow Co.	P O Box 35200	Detroit	MI	48235	Ben C Maibach III	248-351-4500	S	727	1.3
NCS HealthCare Inc.	3201 Enterprise	Cleveland	OH	44122	Kevin B Shaw	216-514-3350	P	718	4.2
U.S. Xpress Enterprises Inc.	4080 Jenkins Rd	Chattanooga	TN	37421	Patrick E Quinn	423-510-3000	P	708	7.2
Barnes-Jewish Inc.	216 S Kingshighway	St. Louis	MO	63110	Peter Slavin	314-454-7000	S	689*	7.2
Spectrum Healthcare Services	12647 Olive Blvd	St. Louis	MO	63141	Richard H Miles	314-878-2280	R	667*	6.0
Richfield Hospitality Services Inc.	5775 DTC Blvd	Englewood	CO	80111	Tom O'Leary	303-220-2000	S	655*	13.0
General Electric Capital Fleet	3 Capital Dr	Eden Prairie	MN	55344	Rick Smith	612-828-1000	S	627*	2.2
Prime Hospitality Corp.	P O Box 2700	Fairfield	NJ	07004	AF Petrocelli	973-882-1010	P	553	6.8
CSX Technology	550 Water St	Jacksonville	FL	32202	John F Andrews	904-633-1645	D	531*	46.1
Automotive Rentals Inc.	P O Box 5039	Mount Laurel	NJ	08054	Michael Laporta	609-778-1500	S	500*	0.6
Technical Management Services	3250 Wilshire Blvd	Los Angeles	CA	90010	R W Holdsworth	213-383-5000	S	500	0.5
Shorenstein Co.	555 California St	San Francisco	CA	94104	Douglas Shorenstein	415-772-7000	R	486*	0.6
Brasfield & Gorrie General	P O Box 10383	Birmingham	AL	35202	Miller Gorrie	205-328-4000	R	477*	1.5
Trammell Crow Co.	2001 Ross Ave	Dallas	TX	75201	George L Lippe	214-863-3000	P	460	5.1
US Oncology Inc.	16825 Northchase	Houston	TX	77060	Lloyd K Everson	281-873-2674	P	456*	1.3
Boldt Group Inc.	P O Box 373	Appleton	WI	54912	Oscar C Boldt	920-739-7800	R	450*	2.3
Covenant Healthcare Inc.	1126 S 70th St	Milwaukee	WI	53214	John Oliverio	414-456-2400	R	450*	10.0
Perini Building Inc	360 E Coronado Rd	Phoenix	AZ	85004	Craig Shaw	602-256-6777	D	449	0.4
URS Consultants Inc.	100 California St	San Francisco	CA	94111	Martin M Koffel	415-774-2700	P	407	3.3
Oscar J. Boldt Construction Co.	PO Box 419	Appleton	WI	54912	Warren Parsons	920-739-6321	S	402*	2.0
PHH Corp.	307 International Cir	Hunt Valley	MD	21031	Mark E Miller	410-771-3600	S	400*	2.5
Achieve Global Inc.	8875 Hidden River	Tampa	FL	33637	Horst Bergman	813-971-1990	S	366*	0.9
J.A. Jones Management Services	6135 Park South Dr	Charlotte	NC	28210	Al Neffgen	704-553-6600	S	350*	7.5
Medaphis Corp.	2840 Mt Wilkinson	Atlanta	GA	30339	Allen W Ritchie	770-440-5300	P	350	6.6
Shorenstein Realty Services L.P.	555 California St	San Francisco	CA	94104	Michael Lattorgue	415-772-7000	S	328*	0.6
Bayfront St	701 6th St S	St. Petersburg	FL	33701	Sue Brody	727-823-1234	R	320	2.0
First Mental Care	501 Great Circle Rd	Nashville	TN	37228	Jim Smith	615-256-3400	R	317*	0.8
Brown and Root Forest Products	PO Box 35090	Louisville	KY	40232		713-676-3231	S	300	3.0
Melaleuca Inc.	3910 S Yellowstone	Idaho Falls	ID	83402		208-522-0700	R	300*	1.5
PhyAmerica Physician Group Inc.	PO Box 15309	Durham	NC	27704	Steven M Scott	919-383-0355	P	294	1.3
Louisiana Lottery Corp.	P O Box 90008	Baton Rouge	LA	70879	Charles Davis	504-297-2000	R	290	0.2
Evanston Hospital Corp.	1301 Central St	Evanston	IL	60201	Mark R Neaman	847-570-2000	R	288*	3.5
HDS Services	39395 W 12 Mile Rd	Farmington Hills	MI	48331	WW Triplett	248-661-9000	R	280	0.7

Source: Ward's Business Directory of U.S. Private and Public Companies, Volumes 1 and 2, 2000. The company type code used is as follows: P - Public, R - Private, S - Subsidiary, D - Division, J - Joint Venture, A - Affiliate, G - Group, N - Company type not reported. Sales are in millions of dollars, employees are in thousands. An asterisk (*) indicates an estimated sales volume. The symbol < stands for 'less than'. Company names and addresses are truncated, in some cases, to fit into the available space.

LOCATION BY STATE AND REGIONAL CONCENTRATION

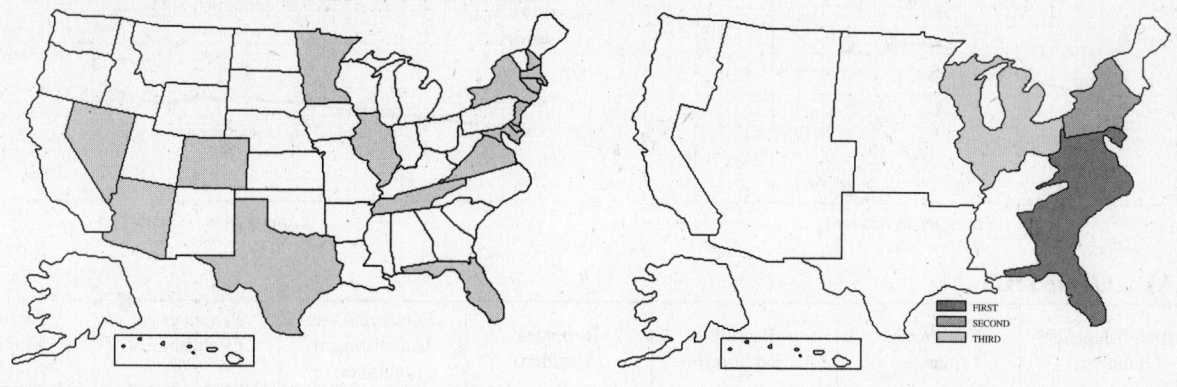

INDUSTRY DATA BY STATE

State	Establishments Total (number)	% of U.S.	Employment Total (number)	% of U.S.	Per Estab.	Payroll Total ($ mil.)	Per Empl. ($)	Revenues Total ($ mil.)	% of U.S.	Per Estab. ($)
California	2,862	11.7	38,342	11.3	13	1,374.1	35,838	3,250.5	11.6	1,135,730
Texas	1,995	8.1	30,720	9.1	15	1,159.8	37,754	2,635.1	9.4	1,320,868
New York	1,949	7.9	24,698	7.3	13	1,091.4	44,191	2,615.1	9.3	1,341,767
Florida	2,028	8.3	21,929	6.5	11	685.0	31,236	1,700.7	6.1	838,602
Illinois	1,248	5.1	17,910	5.3	14	700.2	39,093	1,696.5	6.0	1,359,389
New Jersey	1,003	4.1	15,367	4.5	15	598.2	38,925	1,343.8	4.8	1,339,776
Pennsylvania	922	3.8	13,752	4.1	15	524.5	38,137	1,221.8	4.4	1,325,138
Michigan	700	2.9	13,464	4.0	19	413.0	30,678	1,017.0	3.6	1,452,786
Ohio	978	4.0	13,072	3.9	13	423.4	32,393	960.3	3.4	981,920
Maryland	609	2.5	10,677	3.2	18	359.3	33,650	829.6	3.0	1,362,166
Virginia	642	2.6	9,831	2.9	15	351.9	35,797	793.2	2.8	1,235,579
Massachusetts	615	2.5	9,403	2.8	15	378.0	40,202	788.9	2.8	1,282,709
Tennessee	508	2.1	8,461	2.5	17	314.9	37,217	739.9	2.6	1,456,557
Georgia	649	2.6	11,242	3.3	17	317.3	28,223	738.1	2.6	1,137,337
Indiana	424	1.7	6,701	2.0	16	235.6	35,158	629.2	2.2	1,484,031
Colorado	537	2.2	6,914	2.0	13	307.0	44,399	628.1	2.2	1,169,631
Minnesota	395	1.6	5,278	1.6	13	202.3	38,320	575.4	2.1	1,456,648
North Carolina	494	2.0	7,541	2.2	15	236.1	31,312	478.4	1.7	968,447
Arizona	447	1.8	8,502	2.5	19	190.4	22,400	477.6	1.7	1,068,416
Connecticut	302	1.2	4,096	1.2	14	145.5	35,521	352.8	1.3	1,168,288
Missouri	390	1.6	4,199	1.2	11	125.0	29,768	349.9	1.2	897,282
Louisiana	347	1.4	4,882	1.4	14	159.8	32,723	335.7	1.2	967,455
Washington	410	1.7	3,982	1.2	10	138.8	34,857	318.4	1.1	776,629
Wisconsin	308	1.3	4,882	1.4	16	128.5	26,321	313.6	1.1	1,018,318
D.C.	152	0.6	2,600	0.8	17	98.1	37,719	252.9	0.9	1,664,086
Alabama	266	1.1	2,898	0.9	11	111.7	38,553	249.5	0.9	938,128
South Carolina	225	0.9	3,454	1.0	15	126.0	36,489	249.1	0.9	1,107,093
Oregon	238	1.0	3,097	0.9	13	94.7	30,568	238.3	0.8	1,001,113
Kansas	239	1.0	3,385	1.0	14	104.9	30,995	235.2	0.8	984,084
Nevada	255	1.0	3,247	1.0	13	104.4	32,153	215.4	0.8	844,769
Kentucky	235	1.0	2,072	0.6	9	65.1	31,438	210.4	0.7	895,306
Oklahoma	292	1.2	2,199	0.6	8	60.2	27,363	163.2	0.6	558,860
New Hampshire	139	0.6	1,612	0.5	12	60.7	37,639	144.8	0.5	1,042,065
Iowa	198	0.8	2,100	0.6	11	71.6	34,110	137.9	0.5	696,389
Nebraska	110	0.4	1,502	0.4	14	57.4	38,246	137.0	0.5	1,245,718
Rhode Island	89	0.4	1,388	0.4	16	56.8	40,930	126.1	0.4	1,416,876
Utah	204	0.8	1,616	0.5	8	52.6	32,574	120.7	0.4	591,691
West Virginia	118	0.5	1,523	0.5	13	46.8	30,726	99.3	0.4	841,220
Mississippi	124	0.5	1,949	0.6	16	44.5	22,828	96.7	0.3	779,968
Hawaii	109	0.4	1,568	0.5	14	45.7	29,158	95.5	0.3	875,780
Delaware	96	0.4	1,037	0.3	11	42.7	41,160	93.4	0.3	973,167
Arkansas	135	0.6	972	0.3	7	31.1	32,045	73.7	0.3	546,074
Maine	97	0.4	779	0.2	8	26.1	33,558	67.2	0.2	693,031
Idaho	81	0.3	820	0.2	10	23.0	28,048	56.3	0.2	695,506
New Mexico	97	0.4	609	0.2	6	17.4	28,614	42.4	0.2	437,454
Vermont	44	0.2	325	0.1	7	11.6	35,662	37.7	0.1	856,614
North Dakota	29	0.1	786	0.2	27	24.2	30,796	35.5	0.1	1,222,414
Alaska	53	0.2	291	0.1	5	9.9	34,079	27.7	0.1	523,189
South Dakota	48	0.2	292	0.1	6	9.3	31,849	25.9	0.1	539,625
Montana	65	0.3	290	0.1	4	9.8	33,779	20.5	0.1	314,769
Wyoming	37	0.2	130	0.0	4	4.6	35,054	12.2	0.1	330,892

Source: 1997 *Economic Census*. The states are in descending order of revenues or establishments (if revenue data are missing for the majority). The symbol (D) appears when data are withheld to prevent disclosure of competitive information. States marked with (D) are sorted by number of establishments. A dash (-) indicates that the data element cannot be calculated. * indicates the midpoint of a range; 175, for example is the range 100-249. Shaded *states* on the state map indicate those states which have proportionately greater representation in the industry than would be indicated by the state's population; the ratio is based on total revenues or number of establishments. Shaded *regions* indicate where the industry is regionally most concentrated.

NAICS 561210 - FACILITIES SUPPORT SERVICES*

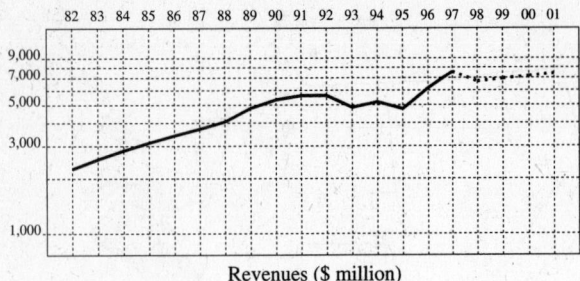

Revenues ($ million)

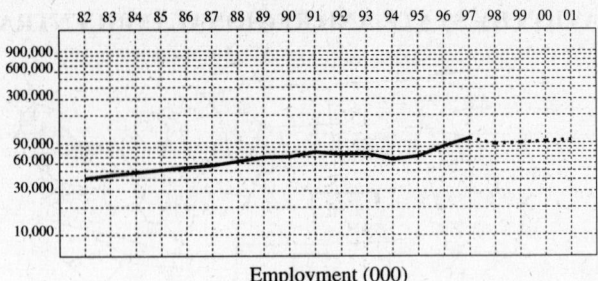

Employment (000)

GENERAL STATISTICS

Year	Establishments (number)	Employment (number)	Payroll ($ million)	Revenues ($ million)	Employees per Establishment (number)	Revenues per Establishment ($)	Payroll per Employee ($)
1982	295	41,348	974.0	2,253.0	140.2	7,637,288	23,556
1983	326 e	44,447 e	1,096.0 e	2,544.0 e	136.3 e	7,803,681 e	24,659 e
1984	358 e	47,546 e	1,219.0 e	2,835.0 e	132.8 e	7,918,994 e	25,638 e
1985	389 e	50,645 e	1,342.0 e	3,126.0 e	130.2 e	8,035,990 e	26,498 e
1986	421 e	53,744 e	1,464.0 e	3,417.0 e	127.7 e	8,116,390 e	27,240 e
1987	452	56,843	1,586.0	3,708.0	125.8	8,203,540	27,901
1988	791	62,758	1,684.0	4,059.0	79.3	5,131,479	26,833
1989	643	69,407	1,970.0	4,803.0	107.9	7,469,673	28,383
1990	675	70,242	2,177.0	5,336.0	104.1	7,905,185	30,993
1991	799	78,891	2,447.0	5,617.0	98.7	7,030,038	31,017
1992	904	74,976	2,381.0	5,625.0	82.9	6,222,345	31,757
1993	972	76,281	2,273.0	4,851.0	78.5	4,990,741	29,798
1994	882	65,905	2,002.0	5,191.0	74.7	5,885,488	30,377
1995	1,206	71,338	2,291.0	4,758.0	59.2	3,945,274	32,115
1996	1,848 e	91,738 e	2,786.0 e	6,167.0 e	49.6 e	3,337,121 e	30,369 e
1997	2,490	112,137	3,280.0	7,576.0	45.0	3,042,570	29,250
1998	1,971 p	96,605 p	2,988.0 p	6,694.0 p	49.0 p	3,396,246 p	30,930 p
1999	2,123 p	100,122 p	3,109.0 p	6,936.0 p	47.2 p	3,267,075 p	31,052 p
2000	2,274 p	103,640 p	3,230.0 p	7,178.0 p	45.6 p	3,156,552 p	31,166 p
2001	2,426 p	107,157 p	3,351.0 p	7,419.0 p	44.2 p	3,058,120 p	31,272 p

Sources: Economic Census of the United States, 1982, 1987, 1992, 1997. Establishment counts, employment, and payroll are from *County Business Patterns* for non-Census years. In non-Census years, industries in the Manufacturing range under SIC coding include data from the *Annual Survey of Manufactures* (*ASM*); those in the old Services range include data from the *Services Annual Survey* (*SAS*). Values followed by a 'p' are projections by the editors. Extrapolations are marked by 'e'. Data are the most recent available at this level of detail.

INDICES OF CHANGE

Year	Establishments (number)	Employment (number)	Payroll ($ million)	Revenues ($ million)	Employees per Establishment (number)	Revenues per Establishment ($)	Payroll per Employee ($)
1982	11.8	36.9	29.7	29.7	311.2	251.0	80.5
1987	18.2	50.7	48.4	48.9	279.2	269.6	95.4
1992	36.3	66.9	72.6	74.2	184.2	204.5	108.6
1993	39.0	68.0	69.3	64.0	174.3	164.0	101.9
1994	35.4	58.8	61.0	68.5	165.9	193.4	103.9
1995	48.4	63.6	69.8	62.8	131.3	129.7	109.8
1996	74.2 e	81.8 e	84.9 e	81.4 e	110.2 e	109.7 e	103.8 e
1997	100.0	100.0	100.0	100.0	100.0	100.0	100.0
1998	79.2 p	86.1 p	91.1 p	88.4 p	108.8 p	111.6 p	105.7 p
1999	85.3 p	89.3 p	94.8 p	91.6 p	104.7 p	107.4 p	106.2 p
2000	91.3 p	92.4 p	98.5 p	94.7 p	101.2 p	103.7 p	106.5 p
2001	97.4 p	95.6 p	102.2 p	97.9 p	98.1 p	100.5 p	106.9 p

Sources: Same as General Statistics. The values shown reflect change from the base year, 1997. Values above 100 mean greater than 1997, values below 100 mean less than 1997, and a value of 100 in the 1982-96 or 1998-2001 period means same as 1997. Values followed by a 'p' are projections by the editors; 'e' stands for extrapolation. Data are the most recent available at this level of detail.

SELECTED RATIOS

For 1997	Avg. of Information	Analyzed Industry	Index	For 1997	Avg. of Information	Analyzed Industry	Index
Employees per establishment	27	45	169	Payroll per establishment	496,890	1,317,269	265
Revenue per establishment	1,070,709	3,042,570	284	Payroll as % of revenue	46	43	93
Revenue per employee	40,278	67,560	168	Payroll per employee	18,692	29,250	156

Sources: Same as General Statistics. The 'Average' column represents the average for the industry sector, in 1997, where the currently shown industry is classified. The Index shows the relationship between the Average and the Analyzed Industry. For example, 100 means that they are equal; 500 that the Analyzed Industry is five times the average; 50 means that the Analyzed Industry is half the national average. The abbreviation 'na' is used to show that data are 'not available'.

*Equivalent to SIC 8744.

LEADING COMPANIES   Number shown: **27**   Total sales ($ mil): **7,477**   Total employment (000): **127.5**

Company Name	Address				CEO Name	Phone	Co. Type	Sales ($ mil)	Empl. (000)
Johnson Controls World Services	7315 N Atlantic Ave	Cape Canaveral	FL	32920		407-784-7100	P	3,380*	65.0
Ogden Corp.	2 Pennsylvania Plz	New York	NY	10121	Scott G Mackin	212-868-6100	P	1,692	22.0
Corrections Corporation	10 Burton Hills Blvd	Nashville	TN	37215	Doctor R Crants	615-263-0200	P	662	13.2
Wackenhut Corrections Corp.	4200 Wackenhut Dr	Palm Bch Grdns	FL	33410	Dr George C Zoley	561-622-5656	P	313	8.0
Bionetics Corp.	11833 Canon Blvd	Newport News	VA	23606	Charles Stern	757-873-0900	R	208*	1.3
Wyle Laboratories Inc.	128 Maryland St	El Segundo	CA	90245	Robert Rieth	310-322-1763	R	175*	1.0
MPW Industrial Services Group	PO Box 10	Hebron	OH	43025	Monte R Black	740-927-8790	P	147	2.1
Amtech Engineering Services	5300 S Eastern Ave	Los Angeles	CA	90040	James C Scranton	213-234-2001	D	133*	2.0
Cornell Corrections Inc.	1700 W Loop South	Houston	TX	77027	Steven W Logan	713-623-0790	P	123	3.0
Correctional Services Corp.	1819 Main St	Sarasota	FL	34236	James F Slattery	941-953-9198	P	98	3.8
Comarco Inc.	1551 N Tustin Ave	Santa Ana	CA	92705	Don M Bailey	714-796-1808	P	92	1.2
Day & Zimmermann Howthorne	PO Box 15	Hawthorne	NV	89415		702-945-7658	R	57	0.6
Canisco Resources Inc.	300 Delaware Ave	Wilmington	DE	19801	Teddy Mansfield	302-777-5050	P	52	0.5
Compex Legal Services Inc.	841 Apollo St	El Segundo	CA	90245	Jeffrey Bachmann	310-726-0000	R	51*	0.5
Brown-Eagle Group Inc.	5330 Dijon Dr	Baton Rouge	LA	70808	Lela Wilkes	225-769-1111	R	45*	0.5
Antarctic Support Associates	61 Inverness Dr E	Englewood	CO	80112		303-790-8606	S	41*	0.6
Haley and Aldrich Inc.	465 Medford St	Boston	MA	02129	Bruce E Beverly	617-886-7400	R	41	0.4
Safety Clean	PO Box 337	Bridgeport	NJ	08014	Larry Walker	609-467-3100	S	30*	0.1
UXB International Inc.	21641 Beaumeade	Ashburn	VA	20147	R H Dugger III	703-724-9600	R	27	0.5
On-Site Sourcing Inc.	1111 N 19th St	Arlington	VA	22209	Christopher J Weiler	703-276-1123	P	26*	0.5
Pink Business Interiors Inc.	5825 Excelsior Blvd	St. Louis Pk.	MN	55416	Bye Barsness	612-915-3100	R	22*	<0.1
Ogden Services Corp	2 Penn Plz	New York	NY	10121	Scott Mackin	212-868-6000	S	20*	0.2
KRA Corp.	1010 Wayne Ave	Silver Spring	MD	20910	K R Atterbeary	301-495-1591	R	14*	0.2
HAZMED Inc.	10001 Derekwood	Lanham	MD	20706		301-577-9339	N	9	0.1
Geotechnical Services Inc.	7050 S 110th St	La Vista	NE	68128		402-339-6104	N	8	0.1
Avalon Correctional Services Inc.	P O Box 57012	Oklahoma City	OK	73157	Donald E Smith	405-752-8802	P	8	0.3
Killam Management	27 Bleeker St	Millburn	NJ	07041	Nick De Michiolo	973-379-6147	D	3*	<0.1

Source: Ward's Business Directory of U.S. Private and Public Companies, Volumes 1 and 2, 2000. The company type code used is as follows: P - Public, R - Private, S - Subsidiary, D - Division, J - Joint Venture, A - Affiliate, G - Group, N - Company type not reported. Sales are in millions of dollars, employees are in thousands. An asterisk (*) indicates an estimated sales volume. The symbol < stands for 'less than'. Company names and addresses are truncated, in some cases, to fit into the available space.

LOCATION BY STATE AND REGIONAL CONCENTRATION

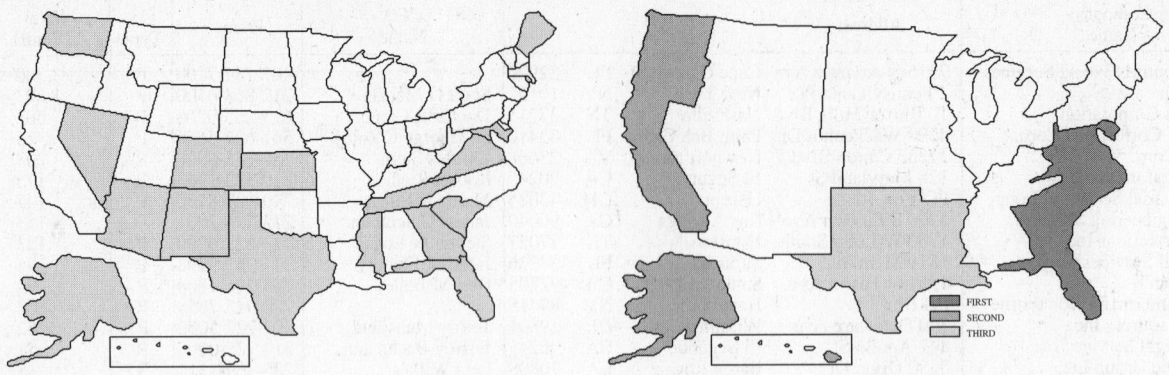

FIRST
SECOND
THIRD

INDUSTRY DATA BY STATE

State	Establishments Total (number)	% of U.S.	Employment Total (number)	% of U.S.	Per Estab.	Payroll Total ($ mil.)	Per Empl. ($)	Revenues Total ($ mil.)	% of U.S.	Per Estab. ($)
Florida	136	5.5	13,793	12.3	101	430.2	31,187	871.1	11.5	6,405,257
California	310	12.4	11,392	10.2	37	337.2	29,598	779.3	10.3	2,513,777
Texas	191	7.7	10,460	9.3	55	299.8	28,661	723.7	9.6	3,788,743
New York	156	6.3	6,627	5.9	42	188.6	28,457	428.4	5.7	2,745,942
Virginia	105	4.2	5,417	4.8	52	165.8	30,604	401.1	5.3	3,820,390
Colorado	52	2.1	4,954	4.4	95	154.2	31,130	384.0	5.1	7,385,577
Tennessee	71	2.9	4,057	3.6	57	124.2	30,603	279.3	3.7	3,933,986
South Carolina	27	1.1	3,808	3.4	141	100.9	26,488	262.5	3.5	9,722,370
Maryland	79	3.2	4,038	3.6	51	118.1	29,254	261.3	3.4	3,307,392
Ohio	84	3.4	2,963	2.6	35	91.5	30,869	229.9	3.0	2,736,417
Georgia	65	2.6	2,497	2.2	38	86.5	34,656	204.5	2.7	3,145,892
New Jersey	84	3.4	2,796	2.5	33	99.6	35,606	184.2	2.4	2,192,583
Pennsylvania	125	5.0	2,956	2.6	24	82.0	27,746	173.6	2.3	1,389,024
New Mexico	26	1.0	2,962	2.6	114	85.0	28,702	163.7	2.2	6,296,462
Washington	31	1.2	1,484	1.3	48	47.1	31,749	163.6	2.2	5,277,935
Illinois	113	4.5	2,273	2.0	20	67.6	29,757	142.0	1.9	1,257,009
Arizona	47	1.9	1,899	1.7	40	45.1	23,765	131.6	1.7	2,799,085
Alaska	25	1.0	1,323	1.2	53	53.2	40,224	127.6	1.7	5,103,320
North Carolina	61	2.4	2,712	2.4	44	58.7	21,645	122.0	1.6	1,999,869
Massachusetts	55	2.2	1,972	1.8	36	54.3	27,540	115.6	1.5	2,102,345
Indiana	43	1.7	1,363	1.2	32	31.9	23,374	99.4	1.3	2,311,698
D.C.	40	1.6	1,781	1.6	45	55.2	31,008	99.0	1.3	2,473,775
Mississippi	31	1.2	1,299	1.2	42	33.7	25,907	94.9	1.3	3,061,065
Michigan	51	2.0	1,106	1.0	22	40.0	36,140	88.6	1.2	1,737,647
Connecticut	33	1.3	1,391	1.2	42	34.0	24,410	88.4	1.2	2,680,182
Alabama	26	1.0	1,389	1.2	53	39.3	28,305	87.2	1.2	3,355,538
Oklahoma	38	1.5	1,118	1.0	29	27.9	24,984	83.1	1.1	2,186,105
Maine	18	0.7	459	0.4	25	16.8	36,706	80.4	1.1	4,467,722
Kansas	28	1.1	2,456	2.2	88	32.6	13,291	80.2	1.1	2,863,464
Missouri	32	1.3	1,178	1.1	37	35.3	29,981	68.6	0.9	2,142,500
Minnesota	53	2.1	1,040	0.9	20	29.2	28,118	62.6	0.8	1,180,698
Nevada	13	0.5	970	0.9	75	31.8	32,805	52.6	0.7	4,047,462
Wisconsin	46	1.8	661	0.6	14	16.1	24,410	45.9	0.6	998,413
Utah	17	0.7	555	0.5	33	16.7	30,139	37.5	0.5	2,206,294
Rhode Island	15	0.6	435	0.4	29	15.9	36,531	30.6	0.4	2,040,667
Kentucky	22	0.9	516	0.5	23	10.9	21,097	30.0	0.4	1,361,864
Oregon	18	0.7	202	0.2	11	6.3	31,381	17.8	0.2	991,278
Delaware	7	0.3	103	0.1	15	5.7	55,553	16.5	0.2	2,362,857
Hawaii	7	0.3	234	0.2	33	8.7	37,333	16.3	0.2	2,334,857
Iowa	11	0.4	612	0.5	56	5.0	8,131	13.4	0.2	1,214,727
Nebraska	11	0.4	190	0.2	17	7.8	41,016	12.4	0.2	1,123,909
West Virginia	13	0.5	155	0.1	12	4.9	31,523	9.4	0.1	720,769
New Hampshire	6	0.2	171	0.2	28	4.2	24,269	9.1	0.1	1,522,833
Montana	5	0.2	83	0.1	17	2.5	30,723	5.5	0.1	1,101,000
Arkansas	5	0.2	111	0.1	22	2.0	18,126	4.3	0.1	870,000
Wyoming	3	0.1	19	0.0	6	0.4	21,474	2.2	0.0	720,000
South Dakota	5	0.2	31	0.0	6	0.9	29,710	1.9	0.0	370,600
Louisiana	40	1.6	1,750*	-	-	(D)	-	(D)	-	-
Idaho	4	0.2	750*	-	-	(D)	-	(D)	-	-
North Dakota	3	0.1	60*	-	-	(D)	-	(D)	-	-
Vermont	3	0.1	175*	-	-	(D)	-	(D)	-	-

Source: 1997 *Economic Census*. The states are in descending order of revenues or establishments (if revenue data are missing for the majority). The symbol (D) appears when data are withheld to prevent disclosure of competitive information. States marked with (D) are sorted by number of establishments. A dash (-) indicates that the data element cannot be calculated. * indicates the midpoint of a range; 175, for example is the range 100-249. Shaded *states* on the state map indicate those states which have proportionately greater representation in the industry than would be indicated by the state's population; the ratio is based on total revenues or number of establishments. Shaded *regions* indicate where the industry is regionally most concentrated.

NAICS 561310 - EMPLOYMENT PLACEMENT AGENCIES

GENERAL STATISTICS

Year	Establishments (number)	Employment (number)	Payroll ($ million)	Revenues ($ million)	Employees per Establishment (number)	Revenues per Establishment ($)	Payroll per Employee ($)
1997	6,281	113,896	2,647.0	4,787.0	18.1	762,140	23,241

Source: Economic Census of the United States, 1997. This is a newly defined industry. Data for prior years were unavailable at the time of publication but may become available over time.

INDICES OF CHANGE

Year	Establishments (number)	Employment (number)	Payroll ($ million)	Revenues ($ million)	Employees per Establishment (number)	Revenues per Establishment ($)	Payroll per Employee ($)
1997	100.0	100.0	100.0	100.0	100.0	100.0	100.0

Sources: Same as General Statistics. The values shown reflect change from the base year, 1997. Values above 100 mean greater than 1997, values below 100 mean less than 1997, and a value of 100 in the 1982-96 or 1998-2001 period means same as 1997. Values followed by a 'p' are projections by the editors; 'e' stands for extrapolation. Data are the most recent available at this level of detail.

SIC INDUSTRIES RELATED TO NAICS 561310

Each new NAICS code represents an industry that used to be part of an SIC or a part of several SIC industries. Data in this table are shown to provide transitional information for these cases. All available data for the precursor SIC(s) are shown. Even if only a part of an SIC is included in the NAICS, *all* data for the SIC are reproduced. If the SIC industry is not marked as being a part (pt) of the NAICS, the entire industry is embedded in the NAICS data. The SIC composition of the new industry provides some hints of the relative importance of its "ancestors." Data marked with a 'p' are projected. Projections begin with 1982 data. Data earlier than 1990 are not shown but are reflected in the projections.

SIC	Industry	1990	1991	1992	1993	1994	1995	1996	1997
7299	**Miscellaneous Personal Services, nec (pt)**								
	Establishments (number)	15,086	15,775	16,017	16,862	17,296	17,740	18,650p	19,294p
	Employment (thousands)	116.4	114.7	105.6	99.6	97.2	99.4	106.1p	106.9p
	Revenues ($ million)	-	-	3,885.0	-	-	-	-	-
7361	**Employment Agencies (pt)**								
	Establishments (number)	12,846	12,750	12,146	12,423	12,474	13,150	13,167p	13,330p
	Employment (thousands)	246.9	261.2	132.8	174.5	199.6	249.3	244.3p	254.7p
	Revenues ($ million)	6,160.0	5,153.0	4,981.0	5,624.0	6,541.0	7,730.0	8,945.0	8,171.2p
7819	**Services Allied to Motion Pictures (pt)**								
	Establishments (number)	2,984	2,955	3,895	3,799	3,691	3,289	3,584p	3,622p
	Employment (thousands)	113.1	102.4	162.2	158.8	130.9	136.7	160.9p	169.5p
	Revenues ($ million)	-	-	7,514.7	-	-	-	-	-
7922	**Theatrical Producers & Services (pt)**								
	Establishments (number)	4,470	4,992	5,924	6,229	6,323	6,428	6,542p	6,792p
	Employment (thousands)	63.9	63.1	69.5	88.8	77.8	79.3	87.3p	91.2p
	Revenues ($ million)	-	-	5,730.5	4,396.6p	4,647.8p	4,899.0p	5,150.2p	5,401.4p

Source: Economic Census of the United States, 1992, annual surveys of economic sectors conducted by the Bureau of the Census, and estimates or projections based on the 1982-1992 period; not all data are shown. 'e' marks estimates made by the editors; 'p' indicates projections based on time series. A dash (-) indicates that data for this SIC or year were not available. The abbreviation (pt) next to the industry name indicates that only a part of the industry is present within the NAICS data. If no (pt) is shown, the entire industry is contained within the NAICS data.

SELECTED RATIOS

For 1997	Avg. of Information	Analyzed Industry	Index	For 1997	Avg. of Information	Analyzed Industry	Index
Employees per establishment	27	18	68	Payroll per establishment	496,890	421,430	85
Revenue per establishment	1,070,709	762,140	71	Payroll as % of revenue	46	55	119
Revenue per employee	40,278	42,030	104	Payroll per employee	18,692	23,241	124

Sources: Same as General Statistics. The 'Average' column represents the average for the industry sector, in 1997, where the currently shown industry is classified. The Index shows the relationship between the Average and the Analyzed Industry. For example, 100 means that they are equal; 500 that the Analyzed Industry is five times the average; 50 means that the Analyzed Industry is half the national average. The abbreviation 'na' is used to show that data are 'not available'.

LEADING COMPANIES   Number shown: **75**   Total sales ($ mil): **25,060**   Total employment (000): **148.9**

Company Name	Address				CEO Name	Phone	Co. Type	Sales ($ mil)	Empl. (000)
Spectra International	3200 N Hayden Rd	Scottsdale	AZ	85251	Sybil Goldberg	480-481-0411	R	13,636*	100.0
Management Recruiters Intern	200 Public Squ	Cleveland	OH	44114	Allen Salikof	216-696-1122	S	3,032*	4.5
Personnel Group of America Inc.	6302 Fairview Rd	Charlotte	NC	28210	Edward P Drudge Jr	704-442-5100	P	918	5.4
TAC Worldwide Cos.	109 Oak St	Newton U Fls	MA	02164	Anthony J Balsamo	617-969-5100	R	737	1.1
Travcorps Corp.	40 Eastern Ave	Malden	MA	02148	Bruce Cerullo	781-322-2600	R	666*	1.0
Labor Ready Inc.	1016 S 28th St	Tacoma	WA	98409	Glenn A Welstad	253-383-9101	P	607	2.3
Butler International Inc.	110 Summit Ave	Montvale	NJ	07645	Edward M Kopko	201-573-8000	P	444	5.6
Training Delivery Services L.P.	4079 Ingot St	Fremont	CA	94538	William Ostler	510-249-0700	S	422*	0.8
Lauer Sbarbaro Associates	30 N La Salle St	Chicago	IL	60602	Richard Sbarbaro	312-372-7050	R	339*	0.5
Alternative Resources Corp.	100 Tri-State Intl	Lincolnshire	IL	60069	Raymond R Hipp	847-317-1000	P	339	0.8
Accountants on Call	Park 80 W Plz 2	Saddle Brook	NJ	07663	Diane O'Meally	201-843-0006	D	312*	0.9
Headway Corporate Resources Inc	850 3rd Ave	New York	NY	10022	Gary S Goldstein	212-508-3500	P	291	9.4
Spencer Stuart and Associates Inc.	401 N Michigan	Chicago	IL	60611	J E Griesedieck Jr	312-822-0088	R	239	0.5
HealthStaffers Inc.	5636 N Broadway	Chicago	IL	60660	Rose Houston	773-561-5400	R	237*	0.4
Heidrick and Struggles Inc.	233 S Wacker Dr	Chicago	IL	60606	Patrick S Pittard	312-372-8811	R	233*	1.0
Russell Reynolds Associates Inc.	200 Park Ave	New York	NY	10166	Hobson Brown Jr	212-351-2000	R	230	0.7
CareMed Chicago	322 S Green St	Chicago	IL	60607	Dan Woods	312-738-8622	R	213*	0.3
Certified Personnel Services	1600 Strawberry	Pasadena	TX	77502		713-477-0321	R	199*	0.3
Office Specialists Inc.	1 Corporate Way	Peabody	MA	01960	Lawrence E Derito	978-538-9500	S	175*	0.4
Interim Healthcare Inc.	141 Providence Rd	Charlotte	NC	28207	Nick Leone	704-372-8230	R	147*	0.7
Career Blazers Inc.	222 W Las Colinas	Irving	TX	75039	Tom Bickes	972-432-3000	R	114*	1.2
Intertec Design Inc.	2500 McClellan	Pennsauken	NJ	08109	Leon Kopyt	609-486-1777	S	114*	3.2
Lee Hecht Harrison Inc.	50 Tice Blvd	Woodcliff Lake	NJ	07675	Stephen G Harrison	201-930-9333	S	100	0.6
ATC Nursing Service Texas Inc.	1895 Phoenix Blvd	Atlanta	GA	30349		770-437-3800	R	68*	0.1
Winston Resources Inc.	535 5th Ave	New York	NY	10017	Seymour Kugler	212-557-5000	P	61	0.1
ASI Solutions Inc.	780 Third Ave	New York	NY	10017	Bernard F Reynolds	212-319-8400	P	60	0.5
Robert Lee Brown Inc.	435 Elm St	Cincinnati	OH	45202	Robert Brown	513-651-1111	R	59*	0.1
Star Multi Care Services Inc.	99 RR Sta Plz	Hicksville	NY	11801	Stephen Sternbach	516-938-2016	P	58	0.3
Solomon-Page Group Ltd.	1140 Av Americas	New York	NY	10036	Scott Page	212-403-6100	P	56	0.2
Richard, Wayne and Roberts	24 Greenway Plz	Houston	TX	77046		713-629-6681	R	53*	<0.1
Romac International	5429 LBJ Hwy	Dallas	TX	75240		972-387-2200	D	53*	<0.1
Search West Inc.	2049 Century Park E	Los Angeles	CA	90067	Bob Cowan	310-203-9797	R	48	<0.1
Chipton-Ross Inc.	343 Main St	El Segundo	CA	90245	Sharon King	310-414-7800	R	44*	0.8
Diversified Corporate Resources	12801 N Cen Expwy	Dallas	TX	75243	M Ted Dillard	972-458-8500	P	42	0.4
Infotech Contracts Services Inc.	400-1 Totten Pond	Waltham	MA	02154	Gary LaFave	781-890-7007	S	42	0.4
General Employment Enterprises	1 Tower Ln	Oakbrk Ter	IL	60181	Herbert F Imhoff	630-954-0400	P	40	0.5
Amedisys Inc.	3029 S Shrwd Frst	Baton Rouge	LA	70816	William F Borne	225-292-2031	P	38	1.6
Isaacson, Miller Inc.	334 Boylston St	Boston	MA	02116		617-262-6500	R	37*	<0.1
Accountants Overload	10990 Wilshire	Los Angeles	CA	90024	Richard Lewis	310-478-8883	R	34*	<0.1
Heuristics Search Inc.	160 W Santa Clara	San Jose	CA	95113	Elizabeth Patrick	408-748-1500	R	33*	<0.1
S.E.S. Staffing Solutions	524 Dolphin St	Baltimore	MD	21217		410-486-4330	R	33*	<0.1
SEEK Inc.	PO Box 148	Grafton	WI	53024	Ray Odya	262-377-8888	R	31	0.1
Spencer Reed Group	6900 College Blvd	Overland Park	KS	66211	Dick Plodzien	913-663-4400	R	29	0.2
Ward Howell International Inc.	99 Park Ave	New York	NY	10016		212-697-3730	N	25	0.2
B.M. Sullivan Inc.	40 Wall St	New York	NY	10005	Brian M Sullivan	212-699-3000	R	24*	<0.1
DHR International Inc.	10 S Riverside Plz	Chicago	IL	60606	David H Hoffmann	312-782-1581	R	24*	0.1
JPM International Enterprises	26060 Acero, #100	Mission Viejo	CA	92691	JP Meehan	949-699-4300	R	22	<0.1
B and B Employment Inc.	668 N 44th St	Phoenix	AZ	85008	Paul Smith	602-277-3381	R	20*	<0.1
Unique International	1700 K-St NW	Washington	DC	20006	Rose Atwood	202-887-0777	R	20*	<0.1
Rankin Technology Group Inc.	2432 W Peoria Ave	Phoenix	AZ	85029	Larry Thacker	602-997-6996	R	19*	<0.1
Whitney Partners Inc.	850 3rd Ave	New York	NY	10022	Gary S Goldstein	212-508-3500	S	18*	<0.1
Winter, Wyman and Co.	950 Winter St	Waltham	MA	02451	Kevin Steele	781-890-7000	R	18*	0.2
Challenger, Gray & Christmas Inc.	150 S Wacker Dr	Chicago	IL	60606		312-332-5790	N	17	<0.1
Entegee Engineering Technical	5309 Victoria Ave	Davenport	IA	52807	Derek Dewan	319-359-7042	S	16	<0.1
G and A Staff Sourcing	5847 San Felipe	Houston	TX	77057		713-784-1181	R	13*	<0.1
Professional Placement Inc.	3900 E Camelback	Phoenix	AZ	85018	Wayne Calhoun	602-955-0870	R	13*	<0.1
Ramsey/Beirne Associates	500 Executive Blvd	Ossining	NY	10562	James Chung	914-762-2012	R	13*	<0.1
Robert Shields and Associates	1560 W Bay Area	Friendswood	TX	77546		281-488-7961	R	13*	<0.1
Advanced Resources Inc.	6250 River Rd	Rosemont	IL	60018		847-518-9222	R	12	<0.1
Lynch Miller Moore O'Hara Inc.	303 W Madison	Chicago	IL	60606	Michael Lynch	312-629-0808	R	11*	<0.1
Forty Plus of New York Inc.	15 Maiden Ln	New York	NY	10038		212-233-6086	R	10*	<0.1
Medstaff Contract Nursing Inc.	1337-A 100 Oaks	Charlotte	NC	28217	Richard C Davis	704-523-1524	R	10	0.5
Personnel Resource Corp.	3829 N 3rd St	Phoenix	AZ	85012	Steven S Swartz	602-248-0010	R	10*	<0.1
Rusher, Losavio and LoPresto	2479 E Bayshore	Palo Alto	CA	94303	Bill Rusher	650-494-0883	R	10*	<0.1
Harrison Personnel Services Inc.	1800 St James Pl	Houston	TX	77056	JB Harrison	713-960-9906	R	8*	<0.1
Ackerman Johnson Inc.	333 N S Houston E	Houston	TX	77060	Frederick W Stang	281-999-8879	R	7*	<0.1
Allerton Heneghan and O'Neill	70 W Madison St	Chicago	IL	60602	Donald Allerton	312-263-1075	R	7*	<0.1
A.G. Fishkin and Associates Inc.	P O Box 34413	Bethesda	MD	20827	Anita Fishkin	301-983-0303	R	5*	<0.1
Accent Human Resource	2850 E Camelback	Phoenix	AZ	85016	Cathy Staudohar	602-955-2222	R	5*	<0.1
Creative Employment	219 N Milwaukee St	Milwaukee	WI	53202	Laura Owens-Johnson	414-277-8506	R	5*	<0.1
Howard-Sloan-Koller Group	353 Lexington	New York	NY	10016		212-661-5250	N	5	<0.1
Loan Administration Network Inc.	18872 MacArthur	Irvine	CA	92612			R	5	<0.1
Norman Broadbent International	200 Park Ave	New York	NY	10166		212-953-6990	N	5	<0.1
David Gomez and Associates Inc.	20 N Clark	Chicago	IL	60602	David Gomez	312-346-5525	R	4	<0.1
Ken Leiner Associates	11510 Georgia Ave	Wheaton	MD	20902	Ken Leiner	301-933-8800	R	4	<0.1

Source: Ward's Business Directory of U.S. Private and Public Companies, Volumes 1 and 2, 2000. The company type code used is as follows: P - Public, R - Private, S - Subsidiary, D - Division, J - Joint Venture, A - Affiliate, G - Group, N - Company type not reported. Sales are in millions of dollars, employees are in thousands. An asterisk (*) indicates an estimated sales volume. The symbol < stands for 'less than'. Company names and addresses are truncated, in some cases, to fit into the available space.

LOCATION BY STATE AND REGIONAL CONCENTRATION

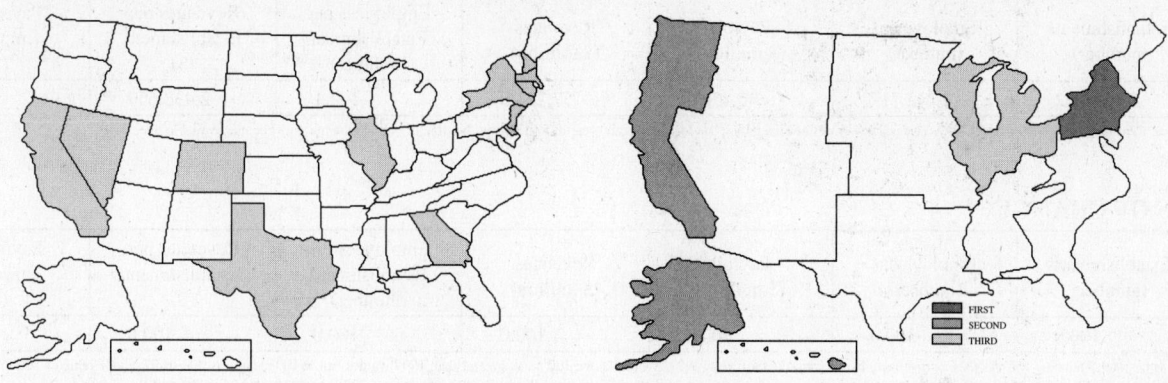

FIRST
SECOND
THIRD

INDUSTRY DATA BY STATE

State	Establishments Total (number)	% of U.S.	Employment Total (number)	% of U.S.	Per Estab.	Payroll Total ($ mil.)	Per Empl. ($)	Revenues Total ($ mil.)	% of U.S.	Per Estab. ($)
California	849	13.5	16,523	14.5	19	440.6	26,663	745.0	15.6	877,489
New York	676	10.8	10,830	9.5	16	315.0	29,082	671.7	14.0	993,679
Texas	483	7.7	10,257	9.0	21	265.0	25,839	431.4	9.0	893,101
Illinois	361	5.7	6,879	6.0	19	144.0	20,927	257.1	5.4	712,197
New Jersey	250	4.0	4,149	3.6	17	117.5	28,321	244.4	5.1	977,796
Massachusetts	219	3.5	4,554	4.0	21	116.7	25,635	207.1	4.3	945,598
Pennsylvania	207	3.3	4,350	3.8	21	90.7	20,844	169.6	3.5	819,309
Ohio	206	3.3	3,117	2.7	15	85.2	27,325	158.2	3.3	768,170
Georgia	197	3.1	3,028	2.7	15	83.3	27,522	145.1	3.0	736,497
Florida	351	5.6	2,028	1.8	6	57.3	28,238	123.5	2.6	351,835
Michigan	196	3.1	4,040	3.5	21	73.1	18,091	119.9	2.5	611,898
North Carolina	146	2.3	3,869	3.4	27	57.6	14,876	103.3	2.2	707,740
Connecticut	133	2.1	2,658	2.3	20	63.6	23,918	103.0	2.2	774,782
Indiana	101	1.6	1,408	1.2	14	38.2	27,114	91.5	1.9	905,842
Washington	117	1.9	2,301	2.0	20	49.6	21,551	87.6	1.8	749,094
Virginia	125	2.0	1,641	1.4	13	45.4	27,692	81.5	1.7	651,952
Minnesota	124	2.0	1,616	1.4	13	37.4	23,121	74.8	1.6	603,524
Maryland	129	2.1	1,389	1.2	11	38.6	27,813	74.3	1.6	575,798
Colorado	115	1.8	1,972	1.7	17	44.1	22,362	74.2	1.6	645,287
Tennessee	111	1.8	3,448	3.0	31	47.6	13,807	70.7	1.5	636,937
Wisconsin	105	1.7	2,049	1.8	20	44.6	21,766	69.0	1.4	657,171
Arizona	94	1.5	1,928	1.7	21	42.7	22,157	64.5	1.3	685,702
New Hampshire	34	0.5	576	0.5	17	18.9	32,774	57.2	1.2	1,681,000
Louisiana	103	1.6	1,966	1.7	19	33.8	17,180	56.7	1.2	550,049
Missouri	102	1.6	1,143	1.0	11	31.5	27,550	56.2	1.2	551,284
South Carolina	66	1.1	2,204	1.9	33	33.4	15,161	50.8	1.1	770,273
Mississippi	47	0.7	1,293	1.1	28	25.0	19,321	36.0	0.8	765,723
Kentucky	51	0.8	1,719	1.5	34	23.1	13,418	35.5	0.7	696,471
Oregon	52	0.8	1,022	0.9	20	19.2	18,816	34.9	0.7	671,942
Alabama	76	1.2	2,382	2.1	31	23.3	9,765	34.6	0.7	455,579
Nevada	39	0.6	245	0.2	6	21.0	85,722	33.3	0.7	854,410
Utah	25	0.4	419	0.4	17	11.8	28,169	28.1	0.6	1,123,920
Oklahoma	42	0.7	863	0.8	21	14.2	16,477	26.4	0.6	629,167
Delaware	22	0.4	544	0.5	25	9.4	17,292	25.3	0.5	1,150,318
Iowa	34	0.5	858	0.8	25	9.0	10,491	18.5	0.4	544,765
Arkansas	37	0.6	503	0.4	14	8.6	17,093	14.9	0.3	401,405
Nebraska	25	0.4	263	0.2	11	4.6	17,529	7.8	0.2	312,440
Hawaii	14	0.2	192	0.2	14	3.6	18,896	6.4	0.1	457,500
Maine	19	0.3	277	0.2	15	2.9	10,296	5.0	0.1	265,316
New Mexico	13	0.2	340	0.3	26	2.4	7,115	4.8	0.1	372,923
Idaho	17	0.3	420	0.4	25	2.8	6,690	4.7	0.1	275,235
Montana	14	0.2	448	0.4	32	2.2	4,875	4.2	0.1	296,857
West Virginia	10	0.2	33	0.0	3	1.3	40,152	2.6	0.1	260,500
Alaska	4	0.1	41	0.0	10	0.7	17,390	1.4	0.0	357,250
North Dakota	7	0.1	30	0.0	4	0.5	16,433	0.8	0.0	120,429
D.C.	42	0.7	750*	-	-	(D)	-	(D)	-	-
Kansas	41	0.7	375*	-	-	(D)	-	(D)	-	-
Rhode Island	34	0.5	750*	-	-	(D)	-	(D)	-	-
South Dakota	6	0.1	60*	-	-	(D)	-	(D)	-	-
Vermont	5	0.1	10*	-	-	(D)	-	(D)	-	-
Wyoming	5	0.1	10*	-	-	(D)	-	(D)	-	-

Source: 1997 Economic Census. The states are in descending order of revenues or establishments (if revenue data are missing for the majority). The symbol (D) appears when data are withheld to prevent disclosure of competitive information. States marked with (D) are sorted by number of establishments. A dash (-) indicates that the data element cannot be calculated. * indicates the midpoint of a range; 175, for example is the range 100-249. Shaded states on the state map indicate those states which have proportionately greater representation in the industry than would be indicated by the state's population; the ratio is based on total revenues or number of establishments. Shaded regions indicate where the industry is regionally most concentrated.

413

NAICS 561320 - TEMPORARY HELP SERVICES

GENERAL STATISTICS

Year	Establishments (number)	Employment (number)	Payroll ($ million)	Revenues ($ million)	Employees per Establishment (number)	Revenues per Establishment ($)	Payroll per Employee ($)
1997	23,522	2,612,719	40,256.0	57,221.0	111.1	2,432,659	15,408

Source: Economic Census of the United States, 1997. This is a newly defined industry. Data for prior years were unavailable at the time of publication but may become available over time.

INDICES OF CHANGE

Year	Establishments (number)	Employment (number)	Payroll ($ million)	Revenues ($ million)	Employees per Establishment (number)	Revenues per Establishment ($)	Payroll per Employee ($)
1997	100.0	100.0	100.0	100.0	100.0	100.0	100.0

Sources: Same as General Statistics. The values shown reflect change from the base year, 1997. Values above 100 mean greater than 1997, values below 100 mean less than 1997, and a value of 100 in the 1982-96 or 1998-2001 period means same as 1997. Values followed by a 'p' are projections by the editors; 'e' stands for extrapolation. Data are the most recent available at this level of detail.

SIC INDUSTRIES RELATED TO NAICS 561320

Each new NAICS code represents an industry that used to be part of an SIC or a part of several SIC industries. Data in this table are shown to provide transitional information for these cases. All available data for the precursor SIC(s) are shown. Even if only a part of an SIC is included in the NAICS, *all* data for the SIC are reproduced. If the SIC industry is not marked as being a part (pt) of the NAICS, the entire industry is embedded in the NAICS data. The SIC composition of the new industry provides some hints of the relative importance of its "ancestors." Data marked with a 'p' are projected. Projections begin with 1982 data. Data earlier than 1990 are not shown but are reflected in the projections.

SIC	Industry	1990	1991	1992	1993	1994	1995	1996	1997
7363	**Help Supply Services (pt)**								
	Establishments (number)	13,306	14,188	19,020	19,579	20,544	22,235	22,177p	23,315p
	Employment (thousands)	1,210.3	1,230.4	1,841.9	1,816.9	2,097.6	2,397.2	2,231.8p	2,357.7p
	Revenues ($ million)	26,380.0	28,292.0	33,729.0	36,525.0	41,443.0	51,637.0	59,573.0	58,292.4p

Source: Economic Census of the United States, 1992, annual surveys of economic sectors conducted by the Bureau of the Census, and estimates or projections based on the 1982-1992 period; not all data are shown. 'e' marks estimates made by the editors; 'p' indicates projections based on time series. A dash (-) indicates that data for this SIC or year were not available. The abbreviation (pt) next to the industry name indicates that only a part of the industry is present within the NAICS data. If no (pt) is shown, the entire industry is contained within the NAICS data.

SELECTED RATIOS

For 1997	Avg. of Information	Analyzed Industry	Index	For 1997	Avg. of Information	Analyzed Industry	Index
Employees per establishment	27	111	418	Payroll per establishment	496,890	1,711,419	344
Revenue per establishment	1,070,709	2,432,659	227	Payroll as % of revenue	46	70	152
Revenue per employee	40,278	21,901	54	Payroll per employee	18,692	15,408	82

Sources: Same as General Statistics. The 'Average' column represents the average for the industry sector, in 1997, where the currently shown industry is classified. The Index shows the relationship between the Average and the Analyzed Industry. For example, 100 means that they are equal; 500 that the Analyzed Industry is five times the average; 50 means that the Analyzed Industry is half the national average. The abbreviation 'na' is used to show that data are 'not available'.

LEADING COMPANIES   Number shown: **75**   Total sales ($ mil): **48,544**   Total employment (000): **2,848.9**

Company Name	Address				CEO Name	Phone	Co. Type	Sales ($ mil)	Empl. (000)
Manpower Inc.	PO Box 2053	Milwaukee	WI	53201	Jeffrey A. Joerres	414-961-1000	P	8,814	15.0
Olsten Corp.	175 Broad Hollow	Melville	NY	11747	E H Blechschmidt	516-844-7800	P	4,603*	700.8
Kelly Services Inc.	999 W Big Beaver	Troy	MI	48084	Terence E Adderley	248-362-4444	P	4,269	800.0
Olsten Staffing Services	175 Broad Hollow	Melville	NY	11747		516-844-7800	S	3,283*	11.7
Staff Leasing Inc.	600-301 Bld W	Bradenton	FL	34205	Charles S Craig	941-748-4540	P	2,375	128.3
Volt Information Sciences Inc.	1221 Av Americas	New York	NY	10036	William Shaw	212-704-2400	P	2,141	38.7
Robert Half International Inc.	2884 Sand Hill Rd	Menlo Park	CA	94025	Harold M Messmer Jr	650-234-6000	P	2,081	185.2
Interim Services Inc.	2050 Spectrum Blvd	Fort Lauderdale	FL	33309	Raymond Marcy	954-938-7600	P	1,890	381.0
CDI Corp.	1717 Arch St	Philadelphia	PA	19103	Walter Garrison	215-569-2200	P	1,540	31.0
Norrell Corp.	3535 Piedmont N E	Atlanta	GA	30305	C Douglas Miller	404-240-3000	P	1,410	236.5
Adecco Employment Services Inc.	100 Redwood Shores	Redwood City	CA	94065	Debbie Pond' Heide	650-610-1000	R	1,300*	2.5
StaffMark Inc.	302 E Millsap Rd	Fayetteville	AR	72701	Clete T Brewer	501-973-6000	P	1,221	35.0
Volt Management Corp.	1221 Av Americas	New York	NY	10020	William Shaw	212-704-2400	S	1,000	31.0
Employee Solutions Inc.	6225 N 24 St	Phoenix	AZ	85016	Quentin P Smith Jr	602-955-5556	P	969	0.4
Metamor Worldwide Inc.	4400 Post Oak	Houston	TX	77027	Peter T Dameris	713-548-3400	P	850	9.0
Kforce.com Inc.	120 W Hyde Park Pl	Tampa	FL	33606	David L Dunkel	813-251-1700	P	680	7.7
Spectrum Healthcare Services	12647 Olive Blvd	St. Louis	MO	63141	Richard H Miles	314-878-2280	R	667*	6.0
Westaff Inc	301Lennon Ln	Walnut Creek	CA	94598	Michael K PhippenE	925-930-5300	P	600	37.0
OutSource International Inc.	1144 E Newport	Deerfield Beach	FL	33442	Paul Burrell	954-418-6400	P	565	37.0
RemedyTemp Inc.	101 Enterprise	Aliso Viejo	CA	92656	Paul Mikes	949-425-7600	P	514	0.5
Volt Technical Services	1221 Av Americas	New York	NY	10020		212-704-2400	S	500	3.0
Westaff Inc.	P O Box 9280	Walnut Creek	CA	94598	Michael K Phippen	925-930-5300	P	482*	1.0
AHL Services Inc.	3353 Peachtree N E	Atlanta	GA	30326	Frank Argenbright Jr	404-267-2222	P	476	13.0
COMFORCE Corp.	415 Crossways	Woodbury	NY	11797	John C Fanning	516-437-3300	P	459	8.0
Staff Builders Inc.	1983 Marcus Ave	Lake Success	NY	11042	David Savitsky	516-358-1000	P	438	4.0
Altres Inc.	711 Kapiolani Blvd	Honolulu	HI	96813	Barron Guss	808-591-4990	R	393*	16.0
SOS Staffing Services Inc.	1415 S Main St	Salt Lake City	UT	84115	Peter R Sollenne	801-484-4400	P	371	1.4
B and M Associates Inc.	18 Commerce Way	Woburn	MA	01801	L R McCormack	781-938-9120	R	341*	1.2
RCM Technologies Inc.	2500 McClellan	Pennsauken	NJ	08109	Leon Kopyt	856-486-1777	P	313	4.6
Barrett Business Services Inc.	4724 SW Macadam	Portland	OR	97201	William W Sherertz	503-220-0988	P	303	19.4
Professional Staff Management	859 W South Jordan	South Jordan	UT	84095	William J Miller	801-984-1700	R	241	6.0
Hall Kinion and Associates Inc.	185 Berry Street	San Francisco	CA	94107	Brenda C Hall	415-974-1300	P	181	1.2
Echelon Service Co.	7604 York Rd	Baltimore	MD	21204	Eugene Hartman	410-321-8254	R	168*	0.2
GTS Duratek Corp.	10100 Old Columbia	Columbia	MD	21046	Robert Prince	410-312-5100	P	160	1.0
On Assignment Inc.	26651 W Agoura Rd	Calabasas	CA	91302	H Tom Buelter	818-878-7900	P	159	13.2
Service Temporaries Inc.	5921 W 12th	Little Rock	AR	72214	Rebecca Addison	501-666-6894	R	142*	0.5
Perfusion Services of Baxter	16818 Via Campo	San Diego	CA	92127	Jack DeVaney	858-485-5599	S	140*	1.0
MATRIX Resources Inc.	115 Perimeter Center	Atlanta	GA	30346		770-677-2400	R	135	0.8
Employers Resource Management	888 N Cole Rd	Boise	ID	83704	George Gersema	208-376-3000	R	132	<0.1
Kelly Staff Leasing Inc.	999 W Big Beaver	Troy	MI	48084	Terence E Adderley	248-362-4444	S	120*	3.0
Pro Staff Personnel Services	4455 Alpha Rd	Dallas	TX	75244	Jeff Dobbs	972-661-1600	R	120*	1.0
National TechTeam Inc.	835 Mason St	Dearborn	MI	48124	Harry A Lewis	313-277-2277	P	117	2.6
L.J. Gonzer Associates	1225 Raymond Blvd	Newark	NJ	07102	Lawrence J Gonzer	973-624-5600	R	111*	0.4
Modern Engineering Inc.	2401 Big Beaver Rd	Troy	MI	48084	George Kubicke	248-458-6000	S	110	1.7
Nursefinders Inc.	1701 E Lamar Blvd	Arlington	TX	76006	Richard L Peranton	817-460-1181	S	110*	0.3
MedTeams	725 American Ave	Waukesha	WI	53188		262-928-2573	R	107*	0.4
Vincam Group Inc.	2850 Douglas Rd	Coral Gables	FL	33134	John Carlen	305-460-2350	P	103	0.6
Employee Solutions II Inc.	6225 N 24St	Phoenix	AZ	85016	Marvin Brody	602-955-5556	S	97*	0.4
Consolidated Technology Group	9 Great Neck CT	Huntington	NY	11743	Seymour Richter	212-488-8484	P	93	1.0
Personnel Management Inc.	1499 Windhorst	Greenwood	IN	46143	Gary F Hentschel	317-888-4400	P	85	35.0
Northwest Administrators Inc.	2323 Eastlake Ave E	Seattle	WA	98102	Chris R Hughes	206-329-4900	R	76*	0.3
Joule Inc.	1245 Rte 1, S	Edison	NJ	08837	Emanuel N Logothetis	732-548-5444	P	68	2.8
Trans Global Services Inc.	1393 Veterans Mem	Hauppauge	NY	11788	Joseph G Sicinski	516-724-0006	P	67	0.7
Ford Models Inc.	114 Green St	New York	NY	10012	Katie Ford	212-219-6500	R	63*	0.1
ATR/Norrell Information Services	1651 Old Meadow	McLean	VA	22102		703-917-7800	S	58*	1.0
Trialon Corp.	PO Box 190199	Burton	MI	48519	Patricia L Crowder	810-742-8500	R	57*	0.2
Accord Human Resources Inc.	201 Park Ave	Oklahoma	OK	73102	Dale Hagman	405-232-9888	R	50*	<0.1
Interim Financial Solutions	2050 Spectrum Blvd	Fort Lauderdale	FL	33309	Eric Archer	954-938-7600	S	47	0.2
Consultis Inc.	1615 S Federal Hwy	Boca Raton	FL	33432	Barbara Fleming	561-362-9104	R	46	3.2
H.C. Watson Corp.	300 Rosewood Dr	Danvers	MA	01923	James Watson	978-777-9090	R	43*	0.2
Entech Personnel Services Inc.	363 W Big Beaver	Troy	MI	48084	Janet Sparks	248-528-1444	R	42	<0.1
Peak Technical Services Inc.	3424 William Penn	Pittsburgh	PA	15235	J Salvucci	412-825-3900	R	42*	<0.1
Contract Professionals Inc.	4141 W Walton	Waterford	MI	48329	Steven E York	248-673-3800	R	41	0.7
Certified Temporary Services Inc.	16951 Feathercraft	Pasadena	TX	77508	Thomas W Warren	281-280-9500	R	38*	<0.1
TRC Temporary Services Inc.	PO Box 888524	Atlanta	GA	30356	Roy Cannon	770-392-1411	R	37*	0.1
Lab Support Inc.	26651 W Agoura Rd	Calabasas	CA	91302		818-878-7900	D	35*	<0.1
CDI Managed CADD Services	50 Payson Ave	Easthampton	MA	01027		413-529-2400	D	32*	0.5
Security Personnel Inc.	8516-18 W Capitol	Milwaukee	WI	53222	Glen Erdman	414-464-5300	R	31*	0.1
Intellimark IT Business Solutions	1350 Treat Blvd	Walnut Creek	CA	94596	Paul Sharps	925-946-0601	D	30	0.5
Office Mates 5 Daystar	1511N Westshore	Tampa	FL	33607		813-281-1918	S	30*	0.1
Advanced Health Management	555 White Plains Rd	Tarrytown	NY	10591	Jon Edelson	914-524-4200	P	29*	0.1
TemPositions Group of Cos.	420 Lexington Ave	New York	NY	10170	James Essey	212-490-7400	R	28*	0.1
Energy Services Group Intern. Inc.	8979 Pocahontas	Williamsburg	VA	23185	Gerald Clarke	757-887-1500	R	25*	0.2
Imprimis Group Inc.	5550 LBJ Fwy	Dallas	TX	75240	Valerie Freeman	972-419-1700	R	24*	<0.1
Human Resources Alternatives Inc	6 Teri Lane	Burlington	NJ	08016	Davie Fried	609-387-8828	R	23	1.4

Source: Ward's Business Directory of U.S. Private and Public Companies, Volumes 1 and 2, 2000. The company type code used is as follows: P - Public, R - Private, S - Subsidiary, D - Division, J - Joint Venture, A - Affiliate, G - Group, N - Company type not reported. Sales are in millions of dollars, employees are in thousands. An asterisk (*) indicates an estimated sales volume. The symbol < stands for 'less than'. Company names and addresses are truncated, in some cases, to fit into the available space.

LOCATION BY STATE AND REGIONAL CONCENTRATION

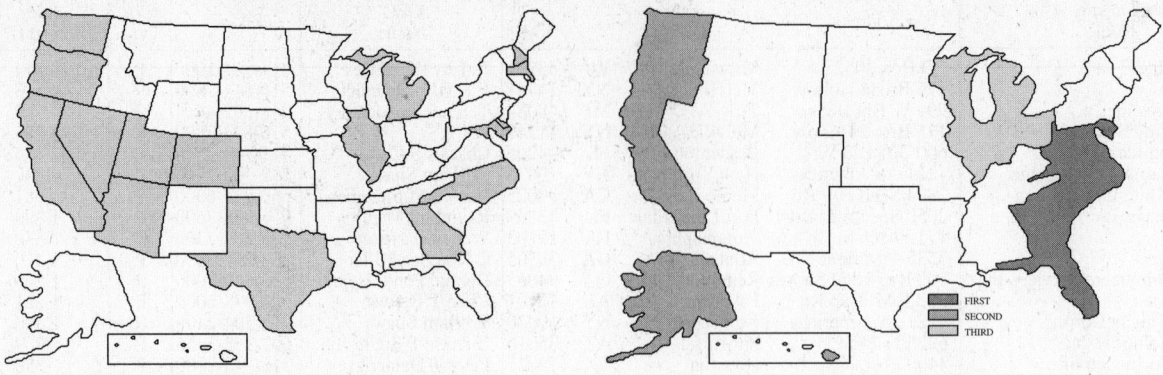

FIRST
SECOND
THIRD

INDUSTRY DATA BY STATE

State	Establishments Total (number)	% of U.S.	Employment Total (number)	% of U.S.	Per Estab.	Payroll Total ($ mil.)	Per Empl. ($)	Revenues Total ($ mil.)	% of U.S.	Per Estab. ($)
California	2,844	12.1	364,549	14.0	128	6,083.0	16,686	8,665.3	15.1	3,046,868
Texas	1,925	8.2	218,953	8.4	114	3,562.3	16,270	5,062.7	8.8	2,629,968
New York	1,201	5.1	136,920	5.2	114	2,603.1	19,012	3,798.5	6.6	3,162,785
Florida	1,506	6.4	144,268	5.5	96	1,957.7	13,570	2,880.0	5.0	1,912,368
Michigan	1,099	4.7	119,475	4.6	109	2,008.4	16,811	2,753.0	4.8	2,505,030
Illinois	1,173	5.0	137,713	5.3	117	1,850.2	13,435	2,746.6	4.8	2,341,479
Georgia	913	3.9	95,922	3.7	105	1,543.2	16,088	2,203.6	3.9	2,413,552
Massachusetts	684	2.9	67,628	2.6	99	1,465.9	21,676	2,183.5	3.8	3,192,235
Ohio	1,064	4.5	115,799	4.4	109	1,567.5	13,536	2,180.8	3.8	2,049,666
Maryland	430	1.8	76,882	2.9	179	1,655.3	21,531	2,095.9	3.7	4,874,107
Pennsylvania	883	3.8	78,947	3.0	89	1,267.3	16,052	1,837.8	3.2	2,081,360
North Carolina	754	3.2	85,621	3.3	114	1,266.3	14,790	1,799.3	3.1	2,386,308
New Jersey	685	2.9	69,353	2.7	101	1,147.5	16,546	1,710.6	3.0	2,497,184
Washington	407	1.7	43,953	1.7	108	1,033.0	23,503	1,326.4	2.3	3,258,961
Virginia	550	2.3	57,856	2.2	105	900.0	15,555	1,291.0	2.3	2,347,264
Arizona	466	2.0	56,011	2.1	120	799.2	14,268	1,088.9	1.9	2,336,590
Colorado	519	2.2	46,601	1.8	90	695.3	14,919	1,029.3	1.8	1,983,320
Minnesota	463	2.0	50,803	1.9	110	706.7	13,910	993.9	1.7	2,146,600
Tennessee	515	2.2	53,770	2.1	104	672.1	12,499	964.8	1.7	1,873,355
Wisconsin	455	1.9	58,360	2.2	128	635.4	10,888	908.9	1.6	1,997,521
Indiana	527	2.2	49,101	1.9	93	601.2	12,244	819.9	1.4	1,555,808
Missouri	452	1.9	40,456	1.5	90	542.5	13,410	762.9	1.3	1,687,841
South Carolina	318	1.4	43,106	1.6	136	535.8	12,430	731.7	1.3	2,301,041
Connecticut	319	1.4	26,554	1.0	83	481.1	18,117	704.4	1.2	2,208,285
Oregon	339	1.4	32,801	1.3	97	501.0	15,272	695.3	1.2	2,050,897
Louisiana	293	1.2	38,609	1.5	132	378.9	9,814	545.7	1.0	1,862,287
Kansas	203	0.9	27,854	1.1	137	371.4	13,334	502.7	0.9	2,476,305
Oklahoma	239	1.0	29,265	1.1	122	338.7	11,575	491.8	0.9	2,057,762
Kentucky	268	1.1	36,229	1.4	135	351.8	9,710	488.4	0.9	1,822,552
Alabama	247	1.1	33,749	1.3	137	339.5	10,061	463.1	0.8	1,874,960
Utah	149	0.6	20,369	0.8	137	264.4	12,981	437.0	0.8	2,932,564
New Hampshire	127	0.5	12,605	0.5	99	264.2	20,958	433.8	0.8	3,415,961
Nevada	166	0.7	11,926	0.5	72	231.5	19,410	317.4	0.6	1,912,018
Arkansas	166	0.7	21,543	0.8	130	211.6	9,822	295.5	0.5	1,780,199
Iowa	146	0.6	16,304	0.6	112	185.1	11,355	259.7	0.5	1,779,055
D.C.	93	0.4	9,976	0.4	107	159.3	15,972	231.2	0.4	2,485,624
Delaware	83	0.4	10,151	0.4	122	160.8	15,844	219.1	0.4	2,639,807
Mississippi	98	0.4	10,365	0.4	106	131.8	12,720	185.9	0.3	1,896,694
New Mexico	104	0.4	9,747	0.4	94	119.8	12,293	176.6	0.3	1,697,721
West Virginia	79	0.3	6,730	0.3	85	112.8	16,761	161.6	0.3	2,045,405
Nebraska	94	0.4	9,334	0.4	99	111.9	11,994	154.2	0.3	1,640,915
Rhode Island	93	0.4	9,126	0.3	98	106.9	11,710	148.2	0.3	1,594,000
Idaho	68	0.3	5,900	0.2	87	83.8	14,208	118.3	0.2	1,739,265
Maine	69	0.3	6,997	0.3	101	77.5	11,073	104.0	0.2	1,507,942
Vermont	38	0.2	2,035	0.1	54	32.4	15,921	52.6	0.1	1,382,921
Hawaii	48	0.2	2,732	0.1	57	33.2	12,135	48.6	0.1	1,012,917
Montana	47	0.2	3,260	0.1	69	30.2	9,249	44.0	0.1	935,553
Alaska	23	0.1	1,098	0.0	48	24.9	22,683	33.1	0.1	1,439,391
South Dakota	38	0.2	2,465	0.1	65	19.5	7,899	26.5	0.0	697,553
North Dakota	22	0.1	1,535	0.1	70	17.5	11,405	25.7	0.0	1,167,409
Wyoming	30	0.1	1,413	0.1	47	16.1	11,368	21.3	0.0	710,567

Source: 1997 *Economic Census*. The states are in descending order of revenues or establishments (if revenue data are missing for the majority). The symbol (D) appears when data are withheld to prevent disclosure of competitive information. States marked with (D) are sorted by number of establishments. A dash (-) indicates that the data element cannot be calculated. * indicates the midpoint of a range; 175, for example is the range 100-249. Shaded *states* on the state map indicate those states which have proportionately greater representation in the industry than would be indicated by the state's population; the ratio is based on total revenues or number of establishments. Shaded *regions* indicate where the industry is regionally most concentrated.

NAICS 561330 - EMPLOYEE LEASING SERVICES

GENERAL STATISTICS

Year	Establishments (number)	Employment (number)	Payroll ($ million)	Revenues ($ million)	Employees per Establishment (number)	Revenues per Establishment ($)	Payroll per Employee ($)
1997	4,766	895,411	19,224.0	24,125.0	187.9	5,061,897	21,469

Source: Economic Census of the United States, 1997. This is a newly defined industry. Data for prior years were unavailable at the time of publication but may become available over time.

INDICES OF CHANGE

Year	Establishments (number)	Employment (number)	Payroll ($ million)	Revenues ($ million)	Employees per Establishment (number)	Revenues per Establishment ($)	Payroll per Employee ($)
1997	100.0	100.0	100.0	100.0	100.0	100.0	100.0

Sources: Same as General Statistics. The values shown reflect change from the base year, 1997. Values above 100 mean greater than 1997, values below 100 mean less than 1997, and a value of 100 in the 1982-96 or 1998-2001 period means same as 1997. Values followed by a 'p' are projections by the editors; 'e' stands for extrapolation. Data are the most recent available at this level of detail.

SIC INDUSTRIES RELATED TO NAICS 561330

Each new NAICS code represents an industry that used to be part of an SIC or a part of several SIC industries. Data in this table are shown to provide transitional information for these cases. All available data for the precursor SIC(s) are shown. Even if only a part of an SIC is included in the NAICS, *all* data for the SIC are reproduced. If the SIC industry is not marked as being a part (pt) of the NAICS, the entire industry is embedded in the NAICS data. The SIC composition of the new industry provides some hints of the relative importance of its "ancestors." Data marked with a 'p' are projected. Projections begin with 1982 data. Data earlier than 1990 are not shown but are reflected in the projections.

SIC	Industry	1990	1991	1992	1993	1994	1995	1996	1997
7363	**Help Supply Services (pt)**								
	Establishments (number)	13,306	14,188	19,020	19,579	20,544	22,235	22,177p	23,315p
	Employment (thousands)	1,210.3	1,230.4	1,841.9	1,816.9	2,097.6	2,397.2	2,231.8p	2,357.7p
	Revenues ($ million)	26,380.0	28,292.0	33,729.0	36,525.0	41,443.0	51,637.0	59,573.0	58,292.4p

Source: Economic Census of the United States, 1992, annual surveys of economic sectors conducted by the Bureau of the Census, and estimates or projections based on the 1982-1992 period; not all data are shown. 'e' marks estimates made by the editors; 'p' indicates projections based on time series. A dash (-) indicates that data for this SIC or year were not available. The abbreviation (pt) next to the industry name indicates that only a part of the industry is present within the NAICS data. If no (pt) is shown, the entire industry is contained within the NAICS data.

SELECTED RATIOS

For 1997	Avg. of Information	Analyzed Industry	Index	For 1997	Avg. of Information	Analyzed Industry	Index
Employees per establishment	27	188	707	Payroll per establishment	496,890	4,033,571	812
Revenue per establishment	1,070,709	5,061,897	473	Payroll as % of revenue	46	80	172
Revenue per employee	40,278	26,943	67	Payroll per employee	18,692	21,469	115

Sources: Same as General Statistics. The 'Average' column represents the average for the industry sector, in 1997, where the currently shown industry is classified. The Index shows the relationship between the Average and the Analyzed Industry. For example, 100 means that they are equal; 500 that the Analyzed Industry is five times the average; 50 means that the Analyzed Industry is half the national average. The abbreviation 'na' is used to show that data are 'not available'.

LEADING COMPANIES

No company data available for this industry.

LOCATION BY STATE AND REGIONAL CONCENTRATION

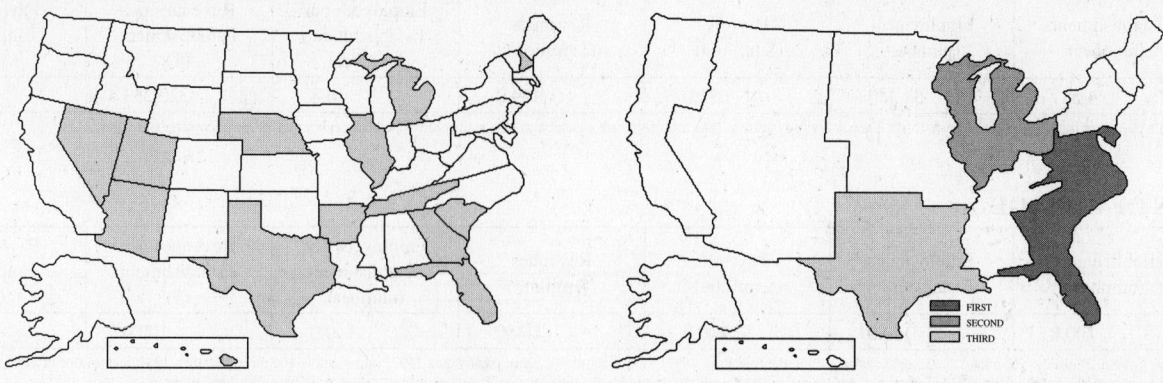

FIRST
SECOND
THIRD

INDUSTRY DATA BY STATE

State	Establishments Total (number)	Establishments % of U.S.	Employment Total (number)	Employment % of U.S.	Employment Per Estab.	Payroll Total ($ mil.)	Payroll Per Empl. ($)	Revenues Total ($ mil.)	Revenues % of U.S.	Revenues Per Estab. ($)
Florida	408	8.6	199,646	22.3	489	3,626.7	18,165	4,497.5	18.6	11,023,314
Texas	464	9.7	106,126	11.9	229	2,726.0	25,686	3,398.4	14.1	7,324,190
California	476	10.0	68,456	7.6	144	1,651.1	24,118	1,991.2	8.3	4,183,183
Illinois	257	5.4	39,870	4.5	155	1,041.8	26,130	1,508.7	6.3	5,870,553
Michigan	405	8.5	40,063	4.5	99	1,173.3	29,287	1,397.0	5.8	3,449,299
Georgia	147	3.1	64,544	7.2	439	1,114.5	17,267	1,282.1	5.3	8,721,939
Arizona	87	1.8	55,618	6.2	639	922.5	16,587	1,056.3	4.4	12,141,713
Ohio	249	5.2	22,565	2.5	91	526.6	23,336	672.9	2.8	2,702,550
New York	214	4.5	25,436	2.8	119	514.1	20,210	640.8	2.7	2,994,374
Utah	70	1.5	19,438	2.2	278	395.8	20,361	554.7	2.3	7,924,029
New Jersey	144	3.0	13,726	1.5	95	388.4	28,300	548.4	2.3	3,808,146
Indiana	113	2.4	15,767	1.8	140	406.4	25,778	539.3	2.2	4,772,637
Tennessee	128	2.7	15,444	1.7	121	370.5	23,987	481.4	2.0	3,761,211
South Carolina	57	1.2	19,646	2.2	345	373.6	19,014	467.8	1.9	8,206,544
Alabama	65	1.4	14,780	1.7	227	306.1	20,709	364.0	1.5	5,599,262
Nebraska	34	0.7	9,581	1.1	282	281.6	29,390	344.0	1.4	10,118,559
North Carolina	85	1.8	13,270	1.5	156	242.6	18,283	337.3	1.4	3,968,306
Massachusetts	89	1.9	7,944	0.9	89	215.5	27,124	312.4	1.3	3,510,652
Minnesota	65	1.4	11,106	1.2	171	234.3	21,097	309.0	1.3	4,753,077
Colorado	84	1.8	9,712	1.1	116	227.3	23,401	267.1	1.1	3,179,357
Arkansas	33	0.7	11,894	1.3	360	217.4	18,275	250.4	1.0	7,587,515
Maryland	63	1.3	7,689	0.9	122	198.3	25,785	244.5	1.0	3,881,429
Oregon	66	1.4	12,401	1.4	188	181.6	14,641	241.0	1.0	3,651,545
Virginia	102	2.1	9,401	1.0	92	178.2	18,956	232.2	1.0	2,276,569
Pennsylvania	146	3.1	10,127	1.1	69	154.3	15,238	200.6	0.8	1,374,253
Missouri	80	1.7	6,276	0.7	78	156.5	24,931	198.1	0.8	2,476,625
Oklahoma	45	0.9	6,017	0.7	134	150.5	25,017	179.8	0.7	3,996,000
New Hampshire	11	0.2	6,905	0.8	628	140.5	20,348	172.4	0.7	15,673,636
Mississippi	38	0.8	6,157	0.7	162	127.1	20,641	151.2	0.6	3,978,316
Hawaii	19	0.4	5,641	0.6	297	100.3	17,779	136.6	0.6	7,190,789
Nevada	32	0.7	3,479	0.4	109	87.0	25,005	134.1	0.6	4,189,469
Louisiana	78	1.6	5,003	0.6	64	98.2	19,632	130.2	0.5	1,669,295
Iowa	38	0.8	4,294	0.5	113	95.6	22,252	124.2	0.5	3,268,658
Wisconsin	71	1.5	4,326	0.5	61	83.9	19,404	100.9	0.4	1,420,845
New Mexico	21	0.4	4,640	0.5	221	87.8	18,923	100.7	0.4	4,794,238
Washington	55	1.2	2,247	0.3	41	59.3	26,390	85.1	0.4	1,547,309
Connecticut	33	0.7	1,741	0.2	53	41.3	23,713	53.5	0.2	1,621,848
West Virginia	33	0.7	1,162	0.1	35	30.0	25,806	47.1	0.2	1,427,515
Kentucky	43	0.9	1,886	0.2	44	26.4	13,998	36.6	0.2	851,698
Idaho	16	0.3	890	0.1	56	21.4	24,038	25.4	0.1	1,586,000
Alaska	8	0.2	475	0.1	59	15.1	31,802	24.6	0.1	3,079,375
Maine	21	0.4	911	0.1	43	18.4	20,161	23.1	0.1	1,100,952
Delaware	11	0.2	294	0.0	27	2.6	8,915	4.3	0.0	392,727
Montana	9	0.2	212	0.0	24	2.6	12,443	3.4	0.0	377,222
North Dakota	3	0.1	110	0.0	37	0.7	6,482	1.0	0.0	329,000
Kansas	22	0.5	3,750*	-	-	(D)	-	(D)	-	-
Rhode Island	16	0.3	3,750*	-	-	(D)	-	(D)	-	-
D.C.	4	0.1	60*	-	-	(D)	-	(D)	-	-
Vermont	4	0.1	60*	-	-	(D)	-	(D)	-	-
South Dakota	3	0.1	375*	-	-	(D)	-	(D)	-	-
Wyoming	1	-	10*	-	-	(D)	-	(D)	-	-

Source: 1997 *Economic Census*. The states are in descending order of revenues or establishments (if revenue data are missing for the majority). The symbol (D) appears when data are withheld to prevent disclosure of competitive information. States marked with (D) are sorted by number of establishments. A dash (-) indicates that the data element cannot be calculated. * indicates the midpoint of a range; 175, for example is the range 100-249. Shaded *states* on the state map indicate those states which have proportionately greater representation in the industry than would be indicated by the state's population; the ratio is based on total revenues or number of establishments. Shaded *regions* indicate where the industry is regionally most concentrated.

NAICS 561410 - DOCUMENT PREPARATION SERVICES

GENERAL STATISTICS

Year	Establishments (number)	Employment (number)	Payroll ($ million)	Revenues ($ million)	Employees per Establishment (number)	Revenues per Establishment ($)	Payroll per Employee ($)
1997	4,587	31,380	625.0	1,469.0	6.8	320,253	19,917

Source: *Economic Census of the United States*, 1997. This is a newly defined industry. Data for prior years were unavailable at the time of publication but may become available over time.

INDICES OF CHANGE

Year	Establishments (number)	Employment (number)	Payroll ($ million)	Revenues ($ million)	Employees per Establishment (number)	Revenues per Establishment ($)	Payroll per Employee ($)
1997	100.0	100.0	100.0	100.0	100.0	100.0	100.0

Sources: Same as General Statistics. The values shown reflect change from the base year, 1997. Values above 100 mean greater than 1997, values below 100 mean less than 1997, and a value of 100 in the 1982-96 or 1998-2001 period means same as 1997. Values followed by a 'p' are projections by the editors; 'e' stands for extrapolation. Data are the most recent available at this level of detail.

SIC INDUSTRIES RELATED TO NAICS 561410

Each new NAICS code represents an industry that used to be part of an SIC or a part of several SIC industries. Data in this table are shown to provide transitional information for these cases. All available data for the precursor SIC(s) are shown. Even if only a part of an SIC is included in the NAICS, *all* data for the SIC are reproduced. If the SIC industry is not marked as being a part (pt) of the NAICS, the entire industry is embedded in the NAICS data. The SIC composition of the new industry provides some hints of the relative importance of its "ancestors." Data marked with a 'p' are projected. Projections begin with 1982 data. Data earlier than 1990 are not shown but are reflected in the projections.

SIC	Industry	1990	1991	1992	1993	1994	1995	1996	1997
2741	**Miscellaneous Publishing (pt)**								
	Establishments (number)	-	-	3,390	-	-	-	-	-
	Employment (thousands)	65.2	65.0	65.4	66.6	71.2	67.4	68.8	-
	Value of Shipments ($ million)	8,874.7	9,762.0	10,977.1	11,806.6	12,332.4	11,992.1	12,510.5	14,309.8*p*
7338	**Secretarial & Court Reporting (pt)**								
	Establishments (number)	5,088	5,584	6,746	7,139	7,349	7,523	7,917*p*	8,294*p*
	Employment (thousands)	25.4	27.7	30.2	32.1	33.0	36.0	37.0*p*	38.7*p*
	Revenues ($ million)	-	-	-	-	-	2,537.0	2,649.0	-
7389	**Business Services, nec (pt)**								
	Establishments (number)	44,079	50,252	52,375	56,829	60,725	53,596	60,893*p*	63,269*p*
	Employment (thousands)	489.6	550.4	523.6	607.9	648.7	623.0	680.2*p*	710.9*p*
	Revenues ($ million)	-	-	32,885.9	-	-	-	-	-

Source: *Economic Census of the United States*, 1992, annual surveys of economic sectors conducted by the Bureau of the Census, and estimates or projections based on the 1982-1992 period; not all data are shown. 'e' marks estimates made by the editors; 'p' indicates projections based on time series. A dash (-) indicates that data for this SIC or year were not available. The abbreviation (pt) next to the industry name indicates that only a part of the industry is present within the NAICS data. If no (pt) is shown, the entire industry is contained within the NAICS data.

SELECTED RATIOS

For 1997	Avg. of Information	Analyzed Industry	Index	For 1997	Avg. of Information	Analyzed Industry	Index
Employees per establishment	27	7	26	Payroll per establishment	496,890	136,255	27
Revenue per establishment	1,070,709	320,253	30	Payroll as % of revenue	46	43	92
Revenue per employee	40,278	46,813	116	Payroll per employee	18,692	19,917	107

Sources: Same as General Statistics. The 'Average' column represents the average for the industry sector, in 1997, where the currently shown industry is classified. The Index shows the relationship between the Average and the Analyzed Industry. For example, 100 means that they are equal; 500 that the Analyzed Industry is five times the average; 50 means that the Analyzed Industry is half the national average. The abbreviation 'na' is used to show that data are 'not available'.

LEADING COMPANIES   Number shown: **11**   Total sales ($ mil): **199**   Total employment (000): **1.5**

Company Name	Address				CEO Name	Phone	Co. Type	Sales ($ mil)	Empl. (000)
Esquire Communications Ltd.	750 B	San Diego	CA	92101	Malcolm L. Elvey	619-515-0811	P	111	0.7
Compex Legal Services Inc.	841 Apollo St	El Segundo	CA	90245	Jeffrey Bachmann	310-726-0000	R	51*	0.5
Kiplinger Washington Editors Inc.	1729 H St NW	Washington	DC	20006	Austin Kiplinger	202-887-6400	R	20*	0.2
Corecomm Inc.	9430 Research Blvd	Austin	TX	78759		512-343-1747	N	6	0.1
Alderson Reporting Company Inc.	1111 14th St N W	Washington	DC	20005	Ira Sharp	202-628-9300	R	5*	<0.1
Office Alternative Company Inc.	3621 Secor Rd	Toledo	OH	43606	Greg Cooke	419-882-9255	R	2*	<0.1
Official Reporters Inc.	211 Liberty St #2	Jacksonville	FL	32202		904-358-2090	R	2*	<0.1
SM Berger and Co.	3201 Enterprise Pky	Beachwood	OH	44122		216-464-6400	N	1	<0.1
Gelles-Cole Literary Enterprises	12 Turner Rd	Pearl River	NY	10965		914-735-1913	N	0	<0.1
Dale Ollila	975 SW 193rd Ct	Beaverton	OR	97006		503-645-7064	N	0	<0.1
Write Job	538 W Sunnyoaks	Campbell	CA	95008		408-370-2855	N	0	<0.1

Source: *Ward's Business Directory of U.S. Private and Public Companies*, Volumes 1 and 2, 2000. The company type code used is as follows: P - Public, R - Private, S - Subsidiary, D - Division, J - Joint Venture, A - Affiliate, G - Group, N - Company type not reported. Sales are in millions of dollars, employees are in thousands. An asterisk (*) indicates an estimated sales volume. The symbol < stands for 'less than'. Company names and addresses are truncated, in some cases, to fit into the available space.

LOCATION BY STATE AND REGIONAL CONCENTRATION

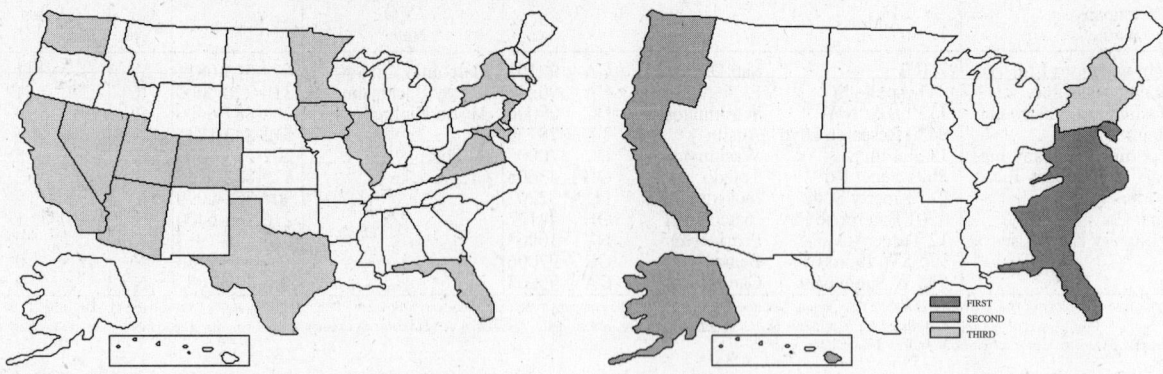

FIRST
SECOND
THIRD

INDUSTRY DATA BY STATE

State	Establishments Total (number)	% of U.S.	Employment Total (number)	% of U.S.	Per Estab.	Payroll Total ($ mil.)	Per Empl. ($)	Revenues Total ($ mil.)	% of U.S.	Per Estab. ($)
California	545	11.9	3,549	11.3	7	87.6	24,680	214.5	14.6	393,516
New York	259	5.6	1,729	5.5	7	45.3	26,199	130.9	8.9	505,320
Texas	314	6.8	2,441	7.8	8	54.9	22,504	129.1	8.8	411,303
Florida	425	9.3	2,119	6.8	5	43.9	20,737	92.7	6.3	218,009
Illinois	240	5.2	1,782	5.7	7	28.1	15,741	78.2	5.3	325,892
New Jersey	170	3.7	1,585	5.1	9	29.8	18,812	68.5	4.7	403,053
Virginia	128	2.8	1,120	3.6	9	25.2	22,456	57.0	3.9	444,930
Pennsylvania	134	2.9	1,189	3.8	9	21.9	18,421	51.4	3.5	383,634
Colorado	120	2.6	987	3.1	8	23.3	23,611	43.4	3.0	361,908
Michigan	141	3.1	1,121	3.6	8	22.0	19,662	42.5	2.9	301,071
Ohio	141	3.1	1,154	3.7	8	18.1	15,724	41.4	2.8	293,624
Arizona	107	2.3	862	2.7	8	15.8	18,376	40.2	2.7	375,617
Georgia	120	2.6	809	2.6	7	19.4	23,949	37.8	2.6	314,900
Maryland	103	2.2	882	2.8	9	18.9	21,380	36.1	2.5	350,757
North Carolina	120	2.6	640	2.0	5	12.1	18,916	31.2	2.1	260,350
Massachusetts	95	2.1	1,201	3.8	13	13.8	11,497	31.0	2.1	326,316
Minnesota	132	2.9	851	2.7	6	14.2	16,745	30.6	2.1	231,652
Washington	148	3.2	870	2.8	6	13.9	15,929	30.5	2.1	206,209
Wisconsin	92	2.0	574	1.8	6	11.0	19,157	24.0	1.6	260,424
Tennessee	56	1.2	511	1.6	9	10.8	21,041	23.5	1.6	420,518
Missouri	88	1.9	461	1.5	5	7.8	16,879	22.1	1.5	250,614
Indiana	79	1.7	348	1.1	4	6.8	19,644	19.1	1.3	241,278
Iowa	26	0.6	307	1.0	12	5.6	18,280	17.2	1.2	662,769
Louisiana	56	1.2	430	1.4	8	5.5	12,763	16.6	1.1	295,625
Oregon	94	2.0	327	1.0	3	5.6	17,003	14.2	1.0	150,649
Utah	33	0.7	394	1.3	12	4.9	12,556	12.9	0.9	390,515
Nevada	42	0.9	336	1.1	8	6.7	20,012	12.8	0.9	304,643
Kentucky	35	0.8	221	0.7	6	3.9	17,769	9.2	0.6	263,086
Alabama	40	0.9	201	0.6	5	3.3	16,637	8.5	0.6	213,125
Rhode Island	19	0.4	190	0.6	10	5.3	27,958	8.5	0.6	447,263
South Carolina	49	1.1	172	0.5	4	3.7	21,331	8.2	0.6	166,592
Oklahoma	47	1.0	128	0.4	3	2.3	17,938	7.1	0.5	151,702
Arkansas	37	0.8	189	0.6	5	3.0	15,624	6.0	0.4	162,378
D.C.	18	0.4	35	0.1	2	1.9	55,000	5.7	0.4	318,389
Maine	27	0.6	155	0.5	6	2.6	16,961	5.4	0.4	199,926
New Hampshire	29	0.6	133	0.4	5	2.1	15,789	5.3	0.4	184,414
West Virginia	20	0.4	154	0.5	8	3.3	21,331	5.2	0.4	259,150
Mississippi	21	0.5	174	0.6	8	2.3	13,167	5.1	0.3	242,190
Nebraska	21	0.5	118	0.4	6	1.8	15,102	3.6	0.2	169,905
Alaska	18	0.4	52	0.2	3	1.0	18,615	3.4	0.2	188,111
Idaho	16	0.3	101	0.3	6	1.3	12,396	3.4	0.2	209,563
Vermont	10	0.2	90	0.3	9	1.4	15,867	2.8	0.2	277,100
New Mexico	16	0.3	44	0.1	3	0.6	13,386	2.4	0.2	148,812
Delaware	11	0.2	25	0.1	2	0.6	25,120	2.0	0.1	178,818
Montana	19	0.4	42	0.1	2	0.6	14,857	1.5	0.1	80,684
Wyoming	7	0.2	12	0.0	2	0.4	35,500	1.4	0.1	201,714
North Dakota	6	0.1	36	0.1	6	0.7	20,278	1.4	0.1	236,500
South Dakota	7	0.2	14	0.0	2	0.3	20,857	0.6	0.0	80,857
Connecticut	52	1.1	175*	-	-	(D)	-	(D)	-	-
Kansas	44	1.0	175*	-	-	(D)	-	(D)	-	-
Hawaii	10	0.2	60*	-	-	(D)	-	(D)	-	-

Source: 1997 *Economic Census*. The states are in descending order of revenues or establishments (if revenue data are missing for the majority). The symbol (D) appears when data are withheld to prevent disclosure of competitive information. States marked with (D) are sorted by number of establishments. A dash (-) indicates that the data element cannot be calculated. * indicates the midpoint of a range; 175, for example is the range 100-249. Shaded *states* on the state map indicate those states which have proportionately greater representation in the industry than would be indicated by the state's population; the ratio is based on total revenues or number of establishments. Shaded *regions* indicate where the industry is regionally most concentrated.

NAICS 561421 - TELEPHONE ANSWERING SERVICES

GENERAL STATISTICS

Year	Establishments (number)	Employment (number)	Payroll ($ million)	Revenues ($ million)	Employees per Establishment (number)	Revenues per Establishment ($)	Payroll per Employee ($)
1997	3,102	56,758	1,106.0	3,810.0	18.3	1,228,240	19,486

Source: *Economic Census of the United States*, 1997. This is a newly defined industry. Data for prior years were unavailable at the time of publication but may become available over time.

INDICES OF CHANGE

Year	Establishments (number)	Employment (number)	Payroll ($ million)	Revenues ($ million)	Employees per Establishment (number)	Revenues per Establishment ($)	Payroll per Employee ($)
1997	100.0	100.0	100.0	100.0	100.0	100.0	100.0

Sources: Same as General Statistics. The values shown reflect change from the base year, 1997. Values above 100 mean greater than 1997, values below 100 mean less than 1997, and a value of 100 in the 1982-96 or 1998-2001 period means same as 1997. Values followed by a 'p' are projections by the editors; 'e' stands for extrapolation. Data are the most recent available at this level of detail.

SIC INDUSTRIES RELATED TO NAICS 561421

Each new NAICS code represents an industry that used to be part of an SIC or a part of several SIC industries. Data in this table are shown to provide transitional information for these cases. All available data for the precursor SIC(s) are shown. Even if only a part of an SIC is included in the NAICS, *all* data for the SIC are reproduced. If the SIC industry is not marked as being a part (pt) of the NAICS, the entire industry is embedded in the NAICS data. The SIC composition of the new industry provides some hints of the relative importance of its "ancestors." Data marked with a 'p' are projected. Projections begin with 1982 data. Data earlier than 1990 are not shown but are reflected in the projections.

SIC	Industry	1990	1991	1992	1993	1994	1995	1996	1997
7389	**Business Services, nec (pt)**								
	Establishments (number)	44,079	50,252	52,375	56,829	60,725	53,596	60,893p	63,269p
	Employment (thousands)	489.6	550.4	523.6	607.9	648.7	623.0	680.2p	710.9p
	Revenues ($ million)	-	-	32,885.9	-	-	-	-	-

Source: *Economic Census of the United States*, 1992, annual surveys of economic sectors conducted by the Bureau of the Census, and estimates or projections based on the 1982-1992 period; not all data are shown. 'e' marks estimates made by the editors; 'p' indicates projections based on time series. A dash (-) indicates that data for this SIC or year were not available. The abbreviation (pt) next to the industry name indicates that only a part of the industry is present within the NAICS data. If no (pt) is shown, the entire industry is contained within the NAICS data.

SELECTED RATIOS

For 1997	Avg. of Information	Analyzed Industry	Index	For 1997	Avg. of Information	Analyzed Industry	Index
Employees per establishment	27	18	69	Payroll per establishment	496,890	356,544	72
Revenue per establishment	1,070,709	1,228,240	115	Payroll as % of revenue	46	29	63
Revenue per employee	40,278	67,127	167	Payroll per employee	18,692	19,486	104

Sources: Same as General Statistics. The 'Average' column represents the average for the industry sector, in 1997, where the currently shown industry is classified. The Index shows the relationship between the Average and the Analyzed Industry. For example, 100 means that they are equal; 500 that the Analyzed Industry is five times the average; 50 means that the Analyzed Industry is half the national average. The abbreviation 'na' is used to show that data are 'not available'.

LEADING COMPANIES

No company data available for this industry.

LOCATION BY STATE AND REGIONAL CONCENTRATION

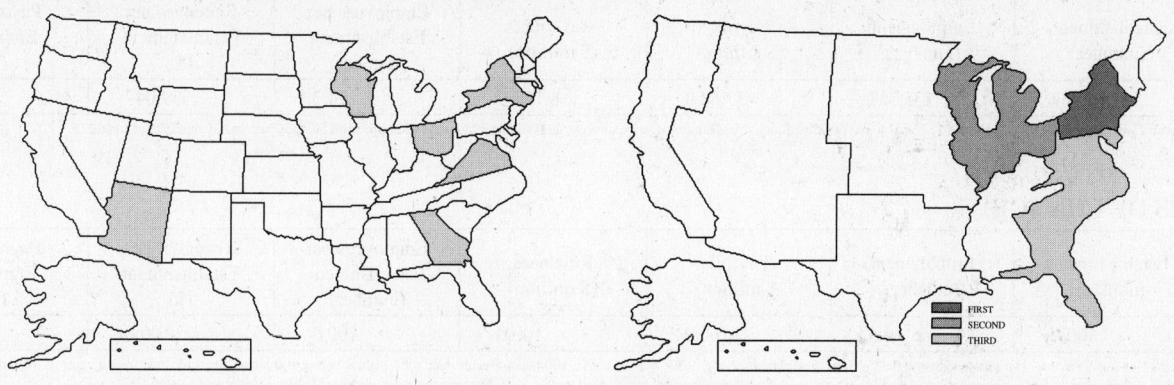

INDUSTRY DATA BY STATE

State	Establishments Total (number)	% of U.S.	Employment Total (number)	% of U.S.	Per Estab.	Payroll Total ($ mil.)	Per Empl. ($)	Revenues Total ($ mil.)	% of U.S.	Per Estab. ($)
New York	200	6.4	3,695	6.5	18	110.6	29,923	892.7	23.4	4,463,605
California	445	14.3	6,744	11.9	15	126.5	18,751	334.7	8.8	752,088
Ohio	115	3.7	3,150	5.5	27	66.1	20,994	185.2	4.9	1,610,296
Pennsylvania	145	4.7	3,153	5.6	22	51.0	16,178	163.1	4.3	1,125,007
Texas	263	8.5	3,625	6.4	14	61.3	16,913	161.0	4.2	612,042
Illinois	114	3.7	1,777	3.1	16	35.3	19,890	159.0	4.2	1,394,886
Wisconsin	40	1.3	1,018	1.8	25	23.5	23,053	150.8	4.0	3,768,925
Florida	203	6.5	3,797	6.7	19	61.7	16,250	135.6	3.6	668,044
Georgia	90	2.9	2,772	4.9	31	47.3	17,058	127.6	3.3	1,417,444
Virginia	67	2.2	1,877	3.3	28	40.9	21,803	103.1	2.7	1,538,746
Arizona	71	2.3	2,760	4.9	39	46.5	16,843	93.2	2.4	1,313,183
New Jersey	110	3.5	1,223	2.2	11	33.4	27,299	73.9	1.9	672,209
Massachusetts	102	3.3	1,305	2.3	13	18.5	14,211	54.2	1.4	531,725
Tennessee	48	1.5	1,035	1.8	22	17.7	17,085	53.5	1.4	1,114,250
Missouri	46	1.5	1,058	1.9	23	13.9	13,172	35.8	0.9	779,239
Oregon	56	1.8	703	1.2	13	16.3	23,119	35.8	0.9	639,607
North Carolina	67	2.2	1,188	2.1	18	17.9	15,095	31.9	0.8	475,687
Michigan	90	2.9	858	1.5	10	13.1	15,238	30.0	0.8	333,522
South Carolina	27	0.9	1,128	2.0	42	16.6	14,737	28.1	0.7	1,041,111
Maryland	50	1.6	816	1.4	16	12.5	15,260	26.7	0.7	534,460
Colorado	57	1.8	699	1.2	12	11.8	16,867	25.6	0.7	449,386
Connecticut	60	1.9	799	1.4	13	11.6	14,573	25.0	0.7	415,983
Washington	43	1.4	463	0.8	11	8.6	18,516	19.5	0.5	454,163
Minnesota	42	1.4	518	0.9	12	7.6	14,670	16.3	0.4	388,619
Nebraska	14	0.5	214	0.4	15	4.9	22,696	15.3	0.4	1,090,929
Iowa	24	0.8	305	0.5	13	4.5	14,839	14.1	0.4	586,375
Nevada	28	0.9	408	0.7	15	5.5	13,426	12.5	0.3	448,143
Kansas	29	0.9	368	0.6	13	5.5	14,826	11.4	0.3	394,276
Kentucky	28	0.9	314	0.6	11	4.8	15,331	9.7	0.3	344,964
Alabama	33	1.1	345	0.6	10	3.9	11,348	8.7	0.2	263,152
Oklahoma	39	1.3	252	0.4	6	3.5	13,730	8.3	0.2	213,795
D.C.	8	0.3	91	0.2	11	3.4	37,363	7.3	0.2	914,375
Mississippi	18	0.6	211	0.4	12	2.8	13,483	6.4	0.2	354,778
Maine	15	0.5	173	0.3	12	2.7	15,676	5.4	0.1	363,200
Arkansas	18	0.6	182	0.3	10	2.4	13,302	5.4	0.1	300,222
New Hampshire	20	0.6	154	0.3	8	2.2	14,344	4.6	0.1	228,750
Idaho	14	0.5	108	0.2	8	1.7	15,343	3.8	0.1	273,071
Montana	11	0.4	138	0.2	13	1.6	11,297	3.3	0.1	300,273
West Virginia	12	0.4	91	0.2	8	1.2	13,077	3.2	0.1	269,583
New Mexico	15	0.5	93	0.2	6	1.2	13,194	3.2	0.1	211,333
Alaska	10	0.3	46	0.1	5	0.8	17,696	1.7	0.0	166,200
Vermont	10	0.3	68	0.1	7	0.8	12,309	1.6	0.0	156,800
North Dakota	7	0.2	50	0.1	7	0.5	9,060	0.9	0.0	132,000
South Dakota	5	0.2	25	0.0	5	0.2	7,720	0.5	0.0	91,800
Indiana	51	1.6	3,750*	-	-	(D)	-	(D)	-	-
Louisiana	50	1.6	750*	-	-	(D)	-	(D)	-	-
Utah	25	0.8	375*	-	-	(D)	-	(D)	-	-
Rhode Island	21	0.7	175*	-	-	(D)	-	(D)	-	-
Hawaii	18	0.6	3,750*	-	-	(D)	-	(D)	-	-
Wyoming	18	0.6	60*	-	-	(D)	-	(D)	-	-
Delaware	10	0.3	60*	-	-	(D)	-	(D)	-	-

Source: 1997 *Economic Census*. The states are in descending order of revenues or establishments (if revenue data are missing for the majority). The symbol (D) appears when data are withheld to prevent disclosure of competitive information. States marked with (D) are sorted by number of establishments. A dash (-) indicates that the data element cannot be calculated. * indicates the midpoint of a range; 175, for example is the range 100-249. Shaded *states* on the state map indicate those states which have proportionately greater representation in the industry than would be indicated by the state's population; the ratio is based on total revenues or number of establishments. Shaded *regions* indicate where the industry is regionally most concentrated.

NAICS 561422 - TELEMARKETING BUREAUS

GENERAL STATISTICS

Year	Establishments (number)	Employment (number)	Payroll ($ million)	Revenues ($ million)	Employees per Establishment (number)	Revenues per Establishment ($)	Payroll per Employee ($)
1997	3,169	235,557	3,468.0	8,173.0	74.3	2,579,047	14,723

Source: Economic Census of the United States, 1997. This is a newly defined industry. Data for prior years were unavailable at the time of publication but may become available over time.

INDICES OF CHANGE

Year	Establishments (number)	Employment (number)	Payroll ($ million)	Revenues ($ million)	Employees per Establishment (number)	Revenues per Establishment ($)	Payroll per Employee ($)
1997	100.0	100.0	100.0	100.0	100.0	100.0	100.0

Sources: Same as General Statistics. The values shown reflect change from the base year, 1997. Values above 100 mean greater than 1997, values below 100 mean less than 1997, and a value of 100 in the 1982-96 or 1998-2001 period means same as 1997. Values followed by a 'p' are projections by the editors; 'e' stands for extrapolation. Data are the most recent available at this level of detail.

SIC INDUSTRIES RELATED TO NAICS 561422

Each new NAICS code represents an industry that used to be part of an SIC or a part of several SIC industries. Data in this table are shown to provide transitional information for these cases. All available data for the precursor SIC(s) are shown. Even if only a part of an SIC is included in the NAICS, *all* data for the SIC are reproduced. If the SIC industry is not marked as being a part (pt) of the NAICS, the entire industry is embedded in the NAICS data. The SIC composition of the new industry provides some hints of the relative importance of its "ancestors." Data marked with a 'p' are projected. Projections begin with 1982 data. Data earlier than 1990 are not shown but are reflected in the projections.

SIC	Industry	1990	1991	1992	1993	1994	1995	1996	1997
7389	**Business Services, nec (pt)**								
	Establishments (number)	44,079	50,252	52,375	56,829	60,725	53,596	60,893p	63,269p
	Employment (thousands)	489.6	550.4	523.6	607.9	648.7	623.0	680.2p	710.9p
	Revenues ($ million)	-	-	32,885.9	-	-	-	-	-

Source: Economic Census of the United States, 1992, annual surveys of economic sectors conducted by the Bureau of the Census, and estimates or projections based on the 1982-1992 period; not all data are shown. 'e' marks estimates made by the editors; 'p' indicates projections based on time series. A dash (-) indicates that data for this SIC or year were not available. The abbreviation (pt) next to the industry name indicates that only a part of the industry is present within the NAICS data. If no (pt) is shown, the entire industry is contained within the NAICS data.

SELECTED RATIOS

For 1997	Avg. of Information	Analyzed Industry	Index	For 1997	Avg. of Information	Analyzed Industry	Index
Employees per establishment	27	74	280	Payroll per establishment	496,890	1,094,352	220
Revenue per establishment	1,070,709	2,579,047	241	Payroll as % of revenue	46	42	91
Revenue per employee	40,278	34,696	86	Payroll per employee	18,692	14,723	79

Sources: Same as General Statistics. The 'Average' column represents the average for the industry sector, in 1997, where the currently shown industry is classified. The Index shows the relationship between the Average and the Analyzed Industry. For example, 100 means that they are equal; 500 that the Analyzed Industry is five times the average; 50 means that the Analyzed Industry is half the national average. The abbreviation 'na' is used to show that data are 'not available'.

LEADING COMPANIES

No company data available for this industry.

LOCATION BY STATE AND REGIONAL CONCENTRATION

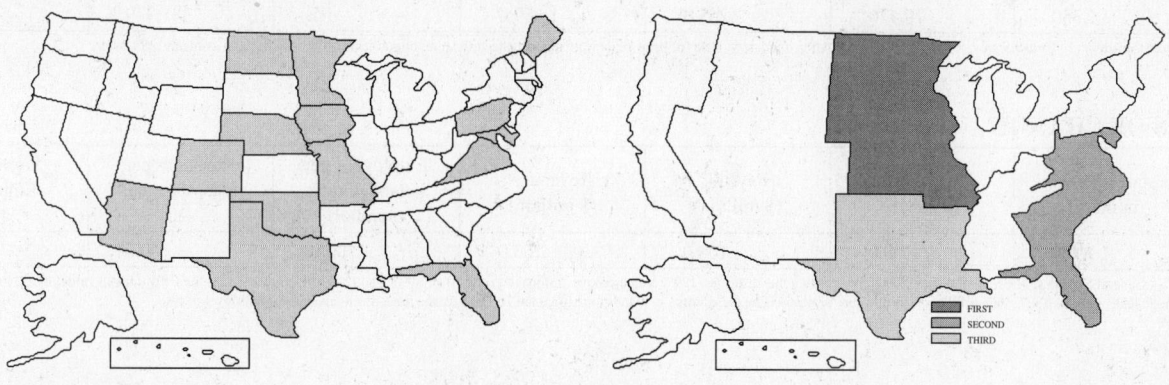

FIRST
SECOND
THIRD

INDUSTRY DATA BY STATE

State	Establishments Total (number)	Establishments % of U.S.	Employment Total (number)	Employment % of U.S.	Employment Per Estab.	Payroll Total ($ mil.)	Payroll Per Empl. ($)	Revenues Total ($ mil.)	Revenues % of U.S.	Revenues Per Estab. ($)
Texas	215	6.8	31,558	13.4	147	441.6	13,993	901.6	11.0	4,193,414
Florida	288	9.1	14,465	6.1	50	302.3	20,897	655.6	8.0	2,276,524
California	296	9.3	12,443	5.3	42	225.0	18,081	539.4	6.6	1,822,412
Missouri	69	2.2	7,427	3.2	108	147.9	19,920	502.5	6.1	7,282,261
Pennsylvania	143	4.5	10,761	4.6	75	141.7	13,171	438.3	5.4	3,064,923
Nebraska	71	2.2	13,834	5.9	195	207.2	14,976	430.8	5.3	6,067,380
Illinois	160	5.0	10,438	4.4	65	163.4	15,652	371.7	4.5	2,323,100
Colorado	85	2.7	11,058	4.7	130	162.1	14,660	356.0	4.4	4,188,824
Maine	15	0.5	3,136	1.3	209	87.6	27,936	331.0	4.1	22,066,600
Iowa	104	3.3	11,901	5.1	114	153.2	12,869	297.2	3.6	2,857,221
Ohio	118	3.7	7,327	3.1	62	99.9	13,629	243.2	3.0	2,061,364
Virginia	63	2.0	7,024	3.0	111	105.2	14,977	241.8	3.0	3,838,778
New Jersey	106	3.3	6,858	2.9	65	91.2	13,305	226.6	2.8	2,137,443
New York	173	5.5	4,811	2.0	28	79.8	16,586	221.0	2.7	1,277,595
Georgia	83	2.6	4,183	1.8	50	65.5	15,664	204.9	2.5	2,469,229
Arizona	100	3.2	8,694	3.7	87	107.9	12,409	194.3	2.4	1,943,390
Maryland	59	1.9	9,231	3.9	156	115.2	12,477	194.3	2.4	3,292,881
Michigan	63	2.0	3,162	1.3	50	43.1	13,617	167.1	2.0	2,652,143
Minnesota	81	2.6	5,781	2.5	71	81.8	14,155	163.3	2.0	2,016,630
Oklahoma	51	1.6	5,894	2.5	116	54.7	9,274	109.5	1.3	2,146,588
Wisconsin	56	1.8	3,720	1.6	66	49.8	13,382	102.4	1.3	1,827,786
Tennessee	52	1.6	3,182	1.4	61	48.6	15,267	95.0	1.2	1,827,673
Connecticut	34	1.1	1,126	0.5	33	23.1	20,501	93.6	1.1	2,753,471
North Carolina	59	1.9	2,907	1.2	49	44.5	15,295	78.1	1.0	1,323,932
Massachusetts	67	2.1	2,575	1.1	38	29.9	11,629	77.2	0.9	1,151,761
Washington	72	2.3	3,802	1.6	53	36.8	9,685	74.6	0.9	1,035,958
Oregon	48	1.5	1,858	0.8	39	26.7	14,397	71.5	0.9	1,490,062
Kansas	41	1.3	4,106	1.7	100	36.3	8,849	70.0	0.9	1,706,415
West Virginia	16	0.5	1,492	0.6	93	10.5	7,014	49.2	0.6	3,072,938
Arkansas	9	0.3	1,142	0.5	127	14.9	13,005	48.5	0.6	5,392,444
North Dakota	25	0.8	1,657	0.7	66	22.5	13,561	46.2	0.6	1,849,120
South Carolina	22	0.7	1,436	0.6	65	20.8	14,458	39.0	0.5	1,771,364
New Hampshire	17	0.5	565	0.2	33	13.9	24,632	31.3	0.4	1,841,765
Nevada	24	0.8	516	0.2	22	9.6	18,578	28.3	0.3	1,178,500
Alabama	46	1.5	911	0.4	20	11.6	12,760	26.4	0.3	574,783
Kentucky	22	0.7	499	0.2	23	5.5	11,078	14.7	0.2	667,864
South Dakota	7	0.2	836	0.4	119	6.6	7,842	13.7	0.2	1,957,286
Idaho	13	0.4	432	0.2	33	4.0	9,366	8.7	0.1	670,846
D.C.	6	0.2	38	0.0	6	1.3	34,447	6.6	0.1	1,105,000
Montana	12	0.4	330	0.1	28	2.1	6,452	5.3	0.1	438,667
New Mexico	15	0.5	129	0.1	9	2.1	16,457	5.3	0.1	350,533
Mississippi	9	0.3	182	0.1	20	1.1	5,978	2.6	0.0	283,667
Vermont	7	0.2	24	0.0	3	0.8	33,750	1.8	0.0	250,000
Indiana	56	1.8	3,750*	-	-	(D)	-	(D)	-	-
Utah	30	0.9	7,500*	-	-	(D)	-	(D)	-	-
Louisiana	29	0.9	750*	-	-	(D)	-	(D)	-	-
Delaware	12	0.4	1,750*	-	-	(D)	-	(D)	-	-
Hawaii	9	0.3	60*	-	-	(D)	-	(D)	-	-
Rhode Island	6	0.2	375*	-	-	(D)	-	(D)	-	-
Wyoming	5	0.2	175*	-	-	(D)	-	(D)	-	-

Source: 1997 *Economic Census*. The states are in descending order of revenues or establishments (if revenue data are missing for the majority). The symbol (D) appears when data are withheld to prevent disclosure of competitive information. States marked with (D) are sorted by number of establishments. A dash (-) indicates that the data element cannot be calculated. * indicates the midpoint of a range; 175, for example is the range 100-249. Shaded *states* on the state map indicate those states which have proportionately greater representation in the industry than would be indicated by the state's population; the ratio is based on total revenues or number of establishments. Shaded *regions* indicate where the industry is regionally most concentrated.

427

NAICS 561431 - PRIVATE MAIL CENTERS

GENERAL STATISTICS

Year	Establishments (number)	Employment (number)	Payroll ($ million)	Revenues ($ million)	Employees per Establishment (number)	Revenues per Establishment ($)	Payroll per Employee ($)
1997	4,350	19,476	265.0	1,659.0	4.5	381,379	13,606

Source: *Economic Census of the United States*, 1997. This is a newly defined industry. Data for prior years were unavailable at the time of publication but may become available over time.

INDICES OF CHANGE

Year	Establishments (number)	Employment (number)	Payroll ($ million)	Revenues ($ million)	Employees per Establishment (number)	Revenues per Establishment ($)	Payroll per Employee ($)
1997	100.0	100.0	100.0	100.0	100.0	100.0	100.0

Sources: Same as General Statistics. The values shown reflect change from the base year, 1997. Values above 100 mean greater than 1997, values below 100 mean less than 1997, and a value of 100 in the 1982-96 or 1998-2001 period means same as 1997. Values followed by a 'p' are projections by the editors; 'e' stands for extrapolation. Data are the most recent available at this level of detail.

SIC INDUSTRIES RELATED TO NAICS 561431

Each new NAICS code represents an industry that used to be part of an SIC or a part of several SIC industries. Data in this table are shown to provide transitional information for these cases. All available data for the precursor SIC(s) are shown. Even if only a part of an SIC is included in the NAICS, *all* data for the SIC are reproduced. If the SIC industry is not marked as being a part (pt) of the NAICS, the entire industry is embedded in the NAICS data. The SIC composition of the new industry provides some hints of the relative importance of its "ancestors." Data marked with a 'p' are projected. Projections begin with 1982 data. Data earlier than 1990 are not shown but are reflected in the projections.

SIC	Industry	1990	1991	1992	1993	1994	1995	1996	1997
7389	**Business Services, nec (pt)**								
	Establishments (number)	44,079	50,252	52,375	56,829	60,725	53,596	60,893p	63,269p
	Employment (thousands)	489.6	550.4	523.6	607.9	648.7	623.0	680.2p	710.9p
	Revenues ($ million)	-	-	32,885.9	-	-	-	-	-

Source: *Economic Census of the United States*, 1992, annual surveys of economic sectors conducted by the Bureau of the Census, and estimates or projections based on the 1982-1992 period; not all data are shown. 'e' marks estimates made by the editors; 'p' indicates projections based on time series. A dash (-) indicates that data for this SIC or year were not available. The abbreviation (pt) next to the industry name indicates that only a part of the industry is present within the NAICS data. If no (pt) is shown, the entire industry is contained within the NAICS data.

SELECTED RATIOS

For 1997	Avg. of Information	Analyzed Industry	Index	For 1997	Avg. of Information	Analyzed Industry	Index
Employees per establishment	27	4	17	Payroll per establishment	496,890	60,920	12
Revenue per establishment	1,070,709	381,379	36	Payroll as % of revenue	46	16	34
Revenue per employee	40,278	85,182	211	Payroll per employee	18,692	13,606	73

Sources: Same as General Statistics. The 'Average' column represents the average for the industry sector, in 1997, where the currently shown industry is classified. The Index shows the relationship between the Average and the Analyzed Industry. For example, 100 means that they are equal; 500 that the Analyzed Industry is five times the average; 50 means that the Analyzed Industry is half the national average. The abbreviation 'na' is used to show that data are 'not available'.

LEADING COMPANIES

No company data available for this industry.

LOCATION BY STATE AND REGIONAL CONCENTRATION

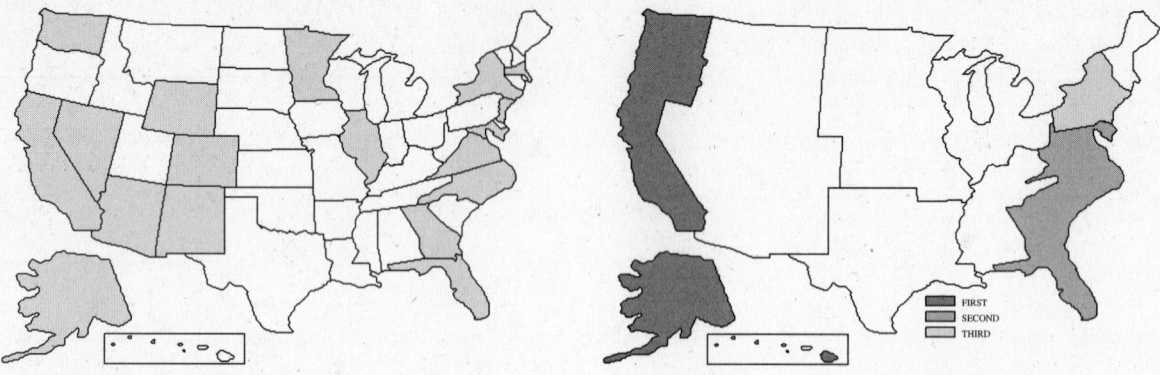

FIRST
SECOND
THIRD

INDUSTRY DATA BY STATE

State	Establishments Total (number)	% of U.S.	Employment Total (number)	% of U.S.	Per Estab.	Payroll Total ($ mil.)	Per Empl. ($)	Revenues Total ($ mil.)	% of U.S.	Per Estab. ($)
California	796	18.3	2,930	15.0	4	35.3	12,054	297.0	17.9	373,121
Florida	363	8.3	1,323	6.8	4	15.6	11,769	122.7	7.4	337,967
New York	191	4.4	1,418	7.3	7	21.7	15,294	119.6	7.2	626,241
Texas	354	8.1	1,473	7.6	4	17.7	12,001	106.3	6.4	300,415
Illinois	138	3.2	852	4.4	6	12.7	14,900	83.1	5.0	602,116
North Carolina	134	3.1	666	3.4	5	8.9	13,365	62.0	3.7	462,679
Minnesota	69	1.6	484	2.5	7	10.6	22,000	57.3	3.5	830,058
Georgia	162	3.7	576	3.0	4	8.4	14,623	55.0	3.3	339,253
New Jersey	116	2.7	771	4.0	7	13.2	17,169	53.8	3.2	463,509
Washington	144	3.3	618	3.2	4	7.4	11,977	50.6	3.0	351,417
Maryland	104	2.4	646	3.3	6	8.1	12,485	48.3	2.9	464,644
Massachusetts	92	2.1	438	2.2	5	9.8	22,324	47.7	2.9	518,663
Virginia	103	2.4	459	2.4	4	11.2	24,495	45.8	2.8	444,670
Colorado	137	3.1	490	2.5	4	6.3	12,863	44.7	2.7	326,372
Michigan	80	1.8	765	3.9	10	9.0	11,824	39.8	2.4	497,188
Arizona	130	3.0	400	2.1	3	4.9	12,195	36.2	2.2	278,485
Pennsylvania	99	2.3	428	2.2	4	5.9	13,895	34.9	2.1	352,101
Nevada	75	1.7	259	1.3	3	2.9	11,286	34.6	2.1	460,747
Ohio	116	2.7	486	2.5	4	7.6	15,578	31.7	1.9	273,440
Missouri	73	1.7	438	2.2	6	6.4	14,701	29.6	1.8	406,027
Indiana	55	1.3	299	1.5	5	4.0	13,502	28.5	1.7	517,909
Oregon	79	1.8	247	1.3	3	2.4	9,850	17.4	1.1	220,658
Connecticut	42	1.0	128	0.7	3	2.7	21,219	16.3	1.0	386,905
Kansas	36	0.8	250	1.3	7	2.4	9,496	14.3	0.9	396,222
New Mexico	45	1.0	194	1.0	4	2.7	13,845	14.1	0.8	312,311
Tennessee	57	1.3	210	1.1	4	2.5	11,914	13.7	0.8	240,509
South Carolina	48	1.1	220	1.1	5	2.5	11,177	12.6	0.8	263,042
Iowa	31	0.7	162	0.8	5	2.2	13,352	11.9	0.7	383,129
Alabama	39	0.9	141	0.7	4	1.7	12,007	10.1	0.6	258,769
Utah	34	0.8	127	0.7	4	1.3	10,220	10.1	0.6	296,118
Oklahoma	45	1.0	145	0.7	3	1.3	9,131	10.1	0.6	225,244
Louisiana	37	0.9	146	0.7	4	1.6	10,925	9.3	0.6	252,676
Wisconsin	32	0.7	108	0.6	3	1.3	11,593	7.3	0.4	228,656
Arkansas	23	0.5	118	0.6	5	1.0	8,881	7.1	0.4	310,609
Hawaii	18	0.4	68	0.3	4	0.8	11,500	6.7	0.4	372,056
New Hampshire	20	0.5	90	0.5	5	1.5	16,267	6.6	0.4	327,600
Idaho	22	0.5	68	0.3	3	0.6	8,647	6.4	0.4	289,182
Kentucky	28	0.6	122	0.6	4	1.0	8,139	6.0	0.4	213,964
Alaska	11	0.3	48	0.2	4	0.7	15,583	5.9	0.4	540,455
Nebraska	23	0.5	91	0.5	4	0.7	7,923	5.3	0.3	230,957
Maine	22	0.5	66	0.3	3	0.8	11,682	5.3	0.3	239,545
Montana	23	0.5	79	0.4	3	0.8	10,291	5.3	0.3	230,478
West Virginia	11	0.3	80	0.4	7	0.8	9,462	4.6	0.3	415,182
D.C.	12	0.3	60	0.3	5	1.0	15,950	4.3	0.3	359,333
Vermont	5	0.1	66	0.3	13	0.7	9,909	3.9	0.2	783,400
Wyoming	13	0.3	55	0.3	4	0.5	8,509	3.5	0.2	270,385
Rhode Island	17	0.4	42	0.2	2	0.5	12,405	3.4	0.2	202,353
Delaware	14	0.3	25	0.1	2	0.4	17,600	2.5	0.1	175,357
Mississippi	15	0.3	30	0.2	2	0.3	9,800	2.4	0.1	161,333
North Dakota	12	0.3	45	0.2	4	0.4	9,600	2.1	0.1	175,500
South Dakota	5	0.1	26	0.1	5	0.2	7,577	1.7	0.1	347,600

Source: 1997 *Economic Census*. The states are in descending order of revenues or establishments (if revenue data are missing for the majority). The symbol (D) appears when data are withheld to prevent disclosure of competitive information. States marked with (D) are sorted by number of establishments. A dash (-) indicates that the data element cannot be calculated. * indicates the midpoint of a range; 175, for example is the range 100-249. Shaded *states* on the state map indicate those states which have proportionately greater representation in the industry than would be indicated by the state's population; the ratio is based on total revenues or number of establishments. Shaded *regions* indicate where the industry is regionally most concentrated.

NAICS 561439 - BUSINESS SERVICE CENTERS (INCLUDING COPY SHOPS) NEC

GENERAL STATISTICS

Year	Establishments (number)	Employment (number)	Payroll ($ million)	Revenues ($ million)	Employees per Establishment (number)	Revenues per Establishment ($)	Payroll per Employee ($)
1997	5,780	87,221	1,811.0	6,844.0	15.1	1,184,083	20,763

Source: *Economic Census of the United States*, 1997. This is a newly defined industry. Data for prior years were unavailable at the time of publication but may become available over time.

INDICES OF CHANGE

Year	Establishments (number)	Employment (number)	Payroll ($ million)	Revenues ($ million)	Employees per Establishment (number)	Revenues per Establishment ($)	Payroll per Employee ($)
1997	100.0	100.0	100.0	100.0	100.0	100.0	100.0

Sources: Same as General Statistics. The values shown reflect change from the base year, 1997. Values above 100 mean greater than 1997, values below 100 mean less than 1997, and a value of 100 in the 1982-96 or 1998-2001 period means same as 1997. Values followed by a 'p' are projections by the editors; 'e' stands for extrapolation. Data are the most recent available at this level of detail.

SIC INDUSTRIES RELATED TO NAICS 561439

Each new NAICS code represents an industry that used to be part of an SIC or a part of several SIC industries. Data in this table are shown to provide transitional information for these cases. All available data for the precursor SIC(s) are shown. Even if only a part of an SIC is included in the NAICS, *all* data for the SIC are reproduced. If the SIC industry is not marked as being a part (pt) of the NAICS, the entire industry is embedded in the NAICS data. The SIC composition of the new industry provides some hints of the relative importance of its "ancestors." Data marked with a 'p' are projected. Projections begin with 1982 data. Data earlier than 1990 are not shown but are reflected in the projections.

SIC	Industry	1990	1991	1992	1993	1994	1995	1996	1997
7334	**Photocopying & Duplicating Services (pt)**								
	Establishments (number)	4,278	4,517	4,949	5,065	5,088	5,141	5,278p	5,400p
	Employment (thousands)	49.6	53.2	58.1	65.1	71.6	79.4	81.2p	86.3p
	Revenues ($ million)	-	-	-	-	-	5,607.0	5,674.0	-
7389	**Business Services, nec (pt)**								
	Establishments (number)	44,079	50,252	52,375	56,829	60,725	53,596	60,893p	63,269p
	Employment (thousands)	489.6	550.4	523.6	607.9	648.7	623.0	680.2p	710.9p
	Revenues ($ million)	-	-	32,885.9	-	-	-	-	-

Source: *Economic Census of the United States*, 1992, annual surveys of economic sectors conducted by the Bureau of the Census, and estimates or projections based on the 1982-1992 period; not all data are shown. 'e' marks estimates made by the editors; 'p' indicates projections based on time series. A dash (-) indicates that data for this SIC or year were not available. The abbreviation (pt) next to the industry name indicates that only a part of the industry is present within the NAICS data. If no (pt) is shown, the entire industry is contained within the NAICS data.

SELECTED RATIOS

For 1997	Avg. of Information	Analyzed Industry	Index	For 1997	Avg. of Information	Analyzed Industry	Index
Employees per establishment	27	15	57	Payroll per establishment	496,890	313,322	63
Revenue per establishment	1,070,709	1,184,083	111	Payroll as % of revenue	46	26	57
Revenue per employee	40,278	78,467	195	Payroll per employee	18,692	20,763	111

Sources: Same as General Statistics. The 'Average' column represents the average for the industry sector, in 1997, where the currently shown industry is classified. The Index shows the relationship between the Average and the Analyzed Industry. For example, 100 means that they are equal; 500 that the Analyzed Industry is five times the average; 50 means that the Analyzed Industry is half the national average. The abbreviation 'na' is used to show that data are 'not available'.

LEADING COMPANIES   Number shown: **32**   Total sales ($ mil): **8,303**   Total employment (000): **77.5**

Company Name	Address				CEO Name	Phone	Co. Type	Sales ($ mil)	Empl. (000)
IKON Office Solutions Inc.	PO Box 834	Valley Forge	PA	19482	James Forese	610-296-8000	P	5,522	39.4
Kinko's Inc.	P O Box 8000	Ventura	CA	93002	Joe Hardin Jj	805-652-4000	R	1,534*	24.0
Merrill Corp.	1 Merrill Cir	Saint Paul	MN	55108	John W Castro	651-646-4501	R	510	3.4
Smart Corp. (Alpharetta, Georgia)	120 Bluegrass Vly	Alpharetta	GA	30005	Tom Brown	770-360-1700	R	221*	3.0
HCC Health Information	226 Arpt Pkwy	San Jose	CA	95110		408-453-1600	S	119*	3.8
TRM Copy Centers Corp.	5208 NE 122nd Ave	Portland	OR	97230	Edward E Cohen	503-257-8766	P	68	0.6
Charrette Corp.	31 Olympia Ave	Woburn	MA	01888	Jack Ford	781-935-6000	R	65	0.7
Compex Legal Services Inc.	841 Apollo St	El Segundo	CA	90245	Jeffrey Bachmann	310-726-0000	R	51*	0.5
FOCUS Direct Inc.	PO Box 17568	San Antonio	TX	78217	Fred Lederman	210-805-9185	R	47	0.5
EMC Corp. (St. Paul, Minnesota)	875 Montreal Way	Saint Paul	MN	55102	David Feinberg	612-290-2800	P	33	0.2
On-Site Sourcing Inc.	1111 N 19th St	Arlington	VA	22209	Christopher J Weiler	703-276-1123	P	26*	0.5
Lazerquick	27375 SW Parkway	Wilsonville	OR	97070	Dave Buel	503-682-1322	R	20	0.3
W & K Consulting Engineers Inc.	PO Box 1345	Eureka	CA	95502	John C Goble	707-443-8326	R	14	0.1
Ginny's Printing and Copying Inc.	1501 W Anderson	Austin	TX	78757	Elizabeth Bradshaw	512-454-6874	R	10	0.1
Campbell Blueprint & Supply Inc.	3124 Broad Ave	Memphis	TN	38112	Richard Campbell	901-327-7385	R	9*	<0.1
Cushing and Company Inc.	325 W Huron St	Chicago	IL	60610	Cathleen Duff	312-266-8228	R	9	<0.1
TCH Group	9801 Old Winery Pl	Sacramento	CA	95827		916-369-6885	P	8*	<0.1
Business Express of Boulder Inc.	1904 Pearl St	Boulder	CO	80302		303-443-9300	S	7*	<0.1
Commercial Graphics Corp.	3014 W 7th St	Los Angeles	CA	90005	James Cherry	213-381-5273	R	7*	<0.1
Image Sensing Systems Inc.	1600 University W	St. Paul	MN	55104	Panos Michalopoulos	651-642-9904	P	5	<0.1
Center Copy	333 W Coffax	Denver	CO	80204	Robert Parella	303-260-7488	R	3*	<0.1
Reprographics Inc.	19 S Wabash Ave	Chicago	IL	60603	Phil Shelton	312-782-2226	S	3*	<0.1
Printing Prep Inc.	12 E Tupper St	Buffalo	NY	14203	Harold Leader	716-852-5011	R	2	<0.1
Illinois Blueprint Corp.	800 S W Jefferson	Peoria	IL	61605	Lynette Smith	309-676-1300	R	2*	<0.1
Valliant Company Inc.	PO Box 2127	Albuquerque	NM	87103	Michael Canfield	505-247-4175	R	2	<0.1
Consolidated Software Services	2365 Paragon Dr	San Jose	CA	95131	Michael S Brown	408-451-0620	R	1	<0.1
Dynamic Reprographics Inc.	1002 W 12th St	Austin	TX	78703	Lisa Tipps	512-474-8842	R	1*	<0.1
HB Digital Arts and HB Blueprint	1615 Alabama St	Huntington Bch	CA	92648	Kristy Selleck	714-536-3939	R	1*	<0.1
On-Line Copy Corp.	48815 Kato Rd	Fremont	CA	94538	Larry Muzinich	510-226-6810	R	1	<0.1
Rapid Print Inc.	6202 NE Hwy 99	Vancouver	WA	98665	Ron McDonald	360-695-6400	R	1*	<0.1
U-Bild Newspaper Features	PO Box 2383	Van Nuys	CA	91409	Kevin Taylor	818-785-6368	R	1*	<0.1
African American Corp.	353 SW Oak St	Portland	OR	97204	Colleen MacKintosh	503-222-2942	R	1	<0.1

Source: Ward's Business Directory of U.S. Private and Public Companies, Volumes 1 and 2, 2000. The company type code used is as follows: P - Public, R - Private, S - Subsidiary, D - Division, J - Joint Venture, A - Affiliate, G - Group, N - Company type not reported. Sales are in millions of dollars, employees are in thousands. An asterisk (*) indicates an estimated sales volume. The symbol < stands for 'less than'. Company names and addresses are truncated, in some cases, to fit into the available space.

LOCATION BY STATE AND REGIONAL CONCENTRATION

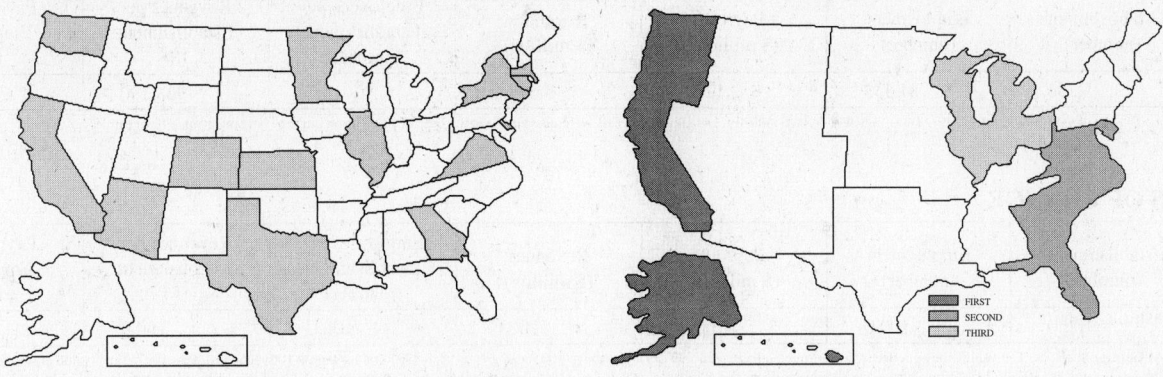

FIRST
SECOND
THIRD

INDUSTRY DATA BY STATE

State	Establishments		Employment			Payroll		Revenues		
	Total (number)	% of U.S.	Total (number)	% of U.S.	Per Estab.	Total ($ mil.)	Per Empl. ($)	Total ($ mil.)	% of U.S.	Per Estab. ($)
California	1,163	20.1	16,945	19.4	15	362.1	21,371	1,339.6	19.6	1,151,832
Texas	445	7.7	6,597	7.6	15	150.0	22,745	551.8	8.1	1,239,978
New York	420	7.3	6,415	7.4	15	172.0	26,814	515.1	7.5	1,226,405
Illinois	248	4.3	3,992	4.6	16	90.2	22,602	364.2	5.3	1,468,710
Pennsylvania	179	3.1	3,371	3.9	19	63.1	18,710	299.2	4.4	1,671,475
Georgia	138	2.4	5,711	6.5	41	109.1	19,097	297.3	4.3	2,154,471
Florida	354	6.1	3,982	4.6	11	83.4	20,939	297.2	4.3	839,619
Ohio	169	2.9	2,744	3.1	16	48.6	17,729	235.9	3.4	1,395,574
Michigan	135	2.3	3,112	3.6	23	64.1	20,588	216.9	3.2	1,606,452
Washington	129	2.2	1,953	2.2	15	39.2	20,076	206.8	3.0	1,602,946
Virginia	166	2.9	2,464	2.8	15	54.3	22,052	197.6	2.9	1,190,440
Massachusetts	140	2.4	2,226	2.6	16	57.2	25,676	183.8	2.7	1,312,914
Minnesota	86	1.5	2,053	2.4	24	36.9	17,972	174.2	2.5	2,025,651
Colorado	131	2.3	1,882	2.2	14	34.2	18,162	161.2	2.4	1,230,908
New Jersey	138	2.4	1,977	2.3	14	48.1	24,319	155.9	2.3	1,129,725
Arizona	115	2.0	1,721	2.0	15	36.1	20,951	153.9	2.2	1,338,548
Missouri	115	2.0	1,761	2.0	15	32.9	18,658	125.0	1.8	1,087,017
Tennessee	116	2.0	1,406	1.6	12	26.4	18,805	112.1	1.6	966,345
Louisiana	85	1.5	1,172	1.3	14	21.3	18,139	109.9	1.6	1,293,247
North Carolina	104	1.8	1,349	1.5	13	26.7	19,818	106.0	1.5	1,019,442
Indiana	73	1.3	1,092	1.3	15	22.5	20,563	104.2	1.5	1,427,685
Connecticut	75	1.3	849	1.0	11	21.1	24,800	100.7	1.5	1,342,213
Maryland	105	1.8	1,187	1.4	11	25.5	21,446	97.6	1.4	929,305
Kansas	47	0.8	727	0.8	15	14.0	19,275	90.5	1.3	1,926,426
Oregon	89	1.5	1,036	1.2	12	18.8	18,176	70.4	1.0	791,472
Wisconsin	81	1.4	883	1.0	11	18.6	21,016	69.7	1.0	860,741
D.C.	53	0.9	1,007	1.2	19	21.3	21,111	57.1	0.8	1,077,340
Oklahoma	70	1.2	845	1.0	12	11.7	13,862	49.9	0.7	712,600
Utah	65	1.1	931	1.1	14	10.9	11,662	48.2	0.7	742,031
Alabama	50	0.9	501	0.6	10	10.3	20,579	38.7	0.6	774,700
Nevada	39	0.7	562	0.6	14	9.7	17,180	34.2	0.5	877,974
Kentucky	35	0.6	553	0.6	16	7.4	13,362	32.2	0.5	920,257
South Carolina	36	0.6	470	0.5	13	7.2	15,323	27.9	0.4	774,000
New Mexico	37	0.6	389	0.4	11	6.7	17,147	27.1	0.4	733,243
Nebraska	30	0.5	350	0.4	12	4.8	13,620	21.1	0.3	703,967
Arkansas	37	0.6	428	0.5	12	4.1	9,549	17.8	0.3	481,297
Delaware	23	0.4	277	0.3	12	4.6	16,747	17.4	0.3	755,174
New Hampshire	23	0.4	236	0.3	10	4.1	17,479	16.1	0.2	702,087
Hawaii	25	0.4	301	0.3	12	4.4	14,551	15.8	0.2	631,920
Rhode Island	21	0.4	270	0.3	13	5.7	21,278	15.8	0.2	751,857
Alaska	27	0.5	234	0.3	9	4.0	17,021	14.9	0.2	550,370
Iowa	30	0.5	235	0.3	8	3.4	14,366	14.5	0.2	482,267
Idaho	20	0.3	205	0.2	10	3.0	14,868	12.4	0.2	622,350
Maine	19	0.3	127	0.1	7	2.4	19,047	9.4	0.1	492,737
Mississippi	24	0.4	138	0.2	6	2.2	15,725	8.2	0.1	342,375
Montana	14	0.2	148	0.2	11	1.9	12,622	7.0	0.1	499,000
West Virginia	22	0.4	164	0.2	7	2.0	12,018	6.8	0.1	309,727
Wyoming	14	0.2	115	0.1	8	1.4	12,017	5.9	0.1	421,786
Vermont	10	0.2	46	0.1	5	1.0	21,130	4.9	0.1	490,400
South Dakota	6	0.1	36	0.0	6	0.5	14,333	2.1	0.0	343,000
North Dakota	4	0.1	46	0.1	11	0.6	13,239	1.9	0.0	486,750

Source: 1997 *Economic Census*. The states are in descending order of revenues or establishments (if revenue data are missing for the majority). The symbol (D) appears when data are withheld to prevent disclosure of competitive information. States marked with (D) are sorted by number of establishments. A dash (-) indicates that the data element cannot be calculated. * indicates the midpoint of a range; 175, for example is the range 100-249. Shaded *states* on the state map indicate those states which have proportionately greater representation in the industry than would be indicated by the state's population; the ratio is based on total revenues or number of establishments. Shaded *regions* indicate where the industry is regionally most concentrated.

NAICS 561440 - COLLECTION AGENCIES

GENERAL STATISTICS

Year	Establishments (number)	Employment (number)	Payroll ($ million)	Revenues ($ million)	Employees per Establishment (number)	Revenues per Establishment ($)	Payroll per Employee ($)
1997	5,250	84,333	2,128.0	5,083.0	16.1	968,190	25,233

Source: *Economic Census of the United States*, 1997. This is a newly defined industry. Data for prior years were unavailable at the time of publication but may become available over time.

INDICES OF CHANGE

Year	Establishments (number)	Employment (number)	Payroll ($ million)	Revenues ($ million)	Employees per Establishment (number)	Revenues per Establishment ($)	Payroll per Employee ($)
1997	100.0	100.0	100.0	100.0	100.0	100.0	100.0

Sources: Same as General Statistics. The values shown reflect change from the base year, 1997. Values above 100 mean greater than 1997, values below 100 mean less than 1997, and a value of 100 in the 1982-96 or 1998-2001 period means same as 1997. Values followed by a 'p' are projections by the editors; 'e' stands for extrapolation. Data are the most recent available at this level of detail.

SIC INDUSTRIES RELATED TO NAICS 561440

Each new NAICS code represents an industry that used to be part of an SIC or a part of several SIC industries. Data in this table are shown to provide transitional information for these cases. All available data for the precursor SIC(s) are shown. Even if only a part of an SIC is included in the NAICS, *all* data for the SIC are reproduced. If the SIC industry is not marked as being a part (pt) of the NAICS, the entire industry is embedded in the NAICS data. The SIC composition of the new industry provides some hints of the relative importance of its "ancestors." Data marked with a 'p' are projected. Projections begin with 1982 data. Data earlier than 1990 are not shown but are reflected in the projections.

SIC	Industry	1990	1991	1992	1993	1994	1995	1996	1997
7322	**Adjustment & Collection Services**								
	Establishments (number)	4,630	4,821	5,814	5,753	5,649	5,542	5,812p	5,934p
	Employment (thousands)	60.5	65.9	71.9	76.1	76.0	78.9	84.3p	88.0p
	Revenues ($ million)	-	-	-	-	-	4,378.0	4,708.0	-
7389	**Business Services, nec (pt)**								
	Establishments (number)	44,079	50,252	52,375	56,829	60,725	53,596	60,893p	63,269p
	Employment (thousands)	489.6	550.4	523.6	607.9	648.7	623.0	680.2p	710.9p
	Revenues ($ million)	-	-	32,885.9	-	-	-	-	-

Source: *Economic Census of the United States*, 1992, annual surveys of economic sectors conducted by the Bureau of the Census, and estimates or projections based on the 1982-1992 period; not all data are shown. 'e' marks estimates made by the editors; 'p' indicates projections based on time series. A dash (-) indicates that data for this SIC or year were not available. The abbreviation (pt) next to the industry name indicates that only a part of the industry is present within the NAICS data. If no (pt) is shown, the entire industry is contained within the NAICS data.

SELECTED RATIOS

For 1997	Avg. of Information	Analyzed Industry	Index	For 1997	Avg. of Information	Analyzed Industry	Index
Employees per establishment	27	16	60	Payroll per establishment	496,890	405,333	82
Revenue per establishment	1,070,709	968,190	90	Payroll as % of revenue	46	42	90
Revenue per employee	40,278	60,273	150	Payroll per employee	18,692	25,233	135

Sources: Same as General Statistics. The 'Average' column represents the average for the industry sector, in 1997, where the currently shown industry is classified. The Index shows the relationship between the Average and the Analyzed Industry. For example, 100 means that they are equal; 500 that the Analyzed Industry is five times the average; 50 means that the Analyzed Industry is half the national average. The abbreviation 'na' is used to show that data are 'not available'.

LEADING COMPANIES   Number shown: **37**   Total sales ($ mil): **1,194**   Total employment (000): **14.2**

Company Name	Address				CEO Name	Phone	Co. Type	Sales ($ mil)	Empl. (000)
NCO Group Inc.	515 Pennsylvania	Fort Washington	PA	19034	Michael J. Barrist	215-793-9300	P	492	7.0
Union Corp.	390 S Woods Mill	Chesterfield	MO	63017	Timothy G Beffa	314-576-0022	P	122	2.0
Allied Bond & Collection Agency	1 Allied Dr	Trevose	PA	19053	Scheldon Zucker	215-639-2100	S	95	0.7
JDR Recovery Corp.	500 N Franklin Tpk	Ramsey	NJ	07446	Neil Hanley	201-818-3800	S	74*	0.9
Transworld Systems Inc.	5880 Commerce	Rohnert Park	CA	94928	George M Macaulay	707-584-4225	S	66	0.4
Healthcare Recoveries Inc.	1400 Watterson Twr	Louisville	KY	40218	Patrick B McGinnis	502-454-1340	P	49	0.5
FMA Enterprises Inc.	11811 N Fwy	Houston	TX	77060	Frank M Souto	281-931-5050	R	39*	0.3
Colonial Commercial Corp.	3601 Hempstead	Levittown	NY	11756	Bernard Korn	516-796-8400	P	25	<0.1
Hospital Billing & Collection	118 Lukens Dr	New Castle	DE	19720	Frank Brynes	302-352-8000	R	24*	0.3
Pioneer Credit Recovery Inc.	674 W Main	Arcade	NY	14009	K Mersmann-Baluf	716-492-5333	R	24*	0.2
Milliken and Michaels Inc.	3850 N Causeway	Metairie	LA	70002	Lou Molettiere	504-834-9900	R	23*	0.2
Source Information Management	11644 Lilburn	Saint Louis	MO	63146	S Leslie Flegel	314-995-9040	P	21	0.5
Region Interstate Billing Inc.	PO Box 2250	Decatur	AL	35602	Paul Crawford	256-260-1190	S	20*	0.1
OSI	8000 Arlington	Jacksonville	FL	32211	Timothy Beffn	314-576-1861	S	15*	0.2
Telecom Services Div.	1500 N W 49th St	Fort Lauderdale	FL	33309		954-491-7800	D	12*	<0.1
Mid-Continent Agencies Inc.	3701 W Algonquin	Roll Meadows	IL	60008	Les Kirschbaum	847-797-1600	D	10	0.2
Continental Credit Adjustors Inc.	P O Box 771748	Houston	TX	77215		713-780-7030	R	9*	<0.1
Health Management Systems	10381 Placerville	Rancho Cordova	CA	95670		916-414-5500	S	8	0.1
Modern Systems International	P O Box 1450	Ellicott City	MD	21041	C F McDonaugh	410-461-0727	R	8*	<0.1
R.C. Wilson Co.	126 S Main St	St. Charles	MO	63301	Micheal Barrist	314-946-6700	S	8*	<0.1
Amsher Collection Services Inc.	1816 3rd Ave N	Birmingham	AL	35203	David Sher	205-322-4110	R	7*	<0.1
People Locator Inc.	P O Box 100699	Fort Lauderdale	FL	33310	Carl D MacBride	954-771-1699	R	7*	<0.1
American Soceity of Travel	1101 King St	Alexandria	VA	22314	Joseph Galloway	703-739-2782	R	6	<0.1
Intercontinental Acceptance Corp.	P O Box 24047	Denver	CO	80224	Joe R Kerr	303-691-6050	R	5	<0.1
Leib and Company Inc.	20000 Horizon Way	Mount Laurel	NJ	08054	Robert Leib	856-439-0555	R	5*	<0.1
CIC Plan Inc.	304 15th St	Des Moines	IA	50309	Doug Phipps	515-243-3113	R	4	<0.1
Betz/Mitchell Associates Inc.	265 Post Ave	Westbury	NY	11590	Joseph Betz	516-745-0161	R	2*	<0.1
Northern California Collection	P O Box 13765	Sacramento	CA	95853	Lawrence Cassidy	916-929-7811	R	2	<0.1
Physicians Professional Billings	110 Old Padonia Rd	Cockeysville	MD	21030	Glen gner	410-825-5626	R	2*	<0.1
Universal Collection Systems	PO Box 11597	Memphis	TN	38111	Larry Pritchett	901-452-8900	R	2	<0.1
URDCO Inc.	PO Box 688	Falls Church	VA	22040		703-237-8600	R	2*	<0.1
Friedman and Associates	100 Owings Ct	Reisterstown	MD	21136		410-526-4500	R	1	<0.1
Medical Credit Bureau Inc.	234 E Gray St	Louisville	KY	40202	Russell F Davidson	502-583-0957	R	1	<0.1
Commtrak Corp.	P O Box 1100	Rehoboth Beach	DE	19971	Gene Wilson	302-644-1600	R	1*	<0.1
T.H. Lehman and Company Inc.	4900 Woodway Dr	Houston	TX	77056		713-621-8404	P	1*	<0.1
Affiliated Management Services	P O Box 40047	Overland Park	KS	66204		913-649-7762	R	1*	<0.1
First Financial Services	P O Box 816	Frankfort	IL	60423	Chuck Patterson	708-747-6875	R	1	<0.1

Source: *Ward's Business Directory of U.S. Private and Public Companies*, Volumes 1 and 2, 2000. The company type code used is as follows: P - Public, R - Private, S - Subsidiary, D - Division, J - Joint Venture, A - Affiliate, G - Group, N - Company type not reported. Sales are in millions of dollars, employees are in thousands. An asterisk (*) indicates an estimated sales volume. The symbol < stands for 'less than'. Company names and addresses are truncated, in some cases, to fit into the available space.

LOCATION BY STATE AND REGIONAL CONCENTRATION

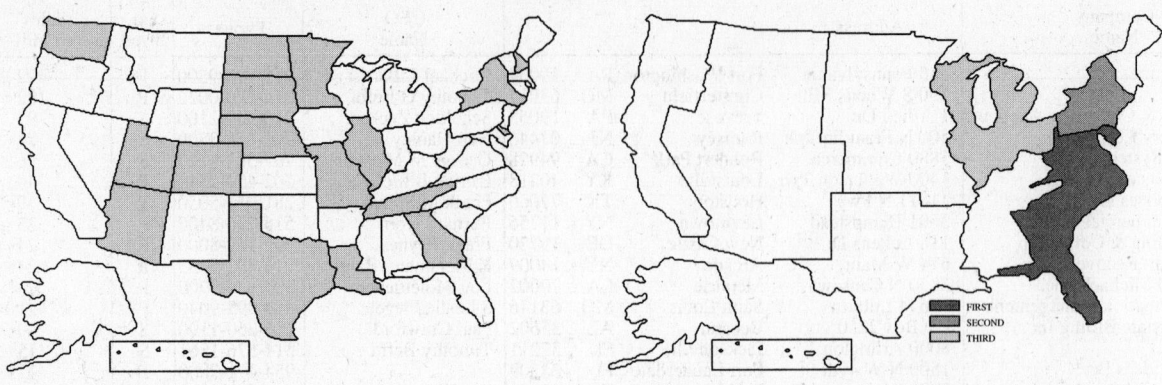

INDUSTRY DATA BY STATE

State	Establishments Total (number)	% of U.S.	Employment Total (number)	% of U.S.	Per Estab.	Payroll Total ($ mil.)	Per Empl. ($)	Revenues Total ($ mil.)	% of U.S.	Per Estab. ($)
California	511	9.7	8,445	10.0	17	228.1	27,014	525.9	10.3	1,029,168
New York	341	6.5	5,807	6.9	17	175.9	30,296	424.0	8.3	1,243,390
Texas	347	6.6	6,665	7.9	19	164.0	24,600	395.7	7.8	1,140,392
Georgia	214	4.1	3,876	4.6	18	105.9	27,335	354.9	7.0	1,658,561
Illinois	243	4.6	4,588	5.4	19	117.8	25,682	266.5	5.2	1,096,601
Florida	322	6.1	4,372	5.2	14	109.7	25,085	253.8	5.0	788,053
Ohio	199	3.8	3,436	4.1	17	80.4	23,394	214.8	4.2	1,079,362
Pennsylvania	231	4.4	3,814	4.5	17	90.2	23,654	200.0	3.9	866,009
Minnesota	125	2.4	3,585	4.3	29	90.2	25,174	192.6	3.8	1,540,992
New Jersey	186	3.5	2,485	2.9	13	68.0	27,353	147.1	2.9	791,065
Arizona	107	2.0	2,589	3.1	24	67.3	25,998	139.9	2.8	1,307,150
Missouri	119	2.3	2,255	2.7	19	54.0	23,937	133.5	2.6	1,122,193
Tennessee	124	2.4	2,322	2.8	19	62.5	26,931	125.8	2.5	1,014,452
Washington	150	2.9	2,320	2.8	15	53.1	22,899	115.6	2.3	770,507
North Carolina	75	1.4	1,635	1.9	22	41.2	25,180	113.5	2.2	1,512,800
Louisiana	102	1.9	1,625	1.9	16	55.2	33,981	107.6	2.1	1,055,167
Michigan	126	2.4	1,774	2.1	14	44.9	25,304	104.6	2.1	830,175
Massachusetts	99	1.9	1,546	1.8	16	42.1	27,229	99.8	2.0	1,008,515
Colorado	122	2.3	1,710	2.0	14	39.0	22,806	97.6	1.9	799,721
Wisconsin	95	1.8	1,194	1.4	13	32.9	27,586	85.5	1.7	900,095
Indiana	139	2.6	1,501	1.8	11	33.2	22,151	82.7	1.6	594,676
Virginia	95	1.8	1,759	2.1	19	33.5	19,067	72.5	1.4	762,968
Maryland	90	1.7	1,160	1.4	13	25.7	22,159	68.9	1.4	765,667
Kentucky	70	1.3	984	1.2	14	25.6	26,048	56.9	1.1	812,900
Oregon	87	1.7	997	1.2	11	24.0	24,045	56.7	1.1	651,483
Oklahoma	83	1.6	996	1.2	12	20.6	20,646	50.1	1.0	603,566
Nebraska	51	1.0	783	0.9	15	17.3	22,091	49.0	1.0	961,725
Alabama	53	1.0	953	1.1	18	18.6	19,491	48.4	1.0	912,321
Iowa	55	1.0	836	1.0	15	19.9	23,780	43.2	0.8	784,782
Utah	64	1.2	711	0.8	11	15.2	21,414	42.9	0.8	669,563
Connecticut	56	1.1	501	0.6	9	15.0	29,944	40.5	0.8	723,589
Delaware	26	0.5	590	0.7	23	17.0	28,744	35.5	0.7	1,366,731
New Hampshire	20	0.4	578	0.7	29	13.5	23,310	32.4	0.6	1,621,000
Arkansas	67	1.3	692	0.8	10	12.6	18,277	28.2	0.6	420,731
Mississippi	50	1.0	487	0.6	10	9.9	20,378	26.8	0.5	536,380
South Carolina	40	0.8	443	0.5	11	10.2	23,129	26.7	0.5	667,825
South Dakota	35	0.7	446	0.5	13	10.2	22,816	23.4	0.5	669,857
North Dakota	27	0.5	365	0.4	14	8.9	24,386	18.9	0.4	701,444
Nevada	30	0.6	328	0.4	11	7.6	23,110	17.4	0.3	579,967
Idaho	46	0.9	341	0.4	7	6.0	17,487	16.4	0.3	356,674
New Mexico	30	0.6	331	0.4	11	6.6	19,985	14.2	0.3	472,200
Montana	34	0.6	217	0.3	6	5.3	24,281	13.7	0.3	404,206
Alaska	19	0.4	188	0.2	10	4.2	22,489	10.2	0.2	535,789
Hawaii	20	0.4	222	0.3	11	4.3	19,554	10.1	0.2	504,800
West Virginia	23	0.4	244	0.3	11	3.7	15,041	8.4	0.2	365,087
Wyoming	17	0.3	127	0.2	7	2.7	21,567	6.7	0.1	391,882
Maine	11	0.2	93	0.1	8	2.7	29,161	5.7	0.1	519,091
Vermont	7	0.1	59	0.1	8	1.2	20,814	4.1	0.1	589,857
Kansas	57	1.1	1,750*	-	-	(D)	-	(D)	-	-
Rhode Island	8	0.2	60*	-	-	(D)	-	(D)	-	-
D.C.	2	-	10*	-	-	(D)	-	(D)	-	-

Source: 1997 *Economic Census*. The states are in descending order of revenues or establishments (if revenue data are missing for the majority). The symbol (D) appears when data are withheld to prevent disclosure of competitive information. States marked with (D) are sorted by number of establishments. A dash (-) indicates that the data element cannot be calculated. * indicates the midpoint of a range; 175, for example is the range 100-249. Shaded *states* on the state map indicate those states which have proportionately greater representation in the industry than would be indicated by the state's population; the ratio is based on total revenues or number of establishments. Shaded *regions* indicate where the industry is regionally most concentrated.

NAICS 561450 - CREDIT BUREAUS*

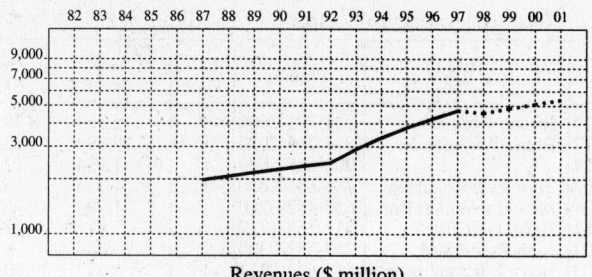

Revenues ($ million)

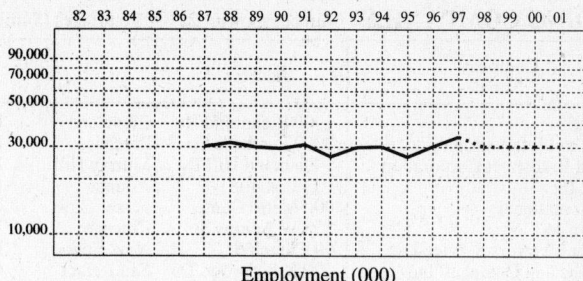

Employment (000)

GENERAL STATISTICS

Year	Establishments (number)	Employment (number)	Payroll ($ million)	Revenues ($ million)	Employees per Establishment (number)	Revenues per Establishment ($)	Payroll per Employee ($)
1982	-	-	-	-	-	-	-
1983	-	-	-	-	-	-	-
1984	-	-	-	-	-	-	-
1985	-	-	-	-	-	-	-
1986	-	-	-	-	-	-	-
1987	1,873	30,186	525.0	1,979.0	16.1	1,056,594	17,392
1988	1,825	31,686	583.0	2,073.0 e	17.4	1,135,890	18,399
1989	1,696	29,932	647.0	2,168.0 e	17.6	1,278,302	21,616
1990	1,663	29,425	689.0	2,262.0 e	17.7	1,360,192	23,415
1991	1,710	30,876	757.0	2,357.0 e	18.1	1,378,363	24,517
1992	1,658	26,585	599.0	2,451.0	16.0	1,478,287	22,532
1993	1,669	29,836	760.0	2,900.0 e	17.9	1,737,567	25,473
1994	1,688	30,131	742.0	3,350.0 e	17.9	1,984,597	24,626
1995	1,645	26,564	750.0	3,800.0 e	16.1	2,310,030	28,234
1996	1,617 e	30,355 e	958.0 e	4,249.0 e	18.8 e	2,627,706 e	31,560 e
1997	1,588	34,146	1,165.0	4,699.0	21.5	2,959,068	34,118
1998	1,563 p	30,233 p	1,022.0 p	4,567.0 p	19.3 p	2,921,945 p	33,804 p
1999	1,541 p	30,277 p	1,069.0 p	4,839.0 p	19.6 p	3,140,169 p	35,307 p
2000	1,519 p	30,320 p	1,115.0 p	5,111.0 p	20.0 p	3,364,714 p	36,774 p
2001	1,497 p	30,363 p	1,162.0 p	5,383.0 p	20.3 p	3,595,858 p	38,270 p

Sources: Economic Census of the United States, 1982, 1987, 1992, 1997. Establishment counts, employment, and payroll are from County Business Patterns for non-Census years. In non-Census years, industries in the Manufacturing range under SIC coding include data from the Annual Survey of Manufactures (ASM); those in the old Services range include data from the Services Annual Survey (SAS). Values followed by a 'p' are projections by the editors. Extrapolations are marked by 'e'. Data are the most recent available at this level of detail.

INDICES OF CHANGE

Year	Establishments (number)	Employment (number)	Payroll ($ million)	Revenues ($ million)	Employees per Establishment (number)	Revenues per Establishment ($)	Payroll per Employee ($)
1982	-	-	-	-	-	-	-
1987	117.9	88.4	45.1	42.1	75.0	35.7	51.0
1992	104.4	77.9	51.4	52.2	74.6	50.0	66.0
1993	105.1	87.4	65.2	61.7 e	83.1	58.7	74.7
1994	106.3	88.2	63.7	71.3 e	83.0	67.1	72.2
1995	103.6	77.8	64.4	80.9 e	75.1	78.1	82.8
1996	101.8 e	88.9 e	82.2 e	90.4 e	87.3 e	88.8 e	92.5 e
1997	100.0	100.0	100.0	100.0	100.0	100.0	100.0
1998	98.4 p	88.5 p	87.7 p	97.2 p	90.0 p	98.7 p	99.1 p
1999	97.0 p	88.7 p	91.8 p	103.0 p	91.4 p	106.1 p	103.5 p
2000	95.7 p	88.8 p	95.7 p	108.8 p	92.8 p	113.7 p	107.8 p
2001	94.3 p	88.9 p	99.7 p	114.6 p	94.3 p	121.5 p	112.2 p

Sources: Same as General Statistics. The values shown reflect change from the base year, 1997. Values above 100 mean greater than 1997, values below 100 mean less than 1997, and a value of 100 in the 1982-96 or 1998-2001 period means same as 1997. Values followed by a 'p' are projections by the editors; 'e' stands for extrapolation. Data are the most recent available at this level of detail.

SELECTED RATIOS

For 1997	Avg. of Information	Analyzed Industry	Index	For 1997	Avg. of Information	Analyzed Industry	Index
Employees per establishment	27	22	81	Payroll per establishment	496,890	733,627	148
Revenue per establishment	1,070,709	2,959,068	276	Payroll as % of revenue	46	25	53
Revenue per employee	40,278	137,615	342	Payroll per employee	18,692	34,118	183

Sources: Same as General Statistics. The 'Average' column represents the average for the industry sector, in 1997, where the currently shown industry is classified. The Index shows the relationship between the Average and the Analyzed Industry. For example, 100 means that they are equal; 500 that the Analyzed Industry is five times the average; 50 means that the Analyzed Industry is half the national average. The abbreviation 'na' is used to show that data are 'not available'.

*Equivalent to SIC 7323.

LEADING COMPANIES Number shown: **25** Total sales ($ mil): **35,093** Total employment (000): **118.5**

Company Name	Address				CEO Name	Phone	Co. Type	Sales ($ mil)	Empl. (000)
TRW Inc.	1900 Richmond Rd	Cleveland	OH	44124	Joseph Gorman	216-291-7000	P	16,969	78.0
MasterCard International Inc.	2000 Purchase St	Purchase	NY	10577	Robert W Selander	914-249-2000	R	10,899	2.4
Dun and Bradstreet Corporation	1 Diamond Hill Rd	Murray Hill	NJ	07974		908-665-5000	P	1,934	12.5
Equifax Inc.	P O Box 4081	Atlanta	GA	30302	Thomas F Chapman	404-885-8000	P	1,773	13.0
Visa International	900 Metro Center	Foster City	CA	94404	Malcolm Williamson	650-432-3200	R	1,700*	5.0
Trans Union Corp.	555 W Adams St	Chicago	IL	60661	Harry Gambill	312-258-1717	S	712*	3.5
Moody's Investors Service Inc.	99 Church St	New York	NY	10007	John Rutherfurd	212-553-0300	S	430	1.5
Fair, Isaac and Company Inc.	120 N Redwood Dr	San Rafael	CA	94903	Larry E Rosenberger	415-472-2211	P	277	0.0
Duff and Phelps Credit Rating Co.	55 E Monroe St	Chicago	IL	60603	Philip T Maffei	312-368-3100	P	92	0.3
SafeCard Services	3001 E Pershing	Cheyenne	WY	82001		307-771-2700	D	86*	0.6
Official Information Co.	250 W 57th St	New York	NY	10109	Ian L M Thomas	212-247-5160	R	81	0.6
Equifax Credit Information	1600 Peachtree	Atlanta	GA	30303		404-885-8000	S	44*	0.2
Credit Data Southwest Inc.	P O Box 2070	Phoenix	AZ	85001	E Clark Huber	602-252-6951	R	29*	0.2
CSC Credit Services Inc.	652 N S Houston	Houston	TX	77060	Bob Denny	281-878-1900	S	16*	0.5
National Information Bureau Ltd.	14 Washington Rd	Princetn Jctn	NJ	08550	Phillip Burgess	609-936-2937	R	15	0.1
LaSalle Business Credit Inc.	135 S LaSalle St	Chicago	IL	60603	Michael D Sharkey	312-263-5454	S	10*	<0.1
Credit Bureau of Baton Rouge Inc.	P O Box 1427	Baton Rouge	LA	70821	Steve Uffman	225-926-6161	R	9*	<0.1
National Tenant Network Inc.	PO Box 1664	Lake Grove	OR	97035	Dennis J Harrington	503-635-1118	R	5*	<0.1
American Tenant Screen Inc.	131 N Narberth Ave	Narberth	PA	19072	Tom Ivory	215-664-2323	R	4*	<0.1
FactaulData	2150 N 107 St	Bellevue	WA	98008	Mike Cahill	206-365-0302	R	2*	<0.1
First Stone Credit Consulting	4416 Spring Valley	Dallas	TX	75244		972-235-1188	R	2*	<0.1
Walnut Financial Services Inc.	8000 Twrs Cres	Vienna	VA	22182	Joel S Kanter	703-448-3771	P	2	<0.1
Kreller Business Information	817 Main St	Cincinnati	OH	45202	JOseph Davidoski	513-723-8900	S	1	<0.1
Health Care Resources Inc.	2755 E Desert Inn	Las Vegas	NV	89121		702-735-5525	R	1*	<0.1
Pathfinder Data Systems Inc.	2104 Oak Ave	Manhattan Bch	CA	90266	Jeffrey G Hunter	310-546-6333	R	0	<0.1

Source: Ward's Business Directory of U.S. Private and Public Companies, Volumes 1 and 2, 2000. The company type code used is as follows: P - Public, R - Private, S - Subsidiary, D - Division, J - Joint Venture, A - Affiliate, G - Group, N - Company type not reported. Sales are in millions of dollars, employees are in thousands. An asterisk (*) indicates an estimated sales volume. The symbol < stands for 'less than'. Company names and addresses are truncated, in some cases, to fit into the available space.

LOCATION BY STATE AND REGIONAL CONCENTRATION

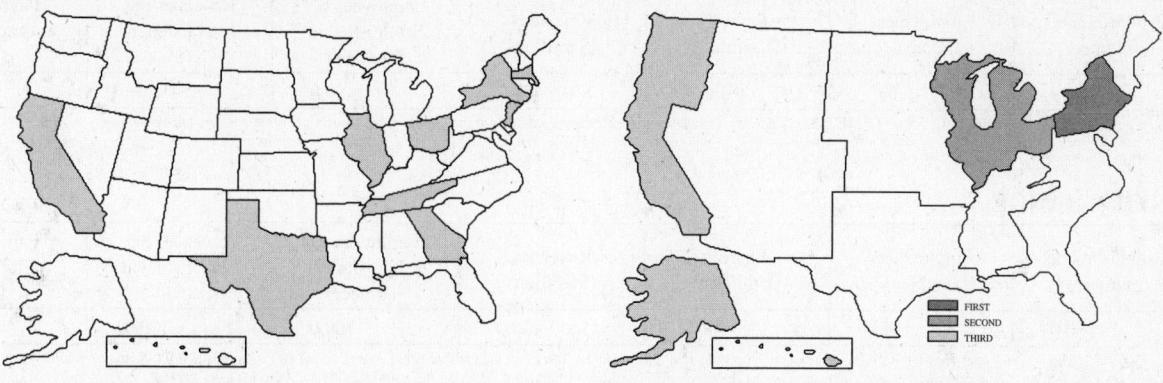

INDUSTRY DATA BY STATE

State	Establishments Total (number)	Establishments % of U.S.	Employment Total (number)	Employment % of U.S.	Employment Per Estab.	Payroll Total ($ mil.)	Payroll Per Empl. ($)	Revenues Total ($ mil.)	Revenues % of U.S.	Revenues Per Estab. ($)
California	193	12.2	4,182	12.2	22	167.3	40,013	700.8	14.9	3,631,212
New York	100	6.3	2,539	7.4	25	163.7	64,466	610.5	13.0	6,104,520
Texas	133	8.4	4,513	13.2	34	147.0	32,565	547.5	11.7	4,116,632
Illinois	73	4.6	2,304	6.7	32	99.0	42,953	495.9	10.6	6,793,288
New Jersey	50	3.1	3,269	9.6	65	103.9	31,788	333.2	7.1	6,664,120
Ohio	58	3.7	2,830	8.3	49	65.8	23,239	253.9	5.4	4,378,155
Georgia	63	4.0	1,392	4.1	22	53.4	38,389	230.6	4.9	3,660,857
Pennsylvania	45	2.8	1,193	3.5	27	35.0	29,319	175.5	3.7	3,898,911
Florida	112	7.1	1,363	4.0	12	35.8	26,255	144.3	3.1	1,288,437
Massachusetts	23	1.4	518	1.5	23	24.3	46,867	115.2	2.5	5,008,348
Tennessee	41	2.6	555	1.6	14	15.2	27,371	96.3	2.1	2,349,951
North Carolina	34	2.1	873	2.6	26	23.4	26,844	81.5	1.7	2,398,500
Michigan	40	2.5	644	1.9	16	23.2	36,064	81.2	1.7	2,028,850
Minnesota	31	2.0	650	1.9	21	16.3	25,026	78.0	1.7	2,515,871
Maryland	27	1.7	382	1.1	14	12.4	32,482	59.3	1.3	2,196,111
Oregon	23	1.4	439	1.3	19	10.5	23,986	51.9	1.1	2,256,478
Connecticut	17	1.1	381	1.1	22	16.6	43,622	51.1	1.1	3,006,059
Virginia	21	1.3	237	0.7	11	9.2	38,987	49.3	1.0	2,346,286
Arizona	32	2.0	467	1.4	15	13.2	28,358	42.5	0.9	1,329,125
Washington	36	2.3	444	1.3	12	12.1	27,270	41.9	0.9	1,163,833
Missouri	29	1.8	308	0.9	11	9.6	31,071	40.2	0.9	1,386,897
Kansas	24	1.5	435	1.3	18	9.8	22,513	35.7	0.8	1,488,292
Louisiana	24	1.5	357	1.0	15	10.3	28,964	31.9	0.7	1,328,875
Colorado	34	2.1	728	2.1	21	8.3	11,462	30.4	0.6	893,471
Indiana	27	1.7	270	0.8	10	7.0	26,074	29.4	0.6	1,087,704
Utah	21	1.3	315	0.9	15	7.3	23,302	25.1	0.5	1,194,857
Alabama	25	1.6	272	0.8	11	6.4	23,537	23.7	0.5	948,560
South Carolina	16	1.0	103	0.3	6	2.5	24,680	23.3	0.5	1,458,437
Wisconsin	20	1.3	233	0.7	12	6.6	28,189	22.8	0.5	1,142,250
Oklahoma	25	1.6	174	0.5	7	4.1	23,437	21.0	0.4	838,160
Iowa	14	0.9	163	0.5	12	4.2	25,521	18.0	0.4	1,284,786
Kentucky	20	1.3	195	0.6	10	4.3	21,800	17.7	0.4	886,500
Nebraska	11	0.7	50	0.1	5	1.7	33,620	15.4	0.3	1,396,182
Mississippi	12	0.8	119	0.3	10	2.7	22,891	13.0	0.3	1,084,667
Nevada	22	1.4	156	0.5	7	4.1	26,224	12.4	0.3	564,818
New Hampshire	6	0.4	71	0.2	12	1.9	26,944	9.6	0.2	1,606,167
New Mexico	14	0.9	122	0.4	9	2.6	21,377	9.3	0.2	661,000
Maine	6	0.4	93	0.3	15	3.1	33,355	9.2	0.2	1,535,500
Idaho	9	0.6	136	0.4	15	4.1	29,978	9.1	0.2	1,012,667
West Virginia	9	0.6	96	0.3	11	1.7	17,417	7.5	0.2	833,889
Arkansas	15	0.9	83	0.2	6	1.8	21,807	5.4	0.1	361,067
Alaska	5	0.3	30	0.1	6	0.8	27,233	4.3	0.1	855,400
Wyoming	6	0.4	77	0.2	13	1.5	19,766	2.9	0.1	477,333
Montana	8	0.5	27	0.1	3	0.6	20,741	1.9	0.0	243,250
Rhode Island	12	0.8	175*	-	-	(D)	-	(D)	-	-
Delaware	6	0.4	60*	-	-	(D)	-	(D)	-	-
Hawaii	5	0.3	60*	-	-	(D)	-	(D)	-	-
North Dakota	4	0.3	60*	-	-	(D)	-	(D)	-	-
South Dakota	3	0.2	60*	-	-	(D)	-	(D)	-	-
D.C.	2	0.1	10*	-	-	(D)	-	(D)	-	-
Vermont	2	0.1	60*	-	-	(D)	-	(D)	-	-

Source: 1997 *Economic Census.* The states are in descending order of revenues or establishments (if revenue data are missing for the majority). The symbol (D) appears when data are withheld to prevent disclosure of competitive information. States marked with (D) are sorted by number of establishments. A dash (-) indicates that the data element cannot be calculated. * indicates the midpoint of a range; 175, for example is the range 100-249. Shaded *states* on the state map indicate those states which have proportionately greater representation in the industry than would be indicated by the state's population; the ratio is based on total revenues or number of establishments. Shaded *regions* indicate where the industry is regionally most concentrated.

NAICS 561491 - REPOSSESSION SERVICES

GENERAL STATISTICS

Year	Establishments (number)	Employment (number)	Payroll ($ million)	Revenues ($ million)	Employees per Establishment (number)	Revenues per Establishment ($)	Payroll per Employee ($)
1997	899	5,692	141.0	487.0	6.3	541,713	24,772

Source: *Economic Census of the United States*, 1997. This is a newly defined industry. Data for prior years were unavailable at the time of publication but may become available over time.

INDICES OF CHANGE

Year	Establishments (number)	Employment (number)	Payroll ($ million)	Revenues ($ million)	Employees per Establishment (number)	Revenues per Establishment ($)	Payroll per Employee ($)
1997	100.0	100.0	100.0	100.0	100.0	100.0	100.0

Sources: Same as General Statistics. The values shown reflect change from the base year, 1997. Values above 100 mean greater than 1997, values below 100 mean less than 1997, and a value of 100 in the 1982-96 or 1998-2001 period means same as 1997. Values followed by a 'p' are projections by the editors; 'e' stands for extrapolation. Data are the most recent available at this level of detail.

SIC INDUSTRIES RELATED TO NAICS 561491

Each new NAICS code represents an industry that used to be part of an SIC or a part of several SIC industries. Data in this table are shown to provide transitional information for these cases. All available data for the precursor SIC(s) are shown. Even if only a part of an SIC is included in the NAICS, *all* data for the SIC are reproduced. If the SIC industry is not marked as being a part (pt) of the NAICS, the entire industry is embedded in the NAICS data. The SIC composition of the new industry provides some hints of the relative importance of its "ancestors." Data marked with a 'p' are projected. Projections begin with 1982 data. Data earlier than 1990 are not shown but are reflected in the projections.

SIC	Industry	1990	1991	1992	1993	1994	1995	1996	1997
7389	**Business Services, nec (pt)**								
	Establishments (number)	44,079	50,252	52,375	56,829	60,725	53,596	60,893p	63,269p
	Employment (thousands)	489.6	550.4	523.6	607.9	648.7	623.0	680.2p	710.9p
	Revenues ($ million)	-	-	32,885.9	-	-	-	-	-

Source: *Economic Census of the United States*, 1992, annual surveys of economic sectors conducted by the Bureau of the Census, and estimates or projections based on the 1982-1992 period; not all data are shown. 'e' marks estimates made by the editors; 'p' indicates projections based on time series. A dash (-) indicates that data for this SIC or year were not available. The abbreviation (pt) next to the industry name indicates that only a part of the industry is present within the NAICS data. If no (pt) is shown, the entire industry is contained within the NAICS data.

SELECTED RATIOS

For 1997	Avg. of Information	Analyzed Industry	Index	For 1997	Avg. of Information	Analyzed Industry	Index
Employees per establishment	27	6	24	Payroll per establishment	496,890	156,841	32
Revenue per establishment	1,070,709	541,713	51	Payroll as % of revenue	46	29	62
Revenue per employee	40,278	85,559	212	Payroll per employee	18,692	24,772	133

Sources: Same as General Statistics. The 'Average' column represents the average for the industry sector, in 1997, where the currently shown industry is classified. The Index shows the relationship between the Average and the Analyzed Industry. For example, 100 means that they are equal; 500 that the Analyzed Industry is five times the average; 50 means that the Analyzed Industry is half the national average. The abbreviation 'na' is used to show that data are 'not available'.

LEADING COMPANIES

No company data available for this industry.

LOCATION BY STATE AND REGIONAL CONCENTRATION

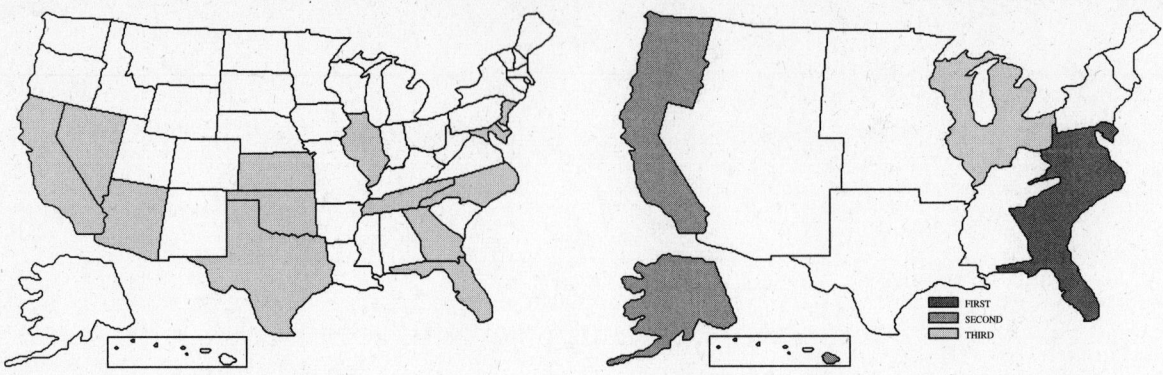

INDUSTRY DATA BY STATE

State	Establishments Total (number)	Establishments % of U.S.	Employment Total (number)	Employment % of U.S.	Employment Per Estab.	Payroll Total ($ mil.)	Payroll Per Empl. ($)	Revenues Total ($ mil.)	Revenues % of U.S.	Revenues Per Estab. ($)
California	127	14.1	866	15.2	7	22.9	26,433	68.3	14.0	537,835
Texas	82	9.1	517	9.1	6	12.1	23,412	44.8	9.2	546,476
Florida	68	7.6	294	5.2	4	7.2	24,320	29.7	6.1	436,868
Arizona	14	1.6	505	8.9	36	10.1	20,085	28.6	5.9	2,045,214
New York	53	5.9	303	5.3	6	7.7	25,290	26.1	5.4	492,094
Georgia	41	4.6	155	2.7	4	4.1	26,329	22.8	4.7	556,098
Illinois	33	3.7	240	4.2	7	8.0	33,350	22.7	4.7	689,061
Maryland	17	1.9	149	2.6	9	3.8	25,255	18.7	3.8	1,100,706
New Jersey	30	3.3	174	3.1	6	4.8	27,770	18.3	3.8	609,367
Tennessee	23	2.6	193	3.4	8	6.6	34,306	17.1	3.5	745,174
Kansas	11	1.2	112	2.0	10	2.4	21,125	14.2	2.9	1,288,727
Ohio	28	3.1	263	4.6	9	5.5	20,821	14.1	2.9	504,500
North Carolina	31	3.4	180	3.2	6	5.0	27,544	13.0	2.7	420,613
Michigan	27	3.0	152	2.7	6	3.9	25,553	12.9	2.6	476,815
Virginia	26	2.9	165	2.9	6	4.3	25,818	12.4	2.5	475,692
Massachusetts	13	1.4	72	1.3	6	3.5	47,986	9.2	1.9	710,385
Indiana	17	1.9	80	1.4	5	2.1	26,325	8.1	1.7	476,647
Pennsylvania	24	2.7	94	1.7	4	2.0	21,468	7.8	1.6	324,125
Washington	16	1.8	78	1.4	5	1.9	24,731	6.8	1.4	424,375
Oklahoma	15	1.7	69	1.2	5	1.6	23,058	6.4	1.3	426,800
Alabama	16	1.8	83	1.5	5	2.1	25,265	6.4	1.3	400,063
Missouri	16	1.8	94	1.7	6	2.2	23,223	6.4	1.3	397,375
Minnesota	7	0.8	41	0.7	6	1.0	24,122	5.5	1.1	781,143
Colorado	15	1.7	60	1.1	4	1.3	22,367	5.5	1.1	363,400
South Carolina	14	1.6	96	1.7	7	1.9	19,500	5.3	1.1	379,357
Nevada	15	1.7	78	1.4	5	1.7	22,154	4.7	1.0	316,000
Utah	14	1.6	80	1.4	6	1.0	12,325	3.4	0.7	241,929
Oregon	14	1.6	45	0.8	3	0.9	19,489	3.2	0.7	229,214
Mississippi	5	0.6	26	0.5	5	0.7	25,192	3.1	0.6	628,000
New Mexico	11	1.2	43	0.8	4	0.8	18,907	3.1	0.6	284,000
Kentucky	8	0.9	31	0.5	4	0.9	30,129	3.1	0.6	389,750
Iowa	4	0.4	43	0.8	11	0.7	15,465	1.5	0.3	381,000
Wisconsin	4	0.4	19	0.3	5	0.5	28,684	1.4	0.3	342,750
Maine	4	0.4	11	0.2	3	0.3	24,818	1.2	0.2	288,000
Idaho	7	0.8	14	0.2	2	0.3	18,786	0.9	0.2	134,143
Montana	4	0.4	18	0.3	5	0.2	13,500	0.9	0.2	222,250
Nebraska	4	0.4	12	0.2	3	0.2	16,583	0.8	0.2	198,500
Delaware	4	0.4	42	0.7	10	0.2	5,214	0.6	0.1	138,500
Vermont	3	0.3	6	0.1	2	0.1	12,667	0.3	0.1	83,333
Louisiana	8	0.9	60*	-	-	(D)	-	(D)	-	-
Arkansas	6	0.7	60*	-	-	(D)	-	(D)	-	-
Connecticut	6	0.7	60*	-	-	(D)	-	(D)	-	-
New Hampshire	3	0.3	10*	-	-	(D)	-	(D)	-	-
Alaska	2	0.2	10*	-	-	(D)	-	(D)	-	-
West Virginia	2	0.2	10*	-	-	(D)	-	(D)	-	-
Wyoming	2	0.2	10*	-	-	(D)	-	(D)	-	-
D.C.	1	0.1	10*	-	-	(D)	-	(D)	-	-
Hawaii	1	0.1	10*	-	-	(D)	-	(D)	-	-
North Dakota	1	0.1	10*	-	-	(D)	-	(D)	-	-
Rhode Island	1	0.1	10*	-	-	(D)	-	(D)	-	-
South Dakota	1	0.1	10*	-	-	(D)	-	(D)	-	-

Source: 1997 *Economic Census*. The states are in descending order of revenues or establishments (if revenue data are missing for the majority). The symbol (D) appears when data are withheld to prevent disclosure of competitive information. States marked with (D) are sorted by number of establishments. A dash (-) indicates that the data element cannot be calculated. * indicates the midpoint of a range; 175, for example is the range 100-249. Shaded *states* on the state map indicate those states which have proportionately greater representation in the industry than would be indicated by the state's population; the ratio is based on total revenues or number of establishments. Shaded *regions* indicate where the industry is regionally most concentrated.

NAICS 561492 - COURT REPORTING AND STENOTYPE SERVICES

GENERAL STATISTICS

Year	Establishments (number)	Employment (number)	Payroll ($ million)	Revenues ($ million)	Employees per Establishment (number)	Revenues per Establishment ($)	Payroll per Employee ($)
1997	3,097	15,447	411.0	1,349.0	5.0	435,583	26,607

Source: Economic Census of the United States, 1997. This is a newly defined industry. Data for prior years were unavailable at the time of publication but may become available over time.

INDICES OF CHANGE

Year	Establishments (number)	Employment (number)	Payroll ($ million)	Revenues ($ million)	Employees per Establishment (number)	Revenues per Establishment ($)	Payroll per Employee ($)
1997	100.0	100.0	100.0	100.0	100.0	100.0	100.0

Sources: Same as General Statistics. The values shown reflect change from the base year, 1997. Values above 100 mean greater than 1997, values below 100 mean less than 1997, and a value of 100 in the 1982-96 or 1998-2001 period means same as 1997. Values followed by a 'p' are projections by the editors; 'e' stands for extrapolation. Data are the most recent available at this level of detail.

SIC INDUSTRIES RELATED TO NAICS 561492

Each new NAICS code represents an industry that used to be part of an SIC or a part of several SIC industries. Data in this table are shown to provide transitional information for these cases. All available data for the precursor SIC(s) are shown. Even if only a part of an SIC is included in the NAICS, *all* data for the SIC are reproduced. If the SIC industry is not marked as being a part (pt) of the NAICS, the entire industry is embedded in the NAICS data. The SIC composition of the new industry provides some hints of the relative importance of its "ancestors." Data marked with a 'p' are projected. Projections begin with 1982 data. Data earlier than 1990 are not shown but are reflected in the projections.

SIC	Industry	1990	1991	1992	1993	1994	1995	1996	1997
7338	**Secretarial & Court Reporting (pt)**								
	Establishments (number)	5,088	5,584	6,746	7,139	7,349	7,523	7,917p	8,294p
	Employment (thousands)	25.4	27.7	30.2	32.1	33.0	36.0	37.0p	38.7p
	Revenues ($ million)	-	-	-	-	-	2,537.0	2,649.0	-

Source: Economic Census of the United States, 1992, annual surveys of economic sectors conducted by the Bureau of the Census, and estimates or projections based on the 1982-1992 period; not all data are shown. 'e' marks estimates made by the editors; 'p' indicates projections based on time series. A dash (-) indicates that data for this SIC or year were not available. The abbreviation (pt) next to the industry name indicates that only a part of the industry is present within the NAICS data. If no (pt) is shown, the entire industry is contained within the NAICS data.

SELECTED RATIOS

For 1997	Avg. of Information	Analyzed Industry	Index	For 1997	Avg. of Information	Analyzed Industry	Index
Employees per establishment	27	5	19	Payroll per establishment	496,890	132,709	27
Revenue per establishment	1,070,709	435,583	41	Payroll as % of revenue	46	30	66
Revenue per employee	40,278	87,331	217	Payroll per employee	18,692	26,607	142

Sources: Same as General Statistics. The 'Average' column represents the average for the industry sector, in 1997, where the currently shown industry is classified. The Index shows the relationship between the Average and the Analyzed Industry. For example, 100 means that they are equal; 500 that the Analyzed Industry is five times the average; 50 means that the Analyzed Industry is half the national average. The abbreviation 'na' is used to show that data are 'not available'.

LEADING COMPANIES

No company data available for this industry.

LOCATION BY STATE AND REGIONAL CONCENTRATION

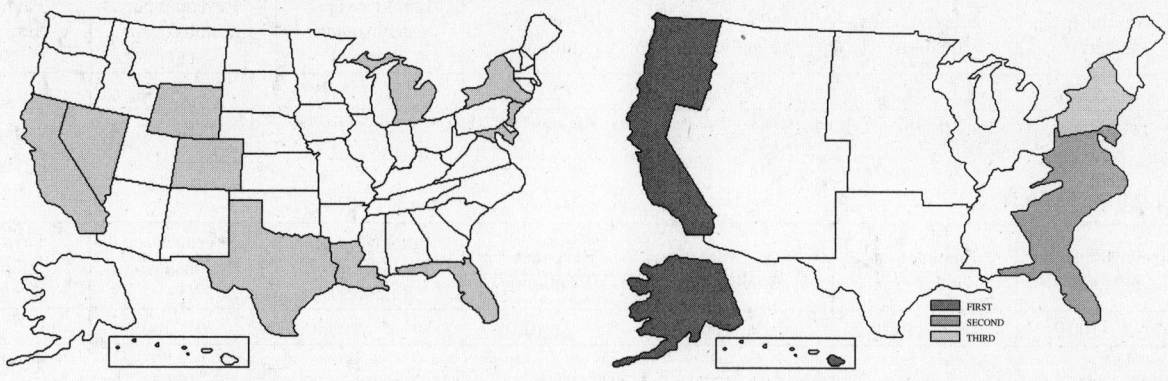

INDUSTRY DATA BY STATE

State	Establishments Total (number)	% of U.S.	Employment Total (number)	% of U.S.	Per Estab.	Payroll Total ($ mil.)	Per Empl. ($)	Revenues Total ($ mil.)	% of U.S.	Per Estab. ($)
California	381	12.3	2,675	17.3	7	68.9	25,740	252.9	18.8	663,869
Florida	428	13.8	1,365	8.8	3	34.9	25,536	132.1	9.8	308,614
Texas	258	8.3	1,644	10.6	6	48.6	29,538	128.9	9.6	499,686
New York	145	4.7	1,163	7.5	8	33.6	28,900	123.7	9.2	852,766
Pennsylvania	102	3.3	762	4.9	7	19.7	25,913	57.9	4.3	567,990
Illinois	141	4.6	466	3.0	3	12.6	26,968	56.3	4.2	399,454
New Jersey	83	2.7	395	2.6	5	15.4	39,046	55.8	4.1	672,253
Michigan	119	3.8	487	3.2	4	14.9	30,641	51.1	3.8	429,697
Ohio	99	3.2	660	4.3	7	19.2	29,156	46.2	3.4	466,778
Maryland	44	1.4	344	2.2	8	8.2	23,927	31.0	2.3	703,727
Louisiana	85	2.7	204	1.3	2	5.1	24,882	27.6	2.0	324,541
Massachusetts	44	1.4	132	0.9	3	5.3	40,439	26.8	2.0	608,318
Georgia	79	2.6	451	2.9	6	12.7	28,111	26.2	1.9	331,734
D.C.	17	0.5	386	2.5	23	13.0	33,785	25.7	1.9	1,511,824
Virginia	77	2.5	280	1.8	4	7.8	27,914	22.5	1.7	292,312
Alabama	35	1.1	143	0.9	4	4.7	33,098	21.9	1.6	625,143
Colorado	53	1.7	378	2.4	7	11.0	29,167	20.6	1.5	388,321
Arizona	76	2.5	146	0.9	2	3.4	23,562	18.1	1.3	238,171
Washington	62	2.0	224	1.5	4	4.6	20,415	16.1	1.2	260,242
Missouri	43	1.4	177	1.1	4	5.2	29,650	14.8	1.1	344,233
Nevada	24	0.8	74	0.5	3	1.6	22,041	14.2	1.1	593,042
Minnesota	62	2.0	165	1.1	3	3.3	20,061	13.5	1.0	217,823
Wisconsin	41	1.3	262	1.7	6	7.0	26,737	12.4	0.9	302,561
Oklahoma	68	2.2	108	0.7	2	2.3	21,657	11.9	0.9	175,706
Indiana	42	1.4	103	0.7	2	2.6	25,146	11.9	0.9	283,714
North Carolina	53	1.7	188	1.2	4	3.4	18,106	11.5	0.9	217,038
Tennessee	35	1.1	122	0.8	3	3.0	24,451	8.8	0.7	250,600
Oregon	24	0.8	153	1.0	6	3.9	25,575	7.9	0.6	328,708
New Mexico	30	1.0	117	0.8	4	2.9	24,906	7.8	0.6	258,367
Kentucky	34	1.1	524	3.4	15	3.0	5,656	7.5	0.6	220,676
Iowa	28	0.9	153	1.0	5	3.3	21,837	6.6	0.5	235,821
South Carolina	26	0.8	94	0.6	4	1.9	19,681	6.1	0.4	232,808
West Virginia	21	0.7	78	0.5	4	2.4	31,308	5.0	0.4	236,952
Utah	24	0.8	74	0.5	3	1.2	16,689	4.9	0.4	205,583
Nebraska	19	0.6	76	0.5	4	1.3	17,553	2.9	0.2	152,105
Idaho	10	0.3	37	0.2	4	0.6	16,216	2.8	0.2	279,500
Wyoming	11	0.4	45	0.3	4	1.1	23,533	2.2	0.2	196,636
Kansas	29	0.9	175*	-	-	(D)	-	(D)	-	-
Connecticut	17	0.5	60*	-	-	(D)	-	(D)	-	-
Maine	16	0.5	60*	-	-	(D)	-	(D)	-	-
Mississippi	16	0.5	60*	-	-	(D)	-	(D)	-	-
Montana	14	0.5	60*	-	-	(D)	-	(D)	-	-
Alaska	13	0.4	60*	-	-	(D)	-	(D)	-	-
Hawaii	13	0.4	60*	-	-	(D)	-	(D)	-	-
Arkansas	12	0.4	60*	-	-	(D)	-	(D)	-	-
Rhode Island	11	0.4	60*	-	-	(D)	-	(D)	-	-
Delaware	7	0.2	60*	-	-	(D)	-	(D)	-	-
North Dakota	7	0.2	10*	-	-	(D)	-	(D)	-	-
South Dakota	7	0.2	10*	-	-	(D)	-	(D)	-	-
Vermont	7	0.2	60*	-	-	(D)	-	(D)	-	-
New Hampshire	5	0.2	10*	-	-	(D)	-	(D)	-	-

Source: 1997 *Economic Census*. The states are in descending order of revenues or establishments (if revenue data are missing for the majority). The symbol (D) appears when data are withheld to prevent disclosure of competitive information. States marked with (D) are sorted by number of establishments. A dash (-) indicates that the data element cannot be calculated. * indicates the midpoint of a range; 175, for example is the range 100-249. Shaded *states* on the state map indicate those states which have proportionately greater representation in the industry than would be indicated by the state's population; the ratio is based on total revenues or number of establishments. Shaded *regions* indicate where the industry is regionally most concentrated.

NAICS 561499 - BUSINESS SUPPORT SERVICES NEC

GENERAL STATISTICS

Year	Establishments (number)	Employment (number)	Payroll ($ million)	Revenues ($ million)	Employees per Establishment (number)	Revenues per Establishment ($)	Payroll per Employee ($)
1997	1,098	34,565	780.0	2,453.0	31.5	2,234,062	22,566

Source: *Economic Census of the United States*, 1997. This is a newly defined industry. Data for prior years were unavailable at the time of publication but may become available over time.

INDICES OF CHANGE

Year	Establishments (number)	Employment (number)	Payroll ($ million)	Revenues ($ million)	Employees per Establishment (number)	Revenues per Establishment ($)	Payroll per Employee ($)
1997	100.0	100.0	100.0	100.0	100.0	100.0	100.0

Sources: Same as General Statistics. The values shown reflect change from the base year, 1997. Values above 100 mean greater than 1997, values below 100 mean less than 1997, and a value of 100 in the 1982-96 or 1998-2001 period means same as 1997. Values followed by a 'p' are projections by the editors; 'e' stands for extrapolation. Data are the most recent available at this level of detail.

SIC INDUSTRIES RELATED TO NAICS 561499

Each new NAICS code represents an industry that used to be part of an SIC or a part of several SIC industries. Data in this table are shown to provide transitional information for these cases. All available data for the precursor SIC(s) are shown. Even if only a part of an SIC is included in the NAICS, *all* data for the SIC are reproduced. If the SIC industry is not marked as being a part (pt) of the NAICS, the entire industry is embedded in the NAICS data. The SIC composition of the new industry provides some hints of the relative importance of its "ancestors." Data marked with a 'p' are projected. Projections begin with 1982 data. Data earlier than 1990 are not shown but are reflected in the projections.

SIC	Industry	1990	1991	1992	1993	1994	1995	1996	1997
7389	**Business Services, nec (pt)**								
	Establishments (number)	44,079	50,252	52,375	56,829	60,725	53,596	60,893*p*	63,269*p*
	Employment (thousands)	489.6	550.4	523.6	607.9	648.7	623.0	680.2*p*	710.9*p*
	Revenues ($ million)	-	-	32,885.9	-	-	-	-	-

Source: *Economic Census of the United States*, 1992, annual surveys of economic sectors conducted by the Bureau of the Census, and estimates or projections based on the 1982-1992 period; not all data are shown. 'e' marks estimates made by the editors; 'p' indicates projections based on time series. A dash (-) indicates that data for this SIC or year were not available. The abbreviation (pt) next to the industry name indicates that only a part of the industry is present within the NAICS data. If no (pt) is shown, the entire industry is contained within the NAICS data.

SELECTED RATIOS

For 1997	Avg. of Information	Analyzed Industry	Index	For 1997	Avg. of Information	Analyzed Industry	Index
Employees per establishment	27	31	118	Payroll per establishment	496,890	710,383	143
Revenue per establishment	1,070,709	2,234,062	209	Payroll as % of revenue	46	32	69
Revenue per employee	40,278	70,968	176	Payroll per employee	18,692	22,566	121

Sources: Same as General Statistics. The 'Average' column represents the average for the industry sector, in 1997, where the currently shown industry is classified. The Index shows the relationship between the Average and the Analyzed Industry. For example, 100 means that they are equal; 500 that the Analyzed Industry is five times the average; 50 means that the Analyzed Industry is half the national average. The abbreviation 'na' is used to show that data are 'not available'.

LEADING COMPANIES
No company data available for this industry.

LOCATION BY STATE AND REGIONAL CONCENTRATION

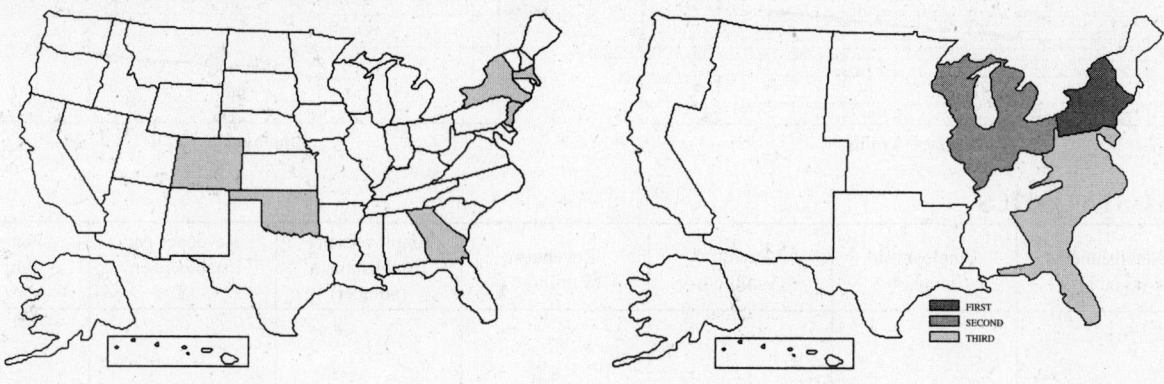

FIRST
SECOND
THIRD

INDUSTRY DATA BY STATE

State	Establishments Total (number)	% of U.S.	Employment Total (number)	% of U.S.	Per Estab.	Payroll Total ($ mil.)	Per Empl. ($)	Revenues Total ($ mil.)	% of U.S.	Per Estab. ($)
New York	82	7.5	3,284	9.5	40	58.1	17,688	191.4	7.8	2,333,585
California	142	12.9	1,898	5.5	13	48.4	25,477	182.3	7.4	1,283,972
New Jersey	46	4.2	957	2.8	21	28.8	30,133	172.2	7.0	3,743,043
Illinois	53	4.8	1,767	5.1	33	37.6	21,273	108.8	4.4	2,053,755
Texas	73	6.6	2,242	6.5	31	41.4	18,468	107.1	4.4	1,467,589
Colorado	30	2.7	872	2.5	29	28.9	33,100	95.6	3.9	3,185,233
Georgia	30	2.7	720	2.1	24	22.4	31,043	91.5	3.7	3,050,300
Massachusetts	30	2.7	640	1.9	21	29.9	46,675	87.4	3.6	2,911,833
Florida	71	6.5	899	2.6	13	16.7	18,552	66.4	2.7	934,676
Ohio	38	3.5	1,072	3.1	28	22.4	20,905	63.4	2.6	1,669,000
Oklahoma	15	1.4	537	1.6	36	13.7	25,601	57.6	2.3	3,839,267
Wisconsin	18	1.6	556	1.6	31	11.8	21,302	44.9	1.8	2,492,444
Virginia	29	2.6	705	2.0	24	18.1	25,606	41.9	1.7	1,446,000
Tennessee	21	1.9	977	2.8	47	18.7	19,126	41.3	1.7	1,967,286
Michigan	29	2.6	293	0.8	10	9.0	30,556	41.2	1.7	1,420,931
Washington	27	2.5	455	1.3	17	11.2	24,514	39.8	1.6	1,475,148
Maryland	27	2.5	335	1.0	12	9.7	28,842	37.0	1.5	1,371,852
Minnesota	20	1.8	658	1.9	33	13.7	20,798	35.2	1.4	1,759,400
Arizona	19	1.7	410	1.2	22	10.6	25,971	28.0	1.1	1,471,474
Pennsylvania	41	3.7	564	1.6	14	9.7	17,191	25.6	1.0	623,512
Missouri	21	1.9	350	1.0	17	5.0	14,400	22.5	0.9	1,072,762
Kentucky	12	1.1	341	1.0	28	5.7	16,754	20.8	0.8	1,730,500
Indiana	20	1.8	225	0.7	11	3.5	15,716	17.8	0.7	889,500
Nebraska	9	0.8	186	0.5	21	3.8	20,570	13.4	0.5	1,487,889
North Carolina	20	1.8	290	0.8	15	3.4	11,752	12.5	0.5	626,600
Iowa	11	1.0	219	0.6	20	3.5	15,808	12.2	0.5	1,112,182
Alabama	7	0.6	252	0.7	36	3.7	14,623	11.9	0.5	1,706,429
Oregon	15	1.4	207	0.6	14	3.6	17,232	11.6	0.5	770,333
Nevada	12	1.1	126	0.4	10	1.9	14,937	8.0	0.3	664,917
New Mexico	10	0.9	67	0.2	7	1.1	16,373	7.2	0.3	720,300
Idaho	5	0.5	83	0.2	17	1.4	16,325	6.1	0.2	1,214,000
Rhode Island	7	0.6	71	0.2	10	1.3	18,958	4.0	0.2	565,571
Utah	5	0.5	50	0.1	10	1.1	21,040	2.8	0.1	563,400
Vermont	5	0.5	45	0.1	9	0.9	19,533	1.9	0.1	370,800
South Carolina	9	0.8	50	0.1	6	0.7	14,180	1.6	0.1	182,222
Connecticut	21	1.9	17,500*	-	-	(D)	-	(D)	-	-
Kansas	16	1.5	750*	-	-	(D)	-	(D)	-	-
Louisiana	11	1.0	60*	-	-	(D)	-	(D)	-	-
New Hampshire	7	0.6	60*	-	-	(D)	-	(D)	-	-
Arkansas	6	0.5	60*	-	-	(D)	-	(D)	-	-
D.C.	5	0.5	60*	-	-	(D)	-	(D)	-	-
Hawaii	4	0.4	175*	-	-	(D)	-	(D)	-	-
West Virginia	4	0.4	60*	-	-	(D)	-	(D)	-	-
Mississippi	3	0.3	60*	-	-	(D)	-	(D)	-	-
North Dakota	3	0.3	375*	-	-	(D)	-	(D)	-	-
South Dakota	3	0.3	60*	-	-	(D)	-	(D)	-	-
Delaware	2	0.2	60*	-	-	(D)	-	(D)	-	-
Maine	2	0.2	10*	-	-	(D)	-	(D)	-	-
Montana	1	0.1	10*	-	-	(D)	-	(D)	-	-
Wyoming	1	0.1	10*	-	-	(D)	-	(D)	-	-

Source: 1997 *Economic Census*. The states are in descending order of revenues or establishments (if revenue data are missing for the majority). The symbol (D) appears when data are withheld to prevent disclosure of competitive information. States marked with (D) are sorted by number of establishments. A dash (-) indicates that the data element cannot be calculated. * indicates the midpoint of a range; 175, for example is the range 100-249. Shaded *states* on the state map indicate those states which have proportionately greater representation in the industry than would be indicated by the state's population; the ratio is based on total revenues or number of establishments. Shaded *regions* indicate where the industry is regionally most concentrated.

NAICS 561510 - TRAVEL AGENCIES*

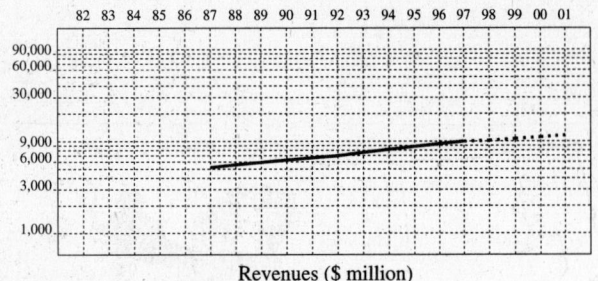

Revenues ($ million)

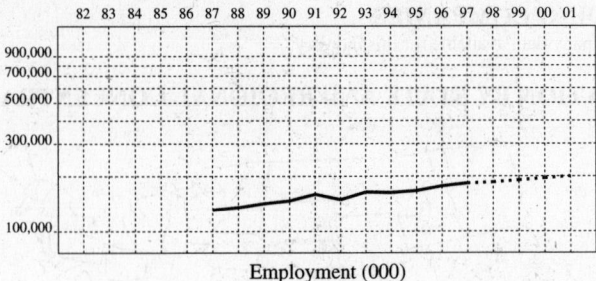

Employment (000)

GENERAL STATISTICS

Year	Establishments (number)	Employment (number)	Payroll ($ million)	Revenues ($ million)	Employees per Establishment (number)	Revenues per Establishment ($)	Payroll per Employee ($)
1982	-	-	-	-	-	-	-
1983	-	-	-	-	-	-	-
1984	-	-	-	-	-	-	-
1985	-	-	-	-	-	-	-
1986	-	-	-	-	-	-	-
1987	23,185	131,131	2,010.0	5,220.0	5.7	225,146	15,328
1988	22,609	135,030	2,435.0	5,569.0	6.0	246,318	18,033
1989	22,847	141,953	2,496.0	5,918.0	6.2	259,027	17,583
1990	22,737	146,877	2,759.0	6,266.0	6.5	275,586	18,784
1991	24,266	159,475	3,099.0	6,615.0	6.6	272,604	19,433
1992	27,688	149,140	2,836.0	6,964.0	5.4	251,517	19,016
1993	27,900	163,844	3,454.0	7,567.0 e	5.9	271,219	21,081
1994	28,118	162,795	3,521.0	8,170.0 e	5.8	290,561	21,628
1995	28,099	166,613	3,642.0	8,772.0 e	5.9	312,182	21,859
1996	28,735	176,699	4,471.0	9,375.0 e	6.1	326,257	25,303
1997	29,332	183,178	4,464.0	9,977.0	6.2	340,140	24,370
1998	30,614 p	185,363 p	4,602.0 p	10,165.0 p	6.1 p	332,038 p	24,827 p
1999	31,390 p	190,246 p	4,836.0 p	10,640.0 p	6.1 p	338,961 p	25,420 p
2000	32,166 p	195,128 p	5,070.0 p	11,116.0 p	6.1 p	345,582 p	25,983 p
2001	32,943 p	200,011 p	5,304.0 p	11,592.0 p	6.1 p	351,881 p	26,519 p

Sources: *Economic Census of the United States*, 1982, 1987, 1992, 1997. Establishment counts, employment, and payroll are from *County Business Patterns* for non-Census years. In non-Census years, industries in the Manufacturing range under SIC coding include data from the *Annual Survey of Manufactures* (ASM); those in the old Services range include data from the *Services Annual Survey* (SAS). Values followed by a 'p' are projections by the editors. Extrapolations are marked by 'e'. Data are the most recent available at this level of detail.

INDICES OF CHANGE

Year	Establishments (number)	Employment (number)	Payroll ($ million)	Revenues ($ million)	Employees per Establishment (number)	Revenues per Establishment ($)	Payroll per Employee ($)
1982	-	-	-	-	-	-	-
1987	79.0	71.6	45.0	52.3	90.6	66.2	62.9
1992	94.4	81.4	63.5	69.8	86.3	73.9	78.0
1993	95.1	89.4	77.4	75.8 e	94.0	79.7	86.5
1994	95.9	88.9	78.9	81.9 e	92.7	85.4	88.8
1995	95.8	91.0	81.6	87.9 e	94.9	91.8	89.7
1996	98.0	96.5	100.2	94.0 e	98.5	95.9	103.8
1997	100.0	100.0	100.0	100.0	100.0	100.0	100.0
1998	104.4 p	101.2 p	103.1 p	101.9 p	97.0 p	97.6 p	101.9 p
1999	107.0 p	103.9 p	108.3 p	106.6 p	97.0 p	99.7 p	104.3 p
2000	109.7 p	106.5 p	113.6 p	111.4 p	97.1 p	101.6 p	106.6 p
2001	112.3 p	109.2 p	118.8 p	116.2 p	97.2 p	103.5 p	108.8 p

Sources: Same as General Statistics. The values shown reflect change from the base year, 1997. Values above 100 mean greater than 1997, values below 100 mean less than 1997, and a value of 100 in the 1982-96 or 1998-2001 period means same as 1997. Values followed by a 'p' are projections by the editors; 'e' stands for extrapolation. Data are the most recent available at this level of detail.

SELECTED RATIOS

For 1997	Avg. of Information	Analyzed Industry	Index	For 1997	Avg. of Information	Analyzed Industry	Index
Employees per establishment	27	6	23	Payroll per establishment	496,890	152,189	31
Revenue per establishment	1,070,709	340,140	32	Payroll as % of revenue	46	45	96
Revenue per employee	40,278	54,466	135	Payroll per employee	18,692	24,370	130

Sources: Same as General Statistics. The 'Average' column represents the average for the industry sector, in 1997, where the currently shown industry is classified. The Index shows the relationship between the Average and the Analyzed Industry. For example, 100 means that they are equal; 500 that the Analyzed Industry is five times the average; 50 means that the Analyzed Industry is half the national average. The abbreviation 'na' is used to show that data are 'not available'.

*Equivalent to SIC 4724.

LEADING COMPANIES   Number shown: **18**   Total sales ($ mil): **24,378**   Total employment (000): **86.8**

Company Name	Address				CEO Name	Phone	Co. Type	Sales ($ mil)	Empl. (000)
American Express Company	AmEx Twr	New York	NY	10285	Ken Chenault	212-640-2000	S	15,428*	65.0
World Travel Partners L.P.	1055 Lenox Park	Atlanta	GA	30319	John Alexander	404-841-6600	R	3,300	5.0
Vacation Break U.S.A. Inc.	6400 N Andrews	Fort Lauderdale	FL	33309	Jim Berk	954-351-8500	D	1,715*	1.8
Galileo International Inc.	9700 W Higgins Rd	Rosemont	IL	60018	James E Barlett	847-518-4000	P	1,526	3.0
Amtran Inc.	P O Box 51609	Indianapolis	IN	46251	John P Tague	317-247-4000	P	1,122	7.0
Northwestern Travel Management	7250 Metro Blvd	Minneapolis	MN	55431	John Noble	612-921-3700	R	700*	0.7
Rail Europe Holding	500 Mamaroneck	Harrison	NY	10528		914-682-2999	R	191*	0.2
Robustelli Corporate Services Ltd.	460 Summer St	Stamford	CT	06901	Rick Robustelli	203-352-0500	R	94*	0.2
AAA Auto Club South	1515 N W Shore	Tampa	FL	33607	Robert R Sharp	813-289-5000	R	90*	3.0
Travel Industry Services Inc.	1106 Clayton Ln	Austin	TX	78723	Damir Bogdanic	512-467-1707	R	52	0.2
Worldwide Assistance Services	1133 15th St	Washington	DC	20005	John Shanley	202-331-1609	R	48*	<0.1
Dozano Enterprises Inc.	320 S W Stark St	Portland	OR	97204	Sho G Dozano	503-223-6245	R	47*	0.2
Rainbow Holding Company Inc.	PO Box 60128	Oklahoma City	OK	73146	Jay Musgrove	405-528-5741	R	19*	<0.1
Vasquez Group Inc.	100 S Greenleaf Ave	Gurnee	IL	60031	Mary Vasquez	847-249-1900	R	16	0.2
Travelocity.com	747 Front St	San Francisco	CA	94111	Kenneth J Orton	415-439-1200	P	14*	0.2
Leading Travel Agencies Group	5454 Wisconsin	Chevy Chase	MD	20815		301-656-1300	R	12*	<0.1
Gary Musick Productions Inc.	PO Box 1000	Page	AZ	86040	Gary S Musick	615-259-2400	R	3	<0.1
Local Arrangements Ltd.	515 E Houston	San Antonio	TX	78205	Marie Pauerstein	210-224-3061	R	1*	<0.1

Source: *Ward's Business Directory of U.S. Private and Public Companies*, Volumes 1 and 2, 2000. The company type code used is as follows: P - Public, R - Private, S - Subsidiary, D - Division, J - Joint Venture, A - Affiliate, G - Group, N - Company type not reported. Sales are in millions of dollars, employees are in thousands. An asterisk (*) indicates an estimated sales volume. The symbol < stands for 'less than'. Company names and addresses are truncated, in some cases, to fit into the available space.

LOCATION BY STATE AND REGIONAL CONCENTRATION

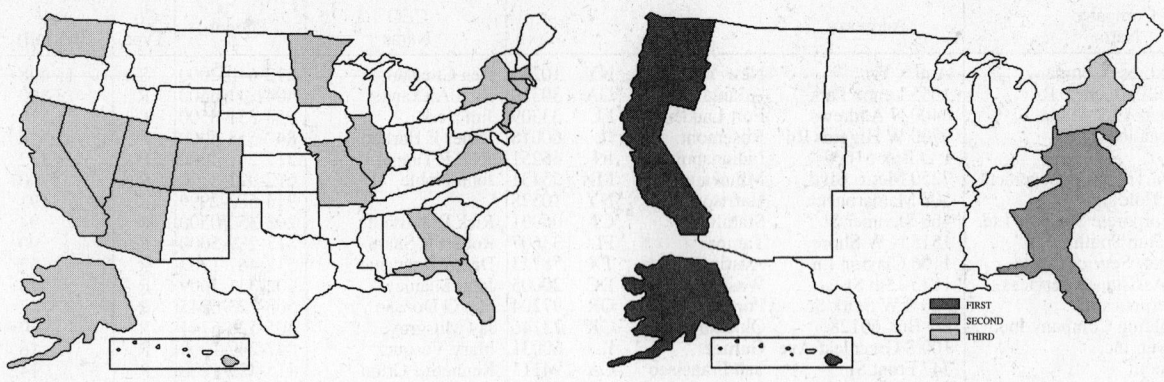

FIRST
SECOND
THIRD

INDUSTRY DATA BY STATE

State	Establishments Total (number)	% of U.S.	Employment Total (number)	% of U.S.	Per Estab.	Payroll Total ($ mil.)	Per Empl. ($)	Revenues Total ($ mil.)	% of U.S.	Per Estab. ($)
California	4,145	14.1	23,798	13.0	6	624.8	26,253	1,380.3	13.8	333,014
New York	2,817	9.6	15,664	8.6	6	481.6	30,743	975.6	9.8	346,332
Florida	2,386	8.1	13,509	7.4	6	304.4	22,535	707.8	7.1	296,636
Illinois	1,547	5.3	10,415	5.7	7	267.4	25,675	674.3	6.8	435,896
Texas	1,749	6.0	11,674	6.4	7	290.6	24,890	620.0	6.2	354,500
New Jersey	1,262	4.3	6,488	3.5	5	166.1	25,606	374.4	3.8	296,651
Pennsylvania	1,026	3.5	6,049	3.3	6	142.6	23,579	334.6	3.4	326,115
Massachusetts	1,041	3.5	6,495	3.5	6	141.1	21,718	326.6	3.3	313,761
Michigan	891	3.0	5,433	3.0	6	117.9	21,700	310.9	3.1	348,925
Missouri	450	1.5	4,032	2.2	9	93.0	23,065	305.4	3.1	678,758
Ohio	878	3.0	5,031	2.7	6	107.6	21,395	291.9	2.9	332,429
Arizona	556	1.9	7,155	3.9	13	185.0	25,856	283.8	2.8	510,433
Georgia	646	2.2	5,028	2.7	8	148.2	29,470	279.7	2.8	433,025
Virginia	640	2.2	4,631	2.5	7	122.9	26,543	265.1	2.7	414,269
Washington	789	2.7	5,105	2.8	6	99.8	19,546	229.8	2.3	291,199
Colorado	640	2.2	4,461	2.4	7	117.3	26,304	217.9	2.2	340,508
Minnesota	566	1.9	3,947	2.2	7	91.5	23,186	205.7	2.1	363,475
Hawaii	362	1.2	2,845	1.6	8	70.9	24,936	201.9	2.0	557,657
Connecticut	527	1.8	3,120	1.7	6	88.0	28,200	185.7	1.9	352,351
Maryland	493	1.7	2,836	1.5	6	59.6	21,011	154.4	1.5	313,276
North Carolina	511	1.7	3,017	1.6	6	66.0	21,872	150.1	1.5	293,781
Tennessee	363	1.2	2,547	1.4	7	66.5	26,104	137.9	1.4	379,895
Wisconsin	515	1.8	3,141	1.7	6	59.3	18,866	128.8	1.3	250,039
Oregon	421	1.4	2,450	1.3	6	53.2	21,709	107.8	1.1	255,950
Indiana	382	1.3	2,090	1.1	5	41.4	19,789	94.2	0.9	246,660
D.C.	236	0.8	1,431	0.8	6	43.3	30,272	90.4	0.9	383,025
Nevada	201	0.7	1,878	1.0	9	37.9	20,167	87.6	0.9	435,682
Louisiana	254	0.9	1,352	0.7	5	28.8	21,277	79.2	0.8	311,650
Utah	193	0.7	1,836	1.0	10	37.9	20,639	75.5	0.8	390,984
South Carolina	212	0.7	1,070	0.6	5	22.2	20,760	60.0	0.6	283,061
Alabama	183	0.6	1,178	0.6	6	24.3	20,635	58.5	0.6	319,585
Oklahoma	244	0.8	1,040	0.6	4	20.4	19,660	54.1	0.5	221,787
Kansas	216	0.7	1,300	0.7	6	26.8	20,648	53.8	0.5	248,921
Kentucky	188	0.6	1,051	0.6	6	18.1	17,260	50.9	0.5	270,590
Iowa	198	0.7	979	0.5	5	18.2	18,556	43.5	0.4	219,924
Nebraska	136	0.5	1,119	0.6	8	20.0	17,915	41.9	0.4	308,301
Alaska	138	0.5	918	0.5	7	19.5	21,212	40.5	0.4	293,428
Delaware	62	0.2	576	0.3	9	16.8	29,151	37.9	0.4	611,565
New Hampshire	167	0.6	726	0.4	4	17.1	23,500	32.2	0.3	192,850
New Mexico	134	0.5	825	0.5	6	14.9	18,018	31.9	0.3	238,015
Rhode Island	134	0.5	566	0.3	4	12.0	21,159	25.3	0.3	188,649
Idaho	90	0.3	606	0.3	7	11.2	18,543	24.8	0.2	275,089
Mississippi	101	0.3	514	0.3	5	10.2	19,780	24.6	0.2	243,277
Arkansas	127	0.4	583	0.3	5	9.8	16,815	22.0	0.2	173,622
Maine	124	0.4	491	0.3	4	9.0	18,232	19.7	0.2	158,903
Montana	109	0.4	474	0.3	4	7.8	16,371	17.6	0.2	161,275
Vermont	64	0.2	394	0.2	6	8.7	22,178	17.2	0.2	269,469
North Dakota	55	0.2	502	0.3	9	7.2	14,307	13.1	0.1	238,636
South Dakota	57	0.2	328	0.2	6	6.2	18,936	11.2	0.1	196,351
Wyoming	51	0.2	255	0.1	5	4.7	18,420	9.8	0.1	192,216
West Virginia	55	0.2	225	0.1	4	4.4	19,418	9.2	0.1	168,109

Source: 1997 *Economic Census*. The states are in descending order of revenues or establishments (if revenue data are missing for the majority). The symbol (D) appears when data are withheld to prevent disclosure of competitive information. States marked with (D) are sorted by number of establishments. A dash (-) indicates that the data element cannot be calculated. * indicates the midpoint of a range; 175, for example is the range 100-249. Shaded *states* on the state map indicate those states which have proportionately greater representation in the industry than would be indicated by the state's population; the ratio is based on total revenues or number of establishments. Shaded *regions* indicate where the industry is regionally most concentrated.

NAICS 561520 - TOUR OPERATORS*

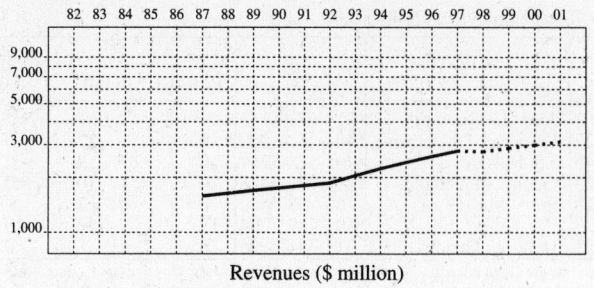

Revenues ($ million)

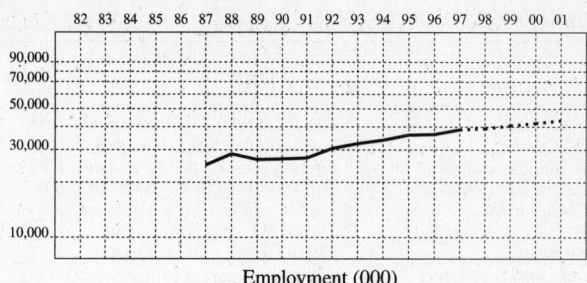

Employment (000)

GENERAL STATISTICS

Year	Establishments (number)	Employment (number)	Payroll ($ million)	Revenues ($ million)	Employees per Establishment (number)	Revenues per Establishment ($)	Payroll per Employee ($)
1982	-	-	-	-	-	-	-
1983	-	-	-	-	-	-	-
1984	-	-	-	-	-	-	-
1985	-	-	-	-	-	-	-
1986	-	-	-	-	-	-	-
1987	2,492	24,821	449.0	1,583.0	10.0	635,233	18,090
1988	2,464	28,488	559.0	1,640.0	11.6	665,584	19,622
1989	2,200	26,559	539.0	1,696.0	12.1	770,909	20,294
1990	2,239	26,762	582.0	1,752.0	12.0	782,492	21,747
1991	2,381	27,068	596.0	1,808.0	11.4	759,345	22,019
1992	3,008	30,519	690.0	1,865.0	10.1	620,013	22,609
1993	3,023	32,416	744.0	2,048.0 e	10.7	677,473	22,952
1994	3,020	33,843	794.0	2,232.0 e	11.2	739,073	23,461
1995	3,051	36,121	899.0	2,415.0 e	11.8	791,544	24,889
1996	3,220	36,416	936.0	2,599.0 e	11.3	807,143	25,703
1997	3,501	38,574	1,034.0	2,782.0	11.0	794,630	26,806
1998	3,481 p	39,163 p	1,043.0 p	2,758.0 p	11.3 p	792,301 p	26,632 p
1999	3,598 p	40,514 p	1,099.0 p	2,878.0 p	11.3 p	799,889 p	27,126 p
2000	3,715 p	41,866 p	1,154.0 p	2,997.0 p	11.3 p	806,729 p	27,564 p
2001	3,831 p	43,218 p	1,209.0 p	3,117.0 p	11.3 p	813,626 p	27,974 p

Sources: Economic Census of the United States, 1982, 1987, 1992, 1997. Establishment counts, employment, and payroll are from *County Business Patterns* for non-Census years. In non-Census years, industries in the Manufacturing range under SIC coding include data from the *Annual Survey of Manufactures* (*ASM*); those in the old Services range include data from the *Services Annual Survey* (*SAS*). Values followed by a 'p' are projections by the editors. Extrapolations are marked by 'e'. Data are the most recent available at this level of detail.

INDICES OF CHANGE

Year	Establishments (number)	Employment (number)	Payroll ($ million)	Revenues ($ million)	Employees per Establishment (number)	Revenues per Establishment ($)	Payroll per Employee ($)
1982	-	-	-	-	-	-	-
1987	71.2	64.3	43.4	56.9	90.4	79.9	67.5
1992	85.9	79.1	66.7	67.0	92.1	78.0	84.3
1993	86.3	84.0	72.0	73.6 e	97.3	85.3	85.6
1994	86.3	87.7	76.8	80.2 e	101.7	93.0	87.5
1995	87.1	93.6	86.9	86.8 e	107.5	99.6	92.8
1996	92.0	94.4	90.5	93.4 e	102.6	101.6	95.9
1997	100.0	100.0	100.0	100.0	100.0	100.0	100.0
1998	99.4 p	101.5 p	100.9 p	99.1 p	102.1 p	99.7 p	99.4 p
1999	102.8 p	105.0 p	106.3 p	103.5 p	102.2 p	100.7 p	101.2 p
2000	106.1 p	108.5 p	111.6 p	107.7 p	102.3 p	101.5 p	102.8 p
2001	109.4 p	112.0 p	116.9 p	112.0 p	102.4 p	102.4 p	104.4 p

Sources: Same as General Statistics. The values shown reflect change from the base year, 1997. Values above 100 mean greater than 1997, values below 100 mean less than 1997, and a value of 100 in the 1982-96 or 1998-2001 period means same as 1997. Values followed by a 'p' are projections by the editors; 'e' stands for extrapolation. Data are the most recent available at this level of detail.

SELECTED RATIOS

For 1997	Avg. of Information	Analyzed Industry	Index	For 1997	Avg. of Information	Analyzed Industry	Index
Employees per establishment	27	11	41	Payroll per establishment	496,890	295,344	59
Revenue per establishment	1,070,709	794,630	74	Payroll as % of revenue	46	37	80
Revenue per employee	40,278	72,121	179	Payroll per employee	18,692	26,806	143

Sources: Same as General Statistics. The 'Average' column represents the average for the industry sector, in 1997, where the currently shown industry is classified. The Index shows the relationship between the Average and the Analyzed Industry. For example, 100 means that they are equal; 500 that the Analyzed Industry is five times the average; 50 means that the Analyzed Industry is half the national average. The abbreviation 'na' is used to show that data are 'not available'.

*Equivalent to SIC 4725.

LEADING COMPANIES   Number shown: **7**   Total sales ($ mil): **1,132**   Total employment (000): **3.0**

Company Name	Address				CEO Name	Phone	Co. Type	Sales ($ mil)	Empl. (000)
President Casinos Inc.	802 N 1st St	St. Louis	MO	63102	John S. Aylsworth	314-621-1111	R	1,067*	2.8
Park Holdings Inc.	2060 Mount Paran	Atlanta	GA	30327	Frederick D Clemente	404-264-1000	R	27*	<0.1
Rainbow Holding Company Inc.	PO Box 60128	Oklahoma City	OK	73146	Jay Musgrove	405-528-5741	R	19*	<0.1
InnerAsia Travel Group Inc.	2627 Lombard St	San Francisco	CA	94123	George Doubleday	415-922-0448	R	10*	<0.1
Global Outdoors Inc.	P O Box 3040	Fallbrook	CA	92028	Perry Massie	760-728-6620	P	7	<0.1
Kaufmann's Streamborn Inc.	8861 SW Comm'l	Tigard	OR	97223		503-639-7004	R	2	<0.1
PlanItDetroit LLC	18430 Fairway Dr	Detroit	MI	48221	Deborah Geddes	313-341-6808	R	1*	<0.1

Source: *Ward's Business Directory of U.S. Private and Public Companies*, Volumes 1 and 2, 2000. The company type code used is as follows: P - Public, R - Private, S - Subsidiary, D - Division, J - Joint Venture, A - Affiliate, G - Group, N - Company type not reported. Sales are in millions of dollars, employees are in thousands. An asterisk (*) indicates an estimated sales volume. The symbol < stands for 'less than'. Company names and addresses are truncated, in some cases, to fit into the available space.

LOCATION BY STATE AND REGIONAL CONCENTRATION

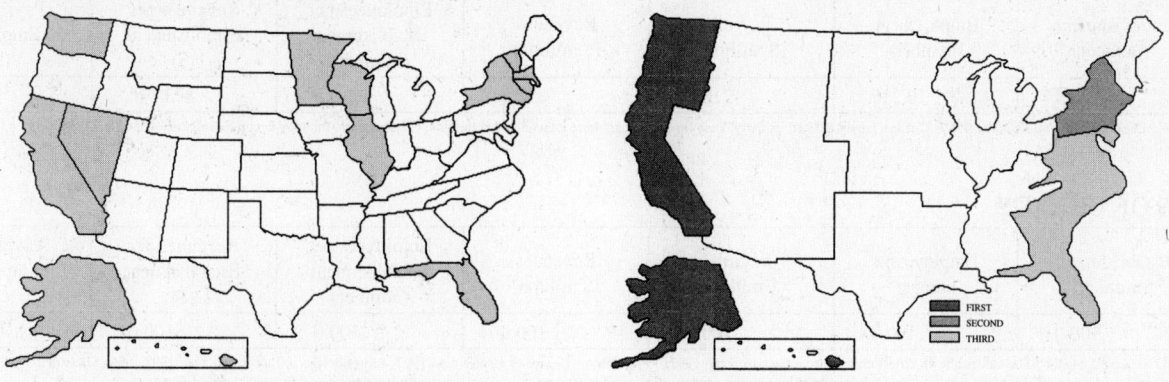

FIRST
SECOND
THIRD

INDUSTRY DATA BY STATE

State	Establishments Total (number)	Establishments % of U.S.	Employment Total (number)	Employment % of U.S.	Employment Per Estab.	Payroll Total ($ mil.)	Payroll Per Empl. ($)	Revenues Total ($ mil.)	Revenues % of U.S.	Revenues Per Estab. ($)
California	553	15.8	7,352	19.1	13	198.6	27,019	515.6	18.5	932,295
New York	386	11.0	3,405	8.8	9	119.1	34,969	309.1	11.1	800,850
Florida	402	11.5	4,319	11.2	11	97.4	22,554	269.5	9.7	670,363
Massachusetts	97	2.8	1,958	5.1	20	63.8	32,559	189.3	6.8	1,951,753
Illinois	153	4.4	2,396	6.2	16	63.8	26,615	156.2	5.6	1,020,752
Hawaii	180	5.1	2,440	6.3	14	61.3	25,118	151.1	5.4	839,661
Washington	87	2.5	1,543	4.0	18	51.0	33,047	122.7	4.4	1,410,080
Pennsylvania	126	3.6	1,311	3.4	10	41.3	31,513	115.5	4.2	917,024
Minnesota	68	1.9	1,416	3.7	21	26.2	18,469	73.1	2.6	1,075,279
Wisconsin	56	1.6	1,093	2.8	20	26.1	23,884	72.2	2.6	1,289,214
Michigan	85	2.4	857	2.2	10	21.5	25,092	68.6	2.5	807,247
New Jersey	120	3.4	874	2.3	7	29.2	33,363	64.4	2.3	536,292
Connecticut	33	0.9	366	0.9	11	17.7	48,240	63.1	2.3	1,911,000
Texas	142	4.1	1,120	2.9	8	21.9	19,564	61.8	2.2	434,915
Virginia	71	2.0	668	1.7	9	18.9	28,220	49.0	1.8	689,662
Nevada	54	1.5	663	1.7	12	16.7	25,134	47.9	1.7	886,278
Missouri	60	1.7	327	0.8	5	9.9	30,306	43.1	1.5	718,000
Arizona	78	2.2	854	2.2	11	18.9	22,107	34.9	1.3	447,167
Ohio	62	1.8	377	1.0	6	5.9	15,753	23.4	0.8	377,887
Kansas	20	0.6	262	0.7	13	6.5	24,958	21.6	0.8	1,080,350
Alaska	51	1.5	103	0.3	2	7.6	74,000	18.9	0.7	370,000
D.C.	18	0.5	263	0.7	15	9.0	34,103	18.8	0.7	1,046,611
Alabama	13	0.4	97	0.3	7	2.7	27,794	18.2	0.7	1,400,077
Maryland	34	1.0	233	0.6	7	4.7	19,957	17.5	0.6	513,500
Georgia	49	1.4	311	0.8	6	7.4	23,678	16.8	0.6	343,612
Oregon	34	1.0	318	0.8	9	7.3	22,906	16.5	0.6	484,559
North Carolina	49	1.4	315	0.8	6	6.2	19,540	15.3	0.5	311,367
Kentucky	10	0.3	143	0.4	14	2.4	16,741	13.0	0.5	1,296,400
Utah	39	1.1	164	0.4	4	3.7	22,421	12.7	0.5	324,872
New Mexico	14	0.4	350	0.9	25	4.8	13,857	12.0	0.4	859,286
Vermont	14	0.4	46	0.1	3	1.6	35,239	10.6	0.4	758,643
South Carolina	33	0.9	106	0.3	3	2.1	20,217	9.4	0.3	285,909
Tennessee	41	1.2	210	0.5	5	3.3	15,938	8.8	0.3	214,707
New Hampshire	12	0.3	75	0.2	6	2.0	26,040	5.0	0.2	414,167
Indiana	23	0.7	83	0.2	4	1.7	20,542	4.4	0.2	190,696
Nebraska	13	0.4	83	0.2	6	1.1	13,193	4.0	0.1	308,077
Iowa	16	0.5	61	0.2	4	1.3	21,311	2.5	0.1	154,437
Mississippi	8	0.2	67	0.2	8	0.6	9,164	1.6	0.1	194,000
Wyoming	10	0.3	35	0.1	4	0.6	17,029	1.5	0.1	147,300
Montana	7	0.2	22	0.1	3	0.3	15,591	1.3	0.0	187,143
Idaho	6	0.2	22	0.1	4	0.3	14,864	1.1	0.0	182,000
North Dakota	6	0.2	17	0.0	3	0.4	22,000	0.8	0.0	136,333
West Virginia	4	0.1	5	0.0	1	0.3	52,800	0.6	0.0	137,500
Arkansas	6	0.2	6	0.0	1	0.2	40,500	0.5	0.0	77,333
South Dakota	4	0.1	8	0.0	2	0.2	23,750	0.4	0.0	109,250
Colorado	78	2.2	750*	-	-	(D)	-	(D)	-	-
Louisiana	39	1.1	375*	-	-	(D)	-	(D)	-	-
Maine	12	0.3	10*	-	-	(D)	-	(D)	-	-
Oklahoma	11	0.3	375*	-	-	(D)	-	(D)	-	-
Rhode Island	8	0.2	375*	-	-	(D)	-	(D)	-	-
Delaware	6	0.2	60*	-	-	(D)	-	(D)	-	-

Source: 1997 *Economic Census*. The states are in descending order of revenues or establishments (if revenue data are missing for the majority). The symbol (D) appears when data are withheld to prevent disclosure of competitive information. States marked with (D) are sorted by number of establishments. A dash (-) indicates that the data element cannot be calculated. * indicates the midpoint of a range; 175, for example is the range 100-249. Shaded *states* on the state map indicate those states which have proportionately greater representation in the industry than would be indicated by the state's population; the ratio is based on total revenues or number of establishments. Shaded *regions* indicate where the industry is regionally most concentrated.

NAICS 561591 - CONVENTION AND VISITORS BUREAUS

GENERAL STATISTICS

Year	Establishments (number)	Employment (number)	Payroll ($ million)	Revenues ($ million)	Employees per Establishment (number)	Revenues per Establishment ($)	Payroll per Employee ($)
1997	975	10,236	218.0	852.0	10.5	873,846	21,297

Source: *Economic Census of the United States*, 1997. This is a newly defined industry. Data for prior years were unavailable at the time of publication but may become available over time.

INDICES OF CHANGE

Year	Establishments (number)	Employment (number)	Payroll ($ million)	Revenues ($ million)	Employees per Establishment (number)	Revenues per Establishment ($)	Payroll per Employee ($)
1997	100.0	100.0	100.0	100.0	100.0	100.0	100.0

Sources: Same as General Statistics. The values shown reflect change from the base year, 1997. Values above 100 mean greater than 1997, values below 100 mean less than 1997, and a value of 100 in the 1982-96 or 1998-2001 period means same as 1997. Values followed by a 'p' are projections by the editors; 'e' stands for extrapolation. Data are the most recent available at this level of detail.

SIC INDUSTRIES RELATED TO NAICS 561591

Each new NAICS code represents an industry that used to be part of an SIC or a part of several SIC industries. Data in this table are shown to provide transitional information for these cases. All available data for the precursor SIC(s) are shown. Even if only a part of an SIC is included in the NAICS, *all* data for the SIC are reproduced. If the SIC industry is not marked as being a part (pt) of the NAICS, the entire industry is embedded in the NAICS data. The SIC composition of the new industry provides some hints of the relative importance of its "ancestors." Data marked with a 'p' are projected. Projections begin with 1982 data. Data earlier than 1990 are not shown but are reflected in the projections.

SIC	Industry	1990	1991	1992	1993	1994	1995	1996	1997
7389	**Business Services, nec (pt)**								
	Establishments (number)	44,079	50,252	52,375	56,829	60,725	53,596	60,893*p*	63,269*p*
	Employment (thousands)	489.6	550.4	523.6	607.9	648.7	623.0	680.2*p*	710.9*p*
	Revenues ($ million)	-	-	32,885.9	-	-	-	-	-

Source: *Economic Census of the United States*, 1992, annual surveys of economic sectors conducted by the Bureau of the Census, and estimates or projections based on the 1982-1992 period; not all data are shown. 'e' marks estimates made by the editors; 'p' indicates projections based on time series. A dash (-) indicates that data for this SIC or year were not available. The abbreviation (pt) next to the industry name indicates that only a part of the industry is present within the NAICS data. If no (pt) is shown, the entire industry is contained within the NAICS data.

SELECTED RATIOS

For 1997	Avg. of Information	Analyzed Industry	Index	For 1997	Avg. of Information	Analyzed Industry	Index
Employees per establishment	27	10	39	Payroll per establishment	496,890	223,590	45
Revenue per establishment	1,070,709	873,846	82	Payroll as % of revenue	46	26	55
Revenue per employee	40,278	83,236	207	Payroll per employee	18,692	21,297	114

Sources: Same as General Statistics. The 'Average' column represents the average for the industry sector, in 1997, where the currently shown industry is classified. The Index shows the relationship between the Average and the Analyzed Industry. For example, 100 means that they are equal; 500 that the Analyzed Industry is five times the average; 50 means that the Analyzed Industry is half the national average. The abbreviation 'na' is used to show that data are 'not available'.

LEADING COMPANIES

No company data available for this industry.

LOCATION BY STATE AND REGIONAL CONCENTRATION

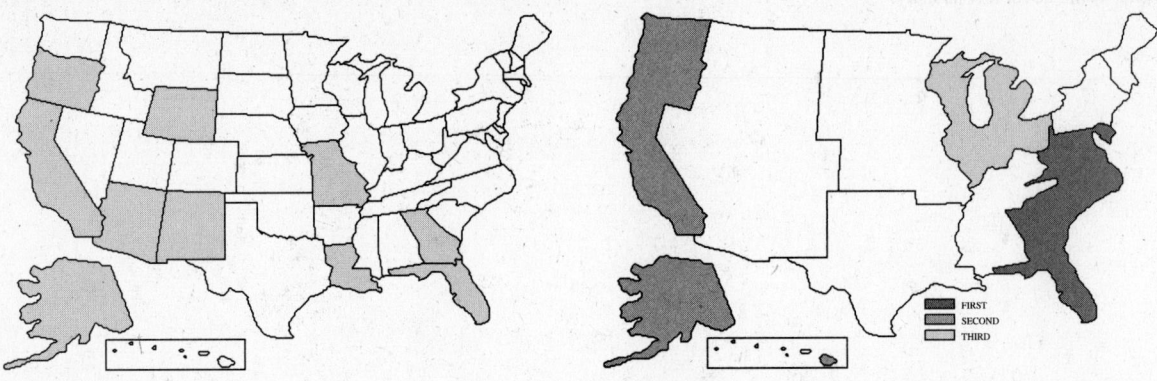

FIRST
SECOND
THIRD

INDUSTRY DATA BY STATE

State	Establishments Total (number)	% of U.S.	Employment Total (number)	% of U.S.	Per Estab.	Payroll Total ($ mil.)	Per Empl. ($)	Revenues Total ($ mil.)	% of U.S.	Per Estab. ($)
California	117	12.0	1,608	15.7	14	32.3	20,060	114.5	13.4	978,222
Florida	47	4.8	824	8.1	18	19.0	23,006	97.4	11.4	2,071,745
New York	44	4.5	342	3.3	8	10.9	31,977	41.7	4.9	948,568
Georgia	24	2.5	277	2.7	12	7.8	28,253	40.4	4.7	1,683,667
Texas	44	4.5	529	5.2	12	11.2	21,117	37.9	4.4	860,932
Ohio	49	5.0	487	4.8	10	9.8	20,205	36.8	4.3	750,327
Pennsylvania	42	4.3	399	3.9	10	8.0	20,018	31.9	3.7	760,452
Illinois	51	5.2	334	3.3	7	7.8	23,434	26.2	3.1	513,255
Michigan	39	4.0	418	4.1	11	7.1	17,048	25.2	3.0	644,974
Louisiana	12	1.2	389	3.8	32	4.7	12,139	20.5	2.4	1,709,583
Missouri	14	1.4	468	4.6	33	9.7	20,782	19.3	2.3	1,376,071
North Carolina	25	2.6	285	2.8	11	5.9	20,807	18.6	2.2	743,320
Arizona	22	2.3	335	3.3	15	6.0	17,839	18.5	2.2	843,000
Indiana	30	3.1	139	1.4	5	4.2	30,345	16.5	1.9	548,667
Washington	28	2.9	263	2.6	9	6.7	25,567	16.3	1.9	582,643
Wisconsin	18	1.8	198	1.9	11	3.9	19,561	15.7	1.8	869,611
New Jersey	14	1.4	367	3.6	26	6.8	18,537	14.8	1.7	1,057,000
Maryland	17	1.7	235	2.3	14	4.1	17,651	14.3	1.7	838,471
Minnesota	32	3.3	180	1.8	6	4.4	24,333	13.9	1.6	433,469
Massachusetts	11	1.1	102	1.0	9	3.3	31,922	13.2	1.5	1,196,455
Alaska	12	1.2	109	1.1	9	3.1	28,706	10.6	1.2	885,750
Tennessee	11	1.1	170	1.7	15	2.8	16,347	10.1	1.2	922,545
Oregon	18	1.8	133	1.3	7	3.4	25,489	9.9	1.2	550,111
D.C.	10	1.0	118	1.2	12	2.1	17,712	9.7	1.1	974,500
Alabama	10	1.0	122	1.2	12	2.7	22,164	9.5	1.1	948,800
Connecticut	14	1.4	79	0.8	6	2.1	26,785	8.5	1.0	604,929
New Mexico	11	1.1	95	0.9	9	2.0	21,063	7.0	0.8	633,545
South Carolina	13	1.3	100	1.0	8	1.6	15,950	5.2	0.6	397,308
Virginia	15	1.5	90	0.9	6	1.5	16,789	3.8	0.4	252,133
Kansas	8	0.8	37	0.4	5	0.7	19,622	2.5	0.3	310,375
West Virginia	15	1.5	44	0.4	3	0.7	15,864	2.5	0.3	166,600
Kentucky	13	1.3	33	0.3	3	0.6	16,818	2.4	0.3	183,538
Wyoming	13	1.3	31	0.3	2	0.4	12,774	1.9	0.2	142,769
Montana	10	1.0	24	0.2	2	0.4	18,000	1.8	0.2	179,200
Mississippi	5	0.5	13	0.1	3	0.2	16,615	0.9	0.1	170,400
Colorado	24	2.5	375*	-	-	(D)	-	(D)	-	-
Hawaii	13	1.3	175*	-	-	(D)	-	(D)	-	-
Iowa	13	1.3	60*	-	-	(D)	-	(D)	-	-
Oklahoma	12	1.2	60*	-	-	(D)	-	(D)	-	-
Maine	7	0.7	60*	-	-	(D)	-	(D)	-	-
Nevada	7	0.7	60*	-	-	(D)	-	(D)	-	-
Utah	7	0.7	175*	-	-	(D)	-	(D)	-	-
Delaware	5	0.5	10*	-	-	(D)	-	(D)	-	-
Idaho	5	0.5	60*	-	-	(D)	-	(D)	-	-
North Dakota	5	0.5	60*	-	-	(D)	-	(D)	-	-
Rhode Island	5	0.5	60*	-	-	(D)	-	(D)	-	-
South Dakota	4	0.4	10*	-	-	(D)	-	(D)	-	-
Vermont	4	0.4	60*	-	-	(D)	-	(D)	-	-
Arkansas	3	0.3	10*	-	-	(D)	-	(D)	-	-
New Hampshire	2	0.2	10*	-	-	(D)	-	(D)	-	-
Nebraska	1	0.1	10*	-	-	(D)	-	(D)	-	-

Source: 1997 *Economic Census*. The states are in descending order of revenues or establishments (if revenue data are missing for the majority). The symbol (D) appears when data are withheld to prevent disclosure of competitive information. States marked with (D) are sorted by number of establishments. A dash (-) indicates that the data element cannot be calculated. * indicates the midpoint of a range; 175, for example is the range 100-249. Shaded *states* on the state map indicate those states which have proportionately greater representation in the industry than would be indicated by the state's population; the ratio is based on total revenues or number of establishments. Shaded *regions* indicate where the industry is regionally most concentrated.

NAICS 561599 - TRAVEL ARRANGEMENT AND RESERVATION SERVICES NEC

GENERAL STATISTICS

Year	Establishments (number)	Employment (number)	Payroll ($ million)	Revenues ($ million)	Employees per Establishment (number)	Revenues per Establishment ($)	Payroll per Employee ($)
1997	2,770	68,516	1,983.0	7,872.0	24.7	2,841,877	28,942

Source: Economic Census of the United States, 1997. This is a newly defined industry. Data for prior years were unavailable at the time of publication but may become available over time.

INDICES OF CHANGE

Year	Establishments (number)	Employment (number)	Payroll ($ million)	Revenues ($ million)	Employees per Establishment (number)	Revenues per Establishment ($)	Payroll per Employee ($)
1997	100.0	100.0	100.0	100.0	100.0	100.0	100.0

Sources: Same as General Statistics. The values shown reflect change from the base year, 1997. Values above 100 mean greater than 1997, values below 100 mean less than 1997, and a value of 100 in the 1982-96 or 1998-2001 period means same as 1997. Values followed by a 'p' are projections by the editors; 'e' stands for extrapolation. Data are the most recent available at this level of detail.

SIC INDUSTRIES RELATED TO NAICS 561599

Each new NAICS code represents an industry that used to be part of an SIC or a part of several SIC industries. Data in this table are shown to provide transitional information for these cases. All available data for the precursor SIC(s) are shown. Even if only a part of an SIC is included in the NAICS, *all* data for the SIC are reproduced. If the SIC industry is not marked as being a part (pt) of the NAICS, the entire industry is embedded in the NAICS data. The SIC composition of the new industry provides some hints of the relative importance of its "ancestors." Data marked with a 'p' are projected. Projections begin with 1982 data. Data earlier than 1990 are not shown but are reflected in the projections.

SIC	Industry	1990	1991	1992	1993	1994	1995	1996	1997
4729	**Miscellaneous Transportation Arrangement, nec (pt)**								
	Establishments (number)	1,320	1,306	1,097	1,022	910	871	852	658p
	Employment (thousands)	14.6	14.8	13.3	12.1	10.7	10.8	9.7	11.1p
	Revenues ($ million)	1,241.5e	1,492.6e	1,743.7	1,994.7p	2,245.8p	2,496.9p	2,748.0p	2,999.1p
7389	**Business Services, nec (pt)**								
	Establishments (number)	44,079	50,252	52,375	56,829	60,725	53,596	60,893p	63,269p
	Employment (thousands)	489.6	550.4	523.6	607.9	648.7	623.0	680.2p	710.9p
	Revenues ($ million)	-	-	32,885.9	-	-	-	-	-
7922	**Theatrical Producers & Services (pt)**								
	Establishments (number)	4,470	4,992	5,924	6,229	6,323	6,428	6,542p	6,792p
	Employment (thousands)	63.9	63.1	69.5	88.8	77.8	79.3	87.3p	91.2p
	Revenues ($ million)	-	-	5,730.5	4,396.6p	4,647.8p	4,899.0p	5,150.2p	5,401.4p
7999	**Amusement & Recreation nec (pt)**								
	Establishments (number)	-	-	21,717	-	-	-	-	-
	Employment (thousands)	-	-	215.8	-	-	-	-	-
	Revenues ($ million)	-	-	10,430.3	-	-	-	-	-
8699	**Membership Organizations, nec (pt)**								
	Establishments (number)	9,670	10,125	10,596	10,695	10,666	10,760	11,062p	11,247p
	Employment (thousands)	87.7	91.9	91.4	95.7	96.0	101.7	103.3p	105.9p
	Revenues ($ million)	-	-	6,267.8	-	-	-	-	-

Source: Economic Census of the United States, 1992, annual surveys of economic sectors conducted by the Bureau of the Census, and estimates or projections based on the 1982-1992 period; not all data are shown. 'e' marks estimates made by the editors; 'p' indicates projections based on time series. A dash (-) indicates that data for this SIC or year were not available. The abbreviation (pt) next to the industry name indicates that only a part of the industry is present within the NAICS data. If no (pt) is shown, the entire industry is contained within the NAICS data.

SELECTED RATIOS

For 1997	Avg. of Information	Analyzed Industry	Index	For 1997	Avg. of Information	Analyzed Industry	Index
Employees per establishment	27	25	93	Payroll per establishment	496,890	715,884	144
Revenue per establishment	1,070,709	2,841,877	265	Payroll as % of revenue	46	25	54
Revenue per employee	40,278	114,893	285	Payroll per employee	18,692	28,942	155

Sources: Same as General Statistics. The 'Average' column represents the average for the industry sector, in 1997, where the currently shown industry is classified. The Index shows the relationship between the Average and the Analyzed Industry. For example, 100 means that they are equal; 500 that the Analyzed Industry is five times the average; 50 means that the Analyzed Industry is half the national average. The abbreviation 'na' is used to show that data are 'not available'.

LEADING COMPANIES   Number shown: **1**   Total sales ($ mil): **3**   Total employment (000): **0.0**

Company Name	Address				CEO Name	Phone	Co. Type	Sales ($ mil)	Empl. (000)
Ran Decisions Inc.	4715-C Town Center	Co Springs	CO	80916	Randy Petersen	719-597-8899	R	3	<0.1

Source: *Ward's Business Directory of U.S. Private and Public Companies*, Volumes 1 and 2, 2000. The company type code used is as follows: P - Public, R - Private, S - Subsidiary, D - Division, J - Joint Venture, A - Affiliate, G - Group, N - Company type not reported. Sales are in millions of dollars, employees are in thousands. An asterisk (*) indicates an estimated sales volume. The symbol < stands for 'less than'. Company names and addresses are truncated, in some cases, to fit into the available space.

LOCATION BY STATE AND REGIONAL CONCENTRATION

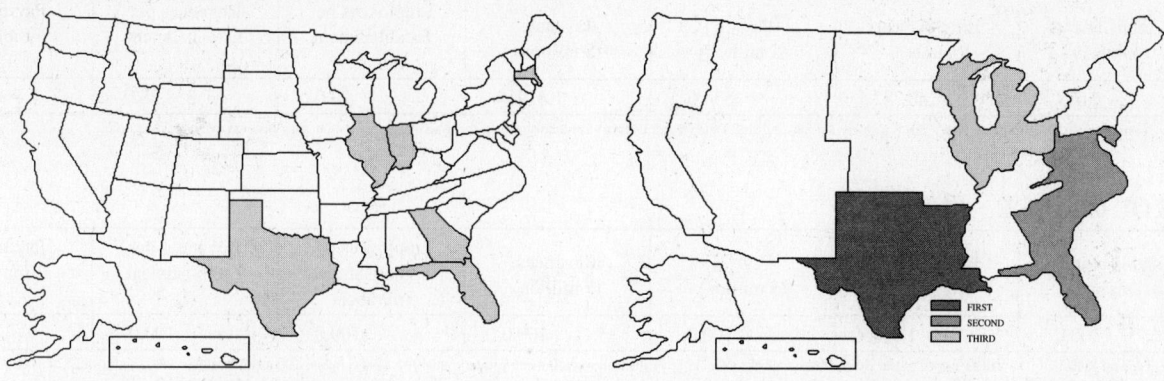

INDUSTRY DATA BY STATE

State	Establishments Total (number)	% of U.S.	Employment Total (number)	% of U.S.	Per Estab.	Payroll Total ($ mil.)	Per Empl. ($)	Revenues Total ($ mil.)	% of U.S.	Per Estab. ($)
Texas	146	5.3	9,752	14.2	67	392.4	40,241	1,547.8	19.7	10,601,212
California	373	13.5	9,603	14.0	26	303.5	31,608	649.9	8.3	1,742,303
Florida	226	8.2	6,230	9.1	28	159.6	25,621	515.5	6.5	2,280,947
Illinois	136	4.9	2,604	3.8	19	69.1	26,533	508.8	6.5	3,741,044
Georgia	60	2.2	2,621	3.8	44	87.3	33,293	507.1	6.4	8,452,500
New York	223	8.1	3,763	5.5	17	104.9	27,879	393.5	5.0	1,764,399
Indiana	58	2.1	2,399	3.5	41	70.2	29,245	236.6	3.0	4,079,897
Massachusetts	81	2.9	2,315	3.4	29	49.3	21,292	219.0	2.8	2,703,296
Pennsylvania	144	5.2	2,691	3.9	19	57.5	21,349	193.9	2.5	1,346,312
Ohio	144	5.2	2,149	3.1	15	47.3	22,002	164.8	2.1	1,144,493
New Jersey	121	4.4	1,818	2.7	15	43.2	23,752	156.8	2.0	1,295,636
Missouri	78	2.8	1,539	2.2	20	49.1	31,921	147.3	1.9	1,888,615
Arizona	44	1.6	1,578	2.3	36	40.6	25,730	112.2	1.4	2,549,159
Michigan	42	1.5	1,215	1.8	29	16.1	13,258	100.8	1.3	2,400,452
Maryland	50	1.8	836	1.2	17	20.5	24,517	91.4	1.2	1,828,960
Connecticut	53	1.9	605	0.9	11	19.4	32,005	86.9	1.1	1,638,698
Virginia	69	2.5	1,158	1.7	17	27.4	23,673	85.0	1.1	1,232,304
Washington	55	2.0	931	1.4	17	22.7	24,425	70.8	0.9	1,286,382
Wisconsin	17	0.6	273	0.4	16	6.9	25,352	67.6	0.9	3,976,529
Tennessee	30	1.1	1,237	1.8	41	43.4	35,100	60.7	0.8	2,022,667
Minnesota	35	1.3	1,067	1.6	30	17.9	16,801	59.5	0.8	1,699,286
Oregon	26	0.9	295	0.4	11	7.6	25,824	57.4	0.7	2,207,077
Kansas	20	0.7	1,112	1.6	56	16.5	14,880	30.8	0.4	1,537,500
Kentucky	17	0.6	393	0.6	23	10.5	26,654	28.0	0.4	1,645,941
D.C.	19	0.7	138	0.2	7	5.1	37,109	19.8	0.3	1,042,000
South Carolina	26	0.9	319	0.5	12	4.5	14,166	18.8	0.2	722,885
North Carolina	28	1.0	140	0.2	5	3.7	26,121	17.2	0.2	615,000
Alabama	28	1.0	283	0.4	10	4.2	14,827	14.3	0.2	509,036
Delaware	12	0.4	98	0.1	8	2.4	24,633	12.1	0.2	1,011,333
Rhode Island	18	0.6	176	0.3	10	4.0	22,636	8.7	0.1	483,111
Montana	13	0.5	116	0.2	9	2.1	18,500	7.2	0.1	550,385
West Virginia	21	0.8	151	0.2	7	3.5	22,987	6.6	0.1	315,619
Alaska	9	0.3	46	0.1	5	2.0	43,935	4.5	0.1	499,667
Wyoming	8	0.3	42	0.1	5	0.5	12,071	3.1	0.0	382,500
New Mexico	11	0.4	70	0.1	6	0.8	11,729	2.6	0.0	237,364
Mississippi	15	0.5	69	0.1	5	0.4	6,348	2.2	0.0	144,667
Colorado	68	2.5	1,750*	-	-	(D)	-	(D)	-	-
Hawaii	42	1.5	750*	-	-	(D)	-	(D)	-	-
Iowa	37	1.3	375*	-	-	(D)	-	(D)	-	-
Louisiana	30	1.1	175*	-	-	(D)	-	(D)	-	-
Nevada	28	1.0	175*	-	-	(D)	-	(D)	-	-
Oklahoma	24	0.9	3,750*	-	-	(D)	-	(D)	-	-
Nebraska	17	0.6	750*	-	-	(D)	-	(D)	-	-
Arkansas	13	0.5	60*	-	-	(D)	-	(D)	-	-
New Hampshire	12	0.4	60*	-	-	(D)	-	(D)	-	-
Utah	12	0.4	375*	-	-	(D)	-	(D)	-	-
Maine	10	0.4	375*	-	-	(D)	-	(D)	-	-
North Dakota	9	0.3	175*	-	-	(D)	-	(D)	-	-
Idaho	7	0.3	60*	-	-	(D)	-	(D)	-	-
South Dakota	3	0.1	375*	-	-	(D)	-	(D)	-	-
Vermont	2	0.1	10*	-	-	(D)	-	(D)	-	-

Source: 1997 *Economic Census*. The states are in descending order of revenues or establishments (if revenue data are missing for the majority). The symbol (D) appears when data are withheld to prevent disclosure of competitive information. States marked with (D) are sorted by number of establishments. A dash (-) indicates that the data element cannot be calculated. * indicates the midpoint of a range; 175, for example is the range 100-249. Shaded *states* on the state map indicate those states which have proportionately greater representation in the industry than would be indicated by the state's population; the ratio is based on total revenues or number of establishments. Shaded *regions* indicate where the industry is regionally most concentrated.

NAICS 561611 - INVESTIGATION SERVICES

GENERAL STATISTICS

Year	Establishments (number)	Employment (number)	Payroll ($ million)	Revenues ($ million)	Employees per Establishment (number)	Revenues per Establishment ($)	Payroll per Employee ($)
1997	5,077	50,782	834.0	1,819.0	10.0	358,282	16,423

Source: *Economic Census of the United States*, 1997. This is a newly defined industry. Data for prior years were unavailable at the time of publication but may become available over time.

INDICES OF CHANGE

Year	Establishments (number)	Employment (number)	Payroll ($ million)	Revenues ($ million)	Employees per Establishment (number)	Revenues per Establishment ($)	Payroll per Employee ($)
1997	100.0	100.0	100.0	100.0	100.0	100.0	100.0

Sources: Same as General Statistics. The values shown reflect change from the base year, 1997. Values above 100 mean greater than 1997, values below 100 mean less than 1997, and a value of 100 in the 1982-96 or 1998-2001 period means same as 1997. Values followed by a 'p' are projections by the editors; 'e' stands for extrapolation. Data are the most recent available at this level of detail.

SIC INDUSTRIES RELATED TO NAICS 561611

Each new NAICS code represents an industry that used to be part of an SIC or a part of several SIC industries. Data in this table are shown to provide transitional information for these cases. All available data for the precursor SIC(s) are shown. Even if only a part of an SIC is included in the NAICS, *all* data for the SIC are reproduced. If the SIC industry is not marked as being a part (pt) of the NAICS, the entire industry is embedded in the NAICS data. The SIC composition of the new industry provides some hints of the relative importance of its "ancestors." Data marked with a 'p' are projected. Projections begin with 1982 data. Data earlier than 1990 are not shown but are reflected in the projections.

SIC	Industry	1990	1991	1992	1993	1994	1995	1996	1997
7381	**Detective & Armored Car Services (pt)**								
	Establishments (number)	9,417	10,249	11,578	11,749	11,995	12,384	12,669*p*	13,070*p*
	Employment (thousands)	467.3	474.2	482.4	489.8	500.3	533.6	531.9*p*	543.7*p*
	Revenues ($ million)	9,018.0	9,555.0	9,670.0	10,250.0	10,766.0	11,935.0	13,474.0	13,413.1*p*

Source: *Economic Census of the United States*, 1992, annual surveys of economic sectors conducted by the Bureau of the Census, and estimates or projections based on the 1982-1992 period; not all data are shown. 'e' marks estimates made by the editors; 'p' indicates projections based on time series. A dash (-) indicates that data for this SIC or year were not available. The abbreviation (pt) next to the industry name indicates that only a part of the industry is present within the NAICS data. If no (pt) is shown, the entire industry is contained within the NAICS data.

SELECTED RATIOS

For 1997	Avg. of Information	Analyzed Industry	Index	For 1997	Avg. of Information	Analyzed Industry	Index
Employees per establishment	27	10	38	Payroll per establishment	496,890	164,270	33
Revenue per establishment	1,070,709	358,282	33	Payroll as % of revenue	46	46	99
Revenue per employee	40,278	35,820	89	Payroll per employee	18,692	16,423	88

Sources: Same as General Statistics. The 'Average' column represents the average for the industry sector, in 1997, where the currently shown industry is classified. The Index shows the relationship between the Average and the Analyzed Industry. For example, 100 means that they are equal; 500 that the Analyzed Industry is five times the average; 50 means that the Analyzed Industry is half the national average. The abbreviation 'na' is used to show that data are 'not available'.

LEADING COMPANIES   Number shown: **53**   Total sales ($ mil): **13,968**   Total employment (000): **460.3**

Company Name	Address				CEO Name	Phone	Co. Type	Sales ($ mil)	Empl. (000)
Pittston Co.	PO Box 4229	Glen Allen	VA	23058	Michael T. Dan	804-553-3600	R	3,747	41.0
Wackenhut Corp.	4200 Wackenhut Dr	Palm Bch Grdns	FL	33410	George R Wackenhut	561-622-5656	P	1,755	70.0
Burns Intern	2 Campus Dr	Parsippany	NJ	07054	John D O'Brien	973-267-5300	S	1,323	75.0
Burns International Services Corp.	200 S Michigan Ave	Chicago	IL	60604	John A Edwardson	312-322-8500	P	1,323	73.0
Brink's Inc.	1 Thorndal Cir	Darien	CT	06820	Michael T Dan	203-662-7800	S	1,100*	9.0
Pinkerton's Inc.	4330 Park Terr Dr	Westlake Village	CA	91361	Denis R Brown	818-380-8800	P	1,009	48.0
Barton Protective Services Inc.	11 Piedmont Ctr	Atlanta	GA	30305	C Barton-Rice Sr	404-266-1038	R	431*	7.0
American Protective Services Inc.	P O Box 6757	Oakland	CA	94603	Dwight Pedersen	510-568-0276	R	336	17.5
Guardsmark Inc.	P O Box 45	Memphis	TN	38101	Ira A Lipman	901-522-6000	R	300	13.0
Akal Security Inc.	P O Box 1197	Santa Cruz	NM	87567	Sopurkh K Khalsa	505-753-7832	R	246*	4.0
U.S. Security Associates Inc.	200 Mansell Ct	Covington	GA	30016	Charles Schneider	770-625-1500	R	235	16.0
ITS	PO Box 318029	Cleveland	OH	44131	Mark D Thompson	216-642-4522	R	227	15.5
Allied Security Inc.	2840 Library Rd	Pittsburgh	PA	15234	Neal H Holmes	412-884-2636	R	200	9.0
Stanley Smith Security Inc.	3355 Cherry Ridge	San Antonio	TX	78230	Michael Schroeder	210-349-6321	S	154	7.0
First Security Service Corp.	1 Harborside Dr	Boston	MA	02128	Robert Johnson	617-568-8700	R	138*	5.5
ATI Systems International Inc.	3220 Winona Ave	Burbank	CA	91504	Richard Irvin	818-845-8883	R	110*	4.9
A and R Security Services Inc.	2552 W 135th St	Blue Island	IL	60406	VL Ruffolo	708-389-3830	R	100*	1.2
MVM Inc.	8301 Greensboro Dr	McLean	VA	22102	Dario O Marquez Jr	703-790-3138	R	99*	1.6
Armored Transport Inc.	1612 W Pico Blvd	Los Angeles	CA	90015	Gregory Irvin	213-383-3611	S	97*	4.0
American Commercial Security	50 Fremont St	San Francisco	CA	94105	Dennis Hooper	415-597-4500	D	92	5.7
Pedus Services Inc.	PO Box 513617	Los Angeles	CA	90051	Richard G Jackson	213-386-8480	R	90	4.0
Vance International Inc.	10467 White Granite	Oakton	VA	22124	Charles F Vince	703-385-6754	R	85	3.0
Professional Security Bureau Ltd.	88 Park Ave	Nutley	NJ	07110	Richard Rockwell	973-661-9000	R	68	4.8
Nana Development Corp.	1001 E Benson Blvd	Anchorage	AK	99508		907-265-4100	S	65	1.3
Command Security Corp.	PO Box 340	Lagrangeville	NY	12540	Franklyn H Snitow	914-454-3703	P	58	3.1
Kent Security Services	14600 Biscayne	Miami	FL	33181	Shlom Alexander	305-919-9400	R	54*	0.9
CSG Security Services Inc.	PO Box 11629	Phoenix	AZ	85061	Michael Shetler	602-264-4193	R	53*	0.9
General Security Services Corp.	9110 Meadowview	Bloomington	MN	55425	Whitney Miller	612-858-5000	R	50	1.1
Levy Security Consultants Ltd.	230 E Ohio St	Chicago	IL	60611	David P Bergsma	312-649-9204	R	42*	0.7
SOS Security Inc.	1 Security Plz	Parsippany	NJ	07054		973-402-6600	R	40	2.0
Pay-O-Matic Corp.	160 Oak Dr	Syosset	NY	11791	Rayman Mustafa	516-496-4900	P	35*	0.6
Budd Group	2325 S Stratford Rd	Winston-Salem	NC	27103	Joseph R Budd	336-765-7690	R	34	2.5
Per Mar Security & Research Corp	PO Box 4227	Davenport	IA	52808	Michael Duffy	319-359-3200	R	34	2.0
Kroll Associates Inc.	900 Third Ave	New York	NY	10022	Jules Kroll	212-593-1000	R	33	0.4
Weiser Security Services Inc.	2600 S Loop W	Houston	TX	77054		281-999-9945	D	25*	0.4
Tri-County Security Inc.	22932 Woodward	Ferndale	MI	48220	Lumduen Tode	248-545-7100	R	24*	0.4
Western Security Systems	6850 Vannuys	Van Nuys	CA	91405		310-324-4981	R	24*	0.4
APG Security Inc.	10170 Mississippi	Denver	CO	80231	Anthony J Pisani	303-751-1000	R	22*	1.2
Boyd and Associates	6319 Colfax Ave	N. Hollywood	CA	91606	Daniel Boyd	818-752-1888	R	15*	0.3
Langner Security Services	2501 Cherry Ave	Long Beach	CA	90806	Roger Langner	562-490-3310	R	15*	0.6
Northwest Protective Service Inc.	2700 Elliott Ave	Seattle	WA	98121	James Stumbles	206-448-4040	R	15*	0.3
Firstwatch Corp.	1819 Hinton St	Dallas	TX	75235	Tim Yarbro	214-630-6636	R	9*	0.2
Dale System Inc.	1101 Stewart Ave	Garden City	NY	11530	Harvey M Yaffe	516-794-2800	P	7	0.2
Preferred Security Services	11757 Katy Fwy	Houston	TX	77079	John Cronin	281-497-7333	R	7	0.2
TEK Industries Inc.	71 Utopia Rd	Manchester	CT	06040	Mark Matheny	860-647-8738	R	7*	<0.1
Record Search Inc.	6365 Taft St	Hollywood	FL	33024	Robin Taylor	954-989-9965	R	7	0.1
Quality Security Service Inc.	8700 Commerce	Houston	TX	77036	Paul Weekly	713-988-2918	R	5*	<0.1
RJD Security Inc.	25 Genessee St	Buffalo	NY	14203		716-855-1766	D	5*	0.6
Safeguard Security Services	16117 N 76th St	Scottsdale	AZ	85260		602-609-6200	R	5*	<0.1
Michael G	237 Park Ave	New York	NY	10017	Michael G Kessler	212-286-9100	R	4	<0.1
Air Security International Inc.	2925 Briarpark Dr	Houston	TX	77042	Issy Boim	713-430-7300	S	3*	<0.1
Armadillo Security Service	7401 Gulf Fwy	Houston	TX	77017	Carl Maynard	713-645-2711	R	3*	<0.1
San-Val Corp.	P O Box 12710	Palm Desert	CA	92255	Robert Sandiford	760-568-5592	R	3*	<0.1

Source: Ward's Business Directory of U.S. Private and Public Companies, Volumes 1 and 2, 2000. The company type code used is as follows: P - Public, R - Private, S - Subsidiary, D - Division, J - Joint Venture, A - Affiliate, G - Group, N - Company type not reported. Sales are in millions of dollars, employees are in thousands. An asterisk (*) indicates an estimated sales volume. The symbol < stands for 'less than'. Company names and addresses are truncated, in some cases, to fit into the available space.

LOCATION BY STATE AND REGIONAL CONCENTRATION

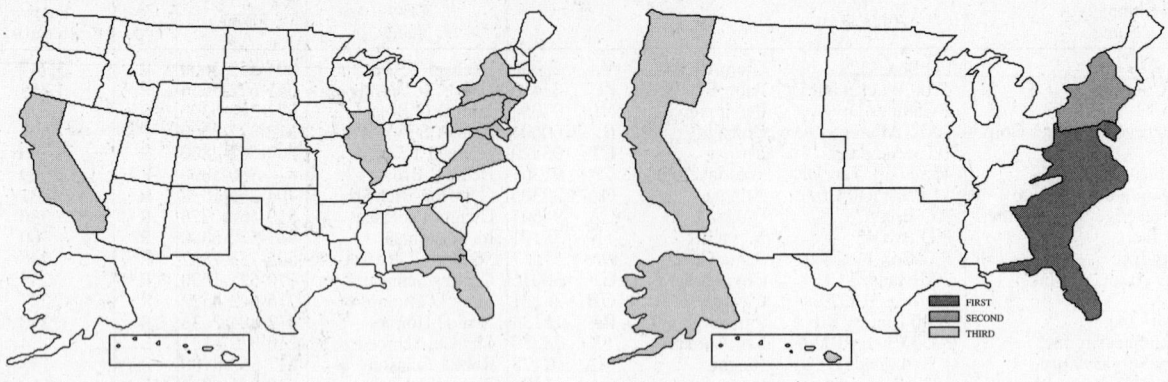

INDUSTRY DATA BY STATE

State	Establishments Total (number)	% of U.S.	Employment Total (number)	% of U.S.	Per Estab.	Payroll Total ($ mil.)	Per Empl. ($)	Revenues Total ($ mil.)	% of U.S.	Per Estab. ($)
California	741	14.6	7,071	13.9	10	128.4	18,153	305.5	16.8	412,275
New York	435	8.6	5,452	10.7	13	92.0	16,875	193.3	10.6	444,336
Florida	524	10.3	4,111	8.1	8	72.3	17,590	179.0	9.8	341,676
Illinois	219	4.3	3,694	7.3	17	61.0	16,523	124.6	6.9	569,009
Texas	347	6.8	2,782	5.5	8	46.4	16,686	106.8	5.9	307,896
Pennsylvania	182	3.6	2,374	4.7	13	47.6	20,035	90.1	5.0	494,874
New Jersey	166	3.3	2,404	4.7	14	41.8	17,392	72.0	4.0	433,687
Maryland	130	2.6	1,340	2.6	10	27.7	20,704	67.8	3.7	521,885
Ohio	165	3.2	2,055	4.0	12	29.1	14,182	62.8	3.5	380,739
Georgia	111	2.2	2,257	4.4	20	31.7	14,067	55.5	3.1	500,045
Michigan	162	3.2	1,379	2.7	9	23.9	17,361	54.3	3.0	335,006
Virginia	152	3.0	1,168	2.3	8	20.5	17,563	51.6	2.8	339,454
Massachusetts	112	2.2	833	1.6	7	15.6	18,776	37.2	2.0	332,429
North Carolina	99	1.9	913	1.8	9	16.3	17,875	30.1	1.7	303,798
Indiana	91	1.8	1,238	2.4	14	12.4	10,050	25.9	1.4	284,231
Louisiana	84	1.7	621	1.2	7	9.1	14,591	24.1	1.3	286,464
Missouri	78	1.5	590	1.2	8	9.9	16,831	23.8	1.3	304,577
Minnesota	74	1.5	714	1.4	10	10.1	14,092	23.1	1.3	312,473
Washington	98	1.9	531	1.0	5	10.0	18,906	22.6	1.2	230,735
Arizona	101	2.0	465	0.9	5	7.8	16,733	18.7	1.0	184,891
Wisconsin	79	1.6	653	1.3	8	8.6	13,205	16.4	0.9	207,342
Alabama	71	1.4	596	1.2	8	6.6	11,153	14.3	0.8	200,789
Nevada	41	0.8	205	0.4	5	3.0	14,717	8.6	0.5	209,463
Iowa	24	0.5	416	0.8	17	4.3	10,255	7.6	0.4	314,833
Kansas	27	0.5	265	0.5	10	3.5	13,215	7.1	0.4	261,889
Oregon	59	1.2	203	0.4	3	2.9	14,345	6.6	0.4	111,373
Kentucky	33	0.6	215	0.4	7	2.9	13,558	6.5	0.4	197,879
Maine	19	0.4	283	0.6	15	3.2	11,481	5.4	0.3	283,053
Arkansas	16	0.3	82	0.2	5	1.4	17,463	4.5	0.2	283,125
Nebraska	22	0.4	201	0.4	9	2.1	10,348	4.3	0.2	195,773
Rhode Island	19	0.4	68	0.1	4	1.4	21,044	3.8	0.2	200,053
Delaware	11	0.2	163	0.3	15	2.2	13,669	3.4	0.2	311,545
Utah	20	0.4	76	0.1	4	0.7	8,987	2.4	0.1	120,650
Wyoming	8	0.2	21	0.0	3	0.2	10,143	0.5	0.0	66,500
Alaska	7	0.1	24	0.0	3	0.2	7,500	0.5	0.0	68,000
Colorado	102	2.0	750*	-	-	(D)	-	(D)	-	-
Tennessee	75	1.5	1,750*	-	-	(D)	-	(D)	-	-
Oklahoma	56	1.1	375*	-	-	(D)	-	(D)	-	-
South Carolina	52	1.0	375*	-	-	(D)	-	(D)	-	-
Connecticut	51	1.0	375*	-	-	(D)	-	(D)	-	-
West Virginia	34	0.7	175*	-	-	(D)	-	(D)	-	-
Mississippi	32	0.6	375*	-	-	(D)	-	(D)	-	-
New Mexico	28	0.6	375*	-	-	(D)	-	(D)	-	-
New Hampshire	23	0.5	60*	-	-	(D)	-	(D)	-	-
D.C.	19	0.4	750*	-	-	(D)	-	(D)	-	-
Hawaii	16	0.3	175*	-	-	(D)	-	(D)	-	-
Idaho	15	0.3	60*	-	-	(D)	-	(D)	-	-
South Dakota	15	0.3	175*	-	-	(D)	-	(D)	-	-
Montana	13	0.3	60*	-	-	(D)	-	(D)	-	-
North Dakota	11	0.2	60*	-	-	(D)	-	(D)	-	-
Vermont	8	0.2	10*	-	-	(D)	-	(D)	-	-

Source: 1997 *Economic Census*. The states are in descending order of revenues or establishments (if revenue data are missing for the majority). The symbol (D) appears when data are withheld to prevent disclosure of competitive information. States marked with (D) are sorted by number of establishments. A dash (-) indicates that the data element cannot be calculated. * indicates the midpoint of a range; 175, for example is the range 100-249. Shaded *states* on the state map indicate those states which have proportionately greater representation in the industry than would be indicated by the state's population; the ratio is based on total revenues or number of establishments. Shaded *regions* indicate where the industry is regionally most concentrated.

NAICS 561612 - SECURITY GUARDS AND PATROL SERVICES

GENERAL STATISTICS

Year	Establishments (number)	Employment (number)	Payroll ($ million)	Revenues ($ million)	Employees per Establishment (number)	Revenues per Establishment ($)	Payroll per Employee ($)
1997	6,644	476,995	6,256.0	9,133.0	71.8	1,374,624	13,115

Source: Economic Census of the United States, 1997. This is a newly defined industry. Data for prior years were unavailable at the time of publication but may become available over time.

INDICES OF CHANGE

Year	Establishments (number)	Employment (number)	Payroll ($ million)	Revenues ($ million)	Employees per Establishment (number)	Revenues per Establishment ($)	Payroll per Employee ($)
1997	100.0	100.0	100.0	100.0	100.0	100.0	100.0

Sources: Same as General Statistics. The values shown reflect change from the base year, 1997. Values above 100 mean greater than 1997, values below 100 mean less than 1997, and a value of 100 in the 1982-96 or 1998-2001 period means same as 1997. Values followed by a 'p' are projections by the editors; 'e' stands for extrapolation. Data are the most recent available at this level of detail.

SIC INDUSTRIES RELATED TO NAICS 561612

Each new NAICS code represents an industry that used to be part of an SIC or a part of several SIC industries. Data in this table are shown to provide transitional information for these cases. All available data for the precursor SIC(s) are shown. Even if only a part of an SIC is included in the NAICS, *all* data for the SIC are reproduced. If the SIC industry is not marked as being a part (pt) of the NAICS, the entire industry is embedded in the NAICS data. The SIC composition of the new industry provides some hints of the relative importance of its "ancestors." Data marked with a 'p' are projected. Projections begin with 1982 data. Data earlier than 1990 are not shown but are reflected in the projections.

SIC	Industry	1990	1991	1992	1993	1994	1995	1996	1997
7381	**Detective & Armored Car Services (pt)**								
	Establishments (number)	9,417	10,249	11,578	11,749	11,995	12,384	12,669p	13,070p
	Employment (thousands)	467.3	474.2	482.4	489.8	500.3	533.6	531.9p	543.7p
	Revenues ($ million)	9,018.0	9,555.0	9,670.0	10,250.0	10,766.0	11,935.0	13,474.0	13,413.1p

Source: Economic Census of the United States, 1992, annual surveys of economic sectors conducted by the Bureau of the Census, and estimates or projections based on the 1982-1992 period; not all data are shown. 'e' marks estimates made by the editors; 'p' indicates projections based on time series. A dash (-) indicates that data for this SIC or year were not available. The abbreviation (pt) next to the industry name indicates that only a part of the industry is present within the NAICS data. If no (pt) is shown, the entire industry is contained within the NAICS data.

SELECTED RATIOS

For 1997	Avg. of Information	Analyzed Industry	Index	For 1997	Avg. of Information	Analyzed Industry	Index
Employees per establishment	27	72	270	Payroll per establishment	496,890	941,601	189
Revenue per establishment	1,070,709	1,374,624	128	Payroll as % of revenue	46	68	148
Revenue per employee	40,278	19,147	48	Payroll per employee	18,692	13,115	70

Sources: Same as General Statistics. The 'Average' column represents the average for the industry sector, in 1997, where the currently shown industry is classified. The Index shows the relationship between the Average and the Analyzed Industry. For example, 100 means that they are equal; 500 that the Analyzed Industry is five times the average; 50 means that the Analyzed Industry is half the national average. The abbreviation 'na' is used to show that data are 'not available'.

LEADING COMPANIES

No company data available for this industry.

LOCATION BY STATE AND REGIONAL CONCENTRATION

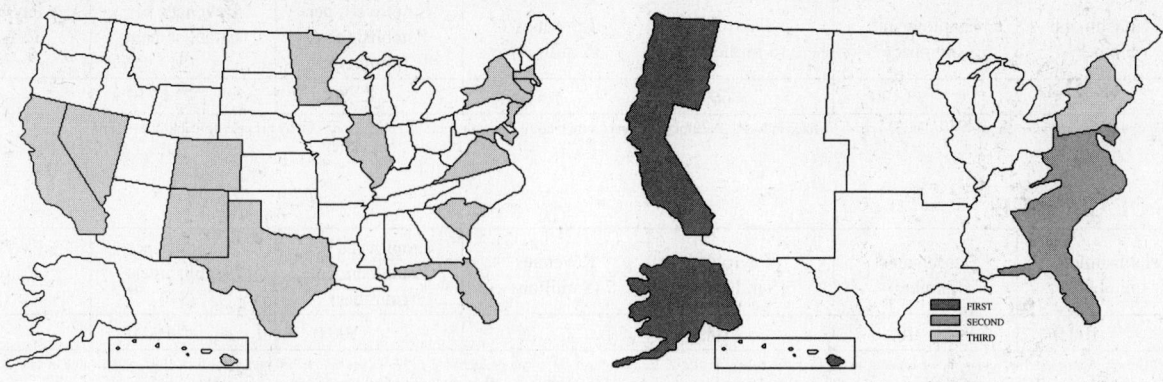

INDUSTRY DATA BY STATE

State	Establishments Total (number)	Establishments % of U.S.	Employment Total (number)	Employment % of U.S.	Employment Per Estab.	Payroll Total ($ mil.)	Payroll Per Empl. ($)	Revenues Total ($ mil.)	Revenues % of U.S.	Revenues Per Estab. ($)
California	1,122	16.9	81,672	17.1	73	1,058.9	12,965	1,606.0	17.6	1,431,348
New York	493	7.4	47,914	10.0	97	702.9	14,671	1,006.6	11.0	2,041,846
Texas	499	7.5	33,736	7.1	68	443.4	13,144	673.7	7.4	1,350,188
Florida	474	7.1	29,103	6.1	61	377.8	12,983	548.1	6.0	1,156,251
Illinois	243	3.7	23,737	5.0	98	328.6	13,843	495.2	5.4	2,037,971
Pennsylvania	213	3.2	18,801	3.9	88	245.5	13,059	364.0	4.0	1,708,991
Virginia	166	2.5	16,062	3.4	97	225.2	14,019	342.0	3.7	2,060,386
New Jersey	162	2.4	16,832	3.5	104	242.7	14,417	328.4	3.6	2,027,451
Massachusetts	169	2.5	15,560	3.3	92	173.6	11,156	247.2	2.7	1,462,444
Michigan	185	2.8	14,033	2.9	76	168.7	12,024	241.3	2.6	1,304,081
Ohio	210	3.2	14,639	3.1	70	168.8	11,529	233.9	2.6	1,113,762
Georgia	178	2.7	13,594	2.8	76	152.7	11,233	225.6	2.5	1,267,354
Maryland	104	1.6	10,222	2.1	98	132.8	12,995	202.5	2.2	1,947,298
Minnesota	69	1.0	10,150	2.1	147	151.9	14,963	199.5	2.2	2,891,406
South Carolina	86	1.3	7,459	1.6	87	132.0	17,695	192.2	2.1	2,234,744
North Carolina	164	2.5	11,315	2.4	69	137.3	12,139	183.1	2.0	1,116,396
Tennessee	135	2.0	9,138	1.9	68	115.4	12,625	159.0	1.7	1,177,904
Colorado	92	1.4	6,412	1.3	70	101.2	15,776	154.6	1.7	1,680,152
Louisiana	131	2.0	8,294	1.7	63	96.0	11,580	136.6	1.5	1,043,038
Connecticut	56	0.8	6,023	1.3	108	87.8	14,571	120.2	1.3	2,146,875
Indiana	128	1.9	6,427	1.3	50	73.9	11,504	110.7	1.2	864,813
Washington	123	1.9	6,015	1.3	49	76.9	12,789	110.3	1.2	896,569
Missouri	133	2.0	5,723	1.2	43	76.4	13,356	107.6	1.2	809,075
Nevada	53	0.8	5,156	1.1	97	69.9	13,563	105.2	1.2	1,985,340
Arizona	105	1.6	5,700	1.2	54	66.5	11,674	98.1	1.1	934,181
New Mexico	59	0.9	3,048	0.6	52	56.8	18,635	82.5	0.9	1,398,475
Hawaii	47	0.7	4,521	0.9	96	55.5	12,282	80.5	0.9	1,712,426
Kentucky	96	1.4	4,486	0.9	47	48.7	10,849	71.0	0.8	739,208
Oregon	85	1.3	3,400	0.7	40	46.3	13,626	70.1	0.8	825,247
Alabama	100	1.5	5,227	1.1	52	50.5	9,661	69.6	0.8	695,880
Mississippi	73	1.1	4,682	1.0	64	46.6	9,944	68.4	0.7	937,548
Wisconsin	84	1.3	3,877	0.8	46	44.6	11,504	60.0	0.7	714,560
Oklahoma	85	1.3	3,829	0.8	45	40.6	10,605	57.0	0.6	671,141
Arkansas	43	0.6	2,798	0.6	65	29.7	10,633	43.3	0.5	1,006,209
Iowa	61	0.9	1,991	0.4	33	23.3	11,711	33.6	0.4	550,361
West Virginia	60	0.9	1,840	0.4	31	20.8	11,316	32.8	0.4	546,650
Kansas	61	0.9	1,992	0.4	33	17.6	8,819	31.0	0.3	508,508
Rhode Island	25	0.4	1,430	0.3	57	19.8	13,829	28.2	0.3	1,126,640
Utah	28	0.4	1,337	0.3	48	18.3	13,681	26.1	0.3	930,571
Nebraska	50	0.8	1,547	0.3	31	18.2	11,767	24.8	0.3	496,140
D.C.	30	0.5	956	0.2	32	17.1	17,839	24.5	0.3	816,333
Maine	25	0.4	775	0.2	31	12.1	15,554	17.0	0.2	680,880
New Hampshire	15	0.2	709	0.1	47	11.0	15,539	15.9	0.2	1,061,933
Idaho	24	0.4	765	0.2	32	8.4	10,987	14.7	0.2	613,792
Montana	21	0.3	590	0.1	28	7.0	11,937	11.2	0.1	535,095
Vermont	10	0.2	590	0.1	59	5.7	9,619	7.5	0.1	746,800
North Dakota	10	0.2	322	0.1	32	3.8	11,913	5.1	0.1	511,300
Wyoming	13	0.2	195	0.0	15	2.2	11,528	3.5	0.0	270,462
South Dakota	11	0.2	200	0.0	18	1.5	7,635	2.2	0.0	200,818
Delaware	20	0.3	1,750*	-	-	(D)	-	(D)	-	-
Alaska	15	0.2	750*	-	-	(D)	-	(D)	-	-

Source: 1997 *Economic Census*. The states are in descending order of revenues or establishments (if revenue data are missing for the majority). The symbol (D) appears when data are withheld to prevent disclosure of competitive information. States marked with (D) are sorted by number of establishments. A dash (-) indicates that the data element cannot be calculated. * indicates the midpoint of a range; 175, for example is the range 100-249. Shaded *states* on the state map indicate those states which have proportionately greater representation in the industry than would be indicated by the state's population; the ratio is based on total revenues or number of establishments. Shaded *regions* indicate where the industry is regionally most concentrated.

465

NAICS 561613 - ARMORED CAR SERVICES

GENERAL STATISTICS

Year	Establishments (number)	Employment (number)	Payroll ($ million)	Revenues ($ million)	Employees per Establishment (number)	Revenues per Establishment ($)	Payroll per Employee ($)
1997	818	33,199	669.0	1,419.0	40.6	1,734,719	20,151

Source: Economic Census of the United States, 1997. This is a newly defined industry. Data for prior years were unavailable at the time of publication but may become available over time.

INDICES OF CHANGE

Year	Establishments (number)	Employment (number)	Payroll ($ million)	Revenues ($ million)	Employees per Establishment (number)	Revenues per Establishment ($)	Payroll per Employee ($)
1997	100.0	100.0	100.0	100.0	100.0	100.0	100.0

Sources: Same as General Statistics. The values shown reflect change from the base year, 1997. Values above 100 mean greater than 1997, values below 100 mean less than 1997, and a value of 100 in the 1982-96 or 1998-2001 period means same as 1997. Values followed by a 'p' are projections by the editors; 'e' stands for extrapolation. Data are the most recent available at this level of detail.

SIC INDUSTRIES RELATED TO NAICS 561613

Each new NAICS code represents an industry that used to be part of an SIC or a part of several SIC industries. Data in this table are shown to provide transitional information for these cases. All available data for the precursor SIC(s) are shown. Even if only a part of an SIC is included in the NAICS, *all* data for the SIC are reproduced. If the SIC industry is not marked as being a part (pt) of the NAICS, the entire industry is embedded in the NAICS data. The SIC composition of the new industry provides some hints of the relative importance of its "ancestors." Data marked with a 'p' are projected. Projections begin with 1982 data. Data earlier than 1990 are not shown but are reflected in the projections.

SIC	Industry	1990	1991	1992	1993	1994	1995	1996	1997
7381	**Detective & Armored Car Services (pt)**								
	Establishments (number)	9,417	10,249	11,578	11,749	11,995	12,384	12,669p	13,070p
	Employment (thousands)	467.3	474.2	482.4	489.8	500.3	533.6	531.9p	543.7p
	Revenues ($ million)	9,018.0	9,555.0	9,670.0	10,250.0	10,766.0	11,935.0	13,474.0	13,413.1p

Source: Economic Census of the United States, 1992, annual surveys of economic sectors conducted by the Bureau of the Census, and estimates or projections based on the 1982-1992 period; not all data are shown. 'e' marks estimates made by the editors; 'p' indicates projections based on time series. A dash (-) indicates that data for this SIC or year were not available. The abbreviation (pt) next to the industry name indicates that only a part of the industry is present within the NAICS data. If no (pt) is shown, the entire industry is contained within the NAICS data.

SELECTED RATIOS

For 1997	Avg. of Information	Analyzed Industry	Index	For 1997	Avg. of Information	Analyzed Industry	Index
Employees per establishment	27	41	153	Payroll per establishment	496,890	817,848	165
Revenue per establishment	1,070,709	1,734,719	162	Payroll as % of revenue	46	47	102
Revenue per employee	40,278	42,742	106	Payroll per employee	18,692	20,151	108

Sources: Same as General Statistics. The 'Average' column represents the average for the industry sector, in 1997, where the currently shown industry is classified. The Index shows the relationship between the Average and the Analyzed Industry. For example, 100 means that they are equal; 500 that the Analyzed Industry is five times the average; 50 means that the Analyzed Industry is half the national average. The abbreviation 'na' is used to show that data are 'not available'.

LEADING COMPANIES

No company data available for this industry.

LOCATION BY STATE AND REGIONAL CONCENTRATION

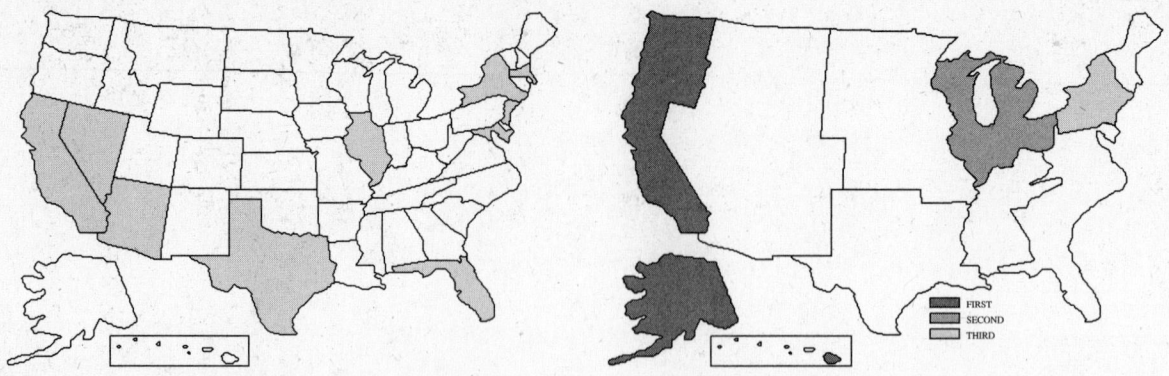

INDUSTRY DATA BY STATE

State	Establishments Total (number)	% of U.S.	Employment Total (number)	% of U.S.	Per Estab.	Payroll Total ($ mil.)	Per Empl. ($)	Revenues Total ($ mil.)	% of U.S.	Per Estab. ($)
California	90	11.0	4,234	12.8	47	101.6	24,000	221.0	15.6	2,455,211
New York	55	6.7	2,385	7.2	43	55.5	23,260	113.6	8.0	2,064,564
Texas	67	8.2	2,139	6.4	32	50.7	23,725	111.8	7.9	1,669,373
Illinois	31	3.8	3,535	10.6	114	66.6	18,839	110.7	7.8	3,570,968
Florida	48	5.9	1,656	5.0	35	32.5	19,649	76.4	5.4	1,591,979
New Jersey	22	2.7	1,243	3.7	57	29.5	23,760	58.3	4.1	2,649,091
Ohio	32	3.9	1,858	5.6	58	26.6	14,320	56.8	4.0	1,775,844
Maryland	16	2.0	1,057	3.2	66	14.6	13,843	35.8	2.5	2,234,437
Arizona	14	1.7	492	1.5	35	15.4	31,289	35.7	2.5	2,549,357
Massachusetts	20	2.4	819	2.5	41	16.5	20,145	35.6	2.5	1,782,300
Virginia	18	2.2	593	1.8	33	13.1	22,054	32.1	2.3	1,781,222
Pennsylvania	27	3.3	913	2.8	34	16.1	17,612	30.8	2.2	1,139,704
Michigan	23	2.8	543	1.6	24	14.9	27,357	28.9	2.0	1,256,174
North Carolina	16	2.0	672	2.0	42	12.8	19,012	28.1	2.0	1,755,375
Georgia	26	3.2	722	2.2	28	12.4	17,163	24.6	1.7	946,269
Washington	18	2.2	409	1.2	23	9.6	23,545	24.0	1.7	1,335,667
Indiana	17	2.1	553	1.7	33	11.3	20,514	23.5	1.7	1,379,647
Missouri	24	2.9	641	1.9	27	11.0	17,164	22.3	1.6	931,167
Louisiana	17	2.1	623	1.9	37	9.9	15,839	21.6	1.5	1,268,765
Wisconsin	15	1.8	482	1.5	32	9.7	20,207	19.4	1.4	1,290,267
Nevada	5	0.6	266	0.8	53	6.3	23,808	14.5	1.0	2,893,000
Alabama	13	1.6	386	1.2	30	5.3	13,858	12.0	0.8	919,615
Minnesota	13	1.6	264	0.8	20	5.1	19,470	11.2	0.8	861,462
Utah	5	0.6	235	0.7	47	4.7	20,038	9.8	0.7	1,969,600
Oregon	7	0.9	221	0.7	32	4.9	22,054	9.7	0.7	1,385,857
Iowa	14	1.7	297	0.9	21	4.7	15,734	9.2	0.6	658,643
Kentucky	7	0.9	199	0.6	28	5.0	25,151	9.0	0.6	1,291,857
Kansas	11	1.3	257	0.8	23	3.0	11,821	6.3	0.4	571,182
Maine	6	0.7	161	0.5	27	2.3	13,981	5.9	0.4	989,500
Arkansas	10	1.2	343	1.0	34	2.8	8,292	5.0	0.4	499,700
Nebraska	10	1.2	219	0.7	22	2.2	10,151	4.9	0.3	485,600
Rhode Island	3	0.4	90	0.3	30	2.3	25,089	4.7	0.3	1,552,000
Wyoming	4	0.5	30	0.1	8	0.2	6,133	0.4	0.0	100,750
Tennessee	18	2.2	750*	-	-	(D)	-	(D)	-	-
Connecticut	11	1.3	375*	-	-	(D)	-	(D)	-	-
South Carolina	11	1.3	750*	-	-	(D)	-	(D)	-	-
Oklahoma	10	1.2	175*	-	-	(D)	-	(D)	-	-
Colorado	9	1.1	750*	-	-	(D)	-	(D)	-	-
Montana	9	1.1	175*	-	-	(D)	-	(D)	-	-
Hawaii	7	0.9	175*	-	-	(D)	-	(D)	-	-
Mississippi	6	0.7	175*	-	-	(D)	-	(D)	-	-
West Virginia	6	0.7	175*	-	-	(D)	-	(D)	-	-
D.C.	5	0.6	375*	-	-	(D)	-	(D)	-	-
New Mexico	4	0.5	60*	-	-	(D)	-	(D)	-	-
North Dakota	4	0.5	60*	-	-	(D)	-	(D)	-	-
Delaware	3	0.4	375*	-	-	(D)	-	(D)	-	-
Idaho	3	0.4	175*	-	-	(D)	-	(D)	-	-
Alaska	2	0.2	60*	-	-	(D)	-	(D)	-	-
New Hampshire	2	0.2	60*	-	-	(D)	-	(D)	-	-
South Dakota	2	0.2	60*	-	-	(D)	-	(D)	-	-
Vermont	2	0.2	60*	-	-	(D)	-	(D)	-	-

Source: 1997 *Economic Census*. The states are in descending order of revenues or establishments (if revenue data are missing for the majority). The symbol (D) appears when data are withheld to prevent disclosure of competitive information. States marked with (D) are sorted by number of establishments. A dash (-) indicates that the data element cannot be calculated. * indicates the midpoint of a range; 175, for example is the range 100-249. Shaded *states* on the state map indicate those states which have proportionately greater representation in the industry than would be indicated by the state's population; the ratio is based on total revenues or number of establishments. Shaded *regions* indicate where the industry is regionally most concentrated.

NAICS 561621 - SECURITY SYSTEMS SERVICES (EXCEPT LOCKSMITHS)*

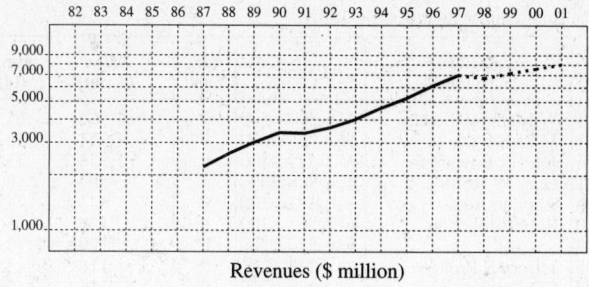

Revenues ($ million)

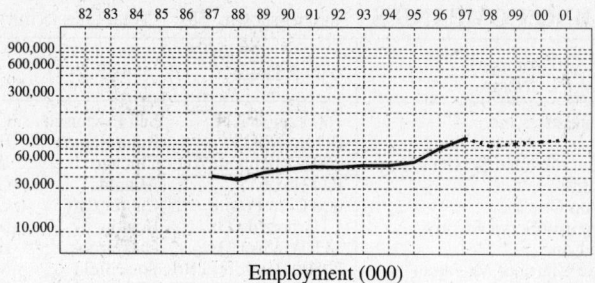

Employment (000)

GENERAL STATISTICS

Year	Establishments (number)	Employment (number)	Payroll ($ million)	Revenues ($ million)	Employees per Establishment (number)	Revenues per Establishment ($)	Payroll per Employee ($)
1982	-	-	-	-	-	-	-
1983	-	-	-	-	-	-	-
1984	-	-	-	-	-	-	-
1985	-	-	-	-	-	-	-
1986	-	-	-	-	-	-	-
1987	2,451	41,214	781.0	2,218.0	16.8	904,937	18,950
1988	2,243	37,400	738.0	2,614.0 e	16.7	1,165,403	19,733
1989	2,146	44,825	999.0	3,010.0 e	20.9	1,402,610	22,287
1990	2,264	48,898	1,078.0	3,406.0	21.6	1,504,417	22,046
1991	2,534	52,218	1,151.0	3,381.0	20.6	1,334,254	22,042
1992	2,968	51,755	1,183.0	3,629.0	17.4	1,222,709	22,858
1993	3,075	53,977	1,302.0	4,027.0	17.6	1,309,593	24,121
1994	3,070	54,129	1,376.0	4,642.0	17.6	1,512,052	25,421
1995	3,190	58,896	1,555.0	5,259.0	18.5	1,648,589	26,402
1996	4,173 e	83,155 e	2,079.0 e	6,126.0 e	19.9 e	1,468,009 e	25,002 e
1997	5,156	107,414	2,603.0	6,992.0	20.8	1,356,090	24,233
1998	4,472 p	88,632 p	2,270.0 p	6,725.0 p	19.8 p	1,503,801 p	25,612 p
1999	4,713 p	93,800 p	2,424.0 p	7,159.0 p	19.9 p	1,518,990 p	25,842 p
2000	4,954 p	98,968 p	2,577.0 p	7,594.0 p	20.0 p	1,532,903 p	26,039 p
2001	5,195 p	104,135 p	2,731.0 p	8,028.0 p	20.0 p	1,545,332 p	26,226 p

Sources: Economic Census of the United States, 1982, 1987, 1992, 1997. Establishment counts, employment, and payroll are from *County Business Patterns* for non-Census years. In non-Census years, industries in the Manufacturing range under SIC coding include data from the *Annual Survey of Manufactures (ASM)*; those in the old Services range include data from the *Services Annual Survey (SAS)*. Values followed by a 'p' are projections by the editors. Extrapolations are marked by 'e'. Data are the most recent available at this level of detail.

INDICES OF CHANGE

Year	Establishments (number)	Employment (number)	Payroll ($ million)	Revenues ($ million)	Employees per Establishment (number)	Revenues per Establishment ($)	Payroll per Employee ($)
1982	-	-	-	-	-	-	-
1987	47.5	38.4	30.0	31.7	80.7	66.7	78.2
1992	57.6	48.2	45.4	51.9	83.7	90.2	94.3
1993	59.6	50.3	50.0	57.6	84.3	96.6	99.5
1994	59.5	50.4	52.9	66.4	84.6	111.5	104.9
1995	61.9	54.8	59.7	75.2	88.6	121.6	109.0
1996	80.9 e	77.4 e	79.9 e	87.6 e	95.7 e	108.3 e	103.2 e
1997	100.0	100.0	100.0	100.0	100.0	100.0	100.0
1998	86.7 p	82.5 p	87.2 p	96.2 p	95.1 p	110.9 p	105.7 p
1999	91.4 p	87.3 p	93.1 p	102.4 p	95.5 p	112.0 p	106.6 p
2000	96.1 p	92.1 p	99.0 p	108.6 p	95.9 p	113.0 p	107.4 p
2001	100.8 p	96.9 p	104.9 p	114.8 p	96.2 p	114.0 p	108.2 p

Sources: Same as General Statistics. The values shown reflect change from the base year, 1997. Values above 100 mean greater than 1997, values below 100 mean less than 1997, and a value of 100 in the 1982-96 or 1998-2001 period means same as 1997. Values followed by a 'p' are projections by the editors; 'e' stands for extrapolation. Data are the most recent available at this level of detail.

SELECTED RATIOS

For 1997	Avg. of Information	Analyzed Industry	Index	For 1997	Avg. of Information	Analyzed Industry	Index
Employees per establishment	27	21	78	Payroll per establishment	496,890	504,849	102
Revenue per establishment	1,070,709	1,356,090	127	Payroll as % of revenue	46	37	80
Revenue per employee	40,278	65,094	162	Payroll per employee	18,692	24,233	130

Sources: Same as General Statistics. The 'Average' column represents the average for the industry sector, in 1997, where the currently shown industry is classified. The Index shows the relationship between the Average and the Analyzed Industry. For example, 100 means that they are equal; 500 that the Analyzed Industry is five times the average; 50 means that the Analyzed Industry is half the national average. The abbreviation 'na' is used to show that data are 'not available'.

*Equivalent to SIC 7382.

LEADING COMPANIES Number shown: **58** Total sales ($ mil): **6,743** Total employment (000): **183.1**

Company Name	Address				CEO Name	Phone	Co. Type	Sales ($ mil)	Empl. (000)
ABM Industries Inc.	160 Pacific Ave	San Francisco	CA	94111	William W. Steele	415-597-4500	P	1,502	55.0
ADT Ltd.	PO Box 5035	Boca Raton	FL	33431	Mike Snyder	561-988-3600	P	1,331	12.5
Burns International Services Corp.	200 S Michigan Ave	Chicago	IL	60604	John A Edwardson	312-322-8500	P	1,323	73.0
Rollins Inc.	P O Box 647	Atlanta	GA	30301	Gary W Rollins	404-888-2000	P	587	8.9
Protection One Inc.	600 Corp Pointe	Culver City	CA	90230	Annette Beck	310-342-6300	P	421	4.6
First Security Service Corp.	1 Harborside Dr	Boston	MA	02128	Robert Johnson	617-568-8700	R	138*	5.5
SecurityLink	111 Windsor Dr	Oak Brook	IL	60523		630-572-1200	R	129*	0.8
Guardian Alarm of Michigan	20800 Southfield Rd	Southfield	MI	48075	Jeffery S Prough	248-423-1000	R	116*	3.0
Jacobus Energy Inc.	11815 W Bradley Rd	Milwaukee	WI	53224	CD Jacobus	414-359-0700	R	116*	0.2
Westec Security Group Inc.	100 Bayview Cir	Newport Beach	CA	92660	Michael Kaye	949-725-6600	R	110*	3.0
A and R Security Services Inc.	2552 W 135th St	Blue Island	IL	60406	VL Ruffolo	708-389-3830	R	100*	1.2
MVM Inc.	8301 Greensboro Dr	McLean	VA	22102	Dario O Marquez Jr	703-790-3138	R	99*	1.6
Protection One Alarm Monitoring	6011 Bristol Pkwy	Culver City	CA	90230	J M Mackenzie Jr	310-342-6300	S	98	0.9
BI Inc.	6400 Lookout Rd	Boulder	CO	80301	David J Hunter	303-218-1000	P	68	0.9
Lifeline Systems Inc.	640 Mem Dr	Cambridge	MA	02139	Ronald Feinstein	508-988-100	P	64	0.6
General Security Services Corp.	9110 Meadowview	Bloomington	MN	55425	Whitney Miller	612-858-5000	R	50	1.1
Doyle Group Inc.	1806 East Ave	Rochester	NY	14610	John G Doyle Jr	716-244-3400	R	48	3.6
RFI Communications & Security	360 Turtle Creek Ct	San Jose	CA	95125	Larry Reece	408-298-5400	R	41*	0.3
Guardian Protection Services Inc.	650 Ridge Rd	Pittsburgh	PA	15205	Russ Cersosimo	412-788-2580	R	40*	0.5
Per Mar Security & Research Corp	PO Box 4227	Davenport	IA	52808	Michael Duffy	319-359-3200	R	34	2.0
Bay Alarm Corp.	925 Ygnacio Valley	Walnut Creek	CA	94596	Ed Jenks	925-935-1100	R	31*	0.6
Smith Alarm Systems	7777 Carpenter Fwy	Dallas	TX	75247	Charles May	214-631-3300	R	31*	0.2
Reliable Fire Equipment Co.	12845 S Cicero Ave	Alsip	IL	60803	Ernest E Horvath	708-597-4600	R	30*	0.1
Silent Watchman Div.	2461 McGaw Rd	Columbus	OH	43207		614-491-5200	D	25*	0.3
Covington Electric Cooperative	P O Box 1357	Andalusia	AL	36420		334-222-4121	R	22*	0.1
Spectrum Financial System Inc.	163 McKenzie Rd	Mooresville	NC	28115	Vennie A Pent	704-663-4466	R	18	0.1
ITI Technologies, Inc.	2266 N 2nd St	North St. Paul	MN	55109		651-777-2690	P	18	0.6
Chubb Security Systems Inc.	1000 Metric #200	Austin	TX	78758	Philip Like	512-977-5100	R	17*	0.2
Doyle Security Systems	1806 East Ave	Rochester	NY	14610	Michael H Cooper	716-232-7002	D	12	0.1
ATX Technologies Inc.	10010 San Pedro	San Antonio	TX	78216	Steven W Riebel	210-979-4999	R	10*	0.1
UAC Security Systems Inc.	996 Scripps Lake Dr	San Diego	CA	92131	Earl Coleman	619-271-1762	S	10	<0.1
Firstwatch Corp.	1819 Hinton St	Dallas	TX	75235	Tim Yarbro	214-630-6636	R	9*	0.2
Delmarva Systems Corp.	1100 First State Blvd	Newport	DE	19804	Carl Thomas	302-992-7950	R	8*	<0.1
Security One Systems	5747 N Andrews	Fort Lauderdale	FL	33309	Robert Newman	954-351-1111	R	8*	<0.1
Sonitrol Communications Corp.	100 Constitution Plz	Hartford	CT	06103	DM Curtiss	860-247-4500	R	8*	<0.1
AAA Security Systems Inc.	10401 Hickman Rd	Des Moines	IA	50322	Tom Skeens	515-254-1161	R	7*	<0.1
Dale System Inc.	1101 Stewart Ave	Garden City	NY	11530	Harvey M Yaffe	516-794-2800	P	7	0.2
Emergency 24 Inc.	4179 W Irving	Chicago	IL	60641	Dante Monteverde	773-777-0707	R	7	0.1
Marine Electric Systems Inc.	PO Box 1135	Clifton	NJ	07014	H Epstein	973-471-6800	R	7	<0.1
Guardian International Inc.	22570 Markey Ct	Dulles	VA	20166	Andrew Moorer	703-444-9894	P	6	<0.1
Crime Alert Alarm Co.	690 Lenfest Rd	San Jose	CA	95133	Jeff Rodriguez	408-729-6200	R	5*	<0.1
Safeguard Security Services	16117 N 76th St	Scottsdale	AZ	85260		602-609-6200	R	5*	<0.1
Videotronix Inc.	1103 W Burnsville	Burnsville	MN	55337	John Morris	612-894-5343	R	5	<0.1
New England Security Inc.	PO Box 562	Westerly	RI	02891	Jeffery A Morrone	401-596-0660	R	4*	<0.1
Byte Brothers Inc.	1309 N 30th St	Renton	WA	98056	Darrell Igelmund	425-271-9567	R	2*	<0.1
Electro-Com Corp.	15324 Mack Ave	GrPointe Pk	MI	48224	CB Raudabaugh	313-821-5595	R	2*	<0.1
Huffman Security Company Inc.	1312 Lonedell Rd	Arnold	MO	63010	Rex Huffman	314-282-7233	R	2*	<0.1
Seatronics Inc.	1501 15th St	Auburn	WA	98001	JK Deonigi	253-939-6060	R	2*	<0.1
Fredriksen & Sons Fire Equipment	760 Thomas Dr	Bensenville	IL	60106	R Fredriksen	630-595-9500	R	2	<0.1
D/A Mid South Inc.	9000 Jameel, #100	Houston	TX	77040	Richard J Gunn	713-895-0090	R	2	<0.1
BABYWATCH Corp.	50 A S Main St	Spring Valley	NY	10977	Jordan P Heilweil		R	1*	<0.1
General Sound (Texas) Co.	P O Box 832367	Richardson	TX	75083	Joe A Durham	972-231-2541	R	1	<0.1
Guardian Technology Inc.	2500 Brookpark Rd	Cleveland	OH	44134	TJ Bower	216-741-6000	S	1*	<0.1
Pinkerton Systems Intergration	1301 Clover Dr S	Bloomington	MN	55420	Tony RA Grimes	612-888-6800	R	1*	<0.1
Albany Security Company Co.	31 Crammond St	Albany	NY	12205	Maurice DeMontozon	518-489-6750	R	1*	<0.1
Steven R. Keller & Associates Inc.	22 Foxfords Chase	Ormond Beach	FL	32174		904-673-9973	N	1	<0.1
Predictive Maintenance Inspection	PO Box 429	Madison	AL	35758	F Scott Hoover	256-721-0100	R	0	<0.1
Alarm Masters	10569 W Arpt Blvd	Stafford	TX	77477	Charles Turner	281-933-3900	R	0*	<0.1

Source: Ward's Business Directory of U.S. Private and Public Companies, Volumes 1 and 2, 2000. The company type code used is as follows: P - Public, R - Private, S - Subsidiary, D - Division, J - Joint Venture, A - Affiliate, G - Group, N - Company type not reported. Sales are in millions of dollars, employees are in thousands. An asterisk (*) indicates an estimated sales volume. The symbol < stands for 'less than'. Company names and addresses are truncated, in some cases, to fit into the available space.

LOCATION BY STATE AND REGIONAL CONCENTRATION

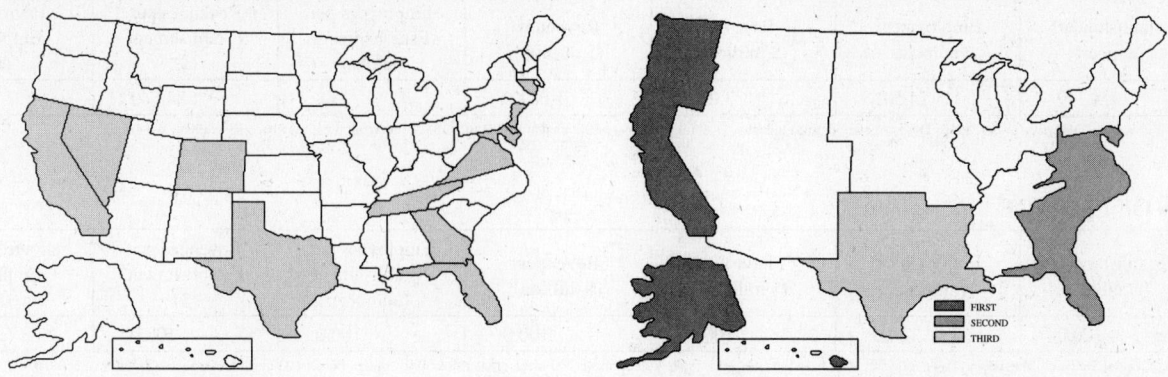

INDUSTRY DATA BY STATE

State	Establishments Total (number)	Establishments % of U.S.	Employment Total (number)	Employment % of U.S.	Employment Per Estab.	Payroll Total ($ mil.)	Payroll Per Empl. ($)	Revenues Total ($ mil.)	Revenues % of U.S.	Revenues Per Estab. ($)
California	640	12.4	16,525	15.4	26	389.5	23,571	1,138.9	16.3	1,779,523
Texas	365	7.1	10,537	9.8	29	249.0	23,632	921.1	13.2	2,523,471
Florida	409	7.9	7,609	7.1	19	172.0	22,606	466.4	6.7	1,140,399
New York	386	7.5	5,758	5.4	15	162.2	28,172	440.3	6.3	1,140,640
Illinois	203	3.9	4,178	3.9	21	122.1	29,222	292.4	4.2	1,440,300
New Jersey	202	3.9	4,320	4.0	21	111.8	25,875	287.4	4.1	1,422,896
Ohio	184	3.6	5,187	4.8	28	120.8	23,298	283.8	4.1	1,542,266
Pennsylvania	184	3.6	3,819	3.6	21	102.9	26,951	244.6	3.5	1,329,408
Michigan	152	2.9	3,723	3.5	24	98.7	26,513	215.7	3.1	1,419,039
Georgia	209	4.1	2,554	2.4	12	75.7	29,622	194.2	2.8	928,990
Virginia	140	2.7	2,830	2.6	20	76.4	27,002	188.9	2.7	1,349,179
Maryland	160	3.1	2,562	2.4	16	66.0	25,749	173.7	2.5	1,085,625
Tennessee	122	2.4	2,154	2.0	18	56.0	25,983	146.8	2.1	1,202,926
Massachusetts	128	2.5	2,139	2.0	17	55.6	25,971	146.0	2.1	1,140,828
Connecticut	78	1.5	1,901	1.8	24	53.7	28,225	145.8	2.1	1,869,782
Washington	78	1.5	1,807	1.7	23	52.7	29,152	140.4	2.0	1,799,859
North Carolina	137	2.7	1,625	1.5	12	50.5	31,049	137.3	2.0	1,002,058
Colorado	105	2.0	2,093	1.9	20	53.3	25,476	112.8	1.6	1,074,505
Arizona	97	1.9	2,381	2.2	25	49.2	20,667	107.6	1.5	1,108,835
Missouri	89	1.7	1,656	1.5	19	39.2	23,680	103.5	1.5	1,162,584
Alabama	81	1.6	2,162	2.0	27	42.6	19,724	97.1	1.4	1,198,370
Indiana	92	1.8	2,178	2.0	24	42.5	19,490	95.9	1.4	1,041,880
Louisiana	80	1.6	1,430	1.3	18	33.7	23,568	86.6	1.2	1,083,113
Wisconsin	63	1.2	3,881	3.6	62	42.3	10,892	85.7	1.2	1,360,873
Minnesota	61	1.2	1,173	1.1	19	30.6	26,130	70.2	1.0	1,151,295
South Carolina	79	1.5	925	0.9	12	24.7	26,711	69.0	1.0	872,886
Oregon	69	1.3	1,169	1.1	17	26.4	22,555	68.4	1.0	991,449
Oklahoma	61	1.2	1,195	1.1	20	23.9	20,013	64.1	0.9	1,051,148
Kentucky	46	0.9	861	0.8	19	18.5	21,537	44.8	0.6	973,761
Nevada	37	0.7	520	0.5	14	16.8	32,327	43.9	0.6	1,187,676
Nebraska	31	0.6	628	0.6	20	11.3	18,005	38.8	0.6	1,252,258
Delaware	20	0.4	393	0.4	20	11.2	28,499	35.0	0.5	1,752,200
Iowa	31	0.6	942	0.9	30	16.9	17,986	34.3	0.5	1,105,065
Mississippi	28	0.5	449	0.4	16	10.2	22,826	26.3	0.4	940,071
Arkansas	37	0.7	392	0.4	11	8.9	22,635	25.3	0.4	684,081
New Mexico	35	0.7	534	0.5	15	10.7	19,961	23.9	0.3	683,514
Utah	16	0.3	430	0.4	27	9.5	22,130	19.5	0.3	1,221,563
Rhode Island	31	0.6	265	0.2	9	6.2	23,351	18.3	0.3	591,129
Hawaii	13	0.3	199	0.2	15	6.8	34,045	15.5	0.2	1,194,538
New Hampshire	27	0.5	173	0.2	6	5.5	31,769	14.8	0.2	547,815
Maine	13	0.3	188	0.2	14	5.1	27,367	14.6	0.2	1,125,462
Idaho	12	0.2	85	0.1	7	1.8	20,706	8.6	0.1	720,167
West Virginia	16	0.3	255	0.2	16	4.2	16,643	7.8	0.1	487,312
South Dakota	10	0.2	86	0.1	9	2.1	23,965	5.4	0.1	539,300
Montana	10	0.2	122	0.1	12	2.4	20,016	5.3	0.1	534,200
North Dakota	7	0.1	35	0.0	5	0.5	14,457	3.0	0.0	429,143
Wyoming	10	0.2	77	0.1	8	1.2	15,987	2.5	0.0	254,100
Vermont	9	0.2	34	0.0	4	0.8	22,088	2.1	0.0	230,000
Kansas	52	1.0	1,750*	-	-	(D)	-	(D)	-	-
Alaska	6	0.1	60*	-	-	(D)	-	(D)	-	-
D.C.	5	0.1	60*	-	-	(D)	-	(D)	-	-

Source: 1997 *Economic Census.* The states are in descending order of revenues or establishments (if revenue data are missing for the majority). The symbol (D) appears when data are withheld to prevent disclosure of competitive information. States marked with (D) are sorted by number of establishments. A dash (-) indicates that the data element cannot be calculated. * indicates the midpoint of a range; 175, for example is the range 100-249. Shaded *states* on the state map indicate those states which have proportionately greater representation in the industry than would be indicated by the state's population; the ratio is based on total revenues or number of establishments. Shaded *regions* indicate where the industry is regionally most concentrated.

NAICS 561622 - LOCKSMITHS

GENERAL STATISTICS

Year	Establishments (number)	Employment (number)	Payroll ($ million)	Revenues ($ million)	Employees per Establishment (number)	Revenues per Establishment ($)	Payroll per Employee ($)
1997	3,799	14,501	336.0	1,081.0	3.8	284,549	23,171

Source: Economic Census of the United States, 1997. This is a newly defined industry. Data for prior years were unavailable at the time of publication but may become available over time.

INDICES OF CHANGE

Year	Establishments (number)	Employment (number)	Payroll ($ million)	Revenues ($ million)	Employees per Establishment (number)	Revenues per Establishment ($)	Payroll per Employee ($)
1997	100.0	100.0	100.0	100.0	100.0	100.0	100.0

Sources: Same as General Statistics. The values shown reflect change from the base year, 1997. Values above 100 mean greater than 1997, values below 100 mean less than 1997, and a value of 100 in the 1982-96 or 1998-2001 period means same as 1997. Values followed by a 'p' are projections by the editors; 'e' stands for extrapolation. Data are the most recent available at this level of detail.

SIC INDUSTRIES RELATED TO NAICS 561622

Each new NAICS code represents an industry that used to be part of an SIC or a part of several SIC industries. Data in this table are shown to provide transitional information for these cases. All available data for the precursor SIC(s) are shown. Even if only a part of an SIC is included in the NAICS, *all* data for the SIC are reproduced. If the SIC industry is not marked as being a part (pt) of the NAICS, the entire industry is embedded in the NAICS data. The SIC composition of the new industry provides some hints of the relative importance of its "ancestors." Data marked with a 'p' are projected. Projections begin with 1982 data. Data earlier than 1990 are not shown but are reflected in the projections.

SIC	Industry	1990	1991	1992	1993	1994	1995	1996	1997
7699	**Repair Services, nec (pt)**								
	Establishments (number)	27,822	29,303	34,103	34,618	34,136	34,391	35,001p	35,792p
	Employment (thousands)	181.0	181.4	191.0	201.5	207.4	220.2	219.6p	226.2p
	Revenues ($ million)	-	-	15,059.4	15,563.6p	16,427.9p	17,292.2p	18,156.5p	19,020.8p

Source: Economic Census of the United States, 1992, annual surveys of economic sectors conducted by the Bureau of the Census, and estimates or projections based on the 1982-1992 period; not all data are shown. 'e' marks estimates made by the editors; 'p' indicates projections based on time series. A dash (-) indicates that data for this SIC or year were not available. The abbreviation (pt) next to the industry name indicates that only a part of the industry is present within the NAICS data. If no (pt) is shown, the entire industry is contained within the NAICS data.

SELECTED RATIOS

For 1997	Avg. of Information	Analyzed Industry	Index	For 1997	Avg. of Information	Analyzed Industry	Index
Employees per establishment	27	4	14	Payroll per establishment	496,890	88,444	18
Revenue per establishment	1,070,709	284,549	27	Payroll as % of revenue	46	31	67
Revenue per employee	40,278	74,547	185	Payroll per employee	18,692	23,171	124

Sources: Same as General Statistics. The 'Average' column represents the average for the industry sector, in 1997, where the currently shown industry is classified. The Index shows the relationship between the Average and the Analyzed Industry. For example, 100 means that they are equal; 500 that the Analyzed Industry is five times the average; 50 means that the Analyzed Industry is half the national average. The abbreviation 'na' is used to show that data are 'not available'.

LEADING COMPANIES
No company data available for this industry.

LOCATION BY STATE AND REGIONAL CONCENTRATION

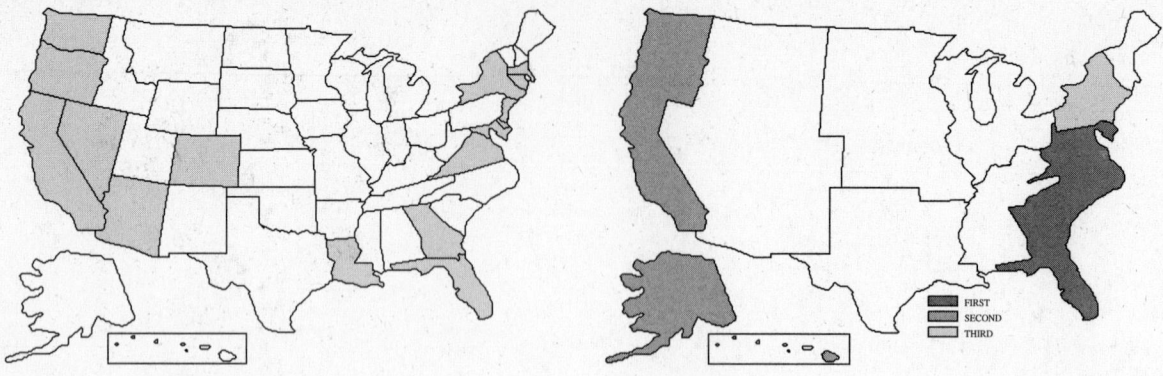

FIRST
SECOND
THIRD

INDUSTRY DATA BY STATE

State	Establishments Total (number)	Establishments % of U.S.	Employment Total (number)	Employment % of U.S.	Employment Per Estab.	Payroll Total ($ mil.)	Payroll Per Empl. ($)	Revenues Total ($ mil.)	Revenues % of U.S.	Revenues Per Estab. ($)
California	462	12.2	1,747	12.0	4	42.7	24,460	145.6	13.5	315,221
New York	304	8.0	1,307	9.0	4	29.7	22,756	99.6	9.2	327,717
Florida	334	8.8	1,273	8.8	4	24.8	19,501	75.6	7.0	226,237
Texas	255	6.7	871	6.0	3	20.3	23,341	63.4	5.9	248,761
Illinois	145	3.8	577	4.0	4	14.7	25,536	47.0	4.3	323,828
New Jersey	127	3.3	489	3.4	4	14.3	29,147	44.6	4.1	351,126
Virginia	117	3.1	524	3.6	4	13.0	24,863	40.0	3.7	342,103
Pennsylvania	116	3.1	529	3.6	5	11.3	21,393	39.9	3.7	344,181
Michigan	106	2.8	425	2.9	4	11.3	26,553	38.4	3.6	362,292
Ohio	115	3.0	441	3.0	4	13.7	31,088	36.0	3.3	313,130
Georgia	106	2.8	411	2.8	4	9.2	22,297	29.8	2.8	281,274
Nevada	33	0.9	257	1.8	8	7.5	28,992	26.1	2.4	789,848
Massachusetts	81	2.1	311	2.1	4	8.3	26,749	25.9	2.4	319,284
Maryland	75	2.0	319	2.2	4	8.6	26,850	25.6	2.4	341,133
Washington	94	2.5	323	2.2	3	8.2	25,238	24.5	2.3	260,351
Colorado	94	2.5	368	2.5	4	7.6	20,674	23.5	2.2	249,926
Connecticut	39	1.0	179	1.2	5	5.3	29,782	20.7	1.9	532,000
Missouri	75	2.0	274	1.9	4	7.0	25,606	20.4	1.9	272,227
Louisiana	72	1.9	334	2.3	5	6.6	19,829	19.5	1.8	271,222
North Carolina	91	2.4	274	1.9	3	5.8	21,201	19.1	1.8	209,560
Wisconsin	62	1.6	230	1.6	4	6.0	26,113	17.2	1.6	277,500
Alabama	59	1.6	238	1.6	4	5.0	21,172	17.0	1.6	287,424
Arizona	81	2.1	253	1.7	3	5.1	20,281	16.8	1.6	207,630
Minnesota	62	1.6	189	1.3	3	4.3	22,910	14.2	1.3	229,210
Oregon	55	1.4	219	1.5	4	4.4	20,114	13.5	1.2	245,327
South Carolina	54	1.4	201	1.4	4	4.1	20,433	13.0	1.2	240,148
Indiana	53	1.4	188	1.3	4	3.7	19,734	11.4	1.1	214,396
Tennessee	53	1.4	173	1.2	3	3.1	18,202	9.5	0.9	179,491
Oklahoma	55	1.4	165	1.1	3	2.6	16,048	8.7	0.8	158,455
Utah	29	0.8	110	0.8	4	2.5	22,273	7.8	0.7	268,138
Iowa	32	0.8	112	0.8	4	2.1	18,393	7.3	0.7	228,750
Kentucky	32	0.8	102	0.7	3	1.8	18,078	6.8	0.6	213,469
Arkansas	29	0.8	142	1.0	5	2.4	16,775	6.8	0.6	233,828
New Mexico	38	1.0	106	0.7	3	2.0	18,972	6.7	0.6	176,816
Nebraska	27	0.7	75	0.5	3	2.0	26,747	6.5	0.6	239,593
Mississippi	32	0.8	95	0.7	3	1.5	16,284	6.1	0.6	191,406
New Hampshire	19	0.5	62	0.4	3	1.5	23,823	4.8	0.4	252,158
Hawaii	18	0.5	60	0.4	3	1.3	22,000	4.6	0.4	253,833
Delaware	11	0.3	60	0.4	5	1.2	20,467	3.6	0.3	324,364
Rhode Island	19	0.5	54	0.4	3	1.1	19,907	3.6	0.3	187,316
Idaho	17	0.4	50	0.3	3	0.9	18,360	3.5	0.3	203,941
Maine	18	0.5	55	0.4	3	0.9	15,945	3.1	0.3	170,167
West Virginia	12	0.3	37	0.3	3	0.7	17,892	3.0	0.3	250,333
Montana	10	0.3	39	0.3	4	0.7	16,872	2.6	0.2	256,700
North Dakota	10	0.3	35	0.2	4	0.5	13,571	2.2	0.2	215,200
South Dakota	6	0.2	29	0.2	5	0.5	17,966	1.8	0.2	305,333
Vermont	9	0.2	17	0.1	2	0.3	16,824	1.1	0.1	120,667
Wyoming	7	0.2	9	0.1	1	0.1	14,222	0.5	0.0	70,857
Kansas	35	0.9	175*	-	-	(D)	-	(D)	-	-
Alaska	7	0.2	60*	-	-	(D)	-	(D)	-	-
D.C.	7	0.2	60*	-	-	(D)	-	(D)	-	-

Source: 1997 *Economic Census*. The states are in descending order of revenues or establishments (if revenue data are missing for the majority). The symbol (D) appears when data are withheld to prevent disclosure of competitive information. States marked with (D) are sorted by number of establishments. A dash (-) indicates that the data element cannot be calculated. * indicates the midpoint of a range; 175, for example is the range 100-249. Shaded *states* on the state map indicate those states which have proportionately greater representation in the industry than would be indicated by the state's population; the ratio is based on total revenues or number of establishments. Shaded *regions* indicate where the industry is regionally most concentrated.

NAICS 561710 - EXTERMINATING AND PEST CONTROL SERVICES

GENERAL STATISTICS

Year	Establishments (number)	Employment (number)	Payroll ($ million)	Revenues ($ million)	Employees per Establishment (number)	Revenues per Establishment ($)	Payroll per Employee ($)
1997	11,062	81,214	1,930.0	4,911.0	7.3	443,952	23,764

Source: Economic Census of the United States, 1997. This is a newly defined industry. Data for prior years were unavailable at the time of publication but may become available over time.

INDICES OF CHANGE

Year	Establishments (number)	Employment (number)	Payroll ($ million)	Revenues ($ million)	Employees per Establishment (number)	Revenues per Establishment ($)	Payroll per Employee ($)
1997	100.0	100.0	100.0	100.0	100.0	100.0	100.0

Sources: Same as General Statistics. The values shown reflect change from the base year, 1997. Values above 100 mean greater than 1997, values below 100 mean less than 1997, and a value of 100 in the 1982-96 or 1998-2001 period means same as 1997. Values followed by a 'p' are projections by the editors; 'e' stands for extrapolation. Data are the most recent available at this level of detail.

SIC INDUSTRIES RELATED TO NAICS 561710

Each new NAICS code represents an industry that used to be part of an SIC or a part of several SIC industries. Data in this table are shown to provide transitional information for these cases. All available data for the precursor SIC(s) are shown. Even if only a part of an SIC is included in the NAICS, *all* data for the SIC are reproduced. If the SIC industry is not marked as being a part (pt) of the NAICS, the entire industry is embedded in the NAICS data. The SIC composition of the new industry provides some hints of the relative importance of its "ancestors." Data marked with a 'p' are projected. Projections begin with 1982 data. Data earlier than 1990 are not shown but are reflected in the projections.

SIC	Industry	1990	1991	1992	1993	1994	1995	1996	1997
4959	**Sanitary Services, nec (pt)**								
	Establishments (number)	-	-	1,277	-	-	-	-	-
	Employment (thousands)	-	-	8.1	-	-	-	-	-
	Revenues ($ million)	-	-	702.4	-	-	-	-	-
7342	**Disinfecting & Exterminating (pt)**								
	Establishments (number)	9,073	9,591	10,300	10,608	10,716	10,922	11,161p	11,418p
	Employment (thousands)	68.9	68.4	70.5	75.8	76.2	78.3	81.3p	83.4p
	Revenues ($ million)	4,526.0	4,811.0	4,928.0	5,044.0	5,333.0	5,848.0	6,289.0	6,510.8p

Source: Economic Census of the United States, 1992, annual surveys of economic sectors conducted by the Bureau of the Census, and estimates or projections based on the 1982-1992 period; not all data are shown. 'e' marks estimates made by the editors; 'p' indicates projections based on time series. A dash (-) indicates that data for this SIC or year were not available. The abbreviation (pt) next to the industry name indicates that only a part of the industry is present within the NAICS data. If no (pt) is shown, the entire industry is contained within the NAICS data.

SELECTED RATIOS

For 1997	Avg. of Information	Analyzed Industry	Index	For 1997	Avg. of Information	Analyzed Industry	Index
Employees per establishment	27	7	28	Payroll per establishment	496,890	174,471	35
Revenue per establishment	1,070,709	443,952	41	Payroll as % of revenue	46	39	85
Revenue per employee	40,278	60,470	150	Payroll per employee	18,692	23,764	127

Sources: Same as General Statistics. The 'Average' column represents the average for the industry sector, in 1997, where the currently shown industry is classified. The Index shows the relationship between the Average and the Analyzed Industry. For example, 100 means that they are equal; 500 that the Analyzed Industry is five times the average; 50 means that the Analyzed Industry is half the national average. The abbreviation 'na' is used to show that data are 'not available'.

LEADING COMPANIES   Number shown: **11**   Total sales ($ mil): **2,922**   Total employment (000): **44.2**

Company Name	Address				CEO Name	Phone	Co. Type	Sales ($ mil)	Empl. (000)
ServiceMaster Consumer Services	860 Ridge Lake	Memphis	TN	38120	Carlos Cantu	901-684-7500	S	910*	15.0
Rollins Inc.	P O Box 647	Atlanta	GA	30301	Gary W Rollins	404-888-2000	P	587	8.9
Orkin Exterminating Inc.	2170 Piedmont	Atlanta	GA	30324	R Randall Rollins	404-888-2000	S	555	8.0
Terminix International L.P.	860 Ridge Lake	Memphis	TN	38120	Carlos H Cantu	901-766-1333	S	413*	6.7
Ecolab Inc. Pest Elimination Div.	370 Wabasha St N	Saint Paul	MN	55102		651-293-2233	S	201*	1.3
Truly Nolen of America Inc.	PO Box 43550	Tucson	AZ	85733	Scott Nolen	520-321-4200	R	61*	1.0
Western Exterminator Co.	1732 Kaiser Ave	Irvine	CA	92614	Roy Ashton	949-261-2440	R	51*	0.8
Cook's Pest Control Inc.	PO Box 669	Decatur	AL	35602	Jim Aycock	256-355-3285	R	50	0.9
Terminix Service Inc.	PO Box 2627	Columbia	SC	29202	Thomas P Knox Jr	803-772-1783	R	36*	0.6
Massey Services Inc.	610 N Wymore Rd	Maitland	FL	32751	Harvey Massey	407-645-2500	R	30	0.5
Dodson Brothers Exterminating	3712 Campbell Ave	Lynchburg	VA	24501	Bertram F Dodson Jr	804-847-9051	R	29*	0.5

Source: Ward's Business Directory of U.S. Private and Public Companies, Volumes 1 and 2, 2000. The company type code used is as follows: P - Public, R - Private, S - Subsidiary, D - Division, J - Joint Venture, A - Affiliate, G - Group, N - Company type not reported. Sales are in millions of dollars, employees are in thousands. An asterisk (*) indicates an estimated sales volume. The symbol < stands for 'less than'. Company names and addresses are truncated, in some cases, to fit into the available space.

LOCATION BY STATE AND REGIONAL CONCENTRATION

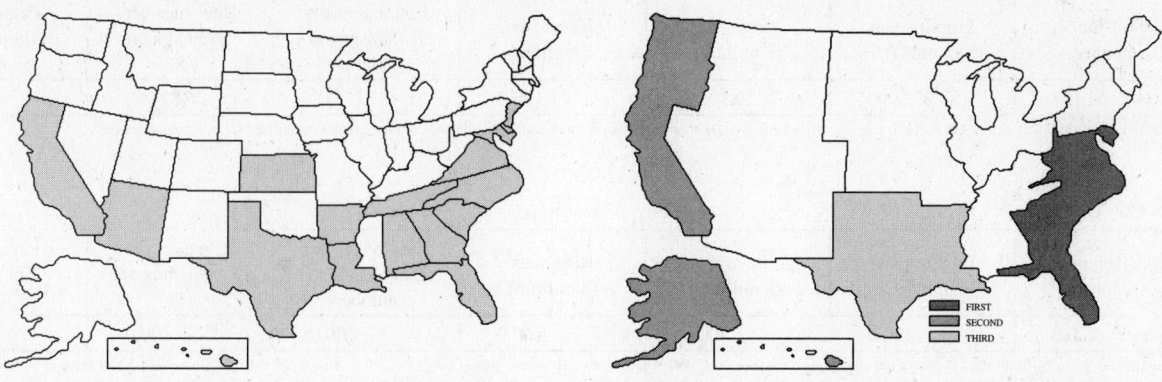

INDUSTRY DATA BY STATE

State	Establishments Total (number)	% of U.S.	Employment Total (number)	% of U.S.	Per Estab.	Payroll Total ($ mil.)	Per Empl. ($)	Revenues Total ($ mil.)	% of U.S.	Per Estab. ($)
California	1,258	11.4	12,275	15.1	10	331.4	27,000	866.1	17.6	688,479
Florida	1,558	14.1	12,147	15.0	8	280.1	23,063	705.8	14.4	453,003
Texas	994	9.0	6,074	7.5	6	134.7	22,176	359.0	7.3	361,198
Georgia	480	4.3	4,076	5.0	8	95.6	23,465	231.8	4.7	482,852
New York	542	4.9	2,869	3.5	5	75.6	26,344	178.1	3.6	328,542
North Carolina	351	3.2	3,149	3.9	9	67.7	21,514	163.0	3.3	464,288
New Jersey	369	3.3	2,284	2.8	6	63.0	27,601	155.7	3.2	421,851
Tennessee	264	2.4	2,371	2.9	9	52.3	22,071	147.2	3.0	557,648
Pennsylvania	302	2.7	2,312	2.8	8	58.9	25,461	144.6	2.9	478,695
Arizona	334	3.0	2,444	3.0	7	53.5	21,890	139.3	2.8	417,036
Virginia	280	2.5	2,385	2.9	9	56.3	23,589	135.0	2.7	482,064
Illinois	327	3.0	2,173	2.7	7	53.2	24,481	133.2	2.7	407,394
Alabama	298	2.7	2,295	2.8	8	49.1	21,386	132.9	2.7	446,030
Louisiana	271	2.4	2,105	2.6	8	45.3	21,527	119.6	2.4	441,384
Ohio	256	2.3	1,860	2.3	7	44.6	23,985	110.0	2.2	429,598
Maryland	190	1.7	1,716	2.1	9	46.3	26,959	108.2	2.2	569,726
South Carolina	260	2.4	1,947	2.4	7	41.3	21,207	104.1	2.1	400,442
Missouri	265	2.4	1,368	1.7	5	31.9	23,337	86.8	1.8	327,419
Massachusetts	187	1.7	1,022	1.3	5	29.6	29,001	72.0	1.5	385,128
Indiana	176	1.6	1,249	1.5	7	26.9	21,557	69.5	1.4	395,063
Michigan	166	1.5	1,063	1.3	6	25.4	23,901	65.3	1.3	393,633
Arkansas	152	1.4	1,200	1.5	8	22.7	18,918	63.1	1.3	414,895
Kentucky	144	1.3	1,125	1.4	8	21.9	19,441	54.5	1.1	378,743
Oklahoma	179	1.6	915	1.1	5	17.4	18,980	50.4	1.0	281,503
Mississippi	158	1.4	944	1.2	6	18.7	19,859	50.3	1.0	318,196
Kansas	137	1.2	1,056	1.3	8	18.9	17,891	49.2	1.0	358,898
Washington	131	1.2	718	0.9	5	19.3	26,937	46.9	1.0	358,298
Hawaii	64	0.6	618	0.8	10	15.7	25,421	42.8	0.9	668,984
Connecticut	100	0.9	491	0.6	5	14.6	29,684	34.1	0.7	341,440
Minnesota	45	0.4	414	0.5	9	15.2	36,833	34.0	0.7	755,000
Wisconsin	66	0.6	493	0.6	7	14.5	29,391	32.3	0.7	489,712
Iowa	98	0.9	506	0.6	5	11.4	22,573	30.3	0.6	309,673
Nevada	85	0.8	446	0.5	5	10.2	22,892	24.7	0.5	291,153
Colorado	62	0.6	467	0.6	8	10.8	23,094	24.7	0.5	398,129
West Virginia	54	0.5	489	0.6	9	9.5	19,346	24.4	0.5	452,111
Oregon	104	0.9	436	0.5	4	8.2	18,917	23.9	0.5	229,702
Nebraska	74	0.7	331	0.4	4	8.1	24,414	19.4	0.4	262,743
New Mexico	64	0.6	327	0.4	5	5.6	17,174	15.2	0.3	237,875
Delaware	44	0.4	270	0.3	6	5.6	20,733	14.9	0.3	338,318
Rhode Island	37	0.3	240	0.3	6	6.0	24,800	13.5	0.3	364,189
Utah	30	0.3	119	0.1	4	2.8	23,319	7.5	0.2	251,000
Maine	18	0.2	103	0.1	6	2.5	24,291	6.9	0.1	384,444
New Hampshire	19	0.2	83	0.1	4	2.3	27,819	6.1	0.1	322,053
Idaho	19	0.2	100	0.1	5	1.8	17,620	5.1	0.1	268,842
Vermont	16	0.1	29	0.0	2	0.8	28,828	2.5	0.1	154,125
Montana	8	0.1	35	0.0	4	0.8	23,971	2.1	0.0	260,375
Alaska	7	0.1	14	0.0	2	0.4	31,571	1.2	0.0	176,143
Wyoming	6	0.1	15	0.0	3	0.4	26,800	1.1	0.0	185,167
South Dakota	7	0.1	11	0.0	2	0.2	18,364	0.6	0.0	84,143
D.C.	4	-	10*	-	-	(D)	-	(D)	-	-
North Dakota	2	-	10*	-	-	(D)	-	(D)	-	-

Source: 1997 *Economic Census.* The states are in descending order of revenues or establishments (if revenue data are missing for the majority). The symbol (D) appears when data are withheld to prevent disclosure of competitive information. States marked with (D) are sorted by number of establishments. A dash (-) indicates that the data element cannot be calculated. * indicates the midpoint of a range; 175, for example is the range 100-249. Shaded *states* on the state map indicate those states which have proportionately greater representation in the industry than would be indicated by the state's population; the ratio is based on total revenues or number of establishments. Shaded *regions* indicate where the industry is regionally most concentrated.

NAICS 561720 - JANITORIAL SERVICES

GENERAL STATISTICS

Year	Establishments (number)	Employment (number)	Payroll ($ million)	Revenues ($ million)	Employees per Establishment (number)	Revenues per Establishment ($)	Payroll per Employee ($)
1997	55,157	892,290	10,106.0	21,128.0	16.2	383,052	11,326

Source: Economic Census of the United States, 1997. This is a newly defined industry. Data for prior years were unavailable at the time of publication but may become available over time.

INDICES OF CHANGE

Year	Establishments (number)	Employment (number)	Payroll ($ million)	Revenues ($ million)	Employees per Establishment (number)	Revenues per Establishment ($)	Payroll per Employee ($)
1997	100.0	100.0	100.0	100.0	100.0	100.0	100.0

Sources: Same as General Statistics. The values shown reflect change from the base year, 1997. Values above 100 mean greater than 1997, values below 100 mean less than 1997, and a value of 100 in the 1982-96 or 1998-2001 period means same as 1997. Values followed by a 'p' are projections by the editors; 'e' stands for extrapolation. Data are the most recent available at this level of detail.

SIC INDUSTRIES RELATED TO NAICS 561720

Each new NAICS code represents an industry that used to be part of an SIC or a part of several SIC industries. Data in this table are shown to provide transitional information for these cases. All available data for the precursor SIC(s) are shown. Even if only a part of an SIC is included in the NAICS, *all* data for the SIC are reproduced. If the SIC industry is not marked as being a part (pt) of the NAICS, the entire industry is embedded in the NAICS data. The SIC composition of the new industry provides some hints of the relative importance of its "ancestors." Data marked with a 'p' are projected. Projections begin with 1982 data. Data earlier than 1990 are not shown but are reflected in the projections.

SIC	Industry	1990	1991	1992	1993	1994	1995	1996	1997
1799	**Special Trade Contractors, n.e.c.**								
	Establishments (number)	22,471	22,634	25,270	27,296	26,150e	26,601e	27,060e	27,527e
	Employment (thousands)	197.0	186.3	204.3	207.1	216.9e	223.4e	230.2e	237.1e
	Revenues ($ million)	12,936.7e	13,535.6e	14,162.3	14,818.0e	15,504.1e	16,221.9e	16,973.0e	17,758.8e
4581	**Airports, Flying Fields and Services (pt)**								
	Establishments (number)	2,777	2,968	3,252	3,382	3,503	3,629	4,014	3,958p
	Employment (thousands)	84.3	83.9	80.0	90.8	90.2	96.6	104.6	103.5p
	Revenues ($ million)	-	-	6,167.6	-	-	-	-	-
7342	**Disinfecting & Exterminating (pt)**								
	Establishments (number)	9,073	9,591	10,300	10,608	10,716	10,922	11,161p	11,418p
	Employment (thousands)	68.9	68.4	70.5	75.8	76.2	78.3	81.3p	83.4p
	Revenues ($ million)	4,526.0	4,811.0	4,928.0	5,044.0	5,333.0	5,848.0	6,289.0	6,510.8p
7349	**Building Maintenance Services, nec (pt)**								
	Establishments (number)	38,557	42,431	47,349	49,278	49,914	50,415	53,847p	56,034p
	Employment (thousands)	729.5	735.3	747.4	786.7	798.9	821.1	835.3p	854.1p
	Revenues ($ million)	17,817.0	17,613.0	18,658.0	18,432.0	20,385.0	21,603.0	24,211.0	24,367.8p

Source: Economic Census of the United States, 1992, annual surveys of economic sectors conducted by the Bureau of the Census, and estimates or projections based on the 1982-1992 period; not all data are shown. 'e' marks estimates made by the editors; 'p' indicates projections based on time series. A dash (-) indicates that data for this SIC or year were not available. The abbreviation (pt) next to the industry name indicates that only a part of the industry is present within the NAICS data. If no (pt) is shown, the entire industry is contained within the NAICS data.

SELECTED RATIOS

For 1997	Avg. of Information	Analyzed Industry	Index	For 1997	Avg. of Information	Analyzed Industry	Index
Employees per establishment	27	16	61	Payroll per establishment	496,890	183,222	37
Revenue per establishment	1,070,709	383,052	36	Payroll as % of revenue	46	48	103
Revenue per employee	40,278	23,678	59	Payroll per employee	18,692	11,326	61

Sources: Same as General Statistics. The 'Average' column represents the average for the industry sector, in 1997, where the currently shown industry is classified. The Index shows the relationship between the Average and the Analyzed Industry. For example, 100 means that they are equal; 500 that the Analyzed Industry is five times the average; 50 means that the Analyzed Industry is half the national average. The abbreviation 'na' is used to show that data are 'not available'.

LEADING COMPANIES   Number shown: **53**   Total sales ($ mil): **25,511**   Total employment (000): **453.3**

Company Name	Address				CEO Name	Phone	Co. Type	Sales ($ mil)	Empl. (000)
ServiceMaster Co.	1 ServiceMaster	Downers Grove	IL	60515	C. William Pollard	630-271-1300	P	5,704	51.7
Marriott Intern	Marriott Dr	Washington	DC	20058		202-380-9000	D	4,443*	72.0
Jacobs Engineering Group Inc.	PO Box 7084	Pasadena	CA	91109	Joseph Jacobs	626-578-3500	P	2,875	15.9
Ecolab Inc.	Ecolab Center	St. Paul	MN	55102	Allan L Schuman	651-293-2233	P	1,888	12.0
Ogden Corp.	2 Pennsylvania Plz	New York	NY	10121	Scott G Mackin	212-868-6100	P	1,692	22.0
ABM Industries Inc.	160 Pacific Ave	San Francisco	CA	94111	William W Steele	415-597-4500	P	1,502	55.0
ABM Janitorial Services	50 Fremont St	San Francisco	CA	94105	John F Egan	415-597-4250	D	912*	52.0
ServiceMaster Consumer Services	860 Ridge Lake	Memphis	TN	38120	Carlos Cantu	901-684-7500	S	910*	15.0
Excel Enterprises Inc.	1534 High St	Richmond	VA	23220	Ray Gross	804-782-9440	D	900	40.0
One Source	1600 Parkwood Cir	Atlanta	GA	30339	Ray Grass	770-436-9900	S	794*	36.0
Unicco Service Co.	4 Copley Pl	Boston	MA	02116	Steven C Kletjian	617-859-1000	R	491	19.0
Associated Building Services Co.	1910 Napoleon	Houston	TX	77003	BL Gershen	713-227-1261	R	416*	3.0
Laro Service Systems Inc.	271 Skip Ln	Bay Shore	NY	11706	Robert Bertuglia	516-667-0900	R	353*	2.5
Admiral Maintenance Service L	730 N Cicero	Chicago	IL	60644		847-675-6000	R	323*	2.3
Pedus Building Services Inc.	15700 Export Plaza	Houston	TX	77018		713-697-9600	R	275*	2.0
Aircraft Service International Inc.	1815 Griffin Rd	Dania	FL	33004	Steve Townes	954-926-2000	S	220	3.2
Healthcare Services Group Inc.	2643 Huntingdon	Huntngdn Val	PA	19006	Thomas A Cook	215-938-1661	P	205	10.8
Holmes and Narver Services Inc.	999 Town & C	Orange	CA	92868	Robert L Murphy	714-567-2400	S	152	2.2
C.H. Heist Corp.	810 N Belcher Rd	Clearwater	FL	33758	W David Foster	727-461-5656	P	136	4.0
Initial Contract Services USA	4067 Ind Park Dr	Norcross	GA	30071	Edward S Fleury	770-476-2590	D	130	5.0
Acme Building Maintenance Inc.	P O Box 158	Alviso	CA	95002	Henry Sanchez	408-263-5911	R	128*	0.9
Servpro Industries Inc.	PO Box 1978	Gallatin	TN	37066	Randall Isaacson	615-451-0200	R	103	<0.1
Jani-King Leasing Corp.	16885 Dallas Pkwy	Dallas	TX	75248	Jim Cavanaugh	972-991-0900	R	100	4.0
Royal Services Inc.	PO Box 40665	Jacksonville	FL	32203	Percy Rosenbloom	904-355-2741	R	99*	0.7
Pedus Services Inc.	PO Box 513617	Los Angeles	CA	90051	Richard G Jackson	213-386-8480	R	90	4.0
Coverall North America Inc.	500 W Cypress	Ft. Lauderdale	FL	33309	Phil Kuber	954-351-1110	R	86	0.5
ISS Building Maintenance Inc.	220 S Spruce Ave	S. San Francisco	CA	94080	Sven Ipsen	650-871-6740	S	74*	2.3
PRIDE Industries Inc.	1 Sierra Gate Plz	Roseville	CA	95678		916-783-5266	R	60	2.9
Wyatt Field Service Co.	P O Box 3052	Houston	TX	77253	Frank L Rister	713-956-2020	S	50*	0.5
BMS Enterprises Inc.	308 Arthur St	Fort Worth	TX	76107	W G Blackman III	817-810-9200	R	41*	0.3
Faulk Co.	1701 River Run Rd	Fort Worth	TX	76107	Tim Faulk	817-332-9157	R	41*	0.3
Molly Maid Inc.	1340 Eisenhower Pl	Ann Arbor	MI	48108	Linda Burzýnski	734-975-1000	R	35*	<0.1
Budd Group	2325 S Stratford Rd	Winston-Salem	NC	27103	Joseph R Budd	336-765-7690	R	34	2.5
Help At Home Inc.	223 W Jackson	Chicago	IL	60606	Joel Davis	312-663-4244	P	28	0.2
General Building Maintenance Inc	3835 Presid'l Pky	Atlanta	GA	30340	Don Kim	404-458-1900	R	28	0.6
J and E Associates	6031 S Loop E	Houston	TX	77033	James Harris	713-640-1177	R	27*	0.2
Clean-Tech Co.	2815 Olive St	St. Louis	MO	63103	James Fiala	314-652-2388	R	26*	2.1
Valley Systems Inc.	11580 Lafayette	Canal Fulton	OH	44614	Ed Strickland	330-854-4526	P	24	0.4
Texas Maintenance Systems Inc.	9106 Bellflower	Houston	TX	77063		713-782-7066	R	23*	0.2
Help At Home Inc. (Subsidiary)	223 W Jackson	Chicago	IL	60606	Louis Goldstein	312-461-9000	S	17*	3.0
Preferred Building Services Inc.	11757 Katy Fwy	Houston	TX	77079	John Cornon	281-497-7333	R	14*	0.1
Professional Polish Inc.	5450 E Loop 820 S	Fort Worth	TX	76119	Sid Cavanaugh	817-572-7353	R	14*	0.1
Centennial One Inc.	851 Brightseat Rd	Landover	MD	20785	Lillian Lincoln	301-808-6700	R	13*	1.0
Mitch Murch's Maintenance	2827 Clark Ave	St. Louis	MO	63103	Mitch Murch	314-535-2100	R	12*	<0.1
GSF Safeway L.L.C.	107 S Pennsylvania	Indianapolis	IN	46204		317-262-1133	S	8*	0.6
Majestic Cleaning Services Inc.	1000 Post & Pad	Grand Prairie	TX	75050	Peter Salonikidis	972-660-5440	R	4*	<0.1
Luminare Service Inc.	6925 Hawthorn	Indianapolis	IN	46220	Charles Ryerson	317-578-0448	R	3	<0.1
Kover Group Inc.	9680 Sweet Valley	Valley View	OH	44125	Phillip W Kubec	216-524-2560	S	2*	<0.1
United Services Associates Inc.	1728 20th St W	Birmingham	AL	35218	John W Nixon Jr	205-785-3154	R	2*	0.2
Al Mar Building Maintenance Inc.	200 S Fielder Dr	Arlington	TX	76013	Rhodi Aceveto	817-261-3824	R	1*	<0.1
JESCO Industrial Services Inc.	P O Box 1147	Calvert City	KY	42029		270-395-7226	S	1*	<0.1
Nelly's Janitorial PS Inc.	5609 Watauga Rd	Fort Worth	TX	76148	Maria Sanchez	817-498-9011	R	1*	<0.1
One Source (Houtson, Texas)	100 McGowen	Houston	TX	77006		713-526-8971	D	1*	<0.1

Source: Ward's Business Directory of U.S. Private and Public Companies, Volumes 1 and 2, 2000. The company type code used is as follows: P - Public, R - Private, S - Subsidiary, D - Division, J - Joint Venture, A - Affiliate, G - Group, N - Company type not reported. Sales are in millions of dollars, employees are in thousands. An asterisk (*) indicates an estimated sales volume. The symbol < stands for 'less than'. Company names and addresses are truncated, in some cases, to fit into the available space.

LOCATION BY STATE AND REGIONAL CONCENTRATION

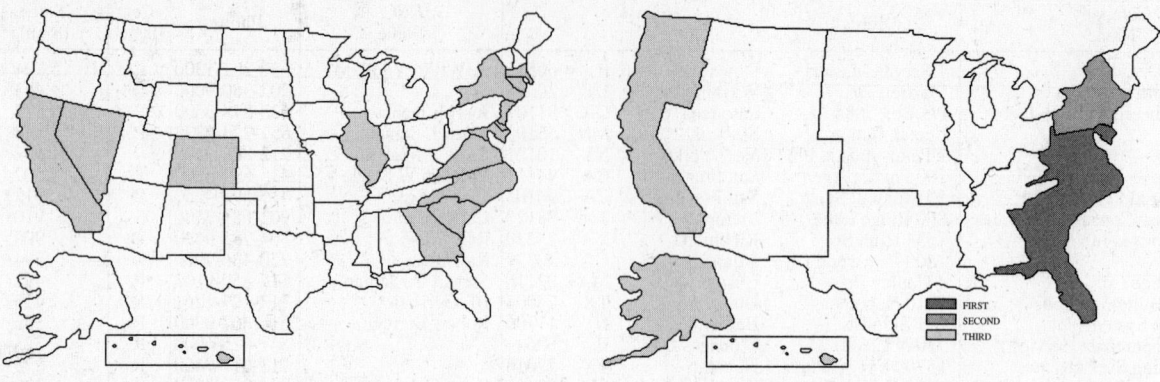

FIRST
SECOND
THIRD

INDUSTRY DATA BY STATE

State	Establishments Total (number)	% of U.S.	Employment Total (number)	% of U.S.	Per Estab.	Payroll Total ($ mil.)	Per Empl. ($)	Revenues Total ($ mil.)	% of U.S.	Per Estab. ($)
California	5,311	9.6	90,032	10.1	17	1,148.9	12,761	2,623.5	12.4	493,976
New York	2,676	4.9	62,299	7.0	23	1,135.4	18,225	2,060.8	9.8	770,114
Texas	3,092	5.6	62,869	7.0	20	659.7	10,494	1,451.8	6.9	469,548
Illinois	2,609	4.7	45,622	5.1	17	634.0	13,898	1,265.7	6.0	485,135
Pennsylvania	2,160	3.9	47,704	5.3	22	508.0	10,649	989.6	4.7	458,157
New Jersey	1,888	3.4	39,260	4.4	21	508.4	12,949	955.5	4.5	506,117
North Carolina	1,902	3.4	24,379	2.7	13	243.1	9,974	906.1	4.3	476,392
Florida	3,582	6.5	39,461	4.4	11	366.1	9,277	876.7	4.1	244,764
Ohio	2,437	4.4	41,653	4.7	17	403.5	9,686	806.3	3.8	330,839
Virginia	1,913	3.5	35,626	4.0	19	337.5	9,474	668.6	3.2	349,481
Massachusetts	1,343	2.4	28,176	3.2	21	340.0	12,066	632.3	3.0	470,809
Michigan	2,057	3.7	26,829	3.0	13	297.8	11,100	608.8	2.9	295,961
Georgia	1,413	2.6	21,604	2.4	15	247.3	11,448	567.4	2.7	401,553
Maryland	1,392	2.5	28,756	3.2	21	285.6	9,931	552.7	2.6	397,045
Missouri	1,226	2.2	23,417	2.6	19	217.5	9,289	422.0	2.0	344,235
Washington	1,492	2.7	13,232	1.5	9	166.1	12,552	376.1	1.8	252,108
Colorado	1,208	2.2	15,615	1.7	13	169.3	10,840	362.3	1.7	299,901
South Carolina	887	1.6	19,451	2.2	22	206.3	10,604	350.0	1.7	394,625
Tennessee	1,135	2.1	17,552	2.0	15	161.0	9,173	346.9	1.6	305,614
Minnesota	1,081	2.0	15,175	1.7	14	165.5	10,904	321.5	1.5	297,379
Arizona	1,017	1.8	15,034	1.7	15	154.7	10,288	308.8	1.5	303,602
Connecticut	800	1.5	14,323	1.6	18	162.7	11,362	304.4	1.4	380,466
Indiana	1,195	2.2	15,487	1.7	13	146.2	9,440	288.9	1.4	241,790
Wisconsin	1,229	2.2	16,676	1.9	14	145.2	8,709	284.7	1.3	231,644
Louisiana	611	1.1	12,253	1.4	20	114.2	9,323	275.4	1.3	450,678
Kentucky	699	1.3	12,252	1.4	18	117.1	9,561	228.4	1.1	326,795
Alabama	679	1.2	11,261	1.3	17	104.3	9,260	201.7	1.0	297,113
Oregon	792	1.4	7,676	0.9	10	92.0	11,988	200.5	0.9	253,122
Oklahoma	570	1.0	9,196	1.0	16	101.9	11,076	190.8	0.9	334,767
Iowa	570	1.0	6,435	0.7	11	67.5	10,488	181.6	0.9	318,516
Utah	467	0.8	7,138	0.8	15	61.1	8,566	139.7	0.7	299,139
Kansas	623	1.1	7,120	0.8	11	66.0	9,266	136.9	0.6	219,819
Nevada	475	0.9	4,481	0.5	9	47.5	10,589	118.0	0.6	248,488
Nebraska	425	0.8	5,653	0.6	13	49.1	8,678	110.2	0.5	259,219
D.C.	119	0.2	5,218	0.6	44	64.4	12,333	109.1	0.5	916,387
Hawaii	243	0.4	3,838	0.4	16	49.8	12,987	102.9	0.5	423,605
Mississippi	347	0.6	4,541	0.5	13	35.0	7,712	81.8	0.4	235,769
Arkansas	384	0.7	4,192	0.5	11	35.7	8,515	78.1	0.4	203,440
Delaware	225	0.4	4,891	0.5	22	43.3	8,859	77.5	0.4	344,649
Rhode Island	260	0.5	3,150	0.4	12	34.1	10,827	73.8	0.3	283,969
New Hampshire	355	0.6	3,215	0.4	9	30.6	9,504	70.7	0.3	199,290
Idaho	310	0.6	3,381	0.4	11	29.0	8,588	64.5	0.3	207,910
Maine	303	0.5	2,482	0.3	8	25.2	10,141	55.6	0.3	183,545
New Mexico	336	0.6	2,663	0.3	8	24.5	9,203	53.3	0.3	158,723
Alaska	214	0.4	1,721	0.2	8	21.9	12,701	50.3	0.2	235,033
West Virginia	236	0.4	2,628	0.3	11	25.3	9,645	49.4	0.2	209,314
North Dakota	148	0.3	1,652	0.2	11	12.5	7,594	37.5	0.2	253,473
Montana	241	0.4	1,386	0.2	6	13.8	9,956	33.7	0.2	140,000
Vermont	165	0.3	1,184	0.1	7	12.9	10,889	30.9	0.1	187,085
South Dakota	154	0.3	1,416	0.2	9	9.9	6,989	22.9	0.1	148,838
Wyoming	161	0.3	1,035	0.1	6	7.8	7,559	21.1	0.1	130,783

Source: 1997 *Economic Census*. The states are in descending order of revenues or establishments (if revenue data are missing for the majority). The symbol (D) appears when data are withheld to prevent disclosure of competitive information. States marked with (D) are sorted by number of establishments. A dash (-) indicates that the data element cannot be calculated. * indicates the midpoint of a range; 175, for example is the range 100-249. Shaded *states* on the state map indicate those states which have proportionately greater representation in the industry than would be indicated by the state's population; the ratio is based on total revenues or number of establishments. Shaded *regions* indicate where the industry is regionally most concentrated.

NAICS 561740 - CARPET AND UPHOLSTERY CLEANING SERVICES*

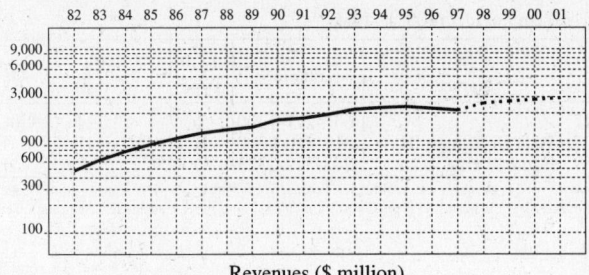

Revenues ($ million)

Employment (000)

GENERAL STATISTICS

Year	Establishments (number)	Employment (number)	Payroll ($ million)	Revenues ($ million)	Employees per Establishment (number)	Revenues per Establishment ($)	Payroll per Employee ($)
1982	4,287	19,065	164.0	479.0	4.4	111,733	8,602
1983	4,593 e	21,606 e	193.0 e	627.0 e	4.7 e	136,512 e	8,933 e
1984	4,899 e	24,148 e	223.0 e	776.0 e	4.9 e	158,400 e	9,235 e
1985	5,204 e	26,689 e	253.0 e	924.0 e	5.1 e	177,556 e	9,480 e
1986	5,510 e	29,231 e	283.0 e	1,072.0 e	5.3 e	194,555 e	9,682 e
1987	5,816	31,772	312.0	1,220.0	5.5	209,766	9,820
1988	5,351	26,900	309.0	1,326.0	5.0	247,804	11,487
1989	5,306	28,780	352.0	1,410.0	5.4	265,737	12,231
1990	5,629	30,512	383.0	1,692.0	5.4	300,586	12,552
1991	6,477	33,424	430.0	1,764.0	5.2	272,348	12,865
1992	7,693	39,318	478.0	1,946.0	5.1	252,957	12,157
1993	8,024	38,852	539.0	2,200.0	4.8	274,177	13,873
1994	8,289	39,576	584.0	2,292.0	4.8	276,511	14,756
1995	8,405	41,120	627.0	2,353.0	4.9	279,952	15,248
1996	8,844 e	44,092 e	678.0 e	2,254.0 e	5.0 e	254,862 e	15,377 e
1997	9,282	47,065	730.0	2,156.0	5.1	232,278	15,510
1998	9,781 p	47,718 p	760.0 p	2,575.0 p	4.9 p	263,266 p	15,927 p
1999	10,213 p	49,589 p	805.0 p	2,692.0 p	4.9 p	263,586 p	16,233 p
2000	10,644 p	51,460 p	849.0 p	2,809.0 p	4.8 p	263,905 p	16,498 p
2001	11,076 p	53,331 p	894.0 p	2,926.0 p	4.8 p	264,175 p	16,763 p

Sources: Economic Census of the United States, 1982, 1987, 1992, 1997. Establishment counts, employment, and payroll are from *County Business Patterns* for non-Census years. In non-Census years, industries in the Manufacturing range under SIC coding include data from the *Annual Survey of Manufactures* (*ASM*); those in the old Services range include data from the *Services Annual Survey* (*SAS*). Values followed by a 'p' are projections by the editors. Extrapolations are marked by 'e'. Data are the most recent available at this level of detail.

INDICES OF CHANGE

Year	Establishments (number)	Employment (number)	Payroll ($ million)	Revenues ($ million)	Employees per Establishment (number)	Revenues per Establishment ($)	Payroll per Employee ($)
1982	46.2	40.5	22.5	22.2	87.7	48.1	55.5
1987	62.7	67.5	42.7	56.6	107.7	90.3	63.3
1992	82.9	83.5	65.5	90.3	100.8	108.9	78.4
1993	86.4	82.5	73.8	102.0	95.5	118.0	89.4
1994	89.3	84.1	80.0	106.3	94.2	119.0	95.1
1995	90.6	87.4	85.9	109.1	96.5	120.5	98.3
1996	95.3 e	93.7 e	92.9 e	104.5 e	98.3 e	109.7 e	99.1 e
1997	100.0	100.0	100.0	100.0	100.0	100.0	100.0
1998	105.4 p	101.4 p	104.1 p	119.4 p	96.2 p	113.3 p	102.7 p
1999	110.0 p	105.4 p	110.3 p	124.9 p	95.8 p	113.5 p	104.7 p
2000	114.7 p	109.3 p	116.3 p	130.3 p	95.3 p	113.6 p	106.4 p
2001	119.3 p	113.3 p	122.5 p	135.7 p	95.0 p	113.7 p	108.1 p

Sources: Same as General Statistics. The values shown reflect change from the base year, 1997. Values above 100 mean greater than 1997, values below 100 mean less than 1997, and a value of 100 in the 1982-96 or 1998-2001 period means same as 1997. Values followed by a 'p' are projections by the editors; 'e' stands for extrapolation. Data are the most recent available at this level of detail.

SELECTED RATIOS

For 1997	Avg. of Information	Analyzed Industry	Index	For 1997	Avg. of Information	Analyzed Industry	Index
Employees per establishment	27	5	19	Payroll per establishment	496,890	78,647	16
Revenue per establishment	1,070,709	232,278	22	Payroll as % of revenue	46	34	73
Revenue per employee	40,278	45,809	114	Payroll per employee	18,692	15,510	83

Sources: Same as General Statistics. The 'Average' column represents the average for the industry sector, in 1997, where the currently shown industry is classified. The Index shows the relationship between the Average and the Analyzed Industry. For example, 100 means that they are equal; 500 that the Analyzed Industry is five times the average; 50 means that the Analyzed Industry is half the national average. The abbreviation 'na' is used to show that data are 'not available'.

*Equivalent to SIC 7217.

LEADING COMPANIES   Number shown: **3**   Total sales ($ mil): **772**   Total employment (000): **14.4**

Company Name	Address				CEO Name	Phone	Co. Type	Sales ($ mil)	Empl. (000)
ServiceMaster Management	2300 Warrenville Rd	Downers Grove	IL	60515		630-271-1300	S	724*	14.0
BMS Enterprises Inc.	308 Arthur St	Fort Worth	TX	76107	W G Blackman III	817-810-9200	R	41*	0.3
Hagopian Cleaning Services Inc.	1400 W 8 Mile Rd	Oak Park	MI	48237	Edmond Hagopian	248-399-2323	D	7*	0.1

Source: *Ward's Business Directory of U.S. Private and Public Companies*, Volumes 1 and 2, 2000. The company type code used is as follows: P - Public, R - Private, S - Subsidiary, D - Division, J - Joint Venture, A - Affiliate, G - Group, N - Company type not reported. Sales are in millions of dollars, employees are in thousands. An asterisk (*) indicates an estimated sales volume. The symbol < stands for 'less than'. Company names and addresses are truncated, in some cases, to fit into the available space.

LOCATION BY STATE AND REGIONAL CONCENTRATION

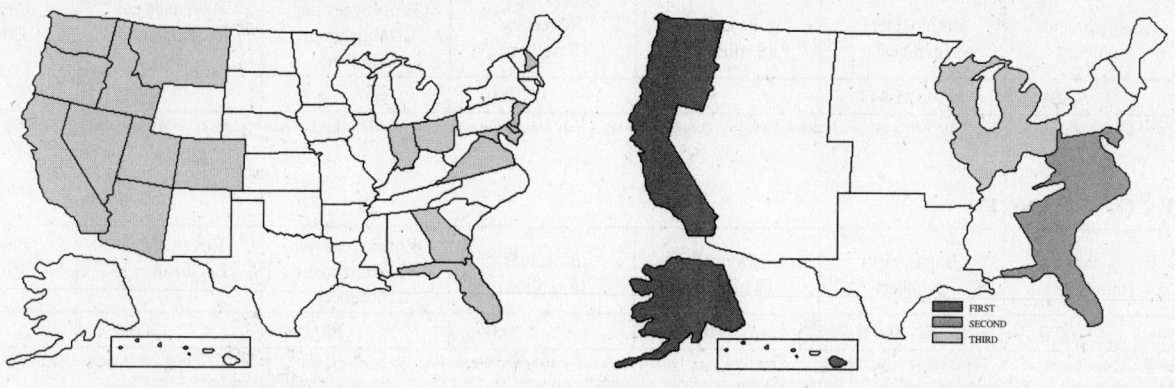

INDUSTRY DATA BY STATE

State	Establishments Total (number)	% of U.S.	Employment Total (number)	% of U.S.	Per Estab.	Payroll Total ($ mil.)	Per Empl. ($)	Revenues Total ($ mil.)	% of U.S.	Per Estab. ($)
California	1,050	11.3	5,285	11.2	5	98.2	18,572	326.9	15.2	311,286
Florida	763	8.2	3,061	6.5	4	52.4	17,123	156.8	7.3	205,558
Texas	576	6.2	2,955	6.3	5	43.6	14,765	131.8	6.1	228,807
New York	387	4.2	2,226	4.7	6	41.9	18,815	117.2	5.4	302,798
Ohio	410	4.4	2,495	5.3	6	37.1	14,864	97.1	4.5	236,863
Illinois	418	4.5	1,848	3.9	4	32.2	17,405	87.7	4.1	209,883
New Jersey	248	2.7	1,311	2.8	5	22.1	16,844	76.7	3.6	309,331
Michigan	348	3.7	1,519	3.2	4	27.0	17,786	74.6	3.5	214,250
Pennsylvania	271	2.9	2,031	4.3	7	27.6	13,586	72.9	3.4	268,838
Virginia	254	2.7	1,648	3.5	6	23.8	14,436	67.1	3.1	264,016
Georgia	247	2.7	1,354	2.9	5	20.3	14,965	63.4	2.9	256,486
Washington	250	2.7	1,229	2.6	5	19.6	15,940	61.0	2.8	243,888
Colorado	260	2.8	1,247	2.6	5	21.8	17,461	59.7	2.8	229,738
Arizona	252	2.7	1,254	2.7	5	18.9	15,054	57.6	2.7	228,401
Indiana	259	2.8	1,323	2.8	5	20.9	15,766	57.4	2.7	221,429
North Carolina	255	2.7	1,119	2.4	4	17.1	15,312	48.3	2.2	189,278
Maryland	192	2.1	1,084	2.3	6	16.8	15,477	47.8	2.2	249,198
Massachusetts	182	2.0	974	2.1	5	14.9	15,285	45.8	2.1	251,588
Missouri	221	2.4	1,313	2.8	6	16.9	12,847	43.5	2.0	196,995
Tennessee	171	1.8	972	2.1	6	13.6	14,025	38.2	1.8	223,509
Oregon	146	1.6	660	1.4	5	11.7	17,744	33.2	1.5	227,192
Wisconsin	181	2.0	1,121	2.4	6	12.1	10,814	30.3	1.4	167,227
Minnesota	145	1.6	696	1.5	5	10.6	15,217	30.1	1.4	207,759
South Carolina	143	1.5	658	1.4	5	8.5	12,857	25.9	1.2	181,210
Kentucky	103	1.1	614	1.3	6	8.9	14,466	24.5	1.1	238,078
Iowa	111	1.2	597	1.3	5	6.4	10,762	22.7	1.1	204,198
Connecticut	86	0.9	351	0.7	4	7.6	21,755	22.0	1.0	255,837
Alabama	134	1.4	568	1.2	4	7.4	13,030	21.3	1.0	158,769
Kansas	105	1.1	680	1.4	6	8.2	12,012	20.3	0.9	193,390
Nevada	87	0.9	404	0.9	5	6.3	15,629	19.4	0.9	222,782
Utah	85	0.9	380	0.8	4	5.2	13,782	18.4	0.9	216,459
Oklahoma	108	1.2	461	1.0	4	5.2	11,260	15.3	0.7	141,509
Idaho	63	0.7	295	0.6	5	3.4	11,631	12.7	0.6	200,984
Mississippi	69	0.7	334	0.7	5	3.7	11,072	12.0	0.6	174,536
New Hampshire	52	0.6	248	0.5	5	3.3	13,423	10.1	0.5	194,077
Nebraska	68	0.7	249	0.5	4	3.1	12,365	9.4	0.4	137,735
West Virginia	51	0.5	254	0.5	5	2.9	11,354	9.0	0.4	176,451
New Mexico	53	0.6	163	0.3	3	2.5	15,626	8.9	0.4	168,094
Arkansas	64	0.7	242	0.5	4	2.4	9,785	8.0	0.4	124,719
Montana	44	0.5	222	0.5	5	2.3	10,216	7.8	0.4	177,432
Hawaii	26	0.3	129	0.3	5	2.3	17,651	6.8	0.3	263,115
Rhode Island	27	0.3	86	0.2	3	1.6	18,326	6.3	0.3	234,444
Delaware	26	0.3	118	0.3	5	2.3	19,381	6.2	0.3	237,308
South Dakota	47	0.5	154	0.3	3	1.5	9,812	5.3	0.2	112,426
North Dakota	38	0.4	189	0.4	5	1.7	8,836	5.3	0.2	139,026
Maine	39	0.4	121	0.3	3	1.7	13,727	5.1	0.2	131,462
Alaska	22	0.2	102	0.2	5	1.5	14,853	4.4	0.2	199,500
Vermont	23	0.2	59	0.1	3	0.8	13,068	2.5	0.1	109,348
Wyoming	26	0.3	95	0.2	4	0.7	7,295	2.4	0.1	91,885
Louisiana	91	1.0	375*	-	-	(D)	-	(D)	-	-
D.C.	5	0.1	175*	-	-	(D)	-	(D)	-	-

Source: 1997 *Economic Census*. The states are in descending order of revenues or establishments (if revenue data are missing for the majority). The symbol (D) appears when data are withheld to prevent disclosure of competitive information. States marked with (D) are sorted by number of establishments. A dash (-) indicates that the data element cannot be calculated. * indicates the midpoint of a range; 175, for example is the range 100-249. Shaded *states* on the state map indicate those states which have proportionately greater representation in the industry than would be indicated by the state's population; the ratio is based on total revenues or number of establishments. Shaded *regions* indicate where the industry is regionally most concentrated.

NAICS 561790 - SERVICES TO BUILDINGS AND DWELLINGS NEC

GENERAL STATISTICS

Year	Establishments (number)	Employment (number)	Payroll ($ million)	Revenues ($ million)	Employees per Establishment (number)	Revenues per Establishment ($)	Payroll per Employee ($)
1997	5,306	25,447	551.0	1,720.0	4.8	324,161	21,653

Source: Economic Census of the United States, 1997. This is a newly defined industry. Data for prior years were unavailable at the time of publication but may become available over time.

INDICES OF CHANGE

Year	Establishments (number)	Employment (number)	Payroll ($ million)	Revenues ($ million)	Employees per Establishment (number)	Revenues per Establishment ($)	Payroll per Employee ($)
1997	100.0	100.0	100.0	100.0	100.0	100.0	100.0

Sources: Same as General Statistics. The values shown reflect change from the base year, 1997. Values above 100 mean greater than 1997, values below 100 mean less than 1997, and a value of 100 in the 1982-96 or 1998-2001 period means same as 1997. Values followed by a 'p' are projections by the editors; 'e' stands for extrapolation. Data are the most recent available at this level of detail.

SIC INDUSTRIES RELATED TO NAICS 561790

Each new NAICS code represents an industry that used to be part of an SIC or a part of several SIC industries. Data in this table are shown to provide transitional information for these cases. All available data for the precursor SIC(s) are shown. Even if only a part of an SIC is included in the NAICS, *all* data for the SIC are reproduced. If the SIC industry is not marked as being a part (pt) of the NAICS, the entire industry is embedded in the NAICS data. The SIC composition of the new industry provides some hints of the relative importance of its "ancestors." Data marked with a 'p' are projected. Projections begin with 1982 data. Data earlier than 1990 are not shown but are reflected in the projections.

SIC	Industry	1990	1991	1992	1993	1994	1995	1996	1997
4959	**Sanitary Services, nec (pt)**								
	Establishments (number)	-	-	1,277	-	-	-	-	-
	Employment (thousands)	-	-	8.1	-	-	-	-	-
	Revenues ($ million)	-	-	702.4	-	-	-	-	-
7349	**Building Maintenance Services, nec (pt)**								
	Establishments (number)	38,557	42,431	47,349	49,278	49,914	50,415	53,847p	56,034p
	Employment (thousands)	729.5	735.3	747.4	786.7	798.9	821.1	835.3p	854.1p
	Revenues ($ million)	17,817.0	17,613.0	18,658.0	18,432.0	20,385.0	21,603.0	24,211.0	24,367.8p
7389	**Business Services, nec (pt)**								
	Establishments (number)	44,079	50,252	52,375	56,829	60,725	53,596	60,893p	63,269p
	Employment (thousands)	489.6	550.4	523.6	607.9	648.7	623.0	680.2p	710.9p
	Revenues ($ million)	-	-	32,885.9	-	-	-	-	-
7699	**Repair Services, nec (pt)**								
	Establishments (number)	27,822	29,303	34,103	34,618	34,136	34,391	35,001p	35,792p
	Employment (thousands)	181.0	181.4	191.0	201.5	207.4	220.2	219.6p	226.2p
	Revenues ($ million)	-	-	15,059.4	15,563.6p	16,427.9p	17,292.2p	18,156.5p	19,020.8p

Source: Economic Census of the United States, 1992, annual surveys of economic sectors conducted by the Bureau of the Census, and estimates or projections based on the 1982-1992 period; not all data are shown. 'e' marks estimates made by the editors; 'p' indicates projections based on time series. A dash (-) indicates that data for this SIC or year were not available. The abbreviation (pt) next to the industry name indicates that only a part of the industry is present within the NAICS data. If no (pt) is shown, the entire industry is contained within the NAICS data.

SELECTED RATIOS

For 1997	Avg. of Information	Analyzed Industry	Index	For 1997	Avg. of Information	Analyzed Industry	Index
Employees per establishment	27	5	18	Payroll per establishment	496,890	103,845	21
Revenue per establishment	1,070,709	324,161	30	Payroll as % of revenue	46	32	69
Revenue per employee	40,278	67,591	168	Payroll per employee	18,692	21,653	116

Sources: Same as General Statistics. The 'Average' column represents the average for the industry sector, in 1997, where the currently shown industry is classified. The Index shows the relationship between the Average and the Analyzed Industry. For example, 100 means that they are equal; 500 that the Analyzed Industry is five times the average; 50 means that the Analyzed Industry is half the national average. The abbreviation 'na' is used to show that data are 'not available'.

LEADING COMPANIES

No company data available for this industry.

LOCATION BY STATE AND REGIONAL CONCENTRATION

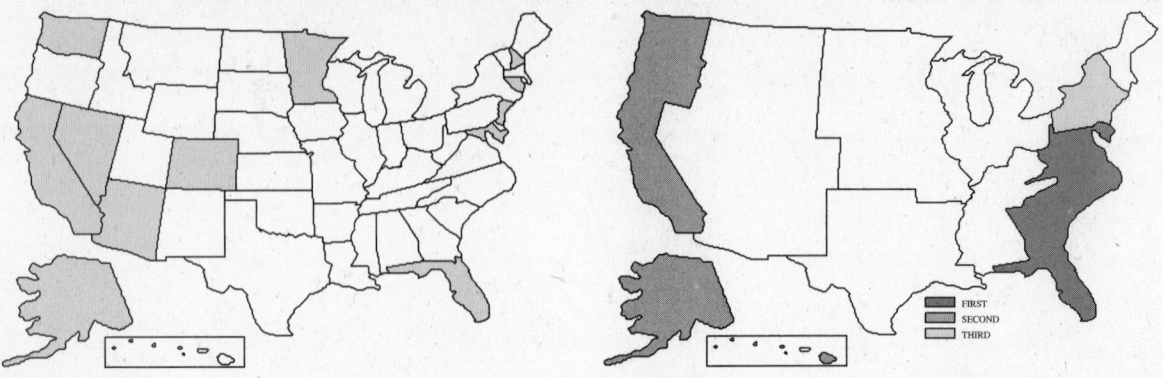

INDUSTRY DATA BY STATE

State	Establishments Total (number)	% of U.S.	Employment Total (number)	% of U.S.	Per Estab.	Payroll Total ($ mil.)	Per Empl. ($)	Revenues Total ($ mil.)	% of U.S.	Per Estab. ($)
California	734	13.8	4,100	16.1	6	95.1	23,191	303.5	17.6	413,508
Florida	772	14.5	3,213	12.6	4	64.6	20,101	208.1	12.1	269,615
Texas	343	6.5	1,896	7.5	6	39.3	20,710	117.9	6.9	343,589
New York	312	5.9	1,574	6.2	5	35.4	22,513	108.1	6.3	346,369
Illinois	175	3.3	1,003	3.9	6	21.4	21,346	68.5	4.0	391,166
Pennsylvania	164	3.1	942	3.7	6	21.4	22,707	63.0	3.7	383,951
Maryland	117	2.2	725	2.8	6	20.8	28,646	57.5	3.3	491,846
New Jersey	186	3.5	609	2.4	3	19.1	31,399	56.2	3.3	302,231
Michigan	187	3.5	757	3.0	4	17.2	22,769	55.7	3.2	298,107
Arizona	188	3.5	894	3.5	5	15.7	17,521	47.3	2.8	251,819
Ohio	130	2.5	653	2.6	5	15.9	24,346	45.9	2.7	352,854
Washington	99	1.9	654	2.6	7	16.4	25,063	45.8	2.7	462,596
Colorado	106	2.0	606	2.4	6	11.5	19,043	44.4	2.6	418,849
Connecticut	102	1.9	314	1.2	3	13.9	44,341	44.2	2.6	433,784
Massachusetts	129	2.4	422	1.7	3	12.4	29,353	38.1	2.2	295,256
Georgia	126	2.4	660	2.6	5	11.0	16,648	37.1	2.2	294,833
Virginia	113	2.1	553	2.2	5	13.5	24,474	35.0	2.0	309,398
Minnesota	94	1.8	597	2.3	6	10.8	18,084	30.9	1.8	328,287
Missouri	87	1.6	345	1.4	4	7.8	22,591	23.4	1.4	269,184
Nevada	79	1.5	391	1.5	5	7.2	18,299	22.6	1.3	285,924
Wisconsin	81	1.5	436	1.7	5	5.7	13,163	21.2	1.2	261,728
Indiana	74	1.4	443	1.7	6	6.7	15,122	20.0	1.2	270,824
Alabama	49	0.9	286	1.1	6	6.6	22,944	19.8	1.2	404,959
Tennessee	63	1.2	320	1.3	5	5.6	17,609	18.7	1.1	296,127
North Carolina	104	2.0	265	1.0	3	5.5	20,725	18.4	1.1	176,471
South Carolina	48	0.9	248	1.0	5	5.3	21,383	17.3	1.0	359,771
Oregon	52	1.0	246	1.0	5	5.7	23,159	16.3	1.0	314,327
Kansas	41	0.8	225	0.9	5	4.2	18,644	13.5	0.8	328,122
Oklahoma	44	0.8	167	0.7	4	2.7	16,126	9.9	0.6	224,545
Kentucky	40	0.8	204	0.8	5	2.9	14,304	9.9	0.6	247,800
Iowa	32	0.6	198	0.8	6	3.3	16,414	9.2	0.5	286,656
New Hampshire	30	0.6	102	0.4	3	2.6	25,794	8.5	0.5	284,833
Nebraska	27	0.5	129	0.5	5	2.4	18,326	7.4	0.4	273,148
Utah	24	0.5	127	0.5	5	2.6	20,260	7.3	0.4	302,708
Alaska	28	0.5	74	0.3	3	1.7	22,622	7.1	0.4	252,214
Arkansas	28	0.5	70	0.3	3	1.5	22,071	5.6	0.3	198,857
Idaho	28	0.5	91	0.4	3	1.4	15,121	5.1	0.3	183,607
Mississippi	23	0.4	102	0.4	4	1.1	10,676	4.8	0.3	207,609
Rhode Island	13	0.2	50	0.2	4	1.2	24,380	4.6	0.3	353,231
Hawaii	20	0.4	63	0.2	3	1.5	23,317	4.6	0.3	227,600
Delaware	14	0.3	32	0.1	2	1.0	32,313	4.2	0.2	300,714
Maine	29	0.5	90	0.4	3	1.3	14,067	4.1	0.2	142,793
West Virginia	15	0.3	53	0.2	4	0.8	14,623	3.0	0.2	203,000
Montana	17	0.3	80	0.3	5	0.7	9,225	2.6	0.2	152,471
New Mexico	21	0.4	64	0.3	3	0.6	9,594	2.2	0.1	106,762
Wyoming	12	0.2	39	0.2	3	0.4	10,538	2.1	0.1	171,417
South Dakota	16	0.3	84	0.3	5	0.7	7,869	1.9	0.1	121,250
Vermont	21	0.4	25	0.1	1	0.4	14,040	1.7	0.1	81,714
Louisiana	53	1.0	175*	-	-	(D)	-	(D)	-	-
North Dakota	12	0.2	60*	-	-	(D)	-	(D)	-	-
D.C.	4	0.1	10*	-	-	(D)	-	(D)	-	-

Source: 1997 *Economic Census*. The states are in descending order of revenues or establishments (if revenue data are missing for the majority). The symbol (D) appears when data are withheld to prevent disclosure of competitive information. States marked with (D) are sorted by number of establishments. A dash (-) indicates that the data element cannot be calculated. * indicates the midpoint of a range; 175, for example is the range 100-249. Shaded *states* on the state map indicate those states which have proportionately greater representation in the industry than would be indicated by the state's population; the ratio is based on total revenues or number of establishments. Shaded *regions* indicate where the industry is regionally most concentrated.

NAICS 561910 - PACKAGING AND LABELING SERVICES

GENERAL STATISTICS

Year	Establishments (number)	Employment (number)	Payroll ($ million)	Revenues ($ million)	Employees per Establishment (number)	Revenues per Establishment ($)	Payroll per Employee ($)
1997	2,331	56,658	1,073.0	4,015.0	24.3	1,722,437	18,938

Source: Economic Census of the United States, 1997. This is a newly defined industry. Data for prior years were unavailable at the time of publication but may become available over time.

INDICES OF CHANGE

Year	Establishments (number)	Employment (number)	Payroll ($ million)	Revenues ($ million)	Employees per Establishment (number)	Revenues per Establishment ($)	Payroll per Employee ($)
1997	100.0	100.0	100.0	100.0	100.0	100.0	100.0

Sources: Same as General Statistics. The values shown reflect change from the base year, 1997. Values above 100 mean greater than 1997, values below 100 mean less than 1997, and a value of 100 in the 1982-96 or 1998-2001 period means same as 1997. Values followed by a 'p' are projections by the editors; 'e' stands for extrapolation. Data are the most recent available at this level of detail.

SIC INDUSTRIES RELATED TO NAICS 561910

Each new NAICS code represents an industry that used to be part of an SIC or a part of several SIC industries. Data in this table are shown to provide transitional information for these cases. All available data for the precursor SIC(s) are shown. Even if only a part of an SIC is included in the NAICS, *all* data for the SIC are reproduced. If the SIC industry is not marked as being a part (pt) of the NAICS, the entire industry is embedded in the NAICS data. The SIC composition of the new industry provides some hints of the relative importance of its "ancestors." Data marked with a 'p' are projected. Projections begin with 1982 data. Data earlier than 1990 are not shown but are reflected in the projections.

SIC	Industry	1990	1991	1992	1993	1994	1995	1996	1997
7389	**Business Services, nec (pt)**								
	Establishments (number)	44,079	50,252	52,375	56,829	60,725	53,596	60,893*p*	63,269*p*
	Employment (thousands)	489.6	550.4	523.6	607.9	648.7	623.0	680.2*p*	710.9*p*
	Revenues ($ million)	-	-	32,885.9	-	-	-	-	-

Source: Economic Census of the United States, 1992, annual surveys of economic sectors conducted by the Bureau of the Census, and estimates or projections based on the 1982-1992 period; not all data are shown. 'e' marks estimates made by the editors; 'p' indicates projections based on time series. A dash (-) indicates that data for this SIC or year were not available. The abbreviation (pt) next to the industry name indicates that only a part of the industry is present within the NAICS data. If no (pt) is shown, the entire industry is contained within the NAICS data.

SELECTED RATIOS

For 1997	Avg. of Information	Analyzed Industry	Index	For 1997	Avg. of Information	Analyzed Industry	Index
Employees per establishment	27	24	91	Payroll per establishment	496,890	460,317	93
Revenue per establishment	1,070,709	1,722,437	161	Payroll as % of revenue	46	27	58
Revenue per employee	40,278	70,864	176	Payroll per employee	18,692	18,938	101

Sources: Same as General Statistics. The 'Average' column represents the average for the industry sector, in 1997, where the currently shown industry is classified. The Index shows the relationship between the Average and the Analyzed Industry. For example, 100 means that they are equal; 500 that the Analyzed Industry is five times the average; 50 means that the Analyzed Industry is half the national average. The abbreviation 'na' is used to show that data are 'not available'.

LEADING COMPANIES

No company data available for this industry.

LOCATION BY STATE AND REGIONAL CONCENTRATION

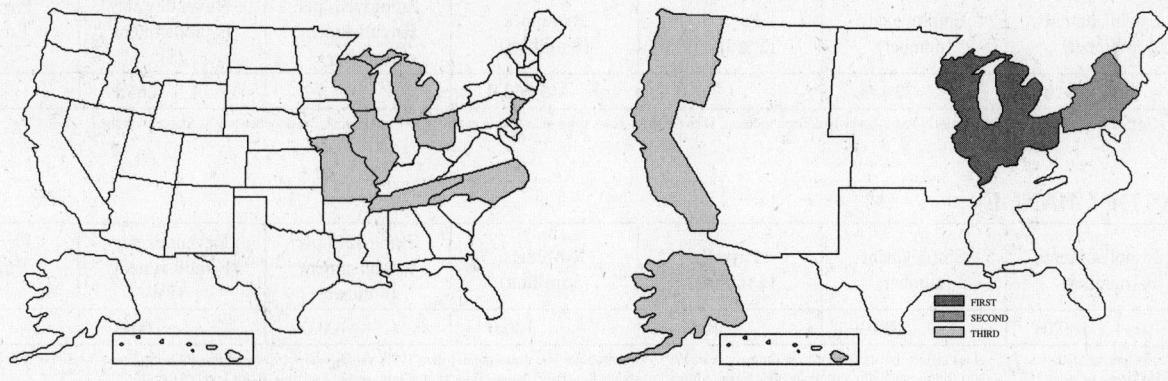

FIRST
SECOND
THIRD

INDUSTRY DATA BY STATE

State	Establishments Total (number)	% of U.S.	Employment Total (number)	% of U.S.	Per Estab.	Payroll Total ($ mil.)	Per Empl. ($)	Revenues Total ($ mil.)	% of U.S.	Per Estab. ($)
Illinois	173	7.4	6,275	11.1	36	140.5	22,389	603.9	15.0	3,490,757
California	305	13.1	5,919	10.4	19	120.6	20,377	477.4	11.9	1,565,262
New Jersey	168	7.2	7,026	12.4	42	137.6	19,583	438.8	10.9	2,612,036
Michigan	101	4.3	3,311	5.8	33	83.9	25,334	414.9	10.3	4,107,792
Ohio	143	6.1	3,965	7.0	28	61.5	15,520	233.3	5.8	1,631,671
New York	163	7.0	5,683	10.0	35	85.8	15,101	230.9	5.8	1,416,761
Wisconsin	57	2.4	2,366	4.2	42	36.2	15,311	212.1	5.3	3,720,649
Pennsylvania	87	3.7	4,664	8.2	54	77.0	16,519	186.8	4.7	2,146,586
Missouri	52	2.2	1,656	2.9	32	32.1	19,402	153.8	3.8	2,958,404
Texas	135	5.8	1,966	3.5	15	43.3	22,035	136.6	3.4	1,012,015
North Carolina	86	3.7	2,188	3.9	25	37.3	17,039	130.5	3.3	1,517,674
Tennessee	40	1.7	1,218	2.1	30	22.7	18,599	89.0	2.2	2,224,025
Indiana	50	2.1	1,722	3.0	34	26.5	15,409	73.6	1.8	1,472,640
Florida	115	4.9	738	1.3	6	13.5	18,287	63.1	1.6	548,730
Minnesota	56	2.4	1,231	2.2	22	18.6	15,106	61.8	1.5	1,103,911
Massachusetts	63	2.7	788	1.4	13	17.4	22,056	55.1	1.4	874,429
Connecticut	39	1.7	637	1.1	16	15.8	24,780	49.7	1.2	1,274,410
Georgia	64	2.7	593	1.0	9	12.1	20,329	48.2	1.2	753,156
Kentucky	33	1.4	530	0.9	16	12.5	23,668	46.6	1.2	1,412,394
Virginia	43	1.8	644	1.1	15	11.4	17,741	31.9	0.8	741,791
Arizona	27	1.2	226	0.4	8	4.7	20,615	29.0	0.7	1,074,000
Alabama	26	1.1	379	0.7	15	9.3	24,435	26.8	0.7	1,029,962
Maryland	30	1.3	337	0.6	11	6.3	18,727	19.9	0.5	664,333
Washington	30	1.3	324	0.6	11	5.4	16,620	19.7	0.5	657,167
Iowa	9	0.4	319	0.6	35	3.4	10,621	15.9	0.4	1,770,889
Louisiana	20	0.9	196	0.3	10	4.0	20,526	15.2	0.4	762,400
South Carolina	17	0.7	194	0.3	11	3.3	17,186	11.1	0.3	652,235
Oregon	20	0.9	135	0.2	7	3.8	28,074	10.5	0.3	523,150
Utah	16	0.7	115	0.2	7	1.3	11,643	8.6	0.2	539,000
Colorado	31	1.3	124	0.2	4	2.5	20,161	8.5	0.2	274,000
Oklahoma	22	0.9	155	0.3	7	2.4	15,516	8.4	0.2	380,182
Kansas	14	0.6	131	0.2	9	2.3	17,733	8.2	0.2	588,071
Arkansas	8	0.3	58	0.1	7	0.9	15,690	4.1	0.1	509,125
Montana	3	0.1	20	0.0	7	0.2	11,850	2.5	0.1	841,667
West Virginia	4	0.2	15	0.0	4	0.2	15,867	2.2	0.1	552,750
New Hampshire	3	0.1	46	0.1	15	1.2	25,370	2.2	0.1	747,667
Idaho	10	0.4	18	0.0	2	0.3	14,833	1.8	0.0	184,200
Mississippi	7	0.3	17	0.0	2	0.4	24,471	1.6	0.0	227,143
New Mexico	9	0.4	29	0.1	3	0.3	9,655	1.5	0.0	169,556
Vermont	7	0.3	33	0.1	5	0.2	6,242	0.8	0.0	118,429
Rhode Island	13	0.6	375*	-	-	(D)	-	(D)	-	-
Nevada	10	0.4	60*	-	-	(D)	-	(D)	-	-
Nebraska	5	0.2	60*	-	-	(D)	-	(D)	-	-
Delaware	4	0.2	60*	-	-	(D)	-	(D)	-	-
Hawaii	3	0.1	10*	-	-	(D)	-	(D)	-	-
North Dakota	3	0.1	10*	-	-	(D)	-	(D)	-	-
D.C.	2	0.1	10*	-	-	(D)	-	(D)	-	-
South Dakota	2	0.1	10*	-	-	(D)	-	(D)	-	-
Alaska	1	-	10*	-	-	(D)	-	(D)	-	-
Maine	1	-	10*	-	-	(D)	-	(D)	-	-
Wyoming	1	-	10*	-	-	(D)	-	(D)	-	-

Source: 1997 *Economic Census*. The states are in descending order of revenues or establishments (if revenue data are missing for the majority). The symbol (D) appears when data are withheld to prevent disclosure of competitive information. States marked with (D) are sorted by number of establishments. A dash (-) indicates that the data element cannot be calculated. * indicates the midpoint of a range; 175, for example is the range 100-249. Shaded *states* on the state map indicate those states which have proportionately greater representation in the industry than would be indicated by the state's population; the ratio is based on total revenues or number of establishments. Shaded *regions* indicate where the industry is regionally most concentrated.

NAICS 561920 - CONVENTION AND TRADE SHOW ORGANIZERS

GENERAL STATISTICS

Year	Establishments (number)	Employment (number)	Payroll ($ million)	Revenues ($ million)	Employees per Establishment (number)	Revenues per Establishment ($)	Payroll per Employee ($)
1997	3,978	72,443	1,733.0	6,260.0	18.2	1,573,655	23,922

Source: *Economic Census of the United States*, 1997. This is a newly defined industry. Data for prior years were unavailable at the time of publication but may become available over time.

INDICES OF CHANGE

Year	Establishments (number)	Employment (number)	Payroll ($ million)	Revenues ($ million)	Employees per Establishment (number)	Revenues per Establishment ($)	Payroll per Employee ($)
1997	100.0	100.0	100.0	100.0	100.0	100.0	100.0

Sources: Same as General Statistics. The values shown reflect change from the base year, 1997. Values above 100 mean greater than 1997, values below 100 mean less than 1997, and a value of 100 in the 1982-96 or 1998-2001 period means same as 1997. Values followed by a 'p' are projections by the editors; 'e' stands for extrapolation. Data are the most recent available at this level of detail.

SIC INDUSTRIES RELATED TO NAICS 561920

Each new NAICS code represents an industry that used to be part of an SIC or a part of several SIC industries. Data in this table are shown to provide transitional information for these cases. All available data for the precursor SIC(s) are shown. Even if only a part of an SIC is included in the NAICS, *all* data for the SIC are reproduced. If the SIC industry is not marked as being a part (pt) of the NAICS, the entire industry is embedded in the NAICS data. The SIC composition of the new industry provides some hints of the relative importance of its "ancestors." Data marked with a 'p' are projected. Projections begin with 1982 data. Data earlier than 1990 are not shown but are reflected in the projections.

SIC	Industry	1990	1991	1992	1993	1994	1995	1996	1997
7389	**Business Services, nec (pt)**								
	Establishments (number)	44,079	50,252	52,375	56,829	60,725	53,596	60,893p	63,269p
	Employment (thousands)	489.6	550.4	523.6	607.9	648.7	623.0	680.2p	710.9p
	Revenues ($ million)	-	-	32,885.9	-	-	-	-	-

Source: *Economic Census of the United States*, 1992, annual surveys of economic sectors conducted by the Bureau of the Census, and estimates or projections based on the 1982-1992 period; not all data are shown. 'e' marks estimates made by the editors; 'p' indicates projections based on time series. A dash (-) indicates that data for this SIC or year were not available. The abbreviation (pt) next to the industry name indicates that only a part of the industry is present within the NAICS data. If no (pt) is shown, the entire industry is contained within the NAICS data.

SELECTED RATIOS

For 1997	Avg. of Information	Analyzed Industry	Index	For 1997	Avg. of Information	Analyzed Industry	Index
Employees per establishment	27	18	69	Payroll per establishment	496,890	435,646	88
Revenue per establishment	1,070,709	1,573,655	147	Payroll as % of revenue	46	28	60
Revenue per employee	40,278	86,413	215	Payroll per employee	18,692	23,922	128

Sources: Same as General Statistics. The 'Average' column represents the average for the industry sector, in 1997, where the currently shown industry is classified. The Index shows the relationship between the Average and the Analyzed Industry. For example, 100 means that they are equal; 500 that the Analyzed Industry is five times the average; 50 means that the Analyzed Industry is half the national average. The abbreviation 'na' is used to show that data are 'not available'.

LEADING COMPANIES

No company data available for this industry.

LOCATION BY STATE AND REGIONAL CONCENTRATION

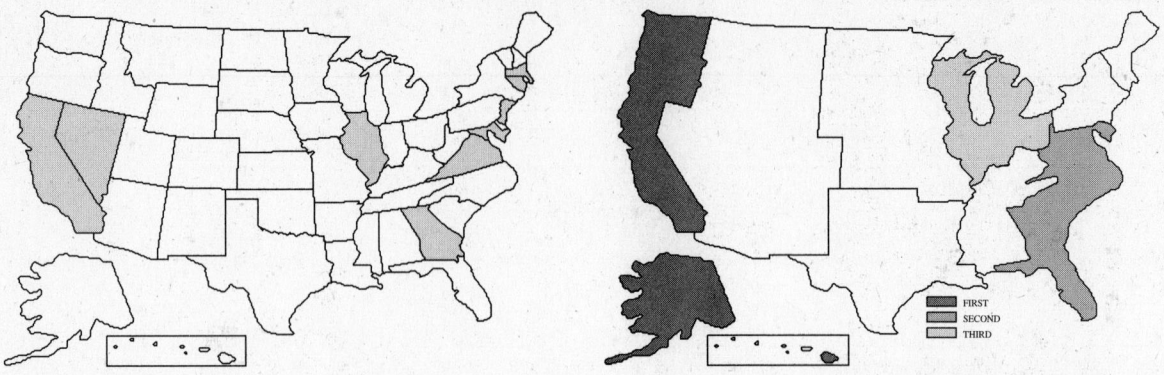

FIRST
SECOND
THIRD

INDUSTRY DATA BY STATE

State	Establishments Total (number)	% of U.S.	Employment Total (number)	% of U.S.	Per Estab.	Payroll Total ($ mil.)	Per Empl. ($)	Revenues Total ($ mil.)	% of U.S.	Per Estab. ($)
California	637	16.0	12,456	17.2	20	288.1	23,127	1,087.5	17.4	1,707,154
Illinois	287	7.2	5,696	7.9	20	184.0	32,308	560.5	9.0	1,952,934
Massachusetts	153	3.8	3,690	5.1	24	109.6	29,697	515.2	8.2	3,367,373
New York	318	8.0	4,465	6.2	14	126.5	28,333	442.4	7.1	1,391,041
New Jersey	144	3.6	2,259	3.1	16	84.7	37,513	322.4	5.2	2,239,097
Florida	288	7.2	3,540	4.9	12	75.6	21,356	306.6	4.9	1,064,726
Georgia	162	4.1	7,910	10.9	49	94.9	12,002	284.8	4.5	1,758,185
Connecticut	52	1.3	1,039	1.4	20	56.7	54,605	263.5	4.2	5,067,769
Texas	212	5.3	4,826	6.7	23	84.3	17,459	262.4	4.2	1,237,500
Nevada	86	2.2	6,391	8.8	74	111.9	17,512	262.3	4.2	3,049,512
Virginia	109	2.7	1,402	1.9	13	51.0	36,350	235.7	3.8	2,162,789
Maryland	100	2.5	1,243	1.7	12	46.6	37,479	152.5	2.4	1,525,460
Ohio	114	2.9	1,210	1.7	11	33.6	27,775	128.8	2.1	1,130,105
Michigan	75	1.9	1,136	1.6	15	37.7	33,169	119.6	1.9	1,594,907
Pennsylvania	113	2.8	1,492	2.1	13	37.7	25,288	118.4	1.9	1,047,398
Washington	93	2.3	1,359	1.9	15	37.3	27,443	112.4	1.8	1,208,860
North Carolina	93	2.3	855	1.2	9	22.7	26,567	93.6	1.5	1,006,172
Minnesota	80	2.0	735	1.0	9	25.8	35,088	87.6	1.4	1,094,475
Colorado	92	2.3	792	1.1	9	19.4	24,437	84.3	1.3	915,761
Louisiana	54	1.4	1,365	1.9	25	17.8	13,011	75.2	1.2	1,392,019
Oregon	60	1.5	631	0.9	11	21.3	33,707	68.3	1.1	1,139,000
Missouri	64	1.6	1,099	1.5	17	21.4	19,493	65.9	1.1	1,029,656
Tennessee	51	1.3	623	0.9	12	19.8	31,796	61.6	1.0	1,207,431
Indiana	52	1.3	677	0.9	13	13.8	20,434	51.9	0.8	997,615
Arizona	78	2.0	555	0.8	7	10.5	18,854	50.9	0.8	651,936
South Carolina	31	0.8	474	0.7	15	9.4	19,753	46.7	0.7	1,507,355
Wisconsin	47	1.2	475	0.7	10	10.9	23,053	41.1	0.7	874,894
Kentucky	33	0.8	367	0.5	11	8.2	22,371	33.5	0.5	1,013,727
Utah	29	0.7	136	0.2	5	5.5	40,301	22.9	0.4	789,448
Rhode Island	15	0.4	108	0.1	7	2.4	22,083	21.6	0.3	1,437,200
Alabama	17	0.4	219	0.3	13	5.9	26,753	17.8	0.3	1,049,000
Maine	9	0.2	128	0.2	14	4.0	31,586	14.8	0.2	1,644,000
Iowa	27	0.7	201	0.3	7	3.3	16,552	14.2	0.2	526,333
Mississippi	15	0.4	964	1.3	64	2.7	2,803	14.1	0.2	937,000
Oklahoma	18	0.5	179	0.2	10	4.6	25,737	14.0	0.2	775,667
Hawaii	22	0.6	289	0.4	13	4.1	14,187	10.3	0.2	469,091
New Hampshire	11	0.3	25	0.0	2	1.7	66,560	8.3	0.1	756,000
Idaho	6	0.2	61	0.1	10	1.4	22,934	7.7	0.1	1,285,000
New Mexico	11	0.3	128	0.2	12	3.3	25,469	7.0	0.1	636,727
Alaska	9	0.2	51	0.1	6	1.0	20,176	4.5	0.1	495,000
Delaware	10	0.3	41	0.1	4	1.0	24,268	4.4	0.1	439,400
Arkansas	11	0.3	32	0.0	3	0.5	14,656	2.9	0.0	266,182
Montana	10	0.3	41	0.1	4	0.7	18,049	2.6	0.0	256,100
West Virginia	3	0.1	9	0.0	3	0.1	16,556	0.5	0.0	151,000
D.C.	30	0.8	375*	-	-	(D)	-	(D)	-	-
Kansas	23	0.6	175*	-	-	(D)	-	(D)	-	-
Nebraska	15	0.4	375*	-	-	(D)	-	(D)	-	-
Vermont	3	0.1	10*	-	-	(D)	-	(D)	-	-
Wyoming	3	0.1	10*	-	-	(D)	-	(D)	-	-
South Dakota	2	0.1	10*	-	-	(D)	-	(D)	-	-
North Dakota	1	-	10*	-	-	(D)	-	(D)	-	-

Source: 1997 *Economic Census*. The states are in descending order of revenues or establishments (if revenue data are missing for the majority). The symbol (D) appears when data are withheld to prevent disclosure of competitive information. States marked with (D) are sorted by number of establishments. A dash (-) indicates that the data element cannot be calculated. * indicates the midpoint of a range; 175, for example is the range 100-249. Shaded *states* on the state map indicate those states which have proportionately greater representation in the industry than would be indicated by the state's population; the ratio is based on total revenues or number of establishments. Shaded *regions* indicate where the industry is regionally most concentrated.

NAICS 561990 - SUPPORT SERVICES NEC

GENERAL STATISTICS

Year	Establishments (number)	Employment (number)	Payroll ($ million)	Revenues ($ million)	Employees per Establishment (number)	Revenues per Establishment ($)	Payroll per Employee ($)
1997	20,321	231,022	4,639.0	16,683.0	11.4	820,973	20,080

Source: Economic Census of the United States, 1997. This is a newly defined industry. Data for prior years were unavailable at the time of publication but may become available over time.

INDICES OF CHANGE

Year	Establishments (number)	Employment (number)	Payroll ($ million)	Revenues ($ million)	Employees per Establishment (number)	Revenues per Establishment ($)	Payroll per Employee ($)
1997	100.0	100.0	100.0	100.0	100.0	100.0	100.0

Sources: Same as General Statistics. The values shown reflect change from the base year, 1997. Values above 100 mean greater than 1997, values below 100 mean less than 1997, and a value of 100 in the 1982-96 or 1998-2001 period means same as 1997. Values followed by a 'p' are projections by the editors; 'e' stands for extrapolation. Data are the most recent available at this level of detail.

SIC INDUSTRIES RELATED TO NAICS 561990

Each new NAICS code represents an industry that used to be part of an SIC or a part of several SIC industries. Data in this table are shown to provide transitional information for these cases. All available data for the precursor SIC(s) are shown. Even if only a part of an SIC is included in the NAICS, *all* data for the SIC are reproduced. If the SIC industry is not marked as being a part (pt) of the NAICS, the entire industry is embedded in the NAICS data. The SIC composition of the new industry provides some hints of the relative importance of its "ancestors." Data marked with a 'p' are projected. Projections begin with 1982 data. Data earlier than 1990 are not shown but are reflected in the projections.

SIC	Industry	1990	1991	1992	1993	1994	1995	1996	1997
7389	**Business Services, nec (pt)**								
	Establishments (number)	44,079	50,252	52,375	56,829	60,725	53,596	60,893p	63,269p
	Employment (thousands)	489.6	550.4	523.6	607.9	648.7	623.0	680.2p	710.9p
	Revenues ($ million)	-	-	32,885.9	-	-	-	-	-

Source: Economic Census of the United States, 1992, annual surveys of economic sectors conducted by the Bureau of the Census, and estimates or projections based on the 1982-1992 period; not all data are shown. 'e' marks estimates made by the editors; 'p' indicates projections based on time series. A dash (-) indicates that data for this SIC or year were not available. The abbreviation (pt) next to the industry name indicates that only a part of the industry is present within the NAICS data. If no (pt) is shown, the entire industry is contained within the NAICS data.

SELECTED RATIOS

For 1997	Avg. of Information	Analyzed Industry	Index	For 1997	Avg. of Information	Analyzed Industry	Index
Employees per establishment	27	11	43	Payroll per establishment	496,890	228,286	46
Revenue per establishment	1,070,709	820,973	77	Payroll as % of revenue	46	28	60
Revenue per employee	40,278	72,214	179	Payroll per employee	18,692	20,080	107

Sources: Same as General Statistics. The 'Average' column represents the average for the industry sector, in 1997, where the currently shown industry is classified. The Index shows the relationship between the Average and the Analyzed Industry. For example, 100 means that they are equal; 500 that the Analyzed Industry is five times the average; 50 means that the Analyzed Industry is half the national average. The abbreviation 'na' is used to show that data are 'not available'.

LEADING COMPANIES

No company data available for this industry.

LOCATION BY STATE AND REGIONAL CONCENTRATION

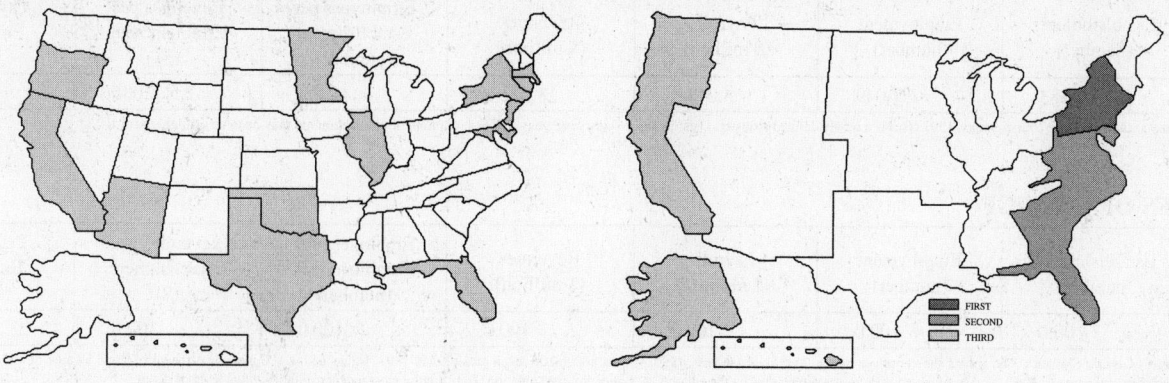

FIRST
SECOND
THIRD

INDUSTRY DATA BY STATE

State	Establishments Total (number)	% of U.S.	Employment Total (number)	% of U.S.	Per Estab.	Payroll Total ($ mil.)	Per Empl. ($)	Revenues Total ($ mil.)	% of U.S.	Per Estab. ($)
California	2,411	11.9	26,615	11.5	11	561.7	21,105	2,191.7	13.1	909,043
New York	1,429	7.0	14,395	6.2	10	383.6	26,650	1,573.5	9.4	1,101,146
Texas	1,333	6.6	19,105	8.3	14	396.4	20,747	1,349.0	8.1	1,012,017
Florida	1,409	6.9	14,338	6.2	10	264.7	18,459	966.2	5.8	685,712
Illinois	1,059	5.2	12,239	5.3	12	251.5	20,550	915.3	5.5	864,262
Pennsylvania	814	4.0	10,633	4.6	13	210.3	19,777	768.2	4.6	943,688
New Jersey	692	3.4	8,207	3.6	12	189.2	23,054	644.1	3.9	930,837
Ohio	741	3.6	10,765	4.7	15	199.6	18,545	591.5	3.5	798,202
Minnesota	490	2.4	5,998	2.6	12	133.0	22,174	540.3	3.2	1,102,602
Arizona	397	2.0	6,370	2.8	16	122.1	19,174	489.4	2.9	1,232,632
Massachusetts	479	2.4	5,716	2.5	12	130.9	22,903	480.2	2.9	1,002,507
Michigan	617	3.0	6,756	2.9	11	131.2	19,413	429.6	2.6	696,241
Georgia	478	2.4	5,829	2.5	12	116.7	20,013	423.8	2.5	886,651
Virginia	448	2.2	5,466	2.4	12	121.6	22,246	400.8	2.4	894,748
North Carolina	515	2.5	7,030	3.0	14	110.8	15,764	391.1	2.3	759,499
Indiana	457	2.2	6,216	2.7	14	122.4	19,688	362.1	2.2	792,451
Maryland	381	1.9	5,162	2.2	14	99.5	19,281	338.8	2.0	889,176
Connecticut	275	1.4	4,352	1.9	16	108.1	24,849	260.4	1.6	946,836
Wisconsin	366	1.8	3,587	1.6	10	56.7	15,817	242.0	1.5	661,068
Oklahoma	352	1.7	3,122	1.4	9	52.9	16,934	241.9	1.4	687,080
Washington	468	2.3	3,554	1.5	8	64.2	18,050	226.5	1.4	484,071
Missouri	428	2.1	3,643	1.6	9	59.1	16,213	210.4	1.3	491,472
Tennessee	306	1.5	3,164	1.4	10	54.1	17,089	207.8	1.2	679,170
Oregon	260	1.3	2,572	1.1	10	41.7	16,230	199.8	1.2	768,350
Colorado	358	1.8	3,372	1.5	9	59.1	17,523	198.2	1.2	553,723
D.C.	113	0.6	861	0.4	8	45.0	52,247	144.8	0.9	1,281,239
Iowa	300	1.5	2,618	1.1	9	40.2	15,356	127.8	0.8	425,943
South Carolina	182	0.9	1,660	0.7	9	26.4	15,908	120.2	0.7	660,522
Kentucky	233	1.1	2,281	1.0	10	38.7	16,947	120.1	0.7	515,288
Alabama	214	1.1	2,487	1.1	12	37.3	14,983	117.6	0.7	549,612
Mississippi	134	0.7	1,177	0.5	9	24.8	21,048	86.4	0.5	644,470
Nebraska	138	0.7	1,424	0.6	10	19.3	13,583	76.7	0.5	555,862
Utah	127	0.6	1,584	0.7	12	24.3	15,348	74.0	0.4	582,693
New Hampshire	113	0.6	1,020	0.4	9	23.4	22,908	72.5	0.4	641,619
Arkansas	133	0.7	1,299	0.6	10	19.0	14,588	68.0	0.4	511,083
New Mexico	139	0.7	983	0.4	7	16.2	16,450	62.7	0.4	451,050
West Virginia	92	0.5	1,104	0.5	12	17.6	15,927	48.4	0.3	526,359
Montana	93	0.5	575	0.2	6	7.0	12,200	34.9	0.2	375,774
South Dakota	80	0.4	633	0.3	8	9.3	14,662	31.9	0.2	398,738
North Dakota	61	0.3	371	0.2	6	6.1	16,404	18.4	0.1	300,902
Vermont	67	0.3	387	0.2	6	5.5	14,235	18.0	0.1	268,701
Wyoming	43	0.2	104	0.0	2	1.7	16,615	8.3	0.0	193,674
Louisiana	247	1.2	3,750*	-	-	(D)	-	(D)	-	-
Kansas	227	1.1	1,750*	-	-	(D)	-	(D)	-	-
Nevada	167	0.8	1,750*	-	-	(D)	-	(D)	-	-
Maine	102	0.5	1,750*	-	-	(D)	-	(D)	-	-
Idaho	81	0.4	750*	-	-	(D)	-	(D)	-	-
Rhode Island	79	0.4	750*	-	-	(D)	-	(D)	-	-
Delaware	73	0.4	1,750*	-	-	(D)	-	(D)	-	-
Hawaii	62	0.3	750*	-	-	(D)	-	(D)	-	-
Alaska	58	0.3	375*	-	-	(D)	-	(D)	-	-

Source: 1997 *Economic Census*. The states are in descending order of revenues or establishments (if revenue data are missing for the majority). The symbol (D) appears when data are withheld to prevent disclosure of competitive information. States marked with (D) are sorted by number of establishments. A dash (-) indicates that the data element cannot be calculated. * indicates the midpoint of a range; 175, for example is the range 100-249. Shaded *states* on the state map indicate those states which have proportionately greater representation in the industry than would be indicated by the state's population; the ratio is based on total revenues or number of establishments. Shaded *regions* indicate where the industry is regionally most concentrated.

NAICS 562111 - SOLID WASTE COLLECTION

GENERAL STATISTICS

Year	Establishments (number)	Employment (number)	Payroll ($ million)	Revenues ($ million)	Employees per Establishment (number)	Revenues per Establishment ($)	Payroll per Employee ($)
1997	7,083	137,049	4,048.0	18,211.0	19.3	2,571,086	29,537

Source: *Economic Census of the United States*, 1997. This is a newly defined industry. Data for prior years were unavailable at the time of publication but may become available over time.

INDICES OF CHANGE

Year	Establishments (number)	Employment (number)	Payroll ($ million)	Revenues ($ million)	Employees per Establishment (number)	Revenues per Establishment ($)	Payroll per Employee ($)
1997	100.0	100.0	100.0	100.0	100.0	100.0	100.0

Sources: Same as General Statistics. The values shown reflect change from the base year, 1997. Values above 100 mean greater than 1997, values below 100 mean less than 1997, and a value of 100 in the 1982-96 or 1998-2001 period means same as 1997. Values followed by a 'p' are projections by the editors; 'e' stands for extrapolation. Data are the most recent available at this level of detail.

SIC INDUSTRIES RELATED TO NAICS 562111

Each new NAICS code represents an industry that used to be part of an SIC or a part of several SIC industries. Data in this table are shown to provide transitional information for these cases. All available data for the precursor SIC(s) are shown. Even if only a part of an SIC is included in the NAICS, *all* data for the SIC are reproduced. If the SIC industry is not marked as being a part (pt) of the NAICS, the entire industry is embedded in the NAICS data. The SIC composition of the new industry provides some hints of the relative importance of its "ancestors." Data marked with a 'p' are projected. Projections begin with 1982 data. Data earlier than 1990 are not shown but are reflected in the projections.

SIC	Industry	1990	1991	1992	1993	1994	1995	1996	1997
4212	**Local Trucking Without Storage (pt)**								
	Establishments (number)	48,279*e*	49,075*e*	49,870	50,665*p*	51,461*p*	52,256*p*	53,052*p*	53,847*p*
	Employment (thousands)	332.7*e*	343.7*e*	354.7	365.7*p*	376.7*p*	387.7*p*	398.7*p*	409.7*p*
	Revenues ($ million)	31,397.0	30,890.0	33,554.4	36,648.0	40,903.0	43,830.0	46,589.0	49,972.0

Source: *Economic Census of the United States*, 1992, annual surveys of economic sectors conducted by the Bureau of the Census, and estimates or projections based on the 1982-1992 period; not all data are shown. 'e' marks estimates made by the editors; 'p' indicates projections based on time series. A dash (-) indicates that data for this SIC or year were not available. The abbreviation (pt) next to the industry name indicates that only a part of the industry is present within the NAICS data. If no (pt) is shown, the entire industry is contained within the NAICS data.

SELECTED RATIOS

For 1997	Avg. of Information	Analyzed Industry	Index	For 1997	Avg. of Information	Analyzed Industry	Index
Employees per establishment	27	19	73	Payroll per establishment	496,890	571,509	115
Revenue per establishment	1,070,709	2,571,086	240	Payroll as % of revenue	46	22	48
Revenue per employee	40,278	132,879	330	Payroll per employee	18,692	29,537	158

Sources: Same as General Statistics. The 'Average' column represents the average for the industry sector, in 1997, where the currently shown industry is classified. The Index shows the relationship between the Average and the Analyzed Industry. For example, 100 means that they are equal; 500 that the Analyzed Industry is five times the average; 50 means that the Analyzed Industry is half the national average. The abbreviation 'na' is used to show that data are 'not available'.

LEADING COMPANIES   Number shown: **33**   Total sales ($ mil): **51,021**   Total employment (000): **204.4**

Company Name	Address				CEO Name	Phone	Co. Type	Sales ($ mil)	Empl. (000)
Waste Management Inc.	1001 Fannin St	Houston	TX	77002	A. Maurice Myers	713-512-6200	P	22,715	68.0
AutoNation Inc.	110 SE 6th St	Fort Lauderdale	FL	33301	John Costello	954-769-6000	P	20,112	42.0
Browning-Ferris Industries Inc.	PO Box 3151	Houston	TX	77253	Donald Stager	281-870-8100	P	4,746	26.0
Waste Management Holdings	700 E Butterfield Rd	Lombard	IL	60148	Robert S Miller	630-572-8800	P	2,145	58.9
Thermo TerraTech Inc.	P O Box 9046	Waltham	MA	02254	John P Appleton	781-370-1500	P	300*	2.7
Heritage Environmental Services	7901 W Morris St	Indianapolis	IN	46231	Kenneth Price	317-243-0811	R	150	0.9
Clean Harbors Environmental	PO Box 850327	Braintree	MA	02185	Alan S McKim	781-849-1800	P	146	1.2
Environmental Quality Co.	36255 Michigan Ave	Wayne	MI	48184	Mcihael Farrantino	734-329-8000	R	100	0.5
EarthTech	2233 Tomlynn St	Richmond	VA	23230	Brian Redd	804-358-5858	S	70*	0.3
American Ecology Corp.	805 W Idaho St	Boise	ID	83702	Jack Lemley	208-331-8400	P	62	0.3
Kimmins Corp.	1501 2nd Ave E	Tampa	FL	33605	Francis M Williams	813-248-3878	P	59	0.7
GZA GeoEnvironmental Inc.	320 Needham St	Newton U Fls	MA	02164	Andrew P Pajak	617-969-0050	S	59	0.2
Coulter Companies Inc.	P O Box 9071	Peoria	IL	61612	Royal J Coulter	309-688-0760	R	55*	0.4
Kaiser Ventures Inc.	3633 E Inland	Ontario	CA	91764	Richard E Stoddard	909-483-8500	P	52	<0.1
Synagro Technologies Inc.	1800 Bering	Houston	TX	77057	Ross Patten	713-369-1700	P	30	0.3
UXB International Inc.	21641 Beaumeade	Ashburn	VA	20147	R H Dugger III	703-724-9600	R	27	0.5
EarthCare Co.	14901 Quorum Dr	Dallas	TX	75240	Harry Habits	972-858-6025	P	26	0.2
American Ecology Recycle Center	109 Flint Rd	Oak Ridge	TN	37830		423-482-5523	S	25	0.1
Med/Waste Inc.	6175 153rd St	Miami Lakes	FL	33014	Carlos Camps	305-819-8877	P	25	0.4
Waste Systems International Inc.	420 Bedford St	Lexington	MA	02420	Philip Strauss	781-862-3000	P	21	0.3
Environmental Enterprises Inc.	10163 C-Dayton	Cincinnati	OH	45241	Daniel McCabe	513-772-2818	R	18	0.2
Waste Microbes Inc.	4901 Milwee St	Houston	TX	77092	Joseph Jennings	713-956-4001	R	12*	<0.1
Land, Air, Water Environmental	P O Box 372	Center Moriches	NY	11934	Christine Lamprecht	516-874-2112	R	11*	<0.1
WRR Environmental Services Inc.	5200 State Road 93	Eau Claire	WI	54701	James Hagar	715-834-9624	S	11	0.1
Marisol Inc.	213 W Union Ave	Bound Brook	NJ	08805	James R Nerger	732-469-5100	R	10*	<0.1
Montgomery Watson Constructors	370 Interlocken Blvd	Broomfield	CO	80021	Phil Hall	303-439-2800	S	10	<0.1
All Chemical Disposal Inc.	21 Great Oaks Blvd	San Jose	CA	95119	Fred Murabito	408-363-1660	R	9*	<0.1
Infinity Inc.	211 W 14th St	Chanute	KS	66720	Stanton E Ross	316-431-6200	P	5	<0.1
KTI Inc.	7000 Boulevard E	Guttenberg	NJ	07093	Martin Sergi	201-854-7777	P	4*	<0.1
FulCircle Recyclers Inc.	509 Manida St	Bronx	NY	10474	Brian Jantzen	718-328-4667	S	3	<0.1
Indiana Fiber Recycling Inc.	4400 New Haven	Fort Wayne	IN	46803	Randy C Aumsbaugh	219-749-6100	R	3	<0.1
Chemfix Technologies Inc.	3500 N Causeway	Metairie	LA	70002	David L Donaldson	504-831-3600	P	1	<0.1
Environmental Response Inc.	2131 Murfreesboro	Nashville	TN	37217	RT McDaniel	615-399-1300	R	1	<0.1

Source: Ward's Business Directory of U.S. Private and Public Companies, Volumes 1 and 2, 2000. The company type code used is as follows: P - Public, R - Private, S - Subsidiary, D - Division, J - Joint Venture, A - Affiliate, G - Group, N - Company type not reported. Sales are in millions of dollars, employees are in thousands. An asterisk (*) indicates an estimated sales volume. The symbol < stands for 'less than'. Company names and addresses are truncated, in some cases, to fit into the available space.

LOCATION BY STATE AND REGIONAL CONCENTRATION

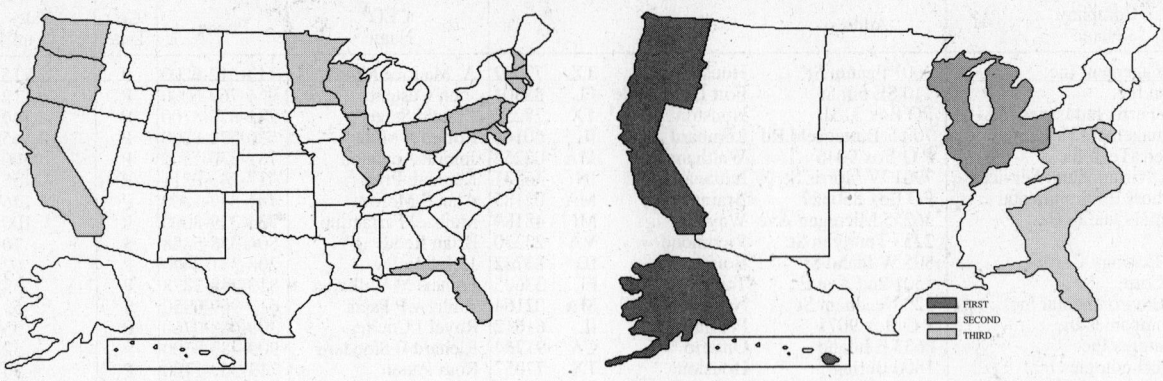

FIRST
SECOND
THIRD

INDUSTRY DATA BY STATE

State	Establishments Total (number)	Establishments % of U.S.	Employment Total (number)	Employment % of U.S.	Employment Per Estab.	Payroll Total ($ mil.)	Payroll Per Empl. ($)	Revenues Total ($ mil.)	Revenues % of U.S.	Revenues Per Estab. ($)
California	492	6.9	17,659	12.9	36	607.5	34,401	2,799.1	15.4	5,689,319
New York	609	8.6	8,899	6.5	15	265.7	29,856	1,135.9	6.2	1,865,122
Florida	176	2.5	7,039	5.1	40	198.7	28,234	1,069.8	5.9	6,078,335
Illinois	335	4.7	6,869	5.0	21	241.2	35,112	1,021.5	5.6	3,049,215
Texas	255	3.6	7,145	5.2	28	194.2	27,173	895.8	4.9	3,513,047
Pennsylvania	372	5.3	6,105	4.5	16	164.4	26,927	874.2	4.8	2,349,930
New Jersey	292	4.1	4,901	3.6	17	175.9	35,898	865.7	4.8	2,964,767
Ohio	306	4.3	7,962	5.8	26	213.3	26,790	838.2	4.6	2,739,330
Michigan	207	2.9	4,802	3.5	23	154.4	32,144	671.9	3.7	3,246,058
Massachusetts	163	2.3	3,466	2.5	21	117.5	33,909	549.1	3.0	3,368,515
Maryland	170	2.4	3,908	2.9	23	116.6	29,845	478.3	2.6	2,813,765
Washington	117	1.7	2,619	1.9	22	85.4	32,619	461.2	2.5	3,942,256
Georgia	208	2.9	3,248	2.4	16	93.9	28,912	437.3	2.4	2,102,255
Connecticut	155	2.2	2,195	1.6	14	87.6	39,892	422.3	2.3	2,724,361
Wisconsin	103	1.5	2,889	2.1	28	90.4	31,290	392.0	2.2	3,805,408
North Carolina	174	2.5	3,254	2.4	19	89.7	27,569	389.3	2.1	2,237,437
Virginia	165	2.3	3,308	2.4	20	87.6	26,494	374.6	2.1	2,270,448
Minnesota	285	4.0	3,128	2.3	11	94.3	30,152	370.1	2.0	1,298,460
Oregon	194	2.7	2,575	1.9	13	78.8	30,619	353.3	1.9	1,821,186
Indiana	137	1.9	3,283	2.4	24	81.1	24,713	348.6	1.9	2,544,182
Missouri	183	2.6	2,512	1.8	14	67.9	27,014	300.5	1.7	1,642,213
Tennessee	94	1.3	2,018	1.5	21	54.4	26,958	268.5	1.5	2,856,894
Kentucky	107	1.5	1,868	1.4	17	48.7	26,044	242.9	1.3	2,270,159
Louisiana	65	0.9	2,068	1.5	32	51.7	24,986	224.4	1.2	3,452,215
Colorado	106	1.5	2,090	1.5	20	53.9	25,789	209.5	1.2	1,976,415
South Carolina	85	1.2	1,483	1.1	17	48.7	32,872	207.2	1.1	2,437,529
Arizona	79	1.1	1,588	1.2	20	42.6	26,816	166.8	0.9	2,111,785
Mississippi	41	0.6	1,114	0.8	27	30.7	27,566	136.5	0.7	3,328,098
Iowa	184	2.6	1,549	1.1	8	30.0	19,396	135.5	0.7	736,424
West Virginia	97	1.4	1,248	0.9	13	25.8	20,659	112.4	0.6	1,158,577
Nebraska	132	1.9	1,277	0.9	10	29.0	22,692	110.2	0.6	835,159
New Hampshire	48	0.7	637	0.5	13	21.1	33,140	107.3	0.6	2,236,271
Oklahoma	99	1.4	1,109	0.8	11	25.3	22,847	90.3	0.5	911,990
Arkansas	75	1.1	820	0.6	11	18.8	22,968	82.8	0.5	1,104,360
Utah	43	0.6	611	0.4	14	11.7	19,160	57.4	0.3	1,334,953
New Mexico	23	0.3	341	0.2	15	8.3	24,211	51.1	0.3	2,220,739
Maine	94	1.3	498	0.4	5	10.9	21,980	45.9	0.3	487,830
Alaska	31	0.4	300	0.2	10	14.5	48,377	44.7	0.2	1,442,645
Idaho	46	0.6	563	0.4	12	13.5	24,034	43.8	0.2	951,913
Vermont	49	0.7	428	0.3	9	10.9	25,362	43.6	0.2	889,633
North Dakota	38	0.5	198	0.1	5	3.9	19,747	17.2	0.1	453,711
Wyoming	26	0.4	132	0.1	5	2.2	16,545	9.2	0.1	355,615
Kansas	129	1.8	1,750*	-	-	(D)	-	(D)	-	-
Alabama	74	1.0	1,750*	-	-	(D)	-	(D)	-	-
South Dakota	62	0.9	375*	-	-	(D)	-	(D)	-	-
Rhode Island	38	0.5	375*	-	-	(D)	-	(D)	-	-
Delaware	31	0.4	375*	-	-	(D)	-	(D)	-	-
Montana	31	0.4	375*	-	-	(D)	-	(D)	-	-
Hawaii	27	0.4	375*	-	-	(D)	-	(D)	-	-
Nevada	21	0.3	1,750*	-	-	(D)	-	(D)	-	-
D.C.	10	0.1	60*	-	-	(D)	-	(D)	-	-

Source: 1997 *Economic Census.* The states are in descending order of revenues or establishments (if revenue data are missing for the majority). The symbol (D) appears when data are withheld to prevent disclosure of competitive information. States marked with (D) are sorted by number of establishments. A dash (-) indicates that the data element cannot be calculated. * indicates the midpoint of a range; 175, for example is the range 100-249. Shaded *states* on the state map indicate those states which have proportionately greater representation in the industry than would be indicated by the state's population; the ratio is based on total revenues or number of establishments. Shaded *regions* indicate where the industry is regionally most concentrated.

NAICS 562112 - HAZARDOUS WASTE COLLECTION

GENERAL STATISTICS

Year	Establishments (number)	Employment (number)	Payroll ($ million)	Revenues ($ million)	Employees per Establishment (number)	Revenues per Establishment ($)	Payroll per Employee ($)
1997	414	8,468	317.0	1,096.0	20.5	2,647,343	37,435

Source: *Economic Census of the United States*, 1997. This is a newly defined industry. Data for prior years were unavailable at the time of publication but may become available over time.

INDICES OF CHANGE

Year	Establishments (number)	Employment (number)	Payroll ($ million)	Revenues ($ million)	Employees per Establishment (number)	Revenues per Establishment ($)	Payroll per Employee ($)
1997	100.0	100.0	100.0	100.0	100.0	100.0	100.0

Sources: Same as General Statistics. The values shown reflect change from the base year, 1997. Values above 100 mean greater than 1997, values below 100 mean less than 1997, and a value of 100 in the 1982-96 or 1998-2001 period means same as 1997. Values followed by a 'p' are projections by the editors; 'e' stands for extrapolation. Data are the most recent available at this level of detail.

SIC INDUSTRIES RELATED TO NAICS 562112

Each new NAICS code represents an industry that used to be part of an SIC or a part of several SIC industries. Data in this table are shown to provide transitional information for these cases. All available data for the precursor SIC(s) are shown. Even if only a part of an SIC is included in the NAICS, *all* data for the SIC are reproduced. If the SIC industry is not marked as being a part (pt) of the NAICS, the entire industry is embedded in the NAICS data. The SIC composition of the new industry provides some hints of the relative importance of its "ancestors." Data marked with a 'p' are projected. Projections begin with 1982 data. Data earlier than 1990 are not shown but are reflected in the projections.

SIC	Industry	1990	1991	1992	1993	1994	1995	1996	1997
4212	**Local Trucking Without Storage (pt)**								
	Establishments (number)	48,279e	49,075e	49,870	50,665p	51,461p	52,256p	53,052p	53,847p
	Employment (thousands)	332.7e	343.7e	354.7	365.7p	376.7p	387.7p	398.7p	409.7p
	Revenues ($ million)	31,397.0	30,890.0	33,554.4	36,648.0	40,903.0	43,830.0	46,589.0	49,972.0

Source: *Economic Census of the United States*, 1992, annual surveys of economic sectors conducted by the Bureau of the Census, and estimates or projections based on the 1982-1992 period; not all data are shown. 'e' marks estimates made by the editors; 'p' indicates projections based on time series. A dash (-) indicates that data for this SIC or year were not available. The abbreviation (pt) next to the industry name indicates that only a part of the industry is present within the NAICS data. If no (pt) is shown, the entire industry is contained within the NAICS data.

SELECTED RATIOS

For 1997	Avg. of Information	Analyzed Industry	Index	For 1997	Avg. of Information	Analyzed Industry	Index
Employees per establishment	27	20	77	Payroll per establishment	496,890	765,700	154
Revenue per establishment	1,070,709	2,647,343	247	Payroll as % of revenue	46	29	62
Revenue per employee	40,278	129,428	321	Payroll per employee	18,692	37,435	200

Sources: Same as General Statistics. The 'Average' column represents the average for the industry sector, in 1997, where the currently shown industry is classified. The Index shows the relationship between the Average and the Analyzed Industry. For example, 100 means that they are equal; 500 that the Analyzed Industry is five times the average; 50 means that the Analyzed Industry is half the national average. The abbreviation 'na' is used to show that data are 'not available'.

LEADING COMPANIES

No company data available for this industry.

LOCATION BY STATE AND REGIONAL CONCENTRATION

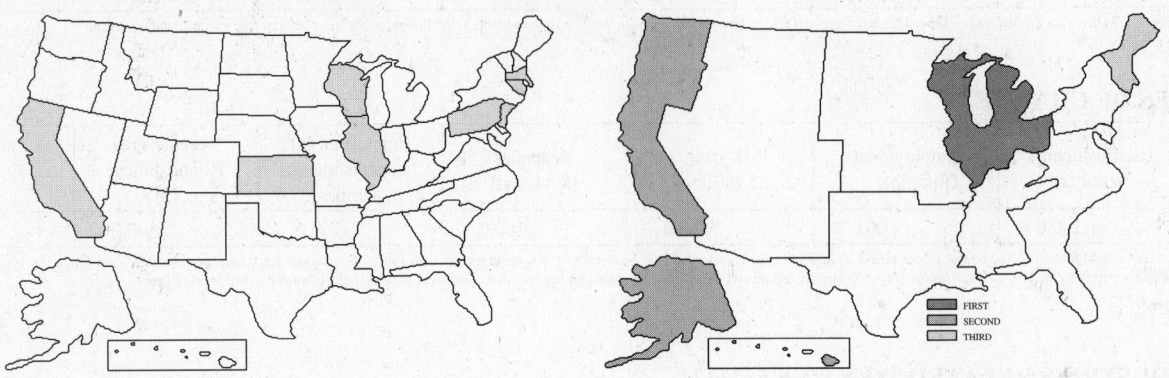

FIRST
SECOND
THIRD

INDUSTRY DATA BY STATE

State	Establishments Total (number)	Establishments % of U.S.	Employment Total (number)	Employment % of U.S.	Employment Per Estab.	Payroll Total ($ mil.)	Payroll Per Empl. ($)	Revenues Total ($ mil.)	Revenues % of U.S.	Revenues Per Estab. ($)
California	73	17.6	1,015	12.0	14	40.2	39,604	147.7	13.5	2,022,781
Massachusetts	16	3.9	1,565	18.5	98	66.3	42,354	139.4	12.7	8,711,812
Illinois	18	4.3	665	7.9	37	21.0	31,642	95.7	8.7	5,317,278
New Jersey	22	5.3	396	4.7	18	16.1	40,535	69.6	6.4	3,164,818
Pennsylvania	16	3.9	466	5.5	29	16.6	35,549	53.8	4.9	3,363,375
Michigan	12	2.9	207	2.4	17	11.1	53,444	35.6	3.3	2,968,083
New York	15	3.6	241	2.8	16	8.0	33,303	33.8	3.1	2,251,000
Texas	25	6.0	291	3.4	12	8.4	28,814	32.5	3.0	1,298,440
Wisconsin	9	2.2	235	2.8	26	9.5	40,447	31.1	2.8	3,460,111
Ohio	14	3.4	170	2.0	12	7.5	43,959	26.1	2.4	1,864,000
Connecticut	10	2.4	104	1.2	10	7.2	69,433	19.3	1.8	1,934,400
Florida	13	3.1	131	1.5	10	4.5	34,466	18.6	1.7	1,433,615
Georgia	13	3.1	124	1.5	10	4.0	32,032	15.4	1.4	1,186,308
Virginia	15	3.6	139	1.6	9	4.1	29,460	15.2	1.4	1,011,000
Indiana	8	1.9	110	1.3	14	4.7	42,764	14.9	1.4	1,861,250
Kansas	8	1.9	148	1.7	19	4.4	29,574	14.8	1.3	1,847,500
Arizona	5	1.2	126	1.5	25	3.6	28,857	14.2	1.3	2,833,600
Washington	9	2.2	80	0.9	9	2.4	29,400	13.9	1.3	1,541,333
South Carolina	7	1.7	86	1.0	12	3.3	37,826	13.1	1.2	1,873,857
North Carolina	9	2.2	78	0.9	9	1.7	21,449	8.4	0.8	932,556
Kentucky	6	1.4	73	0.9	12	2.5	34,836	5.6	0.5	935,333
Tennessee	7	1.7	36	0.4	5	0.8	22,417	3.9	0.4	557,286
Oregon	4	1.0	50	0.6	13	1.9	37,080	3.3	0.3	820,750
Louisiana	8	1.9	39	0.5	5	0.7	17,897	3.2	0.3	397,875
Maryland	3	0.7	10	0.1	3	0.4	35,900	1.1	0.1	374,333
Minnesota	12	2.9	175*	-	-	(D)	-	(D)	-	-
Alabama	7	1.7	375*	-	-	(D)	-	(D)	-	-
Colorado	6	1.4	175*	-	-	(D)	-	(D)	-	-
Oklahoma	6	1.4	60*	-	-	(D)	-	(D)	-	-
North Dakota	5	1.2	10*	-	-	(D)	-	(D)	-	-
Missouri	4	1.0	60*	-	-	(D)	-	(D)	-	-
New Mexico	4	1.0	750*	-	-	(D)	-	(D)	-	-
Vermont	4	1.0	60*	-	-	(D)	-	(D)	-	-
Utah	3	0.7	60*	-	-	(D)	-	(D)	-	-
Arkansas	2	0.5	10*	-	-	(D)	-	(D)	-	-
Idaho	2	0.5	10*	-	-	(D)	-	(D)	-	-
Maine	2	0.5	10*	-	-	(D)	-	(D)	-	-
Montana	2	0.5	10*	-	-	(D)	-	(D)	-	-
New Hampshire	2	0.5	60*	-	-	(D)	-	(D)	-	-
West Virginia	2	0.5	10*	-	-	(D)	-	(D)	-	-
Delaware	1	0.2	60*	-	-	(D)	-	(D)	-	-
Hawaii	1	0.2	10*	-	-	(D)	-	(D)	-	-
Mississippi	1	0.2	10*	-	-	(D)	-	(D)	-	-
Nebraska	1	0.2	10*	-	-	(D)	-	(D)	-	-
Nevada	1	0.2	60*	-	-	(D)	-	(D)	-	-
Wyoming	1	0.2	10*	-	-	(D)	-	(D)	-	-

Source: 1997 Economic Census. The states are in descending order of revenues or establishments (if revenue data are missing for the majority). The symbol (D) appears when data are withheld to prevent disclosure of competitive information. States marked with (D) are sorted by number of establishments. A dash (-) indicates that the data element cannot be calculated. * indicates the midpoint of a range; 175, for example is the range 100-249. Shaded *states* on the state map indicate those states which have proportionately greater representation in the industry than would be indicated by the state's population; the ratio is based on total revenues or number of establishments. Shaded *regions* indicate where the industry is regionally most concentrated.

NAICS 562119 - WASTE COLLECTION NEC

GENERAL STATISTICS

Year	Establishments (number)	Employment (number)	Payroll ($ million)	Revenues ($ million)	Employees per Establishment (number)	Revenues per Establishment ($)	Payroll per Employee ($)
1997	827	7,227	201.0	838.0	8.7	1,013,301	27,812

Source: Economic Census of the United States, 1997. This is a newly defined industry. Data for prior years were unavailable at the time of publication but may become available over time.

INDICES OF CHANGE

Year	Establishments (number)	Employment (number)	Payroll ($ million)	Revenues ($ million)	Employees per Establishment (number)	Revenues per Establishment ($)	Payroll per Employee ($)
1997	100.0	100.0	100.0	100.0	100.0	100.0	100.0

Sources: Same as General Statistics. The values shown reflect change from the base year, 1997. Values above 100 mean greater than 1997, values below 100 mean less than 1997, and a value of 100 in the 1982-96 or 1998-2001 period means same as 1997. Values followed by a 'p' are projections by the editors; 'e' stands for extrapolation. Data are the most recent available at this level of detail.

SIC INDUSTRIES RELATED TO NAICS 562119

Each new NAICS code represents an industry that used to be part of an SIC or a part of several SIC industries. Data in this table are shown to provide transitional information for these cases. All available data for the precursor SIC(s) are shown. Even if only a part of an SIC is included in the NAICS, *all* data for the SIC are reproduced. If the SIC industry is not marked as being a part (pt) of the NAICS, the entire industry is embedded in the NAICS data. The SIC composition of the new industry provides some hints of the relative importance of its "ancestors." Data marked with a 'p' are projected. Projections begin with 1982 data. Data earlier than 1990 are not shown but are reflected in the projections.

SIC	Industry	1990	1991	1992	1993	1994	1995	1996	1997
4212	**Local Trucking Without Storage (pt)**								
	Establishments (number)	48,279e	49,075e	49,870	50,665p	51,461p	52,256p	53,052p	53,847p
	Employment (thousands)	332.7e	343.7e	354.7	365.7p	376.7p	387.7p	398.7p	409.7p
	Revenues ($ million)	31,397.0	30,890.0	33,554.4	36,648.0	40,903.0	43,830.0	46,589.0	49,972.0

Source: Economic Census of the United States, 1992, annual surveys of economic sectors conducted by the Bureau of the Census, and estimates or projections based on the 1982-1992 period; not all data are shown. 'e' marks estimates made by the editors; 'p' indicates projections based on time series. A dash (-) indicates that data for this SIC or year were not available. The abbreviation (pt) next to the industry name indicates that only a part of the industry is present within the NAICS data. If no (pt) is shown, the entire industry is contained within the NAICS data.

SELECTED RATIOS

For 1997	Avg. of Information	Analyzed Industry	Index	For 1997	Avg. of Information	Analyzed Industry	Index
Employees per establishment	27	9	33	Payroll per establishment	496,890	243,047	49
Revenue per establishment	1,070,709	1,013,301	95	Payroll as % of revenue	46	24	52
Revenue per employee	40,278	115,954	288	Payroll per employee	18,692	27,812	149

Sources: Same as General Statistics. The 'Average' column represents the average for the industry sector, in 1997, where the currently shown industry is classified. The Index shows the relationship between the Average and the Analyzed Industry. For example, 100 means that they are equal; 500 that the Analyzed Industry is five times the average; 50 means that the Analyzed Industry is half the national average. The abbreviation 'na' is used to show that data are 'not available'.

LEADING COMPANIES

No company data available for this industry.

LOCATION BY STATE AND REGIONAL CONCENTRATION

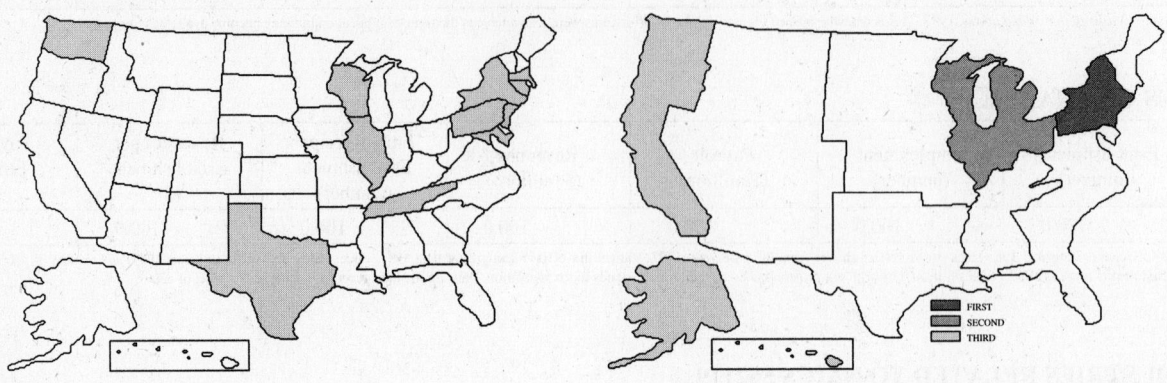

FIRST
SECOND
THIRD

INDUSTRY DATA BY STATE

State	Establishments Total (number)	% of U.S.	Employment Total (number)	% of U.S.	Per Estab.	Payroll Total ($ mil.)	Per Empl. ($)	Revenues Total ($ mil.)	% of U.S.	Per Estab. ($)
New York	75	9.1	699	9.7	9	24.6	35,235	104.9	12.5	1,398,093
Pennsylvania	35	4.2	339	4.7	10	8.6	25,227	104.7	12.5	2,990,800
California	64	7.7	730	10.1	11	23.7	32,466	94.7	11.3	1,480,250
Texas	59	7.1	646	8.9	11	16.7	25,875	59.5	7.1	1,008,169
Illinois	39	4.7	408	5.6	10	13.8	33,725	45.6	5.4	1,169,128
New Jersey	28	3.4	542	7.5	19	14.0	25,753	35.0	4.2	1,250,714
Connecticut	14	1.7	230	3.2	16	8.1	35,396	30.3	3.6	2,166,000
Florida	59	7.1	371	5.1	6	8.8	23,655	28.0	3.3	475,322
Ohio	42	5.1	228	3.2	5	7.3	32,215	25.4	3.0	605,762
Tennessee	11	1.3	164	2.3	15	4.7	28,701	25.3	3.0	2,302,000
Massachusetts	24	2.9	138	1.9	6	4.6	33,210	23.0	2.8	959,792
Wisconsin	20	2.4	229	3.2	11	5.3	22,974	21.9	2.6	1,093,650
Maryland	14	1.7	180	2.5	13	5.1	28,156	20.0	2.4	1,430,143
Michigan	36	4.4	191	2.6	5	5.5	28,911	19.6	2.3	545,361
North Carolina	18	2.2	221	3.1	12	4.4	20,059	17.7	2.1	981,444
Washington	19	2.3	175	2.4	9	5.0	28,291	17.3	2.1	908,632
Indiana	13	1.6	165	2.3	13	3.3	20,212	13.7	1.6	1,056,462
Louisiana	14	1.7	201	2.8	14	2.9	14,617	13.6	1.6	972,000
Georgia	21	2.5	93	1.3	4	2.3	25,022	11.8	1.4	562,333
Iowa	12	1.5	110	1.5	9	2.7	24,682	8.6	1.0	719,167
Oregon	10	1.2	75	1.0	8	2.1	28,413	8.6	1.0	856,900
Arizona	10	1.2	51	0.7	5	1.7	33,431	5.6	0.7	564,800
Virginia	14	1.7	39	0.5	3	0.9	22,179	4.5	0.5	320,571
Alabama	7	0.8	76	1.1	11	1.9	25,316	3.6	0.4	509,714
South Carolina	6	0.7	48	0.7	8	0.9	17,979	2.5	0.3	413,500
Kentucky	8	1.0	18	0.2	2	0.3	14,611	0.9	0.1	112,750
Minnesota	28	3.4	175*	-	-	(D)	-	(D)	-	-
Missouri	19	2.3	175*	-	-	(D)	-	(D)	-	-
Colorado	17	2.1	60*	-	-	(D)	-	(D)	-	-
Oklahoma	13	1.6	60*	-	-	(D)	-	(D)	-	-
Arkansas	10	1.2	10*	-	-	(D)	-	(D)	-	-
Nebraska	8	1.0	60*	-	-	(D)	-	(D)	-	-
New Mexico	7	0.8	60*	-	-	(D)	-	(D)	-	-
Kansas	6	0.7	10*	-	-	(D)	-	(D)	-	-
Maine	6	0.7	10*	-	-	(D)	-	(D)	-	-
Mississippi	6	0.7	60*	-	-	(D)	-	(D)	-	-
Utah	6	0.7	60*	-	-	(D)	-	(D)	-	-
Rhode Island	5	0.6	60*	-	-	(D)	-	(D)	-	-
Idaho	4	0.5	60*	-	-	(D)	-	(D)	-	-
West Virginia	4	0.5	60*	-	-	(D)	-	(D)	-	-
New Hampshire	3	0.4	60*	-	-	(D)	-	(D)	-	-
Vermont	3	0.4	60*	-	-	(D)	-	(D)	-	-
Montana	2	0.2	10*	-	-	(D)	-	(D)	-	-
North Dakota	2	0.2	10*	-	-	(D)	-	(D)	-	-
South Dakota	2	0.2	10*	-	-	(D)	-	(D)	-	-
Wyoming	2	0.2	10*	-	-	(D)	-	(D)	-	-
Delaware	1	0.1	10*	-	-	(D)	-	(D)	-	-
Nevada	1	0.1	10*	-	-	(D)	-	(D)	-	-

Source: 1997 *Economic Census*. The states are in descending order of revenues or establishments (if revenue data are missing for the majority). The symbol (D) appears when data are withheld to prevent disclosure of competitive information. States marked with (D) are sorted by number of establishments. A dash (-) indicates that the data element cannot be calculated. * indicates the midpoint of a range; 175, for example is the range 100-249. Shaded *states* on the state map indicate those states which have proportionately greater representation in the industry than would be indicated by the state's population; the ratio is based on total revenues or number of establishments. Shaded *regions* indicate where the industry is regionally most concentrated.

NAICS 562211 - HAZARDOUS WASTE TREATMENT AND DISPOSAL

GENERAL STATISTICS

Year	Establishments (number)	Employment (number)	Payroll ($ million)	Revenues ($ million)	Employees per Establishment (number)	Revenues per Establishment ($)	Payroll per Employee ($)
1997	512	17,816	745.0	2,878.0	34.8	5,621,094	41,816

Source: Economic Census of the United States, 1997. This is a newly defined industry. Data for prior years were unavailable at the time of publication but may become available over time.

INDICES OF CHANGE

Year	Establishments (number)	Employment (number)	Payroll ($ million)	Revenues ($ million)	Employees per Establishment (number)	Revenues per Establishment ($)	Payroll per Employee ($)
1997	100.0	100.0	100.0	100.0	100.0	100.0	100.0

Sources: Same as General Statistics. The values shown reflect change from the base year, 1997. Values above 100 mean greater than 1997, values below 100 mean less than 1997, and a value of 100 in the 1982-96 or 1998-2001 period means same as 1997. Values followed by a 'p' are projections by the editors; 'e' stands for extrapolation. Data are the most recent available at this level of detail.

SIC INDUSTRIES RELATED TO NAICS 562211

Each new NAICS code represents an industry that used to be part of an SIC or a part of several SIC industries. Data in this table are shown to provide transitional information for these cases. All available data for the precursor SIC(s) are shown. Even if only a part of an SIC is included in the NAICS, *all* data for the SIC are reproduced. If the SIC industry is not marked as being a part (pt) of the NAICS, the entire industry is embedded in the NAICS data. The SIC composition of the new industry provides some hints of the relative importance of its "ancestors." Data marked with a 'p' are projected. Projections begin with 1982 data. Data earlier than 1990 are not shown but are reflected in the projections.

SIC	Industry	1990	1991	1992	1993	1994	1995	1996	1997
4953	**Refuse Systems (pt)**								
	Establishments (number)	-	-	3,317	-	-	-	-	-
	Employment (thousands)	-	-	80.9	-	-	-	-	-
	Revenues ($ million)	-	-	14,101.7	-	-	-	-	-

Source: Economic Census of the United States, 1992, annual surveys of economic sectors conducted by the Bureau of the Census, and estimates or projections based on the 1982-1992 period; not all data are shown. 'e' marks estimates made by the editors; 'p' indicates projections based on time series. A dash (-) indicates that data for this SIC or year were not available. The abbreviation (pt) next to the industry name indicates that only a part of the industry is present within the NAICS data. If no (pt) is shown, the entire industry is contained within the NAICS data.

SELECTED RATIOS

For 1997	Avg. of Information	Analyzed Industry	Index	For 1997	Avg. of Information	Analyzed Industry	Index
Employees per establishment	27	35	131	Payroll per establishment	496,890	1,455,078	293
Revenue per establishment	1,070,709	5,621,094	525	Payroll as % of revenue	46	26	56
Revenue per employee	40,278	161,540	401	Payroll per employee	18,692	41,816	224

Sources: Same as General Statistics. The 'Average' column represents the average for the industry sector, in 1997, where the currently shown industry is classified. The Index shows the relationship between the Average and the Analyzed Industry. For example, 100 means that they are equal; 500 that the Analyzed Industry is five times the average; 50 means that the Analyzed Industry is half the national average. The abbreviation 'na' is used to show that data are 'not available'.

LEADING COMPANIES
No company data available for this industry.

LOCATION BY STATE AND REGIONAL CONCENTRATION

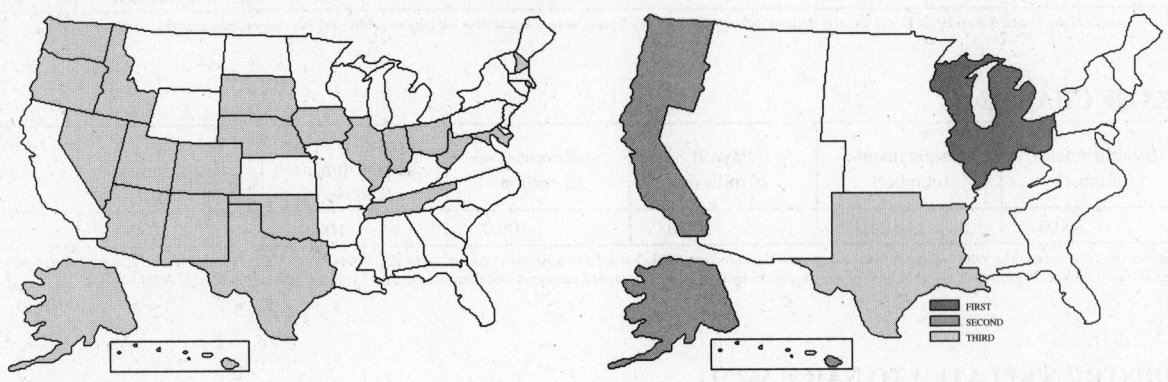

FIRST
SECOND
THIRD

INDUSTRY DATA BY STATE

State	Establishments Total (number)	Establishments % of U.S.	Employment Total (number)	Employment % of U.S.	Employment Per Estab.	Payroll Total ($ mil.)	Payroll Per Empl. ($)	Revenues Total ($ mil.)	Revenues % of U.S.	Revenues Per Estab. ($)
California	57	11.1	1,684	9.5	30	56.0	33,257	262.2	9.1	4,600,246
Illinois	30	5.9	924	5.2	31	37.8	40,859	212.5	7.4	7,084,367
Ohio	26	5.1	1,268	7.1	49	50.9	40,146	208.8	7.3	8,029,385
Michigan	19	3.7	840	4.7	44	36.3	43,269	195.4	6.8	10,281,842
Texas	55	10.7	1,624	9.1	30	61.3	37,749	182.6	6.3	3,319,327
Tennessee	11	2.1	1,082	6.1	98	44.5	41,131	121.3	4.2	11,030,364
Pennsylvania	23	4.5	744	4.2	32	32.1	43,180	116.5	4.0	5,064,348
Utah	7	1.4	865	4.9	124	36.7	42,455	88.1	3.1	12,582,714
Maryland	14	2.7	372	2.1	27	43.6	117,083	83.7	2.9	5,980,071
North Carolina	12	2.3	414	2.3	35	14.5	34,908	83.7	2.9	6,975,500
Indiana	15	2.9	639	3.6	43	28.8	45,075	81.8	2.8	5,451,467
South Carolina	7	1.4	349	2.0	50	12.9	37,037	68.8	2.4	9,830,000
Oregon	8	1.6	133	0.7	17	4.3	31,985	22.0	0.8	2,745,000
Colorado	7	1.4	121	0.7	17	3.6	30,157	21.0	0.7	2,994,571
Georgia	11	2.1	189	1.1	17	5.6	29,735	14.0	0.5	1,276,909
Arizona	9	1.8	90	0.5	10	2.8	31,389	9.8	0.3	1,083,667
Oklahoma	8	1.6	52	0.3	7	1.8	34,519	6.8	0.2	849,625
Mississippi	4	0.8	46	0.3	11	1.5	33,283	5.8	0.2	1,454,750
Minnesota	6	1.2	54	0.3	9	1.1	19,630	2.9	0.1	479,167
New York	29	5.7	1,750*	-	-	(D)	-	(D)	-	-
Florida	20	3.9	750*	-	-	(D)	-	(D)	-	-
Washington	15	2.9	750*	-	-	(D)	-	(D)	-	-
Nevada	14	2.7	375*	-	-	(D)	-	(D)	-	-
Massachusetts	12	2.3	175*	-	-	(D)	-	(D)	-	-
Louisiana	8	1.6	60*	-	-	(D)	-	(D)	-	-
Missouri	7	1.4	175*	-	-	(D)	-	(D)	-	-
New Mexico	7	1.4	175*	-	-	(D)	-	(D)	-	-
Alabama	6	1.2	175*	-	-	(D)	-	(D)	-	-
Iowa	6	1.2	60*	-	-	(D)	-	(D)	-	-
New Jersey	6	1.2	375*	-	-	(D)	-	(D)	-	-
Nebraska	5	1.0	175*	-	-	(D)	-	(D)	-	-
Wisconsin	5	1.0	175*	-	-	(D)	-	(D)	-	-
Alaska	4	0.8	10*	-	-	(D)	-	(D)	-	-
Connecticut	4	0.8	175*	-	-	(D)	-	(D)	-	-
Hawaii	4	0.8	60*	-	-	(D)	-	(D)	-	-
Idaho	4	0.8	375*	-	-	(D)	-	(D)	-	-
Kentucky	4	0.8	175*	-	-	(D)	-	(D)	-	-
West Virginia	4	0.8	10*	-	-	(D)	-	(D)	-	-
Arkansas	3	0.6	750*	-	-	(D)	-	(D)	-	-
Kansas	3	0.6	60*	-	-	(D)	-	(D)	-	-
New Hampshire	3	0.6	60*	-	-	(D)	-	(D)	-	-
Virginia	3	0.6	60*	-	-	(D)	-	(D)	-	-
Rhode Island	2	0.4	60*	-	-	(D)	-	(D)	-	-
South Dakota	2	0.4	60*	-	-	(D)	-	(D)	-	-
Maine	1	0.2	60*	-	-	(D)	-	(D)	-	-
Montana	1	0.2	10*	-	-	(D)	-	(D)	-	-
Vermont	1	0.2	60*	-	-	(D)	-	(D)	-	-

Source: 1997 *Economic Census*. The states are in descending order of revenues or establishments (if revenue data are missing for the majority). The symbol (D) appears when data are withheld to prevent disclosure of competitive information. States marked with (D) are sorted by number of establishments. A dash (-) indicates that the data element cannot be calculated. * indicates the midpoint of a range; 175, for example is the range 100-249. Shaded *states* on the state map indicate those states which have proportionately greater representation in the industry than would be indicated by the state's population; the ratio is based on total revenues or number of establishments. Shaded *regions* indicate where the industry is regionally most concentrated.

NAICS 562212 - SOLID WASTE LANDFILL

GENERAL STATISTICS

Year	Establishments (number)	Employment (number)	Payroll ($ million)	Revenues ($ million)	Employees per Establishment (number)	Revenues per Establishment ($)	Payroll per Employee ($)
1997	1,403	27,454	887.0	5,493.0	19.6	3,915,182	32,309

Source: Economic Census of the United States, 1997. This is a newly defined industry. Data for prior years were unavailable at the time of publication but may become available over time.

INDICES OF CHANGE

Year	Establishments (number)	Employment (number)	Payroll ($ million)	Revenues ($ million)	Employees per Establishment (number)	Revenues per Establishment ($)	Payroll per Employee ($)
1997	100.0	100.0	100.0	100.0	100.0	100.0	100.0

Sources: Same as General Statistics. The values shown reflect change from the base year, 1997. Values above 100 mean greater than 1997, values below 100 mean less than 1997, and a value of 100 in the 1982-96 or 1998-2001 period means same as 1997. Values followed by a 'p' are projections by the editors; 'e' stands for extrapolation. Data are the most recent available at this level of detail.

SIC INDUSTRIES RELATED TO NAICS 562212

Each new NAICS code represents an industry that used to be part of an SIC or a part of several SIC industries. Data in this table are shown to provide transitional information for these cases. All available data for the precursor SIC(s) are shown. Even if only a part of an SIC is included in the NAICS, *all* data for the SIC are reproduced. If the SIC industry is not marked as being a part (pt) of the NAICS, the entire industry is embedded in the NAICS data. The SIC composition of the new industry provides some hints of the relative importance of its "ancestors." Data marked with a 'p' are projected. Projections begin with 1982 data. Data earlier than 1990 are not shown but are reflected in the projections.

SIC	Industry	1990	1991	1992	1993	1994	1995	1996	1997
4953	**Refuse Systems (pt)**								
	Establishments (number)	-	-	3,317	-	-	-	-	-
	Employment (thousands)	-	-	80.9	-	-	-	-	-
	Revenues ($ million)	-	-	14,101.7	-	-	-	-	-

Source: Economic Census of the United States, 1992, annual surveys of economic sectors conducted by the Bureau of the Census, and estimates or projections based on the 1982-1992 period; not all data are shown. 'e' marks estimates made by the editors; 'p' indicates projections based on time series. A dash (-) indicates that data for this SIC or year were not available. The abbreviation (pt) next to the industry name indicates that only a part of the industry is present within the NAICS data. If no (pt) is shown, the entire industry is contained within the NAICS data.

SELECTED RATIOS

For 1997	Avg. of Information	Analyzed Industry	Index	For 1997	Avg. of Information	Analyzed Industry	Index
Employees per establishment	27	20	74	Payroll per establishment	496,890	632,217	127
Revenue per establishment	1,070,709	3,915,182	366	Payroll as % of revenue	46	16	35
Revenue per employee	40,278	200,080	497	Payroll per employee	18,692	32,309	173

Sources: Same as General Statistics. The 'Average' column represents the average for the industry sector, in 1997, where the currently shown industry is classified. The Index shows the relationship between the Average and the Analyzed Industry. For example, 100 means that they are equal; 500 that the Analyzed Industry is five times the average; 50 means that the Analyzed Industry is half the national average. The abbreviation 'na' is used to show that data are 'not available'.

LEADING COMPANIES
No company data available for this industry.

LOCATION BY STATE AND REGIONAL CONCENTRATION

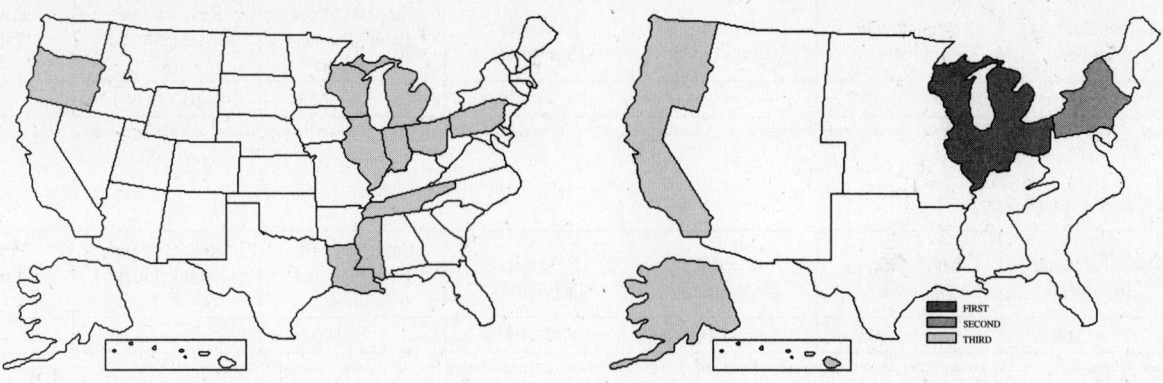

INDUSTRY DATA BY STATE

State	Establishments Total (number)	% of U.S.	Employment Total (number)	% of U.S.	Per Estab.	Payroll Total ($ mil.)	Per Empl. ($)	Revenues Total ($ mil.)	% of U.S.	Per Estab. ($)
California	118	8.4	3,603	13.1	31	128.9	35,763	658.4	12.0	5,579,737
Pennsylvania	61	4.3	2,347	8.5	38	85.8	36,577	574.7	10.5	9,421,885
Illinois	85	6.1	1,426	5.2	17	56.0	39,268	396.2	7.2	4,660,953
Texas	83	5.9	1,927	7.0	23	54.0	28,027	356.6	6.5	4,295,831
Ohio	74	5.3	1,338	4.9	18	43.2	32,270	317.4	5.8	4,289,068
Michigan	51	3.6	1,628	5.9	32	57.5	35,305	301.8	5.5	5,917,353
New York	50	3.6	719	2.6	14	39.4	54,839	243.5	4.4	4,869,640
Indiana	38	2.7	941	3.4	25	29.6	31,423	155.0	2.8	4,079,789
Florida	53	3.8	866	3.2	16	23.3	26,849	150.9	2.7	2,847,396
Tennessee	38	2.7	1,370	5.0	36	20.4	14,862	144.8	2.6	3,811,526
Wisconsin	25	1.8	514	1.9	21	16.4	31,926	140.5	2.6	5,621,640
New Jersey	21	1.5	555	2.0	26	23.1	41,614	131.0	2.4	6,238,095
Georgia	31	2.2	466	1.7	15	13.6	29,135	122.9	2.2	3,963,161
Massachusetts	32	2.3	454	1.7	14	16.1	35,562	111.4	2.0	3,481,563
North Carolina	51	3.6	444	1.6	9	12.3	27,687	95.9	1.7	1,880,647
Louisiana	26	1.9	405	1.5	16	12.8	31,536	94.8	1.7	3,645,192
Oregon	21	1.5	371	1.4	18	10.8	29,054	84.7	1.5	4,031,810
Minnesota	34	2.4	422	1.5	12	15.0	35,438	82.1	1.5	2,415,941
Mississippi	24	1.7	287	1.0	12	7.8	27,233	76.6	1.4	3,193,458
Connecticut	17	1.2	343	1.2	20	18.1	52,784	66.6	1.2	3,916,647
Missouri	36	2.6	303	1.1	8	7.5	24,677	56.7	1.0	1,573,778
Maryland	24	1.7	309	1.1	13	8.5	27,544	54.1	1.0	2,254,583
Alabama	19	1.4	223	0.8	12	7.8	35,197	50.3	0.9	2,649,737
Oklahoma	26	1.9	307	1.1	12	7.0	22,814	49.2	0.9	1,890,500
Arizona	27	1.9	339	1.2	13	8.7	25,684	48.8	0.9	1,808,370
West Virginia	19	1.4	295	1.1	16	6.7	22,583	35.5	0.6	1,869,947
Hawaii	8	0.6	84	0.3	10	2.1	24,655	22.8	0.4	2,852,500
Nebraska	18	1.3	154	0.6	9	3.3	21,558	21.4	0.4	1,188,333
Iowa	19	1.4	130	0.5	7	2.5	19,385	12.3	0.2	647,684
Wyoming	6	0.4	39	0.1	7	0.8	19,974	3.2	0.1	528,333
North Dakota	7	0.5	19	0.1	3	0.4	21,474	2.7	0.0	387,000
Alaska	5	0.4	15	0.1	3	0.4	26,200	1.5	0.0	299,600
Colorado	31	2.2	750*	-	-	(D)	-	(D)	-	-
Virginia	31	2.2	1,750*	-	-	(D)	-	(D)	-	-
Arkansas	29	2.1	175*	-	-	(D)	-	(D)	-	-
Washington	29	2.1	375*	-	-	(D)	-	(D)	-	-
Kentucky	23	1.6	375*	-	-	(D)	-	(D)	-	-
Kansas	20	1.4	175*	-	-	(D)	-	(D)	-	-
South Carolina	17	1.2	375*	-	-	(D)	-	(D)	-	-
Nevada	11	0.8	375*	-	-	(D)	-	(D)	-	-
New Mexico	11	0.8	175*	-	-	(D)	-	(D)	-	-
Montana	10	0.7	60*	-	-	(D)	-	(D)	-	-
New Hampshire	8	0.6	175*	-	-	(D)	-	(D)	-	-
Rhode Island	7	0.5	175*	-	-	(D)	-	(D)	-	-
South Dakota	6	0.4	10*	-	-	(D)	-	(D)	-	-
Vermont	6	0.4	60*	-	-	(D)	-	(D)	-	-
Idaho	5	0.4	60*	-	-	(D)	-	(D)	-	-
Utah	5	0.4	60*	-	-	(D)	-	(D)	-	-
Maine	4	0.3	60*	-	-	(D)	-	(D)	-	-
Delaware	2	0.1	175*	-	-	(D)	-	(D)	-	-
D.C.	1	0.1	60*	-	-	(D)	-	(D)	-	-

Source: 1997 *Economic Census*. The states are in descending order of revenues or establishments (if revenue data are missing for the majority). The symbol (D) appears when data are withheld to prevent disclosure of competitive information. States marked with (D) are sorted by number of establishments. A dash (-) indicates that the data element cannot be calculated. * indicates the midpoint of a range; 175, for example is the range 100-249. Shaded *states* on the state map indicate those states which have proportionately greater representation in the industry than would be indicated by the state's population; the ratio is based on total revenues or number of establishments. Shaded *regions* indicate where the industry is regionally most concentrated.

507

NAICS 562213 - SOLID WASTE COMBUSTORS AND INCINERATORS

GENERAL STATISTICS

Year	Establishments (number)	Employment (number)	Payroll ($ million)	Revenues ($ million)	Employees per Establishment (number)	Revenues per Establishment ($)	Payroll per Employee ($)
1997	105	2,976	133.0	1,129.0	28.3	10,752,381	44,691

Source: Economic Census of the United States, 1997. This is a newly defined industry. Data for prior years were unavailable at the time of publication but may become available over time.

INDICES OF CHANGE

Year	Establishments (number)	Employment (number)	Payroll ($ million)	Revenues ($ million)	Employees per Establishment (number)	Revenues per Establishment ($)	Payroll per Employee ($)
1997	100.0	100.0	100.0	100.0	100.0	100.0	100.0

Sources: Same as General Statistics. The values shown reflect change from the base year, 1997. Values above 100 mean greater than 1997, values below 100 mean less than 1997, and a value of 100 in the 1982-96 or 1998-2001 period means same as 1997. Values followed by a 'p' are projections by the editors; 'e' stands for extrapolation. Data are the most recent available at this level of detail.

SIC INDUSTRIES RELATED TO NAICS 562213

Each new NAICS code represents an industry that used to be part of an SIC or a part of several SIC industries. Data in this table are shown to provide transitional information for these cases. All available data for the precursor SIC(s) are shown. Even if only a part of an SIC is included in the NAICS, *all* data for the SIC are reproduced. If the SIC industry is not marked as being a part (pt) of the NAICS, the entire industry is embedded in the NAICS data. The SIC composition of the new industry provides some hints of the relative importance of its "ancestors." Data marked with a 'p' are projected. Projections begin with 1982 data. Data earlier than 1990 are not shown but are reflected in the projections.

SIC	Industry	1990	1991	1992	1993	1994	1995	1996	1997
4953	**Refuse Systems (pt)**								
	Establishments (number)	-	-	3,317	-	-	-	-	-
	Employment (thousands)	-	-	80.9	-	-	-	-	-
	Revenues ($ million)	-	-	14,101.7	-	-	-	-	-

Source: Economic Census of the United States, 1992, annual surveys of economic sectors conducted by the Bureau of the Census, and estimates or projections based on the 1982-1992 period; not all data are shown. 'e' marks estimates made by the editors; 'p' indicates projections based on time series. A dash (-) indicates that data for this SIC or year were not available. The abbreviation (pt) next to the industry name indicates that only a part of the industry is present within the NAICS data. If no (pt) is shown, the entire industry is contained within the NAICS data.

SELECTED RATIOS

For 1997	Avg. of Information	Analyzed Industry	Index	For 1997	Avg. of Information	Analyzed Industry	Index
Employees per establishment	27	28	107	Payroll per establishment	496,890	1,266,667	255
Revenue per establishment	1,070,709	10,752,381	1,004	Payroll as % of revenue	46	12	25
Revenue per employee	40,278	379,368	942	Payroll per employee	18,692	44,691	239

Sources: Same as General Statistics. The 'Average' column represents the average for the industry sector, in 1997, where the currently shown industry is classified. The Index shows the relationship between the Average and the Analyzed Industry. For example, 100 means that they are equal; 500 that the Analyzed Industry is five times the average; 50 means that the Analyzed Industry is half the national average. The abbreviation 'na' is used to show that data are 'not available'.

LEADING COMPANIES
No company data available for this industry.

LOCATION BY STATE AND REGIONAL CONCENTRATION

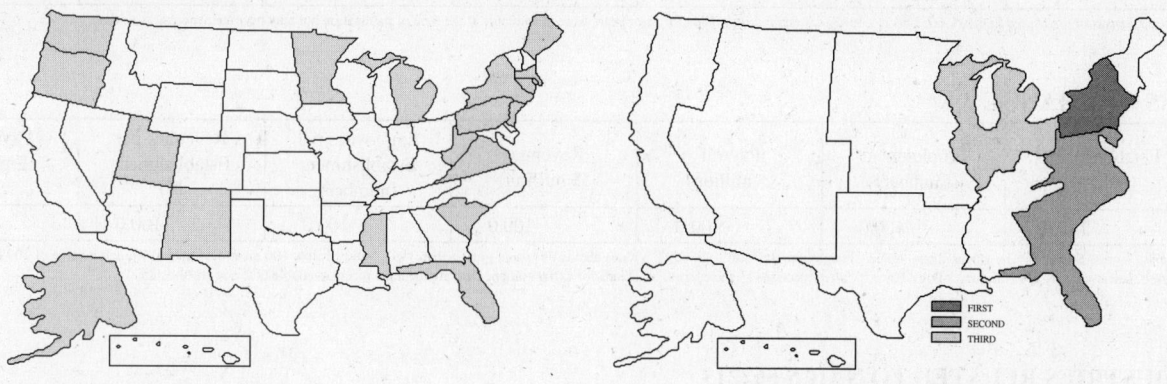

FIRST
SECOND
THIRD

INDUSTRY DATA BY STATE

State	Establishments Total (number)	% of U.S.	Employment Total (number)	% of U.S.	Per Estab.	Payroll Total ($ mil.)	Per Empl. ($)	Revenues Total ($ mil.)	% of U.S.	Per Estab. ($)
New York	11	10.5	350	11.8	32	19.4	55,386	226.5	20.1	20,594,636
Pennsylvania	12	11.4	251	8.4	21	14.8	58,801	149.0	13.2	12,412,833
New Jersey	5	4.8	149	5.0	30	8.4	56,255	88.7	7.9	17,744,600
Minnesota	5	4.8	37	1.2	7	1.2	32,000	4.9	0.4	981,400
Ohio	4	3.8	37	1.2	9	1.0	27,649	2.2	0.2	548,500
Texas	4	3.8	21	0.7	5	0.4	20,714	1.9	0.2	464,250
Florida	10	9.5	375*	-	-	(D)	-	(D)	-	-
Massachusetts	6	5.7	375*	-	-	(D)	-	(D)	-	-
Connecticut	5	4.8	60*	-	-	(D)	-	(D)	-	-
Michigan	4	3.8	60*	-	-	(D)	-	(D)	-	-
Washington	4	3.8	375*	-	-	(D)	-	(D)	-	-
California	3	2.9	10*	-	-	(D)	-	(D)	-	-
South Carolina	3	2.9	60*	-	-	(D)	-	(D)	-	-
Virginia	3	2.9	60*	-	-	(D)	-	(D)	-	-
Illinois	2	1.9	10*	-	-	(D)	-	(D)	-	-
Indiana	2	1.9	10*	-	-	(D)	-	(D)	-	-
Maryland	2	1.9	175*	-	-	(D)	-	(D)	-	-
Mississippi	2	1.9	10*	-	-	(D)	-	(D)	-	-
Oregon	2	1.9	10*	-	-	(D)	-	(D)	-	-
Tennessee	2	1.9	60*	-	-	(D)	-	(D)	-	-
Utah	2	1.9	175*	-	-	(D)	-	(D)	-	-
Alabama	1	1.0	60*	-	-	(D)	-	(D)	-	-
Alaska	1	1.0	10*	-	-	(D)	-	(D)	-	-
Georgia	1	1.0	10*	-	-	(D)	-	(D)	-	-
Iowa	1	1.0	10*	-	-	(D)	-	(D)	-	-
Kentucky	1	1.0	10*	-	-	(D)	-	(D)	-	-
Maine	1	1.0	60*	-	-	(D)	-	(D)	-	-
New Mexico	1	1.0	10*	-	-	(D)	-	(D)	-	-
North Carolina	1	1.0	10*	-	-	(D)	-	(D)	-	-
Oklahoma	1	1.0	10*	-	-	(D)	-	(D)	-	-
Rhode Island	1	1.0	60*	-	-	(D)	-	(D)	-	-
West Virginia	1	1.0	60*	-	-	(D)	-	(D)	-	-
Wisconsin	1	1.0	10*	-	-	(D)	-	(D)	-	-

Source: 1997 *Economic Census*. The states are in descending order of revenues or establishments (if revenue data are missing for the majority). The symbol (D) appears when data are withheld to prevent disclosure of competitive information. States marked with (D) are sorted by number of establishments. A dash (-) indicates that the data element cannot be calculated. * indicates the midpoint of a range; 175, for example is the range 100-249. Shaded *states* on the state map indicate those states which have proportionately greater representation in the industry than would be indicated by the state's population; the ratio is based on total revenues or number of establishments. Shaded *regions* indicate where the industry is regionally most concentrated.

NAICS 562219 - NONHAZARDOUS WASTE TREATMENT AND DISPOSAL NEC

GENERAL STATISTICS

Year	Establishments (number)	Employment (number)	Payroll ($ million)	Revenues ($ million)	Employees per Establishment (number)	Revenues per Establishment ($)	Payroll per Employee ($)
1997	294	5,082	168.0	751.0	17.3	2,554,422	33,058

Source: Economic Census of the United States, 1997. This is a newly defined industry. Data for prior years were unavailable at the time of publication but may become available over time.

INDICES OF CHANGE

Year	Establishments (number)	Employment (number)	Payroll ($ million)	Revenues ($ million)	Employees per Establishment (number)	Revenues per Establishment ($)	Payroll per Employee ($)
1997	100.0	100.0	100.0	100.0	100.0	100.0	100.0

Sources: Same as General Statistics. The values shown reflect change from the base year, 1997. Values above 100 mean greater than 1997, values below 100 mean less than 1997, and a value of 100 in the 1982-96 or 1998-2001 period means same as 1997. Values followed by a 'p' are projections by the editors; 'e' stands for extrapolation. Data are the most recent available at this level of detail.

SIC INDUSTRIES RELATED TO NAICS 562219

Each new NAICS code represents an industry that used to be part of an SIC or a part of several SIC industries. Data in this table are shown to provide transitional information for these cases. All available data for the precursor SIC(s) are shown. Even if only a part of an SIC is included in the NAICS, *all* data for the SIC are reproduced. If the SIC industry is not marked as being a part (pt) of the NAICS, the entire industry is embedded in the NAICS data. The SIC composition of the new industry provides some hints of the relative importance of its "ancestors." Data marked with a 'p' are projected. Projections begin with 1982 data. Data earlier than 1990 are not shown but are reflected in the projections.

SIC	Industry	1990	1991	1992	1993	1994	1995	1996	1997
4953	**Refuse Systems (pt)**								
	Establishments (number)	-	-	3,317	-	-	-	-	-
	Employment (thousands)	-	-	80.9	-	-	-	-	-
	Revenues ($ million)	-	-	14,101.7	-	-	-	-	-

Source: Economic Census of the United States, 1992, annual surveys of economic sectors conducted by the Bureau of the Census, and estimates or projections based on the 1982-1992 period; not all data are shown. 'e' marks estimates made by the editors; 'p' indicates projections based on time series. A dash (-) indicates that data for this SIC or year were not available. The abbreviation (pt) next to the industry name indicates that only a part of the industry is present within the NAICS data. If no (pt) is shown, the entire industry is contained within the NAICS data.

SELECTED RATIOS

For 1997	Avg. of Information	Analyzed Industry	Index	For 1997	Avg. of Information	Analyzed Industry	Index
Employees per establishment	27	17	65	Payroll per establishment	496,890	571,429	115
Revenue per establishment	1,070,709	2,554,422	239	Payroll as % of revenue	46	22	48
Revenue per employee	40,278	147,776	367	Payroll per employee	18,692	33,058	177

Sources: Same as General Statistics. The 'Average' column represents the average for the industry sector, in 1997, where the currently shown industry is classified. The Index shows the relationship between the Average and the Analyzed Industry. For example, 100 means that they are equal; 500 that the Analyzed Industry is five times the average; 50 means that the Analyzed Industry is half the national average. The abbreviation 'na' is used to show that data are 'not available'.

LEADING COMPANIES

No company data available for this industry.

LOCATION BY STATE AND REGIONAL CONCENTRATION

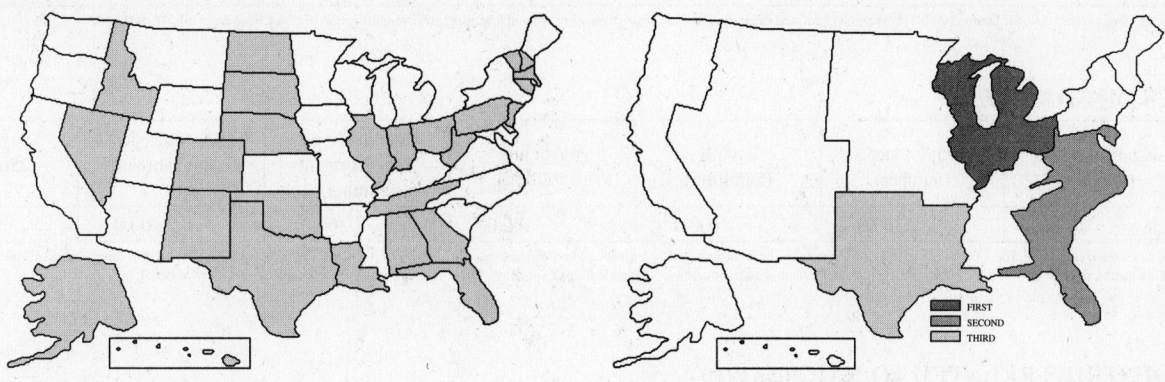

FIRST
SECOND
THIRD

INDUSTRY DATA BY STATE

State	Establishments Total (number)	% of U.S.	Employment Total (number)	% of U.S.	Per Estab.	Payroll Total ($ mil.)	Per Empl. ($)	Revenues Total ($ mil.)	% of U.S.	Per Estab. ($)
Texas	24	8.2	699	13.8	29	34.9	49,976	107.3	14.3	4,470,500
Ohio	17	5.8	376	7.4	22	11.4	30,247	53.6	7.1	3,150,294
Pennsylvania	16	5.4	406	8.0	25	11.6	28,667	39.4	5.2	2,463,125
West Virginia	3	1.0	31	0.6	10	0.6	19,935	2.5	0.3	820,333
Arizona	3	1.0	32	0.6	11	0.8	24,344	1.8	0.2	587,667
Minnesota	3	1.0	7	0.1	2	0.3	37,714	1.4	0.2	458,667
Connecticut	6	2.0	7	0.1	1	0.1	20,143	0.8	0.1	136,667
North Dakota	3	1.0	6	0.1	2	0.2	32,667	0.6	0.1	184,000
California	30	10.2	375*	-	-	(D)	-	(D)	-	-
Florida	17	5.8	375*	-	-	(D)	-	(D)	-	-
Illinois	14	4.8	175*	-	-	(D)	-	(D)	-	-
Indiana	14	4.8	175*	-	-	(D)	-	(D)	-	-
Louisiana	11	3.7	375*	-	-	(D)	-	(D)	-	-
New York	11	3.7	750*	-	-	(D)	-	(D)	-	-
New Jersey	10	3.4	175*	-	-	(D)	-	(D)	-	-
Massachusetts	9	3.1	60*	-	-	(D)	-	(D)	-	-
Michigan	9	3.1	175*	-	-	(D)	-	(D)	-	-
Colorado	8	2.7	60*	-	-	(D)	-	(D)	-	-
Georgia	8	2.7	60*	-	-	(D)	-	(D)	-	-
Alabama	7	2.4	60*	-	-	(D)	-	(D)	-	-
North Carolina	7	2.4	60*	-	-	(D)	-	(D)	-	-
Oklahoma	7	2.4	60*	-	-	(D)	-	(D)	-	-
Tennessee	6	2.0	60*	-	-	(D)	-	(D)	-	-
Maryland	5	1.7	60*	-	-	(D)	-	(D)	-	-
Idaho	4	1.4	10*	-	-	(D)	-	(D)	-	-
Missouri	4	1.4	10*	-	-	(D)	-	(D)	-	-
Nebraska	4	1.4	10*	-	-	(D)	-	(D)	-	-
Hawaii	3	1.0	60*	-	-	(D)	-	(D)	-	-
Mississippi	3	1.0	10*	-	-	(D)	-	(D)	-	-
Oregon	3	1.0	10*	-	-	(D)	-	(D)	-	-
Washington	3	1.0	60*	-	-	(D)	-	(D)	-	-
Wisconsin	3	1.0	60*	-	-	(D)	-	(D)	-	-
Nevada	2	0.7	10*	-	-	(D)	-	(D)	-	-
New Hampshire	2	0.7	10*	-	-	(D)	-	(D)	-	-
New Mexico	2	0.7	60*	-	-	(D)	-	(D)	-	-
South Carolina	2	0.7	10*	-	-	(D)	-	(D)	-	-
Utah	2	0.7	10*	-	-	(D)	-	(D)	-	-
Vermont	2	0.7	60*	-	-	(D)	-	(D)	-	-
Alaska	1	0.3	60*	-	-	(D)	-	(D)	-	-
Iowa	1	0.3	10*	-	-	(D)	-	(D)	-	-
Kentucky	1	0.3	10*	-	-	(D)	-	(D)	-	-
Maine	1	0.3	10*	-	-	(D)	-	(D)	-	-
Montana	1	0.3	10*	-	-	(D)	-	(D)	-	-
South Dakota	1	0.3	60*	-	-	(D)	-	(D)	-	-
Virginia	1	0.3	175*	-	-	(D)	-	(D)	-	-

Source: 1997 *Economic Census*. The states are in descending order of revenues or establishments (if revenue data are missing for the majority). The symbol (D) appears when data are withheld to prevent disclosure of competitive information. States marked with (D) are sorted by number of establishments. A dash (-) indicates that the data element cannot be calculated. * indicates the midpoint of a range; 175, for example is the range 100-249. Shaded *states* on the state map indicate those states which have proportionately greater representation in the industry than would be indicated by the state's population; the ratio is based on total revenues or number of establishments. Shaded *regions* indicate where the industry is regionally most concentrated.

NAICS 562910 - REMEDIATION SERVICES

GENERAL STATISTICS

Year	Establishments (number)	Employment (number)	Payroll ($ million)	Revenues ($ million)	Employees per Establishment (number)	Revenues per Establishment ($)	Payroll per Employee ($)
1997	1,677	40,994	1,500.0	5,690.0	24.4	3,392,964	36,591

Source: Economic Census of the United States, 1997. This is a newly defined industry. Data for prior years were unavailable at the time of publication but may become available over time.

INDICES OF CHANGE

Year	Establishments (number)	Employment (number)	Payroll ($ million)	Revenues ($ million)	Employees per Establishment (number)	Revenues per Establishment ($)	Payroll per Employee ($)
1997	100.0	100.0	100.0	100.0	100.0	100.0	100.0

Sources: Same as General Statistics. The values shown reflect change from the base year, 1997. Values above 100 mean greater than 1997, values below 100 mean less than 1997, and a value of 100 in the 1982-96 or 1998-2001 period means same as 1997. Values followed by a 'p' are projections by the editors; 'e' stands for extrapolation. Data are the most recent available at this level of detail.

SIC INDUSTRIES RELATED TO NAICS 562910

Each new NAICS code represents an industry that used to be part of an SIC or a part of several SIC industries. Data in this table are shown to provide transitional information for these cases. All available data for the precursor SIC(s) are shown. Even if only a part of an SIC is included in the NAICS, *all* data for the SIC are reproduced. If the SIC industry is not marked as being a part (pt) of the NAICS, the entire industry is embedded in the NAICS data. The SIC composition of the new industry provides some hints of the relative importance of its "ancestors." Data marked with a 'p' are projected. Projections begin with 1982 data. Data earlier than 1990 are not shown but are reflected in the projections.

SIC	Industry	1990	1991	1992	1993	1994	1995	1996	1997
1799	**Special Trade Contractors, n.e.c.**								
	Establishments (number)	22,471	22,634	25,270	27,296	26,150e	26,601e	27,060e	27,527e
	Employment (thousands)	197.0	186.3	204.3	207.1	216.9e	223.4e	230.2e	237.1e
	Revenues ($ million)	12,936.7e	13,535.6e	14,162.3	14,818.0e	15,504.1e	16,221.9e	16,973.0e	17,758.8e
4959	**Sanitary Services, nec (pt)**								
	Establishments (number)	-	-	1,277	-	-	-	-	-
	Employment (thousands)	-	-	8.1	-	-	-	-	-
	Revenues ($ million)	-	-	702.4	-	-	-	-	-

Source: Economic Census of the United States, 1992, annual surveys of economic sectors conducted by the Bureau of the Census, and estimates or projections based on the 1982-1992 period; not all data are shown. 'e' marks estimates made by the editors; 'p' indicates projections based on time series. A dash (-) indicates that data for this SIC or year were not available. The abbreviation (pt) next to the industry name indicates that only a part of the industry is present within the NAICS data. If no (pt) is shown, the entire industry is contained within the NAICS data.

SELECTED RATIOS

For 1997	Avg. of Information	Analyzed Industry	Index	For 1997	Avg. of Information	Analyzed Industry	Index
Employees per establishment	27	24	92	Payroll per establishment	496,890	894,454	180
Revenue per establishment	1,070,709	3,392,964	317	Payroll as % of revenue	46	26	57
Revenue per employee	40,278	138,801	345	Payroll per employee	18,692	36,591	196

Sources: Same as General Statistics. The 'Average' column represents the average for the industry sector, in 1997, where the currently shown industry is classified. The Index shows the relationship between the Average and the Analyzed Industry. For example, 100 means that they are equal; 500 that the Analyzed Industry is five times the average; 50 means that the Analyzed Industry is half the national average. The abbreviation 'na' is used to show that data are 'not available'.

LEADING COMPANIES
No company data available for this industry.

LOCATION BY STATE AND REGIONAL CONCENTRATION

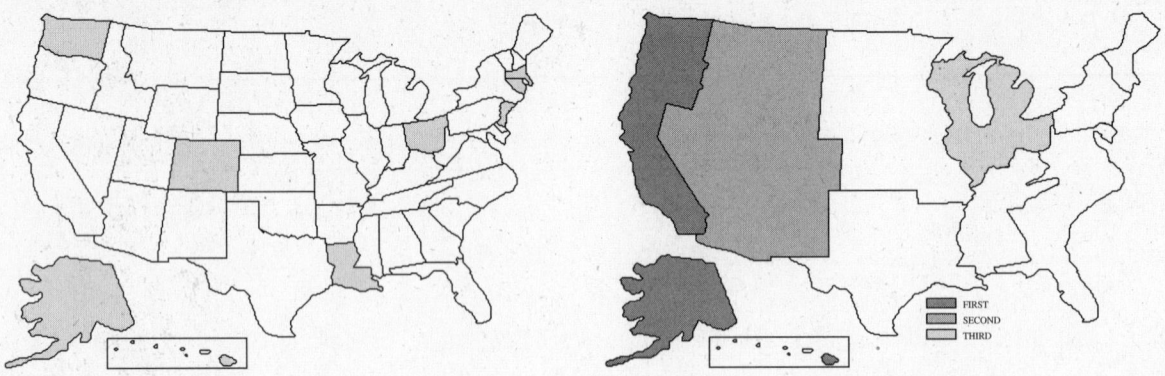

INDUSTRY DATA BY STATE

State	Establishments Total (number)	% of U.S.	Employment Total (number)	% of U.S.	Per Estab.	Payroll Total ($ mil.)	Per Empl. ($)	Revenues Total ($ mil.)	% of U.S.	Per Estab. ($)
Washington	38	2.3	4,217	10.3	111	204.2	48,428	1,134.8	19.9	29,862,158
Colorado	40	2.4	3,434	8.4	86	188.5	54,887	853.2	15.0	21,329,875
California	171	10.2	4,193	10.2	25	135.0	32,199	433.2	7.6	2,533,146
Ohio	59	3.5	2,812	6.9	48	108.6	38,622	346.1	6.1	5,866,644
New York	109	6.5	2,818	6.9	26	78.4	27,835	244.3	4.3	2,241,468
Texas	96	5.7	2,083	5.1	22	71.7	34,418	236.6	4.2	2,464,771
New Jersey	92	5.5	1,592	3.9	17	58.2	36,541	218.8	3.8	2,378,772
Massachusetts	49	2.9	1,061	2.6	22	41.2	38,839	172.7	3.0	3,524,939
Florida	85	5.1	1,540	3.8	18	46.7	30,353	169.2	3.0	1,990,012
Illinois	64	3.8	1,486	3.6	23	54.0	36,338	164.7	2.9	2,573,094
Pennsylvania	85	5.1	1,500	3.7	18	52.7	35,150	164.4	2.9	1,933,565
Georgia	46	2.7	634	1.5	14	24.3	38,265	119.5	2.1	2,598,913
Louisiana	44	2.6	847	2.1	19	24.2	28,557	116.3	2.0	2,642,227
North Carolina	60	3.6	1,665	4.1	28	43.9	26,395	115.7	2.0	1,927,650
Missouri	57	3.4	1,074	2.6	19	35.9	33,414	110.2	1.9	1,933,719
Indiana	37	2.2	964	2.4	26	31.1	32,305	95.1	1.7	2,570,135
Maryland	39	2.3	913	2.2	23	30.5	33,396	93.6	1.6	2,399,846
Virginia	35	2.1	883	2.2	25	26.4	29,942	92.1	1.6	2,630,257
Tennessee	29	1.7	743	1.8	26	25.1	33,771	90.9	1.6	3,132,966
Connecticut	31	1.8	566	1.4	18	24.7	43,617	90.8	1.6	2,928,323
Michigan	45	2.7	662	1.6	15	19.5	29,518	68.5	1.2	1,521,800
Hawaii	16	1.0	323	0.8	20	16.0	49,628	58.1	1.0	3,630,250
Minnesota	30	1.8	359	0.9	12	15.7	43,830	54.3	1.0	1,808,767
Alaska	17	1.0	341	0.8	20	18.5	54,296	48.5	0.9	2,850,059
Wisconsin	25	1.5	400	1.0	16	12.4	30,893	39.5	0.7	1,581,680
Arizona	18	1.1	420	1.0	23	12.5	29,831	37.9	0.7	2,107,889
Alabama	16	1.0	304	0.7	19	8.4	27,530	31.0	0.5	1,936,250
South Carolina	16	1.0	379	0.9	24	12.3	32,541	28.2	0.5	1,764,063
Oklahoma	19	1.1	428	1.0	23	9.0	21,007	25.9	0.5	1,361,737
Oregon	21	1.3	180	0.4	9	5.0	27,872	21.9	0.4	1,043,524
Kansas	12	0.7	192	0.5	16	7.1	36,766	21.3	0.4	1,773,750
Utah	18	1.1	288	0.7	16	5.0	17,236	20.0	0.4	1,110,889
Nevada	12	0.7	139	0.3	12	4.7	34,137	16.8	0.3	1,402,083
New Mexico	12	0.7	150	0.4	13	3.9	26,200	16.7	0.3	1,395,167
Kentucky	16	1.0	151	0.4	9	4.7	31,364	15.6	0.3	977,687
New Hampshire	10	0.6	103	0.3	10	4.0	39,243	13.8	0.2	1,375,000
Maine	12	0.7	158	0.4	13	5.1	32,494	13.2	0.2	1,104,083
Nebraska	5	0.3	96	0.2	19	4.2	43,594	13.0	0.2	2,603,600
Rhode Island	10	0.6	96	0.2	10	3.3	34,469	11.9	0.2	1,191,500
Iowa	14	0.8	147	0.4	10	4.3	29,313	11.3	0.2	809,071
Delaware	10	0.6	130	0.3	13	4.3	33,131	10.6	0.2	1,056,200
Arkansas	10	0.6	129	0.3	13	2.3	18,217	7.3	0.1	733,500
Montana	5	0.3	87	0.2	17	2.2	25,126	6.4	0.1	1,271,000
Mississippi	11	0.7	56	0.1	5	1.5	26,714	6.3	0.1	575,091
West Virginia	7	0.4	57	0.1	8	1.3	22,035	5.5	0.1	791,286
Idaho	9	0.5	60	0.1	7	1.6	26,017	4.5	0.1	501,889
Vermont	4	0.2	43	0.1	11	1.4	32,279	3.2	0.1	798,750
North Dakota	4	0.2	6	0.0	2	0.1	10,500	0.3	0.0	73,500
South Dakota	3	0.2	60*	-	-	(D)	-	(D)	-	-
D.C.	2	0.1	10*	-	-	(D)	-	(D)	-	-
Wyoming	2	0.1	10*	-	-	(D)	-	(D)	-	-

Source: 1997 *Economic Census*. The states are in descending order of revenues or establishments (if revenue data are missing for the majority). The symbol (D) appears when data are withheld to prevent disclosure of competitive information. States marked with (D) are sorted by number of establishments. A dash (-) indicates that the data element cannot be calculated. * indicates the midpoint of a range; 175, for example is the range 100-249. Shaded *states* on the state map indicate those states which have proportionately greater representation in the industry than would be indicated by the state's population; the ratio is based on total revenues or number of establishments. Shaded *regions* indicate where the industry is regionally most concentrated.

NAICS 562920 - MATERIALS RECOVERY FACILITY

GENERAL STATISTICS

Year	Establishments (number)	Employment (number)	Payroll ($ million)	Revenues ($ million)	Employees per Establishment (number)	Revenues per Establishment ($)	Payroll per Employee ($)
1997	765	10,846	283.0	1,299.0	14.2	1,698,039	26,093

Source: Economic Census of the United States, 1997. This is a newly defined industry. Data for prior years were unavailable at the time of publication but may become available over time.

INDICES OF CHANGE

Year	Establishments (number)	Employment (number)	Payroll ($ million)	Revenues ($ million)	Employees per Establishment (number)	Revenues per Establishment ($)	Payroll per Employee ($)
1997	100.0	100.0	100.0	100.0	100.0	100.0	100.0

Sources: Same as General Statistics. The values shown reflect change from the base year, 1997. Values above 100 mean greater than 1997, values below 100 mean less than 1997, and a value of 100 in the 1982-96 or 1998-2001 period means same as 1997. Values followed by a 'p' are projections by the editors; 'e' stands for extrapolation. Data are the most recent available at this level of detail.

SIC INDUSTRIES RELATED TO NAICS 562920

Each new NAICS code represents an industry that used to be part of an SIC or a part of several SIC industries. Data in this table are shown to provide transitional information for these cases. All available data for the precursor SIC(s) are shown. Even if only a part of an SIC is included in the NAICS, *all* data for the SIC are reproduced. If the SIC industry is not marked as being a part (pt) of the NAICS, the entire industry is embedded in the NAICS data. The SIC composition of the new industry provides some hints of the relative importance of its "ancestors." Data marked with a 'p' are projected. Projections begin with 1982 data. Data earlier than 1990 are not shown but are reflected in the projections.

SIC	Industry	1990	1991	1992	1993	1994	1995	1996	1997
4953	**Refuse Systems (pt)**								
	Establishments (number)	-	-	3,317	-	-	-	-	-
	Employment (thousands)	-	-	80.9	-	-	-	-	-
	Revenues ($ million)	-	-	14,101.7	-	-	-	-	-

Source: Economic Census of the United States, 1992, annual surveys of economic sectors conducted by the Bureau of the Census, and estimates or projections based on the 1982-1992 period; not all data are shown. 'e' marks estimates made by the editors; 'p' indicates projections based on time series. A dash (-) indicates that data for this SIC or year were not available. The abbreviation (pt) next to the industry name indicates that only a part of the industry is present within the NAICS data. If no (pt) is shown, the entire industry is contained within the NAICS data.

SELECTED RATIOS

For 1997	Avg. of Information	Analyzed Industry	Index	For 1997	Avg. of Information	Analyzed Industry	Index
Employees per establishment	27	14	53	Payroll per establishment	496,890	369,935	74
Revenue per establishment	1,070,709	1,698,039	159	Payroll as % of revenue	46	22	47
Revenue per employee	40,278	119,768	297	Payroll per employee	18,692	26,093	140

Sources: Same as General Statistics. The 'Average' column represents the average for the industry sector, in 1997, where the currently shown industry is classified. The Index shows the relationship between the Average and the Analyzed Industry. For example, 100 means that they are equal; 500 that the Analyzed Industry is five times the average; 50 means that the Analyzed Industry is half the national average. The abbreviation 'na' is used to show that data are 'not available'.

LEADING COMPANIES
No company data available for this industry.

LOCATION BY STATE AND REGIONAL CONCENTRATION

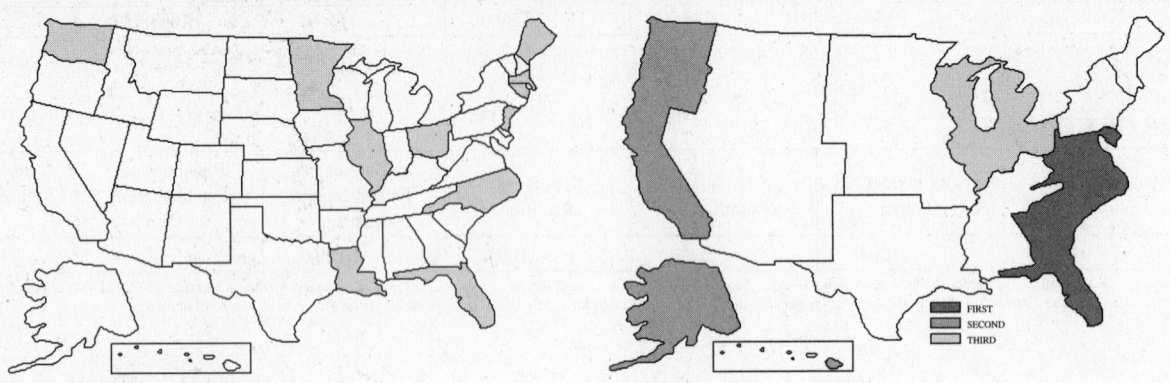

FIRST
SECOND
THIRD

INDUSTRY DATA BY STATE

State	Establishments Total (number)	Establishments % of U.S.	Employment Total (number)	Employment % of U.S.	Employment Per Estab.	Payroll Total ($ mil.)	Payroll Per Empl. ($)	Revenues Total ($ mil.)	Revenues % of U.S.	Revenues Per Estab. ($)
California	83	10.8	1,030	9.5	12	24.9	24,194	114.3	8.8	1,377,590
Florida	47	6.1	913	8.4	19	23.1	25,332	92.5	7.1	1,967,766
Minnesota	21	2.7	494	4.6	24	16.2	32,769	76.8	5.9	3,654,905
New York	47	6.1	583	5.4	12	14.8	25,340	73.7	5.7	1,568,809
North Carolina	22	2.9	690	6.4	31	15.4	22,280	73.2	5.6	3,326,227
Washington	19	2.5	294	2.7	15	9.7	32,827	70.9	5.5	3,729,947
Ohio	23	3.0	680	6.3	30	19.0	27,966	66.9	5.1	2,907,217
Massachusetts	30	3.9	563	5.2	19	14.7	26,174	62.6	4.8	2,088,133
Illinois	30	3.9	729	6.7	24	19.3	26,422	59.4	4.6	1,979,500
Texas	44	5.8	529	4.9	12	9.5	17,879	57.8	4.4	1,313,023
New Jersey	33	4.3	464	4.3	14	10.6	22,813	51.2	3.9	1,552,545
Pennsylvania	30	3.9	268	2.5	9	6.1	22,869	27.0	2.1	900,400
Maine	25	3.3	196	1.8	8	4.9	24,765	26.9	2.1	1,075,760
Michigan	32	4.2	174	1.6	5	6.2	35,724	26.4	2.0	823,594
Maryland	10	1.3	124	1.1	12	4.2	33,903	24.0	1.8	2,401,200
Louisiana	8	1.0	203	1.9	25	5.0	24,537	23.0	1.8	2,878,875
Connecticut	12	1.6	160	1.5	13	7.0	43,600	22.7	1.7	1,888,417
Tennessee	12	1.6	153	1.4	13	3.5	22,895	19.2	1.5	1,597,167
Kentucky	7	0.9	218	2.0	31	6.5	29,839	18.1	1.4	2,587,143
Georgia	21	2.7	187	1.7	9	5.1	27,481	18.0	1.4	857,190
Wisconsin	27	3.5	262	2.4	10	4.8	18,496	17.3	1.3	639,296
Arizona	12	1.6	171	1.6	14	4.2	24,608	16.7	1.3	1,388,917
South Carolina	8	1.0	65	0.6	8	2.6	39,908	14.7	1.1	1,842,750
Oregon	9	1.2	164	1.5	18	2.3	13,750	13.1	1.0	1,451,333
Indiana	12	1.6	66	0.6	6	2.3	35,167	12.8	1.0	1,069,000
Virginia	15	2.0	133	1.2	9	3.2	23,684	11.5	0.9	768,200
Oklahoma	7	0.9	58	0.5	8	1.5	25,724	11.4	0.9	1,625,571
Iowa	15	2.0	89	0.8	6	2.0	22,146	9.8	0.8	654,067
Missouri	20	2.6	72	0.7	4	1.5	20,417	7.3	0.6	363,250
Alabama	8	1.0	50	0.5	6	0.8	15,000	4.5	0.3	560,000
New Hampshire	10	1.3	43	0.4	4	1.0	23,860	4.4	0.3	438,200
West Virginia	6	0.8	24	0.2	4	0.5	20,542	3.4	0.3	573,333
New Mexico	5	0.7	26	0.2	5	0.5	20,423	3.1	0.2	615,200
Arkansas	5	0.7	37	0.3	7	0.7	18,703	2.9	0.2	585,800
South Dakota	5	0.7	29	0.3	6	0.4	12,517	2.8	0.2	552,200
Mississippi	4	0.5	51	0.5	13	0.3	6,627	1.7	0.1	433,750
Colorado	11	1.4	750*	-	-	(D)	-	(D)	-	-
Kansas	8	1.0	10*	-	-	(D)	-	(D)	-	-
Delaware	4	0.5	10*	-	-	(D)	-	(D)	-	-
Nebraska	3	0.4	60*	-	-	(D)	-	(D)	-	-
North Dakota	3	0.4	60*	-	-	(D)	-	(D)	-	-
Rhode Island	3	0.4	60*	-	-	(D)	-	(D)	-	-
Hawaii	2	0.3	10*	-	-	(D)	-	(D)	-	-
Montana	2	0.3	10*	-	-	(D)	-	(D)	-	-
Alaska	1	0.1	10*	-	-	(D)	-	(D)	-	-
Idaho	1	0.1	10*	-	-	(D)	-	(D)	-	-
Utah	1	0.1	60*	-	-	(D)	-	(D)	-	-
Vermont	1	0.1	10*	-	-	(D)	-	(D)	-	-
Wyoming	1	0.1	10*	-	-	(D)	-	(D)	-	-

Source: 1997 *Economic Census*. The states are in descending order of revenues or establishments (if revenue data are missing for the majority). The symbol (D) appears when data are withheld to prevent disclosure of competitive information. States marked with (D) are sorted by number of establishments. A dash (-) indicates that the data element cannot be calculated. * indicates the midpoint of a range; 175, for example is the range 100-249. Shaded *states* on the state map indicate those states which have proportionately greater representation in the industry than would be indicated by the state's population; the ratio is based on total revenues or number of establishments. Shaded *regions* indicate where the industry is regionally most concentrated.

NAICS 562991 - SEPTIC TANK AND RELATED SERVICES

GENERAL STATISTICS

Year	Establishments (number)	Employment (number)	Payroll ($ million)	Revenues ($ million)	Employees per Establishment (number)	Revenues per Establishment ($)	Payroll per Employee ($)
1997	3,101	19,977	514.0	1,581.0	6.4	509,836	25,730

Source: Economic Census of the United States, 1997. This is a newly defined industry. Data for prior years were unavailable at the time of publication but may become available over time.

INDICES OF CHANGE

Year	Establishments (number)	Employment (number)	Payroll ($ million)	Revenues ($ million)	Employees per Establishment (number)	Revenues per Establishment ($)	Payroll per Employee ($)
1997	100.0	100.0	100.0	100.0	100.0	100.0	100.0

Sources: Same as General Statistics. The values shown reflect change from the base year, 1997. Values above 100 mean greater than 1997, values below 100 mean less than 1997, and a value of 100 in the 1982-96 or 1998-2001 period means same as 1997. Values followed by a 'p' are projections by the editors; 'e' stands for extrapolation. Data are the most recent available at this level of detail.

SIC INDUSTRIES RELATED TO NAICS 562991

Each new NAICS code represents an industry that used to be part of an SIC or a part of several SIC industries. Data in this table are shown to provide transitional information for these cases. All available data for the precursor SIC(s) are shown. Even if only a part of an SIC is included in the NAICS, *all* data for the SIC are reproduced. If the SIC industry is not marked as being a part (pt) of the NAICS, the entire industry is embedded in the NAICS data. The SIC composition of the new industry provides some hints of the relative importance of its "ancestors." Data marked with a 'p' are projected. Projections begin with 1982 data. Data earlier than 1990 are not shown but are reflected in the projections.

SIC	Industry	1990	1991	1992	1993	1994	1995	1996	1997
7359	**Equipment Rental & Leasing, nec (pt)**								
	Establishments (number)	16,213	16,430	17,687	17,439	17,564	17,607	17,431p	17,486p
	Employment (thousands)	145.6	143.2	134.1	139.9	143.8	151.3	148.8p	150.4p
	Revenues ($ million)	15,481.0	15,265.0	15,482.0	16,816.0	18,607.0	20,677.0	20,949.0	21,947.1p
7699	**Repair Services, nec (pt)**								
	Establishments (number)	27,822	29,303	34,103	34,618	34,136	34,391	35,001p	35,792p
	Employment (thousands)	181.0	181.4	191.0	201.5	207.4	220.2	219.6p	226.2p
	Revenues ($ million)	-	-	15,059.4	15,563.6p	16,427.9p	17,292.2p	18,156.5p	19,020.8p

Source: Economic Census of the United States, 1992, annual surveys of economic sectors conducted by the Bureau of the Census, and estimates or projections based on the 1982-1992 period; not all data are shown. 'e' marks estimates made by the editors; 'p' indicates projections based on time series. A dash (-) indicates that data for this SIC or year were not available. The abbreviation (pt) next to the industry name indicates that only a part of the industry is present within the NAICS data. If no (pt) is shown, the entire industry is contained within the NAICS data.

SELECTED RATIOS

For 1997	Avg. of Information	Analyzed Industry	Index	For 1997	Avg. of Information	Analyzed Industry	Index
Employees per establishment	27	6	24	Payroll per establishment	496,890	165,753	33
Revenue per establishment	1,070,709	509,836	48	Payroll as % of revenue	46	33	70
Revenue per employee	40,278	79,141	196	Payroll per employee	18,692	25,730	138

Sources: Same as General Statistics. The 'Average' column represents the average for the industry sector, in 1997, where the currently shown industry is classified. The Index shows the relationship between the Average and the Analyzed Industry. For example, 100 means that they are equal; 500 that the Analyzed Industry is five times the average; 50 means that the Analyzed Industry is half the national average. The abbreviation 'na' is used to show that data are 'not available'.

LEADING COMPANIES

No company data available for this industry.

LOCATION BY STATE AND REGIONAL CONCENTRATION

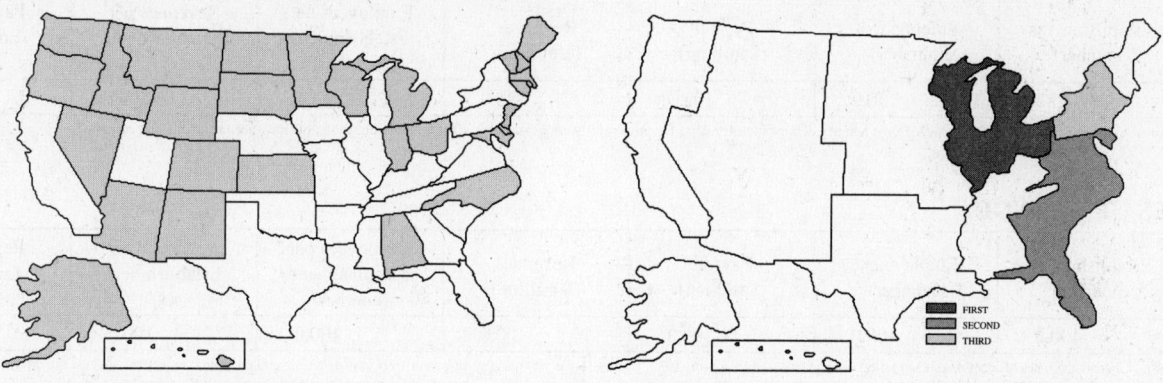

INDUSTRY DATA BY STATE

State	Establishments		Employment			Payroll		Revenues		
	Total (number)	% of U.S.	Total (number)	% of U.S.	Per Estab.	Total ($ mil.)	Per Empl. ($)	Total ($ mil.)	% of U.S.	Per Estab. ($)
California	241	7.8	2,327	11.6	10	57.6	24,762	172.0	10.9	713,768
New York	214	6.9	1,420	7.1	7	38.8	27,343	122.6	7.8	572,715
New Jersey	99	3.2	823	4.1	8	26.5	32,208	82.7	5.2	835,455
Florida	153	4.9	1,106	5.5	7	25.3	22,831	80.8	5.1	528,033
Texas	143	4.6	945	4.7	7	21.9	23,131	69.1	4.4	482,867
Illinois	131	4.2	821	4.1	6	24.8	30,152	65.9	4.2	502,809
Massachusetts	110	3.5	532	2.7	5	16.4	30,776	54.8	3.5	497,964
Wisconsin	124	4.0	531	2.7	4	15.7	29,480	51.2	3.2	412,710
Michigan	128	4.1	560	2.8	4	12.4	22,163	38.3	2.4	298,844
Tennessee	52	1.7	374	1.9	7	8.8	23,481	31.7	2.0	609,673
Arizona	57	1.8	375	1.9	7	10.1	26,949	29.1	1.8	510,333
Alabama	52	1.7	349	1.7	7	7.9	22,585	25.6	1.6	493,135
Minnesota	68	2.2	328	1.6	5	8.7	26,561	25.5	1.6	374,485
Iowa	34	1.1	128	0.6	4	2.9	22,687	8.6	0.5	251,853
Delaware	15	0.5	79	0.4	5	1.9	23,823	5.6	0.4	371,867
Nebraska	14	0.5	81	0.4	6	2.0	24,432	4.8	0.3	344,786
West Virginia	20	0.6	86	0.4	4	1.3	15,372	4.5	0.3	226,800
Ohio	147	4.7	1,750*	-	-	(D)	-	(D)	-	-
Pennsylvania	119	3.8	1,750*	-	-	(D)	-	(D)	-	-
Indiana	93	3.0	750*	-	-	(D)	-	(D)	-	-
North Carolina	92	3.0	750*	-	-	(D)	-	(D)	-	-
Washington	84	2.7	375*	-	-	(D)	-	(D)	-	-
Virginia	77	2.5	375*	-	-	(D)	-	(D)	-	-
Connecticut	65	2.1	375*	-	-	(D)	-	(D)	-	-
Maryland	62	2.0	375*	-	-	(D)	-	(D)	-	-
Georgia	61	2.0	375*	-	-	(D)	-	(D)	-	-
Oregon	60	1.9	375*	-	-	(D)	-	(D)	-	-
Colorado	59	1.9	375*	-	-	(D)	-	(D)	-	-
Missouri	42	1.4	375*	-	-	(D)	-	(D)	-	-
Kansas	34	1.1	175*	-	-	(D)	-	(D)	-	-
Kentucky	34	1.1	175*	-	-	(D)	-	(D)	-	-
New Mexico	33	1.1	175*	-	-	(D)	-	(D)	-	-
South Carolina	33	1.1	175*	-	-	(D)	-	(D)	-	-
Louisiana	31	1.0	175*	-	-	(D)	-	(D)	-	-
New Hampshire	31	1.0	60*	-	-	(D)	-	(D)	-	-
Arkansas	27	0.9	175*	-	-	(D)	-	(D)	-	-
Maine	26	0.8	175*	-	-	(D)	-	(D)	-	-
Idaho	25	0.8	175*	-	-	(D)	-	(D)	-	-
Hawaii	22	0.7	175*	-	-	(D)	-	(D)	-	-
Oklahoma	22	0.7	175*	-	-	(D)	-	(D)	-	-
Nevada	21	0.7	175*	-	-	(D)	-	(D)	-	-
Alaska	19	0.6	60*	-	-	(D)	-	(D)	-	-
Mississippi	19	0.6	60*	-	-	(D)	-	(D)	-	-
Rhode Island	18	0.6	60*	-	-	(D)	-	(D)	-	-
Utah	17	0.5	175*	-	-	(D)	-	(D)	-	-
Montana	16	0.5	60*	-	-	(D)	-	(D)	-	-
Vermont	15	0.5	60*	-	-	(D)	-	(D)	-	-
South Dakota	14	0.5	60*	-	-	(D)	-	(D)	-	-
Wyoming	14	0.5	60*	-	-	(D)	-	(D)	-	-
North Dakota	12	0.4	60*	-	-	(D)	-	(D)	-	-
D.C.	2	0.1	60*	-	-	(D)	-	(D)	-	-

Source: 1997 *Economic Census*. The states are in descending order of revenues or establishments (if revenue data are missing for the majority). The symbol (D) appears when data are withheld to prevent disclosure of competitive information. States marked with (D) are sorted by number of establishments. A dash (-) indicates that the data element cannot be calculated. * indicates the midpoint of a range; 175, for example is the range 100-249. Shaded *states* on the state map indicate those states which have proportionately greater representation in the industry than would be indicated by the state's population; the ratio is based on total revenues or number of establishments. Shaded *regions* indicate where the industry is regionally most concentrated.

NAICS 562998 - MISCELLANEOUS WASTE MANAGEMENT SERVICES NEC

GENERAL STATISTICS

Year	Establishments (number)	Employment (number)	Payroll ($ million)	Revenues ($ million)	Employees per Establishment (number)	Revenues per Establishment ($)	Payroll per Employee ($)
1997	187	2,819	102.0	380.0	15.1	2,032,086	36,183

Source: *Economic Census of the United States*, 1997. This is a newly defined industry. Data for prior years were unavailable at the time of publication but may become available over time.

INDICES OF CHANGE

Year	Establishments (number)	Employment (number)	Payroll ($ million)	Revenues ($ million)	Employees per Establishment (number)	Revenues per Establishment ($)	Payroll per Employee ($)
1997	100.0	100.0	100.0	100.0	100.0	100.0	100.0

Sources: Same as General Statistics. The values shown reflect change from the base year, 1997. Values above 100 mean greater than 1997, values below 100 mean less than 1997, and a value of 100 in the 1982-96 or 1998-2001 period means same as 1997. Values followed by a 'p' are projections by the editors; 'e' stands for extrapolation. Data are the most recent available at this level of detail.

SIC INDUSTRIES RELATED TO NAICS 562998

Each new NAICS code represents an industry that used to be part of an SIC or a part of several SIC industries. Data in this table are shown to provide transitional information for these cases. All available data for the precursor SIC(s) are shown. Even if only a part of an SIC is included in the NAICS, *all* data for the SIC are reproduced. If the SIC industry is not marked as being a part (pt) of the NAICS, the entire industry is embedded in the NAICS data. The SIC composition of the new industry provides some hints of the relative importance of its "ancestors." Data marked with a 'p' are projected. Projections begin with 1982 data. Data earlier than 1990 are not shown but are reflected in the projections.

SIC	Industry	1990	1991	1992	1993	1994	1995	1996	1997
4959	**Sanitary Services, nec (pt)**								
	Establishments (number)	-	-	1,277	-	-	-	-	-
	Employment (thousands)	-	-	8.1	-	-	-	-	-
	Revenues ($ million)	-	-	702.4	-	-	-	-	-
7699	**Repair Services, nec (pt)**								
	Establishments (number)	27,822	29,303	34,103	34,618	34,136	34,391	35,001p	35,792p
	Employment (thousands)	181.0	181.4	191.0	201.5	207.4	220.2	219.6p	226.2p
	Revenues ($ million)	-	-	15,059.4	15,563.6p	16,427.9p	17,292.2p	18,156.5p	19,020.8p

Source: *Economic Census of the United States*, 1992, annual surveys of economic sectors conducted by the Bureau of the Census, and estimates or projections based on the 1982-1992 period; not all data are shown. 'e' marks estimates made by the editors; 'p' indicates projections based on time series. A dash (-) indicates that data for this SIC or year were not available. The abbreviation (pt) next to the industry name indicates that only a part of the industry is present within the NAICS data. If no (pt) is shown, the entire industry is contained within the NAICS data.

SELECTED RATIOS

For 1997	Avg. of Information	Analyzed Industry	Index	For 1997	Avg. of Information	Analyzed Industry	Index
Employees per establishment	27	15	57	Payroll per establishment	496,890	545,455	110
Revenue per establishment	1,070,709	2,032,086	190	Payroll as % of revenue	46	27	58
Revenue per employee	40,278	134,800	335	Payroll per employee	18,692	36,183	194

Sources: Same as General Statistics. The 'Average' column represents the average for the industry sector, in 1997, where the currently shown industry is classified. The Index shows the relationship between the Average and the Analyzed Industry. For example, 100 means that they are equal; 500 that the Analyzed Industry is five times the average; 50 means that the Analyzed Industry is half the national average. The abbreviation 'na' is used to show that data are 'not available'.

LEADING COMPANIES   Number shown: 5   Total sales ($ mil): 2,439   Total employment (000): 61.2

Company Name	Address				CEO Name	Phone	Co. Type	Sales ($ mil)	Empl. (000)
Waste Management Holdings	700 E Butterfield Rd	Lombard	IL	60148	Robert S. Miller	630-572-8800	P	2,145	58.9
Clean Harbors Environmental	PO Box 850327	Braintree	MA	02185	Alan S McKim	781-849-1800	P	146	1.2
Marine Pollution Control Corp.	8631 W Jefferson	Detroit	MI	48209	David Usher	313-849-2333	R	75	<0.1
Waste Connections	620 Coolidge Drive	Folsom	CA	95630	Ronald J Mittelstaedt	916-608-8200	P	54	0.9
Remediation Technologies Inc.	9 Damon Mill S	Concord	MA	01742	John P Appleton	978-371-1422	D	19*	<0.1

Source: *Ward's Business Directory of U.S. Private and Public Companies*, Volumes 1 and 2, 2000. The company type code used is as follows: P - Public, R - Private, S - Subsidiary, D - Division, J - Joint Venture, A - Affiliate, G - Group, N - Company type not reported. Sales are in millions of dollars, employees are in thousands. An asterisk (*) indicates an estimated sales volume. The symbol < stands for 'less than'. Company names and addresses are truncated, in some cases, to fit into the available space.

LOCATION BY STATE AND REGIONAL CONCENTRATION

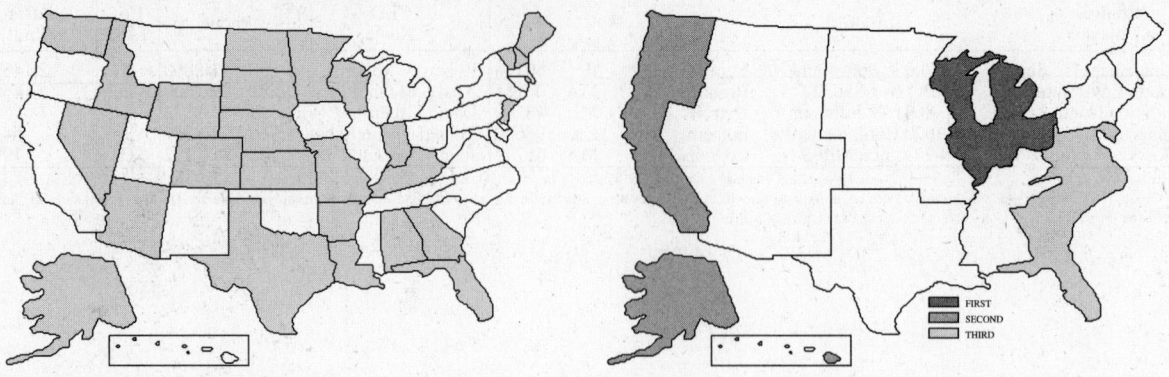

INDUSTRY DATA BY STATE

State	Establishments Total (number)	% of U.S.	Employment Total (number)	% of U.S.	Per Estab.	Payroll Total ($ mil.)	Per Empl. ($)	Revenues Total ($ mil.)	% of U.S.	Per Estab. ($)
New Jersey	11	5.9	416	14.8	38	18.0	43,264	59.9	15.8	5,447,182
Wisconsin	9	4.8	171	6.1	19	5.4	31,526	34.3	9.0	3,810,778
Texas	13	7.0	210	7.4	16	8.0	38,090	21.7	5.7	1,668,077
Florida	13	7.0	245	8.7	19	6.7	27,237	20.0	5.3	1,541,538
New York	6	3.2	92	3.3	15	2.9	31,261	15.6	4.1	2,605,333
Michigan	7	3.7	105	3.7	15	3.9	36,952	12.8	3.4	1,835,286
California	12	6.4	126	4.5	10	2.3	18,532	12.2	3.2	1,014,667
Illinois	5	2.7	109	3.9	22	3.8	35,220	9.7	2.6	1,941,000
Massachusetts	4	2.1	34	1.2	9	2.1	61,088	6.5	1.7	1,616,750
Minnesota	4	2.1	75	2.7	19	1.6	20,733	4.2	1.1	1,061,000
Arizona	5	2.7	35	1.2	7	1.0	27,171	2.5	0.7	502,000
Alabama	4	2.1	7	0.2	2	0.1	21,286	0.6	0.2	155,250
Tennessee	3	1.6	6	0.2	2	0.1	22,833	0.4	0.1	122,667
Missouri	8	4.3	175*	-	-	(D)	-	(D)	-	-
Ohio	7	3.7	175*	-	-	(D)	-	(D)	-	-
Washington	7	3.7	60*	-	-	(D)	-	(D)	-	-
Indiana	6	3.2	60*	-	-	(D)	-	(D)	-	-
Louisiana	6	3.2	175*	-	-	(D)	-	(D)	-	-
Alaska	5	2.7	10*	-	-	(D)	-	(D)	-	-
Georgia	5	2.7	175*	-	-	(D)	-	(D)	-	-
Pennsylvania	5	2.7	60*	-	-	(D)	-	(D)	-	-
Colorado	4	2.1	60*	-	-	(D)	-	(D)	-	-
Kentucky	3	1.6	10*	-	-	(D)	-	(D)	-	-
Maryland	3	1.6	60*	-	-	(D)	-	(D)	-	-
Arkansas	2	1.1	10*	-	-	(D)	-	(D)	-	-
Connecticut	2	1.1	10*	-	-	(D)	-	(D)	-	-
Kansas	2	1.1	10*	-	-	(D)	-	(D)	-	-
Nebraska	2	1.1	10*	-	-	(D)	-	(D)	-	-
Nevada	2	1.1	10*	-	-	(D)	-	(D)	-	-
North Carolina	2	1.1	60*	-	-	(D)	-	(D)	-	-
North Dakota	2	1.1	10*	-	-	(D)	-	(D)	-	-
Oklahoma	2	1.1	60*	-	-	(D)	-	(D)	-	-
Oregon	2	1.1	10*	-	-	(D)	-	(D)	-	-
Rhode Island	2	1.1	60*	-	-	(D)	-	(D)	-	-
Virginia	2	1.1	10*	-	-	(D)	-	(D)	-	-
Idaho	1	0.5	10*	-	-	(D)	-	(D)	-	-
Maine	1	0.5	60*	-	-	(D)	-	(D)	-	-
Mississippi	1	0.5	10*	-	-	(D)	-	(D)	-	-
New Hampshire	1	0.5	10*	-	-	(D)	-	(D)	-	-
New Mexico	1	0.5	10*	-	-	(D)	-	(D)	-	-
South Carolina	1	0.5	10*	-	-	(D)	-	(D)	-	-
South Dakota	1	0.5	10*	-	-	(D)	-	(D)	-	-
Utah	1	0.5	60*	-	-	(D)	-	(D)	-	-
Vermont	1	0.5	10*	-	-	(D)	-	(D)	-	-
Wyoming	1	0.5	10*	-	-	(D)	-	(D)	-	-

Source: 1997 *Economic Census*. The states are in descending order of revenues or establishments (if revenue data are missing for the majority). The symbol (D) appears when data are withheld to prevent disclosure of competitive information. States marked with (D) are sorted by number of establishments. A dash (-) indicates that the data element cannot be calculated. * indicates the midpoint of a range; 175, for example is the range 100-249. Shaded *states* on the state map indicate those states which have proportionately greater representation in the industry than would be indicated by the state's population; the ratio is based on total revenues or number of establishments. Shaded *regions* indicate where the industry is regionally most concentrated.

Part VII

EDUCATION SERVICES

NAICS 611410 - BUSINESS AND SECRETARIAL SCHOOLS*

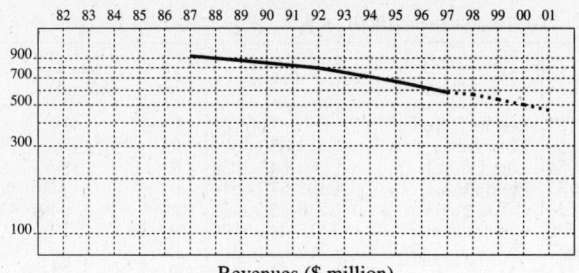

Revenues ($ million)

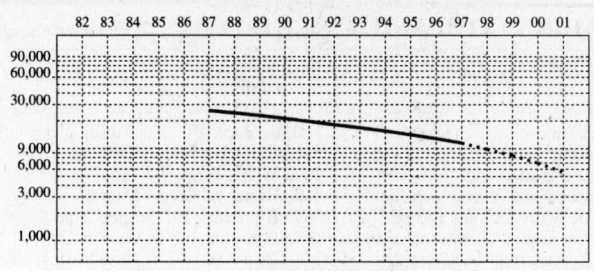

Employment (000)

GENERAL STATISTICS

Year	Establishments (number)	Employment (number)	Payroll ($ million)	Revenues ($ million)	Employees per Establishment (number)	Revenues per Establishment ($)	Payroll per Employee ($)
1982	-	-	-	-	-	-	-
1983	-	-	-	-	-	-	-
1984	-	-	-	-	-	-	-
1985	-	-	-	-	-	-	-
1986	-	-	-	-	-	-	-
1987	937	25,804	385.0	924.0	27.5	986,126	14,920
1988	930 e	24,264 e	369.0 e	898.0 e	26.1 e	965,591 e	15,208 e
1989	923 e	22,724 e	353.0 e	873.0 e	24.6 e	945,829 e	15,534 e
1990	915 e	21,184 e	336.0 e	847.0 e	23.2 e	925,683 e	15,861 e
1991	908 e	19,644 e	320.0 e	821.0 e	21.6 e	904,185 e	16,290 e
1992	901	18,104	303.0	796.0	20.1	883,463	16,737
1993	845 e	16,790 e	288.0 e	753.0 e	19.9 e	891,124 e	17,153 e
1994	788 e	15,475 e	273.0 e	711.0 e	19.6 e	902,284 e	17,641 e
1995	732 e	14,161 e	258.0 e	668.0 e	19.3 e	912,568 e	18,219 e
1996	675 e	12,846 e	242.0 e	626.0 e	19.0 e	927,407 e	18,839 e
1997	619	11,532	227.0	584.0	18.6	943,457	19,684
1998	643 p	9,848 p	210.0 p	569.0 p	15.3 p	884,914 p	21,324 p
1999	611 p	8,421 p	194.0 p	535.0 p	13.8 p	875,614 p	23,038 p
2000	579 p	6,994 p	178.0 p	501.0 p	12.1 p	865,285 p	25,450 p
2001	548 p	5,567 p	162.0 p	467.0 p	10.2 p	852,190 p	29,100 p

Sources: *Economic Census of the United States*, 1982, 1987, 1992, 1997. Establishment counts, employment, and payroll are from *County Business Patterns* for non-Census years. In non-Census years, industries in the Manufacturing range under SIC coding include data from the *Annual Survey of Manufactures* (*ASM*); those in the old Services range include data from the *Services Annual Survey* (*SAS*). Values followed by a 'p' are projections by the editors. Extrapolations are marked by 'e'. Data are the most recent available at this level of detail.

INDICES OF CHANGE

Year	Establishments (number)	Employment (number)	Payroll ($ million)	Revenues ($ million)	Employees per Establishment (number)	Revenues per Establishment ($)	Payroll per Employee ($)
1982	-	-	-	-	-	-	-
1987	151.4	223.8	169.6	158.2	147.8	104.5	75.8
1992	145.6	157.0	133.5	136.3	107.9	93.6	85.0
1993	136.5 e	145.6 e	126.9 e	128.9 e	106.7 e	94.5 e	87.1 e
1994	127.3 e	134.2 e	120.3 e	121.7 e	105.4 e	95.6 e	89.6 e
1995	118.3 e	122.8 e	113.7 e	114.4 e	103.8 e	96.7 e	92.6 e
1996	109.0 e	111.4 e	106.6 e	107.2 e	102.2 e	98.3 e	95.7 e
1997	100.0	100.0	100.0	100.0	100.0	100.0	100.0
1998	103.9 p	85.4 p	92.5 p	97.4 p	82.2 p	93.8 p	108.3 p
1999	98.7 p	73.0 p	85.5 p	91.6 p	74.0 p	92.8 p	117.0 p
2000	93.5 p	60.6 p	78.4 p	85.8 p	64.8 p	91.7 p	129.3 p
2001	88.5 p	48.3 p	71.4 p	80.0 p	54.5 p	90.3 p	147.8 p

Sources: Same as General Statistics. The values shown reflect change from the base year, 1997. Values above 100 mean greater than 1997, values below 100 mean less than 1997, and a value of 100 in the 1982-96 or 1998-2001 period means same as 1997. Values followed by a 'p' are projections by the editors; 'e' stands for extrapolation. Data are the most recent available at this level of detail.

SELECTED RATIOS

For 1997	Avg. of Information	Analyzed Industry	Index	For 1997	Avg. of Information	Analyzed Industry	Index
Employees per establishment	8	19	238	Payroll per establishment	155,475	366,721	236
Revenue per establishment	499,292	943,457	189	Payroll as % of revenue	31	39	125
Revenue per employee	63,659	50,642	80	Payroll per employee	19,823	19,684	99

Sources: Same as General Statistics. The 'Average' column represents the average for the industry sector, in 1997, where the currently shown industry is classified. The Index shows the relationship between the Average and the Analyzed Industry. For example, 100 means that they are equal; 500 that the Analyzed Industry is five times the average; 50 means that the Analyzed Industry is half the national average. The abbreviation 'na' is used to show that data are 'not available'.

LEADING COMPANIES　　Number shown: **9**　　Total sales ($ mil): **1,128**　　Total employment (000): **6.9**

Company Name	Address				CEO Name	Phone	Co. Type	Sales ($ mil)	Empl. (000)
DeVry Inc.	1 Tower Lane	Oakbrk Ter	IL	60181	Dennis J. Keller	630-571-7700	P	419	3.2
Automanage Inc.	5816 Dixie Hwy	Fairfield	OH	45014	Mike Dever	513-870-5000	R	255	0.4
O/E Automation Inc.	3290 W Big Beaver	Troy	MI	48084	Tom Doonan	248-643-2035	R	184*	0.8
Whitman Education Group Inc.	4400 Biscayne Blvd	Miami	FL	33137	Phillip Frost	305-575-6510	P	74	1.1
Monroe @crs-Orleans BOCES	3599 Big Ridge Rd	Spencerport	NY	14559	C Tod Eagle	716-352-2412	R	64*	0.5
Dale Carnegie and Associates Inc.	1475 Franklin Ave	Garden City	NY	11530	Oliver Crom	516-248-5100	R	50*	0.3
Dun & Bradstreet Business	711 Third Ave	New York	NY	10017		212-692-6400	D	30	<0.1
Keller Graduate School	One Tower Ln	Oakbrk Ter	IL	60181		630-574-1960	S	27*	0.3
Dearborn Financial Publishing Inc.	155 N Wacker Dr	Chicago	IL	60606	Dennis Blitz	312-836-4400	S	25*	0.3

Source: *Ward's Business Directory of U.S. Private and Public Companies*, Volumes 1 and 2, 2000. The company type code used is as follows: P - Public, R - Private, S - Subsidiary, D - Division, J - Joint Venture, A - Affiliate, G - Group, N - Company type not reported. Sales are in millions of dollars, employees are in thousands. An asterisk (*) indicates an estimated sales volume. The symbol < stands for 'less than'. Company names and addresses are truncated, in some cases, to fit into the available space.

LOCATION BY STATE AND REGIONAL CONCENTRATION

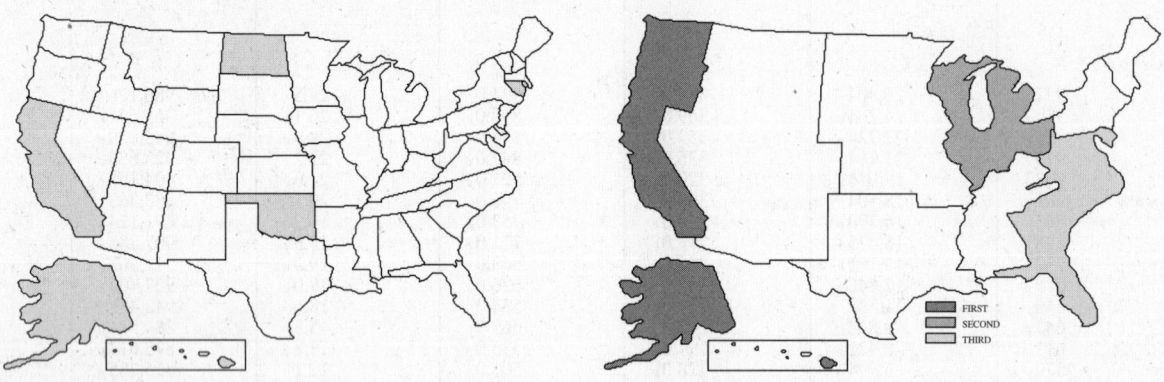

INDUSTRY DATA BY STATE

State	Establishments		Employment			Payroll		Revenues		
	Total (number)	% of U.S.	Total (number)	% of U.S.	Per Estab.	Total ($ mil.)	Per Empl. ($)	Total ($ mil.)	% of U.S.	Per Estab. ($)
California	86	13.9	1,318	11.4	15	29.1	22,064	76.1	13.0	884,849
Connecticut	18	2.9	577	5.0	32	9.9	17,232	22.3	3.8	1,240,167
Michigan	16	2.6	337	2.9	21	5.5	16,217	14.7	2.5	921,562
Illinois	20	3.2	320	2.8	16	4.6	14,291	11.4	2.0	572,000
Rhode Island	11	1.8	194	1.7	18	4.2	21,742	10.8	1.8	977,273
North Carolina	9	1.5	122	1.1	14	3.6	29,443	10.5	1.8	1,169,222
Georgia	12	1.9	181	1.6	15	3.3	18,381	9.3	1.6	778,917
Arizona	9	1.5	233	2.0	26	3.5	14,948	8.4	1.4	930,444
Oklahoma	9	1.5	146	1.3	16	2.2	15,055	5.2	0.9	582,889
Indiana	12	1.9	116	1.0	10	1.8	15,793	4.3	0.7	358,750
Tennessee	6	1.0	68	0.6	11	1.6	23,897	4.2	0.7	700,667
Washington	8	1.3	62	0.5	8	1.7	27,290	3.0	0.5	378,750
Alabama	8	1.3	99	0.9	12	1.2	11,727	2.4	0.4	305,625
Nebraska	3	0.5	27	0.2	9	0.4	13,148	1.2	0.2	399,667
Maryland	7	1.1	175*	-	-	(D)	-	(D)	-	-
Kentucky	6	1.0	175*	-	-	(D)	-	(D)	-	-
Utah	4	0.6	60*	-	-	(D)	-	(D)	-	-
West Virginia	4	0.6	60*	-	-	(D)	-	(D)	-	-
Arkansas	3	0.5	60*	-	-	(D)	-	(D)	-	-
Hawaii	3	0.5	10*	-	-	(D)	-	(D)	-	-
Kansas	3	0.5	60*	-	-	(D)	-	(D)	-	-
North Dakota	3	0.5	10*	-	-	(D)	-	(D)	-	-
Alaska	2	0.3	10*	-	-	(D)	-	(D)	-	-
Maine	2	0.3	10*	-	-	(D)	-	(D)	-	-
New Mexico	2	0.3	60*	-	-	(D)	-	(D)	-	-
Delaware	1	0.2	10*	-	-	(D)	-	(D)	-	-
Mississippi	1	0.2	10*	-	-	(D)	-	(D)	-	-
Montana	1	0.2	10*	-	-	(D)	-	(D)	-	-
Vermont	1	0.2	10*	-	-	(D)	-	(D)	-	-
Wisconsin	1	0.2	10*	-	-	(D)	-	(D)	-	-

Source: 1997 *Economic Census*. The states are in descending order of revenues or establishments (if revenue data are missing for the majority). The symbol (D) appears when data are withheld to prevent disclosure of competitive information. States marked with (D) are sorted by number of establishments. A dash (-) indicates that the data element cannot be calculated. * indicates the midpoint of a range; 175, for example is the range 100-249. Shaded *states* on the state map indicate those states which have proportionately greater representation in the industry than would be indicated by the state's population; the ratio is based on total revenues or number of establishments. Shaded *regions* indicate where the industry is regionally most concentrated.

NAICS 611420 - COMPUTER TRAINING

GENERAL STATISTICS

Year	Establishments (number)	Employment (number)	Payroll ($ million)	Revenues ($ million)	Employees per Establishment (number)	Revenues per Establishment ($)	Payroll per Employee ($)
1997	2,840	29,234	979.0	2,546.0	10.3	896,479	33,488

Source: *Economic Census of the United States*, 1997. This is a newly defined industry. Data for prior years were unavailable at the time of publication but may become available over time.

INDICES OF CHANGE

Year	Establishments (number)	Employment (number)	Payroll ($ million)	Revenues ($ million)	Employees per Establishment (number)	Revenues per Establishment ($)	Payroll per Employee ($)
1997	100.0	100.0	100.0	100.0	100.0	100.0	100.0

Sources: Same as General Statistics. The values shown reflect change from the base year, 1997. Values above 100 mean greater than 1997, values below 100 mean less than 1997, and a value of 100 in the 1982-96 or 1998-2001 period means same as 1997. Values followed by a 'p' are projections by the editors; 'e' stands for extrapolation. Data are the most recent available at this level of detail.

SIC INDUSTRIES RELATED TO NAICS 611420

Each new NAICS code represents an industry that used to be part of an SIC or a part of several SIC industries. Data in this table are shown to provide transitional information for these cases. All available data for the precursor SIC(s) are shown. Even if only a part of an SIC is included in the NAICS, *all* data for the SIC are reproduced. If the SIC industry is not marked as being a part (pt) of the NAICS, the entire industry is embedded in the NAICS data. The SIC composition of the new industry provides some hints of the relative importance of its "ancestors." Data marked with a 'p' are projected. Projections begin with 1982 data. Data earlier than 1990 are not shown but are reflected in the projections.

SIC	Industry	1990	1991	1992	1993	1994	1995	1996	1997
8243	**Data Processing Schools (pt)**								
	Establishments (number)	-	-	1,400	-	-	-	-	-
	Employment (thousands)	-	-	11.5	-	-	-	-	-
	Revenues ($ million)	-	-	898.9	-	-	-	-	-

Source: *Economic Census of the United States*, 1992, annual surveys of economic sectors conducted by the Bureau of the Census, and estimates or projections based on the 1982-1992 period; not all data are shown. 'e' marks estimates made by the editors; 'p' indicates projections based on time series. A dash (-) indicates that data for this SIC or year were not available. The abbreviation (pt) next to the industry name indicates that only a part of the industry is present within the NAICS data. If no (pt) is shown, the entire industry is contained within the NAICS data.

SELECTED RATIOS

For 1997	Avg. of Information	Analyzed Industry	Index	For 1997	Avg. of Information	Analyzed Industry	Index
Employees per establishment	8	10	131	Payroll per establishment	155,475	344,718	222
Revenue per establishment	499,292	896,479	180	Payroll as % of revenue	31	38	123
Revenue per employee	63,659	87,090	137	Payroll per employee	19,823	33,488	169

Sources: Same as General Statistics. The 'Average' column represents the average for the industry sector, in 1997, where the currently shown industry is classified. The Index shows the relationship between the Average and the Analyzed Industry. For example, 100 means that they are equal; 500 that the Analyzed Industry is five times the average; 50 means that the Analyzed Industry is half the national average. The abbreviation 'na' is used to show that data are 'not available'.

LEADING COMPANIES   Number shown: **42**   Total sales ($ mil): **13,876**   Total employment (000): **47.4**

Company Name	Address				CEO Name	Phone	Co. Type	Sales ($ mil)	Empl. (000)
CompUSA Inc.	14951 N Dallas	Dallas	TX	75240	Harold Compton	972-982-4000	P	6,321	19.7
Global Training Network Inc.	2500 Weston Rd	Weston	FL	33331	Paul Garcia	954-385-4300	R	2,550*	1.8
Computer City	100 Throckmorton	Fort Worth	TX	76102	Nathan Morton	817-878-6900	D	1,904*	7.0
Telcordia Technologies	445 South St	Morristown	NJ	07960	Richard C Smith	973-829-2000	S	925*	5.3
Acme Training Inc.	333 Third St	Laguna Beach	CA	92651		714-497-1318	N	500	<0.1
DeVry Inc.	1 Tower Lane	Oakbrk Ter	IL	60181	Dennis J Keller	630-571-7700	P	419	3.2
Learning Tree International Inc.	6053 W Century	Los Angeles	CA	90045	David C Collins	310-417-9700	P	189	0.5
O/E Automation Inc.	3290 W Big Beaver	Troy	MI	48084	Tom Doonan	248-643-2035	R	184*	0.8
Computer Learning Centers Inc.	11350 Random Hills	Fairfax	VA	22030	John L Corse	703-359-9333	P	144	2.1
RWD Technologies Inc.	10480 Patuxent	Columbia	MD	21044	John H Beakes	410-730-4377	P	124	1.0
National TechTeam Inc.	835 Mason St	Dearborn	MI	48124	Harry A Lewis	313-277-2277	P	117	2.6
ComputerWare	605 W California	Sunnyvale	CA	94086	Ron Dupler	408-328-1000	R	110*	0.2
Lewan and Associates Inc.	P O Box 22855	Denver	CO	80222	Paul R Lewan	303-759-5440	R	100	0.5
Wave Technologies Intern. Inc.	10845 Olive Street	St. Louis	MO	63141	Kenneth W Kousky	314-995-5767	P	37	0.2
Consilium Inc.	485 Clyde Ave	Mountain View	CA	94043	Stephen S Schwartz	650-691-6100	S	32*	0.2
Dynamic Graphics Inc.	PO Box 1901	Peoria	IL	61656	Jayne Mueller	309-688-8800	R	22*	0.2
Project Management Solutions Inc	5774 Hendrickson	Franklin	OH	45005	J Kent Crawford	513-422-2114	R	18*	<0.1
PC Professor Computer Training	7056 Beracasa Way	Boca Raton	FL	33433	Howard Fellman	561-750-7879	P	17*	0.1
Real Software Systems	21031 Warner Blvd	Woodland Hills	CA	91302	David Alola	818-313-8000	R	16*	<0.1
Cyntergy Corp.	656 Quince Orchard	Gaithersburg	MD	20878	Robert Grimes	301-926-3400	R	14*	0.8
PB Inc.	4615 Hawkins NE	Albuquerque	NM	87109	Filiberto Pacheco	505-296-4188	R	13*	<0.1
Canterbury Information	1600 Medford Plz	Medford	NJ	08055	Stanton M Pikus	609-953-0044	P	12	<0.1
Digital Consulting & Software	1 Sugar Creek Ctr	Sugar Land	TX	77478	Patricia M Patterson	281-242-9181	R	12*	0.2
DTI Technologies Inc.	10 Comm Pk	Bedford	NH	03110	Dan Doland	603-626-7799	R	12*	<0.1
ExecuTrain Corp.	4800 N Point Pkwy	Alpharetta	GA	30022	Axel Leblois	770-667-7700	R	10*	0.1
Heath Kit Co.	455 Riverview Dr	Benton Harbor	MI	49022	Don Desroches	616-925-6000	R	10	<0.1
Systems Service Enterprises Inc.	795 Office Pkwy	St. Louis	MO	63141	Susan S Elliott	314-997-4700	R	9	0.1
Jacobson Computer Inc.	5610 Monroe St	Sylvania	OH	43560	Gary Jacobson	419-885-0082	R	8*	<0.1
SolArc Inc.	4500 S Garnett Rd	Tulsa	OK	74146	David Dunkin	918-665-0883	R	7	<0.1
OneOnOne Computer Training	2055 Army Trail Rd	Addison	IL	60101	Lee McFadden	630-628-0500	S	6	<0.1
SRA Technology Training Co.	1 Main St	Cambridge	MA	02142	William J Terpstra	630-571-1500	S	6	<0.1
Attorney Software Inc.	742 Washington	Marina Del Rey	CA	90292	Eric Jackson	310-578-9200	R	4*	<0.1
InfoSource Inc.	6947 University	Winter Park	FL	32792	Thomas Warrner	407-677-0300	S	4*	<0.1
Ascolta Training Co.	2351 McGaw Ave	Irvine	CA	92614	Irene Kinoshita	949-852-8811	R	3*	<0.1
Group 3 Consultants Inc.	1411 S W Morrison	Portland	OR	97205	Gudrun K Granhom	503-224-4961	R	3	<0.1
THEOS Software Corp.	1801 Oakland Blvd	Walnut Creek	CA	94596	Timothy Williams	925-935-1118	R	3*	<0.1
Verio	4390 Rte 1 N	Princeton	NJ	08540	Drew Clark	609-514-3800	D	3*	<0.1
Array Inc.	43 W Mundhank Rd	Barrington	IL	60010		847-426-0060	N	2	<0.1
Testware Associates Inc.	1904 Marshall St	St. Paul	MN	55104	Karen Bishop-Stone	651-647-6509	R	2*	<0.1
CompuCad Inc.	4180 Via Real	Carpinteria	CA	93013	Dennis Brown	805-566-6642	R	1	<0.1
CheckPOINT	17 W 240 22nd St	Oakbrk Ter	IL	60181	Greg Hennessey	630-279-9030	D	1*	<0.1
MindWorks Professional	4141 N Granite Reef	Scottsdale	AZ	85251	Jim Gardner	480-874-1500	S	1*	<0.1

Source: *Ward's Business Directory of U.S. Private and Public Companies*, Volumes 1 and 2, 2000. The company type code used is as follows: P - Public, R - Private, S - Subsidiary, D - Division, J - Joint Venture, A - Affiliate, G - Group, N - Company type not reported. Sales are in millions of dollars, employees are in thousands. An asterisk (*) indicates an estimated sales volume. The symbol < stands for 'less than'. Company names and addresses are truncated, in some cases, to fit into the available space.

LOCATION BY STATE AND REGIONAL CONCENTRATION

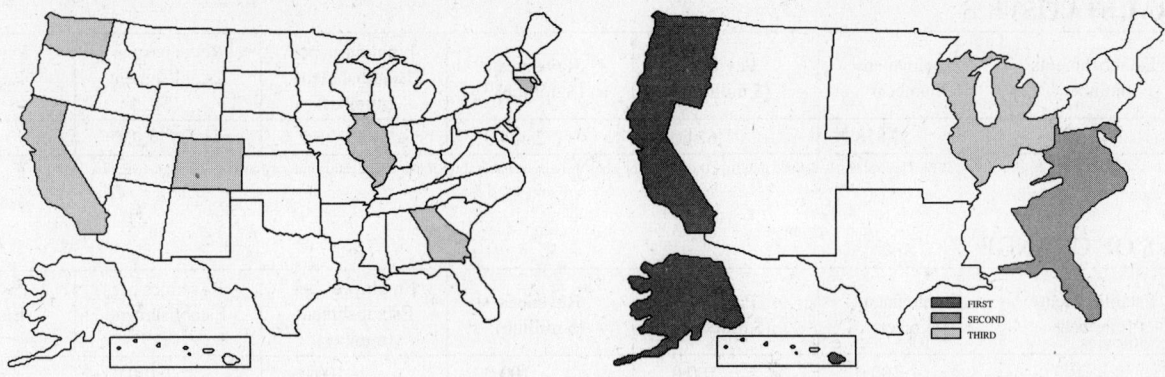

INDUSTRY DATA BY STATE

State	Establishments Total (number)	Establishments % of U.S.	Employment Total (number)	Employment % of U.S.	Employment Per Estab.	Payroll Total ($ mil.)	Payroll Per Empl. ($)	Revenues Total ($ mil.)	Revenues % of U.S.	Revenues Per Estab. ($)
California	358	12.6	4,694	16.1	13	162.0	34,519	391.1	15.4	1,092,542
Illinois	138	4.9	1,645	5.6	12	54.4	33,041	140.2	5.5	1,015,913
Florida	151	5.3	1,154	3.9	8	38.8	33,648	112.1	4.4	742,338
Georgia	109	3.8	965	3.3	9	32.4	33,601	84.4	3.3	774,385
Washington	90	3.2	738	2.5	8	23.1	31,362	62.9	2.5	698,744
North Carolina	80	2.8	736	2.5	9	23.5	31,969	62.2	2.4	777,737
Connecticut	51	1.8	781	2.7	15	29.7	38,033	54.5	2.1	1,069,157
Ohio	86	3.0	611	2.1	7	18.5	30,229	43.9	1.7	510,256
Colorado	76	2.7	409	1.4	5	17.1	41,861	41.9	1.6	551,079
Louisiana	35	1.2	248	0.8	7	6.3	25,528	16.9	0.7	483,829
Indiana	43	1.5	230	0.8	5	6.1	26,561	15.0	0.6	349,093
Alabama	21	0.7	188	0.6	9	5.0	26,505	14.2	0.6	678,286
Kentucky	20	0.7	139	0.5	7	4.3	31,029	10.1	0.4	504,350
South Carolina	23	0.8	112	0.4	5	2.8	24,750	7.5	0.3	325,217
Nebraska	7	0.2	69	0.2	10	2.4	35,391	5.1	0.2	734,143
Iowa	15	0.5	54	0.2	4	1.3	24,741	3.4	0.1	226,400
Alaska	4	0.1	9	0.0	2	0.2	19,000	0.6	0.0	156,000
Wisconsin	32	1.1	375*	-	-	(D)	-	(D)	-	-
Kansas	22	0.8	375*	-	-	(D)	-	(D)	-	-
Nevada	22	0.8	175*	-	-	(D)	-	(D)	-	-
Arkansas	12	0.4	60*	-	-	(D)	-	(D)	-	-
Hawaii	10	0.4	60*	-	-	(D)	-	(D)	-	-
Mississippi	9	0.3	60*	-	-	(D)	-	(D)	-	-
Rhode Island	9	0.3	60*	-	-	(D)	-	(D)	-	-
Idaho	7	0.2	10*	-	-	(D)	-	(D)	-	-
Maine	6	0.2	10*	-	-	(D)	-	(D)	-	-
Montana	6	0.2	10*	-	-	(D)	-	(D)	-	-
Vermont	5	0.2	60*	-	-	(D)	-	(D)	-	-
South Dakota	4	0.1	60*	-	-	(D)	-	(D)	-	-
North Dakota	1	-	10*	-	-	(D)	-	(D)	-	-
Wyoming	1	-	10*	-	-	(D)	-	(D)	-	-

Source: 1997 *Economic Census*. The states are in descending order of revenues or establishments (if revenue data are missing for the majority). The symbol (D) appears when data are withheld to prevent disclosure of competitive information. States marked with (D) are sorted by number of establishments. A dash (-) indicates that the data element cannot be calculated. * indicates the midpoint of a range; 175, for example is the range 100-249. Shaded *states* on the state map indicate those states which have proportionately greater representation in the industry than would be indicated by the state's population; the ratio is based on total revenues or number of establishments. Shaded *regions* indicate where the industry is regionally most concentrated.

NAICS 611430 - PROFESSIONAL AND MANAGEMENT DEVELOPMENT TRAINING

GENERAL STATISTICS

Year	Establishments (number)	Employment (number)	Payroll ($ million)	Revenues ($ million)	Employees per Establishment (number)	Revenues per Establishment ($)	Payroll per Employee ($)
1997	3,116	17,878	624.0	2,424.0	5.7	777,920	34,903

Source: *Economic Census of the United States*, 1997. This is a newly defined industry. Data for prior years were unavailable at the time of publication but may become available over time.

INDICES OF CHANGE

Year	Establishments (number)	Employment (number)	Payroll ($ million)	Revenues ($ million)	Employees per Establishment (number)	Revenues per Establishment ($)	Payroll per Employee ($)
1997	100.0	100.0	100.0	100.0	100.0	100.0	100.0

Sources: Same as General Statistics. The values shown reflect change from the base year, 1997. Values above 100 mean greater than 1997, values below 100 mean less than 1997, and a value of 100 in the 1982-96 or 1998-2001 period means same as 1997. Values followed by a 'p' are projections by the editors; 'e' stands for extrapolation. Data are the most recent available at this level of detail.

SIC INDUSTRIES RELATED TO NAICS 611430

Each new NAICS code represents an industry that used to be part of an SIC or a part of several SIC industries. Data in this table are shown to provide transitional information for these cases. All available data for the precursor SIC(s) are shown. Even if only a part of an SIC is included in the NAICS, *all* data for the SIC are reproduced. If the SIC industry is not marked as being a part (pt) of the NAICS, the entire industry is embedded in the NAICS data. The SIC composition of the new industry provides some hints of the relative importance of its "ancestors." Data marked with a 'p' are projected. Projections begin with 1982 data. Data earlier than 1990 are not shown but are reflected in the projections.

SIC	Industry	1990	1991	1992	1993	1994	1995	1996	1997
8299	**Schools & Educational Services, nec (pt)**								
	Establishments (number)	-	-	13,547	13,711	14,512	15,313	16,115p	16,916p
	Employment (thousands)	-	-	106.1	115.6	123.3	131.0	138.8p	146.5p
	Revenues ($ million)	-	-	5,217.2	3,378.0p	3,608.1p	3,838.1p	4,068.1p	4,298.2p

Source: *Economic Census of the United States*, 1992, annual surveys of economic sectors conducted by the Bureau of the Census, and estimates or projections based on the 1982-1992 period; not all data are shown. 'e' marks estimates made by the editors; 'p' indicates projections based on time series. A dash (-) indicates that data for this SIC or year were not available. The abbreviation (pt) next to the industry name indicates that only a part of the industry is present within the NAICS data. If no (pt) is shown, the entire industry is contained within the NAICS data.

SELECTED RATIOS

For 1997	Avg. of Information	Analyzed Industry	Index	For 1997	Avg. of Information	Analyzed Industry	Index
Employees per establishment	8	6	73	Payroll per establishment	155,475	200,257	129
Revenue per establishment	499,292	777,920	156	Payroll as % of revenue	31	26	83
Revenue per employee	63,659	135,586	213	Payroll per employee	19,823	34,903	176

Sources: Same as General Statistics. The 'Average' column represents the average for the industry sector, in 1997, where the currently shown industry is classified. The Index shows the relationship between the Average and the Analyzed Industry. For example, 100 means that they are equal; 500 that the Analyzed Industry is five times the average; 50 means that the Analyzed Industry is half the national average. The abbreviation 'na' is used to show that data are 'not available'.

LEADING COMPANIES

No company data available for this industry.

LOCATION BY STATE AND REGIONAL CONCENTRATION

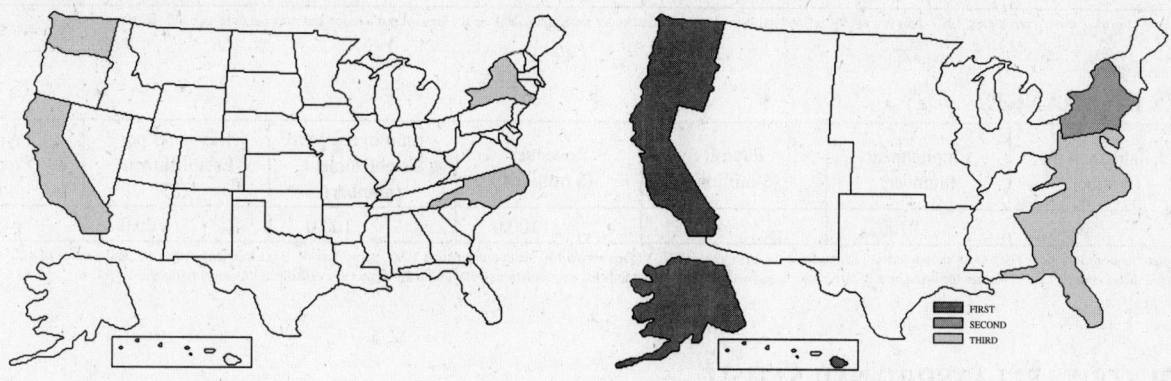

FIRST
SECOND
THIRD

INDUSTRY DATA BY STATE

State	Establishments Total (number)	Establishments % of U.S.	Employment Total (number)	Employment % of U.S.	Employment Per Estab.	Payroll Total ($ mil.)	Payroll Per Empl. ($)	Revenues Total ($ mil.)	Revenues % of U.S.	Revenues Per Estab. ($)
California	371	11.9	2,744	15.3	7	93.6	34,117	366.6	15.1	988,024
New York	173	5.6	1,510	8.4	9	54.1	35,838	295.0	12.2	1,705,150
Texas	217	7.0	1,307	7.3	6	39.2	30,001	125.0	5.2	576,203
Illinois	139	4.5	589	3.3	4	23.9	40,611	96.3	4.0	692,993
North Carolina	65	2.1	247	1.4	4	14.0	56,684	86.4	3.6	1,329,154
Georgia	98	3.1	401	2.2	4	21.3	53,032	61.2	2.5	624,061
Washington	118	3.8	502	2.8	4	14.1	28,114	54.4	2.2	460,949
Connecticut	50	1.6	269	1.5	5	11.2	41,684	30.0	1.2	600,060
Arizona	55	1.8	236	1.3	4	5.4	22,936	15.9	0.7	288,418
Louisiana	29	0.9	125	0.7	4	3.5	28,368	13.7	0.6	470,759
Nebraska	19	0.6	185	1.0	10	4.7	25,416	11.8	0.5	619,421
Tennessee	32	1.0	117	0.7	4	2.8	23,940	8.7	0.4	273,063
South Carolina	22	0.7	84	0.5	4	1.9	22,571	8.0	0.3	364,364
New Mexico	22	0.7	81	0.5	4	2.3	28,420	6.2	0.3	283,364
Hawaii	14	0.4	138	0.8	10	3.7	26,920	5.8	0.2	411,286
Maine	3	0.1	24	0.1	8	0.7	27,125	3.5	0.1	1,161,333
Alabama	14	0.4	59	0.3	4	0.9	14,424	2.5	0.1	181,857
Wyoming	7	0.2	10*	-	-	(D)	-	(D)	-	-
Alaska	3	0.1	10*	-	-	(D)	-	(D)	-	-
South Dakota	3	0.1	10*	-	-	(D)	-	(D)	-	-

Source: 1997 *Economic Census*. The states are in descending order of revenues or establishments (if revenue data are missing for the majority). The symbol (D) appears when data are withheld to prevent disclosure of competitive information. States marked with (D) are sorted by number of establishments. A dash (-) indicates that the data element cannot be calculated. * indicates the midpoint of a range; 175, for example is the range 100-249. Shaded *states* on the state map indicate those states which have proportionately greater representation in the industry than would be indicated by the state's population; the ratio is based on total revenues or number of establishments. Shaded *regions* indicate where the industry is regionally most concentrated.

NAICS 611511 - COSMETOLOGY AND BARBER SCHOOLS

GENERAL STATISTICS

Year	Establishments (number)	Employment (number)	Payroll ($ million)	Revenues ($ million)	Employees per Establishment (number)	Revenues per Establishment ($)	Payroll per Employee ($)
1997	1,805	10,289	160.0	454.0	5.7	251,524	15,551

Source: *Economic Census of the United States*, 1997. This is a newly defined industry. Data for prior years were unavailable at the time of publication but may become available over time.

INDICES OF CHANGE

Year	Establishments (number)	Employment (number)	Payroll ($ million)	Revenues ($ million)	Employees per Establishment (number)	Revenues per Establishment ($)	Payroll per Employee ($)
1997	100.0	100.0	100.0	100.0	100.0	100.0	100.0

Sources: Same as General Statistics. The values shown reflect change from the base year, 1997. Values above 100 mean greater than 1997, values below 100 mean less than 1997, and a value of 100 in the 1982-96 or 1998-2001 period means same as 1997. Values followed by a 'p' are projections by the editors; 'e' stands for extrapolation. Data are the most recent available at this level of detail.

SIC INDUSTRIES RELATED TO NAICS 611511

Each new NAICS code represents an industry that used to be part of an SIC or a part of several SIC industries. Data in this table are shown to provide transitional information for these cases. All available data for the precursor SIC(s) are shown. Even if only a part of an SIC is included in the NAICS, *all* data for the SIC are reproduced. If the SIC industry is not marked as being a part (pt) of the NAICS, the entire industry is embedded in the NAICS data. The SIC composition of the new industry provides some hints of the relative importance of its "ancestors." Data marked with a 'p' are projected. Projections begin with 1982 data. Data earlier than 1990 are not shown but are reflected in the projections.

SIC	Industry	1990	1991	1992	1993	1994	1995	1996	1997
7231	**Beauty Shops (pt)**								
	Establishments (number)	76,148	78,588	82,768	83,238	82,478	81,696	82,042p	82,459p
	Employment (thousands)	371.0	374.3	387.2	396.7	388.9	394.6	412.8p	419.9p
	Revenues ($ million)	12,841.0	13,138.0	14,436.0	14,608.0	15,152.0	16,382.0	16,900.0	17,637.7p
7241	**Barber Shops (pt)**								
	Establishments (number)	5,115	5,053	4,902	4,806	4,629	4,474	3,666p	3,356p
	Employment (thousands)	16.4	16.1	14.5	14.9	14.2	14.1	13.1p	12.5p
	Revenues ($ million)	1,439.0	1,466.0	1,515.0	1,514.0	1,558.0	1,609.0	1,590.0	1,689.5p

Source: *Economic Census of the United States*, 1992, annual surveys of economic sectors conducted by the Bureau of the Census, and estimates or projections based on the 1982-1992 period; not all data are shown. 'e' marks estimates made by the editors; 'p' indicates projections based on time series. A dash (-) indicates that data for this SIC or year were not available. The abbreviation (pt) next to the industry name indicates that only a part of the industry is present within the NAICS data. If no (pt) is shown, the entire industry is contained within the NAICS data.

SELECTED RATIOS

For 1997	Avg. of Information	Analyzed Industry	Index	For 1997	Avg. of Information	Analyzed Industry	Index
Employees per establishment	8	6	73	Payroll per establishment	155,475	88,643	57
Revenue per establishment	499,292	251,524	50	Payroll as % of revenue	31	35	113
Revenue per employee	63,659	44,125	69	Payroll per employee	19,823	15,551	78

Sources: Same as General Statistics. The 'Average' column represents the average for the industry sector, in 1997, where the currently shown industry is classified. The Index shows the relationship between the Average and the Analyzed Industry. For example, 100 means that they are equal; 500 that the Analyzed Industry is five times the average; 50 means that the Analyzed Industry is half the national average. The abbreviation 'na' is used to show that data are 'not available'.

LEADING COMPANIES   Number shown: 25   Total sales ($ mil): 2,433   Total employment (000): 20.0

Company Name	Address				CEO Name	Phone	Co. Type	Sales ($ mil)	Empl. (000)
Comair Holdings Inc.	P O Box 75021	Cincinnati	OH	45275	David R. Mueller	606-767-2550	P	763	4.4
FlightSafety International Inc.	La Guardia	Flushing	NY	11371	Albert Ueltschi	718-565-4100	S	363*	2.5
UNC Aviation Services	175 Adm Cochrane	Annapolis	MD	21401		410-266-1380	S	300	4.5
ITT Educational Services Inc.	PO Box 50466	Indianapolis	IN	46250	Rene R Champagne	317-594-9499	P	291	3.1
O/E Automation Inc.	3290 W Big Beaver	Troy	MI	48084	Tom Doonan	248-643-2035	R	184*	0.8
ICS Learning Systems Inc.	925 Oak St	Scranton	PA	18515	Robert V Antonucci	570-342-7701	S	128	0.9
Lincoln Technical Institute Inc.	200 Executive Dr	West Orange	NJ	07052	Lawrence E Brown	973-736-9340	R	102*	0.8
Whitman Education Group Inc.	4400 Biscayne Blvd	Miami	FL	33137	Phillip Frost	305-575-6510	P	74	1.1
Monroe @crs-Orleans BOCES	3599 Big Ridge Rd	Spencerport	NY	14559	C Tod Eagle	716-352-2412	R	64*	0.5
Instructional Systems Div.	8900 Trinity Blvd	Hurst	TX	76053		817-276-7500	D	26*	0.2
Motorcycle Mechanics Institute	2844 W Deer Valley	Phoenix	AZ	85027	Robert Hartman	623-869-9644	D	25*	0.2
Airline Training Center Arizona	1658 S Litchfield Rd	Goodyear	AZ	85338	Mr Lothar Martin	623-932-1600	S	20*	0.2
American Conservatory Theater	30 Grant Ave	San Francisco	CA	94108		415-834-3200	R	20*	0.2
Sylvan Prometric	7600 France Ave S	Edina	MN	55410	Steve Hoffman	612-220-5000	R	15*	0.1
New York Restaurant School	75 Varick St	New York	NY	10013	Michael R Iannacone	212-226-5500	R	13*	0.1
Sierra Academy of Aeronautics	PO Box 2429	Oakland	CA	94614	Skip Everett	510-568-6100	R	13*	0.2
Canterbury Information	1600 Medford Plz	Medford	NJ	08055	Stanton M Pikus	609-953-0044	P	12	<0.1
Schemers Inc.	2136 N E 68th St	Ft. Lauderdale	FL	33308	Terry Kaufman	954-776-7376	R	6*	<0.1
Computer Data Inc.	25786 Commerce Dr	Madison Heights	MI	48071	James T Weyand	248-544-9900	R	3*	<0.1
Megatech Corp.	555 Woburn St	Tewksbury	MA	01876	Vahan V Basmajian	978-937-9600	P	3*	<0.1
Republic Industries Inc.	P O Box 5565	Wilmington	NC	28403	David A Nugent	910-343-1664	R	3	<0.1
Wilderness Alternative School Inc.	200 Hubbart Dam	Marion	MT	59925	John Brekke	406-854-2832	R	2	<0.1
Natural Health Trends Corp.	250 Park Ave	New York	NY	10177	Joseph Grace	212-490-6609	P	1	<0.1
Educational Self Development Inc.	315 S Maple Ave	Greensburg	PA	15601	Charles H Trafford	724-837-4900	R	1	<0.1
Tectrix Inc.	10025 Warfield	Columbia	MD	21044	Kirsten Sitnick	410-715-1300	R	1	<0.1

Source: *Ward's Business Directory of U.S. Private and Public Companies*, Volumes 1 and 2, 2000. The company type code used is as follows: P - Public, R - Private, S - Subsidiary, D - Division, J - Joint Venture, A - Affiliate, G - Group, N - Company type not reported. Sales are in millions of dollars, employees are in thousands. An asterisk (*) indicates an estimated sales volume. The symbol < stands for 'less than'. Company names and addresses are truncated, in some cases, to fit into the available space.

LOCATION BY STATE AND REGIONAL CONCENTRATION

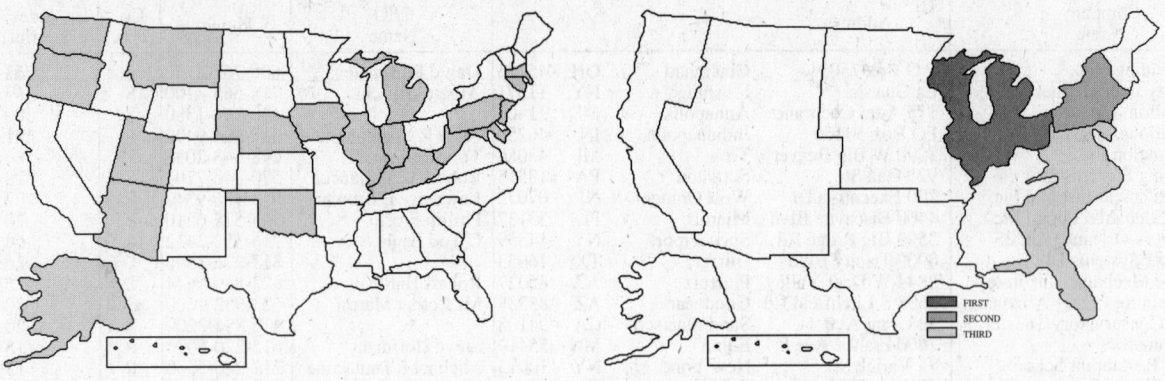

INDUSTRY DATA BY STATE

State	Establishments Total (number)	Establishments % of U.S.	Employment Total (number)	Employment % of U.S.	Employment Per Estab.	Payroll Total ($ mil.)	Payroll Per Empl. ($)	Revenues Total ($ mil.)	Revenues % of U.S.	Revenues Per Estab. ($)
Texas	127	7.0	686	6.7	5	11.0	16,069	30.7	6.8	241,559
Pennsylvania	82	4.5	532	5.2	6	7.9	14,782	25.9	5.7	316,341
New York	93	5.2	528	5.1	6	8.5	16,072	24.1	5.3	259,387
Illinois	78	4.3	509	4.9	7	8.4	16,491	21.4	4.7	274,000
Ohio	76	4.2	471	4.6	6	6.8	14,355	18.5	4.1	243,645
Michigan	71	3.9	452	4.4	6	6.3	13,865	17.4	3.8	245,127
Florida	89	4.9	442	4.3	5	6.1	13,753	17.1	3.8	192,169
New Jersey	50	2.8	349	3.4	7	5.7	16,264	16.0	3.5	320,560
Massachusetts	41	2.3	347	3.4	8	5.3	15,366	15.1	3.3	367,244
Connecticut	33	1.8	245	2.4	7	5.6	22,996	14.1	3.1	428,091
Maryland	41	2.3	244	2.4	6	4.0	16,426	11.4	2.5	277,439
Washington	43	2.4	244	2.4	6	3.4	13,926	11.3	2.5	262,326
North Carolina	45	2.5	240	2.3	5	4.6	19,354	10.9	2.4	243,156
Indiana	53	2.9	268	2.6	5	4.0	14,869	10.7	2.4	202,755
Missouri	48	2.7	240	2.3	5	3.5	14,463	8.7	1.9	180,563
Kentucky	44	2.4	211	2.1	5	3.1	14,900	8.3	1.8	187,682
Iowa	20	1.1	158	1.5	8	2.9	18,430	8.0	1.8	400,550
Oregon	31	1.7	178	1.7	6	2.5	14,270	7.8	1.7	251,774
Arizona	26	1.4	137	1.3	5	2.7	19,650	7.2	1.6	275,923
Georgia	41	2.3	160	1.6	4	2.7	17,169	7.1	1.6	173,878
Wisconsin	20	1.1	122	1.2	6	2.2	18,115	6.7	1.5	334,150
Virginia	42	2.3	149	1.4	4	2.0	13,255	6.1	1.3	145,667
Oklahoma	34	1.9	124	1.2	4	1.6	13,185	6.0	1.3	175,235
Nebraska	16	0.9	102	1.0	6	1.8	17,794	5.6	1.2	351,688
Minnesota	19	1.1	115	1.1	6	1.9	16,278	5.6	1.2	294,474
Louisiana	35	1.9	141	1.4	4	1.8	12,794	5.3	1.2	151,257
Utah	20	1.1	135	1.3	7	1.8	13,252	5.1	1.1	252,950
Arkansas	30	1.7	100	1.0	3	1.3	13,210	4.1	0.9	136,967
West Virginia	12	0.7	100	1.0	8	1.3	12,730	3.5	0.8	288,167
Mississippi	20	1.1	74	0.7	4	1.2	15,892	3.4	0.8	172,300
Montana	10	0.6	33	0.3	3	0.5	15,303	1.7	0.4	166,500
Maine	7	0.4	26	0.3	4	0.5	20,346	1.5	0.3	217,571
Alaska	5	0.3	28	0.3	6	0.5	19,179	1.4	0.3	288,600
Vermont	4	0.2	21	0.2	5	0.4	16,714	1.0	0.2	242,000
South Carolina	30	1.7	175*	-	-	(D)	-	(D)	-	-
Colorado	29	1.6	175*	-	-	(D)	-	(D)	-	-
Alabama	18	1.0	60*	-	-	(D)	-	(D)	-	-
Kansas	17	0.9	175*	-	-	(D)	-	(D)	-	-
New Hampshire	14	0.8	60*	-	-	(D)	-	(D)	-	-
Idaho	11	0.6	60*	-	-	(D)	-	(D)	-	-
Nevada	8	0.4	60*	-	-	(D)	-	(D)	-	-
New Mexico	8	0.4	60*	-	-	(D)	-	(D)	-	-
Wyoming	7	0.4	10*	-	-	(D)	-	(D)	-	-
Rhode Island	6	0.3	60*	-	-	(D)	-	(D)	-	-
North Dakota	5	0.3	60*	-	-	(D)	-	(D)	-	-
South Dakota	5	0.3	60*	-	-	(D)	-	(D)	-	-
Delaware	4	0.2	60*	-	-	(D)	-	(D)	-	-
D.C.	3	0.2	60*	-	-	(D)	-	(D)	-	-
Hawaii	2	0.1	10*	-	-	(D)	-	(D)	-	-

Source: 1997 *Economic Census*. The states are in descending order of revenues or establishments (if revenue data are missing for the majority). The symbol (D) appears when data are withheld to prevent disclosure of competitive information. States marked with (D) are sorted by number of establishments. A dash (-) indicates that the data element cannot be calculated. * indicates the midpoint of a range; 175, for example is the range 100-249. Shaded *states* on the state map indicate those states which have proportionately greater representation in the industry than would be indicated by the state's population; the ratio is based on total revenues or number of establishments. Shaded *regions* indicate where the industry is regionally most concentrated.

NAICS 611512 - FLIGHT TRAINING

GENERAL STATISTICS

Year	Establishments (number)	Employment (number)	Payroll ($ million)	Revenues ($ million)	Employees per Establishment (number)	Revenues per Establishment ($)	Payroll per Employee ($)
1997	849	12,260	261.0	921.0	14.4	1,084,806	21,289

Source: Economic Census of the United States, 1997. This is a newly defined industry. Data for prior years were unavailable at the time of publication but may become available over time.

INDICES OF CHANGE

Year	Establishments (number)	Employment (number)	Payroll ($ million)	Revenues ($ million)	Employees per Establishment (number)	Revenues per Establishment ($)	Payroll per Employee ($)
1997	100.0	100.0	100.0	100.0	100.0	100.0	100.0

Sources: Same as General Statistics. The values shown reflect change from the base year, 1997. Values above 100 mean greater than 1997, values below 100 mean less than 1997, and a value of 100 in the 1982-96 or 1998-2001 period means same as 1997. Values followed by a 'p' are projections by the editors; 'e' stands for extrapolation. Data are the most recent available at this level of detail.

SIC INDUSTRIES RELATED TO NAICS 611512

Each new NAICS code represents an industry that used to be part of an SIC or a part of several SIC industries. Data in this table are shown to provide transitional information for these cases. All available data for the precursor SIC(s) are shown. Even if only a part of an SIC is included in the NAICS, *all* data for the SIC are reproduced. If the SIC industry is not marked as being a part (pt) of the NAICS, the entire industry is embedded in the NAICS data. The SIC composition of the new industry provides some hints of the relative importance of its "ancestors." Data marked with a 'p' are projected. Projections begin with 1982 data. Data earlier than 1990 are not shown but are reflected in the projections.

SIC	Industry	1990	1991	1992	1993	1994	1995	1996	1997
8249	**Vocational Schools, nec (pt)**								
	Establishments (number)	-	-	3,366	-	-	-	-	-
	Employment (thousands)	-	-	43.6	-	-	-	-	-
	Revenues ($ million)	-	-	2,746.2	-	-	-	-	-
8299	**Schools & Educational Services, nec (pt)**								
	Establishments (number)	-	-	13,547	13,711	14,512	15,313	16,115p	16,916p
	Employment (thousands)	-	-	106.1	115.6	123.3	131.0	138.8p	146.5p
	Revenues ($ million)	-	-	5,217.2	3,378.0p	3,608.1p	3,838.1p	4,068.1p	4,298.2p

Source: Economic Census of the United States, 1992, annual surveys of economic sectors conducted by the Bureau of the Census, and estimates or projections based on the 1982-1992 period; not all data are shown. 'e' marks estimates made by the editors; 'p' indicates projections based on time series. A dash (-) indicates that data for this SIC or year were not available. The abbreviation (pt) next to the industry name indicates that only a part of the industry is present within the NAICS data. If no (pt) is shown, the entire industry is contained within the NAICS data.

SELECTED RATIOS

For 1997	Avg. of Information	Analyzed Industry	Index	For 1997	Avg. of Information	Analyzed Industry	Index
Employees per establishment	8	14	184	Payroll per establishment	155,475	307,420	198
Revenue per establishment	499,292	1,084,806	217	Payroll as % of revenue	31	28	91
Revenue per employee	63,659	75,122	118	Payroll per employee	19,823	21,289	107

Sources: Same as General Statistics. The 'Average' column represents the average for the industry sector, in 1997, where the currently shown industry is classified. The Index shows the relationship between the Average and the Analyzed Industry. For example, 100 means that they are equal; 500 that the Analyzed Industry is five times the average; 50 means that the Analyzed Industry is half the national average. The abbreviation 'na' is used to show that data are 'not available'.

LEADING COMPANIES

No company data available for this industry.

LOCATION BY STATE AND REGIONAL CONCENTRATION

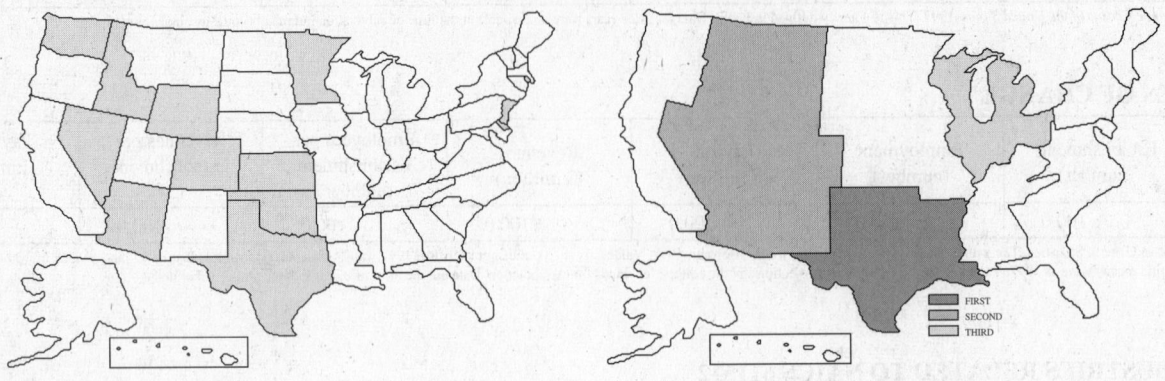

FIRST
SECOND
THIRD

INDUSTRY DATA BY STATE

State	Establishments		Employment			Payroll		Revenues		
	Total (number)	% of U.S.	Total (number)	% of U.S.	Per Estab.	Total ($ mil.)	Per Empl. ($)	Total ($ mil.)	% of U.S.	Per Estab. ($)
Texas	87	10.2	1,456	11.9	17	29.0	19,939	103.7	11.3	1,191,644
Arizona	28	3.3	531	4.3	19	12.2	22,913	50.9	5.5	1,818,250
New Jersey	27	3.2	313	2.6	12	7.8	24,815	34.3	3.7	1,270,407
Washington	30	3.5	281	2.3	9	6.6	23,555	31.8	3.5	1,060,400
Colorado	26	3.1	203	1.7	8	4.7	23,394	17.8	1.9	683,500
Missouri	13	1.5	219	1.8	17	4.6	20,785	17.1	1.9	1,312,692
Minnesota	21	2.5	258	2.1	12	4.4	17,097	14.3	1.6	681,810
Ohio	27	3.2	174	1.4	6	3.0	17,057	13.1	1.4	484,815
Illinois	36	4.2	246	2.0	7	3.1	12,654	13.0	1.4	360,667
Connecticut	7	0.8	52	0.4	7	2.0	37,712	7.1	0.8	1,013,857
South Carolina	6	0.7	92	0.8	15	1.8	19,283	6.0	0.7	1,007,667
Indiana	11	1.3	136	1.1	12	1.7	12,368	5.2	0.6	474,818
Utah	6	0.7	54	0.4	9	1.0	18,537	4.8	0.5	807,333
North Carolina	9	1.1	28	0.2	3	0.5	18,786	2.2	0.2	243,000
Nevada	6	0.7	38	0.3	6	0.5	12,921	1.6	0.2	271,167
Kansas	15	1.8	750*	-	-	(D)	-	(D)	-	-
Oklahoma	14	1.6	375*	-	-	(D)	-	(D)	-	-
Maryland	13	1.5	175*	-	-	(D)	-	(D)	-	-
Idaho	8	0.9	60*	-	-	(D)	-	(D)	-	-
Louisiana	7	0.8	60*	-	-	(D)	-	(D)	-	-
Alabama	4	0.5	175*	-	-	(D)	-	(D)	-	-
Delaware	4	0.5	175*	-	-	(D)	-	(D)	-	-
Mississippi	4	0.5	60*	-	-	(D)	-	(D)	-	-
New Mexico	4	0.5	10*	-	-	(D)	-	(D)	-	-
Maine	3	0.4	10*	-	-	(D)	-	(D)	-	-
New Hampshire	3	0.4	60*	-	-	(D)	-	(D)	-	-
Rhode Island	3	0.4	10*	-	-	(D)	-	(D)	-	-
Iowa	2	0.2	10*	-	-	(D)	-	(D)	-	-
Montana	2	0.2	10*	-	-	(D)	-	(D)	-	-
Nebraska	2	0.2	10*	-	-	(D)	-	(D)	-	-
Vermont	2	0.2	10*	-	-	(D)	-	(D)	-	-
West Virginia	2	0.2	10*	-	-	(D)	-	(D)	-	-
Wyoming	2	0.2	10*	-	-	(D)	-	(D)	-	-
South Dakota	1	0.1	10*	-	-	(D)	-	(D)	-	-

Source: 1997 *Economic Census*. The states are in descending order of revenues or establishments (if revenue data are missing for the majority). The symbol (D) appears when data are withheld to prevent disclosure of competitive information. States marked with (D) are sorted by number of establishments. A dash (-) indicates that the data element cannot be calculated. * indicates the midpoint of a range; 175, for example is the range 100-249. Shaded *states* on the state map indicate those states which have proportionately greater representation in the industry than would be indicated by the state's population; the ratio is based on total revenues or number of establishments. Shaded *regions* indicate where the industry is regionally most concentrated.

NAICS 611513 - APPRENTICESHIP TRAINING

GENERAL STATISTICS

Year	Establishments (number)	Employment (number)	Payroll ($ million)	Revenues ($ million)	Employees per Establishment (number)	Revenues per Establishment ($)	Payroll per Employee ($)
1997	1,157	7,497	140.0	422.0	6.5	364,736	18,674

Source: Economic Census of the United States, 1997. This is a newly defined industry. Data for prior years were unavailable at the time of publication but may become available over time.

INDICES OF CHANGE

Year	Establishments (number)	Employment (number)	Payroll ($ million)	Revenues ($ million)	Employees per Establishment (number)	Revenues per Establishment ($)	Payroll per Employee ($)
1997	100.0	100.0	100.0	100.0	100.0	100.0	100.0

Sources: Same as General Statistics. The values shown reflect change from the base year, 1997. Values above 100 mean greater than 1997, values below 100 mean less than 1997, and a value of 100 in the 1982-96 or 1998-2001 period means same as 1997. Values followed by a 'p' are projections by the editors; 'e' stands for extrapolation. Data are the most recent available at this level of detail.

SIC INDUSTRIES RELATED TO NAICS 611513

Each new NAICS code represents an industry that used to be part of an SIC or a part of several SIC industries. Data in this table are shown to provide transitional information for these cases. All available data for the precursor SIC(s) are shown. Even if only a part of an SIC is included in the NAICS, *all* data for the SIC are reproduced. If the SIC industry is not marked as being a part (pt) of the NAICS, the entire industry is embedded in the NAICS data. The SIC composition of the new industry provides some hints of the relative importance of its "ancestors." Data marked with a 'p' are projected. Projections begin with 1982 data. Data earlier than 1990 are not shown but are reflected in the projections.

SIC	Industry	1990	1991	1992	1993	1994	1995	1996	1997
8249	**Vocational Schools, nec (pt)**								
	Establishments (number)	-	-	3,366	-	-	-	-	-
	Employment (thousands)	-	-	43.6	-	-	-	-	-
	Revenues ($ million)	-	-	2,746.2	-	-	-	-	-

Source: Economic Census of the United States, 1992, annual surveys of economic sectors conducted by the Bureau of the Census, and estimates or projections based on the 1982-1992 period; not all data are shown. 'e' marks estimates made by the editors; 'p' indicates projections based on time series. A dash (-) indicates that data for this SIC or year were not available. The abbreviation (pt) next to the industry name indicates that only a part of the industry is present within the NAICS data. If no (pt) is shown, the entire industry is contained within the NAICS data.

SELECTED RATIOS

For 1997	Avg. of Information	Analyzed Industry	Index	For 1997	Avg. of Information	Analyzed Industry	Index
Employees per establishment	8	6	83	Payroll per establishment	155,475	121,003	78
Revenue per establishment	499,292	364,736	73	Payroll as % of revenue	31	33	107
Revenue per employee	63,659	56,289	88	Payroll per employee	19,823	18,674	94

Sources: Same as General Statistics. The 'Average' column represents the average for the industry sector, in 1997, where the currently shown industry is classified. The Index shows the relationship between the Average and the Analyzed Industry. For example, 100 means that they are equal; 500 that the Analyzed Industry is five times the average; 50 means that the Analyzed Industry is half the national average. The abbreviation 'na' is used to show that data are 'not available'.

LEADING COMPANIES

No company data available for this industry.

REPRESENTATIVE NONPROFIT ORGANIZATIONS

Organization Name	Address				Phone	Income Range ($ mil)
American Line BLDRS Apprenticeship Training Joint Committee	PO Box 370	Medway	OH	45341		1-5
Arizona Carpenters Joint Apprenticeship Training Fund	2625 W Holly	Phoenix	AZ	85009		1-5
Burt Reynolds Institute for Theatre Training Inc	201 Clematis Street	West Palm Beach	FL	33401		1-5
Carpenters Apprenticeship and Training TR Fund for No Calif	444 Hegenberger Rd	Oakland	CA	94621		5-9
Central Minnesota Jobs and Training Services Inc	PO Box 116	Monticello	MN	55362		5-9
Chicago & Vicinity Laborers	PO Box 88658	Carol Stream	IL	60188		20-29
Consorcio Caguas Guayama	Apartado 8518	Caguas	PR	00726		5-9
Construction Education Foundation	2900 W Story Rd	Irving	TX	75038		1-5
East Central Private Industry Council Inc	PO Box 1081	Muncie	IN	47308	765-741-5863	1-5
Employment & Training Services Inc	2809 Forrest Home Rd	Jonesboro	AR	72401	870-932-5340	1-5
Genesis Medical Education Foundation Inc	1345 W Central Park	Davenport	IA	52804		1-5
Greenwich Services Inc	910 E Church LN	Philadelphia	PA	19138	215-848-8500	10-19
Hawaii Drywall & Carpenters Training Trust Fund	1199 Dillingham Blvd	Honolulu	HI	96817		1-5
Home Builders Institute	1090 Vermont Ave	Washington	DC	20005	202-371-0600	10-19
International Union of Operating Engineers	PO Box 2626	Huntington	WV	25726	304-763-3580	1-5
Ironworkers District Council of New England Pension Fund	161 Granite Ave 2nd FL	Dorchester	MA	02124		10-19
Maine Career Advantage	323 State St	Augusta	ME	04330		1-5
Milwaukee Electrical Joint Apprenticeship and Training Plan	3303 S 103rd St	Milwaukee	WI	53227		1-5
N J A T C	301 Prince Georges Blvd	Uppr Marlboro	MD	20774		10-19
Plumbers & Steamfitters Local 375	3568 Geraghty St	Fairbanks	AK	99709	907-479-4154	5-9
Sheet Metal Workers International Association	110 114 Old Forge Rd	Rocky Hill	CT	06067		1-5
Sheet Metal Workers Local 88 Training Fund	2540 Marco St	Las Vegas	NV	89115	702-632-0314	1-5
Thomas Shortman Training Schol & Safety Fund Local 32B-J	101 Ave Americas	New York	NY	10013		20-29
United Association Training Trust Fund	20220 SW Teton	Tualatin	OR	97062		5-9
West Central Georgia Private Industry Council	1435 N Expressway	Griffin	GA	30223		1-5

Source: *National Directory of Nonprofit Organizations*, 2000, Volumes 1 and 2, The Taft Group. The table shows a selection of organizations for illustration and does not constitute a complete selection from the source. The organizations are arranged in alphabetical order.

LOCATION BY STATE AND REGIONAL CONCENTRATION

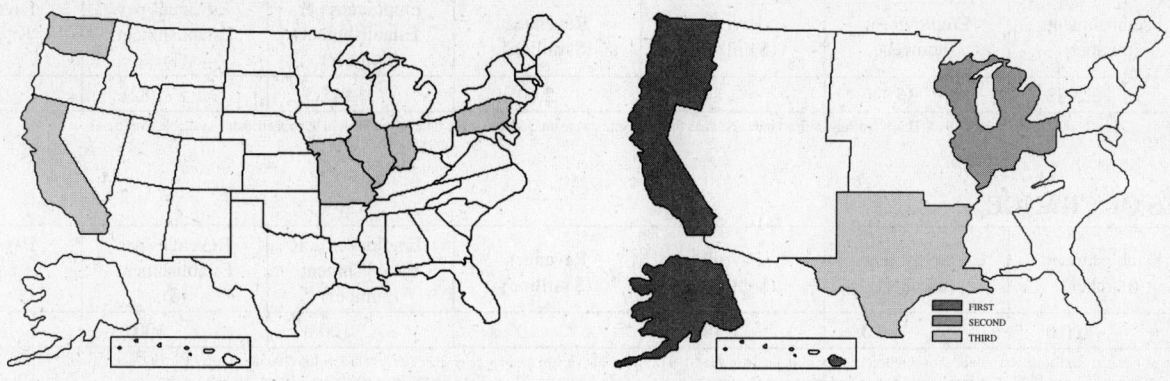

INDUSTRY DATA BY STATE

State	Establishments Total (number)	% of U.S.	Employment Total (number)	% of U.S.	Per Estab.	Payroll Total ($ mil.)	Per Empl. ($)	Revenues Total ($ mil.)	% of U.S.	Per Estab. ($)
California	122	10.5	1,003	13.4	8	24.3	24,236	76.9	18.2	630,098
Illinois	70	6.1	586	7.8	8	13.5	22,976	34.5	8.2	493,029
Texas	54	4.7	437	5.8	8	9.7	22,181	27.0	6.4	499,926
Pennsylvania	55	4.8	333	4.4	6	6.2	18,748	21.1	5.0	383,673
Ohio	64	5.5	460	6.1	7	5.4	11,835	15.3	3.6	238,453
Washington	46	4.0	232	3.1	5	5.2	22,478	14.8	3.5	322,522
Indiana	34	2.9	313	4.2	9	4.8	15,339	14.0	3.3	412,588
Missouri	29	2.5	226	3.0	8	4.3	18,881	13.1	3.1	452,931
Arizona	20	1.7	83	1.1	4	1.6	19,446	5.8	1.4	291,550
Minnesota	18	1.6	95	1.3	5	1.3	13,611	5.1	1.2	281,667
Colorado	15	1.3	83	1.1	6	1.1	13,337	3.7	0.9	246,933
New Mexico	10	0.9	71	0.9	7	1.1	15,704	2.6	0.6	264,100
Virginia	9	0.8	18	0.2	2	1.0	57,389	1.9	0.5	211,333
Alabama	13	1.1	62	0.8	5	0.7	11,968	1.9	0.4	143,462
Connecticut	9	0.8	23	0.3	3	0.5	21,000	1.5	0.4	164,667
North Carolina	9	0.8	25	0.3	3	0.5	18,400	1.1	0.2	117,111
Utah	3	0.3	15	0.2	5	0.2	14,067	0.6	0.1	200,667
South Carolina	4	0.3	8	0.1	2	0.1	17,375	0.3	0.1	69,750
Alaska	9	0.8	60*	-	-	(D)	-	(D)	-	-
D.C.	6	0.5	60*	-	-	(D)	-	(D)	-	-
Maine	4	0.3	60*	-	-	(D)	-	(D)	-	-
Idaho	3	0.3	10*	-	-	(D)	-	(D)	-	-
Vermont	3	0.3	10*	-	-	(D)	-	(D)	-	-
Mississippi	2	0.2	10*	-	-	(D)	-	(D)	-	-
North Dakota	2	0.2	10*	-	-	(D)	-	(D)	-	-
Rhode Island	2	0.2	10*	-	-	(D)	-	(D)	-	-
South Dakota	1	0.1	10*	-	-	(D)	-	(D)	-	-

Source: 1997 *Economic Census*. The states are in descending order of revenues or establishments (if revenue data are missing for the majority). The symbol (D) appears when data are withheld to prevent disclosure of competitive information. States marked with (D) are sorted by number of establishments. A dash (-) indicates that the data element cannot be calculated. * indicates the midpoint of a range; 175, for example is the range 100-249. Shaded *states* on the state map indicate those states which have proportionately greater representation in the industry than would be indicated by the state's population; the ratio is based on total revenues or number of establishments. Shaded *regions* indicate where the industry is regionally most concentrated.

NAICS 611519 - TRADE AND TECHNICAL SCHOOLS NEC

GENERAL STATISTICS

Year	Establishments (number)	Employment (number)	Payroll ($ million)	Revenues ($ million)	Employees per Establishment (number)	Revenues per Establishment ($)	Payroll per Employee ($)
1997	2,988	36,830	843.0	2,605.0	12.3	871,821	22,889

Source: Economic Census of the United States, 1997. This is a newly defined industry. Data for prior years were unavailable at the time of publication but may become available over time.

INDICES OF CHANGE

Year	Establishments (number)	Employment (number)	Payroll ($ million)	Revenues ($ million)	Employees per Establishment (number)	Revenues per Establishment ($)	Payroll per Employee ($)
1997	100.0	100.0	100.0	100.0	100.0	100.0	100.0

Sources: Same as General Statistics. The values shown reflect change from the base year, 1997. Values above 100 mean greater than 1997, values below 100 mean less than 1997, and a value of 100 in the 1982-96 or 1998-2001 period means same as 1997. Values followed by a 'p' are projections by the editors; 'e' stands for extrapolation. Data are the most recent available at this level of detail.

SIC INDUSTRIES RELATED TO NAICS 611519

Each new NAICS code represents an industry that used to be part of an SIC or a part of several SIC industries. Data in this table are shown to provide transitional information for these cases. All available data for the precursor SIC(s) are shown. Even if only a part of an SIC is included in the NAICS, *all* data for the SIC are reproduced. If the SIC industry is not marked as being a part (pt) of the NAICS, the entire industry is embedded in the NAICS data. The SIC composition of the new industry provides some hints of the relative importance of its "ancestors." Data marked with a 'p' are projected. Projections begin with 1982 data. Data earlier than 1990 are not shown but are reflected in the projections.

SIC	Industry	1990	1991	1992	1993	1994	1995	1996	1997
8243	**Data Processing Schools (pt)**								
	Establishments (number)	-	-	1,400	-	-	-	-	-
	Employment (thousands)	-	-	11.5	-	-	-	-	-
	Revenues ($ million)	-	-	898.9	-	-	-	-	-
8249	**Vocational Schools, nec (pt)**								
	Establishments (number)	-	-	3,366	-	-	-	-	-
	Employment (thousands)	-	-	43.6	-	-	-	-	-
	Revenues ($ million)	-	-	2,746.2	-	-	-	-	-
8299	**Schools & Educational Services, nec (pt)**								
	Establishments (number)	-	-	13,547	13,711	14,512	15,313	16,115p	16,916p
	Employment (thousands)	-	-	106.1	115.6	123.3	131.0	138.8p	146.5p
	Revenues ($ million)	-	-	5,217.2	3,378.0p	3,608.1p	3,838.1p	4,068.1p	4,298.2p

Source: Economic Census of the United States, 1992, annual surveys of economic sectors conducted by the Bureau of the Census, and estimates or projections based on the 1982-1992 period; not all data are shown. 'e' marks estimates made by the editors; 'p' indicates projections based on time series. A dash (-) indicates that data for this SIC or year were not available. The abbreviation (pt) next to the industry name indicates that only a part of the industry is present within the NAICS data. If no (pt) is shown, the entire industry is contained within the NAICS data.

SELECTED RATIOS

For 1997	Avg. of Information	Analyzed Industry	Index	For 1997	Avg. of Information	Analyzed Industry	Index
Employees per establishment	8	12	157	Payroll per establishment	155,475	282,129	181
Revenue per establishment	499,292	871,821	175	Payroll as % of revenue	31	32	104
Revenue per employee	63,659	70,730	111	Payroll per employee	19,823	22,889	115

Sources: Same as General Statistics. The 'Average' column represents the average for the industry sector, in 1997, where the currently shown industry is classified. The Index shows the relationship between the Average and the Analyzed Industry. For example, 100 means that they are equal; 500 that the Analyzed Industry is five times the average; 50 means that the Analyzed Industry is half the national average. The abbreviation 'na' is used to show that data are 'not available'.

LEADING COMPANIES

No company data available for this industry.

REPRESENTATIVE NONPROFIT ORGANIZATIONS

Organization Name	Address				Phone	Income Range ($ mil)
Abilene Christian University	Acu Box 29106	Abilene	TX	79699		50+
Act Inc	PO Box 168	Iowa City	IA	52243		50+
Agnes Scott College	141 E College Ave	Decatur	GA	30030		50+
Alta California Regional Center Inc	2031 Howe Ave Ste 100	Sacramento	CA	95825	916-614-0400	50+
American Academy of Family Physicians	11400 Tomahawk Creek	Leawood	KS	66211	913-541-0006	50+
American Academy of Orthopedic Surgeons	6300 N River Rd	Rosemont	IL	60018	847-698-1635	50+
American Arbitration Association	335 Madison Ave	New York	NY	10017	212-484-4034	50+
American Association for the Advancement of Science	1200 New York Ave NW	Washington	DC	20005	202-216-0743	50+
American Association of University Women	60 Split Rock Rd	Boonton	NJ	07005		50+
American College of Cardiology Inc	9111 Old Georgetown Rd	Bethesda	MD	20814		50+
American Printing House for the Blind Inc	1839 Frankfort Ave	Louisville	KY	40206	502-895-2405	50+
Arizona State University Foundation	707 S College	Tempe	AZ	85281	480-965-3759	50+
Armand Hammer United World College of the American West	PO Box 248	Montezuma	NM	87731	505-454-4200	50+
Association for Computing Machinery	900 Arkadelphia Rd	Birmingham	AL	35254		50+
Aurora Medical Centers of Sheboygan County Inc	PO Box 343910	Milwaukee	WI	53234		50+
Baldwin-Wallace College	275 Eastland Rd	Berea	OH	44017	440-826-2253	50+
Berklee College of Music Inc	1140 Boylston St	Boston	MA	02215	617-266-1400	50+
Bethune Cookman College	640 Mary M Bethune	Daytona Beach	FL	32114	904-255-1401	50+
Bowdoin College	5400 College Sta	Brunswick	ME	04011		50+
Bridgeport Hospital	267 Grant St	Bridgeport	CT	06610	203-384-4444	50+
Bryant College of Business Administration	450 Douglas Pike	Smithfield	RI	02917	401-232-6000	50+
Bush Foundation	E 900 1st Nat Bank Bldg	St Paul	MN	55101	651-227-0891	50+
Center for Creative Leadership	PO Box 26300	Greensboro	NC	27438	910-288-7210	50+
Community Medical Center	1822 Mulberry St	Scranton	PA	18510	570-969-8375	50+
Compassion International Incorporated	PO Box 7000	Colorado Springs	CO	80933	719-594-9900	50+
Delaware State College	1200 N Dupont Hwy	Dover	DE	19901	302-857-6353	50+
Delta Dental Plan of Missouri	8390 Delmar Blvd	St Louis	MO	63124		50+
Detroit Osteopathic Hospital Corporation	PO Box 5153	Southfield	MI	48086		50+
Educational Corporation Mukogawa Gakuin	1800 Seafirst Financial	Spokane	WA	99201		50+
Endowment Assoc of the College of WM & Mary in VA Incorp	PO Box 8795	Williamsburg	VA	23187		50+
Fletcher Allen Health Care Inc	111 Colchester Ave	Burlington	VT	05401	802-656-2434	50+
George W Donaghey Foundation	7th and Main	Little Rock	AR	72201		20-29
Hastings College	7th and Turner	Hastings	NE	68901		20-29
Inter American University of Puerto Rico	PO Box 363255	San Juan	PR	00936		50+
Iolani School	563 Kamoku St	Honolulu	HI	96826	808-949-5355	50+
Jackson State University	1325 Lynch St	Jackson	MS	39203		50+
Kawerak Inc	PO Box 948	Nome	AK	99762	907-443-5231	10-19
Linfield College	900 SE Baker St	McMinnville	OR	97128	503-434-2200	50+
Meadows School	8601 Scholar LN	Las Vegas	NV	89128	702-254-1610	10-19
Medcenter One	300 N 7th St	Bismarck	ND	58501		50+
National Collegiate Athletic Association	PO Box 6222	Indianapolis	IN	46206		50+
New Hampshire Charitable Foundation	37 Pleasant St	Concord	NH	03301		30-39
New Orleans Museum of Art	PO Box 19123	New Orleans	LA	70179	504-488-2631	30-39
Oklahoma City University	2501 N Blackwelder	Oklahoma City	OK	73106	405-521-5000	50+
Rapid City Regional Hospital Inc	353 Fairmont Blvd	Rapid City	SD	57701	605-341-8222	50+
Rhodes College	2000 N Parkway	Memphis	TN	38112	901-726-3000	50+
St Croix Country Day School Inc	RR 1 Box 6199 Kingshill	St Croix	VI	00850		1-5
United Hospital Center Inc	PO Box 1680	Clarksburg	WV	26302		50+
University of Idaho Foundation Inc	PO Box 443143	Moscow	ID	83844		50+
University of Montana Foundation	600 Connell Ave	Missoula	MT	59807		20-29
University of South Carolina Educational Foundation	900 Assembly St 4th FL	Columbia	SC	29201		50+
University of Wyoming Foundation	1200 Ivinson Ave	Laramie	WY	82070	307-766-6300	50+
Westminster College	1840 S 1300 E	Salt Lake City	UT	84105	801-484-7651	30-39

Source: National Directory of Nonprofit Organizations, 2000, Volumes 1 and 2, The Taft Group. The table shows a selection of organizations for illustration and does not constitute a complete selection from the source. The organizations are arranged in alphabetical order.

LOCATION BY STATE AND REGIONAL CONCENTRATION

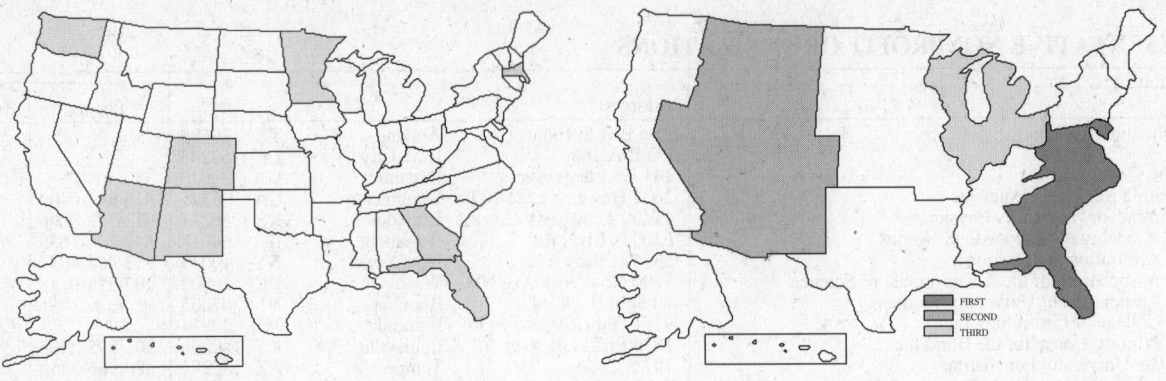

INDUSTRY DATA BY STATE

State	Establishments Total (number)	Establishments % of U.S.	Employment Total (number)	Employment % of U.S.	Employment Per Estab.	Payroll Total ($ mil.)	Payroll Per Empl. ($)	Revenues Total ($ mil.)	Revenues % of U.S.	Revenues Per Estab. ($)
Florida	214	7.2	2,712	7.4	13	56.8	20,928	191.7	7.4	895,636
New York	193	6.5	2,384	6.5	12	60.1	25,206	159.3	6.1	825,244
Texas	181	6.1	2,267	6.2	13	46.3	20,422	141.3	5.4	780,475
Colorado	92	3.1	1,806	4.9	20	50.3	27,837	141.1	5.4	1,534,185
Georgia	69	2.3	1,260	3.4	18	29.3	23,281	98.0	3.8	1,420,000
Illinois	116	3.9	1,627	4.4	14	31.7	19,471	84.3	3.2	726,974
Arizona	70	2.3	1,140	3.1	16	31.0	27,155	79.8	3.1	1,140,314
Massachusetts	84	2.8	1,125	3.1	13	22.6	20,089	71.4	2.7	849,571
Minnesota	39	1.3	688	1.9	18	15.2	22,081	67.6	2.6	1,734,026
Washington	75	2.5	1,087	3.0	14	18.0	16,580	56.3	2.2	750,400
Ohio	115	3.8	1,341	3.6	12	23.5	17,516	56.2	2.2	489,096
Missouri	58	1.9	664	1.8	11	13.5	20,367	50.9	2.0	877,241
Maryland	49	1.6	981	2.7	20	19.8	20,166	49.5	1.9	1,009,939
Michigan	84	2.8	584	1.6	7	13.2	22,642	35.6	1.4	423,583
Virginia	74	2.5	610	1.7	8	12.0	19,662	28.8	1.1	389,581
Louisiana	42	1.4	546	1.5	13	9.3	17,112	28.8	1.1	686,381
Oklahoma	40	1.3	419	1.1	10	11.2	26,714	27.9	1.1	696,575
Indiana	50	1.7	376	1.0	8	10.3	27,495	27.3	1.0	545,620
Alabama	23	0.8	427	1.2	19	19.2	44,890	25.1	1.0	1,092,261
North Carolina	52	1.7	335	0.9	6	8.2	24,379	23.8	0.9	457,788
New Mexico	30	1.0	347	0.9	12	7.1	20,326	20.1	0.8	668,467
Wisconsin	44	1.5	309	0.8	7	5.2	16,809	15.4	0.6	350,750
Kentucky	29	1.0	172	0.5	6	3.7	21,773	11.7	0.4	404,103
Alaska	15	0.5	284	0.8	19	2.5	8,852	5.9	0.2	395,333
Kansas	4	0.1	133	0.4	33	2.2	16,489	5.1	0.2	1,280,750
Hawaii	11	0.4	55	0.1	5	0.9	16,455	3.7	0.1	336,273
Iowa	9	0.3	37	0.1	4	0.5	13,757	1.7	0.1	192,333
Idaho	10	0.3	60*	-	-	(D)	-	(D)	-	-
South Dakota	1	-	10*	-	-	(D)	-	(D)	-	-

Source: 1997 Economic Census. The states are in descending order of revenues or establishments (if revenue data are missing for the majority). The symbol (D) appears when data are withheld to prevent disclosure of competitive information. States marked with (D) are sorted by number of establishments. A dash (-) indicates that the data element cannot be calculated. * indicates the midpoint of a range; 175, for example is the range 100-249. Shaded *states* on the state map indicate those states which have proportionately greater representation in the industry than would be indicated by the state's population; the ratio is based on total revenues or number of establishments. Shaded *regions* indicate where the industry is regionally most concentrated.

NAICS 611610 - FINE ARTS SCHOOLS

GENERAL STATISTICS

Year	Establishments (number)	Employment (number)	Payroll ($ million)	Revenues ($ million)	Employees per Establishment (number)	Revenues per Establishment ($)	Payroll per Employee ($)
1997	7,254	43,252	418.0	1,343.0	6.0	185,139	9,664

Source: *Economic Census of the United States*, 1997. This is a newly defined industry. Data for prior years were unavailable at the time of publication but may become available over time.

INDICES OF CHANGE

Year	Establishments (number)	Employment (number)	Payroll ($ million)	Revenues ($ million)	Employees per Establishment (number)	Revenues per Establishment ($)	Payroll per Employee ($)
1997	100.0	100.0	100.0	100.0	100.0	100.0	100.0

Sources: Same as General Statistics. The values shown reflect change from the base year, 1997. Values above 100 mean greater than 1997, values below 100 mean less than 1997, and a value of 100 in the 1982-96 or 1998-2001 period means same as 1997. Values followed by a 'p' are projections by the editors; 'e' stands for extrapolation. Data are the most recent available at this level of detail.

SIC INDUSTRIES RELATED TO NAICS 611610

Each new NAICS code represents an industry that used to be part of an SIC or a part of several SIC industries. Data in this table are shown to provide transitional information for these cases. All available data for the precursor SIC(s) are shown. Even if only a part of an SIC is included in the NAICS, *all* data for the SIC are reproduced. If the SIC industry is not marked as being a part (pt) of the NAICS, the entire industry is embedded in the NAICS data. The SIC composition of the new industry provides some hints of the relative importance of its "ancestors." Data marked with a 'p' are projected. Projections begin with 1982 data. Data earlier than 1990 are not shown but are reflected in the projections.

SIC	Industry	1990	1991	1992	1993	1994	1995	1996	1997
7911	**Dance Studios, Schools, & Halls (pt)**								
	Establishments (number)	4,022	4,371	-	5,133	5,255	5,297	5,141p	5,254p
	Employment (thousands)	20.6	21.7	-	24.6	24.4	25.3	25.0p	25.6p
	Revenues ($ million)	626.0	662.0	784.0	880.0	906.0	947.0	1,036.0	1,042.5p
8299	**Schools & Educational Services, nec (pt)**								
	Establishments (number)	-	-	13,547	13,711	14,512	15,313	16,115p	16,916p
	Employment (thousands)	-	-	106.1	115.6	123.3	131.0	138.8p	146.5p
	Revenues ($ million)	-	-	5,217.2	3,378.0p	3,608.1p	3,838.1p	4,068.1p	4,298.2p

Source: *Economic Census of the United States*, 1992, annual surveys of economic sectors conducted by the Bureau of the Census, and estimates or projections based on the 1982-1992 period; not all data are shown. 'e' marks estimates made by the editors; 'p' indicates projections based on time series. A dash (-) indicates that data for this SIC or year were not available. The abbreviation (pt) next to the industry name indicates that only a part of the industry is present within the NAICS data. If no (pt) is shown, the entire industry is contained within the NAICS data.

SELECTED RATIOS

For 1997	Avg. of Information	Analyzed Industry	Index	For 1997	Avg. of Information	Analyzed Industry	Index
Employees per establishment	8	6	76	Payroll per establishment	155,475	57,623	37
Revenue per establishment	499,292	185,139	37	Payroll as % of revenue	31	31	100
Revenue per employee	63,659	31,051	49	Payroll per employee	19,823	9,664	49

Sources: Same as General Statistics. The 'Average' column represents the average for the industry sector, in 1997, where the currently shown industry is classified. The Index shows the relationship between the Average and the Analyzed Industry. For example, 100 means that they are equal; 500 that the Analyzed Industry is five times the average; 50 means that the Analyzed Industry is half the national average. The abbreviation 'na' is used to show that data are 'not available'.

LEADING COMPANIES

No company data available for this industry.

LOCATION BY STATE AND REGIONAL CONCENTRATION

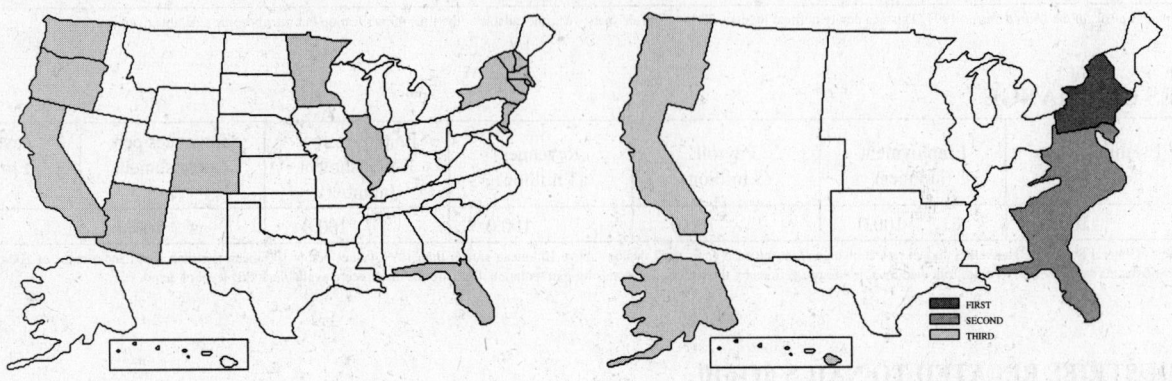

FIRST
SECOND
THIRD

INDUSTRY DATA BY STATE

State	Establishments Total (number)	% of U.S.	Employment Total (number)	% of U.S.	Per Estab.	Payroll Total ($ mil.)	Per Empl. ($)	Revenues Total ($ mil.)	% of U.S.	Per Estab. ($)
New York	634	8.7	4,712	10.9	7	62.2	13,202	171.9	12.8	271,096
California	752	10.4	5,540	12.8	7	54.1	9,771	166.7	12.4	221,733
Texas	446	6.1	2,449	5.7	5	24.4	9,965	86.1	6.4	192,984
Florida	432	6.0	1,970	4.6	5	22.2	11,286	79.6	5.9	184,234
Illinois	312	4.3	2,182	5.0	7	20.9	9,577	66.1	4.9	211,962
New Jersey	358	4.9	2,055	4.8	6	21.2	10,329	64.3	4.8	179,492
Pennsylvania	315	4.3	2,039	4.7	6	17.3	8,498	53.7	4.0	170,594
Massachusetts	247	3.4	1,679	3.9	7	17.6	10,454	51.3	3.8	207,704
Ohio	281	3.9	1,537	3.6	5	12.0	7,835	37.7	2.8	134,174
Minnesota	142	2.0	968	2.2	7	8.7	9,032	34.0	2.5	239,232
North Carolina	217	3.0	1,078	2.5	5	10.2	9,497	33.3	2.5	153,230
Virginia	220	3.0	1,190	2.8	5	11.4	9,557	32.5	2.4	147,841
Washington	166	2.3	937	2.2	6	7.9	8,424	30.8	2.3	185,584
Michigan	221	3.0	1,086	2.5	5	8.4	7,690	30.8	2.3	139,217
Georgia	198	2.7	986	2.3	5	8.8	8,922	30.2	2.2	152,323
Colorado	111	1.5	624	1.4	6	5.3	8,502	25.4	1.9	228,775
Maryland	129	1.8	669	1.5	5	7.5	11,160	25.0	1.9	194,132
Connecticut	127	1.8	868	2.0	7	9.2	10,619	24.9	1.9	196,323
Missouri	149	2.1	932	2.2	6	6.9	7,389	23.5	1.7	157,523
Arizona	100	1.4	683	1.6	7	7.9	11,537	21.9	1.6	219,200
Tennessee	120	1.7	551	1.3	5	6.4	11,617	20.8	1.6	173,675
D.C.	21	0.3	430	1.0	20	8.1	18,816	20.2	1.5	963,619
Wisconsin	131	1.8	621	1.4	5	4.9	7,884	18.2	1.4	138,962
Oregon	69	1.0	700	1.6	10	6.1	8,670	17.3	1.3	250,841
Alabama	108	1.5	521	1.2	5	4.0	7,595	13.8	1.0	128,037
South Carolina	101	1.4	489	1.1	5	2.8	5,828	13.5	1.0	133,990
Indiana	141	1.9	767	1.8	5	4.2	5,506	13.4	1.0	95,326
Louisiana	89	1.2	368	0.9	4	2.5	6,861	12.9	1.0	144,865
Kansas	74	1.0	427	1.0	6	3.1	7,180	10.8	0.8	145,703
Oklahoma	72	1.0	280	0.6	4	2.0	7,004	10.7	0.8	148,611
Vermont	32	0.4	158	0.4	5	2.1	13,310	8.5	0.6	266,000
Kentucky	84	1.2	326	0.8	4	2.2	6,675	8.1	0.6	96,774
Delaware	26	0.4	282	0.7	11	2.8	10,000	8.0	0.6	305,846
New Hampshire	42	0.6	230	0.5	5	2.3	10,035	6.9	0.5	163,405
New Mexico	50	0.7	202	0.5	4	1.8	8,807	6.1	0.5	121,880
Rhode Island	43	0.6	304	0.7	7	2.3	7,651	6.0	0.4	139,721
Nevada	30	0.4	212	0.5	7	1.5	6,991	5.4	0.4	181,200
Arkansas	54	0.7	213	0.5	4	1.4	6,408	5.1	0.4	95,111
Hawaii	30	0.4	123	0.3	4	1.6	12,797	4.7	0.3	155,167
Nebraska	43	0.6	216	0.5	5	1.2	5,505	4.6	0.3	106,535
Maine	31	0.4	153	0.4	5	1.3	8,170	3.9	0.3	126,194
Mississippi	42	0.6	135	0.3	3	0.6	4,096	2.9	0.2	69,262
Idaho	22	0.3	93	0.2	4	0.5	5,860	2.8	0.2	127,318
West Virginia	21	0.3	92	0.2	4	0.9	9,859	2.2	0.2	106,238
Alaska	14	0.2	56	0.1	4	0.5	8,518	1.2	0.1	87,357
Montana	15	0.2	70	0.2	5	0.2	3,043	1.0	0.1	64,600

Source: 1997 *Economic Census*. The states are in descending order of revenues or establishments (if revenue data are missing for the majority). The symbol (D) appears when data are withheld to prevent disclosure of competitive information. States marked with (D) are sorted by number of establishments. A dash (-) indicates that the data element cannot be calculated. * indicates the midpoint of a range; 175, for example is the range 100-249. Shaded *states* on the state map indicate those states which have proportionately greater representation in the industry than would be indicated by the state's population; the ratio is based on total revenues or number of establishments. Shaded *regions* indicate where the industry is regionally most concentrated.

NAICS 611620 - SPORTS AND RECREATION INSTRUCTION

GENERAL STATISTICS

Year	Establishments (number)	Employment (number)	Payroll ($ million)	Revenues ($ million)	Employees per Establishment (number)	Revenues per Establishment ($)	Payroll per Employee ($)
1997	6,423	37,547	422.0	1,426.0	5.8	222,015	11,239

Source: Economic Census of the United States, 1997. This is a newly defined industry. Data for prior years were unavailable at the time of publication but may become available over time.

INDICES OF CHANGE

Year	Establishments (number)	Employment (number)	Payroll ($ million)	Revenues ($ million)	Employees per Establishment (number)	Revenues per Establishment ($)	Payroll per Employee ($)
1997	100.0	100.0	100.0	100.0	100.0	100.0	100.0

Sources: Same as General Statistics. The values shown reflect change from the base year, 1997. Values above 100 mean greater than 1997, values below 100 mean less than 1997, and a value of 100 in the 1982-96 or 1998-2001 period means same as 1997. Values followed by a 'p' are projections by the editors; 'e' stands for extrapolation. Data are the most recent available at this level of detail.

SIC INDUSTRIES RELATED TO NAICS 611620

Each new NAICS code represents an industry that used to be part of an SIC or a part of several SIC industries. Data in this table are shown to provide transitional information for these cases. All available data for the precursor SIC(s) are shown. Even if only a part of an SIC is included in the NAICS, *all* data for the SIC are reproduced. If the SIC industry is not marked as being a part (pt) of the NAICS, the entire industry is embedded in the NAICS data. The SIC composition of the new industry provides some hints of the relative importance of its "ancestors." Data marked with a 'p' are projected. Projections begin with 1982 data. Data earlier than 1990 are not shown but are reflected in the projections.

SIC	Industry	1990	1991	1992	1993	1994	1995	1996	1997
7999	**Amusement & Recreation nec (pt)**								
	Establishments (number)	-	-	21,717	-	-	-	-	-
	Employment (thousands)	-	-	215.8	-	-	-	-	-
	Revenues ($ million)	-	-	10,430.3	-	-	-	-	-
8299	**Schools & Educational Services, nec (pt)**								
	Establishments (number)	-	-	13,547	13,711	14,512	15,313	16,115p	16,916p
	Employment (thousands)	-	-	106.1	115.6	123.3	131.0	138.8p	146.5p
	Revenues ($ million)	-	-	5,217.2	3,378.0p	3,608.1p	3,838.1p	4,068.1p	4,298.2p

Source: Economic Census of the United States, 1992, annual surveys of economic sectors conducted by the Bureau of the Census, and estimates or projections based on the 1982-1992 period; not all data are shown. 'e' marks estimates made by the editors; 'p' indicates projections based on time series. A dash (-) indicates that data for this SIC or year were not available. The abbreviation (pt) next to the industry name indicates that only a part of the industry is present within the NAICS data. If no (pt) is shown, the entire industry is contained within the NAICS data.

SELECTED RATIOS

For 1997	Avg. of Information	Analyzed Industry	Index	For 1997	Avg. of Information	Analyzed Industry	Index
Employees per establishment	8	6	75	Payroll per establishment	155,475	65,701	42
Revenue per establishment	499,292	222,015	44	Payroll as % of revenue	31	30	95
Revenue per employee	63,659	37,979	60	Payroll per employee	19,823	11,239	57

Sources: Same as General Statistics. The 'Average' column represents the average for the industry sector, in 1997, where the currently shown industry is classified. The Index shows the relationship between the Average and the Analyzed Industry. For example, 100 means that they are equal; 500 that the Analyzed Industry is five times the average; 50 means that the Analyzed Industry is half the national average. The abbreviation 'na' is used to show that data are 'not available'.

LEADING COMPANIES

No company data available for this industry.

LOCATION BY STATE AND REGIONAL CONCENTRATION

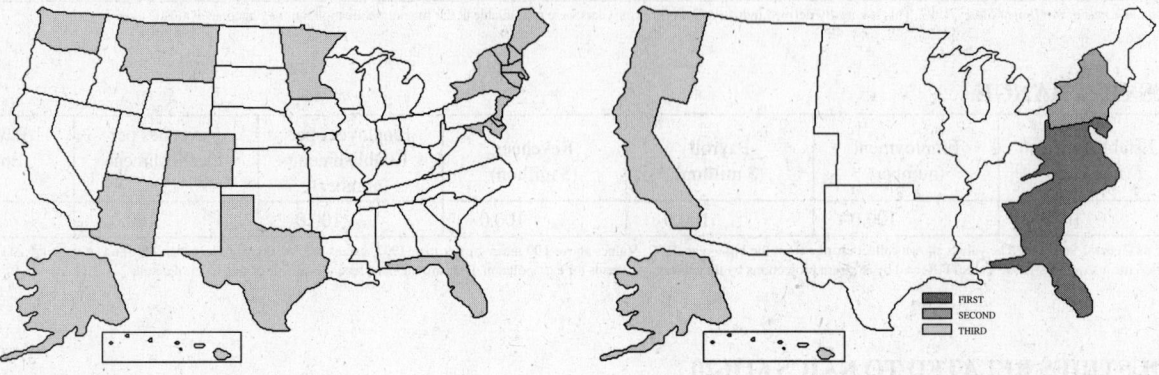

FIRST
SECOND
THIRD

INDUSTRY DATA BY STATE

State	Establishments Total (number)	Establishments % of U.S.	Employment Total (number)	Employment % of U.S.	Employment Per Estab.	Payroll Total ($ mil.)	Payroll Per Empl. ($)	Revenues Total ($ mil.)	Revenues % of U.S.	Revenues Per Estab. ($)
California	693	10.8	4,320	11.5	6	52.1	12,068	173.2	12.1	249,947
New York	484	7.5	2,859	7.6	6	40.6	14,189	143.3	10.0	296,143
Florida	488	7.6	2,363	6.3	5	42.5	17,977	133.4	9.4	273,443
Texas	373	5.8	2,472	6.6	7	27.6	11,164	105.3	7.4	282,249
New Jersey	270	4.2	1,364	3.6	5	19.2	14,043	63.2	4.4	234,204
Pennsylvania	228	3.5	1,454	3.9	6	17.9	12,337	60.9	4.3	267,092
Illinois	213	3.3	1,422	3.8	7	15.6	10,992	51.2	3.6	240,479
Massachusetts	225	3.5	1,135	3.0	5	15.4	13,527	49.9	3.5	221,782
Colorado	181	2.8	1,011	2.7	6	11.4	11,239	40.7	2.9	224,773
Connecticut	108	1.7	616	1.6	6	14.2	23,073	38.5	2.7	356,574
Ohio	189	2.9	1,026	2.7	5	10.4	10,129	38.4	2.7	203,254
Washington	214	3.3	2,470	6.6	12	12.6	5,099	37.7	2.6	176,196
Maryland	165	2.6	970	2.6	6	11.5	11,824	36.0	2.5	218,206
Virginia	189	2.9	1,069	2.8	6	10.7	10,040	35.5	2.5	187,968
Georgia	153	2.4	760	2.0	5	8.1	10,605	31.9	2.2	208,824
North Carolina	161	2.5	852	2.3	5	9.4	11,070	30.8	2.2	191,391
Minnesota	137	2.1	826	2.2	6	8.1	9,788	28.8	2.0	210,474
Michigan	141	2.2	672	1.8	5	7.4	10,999	28.3	2.0	201,057
Arizona	97	1.5	571	1.5	6	7.3	12,842	24.5	1.7	252,577
Wisconsin	132	2.1	924	2.5	7	6.7	7,247	24.4	1.7	184,538
Indiana	121	1.9	749	2.0	6	5.6	7,526	18.6	1.3	153,760
Hawaii	71	1.1	321	0.9	5	5.6	17,511	18.6	1.3	261,873
Missouri	113	1.8	776	2.1	7	5.1	6,518	17.3	1.2	153,000
South Carolina	93	1.4	592	1.6	6	4.8	8,191	17.1	1.2	184,355
Oregon	92	1.4	302	0.8	3	3.9	12,801	14.3	1.0	155,804
Tennessee	96	1.5	389	1.0	4	4.1	10,488	13.5	0.9	141,135
Louisiana	59	0.9	396	1.1	7	3.4	8,634	11.0	0.8	186,254
Maine	58	0.9	138	0.4	2	3.0	21,899	10.9	0.8	188,086
New Hampshire	59	0.9	302	0.8	5	3.1	10,364	10.7	0.8	181,678
Oklahoma	54	0.8	365	1.0	7	3.0	8,323	10.3	0.7	191,648
Utah	52	0.8	364	1.0	7	2.8	7,673	10.1	0.7	195,038
Kentucky	69	1.1	368	1.0	5	2.4	6,609	8.5	0.6	123,855
Alabama	60	0.9	235	0.6	4	1.9	8,183	7.5	0.5	125,517
Kansas	59	0.9	260	0.7	4	2.1	8,208	7.0	0.5	119,051
New Mexico	43	0.7	223	0.6	5	2.8	12,381	6.8	0.5	157,698
Rhode Island	37	0.6	111	0.3	3	1.7	15,441	6.7	0.5	180,892
Montana	53	0.8	386	1.0	7	1.5	4,008	6.0	0.4	112,585
Alaska	26	0.4	120	0.3	5	0.8	6,742	4.8	0.3	182,962
Arkansas	34	0.5	214	0.6	6	1.5	6,836	4.1	0.3	119,118
Vermont	29	0.5	101	0.3	3	1.0	10,129	3.8	0.3	132,000
Delaware	21	0.3	86	0.2	4	1.2	13,477	3.6	0.3	172,714
North Dakota	25	0.4	234	0.6	9	1.1	4,534	3.1	0.2	124,080
West Virginia	18	0.3	71	0.2	4	1.3	17,845	2.3	0.2	126,278
Wyoming	14	0.2	71	0.2	5	0.5	7,620	1.3	0.1	93,786
South Dakota	11	0.2	43	0.1	4	0.2	5,302	0.9	0.1	80,818

Source: 1997 *Economic Census*. The states are in descending order of revenues or establishments (if revenue data are missing for the majority). The symbol (D) appears when data are withheld to prevent disclosure of competitive information. States marked with (D) are sorted by number of establishments. A dash (-) indicates that the data element cannot be calculated. * indicates the midpoint of a range; 175, for example is the range 100-249. Shaded *states* on the state map indicate those states which have proportionately greater representation in the industry than would be indicated by the state's population; the ratio is based on total revenues or number of establishments. Shaded *regions* indicate where the industry is regionally most concentrated.

NAICS 611630 - LANGUAGE SCHOOLS

GENERAL STATISTICS

Year	Establishments (number)	Employment (number)	Payroll ($ million)	Revenues ($ million)	Employees per Establishment (number)	Revenues per Establishment ($)	Payroll per Employee ($)
1997	854	11,836	152.0	489.0	13.9	572,600	12,842

Source: Economic Census of the United States, 1997. This is a newly defined industry. Data for prior years were unavailable at the time of publication but may become available over time.

INDICES OF CHANGE

Year	Establishments (number)	Employment (number)	Payroll ($ million)	Revenues ($ million)	Employees per Establishment (number)	Revenues per Establishment ($)	Payroll per Employee ($)
1997	100.0	100.0	100.0	100.0	100.0	100.0	100.0

Sources: Same as General Statistics. The values shown reflect change from the base year, 1997. Values above 100 mean greater than 1997, values below 100 mean less than 1997, and a value of 100 in the 1982-96 or 1998-2001 period means same as 1997. Values followed by a 'p' are projections by the editors; 'e' stands for extrapolation. Data are the most recent available at this level of detail.

SIC INDUSTRIES RELATED TO NAICS 611630

Each new NAICS code represents an industry that used to be part of an SIC or a part of several SIC industries. Data in this table are shown to provide transitional information for these cases. All available data for the precursor SIC(s) are shown. Even if only a part of an SIC is included in the NAICS, *all* data for the SIC are reproduced. If the SIC industry is not marked as being a part (pt) of the NAICS, the entire industry is embedded in the NAICS data. The SIC composition of the new industry provides some hints of the relative importance of its "ancestors." Data marked with a 'p' are projected. Projections begin with 1982 data. Data earlier than 1990 are not shown but are reflected in the projections.

SIC	Industry	1990	1991	1992	1993	1994	1995	1996	1997
8299	**Schools & Educational Services, nec (pt)**								
	Establishments (number)	-	-	13,547	13,711	14,512	15,313	16,115p	16,916p
	Employment (thousands)	-	-	106.1	115.6	123.3	131.0	138.8p	146.5p
	Revenues ($ million)	-	-	5,217.2	3,378.0p	3,608.1p	3,838.1p	4,068.1p	4,298.2p

Source: Economic Census of the United States, 1992, annual surveys of economic sectors conducted by the Bureau of the Census, and estimates or projections based on the 1982-1992 period; not all data are shown. 'e' marks estimates made by the editors; 'p' indicates projections based on time series. A dash (-) indicates that data for this SIC or year were not available. The abbreviation (pt) next to the industry name indicates that only a part of the industry is present within the NAICS data. If no (pt) is shown, the entire industry is contained within the NAICS data.

SELECTED RATIOS

For 1997	Avg. of Information	Analyzed Industry	Index	For 1997	Avg. of Information	Analyzed Industry	Index
Employees per establishment	8	14	177	Payroll per establishment	155,475	177,986	114
Revenue per establishment	499,292	572,600	115	Payroll as % of revenue	31	31	100
Revenue per employee	63,659	41,315	65	Payroll per employee	19,823	12,842	65

Sources: Same as General Statistics. The 'Average' column represents the average for the industry sector, in 1997, where the currently shown industry is classified. The Index shows the relationship between the Average and the Analyzed Industry. For example, 100 means that they are equal; 500 that the Analyzed Industry is five times the average; 50 means that the Analyzed Industry is half the national average. The abbreviation 'na' is used to show that data are 'not available'.

LEADING COMPANIES
No company data available for this industry.

LOCATION BY STATE AND REGIONAL CONCENTRATION

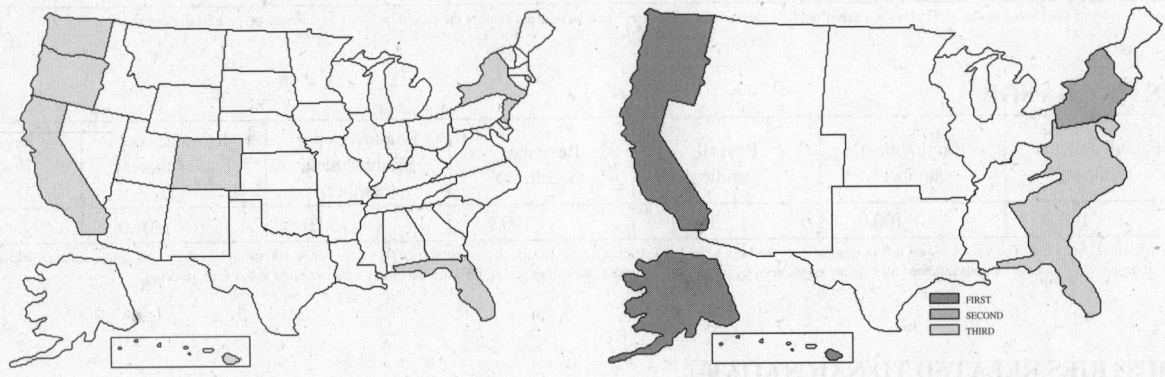

FIRST
SECOND
THIRD

INDUSTRY DATA BY STATE

State	Establishments		Employment			Payroll		Revenues		
	Total (number)	% of U.S.	Total (number)	% of U.S.	Per Estab.	Total ($ mil.)	Per Empl. ($)	Total ($ mil.)	% of U.S.	Per Estab. ($)
California	210	24.6	3,175	26.8	15	35.2	11,079	127.1	26.0	605,257
New York	74	8.7	1,612	13.6	22	26.7	16,536	75.4	15.4	1,018,811
New Jersey	44	5.2	597	5.0	14	11.9	19,987	59.0	12.1	1,340,523
Florida	45	5.3	661	5.6	15	9.3	14,050	36.2	7.4	804,289
Texas	50	5.9	666	5.6	13	7.0	10,557	18.0	3.7	360,420
Washington	46	5.4	630	5.3	14	4.7	7,451	11.9	2.4	259,587
Pennsylvania	29	3.4	267	2.3	9	3.3	12,494	9.1	1.9	313,586
Ohio	11	1.3	308	2.6	28	2.9	9,529	7.6	1.6	690,636
Colorado	21	2.5	284	2.4	14	3.2	11,204	7.4	1.5	350,571
D.C.	5	0.6	162	1.4	32	2.4	15,000	7.2	1.5	1,437,800
Oregon	14	1.6	153	1.3	11	2.5	16,608	6.7	1.4	478,929
Georgia	13	1.5	200	1.7	15	2.6	13,100	6.1	1.2	469,308
Hawaii	26	3.0	218	1.8	8	2.6	11,963	5.6	1.2	216,231
Connecticut	12	1.4	86	0.7	7	1.3	15,500	3.4	0.7	286,583
Wisconsin	11	1.3	94	0.8	9	1.3	13,489	2.8	0.6	258,727
Arizona	7	0.8	80	0.7	11	0.6	7,438	1.9	0.4	266,429
Tennessee	7	0.8	45	0.4	6	0.7	16,422	1.6	0.3	225,429
North Carolina	8	0.9	59	0.5	7	0.7	11,424	1.5	0.3	190,250
South Carolina	4	0.5	45	0.4	11	0.4	9,889	1.1	0.2	274,000
Oklahoma	3	0.4	20	0.2	7	0.4	17,750	0.8	0.2	271,667
Nevada	6	0.7	38	0.3	6	0.4	11,237	0.8	0.2	126,333
Alaska	3	0.4	3	0.0	1	-	8,000	0.1	0.0	43,667
Alabama	3	0.4	10*	-	-	(D)	-	(D)	-	-
West Virginia	3	0.4	10*	-	-	(D)	-	(D)	-	-
Maine	2	0.2	10*	-	-	(D)	-	(D)	-	-
Arkansas	1	0.1	10*	-	-	(D)	-	(D)	-	-
Delaware	1	0.1	10*	-	-	(D)	-	(D)	-	-
Kansas	1	0.1	10*	-	-	(D)	-	(D)	-	-
Kentucky	1	0.1	10*	-	-	(D)	-	(D)	-	-
Rhode Island	1	0.1	10*	-	-	(D)	-	(D)	-	-
South Dakota	1	0.1	10*	-	-	(D)	-	(D)	-	-

Source: 1997 *Economic Census*. The states are in descending order of revenues or establishments (if revenue data are missing for the majority). The symbol (D) appears when data are withheld to prevent disclosure of competitive information. States marked with (D) are sorted by number of establishments. A dash (-) indicates that the data element cannot be calculated. * indicates the midpoint of a range; 175, for example is the range 100-249. Shaded *states* on the state map indicate those states which have proportionately greater representation in the industry than would be indicated by the state's population; the ratio is based on total revenues or number of establishments. Shaded *regions* indicate where the industry is regionally most concentrated.

NAICS 611691 - EXAM PREPARATION AND TUTORING

GENERAL STATISTICS

Year	Establishments (number)	Employment (number)	Payroll ($ million)	Revenues ($ million)	Employees per Establishment (number)	Revenues per Establishment ($)	Payroll per Employee ($)
1997	2,630	22,664	291.0	815.0	8.6	309,886	12,840

Source: Economic Census of the United States, 1997. This is a newly defined industry. Data for prior years were unavailable at the time of publication but may become available over time.

INDICES OF CHANGE

Year	Establishments (number)	Employment (number)	Payroll ($ million)	Revenues ($ million)	Employees per Establishment (number)	Revenues per Establishment ($)	Payroll per Employee ($)
1997	100.0	100.0	100.0	100.0	100.0	100.0	100.0

Sources: Same as General Statistics. The values shown reflect change from the base year, 1997. Values above 100 mean greater than 1997, values below 100 mean less than 1997, and a value of 100 in the 1982-96 or 1998-2001 period means same as 1997. Values followed by a 'p' are projections by the editors; 'e' stands for extrapolation. Data are the most recent available at this level of detail.

SIC INDUSTRIES RELATED TO NAICS 611691

Each new NAICS code represents an industry that used to be part of an SIC or a part of several SIC industries. Data in this table are shown to provide transitional information for these cases. All available data for the precursor SIC(s) are shown. Even if only a part of an SIC is included in the NAICS, *all* data for the SIC are reproduced. If the SIC industry is not marked as being a part (pt) of the NAICS, the entire industry is embedded in the NAICS data. The SIC composition of the new industry provides some hints of the relative importance of its "ancestors." Data marked with a 'p' are projected. Projections begin with 1982 data. Data earlier than 1990 are not shown but are reflected in the projections.

SIC	Industry	1990	1991	1992	1993	1994	1995	1996	1997
8299	**Schools & Educational Services, nec (pt)**								
	Establishments (number)	-	-	13,547	13,711	14,512	15,313	16,115p	16,916p
	Employment (thousands)	-	-	106.1	115.6	123.3	131.0	138.8p	146.5p
	Revenues ($ million)	-	-	5,217.2	3,378.0p	3,608.1p	3,838.1p	4,068.1p	4,298.2p

Source: Economic Census of the United States, 1992, annual surveys of economic sectors conducted by the Bureau of the Census, and estimates or projections based on the 1982-1992 period; not all data are shown. 'e' marks estimates made by the editors; 'p' indicates projections based on time series. A dash (-) indicates that data for this SIC or year were not available. The abbreviation (pt) next to the industry name indicates that only a part of the industry is present within the NAICS data. If no (pt) is shown, the entire industry is contained within the NAICS data.

SELECTED RATIOS

For 1997	Avg. of Information	Analyzed Industry	Index	For 1997	Avg. of Information	Analyzed Industry	Index
Employees per establishment	8	9	110	Payroll per establishment	155,475	110,646	71
Revenue per establishment	499,292	309,886	62	Payroll as % of revenue	31	36	115
Revenue per employee	63,659	35,960	56	Payroll per employee	19,823	12,840	65

Sources: Same as General Statistics. The 'Average' column represents the average for the industry sector, in 1997, where the currently shown industry is classified. The Index shows the relationship between the Average and the Analyzed Industry. For example, 100 means that they are equal; 500 that the Analyzed Industry is five times the average; 50 means that the Analyzed Industry is half the national average. The abbreviation 'na' is used to show that data are 'not available'.

LEADING COMPANIES

No company data available for this industry.

LOCATION BY STATE AND REGIONAL CONCENTRATION

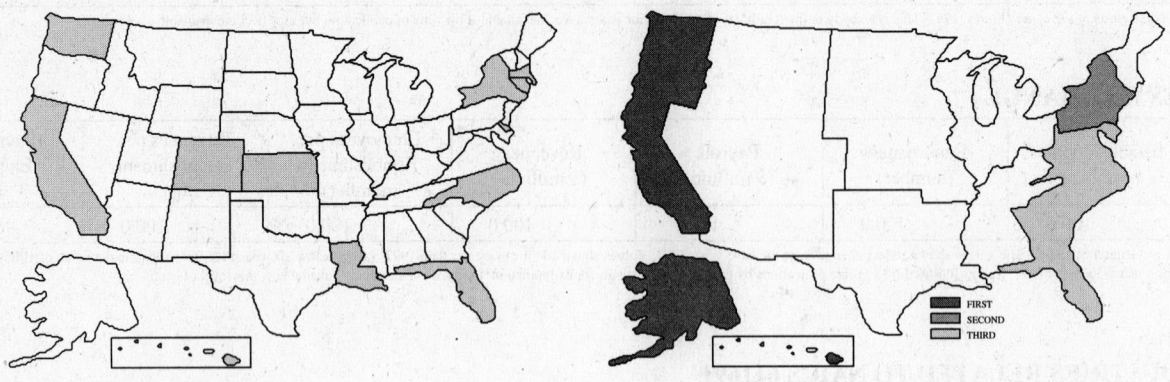

FIRST
SECOND
THIRD

INDUSTRY DATA BY STATE

State	Establishments Total (number)	% of U.S.	Employment Total (number)	% of U.S.	Per Estab.	Payroll Total ($ mil.)	Per Empl. ($)	Revenues Total ($ mil.)	% of U.S.	Per Estab. ($)
California	484	18.4	4,211	18.6	9	42.9	10,193	133.1	16.3	274,919
New York	210	8.0	2,187	9.6	10	50.3	23,005	111.2	13.6	529,348
Texas	146	5.6	1,381	6.1	9	22.0	15,953	53.5	6.6	366,534
Florida	156	5.9	1,298	5.7	8	17.6	13,549	50.7	6.2	325,244
Illinois	114	4.3	814	3.6	7	11.6	14,299	31.5	3.9	276,719
Massachusetts	60	2.3	761	3.4	13	9.4	12,377	26.1	3.2	434,200
North Carolina	64	2.4	637	2.8	10	6.6	10,396	24.6	3.0	384,813
Pennsylvania	80	3.0	733	3.2	9	6.5	8,930	21.6	2.6	270,050
Washington	75	2.9	583	2.6	8	10.4	17,916	21.0	2.6	279,547
Louisiana	33	1.3	518	2.3	16	7.4	14,199	19.8	2.4	601,212
Michigan	65	2.5	597	2.6	9	5.8	9,675	16.5	2.0	254,031
Ohio	90	3.4	776	3.4	9	5.9	7,544	15.9	2.0	177,189
Colorado	40	1.5	325	1.4	8	4.1	12,760	14.2	1.7	355,425
Georgia	62	2.4	411	1.8	7	4.3	10,523	13.8	1.7	223,258
Kansas	17	0.6	239	1.1	14	2.9	12,033	12.6	1.5	742,412
Virginia	81	3.1	475	2.1	6	4.4	9,225	11.7	1.4	144,975
Connecticut	35	1.3	244	1.1	7	3.4	13,742	11.4	1.4	325,286
Arizona	41	1.6	237	1.0	6	3.3	13,726	9.5	1.2	230,805
Missouri	50	1.9	317	1.4	6	3.7	11,546	9.5	1.2	189,200
Tennessee	38	1.4	271	1.2	7	2.9	10,712	7.6	0.9	199,421
Indiana	42	1.6	270	1.2	6	2.1	7,930	7.2	0.9	172,571
South Carolina	29	1.1	189	0.8	7	2.1	10,852	5.7	0.7	197,552
Wisconsin	28	1.1	271	1.2	10	2.5	9,236	5.7	0.7	202,071
Kentucky	30	1.1	184	0.8	6	1.6	8,777	5.1	0.6	171,133
Hawaii	31	1.2	220	1.0	7	1.5	6,959	5.1	0.6	164,935
Oregon	28	1.1	157	0.7	6	1.6	10,185	5.0	0.6	178,393
Oklahoma	17	0.6	102	0.5	6	0.9	9,137	3.7	0.5	220,176
Nevada	14	0.5	52	0.2	4	1.1	20,423	3.3	0.4	232,857
Delaware	9	0.3	141	0.6	16	1.0	7,305	2.7	0.3	302,778
West Virginia	11	0.4	59	0.3	5	0.4	6,525	1.3	0.2	118,273
Arkansas	12	0.5	33	0.1	3	0.4	12,333	0.8	0.1	67,500
Iowa	11	0.4	175*	-	-	(D)	-	(D)	-	-
Idaho	7	0.3	10*	-	-	(D)	-	(D)	-	-
North Dakota	1	-	10*	-	-	(D)	-	(D)	-	-
Wyoming	1	-	10*	-	-	(D)	-	(D)	-	-

Source: 1997 *Economic Census*. The states are in descending order of revenues or establishments (if revenue data are missing for the majority). The symbol (D) appears when data are withheld to prevent disclosure of competitive information. States marked with (D) are sorted by number of establishments. A dash (-) indicates that the data element cannot be calculated. * indicates the midpoint of a range; 175, for example is the range 100-249. Shaded *states* on the state map indicate those states which have proportionately greater representation in the industry than would be indicated by the state's population; the ratio is based on total revenues or number of establishments. Shaded *regions* indicate where the industry is regionally most concentrated.

NAICS 611692 - AUTOMOBILE DRIVING SCHOOLS

GENERAL STATISTICS

Year	Establishments (number)	Employment (number)	Payroll ($ million)	Revenues ($ million)	Employees per Establishment (number)	Revenues per Establishment ($)	Payroll per Employee ($)
1997	1,719	9,713	125.0	362.0	5.7	210,588	12,869

Source: *Economic Census of the United States*, 1997. This is a newly defined industry. Data for prior years were unavailable at the time of publication but may become available over time.

INDICES OF CHANGE

Year	Establishments (number)	Employment (number)	Payroll ($ million)	Revenues ($ million)	Employees per Establishment (number)	Revenues per Establishment ($)	Payroll per Employee ($)
1997	100.0	100.0	100.0	100.0	100.0	100.0	100.0

Sources: Same as General Statistics. The values shown reflect change from the base year, 1997. Values above 100 mean greater than 1997, values below 100 mean less than 1997, and a value of 100 in the 1982-96 or 1998-2001 period means same as 1997. Values followed by a 'p' are projections by the editors; 'e' stands for extrapolation. Data are the most recent available at this level of detail.

SIC INDUSTRIES RELATED TO NAICS 611692

Each new NAICS code represents an industry that used to be part of an SIC or a part of several SIC industries. Data in this table are shown to provide transitional information for these cases. All available data for the precursor SIC(s) are shown. Even if only a part of an SIC is included in the NAICS, *all* data for the SIC are reproduced. If the SIC industry is not marked as being a part (pt) of the NAICS, the entire industry is embedded in the NAICS data. The SIC composition of the new industry provides some hints of the relative importance of its "ancestors." Data marked with a 'p' are projected. Projections begin with 1982 data. Data earlier than 1990 are not shown but are reflected in the projections.

SIC	Industry	1990	1991	1992	1993	1994	1995	1996	1997
8299	**Schools & Educational Services, nec (pt)**								
	Establishments (number)	-	-	13,547	13,711	14,512	15,313	16,115p	16,916p
	Employment (thousands)	-	-	106.1	115.6	123.3	131.0	138.8p	146.5p
	Revenues ($ million)	-	-	5,217.2	3,378.0p	3,608.1p	3,838.1p	4,068.1p	4,298.2p

Source: *Economic Census of the United States*, 1992, annual surveys of economic sectors conducted by the Bureau of the Census, and estimates or projections based on the 1982-1992 period; not all data are shown. 'e' marks estimates made by the editors; 'p' indicates projections based on time series. A dash (-) indicates that data for this SIC or year were not available. The abbreviation (pt) next to the industry name indicates that only a part of the industry is present within the NAICS data. If no (pt) is shown, the entire industry is contained within the NAICS data.

SELECTED RATIOS

For 1997	Avg. of Information	Analyzed Industry	Index	For 1997	Avg. of Information	Analyzed Industry	Index
Employees per establishment	8	6	72	Payroll per establishment	155,475	72,717	47
Revenue per establishment	499,292	210,588	42	Payroll as % of revenue	31	35	111
Revenue per employee	63,659	37,270	59	Payroll per employee	19,823	12,869	65

Sources: Same as General Statistics. The 'Average' column represents the average for the industry sector, in 1997, where the currently shown industry is classified. The Index shows the relationship between the Average and the Analyzed Industry. For example, 100 means that they are equal; 500 that the Analyzed Industry is five times the average; 50 means that the Analyzed Industry is half the national average. The abbreviation 'na' is used to show that data are 'not available'.

LEADING COMPANIES

No company data available for this industry.

LOCATION BY STATE AND REGIONAL CONCENTRATION

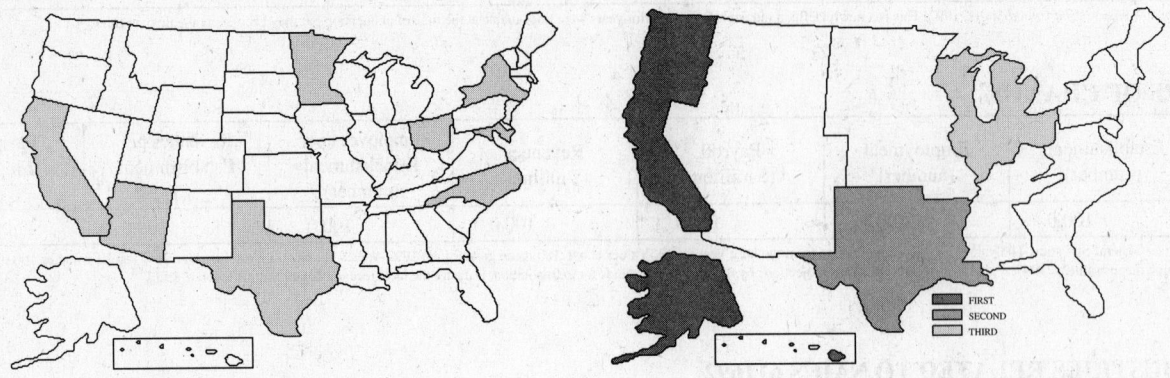

FIRST
SECOND
THIRD

INDUSTRY DATA BY STATE

State	Establishments Total (number)	Establishments % of U.S.	Employment Total (number)	Employment % of U.S.	Employment Per Estab.	Payroll Total ($ mil.)	Payroll Per Empl. ($)	Revenues Total ($ mil.)	Revenues % of U.S.	Revenues Per Estab. ($)
California	268	15.6	1,554	16.0	6	18.8	12,102	51.7	14.3	192,862
Texas	187	10.9	1,321	13.6	7	13.4	10,111	39.6	10.9	211,684
New York	202	11.8	818	8.4	4	9.9	12,077	31.9	8.8	158,139
Ohio	107	6.2	831	8.6	8	8.6	10,326	19.0	5.3	177,729
North Carolina	32	1.9	418	4.3	13	7.1	16,902	13.3	3.7	416,375
Illinois	51	3.0	183	1.9	4	3.5	18,973	9.1	2.5	178,431
Maryland	48	2.8	283	2.9	6	3.5	12,364	8.4	2.3	175,458
Minnesota	56	3.3	299	3.1	5	3.1	10,261	8.2	2.3	146,286
Arizona	12	0.7	106	1.1	9	2.9	26,906	8.0	2.2	669,833
Washington	38	2.2	224	2.3	6	2.2	9,728	6.2	1.7	163,763
Wisconsin	41	2.4	241	2.5	6	2.4	10,050	5.7	1.6	138,829
Virginia	41	2.4	181	1.9	4	1.6	8,691	4.4	1.2	106,146
Oregon	9	0.5	51	0.5	6	0.6	11,667	1.6	0.4	178,000
Missouri	7	0.4	26	0.3	4	0.7	28,577	1.3	0.4	190,429
Kentucky	10	0.6	35	0.4	4	0.4	10,514	1.0	0.3	96,600
Utah	6	0.3	31	0.3	5	0.3	9,935	0.7	0.2	119,833
Iowa	4	0.2	17	0.2	4	0.2	13,176	0.5	0.2	135,750
Vermont	5	0.3	5	0.1	1	0.1	20,800	0.3	0.1	61,600
Alabama	3	0.2	12	0.1	4	0.1	4,500	0.2	0.1	65,333
New Hampshire	17	1.0	60*	-	-	(D)	-	(D)	-	-
Kansas	8	0.5	60*	-	-	(D)	-	(D)	-	-
Rhode Island	5	0.3	10*	-	-	(D)	-	(D)	-	-
Delaware	4	0.2	10*	-	-	(D)	-	(D)	-	-
Nebraska	4	0.2	10*	-	-	(D)	-	(D)	-	-
West Virginia	4	0.2	60*	-	-	(D)	-	(D)	-	-
Idaho	3	0.2	10*	-	-	(D)	-	(D)	-	-
North Dakota	3	0.2	10*	-	-	(D)	-	(D)	-	-
D.C.	2	0.1	10*	-	-	(D)	-	(D)	-	-
Mississippi	2	0.1	60*	-	-	(D)	-	(D)	-	-
Arkansas	1	0.1	10*	-	-	(D)	-	(D)	-	-

Source: 1997 *Economic Census*. The states are in descending order of revenues or establishments (if revenue data are missing for the majority). The symbol (D) appears when data are withheld to prevent disclosure of competitive information. States marked with (D) are sorted by number of establishments. A dash (-) indicates that the data element cannot be calculated. * indicates the midpoint of a range; 175, for example is the range 100-249. Shaded *states* on the state map indicate those states which have proportionately greater representation in the industry than would be indicated by the state's population; the ratio is based on total revenues or number of establishments. Shaded *regions* indicate where the industry is regionally most concentrated.

NAICS 611699 - MISCELLANEOUS SCHOOLS AND INSTRUCTION NEC

GENERAL STATISTICS

Year	Establishments (number)	Employment (number)	Payroll ($ million)	Revenues ($ million)	Employees per Establishment (number)	Revenues per Establishment ($)	Payroll per Employee ($)
1997	4,884	40,339	836.0	2,692.0	8.3	551,188	20,724

Source: *Economic Census of the United States*, 1997. This is a newly defined industry. Data for prior years were unavailable at the time of publication but may become available over time.

INDICES OF CHANGE

Year	Establishments (number)	Employment (number)	Payroll ($ million)	Revenues ($ million)	Employees per Establishment (number)	Revenues per Establishment ($)	Payroll per Employee ($)
1997	100.0	100.0	100.0	100.0	100.0	100.0	100.0

Sources: Same as General Statistics. The values shown reflect change from the base year, 1997. Values above 100 mean greater than 1997, values below 100 mean less than 1997, and a value of 100 in the 1982-96 or 1998-2001 period means same as 1997. Values followed by a 'p' are projections by the editors; 'e' stands for extrapolation. Data are the most recent available at this level of detail.

SIC INDUSTRIES RELATED TO NAICS 611699

Each new NAICS code represents an industry that used to be part of an SIC or a part of several SIC industries. Data in this table are shown to provide transitional information for these cases. All available data for the precursor SIC(s) are shown. Even if only a part of an SIC is included in the NAICS, *all* data for the SIC are reproduced. If the SIC industry is not marked as being a part (pt) of the NAICS, the entire industry is embedded in the NAICS data. The SIC composition of the new industry provides some hints of the relative importance of its "ancestors." Data marked with a 'p' are projected. Projections begin with 1982 data. Data earlier than 1990 are not shown but are reflected in the projections.

SIC	Industry	1990	1991	1992	1993	1994	1995	1996	1997
7999	**Amusement & Recreation nec (pt)**								
	Establishments (number)	-	-	21,717	-	-	-	-	-
	Employment (thousands)	-	-	215.8	-	-	-	-	-
	Revenues ($ million)	-	-	10,430.3	-	-	-	-	-
8299	**Schools & Educational Services, nec (pt)**								
	Establishments (number)	-	-	13,547	13,711	14,512	15,313	16,115p	16,916p
	Employment (thousands)	-	-	106.1	115.6	123.3	131.0	138.8p	146.5p
	Revenues ($ million)	-	-	5,217.2	3,378.0p	3,608.1p	3,838.1p	4,068.1p	4,298.2p

Source: *Economic Census of the United States*, 1992, annual surveys of economic sectors conducted by the Bureau of the Census, and estimates or projections based on the 1982-1992 period; not all data are shown. 'e' marks estimates made by the editors; 'p' indicates projections based on time series. A dash (-) indicates that data for this SIC or year were not available. The abbreviation (pt) next to the industry name indicates that only a part of the industry is present within the NAICS data. If no (pt) is shown, the entire industry is contained within the NAICS data.

SELECTED RATIOS

For 1997	Avg. of Information	Analyzed Industry	Index	For 1997	Avg. of Information	Analyzed Industry	Index
Employees per establishment	8	8	105	Payroll per establishment	155,475	171,171	110
Revenue per establishment	499,292	551,188	110	Payroll as % of revenue	31	31	100
Revenue per employee	63,659	66,734	105	Payroll per employee	19,823	20,724	105

Sources: Same as General Statistics. The 'Average' column represents the average for the industry sector, in 1997, where the currently shown industry is classified. The Index shows the relationship between the Average and the Analyzed Industry. For example, 100 means that they are equal; 500 that the Analyzed Industry is five times the average; 50 means that the Analyzed Industry is half the national average. The abbreviation 'na' is used to show that data are 'not available'.

LEADING COMPANIES   Number shown: **23**   Total sales ($ mil): **877**   Total employment (000): **11.1**

Company Name	Address				CEO Name	Phone	Co. Type	Sales ($ mil)	Empl. (000)
Berlitz International Inc.	400 Alexander Park	Princeton	NJ	08540	Hiromasa Yokoi	609-514-9650	P	437	6.0
Youth Services International Inc.	1819 Main St	Sarasota	FL	34236	James Irving	941-953-9199	P	108	1.8
CareerTrack Inc.	PO Box 2951	Shaw Msn	KS	66201	Josh Klarin	303-447-2323	S	90	0.4
SimuFlite Training International	P O Box 619119	Dallas	TX	75261	Jeff Roberts	972-456-8000	D	42*	0.2
Ambassadors International Inc.	110 S Ferrall St	Spokane	WA	99202	Norman Gritsch	509-534-6200	P	40	0.4
Kansas City Aviation Center Inc.	P O Box 1850	Olathe	KS	66063	David Armacost	913-782-0530	S	26	0.1
California Culinary Academy Inc.	625 Polk St	San Francisco	CA	94102	Keith Keogh	415-771-3536	P	18	0.2
Education Collaborative	20 Kent St	Brookline	MA	02445	Thomas Scott	617-738-5600	R	18	0.5
Ambassador Programs Inc.	110 S Ferrall St	Spokane	WA	99202	Jeffrey D Thomas	509-534-6200	S	17	0.1
Art Instruction Schools	3309 Broadway	Minneapolis	MN	55413		612-362-5075	D	16*	0.1
Diplomatic Language Services Inc	1117 N 19th St	Arlington	VA	22209	John B Ratliff III	703-243-4855	R	13*	0.1
Skip Barber Group	29 Brook St	Lakeville	CT	06039	Skip Barber	860-435-1300	R	13	0.1
Comair Aviation Academy Inc.	2700 Flightline Ave	Sanford	FL	32773	Gary Green	407-330-7020	P	12	0.3
Imperial Tutoring Inc.	10341 Lawler Ave	Oak Lawn	IL	60453	Edward E Gordon	708-636-8852	S	11*	0.2
Kaplan Educational Center Inc.	888 7th Ave	New York	NY	10106	Jonathan Grayer	212-492-5800	S	6*	0.4
Merex Corp.	1270 E Broadway	Tempe	AZ	85282	Ray Karesky	602-921-7077	R	3*	<0.1
TRACOM Corp.	8773 S Ridgeline	Highlnds Rch	CO	80126		303-470-4900	S	3*	<0.1
As You Wish Ceramics Inc.	1938 Pearl St	Boulder	CO	80302		303-443-3469	R	2*	<0.1
Be Bilingual Inc.	7670 Woodway	Houston	TX	77063	Elizabeth Phrush	713-789-6338	R	1*	<0.1
Touch of Nature Environmental	SIU 6888	Carbondale	IL	62901		618-453-1121	N	1	<0.1
World Intercultural Network	3372 Cortese Dr	Los Alamitos	CA	90720		562-430-5536	N	1	<0.1
National Institute for Educational	2402 Michelson	Irvine	CA	92612		714-833-7867	N	0	<0.1
Thomas Hedden	555 Forest Ave	Palo Alto	CA	94301		415-323-6752	N	0	<0.1

Source: Ward's Business Directory of U.S. Private and Public Companies, Volumes 1 and 2, 2000. The company type code used is as follows: P - Public, R - Private, S - Subsidiary, D - Division, J - Joint Venture, A - Affiliate, G - Group, N - Company type not reported. Sales are in millions of dollars, employees are in thousands. An asterisk (*) indicates an estimated sales volume. The symbol < stands for 'less than'. Company names and addresses are truncated, in some cases, to fit into the available space.

REPRESENTATIVE NONPROFIT ORGANIZATIONS

Organization Name	Address				Phone	Income Range ($ mil)
Acton Institute for the Study of Religion and Liberty	161 Ottawa Ave NW	Grand Rapids	MI	49503	616-454-3080	1-5
American Secondary Schools for Internatl Students & Teachers	40 General Miller Rd	Peterborough	NH	03458		1-5
Asia Society	725 Park Ave	New York	NY	10021	212-288-6400	50+
Associated Kyoto Program Inc	237 High St	Middletown	CT	06459		1-5
Australearn	110 16th St Third Floor	Denver	CO	80202		1-5
Bucks County Organization for Intercultural Advancement	PO Box 5910	Princeton	NJ	08543		1-5
Chinese Community Center Inc	5855 Sovereign Dr	Houston	TX	77036	713-271-6100	1-5
Ef Intercultural Foundation Inc	One Education St	Cambridge	MA	02141		5-9
Friendship Force Inc	34 Peachtree St	Atlanta	GA	30303	404-522-9490	5-9
Institute for Study Abroad Inc	1100 W 42nd St	Indianapolis	IN	46208		20-29
International Cultural Foundation Inc	51 Monroe St Ste 1201	Rockville	MD	20850	301-762-1280	5-9
International Research and Exchanges Board Inc	1616 H St NW	Washington	DC	20006	202-661-3500	20-29
Little Company of Mary Hospital Inc	2800 W 95th St	Evergreen Park	IL	60805	708-422-0110	50+
Long Home	200 W End Ave	Lancaster	PA	17603	717-397-3926	1-5
Nacel Open Door Inc	3410 Federal Dr 101	Eagan	MN	55122		5-9
Oberlin Shansi Memorial Association	103 Peters Hall	Oberlin	OH	44074		10-19
Project Harmony Inc	5197 Main St Unit 6	Waitsfield	VT	05673	802-496-4545	1-5
Scientific Environmental Research Foundation	8806 Surrey CT	Alexandria	VA	22309		1-5
Shinnyo-En Foundation	201 Mission St 2450	San Francisco	CA	94105	415-777-1977	40-49
West Virginia Symphony Orchestra Inc	1210 Virginia St E	Charleston	WV	25301	304-342-0151	1-5
World Trade Center of Mississippi Inc	PO Box 1842	Gulfport	MS	39502		1-5

Source: National Directory of Nonprofit Organizations, 2000, Volumes 1 and 2, The Taft Group. The table shows a selection of organizations for illustration and does not constitute a complete selection from the source. The organizations are arranged in alphabetical order.

LOCATION BY STATE AND REGIONAL CONCENTRATION

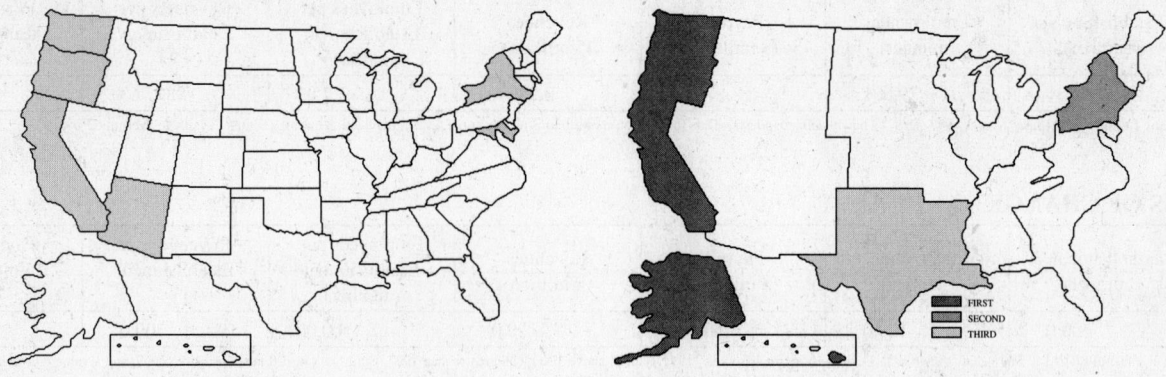

INDUSTRY DATA BY STATE

State	Establishments Total (number)	Establishments % of U.S.	Employment Total (number)	Employment % of U.S.	Employment Per Estab.	Payroll Total ($ mil.)	Payroll Per Empl. ($)	Revenues Total ($ mil.)	Revenues % of U.S.	Revenues Per Estab. ($)
California	792	16.2	7,017	17.4	9	145.9	20,792	486.4	18.1	614,130
New York	349	7.1	3,404	8.4	10	89.2	26,205	303.4	11.3	869,410
Texas	279	5.7	2,648	6.6	9	49.4	18,649	137.5	5.1	492,824
Washington	144	2.9	1,251	3.1	9	28.7	22,955	136.6	5.1	948,417
Maryland	95	1.9	982	2.4	10	28.7	29,214	81.7	3.0	860,000
Illinois	161	3.3	1,471	3.6	9	25.7	17,468	69.8	2.6	433,671
Oregon	79	1.6	691	1.7	9	11.8	17,093	65.4	2.4	827,696
Arizona	105	2.1	917	2.3	9	20.8	22,628	58.2	2.2	553,981
Minnesota	96	2.0	660	1.6	7	14.4	21,842	39.7	1.5	413,646
Wisconsin	47	1.0	415	1.0	9	8.8	21,251	23.4	0.9	498,340
Alabama	42	0.9	363	0.9	9	5.9	16,129	17.9	0.7	426,548
Louisiana	64	1.3	384	1.0	6	4.2	10,896	12.8	0.5	200,719
Kansas	46	0.9	379	0.9	8	5.7	14,953	11.6	0.4	252,609
South Carolina	21	0.4	117	0.3	6	2.2	19,120	7.9	0.3	375,762
West Virginia	18	0.4	126	0.3	7	2.3	18,484	7.9	0.3	437,611
New Hampshire	15	0.3	120	0.3	8	2.4	20,283	7.8	0.3	518,000
Rhode Island	21	0.4	189	0.5	9	2.8	14,836	7.3	0.3	348,476
Mississippi	22	0.5	91	0.2	4	1.7	18,308	5.5	0.2	250,727
Nevada	15	0.3	35	0.1	2	1.2	35,057	4.5	0.2	299,400
Idaho	25	0.5	138	0.3	6	1.6	11,333	4.1	0.2	163,080
Montana	19	0.4	113	0.3	6	1.2	10,637	3.6	0.1	191,000
Nebraska	13	0.3	60	0.1	5	0.7	11,250	2.4	0.1	183,231

Source: 1997 *Economic Census*. The states are in descending order of revenues or establishments (if revenue data are missing for the majority). The symbol (D) appears when data are withheld to prevent disclosure of competitive information. States marked with (D) are sorted by number of establishments. A dash (-) indicates that the data element cannot be calculated. * indicates the midpoint of a range; 175, for example is the range 100-249. Shaded *states* on the state map indicate those states which have proportionately greater representation in the industry than would be indicated by the state's population; the ratio is based on total revenues or number of establishments. Shaded *regions* indicate where the industry is regionally most concentrated.

NAICS 611710 - EDUCATIONAL SUPPORT SERVICES

GENERAL STATISTICS

Year	Establishments (number)	Employment (number)	Payroll ($ million)	Revenues ($ million)	Employees per Establishment (number)	Revenues per Establishment ($)	Payroll per Employee ($)
1997	3,751	29,601	879.0	3,330.0	7.9	887,763	29,695

Source: *Economic Census of the United States*, 1997. This is a newly defined industry. Data for prior years were unavailable at the time of publication but may become available over time.

INDICES OF CHANGE

Year	Establishments (number)	Employment (number)	Payroll ($ million)	Revenues ($ million)	Employees per Establishment (number)	Revenues per Establishment ($)	Payroll per Employee ($)
1997	100.0	100.0	100.0	100.0	100.0	100.0	100.0

Sources: Same as General Statistics. The values shown reflect change from the base year, 1997. Values above 100 mean greater than 1997, values below 100 mean less than 1997, and a value of 100 in the 1982-96 or 1998-2001 period means same as 1997. Values followed by a 'p' are projections by the editors; 'e' stands for extrapolation. Data are the most recent available at this level of detail.

SIC INDUSTRIES RELATED TO NAICS 611710

Each new NAICS code represents an industry that used to be part of an SIC or a part of several SIC industries. Data in this table are shown to provide transitional information for these cases. All available data for the precursor SIC(s) are shown. Even if only a part of an SIC is included in the NAICS, *all* data for the SIC are reproduced. If the SIC industry is not marked as being a part (pt) of the NAICS, the entire industry is embedded in the NAICS data. The SIC composition of the new industry provides some hints of the relative importance of its "ancestors." Data marked with a 'p' are projected. Projections begin with 1982 data. Data earlier than 1990 are not shown but are reflected in the projections.

SIC	Industry	1990	1991	1992	1993	1994	1995	1996	1997
8299	**Schools & Educational Services, nec (pt)**								
	Establishments (number)	-	-	13,547	13,711	14,512	15,313	16,115p	16,916p
	Employment (thousands)	-	-	106.1	115.6	123.3	131.0	138.8p	146.5p
	Revenues ($ million)	-	-	5,217.2	3,378.0p	3,608.1p	3,838.1p	4,068.1p	4,298.2p
8748	**Business Consulting Services, nec (pt)**								
	Establishments (number)	8,819	11,146	13,322	15,561	16,966	18,772	19,284p	20,712p
	Employment (thousands)	70.8	77.9	62.1	72.6	78.6	92.8	87.5p	90.8p
	Revenues ($ million)	6,278.0	6,714.0	7,710.0	8,832.0	9,843.0	12,016.0	13,997.0	14,469.1p

Source: *Economic Census of the United States*, 1992, annual surveys of economic sectors conducted by the Bureau of the Census, and estimates or projections based on the 1982-1992 period; not all data are shown. 'e' marks estimates made by the editors; 'p' indicates projections based on time series. A dash (-) indicates that data for this SIC or year were not available. The abbreviation (pt) next to the industry name indicates that only a part of the industry is present within the NAICS data. If no (pt) is shown, the entire industry is contained within the NAICS data.

SELECTED RATIOS

For 1997	Avg. of Information	Analyzed Industry	Index	For 1997	Avg. of Information	Analyzed Industry	Index
Employees per establishment	8	8	101	Payroll per establishment	155,475	234,338	151
Revenue per establishment	499,292	887,763	178	Payroll as % of revenue	31	26	85
Revenue per employee	63,659	112,496	177	Payroll per employee	19,823	29,695	150

Sources: Same as General Statistics. The 'Average' column represents the average for the industry sector, in 1997, where the currently shown industry is classified. The Index shows the relationship between the Average and the Analyzed Industry. For example, 100 means that they are equal; 500 that the Analyzed Industry is five times the average; 50 means that the Analyzed Industry is half the national average. The abbreviation 'na' is used to show that data are 'not available'.

LEADING COMPANIES

No company data available for this industry.

LOCATION BY STATE AND REGIONAL CONCENTRATION

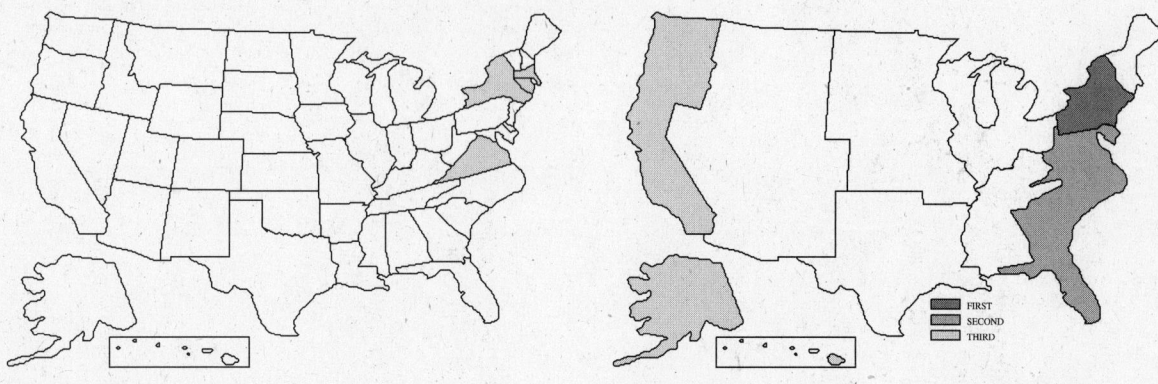

FIRST
SECOND
THIRD

INDUSTRY DATA BY STATE

State	Establishments Total (number)	% of U.S.	Employment Total (number)	% of U.S.	Per Estab.	Payroll Total ($ mil.)	Per Empl. ($)	Revenues Total ($ mil.)	% of U.S.	Per Estab. ($)
New York	290	7.7	3,131	10.6	11	102.1	32,594	615.3	18.5	2,121,817
California	500	13.3	3,320	11.2	7	101.2	30,470	309.7	9.3	619,454
D.C.	78	2.1	1,680	5.7	22	61.2	36,436	304.5	9.1	3,903,449
Texas	231	6.2	2,010	6.8	9	46.9	23,352	133.9	4.0	579,481
Pennsylvania	99	2.6	1,052	3.6	11	33.1	31,481	132.0	4.0	1,333,273
Massachusetts	149	4.0	1,286	4.3	9	37.1	28,825	131.8	4.0	884,557
Virginia	119	3.2	573	1.9	5	24.2	42,265	112.0	3.4	941,261
Connecticut	63	1.7	481	1.6	8	16.8	34,994	97.7	2.9	1,550,397
Illinois	177	4.7	1,064	3.6	6	28.3	26,587	89.2	2.7	504,209
Florida	215	5.7	1,160	3.9	5	22.5	19,412	75.6	2.3	351,423
Michigan	106	2.8	750	2.5	7	24.5	32,627	58.3	1.8	550,085
Washington	104	2.8	440	1.5	4	10.8	24,477	53.8	1.6	517,481
Ohio	121	3.2	716	2.4	6	18.7	26,145	48.8	1.5	403,446
Maryland	95	2.5	419	1.4	4	15.9	38,050	43.0	1.3	452,705
Georgia	86	2.3	432	1.5	5	13.8	31,889	42.0	1.3	488,209
Minnesota	79	2.1	416	1.4	5	9.0	21,697	40.8	1.2	516,886
North Carolina	96	2.6	1,492	5.0	16	15.5	10,410	40.5	1.2	422,188
Colorado	117	3.1	733	2.5	6	14.0	19,068	37.9	1.1	323,838
Oregon	68	1.8	309	1.0	5	8.9	28,845	23.1	0.7	339,632
Missouri	50	1.3	163	0.6	3	3.8	23,460	18.5	0.6	369,760
Indiana	47	1.3	405	1.4	9	6.3	15,474	14.0	0.4	297,447
Oklahoma	28	0.7	144	0.5	5	3.4	23,479	10.9	0.3	390,357
Hawaii	18	0.5	97	0.3	5	2.8	29,206	9.2	0.3	512,389
Kentucky	29	0.8	188	0.6	6	3.2	17,074	8.5	0.3	293,862
Louisiana	30	0.8	113	0.4	4	2.4	21,327	7.2	0.2	239,867
Montana	6	0.2	33	0.1	6	1.1	33,364	3.2	0.1	527,333
Idaho	8	0.2	31	0.1	4	0.8	25,581	1.8	0.1	225,125
North Dakota	4	0.1	10*	-	-	(D)	-	(D)	-	-
Wyoming	3	0.1	10*	-	-	(D)	-	(D)	-	-

Source: 1997 Economic Census. The states are in descending order of revenues or establishments (if revenue data are missing for the majority). The symbol (D) appears when data are withheld to prevent disclosure of competitive information. States marked with (D) are sorted by number of establishments. A dash (-) indicates that the data element cannot be calculated. * indicates the midpoint of a range; 175, for example is the range 100-249. Shaded *states* on the state map indicate those states which have proportionately greater representation in the industry than would be indicated by the state's population; the ratio is based on total revenues or number of establishments. Shaded *regions* indicate where the industry is regionally most concentrated.

Part VIII

HEALTH CARE AND SOCIAL ASSISTANCE

NAICS 621111 - OFFICES OF PHYSICIANS (EXCEPT MENTAL HEALTH SPECIALISTS)

GENERAL STATISTICS

Year	Establishments (number)	Employment (number)	Payroll ($ million)	Revenues ($ million)	Employees per Establishment (number)	Revenues per Establishment ($)	Payroll per Employee ($)
1997	185,094	1,536,459	83,482.0	168,252.0	8.3	909,008	54,334

Source: Economic Census of the United States, 1997. This is a newly defined industry. Data for prior years were unavailable at the time of publication but may become available over time.

INDICES OF CHANGE

Year	Establishments (number)	Employment (number)	Payroll ($ million)	Revenues ($ million)	Employees per Establishment (number)	Revenues per Establishment ($)	Payroll per Employee ($)
1997	100.0	100.0	100.0	100.0	100.0	100.0	100.0

Sources: Same as General Statistics. The values shown reflect change from the base year, 1997. Values above 100 mean greater than 1997, values below 100 mean less than 1997, and a value of 100 in the 1982-96 or 1998-2001 period means same as 1997. Values followed by a 'p' are projections by the editors; 'e' stands for extrapolation. Data are the most recent available at this level of detail.

SIC INDUSTRIES RELATED TO NAICS 621111

Each new NAICS code represents an industry that used to be part of an SIC or a part of several SIC industries. Data in this table are shown to provide transitional information for these cases. All available data for the precursor SIC(s) are shown. Even if only a part of an SIC is included in the NAICS, *all* data for the SIC are reproduced. If the SIC industry is not marked as being a part (pt) of the NAICS, the entire industry is embedded in the NAICS data. The SIC composition of the new industry provides some hints of the relative importance of its "ancestors." Data marked with a 'p' are projected. Projections begin with 1982 data. Data earlier than 1990 are not shown but are reflected in the projections.

SIC	Industry	1990	1991	1992	1993	1994	1995	1996	1997
8011	**Offices of Physicians (pt)**								
	Establishments (number)	193,620	195,610	197,701	200,590	198,538	194,288	198,532p	199,126p
	Employment (thousands)	1,387.2	1,454.0	1,356.7	1,577.1	1,621.4	1,663.9	1,730.5p	1,793.6p
	Revenues ($ million)	128,871.0	138,576.0	151,824.0	154,242.0	159,616.0	167,969.0	173,483.0	186,612.0p
8031	**Offices of Osteopathic Physicians (pt)**								
	Establishments (number)	7,087	7,161	8,708	8,554	8,385	8,022	8,374p	8,496p
	Employment (thousands)	37.9	39.8	47.0	48.9	48.9	49.0	50.8p	52.5p
	Revenues ($ million)	3,254.0	3,584.0	4,008.0	4,159.0	4,354.0	4,698.0	4,760.0	4,995.7p

Source: Economic Census of the United States, 1992, annual surveys of economic sectors conducted by the Bureau of the Census, and estimates or projections based on the 1982-1992 period; not all data are shown. 'e' marks estimates made by the editors; 'p' indicates projections based on time series. A dash (-) indicates that data for this SIC or year were not available. The abbreviation (pt) next to the industry name indicates that only a part of the industry is present within the NAICS data. If no (pt) is shown, the entire industry is contained within the NAICS data.

SELECTED RATIOS

For 1997	Avg. of Information	Analyzed Industry	Index	For 1997	Avg. of Information	Analyzed Industry	Index
Employees per establishment	21	8	40	Payroll per establishment	585,591	451,025	77
Revenue per establishment	1,370,364	909,008	66	Payroll as % of revenue	43	50	116
Revenue per employee	65,262	109,506	168	Payroll per employee	27,888	54,334	195

Sources: Same as General Statistics. The 'Average' column represents the average for the industry sector, in 1997, where the currently shown industry is classified. The Index shows the relationship between the Average and the Analyzed Industry. For example, 100 means that they are equal; 500 that the Analyzed Industry is five times the average; 50 means that the Analyzed Industry is half the national average. The abbreviation 'na' is used to show that data are 'not available'.

LEADING COMPANIES   Number shown: **60**   Total sales ($ mil): **28,105**   Total employment (000): **124.4**

Company Name	Address				CEO Name	Phone	Co. Type	Sales ($ mil)	Empl. (000)
UnitedHealth Group	PO Box 1459	Minneapolis	MN	55440	W. W. McGuire, M.D.	612-936-1300	P	17,106	29.2
HEALTHSOUTH Corp.	1 Healthsouth Pkwy	Birmingham	AL	35243	James P Bennett	205-967-7116	P	4,006	32.6
Scottsdale Healthcare	7301 E 2nd St	Scottsdale	AZ	85251		480-481-4545	D	2,247*	16.0
PhyCor Inc.	30 Burton Hills	Nashville	TN	37215	Thompson S Dent	615-665-9066	P	1,513	21.7
Marshfield Clinic	1000 N Oak Ave	Marshfield	WI	54449		715-387-5511	R	589*	4.2
North Carolina Kids Pediatric	2605 Blue Ridge Rd	Raleigh	NC	27607	James Albright	919-881-9009	R	421*	3.0
Physician Health Services	120 Hawley Ln	Trumbull	CT	06611	Karen Coughlin	203-381-6400	R	281*	2.0
MedCath Inc.	7621 Little Ave	Charlotte	NC	28226	Stephen R Puckett	704-541-3228	R	200	2.0
Pediatrix Medical Group Inc.	PO Box 559001	Fort Lauderdale	FL	33355	Roger J Medel	954-384-0175	P	185	0.9
MacGregor Medical Association	2550 Holly Hall	Houston	TX	77054	James R Birge	713-741-2273	R	166*	1.2
Deaconess Billings Clinic	2800 10th Ave N	Billings	MT	59101	Nicholas Wolter	406-256-2500	R	153	2.1
Woodland Health Care	1207 Fairchild Ct	Woodland	CA	95695	Margaret Cleary	530-666-1631	R	126*	1.0
Aspen Medical Group P.A.	1020 Bandana W	St. Paul	MN	55108	Tom Holets	612-642-2700	R	106*	0.9
Vision America Inc.	5350 Poplar Ave	Memphis	TN	38119	Thomas P Lewis	901-683-7868	P	97	0.7
Diagnostic Clinic Medical Group	1551 W Bay Dr	Largo	FL	33770		813-581-8767	S	84*	0.7
AmSurg Corp.	20 Burton Hills	Nashville	TN	37215	Thomas Cigarran	615-665-1283	P	80	0.3
Molina Medical Centers	1 Golden Shore Dr	Long Beach	CA	90802	J Mario Molina	562-435-3666	R	60*	0.5
Camino Medical Group Inc.	301 Old SF	Sunnyvale	CA	94086	Kathy Rowan	408-739-6000	R	47	0.6
Premier Practice Management	100 10th St N W	Atlanta	GA	30309	Benjamin A Breier	404-897-6816	S	43*	0.4
Kauai Medical Clinic	3-3420 Kuhio Hwy	Lihue	HI	96766	Lee A Evslin	808-245-1500	R	42*	0.3
PAPP Clinic P.C.	PO Box 609	Newnan	GA	30264	Charles Wilson	770-253-6616	S	42*	0.3
IntegraMed America Inc.	1 Manhattanville Rd	Purchase	NY	10577	Gerardo Canet	914-253-8000	P	39	0.4
Galichia Medical Group P.A.	PO Box 47668	Wichita	KS	67214		316-684-3838	R	35*	0.3
Houston Eye Associates	2855 Gramercy St	Houston	TX	77025	Robert B Wilkins MD	713-668-6828	R	35*	0.2
LCA-Vision Inc.	7840 Montgomery	Cincinnati	OH	45236	Dr Stephen Joffe	513-792-9292	P	35	0.1
Managed HealthCare Northwest	2701 NW Vaughn	Portland	OR	97210	Delores Russel	503-224-0409	S	34*	<0.1
Paradigm Health Corp.	1001 Galaxy Way	Concord	CA	94520	Michael Grisham	925-676-2300	R	34*	0.1
Buffalo Cardiology & Pulmonary	P O Box 9060	Williamsville	NY	14231		716-634-5100	R	28*	0.2
Georgia Cancer Specialists P.C.	2712 Lawrenceville	Decatur	GA	30033		770-496-5555	R	28*	0.2
Tidewater Physicians	12388 Warwick	Newport News	VA	23606		757-596-5971	R	28*	0.2
Mid-America Cardiology	4901 Main, Ste 302	Kansas City	MO	64112	Tracy Rasmussen	816-531-5510	R	27*	0.2
Joliet Medical Group Ltd.	2100 Glenwood Ave	Joliet	IL	60435		815-725-2121	R	24*	0.2
Honolulu Medical Group Inc.	550 S Beretania St	Honolulu	HI	96813	Richard L Littenberg	808-537-2211	R	22*	0.2
JSA Healthcare Corp.	111 2nd Ave N E	St. Petersburg	FL	33701	Gary Damkoehler	727-824-0780	R	16*	0.4
West Alabama Health Services Inc	P O Box 599	Eutaw	AL	35462		205-372-4770	R	16	0.3
Koch Eye Associates	566 Tollgate Rd	Warwick	RI	02886		401-738-4800	R	14*	0.1
Eye Health Services Inc.	541 Main St	S. Weymouth	MA	02190	Eric Johnson	781-331-3900	R	13*	0.2
Gila Health Plan Inc.	P O Drawer L	Claypool	AZ	85532	Arthur A Bejarano	520-473-4441	R	9	<0.1
Ortho-Kinetics Inc.	PO Box 1647	Waukesha	WI	53187		414-542-6060	R	7*	<0.1
J.A. Ditty and Associates Inc.	1709 John R Rd	Troy	MI	48083	Jeff A Ditty	248-680-0080	R	7*	<0.1
Medical Park Family Care	2211 E Nor Lights	Anchorage	AK	99508		907-279-8486	R	7*	<0.1
Southern Arizona Anesthesia	3390 N Campbell	Tucson	AZ	85719	David Joseph	520-795-7650	R	7*	<0.1
San Ramon Valley Imaging	3160 Crow Canyon	San Ramon	CA	94583	John Buckhalter	925-866-9447	R	5*	<0.1
St. Louis Eye Clinic Optical	4530 Hampton Ave	St. Louis	MO	63109	KV Rednem	314-352-9800	R	5	<0.1
Cardiology Center of Cincinnati	10525 Montgomery	Cincinnati	OH	45242		513-745-9800	R	4*	<0.1
Dermatology Associates	5555 Peachtree	Atlanta	GA	30342	Edmond Griffin	404-256-4457	R	4	<0.1
East County Urgent Care	1625 E Main St	El Cajon	CA	92021	Jack Wolfe	619-442-9896	R	4*	<0.1
Reproductive Health Associates P	360 Sherman St	St. Paul	MN	55102	Theodor Nagel MD	651-222-8666	R	4*	<0.1
Med7 Urgent Care Center Medical	4156 Manzanita	Carmichael	CA	95608	Meryl O'Brien	916-488-6337	R	3*	<0.1
Samaritan Family Practice	2460 Samaritan Dr	San Jose	CA	95124		408-358-1911	S	3*	<0.1
Thomas Stern, MD	2636 Telegraph Ave	Berkeley	CA	94704		510-841-1647	N	3	<0.1
U.S. Occupational Health Inc.	205 W Randolph St	Chicago	IL	60606		312-641-1449	R	3*	<0.1
Cosmetic & Plastic Surgery	1235 Old York Rd	Abington	PA	19001	James Slavin	215-572-7200	R	1	<0.1
DR Systems Inc.	9369 Carroll Park Dr	San Diego	CA	92121	Murray A Reicher	619-625-3344	R	1*	<0.1
Georgia Plastic Surgery P.C.	2665 N Decatur Rd	Atlanta	GA	30301		404-292-5600	R	1*	<0.1
Houston Eye and Laser Center Inc.	902 Frostwood St	Houston	TX	77024	HT Youens	713-461-2646	R	1*	<0.1
Infertility Center Inc.	2601 E Fortune	Indianapolis	IN	46241	Jane Virro	317-243-8793	R	1*	<0.1
Sports & Orthopedic Physical	825 Nicollet Mall	Minneapolis	MN	55402		612-338-7462	S	1	<0.1
Women's Specialists of Houston	7515 S Main St	Houston	TX	77030	Mark Gottesman	713-797-9277	R	1*	<0.1
X-Ray Ltd.	1014 N CClub	Tucson	AZ	85716	Fred Brickman	520-795-9042	R	1*	<0.1

Source: Ward's Business Directory of U.S. Private and Public Companies, Volumes 1 and 2, 2000. The company type code used is as follows: P - Public, R - Private, S - Subsidiary, D - Division, J - Joint Venture, A - Affiliate, G - Group, N - Company type not reported. Sales are in millions of dollars, employees are in thousands. An asterisk (*) indicates an estimated sales volume. The symbol < stands for 'less than'. Company names and addresses are truncated, in some cases, to fit into the available space.

REPRESENTATIVE NONPROFIT ORGANIZATIONS

Organization Name	Address				Phone	Income Range ($ mil)
Alliance Primary Care	700 W Pete Rose Way	Cincinnati	OH	45203	513-631-1268	30-39
Aspen Medical Group PA	1021 Bandana Blvd E	St Paul	MN	55108		50+
Association of University Physicians	2324 Eastlake Ave E	Seattle	WA	98102		50+
CHW Medical Foundation	10540 White Rock	Rncho Cordova	CA	95670	916-536-3530	50+
Caritas Medical Group Inc	736 Cambridge St	Brighton	MA	02135	617-254-7377	50+
Central Vermont Physician Practice Corporation	PO Box 547	Barre	VT	05641		5-9
Community Foundation of Greater Flint	502 Church St	Flint	MI	48502	810-767-8270	40-49
Cytogenetics Foundation	12717 Davenport Plz	Omaha	NE	68154		1-5
Dartmouth-Hitchcock Clinic	1 Medical Center Dr	Lebanon	NH	03756	603-650-5000	50+
Deaconess Health Services Corporation	5501 N Portland Ave	Oklahoma City	OK	73112	405-604-6138	1-5
Duke University Affiliated Physicans Inc	Duke University	Durham	NC	27710		20-29
Emergency Physicians Services	4 White St	Rockland	ME	04841		1-5
Florida Clinical Practice Association Inc	Box J 354	Gainesville	FL	32602		50+
GHC Partners in Health Inc	701grove Rd	Greenville	SC	29605		10-19
Hmsa Foundation	PO Box 860	Honolulu	HI	96808		1-5
Jefferson University Physicians	1025 Walnut St	Philadelphia	PA	19107		50+
Johns Hopkins Bayview Physicians PA	333 Cassell Dr	Baltimore	MD	21224		50+
Kansas University Physicians Inc	3901 Rainbow Blvd	Kansas City	KS	66160	913-588-6118	30-39
Louisiana State University of Medicine in New Orleans	2020 Gravier St	New Orleans	LA	70112	504-568-6836	40-49
Medical Foundation Inc Non Profit Organization	PO Box 5187	Meridian	MS	39302		10-19
Methodist Medical Group Inc	1633 N Capitol Ave	Indianapolis	IN	46202	317-929-2222	50+
Mill Hill Medical Consultants Inc	50 Ridgefield Ave 218	Bridgeport	CT	06610	203-384-3394	5-9
Northeast Iowa Medical Education Foundation Inc	2055 Kimball Ave	Waterloo	IA	50702		1-5
Northwest Health Services Inc	502 State St	Mound City	MO	64470	660-442-5464	5-9
Pediatric Faculty Association Inc	601 Childrens LN	Norfoljk	VA	23507	757-668-7500	10-19
Physicians Practice Group	1499 Walton Way	Augusta	GA	30901		50+
Rochester Individual Practice Association Inc	2000 Winton Rd S Bldg 1	Rochester	NY	14618		50+
Siu Physicians & Surgeons Inc	PO Box 19620	Springfield	IL	62794		30-39
St Joseph Physician Group	7850 Jefferson St NE	Albuquerque	NM	87109	505-727-4497	10-19
Surgery Departmental Association Inc	550 S Jackson	Louisville	KY	40202		1-5
The Burnett Foundation	801 Cherry St	Fort Worth	TX	76102	817-877-3344	30-39
UT Medical Group Inc	66 N Pauline	Memphis	TN	38105	901-448-6610	50+
University Medicine Foundation Inc	178 Norwood Ave	Cranston	RI	02905		20-29
University Physician Associates of New Jersey	30 Bergen St RM 1202	Newark	NJ	07107		30-39
University Physicians Inc	575 E River Rd	Tucson	AZ	85704	520-321-7295	50+
University Radiologists P C	3181 SW Jackson Park	Portland	OR	97201		1-5
University of Nevada School of Medicine	2040 W Charleston Blvd	Las Vegas	NV	89102		5-9
University of Wisconsin Medical Foundation Inc	8007 Excelsior Dr	Madison	WI	53717	608-833-6090	50+

Source: National Directory of Nonprofit Organizations, 2000, Volumes 1 and 2, The Taft Group. The table shows a selection of organizations for illustration and does not constitute a complete selection from the source. The organizations are arranged in alphabetical order.

LOCATION BY STATE AND REGIONAL CONCENTRATION

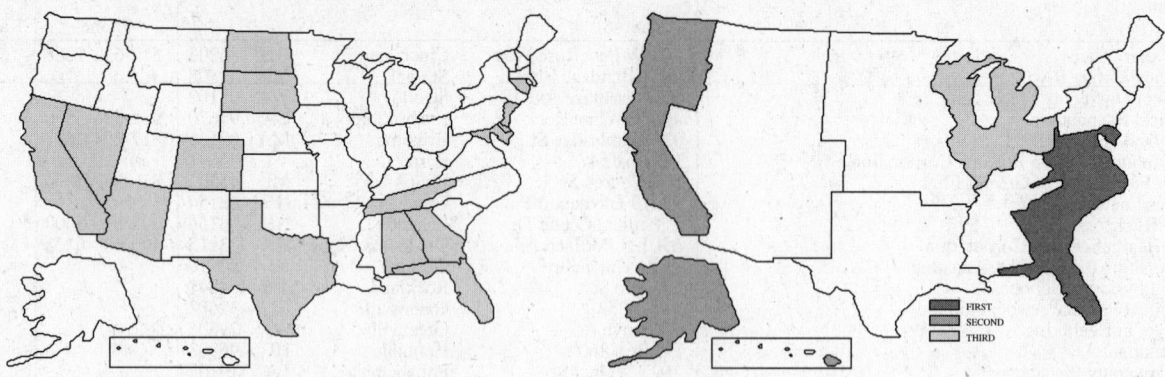

FIRST
SECOND
THIRD

INDUSTRY DATA BY STATE

State	Establishments Total (number)	% of U.S.	Employment Total (number)	% of U.S.	Per Estab.	Payroll Total ($ mil.)	Per Empl. ($)	Revenues Total ($ mil.)	% of U.S.	Per Estab. ($)
California	24,079	13.0	179,539	11.7	7	9,488.1	52,847	22,317.5	13.3	926,843
Texas	14,041	7.6	98,975	6.4	7	5,791.9	58,519	12,439.4	7.4	885,931
New York	15,137	8.2	102,563	6.7	7	5,330.9	51,977	11,966.0	7.1	790,511
Florida	13,784	7.4	108,789	7.1	8	5,807.9	53,386	11,676.1	6.9	847,079
Pennsylvania	9,078	4.9	77,654	5.1	9	4,019.5	51,761	7,594.7	4.5	836,601
Illinois	7,440	4.0	61,477	4.0	8	3,675.2	59,782	7,233.1	4.3	972,190
Ohio	7,573	4.1	66,974	4.4	9	3,771.2	56,309	6,785.4	4.0	896,004
New Jersey	7,644	4.1	51,458	3.3	7	2,980.6	57,923	6,087.7	3.6	796,404
Michigan	6,234	3.4	53,249	3.5	9	2,832.8	53,200	5,137.6	3.1	824,127
Georgia	5,081	2.7	40,475	2.6	8	2,429.7	60,029	4,785.3	2.8	941,810
North Carolina	3,858	2.1	38,852	2.5	10	2,247.5	57,848	4,271.9	2.5	1,107,277
Tennessee	3,620	2.0	37,671	2.5	10	2,133.8	56,642	4,137.6	2.5	1,142,983
Virginia	4,277	2.3	40,927	2.7	10	2,097.7	51,256	3,983.3	2.4	931,328
Massachusetts	3,844	2.1	33,637	2.2	9	1,884.4	56,023	3,574.5	2.1	929,882
Indiana	3,387	1.8	34,140	2.2	10	1,771.5	51,890	3,475.9	2.1	1,026,262
Maryland	4,343	2.3	34,413	2.2	8	1,688.1	49,053	3,354.1	2.0	772,308
Missouri	3,160	1.7	27,870	1.8	9	1,640.9	58,878	3,134.3	1.9	991,859
Wisconsin	2,198	1.2	29,623	1.9	13	1,738.9	58,699	3,049.6	1.8	1,387,465
Washington	3,058	1.7	30,354	2.0	10	1,400.2	46,128	2,818.1	1.7	921,563
Alabama	2,694	1.5	25,473	1.7	9	1,457.4	57,215	2,780.8	1.7	1,032,237
Louisiana	3,051	1.6	24,550	1.6	8	1,249.0	50,874	2,741.8	1.6	898,652
Arizona	3,269	1.8	24,056	1.6	7	1,331.1	55,335	2,684.4	1.6	821,155
Connecticut	2,661	1.4	22,538	1.5	8	1,351.5	59,965	2,616.3	1.6	983,190
Minnesota	1,217	0.7	25,565	1.7	21	1,378.4	53,919	2,367.3	1.4	1,945,223
Kentucky	2,474	1.3	23,199	1.5	9	1,230.4	53,035	2,342.1	1.4	946,675
Colorado	2,586	1.4	20,669	1.3	8	1,179.8	57,082	2,286.4	1.4	884,159
South Carolina	2,216	1.2	19,896	1.3	9	1,117.2	56,151	2,055.1	1.2	927,371
Oregon	2,040	1.1	19,487	1.3	10	917.1	47,061	1,862.4	1.1	912,940
Oklahoma	2,189	1.2	17,276	1.1	8	922.1	53,377	1,812.5	1.1	828,010
Kansas	1,368	0.7	17,209	1.1	13	816.7	47,460	1,566.6	0.9	1,145,207
Iowa	1,283	0.7	14,601	1.0	11	807.1	55,280	1,465.1	0.9	1,141,907
Arkansas	1,645	0.9	14,149	0.9	9	745.9	52,718	1,402.8	0.8	852,739
Mississippi	1,520	0.8	12,818	0.8	8	689.0	53,751	1,392.6	0.8	916,212
Nevada	1,335	0.7	9,910	0.6	7	552.3	55,730	1,220.7	0.7	914,356
West Virginia	1,415	0.8	10,995	0.7	8	537.7	48,905	1,124.0	0.7	794,372
Utah	1,219	0.7	10,296	0.7	8	507.5	49,290	1,039.8	0.6	853,007
Nebraska	774	0.4	8,820	0.6	11	484.2	54,900	882.2	0.5	1,139,752
Hawaii	1,022	0.6	6,035	0.4	6	355.2	58,857	720.7	0.4	705,161
Maine	838	0.5	6,384	0.4	8	350.3	54,878	635.2	0.4	757,973
New Mexico	941	0.5	6,974	0.5	7	309.3	44,354	626.2	0.4	665,430
New Hampshire	656	0.4	6,314	0.4	10	376.7	59,654	613.8	0.4	935,678
Idaho	752	0.4	5,946	0.4	8	308.6	51,894	600.7	0.4	798,831
Rhode Island	764	0.4	5,163	0.3	7	256.2	49,630	525.6	0.3	687,948
Delaware	572	0.3	4,473	0.3	8	270.5	60,471	500.6	0.3	875,135
D.C.	587	0.3	3,563	0.2	6	221.2	62,075	462.4	0.3	787,712
Montana	586	0.3	4,353	0.3	7	219.3	50,382	438.8	0.3	748,833
North Dakota	191	0.1	4,537	0.3	24	203.2	44,780	427.8	0.3	2,239,607
South Dakota	332	0.2	4,332	0.3	13	221.6	51,158	424.2	0.3	1,277,780
Alaska	356	0.2	2,698	0.2	8	154.8	57,377	316.6	0.2	889,371
Vermont	360	0.2	3,285	0.2	9	122.8	37,377	278.8	0.2	774,319
Wyoming	345	0.2	2,255	0.1	7	107.1	47,498	215.6	0.1	624,939

Source: 1997 *Economic Census*. The states are in descending order of revenues or establishments (if revenue data are missing for the majority). The symbol (D) appears when data are withheld to prevent disclosure of competitive information. States marked with (D) are sorted by number of establishments. A dash (-) indicates that the data element cannot be calculated. * indicates the midpoint of a range; 175, for example is the range 100-249. Shaded *states* on the state map indicate those states which have proportionately greater representation in the industry than would be indicated by the state's population; the ratio is based on total revenues or number of establishments. Shaded *regions* indicate where the industry is regionally most concentrated.

NAICS 621112 - OFFICES OF PHYSICIANS, MENTAL HEALTH SPECIALISTS

GENERAL STATISTICS

Year	Establishments (number)	Employment (number)	Payroll ($ million)	Revenues ($ million)	Employees per Establishment (number)	Revenues per Establishment ($)	Payroll per Employee ($)
1997	10,355	34,686	1,494.0	3,377.0	3.3	326,123	43,072

Source: Economic Census of the United States, 1997. This is a newly defined industry. Data for prior years were unavailable at the time of publication but may become available over time.

INDICES OF CHANGE

Year	Establishments (number)	Employment (number)	Payroll ($ million)	Revenues ($ million)	Employees per Establishment (number)	Revenues per Establishment ($)	Payroll per Employee ($)
1997	100.0	100.0	100.0	100.0	100.0	100.0	100.0

Sources: Same as General Statistics. The values shown reflect change from the base year, 1997. Values above 100 mean greater than 1997, values below 100 mean less than 1997, and a value of 100 in the 1982-96 or 1998-2001 period means same as 1997. Values followed by a 'p' are projections by the editors; 'e' stands for extrapolation. Data are the most recent available at this level of detail.

SIC INDUSTRIES RELATED TO NAICS 621112

Each new NAICS code represents an industry that used to be part of an SIC or a part of several SIC industries. Data in this table are shown to provide transitional information for these cases. All available data for the precursor SIC(s) are shown. Even if only a part of an SIC is included in the NAICS, *all* data for the SIC are reproduced. If the SIC industry is not marked as being a part (pt) of the NAICS, the entire industry is embedded in the NAICS data. The SIC composition of the new industry provides some hints of the relative importance of its "ancestors." Data marked with a 'p' are projected. Projections begin with 1982 data. Data earlier than 1990 are not shown but are reflected in the projections.

SIC	Industry	1990	1991	1992	1993	1994	1995	1996	1997
8011	**Offices of Physicians (pt)**								
	Establishments (number)	193,620	195,610	197,701	200,590	198,538	194,288	198,532p	199,126p
	Employment (thousands)	1,387.2	1,454.0	1,356.7	1,577.1	1,621.4	1,663.9	1,730.5p	1,793.6p
	Revenues ($ million)	128,871.0	138,576.0	151,824.0	154,242.0	159,616.0	167,969.0	173,483.0	186,612.0p
8031	**Offices of Osteopathic Physicians (pt)**								
	Establishments (number)	7,087	7,161	8,708	8,554	8,385	8,022	8,374p	8,496p
	Employment (thousands)	37.9	39.8	47.0	48.9	48.9	49.0	50.8p	52.5p
	Revenues ($ million)	3,254.0	3,584.0	4,008.0	4,159.0	4,354.0	4,698.0	4,760.0	4,995.7p

Source: Economic Census of the United States, 1992, annual surveys of economic sectors conducted by the Bureau of the Census, and estimates or projections based on the 1982-1992 period; not all data are shown. 'e' marks estimates made by the editors; 'p' indicates projections based on time series. A dash (-) indicates that data for this SIC or year were not available. The abbreviation (pt) next to the industry name indicates that only a part of the industry is present within the NAICS data. If no (pt) is shown, the entire industry is contained within the NAICS data.

SELECTED RATIOS

For 1997	Avg. of Information	Analyzed Industry	Index	For 1997	Avg. of Information	Analyzed Industry	Index
Employees per establishment	21	3	16	Payroll per establishment	585,591	144,278	25
Revenue per establishment	1,370,364	326,123	24	Payroll as % of revenue	43	44	104
Revenue per employee	65,262	97,359	149	Payroll per employee	27,888	43,072	154

Sources: Same as General Statistics. The 'Average' column represents the average for the industry sector, in 1997, where the currently shown industry is classified. The Index shows the relationship between the Average and the Analyzed Industry. For example, 100 means that they are equal; 500 that the Analyzed Industry is five times the average; 50 means that the Analyzed Industry is half the national average. The abbreviation 'na' is used to show that data are 'not available'.

LEADING COMPANIES

No company data available for this industry.

LOCATION BY STATE AND REGIONAL CONCENTRATION

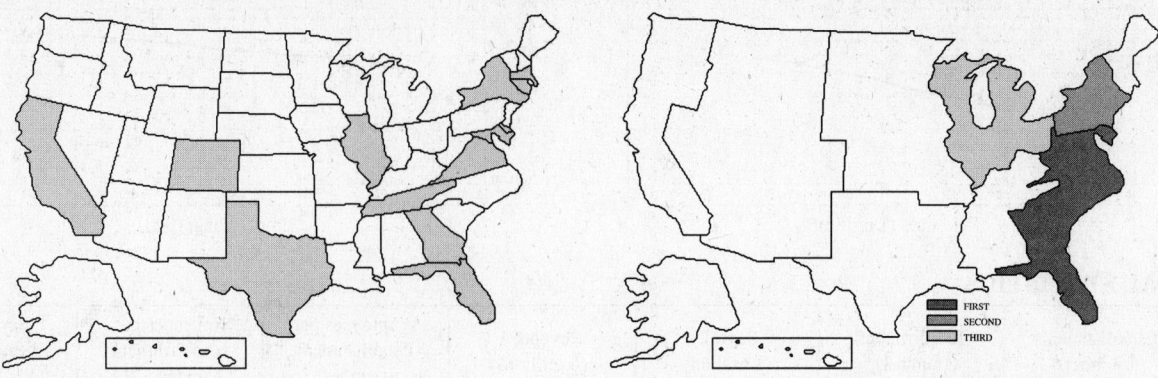

FIRST
SECOND
THIRD

INDUSTRY DATA BY STATE

State	Establishments Total (number)	% of U.S.	Employment Total (number)	% of U.S.	Per Estab.	Payroll Total ($ mil.)	Per Empl. ($)	Revenues Total ($ mil.)	% of U.S.	Per Estab. ($)
California	1,456	14.1	3,644	10.5	3	179.7	49,316	425.7	12.6	292,387
Texas	785	7.6	2,613	7.5	3	115.9	44,344	300.4	8.9	382,724
New York	876	8.5	2,079	6.0	2	100.1	48,162	272.0	8.1	310,526
Florida	793	7.7	2,804	8.1	4	110.9	39,543	258.0	7.6	325,400
Illinois	487	4.7	1,857	5.4	4	91.3	49,150	179.9	5.3	369,343
Pennsylvania	417	4.0	1,648	4.8	4	68.5	41,587	141.1	4.2	338,477
Ohio	358	3.5	1,406	4.1	4	57.4	40,854	126.0	3.7	351,838
Georgia	317	3.1	1,328	3.8	4	58.8	44,264	117.1	3.5	369,300
Michigan	346	3.3	1,240	3.6	4	54.5	43,940	107.5	3.2	310,812
New Jersey	346	3.3	888	2.6	3	41.2	46,366	102.9	3.0	297,289
Maryland	296	2.9	1,002	2.9	3	44.0	43,935	100.1	3.0	338,152
Virginia	292	2.8	1,130	3.3	4	45.9	40,614	94.3	2.8	322,822
Massachusetts	260	2.5	1,113	3.2	4	42.7	38,363	93.3	2.8	358,869
Tennessee	183	1.8	809	2.3	4	32.1	39,644	81.8	2.4	446,787
North Carolina	213	2.1	951	2.7	4	34.6	36,419	71.1	2.1	333,676
Connecticut	204	2.0	700	2.0	3	31.7	45,253	68.8	2.0	337,020
Colorado	195	1.9	684	2.0	4	31.4	45,944	60.4	1.8	309,656
Missouri	197	1.9	744	2.1	4	30.4	40,926	57.4	1.7	291,208
Wisconsin	141	1.4	694	2.0	5	30.4	43,775	53.1	1.6	376,645
Louisiana	161	1.6	591	1.7	4	20.3	34,428	48.4	1.4	300,509
Kentucky	121	1.2	492	1.4	4	19.4	39,411	48.2	1.4	398,281
Alabama	103	1.0	522	1.5	5	20.9	39,966	45.4	1.3	441,068
Minnesota	100	1.0	427	1.2	4	21.6	50,644	44.5	1.3	445,160
Washington	185	1.8	512	1.5	3	19.0	37,129	41.3	1.2	223,470
Indiana	131	1.3	438	1.3	3	17.9	40,909	39.0	1.2	298,015
Arizona	143	1.4	351	1.0	2	15.6	44,524	37.3	1.1	260,517
Iowa	65	0.6	414	1.2	6	17.8	42,918	31.9	0.9	491,538
South Carolina	110	1.1	388	1.1	4	14.3	36,755	31.2	0.9	283,209
Arkansas	67	0.6	293	0.8	4	13.3	45,498	29.6	0.9	441,343
Oklahoma	106	1.0	293	0.8	3	12.0	40,884	27.0	0.8	255,066
Kansas	78	0.8	269	0.8	3	10.0	37,004	23.7	0.7	303,590
Mississippi	76	0.7	237	0.7	3	7.0	29,671	21.9	0.6	287,842
Oregon	112	1.1	205	0.6	2	8.8	43,083	20.9	0.6	186,420
West Virginia	47	0.5	250	0.7	5	8.0	32,192	19.4	0.6	412,383
D.C.	80	0.8	114	0.3	1	7.7	67,939	16.9	0.5	211,738
Utah	56	0.5	199	0.6	4	6.6	33,166	14.8	0.4	263,661
New Hampshire	38	0.4	200	0.6	5	6.0	29,765	14.6	0.4	385,211
Delaware	32	0.3	135	0.4	4	5.3	39,615	12.7	0.4	395,438
Idaho	41	0.4	115	0.3	3	5.1	44,748	12.4	0.4	302,195
Nevada	37	0.4	113	0.3	3	4.6	40,372	12.1	0.4	326,297
Rhode Island	41	0.4	130	0.4	3	5.3	40,808	11.8	0.3	288,024
Maine	34	0.3	115	0.3	3	5.6	48,296	11.0	0.3	324,206
Hawaii	54	0.5	90	0.3	2	3.9	43,856	10.6	0.3	196,315
Nebraska	44	0.4	118	0.3	3	4.1	34,559	10.0	0.3	227,568
New Mexico	51	0.5	97	0.3	2	3.7	38,268	8.3	0.2	162,000
Alaska	13	0.1	65	0.2	5	2.3	34,785	4.6	0.1	353,923
South Dakota	10	0.1	51	0.1	5	2.4	47,863	4.5	0.1	453,100
Montana	18	0.2	36	0.1	2	1.3	36,528	4.3	0.1	240,778
Vermont	21	0.2	22	0.1	1	1.2	53,591	3.4	0.1	162,905
North Dakota	8	0.1	42	0.1	5	1.3	31,571	3.0	0.1	378,625
Wyoming	10	0.1	28	0.1	3	0.5	16,571	1.8	0.1	176,100

Source: 1997 *Economic Census*. The states are in descending order of revenues or establishments (if revenue data are missing for the majority). The symbol (D) appears when data are withheld to prevent disclosure of competitive information. States marked with (D) are sorted by number of establishments. A dash (-) indicates that the data element cannot be calculated. * indicates the midpoint of a range; 175, for example is the range 100-249. Shaded *states* on the state map indicate those states which have proportionately greater representation in the industry than would be indicated by the state's population; the ratio is based on total revenues or number of establishments. Shaded *regions* indicate where the industry is regionally most concentrated.

NAICS 621210 - OFFICES OF DENTISTS*

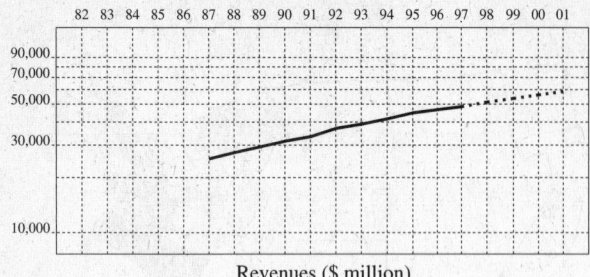

Revenues ($ million)

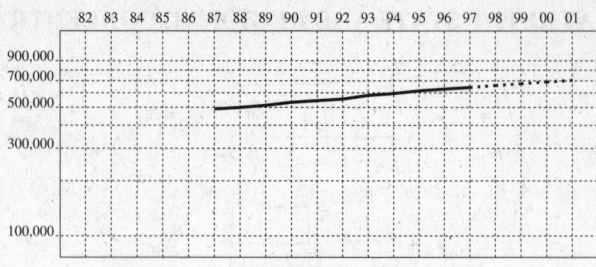

Employment (000)

GENERAL STATISTICS

Year	Establishments (number)	Employment (number)	Payroll ($ million)	Revenues ($ million)	Employees per Establishment (number)	Revenues per Establishment ($)	Payroll per Employee ($)
1982	-	-	-	-	-	-	-
1983	-	-	-	-	-	-	-
1984	-	-	-	-	-	-	-
1985	-	-	-	-	-	-	-
1986	-	-	-	-	-	-	-
1987	104,151	491,536	8,760.0	25,258.0	4.7	242,513	17,822
1988	102,241	499,440	9,958.0	27,325.0	4.9	267,261	19,938
1989	103,279	512,894	10,588.0	29,297.0	5.0	283,669	20,644
1990	104,654	533,248	11,618.0	31,502.0	5.1	301,011	21,787
1991	106,362	544,472	12,321.0	33,279.0	5.1	312,884	22,629
1992	108,804	554,589	13,039.0	36,939.0	5.1	339,500	23,511
1993	109,818	581,378	14,171.0	38,946.0	5.3	354,641	24,375
1994	110,559	594,259	14,997.0	41,663.0	5.4	376,840	25,236
1995	111,204	615,303	16,139.0	44,909.0	5.5	403,843	26,229
1996	112,691 e	628,488 e	17,183.0 e	46,695.0 e	5.6 e	414,363 e	27,340 e
1997	114,178	641,674	18,227.0	48,482.0	5.6	424,618	28,405
1998	115,139 p	657,918 p	18,900.0 p	51,287.0 p	5.7 p	445,436 p	28,727 p
1999	116,329 p	673,673 p	19,823.0 p	53,709.0 p	5.8 p	461,699 p	29,425 p
2000	117,520 p	689,428 p	20,745.0 p	56,131.0 p	5.9 p	477,629 p	30,090 p
2001	118,711 p	705,183 p	21,668.0 p	58,553.0 p	5.9 p	493,240 p	30,727 p

Sources: *Economic Census of the United States*, 1982, 1987, 1992, 1997. Establishment counts, employment, and payroll are from *County Business Patterns* for non-Census years. In non-Census years, industries in the Manufacturing range under SIC coding include data from the *Annual Survey of Manufactures* (*ASM*); those in the old Services range include data from the *Services Annual Survey* (*SAS*). Values followed by a 'p' are projections by the editors. Extrapolations are marked by 'e'. Data are the most recent available at this level of detail.

INDICES OF CHANGE

Year	Establishments (number)	Employment (number)	Payroll ($ million)	Revenues ($ million)	Employees per Establishment (number)	Revenues per Establishment ($)	Payroll per Employee ($)
1982	-	-	-	-	-	-	-
1987	91.2	76.6	48.1	52.1	84.0	57.1	62.7
1992	95.3	86.4	71.5	76.2	90.7	80.0	82.8
1993	96.2	90.6	77.7	80.3	94.2	83.5	85.8
1994	96.8	92.6	82.3	85.9	95.6	88.7	88.8
1995	97.4	95.9	88.5	92.6	98.5	95.1	92.3
1996	98.7 e	97.9 e	94.3 e	96.3 e	99.2 e	97.6 e	96.3 e
1997	100.0	100.0	100.0	100.0	100.0	100.0	100.0
1998	100.8 p	102.5 p	103.7 p	105.8 p	101.7 p	104.9 p	101.1 p
1999	101.9 p	105.0 p	108.8 p	110.8 p	103.0 p	108.7 p	103.6 p
2000	102.9 p	107.4 p	113.8 p	115.8 p	104.4 p	112.5 p	105.9 p
2001	104.0 p	109.9 p	118.9 p	120.8 p	105.7 p	116.2 p	108.2 p

Sources: Same as General Statistics. The values shown reflect change from the base year, 1997. Values above 100 mean greater than 1997, values below 100 mean less than 1997, and a value of 100 in the 1982-96 or 1998-2001 period means same as 1997. Values followed by a 'p' are projections by the editors; 'e' stands for extrapolation. Data are the most recent available at this level of detail.

SELECTED RATIOS

For 1997	Avg. of Information	Analyzed Industry	Index	For 1997	Avg. of Information	Analyzed Industry	Index
Employees per establishment	21	6	27	Payroll per establishment	585,591	159,637	27
Revenue per establishment	1,370,364	424,618	31	Payroll as % of revenue	43	38	88
Revenue per employee	65,262	75,556	116	Payroll per employee	27,888	28,405	102

Sources: Same as General Statistics. The 'Average' column represents the average for the industry sector, in 1997, where the currently shown industry is classified. The Index shows the relationship between the Average and the Analyzed Industry. For example, 100 means that they are equal; 500 that the Analyzed Industry is five times the average; 50 means that the Analyzed Industry is half the national average. The abbreviation 'na' is used to show that data are 'not available'.

*Equivalent to SIC 8021.

LEADING COMPANIES   Number shown: **12**   Total sales ($ mil): **1,287**   Total employment (000): **5.6**

Company Name	Address				CEO Name	Phone	Co. Type	Sales ($ mil)	Empl. (000)
Dental Services of America Inc.	2260 S W 8th St	Miami	FL	33135	Luis Cruz	305-642-9090	P	749	<0.1
Orthodontic Centers of America	5000 Sawgrass	Pte Vedra Bch	FL	32082	Geoffrey Faux	904-280-4500	P	226	2.1
Safeguard Health Enterprises Inc.	P O Box 3210	Anaheim	CA	92803	Steven J Baileys	949-425-4300	P	97	0.3
Castle Dental Center Inc.	1360 Post Oak Blvd	Houston	TX	77056	Jack H Castle Jr	713-479-8000	P	75	1.2
Apple Orthodontix Inc.	2777 Allen Pkwy	Houston	TX	77019	A Stone Douglass	281-698-2500	P	48*	0.7
Coast Dental Services Inc.	2502 Rocky Pt Dr N	Tampa	FL	33607	Adam Diasti	813-288-1999	P	35	0.6
Rx Medical Services Corp.	888 E Las Olas	Fort Lauderdale	FL	33301	Mihael L Goldberg	954-462-1711	P	20	0.3
Princeton Dental Management	7421 W 100th Pl	Bridgeview	IL	60455	Frank Leonard Laport	708-974-4000	P	12	0.2
HealthDrive Medical & Dental	25 Needham St	Newton	MA	02461	Steven Charlap	617-964-6681	R	11*	0.2
Mark R. Morin D.D.S. P.C.	19178 W 10 Mile Rd	Southfield	MI	48075	Dr Mark R Morin	248-354-1555	R	10*	<0.1
Adult & Implant Dentistry	1350 W Gonzalez	Oxnard	CA	93030	Richard A Gagne	805-485-2777	R	3*	<0.1
Prosthodontics Intermedica	467 Pennsylvania	Fort Washington	PA	19034	Thomas J Balshi	215-646-6334	R	1	<0.1

Source: Ward's Business Directory of U.S. Private and Public Companies, Volumes 1 and 2, 2000. The company type code used is as follows: P - Public, R - Private, S - Subsidiary, D - Division, J - Joint Venture, A - Affiliate, G - Group, N - Company type not reported. Sales are in millions of dollars, employees are in thousands. An asterisk (*) indicates an estimated sales volume. The symbol < stands for 'less than'. Company names and addresses are truncated, in some cases, to fit into the available space.

LOCATION BY STATE AND REGIONAL CONCENTRATION

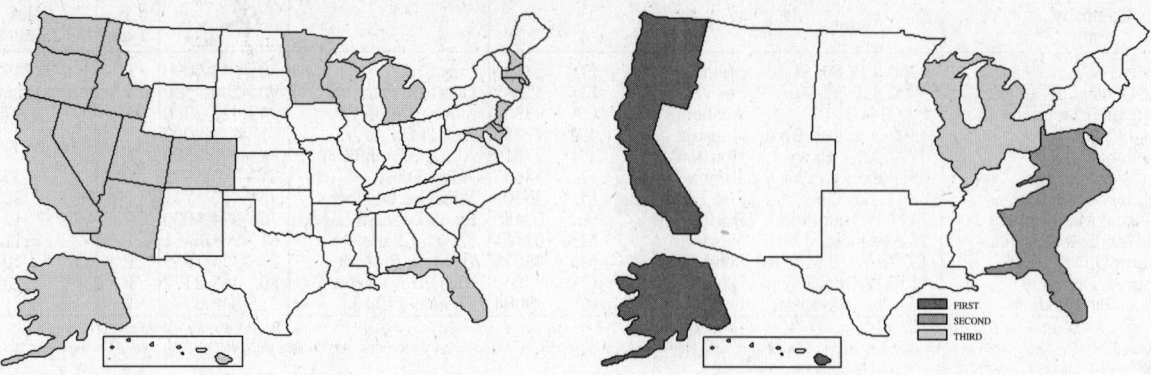

FIRST
SECOND
THIRD

INDUSTRY DATA BY STATE

State	Establishments Total (number)	% of U.S.	Employment Total (number)	% of U.S.	Per Estab.	Payroll Total ($ mil.)	Per Empl. ($)	Revenues Total ($ mil.)	% of U.S.	Per Estab. ($)
California	16,269	14.2	90,084	14.0	6	2,527.3	28,054	7,262.1	15.0	446,376
New York	8,694	7.6	41,912	6.5	5	1,094.3	26,110	3,365.1	6.9	387,060
Texas	6,691	5.9	35,291	5.5	5	1,036.8	29,379	2,811.1	5.8	420,133
Florida	6,182	5.4	34,667	5.4	6	1,064.9	30,718	2,677.4	5.5	433,095
Pennsylvania	5,433	4.8	29,121	4.5	5	735.6	25,259	2,040.2	4.2	375,515
Illinois	5,383	4.7	28,691	4.5	5	787.2	27,439	2,032.9	4.2	377,649
Michigan	4,352	3.8	28,894	4.5	7	829.8	28,718	1,960.3	4.0	450,436
New Jersey	4,272	3.7	22,908	3.6	5	679.8	29,674	1,803.1	3.7	422,076
Ohio	4,519	4.0	26,239	4.1	6	710.8	27,090	1,778.7	3.7	393,602
Washington	2,827	2.5	18,772	2.9	7	588.4	31,344	1,554.2	3.2	549,787
Massachusetts	2,929	2.6	17,635	2.7	6	508.0	28,805	1,343.0	2.8	458,523
Georgia	2,574	2.3	16,000	2.5	6	484.2	30,262	1,228.1	2.5	477,108
North Carolina	2,323	2.0	14,524	2.3	6	481.7	33,162	1,171.8	2.4	504,422
Virginia	2,645	2.3	15,078	2.3	6	475.0	31,506	1,136.0	2.3	429,474
Wisconsin	2,203	1.9	14,366	2.2	7	424.8	29,568	979.2	2.0	444,465
Maryland	2,371	2.1	13,001	2.0	5	384.3	29,556	952.5	2.0	401,741
Minnesota	2,002	1.8	12,504	1.9	6	383.5	30,667	942.8	1.9	470,948
Indiana	2,208	1.9	12,865	2.0	6	338.1	26,282	902.9	1.9	408,918
Colorado	2,042	1.8	10,694	1.7	5	327.5	30,625	833.3	1.7	408,087
Connecticut	1,774	1.6	9,998	1.6	6	309.7	30,981	826.4	1.7	465,831
Tennessee	2,050	1.8	10,806	1.7	5	281.8	26,080	814.0	1.7	397,068
Oregon	1,680	1.5	10,227	1.6	6	298.2	29,154	810.4	1.7	482,404
Missouri	2,052	1.8	11,112	1.7	5	306.6	27,590	783.7	1.6	381,919
Arizona	1,641	1.4	9,712	1.5	6	306.7	31,577	758.6	1.6	462,255
Louisiana	1,541	1.3	8,934	1.4	6	221.2	24,763	642.7	1.3	417,048
Alabama	1,356	1.2	7,928	1.2	6	219.8	27,725	585.7	1.2	431,956
South Carolina	1,216	1.1	7,219	1.1	6	213.6	29,591	531.7	1.1	437,257
Kentucky	1,516	1.3	7,431	1.2	5	172.2	23,178	479.8	1.0	316,495
Oklahoma	1,268	1.1	6,461	1.0	5	164.5	25,467	455.4	0.9	359,185
Iowa	1,113	1.0	6,202	1.0	6	163.7	26,391	430.8	0.9	387,052
Kansas	1,012	0.9	6,098	1.0	6	164.3	26,939	428.6	0.9	423,526
Utah	1,088	1.0	5,904	0.9	5	135.8	23,007	402.2	0.8	369,642
Arkansas	898	0.8	4,805	0.7	5	124.3	25,865	348.0	0.7	387,532
Nevada	575	0.5	3,649	0.6	6	132.9	36,411	328.7	0.7	571,610
Mississippi	780	0.7	3,941	0.6	5	104.5	26,522	290.0	0.6	371,849
Hawaii	657	0.6	3,266	0.5	5	101.5	31,066	267.6	0.6	407,301
Nebraska	754	0.7	3,814	0.6	5	94.1	24,660	252.5	0.5	334,887
New Hampshire	533	0.5	3,266	0.5	6	97.2	29,761	248.1	0.5	465,538
New Mexico	557	0.5	3,207	0.5	6	90.6	28,260	232.9	0.5	418,052
Idaho	502	0.4	3,226	0.5	6	80.9	25,085	226.8	0.5	451,837
Maine	462	0.4	2,824	0.4	6	80.6	28,544	205.3	0.4	444,325
West Virginia	588	0.5	3,082	0.5	5	62.1	20,141	200.4	0.4	340,733
Rhode Island	410	0.4	2,596	0.4	6	71.3	27,463	193.4	0.4	471,659
Alaska	292	0.3	1,867	0.3	6	58.3	31,231	158.5	0.3	542,873
Delaware	218	0.2	1,774	0.3	6	67.5	38,054	142.3	0.3	652,550
Montana	419	0.4	2,075	0.3	5	47.8	23,038	138.7	0.3	331,012
D.C.	329	0.3	1,339	0.2	4	51.9	38,782	135.7	0.3	412,602
Vermont	256	0.2	1,635	0.3	6	42.1	25,719	110.9	0.2	433,270
South Dakota	267	0.2	1,555	0.2	6	37.1	23,841	109.5	0.2	410,041
North Dakota	246	0.2	1,376	0.2	6	37.3	27,131	98.8	0.2	401,634
Wyoming	209	0.2	1,099	0.2	5	24.8	22,556	69.3	0.1	331,732

Source: 1997 *Economic Census*. The states are in descending order of revenues or establishments (if revenue data are missing for the majority). The symbol (D) appears when data are withheld to prevent disclosure of competitive information. States marked with (D) are sorted by number of establishments. A dash (-) indicates that the data element cannot be calculated. * indicates the midpoint of a range; 175, for example is the range 100-249. Shaded *states* on the state map indicate those states which have proportionately greater representation in the industry than would be indicated by the state's population; the ratio is based on total revenues or number of establishments. Shaded *regions* indicate where the industry is regionally most concentrated.

NAICS 621310 - OFFICES OF CHIROPRACTORS*

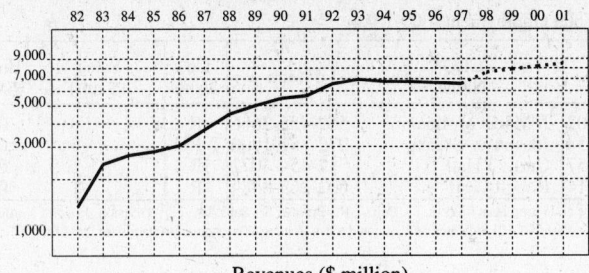

Revenues ($ million)

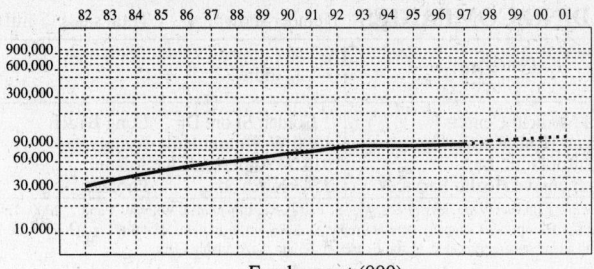

Employment (000)

GENERAL STATISTICS

Year	Establishments (number)	Employment (number)	Payroll ($ million)	Revenues ($ million)	Employees per Establishment (number)	Revenues per Establishment ($)	Payroll per Employee ($)
1982	12,937	32,538	372.0	1,413.0	2.5	109,222	11,433
1983	14,363 e	37,639 e	477.0 e	2,413.0	2.6 e	168,001 e	12,673 e
1984	15,788 e	42,739 e	583.0 e	2,689.0	2.7 e	170,319 e	13,641 e
1985	17,214 e	47,840 e	689.0 e	2,818.0	2.8 e	163,704 e	14,402 e
1986	18,639 e	52,940 e	794.0 e	3,038.0	2.8 e	162,992 e	14,998 e
1987	20,065	58,041	900.0	3,707.0	2.9	184,750	15,506
1988	20,056	60,987	1,049.0	4,510.0	3.0	224,870	17,200
1989	21,701	66,694	1,180.0	5,005.0	3.1	230,635	17,693
1990	22,899	73,020	1,318.0	5,467.0	3.2	238,744	18,050
1991	24,572	77,158	1,460.0	5,647.0	3.1	229,814	18,922
1992	27,329	84,730	1,652.0	6,555.0	3.1	239,855	19,497
1993	28,288	89,177	1,744.0	6,936.0	3.2	245,192	19,557
1994	28,768	89,121	1,737.0	6,757.0	3.1	234,879	19,490
1995	29,022	89,063	1,766.0	6,742.0	3.1	232,307	19,829
1996	29,755 e	90,381 e	1,826.0 e	6,656.0 e	3.0 e	223,693 e	20,203 e
1997	30,487	91,700	1,886.0	6,570.0	3.0	215,502	20,567
1998	32,721 p	100,763 p	2,097.0 p	7,613.0 p	3.1 p	232,664 p	20,811 p
1999	33,888 p	104,374 p	2,197.0 p	7,903.0 p	3.1 p	233,209 p	21,049 p
2000	35,055 p	107,985 p	2,296.0 p	8,194.0 p	3.1 p	233,747 p	21,262 p
2001	36,221 p	111,596 p	2,395.0 p	8,485.0 p	3.1 p	234,256 p	21,461 p

Sources: Economic Census of the United States, 1982, 1987, 1992, 1997. Establishment counts, employment, and payroll are from County Business Patterns for non-Census years. In non-Census years, industries in the Manufacturing range under SIC coding include data from the Annual Survey of Manufactures (ASM); those in the old Services range include data from the Services Annual Survey (SAS). Values followed by a 'p' are projections by the editors. Extrapolations are marked by 'e'. Data are the most recent available at this level of detail.

INDICES OF CHANGE

Year	Establishments (number)	Employment (number)	Payroll ($ million)	Revenues ($ million)	Employees per Establishment (number)	Revenues per Establishment ($)	Payroll per Employee ($)
1982	42.4	35.5	19.7	21.5	83.6	50.7	55.6
1987	65.8	63.3	47.7	56.4	96.2	85.7	75.4
1992	89.6	92.4	87.6	99.8	103.1	111.3	94.8
1993	92.8	97.2	92.5	105.6	104.8	113.8	95.1
1994	94.4	97.2	92.1	102.8	103.0	109.0	94.8
1995	95.2	97.1	93.6	102.6	102.0	107.8	96.4
1996	97.6 e	98.6 e	96.8 e	101.3 e	101.0 e	103.8 e	98.2 e
1997	100.0	100.0	100.0	100.0	100.0	100.0	100.0
1998	107.3 p	109.9 p	111.2 p	115.9 p	102.4 p	108.0 p	101.2 p
1999	111.2 p	113.8 p	116.5 p	120.3 p	102.4 p	108.2 p	102.3 p
2000	115.0 p	117.8 p	121.7 p	124.7 p	102.4 p	108.5 p	103.4 p
2001	118.8 p	121.7 p	127.0 p	129.1 p	102.4 p	108.7 p	104.3 p

Sources: Same as General Statistics. The values shown reflect change from the base year, 1997. Values above 100 mean greater than 1997, values below 100 mean less than 1997, and a value of 100 in the 1982-96 or 1998-2001 period means same as 1997. Values followed by a 'p' are projections by the editors; 'e' stands for extrapolation. Data are the most recent available at this level of detail.

SELECTED RATIOS

For 1997	Avg. of Information	Analyzed Industry	Index	For 1997	Avg. of Information	Analyzed Industry	Index
Employees per establishment	21	3	14	Payroll per establishment	585,591	61,862	11
Revenue per establishment	1,370,364	215,502	16	Payroll as % of revenue	43	29	67
Revenue per employee	65,262	71,647	110	Payroll per employee	27,888	20,567	74

Sources: Same as General Statistics. The 'Average' column represents the average for the industry sector, in 1997, where the currently shown industry is classified. The Index shows the relationship between the Average and the Analyzed Industry. For example, 100 means that they are equal; 500 that the Analyzed Industry is five times the average; 50 means that the Analyzed Industry is half the national average. The abbreviation 'na' is used to show that data are 'not available'.

*Equivalent to SIC 8041.

LEADING COMPANIES   Number shown: **4**   Total sales ($ mil): **67**   Total employment (000): **0.6**

Company Name	Address				CEO Name	Phone	Co. Type	Sales ($ mil)	Empl. (000)
Molina Medical Centers	1 Golden Shore Dr	Long Beach	CA	90802	J. Mario Molina	562-435-3666	R	60*	0.5
American HealthChoice Inc.	1300 W Walnut Hill	Irving	TX	75038	Joseph W Stucki	972-751-1900	P	5	<0.1
Hall Chiropractic Inc.	914 W Anderson Ln	Austin	TX	78757	Curtis J Hall	512-454-4072	R	2	<0.1
Comprehensive Health Services	3543 N 7th St	Phoenix	AZ	85014	Robert Gear	602-263-8484	R	1	<0.1

Source: *Ward's Business Directory of U.S. Private and Public Companies*, Volumes 1 and 2, 2000. The company type code used is as follows: P - Public, R - Private, S - Subsidiary, D - Division, J - Joint Venture, A - Affiliate, G - Group, N - Company type not reported. Sales are in millions of dollars, employees are in thousands. An asterisk (*) indicates an estimated sales volume. The symbol < stands for 'less than'. Company names and addresses are truncated, in some cases, to fit into the available space.

LOCATION BY STATE AND REGIONAL CONCENTRATION

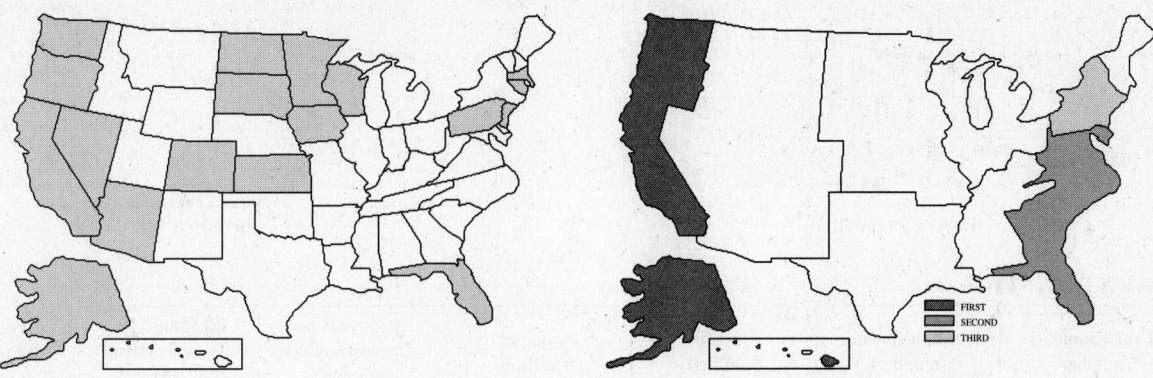

FIRST
SECOND
THIRD

INDUSTRY DATA BY STATE

State	Establishments		Employment			Payroll		Revenues		
	Total (number)	% of U.S.	Total (number)	% of U.S.	Per Estab.	Total ($ mil.)	Per Empl. ($)	Total ($ mil.)	% of U.S.	Per Estab. ($)
California	4,111	13.5	11,098	12.1	3	197.0	17,749	854.3	13.0	207,802
Florida	1,963	6.4	6,814	7.4	3	164.3	24,116	497.5	7.6	253,436
New Jersey	1,415	4.6	4,457	4.9	3	114.6	25,717	382.2	5.8	270,092
Texas	1,705	5.6	5,034	5.5	3	109.5	21,753	381.2	5.8	223,595
New York	1,915	6.3	5,169	5.6	3	91.3	17,665	378.4	5.8	197,617
Pennsylvania	1,582	5.2	5,133	5.6	3	97.6	19,007	338.5	5.2	213,952
Ohio	1,070	3.5	4,187	4.6	4	95.3	22,767	280.1	4.3	261,757
Illinois	1,275	4.2	4,185	4.6	3	84.5	20,195	276.9	4.2	217,137
Michigan	1,015	3.3	3,086	3.4	3	59.7	19,335	195.8	3.0	192,928
Minnesota	885	2.9	3,152	3.4	4	61.2	19,418	194.6	3.0	219,899
Wisconsin	802	2.6	2,897	3.2	4	72.8	25,128	194.3	3.0	242,330
Washington	921	3.0	2,331	2.5	3	43.3	18,596	179.1	2.7	194,488
Massachusetts	642	2.1	2,183	2.4	3	52.1	23,880	172.1	2.6	268,051
Georgia	829	2.7	2,303	2.5	3	46.7	20,261	157.5	2.4	189,999
North Carolina	597	2.0	1,746	1.9	3	44.3	25,355	148.9	2.3	249,496
Arizona	742	2.4	2,054	2.2	3	41.1	19,988	148.9	2.3	200,625
Colorado	634	2.1	1,587	1.7	3	32.8	20,640	118.1	1.8	186,226
Virginia	491	1.6	1,593	1.7	3	37.8	23,719	107.5	1.6	218,886
Indiana	519	1.7	1,721	1.9	3	33.5	19,443	105.5	1.6	203,208
Connecticut	384	1.3	1,238	1.4	3	29.4	23,721	105.2	1.6	274,078
Missouri	642	2.1	1,573	1.7	2	26.1	16,598	98.3	1.5	153,086
Iowa	545	1.8	1,490	1.6	3	23.9	16,009	92.3	1.4	169,303
Tennessee	437	1.4	1,205	1.3	3	23.6	19,547	86.8	1.3	198,721
Oregon	478	1.6	1,191	1.3	2	20.4	17,116	84.1	1.3	176,025
South Carolina	392	1.3	1,035	1.1	3	22.5	21,780	78.5	1.2	200,171
Maryland	273	0.9	968	1.1	4	24.5	25,305	75.6	1.2	276,971
Louisiana	294	1.0	1,035	1.1	4	21.8	21,062	73.4	1.1	249,830
Kentucky	343	1.1	1,029	1.1	3	21.8	21,194	72.4	1.1	211,085
Oklahoma	341	1.1	999	1.1	3	19.0	19,029	67.9	1.0	198,977
Kansas	369	1.2	1,053	1.1	3	19.4	18,412	65.1	1.0	176,463
Alabama	319	1.0	843	0.9	3	16.2	19,206	56.6	0.9	177,354
Nevada	205	0.7	592	0.6	3	14.6	24,701	50.8	0.8	247,868
Arkansas	247	0.8	684	0.7	3	12.8	18,730	44.1	0.7	178,737
Nebraska	201	0.7	576	0.6	3	10.6	18,460	40.8	0.6	203,184
Utah	197	0.6	584	0.6	3	7.8	13,300	33.3	0.5	168,807
West Virginia	125	0.4	462	0.5	4	9.2	19,814	31.7	0.5	253,968
New Mexico	182	0.6	482	0.5	3	8.7	17,956	29.9	0.5	164,286
New Hampshire	131	0.4	333	0.4	3	6.1	18,456	26.7	0.4	204,153
South Dakota	133	0.4	436	0.5	3	7.1	16,211	26.2	0.4	196,677
Maine	143	0.5	373	0.4	3	6.6	17,788	26.2	0.4	183,161
Idaho	160	0.5	416	0.5	3	6.4	15,389	26.1	0.4	162,950
Mississippi	131	0.4	352	0.4	3	6.1	17,437	23.4	0.4	178,626
Alaska	81	0.3	248	0.3	3	7.8	31,585	23.2	0.4	286,926
Hawaii	95	0.3	263	0.3	3	6.1	23,038	20.1	0.3	212,095
Montana	136	0.4	364	0.4	3	4.7	12,975	20.0	0.3	147,213
North Dakota	104	0.3	319	0.3	3	5.9	18,618	19.5	0.3	187,288
Rhode Island	90	0.3	270	0.3	3	5.4	20,130	18.2	0.3	201,900
Delaware	60	0.2	220	0.2	4	6.2	28,341	15.8	0.2	263,567
Vermont	73	0.2	179	0.2	2	2.9	16,078	13.5	0.2	184,438
Wyoming	51	0.2	132	0.1	3	2.3	17,152	8.9	0.1	174,451
D.C.	12	-	26	0.0	2	1.0	38,154	4.0	0.1	332,500

Source: 1997 *Economic Census*. The states are in descending order of revenues or establishments (if revenue data are missing for the majority). The symbol (D) appears when data are withheld to prevent disclosure of competitive information. States marked with (D) are sorted by number of establishments. A dash (-) indicates that the data element cannot be calculated. * indicates the midpoint of a range; 175, for example is the range 100-249. Shaded *states* on the state map indicate those states which have proportionately greater representation in the industry than would be indicated by the state's population; the ratio is based on total revenues or number of establishments. Shaded *regions* indicate where the industry is regionally most concentrated.

NAICS 621320 - OFFICES OF OPTOMETRISTS*

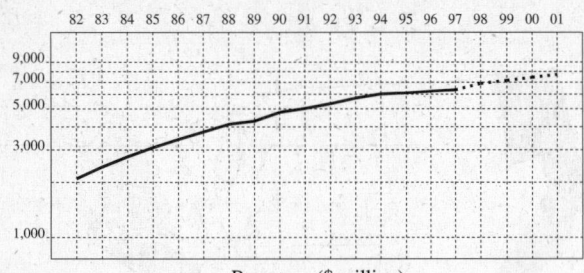
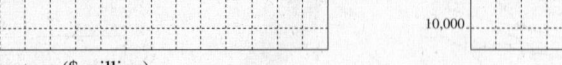
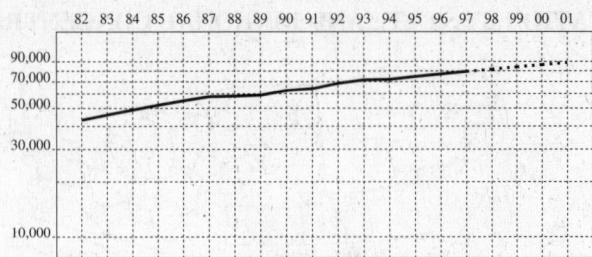

Revenues ($ million)   Employment (000)

GENERAL STATISTICS

Year	Establishments (number)	Employment (number)	Payroll ($ million)	Revenues ($ million)	Employees per Establishment (number)	Revenues per Establishment ($)	Payroll per Employee ($)
1982	15,013	43,227	514.0	2,091.0	2.9	139,279	11,891
1983	15,205 e	46,162 e	590.0 e	2,424.0 e	3.0 e	159,421 e	12,781 e
1984	15,397 e	49,096 e	666.0 e	2,757.0 e	3.2 e	179,061 e	13,565 e
1985	15,588 e	52,031 e	742.0 e	3,089.0 e	3.3 e	198,165 e	14,261 e
1986	15,780 e	54,965 e	818.0 e	3,422.0 e	3.5 e	216,857 e	14,882 e
1987	15,972	57,900	893.0	3,755.0	3.6	235,099	15,423
1988	15,291	58,253	964.0	4,133.0	3.8	270,290	16,549
1989	15,049	58,893	1,008.0	4,296.0	3.9	285,467	17,116
1990	15,320	62,604	1,116.0	4,799.0	4.1	313,251	17,826
1991	15,425	64,078	1,181.0	5,028.0	4.2	325,964	18,431
1992	17,135	68,596	1,301.0	5,333.0	4.0	311,234	18,966
1993	17,054	71,672	1,383.0	5,715.0	4.2	335,112	19,296
1994	17,080	72,027	1,442.0	6,021.0	4.2	352,518	20,020
1995	17,028	74,658	1,539.0	6,113.0	4.4	358,997	20,614
1996	17,452 e	77,102 e	1,656.0 e	6,237.0 e	4.4 e	357,380 e	21,478 e
1997	17,875	79,545	1,773.0	6,362.0	4.5	355,916	22,289
1998	18,021 p	81,795 p	1,820.0 p	6,892.0 p	4.5 p	382,443 p	22,251 p
1999	18,287 p	84,134 p	1,908.0 p	7,165.0 p	4.6 p	391,808 p	22,678 p
2000	18,552 p	86,474 p	1,995.0 p	7,438.0 p	4.7 p	400,927 p	23,071 p
2001	18,818 p	88,813 p	2,083.0 p	7,711.0 p	4.7 p	409,767 p	23,454 p

Sources: Economic Census of the United States, 1982, 1987, 1992, 1997. Establishment counts, employment, and payroll are from County Business Patterns for non-Census years. In non-Census years, industries in the Manufacturing range under SIC coding include data from the Annual Survey of Manufactures (ASM); those in the old Services range include data from the Services Annual Survey (SAS). Values followed by a 'p' are projections by the editors. Extrapolations are marked by 'e'. Data are the most recent available at this level of detail.

INDICES OF CHANGE

Year	Establishments (number)	Employment (number)	Payroll ($ million)	Revenues ($ million)	Employees per Establishment (number)	Revenues per Establishment ($)	Payroll per Employee ($)
1982	84.0	54.3	29.0	32.9	64.7	39.1	53.3
1987	89.4	72.8	50.4	59.0	81.5	66.1	69.2
1992	95.9	86.2	73.4	83.8	90.0	87.4	85.1
1993	95.4	90.1	78.0	89.8	94.4	94.2	86.6
1994	95.6	90.5	81.3	94.6	94.8	99.0	89.8
1995	95.3	93.9	86.8	96.1	98.5	100.9	92.5
1996	97.6 e	96.9 e	93.4 e	98.0 e	99.3 e	100.4 e	96.4 e
1997	100.0	100.0	100.0	100.0	100.0	100.0	100.0
1998	100.8 p	102.8 p	102.7 p	108.3 p	102.0 p	107.5 p	99.8 p
1999	102.3 p	105.8 p	107.6 p	112.6 p	103.4 p	110.1 p	101.7 p
2000	103.8 p	108.7 p	112.5 p	116.9 p	104.7 p	112.6 p	103.5 p
2001	105.3 p	111.7 p	117.5 p	121.2 p	106.1 p	115.1 p	105.2 p

Sources: Same as General Statistics. The values shown reflect change from the base year, 1997. Values above 100 mean greater than 1997, values below 100 mean less than 1997, and a value of 100 in the 1982-96 or 1998-2001 period means same as 1997. Values followed by a 'p' are projections by the editors; 'e' stands for extrapolation. Data are the most recent available at this level of detail.

SELECTED RATIOS

For 1997	Avg. of Information	Analyzed Industry	Index	For 1997	Avg. of Information	Analyzed Industry	Index
Employees per establishment	21	4	21	Payroll per establishment	585,591	99,189	17
Revenue per establishment	1,370,364	355,916	26	Payroll as % of revenue	43	28	65
Revenue per employee	65,262	79,980	123	Payroll per employee	27,888	22,289	80

Sources: Same as General Statistics. The 'Average' column represents the average for the industry sector, in 1997, where the currently shown industry is classified. The Index shows the relationship between the Average and the Analyzed Industry. For example, 100 means that they are equal; 500 that the Analyzed Industry is five times the average; 50 means that the Analyzed Industry is half the national average. The abbreviation 'na' is used to show that data are 'not available'.

*Equivalent to SIC 8042.

LEADING COMPANIES   Number shown: **5**   Total sales ($ mil): **296**   Total employment (000): **3.0**

Company Name	Address				CEO Name	Phone	Co. Type	Sales ($ mil)	Empl. (000)
Vision Twenty-One Inc.	7209 Bryan Dairy	Largo	FL	33777	Theodore N. Gillette	727-545-4300	P	223	2.3
Molina Medical Centers	1 Golden Shore Dr	Long Beach	CA	90802	J Mario Molina	562-435-3666	R	60*	0.5
HealthDrive Medical & Dental	25 Needham St	Newton	MA	02461	Steven Charlap	617-964-6681	R	11*	0.2
Gary Hall Eye Surgery Institute	2501 N 32nd St	Phoenix	AZ	85008	Gary Hall	602-957-6799	R	1*	<0.1
Robert M. Kershner, M.D., P.C.	1925 W Or Grove	Tucson	AZ	85704	Robert M Kershner	520-797-2020	R	1*	<0.1

Source: *Ward's Business Directory of U.S. Private and Public Companies*, Volumes 1 and 2, 2000. The company type code used is as follows: P - Public, R - Private, S - Subsidiary, D - Division, J - Joint Venture, A - Affiliate, G - Group, N - Company type not reported. Sales are in millions of dollars, employees are in thousands. An asterisk (*) indicates an estimated sales volume. The symbol < stands for 'less than'. Company names and addresses are truncated, in some cases, to fit into the available space.

LOCATION BY STATE AND REGIONAL CONCENTRATION

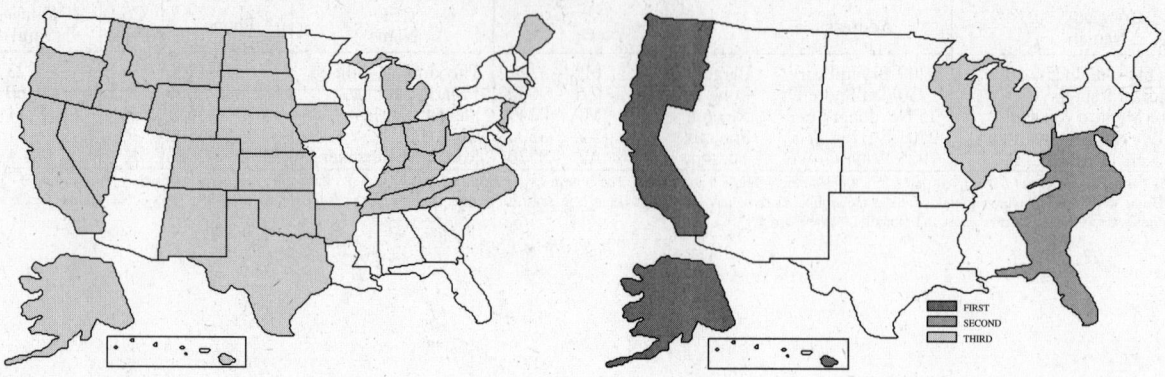

INDUSTRY DATA BY STATE

State	Establishments Total (number)	% of U.S.	Employment Total (number)	% of U.S.	Per Estab.	Payroll Total ($ mil.)	Per Empl. ($)	Revenues Total ($ mil.)	% of U.S.	Per Estab. ($)
California	2,448	13.7	10,281	12.9	4	218.6	21,266	894.0	14.1	365,185
Texas	1,225	6.9	5,613	7.1	5	132.9	23,670	464.5	7.3	379,148
North Carolina	590	3.3	3,544	4.5	6	90.5	25,523	326.6	5.1	553,551
Florida	898	5.0	3,743	4.7	4	98.0	26,183	296.1	4.7	329,703
Ohio	861	4.8	3,843	4.8	4	83.1	21,633	290.1	4.6	336,934
Pennsylvania	928	5.2	3,859	4.9	4	76.8	19,898	285.7	4.5	307,887
Illinois	699	3.9	3,397	4.3	5	74.8	22,032	254.4	4.0	363,977
New York	750	4.2	2,978	3.7	4	65.8	22,108	248.1	3.9	330,811
Michigan	585	3.3	3,014	3.8	5	74.2	24,623	242.1	3.8	413,860
New Jersey	589	3.3	2,526	3.2	4	54.3	21,500	198.3	3.1	336,674
Indiana	510	2.9	2,458	3.1	5	53.2	21,646	192.7	3.0	377,867
Virginia	426	2.4	1,837	2.3	4	41.9	22,813	140.2	2.2	329,183
Tennessee	392	2.2	1,715	2.2	4	35.2	20,525	139.5	2.2	355,946
Georgia	384	2.1	1,655	2.1	4	41.1	24,830	130.2	2.0	339,049
Washington	379	2.1	1,619	2.0	4	34.3	21,183	130.0	2.0	343,005
Massachusetts	381	2.1	1,620	2.0	4	34.5	21,282	122.8	1.9	322,428
Wisconsin	332	1.9	1,607	2.0	5	34.1	21,227	116.9	1.8	352,157
Oklahoma	342	1.9	1,393	1.8	4	26.0	18,677	106.8	1.7	312,383
Iowa	277	1.5	1,424	1.8	5	31.6	22,198	106.3	1.7	383,809
Kansas	257	1.4	1,327	1.7	5	27.6	20,815	105.7	1.7	411,206
Missouri	297	1.7	1,354	1.7	5	30.7	22,656	100.4	1.6	338,185
Colorado	285	1.6	1,314	1.7	5	31.7	24,162	98.4	1.5	345,175
Minnesota	267	1.5	1,304	1.6	5	29.4	22,564	96.6	1.5	361,884
Maryland	255	1.4	1,252	1.6	5	30.3	24,222	96.0	1.5	376,620
Kentucky	262	1.5	1,237	1.6	5	26.8	21,627	94.5	1.5	360,771
Arizona	212	1.2	988	1.2	5	28.1	28,442	83.8	1.3	395,156
Oregon	239	1.3	985	1.2	4	19.6	19,884	77.5	1.2	324,163
Alabama	244	1.4	981	1.2	4	19.6	19,967	75.9	1.2	311,020
Connecticut	221	1.2	844	1.1	4	19.9	23,540	75.8	1.2	343,045
Arkansas	203	1.1	884	1.1	4	16.5	18,657	68.0	1.1	334,926
South Carolina	205	1.1	782	1.0	4	18.9	24,231	63.8	1.0	311,405
Louisiana	188	1.1	829	1.0	4	17.0	20,532	59.1	0.9	314,340
Nebraska	135	0.8	766	1.0	6	16.2	21,161	51.7	0.8	383,185
Nevada	124	0.7	529	0.7	4	15.6	29,571	48.9	0.8	394,274
West Virginia	161	0.9	652	0.8	4	11.3	17,399	48.5	0.8	301,522
Mississippi	150	0.8	611	0.8	4	11.6	18,920	46.7	0.7	311,207
Maine	120	0.7	503	0.6	4	10.9	21,736	43.6	0.7	363,492
New Mexico	116	0.6	542	0.7	5	11.3	20,828	42.4	0.7	365,509
Idaho	124	0.7	478	0.6	4	8.3	17,316	34.1	0.5	275,210
Hawaii	111	0.6	363	0.5	3	7.8	21,366	30.9	0.5	277,991
Utah	90	0.5	376	0.5	4	7.3	19,335	28.1	0.4	312,778
Montana	91	0.5	395	0.5	4	6.7	16,904	27.9	0.4	306,407
New Hampshire	77	0.4	323	0.4	4	7.5	23,232	27.2	0.4	353,312
South Dakota	74	0.4	316	0.4	4	6.3	19,946	25.9	0.4	350,622
Rhode Island	90	0.5	331	0.4	4	7.0	21,221	24.2	0.4	269,167
North Dakota	65	0.4	293	0.4	5	6.9	23,433	22.8	0.4	351,462
Wyoming	60	0.3	268	0.3	4	5.6	20,761	21.7	0.3	361,400
Delaware	48	0.3	231	0.3	5	6.2	26,861	20.6	0.3	429,896
Alaska	46	0.3	171	0.2	4	5.7	33,088	17.3	0.3	375,065
Vermont	46	0.3	133	0.2	3	2.7	20,090	13.5	0.2	293,435
D.C.	16	0.1	57	0.1	4	1.5	26,807	4.7	0.1	292,625

Source: 1997 *Economic Census*. The states are in descending order of revenues or establishments (if revenue data are missing for the majority). The symbol (D) appears when data are withheld to prevent disclosure of competitive information. States marked with (D) are sorted by number of establishments. A dash (-) indicates that the data element cannot be calculated. * indicates the midpoint of a range; 175, for example is the range 100-249. Shaded *states* on the state map indicate those states which have proportionately greater representation in the industry than would be indicated by the state's population; the ratio is based on total revenues or number of establishments. Shaded *regions* indicate where the industry is regionally most concentrated.

NAICS 621330 - OFFICES OF MENTAL HEALTH PRACTITIONERS (EXCEPT PHYSICIANS)

GENERAL STATISTICS

Year	Establishments (number)	Employment (number)	Payroll ($ million)	Revenues ($ million)	Employees per Establishment (number)	Revenues per Establishment ($)	Payroll per Employee ($)
1997	11,750	38,427	948.0	2,505.0	3.3	213,191	24,670

Source: Economic Census of the United States, 1997. This is a newly defined industry. Data for prior years were unavailable at the time of publication but may become available over time.

INDICES OF CHANGE

Year	Establishments (number)	Employment (number)	Payroll ($ million)	Revenues ($ million)	Employees per Establishment (number)	Revenues per Establishment ($)	Payroll per Employee ($)
1997	100.0	100.0	100.0	100.0	100.0	100.0	100.0

Sources: Same as General Statistics. The values shown reflect change from the base year, 1997. Values above 100 mean greater than 1997, values below 100 mean less than 1997, and a value of 100 in the 1982-96 or 1998-2001 period means same as 1997. Values followed by a 'p' are projections by the editors; 'e' stands for extrapolation. Data are the most recent available at this level of detail.

SIC INDUSTRIES RELATED TO NAICS 621330

Each new NAICS code represents an industry that used to be part of an SIC or a part of several SIC industries. Data in this table are shown to provide transitional information for these cases. All available data for the precursor SIC(s) are shown. Even if only a part of an SIC is included in the NAICS, *all* data for the SIC are reproduced. If the SIC industry is not marked as being a part (pt) of the NAICS, the entire industry is embedded in the NAICS data. The SIC composition of the new industry provides some hints of the relative importance of its "ancestors." Data marked with a 'p' are projected. Projections begin with 1982 data. Data earlier than 1990 are not shown but are reflected in the projections.

SIC	Industry	1990	1991	1992	1993	1994	1995	1996	1997
8049	**Offices of Health Practitioners, nec (pt)**								
	Establishments (number)	14,968	16,957	22,260	23,992	24,817	25,445	28,554p	30,601p
	Employment (thousands)	82.0	91.6	103.5	123.9	126.3	142.1	153.0p	164.9p
	Revenues ($ million)	-	-	6,148.1	-	-	-	-	-

Source: Economic Census of the United States, 1992, annual surveys of economic sectors conducted by the Bureau of the Census, and estimates or projections based on the 1982-1992 period; not all data are shown. 'e' marks estimates made by the editors; 'p' indicates projections based on time series. A dash (-) indicates that data for this SIC or year were not available. The abbreviation (pt) next to the industry name indicates that only a part of the industry is present within the NAICS data. If no (pt) is shown, the entire industry is contained within the NAICS data.

SELECTED RATIOS

For 1997	Avg. of Information	Analyzed Industry	Index	For 1997	Avg. of Information	Analyzed Industry	Index
Employees per establishment	21	3	16	Payroll per establishment	585,591	80,681	14
Revenue per establishment	1,370,364	213,191	16	Payroll as % of revenue	43	38	89
Revenue per employee	65,262	65,189	100	Payroll per employee	27,888	24,670	88

Sources: Same as General Statistics. The 'Average' column represents the average for the industry sector, in 1997, where the currently shown industry is classified. The Index shows the relationship between the Average and the Analyzed Industry. For example, 100 means that they are equal; 500 that the Analyzed Industry is five times the average; 50 means that the Analyzed Industry is half the national average. The abbreviation 'na' is used to show that data are 'not available'.

LEADING COMPANIES

No company data available for this industry.

LOCATION BY STATE AND REGIONAL CONCENTRATION

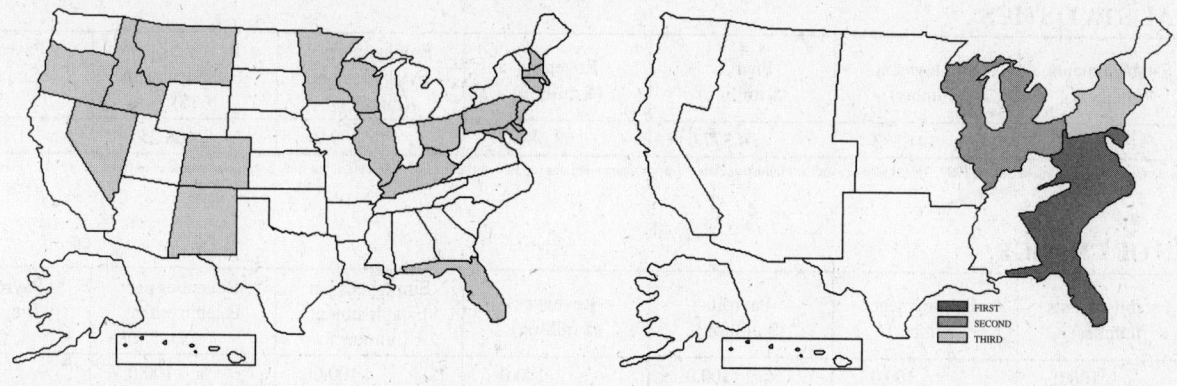

INDUSTRY DATA BY STATE

State	Establishments Total (number)	Establishments % of U.S.	Employment Total (number)	Employment % of U.S.	Employment Per Estab.	Payroll Total ($ mil.)	Payroll Per Empl. ($)	Revenues Total ($ mil.)	Revenues % of U.S.	Revenues Per Estab. ($)
California	1,807	15.4	4,238	11.0	2	90.9	21,437	289.6	11.6	160,288
Florida	961	8.2	2,564	6.7	3	65.7	25,629	182.4	7.3	189,825
New York	652	5.5	1,904	5.0	3	56.8	29,839	167.2	6.7	256,508
Texas	805	6.9	2,384	6.2	3	56.7	23,767	149.5	6.0	185,760
Pennsylvania	423	3.6	2,349	6.1	6	50.5	21,505	131.1	5.2	309,905
Ohio	464	3.9	2,105	5.5	5	51.5	24,466	117.9	4.7	254,153
Illinois	465	4.0	1,904	5.0	4	49.1	25,805	116.1	4.6	249,742
Maryland	272	2.3	1,430	3.7	5	44.9	31,427	101.7	4.1	374,048
New Jersey	355	3.0	1,281	3.3	4	39.4	30,723	96.9	3.9	272,896
Michigan	436	3.7	1,350	3.5	3	37.6	27,867	92.5	3.7	212,197
Massachusetts	247	2.1	1,116	2.9	5	28.4	25,483	91.5	3.7	370,587
Georgia	341	2.9	894	2.3	3	22.3	24,940	64.3	2.6	188,490
Virginia	318	2.7	1,055	2.7	3	27.3	25,859	60.0	2.4	188,755
Colorado	335	2.9	964	2.5	3	23.1	23,968	59.9	2.4	178,922
Wisconsin	219	1.9	1,271	3.3	6	27.7	21,794	58.9	2.3	268,749
Connecticut	162	1.4	408	1.1	3	12.9	31,630	49.7	2.0	306,636
Kentucky	114	1.0	452	1.2	4	9.7	21,540	49.4	2.0	433,132
Minnesota	223	1.9	835	2.2	4	21.8	26,149	48.6	1.9	217,978
North Carolina	248	2.1	736	1.9	3	19.1	26,003	46.6	1.9	187,972
Missouri	226	1.9	690	1.8	3	16.2	23,503	39.9	1.6	176,535
Washington	235	2.0	717	1.9	3	16.6	23,216	38.1	1.5	161,979
Arizona	242	2.1	587	1.5	2	14.3	24,405	36.9	1.5	152,450
Tennessee	209	1.8	545	1.4	3	12.7	23,327	33.5	1.3	160,459
Indiana	147	1.3	583	1.5	4	13.9	23,895	33.1	1.3	224,905
Oregon	189	1.6	608	1.6	3	14.2	23,368	32.6	1.3	172,561
Louisiana	158	1.3	520	1.4	3	13.3	25,600	30.1	1.2	190,430
Oklahoma	138	1.2	730	1.9	5	10.7	14,611	26.9	1.1	194,775
Alabama	110	0.9	235	0.6	2	5.7	24,153	21.1	0.8	191,964
New Mexico	110	0.9	399	1.0	4	7.1	17,822	18.1	0.7	164,382
Nevada	52	0.4	220	0.6	4	7.8	35,359	16.8	0.7	323,904
South Carolina	87	0.7	263	0.7	3	7.3	27,586	16.7	0.7	192,103
D.C.	52	0.4	143	0.4	3	6.2	43,573	16.4	0.7	314,788
Iowa	73	0.6	310	0.8	4	5.9	19,119	15.3	0.6	209,753
New Hampshire	55	0.5	236	0.6	4	5.9	25,212	13.8	0.5	250,055
Arkansas	85	0.7	192	0.5	2	5.2	27,005	13.3	0.5	156,353
Utah	97	0.8	247	0.6	3	4.7	18,830	12.8	0.5	132,113
Nebraska	62	0.5	217	0.6	4	4.4	20,143	12.8	0.5	206,452
Idaho	49	0.4	240	0.6	5	5.3	22,071	12.4	0.5	252,082
West Virginia	41	0.3	168	0.4	4	3.4	20,494	10.1	0.4	245,829
Maine	73	0.6	200	0.5	3	4.0	19,775	9.5	0.4	130,000
Delaware	32	0.3	170	0.4	5	4.0	23,500	9.5	0.4	298,406
Montana	46	0.4	132	0.3	3	3.5	26,356	9.0	0.4	194,674
Hawaii	52	0.4	155	0.4	3	3.3	21,265	8.5	0.3	163,923
Mississippi	43	0.4	79	0.2	2	2.1	25,962	5.9	0.2	136,163
Alaska	19	0.2	69	0.2	4	2.0	29,696	5.7	0.2	298,211
Vermont	46	0.4	70	0.2	2	1.7	24,014	4.9	0.2	105,717
South Dakota	22	0.2	85	0.2	4	1.7	20,553	4.4	0.2	198,318
Wyoming	22	0.2	52	0.1	2	1.0	18,365	2.6	0.1	120,273
North Dakota	15	0.1	48	0.1	3	1.4	29,458	2.5	0.1	165,333
Kansas	95	0.8	175*	-	-	(D)	-	(D)	-	-
Rhode Island	21	0.2	60*	-	-	(D)	-	(D)	-	-

Source: 1997 Economic Census. The states are in descending order of revenues or establishments (if revenue data are missing for the majority). The symbol (D) appears when data are withheld to prevent disclosure of competitive information. States marked with (D) are sorted by number of establishments. A dash (-) indicates that the data element cannot be calculated. * indicates the midpoint of a range; 175, for example is the range 100-249. Shaded *states* on the state map indicate those states which have proportionately greater representation in the industry than would be indicated by the state's population; the ratio is based on total revenues or number of establishments. Shaded *regions* indicate where the industry is regionally most concentrated.

NAICS 621340 - OFFICES OF PHYSICAL, OCCUPATIONAL, AND SPEECH THERAPISTS AND AUDIOLOGISTS

GENERAL STATISTICS

Year	Establishments (number)	Employment (number)	Payroll ($ million)	Revenues ($ million)	Employees per Establishment (number)	Revenues per Establishment ($)	Payroll per Employee ($)
1997	14,277	141,533	4,377.0	8,684.0	9.9	608,251	30,926

Source: Economic Census of the United States, 1997. This is a newly defined industry. Data for prior years were unavailable at the time of publication but may become available over time.

INDICES OF CHANGE

Year	Establishments (number)	Employment (number)	Payroll ($ million)	Revenues ($ million)	Employees per Establishment (number)	Revenues per Establishment ($)	Payroll per Employee ($)
1997	100.0	100.0	100.0	100.0	100.0	100.0	100.0

Sources: Same as General Statistics. The values shown reflect change from the base year, 1997. Values above 100 mean greater than 1997, values below 100 mean less than 1997, and a value of 100 in the 1982-96 or 1998-2001 period means same as 1997. Values followed by a 'p' are projections by the editors; 'e' stands for extrapolation. Data are the most recent available at this level of detail.

SIC INDUSTRIES RELATED TO NAICS 621340

Each new NAICS code represents an industry that used to be part of an SIC or a part of several SIC industries. Data in this table are shown to provide transitional information for these cases. All available data for the precursor SIC(s) are shown. Even if only a part of an SIC is included in the NAICS, *all* data for the SIC are reproduced. If the SIC industry is not marked as being a part (pt) of the NAICS, the entire industry is embedded in the NAICS data. The SIC composition of the new industry provides some hints of the relative importance of its "ancestors." Data marked with a 'p' are projected. Projections begin with 1982 data. Data earlier than 1990 are not shown but are reflected in the projections.

SIC	Industry	1990	1991	1992	1993	1994	1995	1996	1997
8049	**Offices of Health Practitioners, nec (pt)**								
	Establishments (number)	14,968	16,957	22,260	23,992	24,817	25,445	28,554p	30,601p
	Employment (thousands)	82.0	91.6	103.5	123.9	126.3	142.1	153.0p	164.9p
	Revenues ($ million)	-	-	6,148.1	-	-	-	-	-

Source: Economic Census of the United States, 1992, annual surveys of economic sectors conducted by the Bureau of the Census, and estimates or projections based on the 1982-1992 period; not all data are shown. 'e' marks estimates made by the editors; 'p' indicates projections based on time series. A dash (-) indicates that data for this SIC or year were not available. The abbreviation (pt) next to the industry name indicates that only a part of the industry is present within the NAICS data. If no (pt) is shown, the entire industry is contained within the NAICS data.

SELECTED RATIOS

For 1997	Avg. of Information	Analyzed Industry	Index	For 1997	Avg. of Information	Analyzed Industry	Index
Employees per establishment	21	10	47	Payroll per establishment	585,591	306,577	52
Revenue per establishment	1,370,364	608,251	44	Payroll as % of revenue	43	50	118
Revenue per employee	65,262	61,357	94	Payroll per employee	27,888	30,926	111

Sources: Same as General Statistics. The 'Average' column represents the average for the industry sector, in 1997, where the currently shown industry is classified. The Index shows the relationship between the Average and the Analyzed Industry. For example, 100 means that they are equal; 500 that the Analyzed Industry is five times the average; 50 means that the Analyzed Industry is half the national average. The abbreviation 'na' is used to show that data are 'not available'.

LEADING COMPANIES
No company data available for this industry.

LOCATION BY STATE AND REGIONAL CONCENTRATION

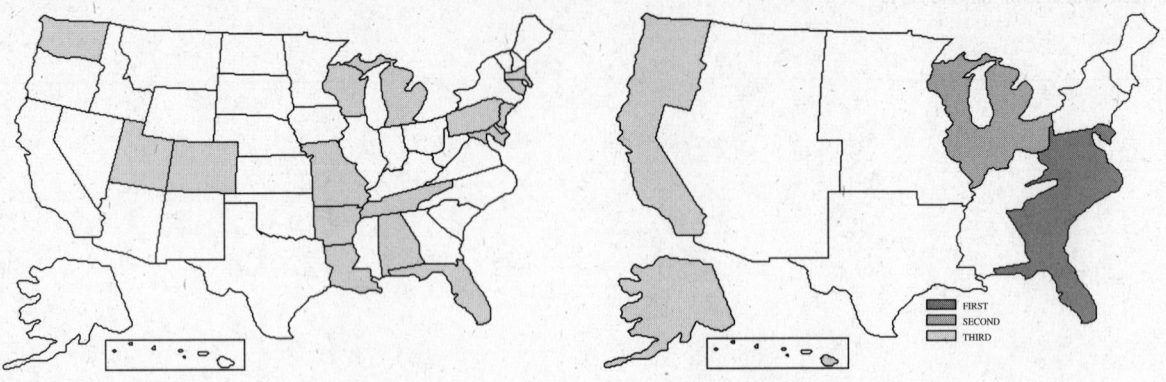

INDUSTRY DATA BY STATE

State	Establishments Total (number)	% of U.S.	Employment Total (number)	% of U.S.	Per Estab.	Payroll Total ($ mil.)	Per Empl. ($)	Revenues Total ($ mil.)	% of U.S.	Per Estab. ($)
California	1,688	11.8	14,835	10.5	9	425.1	28,655	881.1	10.1	521,958
Florida	1,070	7.5	11,132	7.9	10	358.7	32,223	709.2	8.2	662,804
Texas	814	5.7	8,588	6.1	11	264.7	30,821	564.0	6.5	692,915
Pennsylvania	801	5.6	8,019	5.7	10	284.4	35,462	504.9	5.8	630,380
New York	1,042	7.3	6,705	4.7	6	188.7	28,144	430.6	5.0	413,198
Michigan	504	3.5	5,790	4.1	11	195.8	33,808	399.6	4.6	792,952
Ohio	537	3.8	6,340	4.5	12	181.3	28,592	329.8	3.8	614,227
Illinois	451	3.2	5,392	3.8	12	172.7	32,035	321.1	3.7	712,020
Massachusetts	348	2.4	4,943	3.5	14	178.8	36,173	319.3	3.7	917,394
New Jersey	520	3.6	3,953	2.8	8	128.0	32,389	270.2	3.1	519,625
Maryland	363	2.5	3,591	2.5	10	120.6	33,596	235.7	2.7	649,234
Connecticut	204	1.4	2,615	1.8	13	86.6	33,100	232.6	2.7	1,140,284
Tennessee	199	1.4	3,793	2.7	19	126.3	33,292	225.7	2.6	1,134,317
Missouri	287	2.0	3,770	2.7	13	115.2	30,563	212.4	2.4	740,202
Washington	402	2.8	3,212	2.3	8	91.1	28,362	205.1	2.4	510,087
Georgia	339	2.4	3,470	2.5	10	101.4	29,225	202.6	2.3	597,767
Virginia	302	2.1	3,636	2.6	12	110.0	30,249	198.1	2.3	656,079
Wisconsin	231	1.6	3,300	2.3	14	96.0	29,102	180.8	2.1	782,879
Indiana	251	1.8	3,123	2.2	12	99.8	31,955	175.8	2.0	700,530
North Carolina	324	2.3	2,997	2.1	9	86.4	28,817	170.3	2.0	525,679
Louisiana	278	1.9	2,756	1.9	10	85.9	31,180	167.6	1.9	602,831
Alabama	141	1.0	2,736	1.9	19	87.6	32,015	150.4	1.7	1,066,376
Colorado	321	2.2	2,152	1.5	7	69.9	32,474	143.8	1.7	447,888
Arizona	318	2.2	2,149	1.5	7	62.3	28,978	132.9	1.5	417,984
Minnesota	220	1.5	2,085	1.5	9	60.9	29,220	130.0	1.5	591,109
Kentucky	179	1.3	2,099	1.5	12	59.2	28,182	110.0	1.3	614,721
South Carolina	125	0.9	1,537	1.1	12	55.9	36,373	108.6	1.3	868,440
Arkansas	180	1.3	1,627	1.1	9	54.6	33,556	102.2	1.2	567,583
Oklahoma	158	1.1	1,485	1.0	9	43.3	29,139	90.1	1.0	570,171
Utah	117	0.8	1,934	1.4	17	52.4	27,082	89.5	1.0	765,043
Oregon	188	1.3	1,450	1.0	8	40.3	27,776	88.9	1.0	472,989
Iowa	135	0.9	1,290	0.9	10	36.3	28,134	69.1	0.8	511,622
Mississippi	87	0.6	1,122	0.8	13	32.7	29,124	65.4	0.8	752,000
Kansas	96	0.7	1,119	0.8	12	32.1	28,688	60.2	0.7	626,625
Nevada	97	0.7	643	0.5	7	21.4	33,288	45.3	0.5	466,948
Maine	81	0.6	571	0.4	7	18.3	32,095	38.4	0.4	474,198
New Mexico	104	0.7	730	0.5	7	19.7	26,955	38.3	0.4	367,990
Nebraska	83	0.6	615	0.4	7	17.6	28,615	36.9	0.4	444,253
West Virginia	84	0.6	473	0.3	6	13.9	29,400	35.1	0.4	418,226
Idaho	82	0.6	632	0.4	8	15.5	24,486	32.7	0.4	398,488
Rhode Island	42	0.3	408	0.3	10	13.9	34,081	26.7	0.3	635,571
Delaware	65	0.5	341	0.2	5	10.8	31,713	24.2	0.3	371,554
Hawaii	69	0.5	408	0.3	6	11.0	27,081	24.1	0.3	348,899
New Hampshire	71	0.5	393	0.3	6	11.7	29,697	23.0	0.3	324,507
Montana	68	0.5	259	0.2	4	5.9	22,911	14.6	0.2	215,118
North Dakota	28	0.2	352	0.2	13	8.4	23,767	14.6	0.2	522,214
South Dakota	39	0.3	211	0.1	5	5.8	27,389	11.8	0.1	301,718
Vermont	42	0.3	225	0.2	5	6.2	27,578	11.5	0.1	273,214
Alaska	44	0.3	187	0.1	4	3.7	19,968	10.1	0.1	230,136
D.C.	23	0.2	142	0.1	6	4.4	30,789	10.0	0.1	435,913
Wyoming	35	0.2	198	0.1	6	3.8	19,020	9.0	0.1	258,200

Source: 1997 *Economic Census*. The states are in descending order of revenues or establishments (if revenue data are missing for the majority). The symbol (D) appears when data are withheld to prevent disclosure of competitive information. States marked with (D) are sorted by number of establishments. A dash (-) indicates that the data element cannot be calculated. * indicates the midpoint of a range; 175, for example is the range 100-249. Shaded *states* on the state map indicate those states which have proportionately greater representation in the industry than would be indicated by the state's population; the ratio is based on total revenues or number of establishments. Shaded *regions* indicate where the industry is regionally most concentrated.

NAICS 621391 - OFFICES OF PODIATRISTS*

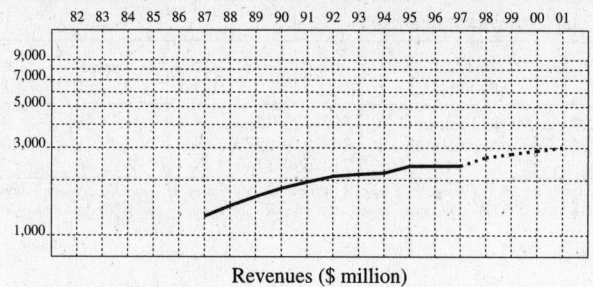

Revenues ($ million)

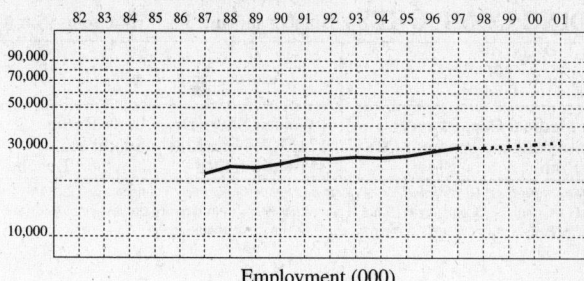

Employment (000)

GENERAL STATISTICS

Year	Establishments (number)	Employment (number)	Payroll ($ million)	Revenues ($ million)	Employees per Establishment (number)	Revenues per Establishment ($)	Payroll per Employee ($)
1982	-	-	-	-	-	-	-
1983	-	-	-	-	-	-	-
1984	-	-	-	-	-	-	-
1985	-	-	-	-	-	-	-
1986	-	-	-	-	-	-	-
1987	7,474	21,969	404.0	1,278.0	2.9	170,993	18,390
1988	7,487	24,025	502.0	1,456.0 e	3.2	194,470	20,895
1989	6,993	23,696	515.0	1,633.0 e	3.4	233,519	21,734
1990	7,132	24,863	576.0	1,811.0	3.5	253,926	23,167
1991	7,246	26,580	620.0	1,957.0	3.7	270,080	23,326
1992	7,948	26,429	624.0	2,102.0	3.3	264,469	23,610
1993	7,937	27,044	644.0	2,156.0	3.4	271,639	23,813
1994	7,981	26,805	653.0	2,190.0	3.4	274,402	24,361
1995	7,954	27,434	715.0	2,388.0	3.4	300,226	26,063
1996	8,308 e	28,953 e	743.0 e	2,391.0 e	3.5 e	287,795 e	25,662 e
1997	8,662	30,472	771.0	2,393.0	3.5	276,264	25,302
1998	8,529 p	30,449 p	810.0 p	2,662.0 p	3.6 p	312,112 p	26,602 p
1999	8,661 p	31,157 p	843.0 p	2,776.0 p	3.6 p	320,517 p	27,057 p
2000	8,793 p	31,864 p	875.0 p	2,890.0 p	3.6 p	328,671 p	27,460 p
2001	8,924 p	32,571 p	908.0 p	3,004.0 p	3.6 p	336,620 p	27,878 p

Sources: *Economic Census of the United States*, 1982, 1987, 1992, 1997. Establishment counts, employment, and payroll are from *County Business Patterns* for non-Census years. In non-Census years, industries in the Manufacturing range under SIC coding include data from the *Annual Survey of Manufactures* (*ASM*); those in the old Services range include data from the *Services Annual Survey* (*SAS*). Values followed by a 'p' are projections by the editors. Extrapolations are marked by 'e'. Data are the most recent available at this level of detail.

INDICES OF CHANGE

Year	Establishments (number)	Employment (number)	Payroll ($ million)	Revenues ($ million)	Employees per Establishment (number)	Revenues per Establishment ($)	Payroll per Employee ($)
1982	-	-	-	-	-	-	-
1987	86.3	72.1	52.4	53.4	83.6	61.9	72.7
1992	91.8	86.7	80.9	87.8	94.5	95.7	93.3
1993	91.6	88.8	83.5	90.1	96.9	98.3	94.1
1994	92.1	88.0	84.7	91.5	95.5	99.3	96.3
1995	91.8	90.0	92.7	99.8	98.0	108.7	103.0
1996	95.9 e	95.0 e	96.4 e	99.9 e	99.1 e	104.2 e	101.4 e
1997	100.0	100.0	100.0	100.0	100.0	100.0	100.0
1998	98.5 p	99.9 p	105.1 p	111.2 p	101.5 p	113.0 p	105.1 p
1999	100.0 p	102.2 p	109.3 p	116.0 p	102.3 p	116.0 p	106.9 p
2000	101.5 p	104.6 p	113.5 p	120.8 p	103.0 p	119.0 p	108.5 p
2001	103.0 p	106.9 p	117.8 p	125.5 p	103.8 p	121.8 p	110.2 p

Sources: Same as General Statistics. The values shown reflect change from the base year, 1997. Values above 100 mean greater than 1997, values below 100 mean less than 1997, and a value of 100 in the 1982-96 or 1998-2001 period means same as 1997. Values followed by a 'p' are projections by the editors; 'e' stands for extrapolation. Data are the most recent available at this level of detail.

SELECTED RATIOS

For 1997	Avg. of Information	Analyzed Industry	Index	For 1997	Avg. of Information	Analyzed Industry	Index
Employees per establishment	21	4	17	Payroll per establishment	585,591	89,009	15
Revenue per establishment	1,370,364	276,264	20	Payroll as % of revenue	43	32	75
Revenue per employee	65,262	78,531	120	Payroll per employee	27,888	25,302	91

Sources: Same as General Statistics. The 'Average' column represents the average for the industry sector, in 1997, where the currently shown industry is classified. The Index shows the relationship between the Average and the Analyzed Industry. For example, 100 means that they are equal; 500 that the Analyzed Industry is five times the average; 50 means that the Analyzed Industry is half the national average. The abbreviation 'na' is used to show that data are 'not available'.

*Equivalent to SIC 8043.

LEADING COMPANIES   Number shown: **3**   Total sales ($ mil): **72**   Total employment (000): **0.5**

Company Name	Address				CEO Name	Phone	Co. Type	Sales ($ mil)	Empl. (000)
Molina Medical Centers	1 Golden Shore Dr	Long Beach	CA	90802	J. Mario Molina	562-435-3666	R	60*	0.5
National Foot Care Program Inc.	17117 W Nine Mile	Southfield	MI	48075	William Hoffman	248-559-2579	R	12	<0.1
Ivar E. Roth	351 Hospital Rd	Newport Beach	CA	92663		714-650-1147	N	0	<0.1

Source: *Ward's Business Directory of U.S. Private and Public Companies*, Volumes 1 and 2, 2000. The company type code used is as follows: P - Public, R - Private, S - Subsidiary, D - Division, J - Joint Venture, A - Affiliate, G - Group, N - Company type not reported. Sales are in millions of dollars, employees are in thousands. An asterisk (*) indicates an estimated sales volume. The symbol < stands for 'less than'. Company names and addresses are truncated, in some cases, to fit into the available space.

LOCATION BY STATE AND REGIONAL CONCENTRATION

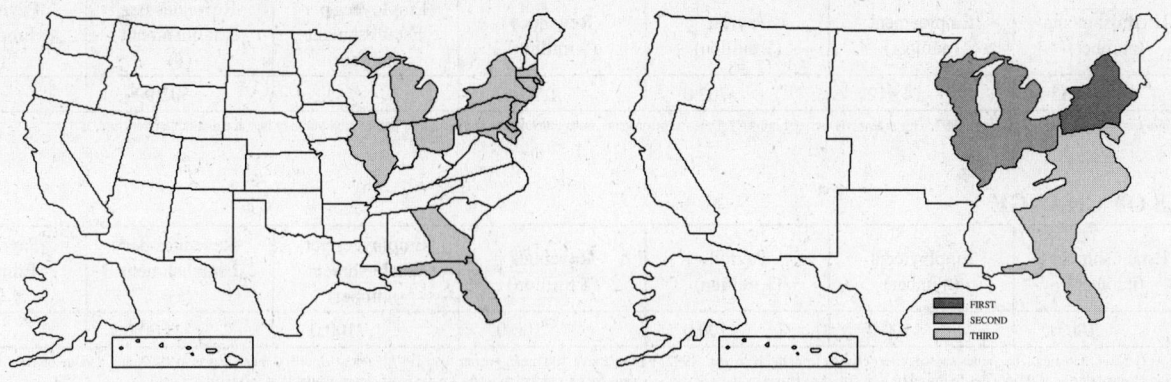

INDUSTRY DATA BY STATE

State	Establishments Total (number)	% of U.S.	Employment Total (number)	% of U.S.	Per Estab.	Payroll Total ($ mil.)	Per Empl. ($)	Revenues Total ($ mil.)	% of U.S.	Per Estab. ($)
New York	1,087	12.5	3,414	11.2	3	70.7	20,707	286.5	12.0	263,598
California	825	9.5	2,418	7.9	3	59.8	24,751	214.0	8.9	259,345
Florida	613	7.1	2,459	8.1	4	70.0	28,473	185.4	7.7	302,406
Pennsylvania	663	7.7	2,270	7.4	3	46.3	20,385	157.2	6.6	237,143
New Jersey	531	6.1	1,767	5.8	3	37.1	20,971	143.2	6.0	269,695
Illinois	489	5.6	1,632	5.4	3	42.9	26,257	133.3	5.6	272,589
Michigan	421	4.9	1,868	6.1	4	53.8	28,812	133.0	5.6	315,917
Texas	427	4.9	1,369	4.5	3	40.1	29,315	125.4	5.2	293,780
Ohio	495	5.7	1,748	5.7	4	43.5	24,902	125.0	5.2	252,465
Georgia	175	2.0	770	2.5	4	26.1	33,887	71.0	3.0	405,886
Maryland	222	2.6	903	3.0	4	24.6	27,292	61.3	2.6	276,050
Massachusetts	230	2.7	718	2.4	3	17.8	24,742	60.8	2.5	264,535
Virginia	200	2.3	740	2.4	4	20.4	27,558	54.2	2.3	270,885
Connecticut	158	1.8	569	1.9	4	17.4	30,557	47.5	2.0	300,620
Indiana	174	2.0	613	2.0	4	14.8	24,217	45.6	1.9	261,885
North Carolina	141	1.6	590	1.9	4	15.8	26,780	44.6	1.9	316,262
Washington	169	2.0	539	1.8	3	11.1	20,551	40.8	1.7	241,538
Wisconsin	121	1.4	512	1.7	4	13.8	26,900	37.2	1.6	307,331
Missouri	117	1.4	397	1.3	3	11.0	27,776	32.8	1.4	280,658
Arizona	118	1.4	427	1.4	4	11.4	26,681	31.8	1.3	269,695
Tennessee	109	1.3	383	1.3	4	9.6	25,107	30.5	1.3	279,596
Colorado	93	1.1	356	1.2	4	10.1	28,486	26.9	1.1	289,624
Alabama	61	0.7	305	1.0	5	9.6	31,361	22.1	0.9	361,639
Iowa	81	0.9	312	1.0	4	8.0	25,526	21.1	0.9	260,049
Kentucky	62	0.7	225	0.7	4	7.3	32,382	19.4	0.8	313,387
Louisiana	53	0.6	231	0.8	4	6.2	26,931	18.2	0.8	342,849
Minnesota	59	0.7	234	0.8	4	6.6	28,188	17.3	0.7	293,712
Oregon	63	0.7	183	0.6	3	4.0	21,918	16.8	0.7	266,476
Oklahoma	57	0.7	214	0.7	4	5.5	25,687	16.0	0.7	280,842
South Carolina	47	0.5	198	0.6	4	5.8	29,242	15.3	0.6	324,851
Rhode Island	48	0.6	204	0.7	4	4.8	23,480	13.7	0.6	286,125
Kansas	54	0.6	164	0.5	3	4.1	25,280	13.7	0.6	253,352
Utah	58	0.7	213	0.7	4	3.2	15,183	12.3	0.5	211,759
New Mexico	45	0.5	162	0.5	4	3.4	20,951	11.0	0.5	243,733
Nevada	34	0.4	114	0.4	3	3.1	27,482	10.6	0.4	312,500
Nebraska	42	0.5	143	0.5	3	4.5	31,699	10.5	0.4	250,976
Arkansas	29	0.3	147	0.5	5	5.0	34,163	10.4	0.4	358,138
Maine	42	0.5	120	0.4	3	3.1	25,542	9.4	0.4	223,095
West Virginia	36	0.4	104	0.3	3	1.7	16,510	9.0	0.4	248,889
New Hampshire	31	0.4	116	0.4	4	2.7	22,991	8.8	0.4	284,516
D.C.	31	0.4	83	0.3	3	2.8	33,578	8.1	0.3	260,065
Delaware	21	0.2	98	0.3	5	3.0	30,102	7.2	0.3	344,952
Mississippi	27	0.3	106	0.3	4	2.0	18,425	7.2	0.3	264,963
Idaho	20	0.2	102	0.3	5	2.0	19,765	6.8	0.3	340,900
Montana	25	0.3	62	0.2	2	1.3	20,548	5.3	0.2	210,280
Hawaii	13	0.2	37	0.1	3	0.7	19,649	3.7	0.2	284,000
Alaska	8	0.1	28	0.1	4	0.7	24,643	3.4	0.1	422,375
South Dakota	13	0.2	37	0.1	3	0.6	16,757	2.7	0.1	208,615
Vermont	10	0.1	24	0.1	2	0.5	20,333	2.2	0.1	224,100
North Dakota	6	0.1	27	0.1	5	0.6	21,852	1.8	0.1	292,333
Wyoming	8	0.1	17	0.1	2	0.3	14,882	1.6	0.1	195,375

Source: 1997 *Economic Census*. The states are in descending order of revenues or establishments (if revenue data are missing for the majority). The symbol (D) appears when data are withheld to prevent disclosure of competitive information. States marked with (D) are sorted by number of establishments. A dash (-) indicates that the data element cannot be calculated. * indicates the midpoint of a range; 175, for example is the range 100-249. Shaded *states* on the state map indicate those states which have proportionately greater representation in the industry than would be indicated by the state's population; the ratio is based on total revenues or number of establishments. Shaded *regions* indicate where the industry is regionally most concentrated.

NAICS 621399 - OFFICES OF ALL HEALTH PRACTITIONERS NEC

GENERAL STATISTICS

Year	Establishments (number)	Employment (number)	Payroll ($ million)	Revenues ($ million)	Employees per Establishment (number)	Revenues per Establishment ($)	Payroll per Employee ($)
1997	5,835	24,912	702.0	1,768.0	4.3	302,999	28,179

Source: Economic Census of the United States, 1997. This is a newly defined industry. Data for prior years were unavailable at the time of publication but may become available over time.

INDICES OF CHANGE

Year	Establishments (number)	Employment (number)	Payroll ($ million)	Revenues ($ million)	Employees per Establishment (number)	Revenues per Establishment ($)	Payroll per Employee ($)
1997	100.0	100.0	100.0	100.0	100.0	100.0	100.0

Sources: Same as General Statistics. The values shown reflect change from the base year, 1997. Values above 100 mean greater than 1997, values below 100 mean less than 1997, and a value of 100 in the 1982-96 or 1998-2001 period means same as 1997. Values followed by a 'p' are projections by the editors; 'e' stands for extrapolation. Data are the most recent available at this level of detail.

SIC INDUSTRIES RELATED TO NAICS 621399

Each new NAICS code represents an industry that used to be part of an SIC or a part of several SIC industries. Data in this table are shown to provide transitional information for these cases. All available data for the precursor SIC(s) are shown. Even if only a part of an SIC is included in the NAICS, *all* data for the SIC are reproduced. If the SIC industry is not marked as being a part (pt) of the NAICS, the entire industry is embedded in the NAICS data. The SIC composition of the new industry provides some hints of the relative importance of its "ancestors." Data marked with a 'p' are projected. Projections begin with 1982 data. Data earlier than 1990 are not shown but are reflected in the projections.

SIC	Industry	1990	1991	1992	1993	1994	1995	1996	1997
8049	**Offices of Health Practitioners, nec (pt)**								
	Establishments (number)	14,968	16,957	22,260	23,992	24,817	25,445	28,554p	30,601p
	Employment (thousands)	82.0	91.6	103.5	123.9	126.3	142.1	153.0p	164.9p
	Revenues ($ million)	-	-	6,148.1	-	-	-	-	-

Source: Economic Census of the United States, 1992, annual surveys of economic sectors conducted by the Bureau of the Census, and estimates or projections based on the 1982-1992 period; not all data are shown. 'e' marks estimates made by the editors; 'p' indicates projections based on time series. A dash (-) indicates that data for this SIC or year were not available. The abbreviation (pt) next to the industry name indicates that only a part of the industry is present within the NAICS data. If no (pt) is shown, the entire industry is contained within the NAICS data.

SELECTED RATIOS

For 1997	Avg. of Information	Analyzed Industry	Index	For 1997	Avg. of Information	Analyzed Industry	Index
Employees per establishment	21	4	20	Payroll per establishment	585,591	120,308	21
Revenue per establishment	1,370,364	302,999	22	Payroll as % of revenue	43	40	93
Revenue per employee	65,262	70,970	109	Payroll per employee	27,888	28,179	101

Sources: Same as General Statistics. The 'Average' column represents the average for the industry sector, in 1997, where the currently shown industry is classified. The Index shows the relationship between the Average and the Analyzed Industry. For example, 100 means that they are equal; 500 that the Analyzed Industry is five times the average; 50 means that the Analyzed Industry is half the national average. The abbreviation 'na' is used to show that data are 'not available'.

LEADING COMPANIES Number shown: 25 Total sales ($ mil): 774 Total employment (000): 14.7

Company Name	Address				CEO Name	Phone	Co. Type	Sales ($ mil)	Empl. (000)
Rehabworks Inc.	910 Ridgebrook Rd	Sparks Glencoe	MD	21152		410-773-2555	R	360*	8.0
Curative Health Services Inc.	150 Motor Pkwy	Hauppauge	NY	11788	John Vakoutis	516-232-7000	P	104	0.7
American Healthways Inc.	3841 Green Hls	Nashville	TN	37215	Thomas G Cigarran	615-665-1122	P	50	0.6
Comprehensive Care Corp.	4200 W Cypress	Tampa	FL	33607	Chriss W Street	813-876-5036	P	46	0.3
U.S. Physical Therapy Inc.	3040 Post Oak Blvd	Houston	TX	77056	Roy W Spradlin	713-297-9050	P	44	0.7
Diabetes Treatment Centers	1 Burton Hills Blvd	Nashville	TN	37215	Thomas G Cigarran	615-665-1122	S	41	0.7
National Home Health Care Corp.	700 White Plains	Scarsdale	NY	10583	Frederick H Fialkow	914-722-9000	P	38	1.9
In-House Rehab Corp.	325 W Main St	Louisville	KY	40202	David V Hall	502-568-8963	R	14*	0.4
Diagnostic Imaging Services Inc.	1516 Cotner Ave	Los Angeles	CA	90025	Norman Hames	310-479-0399	S	13	<0.1
OptimumCare Corp.	30011 Ivy Glenn Dr	Laguna Niguel	CA	92677	Edward A Johnson	949-495-1100	P	13	0.2
Burger Physical Therapy Services	1301 E Bidwell St	Folsom	CA	95630	Carol Burger	916-983-5915	S	12*	0.3
Burger Physical Therapy	1301 E Bidwell	Folsom	CA	95630	Carol Burger	916-983-5900	S	10*	0.1
Plus One Holdings Inc.	90 West St	New York	NY	10006	Micheal A Motta	212-791-2300	R	9	0.3
Ambulatory Healthcare	7960 Donagan Dr	Manassas	VA	20109	William Danielczyk	703-361-9731	R	4	0.1
Medical Advisory Systems Inc.	8050 S Maryland	Owings	MD	20736	Thomas M Hall	301-855-8070	P	3	<0.1
Corporate Psychology Resources	233 Peachtree	Atlanta	GA	30303	Frank M Merritt	404-266-9368	R	2*	<0.1
FEI Behavioral Health	11700 W Lake	Milwaukee	WI	53224		414-359-1055	R	2*	<0.1
Genesis Elder Care/Rehabilitation	101 E East State St	Kennett Square	PA	19348		610-444-6350	D	2*	<0.1
St. Charles Sports & Physical	263 Centre Pointe	St. Peters	MO	63376	Dennis Roth	314-441-7500	R	2*	<0.1
Aquatic Rehabilitation Center Inc.	10567 Montgomery	Cincinnati	OH	45242	Stephen Kempf	513-793-5525	R	1*	<0.1
BaySport Inc.	196 N 3rd St	San Jose	CA	95112		408-287-8288	R	1	<0.1
MDA Consulting Group Inc.	150 S 5th St	Minneapolis	MN	55402	Sandra L Davis	612-332-8182	R	1*	<0.1
Comprehensive Health Services	3543 N 7th St	Phoenix	AZ	85014	Robert Gear	602-263-8484	R	1	<0.1
HEALTHSOUTH Cascade	9260-B S E Stark St	Portland	OR	97216		503-253-2662	D	0*	<0.1
Nutrition Consultants Inc.	1643-B Owen Dr	Fayetteville	NC	28304		910-483-4202	N	0	<0.1

Source: Ward's Business Directory of U.S. Private and Public Companies, Volumes 1 and 2, 2000. The company type code used is as follows: P - Public, R - Private, S - Subsidiary, D - Division, J - Joint Venture, A - Affiliate, G - Group, N - Company type not reported. Sales are in millions of dollars, employees are in thousands. An asterisk (*) indicates an estimated sales volume. The symbol < stands for 'less than'. Company names and addresses are truncated, in some cases, to fit into the available space.

LOCATION BY STATE AND REGIONAL CONCENTRATION

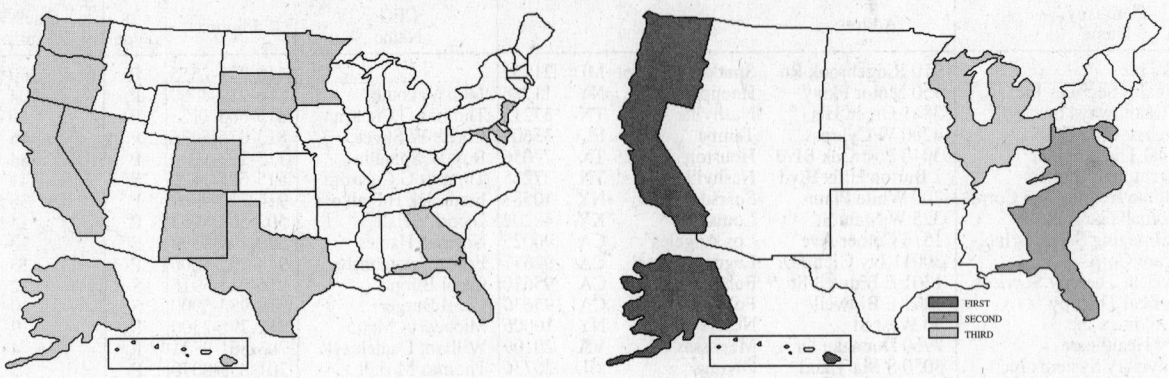

INDUSTRY DATA BY STATE

State	Establishments Total (number)	% of U.S.	Employment Total (number)	% of U.S.	Per Estab.	Payroll Total ($ mil.)	Per Empl. ($)	Revenues Total ($ mil.)	% of U.S.	Per Estab. ($)
California	792	13.6	4,151	16.7	5	111.6	26,894	323.0	18.3	407,880
Texas	468	8.0	2,301	9.2	5	65.0	28,262	159.7	9.0	341,158
Florida	659	11.3	1,776	7.1	3	49.6	27,908	131.6	7.4	199,634
New York	256	4.4	1,110	4.5	4	29.8	26,868	80.8	4.6	315,539
Pennsylvania	169	2.9	901	3.6	5	27.5	30,508	71.1	4.0	420,462
Minnesota	113	1.9	805	3.2	7	29.8	37,042	67.8	3.8	600,381
Illinois	170	2.9	984	3.9	6	32.8	33,384	65.8	3.7	387,312
Washington	280	4.8	933	3.7	3	22.2	23,811	61.3	3.5	219,050
New Jersey	147	2.5	594	2.4	4	20.4	34,407	56.8	3.2	386,429
Ohio	149	2.6	1,071	4.3	7	26.2	24,452	52.4	3.0	351,483
Michigan	180	3.1	839	3.4	5	21.5	25,621	52.1	2.9	289,500
Georgia	135	2.3	751	3.0	6	23.4	31,133	52.0	2.9	384,933
Maryland	128	2.2	619	2.5	5	15.2	24,528	40.5	2.3	316,727
Colorado	161	2.8	477	1.9	3	13.1	27,493	38.2	2.2	237,106
North Carolina	113	1.9	803	3.2	7	15.3	19,098	34.0	1.9	301,142
Tennessee	91	1.6	379	1.5	4	16.1	42,412	33.5	1.9	367,802
Indiana	85	1.5	554	2.2	7	10.8	19,408	27.7	1.6	326,294
Arizona	126	2.2	350	1.4	3	10.4	29,606	26.1	1.5	206,944
Wisconsin	79	1.4	375	1.5	5	9.0	24,024	25.2	1.4	318,405
Oregon	145	2.5	380	1.5	3	7.5	19,766	24.9	1.4	171,669
Massachusetts	101	1.7	297	1.2	3	8.7	29,330	24.5	1.4	242,505
Missouri	78	1.3	281	1.1	4	8.8	31,317	20.9	1.2	268,551
Virginia	86	1.5	230	0.9	3	6.8	29,683	20.7	1.2	241,128
Kentucky	57	1.0	245	1.0	4	7.5	30,682	19.3	1.1	339,404
Oklahoma	89	1.5	228	0.9	3	8.4	36,912	19.3	1.1	216,337
Alabama	61	1.0	247	1.0	4	10.3	41,607	19.0	1.1	311,016
Louisiana	82	1.4	346	1.4	4	8.5	24,616	18.5	1.0	225,110
South Carolina	63	1.1	354	1.4	6	9.6	27,237	18.0	1.0	285,413
Arkansas	46	0.8	135	0.5	3	7.0	51,911	15.7	0.9	341,087
Connecticut	54	0.9	171	0.7	3	3.7	21,655	14.5	0.8	267,833
New Mexico	83	1.4	198	0.8	2	5.0	25,177	13.3	0.8	160,337
Nevada	36	0.6	107	0.4	3	3.9	36,701	13.0	0.7	362,472
Utah	58	1.0	170	0.7	3	4.7	27,547	12.7	0.7	219,466
Iowa	38	0.7	102	0.4	3	5.5	53,549	10.6	0.6	278,526
Nebraska	26	0.4	66	0.3	3	4.5	68,803	8.9	0.5	341,231
Hawaii	40	0.7	133	0.5	3	3.1	22,992	8.8	0.5	219,150
Mississippi	33	0.6	191	0.8	6	3.5	18,084	8.2	0.5	247,758
Maine	33	0.6	153	0.6	5	3.4	22,078	7.8	0.4	236,788
Alaska	34	0.6	109	0.4	3	2.7	24,349	7.2	0.4	212,029
Montana	37	0.6	73	0.3	2	2.2	29,973	6.2	0.3	166,946
South Dakota	18	0.3	64	0.3	4	2.9	44,688	5.7	0.3	316,556
Idaho	25	0.4	75	0.3	3	2.1	28,253	4.5	0.3	178,560
West Virginia	14	0.2	77	0.3	6	2.4	31,429	4.4	0.2	313,357
New Hampshire	17	0.3	71	0.3	4	1.7	23,507	3.5	0.2	208,647
D.C.	16	0.3	42	0.2	3	1.4	34,333	3.2	0.2	200,125
Delaware	15	0.3	45	0.2	3	0.6	12,533	2.5	0.1	168,267
North Dakota	16	0.3	36	0.1	2	0.7	20,278	2.5	0.1	154,500
Wyoming	18	0.3	32	0.1	2	0.7	21,281	2.1	0.1	119,333
Vermont	18	0.3	32	0.1	2	0.6	19,656	2.1	0.1	119,056
Kansas	75	1.3	375*	-	-	(D)	-	(D)	-	-
Rhode Island	22	0.4	175*	-	-	(D)	-	(D)	-	-

Source: 1997 *Economic Census*. The states are in descending order of revenues or establishments (if revenue data are missing for the majority). The symbol (D) appears when data are withheld to prevent disclosure of competitive information. States marked with (D) are sorted by number of establishments. A dash (-) indicates that the data element cannot be calculated. * indicates the midpoint of a range; 175, for example is the range 100-249. Shaded *states* on the state map indicate those states which have proportionately greater representation in the industry than would be indicated by the state's population; the ratio is based on total revenues or number of establishments. Shaded *regions* indicate where the industry is regionally most concentrated.

NAICS 621410 - FAMILY PLANNING CENTERS

GENERAL STATISTICS

Year	Establishments (number)	Employment (number)	Payroll ($ million)	Revenues ($ million)	Employees per Establishment (number)	Revenues per Establishment ($)	Payroll per Employee ($)
1997	1,833	18,122	392.0	946.0	9.9	516,094	21,631

Source: Economic Census of the United States, 1997. This is a newly defined industry. Data for prior years were unavailable at the time of publication but may become available over time.

INDICES OF CHANGE

Year	Establishments (number)	Employment (number)	Payroll ($ million)	Revenues ($ million)	Employees per Establishment (number)	Revenues per Establishment ($)	Payroll per Employee ($)
1997	100.0	100.0	100.0	100.0	100.0	100.0	100.0

Sources: Same as General Statistics. The values shown reflect change from the base year, 1997. Values above 100 mean greater than 1997, values below 100 mean less than 1997, and a value of 100 in the 1982-96 or 1998-2001 period means same as 1997. Values followed by a 'p' are projections by the editors; 'e' stands for extrapolation. Data are the most recent available at this level of detail.

SIC INDUSTRIES RELATED TO NAICS 621410

Each new NAICS code represents an industry that used to be part of an SIC or a part of several SIC industries. Data in this table are shown to provide transitional information for these cases. All available data for the precursor SIC(s) are shown. Even if only a part of an SIC is included in the NAICS, *all* data for the SIC are reproduced. If the SIC industry is not marked as being a part (pt) of the NAICS, the entire industry is embedded in the NAICS data. The SIC composition of the new industry provides some hints of the relative importance of its "ancestors." Data marked with a 'p' are projected. Projections begin with 1982 data. Data earlier than 1990 are not shown but are reflected in the projections.

SIC	Industry	1990	1991	1992	1993	1994	1995	1996	1997
8093	**Specialty Outpatient Facilities, nec (pt)**								
	Establishments (number)	-	-	11,623	-	-	-	-	-
	Employment (thousands)	-	-	178.9	-	-	-	-	-
	Revenues ($ million)	5,326.0	6,508.0	6,476.0	6,999.0	7,965.0	8,616.0	9,586.0	9,994.4p
8099	**Health & Allied Services, nec (pt)**								
	Establishments (number)	-	-	5,011	-	-	-	-	-
	Employment (thousands)	-	-	71.9	-	-	-	-	-
	Revenues ($ million)	-	-	5,022.6	-	-	-	-	-

Source: Economic Census of the United States, 1992, annual surveys of economic sectors conducted by the Bureau of the Census, and estimates or projections based on the 1982-1992 period; not all data are shown. 'e' marks estimates made by the editors; 'p' indicates projections based on time series. A dash (-) indicates that data for this SIC or year were not available. The abbreviation (pt) next to the industry name indicates that only a part of the industry is present within the NAICS data. If no (pt) is shown, the entire industry is contained within the NAICS data.

SELECTED RATIOS

For 1997	Avg. of Information	Analyzed Industry	Index	For 1997	Avg. of Information	Analyzed Industry	Index
Employees per establishment	21	10	47	Payroll per establishment	585,591	213,857	37
Revenue per establishment	1,370,364	516,094	38	Payroll as % of revenue	43	41	97
Revenue per employee	65,262	52,202	80	Payroll per employee	27,888	21,631	78

Sources: Same as General Statistics. The 'Average' column represents the average for the industry sector, in 1997, where the currently shown industry is classified. The Index shows the relationship between the Average and the Analyzed Industry. For example, 100 means that they are equal; 500 that the Analyzed Industry is five times the average; 50 means that the Analyzed Industry is half the national average. The abbreviation 'na' is used to show that data are 'not available'.

LEADING COMPANIES

No company data available for this industry.

LOCATION BY STATE AND REGIONAL CONCENTRATION

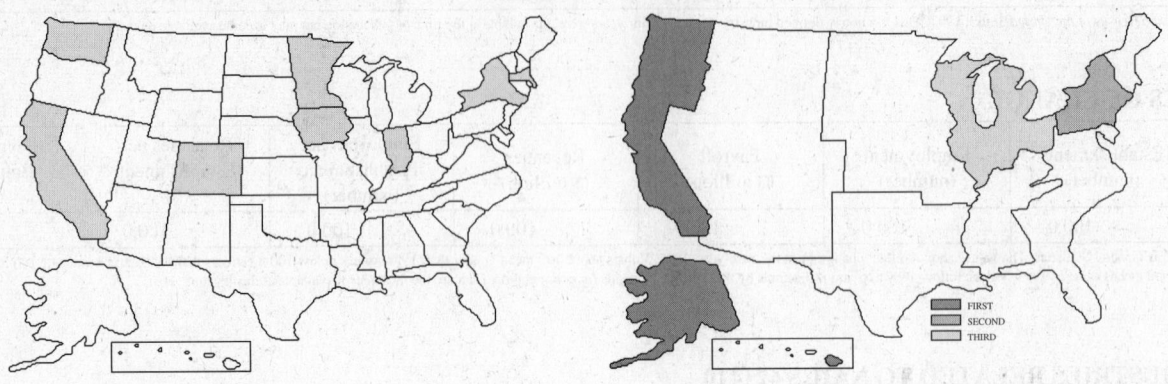

FIRST
SECOND
THIRD

INDUSTRY DATA BY STATE

State	Establishments Total (number)	Establishments % of U.S.	Employment Total (number)	Employment % of U.S.	Employment Per Estab.	Payroll Total ($ mil.)	Payroll Per Empl. ($)	Revenues Total ($ mil.)	Revenues % of U.S.	Revenues Per Estab. ($)
California	203	11.1	2,938	16.2	14	76.9	26,176	205.5	21.7	1,012,468
New York	137	7.5	2,179	12.0	16	59.8	27,462	128.1	13.5	935,307
Texas	158	8.6	1,033	5.7	7	22.8	22,111	58.2	6.2	368,165
Pennsylvania	103	5.6	820	4.5	8	16.6	20,271	37.7	4.0	366,204
Ohio	114	6.2	837	4.6	7	14.4	17,171	32.7	3.5	287,193
Florida	93	5.1	787	4.3	8	11.4	14,440	32.6	3.5	350,903
Massachusetts	37	2.0	741	4.1	20	13.6	18,306	30.5	3.2	823,865
Illinois	39	2.1	493	2.7	13	11.9	24,126	26.0	2.7	666,103
Washington	53	2.9	556	3.1	10	12.4	22,317	25.5	2.7	481,019
Indiana	77	4.2	476	2.6	6	9.5	19,941	22.7	2.4	294,195
North Carolina	41	2.2	367	2.0	9	6.5	17,820	20.6	2.2	503,049
Michigan	52	2.8	416	2.3	8	9.8	23,647	20.1	2.1	386,038
Wisconsin	59	3.2	452	2.5	8	8.4	18,639	18.3	1.9	309,542
Georgia	33	1.8	269	1.5	8	6.8	25,435	17.8	1.9	538,909
Minnesota	43	2.3	506	2.8	12	8.3	16,439	17.5	1.8	406,674
Colorado	7	0.4	150	0.8	21	7.7	51,567	15.5	1.6	2,214,143
Maryland	28	1.5	300	1.7	11	5.1	17,087	14.6	1.5	521,000
Missouri	29	1.6	247	1.4	9	4.0	16,259	14.6	1.5	503,690
Iowa	40	2.2	352	1.9	9	6.4	18,307	14.2	1.5	354,775
Arizona	33	1.8	230	1.3	7	4.4	19,200	11.7	1.2	354,182
Tennessee	25	1.4	209	1.2	8	4.2	20,067	10.6	1.1	425,880
Connecticut	13	0.7	127	0.7	10	2.4	19,283	10.3	1.1	794,231
Virginia	25	1.4	209	1.2	8	3.3	15,995	9.7	1.0	389,360
Oklahoma	22	1.2	175	1.0	8	3.1	17,743	8.6	0.9	390,227
Alabama	14	0.8	116	0.6	8	1.6	13,733	5.6	0.6	398,214
Nebraska	13	0.7	152	0.8	12	2.6	16,803	5.1	0.5	392,231
Kansas	16	0.9	111	0.6	7	1.8	16,252	4.3	0.5	266,125
Kentucky	19	1.0	81	0.4	4	1.3	16,346	3.4	0.4	178,368
Louisiana	6	0.3	41	0.2	7	0.5	12,805	2.7	0.3	455,500
West Virginia	4	0.2	46	0.3	11	1.2	27,000	2.4	0.3	599,500
Alaska	8	0.4	37	0.2	5	0.7	17,838	1.5	0.2	182,125
Oregon	8	0.4	18	0.1	2	0.2	12,056	1.4	0.1	170,875
South Dakota	4	0.2	48	0.3	12	0.5	10,479	1.3	0.1	335,750
Wyoming	7	0.4	29	0.2	4	0.5	17,724	1.0	0.1	141,286
Arkansas	6	0.3	17	0.1	3	0.2	13,529	0.5	0.0	77,667
New Hampshire	16	0.9	175*	-	-	(D)	-	(D)	-	-
Hawaii	6	0.3	60*	-	-	(D)	-	(D)	-	-
North Dakota	3	0.2	60*	-	-	(D)	-	(D)	-	-

Source: 1997 *Economic Census*. The states are in descending order of revenues or establishments (if revenue data are missing for the majority). The symbol (D) appears when data are withheld to prevent disclosure of competitive information. States marked with (D) are sorted by number of establishments. A dash (-) indicates that the data element cannot be calculated. * indicates the midpoint of a range; 175, for example is the range 100-249. Shaded *states* on the state map indicate those states which have proportionately greater representation in the industry than would be indicated by the state's population; the ratio is based on total revenues or number of establishments. Shaded *regions* indicate where the industry is regionally most concentrated.

NAICS 621420 - OUTPATIENT MENTAL HEALTH AND SUBSTANCE ABUSE CENTERS

GENERAL STATISTICS

Year	Establishments (number)	Employment (number)	Payroll ($ million)	Revenues ($ million)	Employees per Establishment (number)	Revenues per Establishment ($)	Payroll per Employee ($)
1997	6,294	125,097	2,998.0	6,219.0	19.9	988,084	23,965

Source: Economic Census of the United States, 1997. This is a newly defined industry. Data for prior years were unavailable at the time of publication but may become available over time.

INDICES OF CHANGE

Year	Establishments (number)	Employment (number)	Payroll ($ million)	Revenues ($ million)	Employees per Establishment (number)	Revenues per Establishment ($)	Payroll per Employee ($)
1997	100.0	100.0	100.0	100.0	100.0	100.0	100.0

Sources: Same as General Statistics. The values shown reflect change from the base year, 1997. Values above 100 mean greater than 1997, values below 100 mean less than 1997, and a value of 100 in the 1982-96 or 1998-2001 period means same as 1997. Values followed by a 'p' are projections by the editors; 'e' stands for extrapolation. Data are the most recent available at this level of detail.

SIC INDUSTRIES RELATED TO NAICS 621420

Each new NAICS code represents an industry that used to be part of an SIC or a part of several SIC industries. Data in this table are shown to provide transitional information for these cases. All available data for the precursor SIC(s) are shown. Even if only a part of an SIC is included in the NAICS, *all* data for the SIC are reproduced. If the SIC industry is not marked as being a part (pt) of the NAICS, the entire industry is embedded in the NAICS data. The SIC composition of the new industry provides some hints of the relative importance of its "ancestors." Data marked with a 'p' are projected. Projections begin with 1982 data. Data earlier than 1990 are not shown but are reflected in the projections.

SIC	Industry	1990	1991	1992	1993	1994	1995	1996	1997
8093	**Specialty Outpatient Facilities, nec (pt)**								
	Establishments (number)	-	-	11,623	-	-	-	-	-
	Employment (thousands)	-	-	178.9	-	-	-	-	-
	Revenues ($ million)	5,326.0	6,508.0	6,476.0	6,999.0	7,965.0	8,616.0	9,586.0	9,994.4$_p$

Source: Economic Census of the United States, 1992, annual surveys of economic sectors conducted by the Bureau of the Census, and estimates or projections based on the 1982-1992 period; not all data are shown. 'e' marks estimates made by the editors; 'p' indicates projections based on time series. A dash (-) indicates that data for this SIC or year were not available. The abbreviation (pt) next to the industry name indicates that only a part of the industry is present within the NAICS data. If no (pt) is shown, the entire industry is contained within the NAICS data.

SELECTED RATIOS

For 1997	Avg. of Information	Analyzed Industry	Index	For 1997	Avg. of Information	Analyzed Industry	Index
Employees per establishment	21	20	95	Payroll per establishment	585,591	476,327	81
Revenue per establishment	1,370,364	988,084	72	Payroll as % of revenue	43	48	113
Revenue per employee	65,262	49,713	76	Payroll per employee	27,888	23,965	86

Sources: Same as General Statistics. The 'Average' column represents the average for the industry sector, in 1997, where the currently shown industry is classified. The Index shows the relationship between the Average and the Analyzed Industry. For example, 100 means that they are equal; 500 that the Analyzed Industry is five times the average; 50 means that the Analyzed Industry is half the national average. The abbreviation 'na' is used to show that data are 'not available'.

LEADING COMPANIES

No company data available for this industry.

LOCATION BY STATE AND REGIONAL CONCENTRATION

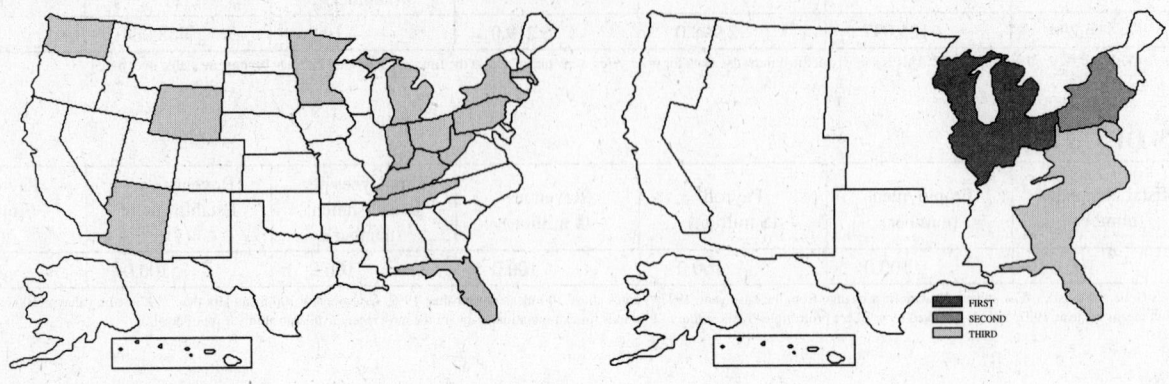

FIRST
SECOND
THIRD

INDUSTRY DATA BY STATE

State	Establishments		Employment			Payroll		Revenues		
	Total (number)	% of U.S.	Total (number)	% of U.S.	Per Estab.	Total ($ mil.)	Per Empl. ($)	Total ($ mil.)	% of U.S.	Per Estab. ($)
New York	422	6.7	9,549	7.6	23	252.2	26,414	517.0	8.3	1,225,204
Florida	404	6.4	9,375	7.5	23	213.2	22,737	456.4	7.3	1,129,750
California	575	9.1	7,367	5.9	13	188.2	25,547	418.6	6.7	728,031
Pennsylvania	270	4.3	9,146	7.3	34	204.2	22,323	377.4	6.1	1,397,856
Ohio	297	4.7	6,761	5.4	23	173.0	25,595	315.7	5.1	1,063,020
Arizona	139	2.2	3,175	2.5	23	79.8	25,120	310.6	5.0	2,234,626
Minnesota	199	3.2	4,241	3.4	21	113.3	26,722	268.6	4.3	1,349,633
Michigan	233	3.7	4,371	3.5	19	107.0	24,490	263.2	4.2	1,129,592
Texas	291	4.6	4,392	3.5	15	107.2	24,406	243.4	3.9	836,282
Illinois	244	3.9	4,941	3.9	20	123.9	25,071	230.5	3.7	944,492
Massachusetts	203	3.2	5,041	4.0	25	122.8	24,351	223.9	3.6	1,102,764
Indiana	177	2.8	3,358	2.7	19	92.4	27,502	189.4	3.0	1,069,876
Washington	185	2.9	3,725	3.0	20	94.5	25,373	172.5	2.8	932,573
Kentucky	206	3.3	3,921	3.1	19	85.5	21,809	167.8	2.7	814,631
Tennessee	130	2.1	2,960	2.4	23	68.8	23,259	153.8	2.5	1,183,315
Maryland	108	1.7	1,938	1.5	18	46.3	23,879	103.4	1.7	957,843
West Virginia	80	1.3	2,719	2.2	34	47.1	17,304	101.3	1.6	1,266,425
Missouri	103	1.6	2,579	2.1	25	53.1	20,605	98.4	1.6	955,204
Georgia	107	1.7	1,740	1.4	16	35.0	20,091	78.4	1.3	733,000
Alabama	98	1.6	2,005	1.6	20	37.4	18,647	73.4	1.2	749,041
Oklahoma	107	1.7	1,725	1.4	16	37.2	21,548	71.8	1.2	671,131
North Carolina	101	1.6	1,358	1.1	13	30.9	22,732	64.2	1.0	635,970
Virginia	84	1.3	996	0.8	12	26.8	26,945	54.1	0.9	644,417
Iowa	80	1.3	1,362	1.1	17	31.6	23,173	52.6	0.8	657,188
Wisconsin	114	1.8	1,024	0.8	9	21.4	20,923	43.1	0.7	378,026
Nebraska	28	0.4	295	0.2	11	8.5	28,668	20.9	0.3	745,714
Louisiana	60	1.0	317	0.3	5	6.6	20,675	14.9	0.2	248,950
South Dakota	28	0.4	424	0.3	15	7.7	18,248	13.9	0.2	496,464
Wyoming	17	0.3	332	0.3	20	7.9	23,732	11.1	0.2	650,118

Source: 1997 *Economic Census*. The states are in descending order of revenues or establishments (if revenue data are missing for the majority). The symbol (D) appears when data are withheld to prevent disclosure of competitive information. States marked with (D) are sorted by number of establishments. A dash (-) indicates that the data element cannot be calculated. * indicates the midpoint of a range; 175, for example is the range 100-249. Shaded *states* on the state map indicate those states which have proportionately greater representation in the industry than would be indicated by the state's population; the ratio is based on total revenues or number of establishments. Shaded *regions* indicate where the industry is regionally most concentrated.

NAICS 621491 - HMO MEDICAL CENTERS

GENERAL STATISTICS

Year	Establishments (number)	Employment (number)	Payroll ($ million)	Revenues ($ million)	Employees per Establishment (number)	Revenues per Establishment ($)	Payroll per Employee ($)
1997	772	58,247	2,405.0	13,999.0	75.4	18,133,420	41,290

Source: Economic Census of the United States, 1997. This is a newly defined industry. Data for prior years were unavailable at the time of publication but may become available over time.

INDICES OF CHANGE

Year	Establishments (number)	Employment (number)	Payroll ($ million)	Revenues ($ million)	Employees per Establishment (number)	Revenues per Establishment ($)	Payroll per Employee ($)
1997	100.0	100.0	100.0	100.0	100.0	100.0	100.0

Sources: Same as General Statistics. The values shown reflect change from the base year, 1997. Values above 100 mean greater than 1997, values below 100 mean less than 1997, and a value of 100 in the 1982-96 or 1998-2001 period means same as 1997. Values followed by a 'p' are projections by the editors; 'e' stands for extrapolation. Data are the most recent available at this level of detail.

SIC INDUSTRIES RELATED TO NAICS 621491

Each new NAICS code represents an industry that used to be part of an SIC or a part of several SIC industries. Data in this table are shown to provide transitional information for these cases. All available data for the precursor SIC(s) are shown. Even if only a part of an SIC is included in the NAICS, *all* data for the SIC are reproduced. If the SIC industry is not marked as being a part (pt) of the NAICS, the entire industry is embedded in the NAICS data. The SIC composition of the new industry provides some hints of the relative importance of its "ancestors." Data marked with a 'p' are projected. Projections begin with 1982 data. Data earlier than 1990 are not shown but are reflected in the projections.

SIC	Industry	1990	1991	1992	1993	1994	1995	1996	1997
8011	**Offices of Physicians (pt)**								
	Establishments (number)	193,620	195,610	197,701	200,590	198,538	194,288	198,532p	199,126p
	Employment (thousands)	1,387.2	1,454.0	1,356.7	1,577.1	1,621.4	1,663.9	1,730.5p	1,793.6p
	Revenues ($ million)	128,871.0	138,576.0	151,824.0	154,242.0	159,616.0	167,969.0	173,483.0	186,612.0p

Source: Economic Census of the United States, 1992, annual surveys of economic sectors conducted by the Bureau of the Census, and estimates or projections based on the 1982-1992 period; not all data are shown. 'e' marks estimates made by the editors; 'p' indicates projections based on time series. A dash (-) indicates that data for this SIC or year were not available. The abbreviation (pt) next to the industry name indicates that only a part of the industry is present within the NAICS data. If no (pt) is shown, the entire industry is contained within the NAICS data.

SELECTED RATIOS

For 1997	Avg. of Information	Analyzed Industry	Index	For 1997	Avg. of Information	Analyzed Industry	Index
Employees per establishment	21	75	359	Payroll per establishment	585,591	3,115,285	532
Revenue per establishment	1,370,364	18,133,420	1,323	Payroll as % of revenue	43	17	40
Revenue per employee	65,262	240,339	368	Payroll per employee	27,888	41,290	148

Sources: Same as General Statistics. The 'Average' column represents the average for the industry sector, in 1997, where the currently shown industry is classified. The Index shows the relationship between the Average and the Analyzed Industry. For example, 100 means that they are equal; 500 that the Analyzed Industry is five times the average; 50 means that the Analyzed Industry is half the national average. The abbreviation 'na' is used to show that data are 'not available'.

LEADING COMPANIES
No company data available for this industry.

LOCATION BY STATE AND REGIONAL CONCENTRATION

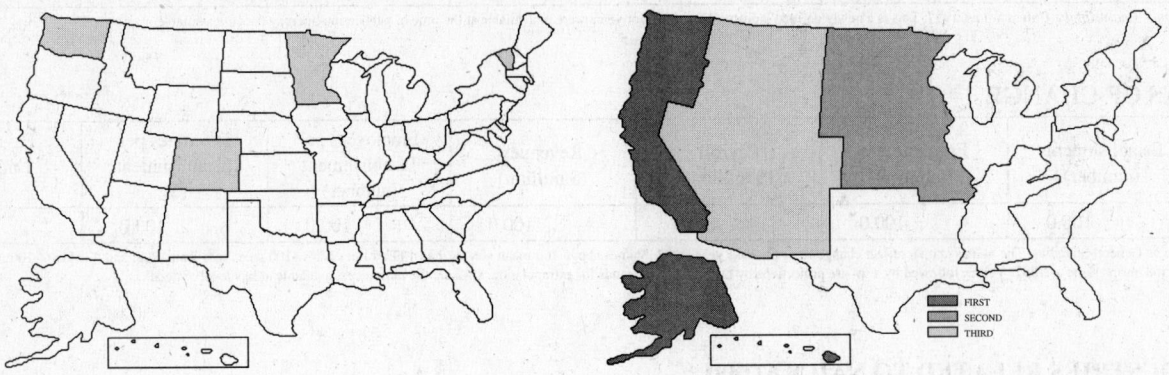

FIRST
SECOND
THIRD

INDUSTRY DATA BY STATE

State	Establishments		Employment			Payroll		Revenues		
	Total (number)	% of U.S.	Total (number)	% of U.S.	Per Estab.	Total ($ mil.)	Per Empl. ($)	Total ($ mil.)	% of U.S.	Per Estab. ($)
Washington	49	6.3	7,500*	-	-	(D)	-	(D)	-	-
Minnesota	29	3.8	3,750*	-	-	(D)	-	(D)	-	-
Colorado	19	2.5	1,750*	-	-	(D)	-	(D)	-	-
Vermont	13	1.7	375*	-	-	(D)	-	(D)	-	-
Wisconsin	12	1.6	1,750*	-	-	(D)	-	(D)	-	-
Texas	9	1.2	750*	-	-	(D)	-	(D)	-	-
Connecticut	6	0.8	375*	-	-	(D)	-	(D)	-	-
Tennessee	4	0.5	175*	-	-	(D)	-	(D)	-	-
Arizona	1	0.1	175*	-	-	(D)	-	(D)	-	-
D.C.	1	0.1	175*	-	-	(D)	-	(D)	-	-
Idaho	1	0.1	60*	-	-	(D)	-	(D)	-	-
New Hampshire	1	0.1	60*	-	-	(D)	-	(D)	-	-

Source: 1997 *Economic Census*. The states are in descending order of revenues or establishments (if revenue data are missing for the majority). The symbol (D) appears when data are withheld to prevent disclosure of competitive information. States marked with (D) are sorted by number of establishments. A dash (-) indicates that the data element cannot be calculated. * indicates the midpoint of a range; 175, for example is the range 100-249. Shaded *states* on the state map indicate those states which have proportionately greater representation in the industry than would be indicated by the state's population; the ratio is based on total revenues or number of establishments. Shaded *regions* indicate where the industry is regionally most concentrated.

NAICS 621492 - KIDNEY DIALYSIS CENTERS*

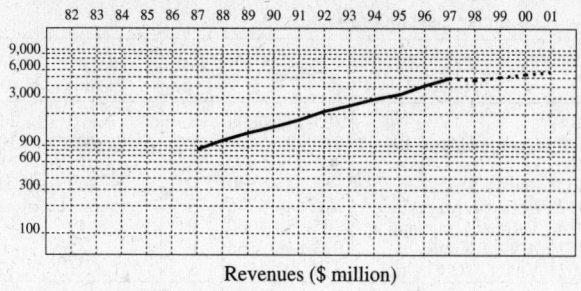

Revenues ($ million)

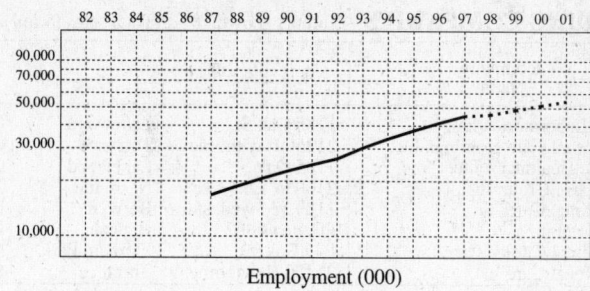

Employment (000)

GENERAL STATISTICS

Year	Establishments (number)	Employment (number)	Payroll ($ million)	Revenues ($ million)	Employees per Establishment (number)	Revenues per Establishment ($)	Payroll per Employee ($)
1982	-	-	-	-	-	-	-
1983	-	-	-	-	-	-	-
1984	-	-	-	-	-	-	-
1985	-	-	-	-	-	-	-
1986	-	-	-	-	-	-	-
1987	839	16,808	317.0	825.0	20.0	983,313	18,860
1988	934 e	18,747 e	392.0 e	1,033.0 e	20.1 e	1,105,996 e	20,910 e
1989	1,029 e	20,686 e	467.0 e	1,242.0 e	20.1 e	1,206,997 e	22,576 e
1990	1,125 e	22,626 e	542.0 e	1,451.0	20.1 e	1,289,778 e	23,955 e
1991	1,220 e	24,565 e	617.0 e	1,717.0	20.1 e	1,407,377 e	25,117 e
1992	1,315	26,504	692.0	2,140.0	20.2	1,627,376	26,109
1993	1,495 e	30,231 e	821.0 e	2,468.0	20.2 e	1,650,836 e	27,158 e
1994	1,675 e	33,959 e	951.0 e	2,898.0	20.3 e	1,730,149 e	28,004 e
1995	1,854 e	37,686 e	1,081.0 e	3,259.0	20.3 e	1,757,821 e	28,684 e
1996	2,034 e	41,414 e	1,211.0 e	4,077.0 e	20.4 e	2,004,425 e	29,241 e
1997	2,214	45,141	1,341.0	4,895.0	20.4	2,210,930	29,707
1998	2,255 p	45,942 p	1,381.0 p	4,667.0 p	20.4 p	2,069,623 p	30,060 p
1999	2,393 p	48,776 p	1,484.0 p	5,051.0 p	20.4 p	2,110,740 p	30,425 p
2000	2,530 p	51,609 p	1,586.0 p	5,434.0 p	20.4 p	2,147,826 p	30,731 p
2001	2,668 p	54,442 p	1,689.0 p	5,818.0 p	20.4 p	2,180,660 p	31,024 p

Sources: *Economic Census of the United States*, 1982, 1987, 1992, 1997. Establishment counts, employment, and payroll are from *County Business Patterns* for non-Census years. In non-Census years, industries in the Manufacturing range under SIC coding include data from the *Annual Survey of Manufactures* (ASM); those in the old Services range include data from the *Services Annual Survey* (SAS). Values followed by a 'p' are projections by the editors. Extrapolations are marked by 'e'. Data are the most recent available at this level of detail.

INDICES OF CHANGE

Year	Establishments (number)	Employment (number)	Payroll ($ million)	Revenues ($ million)	Employees per Establishment (number)	Revenues per Establishment ($)	Payroll per Employee ($)
1982	-	-	-	-	-	-	-
1987	37.9	37.2	23.6	16.9	98.3	44.5	63.5
1992	59.4	58.7	51.6	43.7	98.9	73.6	87.9
1993	67.5 e	67.0 e	61.2 e	50.4	99.2 e	74.7 e	91.4 e
1994	75.7 e	75.2 e	70.9 e	59.2	99.4 e	78.3 e	94.3 e
1995	83.7 e	83.5 e	80.6 e	66.6	99.7 e	79.5 e	96.6 e
1996	91.9 e	91.7 e	90.3 e	83.3 e	99.9 e	90.7 e	98.4 e
1997	100.0	100.0	100.0	100.0	100.0	100.0	100.0
1998	101.9 p	101.8 p	103.0 p	95.3 p	99.9 p	93.6 p	101.2 p
1999	108.1 p	108.1 p	110.7 p	103.2 p	100.0 p	95.5 p	102.4 p
2000	114.3 p	114.3 p	118.3 p	111.0 p	100.0 p	97.1 p	103.4 p
2001	120.5 p	120.6 p	126.0 p	118.9 p	100.1 p	98.6 p	104.4 p

Sources: Same as General Statistics. The values shown reflect change from the base year, 1997. Values above 100 mean greater than 1997, values below 100 mean less than 1997, and a value of 100 in the 1982-96 or 1998-2001 period means same as 1997. Values followed by a 'p' are projections by the editors; 'e' stands for extrapolation. Data are the most recent available at this level of detail.

SELECTED RATIOS

For 1997	Avg. of Information	Analyzed Industry	Index	For 1997	Avg. of Information	Analyzed Industry	Index
Employees per establishment	21	20	97	Payroll per establishment	585,591	605,691	103
Revenue per establishment	1,370,364	2,210,930	161	Payroll as % of revenue	43	27	64
Revenue per employee	65,262	108,438	166	Payroll per employee	27,888	29,707	107

Sources: Same as General Statistics. The 'Average' column represents the average for the industry sector, in 1997, where the currently shown industry is classified. The Index shows the relationship between the Average and the Analyzed Industry. For example, 100 means that they are equal; 500 that the Analyzed Industry is five times the average; 50 means that the Analyzed Industry is half the national average. The abbreviation 'na' is used to show that data are 'not available'.

*Equivalent to SIC 8092.

LEADING COMPANIES   Number shown: **8**   Total sales ($ mil): **4,687**   Total employment (000): **49.4**

Company Name	Address				CEO Name	Phone	Co. Type	Sales ($ mil)	Empl. (000)
COBE Laboratories Inc.	1185 Oak St	Lakewood	CO	80215		303-232-6800	S	1,720*	11.0
Total Renal Care Holdings Inc.	21250 Hawthorne	Torrance	CA	90503	George Deltuff III	310-792-2600	P	1,205	12.3
Gambro Healthcare Inc.	1185 Oak St	Lakewood	CO	80215		303-232-6800	S	1,018*	8.0
Renal Care Group Inc.	2100 W End Ave	Nashville	TN	37203	Sam A Brooks Jr	615-345-5500	P	369	3.5
Total Renal Care	1180 W Swedesford	Berwyn	PA	19312	Robert L Mayer Jr	610-644-4796	S	323	2.0
Medicore Inc.	PO Box 4862	Hialeah	FL	33014	Thomas Langbein	305-558-4000	P	49	0.6
Continental Choice Care Inc.	P O Box 99	Florham Park	NJ	07932	Alvin S Trenk	973-898-9666	P	1	<0.1
Total Renal Care Inc.	21250 Hawthorne	Torrance	CA	90503	Victor MG Chaltiel	310-792-2600	S	1	12.0

Source: *Ward's Business Directory of U.S. Private and Public Companies*, Volumes 1 and 2, 2000. The company type code used is as follows: P - Public, R - Private, S - Subsidiary, D - Division, J - Joint Venture, A - Affiliate, G - Group, N - Company type not reported. Sales are in millions of dollars, employees are in thousands. An asterisk (*) indicates an estimated sales volume. The symbol < stands for 'less than'. Company names and addresses are truncated, in some cases, to fit into the available space.

LOCATION BY STATE AND REGIONAL CONCENTRATION

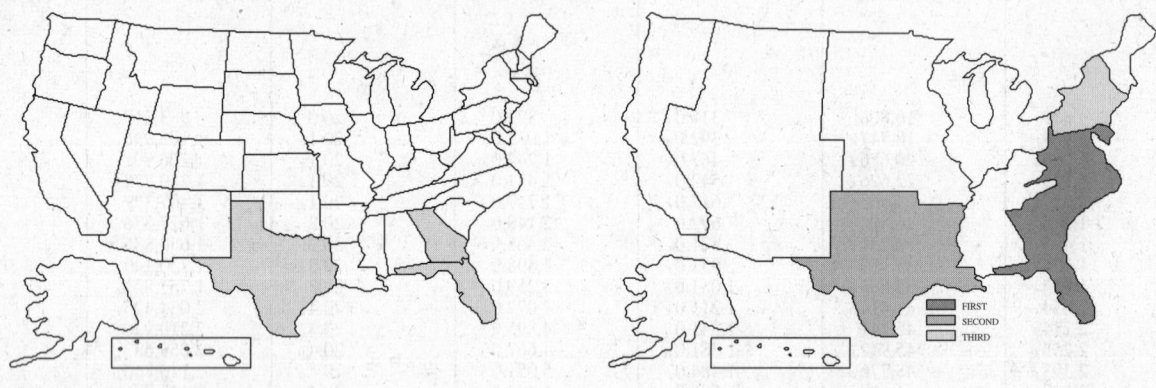

INDUSTRY DATA BY STATE

State	Establishments Total (number)	% of U.S.	Employment Total (number)	% of U.S.	Per Estab.	Payroll Total ($ mil.)	Per Empl. ($)	Revenues Total ($ mil.)	% of U.S.	Per Estab. ($)
Texas	197	8.9	4,330	9.6	22	120.5	27,823	450.2	9.2	2,285,137
Florida	180	8.1	3,460	7.7	19	96.3	27,835	349.2	7.1	1,939,756
New York	67	3.0	2,316	5.1	35	82.9	35,791	235.9	4.8	3,521,149
Illinois	68	3.1	1,810	4.0	27	50.8	28,056	200.3	4.1	2,945,868
Georgia	84	3.8	1,640	3.6	20	44.5	27,129	193.9	4.0	2,307,762
Minnesota	53	2.4	406	0.9	8	16.5	40,638	56.0	1.1	1,056,453
D.C.	18	0.8	376	0.8	21	13.0	34,503	43.5	0.9	2,414,167
Kansas	30	1.4	347	0.8	12	9.8	28,346	42.0	0.9	1,399,933
Oklahoma	29	1.3	310	0.7	11	8.9	28,568	37.9	0.8	1,307,345
Wisconsin	12	0.5	235	0.5	20	6.4	27,085	27.5	0.6	2,293,583
Iowa	8	0.4	79	0.2	10	3.0	37,367	10.4	0.2	1,295,750
West Virginia	10	0.5	175*	-	-	(D)	-	(D)	-	-
Delaware	6	0.3	175*	-	-	(D)	-	(D)	-	-
Nevada	5	0.2	175*	-	-	(D)	-	(D)	-	-
New Hampshire	4	0.2	60*	-	-	(D)	-	(D)	-	-
South Dakota	4	0.2	60*	-	-	(D)	-	(D)	-	-
Maine	3	0.1	60*	-	-	(D)	-	(D)	-	-
Alaska	2	0.1	60*	-	-	(D)	-	(D)	-	-
Idaho	2	0.1	60*	-	-	(D)	-	(D)	-	-
Utah	2	0.1	10*	-	-	(D)	-	(D)	-	-
Wyoming	2	0.1	60*	-	-	(D)	-	(D)	-	-
Montana	1	-	10*	-	-	(D)	-	(D)	-	-

Source: 1997 *Economic Census*. The states are in descending order of revenues or establishments (if revenue data are missing for the majority). The symbol (D) appears when data are withheld to prevent disclosure of competitive information. States marked with (D) are sorted by number of establishments. A dash (-) indicates that the data element cannot be calculated. * indicates the midpoint of a range; 175, for example is the range 100-249. Shaded *states* on the state map indicate those states which have proportionately greater representation in the industry than would be indicated by the state's population; the ratio is based on total revenues or number of establishments. Shaded *regions* indicate where the industry is regionally most concentrated.

NAICS 621493 - FREESTANDING AMBULATORY SURGICAL AND EMERGENCY CENTERS

GENERAL STATISTICS

Year	Establishments (number)	Employment (number)	Payroll ($ million)	Revenues ($ million)	Employees per Establishment (number)	Revenues per Establishment ($)	Payroll per Employee ($)
1997	2,402	42,416	1,524.0	4,761.0	17.7	1,982,098	35,930

Source: Economic Census of the United States, 1997. This is a newly defined industry. Data for prior years were unavailable at the time of publication but may become available over time.

INDICES OF CHANGE

Year	Establishments (number)	Employment (number)	Payroll ($ million)	Revenues ($ million)	Employees per Establishment (number)	Revenues per Establishment ($)	Payroll per Employee ($)
1997	100.0	100.0	100.0	100.0	100.0	100.0	100.0

Sources: Same as General Statistics. The values shown reflect change from the base year, 1997. Values above 100 mean greater than 1997, values below 100 mean less than 1997, and a value of 100 in the 1982-96 or 1998-2001 period means same as 1997. Values followed by a 'p' are projections by the editors; 'e' stands for extrapolation. Data are the most recent available at this level of detail.

SIC INDUSTRIES RELATED TO NAICS 621493

Each new NAICS code represents an industry that used to be part of an SIC or a part of several SIC industries. Data in this table are shown to provide transitional information for these cases. All available data for the precursor SIC(s) are shown. Even if only a part of an SIC is included in the NAICS, *all* data for the SIC are reproduced. If the SIC industry is not marked as being a part (pt) of the NAICS, the entire industry is embedded in the NAICS data. The SIC composition of the new industry provides some hints of the relative importance of its "ancestors." Data marked with a 'p' are projected. Projections begin with 1982 data. Data earlier than 1990 are not shown but are reflected in the projections.

SIC	Industry	1990	1991	1992	1993	1994	1995	1996	1997
8011	**Offices of Physicians (pt)**								
	Establishments (number)	193,620	195,610	197,701	200,590	198,538	194,288	198,532p	199,126p
	Employment (thousands)	1,387.2	1,454.0	1,356.7	1,577.1	1,621.4	1,663.9	1,730.5p	1,793.6p
	Revenues ($ million)	128,871.0	138,576.0	151,824.0	154,242.0	159,616.0	167,969.0	173,483.0	186,612.0p

Source: Economic Census of the United States, 1992, annual surveys of economic sectors conducted by the Bureau of the Census, and estimates or projections based on the 1982-1992 period; not all data are shown. 'e' marks estimates made by the editors; 'p' indicates projections based on time series. A dash (-) indicates that data for this SIC or year were not available. The abbreviation (pt) next to the industry name indicates that only a part of the industry is present within the NAICS data. If no (pt) is shown, the entire industry is contained within the NAICS data.

SELECTED RATIOS

For 1997	Avg. of Information	Analyzed Industry	Index	For 1997	Avg. of Information	Analyzed Industry	Index
Employees per establishment	21	18	84	Payroll per establishment	585,591	634,471	108
Revenue per establishment	1,370,364	1,982,098	145	Payroll as % of revenue	43	32	75
Revenue per employee	65,262	112,245	172	Payroll per employee	27,888	35,930	129

Sources: Same as General Statistics. The 'Average' column represents the average for the industry sector, in 1997, where the currently shown industry is classified. The Index shows the relationship between the Average and the Analyzed Industry. For example, 100 means that they are equal; 500 that the Analyzed Industry is five times the average; 50 means that the Analyzed Industry is half the national average. The abbreviation 'na' is used to show that data are 'not available'.

LEADING COMPANIES
No company data available for this industry.

LOCATION BY STATE AND REGIONAL CONCENTRATION

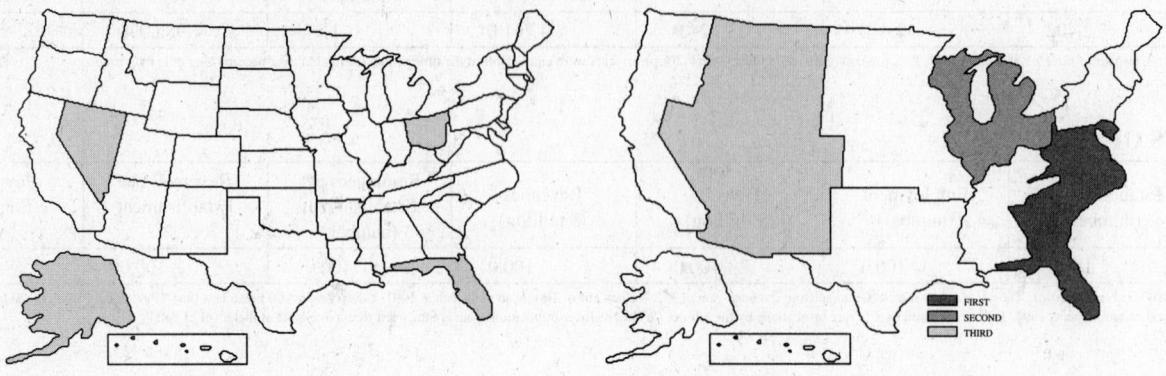

FIRST
SECOND
THIRD

INDUSTRY DATA BY STATE

State	Establishments		Employment			Payroll		Revenues		
	Total (number)	% of U.S.	Total (number)	% of U.S.	Per Estab.	Total ($ mil.)	Per Empl. ($)	Total ($ mil.)	% of U.S.	Per Estab. ($)
Florida	234	9.7	4,378	10.3	19	146.9	33,560	500.6	10.5	2,139,393
Ohio	131	5.5	2,125	5.0	16	75.0	35,310	218.2	4.6	1,665,763
Wisconsin	34	1.4	798	1.9	23	32.4	40,637	90.7	1.9	2,668,559
Nevada	27	1.1	700	1.7	26	29.1	41,551	85.0	1.8	3,149,185
Colorado	26	1.1	514	1.2	20	14.5	28,265	63.0	1.3	2,421,731
Oklahoma	29	1.2	377	0.9	13	13.3	35,273	48.6	1.0	1,676,828
West Virginia	14	0.6	229	0.5	16	7.6	33,017	27.7	0.6	1,976,857
Alaska	8	0.3	135	0.3	17	5.1	37,867	15.7	0.3	1,968,375
Montana	14	0.6	128	0.3	9	4.6	35,844	11.7	0.2	836,000
Hawaii	10	0.4	107	0.3	11	6.6	62,112	11.3	0.2	1,130,200
North Dakota	6	0.2	74	0.2	12	1.9	25,446	5.6	0.1	936,667
Wyoming	4	0.2	15	0.0	4	0.4	26,133	1.8	0.0	447,500
Kansas	11	0.5	175*	-	-	(D)	-	(D)	-	-
Nebraska	10	0.4	175*	-	-	(D)	-	(D)	-	-
South Dakota	7	0.3	60*	-	-	(D)	-	(D)	-	-
New Mexico	5	0.2	375*	-	-	(D)	-	(D)	-	-
D.C.	2	0.1	60*	-	-	(D)	-	(D)	-	-
Vermont	1	-	10*	-	-	(D)	-	(D)	-	-

Source: 1997 *Economic Census*. The states are in descending order of revenues or establishments (if revenue data are missing for the majority). The symbol (D) appears when data are withheld to prevent disclosure of competitive information. States marked with (D) are sorted by number of establishments. A dash (-) indicates that the data element cannot be calculated. * indicates the midpoint of a range; 175, for example is the range 100-249. Shaded *states* on the state map indicate those states which have proportionately greater representation in the industry than would be indicated by the state's population; the ratio is based on total revenues or number of establishments. Shaded *regions* indicate where the industry is regionally most concentrated.

NAICS 621498 - OUTPATIENT CARE CENTERS NEC

GENERAL STATISTICS

Year	Establishments (number)	Employment (number)	Payroll ($ million)	Revenues ($ million)	Employees per Establishment (number)	Revenues per Establishment ($)	Payroll per Employee ($)
1997	8,253	231,287	8,000.0	18,049.0	28.0	2,186,962	34,589

Source: Economic Census of the United States, 1997. This is a newly defined industry. Data for prior years were unavailable at the time of publication but may become available over time.

INDICES OF CHANGE

Year	Establishments (number)	Employment (number)	Payroll ($ million)	Revenues ($ million)	Employees per Establishment (number)	Revenues per Establishment ($)	Payroll per Employee ($)
1997	100.0	100.0	100.0	100.0	100.0	100.0	100.0

Sources: Same as General Statistics. The values shown reflect change from the base year, 1997. Values above 100 mean greater than 1997, values below 100 mean less than 1997, and a value of 100 in the 1982-96 or 1998-2001 period means same as 1997. Values followed by a 'p' are projections by the editors; 'e' stands for extrapolation. Data are the most recent available at this level of detail.

SIC INDUSTRIES RELATED TO NAICS 621498

Each new NAICS code represents an industry that used to be part of an SIC or a part of several SIC industries. Data in this table are shown to provide transitional information for these cases. All available data for the precursor SIC(s) are shown. Even if only a part of an SIC is included in the NAICS, *all* data for the SIC are reproduced. If the SIC industry is not marked as being a part (pt) of the NAICS, the entire industry is embedded in the NAICS data. The SIC composition of the new industry provides some hints of the relative importance of its "ancestors." Data marked with a 'p' are projected. Projections begin with 1982 data. Data earlier than 1990 are not shown but are reflected in the projections.

SIC	Industry	1990	1991	1992	1993	1994	1995	1996	1997
8093	**Specialty Outpatient Facilities, nec (pt)**								
	Establishments (number)	-	-	11,623	-	-	-	-	-
	Employment (thousands)	-	-	178.9	-	-	-	-	-
	Revenues ($ million)	5,326.0	6,508.0	6,476.0	6,999.0	7,965.0	8,616.0	9,586.0	9,994.4p

Source: Economic Census of the United States, 1992, annual surveys of economic sectors conducted by the Bureau of the Census, and estimates or projections based on the 1982-1992 period; not all data are shown. 'e' marks estimates made by the editors; 'p' indicates projections based on time series. A dash (-) indicates that data for this SIC or year were not available. The abbreviation (pt) next to the industry name indicates that only a part of the industry is present within the NAICS data. If no (pt) is shown, the entire industry is contained within the NAICS data.

SELECTED RATIOS

For 1997	Avg. of Information	Analyzed Industry	Index	For 1997	Avg. of Information	Analyzed Industry	Index
Employees per establishment	21	28	133	Payroll per establishment	585,591	969,344	166
Revenue per establishment	1,370,364	2,186,962	160	Payroll as % of revenue	43	44	104
Revenue per employee	65,262	78,037	120	Payroll per employee	27,888	34,589	124

Sources: Same as General Statistics. The 'Average' column represents the average for the industry sector, in 1997, where the currently shown industry is classified. The Index shows the relationship between the Average and the Analyzed Industry. For example, 100 means that they are equal; 500 that the Analyzed Industry is five times the average; 50 means that the Analyzed Industry is half the national average. The abbreviation 'na' is used to show that data are 'not available'.

LEADING COMPANIES   Number shown: **47**   Total sales ($ mil): **9,317**   Total employment (000): **119.1**

Company Name	Address				CEO Name	Phone	Co. Type	Sales ($ mil)	Empl. (000)
HEALTHSOUTH Corp.	1 Healthsouth Pkwy	Birmingham	AL	35243	James P. Bennett	205-967-7116	P	4,006	32.6
Vencor Inc.	3300 Aegon Ctr	Louisville	KY	40202	Edward Kuntz	502-569-7300	P	2,999	57.0
Physician Reliance Network Inc.	1901 Grandview	El Paso	TX	79902	Lloyd K Everson	281-873-2674	P	456	1.3
Physicians Resource Group Inc.	14800 Landmark	Dallas	TX	75240	David Meyer	972-892-7200	P	404	4.9
RehabCare Group Inc.	7733 Forsyth Blvd	St. Louis	MO	63105	Alan C Henderson	314-863-7422	P	207	7.5
Hanger Orthopedic Group Inc.	7700 O Grgtwn	Bethesda	MD	20814	Ivan R Sabel	301-986-0701	P	188	1.4
Response Oncology Inc.	1805 Moriah Woods	Memphis	TN	38117	A M LaMacchia	901-761-7000	P	128	0.7
America Service Group Inc.	105 Westpark Dr	Brentwood	TN	37027	Michael Catalano	615-373-3100	P	113	3.0
National Surgery Centers Inc.	30 S Wacker Dr	Chicago	IL	60606	E Timothy Geary	312-655-1400	P	94	0.7
Consolidated Technology Group	9 Great Neck CT	Huntington	NY	11743	Seymour Richter	212-488-8484	P	93	1.0
Surgical Health Corp.	1 Health S Pky	Birmingham	AL	35243	Richard Scrushy	205-969-4773	S	75*	0.9
Landmark Medical Center	115 Cass Ave	Woonsocket	RI	02895		401-769-4100	S	70*	0.9
TME Inc.	333 N S Houston E	Houston	TX	77060	Cherrill Farnsworth	281-931-9573	S	50*	0.2
Pacific Rehabilitation & Sports	1 S W Columbia St	Portland	OR	97258	John A Elorriaga	503-222-4191	P	44*	0.5
Northstar Health Services Inc.	PO Box 1289	Indiana	PA	15701	Thomas W Zaucha	724-349-7500	P	33*	0.6
Integra Inc.	1060 First Ave	King of Prussia	PA	19406	Eric Anderson	610-992-2600	P	33	<0.1
Watson Clinic L.L.P.	P O Box 95000	Lakeland	FL	33804	Glen A Barden	941-680-7000	R	31*	1.0
Universal Standard Healthcare Inc.	26500 Northwestern	Southfield	MI	48076	Robert Helbling	248-386-5314	P	25	<0.1
United Behavioral Health	425 Market St	San Francisco	CA	94105	Saul Feldman	415-547-5000	S	25	0.8
Complete Wellness Centers Inc.	725 Indep S E	Washington	DC	20003	Joseph J Raymond Jr	202-543-6800	P	24	0.4
MHM Services Inc.	8000 Twrs Cres	Vienna	VA	22182	Michael S Pinkert	703-749-4600	P	21*	0.2
Wendt-Bristol Co.	2 Nationwide Plz	Columbus	OH	43215	Sheldon Gold	614-221-6000	S	21	0.2
PHC Inc.	200 Lake St	Peabody	MA	01960	Bruce A Shear	978-536-2777	P	19	0.3
Lakeside Alternatives Inc.	434 W Kennedy	Orlando	FL	32810	Duane Zimmerman	407-875-3700	R	19*	0.5
Mt. Carmel Health	5700 W Layton Ave	Milwaukee	WI	53220		414-281-7200	S	18*	0.7
Cancer Treatment Holdings Inc.	4491 S State Rd 7	Fort Lauderdale	FL	33314	Ullrich Klamm	954-321-9555	P	17	0.3
Medical Alliance Inc.	2445 Gateway	Irving	TX	75063	Paul R Herchman	972-580-8999	P	16	0.1
Rehabilitation Institute	3011 Baltimore Ave	Kansas City	MO	64108	Ronald L Herrick	816-751-7000	S	14	0.3
Integrated Orthopaedics Inc.	5858 Westheimer	Houston	TX	77056	Jose E Kauachi	713-225-5464	P	12*	0.1
Contact Behavioral Health	1400 E Southern	Tempe	AZ	85282	Larry Frazier	602-730-3023	D	11	<0.1
Delaware Curative Workshop Inc.	1600 Washington St	Wilmington	DE	19802	Guy Brown	302-656-2521	R	9*	0.1
Wendt-Bristol Health Services	2 Nationwide Plz	Columbus	OH	43215	Sheldon A Gold	614-221-6000	P	8*	0.2
Alamo Group Inc.	4242 Medical Dr	San Antonio	TX	78229		210-614-8400	R	5*	<0.1
Upshaw and Associates	10680 Barkley St	Overland Park	KS	66212	Joan Upshaw	913-648-2888	R	5	<0.1
Ambulatory Healthcare	7960 Donagan Dr	Manassas	VA	20109	William Danielczyk	703-361-9731	R	4	0.1
Renaissance West Community	13940 Tireman St	Detroit	MI	48228	Daisy Barlow-Smith	313-581-9070	R	4*	<0.1
Pacific Sports Medicine	3315 S 23rd St	Tacoma	WA	98405	Joanne Madasky	253-572-8326	R	3*	<0.1
Glass Substance Abuse Programs	821 N Utah St	Baltimore	MD	21201	Herman Jones	410-225-0594	D	2*	<0.1
Unipsych Corp.	7777 Davie Rd Ext	Hollywood	FL	33024		954-704-8686	R	2*	<0.1
Wilderness Alternative School Inc.	200 Hubbart Dam	Marion	MT	59925	John Brekke	406-854-2832	R	2	<0.1
Change Point Inc.	P O Box 92067	Portland	OR	97292	Richard Drandoff	503-253-5954	R	2	<0.1
Behavioral Science Center Inc.	2316 Kemper Ln	Cincinnati	OH	45206	William C Wester II	513-221-8545	R	1*	<0.1
Institute for Cognitive Prosthetics	33 Rock Hill Rd	Bala Cynwyd	PA	19004	Elliot Cole	610-664-3585	R	1*	<0.1
Main Line Reproductive Science	950 W Valley Rd	Wayne	PA	19087		610-964-9663	R	1*	<0.1
Michigan Hand Rehabilitation	23500 Park St	Dearborn	MI	48124		313-791-0616	D	1*	<0.1
Horus Global HealthNet	94-D Main St	Hilton Hd Isl	SC	29926	Bernard C Ouellette	843-342-2391	R	1	<0.1
Preventive Lifestyles Inc.	7546 14th Ave N E	Seattle	WA	98115	Bobette S Jones	206-525-2929	R	0	<0.1

Source: Ward's Business Directory of U.S. Private and Public Companies, Volumes 1 and 2, 2000. The company type code used is as follows: P - Public, R - Private, S - Subsidiary, D - Division, J - Joint Venture, A - Affiliate, G - Group, N - Company type not reported. Sales are in millions of dollars, employees are in thousands. An asterisk (*) indicates an estimated sales volume. The symbol < stands for 'less than'. Company names and addresses are truncated, in some cases, to fit into the available space.

LOCATION BY STATE AND REGIONAL CONCENTRATION

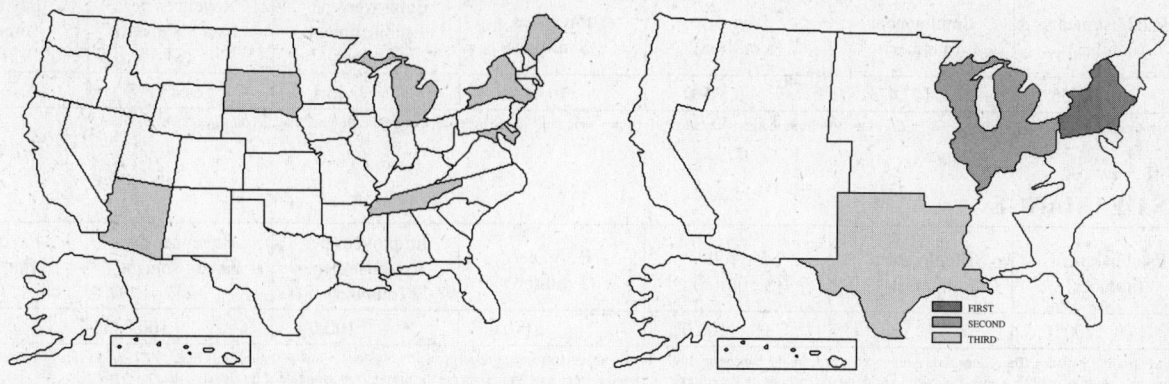

FIRST
SECOND
THIRD

INDUSTRY DATA BY STATE

State	Establishments		Employment			Payroll		Revenues		
	Total (number)	% of U.S.	Total (number)	% of U.S.	Per Estab.	Total ($ mil.)	Per Empl. ($)	Total ($ mil.)	% of U.S.	Per Estab. ($)
New York	495	6.0	19,840	8.6	40	677.2	34,134	1,314.2	7.3	2,654,976
Texas	596	7.2	10,553	4.6	18	357.5	33,881	907.7	5.0	1,522,985
Michigan	295	3.6	9,588	4.1	33	338.6	35,315	776.3	4.3	2,631,458
Illinois	301	3.6	8,239	3.6	27	274.5	33,319	706.7	3.9	2,347,734
Pennsylvania	370	4.5	8,756	3.8	24	280.2	32,002	671.8	3.7	1,815,559
Tennessee	226	2.7	6,247	2.7	28	180.3	28,867	450.4	2.5	1,993,088
Ohio	279	3.4	6,421	2.8	23	179.3	27,931	401.7	2.2	1,439,853
Maryland	194	2.4	3,584	1.5	18	122.0	34,044	369.9	2.0	1,906,866
North Carolina	191	2.3	4,798	2.1	25	160.7	33,496	364.4	2.0	1,907,822
Arizona	132	1.6	4,193	1.8	32	166.1	39,603	360.6	2.0	2,732,091
New Jersey	259	3.1	4,122	1.8	16	138.7	33,649	335.1	1.9	1,293,768
Missouri	234	2.8	3,654	1.6	16	112.9	30,911	277.1	1.5	1,184,179
Massachusetts	115	1.4	2,585	1.1	22	92.9	35,943	202.9	1.1	1,764,043
Indiana	125	1.5	3,687	1.6	29	92.7	25,136	201.9	1.1	1,615,448
Kentucky	109	1.3	2,519	1.1	23	76.4	30,316	153.6	0.9	1,408,817
Oklahoma	77	0.9	1,701	0.7	22	64.6	37,975	147.0	0.8	1,908,584
South Carolina	102	1.2	2,097	0.9	21	60.9	29,043	142.9	0.8	1,400,549
Maine	79	1.0	1,558	0.7	20	45.9	29,457	139.9	0.8	1,771,000
Louisiana	119	1.4	1,287	0.6	11	45.8	35,598	100.8	0.6	847,462
South Dakota	33	0.4	1,130	0.5	34	43.9	38,849	84.7	0.5	2,565,212
Arkansas	27	0.3	333	0.1	12	9.5	28,514	23.6	0.1	872,296
North Dakota	23	0.3	271	0.1	12	11.0	40,524	17.8	0.1	775,130

Source: 1997 *Economic Census.* The states are in descending order of revenues or establishments (if revenue data are missing for the majority). The symbol (D) appears when data are withheld to prevent disclosure of competitive information. States marked with (D) are sorted by number of establishments. A dash (-) indicates that the data element cannot be calculated. * indicates the midpoint of a range; 175, for example is the range 100-249. Shaded *states* on the state map indicate those states which have proportionately greater representation in the industry than would be indicated by the state's population; the ratio is based on total revenues or number of establishments. Shaded *regions* indicate where the industry is regionally most concentrated.

NAICS 621511 - MEDICAL LABORATORIES

GENERAL STATISTICS

Year	Establishments (number)	Employment (number)	Payroll ($ million)	Revenues ($ million)	Employees per Establishment (number)	Revenues per Establishment ($)	Payroll per Employee ($)
1997	4,655	107,474	3,519.0	10,444.0	23.1	2,243,609	32,743

Source: Economic Census of the United States, 1997. This is a newly defined industry. Data for prior years were unavailable at the time of publication but may become available over time.

INDICES OF CHANGE

Year	Establishments (number)	Employment (number)	Payroll ($ million)	Revenues ($ million)	Employees per Establishment (number)	Revenues per Establishment ($)	Payroll per Employee ($)
1997	100.0	100.0	100.0	100.0	100.0	100.0	100.0

Sources: Same as General Statistics. The values shown reflect change from the base year, 1997. Values above 100 mean greater than 1997, values below 100 mean less than 1997, and a value of 100 in the 1982-96 or 1998-2001 period means same as 1997. Values followed by a 'p' are projections by the editors; 'e' stands for extrapolation. Data are the most recent available at this level of detail.

SIC INDUSTRIES RELATED TO NAICS 621511

Each new NAICS code represents an industry that used to be part of an SIC or a part of several SIC industries. Data in this table are shown to provide transitional information for these cases. All available data for the precursor SIC(s) are shown. Even if only a part of an SIC is included in the NAICS, *all* data for the SIC are reproduced. If the SIC industry is not marked as being a part (pt) of the NAICS, the entire industry is embedded in the NAICS data. The SIC composition of the new industry provides some hints of the relative importance of its "ancestors." Data marked with a 'p' are projected. Projections begin with 1982 data. Data earlier than 1990 are not shown but are reflected in the projections.

SIC	Industry	1990	1991	1992	1993	1994	1995	1996	1997
8071	**Medical Laboratories (pt)**								
	Establishments (number)	7,134	7,269	8,434	8,442	8,772	8,568	9,076p	9,345p
	Employment (thousands)	118.4	130.1	138.8	147.2	150.9	155.7	165.3p	172.8p
	Revenues ($ million)	9,996.0	11,458.0	12,882.0	12,735.0	13,007.0	12,909.0	13,266.0	16,570.2p

Source: Economic Census of the United States, 1992, annual surveys of economic sectors conducted by the Bureau of the Census, and estimates or projections based on the 1982-1992 period; not all data are shown. 'e' marks estimates made by the editors; 'p' indicates projections based on time series. A dash (-) indicates that data for this SIC or year were not available. The abbreviation (pt) next to the industry name indicates that only a part of the industry is present within the NAICS data. If no (pt) is shown, the entire industry is contained within the NAICS data.

SELECTED RATIOS

For 1997	Avg. of Information	Analyzed Industry	Index	For 1997	Avg. of Information	Analyzed Industry	Index
Employees per establishment	21	23	110	Payroll per establishment	585,591	755,961	129
Revenue per establishment	1,370,364	2,243,609	164	Payroll as % of revenue	43	34	79
Revenue per employee	65,262	97,177	149	Payroll per employee	27,888	32,743	117

Sources: Same as General Statistics. The 'Average' column represents the average for the industry sector, in 1997, where the currently shown industry is classified. The Index shows the relationship between the Average and the Analyzed Industry. For example, 100 means that they are equal; 500 that the Analyzed Industry is five times the average; 50 means that the Analyzed Industry is half the national average. The abbreviation 'na' is used to show that data are 'not available'.

LEADING COMPANIES　Number shown: **2**　Total sales ($ mil): **15**　Total employment (000): **0.2**

Company Name	Address				CEO Name	Phone	Co. Type	Sales ($ mil)	Empl. (000)
Metropolitan Health Network Inc.	5100 Town Ctr	Boca Raton	FL	33486	Noel J. Guillama	561-416-9484	P	14	0.1
North American Scientific Inc.	20200 Sunburst St	Chatsworth	GA	91311	L Michael Cotrer	818-734-8600	N	1	<0.1

Source: Ward's Business Directory of U.S. Private and Public Companies, Volumes 1 and 2, 2000. The company type code used is as follows: P - Public, R - Private, S - Subsidiary, D - Division, J - Joint Venture, A - Affiliate, G - Group, N - Company type not reported. Sales are in millions of dollars, employees are in thousands. An asterisk (*) indicates an estimated sales volume. The symbol < stands for 'less than'. Company names and addresses are truncated, in some cases, to fit into the available space.

REPRESENTATIVE NONPROFIT ORGANIZATIONS

Organization Name	Address				Phone	Income Range ($ mil)
Alfred E Mann Institute for Biomedical Engineering, USC	USC UGB 203	Los Angeles	CA	90089		50+
Allen Lovelace Moore and Blanche Davis Moore Foundation	800 N Shoreline	Corpus Christi	TX	78401		5-9
American Academy of Family Physicians Foundation	8880 Ward Pky	Kansas City	MO	64114	816-333-9700	1-5
American Paralysis Association	500 Morris Ave	Springfield	NJ	07081	973-379-2690	5-9
American Psychological Society	1010 Vermont Ave NW	Washington	DC	20005	202-783-2077	1-5
Arizona Mexico Border Health Foundation	2501 E Elm St	Tucson	AZ	85716	520-795-9756	1-5
Baystate Health System Inc	759 Chestnut St	Springfield	MA	01199	413-784-4293	10-19
Benjamin Franklin Literary & Medical Society Inc	PO Box 567	Indianapolis	IN	46206		10-19
Black Hills Regional Eye Institute	2800 S 3rd St	Rapid City	SD	57701		5-9
Blue Cross and Blue Shield of Michigan Foundation	600 Lafayette E Mc X520	Detroit	MI	48226	313-225-9000	40-49
Brain Injury Association of Washington	16315 NE 87th Apt B 4	Redmond	WA	98052	425-895-0047	1-5
Christine M Kleinert Institute for Hand & Micro Surgery Inc	225 Abraham Flexner Way	Louisville	KY	40202		1-5
Dean Foundation for Health Research and Education Inc	2711 Allen Blvd	Middleton	WI	53562	608-827-2316	5-9
Delco Systems Services Inc	100 W Sproul Rd	Springfield	PA	19064		10-19
Foundation for Medical Excellence	Bldg 2 Ste 100	Lakea Oswego	OR	97035		1-5
Howard Hughes Medical Institute	4000 Jones Bridge Rd	Chevy Chase	MD	20815	301-215-8500	50+
Inova Physical Rehabilitation Services	2990 Telestar CT	Falls Church	VA	22042		5-9
Institute for Medical Research Inc	VA Medical Center 151	Durham	NC	27705		1-5
Iowa Statewide Organ Procurement Organization	2732 Northgate Dr	Iowa City	IA	52245		1-5
Jcaho Surveyor and QHR Consultant Corporation	One Renaissance Blvd	Oakbrook Ter	IL	60181		20-29
Maine Medical Assessment Foundation	PO Box 249	Manchester	ME	04351		1-5
Medical Research Associates PC	Munger Pavilion NY Med	Valhalla	NY	10595		10-19
Metatherapy Institute Inc	PO Box 1330	Homestead	FL	33090	305-247-4515	1-5
Methodist Healthcare-Central Mississippi Medical Associates	1850 Chadwick Drive	Jackson	MS	39204	601-376-2561	5-9
Midwest Transplant Network Inc	1900 W 47th PL Ste 400	Westwood	KS	66205		10-19
Nebraska Organ Retrieval System	5725 F St	Omaha	NE	68117	402-553-7952	1-5
Pacific Health Research Institute	846 S Hotel St Ste 303	Honolulu	HI	96813	808-524-3595	1-5
Pennington Medical Foundation	6400 Perkins Rd	Baton Rouge	LA	70808		5-9
Richard Seth Staley Educational Foundation	916 W Smuggler St	Aspen	CO	81611		5-9
Richland Memorial Hospital Foundation	Five Richland Medical	Columbia	SC	29203	803-434-7020	10-19
Robert W Woodruff Health Sciences Center Fund Inc	50 Hurt Plaza	Atlanta	GA	30303	404-522-6755	50+
Saint Ann Foundation	2531 E 22nd St	Cleveland	OH	44115		50+
Stratis Health	2901 Metro Dr	Bloomington	MN	55425	952-854-3306	5-9
Tang Foundation	3773 H Hughes Pky	Las Vegas	NV	89109		1-5
University Physicians Foundation Inc	164 Summit Ave	Providence	RI	02906		10-19
William K Warren Medical Research Center Inc	PO Box 470372	Tulsa	OK	74147		20-29

Source: National Directory of Nonprofit Organizations, 2000, Volumes 1 and 2, The Taft Group. The table shows a selection of organizations for illustration and does not constitute a complete selection from the source. The organizations are arranged in alphabetical order.

LOCATION BY STATE AND REGIONAL CONCENTRATION

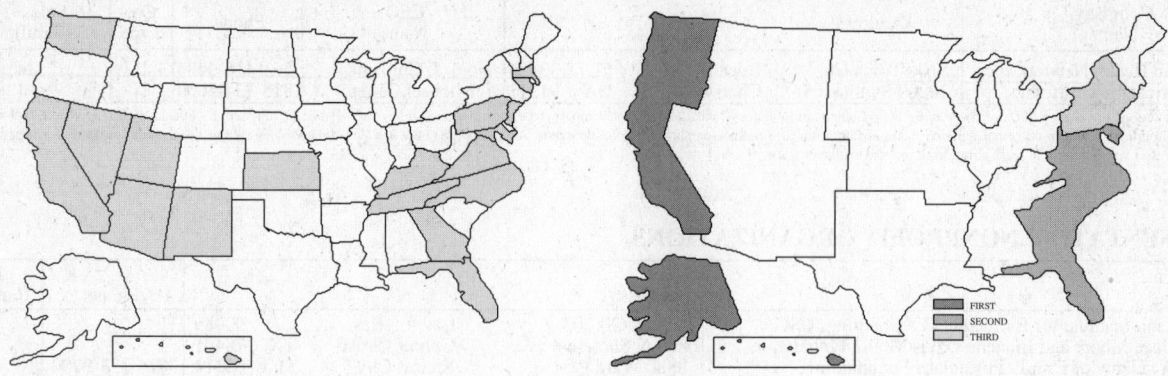

INDUSTRY DATA BY STATE

State	Establishments Total (number)	Establishments % of U.S.	Employment Total (number)	Employment % of U.S.	Employment Per Estab.	Payroll Total ($ mil.)	Payroll Per Empl. ($)	Revenues Total ($ mil.)	Revenues % of U.S.	Revenues Per Estab. ($)
California	1,032	22.2	16,279	15.1	16	558.3	34,295	1,636.7	15.7	1,585,921
Texas	303	6.5	7,132	6.6	24	236.7	33,192	694.0	6.6	2,290,525
New York	294	6.3	6,680	6.2	23	224.1	33,546	598.3	5.7	2,035,119
Florida	312	6.7	5,681	5.3	18	179.5	31,595	565.5	5.4	1,812,596
Pennsylvania	208	4.5	5,525	5.1	27	187.7	33,965	538.8	5.2	2,590,163
New Jersey	130	2.8	4,522	4.2	35	172.1	38,053	530.3	5.1	4,079,062
Maryland	110	2.4	3,091	2.9	28	94.6	30,613	390.9	3.7	3,553,218
Virginia	62	1.3	2,940	2.7	47	107.4	36,534	362.3	3.5	5,843,258
North Carolina	87	1.9	2,730	2.5	31	100.3	36,747	326.4	3.1	3,752,103
Georgia	113	2.4	2,869	2.7	25	99.4	34,630	292.2	2.8	2,585,814
Illinois	162	3.5	3,496	3.3	22	104.0	29,761	291.0	2.8	1,796,426
Washington	85	1.8	2,941	2.7	35	101.3	34,447	280.0	2.7	3,294,000
Ohio	128	2.7	3,105	2.9	24	90.4	29,119	271.0	2.6	2,116,875
Michigan	101	2.2	2,974	2.8	29	97.2	32,672	269.4	2.6	2,667,762
Massachusetts	107	2.3	3,004	2.8	28	95.0	31,622	265.2	2.5	2,478,364
Tennessee	85	1.8	3,078	2.9	36	89.7	29,147	263.4	2.5	3,098,929
Arizona	77	1.7	2,105	2.0	27	73.4	34,868	209.7	2.0	2,722,818
Missouri	71	1.5	1,962	1.8	28	68.9	35,128	204.5	2.0	2,880,944
Connecticut	109	2.3	2,053	1.9	19	73.6	35,853	204.5	2.0	1,876,138
Kentucky	57	1.2	1,360	1.3	24	54.3	39,954	179.6	1.7	3,150,211
Indiana	76	1.6	1,736	1.6	23	55.0	31,687	170.4	1.6	2,241,461
Kansas	40	0.9	1,468	1.4	37	48.5	33,048	166.9	1.6	4,172,675
Utah	33	0.7	1,661	1.5	50	48.6	29,277	152.0	1.5	4,604,939
Nevada	31	0.7	1,305	1.2	42	51.6	39,577	133.5	1.3	4,305,710
Wisconsin	48	1.0	1,711	1.6	36	45.6	26,676	129.3	1.2	2,694,167
Alabama	59	1.3	1,572	1.5	27	40.9	25,995	124.2	1.2	2,105,254
Oklahoma	56	1.2	1,203	1.1	21	40.0	33,214	121.6	1.2	2,171,732
Oregon	44	0.9	1,325	1.2	30	41.4	31,236	119.9	1.1	2,724,250
Hawaii	25	0.5	1,100	1.0	44	35.4	32,192	117.3	1.1	4,690,880
Colorado	51	1.1	1,399	1.3	27	38.5	27,516	103.7	1.0	2,034,176
Minnesota	34	0.7	640	0.6	19	27.2	42,572	72.1	0.7	2,120,059
New Mexico	44	0.9	1,238	1.2	28	28.2	22,775	71.7	0.7	1,629,636
Nebraska	40	0.9	755	0.7	19	20.6	27,297	64.8	0.6	1,619,325
Mississippi	32	0.7	828	0.8	26	20.7	25,041	56.5	0.5	1,765,438
Iowa	29	0.6	716	0.7	25	19.8	27,694	53.4	0.5	1,840,000
Arkansas	40	0.9	604	0.6	15	17.9	29,694	49.1	0.5	1,228,000
South Carolina	38	0.8	450	0.4	12	12.6	27,998	37.7	0.4	991,342
New Hampshire	37	0.8	497	0.5	13	13.8	27,851	33.2	0.3	896,027
Maine	14	0.3	401	0.4	29	10.4	25,960	31.9	0.3	2,278,429
Delaware	29	0.6	445	0.4	15	10.2	22,856	24.8	0.2	853,483
West Virginia	25	0.5	210	0.2	8	6.7	31,957	22.9	0.2	915,880
Rhode Island	50	1.1	413	0.4	8	9.4	22,683	21.2	0.2	423,240
Idaho	17	0.4	222	0.2	13	6.6	29,892	20.9	0.2	1,231,412
South Dakota	14	0.3	174	0.2	12	10.1	58,098	18.3	0.2	1,305,643
Montana	10	0.2	189	0.2	19	4.7	24,709	11.8	0.1	1,175,300
Alaska	11	0.2	103	0.1	9	4.9	47,427	10.4	0.1	945,636
Wyoming	9	0.2	147	0.1	16	4.0	27,156	9.0	0.1	1,000,000
Vermont	5	0.1	43	0.0	9	1.0	22,767	3.4	0.0	670,600
Louisiana	69	1.5	1,750*	-	-	(D)	-	(D)	-	-
D.C.	7	0.2	60*	-	-	(D)	-	(D)	-	-
North Dakota	5	0.1	60*	-	-	(D)	-	(D)	-	-

Source: 1997 *Economic Census*. The states are in descending order of revenues or establishments (if revenue data are missing for the majority). The symbol (D) appears when data are withheld to prevent disclosure of competitive information. States marked with (D) are sorted by number of establishments. A dash (-) indicates that the data element cannot be calculated. * indicates the midpoint of a range; 175, for example is the range 100-249. Shaded *states* on the state map indicate those states which have proportionately greater representation in the industry than would be indicated by the state's population; the ratio is based on total revenues or number of establishments. Shaded *regions* indicate where the industry is regionally most concentrated.

NAICS 621512 - DIAGNOSTIC IMAGING CENTERS

GENERAL STATISTICS

Year	Establishments (number)	Employment (number)	Payroll ($ million)	Revenues ($ million)	Employees per Establishment (number)	Revenues per Establishment ($)	Payroll per Employee ($)
1997	4,421	43,864	1,882.0	5,874.0	9.9	1,328,659	42,905

Source: Economic Census of the United States, 1997. This is a newly defined industry. Data for prior years were unavailable at the time of publication but may become available over time.

INDICES OF CHANGE

Year	Establishments (number)	Employment (number)	Payroll ($ million)	Revenues ($ million)	Employees per Establishment (number)	Revenues per Establishment ($)	Payroll per Employee ($)
1997	100.0	100.0	100.0	100.0	100.0	100.0	100.0

Sources: Same as General Statistics. The values shown reflect change from the base year, 1997. Values above 100 mean greater than 1997, values below 100 mean less than 1997, and a value of 100 in the 1982-96 or 1998-2001 period means same as 1997. Values followed by a 'p' are projections by the editors; 'e' stands for extrapolation. Data are the most recent available at this level of detail.

SIC INDUSTRIES RELATED TO NAICS 621512

Each new NAICS code represents an industry that used to be part of an SIC or a part of several SIC industries. Data in this table are shown to provide transitional information for these cases. All available data for the precursor SIC(s) are shown. Even if only a part of an SIC is included in the NAICS, *all* data for the SIC are reproduced. If the SIC industry is not marked as being a part (pt) of the NAICS, the entire industry is embedded in the NAICS data. The SIC composition of the new industry provides some hints of the relative importance of its "ancestors." Data marked with a 'p' are projected. Projections begin with 1982 data. Data earlier than 1990 are not shown but are reflected in the projections.

SIC	Industry	1990	1991	1992	1993	1994	1995	1996	1997
8071	**Medical Laboratories (pt)**								
	Establishments (number)	7,134	7,269	8,434	8,442	8,772	8,568	9,076p	9,345p
	Employment (thousands)	118.4	130.1	138.8	147.2	150.9	155.7	165.3p	172.8p
	Revenues ($ million)	9,996.0	11,458.0	12,882.0	12,735.0	13,007.0	12,909.0	13,266.0	16,570.2p

Source: Economic Census of the United States, 1992, annual surveys of economic sectors conducted by the Bureau of the Census, and estimates or projections based on the 1982-1992 period; not all data are shown. 'e' marks estimates made by the editors; 'p' indicates projections based on time series. A dash (-) indicates that data for this SIC or year were not available. The abbreviation (pt) next to the industry name indicates that only a part of the industry is present within the NAICS data. If no (pt) is shown, the entire industry is contained within the NAICS data.

SELECTED RATIOS

For 1997	Avg. of Information	Analyzed Industry	Index	For 1997	Avg. of Information	Analyzed Industry	Index
Employees per establishment	21	10	47	Payroll per establishment	585,591	425,696	73
Revenue per establishment	1,370,364	1,328,659	97	Payroll as % of revenue	43	32	75
Revenue per employee	65,262	133,914	205	Payroll per employee	27,888	42,905	154

Sources: Same as General Statistics. The 'Average' column represents the average for the industry sector, in 1997, where the currently shown industry is classified. The Index shows the relationship between the Average and the Analyzed Industry. For example, 100 means that they are equal; 500 that the Analyzed Industry is five times the average; 50 means that the Analyzed Industry is half the national average. The abbreviation 'na' is used to show that data are 'not available'.

LEADING COMPANIES

No company data available for this industry.

LOCATION BY STATE AND REGIONAL CONCENTRATION

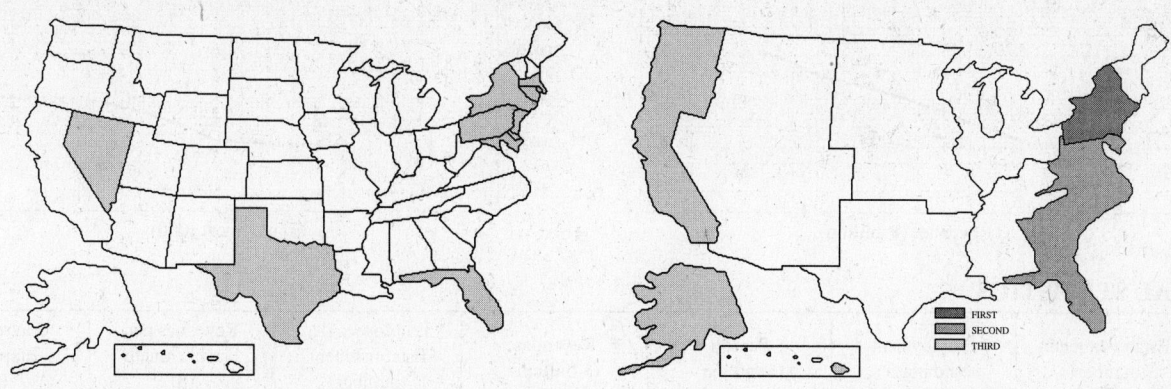

FIRST
SECOND
THIRD

INDUSTRY DATA BY STATE

State	Establishments Total (number)	Establishments % of U.S.	Employment Total (number)	Employment % of U.S.	Employment Per Estab.	Payroll Total ($ mil.)	Payroll Per Empl. ($)	Revenues Total ($ mil.)	Revenues % of U.S.	Revenues Per Estab. ($)
New York	466	10.5	5,579	12.7	12	259.1	46,433	723.3	12.3	1,552,202
California	523	11.8	4,945	11.3	9	180.1	36,424	633.0	10.8	1,210,279
New Jersey	225	5.1	2,971	6.8	13	138.9	46,740	514.0	8.8	2,284,658
Florida	497	11.2	3,999	9.1	8	152.6	38,150	498.6	8.5	1,003,278
Texas	301	6.8	2,767	6.3	9	125.1	45,196	408.3	7.0	1,356,505
Pennsylvania	260	5.9	2,460	5.6	9	101.6	41,317	322.1	5.5	1,238,942
Massachusetts	113	2.6	1,546	3.5	14	74.9	48,454	208.2	3.5	1,842,885
Maryland	134	3.0	1,768	4.0	13	50.1	28,334	196.7	3.3	1,467,955
Michigan	136	3.1	1,656	3.8	12	73.0	44,081	188.0	3.2	1,382,507
Illinois	171	3.9	1,189	2.7	7	53.0	44,559	173.7	3.0	1,015,678
Ohio	143	3.2	1,238	2.8	9	48.6	39,278	152.2	2.6	1,064,517
Connecticut	93	2.1	1,370	3.1	15	62.4	45,525	140.6	2.4	1,512,344
Washington	95	2.1	878	2.0	9	47.0	53,555	119.2	2.0	1,254,337
Tennessee	72	1.6	681	1.6	9	44.3	65,115	109.6	1.9	1,522,833
North Carolina	59	1.3	738	1.7	13	34.3	46,485	93.2	1.6	1,579,220
Wisconsin	43	1.0	983	2.2	23	40.8	41,546	90.4	1.5	2,102,419
Missouri	57	1.3	612	1.4	11	26.1	42,626	85.7	1.5	1,504,316
Georgia	92	2.1	641	1.5	7	20.7	32,285	75.9	1.3	825,087
Arizona	88	2.0	692	1.6	8	19.8	28,594	74.3	1.3	843,909
Indiana	76	1.7	576	1.3	8	22.8	39,524	72.3	1.2	951,026
Virginia	72	1.6	517	1.2	7	21.4	41,364	67.1	1.1	931,542
Kentucky	49	1.1	364	0.8	7	18.3	50,261	65.1	1.1	1,329,265
Alabama	53	1.2	440	1.0	8	17.4	39,568	64.8	1.1	1,223,566
Oregon	35	0.8	394	0.9	11	14.5	36,827	59.1	1.0	1,689,086
Nevada	23	0.5	401	0.9	17	17.0	42,289	58.9	1.0	2,559,565
Delaware	18	0.4	251	0.6	14	12.3	49,024	58.1	1.0	3,228,889
Colorado	58	1.3	482	1.1	8	14.5	30,035	56.5	1.0	973,293
Rhode Island	28	0.6	284	0.6	10	18.2	64,035	48.6	0.8	1,734,107
South Carolina	31	0.7	270	0.6	9	9.0	33,181	42.2	0.7	1,361,161
Kansas	31	0.7	238	0.5	8	16.8	70,458	42.2	0.7	1,360,613
Minnesota	27	0.6	354	0.8	13	24.3	68,627	38.3	0.7	1,417,000
Oklahoma	41	0.9	277	0.6	7	12.7	45,711	34.3	0.6	836,244
Arkansas	22	0.5	226	0.5	10	10.7	47,473	29.4	0.5	1,338,409
Iowa	27	0.6	186	0.4	7	9.3	50,134	28.3	0.5	1,048,889
Maine	14	0.3	130	0.3	9	6.4	48,954	22.8	0.4	1,628,000
New Mexico	23	0.5	144	0.3	6	4.8	33,326	22.5	0.4	976,391
Hawaii	17	0.4	164	0.4	10	9.8	59,750	22.2	0.4	1,304,647
Idaho	16	0.4	139	0.3	9	5.8	41,849	19.6	0.3	1,226,937
Utah	14	0.3	87	0.2	6	10.5	120,667	15.0	0.3	1,069,571
Mississippi	21	0.5	94	0.2	4	3.1	33,117	14.9	0.3	710,714
West Virginia	18	0.4	100	0.2	6	4.5	45,450	14.2	0.2	786,556
New Hampshire	10	0.2	78	0.2	8	2.7	35,013	8.3	0.1	834,500
Nebraska	11	0.2	27	0.1	2	2.2	80,370	7.3	0.1	662,455
Alaska	7	0.2	50	0.1	7	2.5	49,760	7.1	0.1	1,008,286
South Dakota	4	0.1	64	0.1	16	2.5	39,797	6.8	0.1	1,701,000
Montana	14	0.3	47	0.1	3	1.0	20,617	3.4	0.1	244,214
Vermont	7	0.2	17	0.0	2	1.9	114,176	3.3	0.1	464,857
Wyoming	6	0.1	19	0.0	3	1.2	61,105	3.1	0.1	519,833
Louisiana	63	1.4	375*	-	-	(D)	-	(D)	-	-
D.C.	11	0.2	175*	-	-	(D)	-	(D)	-	-
North Dakota	6	0.1	175*	-	-	(D)	-	(D)	-	-

Source: 1997 *Economic Census*. The states are in descending order of revenues or establishments (if revenue data are missing for the majority). The symbol (D) appears when data are withheld to prevent disclosure of competitive information. States marked with (D) are sorted by number of establishments. A dash (-) indicates that the data element cannot be calculated. * indicates the midpoint of a range; 175, for example is the range 100-249. Shaded *states* on the state map indicate those states which have proportionately greater representation in the industry than would be indicated by the state's population; the ratio is based on total revenues or number of establishments. Shaded *regions* indicate where the industry is regionally most concentrated.

NAICS 621610 - HOME HEALTH CARE SERVICES*

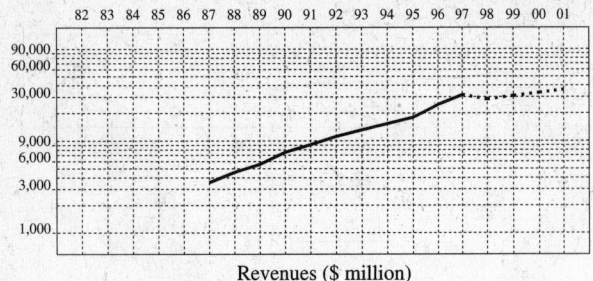

Revenues ($ million)

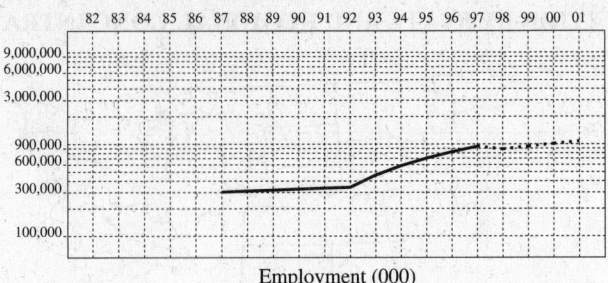

Employment (000)

GENERAL STATISTICS

Year	Establishments (number)	Employment (number)	Payroll ($ million)	Revenues ($ million)	Employees per Establishment (number)	Revenues per Establishment ($)	Payroll per Employee ($)
1982	-	-	-	-	-	-	-
1983	-	-	-	-	-	-	-
1984	-	-	-	-	-	-	-
1985	-	-	-	-	-	-	-
1986	-	-	-	-	-	-	-
1987	6,849	303,535	2,820.0	3,549.0	44.3	518,178	9,291
1988	7,088 e	311,206 e	3,227.0 e	4,589.0	43.9 e	647,432 e	10,369 e
1989	7,327 e	318,877 e	3,633.0 e	5,595.0	43.5 e	763,614 e	11,393 e
1990	7,567 e	326,547 e	4,040.0 e	7,556.0	43.2 e	998,546 e	12,372 e
1991	7,806 e	334,218 e	4,446.0 e	9,129.0	42.8 e	1,169,485 e	13,303 e
1992	8,045	341,889	4,853.0	11,208.0	42.5	1,393,163	14,195
1993	10,374 e	463,309 e	7,156.0 e	13,178.0	44.7 e	1,270,291 e	15,445 e
1994	12,703 e	584,729 e	9,459.0 e	15,394.0	46.0 e	1,211,840 e	16,177 e
1995	15,032 e	706,149 e	11,761.0 e	17,987.0	47.0 e	1,196,581 e	16,655 e
1996	17,361 e	827,569 e	14,064.0 e	24,783.0 e	47.7 e	1,427,510 e	16,994 e
1997	19,690	948,989	16,367.0	31,578.0	48.2	1,603,758	17,247
1998	18,599 p	884,274 p	15,567.0 p	28,294.0 p	47.5 p	1,521,265 p	17,604 p
1999	19,883 p	948,819 p	16,922.0 p	30,820.0 p	47.7 p	1,550,068 p	17,835 p
2000	21,168 p	1,013,365 p	18,277.0 p	33,346.0 p	47.9 p	1,575,302 p	18,036 p
2001	22,452 p	1,077,910 p	19,631.0 p	35,871.0 p	48.0 p	1,597,675 p	18,212 p

Sources: *Economic Census of the United States*, 1982, 1987, 1992, 1997. Establishment counts, employment, and payroll are from *County Business Patterns* for non-Census years. In non-Census years, industries in the Manufacturing range under SIC coding include data from the *Annual Survey of Manufactures* (*ASM*); those in the old Services range include data from the *Services Annual Survey* (*SAS*). Values followed by a 'p' are projections by the editors. Extrapolations are marked by 'e'. Data are the most recent available at this level of detail.

INDICES OF CHANGE

Year	Establishments (number)	Employment (number)	Payroll ($ million)	Revenues ($ million)	Employees per Establishment (number)	Revenues per Establishment ($)	Payroll per Employee ($)
1982	-	-	-	-	-	-	-
1987	34.8	32.0	17.2	11.2	92.0	32.3	53.9
1992	40.9	36.0	29.7	35.5	88.2	86.9	82.3
1993	52.7 e	48.8 e	43.7 e	41.7	92.7 e	79.2 e	89.6 e
1994	64.5 e	61.6 e	57.8 e	48.7	95.5 e	75.6 e	93.8 e
1995	76.3 e	74.4 e	71.9 e	57.0	97.5 e	74.6 e	96.6 e
1996	88.2 e	87.2 e	85.9 e	78.5 e	98.9 e	89.0 e	98.5 e
1997	100.0	100.0	100.0	100.0	100.0	100.0	100.0
1998	94.5 p	93.2 p	95.1 p	89.6 p	98.6 p	94.9 p	102.1 p
1999	101.0 p	100.0 p	103.4 p	97.6 p	99.0 p	96.7 p	103.4 p
2000	107.5 p	106.8 p	111.7 p	105.6 p	99.3 p	98.2 p	104.6 p
2001	114.0 p	113.6 p	119.9 p	113.6 p	99.6 p	99.6 p	105.6 p

Sources: Same as General Statistics. The values shown reflect change from the base year, 1997. Values above 100 mean greater than 1997, values below 100 mean less than 1997, and a value of 100 in the 1982-96 or 1998-2001 period means same as 1997. Values followed by a 'p' are projections by the editors; 'e' stands for extrapolation. Data are the most recent available at this level of detail.

SELECTED RATIOS

For 1997	Avg. of Information	Analyzed Industry	Index	For 1997	Avg. of Information	Analyzed Industry	Index
Employees per establishment	21	48	230	Payroll per establishment	585,591	831,234	142
Revenue per establishment	1,370,364	1,603,758	117	Payroll as % of revenue	43	52	121
Revenue per employee	65,262	33,275	51	Payroll per employee	27,888	17,247	62

Sources: Same as General Statistics. The 'Average' column represents the average for the industry sector, in 1997, where the currently shown industry is classified. The Index shows the relationship between the Average and the Analyzed Industry. For example, 100 means that they are equal; 500 that the Analyzed Industry is five times the average; 50 means that the Analyzed Industry is half the national average. The abbreviation 'na' is used to show that data are 'not available'.

*Equivalent to SIC 8082.

LEADING COMPANIES　　Number shown: **75**　　Total sales ($ mil): **21,399**　　Total employment (000): **374.3**

Company Name	Address				CEO Name	Phone	Co. Type	Sales ($ mil)	Empl. (000)
Vencor Inc.	3300 Aegon Ctr	Louisville	KY	40202	Edward Kuntz	502-569-7300	P	2,999	57.0
Integrated Health Services Inc.	10065 Red Run Blvd	Owings Mills	MD	21117	Lawrence P Cirka	410-773-1000	P	2,972	84.0
Beverly Enterprises Inc.	PO Box 3324	Fort Smith	AR	72913	David R Banks	501-452-6712	P	2,774*	73.0
Sierra Health Services Inc.	PO Box 15645	Las Vegas	NV	89114	Erin E MacDonald	702-242-7000	P	1,284	4.7
Wilmac Corp.	P O Box 5047	York	PA	17405	Karen McCormack	717-854-7857	R	1,241*	1.5
Methodist Healthcare	1211 Union Ave	Memphis	TN	38104	Maurice Elliot	901-726-2300	R	1,084*	13.0
Helix Health Inc.	2330 W Joppa Rd	Lutherville	MD	21093	John McDaniel	410-847-6700	R	1,010*	18.0
Paracelsus Healthcare Corp.	515 W Greens Rd	Houston	TX	77067	Ronald R Patterson	281-774-5100	P	664	7.0
Medstar Health	100 Irving St	Washington	DC	20010	John P McDaniel	202-877-7000	R	634*	6.0
Coram Healthcare Corp.	1125 17th St	Denver	CO	80202	Donald Amaral	303-292-4973	P	526	3.6
Parkview Home Health Services	2270 Lake Ave	Fort Wayne	IN	46805		219-422-9911	R	501*	5.0
Lincare Holdings Inc.	19337 U S 19 N	Clearwater	FL	34624	John P Byrnes	727-530-7700	P	487	4.2
Chemed Corp.	2600 Chemed Ctr	Cincinnati	OH	45202	Edward L Hutton	513-762-6900	P	454	7.7
RoTech Medical Corp.	PO Box 536576	Orlando	FL	32853	Stephen P Griggs	407-841-2115	P	423	0.8
American HomePatient Inc.	5200 Maryland Way	Brentwood	TN	37027	Joseph F Furlong III	615-221-8884	P	404	4.8
PSA Health HomeCare L.P.	310 Technology	Norcross	GA	30092	Joseph Sansone	770-441-1580	S	300	3.5
Pittsburgh Mercy Health System	1400 Locust St	Pittsburgh	PA	15219	Joanne M Andiorio	412-232-8275	R	290*	3.5
Pediatric Services of America Inc.	310 Technology	Norcross	GA	30092	Joseph D Sansone	770-441-1580	P	214	5.0
CareMed Chicago	322 S Green St	Chicago	IL	60607	Dan Woods	312-738-8622	R	213*	0.3
Columbia Health System Inc.	2025 E Newport Ave	Milwaukee	WI	53211	John F Schuler	414-961-3300	R	196	1.4
Housecall Medical Resources Inc.	1000 Abernathy Rd	Atlanta	GA	30328	L Dolomantono	423-292-6000	R	192	2.3
Home Health Corporation	2200 Renaissance	King of Prussia	PA	19406	David S Gellar	610-272-1717	P	174	3.1
United Health Services Inc.	10-42 Mitchell Ave	Binghamton	NY	13903	Mark T O'Neal	607-762-2200	R	160*	3.5
Transworld HealthCare Inc.	555 Madison Ave	New York	NY	10022	Timothy M Aitken	212-750-0064	P	155	0.5
National Health Care Affiliates	651 Delaware Ave	Buffalo	NY	14202	Mark E Hamister	716-881-4425	R	140*	4.0
South Hills Health System	P O Box 18119	Pittsburgh	PA	15236	William R Jennings	412-469-5000	R	139*	27.7
VITAS Healthcare Corp.	100 S Biscayne	Miami	FL	33131	Hugh Westbrook	305-374-4143	R	136*	4.0
Matria Healthcare Inc.	1850 Parkway Pl	Marietta	GA	30067	Donald R Millard	770-767-4500	P	135	1.2
HealthCor Holdings Inc.	8150 N Cen Expwy	Dallas	TX	75206	Michael D Ayres	214-692-4663	R	119	<0.1
Option Care Inc.	100 Corporate N	Bannockburn	IL	60015	Michael Rusnak	847-615-1690	P	114	1.1
In Home Health Inc.	601 Carlson Pkwy	Minnetonka	MN	55305	Wolfgang von Maack	612-449-7500	P	97	2.1
Lincare Inc.	19337 U S 19 N	Clearwater	FL	33764	Don Byrnes	813-530-7700	S	87*	1.0
IVonyx Inc.	17852 N Laurel	Livonia	MI	48152	Richard A Breakie	734-462-9290	R	80*	0.3
United Professional Cos.	3724 W Wisconsin	Milwaukee	WI	53208		414-342-9292	S	72	0.8
Visiting Nurse Association	75 Arlington St	Boston	MA	02116		617-426-5555	R	65*	1.5
Kuala Healthcare Inc.	910 Sylvan Ave	Englewd Clfs	NJ	07632	Jack Rosen	201-567-4600	P	64	1.0
Professional Medical Services Inc.	3611 Queen Palm Dr	Tampa	FL	33619	C Arnold Renschler	813-626-7788	D	52*	0.4
Horizon Homecare & Hospice Inc.	8949 N Deerbrook	Milwaukee	WI	53223		414-365-8300	R	48*	0.6
U.S. Homecare Corp.	2 Hartford Sq, W	Hartford	CT	06106	Sophia V Bilinsky	860-278-7242	P	48	3.0
SpectraCare Inc.	240 Whittington	Louisville	KY	40222	Richard Hogan	502-429-4550	R	44	0.4
Allied Home Health	2603 Dunstan	Houston	TX	77005	Helen Dichoso	713-522-5773	R	40*	0.4
National Home Health Care Corp.	700 White Plains	Scarsdale	NY	10583	Frederick H Fialkow	914-722-9000	P	38	1.9
Archbold Health Services Inc.	400 Old Albany Rd	Thomasville	GA	31792	Ken E Beverly	912-227-6800	R	35	0.1
HealthSphere of America Inc.	5135 Covington	Memphis	TN	38134	Kyle Altman	901-386-5082	R	35*	0.4
Alpha Christian Registry Inc.	75 S Stolp Ave	Aurora	IL	60506	Marjorie Mickle	630-892-1111	R	33*	0.4
PharmaThera Inc.	1785 Nonconnah	Memphis	TN	38132		901-348-8200	R	30	0.2
Trinity Health Care Services	1049 Cresthaven Rd	Memphis	TN	38119	Karen O'Connell	901-767-6767	R	30*	0.3
Visiting Nurse Association	2905 Sackett St	Houston	TX	77098		713-520-8115	S	28*	0.2
Infu-Tech Inc.	910 Sylvan Ave	Englewd Clfs	NJ	07632	Jack Rosen	201-567-4600	P	27	0.1
Lifeline Home Health Services	4301 Saturn Rd	Garland	TX	75041	Deanna K Beauchamp	972-864-4900	R	26*	0.3
HomeCall Inc.	92 Tom Johnson Dr	Frederick	MD	21702	Artie R Esworthy Jr	301-663-8818	S	25	0.8
Wendt-Bristol Co.	2 Nationwide Plz	Columbus	OH	43215	Sheldon Gold	614-221-6000	S	21	0.2
Dynacq International Inc.	10304 I-10 E	Houston	TX	77029	Chiu M Chan	713-673-6432	P	20	0.1
New York Health Care Inc.	1850 McDonald Ave	Brooklyn	NY	11223	Jerry Braun	718-375-6700	P	20	1.3
Home-Bound Medical Care Inc.	2165 Spicer Cr #1	Memphis	TN	38134	Kyle Altman	901-386-5061	S	20	0.6
Proffessional Nursing Services	3421 N Causeway	Metairie	LA	70002		504-832-1679	D	20*	0.2
Mt. Carmel Health	5700 W Layton Ave	Milwaukee	WI	53220		414-281-7200	S	18*	0.7
ATS Health Services	5161 Beach Blvd	Jacksonville	FL	32207	Mark Pass	904-398-9098	D	13*	0.1
Caremark Therapeutic Services	1127 Bryn Mawr	Redlands	CA	92374	John Arlotta	909-796-7171	D	13*	0.2
Castle Home Health Inc.	201 S Wilcox St	Castle Rock	CO	80104		303-660-8474	D	13*	0.4
IVonyx/Complete Infusion Care	12407 Stark Rd	Livonia	MI	48150		734-261-7730	S	13*	<0.1
The Center for Hospice	225 Como Park Blvd	Buffalo	NY	14227	Donald Schumacher	716-686-1900	R	13*	0.3
Supplemental Health Care	2829 Sheridan Dr	Tonawanda	NY	14150	Leo R Blatz	716-832-8986	R	10*	1.0
Visiting Nurse & Hospice Care Of	1029 E main St	Stamford	CT	06902	Janet Casey	203-325-7200	R	10*	0.1
Cooperative Home Care	349 E 149th St	Bronx	NY	10451	Rick Surpin	718-993-7104	R	9*	0.5
Visiting Nurse Service Inc.	4701 N Keystone	Indianapolis	IN	46205	John Pipas	317-722-8200	R	7	0.2
American Nursing Care Inc.	300 Teche Center	Milford	OH	45150	Tom Karpinski	513-576-0262	R	6*	<0.1
HomeCall Inc	92 Thomas Johnson	Frederick	MD	21702	Gretchen Murzda	410-644-0105	R	6*	<0.1
Older Adults Care Management	520 S Cam Real	San Mateo	CA	94402	Rita Ghatak	650-329-1411	R	6*	0.2
Home Health Care of Mississippi	PO Box 1956	Hattiesburg	MS	39403	WA Payne	601-544-2900	S	5*	0.1
Home Health Outreach	1460 Walton Blvd	Rochester Hills	MI	48309		248-656-6757	R	5*	0.2
Ridgaway Philips Co.	909 Sumneytown	Spring House	PA	19477	Jacqueline Moore	215-643-1200	R	5	<0.1
Home Health Plus Inc.	6160 N Cicero Ave	Chicago	IL	60646	Wolfgang Von Mazek	773-545-6696	S	3*	<0.1
Accent on Independence	1728 Race St	Denver	CO	80206	Carol Bouchard	303-331-0818	R	2	<0.1
Medical Team Inc.	1930 Newton Sq	Reston	VA	20190	Leslie Pembrook	703-435-9500	R	2*	<0.1

Source: *Ward's Business Directory of U.S. Private and Public Companies*, Volumes 1 and 2, 2000. The company type code used is as follows: P - Public, R - Private, S - Subsidiary, D - Division, J - Joint Venture, A - Affiliate, G - Group, N - Company type not reported. Sales are in millions of dollars, employees are in thousands. An asterisk (*) indicates an estimated sales volume. The symbol < stands for 'less than'. Company names and addresses are truncated, in some cases, to fit into the available space.

LOCATION BY STATE AND REGIONAL CONCENTRATION

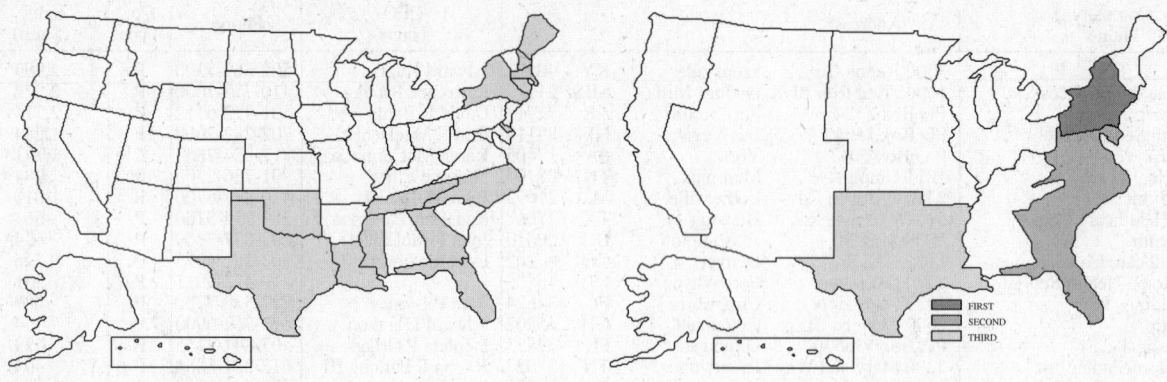

INDUSTRY DATA BY STATE

State	Establishments Total (number)	% of U.S.	Employment Total (number)	% of U.S.	Per Estab.	Payroll Total ($ mil.)	Per Empl. ($)	Revenues Total ($ mil.)	% of U.S.	Per Estab. ($)
New York	1,061	5.4	135,109	14.2	127	2,260.4	16,730	4,026.6	12.8	3,795,103
Texas	2,660	13.5	141,161	14.9	53	1,963.6	13,910	3,647.8	11.6	1,371,344
Florida	1,462	7.4	61,976	6.5	42	1,214.4	19,595	2,534.4	8.0	1,733,536
California	1,639	8.3	58,363	6.2	36	1,107.5	18,976	2,197.9	7.0	1,340,996
Pennsylvania	808	4.1	33,670	3.5	42	635.1	18,861	1,243.9	3.9	1,539,530
Massachusetts	483	2.5	36,449	3.8	75	690.4	18,942	1,213.7	3.8	2,512,810
Ohio	802	4.1	36,649	3.9	46	580.2	15,832	1,154.4	3.7	1,439,431
Illinois	657	3.3	31,314	3.3	48	538.6	17,201	1,073.1	3.4	1,633,381
Michigan	721	3.7	27,866	2.9	39	517.3	18,563	1,011.0	3.2	1,402,225
New Jersey	449	2.3	29,490	3.1	66	517.0	17,531	940.4	3.0	2,094,385
Georgia	562	2.9	18,700	2.0	33	398.0	21,284	860.2	2.7	1,530,562
North Carolina	494	2.5	26,241	2.8	53	426.8	16,264	845.3	2.7	1,711,176
Tennessee	501	2.5	18,902	2.0	38	391.2	20,695	831.1	2.6	1,658,910
Louisiana	625	3.2	21,492	2.3	34	432.8	20,139	823.7	2.6	1,317,914
Connecticut	265	1.3	20,905	2.2	79	384.2	18,381	646.4	2.0	2,439,264
Missouri	431	2.2	18,099	1.9	42	295.6	16,333	581.0	1.8	1,347,995
Indiana	417	2.1	17,652	1.9	42	274.0	15,521	513.5	1.6	1,231,460
Oklahoma	528	2.7	14,259	1.5	27	280.2	19,651	511.7	1.6	969,045
Virginia	421	2.1	15,839	1.7	38	277.3	17,506	507.8	1.6	1,206,081
Alabama	279	1.4	10,520	1.1	38	210.2	19,981	459.8	1.5	1,647,857
Minnesota	353	1.8	18,299	1.9	52	233.1	12,738	415.5	1.3	1,177,110
Kentucky	219	1.1	8,766	0.9	40	187.2	21,360	405.7	1.3	1,852,434
Mississippi	178	0.9	6,901	0.7	39	162.2	23,498	396.2	1.3	2,225,888
Arizona	274	1.4	9,779	1.0	36	181.8	18,587	391.0	1.2	1,426,964
Maryland	272	1.4	9,305	1.0	34	182.3	19,591	386.5	1.2	1,421,110
Washington	266	1.4	11,803	1.2	44	203.5	17,243	377.9	1.2	1,420,722
Wisconsin	316	1.6	13,692	1.4	43	213.8	15,617	358.0	1.1	1,132,778
Colorado	283	1.4	10,984	1.2	39	167.0	15,205	343.4	1.1	1,213,314
South Carolina	182	0.9	6,454	0.7	35	126.3	19,563	255.5	0.8	1,403,687
Kansas	240	1.2	7,198	0.8	30	124.6	17,310	252.5	0.8	1,051,879
Maine	132	0.7	5,361	0.6	41	107.8	20,100	197.2	0.6	1,493,818
West Virginia	125	0.6	5,102	0.5	41	84.6	16,588	186.4	0.6	1,491,048
Iowa	194	1.0	6,471	0.7	33	89.5	13,838	180.4	0.6	929,943
Oregon	171	0.9	3,944	0.4	23	75.9	19,245	179.4	0.6	1,049,363
Arkansas	102	0.5	4,963	0.5	49	85.6	17,257	174.6	0.6	1,711,608
Nevada	104	0.5	3,322	0.4	32	68.9	20,755	161.6	0.5	1,553,846
Utah	113	0.6	4,385	0.5	39	68.9	15,705	158.7	0.5	1,404,301
New Hampshire	98	0.5	6,019	0.6	61	91.9	15,274	156.7	0.5	1,599,367
New Mexico	125	0.6	3,469	0.4	28	57.7	16,644	116.8	0.4	934,552
Delaware	44	0.2	2,638	0.3	60	52.8	20,016	91.8	0.3	2,086,705
Vermont	48	0.2	2,513	0.3	52	45.2	17,990	74.0	0.2	1,541,125
Nebraska	63	0.3	2,105	0.2	33	28.4	13,498	69.5	0.2	1,102,667
Hawaii	44	0.2	1,627	0.2	37	29.2	17,945	64.1	0.2	1,456,864
D.C.	28	0.1	2,215	0.2	79	33.0	14,898	58.8	0.2	2,100,357
Montana	54	0.3	2,680	0.3	50	27.7	10,325	48.7	0.2	902,111
Wyoming	28	0.1	471	0.0	17	9.1	19,219	18.3	0.1	654,536
Alaska	23	0.1	401	0.0	17	7.9	19,586	14.4	0.0	627,087
South Dakota	27	0.1	598	0.1	22	7.3	12,288	13.6	0.0	504,000
North Dakota	21	0.1	387	0.0	18	4.2	10,964	6.9	0.0	328,238

Source: 1997 *Economic Census*. The states are in descending order of revenues or establishments (if revenue data are missing for the majority). The symbol (D) appears when data are withheld to prevent disclosure of competitive information. States marked with (D) are sorted by number of establishments. A dash (-) indicates that the data element cannot be calculated. * indicates the midpoint of a range; 175, for example is the range 100-249. Shaded *states* on the state map indicate those states which have proportionately greater representation in the industry than would be indicated by the state's population; the ratio is based on total revenues or number of establishments. Shaded *regions* indicate where the industry is regionally most concentrated.

NAICS 621910 - AMBULANCE SERVICES

GENERAL STATISTICS

Year	Establishments (number)	Employment (number)	Payroll ($ million)	Revenues ($ million)	Employees per Establishment (number)	Revenues per Establishment ($)	Payroll per Employee ($)
1997	3,485	111,226	2,123.0	5,027.0	31.9	1,442,468	19,087

Source: *Economic Census of the United States*, 1997. This is a newly defined industry. Data for prior years were unavailable at the time of publication but may become available over time.

INDICES OF CHANGE

Year	Establishments (number)	Employment (number)	Payroll ($ million)	Revenues ($ million)	Employees per Establishment (number)	Revenues per Establishment ($)	Payroll per Employee ($)
1997	100.0	100.0	100.0	100.0	100.0	100.0	100.0

Sources: Same as General Statistics. The values shown reflect change from the base year, 1997. Values above 100 mean greater than 1997, values below 100 mean less than 1997, and a value of 100 in the 1982-96 or 1998-2001 period means same as 1997. Values followed by a 'p' are projections by the editors; 'e' stands for extrapolation. Data are the most recent available at this level of detail.

SIC INDUSTRIES RELATED TO NAICS 621910

Each new NAICS code represents an industry that used to be part of an SIC or a part of several SIC industries. Data in this table are shown to provide transitional information for these cases. All available data for the precursor SIC(s) are shown. Even if only a part of an SIC is included in the NAICS, *all* data for the SIC are reproduced. If the SIC industry is not marked as being a part (pt) of the NAICS, the entire industry is embedded in the NAICS data. The SIC composition of the new industry provides some hints of the relative importance of its "ancestors." Data marked with a 'p' are projected. Projections begin with 1982 data. Data earlier than 1990 are not shown but are reflected in the projections.

SIC	Industry	1990	1991	1992	1993	1994	1995	1996	1997
4119	**Local Passenger Transportation, nec (pt)**								
	Establishments (number)	5,187	5,991	7,140	7,652	7,915	7,800	8,305	8,988*p*
	Employment (thousands)	94.0	94.6	115.6	124.4	130.7	139.0	149.0	156.0*p*
	Revenues ($ million)	-	-	4,604.0	-	-	-	-	-
4522	**Air Transportation, Nonscheduled (pt)**								
	Establishments (number)	928	1,441	1,791	1,714	1,692	1,621	1,831	2,052*p*
	Employment (thousands)	15.3	20.5	23.1	24.4	29.1	27.7	28.8	33.2*p*
	Revenues ($ million)	-	-	3,432.7	-	-	-	-	-

Source: *Economic Census of the United States*, 1992, annual surveys of economic sectors conducted by the Bureau of the Census, and estimates or projections based on the 1982-1992 period; not all data are shown. 'e' marks estimates made by the editors; 'p' indicates projections based on time series. A dash (-) indicates that data for this SIC or year were not available. The abbreviation (pt) next to the industry name indicates that only a part of the industry is present within the NAICS data. If no (pt) is shown, the entire industry is contained within the NAICS data.

SELECTED RATIOS

For 1997	Avg. of Information	Analyzed Industry	Index	For 1997	Avg. of Information	Analyzed Industry	Index
Employees per establishment	21	32	152	Payroll per establishment	585,591	609,182	104
Revenue per establishment	1,370,364	1,442,468	105	Payroll as % of revenue	43	42	99
Revenue per employee	65,262	45,196	69	Payroll per employee	27,888	19,087	68

Sources: Same as General Statistics. The 'Average' column represents the average for the industry sector, in 1997, where the currently shown industry is classified. The Index shows the relationship between the Average and the Analyzed Industry. For example, 100 means that they are equal; 500 that the Analyzed Industry is five times the average; 50 means that the Analyzed Industry is half the national average. The abbreviation 'na' is used to show that data are 'not available'.

LEADING COMPANIES

No company data available for this industry.

LOCATION BY STATE AND REGIONAL CONCENTRATION

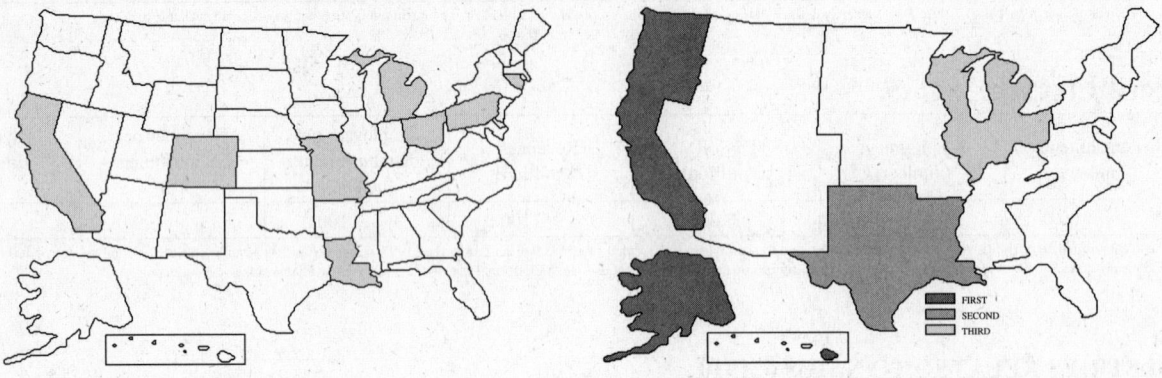

FIRST
SECOND
THIRD

INDUSTRY DATA BY STATE

State	Establishments Total (number)	% of U.S.	Employment Total (number)	% of U.S.	Per Estab.	Payroll Total ($ mil.)	Per Empl. ($)	Revenues Total ($ mil.)	% of U.S.	Per Estab. ($)
California	291	8.4	12,562	11.3	43	292.3	23,265	718.7	14.3	2,469,818
Pennsylvania	392	11.2	11,108	10.0	28	166.8	15,016	406.4	8.1	1,036,847
Texas	228	6.5	6,253	5.6	27	129.3	20,684	327.8	6.5	1,437,522
Ohio	165	4.7	6,522	5.9	40	117.1	17,958	254.5	5.1	1,542,279
Michigan	122	3.5	4,989	4.5	41	94.8	19,002	199.1	4.0	1,631,730
Florida	96	2.8	3,554	3.2	37	74.9	21,066	198.9	4.0	2,071,479
Colorado	32	0.9	2,119	1.9	66	49.3	23,253	175.3	3.5	5,477,406
Louisiana	38	1.1	2,654	2.4	70	62.5	23,534	147.3	2.9	3,877,237
Connecticut	24	0.7	2,392	2.2	100	58.3	24,363	138.2	2.7	5,759,833
Missouri	47	1.3	1,719	1.5	37	34.7	20,202	105.0	2.1	2,233,426
Minnesota	56	1.6	1,779	1.6	32	34.8	19,586	83.5	1.7	1,490,482
Alabama	81	2.3	2,217	2.0	27	35.9	16,197	81.0	1.6	1,000,506
Tennessee	59	1.7	1,654	1.5	28	25.2	15,226	53.2	1.1	902,492
Oregon	21	0.6	944	0.8	45	20.3	21,526	49.2	1.0	2,342,476
Kentucky	63	1.8	1,553	1.4	25	22.1	14,241	48.9	1.0	775,524
Arkansas	60	1.7	1,275	1.1	21	20.2	15,851	46.4	0.9	773,867
North Carolina	76	2.2	1,150	1.0	15	18.2	15,824	42.1	0.8	553,947
West Virginia	56	1.6	1,103	1.0	20	15.2	13,776	31.2	0.6	557,464
Oklahoma	27	0.8	745	0.7	28	13.6	18,192	27.4	0.5	1,013,037
South Carolina	42	1.2	756	0.7	18	13.4	17,701	25.7	0.5	610,786
Utah	11	0.3	425	0.4	39	8.7	20,393	24.8	0.5	2,255,364
Iowa	44	1.3	687	0.6	16	8.0	11,603	19.7	0.4	446,614
South Dakota	20	0.6	147	0.1	7	2.8	19,238	5.5	0.1	274,300
Alaska	5	0.1	36	0.0	7	1.2	34,639	3.4	0.1	686,600
North Dakota	17	0.5	216	0.2	13	1.1	5,111	2.4	0.0	139,176
Wyoming	4	0.1	47	0.0	12	0.6	13,681	1.4	0.0	351,500
Hawaii	7	0.2	375*	-	-	(D)	-	(D)	-	-
D.C.	3	0.1	60*	-	-	(D)	-	(D)	-	-

Source: 1997 *Economic Census*. The states are in descending order of revenues or establishments (if revenue data are missing for the majority). The symbol (D) appears when data are withheld to prevent disclosure of competitive information. States marked with (D) are sorted by number of establishments. A dash (-) indicates that the data element cannot be calculated. * indicates the midpoint of a range; 175, for example is the range 100-249. Shaded *states* on the state map indicate those states which have proportionately greater representation in the industry than would be indicated by the state's population; the ratio is based on total revenues or number of establishments. Shaded *regions* indicate where the industry is regionally most concentrated.

NAICS 621991 - BLOOD AND ORGAN BANKS

GENERAL STATISTICS

Year	Establishments (number)	Employment (number)	Payroll ($ million)	Revenues ($ million)	Employees per Establishment (number)	Revenues per Establishment ($)	Payroll per Employee ($)
1997	1,230	42,997	1,186.0	3,868.0	35.0	3,144,715	27,583

Source: *Economic Census of the United States*, 1997. This is a newly defined industry. Data for prior years were unavailable at the time of publication but may become available over time.

INDICES OF CHANGE

Year	Establishments (number)	Employment (number)	Payroll ($ million)	Revenues ($ million)	Employees per Establishment (number)	Revenues per Establishment ($)	Payroll per Employee ($)
1997	100.0	100.0	100.0	100.0	100.0	100.0	100.0

Sources: Same as General Statistics. The values shown reflect change from the base year, 1997. Values above 100 mean greater than 1997, values below 100 mean less than 1997, and a value of 100 in the 1982-96 or 1998-2001 period means same as 1997. Values followed by a 'p' are projections by the editors; 'e' stands for extrapolation. Data are the most recent available at this level of detail.

SIC INDUSTRIES RELATED TO NAICS 621991

Each new NAICS code represents an industry that used to be part of an SIC or a part of several SIC industries. Data in this table are shown to provide transitional information for these cases. All available data for the precursor SIC(s) are shown. Even if only a part of an SIC is included in the NAICS, *all* data for the SIC are reproduced. If the SIC industry is not marked as being a part (pt) of the NAICS, the entire industry is embedded in the NAICS data. The SIC composition of the new industry provides some hints of the relative importance of its "ancestors." Data marked with a 'p' are projected. Projections begin with 1982 data. Data earlier than 1990 are not shown but are reflected in the projections.

SIC	Industry	1990	1991	1992	1993	1994	1995	1996	1997
8099	**Health & Allied Services, nec (pt)**								
	Establishments (number)	-	-	5,011	-	-	-	-	-
	Employment (thousands)	-	-	71.9	-	-	-	-	-
	Revenues ($ million)	-	-	5,022.6	-	-	-	-	-

Source: *Economic Census of the United States*, 1992, annual surveys of economic sectors conducted by the Bureau of the Census, and estimates or projections based on the 1982-1992 period; not all data are shown. 'e' marks estimates made by the editors; 'p' indicates projections based on time series. A dash (-) indicates that data for this SIC or year were not available. The abbreviation (pt) next to the industry name indicates that only a part of the industry is present within the NAICS data. If no (pt) is shown, the entire industry is contained within the NAICS data.

SELECTED RATIOS

For 1997	Avg. of Information	Analyzed Industry	Index	For 1997	Avg. of Information	Analyzed Industry	Index
Employees per establishment	21	35	166	Payroll per establishment	585,591	964,228	165
Revenue per establishment	1,370,364	3,144,715	229	Payroll as % of revenue	43	31	72
Revenue per employee	65,262	89,960	138	Payroll per employee	27,888	27,583	99

Sources: Same as General Statistics. The 'Average' column represents the average for the industry sector, in 1997, where the currently shown industry is classified. The Index shows the relationship between the Average and the Analyzed Industry. For example, 100 means that they are equal; 500 that the Analyzed Industry is five times the average; 50 means that the Analyzed Industry is half the national average. The abbreviation 'na' is used to show that data are 'not available'.

LEADING COMPANIES

No company data available for this industry.

REPRESENTATIVE NONPROFIT ORGANIZATIONS

Organization Name	Address				Phone	Income Range ($ mil)
Astraea Inc	2201 Westwood Ave	Richmond	VA	23230		5-9
Blood Assurance Inc	700 E Third St	Chattanooga	TN	37403	423-756-0966	5-9
Blood Center for Southeast Louisiana	312 S Galvez St	New Orleans	LA	70119	504-524-1322	10-19
Blood Systems Inc	PO Box 1867	Scottsdale	AZ	85252		50+
Carolina-Georgia Blood Center 208	515 Grove Rd	Greenville	SC	29605	864-255-5000	5-9
Central California Blood Bank	3445 N First St	Fresno	CA	93726	559-224-2900	5-9
Central Kentucky Blood Center Inc	330 Waller Ave	Lexington	KY	40504		10-19
Community Blood Bank of Erie County	2646 Peach St	Erie	PA	16508	814-456-4206	1-5
Community Blood Center	349 S Main St	Dayton	OH	45402	937-461-3450	20-29
Florida Blood Services Inc	PO Box 22500	St Petersburg	FL	33742		30-39
Greater Metropolitan Community Blood Service Inc	1150 Yonkers Ave	Yonkers	NY	10704		10-19
Gulf Coast Regional Blood Center	1400 La Concha	Houston	TX	77054		40-49
Lifesource	1205 N Milwaukee Ave	Glenview	IL	60025	847-298-9660	30-39
Mississippi Blood Services Inc	1995 Lakeland Dr	Jackson	MS	39216	601-981-3232	5-9
Oklahoma Blood Institute	1001 N Lincoln Blvd	Oklahoma City	OK	73104	405-297-5700	20-29
Puget Sound Blood Center and Blood Program	921 Terry Ave	Seattle	WA	98104	206-292-6500	50+
Southeast Iowa Blood Center	1005 E Pennsylvania	Ottumwa	IA	52501	515-682-8149	1-5
Walter L Shepeard Community Blood Center Inc	1533 Wrightsboro Rd	Augusta	GA	30904		1-5

Source: *National Directory of Nonprofit Organizations*, 2000, Volumes 1 and 2, The Taft Group. The table shows a selection of organizations for illustration and does not constitute a complete selection from the source. The organizations are arranged in alphabetical order.

LOCATION BY STATE AND REGIONAL CONCENTRATION

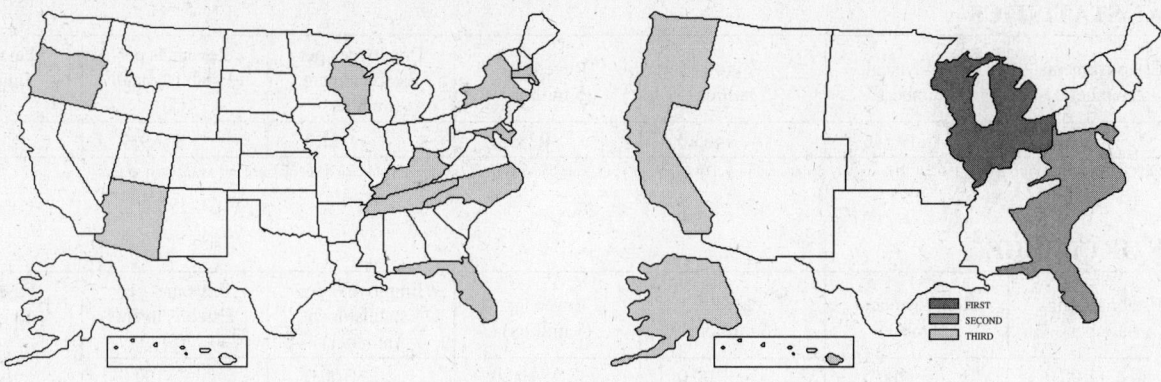

INDUSTRY DATA BY STATE

State	Establishments		Employment			Payroll		Revenues		
	Total (number)	% of U.S.	Total (number)	% of U.S.	Per Estab.	Total ($ mil.)	Per Empl. ($)	Total ($ mil.)	% of U.S.	Per Estab. ($)
California	133	10.8	4,376	10.2	33	133.7	30,548	369.7	9.6	2,779,759
New York	26	2.1	2,384	5.5	92	91.2	38,252	279.0	7.2	10,730,000
Texas	104	8.5	2,906	6.8	28	72.2	24,856	238.6	6.2	2,294,010
Florida	123	10.0	2,914	6.8	24	69.7	23,920	233.1	6.0	1,895,480
Ohio	55	4.5	1,996	4.6	36	50.5	25,319	160.5	4.2	2,918,727
Massachusetts	18	1.5	984	2.3	55	38.3	38,947	128.4	3.3	7,133,167
Illinois	46	3.7	1,666	3.9	36	41.8	25,078	123.6	3.2	2,687,543
Wisconsin	41	3.3	1,476	3.4	36	31.1	21,054	120.2	3.1	2,931,585
North Carolina	34	2.8	1,196	2.8	35	31.6	26,392	115.1	3.0	3,385,441
Tennessee	35	2.8	1,146	2.7	33	31.3	27,278	108.6	2.8	3,101,743
Arizona	23	1.9	1,159	2.7	50	34.1	29,405	91.0	2.4	3,955,130
Maryland	16	1.3	927	2.2	58	31.1	33,589	85.1	2.2	5,321,250
Indiana	41	3.3	1,105	2.6	27	27.6	24,959	79.8	2.1	1,946,829
Kentucky	21	1.7	741	1.7	35	17.6	23,718	56.7	1.5	2,701,429
Colorado	23	1.9	497	1.2	22	13.4	26,960	46.6	1.2	2,025,783
Oregon	13	1.1	666	1.5	51	15.5	23,231	44.7	1.2	3,441,692
Iowa	20	1.6	593	1.4	30	13.7	23,040	43.1	1.1	2,155,450
Alabama	22	1.8	509	1.2	23	9.9	19,481	37.8	1.0	1,717,818
Arkansas	14	1.1	402	0.9	29	8.7	21,622	31.0	0.8	2,213,714
Louisiana	19	1.5	227	0.5	12	3.6	15,674	18.6	0.5	981,526
Delaware	5	0.4	175*	-	-	(D)	-	(D)	-	-
Montana	2	0.2	60*	-	-	(D)	-	(D)	-	-
New Hampshire	2	0.2	10*	-	-	(D)	-	(D)	-	-
D.C.	1	0.1	10*	-	-	(D)	-	(D)	-	-
Vermont	1	0.1	10*	-	-	(D)	-	(D)	-	-

Source: 1997 *Economic Census*. The states are in descending order of revenues or establishments (if revenue data are missing for the majority). The symbol (D) appears when data are withheld to prevent disclosure of competitive information. States marked with (D) are sorted by number of establishments. A dash (-) indicates that the data element cannot be calculated. * indicates the midpoint of a range; 175, for example is the range 100-249. Shaded *states* on the state map indicate those states which have proportionately greater representation in the industry than would be indicated by the state's population; the ratio is based on total revenues or number of establishments. Shaded *regions* indicate where the industry is regionally most concentrated.

NAICS 621999 - MISCELLANEOUS AMBULATORY HEALTH CARE SERVICES NEC

GENERAL STATISTICS

Year	Establishments (number)	Employment (number)	Payroll ($ million)	Revenues ($ million)	Employees per Establishment (number)	Revenues per Establishment ($)	Payroll per Employee ($)
1997	1,619	19,346	465.0	1,389.0	11.9	857,937	24,036

Source: *Economic Census of the United States*, 1997. This is a newly defined industry. Data for prior years were unavailable at the time of publication but may become available over time.

INDICES OF CHANGE

Year	Establishments (number)	Employment (number)	Payroll ($ million)	Revenues ($ million)	Employees per Establishment (number)	Revenues per Establishment ($)	Payroll per Employee ($)
1997	100.0	100.0	100.0	100.0	100.0	100.0	100.0

Sources: Same as General Statistics. The values shown reflect change from the base year, 1997. Values above 100 mean greater than 1997, values below 100 mean less than 1997, and a value of 100 in the 1982-96 or 1998-2001 period means same as 1997. Values followed by a 'p' are projections by the editors; 'e' stands for extrapolation. Data are the most recent available at this level of detail.

SIC INDUSTRIES RELATED TO NAICS 621999

Each new NAICS code represents an industry that used to be part of an SIC or a part of several SIC industries. Data in this table are shown to provide transitional information for these cases. All available data for the precursor SIC(s) are shown. Even if only a part of an SIC is included in the NAICS, *all* data for the SIC are reproduced. If the SIC industry is not marked as being a part (pt) of the NAICS, the entire industry is embedded in the NAICS data. The SIC composition of the new industry provides some hints of the relative importance of its "ancestors." Data marked with a 'p' are projected. Projections begin with 1982 data. Data earlier than 1990 are not shown but are reflected in the projections.

SIC	Industry	1990	1991	1992	1993	1994	1995	1996	1997
8099	**Health & Allied Services, nec (pt)**								
	Establishments (number)	-	-	5,011	-	-	-	-	-
	Employment (thousands)	-	-	71.9	-	-	-	-	-
	Revenues ($ million)	-	-	5,022.6	-	-	-	-	-

Source: *Economic Census of the United States*, 1992; annual surveys of economic sectors conducted by the Bureau of the Census, and estimates or projections based on the 1982-1992 period; not all data are shown. 'e' marks estimates made by the editors; 'p' indicates projections based on time series. A dash (-) indicates that data for this SIC or year were not available. The abbreviation (pt) next to the industry name indicates that only a part of the industry is present within the NAICS data. If no (pt) is shown, the entire industry is contained within the NAICS data.

SELECTED RATIOS

For 1997	Avg. of Information	Analyzed Industry	Index	For 1997	Avg. of Information	Analyzed Industry	Index
Employees per establishment	21	12	57	Payroll per establishment	585,591	287,214	49
Revenue per establishment	1,370,364	857,937	63	Payroll as % of revenue	43	33	78
Revenue per employee	65,262	71,798	110	Payroll per employee	27,888	24,036	86

Sources: Same as General Statistics. The 'Average' column represents the average for the industry sector, in 1997, where the currently shown industry is classified. The Index shows the relationship between the Average and the Analyzed Industry. For example, 100 means that they are equal; 500 that the Analyzed Industry is five times the average; 50 means that the Analyzed Industry is half the national average. The abbreviation 'na' is used to show that data are 'not available'.

LEADING COMPANIES   Number shown: **75**   Total sales ($ mil): **14,431**   Total employment (000): **105.1**

Company Name	Address				CEO Name	Phone	Co. Type	Sales ($ mil)	Empl. (000)
Physicians' Specialty Corp.	1150 Lake Hearn Dr	Atlanta	GA	30342	Ramie A. Tritt, M.D.	404-256-7535	R	5,010*	0.5
Coventry Health Care Inc.	6705 Rockledge Dr	Bethesda	MD	20817	Alan F Wise	301-581-0600	P	2,110	3.0
Medstar Health Corp.	5565 Sterrett Pl	Columbia	MD	21044	John P McDaniel	410-772-6300	R	1,800	19.0
NovaCare Inc.	1016 W 9th Ave	King Of Prussia	PA	19406	Timothy Foster	610-992-7200	P	1,478	54.8
Hooper Holmes Inc.	170 Mount Airy Rd	Basking Ridge	NJ	07920	James M McNamee	908-766-5000	P	1,185	1.6
Advance ParadigM Inc.	P O Box 542906	Irving	TX	75062	David D Halbert	972-830-6199	P	775	0.9
Vitalink Pharmacy Services Inc.	1250 E Diehl Rd	Naperville	IL	60563	Stewart Bainum Jr	630-245-4800	P	274	3.3
Alliance Imaging Inc.	1065 N PacifiCenter	Anaheim	CA	92806	Vincent S Pino	714-688-7100	S	199	1.6
CorVel Corp.	2010 Main St	Irvine	CA	92614	V Gordon Clemons	949-851-1473	P	166	2.5
Horizon Health Corp.	1500 Waters Ridge	Lewisville	TX	75057	James W McAtee	972-420-8200	P	146	1.5
Monarch Dental Corp.	4201 Spring Valley	Dallas	TX	75244	Gary W Cage	972-702-7446	P	130	1.8
Suncare Respiratory Services Inc.	106 E College Ave	Tallahassee	FL	32301	Tom R Futch	850-577-0090	S	112*	4.5
Raytel Medical Corp.	2755 Campus Dr	San Mateo	CA	94403	Richard F Bader	650-349-0800	P	108	0.8
HEARx Ltd.	1250 Northpoint	W. Palm Beach	FL	33407	Paul A Brown	561-478-8770	P	84*	0.3
Ceres Group Incorp.	17800 Royalton Rd	Cleveland	OH	44136	Peter W Nauert	440-572-2400	R	82*	0.5
United Professional Cos.	3724 W Wisconsin	Milwaukee	WI	53208		414-342-9292	S	72	0.8
CryoLife Inc.	1655 Roberts Blvd	Kennesaw	GA	30144	Steven G Anderson	770-419-3355	P	61	0.4
SteriGenics International	2001 Spring Break	oak Brook	IL	60523	Kevin Swan	630-571-1280	P	54	0.3
Sterile Recoveries Inc.	28100 U S 19 N	Clearwater	FL	33761	Richard T Isel	727-726-4421	P	52	1.0
Medicode Inc.	PO Box 27358	Salt Lake City	UT	84127	Gene Cattarina	801-536-1000	R	50	0.3
Treimier	PO Box 668800	Charlotte	NC	28266		704-529-3300	N	50	0.6
CORE Inc.	18881 Von Karman	Irvine	CA	92612	G C Carpenter IV	949-442-2100	P	46	0.9
Transcriptions Ltd.	15 Henry Ave	Feasterville	PA	19053	David Cohen	215-322-1660	S	45	0.5
Gulf Coast Regional Blood Center	1400 La Concha Ln	Houston	TX	77054		713-790-1200	R	37	0.5
Lighthouse International	111 E 59th St	New York	NY	10022	Barbara Silverstone	212-821-9200	R	35*	0.3
Concord Resources Group Inc.	1835 Market St	Philadelphia	PA	19103	Stephen Rosenzweig	215-563-5555	S	27*	<0.1
Griffith Micro Science Inc.	2001 Spring Rd	Oak Brook	IL	60523	Kevin Swan	630-571-1280	S	26*	0.1
Respiratory Care Services	705 Juniper St	Atlanta	GA	30365	Ailene Miller	404-873-2871	D	22*	0.3
Call Connect	5720 Flatiron Pkwy	Boulder	CO	80301	David Shanks	303-442-1111	R	20*	0.3
Healthcare Corp.	30 Burton Hills	Nashville	TN	37215	Robert I Falk	615-665-9900	R	20*	0.2
Johnson, Bassin and Shaw Inc.	8630 Fenton St	Silver Spring	MD	20910		301-495-1080	N	18	0.1
HemaCare Corp.	4954 Van Nuys Blvd	Sherman Oaks	CA	91403	William D Nicely	818-968-3883	P	13	0.2
Medex Assistance Corp.	9515 Deereco Rd	Timonium	MD	21093	Philip H Dell	410-453-6300	S	13*	0.1
Athena Diagnostics Inc.	377 Plantation St	Worcester	MA	01605	Robert F Flaherty	508-756-2886	R	10*	<0.1
Health Care Excellence Inc.	600 New Hampshire	Washington	DC	20037	Don Hernley	202-625-3200	R	10	0.1
Medical Sterilization Inc.	225 Underhill Blvd	Syosset	NY	11791	D Michael Deignan	516-496-8822	P	10*	0.1
Health Management Inc.	9100 Southwest	Houston	TX	77074	John Goodman	713-541-2727	R	9	<0.1
Blood Bank of Delaware Inc.	100 Hygeia Dr	Newark	DE	19713	Robert L Travis	302-737-8400	R	7*	0.2
Hospice Homecare Inc.	8135 Beechmont	Cincinnati	OH	45255		513-474-2550	R	6*	<0.1
Mattson Jack Group Inc.	11960 Westline Ind	St. Louis	MO	63146		314-469-7600	N	5	<0.1
Bio-Imaging Technologies Inc.	830 Bear Tavern Rd	West Trenton	NJ	08628	Mark Weinstein	609-883-2000	P	4	<0.1
American Corporate Health	559 W Uwchlan	Exton	PA	19341	Richard Robson	610-594-2110	R	4*	<0.1
Lauren Corp.	1670 Broadway	Denver	CO	80202	Thomas H Fortner	303-813-9505	R	4*	<0.1
KAI	6001 Montrose Rd	Rockville	MD	20852		301-770-2730	N	3	<0.1
Pharma-Care Inc.	35 Walnut Ave	Clark	NJ	07066	Harlan Martin	732-574-9015	R	3*	<0.1
Xytex Corp.	1100 Emmett St	Augusta	GA	30904	Armand M Karow	706-733-0130	R	3*	<0.1
RTI Inc.	301 Antone	Sunland Park	NM	88063	Rick E Bacchus	505-589-5431	P	3	0.2
Better Life Institute Inc.	220 Lyon St NW	Grand Rapids	MI	49503	Patricia M Zifferblatt	616-776-6490	R	2*	<0.1
Dickson Gabbay Corp.	1205 Westlakes Dr	Berwyn	PA	19312		610-640-2035	N	2	<0.1
Obesity Treatment Center Inc.	1325 Howe Ave	Sacramento	CA	95825	Caroline Goddard	916-925-0300	R	2*	<0.1
The DRB Group Inc.	1661 Commerce	St. Petersburg	FL	33716		813-568-0088	N	2	<0.1
Adcare Health Systems Inc.	5057 Troy Rd	Springfield	OH	45502		937-964-8974	N	2	<0.1
Creative Medical Communications	240 W 98th St	New York	NY	10025		212-864-8074	N	2	<0.1
Institute for Alternative Futures	100 N Pitt St	Alexandria	VA	22314		703-684-5880	N	2	<0.1
Micro Management Technologies	165 Winchester St	Brookline	MA	02146		617-731-3737	N	2	<0.1
Morrisy and Company Inc.	3840 Park Ave	Edison	NJ	08820		732-906-9313	N	1	<0.1
Bill Miller and Associates Inc.	12696 Pacato Cir N	San Diego	CA	92128		619-487-2455	N	1	<0.1
Biogenetics Corp.	P O Box 1290	Mountainside	NJ	07092	Albert Anouna	908-654-8836	R	1*	<0.1
Garrett Associates Inc.	PO Box 53359	Atlanta	GA	30355		404-364-0001	N	1	<0.1
Idant Laboratories Div.	350 5th Ave	New York	NY	10118	Joseph Feldschuh	212-244-0555	D	1*	<0.1
Managed Health Consultants Inc.	100 Grandview Rd	Braintree	MA	02184		781-356-4994	N	1	<0.1
Menlo Biomedical Associates Inc.	1836 17th Ave	Santa Cruz	CA	95062	Frank Von Richter	831-475-6244	R	1*	<0.1
Northwest Physicians Inc.	5555 Arpt Hwy	Toledo	OH	43615		419-868-5230	R	1*	<0.1
SRS International Corp.	1625 K St N W	Washington	DC	20006	John Todhunter	202-223-0157	R	1	<0.1
Health Consultants Inc.	420-D Madison St	Clarksville	TN	37040		931-552-4655	N	1	<0.1
Koffel Associates Inc.	3300 N Ridge Rd	Ellicott City	MD	21043		410-750-2246	N	1	<0.1
Pharm Rx Consultants Inc.	1238 Stuivesant	Union	NJ	07083	I Barton Frenchman	908-686-2063	N	1	<0.1
Health Resource Inc.	564 Locust Ave	Conway	AR	72032	Jan Guthrie	501-329-5272	R	1	<0.1
Wellness Group Inc.	29201 Telegraph Rd	Southfield	MI	48034		248-351-7890	N	1	<0.1
Alcor Life Extension Foundation	7895 E Acoma Rd	Scottsdale	AZ	85260	Fred Chamberlain	480-905-1906	R	1	<0.1
Criterion Systems Inc.	100 Crother Rd	Applegate	CA	95703		916-878-6689	N	1	<0.1
CSI	15425 N Freeway	Houston	TX	77090		281-872-0984	N	1	<0.1
Medical Marketing Inc.	507 N New York	Winter Park	FL	32789	Andrea Eliscu	407-629-0062	R	1	<0.1
MEDIVAN Inc.	4953 S Packard Ave	Cudahy	WI	53110	Judith A Geiger	414-483-8267	R	1	<0.1
NCES Inc.	1904 E 123rd	Olathe	KS	66061		913-782-4385	N	0	<0.1

Source: Ward's Business Directory of U.S. Private and Public Companies, Volumes 1 and 2, 2000. The company type code used is as follows: P - Public, R - Private, S - Subsidiary, D - Division, J - Joint Venture, A - Affiliate, G - Group, N - Company type not reported. Sales are in millions of dollars, employees are in thousands. An asterisk (*) indicates an estimated sales volume. The symbol < stands for 'less than'. Company names and addresses are truncated, in some cases, to fit into the available space.

REPRESENTATIVE NONPROFIT ORGANIZATIONS

Organization Name	Address				Phone	Income Range ($ mil)
1115 Health and Benefits Fund	761 Merrick Ave	Westbury	NY	11590		50+
Allegheny Health Education & Research Foundation	320 E North Ave	Pittsburgh	PA	15212	412-359-3141	50+
Allina Health System	5640 Smetana Dr	Minneapolis	MN	55420		50+
Arkansas Community Health and Education Foundation	6701 W 12th St	Little Rock	AR	72204	501-221-0404	10-19
Aultman Health Services Association	2600 Sixth St SW	Canton	OH	44710		50+
Aurora Health Care Inc	3000 W Montana St	Milwaukee	WI	53215		50+
BJC Health System	4444 Forest Park Ave	St Louis	MO	63108	314-286-2000	50+
Baptist Memorial Health Care Corp	899 Madison Ave	Memphis	TN	38103		50+
Baylor Health Care System	3500 Gaston Ave	Dallas	TX	75246	214-820-7676	50+
Blodget Memorial Medical Center	1840 Wealthy St SE	Grand Rapids	MI	49506	616-774-7444	50+
California Endowment	21650 Oxnard St	Woodland Hills	CA	91367	818-703-3311	50+
Camuy Health Services Inc	PO Box 660	Camuy	PR	00627		5-9
Capital Plan	2140 Centerville PL	Tallahassee	FL	32308		50+
Charlotte-Mecklenburg Health Services Foundation Inc	PO Box 34725	Charlotte	NC	28234		50+
Chester County Hospital & Nursing Center Inc	Great Falls Rd	Chester	SC	29706	803-581-3151	20-29
Colorado Dental Service Inc	4582 S Ulster St	Denver	CO	80237		50+
Cooley Dickinson Hospital	30 Locust St	Northampton	MA	01060	413-582-2000	50+
Delaware Hospice Inc	3519 Silverside Rd	Wilmington	DE	19810	302-478-5707	5-9
Delta Dental Plan of Idaho Inc	200 N 4th	Boise	ID	83702	208-344-4546	20-29
Delta Dental Plan of Iowa	2401 SE Tones Dr 13	Ankeny	IA	50021		50+
Delta Dental Plan of New Jersey	PO Box 222	Parsippany	NJ	07054	973-285-4000	50+
Delta Dental Plan of New Mexico Inc	2500 Louisiana Blvd NE	Albuquerque	NM	87110	505-883-4777	30-39
Delta Dental Plan of Virginia	4818 Starkey Rd S W	Roanoke	VA	24014	540-989-8000	50+
Delta Dental Plan of Wyoming	320 W 25th St	Cheyenne	WY	82001	307-632-3313	5-9
Eastern Maine Healthcare Endowment Inc	PO Box 404	Bangor	ME	04402	207-973-7000	40-49
Egleston Childrens Hospital at Emory University Inc	1405 Clifton Rd NE	Atlanta	GA	30322		50+
Enh Faculty Practice Associates	1301 Central St	Evanston	IL	60201		50+
Fraser Hall	2902 S Univ Dr	Fargo	ND	58103		1-5
General Health System	5757 Corporate Blvd	Baton Rouge	LA	70808		40-49
Greater Baltimore Medical Center	6701 N Charles St	Baltimore	MD	21204		50+
Greater Waterbury Health Network Inc	64 Robbins St	Waterbury	CT	06708		50+
Health Plan Partners	55 Merchant St 24th Flr	Honolulu	HI	96813		30-39
Hometown Health Plan Inc	400 S Wells Ave	Reno	NV	89502		50+
Hospice of the Bluegrass Inc	2312 Alexandria Dr	Lexington	KY	40504	859-276-5344	20-29
Ihc Health Plans Inc	4646 Lake Park Blvd	Salt Lake Cty	UT	84120	801-442-5000	50+
Infirmary Health System Inc	PO Box 2226	Mobile	AL	36652		40-49
Integris Homecare Inc	3366 NW Expressway	Oklahoma City	OK	73112		5-9
Lifespan Corporation	167 Point St	Providence	RI	02903	401-444-3500	50+
Lutheran Health Foundation of Indiana Inc	3024 Fairfield Ave	Fort Wayne	IN	46807	219-458-2374	50+
Newton Healthcare Corporation	PO Box 308	Newton	KS	67114		40-49
North Mississippi Health Services Inc	830 S Gloster	Tupelo	MS	38801	662-841-3235	10-19
Northwest Horizons Inc	350 Conway Dr	Kalispell	MT	59901		5-9
Norton Sound Health Corporation	PO Box 966	Nome	AK	99762	907-443-3311	40-49
Optima Health Inc	286 Commercial St	Manchester	NH	03101		20-29
Premera Healthplus	PO Box 327 Mailstop 350	Seattle	WA	98111		50+
Self-Insurance Trust of Washington Hospital Center	100 Irving St NW	Washington	DC	20010		50+
Sioux Valley Health Network	PO Box 5039	Sioux Falls	SD	57117	605-333-2220	30-39
Sisters of Providence Good Health Plan of Oregon Inc	1235 NE 47th	Portland	OR	97213	503-215-4321	50+
Southwest Catholic Health Network Corporation	2800 N Central Ave	Phoenix	AZ	85004		50+
Southwestern Vermont Medical Center Inc	100 Hospital Dr E	Bennington	VT	05201	802-442-6361	40-49
Visiting Nurse Assocation of the Midlands	1941 S 42nd St	Omaha	NE	68105	402-342-5566	10-19
West Virginia University Medical Corporation	330 Scott Ave	Morgantown	WV	26508		50+

Source: National Directory of Nonprofit Organizations, 2000, Volumes 1 and 2, The Taft Group. The table shows a selection of organizations for illustration and does not constitute a complete selection from the source. The organizations are arranged in alphabetical order.

LOCATION BY STATE AND REGIONAL CONCENTRATION

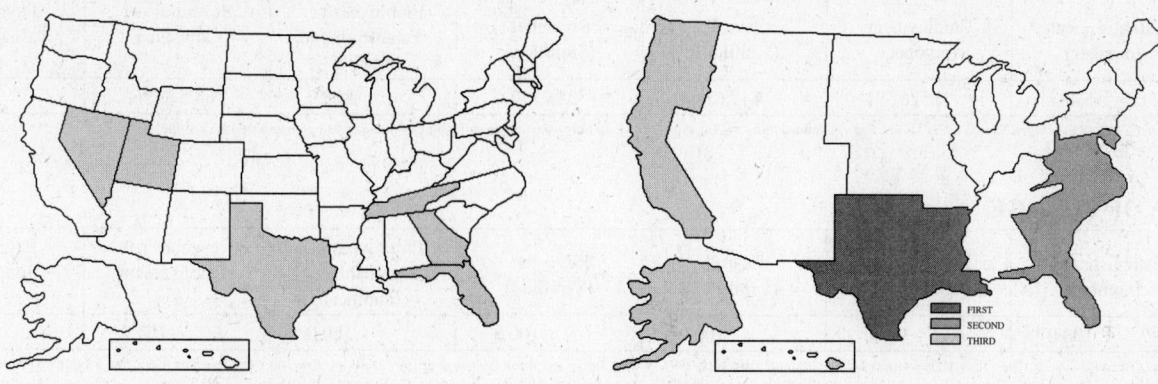

INDUSTRY DATA BY STATE

State	Establishments		Employment			Payroll		Revenues		
	Total (number)	% of U.S.	Total (number)	% of U.S.	Per Estab.	Total ($ mil.)	Per Empl. ($)	Total ($ mil.)	% of U.S.	Per Estab. ($)
Texas	152	9.4	2,152	11.1	14	54.7	25,428	181.9	13.1	1,196,454
California	172	10.6	1,795	9.3	10	48.2	26,873	138.5	10.0	805,076
Florida	142	8.8	1,502	7.8	11	37.8	25,200	119.2	8.6	839,761
Tennessee	37	2.3	535	2.8	14	12.8	23,880	39.9	2.9	1,077,486
Georgia	42	2.6	509	2.6	12	13.8	27,081	39.5	2.8	940,143
Ohio	58	3.6	436	2.3	8	10.6	24,360	29.2	2.1	502,776
North Carolina	34	2.1	300	1.6	9	7.8	25,967	24.5	1.8	719,529
Utah	19	1.2	360	1.9	19	6.5	17,981	20.3	1.5	1,071,000
Kentucky	26	1.6	378	2.0	15	8.3	21,923	19.5	1.4	748,654
Nevada	15	0.9	288	1.5	19	5.4	18,597	14.8	1.1	987,800
Alabama	19	1.2	194	1.0	10	3.9	20,242	11.5	0.8	602,684
Kansas	19	1.2	227	1.2	12	3.0	13,159	8.2	0.6	430,579
Iowa	15	0.9	195	1.0	13	2.8	14,410	6.3	0.5	423,133
Oklahoma	16	1.0	99	0.5	6	2.1	21,384	5.1	0.4	318,938
Arkansas	11	0.7	67	0.3	6	1.6	23,343	4.2	0.3	384,636
Mississippi	11	0.7	87	0.4	8	1.5	16,954	3.9	0.3	354,182
Delaware	8	0.5	61	0.3	8	1.4	23,164	3.4	0.2	422,375
Maryland	22	1.4	375*	-	-	(D)	-	(D)	-	-
Connecticut	11	0.7	175*	-	-	(D)	-	(D)	-	-
Rhode Island	5	0.3	60*	-	-	(D)	-	(D)	-	-
South Dakota	4	0.2	10*	-	-	(D)	-	(D)	-	-
Montana	3	0.2	60*	-	-	(D)	-	(D)	-	-
North Dakota	3	0.2	10*	-	-	(D)	-	(D)	-	-
Idaho	2	0.1	60*	-	-	(D)	-	(D)	-	-

Source: 1997 *Economic Census*. The states are in descending order of revenues or establishments (if revenue data are missing for the majority). The symbol (D) appears when data are withheld to prevent disclosure of competitive information. States marked with (D) are sorted by number of establishments. A dash (-) indicates that the data element cannot be calculated. * indicates the midpoint of a range; 175, for example is the range 100-249. Shaded *states* on the state map indicate those states which have proportionately greater representation in the industry than would be indicated by the state's population; the ratio is based on total revenues or number of establishments. Shaded *regions* indicate where the industry is regionally most concentrated.

NAICS 622110 - GENERAL MEDICAL AND SURGICAL HOSPITALS

GENERAL STATISTICS

Year	Establishments (number)	Employment (number)	Payroll ($ million)	Revenues ($ million)	Employees per Establishment (number)	Revenues per Establishment ($)	Payroll per Employee ($)
1997	5,487	4,526,591	142,624.0	354,133.0	825.0	64,540,368	31,508

Source: Economic Census of the United States, 1997. This is a newly defined industry. Data for prior years were unavailable at the time of publication but may become available over time.

INDICES OF CHANGE

Year	Establishments (number)	Employment (number)	Payroll ($ million)	Revenues ($ million)	Employees per Establishment (number)	Revenues per Establishment ($)	Payroll per Employee ($)
1997	100.0	100.0	100.0	100.0	100.0	100.0	100.0

Sources: Same as General Statistics. The values shown reflect change from the base year, 1997. Values above 100 mean greater than 1997, values below 100 mean less than 1997, and a value of 100 in the 1982-96 or 1998-2001 period means same as 1997. Values followed by a 'p' are projections by the editors; 'e' stands for extrapolation. Data are the most recent available at this level of detail.

SIC INDUSTRIES RELATED TO NAICS 622110

Each new NAICS code represents an industry that used to be part of an SIC or a part of several SIC industries. Data in this table are shown to provide transitional information for these cases. All available data for the precursor SIC(s) are shown. Even if only a part of an SIC is included in the NAICS, *all* data for the SIC are reproduced. If the SIC industry is not marked as being a part (pt) of the NAICS, the entire industry is embedded in the NAICS data. The SIC composition of the new industry provides some hints of the relative importance of its "ancestors." Data marked with a 'p' are projected. Projections begin with 1982 data. Data earlier than 1990 are not shown but are reflected in the projections.

SIC	Industry	1990	1991	1992	1993	1994	1995	1996	1997
8062	**General Medical & Surgical Hospitals**								
	Establishments (number)	-	-	5,624	-	-	-	-	-
	Employment (thousands)	-	-	4,411.0	-	-	-	-	-
	Revenues ($ million)	20,442.0	22,220.0	24,162.0	26,683.0	27,993.0	30,704.0	36,496.0	36,808.7p
8069	**Specialty Hospitals, Ex Psychiatric (pt)**								
	Establishments (number)	-	-	577	-	-	-	-	-
	Employment (thousands)	-	-	266.0	-	-	-	-	-
	Revenues ($ million)	1,916.0	2,185.0	2,525.0	2,918.0	3,386.0	3,866.0	4,665.0	3,249.9p

Source: Economic Census of the United States, 1992, annual surveys of economic sectors conducted by the Bureau of the Census, and estimates or projections based on the 1982-1992 period; not all data are shown. 'e' marks estimates made by the editors; 'p' indicates projections based on time series. A dash (-) indicates that data for this SIC or year were not available. The abbreviation (pt) next to the industry name indicates that only a part of the industry is present within the NAICS data. If no (pt) is shown, the entire industry is contained within the NAICS data.

SELECTED RATIOS

For 1997	Avg. of Information	Analyzed Industry	Index	For 1997	Avg. of Information	Analyzed Industry	Index
Employees per establishment	21	825	3,929	Payroll per establishment	585,591	25,993,075	4,439
Revenue per establishment	1,370,364	64,540,368	4,710	Payroll as % of revenue	43	40	94
Revenue per employee	65,262	78,234	120	Payroll per employee	27,888	31,508	113

Sources: Same as General Statistics. The 'Average' column represents the average for the industry sector, in 1997, where the currently shown industry is classified. The Index shows the relationship between the Average and the Analyzed Industry. For example, 100 means that they are equal; 500 that the Analyzed Industry is five times the average; 50 means that the Analyzed Industry is half the national average. The abbreviation 'na' is used to show that data are 'not available'.

LEADING COMPANIES   Number shown: **64**   Total sales ($ mil): **82,475**   Total employment (000): **1,060.1**

Company Name	Address				CEO Name	Phone	Co. Type	Sales ($ mil)	Empl. (000)
Columbia/HCA Healthcare Corp.	1 Park Plaza	Nashville	TN	37203	Jack O. Bovender Jr.	615-344-9551	P	18,618	260.0
Tenet Healthcare Corp.	PO Box 4070	Santa Monica	CA	90404	Jeffery C Barbakow	805-563-7000	P	10,880	126.0
Banner Health System	1441 N 12th St	Phoenix	AZ	85006	John Casey	602-495-4000	R	10,013*	120.0
Tenet HealthSystem Holdings Inc.	PO Box 809088	Dallas	TX	75380	Jeffrey C Barbakow	972-789-2200	S	9,895	116.8
Vencor Inc.	3300 Aegon Ctr	Louisville	KY	40202	Edward Kuntz	502-569-7300	P	2,999	57.0
Mercy Health Services	34605 12 Mile Rd	Farmington Hills	MI	48331	Judy Pelham	248-489-6000	R	2,534	26.4
Intermountain Health Care Inc.	36 S State St	Salt Lake City	UT	84111	Scott Parker	801-442-2000	R	2,009	22.0
Universal Health Services Inc.	PO Box 61558	King of Prussia	PA	19406	Alan B Miller	610-768-3300	P	1,874	19.2
Quorum Health Group Inc.	103 Continental Pl	Brentwood	TN	37027	James E Dalton Jr	615-371-7979	P	1,653	20.9
Advocate HealthCare	2025 Windsor Dr	Oak Brook	IL	60523	Richard R Risk	630-572-9393	R	1,636*	21.0
Banner Health Arizona	1441 N 12th St	Phoenix	AZ	85006	James C Crews	602-495-4000	R	1,364*	22.0
Catholic Health Initiatives	One MacIntyre Dr	Aston	PA	19014	William Foley	610-358-3950	D	1,200	12.0
Herrick Memorial Hospital Inc.	500 E Pottawatamie	Tecumseh	MI	49286	John Robertstad	517-423-2141	R	1,157*	14.0
Methodist Healthcare	1211 Union Ave	Memphis	TN	38104	Maurice Elliot	901-726-2300	R	1,084*	13.0
Baptist Health Systems	6855 Red Rd	Coral Gables	FL	33143	George E Cadman III		R	1,036	7.5
Helix Health Inc.	2330 W Joppa Rd	Lutherville	MD	21093	John McDaniel	410-847-6700	R	1,010*	18.0
Memorial Health Services Inc.	2801 Atlantic Ave	Long Beach	CA	90806	Tom Collins	562-933-2000	R	980*	4.2
Community Health Systems Inc.	P O Box 217	Brentwood	TN	37024	Wayne Smith	615-373-9600	S	840	12.0
Bon Secours Health System Inc.	1505 Marriottsville	Marriottsville	MD	21104	Christopher Carney	410-442-5511	R	834*	10.0
Oakwood Healthcare System Inc.	P O Box 2500	Dearborn	MI	48123	Gerald D Fitzgerald	313-593-7000	R	751*	9.0
Aurora Health Care Inc.	P O Box 343910	Milwaukee	WI	53234	G Edwin Howe	414-647-3493	R	750*	9.0
Wheaton Franciscan Services Inc.	P O Box 667	Wheaton	IL	60189	Wilfred F Loebig Jr	630-462-9271	R	750	13.0
Sharp Healthcare	3131 Berger Ave	San Diego	CA	92123	Mike Murphy	619-541-4045	R	708	10.0
Paracelsus Healthcare Corp.	515 W Greens Rd	Houston	TX	77067	Ronald R Patterson	281-774-5100	P	664	7.0
Medstar Health	100 Irving St	Washington	DC	20010	John P McDaniel	202-877-7000	R	634*	6.0
Ancilla Systems Inc.	1000 S Lake	Hobart	IN	46342	William O Harkins	219-947-8500	R	607*	4.3
Norton Healthcare	P O Box 35070	Louisville	KY	40232	Stephen A Williams	502-629-6000	R	498*	7.5
PEACEHEALTH	15325 S E 30th Pl	Bellevue	WA	98007	John Hayward	425-747-1711	R	492*	6.0
University Health Inc.	1350 Walton Wy	Augusta	GA	30901	J Larry Read	706-722-9011	R	350	3.4
Straub Clinic and Hospital Inc.	888 S King St	Honolulu	HI	96813	Jonathan G Grimes	808-522-4000	R	333	1.8
St. Francis Regional Medical	929 N St Francis St	Wichita	KS	67214	Randy Nyp	316-268-5000	R	332*	4.0
Pittsburgh Mercy Health System	1400 Locust St	Pittsburgh	PA	15219	Joanne M Andiorio	412-232-8275	R	290*	3.5
Santa Rosa Health Care Corp.	519 W Houston St	San Antonio	TX	78207	Bill Filnagson	210-704-2111	R	265*	3.2
Munson Medical Center	1105 6th St	Traverse City	MI	49684	Ralph Cerny	616-922-9000	R	252*	3.0
Unity Health System	1565 Long Pond Rd	Rochester	NY	14626	Timothy McCormick	716-464-3743	R	235	2.0
St. Joseph's Hospital	350 W Thomas Rd	Phoenix	AZ	85013	William Foley	602-406-3000	D	230*	2.8
Horizon Health System	PO Box 5153	Southfield	MI	48086	Thomas Caufield	248-746-4300	R	209*	2.5
Citrus Valley Health Partners Inc.	140 W College St	Covina	CA	91723	Peter Makowski	626-331-7331	R	204*	2.0
John C. Lincoln Health Network	9200 N 3rd St	Phoenix	AZ	85020	Dan Coleman	602-870-6309	R	199*	2.8
Memorial Medical Center	800 N Rutledge St	Springfield	IL	62781	Robert Clarke	217-788-3000	R	175*	2.1
Children's Hospital of the King's	601 Children's Ln	Norfolk	VA	23507	Robert I Bonar	757-668-7000	R	167*	2.0
Fairview Riverside Medical	2450 Riverside	Minneapolis	MN	55454		612-672-6000	R	166*	2.0
John Muir Medical Center Inc.	1601 Ygnacio Valley	Walnut Creek	CA	94598	J Kendall Anderson	925-939-3000	R	163	1.9
United Health Services Inc.	10-42 Mitchell Ave	Binghamton	NY	13903	Mark T O'Neal	607-762-2200	R	160*	3.5
BJC Health System	4444 Forest	St. Louis	MO	63108	Fred L Brown	314-362-5000	R	151*	2.1
South Hills Health System	P O Box 18119	Pittsburgh	PA	15236	William R Jennings	412-469-5000	R	139*	27.7
Beebe Medical Center	424 Savannah Rd	Lewes	DE	19958	Jeffrey M Fried	302-645-3300	R	115	1.0
Charlton Memorial Hospital	363 Highland Ave	Fall River	MA	02720	Dr Ronald Goodstead	508-679-3131	S	91*	1.1
St. Luke's Hospital of New	101 Page St	New Bedford	MA	02740		508-997-1515	R	83*	1.0
Landmark Medical Center	115 Cass Ave	Woonsocket	RI	02895	Gary Gaube	401-769-4100	S	70*	0.9
Loudoun Healthcare Inc.	44045 Riverside	Leesburg	VA	20176	GT Ecker	703-777-3300	R	70	0.9
Medical Center-Independence	17203 E 23rd St	Independence	MO	64057	Kent Howard	816-478-5000	S	70	0.4
Nanticoke Memorial Hospital Inc.	801 Middleford Rd	Seaford	DE	19973	EH Hancock	302-629-6611	R	70*	0.6
NewCare Health Corp.	6000 Lake Forrest	Atlanta	GA	30328	Chris Brogdon	404-252-2923	R	66	2.7
Whittier Hospital Medical Center	9080 Colima Rd	Whittier	CA	90605		562-945-3561	P	66*	0.8
Broadlawns Medical Center	1801 Hickman Rd	Des Moines	IA	50314	Willis Fry	515-282-2200	R	62*	1.0
Milford Memorial Hospital Inc.	PO Box 199	Milford	DE	19963	Dennis Klima	302-422-3311	R	62*	0.8
Southern Ohio Medicare Center	1805 27th St	Portsmouth	OH	45662	Randal M Arnett	740-354-5000	R	58	2.0
Genesis Health Inc.	3627 University S	Jacksonville	FL	32216	Brooks Brown	904-391-1200	R	42	0.6
MedSpan	225 Asylum St	Hartford	CT	06103		860-616-2200	R	37	0.1
Rx Medical Services Corp.	888 E Las Olas	Fort Lauderdale	FL	33301	Mihael L Goldberg	954-462-1711	P	20	0.3
Cataract Eye Center	2322 E 22nd St	Cleveland	OH	44115	Samuel M Salmon	216-363-2718	R	2*	<0.1
Lovejoy Surgicenter Inc.	933 N W 25th Ave	Portland	OR	97210	Allene Klass	503-221-1870	R	1*	<0.1
UniHealth America	3400 Riverside Dr	Burbank	CA	91505	David Carpenter	818-238-6000	R	1*	<0.1

Source: Ward's Business Directory of U.S. Private and Public Companies, Volumes 1 and 2, 2000. The company type code used is as follows: P - Public, R - Private, S - Subsidiary, D - Division, J - Joint Venture, A - Affiliate, G - Group, N - Company type not reported. Sales are in millions of dollars, employees are in thousands. An asterisk (*) indicates an estimated sales volume. The symbol < stands for 'less than'. Company names and addresses are truncated, in some cases, to fit into the available space.

REPRESENTATIVE NONPROFIT ORGANIZATIONS

Organization Name	Address				Phone	Income Range ($ mil)
Abington Memorial Hospital	1200 Old York Rd	Abington	PA	19001		50+
Adventist Health Clearlake Hospital Inc	PO Box 6710	Clearlake	CA	95422		50+
Advocate Health and Hospitals Corporation	2025 Windsor Dr	Oak Brook	IL	60523	630-572-9393	50+
Ahs Hospital Corp	325 Columbia Turnpike	Florham Park	NJ	07932		50+
Akron General Medical Center	400 Wabash Ave	Akron	OH	44307	330-384-6699	50+
Alamance Regional Medical Center	PO Box 202	Burlington	NC	27216	910-538-7000	50+
Albany Medical Center Hospital	43 New Scotland Ave	Albany	NY	12208	518-262-4317	50+
Albert Lea Medical Center	404 Fountain St	Albert Lea	MN	56007	507-373-2384	50+
Alexandria Hospital Inc Accounting Dept	4320 Seminary Rd	Alexandria	VA	22304	703-504-7867	50+
All Childrens Hospital Inc	801 Sixth St S	St Petersburg	FL	33701		50+
Allen Memorial Hospital Corporation	1825 Logan Ave	Waterloo	IA	50703		50+
Altru Health System	1200 S Columbia Rd	Grand Forks	ND	58201		50+
Amarillo Hospital District	PO Box 868	Amarillo	TX	79105	806-379-8540	50+
Ancilla Health Care Inc	215 W 4th St	Mishawaka	IN	46544	219-259-2431	50+
Anderson Area Medical Center	800 N Fant St	Anderson	SC	29621		50+
Anderson Infirmary Benevolent Association Inc	2124 14th St	Meridan	MS	39301		50+
Anna Jaques Hospital	25 Highland Ave	Newburyport	MA	01950	978-465-6580	50+
Appalachian Regional Healthcare Inc	PO Box 8086	Lexington	KY	40533		50+
Appleton Medical Center	PO Box 8025	Appleton	WI	54913	920-749-1717	50+
Arkansas Childrens Hospital	800 Marshall	Little Rock	AR	72202	501-320-1004	50+
Aroostook Medical Center	PO Box 151	Presque Isle	ME	04769	207-768-4000	50+
Asante Health System	2650 Siskiyou Blvd	Medford	OR	97504	541-770-5042	50+
Athens Regional Medical Center Inc	1199 Prince Ave	Athens	GA	30606	706-549-9977	50+
Audrain Health Care Inc	620 E Monroe	Mexico	MO	65265	573-473-3800	50+
Avera St Lukes	305 S State St	Aberdeen	SD	57401		50+
Baptist Health System Inc	PO Box 830605	Birmingham	AL	35283	205-715-5000	50+
Baptist Hospital Inc	2000 Church St	Nashville	TN	37236	615-329-5438	50+
Battle Creek Health System	300 North Ave	Battle Creek	MI	49017	616-966-8000	50+
Bayhealth Medical Center Inc	640 S State St	Dover	DE	19901	302-674-4700	50+
Bluefield Regional Medical Center	500 Cherry St	Bluefield	WV	24701	304-327-1100	50+
Bon Secours Hospital Inc	2000 W Baltimore St	Baltimore	MD	21223	410-362-3053	50+
Bozeman Deaconess Health Services	915 Highland Blvd	Bozeman	MT	59715	406-585-5000	50+
Bradley Memorial Hospital & Health Center Inc	81 Meriden Ave CT	Southington	CT	06489	860-276-5000	50+
Catholic Health Initiatives Mountain Region	2525 S Downing St	Denver	CO	80210		50+
Catholic Healthcare West Arizona	350 W Thomas Rd	Phoenix	AZ	85013		50+
Catholic Medical Center	286 Commercial St	Manchester	NH	03101	603-626-2535	50+
Central Washington Health Services Association	PO Box 1887	Wenatchee	WA	98807		50+
Childrens Hospital Inc	200 Henry Clay Ave	New Orleans	LA	70118		50+
Childrens Hospital	111 Michigan Ave NW	Washigton	DC	20010		50+
Childrens Memorial Hospital Incorporated	8301 Dodge	Omaha	NE	68114	402-000-1111	50+
Deaconess Hospital	5501 N Portland	Oklahoma City	OK	73112	405-604-4382	50+
G N Wilcox Memorial Hospital	3420 Kuhio Hwy	Lithue	HI	96766		50+
Hays Medical Center Inc	PO Box 8100	Hays	KS	67601		50+
Hospital Auxilio Mutuo Inc	PO Box 191227	San Juan	PR	00919		50+
Ihc Health Services Inc	36 S State St Ste 2300	Salt Lake Cty	UT	84111	801-442-3946	50+
Kent County Memorial Hospital	455 Toll Gate Rd	Warwick	RI	02886	401-737-7000	50+
Memorial Medical Center Inc	2450 S Telshor Blvd	Las Cruces	NM	88011	505-521-2286	50+
Rutland Hospital Inc	160 Allen St	Rutland	VT	05701		50+
St Lukes Regional Medical Center	190 E Bannock	Boise	ID	83712	208-381-3088	50+
St Marys Regional Medical Center	235 W Sixth St	Reno	NV	89520		50+
Wyoming Medical Center Inc	1233 E 2nd	Casper	WY	82601	307-577-7910	50+
Yukon-Kuskokwim Health Corporation	PO Box 528	Bethel	AK	99559	907-557-5541	50+

Source: National Directory of Nonprofit Organizations, 2000, Volumes 1 and 2, The Taft Group. The table shows a selection of organizations for illustration and does not constitute a complete selection from the source. The organizations are arranged in alphabetical order.

LOCATION BY STATE AND REGIONAL CONCENTRATION

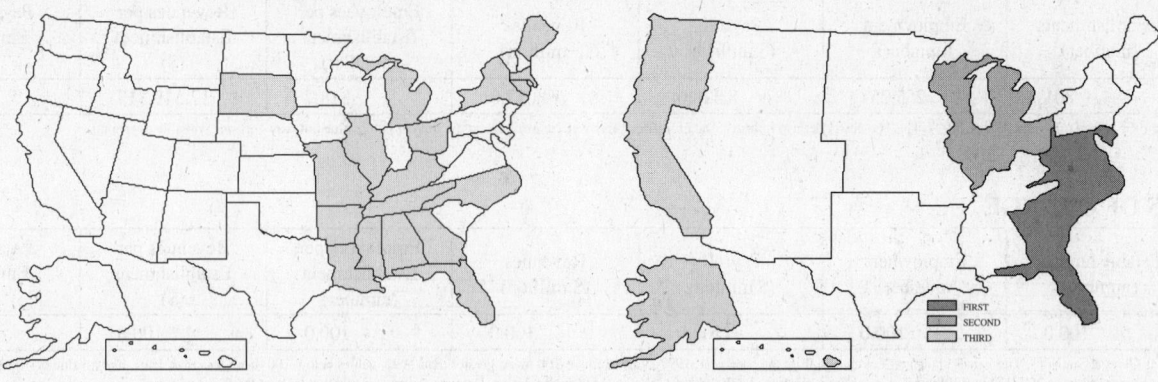

FIRST
SECOND
THIRD

INDUSTRY DATA BY STATE

State	Establishments		Employment			Payroll		Revenues		
	Total (number)	% of U.S.	Total (number)	% of U.S.	Per Estab.	Total ($ mil.)	Per Empl. ($)	Total ($ mil.)	% of U.S.	Per Estab. ($)
California	450	8.2	392,213	8.7	872	14,110.4	35,976	34,091.7	9.6	75,759,371
New York	245	4.5	372,329	8.2	1,520	14,294.3	38,392	30,173.1	8.5	123,155,576
Texas	421	7.7	276,497	6.1	657	8,038.1	29,071	22,343.0	6.3	53,071,271
Florida	235	4.3	242,204	5.4	1,031	7,323.3	30,236	19,997.8	5.6	85,097,221
Illinois	213	3.9	221,379	4.9	1,039	6,758.1	30,527	17,669.8	5.0	82,956,728
Ohio	189	3.4	206,544	4.6	1,093	6,463.9	31,296	15,749.4	4.4	83,330,333
Michigan	170	3.1	182,163	4.0	1,072	5,939.4	32,605	13,997.4	4.0	82,337,588
New Jersey	96	1.7	132,204	2.9	1,377	4,695.0	35,513	10,593.6	3.0	110,349,698
North Carolina	131	2.4	122,154	2.7	932	3,690.7	30,213	9,766.0	2.8	74,549,870
Georgia	164	3.0	120,076	2.7	732	3,450.4	28,735	9,716.3	2.7	59,245,524
Massachusetts	88	1.6	124,214	2.7	1,412	4,065.8	32,732	9,374.2	2.6	106,524,648
Missouri	136	2.5	122,830	2.7	903	3,511.0	28,584	8,674.2	2.4	63,781,162
Tennessee	139	2.5	101,973	2.3	734	3,134.7	30,741	8,262.0	2.3	59,438,748
Virginia	102	1.9	95,609	2.1	937	2,927.2	30,617	7,950.3	2.2	77,944,049
Indiana	122	2.2	103,796	2.3	851	2,978.1	28,692	7,714.7	2.2	63,235,254
Louisiana	136	2.5	93,426	2.1	687	2,562.3	27,426	6,598.7	1.9	48,519,596
Maryland	59	1.1	78,702	1.7	1,334	2,427.7	30,846	6,067.7	1.7	102,842,644
Alabama	118	2.2	78,929	1.7	669	2,272.8	28,796	6,001.3	1.7	50,858,585
Washington	100	1.8	76,344	1.7	763	2,631.5	34,469	5,969.1	1.7	59,690,720
Minnesota	146	2.7	79,811	1.8	547	2,357.4	29,537	5,591.5	1.6	38,298,041
Kentucky	108	2.0	71,922	1.6	666	1,976.4	27,480	5,342.4	1.5	49,466,907
South Carolina	73	1.3	62,918	1.4	862	1,835.5	29,173	4,878.5	1.4	66,828,534
Connecticut	36	0.7	55,669	1.2	1,546	1,972.8	35,439	4,471.7	1.3	124,213,333
Mississippi	106	1.9	57,447	1.3	542	1,523.0	26,512	4,088.1	1.2	38,566,868
Iowa	120	2.2	61,936	1.4	516	1,555.1	25,109	3,910.5	1.1	32,587,742
Oklahoma	124	2.3	56,571	1.2	456	1,495.2	26,431	3,909.6	1.1	31,528,637
Arkansas	85	1.5	47,270	1.0	556	1,216.8	25,741	3,398.3	1.0	39,979,506
Kansas	127	2.3	41,965	0.9	330	1,136.5	27,081	2,758.2	0.8	21,717,874
Utah	42	0.8	27,044	0.6	644	765.3	28,298	2,098.8	0.6	49,971,262
New Mexico	48	0.9	24,310	0.5	506	785.6	32,316	1,854.2	0.5	38,628,750
Maine	39	0.7	22,056	0.5	566	639.1	28,977	1,636.3	0.5	41,955,436
Rhode Island	14	0.3	16,954	0.4	1,211	644.1	37,990	1,477.0	0.4	105,499,643
Hawaii	21	0.4	14,515	0.3	691	509.8	35,119	1,259.8	0.4	59,989,762
South Dakota	59	1.1	19,717	0.4	334	551.9	27,993	1,259.2	0.4	21,342,576
Montana	53	1.0	16,171	0.4	305	432.3	26,734	1,068.7	0.3	20,163,792
Idaho	41	0.7	14,779	0.3	360	419.1	28,354	1,019.7	0.3	24,871,732
Vermont	15	0.3	7,500*	-	-	(D)	-	(D)	-	-
Delaware	11	0.2	17,500*	-	-	(D)	-	(D)	-	-

Source: 1997 *Economic Census*. The states are in descending order of revenues or establishments (if revenue data are missing for the majority). The symbol (D) appears when data are withheld to prevent disclosure of competitive information. States marked with (D) are sorted by number of establishments. A dash (-) indicates that the data element cannot be calculated. * indicates the midpoint of a range; 175, for example is the range 100-249. Shaded *states* on the state map indicate those states which have proportionately greater representation in the industry than would be indicated by the state's population; the ratio is based on total revenues or number of establishments. Shaded *regions* indicate where the industry is regionally most concentrated.

623

NAICS 622210 - PSYCHIATRIC AND SUBSTANCE ABUSE HOSPITALS

GENERAL STATISTICS

Year	Establishments (number)	Employment (number)	Payroll ($ million)	Revenues ($ million)	Employees per Establishment (number)	Revenues per Establishment ($)	Payroll per Employee ($)
1997	801	255,257	8,328.0	14,057.0	318.7	17,549,313	32,626

Source: Economic Census of the United States, 1997. This is a newly defined industry. Data for prior years were unavailable at the time of publication but may become available over time.

INDICES OF CHANGE

Year	Establishments (number)	Employment (number)	Payroll ($ million)	Revenues ($ million)	Employees per Establishment (number)	Revenues per Establishment ($)	Payroll per Employee ($)
1997	100.0	100.0	100.0	100.0	100.0	100.0	100.0

Sources: Same as General Statistics. The values shown reflect change from the base year, 1997. Values above 100 mean greater than 1997, values below 100 mean less than 1997, and a value of 100 in the 1982-96 or 1998-2001 period means same as 1997. Values followed by a 'p' are projections by the editors; 'e' stands for extrapolation. Data are the most recent available at this level of detail.

SIC INDUSTRIES RELATED TO NAICS 622210

Each new NAICS code represents an industry that used to be part of an SIC or a part of several SIC industries. Data in this table are shown to provide transitional information for these cases. All available data for the precursor SIC(s) are shown. Even if only a part of an SIC is included in the NAICS, *all* data for the SIC are reproduced. If the SIC industry is not marked as being a part (pt) of the NAICS, the entire industry is embedded in the NAICS data. The SIC composition of the new industry provides some hints of the relative importance of its "ancestors." Data marked with a 'p' are projected. Projections begin with 1982 data. Data earlier than 1990 are not shown but are reflected in the projections.

SIC	Industry	1990	1991	1992	1993	1994	1995	1996	1997
8063	**Psychiatric Hospitals**								
	Establishments (number)	-	-	919	-	-	-	-	-
	Employment (thousands)	-	-	317.4	-	-	-	-	-
	Revenues ($ million)	4,129.0	4,402.0	4,396.0	3,730.0	3,764.0	3,847.0	3,508.0	3,453.0p
8069	**Specialty Hospitals, Ex Psychiatric (pt)**								
	Establishments (number)	-	-	577	-	-	-	-	-
	Employment (thousands)	-	-	266.0	-	-	-	-	-
	Revenues ($ million)	1,916.0	2,185.0	2,525.0	2,918.0	3,386.0	3,866.0	4,665.0	3,249.9p

Source: Economic Census of the United States, 1992, annual surveys of economic sectors conducted by the Bureau of the Census, and estimates or projections based on the 1982-1992 period; not all data are shown. 'e' marks estimates made by the editors; 'p' indicates projections based on time series. A dash (-) indicates that data for this SIC or year were not available. The abbreviation (pt) next to the industry name indicates that only a part of the industry is present within the NAICS data. If no (pt) is shown, the entire industry is contained within the NAICS data.

SELECTED RATIOS

For 1997	Avg. of Information	Analyzed Industry	Index	For 1997	Avg. of Information	Analyzed Industry	Index
Employees per establishment	21	319	1,518	Payroll per establishment	585,591	10,397,004	1,775
Revenue per establishment	1,370,364	17,549,313	1,281	Payroll as % of revenue	43	59	139
Revenue per employee	65,262	55,070	84	Payroll per employee	27,888	32,626	117

Sources: Same as General Statistics. The 'Average' column represents the average for the industry sector, in 1997, where the currently shown industry is classified. The Index shows the relationship between the Average and the Analyzed Industry. For example, 100 means that they are equal; 500 that the Analyzed Industry is five times the average; 50 means that the Analyzed Industry is half the national average. The abbreviation 'na' is used to show that data are 'not available'.

LEADING COMPANIES   Number shown: **22**   Total sales ($ mil): **35,741**   Total employment (000): **453.6**

Company Name	Address				CEO Name	Phone	Co. Type	Sales ($ mil)	Empl. (000)
Columbia/HCA Healthcare Corp.	1 Park Plaza	Nashville	TN	37203	Jack O. Bovender Jr.	615-344-9551	P	18,618	260.0
Tenet Healthcare Corp.	PO Box 4070	Santa Monica	CA	90404	Jeffery C Barbakow	805-563-7000	P	10,880	126.0
Intermountain Health Care Inc.	36 S State St	Salt Lake City	UT	84111	Scott Parker	801-442-2000	R	2,009	22.0
Universal Health Services Inc.	PO Box 61558	King of Prussia	PA	19406	Alan B Miller	610-768-3300	P	1,874	19.2
Magellan Health Services Inc.	6950 Columbia	Columbia	MD	21046	Henry T Harbin, MD	410-953-1000	P	1,345	11.6
Pittsburgh Mercy Health System	1400 Locust St	Pittsburgh	PA	15219	Joanne M Andiorio	412-232-8275	R	290*	3.5
FHC Health Systems	240 Corporate Blvd	Norfolk	VA	23502	Ronald I Dozoretz	757-459-5100	R	184*	4.0
Cooper Companies Inc.	10 Farraday	Irvine	CA	92618	A Thomas Bender	925-597-4700	P	165	1.9
Ramsay Youth Services Inc.	Columbus Center	Coral Gables	FL	33134	Luis E Lamela	305-569-6993	P	155	2.8
Comprehensive Care Corp.	4200 W Cypress	Tampa	FL	33607	Chriss W Street	813-876-5036	P	46	0.3
Comprehensive Behavioral Care	4200 W Cypress St	Tampa	FL	33607	Chris Street	813-876-5036	S	24*	<0.1
Vencor Hospital East Inc.	601 S Carlin Sprgs	Arlington	VA	22204	Robert Davis	703-671-1200	S	23*	0.6
MHM Services Inc.	8000 Twrs Cres	Vienna	VA	22182	Michael S Pinkert	703-749-4600	P	21*	0.2
Mount Rogers Community Service	770 W Ridge Rd	Wytheville	VA	24382		540-228-2158	R	21*	0.4
PHC Inc.	200 Lake St	Peabody	MA	01960	Bruce A Shear	978-536-2777	P	19	0.3
Intelligent Systems Corp.	4355 Shackleford Rd	Norcross	GA	30093	J Leland Strange	770-381-2900	P	18	<0.1
Charter Behavioral Health	4004 N Riverside Dr	Tampa	FL	33603	James Hill	727-587-6000	S	13*	0.2
Charter Behavior Health Systems	101 Cirby Hills Dr	Roseville	CA	95678	Tom Pinizzotto	916-969-3333	S	10*	0.1
Charter Behavioral Health System	206 Park Place Blvd	Kissimmee	FL	34741	Daniel J Kearney	407-846-0444	R	9*	0.1
Rock Creek Center L.P.	40 Timberline Dr	Lemont	IL	60439	Wendy Mamoon	630-257-3636	R	9*	0.1
Rye Hospital Center	754 Boston Post Rd	Rye	NY	10580		914-967-4567	R	6*	<0.1
Glass Health Systems	3635 Old Court Rd	Baltimore	MD	21208	Dr Sheldon Glass MD	410-484-2700	R	1*	<0.1

Source: *Ward's Business Directory of U.S. Private and Public Companies*, Volumes 1 and 2, 2000. The company type code used is as follows: P - Public, R - Private, S - Subsidiary, D - Division, J - Joint Venture, A - Affiliate, G - Group, N - Company type not reported. Sales are in millions of dollars, employees are in thousands. An asterisk (*) indicates an estimated sales volume. The symbol < stands for 'less than'. Company names and addresses are truncated, in some cases, to fit into the available space.

REPRESENTATIVE NONPROFIT ORGANIZATIONS

Organization Name	Address				Phone	Income Range ($ mil)
Abbe Center for Community Care Inc	3150 E Avenue NW	Cedar Rapids	IA	52405		5-9
Adults and Children with Learning and Dev Disabilities Inc	807 S Oyster Bay Rd	Bethpage	NY	11714	516-822-0028	20-29
Albany County Association for Retarded Children Inc	1150 N Third	Laramie	WY	82070	307-721-2511	1-5
Anchorage Community Mental Health Services Inc	4020 Folker St	Anchorage	AK	99508		10-19
Anderson Youth Association	2300 Standridge Rd	Anderson	SC	29625	864-225-1628	5-9
Arc in Hawaii	3989 Diamond Head Rd	Honolulu	HI	96816		5-9
Arkansas Community Mental Health Center Inc	PO Box 5080	Jonesboro	AR	72403		10-19
Ayudantes Inc	PO Box 6108	Santa Fe	NM	87502		1-5
Baltimore Mental Health Systems Inc	201 E Baltimore St	Baltimore	MD	21202	410-837-2647	20-29
Bear River Mental Health Services Inc	PO Box 683	Logan	UT	84323		1-5
Behavioral Health Specialists Inc	600 S 13	Norfolk	NE	68701	402-370-3140	1-5
Behavioral Healthcare Inc	6801 S Yosemite St	Englewood	CO	80112	303-889-4805	20-29
Behaviorcorp Inc	PO Box 1129	Carmel	IN	46082	317-574-0055	10-19
Bellin Psychiatric Center	301 E Saint Joseph St	Green Bay	WI	54301	920-433-3630	5-9
Citrus Health Network Inc	4175 W 20th Ave	Hialeah	FL	33012	305-825-0300	20-29
Clay County Residence Inc	725 Center Ave	Moorhead	MN	56560	218-236-6730	1-5
Coleman Professional Services Inc	5982 Rhodes Rd	Kent	OH	44240	330-673-1347	10-19
Community Connections	801 Pennsylvania Ave SE	Washington	DC	20003		5-9
Community Living Options Inc	239 S Cherry St	Galesburg	IL	61401		20-29
Community Living Services Inc	35425 Michigan Ave W	Wayne	MI	48184	734-467-7600	50+
Community Mental Health Affil Inc	300 Main St	Bristol	CT	06010	860-583-9937	5-9
Community Systems Inc	8500 Leesburg Pike 207	Vienna	VA	22182		5-9
Compass Health	PO Box 3810	Everett	WA	98203		20-29
Cope Behavioral Services Inc	85 W Franklin	Tucson	AZ	85701	520-792-3293	10-19
East Alabama Mental Health - Mental Retardation Board	2506 Lambert Dr	Opelika	AL	36801		10-19
Family Counseling Center Inc	PO Box 71	Kennett	MO	63857	573-888-5925	5-9
Fellowship Health Resources Inc	25 Blackstone Valley PL	Lincoln	RI	02865	401-333-3980	10-19
Foothills Area Program	301 S King St	Morganton	NC	28655		20-29
Greater Oregon Behavioral Health Inc	400 E Scenic Dr	The Dalles	OR	97058	541-298-2101	10-19
Health and Education Services Inc	131 Rantoul St	Beverly	MA	01915	978-927-4506	20-29
Keystone Service Systems Inc	310 N 2nd St	Harrisburg	PA	17101	717-232-7509	20-29
Life Management Center	PO Box 9997	El Paso	TX	79990		30-39
Mental Health Cooperative Inc	275 Cumberland Bend	Nashville	TN	37228	615-726-3340	5-9
Northern Kentucky Mental Health	503 Farrell Dr	Covington	KY	41011		20-29
Parkside Inc	1620 E 12th St	Tulsa	OK	74120	918-588-8803	10-19
Pawnee Mental Health Service Inc	2001 Claflin	Manhattan	KS	66502	785-587-4300	10-19
Programs for Parents Inc	74 Porter PL	Montclair	NJ	07042		20-29
Red River Human Services Foundation	2506 35th Ave S	Fargo	ND	58104	701-235-0971	5-9
Region 12 Commission on Mental Health & Retardation	103 S 19th Ave	Hattiesburg	MS	39401		10-19
Seneca Health Sercvices Inc	1305 Webster Rd	Summersville	WV	26651	304-872-6503	10-19
South Central L A Reg Central	2160 W Adams Blvd	Los Angeles	CA	90018	323-734-1884	40-49
Tri-County Mental Health Services	PO Box 2008	Lewiston	ME	04241	207-783-9141	10-19
Upper Valley Services Inc	PO Box 4409	White Riv JCT	VT	05001		5-9
Western Montana Mental Health Center	T9 Fort Missoula	Missoula	MT	59804		10-19
Westside Habilitation Center	PO Box 226	Alexandria	LA	71309		5-9

Source: National Directory of Nonprofit Organizations, 2000, Volumes 1 and 2, The Taft Group. The table shows a selection of organizations for illustration and does not constitute a complete selection from the source. The organizations are arranged in alphabetical order.

LOCATION BY STATE AND REGIONAL CONCENTRATION

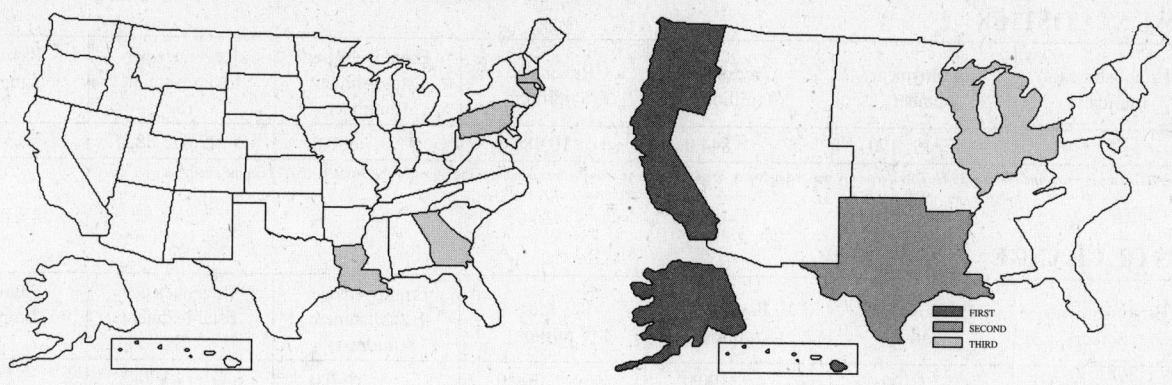

INDUSTRY DATA BY STATE

State	Establishments		Employment			Payroll		Revenues		
	Total (number)	% of U.S.	Total (number)	% of U.S.	Per Estab.	Total ($ mil.)	Per Empl. ($)	Total ($ mil.)	% of U.S.	Per Estab. ($)
California	60	7.5	15,611	6.1	260	558.4	35,772	995.1	7.1	16,585,183
Pennsylvania	42	5.2	14,241	5.6	339	536.7	37,684	898.2	6.4	21,386,310
Texas	66	8.2	17,139	6.7	260	420.7	24,544	757.2	5.4	11,473,348
Illinois	26	3.2	9,206	3.6	354	359.7	39,068	552.4	3.9	21,247,346
Massachusetts	28	3.5	9,170	3.6	328	318.2	34,696	550.1	3.9	19,646,250
Florida	46	5.7	10,501	4.1	228	287.9	27,414	502.3	3.6	10,919,348
Michigan	22	2.7	7,277	2.9	331	278.5	38,267	451.1	3.2	20,503,409
Georgia	31	3.9	7,751	3.0	250	225.5	29,095	427.2	3.0	13,780,387
Louisiana	28	3.5	5,335	2.1	191	137.3	25,742	272.9	1.9	9,747,607
Connecticut	11	1.4	3,690	1.4	335	154.7	41,922	222.6	1.6	20,238,091
Washington	9	1.1	3,340	1.3	371	122.2	36,578	188.7	1.3	20,968,556
Colorado	9	1.1	2,893	1.1	321	107.7	37,234	176.9	1.3	19,656,778
Hawaii	3	0.4	1,053	0.4	351	36.7	34,889	62.7	0.4	20,898,000
West Virginia	3	0.4	798	0.3	266	18.1	22,662	38.3	0.3	12,758,333
Iowa	5	0.6	1,750*	-	-	(D)	-	(D)	-	-
D.C.	2	0.2	375*	-	-	(D)	-	(D)	-	-
Rhode Island	2	0.2	750*	-	-	(D)	-	(D)	-	-
South Dakota	2	0.2	175*	-	-	(D)	-	(D)	-	-
Vermont	2	0.2	750*	-	-	(D)	-	(D)	-	-
North Dakota	1	0.1	750*	-	-	(D)	-	(D)	-	-

Source: 1997 *Economic Census.* The states are in descending order of revenues or establishments (if revenue data are missing for the majority). The symbol (D) appears when data are withheld to prevent disclosure of competitive information. States marked with (D) are sorted by number of establishments. A dash (-) indicates that the data element cannot be calculated. * indicates the midpoint of a range; 175, for example is the range 100-249. Shaded *states* on the state map indicate those states which have proportionately greater representation in the industry than would be indicated by the state's population; the ratio is based on total revenues or number of establishments. Shaded *regions* indicate where the industry is regionally most concentrated.

NAICS 622310 - SPECIALTY (EXCEPT PSYCHIATRIC AND SUBSTANCE ABUSE) HOSPITALS

GENERAL STATISTICS

Year	Establishments (number)	Employment (number)	Payroll ($ million)	Revenues ($ million)	Employees per Establishment (number)	Revenues per Establishment ($)	Payroll per Employee ($)
1997	397	151,190	4,844.0	10,988.0	380.8	27,677,582	32,039

Source: *Economic Census of the United States*, 1997. This is a newly defined industry. Data for prior years were unavailable at the time of publication but may become available over time.

INDICES OF CHANGE

Year	Establishments (number)	Employment (number)	Payroll ($ million)	Revenues ($ million)	Employees per Establishment (number)	Revenues per Establishment ($)	Payroll per Employee ($)
1997	100.0	100.0	100.0	100.0	100.0	100.0	100.0

Sources: Same as General Statistics. The values shown reflect change from the base year, 1997. Values above 100 mean greater than 1997, values below 100 mean less than 1997, and a value of 100 in the 1982-96 or 1998-2001 period means same as 1997. Values followed by a 'p' are projections by the editors; 'e' stands for extrapolation. Data are the most recent available at this level of detail.

SIC INDUSTRIES RELATED TO NAICS 622310

Each new NAICS code represents an industry that used to be part of an SIC or a part of several SIC industries. Data in this table are shown to provide transitional information for these cases. All available data for the precursor SIC(s) are shown. Even if only a part of an SIC is included in the NAICS, *all* data for the SIC are reproduced. If the SIC industry is not marked as being a part (pt) of the NAICS, the entire industry is embedded in the NAICS data. The SIC composition of the new industry provides some hints of the relative importance of its "ancestors." Data marked with a 'p' are projected. Projections begin with 1982 data. Data earlier than 1990 are not shown but are reflected in the projections.

SIC	Industry	1990	1991	1992	1993	1994	1995	1996	1997
8069	**Specialty Hospitals, Ex Psychiatric (pt)**								
	Establishments (number)	-	-	577	-	-	-	-	-
	Employment (thousands)	-	-	266.0	-	-	-	-	-
	Revenues ($ million)	1,916.0	2,185.0	2,525.0	2,918.0	3,386.0	3,866.0	4,665.0	3,249.9p

Source: *Economic Census of the United States*, 1992, annual surveys of economic sectors conducted by the Bureau of the Census, and estimates or projections based on the 1982-1992 period; not all data are shown. 'e' marks estimates made by the editors; 'p' indicates projections based on time series. A dash (-) indicates that data for this SIC or year were not available. The abbreviation (pt) next to the industry name indicates that only a part of the industry is present within the NAICS data. If no (pt) is shown, the entire industry is contained within the NAICS data.

SELECTED RATIOS

For 1997	Avg. of Information	Analyzed Industry	Index	For 1997	Avg. of Information	Analyzed Industry	Index
Employees per establishment	21	381	1,814	Payroll per establishment	585,591	12,201,511	2,084
Revenue per establishment	1,370,364	27,677,582	2,020	Payroll as % of revenue	43	44	103
Revenue per employee	65,262	72,677	111	Payroll per employee	27,888	32,039	115

Sources: Same as General Statistics. The 'Average' column represents the average for the industry sector, in 1997, where the currently shown industry is classified. The Index shows the relationship between the Average and the Analyzed Industry. For example, 100 means that they are equal; 500 that the Analyzed Industry is five times the average; 50 means that the Analyzed Industry is half the national average. The abbreviation 'na' is used to show that data are 'not available'.

LEADING COMPANIES   Number shown: **24**   Total sales ($ mil): **50,645**   Total employment (000): **718.7**

Company Name	Address				CEO Name	Phone	Co. Type	Sales ($ mil)	Empl. (000)
Columbia/HCA Healthcare Corp.	1 Park Plaza	Nashville	TN	37203	Jack O. Bovender Jr.	615-344-9551	P	18,618	260.0
Tenet Healthcare Corp.	PO Box 4070	Santa Monica	CA	90404	Jeffery C Barbakow	805-563-7000	P	10,880	126.0
Tenet HealthSystem Holdings Inc.	PO Box 809088	Dallas	TX	75380	Jeffery C Barbakow	972-789-2200	S	9,895	116.8
Sun Healthcare Group Inc.	101 Sun Ave N E	Albuquerque	NM	87109	Andrew L Turner	505-821-3355	P	3,089	80.7
Beverly Enterprises Inc.	PO Box 3324	Fort Smith	AR	72913	David R Banks	501-452-6712	P	2,774*	73.0
Intermountain Health Care Inc.	36 S State St	Salt Lake City	UT	84111	Scott Parker	801-442-2000	R	2,009	22.0
Bon Secours Health System Inc.	1505 Marriottsville	Marriottsville	MD	21104	Christopher Carney	410-442-5511	R	834*	10.0
Paracelsus Healthcare Corp.	515 W Greens Rd	Houston	TX	77067	Ronald R Patterson	281-774-5100	P	664	7.0
Medstar Health	100 Irving St	Washington	DC	20010	John P McDaniel	202-877-7000	R	634*	6.0
Bronson Healthcare Group	1 Healthcare Plz	Kalamazoo	MI	49007	Frank J Sardone	616-341-6000	R	300	3.0
Columbia Health System Inc.	2025 E Newport Ave	Milwaukee	WI	53211	John F Schuler	414-961-3300	R	196	1.4
FHC Health Systems	240 Corporate Blvd	Norfolk	VA	23502	Ronald I Dozoretz	757-459-5100	R	184*	4.0
Le Bonheur Health Systems Inc.	50 N Dunlap St	Memphis	TN	38103	Jim Smirling	901-572-3000	S	119*	1.4
Lab Holdings Inc.	PO Box 7568	Shaw Msn	KS	66207	W Thomas Grant II	913-652-1000	P	102*	0.9
Allied Services	PO Box 1103	Scranton	PA	18501	James Brady	717-348-1300	R	83	2.5
Southboro Medical Group Inc.	24 Newton St	Southborough	MA	01772		508-481-5500	R	50*	0.4
ReMed Recovery Care Centers	625 Ridge Pike	Conshohocken	PA	19428	Ross Rieder	610-834-1300	R	47*	0.4
Craig Hospital	3425 S Clarkson St	Englewood	CO	80110	Dennis O'Malley	303-789-8000	R	44*	0.6
NextHealth Inc.	16600 N Lg Oro	Tucson	AZ	85739	W T O'Donnell Jr	520-792-5800	P	30	0.3
Butler Hospital	345 Blackstone Blvd	Providence	RI	02906	Patricia Recupero	401-455-6200	R	23	0.7
Vencor Hospital East Inc.	601 S Carlin Sprgs	Arlington	VA	22204	Robert Davis	703-671-1200	S	23*	0.6
Mount Rogers Community Service	770 W Ridge Rd	Wytheville	VA	24382		540-228-2158	R	21*	0.4
MD Anderson Cancer Center	1561 W Fairbanks	Winter Park	FL	32789	Aarince Brown	407-628-0991	R	16*	0.1
MileStone Healthcare	2501 Cedar Sprgs	Dallas	TX	75201	Charles Allen	214-871-9600	S	11*	0.5

Source: *Ward's Business Directory of U.S. Private and Public Companies*, Volumes 1 and 2, 2000. The company type code used is as follows: P - Public, R - Private, S - Subsidiary, D - Division, J - Joint Venture, A - Affiliate, G - Group, N - Company type not reported. Sales are in millions of dollars, employees are in thousands. An asterisk (*) indicates an estimated sales volume. The symbol < stands for 'less than'. Company names and addresses are truncated, in some cases, to fit into the available space.

LOCATION BY STATE AND REGIONAL CONCENTRATION

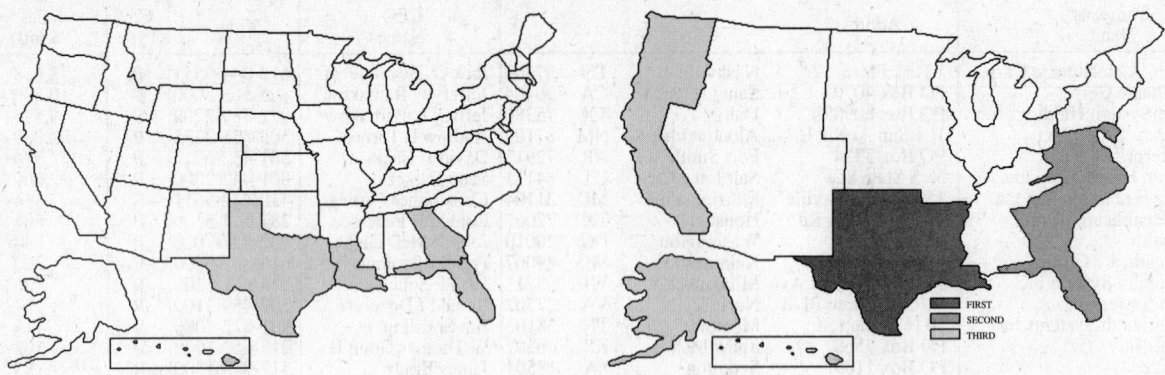

INDUSTRY DATA BY STATE

State	Establishments Total (number)	Establishments % of U.S.	Employment Total (number)	Employment % of U.S.	Employment Per Estab.	Payroll Total ($ mil.)	Payroll Per Empl. ($)	Revenues Total ($ mil.)	Revenues % of U.S.	Revenues Per Estab. ($)
Texas	52	13.1	19,682	13.0	378	568.1	28,864	1,402.7	12.8	26,975,673
California	29	7.3	9,408	6.2	324	333.9	35,493	642.4	5.8	22,151,483
Florida	24	6.0	8,073	5.3	336	221.1	27,382	617.0	5.6	25,708,333
Georgia	11	2.8	6,799	4.5	618	210.1	30,896	480.4	4.4	43,675,182
Louisiana	24	6.0	5,391	3.6	225	147.0	27,268	372.7	3.4	15,528,250
Illinois	5	1.3	3,833	2.5	767	146.3	38,159	293.6	2.7	58,724,400
Hawaii	4	1.0	2,308	1.5	577	78.2	33,887	205.4	1.9	51,345,750
Michigan	12	3.0	2,114	1.4	176	57.2	27,048	131.7	1.2	10,976,583
Connecticut	3	0.8	1,364	0.9	455	58.5	42,921	103.2	0.9	34,395,667
Indiana	8	2.0	1,421	0.9	178	35.9	25,244	90.2	0.8	11,270,625
Nebraska	3	0.8	1,625	1.1	542	42.7	26,307	70.2	0.6	23,402,333
Washington	4	1.0	679	0.4	170	23.3	34,330	39.7	0.4	9,915,000
Arizona	5	1.3	565	0.4	113	12.5	22,181	30.9	0.3	6,187,400
Nevada	4	1.0	750*	-	-	(D)	-	(D)	-	-
Minnesota	3	0.8	750*	-	-	(D)	-	(D)	-	-
D.C.	2	0.5	1,750*	-	-	(D)	-	(D)	-	-
Idaho	2	0.5	750*	-	-	(D)	-	(D)	-	-
Iowa	2	0.5	750*	-	-	(D)	-	(D)	-	-
Mississippi	2	0.5	175*	-	-	(D)	-	(D)	-	-
West Virginia	2	0.5	375*	-	-	(D)	-	(D)	-	-
Alaska	1	0.3	60*	-	-	(D)	-	(D)	-	-
Maine	1	0.3	375*	-	-	(D)	-	(D)	-	-
Oregon	1	0.3	375*	-	-	(D)	-	(D)	-	-
South Dakota	1	0.3	10*	-	-	(D)	-	(D)	-	-
Wisconsin	1	0.3	375*	-	-	(D)	-	(D)	-	-
Wyoming	1	0.3	60*	-	-	(D)	-	(D)	-	-

Source: 1997 *Economic Census*. The states are in descending order of revenues or establishments (if revenue data are missing for the majority). The symbol (D) appears when data are withheld to prevent disclosure of competitive information. States marked with (D) are sorted by number of establishments. A dash (-) indicates that the data element cannot be calculated. * indicates the midpoint of a range; 175, for example is the range 100-249. Shaded *states* on the state map indicate those states which have proportionately greater representation in the industry than would be indicated by the state's population; the ratio is based on total revenues or number of establishments. Shaded *regions* indicate where the industry is regionally most concentrated.

NAICS 623110 - NURSING CARE FACILITIES

GENERAL STATISTICS

Year	Establishments (number)	Employment (number)	Payroll ($ million)	Revenues ($ million)	Employees per Establishment (number)	Revenues per Establishment ($)	Payroll per Employee ($)
1997	15,605	1,557,162	27,589.0	59,734.0	99.8	3,827,876	17,717

Source: Economic Census of the United States, 1997. This is a newly defined industry. Data for prior years were unavailable at the time of publication but may become available over time.

INDICES OF CHANGE

Year	Establishments (number)	Employment (number)	Payroll ($ million)	Revenues ($ million)	Employees per Establishment (number)	Revenues per Establishment ($)	Payroll per Employee ($)
1997	100.0	100.0	100.0	100.0	100.0	100.0	100.0

Sources: Same as General Statistics. The values shown reflect change from the base year, 1997. Values above 100 mean greater than 1997, values below 100 mean less than 1997, and a value of 100 in the 1982-96 or 1998-2001 period means same as 1997. Values followed by a 'p' are projections by the editors; 'e' stands for extrapolation. Data are the most recent available at this level of detail.

SIC INDUSTRIES RELATED TO NAICS 623110

Each new NAICS code represents an industry that used to be part of an SIC or a part of several SIC industries. Data in this table are shown to provide transitional information for these cases. All available data for the precursor SIC(s) are shown. Even if only a part of an SIC is included in the NAICS, *all* data for the SIC are reproduced. If the SIC industry is not marked as being a part (pt) of the NAICS, the entire industry is embedded in the NAICS data. The SIC composition of the new industry provides some hints of the relative importance of its "ancestors." Data marked with a 'p' are projected. Projections begin with 1982 data. Data earlier than 1990 are not shown but are reflected in the projections.

SIC	Industry	1990	1991	1992	1993	1994	1995	1996	1997
8051	**Skilled Nursing Care Facilities (pt)**								
	Establishments (number)	-	-	12,965	-	-	-	-	-
	Employment (thousands)	-	-	1,305.1	-	-	-	-	-
	Revenues ($ million)	-	-	40,480.9	-	-	-	-	-
8052	**Intermediate Care Facilities (pt)**								
	Establishments (number)	-	-	6,166	-	-	-	-	-
	Employment (thousands)	-	-	278.2	-	-	-	-	-
	Revenues ($ million)	-	-	7,156.7	-	-	-	-	-
8059	**Nursing & Personal Care, nec (pt)**								
	Establishments (number)	-	-	1,748	-	-	-	-	-
	Employment (thousands)	-	-	49.5	-	-	-	-	-
	Revenues ($ million)	-	-	1,572.5	-	-	-	-	-

Source: Economic Census of the United States, 1992, annual surveys of economic sectors conducted by the Bureau of the Census, and estimates or projections based on the 1982-1992 period; not all data are shown. 'e' marks estimates made by the editors; 'p' indicates projections based on time series. A dash (-) indicates that data for this SIC or year were not available. The abbreviation (pt) next to the industry name indicates that only a part of the industry is present within the NAICS data. If no (pt) is shown, the entire industry is contained within the NAICS data.

SELECTED RATIOS

For 1997	Avg. of Information	Analyzed Industry	Index	For 1997	Avg. of Information	Analyzed Industry	Index
Employees per establishment	21	100	475	Payroll per establishment	585,591	1,767,959	302
Revenue per establishment	1,370,364	3,827,876	279	Payroll as % of revenue	43	46	108
Revenue per employee	65,262	38,361	59	Payroll per employee	27,888	17,717	64

Sources: Same as General Statistics. The 'Average' column represents the average for the industry sector, in 1997, where the currently shown industry is classified. The Index shows the relationship between the Average and the Analyzed Industry. For example, 100 means that they are equal; 500 that the Analyzed Industry is five times the average; 50 means that the Analyzed Industry is half the national average. The abbreviation 'na' is used to show that data are 'not available'.

LEADING COMPANIES   Number shown: **75**   Total sales ($ mil): **40,596**   Total employment (000): **818.5**

Company Name	Address			CEO Name	Phone	Co. Type	Sales ($ mil)	Empl. (000)
Marriott International Inc.	10400 Fernwood Rd	Bethesda	MD 20817	J.W. Marriott Jr.	301-380-3000	P	7,968	133.0
Sun Healthcare Group Inc.	101 Sun Ave N E	Albuquerque	NM 87109	Andrew L Turner	505-821-3355	P	3,089	80.7
Integrated Health Services Inc.	10065 Red Run Blvd	Owings Mills	MD 21117	Lawrence P Cirka	410-773-1000	P	2,972	84.0
Beverly Enterprises Inc.	PO Box 3324	Fort Smith	AR 72913	David R Banks	501-452-6712	P	2,774*	73.0
Life Care Centers of America Inc.	PO Box 3480	Cleveland	TN 37320	Michael Waddell	423-472-9585	R	2,375*	25.0
HCR Manor Care Inc.	333 N Summit St	Toledo	OH 43604	Paul A Ormond	419-252-5500	P	2,209	55.0
Mariner Post-Acute Network Inc.	1 Ravinia Dr	Atlanta	GA 30346	F 'butch' Cash	678-443-7000	P	2,036	65.0
Genesis Health Ventures Inc.	101 E State St	Kennett Square	PA 19348	Richard R Howard	610-444-6350	P	1,866	48.0
Manor Care Inc.	11555 Darnestown	Gaithersburg	MD 20878	Stewart Bainum Jr	301-979-4000	S	1,359	31.5
Magellan Health Services Inc.	6950 Columbia	Columbia	MD 21046	Henry T Harbin, MD	410-953-1000	P	1,345	11.6
Wilmac Corp.	P O Box 5047	York	PA 17405	Karen McCormack	717-854-7857	R	1,241*	1.5
Catholic Health Initiatives	One MacIntyre Dr	Aston	PA 19014	William Foley	610-358-3950	D	1,200	12.0
Helix Health Inc.	2330 W Joppa Rd	Lutherville	MD 21093	John McDaniel	410-847-6700	R	1,010*	18.0
Memorial Health Services Inc.	2801 Atlantic Ave	Long Beach	CA 90806	Tom Collins	562-933-2000	R	980*	4.2
United Health Inc.	105 W Michigan St	Milwaukee	WI 53203	J Wesley Carter	414-271-9696	S	900	17.0
Bon Secours Health System Inc.	1505 Marriottsville	Marriottsville	MD 21104	Christopher Carney	410-442-5511	R	834*	10.0
Wheaton Franciscan Services Inc.	P O Box 667	Wheaton	IL 60189	Wilfred F Loebig Jr	630-462-9271	R	750	13.0
Medstar Health	100 Irving St	Washington	DC 20010	John P McDaniel	202-877-7000	R	634*	6.0
National HealthCare Corp.	P O Box 1398	Murfreesboro	TN 37133	W Andrew Adams	615-890-2020	P	441	16.0
Centennial HealthCare Corp.	400 Perimeter	Atlanta	GA 30346	Stephen Eaton	770-698-9040	P	358	10.0
Harborside Healthcare Corp.	470 Atlantic Ave	Boston	MA 02210	Stephen L Guillard	617-556-1515	R	300	7.8
Pittsburgh Mercy Health System	1400 Locust St	Pittsburgh	PA 15219	Joanne M Andiorio	412-232-8275	R	290*	3.5
RehabCare Group Inc.	7733 Forsyth Blvd	St. Louis	MO 63105	Alan C Henderson	314-863-7422	P	207	7.5
Advocat Inc.	277 Mallory Station	Franklin	TN 37067	C W Birkett, MD	615-771-7575	P	205	5.2
Carondelet Health Corp.	1000 Carondelet Dr	Kansas City	MO 64114	George Zara	816-942-4400	R	200*	1.5
Summit Care Corp.	2600 W Magnolia	Burbank	CA 91505	D G Schumacher Jr	818-841-8750	P	198	4.2
RainTree Healthcare Corp.	15300 N 90th	Scottsdale	AZ 85258	Michael A Jeffries	602-423-1954	R	184	3.7
Res-Care Inc	10140 Linn Station	Louisville	KY 40223	Ronald Geary	502-394-2100	D	175*	7.3
Sunrise Assisted Living Inc.	7901 Westpark Dr	McLean	VA 22102	David W Faeder	703-273-7500	P	169	5.2
Emeritus Corp.	3131 Elliott Ave	Seattle	WA 98121	Daniel R Baty	206-298-2909	P	152	5.1
CareMatrix Corp.	197 1st Ave	Needham	MA 02494	marc Benson	781-433-1000	P	147	2.3
American Retirement Corp.	111 Westwood Place	Brentwood	TN 37027	WE Sheriff	615-221-2250	P	142	5.2
National Health Care Affiliates	651 Delaware Ave	Buffalo	NY 14202	Mark E Hamister	716-881-4425	R	140*	4.0
ARV Assisted Living Inc.	245 Fischer Ave	Costa Mesa	CA 92626	Gary L Davidson	714-751-7400	P	129	3.4
Horizon West Inc.	4020 Sierra College	Rocklin	CA 95677	Ellen Kuykendall	916-624-6230	R	110	3.5
Caretenders Health Corp.	100 Mallard Creek	Louisville	KY 40207	William B Yarmuth	502-899-5355	P	97	3.4
Algood Healthcare Inc.	409A Pleasant Home	Augusta	GA 30919	Thelma Algood	706-855-1773	R	93*	0.7
Guardian Postacute Services Inc.	5725 Paradise Dr	Corte Madera	CA 94925	Robert Peirce	415-945-2200	R	90*	2.2
Assisted Living Concepts Inc.	11835 NE G Widing	Portland	OR 97220	Richard Ladd	503-252-6233	R	89	3.6
Prestige Care Inc.	501 SE Col Shrs	Vancouver	WA 98661	Phil Fogg	503-253-9650	R	87*	1.9
Lifemark Corp.	7600 N 16th St	Phoenix	AZ 85020	Rhonda Brede	602-331-5100	P	85	0.8
Balanced Care Corp.	1215 Manor Dr	Mechanicsburg	PA 17055	Brad E Hollinger	717-796-6100	P	78	2.9
Golden State Health Centers Inc.	13347 Ventura Blvd	Van Nuys	CA 91423	David B Weiss	818-986-1550	R	75	2.4
NewCare Health Corp.	6000 Lake Forrest	Atlanta	GA 30328	Chris Brogdon	404-252-2923	R	66	2.7
Kuala Healthcare Inc.	910 Sylvan Ave	Englewd Clfs	NJ 07632	Jack Rosen	201-567-4600	P	64	1.0
Greenbriar Corp.	4265 Kellway Cir	Dallas	TX 75244	James R Gilley	972-407-8400	P	53	1.2
VNA/Advanced Home Care	2100 Wherle Dr	Williamsville	NY 14221	Lawrence Zielinski	716-635-0100	R	53*	0.4
Health Care Lodges Inc.	P O Box 509	Coffeyville	KS 67337	Larry Fisher	316-251-6700	R	51	2.5
Meritcare Inc.	625 Stanwix St	Pittsburgh	PA 15222	Thomas Konig	412-201-2040	S	50	1.0
Hallmark Nursing Centre Inc.	526 Altamont Ave	Schenectady	NY 12303	James Durante	518-346-6121	R	47*	1.0
Fairview Ministries Inc.	250 Village Dr	Downers Grove	IL 60516	WP Ringdahl	630-769-6000	R	39*	0.3
Kendall Healthcare Properties Inc.	11355 SW 84th	Miami	FL 33173	Avi Bittan	305-270-7000	R	35	0.6
Paradise Pines	11565 Harts Rd	Jacksonville	FL 32218		904-751-1834	S	35*	0.2
Eger Health Care & Rehabilitation	140 Meisner Ave	Staten Island	NY 10306	Adeline M Conroy	718-979-1800	R	32	0.7
Visiting Nurse Association	2905 Sackett St	Houston	TX 77098		713-520-8115	S	28*	0.2
Iatros Health Network Inc.	4514 Travis Street	Dallas	TX 75205	Ronald Lusk	214-599-9777	P	27	0.2
Spectrum Comprehensive Care Inc	12300 Ford Rd	Dallas	TX 75234	Robert Helms	972-243-6279	R	21*	0.1
Wendt-Bristol Co.	2 Nationwide Plz	Columbus	OH 43215	Sheldon Gold	614-221-6000	S	21	0.2
Evergreen House Health Center	1 Evergreen Dr	East Providence	RI 02914		401-438-3250	S	19*	0.2
Mt. Carmel Health	5700 W Layton Ave	Milwaukee	WI 53220		414-281-7200	S	18*	0.7
Five Star Corp.	4700 84th St	Urbandale	IA 50322	Rod Bailey	515-223-1133	R	15	0.6
Tamba Oaks Health Care	5010 N 40th St	Tampa	FL 33610		813-626-3641	R	15*	0.1
Woonsocket Health	262 Poplar St	Woonsocket	RI 02895		401-765-2100	R	14*	0.3
OptimumCare Corp.	30011 Ivy Glenn Dr	Laguna Niguel	CA 92677	Edward A Johnson	949-495-1100	P	13	0.2
DCC Inc.	400 Nyala Farms Rd	Westport	CT 06880	Peter G Burki	203-226-2680	R	12	0.2
Friendship Manor Homes	725 Lois Dr	Sun Prairie	WI 53590		715-256-0202	R	11	0.7
Franciscan Villa	3601 S Chicago Ave	S. Milwaukee	WI 53172	Roger DeMark	414-764-4100	S	10*	0.3
Oakhill Nursing & Rehabilitation	544 Pleasant St	Pawtucket	RI 02860		401-725-8888	S	9*	0.2
Mann Health Services Inc.	5413 Northland Dr	Atlanta	GA 30342	Charles H Mann III	404-250-9300	R	8	<0.1
Marian Franciscan Center Inc.	9632 W Appleton	Milwaukee	WI 53225	James G Gresham	414-461-8850	S	8*	0.3
Mid-America Health Centers	120 S Market St	Wichita	KS 67202	Paul Wurth	316-262-4206	R	8*	<0.1
Wendt-Bristol Health Services	2 Nationwide Plz	Columbus	OH 43215	Sheldon A Gold	614-221-6000	P	8*	0.2
TORCH Health Care Inc.	6311 N O'Connor	Irving	TX 75039		972-501-9210	R	8	0.4
Ingleside Care Center	6525 Lancaster Pike	Hockessin	DE 19707	Carol A Berster	302-998-0181	S	7	0.1
Friendly Home Inc.	303 Rhodes Ave	Woonsocket	RI 02895		401-769-7220	R	6*	0.2

Source: Ward's Business Directory of U.S. Private and Public Companies, Volumes 1 and 2, 2000. The company type code used is as follows: P - Public, R - Private, S - Subsidiary, D - Division, J - Joint Venture, A - Affiliate, G - Group, N - Company type not reported. Sales are in millions of dollars, employees are in thousands. An asterisk (*) indicates an estimated sales volume. The symbol < stands for 'less than'. Company names and addresses are truncated, in some cases, to fit into the available space.

LOCATION BY STATE AND REGIONAL CONCENTRATION

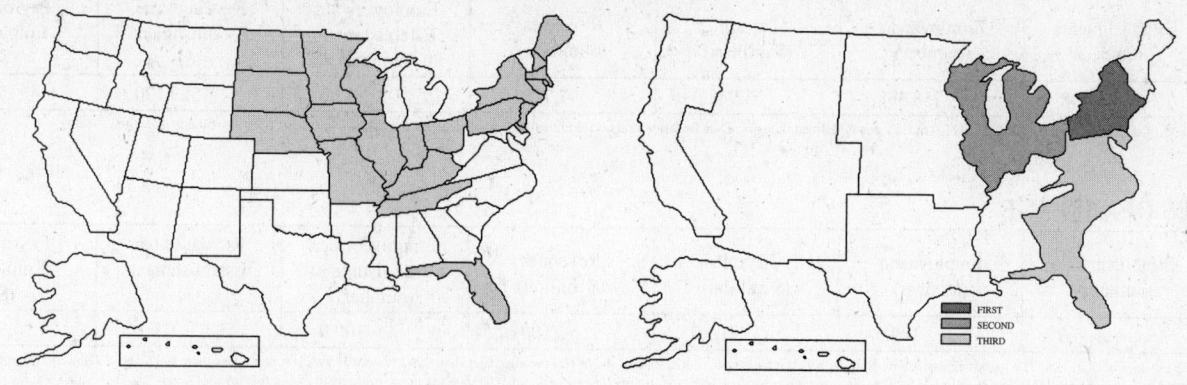

FIRST
SECOND
THIRD

INDUSTRY DATA BY STATE

State	Establishments Total (number)	% of U.S.	Employment Total (number)	% of U.S.	Per Estab.	Payroll Total ($ mil.)	Per Empl. ($)	Revenues Total ($ mil.)	% of U.S.	Per Estab. ($)
New York	624	4.0	118,515	7.6	190	2,849.1	24,040	6,193.3	10.4	9,925,175
California	1,338	8.6	103,743	6.7	78	1,886.8	18,187	4,142.5	6.9	3,096,038
Florida	721	4.6	74,930	4.8	104	1,468.5	19,598	3,512.4	5.9	4,871,634
Ohio	863	5.5	89,326	5.7	104	1,539.3	17,232	3,325.0	5.6	3,852,788
Pennsylvania	652	4.2	69,919	4.5	107	1,369.5	19,586	3,115.3	5.2	4,778,040
Texas	1,234	7.9	91,181	5.9	74	1,332.1	14,609	3,015.1	5.0	2,443,331
Massachusetts	569	3.6	69,488	4.5	122	1,466.9	21,109	2,888.0	4.8	5,075,525
Illinois	751	4.8	75,697	4.9	101	1,202.3	15,883	2,742.7	4.6	3,652,003
New Jersey	330	2.1	44,330	2.8	134	982.5	22,164	2,259.2	3.8	6,846,112
Connecticut	273	1.7	40,141	2.6	147	954.3	23,775	1,875.1	3.1	6,868,421
Michigan	415	2.7	44,388	2.9	107	758.2	17,082	1,599.0	2.7	3,853,118
Indiana	533	3.4	42,128	2.7	79	704.9	16,732	1,520.8	2.5	2,853,236
North Carolina	402	2.6	41,852	2.7	104	714.0	17,060	1,483.9	2.5	3,691,236
Tennessee	342	2.2	38,875	2.5	114	628.9	16,179	1,442.3	2.4	4,217,117
Wisconsin	365	2.3	40,297	2.6	110	689.4	17,109	1,432.3	2.4	3,924,244
Missouri	507	3.2	41,715	2.7	82	622.7	14,928	1,417.4	2.4	2,795,720
Minnesota	369	2.4	44,885	2.9	122	755.9	16,840	1,410.8	2.4	3,823,328
Georgia	384	2.5	34,029	2.2	89	528.6	15,535	1,241.7	2.1	3,233,563
Maryland	214	1.4	29,320	1.9	137	541.0	18,452	1,163.9	1.9	5,438,617
Washington	289	1.9	28,029	1.8	97	526.1	18,769	1,051.8	1.8	3,639,388
Virginia	242	1.6	27,955	1.8	116	461.8	16,518	1,030.5	1.7	4,258,302
Kentucky	290	1.9	29,931	1.9	103	457.8	15,296	1,029.9	1.7	3,551,455
Alabama	204	1.3	23,022	1.5	113	379.9	16,502	827.4	1.4	4,055,971
Iowa	385	2.5	28,525	1.8	74	404.2	14,169	791.8	1.3	2,056,644
Louisiana	294	1.9	26,735	1.7	91	340.3	12,728	783.7	1.3	2,665,806
Colorado	182	1.2	18,201	1.2	100	323.0	17,749	720.8	1.2	3,960,632
Oklahoma	391	2.5	24,555	1.6	63	303.0	12,338	659.0	1.1	1,685,327
Arizona	157	1.0	16,150	1.0	103	288.3	17,852	623.1	1.0	3,968,904
Arkansas	241	1.5	18,979	1.2	79	253.8	13,373	561.9	0.9	2,331,685
South Carolina	156	1.0	14,653	0.9	94	240.9	16,439	537.7	0.9	3,446,731
Oregon	177	1.1	16,347	1.0	92	243.6	14,903	478.7	0.8	2,704,503
Mississippi	178	1.1	13,898	0.9	78	207.8	14,951	462.5	0.8	2,598,264
Nebraska	167	1.1	15,076	1.0	90	244.2	16,196	453.5	0.8	2,715,269
Rhode Island	93	0.6	10,896	0.7	117	194.1	17,818	397.0	0.7	4,269,129
West Virginia	124	0.8	10,941	0.7	88	158.0	14,439	383.6	0.6	3,093,411
Maine	129	0.8	11,635	0.7	90	183.3	15,755	363.0	0.6	2,814,287
New Hampshire	73	0.5	7,287	0.5	100	135.3	18,561	299.5	0.5	4,103,110
Utah	91	0.6	7,699	0.5	85	107.8	14,005	233.2	0.4	2,562,264
South Dakota	98	0.6	7,962	0.5	81	112.9	14,181	211.0	0.4	2,152,796
North Dakota	71	0.5	8,204	0.5	116	107.3	13,076	191.4	0.3	2,695,423
Idaho	62	0.4	5,565	0.4	90	84.3	15,146	176.0	0.3	2,838,129
Montana	72	0.5	5,202	0.3	72	83.3	16,015	161.9	0.3	2,248,528
New Mexico	64	0.4	5,641	0.4	88	86.7	15,373	161.2	0.3	2,518,313
Hawaii	27	0.2	2,817	0.2	104	71.5	25,370	157.2	0.3	5,821,778
Delaware	40	0.3	4,024	0.3	101	70.3	17,465	156.9	0.3	3,923,575
Vermont	47	0.3	4,008	0.3	85	71.1	17,747	138.5	0.2	2,946,745
D.C.	16	0.1	2,174	0.1	136	50.9	23,417	122.0	0.2	7,627,375
Wyoming	20	0.1	2,289	0.1	114	34.4	15,040	75.1	0.1	3,755,500
Alaska	4	-	561	0.0	140	15.2	27,046	28.3	0.0	7,073,250

Source: 1997 *Economic Census*. The states are in descending order of revenues or establishments (if revenue data are missing for the majority). The symbol (D) appears when data are withheld to prevent disclosure of competitive information. States marked with (D) are sorted by number of establishments. A dash (-) indicates that the data element cannot be calculated. * indicates the midpoint of a range; 175, for example is the range 100-249. Shaded *states* on the state map indicate those states which have proportionately greater representation in the industry than would be indicated by the state's population; the ratio is based on total revenues or number of establishments. Shaded *regions* indicate where the industry is regionally most concentrated.

NAICS 623210 - RESIDENTIAL MENTAL RETARDATION FACILITIES

GENERAL STATISTICS

Year	Establishments (number)	Employment (number)	Payroll ($ million)	Revenues ($ million)	Employees per Establishment (number)	Revenues per Establishment ($)	Payroll per Employee ($)
1997	14,698	258,368	3,948.0	7,777.0	17.6	529,120	15,281

Source: Economic Census of the United States, 1997. This is a newly defined industry. Data for prior years were unavailable at the time of publication but may become available over time.

INDICES OF CHANGE

Year	Establishments (number)	Employment (number)	Payroll ($ million)	Revenues ($ million)	Employees per Establishment (number)	Revenues per Establishment ($)	Payroll per Employee ($)
1997	100.0	100.0	100.0	100.0	100.0	100.0	100.0

Sources: Same as General Statistics. The values shown reflect change from the base year, 1997. Values above 100 mean greater than 1997, values below 100 mean less than 1997, and a value of 100 in the 1982-96 or 1998-2001 period means same as 1997. Values followed by a 'p' are projections by the editors; 'e' stands for extrapolation. Data are the most recent available at this level of detail.

SIC INDUSTRIES RELATED TO NAICS 623210

Each new NAICS code represents an industry that used to be part of an SIC or a part of several SIC industries. Data in this table are shown to provide transitional information for these cases. All available data for the precursor SIC(s) are shown. Even if only a part of an SIC is included in the NAICS, *all* data for the SIC are reproduced. If the SIC industry is not marked as being a part (pt) of the NAICS, the entire industry is embedded in the NAICS data. The SIC composition of the new industry provides some hints of the relative importance of its "ancestors." Data marked with a 'p' are projected. Projections begin with 1982 data. Data earlier than 1990 are not shown but are reflected in the projections.

SIC	Industry	1990	1991	1992	1993	1994	1995	1996	1997
8051	**Skilled Nursing Care Facilities (pt)**								
	Establishments (number)	-	-	12,965	-	-	-	-	-
	Employment (thousands)	-	-	1,305.1	-	-	-	-	-
	Revenues ($ million)	-	-	40,480.9	-	-	-	-	-
8052	**Intermediate Care Facilities (pt)**								
	Establishments (number)	-	-	6,166	-	-	-	-	-
	Employment (thousands)	-	-	278.2	-	-	-	-	-
	Revenues ($ million)	-	-	7,156.7	-	-	-	-	-
8059	**Nursing & Personal Care, nec (pt)**								
	Establishments (number)	-	-	1,748	-	-	-	-	-
	Employment (thousands)	-	-	49.5	-	-	-	-	-
	Revenues ($ million)	-	-	1,572.5	-	-	-	-	-
8361	**Residential Care (pt)**								
	Establishments (number)	20,967	22,267	27,143	27,912	28,937	29,937	31,850p	33,440p
	Employment (thousands)	416.8	449.7	457.3	491.1	518.2	549.9	571.8p	598.0p
	Revenues ($ million)	4,626.0	4,934.0	4,853.0	5,421.0	5,905.0	6,437.0	7,244.0	7,377.7p

Source: Economic Census of the United States, 1992, annual surveys of economic sectors conducted by the Bureau of the Census, and estimates or projections based on the 1982-1992 period; not all data are shown. 'e' marks estimates made by the editors; 'p' indicates projections based on time series. A dash (-) indicates that data for this SIC or year were not available. The abbreviation (pt) next to the industry name indicates that only a part of the industry is present within the NAICS data. If no (pt) is shown, the entire industry is contained within the NAICS data.

SELECTED RATIOS

For 1997	Avg. of Information	Analyzed Industry	Index	For 1997	Avg. of Information	Analyzed Industry	Index
Employees per establishment	21	18	84	Payroll per establishment	585,591	268,608	46
Revenue per establishment	1,370,364	529,120	39	Payroll as % of revenue	43	51	119
Revenue per employee	65,262	30,100	46	Payroll per employee	27,888	15,281	55

Sources: Same as General Statistics. The 'Average' column represents the average for the industry sector, in 1997, where the currently shown industry is classified. The Index shows the relationship between the Average and the Analyzed Industry. For example, 100 means that they are equal; 500 that the Analyzed Industry is five times the average; 50 means that the Analyzed Industry is half the national average. The abbreviation 'na' is used to show that data are 'not available'.

LEADING COMPANIES

No company data available for this industry.

LOCATION BY STATE AND REGIONAL CONCENTRATION

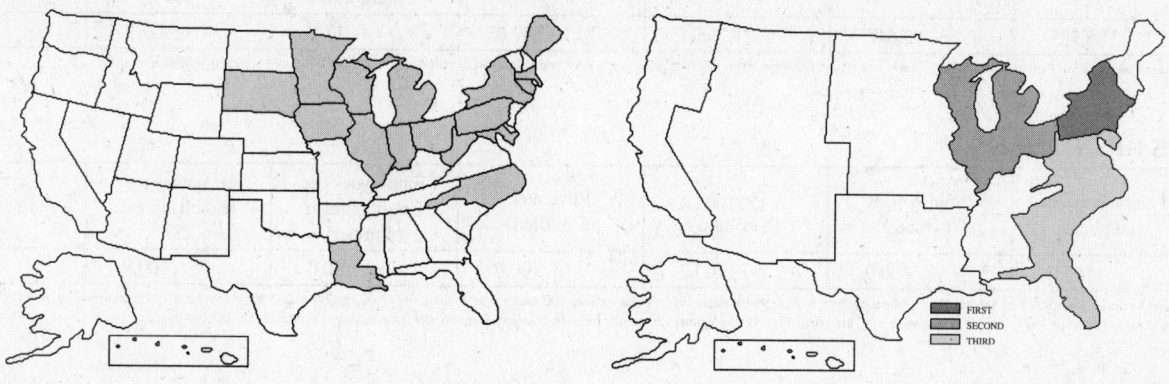

FIRST
SECOND
THIRD

INDUSTRY DATA BY STATE

State	Establishments Total (number)	% of U.S.	Employment Total (number)	% of U.S.	Per Estab.	Payroll Total ($ mil.)	Per Empl. ($)	Revenues Total ($ mil.)	% of U.S.	Per Estab. ($)
New York	1,329	9.0	26,263	10.2	20	449.3	17,109	939.1	12.1	706,612
Pennsylvania	1,143	7.8	21,113	8.2	18	388.4	18,397	703.6	9.0	615,560
California	1,320	9.0	16,266	6.3	12	220.7	13,566	499.3	6.4	378,293
Ohio	717	4.9	14,140	5.5	20	219.7	15,540	428.0	5.5	596,887
Illinois	516	3.5	12,877	5.0	25	194.7	15,120	410.4	5.3	795,314
Michigan	1,193	8.1	13,227	5.1	11	202.7	15,324	341.7	4.4	286,399
Minnesota	914	6.2	14,230	5.5	16	194.8	13,687	339.7	4.4	371,688
Texas	573	3.9	10,252	4.0	18	143.9	14,040	329.6	4.2	575,175
Massachusetts	675	4.6	9,360	3.6	14	158.3	16,911	290.8	3.7	430,809
Florida	341	2.3	8,684	3.4	25	127.4	14,671	264.1	3.4	774,437
North Carolina	490	3.3	8,516	3.3	17	128.1	15,037	244.4	3.1	498,855
Indiana	386	2.6	5,854	2.3	15	92.6	15,815	222.1	2.9	575,513
Wisconsin	492	3.3	6,900	2.7	14	100.1	14,509	188.0	2.4	382,104
Iowa	335	2.3	7,329	2.8	22	100.9	13,761	179.9	2.3	536,899
New Jersey	233	1.6	5,181	2.0	22	91.4	17,645	171.1	2.2	734,395
Maryland	363	2.5	5,768	2.2	16	91.3	15,834	169.2	2.2	466,047
Louisiana	283	1.9	5,997	2.3	21	71.2	11,865	168.5	2.2	595,399
Connecticut	185	1.3	4,674	1.8	25	92.5	19,784	166.7	2.1	901,286
Missouri	308	2.1	5,469	2.1	18	78.9	14,423	147.1	1.9	477,536
Oklahoma	87	0.6	3,904	1.5	45	51.4	13,159	96.3	1.2	1,106,448
Tennessee	223	1.5	3,187	1.2	14	47.9	15,017	94.4	1.2	423,493
Colorado	123	0.8	2,557	1.0	21	30.8	12,026	88.9	1.1	723,146
South Carolina	200	1.4	3,158	1.2	16	44.9	14,225	87.7	1.1	438,615
Oregon	289	2.0	3,281	1.3	11	47.7	14,533	85.3	1.1	295,221
West Virginia	145	1.0	2,873	1.1	20	36.9	12,852	78.2	1.0	539,476
Arizona	180	1.2	2,670	1.0	15	41.5	15,561	75.6	1.0	419,939
Maine	120	0.8	2,724	1.1	23	38.3	14,061	68.8	0.9	573,300
Washington	141	1.0	2,441	0.9	17	37.4	15,303	62.4	0.8	442,489
D.C.	85	0.6	1,600	0.6	19	28.8	18,026	61.9	0.8	727,871
Georgia	91	0.6	1,652	0.6	18	25.8	15,596	56.7	0.7	622,923
Virginia	116	0.8	1,701	0.7	15	27.2	16,005	51.7	0.7	445,414
Utah	94	0.6	2,438	0.9	26	30.9	12,670	50.2	0.6	534,330
Arkansas	65	0.4	1,691	0.7	26	19.9	11,743	45.7	0.6	702,938
Nebraska	77	0.5	2,140	0.8	28	25.7	12,029	43.3	0.6	562,649
Alabama	113	0.8	1,682	0.7	15	19.9	11,809	42.0	0.5	371,991
Mississippi	20	0.1	1,029	0.4	51	12.5	12,145	31.9	0.4	1,595,750
South Dakota	28	0.2	1,104	0.4	39	17.0	15,377	28.1	0.4	1,003,607
New Hampshire	47	0.3	636	0.2	14	9.4	14,734	26.2	0.3	556,809
Idaho	49	0.3	1,165	0.5	24	13.9	11,959	25.4	0.3	518,592
New Mexico	11	0.1	882	0.3	80	11.6	13,101	25.0	0.3	2,272,455
Kentucky	54	0.4	806	0.3	15	13.1	16,244	23.7	0.3	439,370
Alaska	44	0.3	315	0.1	7	6.9	21,997	16.0	0.2	363,136
Kansas	20	0.1	558	0.2	28	7.8	13,952	13.2	0.2	658,100
Hawaii	7	-	296	0.1	42	4.0	13,351	7.5	0.1	1,070,143
Vermont	8	0.1	160	0.1	20	3.0	19,019	5.4	0.1	678,625

Source: 1997 *Economic Census*. The states are in descending order of revenues or establishments (if revenue data are missing for the majority). The symbol (D) appears when data are withheld to prevent disclosure of competitive information. States marked with (D) are sorted by number of establishments. A dash (-) indicates that the data element cannot be calculated. * indicates the midpoint of a range; 175, for example is the range 100-249. Shaded *states* on the state map indicate those states which have proportionately greater representation in the industry than would be indicated by the state's population; the ratio is based on total revenues or number of establishments. Shaded *regions* indicate where the industry is regionally most concentrated.

NAICS 623220 - RESIDENTIAL MENTAL HEALTH AND SUBSTANCE ABUSE FACILITIES

GENERAL STATISTICS

Year	Establishments (number)	Employment (number)	Payroll ($ million)	Revenues ($ million)	Employees per Establishment (number)	Revenues per Establishment ($)	Payroll per Employee ($)
1997	5,535	97,647	1,796.0	3,817.0	17.6	689,612	18,393

Source: Economic Census of the United States, 1997. This is a newly defined industry. Data for prior years were unavailable at the time of publication but may become available over time.

INDICES OF CHANGE

Year	Establishments (number)	Employment (number)	Payroll ($ million)	Revenues ($ million)	Employees per Establishment (number)	Revenues per Establishment ($)	Payroll per Employee ($)
1997	100.0	100.0	100.0	100.0	100.0	100.0	100.0

Sources: Same as General Statistics. The values shown reflect change from the base year, 1997. Values above 100 mean greater than 1997, values below 100 mean less than 1997, and a value of 100 in the 1982-96 or 1998-2001 period means same as 1997. Values followed by a 'p' are projections by the editors; 'e' stands for extrapolation. Data are the most recent available at this level of detail.

SIC INDUSTRIES RELATED TO NAICS 623220

Each new NAICS code represents an industry that used to be part of an SIC or a part of several SIC industries. Data in this table are shown to provide transitional information for these cases. All available data for the precursor SIC(s) are shown. Even if only a part of an SIC is included in the NAICS, *all* data for the SIC are reproduced. If the SIC industry is not marked as being a part (pt) of the NAICS, the entire industry is embedded in the NAICS data. The SIC composition of the new industry provides some hints of the relative importance of its "ancestors." Data marked with a 'p' are projected. Projections begin with 1982 data. Data earlier than 1990 are not shown but are reflected in the projections.

SIC	Industry	1990	1991	1992	1993	1994	1995	1996	1997
8059	**Nursing & Personal Care, nec (pt)**								
	Establishments (number)	-	-	1,748	-	-	-	-	-
	Employment (thousands)	-	-	49.5	-	-	-	-	-
	Revenues ($ million)	-	-	1,572.5	-	-	-	-	-
8361	**Residential Care (pt)**								
	Establishments (number)	20,967	22,267	27,143	27,912	28,937	29,937	31,850p	33,440p
	Employment (thousands)	416.8	449.7	457.3	491.1	518.2	549.9	571.8p	598.0p
	Revenues ($ million)	4,626.0	4,934.0	4,853.0	5,421.0	5,905.0	6,437.0	7,244.0	7,377.7p

Source: Economic Census of the United States, 1992, annual surveys of economic sectors conducted by the Bureau of the Census, and estimates or projections based on the 1982-1992 period; not all data are shown. 'e' marks estimates made by the editors; 'p' indicates projections based on time series. A dash (-) indicates that data for this SIC or year were not available. The abbreviation (pt) next to the industry name indicates that only a part of the industry is present within the NAICS data. If no (pt) is shown, the entire industry is contained within the NAICS data.

SELECTED RATIOS

For 1997	Avg. of Information	Analyzed Industry	Index	For 1997	Avg. of Information	Analyzed Industry	Index
Employees per establishment	21	18	84	Payroll per establishment	585,591	324,481	55
Revenue per establishment	1,370,364	689,612	50	Payroll as % of revenue	43	47	110
Revenue per employee	65,262	39,090	60	Payroll per employee	27,888	18,393	66

Sources: Same as General Statistics. The 'Average' column represents the average for the industry sector, in 1997, where the currently shown industry is classified. The Index shows the relationship between the Average and the Analyzed Industry. For example, 100 means that they are equal; 500 that the Analyzed Industry is five times the average; 50 means that the Analyzed Industry is half the national average. The abbreviation 'na' is used to show that data are 'not available'.

LEADING COMPANIES

No company data available for this industry.

REPRESENTATIVE NONPROFIT ORGANIZATIONS

Organization Name	Address				Phone	Income Range ($ mil)
12 & 12 Inc	6333 E Skelly Dr	Tulsa	OK	74135	918-664-4224	1-5
A Program Planned for Life Enrichment Inc	153 Main St	Smithtown	NY	11787	631-979-7300	10-19
African American Family Services Inc	2616 Nicollet Ave S	Minneapolis	MN	55408		1-5
Agency for Community Treatment Services Inc	4612 N 56th St	Tampa	FL	33610	813-246-4899	10-19
Aiken County Commission on Alcohol and Drug Abuse	1105 Gregg Hwy	Aiken	SC	29801	803-642-1690	1-5
Alcoholism Recovery Services Inc	2701 Jefferson Ave SW	Birmingham	AL	35211	205-785-5787	1-5
Alternatives Incorporated	2013 Cunningham Dr	Hampton	VA	23666	757-838-2330	1-5
Arapahoe House Inc	8801 Lipan St	Thornton	CO	80260	303-657-3700	10-19
Area Five Agency on Aging & Community Services	1801 Smith St	Logansport	IN	46947	219-722-4451	10-19
Ashley Inc	800 Tydings LN	Hvre De Grace	MD	21078	410-575-7234	10-19
Behavioral Connections of Wood County Inc	315 Thurstin Ave	Bowling Green	OH	43402	419-352-5387	5-9
Best Foundation for a Drug Free Tomorrow	725 S Figueroa St	Los Angeles	CA	90017	213-253-5470	10-19
Big Island Substance Abuse Council	1420 Kilauea Ave	Hilo	HI	96720	808-935-4927	1-5
Blueridge Health Services Inc	PO Box 151	Portland	CT	06480		10-19
Brandywine Counseling Inc	2713 Lancaster Ave	Wilmington	DE	19805	302-656-2348	1-5
Bridgeway Counseling Service Inc	120 First Capitol Dr	St Charles	MO	63301	636-940-2283	1-5
Caritas House	166 Pawtucket Ave	Pawtucket	RI	02860	401-725-5570	1-5
Caritas	1234 S Michigan Ave	Chicago	IL	60605		20-29
Carrier Foundation	PO Box 147	Belle Mead	NJ	08502	908-281-1000	30-39
Cenla Chemical Dependency Council Inc	PO Box 4582	Pineville	LA	71361		1-5
Center for Alcohol & Drug Treatment	PO Box 950	Wenatchee	WA	98807	509-662-9673	1-5
Central Arkansas Substance Abuse Programs Inc	1509 Mart Dr	Little Rock	AR	72202		1-5
Clear Brook Inc	1003 Wyoming Ave	Forty Fort	PA	18704	570-288-6692	10-19
Comprehensive Options for Drug Abusers Inc	1027 E Burnside	Portland	OR	97214		5-9
Crossroads for Women Inc	66 Pearl St	Portland	ME	04101	207-773-9931	1-5
Dccca Inc	3312 Clinton Pkwy	Lawrence	KS	66047	785-841-4138	10-19
Delancey Street/New Mexico Inc	P O Box 1240	San Juan Pueblo	NM	87566	505-852-4291	1-5
Door to Recovery Inc	4910 Dacoma	Houston	TX	77092	713-956-2099	5-9
Fairbanks Native Association	201 1st Ave	Fairbanks	AK	99701	907-452-1648	10-19
Family Life Services of New England Inc	72 Main St	Vergennes	VT	05491	802-877-3166	1-5
Hegira Programs Inc	8623 N Wayne Rd	Westland	MI	48185		10-19
Honac Inc	2762 Watson Blvd	Warner Robins	GA	31093		1-5
Intertribal Addictions Recovery Organization Inc	1000 Decker Rd	Sheridan	WY	82801		1-5
Island View Academy Inc	2651 W 2700 S	Syracuse	UT	84075	801-773-0200	1-5
Ministry Behavorial Health of St Michaels Hospital Inc	PO Box 8004	Stevens Point	WI	54481	715-344-4611	1-5
Native American Heritage Association	410 Sheridan Lake Rd	Rapid City	SD	57702	605-341-9110	5-9
Nova Therapeutic Community Inc	3483 Larimore Ave	Omaha	NE	68111	402-455-8303	1-5
Pavillon International	PO Box 189	Mill Springs	NC	28756	828-625-8210	5-9
Port of Hope Centers Inc	PO Box 7823	Boise	ID	83707	208-342-0633	1-5
Prehab of Arizona Inc	PO Drawer G	Mesa	AZ	85201	480-464-9669	10-19
Recovery Lodge Inc	PO Box 10545	Jackson	MS	39289	601-922-0802	1-5
South Middlesex Opportunity Council Inc	300 Howard St	Framingham	MA	01702	508-872-4853	20-29
St Lukes Health Resources	2720 Stone Park Blvd	Sioux City	IA	51104	712-279-3141	20-29
T J Mahoney and Associates Inc	3900 Paradise Rd	Las Vegas	NV	89109		1-5
The Helen Ross McNabb Center	1520 Cherokee Trail	Knoxville	TN	37920	865-637-9711	10-19
The Morton Center Inc	982 Eastern Pkwy	Louisville	KY	40217	502-636-1448	1-5

Source: National Directory of Nonprofit Organizations, 2000, Volumes 1 and 2, The Taft Group. The table shows a selection of organizations for illustration and does not constitute a complete selection from the source. The organizations are arranged in alphabetical order.

LOCATION BY STATE AND REGIONAL CONCENTRATION

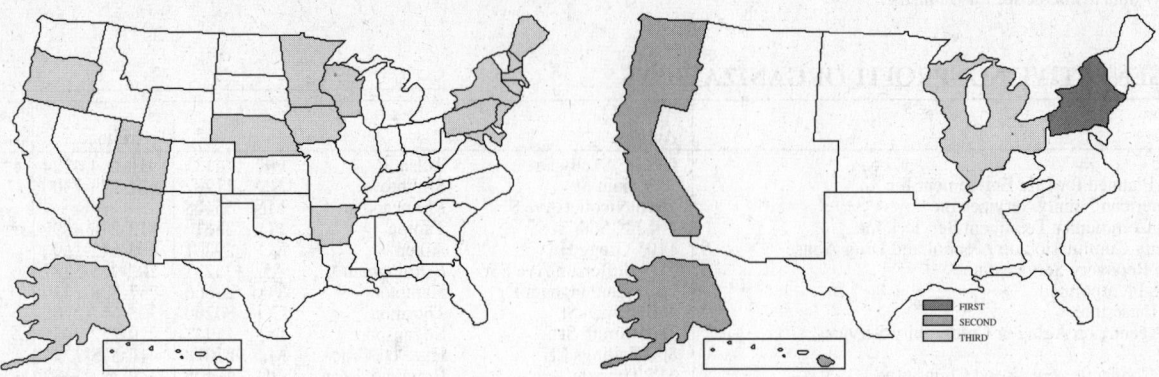

INDUSTRY DATA BY STATE

State	Establishments Total (number)	% of U.S.	Employment Total (number)	% of U.S.	Per Estab.	Payroll Total ($ mil.)	Per Empl. ($)	Revenues Total ($ mil.)	% of U.S.	Per Estab. ($)
New York	521	9.4	10,510	10.8	20	231.4	22,017	481.9	12.6	924,948
California	798	14.4	11,121	11.4	14	198.4	17,841	451.2	11.8	565,381
Pennsylvania	281	5.1	6,426	6.6	23	121.5	18,906	260.9	6.8	928,605
Massachusetts	356	6.4	6,058	6.2	17	110.5	18,248	204.6	5.4	574,579
Florida	238	4.3	4,229	4.3	18	78.0	18,449	186.7	4.9	784,416
New Jersey	125	2.3	3,662	3.8	29	72.6	19,830	146.8	3.8	1,174,120
Illinois	192	3.5	3,398	3.5	18	61.8	18,180	146.4	3.8	762,693
Texas	198	3.6	3,403	3.5	17	59.9	17,615	139.9	3.7	706,606
Michigan	311	5.6	3,654	3.7	12	59.9	16,406	133.8	3.5	430,312
Ohio	171	3.1	2,691	2.8	16	46.3	17,223	100.9	2.6	590,117
Iowa	99	1.8	3,255	3.3	33	54.0	16,578	96.1	2.5	971,162
Wisconsin	172	3.1	2,723	2.8	16	43.9	16,128	87.5	2.3	508,535
Minnesota	134	2.4	2,354	2.4	18	39.8	16,887	85.3	2.2	636,291
Arizona	80	1.4	1,683	1.7	21	38.0	22,552	85.1	2.2	1,064,000
Maryland	75	1.4	1,919	2.0	26	35.7	18,623	79.6	2.1	1,061,547
Connecticut	88	1.6	1,787	1.8	20	39.1	21,881	74.5	2.0	846,136
Washington	105	1.9	1,955	2.0	19	36.0	18,391	73.4	1.9	698,610
North Carolina	149	2.7	1,919	2.0	13	31.0	16,141	68.8	1.8	461,638
Tennessee	77	1.4	1,717	1.8	22	34.6	20,135	68.4	1.8	888,494
Indiana	107	1.9	1,526	1.6	14	25.0	16,383	64.2	1.7	600,439
Missouri	125	2.3	2,136	2.2	17	29.2	13,689	61.4	1.6	491,568
Oregon	91	1.6	1,809	1.9	20	31.5	17,401	59.7	1.6	656,484
Georgia	45	0.8	1,521	1.6	34	24.2	15,884	56.0	1.5	1,244,111
Virginia	74	1.3	1,138	1.2	15	22.0	19,303	45.7	1.2	617,932
Arkansas	33	0.6	1,091	1.1	33	24.8	22,735	45.0	1.2	1,365,121
Colorado	73	1.3	986	1.0	14	19.8	20,103	43.0	1.1	589,699
Maine	103	1.9	1,178	1.2	11	21.8	18,480	41.7	1.1	405,282
Oklahoma	72	1.3	1,198	1.2	17	15.0	12,553	36.4	1.0	505,972
Utah	32	0.6	602	0.6	19	15.5	25,664	31.4	0.8	981,187
Louisiana	59	1.1	818	0.8	14	13.9	17,029	28.4	0.7	480,644
Nebraska	43	0.8	729	0.7	17	12.8	17,594	28.2	0.7	655,465
South Carolina	34	0.6	711	0.7	21	12.4	17,494	27.6	0.7	811,765
Alabama	54	1.0	695	0.7	13	11.7	16,770	25.5	0.7	472,537
New Hampshire	42	0.8	478	0.5	11	10.4	21,669	21.2	0.6	503,619
D.C.	34	0.6	601	0.6	18	10.9	18,166	21.2	0.6	624,324
West Virginia	39	0.7	698	0.7	18	10.0	14,383	19.7	0.5	506,256
Alaska	10	0.2	276	0.3	28	6.1	21,938	15.0	0.4	1,502,200
Delaware	15	0.3	167	0.2	11	4.0	24,078	7.2	0.2	480,000
Mississippi	18	0.3	147	0.2	8	2.1	14,415	5.3	0.1	292,333
Idaho	19	0.3	116	0.1	6	1.7	14,276	4.8	0.1	252,842
New Mexico	7	0.1	127	0.1	18	2.0	15,488	3.3	0.1	468,571
Nevada	7	0.1	107	0.1	15	1.4	13,187	3.3	0.1	464,571
Wyoming	11	0.2	375 *	-	-	(D)	-	(D)	-	-

Source: 1997 *Economic Census*. The states are in descending order of revenues or establishments (if revenue data are missing for the majority). The symbol (D) appears when data are withheld to prevent disclosure of competitive information. States marked with (D) are sorted by number of establishments. A dash (-) indicates that the data element cannot be calculated. * indicates the midpoint of a range; 175, for example is the range 100-249. Shaded *states* on the state map indicate those states which have proportionately greater representation in the industry than would be indicated by the state's population; the ratio is based on total revenues or number of establishments. Shaded *regions* indicate where the industry is regionally most concentrated.

NAICS 623311 - CONTINUING CARE RETIREMENT COMMUNITIES

GENERAL STATISTICS

Year	Establishments (number)	Employment (number)	Payroll ($ million)	Revenues ($ million)	Employees per Establishment (number)	Revenues per Establishment ($)	Payroll per Employee ($)
1997	2,995	242,319	3,931.0	9,841.0	80.9	3,285,810	16,222

Source: Economic Census of the United States, 1997. This is a newly defined industry. Data for prior years were unavailable at the time of publication but may become available over time.

INDICES OF CHANGE

Year	Establishments (number)	Employment (number)	Payroll ($ million)	Revenues ($ million)	Employees per Establishment (number)	Revenues per Establishment ($)	Payroll per Employee ($)
1997	100.0	100.0	100.0	100.0	100.0	100.0	100.0

Sources: Same as General Statistics. The values shown reflect change from the base year, 1997. Values above 100 mean greater than 1997, values below 100 mean less than 1997, and a value of 100 in the 1982-96 or 1998-2001 period means same as 1997. Values followed by a 'p' are projections by the editors; 'e' stands for extrapolation. Data are the most recent available at this level of detail.

SIC INDUSTRIES RELATED TO NAICS 623311

Each new NAICS code represents an industry that used to be part of an SIC or a part of several SIC industries. Data in this table are shown to provide transitional information for these cases. All available data for the precursor SIC(s) are shown. Even if only a part of an SIC is included in the NAICS, *all* data for the SIC are reproduced. If the SIC industry is not marked as being a part (pt) of the NAICS, the entire industry is embedded in the NAICS data. The SIC composition of the new industry provides some hints of the relative importance of its "ancestors." Data marked with a 'p' are projected. Projections begin with 1982 data. Data earlier than 1990 are not shown but are reflected in the projections.

SIC	Industry	1990	1991	1992	1993	1994	1995	1996	1997
8051	**Skilled Nursing Care Facilities (pt)**								
	Establishments (number)	-	-	12,965	-	-	-	-	-
	Employment (thousands)	-	-	1,305.1	-	-	-	-	-
	Revenues ($ million)	-	-	40,480.9	-	-	-	-	-
8052	**Intermediate Care Facilities (pt)**								
	Establishments (number)	-	-	6,166	-	-	-	-	-
	Employment (thousands)	-	-	278.2	-	-	-	-	-
	Revenues ($ million)	-	-	7,156.7	-	-	-	-	-
8059	**Nursing & Personal Care, nec (pt)**								
	Establishments (number)	-	-	1,748	-	-	-	-	-
	Employment (thousands)	-	-	49.5	-	-	-	-	-
	Revenues ($ million)	-	-	1,572.5	-	-	-	-	-

Source: Economic Census of the United States, 1992, annual surveys of economic sectors conducted by the Bureau of the Census, and estimates or projections based on the 1982-1992 period; not all data are shown. 'e' marks estimates made by the editors; 'p' indicates projections based on time series. A dash (-) indicates that data for this SIC or year were not available. The abbreviation (pt) next to the industry name indicates that only a part of the industry is present within the NAICS data. If no (pt) is shown, the entire industry is contained within the NAICS data.

SELECTED RATIOS

For 1997	Avg. of Information	Analyzed Industry	Index	For 1997	Avg. of Information	Analyzed Industry	Index
Employees per establishment	21	81	385	Payroll per establishment	585,591	1,312,521	224
Revenue per establishment	1,370,364	3,285,810	240	Payroll as % of revenue	43	40	93
Revenue per employee	65,262	40,612	62	Payroll per employee	27,888	16,222	58

Sources: Same as General Statistics. The 'Average' column represents the average for the industry sector, in 1997, where the currently shown industry is classified. The Index shows the relationship between the Average and the Analyzed Industry. For example, 100 means that they are equal; 500 that the Analyzed Industry is five times the average; 50 means that the Analyzed Industry is half the national average. The abbreviation 'na' is used to show that data are 'not available'.

LEADING COMPANIES

No company data available for this industry.

REPRESENTATIVE NONPROFIT ORGANIZATIONS

Organization Name	Address				Phone	Income Range ($ mil)
Advanced Living Technologies Inc	215 SE 4th St	Evansville	IN	47713		10-19
Arcadia Retirement Residence	1434 Punahou Street	Honolulu	HI	96822	808-941-0941	10-19
Arizona Baptist Retirement Center Inc	PO Box 33099	Phoenix	AZ	85067		10-19
Army Retirement Residence Foundation San Antonio	7400 Crestway	San Antonio	TX	78239		50+
Augusta Resource Center on Aging Inc	4275 Owens Rd	Evans	GA	30809		10-19
B C B U Inc	2277 Fort Union Blvd	Salt Lake Cty	UT	84121		10-19
Baptist Outreach Services Corp	PO Box 11010	Montgomery	AL	36111		5-9
Bethel Lutheran Home	1001 S Egan	Madison	SD	57042	605-256-4539	1-5
Bnai Brith Senior Citizen Housing Inc	8000 Society Dr	Claymont	DE	19703		1-5
Butterfield Trail Village Incorporated	1923 E Joyce St	Fayetteville	AR	72703	501-442-7220	5-9
Central Boston Elder Services Inc	812 Huntington Ave	Boston	MA	02115	617-277-7416	10-19
Christian Retirement Homes Inc	6315 O St	Lincoln	NE	68510		1-5
Church Homes Inc Congregational	705 New Britain Ave	Hartford	CT	06106	860-947-2369	30-39
Citizens Memorial Health Care Foundation	1500 N Oakland Ave	Bolivar	MO	65613	417-326-3585	10-19
Edgewood Summit Inc	300 Baker LN	Charleston	WV	25302	304-346-2323	1-5
Ehs Home Health Care Service Inc	2025 Windsor Dr	Oak Brook	IL	60523	630-572-9393	20-29
Elderplan Inc	6323 Seventh Ave 3rd Flr	Brooklyn	NY	11220	718-921-7898	50+
Elyria United Methodist Village	807 West Ave	Elyria	OH	44035	440-284-9000	30-39
Episcopal Housing Foundation of Rhode Island	275 N Main St	Providence	RI	02903	401-434-5012	1-5
Good Samaritan Outreach Services	PO Box 1247	Puyallup	WA	98371	253-848-6661	20-29
Greater Southeast Community Center for the Aging	1380 Southern Ave SE	Washington	DC	20032	202-574-6757	5-9
Heritage Place Inc	702 W Walnut	Coeur Dalene	ID	83814	208-664-2680	1-5
Kendal at Hanover	80 Lyme Rd	Hanover	NH	03755		10-19
Lakeshore Estate Inc	8044 Coley Davis Rd	Nashville	TN	37221		10-19
Life Care Retirement Communities Inc	100 E Grand Ave Ste 230	Des Moines	IA	50309	515-288-5805	50+
Masonic Charity Foundation of Oklahoma	PO Box 2406	Edmond	OK	73083		10-19
Meriter Retirement Services Inc	110 S Henry St	Madison	WI	53703	608-283-2000	10-19
Missoula Manor Homes	909 W Central	Missoula	MT	59801	406-728-3210	1-5
Mountain Home Health Care Inc	PO Box 2566	Taos	NM	87571		1-5
National Lutheran Home for the Aged	9701 Veirs Dr	Rockville	MD	20850	301-424-9560	50+
Oakwood Health Promotions Inc	16351 Rotunda Dr	Dearborn	MI	48120	313-253-6009	20-29
Oregon Baptist Retirement Home	1825 NE 108th Ave	Portland	OR	97220	503-255-7160	1-5
Pacific Homes Corp	2835 N Naomi St Ste 300	Burbank	CA	91504		50+
Presbyterian Home Care Centers Inc	3220 Lake Johanna Blvd	St Paul	MN	55112	651-631-6000	10-19
Presbyterian Homes and Services of KY Inc	PO Box 18067	Louisville	KY	40261	502-499-3300	10-19
Presbyterian Manors Inc	PO Box 20440	Wichita	KS	67208	316-685-1100	50+
Presbyterian Retirement Communities Inc	80 W Lucerne Cir	Orlando	FL	32801	407-839-5050	50+
Souris Valley Care Center Inc	RT 2 Box 66E	Velva	ND	58790	701-338-2072	1-5
South Carolina Episcopal Home at Still Hopes	One Still Hopes Dr	W Columbia	SC	29169		5-9
Southern Healthcare Systems Inc	17617 S Harrels Ferry Rd	Baton Rouge	LA	70816		30-39
Southwestern Vermont Council on Aging Inc	1 Scale Ave Unit 108	Rutland	VT	05701	802-773-4333	1-5
Springmoor Inc	812 Springmoor Dr	Raleigh	NC	27615		20-29
Sta-Home Hospice Inc	105 N Van Buren	Carthage	MS	39051	601-267-8333	1-5
Total Longterm Care Inc	303 E 17th Ave Ste 650	Denver	CO	80203	303-869-4664	5-9
United Methodist Homes of New Jersey	3311 Hwy 33	Neptune	NJ	07753	732-922-9800	20-29
Western Area Agency on Aging Inc	PO Box 659	Lewiston	ME	04243		30-39
Westminster-Canterbury of Winchester Inc	300 W-Canterbury Dr	Winchester	VA	22603	540-665-0156	10-19
Willow Valley Manor	600 Willow Valley Square	Lancaster	PA	17602	717-464-5478	40-49

Source: *National Directory of Nonprofit Organizations*, 2000, Volumes 1 and 2, The Taft Group. The table shows a selection of organizations for illustration and does not constitute a complete selection from the source. The organizations are arranged in alphabetical order.

LOCATION BY STATE AND REGIONAL CONCENTRATION

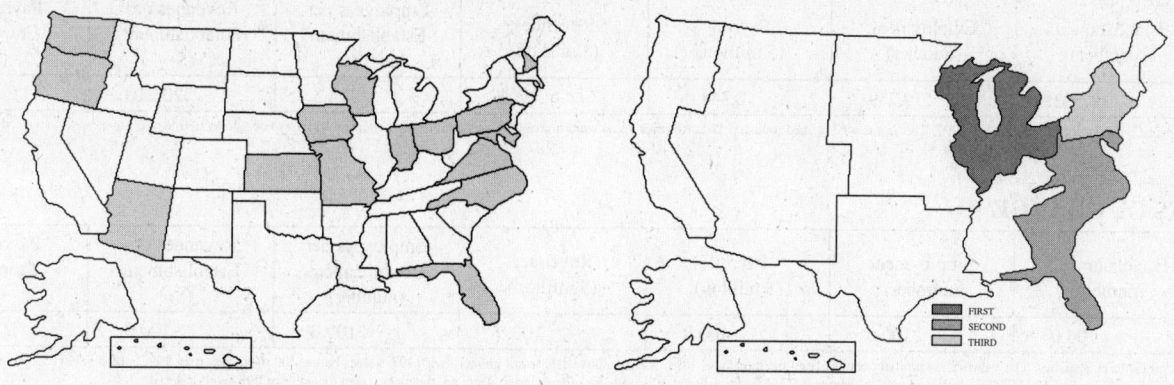

INDUSTRY DATA BY STATE

State	Establishments Total (number)	% of U.S.	Employment Total (number)	% of U.S.	Per Estab.	Payroll Total ($ mil.)	Per Empl. ($)	Revenues Total ($ mil.)	% of U.S.	Per Estab. ($)
Pennsylvania	246	8.2	31,743	13.1	129	551.8	17,384	1,379.6	14.0	5,608,053
California	268	8.9	19,391	8.0	72	322.0	16,605	851.8	8.7	3,178,403
Ohio	202	6.7	20,764	8.6	103	350.1	16,860	814.3	8.3	4,031,168
Florida	163	5.4	15,922	6.6	98	259.7	16,314	746.2	7.6	4,578,117
Illinois	91	3.0	10,756	4.4	118	174.5	16,225	447.1	4.5	4,913,582
Texas	168	5.6	9,973	4.1	59	150.1	15,047	393.8	4.0	2,343,851
North Carolina	99	3.3	8,829	3.6	89	145.8	16,515	378.9	3.9	3,827,000
Michigan	94	3.1	9,153	3.8	97	136.2	14,880	330.3	3.4	3,513,543
Virginia	79	2.6	8,021	3.3	102	123.3	15,375	326.3	3.3	4,130,278
Indiana	88	2.9	8,547	3.5	97	141.0	16,497	312.3	3.2	3,548,477
Maryland	43	1.4	6,149	2.5	143	104.3	16,964	308.2	3.1	7,167,116
Missouri	137	4.6	7,730	3.2	56	115.8	14,987	273.3	2.8	1,994,803
New Jersey	67	2.2	4,826	2.0	72	98.9	20,487	263.8	2.7	3,936,582
Washington	110	3.7	6,577	2.7	60	113.0	17,175	260.9	2.7	2,371,618
Kansas	72	2.4	7,042	2.9	98	105.4	14,971	242.9	2.5	3,373,611
Wisconsin	91	3.0	6,240	2.6	69	103.7	16,614	211.1	2.1	2,319,648
New York	48	1.6	3,826	1.6	80	76.4	19,979	191.5	1.9	3,988,937
Arizona	50	1.7	3,719	1.5	74	63.8	17,161	166.6	1.7	3,332,700
Iowa	60	2.0	5,011	2.1	84	72.8	14,529	153.4	1.6	2,556,283
Massachusetts	64	2.1	3,496	1.4	55	57.8	16,541	150.8	1.5	2,355,813
Oregon	99	3.3	3,928	1.6	40	55.9	14,220	146.6	1.5	1,480,687
Tennessee	26	0.9	3,092	1.3	119	48.1	15,559	127.1	1.3	4,890,231
Minnesota	68	2.3	3,950	1.6	58	58.4	14,785	126.2	1.3	1,855,353
Connecticut	20	0.7	2,029	0.8	101	40.1	19,768	123.0	1.2	6,149,750
Georgia	60	2.0	2,813	1.2	47	38.9	13,839	107.5	1.1	1,791,733
Alabama	35	1.2	2,364	1.0	68	36.5	15,437	91.7	0.9	2,620,629
South Carolina	43	1.4	2,503	1.0	58	35.7	14,282	89.7	0.9	2,086,000
Colorado	24	0.8	2,326	1.0	97	34.4	14,804	84.3	0.9	3,512,833
Oklahoma	41	1.4	2,490	1.0	61	35.6	14,313	77.6	0.8	1,893,537
New Hampshire	23	0.8	1,651	0.7	72	27.6	16,718	75.3	0.8	3,275,174
Louisiana	34	1.1	2,165	0.9	64	26.1	12,075	58.3	0.6	1,713,676
Nebraska	26	0.9	1,685	0.7	65	24.3	14,427	56.9	0.6	2,187,231
Kentucky	26	0.9	1,736	0.7	67	25.8	14,836	53.8	0.5	2,069,462
Arkansas	25	0.8	1,390	0.6	56	17.7	12,749	44.4	0.5	1,777,000
Maine	23	0.8	1,258	0.5	55	19.3	15,378	37.2	0.4	1,619,304
West Virginia	20	0.7	793	0.3	40	11.1	13,958	31.6	0.3	1,579,900
New Mexico	14	0.5	862	0.4	62	14.2	16,454	31.3	0.3	2,234,929
Montana	18	0.6	782	0.3	43	10.9	13,951	24.0	0.2	1,331,333
South Dakota	14	0.5	827	0.3	59	12.0	14,563	23.0	0.2	1,645,929
Idaho	25	0.8	478	0.2	19	7.4	15,418	18.3	0.2	731,080
Mississippi	3	0.1	382	0.2	127	6.0	15,694	13.7	0.1	4,561,000
Nevada	7	0.2	64	0.0	9	1.1	16,781	2.7	0.0	387,714
Alaska	1	-	10*	-	-	(D)	-	(D)	-	-
Hawaii	1	-	175*	-	-	(D)	-	(D)	-	-

Source: 1997 *Economic Census*. The states are in descending order of revenues or establishments (if revenue data are missing for the majority). The symbol (D) appears when data are withheld to prevent disclosure of competitive information. States marked with (D) are sorted by number of establishments. A dash (-) indicates that the data element cannot be calculated. * indicates the midpoint of a range; 175, for example is the range 100-249. Shaded *states* on the state map indicate those states which have proportionately greater representation in the industry than would be indicated by the state's population; the ratio is based on total revenues or number of establishments. Shaded *regions* indicate where the industry is regionally most concentrated.

NAICS 623312 - HOMES FOR THE ELDERLY

GENERAL STATISTICS

Year	Establishments (number)	Employment (number)	Payroll ($ million)	Revenues ($ million)	Employees per Establishment (number)	Revenues per Establishment ($)	Payroll per Employee ($)
1997	12,593	179,759	2,344.0	6,551.0	14.3	520,210	13,040

Source: *Economic Census of the United States*, 1997. This is a newly defined industry. Data for prior years were unavailable at the time of publication but may become available over time.

INDICES OF CHANGE

Year	Establishments (number)	Employment (number)	Payroll ($ million)	Revenues ($ million)	Employees per Establishment (number)	Revenues per Establishment ($)	Payroll per Employee ($)
1997	100.0	100.0	100.0	100.0	100.0	100.0	100.0

Sources: Same as General Statistics. The values shown reflect change from the base year, 1997. Values above 100 mean greater than 1997, values below 100 mean less than 1997, and a value of 100 in the 1982-96 or 1998-2001 period means same as 1997. Values followed by a 'p' are projections by the editors; 'e' stands for extrapolation. Data are the most recent available at this level of detail.

SIC INDUSTRIES RELATED TO NAICS 623312

Each new NAICS code represents an industry that used to be part of an SIC or a part of several SIC industries. Data in this table are shown to provide transitional information for these cases. All available data for the precursor SIC(s) are shown. Even if only a part of an SIC is included in the NAICS, *all* data for the SIC are reproduced. If the SIC industry is not marked as being a part (pt) of the NAICS, the entire industry is embedded in the NAICS data. The SIC composition of the new industry provides some hints of the relative importance of its "ancestors." Data marked with a 'p' are projected. Projections begin with 1982 data. Data earlier than 1990 are not shown but are reflected in the projections.

SIC	Industry	1990	1991	1992	1993	1994	1995	1996	1997
8361	**Residential Care (pt)**								
	Establishments (number)	20,967	22,267	27,143	27,912	28,937	29,937	31,850p	33,440p
	Employment (thousands)	416.8	449.7	457.3	491.1	518.2	549.9	571.8p	598.0p
	Revenues ($ million)	4,626.0	4,934.0	4,853.0	5,421.0	5,905.0	6,437.0	7,244.0	7,377.7p

Source: *Economic Census of the United States*, 1992, annual surveys of economic sectors conducted by the Bureau of the Census, and estimates or projections based on the 1982-1992 period; not all data are shown. 'e' marks estimates made by the editors; 'p' indicates projections based on time series. A dash (-) indicates that data for this SIC or year were not available. The abbreviation (pt) next to the industry name indicates that only a part of the industry is present within the NAICS data. If no (pt) is shown, the entire industry is contained within the NAICS data.

SELECTED RATIOS

For 1997	Avg. of Information	Analyzed Industry	Index	For 1997	Avg. of Information	Analyzed Industry	Index
Employees per establishment	21	14	68	Payroll per establishment	585,591	186,135	32
Revenue per establishment	1,370,364	520,210	38	Payroll as % of revenue	43	36	84
Revenue per employee	65,262	36,443	56	Payroll per employee	27,888	13,040	47

Sources: Same as General Statistics. The 'Average' column represents the average for the industry sector, in 1997, where the currently shown industry is classified. The Index shows the relationship between the Average and the Analyzed Industry. For example, 100 means that they are equal; 500 that the Analyzed Industry is five times the average; 50 means that the Analyzed Industry is half the national average. The abbreviation 'na' is used to show that data are 'not available'.

LEADING COMPANIES Number shown: 1   Total sales ($ mil): 553   Total employment (000): 0.0

Company Name	Address				CEO Name	Phone	Co. Type	Sales ($ mil)	Empl. (000)
ResCare Inc.	10140 Linn Station	Louisville	KY	40223	Ronald G Geary	502-394-2100	P	553	0.0

Source: Ward's Business Directory of U.S. Private and Public Companies, Volumes 1 and 2, 2000. The company type code used is as follows: P - Public, R - Private, S - Subsidiary, D - Division, J - Joint Venture, A - Affiliate, G - Group, N - Company type not reported. Sales are in millions of dollars, employees are in thousands. An asterisk (*) indicates an estimated sales volume. The symbol < stands for 'less than'. Company names and addresses are truncated, in some cases, to fit into the available space.

REPRESENTATIVE NONPROFIT ORGANIZATIONS

Organization Name	Address				Phone	Income Range ($ mil)
Adult Communities Total Services Inc	PO Box 90	W Point	PA	19486	215-661-8330	50+
Altergarten Las Teresas II Inc	901 Calle Azabache	San Juan	PR	00924		1-5
American Baptist Homes of the Midwest	11985 Technology Dr	Eden Prairie	MN	55344	952-941-3175	50+
American Baptist Homes of the West	6120 Stoneridge Mall	Pleasanton	CA	94588	925-635-7600	50+
Army Distaff Foundation Inc	6200 Oregon Ave NW	Washington	DC	20015	202-541-0105	10-19
Arthur B Hodges Center Inc	500 Morris St	Charleston	WV	25301	304-345-6560	5-9
Asbury Methodist Village Inc	201 Russell Ave	Gaithersburg	MD	20877	301-216-4100	50+
Baptist Homes of Indiana Inc	PO Box 453	Zionsville	IN	46077		20-29
Baptist Retirement Homes of North Carolina Incorporated	PO Box 11024	Winston Salem	NC	27116		10-19
Beatitudes Campus of Care	1610 W Glendale Ave	Phoenix	AZ	85021	602-995-2611	10-19
Bethany Home Association of Lindsborg Kansas	321 N Chestnut	Lindsborg	KS	67456	785-227-2721	5-9
Bradley Home for the Aged	320 Colony St	Meriden	CT	06451	203-235-5716	20-29
C C Young Memorial Home	4829 W Lawther Dr	Dallas	TX	75214	214-827-8080	40-49
Care Initiatives Inc	1611 Westlakes Pkwy	W Des Moines	IA	50266	515-224-4442	50+
Caroline Kline Galland Home	7500 Seward Park Ave S	Seattle	WA	98118		10-19
Christian & Missionary Alliance Foundation Inc	15000 Shell Point Blvd	Fort Myers	FL	33908		50+
Eastern Idaho Special Services Agency	PO Box 51098	Idaho Falls	ID	83405		1-5
El Castillo Retirement Residences	250 E Alameda	Santa Fe	NM	87501		1-5
Friendship Manor Corporation	2929 Third Ave N Ste 538	Billings	MT	59101		1-5
General Assembly of the Christian Church Disciples of Christ	11780 Borman Dr Ste 200	St Louis	MO	63146		50+
General Living Centers Inc	5757 Corporate Blvd	Baton Rouge	LA	70808	225-344-3551	20-29
Hebrew Home for the Aged	5901 Palisade Ave	Bronx	NY	10471	718-549-8700	50+
Hospice Ministries Inc	450 Towne Center Blvd	Ridgeland	MS	39157	601-366-9881	5-9
Ingleside Homes Inc	1010 N Broom St	Wilmington	DE	19806	302-575-0283	10-19
Jenkins Living Center Inc	215 S Maple St	Watertown	SD	57201	605-886-5777	5-9
Long Term Care Foundation	2230 Ashley Crossing Dr	Charleston	SC	29414		50+
Looking Upwards Inc	438 E Main Rd	Middletown	RI	02842		5-9
Lunalilo Home	501 Kekauluohi St	Honolulu	HI	96825	808-395-1000	1-5
Lutheran Social Services of Michigan	8131 E Jefferson Ave	Detroit	MI	48214	313-823-7700	50+
Lutheran Social Services of Wisconsin and Upper Michigan	647 W Virginia St Ste 300	Milwaukee	WI	53204	414-281-4400	50+
Madonna Rehabilitation Hospital	5401 South St	Lincoln	NE	68506	402-489-7102	30-39
Maine Veterans Home	Civic Center PL	Augusta	ME	04330	207-622-2454	20-29
Masonic Home Inc	PO Box 1000	Charlton	MA	01507	508-248-7344	50+
Masonic Home	PO Box 5168	Manchester	NH	03108		5-9
McKendree Village Inc	4343 47 Lebanon Rd	Hermitage	TN	37076		20-29
Mega Care Inc	695 Chestnut St	Union	NJ	07083		30-39
Mission Health Services	2598 E 3650 N	Layton	UT	84040		10-19
Northside Operating Co	5700 N Ashland Ave	Chicago	IL	60660		50+
Otterbein Homes	580 N State RT 741	Lebanon	OH	45036		50+
Parkway Village Inc	14300 Chenal Pkwy	Little Rock	AR	72211	501-202-1664	5-9
Resource Healthcare of America Inc	3060 Peachtree Rd NW	Atlanta	GA	30305	404-364-2900	50+
Riverton Sertoma Foundation	PO Box 846	Riverton	WY	82501	307-856-4782	1-5
Rogue Valley Manor	1200 Mira Mar	Medford	OR	97504	541-858-6800	10-19
Shalom Park	14800 E Belleview Dr	Aurora	CO	80015		10-19
Sierra Assisted Living Foundation Inc	1187 B High School St	Gardnerville	NV	89410		1-5
St Charles Care Center Inc	500 Farrell Dr	Covington	KY	41011	859-331-3224	10-19
St Simeons Episcopal Home	3701 N Cincinnati	Tulsa	OK	74106	918-425-3583	5-9
Trinity Homes	PO Box 5030	Minot	ND	58702	701-857-5082	10-19
Virginia United Methodist Homes Inc	7113 Three Chopt Rd	Richmond	VA	23226	804-673-1031	40-49
Wake Robin Corp	200 Wake Robin Dr	Shelburne	VT	05482	802-985-9400	10-19
Wesley Scott Place a Methodist Home for the Aging Inc	1520 Cooper Hill Rd	Birmingham	AL	35210		20-29

Source: National Directory of Nonprofit Organizations, 2000, Volumes 1 and 2, The Taft Group. The table shows a selection of organizations for illustration and does not constitute a complete selection from the source. The organizations are arranged in alphabetical order.

LOCATION BY STATE AND REGIONAL CONCENTRATION

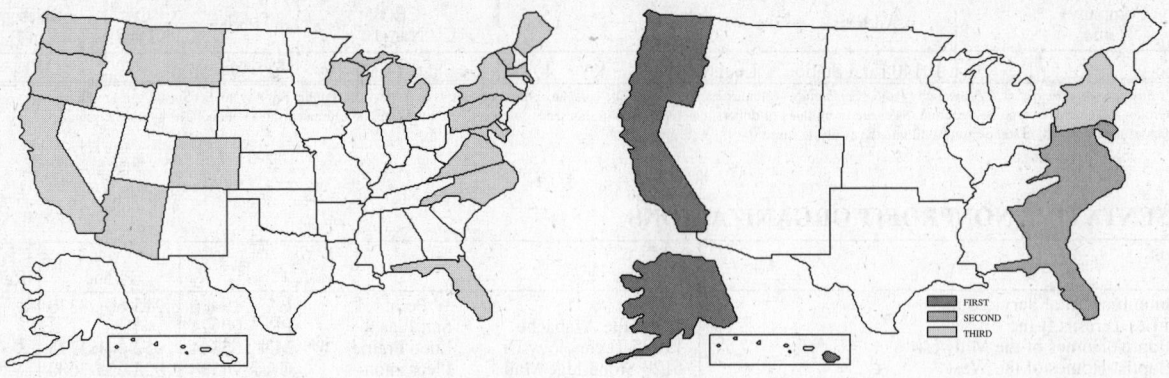

INDUSTRY DATA BY STATE

State	Establishments Total (number)	Establishments % of U.S.	Employment Total (number)	Employment % of U.S.	Employment Per Estab.	Payroll Total ($ mil.)	Payroll Per Empl. ($)	Revenues Total ($ mil.)	Revenues % of U.S.	Revenues Per Estab. ($)
California	2,139	17.0	23,635	13.1	11	308.6	13,057	965.8	14.7	451,503
New York	588	4.7	14,448	8.0	25	239.0	16,540	649.6	9.9	1,104,692
Florida	796	6.3	11,747	6.5	15	164.5	14,007	500.7	7.6	628,984
Pennsylvania	699	5.6	11,509	6.4	16	141.9	12,332	363.0	5.5	519,272
Texas	434	3.4	7,458	4.1	17	93.4	12,517	305.7	4.7	704,348
Michigan	715	5.7	8,880	4.9	12	110.4	12,431	296.2	4.5	414,239
Washington	684	5.4	7,016	3.9	10	89.5	12,755	295.3	4.5	431,661
North Carolina	535	4.2	10,446	5.8	20	110.1	10,540	278.8	4.3	521,067
Massachusetts	330	2.6	6,149	3.4	19	89.8	14,597	222.9	3.4	675,458
Illinois	247	2.0	4,861	2.7	20	75.6	15,552	201.8	3.1	816,984
Virginia	314	2.5	6,139	3.4	20	70.8	11,535	194.2	3.0	618,484
Oregon	652	5.2	4,942	2.7	8	56.0	11,332	178.9	2.7	274,356
New Jersey	159	1.3	3,567	2.0	22	61.7	17,293	159.9	2.4	1,005,761
Ohio	270	2.1	4,247	2.4	16	63.1	14,866	154.4	2.4	571,759
Maryland	230	1.8	3,998	2.2	17	55.9	13,991	151.0	2.3	656,622
Wisconsin	475	3.8	5,615	3.1	12	62.9	11,194	148.1	2.3	311,796
Arizona	315	2.5	3,329	1.9	11	41.9	12,597	121.0	1.8	384,089
Georgia	255	2.0	3,358	1.9	13	41.9	12,476	109.2	1.7	428,341
Tennessee	173	1.4	2,711	1.5	16	32.1	11,829	96.9	1.5	560,324
Colorado	158	1.3	2,548	1.4	16	30.5	11,976	93.4	1.4	591,000
Missouri	265	2.1	2,847	1.6	11	31.6	11,107	87.6	1.3	330,411
Connecticut	119	0.9	1,835	1.0	15	30.7	16,756	77.1	1.2	648,143
South Carolina	162	1.3	2,742	1.5	17	30.0	10,923	74.1	1.1	457,457
Minnesota	211	1.7	2,603	1.4	12	30.2	11,606	73.2	1.1	346,905
Maine	123	1.0	1,953	1.1	16	24.5	12,567	55.8	0.9	453,325
Kansas	84	0.7	1,781	1.0	21	19.9	11,197	48.9	0.7	581,702
Kentucky	83	0.7	1,387	0.8	17	16.9	12,150	47.0	0.7	566,807
Alabama	131	1.0	1,383	0.8	11	17.2	12,411	46.0	0.7	350,794
Oklahoma	64	0.5	1,137	0.6	18	14.2	12,499	38.3	0.6	598,891
Arkansas	82	0.7	824	0.5	10	8.8	10,698	29.5	0.5	360,305
Mississippi	97	0.8	971	0.5	10	11.3	11,677	28.8	0.4	297,247
Idaho	90	0.7	996	0.6	11	10.6	10,668	28.0	0.4	310,611
New Mexico	56	0.4	763	0.4	14	9.0	11,733	24.7	0.4	441,732
Vermont	64	0.5	818	0.5	13	10.4	12,740	24.1	0.4	376,844
Montana	55	0.4	760	0.4	14	8.3	10,867	23.9	0.4	434,582
West Virginia	70	0.6	715	0.4	10	7.7	10,794	22.7	0.3	323,929
Nebraska	50	0.4	685	0.4	14	7.2	10,575	22.3	0.3	445,620
New Hampshire	69	0.5	687	0.4	10	8.3	12,074	22.1	0.3	320,855
Nevada	57	0.5	448	0.2	8	5.4	12,092	21.2	0.3	371,246
Utah	46	0.4	688	0.4	15	6.6	9,626	20.7	0.3	450,652
North Dakota	27	0.2	584	0.3	22	5.8	9,974	15.8	0.2	583,481
Alaska	19	0.2	274	0.2	14	5.4	19,715	12.3	0.2	646,684
South Dakota	61	0.5	500	0.3	8	4.7	9,478	12.3	0.2	201,148

Source: 1997 *Economic Census*. The states are in descending order of revenues or establishments (if revenue data are missing for the majority). The symbol (D) appears when data are withheld to prevent disclosure of competitive information. States marked with (D) are sorted by number of establishments. A dash (-) indicates that the data element cannot be calculated. * indicates the midpoint of a range; 175, for example is the range 100-249. Shaded *states* on the state map indicate those states which have proportionately greater representation in the industry than would be indicated by the state's population; the ratio is based on total revenues or number of establishments. Shaded *regions* indicate where the industry is regionally most concentrated.

NAICS 623990 - RESIDENTIAL CARE FACILITIES NEC

GENERAL STATISTICS

Year	Establishments (number)	Employment (number)	Payroll ($ million)	Revenues ($ million)	Employees per Establishment (number)	Revenues per Establishment ($)	Payroll per Employee ($)
1997	5,933	135,468	2,544.0	5,360.0	22.8	903,422	18,779

Source: Economic Census of the United States, 1997. This is a newly defined industry. Data for prior years were unavailable at the time of publication but may become available over time.

INDICES OF CHANGE

Year	Establishments (number)	Employment (number)	Payroll ($ million)	Revenues ($ million)	Employees per Establishment (number)	Revenues per Establishment ($)	Payroll per Employee ($)
1997	100.0	100.0	100.0	100.0	100.0	100.0	100.0

Sources: Same as General Statistics. The values shown reflect change from the base year, 1997. Values above 100 mean greater than 1997, values below 100 mean less than 1997, and a value of 100 in the 1982-96 or 1998-2001 period means same as 1997. Values followed by a 'p' are projections by the editors; 'e' stands for extrapolation. Data are the most recent available at this level of detail.

SIC INDUSTRIES RELATED TO NAICS 623990

Each new NAICS code represents an industry that used to be part of an SIC or a part of several SIC industries. Data in this table are shown to provide transitional information for these cases. All available data for the precursor SIC(s) are shown. Even if only a part of an SIC is included in the NAICS, *all* data for the SIC are reproduced. If the SIC industry is not marked as being a part (pt) of the NAICS, the entire industry is embedded in the NAICS data. The SIC composition of the new industry provides some hints of the relative importance of its "ancestors." Data marked with a 'p' are projected. Projections begin with 1982 data. Data earlier than 1990 are not shown but are reflected in the projections.

SIC	Industry	1990	1991	1992	1993	1994	1995	1996	1997
8361	**Residential Care (pt)**								
	Establishments (number)	20,967	22,267	27,143	27,912	28,937	29,937	31,850p	33,440p
	Employment (thousands)	416.8	449.7	457.3	491.1	518.2	549.9	571.8p	598.0p
	Revenues ($ million)	4,626.0	4,934.0	4,853.0	5,421.0	5,905.0	6,437.0	7,244.0	7,377.7p

Source: Economic Census of the United States, 1992, annual surveys of economic sectors conducted by the Bureau of the Census, and estimates or projections based on the 1982-1992 period; not all data are shown. 'e' marks estimates made by the editors; 'p' indicates projections based on time series. A dash (-) indicates that data for this SIC or year were not available. The abbreviation (pt) next to the industry name indicates that only a part of the industry is present within the NAICS data. If no (pt) is shown, the entire industry is contained within the NAICS data.

SELECTED RATIOS

For 1997	Avg. of Information	Analyzed Industry	Index	For 1997	Avg. of Information	Analyzed Industry	Index
Employees per establishment	21	23	109	Payroll per establishment	585,591	428,788	73
Revenue per establishment	1,370,364	903,422	66	Payroll as % of revenue	43	47	111
Revenue per employee	65,262	39,567	61	Payroll per employee	27,888	18,779	67

Sources: Same as General Statistics. The 'Average' column represents the average for the industry sector, in 1997, where the currently shown industry is classified. The Index shows the relationship between the Average and the Analyzed Industry. For example, 100 means that they are equal; 500 that the Analyzed Industry is five times the average; 50 means that the Analyzed Industry is half the national average. The abbreviation 'na' is used to show that data are 'not available'.

LEADING COMPANIES   Number shown: **12**   Total sales ($ mil): **3,356**   Total employment (000): **92.2**

Company Name	Address				CEO Name	Phone	Co. Type	Sales ($ mil)	Empl. (000)
HRC Manor Care Inc.	333 N Summit St	Toledo	OH	43604	Paul A. Ormond	419-252-5500	P	2,209	55.0
Res-Care Inc.	10140 Linn Station	Louisville	KY	40223	Ronald G Geary	502-394-2100	P	523	18.5
Alterra Healthcare Corp.	450 N Sunnyslope	Brookfield	WI	53005	William F Lasky	262-789-9565	P	244	6.6
Res-Care Inc	10140 Linn Station	Louisville	KY	40223	Ronald Geary	502-394-2100	D	175*	7.3
Brookdale Living Communities	77 W Wacker Dr	Chicago	IL	60601	Michael W Reschke	312-977-3700	P	78	1.7
Res-Care Inc. Youth Services Div.	10140 Linn Station	Louisville	KY	40223		502-394-2100	D	43*	0.8
Golden Rain Foundation	P O Box 2070	Walnut Creek	CA	94595		925-988-7700	R	33*	0.5
Hazelden Foundation	P O Box 11	Center City	MN	55012	Jerry W Spicer	612-257-4010	R	28*	0.9
Comprehensive Systems Inc.	PO Box 457	Charles City	IA	50616		515-228-4842	R	10*	0.5
Franciscan Villa	3601 S Chicago Ave	S. Milwaukee	WI	53172	Roger DeMark	414-764-4100	S	10*	0.3
Community Alternatives	121 S Broadview	Cape Girardeau	MO	63701	Ron Geary	573-334-1088	S	2*	<0.1
Retirement Communities	3155 Hickory Hill	Memphis	TN	38115	Charles S Trammell Jr	901-794-2598	R	1*	<0.1

Source: Ward's Business Directory of U.S. Private and Public Companies, Volumes 1 and 2, 2000. The company type code used is as follows: P - Public, R - Private, S - Subsidiary, D - Division, J - Joint Venture, A - Affiliate, G - Group, N - Company type not reported. Sales are in millions of dollars, employees are in thousands. An asterisk (*) indicates an estimated sales volume. The symbol < stands for 'less than'. Company names and addresses are truncated, in some cases, to fit into the available space.

REPRESENTATIVE NONPROFIT ORGANIZATIONS

Organization Name	Address				Phone	Income Range ($ mil)
Alabama Youth Home Inc	PO Box 66	Westover	AL	35185	205-678-7734	1-5
Arrow Project	350 N Sam Houston Pky	Houston	TX	77060	281-931-1190	10-19
Arrowhead Ranch	12200 104th St	Coal Valley	IL	61240	309-799-7044	5-9
Board of Child Care, Methodist Church Inc	3300 Gaither Rd	Baltimore	MD	21244	410-922-2100	10-19
Bonnie Brae	3415 Valley Rd	Liberty Corner	NJ	07938		10-19
Boys Hope & Girls Hope	12120 Bridgeton Square	Bridgeton	MO	63044	314-298-1250	10-19
Boys and Girls Home of Nebraska Inc	PO Box 1197	Sioux City	IA	51102	712-258-2470	5-9
Burlington United Methodist Family Services Inc	PO Box 69	Burlington	WV	26710		5-9
Care Development	970 Illinois Ave	Bangor	ME	04401	207-945-4240	10-19
Children First Inc	2460 Terry Rd Ste 27Q	Jackson	MS	39204		5-9
Childrens Home Inc	5515 Old Walcott Rd	Paragould	AR	72450	870-239-4031	1-5
Childrens Home of Virginia Baptists Inc	6900 Hickory Rd	Petersburg	VA	23803	804-590-2080	1-5
Christian Family Care Agency Inc	3603 N 7th Ave	Phoenix	AZ	85013	602-234-1935	1-5
Consuelo Zobel Alger Foundation	110 N Hotel St	Honolulu	HI	96817	808-532-3939	10-19
Covenant House Alaska	PO Box 104640	Anchorage	AK	99510		1-5
Covenant House Florida Inc	733 Breakers Ave	Ft Lauderdale	FL	33304	954-561-5559	10-19
Covenant House Washington D C	1015 15th St NW	Washington	DC	20005		1-5
Elizabeth W Murphey School Inc	42 Kings Hwy E	Dover	DE	19901	302-734-7478	1-5
Epworth Village Inc	PO Box 503	York	NE	68467		1-5
Familiesfirst Inc	2100 5th St	Davis	CA	95616	530-753-0220	30-39
Family AIDS Center for Treatment and Support Facts	18 Parkis Ave	Providence	RI	02907	401-521-3603	1-5
Georgia Sheriffs Youth Homes Inc	PO Box 1000	Stockbridge	GA	30281	770-914-1076	10-19
Grace Enterprises	19537 Chiwawa Loop Rd	Leavenworth	WA	98826		1-5
Graham-Windham	33 Irving PL	New York	NY	10003	212-529-6445	30-39
Gulf Coast Teaching Family Services Incorporated	401 Whitney Ave	Gretna	LA	70056	504-361-9950	10-19
Home of the Innocents	485 E Gray St	Louisville	KY	40202	502-561-6600	10-19
Hope House Inc	11461 Lone Star Rd	Nampa	ID	83651	208-466-4673	1-5
Kansas Childrens Service League	1365 N Custer	Wichita	KS	67203	316-942-4261	20-29
Kids Crossing Inc	125 Swope Ave	Colorado SPGS	CO	80909	719-632-4771	5-9
Kidspeace National Centers for Kids in Crisis Inc	3438 RT 309	Orefield	PA	18069		50+
Lighthouse Youth Services Inc	1501 Madison Rd	Cincinnati	OH	45206	513-221-3350	10-19
Living in Safe Alternative Incorporated	159 Old Bound Line Rd	Wolcott	CT	06716		1-5
Looking Glass Youth and Family Services Inc	72 B Centennial Loop	Eugene	OR	97401	541-686-2688	5-9
New Life Homes Inc	PO Box 15676	Chattanooga	TN	37415	423-877-7897	1-5
Oikos Incorporated	PO Box 11491	Reno	NV	89510		1-5
Orchards Childrens Services Inc	30215 Southfield Rd	Southfield	MI	48076	248-258-2099	20-29
Orion House Inc	PO Box 175	Newport	NH	03773	603-863-1114	1-5
Our Home Inc	334 3rd St SW	Huron	SD	57350	605-352-1554	1-5
Pleasant Run Childrens Home Inc	2400 N Tibbs Ave	Indianapolis	IN	46222	317-693-9222	5-9
Sand Springs Home	PO Box 278	Sand Springs	OK	74063	918-245-1391	5-9
St Aemilian-Lakeside Inc	8901 W Capitol Dr	Milwaukee	WI	53222	414-463-1880	5-9
St James Home of Duluth Inc	4321 Allendale Ave	Duluth	MN	55803		5-9
The Methodist Home for Children Inc	PO Box 10917	Raleigh	NC	27605	919-828-0345	20-29
Thornwell Home for Children	PO Box 60	Clinton	SC	29325	864-833-1232	10-19
Wayside Youth & Family Support Network	75 Fountain St	Framingham	MA	01702	508-620-7963	10-19
Youth Development Inc	6301 Central Ave NW	Albuquerque	NM	87105	505-831-6038	10-19

Source: National Directory of Nonprofit Organizations, 2000, Volumes 1 and 2, The Taft Group. The table shows a selection of organizations for illustration and does not constitute a complete selection from the source. The organizations are arranged in alphabetical order.

LOCATION BY STATE AND REGIONAL CONCENTRATION

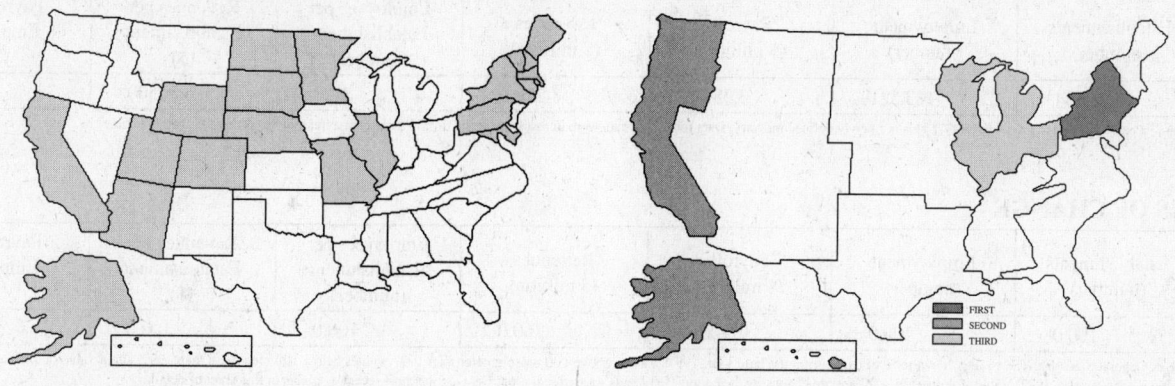

INDUSTRY DATA BY STATE

State	Establishments Total (number)	% of U.S.	Employment Total (number)	% of U.S.	Per Estab.	Payroll Total ($ mil.)	Per Empl. ($)	Revenues Total ($ mil.)	% of U.S.	Per Estab. ($)
California	1,048	17.7	21,209	15.7	20	390.0	18,391	792.6	14.8	756,336
New York	377	6.4	12,318	9.1	33	288.6	23,429	583.0	10.9	1,546,520
Pennsylvania	241	4.1	7,108	5.2	29	142.8	20,096	311.9	5.8	1,294,058
Illinois	184	3.1	6,256	4.6	34	141.6	22,634	260.3	4.9	1,414,560
Texas	250	4.2	6,263	4.6	25	112.2	17,911	259.0	4.8	1,036,184
Massachusetts	205	3.5	5,521	4.1	27	113.5	20,561	217.1	4.1	1,059,205
Michigan	240	4.0	4,746	3.5	20	92.0	19,392	197.7	3.7	823,913
Florida	234	3.9	5,231	3.9	22	92.8	17,744	189.2	3.5	808,457
Arizona	132	2.2	4,252	3.1	32	77.7	18,281	167.3	3.1	1,267,288
Ohio	167	2.8	4,168	3.1	25	74.9	17,970	159.3	3.0	954,162
Missouri	120	2.0	4,056	3.0	34	65.3	16,105	138.2	2.6	1,151,858
Nebraska	26	0.4	1,591	1.2	61	37.1	23,341	129.0	2.4	4,959,885
Maryland	126	2.1	3,124	2.3	25	61.6	19,706	121.2	2.3	962,270
North Carolina	137	2.3	2,658	2.0	19	46.1	17,332	110.2	2.1	804,620
Colorado	106	1.8	2,601	1.9	25	50.1	19,263	106.0	2.0	999,726
Minnesota	152	2.6	3,029	2.2	20	53.5	17,657	98.3	1.8	647,007
Tennessee	164	2.8	2,422	1.8	15	36.5	15,053	86.5	1.6	527,524
Wisconsin	154	2.6	2,182	1.6	14	38.1	17,449	78.6	1.5	510,506
Connecticut	75	1.3	1,792	1.3	24	40.6	22,684	77.6	1.4	1,034,413
Georgia	99	1.7	1,844	1.4	19	30.7	16,672	71.5	1.3	721,909
Kentucky	58	1.0	1,698	1.3	29	29.0	17,102	66.2	1.2	1,141,776
New Jersey	92	1.6	1,660	1.2	18	33.7	20,320	66.1	1.2	718,609
Washington	118	2.0	1,659	1.2	14	32.4	19,516	65.3	1.2	553,042
South Carolina	73	1.2	1,777	1.3	24	28.0	15,768	62.1	1.2	850,534
Virginia	95	1.6	1,613	1.2	17	22.1	13,686	61.0	1.1	641,905
Alabama	84	1.4	1,395	1.0	17	20.9	15,003	50.9	1.0	606,250
Oklahoma	117	2.0	1,617	1.2	14	22.3	13,773	49.3	0.9	421,393
Utah	26	0.4	1,278	0.9	49	18.5	14,442	41.7	0.8	1,603,231
Oregon	138	2.3	1,104	0.8	8	17.3	15,655	36.0	0.7	261,116
West Virginia	45	0.8	1,013	0.7	23	16.3	16,134	32.2	0.6	716,400
New Hampshire	43	0.7	821	0.6	19	16.3	19,821	32.2	0.6	748,442
Maine	54	0.9	626	0.5	12	12.7	20,299	30.8	0.6	570,296
New Mexico	39	0.7	755	0.6	19	12.8	16,948	29.4	0.5	754,718
Rhode Island	42	0.7	877	0.6	21	15.2	17,373	29.3	0.5	697,881
Mississippi	24	0.4	471	0.3	20	7.4	15,777	22.5	0.4	936,708
Arkansas	51	0.9	591	0.4	12	8.7	14,766	22.1	0.4	433,255
South Dakota	19	0.3	581	0.4	31	9.3	15,988	20.0	0.4	1,050,842
D.C.	41	0.7	597	0.4	15	10.5	17,625	19.6	0.4	479,098
Vermont	21	0.4	436	0.3	21	7.0	16,122	19.2	0.4	913,810
North Dakota	18	0.3	529	0.4	29	8.9	16,767	16.5	0.3	916,333
Montana	31	0.5	437	0.3	14	7.6	17,371	14.7	0.3	473,000
Alaska	13	0.2	331	0.2	25	7.5	22,644	13.7	0.3	1,055,231
Idaho	22	0.4	416	0.3	19	6.4	15,337	13.6	0.3	618,000
Nevada	20	0.3	362	0.3	18	6.5	17,854	13.2	0.2	661,100
Wyoming	14	0.2	311	0.2	22	4.8	15,431	10.1	0.2	723,714

Source: 1997 Economic Census. The states are in descending order of revenues or establishments (if revenue data are missing for the majority). The symbol (D) appears when data are withheld to prevent disclosure of competitive information. States marked with (D) are sorted by number of establishments. A dash (-) indicates that the data element cannot be calculated. * indicates the midpoint of a range; 175, for example is the range 100-249. Shaded *states* on the state map indicate those states which have proportionately greater representation in the industry than would be indicated by the state's population; the ratio is based on total revenues or number of establishments. Shaded *regions* indicate where the industry is regionally most concentrated.

NAICS 624110 - CHILD AND YOUTH SERVICES

GENERAL STATISTICS

Year	Establishments (number)	Employment (number)	Payroll ($ million)	Revenues ($ million)	Employees per Establishment (number)	Revenues per Establishment ($)	Payroll per Employee ($)
1997	12,734	183,521	3,381.0	8,258.0	14.4	648,500	18,423

Source: Economic Census of the United States, 1997. This is a newly defined industry. Data for prior years were unavailable at the time of publication but may become available over time.

INDICES OF CHANGE

Year	Establishments (number)	Employment (number)	Payroll ($ million)	Revenues ($ million)	Employees per Establishment (number)	Revenues per Establishment ($)	Payroll per Employee ($)
1997	100.0	100.0	100.0	100.0	100.0	100.0	100.0

Sources: Same as General Statistics. The values shown reflect change from the base year, 1997. Values above 100 mean greater than 1997, values below 100 mean less than 1997, and a value of 100 in the 1982-96 or 1998-2001 period means same as 1997. Values followed by a 'p' are projections by the editors; 'e' stands for extrapolation. Data are the most recent available at this level of detail.

SIC INDUSTRIES RELATED TO NAICS 624110

Each new NAICS code represents an industry that used to be part of an SIC or a part of several SIC industries. Data in this table are shown to provide transitional information for these cases. All available data for the precursor SIC(s) are shown. Even if only a part of an SIC is included in the NAICS, *all* data for the SIC are reproduced. If the SIC industry is not marked as being a part (pt) of the NAICS, the entire industry is embedded in the NAICS data. The SIC composition of the new industry provides some hints of the relative importance of its "ancestors." Data marked with a 'p' are projected. Projections begin with 1982 data. Data earlier than 1990 are not shown but are reflected in the projections.

SIC	Industry	1990	1991	1992	1993	1994	1995	1996	1997
8322	**Individual & Family Services (pt)**								
	Establishments (number)	27,580	29,630	36,232	36,795	37,138	37,311	40,418p	42,214p
	Employment (thousands)	408.4	440.7	476.8	506.6	536.5	570.4	595.7p	625.7p
	Revenues ($ million)	-	-	17,740.0	-	-	-		

Source: Economic Census of the United States, 1992, annual surveys of economic sectors conducted by the Bureau of the Census, and estimates or projections based on the 1982-1992 period; not all data are shown. 'e' marks estimates made by the editors; 'p' indicates projections based on time series. A dash (-) indicates that data for this SIC or year were not available. The abbreviation (pt) next to the industry name indicates that only a part of the industry is present within the NAICS data. If no (pt) is shown, the entire industry is contained within the NAICS data.

SELECTED RATIOS

For 1997	Avg. of Information	Analyzed Industry	Index	For 1997	Avg. of Information	Analyzed Industry	Index
Employees per establishment	21	14	69	Payroll per establishment	585,591	265,510	45
Revenue per establishment	1,370,364	648,500	47	Payroll as % of revenue	43	41	96
Revenue per employee	65,262	44,998	69	Payroll per employee	27,888	18,423	66

Sources: Same as General Statistics. The 'Average' column represents the average for the industry sector, in 1997, where the currently shown industry is classified. The Index shows the relationship between the Average and the Analyzed Industry. For example, 100 means that they are equal; 500 that the Analyzed Industry is five times the average; 50 means that the Analyzed Industry is half the national average. The abbreviation 'na' is used to show that data are 'not available'.

LEADING COMPANIES

No company data available for this industry.

LOCATION BY STATE AND REGIONAL CONCENTRATION

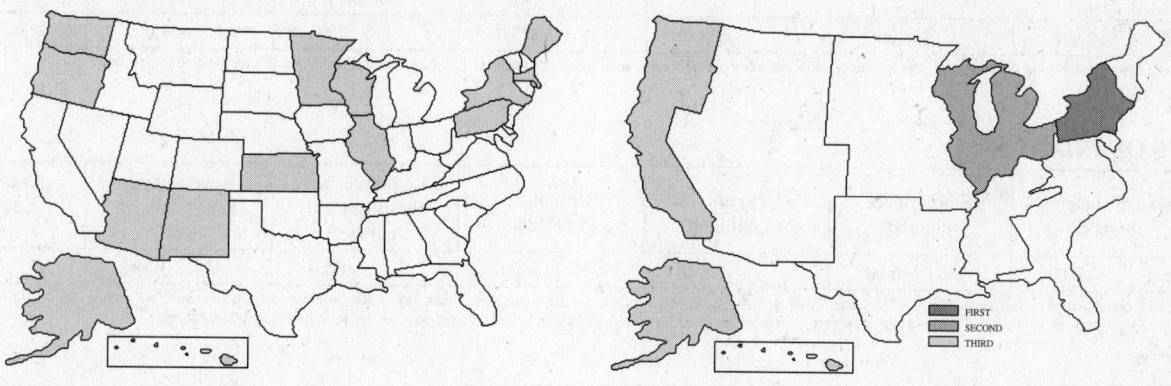

FIRST
SECOND
THIRD

INDUSTRY DATA BY STATE

State	Establishments Total (number)	Establishments % of U.S.	Employment Total (number)	Employment % of U.S.	Employment Per Estab.	Payroll Total ($ mil.)	Payroll Per Empl. ($)	Revenues Total ($ mil.)	Revenues % of U.S.	Revenues Per Estab. ($)
New York	942	7.4	22,175	12.1	24	466.7	21,047	1,102.4	13.3	1,170,232
California	1,468	11.5	20,443	11.1	14	383.2	18,743	980.0	11.9	667,550
Illinois	639	5.0	11,950	6.5	19	235.7	19,725	540.1	6.5	845,202
Pennsylvania	654	5.1	10,686	5.8	16	202.3	18,934	478.8	5.8	732,049
Texas	823	6.5	10,683	5.8	13	177.9	16,653	420.1	5.1	510,400
Florida	598	4.7	8,650	4.7	14	151.0	17,452	357.9	4.3	598,490
Massachusetts	399	3.1	8,211	4.5	21	142.8	17,387	317.3	3.8	795,193
Ohio	449	3.5	6,477	3.5	14	122.7	18,942	313.7	3.8	698,570
Michigan	406	3.2	5,776	3.1	14	109.3	18,924	270.0	3.3	665,143
Washington	304	2.4	4,353	2.4	14	75.1	17,245	174.0	2.1	572,421
Wisconsin	356	2.8	3,914	2.1	11	72.6	18,547	171.5	2.1	481,694
Indiana	340	2.7	4,284	2.3	13	69.4	16,203	163.8	2.0	481,835
Minnesota	259	2.0	3,333	1.8	13	60.9	18,286	161.2	2.0	622,494
Georgia	267	2.1	2,970	1.6	11	57.4	19,310	160.9	1.9	602,610
Oregon	227	1.8	3,001	1.6	13	53.6	17,855	151.3	1.8	666,670
New Jersey	268	2.1	3,465	1.9	13	68.6	19,787	148.7	1.8	554,765
North Carolina	301	2.4	3,254	1.8	11	53.5	16,452	136.3	1.7	452,944
Arizona	200	1.6	3,602	2.0	18	62.4	17,317	135.7	1.6	678,355
Virginia	240	1.9	2,495	1.4	10	52.4	21,002	128.9	1.6	537,021
Kansas	173	1.4	2,505	1.4	14	44.2	17,656	115.8	1.4	669,173
Maryland	173	1.4	2,618	1.4	15	50.7	19,365	115.5	1.4	667,728
Alabama	171	1.3	1,751	1.0	10	29.2	16,684	106.1	1.3	620,351
Missouri	181	1.4	2,332	1.3	13	40.7	17,460	97.5	1.2	538,547
Tennessee	198	1.6	2,155	1.2	11	40.9	18,963	92.6	1.1	467,475
Connecticut	186	1.5	2,174	1.2	12	39.5	18,181	88.8	1.1	477,215
Rhode Island	59	0.5	1,512	0.8	26	29.9	19,791	86.1	1.0	1,458,966
Maine	102	0.8	1,884	1.0	18	34.1	18,082	73.1	0.9	716,363
Oklahoma	170	1.3	1,629	0.9	10	29.6	18,145	69.1	0.8	406,188
Louisiana	163	1.3	2,163	1.2	13	29.3	13,550	67.3	0.8	413,166
New Mexico	129	1.0	1,795	1.0	14	28.3	15,757	66.1	0.8	512,488
Utah	91	0.7	1,205	0.7	13	25.9	21,520	55.7	0.7	612,121
Hawaii	82	0.6	999	0.5	12	24.8	24,793	53.0	0.6	646,341
Iowa	128	1.0	1,279	0.7	10	19.4	15,188	46.7	0.6	364,641
South Carolina	136	1.1	1,141	0.6	8	18.4	16,117	44.6	0.5	327,846
Arkansas	117	0.9	1,163	0.6	10	18.6	15,991	41.1	0.5	351,684
West Virginia	104	0.8	879	0.5	8	14.5	16,474	35.3	0.4	339,865
Mississippi	79	0.6	819	0.4	10	14.1	17,232	31.6	0.4	400,443
Alaska	45	0.4	841	0.5	19	14.0	16,591	28.1	0.3	623,733
Idaho	86	0.7	680	0.4	8	11.5	16,978	26.7	0.3	310,047
Vermont	45	0.4	428	0.2	10	8.8	20,668	20.6	0.2	458,556
North Dakota	51	0.4	637	0.3	12	6.4	10,003	19.0	0.2	373,529
Montana	60	0.5	408	0.2	7	6.0	14,593	16.6	0.2	276,467
Delaware	38	0.3	352	0.2	9	6.5	18,597	14.4	0.2	379,842
South Dakota	46	0.4	400	0.2	9	5.6	13,947	13.8	0.2	300,739

Source: 1997 Economic Census. The states are in descending order of revenues or establishments (if revenue data are missing for the majority). The symbol (D) appears when data are withheld to prevent disclosure of competitive information. States marked with (D) are sorted by number of establishments. A dash (-) indicates that the data element cannot be calculated. * indicates the midpoint of a range; 175, for example is the range 100-249. Shaded states on the state map indicate those states which have proportionately greater representation in the industry than would be indicated by the state's population; the ratio is based on total revenues or number of establishments. Shaded regions indicate where the industry is regionally most concentrated.

NAICS 624120 - SERVICES FOR THE ELDERLY AND PERSONS WITH DISABILITIES

GENERAL STATISTICS

Year	Establishments (number)	Employment (number)	Payroll ($ million)	Revenues ($ million)	Employees per Establishment (number)	Revenues per Establishment ($)	Payroll per Employee ($)
1997	12,936	258,906	3,654.0	9,025.0	20.0	697,665	14,113

Source: Economic Census of the United States, 1997. This is a newly defined industry. Data for prior years were unavailable at the time of publication but may become available over time.

INDICES OF CHANGE

Year	Establishments (number)	Employment (number)	Payroll ($ million)	Revenues ($ million)	Employees per Establishment (number)	Revenues per Establishment ($)	Payroll per Employee ($)
1997	100.0	100.0	100.0	100.0	100.0	100.0	100.0

Sources: Same as General Statistics. The values shown reflect change from the base year, 1997. Values above 100 mean greater than 1997, values below 100 mean less than 1997, and a value of 100 in the 1982-96 or 1998-2001 period means same as 1997. Values followed by a 'p' are projections by the editors; 'e' stands for extrapolation. Data are the most recent available at this level of detail.

SIC INDUSTRIES RELATED TO NAICS 624120

Each new NAICS code represents an industry that used to be part of an SIC or a part of several SIC industries. Data in this table are shown to provide transitional information for these cases. All available data for the precursor SIC(s) are shown. Even if only a part of an SIC is included in the NAICS, *all* data for the SIC are reproduced. If the SIC industry is not marked as being a part (pt) of the NAICS, the entire industry is embedded in the NAICS data. The SIC composition of the new industry provides some hints of the relative importance of its "ancestors." Data marked with a 'p' are projected. Projections begin with 1982 data. Data earlier than 1990 are not shown but are reflected in the projections.

SIC	Industry	1990	1991	1992	1993	1994	1995	1996	1997
8322	**Individual & Family Services (pt)**								
	Establishments (number)	27,580	29,630	36,232	36,795	37,138	37,311	40,418p	42,214p
	Employment (thousands)	408.4	440.7	476.8	506.6	536.5	570.4	595.7p	625.7p
	Revenues ($ million)	-	-	17,740.0	-	-	-	-	-

Source: Economic Census of the United States, 1992, annual surveys of economic sectors conducted by the Bureau of the Census, and estimates or projections based on the 1982-1992 period; not all data are shown. 'e' marks estimates made by the editors; 'p' indicates projections based on time series. A dash (-) indicates that data for this SIC or year were not available. The abbreviation (pt) next to the industry name indicates that only a part of the industry is present within the NAICS data. If no (pt) is shown, the entire industry is contained within the NAICS data.

SELECTED RATIOS

For 1997	Avg. of Information	Analyzed Industry	Index	For 1997	Avg. of Information	Analyzed Industry	Index
Employees per establishment	21	20	95	Payroll per establishment	585,591	282,468	48
Revenue per establishment	1,370,364	697,665	51	Payroll as % of revenue	43	40	95
Revenue per employee	65,262	34,858	53	Payroll per employee	27,888	14,113	51

Sources: Same as General Statistics. The 'Average' column represents the average for the industry sector, in 1997, where the currently shown industry is classified. The Index shows the relationship between the Average and the Analyzed Industry. For example, 100 means that they are equal; 500 that the Analyzed Industry is five times the average; 50 means that the Analyzed Industry is half the national average. The abbreviation 'na' is used to show that data are 'not available'.

LEADING COMPANIES
No company data available for this industry.

LOCATION BY STATE AND REGIONAL CONCENTRATION

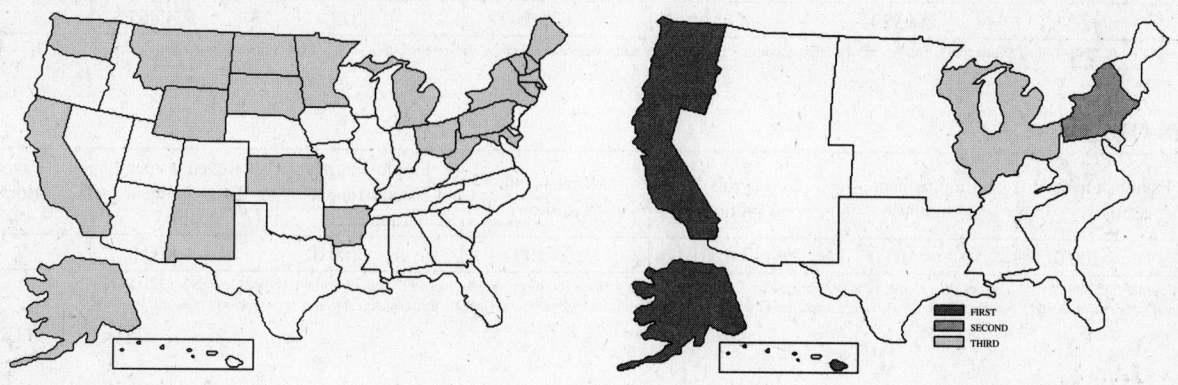

FIRST
SECOND
THIRD

INDUSTRY DATA BY STATE

State	Establishments Total (number)	% of U.S.	Employment Total (number)	% of U.S.	Per Estab.	Payroll Total ($ mil.)	Per Empl. ($)	Revenues Total ($ mil.)	% of U.S.	Per Estab. ($)
California	1,401	10.8	27,042	10.4	19	436.6	16,146	1,520.6	16.8	1,085,385
New York	1,067	8.2	30,923	11.9	29	541.8	17,522	1,126.1	12.5	1,055,427
Michigan	360	2.8	7,754	3.0	22	145.0	18,696	531.4	5.9	1,476,142
Pennsylvania	760	5.9	13,146	5.1	17	184.7	14,047	440.6	4.9	579,739
Ohio	466	3.6	10,142	3.9	22	137.2	13,529	407.6	4.5	874,723
Illinois	509	3.9	14,126	5.5	28	177.1	12,540	388.4	4.3	763,114
Massachusetts	420	3.2	10,361	4.0	25	154.2	14,886	365.8	4.1	870,857
Florida	519	4.0	8,196	3.2	16	123.7	15,091	308.0	3.4	593,482
Maryland	228	1.8	6,928	2.7	30	105.7	15,256	294.0	3.3	1,289,325
Texas	695	5.4	7,924	3.1	11	106.8	13,480	250.0	2.8	359,681
Connecticut	198	1.5	4,112	1.6	21	74.4	18,091	202.9	2.2	1,024,606
Washington	312	2.4	5,980	2.3	19	93.1	15,566	191.5	2.1	613,782
New Jersey	270	2.1	5,580	2.2	21	89.7	16,083	188.0	2.1	696,148
Minnesota	354	2.7	7,126	2.8	20	84.8	11,907	170.5	1.9	481,766
Wisconsin	343	2.7	6,473	2.5	19	77.7	12,008	165.1	1.8	481,277
Indiana	233	1.8	5,855	2.3	25	67.9	11,598	163.8	1.8	702,871
Arkansas	169	1.3	6,296	2.4	37	67.4	10,705	149.2	1.7	882,811
Missouri	375	2.9	6,141	2.4	16	71.1	11,581	149.2	1.7	397,931
Colorado	108	0.8	3,487	1.3	32	47.4	13,599	113.3	1.3	1,049,398
Tennessee	248	1.9	4,555	1.8	18	53.5	11,737	112.7	1.2	454,508
Virginia	254	2.0	4,325	1.7	17	49.0	11,331	107.4	1.2	422,654
West Virginia	146	1.1	5,022	1.9	34	53.7	10,685	105.4	1.2	721,596
Louisiana	249	1.9	5,549	2.1	22	51.2	9,234	101.3	1.1	406,683
New Hampshire	62	0.5	1,735	0.7	28	26.4	15,193	98.1	1.1	1,581,855
Arizona	171	1.3	2,921	1.1	17	36.9	12,644	94.2	1.0	551,006
Kansas	196	1.5	3,755	1.5	19	46.2	12,303	88.7	1.0	452,668
Kentucky	200	1.5	3,182	1.2	16	37.8	11,890	88.3	1.0	441,675
North Carolina	231	1.8	2,932	1.1	13	40.3	13,733	87.1	1.0	377,190
Georgia	165	1.3	2,593	1.0	16	38.2	14,725	82.2	0.9	498,036
Oregon	244	1.9	2,692	1.0	11	37.4	13,876	80.9	0.9	331,447
South Carolina	183	1.4	2,755	1.1	15	35.2	12,777	79.0	0.9	431,475
Maine	118	0.9	3,199	1.2	27	39.7	12,399	78.5	0.9	665,102
Iowa	209	1.6	3,855	1.5	18	32.2	8,351	73.9	0.8	353,593
Alabama	151	1.2	1,757	0.7	12	24.4	13,864	67.9	0.8	449,616
New Mexico	77	0.6	1,961	0.8	25	25.3	12,887	59.6	0.7	774,013
Oklahoma	164	1.3	2,126	0.8	13	27.8	13,056	48.7	0.5	296,750
Hawaii	70	0.5	1,341	0.5	19	18.7	13,927	38.8	0.4	554,871
North Dakota	66	0.5	1,661	0.6	25	17.9	10,806	34.4	0.4	521,000
Montana	84	0.6	1,481	0.6	18	15.5	10,437	34.0	0.4	404,893
South Dakota	43	0.3	1,342	0.5	31	16.0	11,902	33.0	0.4	766,535
Rhode Island	55	0.4	970	0.4	18	15.0	15,427	32.9	0.4	597,327
Vermont	78	0.6	697	0.3	9	11.3	16,166	29.1	0.3	373,333
Nebraska	102	0.8	878	0.3	9	12.1	13,746	27.7	0.3	272,049
Alaska	50	0.4	789	0.3	16	13.2	16,711	24.9	0.3	497,460
Idaho	80	0.6	930	0.4	12	9.4	10,103	18.4	0.2	229,662
Wyoming	51	0.4	989	0.4	19	10.4	10,471	18.1	0.2	355,451
Nevada	26	0.2	953	0.4	37	10.8	11,332	17.7	0.2	679,038
Delaware	43	0.3	518	0.2	12	6.8	13,031	17.0	0.2	395,651
Mississippi	50	0.4	619	0.2	12	8.0	12,847	16.6	0.2	332,820
Utah	35	0.3	462	0.2	13	6.9	14,942	14.1	0.2	403,514

Source: 1997 Economic Census. The states are in descending order of revenues or establishments (if revenue data are missing for the majority). The symbol (D) appears when data are withheld to prevent disclosure of competitive information. States marked with (D) are sorted by number of establishments. A dash (-) indicates that the data element cannot be calculated. * indicates the midpoint of a range; 175, for example is the range 100-249. Shaded *states* on the state map indicate those states which have proportionately greater representation in the industry than would be indicated by the state's population; the ratio is based on total revenues or number of establishments. Shaded *regions* indicate where the industry is regionally most concentrated.

NAICS 624190 - INDIVIDUAL AND FAMILY SERVICES NEC

GENERAL STATISTICS

Year	Establishments (number)	Employment (number)	Payroll ($ million)	Revenues ($ million)	Employees per Establishment (number)	Revenues per Establishment ($)	Payroll per Employee ($)
1997	20,537	268,929	4,858.0	11,806.0	13.1	574,865	18,064

Source: Economic Census of the United States, 1997. This is a newly defined industry. Data for prior years were unavailable at the time of publication but may become available over time.

INDICES OF CHANGE

Year	Establishments (number)	Employment (number)	Payroll ($ million)	Revenues ($ million)	Employees per Establishment (number)	Revenues per Establishment ($)	Payroll per Employee ($)
1997	100.0	100.0	100.0	100.0	100.0	100.0	100.0

Sources: Same as General Statistics. The values shown reflect change from the base year, 1997. Values above 100 mean greater than 1997, values below 100 mean less than 1997, and a value of 100 in the 1982-96 or 1998-2001 period means same as 1997. Values followed by a 'p' are projections by the editors; 'e' stands for extrapolation. Data are the most recent available at this level of detail.

SIC INDUSTRIES RELATED TO NAICS 624190

Each new NAICS code represents an industry that used to be part of an SIC or a part of several SIC industries. Data in this table are shown to provide transitional information for these cases. All available data for the precursor SIC(s) are shown. Even if only a part of an SIC is included in the NAICS, *all* data for the SIC are reproduced. If the SIC industry is not marked as being a part (pt) of the NAICS, the entire industry is embedded in the NAICS data. The SIC composition of the new industry provides some hints of the relative importance of its "ancestors." Data marked with a 'p' are projected. Projections begin with 1982 data. Data earlier than 1990 are not shown but are reflected in the projections.

SIC	Industry	1990	1991	1992	1993	1994	1995	1996	1997
8322	**Individual & Family Services (pt)**								
	Establishments (number)	27,580	29,630	36,232	36,795	37,138	37,311	40,418p	42,214p
	Employment (thousands)	408.4	440.7	476.8	506.6	536.5	570.4	595.7p	625.7p
	Revenues ($ million)	-	-	17,740.0	-	-	-	-	-

Source: Economic Census of the United States, 1992, annual surveys of economic sectors conducted by the Bureau of the Census, and estimates or projections based on the 1982-1992 period; not all data are shown. 'e' marks estimates made by the editors; 'p' indicates projections based on time series. A dash (-) indicates that data for this SIC or year were not available. The abbreviation (pt) next to the industry name indicates that only a part of the industry is present within the NAICS data. If no (pt) is shown, the entire industry is contained within the NAICS data.

SELECTED RATIOS

For 1997	Avg. of Information	Analyzed Industry	Index	For 1997	Avg. of Information	Analyzed Industry	Index
Employees per establishment	21	13	62	Payroll per establishment	585,591	236,549	40
Revenue per establishment	1,370,364	574,865	42	Payroll as % of revenue	43	41	96
Revenue per employee	65,262	43,900	67	Payroll per employee	27,888	18,064	65

Sources: Same as General Statistics. The 'Average' column represents the average for the industry sector, in 1997, where the currently shown industry is classified. The Index shows the relationship between the Average and the Analyzed Industry. For example, 100 means that they are equal; 500 that the Analyzed Industry is five times the average; 50 means that the Analyzed Industry is half the national average. The abbreviation 'na' is used to show that data are 'not available'.

LEADING COMPANIES   Number shown: **2**   Total sales ($ mil): **125**   Total employment (000): **3.2**

Company Name	Address				CEO Name	Phone	Co. Type	Sales ($ mil)	Empl. (000)
Children's Comprehensive	3401 West End Ave	Nashville	TN	37203	William J. Ballard	615-250-0000	P	116	2.8
Almost Family	9337 Liberty Rd	Randallstown	MD	21133	Mary Yarmuth	410-655-9900	S	9*	0.4

Source: Ward's Business Directory of U.S. Private and Public Companies, Volumes 1 and 2, 2000. The company type code used is as follows: P - Public, R - Private, S - Subsidiary, D - Division, J - Joint Venture, A - Affiliate, G - Group, N - Company type not reported. Sales are in millions of dollars, employees are in thousands. An asterisk (*) indicates an estimated sales volume. The symbol < stands for 'less than'. Company names and addresses are truncated, in some cases, to fit into the available space.

REPRESENTATIVE NONPROFIT ORGANIZATIONS

Organization Name	Address				Phone	Income Range ($ mil)
Accion Social De Puerto Rico Inc	Apartado 3930	Guaynabo	PR	00970		5-9
Action for Boston Community Development	178 Tremont St	Boston	MA	02111		50+
Aging Community Coordinated Enterprises	PO Box 4666	Medford	OR	97501		5-9
Alive Hospice Inc	PO Box 23588	Nashville	TN	37202	615-327-1085	10-19
Alliance Community Hospital	264 E Rice St	Alliance	OH	44601	330-829-4000	50+
Alphapointe Association for the Bli ND	1844 Broadway St	Kansas City	MO	64108	816-421-5848	10-19
American Association of Retired Persons	601 E St NW A1-350	Washington	DC	20049		50+
Appleton Prison Corporation	PO Box 34	Appleton	MN	56208		50+
Arc Inc	PO Box 1016	Boise	ID	83701	208-343-5583	1-5
Area Agency on Aging Region I Inc	1366 E Thomas Rd	Phoenix	AZ	85014	602-264-2255	10-19
Area Agency on Aging of Southeast Arkansas Inc	PO Box 8569	Pine Bluff	AR	71611		10-19
Areawide Aging Agency Inc	3200 NW 48th Ste 104	Oklahoma City	OK	73112	405-942-8500	5-9
Aware Inc	118 E 7th St	Anaconda	MT	59711	406-563-8117	5-9
Bethphage	4980 South 118th St	Omaha	NE	68137	402-896-3884	50+
Central Valley Regional Center Inc	5168 N Blythe Ave	Fresno	CA	93722	559-276-4300	50+
Child Care Resources Inc	700 Kenilworth Ave	Charlotte	NC	28204	704-376-6697	40-49
Childcare Resources for Jefferson Shelby and Walker Counties	1904 1st Ave N	Birmingham	AL	35203	205-252-1991	10-19
Children and Families of Iowa	1111 University	Des Moines	IA	50314	515-288-1981	10-19
Christiana Care Home Health and Community Services Inc	One Reads Way Ste 100	New Castle	DE	19720	302-323-8212	30-39
Comm-Care Corporation	763 Avery Blvd N	Ridgeland	MS	39157		30-39
Communicare Inc	1311 N Dixie Ave	Elizabethtown	KY	42701	270-765-2605	10-19
Community Entry Services Inc	2441 Peck Ave	Riverton	WY	82501	307-332-7616	5-9
Community and Econ Dev Assoc of Cook County Inc	208 S Lasalle STR 1900	Chicago	IL	60604	312-207-5444	50+
Connecticut Childrens Medical Center	282 Washington St	Hartford	CT	06106	860-545-9195	50+
Crane Fund	4740 NW 97th PL	Miami	FL	33178		50+
Denver Options Inc	5250 Leetsdale Dr Ste 200	Denver	CO	80246	303-753-6688	20-29
District Council 37 Health and Security Fund	125 Barclay St	New York	NY	10007	212-815-1000	50+
Easter Seals New Hampshire Inc	555 Auburn Street	Manchester	NH	03103	603-623-8863	20-29
Economic Opportunity Board of Clark County	2228 Comstock Dr	Las Vegas	NV	89030	702-647-2010	20-29
Genus Credit Management Corporation	5950 Symphony Woods	Columbia	MD	21044	410-997-0040	50+
Goodwill Industries of Central Indiana Inc	1635 W Michigan St	Indianapolis	IN	46222	317-692-2539	20-29
Goodwill Industries of New Mexico	5000 San Mateo NE	Albuquerque	NM	87109	505-881-6792	5-9
Goodwill Industries of Northern New England	PO Box 8600	Portland	ME	04104	207-874-9543	20-29
Goodwill Industries of SE Wisc & Metro Chicago	6055 N 91st St	Milwaukee	WI	53225	414-358-4260	50+
Hawaii Carpenters Apprenticeship Training Trust Fund	1199 Dillingham	Honolulu	HI	96817		5-9
Health Care and Rehabilitation Services of SE Vermont	1 Hospital CT	Bellows Falls	VT	05101	802-463-3947	10-19
Hitchcock Rehabilitation Center Inc	690 Medical Park Dr	Aiken	SC	29801	803-648-8344	5-9
Hope Community Resources Inc	540 W Intern Airport	Anchorage	AK	99518	907-561-5335	10-19
Hrsa-Ila Welfare Fund	1355 Intern Terminal	Norfolk	VA	23505	757-423-3090	50+
Louisiana Assn for the Blind Inc	1750 Claiborne Ave	Shreveport	LA	71103	318-635-6471	10-19
Map International	PO Box 215000	Brunswick	GA	31521		50+
North Dakota Association for the Disabled	1913 S Washington St	Grand Forks	ND	58201	701-775-5577	20-29
Parent Child Incorporated of San Antonio & Bexar County	1000 Harriman PL	San Antonio	TX	78207	210-226-6232	30-39
Philadelphia Corporation for Aging	642 N Broad St	Philadelphia	PA	19130	215-765-9033	50+
Pioneer Human Services	PO Box 18377	Seattle	WA	98118	206-725-6207	40-49
Rockhurst College Continuing Education	6901 W 63rd St	Shawnee Mission	KS	66202		50+
Shawnee Hills Inc	511 Morris St	Charleston	WV	25301	304-345-4800	30-39
South Dakota Association of the Deaf	102 N Krohn PL	Sioux Falls	SD	57103	605-367-5200	20-29
The Easter Seal Society of New Jersey Inc	1 Kimberly Rd	E Brunswick	NJ	08816	732-257-6662	30-39
UAW-GM Center for Human Resources	2630 Featherstone Rd	Auburn Hills	MI	48326	248-377-2400	50+
VNA Inc	32 Branch Ave	Providence	RI	02904	401-444-9700	30-39
Valley Mental Health Incorporated	5965 S 900 E Ste 310	Salt Lake City	UT	84121	801-263-7100	50+

Source: National Directory of Nonprofit Organizations, 2000, Volumes 1 and 2, The Taft Group. The table shows a selection of organizations for illustration and does not constitute a complete selection from the source. The organizations are arranged in alphabetical order.

LOCATION BY STATE AND REGIONAL CONCENTRATION

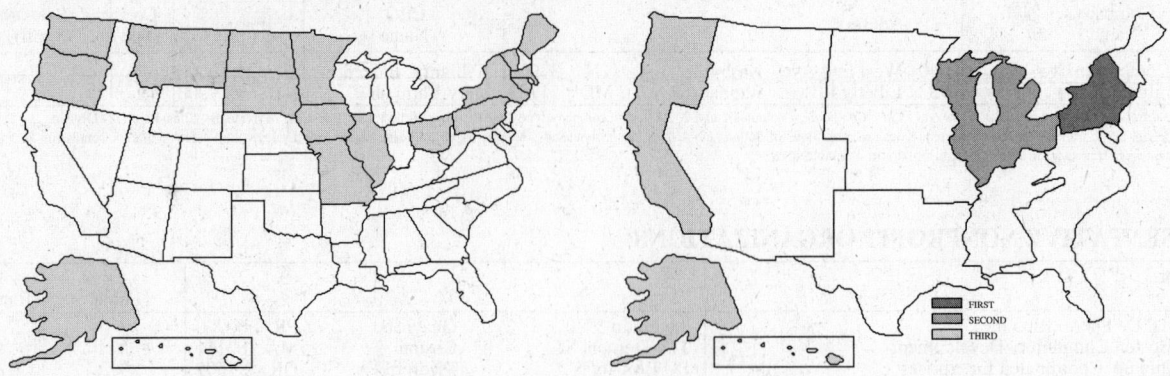

INDUSTRY DATA BY STATE

State	Establishments Total (number)	Establishments % of U.S.	Employment Total (number)	Employment % of U.S.	Employment Per Estab.	Payroll Total ($ mil.)	Payroll Per Empl. ($)	Revenues Total ($ mil.)	Revenues % of U.S.	Revenues Per Estab. ($)
New York	1,568	7.6	30,822	11.5	20	609.1	19,761	1,396.0	11.8	890,311
California	2,148	10.5	24,099	9.0	11	443.0	18,383	1,213.9	10.3	565,139
Illinois	948	4.6	15,999	5.9	17	309.3	19,335	884.5	7.5	933,045
Pennsylvania	968	4.7	15,557	5.8	16	285.4	18,344	646.0	5.5	667,394
Ohio	735	3.6	13,491	5.0	18	242.8	17,999	556.7	4.7	757,405
Texas	1,179	5.7	13,748	5.1	12	219.0	15,927	520.4	4.4	441,403
Florida	1,003	4.9	12,064	4.5	12	217.2	18,002	511.9	4.3	510,323
Massachusetts	585	2.8	9,853	3.7	17	218.6	22,182	497.8	4.2	850,935
Michigan	723	3.5	9,788	3.6	14	169.7	17,333	390.0	3.3	539,419
Minnesota	504	2.5	8,331	3.1	17	146.6	17,597	364.9	3.1	723,964
New Jersey	483	2.4	6,801	2.5	14	134.0	19,697	299.7	2.5	620,499
Washington	581	2.8	7,523	2.8	13	130.7	17,370	293.2	2.5	504,675
Connecticut	249	1.2	5,008	1.9	20	104.9	20,955	248.6	2.1	998,297
Missouri	542	2.6	6,264	2.3	12	101.0	16,118	248.5	2.1	458,402
Wisconsin	532	2.6	6,294	2.3	12	105.8	16,808	229.7	1.9	431,788
Indiana	418	2.0	5,714	2.1	14	91.1	15,950	227.9	1.9	545,153
North Carolina	490	2.4	4,998	1.9	10	88.5	17,710	226.8	1.9	462,822
Maryland	368	1.8	4,060	1.5	11	83.1	20,477	221.8	1.9	602,625
Virginia	466	2.3	3,863	1.4	8	69.2	17,903	201.6	1.7	432,639
Georgia	429	2.1	4,533	1.7	11	78.1	17,228	186.3	1.6	434,354
Arizona	355	1.7	4,482	1.7	13	76.6	17,097	181.9	1.5	512,268
Iowa	372	1.8	3,630	1.3	10	63.3	17,432	165.1	1.4	443,788
Kentucky	311	1.5	3,913	1.5	13	63.8	16,298	151.7	1.3	487,723
D.C.	137	0.7	1,653	0.6	12	40.3	24,393	149.5	1.3	1,091,372
Oregon	325	1.6	3,154	1.2	10	56.7	17,981	138.4	1.2	425,914
Colorado	418	2.0	3,131	1.2	7	54.4	17,378	130.0	1.1	311,081
Louisiana	310	1.5	3,974	1.5	13	58.2	14,641	128.8	1.1	415,519
Maine	163	0.8	2,441	0.9	15	52.1	21,335	126.0	1.1	772,828
Oklahoma	255	1.2	2,904	1.1	11	43.0	14,815	107.6	0.9	421,910
Tennessee	283	1.4	2,916	1.1	10	39.9	13,694	98.4	0.8	347,611
Alaska	75	0.4	1,397	0.5	19	35.0	25,054	85.5	0.7	1,140,613
Alabama	228	1.1	2,087	0.8	9	35.4	16,939	84.1	0.7	368,882
New Mexico	170	0.8	2,134	0.8	13	29.4	13,758	73.0	0.6	429,329
Mississippi	129	0.6	1,620	0.6	13	23.5	14,501	60.5	0.5	468,915
Arkansas	201	1.0	1,612	0.6	8	27.1	16,839	57.9	0.5	288,204
Nebraska	144	0.7	1,219	0.5	8	20.9	17,174	57.2	0.5	397,556
Kansas	189	0.9	1,407	0.5	7	23.2	16,466	55.3	0.5	292,481
Vermont	108	0.5	1,241	0.5	11	24.8	19,953	54.1	0.5	501,167
South Carolina	187	0.9	1,450	0.5	8	22.2	15,330	52.7	0.4	281,701
Montana	113	0.6	1,386	0.5	12	20.6	14,899	47.2	0.4	417,681
West Virginia	133	0.6	1,499	0.6	11	20.3	13,556	46.7	0.4	351,015
South Dakota	107	0.5	1,337	0.5	12	20.0	14,924	42.1	0.4	393,224
Rhode Island	59	0.3	1,017	0.4	17	17.0	16,687	37.4	0.3	633,881
Idaho	124	0.6	888	0.3	7	13.3	15,008	33.2	0.3	267,790
North Dakota	48	0.2	1,172	0.4	24	13.6	11,617	30.1	0.3	627,896
Nevada	78	0.4	628	0.2	8	11.4	18,137	27.4	0.2	351,692
Wyoming	44	0.2	653	0.2	15	9.3	14,208	17.0	0.1	387,364

Source: 1997 *Economic Census*. The states are in descending order of revenues or establishments (if revenue data are missing for the majority). The symbol (D) appears when data are withheld to prevent disclosure of competitive information. States marked with (D) are sorted by number of establishments. A dash (-) indicates that the data element cannot be calculated. * indicates the midpoint of a range; 175, for example is the range 100-249. Shaded *states* on the state map indicate those states which have proportionately greater representation in the industry than would be indicated by the state's population; the ratio is based on total revenues or number of establishments. Shaded *regions* indicate where the industry is regionally most concentrated.

NAICS 624210 - COMMUNITY FOOD SERVICES

GENERAL STATISTICS

Year	Establishments (number)	Employment (number)	Payroll ($ million)	Revenues ($ million)	Employees per Establishment (number)	Revenues per Establishment ($)	Payroll per Employee ($)
1997	3,083	23,305	328.0	1,615.0	7.6	523,840	14,074

Source: *Economic Census of the United States*, 1997. This is a newly defined industry. Data for prior years were unavailable at the time of publication but may become available over time.

INDICES OF CHANGE

Year	Establishments (number)	Employment (number)	Payroll ($ million)	Revenues ($ million)	Employees per Establishment (number)	Revenues per Establishment ($)	Payroll per Employee ($)
1997	100.0	100.0	100.0	100.0	100.0	100.0	100.0

Sources: Same as General Statistics. The values shown reflect change from the base year, 1997. Values above 100 mean greater than 1997, values below 100 mean less than 1997, and a value of 100 in the 1982-96 or 1998-2001 period means same as 1997. Values followed by a 'p' are projections by the editors; 'e' stands for extrapolation. Data are the most recent available at this level of detail.

SIC INDUSTRIES RELATED TO NAICS 624210

Each new NAICS code represents an industry that used to be part of an SIC or a part of several SIC industries. Data in this table are shown to provide transitional information for these cases. All available data for the precursor SIC(s) are shown. Even if only a part of an SIC is included in the NAICS, *all* data for the SIC are reproduced. If the SIC industry is not marked as being a part (pt) of the NAICS, the entire industry is embedded in the NAICS data. The SIC composition of the new industry provides some hints of the relative importance of its "ancestors." Data marked with a 'p' are projected. Projections begin with 1982 data. Data earlier than 1990 are not shown but are reflected in the projections.

SIC	Industry	1990	1991	1992	1993	1994	1995	1996	1997
8322	**Individual & Family Services (pt)**								
	Establishments (number)	27,580	29,630	36,232	36,795	37,138	37,311	40,418*p*	42,214*p*
	Employment (thousands)	408.4	440.7	476.8	506.6	536.5	570.4	595.7*p*	625.7*p*
	Revenues ($ million)	-	-	17,740.0	-	-	-	-	-

Source: *Economic Census of the United States*, 1992, annual surveys of economic sectors conducted by the Bureau of the Census, and estimates or projections based on the 1982-1992 period; not all data are shown. 'e' marks estimates made by the editors; 'p' indicates projections based on time series. A dash (-) indicates that data for this SIC or year were not available. The abbreviation (pt) next to the industry name indicates that only a part of the industry is present within the NAICS data. If no (pt) is shown, the entire industry is contained within the NAICS data.

SELECTED RATIOS

For 1997	Avg. of Information	Analyzed Industry	Index	For 1997	Avg. of Information	Analyzed Industry	Index
Employees per establishment	21	8	36	Payroll per establishment	585,591	106,390	18
Revenue per establishment	1,370,364	523,840	38	Payroll as % of revenue	43	20	48
Revenue per employee	65,262	69,298	106	Payroll per employee	27,888	14,074	50

Sources: Same as General Statistics. The 'Average' column represents the average for the industry sector, in 1997, where the currently shown industry is classified. The Index shows the relationship between the Average and the Analyzed Industry. For example, 100 means that they are equal; 500 that the Analyzed Industry is five times the average; 50 means that the Analyzed Industry is half the national average. The abbreviation 'na' is used to show that data are 'not available'.

LEADING COMPANIES
No company data available for this industry.

LOCATION BY STATE AND REGIONAL CONCENTRATION

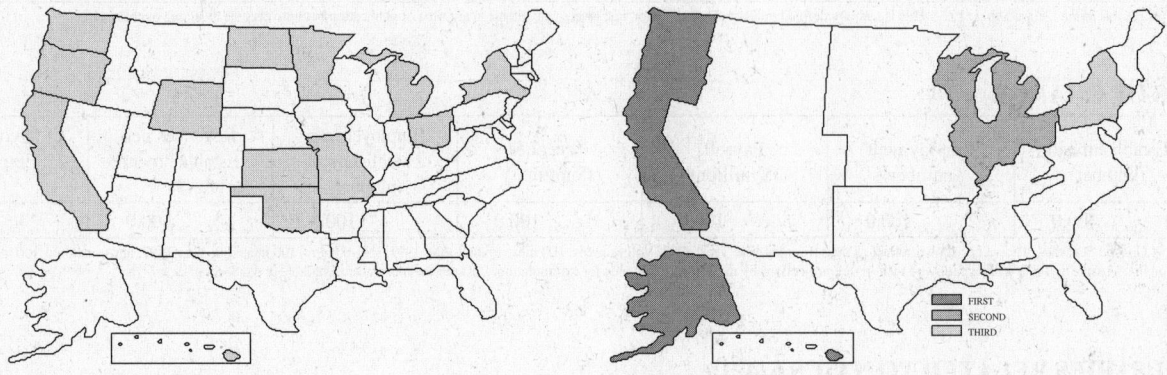

FIRST
SECOND
THIRD

INDUSTRY DATA BY STATE

State	Establishments		Employment			Payroll		Revenues		
	Total (number)	% of U.S.	Total (number)	% of U.S.	Per Estab.	Total ($ mil.)	Per Empl. ($)	Total ($ mil.)	% of U.S.	Per Estab. ($)
California	310	10.1	2,527	10.8	8	42.1	16,645	246.5	15.3	795,190
New York	227	7.4	2,398	10.3	11	38.3	15,955	151.5	9.4	667,189
Minnesota	118	3.8	838	3.6	7	10.8	12,844	70.8	4.4	600,144
Ohio	119	3.9	877	3.8	7	12.0	13,702	70.8	4.4	595,059
Illinois	78	2.5	747	3.2	10	12.8	17,190	67.7	4.2	868,423
Michigan	96	3.1	710	3.0	7	10.7	15,061	64.3	4.0	669,479
Oregon	39	1.3	279	1.2	7	4.4	15,803	38.4	2.4	983,718
Missouri	129	4.2	787	3.4	6	10.0	12,742	38.0	2.4	294,860
Washington	112	3.6	754	3.2	7	9.7	12,837	36.1	2.2	322,679
Oklahoma	100	3.2	650	2.8	7	7.5	11,503	27.5	1.7	275,490
Indiana	60	1.9	356	1.5	6	4.9	13,770	27.0	1.7	449,433
D.C.	10	0.3	160	0.7	16	3.9	24,388	24.3	1.5	2,432,800
Wisconsin	42	1.4	215	0.9	5	2.8	13,093	23.7	1.5	564,500
North Carolina	40	1.3	261	1.1	7	4.2	16,080	23.0	1.4	574,475
Kansas	145	4.7	659	2.8	5	4.4	6,687	16.5	1.0	113,821
South Carolina	28	0.9	233	1.0	8	3.3	14,305	14.0	0.9	500,393
Hawaii	8	0.3	59	0.3	7	1.1	18,763	13.3	0.8	1,656,875
Louisiana	28	0.9	251	1.1	9	3.6	14,474	12.1	0.8	433,536
Kentucky	29	0.9	331	1.4	11	3.8	11,538	10.8	0.7	373,379
Alabama	33	1.1	249	1.1	8	3.6	14,373	9.2	0.6	279,333
Tennessee	41	1.3	192	0.8	5	2.8	14,365	8.1	0.5	196,927
Arkansas	36	1.2	398	1.7	11	3.1	7,769	7.9	0.5	220,222
North Dakota	15	0.5	181	0.8	12	1.4	7,691	5.0	0.3	336,533
Mississippi	16	0.5	142	0.6	9	1.5	10,268	4.8	0.3	299,375
West Virginia	21	0.7	94	0.4	4	0.8	8,117	2.8	0.2	131,429
Wyoming	12	0.4	74	0.3	6	0.9	12,405	2.6	0.2	218,167
Georgia	41	1.3	175*	-	-	(D)	-	(D)	-	-
Rhode Island	12	0.4	175*	-	-	(D)	-	(D)	-	-
Delaware	6	0.2	175*	-	-	(D)	-	(D)	-	-

Source: 1997 *Economic Census*. The states are in descending order of revenues or establishments (if revenue data are missing for the majority). The symbol (D) appears when data are withheld to prevent disclosure of competitive information. States marked with (D) are sorted by number of establishments. A dash (-) indicates that the data element cannot be calculated. * indicates the midpoint of a range; 175, for example is the range 100-249. Shaded *states* on the state map indicate those states which have proportionately greater representation in the industry than would be indicated by the state's population; the ratio is based on total revenues or number of establishments. Shaded *regions* indicate where the industry is regionally most concentrated.

NAICS 624221 - TEMPORARY SHELTERS

GENERAL STATISTICS

Year	Establishments (number)	Employment (number)	Payroll ($ million)	Revenues ($ million)	Employees per Establishment (number)	Revenues per Establishment ($)	Payroll per Employee ($)
1997	2,595	40,136	676.0	1,549.0	15.5	596,917	16,843

Source: Economic Census of the United States, 1997. This is a newly defined industry. Data for prior years were unavailable at the time of publication but may become available over time.

INDICES OF CHANGE

Year	Establishments (number)	Employment (number)	Payroll ($ million)	Revenues ($ million)	Employees per Establishment (number)	Revenues per Establishment ($)	Payroll per Employee ($)
1997	100.0	100.0	100.0	100.0	100.0	100.0	100.0

Sources: Same as General Statistics. The values shown reflect change from the base year, 1997. Values above 100 mean greater than 1997, values below 100 mean less than 1997, and a value of 100 in the 1982-96 or 1998-2001 period means same as 1997. Values followed by a 'p' are projections by the editors; 'e' stands for extrapolation. Data are the most recent available at this level of detail.

SIC INDUSTRIES RELATED TO NAICS 624221

Each new NAICS code represents an industry that used to be part of an SIC or a part of several SIC industries. Data in this table are shown to provide transitional information for these cases. All available data for the precursor SIC(s) are shown. Even if only a part of an SIC is included in the NAICS, *all* data for the SIC are reproduced. If the SIC industry is not marked as being a part (pt) of the NAICS, the entire industry is embedded in the NAICS data. The SIC composition of the new industry provides some hints of the relative importance of its "ancestors." Data marked with a 'p' are projected. Projections begin with 1982 data. Data earlier than 1990 are not shown but are reflected in the projections.

SIC	Industry	1990	1991	1992	1993	1994	1995	1996	1997
8322	**Individual & Family Services (pt)**								
	Establishments (number)	27,580	29,630	36,232	36,795	37,138	37,311	40,418*p*	42,214*p*
	Employment (thousands)	408.4	440.7	476.8	506.6	536.5	570.4	595.7*p*	625.7*p*
	Revenues ($ million)	-	-	17,740.0	-	-	-	-	-

Source: Economic Census of the United States, 1992, annual surveys of economic sectors conducted by the Bureau of the Census, and estimates or projections based on the 1982-1992 period; not all data are shown. 'e' marks estimates made by the editors; 'p' indicates projections based on time series. A dash (-) indicates that data for this SIC or year were not available. The abbreviation (pt) next to the industry name indicates that only a part of the industry is present within the NAICS data. If no (pt) is shown, the entire industry is contained within the NAICS data.

SELECTED RATIOS

For 1997	Avg. of Information	Analyzed Industry	Index	For 1997	Avg. of Information	Analyzed Industry	Index
Employees per establishment	21	15	74	Payroll per establishment	585,591	260,501	44
Revenue per establishment	1,370,364	596,917	44	Payroll as % of revenue	43	44	102
Revenue per employee	65,262	38,594	59	Payroll per employee	27,888	16,843	60

Sources: Same as General Statistics. The 'Average' column represents the average for the industry sector, in 1997, where the currently shown industry is classified. The Index shows the relationship between the Average and the Analyzed Industry. For example, 100 means that they are equal; 500 that the Analyzed Industry is five times the average; 50 means that the Analyzed Industry is half the national average. The abbreviation 'na' is used to show that data are 'not available'.

LEADING COMPANIES

No company data available for this industry.

LOCATION BY STATE AND REGIONAL CONCENTRATION

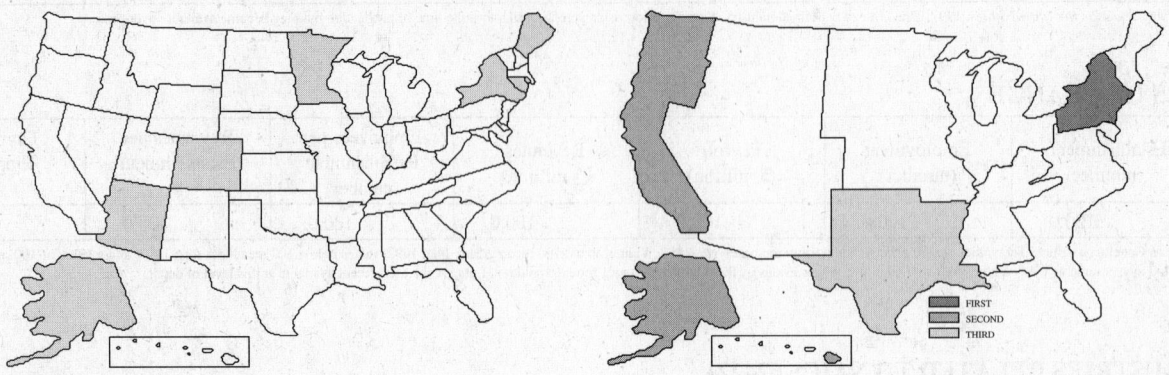

FIRST
SECOND
THIRD

INDUSTRY DATA BY STATE

State	Establishments Total (number)	Establishments % of U.S.	Employment Total (number)	Employment % of U.S.	Employment Per Estab.	Payroll Total ($ mil.)	Payroll Per Empl. ($)	Revenues Total ($ mil.)	Revenues % of U.S.	Revenues Per Estab. ($)
New York	181	7.0	4,123	10.3	23	84.9	20,598	212.2	13.7	1,172,304
California	242	9.3	3,897	9.7	16	69.8	17,905	167.5	10.8	692,293
Texas	143	5.5	2,523	6.3	18	40.1	15,900	87.4	5.6	611,203
Minnesota	41	1.6	1,179	2.9	29	20.7	17,592	41.3	2.7	1,008,488
Virginia	75	2.9	1,104	2.8	15	15.6	14,093	35.0	2.3	466,400
Missouri	65	2.5	876	2.2	13	13.0	14,857	29.0	1.9	446,431
Arizona	60	2.3	916	2.3	15	14.1	15,448	28.1	1.8	469,150
Indiana	48	1.8	897	2.2	19	13.3	14,794	27.6	1.8	575,854
Connecticut	36	1.4	506	1.3	14	9.7	19,184	27.5	1.8	763,306
Colorado	39	1.5	751	1.9	19	14.7	19,517	26.9	1.7	689,923
North Carolina	77	3.0	726	1.8	9	11.2	15,483	25.9	1.7	336,753
Wisconsin	56	2.2	793	2.0	14	11.4	14,342	25.5	1.6	455,464
Georgia	64	2.5	711	1.8	11	10.6	14,892	25.4	1.6	396,312
Kentucky	38	1.5	639	1.6	17	10.1	15,759	19.2	1.2	506,395
Tennessee	52	2.0	406	1.0	8	6.2	15,236	17.0	1.1	327,788
Louisiana	34	1.3	429	1.1	13	6.7	15,627	17.0	1.1	498,971
Iowa	33	1.3	471	1.2	14	7.0	14,777	13.9	0.9	420,909
Oklahoma	36	1.4	456	1.1	13	6.3	13,711	13.1	0.8	364,333
South Carolina	31	1.2	407	1.0	13	5.8	14,305	12.8	0.8	412,065
Alaska	19	0.7	346	0.9	18	6.4	18,535	11.3	0.7	593,895
Alabama	27	1.0	303	0.8	11	4.7	15,594	11.0	0.7	407,852
Maine	16	0.6	225	0.6	14	3.3	14,471	9.7	0.6	609,250
Utah	17	0.7	288	0.7	17	3.9	13,444	9.5	0.6	561,235
Rhode Island	15	0.6	258	0.6	17	4.1	15,926	9.0	0.6	598,600
Nevada	11	0.4	157	0.4	14	3.1	19,752	7.6	0.5	694,091
Arkansas	29	1.1	201	0.5	7	2.4	12,000	6.2	0.4	213,448
Mississippi	15	0.6	193	0.5	13	2.5	13,181	5.9	0.4	394,067
Idaho	18	0.7	210	0.5	12	2.8	13,443	5.7	0.4	316,444
Montana	17	0.7	174	0.4	10	2.1	12,121	4.1	0.3	243,294
North Dakota	10	0.4	93	0.2	9	1.5	15,935	3.8	0.2	380,500
South Dakota	15	0.6	120	0.3	8	1.8	14,967	3.5	0.2	232,533
New Hampshire	13	0.5	116	0.3	9	1.4	11,750	3.4	0.2	258,846
Vermont	10	0.4	68	0.2	7	0.9	13,044	2.1	0.1	206,100
Wyoming	11	0.4	60*	-	-	(D)	-	(D)	-	-
Delaware	8	0.3	175*	-	-	(D)	-	(D)	-	-

Source: 1997 *Economic Census.* The states are in descending order of revenues or establishments (if revenue data are missing for the majority). The symbol (D) appears when data are withheld to prevent disclosure of competitive information. States marked with (D) are sorted by number of establishments. A dash (-) indicates that the data element cannot be calculated. * indicates the midpoint of a range; 175, for example is the range 100-249. Shaded *states* on the state map indicate those states which have proportionately greater representation in the industry than would be indicated by the state's population; the ratio is based on total revenues or number of establishments. Shaded *regions* indicate where the industry is regionally most concentrated.

NAICS 624229 - COMMUNITY HOUSING SERVICES NEC

GENERAL STATISTICS

Year	Establishments (number)	Employment (number)	Payroll ($ million)	Revenues ($ million)	Employees per Establishment (number)	Revenues per Establishment ($)	Payroll per Employee ($)
1997	2,309	21,014	424.0	1,479.0	9.1	640,537	20,177

Source: *Economic Census of the United States*, 1997. This is a newly defined industry. Data for prior years were unavailable at the time of publication but may become available over time.

INDICES OF CHANGE

Year	Establishments (number)	Employment (number)	Payroll ($ million)	Revenues ($ million)	Employees per Establishment (number)	Revenues per Establishment ($)	Payroll per Employee ($)
1997	100.0	100.0	100.0	100.0	100.0	100.0	100.0

Sources: Same as General Statistics. The values shown reflect change from the base year, 1997. Values above 100 mean greater than 1997, values below 100 mean less than 1997, and a value of 100 in the 1982-96 or 1998-2001 period means same as 1997. Values followed by a 'p' are projections by the editors; 'e' stands for extrapolation. Data are the most recent available at this level of detail.

SIC INDUSTRIES RELATED TO NAICS 624229

Each new NAICS code represents an industry that used to be part of an SIC or a part of several SIC industries. Data in this table are shown to provide transitional information for these cases. All available data for the precursor SIC(s) are shown. Even if only a part of an SIC is included in the NAICS, *all* data for the SIC are reproduced. If the SIC industry is not marked as being a part (pt) of the NAICS, the entire industry is embedded in the NAICS data. The SIC composition of the new industry provides some hints of the relative importance of its "ancestors." Data marked with a 'p' are projected. Projections begin with 1982 data. Data earlier than 1990 are not shown but are reflected in the projections.

SIC	Industry	1990	1991	1992	1993	1994	1995	1996	1997
8322	**Individual & Family Services (pt)**								
	Establishments (number)	27,580	29,630	36,232	36,795	37,138	37,311	40,418p	42,214p
	Employment (thousands)	408.4	440.7	476.8	506.6	536.5	570.4	595.7p	625.7p
	Revenues ($ million)	-	-	17,740.0	-	-	-	-	-

Source: *Economic Census of the United States*, 1992, annual surveys of economic sectors conducted by the Bureau of the Census, and estimates or projections based on the 1982-1992 period; not all data are shown. 'e' marks estimates made by the editors; 'p' indicates projections based on time series. A dash (-) indicates that data for this SIC or year were not available. The abbreviation (pt) next to the industry name indicates that only a part of the industry is present within the NAICS data. If no (pt) is shown, the entire industry is contained within the NAICS data.

SELECTED RATIOS

For 1997	Avg. of Information	Analyzed Industry	Index	For 1997	Avg. of Information	Analyzed Industry	Index
Employees per establishment	21	9	43	Payroll per establishment	585,591	183,629	31
Revenue per establishment	1,370,364	640,537	47	Payroll as % of revenue	43	29	67
Revenue per employee	65,262	70,382	108	Payroll per employee	27,888	20,177	72

Sources: Same as General Statistics. The 'Average' column represents the average for the industry sector, in 1997, where the currently shown industry is classified. The Index shows the relationship between the Average and the Analyzed Industry. For example, 100 means that they are equal; 500 that the Analyzed Industry is five times the average; 50 means that the Analyzed Industry is half the national average. The abbreviation 'na' is used to show that data are 'not available'.

LEADING COMPANIES

No company data available for this industry.

LOCATION BY STATE AND REGIONAL CONCENTRATION

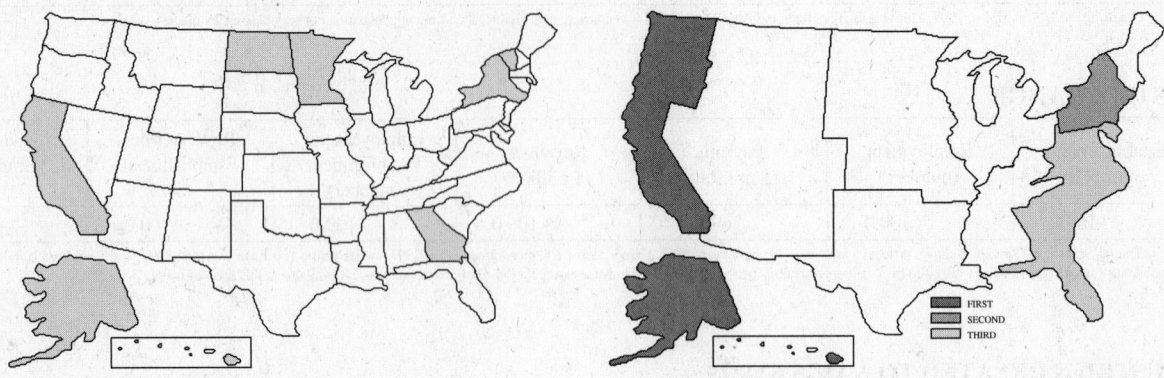

FIRST
SECOND
THIRD

INDUSTRY DATA BY STATE

State	Establishments Total (number)	% of U.S.	Employment Total (number)	% of U.S.	Per Estab.	Payroll Total ($ mil.)	Per Empl. ($)	Revenues Total ($ mil.)	% of U.S.	Per Estab. ($)
California	236	10.2	3,055	14.5	13	64.5	21,118	223.7	15.1	947,911
New York	245	10.6	3,047	14.5	12	64.2	21,067	174.2	11.8	711,073
Georgia	44	1.9	847	4.0	19	11.1	13,109	109.6	7.4	2,490,068
Ohio	82	3.6	753	3.6	9	14.7	19,467	47.7	3.2	581,207
Minnesota	60	2.6	571	2.7	10	11.5	20,154	31.5	2.1	525,833
Tennessee	52	2.3	320	1.5	6	6.1	19,131	28.0	1.9	537,538
Indiana	50	2.2	353	1.7	7	6.5	18,329	22.0	1.5	440,600
Missouri	41	1.8	187	0.9	5	3.9	20,861	14.5	1.0	354,634
North Carolina	54	2.3	174	0.8	3	3.7	21,540	13.7	0.9	252,889
Vermont	18	0.8	148	0.7	8	3.2	21,818	12.0	0.8	666,222
Kentucky	36	1.6	196	0.9	5	3.0	15,546	9.6	0.6	266,417
Alaska	5	0.2	58	0.3	12	1.5	25,362	8.8	0.6	1,767,400
Hawaii	14	0.6	121	0.6	9	2.8	23,322	7.1	0.5	504,214
Alabama	20	0.9	65	0.3	3	1.3	20,062	6.4	0.4	320,150
North Dakota	7	0.3	53	0.3	8	1.7	32,302	4.5	0.3	643,000
South Carolina	17	0.7	56	0.3	3	0.9	16,679	4.4	0.3	256,000
Montana	6	0.3	70	0.3	12	1.1	16,129	4.0	0.3	668,833
Idaho	14	0.6	57	0.3	4	1.2	20,316	3.2	0.2	227,571
Nebraska	15	0.6	62	0.3	4	1.2	19,613	2.9	0.2	195,867
Delaware	9	0.4	59	0.3	7	1.0	17,068	2.7	0.2	303,222
West Virginia	12	0.5	54	0.3	5	0.8	15,241	2.3	0.2	193,250
Mississippi	14	0.6	58	0.3	4	0.6	9,603	1.7	0.1	121,286
Kansas	21	0.9	175*	--	--	(D)	-	(D)	-	-

Source: 1997 *Economic Census*. The states are in descending order of revenues or establishments (if revenue data are missing for the majority). The symbol (D) appears when data are withheld to prevent disclosure of competitive information. States marked with (D) are sorted by number of establishments. A dash (-) indicates that the data element cannot be calculated. * indicates the midpoint of a range; 175, for example is the range 100-249. Shaded *states* on the state map indicate those states which have proportionately greater representation in the industry than would be indicated by the state's population; the ratio is based on total revenues or number of establishments. Shaded *regions* indicate where the industry is regionally most concentrated.

NAICS 624230 - EMERGENCY AND OTHER RELIEF SERVICES

GENERAL STATISTICS

Year	Establishments (number)	Employment (number)	Payroll ($ million)	Revenues ($ million)	Employees per Establishment (number)	Revenues per Establishment ($)	Payroll per Employee ($)
1997	1,963	17,939	340.0	1,553.0	9.1	791,136	18,953

Source: Economic Census of the United States, 1997. This is a newly defined industry. Data for prior years were unavailable at the time of publication but may become available over time.

INDICES OF CHANGE

Year	Establishments (number)	Employment (number)	Payroll ($ million)	Revenues ($ million)	Employees per Establishment (number)	Revenues per Establishment ($)	Payroll per Employee ($)
1997	100.0	100.0	100.0	100.0	100.0	100.0	100.0

Sources: Same as General Statistics. The values shown reflect change from the base year, 1997. Values above 100 mean greater than 1997, values below 100 mean less than 1997, and a value of 100 in the 1982-96 or 1998-2001 period means same as 1997. Values followed by a 'p' are projections by the editors; 'e' stands for extrapolation. Data are the most recent available at this level of detail.

SIC INDUSTRIES RELATED TO NAICS 624230

Each new NAICS code represents an industry that used to be part of an SIC or a part of several SIC industries. Data in this table are shown to provide transitional information for these cases. All available data for the precursor SIC(s) are shown. Even if only a part of an SIC is included in the NAICS, *all* data for the SIC are reproduced. If the SIC industry is not marked as being a part (pt) of the NAICS, the entire industry is embedded in the NAICS data. The SIC composition of the new industry provides some hints of the relative importance of its "ancestors." Data marked with a 'p' are projected. Projections begin with 1982 data. Data earlier than 1990 are not shown but are reflected in the projections.

SIC	Industry	1990	1991	1992	1993	1994	1995	1996	1997
8322	**Individual & Family Services (pt)**								
	Establishments (number)	27,580	29,630	36,232	36,795	37,138	37,311	40,418p	42,214p
	Employment (thousands)	408.4	440.7	476.8	506.6	536.5	570.4	595.7p	625.7p
	Revenues ($ million)	-	-	17,740.0	-	-	-	-	-

Source: Economic Census of the United States, 1992, annual surveys of economic sectors conducted by the Bureau of the Census, and estimates or projections based on the 1982-1992 period; not all data are shown. 'e' marks estimates made by the editors; 'p' indicates projections based on time series. A dash (-) indicates that data for this SIC or year were not available. The abbreviation (pt) next to the industry name indicates that only a part of the industry is present within the NAICS data. If no (pt) is shown, the entire industry is contained within the NAICS data.

SELECTED RATIOS

For 1997	Avg. of Information	Analyzed Industry	Index	For 1997	Avg. of Information	Analyzed Industry	Index
Employees per establishment	21	9	44	Payroll per establishment	585,591	173,204	30
Revenue per establishment	1,370,364	791,136	58	Payroll as % of revenue	43	22	51
Revenue per employee	65,262	86,571	133	Payroll per employee	27,888	18,953	68

Sources: Same as General Statistics. The 'Average' column represents the average for the industry sector, in 1997, where the currently shown industry is classified. The Index shows the relationship between the Average and the Analyzed Industry. For example, 100 means that they are equal; 500 that the Analyzed Industry is five times the average; 50 means that the Analyzed Industry is half the national average. The abbreviation 'na' is used to show that data are 'not available'.

LEADING COMPANIES

No company data available for this industry.

LOCATION BY STATE AND REGIONAL CONCENTRATION

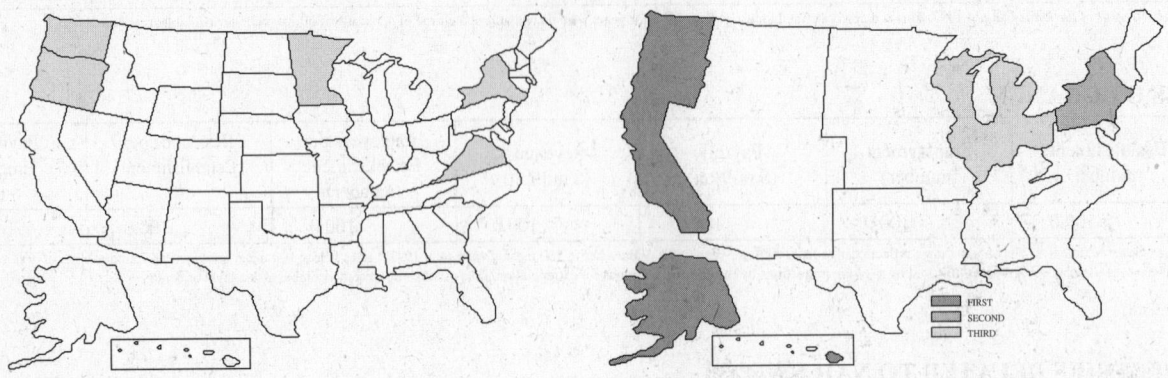

FIRST
SECOND
THIRD

INDUSTRY DATA BY STATE

State	Establishments		Employment			Payroll		Revenues		
	Total (number)	% of U.S.	Total (number)	% of U.S.	Per Estab.	Total ($ mil.)	Per Empl. ($)	Total ($ mil.)	% of U.S.	Per Estab. ($)
New York	117	6.0	2,453	13.7	21	51.9	21,147	169.4	10.9	1,447,641
California	175	8.9	2,061	11.5	12	38.3	18,574	115.2	7.4	658,314
Oregon	28	1.4	552	3.1	20	8.8	15,940	49.5	3.2	1,767,929
Virginia	83	4.2	652	3.6	8	13.4	20,618	44.1	2.8	531,253
Ohio	96	4.9	938	5.2	10	16.1	17,134	40.9	2.6	426,219
Washington	43	2.2	476	2.7	11	8.4	17,626	38.5	2.5	894,814
Minnesota	40	2.0	425	2.4	11	8.0	18,727	31.2	2.0	779,550
North Carolina	81	4.1	484	2.7	6	7.9	16,399	17.5	1.1	216,321
Indiana	69	3.5	435	2.4	6	6.0	13,733	17.0	1.1	246,580
Tennessee	51	2.6	264	1.5	5	4.0	14,962	14.9	1.0	291,510
Wisconsin	41	2.1	339	1.9	8	4.9	14,593	13.0	0.8	316,415
Connecticut	25	1.3	219	1.2	9	4.7	21,320	11.6	0.7	462,560
Missouri	44	2.2	183	1.0	4	2.9	15,579	11.4	0.7	258,114
Alabama	50	2.5	239	1.3	5	4.1	17,029	10.3	0.7	206,880
Hawaii	13	0.7	159	0.9	12	2.6	16,164	5.8	0.4	446,154
Arkansas	25	1.3	113	0.6	5	1.9	17,177	5.4	0.3	216,240
South Carolina	33	1.7	177	1.0	5	2.5	13,983	5.4	0.3	162,455
Iowa	36	1.8	166	0.9	5	2.2	13,072	4.7	0.3	131,333
Nebraska	9	0.5	125	0.7	14	1.2	9,376	3.2	0.2	353,333
Maine	9	0.5	114	0.6	13	1.3	11,737	2.8	0.2	308,667
Mississippi	20	1.0	82	0.5	4	1.1	13,402	2.7	0.2	136,150
West Virginia	19	1.0	88	0.5	5	1.1	12,511	2.6	0.2	135,526
Idaho	12	0.6	87	0.5	7	1.0	11,598	2.5	0.2	206,250
Alaska	8	0.4	55	0.3	7	0.8	15,218	1.9	0.1	231,625
Montana	12	0.6	48	0.3	4	0.6	12,833	1.6	0.1	130,833
Nevada	4	0.2	38	0.2	10	0.6	16,395	1.2	0.1	307,500
South Dakota	12	0.6	39	0.2	3	0.5	12,564	1.2	0.1	99,500
North Dakota	8	0.4	28	0.2	4	0.4	12,750	1.0	0.1	121,500
Wyoming	5	0.3	11	0.1	2	0.2	17,000	0.4	0.0	89,000
Delaware	4	0.2	60*	-	-	(D)	-	(D)	-	-
Rhode Island	3	0.2	60*	-	-	(D)	-	(D)	-	-

Source: 1997 *Economic Census*. The states are in descending order of revenues or establishments (if revenue data are missing for the majority). The symbol (D) appears when data are withheld to prevent disclosure of competitive information. States marked with (D) are sorted by number of establishments. A dash (-) indicates that the data element cannot be calculated. * indicates the midpoint of a range; 175, for example is the range 100-249. Shaded *states* on the state map indicate those states which have proportionately greater representation in the industry than would be indicated by the state's population; the ratio is based on total revenues or number of establishments. Shaded *regions* indicate where the industry is regionally most concentrated.

NAICS 624310 - VOCATIONAL REHABILITATION SERVICES*

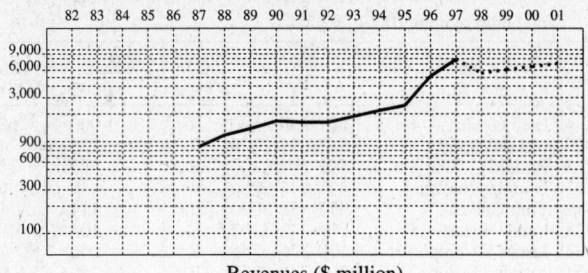

Revenues ($ million)

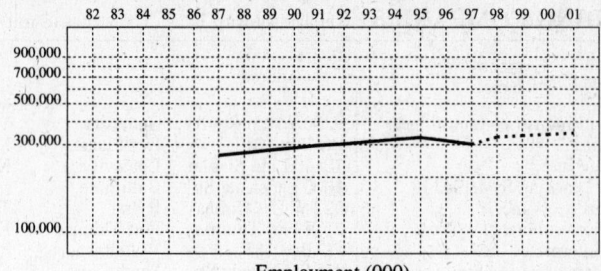

Employment (000)

GENERAL STATISTICS

Year	Establishments (number)	Employment (number)	Payroll ($ million)	Revenues ($ million)	Employees per Establishment (number)	Revenues per Establishment ($)	Payroll per Employee ($)
1982	-	-	-	-	-	-	-
1983	-	-	-	-	-	-	-
1984	-	-	-	-	-	-	-
1985	-	-	-	-	-	-	-
1986	-	-	-	-	-	-	-
1987	6,782	262,344	2,104.0	884.0	38.7	130,345	8,020
1988	6,684	270,618	2,313.0	1,177.0	40.5	176,092	8,547
1989	6,608	280,331	2,512.0	1,384.0	42.4	209,443	8,961
1990	6,925	288,506	2,756.0	1,673.0	41.7	241,588	9,553
1991	7,322	297,523	2,992.0	1,618.0	40.6	220,978	10,056
1992	8,761	302,536	3,258.0	1,620.0	34.5	184,910	10,769
1993	8,742	311,806	3,541.0	1,877.0	35.7	214,711	11,356
1994	8,679	320,108	3,750.0	2,173.0	36.9	250,374	11,715
1995	8,649	327,869	3,947.0	2,468.0	37.9	285,351	12,038
1996	8,433 e	314,806 e	3,858.0 e	5,181.0 e	37.3 e	614,372 e	12,255 e
1997	8,217	301,742	3,769.0	7,894.0	36.7	960,691	12,491
1998	9,176 p	330,409 p	4,328.0 p	5,572.0 p	36.0 p	607,236 p	13,099 p
1999	9,405 p	335,807 p	4,522.0 p	6,078.0 p	35.7 p	646,252 p	13,466 p
2000	9,635 p	341,206 p	4,716.0 p	6,583.0 p	35.4 p	683,238 p	13,822 p
2001	9,864 p	346,604 p	4,910.0 p	7,088.0 p	35.1 p	718,573 p	14,166 p

Sources: Economic Census of the United States, 1982, 1987, 1992, 1997. Establishment counts, employment, and payroll are from County Business Patterns for non-Census years. In non-Census years, industries in the Manufacturing range under SIC coding include data from the Annual Survey of Manufactures (ASM); those in the old Services range include data from the Services Annual Survey (SAS). Values followed by a 'p' are projections by the editors. Extrapolations are marked by 'e'. Data are the most recent available at this level of detail.

INDICES OF CHANGE

Year	Establishments (number)	Employment (number)	Payroll ($ million)	Revenues ($ million)	Employees per Establishment (number)	Revenues per Establishment ($)	Payroll per Employee ($)
1982	-	-	-	-	-	-	-
1987	82.5	86.9	55.8	11.2	105.3	13.6	64.2
1992	106.6	100.3	86.4	20.5	94.0	19.2	86.2
1993	106.4	103.3	94.0	23.8	97.1	22.3	90.9
1994	105.6	106.1	99.5	27.5	100.4	26.1	93.8
1995	105.3	108.7	104.7	31.3	103.2	29.7	96.4
1996	102.6 e	104.3 e	102.4 e	65.6 e	101.7 e	64.0 e	98.1 e
1997	100.0	100.0	100.0	100.0	100.0	100.0	100.0
1998	111.7 p	109.5 p	114.8 p	70.6 p	98.1 p	63.2 p	104.9 p
1999	114.5 p	111.3 p	120.0 p	77.0 p	97.2 p	67.3 p	107.8 p
2000	117.3 p	113.1 p	125.1 p	83.4 p	96.4 p	71.1 p	110.7 p
2001	120.0 p	114.9 p	130.3 p	89.8 p	95.7 p	74.8 p	113.4 p

Sources: Same as General Statistics. The values shown reflect change from the base year, 1997. Values above 100 mean greater than 1997, values below 100 mean less than 1997, and a value of 100 in the 1982-96 or 1998-2001 period means same as 1997. Values followed by a 'p' are projections by the editors; 'e' stands for extrapolation. Data are the most recent available at this level of detail.

SELECTED RATIOS

For 1997	Avg. of Information	Analyzed Industry	Index	For 1997	Avg. of Information	Analyzed Industry	Index
Employees per establishment	21	37	175	Payroll per establishment	585,591	458,683	78
Revenue per establishment	1,370,364	960,691	70	Payroll as % of revenue	43	48	112
Revenue per employee	65,262	26,161	40	Payroll per employee	27,888	12,491	45

Sources: Same as General Statistics. The 'Average' column represents the average for the industry sector, in 1997, where the currently shown industry is classified. The Index shows the relationship between the Average and the Analyzed Industry. For example, 100 means that they are equal; 500 that the Analyzed Industry is five times the average; 50 means that the Analyzed Industry is half the national average. The abbreviation 'na' is used to show that data are 'not available'.

*Equivalent to SIC 8331.

LEADING COMPANIES Number shown: **34** Total sales ($ mil): **3,344** Total employment (000): **97.2**

Company Name	Address				CEO Name	Phone	Co. Type	Sales ($ mil)	Empl. (000)
Goodwill Industries Intern. Inc.	9200 Wisconsin Ave	Bethesda	MD	20814	Fred Grandy	301-530-6500	R	1,000*	60.0
UOP L.L.C.	PO Box 5017	Des Plaines	IL	60017	Mike Winfield	847-391-2000	R	770*	4.0
Res-Care Inc.	10140 Linn Station	Louisville	KY	40223	Ronald G Geary	502-394-2100	P	523	18.5
Sylvan Learning Systems Inc.	1000 Lancaster St	Baltimore	MD	21202	Douglas Becker	410-843-8000	P	440	6.3
Career Blazers Inc.	222 W Las Colinas	Irving	TX	75039	Tom Bickes	972-432-3000	R	114*	1.2
Fort Thomas Financial Corp.	25 N Fort Thomas	Fort Thomas	KY	41075	Larry N Hatfield	606-441-3302	R	104	<0.1
Hope Enterprises Inc.	PO Box 1837	Williamsport	PA	17703	James F Campbell	570-326-3745	R	56*	0.4
Hope Rehabilitation Services	4351 Lafayatte St	Santa Clara	CA	95054	Joseph Campbell	408-749-2850	R	49*	0.4
VisionQuest National Ltd.	PO Box 12906	Tucson	AZ	85732	Steven R Rogers	520-881-3950	R	48	1.1
Res-Care Inc. Youth Services Div.	10140 Linn Station	Louisville	KY	40223		502-394-2100	D	43*	0.8
Tualatin Valley Workshop Inc.	6615 SE Alexander	Hillsboro	OR	97123	Mike Seabaugh	503-649-8571	R	33*	0.3
Southeast Enterprises Pkg	PO Box 9473	Raytown	MO	64133		816-353-2704	R	26*	0.2
Mid-Michigan Industries Inc.	2426 Parkway Dr	Mount Pleasant	MI	48858	M Judith Garland	517-773-6918	R	21*	0.2
Pearl Buck Production Services	4232 W 5th Ave	Eugene	OR	97402		541-484-4666	D	17*	0.1
L C A R	2650 W 35th Ave	Gary	IN	46408		219-884-1138	R	14	0.4
Orion Industries	33926 9th Ave S	Federal Way	WA	98003	Ronald Branham	253-661-7805	R	14*	0.1
Knox County ARC	2830 E Arc Ave	Vincennes	IN	47591		812-886-4312	R	12	0.5
Comprehensive Systems Inc.	PO Box 457	Charles City	IA	50616		515-228-4842	R	10*	0.5
Bibliographical Center	14394 E Evans Ave	Aurora	CO	80014		303-751-6277	R	7*	<0.1
Tri County Industries Inc.	1250 Atlantic Ave	Rocky Mount	NC	27801	Steven Stone	252-977-3800	R	6	0.1
Trico Opportunities Inc.	137 N Hooper St	Kingsford	MI	49802	Dale Frei	906-774-5718	R	4*	0.1
Suncom Industries Inc.	PO Box 46	Northumberland	PA	17857	Peggy Vitale	717-473-8352	R	4	0.1
Southern Indiana Rehabilitation	1579 S Folsomville	Boonville	IN	47601	John Ward	812-897-4840	R	4	0.3
Abilities Services Inc.	PO Box 808	Crawfordsville	IN	47933		765-362-4020	R	3	<0.1
Evansville Association	PO Box 6445	Evansville	IN	47719		812-422-1181	R	3	0.1
Micro Overflow Corp.	1415 N Eagle St	Naperville	IL	60563	Don Dalton	630-778-4080	R	3*	<0.1
Putnam County Comprehensive	630 Tennessee St	Greencastle	IN	46135	Charles Schroeder	765-653-9763	R	3	0.1
SW. Resources Inc.	1007 Mary St	Parkersburg	WV	26101	Michael Cormier	304-428-6344	R	3	<0.1
St Vincent DePaul Rehabiltn	4867 NE M L King	Portland	OR	97211	Roy Soards	503-281-1289	R	3	1.0
Opportunity Workshop	650 Kennedy Rd	Lexington	KY	40511	John Adams	606-254-0576	R	2	<0.1
Cosec International Inc.	8141 E 44th St	Tulsa	OK	74145	Scott Hood	918-622-3903	R	2	<0.1
Rolling Hills Progress Center	201 W Route 64	Lanark	IL	61046		815-493-2321	R	2	0.1
Frankfort Habilitation Inc.	3755 US 127 S	Frankfort	KY	40601		502-227-9529	R	1	<0.1
Verk Consultants Inc.	PO Box 11277	Eugene	OR	97440	Larry H Malmgren	541-687-9170	N	1	<0.1

Source: Ward's Business Directory of U.S. Private and Public Companies, Volumes 1 and 2, 2000. The company type code used is as follows: P - Public, R - Private, S - Subsidiary, D - Division, J - Joint Venture, A - Affiliate, G - Group, N - Company type not reported. Sales are in millions of dollars, employees are in thousands. An asterisk (*) indicates an estimated sales volume. The symbol < stands for 'less than'. Company names and addresses are truncated, in some cases, to fit into the available space.

REPRESENTATIVE NONPROFIT ORGANIZATIONS

Organization Name	Address				Phone	Income Range ($ mil)
A B C Recovery Center Inc	44 374 Palm St	Indio	CA	92201		1-5
Carenet Inc	PO Box 573001	Winston Salem	NC	27157		1-5
Center for Women and Families, Inc	PO Box 1101	Louisville	KY	40201	502-581-7237	1-5
Chi Chi Rodriguez Youth Foundation	3030 McMullen Booth Rd	Clearwater	FL	33761	727-726-8829	1-5
City Lights School Inc	62 T St NE	Washington	DC	20002	202-832-4366	1-5
Go-Getters Inc	716 N Division St	Salisbury	MD	21801	410-548-2371	5-9
Hmong American Partnership	1600 W University Ave	St Paul	MN	55104		1-5
Native American Cultural Center	PO Box 225	Rancocas	NJ	08073		1-5
Northwest Illinois J T P A Inc	24711 Emerson Road	Sterling	IL	61081		1-5
Opportunities Unlimited Incorporated	2705 E Main	Lewiston	ID	83501	208-743-1563	1-5
Project Quest Inc	301 S Frio Ste 400	San Antonio	TX	78207	210-270-4690	1-5
Sojourner Hall for Women Inc	30 Millbank St	Rochester	NY	14619	716-436-7100	1-5
Sullivan & Associates Inc	PO Box 2853	Springfield	MA	01101		5-9
Three Rivers Employment Service	100 Columbus Ave	Pittsburgh	PA	15233	412-323-0100	1-5

Source: National Directory of Nonprofit Organizations, 2000, Volumes 1 and 2, The Taft Group. The table shows a selection of organizations for illustration and does not constitute a complete selection from the source. The organizations are arranged in alphabetical order.

LOCATION BY STATE AND REGIONAL CONCENTRATION

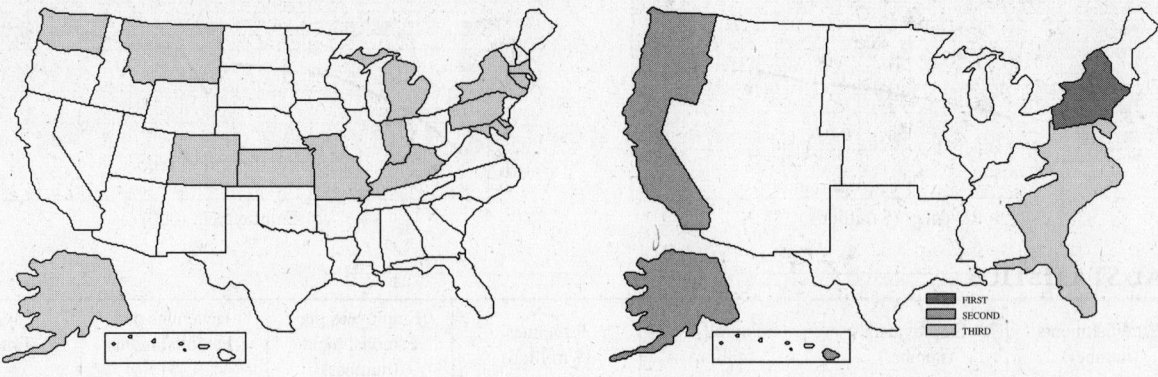

FIRST
SECOND
THIRD

INDUSTRY DATA BY STATE

State	Establishments		Employment			Payroll		Revenues		
	Total (number)	% of U.S.	Total (number)	% of U.S.	Per Estab.	Total ($ mil.)	Per Empl. ($)	Total ($ mil.)	% of U.S.	Per Estab. ($)
California	1,142	13.9	28,358	9.4	25	436.0	15,374	951.5	12.1	833,180
New York	489	6.0	19,998	6.6	41	312.7	15,634	671.3	8.5	1,372,767
Pennsylvania	353	4.3	17,224	5.7	49	207.1	12,022	423.2	5.4	1,198,785
Ohio	338	4.1	21,070	7.0	62	163.9	7,780	337.0	4.3	997,003
Illinois	364	4.4	12,969	4.3	36	170.6	13,157	329.0	4.2	903,841
Florida	296	3.6	11,540	3.8	39	145.3	12,589	314.9	4.0	1,063,834
Texas	363	4.4	10,903	3.6	30	143.9	13,198	312.1	4.0	859,672
Michigan	284	3.5	12,415	4.1	44	143.9	11,593	310.1	3.9	1,091,810
Massachusetts	261	3.2	8,990	3.0	34	123.0	13,687	251.6	3.2	963,812
Indiana	202	2.5	7,372	2.4	36	91.9	12,467	207.8	2.6	1,028,876
Missouri	210	2.6	10,782	3.6	51	90.9	8,429	198.8	2.5	946,571
Washington	291	3.5	6,194	2.1	21	104.1	16,800	197.3	2.5	678,017
Virginia	175	2.1	7,460	2.5	43	95.7	12,823	193.5	2.5	1,105,714
Maryland	158	1.9	5,937	2.0	38	86.2	14,527	173.3	2.2	1,096,627
North Carolina	141	1.7	4,977	1.6	35	68.8	13,831	171.4	2.2	1,215,745
Connecticut	131	1.6	4,206	1.4	32	69.1	16,432	163.1	2.1	1,245,366
New Jersey	136	1.7	6,060	2.0	45	81.1	13,384	161.3	2.0	1,186,324
Georgia	154	1.9	5,277	1.7	34	77.8	14,738	151.6	1.9	984,149
D.C.	65	0.8	4,109	1.4	63	58.8	14,316	117.1	1.5	1,802,092
Kentucky	96	1.2	4,356	1.4	45	56.1	12,883	115.3	1.5	1,200,573
Arizona	144	1.8	4,012	1.3	28	51.6	12,852	107.8	1.4	748,479
Colorado	120	1.5	3,052	1.0	25	39.6	12,981	107.5	1.4	895,700
Kansas	90	1.1	4,278	1.4	48	49.8	11,641	95.4	1.2	1,060,378
Louisiana	127	1.5	4,212	1.4	33	42.5	10,083	93.6	1.2	736,693
Tennessee	119	1.4	2,386	0.8	20	31.3	13,120	75.8	1.0	636,588
Oklahoma	108	1.3	4,482	1.5	42	40.8	9,098	71.3	0.9	660,324
Mississippi	78	0.9	2,154	0.7	28	26.3	12,207	60.2	0.8	771,282
New Mexico	31	0.4	1,937	0.6	62	23.9	12,345	46.7	0.6	1,506,290
Alabama	65	0.8	1,718	0.6	26	22.7	13,223	44.4	0.6	683,169
Alaska	29	0.4	1,082	0.4	37	20.6	19,071	43.8	0.6	1,508,690
South Carolina	90	1.1	2,435	0.8	27	21.9	8,993	42.0	0.5	466,533
Nebraska	85	1.0	1,763	0.6	21	21.4	12,154	37.4	0.5	440,565
Montana	58	0.7	1,346	0.4	23	16.8	12,499	35.3	0.4	609,345
Hawaii	31	0.4	818	0.3	26	14.9	18,249	31.7	0.4	1,022,065
Nevada	39	0.5	944	0.3	24	12.9	13,624	27.9	0.4	715,436
Utah	28	0.3	1,150	0.4	41	15.6	13,579	26.1	0.3	931,250
Delaware	17	0.2	1,236	0.4	73	12.6	10,182	24.6	0.3	1,448,588
Vermont	23	0.3	634	0.2	28	8.5	13,353	18.0	0.2	783,000

Source: 1997 *Economic Census*. The states are in descending order of revenues or establishments (if revenue data are missing for the majority). The symbol (D) appears when data are withheld to prevent disclosure of competitive information. States marked with (D) are sorted by number of establishments. A dash (-) indicates that the data element cannot be calculated. * indicates the midpoint of a range; 175, for example is the range 100-249. Shaded *states* on the state map indicate those states which have proportionately greater representation in the industry than would be indicated by the state's population; the ratio is based on total revenues or number of establishments. Shaded *regions* indicate where the industry is regionally most concentrated.

NAICS 624410 - CHILD DAY CARE SERVICES*

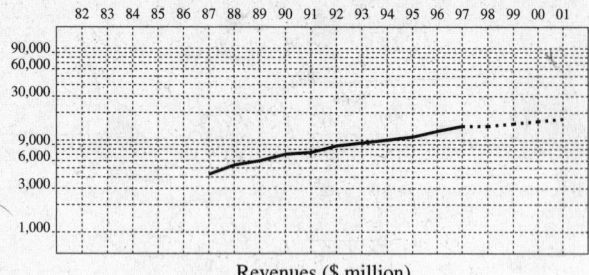

Revenues ($ million)

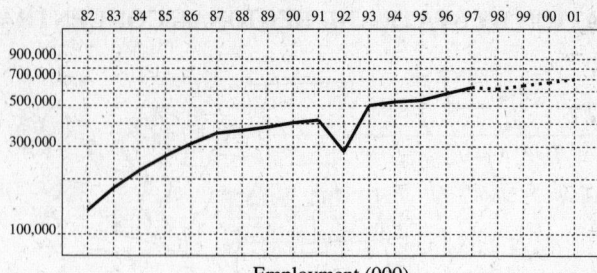

Employment (000)

GENERAL STATISTICS

Year	Establishments (number)	Employment (number)	Payroll ($ million)	Revenues ($ million)	Employees per Establishment (number)	Revenues per Establishment ($)	Payroll per Employee ($)
1982	13,108	135,269	889.0	-	10.3	-	6,572
1983	18,613 e	179,229 e	1,221.0 e	-	9.6 e	-	6,813 e
1984	24,117 e	223,189 e	1,552.0 e	-	9.3 e	-	6,954 e
1985	29,622 e	267,148 e	1,883.0 e	-	9.0 e	-	7,049 e
1986	35,126 e	311,108 e	2,215.0 e	-	8.9 e	-	7,120 e
1987	40,631	355,068	2,546.0	4,284.0	8.7	105,437	7,170
1988	39,172	367,632	2,848.0	5,400.0	9.4	137,854	7,747
1989	38,797	383,423	3,089.0	5,986.0	9.9	154,290	8,056
1990	39,017	405,125	3,433.0	7,064.0	10.4	181,049	8,474
1991	40,758	418,875	3,783.0	7,395.0	10.3	181,437	9,031
1992	35,327	282,675	2,388.0	8,708.0	8.0	246,497	8,448
1993	52,467	502,725	4,793.0	9,352.0	9.6	178,245	9,534
1994	51,191	526,000	5,216.0	10,074.0	10.3	196,792	9,916
1995	49,124	534,985	5,535.0	10,882.0	10.9	221,521	10,346
1996	55,589 e	581,849 e	6,249.0 e	12,529.0 e	10.5 e	225,386 e	10,740 e
1997	62,054	628,712	6,963.0	14,175.0	10.1	228,430	11,075
1998	58,911 p	617,299 p	6,855.0 p	14,203.0 p	10.5 p	241,092 p	11,105 p
1999	61,091 p	644,621 p	7,288.0 p	15,118.0 p	10.6 p	247,467 p	11,306 p
2000	63,271 p	671,943 p	7,721.0 p	16,033.0 p	10.6 p	253,402 p	11,491 p
2001	65,451 p	699,264 p	8,154.0 p	16,947.0 p	10.7 p	258,927 p	11,661 p

Sources: Economic Census of the United States, 1982, 1987, 1992, 1997. Establishment counts, employment, and payroll are from County Business Patterns for non-Census years. In non-Census years, industries in the Manufacturing range under SIC coding include data from the Annual Survey of Manufactures (ASM); those in the old Services range include data from the Services Annual Survey (SAS). Values followed by a 'p' are projections by the editors. Extrapolations are marked by 'e'. Data are the most recent available at this level of detail.

INDICES OF CHANGE

Year	Establishments (number)	Employment (number)	Payroll ($ million)	Revenues ($ million)	Employees per Establishment (number)	Revenues per Establishment ($)	Payroll per Employee ($)
1982	21.1	21.5	12.8	-	101.9	-	59.3
1987	65.5	56.5	36.6	30.2	86.3	46.2	64.7
1992	56.9	45.0	34.3	61.4	79.0	107.9	76.3
1993	84.6	80.0	68.8	66.0	94.6	78.0	86.1
1994	82.5	83.7	74.9	71.1	101.4	86.1	89.5
1995	79.2	85.1	79.5	76.8	107.5	97.0	93.4
1996	89.6 e	92.5 e	89.7 e	88.4 e	103.3 e	98.7 e	97.0 e
1997	100.0	100.0	100.0	100.0	100.0	100.0	100.0
1998	94.9 p	98.2 p	98.4 p	100.2 p	103.4 p	105.5 p	100.3 p
1999	98.4 p	102.5 p	104.7 p	106.7 p	104.1 p	108.3 p	102.1 p
2000	102.0 p	106.9 p	110.9 p	113.1 p	104.8 p	110.9 p	103.8 p
2001	105.5 p	111.2 p	117.1 p	119.6 p	105.4 p	113.4 p	105.3 p

Sources: Same as General Statistics. The values shown reflect change from the base year, 1997. Values above 100 mean greater than 1997, values below 100 mean less than 1997, and a value of 100 in the 1982-96 or 1998-2001 period means same as 1997. Values followed by a 'p' are projections by the editors; 'e' stands for extrapolation. Data are the most recent available at this level of detail.

SELECTED RATIOS

For 1997	Avg. of Information	Analyzed Industry	Index	For 1997	Avg. of Information	Analyzed Industry	Index
Employees per establishment	21	10	48	Payroll per establishment	585,591	112,209	19
Revenue per establishment	1,370,364	228,430	17	Payroll as % of revenue	43	49	115
Revenue per employee	65,262	22,546	35	Payroll per employee	27,888	11,075	40

Sources: Same as General Statistics. The 'Average' column represents the average for the industry sector, in 1997, where the currently shown industry is classified. The Index shows the relationship between the Average and the Analyzed Industry. For example, 100 means that they are equal; 500 that the Analyzed Industry is five times the average; 50 means that the Analyzed Industry is half the national average. The abbreviation 'na' is used to show that data are 'not available'.

*Equivalent to SIC 8351.

LEADING COMPANIES   Number shown: **17**   Total sales ($ mil): **7,880**   Total employment (000): **139.3**

Company Name	Address				CEO Name	Phone	Co. Type	Sales ($ mil)	Empl. (000)
ServiceMaster Co.	1 ServiceMaster	Downers Grove	IL	60515	C. William Pollard	630-271-1300	P	5,704	51.7
KinderCare Learning Centers Inc.	650 NE Holladay	Portland	OR	97232	David J Johnson	503-872-1300	P	633	25.4
La Petite Academy Inc.	8717 W 110th St	Overland Park	KS	66210	James R Kahl	913-345-1250	S	315	12.7
ARAMARK Educational	573 Park Point Dr	Golden	CO	80401	Duane Larson	303-526-3400	S	288*	15.0
Bright Horizons Family Solutions	209 10th Ave S	Nashville	TN	37203	Marguerite Sallee	615-256-9915	S	236*	4.5
Bright Horizons Family Solutions	1 Kendall Sq	Cambridge	MA	02139	Roger H Brown	617-577-8020	P	209	9.4
Childtime Learning Centers Inc.	38345 W 10 Mile	Farmington Hills	MI	48335	George Kellner	248-476-3200	P	113	5.0
Nobel Learning Communities Inc.	1400 N Providence	Media	PA	19063	AJ Clegg	610-891-8200	P	110	3.8
Children's Discovery Centers Inc.	4340 Redwood Hwy	San Rafael	CA	94903	Elanna Yalow	415-444-1600	S	93	4.7
Childtime Childcare Inc.	38345 W 10 Mile	Farmington	MI	48335	Harold A Lewis	248-476-3200	S	74*	4.5
TesseracT Group	9977 N 90th St	Scottsdale	AZ	85258	John Golle	480-767-2300	P	37	1.0
Magic Years Child Care	1849 Charter Ln	Lancaster	PA	17601	Richard A Niglio	610-272-2358	S	31*	0.6
New Horizon Kids Quest Inc.	16355 36th Ave N	Plymouth	MN	55446	Susan Dunkley	612-557-1111	P	16	0.5
Franciscan Villa	3601 S Chicago Ave	S. Milwaukee	WI	53172	Roger DeMark	414-764-4100	S	10*	0.3
Montessori Learning Commons	1123 D St	Sacramento	CA	95814		916-444-9072	R	6*	0.1
New Horizon Enterprises Inc.	3650 Annpls Ln	Plymouth	MN	55447	Sue Dunclay	612-557-1111	R	3*	<0.1
New Life Discovery Schools Inc.	4035 N Valentine	Fresno	CA	93722	Lynette Ferguson	559-226-8687	R	2*	<0.1

Source: *Ward's Business Directory of U.S. Private and Public Companies*, Volumes 1 and 2, 2000. The company type code used is as follows: P - Public, R - Private, S - Subsidiary, D - Division, J - Joint Venture, A - Affiliate, G - Group, N - Company type not reported. Sales are in millions of dollars, employees are in thousands. An asterisk (*) indicates an estimated sales volume. The symbol < stands for 'less than'. Company names and addresses are truncated, in some cases, to fit into the available space.

LOCATION BY STATE AND REGIONAL CONCENTRATION

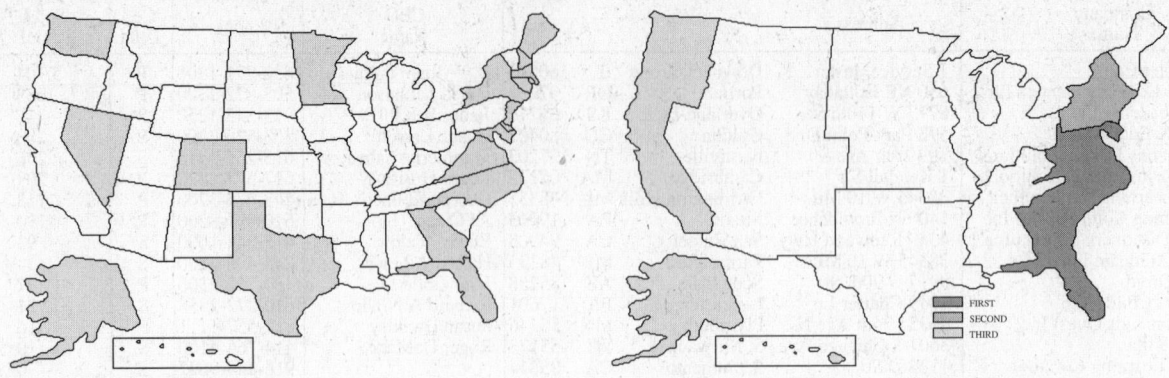

FIRST
SECOND
THIRD

INDUSTRY DATA BY STATE

State	Establishments Total (number)	% of U.S.	Employment Total (number)	% of U.S.	Per Estab.	Payroll Total ($ mil.)	Per Empl. ($)	Revenues Total ($ mil.)	% of U.S.	Per Estab. ($)
California	6,401	10.3	54,752	8.7	9	725.9	13,257	1,585.0	11.2	247,614
New York	3,458	5.6	42,967	6.8	12	640.0	14,896	1,188.6	8.4	343,727
Texas	4,363	7.0	52,721	8.4	12	524.8	9,954	1,122.0	7.9	257,173
Florida	3,132	5.0	33,317	5.3	11	365.4	10,968	775.3	5.5	247,527
Massachusetts	1,676	2.7	19,363	3.1	12	283.8	14,659	621.5	4.4	370,847
Illinois	2,140	3.4	25,095	4.0	12	296.3	11,808	598.0	4.2	279,451
Pennsylvania	2,535	4.1	28,159	4.5	11	306.0	10,867	593.3	4.2	234,037
Georgia	1,924	3.1	26,489	4.2	14	270.4	10,208	552.6	3.9	287,238
New Jersey	1,754	2.8	21,631	3.4	12	280.9	12,987	549.0	3.9	312,985
North Carolina	2,292	3.7	23,984	3.8	10	250.3	10,437	498.8	3.5	217,617
Ohio	1,919	3.1	23,002	3.7	12	245.2	10,659	489.2	3.5	254,932
Virginia	1,483	2.4	18,107	2.9	12	185.8	10,262	368.1	2.6	248,210
Michigan	2,407	3.9	16,783	2.7	7	168.3	10,027	346.8	2.4	144,081
Washington	1,937	3.1	14,029	2.2	7	148.3	10,570	309.1	2.2	159,596
Maryland	1,206	1.9	13,418	2.1	11	161.3	12,019	302.7	2.1	251,008
Tennessee	1,493	2.4	14,451	2.3	10	136.5	9,448	276.0	1.9	184,830
Wisconsin	1,417	2.3	13,931	2.2	10	144.4	10,365	271.6	1.9	191,697
Missouri	1,393	2.2	13,448	2.1	10	130.6	9,714	268.3	1.9	192,616
Minnesota	1,247	2.0	11,087	1.8	9	121.2	10,935	259.8	1.8	208,309
Indiana	1,305	2.1	11,453	1.8	9	112.0	9,780	235.1	1.7	180,152
Connecticut	992	1.6	10,174	1.6	10	124.4	12,222	228.2	1.6	229,996
Colorado	885	1.4	10,310	1.6	12	107.7	10,447	221.0	1.6	249,760
South Carolina	1,044	1.7	9,795	1.6	9	96.6	9,867	195.7	1.4	187,495
Arizona	695	1.1	9,248	1.5	13	86.9	9,397	190.5	1.3	274,083
Louisiana	1,091	1.8	9,312	1.5	9	78.5	8,431	167.0	1.2	153,111
Oklahoma	976	1.6	8,942	1.4	9	78.8	8,816	164.5	1.2	168,529
Alabama	1,045	1.7	9,774	1.6	9	83.0	8,494	164.0	1.2	156,967
Kentucky	843	1.4	8,939	1.4	11	80.7	9,030	156.1	1.1	185,179
Mississippi	757	1.2	6,369	1.0	8	56.9	8,939	119.5	0.8	157,888
Oregon	750	1.2	5,807	0.9	8	58.3	10,038	117.1	0.8	156,101
Iowa	856	1.4	7,011	1.1	8	56.2	8,020	110.3	0.8	128,821
Nevada	282	0.5	3,700	0.6	13	41.3	11,160	97.1	0.7	344,422
Arkansas	636	1.0	5,156	0.8	8	44.8	8,687	88.5	0.6	139,105
New Hampshire	504	0.8	4,030	0.6	8	46.0	11,416	86.5	0.6	171,544
Utah	353	0.6	4,250	0.7	12	37.1	8,728	80.4	0.6	227,660
Maine	536	0.9	2,669	0.4	5	31.0	11,614	74.6	0.5	139,114
Nebraska	547	0.9	4,085	0.6	7	34.4	8,429	69.3	0.5	126,680
New Mexico	277	0.4	2,992	0.5	11	30.8	10,301	61.9	0.4	223,484
Delaware	252	0.4	2,699	0.4	11	31.4	11,622	61.1	0.4	242,460
D.C.	171	0.3	2,164	0.3	13	33.3	15,378	61.0	0.4	356,573
Rhode Island	251	0.4	2,432	0.4	10	29.7	12,209	55.5	0.4	221,179
Hawaii	138	0.2	1,572	0.3	11	21.4	13,607	45.0	0.3	325,768
West Virginia	234	0.4	2,164	0.3	9	19.9	9,177	38.7	0.3	165,466
Kansas	204	0.3	2,262	0.4	11	21.4	9,470	38.5	0.3	188,588
Idaho	310	0.5	2,013	0.3	6	18.7	9,273	38.1	0.3	122,942
Alaska	178	0.3	1,470	0.2	8	18.9	12,852	37.5	0.3	210,646
Montana	360	0.6	1,903	0.3	5	14.8	7,774	32.1	0.2	89,044
South Dakota	237	0.4	1,734	0.3	7	16.3	9,405	31.7	0.2	133,903
Vermont	268	0.4	1,488	0.2	6	15.9	10,683	28.7	0.2	107,116
Wyoming	162	0.3	1,260	0.2	8	11.3	8,944	20.6	0.1	127,352

Source: 1997 *Economic Census*. The states are in descending order of revenues or establishments (if revenue data are missing for the majority). The symbol (D) appears when data are withheld to prevent disclosure of competitive information. States marked with (D) are sorted by number of establishments. A dash (-) indicates that the data element cannot be calculated. * indicates the midpoint of a range; 175, for example is the range 100-249. Shaded *states* on the state map indicate those states which have proportionately greater representation in the industry than would be indicated by the state's population; the ratio is based on total revenues or number of establishments. Shaded *regions* indicate where the industry is regionally most concentrated.

Part IX

ARTS, ENTERTAINMENT, AND RECREATION

NAICS 711110 - THEATER COMPANIES AND DINNER THEATERS

GENERAL STATISTICS

Year	Establishments (number)	Employment (number)	Payroll ($ million)	Revenues ($ million)	Employees per Establishment (number)	Revenues per Establishment ($)	Payroll per Employee ($)
1997	3,247	59,294	1,224.0	4,120.0	18.3	1,268,864	20,643

Source: Economic Census of the United States, 1997. This is a newly defined industry. Data for prior years were unavailable at the time of publication but may become available over time.

INDICES OF CHANGE

Year	Establishments (number)	Employment (number)	Payroll ($ million)	Revenues ($ million)	Employees per Establishment (number)	Revenues per Establishment ($)	Payroll per Employee ($)
1997	100.0	100.0	100.0	100.0	100.0	100.0	100.0

Sources: Same as General Statistics. The values shown reflect change from the base year, 1997. Values above 100 mean greater than 1997, values below 100 mean less than 1997, and a value of 100 in the 1982-96 or 1998-2001 period means same as 1997. Values followed by a 'p' are projections by the editors; 'e' stands for extrapolation. Data are the most recent available at this level of detail.

SIC INDUSTRIES RELATED TO NAICS 711110

Each new NAICS code represents an industry that used to be part of an SIC or a part of several SIC industries. Data in this table are shown to provide transitional information for these cases. All available data for the precursor SIC(s) are shown. Even if only a part of an SIC is included in the NAICS, *all* data for the SIC are reproduced. If the SIC industry is not marked as being a part (pt) of the NAICS, the entire industry is embedded in the NAICS data. The SIC composition of the new industry provides some hints of the relative importance of its "ancestors." Data marked with a 'p' are projected. Projections begin with 1982 data. Data earlier than 1990 are not shown but are reflected in the projections.

SIC	Industry	1990	1991	1992	1993	1994	1995	1996	1997
5812	**Eating places (pt)**								
	Establishments (number)	286,792	280,200	377,760	360,212	367,205	344,854	361,385p	367,752p
	Employment (thousands)	5,700.3	5,459.7	6,243.9	6,346.0	6,477.0	6,568.2	6,822.7p	6,993.9p
	Revenues ($ million)	166,234.6e	175,218.9e	184,203.2	193,580.8p	202,685.3p	211,789.8p	220,894.3p	229,998.8p
7922	**Theatrical Producers & Services (pt)**								
	Establishments (number)	4,470	4,992	5,924	6,229	6,323	6,428	6,542p	6,792p
	Employment (thousands)	63.9	63.1	69.5	88.8	77.8	79.3	87.3p	91.2p
	Revenues ($ million)	-	-	5,730.5	4,396.6p	4,647.8p	4,899.0p	5,150.2p	5,401.4p

Source: Economic Census of the United States, 1992, annual surveys of economic sectors conducted by the Bureau of the Census, and estimates or projections based on the 1982-1992 period; not all data are shown. 'e' marks estimates made by the editors; 'p' indicates projections based on time series. A dash (-) indicates that data for this SIC or year were not available. The abbreviation (pt) next to the industry name indicates that only a part of the industry is present within the NAICS data. If no (pt) is shown, the entire industry is contained within the NAICS data.

SELECTED RATIOS

For 1997	Avg. of Information	Analyzed Industry	Index	For 1997	Avg. of Information	Analyzed Industry	Index
Employees per establishment	16	18	114	Payroll per establishment	330,963	376,963	114
Revenue per establishment	1,057,073	1,268,864	120	Payroll as % of revenue	31	30	95
Revenue per employee	65,958	69,484	105	Payroll per employee	20,651	20,643	100

Sources: Same as General Statistics. The 'Average' column represents the average for the industry sector, in 1997, where the currently shown industry is classified. The Index shows the relationship between the Average and the Analyzed Industry. For example, 100 means that they are equal; 500 that the Analyzed Industry is five times the average; 50 means that the Analyzed Industry is half the national average. The abbreviation 'na' is used to show that data are 'not available'.

LEADING COMPANIES

No company data available for this industry.

REPRESENTATIVE NONPROFIT ORGANIZATIONS

Organization Name	Address				Phone	Income Range ($ mil)
American Cabaret Theatre Inc	401 E Michigan St	Indianapolis	IN	46204	317-631-0334	1-5
American Stage Co Inc	PO Box 1560	St Petersburg	FL	33731		1-5
Arkansas Repertory Theatre Company	PO Box 110	Little Rock	AR	72203		1-5
Ballet Pacifica	1824 Kaiser Ave	Irvine	CA	92614		1-5
Broadway Theatre Guild	161 Ottawa NW	Grand Rapids	MI	49503	616-774-9922	1-5
Childrens Theater Company and School	2400 Third Ave S	Minneapolis	MN	55404	612-874-0500	5-9
Crossroads Incorporated	7 Livingston Ave	New Brunswick	NJ	08901	732-249-5581	1-5
Dance Umbrella Boston Inc	515 Washington St 5th FL	Boston	MA	02111	617-482-7570	1-5
Downtown Cabaret Theatre Company of Bridgeport	263 Golden Hill St	Bridgeport	CT	06604	203-576-1636	1-5
Facets-Multimedia Incorporated	1517 W Fullerton Ave	Chicago	IL	60614	773-281-9075	5-9
Franklin-Simpson Community Arts Council Inc	P O Box 189	Franklin	KY	42135		1-5
Great American Childrens Theatre Co Inc	304 E Florida St	Milwaukee	WI	53204		1-5
Hawaii Theater Center	1130 Bethel St	Honolulu	HI	96813	808-528-5535	1-5
Lyric Theatre of Oklahoma Inc	4444 N Classen Blvd	Oklahoma City	OK	73118	405-524-9310	1-5
MCT Inc	200 N Adams	Missoula	MT	59802		1-5
Music Theatre of Wichita Inc	225 W Douglas	Wichita	KS	67202	316-265-3107	1-5
Nevada Dance Theatre Inc	1555 E Flamingo Road	Las Vegas	NV	89119		1-5
Next Door Inc	PO Box 661	Hood River	OR	97031		1-5
North Carolina Shakerspeare Festival Inc	PO Box 6066	High Point	NC	27262		1-5
North Valley Arts Council	415 Demers Ave	Grand Forks	ND	58201	701-746-4732	1-5
One Reel	1725 Westlake Ave	Seattle	WA	98109		5-9
Pittsburgh Public Theater Corporation	621 Pann Ave	Pittsburgh	PA	15222	412-321-9800	5-9
Playhouse Square Foundation	1501 Euclid Ave 200	Cleveland	OH	44115	216-771-4444	40-49
Rochester Broadway Theatre League Inc	10 Gibbs St	Rochester	NY	14604	716-325-7760	10-19
Salt Lake Acting Company	168 W 500 N	Salt Lake City	UT	84103	801-363-7522	1-5
Scottsdale Cultural Council	7380 E 2nd Street	Scottsdale	AZ	85251	480-874-4610	10-19
Stages St Louis	104 N Clay	St Louis	MO	63122		1-5
Theatre Under the Stars Inc	PO Box 980609	Houston	TX	77098		10-19
Theatre in the Square Inc	11 Whitlock Ave	Marietta	GA	30064	770-422-8369	1-5

Source: National Directory of Nonprofit Organizations, 2000, Volumes 1 and 2, The Taft Group. The table shows a selection of organizations for illustration and does not constitute a complete selection from the source. The organizations are arranged in alphabetical order.

LOCATION BY STATE AND REGIONAL CONCENTRATION

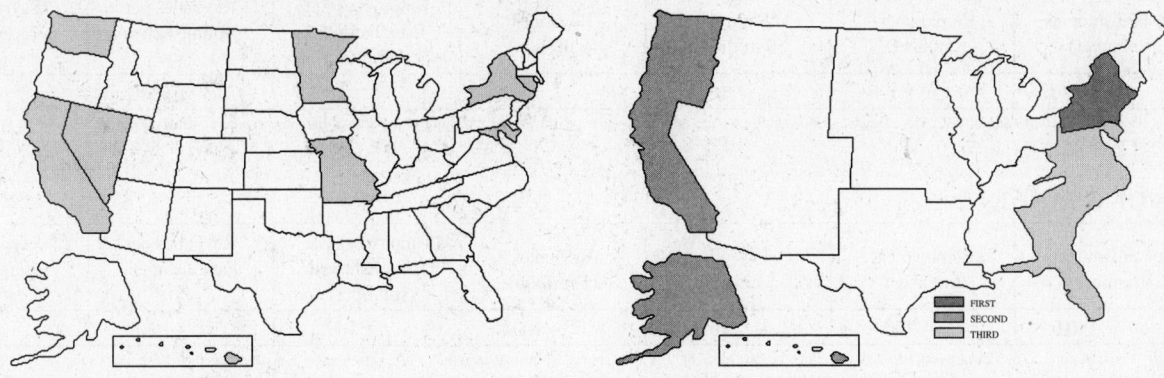

INDUSTRY DATA BY STATE

State	Establishments Total (number)	% of U.S.	Employment Total (number)	% of U.S.	Per Estab.	Payroll Total ($ mil.)	Per Empl. ($)	Revenues Total ($ mil.)	% of U.S.	Per Estab. ($)
New York	596	18.4	13,984	23.6	23	405.2	28,977	1,460.2	35.4	2,449,956
California	478	14.7	9,537	16.1	20	218.8	22,939	568.6	13.8	1,189,462
Texas	143	4.4	2,367	4.0	17	38.9	16,447	209.9	5.1	1,467,650
Illinois	149	4.6	2,747	4.6	18	56.5	20,556	181.5	4.4	1,217,832
Missouri	71	2.2	1,779	3.0	25	37.8	21,262	128.5	3.1	1,810,014
Maryland	58	1.8	1,298	2.2	22	23.3	17,976	118.3	2.9	2,040,517
Minnesota	93	2.9	2,092	3.5	22	30.9	14,748	111.1	2.7	1,194,677
Florida	143	4.4	2,268	3.8	16	30.4	13,389	108.5	2.6	758,497
Pennsylvania	120	3.7	1,712	2.9	14	30.4	17,758	96.5	2.3	804,417
Washington	82	2.5	2,273	3.8	28	29.7	13,051	94.9	2.3	1,157,476
Connecticut	50	1.5	931	1.6	19	19.0	20,427	82.5	2.0	1,649,780
New Jersey	90	2.8	1,233	2.1	14	24.1	19,521	69.5	1.7	771,822
Ohio	75	2.3	1,268	2.1	17	19.7	15,550	62.1	1.5	828,307
Hawaii	25	0.8	906	1.5	36	14.3	15,741	58.6	1.4	2,343,280
Tennessee	43	1.3	989	1.7	23	13.6	13,788	57.3	1.4	1,331,674
D.C.	19	0.6	846	1.4	45	16.6	19,564	49.2	1.2	2,592,000
Wisconsin	54	1.7	1,112	1.9	21	16.4	14,752	48.0	1.2	889,556
Georgia	67	2.1	737	1.2	11	12.2	16,551	44.7	1.1	666,821
South Carolina	25	0.8	778	1.3	31	13.0	16,684	41.2	1.0	1,649,560
Colorado	51	1.6	724	1.2	14	12.7	17,540	40.4	1.0	792,863
Nevada	33	1.0	325	0.5	10	17.5	53,991	39.4	1.0	1,194,394
Arizona	54	1.7	769	1.3	14	9.2	11,990	33.7	0.8	624,444
Indiana	45	1.4	561	0.9	12	8.9	15,929	31.2	0.8	693,644
Oregon	39	1.2	689	1.2	18	13.0	18,849	31.1	0.8	796,821
North Carolina	67	2.1	363	0.6	5	6.9	19,099	24.4	0.6	364,746
Kentucky	30	0.9	536	0.9	18	7.1	13,196	22.9	0.6	764,300
Kansas	23	0.7	387	0.7	17	5.5	14,111	14.4	0.3	625,913
Arkansas	8	0.2	238	0.4	30	4.0	16,756	11.5	0.3	1,436,000
Utah	18	0.6	226	0.4	13	2.7	11,827	9.6	0.2	531,667
Maine	21	0.6	245	0.4	12	2.4	9,641	6.3	0.2	300,810
Iowa	17	0.5	106	0.2	6	1.8	16,528	5.6	0.1	330,824
Delaware	6	0.2	50	0.1	8	0.9	18,080	4.5	0.1	744,667
New Hampshire	12	0.4	59	0.1	5	1.4	23,814	4.1	0.1	338,917
Rhode Island	8	0.2	64	0.1	8	0.9	13,344	3.9	0.1	485,125
Montana	9	0.3	118	0.2	13	1.4	12,195	3.9	0.1	429,889
Idaho	12	0.4	149	0.3	12	0.9	5,960	3.2	0.1	263,500
North Dakota	9	0.3	77	0.1	9	1.0	12,740	1.6	0.0	182,556
South Dakota	6	0.2	7	0.0	1	0.3	45,000	1.1	0.0	182,667

Source: 1997 *Economic Census*. The states are in descending order of revenues or establishments (if revenue data are missing for the majority). The symbol (D) appears when data are withheld to prevent disclosure of competitive information. States marked with (D) are sorted by number of establishments. A dash (-) indicates that the data element cannot be calculated. * indicates the midpoint of a range; 175, for example is the range 100-249. Shaded *states* on the state map indicate those states which have proportionately greater representation in the industry than would be indicated by the state's population; the ratio is based on total revenues or number of establishments. Shaded *regions* indicate where the industry is regionally most concentrated.

NAICS 711120 - DANCE COMPANIES

GENERAL STATISTICS

Year	Establishments (number)	Employment (number)	Payroll ($ million)	Revenues ($ million)	Employees per Establishment (number)	Revenues per Establishment ($)	Payroll per Employee ($)
1997	530	9,170	166.0	433.0	17.3	816,981	18,103

Source: Economic Census of the United States, 1997. This is a newly defined industry. Data for prior years were unavailable at the time of publication but may become available over time.

INDICES OF CHANGE

Year	Establishments (number)	Employment (number)	Payroll ($ million)	Revenues ($ million)	Employees per Establishment (number)	Revenues per Establishment ($)	Payroll per Employee ($)
1997	100.0	100.0	100.0	100.0	100.0	100.0	100.0

Sources: Same as General Statistics. The values shown reflect change from the base year, 1997. Values above 100 mean greater than 1997, values below 100 mean less than 1997, and a value of 100 in the 1982-96 or 1998-2001 period means same as 1997. Values followed by a 'p' are projections by the editors; 'e' stands for extrapolation. Data are the most recent available at this level of detail.

SIC INDUSTRIES RELATED TO NAICS 711120

Each new NAICS code represents an industry that used to be part of an SIC or a part of several SIC industries. Data in this table are shown to provide transitional information for these cases. All available data for the precursor SIC(s) are shown. Even if only a part of an SIC is included in the NAICS, *all* data for the SIC are reproduced. If the SIC industry is not marked as being a part (pt) of the NAICS, the entire industry is embedded in the NAICS data. The SIC composition of the new industry provides some hints of the relative importance of its "ancestors." Data marked with a 'p' are projected. Projections begin with 1982 data. Data earlier than 1990 are not shown but are reflected in the projections.

SIC	Industry	1990	1991	1992	1993	1994	1995	1996	1997
7922	**Theatrical Producers & Services (pt)**								
	Establishments (number)	4,470	4,992	5,924	6,229	6,323	6,428	6,542*p*	6,792*p*
	Employment (thousands)	63.9	63.1	69.5	88.8	77.8	79.3	87.3*p*	91.2*p*
	Revenues ($ million)	-	-	5,730.5	4,396.6*p*	4,647.8*p*	4,899.0*p*	5,150.2*p*	5,401.4*p*

Source: Economic Census of the United States, 1992, annual surveys of economic sectors conducted by the Bureau of the Census, and estimates or projections based on the 1982-1992 period; not all data are shown. 'e' marks estimates made by the editors; 'p' indicates projections based on time series. A dash (-) indicates that data for this SIC or year were not available. The abbreviation (pt) next to the industry name indicates that only a part of the industry is present within the NAICS data. If no (pt) is shown, the entire industry is contained within the NAICS data.

SELECTED RATIOS

For 1997	Avg. of Information	Analyzed Industry	Index	For 1997	Avg. of Information	Analyzed Industry	Index
Employees per establishment	16	17	108	Payroll per establishment	330,963	313,208	95
Revenue per establishment	1,057,073	816,981	77	Payroll as % of revenue	31	38	122
Revenue per employee	65,958	47,219	72	Payroll per employee	20,651	18,103	88

Sources: Same as General Statistics. The 'Average' column represents the average for the industry sector, in 1997, where the currently shown industry is classified. The Index shows the relationship between the Average and the Analyzed Industry. For example, 100 means that they are equal; 500 that the Analyzed Industry is five times the average; 50 means that the Analyzed Industry is half the national average. The abbreviation 'na' is used to show that data are 'not available'.

LEADING COMPANIES

No company data available for this industry.

LOCATION BY STATE AND REGIONAL CONCENTRATION

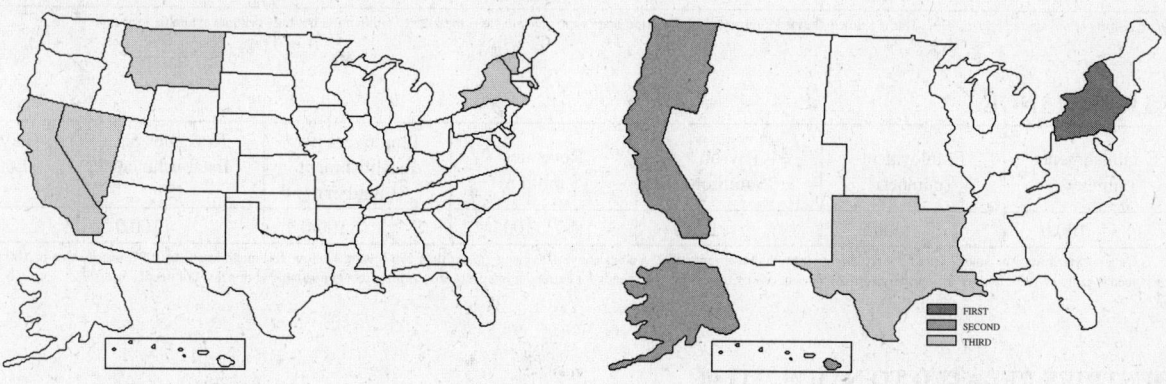

FIRST
SECOND
THIRD

INDUSTRY DATA BY STATE

State	Establishments		Employment			Payroll		Revenues		
	Total (number)	% of U.S.	Total (number)	% of U.S.	Per Estab.	Total ($ mil.)	Per Empl. ($)	Total ($ mil.)	% of U.S.	Per Estab. ($)
New York	107	20.2	1,823	19.9	17	38.9	21,363	105.0	24.3	981,729
California	83	15.7	1,061	11.6	13	27.4	25,839	80.8	18.7	973,157
Texas	22	4.2	717	7.8	33	7.0	9,789	15.5	3.6	705,455
North Carolina	9	1.7	126	1.4	14	1.6	12,476	4.4	1.0	487,000
Alabama	3	0.6	39	0.4	13	0.4	9,000	0.9	0.2	295,333
Louisiana	5	0.9	60*	-	-	(D)	-	(D)	-	-
Arizona	3	0.6	175*	-	-	(D)	-	(D)	-	-
Arkansas	3	0.6	10*	-	-	(D)	-	(D)	-	-
Nevada	3	0.6	60*	-	-	(D)	-	(D)	-	-
Rhode Island	3	0.6	10*	-	-	(D)	-	(D)	-	-
D.C.	2	0.4	60*	-	-	(D)	-	(D)	-	-
Idaho	2	0.4	10*	-	-	(D)	-	(D)	-	-
Kentucky	2	0.4	60*	-	-	(D)	-	(D)	-	-
Maine	2	0.4	10*	-	-	(D)	-	(D)	-	-
Mississippi	2	0.4	60*	-	-	(D)	-	(D)	-	-
Montana	2	0.4	10*	-	-	(D)	-	(D)	-	-
Vermont	2	0.4	10*	-	-	(D)	-	(D)	-	-
West Virginia	2	0.4	10*	-	-	(D)	-	(D)	-	-
Alaska	1	0.2	10*	-	-	(D)	-	(D)	-	-
Delaware	1	0.2	10*	-	-	(D)	-	(D)	-	-

Source: 1997 *Economic Census*. The states are in descending order of revenues or establishments (if revenue data are missing for the majority). The symbol (D) appears when data are withheld to prevent disclosure of competitive information. States marked with (D) are sorted by number of establishments. A dash (-) indicates that the data element cannot be calculated. * indicates the midpoint of a range; 175, for example is the range 100-249. Shaded *states* on the state map indicate those states which have proportionately greater representation in the industry than would be indicated by the state's population; the ratio is based on total revenues or number of establishments. Shaded *regions* indicate where the industry is regionally most concentrated.

NAICS 711130 - MUSICAL GROUPS AND ARTISTS

GENERAL STATISTICS

Year	Establishments (number)	Employment (number)	Payroll ($ million)	Revenues ($ million)	Employees per Establishment (number)	Revenues per Establishment ($)	Payroll per Employee ($)
1997	4,580	46,122	1,134.0	3,326.0	10.1	726,201	24,587

Source: Economic Census of the United States, 1997. This is a newly defined industry. Data for prior years were unavailable at the time of publication but may become available over time.

INDICES OF CHANGE

Year	Establishments (number)	Employment (number)	Payroll ($ million)	Revenues ($ million)	Employees per Establishment (number)	Revenues per Establishment ($)	Payroll per Employee ($)
1997	100.0	100.0	100.0	100.0	100.0	100.0	100.0

Sources: Same as General Statistics. The values shown reflect change from the base year, 1997. Values above 100 mean greater than 1997, values below 100 mean less than 1997, and a value of 100 in the 1982-96 or 1998-2001 period means same as 1997. Values followed by a 'p' are projections by the editors; 'e' stands for extrapolation. Data are the most recent available at this level of detail.

SIC INDUSTRIES RELATED TO NAICS 711130

Each new NAICS code represents an industry that used to be part of an SIC or a part of several SIC industries. Data in this table are shown to provide transitional information for these cases. All available data for the precursor SIC(s) are shown. Even if only a part of an SIC is included in the NAICS, *all* data for the SIC are reproduced. If the SIC industry is not marked as being a part (pt) of the NAICS, the entire industry is embedded in the NAICS data. The SIC composition of the new industry provides some hints of the relative importance of its "ancestors." Data marked with a 'p' are projected. Projections begin with 1982 data. Data earlier than 1990 are not shown but are reflected in the projections.

SIC	Industry	1990	1991	1992	1993	1994	1995	1996	1997
7929	**Entertainers & Entertainment Groups (pt)**								
	Establishments (number)	5,038	5,514	7,251	7,547	7,583	7,922	7,795p	8,080p
	Employment (thousands)	61.2	61.5	72.3	73.2	73.3	73.6	81.8p	85.4p
	Revenues ($ million)	-	-	5,714.7	4,279.9p	4,561.2p	4,842.4p	5,123.6p	5,404.9p

Source: Economic Census of the United States, 1992, annual surveys of economic sectors conducted by the Bureau of the Census, and estimates or projections based on the 1982-1992 period; not all data are shown. 'e' marks estimates made by the editors; 'p' indicates projections based on time series. A dash (-) indicates that data for this SIC or year were not available. The abbreviation (pt) next to the industry name indicates that only a part of the industry is present within the NAICS data. If no (pt) is shown, the entire industry is contained within the NAICS data.

SELECTED RATIOS

For 1997	Avg. of Information	Analyzed Industry	Index	For 1997	Avg. of Information	Analyzed Industry	Index
Employees per establishment	16	10	63	Payroll per establishment	330,963	247,598	75
Revenue per establishment	1,057,073	726,201	69	Payroll as % of revenue	31	34	109
Revenue per employee	65,958	72,113	109	Payroll per employee	20,651	24,587	119

Sources: Same as General Statistics. The 'Average' column represents the average for the industry sector, in 1997, where the currently shown industry is classified. The Index shows the relationship between the Average and the Analyzed Industry. For example, 100 means that they are equal; 500 that the Analyzed Industry is five times the average; 50 means that the Analyzed Industry is half the national average. The abbreviation 'na' is used to show that data are 'not available'.

LEADING COMPANIES Number shown: **2** Total sales ($ mil): **8** Total employment (000): **0.0**

Company Name	Address				CEO Name	Phone	Co. Type	Sales ($ mil)	Empl. (000)
StarShowz International Inc.	1800 W Maple Rd	Troy	MI	48084	Rick Galdi		R	4*	<0.1
Entertainment Properties Trust	One Kansas Pl	Kansas City	MO	64105	Robert L Harris	816-472-1700	N	4	<0.1

Source: Ward's Business Directory of U.S. Private and Public Companies, Volumes 1 and 2, 2000. The company type code used is as follows: P - Public, R - Private, S - Subsidiary, D - Division, J - Joint Venture, A - Affiliate, G - Group, N - Company type not reported. Sales are in millions of dollars, employees are in thousands. An asterisk (*) indicates an estimated sales volume. The symbol < stands for 'less than'. Company names and addresses are truncated, in some cases, to fit into the available space.

LOCATION BY STATE AND REGIONAL CONCENTRATION

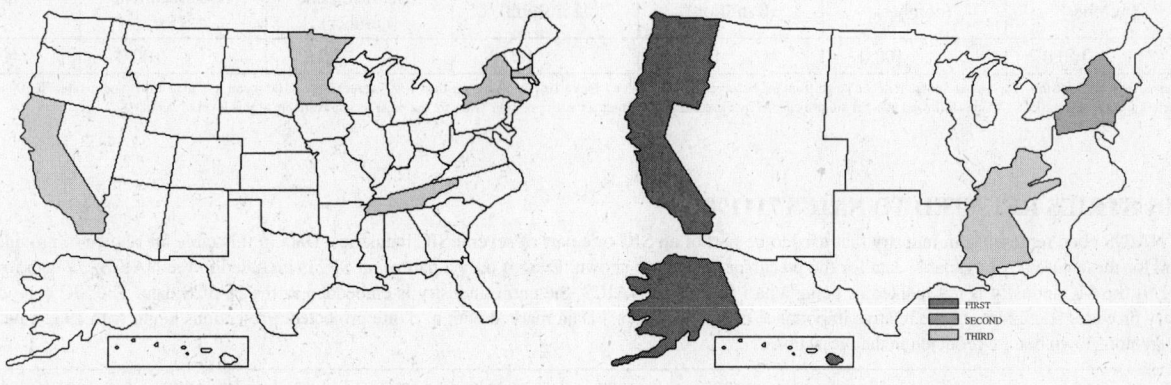

INDUSTRY DATA BY STATE

State	Establishments Total (number)	% of U.S.	Employment Total (number)	% of U.S.	Per Estab.	Payroll Total ($ mil.)	Per Empl. ($)	Revenues Total ($ mil.)	% of U.S.	Per Estab. ($)
California	991	21.6	7,198	15.6	7	280.1	38,915	898.0	27.0	906,195
New York	617	13.5	5,060	11.0	8	131.6	26,000	419.2	12.6	679,389
Tennessee	359	7.8	3,084	6.7	9	118.1	38,290	340.6	10.2	948,710
Texas	203	4.4	2,336	5.1	12	55.2	23,631	163.4	4.9	804,828
Florida	192	4.2	1,697	3.7	9	40.6	23,932	116.3	3.5	605,641
Massachusetts	78	1.7	958	2.1	12	36.3	37,915	103.1	3.1	1,322,128
Ohio	99	2.2	1,995	4.3	20	39.1	19,614	97.8	2.9	988,172
Illinois	176	3.8	2,690	5.8	15	50.8	18,903	95.6	2.9	543,023
Minnesota	99	2.2	1,007	2.2	10	25.5	25,361	92.6	2.8	935,707
Pennsylvania	112	2.4	1,617	3.5	14	38.3	23,692	87.7	2.6	783,205
Georgia	97	2.1	875	1.9	9	24.4	27,938	80.7	2.4	831,722
Indiana	75	1.6	1,096	2.4	15	17.4	15,861	73.7	2.2	983,227
New Jersey	132	2.9	1,009	2.2	8	22.8	22,631	68.8	2.1	521,417
Missouri	73	1.6	1,083	2.3	15	26.3	24,303	63.2	1.9	866,110
Washington	118	2.6	1,028	2.2	9	17.3	16,837	51.4	1.5	435,610
Colorado	62	1.4	890	1.9	14	15.1	16,937	39.4	1.2	635,161
Michigan	35	0.8	1,107	2.4	32	17.2	15,508	37.2	1.1	1,063,743
Wisconsin	102	2.2	859	1.9	8	12.4	14,424	29.8	0.9	292,402
Connecticut	66	1.4	790	1.7	12	11.7	14,780	29.2	0.9	442,197
North Carolina	65	1.4	825	1.8	13	12.2	14,756	27.6	0.8	424,646
Alabama	28	0.6	432	0.9	15	8.7	20,218	22.8	0.7	815,250
Louisiana	50	1.1	607	1.3	12	8.8	14,545	21.2	0.6	424,140
South Carolina	33	0.7	499	1.1	15	5.1	10,184	16.7	0.5	506,455
Oklahoma	34	0.7	376	0.8	11	6.7	17,859	16.6	0.5	488,500
Oregon	29	0.6	345	0.7	12	8.9	25,672	16.3	0.5	561,138
Kentucky	30	0.7	547	1.2	18	6.0	10,892	13.6	0.4	453,600
New Mexico	21	0.5	255	0.6	12	4.0	15,757	11.8	0.4	562,619
Montana	6	0.1	37	0.1	6	0.9	23,541	10.5	0.3	1,752,833
Iowa	24	0.5	658	1.4	27	3.3	4,939	8.3	0.2	343,750
Hawaii	23	0.5	105	0.2	5	1.0	10,000	3.6	0.1	154,609
Kansas	10	0.2	94	0.2	9	0.7	7,074	2.6	0.1	256,000
Utah	13	0.3	30	0.1	2	0.3	9,433	1.4	0.0	110,692
North Dakota	5	0.1	14	0.0	3	0.2	12,857	0.6	0.0	125,000
South Dakota	6	0.1	9	0.0	2	0.1	7,778	0.5	0.0	81,833

Source: 1997 Economic Census. The states are in descending order of revenues or establishments (if revenue data are missing for the majority). The symbol (D) appears when data are withheld to prevent disclosure of competitive information. States marked with (D) are sorted by number of establishments. A dash (-) indicates that the data element cannot be calculated. * indicates the midpoint of a range; 175, for example is the range 100-249. Shaded states on the state map indicate those states which have proportionately greater representation in the industry than would be indicated by the state's population; the ratio is based on total revenues or number of establishments. Shaded regions indicate where the industry is regionally most concentrated.

NAICS 711190 - PERFORMING ARTS COMPANIES NEC

GENERAL STATISTICS

Year	Establishments (number)	Employment (number)	Payroll ($ million)	Revenues ($ million)	Employees per Establishment (number)	Revenues per Establishment ($)	Payroll per Employee ($)
1997	842	7,417	201.0	691.0	8.8	820,665	27,100

Source: Economic Census of the United States, 1997. This is a newly defined industry. Data for prior years were unavailable at the time of publication but may become available over time.

INDICES OF CHANGE

Year	Establishments (number)	Employment (number)	Payroll ($ million)	Revenues ($ million)	Employees per Establishment (number)	Revenues per Establishment ($)	Payroll per Employee ($)
1997	100.0	100.0	100.0	100.0	100.0	100.0	100.0

Sources: Same as General Statistics. The values shown reflect change from the base year, 1997. Values above 100 mean greater than 1997, values below 100 mean less than 1997, and a value of 100 in the 1982-96 or 1998-2001 period means same as 1997. Values followed by a 'p' are projections by the editors; 'e' stands for extrapolation. Data are the most recent available at this level of detail.

SIC INDUSTRIES RELATED TO NAICS 711190

Each new NAICS code represents an industry that used to be part of an SIC or a part of several SIC industries. Data in this table are shown to provide transitional information for these cases. All available data for the precursor SIC(s) are shown. Even if only a part of an SIC is included in the NAICS, *all* data for the SIC are reproduced. If the SIC industry is not marked as being a part (pt) of the NAICS, the entire industry is embedded in the NAICS data. The SIC composition of the new industry provides some hints of the relative importance of its "ancestors." Data marked with a 'p' are projected. Projections begin with 1982 data. Data earlier than 1990 are not shown but are reflected in the projections.

SIC	Industry	1990	1991	1992	1993	1994	1995	1996	1997
7929	**Entertainers & Entertainment Groups (pt)**								
	Establishments (number)	5,038	5,514	7,251	7,547	7,583	7,922	7,795p	8,080p
	Employment (thousands)	61.2	61.5	72.3	73.2	73.3	73.6	81.8p	85.4p
	Revenues ($ million)	-	-	5,714.7	4,279.9p	4,561.2p	4,842.4p	5,123.6p	5,404.9p
7999	**Amusement & Recreation nec (pt)**								
	Establishments (number)	-	-	21,717	-	-	-	-	-
	Employment (thousands)	-	-	215.8	-	-	-	-	-
	Revenues ($ million)	-	-	10,430.3	-	-	-	-	-

Source: Economic Census of the United States, 1992, annual surveys of economic sectors conducted by the Bureau of the Census, and estimates or projections based on the 1982-1992 period; not all data are shown. 'e' marks estimates made by the editors; 'p' indicates projections based on time series. A dash (-) indicates that data for this SIC or year were not available. The abbreviation (pt) next to the industry name indicates that only a part of the industry is present within the NAICS data. If no (pt) is shown, the entire industry is contained within the NAICS data.

SELECTED RATIOS

For 1997	Avg. of Information	Analyzed Industry	Index	For 1997	Avg. of Information	Analyzed Industry	Index
Employees per establishment	16	9	55	Payroll per establishment	330,963	238,717	72
Revenue per establishment	1,057,073	820,665	78	Payroll as % of revenue	31	29	93
Revenue per employee	65,958	93,164	141	Payroll per employee	20,651	27,100	131

Sources: Same as General Statistics. The 'Average' column represents the average for the industry sector, in 1997, where the currently shown industry is classified. The Index shows the relationship between the Average and the Analyzed Industry. For example, 100 means that they are equal; 500 that the Analyzed Industry is five times the average; 50 means that the Analyzed Industry is half the national average. The abbreviation 'na' is used to show that data are 'not available'.

LEADING COMPANIES   Number shown: **9**   Total sales ($ mil): **498**   Total employment (000): **1.7**

Company Name	Address				CEO Name	Phone	Co. Type	Sales ($ mil)	Empl. (000)
Madison Square Garden L.P.	2 Penn Plz	New York	NY	10121	David Checketts	212-465-6000	S	375*	1.0
PACE Inc. (Houston, Texas)	515 Post Oak Blvd	Houston	TX	77027	Brian Becker	713-621-8600	S	41*	0.3
Platinum Entertainment Inc.	2001 Butterfield Rd	Downers Grove	IL	60515	Steve Devick	630-769-0033	P	41	0.1
Cove Marketing Inc.	2024 N King St	Honolulu	HI	96814	Keith Horita	808-842-7911	R	33*	0.2
Chicago City Limits	1105 1st Ave at 61st	New York	NY	10021	Paul Zuckerman	212-888-5233	R	3*	<0.1
Gary Musick Productions Inc.	PO Box 1000	Page	AZ	86040	Gary S Musick	615-259-2400	R	3	<0.1
Celebrity Suppliers	2756 N Gr Vly	Henderson	NV	89014	AJ Sagman	702-451-8090	D	1	<0.1
Cliff Colnot Music Inc.	211 E Ohio St	Chicago	IL	60611	Cliff Colnot	312-527-5015	R	1*	<0.1
Bargemusic Ltd.	Fulton Ferry	Brooklyn	NY	11201		718-624-2083	R	0	<0.1

Source: Ward's Business Directory of U.S. Private and Public Companies, Volumes 1 and 2, 2000. The company type code used is as follows: P - Public, R - Private, S - Subsidiary, D - Division, J - Joint Venture, A - Affiliate, G - Group, N - Company type not reported. Sales are in millions of dollars, employees are in thousands. An asterisk (*) indicates an estimated sales volume. The symbol < stands for 'less than'. Company names and addresses are truncated, in some cases, to fit into the available space.

LOCATION BY STATE AND REGIONAL CONCENTRATION

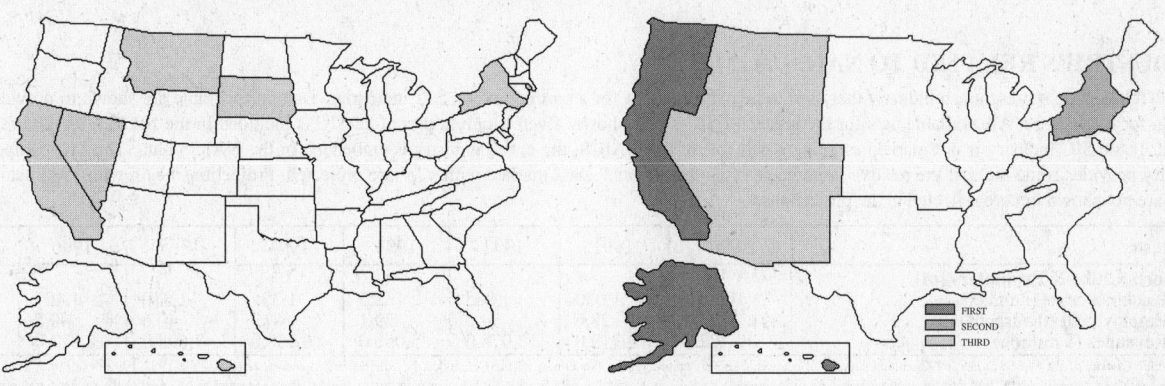

FIRST
SECOND
THIRD

INDUSTRY DATA BY STATE

State	Establishments Total (number)	% of U.S.	Employment Total (number)	% of U.S.	Per Estab.	Payroll Total ($ mil.)	Per Empl. ($)	Revenues Total ($ mil.)	% of U.S.	Per Estab. ($)
California	227	27.0	1,411	19.0	6	59.1	41,863	123.9	17.9	545,709
New York	116	13.8	719	9.7	6	22.2	30,903	80.1	11.6	690,517
Nevada	31	3.7	539	7.3	17	17.3	32,032	41.9	6.1	1,350,258
Arizona	9	1.1	188	2.5	21	4.1	22,005	19.4	2.8	2,160,889
Texas	22	2.6	94	1.3	4	1.7	18,117	8.9	1.3	402,955
North Carolina	7	0.8	18	0.2	3	0.6	30,833	1.9	0.3	270,714
D.C.	3	0.4	16	0.2	5	0.2	9,563	1.2	0.2	400,333
Idaho	3	0.4	4	0.1	1	0.3	77,750	0.7	0.1	249,667
West Virginia	3	0.4	7	0.1	2	0.1	18,857	0.5	0.1	179,667
Iowa	8	1.0	22	0.3	3	0.1	2,682	0.3	0.0	38,375
South Dakota	3	0.4	8	0.1	3	-	1,750	0.1	0.0	41,333
Illinois	24	2.9	375*	-	-	(D)	-	(D)	-	-
Rhode Island	5	0.6	60*	-	-	(D)	-	(D)	-	-
South Carolina	5	0.6	60*	-	-	(D)	-	(D)	-	-
Hawaii	4	0.5	60*	-	-	(D)	-	(D)	-	-
Oklahoma	4	0.5	60*	-	-	(D)	-	(D)	-	-
Montana	3	0.4	10*	-	-	(D)	-	(D)	-	-
Nebraska	2	0.2	10*	-	-	(D)	-	(D)	-	-
Alabama	1	0.1	10*	-	-	(D)	-	(D)	-	-
Arkansas	1	0.1	10*	-	-	(D)	-	(D)	-	-
Kansas	1	0.1	10*	-	-	(D)	-	(D)	-	-
Mississippi	1	0.1	10*	-	-	(D)	-	(D)	-	-
New Hampshire	1	0.1	10*	-	-	(D)	-	(D)	-	-
New Mexico	1	0.1	10*	-	-	(D)	-	(D)	-	-
North Dakota	1	0.1	10*	-	-	(D)	-	(D)	-	-

Source: 1997 *Economic Census*. The states are in descending order of revenues or establishments (if revenue data are missing for the majority). The symbol (D) appears when data are withheld to prevent disclosure of competitive information. States marked with (D) are sorted by number of establishments. A dash (-) indicates that the data element cannot be calculated. * indicates the midpoint of a range; 175, for example is the range 100-249. Shaded *states* on the state map indicate those states which have proportionately greater representation in the industry than would be indicated by the state's population; the ratio is based on total revenues or number of establishments. Shaded *regions* indicate where the industry is regionally most concentrated.

NAICS 711211 - SPORTS TEAMS AND CLUBS

GENERAL STATISTICS

Year	Establishments (number)	Employment (number)	Payroll ($ million)	Revenues ($ million)	Employees per Establishment (number)	Revenues per Establishment ($)	Payroll per Employee ($)
1997	483	33,330	4,922.0	7,809.0	69.0	16,167,702	147,675

Source: Economic Census of the United States, 1997. This is a newly defined industry. Data for prior years were unavailable at the time of publication but may become available over time.

INDICES OF CHANGE

Year	Establishments (number)	Employment (number)	Payroll ($ million)	Revenues ($ million)	Employees per Establishment (number)	Revenues per Establishment ($)	Payroll per Employee ($)
1997	100.0	100.0	100.0	100.0	100.0	100.0	100.0

Sources: Same as General Statistics. The values shown reflect change from the base year, 1997. Values above 100 mean greater than 1997, values below 100 mean less than 1997, and a value of 100 in the 1982-96 or 1998-2001 period means same as 1997. Values followed by a 'p' are projections by the editors; 'e' stands for extrapolation. Data are the most recent available at this level of detail.

SIC INDUSTRIES RELATED TO NAICS 711211

Each new NAICS code represents an industry that used to be part of an SIC or a part of several SIC industries. Data in this table are shown to provide transitional information for these cases. All available data for the precursor SIC(s) are shown. Even if only a part of an SIC is included in the NAICS, *all* data for the SIC are reproduced. If the SIC industry is not marked as being a part (pt) of the NAICS, the entire industry is embedded in the NAICS data. The SIC composition of the new industry provides some hints of the relative importance of its "ancestors." Data marked with a 'p' are projected. Projections begin with 1982 data. Data earlier than 1990 are not shown but are reflected in the projections.

SIC	Industry	1990	1991	1992	1993	1994	1995	1996	1997
7941	**Sports Clubs & Promoters (pt)**								
	Establishments (number)	913	1,030	1,085	1,225	1,335	1,510	1,407p	1,473p
	Employment (thousands)	26.9	28.6	34.2	39.1	40.9	40.6	40.5p	42.1p
	Revenues ($ million)	3,702.0	3,719.0	3,978.0	5,056.0	6,138.0	7,695.0	8,877.0	8,573.4p

Source: Economic Census of the United States, 1992, annual surveys of economic sectors conducted by the Bureau of the Census, and estimates or projections based on the 1982-1992 period; not all data are shown. 'e' marks estimates made by the editors; 'p' indicates projections based on time series. A dash (-) indicates that data for this SIC or year were not available. The abbreviation (pt) next to the industry name indicates that only a part of the industry is present within the NAICS data. If no (pt) is shown, the entire industry is contained within the NAICS data.

SELECTED RATIOS

For 1997	Avg. of Information	Analyzed Industry	Index	For 1997	Avg. of Information	Analyzed Industry	Index
Employees per establishment	16	69	431	Payroll per establishment	330,963	10,190,476	3,079
Revenue per establishment	1,057,073	16,167,702	1,529	Payroll as % of revenue	31	63	201
Revenue per employee	65,958	234,293	355	Payroll per employee	20,651	147,675	715

Sources: Same as General Statistics. The 'Average' column represents the average for the industry sector, in 1997, where the currently shown industry is classified. The Index shows the relationship between the Average and the Analyzed Industry. For example, 100 means that they are equal; 500 that the Analyzed Industry is five times the average; 50 means that the Analyzed Industry is half the national average. The abbreviation 'na' is used to show that data are 'not available'.

LEADING COMPANIES   Number shown: **30**   Total sales ($ mil): **1,851**   Total employment (000): **11.7**

Company Name	Address				CEO Name	Phone	Co. Type	Sales ($ mil)	Empl. (000)
International Management Group	1360 E 9th St	Cleveland	OH	44114	Mark H. McCormack	216-522-1200	R	1,150*	2.1
Boca Resorts	450 E Las Olas Blvd	Fort Lauderdale	FL	33301	Richard H Evans	954-768-1900	P	387	4.8
Los Angeles Dodgers Inc.	1000 Elysian	Los Angeles	CA	90012	Peter O'Malley	323-224-1500	R	82*	1.2
Pittsburgh Associates	600 Stadium Cir	Pittsburgh	PA	15212	kevin mcClatchy	412-323-5000	R	45	0.5
SMG	701 Market St	Philadelphia	PA	19106	Harold Westley	215-592-4100	R	30*	1.4
Detroit Pistons Basketball Co.	2 Championship Dr	Auburn Hills	MI	48326	Tom Wilson	248-377-0100	R	20*	0.3
Bridgestone/Firestone Tire Sales	1 Bridgestone Park	Nashville	TN	37214		615-391-0088	D	18*	0.1
Florida Gaming Corp.	3500 N W 37th Ave	Miami	FL	33142	WB Collett	305-633-6400	P	18	0.4
Millsport Inc.	750 Washington	Stamford	CT	06901	James R Millman	203-977-0500	R	11*	<0.1
ProServ Inc.	1620 L St N W	Washington	DC	20036	William Allard	202-721-7200	S	10	<0.1
Boston Celtics L.P.	151 Merrimac St	Boston	MA	02114	Paul E Gaston	617-523-6050	P	10	<0.1
CAVS/Gund Arena Co.	1 Center Ct	Cleveland	OH	44115	Jim Boland	216-420-2000	R	8*	0.1
Green Bay Packers Inc.	PO Box 10628	Green Bay	WI	54307	Robert Harlan	920-496-5700	R	8*	0.2
Championship Group Inc.	3690 N Peachtree Rd	Atlanta	GA	30341		770-457-5777	R	7*	<0.1
Baseball Jax Inc.	1201 E Duvall St	Jacksonville	FL	32202	Peter Bragan Sr	904-358-2846	R	6*	<0.1
Kemper Lesnik Communications	455 N Ctyfrnt	Chicago	IL	60611	Steven H Lesnik	312-755-3500	R	5*	<0.1
Momentum- IMC	79 5th Ave	New York	NY	10003	Mark Dowley	212-367-4500	S	5*	<0.1
World Classic Productions Inc.	PO Box 10	Whites Creek	TN	37189	George E Runquist	615-876-6100	R	5*	<0.1
Indiana Sports Corp.	201 S Capitol Ave	Indianapolis	IN	46225	Dale Nenburger	317-237-5000	R	4	<0.1
Kansas City Air Show	1915 S Ohio St	Salina	KS	67401		913-384-8930	R	4*	<0.1
Orlando Predators Entertainment	400 W Church St	Orlando	FL	32801	Brett Bouchy	407-648-4444	P	4*	<0.1
Main Events Inc.	811 Totowa Rd	Totowa	NJ	07512	Dino Duva	973-389-9000	R	3*	<0.1
Tom Collins Enterprises Inc.	3500 W 80th St	Minneapolis	MN	55431	Tom Collins	612-831-2237	R	3*	<0.1
Collegiate Licensing Co.	320 Interstate N	Atlanta	GA	30339	Bill Battle	770-956-0520	R	2	<0.1
International Promotions Inc.	1265 S Gilbert Rd	Gilbert	AZ	85296	Stanley Torgerson	480-899-2222	R	2*	<0.1
Sports Marketing of Indiana Corp.	201 S Capitol Ave	Indianapolis	IN	46225	Dale Neuburger	317-237-5000	S	2*	<0.1
Athletic Resource Management	6075 Poplar Ave	Memphis	TN	38119	Kyle Rote Jr	901-763-4900	S	1*	<0.1
Louisville Baseball Club Inc.	P O Box 36407	Louisville	KY	40233	Gary Ulmer	502-367-9121	R	1*	<0.1
Professional Management Inc.	PO Box 8296	Columbia	SC	29202	William Black	803-771-6000	R	1	<0.1
SportStar USA Inc.	6325 Gunpark Dr	Boulder	CO	80301	Michael W Doland	303-530-7811	R	1	<0.1

Source: *Ward's Business Directory of U.S. Private and Public Companies*, Volumes 1 and 2, 2000. The company type code used is as follows: P - Public, R - Private, S - Subsidiary, D - Division, J - Joint Venture, A - Affiliate, G - Group, N - Company type not reported. Sales are in millions of dollars, employees are in thousands. An asterisk (*) indicates an estimated sales volume. The symbol < stands for 'less than'. Company names and addresses are truncated, in some cases, to fit into the available space.

REPRESENTATIVE NONPROFIT ORGANIZATIONS

Organization Name	Address				Phone	Income Range ($ mil)
Amateur Trapshooting Association of America	601 W National Rd	Vandalia	OH	45377	937-898-4638	1-5
Arc of Prince Georges County Inc	1300 Mercantile LN	Landover	MD	20785		5-9
Arena Football League Inc	75 E Wacker Dr Ste 400	Chicago	IL	60601	312-332-5510	1-5
Chippanee Golf Course	6 Marsh Rd	Bristol	CT	06010	860-589-5645	1-5
Club West Wrestling Inc	625 B E Jackson St	Medford	OR	97504		1-5
Dallas Gun Club	PO Box 292848	Lewisville	TX	75029	214-462-0043	1-5
Deep Creek Baseball Association Inc	PO Box 6477	Chesapeake	VA	23323		1-5
Desert Hills Golf Club of Green Valley Inc	2500 S Circulo Lomas	Green Valley	AZ	85614	520-625-5090	1-5
East Coast Hockey League Inc	125 Village Blvd Ste 210	Princeton	NJ	08540	609-452-0770	1-5
Landings Yacht Club Inc	1 Marina Dr	Savannah	GA	31411		1-5
Louisville Soccer Alliance Inc	1503 Sylvan Wynde	Louisville	KY	40205		1-5
Michigan Association of SFS Retailers Employees Benefit Plan	1227 E Chippewa	Mt Pleasant	MI	48858		1-5
National Hockey League	1251 Ave of Americas	New York	NY	10020	212-789-2000	30-39
National Hot Rod Association	2035 Financial Way	Glendora	CA	91741	626-914-4761	50+
North River Yacht Club Inc	PO Box 48999	Tuscaloosa	AL	35404		1-5
Notre Dame Ministry Corporation	320 E Ripa Ave	St Louis	MO	63125	314-544-1015	5-9
Orchard Golf Course Inc	PO Box 21	S Hadley	MA	01075	413-534-3806	1-5
Professional Golfers Association of America	PO Box 109601	Palm Beach Gdns	FL	33420		50+
Racquet Sports Club Inc	One Oxford Center	Pittsburgh	PA	15219		5-9
Roadrunners Soft Ball Association	866 White Point Blvd	Charleston	SC	29412		1-5
Seattle Skating Club Inc	12111 Hwy 99	Edmonds	WA	98020		5-9
Spring Hill Golf Club	700 Spring Hill Rd	Wayzata	MN	55391	952-489-3696	5-9
United States Synchronized Swimming Inc	201 S Capitol Ave 510	Indianapolis	IN	46225	317-237-5050	1-5

Source: *National Directory of Nonprofit Organizations*, 2000, Volumes 1 and 2, The Taft Group. The table shows a selection of organizations for illustration and does not constitute a complete selection from the source. The organizations are arranged in alphabetical order.

LOCATION BY STATE AND REGIONAL CONCENTRATION

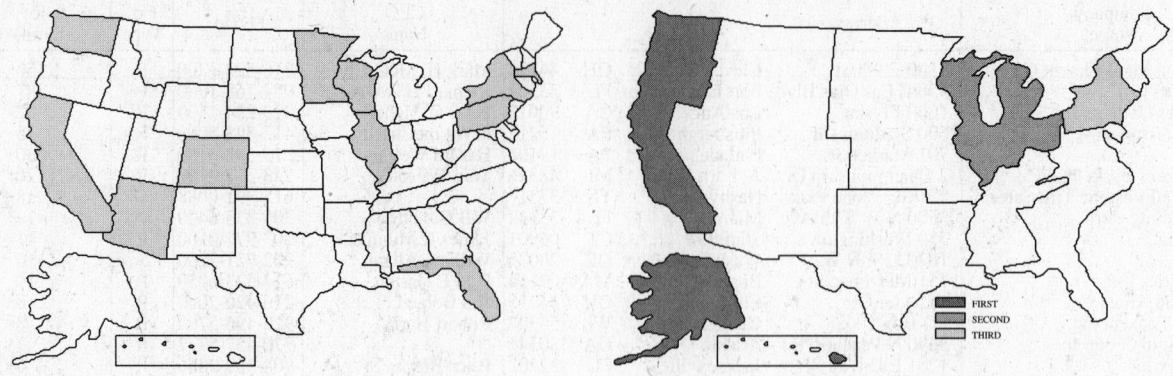

FIRST
SECOND
THIRD

INDUSTRY DATA BY STATE

State	Establishments Total (number)	% of U.S.	Employment Total (number)	% of U.S.	Per Estab.	Payroll Total ($ mil.)	Per Empl. ($)	Revenues Total ($ mil.)	% of U.S.	Per Estab. ($)
California	40	8.3	4,130	12.4	103	711.3	172,223	1,081.6	13.9	27,039,375
New York	50	10.4	2,614	7.8	52	412.2	157,671	711.4	9.1	14,227,820
Florida	36	7.5	3,708	11.1	103	408.6	110,204	590.0	7.6	16,390,028
Texas	31	6.4	2,886	8.7	93	296.1	102,590	515.0	6.6	16,611,968
Pennsylvania	20	4.1	1,911	5.7	96	300.3	157,127	463.8	5.9	23,188,850
Illinois	14	2.9	1,129	3.4	81	288.3	255,360	402.6	5.2	28,759,000
Ohio	13	2.7	2,371	7.1	182	197.8	83,404	330.5	4.2	25,422,692
Michigan	12	2.5	582	1.7	48	149.7	257,270	284.0	3.6	23,670,500
Colorado	7	1.4	534	1.6	76	171.0	320,262	275.1	3.5	39,302,000
Massachusetts	10	2.1	606	1.8	61	183.0	301,926	275.1	3.5	27,509,900
Washington	13	2.7	885	2.7	68	160.7	181,629	237.8	3.0	18,292,615
Arizona	10	2.1	1,047	3.1	105	137.8	131,637	224.7	2.9	22,465,600
Wisconsin	15	3.1	653	2.0	44	140.5	215,124	190.2	2.4	12,677,267
Minnesota	10	2.1	438	1.3	44	98.5	224,916	185.1	2.4	18,514,500
North Carolina	16	3.3	496	1.5	31	91.3	184,087	160.0	2.0	9,998,750
Indiana	10	2.1	811	2.4	81	109.2	134,639	139.5	1.8	13,949,200
Virginia	16	3.3	480	1.4	30	56.9	118,479	100.4	1.3	6,275,500
Louisiana	7	1.4	434	1.3	62	50.6	116,618	88.6	1.1	12,655,286
Oregon	9	1.9	318	1.0	35	44.6	140,189	66.5	0.9	7,390,111
Tennessee	11	2.3	176	0.5	16	43.1	245,165	59.8	0.8	5,436,364
Connecticut	7	1.4	444	1.3	63	36.8	82,905	54.3	0.7	7,756,286
South Carolina	6	1.2	351	1.1	58	2.6	7,436	10.0	0.1	1,671,833
Kansas	4	0.8	268	0.8	67	2.2	8,131	9.9	0.1	2,479,750
Oklahoma	4	0.8	138	0.4	35	3.2	22,964	8.8	0.1	2,208,250
Alabama	4	0.8	248	0.7	62	1.7	7,016	8.3	0.1	2,074,000
Nebraska	3	0.6	98	0.3	33	1.4	14,612	6.2	0.1	2,074,000
Idaho	4	0.8	171	0.5	43	1.2	6,982	4.7	0.1	1,165,000
New Mexico	4	0.8	56	0.2	14	1.4	24,482	4.3	0.1	1,086,500
South Dakota	3	0.6	122	0.4	41	1.0	8,025	3.2	0.0	1,066,000
West Virginia	6	1.2	78	0.2	13	0.9	11,115	2.6	0.0	436,833
Montana	4	0.8	31	0.1	8	0.4	11,968	1.4	0.0	352,750
New Jersey	13	2.7	750*	-	-	(D)	-	(D)	-	-
Iowa	10	2.1	60*	-	-	(D)	-	(D)	-	-
Maryland	10	2.1	750*	-	-	(D)	-	(D)	-	-
Missouri	10	2.1	1,750*	-	-	(D)	-	(D)	-	-
Georgia	9	1.9	1,750*	-	-	(D)	-	(D)	-	-
Nevada	5	1.0	175*	-	-	(D)	-	(D)	-	-
Mississippi	4	0.8	60*	-	-	(D)	-	(D)	-	-
Utah	4	0.8	175*	-	-	(D)	-	(D)	-	-
Alaska	3	0.6	60*	-	-	(D)	-	(D)	-	-
Maine	3	0.6	60*	-	-	(D)	-	(D)	-	-
North Dakota	3	0.6	60*	-	-	(D)	-	(D)	-	-
Kentucky	2	0.4	60*	-	-	(D)	-	(D)	-	-
Rhode Island	2	0.4	60*	-	-	(D)	-	(D)	-	-
Arkansas	1	0.2	10*	-	-	(D)	-	(D)	-	-
Delaware	1	0.2	60*	-	-	(D)	-	(D)	-	-
Hawaii	1	0.2	10*	-	-	(D)	-	(D)	-	-
New Hampshire	1	0.2	10*	-	-	(D)	-	(D)	-	-
Vermont	1	0.2	10*	-	-	(D)	-	(D)	-	-
Wyoming	1	0.2	10*	-	-	(D)	-	(D)	-	-

Source: 1997 *Economic Census*. The states are in descending order of revenues or establishments (if revenue data are missing for the majority). The symbol (D) appears when data are withheld to prevent disclosure of competitive information. States marked with (D) are sorted by number of establishments. A dash (-) indicates that the data element cannot be calculated. * indicates the midpoint of a range; 175, for example is the range 100-249. Shaded *states* on the state map indicate those states which have proportionately greater representation in the industry than would be indicated by the state's population; the ratio is based on total revenues or number of establishments. Shaded *regions* indicate where the industry is regionally most concentrated.

NAICS 711212 - RACETRACKS

GENERAL STATISTICS

Year	Establishments (number)	Employment (number)	Payroll ($ million)	Revenues ($ million)	Employees per Establishment (number)	Revenues per Establishment ($)	Payroll per Employee ($)
1997	807	44,880	797.0	4,142.0	55.6	5,132,590	17,758

Source: Economic Census of the United States, 1997. This is a newly defined industry. Data for prior years were unavailable at the time of publication but may become available over time.

INDICES OF CHANGE

Year	Establishments (number)	Employment (number)	Payroll ($ million)	Revenues ($ million)	Employees per Establishment (number)	Revenues per Establishment ($)	Payroll per Employee ($)
1997	100.0	100.0	100.0	100.0	100.0	100.0	100.0

Sources: Same as General Statistics. The values shown reflect change from the base year, 1997. Values above 100 mean greater than 1997, values below 100 mean less than 1997, and a value of 100 in the 1982-96 or 1998-2001 period means same as 1997. Values followed by a 'p' are projections by the editors; 'e' stands for extrapolation. Data are the most recent available at this level of detail.

SIC INDUSTRIES RELATED TO NAICS 711212

Each new NAICS code represents an industry that used to be part of an SIC or a part of several SIC industries. Data in this table are shown to provide transitional information for these cases. All available data for the precursor SIC(s) are shown. Even if only a part of an SIC is included in the NAICS, *all* data for the SIC are reproduced. If the SIC industry is not marked as being a part (pt) of the NAICS, the entire industry is embedded in the NAICS data. The SIC composition of the new industry provides some hints of the relative importance of its "ancestors." Data marked with a 'p' are projected. Projections begin with 1982 data. Data earlier than 1990 are not shown but are reflected in the projections.

SIC	Industry	1990	1991	1992	1993	1994	1995	1996	1997
7948	**Racing, Including Track Operation (pt)**								
	Establishments (number)	2,339	2,538	2,666	2,742	2,762	2,774	2,824p	2,882p
	Employment (thousands)	52.0	52.9	56.3	53.4	52.4	53.9	56.0p	56.9p
	Revenues ($ million)	4,934.0	4,878.0	5,032.0	4,814.0	4,952.0	5,360.0	5,755.0	5,731.2p

Source: Economic Census of the United States, 1992, annual surveys of economic sectors conducted by the Bureau of the Census, and estimates or projections based on the 1982-1992 period; not all data are shown. 'e' marks estimates made by the editors; 'p' indicates projections based on time series. A dash (-) indicates that data for this SIC or year were not available. The abbreviation (pt) next to the industry name indicates that only a part of the industry is present within the NAICS data. If no (pt) is shown, the entire industry is contained within the NAICS data.

SELECTED RATIOS

For 1997	Avg. of Information	Analyzed Industry	Index	For 1997	Avg. of Information	Analyzed Industry	Index
Employees per establishment	16	56	347	Payroll per establishment	330,963	987,608	298
Revenue per establishment	1,057,073	5,132,590	486	Payroll as % of revenue	31	19	61
Revenue per employee	65,958	92,291	140	Payroll per employee	20,651	17,758	86

Sources: Same as General Statistics. The 'Average' column represents the average for the industry sector, in 1997, where the currently shown industry is classified. The Index shows the relationship between the Average and the Analyzed Industry. For example, 100 means that they are equal; 500 that the Analyzed Industry is five times the average; 50 means that the Analyzed Industry is half the national average. The abbreviation 'na' is used to show that data are 'not available'.

LEADING COMPANIES   Number shown: **49**   Total sales ($ mil): **24,658**   Total employment (000): **73.5**

Company Name	Address				CEO Name	Phone	Co. Type	Sales ($ mil)	Empl. (000)
Westwood Group Inc.	190 VFW Pkwy	Revere	MA	02151	Charles F. Sarkis	781-284-2600	P	10,903*	2.3
Penske Corp.	13400 Outer Dr W	Detroit	MI	48239	Roger S Penske	313-592-5000	R	10,000	34.0
Hollywood Park Inc.	330 N Brand Ave	Glendale	CA	91203	Paul R Alanis	818-662-5900	P	427	8.9
Players International Inc.	1300 Atlantic Ave	Atlantic City	NJ	08401	John Groom	609-449-7777	P	331	3.5
International Speedway Corp.	P O Box 2801	Daytona Beach	FL	32120	Jim France	904-254-2700	P	299	0.4
Speedway Motorsports Inc.	P O Box 600	Concord	NC	28026	O Bruton Smith	704-455-3239	P	230	1.0
Dover Downs Entertainment Inc.	PO Box 843	Dover	DE	19903	Denis McGlynn	302-674-4600	P	208	0.8
Powerhouse Technologies Inc.	2311 S 7th Ave	Bozeman	MT	59715	Michael Eide	406-585-6600	P	201	1.4
New York Racing Association Inc.	P O Box 90	Jamaica	NY	11417	Terry Meyocks	718-641-4700	R	185*	1.5
Delaware Racing Association	777 Deleware Park	Wilmington	DE	19804	William Rickman Sr	302-994-2521	R	161*	1.3
Penn National Gaming Inc.	825 Berkshire Blvd	Wyomissing	PA	19610	William J Bork	610-373-2400	P	154	1.7
Racing Association of Central	PO Box 1000	Altoona	IA	50009	Robert Favinella	515-967-1000	R	152*	1.4
Churchill Downs Inc.	700 Central Ave	Louisville	KY	40208	Thomas H Meeker	502-636-4400	P	147	0.9
Penske Motorsports Inc.	13400 Outer Dr W	Detroit	MI	48239	Gregory W Penske	313-592-5000	P	117	0.2
Sportsystems Corp.	438 Main St	Buffalo	NY	14202	Ron Sultemeier	716-858-5000	S	107*	1.6
Calder Race Course Inc.	P O Box 1808	Opa Locka	FL	33055	C Kenneth Dunn	305-625-1311	S	91*	0.8
Wembley USA Inc.	10750 E Iliff Ave	Aurora	CO	80014	Skip Sherman	303-751-5918	S	79	1.3
Burrillville Racing Association	Old Louisquisset	Lincoln	RI	02865		401-723-3200	S	74*	0.6
Charles Town Races Inc.	Flowing Spring Rd	Charles Town	WV	25414	Jim Buchanan	304-725-7001	R	74*	0.6
Los Angeles Turf Club Inc.	P O Box 60014	Arcadia	CA	91066	William C Baker	626-574-7223	S	70*	1.6
Equus Gaming Company L.P.	650 Munoz Rivera	Hato Rey	PR	00917	James Wilson	787-753-0676	P	69	0.3
Santa Anita Operating Co.	P O Box 60014	Arcadia	CA	91066	Lonny Powell	626-574-7223	S	64*	1.6
American Greyhound Racing Inc.	3801 E Washington	Phoenix	AZ	85034	Daniel A Luciano	602-273-7181	S	56*	0.5
Ruidoso Downs Racing Inc.	PO Box 449	Ruidoso Downs	NM	88346	Greg Hall	505-378-4431	R	56*	0.5
Southland Racing Corp.	PO Box 2088	West Memphis	AR	72303		870-735-3670	S	43*	0.4
United Track Greyhound Racing	6200 Dahlia St	Commerce City	CO	80022	Skip Sherman	303-288-1591	R	43*	0.4
Garden State Race Track Inc.	P O Box 1232	Cherry Hill	NJ	08034		609-488-3838	S	43*	0.6
Fair Grounds Corp.	1751 Gentilly Blvd	New Orleans	LA	70119		504-944-5515	P	42	0.8
Delta Downs Racing Association	PO Box 175	Vinton	LA	70668	Shawn Scott	318-589-7441	R	37*	0.3
Colonial Downs Holdings Inc.	10515 Colonial	New Kent	VA	23124	Jeffrey Pl Jacobs	804-966-7223	P	30	0.5
Atlanta Motor Speedway Inc.	PO Box 500	Hampton	GA	30228		404-946-4211	S	27	<0.1
Dover Downs Intern	P O Box 843	Dover	DE	19903	Denis McGlynn	302-674-4600	S	20	<0.1
Keeneland Association	PO Box 1690	Lexington	KY	40588	James E Bassett III	606-254-3412	R	19*	0.2
Nuevo Sol Turf Club Inc.	P O Box 1	Sunland Park	NM	88063		505-589-1131	S	19*	0.3
Finger Lakes Racing Association	P O Box 25250	Farmington	NY	14425		716-924-3232	S	16*	0.3
Multnomah Kennel Club Inc.	PO Box 9	Fairview	OR	97024	Richard Cummings	503-667-7700	R	10	0.5
Mile High Greyhound Park	6200 Dahlia St	Commerce City	CO	80022	Skip Sherman	303-288-1591	S	9*	<0.1
Mid State Raceway Inc.	PO Box 860	Vernon	NY	13476	Justice M Cheney	315-829-2201	P	7	0.3
Derrick Walker Racing	4035 Championship	Indianapolis	IN	46278	Derrick Walker	317-387-1500	R	6*	<0.1
Oaklawn Jockey Club Inc.	PO Box 699	Hot Springs	AR	71902	Charles J Cella	501-623-4411	R	6	0.1
Team Valor Inc.	P O Box 428	Versailles	KY	40383	Barry Irwin	626-879-0696	R	5	<0.1
Calumet Farm Inc.	3301 Versailles Rd	Lexington	KY	40510	H De Kwiatkowski	606-231-8272	R	4*	<0.1
Hawthorne Race Course	3501 S Laramie Ave	Cicero	IL	60804		708-780-3700	R	4*	<0.1
Lexington Trotters & Breeders	P O Box 420	Lexington	KY	40588	John A Cashman Jr	606-255-0752	R	4*	<0.1
Wichita Greyhound Park	P O Box 277	Valley Center	KS	67147		316-755-4000	R	4*	<0.1
Jefferson County Kennel Club Inc.	P O Box 400	Monticello	FL	32345	Steve Andris	850-997-2561	R	4	0.1
Dogwood Stable Inc.	PO Box 1549	Aiken	SC	29802	Cot Campbell	803-642-2972	R	1*	<0.1
Far West Farms	P O Box 2166	Manhattan Bch	CA	90267	Sandy Arledge	619-755-3088	R	1*	<0.1
Indy Indoor Sports Inc.	6382 W 34th St	Indianapolis	IN	46224	George Klein	317-291-2729	R	1	<0.1

Source: Ward's Business Directory of U.S. Private and Public Companies, Volumes 1 and 2, 2000. The company type code used is as follows: P - Public, R - Private, S - Subsidiary, D - Division, J - Joint Venture, A - Affiliate, G - Group, N - Company type not reported. Sales are in millions of dollars, employees are in thousands. An asterisk (*) indicates an estimated sales volume. The symbol < stands for 'less than'. Company names and addresses are truncated, in some cases, to fit into the available space.

LOCATION BY STATE AND REGIONAL CONCENTRATION

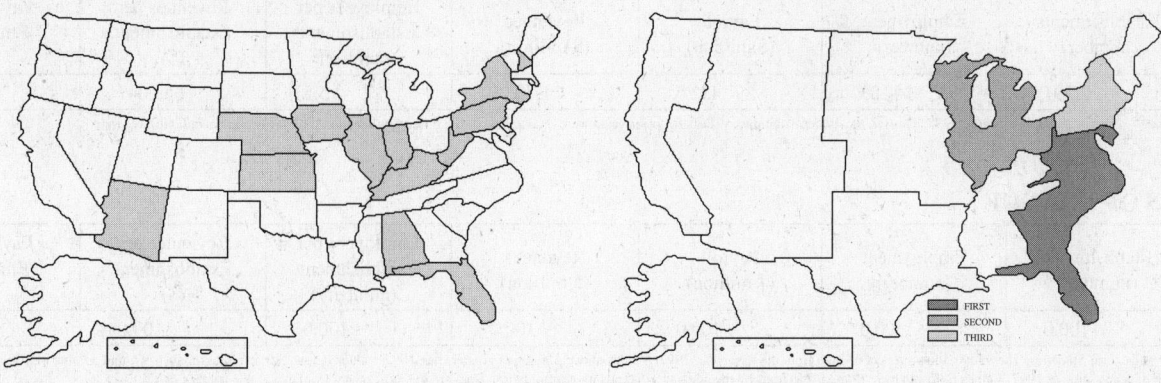

INDUSTRY DATA BY STATE

State	Establishments Total (number)	% of U.S.	Employment Total (number)	% of U.S.	Per Estab.	Payroll Total ($ mil.)	Per Empl. ($)	Revenues Total ($ mil.)	% of U.S.	Per Estab. ($)
Florida	46	5.7	6,107	13.6	133	80.5	13,187	411.9	9.9	8,953,848
California	64	7.9	3,416	7.6	53	103.2	30,221	392.8	9.5	6,136,766
New York	44	5.5	2,222	5.0	51	66.3	29,822	351.8	8.5	7,995,250
Iowa	21	2.6	2,945	6.6	140	53.2	18,080	264.3	6.4	12,587,524
Pennsylvania	41	5.1	2,681	6.0	65	40.4	15,062	233.5	5.6	5,696,049
Illinois	35	4.3	1,400	3.1	40	31.1	22,216	198.4	4.8	5,669,486
Texas	36	4.5	1,850	4.1	51	31.3	16,917	174.8	4.2	4,854,639
Kentucky	15	1.9	1,164	2.6	78	22.4	19,259	164.8	4.0	10,984,933
Michigan	37	4.6	1,158	2.6	31	25.4	21,899	148.6	3.6	4,016,919
Ohio	35	4.3	1,761	3.9	50	27.1	15,390	141.4	3.4	4,040,171
West Virginia	10	1.2	1,629	3.6	163	18.4	11,314	130.2	3.1	13,015,700
Indiana	28	3.5	870	1.9	31	23.2	26,672	128.2	3.1	4,579,893
Alabama	18	2.2	1,223	2.7	68	13.8	11,316	93.5	2.3	5,195,222
Massachusetts	11	1.4	1,109	2.5	101	18.0	16,243	87.9	2.1	7,991,545
New Hampshire	15	1.9	616	1.4	41	14.2	23,071	84.3	2.0	5,616,733
Arizona	14	1.7	1,244	2.8	89	14.1	11,369	75.9	1.8	5,424,929
Kansas	9	1.1	460	1.0	51	6.4	14,017	68.9	1.7	7,659,889
Wisconsin	34	4.2	909	2.0	27	12.8	14,081	64.5	1.6	1,896,353
Virginia	24	3.0	443	1.0	18	9.0	20,264	57.3	1.4	2,385,667
Colorado	15	1.9	620	1.4	41	8.9	14,356	48.1	1.2	3,209,133
Georgia	16	2.0	410	0.9	26	4.6	11,307	42.8	1.0	2,675,813
North Carolina	27	3.3	175	0.4	6	5.9	33,509	41.0	1.0	1,519,111
Tennessee	16	2.0	189	0.4	12	4.1	21,778	38.9	0.9	2,431,313
Louisiana	8	1.0	853	1.9	107	11.7	13,685	38.3	0.9	4,793,000
Washington	15	1.9	510	1.1	34	10.3	20,178	35.5	0.9	2,369,733
Nebraska	14	1.7	504	1.1	36	5.0	9,881	29.0	0.7	2,071,071
Minnesota	15	1.9	191	0.4	13	4.0	21,147	27.4	0.7	1,827,667
Oklahoma	10	1.2	681	1.5	68	10.0	14,648	25.5	0.6	2,546,900
Connecticut	5	0.6	509	1.1	102	5.5	10,731	23.2	0.6	4,634,600
South Carolina	10	1.2	42	0.1	4	1.4	32,786	18.7	0.5	1,871,500
New Mexico	5	0.6	292	0.7	58	5.9	20,127	16.6	0.4	3,310,400
Maine	11	1.4	327	0.7	30	3.2	9,740	12.2	0.3	1,113,545
Idaho	9	1.1	151	0.3	17	2.0	13,358	7.6	0.2	842,333
South Dakota	10	1.2	56	0.1	6	0.4	7,464	3.5	0.1	352,500
Vermont	3	0.4	5	0.0	2	0.5	93,000	1.5	0.0	506,333
Mississippi	5	0.6	49	0.1	10	0.2	4,286	1.4	0.0	288,400
New Jersey	16	2.0	750*	-	-	(D)	-	(D)	-	-
Missouri	15	1.9	10*	-	-	(D)	-	(D)	-	-
Arkansas	10	1.2	1,750*	-	-	(D)	-	(D)	-	-
Maryland	10	1.2	1,750*	-	-	(D)	-	(D)	-	-
Oregon	9	1.1	750*	-	-	(D)	-	(D)	-	-
Delaware	4	0.5	1,750*	-	-	(D)	-	(D)	-	-
Montana	4	0.5	10*	-	-	(D)	-	(D)	-	-
Nevada	3	0.4	375*	-	-	(D)	-	(D)	-	-
Wyoming	3	0.4	60*	-	-	(D)	-	(D)	-	-
North Dakota	1	0.1	10*	-	-	(D)	-	(D)	-	-
Rhode Island	1	0.1	375*	-	-	(D)	-	(D)	-	-

Source: 1997 *Economic Census.* The states are in descending order of revenues or establishments (if revenue data are missing for the majority). The symbol (D) appears when data are withheld to prevent disclosure of competitive information. States marked with (D) are sorted by number of establishments. A dash (-) indicates that the data element cannot be calculated. * indicates the midpoint of a range; 175, for example is the range 100-249. Shaded *states* on the state map indicate those states which have proportionately greater representation in the industry than would be indicated by the state's population; the ratio is based on total revenues or number of establishments. Shaded *regions* indicate where the industry is regionally most concentrated.

NAICS 711219 - SPECTATOR SPORTS NEC

GENERAL STATISTICS

Year	Establishments (number)	Employment (number)	Payroll ($ million)	Revenues ($ million)	Employees per Establishment (number)	Revenues per Establishment ($)	Payroll per Employee ($)
1997	2,591	14,183	432.0	1,705.0	5.5	658,047	30,459

Source: *Economic Census of the United States*, 1997. This is a newly defined industry. Data for prior years were unavailable at the time of publication but may become available over time.

INDICES OF CHANGE

Year	Establishments (number)	Employment (number)	Payroll ($ million)	Revenues ($ million)	Employees per Establishment (number)	Revenues per Establishment ($)	Payroll per Employee ($)
1997	100.0	100.0	100.0	100.0	100.0	100.0	100.0

Sources: Same as General Statistics. The values shown reflect change from the base year, 1997. Values above 100 mean greater than 1997, values below 100 mean less than 1997, and a value of 100 in the 1982-96 or 1998-2001 period means same as 1997. Values followed by a 'p' are projections by the editors; 'e' stands for extrapolation. Data are the most recent available at this level of detail.

SIC INDUSTRIES RELATED TO NAICS 711219

Each new NAICS code represents an industry that used to be part of an SIC or a part of several SIC industries. Data in this table are shown to provide transitional information for these cases. All available data for the precursor SIC(s) are shown. Even if only a part of an SIC is included in the NAICS, *all* data for the SIC are reproduced. If the SIC industry is not marked as being a part (pt) of the NAICS, the entire industry is embedded in the NAICS data. The SIC composition of the new industry provides some hints of the relative importance of its "ancestors." Data marked with a 'p' are projected. Projections begin with 1982 data. Data earlier than 1990 are not shown but are reflected in the projections.

SIC	Industry	1990	1991	1992	1993	1994	1995	1996	1997
7948	**Racing, Including Track Operation (pt)**								
	Establishments (number)	2,339	2,538	2,666	2,742	2,762	2,774	2,824p	2,882p
	Employment (thousands)	52.0	52.9	56.3	53.4	52.4	53.9	56.0p	56.9p
	Revenues ($ million)	4,934.0	4,878.0	5,032.0	4,814.0	4,952.0	5,360.0	5,755.0	5,731.2p
7999	**Amusement & Recreation nec (pt)**								
	Establishments (number)	-	-	21,717	-	-	-	-	-
	Employment (thousands)	-	-	215.8	-	-	-	-	-
	Revenues ($ million)	-	-	10,430.3	-	-	-	-	-

Source: *Economic Census of the United States*, 1992, annual surveys of economic sectors conducted by the Bureau of the Census, and estimates or projections based on the 1982-1992 period; not all data are shown. 'e' marks estimates made by the editors; 'p' indicates projections based on time series. A dash (-) indicates that data for this SIC or year were not available. The abbreviation (pt) next to the industry name indicates that only a part of the industry is present within the NAICS data. If no (pt) is shown, the entire industry is contained within the NAICS data.

SELECTED RATIOS

For 1997	Avg. of Information	Analyzed Industry	Index	For 1997	Avg. of Information	Analyzed Industry	Index
Employees per establishment	16	5	34	Payroll per establishment	330,963	166,731	50
Revenue per establishment	1,057,073	658,047	62	Payroll as % of revenue	31	25	81
Revenue per employee	65,958	120,214	182	Payroll per employee	20,651	30,459	147

Sources: Same as General Statistics. The 'Average' column represents the average for the industry sector, in 1997, where the currently shown industry is classified. The Index shows the relationship between the Average and the Analyzed Industry. For example, 100 means that they are equal; 500 that the Analyzed Industry is five times the average; 50 means that the Analyzed Industry is half the national average. The abbreviation 'na' is used to show that data are 'not available'.

LEADING COMPANIES

No company data available for this industry.

LOCATION BY STATE AND REGIONAL CONCENTRATION

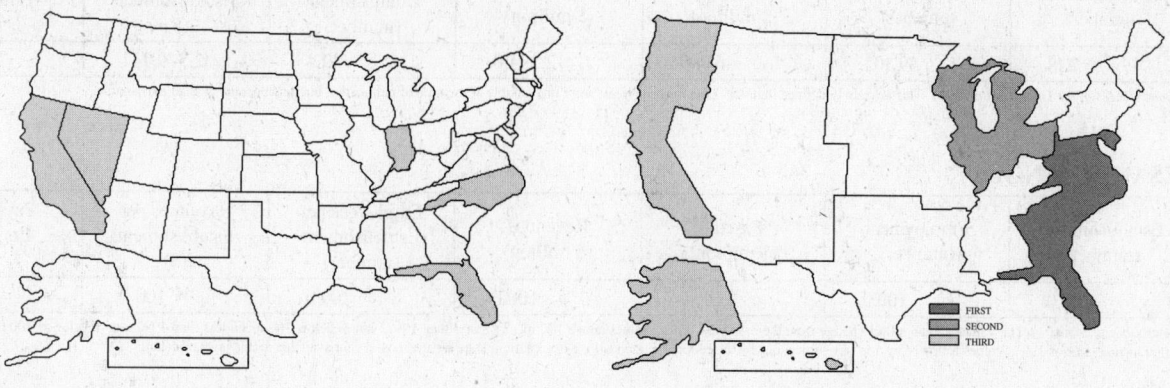

FIRST
SECOND
THIRD

INDUSTRY DATA BY STATE

State	Establishments Total (number)	% of U.S.	Employment Total (number)	% of U.S.	Per Estab.	Payroll Total ($ mil.)	Per Empl. ($)	Revenues Total ($ mil.)	% of U.S.	Per Estab. ($)
North Carolina	167	6.4	1,884	13.3	11	98.6	52,350	365.1	21.4	2,186,413
California	363	14.0	2,517	17.7	7	70.8	28,144	269.8	15.8	743,306
Florida	305	11.8	1,387	9.8	5	44.7	32,239	164.8	9.7	540,416
Indiana	66	2.5	671	4.7	10	32.5	48,368	161.9	9.5	2,452,879
New York	192	7.4	1,269	8.9	7	22.2	17,488	81.1	4.8	422,516
Illinois	134	5.2	648	4.6	5	17.5	27,008	68.8	4.0	513,306
Michigan	61	2.4	314	2.2	5	5.9	18,949	60.5	3.5	991,377
Pennsylvania	73	2.8	369	2.6	5	15.6	42,352	57.7	3.4	790,329
Ohio	101	3.9	451	3.2	4	12.8	28,410	47.5	2.8	470,495
Virginia	43	1.7	230	1.6	5	7.8	34,078	43.1	2.5	1,003,326
Texas	107	4.1	407	2.9	4	8.3	20,432	34.3	2.0	320,346
Colorado	43	1.7	126	0.9	3	9.2	72,786	21.6	1.3	503,163
Nevada	14	0.5	62	0.4	4	6.0	96,565	21.3	1.2	1,521,143
Washington	55	2.1	177	1.2	3	4.4	24,938	20.4	1.2	371,764
Oklahoma	44	1.7	174	1.2	4	5.4	31,086	16.8	1.0	380,750
Louisiana	47	1.8	205	1.4	4	3.3	16,122	13.2	0.8	281,234
South Carolina	34	1.3	214	1.5	6	4.7	21,729	12.3	0.7	362,676
New Mexico	15	0.6	67	0.5	4	3.9	58,060	10.4	0.6	696,333
Tennessee	22	0.8	128	0.9	6	2.6	20,203	9.7	0.6	440,227
Arizona	39	1.5	89	0.6	2	2.2	24,921	8.9	0.5	227,564
Alabama	19	0.7	69	0.5	4	0.9	13,652	6.8	0.4	356,526
Missouri	24	0.9	48	0.3	2	1.1	22,542	6.1	0.4	254,333
Massachusetts	25	1.0	69	0.5	3	1.6	22,551	5.0	0.3	200,680
Wisconsin	27	1.0	78	0.5	3	1.1	14,705	5.0	0.3	184,889
Nebraska	14	0.5	77	0.5	6	1.1	13,766	5.0	0.3	356,214
West Virginia	14	0.5	44	0.3	3	0.6	12,841	3.5	0.2	249,357
Minnesota	17	0.7	32	0.2	2	0.4	12,625	2.8	0.2	164,529
Connecticut	15	0.6	24	0.2	2	0.6	25,750	2.8	0.2	186,200
Idaho	4	0.2	4	0.0	1	0.2	51,000	1.7	0.1	436,500
South Dakota	5	0.2	8	0.1	2	0.2	18,750	1.0	0.1	193,000
Kentucky	114	4.4	750*	-	-	(D)	-	(D)	-	-
New Jersey	98	3.8	375*	-	-	(D)	-	(D)	-	-
Maryland	82	3.2	375*	-	-	(D)	-	(D)	-	-
Georgia	47	1.8	175*	-	-	(D)	-	(D)	-	-
Kansas	30	1.2	60*	-	-	(D)	-	(D)	-	-
Arkansas	25	1.0	175*	-	-	(D)	-	(D)	-	-
Iowa	19	0.7	60*	-	-	(D)	-	(D)	-	-
Delaware	17	0.7	60*	-	-	(D)	-	(D)	-	-
Oregon	15	0.6	60*	-	-	(D)	-	(D)	-	-
Maine	12	0.5	60*	-	-	(D)	-	(D)	-	-
Rhode Island	11	0.4	60*	-	-	(D)	-	(D)	-	-
New Hampshire	10	0.4	10*	-	-	(D)	-	(D)	-	-
North Dakota	4	0.2	10*	-	-	(D)	-	(D)	-	-
Hawaii	3	0.1	10*	-	-	(D)	-	(D)	-	-
Montana	3	0.1	10*	-	-	(D)	-	(D)	-	-
Utah	3	0.1	10*	-	-	(D)	-	(D)	-	-
Vermont	3	0.1	10*	-	-	(D)	-	(D)	-	-
Alaska	2	0.1	10*	-	-	(D)	-	(D)	-	-
Mississippi	2	0.1	10*	-	-	(D)	-	(D)	-	-
Wyoming	2	0.1	10*	-	-	(D)	-	(D)	-	-

Source: 1997 Economic Census. The states are in descending order of revenues or establishments (if revenue data are missing for the majority). The symbol (D) appears when data are withheld to prevent disclosure of competitive information. States marked with (D) are sorted by number of establishments. A dash (-) indicates that the data element cannot be calculated. * indicates the midpoint of a range; 175, for example is the range 100-249. Shaded *states* on the state map indicate those states which have proportionately greater representation in the industry than would be indicated by the state's population; the ratio is based on total revenues or number of establishments. Shaded *regions* indicate where the industry is regionally most concentrated.

NAICS 711310 - PROMOTERS OF PERFORMING ARTS, SPORTS, AND SIMILAR EVENTS WITH FACILITIES

GENERAL STATISTICS

Year	Establishments (number)	Employment (number)	Payroll ($ million)	Revenues ($ million)	Employees per Establishment (number)	Revenues per Establishment ($)	Payroll per Employee ($)
1997	928	39,302	644.0	2,394.0	42.4	2,579,741	16,386

Source: *Economic Census of the United States*, 1997. This is a newly defined industry. Data for prior years were unavailable at the time of publication but may become available over time.

INDICES OF CHANGE

Year	Establishments (number)	Employment (number)	Payroll ($ million)	Revenues ($ million)	Employees per Establishment (number)	Revenues per Establishment ($)	Payroll per Employee ($)
1997	100.0	100.0	100.0	100.0	100.0	100.0	100.0

Sources: Same as General Statistics. The values shown reflect change from the base year, 1997. Values above 100 mean greater than 1997, values below 100 mean less than 1997, and a value of 100 in the 1982-96 or 1998-2001 period means same as 1997. Values followed by a 'p' are projections by the editors; 'e' stands for extrapolation. Data are the most recent available at this level of detail.

SIC INDUSTRIES RELATED TO NAICS 711310

Each new NAICS code represents an industry that used to be part of an SIC or a part of several SIC industries. Data in this table are shown to provide transitional information for these cases. All available data for the precursor SIC(s) are shown. Even if only a part of an SIC is included in the NAICS, *all* data for the SIC are reproduced. If the SIC industry is not marked as being a part (pt) of the NAICS, the entire industry is embedded in the NAICS data. The SIC composition of the new industry provides some hints of the relative importance of its "ancestors." Data marked with a 'p' are projected. Projections begin with 1982 data. Data earlier than 1990 are not shown but are reflected in the projections.

SIC	Industry	1990	1991	1992	1993	1994	1995	1996	1997
6512	**Nonresidential Building Operators (pt)**	-	-	-	-	-	-	-	-
7389	**Business Services, nec (pt)**								
	Establishments (number)	44,079	50,252	52,375	56,829	60,725	53,596	60,893p	63,269p
	Employment (thousands)	489.6	550.4	523.6	607.9	648.7	623.0	680.2p	710.9p
	Revenues ($ million)	-	-	32,885.9	-	-	-	-	-
7922	**Theatrical Producers & Services (pt)**								
	Establishments (number)	4,470	4,992	5,924	6,229	6,323	6,428	6,542p	6,792p
	Employment (thousands)	63.9	63.1	69.5	88.8	77.8	79.3	87.3p	91.2p
	Revenues ($ million)	-	-	5,730.5	4,396.6p	4,647.8p	4,899.0p	5,150.2p	5,401.4p
7941	**Sports Clubs & Promoters (pt)**								
	Establishments (number)	913	1,030	1,085	1,225	1,335	1,510	1,407p	1,473p
	Employment (thousands)	26.9	28.6	34.2	39.1	40.9	40.6	40.5p	42.1p
	Revenues ($ million)	3,702.0	3,719.0	3,978.0	5,056.0	6,138.0	7,695.0	8,877.0	8,573.4p
7999	**Amusement & Recreation nec (pt)**								
	Establishments (number)	-	-	21,717	-	-	-	-	-
	Employment (thousands)	-	-	215.8	-	-	-	-	-
	Revenues ($ million)	-	-	10,430.3	-	-	-	-	-

Source: *Economic Census of the United States*, 1992, annual surveys of economic sectors conducted by the Bureau of the Census, and estimates or projections based on the 1982-1992 period; not all data are shown. 'e' marks estimates made by the editors; 'p' indicates projections based on time series. A dash (-) indicates that data for this SIC or year were not available. The abbreviation (pt) next to the industry name indicates that only a part of the industry is present within the NAICS data. If no (pt) is shown, the entire industry is contained within the NAICS data.

SELECTED RATIOS

For 1997	Avg. of Information	Analyzed Industry	Index	For 1997	Avg. of Information	Analyzed Industry	Index
Employees per establishment	16	42	264	Payroll per establishment	330,963	693,966	210
Revenue per establishment	1,057,073	2,579,741	244	Payroll as % of revenue	31	27	86
Revenue per employee	65,958	60,913	92	Payroll per employee	20,651	16,386	79

Sources: Same as General Statistics. The 'Average' column represents the average for the industry sector, in 1997, where the currently shown industry is classified. The Index shows the relationship between the Average and the Analyzed Industry. For example, 100 means that they are equal; 500 that the Analyzed Industry is five times the average; 50 means that the Analyzed Industry is half the national average. The abbreviation 'na' is used to show that data are 'not available'.

LEADING COMPANIES

No company data available for this industry.

LOCATION BY STATE AND REGIONAL CONCENTRATION

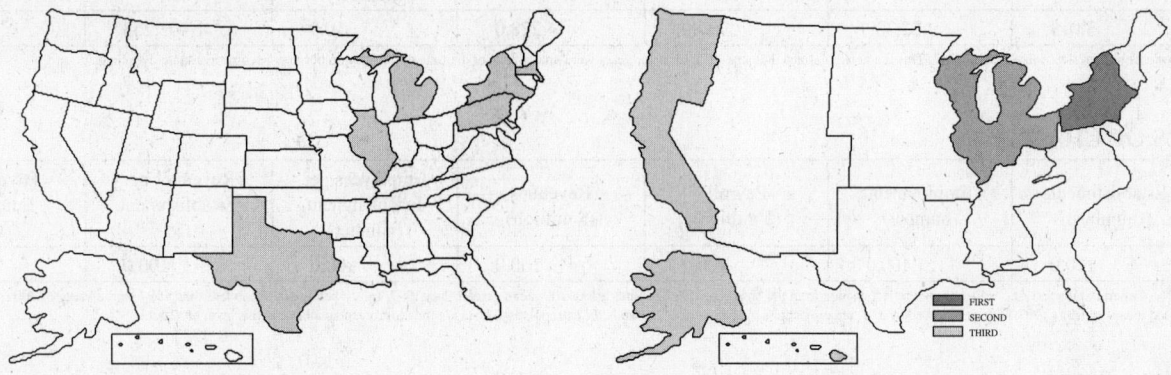

FIRST
SECOND
THIRD

INDUSTRY DATA BY STATE

State	Establishments Total (number)	% of U.S.	Employment Total (number)	% of U.S.	Per Estab.	Payroll Total ($ mil.)	Per Empl. ($)	Revenues Total ($ mil.)	% of U.S.	Per Estab. ($)
New York	127	13.7	7,208	18.3	57	192.7	26,741	422.2	17.6	3,324,567
Texas	57	6.1	1,607	4.1	28	67.7	42,142	187.6	7.8	3,291,807
California	115	12.4	2,617	6.7	23	48.4	18,498	183.0	7.6	1,591,574
Illinois	38	4.1	977	2.5	26	19.1	19,533	139.1	5.8	3,660,421
Massachusetts	27	2.9	2,006	5.1	74	19.7	9,823	126.2	5.3	4,674,593
Florida	51	5.5	3,229	8.2	63	31.0	9,607	120.1	5.0	2,354,824
Pennsylvania	40	4.3	2,079	5.3	52	30.3	14,568	117.5	4.9	2,937,525
Ohio	50	5.4	2,126	5.4	43	22.5	10,570	96.9	4.0	1,937,920
Michigan	33	3.6	3,160	8.0	96	34.0	10,767	96.2	4.0	2,916,333
New Jersey	17	1.8	311	0.8	18	7.8	24,994	62.9	2.6	3,702,176
Arizona	15	1.6	585	1.5	39	8.4	14,344	33.4	1.4	2,225,933
Indiana	16	1.7	177	0.5	11	2.9	16,638	30.3	1.3	1,892,562
Wisconsin	22	2.4	460	1.2	21	6.0	13,017	21.3	0.9	966,000
Alabama	8	0.9	280	0.7	35	1.4	4,893	15.6	0.7	1,946,625
Washington	24	2.6	344	0.9	14	3.1	9,070	12.7	0.5	528,000
Georgia	9	1.0	523	1.3	58	3.5	6,675	11.2	0.5	1,240,778
Oregon	11	1.2	62	0.2	6	1.0	15,984	6.1	0.3	553,818
Oklahoma	5	0.5	33	0.1	7	1.0	29,576	4.2	0.2	835,200
South Carolina	10	1.1	106	0.3	11	1.7	16,274	3.0	0.1	301,500
Maine	6	0.6	19	0.0	3	0.2	12,684	0.9	0.0	157,333
Arkansas	3	0.3	2	0.0	1	-	6,500	0.2	0.0	59,333
Idaho	3	0.3	60*	-	-	(D)	-	(D)	-	-
Mississippi	2	0.2	10*	-	-	(D)	-	(D)	-	-
Rhode Island	2	0.2	60*	-	-	(D)	-	(D)	-	-
Nebraska	1	0.1	10*	-	-	(D)	-	(D)	-	-
West Virginia	1	0.1	10*	-	-	(D)	-	(D)	-	-

Source: 1997 *Economic Census.* The states are in descending order of revenues or establishments (if revenue data are missing for the majority). The symbol (D) appears when data are withheld to prevent disclosure of competitive information. States marked with (D) are sorted by number of establishments. A dash (-) indicates that the data element cannot be calculated. * indicates the midpoint of a range; 175, for example is the range 100-249. Shaded *states* on the state map indicate those states which have proportionately greater representation in the industry than would be indicated by the state's population; the ratio is based on total revenues or number of establishments. Shaded *regions* indicate where the industry is regionally most concentrated.

NAICS 711320 - PROMOTERS OF PERFORMING ARTS, SPORTS, AND SIMILAR EVENTS WITHOUT FACILITIES

GENERAL STATISTICS

Year	Establishments (number)	Employment (number)	Payroll ($ million)	Revenues ($ million)	Employees per Establishment (number)	Revenues per Establishment ($)	Payroll per Employee ($)
1997	3,013	32,739	757.0	4,228.0	10.9	1,403,253	23,122

Source: Economic Census of the United States, 1997. This is a newly defined industry. Data for prior years were unavailable at the time of publication but may become available over time.

INDICES OF CHANGE

Year	Establishments (number)	Employment (number)	Payroll ($ million)	Revenues ($ million)	Employees per Establishment (number)	Revenues per Establishment ($)	Payroll per Employee ($)
1997	100.0	100.0	100.0	100.0	100.0	100.0	100.0

Sources: Same as General Statistics. The values shown reflect change from the base year, 1997. Values above 100 mean greater than 1997, values below 100 mean less than 1997, and a value of 100 in the 1982-96 or 1998-2001 period means same as 1997. Values followed by a 'p' are projections by the editors; 'e' stands for extrapolation. Data are the most recent available at this level of detail.

SIC INDUSTRIES RELATED TO NAICS 711320

Each new NAICS code represents an industry that used to be part of an SIC or a part of several SIC industries. Data in this table are shown to provide transitional information for these cases. All available data for the precursor SIC(s) are shown. Even if only a part of an SIC is included in the NAICS, *all* data for the SIC are reproduced. If the SIC industry is not marked as being a part (pt) of the NAICS, the entire industry is embedded in the NAICS data. The SIC composition of the new industry provides some hints of the relative importance of its "ancestors." Data marked with a 'p' are projected. Projections begin with 1982 data. Data earlier than 1990 are not shown but are reflected in the projections.

SIC	Industry	1990	1991	1992	1993	1994	1995	1996	1997
7389	**Business Services, nec (pt)**								
	Establishments (number)	44,079	50,252	52,375	56,829	60,725	53,596	60,893p	63,269p
	Employment (thousands)	489.6	550.4	523.6	607.9	648.7	623.0	680.2p	710.9p
	Revenues ($ million)	-	-	32,885.9	-	-		-	-
7922	**Theatrical Producers & Services (pt)**								
	Establishments (number)	4,470	4,992	5,924	6,229	6,323	6,428	6,542p	6,792p
	Employment (thousands)	63.9	63.1	69.5	88.8	77.8	79.3	87.3p	91.2p
	Revenues ($ million)	-	-	5,730.5	4,396.6p	4,647.8p	4,899.0p	5,150.2p	5,401.4p
7941	**Sports Clubs & Promoters (pt)**								
	Establishments (number)	913	1,030	1,085	1,225	1,335	1,510	1,407p	1,473p
	Employment (thousands)	26.9	28.6	34.2	39.1	40.9	40.6	40.5p	42.1p
	Revenues ($ million)	3,702.0	3,719.0	3,978.0	5,056.0	6,138.0	7,695.0	8,877.0	8,573.4p
7999	**Amusement & Recreation nec (pt)**								
	Establishments (number)	-	-	21,717	-	-		-	-
	Employment (thousands)	-	-	215.8	-	-		-	-
	Revenues ($ million)	-	-	10,430.3	-	-		-	-

Source: Economic Census of the United States, 1992, annual surveys of economic sectors conducted by the Bureau of the Census, and estimates or projections based on the 1982-1992 period; not all data are shown. 'e' marks estimates made by the editors; 'p' indicates projections based on time series. A dash (-) indicates that data for this SIC or year were not available. The abbreviation (pt) next to the industry name indicates that only a part of the industry is present within the NAICS data. If no (pt) is shown, the entire industry is contained within the NAICS data.

SELECTED RATIOS

For 1997	Avg. of Information	Analyzed Industry	Index	For 1997	Avg. of Information	Analyzed Industry	Index
Employees per establishment	16	11	68	Payroll per establishment	330,963	251,245	76
Revenue per establishment	1,057,073	1,403,253	133	Payroll as % of revenue	31	18	57
Revenue per employee	65,958	129,143	196	Payroll per employee	20,651	23,122	112

Sources: Same as General Statistics. The 'Average' column represents the average for the industry sector, in 1997, where the currently shown industry is classified. The Index shows the relationship between the Average and the Analyzed Industry. For example, 100 means that they are equal; 500 that the Analyzed Industry is five times the average; 50 means that the Analyzed Industry is half the national average. The abbreviation 'na' is used to show that data are 'not available'.

LEADING COMPANIES Number shown: **75**   Total sales ($ mil): **9,141**   Total employment (000): **27.2**

Company Name	Address				CEO Name	Phone	Co. Type	Sales ($ mil)	Empl. (000)
National Broadcasting Inc	30 Rockefeller, #310	New York	NY	10112	Robert C. Wright	212-664-4444	P	5,269	6.5
Opryland Productions Inc.	2802 Opryland Dr	Nashville	TN	37214	Terry London	615-871-6614	S	1,306*	6.0
Hoyts Cinema Corp.	2312 N Salisbury	Salisbury	MD	21801		410-543-0902	R	1,068*	5.0
Feld Entertainment Inc.	8607 Westwood	Vienna	VA	22182	Kenneth Feld	703-448-4000	R	250*	2.5
New Line Home Video Inc.	116 N Robertson	Los Angeles	CA	90048	Stephen Eihorn	310-854-5811	S	218*	1.0
William Morris Agency Inc.	151 El Camino Dr	Beverly Hills	CA	90212	Walter Ziskin	310-859-4000	R	150*	0.7
Reprise Records	3300 Warner Blvd	Burbank	CA	91505		818-846-9090	S	109*	0.5
Atlantic Recording Corp.	1290 Av Americas	New York	NY	10104	Val Azzoli	212-707-2000	D	87*	0.4
Raycom Sports	2815 Coliseum	Charlotte	NC	28217		704-378-4400	P	64	<0.1
Creative Artists Agency Inc.	9830 Wilshire Blvd	Beverly Hills	CA	90212	Richard Lovett	310-288-4545	R	46*	0.5
Elite Model Management Corp.	111 E 22nd St	New York	NY	10010	John Casablancas	212-529-9700	R	46*	<0.1
Carnegie Hall Corp.	881 7th Ave	New York	NY	10019		212-903-9600	R	34*	0.3
Rhino Records Inc.	10635 Santa Monica	Los Angeles	CA	90025	Richard Foos	310-474-4778	R	34*	0.2
Gilmore Entertainment Group L	P O Box 7576	Myrtle Beach	SC	29572	Calvin Gilmore	843-913-1400	R	30*	0.1
On Stage Entertainment Inc.	4625 W Nevso Dr	Las Vegas	NV	89103	David Hope	702-253-1333	P	28	0.6
Bay Area Seating Service Inc.	1855 Gateway Blvd	Concord	CA	94520		925-671-4000	R	25*	0.3
OCC Sports Inc.	605 3rd Ave	New York	NY	10158		212-916-9200	S	25	<0.1
American Conservatory Theater	30 Grant Ave	San Francisco	CA	94108		415-834-3200	R	20*	0.2
Epic Records	2100 Colorado Ave	Santa Monica	CA	90404		310-449-2100	S	20	0.2
United Talent Agency	9560 Wilshire Blvd	Beverly Hills	CA	90212	Jim Berkus	310-273-6700	R	19*	0.2
BRC Imagination Arts	2711 Winona Ave	Burbank	CA	91504	Bob Rogers	818-841-8084	R	18*	<0.1
Jack Rouse Associates Inc.	1014 Vine St	Cincinnati	OH	45202	Jack Rouse	513-381-0055	R	15*	<0.1
Starstruck Entertainment Inc.	P O Box 121996	Nashville	TN	37212	Narvel Blackstock	615-259-0001	R	15*	<0.1
Steppenwolf Theater Co.	1650 N Halsted St	Chicago	IL	60614		312-335-1888	R	15*	<0.1
Higher Octave Music Inc.	23852 Pacific Coast	Malibu	CA	90265	Matt Marshall	310-589-1515	R	14*	<0.1
Broadcast Programming	2211 5th Ave	Seattle	WA	98121	Edie Hilliard	206-728-2741	S	13*	<0.1
Contemporary Productions Inc.	1401 S Brentwood	St. Louis	MO	63144	Steve Schankman	314-962-4000	R	13*	<0.1
MJI Broadcasting	135 w 50th St Fl 8	New York	NY	10020	Joshua Feigenbaum	212-896-5200	R	13*	<0.1
Crossroads V Communications	PO Box 18162	Beverly Hills	CA	90209	John W Hyde	310-282-0871	R	12*	<0.1
Nederlander Organization Inc.	810 7th Ave	New York	NY	10019	James Nederlander	212-262-2400	R	11*	<0.1
Metropolitan Tickets Inc.	531 N Grand Blvd	St. Louis	MO	63103	David R Ray	314-534-1678	R	10*	<0.1
Triangle Talent Inc.	10424 Waterson Tr	Louisville	KY	40299	David H Snowden	502-267-5466	R	10	<0.1
Curtis Brown Ltd.	10 Astor Pl	New York	NY	10003	Perry Knowlton	212-473-5400	R	8*	<0.1
N.S. Bienstock Inc.	1740 Broadway	New York	NY	10019		212-765-3040	R	7*	<0.1
Opryland Theatricals Inc.	2802 Opryland Dr	Nashville	TN	37214		615-871-6614	D	7*	<0.1
Tihati Productions Ltd.	3615 Harding	Honolulu	HI	96816	Jack Thompson	808-735-0292	R	7*	<0.1
R.A. Reed Productions Inc.	955 N Columbia	Portland	OR	97217	RA Reed	503-735-0003	R	7	<0.1
Intern. Renaissance Festivals Ltd.	P O Box 315	Crownsville	MD	21032		410-266-7304	R	6	0.7
Dick Orkin's Creative Services	1140 N La Brea Ave	Hollywood	CA	90038	Dick Orkin	323-462-4966	R	5*	<0.1
Musson Theatrical Inc.	890 Walsh Ave	Santa Clara	CA	95050	Robert Downs	408-986-0210	R	5	<0.1
TM Century Inc.	2002 Academy	Dallas	TX	75234	Robert D Graupner	972-406-6800	P	5	<0.1
James Gang Inc.	2514 Converse	Dallas	TX	75207	James W Beresford	214-630-5656	R	4*	<0.1
Jeff Arthur Productions	4900 Creekside Dr	Clearwater	FL	33760	Jeff Arthur	727-573-5277	R	4*	<0.1
Lyric Opera of Kansas City	1029 Central St	Kansas City	MO	64105		816-471-4933	R	4*	<0.1
Mt. High Entertainment	7965 Vineyard Ave	R. Cucamonga	CA	91730	Michael Scafuto	909-980-8900	R	4	<0.1
One Reel	PO Box 9750	Seattle	WA	98109	Norman Langill	206-281-7788	R	4*	<0.1
T. Skorman Productions Inc.	3660 Maguire Blvd	Orlando	FL	32803	Ted Skorman	407-895-3000	R	4*	<0.1
Theater Communications Group	355 Lexington Ave	New York	NY	10017	John Sullivan	212-697-5230	R	4*	<0.1
Bert Berdis and Company Inc.	1956 N Cahuenga	Los Angeles	CA	90068	Bert Berdis	323-462-7261	R	3*	<0.1
Children's Radio Group	5501 Excelsior Blvd	St. Louis Park	MN	55416	Christopher Dahl	612-925-8840	R	3*	<0.1
Miles Bell and Associates Inc.	707 18th Ave S	Nashville	TN	37203	Miles Bell	615-327-8008	R	3*	<0.1
Professional Sports Planning Inc.	28025 S Harwich Dr	Farmington Hills	MI	48334	Kevin Poston	248-932-1007	R	3*	<0.1
Steven Scott Productions	200 W 57th St	New York	NY	10019	Stuart White	212-757-3299	D	3*	<0.1
Sub Pop Ltd.	1932 1st Ave	Seattle	WA	98101	Jonathan Poneman	206-441-8441	R	3*	<0.1
McDonald/Richards Model	156 5th Ave	New York	NY	10010	Gary Bertalovitz	212-627-3100	R	3	<0.1
Artists Intern. Management Inc.	9850 Sandalfoot	Boca Raton	FL	33428	Steve Green	561-498-1300	R	2	<0.1
Coralie Jr. Theatrical Agency	4789 Vineland Ave	N. Hollywood	CA	91602	Stuart Coralie Jr	818-766-9501	R	2*	<0.1
Delicious Vinyl Inc.	6607 Sunset Blvd	Los Angeles	CA	90028	Michael Ross	323-465-2700	S	2*	<0.1
Jon Koons Productions Inc.	139 Everett Pl	Englewood	NJ	07631	Jon Koons	201-568-7782	R	2*	<0.1
Nationwide Entertainment	2756 N Gr Vly	Henderson	NV	89014	AJ Sagman	702-451-8090	R	2	<0.1
P I A	680 N Lakeshore	Chicago	IL	60611	Brad Saul	312-943-8888	R	2*	<0.1
Smith Gosnell Nicholson	1515 Palisades Dr	Pacific Palisades	CA	90272	Crayton Smith	310-459-0307	R	2*	<0.1
Soundscapes Inc.	3422 Old Cantrell	Little Rock	AR	72202	Brent Walker	501-661-1765	R	2*	<0.1
Talent Plus Inc.	55 Maryland Plz	St. Louis	MO	63108	Sharon Lee-Tucci	314-367-5588	R	2*	<0.1
Tribe	8447 Wilshire Blvd	Beverly Hills	CA	90211		323-782-1220	R	2*	<0.1
Buddy Lee Attractions Inc.	38 Music Sq E	Nashville	TN	37203	Tony Conway	615-244-4336	R	1.	<0.1
Cellar Door	900 NE 26th Ave	Fort Lauderdale	FL	33304	AJ Wasson	954-561-3100	R	1*	<0.1
DiCesare Engler Productions Inc.	2825 Tenn Ave	Pittsburgh	PA	15222	Pat DiCesare	412-562-9900	R	1*	<0.1
Dolores Robinson Entertainment	112 S Almont Dr	Los Angeles	CA	90048	Dolores Robinson	310-777-8777	R	1*	<0.1
Grand Entertainment Group Inc.	20 Music Sq W	Nashville	TN	37203	Joe Meador	615-742-8080	R	1*	<0.1
Herbert H. Breslin Inc.	119 W 57th St	New York	NY	10019	Herbert H Breslin	212-246-5480	R	1*	<0.1
Hi Mote	106 W 71st St	New York	NY	10023	Barney Fields	212-873-2020	R	1*	<0.1
IMAGE Management Group	1009 16th Ave S	Nashville	TN	37212	Johnny Slate	615-327-9050	R	1*	<0.1
Kelley Communications Corp.	100 Conifer Hill Dr	Danvers	MA	01923	Paul Kelley	978-762-4667	R	1*	<0.1
One Nighters Inc.	PO Box 40686	Nashville	TN	37204	Billy Smith	615-383-8412	R	1*	<0.1

Source: Ward's Business Directory of U.S. Private and Public Companies, Volumes 1 and 2, 2000. The company type code used is as follows: P - Public, R - Private, S - Subsidiary, D - Division, J - Joint Venture, A - Affiliate, G - Group, N - Company type not reported. Sales are in millions of dollars, employees are in thousands. An asterisk (*) indicates an estimated sales volume. The symbol < stands for 'less than'. Company names and addresses are truncated, in some cases, to fit into the available space.

REPRESENTATIVE NONPROFIT ORGANIZATIONS

Organization Name	Address				Phone	Income Range ($ mil)
Alabama Sports Foundation	2 Perimeter Park S Ste 310	Birmingham	AL	35243	205-967-8564	1-5
Boomer Esiason Foundation	4720 Montgomery LN	Bethesda	MD	20814		1-5
Brickyard Foundation Inc	4790 W 16th St	Indianapolis	IN	46222		1-5
Capital Sports Foundation Inc	P O Box 81407	Lincoln	NE	68501	402-464-3183	1-5
Celebrity Bowl Charities Incorporated	PO Box 819	Mankato	MN	56002	507-386-1934	5-9
Century Club of San Diego	3333 Camino Del Rio	San Diego	CA	92108	619-281-4653	5-9
Charlotte Steeplechase Association Inc	815 Wood Ridge Center	Charlotte	NC	28217		1-5
Classic Foundation Inc	110 Veterans Blvd Ste 170	Metairie	LA	70005	504-831-4653	5-9
Community Development Services Inc	1544 E Main St	Meriden	CT	06450		1-5
Doral Ryder Open Foundation Inc	4400 NW 87th Ave	Miami	FL	33178		5-9
Fight for Children Inc	1650 Tysons Blvd	McLean	VA	22102		1-5
Henry County High School Athletic Booster Club	221 Chilton CT	Campbells Burg	KY	40011		1-5
Houston Golf Association	1830 S Millbend Dr	The Woodlands	TX	77380	281-367-7999	10-19
Mahoning Valley Sports Charities Inc	1 American Way	Warren	OH	44484		1-5
McDonalds Kids Charities	401 City Ave Ste 800	Bala Cynwyd	PA	19004		5-9
Metro South Golf Charities Inc	100 Eagles Landing	Stockbridge	GA	30281		1-5
Northville Foundation	25 Melville Park Rd	Melville	NY	11747		1-5
Salt Lake Olympic Organizing Committee	257 E 200 S Ste 600	Salt Lake City	UT	84111		20-29
Springhouse Golf Classic Corporation	One Gaylord Dr	Nashville	TN	37214	615-871-7759	5-9
Truckee Meadows Boys & Girls Club Foundation Inc	2680 East 9th Street	Reno	NV	89512	775-331-3605	1-5
Womens International Bowling Congress Inc	5301 S 76th St	Greendale	WI	53129	414-421-9000	10-19

Source: National Directory of Nonprofit Organizations, 2000, Volumes 1 and 2, The Taft Group. The table shows a selection of organizations for illustration and does not constitute a complete selection from the source. The organizations are arranged in alphabetical order.

LOCATION BY STATE AND REGIONAL CONCENTRATION

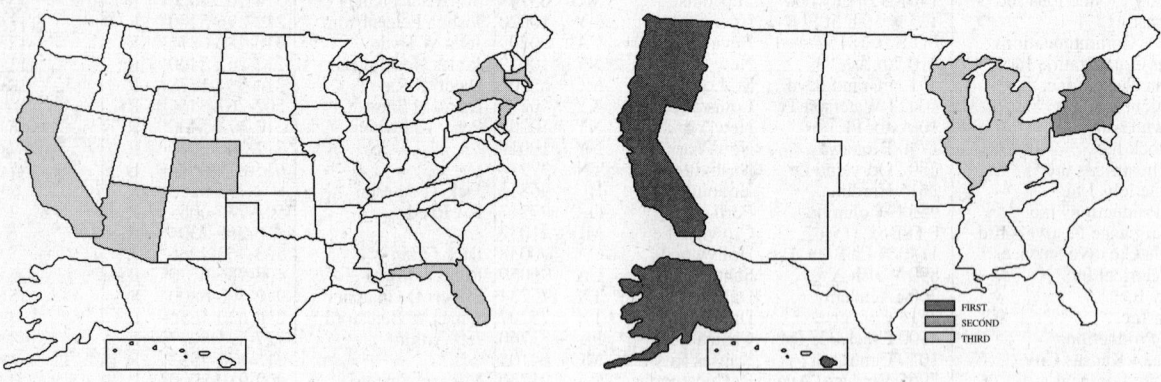

FIRST
SECOND
THIRD

INDUSTRY DATA BY STATE

State	Establishments		Employment			Payroll		Revenues		
	Total (number)	% of U.S.	Total (number)	% of U.S.	Per Estab.	Total ($ mil.)	Per Empl. ($)	Total ($ mil.)	% of U.S.	Per Estab. ($)
California	455	15.1	4,190	12.8	9	214.2	51,121	731.2	17.3	1,607,088
Florida	197	6.5	2,114	6.5	11	49.4	23,359	398.3	9.4	2,021,640
New York	254	8.4	7,273	22.2	29	97.8	13,452	380.3	9.0	1,497,165
Texas	138	4.6	2,158	6.6	16	41.0	18,992	261.1	6.2	1,892,246
New Jersey	70	2.3	447	1.4	6	19.8	44,327	155.9	3.7	2,227,857
Illinois	123	4.1	483	1.5	4	18.0	37,337	155.2	3.7	1,262,008
Ohio	142	4.7	1,176	3.6	8	15.6	13,304	127.0	3.0	894,331
Massachusetts	55	1.8	761	2.3	14	15.8	20,714	123.6	2.9	2,246,655
Michigan	102	3.4	386	1.2	4	14.5	37,637	121.3	2.9	1,189,020
Colorado	55	1.8	672	2.1	12	14.8	21,988	113.4	2.7	2,062,127
Arizona	57	1.9	516	1.6	9	10.9	21,143	109.6	2.6	1,922,053
Pennsylvania	113	3.8	1,748	5.3	15	14.1	8,063	96.0	2.3	849,947
Wisconsin	82	2.7	470	1.4	6	9.4	20,077	64.8	1.5	790,512
Minnesota	35	1.2	196	0.6	6	5.9	30,051	63.2	1.5	1,806,400
Washington	65	2.2	619	1.9	10	14.0	22,627	61.3	1.4	942,462
Indiana	69	2.3	573	1.8	8	7.9	13,775	49.6	1.2	718,145
Oregon	36	1.2	216	0.7	6	5.8	26,894	41.8	1.0	1,160,889
South Carolina	27	0.9	160	0.5	6	4.6	28,906	25.6	0.6	948,630
Alabama	16	0.5	47	0.1	3	1.3	28,319	13.1	0.3	817,188
Nebraska	25	0.8	84	0.3	3	1.4	16,464	8.8	0.2	353,720
North Dakota	9	0.3	29	0.1	3	0.8	26,276	6.9	0.2	771,667
North Carolina	14	0.5	37	0.1	3	0.7	19,595	4.5	0.1	324,143
Rhode Island	5	0.2	31	0.1	6	0.3	10,581	1.5	0.0	293,600

Source: 1997 *Economic Census*. The states are in descending order of revenues or establishments (if revenue data are missing for the majority). The symbol (D) appears when data are withheld to prevent disclosure of competitive information. States marked with (D) are sorted by number of establishments. A dash (-) indicates that the data element cannot be calculated. * indicates the midpoint of a range; 175, for example is the range 100-249. Shaded *states* on the state map indicate those states which have proportionately greater representation in the industry than would be indicated by the state's population; the ratio is based on total revenues or number of establishments. Shaded *regions* indicate where the industry is regionally most concentrated.

NAICS 711410 - AGENTS AND MANAGERS FOR ARTISTS, ATHLETES, ENTERTAINERS AND OTHER PUBLIC FIGURES

GENERAL STATISTICS

Year	Establishments (number)	Employment (number)	Payroll ($ million)	Revenues ($ million)	Employees per Establishment (number)	Revenues per Establishment ($)	Payroll per Employee ($)
1997	2,532	13,239	911.0	2,410.0	5.2	951,817	68,812

Source: Economic Census of the United States, 1997. This is a newly defined industry. Data for prior years were unavailable at the time of publication but may become available over time.

INDICES OF CHANGE

Year	Establishments (number)	Employment (number)	Payroll ($ million)	Revenues ($ million)	Employees per Establishment (number)	Revenues per Establishment ($)	Payroll per Employee ($)
1997	100.0	100.0	100.0	100.0	100.0	100.0	100.0

Sources: Same as General Statistics. The values shown reflect change from the base year, 1997. Values above 100 mean greater than 1997, values below 100 mean less than 1997, and a value of 100 in the 1982-96 or 1998-2001 period means same as 1997. Values followed by a 'p' are projections by the editors; 'e' stands for extrapolation. Data are the most recent available at this level of detail.

SIC INDUSTRIES RELATED TO NAICS 711410

Each new NAICS code represents an industry that used to be part of an SIC or a part of several SIC industries. Data in this table are shown to provide transitional information for these cases. All available data for the precursor SIC(s) are shown. Even if only a part of an SIC is included in the NAICS, *all* data for the SIC are reproduced. If the SIC industry is not marked as being a part (pt) of the NAICS, the entire industry is embedded in the NAICS data. The SIC composition of the new industry provides some hints of the relative importance of its "ancestors." Data marked with a 'p' are projected. Projections begin with 1982 data. Data earlier than 1990 are not shown but are reflected in the projections.

SIC	Industry	1990	1991	1992	1993	1994	1995	1996	1997
7389	**Business Services, nec (pt)**								
	Establishments (number)	44,079	50,252	52,375	56,829	60,725	53,596	60,893p	63,269p
	Employment (thousands)	489.6	550.4	523.6	607.9	648.7	623.0	680.2p	710.9p
	Revenues ($ million)	-	-	32,885.9	-	-	-	-	-
7922	**Theatrical Producers & Services (pt)**								
	Establishments (number)	4,470	4,992	5,924	6,229	6,323	6,428	6,542p	6,792p
	Employment (thousands)	63.9	63.1	69.5	88.8	77.8	79.3	87.3p	91.2p
	Revenues ($ million)	-	-	5,730.5	4,396.6p	4,647.8p	4,899.0p	5,150.2p	5,401.4p
7941	**Sports Clubs & Promoters (pt)**								
	Establishments (number)	913	1,030	1,085	1,225	1,335	1,510	1,407p	1,473p
	Employment (thousands)	26.9	28.6	34.2	39.1	40.9	40.6	40.5p	42.1p
	Revenues ($ million)	3,702.0	3,719.0	3,978.0	5,056.0	6,138.0	7,695.0	8,877.0	8,573.4p

Source: Economic Census of the United States, 1992, annual surveys of economic sectors conducted by the Bureau of the Census, and estimates or projections based on the 1982-1992 period; not all data are shown. 'e' marks estimates made by the editors; 'p' indicates projections based on time series. A dash (-) indicates that data for this SIC or year were not available. The abbreviation (pt) next to the industry name indicates that only a part of the industry is present within the NAICS data. If no (pt) is shown, the entire industry is contained within the NAICS data.

SELECTED RATIOS

For 1997	Avg. of Information	Analyzed Industry	Index	For 1997	Avg. of Information	Analyzed Industry	Index
Employees per establishment	16	5	33	Payroll per establishment	330,963	359,795	109
Revenue per establishment	1,057,073	951,817	90	Payroll as % of revenue	31	38	121
Revenue per employee	65,958	182,038	276	Payroll per employee	20,651	68,812	333

Sources: Same as General Statistics. The 'Average' column represents the average for the industry sector, in 1997, where the currently shown industry is classified. The Index shows the relationship between the Average and the Analyzed Industry. For example, 100 means that they are equal; 500 that the Analyzed Industry is five times the average; 50 means that the Analyzed Industry is half the national average. The abbreviation 'na' is used to show that data are 'not available'.

LEADING COMPANIES

No company data available for this industry.

LOCATION BY STATE AND REGIONAL CONCENTRATION

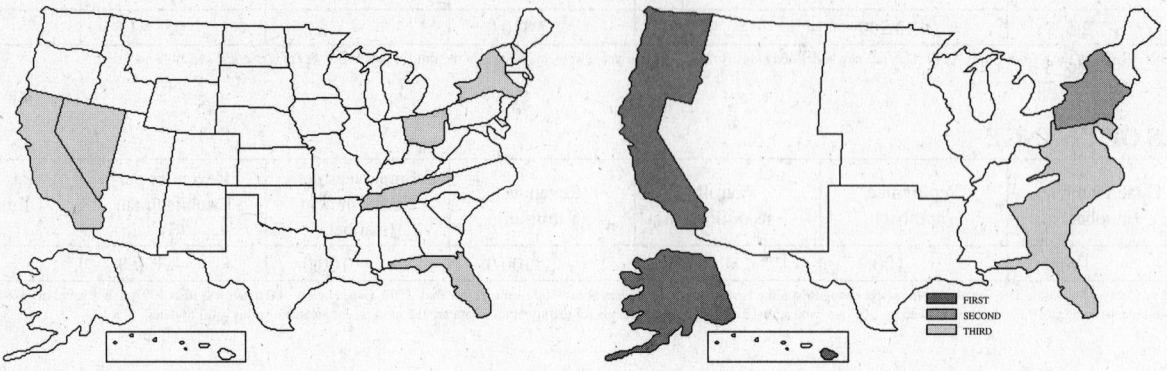

FIRST
SECOND
THIRD

INDUSTRY DATA BY STATE

State	Establishments Total (number)	% of U.S.	Employment Total (number)	% of U.S.	Per Estab.	Payroll Total ($ mil.)	Per Empl. ($)	Revenues Total ($ mil.)	% of U.S.	Per Estab. ($)
California	668	26.4	4,604	34.8	7	455.1	98,839	974.8	40.5	1,459,320
New York	590	23.3	3,368	25.4	6	218.6	64,910	624.1	25.9	1,057,861
Florida	152	6.0	656	5.0	4	22.7	34,677	132.2	5.5	869,579
Ohio	38	1.5	469	3.5	12	22.6	48,154	111.9	4.6	2,944,342
Texas	109	4.3	296	2.2	3	19.8	66,868	62.7	2.6	575,642
New Jersey	73	2.9	443	3.3	6	17.9	40,386	61.4	2.5	840,548
Tennessee	103	4.1	560	4.2	5	32.0	57,141	59.0	2.4	572,874
Illinois	84	3.3	280	2.1	3	18.1	64,796	43.3	1.8	515,226
Massachusetts	64	2.5	235	1.8	4	11.4	48,706	37.2	1.5	581,672
Michigan	46	1.8	170	1.3	4	9.0	52,735	26.8	1.1	581,674
D.C.	13	0.5	60	0.5	5	12.4	207,317	22.9	0.9	1,760,077
Washington	37	1.5	115	0.9	3	4.8	41,635	20.6	0.9	557,514
Connecticut	31	1.2	94	0.7	3	6.7	71,298	20.4	0.8	659,032
Virginia	39	1.5	148	1.1	4	6.4	43,514	19.8	0.8	506,564
Pennsylvania	45	1.8	146	1.1	3	4.4	30,021	17.4	0.7	386,400
North Carolina	36	1.4	142	1.1	4	4.4	30,937	16.6	0.7	461,028
Georgia	41	1.6	129	1.0	3	5.0	39,140	16.1	0.7	392,610
Nevada	35	1.4	104	0.8	3	4.5	43,288	15.4	0.6	440,200
Maryland	24	0.9	89	0.7	4	3.5	39,236	13.1	0.5	544,208
Colorado	25	1.0	80	0.6	3	2.8	34,987	12.9	0.5	515,720
Missouri	26	1.0	91	0.7	4	2.6	28,176	11.0	0.5	422,000
Minnesota	37	1.5	98	0.7	3	2.9	29,439	9.9	0.4	266,541
Oregon	20	0.8	65	0.5	3	3.6	55,877	9.8	0.4	492,150
Arizona	22	0.9	64	0.5	3	2.1	32,094	9.2	0.4	417,045
Hawaii	14	0.6	121	0.9	9	1.8	15,115	6.3	0.3	453,000
Indiana	25	1.0	205	1.5	8	2.6	12,561	6.2	0.3	246,920
Alabama	10	0.4	76	0.6	8	1.5	19,368	5.1	0.2	505,100
Wisconsin	18	0.7	40	0.3	2	1.0	24,875	5.0	0.2	277,222
Montana	7	0.3	23	0.2	3	2.9	127,087	4.0	0.2	566,571
New Mexico	6	0.2	19	0.1	3	0.3	18,211	3.5	0.1	580,000
Oklahoma	11	0.4	49	0.4	4	0.9	19,265	3.1	0.1	279,727
Louisiana	9	0.4	29	0.2	3	0.6	22,276	2.7	0.1	300,444
Kansas	10	0.4	21	0.2	2	0.8	36,476	2.5	0.1	251,300
Kentucky	8	0.3	24	0.2	3	0.6	24,292	2.4	0.1	301,750
South Carolina	12	0.5	28	0.2	2	0.7	23,536	2.1	0.1	175,583
Vermont	5	0.2	12	0.1	2	1.0	84,583	2.1	0.1	422,800
Arkansas	6	0.2	10	0.1	2	0.4	43,900	1.4	0.1	234,333
New Hampshire	3	0.1	16	0.1	5	0.1	8,375	0.7	0.0	244,000
Utah	7	0.3	10*	-	-	(D)	-	(D)	-	-
Nebraska	6	0.2	60*	-	-	(D)	-	(D)	-	-
Maine	4	0.2	10*	-	-	(D)	-	(D)	-	-
Iowa	3	0.1	10*	-	-	(D)	-	(D)	-	-
Mississippi	3	0.1	10*	-	-	(D)	-	(D)	-	-
Rhode Island	2	0.1	10*	-	-	(D)	-	(D)	-	-
Wyoming	2	0.1	10*	-	-	(D)	-	(D)	-	-
Delaware	1	-	10*	-	-	(D)	-	(D)	-	-
Idaho	1	-	10*	-	-	(D)	-	(D)	-	-
North Dakota	1	-	10*	-	-	(D)	-	(D)	-	-

Source: 1997 *Economic Census*. The states are in descending order of revenues or establishments (if revenue data are missing for the majority). The symbol (D) appears when data are withheld to prevent disclosure of competitive information. States marked with (D) are sorted by number of establishments. A dash (-) indicates that the data element cannot be calculated. * indicates the midpoint of a range; 175, for example is the range 100-249. Shaded *states* on the state map indicate those states which have proportionately greater representation in the industry than would be indicated by the state's population; the ratio is based on total revenues or number of establishments. Shaded *regions* indicate where the industry is regionally most concentrated.

NAICS 711510 - INDEPENDENT ARTISTS, WRITERS, AND PERFORMERS

GENERAL STATISTICS

Year	Establishments (number)	Employment (number)	Payroll ($ million)	Revenues ($ million)	Employees per Establishment (number)	Revenues per Establishment ($)	Payroll per Employee ($)
1997	11,013	27,081	3,268.0	6,361.0	2.5	577,590	120,675

Source: Economic Census of the United States, 1997. This is a newly defined industry. Data for prior years were unavailable at the time of publication but may become available over time.

INDICES OF CHANGE

Year	Establishments (number)	Employment (number)	Payroll ($ million)	Revenues ($ million)	Employees per Establishment (number)	Revenues per Establishment ($)	Payroll per Employee ($)
1997	100.0	100.0	100.0	100.0	100.0	100.0	100.0

Sources: Same as General Statistics. The values shown reflect change from the base year, 1997. Values above 100 mean greater than 1997, values below 100 mean less than 1997, and a value of 100 in the 1982-96 or 1998-2001 period means same as 1997. Values followed by a 'p' are projections by the editors; 'e' stands for extrapolation. Data are the most recent available at this level of detail.

SIC INDUSTRIES RELATED TO NAICS 711510

Each new NAICS code represents an industry that used to be part of an SIC or a part of several SIC industries. Data in this table are shown to provide transitional information for these cases. All available data for the precursor SIC(s) are shown. Even if only a part of an SIC is included in the NAICS, *all* data for the SIC are reproduced. If the SIC industry is not marked as being a part (pt) of the NAICS, the entire industry is embedded in the NAICS data. The SIC composition of the new industry provides some hints of the relative importance of its "ancestors." Data marked with a 'p' are projected. Projections begin with 1982 data. Data earlier than 1990 are not shown but are reflected in the projections.

SIC	Industry	1990	1991	1992	1993	1994	1995	1996	1997
7383	**News Syndicates (pt)**								
	Establishments (number)	576	642	598	532	511	512	512p	500p
	Employment (thousands)	10.0	9.5	8.2	8.4	8.5	9.3	8.9p	9.0p
	Revenues ($ million)	-	-	1,020.8					
7641	**Reupholstery & Furniture Repair (pt)**								
	Establishments (number)	6,514	6,515	6,731	6,806	6,735	6,640	6,682p	6,681p
	Employment (thousands)	23.7	22.3	21.2	21.4	21.8	22.2	22.7p	22.7p
	Revenues ($ million)	-	-	980.4	1,060.6p	1,098.8p	1,137.0p	1,175.2p	1,213.4p
7699	**Repair Services, nec (pt)**								
	Establishments (number)	27,822	29,303	34,103	34,618	34,136	34,391	35,001p	35,792p
	Employment (thousands)	181.0	181.4	191.0	201.5	207.4	220.2	219.6p	226.2p
	Revenues ($ million)	-	-	15,059.4	15,563.6p	16,427.9p	17,292.2p	18,156.5p	19,020.8p
7819	**Services Allied to Motion Pictures (pt)**								
	Establishments (number)	2,984	2,955	3,895	3,799	3,691	3,289	3,584p	3,622p
	Employment (thousands)	113.1	102.4	162.2	158.8	130.9	136.7	160.9p	169.5p
	Revenues ($ million)	-	-	7,514.7	-				
7922	**Theatrical Producers & Services (pt)**								
	Establishments (number)	4,470	4,992	5,924	6,229	6,323	6,428	6,542p	6,792p
	Employment (thousands)	63.9	63.1	69.5	88.8	77.8	79.3	87.3p	91.2p
	Revenues ($ million)	-	-	5,730.5	4,396.6p	4,647.8p	4,899.0p	5,150.2p	5,401.4p
7929	**Entertainers & Entertainment Groups (pt)**								
	Establishments (number)	5,038	5,514	7,251	7,547	7,583	7,922	7,795p	8,080p
	Employment (thousands)	61.2	61.5	72.3	73.2	73.3	73.6	81.8p	85.4p
	Revenues ($ million)	-	-	5,714.7	4,279.9p	4,561.2p	4,842.4p	5,123.6p	5,404.9p
8999	**Services, nec (pt)**								
	Establishments (number)	-	-	14,587	-	-	-	-	-
	Employment (thousands)	-	-	81.1	-	-	-	-	-
	Revenues ($ million)	-	-	7,966.2	-	-	-	-	-

Source: Economic Census of the United States, 1992, annual surveys of economic sectors conducted by the Bureau of the Census, and estimates or projections based on the 1982-1992 period; not all data are shown. 'e' marks estimates made by the editors; 'p' indicates projections based on time series. A dash (-) indicates that data for this SIC or year were not available. The abbreviation (pt) next to the industry name indicates that only a part of the industry is present within the NAICS data. If no (pt) is shown, the entire industry is contained within the NAICS data.

SELECTED RATIOS

For 1997	Avg. of Information	Analyzed Industry	Index	For 1997	Avg. of Information	Analyzed Industry	Index
Employees per establishment	16	2	15	Payroll per establishment	330,963	296,740	90
Revenue per establishment	1,057,073	577,590	55	Payroll as % of revenue	31	51	164
Revenue per employee	65,958	234,888	356	Payroll per employee	20,651	120,675	584

Sources: Same as General Statistics. The 'Average' column represents the average for the industry sector, in 1997, where the currently shown industry is classified. The Index shows the relationship between the Average and the Analyzed Industry. For example, 100 means that they are equal; 500 that the Analyzed Industry is five times the average; 50 means that the Analyzed Industry is half the national average. The abbreviation 'na' is used to show that data are 'not available'.

LEADING COMPANIES

No company data available for this industry.

LOCATION BY STATE AND REGIONAL CONCENTRATION

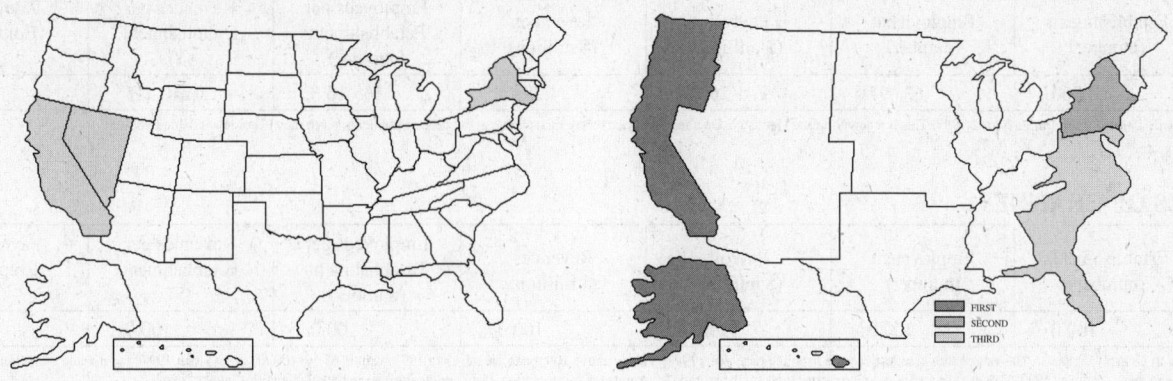

FIRST
SECOND
THIRD

INDUSTRY DATA BY STATE

State	Establishments Total (number)	% of U.S.	Employment Total (number)	% of U.S.	Per Estab.	Payroll Total ($ mil.)	Per Empl. ($)	Revenues Total ($ mil.)	% of U.S.	Per Estab. ($)
California	4,544	41.3	9,025	33.3	2	2,283.4	253,003	3,853.1	60.6	847,957
New York	1,520	13.8	3,036	11.2	2	433.6	142,806	931.4	14.6	612,788
Florida	462	4.2	1,155	4.3	3	37.5	32,455	130.6	2.1	282,734
Texas	294	2.7	1,005	3.7	3	44.2	43,982	127.7	2.0	434,255
New Jersey	284	2.6	578	2.1	2	48.1	83,170	114.4	1.8	402,764
Nevada	76	0.7	441	1.6	6	45.0	102,045	112.3	1.8	1,478,066
Michigan	173	1.6	684	2.5	4	47.4	69,351	88.6	1.4	512,046
Illinois	376	3.4	855	3.2	2	36.3	42,471	84.2	1.3	224,000
Massachusetts	176	1.6	603	2.2	3	21.5	35,624	64.9	1.0	368,977
Minnesota	185	1.7	1,017	3.8	5	19.5	19,132	64.6	1.0	349,422
Virginia	173	1.6	589	2.2	3	16.5	27,944	62.6	1.0	361,925
Washington	169	1.5	537	2.0	3	16.3	30,304	55.1	0.9	325,893
Connecticut	152	1.4	386	1.4	3	24.5	63,547	51.2	0.8	336,875
Pennsylvania	166	1.5	526	1.9	3	17.5	33,329	48.0	0.8	289,145
Maryland	152	1.4	412	1.5	3	16.6	40,197	43.6	0.7	286,612
Georgia	189	1.7	359	1.3	2	14.2	39,632	41.1	0.6	217,317
Tennessee	134	1.2	327	1.2	2	11.3	34,425	40.4	0.6	301,709
Ohio	160	1.5	552	2.0	3	13.6	24,551	36.9	0.6	230,500
Arizona	123	1.1	392	1.4	3	10.2	26,020	35.2	0.6	286,423
Colorado	197	1.8	534	2.0	3	10.2	19,081	35.1	0.6	178,274
Missouri	102	0.9	506	1.9	5	9.9	19,488	33.7	0.5	330,000
North Carolina	118	1.1	332	1.2	3	9.6	28,846	26.3	0.4	222,576
New Mexico	78	0.7	258	1.0	3	8.4	32,659	24.8	0.4	318,397
D.C.	58	0.5	172	0.6	3	9.3	53,808	20.3	0.3	349,534
Utah	62	0.6	186	0.7	3	4.8	25,823	19.6	0.3	315,823
Oregon	101	0.9	183	0.7	2	4.9	26,918	19.5	0.3	192,673
Louisiana	43	0.4	217	0.8	5	4.0	18,263	18.4	0.3	428,698
Wisconsin	114	1.0	530	2.0	5	6.3	11,792	17.0	0.3	148,711
Indiana	82	0.7	213	0.8	3	5.6	26,169	15.1	0.2	184,549
Kansas	39	0.4	136	0.5	3	3.2	23,816	13.4	0.2	343,949
New Hampshire	30	0.3	87	0.3	3	5.8	66,931	11.8	0.2	393,133
South Carolina	42	0.4	197	0.7	5	2.8	14,442	10.1	0.2	240,333
Iowa	58	0.5	136	0.5	2	3.2	23,662	8.2	0.1	142,121
Vermont	42	0.4	70	0.3	2	2.4	34,671	7.0	0.1	166,762
Rhode Island	22	0.2	60	0.2	3	2.9	48,483	6.5	0.1	293,500
Mississippi	14	0.1	30	0.1	2	0.7	22,567	6.3	0.1	453,500
Oklahoma	33	0.3	91	0.3	3	1.4	15,813	5.8	0.1	174,848
Hawaii	27	0.2	59	0.2	2	2.3	38,780	5.7	0.1	211,889
Idaho	27	0.2	30	0.1	1	1.1	37,367	5.4	0.1	198,444
Nebraska	30	0.3	131	0.5	4	2.3	17,443	5.3	0.1	176,533
Alabama	29	0.3	89	0.3	3	1.2	13,562	4.4	0.1	152,414
Wyoming	17	0.2	27	0.1	2	0.9	32,630	3.8	0.1	221,235
Arkansas	18	0.2	74	0.3	4	1.6	22,027	3.1	0.0	174,167
Montana	21	0.2	39	0.1	2	0.6	14,564	2.9	0.0	137,381
Kentucky	28	0.3	35	0.1	1	0.7	19,200	2.2	0.0	77,357
Alaska	10	0.1	21	0.1	2	0.5	24,524	1.6	0.0	162,400
South Dakota	10	0.1	23	0.1	2	0.3	11,174	1.4	0.0	144,300
West Virginia	4	-	5	0.0	1	0.1	28,200	0.5	0.0	121,250
Maine	30	0.3	60*	-	-	(D)	-	(D)	-	-
Delaware	14	0.1	60*	-	-	(D)	-	(D)	-	-
North Dakota	5	-	60*	-	-	(D)	-	(D)	-	-

Source: 1997 *Economic Census*. The states are in descending order of revenues or establishments (if revenue data are missing for the majority). The symbol (D) appears when data are withheld to prevent disclosure of competitive information. States marked with (D) are sorted by number of establishments. A dash (-) indicates that the data element cannot be calculated. * indicates the midpoint of a range; 175, for example is the range 100-249. Shaded *states* on the state map indicate those states which have proportionately greater representation in the industry than would be indicated by the state's population; the ratio is based on total revenues or number of establishments. Shaded *regions* indicate where the industry is regionally most concentrated.

NAICS 712110 - MUSEUMS

GENERAL STATISTICS

Year	Establishments (number)	Employment (number)	Payroll ($ million)	Revenues ($ million)	Employees per Establishment (number)	Revenues per Establishment ($)	Payroll per Employee ($)
1997	3,860	63,097	1,265.0	4,788.0	16.3	1,240,415	20,048

Source: Economic Census of the United States, 1997. This is a newly defined industry. Data for prior years were unavailable at the time of publication but may become available over time.

INDICES OF CHANGE

Year	Establishments (number)	Employment (number)	Payroll ($ million)	Revenues ($ million)	Employees per Establishment (number)	Revenues per Establishment ($)	Payroll per Employee ($)
1997	100.0	100.0	100.0	100.0	100.0	100.0	100.0

Sources: Same as General Statistics. The values shown reflect change from the base year, 1997. Values above 100 mean greater than 1997, values below 100 mean less than 1997, and a value of 100 in the 1982-96 or 1998-2001 period means same as 1997. Values followed by a 'p' are projections by the editors; 'e' stands for extrapolation. Data are the most recent available at this level of detail.

SIC INDUSTRIES RELATED TO NAICS 712110

Each new NAICS code represents an industry that used to be part of an SIC or a part of several SIC industries. Data in this table are shown to provide transitional information for these cases. All available data for the precursor SIC(s) are shown. Even if only a part of an SIC is included in the NAICS, *all* data for the SIC are reproduced. If the SIC industry is not marked as being a part (pt) of the NAICS, the entire industry is embedded in the NAICS data. The SIC composition of the new industry provides some hints of the relative importance of its "ancestors." Data marked with a 'p' are projected. Projections begin with 1982 data. Data earlier than 1990 are not shown but are reflected in the projections.

SIC	Industry	1990	1991	1992	1993	1994	1995	1996	1997
8412	**Museums & Art Galleries (pt)**								
	Establishments (number)	2,838	3,124	3,105	3,150	3,257	3,307	3,419p	3,506p
	Employment (thousands)	52.2	53.8	56.0	58.9	58.9	60.7	63.6p	65.6p
	Revenues ($ million)	-	-	2,737.3	-	-	-	-	-

Source: Economic Census of the United States, 1992, annual surveys of economic sectors conducted by the Bureau of the Census, and estimates or projections based on the 1982-1992 period; not all data are shown. 'e' marks estimates made by the editors; 'p' indicates projections based on time series. A dash (-) indicates that data for this SIC or year were not available. The abbreviation (pt) next to the industry name indicates that only a part of the industry is present within the NAICS data. If no (pt) is shown, the entire industry is contained within the NAICS data.

SELECTED RATIOS

For 1997	Avg. of Information	Analyzed Industry	Index	For 1997	Avg. of Information	Analyzed Industry	Index
Employees per establishment	16	16	102	Payroll per establishment	330,963	327,720	99
Revenue per establishment	1,057,073	1,240,415	117	Payroll as % of revenue	31	26	84
Revenue per employee	65,958	75,883	115	Payroll per employee	20,651	20,048	97

Sources: Same as General Statistics. The 'Average' column represents the average for the industry sector, in 1997, where the currently shown industry is classified. The Index shows the relationship between the Average and the Analyzed Industry. For example, 100 means that they are equal; 500 that the Analyzed Industry is five times the average; 50 means that the Analyzed Industry is half the national average. The abbreviation 'na' is used to show that data are 'not available'.

LEADING COMPANIES

No company data available for this industry.

REPRESENTATIVE NONPROFIT ORGANIZATIONS

Organization Name	Address				Phone	Income Range ($ mil)
Ann Arbor Art Association	117 W Liberty St	Ann Arbor	MI	48104	734-994-8004	1-5
Aperture Foundation Inc	20 E 23rd St	New York	NY	10010	212-505-5555	5-9
Arts Power Inc	39 S Fullerton Ave 3rd Flr	Montclair	NJ	07042	973-744-0909	1-5
Atlantic Center for the Arts Inc	1414 Art Center Ave	New Smyrna Bch	FL	32168		1-5
Bemis Center for Contemporary Arts	724 S 12th St	Omaha	NE	68102	402-341-7130	1-5
Cherry Creek Arts Festival Co	6200 S Syracuse Way	Englewood	CO	80111		1-5
Columbus Museum of Art	480 E Broad St	Columbus	OH	43215	614-221-6801	5-9
Contemporary Arts Center	900 Camp St	New Orleans	LA	70130	504-523-1216	1-5
Crab Tree Farm Foundation Inc	PO Box 218	Lake Bluff	IL	60044		1-5
Degrazia Art & Cultural Foundation Inc	6300 N Swan Rd	Tucson	AZ	85718		1-5
Frick Art & Historical Center Inc	7227 Reynolds St	Pittsburgh	PA	15208	412-371-0600	10-19
Friends of the Festival Inc	PO Box 886	Chattanooga	TN	37401	423-756-2212	1-5
Georgia Okeeffe Foundation	PO Box 40	Abiquiu	NM	87510		1-5
Gwinnett Council for the Arts Inc	6400 Sugarloaf Pkwy	Duluth	GA	30097		1-5
Herbert H Kohl Charities Inc	825 N Jefferson St	Milwaukee	WI	53202		1-5
Kentucky Art and Craft Foundation Inc	609 W Main St	Louisville	KY	40202	502-589-0102	1-5
Menil Foundation Inc	1519 Branard	Houston	TX	77006	713-525-9426	50+
New Hampshire Institute of Art	148 Concord St	Manchester	NH	03104	603-623-0313	10-19
On the Chisholm Trail Association	1000 N 29th St	Duncan	OK	73533		1-5
Robert and Jane Meyerhoff Foundation Inc	1025 Cranbrook Rd	Cockeysville	MD	21030		1-5
Simpson Foundation	PO Box 359	Lafayette	CA	94549		10-19
Spoleto Festival U S A	PO Box 157	Charleston	SC	29402		5-9
Stamford Center for the Arts Inc	307 Atlantic St	Stamford	CT	06901	203-325-4466	5-9
Trust for Museum Exhibitions	1424 16th St NW 600	Washington	DC	20036	202-745-2566	1-5

Source: National Directory of Nonprofit Organizations, 2000, Volumes 1 and 2, The Taft Group. The table shows a selection of organizations for illustration and does not constitute a complete selection from the source. The organizations are arranged in alphabetical order.

LOCATION BY STATE AND REGIONAL CONCENTRATION

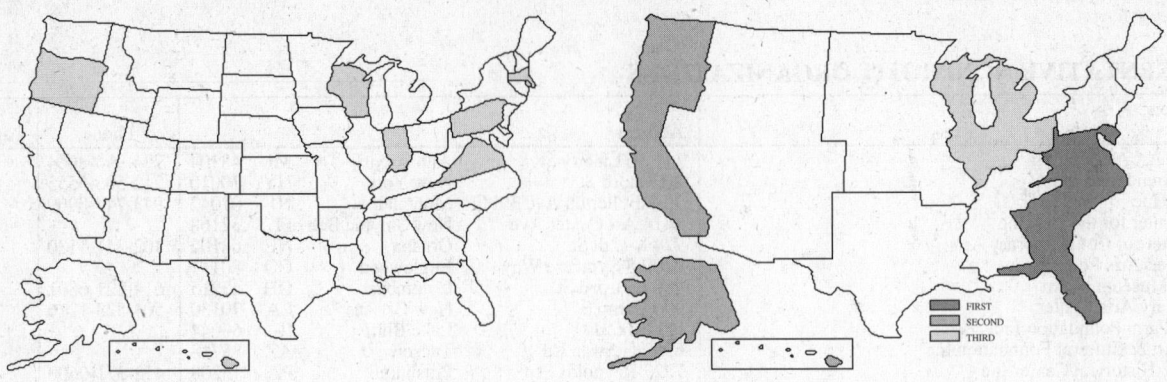

INDUSTRY DATA BY STATE

State	Establishments Total (number)	% of U.S.	Employment Total (number)	% of U.S.	Per Estab.	Payroll Total ($ mil.)	Per Empl. ($)	Revenues Total ($ mil.)	% of U.S.	Per Estab. ($)
California	347	9.0	5,729	9.1	17	130.0	22,697	459.9	9.6	1,325,334
Pennsylvania	151	3.9	3,079	4.9	20	56.9	18,484	257.2	5.4	1,702,987
Virginia	96	2.5	2,749	4.4	29	59.6	21,694	222.2	4.6	2,314,885
Texas	235	6.1	3,870	6.1	16	67.3	17,396	220.9	4.6	939,953
Florida	171	4.4	2,829	4.5	17	48.6	17,194	219.0	4.6	1,280,778
Indiana	67	1.7	1,142	1.8	17	20.5	17,940	185.2	3.9	2,763,672
Massachusetts	164	4.2	2,571	4.1	16	50.2	19,523	164.4	3.4	1,002,146
D.C.	29	0.8	1,186	1.9	41	36.0	30,373	130.2	2.7	4,488,793
Wisconsin	90	2.3	1,121	1.8	12	20.5	18,255	108.9	2.3	1,209,967
Michigan	87	2.3	2,002	3.2	23	30.4	15,176	106.6	2.2	1,225,000
Washington	86	2.2	1,174	1.9	14	20.8	17,707	68.4	1.4	795,674
Georgia	64	1.7	903	1.4	14	17.7	19,648	68.4	1.4	1,068,687
New Jersey	69	1.8	1,190	1.9	17	18.6	15,652	58.2	1.2	843,043
Oregon	60	1.6	877	1.4	15	15.7	17,870	55.5	1.2	925,500
Arizona	63	1.6	838	1.3	13	14.9	17,763	50.7	1.1	805,476
Tennessee	71	1.8	753	1.2	11	12.7	16,922	39.2	0.8	551,789
Hawaii	24	0.6	615	1.0	26	12.2	19,906	37.4	0.8	1,558,083
Colorado	79	2.0	458	0.7	6	7.4	16,181	26.9	0.6	340,127
Iowa	63	1.6	502	0.8	8	7.4	14,647	26.3	0.5	417,587
New Mexico	33	0.9	248	0.4	8	5.0	19,968	21.1	0.4	638,788
Rhode Island	37	1.0	303	0.5	8	5.2	17,218	18.3	0.4	495,432
Nebraska	32	0.8	267	0.4	8	4.4	16,607	15.1	0.3	472,813
Arkansas	31	0.8	157	0.2	5	1.9	12,325	9.9	0.2	318,710
New Hampshire	32	0.8	260	0.4	8	4.1	15,854	9.4	0.2	293,250
Montana	41	1.1	155	0.2	4	2.2	14,032	9.0	0.2	219,268
Nevada	14	0.4	126	0.2	9	2.1	16,310	7.3	0.2	522,500
West Virginia	14	0.4	81	0.1	6	1.6	20,296	7.0	0.1	502,929
Idaho	20	0.5	60	0.1	3	0.9	15,700	5.1	0.1	257,050
Delaware	16	0.4	750*	-	-	(D)	-	(D)	-	-

Source: 1997 *Economic Census*. The states are in descending order of revenues or establishments (if revenue data are missing for the majority). The symbol (D) appears when data are withheld to prevent disclosure of competitive information. States marked with (D) are sorted by number of establishments. A dash (-) indicates that the data element cannot be calculated. * indicates the midpoint of a range; 175, for example is the range 100-249. Shaded *states* on the state map indicate those states which have proportionately greater representation in the industry than would be indicated by the state's population; the ratio is based on total revenues or number of establishments. Shaded *regions* indicate where the industry is regionally most concentrated.

NAICS 712120 - HISTORICAL SITES

GENERAL STATISTICS

Year	Establishments (number)	Employment (number)	Payroll ($ million)	Revenues ($ million)	Employees per Establishment (number)	Revenues per Establishment ($)	Payroll per Employee ($)
1997	892	7,684	111.0	370.0	8.6	414,798	14,446

Source: *Economic Census of the United States*, 1997. This is a newly defined industry. Data for prior years were unavailable at the time of publication but may become available over time.

INDICES OF CHANGE

Year	Establishments (number)	Employment (number)	Payroll ($ million)	Revenues ($ million)	Employees per Establishment (number)	Revenues per Establishment ($)	Payroll per Employee ($)
1997	100.0	100.0	100.0	100.0	100.0	100.0	100.0

Sources: Same as General Statistics. The values shown reflect change from the base year, 1997. Values above 100 mean greater than 1997, values below 100 mean less than 1997, and a value of 100 in the 1982-96 or 1998-2001 period means same as 1997. Values followed by a 'p' are projections by the editors; 'e' stands for extrapolation. Data are the most recent available at this level of detail.

SIC INDUSTRIES RELATED TO NAICS 712120

Each new NAICS code represents an industry that used to be part of an SIC or a part of several SIC industries. Data in this table are shown to provide transitional information for these cases. All available data for the precursor SIC(s) are shown. Even if only a part of an SIC is included in the NAICS, *all* data for the SIC are reproduced. If the SIC industry is not marked as being a part (pt) of the NAICS, the entire industry is embedded in the NAICS data. The SIC composition of the new industry provides some hints of the relative importance of its "ancestors." Data marked with a 'p' are projected. Projections begin with 1982 data. Data earlier than 1990 are not shown but are reflected in the projections.

SIC	Industry	1990	1991	1992	1993	1994	1995	1996	1997
8412	**Museums & Art Galleries (pt)**								
	Establishments (number)	2,838	3,124	3,105	3,150	3,257	3,307	3,419*p*	3,506*p*
	Employment (thousands)	52.2	53.8	56.0	58.9	58.9	60.7	63.6*p*	65.6*p*
	Revenues ($ million)	-	-	2,737.3	-	-	-	-	-

Source: *Economic Census of the United States*, 1992, annual surveys of economic sectors conducted by the Bureau of the Census, and estimates or projections based on the 1982-1992 period; not all data are shown. 'e' marks estimates made by the editors; 'p' indicates projections based on time series. A dash (-) indicates that data for this SIC or year were not available. The abbreviation (pt) next to the industry name indicates that only a part of the industry is present within the NAICS data. If no (pt) is shown, the entire industry is contained within the NAICS data.

SELECTED RATIOS

For 1997	Avg. of Information	Analyzed Industry	Index	For 1997	Avg. of Information	Analyzed Industry	Index
Employees per establishment	16	9	54	Payroll per establishment	330,963	124,439	38
Revenue per establishment	1,057,073	414,798	39	Payroll as % of revenue	31	30	96
Revenue per employee	65,958	48,152	73	Payroll per employee	20,651	14,446	70

Sources: Same as General Statistics. The 'Average' column represents the average for the industry sector, in 1997, where the currently shown industry is classified. The Index shows the relationship between the Average and the Analyzed Industry. For example, 100 means that they are equal; 500 that the Analyzed Industry is five times the average; 50 means that the Analyzed Industry is half the national average. The abbreviation 'na' is used to show that data are 'not available'.

LEADING COMPANIES
No company data available for this industry.

REPRESENTATIVE NONPROFIT ORGANIZATIONS

Organization Name	Address				Phone	Income Range ($ mil)
Air Force Museum Foundation Inc	Box 33624 Amc Branch	Wright Pat	OH	45433	937-258-1218	5-9
Alabama Historic Ironworks Commission	12632 Confederate Pky	McCalla	AL	35111		1-5
Arizona Memorial Museum Association	1 Arizona Memorial PL	Honolulu	HI	96818	808-422-2771	1-5
Aspen Historical Society	620 W Bleeker	Aspen	CO	81611	970-925-3721	1-5
Association for the Preservation of Tennessee Antiquities	110 Leake Ave	Nashville	TN	37205		1-5
Atlanta Landmarks Inc	660 Peachtree St	Atlanta	GA	30365		5-9
Cathedral Heritage Foundation Inc	429 W M Ali Blvd	Louisville	KY	40202	502-583-3100	1-5
Center for American Archeology	PO Box 22	Kampsville	IL	62053		1-5
Classical American Homes Preservation TR	1 Pershing Plz	Jersey City	NJ	07399		5-9
Columbia River Maritime Museum Inc	1792 Marine Dr	Astoria	OR	97103	503-325-2323	1-5
Compass Square & Star Inc	PO Box 220216	St Louis	MO	63122		1-5
Connecticut Historical Society	One Elizabeth Street	Hartford	CT	06105	860-236-5621	40-49
Crete Bicentennial Society Crete Nebraska	13th and Redwood Ave	Crete	NE	68333		1-5
Delaware Performing Arts Center Inc	PO Box 3697	Greenville	DE	19807		1-5
Dewitt Wallace Fund for Colonial Williamsburg	2 Park Ave 23rd Flr	New York	NY	10016	212-251-9700	10-19
Edsel and Eleanor Ford House	1100 Lake Shore Drive	Grosse Pointe	MI	48236	313-884-4222	5-9
Ensign Peak Foundation	736 Northview Cir	Salt Lake Cty	UT	84103		1-5
Fort Abraham Lincoln Foundation	401 W Main	Mandan	ND	58554	701-663-4758	1-5
General Society of Colonial Wars	1426 Maryland Ave	Baltimore	MD	21201		1-5
Heritage Hill Foundation	2640 S Webster Ave	Green Bay	WI	54301	920-448-5150	1-5
Historic Landmarks Foundation of Indiana Inc	340 W Michigan St	Indianapolis	IN	46202	317-639-4534	40-49
Historic Pensacola Inc	120 Church St	Pensacola	FL	32501		1-5
Historic Wichita-Sedgwick County Inc	1871 Sim Park Dr	Wichita	KS	67203		1-5
Iditarod Trail Committee Inc	PO Box 870800	Wasilla	AK	99687	907-376-5155	1-5
Jefferson Davis Shrine Beauvoir Shrine	2244 Beach Blvd	Biloxi	MS	39531	228-388-1313	1-5
Linn County Historical Society	615 1st Ave SE	Cedar Rapids	IA	52401		1-5
Logan County Historical Society Inc	PO Box 1512	Guthrie	OK	73044		1-5
Maine Historical Society	485 Congress St	Portland	ME	04101	207-774-1822	5-9
Massachusetts Historical Society	1154 Boylston St	Boston	MA	02215	617-536-1608	10-19
Minnesota Historical Society	345 Kellogg Blvd W	St Paul	MN	55102	651-296-2143	40-49
Mount Vernon Ladies Association of the Union	PO Box 110	Mount Vernon	VA	22121	703-780-0011	50+
National Trust for Historic Preservation in the United States	1785 Mass Ave NW	Washington	DC	20036	202-588-6000	50+
Panhandle-Plains Historical Society	Wtamu Box 60967	Canyon	TX	79016	806-651-2260	5-9
Penns Landing Corporation	121 N Columbus Blvd	Philadelphia	PA	19106	215-629-3200	10-19
Preservation Society of Newport County	424 Bellevue Ave	Newport	RI	02840	401-847-1000	20-29
School of American Research	PO Box 2188	Santa Fe	NM	87504		50+
Southwest Parks & Monuments Association	221 N CT	Tucson	AZ	85701	520-622-1999	5-9
Survivors of the Shoah Visual History Foundation	10345 W Olympic Blvd	Los Angeles	CA	90064		10-19
The Historic Preservation Foundation of North Carolina Inc	PO Box 27644	Raleigh	NC	27611		5-9
The Wyoming Territorial Prison Corporation	975 Snowy Range Rd	Laramie	WY	82070		1-5
University of South Carolina Development Foundation	900 Assembly St Ste 404	Columbia	SC	29201		30-39

Source: National Directory of Nonprofit Organizations, 2000, Volumes 1 and 2, The Taft Group. The table shows a selection of organizations for illustration and does not constitute a complete selection from the source. The organizations are arranged in alphabetical order.

LOCATION BY STATE AND REGIONAL CONCENTRATION

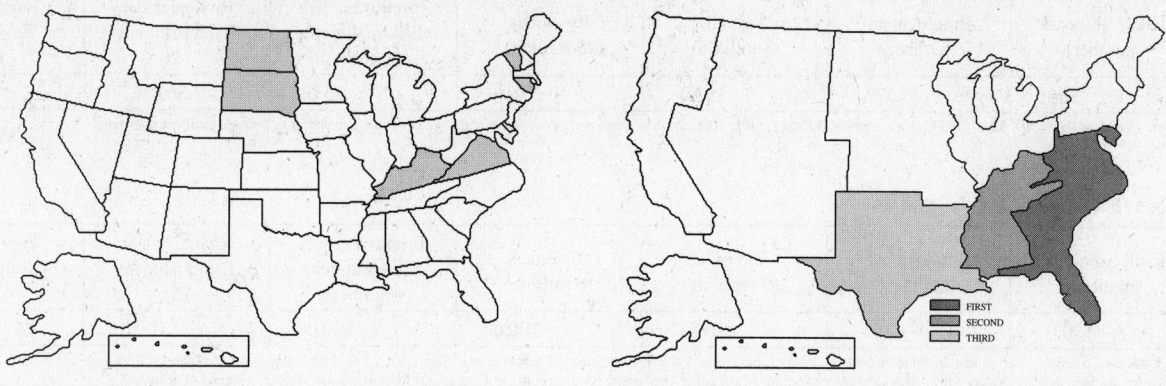

FIRST
SECOND
THIRD

INDUSTRY DATA BY STATE

State	Establishments Total (number)	% of U.S.	Employment Total (number)	% of U.S.	Per Estab.	Payroll Total ($ mil.)	Per Empl. ($)	Revenues Total ($ mil.)	% of U.S.	Per Estab. ($)
Virginia	32	3.6	768	10.0	24	12.4	16,113	42.1	11.4	1,314,375
Kentucky	11	1.2	199	2.6	18	3.1	15,673	12.5	3.4	1,137,818
Texas	36	4.0	235	3.1	7	3.0	12,979	9.6	2.6	265,667
Wisconsin	21	2.4	72	0.9	3	1.6	21,903	6.5	1.8	309,476
Florida	18	2.0	124	1.6	7	1.8	14,798	6.2	1.7	345,056
Georgia	16	1.8	132	1.7	8	1.4	10,932	6.0	1.6	373,750
Connecticut	17	1.9	94	1.2	6	1.1	11,894	5.5	1.5	325,412
Tennessee	12	1.3	145	1.9	12	1.7	11,959	4.2	1.1	348,417
South Dakota	5	0.6	54	0.7	11	1.0	18,741	3.9	1.1	782,800
Washington	16	1.8	65	0.8	4	1.2	18,000	3.4	0.9	209,687
Vermont	7	0.8	31	0.4	4	0.7	22,323	3.3	0.9	475,286
Iowa	21	2.4	69	0.9	3	0.7	9,493	2.2	0.6	104,905
Alabama	7	0.8	57	0.7	8	0.7	11,509	1.9	0.5	269,571
North Dakota	6	0.7	17	0.2	3	0.1	8,000	0.9	0.3	157,167
Oregon	8	0.9	16	0.2	2	0.3	16,000	0.7	0.2	83,500
Wyoming	3	0.3	4	0.1	1	0.1	22,250	0.4	0.1	149,000
New Jersey	20	2.2	175*	-	-	(D)	-	(D)	-	-
Montana	9	1.0	10*	-	-	(D)	-	(D)	-	-
Nebraska	9	1.0	60*	-	-	(D)	-	(D)	-	-
Oklahoma	8	0.9	60*	-	-	(D)	-	(D)	-	-
Delaware	4	0.4	60*	-	-	(D)	-	(D)	-	-
D.C.	4	0.4	60*	-	-	(D)	-	(D)	-	-
Rhode Island	4	0.4	10*	-	-	(D)	-	(D)	-	-
West Virginia	3	0.3	10*	-	-	(D)	-	(D)	-	-
Utah	1	0.1	10*	-	-	(D)	-	(D)	-	-

Source: 1997 Economic Census. The states are in descending order of revenues or establishments (if revenue data are missing for the majority). The symbol (D) appears when data are withheld to prevent disclosure of competitive information. States marked with (D) are sorted by number of establishments. A dash (-) indicates that the data element cannot be calculated. * indicates the midpoint of a range; 175, for example is the range 100-249. Shaded *states* on the state map indicate those states which have proportionately greater representation in the industry than would be indicated by the state's population; the ratio is based on total revenues or number of establishments. Shaded *regions* indicate where the industry is regionally most concentrated.

NAICS 712130 - ZOOS AND BOTANICAL GARDENS

GENERAL STATISTICS

Year	Establishments (number)	Employment (number)	Payroll ($ million)	Revenues ($ million)	Employees per Establishment (number)	Revenues per Establishment ($)	Payroll per Employee ($)
1997	386	17,372	393.0	1,376.0	45.0	3,564,767	22,623

Source: *Economic Census of the United States*, 1997. This is a newly defined industry. Data for prior years were unavailable at the time of publication but may become available over time.

INDICES OF CHANGE

Year	Establishments (number)	Employment (number)	Payroll ($ million)	Revenues ($ million)	Employees per Establishment (number)	Revenues per Establishment ($)	Payroll per Employee ($)
1997	100.0	100.0	100.0	100.0	100.0	100.0	100.0

Sources: Same as General Statistics. The values shown reflect change from the base year, 1997. Values above 100 mean greater than 1997, values below 100 mean less than 1997, and a value of 100 in the 1982-96 or 1998-2001 period means same as 1997. Values followed by a 'p' are projections by the editors; 'e' stands for extrapolation. Data are the most recent available at this level of detail.

SIC INDUSTRIES RELATED TO NAICS 712130

Each new NAICS code represents an industry that used to be part of an SIC or a part of several SIC industries. Data in this table are shown to provide transitional information for these cases. All available data for the precursor SIC(s) are shown. Even if only a part of an SIC is included in the NAICS, *all* data for the SIC are reproduced. If the SIC industry is not marked as being a part (pt) of the NAICS, the entire industry is embedded in the NAICS data. The SIC composition of the new industry provides some hints of the relative importance of its "ancestors." Data marked with a 'p' are projected. Projections begin with 1982 data. Data earlier than 1990 are not shown but are reflected in the projections.

SIC	Industry	1990	1991	1992	1993	1994	1995	1996	1997
8422	**Botanical & Zoological Gardens (pt)**								
	Establishments (number)	317	389	448	455	454	473	519*p*	547*p*
	Employment (thousands)	11.4	12.3	13.6	15.0	14.9	15.3	16.6*p*	17.4*p*
	Revenues ($ million)	-	-	652.9	-	-	-	-	-

Source: *Economic Census of the United States*, 1992, annual surveys of economic sectors conducted by the Bureau of the Census, and estimates or projections based on the 1982-1992 period; not all data are shown. 'e' marks estimates made by the editors; 'p' indicates projections based on time series. A dash (-) indicates that data for this SIC or year were not available. The abbreviation (pt) next to the industry name indicates that only a part of the industry is present within the NAICS data. If no (pt) is shown, the entire industry is contained within the NAICS data.

SELECTED RATIOS

For 1997	Avg. of Information	Analyzed Industry	Index	For 1997	Avg. of Information	Analyzed Industry	Index
Employees per establishment	16	45	281	Payroll per establishment	330,963	1,018,135	308
Revenue per establishment	1,057,073	3,564,767	337	Payroll as % of revenue	31	29	91
Revenue per employee	65,958	79,208	120	Payroll per employee	20,651	22,623	110

Sources: Same as General Statistics. The 'Average' column represents the average for the industry sector, in 1997, where the currently shown industry is classified. The Index shows the relationship between the Average and the Analyzed Industry. For example, 100 means that they are equal; 500 that the Analyzed Industry is five times the average; 50 means that the Analyzed Industry is half the national average. The abbreviation 'na' is used to show that data are 'not available'.

LEADING COMPANIES Number shown: **1**   Total sales ($ mil): **20**   Total employment (000): **0.6**

Company Name	Address				CEO Name	Phone	Co. Type	Sales ($ mil)	Empl. (000)
Florida Cypress Gardens Inc.	PO Box 1	Cypress Gardens	FL	33884	William Reynolds	863-324-2111	R	20*	0.6

Source: Ward's Business Directory of U.S. Private and Public Companies, Volumes 1 and 2, 2000. The company type code used is as follows: P - Public, R - Private, S - Subsidiary, D - Division, J - Joint Venture, A - Affiliate, G - Group, N - Company type not reported. Sales are in millions of dollars, employees are in thousands. An asterisk (*) indicates an estimated sales volume. The symbol < stands for 'less than'. Company names and addresses are truncated, in some cases, to fit into the available space.

REPRESENTATIVE NONPROFIT ORGANIZATIONS

Organization Name	Address				Phone	Income Range ($ mil)
Air Force Heritage Foundation of Utah Inc	PO Box 612	Roy	UT	84067		1-5
American Museum of Natural History	79th & Central Pk W	New York	NY	10024		50+
Arkansas Museum of Science & History	501 E Markham Ste 150	Little Rock	AR	72201		1-5
Atlanta-Fulton County Zoo Inc	800 Cherokee Avenue	Atlanta	GA	30315	404-624-5600	10-19
Audubon Institute Foundation	PO Box 4327	New Orleans	LA	70178		1-5
Barber Vintage Motorsport Museum	27 Inverness Center Pkwy	Birmingham	AL	35242	205-252-8377	5-9
Bishop Museum	1525 Bernice St	Honolulu	HI	96817		10-19
Buffalo Bill Memorial Association	720 Sheridan Ave	Cody	WY	82414	307-587-3243	20-29
Burt County Museum Inc	319 N 13th St	Tekamah	NE	68061	402-374-1505	1-5
Charleston Museum	360 Meeting St	Charleston	SC	29403	843-722-2996	1-5
Childrens Museum of Indianapolis Incorporated	3000 N Meridian St	Indianapolis	IN	46208	317-924-5431	50+
Cleveland Museum of Art	11150 East Blvd	Cleveland	OH	44106	216-421-7340	50+
Country Music Foundation Inc	4 Music SQ E	Nashville	TN	37203	615-256-1639	10-19
Denver Museum of Natural History	2001 Colorado Blvd	Denver	CO	80205		20-29
Eleutherian Mills-Hagley Foundation Inc	PO Box 3630	Wilmington	DE	19807	302-658-2400	50+
Experience Music Project	110 110th Ave NE	Bellevue	WA	98004	425-450-1997	50+
Exploration Place Inc	300 N McLean Blvd	Wichita	KS	67203	316-263-3373	5-9
Fine Arts Museums Foundation	233 Post St 5th Flr	San Francisco	CA	94108		50+
Heard Museum	2301 N Central	Phoenix	AZ	85004	602-252-8840	10-19
Henry Morrison Flagler Museum	PO Box 969	Palm Beach	FL	33480	561-655-2833	50+
Heritage Center Foundation	171 W Michigan Ave	Battle Creek	MI	49017		10-19
Houston Museum of Natural Science	1 Herman Circle Dr	Houston	TX	77030	713-639-4629	20-29
Hubbard Museum	PO Box 40	Ruidoso Downs	NM	88346	505-378-4142	1-5
Huntington Museum of Art Inc	2033 McCoy Rd	Huntington	WV	25701	304-529-2701	5-9
International Wolf Center	5930 Brooklyn Blvd	Brooklyn Center	MN	55429	763-560-7374	1-5
Jackson Zoological Park	2918 W Capitol St	Jackson	MS	39209		1-5
Katharine Matthies Foundation	PO Box 6767	Providence	RI	02940		1-5
Kemper Museum Operating Foundation	4420 Warwick Blvd	Kansas City	MO	64111	816-561-3737	1-5
Lied Discovery Childrens Museum	833 N Las Vegas Blvd	Las Vegas	NV	89101	702-382-5437	1-5
Milwaukee Public Museum Inc	800 W Wells St	Milwaukee	WI	53233	414-278-2795	10-19
Museum of Science and Industry	57th St and Lake Shore Dr	Chicago	IL	60637		50+
Museum of Science	Science Park	Boston	MA	02114		50+
National Aquarium in Baltimore Inc	Pier 3 501 E Pratt St	Baltimore	MD	21202	410-576-3800	20-29
National Film Preserve Ltd	379 State St	Portsmouth	NH	03801		1-5
Newark Museum Association	49 Washington St	Newark	NJ	07102	973-596-6622	10-19
Oklahoma City Art Museum Inc	3113 Pershing Blvd	Oklahoma Ciy	OK	73107	405-946-4477	10-19
Oregon Coast Aquarium Inc	2820 SE Ferry Slip Rd	Newport	OR	97365	541-867-3474	5-9
Paris Gibson Square Incorporated	1400 First Ave N	Great Falls	MT	59401	406-727-8255	1-5
Plains Art Museum	PO Box 2338	Fargo	ND	58108		10-19
Portland Museum of Art	7 Congress SQ	Portland	ME	04101	207-775-6148	10-19
Richard C Von Hess Foundation	1650 Market St Ste 1200	Philadelphia	PA	19103		20-29
Salisbury House Foundation	4025 Tonawanda Dr	Des Moines	IA	50312	515-274-1777	10-19
Sea Research Foundation Inc	55 Coogan Blvd	Mystic	CT	06355		20-29
Shelburne Museum Incorporated	Us RT 7 Box 10	Shelburne	VT	05482		30-39
Shrine to Music Museum Inc	414 E Clark	Vermillion	SD	57069	605-677-5306	1-5
St Marks Incorporated	200 Clanton Rd	Charlotte	NC	28217	704-523-0100	10-19
The Chrysler Museum Inc	245 W Olney Rd	Norfolk	VA	23510	757-664-6200	20-29
The Louisville Science Center Inc	727 W Main St	Louisville	KY	40202	502-561-6100	5-9
Trustees of the Corcoran Gallery of Art	500 Seventeenth St NW	Washington	DC	20006	202-639-1700	50+

Source: National Directory of Nonprofit Organizations, 2000, Volumes 1 and 2, The Taft Group. The table shows a selection of organizations for illustration and does not constitute a complete selection from the source. The organizations are arranged in alphabetical order.

LOCATION BY STATE AND REGIONAL CONCENTRATION

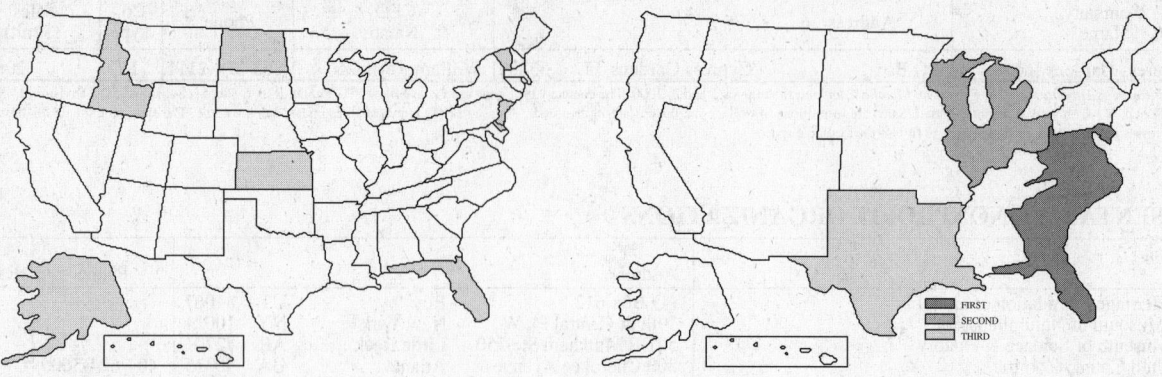

INDUSTRY DATA BY STATE

State	Establishments Total (number)	% of U.S.	Employment Total (number)	% of U.S.	Per Estab.	Payroll Total ($ mil.)	Per Empl. ($)	Revenues Total ($ mil.)	% of U.S.	Per Estab. ($)
Illinois	12	3.1	1,658	9.5	138	44.1	26,590	104.5	7.6	8,711,833
Texas	20	5.2	1,455	8.4	73	24.4	16,737	99.0	7.2	4,948,600
Florida	28	7.3	1,173	6.8	42	25.8	21,957	63.9	4.6	2,281,929
Ohio	13	3.4	930	5.4	72	16.9	18,152	42.6	3.1	3,274,769
Arizona	5	1.3	312	1.8	62	7.2	22,968	19.7	1.4	3,946,400
New Jersey	12	3.1	226	1.3	19	5.0	22,248	14.2	1.0	1,180,583
Kansas	4	1.0	170	1.0	43	4.0	23,441	9.7	0.7	2,428,750
Alabama	4	1.0	143	0.8	36	1.5	10,832	5.0	0.4	1,252,500
Maryland	5	1.3	750*	-	-	(D)	-	(D)	-	-
North Dakota	3	0.8	10*	-	-	(D)	-	(D)	-	-
Oklahoma	3	0.8	60*	-	-	(D)	-	(D)	-	-
Alaska	2	0.5	60*	-	-	(D)	-	(D)	-	-
Idaho	2	0.5	10*	-	-	(D)	-	(D)	-	-
Mississippi	2	0.5	60*	-	-	(D)	-	(D)	-	-
Nevada	2	0.5	10*	-	-	(D)	-	(D)	-	-
Delaware	1	0.3	10*	-	-	(D)	-	(D)	-	-
Montana	1	0.3	10*	-	-	(D)	-	(D)	-	-
New Mexico	1	0.3	10*	-	-	(D)	-	(D)	-	-
Rhode Island	1	0.3	60*	-	-	(D)	-	(D)	-	-
Utah	1	0.3	175*	-	-	(D)	-	(D)	-	-
Vermont	1	0.3	10*	-	-	(D)	-	(D)	-	-

Source: 1997 Economic Census. The states are in descending order of revenues or establishments (if revenue data are missing for the majority). The symbol (D) appears when data are withheld to prevent disclosure of competitive information. States marked with (D) are sorted by number of establishments. A dash (-) indicates that the data element cannot be calculated. * indicates the midpoint of a range; 175, for example is the range 100-249. Shaded states on the state map indicate those states which have proportionately greater representation in the industry than would be indicated by the state's population; the ratio is based on total revenues or number of establishments. Shaded regions indicate where the industry is regionally most concentrated.

NAICS 712190 - NATURE PARKS AND OTHER SIMILAR INSTITUTIONS

GENERAL STATISTICS

Year	Establishments (number)	Employment (number)	Payroll ($ million)	Revenues ($ million)	Employees per Establishment (number)	Revenues per Establishment ($)	Payroll per Employee ($)
1997	442	3,623	68.0	230.0	8.2	520,362	18,769

Source: Economic Census of the United States, 1997. This is a newly defined industry. Data for prior years were unavailable at the time of publication but may become available over time.

INDICES OF CHANGE

Year	Establishments (number)	Employment (number)	Payroll ($ million)	Revenues ($ million)	Employees per Establishment (number)	Revenues per Establishment ($)	Payroll per Employee ($)
1997	100.0	100.0	100.0	100.0	100.0	100.0	100.0

Sources: Same as General Statistics. The values shown reflect change from the base year, 1997. Values above 100 mean greater than 1997, values below 100 mean less than 1997, and a value of 100 in the 1982-96 or 1998-2001 period means same as 1997. Values followed by a 'p' are projections by the editors; 'e' stands for extrapolation. Data are the most recent available at this level of detail.

SIC INDUSTRIES RELATED TO NAICS 712190

Each new NAICS code represents an industry that used to be part of an SIC or a part of several SIC industries. Data in this table are shown to provide transitional information for these cases. All available data for the precursor SIC(s) are shown. Even if only a part of an SIC is included in the NAICS, *all* data for the SIC are reproduced. If the SIC industry is not marked as being a part (pt) of the NAICS, the entire industry is embedded in the NAICS data. The SIC composition of the new industry provides some hints of the relative importance of its "ancestors." Data marked with a 'p' are projected. Projections begin with 1982 data. Data earlier than 1990 are not shown but are reflected in the projections.

SIC	Industry	1990	1991	1992	1993	1994	1995	1996	1997
7999	**Amusement & Recreation nec (pt)**								
	Establishments (number)	-	-	21,717	-	-	-	-	-
	Employment (thousands)	-	-	215.8	-	-	-	-	-
	Revenues ($ million)	-	-	10,430.3	-	-	-	-	-
8422	**Botanical & Zoological Gardens (pt)**								
	Establishments (number)	317	389	448	455	454	473	519*p*	547*p*
	Employment (thousands)	11.4	12.3	13.6	15.0	14.9	15.3	16.6*p*	17.4*p*
	Revenues ($ million)	-	-	652.9	-	-	-	-	-

Source: Economic Census of the United States, 1992, annual surveys of economic sectors conducted by the Bureau of the Census, and estimates or projections based on the 1982-1992 period; not all data are shown. 'e' marks estimates made by the editors; 'p' indicates projections based on time series. A dash (-) indicates that data for this SIC or year were not available. The abbreviation (pt) next to the industry name indicates that only a part of the industry is present within the NAICS data. If no (pt) is shown, the entire industry is contained within the NAICS data.

SELECTED RATIOS

For 1997	Avg. of Information	Analyzed Industry	Index	For 1997	Avg. of Information	Analyzed Industry	Index
Employees per establishment	16	8	51	Payroll per establishment	330,963	153,846	46
Revenue per establishment	1,057,073	520,362	49	Payroll as % of revenue	31	30	94
Revenue per employee	65,958	63,483	96	Payroll per employee	20,651	18,769	91

Sources: Same as General Statistics. The 'Average' column represents the average for the industry sector, in 1997, where the currently shown industry is classified. The Index shows the relationship between the Average and the Analyzed Industry. For example, 100 means that they are equal; 500 that the Analyzed Industry is five times the average; 50 means that the Analyzed Industry is half the national average. The abbreviation 'na' is used to show that data are 'not available'.

LEADING COMPANIES

No company data available for this industry.

LOCATION BY STATE AND REGIONAL CONCENTRATION

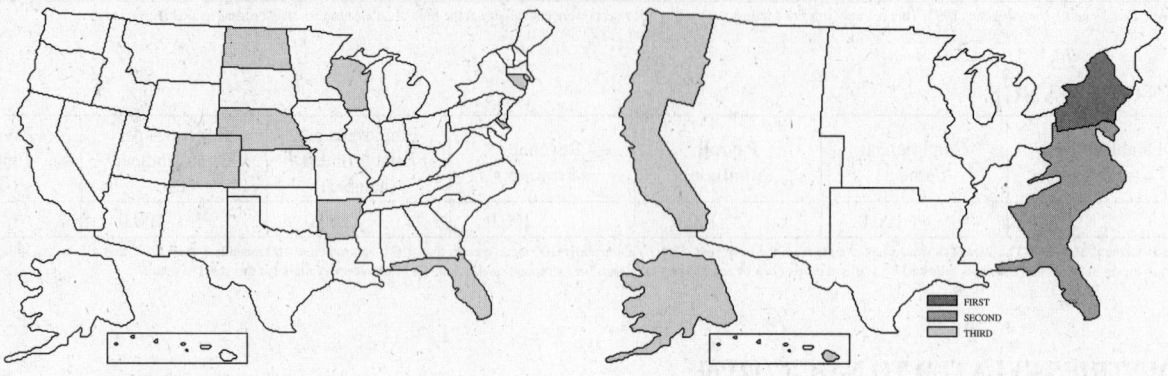

FIRST
SECOND
THIRD

INDUSTRY DATA BY STATE

State	Establishments Total (number)	% of U.S.	Employment Total (number)	% of U.S.	Per Estab.	Payroll Total ($ mil.)	Per Empl. ($)	Revenues Total ($ mil.)	% of U.S.	Per Estab. ($)
Florida	29	6.6	372	10.3	13	7.2	19,290	27.8	12.1	959,759
Colorado	15	3.4	195	5.4	13	3.4	17,667	15.5	6.8	1,036,267
New York	27	6.1	228	6.3	8	5.4	23,838	14.1	6.1	521,593
California	39	8.8	145	4.0	4	3.7	25,607	13.3	5.8	341,974
Connecticut	22	5.0	160	4.4	7	3.5	22,156	11.5	5.0	520,818
Texas	28	6.3	213	5.9	8	3.0	14,230	9.7	4.2	345,036
Ohio	18	4.1	96	2.6	5	2.0	20,438	6.0	2.6	333,222
Pennsylvania	18	4.1	93	2.6	5	1.4	15,548	5.7	2.5	318,111
Wisconsin	19	4.3	59	1.6	3	1.2	20,136	4.9	2.1	256,211
Georgia	4	0.9	39	1.1	10	0.7	17,103	1.4	0.6	352,500
Alabama	4	0.9	34	0.9	9	0.4	10,941	0.9	0.4	217,250
Arkansas	8	1.8	20	0.6	3	0.2	10,500	0.9	0.4	108,125
Kentucky	5	1.1	10*	-	-	(D)	-	(D)	-	-
Nebraska	4	0.9	60*	-	-	(D)	-	(D)	-	-
South Carolina	4	0.9	10*	-	-	(D)	-	(D)	-	-
Delaware	2	0.5	10*	-	-	(D)	-	(D)	-	-
D.C.	2	0.5	10*	-	-	(D)	-	(D)	-	-
Louisiana	2	0.5	60*	-	-	(D)	-	(D)	-	-
Nevada	2	0.5	10*	-	-	(D)	-	(D)	-	-
New Jersey	2	0.5	60*	-	-	(D)	-	(D)	-	-
North Dakota	2	0.5	10*	-	-	(D)	-	(D)	-	-
Rhode Island	2	0.5	10*	-	-	(D)	-	(D)	-	-
Alaska	1	0.2	10*	-	-	(D)	-	(D)	-	-
Kansas	1	0.2	10*	-	-	(D)	-	(D)	-	-
Mississippi	1	0.2	10*	-	-	(D)	-	(D)	-	-
Montana	1	0.2	10*	-	-	(D)	-	(D)	-	-

Source: 1997 *Economic Census.* The states are in descending order of revenues or establishments (if revenue data are missing for the majority). The symbol (D) appears when data are withheld to prevent disclosure of competitive information. States marked with (D) are sorted by number of establishments. A dash (-) indicates that the data element cannot be calculated. * indicates the midpoint of a range; 175, for example is the range 100-249. Shaded *states* on the state map indicate those states which have proportionately greater representation in the industry than would be indicated by the state's population; the ratio is based on total revenues or number of establishments. Shaded *regions* indicate where the industry is regionally most concentrated.

NAICS 713110 - AMUSEMENT AND THEME PARKS*

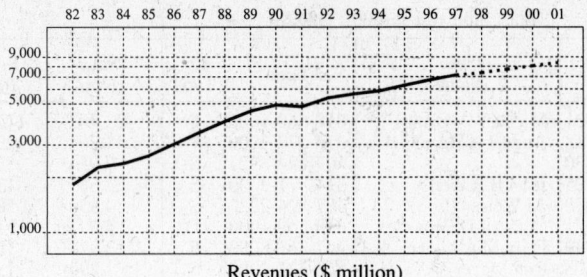

Revenues ($ million)

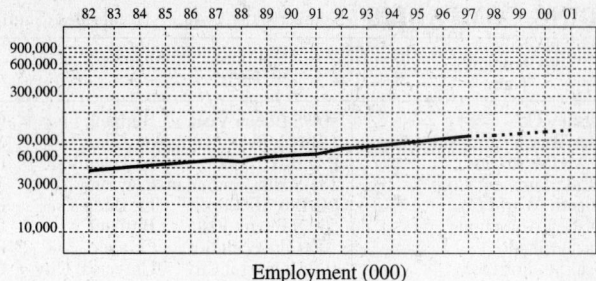

Employment (000)

GENERAL STATISTICS

Year	Establishments (number)	Employment (number)	Payroll ($ million)	Revenues ($ million)	Employees per Establishment (number)	Revenues per Establishment ($)	Payroll per Employee ($)
1982	491	46,464	603.0	1,824.0	94.6	3,714,868	12,978
1983	542 e	49,254 e	646.0 e	2,268.0	90.9 e	4,184,502 e	13,116 e
1984	592 e	52,044 e	690.0 e	2,380.0	87.9 e	4,020,270 e	13,258 e
1985	643 e	54,834 e	733.0 e	2,619.0	85.3 e	4,073,095 e	13,368 e
1986	693 e	57,624 e	776.0 e	3,025.0	83.2 e	4,365,079 e	13,467 e
1987	744	60,414	820.0	3,505.0	81.2	4,711,022	13,573
1988	754	58,581	876.0	4,017.0	77.7	5,327,586	14,954
1989	703	65,341	991.0	4,562.0	92.9	6,489,331	15,167
1990	695	68,593	1,060.0	4,922.0	98.7	7,082,014	15,453
1991	747	70,552	1,092.0	4,820.0	94.4	6,452,477	15,478
1992	825	80,745	1,298.0	5,366.0	97.9	6,504,242	16,075
1993	925	84,923	1,382.0	5,641.0	91.8	6,098,378	16,274
1994	916	90,221	1,448.0	5,858.0	98.5	6,395,197	16,049
1995	1,010	96,331	1,508.0	6,298.0	95.4	6,235,644	15,654
1996	809 e	103,560 e	1,599.0 e	6,735.0 e	128.0 e	8,325,093 e	15,440 e
1997	607	110,789	1,690.0	7,172.0	182.5	11,815,486	15,254
1998	853 p	112,680 p	1,789.0 p	7,378.0 p	132.1 p	8,649,472 p	15,877 p
1999	863 p	117,975 p	1,879.0 p	7,715.0 p	136.7 p	8,939,745 p	15,927 p
2000	872 p	123,269 p	1,968.0 p	8,053.0 p	141.4 p	9,235,092 p	15,965 p
2001	882 p.	128,564 p	2,058.0 p	8,390.0 p	145.8 p	9,512,472 p	16,008 p

Sources: Economic Census of the United States, 1982, 1987, 1992, 1997. Establishment counts, employment, and payroll are from *County Business Patterns* for non-Census years. In non-Census years, industries in the Manufacturing range under SIC coding include data from the *Annual Survey of Manufactures* (*ASM*); those in the old Services range include data from the *Services Annual Survey* (*SAS*). Values followed by a 'p' are projections by the editors. Extrapolations are marked by an 'e'. Data are the most recent available at this level of detail.

INDICES OF CHANGE

Year	Establishments (number)	Employment (number)	Payroll ($ million)	Revenues ($ million)	Employees per Establishment (number)	Revenues per Establishment ($)	Payroll per Employee ($)
1982	80.9	41.9	35.7	25.4	51.8	31.4	85.1
1987	122.6	54.5	48.5	48.9	44.5	39.9	89.0
1992	135.9	72.9	76.8	74.8	53.6	55.0	105.4
1993	152.4	76.7	81.8	78.7	50.3	51.6	106.7
1994	150.9	81.4	85.7	81.7	54.0	54.1	105.2
1995	166.4	86.9	89.2	87.8	52.3	52.8	102.6
1996	133.3 e	93.5 e	94.6 e	93.9 e	70.1 e	70.5 e	101.2 e
1997	100.0	100.0	100.0	100.0	100.0	100.0	100.0
1998	140.5 p	101.7 p	105.9 p	102.9 p	72.4 p	73.2 p	104.1 p
1999	142.2 p	106.5 p	111.2 p	107.6 p	74.9 p	75.7 p	104.4 p
2000	143.7 p	111.3 p	116.4 p	112.3 p	77.5 p	78.2 p	104.7 p
2001	145.3 p	116.0 p	121.8 p	117.0 p	79.9 p	80.5 p	104.9 p

Sources: Same as General Statistics. The values shown reflect change from the base year, 1997. Values above 100 mean greater than 1997, values below 100 mean less than 1997, and a value of 100 in the 1982-96 or 1998-2001 period means same as 1997. Values followed by a 'p' are projections by the editors; 'e' stands for extrapolation. Data are the most recent available at this level of detail.

SELECTED RATIOS

For 1997	Avg. of Information	Analyzed Industry	Index	For 1997	Avg. of Information	Analyzed Industry	Index
Employees per establishment	16	183	1,139	Payroll per establishment	330,963	2,784,185	841
Revenue per establishment	1,057,073	11,815,486	1,118	Payroll as % of revenue	31	24	75
Revenue per employee	65,958	64,736	98	Payroll per employee	20,651	15,254	74

Sources: Same as General Statistics. The 'Average' column represents the average for the industry sector, in 1997, where the currently shown industry is classified. The Index shows the relationship between the Average and the Analyzed Industry. For example, 100 means that they are equal; 500 that the Analyzed Industry is five times the average; 50 means that the Analyzed Industry is half the national average. The abbreviation 'na' is used to show that data are 'not available'.

---

*Equivalent to SIC 7996.

LEADING COMPANIES   Number shown: **46**   Total sales ($ mil): **68,882**   Total employment (000): **354.8**

Company Name	Address			CEO Name	Phone	Co. Type	Sales ($ mil)	Empl. (000)
Walt Disney Co.	500 S Buena Vista	Burbank	CA 91521	Michael D. Eisner	818-560-1000	P	23,402	117.0
Anheuser-Busch Companies Inc.	1 Busch Pl	St. Louis	MO 63118	August A Busch III	314-577-2000	P	11,704	23.3
Disney-MGM Studios	P O Box 10000	Lk Buen Vst	FL 32830		407-824-4321	S	7,954*	56.0
Busch Entertainment Corp.	231 South Bemisstan	Clayton	MO 63105	John B Roberts	314-577-2000	S	7,535	15.0
Walt Disney World Co.	PO Box 10000	Lk Buen Vst	FL 32830	Al Weiss	407-824-2222	S	4,850*	50.0
Walt Disney Attractions	500 S Buena Vista	Burbank	CA 91521	Michael D Eisner	818-560-1000	D	4,092*	31.0
Universal Orlando	1000 Univ Studios	Orlando	FL 32819	Felix Mussenden	407-363-8000	R	3,376*	12.0
Universal Studios Inc.	100 Universal City	Universal City	CA 91608	Ron Meyer	818-777-1000	S	1,794*	13.0
Six Flags Theme Parks Inc.	400 Interpace Pkwy	Parsippany	NJ 07054		973-402-8100	S	600	0.5
Cedar Fair L.P.	PO Box 5006	Sandusky	OH 44871	Richard L Kinzel	419-626-0830	P	419	5.0
Six Flags Over Texas Inc.	P O Box 90191	Arlington	TX 76004	Steve Calloway	817-640-8900	S	413*	1.3
New Gaylord Entertainment Co.	PO Box 25125	Oklahoma City	OK 73125		405-475-3311	S	340	4.6
Six Flags	9993 Allegheny Rd	Darien Center	NY 14040		716-599-4641	R	298*	2.2
SeaWorld San Diego	500 Sea World Dr	San Diego	CA 92109		619-222-6363	S	257*	3.5
Hershey Entertainment & Resorts	300 Park Blvd	Hershey	PA 17033	J Bruce McKinney	717-534-3131	R	240*	4.0
Funtime Parks Inc.	1060 Aurora Rd	Aurora	OH 44202	Garry Story	330-562-4400	R	215*	1.5
Silver Dollar City Inc.	HCR 1, Box 791	Branson	MO 65616	Mike Bilbo	417-338-2611	R	213*	1.5
Kennywood Entertainment Co.	4800 Kennywood	West Mifflin	PA 15122	H Henninger	412-461-0500	R	162*	1.2
Sea World of Florida Inc.	7007 Sea World Dr	Orlando	FL 32821		407-351-3600	S	160*	2.0
Nickels and Dimes Inc.	4534 Old Denton Rd	Carrollton	TX 75008	Ron Kostelny	972-492-3262	R	148*	1.1
Six Flags California	PO Box 5500	Valencia	CA 91385	Del Holland	805-255-4100	S	99	0.3
Six Flags St. Louis Inc.	P O Box 60	Eureka	MO 63025		314-938-5300	S	59*	0.2
Castle Park Amusement Co.	3500 Polk St	Riverside	CA 92505	Keat LaMasters	909-785-4141	R	57*	0.4
Dutch Wonderland	2249 Lincoln Hwy E	Lancaster	PA 17602	Murl Clark	717-291-1888	R	57*	0.4
Shepherd of the Hills Homestead	5586 W Hwy 76	Branson	MO 65616	Gary Snadon	417-332-1099	R	50*	0.4
Malibu Entertainment Worldwide	717 N Harwood	Dallas	TX 75201	Richard Beckert	201-210-8701	P	46	1.2
PIER 39 L.P.	P O Box 193730	San Francisco	CA 94119	Fritz Arko	415-705-5500	S	45*	0.1
Adventure Lands of America Inc.	PO Box 3355	Des Moines	IA 50316	JF Krantz	515-266-2121	R	33*	0.2
Lagoon Corp.	PO Box 696	Farmington	UT 84025	Alan Freed	801-451-8000	R	30	2.0
Dollywood Co.	1020 Dollywood Ln	Pigeon Forge	TN 37863		865-428-9401	R	28*	0.2
Knott's Berry Farm Foods Inc.	8039 Beach Blvd	Buena Park	CA 90620		714-827-1776	S	23*	0.4
Venice Amusement Corp.	800 Ocean Ter	Seaside Heights	NJ 08751	Robert Bennett	732-793-6488	R	23*	0.2
H.H. Knoebels Sons Inc.	PO Box 317	Elysburg	PA 17824	Richard Knoebel	570-672-2572	R	22*	1.6
Mystery Fun House	5767 Major Blvd	Orlando	FL 32819	David Segal	407-351-3356	R	21*	0.2
Florida Cypress Gardens Inc.	PO Box 1	Cypress Gardens	FL 33884	William Reynolds	863-324-2111	R	20*	0.6
Morey's Piers	3501 Boardwalk	Wildwood	NJ 08260	Wilbert Morey	609-729-0586	R	18	0.3
Gatorland	14501 S Or Blssm	Orlando	FL 32837	Mark McHugh	407-855-5496	R	15*	0.1
Scandia Amusement Park	1155 S Wanamaker	Ontario	CA 91761		909-390-3091	R	14*	0.1
Fun-Plex Inc.	13700 Beachnut St	Houston	TX 77083	Farooq A Khan	281-530-7777	R	14	0.1
Kentucky Kingdom Inc.	P O Box 9287	Louisville	KY 40209	Burke Kieran	502-366-2231	R	10*	0.1
Lakeside Park Co.	4601 Sheridan Blvd	Denver	CO 80212	Rhoda Krasner	303-477-1621	R	9*	<0.1
Santa's Enchanted Forest Inc.	11900 Biscayne	Miami	FL 33181	S Brian Shechtman	305-893-0090	R	7*	<0.1
Adventureland Park	P O Box 3355	Des Moines	IA 50316	John Krantz	515-266-2121	R	4*	<0.1
All Star Amusement Co.	15 Willow Bay Dr	Barrington	IL 60010	Jeff Blomsness	847-382-3330	R	3*	<0.1
Clabrook Farms Inc.	26205 E Hwy 50	Christmas	FL 32709		407-568-2885	R	2*	<0.1
Associates Four Inc.	841 Bishop St	Honolulu	HI 96813		808-536-7091	R	1*	<0.1

Source: Ward's Business Directory of U.S. Private and Public Companies, Volumes 1 and 2, 2000. The company type code used is as follows: P - Public, R - Private, S - Subsidiary, D - Division, J - Joint Venture, A - Affiliate, G - Group, N - Company type not reported. Sales are in millions of dollars, employees are in thousands. An asterisk (*) indicates an estimated sales volume. The symbol < stands for 'less than'. Company names and addresses are truncated, in some cases, to fit into the available space.

LOCATION BY STATE AND REGIONAL CONCENTRATION

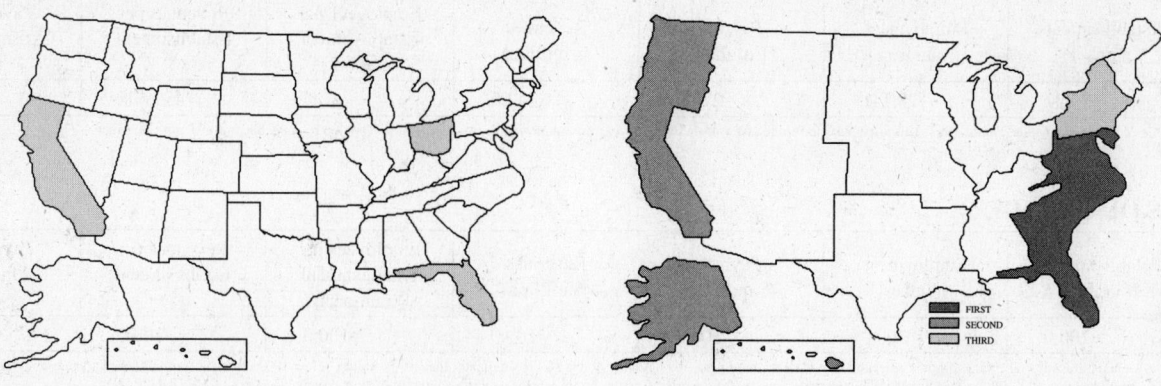

FIRST
SECOND
THIRD

INDUSTRY DATA BY STATE

State	Establishments Total (number)	Establishments % of U.S.	Employment Total (number)	Employment % of U.S.	Employment Per Estab.	Payroll Total ($ mil.)	Payroll Per Empl. ($)	Revenues Total ($ mil.)	Revenues % of U.S.	Revenues Per Estab. ($)
Florida	49	8.1	33,363	30.1	681	555.2	16,642	3,211.7	44.8	65,545,796
California	63	10.4	29,468	26.6	468	469.6	15,936	1,555.6	21.7	24,692,048
Ohio	15	2.5	2,062	1.9	137	84.8	41,129	337.2	4.7	22,478,200
Texas	43	7.1	12,806	11.6	298	100.8	7,869	308.9	4.3	7,184,698
Pennsylvania	33	5.4	1,983	1.8	60	57.2	28,824	205.1	2.9	6,214,212
New Jersey	30	4.9	3,327	3.0	111	43.1	12,943	181.1	2.5	6,036,267
Tennessee	12	2.0	2,166	2.0	181	34.5	15,925	133.9	1.9	11,158,083
Georgia	13	2.1	2,520	2.3	194	27.4	10,883	111.1	1.5	8,546,231
New York	54	8.9	629	0.6	12	21.1	33,618	77.4	1.1	1,433,056
North Carolina	21	3.5	1,913	1.7	91	21.8	11,408	73.4	1.0	3,495,286
Indiana	8	1.3	1,014	0.9	127	17.3	17,099	54.2	0.8	6,780,250
Colorado	8	1.3	191	0.2	24	9.6	50,058	36.4	0.5	4,551,125
New Hampshire	12	2.0	202	0.2	17	13.7	67,906	31.1	0.4	2,592,750
Massachusetts	17	2.8	207	0.2	12	9.2	44,362	29.9	0.4	1,757,824
South Carolina	5	0.8	581	0.5	116	9.0	15,478	28.8	0.4	5,764,800
Maryland	7	1.2	123	0.1	18	6.7	54,089	28.1	0.4	4,021,286
Kentucky	12	2.0	749	0.7	62	6.1	8,130	25.8	0.4	2,148,250
Utah	7	1.2	680	0.6	97	8.4	12,394	24.1	0.3	3,449,857
Oklahoma	7	1.2	292	0.3	42	5.1	17,616	21.0	0.3	3,005,714
Wisconsin	12	2.0	92	0.1	8	5.1	55,272	19.9	0.3	1,662,417
Iowa	4	0.7	63	0.1	16	4.4	69,175	17.2	0.2	4,306,500
Michigan	28	4.6	202	0.2	7	5.4	26,520	16.9	0.2	603,893
Arizona	4	0.7	571	0.5	143	5.3	9,329	16.1	0.2	4,017,750
Washington	8	1.3	146	0.1	18	4.3	29,514	16.0	0.2	2,002,375
Louisiana	10	1.6	271	0.2	27	3.5	12,937	10.7	0.1	1,067,700
Idaho	7	1.2	116	0.1	17	2.6	22,000	7.8	0.1	1,109,714
Oregon	4	0.7	208	0.2	52	2.2	10,774	6.3	0.1	1,585,500
New Mexico	3	0.5	43	0.0	14	1.4	31,721	5.6	0.1	1,853,667
Maine	6	1.0	27	0.0	5	1.7	62,074	5.3	0.1	886,000
Mississippi	9	1.5	133	0.1	15	1.5	11,594	4.9	0.1	543,889
Alabama	5	0.8	60	0.1	12	1.0	16,917	3.9	0.1	786,600
South Dakota	6	1.0	8	0.0	1	0.8	94,625	2.5	0.0	413,000
Montana	5	0.8	2	0.0	-	0.3	126,500	1.3	0.0	261,400
Rhode Island	3	0.5	-	-	-	0.3	-	0.9	0.0	302,667
Minnesota	14	2.3	175*	-	-	(D)	-	(D)	-	-
Missouri	14	2.3	7,500*	-	-	(D)	-	(D)	-	-
Illinois	11	1.8	1,750*	-	-	(D)	-	(D)	-	-
Virginia	6	1.0	7,500*	-	-	(D)	-	(D)	-	-
Connecticut	5	0.8	60*	-	-	(D)	-	(D)	-	-
Nevada	5	0.8	750*	-	-	(D)	-	(D)	-	-
Delaware	4	0.7	10*	-	-	(D)	-	(D)	-	-
Kansas	4	0.7	10*	-	-	(D)	-	(D)	-	-
Hawaii	3	0.5	375*	-	-	(D)	-	(D)	-	-
Arkansas	2	0.3	10*	-	-	(D)	-	(D)	-	-
Nebraska	2	0.3	60*	-	-	(D)	-	(D)	-	-
Vermont	2	0.3	10*	-	-	(D)	-	(D)	-	-
West Virginia	2	0.3	10*	-	-	(D)	-	(D)	-	-
Wyoming	2	0.3	10*	-	-	(D)	-	(D)	-	-
Alaska	1	0.2	10*	-	-	(D)	-	(D)	-	-

Source: 1997 *Economic Census*. The states are in descending order of revenues or establishments (if revenue data are missing for the majority). The symbol (D) appears when data are withheld to prevent disclosure of competitive information. States marked with (D) are sorted by number of establishments. A dash (-) indicates that the data element cannot be calculated. * indicates the midpoint of a range; 175, for example is the range 100-249. Shaded *states* on the state map indicate those states which have proportionately greater representation in the industry than would be indicated by the state's population; the ratio is based on total revenues or number of establishments. Shaded *regions* indicate where the industry is regionally most concentrated.

NAICS 713120 - AMUSEMENT ARCADES

GENERAL STATISTICS

Year	Establishments (number)	Employment (number)	Payroll ($ million)	Revenues ($ million)	Employees per Establishment (number)	Revenues per Establishment ($)	Payroll per Employee ($)
1997	2,737	28,141	272.0	1,247.0	10.3	455,608	9,666

Source: *Economic Census of the United States*, 1997. This is a newly defined industry. Data for prior years were unavailable at the time of publication but may become available over time.

INDICES OF CHANGE

Year	Establishments (number)	Employment (number)	Payroll ($ million)	Revenues ($ million)	Employees per Establishment (number)	Revenues per Establishment ($)	Payroll per Employee ($)
1997	100.0	100.0	100.0	100.0	100.0	100.0	100.0

Sources: Same as General Statistics. The values shown reflect change from the base year, 1997. Values above 100 mean greater than 1997, values below 100 mean less than 1997, and a value of 100 in the 1982-96 or 1998-2001 period means same as 1997. Values followed by a 'p' are projections by the editors; 'e' stands for extrapolation. Data are the most recent available at this level of detail.

SIC INDUSTRIES RELATED TO NAICS 713120

Each new NAICS code represents an industry that used to be part of an SIC or a part of several SIC industries. Data in this table are shown to provide transitional information for these cases. All available data for the precursor SIC(s) are shown. Even if only a part of an SIC is included in the NAICS, *all* data for the SIC are reproduced. If the SIC industry is not marked as being a part (pt) of the NAICS, the entire industry is embedded in the NAICS data. The SIC composition of the new industry provides some hints of the relative importance of its "ancestors." Data marked with a 'p' are projected. Projections begin with 1982 data. Data earlier than 1990 are not shown but are reflected in the projections.

SIC	Industry	1990	1991	1992	1993	1994	1995	1996	1997
7993	**Coin-Operated Amusement Devices (pt)**								
	Establishments (number)	3,932	3,772	4,932	4,826	4,722	4,814	4,090*p*	4,001*p*
	Employment (thousands)	25.2	23.8	28.1	31.0	31.4	57.1	36.9*p*	38.0*p*
	Revenues ($ million)	2,146.0	2,301.0	2,566.0	2,763.0	2,965.0	3,254.0	3,486.0	3,397.7*p*

Source: *Economic Census of the United States*, 1992, annual surveys of economic sectors conducted by the Bureau of the Census, and estimates or projections based on the 1982-1992 period; not all data are shown. 'e' marks estimates made by the editors; 'p' indicates projections based on time series. A dash (-) indicates that data for this SIC or year were not available. The abbreviation (pt) next to the industry name indicates that only a part of the industry is present within the NAICS data. If no (pt) is shown, the entire industry is contained within the NAICS data.

SELECTED RATIOS

For 1997	Avg. of Information	Analyzed Industry	Index	For 1997	Avg. of Information	Analyzed Industry	Index
Employees per establishment	16	10	64	Payroll per establishment	330,963	99,379	30
Revenue per establishment	1,057,073	455,608	43	Payroll as % of revenue	31	22	70
Revenue per employee	65,958	44,313	67	Payroll per employee	20,651	9,666	47

Sources: Same as General Statistics. The 'Average' column represents the average for the industry sector, in 1997, where the currently shown industry is classified. The Index shows the relationship between the Average and the Analyzed Industry. For example, 100 means that they are equal; 500 that the Analyzed Industry is five times the average; 50 means that the Analyzed Industry is half the national average. The abbreviation 'na' is used to show that data are 'not available'.

LEADING COMPANIES   Number shown: **24**   Total sales ($ mil): **3,663**   Total employment (000): **35.8**

Company Name	Address				CEO Name	Phone	Co. Type	Sales ($ mil)	Empl. (000)
Argosy Gaming Co.	219 Piasa St	Alton	IL	62002	William F. Cellini	618-474-7500	P	595	5.1
Isle of Capri Casions Inc.	711 Wash Loop	Biloxi	MS	39530	John M Gallaway	228-436-7000	P	480	6.0
Alliance Gaming Corp.	6601 S Bermuda Rd	Las Vegas	NV	89119	Morris Goldstein	702-270-7600	P	458	2.5
Little Six Inc.	2400 Mystic Lake	Prior Lake	MN	55372		612-445-6000	R	330*	4.0
Hollywood Casino Corp.	13455 Noel Rd	Dallas	TX	75240	Jack E Pratt	972-392-7777	P	269	2.8
Anchor Gaming	815 Pilot Rd	Las Vegas	NV	89119	Stanley E Fulton	702-896-7568	P	249	2.8
President Riverboat Casinos Inc.	802 N 1st St	St. Louis	MO	63102	John S Aylsworth	314-622-3000	P	206	2.8
Barona Casino	1000 Wildcat Cny	Lakeside	CA	92040	Carol Schoen	619-443-2300	R	152*	1.3
Sycuan Gaming Center	5469 Dehesa Rd	El Cajon	CA	92019	Georgia Tucker	619-445-6002	R	135*	1.1
Muckleshoot Indian Casino	2402 Auburn Way S	Auburn	WA	98002		253-804-4444	R	107*	0.9
American Coin Merchandising Inc	5660 Central Ave	Boulder	CO	80301	Randall J Fagundo	303-444-2559	P	98	0.8
Jackpot Enterprises Inc.	1110 Palms Arpt Dr	Las Vegas	NV	89119	Don R Kornstein	702-263-5555	P	96	0.8
Black Hawk Gaming	PO Box 21	Black Hawk	CO	80422	Jeffrey P Jacobs	303-582-1117	P	93	0.9
Dover Downs Inc.	P O Box 843	Dover	DE	19903	Denis McGlynn	302-674-4600	S	81	0.4
Alton Gaming Co.	219 Piasa St	Alton	IL	62002	James B Perry	618-474-7500	S	74	0.8
Lady Luck Casino Hotel	1777 Lady Luck	Bettendorf	IA	52722		319-359-7280	S	69*	1.0
Jubilee Casino	242 S Walnut St	Greenville	MS	38701	Jack O'Donald	601-335-1111	R	58*	0.5
Lucky Eagle Casino	PO Box 610	Rochester	WA	98579	Sherri Clecender	360-273-2000	R	58*	0.5
Rainbow Casino	122 S Water St	Henderson	NV	89015		702-565-9777	R	23*	0.2
Trans World Gaming Corp.	1 Penn Plz	New York	NY	10119	Stanley Kohlenberg	212-563-3355	P	15	0.3
Innovative Gaming Corporation	4750 Turbo Circle	Reno	NV	89502	Edward G Stevenson	775-823-3000	P	9	<0.1
Southern Amusement Co.	3770 Progress Rd	Norfolk	VA	23502	John Lineberry	757-857-6211	R	7*	<0.1
Doc Holiday Inc.	P O Box 639	Central City	CO	80427		303-582-1400	R	3*	<0.1
CCA Companies Inc.	3250 Mary St	Coconut Grove	FL	33133	Dallas R Dempster	305-670-3838	P	1	0.2

Source: *Ward's Business Directory of U.S. Private and Public Companies*, Volumes 1 and 2, 2000. The company type code used is as follows: P - Public, R - Private, S - Subsidiary, D - Division, J - Joint Venture, A - Affiliate, G - Group, N - Company type not reported. Sales are in millions of dollars, employees are in thousands. An asterisk (*) indicates an estimated sales volume. The symbol < stands for 'less than'. Company names and addresses are truncated, in some cases, to fit into the available space.

LOCATION BY STATE AND REGIONAL CONCENTRATION

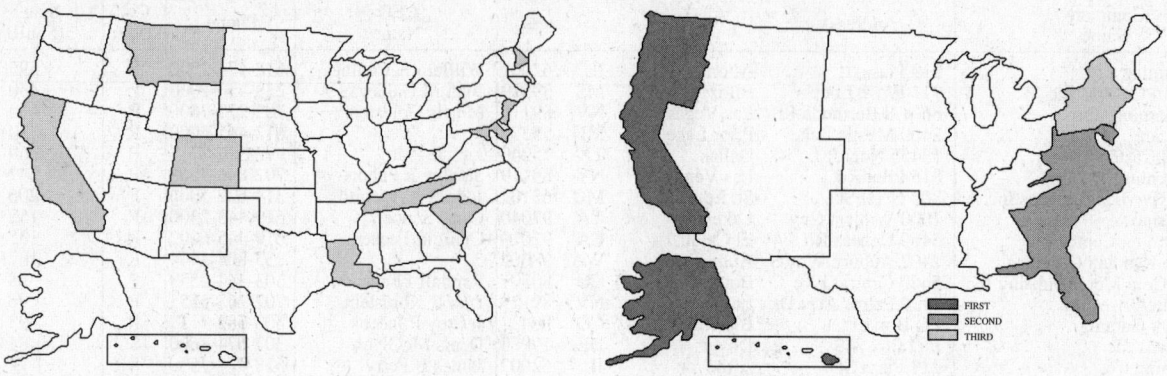

INDUSTRY DATA BY STATE

State	Establishments Total (number)	% of U.S.	Employment Total (number)	% of U.S.	Per Estab.	Payroll Total ($ mil.)	Per Empl. ($)	Revenues Total ($ mil.)	% of U.S.	Per Estab. ($)
California	236	8.6	3,362	11.9	14	36.0	10,695	208.7	16.7	884,521
New York	149	5.4	2,101	7.5	14	23.4	11,160	84.3	6.8	565,872
Texas	190	6.9	2,263	8.0	12	17.6	7,757	72.6	5.8	382,279
South Carolina	107	3.9	951	3.4	9	10.6	11,180	69.8	5.6	652,271
Florida	179	6.5	1,750	6.2	10	16.3	9,295	65.0	5.2	363,050
New Jersey	104	3.8	1,031	3.7	10	15.4	14,957	62.0	5.0	595,942
Ohio	111	4.1	1,257	4.5	11	10.2	8,134	40.4	3.2	364,288
Pennsylvania	120	4.4	1,121	4.0	9	9.2	8,220	39.5	3.2	329,583
Michigan	91	3.3	792	2.8	9	8.6	10,812	37.3	3.0	409,374
Maryland	55	2.0	650	2.3	12	6.7	10,363	27.2	2.2	494,036
Tennessee	85	3.1	778	2.8	9	6.5	8,392	25.3	2.0	298,094
Georgia	69	2.5	659	2.3	10	5.4	8,231	24.8	2.0	359,739
Louisiana	43	1.6	328	1.2	8	3.6	11,088	22.9	1.8	533,651
Indiana	66	2.4	719	2.6	11	5.7	7,882	22.0	1.8	332,712
North Carolina	71	2.6	594	2.1	8	6.1	10,234	21.5	1.7	302,310
Massachusetts	61	2.2	486	1.7	8	5.0	10,368	20.9	1.7	342,689
Washington	47	1.7	461	1.6	10	4.5	9,709	19.6	1.6	417,319
Colorado	53	1.9	437	1.6	8	3.6	8,224	17.0	1.4	321,245
Arizona	30	1.1	553	2.0	18	3.4	6,170	15.2	1.2	507,033
Wisconsin	57	2.1	417	1.5	7	3.4	8,252	14.3	1.1	250,912
Oklahoma	40	1.5	480	1.7	12	4.2	8,690	14.0	1.1	349,425
Oregon	29	1.1	311	1.1	11	2.8	8,907	12.8	1.0	441,931
Alabama	48	1.8	366	1.3	8	2.6	7,191	12.8	1.0	265,958
Iowa	34	1.2	283	1.0	8	2.2	7,873	10.5	0.8	309,971
New Hampshire	20	0.7	208	0.7	10	2.5	12,226	10.5	0.8	522,750
New Mexico	22	0.8	181	0.6	8	1.8	9,851	7.7	0.6	349,409
Kentucky	37	1.4	284	1.0	8	2.0	7,141	7.6	0.6	205,838
Montana	15	0.5	65	0.2	4	1.3	20,292	6.9	0.6	457,867
Mississippi	39	1.4	197	0.7	5	1.3	6,406	6.8	0.5	173,795
Idaho	10	0.4	89	0.3	9	0.9	10,371	4.5	0.4	452,700
Maine	17	0.6	56	0.2	3	1.1	18,839	4.1	0.3	243,588
Utah	18	0.7	167	0.6	9	1.1	6,311	4.0	0.3	223,167
South Dakota	11	0.4	83	0.3	8	0.7	8,217	3.1	0.2	278,455
Rhode Island	8	0.3	69	0.2	9	0.5	7,899	3.0	0.2	369,000
North Dakota	7	0.3	49	0.2	7	0.2	4,735	1.4	0.1	193,571
Illinois	106	3.9	1,750*	-	-	(D)	-	(D)	-	-
Missouri	63	2.3	750*	-	-	(D)	-	(D)	-	-
Virginia	61	2.2	750*	-	-	(D)	-	(D)	-	-
Minnesota	41	1.5	375*	-	-	(D)	-	(D)	-	-
Connecticut	31	1.1	375*	-	-	(D)	-	(D)	-	-
Hawaii	31	1.1	175*	-	-	(D)	-	(D)	-	-
Kansas	28	1.0	375*	-	-	(D)	-	(D)	-	-
Arkansas	20	0.7	175*	-	-	(D)	-	(D)	-	-
Nevada	18	0.7	375*	-	-	(D)	-	(D)	-	-
Nebraska	15	0.5	175*	-	-	(D)	-	(D)	-	-
Wyoming	11	0.4	60*	-	-	(D)	-	(D)	-	-
West Virginia	10	0.4	60*	-	-	(D)	-	(D)	-	-
Delaware	9	0.3	175*	-	-	(D)	-	(D)	-	-
Vermont	8	0.3	60*	-	-	(D)	-	(D)	-	-
Alaska	6	0.2	60*	-	-	(D)	-	(D)	-	-

Source: 1997 Economic Census. The states are in descending order of revenues or establishments (if revenue data are missing for the majority). The symbol (D) appears when data are withheld to prevent disclosure of competitive information. States marked with (D) are sorted by number of establishments. A dash (-) indicates that the data element cannot be calculated. * indicates the midpoint of a range; 175, for example is the range 100-249. Shaded states on the state map indicate those states which have proportionately greater representation in the industry than would be indicated by the state's population; the ratio is based on total revenues or number of establishments. Shaded regions indicate where the industry is regionally most concentrated.

NAICS 713210 - CASINOS (EXCEPT CASINO HOTELS)

GENERAL STATISTICS

Year	Establishments (number)	Employment (number)	Payroll ($ million)	Revenues ($ million)	Employees per Establishment (number)	Revenues per Establishment ($)	Payroll per Employee ($)
1997	447	115,210	2,305.0	10,186.0	257.7	22,787,472	20,007

Source: *Economic Census of the United States*, 1997. This is a newly defined industry. Data for prior years were unavailable at the time of publication but may become available over time.

INDICES OF CHANGE

Year	Establishments (number)	Employment (number)	Payroll ($ million)	Revenues ($ million)	Employees per Establishment (number)	Revenues per Establishment ($)	Payroll per Employee ($)
1997	100.0	100.0	100.0	100.0	100.0	100.0	100.0

Sources: Same as General Statistics. The values shown reflect change from the base year, 1997. Values above 100 mean greater than 1997, values below 100 mean less than 1997, and a value of 100 in the 1982-96 or 1998-2001 period means same as 1997. Values followed by a 'p' are projections by the editors; 'e' stands for extrapolation. Data are the most recent available at this level of detail.

SIC INDUSTRIES RELATED TO NAICS 713210

Each new NAICS code represents an industry that used to be part of an SIC or a part of several SIC industries. Data in this table are shown to provide transitional information for these cases. All available data for the precursor SIC(s) are shown. Even if only a part of an SIC is included in the NAICS, *all* data for the SIC are reproduced. If the SIC industry is not marked as being a part (pt) of the NAICS, the entire industry is embedded in the NAICS data. The SIC composition of the new industry provides some hints of the relative importance of its "ancestors." Data marked with a 'p' are projected. Projections begin with 1982 data. Data earlier than 1990 are not shown but are reflected in the projections.

SIC	Industry	1990	1991	1992	1993	1994	1995	1996	1997
7999	**Amusement & Recreation nec (pt)**								
	Establishments (number)	-	-	21,717	-	-	-	-	-
	Employment (thousands)	-	-	215.8	-	-	-	-	-
	Revenues ($ million)	-	-	10,430.3	-	-	-	-	-

Source: *Economic Census of the United States*, 1992, annual surveys of economic sectors conducted by the Bureau of the Census, and estimates or projections based on the 1982-1992 period; not all data are shown. 'e' marks estimates made by the editors; 'p' indicates projections based on time series. A dash (-) indicates that data for this SIC or year were not available. The abbreviation (pt) next to the industry name indicates that only a part of the industry is present within the NAICS data. If no (pt) is shown, the entire industry is contained within the NAICS data.

SELECTED RATIOS

For 1997	Avg. of Information	Analyzed Industry	Index	For 1997	Avg. of Information	Analyzed Industry	Index
Employees per establishment	16	258	1,608	Payroll per establishment	330,963	5,156,600	1,558
Revenue per establishment	1,057,073	22,787,472	2,156	Payroll as % of revenue	31	23	72
Revenue per employee	65,958	88,412	134	Payroll per employee	20,651	20,007	97

Sources: Same as General Statistics. The 'Average' column represents the average for the industry sector, in 1997, where the currently shown industry is classified. The Index shows the relationship between the Average and the Analyzed Industry. For example, 100 means that they are equal; 500 that the Analyzed Industry is five times the average; 50 means that the Analyzed Industry is half the national average. The abbreviation 'na' is used to show that data are 'not available'.

LEADING COMPANIES

No company data available for this industry.

LOCATION BY STATE AND REGIONAL CONCENTRATION

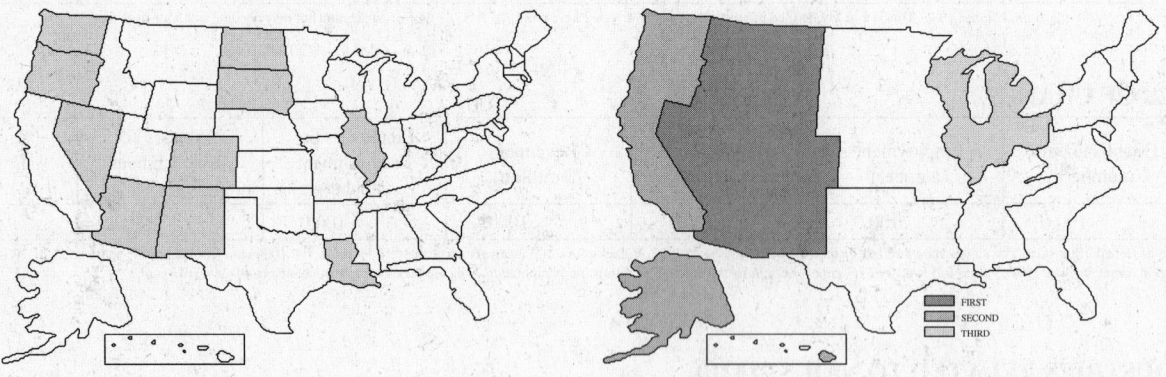

FIRST
SECOND
THIRD

INDUSTRY DATA BY STATE

State	Establishments Total (number)	Establishments % of U.S.	Employment Total (number)	Employment % of U.S.	Employment Per Estab.	Payroll Total ($ mil.)	Payroll Per Empl. ($)	Revenues Total ($ mil.)	Revenues % of U.S.	Revenues Per Estab. ($)
Illinois	10	2.2	9,963	8.6	996	216.7	21,750	1,101.2	10.8	110,117,800
Louisiana	15	3.4	9,634	8.4	642	197.6	20,516	909.6	8.9	60,640,867
California	20	4.5	6,633	5.8	332	124.3	18,746	690.3	6.8	34,517,450
Arizona	8	1.8	2,783	2.4	348	57.9	20,797	600.9	5.9	75,113,125
Nevada	160	35.8	11,336	9.8	71	177.2	15,632	579.8	5.7	3,623,619
Colorado	51	11.4	4,304	3.7	84	89.7	20,845	395.0	3.9	7,745,059
Washington	13	2.9	4,808	4.2	370	105.4	21,931	278.0	2.7	21,383,692
Florida	23	5.1	1,860	1.6	81	40.1	21,533	255.1	2.5	11,091,348
New Mexico	7	1.6	2,528	2.2	361	39.4	15,573	251.1	2.5	35,866,571
Oregon	6	1.3	2,447	2.1	408	56.4	23,045	220.3	2.2	36,717,333
South Dakota	66	14.8	1,852	1.6	28	28.8	15,531	132.4	1.3	2,006,258
North Dakota	3	0.7	1,212	1.1	404	17.7	14,626	96.5	0.9	32,166,667
Mississippi	22	4.9	17,500*	-	-	(D)	-	(D)	-	-
Iowa	9	2.0	3,750*	-	-	(D)	-	(D)	-	-
Missouri	9	2.0	7,500*	-	-	(D)	-	(D)	-	-
Indiana	7	1.6	7,500*	-	-	(D)	-	(D)	-	-
New York	6	1.3	60*	-	-	(D)	-	(D)	-	-
Michigan	4	0.9	1,750*	-	-	(D)	-	(D)	-	-
Connecticut	2	0.4	17,500*	-	-	(D)	-	(D)	-	-
Kansas	2	0.4	750*	-	-	(D)	-	(D)	-	-
Texas	2	0.4	750*	-	-	(D)	-	(D)	-	-
Georgia	1	0.2	60*	-	-	(D)	-	(D)	-	-
North Carolina	1	0.2	10*	-	-	(D)	-	(D)	-	-

Source: 1997 *Economic Census*. The states are in descending order of revenues or establishments (if revenue data are missing for the majority). The symbol (D) appears when data are withheld to prevent disclosure of competitive information. States marked with (D) are sorted by number of establishments. A dash (-) indicates that the data element cannot be calculated. * indicates the midpoint of a range; 175, for example is the range 100-249. Shaded *states* on the state map indicate those states which have proportionately greater representation in the industry than would be indicated by the state's population; the ratio is based on total revenues or number of establishments. Shaded *regions* indicate where the industry is regionally most concentrated.

NAICS 713290 - GAMBLING INDUSTRIES NEC

GENERAL STATISTICS

Year	Establishments (number)	Employment (number)	Payroll ($ million)	Revenues ($ million)	Employees per Establishment (number)	Revenues per Establishment ($)	Payroll per Employee ($)
1997	1,653	53,892	928.0	5,396.0	32.6	3,264,368	17,220

Source: *Economic Census of the United States*, 1997. This is a newly defined industry. Data for prior years were unavailable at the time of publication but may become available over time.

INDICES OF CHANGE

Year	Establishments (number)	Employment (number)	Payroll ($ million)	Revenues ($ million)	Employees per Establishment (number)	Revenues per Establishment ($)	Payroll per Employee ($)
1997	100.0	100.0	100.0	100.0	100.0	100.0	100.0

Sources: Same as General Statistics. The values shown reflect change from the base year, 1997. Values above 100 mean greater than 1997, values below 100 mean less than 1997, and a value of 100 in the 1982-96 or 1998-2001 period means same as 1997. Values followed by a 'p' are projections by the editors; 'e' stands for extrapolation. Data are the most recent available at this level of detail.

SIC INDUSTRIES RELATED TO NAICS 713290

Each new NAICS code represents an industry that used to be part of an SIC or a part of several SIC industries. Data in this table are shown to provide transitional information for these cases. All available data for the precursor SIC(s) are shown. Even if only a part of an SIC is included in the NAICS, *all* data for the SIC are reproduced. If the SIC industry is not marked as being a part (pt) of the NAICS, the entire industry is embedded in the NAICS data. The SIC composition of the new industry provides some hints of the relative importance of its "ancestors." Data marked with a 'p' are projected. Projections begin with 1982 data. Data earlier than 1990 are not shown but are reflected in the projections.

SIC	Industry	1990	1991	1992	1993	1994	1995	1996	1997
7993	**Coin-Operated Amusement Devices (pt)**								
	Establishments (number)	3,932	3,772	4,932	4,826	4,722	4,814	4,090p	4,001p
	Employment (thousands)	25.2	23.8	28.1	31.0	31.4	57.1	36.9p	38.0p
	Revenues ($ million)	2,146.0	2,301.0	2,566.0	2,763.0	2,965.0	3,254.0	3,486.0	3,397.7p
7999	**Amusement & Recreation nec (pt)**								
	Establishments (number)	-	-	21,717	-	-	-	-	-
	Employment (thousands)	-	-	215.8	-	-	-	-	-
	Revenues ($ million)	-	-	10,430.3	-	-	-	-	-

Source: *Economic Census of the United States*, 1992, annual surveys of economic sectors conducted by the Bureau of the Census, and estimates or projections based on the 1982-1992 period; not all data are shown. 'e' marks estimates made by the editors; 'p' indicates projections based on time series. A dash (-) indicates that data for this SIC or year were not available. The abbreviation (pt) next to the industry name indicates that only a part of the industry is present within the NAICS data. If no (pt) is shown, the entire industry is contained within the NAICS data.

SELECTED RATIOS

For 1997	Avg. of Information	Analyzed Industry	Index	For 1997	Avg. of Information	Analyzed Industry	Index
Employees per establishment	16	33	203	Payroll per establishment	330,963	561,404	170
Revenue per establishment	1,057,073	3,264,368	309	Payroll as % of revenue	31	17	55
Revenue per employee	65,958	100,126	152	Payroll per employee	20,651	17,220	83

Sources: Same as General Statistics. The 'Average' column represents the average for the industry sector, in 1997, where the currently shown industry is classified. The Index shows the relationship between the Average and the Analyzed Industry. For example, 100 means that they are equal; 500 that the Analyzed Industry is five times the average; 50 means that the Analyzed Industry is half the national average. The abbreviation 'na' is used to show that data are 'not available'.

LEADING COMPANIES
No company data available for this industry.

LOCATION BY STATE AND REGIONAL CONCENTRATION

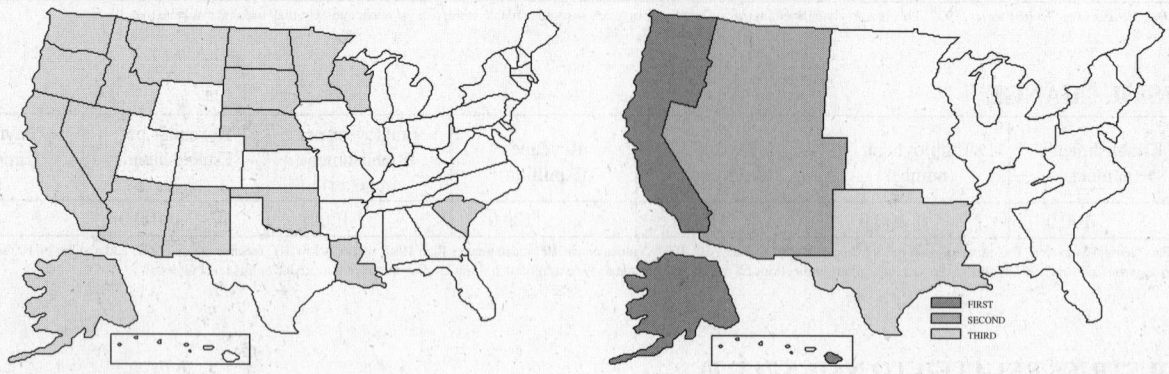

FIRST
SECOND
THIRD

INDUSTRY DATA BY STATE

State	Establishments Total (number)	Establishments % of U.S.	Employment Total (number)	Employment % of U.S.	Employment Per Estab.	Payroll Total ($ mil.)	Payroll Per Empl. ($)	Revenues Total ($ mil.)	Revenues % of U.S.	Revenues Per Estab. ($)
California	138	8.3	16,233	30.1	118	317.6	19,565	1,249.2	23.1	9,052,225
Louisiana	129	7.8	2,459	4.6	19	44.6	18,152	491.0	9.1	3,806,419
Nevada	102	6.2	2,964	5.5	29	60.8	20,526	368.9	6.8	3,616,755
Minnesota	42	2.5	6,402	11.9	152	120.7	18,855	361.2	6.7	8,599,024
Wisconsin	13	0.8	2,012	3.7	155	33.8	16,800	306.0	5.7	23,534,769
Washington	67	4.1	1,778	3.3	27	27.1	15,232	240.5	4.5	3,588,925
Arizona	23	1.4	2,214	4.1	96	37.8	17,062	235.7	4.4	10,248,957
Oklahoma	34	2.1	1,557	2.9	46	21.4	13,771	230.7	4.3	6,784,441
South Carolina	159	9.6	1,799	3.3	11	33.4	18,564	183.8	3.4	1,155,786
Montana	171	10.3	2,354	4.4	14	26.4	11,222	156.6	2.9	915,965
Florida	42	2.5	2,177	4.0	52	31.2	14,324	135.0	2.5	3,214,857
Pennsylvania	44	2.7	528	1.0	12	6.3	11,964	121.7	2.3	2,765,636
Illinois	32	1.9	1,046	1.9	33	16.3	15,622	85.0	1.6	2,656,312
Oregon	22	1.3	896	1.7	41	14.7	16,407	70.2	1.3	3,192,909
Alaska	42	2.5	892	1.7	21	10.1	11,295	68.6	1.3	1,633,762
South Dakota	70	4.2	650	1.2	9	8.9	13,735	64.7	1.2	923,871
Nebraska	34	2.1	686	1.3	20	7.0	10,156	60.6	1.1	1,781,294
New Mexico	14	0.8	518	1.0	37	9.1	17,618	43.8	0.8	3,132,000
Maryland	29	1.8	550	1.0	19	4.6	8,391	38.4	0.7	1,324,828
Idaho	8	0.5	270	0.5	34	4.7	17,315	28.0	0.5	3,502,125
Ohio	18	1.1	114	0.2	6	2.0	17,912	27.4	0.5	1,522,111
Kentucky	20	1.2	399	0.7	20	5.4	13,481	25.2	0.5	1,260,400
North Dakota	54	3.3	511	0.9	9	3.8	7,350	20.6	0.4	381,815
Colorado	22	1.3	231	0.4	10	3.4	14,641	18.1	0.3	823,864
Alabama	5	0.3	191	0.4	38	1.7	9,105	15.0	0.3	2,998,800
D.C.	3	0.2	26	0.0	9	1.9	73,654	5.7	0.1	1,910,667
Wyoming	4	0.2	26	0.0	7	0.2	6,962	3.5	0.1	868,000
Maine	6	0.4	30	0.1	5	0.3	8,900	2.0	0.0	333,333
Arkansas	11	0.7	79	0.1	7	0.6	7,038	2.0	0.0	185,273
Texas	89	5.4	1,750*	-	-	(D)	-	(D)	-	-
North Carolina	53	3.2	175*	-	-	(D)	-	(D)	-	-
New York	26	1.6	375*	-	-	(D)	-	(D)	-	-
Michigan	20	1.2	175*	-	-	(D)	-	(D)	-	-
Georgia	16	1.0	175*	-	-	(D)	-	(D)	-	-
New Jersey	16	1.0	175*	-	-	(D)	-	(D)	-	-
Connecticut	15	0.9	375*	-	-	(D)	-	(D)	-	-
Kansas	15	0.9	175*	-	-	(D)	-	(D)	-	-
Mississippi	10	0.6	750*	-	-	(D)	-	(D)	-	-
Massachusetts	7	0.4	10*	-	-	(D)	-	(D)	-	-
Missouri	5	0.3	60*	-	-	(D)	-	(D)	-	-
Vermont	5	0.3	10*	-	-	(D)	-	(D)	-	-
Iowa	4	0.2	60*	-	-	(D)	-	(D)	-	-
Virginia	4	0.2	60*	-	-	(D)	-	(D)	-	-
Indiana	3	0.2	60*	-	-	(D)	-	(D)	-	-
West Virginia	3	0.2	60*	-	-	(D)	-	(D)	-	-
New Hampshire	2	0.1	10*	-	-	(D)	-	(D)	-	-
Rhode Island	2	0.1	375*	-	-	(D)	-	(D)	-	-

Source: 1997 *Economic Census*. The states are in descending order of revenues or establishments (if revenue data are missing for the majority). The symbol (D) appears when data are withheld to prevent disclosure of competitive information. States marked with (D) are sorted by number of establishments. A dash (-) indicates that the data element cannot be calculated. * indicates the midpoint of a range; 175, for example is the range 100-249. Shaded *states* on the state map indicate those states which have proportionately greater representation in the industry than would be indicated by the state's population; the ratio is based on total revenues or number of establishments. Shaded *regions* indicate where the industry is regionally most concentrated.

NAICS 713910 - GOLF COURSES AND COUNTRY CLUBS

GENERAL STATISTICS

Year	Establishments (number)	Employment (number)	Payroll ($ million)	Revenues ($ million)	Employees per Establishment (number)	Revenues per Establishment ($)	Payroll per Employee ($)
1997	11,758	276,078	5,023.0	14,220.0	23.5	1,209,389	18,194

Source: *Economic Census of the United States*, 1997. This is a newly defined industry. Data for prior years were unavailable at the time of publication but may become available over time.

INDICES OF CHANGE

Year	Establishments (number)	Employment (number)	Payroll ($ million)	Revenues ($ million)	Employees per Establishment (number)	Revenues per Establishment ($)	Payroll per Employee ($)
1997	100.0	100.0	100.0	100.0	100.0	100.0	100.0

Sources: Same as General Statistics. The values shown reflect change from the base year, 1997. Values above 100 mean greater than 1997, values below 100 mean less than 1997, and a value of 100 in the 1982-96 or 1998-2001 period means same as 1997. Values followed by a 'p' are projections by the editors; 'e' stands for extrapolation. Data are the most recent available at this level of detail.

SIC INDUSTRIES RELATED TO NAICS 713910

Each new NAICS code represents an industry that used to be part of an SIC or a part of several SIC industries. Data in this table are shown to provide transitional information for these cases. All available data for the precursor SIC(s) are shown. Even if only a part of an SIC is included in the NAICS, *all* data for the SIC are reproduced. If the SIC industry is not marked as being a part (pt) of the NAICS, the entire industry is embedded in the NAICS data. The SIC composition of the new industry provides some hints of the relative importance of its "ancestors." Data marked with a 'p' are projected. Projections begin with 1982 data. Data earlier than 1990 are not shown but are reflected in the projections.

SIC	Industry	1990	1991	1992	1993	1994	1995	1996	1997
7992	**Public Golf Courses**								
	Establishments (number)	2,789	3,048	3,780	3,943	4,021	4,168	4,081p	4,220p
	Employment (thousands)	29.4	33.2	42.3	46.0	48.0	55.3	51.8p	54.6p
	Revenues ($ million)	2,254.0	2,386.0	2,609.0	2,828.0	3,059.0	3,584.0	3,976.0	4,087.6p
7997	**Membership Sports & Recreation Clubs (pt)**								
	Establishments (number)	13,089	13,560	14,727	14,674	14,624	14,544	14,800p	14,960p
	Employment (thousands)	242.1	247.5	258.6	264.8	268.4	277.7	283.6p	290.5p
	Revenues ($ million)	4,825.0	5,151.0	5,397.0	5,965.0	6,379.0	6,765.0	7,439.0	7,240.3p

Source: *Economic Census of the United States*, 1992, annual surveys of economic sectors conducted by the Bureau of the Census, and estimates or projections based on the 1982-1992 period; not all data are shown. 'e' marks estimates made by the editors; 'p' indicates projections based on time series. A dash (-) indicates that data for this SIC or year were not available. The abbreviation (pt) next to the industry name indicates that only a part of the industry is present within the NAICS data. If no (pt) is shown, the entire industry is contained within the NAICS data.

SELECTED RATIOS

For 1997	Avg. of Information	Analyzed Industry	Index	For 1997	Avg. of Information	Analyzed Industry	Index
Employees per establishment	16	23	147	Payroll per establishment	330,963	427,199	129
Revenue per establishment	1,057,073	1,209,389	114	Payroll as % of revenue	31	35	113
Revenue per employee	65,958	51,507	78	Payroll per employee	20,651	18,194	88

Sources: Same as General Statistics. The 'Average' column represents the average for the industry sector, in 1997, where the currently shown industry is classified. The Index shows the relationship between the Average and the Analyzed Industry. For example, 100 means that they are equal; 500 that the Analyzed Industry is five times the average; 50 means that the Analyzed Industry is half the national average. The abbreviation 'na' is used to show that data are 'not available'.

LEADING COMPANIES　　Number shown: **16**　　Total sales ($ mil): **1,320**　　Total employment (000): **24.0**

Company Name	Address				CEO Name	Phone	Co. Type	Sales ($ mil)	Empl. (000)
American Golf Corp.	2951 28th St	Santa Monica	CA	90405	David G. Price	310-664-4000	R	525	15.0
Rio Hotel and Casino Inc.	3700 W Flamingo	Las Vegas	NV	89103	Anthony A Marnell II	702-252-7733	P	392	5.0
Mount Snow Ltd.	Mountain Rd	Mount Snow	VT	05356	Scott Pierpoint	802-464-3333	S	153*	1.2
Evergreen Alliance Golf Ltd.	8505 Freeport Pkwy	Irving	TX	75063	Larry Corson	972-915-3673	R	71*	0.8
Resort at Squaw Creek	400 Squaw Creek	Olympic Valley	CA	96146		530-583-6300	R	38*	0.3
Peek 'N Peak Recreation Inc.	1405 Olde Rd	Clymer	NY	14724	NJ Cross	716-355-4141	R	37	0.8
Millstein Industries L.L.C.	PO Box K	Youngwood	PA	15697	Jack Millstein	724-925-1300	R	33*	<0.1
Cog Hill Second Inc.	12294 Archer Ave	Lemont	IL	60439	Frank Jemsek	630-257-5872	R	24*	0.3
Waterhouse Properties Inc.	670 Queen St	Honolulu	HI	96813	Edwin Wong	808-592-4800	R	20*	0.2
BSL Golf Corp.	2323 S Shepard Dr	Houston	TX	77019		713-522-4547	R	14*	0.2
Divot Golf Corp.	201 N Franklin St	Tampa	FL	33602	Joseph R Cellura	813-222-0611	P	4	0.1
Rancho Carlsbad	5200 Cam Real	Carlsbad	CA	92008		760-438-0332	R	3*	<0.1
Sunnybrook Golf Bowl	7191 E 17 Mile Rd	Sterling Heights	MI	48313	Randy Shank	810-264-2700	R	3	<0.1
Cocopah Bend RV & Golf Resort	6800 S Strand Ave	Yuma	AZ	85364		520-343-9300	R	1	<0.1
Cherry Creek Golf Course	P O Box 146	Youngwood	PA	15697		724-925-8665	D	1*	<0.1
Dye Designs International Inc.	5500 E Yale Ave	Denver	CO	80222	Perry O Dye	303-759-5353	R	1*	<0.1

Source: *Ward's Business Directory of U.S. Private and Public Companies*, Volumes 1 and 2, 2000. The company type code used is as follows: P - Public, R - Private, S - Subsidiary, D - Division, J - Joint Venture, A - Affiliate, G - Group, N - Company type not reported. Sales are in millions of dollars, employees are in thousands. An asterisk (*) indicates an estimated sales volume. The symbol < stands for 'less than'. Company names and addresses are truncated, in some cases, to fit into the available space.

REPRESENTATIVE NONPROFIT ORGANIZATIONS

Organization Name	Address				Phone	Income Range ($ mil)
Agawam Hunt	15 Roger Williams Ave	Rumford	RI	02916		1-5
Alpine Country Club Corp	80 Anderson Ave	Demarest	NJ	07627	201-768-2121	5-9
Alpine Country Club	4994 W Country Club Dr	Highland	UT	84003	801-226-1736	1-5
Altadena Valley Golf & Country Club	2651 Altavista Dr	Birmingham	AL	35243	205-967-5322	1-5
Andover Golf & Country Club Inc	6450 Todds Rd	Lexington	KY	40509	859-263-3710	1-5
Annandale Inc	PO Box 1939	Madison	MS	39130		1-5
Arrowhead Country Club	3675 Sheridan Lake Rd	Rapid City	SD	57702	605-342-6477	1-5
Astoria Golf & Country Club	PO Box 148	Astoria	OR	97103	503-861-2211	1-5
Augusta Country Club	PO Box 239	Manchester	ME	04351	207-623-3021	1-5
Beechmont Inc	29600 Chagrin Blvd	Cleveland	OH	44122	216-831-9100	5-9
Belle Meade Country Club	815 Belle Meade Blvd	Nashville	TN	37205	615-385-0150	5-9
Belmont Country Club Inc	PO Box 79130	Belmont	MA	02179		5-9
Berry Hills Country Club	1 Berry Hills Rd	Charleston	WV	25314	304-744-1393	1-5
Birmingham Country Club	1750 Saxon	Birmingham	MI	48009	248-723-2815	5-9
Blackhawk Country Club	599 Blackhawk Club Dr	Danville	CA	94506	925-736-6500	10-19
Blue Lakes Country Club Inc	PO Box 582	Twin Falls	ID	83303		1-5
Boca West Country Club	PO Box 3070	Boca Raton	FL	33431	561-483-6300	20-29
Brandywine Country Club	2822 Shipley Rd	Wilmington	DE	19810	302-478-2110	1-5
Briarwood Country Club	355 Deerfield Rd	Deerfield	IL	60015	847-945-2660	5-9
Burlington Country Club Corp	568 S Prospect St	Burlington	VT	05401	802-658-3856	1-5
Burlington Golf Club	2124 Sunnyside	Burlington	IA	52601	319-752-2769	1-5
Cape Fear Country Club Inc	1518 Country Club Rd	Wilmington	NC	28403	910-762-4751	5-9
Capital City Club Inc	7 Harris St NW	Atlanta	GA	30303	404-523-8221	10-19
Casper Country Club	PO Box 50037	Casper	WY	82605	307-237-1078	1-5
Cherry Hills Country Club	4125 S University Blvd	Englewood	CO	80110	303-761-9900	5-9
Chevy Chase Club Inc	6100 Connecticut Ave	Chevy Chase	MD	20815	301-652-4100	10-19
Columbia Club Inc	121 Monument Circle	Indianapolis	IN	46204	317-767-1361	5-9
Country Club of Darien	300 Mansfield Ave	Darien	CT	06820	203-655-9726	5-9
Country Club of Lincoln	3200 S 24th St	Lincoln	NE	68502		1-5
Country Club of Virginia Inc	6031 St Andrews LN	Richmond	VA	23226	804-288-2891	10-19
Crestview Country Club Assoc	1000 N 127th St E	Wichita	KS	67206	316-733-1344	5-9
Dallas Country Club	4100 Beverly Dr	Dallas	TX	75205	214-521-2151	10-19
Edina Country Club	5100 Wooddale Ave S	Edina	MN	55424	952-927-7151	5-9
Fargo Country Club Inc	509 26th Ave S	Fargo	ND	58103	701-237-9122	1-5
Fircrest Golf Club Inc	6520 Regents Blvd	Tacoma	WA	98466	253-564-6756	5-9
Forest Hills Country Club	36 Forest Club Dr	Chesterfield	MO	63005	636-227-5030	5-9
Greenville Country Club	PO Box 9358	Greenville	SC	29604	864-232-6771	5-9
Hilands Golf Club	714 Poly Dr	Billings	MT	59102	406-245-3049	1-5
Hobbs Country Club	PO Box 548	Hobbs	NM	88241	505-393-5167	1-5
Metairie Country Club	580 Woodvine Ave	Metairie	LA	70005	504-833-4671	5-9
Nashua Country Club	Fairway St	Nashua	NH	03060	603-888-0121	1-5
Nassau Country Club	St Andrews LN	Glen Cove	NY	11542	516-676-0554	10-19
National Republican Club of Capitol Hill	300 First St SE	Washington	DC	20003		1-5
Oklahoma City Golf & Country Club	7000 NW Grand Blvd	Oklahoma City	OK	73116		5-9
Phoenix Country Club	2901 N 7th St	Phoenix	AZ	85014	602-263-5208	5-9
Saucon Valley Country Club	2050 Saucon Valley Rd	Bethlehem	PA	18015	610-838-1199	10-19
University of the Ozarks	415 College Ave	Clarksville	AR	72830	501-754-3140	50+
Waialae Country Club	4997 Kahala Ave	Honolulu	HI	96816	808-734-2151	10-19
Westmoor Country Club	400 S Moorland Rd	Brookfield	WI	53005	262-796-7800	5-9

Source: National Directory of Nonprofit Organizations, 2000, Volumes 1 and 2, The Taft Group. The table shows a selection of organizations for illustration and does not constitute a complete selection from the source. The organizations are arranged in alphabetical order.

LOCATION BY STATE AND REGIONAL CONCENTRATION

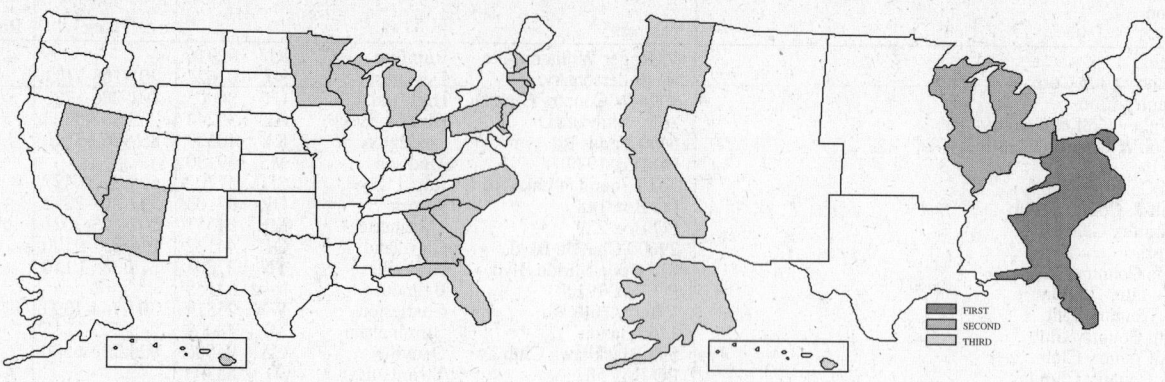

INDUSTRY DATA BY STATE

State	Establishments Total (number)	Establishments % of U.S.	Employment Total (number)	Employment % of U.S.	Employment Per Estab.	Payroll Total ($ mil.)	Payroll Per Empl. ($)	Revenues Total ($ mil.)	Revenues % of U.S.	Revenues Per Estab. ($)
California	717	6.1	31,657	11.5	44	561.3	17,730	1,613.0	11.3	2,249,622
Florida	657	5.6	32,769	11.9	50	504.5	15,396	1,372.5	9.7	2,089,040
Texas	589	5.0	18,611	6.7	32	302.1	16,232	899.8	6.3	1,527,715
New York	699	5.9	10,714	3.9	15	286.3	26,721	810.5	5.7	1,159,492
Pennsylvania	595	5.1	13,686	5.0	23	253.0	18,483	695.2	4.9	1,168,385
Ohio	643	5.5	12,984	4.7	20	230.3	17,738	665.1	4.7	1,034,437
Illinois	501	4.3	11,366	4.1	23	228.3	20,086	620.4	4.4	1,238,315
Michigan	640	5.4	8,248	3.0	13	211.8	25,674	593.4	4.2	927,189
North Carolina	444	3.8	11,123	4.0	25	183.4	16,484	506.5	3.6	1,140,872
New Jersey	227	1.9	6,559	2.4	29	156.6	23,872	456.1	3.2	2,009,313
Georgia	287	2.4	8,507	3.1	30	143.6	16,877	426.5	3.0	1,486,115
South Carolina	277	2.4	8,786	3.2	32	119.6	13,611	400.5	2.8	1,445,996
Massachusetts	301	2.6	5,404	2.0	18	133.4	24,686	385.5	2.7	1,280,625
Arizona	188	1.6	7,560	2.7	40	119.2	15,771	356.6	2.5	1,897,043
Virginia	227	1.9	6,714	2.4	30	104.9	15,622	291.3	2.0	1,283,361
Wisconsin	358	3.0	5,027	1.8	14	95.8	19,052	281.1	2.0	785,115
Maryland	141	1.2	5,235	1.9	37	98.2	18,754	262.8	1.8	1,864,000
Indiana	356	3.0	5,113	1.9	14	90.1	17,620	259.2	1.8	728,208
Minnesota	356	3.0	4,136	1.5	12	88.6	21,418	250.5	1.8	703,654
Connecticut	156	1.3	3,053	1.1	20	92.3	30,234	239.3	1.7	1,534,058
Missouri	262	2.2	4,708	1.7	18	84.7	17,996	227.8	1.6	869,309
Washington	221	1.9	4,017	1.5	18	76.7	19,094	214.1	1.5	968,742
Tennessee	215	1.8	4,599	1.7	21	74.1	16,102	208.7	1.5	970,484
Hawaii	50	0.4	2,532	0.9	51	51.2	20,239	176.0	1.2	3,520,920
Alabama	183	1.6	4,169	1.5	23	65.4	15,699	171.6	1.2	937,481
Colorado	132	1.1	2,958	1.1	22	63.2	21,359	158.5	1.1	1,200,902
Oregon	143	1.2	2,908	1.1	20	51.1	17,562	144.7	1.0	1,012,126
Kentucky	197	1.7	3,280	1.2	17	50.2	15,320	139.7	1.0	709,305
Iowa	309	2.6	2,849	1.0	9	52.8	18,521	137.8	1.0	445,896
Nevada	47	0.4	2,305	0.8	49	42.9	18,611	136.3	1.0	2,899,702
Oklahoma	117	1.0	2,566	0.9	22	37.4	14,573	99.0	0.7	846,137
Arkansas	152	1.3	2,282	0.8	15	33.6	14,721	93.4	0.7	614,283
Nebraska	157	1.3	1,822	0.7	12	30.0	16,451	87.4	0.6	556,389
Mississippi	133	1.1	2,108	0.8	16	27.8	13,203	80.9	0.6	608,316
New Hampshire	72	0.6	944	0.3	13	23.6	25,015	69.5	0.5	965,375
Delaware	32	0.3	1,270	0.5	40	24.8	19,528	59.0	0.4	1,845,156
Rhode Island	53	0.5	1,132	0.4	21	20.7	18,265	58.8	0.4	1,109,830
Louisiana	81	0.7	1,563	0.6	19	18.6	11,930	55.0	0.4	679,432
West Virginia	91	0.8	1,084	0.4	12	17.1	15,733	49.0	0.3	538,879
New Mexico	44	0.4	1,025	0.4	23	16.2	15,759	48.1	0.3	1,092,386
Idaho	71	0.6	738	0.3	10	14.9	20,238	44.3	0.3	623,352
Utah	52	0.4	898	0.3	17	15.9	17,725	40.1	0.3	771,865
Maine	90	0.8	458	0.2	5	13.0	28,452	37.7	0.3	418,822
Montana	67	0.6	489	0.2	7	9.8	20,082	27.1	0.2	403,985
South Dakota	63	0.5	540	0.2	9	9.4	17,341	23.1	0.2	366,714
Vermont	43	0.4	209	0.1	5	7.5	35,923	22.8	0.2	530,302
Wyoming	33	0.3	312	0.1	9	6.2	19,965	18.6	0.1	562,758
North Dakota	66	0.6	328	0.1	5	5.2	15,759	14.4	0.1	218,258
D.C.	5	-	175 *	-	-	(D)	-	(D)	-	-

Source: 1997 *Economic Census*. The states are in descending order of revenues or establishments (if revenue data are missing for the majority). The symbol (D) appears when data are withheld to prevent disclosure of competitive information. States marked with (D) are sorted by number of establishments. A dash (-) indicates that the data element cannot be calculated. * indicates the midpoint of a range; 175, for example is the range 100-249. Shaded *states* on the state map indicate those states which have proportionately greater representation in the industry than would be indicated by the state's population; the ratio is based on total revenues or number of establishments. Shaded *regions* indicate where the industry is regionally most concentrated.

NAICS 713920 - SKIING FACILITIES

GENERAL STATISTICS

Year	Establishments (number)	Employment (number)	Payroll ($ million)	Revenues ($ million)	Employees per Establishment (number)	Revenues per Establishment ($)	Payroll per Employee ($)
1997	379	58,513	431.0	1,341.0	154.4	3,538,259	7,366

Source: *Economic Census of the United States*, 1997. This is a newly defined industry. Data for prior years were unavailable at the time of publication but may become available over time.

INDICES OF CHANGE

Year	Establishments (number)	Employment (number)	Payroll ($ million)	Revenues ($ million)	Employees per Establishment (number)	Revenues per Establishment ($)	Payroll per Employee ($)
1997	100.0	100.0	100.0	100.0	100.0	100.0	100.0

Sources: Same as General Statistics. The values shown reflect change from the base year, 1997. Values above 100 mean greater than 1997, values below 100 mean less than 1997, and a value of 100 in the 1982-96 or 1998-2001 period means same as 1997. Values followed by a 'p' are projections by the editors; 'e' stands for extrapolation. Data are the most recent available at this level of detail.

SIC INDUSTRIES RELATED TO NAICS 713920

Each new NAICS code represents an industry that used to be part of an SIC or a part of several SIC industries. Data in this table are shown to provide transitional information for these cases. All available data for the precursor SIC(s) are shown. Even if only a part of an SIC is included in the NAICS, *all* data for the SIC are reproduced. If the SIC industry is not marked as being a part (pt) of the NAICS, the entire industry is embedded in the NAICS data. The SIC composition of the new industry provides some hints of the relative importance of its "ancestors." Data marked with a 'p' are projected. Projections begin with 1982 data. Data earlier than 1990 are not shown but are reflected in the projections.

SIC	Industry	1990	1991	1992	1993	1994	1995	1996	1997
7999	**Amusement & Recreation nec (pt)**								
	Establishments (number)	-	-	21,717	-	-	-	-	-
	Employment (thousands)	-	-	215.8	-	-	-	-	-
	Revenues ($ million)	-	-	10,430.3	-	-	-	-	-

Source: *Economic Census of the United States*, 1992, annual surveys of economic sectors conducted by the Bureau of the Census, and estimates or projections based on the 1982-1992 period; not all data are shown. 'e' marks estimates made by the editors; 'p' indicates projections based on time series. A dash (-) indicates that data for this SIC or year were not available. The abbreviation (pt) next to the industry name indicates that only a part of the industry is present within the NAICS data. If no (pt) is shown, the entire industry is contained within the NAICS data.

SELECTED RATIOS

For 1997	Avg. of Information	Analyzed Industry	Index	For 1997	Avg. of Information	Analyzed Industry	Index
Employees per establishment	16	154	963	Payroll per establishment	330,963	1,137,203	344
Revenue per establishment	1,057,073	3,538,259	335	Payroll as % of revenue	31	32	103
Revenue per employee	65,958	22,918	35	Payroll per employee	20,651	7,366	36

Sources: Same as General Statistics. The 'Average' column represents the average for the industry sector, in 1997, where the currently shown industry is classified. The Index shows the relationship between the Average and the Analyzed Industry. For example, 100 means that they are equal; 500 that the Analyzed Industry is five times the average; 50 means that the Analyzed Industry is half the national average. The abbreviation 'na' is used to show that data are 'not available'.

LEADING COMPANIES

No company data available for this industry.

LOCATION BY STATE AND REGIONAL CONCENTRATION

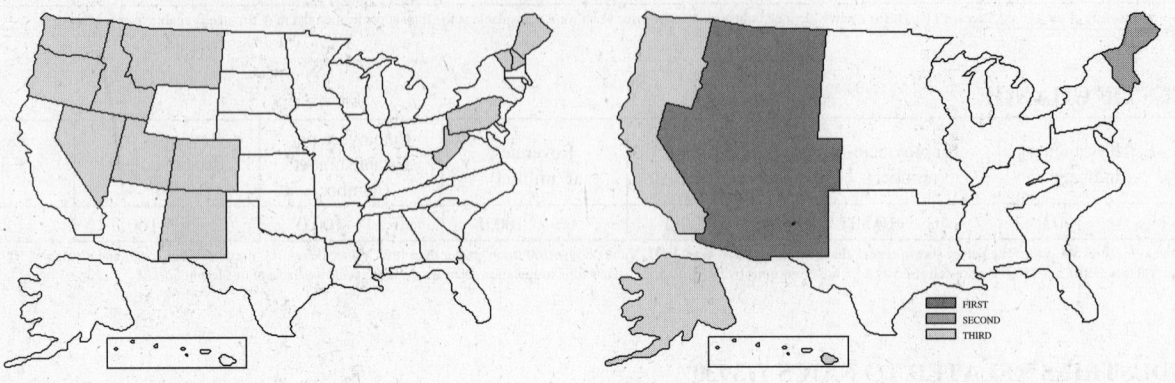

FIRST
SECOND
THIRD

INDUSTRY DATA BY STATE

State	Establishments Total (number)	% of U.S.	Employment Total (number)	% of U.S.	Per Estab.	Payroll Total ($ mil.)	Per Empl. ($)	Revenues Total ($ mil.)	% of U.S.	Per Estab. ($)
Colorado	37	9.8	10,820	18.5	292	148.3	13,710	430.9	32.1	11,646,216
California	34	9.0	6,356	10.9	187	47.6	7,489	145.1	10.8	4,266,765
Vermont	14	3.7	3,804	6.5	272	36.6	9,616	138.2	10.3	9,870,357
Utah	10	2.6	2,914	5.0	291	23.1	7,932	82.2	6.1	8,224,400
Pennsylvania	21	5.5	4,247	7.3	202	19.0	4,467	64.2	4.8	3,057,857
Maine	12	3.2	2,346	4.0	195	17.7	7,566	49.3	3.7	4,105,083
Oregon	12	3.2	2,138	3.7	178	11.8	5,537	40.4	3.0	3,365,583
New Hampshire	13	3.4	2,043	3.5	157	11.8	5,787	40.0	3.0	3,079,923
Washington	19	5.0	2,686	4.6	141	15.1	5,611	34.4	2.6	1,810,474
New York	44	11.6	3,670	6.3	83	12.3	3,341	33.5	2.5	761,432
New Mexico	6	1.6	1,529	2.6	255	8.9	5,827	27.1	2.0	4,522,333
Michigan	13	3.4	1,437	2.5	111	7.4	5,172	23.8	1.8	1,832,692
Minnesota	10	2.6	1,395	2.4	140	7.7	5,498	22.0	1.6	2,197,200
Massachusetts	16	4.2	1,637	2.8	102	5.5	3,356	21.0	1.6	1,311,187
Wisconsin	18	4.7	2,148	3.7	119	6.6	3,057	19.7	1.5	1,092,444
North Carolina	8	2.1	607	1.0	76	5.0	8,310	18.2	1.4	2,269,375
Montana	14	3.7	781	1.3	56	4.1	5,265	14.5	1.1	1,039,286
West Virginia	5	1.3	535	0.9	107	3.5	6,488	12.6	0.9	2,513,400
Ohio	8	2.1	791	1.4	99	4.3	5,378	9.7	0.7	1,212,250
Idaho	12	3.2	832	1.4	69	3.4	4,067	8.8	0.7	729,750
Nevada	4	1.1	371	0.6	93	2.7	7,313	8.5	0.6	2,113,500
Connecticut	6	1.6	1,141	1.9	190	2.9	2,564	6.8	0.5	1,127,333
Iowa	4	1.1	173	0.3	43	1.2	6,786	4.4	0.3	1,095,000
Alaska	5	1.3	128	0.2	26	0.7	5,492	2.0	0.2	405,400
North Dakota	3	0.8	79	0.1	26	0.2	2,101	0.6	0.0	209,333
Wyoming	6	1.6	750*	-	-	(D)	-	(D)	-	-
Missouri	4	1.1	175*	-	-	(D)	-	(D)	-	-
Arizona	3	0.8	375*	-	-	(D)	-	(D)	-	-
Indiana	3	0.8	375*	-	-	(D)	-	(D)	-	-
South Dakota	3	0.8	175*	-	-	(D)	-	(D)	-	-
Tennessee	3	0.8	375*	-	-	(D)	-	(D)	-	-
Illinois	2	0.5	175*	-	-	(D)	-	(D)	-	-
New Jersey	2	0.5	375*	-	-	(D)	-	(D)	-	-
Virginia	2	0.5	750*	-	-	(D)	-	(D)	-	-
Georgia	1	0.3	60*	-	-	(D)	-	(D)	-	-
Maryland	1	0.3	175*	-	-	(D)	-	(D)	-	-
Rhode Island	1	0.3	175*	-	-	(D)	-	(D)	-	-

Source: 1997 Economic Census. The states are in descending order of revenues or establishments (if revenue data are missing for the majority). The symbol (D) appears when data are withheld to prevent disclosure of competitive information. States marked with (D) are sorted by number of establishments. A dash (-) indicates that the data element cannot be calculated. * indicates the midpoint of a range; 175, for example is the range 100-249. Shaded *states* on the state map indicate those states which have proportionately greater representation in the industry than would be indicated by the state's population; the ratio is based on total revenues or number of establishments. Shaded *regions* indicate where the industry is regionally most concentrated.

NAICS 713930 - MARINAS*

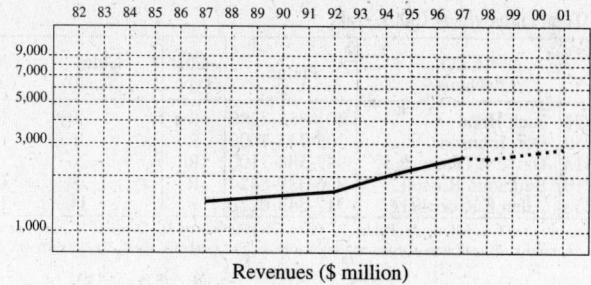

Revenues ($ million)

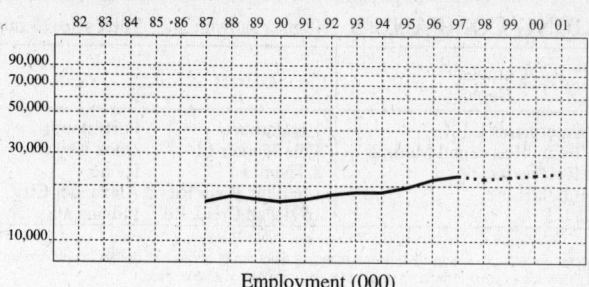

Employment (000)

GENERAL STATISTICS

Year	Establishments (number)	Employment (number)	Payroll ($ million)	Revenues ($ million)	Employees per Establishment (number)	Revenues per Establishment ($)	Payroll per Employee ($)
1982	-	-	-	-	-	-	-
1983	-	-	-	-	-	-	-
1984	-	-	-	-	-	-	-
1985	-	-	-	-	-	-	-
1986	-	-	-	-	-	-	-
1987	2,641	16,433	263.0	1,455.0	6.2	550,928	16,004
1988	2,595	17,608	329.0	1,494.0	6.8	575,723	18,685
1989	2,398	16,968	320.0	1,533.0	7.1	639,283	18,859
1990	2,537	16,443	322.0	1,573.0	6.5	620,024	19,583
1991	2,837	16,915	356.0	1,612.0	6.0	568,206	21,046
1992	3,348	17,913	346.0	1,651.0	5.4	493,130	19,316
1993	3,613	18,476	379.0	1,829.0 e	5.1	506,228	20,513
1994	3,763	18,496	403.0	2,007.0 e	4.9	533,351	21,788
1995	3,772	19,692	432.0	2,185.0 e	5.2	579,268	21,938
1996	4,202	21,733	490.0	2,363.0 e	5.2	562,351	22,546
1997	4,217	22,765	517.0	2,541.0	5.4	602,561	22,710
1998	4,447 p	21,876 p	511.0 p	2,493.0 p	4.9 p	560,603 p	23,359 p
1999	4,644 p	22,440 p	533.0 p	2,601.0 p	4.8 p	560,078 p	23,752 p
2000	4,841 p	23,004 p	555.0 p	2,710.0 p	4.8 p	559,802 p	24,126 p
2001	5,038 p	23,567 p	577.0 p	2,819.0 p	4.7 p	559,547 p	24,483 p

Sources: *Economic Census of the United States*, 1982, 1987, 1992, 1997. Establishment counts, employment, and payroll are from *County Business Patterns* for non-Census years. In non-Census years, industries in the Manufacturing range under SIC coding include data from the *Annual Survey of Manufactures* (*ASM*); those in the old Services range include data from the *Services Annual Survey* (*SAS*). Values followed by a 'p' are projections by the editors. Extrapolations are marked by an 'e'. Data are the most recent available at this level of detail.

INDICES OF CHANGE

Year	Establishments (number)	Employment (number)	Payroll ($ million)	Revenues ($ million)	Employees per Establishment (number)	Revenues per Establishment ($)	Payroll per Employee ($)
1982	-	-	-	-	-	-	-
1987	62.6	72.2	50.9	57.3	115.3	91.4	70.5
1992	79.4	78.7	66.9	65.0	99.1	81.8	85.1
1993	85.7	81.2	73.3	72.0 e	94.7	84.0	90.3
1994	89.2	81.2	77.9	79.0 e	91.0	88.5	95.9
1995	89.4	86.5	83.6	86.0 e	96.7	96.1	96.6
1996	99.6	95.5	94.8	93.0 e	95.8	93.3	99.3
1997	100.0	100.0	100.0	100.0	100.0	100.0	100.0
1998	105.5 p	96.1 p	98.8 p	98.1 p	91.1 p	93.0 p	102.9 p
1999	110.1 p	98.6 p	103.1 p	102.4 p	89.5 p	92.9 p	104.6 p
2000	114.8 p	101.0 p	107.4 p	106.7 p	88.0 p	92.9 p	106.2 p
2001	119.5 p	103.5 p	111.6 p	110.9 p	86.7 p	92.9 p	107.8 p

Sources: Same as General Statistics. The values shown reflect change from the base year, 1997. Values above 100 mean greater than 1997, values below 100 mean less than 1997, and a value of 100 in the 1982-96 or 1998-2001 period means same as 1997. Values followed by a 'p' are projections by the editors; 'e' stands for extrapolation. Data are the most recent available at this level of detail.

SELECTED RATIOS

For 1997	Avg. of Information	Analyzed Industry	Index	For 1997	Avg. of Information	Analyzed Industry	Index
Employees per establishment	16	5	34	Payroll per establishment	330,963	122,599	37
Revenue per establishment	1,057,073	602,561	57	Payroll as % of revenue	31	20	65
Revenue per employee	65,958	111,619	169	Payroll per employee	20,651	22,710	110

Sources: Same as General Statistics. The 'Average' column represents the average for the industry sector, in 1997, where the currently shown industry is classified. The Index shows the relationship between the Average and the Analyzed Industry. For example, 100 means that they are equal; 500 that the Analyzed Industry is five times the average; 50 means that the Analyzed Industry is half the national average. The abbreviation 'na' is used to show that data are 'not available'.

*Equivalent to SIC 4493.

LEADING COMPANIES   Number shown: 5   Total sales ($ mil): 112   Total employment (000): 1.4

Company Name	Address				CEO Name	Phone	Co. Type	Sales ($ mil)	Empl. (000)
Hood Enterprises L.L.C.	1 L Harbor	Portsmouth	RI	02871	Rick Hood	401-683-7280	R	30*	0.2
Hawk's Cay Resort and Marina	Mile Marker 61	Duck Key	FL	33050	Don Johnson	305-743-7000	R	26*	0.2
Seven Resorts Inc.	8 Thomas	Irvine	CA	92618	David A Ohanesian	949-588-7100	R	26	0.7
Russell Lands Inc.	1 Willow Point Rd	Alexander City	AL	35010	Benjamin Russell	256-329-8424	R	19	0.2
Marina L.P.	1691 Fall Creek Rd	Indianapolis	IN	46256	Allen E Rosenberg	317-845-0270	P	11	<0.1

Source: *Ward's Business Directory of U.S. Private and Public Companies*, Volumes 1 and 2, 2000. The company type code used is as follows: P - Public, R - Private, S - Subsidiary, D - Division, J - Joint Venture, A - Affiliate, G - Group, N - Company type not reported. Sales are in millions of dollars, employees are in thousands. An asterisk (*) indicates an estimated sales volume. The symbol < stands for 'less than'. Company names and addresses are truncated, in some cases, to fit into the available space.

LOCATION BY STATE AND REGIONAL CONCENTRATION

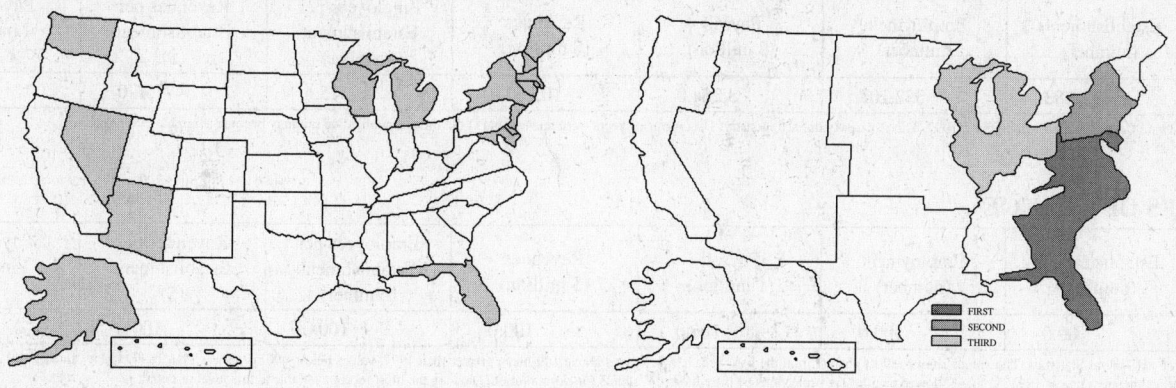

FIRST
SECOND
THIRD

INDUSTRY DATA BY STATE

State	Establishments Total (number)	Establishments % of U.S.	Employment Total (number)	Employment % of U.S.	Employment Per Estab.	Payroll Total ($ mil.)	Payroll Per Empl. ($)	Revenues Total ($ mil.)	Revenues % of U.S.	Revenues Per Estab. ($)
Florida	487	11.5	3,572	15.7	7	69.1	19,345	344.3	13.5	707,074
New York	407	9.7	1,582	6.9	4	47.7	30,124	272.5	10.7	669,627
California	259	6.1	1,906	8.4	7	43.2	22,690	202.8	8.0	782,857
Michigan	232	5.5	1,083	4.8	5	26.9	24,836	141.0	5.5	607,599
Maryland	206	4.9	1,194	5.2	6	26.5	22,193	113.8	4.5	552,223
New Jersey	213	5.1	865	3.8	4	24.2	28,024	112.4	4.4	527,822
Massachusetts	129	3.1	773	3.4	6	22.7	29,413	110.1	4.3	853,767
Texas	194	4.6	1,139	5.0	6	24.5	21,515	106.7	4.2	549,866
Connecticut	113	2.7	699	3.1	6	22.7	32,506	91.0	3.6	805,283
Wisconsin	96	2.3	531	2.3	6	12.7	23,838	75.0	2.9	780,927
Ohio	140	3.3	714	3.1	5	15.8	22,127	74.8	2.9	534,164
Arizona	44	1.0	396	1.7	9	8.3	20,904	59.7	2.4	1,357,795
Virginia	122	2.9	700	3.1	6	13.9	19,801	57.1	2.2	468,098
Washington	124	2.9	706	3.1	6	11.3	16,024	55.0	2.2	443,887
North Carolina	110	2.6	542	2.4	5	11.0	20,231	54.6	2.1	496,573
Illinois	91	2.2	418	1.8	5	11.1	26,548	52.0	2.0	571,297
Missouri	86	2.0	408	1.8	5	8.2	20,181	51.8	2.0	602,837
Georgia	66	1.6	453	2.0	7	9.9	21,817	48.8	1.9	739,697
Maine	85	2.0	454	2.0	5	11.7	25,769	45.7	1.8	538,012
Louisiana	86	2.0	451	2.0	5	9.1	20,100	38.4	1.5	445,977
Rhode Island	53	1.3	344	1.5	6	10.5	30,512	36.6	1.4	690,094
Tennessee	101	2.4	480	2.1	5	7.5	15,604	35.7	1.4	353,139
New Hampshire	42	1.0	201	0.9	5	5.2	25,896	33.7	1.3	801,714
Kentucky	57	1.4	324	1.4	6	7.1	22,052	32.3	1.3	566,000
Indiana	54	1.3	213	0.9	4	4.5	21,183	30.6	1.2	566,352
Minnesota	60	1.4	239	1.0	4	6.5	27,042	30.1	1.2	502,150
Alabama	62	1.5	292	1.3	5	4.7	16,055	28.5	1.1	459,903
South Carolina	66	1.6	379	1.7	6	5.4	14,317	27.3	1.1	413,485
Oklahoma	47	1.1	249	1.1	5	4.2	17,020	22.2	0.9	471,638
Iowa	28	0.7	133	0.6	5	3.3	25,090	18.9	0.7	674,500
Nevada	12	0.3	142	0.6	12	2.9	20,338	16.4	0.6	1,369,750
Pennsylvania	40	0.9	121	0.5	3	2.9	23,595	15.4	0.6	385,050
Arkansas	47	1.1	152	0.7	3	2.4	15,474	13.7	0.5	292,106
Oregon	43	1.0	123	0.5	3	2.4	19,171	11.2	0.4	261,395
Alaska	25	0.6	87	0.4	3	2.5	28,264	10.4	0.4	417,640
Delaware	11	0.3	119	0.5	11	2.3	18,975	8.5	0.3	776,636
Mississippi	18	0.4	127	0.6	7	1.7	13,087	7.8	0.3	434,722
Colorado	27	0.6	52	0.2	2	1.6	30,481	7.3	0.3	271,889
Vermont	12	0.3	51	0.2	4	1.4	27,255	6.0	0.2	500,333
Utah	10	0.2	41	0.2	4	1.2	28,927	5.5	0.2	549,500
Kansas	14	0.3	35	0.2	3	0.8	22,171	5.2	0.2	367,929
Hawaii	10	0.2	65	0.3	7	1.1	16,938	4.2	0.2	415,200
Montana	13	0.3	18	0.1	1	0.9	47,500	4.1	0.2	312,231
Idaho	14	0.3	41	0.2	3	0.6	13,415	4.0	0.2	288,714
South Dakota	5	0.1	27	0.1	5	0.4	16,630	3.9	0.2	787,800
New Mexico	6	0.1	39	0.2	7	0.6	15,154	3.4	0.1	569,833
Nebraska	13	0.3	20	0.1	2	0.5	25,700	3.4	0.1	262,846
D.C.	4	0.1	23	0.1	6	0.5	20,174	1.8	0.1	444,750
North Dakota	7	0.2	10	0.0	1	0.1	9,600	1.3	0.1	183,571
West Virginia	19	0.5	60*	-	-	(D)	-	(D)	-	-
Wyoming	7	0.2	10*	-	-	(D)	-	(D)	-	-

Source: 1997 *Economic Census*. The states are in descending order of revenues or establishments (if revenue data are missing for the majority). The symbol (D) appears when data are withheld to prevent disclosure of competitive information. States marked with (D) are sorted by number of establishments. A dash (-) indicates that the data element cannot be calculated. * indicates the midpoint of a range; 175, for example is the range 100-249. Shaded *states* on the state map indicate those states which have proportionately greater representation in the industry than would be indicated by the state's population; the ratio is based on total revenues or number of establishments. Shaded *regions* indicate where the industry is regionally most concentrated.

NAICS 713940 - FITNESS AND RECREATIONAL SPORTS CENTERS

GENERAL STATISTICS

Year	Establishments (number)	Employment (number)	Payroll ($ million)	Revenues ($ million)	Employees per Establishment (number)	Revenues per Establishment ($)	Payroll per Employee ($)
1997	21,283	332,103	3,264.0	10,162.0	15.6	477,470	9,828

Source: *Economic Census of the United States*, 1997. This is a newly defined industry. Data for prior years were unavailable at the time of publication but may become available over time.

INDICES OF CHANGE

Year	Establishments (number)	Employment (number)	Payroll ($ million)	Revenues ($ million)	Employees per Establishment (number)	Revenues per Establishment ($)	Payroll per Employee ($)
1997	100.0	100.0	100.0	100.0	100.0	100.0	100.0

Sources: Same as General Statistics. The values shown reflect change from the base year, 1997. Values above 100 mean greater than 1997, values below 100 mean less than 1997, and a value of 100 in the 1982-96 or 1998-2001 period means same as 1997. Values followed by a 'p' are projections by the editors; 'e' stands for extrapolation. Data are the most recent available at this level of detail.

SIC INDUSTRIES RELATED TO NAICS 713940

Each new NAICS code represents an industry that used to be part of an SIC or a part of several SIC industries. Data in this table are shown to provide transitional information for these cases. All available data for the precursor SIC(s) are shown. Even if only a part of an SIC is included in the NAICS, *all* data for the SIC are reproduced. If the SIC industry is not marked as being a part (pt) of the NAICS, the entire industry is embedded in the NAICS data. The SIC composition of the new industry provides some hints of the relative importance of its "ancestors." Data marked with a 'p' are projected. Projections begin with 1982 data. Data earlier than 1990 are not shown but are reflected in the projections.

SIC	Industry	1990	1991	1992	1993	1994	1995	1996	1997
7991	**Physical Fitness Facilities**								
	Establishments (number)	7,723	8,098	9,216	9,689	9,813	10,057	9,816p	9,977p
	Employment (thousands)	115.0	119.1	129.9	147.8	154.7	163.1	166.3p	173.9p
	Revenues ($ million)	3,623.0	3,449.0	4,135.0	3,961.0	4,033.0	4,412.0	4,970.0	4,914.5p
7997	**Membership Sports & Recreation Clubs (pt)**								
	Establishments (number)	13,089	13,560	14,727	14,674	14,624	14,544	14,800p	14,960p
	Employment (thousands)	242.1	247.5	258.6	264.8	268.4	277.7	283.6p	290.5p
	Revenues ($ million)	4,825.0	5,151.0	5,397.0	5,965.0	6,379.0	6,765.0	7,439.0	7,240.3p
7999	**Amusement & Recreation nec (pt)**								
	Establishments (number)	-	-	21,717	-	-	-	-	-
	Employment (thousands)	-	-	215.8	-	-	-	-	-
	Revenues ($ million)	-	-	10,430.3	-	-	-	-	-

Source: *Economic Census of the United States*, 1992, annual surveys of economic sectors conducted by the Bureau of the Census, and estimates or projections based on the 1982-1992 period; not all data are shown. 'e' marks estimates made by the editors; 'p' indicates projections based on time series. A dash (-) indicates that data for this SIC or year were not available. The abbreviation (pt) next to the industry name indicates that only a part of the industry is present within the NAICS data. If no (pt) is shown, the entire industry is contained within the NAICS data.

SELECTED RATIOS

For 1997	Avg. of Information	Analyzed Industry	Index	For 1997	Avg. of Information	Analyzed Industry	Index
Employees per establishment	16	16	97	Payroll per establishment	330,963	153,362	46
Revenue per establishment	1,057,073	477,470	45	Payroll as % of revenue	31	32	103
Revenue per employee	65,958	30,599	46	Payroll per employee	20,651	9,828	48

Sources: Same as General Statistics. The 'Average' column represents the average for the industry sector, in 1997, where the currently shown industry is classified. The Index shows the relationship between the Average and the Analyzed Industry. For example, 100 means that they are equal; 500 that the Analyzed Industry is five times the average; 50 means that the Analyzed Industry is half the national average. The abbreviation 'na' is used to show that data are 'not available'.

LEADING COMPANIES   Number shown: **45**   Total sales ($ mil): **2,309**   Total employment (000): **47.0**

Company Name	Address				CEO Name	Phone	Co. Type	Sales ($ mil)	Empl. (000)
Bally Total Fitness Holding Corp.	8700 W Bryn Mawr	Chicago	IL	60631	Lee S. Hillman	773-380-3000	P	728	15.0
Bally Total Fitness Corp.	8700 W Bryn Mawr	Chicago	IL	60631	Artur M Golberg	773-380-3000	S	661*	13.9
Clubsource	235 Montgomery St	San Francisco	CA	94104		415-986-2582	R	148*	1.5
Northwest Racquet Swim	5525 Cedar Lake Rd	St. Louis Park	MN	55416	Marvin Wolfenson	612-546-5474	S	119*	1.2
Club Sports International Inc.	1700 Broadway St	Denver	CO	80290	Burnett W Donoho	303-866-0800	R	115	4.5
Aveda Corp.	4000 Pheasant	Minneapolis	MN	55449	Nicole Rechelbacher	612-783-4000	S	88*	0.5
Sports Club Company Inc.	11100 Santa Monica	Los Angeles	CA	90025	D Michael Talla	310-479-5200	P	82	2.3
WW Group Inc.	P O Box 9072	Farmington Hills	MI	48333	Florine Mark	248-553-8555	R	50	3.0
Worldwide Television	PO Box 583081	Minneapolis	MN	55458		612-649-4811	N	38	<0.1
New York Health & Racquet Club	3 NY Plz	New York	NY	10004	Kevin Sagafi	212-797-1500	R	37*	0.4
Health Fitness Corp.	3500 West 80th St	Bloomington	MN	55431	Loren S Brink	612-831-6830	P	26	2.2
Glenwood Hot Springs Lodge	401 N River Rd	Glenwood Sprgs	CO	81601	Henry A Bosco	970-945-6571	R	23*	0.2
Physicians Weight Loss Centers	395 Sprgside Dr	Akron	OH	44333	Charles E Sekeres	330-666-7952	R	22*	<0.1
Brick Bodies Fitness Services Inc.	201 O Padonia	Cockeysville	MD	21030	Lynn Brick	410-252-8058	R	19*	0.2
Preston Wynne Salon	14567 Big Basin	Saratoga	CA	95070	Peggy Borgman	408-741-5525	R	19*	<0.1
Beverly Hills Weight Loss	20 Arpt Rd	Gilford	NH	03246	Ralph Cutillo	401-683-6620	R	18*	0.2
Denver Athletic Club	1325 Glenarm Pl	Denver	CO	80204	Rick Watson	303-534-1211	R	13*	0.1
Australian Body Works	6331 Roswell Rd	Atlanta	GA	30328	Tony Deleede	678-686-4500	R	11	0.5
Seattle Athletic Club Downtown	2020 Western Ave	Seattle	WA	98121		206-443-1111	R	11*	0.1
Jim Boltin Enterprises Inc.	8320 Hwy 107	Sherwood	AR	72120	Jim Bottin	501-835-4569	R	10*	0.1
Aerobics & Fitness Association	15250 Ventura Blvd	Sherman Oaks	CA	91403	Linda Pfeffer, RN	818-905-0040	R	9	<0.1
Mitchell's Salon and Day Spa Inc.	8118 Montgomery	Cincinnati	OH	45236	Deborah Schmidt	513-793-0900	R	8*	0.2
Ronnie Lotts' Club Fitness	5434 Thornwood Dr	San Jose	CA	95123		408-226-5688	R	8*	<0.1
Corporate Sports Unlimited Inc.	6400 Highlands	Smyrna	GA	30082	Donald Whitney	770-432-0100	R	7*	0.1
Decathlon Hotel and Athletic Club	1700 E 79th St	Bloomington	MN	55425		612-854-7777	R	5	0.1
Albert L Schultz	655 Arastradero Rd	Palo Alto	CA	94303	Sandy Boovad	650-493-9400	R	4*	<0.1
International Wellness	1630 Welton St	Denver	CO	80202	Tom Lyneis	303-623-2100	S	4*	<0.1
Leisure World Health Clubs	9 Collinsport Dr	Collinsville	IL	62234	Mark Lymberopoulos	618-344-3095	R	4*	<0.1
Cincinnati Sports Club	3950 Red Bank Rd	Cincinnati	OH	45227	Tom Sirorini	513-527-4550	R	3*	<0.1
Pro-Robics	3811 NE 45th St	Seattle	WA	98105	Mark Pavlovic	206-524-9246	R	3	<0.1
21st Point	199 E Middlefield	Mountain View	CA	94043	Jim Nelson	650-969-1783	R	2*	<0.1
Keystone Athletic Club	10407 Clayton Rd	St. Louis	MO	63131	Nick Caruso	314-991-2220	R	2*	<0.1
Pinnalle Fitness Centre	1 Post St	San Francisco	CA	94104	John J Bagshaw	415-781-6400	R	2*	<0.1
Racquet Club of Columbus Ltd.	1100 Bethel Rd	Columbus	OH	43220	Jane Hendrix	614-457-5671	R	2*	<0.1
Anthony Snipes	1202 Chambers Rd	St. Louis	MO	63128	Anthony Snipes	314-522-9939	R	1*	<0.1
Fitness Firm	PO Box 2104	Vineyard Haven	MA	02568	Ann Richards Schot	508-693-5533	R	1*	<0.1
Fitness Fleet Inc.	6830 Cloisters Dr	McLean	VA	22101	Frederick A Daniels	703-448-6632	R	1	<0.1
Health Management Corp.	3200 Westown	W. Des Moines	IA	50266	Paul From	515-223-5111	R	1*	<0.1
Osmosis Partners Ltd.	209 Bohemian Hwy	Freestone	CA	95472		707-823-8231	R	1*	<0.1
Workout 4 Life, LLC DBA	2010 Jimmy Durante	Del Mar	CA	92014	David I Garfinkel	858-481-6226	R	1	<0.1
48 West Health and Fitness Club	1020 S 48th Ave	Yakima	WA	98908	Sharlyne R Powell	509-965-0115	R	1	<0.1
Cardiac Carr Co.	34976 Aspenwood	Willoughby	OH	44094	Margaret Carr	440-946-7888	R	1	<0.1
Thrash & Dangle Enterprises Inc.	2810 S Roosevelt St	Tempe	AZ	85282	Paul Diefenderfer	480-921-8322	R	0	<0.1
Gym Time Inc.	1730 E Elliot Rd	Tempe	AZ	85284	Scott Barclay	602-820-3774	R	0	<0.1
Pee Wee Workout Inc.	34976 Aspen Wood	Willoughby	OH	44094	Margaret Carr	440-946-7888	S	0	<0.1

Source: Ward's Business Directory of U.S. Private and Public Companies, Volumes 1 and 2, 2000. The company type code used is as follows: P - Public, R - Private, S - Subsidiary, D - Division, J - Joint Venture, A - Affiliate, G - Group, N - Company type not reported. Sales are in millions of dollars, employees are in thousands. An asterisk (*) indicates an estimated sales volume. The symbol < stands for 'less than'. Company names and addresses are truncated, in some cases, to fit into the available space.

LOCATION BY STATE AND REGIONAL CONCENTRATION

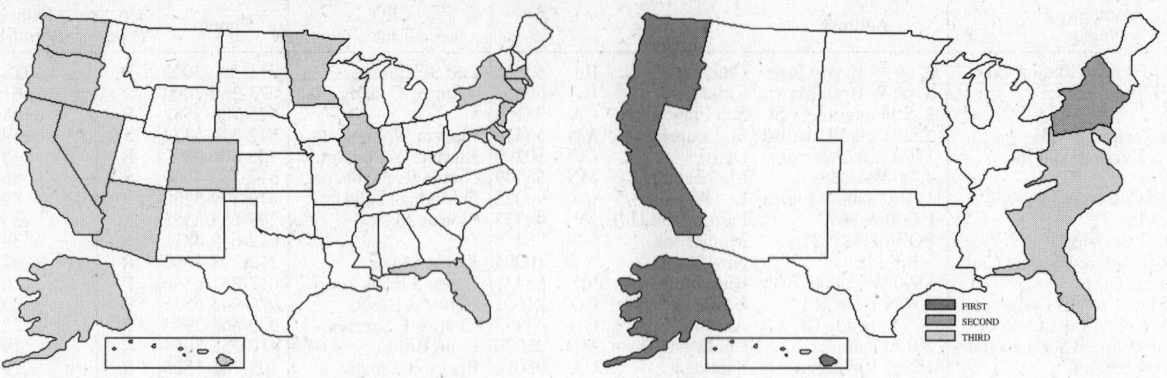

FIRST
SECOND
THIRD

INDUSTRY DATA BY STATE

State	Establishments Total (number)	% of U.S.	Employment Total (number)	% of U.S.	Per Estab.	Payroll Total ($ mil.)	Per Empl. ($)	Revenues Total ($ mil.)	% of U.S.	Per Estab. ($)
California	2,229	10.5	45,857	13.8	21	491.1	10,710	1,596.1	15.7	716,066
New York	1,520	7.1	27,286	8.2	18	330.5	12,112	1,146.7	11.3	754,407
Florida	1,093	5.1	16,926	5.1	15	185.1	10,935	587.3	5.8	537,347
Texas	1,212	5.7	17,736	5.3	15	175.0	9,868	546.4	5.4	450,822
Illinois	831	3.9	14,477	4.4	17	149.6	10,337	487.3	4.8	586,414
Pennsylvania	1,118	5.3	15,869	4.8	14	148.9	9,384	442.4	4.4	395,682
New Jersey	863	4.1	12,744	3.8	15	141.1	11,069	428.7	4.2	496,786
Massachusetts	708	3.3	12,965	3.9	18	142.3	10,978	419.6	4.1	592,664
Ohio	942	4.4	12,590	3.8	13	109.2	8,677	336.8	3.3	357,523
Michigan	682	3.2	9,627	2.9	14	87.4	9,079	288.7	2.8	423,280
Minnesota	364	1.7	10,969	3.3	30	98.9	9,020	261.0	2.6	717,022
Washington	524	2.5	8,602	2.6	16	82.7	9,613	259.3	2.6	494,882
Virginia	655	3.1	8,493	2.6	13	81.2	9,555	256.3	2.5	391,363
Maryland	484	2.3	7,827	2.4	16	75.1	9,599	229.9	2.3	474,936
Georgia	555	2.6	8,773	2.6	16	72.8	8,304	222.8	2.2	401,357
Arizona	277	1.3	6,374	1.9	23	66.2	10,378	214.3	2.1	773,776
Colorado	385	1.8	6,616	2.0	17	68.2	10,311	208.8	2.1	542,262
North Carolina	706	3.3	8,337	2.5	12	72.0	8,630	200.7	2.0	284,254
Connecticut	376	1.8	5,423	1.6	14	64.4	11,874	191.7	1.9	509,904
Wisconsin	376	1.8	7,168	2.2	19	53.0	7,397	150.5	1.5	400,375
Oregon	295	1.4	5,565	1.7	19	53.8	9,662	147.0	1.4	498,454
Missouri	443	2.1	5,271	1.6	12	50.3	9,552	145.5	1.4	328,506
Indiana	422	2.0	6,110	1.8	14	48.3	7,904	137.6	1.4	325,948
Tennessee	336	1.6	3,934	1.2	12	35.7	9,077	99.8	1.0	296,923
Louisiana	296	1.4	3,151	0.9	11	28.1	8,903	88.5	0.9	298,956
South Carolina	305	1.4	3,369	1.0	11	29.6	8,796	85.9	0.8	281,482
Kentucky	288	1.4	3,543	1.1	12	27.5	7,776	84.6	0.8	293,833
Alabama	320	1.5	3,806	1.1	12	28.2	7,400	83.0	0.8	259,297
Kansas	210	1.0	2,640	0.8	13	24.0	9,090	72.9	0.7	347,171
Nevada	90	0.4	2,015	0.6	22	21.8	10,800	68.7	0.7	762,856
Oklahoma	238	1.1	2,782	0.8	12	21.1	7,579	60.1	0.6	252,664
Hawaii	67	0.3	1,229	0.4	18	15.4	12,512	46.4	0.5	692,104
Iowa	195	0.9	2,492	0.8	13	15.7	6,285	45.8	0.5	234,938
Arkansas	192	0.9	1,800	0.5	9	15.1	8,390	45.1	0.4	234,932
New Hampshire	120	0.6	1,896	0.6	16	17.0	8,985	44.4	0.4	370,017
Utah	122	0.6	2,092	0.6	17	14.2	6,774	42.5	0.4	348,197
New Mexico	126	0.6	1,599	0.5	13	13.3	8,290	41.7	0.4	330,976
Maine	154	0.7	1,560	0.5	10	13.7	8,808	38.0	0.4	246,461
Nebraska	121	0.6	1,866	0.6	15	12.4	6,623	36.4	0.4	300,884
D.C.	48	0.2	566	0.2	12	7.7	13,689	32.6	0.3	679,375
Mississippi	174	0.8	1,084	0.3	6	8.9	8,167	31.4	0.3	180,580
Montana	105	0.5	1,485	0.4	14	9.2	6,191	28.9	0.3	274,771
Rhode Island	86	0.4	724	0.2	8	7.6	10,434	27.7	0.3	321,616
Alaska	69	0.3	1,207	0.4	17	8.8	7,302	26.6	0.3	386,072
Idaho	100	0.5	1,247	0.4	12	8.8	7,037	25.8	0.3	257,990
West Virginia	127	0.6	1,238	0.4	10	9.0	7,291	24.0	0.2	188,669
South Dakota	69	0.3	640	0.2	9	4.8	7,528	22.0	0.2	318,797
Vermont	90	0.4	906	0.3	10	6.9	7,668	20.0	0.2	222,533
Delaware	74	0.3	724	0.2	10	5.8	7,978	17.6	0.2	237,676
North Dakota	51	0.2	478	0.1	9	3.8	7,889	9.2	0.1	179,863
Wyoming	50	0.2	425	0.1	9	2.6	6,165	7.4	0.1	148,400

Source: 1997 *Economic Census*. The states are in descending order of revenues or establishments (if revenue data are missing for the majority). The symbol (D) appears when data are withheld to prevent disclosure of competitive information. States marked with (D) are sorted by number of establishments. A dash (-) indicates that the data element cannot be calculated. * indicates the midpoint of a range; 175, for example is the range 100-249. Shaded *states* on the state map indicate those states which have proportionately greater representation in the industry than would be indicated by the state's population; the ratio is based on total revenues or number of establishments. Shaded *regions* indicate where the industry is regionally most concentrated.

NAICS 713950 - BOWLING CENTERS*

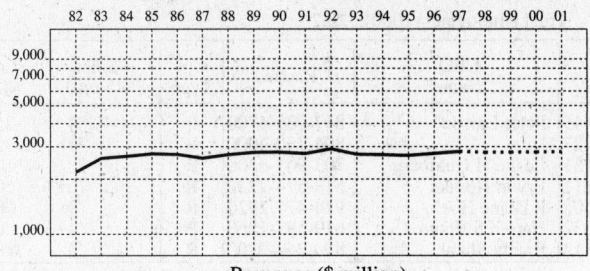

Revenues ($ million)

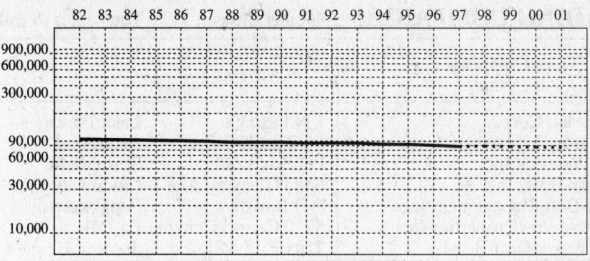

Employment (000)

GENERAL STATISTICS

Year	Establishments (number)	Employment (number)	Payroll ($ million)	Revenues ($ million)	Employees per Establishment (number)	Revenues per Establishment ($)	Payroll per Employee ($)
1982	6,872	105,406	629.0	2,184.0	15.3	317,811	5,967
1983	6,832 e	104,281 e	644.0 e	2,590.0	15.3 e	379,098 e	6,176 e
1984	6,792 e	103,156 e	658.0 e	2,659.0	15.2 e	391,490 e	6,379 e
1985	6,751 e	102,030 e	673.0 e	2,738.0	15.1 e	405,570 e	6,596 e
1986	6,711 e	100,905 e	688.0 e	2,720.0	15.0 e	405,305 e	6,818 e
1987	6,671	99,780	702.0	2,597.0	15.0	389,297	7,035
1988	6,200	97,058	735.0	2,712.0	15.7	437,419	7,573
1989	6,179	97,381	756.0	2,788.0	15.8	451,206	7,763
1990	5,982	97,392	786.0	2,800.0	16.3	468,071	8,070
1991	5,956	95,317	797.0	2,747.0	16.0	461,216	8,362
1992	6,093	95,701	804.0	2,915.0	15.7	478,418	8,401
1993	6,006	95,443	812.0	2,724.0	15.9	453,546	8,508
1994	5,855	92,962	814.0	2,709.0	15.9	462,681	8,756
1995	5,713	92,541	811.0	2,681.0	16.2	469,281	8,764
1996	5,651 e	90,293 e	816.0 e	2,751.0 e	16.0 e	486,816 e	9,037 e
1997	5,590	88,044	821.0	2,821.0	15.8	504,651	9,325
1998	5,489 p	88,774 p	849.0 p	2,790.0 p	16.2 p	508,289 p	9,564 p
1999	5,405 p	87,783 p	860.0 p	2,797.0 p	16.2 p	517,484 p	9,797 p
2000	5,321 p	86,792 p	870.0 p	2,804.0 p	16.3 p	526,969 p	10,024 p
2001	5,238 p	85,802 p	881.0 p	2,811.0 p	16.4 p	536,655 p	10,268 p

Sources: *Economic Census of the United States*, 1982, 1987, 1992, 1997. Establishment counts, employment, and payroll are from *County Business Patterns* for non-Census years. In non-Census years, industries in the Manufacturing range under SIC coding include data from the *Annual Survey of Manufactures* (*ASM*); those in the old Services range include data from the *Services Annual Survey* (*SAS*). Values followed by a 'p' are projections by the editors. Extrapolations are marked by 'e'. Data are the most recent available at this level of detail.

INDICES OF CHANGE

Year	Establishments (number)	Employment (number)	Payroll ($ million)	Revenues ($ million)	Employees per Establishment (number)	Revenues per Establishment ($)	Payroll per Employee ($)
1982	122.9	119.7	76.6	77.4	97.4	63.0	64.0
1987	119.3	113.3	85.5	92.1	95.0	77.1	75.4
1992	109.0	108.7	97.9	103.3	99.7	94.8	90.1
1993	107.4	108.4	98.9	96.6	100.9	89.9	91.2
1994	104.7	105.6	99.1	96.0	100.8	91.7	93.9
1995	102.2	105.1	98.8	95.0	102.8	93.0	94.0
1996	101.1 e	102.6 e	99.4 e	97.5 e	101.4 e	96.5 e	96.9 e
1997	100.0	100.0	100.0	100.0	100.0	100.0	100.0
1998	98.2 p	100.8 p	103.4 p	98.9 p	102.7 p	100.7 p	102.6 p
1999	96.7 p	99.7 p	104.8 p	99.1 p	103.1 p	102.5 p	105.1 p
2000	95.2 p	98.6 p	106.0 p	99.4 p	103.6 p	104.4 p	107.5 p
2001	93.7 p	97.5 p	107.3 p	99.6 p	104.0 p	106.3 p	110.1 p

Sources: Same as General Statistics. The values shown reflect change from the base year, 1997. Values above 100 mean greater than 1997, values below 100 mean less than 1997, and a value of 100 in the 1982-96 or 1998-2001 period means same as 1997. Values followed by a 'p' are projections by the editors; 'e' stands for extrapolation. Data are the most recent available at this level of detail.

SELECTED RATIOS

For 1997	Avg. of Information	Analyzed Industry	Index	For 1997	Avg. of Information	Analyzed Industry	Index
Employees per establishment	16	16	98	Payroll per establishment	330,963	146,869	44
Revenue per establishment	1,057,073	504,651	48	Payroll as % of revenue	31	29	93
Revenue per employee	65,958	32,041	49	Payroll per employee	20,651	9,325	45

Sources: Same as General Statistics. The 'Average' column represents the average for the industry sector, in 1997, where the currently shown industry is classified. The Index shows the relationship between the Average and the Analyzed Industry. For example, 100 means that they are equal; 500 that the Analyzed Industry is five times the average; 50 means that the Analyzed Industry is half the national average. The abbreviation 'na' is used to show that data are 'not available'.

*Equivalent to SIC 7933.

LEADING COMPANIES Number shown: 7   Total sales ($ mil): **4,410**   Total employment (000): **28.7**

Company Name	Address				CEO Name	Phone	Co. Type	Sales ($ mil)	Empl. (000)
Brunswick Corp.	1 N Field Ct	Lake Forest	IL	60045	Peter Larson	847-735-4700	P	4,284	25.5
AMF Bowling Centers Inc.	PO Box 15060	Richmond	VA	23227		804-730-4000	R	73*	2.0
Bowl America Inc.	PO Box 1288	Springfield	VA	22151	Leslie H Goldberg	703-941-6300	P	28	0.8
Western Bowl Inc.	6383 Glenway Ave	Cincinnati	OH	45211	Erwin Hoinke	513-574-2222	R	10*	0.2
Mardi-Bob Management Inc.	P O Box 69	Poughkeepsie	NY	12602	P Diane Hoe	914-471-2920	R	9*	0.2
Sports Arenas Properties Inc.	5230 Carroll Canyon	La Jolla	CA	92037	Harold S Elkan	619-587-1060	P	4*	0.1
Sunnybrook Golf Bowl	7191 E 17 Mile Rd	Sterling Heights	MI	48313	Randy Shank	810-264-2700	R	3	<0.1

Source: Ward's Business Directory of U.S. Private and Public Companies, Volumes 1 and 2, 2000. The company type code used is as follows: P - Public, R - Private, S - Subsidiary, D - Division, J - Joint Venture, A - Affiliate, G - Group, N - Company type not reported. Sales are in millions of dollars, employees are in thousands. An asterisk (*) indicates an estimated sales volume. The symbol < stands for 'less than'. Company names and addresses are truncated, in some cases, to fit into the available space.

LOCATION BY STATE AND REGIONAL CONCENTRATION

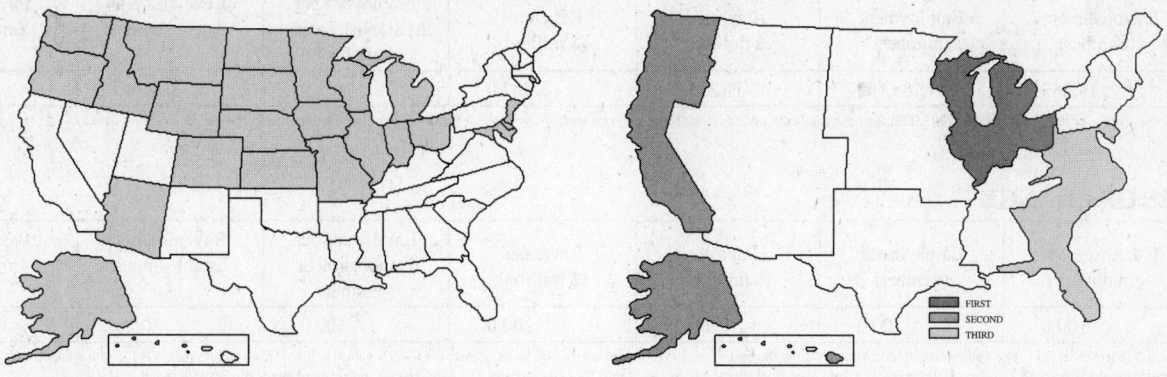

FIRST
SECOND
THIRD

INDUSTRY DATA BY STATE

State	Establishments Total (number)	Establishments % of U.S.	Employment Total (number)	Employment % of U.S.	Employment Per Estab.	Payroll Total ($ mil.)	Payroll Per Empl. ($)	Revenues Total ($ mil.)	Revenues % of U.S.	Revenues Per Estab. ($)
California	303	5.4	7,198	8.2	24	82.3	11,430	253.5	9.0	836,644
Michigan	343	6.1	6,700	7.6	20	57.0	8,511	199.2	7.1	580,697
New York	417	7.5	5,494	6.2	13	53.0	9,644	188.3	6.7	451,597
Illinois	373	6.7	5,397	6.1	14	50.7	9,396	180.8	6.4	484,592
Ohio	386	6.9	5,898	6.7	15	51.1	8,660	175.6	6.2	455,049
Texas	207	3.7	3,805	4.3	18	40.0	10,501	124.8	4.4	603,121
Wisconsin	321	5.7	4,594	5.2	14	30.2	6,574	120.2	4.3	374,592
Pennsylvania	278	5.0	3,378	3.8	12	31.6	9,351	107.6	3.8	387,032
Florida	166	3.0	2,874	3.3	17	29.8	10,381	106.9	3.8	643,825
Washington	120	2.1	2,956	3.4	25	30.3	10,264	99.8	3.5	831,358
New Jersey	121	2.2	2,142	2.4	18	26.2	12,225	88.2	3.1	729,124
Indiana	177	3.2	2,949	3.3	17	25.4	8,625	86.4	3.1	488,175
Minnesota	193	3.5	2,929	3.3	15	22.6	7,713	83.0	2.9	430,269
Virginia	94	1.7	2,082	2.4	22	20.4	9,803	68.8	2.4	731,968
Missouri	144	2.6	2,195	2.5	15	18.6	8,497	63.1	2.2	438,021
Maryland	96	1.7	1,636	1.9	17	17.4	10,650	57.8	2.0	602,167
Colorado	98	1.8	1,592	1.8	16	14.7	9,219	53.5	1.9	546,184
Georgia	72	1.3	1,325	1.5	18	14.7	11,117	52.6	1.9	731,097
North Carolina	86	1.5	1,467	1.7	17	15.2	10,365	50.5	1.8	586,814
Oregon	81	1.4	1,156	1.3	14	12.3	10,653	46.1	1.6	569,074
Iowa	177	3.2	1,721	2.0	10	11.1	6,475	44.4	1.6	250,571
Arizona	64	1.1	1,407	1.6	22	13.2	9,414	44.3	1.6	691,531
Massachusetts	111	2.0	1,282	1.5	12	12.3	9,575	43.0	1.5	387,072
Kansas	99	1.8	1,203	1.4	12	10.7	8,860	38.7	1.4	391,192
Tennessee	64	1.1	1,115	1.3	17	11.2	10,030	34.9	1.2	545,563
Connecticut	51	0.9	890	1.0	17	10.4	11,701	34.2	1.2	669,725
Kentucky	77	1.4	1,133	1.3	15	10.6	9,333	33.9	1.2	440,247
Nebraska	94	1.7	1,120	1.3	12	8.7	7,761	30.6	1.1	325,362
Oklahoma	66	1.2	953	1.1	14	7.8	8,144	25.5	0.9	385,833
South Carolina	49	0.9	681	0.8	14	7.3	10,673	24.9	0.9	508,143
Louisiana	39	0.7	760	0.9	19	7.2	9,486	23.2	0.8	593,795
Alabama	40	0.7	656	0.7	16	6.4	9,784	22.9	0.8	572,550
Montana	55	1.0	627	0.7	11	5.2	8,301	18.7	0.7	339,855
West Virginia	44	0.8	557	0.6	13	5.6	10,065	18.5	0.7	419,909
Utah	37	0.7	698	0.8	19	4.9	7,056	16.0	0.6	433,108
North Dakota	46	0.8	545	0.6	12	3.2	5,939	14.4	0.5	313,522
Idaho	50	0.9	618	0.7	12	4.2	6,796	14.3	0.5	286,960
South Dakota	60	1.1	577	0.7	10	3.6	6,210	14.3	0.5	237,883
Arkansas	46	0.8	457	0.5	10	3.9	8,523	13.4	0.5	291,152
New Mexico	31	0.6	501	0.6	16	4.2	8,311	12.5	0.4	401,742
Hawaii	17	0.3	296	0.3	17	3.7	12,490	12.1	0.4	709,882
Delaware	17	0.3	409	0.5	24	3.5	8,504	11.8	0.4	692,882
Rhode Island	19	0.3	352	0.4	19	3.4	9,625	11.6	0.4	608,368
New Hampshire	26	0.5	271	0.3	10	3.1	11,542	10.6	0.4	409,154
Maine	35	0.6	266	0.3	8	2.3	8,586	10.0	0.4	285,057
Alaska	13	0.2	279	0.3	21	2.8	9,907	9.8	0.3	752,846
Mississippi	26	0.5	273	0.3	10	2.1	7,795	8.5	0.3	326,577
Wyoming	27	0.5	278	0.3	10	1.9	6,835	6.6	0.2	243,296
Vermont	20	0.4	211	0.2	11	1.7	7,924	6.4	0.2	319,900
Nevada	14	0.3	141	0.2	10	1.3	9,482	4.2	0.2	303,214

Source: 1997 *Economic Census*. The states are in descending order of revenues or establishments (if revenue data are missing for the majority). The symbol (D) appears when data are withheld to prevent disclosure of competitive information. States marked with (D) are sorted by number of establishments. A dash (-) indicates that the data element cannot be calculated. * indicates the midpoint of a range; 175, for example is the range 100-249. Shaded *states* on the state map indicate those states which have proportionately greater representation in the industry than would be indicated by the state's population; the ratio is based on total revenues or number of establishments. Shaded *regions* indicate where the industry is regionally most concentrated.

NAICS 713990 - AMUSEMENT AND RECREATION INDUSTRIES NEC

GENERAL STATISTICS

Year	Establishments (number)	Employment (number)	Payroll ($ million)	Revenues ($ million)	Employees per Establishment (number)	Revenues per Establishment ($)	Payroll per Employee ($)
1997	14,283	84,162	1,255.0	5,287.0	5.9	370,160	14,912

Source: Economic Census of the United States, 1997. This is a newly defined industry. Data for prior years were unavailable at the time of publication but may become available over time.

INDICES OF CHANGE

Year	Establishments (number)	Employment (number)	Payroll ($ million)	Revenues ($ million)	Employees per Establishment (number)	Revenues per Establishment ($)	Payroll per Employee ($)
1997	100.0	100.0	100.0	100.0	100.0	100.0	100.0

Sources: Same as General Statistics. The values shown reflect change from the base year, 1997. Values above 100 mean greater than 1997, values below 100 mean less than 1997, and a value of 100 in the 1982-96 or 1998-2001 period means same as 1997. Values followed by a 'p' are projections by the editors; 'e' stands for extrapolation. Data are the most recent available at this level of detail.

SIC INDUSTRIES RELATED TO NAICS 713990

Each new NAICS code represents an industry that used to be part of an SIC or a part of several SIC industries. Data in this table are shown to provide transitional information for these cases. All available data for the precursor SIC(s) are shown. Even if only a part of an SIC is included in the NAICS, *all* data for the SIC are reproduced. If the SIC industry is not marked as being a part (pt) of the NAICS, the entire industry is embedded in the NAICS data. The SIC composition of the new industry provides some hints of the relative importance of its "ancestors." Data marked with a 'p' are projected. Projections begin with 1982 data. Data earlier than 1990 are not shown but are reflected in the projections.

SIC	Industry	1990	1991	1992	1993	1994	1995	1996	1997
7911	**Dance Studios, Schools, & Halls (pt)**								
	Establishments (number)	4,022	4,371	-	5,133	5,255	5,297	5,141*p*	5,254*p*
	Employment (thousands)	20.6	21.7	-	24.6	24.4	25.3	25.0*p*	25.6*p*
	Revenues ($ million)	626.0	662.0	784.0	880.0	906.0	947.0	1,036.0	1,042.5*p*
7993	**Coin-Operated Amusement Devices (pt)**								
	Establishments (number)	3,932	3,772	4,932	4,826	4,722	4,814	4,090*p*	4,001*p*
	Employment (thousands)	25.2	23.8	28.1	31.0	31.4	57.1	36.9*p*	38.0*p*
	Revenues ($ million)	2,146.0	2,301.0	2,566.0	2,763.0	2,965.0	3,254.0	3,486.0	3,397.7*p*
7997	**Membership Sports & Recreation Clubs (pt)**								
	Establishments (number)	13,089	13,560	14,727	14,674	14,624	14,544	14,800*p*	14,960*p*
	Employment (thousands)	242.1	247.5	258.6	264.8	268.4	277.7	283.6*p*	290.5*p*
	Revenues ($ million)	4,825.0	5,151.0	5,397.0	5,965.0	6,379.0	6,765.0	7,439.0	7,240.3*p*
7999	**Amusement & Recreation nec (pt)**								
	Establishments (number)	-	-	21,717	-	-	-	-	-
	Employment (thousands)	-	-	215.8	-	-	-	-	-
	Revenues ($ million)	-	-	10,430.3	-	-	-	-	-

Source: Economic Census of the United States, 1992, annual surveys of economic sectors conducted by the Bureau of the Census, and estimates or projections based on the 1982-1992 period; not all data are shown. 'e' marks estimates made by the editors; 'p' indicates projections based on time series. A dash (-) indicates that data for this SIC or year were not available. The abbreviation (pt) next to the industry name indicates that only a part of the industry is present within the NAICS data. If no (pt) is shown, the entire industry is contained within the NAICS data.

SELECTED RATIOS

For 1997	Avg. of Information	Analyzed Industry	Index	For 1997	Avg. of Information	Analyzed Industry	Index
Employees per establishment	16	6	37	Payroll per establishment	330,963	87,867	27
Revenue per establishment	1,057,073	370,160	35	Payroll as % of revenue	31	24	76
Revenue per employee	65,958	62,819	95	Payroll per employee	20,651	14,912	72

Sources: Same as General Statistics. The 'Average' column represents the average for the industry sector, in 1997, where the currently shown industry is classified. The Index shows the relationship between the Average and the Analyzed Industry. For example, 100 means that they are equal; 500 that the Analyzed Industry is five times the average; 50 means that the Analyzed Industry is half the national average. The abbreviation 'na' is used to show that data are 'not available'.

LEADING COMPANIES   Number shown: **75**   Total sales ($ mil): **5,822**   Total employment (000): **85.0**

Company Name	Address				CEO Name	Phone	Co. Type	Sales ($ mil)	Empl. (000)
Club Corp.	PO Box 819012	Dallas	TX	75381	Robert H. Dedman Jr.	972-243-6191	D	1,070	23.0
GTECH Corp.	55 Technology Way	West Greenwich	RI	02817		401-392-1000	S	808*	5.0
Vail Resorts Inc.	PO Box 7	Vail	CO	81658	Adam M Aron	970-476-5601	P	457	13.2
Ringling Brothers & Barnum	8607 Westwood	Vienna	VA	22182	Kenneth Feld	703-448-4000	S	409*	3.0
Players International Inc.	1300 Atlantic Ave	Atlantic City	NJ	08401	John Groom	609-449-7777	P	331	3.5
World Wrestling Federation	1241 E Main St	Stamford	CT	06902	Linda McMahon	203-352-8600	P	251	0.3
Ticketmaster Corp.	3701 Wilshire Blvd	Los Angeles	CA	90010	Terry Barnes	213-381-2000	S	230	6.6
Vail Associates Inc.	P O Box 7	Vail	CO	81658	Adam M Aron	970-476-5601	S	189*	6.0
Empress Casino Corp.	P O Box 2789	Joliet	IL	60434		815-744-9400	R	180*	2.0
Western Regional Off-Track	700 Ellicott St	Batavia	NY	14020	Martin C Basinait	716-343-1423	R	180	0.5
Big Apple Circus	505 8th Ave	New York	NY	10018		212-268-2500	R	136*	1.0
Treasure Island Inc.	P O Box 75	Red Wing	MN	55066		612-388-0083	R	130	1.4
Family Golf Centers Inc.	538 Broadhollow	Melville	NY	11747	Dominic Chang	516-694-1666	P	122	3.7
Ticketmaster Group Inc.	33701 Wilshire	Los Angeles	CA	90010	Terry Barnes	310-360-6000	S	117*	2.2
Quintel Entertainment Inc.	P O Box 1665	Pearl River	NY	10965	Jay Greenwald	914-620-1212	P	95	<0.1
Peninsula Gaming L.L.C.	P O Box 1683	Dubuque	IA	52001		319-583-7005	R	85*	0.6
New Orleans Saints	5800 Airline Hwy	Metairie	LA	70003	Bill Kuharich	504-733-0255	R	81	0.1
Carson Nugget Inc.	507 N Carson St	Carson City	NV	89701		775-882-1626	R	80*	0.6
United Skates of America Inc.	1317 E Broad St	Columbus	OH	43205	James A Dvorak	614-258-3191	R	74*	0.6
Jillian's Entertainment Holdings	1387 S 4th St	Louisville	US	40208	Steven L Foster	502-638-9008	P	60	2.8
Biltmore Co.	1 N Pack Sq	Asheville	NC	28801	William Cecil	828-255-1776	R	50	0.5
Ponte Vedra Corp.	200 Ponte Vedra	Pte Vedra Bch	FL	32082		904-285-1111	S	50*	0.6
Cumberland Valley Shows Inc.	P O Box 702	Lebanon	TN	37087		615-444-6627	R	40*	0.3
Ray Cammack Shows Inc.	4950 W Southern	Laveen	AZ	85339	Guy Leavitt	602-237-3333	R	40*	0.3
Milwaukee Athletic Club	758 N Broadway	Milwaukee	WI	53202		414-273-5080	R	37*	0.3
South of the Border Inc.	PO Box 8	Hamer	SC	29547	Alan Schafer	843-774-2411	S	33*	0.6
United Shows of America	PO Box 1089	Nolensville	TN	37135	Ed Gregory	615-776-5656	R	33*	0.3
Suffolk Regional Off-Track	5 Davids Dr	Smithtown	NY	11787	Walt Conlon	516-853-1000	R	25	0.5
Arabian Nights	6225 W Irlo Bronson	Kissimmee	FL	34747	Mark M Miller	407-239-9221	R	22*	0.2
Leroy's Horse and Sports Place	675 Grier Dr	Las Vegas	NV	89119	Victor J Salerno	702-735-0101	S	21*	0.2
New Orleans Paddlewheels Inc.	27 Poydras St Wharf	New Orleans	LA	70130	Warren L Reuther Jr	504-529-4567	R	20*	0.2
Orlando Jai Alai	P O Box 300107	Fern Park	FL	32730	Hort Soper	407-339-6221	R	20*	0.2
Tip Top Shows Inc.	P O Box 389	Waupaca	WI	54981	Charlie Larkee	715-258-4200	R	18*	0.1
Oregon Ticket Company Inc.	10 N W 6th Ave	Portland	OR	97209	David Leiken	503-224-0368	R	16*	<0.1
New Horizon Kids Quest Inc.	16355 36th Ave N	Plymouth	MN	55446	Susan Dunkley	612-557-1111	P	16	0.5
Renaissance Entertainment Corp.	275 Century Cr	Louisville	CO	80027	J Stanley Gilbert	303-664-0300	P	15	<0.1
Venture Catalyst Inc.	16868 V Campo	San Diego	CA	92127	LDonald Speer II	858-716-2100	P	15	<0.1
Loon Mountain Recreation Corp.	R R 1, Box 41	Lincoln	NH	03251	George Gillette	603-745-8111	R	15*	0.7
Blue Grass Shows Inc.	PO Box 75244	Tampa	FL	33675	James A Murphy	813-247-4431	R	14*	0.2
Farrow Amusement Company Inc.	PO Box 6747	Jackson	MS	39282	James M Williams	601-371-1203	R	14	0.2
Laurel Highlands River Tours Inc.	P O Box 107	Ohiopyle	PA	15470	Mark McCarty	724-329-8531	R	14*	0.1
American Bingo & Gaming Corp.	1440 Charleston	West Columbia	SC	29169	Daniel Delaney	803-796-7875	P	13	<0.1
Kramer Entertainment Agency Inc	3849 Lake Michigan	Grand Rapids	MI	49544	Robert A Kramer	616-791-0095	R	13*	0.1
McAuley LCX Corp.	8888 Los Coyotes	Buena Park	CA	90621	Charles S McAuley	714-521-6171	R	13*	0.1
Pacer/CATS	355 Inverness Dr	Englewood	CO	80112		303-649-9818	D	13*	0.1
Alta Ski Lifts Company Inc.	PO Box 8007	Alta	UT	84092	Onno Wieringa	801-742-3333	R	12*	0.5
American Wagering Inc.	675 Grier Dr	Las Vegas	NV	89119	Victor J Salerno	702-735-0101	P	10	0.3
Skyline Multimedia Entertainment	350 5th Ave	New York	NY	10118	Jay Berkman	212-564-2224	P	10	0.2
Aerobics & Fitness Association	15250 Ventura Blvd	Sherman Oaks	CA	91403	Linda Pfeffer, RN	818-905-0040	R	9	<0.1
Florida Radio Rental Inc.	2700 Davie Rd	Davie	FL	33314	Richard Pudsey	954-581-4437	R	8*	<0.1
Bear Valley Ski Co.	P O Box 5038	Bear Valley	CA	95223	Jim Bottomley	209-753-2301	R	8	0.3
Royal Gorge of Colorado	P O Box 549	Canon City	CO	81215		719-275-7507	R	8	0.2
McDaniel Brothers Shows Inc.	P O Box 293	Lodi	NJ	07644		973-458-6156	R	7*	<0.1
Nolan Amusement Co.	3600 Moxahall Pl	Zanesville	OH	43701	Rick Nolan	740-452-3398	R	7*	<0.1
AARCEE Party Rentals Inc.	3501 Hwy 100 S	Minneapolis	MN	55416	Richard Nelson	612-922-7233	R	6*	<0.1
Ripley Entertainment Inc.	5728 Major Blvd	Orlando	FL	32819	Robert Masterson	407-345-8010	R	6*	<0.1
Absolute Amusements Rental Inc.	11100 Astronaut	Orlando	FL	32837	David Peters	407-856-3866	R	5*	<0.1
Club Lanai	355 Hukilike St	Kahului	HI	96732	Chuck Forman	808-871-1144	R	5*	<0.1
New Orleans Tourism Marketing	365 Canal St	New Orleans	LA	70130	Robert Bevier	504-524-4784	R	5	<0.1
Riverboat Cruises/Spirit	110 L St	Sacramento	CA	94203	Brian Gerhart	916-552-2933	R	5*	<0.1
Sailboats Inc.	250 Marina Dr	Superior	WI	54880	Jack Culley	715-392-7131	R	5	<0.1
Zambelli Intern	PO Box 1463	New Castle	PA	16103		724-658-6611	R	5*	<0.1
Kissel Brothers Shows Inc.	6003 Squrlwd Crt	Cincinnati	OH	45247	Barbara Kissel	513-741-1080	R	4*	<0.1
Mid-America Festivals	1244 Canterbury Rd	Shakopee	MN	55379	James H Peterson	612-445-7361	R	4	<0.1
Tupelo Furniture Mart	589 N Coley Rd	Tupelo	MS	38801		662-844-1473	R	4*	<0.1
BounceBackTechnologies	707 Bienville Blvd	Ocean Springs	MS	39564	John J Pilger	228-872-5558	P	3	0.3
Air Combat U.S.A. Inc.	P O Box 2726	Fullerton	CA	92837	Mike Blackstone	714-522-7590	R	3*	<0.1
Bates Brothers Amusement Co.	1506 Fewrnwood Rd	Wintersville	OH	43952	Eric Bates	740-266-2950	R	3*	<0.1
Minneapolis Grand Hotel	615 2nd Ave S	Minneapolis	MN	55402		612-339-3655	R	3*	<0.1
Butterfly World Ltd.	3600 W Sample Rd	Coconut Creek	FL	33073		954-977-4434	R	3	<0.1
Cheer Ltd.	118 Ridgeway Dr	Fayetteville	NC	28311	Gwen P Holtsclaw	910-488-2600	R	2	0.2
Davis Amusement Co.	PO Box 1585	Clackamas	OR	97015	Cathy Davis	503-632-6104	R	2	<0.1
Ed Robinson's Diving Adventures	P O Box 616	Kihei	HI	96753	Ed Robinson	808-879-3584	R	2*	<0.1
Golf Academy of Hilton Head	P O Box 5580	Hilton Hd Isl	SC	29938	Raymond Travaglione	843-785-4540	S	2*	<0.1
Grandfather Mountain Inc.	P O Box 129	Linville	NC	28646	Hugh Morton	828-733-2013	R	2*	<0.1

Source: Ward's Business Directory of U.S. Private and Public Companies, Volumes 1 and 2, 2000. The company type code used is as follows: P - Public, R - Private, S - Subsidiary, D - Division, J - Joint Venture, A - Affiliate, G - Group, N - Company type not reported. Sales are in millions of dollars, employees are in thousands. An asterisk (*) indicates an estimated sales volume. The symbol < stands for 'less than'. Company names and addresses are truncated, in some cases, to fit into the available space.

REPRESENTATIVE NONPROFIT ORGANIZATIONS

Organization Name	Address				Phone	Income Range ($ mil)
Academy of Motion Picture Arts & Sciences	8949 Wilshire Blvd	Beverly Hills	CA	90211		40-49
Alaska State Fair Incorporated	2075 Glenn Hwy	Palmer	AK	99645	907-745-4827	1-5
Albergue Olimpico De Puerto Rico	PO Box 2004	Salinas	PR	00751		1-5
Albuquerque International Balloon Fiesta Inc	8309 Washington PL NE	Albuquerque	NM	87113		1-5
American Booksellers Assoc Inc	828 S Broadway	Tarrytown	NY	10591	914-591-2665	50+
American Contract Bridge League Inc	2990 Airways Blvd	Memphis	TN	38116	901-332-5586	10-19
American Hospital Association	One N Franklin	Chicago	IL	60606		50+
American Morgan Horse Association Inc	PO Box 960	Shelburn	VT	05482	802-985-4944	1-5
American Urological Association Incorporated	1120 N Charles St	Baltimore	MD	21201	410-727-1100	30-39
Appaloosa Horse Club	2720 W Pullman Rd	Moscow	ID	83843		5-9
Arizona Sports Foundation	120 S Ash Ave	Tempe	AZ	85281		10-19
Atlanta Athletic Club	Bobby Jones Dr	Duluth	GA	30097	770-448-2166	10-19
Atlantic Coast Conference	PO Drawer Acc	Greensboro	NC	27417		50+
Boys & Girls Club of Pawtucket	1 Moeller PL	Pawtucket	RI	02860	401-722-8840	1-5
Boys and Girls Clubs of Boston Inc	50 Congress St Ste 730	Boston	MA	02109		20-29
Bridger Bowl	15795 Bridger Canyon Rd	Bozeman	MT	59715	406-587-2111	5-9
Capitol Center for the Arts	44 S Main St	Concord	NH	03301	603-224-4077	1-5
Carnegie Hall a Corporation	105 Church Street	Lewisburg	WV	24901	304-645-7917	1-5
Casper Petroleum Club Inc	PO Box 222	Casper	WY	82602	307-234-3588	1-5
Central Indiana Community Foundation Inc	615 N Alabama	Indianapolis	IN	46204	317-634-2423	50+
Clarksdale Country Club	PO Box 1231	Clarksdale	MS	38614	662-624-4170	1-5
Country Club of Little Rock	4200 Country Club Blvd	Little Rock	AR	72207	501-660-4339	5-9
Crazy Horse Memorial Foundation	Ave of the Chiefs	Custer	SD	57730	605-673-4681	1-5
Detroit Symphany Orchestra Hall	3663 Woodward	Detroit	MI	48201		20-29
Eugene and Kristine Hughes Charitable Foundation	136 South Main Ste 404	Salt Lake Cty	UT	84101		1-5
Fargo-Moorhead Family YMCA	400 First Ave S	Fargo	ND	58103		1-5
Gateway Economic Development Corp of Greater Cleveland	758 Bolivar Rd	Cleveland	OH	44115		20-29
Greek Catholic Union of the USA	5400 Tuscarawas Rd	Beaver	PA	15009	724-495-3400	50+
Hall County Livestock Improvement Assn Inc	PO Box 490	Grand Island	NE	68802		20-29
Houston Livestock Show & Rodeo Inc	PO Box 20070	Houston	TX	77225		30-39
J B Speed Art Museum	PO Box 2600	Louisville	KY	40201		50+
Longwood Foundation Inc	100 W 10th St Ste 1109	Wilmington	DE	19801	302-777-1212	50+
Maine Tourism Association	PO Box 2300	Hallowell	ME	04347		1-5
Milwaukee County War Memorial Center Inc	750 N Lincoln Memorial	Milwaukee	WI	53202	414-273-5533	10-19
Missouri Athletic Club	405 Washington Ave	St Louis	MO	63102	314-231-7220	10-19
National Automobile Dealers Association	8400 Westpark Dr	McLean	VA	22102	703-821-7000	50+
National Cable Television Assn	1724 Mass Ave NW	Washington	DC	20036	202-775-3550	50+
New Jersey Performing Arts Center Corporation	One Center St	Newark	NJ	07102		30-39
Outrigger Canoe Club	2909 Kalakaua Ave	Honolulu	HI	96815		5-9
Palmetto Rural Telephone Cooperative Inc	PO Drawer 1577	Walterboro	SC	29488		5-9
Portland Art Museum	1219 SW Park Ave	Portland	OR	97205	503-226-2811	50+
Racing Association of Central Iowa	PO Box 1000	Altoona	IA	50009		50+
Science Museum of Minnesota	120 W Kellogg Blvd	St Paul	MN	55102	651-221-4722	50+
Southeastern Conference	2001 Civic Center Blvd	Birmingham	AL	35203		50+
State Fair of Oklahoma	500 N Land Rush	Oklahoma City	OK	73107	405-948-6700	10-19
Tampa Bay Performing Arts Center	1010 N WC Macinnes PL	Tampa	FL	33602	813-229-7827	30-39
Teamsters Security Fund for Southern Nevada	101 Convention Center	Las Vegas	NV	89109		20-29
United States Olympic Committee	1 Olympic Plz	Colorado SPGS	CO	80909	719-578-4581	50+
University of Kansas Athletic Corporation	Allen Field House	Lawrence	KS	66045	913-864-2700	30-39
Western Washington Fair Association	PO Box 430	Puyallup	WA	98371		20-29
World Trade Center of New Orleans	2 Canal St Ste 2900	New Orleans	LA	70130	504-568-8222	10-19
Young Womens Christian Association of the Hartford Region	135 Broad St	Hartford	CT	06105		10-19

Source: National Directory of Nonprofit Organizations, 2000, Volumes 1 and 2, The Taft Group. The table shows a selection of organizations for illustration and does not constitute a complete selection from the source. The organizations are arranged in alphabetical order.

LOCATION BY STATE AND REGIONAL CONCENTRATION

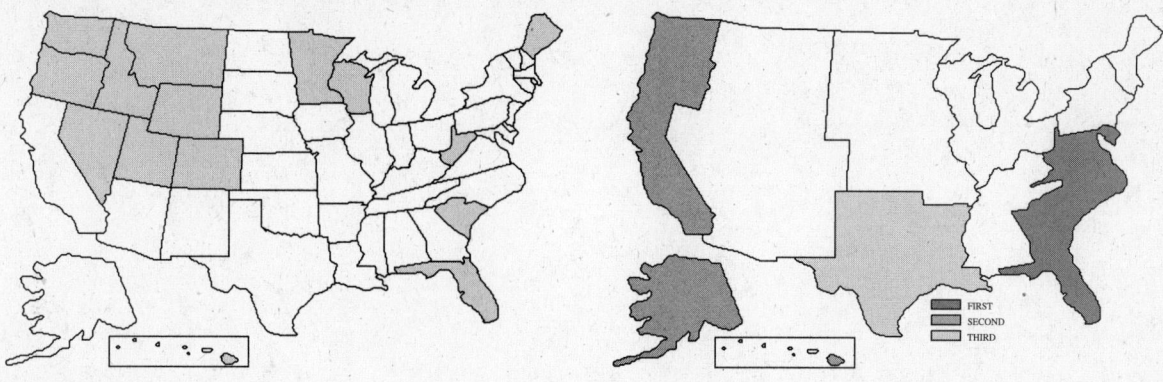

INDUSTRY DATA BY STATE

State	Establishments Total (number)	% of U.S.	Employment Total (number)	% of U.S.	Per Estab.	Payroll Total ($ mil.)	Per Empl. ($)	Revenues Total ($ mil.)	% of U.S.	Per Estab. ($)
California	1,242	8.7	10,329	12.3	8	146.0	14,133	553.2	10.5	445,429
Texas	886	6.2	6,050	7.2	7	74.4	12,295	352.3	6.7	397,585
Florida	878	6.1	5,203	6.2	6	69.9	13,428	296.4	5.6	337,590
South Carolina	307	2.1	2,656	3.2	9	41.6	15,651	247.7	4.7	806,980
Pennsylvania	642	4.5	3,545	4.2	6	55.4	15,629	223.2	4.2	347,623
Ohio	541	3.8	3,001	3.6	6	44.8	14,921	180.8	3.4	334,211
Michigan	461	3.2	2,704	3.2	6	38.3	14,175	147.9	2.8	320,926
Colorado	396	2.8	1,949	2.3	5	31.9	16,349	135.8	2.6	343,018
Wisconsin	319	2.2	1,776	2.1	6	28.0	15,752	131.1	2.5	410,991
Virginia	339	2.4	2,066	2.5	6	29.4	14,215	118.8	2.2	350,407
North Carolina	424	3.0	1,732	2.1	4	26.6	15,386	113.5	2.1	267,583
Washington	353	2.5	2,186	2.6	6	26.4	12,095	113.4	2.1	321,147
Minnesota	349	2.4	2,110	2.5	6	22.6	10,726	101.3	1.9	290,232
Louisiana	164	1.1	794	0.9	5	13.6	17,146	86.4	1.6	526,787
Oregon	243	1.7	1,429	1.7	6	19.2	13,456	80.8	1.5	332,412
Hawaii	115	0.8	1,298	1.5	11	21.6	16,675	70.0	1.3	609,035
Nevada	79	0.6	859	1.0	11	17.4	20,282	62.7	1.2	794,291
Utah	141	1.0	825	1.0	6	16.2	19,587	62.2	1.2	440,794
Connecticut	170	1.2	759	0.9	4	14.3	18,813	58.9	1.1	346,518
Iowa	146	1.0	584	0.7	4	6.8	11,615	55.3	1.0	378,986
Montana	194	1.4	470	0.6	2	8.0	17,074	46.7	0.9	240,691
West Virginia	121	0.8	762	0.9	6	11.0	14,406	46.0	0.9	380,091
Kentucky	158	1.1	761	0.9	5	9.6	12,597	39.0	0.7	246,886
Oklahoma	141	1.0	824	1.0	6	9.5	11,540	38.6	0.7	273,716
Kansas	131	0.9	704	0.8	5	7.3	10,317	30.6	0.6	233,481
Idaho	158	1.1	464	0.6	3	6.5	13,909	29.8	0.6	188,741
Maine	121	0.8	434	0.5	4	7.8	17,908	28.9	0.5	238,711
Alabama	129	0.9	607	0.7	5	7.2	11,799	28.9	0.5	224,279
Nebraska	102	0.7	562	0.7	6	5.4	9,685	27.0	0.5	264,794
Wyoming	119	0.8	350	0.4	3	4.9	14,086	25.9	0.5	217,706
Arkansas	138	1.0	478	0.6	3	5.5	11,431	25.0	0.5	181,145
Mississippi	102	0.7	447	0.5	4	5.6	12,425	21.4	0.4	210,108
Tennessee	26	0.2	384	0.5	15	7.8	20,380	20.8	0.4	800,154
New Mexico	79	0.6	355	0.4	4	4.5	12,707	19.6	0.4	248,013
Delaware	49	0.3	228	0.3	5	2.8	12,132	13.2	0.2	268,490
Illinois	60	0.4	375	0.4	6	3.8	10,224	13.0	0.2	217,000
Georgia	30	0.2	117	0.1	4	2.5	21,111	10.1	0.2	335,333
North Dakota	63	0.4	305	0.4	5	2.5	8,085	9.9	0.2	156,444
Vermont	53	0.4	183	0.2	3	2.3	12,689	9.9	0.2	186,132
Indiana	37	0.3	243	0.3	7	2.5	10,486	8.5	0.2	229,514
Rhode Island	17	0.1	77	0.1	5	1.9	24,701	4.8	0.1	280,824
Missouri	32	0.2	93	0.1	3	0.9	9,140	4.0	0.1	124,375
South Dakota	20	0.1	71	0.1	4	0.7	9,648	2.2	0.0	111,350
New Hampshire	8	0.1	35	0.0	4	0.6	16,514	1.9	0.0	237,625
D.C.	10	0.1	60*	-	-	(D)	-	(D)	-	-

Source: 1997 *Economic Census*. The states are in descending order of revenues or establishments (if revenue data are missing for the majority). The symbol (D) appears when data are withheld to prevent disclosure of competitive information. States marked with (D) are sorted by number of establishments. A dash (-) indicates that the data element cannot be calculated. * indicates the midpoint of a range; 175, for example is the range 100-249. Shaded *states* on the state map indicate those states which have proportionately greater representation in the industry than would be indicated by the state's population; the ratio is based on total revenues or number of establishments. Shaded *regions* indicate where the industry is regionally most concentrated.

Part X

ACCOMMODATION AND FOOD SERVICES

NAICS 721110 - HOTELS (EXCEPT CASINO HOTELS) AND MOTELS

GENERAL STATISTICS

Year	Establishments (number)	Employment (number)	Payroll ($ million)	Revenues ($ million)	Employees per Establishment (number)	Revenues per Establishment ($)	Payroll per Employee ($)
1997	43,188	1,355,660	19,647.0	73,451.0	31.4	1,700,727	14,493

Source: *Economic Census of the United States*, 1997. This is a newly defined industry. Data for prior years were unavailable at the time of publication but may become available over time.

INDICES OF CHANGE

Year	Establishments (number)	Employment (number)	Payroll ($ million)	Revenues ($ million)	Employees per Establishment (number)	Revenues per Establishment ($)	Payroll per Employee ($)
1997	100.0	100.0	100.0	100.0	100.0	100.0	100.0

Sources: Same as General Statistics. The values shown reflect change from the base year, 1997. Values above 100 mean greater than 1997, values below 100 mean less than 1997, and a value of 100 in the 1982-96 or 1998-2001 period means same as 1997. Values followed by a 'p' are projections by the editors; 'e' stands for extrapolation. Data are the most recent available at this level of detail.

SIC INDUSTRIES RELATED TO NAICS 721110

Each new NAICS code represents an industry that used to be part of an SIC or a part of several SIC industries. Data in this table are shown to provide transitional information for these cases. All available data for the precursor SIC(s) are shown. Even if only a part of an SIC is included in the NAICS, *all* data for the SIC are reproduced. If the SIC industry is not marked as being a part (pt) of the NAICS, the entire industry is embedded in the NAICS data. The SIC composition of the new industry provides some hints of the relative importance of its "ancestors." Data marked with a 'p' are projected. Projections begin with 1982 data. Data earlier than 1990 are not shown but are reflected in the projections.

SIC	Industry	1990	1991	1992	1993	1994	1995	1996	1997
7011	**Hotels, Motels (pt)**								
	Establishments (number)	39,247	40,892	41,684	42,597	42,924	43,251	43,163p	43,555p
	Employment (thousands)	1,463.1	1,440.8	1,455.9	1,477.0	1,484.4	1,519.2	1,591.2p	1,622.9p
	Revenues ($ million)	61,991.0	63,082.0	68,508.0	71,519.0	76,696.0	81,104.0	85,720.0	87,807.4p
7041	**Membership-Basis Organization Hotels (pt)**								
	Establishments (number)	2,257	2,279	1,993	1,953	1,886	1,897	1,791p	1,723p
	Employment (thousands)	12.1	12.4	9.6	10.3	9.8	11.1	10.4p	10.3p
	Revenues ($ million)	-	-	433.7	-	-	-		

Source: *Economic Census of the United States*, 1992, annual surveys of economic sectors conducted by the Bureau of the Census, and estimates or projections based on the 1982-1992 period; not all data are shown. 'e' marks estimates made by the editors; 'p' indicates projections based on time series. A dash (-) indicates that data for this SIC or year were not available. The abbreviation (pt) next to the industry name indicates that only a part of the industry is present within the NAICS data. If no (pt) is shown, the entire industry is contained within the NAICS data.

SELECTED RATIOS

For 1997	Avg. of Information	Analyzed Industry	Index	For 1997	Avg. of Information	Analyzed Industry	Index
Employees per establishment	17	31	181	Payroll per establishment	177,969	454,918	256
Revenue per establishment	642,845	1,700,727	265	Payroll as % of revenue	28	27	97
Revenue per employee	37,074	54,181	146	Payroll per employee	10,264	14,493	141

Sources: Same as General Statistics. The 'Average' column represents the average for the industry sector, in 1997, where the currently shown industry is classified. The Index shows the relationship between the Average and the Analyzed Industry. For example, 100 means that they are equal; 500 that the Analyzed Industry is five times the average; 50 means that the Analyzed Industry is half the national average. The abbreviation 'na' is used to show that data are 'not available'.

LEADING COMPANIES   Number shown: **75**   Total sales ($ mil): **100,326**   Total employment (000): **1,310.0**

Company Name	Address			CEO Name	Phone	Co. Type	Sales ($ mil)	Empl. (000)
Carlson Holdings Inc.	PO Box 59159	Minneapolis	MN 55459	Marilyn C. Nelson	612-449-1000	R	22,000	165.0
Radisson Hospitality Worldwide	P O Box 59159	Minneapolis	MN 55459	Brian Stage	612-540-5526	S	9,105*	68.5
Marriott International Inc.	10400 Fernwood Rd	Bethesda	MD 20817	JW Marriott Jr	301-380-3000	P	7,968	133.0
Starwood Hotels & Resorts	777 Westchester	White Plains	NY 10604	Barry S Sternlicht	914-640-8100	P	4,710*	130.0
Hilton International Co.	901 Ponce de Leon	Coral Gables	FL 33134	Howard Friedman	305-444-3444	S	4,565*	40.0
Host Marriott Corp.	10400 Fernwood Rd	Bethesda	MD 20817	Terence C Golden	301-380-9000	P	3,442	0.2
Hyatt Hotels Corp.	200 W Madison St	Chicago	IL 60606	Scott Miller	312-750-1234	S	2,900*	70.0
Mirage Resorts Inc.	3600 Las Vegas S	Las Vegas	NV 89109	Stephen A Wynn	702-791-7111	P	2,403	29.9
Park Place Entertainment	3930 H Hughes	Las Vegas	NV 89109	Stephen F Bollenbach	702-699-5000	P	2,305	42.0
Carlson Companies Inc.	PO Box 59159	Minneapolis	MN 55459	M Carlson Nelson	763-212-5000	S	2,267*	17.0
Harrah's Entertainment Inc.	1023 Cherry Rd	Memphis	TN 38117	Philip G Satre	901-762-8600	P	2,004	37.4
Hilton Hotels Corp.	9336 Civic Center	Beverly Hills	CA 90210	Stephen F Bollenbach	310-278-4321	P	1,769	38.0
Rosewood Corp.	100 Crescent Ct	Dallas	TX 75201		214-871-8400	R	1,689*	1.3
Harrah's	1023 Cherry Rd	Memphis	TN 38117	Philip Satre	901-762-8600	D	1,619*	23.0
Mandalay Resort Group	3950 Las Vegas S	Las Vegas	NV 89119	Michael S Ensign	702-734-0410	P	1,480	27.0
Trump Hotels & Casino Resorts	2500 Boardwalk	Atlantic City	NJ 08401	Nicholas L Ribis	609-441-6060	P	1,404	12.7
MGM Grand Inc.	3799 Las Vegas S	Las Vegas	NV 89109	James F Murren	702-891-3333	P	1,392	6.7
Caesars World Inc.	3570 Las Vegas, S	Las Vegas	NV 89109	Peter G Boynton	702-866-1000	S	1,373	14.0
Promus Hotel Corp.	755 Crossover Ln	Memphis	TN 38117	Norman P Blake Jr	901-374-5000	P	1,062	40.0
Lane Industries Inc.	1200 Shermer Rd	Northbrook	IL 60062	William Lane	847-498-6789	R	1,020	8.6
Boyd Gaming Corp.	2950 S Industrial Rd	Las Vegas	NV 89109	William S Boyd	702-792-7200	P	975	15.0
Station Casinos Inc.	PO Box 29500	Las Vegas	NV 89126	Frank J Fertitta III	702-367-2411	P	943	10.4
Quorum Hotels and Resorts	12770 Merit Dr	Dallas	TX 75251	Tony Farris	972-458-7265	R	871*	2.2
Aztar Corp.	2390 E Camelback	Phoenix	AZ 85016	Paul E Rubeli	602-381-4100	P	806	10.8
Tollman-Hundley Hotels	1886 State Rte 52	Hopewell Jctn	NY 12533	Monty Hundley	914-223-3603	R	796*	7.0
John Q. Hammons Industries Inc.	300 JQ Hammons	Springfield	MO 65806		417-864-4300	R	793*	7.0
Gaylord Entertainment Co	1 Gaylord Dr	Nashville	TN 37214	Carrie London	615-316-6000	R	768*	6.0
BRISTOL Hotels and Resorts	14295 Midway Rd	Addison	TX 75001	John A Beckert	972-391-3910	P	757	14.0
MGM Grand Hotel Inc.	3799 Las Vegas S	Las Vegas	NV 89109	Dan Wade	702-891-3333	S	672*	7.0
Patriot American Hospitality	1950 Stemmons	Dallas	TX 75207	Paul A Nussbaum	214-863-1000	S	649*	22.0
Mirage Casino-Hotel	P O Box 7777	Las Vegas	NV 89177	Mark Schoor	702-791-7111	S	616	6.5
Opryland USA Inc.	2808 Opryland Dr	Nashville	TN 37214	Terry London	615-889-1000	P	609*	4.8
Prime Hospitality Corp.	P O Box 2700	Fairfield	NJ 07004	AF Petrocelli	973-882-1010	P	553	6.8
DJONT Operations L.L.C.	545 E Carpenter	Irving	TX 75062	Thomas J Corcoran Jr	972-444-4900	R	535	0.0
Gaylord Entertainment Co.	1 Gaylord Dr	Nashville	TN 37214	Ek Gaylord II	615-316-6000	P	525	6.2
California Hotel and Casino Inc.	2950 S Industrial Rd	Las Vegas	NV 89109	William S Boyd	702-792-7200	S	524	8.4
Kyo-Ya Company Ltd.	2255 Kalakaua Ave	Honolulu	HI 96815		808-931-8600	S	512*	4.0
Isle of Capri Casinos Inc.	711 Wash Loop	Biloxi	MS 39530	John M Gallaway	228-436-7000	P	480	6.0
Destination Hotels & Resorts Inc.	10333 E Dry Creek	Englewood	CO 80112	John B Platt III	303-799-3830	S	470	6.0
Richfield Holdings Inc.	5775 DTC Blvd	Englewood	CO 80111	Tom O'Leary	303-220-2000	R	436	123.0
Extended Stay America Inc.	450 E Las Olas	Fort Lauderdale	FL 33301	George D Johnson Jr	954-713-1600	P	418	4.6
Pointe Hilton Resorts Inc.	7600 N 16th St	Phoenix	AZ 85020		602-997-7777	R	409*	3.2
Aspen Skiing Co.	PO Box 1248	Aspen	CO 81612	Patrick O' Donnell	970-925-1220	R	407*	3.6
Rio Hotel and Casino Inc.	3700 W Flamingo	Las Vegas	NV 89103	Anthony A Marnell II	702-252-7733	P	392	5.0
Red Roof Inns Inc.	4355 Davidson Rd	Hilliard	OH 43026	Francis W Cash	614-777-1070	P	375	5.9
Benchmark Hospitality Inc.	2170 Buckthorne Pl	The Woodlands	TX 77380	Burt Cabanas	281-367-5757	R	373*	3.3
Sunterra Corp.	1781 Park Center Dr	Orlando	FL 32835	Andrew Gessow	407-532-1000	P	359	6.5
Horseshoe Entertainment L.P.	711 Horseshoe Blvd	Bossier City	LA 71171	Larry Lepinski	318-742-0711	R	358*	2.8
Atlantic City Showboat Inc.	P O Box 840	Atlantic City	NJ 08404	Herb Wolfe	609-343-4000	S	347*	3.5
GNAC Corp.	P O Box 1737	Atlantic City	NJ 08404	Wallis Barr	609-340-7268	S	340*	3.0
Marcus Corp.	250 E Wisconsin	Milwaukee	WI 53202	Stephen H Marcus	414-905-1000	P	333	7.3
John Q. Hammons Hotels Inc.	300 JQ Hammons	Springfield	MO 65806	John Q Hammons	417-864-4300	P	326	8.0
Goodale and Barbieri Cos.	W 201 N River Dr	Spokane	WA 99201		509-459-6100	R	321*	2.5
Harveys Casino Resorts	P O Box 128	Stateline	NV 89449	Charles W Scharer	702-588-2411	R	310	4.1
Adam's Mark Hotels and Resorts	P O Box 419039	St. Louis	MO 63141	Fred S Kummer	314-567-9000	D	309*	6.0
Shilo Corp. Management Offices	11600 S W Shilo Ln	Portland	OR 97225	Mark S Hemstreet	503-641-6565	R	283*	2.5
Boykin Hospitality	45 W Prospect Ave	Cleveland	OH 44115	Robert Boykin	216-241-6375	R	280*	3.5
Shilo Inns Co.	11600 S W Shilo	Portland	OR 97225	Mark S Hemstreet	503-641-6565	S	280*	2.2
Tropicana Casino and Resort	Brigh & Brdwlk	Atlantic City	NJ 08401		609-340-4000	S	280*	4.2
WestCoast Hotels Inc.	600 Stewart St	Seattle	WA 98101	Rodney Olson		R	279*	2.5
Park Place Entertainment Corp.	Bos at Brdwlk	Atlantic City	NJ 08401	Arthur M Goldberg	609-347-7111	S	278*	3.2
Resorts Inc.	1133 Boardwalk	Atlantic City	NJ 08401	George Papanier	609-344-6000	S	277	3.0
Primadonna Resorts Inc.	PO Box 95997	Las Vegas	NV 89193	Gary E Primm	702-382-1212	P	273	3.7
Davidson Hotel Partners L.P.	1755 Lynnfield Rd	Memphis	TN 38119	Wilton D Hill	901-761-4664	R	271*	2.4
Japan Air Lines Development	160 Central Park S	New York	NY 10019	Akira Osawa	212-247-0300	S	271*	1.7
New York-New York Hotel	3790 Las Vegas	Las Vegas	NV 89109		702-740-6969	J	268*	2.1
Lane Hospitality	1200 Shermer	Northbrook	IL 60062	John Rijos	847-498-6789	R	267*	5.0
Ameristar Casinos Inc.	3773 H Hughes	Las Vegas	NV 89109	Craig H Neilsen	702-567-7000	P	264	4.2
Showboat Casino Hotel	P O Box 840	Atlantic City	NJ 08401	Herb Wolfe	609-343-4000	S	263*	3.5
Casino Magic Corp.	711 Casino Magic	Bay St. Louis	MS 39520	Marlin Torguson	228-467-9257	P	262	2.8
Hershey Entertainment & Resorts	300 Park Blvd	Hershey	PA 17033	J Bruce McKinney	717-534-3131	R	240*	4.0
Kemmons Wilson Inc.	1629 Winchester Rd	Memphis	TN 38116	Spence Wilson	901-346-8800	R	225	3.0
Hilton Hawaiian Village	2005 Kalia Rd	Honolulu	HI 96815		808-949-4321	R	224*	1.8
Larken Inc.	P O Box 1808	Cedar Rapids	IA 52406	Larry Cahill	319-366-8201	R	200*	6.1
White Lodging Services Corp.	1000 E 80th Pl	Merrillville	IN 46410	Bruce White	219-769-3267	R	200	2.0

Source: Ward's Business Directory of U.S. Private and Public Companies, Volumes 1 and 2, 2000. The company type code used is as follows: P - Public, R - Private, S - Subsidiary, D - Division, J - Joint Venture, A - Affiliate, G - Group, N - Company type not reported. Sales are in millions of dollars, employees are in thousands. An asterisk (*) indicates an estimated sales volume. The symbol < stands for 'less than'. Company names and addresses are truncated, in some cases, to fit into the available space.

LOCATION BY STATE AND REGIONAL CONCENTRATION

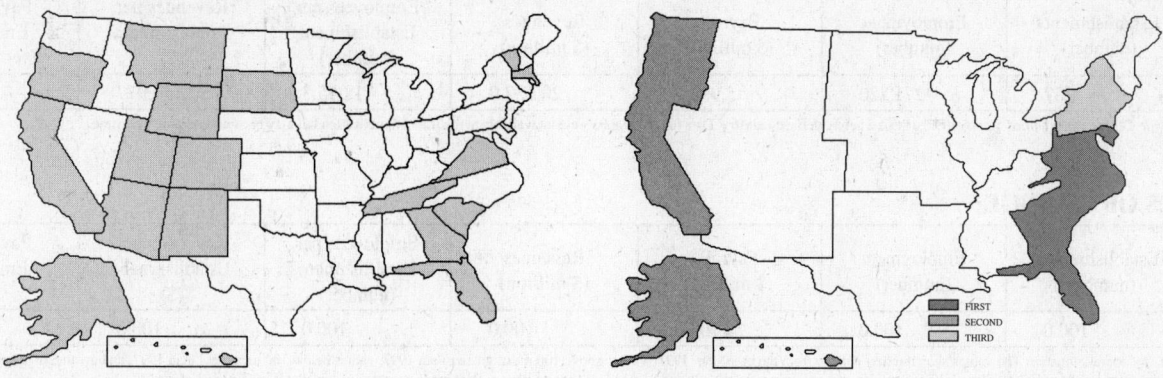

INDUSTRY DATA BY STATE

State	Establishments Total (number)	Establishments % of U.S.	Employment Total (number)	Employment % of U.S.	Employment Per Estab.	Payroll Total ($ mil.)	Payroll Per Empl. ($)	Revenues Total ($ mil.)	Revenues % of U.S.	Revenues Per Estab. ($)
California	4,776	11.1	177,192	13.1	37	2,857.4	16,126	10,541.3	14.4	2,207,133
Florida	3,089	7.2	141,746	10.5	46	2,034.6	14,354	8,479.1	11.5	2,744,920
New York	1,766	4.1	69,946	5.2	40	1,477.1	21,117	5,201.6	7.1	2,945,394
Texas	2,737	6.3	82,340	6.1	30	1,081.5	13,134	4,313.8	5.9	1,576,089
Hawaii	280	0.6	39,990	2.9	143	951.0	23,781	3,020.9	4.1	10,788,811
Illinois	1,173	2.7	50,258	3.7	43	778.4	15,489	2,969.9	4.0	2,531,845
Georgia	1,346	3.1	44,187	3.3	33	596.2	13,493	2,204.6	3.0	1,637,860
Pennsylvania	1,188	2.8	44,549	3.3	37	599.1	13,448	2,106.4	2.9	1,773,086.
Virginia	1,142	2.6	39,151	2.9	34	538.7	13,759	2,023.0	2.8	1,771,475
Arizona	854	2.0	37,371	2.8	44	532.0	14,235	1,992.6	2.7	2,333,297
Massachusetts	739	1.7	27,853	2.1	38	502.4	18,039	1,864.1	2.5	2,522,442
Colorado	1,073	2.5	38,367	2.8	36	514.1	13,401	1,808.6	2.5	1,685,549
North Carolina	1,376	3.2	31,207	2.3	23	403.8	12,940	1,564.9	2.1	1,137,299
Ohio	1,099	2.5	33,793	2.5	31	404.8	11,978	1,564.3	2.1	1,423,370
New Jersey	1,065	2.5	24,104	1.8	23	410.9	17,048	1,531.9	2.1	1,438,376
Tennessee	1,137	2.6	28,928	2.1	25	367.7	12,709	1,483.5	2.0	1,304,706
Michigan	1,315	3.0	29,821	2.2	23	367.9	12,337	1,401.6	1.9	1,065,834
Washington	961	2.2	23,224	1.7	24	339.5	14,620	1,302.3	1.8	1,355,108
Louisiana	549	1.3	22,181	1.6	40	288.8	13,022	1,171.4	1.6	2,133,667
South Carolina	950	2.2	23,117	1.7	24	284.4	12,302	1,130.4	1.5	1,189,863
Minnesota	905	2.1	24,289	1.8	27	305.3	12,568	1,128.2	1.5	1,246,674
Maryland	516	1.2	18,634	1.4	36	284.0	15,242	1,082.6	1.5	2,098,109
D.C.	103	0.2	15,277	1.1	148	346.9	22,706	1,076.3	1.5	10,449,398
Wisconsin	1,063	2.5	24,523	1.8	23	265.2	10,816	959.5	1.3	902,673
Oregon	811	1.9	16,290	1.2	20	214.5	13,169	867.4	1.2	1,069,593
Indiana	658	1.5	19,047	1.4	29	215.9	11,337	801.6	1.1	1,218,233
Kentucky	579	1.3	15,433	1.1	27	172.7	11,190	653.4	0.9	1,128,566
Utah	438	1.0	14,893	1.1	34	168.0	11,278	620.8	0.8	1,417,372
Alabama	607	1.4	13,416	1.0	22	146.6	10,928	575.2	0.8	947,575
Connecticut	284	0.7	10,250	0.8	36	158.9	15,499	572.2	0.8	2,014,901
New Mexico	596	1.4	13,389	1.0	22	142.4	10,636	535.1	0.7	897,864
Iowa	555	1.3	11,680	0.9	21	117.9	10,093	415.9	0.6	749,314
Oklahoma	521	1.2	9,679	0.7	19	96.2	9,937	386.4	0.5	741,578
Arkansas	548	1.3	9,494	0.7	17	97.5	10,272	361.9	0.5	660,314
West Virginia	291	0.7	8,082	0.6	28	109.3	13,526	361.5	0.5	1,242,220
Mississippi	464	1.1	8,481	0.6	18	83.1	9,794	337.5	0.5	727,321
Vermont	314	0.7	8,004	0.6	25	103.0	12,869	335.3	0.5	1,067,990
Maine	545	1.3	6,152	0.5	11	88.9	14,444	328.1	0.4	602,020
Wyoming	371	0.9	7,198	0.5	19	75.8	10,532	306.1	0.4	825,159
Idaho	313	0.7	8,260	0.6	26	83.6	10,127	302.4	0.4	966,054
New Hampshire	314	0.7	6,600	0.5	21	87.0	13,188	291.2	0.4	927,465
Alaska	233	0.5	5,139	0.4	22	79.7	15,516	287.0	0.4	1,231,704
Montana	487	1.1	7,527	0.6	15	76.9	10,219	284.7	0.4	584,587
Nebraska	363	0.8	7,582	0.6	21	78.6	10,372	266.7	0.4	734,686
South Dakota	398	0.9	5,499	0.4	14	50.3	9,142	194.3	0.3	488,254
Rhode Island	109	0.3	2,571	0.2	24	41.9	16,284	158.1	0.2	1,450,018
North Dakota	231	0.5	4,762	0.4	21	40.4	8,492	148.1	0.2	641,238
Delaware	122	0.3	2,317	0.2	19	38.2	16,498	138.5	0.2	1,135,041
Missouri	994	2.3	37,500*	-	-	(D)	-	(D)	-	-
Kansas	463	1.1	7,500*	-	-	(D)	-	(D)	-	-
Nevada	377	0.9	7,500*	-	-	(D)	-	(D)	-	-

Source: 1997 *Economic Census*. The states are in descending order of revenues or establishments (if revenue data are missing for the majority). The symbol (D) appears when data are withheld to prevent disclosure of competitive information. States marked with (D) are sorted by number of establishments. A dash (-) indicates that the data element cannot be calculated. * indicates the midpoint of a range; 175, for example is the range 100-249. Shaded *states* on the state map indicate those states which have proportionately greater representation in the industry than would be indicated by the state's population; the ratio is based on total revenues or number of establishments. Shaded *regions* indicate where the industry is regionally most concentrated.

NAICS 721120 - CASINO HOTELS

GENERAL STATISTICS

Year	Establishments (number)	Employment (number)	Payroll ($ million)	Revenues ($ million)	Employees per Establishment (number)	Revenues per Establishment ($)	Payroll per Employee ($)
1997	257	271,220	5,998.0	20,652.0	1,055.3	80,357,977	22,115

Source: *Economic Census of the United States*, 1997. This is a newly defined industry. Data for prior years were unavailable at the time of publication but may become available over time.

INDICES OF CHANGE

Year	Establishments (number)	Employment (number)	Payroll ($ million)	Revenues ($ million)	Employees per Establishment (number)	Revenues per Establishment ($)	Payroll per Employee ($)
1997	100.0	100.0	100.0	100.0	100.0	100.0	100.0

Sources: Same as General Statistics. The values shown reflect change from the base year, 1997. Values above 100 mean greater than 1997, values below 100 mean less than 1997, and a value of 100 in the 1982-96 or 1998-2001 period means same as 1997. Values followed by a 'p' are projections by the editors; 'e' stands for extrapolation. Data are the most recent available at this level of detail.

SIC INDUSTRIES RELATED TO NAICS 721120

Each new NAICS code represents an industry that used to be part of an SIC or a part of several SIC industries. Data in this table are shown to provide transitional information for these cases. All available data for the precursor SIC(s) are shown. Even if only a part of an SIC is included in the NAICS, *all* data for the SIC are reproduced. If the SIC industry is not marked as being a part (pt) of the NAICS, the entire industry is embedded in the NAICS data. The SIC composition of the new industry provides some hints of the relative importance of its "ancestors." Data marked with a 'p' are projected. Projections begin with 1982 data. Data earlier than 1990 are not shown but are reflected in the projections.

SIC	Industry	1990	1991	1992	1993	1994	1995	1996	1997
7011	**Hotels, Motels (pt)**								
	Establishments (number)	39,247	40,892	41,684	42,597	42,924	43,251	43,163p	43,555p
	Employment (thousands)	1,463.1	1,440.8	1,455.9	1,477.0	1,484.4	1,519.2	1,591.2p	1,622.9p
	Revenues ($ million)	61,991.0	63,082.0	68,508.0	71,519.0	76,696.0	81,104.0	85,720.0	87,807.4p

Source: *Economic Census of the United States*, 1992, annual surveys of economic sectors conducted by the Bureau of the Census, and estimates or projections based on the 1982-1992 period; not all data are shown. 'e' marks estimates made by the editors; 'p' indicates projections based on time series. A dash (-) indicates that data for this SIC or year were not available. The abbreviation (pt) next to the industry name indicates that only a part of the industry is present within the NAICS data. If no (pt) is shown, the entire industry is contained within the NAICS data.

SELECTED RATIOS

For 1997	Avg. of Information	Analyzed Industry	Index	For 1997	Avg. of Information	Analyzed Industry	Index
Employees per establishment	17	1,055	6,086	Payroll per establishment	177,969	23,338,521	13,114
Revenue per establishment	642,845	80,357,977	12,500	Payroll as % of revenue	28	29	105
Revenue per employee	37,074	76,145	205	Payroll per employee	10,264	22,115	215

Sources: Same as General Statistics. The 'Average' column represents the average for the industry sector, in 1997, where the currently shown industry is classified. The Index shows the relationship between the Average and the Analyzed Industry. For example, 100 means that they are equal; 500 that the Analyzed Industry is five times the average; 50 means that the Analyzed Industry is half the national average. The abbreviation 'na' is used to show that data are 'not available'.

LEADING COMPANIES

No company data available for this industry.

LOCATION BY STATE AND REGIONAL CONCENTRATION

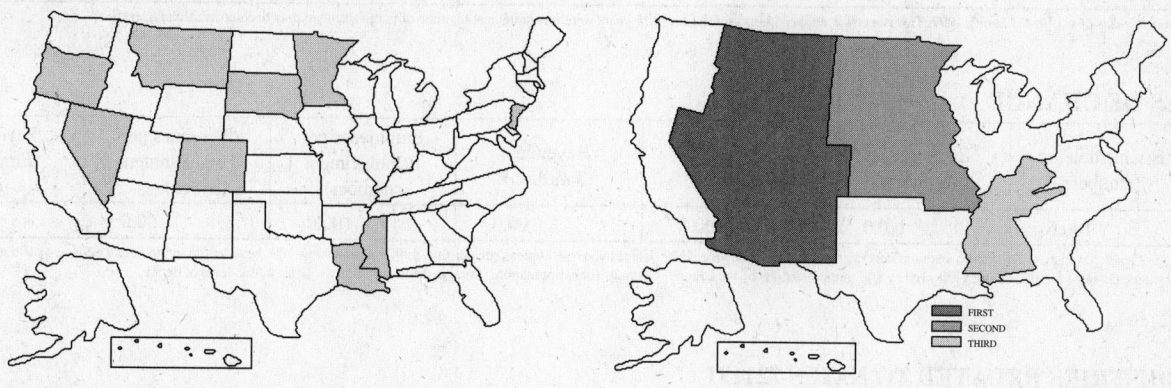

FIRST
SECOND
THIRD

INDUSTRY DATA BY STATE

State	Establishments		Employment			Payroll		Revenues		
	Total (number)	% of U.S.	Total (number)	% of U.S.	Per Estab.	Total ($ mil.)	Per Empl. ($)	Total ($ mil.)	% of U.S.	Per Estab. ($)
Nevada	170	66.1	182,652	67.3	1,074	4,026.2	22,043	12,993.5	62.9	76,432,224
New Jersey	12	4.7	45,955	16.9	3,830	1,214.7	26,431	4,595.3	22.3	382,945,167
Mississippi	11	4.3	14,031	5.2	1,276	265.8	18,941	994.3	4.8	90,388,364
Louisiana	5	1.9	5,392	2.0	1,078	99.5	18,460	415.5	2.0	83,099,200
Minnesota	6	2.3	3,939	1.5	657	68.8	17,476	290.9	1.4	48,483,667
Colorado	14	5.4	2,419	0.9	173	44.0	18,198	175.6	0.9	12,539,857
South Dakota	10	3.9	819	0.3	82	11.4	13,873	57.9	0.3	5,792,700
Oregon	6	2.3	676	0.2	113	12.5	18,519	47.7	0.2	7,954,667
Montana	6	2.3	379	0.1	63	3.9	10,306	11.7	0.1	1,942,667
Missouri	3	1.2	7,500*	-	-	(D)	-	(D)	-	-
Arizona	2	0.8	1,750*	-	-	(D)	-	(D)	-	-
Florida	2	0.8	10*	-	-	(D)	-	(D)	-	-
Wisconsin	2	0.8	750*	-	-	(D)	-	(D)	-	-
California	1	0.4	60*	-	-	(D)	-	(D)	-	-
Idaho	1	0.4	175*	-	-	(D)	-	(D)	-	-
Indiana	1	0.4	1,750*	-	-	(D)	-	(D)	-	-
Iowa	1	0.4	1,750*	-	-	(D)	-	(D)	-	-
Massachusetts	1	0.4	10*	-	-	(D)	-	(D)	-	-
Michigan	1	0.4	375*	-	-	(D)	-	(D)	-	-
South Carolina	1	0.4	10*	-	-	(D)	-	(D)	-	-
Tennessee	1	0.4	1,750*	-	-	(D)	-	(D)	-	-

Source: 1997 *Economic Census*. The states are in descending order of revenues or establishments (if revenue data are missing for the majority). The symbol (D) appears when data are withheld to prevent disclosure of competitive information. States marked with (D) are sorted by number of establishments. A dash (-) indicates that the data element cannot be calculated. * indicates the midpoint of a range; 175, for example is the range 100-249. Shaded *states* on the state map indicate those states which have proportionately greater representation in the industry than would be indicated by the state's population; the ratio is based on total revenues or number of establishments. Shaded *regions* indicate where the industry is regionally most concentrated.

NAICS 721191 - BED AND BREAKFAST INNS

GENERAL STATISTICS

Year	Establishments (number)	Employment (number)	Payroll ($ million)	Revenues ($ million)	Employees per Establishment (number)	Revenues per Establishment ($)	Payroll per Employee ($)
1997	2,898	16,049	169.0	687.0	5.5	237,060	10,530

Source: *Economic Census of the United States*, 1997. This is a newly defined industry. Data for prior years were unavailable at the time of publication but may become available over time.

INDICES OF CHANGE

Year	Establishments (number)	Employment (number)	Payroll ($ million)	Revenues ($ million)	Employees per Establishment (number)	Revenues per Establishment ($)	Payroll per Employee ($)
1997	100.0	100.0	100.0	100.0	100.0	100.0	100.0

Sources: Same as General Statistics. The values shown reflect change from the base year, 1997. Values above 100 mean greater than 1997, values below 100 mean less than 1997, and a value of 100 in the 1982-96 or 1998-2001 period means same as 1997. Values followed by a 'p' are projections by the editors; 'e' stands for extrapolation. Data are the most recent available at this level of detail.

SIC INDUSTRIES RELATED TO NAICS 721191

Each new NAICS code represents an industry that used to be part of an SIC or a part of several SIC industries. Data in this table are shown to provide transitional information for these cases. All available data for the precursor SIC(s) are shown. Even if only a part of an SIC is included in the NAICS, *all* data for the SIC are reproduced. If the SIC industry is not marked as being a part (pt) of the NAICS, the entire industry is embedded in the NAICS data. The SIC composition of the new industry provides some hints of the relative importance of its "ancestors." Data marked with a 'p' are projected. Projections begin with 1982 data. Data earlier than 1990 are not shown but are reflected in the projections.

SIC	Industry	1990	1991	1992	1993	1994	1995	1996	1997
7011	**Hotels, Motels (pt)**								
	Establishments (number)	39,247	40,892	41,684	42,597	42,924	43,251	43,163p	43,555p
	Employment (thousands)	1,463.1	1,440.8	1,455.9	1,477.0	1,484.4	1,519.2	1,591.2p	1,622.9p
	Revenues ($ million)	61,991.0	63,082.0	68,508.0	71,519.0	76,696.0	81,104.0	85,720.0	87,807.4p

Source: *Economic Census of the United States*, 1992, annual surveys of economic sectors conducted by the Bureau of the Census, and estimates or projections based on the 1982-1992 period; not all data are shown. 'e' marks estimates made by the editors; 'p' indicates projections based on time series. A dash (-) indicates that data for this SIC or year were not available. The abbreviation (pt) next to the industry name indicates that only a part of the industry is present within the NAICS data. If no (pt) is shown, the entire industry is contained within the NAICS data.

SELECTED RATIOS

For 1997	Avg. of Information	Analyzed Industry	Index	For 1997	Avg. of Information	Analyzed Industry	Index
Employees per establishment	17	6	32	Payroll per establishment	177,969	58,316	33
Revenue per establishment	642,845	237,060	37	Payroll as % of revenue	28	25	89
Revenue per employee	37,074	42,806	115	Payroll per employee	10,264	10,530	103

Sources: Same as General Statistics. The 'Average' column represents the average for the industry sector, in 1997, where the currently shown industry is classified. The Index shows the relationship between the Average and the Analyzed Industry. For example, 100 means that they are equal; 500 that the Analyzed Industry is five times the average; 50 means that the Analyzed Industry is half the national average. The abbreviation 'na' is used to show that data are 'not available'.

LEADING COMPANIES

No company data available for this industry.

LOCATION BY STATE AND REGIONAL CONCENTRATION

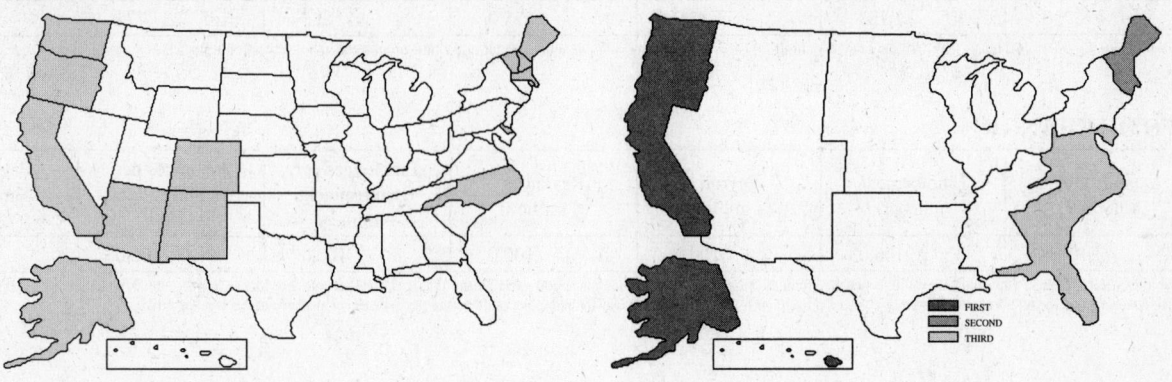

FIRST
SECOND
THIRD

INDUSTRY DATA BY STATE

State	Establishments Total (number)	% of U.S.	Employment Total (number)	% of U.S.	Per Estab.	Payroll Total ($ mil.)	Per Empl. ($)	Revenues Total ($ mil.)	% of U.S.	Per Estab. ($)
California	324	11.2	2,534	15.8	8	28.3	11,180	122.5	17.8	378,034
Massachusetts	167	5.8	621	3.9	4	9.3	14,907	42.0	6.1	251,707
North Carolina	126	4.3	942	5.9	7	10.3	10,882	35.5	5.2	282,071
New York	111	3.8	681	4.2	6	8.7	12,747	34.2	5.0	308,441
Florida	97	3.3	536	3.3	6	6.1	11,397	33.3	4.9	343,670
Vermont	131	4.5	862	5.4	7	8.2	9,498	32.1	4.7	244,924
Maine	152	5.2	440	2.7	3	6.3	14,430	29.4	4.3	193,658
Pennsylvania	103	3.6	785	4.9	8	7.1	9,036	25.4	3.7	246,388
Colorado	97	3.3	556	3.5	6	5.4	9,772	21.5	3.1	221,753
New Hampshire	86	3.0	494	3.1	6	4.7	9,601	18.7	2.7	216,884
Texas	105	3.6	594	3.7	6	4.7	7,941	18.6	2.7	177,162
Washington	106	3.7	405	2.5	4	4.2	10,477	16.9	2.5	159,009
Michigan	90	3.1	444	2.8	5	3.9	8,700	16.4	2.4	182,167
Rhode Island	45	1.6	238	1.5	5	3.8	16,038	15.8	2.3	351,333
Oregon	58	2.0	334	2.1	6	4.3	12,775	15.4	2.2	266,034
Georgia	54	1.9	326	2.0	6	3.1	9,377	13.5	2.0	249,130
Arizona	53	1.8	303	1.9	6	3.1	10,340	11.7	1.7	221,453
New Mexico	63	2.2	225	1.4	4	2.4	10,760	10.7	1.6	170,032
Maryland	37	1.3	196	1.2	5	2.8	14,444	9.7	1.4	262,486
Ohio	49	1.7	124	0.8	3	1.6	12,815	7.0	1.0	143,061
Mississippi	38	1.3	181	1.1	5	1.9	10,243	6.5	0.9	170,105
Louisiana	29	1.0	192	1.2	7	1.4	7,484	5.8	0.8	200,586
Minnesota	44	1.5	181	1.1	4	1.1	6,260	5.0	0.7	113,250
Alaska	44	1.5	39	0.2	1	0.7	16,718	4.9	0.7	112,045
Utah	29	1.0	157	1.0	5	1.1	6,783	4.2	0.6	145,655
Delaware	6	0.2	60	0.4	10	1.1	17,583	2.6	0.4	433,833
Arkansas	25	0.9	50	0.3	2	0.4	8,920	2.2	0.3	87,560
Montana	23	0.8	37	0.2	2	0.2	6,135	1.3	0.2	56,652
South Dakota	5	0.2	8	0.0	2	0.1	8,625	0.4	0.1	77,000
Virginia	90	3.1	750*	-	-	(D)	-	(D)	-	-
New Jersey	75	2.6	375*	-	-	(D)	-	(D)	-	-
Wisconsin	69	2.4	375*	-	-	(D)	-	(D)	-	-
South Carolina	46	1.6	375*	-	-	(D)	-	(D)	-	-
Indiana	42	1.4	375*	-	-	(D)	-	(D)	-	-
Tennessee	36	1.2	175*	-	-	(D)	-	(D)	-	-
Illinois	35	1.2	375*	-	-	(D)	-	(D)	-	-
Missouri	34	1.2	175*	-	-	(D)	-	(D)	-	-
Iowa	27	0.9	175*	-	-	(D)	-	(D)	-	-
West Virginia	21	0.7	60*	-	-	(D)	-	(D)	-	-
Kentucky	19	0.7	60*	-	-	(D)	-	(D)	-	-
Connecticut	17	0.6	175*	-	-	(D)	-	(D)	-	-
Idaho	17	0.6	175*	-	-	(D)	-	(D)	-	-
Kansas	17	0.6	60*	-	-	(D)	-	(D)	-	-
Nebraska	13	0.4	60*	-	-	(D)	-	(D)	-	-
Wyoming	11	0.4	10*	-	-	(D)	-	(D)	-	-
Hawaii	10	0.3	60*	-	-	(D)	-	(D)	-	-
Oklahoma	9	0.3	60*	-	-	(D)	-	(D)	-	-
Alabama	8	0.3	10*	-	-	(D)	-	(D)	-	-
Nevada	4	0.1	60*	-	-	(D)	-	(D)	-	-
North Dakota	1	-	10*	-	-	(D)	-	(D)	-	-

Source: 1997 *Economic Census.* The states are in descending order of revenues or establishments (if revenue data are missing for the majority). The symbol (D) appears when data are withheld to prevent disclosure of competitive information. States marked with (D) are sorted by number of establishments. A dash (-) indicates that the data element cannot be calculated. * indicates the midpoint of a range; 175, for example is the range 100-249. Shaded *states* on the state map indicate those states which have proportionately greater representation in the industry than would be indicated by the state's population; the ratio is based on total revenues or number of establishments. Shaded *regions* indicate where the industry is regionally most concentrated.

NAICS 721199 - TRAVELER ACCOMMODATION NEC

GENERAL STATISTICS

Year	Establishments (number)	Employment (number)	Payroll ($ million)	Revenues ($ million)	Employees per Establishment (number)	Revenues per Establishment ($)	Payroll per Employee ($)
1997	736	2,737	37.0	175.0	3.7	237,772	13,518

Source: Economic Census of the United States, 1997. This is a newly defined industry. Data for prior years were unavailable at the time of publication but may become available over time.

INDICES OF CHANGE

Year	Establishments (number)	Employment (number)	Payroll ($ million)	Revenues ($ million)	Employees per Establishment (number)	Revenues per Establishment ($)	Payroll per Employee ($)
1997	100.0	100.0	100.0	100.0	100.0	100.0	100.0

Sources: Same as General Statistics. The values shown reflect change from the base year, 1997. Values above 100 mean greater than 1997, values below 100 mean less than 1997, and a value of 100 in the 1982-96 or 1998-2001 period means same as 1997. Values followed by a 'p' are projections by the editors; 'e' stands for extrapolation. Data are the most recent available at this level of detail.

SIC INDUSTRIES RELATED TO NAICS 721199

Each new NAICS code represents an industry that used to be part of an SIC or a part of several SIC industries. Data in this table are shown to provide transitional information for these cases. All available data for the precursor SIC(s) are shown. Even if only a part of an SIC is included in the NAICS, *all* data for the SIC are reproduced. If the SIC industry is not marked as being a part (pt) of the NAICS, the entire industry is embedded in the NAICS data. The SIC composition of the new industry provides some hints of the relative importance of its "ancestors." Data marked with a 'p' are projected. Projections begin with 1982 data. Data earlier than 1990 are not shown but are reflected in the projections.

SIC	Industry	1990	1991	1992	1993	1994	1995	1996	1997
7011	**Hotels, Motels (pt)**								
	Establishments (number)	39,247	40,892	41,684	42,597	42,924	43,251	43,163*p*	43,555*p*
	Employment (thousands)	1,463.1	1,440.8	1,455.9	1,477.0	1,484.4	1,519.2	1,591.2*p*	1,622.9*p*
	Revenues ($ million)	61,991.0	63,082.0	68,508.0	71,519.0	76,696.0	81,104.0	85,720.0	87,807.4*p*

Source: Economic Census of the United States, 1992, annual surveys of economic sectors conducted by the Bureau of the Census, and estimates or projections based on the 1982-1992 period; not all data are shown. 'e' marks estimates made by the editors; 'p' indicates projections based on time series. A dash (-) indicates that data for this SIC or year were not available. The abbreviation (pt) next to the industry name indicates that only a part of the industry is present within the NAICS data. If no (pt) is shown, the entire industry is contained within the NAICS data.

SELECTED RATIOS

For 1997	Avg. of Information	Analyzed Industry	Index	For 1997	Avg. of Information	Analyzed Industry	Index
Employees per establishment	17	4	21	Payroll per establishment	177,969	50,272	28
Revenue per establishment	642,845	237,772	37	Payroll as % of revenue	28	21	76
Revenue per employee	37,074	63,939	172	Payroll per employee	10,264	13,518	132

Sources: Same as General Statistics. The 'Average' column represents the average for the industry sector, in 1997, where the currently shown industry is classified. The Index shows the relationship between the Average and the Analyzed Industry. For example, 100 means that they are equal; 500 that the Analyzed Industry is five times the average; 50 means that the Analyzed Industry is half the national average. The abbreviation 'na' is used to show that data are 'not available'.

LEADING COMPANIES

No company data available for this industry.

LOCATION BY STATE AND REGIONAL CONCENTRATION

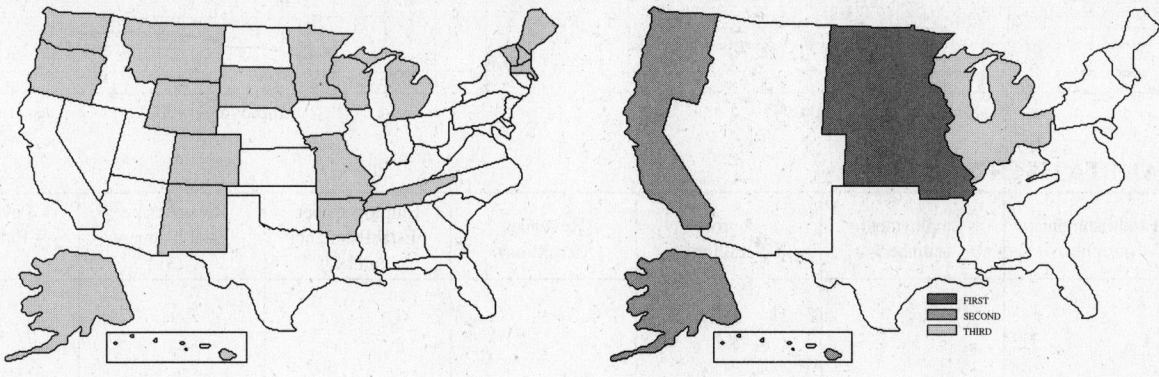

FIRST
SECOND
THIRD

INDUSTRY DATA BY STATE

State	Establishments Total (number)	Establishments % of U.S.	Employment Total (number)	Employment % of U.S.	Employment Per Estab.	Payroll Total ($ mil.)	Payroll Per Empl. ($)	Revenues Total ($ mil.)	Revenues % of U.S.	Revenues Per Estab. ($)
Colorado	51	6.9	177	6.5	3	2.6	14,932	12.4	7.1	243,608
Minnesota	78	10.6	127	4.6	2	1.5	11,906	11.2	6.4	143,603
New York	45	6.1	121	4.4	3	2.0	16,760	10.8	6.2	240,489
Texas	17	2.3	164	6.0	10	1.8	11,244	7.1	4.1	417,647
Washington	24	3.3	163	6.0	7	1.8	11,117	7.0	4.0	292,542
North Carolina	19	2.6	86	3.1	5	1.3	14,814	4.7	2.7	249,526
Michigan	39	5.3	75	2.7	2	1.3	17,467	4.6	2.6	116,923
Maine	33	4.5	38	1.4	1	0.8	22,000	4.5	2.6	137,000
Arkansas	23	3.1	79	2.9	3	0.7	9,114	4.2	2.4	182,609
Pennsylvania	15	2.0	48	1.8	3	0.6	13,125	4.2	2.4	279,867
New Mexico	11	1.5	95	3.5	9	0.9	8,958	3.1	1.7	278,636
Georgia	11	1.5	42	1.5	4	0.6	13,929	2.5	1.4	227,364
Oregon	11	1.5	34	1.2	3	0.3	9,588	1.9	1.1	175,273
New Hampshire	20	2.7	23	0.8	1	0.4	17,000	1.9	1.1	93,750
South Dakota	12	1.6	13	0.5	1	0.3	19,615	1.3	0.8	109,750
Louisiana	4	0.5	30	1.1	8	0.3	8,867	1.2	0.7	303,000
Ohio	11	1.5	26	0.9	2	0.2	9,000	1.2	0.7	105,909
Montana	8	1.1	6	0.2	1	0.1	24,833	0.9	0.5	115,375
Utah	3	0.4	23	0.8	8	0.1	5,696	0.5	0.3	178,667
Alaska	4	0.5	9	0.3	2	0.1	13,222	0.4	0.2	101,500
Vermont	6	0.8	3	0.1	1	-	14,667	0.4	0.2	63,333
California	64	8.7	375*	-	-	(D)	-	(D)	-	-
Wisconsin	50	6.8	60*	-	-	(D)	-	(D)	-	-
Missouri	45	6.1	60*	-	-	(D)	-	(D)	-	-
Tennessee	33	4.5	175*	-	-	(D)	-	(D)	-	-
Florida	22	3.0	60*	-	-	(D)	-	(D)	-	-
Massachusetts	20	2.7	60*	-	-	(D)	-	(D)	-	-
Arizona	8	1.1	60*	-	-	(D)	-	(D)	-	-
Oklahoma	6	0.8	60*	-	-	(D)	-	(D)	-	-
Indiana	5	0.7	10*	-	-	(D)	-	(D)	-	-
Kentucky	5	0.7	10*	-	-	(D)	-	(D)	-	-
Virginia	5	0.7	175*	-	-	(D)	-	(D)	-	-
Wyoming	5	0.7	60*	-	-	(D)	-	(D)	-	-
Hawaii	4	0.5	60*	-	-	(D)	-	(D)	-	-
Idaho	3	0.4	10*	-	-	(D)	-	(D)	-	-
Nevada	3	0.4	10*	-	-	(D)	-	(D)	-	-
Alabama	2	0.3	60*	-	-	(D)	-	(D)	-	-
South Carolina	2	0.3	60*	-	-	(D)	-	(D)	-	-
West Virginia	2	0.3	10*	-	-	(D)	-	(D)	-	-
Connecticut	1	0.1	10*	-	-	(D)	-	(D)	-	-
Illinois	1	0.1	10*	-	-	(D)	-	(D)	-	-
Iowa	1	0.1	10*	-	-	(D)	-	(D)	-	-
Kansas	1	0.1	10*	-	-	(D)	-	(D)	-	-
Nebraska	1	0.1	10*	-	-	(D)	-	(D)	-	-
New Jersey	1	0.1	10*	-	-	(D)	-	(D)	-	-
North Dakota	1	0.1	10*	-	-	(D)	-	(D)	-	-

Source: 1997 Economic Census. The states are in descending order of revenues or establishments (if revenue data are missing for the majority). The symbol (D) appears when data are withheld to prevent disclosure of competitive information. States marked with (D) are sorted by number of establishments. A dash (-) indicates that the data element cannot be calculated. * indicates the midpoint of a range; 175, for example is the range 100-249. Shaded *states* on the state map indicate those states which have proportionately greater representation in the industry than would be indicated by the state's population; the ratio is based on total revenues or number of establishments. Shaded *regions* indicate where the industry is regionally most concentrated.

NAICS 721211 - RV (RECREATIONAL VEHICLE) PARKS AND CAMPGROUNDS*

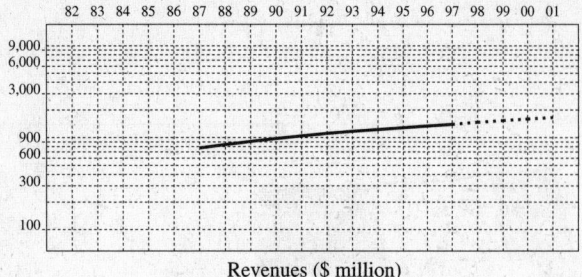

Revenues ($ million)

Employment (000)

GENERAL STATISTICS

Year	Establishments (number)	Employment (number)	Payroll ($ million)	Revenues ($ million)	Employees per Establishment (number)	Revenues per Establishment ($)	Payroll per Employee ($)
1982	-	-	-	-	-	-	-
1983	-	-	-	-	-	-	-
1984	-	-	-	-	-	-	-
1985	-	-	-	-	-	-	-
1986	-	-	-	-	-	-	-
1987	2,859	12,841	145.0	774.0	4.5	270,724	11,292
1988	2,724	11,699	153.0	842.0e	4.3	309,104	13,078
1989	2,723	12,981	186.0	910.0e	4.8	334,190	14,329
1990	2,820	13,537	186.0	978.0e	4.8	346,809	13,740
1991	2,965	13,539	193.0	1,046.0e	4.6	352,782	14,255
1992	3,475	15,419	224.0	1,113.0	4.4	320,288	14,528
1993	3,541	16,035	254.0	1,170.0e	4.5	330,415	15,840
1994	3,611	16,173	264.0	1,226.0e	4.5	339,518	16,324
1995	3,596	16,384	275.0	1,282.0e	4.6	356,507	16,785
1996	3,840e	16,429e	279.0e	1,338.0e	4.3e	348,438e	16,982e
1997	4,085	16,474	283.0	1,394.0	4.0	341,248	17,179
1998	4,133p	17,686p	313.0p	1,470.0p	4.3p	355,674p	17,698p
1999	4,273p	18,187p	329.0p	1,532.0p	4.3p	358,530p	18,090p
2000	4,412p	18,687p	344.0p	1,594.0p	4.2p	361,287p	18,409p
2001	4,552p	19,188p	359.0p	1,656.0p	4.2p	363,796p	18,710p

Sources: Economic Census of the United States, 1982, 1987, 1992, 1997. Establishment counts, employment, and payroll are from *County Business Patterns* for non-Census years. In non-Census years, industries in the Manufacturing range under SIC coding include data from the *Annual Survey of Manufactures* (*ASM*); those in the old Services range include data from the *Services Annual Survey* (*SAS*). Values followed by a 'p' are projections by the editors. Extrapolations are marked by 'e'. Data are the most recent available at this level of detail.

INDICES OF CHANGE

Year	Establishments (number)	Employment (number)	Payroll ($ million)	Revenues ($ million)	Employees per Establishment (number)	Revenues per Establishment ($)	Payroll per Employee ($)
1982	-	-	-	-	-	-	-
1987	70.0	77.9	51.2	55.5	111.4	79.3	65.7
1992	85.1	93.6	79.2	79.8	110.0	93.9	84.6
1993	86.7	97.3	89.8	83.9e	112.3	96.8	92.2
1994	88.4	98.2	93.3	87.9e	111.1	99.5	95.0
1995	88.0	99.5	97.2	92.0e	113.0	104.5	97.7
1996	94.0e	99.7e	98.6e	96.0e	106.1e	102.1e	98.9e
1997	100.0	100.0	100.0	100.0	100.0	100.0	100.0
1998	101.2p	107.4p	110.6p	105.5p	106.1p	104.2p	103.0p
1999	104.6p	110.4p	116.3p	109.9p	105.5p	105.1p	105.3p
2000	108.0p	113.4p	121.6p	114.3p	105.0p	105.9p	107.2p
2001	111.4p	116.5p	126.9p	118.8p	104.5p	106.6p	108.9p

Sources: Same as General Statistics. The values shown reflect change from the base year, 1997. Values above 100 mean greater than 1997, values below 100 mean less than 1997, and a value of 100 in the 1982-96 or 1998-2001 period means same as 1997. Values followed by a 'p' are projections by the editors; 'e' stands for extrapolation. Data are the most recent available at this level of detail.

SELECTED RATIOS

For 1997	Avg. of Information	Analyzed Industry	Index	For 1997	Avg. of Information	Analyzed Industry	Index
Employees per establishment	17	4	23	Payroll per establishment	177,969	69,278	39
Revenue per establishment	642,845	341,248	53	Payroll as % of revenue	28	20	73
Revenue per employee	37,074	84,618	228	Payroll per employee	10,264	17,179	167

Sources: Same as General Statistics. The 'Average' column represents the average for the industry sector, in 1997, where the currently shown industry is classified. The Index shows the relationship between the Average and the Analyzed Industry. For example, 100 means that they are equal; 500 that the Analyzed Industry is five times the average; 50 means that the Analyzed Industry is half the national average. The abbreviation 'na' is used to show that data are 'not available'.

*Equivalent to SIC 7033.

LEADING COMPANIES   Number shown: **12**   Total sales ($ mil): **257**   Total employment (000): **3.8**

Company Name	Address				CEO Name	Phone	Co. Type	Sales ($ mil)	Empl. (000)
Thousand Trails Inc.	2711 LBJ Fwy	Dallas	TX	75234	William J. Shaw	972-243-2228	P	68	0.8
Prairie Land Cooperative	PO Box 99	Windom	MN	56101	Steve Freking	507-831-2527	N	40	<0.1
Adventure Lands of America Inc.	PO Box 3355	Des Moines	IA	50316	JF Krantz	515-266-2121	R	33*	0.2
1000 Trails Inc.	2711 LBJ Fwy	Dallas	TX	75234	Bill Shaw	972-243-2228	S	32*	0.7
Resorts USA Inc.	PO Box 447	Bushkill	PA	18324	Andrew Worthington	570-588-6661	D	27	1.0
KOA Holdings Inc.	550 N 31st St	Billings	MT	59101	Art Peterson	406-248-7444	R	23*	0.4
Kampgrounds of America Inc.	PO Box 30558	Billings	MT	59114	Arthur M Peterson	406-248-7444	S	12*	0.2
Mesa Verde Co.	P O Box 277	Mancos	CO	81328		970-533-7731	S	10*	0.2
Coast to Coast Resorts	64 Inverness Dr E	Englewood	CO	80112	Joe McAdams	303-728-2267	R	8*	0.1
Harold W. Pelton Co.	418 S Town St	Fostoria	OH	44830	Harold W Pelton Sr	419-435-2330	R	2*	<0.1
Cocopah Bend RV & Golf Resort	6800 S Strand Ave	Yuma	AZ	85364		520-343-9300	R	1	<0.1
Marineland Foundation Inc.	9507 Oceanshore	St. Augustine	FL	32086	Dennis LaPorte	904-460-1275	R	1	<0.1

Source: *Ward's Business Directory of U.S. Private and Public Companies*, Volumes 1 and 2, 2000. The company type code used is as follows: P - Public, R - Private, S - Subsidiary, D - Division, J - Joint Venture, A - Affiliate, G - Group, N - Company type not reported. Sales are in millions of dollars, employees are in thousands. An asterisk (*) indicates an estimated sales volume. The symbol < stands for 'less than'. Company names and addresses are truncated, in some cases, to fit into the available space.

LOCATION BY STATE AND REGIONAL CONCENTRATION

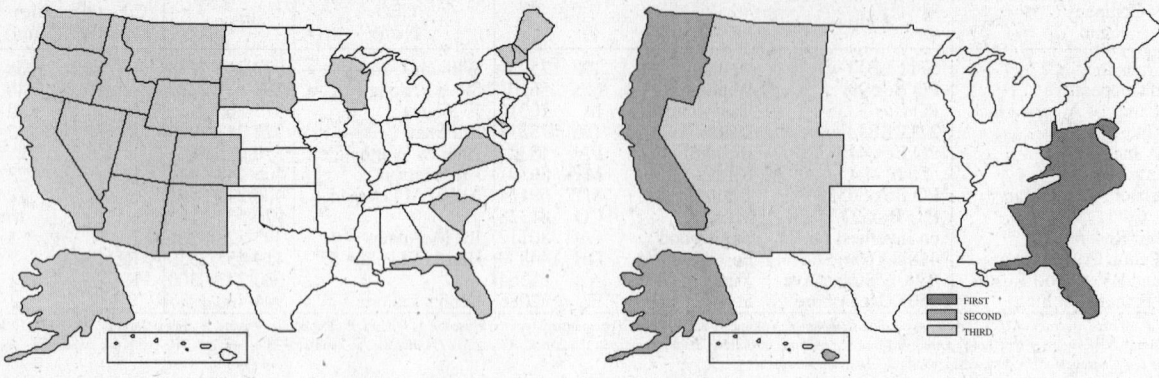

FIRST
SECOND
THIRD

INDUSTRY DATA BY STATE

State	Establishments Total (number)	Establishments % of U.S.	Employment Total (number)	Employment % of U.S.	Employment Per Estab.	Payroll Total ($ mil.)	Payroll Per Empl. ($)	Revenues Total ($ mil.)	Revenues % of U.S.	Revenues Per Estab. ($)
Florida	372	9.1	2,854	17.3	8	42.2	14,795	218.9	15.7	588,409
California	461	11.3	2,781	16.9	6	46.0	16,529	200.6	14.4	435,056
Arizona	176	4.3	1,451	8.8	8	17.6	12,159	110.4	7.9	627,506
Pennsylvania	164	4.0	513	3.1	3	10.4	20,314	56.6	4.1	345,079
South Carolina	30	0.7	450	2.7	15	8.9	19,858	49.5	3.6	1,651,333
Texas	208	5.1	857	5.2	4	10.0	11,667	48.9	3.5	235,135
New York	165	4.0	299	1.8	2	9.3	30,957	43.3	3.1	262,182
Washington	167	4.1	673	4.1	4	11.3	16,762	41.6	3.0	248,874
New Jersey	83	2.0	316	1.9	4	7.8	24,744	39.2	2.8	472,205
Ohio	173	4.2	354	2.1	2	6.5	18,500	36.8	2.6	212,538
Virginia	91	2.2	456	2.8	5	9.9	21,618	36.7	2.6	403,000
Oregon	122	3.0	514	3.1	4	7.8	15,222	35.7	2.6	292,484
Michigan	154	3.8	291	1.8	2	7.7	26,498	34.6	2.5	224,506
Wisconsin	137	3.4	261	1.6	2	5.9	22,571	31.3	2.2	228,672
Maine	111	2.7	155	0.9	1	6.0	38,419	30.1	2.2	271,595
North Carolina	104	2.5	306	1.9	3	5.5	17,843	30.0	2.1	288,106
Massachusetts	64	1.6	136	0.8	2	5.3	38,868	23.3	1.7	364,656
Colorado	80	2.0	162	1.0	2	4.0	24,481	20.8	1.5	260,337
Nevada	42	1.0	303	1.8	7	3.9	12,805	20.6	1.5	490,524
Illinois	72	1.8	200	1.2	3	4.0	20,085	18.8	1.3	260,889
Utah	47	1.2	287	1.7	6	5.2	18,010	18.6	1.3	395,298
New Hampshire	75	1.8	112	0.7	1	3.2	28,545	17.6	1.3	234,440
Indiana	75	1.8	204	1.2	3	3.1	15,088	17.3	1.2	230,147
Tennessee	63	1.5	230	1.4	4	3.2	13,987	17.2	1.2	273,476
Minnesota	98	2.4	154	0.9	2	3.4	22,058	16.6	1.2	169,643
Maryland	32	0.8	171	1.0	5	3.5	20,415	15.2	1.1	474,438
Montana	56	1.4	143	0.9	3	2.2	15,210	13.4	1.0	238,393
Missouri	77	1.9	177	1.1	2	2.7	15,169	13.1	0.9	170,481
Alabama	38	0.9	173	1.1	5	2.1	12,168	11.2	0.8	295,789
New Mexico	55	1.3	172	1.0	3	1.8	10,657	11.2	0.8	202,873
South Dakota	44	1.1	111	0.7	3	2.0	18,063	10.8	0.8	246,091
Connecticut	21	0.5	44	0.3	2	2.0	45,864	9.3	0.7	441,333
Georgia	37	0.9	123	0.7	3	1.7	14,154	8.1	0.6	219,946
Oklahoma	33	0.8	134	0.8	4	2.0	14,799	8.0	0.6	243,606
Kentucky	36	0.9	108	0.7	3	1.3	11,750	8.0	0.6	222,306
Wyoming	36	0.9	53	0.3	1	1.3	24,547	7.9	0.6	219,444
Louisiana	26	0.6	101	0.6	4	1.3	13,307	7.0	0.5	268,154
Delaware	12	0.3	53	0.3	4	1.3	25,094	6.6	0.5	552,917
Idaho	32	0.8	80	0.5	3	1.1	13,913	6.4	0.5	201,000
Alaska	28	0.7	48	0.3	2	1.1	22,625	6.4	0.5	227,107
Mississippi	25	0.6	90	0.5	4	1.3	14,256	5.5	0.4	220,280
Vermont	25	0.6	40	0.2	2	0.8	19,000	4.7	0.3	189,880
West Virginia	17	0.4	58	0.4	3	1.1	19,552	4.1	0.3	243,471
Arkansas	22	0.5	78	0.5	4	1.1	13,756	3.9	0.3	176,682
Rhode Island	16	0.4	21	0.1	1	0.8	35,952	3.8	0.3	238,313
Nebraska	17	0.4	23	0.1	1	0.3	12,217	3.3	0.2	192,941
Iowa	28	0.7	60*	-	-	(D)	-	(D)	-	-
Kansas	26	0.6	60*	-	-	(D)	-	(D)	-	-
North Dakota	10	0.2	10*	-	-	(D)	-	(D)	-	-
Hawaii	2	-	10*	-	-	(D)	-	(D)	-	-

Source: 1997 *Economic Census*. The states are in descending order of revenues or establishments (if revenue data are missing for the majority). The symbol (D) appears when data are withheld to prevent disclosure of competitive information. States marked with (D) are sorted by number of establishments. A dash (-) indicates that the data element cannot be calculated. * indicates the midpoint of a range; 175, for example is the range 100-249. Shaded *states* on the state map indicate those states which have proportionately greater representation in the industry than would be indicated by the state's population; the ratio is based on total revenues or number of establishments. Shaded *regions* indicate where the industry is regionally most concentrated.

NAICS 721214 - RECREATIONAL AND VACATION CAMPS (EXCEPT CAMPGROUNDS)*

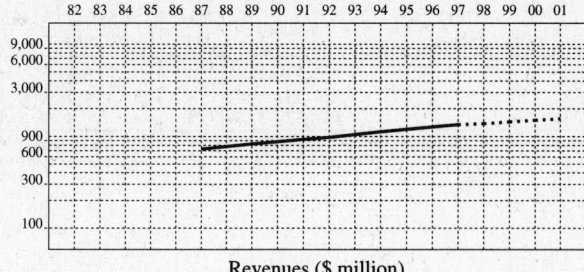

82 83 84 85 86 87 88 89 90 91 92 93 94 95 96 97 98 99 00 01

Revenues ($ million)

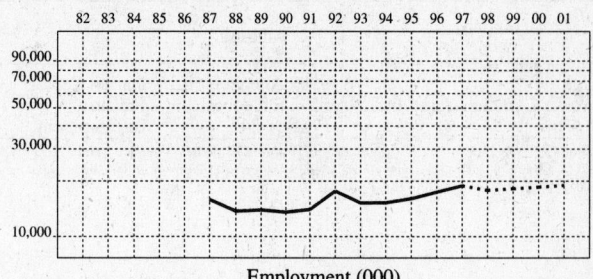

82 83 84 85 86 87 88 89 90 91 92 93 94 95 96 97 98 99 00 01

Employment (000)

GENERAL STATISTICS

Year	Establishments (number)	Employment (number)	Payroll ($ million)	Revenues ($ million)	Employees per Establishment (number)	Revenues per Establishment ($)	Payroll per Employee ($)
1982	-	-	-	-	-	-	-
1983	-	-	-	-	-	-	-
1984	-	-	-	-	-	-	-
1985	-	-	-	-	-	-	-
1986	-	-	-	-	-	-	-
1987	2,846	15,876	189.0	727.0	5.6	255,446	11,905
1988	2,714	13,723	215.0	777.0 e	5.1	286,293	15,667
1989	2,644	13,934	239.0	827.0 e	5.3	312,784	17,152
1990	2,615	13,551	236.0	877.0 e	5.2	335,373	17,416
1991	2,732	14,006	256.0	927.0 e	5.1	339,312	18,278
1992	3,045	17,650	271.0	977.0	5.8	320,854	15,354
1993	3,001	15,217	286.0	1,050.0 e	5.1	349,883	18,795
1994	3,018	15,238	303.0	1,122.0 e	5.0	371,769	19,884
1995	3,039	16,053	330.0	1,195.0 e	5.3	393,221	20,557
1996	3,276 e	17,455 e	356.0 e	1,268.0 e	5.3 e	387,057 e	20,395 e
1997	3,513	18,857	383.0	1,341.0	5.4	381,725	20,311
1998	3,377 p	17,820 p	386.0 p	1,376.0 p	5.3 p	407,462 p	21,661 p
1999	3,448 p	18,191 p	404.0 p	1,438.0 p	5.3 p	417,053 p	22,209 p
2000	3,520 p	18,562 p	422.0 p	1,499.0 p	5.3 p	425,852 p	22,735 p
2001	3,591 p	18,932 p	440.0 p	1,560.0 p	5.3 p	434,419 p	23,241 p

Sources: Economic Census of the United States, 1982, 1987, 1992, 1997. Establishment counts, employment, and payroll are from *County Business Patterns* for non-Census years. In non-Census years, industries in the Manufacturing range under SIC coding include data from the *Annual Survey of Manufactures* (*ASM*); those in the old Services range include data from the *Services Annual Survey* (*SAS*). Values followed by a 'p' are projections by the editors. Extrapolations are marked by 'e'. Data are the most recent available at this level of detail.

INDICES OF CHANGE

Year	Establishments (number)	Employment (number)	Payroll ($ million)	Revenues ($ million)	Employees per Establishment (number)	Revenues per Establishment ($)	Payroll per Employee ($)
1982	-	-	-	-	-	-	-
1987	81.0	84.2	49.3	54.2	103.9	66.9	58.6
1992	86.7	93.6	70.8	72.9	108.0	84.1	75.6
1993	85.4	80.7	74.7	78.3 e	94.5	91.7	92.5
1994	85.9	80.8	79.1	83.7 e	94.1	97.4	97.9
1995	86.5	85.1	86.2	89.1 e	98.4	103.0	101.2
1996	93.3 e	92.6 e	93.0 e	94.6 e	99.3 e	101.4 e	100.4 e
1997	100.0	100.0	100.0	100.0	100.0	100.0	100.0
1998	96.1 p	94.5 p	100.8 p	102.6 p	98.3 p	106.7 p	106.6 p
1999	98.1 p	96.5 p	105.5 p	107.2 p	98.3 p	109.3 p	109.3 p
2000	100.2 p	98.4 p	110.2 p	111.8 p	98.2 p	111.6 p	111.9 p
2001	102.2 p	100.4 p	114.9 p	116.3 p	98.2 p	113.8 p	114.4 p

Sources: Same as General Statistics. The values shown reflect change from the base year, 1997. Values above 100 mean greater than 1997, values below 100 mean less than 1997, and a value of 100 in the 1982-96 or 1998-2001 period means same as 1997. Values followed by a 'p' are projections by the editors; 'e' stands for extrapolation. Data are the most recent available at this level of detail.

SELECTED RATIOS

For 1997	Avg. of Information	Analyzed Industry	Index	For 1997	Avg. of Information	Analyzed Industry	Index
Employees per establishment	17	5	31	Payroll per establishment	177,969	109,024	61
Revenue per establishment	642,845	381,725	59	Payroll as % of revenue	28	29	103
Revenue per employee	37,074	71,114	192	Payroll per employee	10,264	20,311	198

Sources: Same as General Statistics. The 'Average' column represents the average for the industry sector, in 1997, where the currently shown industry is classified. The Index shows the relationship between the Average and the Analyzed Industry. For example, 100 means that they are equal; 500 that the Analyzed Industry is five times the average; 50 means that the Analyzed Industry is half the national average. The abbreviation 'na' is used to show that data are 'not available'.

*Equivalent to SIC 7032.

LEADING COMPANIES Number shown: **3**   Total sales ($ mil): **340**   Total employment (000): **2.6**

Company Name	Address				CEO Name	Phone	Co. Type	Sales ($ mil)	Empl. (000)
Six Flags	9993 Allegheny Rd	Darien Center	NY	14040		716-599-4641	R	298*	2.2
Hume Lake Christian Camp Inc.	6545 E Hedges	Fresno	CA	93727		559-251-6043	R	39*	0.3
A-Bar A Inc.	PO Box 247	Encampment	WY	82325		307-327-5454	S	3	<0.1

Source: *Ward's Business Directory of U.S. Private and Public Companies*, Volumes 1 and 2, 2000. The company type code used is as follows: P - Public, R - Private, S - Subsidiary, D - Division, J - Joint Venture, A - Affiliate, G - Group, N - Company type not reported. Sales are in millions of dollars, employees are in thousands. An asterisk (*) indicates an estimated sales volume. The symbol < stands for 'less than'. Company names and addresses are truncated, in some cases, to fit into the available space.

LOCATION BY STATE AND REGIONAL CONCENTRATION

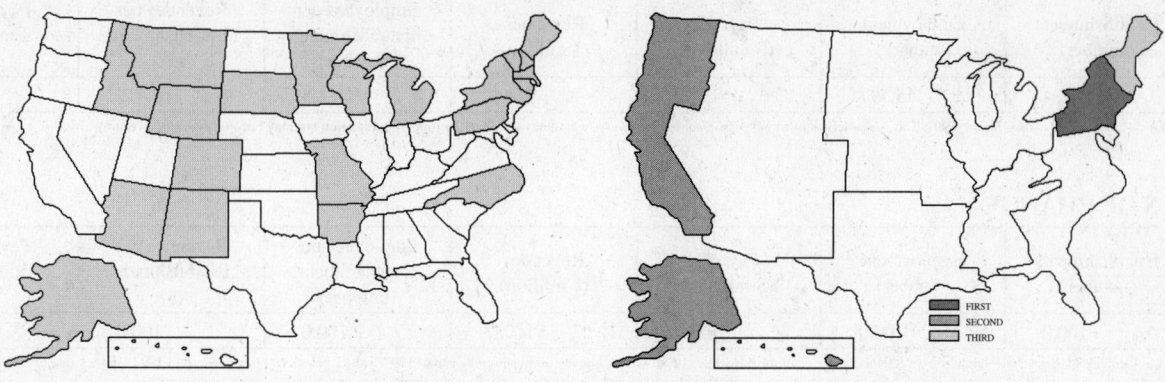

INDUSTRY DATA BY STATE

State	Establishments Total (number)	% of U.S.	Employment Total (number)	% of U.S.	Per Estab.	Payroll Total ($ mil.)	Per Empl. ($)	Revenues Total ($ mil.)	% of U.S.	Per Estab. ($)
New York	246	7.0	1,446	7.7	6	42.5	29,395	153.3	11.4	623,346
Pennsylvania	190	5.4	1,149	6.1	6	25.4	22,135	101.9	7.6	536,084
California	267	7.6	1,558	8.3	6	28.5	18,272	98.7	7.4	369,599
Texas	172	4.9	1,485	7.9	9	21.6	14,516	75.8	5.7	440,465
North Carolina	104	3.0	633	3.4	6	16.4	25,972	53.6	4.0	515,221
Colorado	133	3.8	869	4.6	7	15.1	17,356	52.5	3.9	395,000
Michigan	145	4.1	1,089	5.8	8	17.7	16,280	52.3	3.9	360,821
Wisconsin	137	3.9	754	4.0	6	15.5	20,598	51.3	3.8	374,263
Minnesota	195	5.6	777	4.1	4	12.3	15,820	50.3	3.8	258,128
Massachusetts	83	2.4	489	2.6	6	14.4	29,466	48.0	3.6	578,554
Maine	112	3.2	494	2.6	4	12.2	24,698	47.9	3.6	427,250
Florida	121	3.4	543	2.9	4	9.8	18,127	34.5	2.6	285,182
Alaska	102	2.9	214	1.1	2	8.0	37,402	31.8	2.4	311,892
New Hampshire	69	2.0	398	2.1	6	8.2	20,595	31.1	2.3	451,188
Missouri	79	2.2	392	2.1	5	9.1	23,296	30.4	2.3	385,316
Wyoming	94	2.7	385	2.0	4	8.6	22,449	28.6	2.1	304,191
Connecticut	31	0.9	172	0.9	6	6.7	39,052	26.3	2.0	849,032
New Jersey	43	1.2	349	1.9	8	7.4	21,221	24.7	1.8	575,372
Washington	86	2.4	351	1.9	4	6.9	19,570	23.1	1.7	268,174
Montana	74	2.1	235	1.2	3	7.1	30,204	22.9	1.7	309,973
Arizona	45	1.3	453	2.4	10	6.0	13,349	21.8	1.6	483,711
Georgia	47	1.3	321	1.7	7	5.9	18,517	21.4	1.6	455,170
Illinois	82	2.3	352	1.9	4	5.5	15,722	20.3	1.5	248,049
Ohio	84	2.4	422	2.2	5	6.7	15,827	19.7	1.5	234,976
Alabama	38	1.1	357	1.9	9	6.9	19,193	19.4	1.4	511,395
New Mexico	32	0.9	244	1.3	8	5.8	23,906	17.1	1.3	535,406
Virginia	64	1.8	292	1.5	5	5.1	17,329	16.7	1.2	260,984
Arkansas	41	1.2	271	1.4	7	3.9	14,568	16.7	1.2	406,756
Oregon	50	1.4	245	1.3	5	3.6	14,600	14.4	1.1	288,580
Vermont	43	1.2	139	0.7	3	3.9	27,978	13.1	1.0	305,209
Maryland	39	1.1	163	0.9	4	3.7	22,497	12.2	0.9	311,744
Idaho	48	1.4	144	0.8	3	3.4	23,417	11.9	0.9	248,667
Tennessee	49	1.4	247	1.3	5	2.8	11,437	9.4	0.7	191,429
Kentucky	33	0.9	186	1.0	6	2.3	12,559	9.1	0.7	276,848
South Carolina	26	0.7	122	0.6	5	2.7	22,475	8.8	0.7	336,538
Mississippi	22	0.6	114	0.6	5	1.9	16,316	6.0	0.4	273,455
West Virginia	28	0.8	79	0.4	3	1.9	24,456	5.9	0.4	211,500
Nebraska	25	0.7	79	0.4	3	1.3	16,962	5.1	0.4	205,120
Oklahoma	27	0.8	61	0.3	2	1.2	20,164	5.0	0.4	186,704
Utah	22	0.6	80	0.4	4	1.2	14,387	4.7	0.4	215,591
South Dakota	17	0.5	36	0.2	2	0.7	20,028	4.0	0.3	235,765
Nevada	8	0.2	58	0.3	7	0.7	11,741	1.6	0.1	201,875
Rhode Island	7	0.2	20	0.1	3	0.3	16,300	1.5	0.1	208,857
North Dakota	9	0.3	14	0.1	2	0.4	29,214	1.2	0.1	128,000
Indiana	54	1.5	175*	-	-	(D)	-	(D)	-	-
Iowa	33	0.9	175*	-	-	(D)	-	(D)	-	-
Kansas	26	0.7	60*	-	-	(D)	-	(D)	-	-
Louisiana	24	0.7	175*	-	-	(D)	-	(D)	-	-
Hawaii	4	0.1	10*	-	-	(D)	-	(D)	-	-
Delaware	3	0.1	10*	-	-	(D)	-	(D)	-	-

Source: 1997 *Economic Census*. The states are in descending order of revenues or establishments (if revenue data are missing for the majority). The symbol (D) appears when data are withheld to prevent disclosure of competitive information. States marked with (D) are sorted by number of establishments. A dash (-) indicates that the data element cannot be calculated. * indicates the midpoint of a range; 175, for example is the range 100-249. Shaded *states* on the state map indicate those states which have proportionately greater representation in the industry than would be indicated by the state's population; the ratio is based on total revenues or number of establishments. Shaded *regions* indicate where the industry is regionally most concentrated.

755

NAICS 721310 - ROOMING AND BOARDING HOUSES

GENERAL STATISTICS

Year	Establishments (number)	Employment (number)	Payroll ($ million)	Revenues ($ million)	Employees per Establishment (number)	Revenues per Establishment ($)	Payroll per Employee ($)
1997	3,484	15,597	156.0	754.0	4.5	216,418	10,002

Source: *Economic Census of the United States*, 1997. This is a newly defined industry. Data for prior years were unavailable at the time of publication but may become available over time.

INDICES OF CHANGE

Year	Establishments (number)	Employment (number)	Payroll ($ million)	Revenues ($ million)	Employees per Establishment (number)	Revenues per Establishment ($)	Payroll per Employee ($)
1997	100.0	100.0	100.0	100.0	100.0	100.0	100.0

Sources: Same as General Statistics. The values shown reflect change from the base year, 1997. Values above 100 mean greater than 1997, values below 100 mean less than 1997, and a value of 100 in the 1982-96 or 1998-2001 period means same as 1997. Values followed by a 'p' are projections by the editors; 'e' stands for extrapolation. Data are the most recent available at this level of detail.

SIC INDUSTRIES RELATED TO NAICS 721310

Each new NAICS code represents an industry that used to be part of an SIC or a part of several SIC industries. Data in this table are shown to provide transitional information for these cases. All available data for the precursor SIC(s) are shown. Even if only a part of an SIC is included in the NAICS, *all* data for the SIC are reproduced. If the SIC industry is not marked as being a part (pt) of the NAICS, the entire industry is embedded in the NAICS data. The SIC composition of the new industry provides some hints of the relative importance of its "ancestors." Data marked with a 'p' are projected. Projections begin with 1982 data. Data earlier than 1990 are not shown but are reflected in the projections.

SIC	Industry	1990	1991	1992	1993	1994	1995	1996	1997
7021	**Rooming & Boarding Houses**								
	Establishments (number)	1,585	1,582	1,620	1,634	1,627	1,578	1,560p	1,545p
	Employment (thousands)	8.7	9.0	8.1	8.2	8.2	8.7	8.2p	8.1p
	Revenues ($ million)	-	-	294.6	-	-	-	-	-
7041	**Membership-Basis Organization Hotels (pt)**								
	Establishments (number)	2,257	2,279	1,993	1,953	1,886	1,897	1,791p	1,723p
	Employment (thousands)	12.1	12.4	9.6	10.3	9.8	11.1	10.4p	10.3p
	Revenues ($ million)	-	-	433.7	-	-	-	-	-

Source: *Economic Census of the United States*, 1992, annual surveys of economic sectors conducted by the Bureau of the Census, and estimates or projections based on the 1982-1992 period; not all data are shown. 'e' marks estimates made by the editors; 'p' indicates projections based on time series. A dash (-) indicates that data for this SIC or year were not available. The abbreviation (pt) next to the industry name indicates that only a part of the industry is present within the NAICS data. If no (pt) is shown, the entire industry is contained within the NAICS data.

SELECTED RATIOS

For 1997	Avg. of Information	Analyzed Industry	Index	For 1997	Avg. of Information	Analyzed Industry	Index
Employees per establishment	17	4	26	Payroll per establishment	177,969	44,776	25
Revenue per establishment	642,845	216,418	34	Payroll as % of revenue	28	21	75
Revenue per employee	37,074	48,343	130	Payroll per employee	10,264	10,002	97

Sources: Same as General Statistics. The 'Average' column represents the average for the industry sector, in 1997, where the currently shown industry is classified. The Index shows the relationship between the Average and the Analyzed Industry. For example, 100 means that they are equal; 500 that the Analyzed Industry is five times the average; 50 means that the Analyzed Industry is half the national average. The abbreviation 'na' is used to show that data are 'not available'.

LEADING COMPANIES   Number shown: **2**   Total sales ($ mil): **98**   Total employment (000): **0.4**

Company Name	Address				CEO Name	Phone	Co. Type	Sales ($ mil)	Empl. (000)
BridgeStreet Accommodations Inc	2242 Pinnacle Pky	Twinsburg	OH	44087	John E. Danneberg	330-405-6060	P	96	0.4
Harold W. Pelton Co.	418 S Town St	Fostoria	OH	44830	Harold W Pelton Sr	419-435-2330	R	2*	<0.1

Source: Ward's Business Directory of U.S. Private and Public Companies, Volumes 1 and 2, 2000. The company type code used is as follows: P - Public, R - Private, S - Subsidiary, D - Division, J - Joint Venture, A - Affiliate, G - Group, N - Company type not reported. Sales are in millions of dollars, employees are in thousands. An asterisk (*) indicates an estimated sales volume. The symbol < stands for 'less than'. Company names and addresses are truncated, in some cases, to fit into the available space.

LOCATION BY STATE AND REGIONAL CONCENTRATION

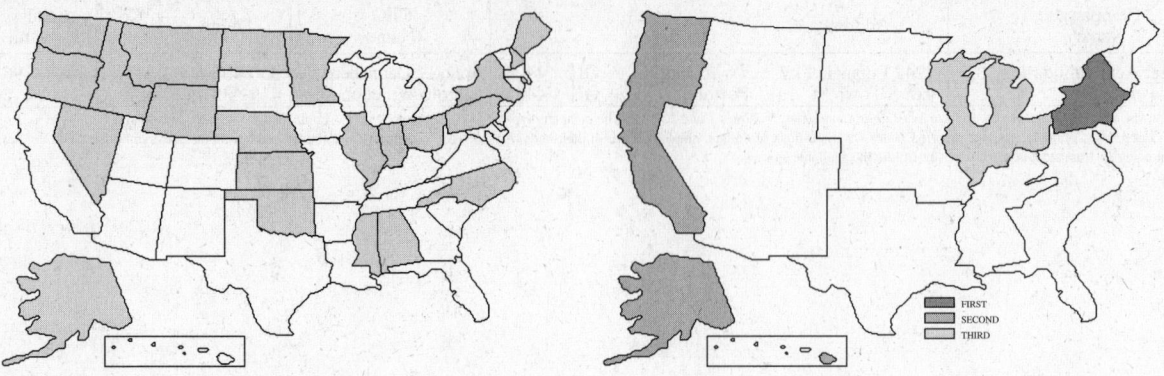

INDUSTRY DATA BY STATE

State	Establishments Total (number)	Establishments % of U.S.	Employment Total (number)	Employment % of U.S.	Employment Per Estab.	Payroll Total ($ mil.)	Payroll Per Empl. ($)	Revenues Total ($ mil.)	Revenues % of U.S.	Revenues Per Estab. ($)
New York	263	7.5	1,349	8.6	5	22.7	16,812	87.6	11.6	333,141
California	406	11.7	1,645	10.5	4	17.3	10,491	82.5	10.9	203,229
Texas	131	3.8	827	5.3	6	9.7	11,750	42.3	5.6	322,847
Illinois	176	5.1	902	5.8	5	8.1	9,004	41.3	5.5	234,386
Pennsylvania	204	5.9	793	5.1	4	8.9	11,277	39.2	5.2	192,225
Indiana	158	4.5	882	5.7	6	5.8	6,563	37.3	4.9	235,867
Ohio	155	4.4	681	4.4	4	6.7	9,815	36.8	4.9	237,671
Florida	140	4.0	803	5.1	6	7.4	9,189	34.5	4.6	246,721
Washington	109	3.1	454	2.9	4	3.7	8,112	23.0	3.0	210,917
North Carolina	80	2.3	464	3.0	6	4.5	9,685	22.3	3.0	279,300
Kansas	106	3.0	480	3.1	5	3.0	6,350	19.1	2.5	180,009
New Jersey	83	2.4	429	2.8	5	5.7	13,217	18.3	2.4	220,000
Minnesota	81	2.3	436	2.8	5	4.9	11,174	18.1	2.4	222,914
Massachusetts	95	2.7	233	1.5	2	2.9	12,622	17.0	2.3	179,221
Oklahoma	69	2.0	335	2.1	5	2.8	8,301	16.2	2.1	234,638
Oregon	84	2.4	402	2.6	5	2.2	5,483	12.8	1.7	152,583
Alabama	58	1.7	269	1.7	5	2.2	8,234	12.7	1.7	218,414
Georgia	60	1.7	191	1.2	3	2.0	10,576	12.0	1.6	199,500
Virginia	53	1.5	181	1.2	3	1.8	10,149	10.3	1.4	194,396
Colorado	53	1.5	253	1.6	5	2.1	8,407	9.5	1.3	179,566
Mississippi	40	1.1	195	1.3	5	1.7	8,513	9.1	1.2	228,600
Wisconsin	58	1.7	268	1.7	5	1.6	5,828	8.3	1.1	142,241
Nebraska	43	1.2	177	1.1	4	1.2	6,565	8.1	1.1	187,372
Arizona	32	0.9	193	1.2	6	2.0	10,301	7.6	1.0	237,094
Maryland	28	0.8	82	0.5	3	1.0	11,634	5.3	0.7	190,250
Maine	44	1.3	134	0.9	3	1.3	9,761	5.3	0.7	120,659
Kentucky	29	0.8	89	0.6	3	0.7	7,966	5.3	0.7	182,759
D.C.	11	0.3	92	0.6	8	1.3	14,174	5.1	0.7	466,182
Arkansas	19	0.5	99	0.6	5	0.9	8,687	4.9	0.7	260,368
Alaska	7	0.2	30	0.2	4	0.4	12,867	4.7	0.6	677,571
Connecticut	20	0.6	134	0.9	7	1.3	9,851	4.6	0.6	230,850
Nevada	16	0.5	95	0.6	6	1.5	15,979	4.6	0.6	284,500
Rhode Island	29	0.8	48	0.3	2	0.5	10,438	3.9	0.5	135,621
Idaho	24	0.7	75	0.5	3	0.5	6,267	3.7	0.5	154,542
New Hampshire	11	0.3	64	0.4	6	0.8	12,203	3.5	0.5	316,182
Montana	28	0.8	86	0.6	3	0.6	7,209	3.0	0.4	106,786
Utah	13	0.4	66	0.4	5	0.6	8,773	2.6	0.3	200,538
North Dakota	25	0.7	48	0.3	2	0.3	6,083	2.3	0.3	90,600
Wyoming	15	0.4	47	0.3	3	0.4	7,915	2.2	0.3	149,200
West Virginia	18	0.5	73	0.5	4	0.7	9,055	2.1	0.3	116,278
South Carolina	16	0.5	60	0.4	4	0.6	10,483	2.1	0.3	129,500
Vermont	13	0.4	40	0.3	3	0.4	9,775	1.8	0.2	136,154
Hawaii	9	0.3	29	0.2	3	0.4	14,862	1.7	0.2	192,111
South Dakota	16	0.5	36	0.2	2	0.2	6,222	1.5	0.2	92,063
New Mexico	10	0.3	40	0.3	4	0.3	8,475	1.3	0.2	125,300
Michigan	102	2.9	375*	-	-	(D)	-	(D)	-	-
Missouri	89	2.6	375*	-	-	(D)	-	(D)	-	-
Iowa	86	2.5	375*	-	-	(D)	-	(D)	-	-
Tennessee	40	1.1	175*	-	-	(D)	-	(D)	-	-
Louisiana	27	0.8	60*	-	-	(D)	-	(D)	-	-
Delaware	2	0.1	10*	-	-	(D)	-	(D)	-	-

Source: 1997 *Economic Census*. The states are in descending order of revenues or establishments (if revenue data are missing for the majority). The symbol (D) appears when data are withheld to prevent disclosure of competitive information. States marked with (D) are sorted by number of establishments. A dash (-) indicates that the data element cannot be calculated. * indicates the midpoint of a range; 175, for example is the range 100-249. Shaded *states* on the state map indicate those states which have proportionately greater representation in the industry than would be indicated by the state's population; the ratio is based on total revenues or number of establishments. Shaded *regions* indicate where the industry is regionally most concentrated.

NAICS 722110 - FULL-SERVICE RESTAURANTS

GENERAL STATISTICS

Year	Establishments (number)	Employment (number)	Payroll ($ million)	Revenues ($ million)	Employees per Establishment (number)	Revenues per Establishment ($)	Payroll per Employee ($)
1997	191,245	3,641,402	34,435.0	112,450.0	19.0	587,989	9,457

Source: *Economic Census of the United States*, 1997. This is a newly defined industry. Data for prior years were unavailable at the time of publication but may become available over time.

INDICES OF CHANGE

Year	Establishments (number)	Employment (number)	Payroll ($ million)	Revenues ($ million)	Employees per Establishment (number)	Revenues per Establishment ($)	Payroll per Employee ($)
1997	100.0	100.0	100.0	100.0	100.0	100.0	100.0

Sources: Same as General Statistics. The values shown reflect change from the base year, 1997. Values above 100 mean greater than 1997, values below 100 mean less than 1997, and a value of 100 in the 1982-96 or 1998-2001 period means same as 1997. Values followed by a 'p' are projections by the editors; 'e' stands for extrapolation. Data are the most recent available at this level of detail.

SIC INDUSTRIES RELATED TO NAICS 722110

Each new NAICS code represents an industry that used to be part of an SIC or a part of several SIC industries. Data in this table are shown to provide transitional information for these cases. All available data for the precursor SIC(s) are shown. Even if only a part of an SIC is included in the NAICS, *all* data for the SIC are reproduced. If the SIC industry is not marked as being a part (pt) of the NAICS, the entire industry is embedded in the NAICS data. The SIC composition of the new industry provides some hints of the relative importance of its "ancestors." Data marked with a 'p' are projected. Projections begin with 1982 data. Data earlier than 1990 are not shown but are reflected in the projections.

SIC	Industry	1990	1991	1992	1993	1994	1995	1996	1997
5461	**Retail bakeries (pt)**								
	Establishments (number)	19,897	20,757	20,418	20,683	21,301	20,248	20,474p	20,444p
	Employment (thousands)	176.4	174.8	157.1	160.7	162.4	153.5	150.8p	147.1p
	Revenues ($ million)	5,180.4e	5,283.7e	5,386.9	5,490.1p	5,593.3p	5,696.6p	5,799.8p	5,903.0p
5812	**Eating places (pt)**								
	Establishments (number)	286,792	280,200	377,760	360,212	367,205	344,854	361,385p	367,752p
	Employment (thousands)	5,700.3	5,459.7	6,243.9	6,346.0	6,477.0	6,568.2	6,822.7p	6,993.9p
	Revenues ($ million)	166,234.6e	175,218.9e	184,203.2	193,580.8p	202,685.3p	211,789.8p	220,894.3p	229,998.8p

Source: *Economic Census of the United States*, 1992, annual surveys of economic sectors conducted by the Bureau of the Census, and estimates or projections based on the 1982-1992 period; not all data are shown. 'e' marks estimates made by the editors; 'p' indicates projections based on time series. A dash (-) indicates that data for this SIC or year were not available. The abbreviation (pt) next to the industry name indicates that only a part of the industry is present within the NAICS data. If no (pt) is shown, the entire industry is contained within the NAICS data.

SELECTED RATIOS

For 1997	Avg. of Information	Analyzed Industry	Index	For 1997	Avg. of Information	Analyzed Industry	Index
Employees per establishment	17	19	110	Payroll per establishment	177,969	180,057	101
Revenue per establishment	642,845	587,989	91	Payroll as % of revenue	28	31	111
Revenue per employee	37,074	30,881	83	Payroll per employee	10,264	9,457	92

Sources: Same as General Statistics. The 'Average' column represents the average for the industry sector, in 1997, where the currently shown industry is classified. The Index shows the relationship between the Average and the Analyzed Industry. For example, 100 means that they are equal; 500 that the Analyzed Industry is five times the average; 50 means that the Analyzed Industry is half the national average. The abbreviation 'na' is used to show that data are 'not available'.

LEADING COMPANIES   Number shown: **75**   Total sales ($ mil): **250,230**   Total employment (000): **3,188.8**

Company Name	Address				CEO Name	Phone	Co. Type	Sales ($ mil)	Empl. (000)
Wal-Mart Stores Inc.	702 SW 8th St	Bentonville	AR	72716	David D. Glass	501-273-4000	P	137,634	825.0
McDonald's Corp.	McDonald's Plz	Oak Brook	IL	60523	Jack M Greenberg	630-623-3000	P	13,259	284.0
Westwood Group Inc.	190 VFW Pkwy	Revere	MA	02151	Charles F Sarkis	781-284-2600	P	10,903*	2.3
Tricon Global Restaurants Inc.	1441 Gardiner Ln	Louisville	KY	40213	David C Novak	502-874-8300	P	8,468	260.0
Taco Bell Corp.	17901 Von Karman	Irvine	CA	92614	Peter C Waller	949-863-4500	S	5,000*	120.0
Pizza Hut Inc.	14841 Dallas Pkwy	Dallas	TX	75240	Michael S Rawlings	972-338-7700	D	4,800	135.0
Marriott Intern	Marriott Dr	Washington	DC	20058		202-380-9000	D	4,443*	72.0
Hardee's Food Systems Inc.	PO Box 1619	Rocky Mount	NC	27802	Rory Murphy	252-977-2000	P	4,300*	43.0
Darden Restaurants Inc.	PO Box 593330	Orlando	FL	32809	Joe R Lee	407-245-4000	P	3,458	116.7
Domino's Pizza Inc.	P O Box 997	Ann Arbor	MI	48106	Thomas Monaghan	734-930-3030	R	3,200	120.0
Compass Group USA Inc.	2400 Yorkmont Rd	Charlotte	NC	28217	Mike Bailey	704-329-4000	R	2,600*	57.0
Viad Corp.	1850 N Central Ave	Phoenix	AZ	85007	Robert Bohannon	602-207-4000	P	2,542	19.8
Burger King Corp.	PO Box 020783	Miami	FL	33102	Dennis Malamatinas	305-378-7011	S	2,158	17.1
Travel Centers of America	24601 Center Ridge	Westlake	OH	44145	Ed Kuhn	440-808-9100	S	2,134*	10.0
CKE Restaurants Inc.	401 W Carl Karcher	Anaheim	CA	92803	William P Foley II	714-774-5796	P	1,892	67.0
Brinker International Inc.	6820 LBJ Fwy	Dallas	TX	75240	Norman E Brinker	972-980-9917	P	1,871	62.3
Ogden Services Corp.	2 Penn Plz	New York	NY	10121	R Richard Ablon	212-868-6000	S	1,750*	39.0
Advantica Restaurant Group Inc.	203 E Main St	Spartanburg	SC	29319	James B Adamson	864-597-8000	P	1,720	54.0
Marsh Supermarkets Inc.	9800 Crosspoint	Indianapolis	IN	46256		317-594-2100	P	1,607	13.4
Viad Corp.	1850 N Central Ave	Phoenix	AZ	85007	Robert Bohannon	602-207-4000	P	1,581	19.8
Jack in the Box Inc.	PO Box 783	San Diego	CA	92112	Robert J Nugent	619-571-2121	P	1,456	37.8
Outback Steakhouse Inc.	550 N Reo	Tampa	FL	33609	Robert D Basham	813-282-1225	P	1,359	36.5
Cracker Barrel Old Country Store	PO Box 787	Lebanon	TN	37088	Dan W Evins	615-444-5533	P	1,317	38.8
Carlson Restaurants Worldwide	PO Box 809062	Dallas	TX	75380	Wallace B Doolin	972-450-5400	S	1,317	42.5
Delaware North Companies Inc.	438 Main St	Buffalo	NY	14202	Jeremy M Jacobs	716-858-5000	R	1,224	25.0
Stouffer Corp.	PO Box 39594	Solon	OH	44139		440-248-3600	D	1,210	21.0
Little Caesar Enterprises Inc.	2211 Woodward	Detroit	MI	48201	Michael Ilitch	313-983-6000	R	1,160	86.0
Denny's Inc.	203 E Main St	Spartanburg	SC	29319	John Romandetti	864-597-8000	S	1,148*	38.5
Valhi Inc.	3 Lincoln Ctr	Dallas	TX	75240	Harold C Simmons	972-233-1700	P	1,059	6.7
TGI Friday's Inc.	PO Box 809062	Dallas	TX	75380	Wallace B Doolin	972-450-5400	S	1,043*	17.0
Shoney's Inc.	PO Box 1260	Nashville	TN	37202	J Michael Bodnar	615-391-5201	P	999	26.0
Jack in the Box Div.	9330 Balboa Ave	San Diego	CA	92123	Robert J Nugent	619-571-2121	D	987	27.0
Bob Evans Farms Inc.	PO Box 7863	Columbus	OH	43207	Daniel Evans	614-491-2225	P	887	3.0
Ground Round Inc.	P O Box 9078	Braintree	MA	02184	Thomas Russo	781-380-3100	S	879*	8.0
Buffets Inc.	10260 Viking Dr	Eden Prairie	MN	55344	Roe H Hatlen	612-942-9760	P	869	24.4
Avado Brands Inc.	Hancock at Wash	Madison	GA	30650	Thomas E DuPree Jr	706-342-4552	P	863	20.3
Papa John's International Inc.	PO Box 99900	Louisville	KY	40269	Blaine Hurst	502-266-5200	P	805	14.3
Ruby Tuesday Inc.	150 W Church Ave	Maryville	TN	37801	Samuel E Beall III	865-379-5700	P	722	27.2
Aramark Sports & Entertainment	1101 Market St	Philadelphia	PA	19107	Charles Gillespie	215-238-3000	S	700*	7.0
Long John Silver's Restaurants	P O Box 11988	Lexington	KY	40579	John M Cranor III	606-388-6000	S	675	18.0
Casino USA Inc.	4700 S Boyle Ave	Vernon	CA	90058	Robert J Emmons	213-589-1054	S	672	2.3
Papa John's International Inc.	PO Box 99900	Louisville	KY	40269	Blaine Hurst	502-266-5200	P	670	14.3
Ryan's Family Steak Houses Inc.	PO Box 100	Greer	SC	29652	Charles D Way	864-879-1000	P	665	19.0
AFC Enterprises Inc.	6 Concourse N E	Atlanta	GA	30328	Frank Belatti	770-391-9500	R	609	18.1
Red Robin International Inc.	5575 DTC Pkwy	Englewood	CO	80111	Mike Snyder	303-846-6000	R	606*	4.5
Galpin Motors Inc.	15505 Roscoe Blvd	North Hills	CA	91343	Bert Boeckmann	818-787-3800	R	561	0.7
RTM Restaurant Group	5995 Barfield Rd	Atlanta	GA	30328	R V Umphenour Jr	404-256-4900	R	535	23.0
Sybra Inc.	9404 Genesee Ave	La Jolla	CA	92037	James R Arabia	858-587-8533	S	534*	3.9
Isle of Capri Casinos Inc.	711 ML King	Biloxi	MS	39530	John M Gallaway	228-436-7000	P	480	6.0
Love's Country Stores Inc.	PO Box 26210	Oklahoma City	OK	73126	Greg Love	405-751-9000	R	478*	2.2
Eateries Inc.	3240 W Britton Rd	Oklahoma City	OK	73120	Vincent F Orza Jr	405-755-3607	P	468*	3.5
Boston Chicken Inc.	PO Box 4086	Golden	CO	80401	J Michael Jenkins	303-278-9500	P	462	12.5
Chi-Chi's Inc.	10200 Linn Station	Louisville	KY	40223	Roger Chamnes	502-426-3900	S	430*	20.0
Popeyes Inc.	5555 Glenridge	Atlanta	GA	30326	Jon Luther	404-459-4450	R	427*	6.2
NPC International Inc.	P O Box 62643	Pittsburg	KS	66762	O Gene Bicknell	316-231-3390	P	401	15.0
Landry's Seafood Restaurants Inc.	1400 Post Oak Blvd	Houston	TX	77056	Tilman J Fertitta	713-850-1010	P	399	14.4
Investors Management Corp.	5151 Glenwood Ave	Raleigh	NC	27612	James H Maynard	919-781-9310	P	391*	14.0
CEC Entertainment Inc.	P O Box 152077	Irving	TX	75015	Richard M Frank	972-258-8507	P	379	13.8
Einstein/Noah Bagel Corp.	14103 Denver West	Golden	CO	80401	Robert M Hartnett	303-215-9300	P	372	11.7
Sbarro Inc.	401 Broad Hollow	Melville	NY	11747	Mario Sbarro	516-715-4100	R	362	7.5
Consolidated Products Inc.	36 S Pennsylvania St	Indianapolis	IN	46204	Alan B Gilman	317-633-4100	P	361	18.6
W.H. Braum Inc.	1900 S Grand St	Amarillo	TX	79103	William Braum	806-374-4413	R	350*	7.9
Phillips Seafood Restaurants Inc.	2004 Philadelphia	Ocean City	MD	21842	Stephen B Philips	410-289-6821	R	337*	2.5
Heart of America Restaurants	1501 River Dr	Moline	IL	61265	Mike Whalen	309-797-9300	R	328*	3.0
Bakers Square Restaurants Inc.	PO Box 16601	Denver	CO	80216	Jay Trungale	303-296-2121	S	325	12.0
Perkins Family Restaurants L.P.	6075 Poplar Ave	Memphis	TN	38119		901-766-6400	R	299	10.5
Kentucky Fried Chicken Corp.	P O Box 32070	Louisville	KY	40232	Jeffrey A Moody	502-874-8300	S	274*	2.0
Restaurant Co.	1 Pierce Pl	Itasca	IL	60143	Donald N Smith	630-250-0471	R	271	9.5
Whataburger Inc.	4600 Parkdale Dr	Corpus Christi	TX	78411	Tom Dobson	361-878-0650	R	264	8.0
Fresh Foods Inc.	PO Box 399	Claremont	NC	28610		828-304-0027	R	258	4.9
Sonic Corp.	101 Park Ave	Oklahoma City	OK	73102	J Clifford Hudson	405-280-7654	P	258	6.0
Krystal Co.	1 Union Sq	Chattanooga	TN	37402	Philip H Sanford	423-757-1550	R	257	9.0
CA One Services Inc.	438 Main St	Buffalo	NY	14202	Charles E Moran Jr	716-858-5000	S	254	2.9
O'Charley's Inc.	3038 Sidco Dr	Nashville	TN	37204	Gregory L Burns	615-256-8500	P	246	8.0
Perkins Restaurants Inc.	6075 Poplar Ave	Memphis	TN	38119	Richard K Arras	901-766-6400	R	246	9.0

Source: *Ward's Business Directory of U.S. Private and Public Companies*, Volumes 1 and 2, 2000. The company type code used is as follows: P - Public, R - Private, S - Subsidiary, D - Division, J - Joint Venture, A - Affiliate, G - Group, N - Company type not reported. Sales are in millions of dollars, employees are in thousands. An asterisk (*) indicates an estimated sales volume. The symbol < stands for 'less than'. Company names and addresses are truncated, in some cases, to fit into the available space.

LOCATION BY STATE AND REGIONAL CONCENTRATION

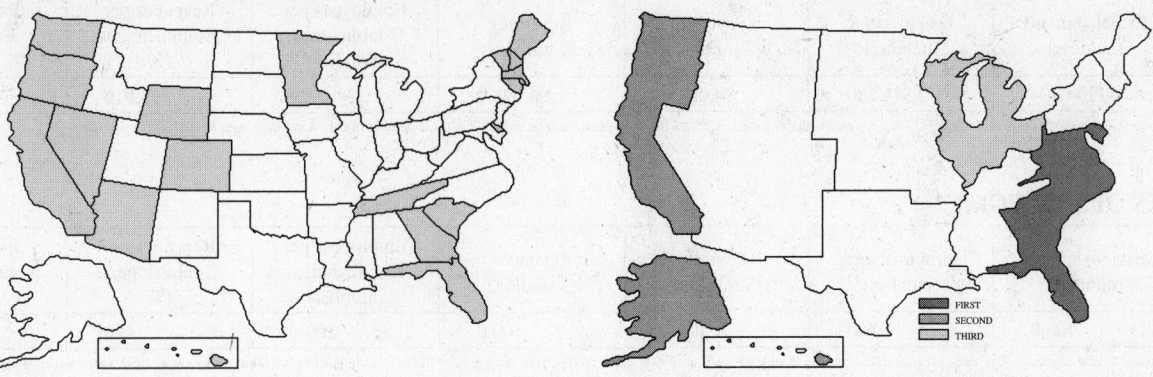

INDUSTRY DATA BY STATE

State	Establishments Total (number)	Establishments % of U.S.	Employment Total (number)	Employment % of U.S.	Employment Per Estab.	Payroll Total ($ mil.)	Payroll Per Empl. ($)	Revenues Total ($ mil.)	Revenues % of U.S.	Revenues Per Estab. ($)
California	22,871	12.0	420,614	11.6	18	4,376.1	10,404	14,401.1	12.8	629,668
Florida	11,989	6.3	253,417	7.0	21	2,371.5	9,358	8,228.1	7.3	686,302
Texas	12,154	6.4	246,145	6.8	20	2,293.1	9,316	7,529.3	6.7	619,490
New York	13,536	7.1	189,076	5.2	14	2,285.3	12,087	7,478.1	6.7	552,458
Illinois	7,434	3.9	148,832	4.1	20	1,437.1	9,656	4,807.6	4.3	646,708
Ohio	6,729	3.5	168,250	4.6	25	1,442.3	8,572	4,522.5	4.0	672,091
Pennsylvania	8,152	4.3	160,786	4.4	20	1,376.7	8,562	4,504.1	4.0	552,515
Michigan	6,387	3.3	139,671	3.8	22	1,198.2	8,579	3,801.1	3.4	595,124
Massachusetts	4,821	2.5	97,564	2.7	20	1,038.8	10,648	3,412.4	3.0	707,811
Georgia	5,306	2.8	104,775	2.9	20	993.9	9,486	3,287.5	2.9	619,581
New Jersey	5,330	2.8	83,155	2.3	16	902.4	10,852	3,091.0	2.7	579,926
North Carolina	5,688	3.0	101,104	2.8	18	898.3	8,885	2,972.3	2.6	522,555
Virginia	4,889	2.6	91,734	2.5	19	846.3	9,225	2,776.6	2.5	567,928
Washington	4,775	2.5	81,278	2.2	17	819.0	10,076	2,581.1	2.3	540,548
Colorado	3,941	2.1	82,182	2.3	21	759.4	9,240	2,372.8	2.1	602,079
Tennessee	3,407	1.8	73,064	2.0	21	710.8	9,728	2,283.9	2.0	670,354
Indiana	3,801	2.0	85,136	2.3	22	711.7	8,360	2,270.2	2.0	597,277
Maryland	3,192	1.7	67,311	1.8	21	659.9	9,804	2,189.6	1.9	685,956
Minnesota	3,367	1.8	75,979	2.1	23	673.7	8,866	2,101.1	1.9	624,036
Arizona	3,256	1.7	71,955	2.0	22	653.2	9,078	2,074.6	1.8	637,154
Missouri	3,561	1.9	73,245	2.0	21	648.1	8,848	2,042.0	1.8	573,422
Wisconsin	4,461	2.3	81,153	2.2	18	624.8	7,699	2,012.6	1.8	451,149
South Carolina	3,062	1.6	54,622	1.5	18	488.5	8,943	1,687.0	1.5	550,959
Oregon	3,194	1.7	52,462	1.4	16	524.0	9,988	1,630.6	1.5	510,507
Louisiana	2,444	1.3	49,608	1.4	20	434.6	8,761	1,431.4	1.3	585,690
Connecticut	2,607	1.4	40,938	1.1	16	436.1	10,653	1,410.1	1.3	540,883
Kentucky	2,145	1.1	46,647	1.3	22	408.7	8,762	1,303.9	1.2	607,882
Alabama	2,459	1.3	41,852	1.1	17	370.1	8,842	1,233.6	1.1	501,659
Hawaii	1,207	0.6	25,170	0.7	21	309.5	12,295	1,002.4	0.9	830,506
Oklahoma	2,282	1.2	38,070	1.0	17	300.8	7,901	986.3	0.9	432,213
Iowa	2,248	1.2	38,997	1.1	17	277.4	7,113	902.3	0.8	401,363
Nevada	1,098	0.6	24,161	0.7	22	262.9	10,879	878.4	0.8	799,968
Kansas	1,864	1.0	33,907	0.9	18	275.4	8,123	868.9	0.8	466,125
Arkansas	1,748	0.9	25,897	0.7	15	204.3	7,889	696.1	0.6	398,204
New Mexico	1,323	0.7	24,603	0.7	19	219.1	8,904	681.1	0.6	514,839
New Hampshire	1,110	0.6	20,594	0.6	19	205.5	9,977	636.1	0.6	573,022
Utah	1,154	0.6	25,748	0.7	22	209.3	8,127	634.1	0.6	549,465
Nebraska	1,296	0.7	24,630	0.7	19	189.7	7,703	595.1	0.5	459,156
Mississippi	1,321	0.7	21,238	0.6	16	168.9	7,953	583.3	0.5	441,545
D.C.	613	0.3	13,605	0.4	22	183.3	13,473	582.8	0.5	950,677
Maine	1,258	0.7	17,494	0.5	14	179.5	10,258	553.3	0.5	439,790
Rhode Island	935	0.5	15,520	0.4	17	147.9	9,530	478.1	0.4	511,350
West Virginia	1,042	0.5	18,138	0.5	17	147.5	8,135	472.3	0.4	453,274
Idaho	1,063	0.6	16,263	0.4	15	132.0	8,115	409.9	0.4	385,573
Delaware	630	0.3	12,826	0.4	20	123.3	9,610	402.4	0.4	638,779
Montana	1,052	0.6	14,644	0.4	14	121.1	8,266	386.6	0.3	367,463
Vermont	675	0.4	10,656	0.3	16	95.3	8,945	284.4	0.3	421,333
South Dakota	722	0.4	10,878	0.3	15	79.4	7,299	266.6	0.2	369,222
Alaska	537	0.3	6,174	0.2	11	75.4	12,220	264.5	0.2	492,579
North Dakota	561	0.3	10,830	0.3	19	74.4	6,870	229.8	0.2	409,708
Wyoming	548	0.3	8,804	0.2	16	70.9	8,051	219.6	0.2	400,695

Source: 1997 *Economic Census*. The states are in descending order of revenues or establishments (if revenue data are missing for the majority). The symbol (D) appears when data are withheld to prevent disclosure of competitive information. States marked with (D) are sorted by number of establishments. A dash (-) indicates that the data element cannot be calculated. * indicates the midpoint of a range; 175, for example is the range 100-249. Shaded *states* on the state map indicate those states which have proportionately greater representation in the industry than would be indicated by the state's population; the ratio is based on total revenues or number of establishments. Shaded *regions* indicate where the industry is regionally most concentrated.

761

NAICS 722211 - LIMITED-SERVICE RESTAURANTS

GENERAL STATISTICS

Year	Establishments (number)	Employment (number)	Payroll ($ million)	Revenues ($ million)	Employees per Establishment (number)	Revenues per Establishment ($)	Payroll per Employee ($)
1997	174,104	2,944,280	24,032.0	94,698.0	16.9	543,916	8,162

Source: Economic Census of the United States, 1997. This is a newly defined industry. Data for prior years were unavailable at the time of publication but may become available over time.

INDICES OF CHANGE

Year	Establishments (number)	Employment (number)	Payroll ($ million)	Revenues ($ million)	Employees per Establishment (number)	Revenues per Establishment ($)	Payroll per Employee ($)
1997	100.0	100.0	100.0	100.0	100.0	100.0	100.0

Sources: Same as General Statistics. The values shown reflect change from the base year, 1997. Values above 100 mean greater than 1997, values below 100 mean less than 1997, and a value of 100 in the 1982-96 or 1998-2001 period means same as 1997. Values followed by a 'p' are projections by the editors; 'e' stands for extrapolation. Data are the most recent available at this level of detail.

SIC INDUSTRIES RELATED TO NAICS 722211

Each new NAICS code represents an industry that used to be part of an SIC or a part of several SIC industries. Data in this table are shown to provide transitional information for these cases. All available data for the precursor SIC(s) are shown. Even if only a part of an SIC is included in the NAICS, *all* data for the SIC are reproduced. If the SIC industry is not marked as being a part (pt) of the NAICS, the entire industry is embedded in the NAICS data. The SIC composition of the new industry provides some hints of the relative importance of its "ancestors." Data marked with a 'p' are projected. Projections begin with 1982 data. Data earlier than 1990 are not shown but are reflected in the projections.

SIC	Industry	1990	1991	1992	1993	1994	1995	1996	1997
5812	**Eating places (pt)**								
	Establishments (number)	286,792	280,200	377,760	360,212	367,205	344,854	361,385*p*	367,752*p*
	Employment (thousands)	5,700.3	5,459.7	6,243.9	6,346.0	6,477.0	6,568.2	6,822.7*p*	6,993.9*p*
	Revenues ($ million)	166,234.6*e*	175,218.9*e*	184,203.2	193,580.8*p*	202,685.3*p*	211,789.8*p*	220,894.3*p*	229,998.8*p*

Source: Economic Census of the United States, 1992, annual surveys of economic sectors conducted by the Bureau of the Census, and estimates or projections based on the 1982-1992 period; not all data are shown. 'e' marks estimates made by the editors; 'p' indicates projections based on time series. A dash (-) indicates that data for this SIC or year were not available. The abbreviation (pt) next to the industry name indicates that only a part of the industry is present within the NAICS data. If no (pt) is shown, the entire industry is contained within the NAICS data.

SELECTED RATIOS

For 1997	Avg. of Information	Analyzed Industry	Index	For 1997	Avg. of Information	Analyzed Industry	Index
Employees per establishment	17	17	98	Payroll per establishment	177,969	138,032	78
Revenue per establishment	642,845	543,916	85	Payroll as % of revenue	28	25	92
Revenue per employee	37,074	32,163	87	Payroll per employee	10,264	8,162	80

Sources: Same as General Statistics. The 'Average' column represents the average for the industry sector, in 1997, where the currently shown industry is classified. The Index shows the relationship between the Average and the Analyzed Industry. For example, 100 means that they are equal; 500 that the Analyzed Industry is five times the average; 50 means that the Analyzed Industry is half the national average. The abbreviation 'na' is used to show that data are 'not available'.

LEADING COMPANIES   Number shown: 75   Total sales ($ mil): 156,120   Total employment (000): 1,059.7

Company Name	Address				CEO Name	Phone	Co. Type	Sales ($ mil)	Empl. (000)
Wal-Mart Stores Inc.	702 SW 8th St	Bentonville	AR	72716	David D. Glass	501-273-4000	P	137,634	825.0
Compass Group USA Inc.	2400 Yorkmont Rd	Charlotte	NC	28217	Mike Bailey	704-329-4000	R	2,600*	57.0
Viad Corp.	1850 N Central Ave	Phoenix	AZ	85007	Robert Bohannon	602-207-4000	P	2,542	19.8
Travel Centers of America	24601 Center Ridge	Westlake	OH	44145	Ed Kuhn	440-808-9100	S	2,134*	10.0
Ogden Services Corp.	2 Penn Plz	New York	NY	10121	R Richard Ablon	212-868-6000	S	1,750*	39.0
Marsh Supermarkets Inc.	9800 Crosspoint	Indianapolis	IN	46256		317-594-2100	P	1,607	13.4
Valhi Inc.	3 Lincoln Ctr	Dallas	TX	75240	Harold C Simmons	972-233-1700	P	1,059	6.7
Aramark Sports & Entertainment	1101 Market St	Philadelphia	PA	19107	Charles Gillespie	215-238-3000	S	700*	7.0
Casino USA Inc.	4700 S Boyle Ave	Vernon	CA	90058	Robert J Emmons	213-589-1054	S	672	2.3
Papa John's International Inc.	PO Box 99900	Louisville	KY	40269	Blaine Hurst	502-266-5200	P	670	14.3
Galpin Motors Inc.	15505 Roscoe Blvd	North Hills	CA	91343	Bert Boeckmann	818-787-3800	R	561	0.7
White Castle System Inc.	PO Box 1498	Columbus	OH	43216	E Ingram	614-228-5781	R	467	11.4
W.H. Braum Inc.	1900 S Grand St	Amarillo	TX	79103	William Braum	806-374-4413	R	350*	7.9
Fresh Foods Inc.	PO Box 399	Claremont	NC	28610		828-304-0027	R	258	4.9
CA One Services Inc.	438 Main St	Buffalo	NY	14202	Charles E Moran Jr	716-858-5000	S	254	2.9
Rainforest Cafe Inc.	720 S 5th St	Hopkins	MN	55343	Lyle Berman	612-945-5400	P	214	6.0
Shirley Oil and Supply Inc.	401 E South St	McLean	IL	61754	Charles G Beeler	309-874-2832	P	212*	0.5
Travel Ports of America Inc.	3495 Winton Pl	Rochester	NY	14623	John M Holahan	716-272-1810	P	212	1.4
Broughton Foods Co.	PO Box 656	Marietta	OH	45750		740-373-4121	R	179	0.9
Z.V. Pate Inc.	PO Box 159	Laurel Hill	NC	28351	David L Burns	910-462-2122	R	176*	0.9
Gas America Services Inc.	PO Box 20	Shirley	IN	47384	Stephanie White	765-737-6501	R	170*	0.6
Chart House Enterprises Inc.	604 N LaSalle	Chicago	IL	60610	Thomas J Walters	312-266-1100	P	145	4.2
Saint Louis Bread Company Inc.	7930 Big Bend	St. Louis	MO	63146	Richard C Postle	314-918-7779	S	116*	3.0
Overhill Farms Inc.	5730 Uplander Way	Culver City	CA	90230		310-641-3680	P	105	0.7
Il Fornaio America Corp.	770 Tamalpais Dr	Corte Madera	CA	94925	Michael Hislop	415-945-0500	P	83	2.3
Dick Clark Productions Inc.	3003 W Olive Ave	Burbank	CA	91510	Richard W Clark	818-841-3003	P	73	0.8
Faber Enterprises Inc.	100 S Wacker Dr	Chicago	IL	60606		312-558-8900	S	65*	1.1
C.L. Swanson Corp.	4501 Femrite Dr	Madison	WI	53716	Jeff Parks	608-221-7640	R	59*	0.4
American Eagle Management Inc.	PO Box 5026	Cordele	GA	31015	Mike Ouimet	912-273-5710	R	55*	0.1
Nation's Foodservice Inc.	11090 San Pablo	El Cerrito	CA	94530	Dale Power	510-237-1952	R	55*	0.5
Biltmore Co.	1 N Pack Sq	Asheville	NC	28801	William Cecil	828-255-1776	R	50	0.5
Burns Bros. Inc.	4800 SW Meadows	Lake Oswego	OR	97035	Bruce Burns	503-238-7393	R	50*	0.3
Busler Enterprises Inc.	PO Box 23610	Evansville	IN	47724	George W Busler	812-424-7511	R	47	0.2
Wynkoop Brewing Co.	1634 18th St	Denver	CO	80202	John Hickenlooper	303-297-2700	R	46*	0.2
Hasslocher Enterprises Inc.	8520 Crownhill Blvd	San Antonio	TX	78209	Robert Hasslocher	210-828-1493	R	45	1.6
Watermarc Food Managment Co.	11111 Wilcrest	Houston	TX	77042	Ghulam Bombaywala	713-783-0500	P	40	1.4
Nebraska Iowa Supply Co.	1160 Lincoln St	Blair	NE	68008	Thomas J Lippincott	402-426-2171	R	40	<0.1
Martin Wine's Ltd.	3827 Baronne St	New Orleans	LA	70115	Dave Gladden	504-899-7411	R	39*	0.3
Sierra Nevada Brewing Co.	1075 E 20th St	Chico	CA	95928	Ken Grossman	530-893-3520	R	35	0.1
Dean and DeLuca Inc.	560 Broadway	New York	NY	10012	Dane Neller	212-431-1691	R	33*	0.5
Bobber Travel Center	PO Box 698	Sullivan	MO	63080	Melvin King	573-468-4166	R	32*	<0.1
Automated Custom Food Services	7700 Brookhollow	Dallas	TX	75235	Steve Errico	214-631-7040	R	31*	0.3
FFP Operating Partners L.P.	2801 Glenda Ave	Fort Worth	TX	76117	Robert J Byrnes	817-838-4700	S	31*	0.1
BOWLIN Outdoor Advertising	150 Louisiana NE	Albuquerque	NM	87108	Michael Bowlin	505-266-5985	P	30	0.3
Chicago Pizza and Brewery Inc.	26131 Marguerite	Mission Viejo	CA	92692	Jerry J Hennessy	949-367-8616	P	30	1.4
Newport Creamery Inc.	PO Box 219	Newport	RI	02840		401-847-0390	R	27	1.5
Monterey Pasta Co.	1528 Moffett St	Salinas	CA	93905	Lance Hewett	408-753-6262	P	26	0.2
Bazaar Del Mundo Inc.	2754 Calhoun St	San Diego	CA	92110	Diane Powers	619-296-6301	R	23	0.7
Robinhood Marine Center Inc.	HC 33 Box 1460	Georgetown	ME	04548	Andrew Varolotis	207-371-2525	R	23	<0.1
Epicurean International Inc.	229 Castro St	Oakland	CA	94607	Seth Jacobson	510-268-0209	R	21*	<0.1
El Gallo Giro Inc.	7148 Pacific Blvd	Huntington Park	CA	90255	Carlos Bonaparte	213-585-4433	R	20	0.3
McMenamins Pubs and Breweries	1624 NW Glisan St	Portland	OR	97209		503-223-0109	R	19*	0.6
Chefs International Inc.	PO Box 1332	Pt Pleas Bch	NJ	08742	Anthony C Papalia	732-295-0350	P	19	0.4
Arnie's Inc.	722 Leonard St NW	Grand Rapids	MI	49504		616-458-1107	R	16	0.3
Delivery Concepts Inc.	2658 Holcomb	Alpharetta	GA	30009	Bob Cotman	404-552-1424	R	16*	0.1
Breckinridge Brewery Denver	2220 Blake St	Denver	CO	80205	Richard Squire	303-297-3644	R	13	<0.1
Red River Barbeque and Grille	7500 Brooktree Rd	Wexford	PA	15090	Ronald Sofranko	724-933-5550	R	12*	<0.1
Summit Station Restaurant	227 E Diamond Ave	Gaithersburg	MD	20877	Jonathan Warner	301-519-9400	R	12*	<0.1
BFX Hospitality Group Corp.	226 Bailey Ave	Fort Worth	TX	76107	Jean-Claude Mathot	817-332-4761	P	11	0.4
Heartland Brewery	35 Union Sq W	New York	NY	10003	John Bloostein	212-645-3400	R	10*	<0.1
National Park Concessions Inc.	PO Box 27	Mammoth Cave	KY	42259	James W Milburn Jr	270-773-2191	R	10*	0.4
Wilton Foods Inc.	1 6 1/2 Station Rd	Goshen	NY	10924	Martin Hoffman	914-294-2801	R	9*	0.3
White Coffee Pot Family Inns Inc.	137 S Warwick Ave	Baltimore	MD	21223	A Katz	410-233-8600	R	8*	<0.1
Clines Corners Operating Co.	1 Yacht Club Dr	Clines Corners	NM	87070	CC Blair	505-472-5488	R	7	<0.1
English Co.	1123 S Division St	Salisbury	MD	21801	R Wayne Strauburg	410-742-9511	R	7*	0.3
Thornton Winery	PO Box 9008	Temecula	CA	92589	John Thornton	909-699-0099	R	7	<0.1
CFN Inc.	4141 Highline Blvd	Oklahoma City	OK	73108	Jerry Wright	405-947-6277	R	6*	0.1
Elliott Bay Book Co.	101 S Main St	Seattle	WA	98104		206-624-6600	R	6*	<0.1
Foss Co.	1224 Washington	Golden	CO	80401	Robert Lowry	303-279-3373	R	6*	<0.1
Frasinetti Winery	7395 Frasinetti Rd	Sacramento	CA	95828		916-383-2444	R	6*	<0.1
Broadway Brewing L.L.C.	2441 Broadway	Denver	CO	80205	John Hickenlooper	303-292-5027	R	5	<0.1
Vavin Inc.	HCR 4, Box 77	Leon	VA	22725	Stephen B Lane	540-547-3707	R	5*	<0.1
Zarda Development Company Inc.	214 N 7 Hwy	Blue Springs	MO	64015	Michael Zarda	816-229-9999	R	5	0.2
Buscemi's International Inc.	30362 Gratiot Ave	Roseville	MI	48066	Anthony P Buscemi	810-296-5560	R	4	<0.1
Mendocino Brewing Inc.	PO Box 400	Hopland	CA	95449	Michael Laybourn	707-744-1015	P	3	<0.1

Source: Ward's Business Directory of U.S. Private and Public Companies, Volumes 1 and 2, 2000. The company type code used is as follows: P - Public, R - Private, S - Subsidiary, D - Division, J - Joint Venture, A - Affiliate, G - Group, N - Company type not reported. Sales are in millions of dollars, employees are in thousands. An asterisk (*) indicates an estimated sales volume. The symbol < stands for 'less than'. Company names and addresses are truncated, in some cases, to fit into the available space.

LOCATION BY STATE AND REGIONAL CONCENTRATION

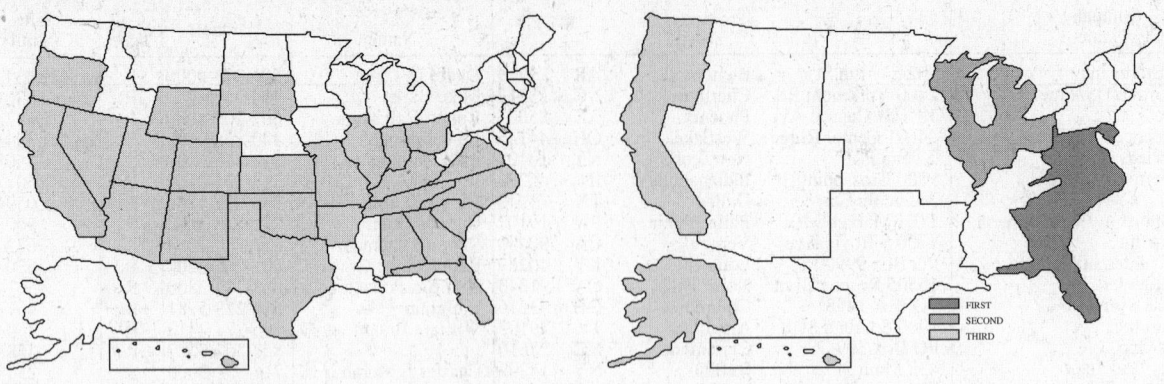

INDUSTRY DATA BY STATE

State	Establishments Total (number)	% of U.S.	Employment Total (number)	% of U.S.	Per Estab.	Payroll Total ($ mil.)	Per Empl. ($)	Revenues Total ($ mil.)	% of U.S.	Per Estab. ($)
California	20,765	11.9	321,176	10.9	15	2,808.0	8,743	11,843.4	12.5	570,354
Texas	12,549	7.2	221,339	7.5	18	1,914.2	8,648	7,550.3	8.0	601,663
Florida	8,299	4.8	155,534	5.3	19	1,236.5	7,950	4,990.6	5.3	601,351
New York	11,448	6.6	117,825	4.0	10	1,098.7	9,324	4,527.4	4.8	395,479
Ohio	7,932	4.6	149,601	5.1	19	1,168.2	7,809	4,515.9	4.8	569,323
Illinois	8,077	4.6	132,102	4.5	16	1,117.6	8,460	4,415.4	4.7	546,659
Michigan	6,068	3.5	107,765	3.7	18	850.7	7,894	3,371.0	3.6	555,533
Georgia	5,079	2.9	100,538	3.4	20	821.9	8,175	3,160.7	3.3	622,301
Pennsylvania	7,063	4.1	97,557	3.3	14	773.4	7,928	3,142.4	3.3	444,905
North Carolina	4,998	2.9	105,362	3.6	21	823.8	7,819	3,121.4	3.3	624,526
Virginia	4,296	2.5	80,208	2.7	19	668.8	8,338	2,539.6	2.7	591,154
Indiana	4,229	2.4	83,690	2.8	20	671.4	8,023	2,506.6	2.6	592,715
Tennessee	3,585	2.1	79,040	2.7	22	596.8	7,551	2,264.9	2.4	631,758
Missouri	3,814	2.2	73,218	2.5	19	585.3	7,994	2,197.9	2.3	576,269
New Jersey	5,068	2.9	52,506	1.8	10	504.3	9,604	2,092.3	2.2	412,842
Washington	3,709	2.1	61,538	2.1	17	501.3	8,145	1,908.5	2.0	514,568
Massachusetts	4,401	2.5	51,215	1.7	12	459.7	8,975	1,872.9	2.0	425,570
Maryland	3,272	1.9	54,130	1.8	17	456.7	8,438	1,785.8	1.9	545,768
Alabama	2,816	1.6	69,409	2.4	25	448.8	6,466	1,720.8	1.8	611,079
Kentucky	2,707	1.6	56,442	1.9	21	452.1	8,010	1,691.9	1.8	625,004
Arizona	2,807	1.6	50,627	1.7	18	410.2	8,103	1,657.4	1.8	590,470
Wisconsin	3,086	1.8	56,464	1.9	18	430.0	7,616	1,606.9	1.7	520,719
Louisiana	2,526	1.5	49,408	1.7	20	371.1	7,511	1,541.8	1.6	610,361
South Carolina	2,581	1.5	59,636	2.0	23	403.5	6,766	1,518.4	1.6	588,286
Minnesota	2,778	1.6	50,195	1.7	18	393.8	7,845	1,473.0	1.6	530,241
Colorado	2,553	1.5	46,316	1.6	18	385.3	8,319	1,459.2	1.5	571,580
Oklahoma	2,478	1.4	43,321	1.5	17	333.9	7,709	1,278.5	1.4	515,954
Oregon	2,290	1.3	38,191	1.3	17	323.0	8,457	1,190.5	1.3	519,855
Kansas	1,933	1.1	35,673	1.2	18	275.1	7,711	1,032.0	1.1	533,880
Mississippi	1,637	0.9	34,923	1.2	21	239.8	6,866	946.5	1.0	578,176
Iowa	1,916	1.1	35,005	1.2	18	255.2	7,292	934.5	1.0	487,741
Arkansas	1,751	1.0	32,327	1.1	18	238.7	7,382	924.4	1.0	527,925
Connecticut	1,850	1.1	24,108	0.8	13	212.4	8,812	858.8	0.9	464,232
Utah	1,434	0.8	26,345	0.9	18	202.0	7,666	803.6	0.8	560,393
Nevada	1,106	0.6	18,548	0.6	17	172.0	9,273	687.0	0.7	621,141
Hawaii	971	0.6	16,230	0.6	17	160.9	9,914	653.7	0.7	673,231
West Virginia	1,161	0.7	20,985	0.7	18	167.7	7,994	648.4	0.7	558,459
New Mexico	1,164	0.7	20,607	0.7	18	164.1	7,963	644.8	0.7	553,911
Nebraska	1,110	0.6	20,396	0.7	18	154.0	7,549	576.0	0.6	518,961
Maine	882	0.5	10,605	0.4	12	94.2	8,884	362.7	0.4	411,248
Idaho	757	0.4	12,304	0.4	16	89.0	7,230	352.4	0.4	465,464
New Hampshire	797	0.5	9,812	0.3	12	84.0	8,562	338.3	0.4	424,414
Montana	678	0.4	9,560	0.3	14	67.1	7,019	266.4	0.3	392,860
Delaware	466	0.3	7,485	0.3	16	65.2	8,717	265.5	0.3	569,813
Rhode Island	689	0.4	7,762	0.3	11	68.7	8,854	263.5	0.3	382,427
D.C.	493	0.3	6,053	0.2	12	63.5	10,496	244.2	0.3	495,262
South Dakota	502	0.3	8,706	0.3	17	62.8	7,211	237.0	0.3	472,018
Alaska	364	0.2	4,862	0.2	13	50.5	10,396	204.8	0.2	562,725
North Dakota	437	0.3	7,100	0.2	16	50.8	7,153	189.8	0.2	434,277
Wyoming	365	0.2	6,282	0.2	17	47.0	7,478	175.7	0.2	481,436
Vermont	366	0.2	4,090	0.1	11	36.2	8,853	134.3	0.1	366,959

Source: 1997 Economic Census. The states are in descending order of revenues or establishments (if revenue data are missing for the majority). The symbol (D) appears when data are withheld to prevent disclosure of competitive information. States marked with (D) are sorted by number of establishments. A dash (-) indicates that the data element cannot be calculated. * indicates the midpoint of a range; 175, for example is the range 100-249. Shaded states on the state map indicate those states which have proportionately greater representation in the industry than would be indicated by the state's population; the ratio is based on total revenues or number of establishments. Shaded regions indicate where the industry is regionally most concentrated.

NAICS 722212 - CAFETERIAS

GENERAL STATISTICS

Year	Establishments (number)	Employment (number)	Payroll ($ million)	Revenues ($ million)	Employees per Establishment (number)	Revenues per Establishment ($)	Payroll per Employee ($)
1997	4,172	72,324	799.0	2,579.0	17.3	618,169	11,048

Source: Economic Census of the United States, 1997. This is a newly defined industry. Data for prior years were unavailable at the time of publication but may become available over time.

INDICES OF CHANGE

Year	Establishments (number)	Employment (number)	Payroll ($ million)	Revenues ($ million)	Employees per Establishment (number)	Revenues per Establishment ($)	Payroll per Employee ($)
1997	100.0	100.0	100.0	100.0	100.0	100.0	100.0

Sources: Same as General Statistics. The values shown reflect change from the base year, 1997. Values above 100 mean greater than 1997, values below 100 mean less than 1997, and a value of 100 in the 1982-96 or 1998-2001 period means same as 1997. Values followed by a 'p' are projections by the editors; 'e' stands for extrapolation. Data are the most recent available at this level of detail.

SIC INDUSTRIES RELATED TO NAICS 722212

Each new NAICS code represents an industry that used to be part of an SIC or a part of several SIC industries. Data in this table are shown to provide transitional information for these cases. All available data for the precursor SIC(s) are shown. Even if only a part of an SIC is included in the NAICS, *all* data for the SIC are reproduced. If the SIC industry is not marked as being a part (pt) of the NAICS, the entire industry is embedded in the NAICS data. The SIC composition of the new industry provides some hints of the relative importance of its "ancestors." Data marked with a 'p' are projected. Projections begin with 1982 data. Data earlier than 1990 are not shown but are reflected in the projections.

SIC	Industry	1990	1991	1992	1993	1994	1995	1996	1997
5812	**Eating places (pt)**								
	Establishments (number)	286,792	280,200	377,760	360,212	367,205	344,854	361,385p	367,752p
	Employment (thousands)	5,700.3	5,459.7	6,243.9	6,346.0	6,477.0	6,568.2	6,822.7p	6,993.9p
	Revenues ($ million)	166,234.6e	175,218.9e	184,203.2	193,580.8p	202,685.3p	211,789.8p	220,894.3p	229,998.8p

Source: Economic Census of the United States, 1992, annual surveys of economic sectors conducted by the Bureau of the Census, and estimates or projections based on the 1982-1992 period; not all data are shown. 'e' marks estimates made by the editors; 'p' indicates projections based on time series. A dash (-) indicates that data for this SIC or year were not available. The abbreviation (pt) next to the industry name indicates that only a part of the industry is present within the NAICS data. If no (pt) is shown, the entire industry is contained within the NAICS data.

SELECTED RATIOS

For 1997	Avg. of Information	Analyzed Industry	Index	For 1997	Avg. of Information	Analyzed Industry	Index
Employees per establishment	17	17	100	Payroll per establishment	177,969	191,515	108
Revenue per establishment	642,845	618,169	96	Payroll as % of revenue	28	31	112
Revenue per employee	37,074	35,659	96	Payroll per employee	10,264	11,048	108

Sources: Same as General Statistics. The 'Average' column represents the average for the industry sector, in 1997, where the currently shown industry is classified. The Index shows the relationship between the Average and the Analyzed Industry. For example, 100 means that they are equal; 500 that the Analyzed Industry is five times the average; 50 means that the Analyzed Industry is half the national average. The abbreviation 'na' is used to show that data are 'not available'.

LEADING COMPANIES   Number shown: **75**   Total sales ($ mil): **158,301**   Total employment (000): **1,094.2**

Company Name	Address				CEO Name	Phone	Co. Type	Sales ($ mil)	Empl. (000)
Wal-Mart Stores Inc.	702 SW 8th St	Bentonville	AR	72716	David D. Glass	501-273-4000	P	137,634	825.0
Compass Group USA Inc.	2400 Yorkmont Rd	Charlotte	NC	28217	Mike Bailey	704-329-4000	R	2,600*	57.0
Viad Corp.	1850 N Central Ave	Phoenix	AZ	85007	Robert Bohannon	602-207-4000	P	2,542	19.8
Travel Centers of America	24601 Center Ridge	Westlake	OH	44145	Ed Kuhn	440-808-9100	S	2,134*	10.0
Ogden Services Corp.	2 Penn Plz	New York	NY	10121	R Richard Ablon	212-868-6000	S	1,750*	39.0
Marsh Supermarkets Inc.	9800 Crosspoint	Indianapolis	IN	46256		317-594-2100	P	1,607	13.4
Cracker Barrel Old Country Store	PO Box 787	Lebanon	TN	37088	Dan W Evins	615-444-5533	P	1,317	38.8
Valhi Inc.	3 Lincoln Ctr	Dallas	TX	75240	Harold C Simmons	972-233-1700	P	1,059	6.7
Bob Evans Farms Inc.	PO Box 7863	Columbus	OH	43207	Daniel Evans	614-491-2225	P	887	3.0
Aramark Sports & Entertainment	1101 Market St	Philadelphia	PA	19107	Charles Gillespie	215-238-3000	S	700*	7.0
Casino USA Inc.	4700 S Boyle Ave	Vernon	CA	90058	Robert J Emmons	213-589-1054	S	672	2.3
Papa John's International Inc.	PO Box 99900	Louisville	KY	40269	Blaine Hurst	502-266-5200	P	670	14.3
Galpin Motors Inc.	15505 Roscoe Blvd	North Hills	CA	91343	Bert Boeckmann	818-787-3800	R	561	0.7
Isle of Capri Casions Inc.	711 ML King	Biloxi	MS	39530	John M Gallaway	228-436-7000	P	480	6.0
W.H. Braum Inc.	1900 S Grand St	Amarillo	TX	79103	William Braum	806-374-4413	R	350*	7.9
Fresh Foods Inc.	PO Box 399	Claremont	NC	28610		828-304-0027	R	258	4.9
CA One Services Inc.	438 Main St	Buffalo	NY	14202	Charles E Moran Jr	716-858-5000	S	254	2.9
Rainforest Cafe Inc.	720 S 5th St	Hopkins	MN	55343	Lyle Berman	612-945-5400	P	214	6.0
Shirley Oil and Supply Inc.	401 E South St	McLean	IL	61754	Charles G Beeler	309-874-2832	R	212*	0.5
Travel Ports of America Inc.	3495 Winton Pl	Rochester	NY	14623	John M Holahan	716-272-1810	P	212	1.4
Broughton Foods Co.	PO Box 656	Marietta	OH	45750		740-373-4121	R	179	0.9
Z.V. Pate Inc.	PO Box 159	Laurel Hill	NC	28351	David L Burns	910-462-2122	R	176*	0.9
Gas America Services Inc.	PO Box 20	Shirley	IN	47384	Stephanie White	765-737-6501	R	170*	0.6
Chart House Enterprises Inc.	604 N LaSalle	Chicago	IL	60610	Thomas J Walters	312-266-1100	P	145	4.2
Saint Louis Bread Company Inc.	7930 Big Bend	St. Louis	MO	63146	Richard C Postle	314-918-7779	S	116*	3.0
Overhill Farms Inc.	5730 Uplander Way	Culver City	CA	90230		310-641-3680	P	105	0.7
Il Fornaio America Corp.	770 Tamalpais Dr	Corte Madera	CA	94925	Michael Hislop	415-945-0500	P	83	2.3
Dick Clark Productions Inc.	3003 W Olive Ave	Burbank	CA	91510	Richard W Clark	818-841-3003	P	73	0.8
Faber Enterprises Inc.	100 S Wacker Dr	Chicago	IL	60606		312-558-8900	S	65*	1.1
C.L. Swanson Corp.	4501 Femrite Dr	Madison	WI	53716	Jeff Parks	608-221-7640	R	59*	0.4
American Eagle Management Inc.	PO Box 5026	Cordele	GA	31015	Mike Ouimet	912-273-5710	R	55*	0.1
Nation's Foodservice Inc.	11090 San Pablo	El Cerrito	CA	94530	Dale Power	510-237-1952	R	55*	0.5
Biltmore Co.	1 N Pack Sq	Asheville	NC	28801	William Cecil	828-255-1776	R	50	0.5
Burns Bros. Inc.	4800 SW Meadows	Lake Oswego	OR	97035	Bruce Burns	503-238-7393	R	50*	0.3
Busler Enterprises Inc.	PO Box 23610	Evansville	IN	47724	George W Busler	812-424-7511	R	47	0.2
Wynkoop Brewing Co.	1634 18th St	Denver	CO	80202	John Hickenlooper	303-297-2700	R	46*	0.2
Hasslocher Enterprises Inc.	8520 Crownhill Blvd	San Antonio	TX	78209	Robert Hasslocher	210-828-1493	R	45	1.6
Watermarc Food Managment Co.	11111 Wilcrest	Houston	TX	77042	Ghulam Bombaywala	713-783-0500	P	40	1.4
Nebraska Iowa Supply Co.	1160 Lincoln St	Blair	NE	68008	Thomas J Lippincott	402-426-2171	R	40	<0.1
Martin Wine's Ltd.	3827 Baronne St	New Orleans	LA	70115	Dave Gladden	504-899-7411	R	39*	0.3
Sierra Nevada Brewing Co.	1075 E 20th St	Chico	CA	95928	Ken Grossman	530-893-3520	R	35	0.1
Dean and DeLuca Inc.	560 Broadway	New York	NY	10012	Dane Neller	212-431-1691	R	33*	0.5
Bobber Travel Center	PO Box 698	Sullivan	MO	63080	Melvin King	573-468-4166	R	32*	<0.1
FFP Operating Partners L.P.	2801 Glenda Ave	Fort Worth	TX	76117	Robert J Byrnes	817-838-4700	S	31*	0.1
BOWLIN Outdoor Advertising	150 Louisiana NE	Albuquerque	NM	87108	Michael Bowlin	505-266-5985	P	30	0.3
Chicago Pizza and Brewery Inc.	26131 Marguerite	Mission Viejo	CA	92692	Jerry J Hennessy	949-367-8616	P	30	1.4
Monterey Pasta Co.	1528 Moffett St	Salinas	CA	93905	Lance Hewett	408-753-6262	P	26	0.2
I-74 Auto Truck Plaza	PO Box 550	Oakwood	IL	61858		217-354-2105	R	25	<0.1
Bazaar Del Mundo Inc.	2754 Calhoun St	San Diego	CA	92110	Diane Powers	619-296-6301	R	23	0.7
Robinhood Marine Center Inc.	HC 33 Box 1460	Georgetown	ME	04548	Andrew Varolotis	207-371-2525	R	23	<0.1
Epicurean International Inc.	229 Castro St	Oakland	CA	94607	Seth Jacobson	510-268-0209	R	21*	<0.1
El Gallo Giro Inc.	7148 Pacific Blvd	Huntington Park	CA	90255	Carlos Bonaparte	213-585-4433	R	20	0.3
McMenamins Pubs and Breweries	1624 NW Glisan St	Portland	OR	97209		503-223-0109	R	19*	0.6
Chefs International Inc.	PO Box 1332	Pt Pleas Bch	NJ	08742	Anthony C Papalia	732-295-0350	P	19	0.4
Arnie's Inc.	722 Leonard St NW	Grand Rapids	MI	49504		616-458-1107	R	16	0.3
Delivery Concepts Inc.	2658 Holcomb	Alpharetta	GA	30009	Bob Cotman	404-552-1424	R	16*	0.1
Breckinridge Brewery Denver	2220 Blake St	Denver	CO	80205	Richard Squire	303-297-3644	R	13	<0.1
Red River Barbeque and Grille	7500 Brooktree Rd	Wexford	PA	15090	Ronald Sofranko	724-933-5550	R	12*	<0.1
Summit Station Restaurant	227 E Diamond Ave	Gaithersburg	MD	20877	Jonathan Warner	301-519-9400	R	12*	<0.1
BFX Hospitality Group Corp.	226 Bailey Ave	Fort Worth	TX	76107	Jean-Claude Mathot	817-332-4761	P	11	0.4
Heartland Brewery	35 Union Sq W	New York	NY	10003	John Bloostein	212-645-3400	R	10*	<0.1
National Park Concessions Inc.	PO Box 27	Mammoth Cave	KY	42259	James W Milburn Jr	270-773-2191	R	10*	0.4
Wilton Foods Inc.	1 6 1/2 Station Rd	Goshen	NY	10924	Martin Hoffman	914-294-2801	R	9*	0.3
White Coffee Pot Family Inns Inc.	137 S Warwick Ave	Baltimore	MD	21223	A Katz	410-233-8600	R	8*	<0.1
Clines Corners Operating Co.	1 Yacht Club Dr	Clines Corners	NM	87070	CC Blair	505-472-5488	R	7	<0.1
English Co.	1123 S Division St	Salisbury	MD	21804	R Wayne Strauburg	410-742-9511	R	7*	0.3
Thornton Winery	PO Box 9008	Temecula	CA	92589	John Thornton	909-699-0099	R	7	0.1
CFN Inc.	4141 Highline Blvd	Oklahoma City	OK	73108	Jerry Wright	405-947-6277	R	6*	0.1
Elliott Bay Book Co.	101 S Main St	Seattle	WA	98104		206-624-6600	R	6*	<0.1
Foss Co.	1224 Washington	Golden	CO	80401	Robert Lowry	303-279-3373	R	6*	<0.1
Frasinetti Winery	7395 Frasinetti Rd	Sacramento	CA	95828		916-383-2444	R	6*	<0.1
Broadway Brewing L.L.C.	2441 Broadway	Denver	CO	80205	John Hickenlooper	303-292-5027	R	5	<0.1
Vavin Inc.	HCR 4, Box 77	Leon	VA	22725	Stephen B Lane	540-547-3707	R	5*	<0.1
Zarda Development Company Inc.	214 N 7 Hwy	Blue Springs	MO	64015	Michael Zarda	816-229-9999	R	5	0.2
Buscemi's International Inc.	30362 Gratiot Ave	Roseville	MI	48066	Anthony P Buscemi	810-296-5560	R	4	<0.1

Source: Ward's Business Directory of U.S. Private and Public Companies, Volumes 1 and 2, 2000. The company type code used is as follows: P - Public, R - Private, S - Subsidiary, D - Division, J - Joint Venture, A - Affiliate, G - Group, N - Company type not reported. Sales are in millions of dollars, employees are in thousands. An asterisk (*) indicates an estimated sales volume. The symbol < stands for 'less than'. Company names and addresses are truncated, in some cases, to fit into the available space.

LOCATION BY STATE AND REGIONAL CONCENTRATION

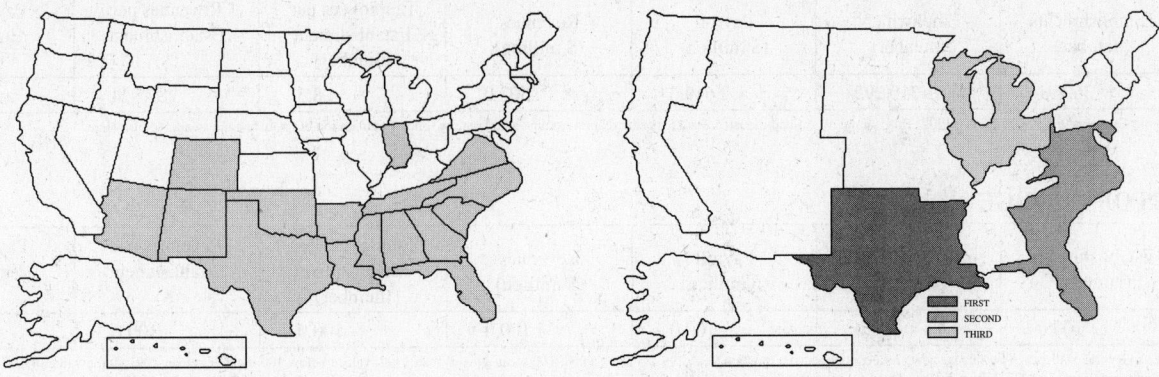

INDUSTRY DATA BY STATE

State	Establishments		Employment			Payroll		Revenues		
	Total (number)	% of U.S.	Total (number)	% of U.S.	Per Estab.	Total ($ mil.)	Per Empl. ($)	Total ($ mil.)	% of U.S.	Per Estab. ($)
Texas	530	12.7	16,340	22.6	31	209.4	12,815	648.8	25.2	1,224,164
Florida	340	8.1	5,665	7.8	17	58.4	10,316	195.2	7.6	574,194
Georgia	218	5.2	4,092	5.7	19	45.2	11,053	148.9	5.8	682,986
California	465	11.1	3,520	4.9	8	37.2	10,578	137.1	5.3	294,944
North Carolina	125	3.0	3,840	5.3	31	44.1	11,478	134.7	5.2	1,077,240
Louisiana	96	2.3	2,695	3.7	28	33.0	12,255	103.4	4.0	1,077,229
Tennessee	125	3.0	2,691	3.7	22	32.4	12,055	97.3	3.8	778,664
Indiana	102	2.4	2,375	3.3	23	25.6	10,760	78.1	3.0	766,020
Virginia	106	2.5	2,169	3.0	20	23.8	10,995	74.2	2.9	700,453
New York	273	6.5	1,825	2.5	7	20.9	11,453	71.9	2.8	263,216
Alabama	94	2.3	1,901	2.6	20	19.3	10,136	64.5	2.5	686,223
Ohio	122	2.9	2,355	3.3	19	17.7	7,501	61.4	2.4	503,156
Arizona	58	1.4	1,845	2.6	32	19.5	10,595	58.0	2.2	1,000,138
South Carolina	53	1.3	1,495	2.1	28	17.8	11,890	54.6	2.1	1,029,453
Michigan	120	2.9	1,603	2.2	13	14.4	9,010	52.6	2.0	438,342
Oklahoma	48	1.2	1,510	2.1	31	16.5	10,921	51.6	2.0	1,075,333
New Mexico	37	0.9	1,291	1.8	35	13.6	10,514	46.7	1.8	1,262,622
Colorado	59	1.4	1,861	2.6	32	14.1	7,563	46.5	1.8	787,525
Missouri	73	1.7	1,426	2.0	20	15.7	10,978	43.1	1.7	590,370
Illinois	117	2.8	1,169	1.6	10	10.1	8,622	38.4	1.5	328,239
Pennsylvania	118	2.8	964	1.3	8	10.1	10,478	35.8	1.4	303,551
New Jersey	140	3.4	680	0.9	5	9.6	14,079	34.6	1.3	246,964
Maryland	77	1.8	682	0.9	9	8.1	11,891	30.7	1.2	398,753
Arkansas	41	1.0	940	1.3	23	9.8	10,476	29.6	1.1	721,878
Mississippi	41	1.0	811	1.1	20	9.2	11,353	29.3	1.1	715,561
Kentucky	45	1.1	962	1.3	21	7.9	8,193	25.5	1.0	566,978
Massachusetts	79	1.9	532	0.7	7	4.8	9,070	19.2	0.7	243,342
Iowa	23	0.6	624	0.9	27	4.7	7,567	15.2	0.6	663,043
D.C.	38	0.9	265	0.4	7	4.2	15,955	14.3	0.6	375,474
Washington	53	1.3	362	0.5	7	3.4	9,309	12.8	0.5	240,943
Oregon	39	0.9	332	0.5	9	3.2	9,738	12.3	0.5	314,333
Minnesota	53	1.3	336	0.5	6	3.6	10,658	12.1	0.5	228,019
West Virginia	16	0.4	383	0.5	24	3.6	9,305	11.5	0.4	719,563
Connecticut	40	1.0	147	0.2	4	2.2	15,116	6.7	0.3	168,450
Montana	15	0.4	212	0.3	14	1.7	7,825	6.2	0.2	414,267
Wisconsin	26	0.6	203	0.3	8	2.1	10,512	5.9	0.2	228,077
Utah	20	0.5	148	0.2	7	1.4	9,689	5.4	0.2	269,200
Nebraska	29	0.7	162	0.2	6	1.2	7,630	5.0	0.2	171,724
Nevada	6	0.1	120	0.2	20	1.3	10,433	4.3	0.2	714,667
New Hampshire	12	0.3	210	0.3	18	1.4	6,429	4.1	0.2	342,583
Vermont	8	0.2	191	0.3	24	1.1	5,916	3.1	0.1	387,375
Hawaii	8	0.2	53	0.1	7	0.9	16,302	2.8	0.1	352,750
Alaska	5	0.1	44	0.1	9	0.8	17,795	2.3	0.1	457,600
Idaho	11	0.3	91	0.1	8	0.6	6,846	2.3	0.1	206,818
Delaware	7	0.2	26	0.0	4	0.6	24,346	2.1	0.1	293,286
Maine	4	0.1	118	0.2	30	0.6	4,669	1.9	0.1	483,750
South Dakota	6	0.1	21	0.0	4	0.2	8,238	0.6	0.0	103,667
North Dakota	3	0.1	9	0.0	3	-	5,222	0.2	0.0	57,000
Kansas	39	0.9	750*	-	-	(D)	-	(D)	-	-
Rhode Island	7	0.2	60*	-	-	(D)	-	(D)	-	-
Wyoming	2	-	60*	-	-	(D)	-	(D)	-	-

Source: 1997 *Economic Census.* The states are in descending order of revenues or establishments (if revenue data are missing for the majority). The symbol (D) appears when data are withheld to prevent disclosure of competitive information. States marked with (D) are sorted by number of establishments. A dash (-) indicates that the data element cannot be calculated. * indicates the midpoint of a range; 175, for example is the range 100-249. Shaded *states* on the state map indicate those states which have proportionately greater representation in the industry than would be indicated by the state's population; the ratio is based on total revenues or number of establishments. Shaded *regions* indicate where the industry is regionally most concentrated.

NAICS 722213 - SNACK AND NONALCOHOLIC BEVERAGE BARS

GENERAL STATISTICS

Year	Establishments (number)	Employment (number)	Payroll ($ million)	Revenues ($ million)	Employees per Establishment (number)	Revenues per Establishment ($)	Payroll per Employee ($)
1997	36,491	310,292	2,649.0	10,503.0	8.5	287,824	8,537

Source: Economic Census of the United States, 1997. This is a newly defined industry. Data for prior years were unavailable at the time of publication but may become available over time.

INDICES OF CHANGE

Year	Establishments (number)	Employment (number)	Payroll ($ million)	Revenues ($ million)	Employees per Establishment (number)	Revenues per Establishment ($)	Payroll per Employee ($)
1997	100.0	100.0	100.0	100.0	100.0	100.0	100.0

Sources: Same as General Statistics. The values shown reflect change from the base year, 1997. Values above 100 mean greater than 1997, values below 100 mean less than 1997, and a value of 100 in the 1982-96 or 1998-2001 period means same as 1997. Values followed by a 'p' are projections by the editors; 'e' stands for extrapolation. Data are the most recent available at this level of detail.

SIC INDUSTRIES RELATED TO NAICS 722213

Each new NAICS code represents an industry that used to be part of an SIC or a part of several SIC industries. Data in this table are shown to provide transitional information for these cases. All available data for the precursor SIC(s) are shown. Even if only a part of an SIC is included in the NAICS, *all* data for the SIC are reproduced. If the SIC industry is not marked as being a part (pt) of the NAICS, the entire industry is embedded in the NAICS data. The SIC composition of the new industry provides some hints of the relative importance of its "ancestors." Data marked with a 'p' are projected. Projections begin with 1982 data. Data earlier than 1990 are not shown but are reflected in the projections.

SIC	Industry	1990	1991	1992	1993	1994	1995	1996	1997
5461	**Retail bakeries (pt)**								
	Establishments (number)	19,897	20,757	20,418	20,683	21,301	20,248	20,474p	20,444p
	Employment (thousands)	176.4	174.8	157.1	160.7	162.4	153.5	150.8p	147.1p
	Revenues ($ million)	5,180.4e	5,283.7e	5,386.9	5,490.1p	5,593.3p	5,696.6p	5,799.8p	5,903.0p
5812	**Eating places (pt)**								
	Establishments (number)	286,792	280,200	377,760	360,212	367,205	344,854	361,385p	367,752p
	Employment (thousands)	5,700.3	5,459.7	6,243.9	6,346.0	6,477.0	6,568.2	6,822.7p	6,993.9p
	Revenues ($ million)	166,234.6e	175,218.9e	184,203.2	193,580.8p	202,685.3p	211,789.8p	220,894.3p	229,998.8p

Source: Economic Census of the United States, 1992, annual surveys of economic sectors conducted by the Bureau of the Census, and estimates or projections based on the 1982-1992 period; not all data are shown. 'e' marks estimates made by the editors; 'p' indicates projections based on time series. A dash (-) indicates that data for this SIC or year were not available. The abbreviation (pt) next to the industry name indicates that only a part of the industry is present within the NAICS data. If no (pt) is shown, the entire industry is contained within the NAICS data.

SELECTED RATIOS

For 1997	Avg. of Information	Analyzed Industry	Index	For 1997	Avg. of Information	Analyzed Industry	Index
Employees per establishment	17	9	49	Payroll per establishment	177,969	72,593	41
Revenue per establishment	642,845	287,824	45	Payroll as % of revenue	28	25	91
Revenue per employee	37,074	33,849	91	Payroll per employee	10,264	8,537	83

Sources: Same as General Statistics. The 'Average' column represents the average for the industry sector, in 1997, where the currently shown industry is classified. The Index shows the relationship between the Average and the Analyzed Industry. For example, 100 means that they are equal; 500 that the Analyzed Industry is five times the average; 50 means that the Analyzed Industry is half the national average. The abbreviation 'na' is used to show that data are 'not available'.

LEADING COMPANIES   Number shown: **75**   Total sales ($ mil): **158,964**   Total employment (000): **1,119.8**

Company Name	Address				CEO Name	Phone	Co. Type	Sales ($ mil)	Empl. (000)
Wal-Mart Stores Inc.	702 SW 8th St	Bentonville	AR	72716	David D. Glass	501-273-4000	P	137,634	825.0
Compass Group USA Inc.	2400 Yorkmont Rd	Charlotte	NC	28217	Mike Bailey	704-329-4000	R	2,600*	57.0
Viad Corp.	1850 N Central Ave	Phoenix	AZ	85007	Robert Bohannon	602-207-4000	P	2,542	19.8
Travel Centers of America	24601 Center Ridge	Westlake	OH	44145	Ed Kuhn	440-808-9100	S	2,134*	10.0
Wendy's International Inc.	PO Box 256	Dublin	OH	43016		614-764-3100	P	1,948	39.0
Ogden Services Corp.	2 Penn Plz	New York	NY	10121	R Richard Ablon	212-868-6000	S	1,750*	39.0
Marsh Supermarkets Inc.	9800 Crosspoint	Indianapolis	IN	46256		317-594-2100	P	1,607	13.4
Valhi Inc.	3 Lincoln Ctr	Dallas	TX	75240	Harold C Simmons	972-233-1700	P	1,059	6.7
Aramark Sports & Entertainment	1101 Market St	Philadelphia	PA	19107	Charles Gillespie	215-238-3000	S	700*	7.0
Casino USA Inc.	4700 S Boyle Ave	Vernon	CA	90058	Robert J Emmons	213-589-1054	S	672	2.3
Papa John's International Inc.	PO Box 99900	Louisville	KY	40269	Blaine Hurst	502-266-5200	P	670	14.3
Friendly Ice Cream Corp.	1855 Boston Rd	Wilbraham	MA	01095	Gerald Sinsigalli	413-543-2400	P	650*	25.0
Galpin Motors Inc.	15505 Roscoe Blvd	North Hills	CA	91343	Bert Boeckmann	818-787-3800	R	561	0.7
W.H. Braum Inc.	1900 S Grand St	Amarillo	TX	79103	William Braum	806-374-4413	R	350*	7.9
Fresh Foods Inc.	PO Box 399	Claremont	NC	28610		828-304-0027	R	258	4.9
CA One Services Inc.	438 Main St	Buffalo	NY	14202	Charles E Moran Jr	716-858-5000	S	254	2.9
Rainforest Cafe Inc.	720 S 5th St	Hopkins	MN	55343	Lyle Berman	612-945-5400	P	214	6.0
Shirley Oil and Supply Inc.	401 E South St	McLean	IL	61754	Charles G Beeler	309-874-2832	R	212*	0.5
Travel Ports of America Inc.	3495 Winton Pl	Rochester	NY	14623	John M Holahan	716-272-1810	P	212	1.4
Ben and Jerry's Homemade Inc.	30 Community Dr	S. Burlington	VT	05403		802-846-1500	P	209	0.8
Broughton Foods Co.	PO Box 656	Marietta	OH	45750		740-373-4121	R	179	0.9
Z.V. Pate Inc.	PO Box 159	Laurel Hill	NC	28351	David L Burns	910-462-2122	R	176*	0.9
Baskin-Robbins USA Co.	PO Box 1200	Glendale	CA	91209		818-956-0031	R	170*	0.8
Gas America Services Inc.	PO Box 20	Shirley	IN	47384	Stephanie White	765-737-6501	R	170*	0.6
Cinnabon Inc.	6 Concourse Pkwy	Atlanta	GA	30328	Kern GIllette	206-548-1032	R	155*	4.5
Chart House Enterprises Inc.	604 N LaSalle	Chicago	IL	60610	Thomas J Walters	312-266-1100	P	145	4.2
Saint Louis Bread Company Inc.	7930 Big Bend	St. Louis	MO	63146	Richard C Postle	314-918-7779	S	116*	3.0
TCBY Enterprises Inc.	425 W Capitol Ave	Little Rock	AR	72201		501-688-8229	P	107	0.4
Overhill Farms Inc.	5730 Uplander Way	Culver City	CA	90230		310-641-3680	P	105	0.7
Il Fornaio America Corp.	770 Tamalpais Dr	Corte Madera	CA	94925	Michael Hislop	415-945-0500	P	83	2.3
Dick Clark Productions Inc.	3003 W Olive Ave	Burbank	CA	91510	Richard W Clark	818-841-3003	P	73	0.8
Faber Enterprises Inc.	100 S Wacker Dr	Chicago	IL	60606		312-558-8900	S	65*	1.1
C.L. Swanson Corp.	4501 Femrite Dr	Madison	WI	53716	Jeff Parks	608-221-7640	R	59*	0.4
American Eagle Management Inc.	PO Box 5026	Cordele	GA	31015	Mike Ouimet	912-273-5710	R	55*	0.1
Nation's Foodservice Inc.	11090 San Pablo	El Cerrito	CA	94530	Dale Power	510-237-1952	R	55*	0.5
Biltmore Co.	1 N Pack Sq	Asheville	NC	28801	William Cecil	828-255-1776	R	50	0.5
Burns Bros. Inc.	4800 SW Meadows	Lake Oswego	OR	97035	Bruce Burns	503-238-7393	R	50*	0.3
Busler Enterprises Inc.	PO Box 23610	Evansville	IN	47724	George W Busler	812-424-7511	R	47	0.2
Wynkoop Brewing Co.	1634 18th St	Denver	CO	80202	John Hickenlooper	303-297-2700	R	46*	0.2
Hasslocher Enterprises Inc.	8520 Crownhill Blvd	San Antonio	TX	78209	Robert Hasslocher	210-828-1493	R	45	1.6
Java City Inc.	717 Del Paso Rd	Sacramento	CA	95834		916-565-5500	R	43	0.8
Watermarc Food Managment Co.	11111 Wilcrest	Houston	TX	77042	Ghulam Bombaywala	713-783-0500	P	40	1.4
Nebraska Iowa Supply Co.	1160 Lincoln St	Blair	NE	68008	Thomas J Lippincott	402-426-2171	R	40	<0.1
Martin Wine's Ltd.	3827 Baronne St	New Orleans	LA	70115	Dave Gladden	504-899-7411	R	39*	0.3
Sierra Nevada Brewing Co.	1075 E 20th St	Chico	CA	95928	Ken Grossman	530-893-3520	R	35	0.1
Skyline Chili Inc.	4180 ThunderbiRd	Fairfield	OH	45014	Kevin McDonnell	513-874-1188	P	35	0.8
Dean and DeLuca Inc.	560 Broadway	New York	NY	10012	Dane Neller	212-431-1691	R	33*	0.5
Bobber Travel Center	PO Box 698	Sullivan	MO	63080	Melvin King	573-468-4166	R	32*	<0.1
Automated Custom Food Services	7700 Brookhollow	Dallas	TX	75235	Steve Errico	214-631-7040	R	31*	0.3
FFP Operating Partners L.P.	2801 Glenda Ave	Fort Worth	TX	76117	Robert J Byrnes	817-838-4700	S	31*	0.1
BOWLIN Outdoor Advertising	150 Louisiana NE	Albuquerque	NM	87108	Michael Bowlin	505-266-5985	P	30	0.3
Chicago Pizza and Brewery Inc.	26131 Marguerite	Mission Viejo	CA	92692	Jerry J Hennessy	949-367-8616	P	30	1.4
Newport Creamery Inc.	PO Box 219	Newport	RI	02840		401-847-0390	R	27	1.5
Monterey Pasta Co.	1528 Moffett St	Salinas	CA	93905	Lance Hewett	408-753-6262	P	26	0.2
I-74 Auto Truck Plaza	PO Box 550	Oakwood	IL	61858		217-354-2105	R	25	<0.1
Bazaar Del Mundo Inc.	2754 Calhoun St	San Diego	CA	92110	Diane Powers	619-296-6301	R	23	0.7
Robinhood Marine Center Inc.	HC 33 Box 1460	Georgetown	ME	04548	Andrew Varolotis	207-371-2525	R	23	<0.1
Epicurean International Inc.	229 Castro St	Oakland	CA	94607	Seth Jacobson	510-268-0209	R	21*	<0.1
El Gallo Giro Inc.	7148 Pacific Blvd	Huntington Park	CA	90255	Carlos Bonaparte	213-585-4433	R	20	0.3
McMenamins Pubs and Breweries	1624 NW Glisan St	Portland	OR	97209		503-223-0109	R	19*	0.6
Chefs International Inc.	PO Box 1332	Pt Pleas Bch	NJ	08742	Anthony C Papalia	732-295-0350	P	19	0.4
Arnie's Inc.	722 Leonard St NW	Grand Rapids	MI	49504		616-458-1107	R	16	0.3
Delivery Concepts Inc.	2658 Holcomb	Alpharetta	GA	30009	Bob Cotman	404-552-1424	R	16*	0.1
Breckinridge Brewery Denver	2220 Blake St	Denver	CO	80205	Richard Squire	303-297-3644	R	13	<0.1
Just Desserts Inc.	1970 Carroll Ave	San Francisco	CA	94124	Elliott Hoffman	415-330-3600	R	13*	0.3
Red River Barbeque and Grille	7500 Brooktree Rd	Wexford	PA	15090	Ronald Sofranko	724-933-5550	R	12*	<0.1
Summit Station Restaurant	227 E Diamond Ave	Gaithersburg	MD	20877	Jonathan Warner	301-519-9400	R	12*	<0.1
BFX Hospitality Group Corp.	226 Bailey Ave	Fort Worth	TX	76107	Jean-Claude Mathot	817-332-4761	P	11	0.4
Heartland Brewery	35 Union Sq W	New York	NY	10003	John Bloostein	212-645-3400	R	10*	<0.1
National Park Concessions Inc.	PO Box 27	Mammoth Cave	KY	42259	James W Milburn Jr	270-773-2191	R	10*	0.4
Wilton Foods Inc.	1 6 1/2 Station Rd	Goshen	NY	10924	Martin Hoffman	914-294-2801	R	9*	0.3
John Conti Coffee Co.	PO Box 18289	Louisville	KY	40261	John Conti	502-499-8600	R	8*	0.1
Kopp's Frozen Custard	18880 W Blmnd	Brookfield	WI	53045	Richard McGuire	414-789-9490	R	8*	<0.1
White Coffee Pot Family Inns Inc.	137 S Warwick Ave	Baltimore	MD	21223	A Katz	410-233-8600	R	8*	<0.1
Clines Corners Operating Co.	1 Yacht Club Dr	Clines Corners	NM	87070	CC Blair	505-472-5488	R	7	<0.1

Source: Ward's Business Directory of U.S. Private and Public Companies, Volumes 1 and 2, 2000. The company type code used is as follows: P - Public, R - Private, S - Subsidiary, D - Division, J - Joint Venture, A - Affiliate, G - Group, N - Company type not reported. Sales are in millions of dollars, employees are in thousands. An asterisk (*) indicates an estimated sales volume. The symbol < stands for 'less than'. Company names and addresses are truncated, in some cases, to fit into the available space.

LOCATION BY STATE AND REGIONAL CONCENTRATION

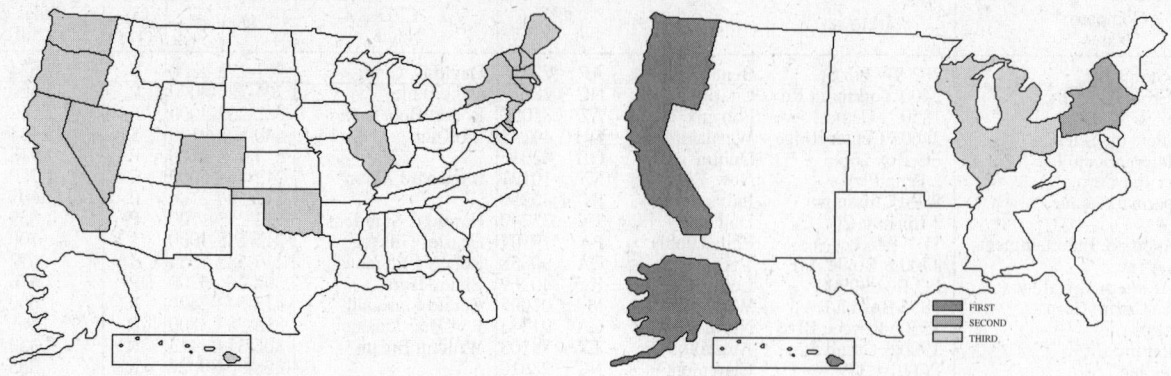

INDUSTRY DATA BY STATE

State	Establishments		Employment			Payroll		Revenues		
	Total (number)	% of U.S.	Total (number)	% of U.S.	Per Estab.	Total ($ mil.)	Per Empl. ($)	Total ($ mil.)	% of U.S.	Per Estab. ($)
California	5,425	14.9	45,662	14.7	8	364.9	7,991	1,619.8	15.4	298,579
New York	3,098	8.5	22,248	7.2	7	222.9	10,018	940.2	9.0	303,501
Massachusetts	1,586	4.3	19,205	6.2	12	191.2	9,954	746.0	7.1	470,388
Texas	1,744	4.8	16,181	5.2	9	131.2	8,111	506.7	4.8	290,515
Illinois	1,601	4.4	13,836	4.5	9	122.5	8,856	498.5	4.7	311,366
New Jersey	1,642	4.5	10,779	3.5	7	112.1	10,402	470.5	4.5	286,548
Pennsylvania	1,749	4.8	12,712	4.1	7	106.1	8,350	424.3	4.0	242,604
Florida	1,606	4.4	12,422	4.0	8	102.2	8,230	418.5	4.0	260,574
Ohio	1,635	4.5	13,082	4.2	8	103.0	7,875	380.3	3.6	232,602
Washington	1,238	3.4	9,196	3.0	7	82.2	8,935	320.0	3.0	258,486
Connecticut	736	2.0	7,768	2.5	11	79.4	10,222	298.1	2.8	405,027
Michigan	1,297	3.6	8,963	2.9	7	73.6	8,211	292.5	2.8	225,503
Oklahoma	437	1.2	6,649	2.1	15	50.2	7,543	214.1	2.0	489,945
Colorado	729	2.0	7,478	2.4	10	54.8	7,328	196.9	1.9	270,099
Minnesota	645	1.8	6,112	2.0	9	48.2	7,891	183.2	1.7	284,088
Maryland	582	1.6	5,382	1.7	9	46.5	8,637	181.2	1.7	311,363
Virginia	583	1.6	5,644	1.8	10	46.7	8,273	175.8	1.7	301,487
Georgia	587	1.6	5,027	1.6	9	43.0	8,561	169.0	1.6	287,865
Missouri	619	1.7	5,426	1.7	9	44.5	8,206	167.0	1.6	269,848
North Carolina	635	1.7	5,050	1.6	8	43.8	8,681	164.2	1.6	258,655
Oregon	615	1.7	4,764	1.5	8	40.4	8,483	162.4	1.5	263,985
Indiana	642	1.8	5,394	1.7	8	41.9	7,770	147.0	1.4	228,935
Arizona	538	1.5	5,039	1.6	9	37.1	7,372	135.2	1.3	251,232
Wisconsin	501	1.4	4,135	1.3	8	30.3	7,327	113.7	1.1	226,914
New Hampshire	297	0.8	3,248	1.0	11	29.3	9,030	113.0	1.1	380,481
Tennessee	369	1.0	2,916	0.9	8	24.2	8,310	88.4	0.8	239,656
Louisiana	349	1.0	2,926	0.9	8	24.8	8,491	84.5	0.8	242,026
Iowa	396	1.1	3,204	1.0	8	20.0	6,228	75.6	0.7	190,952
Utah	266	0.7	2,772	0.9	10	21.8	7,882	73.1	0.7	274,921
Kentucky	278	0.8	2,613	0.8	9	19.9	7,617	71.7	0.7	257,964
Nevada	238	0.7	2,051	0.7	9	17.7	8,610	70.0	0.7	294,277
Hawaii	206	0.6	1,705	0.5	8	16.9	9,926	67.0	0.6	325,204
Maine	283	0.8	1,726	0.6	6	16.6	9,639	64.8	0.6	228,929
South Carolina	287	0.8	2,246	0.7	8	18.5	8,239	64.7	0.6	225,303
D.C.	124	0.3	1,251	0.4	10	13.0	10,421	53.8	0.5	433,556
Arkansas	166	0.5	1,778	0.6	11	13.6	7,666	49.1	0.5	295,584
Alabama	220	0.6	1,675	0.5	8	11.6	6,902	45.3	0.4	205,845
New Mexico	185	0.5	1,533	0.5	8	12.0	7,815	42.2	0.4	228,341
Delaware	136	0.4	1,077	0.3	8	10.4	9,644	42.1	0.4	309,463
Nebraska	237	0.6	1,666	0.5	7	11.8	7,072	41.3	0.4	174,148
Idaho	191	0.5	1,340	0.4	7	8.5	6,333	31.0	0.3	162,539
Vermont	109	0.3	909	0.3	8	8.1	8,939	28.6	0.3	262,477
Mississippi	149	0.4	920	0.3	6	6.8	7,397	28.1	0.3	188,403
Montana	162	0.4	1,105	0.4	7	7.8	7,047	27.6	0.3	170,148
West Virginia	151	0.4	1,081	0.3	7	7.2	6,655	27.0	0.3	178,609
Alaska	118	0.3	621	0.2	5	6.7	10,828	25.1	0.2	212,780
North Dakota	94	0.3	798	0.3	8	5.0	6,262	18.7	0.2	198,670
South Dakota	107	0.3	658	0.2	6	4.3	6,574	15.6	0.1	145,888
Kansas	355	1.0	3,750*	-	-	(D)	-	(D)	-	-
Rhode Island	293	0.8	3,750*	-	-	(D)	-	(D)	-	-
Wyoming	73	0.2	375*	-	-	(D)	-	(D)	-	-

Source: 1997 *Economic Census*. The states are in descending order of revenues or establishments (if revenue data are missing for the majority). The symbol (D) appears when data are withheld to prevent disclosure of competitive information. States marked with (D) are sorted by number of establishments. A dash (-) indicates that the data element cannot be calculated. * indicates the midpoint of a range; 175, for example is the range 100-249. Shaded *states* on the state map indicate those states which have proportionately greater representation in the industry than would be indicated by the state's population; the ratio is based on total revenues or number of establishments. Shaded *regions* indicate where the industry is regionally most concentrated.

NAICS 722310 - FOODSERVICE CONTRACTORS

GENERAL STATISTICS

Year	Establishments (number)	Employment (number)	Payroll ($ million)	Revenues ($ million)	Employees per Establishment (number)	Revenues per Establishment ($)	Payroll per Employee ($)
1997	18,991	361,996	4,617.0	15,160.0	19.1	798,273	12,754

Source: Economic Census of the United States, 1997. This is a newly defined industry. Data for prior years were unavailable at the time of publication but may become available over time.

INDICES OF CHANGE

Year	Establishments (number)	Employment (number)	Payroll ($ million)	Revenues ($ million)	Employees per Establishment (number)	Revenues per Establishment ($)	Payroll per Employee ($)
1997	100.0	100.0	100.0	100.0	100.0	100.0	100.0

Sources: Same as General Statistics. The values shown reflect change from the base year, 1997. Values above 100 mean greater than 1997, values below 100 mean less than 1997, and a value of 100 in the 1982-96 or 1998-2001 period means same as 1997. Values followed by a 'p' are projections by the editors; 'e' stands for extrapolation. Data are the most recent available at this level of detail.

SIC INDUSTRIES RELATED TO NAICS 722310

Each new NAICS code represents an industry that used to be part of an SIC or a part of several SIC industries. Data in this table are shown to provide transitional information for these cases. All available data for the precursor SIC(s) are shown. Even if only a part of an SIC is included in the NAICS, *all* data for the SIC are reproduced. If the SIC industry is not marked as being a part (pt) of the NAICS, the entire industry is embedded in the NAICS data. The SIC composition of the new industry provides some hints of the relative importance of its "ancestors." Data marked with a 'p' are projected. Projections begin with 1982 data. Data earlier than 1990 are not shown but are reflected in the projections.

SIC	Industry	1990	1991	1992	1993	1994	1995	1996	1997
4789	**Miscellaneous Transportation Services (pt)**								
	Establishments (number)	995e	1,009e	1,024	1,039p	1,053p	1,068p	1,082p	1,097p
	Employment (thousands)	17.3e	16.8e	16.4	15.9p	15.5p	15.1p	14.6p	14.2p
	Revenues ($ million)	1,231.2e	1,382.5e	1,533.8	1,685.1p	1,836.4p	1,987.7p	2,139.0p	2,290.3p
5812	**Eating places (pt)**								
	Establishments (number)	286,792	280,200	377,760	360,212	367,205	344,854	361,385p	367,752p
	Employment (thousands)	5,700.3	5,459.7	6,243.9	6,346.0	6,477.0	6,568.2	6,822.7p	6,993.9p
	Revenues ($ million)	166,234.6e	175,218.9e	184,203.2	193,580.8p	202,685.3p	211,789.8p	220,894.3p	229,998.8p

Source: Economic Census of the United States, 1992, annual surveys of economic sectors conducted by the Bureau of the Census, and estimates or projections based on the 1982-1992 period; not all data are shown. 'e' marks estimates made by the editors; 'p' indicates projections based on time series. A dash (-) indicates that data for this SIC or year were not available. The abbreviation (pt) next to the industry name indicates that only a part of the industry is present within the NAICS data. If no (pt) is shown, the entire industry is contained within the NAICS data.

SELECTED RATIOS

For 1997	Avg. of Information	Analyzed Industry	Index	For 1997	Avg. of Information	Analyzed Industry	Index
Employees per establishment	17	19	110	Payroll per establishment	177,969	243,115	137
Revenue per establishment	642,845	798,273	124	Payroll as % of revenue	28	30	110
Revenue per employee	37,074	41,879	113	Payroll per employee	10,264	12,754	124

Sources: Same as General Statistics. The 'Average' column represents the average for the industry sector, in 1997, where the currently shown industry is classified. The Index shows the relationship between the Average and the Analyzed Industry. For example, 100 means that they are equal; 500 that the Analyzed Industry is five times the average; 50 means that the Analyzed Industry is half the national average. The abbreviation 'na' is used to show that data are 'not available'.

LEADING COMPANIES

No company data available for this industry.

LOCATION BY STATE AND REGIONAL CONCENTRATION

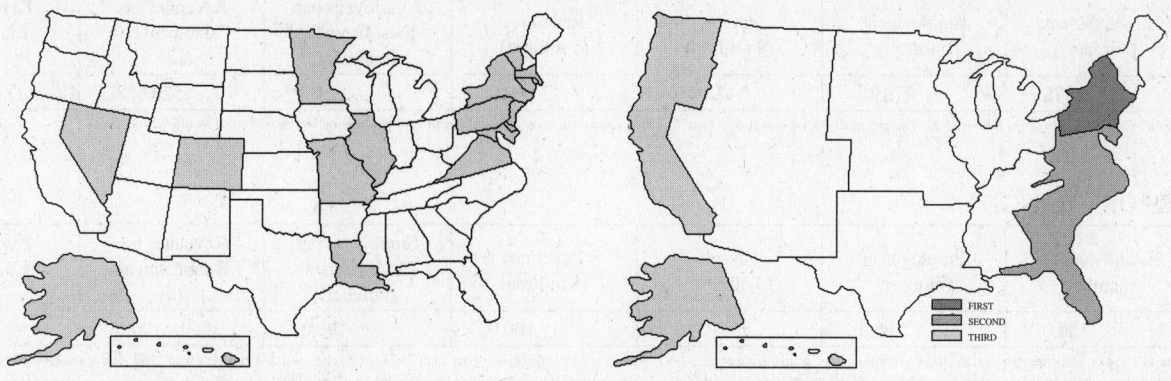

FIRST
SECOND
THIRD

INDUSTRY DATA BY STATE

State	Establishments Total (number)	Establishments % of U.S.	Employment Total (number)	Employment % of U.S.	Employment Per Estab.	Payroll Total ($ mil.)	Payroll Per Empl. ($)	Revenues Total ($ mil.)	Revenues % of U.S.	Revenues Per Estab. ($)
New York	1,947	10.3	36,701	10.1	19	547.9	14,929	1,708.0	11.3	877,223
California	1,368	7.2	33,859	9.4	25	472.9	13,966	1,576.2	10.4	1,152,212
Illinois	1,150	6.1	22,997	6.4	20	301.4	13,107	969.0	6.4	842,569
Pennsylvania	1,079	5.7	23,102	6.4	21	255.0	11,040	849.0	5.6	786,804
Texas	961	5.1	20,653	5.7	21	243.6	11,797	844.9	5.6	879,153
New Jersey	1,235	6.5	19,540	5.4	16	263.8	13,502	794.5	5.2	643,292
Florida	644	3.4	16,990	4.7	26	205.0	12,063	738.3	4.9	1,146,380
Massachusetts	1,082	5.7	16,264	4.5	15	217.0	13,342	720.9	4.8	666,221
Virginia	586	3.1	8,998	2.5	15	131.2	14,581	439.1	2.9	749,316
Michigan	579	3.0	9,868	2.7	17	135.8	13,759	420.9	2.8	726,895
Ohio	633	3.3	10,150	2.8	16	110.9	10,923	409.8	2.7	647,433
Georgia	417	2.2	8,108	2.2	19	118.4	14,598	390.1	2.6	935,547
Connecticut	511	2.7	8,232	2.3	16	107.7	13,084	338.8	2.2	663,082
Missouri	480	2.5	8,220	2.3	17	105.6	12,842	338.4	2.2	705,008
Maryland	370	1.9	7,211	2.0	19	96.8	13,429	331.2	2.2	895,073
North Carolina	648	3.4	8,527	2.4	13	96.9	11,367	325.2	2.1	501,789
Washington	295	1.6	6,393	1.8	22	83.2	13,016	278.3	1.8	943,431
Minnesota	418	2.2	6,431	1.8	15	87.6	13,615	273.1	1.8	653,340
Louisiana	182	1.0	7,421	2.1	41	94.8	12,769	258.0	1.7	1,417,797
Colorado	248	1.3	5,136	1.4	21	58.4	11,372	214.5	1.4	864,730
Tennessee	307	1.6	5,605	1.5	18	63.8	11,389	211.0	1.4	687,163
D.C.	228	1.2	4,135	1.1	18	61.8	14,954	198.2	1.3	869,474
Indiana	309	1.6	5,239	1.4	17	54.0	10,300	197.2	1.3	638,275
Arizona	300	1.6	4,925	1.4	16	57.3	11,640	195.5	1.3	651,607
South Carolina	222	1.2	4,685	1.3	21	49.9	10,661	159.8	1.1	719,730
Kentucky	173	0.9	3,750	1.0	22	48.7	12,995	157.5	1.0	910,590
Wisconsin	314	1.7	5,452	1.5	17	46.1	8,449	149.7	1.0	476,707
Alaska	72	0.4	1,529	0.4	21	52.3	34,237	143.8	0.9	1,997,306
Hawaii	51	0.3	2,267	0.6	44	40.2	17,745	142.8	0.9	2,800,941
Oregon	201	1.1	3,812	1.1	19	38.0	9,969	127.0	0.8	632,020
Kansas	198	1.0	3,093	0.9	16	32.6	10,532	109.1	0.7	551,253
Nevada	42	0.2	2,409	0.7	57	31.9	13,242	106.5	0.7	2,535,643
Alabama	186	1.0	3,293	0.9	18	32.2	9,777	106.3	0.7	571,645
Delaware	109	0.6	1,886	0.5	17	27.8	14,727	98.4	0.6	902,569
Oklahoma	148	0.8	2,940	0.8	20	29.9	10,162	95.3	0.6	644,250
Iowa	172	0.9	2,231	0.6	13	23.8	10,646	87.9	0.6	511,105
Mississippi	124	0.7	2,763	0.8	22	25.8	9,353	81.2	0.5	655,234
Utah	93	0.5	1,493	0.4	16	21.0	14,046	69.2	0.5	743,882
Rhode Island	117	0.6	2,269	0.6	19	20.3	8,948	66.4	0.4	567,479
New Mexico	97	0.5	2,050	0.6	21	18.3	8,905	65.0	0.4	670,021
Nebraska	98	0.5	1,769	0.5	18	17.7	10,010	60.1	0.4	613,765
Arkansas	75	0.4	1,330	0.4	18	11.9	8,977	53.6	0.4	714,507
New Hampshire	121	0.6	1,400	0.4	12	15.8	11,266	50.3	0.3	416,041
West Virginia	76	0.4	1,045	0.3	14	11.7	11,191	41.4	0.3	545,039
Vermont	78	0.4	1,243	0.3	16	12.8	10,289	40.8	0.3	523,603
Maine	79	0.4	1,153	0.3	15	11.5	9,972	37.6	0.2	475,772
Idaho	67	0.4	1,022	0.3	15	9.0	8,806	30.7	0.2	457,836
Montana	32	0.2	702	0.2	22	5.3	7,587	19.2	0.1	598,906
South Dakota	30	0.2	947	0.3	32	5.6	5,947	18.7	0.1	622,833
North Dakota	16	0.1	346	0.1	22	2.4	6,832	6.3	0.0	394,188
Wyoming	22	0.1	303	0.1	14	1.9	6,261	6.0	0.0	273,773

Source: 1997 *Economic Census*. The states are in descending order of revenues or establishments (if revenue data are missing for the majority). The symbol (D) appears when data are withheld to prevent disclosure of competitive information. States marked with (D) are sorted by number of establishments. A dash (-) indicates that the data element cannot be calculated. * indicates the midpoint of a range; 175, for example is the range 100-249. Shaded *states* on the state map indicate those states which have proportionately greater representation in the industry than would be indicated by the state's population; the ratio is based on total revenues or number of establishments. Shaded *regions* indicate where the industry is regionally most concentrated.

NAICS 722320 - CATERERS

GENERAL STATISTICS

Year	Establishments (number)	Employment (number)	Payroll ($ million)	Revenues ($ million)	Employees per Establishment (number)	Revenues per Establishment ($)	Payroll per Employee ($)
1997	6,478	91,191	978.0	3,369.0	14.1	520,068	10,725

Source: *Economic Census of the United States*, 1997. This is a newly defined industry. Data for prior years were unavailable at the time of publication but may become available over time.

INDICES OF CHANGE

Year	Establishments (number)	Employment (number)	Payroll ($ million)	Revenues ($ million)	Employees per Establishment (number)	Revenues per Establishment ($)	Payroll per Employee ($)
1997	100.0	100.0	100.0	100.0	100.0	100.0	100.0

Sources: Same as General Statistics. The values shown reflect change from the base year, 1997. Values above 100 mean greater than 1997, values below 100 mean less than 1997, and a value of 100 in the 1982-96 or 1998-2001 period means same as 1997. Values followed by a 'p' are projections by the editors; 'e' stands for extrapolation. Data are the most recent available at this level of detail.

SIC INDUSTRIES RELATED TO NAICS 722320

Each new NAICS code represents an industry that used to be part of an SIC or a part of several SIC industries. Data in this table are shown to provide transitional information for these cases. All available data for the precursor SIC(s) are shown. Even if only a part of an SIC is included in the NAICS, *all* data for the SIC are reproduced. If the SIC industry is not marked as being a part (pt) of the NAICS, the entire industry is embedded in the NAICS data. The SIC composition of the new industry provides some hints of the relative importance of its "ancestors." Data marked with a 'p' are projected. Projections begin with 1982 data. Data earlier than 1990 are not shown but are reflected in the projections.

SIC	Industry	1990	1991	1992	1993	1994	1995	1996	1997
5812	**Eating places (pt)**								
	Establishments (number)	286,792	280,200	377,760	360,212	367,205	344,854	361,385p	367,752p
	Employment (thousands)	5,700.3	5,459.7	6,243.9	6,346.0	6,477.0	6,568.2	6,822.7p	6,993.9p
	Revenues ($ million)	166,234.6e	175,218.9e	184,203.2	193,580.8p	202,685.3p	211,789.8p	220,894.3p	229,998.8p

Source: *Economic Census of the United States*, 1992, annual surveys of economic sectors conducted by the Bureau of the Census, and estimates or projections based on the 1982-1992 period; not all data are shown. 'e' marks estimates made by the editors; 'p' indicates projections based on time series. A dash (-) indicates that data for this SIC or year were not available. The abbreviation (pt) next to the industry name indicates that only a part of the industry is present within the NAICS data. If no (pt) is shown, the entire industry is contained within the NAICS data.

SELECTED RATIOS

For 1997	Avg. of Information	Analyzed Industry	Index	For 1997	Avg. of Information	Analyzed Industry	Index
Employees per establishment	17	14	81	Payroll per establishment	177,969	150,973	85
Revenue per establishment	642,845	520,068	81	Payroll as % of revenue	28	29	105
Revenue per employee	37,074	36,944	100	Payroll per employee	10,264	10,725	104

Sources: Same as General Statistics. The 'Average' column represents the average for the industry sector, in 1997, where the currently shown industry is classified. The Index shows the relationship between the Average and the Analyzed Industry. For example, 100 means that they are equal; 500 that the Analyzed Industry is five times the average; 50 means that the Analyzed Industry is half the national average. The abbreviation 'na' is used to show that data are 'not available'.

LEADING COMPANIES

No company data available for this industry.

LOCATION BY STATE AND REGIONAL CONCENTRATION

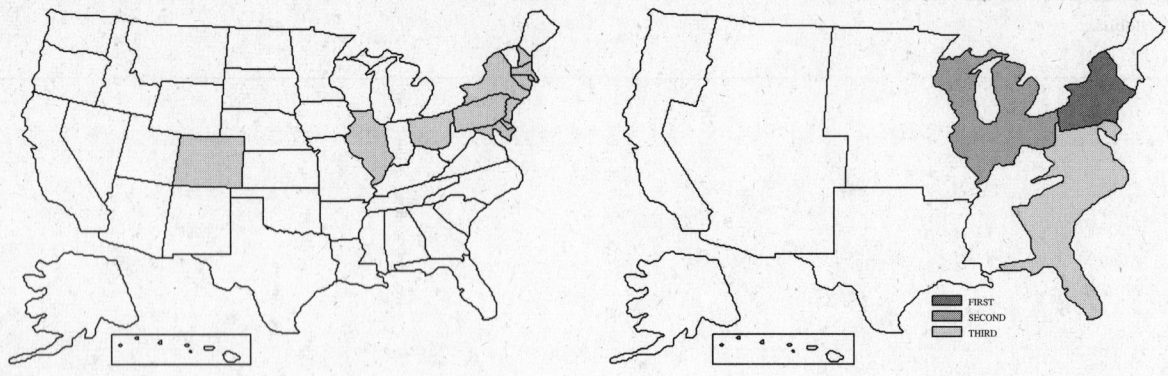

FIRST
SECOND
THIRD

INDUSTRY DATA BY STATE

State	Establishments Total (number)	% of U.S.	Employment Total (number)	% of U.S.	Per Estab.	Payroll Total ($ mil.)	Per Empl. ($)	Revenues Total ($ mil.)	% of U.S.	Per Estab. ($)
New York	731	11.3	13,511	14.8	18	180.3	13,343	594.4	17.6	813,119
California	666	10.3	10,241	11.2	15	109.3	10,668	368.9	10.9	553,845
New Jersey	325	5.0	5,141	5.6	16	71.7	13,941	249.0	7.4	766,003
Illinois	364	5.6	7,181	7.9	20	70.0	9,746	242.4	7.2	665,929
Pennsylvania	388	6.0	5,453	6.0	14	52.1	9,552	182.7	5.4	470,954
Ohio	327	5.0	5,139	5.6	16	43.5	8,467	166.5	4.9	509,110
Maryland	165	2.5	2,952	3.2	18	39.8	13,493	128.9	3.8	780,994
Texas	272	4.2	3,210	3.5	12	34.7	10,805	124.1	3.7	456,346
Massachusetts	234	3.6	3,772	4.1	16	38.6	10,226	122.6	3.6	523,774
Florida	299	4.6	3,673	4.0	12	30.9	8,403	119.9	3.6	401,144
Michigan	267	4.1	3,467	3.8	13	31.9	9,208	113.1	3.4	423,670
Connecticut	171	2.6	1,638	1.8	10	26.6	16,253	84.2	2.5	492,474
Virginia	142	2.2	1,481	1.6	10	18.9	12,758	69.8	2.1	491,754
Indiana	145	2.2	2,146	2.4	15	19.0	8,854	67.6	2.0	466,317
Missouri	152	2.3	2,357	2.6	16	20.7	8,792	67.0	2.0	440,737
Georgia	142	2.2	1,817	2.0	13	16.0	8,806	60.4	1.8	425,261
Wisconsin	144	2.2	2,126	2.3	15	15.3	7,174	53.6	1.6	372,174
Colorado	103	1.6	1,338	1.5	13	15.6	11,684	49.8	1.5	483,340
Minnesota	106	1.6	1,361	1.5	13	15.1	11,096	47.1	1.4	444,349
Louisiana	86	1.3	1,299	1.4	15	11.5	8,868	43.4	1.3	504,081
North Carolina	118	1.8	1,257	1.4	11	13.0	10,356	42.0	1.2	356,042
Arizona	69	1.1	1,110	1.2	16	9.0	8,140	35.0	1.0	507,623
Washington	116	1.8	1,109	1.2	10	10.6	9,582	32.6	1.0	281,216
Tennessee	82	1.3	627	0.7	8	8.0	12,794	29.7	0.9	361,829
Rhode Island	44	0.7	510	0.6	12	6.2	12,188	19.9	0.6	453,364
Oregon	66	1.0	762	0.8	12	6.9	9,068	19.9	0.6	301,924
Kentucky	52	0.8	317	0.3	6	3.9	12,278	18.6	0.6	357,462
South Carolina	64	1.0	547	0.6	9	5.4	9,870	18.3	0.5	285,953
New Hampshire	44	0.7	469	0.5	11	4.9	10,539	18.2	0.5	414,591
Utah	35	0.5	656	0.7	19	4.3	6,617	17.1	0.5	488,486
Alabama	51	0.8	385	0.4	8	3.3	8,504	13.7	0.4	267,843
Delaware	24	0.4	256	0.3	11	4.0	15,445	13.0	0.4	543,292
Iowa	66	1.0	453	0.5	7	3.3	7,227	12.7	0.4	192,758
Hawaii	22	0.3	447	0.5	20	4.2	9,336	12.6	0.4	572,591
Oklahoma	38	0.6	300	0.3	8	2.7	8,910	11.1	0.3	291,289
Maine	41	0.6	241	0.3	6	2.2	9,266	8.9	0.3	216,463
Nebraska	41	0.6	352	0.4	9	2.6	7,259	8.9	0.3	215,927
Nevada	24	0.4	189	0.2	8	1.3	6,667	6.3	0.2	261,208
Alaska	10	0.2	89	0.1	9	2.1	23,674	5.1	0.2	511,400
New Mexico	27	0.4	228	0.3	8	1.3	5,798	4.7	0.1	173,370
Mississippi	22	0.3	139	0.2	6	1.1	7,935	4.0	0.1	183,409
Vermont	17	0.3	126	0.1	7	1.1	8,690	3.7	0.1	216,412
Arkansas	25	0.4	133	0.1	5	1.1	8,053	3.6	0.1	145,440
Idaho	23	0.4	100	0.1	4	0.8	8,320	3.6	0.1	156,261
West Virginia	25	0.4	156	0.2	6	0.8	5,077	3.2	0.1	128,520
North Dakota	8	0.1	64	0.1	8	0.4	6,391	1.7	0.1	215,625
South Dakota	9	0.1	38	0.0	4	0.3	8,816	1.6	0.0	177,444
Montana	10	0.2	41	0.0	4	0.3	6,122	1.3	0.0	127,500
Wyoming	4	0.1	15	0.0	4	-	933	0.1	0.0	22,500
Kansas	49	0.8	375*	-	-	(D)	-	(D)	-	-
D.C.	23	0.4	375*	-	-	(D)	-	(D)	-	-

Source: 1997 *Economic Census*. The states are in descending order of revenues or establishments (if revenue data are missing for the majority). The symbol (D) appears when data are withheld to prevent disclosure of competitive information. States marked with (D) are sorted by number of establishments. A dash (-) indicates that the data element cannot be calculated. * indicates the midpoint of a range; 175, for example is the range 100-249. Shaded *states* on the state map indicate those states which have proportionately greater representation in the industry than would be indicated by the state's population; the ratio is based on total revenues or number of establishments. Shaded *regions* indicate where the industry is regionally most concentrated.

NAICS 722330 - MOBILE FOODSERVICES

GENERAL STATISTICS

Year	Establishments (number)	Employment (number)	Payroll ($ million)	Revenues ($ million)	Employees per Establishment (number)	Revenues per Establishment ($)	Payroll per Employee ($)
1997	2,593	11,683	170.0	879.0	4.5	338,990	14,551

Source: Economic Census of the United States, 1997. This is a newly defined industry. Data for prior years were unavailable at the time of publication but may become available over time.

INDICES OF CHANGE

Year	Establishments (number)	Employment (number)	Payroll ($ million)	Revenues ($ million)	Employees per Establishment (number)	Revenues per Establishment ($)	Payroll per Employee ($)
1997	100.0	100.0	100.0	100.0	100.0	100.0	100.0

Sources: Same as General Statistics. The values shown reflect change from the base year, 1997. Values above 100 mean greater than 1997, values below 100 mean less than 1997, and a value of 100 in the 1982-96 or 1998-2001 period means same as 1997. Values followed by a 'p' are projections by the editors; 'e' stands for extrapolation. Data are the most recent available at this level of detail.

SIC INDUSTRIES RELATED TO NAICS 722330

Each new NAICS code represents an industry that used to be part of an SIC or a part of several SIC industries. Data in this table are shown to provide transitional information for these cases. All available data for the precursor SIC(s) are shown. Even if only a part of an SIC is included in the NAICS, *all* data for the SIC are reproduced. If the SIC industry is not marked as being a part (pt) of the NAICS, the entire industry is embedded in the NAICS data. The SIC composition of the new industry provides some hints of the relative importance of its "ancestors." Data marked with a 'p' are projected. Projections begin with 1982 data. Data earlier than 1990 are not shown but are reflected in the projections.

SIC	Industry	1990	1991	1992	1993	1994	1995	1996	1997
5963	**Direct selling establishments (pt)**								
	Establishments (number)	8,820	8,650	13,641	13,279	13,207	13,388	13,191*p*	13,603*p*
	Employment (thousands)	106.9	103.9	119.4	121.4	119.5	122.9	128.0*p*	131.0*p*
	Revenues ($ million)	9,244.0*e*	9,707.2*e*	10,170.3	11,079.8*p*	11,679.3*p*	12,278.9*p*	12,878.4*p*	13,477.9*p*

Source: Economic Census of the United States, 1992, annual surveys of economic sectors conducted by the Bureau of the Census, and estimates or projections based on the 1982-1992 period; not all data are shown. 'e' marks estimates made by the editors; 'p' indicates projections based on time series. A dash (-) indicates that data for this SIC or year were not available. The abbreviation (pt) next to the industry name indicates that only a part of the industry is present within the NAICS data. If no (pt) is shown, the entire industry is contained within the NAICS data.

SELECTED RATIOS

For 1997	Avg. of Information	Analyzed Industry	Index	For 1997	Avg. of Information	Analyzed Industry	Index
Employees per establishment	17	5	26	Payroll per establishment	177,969	65,561	37
Revenue per establishment	642,845	338,990	53	Payroll as % of revenue	28	19	70
Revenue per employee	37,074	75,238	203	Payroll per employee	10,264	14,551	142

Sources: Same as General Statistics. The 'Average' column represents the average for the industry sector, in 1997, where the currently shown industry is classified. The Index shows the relationship between the Average and the Analyzed Industry. For example, 100 means that they are equal; 500 that the Analyzed Industry is five times the average; 50 means that the Analyzed Industry is half the national average. The abbreviation 'na' is used to show that data are 'not available'.

LEADING COMPANIES

No company data available for this industry.

LOCATION BY STATE AND REGIONAL CONCENTRATION

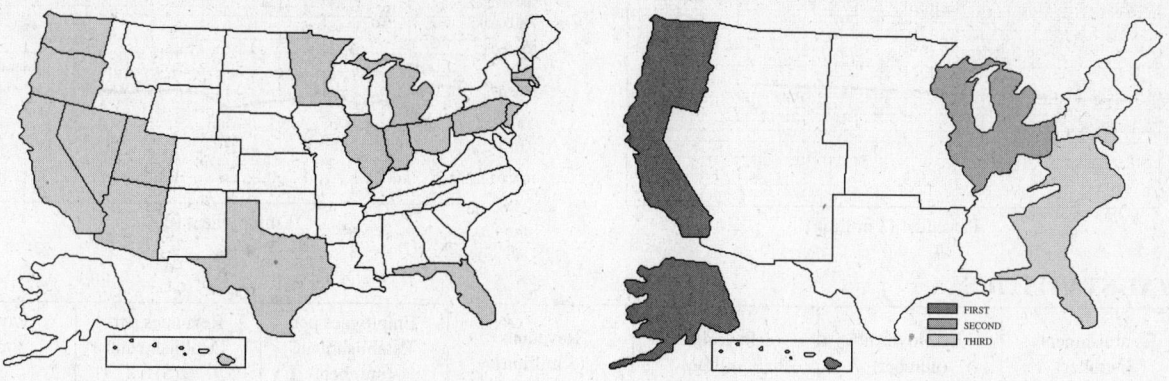

INDUSTRY DATA BY STATE

State	Establishments Total (number)	Establishments % of U.S.	Employment Total (number)	Employment % of U.S.	Employment Per Estab.	Payroll Total ($ mil.)	Payroll Per Empl. ($)	Revenues Total ($ mil.)	Revenues % of U.S.	Revenues Per Estab. ($)
California	397	15.3	1,791	15.3	5	26.5	14,773	144.0	16.4	362,824
Texas	104	4.0	670	5.7	6	11.3	16,854	68.0	7.7	653,375
Ohio	149	5.7	742	6.4	5	11.3	15,240	64.5	7.3	433,148
Florida	170	6.6	647	5.5	4	7.4	11,433	55.9	6.4	328,765
Washington	147	5.7	659	5.6	4	10.9	16,602	50.8	5.8	345,803
Illinois	82	3.2	590	5.1	7	9.7	16,386	47.4	5.4	578,598
Pennsylvania	125	4.8	590	5.1	5	9.6	16,312	45.0	5.1	359,688
New York	152	5.9	459	3.9	3	6.9	15,081	41.7	4.7	274,164
Michigan	72	2.8	429	3.7	6	8.2	19,096	38.2	4.3	531,125
New Jersey	101	3.9	324	2.8	3	6.6	20,435	32.8	3.7	324,594
Indiana	60	2.3	344	2.9	6	4.3	12,419	21.6	2.5	360,217
Massachusetts	62	2.4	305	2.6	5	4.2	13,630	21.2	2.4	342,484
Minnesota	74	2.9	157	1.3	2	3.8	24,369	20.0	2.3	269,986
North Carolina	45	1.7	364	3.1	8	4.4	12,049	17.4	2.0	386,089
Maryland	42	1.6	266	2.3	6	4.4	16,571	16.0	1.8	380,643
Arizona	45	1.7	288	2.5	6	3.2	11,243	14.9	1.7	331,444
Connecticut	42	1.6	168	1.4	4	3.1	18,577	14.9	1.7	354,429
Georgia	45	1.7	178	1.5	4	2.8	15,815	14.4	1.6	318,956
Oregon	70	2.7	216	1.8	3	3.4	15,546	14.1	1.6	201,386
Missouri	39	1.5	180	1.5	5	2.9	16,311	12.7	1.4	325,051
Colorado	56	2.2	218	1.9	4	2.3	10,592	11.2	1.3	199,464
Virginia	59	2.3	158	1.4	3	2.6	16,525	10.9	1.2	185,136
Utah	19	0.7	118	1.0	6	1.6	13,407	8.9	1.0	466,737
Tennessee	23	0.9	213	1.8	9	1.9	8,930	7.5	0.9	326,130
Wisconsin	46	1.8	158	1.4	3	1.6	9,835	7.1	0.8	154,000
Nevada	14	0.5	132	1.1	9	1.3	10,061	6.7	0.8	478,929
Hawaii	23	0.9	132	1.1	6	1.6	12,182	6.7	0.8	291,478
Iowa	27	1.0	58	0.5	2	1.1	19,155	5.8	0.7	214,593
Kentucky	16	0.6	87	0.7	5	1.1	13,218	5.7	0.6	356,438
Oklahoma	21	0.8	91	0.8	4	0.6	6,231	5.4	0.6	255,429
Louisiana	25	1.0	93	0.8	4	1.2	13,183	4.9	0.6	196,560
Mississippi	12	0.5	94	0.8	8	1.2	12,298	4.9	0.6	407,750
Alabama	17	0.7	101	0.9	6	0.9	8,752	4.0	0.5	236,941
Arkansas	10	0.4	43	0.4	4	0.4	9,023	3.2	0.4	318,900
South Carolina	13	0.5	146	1.2	11	0.7	5,048	3.0	0.3	232,692
Maine	23	0.9	37	0.3	2	0.7	19,054	2.9	0.3	126,957
Rhode Island	18	0.7	36	0.3	2	0.6	16,639	2.7	0.3	148,500
Nebraska	10	0.4	52	0.4	5	0.6	11,423	2.6	0.3	256,500
New Hampshire	15	0.6	25	0.2	2	0.4	14,080	2.1	0.2	141,400
North Dakota	13	0.5	13	0.1	1	0.2	17,692	1.7	0.2	133,231
Montana	15	0.6	17	0.1	1	0.4	22,765	1.5	0.2	100,333
New Mexico	8	0.3	15	0.1	2	0.2	14,333	1.4	0.2	171,000
Delaware	8	0.3	20	0.2	3	0.2	8,500	1.4	0.2	170,500
Alaska	14	0.5	112	1.0	8	0.3	2,813	1.3	0.2	94,786
Idaho	13	0.5	5	0.0	-	0.1	29,800	1.2	0.1	92,846
West Virginia	12	0.5	15	0.1	1	0.2	11,733	1.0	0.1	81,917
Wyoming	5	0.2	27	0.2	5	0.2	6,667	0.9	0.1	189,600
South Dakota	8	0.3	21	0.2	3	0.2	8,810	0.9	0.1	115,625
Vermont	8	0.3	3	0.0	-	0.1	23,000	0.6	0.1	73,750
Kansas	17	0.7	60*	-	-	(D)	-	(D)	-	-
D.C.	2	0.1	10*	-	-	(D)	-	(D)	-	-

Source: 1997 *Economic Census.* The states are in descending order of revenues or establishments (if revenue data are missing for the majority). The symbol (D) appears when data are withheld to prevent disclosure of competitive information. States marked with (D) are sorted by number of establishments. A dash (-) indicates that the data element cannot be calculated. * indicates the midpoint of a range; 175, for example is the range 100-249. Shaded *states* on the state map indicate those states which have proportionately greater representation in the industry than would be indicated by the state's population; the ratio is based on total revenues or number of establishments. Shaded *regions* indicate where the industry is regionally most concentrated.

NAICS 722410 - DRINKING PLACES (ALCOHOLIC BEVERAGES)*

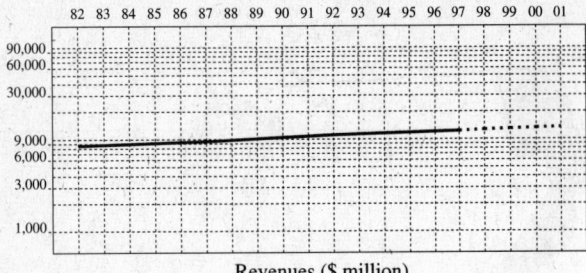

Revenues ($ million)

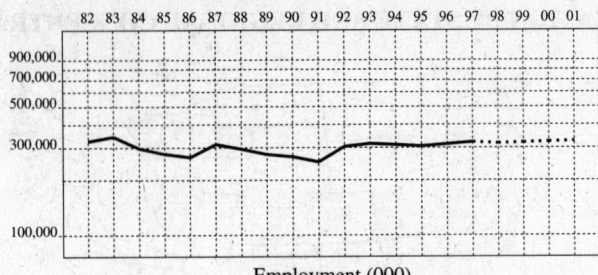

Employment (000)

GENERAL STATISTICS

Year	Establishments (number)	Employment (number)	Payroll ($ million)	Revenues ($ million)	Employees per Establishment (number)	Revenues per Establishment ($)	Payroll per Employee ($)
1982	67,735	324,998	1,721.0	8,565.0	4.8	126,449	5,295
1983	64,884	344,127	1,998.0	8,751.0	5.3	134,871	5,806
1984	58,109	297,249	1,746.0	8,937.0	5.1	153,797	5,874
1985	52,624	277,418	1,704.0	9,123.0	5.3	173,362	6,142
1986	50,205	265,808	1,693.0	9,309.0	5.3	185,420	6,369
1987	58,692	312,831	1,950.0	9,495.0	5.3	161,777	6,233
1988	52,496	294,593	2,025.0	9,819.0	5.6	187,043	6,874
1989	47,197	275,523	1,969.0	10,142.0	5.8	214,887	7,146
1990	43,769	267,283	1,995.0	10,466.0	6.1	239,119	7,464
1991	41,374	250,644	1,957.0	10,790.0	6.1	260,792	7,808
1992	55,848	304,046	2,263.0	11,114.0	5.4	199,004	7,443
1993	52,757	314,340	2,418.0	11,350.0 e	6.0	215,137	7,692
1994	52,874	310,238	2,496.0	11,587.0 e	5.9	219,144	8,045
1995	47,753	304,735	2,506.0	11,823.0 e	6.4	247,587	8,224
1996	50,289 e	313,014 e	2,578.0 e	12,059.0 e	6.2 e	239,794 e	8,236 e
1997	52,825	321,294	2,649.0	12,296.0	6.1	232,769	8,245
1998	50,158 p	316,408 p	2,734.0 p	12,675.0 p	6.3 p	252,701 p	8,641 p
1999	50,095 p	319,619 p	2,814.0 p	12,955.0 p	6.4 p	258,609 p	8,804 p
2000	50,032 p	322,830 p	2,894.0 p	13,235.0 p	6.5 p	264,531 p	8,964 p
2001	49,969 p	326,042 p	2,974.0 p	13,515.0 p	6.5 p	270,468 p	9,122 p

Sources: Economic Census of the United States, 1982, 1987, 1992, 1997. Establishment counts, employment, and payroll are from *County Business Patterns* for non-Census years. In non-Census years, industries in the Manufacturing range under SIC coding include data from the *Annual Survey of Manufactures* (*ASM*); those in the old Services range include data from the *Services Annual Survey* (*SAS*). Values followed by a 'p' are projections by the editors. Extrapolations are marked by 'e'. Data are the most recent available at this level of detail.

INDICES OF CHANGE

Year	Establishments (number)	Employment (number)	Payroll ($ million)	Revenues ($ million)	Employees per Establishment (number)	Revenues per Establishment ($)	Payroll per Employee ($)
1982	128.2	101.2	65.0	69.7	78.9	54.3	64.2
1987	111.1	97.4	73.6	77.2	87.6	69.5	75.6
1992	105.7	94.6	85.4	90.4	89.5	85.5	90.3
1993	99.9	97.8	91.3	92.3 e	98.0	92.4	93.3
1994	100.1	96.6	94.2	94.2 e	96.5	94.1	97.6
1995	90.4	94.8	94.6	96.2 e	104.9	106.4	99.7
1996	95.2 e	97.4 e	97.3 e	98.1 e	102.3 e	103.0 e	99.9 e
1997	100.0	100.0	100.0	100.0	100.0	100.0	100.0
1998	95.0 p	98.5 p	103.2 p	103.1 p	103.7 p	108.6 p	104.8 p
1999	94.8 p	99.5 p	106.2 p	105.4 p	104.9 p	111.1 p	106.8 p
2000	94.7 p	100.5 p	109.2 p	107.6 p	106.1 p	113.6 p	108.7 p
2001	94.6 p	101.5 p	112.3 p	109.9 p	107.3 p	116.2 p	110.6 p

Sources: Same as General Statistics. The values shown reflect change from the base year, 1997. Values above 100 mean greater than 1997, values below 100 mean less than 1997, and a value of 100 in the 1982-96 or 1998-2001 period means same as 1997. Values followed by a 'p' are projections by the editors; 'e' stands for extrapolation. Data are the most recent available at this level of detail.

SELECTED RATIOS

For 1997	Avg. of Information	Analyzed Industry	Index	For 1997	Avg. of Information	Analyzed Industry	Index
Employees per establishment	17	6	35	Payroll per establishment	177,969	50,147	28
Revenue per establishment	642,845	232,769	36	Payroll as % of revenue	28	22	78
Revenue per employee	37,074	38,270	103	Payroll per employee	10,264	8,245	80

Sources: Same as General Statistics. The 'Average' column represents the average for the industry sector, in 1997, where the currently shown industry is classified. The Index shows the relationship between the Average and the Analyzed Industry. For example, 100 means that they are equal; 500 that the Analyzed Industry is five times the average; 50 means that the Analyzed Industry is half the national average. The abbreviation 'na' is used to show that data are 'not available'.

*Equivalent to SIC 5813.

LEADING COMPANIES   Number shown: **11**   Total sales ($ mil): **169**   Total employment (000): **2.4**

Company Name	Address				CEO Name	Phone	Co. Type	Sales ($ mil)	Empl. (000)
Suburban Lodging Corp.	164 Fort Couch Rd	Pittsburgh	PA	15241	Donald F. Bagnato	412-833-5300	R	64*	0.5
Grand Hotel Co.	Grand Ave	Mackinac Island	MI	49757	RD Musser	906-847-3331	R	27	0.6
Simpson Land Company Inc.	P O Box 1099	Solomons	MD	20688	John A Simpson Jr	410-326-6311	R	26*	0.2
Flanigan's Enterprises Inc.	2841 Cypress Creek	Fort Lauderdale	FL	33309	Joseph G Flanigan	954-974-9003	P	22	0.4
McMenamins Pubs and Breweries	1624 NW Glisan St	Portland	OR	97209		503-223-0109	R	19*	0.6
Broadway Brewing L.L.C.	2441 Broadway	Denver	CO	80205	John Hickenlooper	303-292-5027	R	5	<0.1
First Entertainment Holding Corp.	7887 East Bellview	Englewood	CO	80111	Douglas Olson	303-228-1650	P	2	<0.1
Mountain Valley Brewing Co.	122 Orange Ave	Suffern	NY	10901	Lisa M Cantillo	914-357-0101	R	2	<0.1
Sarasota Brewing Co.	6607 Gateway Ave	Sarasota	FL	34231	Jeff Rosenberg	941-925-2337	R	1	<0.1
Cherryland Brewing Co.	341 N 3rd St	Sturgeon Bay	WI	54235	Tom Alberts	920-743-1945	R	1	<0.1
Skyport Lodge Inc.	PO Box 351	Grand Portage	MN	55605	Rick Ryberg	218-387-1411	R	0	<0.1

Source: *Ward's Business Directory of U.S. Private and Public Companies*, Volumes 1 and 2, 2000. The company type code used is as follows: P - Public, R - Private, S - Subsidiary, D - Division, J - Joint Venture, A - Affiliate, G - Group, N - Company type not reported. Sales are in millions of dollars, employees are in thousands. An asterisk (*) indicates an estimated sales volume. The symbol < stands for 'less than'. Company names and addresses are truncated, in some cases, to fit into the available space.

LOCATION BY STATE AND REGIONAL CONCENTRATION

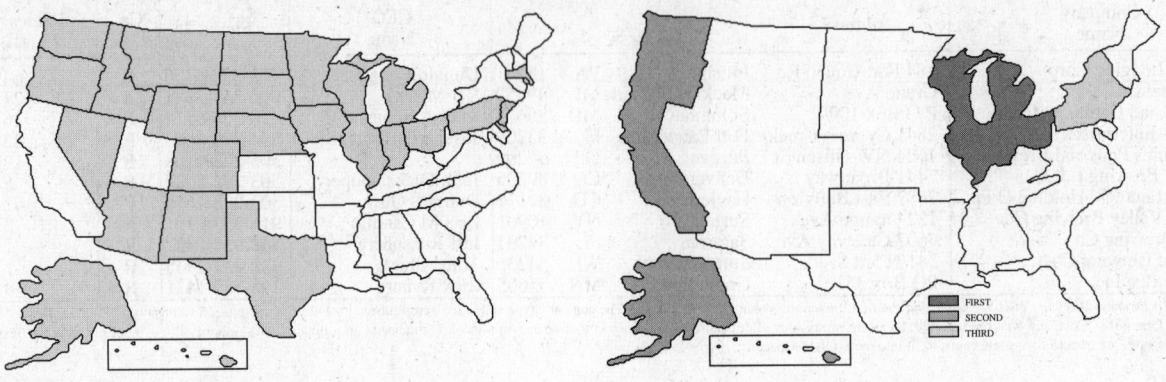

INDUSTRY DATA BY STATE

State	Establishments Total (number)	% of U.S.	Employment Total (number)	% of U.S.	Per Estab.	Payroll Total ($ mil.)	Per Empl. ($)	Revenues Total ($ mil.)	% of U.S.	Per Estab. ($)
California	4,276	8.1	29,710	9.2	7	259.7	8,742	1,103.7	9.0	258,122
Texas	2,476	4.7	27,528	8.6	11	208.6	7,579	920.5	7.5	371,755
New York	4,264	8.1	17,840	5.6	4	176.0	9,863	778.6	6.3	182,606
Illinois	3,620	6.9	18,564	5.8	5	152.2	8,200	750.4	6.1	207,289
Pennsylvania	3,927	7.4	16,157	5.0	4	129.4	8,010	710.3	5.8	180,866
Ohio	3,533	6.7	16,487	5.1	5	120.8	7,326	624.3	5.1	176,698
Florida	1,809	3.4	13,918	4.3	8	124.8	8,966	608.4	4.9	336,306
Michigan	2,322	4.4	15,857	4.9	7	117.0	7,377	524.5	4.3	225,879
Wisconsin	3,158	6.0	13,627	4.2	4	92.6	6,794	512.7	4.2	162,354
New Jersey	1,771	3.4	8,218	2.6	5	86.8	10,568	414.7	3.4	234,177
Washington	1,319	2.5	9,150	2.8	7	84.9	9,281	397.2	3.2	301,121
Massachusetts	1,366	2.6	9,212	2.9	7	85.4	9,271	353.9	2.9	259,102
Minnesota	1,134	2.1	9,013	2.8	8	65.7	7,295	304.2	2.5	268,235
Indiana	1,424	2.7	8,586	2.7	6	70.3	8,182	303.5	2.5	213,136
Colorado	874	1.7	7,794	2.4	9	60.1	7,714	253.7	2.1	290,323
Arizona	846	1.6	7,537	2.3	9	53.2	7,059	238.4	1.9	281,840
Oregon	746	1.4	5,391	1.7	7	52.4	9,729	233.6	1.9	313,071
Nevada	484	0.9	4,003	1.2	8	47.0	11,731	197.3	1.6	407,738
Georgia	480	0.9	4,597	1.4	10	44.4	9,650	197.0	1.6	410,446
Missouri	1,091	2.1	5,574	1.7	5	42.3	7,581	194.1	1.6	177,902
Maryland	697	1.3	4,093	1.3	6	37.4	9,145	184.2	1.5	264,265
Iowa	1,251	2.4	5,069	1.6	4	34.1	6,726	183.4	1.5	146,639
Louisiana	779	1.5	5,452	1.7	7	44.3	8,132	182.9	1.5	234,792
Nebraska	787	1.5	4,100	1.3	5	28.8	7,031	152.7	1.2	194,065
Montana	632	1.2	3,839	1.2	6	30.7	8,008	152.4	1.2	241,100
North Carolina	513	1.0	3,706	1.2	7	27.0	7,294	136.8	1.1	266,620
South Carolina	422	0.8	3,156	1.0	7	28.9	9,170	121.7	1.0	288,424
Connecticut	572	1.1	2,803	0.9	5	23.9	8,539	115.4	0.9	201,741
Kentucky	429	0.8	2,739	0.9	6	20.6	7,531	102.5	0.8	238,935
Kansas	583	1.1	3,205	1.0	5	19.4	6,042	97.1	0.8	166,602
Hawaii	284	0.5	1,974	0.6	7	21.0	10,617	92.9	0.8	327,130
Tennessee	347	0.7	2,096	0.7	6	19.6	9,343	90.0	0.7	259,481
Oklahoma	417	0.8	2,758	0.9	7	19.5	7,055	89.3	0.7	214,252
North Dakota	418	0.8	2,335	0.7	6	14.5	6,205	84.0	0.7	200,986
Alaska	225	0.4	1,677	0.5	7	23.3	13,875	83.2	0.7	369,916
New Mexico	217	0.4	2,642	0.8	12	16.9	6,386	80.5	0.7	371,069
South Dakota	372	0.7	2,340	0.7	6	16.6	7,111	76.8	0.6	206,417
Alabama	361	0.7	1,839	0.6	5	15.3	8,298	72.8	0.6	201,740
Virginia	237	0.4	2,253	0.7	10	17.6	7,832	72.7	0.6	306,945
Rhode Island	308	0.6	1,710	0.5	6	15.5	9,062	71.6	0.6	232,591
Idaho	415	0.8	2,097	0.7	5	13.6	6,474	62.6	0.5	150,957
D.C.	65	0.1	1,640	0.5	25	18.9	11,546	58.2	0.5	895,415
West Virginia	430	0.8	1,346	0.4	3	9.9	7,372	52.2	0.4	121,307
Utah	207	0.4	1,604	0.5	8	11.4	7,079	46.2	0.4	223,213
Wyoming	200	0.4	1,258	0.4	6	8.4	6,653	45.1	0.4	225,645
Delaware	80	0.2	956	0.3	12	8.6	9,045	35.7	0.3	445,688
Maine	147	0.3	837	0.3	6	8.0	9,575	31.9	0.3	216,837
Mississippi	144	0.3	854	0.3	6	6.2	7,231	28.5	0.2	198,132
Vermont	139	0.3	782	0.2	6	6.1	7,863	27.2	0.2	195,734
Arkansas	169	0.3	878	0.3	5	5.5	6,277	26.4	0.2	156,278
New Hampshire	58	0.1	493	0.2	9	4.2	8,566	17.4	0.1	300,690

Source: 1997 *Economic Census*. The states are in descending order of revenues or establishments (if revenue data are missing for the majority). The symbol (D) appears when data are withheld to prevent disclosure of competitive information. States marked with (D) are sorted by number of establishments. A dash (-) indicates that the data element cannot be calculated. * indicates the midpoint of a range; 175, for example is the range 100-249. Shaded *states* on the state map indicate those states which have proportionately greater representation in the industry than would be indicated by the state's population; the ratio is based on total revenues or number of establishments. Shaded *regions* indicate where the industry is regionally most concentrated.

Part XI

OTHER SERVICES

NAICS 811111 - GENERAL AUTOMOTIVE REPAIR*

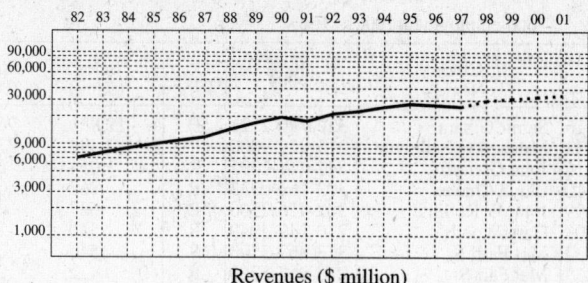

82 83 84 85 86 87 88 89 90 91 92 93 94 95 96 97 98 99 00 01

Revenues ($ million)

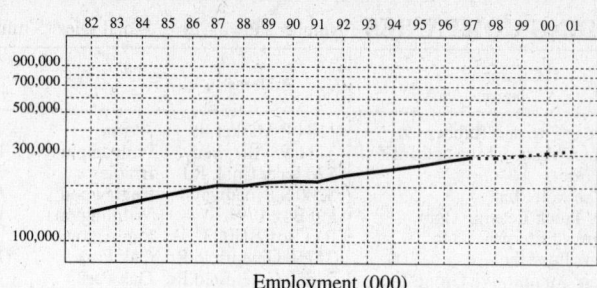

82 83 84 85 86 87 88 89 90 91 92 93 94 95 96 97 98 99 00 01

Employment (000)

GENERAL STATISTICS

Year	Establishments (number)	Employment (number)	Payroll ($ million)	Revenues ($ million)	Employees per Establishment (number)	Revenues per Establishment ($)	Payroll per Employee ($)
1982	43,425	144,054	1,840.0	7,068.0	3.3	162,763	12,773
1983	45,810 e	155,756 e	2,084.0 e	8,029.0 e	3.4 e	175,267 e	13,380 e
1984	48,194 e	167,458 e	2,329.0 e	8,990.0 e	3.5 e	186,538 e	13,908 e
1985	50,579 e	179,160 e	2,573.0 e	9,951.0 e	3.5 e	196,742 e	14,361 e
1986	52,963 e	190,862 e	2,818.0 e	10,912.0 e	3.6 e	206,031 e	14,765 e
1987	55,348	202,564	3,063.0	11,873.0	3.7	214,515	15,121
1988	52,154	201,953	3,354.0	14,456.0 e	3.9	277,179	16,608
1989	54,367	210,952	3,635.0	17,039.0 e	3.9	313,407	17,231
1990	54,796	214,445	3,848.0	19,623.0	3.9	358,110	17,944
1991	57,366	213,658	3,973.0	17,745.0	3.7	309,330	18,595
1992	64,822	229,859	4,406.0	21,322.0	3.5	328,932	19,168
1993	67,338	240,226	4,775.0	22,698.0	3.6	337,076	19,877
1994	68,419	249,981	5,158.0	25,227.0	3.7	368,713	20,634
1995	69,461	262,087	5,515.0	27,347.0	3.8	393,703	21,043
1996	73,606 e	276,361 e	5,977.0 e	26,473.0 e	3.8 e	359,658 e	21,628 e
1997	77,751	290,634	6,439.0	25,599.0	3.7	329,243	22,155
1998	78,511 p	289,649 p	6,546.0 p	29,788.0 p	3.7 p	379,412 p	22,600 p
1999	81,059 p	298,640 p	6,877.0 p	31,277.0 p	3.7 p	385,855 p	23,028 p
2000	83,608 p	307,631 p	7,208.0 p	32,766.0 p	3.7 p	391,900 p	23,431 p
2001	86,156 p	316,622 p	7,539.0 p	34,255.0 p	3.7 p	397,593 p	23,811 p

Sources: Economic Census of the United States, 1982, 1987, 1992, 1997. Establishment counts, employment, and payroll are from *County Business Patterns* for non-Census years. In non-Census years, industries in the Manufacturing range under SIC coding include data from the *Annual Survey of Manufactures* (*ASM*); those in the old Services range include data from the *Services Annual Survey* (*SAS*). Values followed by a 'p' are projections by the editors. Extrapolations are marked by 'e'. Data are the most recent available at this level of detail.

INDICES OF CHANGE

Year	Establishments (number)	Employment (number)	Payroll ($ million)	Revenues ($ million)	Employees per Establishment (number)	Revenues per Establishment ($)	Payroll per Employee ($)
1982	55.9	49.6	28.6	27.6	88.7	49.4	57.7
1987	71.2	69.7	47.6	46.4	97.9	65.2	68.3
1992	83.4	79.1	68.4	83.3	94.9	99.9	86.5
1993	86.6	82.7	74.2	88.7	95.4	102.4	89.7
1994	88.0	86.0	80.1	98.5	97.7	112.0	93.1
1995	89.3	90.2	85.6	106.8	100.9	119.6	95.0
1996	94.7 e	95.1 e	92.8 e	103.4 e	100.4 e	109.2 e	97.6 e
1997	100.0	100.0	100.0	100.0	100.0	100.0	100.0
1998	101.0 p	99.7 p	101.7 p	116.4 p	98.7 p	115.2 p	102.0 p
1999	104.3 p	102.8 p	106.8 p	122.2 p	98.6 p	117.2 p	103.9 p
2000	107.5 p	105.8 p	111.9 p	128.0 p	98.4 p	119.0 p	105.8 p
2001	110.8 p	108.9 p	117.1 p	133.8 p	98.3 p	120.8 p	107.5 p

Sources: Same as General Statistics. The values shown reflect change from the base year, 1997. Values above 100 mean greater than 1997, values below 100 mean less than 1997, and a value of 100 in the 1982-96 or 1998-2001 period means same as 1997. Values followed by a 'p' are projections by the editors; 'e' stands for extrapolation. Data are the most recent available at this level of detail.

SELECTED RATIOS

For 1997	Avg. of Information	Analyzed Industry	Index	For 1997	Avg. of Information	Analyzed Industry	Index
Employees per establishment	6	4	60	Payroll per establishment	126,069	82,816	66
Revenue per establishment	511,622	329,243	64	Payroll as % of revenue	25	25	102
Revenue per employee	81,659	88,080	108	Payroll per employee	20,122	22,155	110

Sources: Same as General Statistics. The 'Average' column represents the average for the industry sector, in 1997, where the currently shown industry is classified. The Index shows the relationship between the Average and the Analyzed Industry. For example, 100 means that they are equal; 500 that the Analyzed Industry is five times the average; 50 means that the Analyzed Industry is half the national average. The abbreviation 'na' is used to show that data are 'not available'.

*Equivalent to SIC 7538.

LEADING COMPANIES   Number shown: **75**   Total sales ($ mil): **24,712**   Total employment (000): **158.4**

Company Name	Address				CEO Name	Phone	Co. Type	Sales ($ mil)	Empl. (000)
Goodyear Tire and Rubber Co.	1144 E Market St	Akron	OH	44316	Samir Gibara	330-796-2121	P	12,881	96.9
Pep Boys-Manny, Moe and Jack	3111 W Allegheny	Philadelphia	PA	19132	Mitchell G Leibovitz	215-229-9000	P	2,399	27.5
Fleet Pride	520 Lake Cook Rd	Bradley	IL	60915	John Greisch	847-444-1095	R	1,054*	2.5
Burt Chevrolet Inc.	5200 S Broadway	Englewood	CO	80110	Lloyd Chavez	303-761-0333	R	867	0.9
Rollins Truck Leasing Corp.	PO Box 1791	Wilmington	DE	19899	John W Rollins	302-426-2700	P	627	4.0
McCombs Enterprises Inc.	P O Box BH003	San Antonio	TX	78201	Gary Woods	210-349-4949	R	540	1.4
Mel Farr Ford Inc.	24750 Greenfield Rd	Oak Park	MI	48237	Mel Farr, Sr	313-967-3700	S	540	0.2
Mel Farr Automotive Group Inc.	24750 Greenfield Rd	Oak Park	MI	48237	Mel Farr Sr	248-967-3700	R	432	0.6
Kirby Corp.	P O Box 1745	Houston	TX	77251	JH Pyne	713-435-1000	P	366	1.3
Pacific Detroit Diesel Allison Co.	5061 N Lagoon Ave	Portland	OR	97217	JR Tyrrell	503-283-0505	R	350*	0.4
Jiffy Lube International Inc.	PO Box 2967	Houston	TX	77252	James M Wheat	713-546-4100	S	329	7.0
Monro Muffler Brake Inc.	200 Holleder Pkwy	Rochester	NY	14615	Robert Gross	716-647-6400	P	193	2.8
PACCAR Automotive Inc.	1400 N 4th St	Renton	WA	98055		425-251-7600	S	186	2.1
Fyda Freightliner Inc.	1250 Walcutt Rd	Columbus	OH	43228	Timothy Fyda	614-851-0002	R	168*	0.1
Cummins Midstates Power Inc.	3762 W Morris St	Indianapolis	IN	46242	Hal A Smitson Jr	317-589-2171	R	162*	0.2
Somerset Tire Service Inc.	PO Box 2001	Bound Brook	NJ	08805	WF Caulin	732-356-8500	R	161*	0.5
Mustang Power Systems	7777 Washington	Houston	TX	77007	F Louis Tucker	713-861-7727	S	148*	0.4
Peach State Trucks Center Inc.	I-85 Jimmy Carter	Norcross	GA	30091	Thomas B Reynolds	770-449-5300	R	136*	0.1
Alaska Sales and Service Inc.	1016 W Nor Lights	Anchorage	AK	99503	Leonard G Bryant	907-279-9641	R	120*	0.3
Capitol Chevrolet Cadillac	PO Box 12456	Salem	OR	97309	Scott Caseber	503-585-4141	R	117*	0.3
Dick Strauss Ford Inc.	10601 Midloth	Richmond	VA	23235	Vincent Sheehy IV	804-794-0500	D	117	0.2
Don Davis Auto Group	P O Box 1587	Arlington	TX	76004	Robert Howard	817-461-1000	R	117*	0.3
Badger Truck Center Inc.	2326 W St Paul Ave	Milwaukee	WI	53201	Paul Schlagenhauf	414-344-9500	R	113*	0.1
W.W. Williams Co.	835 W Goodale Blvd	Columbus	OH	43212	Robert G Peyton	614-228-5000	R	100*	1.1
Cummins Alabama Inc.	PO Box 1147	Birmingham	AL	35201	KB McDonald	205-841-0421	R	99*	0.1
Schaller Oldsmobile Inc.	55 Veterans Dr	New Britain	CT	06051	Arthur Schaller	860-223-2230	R	99*	0.3
Allied Tire Sales Inc.	3320A Maggie Blvd	Orlando	FL	32811		407-648-1555	R	97*	0.5
Alhambra Motors Inc.	1400 W Main St	Alhambra	CA	91801	Gordon H Goudy	626-576-1114	R	93*	0.2
Dobbs Tire and Auto Center Inc.	1983 Brennan Plz	High Ridge	MO	63049	David Dobbs	314-677-2101	R	93*	0.3
Carnegie Body Co.	9500 Brookpark Rd	Cleveland	OH	44129	Howard A Weisblat	216-749-5000	R	86*	<0.1
James Stohlman Corp.	200 S Pickett St	Alexandria	VA	22304	James Stohlman	703-751-9100	R	84*	0.2
Hub City Ford Inc.	P O Box 90670	Lafayette	LA	70509	DE Citron III	318-233-4500	R	76*	0.2
Tom Endicott Buick Inc.	1345 S Federal Hwy	Pompano Beach	FL	33062	Tom Endicott	954-781-7700	R	75	0.1
Tate Chrysler Plymouth Jeep	PO Box 757	Glen Burnie	MD	21061	Creston G Tate	410-761-1560	R	70*	0.2
Mirak Chevrolet Inc.	1125 Mass Ave	Arlington	MA	02174	C Mirak	781-643-8000	R	66*	0.1
Kenworth Sales Company Inc.	P O Box 65829	Salt Lake City	UT	84165	Kyle Treadway	801-487-4161	R	65	0.1
SpeeDee Oil Change and Tune-Up	P O Box 1350	Madisonville	LA	70447	Gary Copp	504-845-1919	R	65	<0.1
Rickenbaugh Cadillac/Volvo	777 Broadway	Denver	CO	80203	Kent Rickenbaugh	303-573-7773	R	62*	0.1
Jones Ford Inc.	P O Box 62829	N. Charleston	SC	29419	David M Walters	843-744-3311	R	61*	0.1
McCarthy Tire Service Co.	P O Box 1125	Wilkes Barre	PA	18703	John D McCarthy Sr	717-822-3151	R	56*	0.2
Lucor Inc.	790 Pershing Rd	Raleigh	NC	27608	Jerry B Conway	919-828-9511	P	55	1.3
Auto Stiegler Inc.	16721 Ventura Blvd	Encino	CA	91316	John M Stiegler	818-788-0234	R	54	0.1
Automaster Motor Company Inc.	Rte 7	Shelburne	VT	05482	JA DuBrul II	802-985-8411	R	52	<0.1
Jack Griffin Ford Inc.	1940 E Main St	Waukesha	WI	53186	Jack A Griffin Jr	414-542-5781	R	52*	0.1
Star Truck Rentals Inc.	3940 Eastern S E	Grand Rapids	MI	49508	Thomas Bylenga	616-243-7033	R	49*	0.2
Holmes Automotive	11206 Hickman Rd	Des Moines	IA	50325	MH Holmes	515-253-3000	R	48	0.2
Omnicor Inc. Richfield Center	2636 Brecksville Rd	Richfield	OH	44286		330-659-9311	D	47*	0.1
Southgate Automotive Inc.	PO Box 1423	Southgate	MI	48195	Walter Oben, Jr	734-282-3636	R	47*	0.1
Sunfair Chevrolet Inc.	P O Box 1262	Yakima	WA	98907	RD Hall	509-248-7600	R	47	0.1
Les Marks Chevrolet-Mazda Inc.	112 S 10th St	La Porte	TX	77571	Les Marks	281-471-2424	R	46*	<0.1
Cunningham Motors Inc.	Hwy 70 W	Lebanon	TN	37087	HB Cunningham	615-444-8370	R	45	<0.1
Don McGill Toyota Inc.	11800 Old Katy Rd	Houston	TX	77079	DR McGill	281-496-2000	R	44	0.2
Smith Detroit Diesel/Allison Inc.	PO Box 27527	Salt Lake City	UT	84127	Mike Smith	801-262-2631	R	42	0.2
Childress Buick Co.	2223 W Camelback	Phoenix	AZ	85015	George Childress	602-249-1133	R	40*	0.1
Cummins Gateway Inc.	7210 Hall St	St. Louis	MO	63147	John Wagner	314-389-5400	R	40	0.2
De Nooyer Brothers Inc.	5800 Stadium Dr	Kalamazoo	MI	49009	William T DeNooyer	616-372-3040	R	40*	<0.1
Sierra Detroit Diesel Allison Inc.	1755 Adams Ave	San Leandro	CA	94577	Darren Jaminson	510-635-8991	S	40	0.2
Harvey Cadillac Co.	2600 28th St S E	Grand Rapids	MI	49512		616-949-1140	R	39	<0.1
Major Cadillac Pontiac GMC	3200 Main St	Kansas City	MO	64111	FL Major III	816-756-3300	R	37*	<0.1
Bay Lincoln Mercury Dodge	641 W 15th St	Panama City	FL	32401	George Gainer	850-785-1591	R	36*	<0.1
Stratham Tire Inc.	17 Portsmouth Ave	Stratham	NH	03885	Lionel Labonte	603-772-3783	R	35*	0.2
Roppel Industries Inc.	829 Logan St	Louisville	KY	40204	Thomas V Roppel	502-581-1004	R	32*	<0.1
Sam Johnson Croos Creek Lincoln	P O Box 43805	Fayetteville	NC	28309	Sam Johnson	910-864-5240	R	30*	<0.1
Bosak Motor Sales Inc.	3111 W Lincoln	Merrillville	IN	46410	Emmett G Bosak	219-738-2323	R	28*	<0.1
Brody Transportation Inc.	621 S Bentalou St	Baltimore	MD	21223	Edward J Brody	410-947-5800	R	26*	<0.1
Gordon Rountree Motors Ltd.	2720 Franklin Ave	Waco	TX	76710		254-756-4461	R	26	<0.1
Jim Barnard Chevrolet Geo Inc.	7101 Buffalo Rd	Churchville	NY	14428	Allyn G Barnard	716-293-2120	R	22	<0.1
Southern Nevada T	1701 Las Vegas S	Las Vegas	NV	89104	Ted Wiens Jr	702-732-2382	R	20*	0.2
Hedahls Auto Parts	P O Box 1038	Bismarck	ND	58502	Richard Hedahls	701-223-8393	R	19	0.2
Fargo Freightliner Inc.	Box 8898	Fargo	ND	58109	Ron Ristvedt	701-293-9133	R	18*	<0.1
KM Inc.	PO Box 5825	Washington	DC	20016	Konrad Murrer	202-364-6360	R	18*	<0.1
Martin Automotive Group Inc.	P O Box 795	Lake Charles	LA	70602		318-433-0506	R	18*	<0.1
Culberson Stowers Inc.	PO Box 1542	Pampa	TX	79066	Richard W Stowers Jr	806-665-1665	R	17*	<0.1
La Crosse Truck Center Inc.	P O Box 1176	La Crosse	WI	54602	Stephen T Heuslein	608-785-0800	R	17*	<0.1
Place Motor Inc.	19 Thompson Rd	Webster	MA	01570	James L Place	508-943-8012	S	16*	<0.1

Source: Ward's Business Directory of U.S. Private and Public Companies, Volumes 1 and 2, 2000. The company type code used is as follows: P - Public, R - Private, S - Subsidiary, D - Division, J - Joint Venture, A - Affiliate, G - Group, N - Company type not reported. Sales are in millions of dollars, employees are in thousands. An asterisk (*) indicates an estimated sales volume. The symbol < stands for 'less than'. Company names and addresses are truncated, in some cases, to fit into the available space.

LOCATION BY STATE AND REGIONAL CONCENTRATION

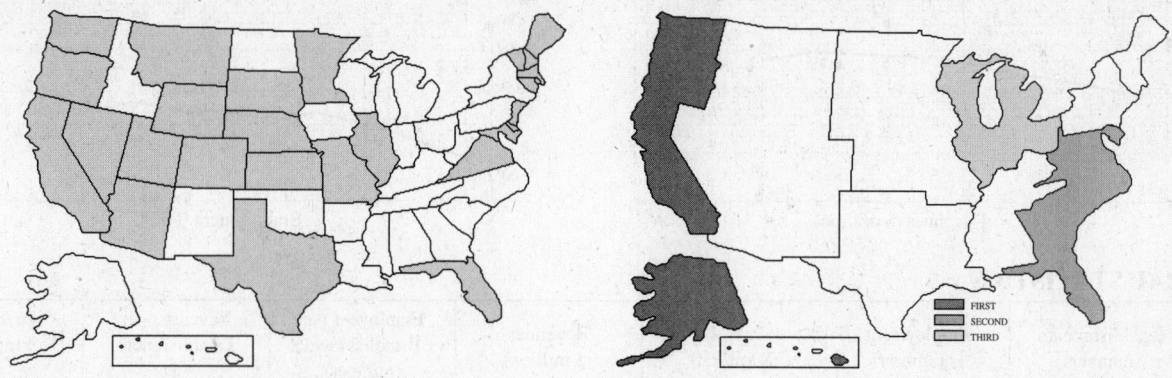

INDUSTRY DATA BY STATE

State	Establishments Total (number)	% of U.S.	Employment Total (number)	% of U.S.	Per Estab.	Payroll Total ($ mil.)	Per Empl. ($)	Revenues Total ($ mil.)	% of U.S.	Per Estab. ($)
California	9,662	12.4	36,259	12.5	4	847.5	23,373	3,564.7	13.9	368,941
Texas	5,271	6.8	21,266	7.3	4	474.7	22,322	1,785.8	7.0	338,802
New York	5,354	6.9	16,178	5.6	3	333.4	20,610	1,479.1	5.8	276,263
Florida	4,552	5.9	16,082	5.5	4	344.8	21,441	1,390.1	5.4	305,376
Illinois	3,249	4.2	13,615	4.7	4	325.5	23,909	1,221.1	4.8	375,851
Pennsylvania	3,999	5.1	13,112	4.5	3	269.5	20,552	1,189.5	4.6	297,439
Ohio	2,776	3.6	11,530	4.0	4	250.9	21,757	928.1	3.6	334,334
New Jersey	2,544	3.3	8,177	2.8	3	205.1	25,082	848.2	3.3	333,415
Michigan	2,443	3.1	9,744	3.4	4	226.6	23,258	842.4	3.3	344,824
Virginia	2,189	2.8	9,076	3.1	4	212.9	23,463	742.8	2.9	339,329
Massachusetts	1,853	2.4	6,353	2.2	3	151.7	23,877	654.8	2.6	353,392
Georgia	1,981	2.5	7,422	2.6	4	168.3	22,681	642.9	2.5	324,517
North Carolina	2,244	2.9	7,701	2.6	3	163.0	21,171	621.8	2.4	277,115
Washington	1,635	2.1	6,462	2.2	4	156.9	24,283	579.1	2.3	354,193
Maryland	1,475	1.9	6,126	2.1	4	153.9	25,128	544.8	2.1	369,357
Indiana	1,587	2.0	6,766	2.3	4	146.9	21,712	536.1	2.1	337,804
Arizona	1,420	1.8	6,344	2.2	4	143.5	22,623	532.6	2.1	375,093
Missouri	1,769	2.3	6,673	2.3	4	142.2	21,311	528.9	2.1	298,980
Minnesota	1,328	1.7	5,604	1.9	4	131.9	23,534	524.1	2.0	394,639
Wisconsin	1,480	1.9	5,585	1.9	4	119.4	21,382	498.1	1.9	336,583
Colorado	1,344	1.7	5,495	1.9	4	132.8	24,165	488.8	1.9	363,690
Connecticut	1,007	1.3	4,163	1.4	4	106.7	25,642	409.9	1.6	407,077
Oregon	1,042	1.3	4,359	1.5	4	104.4	23,943	390.2	1.5	374,448
Louisiana	1,006	1.3	4,091	1.4	4	89.4	21,848	361.8	1.4	359,664
Tennessee	1,256	1.6	4,572	1.6	4	92.1	20,143	358.6	1.4	285,487
Alabama	1,104	1.4	4,036	1.4	4	76.6	18,972	299.5	1.2	271,324
Kentucky	866	1.1	3,222	1.1	4	62.7	19,465	280.2	1.1	323,509
South Carolina	1,017	1.3	3,570	1.2	4	70.9	19,864	276.8	1.1	272,204
Kansas	895	1.2	3,105	1.1	3	65.3	21,043	274.0	1.1	306,122
Iowa	972	1.3	3,171	1.1	3	57.0	17,985	261.8	1.0	269,295
Nebraska	656	0.8	3,141	1.1	5	57.9	18,432	220.4	0.9	335,927
Oklahoma	813	1.0	2,824	1.0	3	54.7	19,386	215.2	0.8	264,694
Utah	567	0.7	2,417	0.8	4	49.5	20,460	199.7	0.8	352,228
Nevada	459	0.6	2,154	0.7	5	52.1	24,172	198.7	0.8	432,932
New Hampshire	499	0.6	1,870	0.6	4	42.1	22,513	186.6	0.7	373,910
Arkansas	658	0.8	2,342	0.8	4	40.6	17,327	179.0	0.7	272,000
Mississippi	674	0.9	2,181	0.8	3	39.3	18,018	165.6	0.6	245,677
New Mexico	517	0.7	1,961	0.7	4	39.4	20,075	148.2	0.6	286,582
Maine	476	0.6	1,346	0.5	3	25.3	18,792	127.5	0.5	267,916
Idaho	346	0.4	1,291	0.4	4	25.4	19,672	105.3	0.4	304,338
Vermont	303	0.4	904	0.3	3	17.7	19,534	98.6	0.4	325,502
Montana	338	0.4	1,088	0.4	3	20.4	18,737	91.7	0.4	271,340
Rhode Island	343	0.4	983	0.3	3	21.6	22,000	90.8	0.4	264,828
West Virginia	442	0.6	1,383	0.5	3	21.7	15,672	89.4	0.3	202,296
South Dakota	286	0.4	968	0.3	3	17.9	18,467	84.5	0.3	295,416
Delaware	213	0.3	908	0.3	4	20.9	22,992	74.6	0.3	350,258
Wyoming	235	0.3	759	0.3	3	15.0	19,747	66.5	0.3	282,838
Hawaii	195	0.3	756	0.3	4	18.5	24,511	65.0	0.3	333,564
Alaska	169	0.2	643	0.2	4	16.9	26,344	63.2	0.2	374,183
North Dakota	187	0.2	687	0.2	4	11.6	16,853	55.7	0.2	297,668
D.C.	55	0.1	175*	-	-	(D)	-	(D)	-	-

Source: 1997 *Economic Census*. The states are in descending order of revenues or establishments (if revenue data are missing for the majority). The symbol (D) appears when data are withheld to prevent disclosure of competitive information. States marked with (D) are sorted by number of establishments. A dash (-) indicates that the data element cannot be calculated. * indicates the midpoint of a range; 175, for example is the range 100-249. Shaded *states* on the state map indicate those states which have proportionately greater representation in the industry than would be indicated by the state's population; the ratio is based on total revenues or number of establishments. Shaded *regions* indicate where the industry is regionally most concentrated.

NAICS 811112 - AUTOMOTIVE EXHAUST SYSTEM REPAIR*

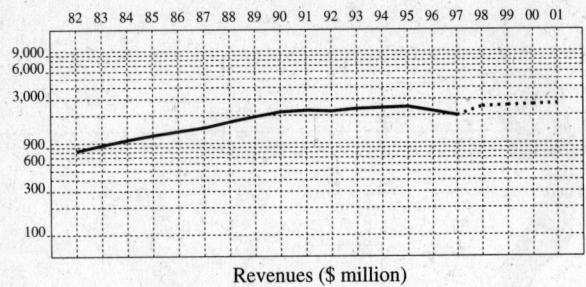

Revenues ($ million)

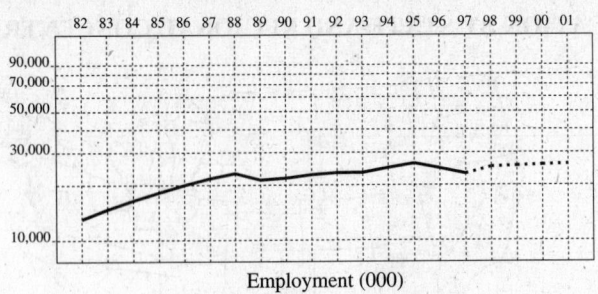

Employment (000)

GENERAL STATISTICS

Year	Establishments (number)	Employment (number)	Payroll ($ million)	Revenues ($ million)	Employees per Establishment (number)	Revenues per Establishment ($)	Payroll per Employee ($)
1982	3,169	13,069	201.0	821.0	4.1	259,072	15,380
1983	3,517 e	14,796 e	235.0 e	950.0 e	4.2 e	270,117 e	15,883 e
1984	3,865 e	16,524 e	270.0 e	1,079.0 e	4.3 e	279,172 e	16,340 e
1985	4,214 e	18,251 e	304.0 e	1,209.0 e	4.3 e	286,901 e	16,657 e
1986	4,562 e	19,979 e	338.0 e	1,338.0 e	4.4 e	293,292 e	16,918 e
1987	4,910	21,706	372.0	1,467.0	4.4	298,778	17,138
1988	4,896	23,122	413.0	1,701.0 e	4.7	347,426	17,862
1989	4,693	21,294	423.0	1,936.0 e	4.5	412,529	19,865
1990	4,651	21,772	453.0	2,171.0	4.7	466,781	20,807
1991	4,837	22,699	464.0	2,260.0	4.7	467,232	20,441
1992	5,521	23,277	483.0	2,211.0	4.2	400,471	20,750
1993	5,389	23,282	509.0	2,353.0	4.3	436,630	21,862
1994	5,502	24,720	557.0	2,408.0	4.5	437,659	22,532
1995	5,511	26,162	578.0	2,457.0	4.7	445,836	22,093
1996	5,381 e	24,588 e	551.0 e	2,221.0 e	4.6 e	412,749 e	22,409 e
1997	5,251	23,015	525.0	1,985.0	4.4	378,023	22,811
1998	5,596 p	25,067 p	595.0 p	2,477.0 p	4.5 p	442,638 p	23,736 p
1999	5,672 p	25,371 p	614.0 p	2,539.0 p	4.5 p	447,638 p	24,201 p
2000	5,748 p	25,676 p	632.0 p	2,601.0 p	4.5 p	452,505 p	24,614 p
2001	5,824 p	25,980 p	651.0 p	2,663.0 p	4.5 p	457,246 p	25,058 p

Sources: *Economic Census of the United States*, 1982, 1987, 1992, 1997. Establishment counts, employment, and payroll are from *County Business Patterns* for non-Census years. In non-Census years, industries in the Manufacturing range under SIC coding include data from the *Annual Survey of Manufactures* (*ASM*); those in the old Services range include data from the *Services Annual Survey* (*SAS*). Values followed by a 'p' are projections by the editors. Extrapolations are marked by 'e'. Data are the most recent available at this level of detail.

INDICES OF CHANGE

Year	Establishments (number)	Employment (number)	Payroll ($ million)	Revenues ($ million)	Employees per Establishment (number)	Revenues per Establishment ($)	Payroll per Employee ($)
1982	60.4	56.8	38.3	41.4	94.1	68.5	67.4
1987	93.5	94.3	70.9	73.9	100.9	79.0	75.1
1992	105.1	101.1	92.0	111.4	96.2	105.9	91.0
1993	102.6	101.2	97.0	118.5	98.6	115.5	95.8
1994	104.8	107.4	106.1	121.3	102.5	115.8	98.8
1995	105.0	113.7	110.1	123.8	108.3	117.9	96.9
1996	102.5 e	106.8 e	105.0 e	111.9 e	104.3 e	109.2 e	98.2 e
1997	100.0	100.0	100.0	100.0	100.0	100.0	100.0
1998	106.6 p	108.9 p	113.3 p	124.8 p	102.2 p	117.1 p	104.1 p
1999	108.0 p	110.2 p	117.0 p	127.9 p	102.1 p	118.4 p	106.1 p
2000	109.5 p	111.6 p	120.4 p	131.0 p	101.9 p	119.7 p	107.9 p
2001	110.9 p	112.9 p	124.0 p	134.2 p	101.8 p	121.0 p	109.8 p

Sources: Same as General Statistics. The values shown reflect change from the base year, 1997. Values above 100 mean greater than 1997, values below 100 mean less than 1997, and a value of 100 in the 1982-96 or 1998-2001 period means same as 1997. Values followed by a 'p' are projections by the editors; 'e' stands for extrapolation. Data are the most recent available at this level of detail.

SELECTED RATIOS

For 1997	Avg. of Information	Analyzed Industry	Index	For 1997	Avg. of Information	Analyzed Industry	Index
Employees per establishment	6	4	70	Payroll per establishment	126,069	99,981	79
Revenue per establishment	511,622	378,023	74	Payroll as % of revenue	25	26	107
Revenue per employee	81,659	86,248	106	Payroll per employee	20,122	22,811	113

Sources: Same as General Statistics. The 'Average' column represents the average for the industry sector, in 1997, where the currently shown industry is classified. The Index shows the relationship between the Average and the Analyzed Industry. For example, 100 means that they are equal; 500 that the Analyzed Industry is five times the average; 50 means that the Analyzed Industry is half the national average. The abbreviation 'na' is used to show that data are 'not available'.

*Equivalent to SIC 7533.

LEADING COMPANIES   Number shown: **5**   Total sales ($ mil): **2,584**   Total employment (000): **11.2**

Company Name	Address				CEO Name	Phone	Co. Type	Sales ($ mil)	Empl. (000)
Whitman Corp.	3501 Algonquin Rd	Roll Meadows	IL	60008	Bruce S. Chelberg	847-818-5000	P	1,635	6.5
Midas International Corp.	1300 N Arl Hght	Itasca	IL	60143		312-565-7500	R	519	1.5
Walt's Radiator and Muffler Inc.	2588 Pacific Hwy E	Tacoma	WA	98424	Stephen Dwinal	253-922-5111	R	201*	0.3
Monro Muffler Brake Inc.	200 Holleder Pkwy	Rochester	NY	14615	Robert Gross	716-647-6400	P	193	2.8
Meineke Discount Muffler Shops	128 S Tryon St	Charlotte	NC	28202	Ken Walker	704-377-8855	R	35	0.1

Source: *Ward's Business Directory of U.S. Private and Public Companies*, Volumes 1 and 2, 2000. The company type code used is as follows: P - Public, R - Private, S - Subsidiary, D - Division, J - Joint Venture, A - Affiliate, G - Group, N - Company type not reported. Sales are in millions of dollars, employees are in thousands. An asterisk (*) indicates an estimated sales volume. The symbol < stands for 'less than'. Company names and addresses are truncated, in some cases, to fit into the available space.

LOCATION BY STATE AND REGIONAL CONCENTRATION

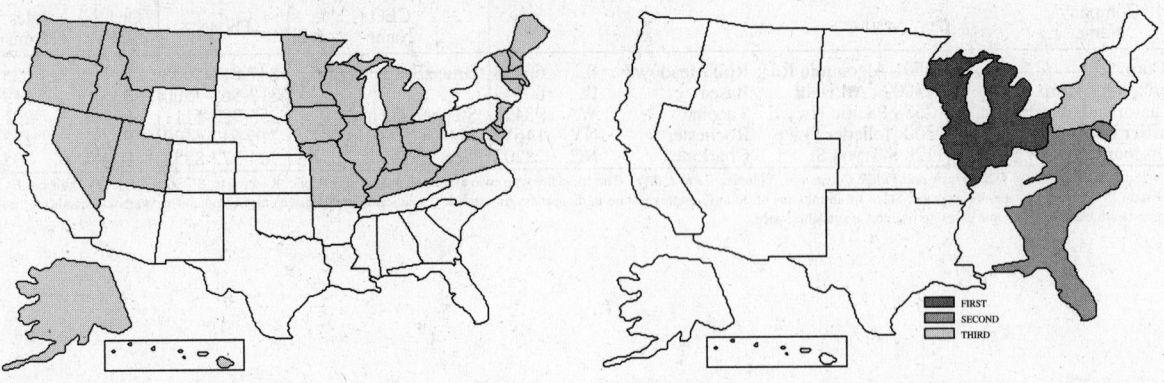

INDUSTRY DATA BY STATE

State	Establishments Total (number)	Establishments % of U.S.	Employment Total (number)	Employment % of U.S.	Employment Per Estab.	Payroll Total ($ mil.)	Payroll Per Empl. ($)	Revenues Total ($ mil.)	Revenues % of U.S.	Revenues Per Estab. ($)
Illinois	323	6.2	1,664	7.2	5	40.2	24,151	146.4	7.4	453,102
California	432	8.2	1,458	6.3	3	34.7	23,784	137.3	6.9	317,829
New York	290	5.5	1,449	6.3	5	34.0	23,451	131.1	6.6	452,066
Michigan	294	5.6	1,389	6.0	5	34.1	24,554	123.8	6.2	421,048
Ohio	301	5.7	1,511	6.6	5	30.5	20,154	115.4	5.8	383,362
Texas	362	6.9	1,252	5.4	3	27.0	21,562	108.6	5.5	300,066
Florida	248	4.7	896	3.9	4	20.1	22,448	81.2	4.1	327,222
New Jersey	148	2.8	761	3.3	5	20.0	26,272	71.7	3.6	484,392
Indiana	174	3.3	938	4.1	5	19.9	21,229	71.2	3.6	408,983
Pennsylvania	163	3.1	801	3.5	5	16.6	20,708	67.1	3.4	411,687
Missouri	182	3.5	833	3.6	5	17.6	21,103	66.9	3.4	367,555
Massachusetts	122	2.3	683	3.0	6	15.4	22,606	62.1	3.1	508,861
Virginia	142	2.7	683	3.0	5	16.0	23,473	55.9	2.8	393,662
Maryland	95	1.8	597	2.6	6	13.5	22,631	51.3	2.6	539,611
Wisconsin	102	1.9	548	2.4	5	11.7	21,307	47.4	2.4	464,637
Connecticut	83	1.6	451	2.0	5	12.0	26,585	45.2	2.3	545,024
North Carolina	141	2.7	547	2.4	4	12.3	22,534	45.2	2.3	320,688
Washington	116	2.2	444	1.9	4	10.9	24,507	41.1	2.1	354,724
Georgia	114	2.2	427	1.9	4	10.6	24,923	39.3	2.0	344,632
Tennessee	138	2.6	478	2.1	3	10.6	22,157	38.4	1.9	278,493
Iowa	91	1.7	402	1.7	4	11.5	28,706	37.9	1.9	416,220
Minnesota	90	1.7	329	1.4	4	8.6	26,164	35.5	1.8	394,222
Kentucky	82	1.6	376	1.6	5	9.5	25,330	33.6	1.7	409,805
Oregon	82	1.6	322	1.4	4	7.6	23,637	26.8	1.3	326,402
Colorado	55	1.0	271	1.2	5	7.0	25,801	23.4	1.2	426,236
Louisiana	86	1.6	280	1.2	3	5.0	17,804	20.7	1.0	241,267
Utah	42	0.8	247	1.1	6	5.8	23,648	20.3	1.0	483,357
Alabama	72	1.4	295	1.3	4	4.8	16,420	20.2	1.0	280,167
Oklahoma	70	1.3	209	0.9	3	4.5	21,574	18.7	0.9	267,614
Arizona	55	1.0	206	0.9	4	5.2	25,408	18.6	0.9	338,400
South Carolina	61	1.2	236	1.0	4	4.8	20,225	17.9	0.9	292,672
Kansas	48	0.9	216	0.9	5	5.4	25,125	16.4	0.8	341,083
Nevada	28	0.5	148	0.6	5	3.8	25,750	13.6	0.7	485,214
Nebraska	31	0.6	142	0.6	5	3.4	24,042	12.2	0.6	394,613
Hawaii	18	0.3	126	0.5	7	2.7	21,048	11.6	0.6	645,778
Mississippi	54	1.0	140	0.6	3	2.3	16,414	10.3	0.5	191,593
Idaho	27	0.5	134	0.6	5	2.4	18,149	10.0	0.5	370,778
Arkansas	54	1.0	134	0.6	2	2.4	17,552	9.8	0.5	181,056
Maine	25	0.5	100	0.4	4	2.3	23,120	9.4	0.5	377,760
New Hampshire	16	0.3	89	0.4	6	2.7	29,787	9.0	0.5	563,563
Montana	29	0.6	94	0.4	3	1.9	20,394	8.5	0.4	291,759
West Virginia	34	0.6	153	0.7	5	2.2	14,118	8.2	0.4	241,029
Delaware	14	0.3	72	0.3	5	1.9	26,306	7.7	0.4	551,429
Alaska	12	0.2	65	0.3	5	2.0	30,985	7.6	0.4	634,167
Rhode Island	22	0.4	100	0.4	5	1.7	17,180	7.3	0.4	333,591
New Mexico	30	0.6	95	0.4	3	1.5	15,874	6.3	0.3	210,267
Vermont	11	0.2	55	0.2	5	1.4	25,164	5.0	0.3	457,455
South Dakota	12	0.2	43	0.2	4	0.9	20,186	3.8	0.2	319,000
North Dakota	15	0.3	67	0.3	4	1.0	14,358	3.8	0.2	250,533
Wyoming	11	0.2	31	0.1	3	0.6	19,903	2.6	0.1	236,727
D.C.	4	0.1	60*	-	-	(D)	-	(D)	-	-

Source: 1997 *Economic Census*. The states are in descending order of revenues or establishments (if revenue data are missing for the majority). The symbol (D) appears when data are withheld to prevent disclosure of competitive information. States marked with (D) are sorted by number of establishments. A dash (-) indicates that the data element cannot be calculated. * indicates the midpoint of a range; 175, for example is the range 100-249. Shaded *states* on the state map indicate those states which have proportionately greater representation in the industry than would be indicated by the state's population; the ratio is based on total revenues or number of establishments. Shaded *regions* indicate where the industry is regionally most concentrated.

NAICS 811113 - AUTOMOTIVE TRANSMISSION REPAIR*

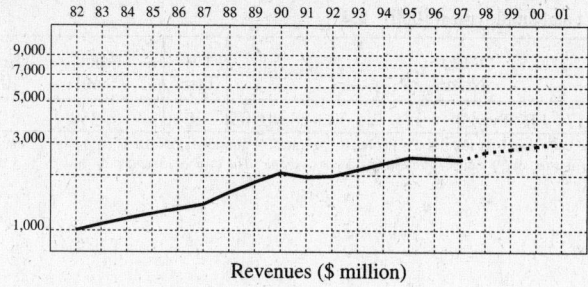

Revenues ($ million)

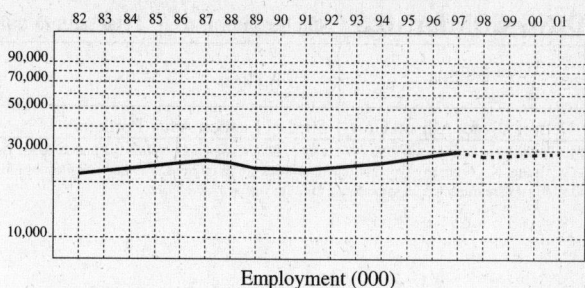

Employment (000)

GENERAL STATISTICS

Year	Establishments (number)	Employment (number)	Payroll ($ million)	Revenues ($ million)	Employees per Establishment (number)	Revenues per Establishment ($)	Payroll per Employee ($)
1982	5,701	22,157	302.0	1,007.0	3.9	176,636	13,630
1983	5,828 e	22,979 e	325.0 e	1,085.0 e	3.9 e	186,170 e	14,143 e
1984	5,955 e	23,800 e	348.0 e	1,162.0 e	4.0 e	195,130 e	14,622 e
1985	6,081 e	24,622 e	371.0 e	1,239.0 e	4.0 e	203,749 e	15,068 e
1986	6,208 e	25,443 e	394.0 e	1,317.0 e	4.1 e	212,146 e	15,486 e
1987	6,335	26,265	417.0	1,394.0	4.1	220,047	15,877
1988	5,932	25,547	440.0	1,618.0 e	4.3	272,758	17,223
1989	5,500	23,894	429.0	1,841.0 e	4.3	334,727	17,954
1990	5,523	23,802	447.0	2,065.0	4.3	373,891	18,780
1991	5,729	23,473	453.0	1,958.0	4.1	341,770	19,299
1992	6,277	24,136	479.0	1,983.0	3.8	315,915	19,846
1993	6,305	24,794	505.0	2,147.0	3.9	340,523	20,368
1994	6,391	25,578	549.0	2,326.0	4.0	363,949	21,464
1995	6,343	26,839	592.0	2,509.0	4.2	395,554	22,057
1996	6,556 e	28,141 e	651.0 e	2,470.0 e	4.3 e	376,754 e	23,134 e
1997	6,768	29,442	709.0	2,432.0	4.4	359,338	24,081
1998	6,669 p	27,808 p	682.0 p	2,685.0 p	4.2 p	402,609 p	24,525 p
1999	6,755 p	28,172 p	710.0 p	2,787.0 p	4.2 p	412,583 p	25,202 p
2000	6,842 p	28,535 p	737.0 p	2,890.0 p	4.2 p	422,391 p	25,828 p
2001	6,928 p	28,898 p	765.0 p	2,993.0 p	4.2 p	432,015 p	26,472 p

Sources: *Economic Census of the United States*, 1982, 1987, 1992, 1997. Establishment counts, employment, and payroll are from *County Business Patterns* for non-Census years. In non-Census years, industries in the Manufacturing range under SIC coding include data from the *Annual Survey of Manufactures* (*ASM*); those in the old Services range include data from the *Services Annual Survey* (*SAS*). Values followed by a 'p' are projections by the editors. Extrapolations are marked by 'e'. Data are the most recent available at this level of detail.

INDICES OF CHANGE

Year	Establishments (number)	Employment (number)	Payroll ($ million)	Revenues ($ million)	Employees per Establishment (number)	Revenues per Establishment ($)	Payroll per Employee ($)
1982	84.2	75.3	42.6	41.4	89.3	49.2	56.6
1987	93.6	89.2	58.8	57.3	95.3	61.2	65.9
1992	92.7	82.0	67.6	81.5	88.4	87.9	82.4
1993	93.2	84.2	71.2	88.3	90.4	94.8	84.6
1994	94.4	86.9	77.4	95.6	92.0	101.3	89.1
1995	93.7	91.2	83.5	103.2	97.3	110.1	91.6
1996	96.9 e	95.6 e	91.8 e	101.6 e	98.7 e	104.8 e	96.1 e
1997	100.0	100.0	100.0	100.0	100.0	100.0	100.0
1998	98.5 p	94.5 p	96.2 p	110.4 p	95.9 p	112.0 p	101.8 p
1999	99.8 p	95.7 p	100.1 p	114.6 p	95.9 p	114.8 p	104.7 p
2000	101.1 p	96.9 p	103.9 p	118.8 p	95.9 p	117.5 p	107.3 p
2001	102.4 p	98.2 p	107.9 p	123.1 p	95.9 p	120.2 p	109.9 p

Sources: Same as General Statistics. The values shown reflect change from the base year, 1997. Values above 100 mean greater than 1997, values below 100 mean less than 1997, and a value of 100 in the 1982-96 or 1998-2001 period means same as 1997. Values followed by a 'p' are projections by the editors; 'e' stands for extrapolation. Data are the most recent available at this level of detail.

SELECTED RATIOS

For 1997	Avg. of Information	Analyzed Industry	Index	For 1997	Avg. of Information	Analyzed Industry	Index
Employees per establishment	6	4	69	Payroll per establishment	126,069	104,758	83
Revenue per establishment	511,622	359,338	70	Payroll as % of revenue	25	29	118
Revenue per employee	81,659	82,603	101	Payroll per employee	20,122	24,081	120

Sources: Same as General Statistics. The 'Average' column represents the average for the industry sector, in 1997, where the currently shown industry is classified. The Index shows the relationship between the Average and the Analyzed Industry. For example, 100 means that they are equal; 500 that the Analyzed Industry is five times the average; 50 means that the Analyzed Industry is half the national average. The abbreviation 'na' is used to show that data are 'not available'.

*Equivalent to SIC 7537.

LEADING COMPANIES   Number shown: **1**   Total sales ($ mil): **350**   Total employment (000): **0.4**

Company Name	Address				CEO Name	Phone	Co. Type	Sales ($ mil)	Empl. (000)
Pacific Detroit Diesel Allison Co.	5061 N Lagoon Ave	Portland	OR	97217	J.R. Tyrrell	503-283-0505	R	350*	0.4

Source: Ward's Business Directory of U.S. Private and Public Companies, Volumes 1 and 2, 2000. The company type code used is as follows: P - Public, R - Private, S - Subsidiary, D - Division, J - Joint Venture, A - Affiliate, G - Group, N - Company type not reported. Sales are in millions of dollars, employees are in thousands. An asterisk (*) indicates an estimated sales volume. The symbol < stands for 'less than'. Company names and addresses are truncated, in some cases, to fit into the available space.

LOCATION BY STATE AND REGIONAL CONCENTRATION

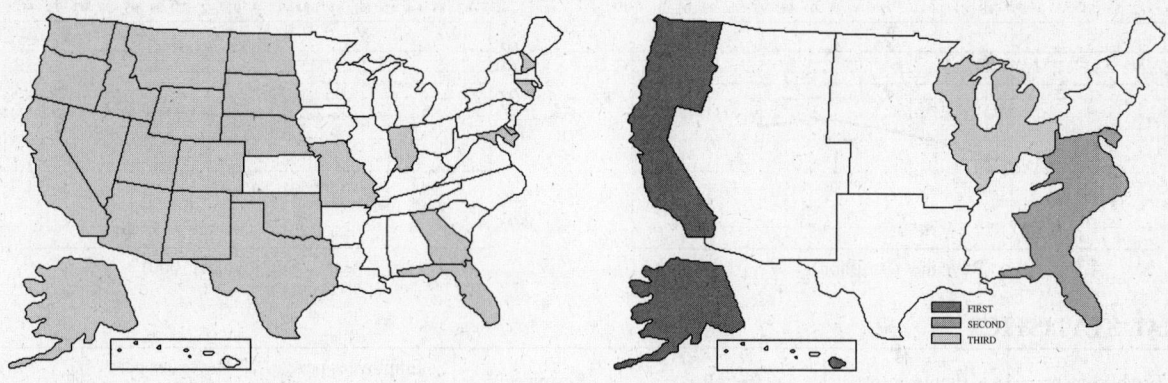

FIRST
SECOND
THIRD

INDUSTRY DATA BY STATE

State	Establishments Total (number)	% of U.S.	Employment Total (number)	% of U.S.	Per Estab.	Payroll Total ($ mil.)	Per Empl. ($)	Revenues Total ($ mil.)	% of U.S.	Per Estab. ($)
California	899	13.3	3,578	12.2	4	88.6	24,757	340.5	14.0	378,751
Texas	586	8.7	2,617	8.9	4	59.9	22,888	198.4	8.2	338,560
Florida	445	6.6	1,691	5.7	4	37.9	22,435	135.4	5.6	304,211
New York	404	6.0	1,672	5.7	4	36.0	21,526	134.2	5.5	332,173
Pennsylvania	270	4.0	1,134	3.9	4	28.7	25,349	97.1	4.0	359,733
Illinois	236	3.5	1,111	3.8	5	28.8	25,905	92.5	3.8	392,097
Ohio	236	3.5	1,049	3.6	4	25.2	24,002	81.1	3.3	343,712
Michigan	232	3.4	974	3.3	4	23.9	24,562	77.5	3.2	333,966
New Jersey	221	3.3	846	2.9	4	21.9	25,915	72.6	3.0	328,719
Georgia	201	3.0	811	2.8	4	20.3	24,991	69.4	2.9	345,493
Washington	155	2.3	859	2.9	6	21.0	24,461	68.5	2.8	441,968
Virginia	154	2.3	736	2.5	5	19.7	26,764	59.0	2.4	383,305
Missouri	170	2.5	751	2.6	4	16.8	22,333	58.0	2.4	341,124
North Carolina	180	2.7	708	2.4	4	16.5	23,254	57.6	2.4	320,267
Indiana	146	2.2	774	2.6	5	18.3	23,695	57.0	2.3	390,493
Maryland	102	1.5	679	2.3	7	20.6	30,368	56.9	2.3	558,265
Arizona	133	2.0	701	2.4	5	17.0	24,315	52.9	2.2	397,759
Colorado	125	1.8	568	1.9	5	14.6	25,755	50.7	2.1	405,560
Tennessee	148	2.2	584	2.0	4	13.1	22,507	46.1	1.9	311,209
Massachusetts	106	1.6	513	1.7	5	13.7	26,614	41.1	1.7	388,085
Minnesota	101	1.5	423	1.4	4	11.4	26,972	41.0	1.7	405,554
Alabama	130	1.9	484	1.6	4	10.3	21,372	37.3	1.5	286,931
Oregon	96	1.4	439	1.5	5	10.3	23,390	35.6	1.5	371,333
Oklahoma	87	1.3	390	1.3	4	8.5	21,846	35.4	1.5	406,598
Connecticut	89	1.3	363	1.2	4	10.3	28,482	33.3	1.4	373,674
Louisiana	111	1.6	487	1.7	4	9.3	19,127	33.2	1.4	299,333
Wisconsin	89	1.3	382	1.3	4	8.9	23,359	32.4	1.3	363,865
South Carolina	97	1.4	368	1.2	4	8.9	24,234	30.4	1.3	313,629
Kentucky	99	1.5	381	1.3	4	8.0	20,929	27.5	1.1	278,263
Utah	50	0.7	314	1.1	6	8.6	27,529	26.2	1.1	524,720
Iowa	51	0.8	259	0.9	5	6.8	26,077	24.3	1.0	476,843
Nevada	59	0.9	265	0.9	4	6.8	25,823	24.2	1.0	410,254
Nebraska	53	0.8	267	0.9	5	7.6	28,506	23.9	1.0	450,491
Kansas	60	0.9	271	0.9	5	6.6	24,339	22.8	0.9	380,550
Mississippi	63	0.9	292	1.0	5	5.7	19,442	19.5	0.8	310,206
New Mexico	49	0.7	250	0.8	5	5.5	21,876	18.6	0.8	379,918
Arkansas	63	0.9	260	0.9	4	5.3	20,500	18.4	0.8	292,825
Idaho	34	0.5	146	0.5	4	3.3	22,623	11.8	0.5	348,294
Montana	27	0.4	137	0.5	5	3.3	24,022	11.7	0.5	432,444
New Hampshire	27	0.4	118	0.4	4	3.1	26,475	11.0	0.5	406,037
Delaware	21	0.3	114	0.4	5	2.8	25,000	8.5	0.4	405,333
Rhode Island	19	0.3	99	0.3	5	2.6	25,889	8.0	0.3	419,526
West Virginia	34	0.5	122	0.4	4	2.0	16,648	8.0	0.3	233,882
North Dakota	17	0.3	90	0.3	5	2.0	22,656	7.9	0.3	464,294
South Dakota	22	0.3	89	0.3	4	1.9	21,787	7.8	0.3	354,455
Hawaii	10	0.1	59	0.2	6	1.7	28,898	7.1	0.3	705,100
Alaska	16	0.2	55	0.2	3	1.5	27,564	6.2	0.3	385,812
Wyoming	11	0.2	46	0.2	4	1.3	28,413	4.5	0.2	405,727
Maine	18	0.3	79	0.3	4	1.1	14,190	4.2	0.2	233,722
Vermont	7	0.1	17	0.1	2	0.4	23,059	2.8	0.1	400,857
D.C.	9	0.1	60*	-	-	(D)	-	(D)	-	-

Source: 1997 *Economic Census*. The states are in descending order of revenues or establishments (if revenue data are missing for the majority). The symbol (D) appears when data are withheld to prevent disclosure of competitive information. States marked with (D) are sorted by number of establishments. A dash (-) indicates that the data element cannot be calculated. * indicates the midpoint of a range; 175, for example is the range 100-249. Shaded *states* on the state map indicate those states which have proportionately greater representation in the industry than would be indicated by the state's population; the ratio is based on total revenues or number of establishments. Shaded *regions* indicate where the industry is regionally most concentrated.

NAICS 811118 - AUTOMOTIVE MECHANICAL AND ELECTRICAL REPAIR AND MAINTENANCE NEC*

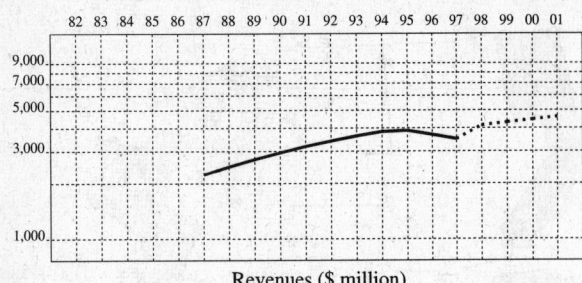

Revenues ($ million)

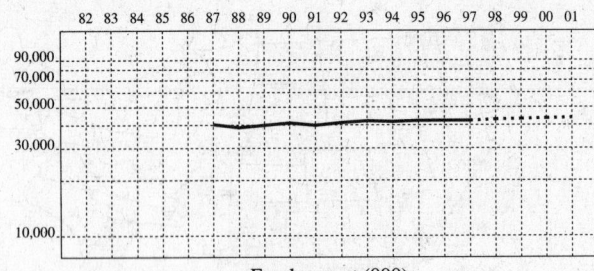

Employment (000)

GENERAL STATISTICS

Year	Establishments (number)	Employment (number)	Payroll ($ million)	Revenues ($ million)	Employees per Establishment (number)	Revenues per Establishment ($)	Payroll per Employee ($)
1982	-	-	-	-	-	-	-
1983	-	-	-	-	-	-	-
1984	-	-	-	-	-	-	-
1985	-	-	-	-	-	-	-
1986	-	-	-	-	-	-	-
1987	9,593	40,302	638.0	2,237.0	4.2	233,191	15,830
1988	9,124	38,798	668.0	2,474.0 e	4.3	271,153	17,217
1989	9,253	39,886	706.0	2,711.0 e	4.3	292,986	17,700
1990	9,521	41,062	750.0	2,948.0	4.3	309,631	18,265
1991	9,701	39,853	759.0	3,190.0	4.1	328,832	19,045
1992	10,305	41,199	788.0	3,408.0	4.0	330,713	19,127
1993	10,149	42,063	843.0	3,629.0	4.1	357,572	20,041
1994	9,931	41,687	870.0	3,827.0	4.2	385,359	20,870
1995	9,668	42,201	898.0	3,876.0	4.4	400,910	21,279
1996	9,671 e	42,217 e	929.0 e	3,685.0 e	4.4 e	381,036 e	22,005 e
1997	9,674	42,234	961.0	3,495.0	4.4	361,278	22,754
1998	9,969 p	42,886 p	995.0 p	4,143.0 p	4.3 p	415,588 p	23,201 p
1999	10,015 p	43,193 p	1,027.0 p	4,296.0 p	4.3 p	428,957 p	23,777 p
2000	10,061 p	43,500 p	1,060.0 p	4,449.0 p	4.3 p	442,203 p	24,368 p
2001	10,108 p	43,806 p	1,092.0 p	4,602.0 p	4.3 p	455,283 p	24,928 p

Sources: Economic Census of the United States, 1982, 1987, 1992, 1997. Establishment counts, employment, and payroll are from *County Business Patterns* for non-Census years. In non-Census years, industries in the Manufacturing range under SIC coding include data from the *Annual Survey of Manufactures* (*ASM*); those in the old Services range include data from the *Services Annual Survey* (*SAS*). Values followed by a 'p' are projections by the editors. Extrapolations are marked by 'e'. Data are the most recent available at this level of detail.

INDICES OF CHANGE

Year	Establishments (number)	Employment (number)	Payroll ($ million)	Revenues ($ million)	Employees per Establishment (number)	Revenues per Establishment ($)	Payroll per Employee ($)
1982	-	-	-	-	-	-	-
1987	99.2	95.4	66.4	64.0	96.2	64.5	69.6
1992	106.5	97.5	82.0	97.5	91.6	91.5	84.1
1993	104.9	99.6	87.7	103.8	94.9	99.0	88.1
1994	102.7	98.7	90.5	109.5	96.2	106.7	91.7
1995	99.9	99.9	93.4	110.9	100.0	111.0	93.5
1996	100.0 e	100.0 e	96.7 e	105.4 e	100.0 e	105.5 e	96.7 e
1997	100.0	100.0	100.0	100.0	100.0	100.0	100.0
1998	103.0 p	101.5 p	103.5 p	118.5 p	98.5 p	115.0 p	102.0 p
1999	103.5 p	102.3 p	106.9 p	122.9 p	98.8 p	118.7 p	104.5 p
2000	104.0 p	103.0 p	110.3 p	127.3 p	99.0 p	122.4 p	107.1 p
2001	104.5 p	103.7 p	113.6 p	131.7 p	99.3 p	126.0 p	109.6 p

Sources: Same as General Statistics. The values shown reflect change from the base year, 1997. Values above 100 mean greater than 1997, values below 100 mean less than 1997, and a value of 100 in the 1982-96 or 1998-2001 period means same as 1997. Values followed by a 'p' are projections by the editors; 'e' stands for extrapolation. Data are the most recent available at this level of detail.

SELECTED RATIOS

For 1997	Avg. of Information	Analyzed Industry	Index	For 1997	Avg. of Information	Analyzed Industry	Index
Employees per establishment	6	4	70	Payroll per establishment	126,069	99,338	79
Revenue per establishment	511,622	361,278	71	Payroll as % of revenue	25	27	112
Revenue per employee	81,659	82,753	101	Payroll per employee	20,122	22,754	113

Sources: Same as General Statistics. The 'Average' column represents the average for the industry sector, in 1997, where the currently shown industry is classified. The Index shows the relationship between the Average and the Analyzed Industry. For example, 100 means that they are equal; 500 that the Analyzed Industry is five times the average; 50 means that the Analyzed Industry is half the national average. The abbreviation 'na' is used to show that data are 'not available'.

*Equivalent to SIC 7539.

LEADING COMPANIES   Number shown: **14**   Total sales ($ mil): **1,486**   Total employment (000): **6.7**

Company Name	Address				CEO Name	Phone	Co. Type	Sales ($ mil)	Empl. (000)
Midas International Corp.	1300 N Arl Hght	Itasca	IL	60143		312-565-7500	R	519	1.5
Walt's Radiator and Muffler Inc.	2588 Pacific Hwy E	Tacoma	WA	98424	Stephen Dwinal	253-922-5111	R	201*	0.3
Monro Muffler Brake Inc.	200 Holleder Pkwy	Rochester	NY	14615	Robert Gross	716-647-6400	P	193	2.8
Cummins Alabama Inc.	PO Box 1147	Birmingham	AL	35201	KB McDonald	205-841-0421	R	99*	0.1
Peck Road Ford Truck Sales Inc.	2450 Kella Ave	Whittier	CA	90601	AW Fraser	562-692-7267	R	94*	0.1
Utility Manufacturing	17295 E Railroad St	City of Industry	CA	91748		626-965-1541	R	72*	0.2
Illinois Auto Electric Co.	656 County Line Rd	Elmhurst	IL	60126	H Bruce Sirotek	630-833-4300	R	63*	0.2
R.B. Matheson Trucking Inc.	10519 E Stockton	Elk Grove	CA	95624	Robert B Matheson	916-685-2330	R	58	1.0
Scholfield Pontiac GMC	7633 E Kellogg	Wichita	KS	67207	Steve Hatchette	316-684-2841	R	47*	0.1
Nixon Power Services Co.	297 Hill Ave	Nashville	TN	37210	Roger Bellman	615-244-0650	R	37*	0.1
Meineke Discount Muffler Shops	128 S Tryon St	Charlotte	NC	28202	Ken Walker	704-377-8855	R	35	0.1
T.J.T. Inc.	PO Box 278	Emmett	ID	83617		208-365-5321	P	35	0.1
Mid-Tenn Ford Truck Sales Inc.	1319 Foster Ave	Nashville	TN	37210	WE Boyte	615-259-2050	R	31	<0.1
Constant Velocity Systems Inc.	22 Corporate Dr	Clifton Park	NY	12065	John O Naumann	518-383-8800	R	2*	<0.1

Source: *Ward's Business Directory of U.S. Private and Public Companies*, Volumes 1 and 2, 2000. The company type code used is as follows: P - Public, R - Private, S - Subsidiary, D - Division, J - Joint Venture, A - Affiliate, G - Group, N - Company type not reported. Sales are in millions of dollars, employees are in thousands. An asterisk (*) indicates an estimated sales volume. The symbol < stands for 'less than'. Company names and addresses are truncated, in some cases, to fit into the available space.

LOCATION BY STATE AND REGIONAL CONCENTRATION

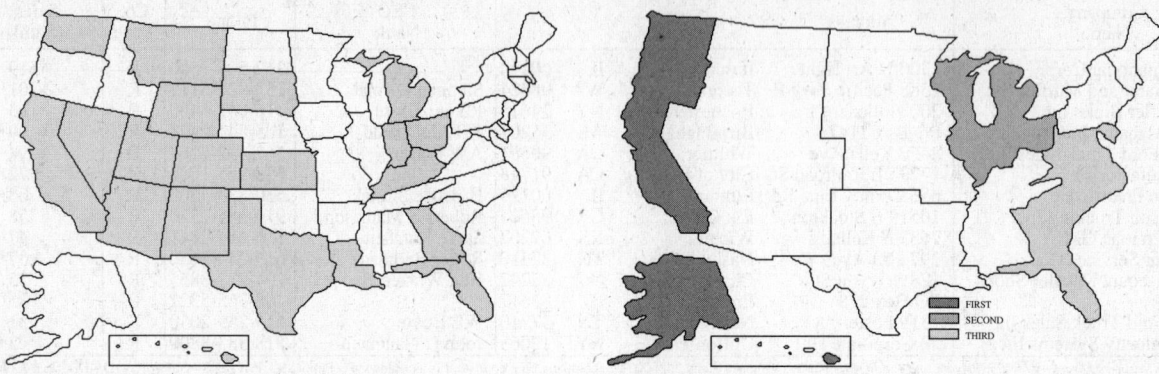

FIRST
SECOND
THIRD

INDUSTRY DATA BY STATE

State	Establishments Total (number)	% of U.S.	Employment Total (number)	% of U.S.	Per Estab.	Payroll Total ($ mil.)	Per Empl. ($)	Revenues Total ($ mil.)	% of U.S.	Per Estab. ($)
California	1,360	14.1	5,674	13.4	4	130.9	23,066	504.2	14.4	370,706
Texas	899	9.3	4,018	9.5	4	81.4	20,270	305.5	8.7	339,799
Florida	657	6.8	2,687	6.4	4	56.0	20,853	206.2	5.9	313,851
Michigan	403	4.2	1,862	4.4	5	47.1	25,313	173.1	5.0	429,459
Ohio	373	3.9	1,982	4.7	5	46.5	23,471	170.3	4.9	456,670
Illinois	360	3.7	1,757	4.2	5	44.7	25,468	155.6	4.5	432,200
New York	435	4.5	1,776	4.2	4	39.4	22,203	146.6	4.2	337,074
Pennsylvania	345	3.6	1,447	3.4	4	31.8	21,972	122.4	3.5	354,643
Georgia	324	3.3	1,397	3.3	4	31.0	22,224	112.9	3.2	348,460
Washington	259	2.7	1,153	2.7	4	27.2	23,552	98.9	2.8	381,934
Indiana	239	2.5	1,222	2.9	5	27.3	22,372	90.7	2.6	379,690
New Jersey	209	2.2	905	2.1	4	23.1	25,551	85.2	2.4	407,895
North Carolina	288	3.0	1,116	2.6	4	23.8	21,324	85.0	2.4	295,142
Virginia	196	2.0	1,072	2.5	5	24.2	22,582	79.4	2.3	404,918
Colorado	177	1.8	811	1.9	5	20.9	25,820	70.0	2.0	395,452
Louisiana	186	1.9	883	2.1	5	19.0	21,524	67.2	1.9	361,237
Wisconsin	144	1.5	708	1.7	5	18.4	26,008	61.9	1.8	430,056
Maryland	123	1.3	685	1.6	6	18.8	27,378	61.0	1.7	495,675
Arizona	187	1.9	827	2.0	4	17.1	20,705	60.6	1.7	324,134
Missouri	191	2.0	768	1.8	4	17.5	22,728	57.7	1.7	301,958
Massachusetts	129	1.3	577	1.4	4	15.5	26,898	57.3	1.6	444,240
Minnesota	149	1.5	656	1.6	4	16.3	24,849	56.4	1.6	378,208
Alabama	159	1.6	706	1.7	4	15.6	22,156	54.0	1.5	339,868
Tennessee	167	1.7	694	1.6	4	15.7	22,679	52.5	1.5	314,174
Kentucky	139	1.4	586	1.4	4	12.3	21,051	50.9	1.5	366,209
South Carolina	141	1.5	548	1.3	4	11.6	21,093	39.6	1.1	280,780
Oklahoma	148	1.5	561	1.3	4	11.1	19,747	39.5	1.1	267,223
Kansas	118	1.2	495	1.2	4	11.4	23,079	37.9	1.1	321,551
Oregon	110	1.1	437	1.0	4	10.5	24,073	37.8	1.1	343,927
New Mexico	81	0.8	411	1.0	5	8.9	21,727	31.5	0.9	388,642
Iowa	93	1.0	385	0.9	4	8.1	21,021	31.2	0.9	335,280
Nevada	73	0.8	331	0.8	5	8.5	25,571	29.7	0.9	407,068
Connecticut	82	0.8	319	0.8	4	8.0	24,931	28.7	0.8	350,280
Utah	67	0.7	303	0.7	5	7.0	23,033	26.3	0.8	392,134
Mississippi	106	1.1	361	0.9	3	6.2	17,307	25.9	0.7	244,538
Arkansas	109	1.1	341	0.8	3	6.4	18,727	24.4	0.7	224,037
Nebraska	51	0.5	238	0.6	5	5.8	24,277	21.2	0.6	416,588
Hawaii	35	0.4	135	0.3	4	4.2	31,185	15.9	0.5	455,057
New Hampshire	28	0.3	141	0.3	5	3.8	26,979	15.6	0.4	558,000
Maine	45	0.5	160	0.4	4	3.9	24,581	14.2	0.4	314,933
West Virginia	38	0.4	179	0.4	5	3.6	20,352	13.0	0.4	343,079
Montana	40	0.4	147	0.3	4	2.9	19,755	12.9	0.4	322,275
South Dakota	40	0.4	156	0.4	4	3.5	22,487	12.4	0.4	309,450
Rhode Island	34	0.4	148	0.4	4	3.1	20,642	11.1	0.3	326,000
Idaho	47	0.5	157	0.4	3	3.0	19,006	11.1	0.3	235,596
Delaware	21	0.2	87	0.2	4	2.2	25,356	7.5	0.2	355,905
North Dakota	24	0.2	63	0.1	3	1.4	22,810	6.5	0.2	271,542
Wyoming	23	0.2	76	0.2	3	1.5	19,684	6.3	0.2	272,435
Alaska	8	0.1	38	0.1	5	1.1	27,658	4.1	0.1	516,750
Vermont	11	0.1	36	0.1	3	0.8	21,361	3.2	0.1	290,545
D.C.	3	-	12	0.0	4	0.3	28,583	1.6	0.0	518,667

Source: 1997 *Economic Census*. The states are in descending order of revenues or establishments (if revenue data are missing for the majority). The symbol (D) appears when data are withheld to prevent disclosure of competitive information. States marked with (D) are sorted by number of establishments. A dash (-) indicates that the data element cannot be calculated. * indicates the midpoint of a range; 175, for example is the range 100-249. Shaded *states* on the state map indicate those states which have proportionately greater representation in the industry than would be indicated by the state's population; the ratio is based on total revenues or number of establishments. Shaded *regions* indicate where the industry is regionally most concentrated.

NAICS 811121 - AUTOMOTIVE BODY, PAINT, AND INTERIOR REPAIR AND MAINTENANCE*

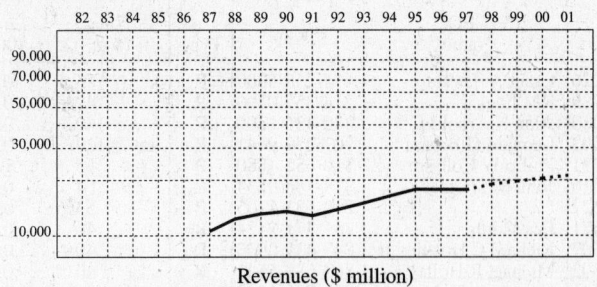

Revenues ($ million)

Employment (000)

GENERAL STATISTICS

Year	Establishments (number)	Employment (number)	Payroll ($ million)	Revenues ($ million)	Employees per Establishment (number)	Revenues per Establishment ($)	Payroll per Employee ($)
1982	-	-	-	-	-	-	-
1983	-	-	-	-	-	-	-
1984	-	-	-	-	-	-	-
1985	-	-	-	-	-	-	-
1986	-	-	-	-	-	-	-
1987	32,951	162,814	2,698.0	10,568.0	4.9	320,719	16,571
1988	30,738	162,172	2,993.0	12,335.0	5.3	401,295	18,456
1989	30,335	161,073	3,076.0	13,135.0	5.3	432,998	19,097
1990	30,502	163,625	3,233.0	13,532.0	5.4	443,643	19,759
1991	31,323	156,032	3,174.0	12,844.0	5.0	410,050	20,342
1992	35,043	165,894	3,445.0	13,876.0	4.7	395,971	20,766
1993	35,074	170,762	3,720.0	15,037.0	4.9	428,722	21,785
1994	35,030	177,811	4,051.0	16,411.0	5.1	468,484	22,783
1995	34,710	185,836	4,347.0	17,807.0	5.4	513,022	23,392
1996	35,140 e	195,504 e	4,760.0 e	17,781.0 e	5.6 e	506,005 e	24,347 e
1997	35,569	205,172	5,172.0	17,755.0	5.8	499,171	25,208
1998	36,399 p	198,564 p	5,084.0 p	18,990.0 p	5.5 p	521,718 p	25,604 p
1999	36,914 p	202,768 p	5,316.0 p	19,715.0 p	5.5 p	534,079 p	26,217 p
2000	37,429 p	206,973 p	5,547.0 p	20,439.0 p	5.5 p	546,074 p	26,801 p
2001	37,944 p	211,178 p	5,778.0 p	21,164.0 p	5.6 p	557,769 p	27,361 p

Sources: *Economic Census of the United States*, 1982, 1987, 1992, 1997. Establishment counts, employment, and payroll are from *County Business Patterns* for non-Census years. In non-Census years, industries in the Manufacturing range under SIC coding include data from the *Annual Survey of Manufactures* (*ASM*); those in the old Services range include data from the *Services Annual Survey* (*SAS*). Values followed by a 'p' are projections by the editors. Extrapolations are marked by 'e'. Data are the most recent available at this level of detail.

INDICES OF CHANGE

Year	Establishments (number)	Employment (number)	Payroll ($ million)	Revenues ($ million)	Employees per Establishment (number)	Revenues per Establishment ($)	Payroll per Employee ($)
1982	-	-	-	-	-	-	-
1987	92.6	79.4	52.2	59.5	85.7	64.3	65.7
1992	98.5	80.9	66.6	78.2	82.1	79.3	82.4
1993	98.6	83.2	71.9	84.7	84.4	85.9	86.4
1994	98.5	86.7	78.3	92.4	88.0	93.9	90.4
1995	97.6	90.6	84.0	100.3	92.8	102.8	92.8
1996	98.8 e	95.3 e	92.0 e	100.1 e	96.5 e	101.4 e	96.6 e
1997	100.0	100.0	100.0	100.0	100.0	100.0	100.0
1998	102.3 p	96.8 p	98.3 p	107.0 p	94.6 p	104.5 p	101.6 p
1999	103.8 p	98.8 p	102.8 p	111.0 p	95.2 p	107.0 p	104.0 p
2000	105.2 p	100.9 p	107.3 p	115.1 p	95.9 p	109.4 p	106.3 p
2001	106.7 p	102.9 p	111.7 p	119.2 p	96.5 p	111.7 p	108.5 p

Sources: Same as General Statistics. The values shown reflect change from the base year, 1997. Values above 100 mean greater than 1997, values below 100 mean less than 1997, and a value of 100 in the 1982-96 or 1998-2001 period means same as 1997. Values followed by a 'p' are projections by the editors; 'e' stands for extrapolation. Data are the most recent available at this level of detail.

SELECTED RATIOS

For 1997	Avg. of Information	Analyzed Industry	Index	For 1997	Avg. of Information	Analyzed Industry	Index
Employees per establishment	6	6	92	Payroll per establishment	126,069	145,408	115
Revenue per establishment	511,622	499,171	98	Payroll as % of revenue	25	29	118
Revenue per employee	81,659	86,537	106	Payroll per employee	20,122	25,208	125

Sources: Same as General Statistics. The 'Average' column represents the average for the industry sector, in 1997, where the currently shown industry is classified. The Index shows the relationship between the Average and the Analyzed Industry. For example, 100 means that they are equal; 500 that the Analyzed Industry is five times the average; 50 means that the Analyzed Industry is half the national average. The abbreviation 'na' is used to show that data are 'not available'.

*Equivalent to SIC 7532.

LEADING COMPANIES   Number shown: 30   Total sales ($ mil): 1,263   Total employment (000): 4.4

Company Name	Address				CEO Name	Phone	Co. Type	Sales ($ mil)	Empl. (000)
Ewald Automotive Group Inc.	2201 N Mayfair Rd	Milwaukee	WI	53226	Craig A. Ewald	414-258-5000	R	165	0.5
John Eagle Lincoln, Mercury	6200 Lemmon Ave	Dallas	TX	75209	RM Eagle	214-357-0700	R	140*	0.3
Wade Ford Inc.	3860 S Cobb Dr	Smyrna	GA	30080	Alan K Arnold	770-436-1200	R	140	0.1
Alaska Sales and Service Inc.	1016 W Nor Lights	Anchorage	AK	99503	Leonard G Bryant	907-279-9641	R	120*	0.3
Earl Scheib Inc.	8737 Wilshire Blvd	Beverly Hills	CA	90211	Philip W Colburn	310-652-4880	P	55	1.2
Auto Stiegler Inc.	16721 Ventura Blvd	Encino	CA	91316	John M Stiegler	818-788-0234	R	54	0.1
Starcraft Automotive Group Inc.	PO Box 1903	Goshen	IN	46527		219-533-1105	P	53	0.6
Les Marks Chevrolet-Mazda Inc.	112 S 10th St	La Porte	TX	77571	Les Marks	281-471-2424	R	46*	<0.1
Hoskins Chevrolet Inc.	P O Box 175	Elk Grove Vill.	IL	60007	Richard C Hoskins Jr	847-439-0900	R	40*	0.1
T. Thomas Chevrolet Inc.	1025 Hwy 98 S	Lakeland	FL	33802	Michael R Holley	863-688-5541	R	40	<0.1
Bay Lincoln Mercury Dodge	641 W 15th St	Panama City	FL	32401	George Gainer	850-785-1591	R	36*	<0.1
Boggus Motor Sales Inc.	PO Box 2318	McAllen	TX	78502	RF Boggus	956-686-7411	R	36*	0.1
Mid-Tenn Ford Truck Sales Inc.	1319 Foster Ave	Nashville	TN	37210	WE Boyte	615-259-2050	R	31	<0.1
Supermarket Drugs & Cosmetics	PO Box 36	Springfield	NJ	07081	Larry Wolf	908-810-9300	N	30	<0.1
Bosak Motor Sales Inc.	3111 W Lincoln	Merrillville	IN	46410	Emmett G Bosak	219-738-2323	R	28*	<0.1
Miracle Auto Painting Inc.	3157 Corporate Pl	Hayward	CA	94545	Lester Thayer	510-887-2211	R	27	<0.1
Custom Coach Corp.	1400 Dublin Rd	Columbus	OH	43215		614-481-8881	S	26*	<0.1
Gordon Rountree Motors Ltd.	2720 Franklin Ave	Waco	TX	76710		254-756-4461	R	26	<0.1
Team Chevrolet Inc.	720 Kingery Expwy	Westmont	IL	60559	J Michael Harris	630-986-8000	R	26*	<0.1
Wolf Chevrolet Sales	PO Box 558	Belvidere	IL	61008	William A Wolf	815-544-3495	R	25	<0.1
Graham Ford L and M Inc.	407 Hwy 46 S	Dickson	TN	37055	John Graham	615-446-2308	R	22*	<0.1
Horace G. Ilderton Inc.	701 S Main St	High Point	NC	27261	Thomas C Ilderton	336-841-6100	R	21*	<0.1
Melton Motors Inc.	15100 Eureka Rd	Southgate	MI	48195	George Melton	734-283-2600	R	21	<0.1
Syd Dorn Chevrolet Inc.	8150 N Lombard	Portland	OR	97203	Syd Dorn	503-286-1641	R	18*	<0.1
Schwartz Ford Company Inc.	1410 Nuttman Ave	Decatur	IN	46733	Steven Schwartz	219-724-3101	R	16*	<0.1
Three-C Body Shop Inc.	2300 Briggs Rd	Columbus	OH	43223	Robert A Juniper Jr	614-274-8245	R	9	<0.1
Lewis Supply Company Inc.	PO Box 24268	Richmond	VA	23224		804-232-7801	N	6	<0.1
Advantage Mobility Outfitters Inc.	3990 2nd St	Wayne	MI	48184	James Bishop	734-595-4400	R	3*	<0.1
New Country Pontiac, GMC	PO Box 552	Mechanicville	NY	12118	Michael Cantanucci	518-664-9851	R	3	<0.1
Elliott's Mini Storage	1430 Golden Belt	Junction City	KS	66441	Eldon Elliott	785-238-2425	R	1*	<0.1

Source: *Ward's Business Directory of U.S. Private and Public Companies*, Volumes 1 and 2, 2000. The company type code used is as follows: P - Public, R - Private, S - Subsidiary, D - Division, J - Joint Venture, A - Affiliate, G - Group, N - Company type not reported. Sales are in millions of dollars, employees are in thousands. An asterisk (*) indicates an estimated sales volume. The symbol < stands for 'less than'. Company names and addresses are truncated, in some cases, to fit into the available space.

LOCATION BY STATE AND REGIONAL CONCENTRATION

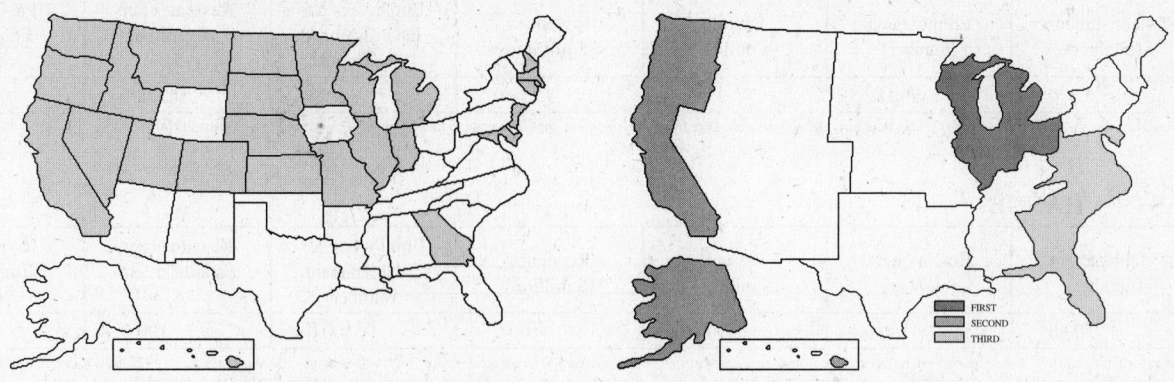

FIRST
SECOND
THIRD

INDUSTRY DATA BY STATE

State	Establishments Total (number)	% of U.S.	Employment Total (number)	% of U.S.	Per Estab.	Payroll Total ($ mil.)	Per Empl. ($)	Revenues Total ($ mil.)	% of U.S.	Per Estab. ($)
California	3,885	10.9	27,665	13.5	7	722.0	26,098	2,462.0	13.9	633,717
Texas	2,078	5.8	13,805	6.7	7	326.4	23,643	1,097.0	6.2	527,899
Illinois	1,756	4.9	11,521	5.6	7	329.3	28,584	1,056.6	6.0	601,729
New York	2,232	6.3	9,708	4.7	4	229.2	23,610	847.1	4.8	379,544
Michigan	1,434	4.0	8,755	4.3	6	245.6	28,058	803.1	4.5	560,012
Florida	1,857	5.2	9,611	4.7	5	216.7	22,550	777.8	4.4	418,866
Pennsylvania	1,735	4.9	8,726	4.3	5	211.3	24,214	775.7	4.4	447,105
Ohio	1,379	3.9	8,161	4.0	6	200.7	24,587	697.6	3.9	505,841
New Jersey	1,235	3.5	6,917	3.4	6	195.9	28,316	666.5	3.8	539,653
Georgia	941	2.6	5,713	2.8	6	150.5	26,339	504.9	2.8	536,594
Massachusetts	1,015	2.9	5,166	2.5	5	134.4	26,012	485.2	2.7	478,039
Indiana	851	2.4	5,669	2.8	7	137.6	24,280	466.1	2.6	547,687
Washington	753	2.1	5,163	2.5	7	143.5	27,802	457.6	2.6	607,760
Minnesota	755	2.1	4,066	2.0	5	110.2	27,104	416.4	2.3	551,460
North Carolina	955	2.7	4,637	2.3	5	117.1	25,250	393.4	2.2	411,979
Virginia	720	2.0	4,502	2.2	6	121.2	26,922	383.0	2.2	531,899
Maryland	575	1.6	4,111	2.0	7	116.5	28,343	369.3	2.1	642,250
Missouri	838	2.4	4,435	2.2	5	114.1	25,728	368.1	2.1	439,279
Wisconsin	855	2.4	4,199	2.0	5	99.1	23,600	356.1	2.0	416,511
Colorado	541	1.5	3,921	1.9	7	104.3	26,601	348.5	2.0	644,179
Tennessee	666	1.9	3,627	1.8	5	91.2	25,137	309.4	1.7	464,503
Oregon	453	1.3	3,045	1.5	7	82.2	26,996	262.0	1.5	578,318
Connecticut	492	1.4	2,734	1.3	6	78.8	28,820	261.9	1.5	532,276
Alabama	581	1.6	3,220	1.6	6	71.0	22,056	253.9	1.4	437,072
Arizona	446	1.3	3,094	1.5	7	78.2	25,272	246.8	1.4	553,354
Louisiana	439	1.2	2,556	1.2	6	56.3	22,040	202.4	1.1	461,105
Kentucky	477	1.3	2,327	1.1	5	51.8	22,275	189.1	1.1	396,541
South Carolina	515	1.4	2,417	1.2	5	52.4	21,679	187.2	1.1	363,452
Kansas	441	1.2	2,132	1.0	5	52.5	24,643	180.8	1.0	409,925
Iowa	538	1.5	2,267	1.1	4	47.7	21,059	180.7	1.0	335,820
Oklahoma	446	1.3	2,376	1.2	5	49.5	20,833	177.3	1.0	397,610
Utah	269	0.8	1,803	0.9	7	43.2	23,937	149.3	0.8	555,041
Mississippi	332	0.9	1,573	0.8	5	36.1	22,920	141.6	0.8	426,581
Arkansas	371	1.0	1,723	0.8	5	34.7	20,150	137.5	0.8	370,663
Nebraska	355	1.0	1,652	0.8	5	36.3	21,990	126.6	0.7	356,580
Nevada	174	0.5	1,374	0.7	8	36.5	26,587	114.3	0.6	656,977
New Hampshire	196	0.6	940	0.5	5	24.5	26,013	88.6	0.5	452,265
Hawaii	141	0.4	1,002	0.5	7	26.1	26,001	87.6	0.5	621,199
New Mexico	208	0.6	1,137	0.6	5	27.0	23,774	85.8	0.5	412,697
Idaho	210	0.6	1,082	0.5	5	24.3	22,435	84.6	0.5	403,067
Montana	176	0.5	1,013	0.5	6	21.1	20,806	78.9	0.4	448,392
Rhode Island	185	0.5	853	0.4	5	20.7	24,252	75.0	0.4	405,297
Maine	187	0.5	795	0.4	4	16.4	20,574	71.1	0.4	380,043
West Virginia	200	0.6	862	0.4	4	16.0	18,556	62.8	0.4	313,835
North Dakota	147	0.4	696	0.3	5	15.0	21,618	58.3	0.3	396,442
South Dakota	169	0.5	630	0.3	4	12.3	19,551	51.5	0.3	304,982
Delaware	94	0.3	501	0.2	5	12.8	25,611	41.3	0.2	439,266
Alaska	69	0.2	395	0.2	6	11.6	29,370	39.5	0.2	572,507
Vermont	88	0.2	358	0.2	4	8.0	22,279	32.5	0.2	368,852
Wyoming	89	0.3	375*	-	-	(D)	-	(D)	-	-
D.C.	25	0.1	175*	-	-	(D)	-	(D)	-	-

Source: 1997 *Economic Census*. The states are in descending order of revenues or establishments (if revenue data are missing for the majority). The symbol (D) appears when data are withheld to prevent disclosure of competitive information. States marked with (D) are sorted by number of establishments. A dash (-) indicates that the data element cannot be calculated. * indicates the midpoint of a range; 175, for example is the range 100-249. Shaded *states* on the state map indicate those states which have proportionately greater representation in the industry than would be indicated by the state's population; the ratio is based on total revenues or number of establishments. Shaded *regions* indicate where the industry is regionally most concentrated.

NAICS 811122 - AUTOMOTIVE GLASS REPLACEMENT SHOPS

GENERAL STATISTICS

Year	Establishments (number)	Employment (number)	Payroll ($ million)	Revenues ($ million)	Employees per Establishment (number)	Revenues per Establishment ($)	Payroll per Employee ($)
1997	5,599	29,187	754.0	3,150.0	5.2	562,600	25,833

Source: Economic Census of the United States, 1997. This is a newly defined industry. Data for prior years were unavailable at the time of publication but may become available over time.

INDICES OF CHANGE

Year	Establishments (number)	Employment (number)	Payroll ($ million)	Revenues ($ million)	Employees per Establishment (number)	Revenues per Establishment ($)	Payroll per Employee ($)
1997	100.0	100.0	100.0	100.0	100.0	100.0	100.0

Sources: Same as General Statistics. The values shown reflect change from the base year, 1997. Values above 100 mean greater than 1997, values below 100 mean less than 1997, and a value of 100 in the 1982-96 or 1998-2001 period means same as 1997. Values followed by a 'p' are projections by the editors; 'e' stands for extrapolation. Data are the most recent available at this level of detail.

SIC INDUSTRIES RELATED TO NAICS 811122

Each new NAICS code represents an industry that used to be part of an SIC or a part of several SIC industries. Data in this table are shown to provide transitional information for these cases. All available data for the precursor SIC(s) are shown. Even if only a part of an SIC is included in the NAICS, *all* data for the SIC are reproduced. If the SIC industry is not marked as being a part (pt) of the NAICS, the entire industry is embedded in the NAICS data. The SIC composition of the new industry provides some hints of the relative importance of its "ancestors." Data marked with a 'p' are projected. Projections begin with 1982 data. Data earlier than 1990 are not shown but are reflected in the projections.

SIC	Industry	1990	1991	1992	1993	1994	1995	1996	1997
7536	**Automotive Glass Replacement Shops**								
	Establishments (number)	3,529	4,335	4,925	4,847	4,938	5,026	5,171p	5,357p
	Employment (thousands)	20.1	20.6	22.2	22.3	22.8	24.2	24.8p	25.6p
	Revenues ($ million)	1,863.0	1,913.0	2,018.0	2,292.0	2,751.0	2,822.0	3,344.0	3,428.1p
7549	**Automotive Services, nec (pt)**								
	Establishments (number)	7,856	8,721	10,906	11,269	11,704	12,058	12,470p	13,093p
	Employment (thousands)	54.2	55.9	67.4	71.2	77.1	85.5	85.8p	90.6p
	Revenues ($ million)	-	-	3,402.8	3,589.4p	3,858.4p	4,127.4p	4,396.4p	4,665.4p

Source: Economic Census of the United States, 1992, annual surveys of economic sectors conducted by the Bureau of the Census, and estimates or projections based on the 1982-1992 period; not all data are shown. 'e' marks estimates made by the editors; 'p' indicates projections based on time series. A dash (-) indicates that data for this SIC or year were not available. The abbreviation (pt) next to the industry name indicates that only a part of the industry is present within the NAICS data. If no (pt) is shown, the entire industry is contained within the NAICS data.

SELECTED RATIOS

For 1997	Avg. of Information	Analyzed Industry	Index	For 1997	Avg. of Information	Analyzed Industry	Index
Employees per establishment	6	5	83	Payroll per establishment	126,069	134,667	107
Revenue per establishment	511,622	562,600	110	Payroll as % of revenue	25	24	97
Revenue per employee	81,659	107,925	132	Payroll per employee	20,122	25,833	128

Sources: Same as General Statistics. The 'Average' column represents the average for the industry sector, in 1997, where the currently shown industry is classified. The Index shows the relationship between the Average and the Analyzed Industry. For example, 100 means that they are equal; 500 that the Analyzed Industry is five times the average; 50 means that the Analyzed Industry is half the national average. The abbreviation 'na' is used to show that data are 'not available'.

LEADING COMPANIES   Number shown: **5**   Total sales ($ mil): **989**   Total employment (000): **7.6**

Company Name	Address				CEO Name	Phone	Co. Type	Sales ($ mil)	Empl. (000)
Safelite Glass Corp.	1105 Schrock Rd	Columbus	OH	43229	John Barlow	614-842-3000	R	877	6.5
Auto Glass Specialists Inc.	PO Box 259500	Madison	WI	53725	Robert R Birkhauser	608-271-5484	R	51	0.6
Speedy Auto Glass Inc.	9675 S E 36th St	Mercer Island	WA	98040		206-232-9500	S	28*	0.3
Guardian Glass Co.	691 Green Crest Dr	Westerville	OH	43081		614-891-3405	D	23*	0.2
Novus Inc.	10425 Hampshire S	Minneapolis	MN	55438		612-944-8000	R	10	<0.1

Source: *Ward's Business Directory of U.S. Private and Public Companies*, Volumes 1 and 2, 2000. The company type code used is as follows: P - Public, R - Private, S - Subsidiary, D - Division, J - Joint Venture, A - Affiliate, G - Group, N - Company type not reported. Sales are in millions of dollars, employees are in thousands. An asterisk (*) indicates an estimated sales volume. The symbol < stands for 'less than'. Company names and addresses are truncated, in some cases, to fit into the available space.

LOCATION BY STATE AND REGIONAL CONCENTRATION

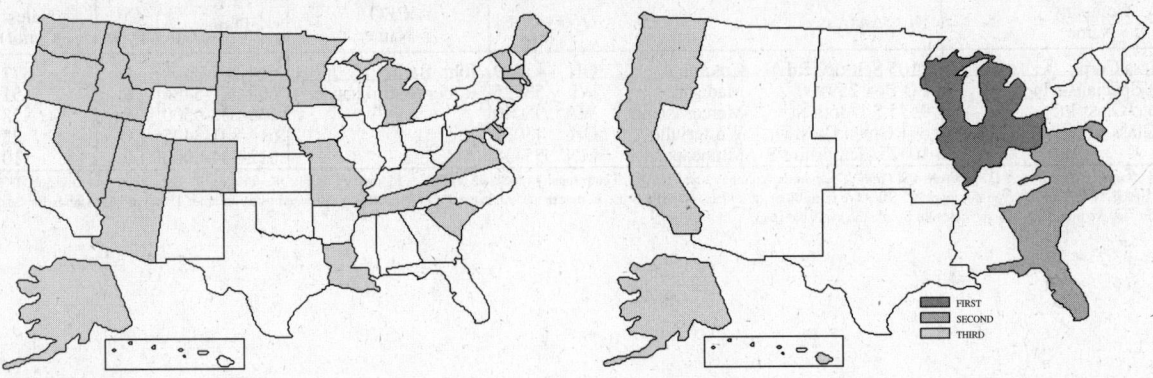

FIRST
SECOND
THIRD

INDUSTRY DATA BY STATE

State	Establishments Total (number)	% of U.S.	Employment Total (number)	% of U.S.	Per Estab.	Payroll Total ($ mil.)	Per Empl. ($)	Revenues Total ($ mil.)	% of U.S.	Per Estab. ($)
California	466	8.3	2,409	8.3	5	65.9	27,339	260.3	8.3	558,624
Michigan	269	4.8	1,746	6.0	6	46.2	26,435	189.1	6.0	702,963
Texas	344	6.1	1,782	6.1	5	43.4	24,354	182.0	5.8	529,186
Florida	241	4.3	1,425	4.9	6	35.6	24,987	150.4	4.8	624,137
New York	270	4.8	1,266	4.3	5	33.4	26,378	137.0	4.3	507,444
Illinois	203	3.6	1,143	3.9	6	32.5	28,437	134.1	4.3	660,458
Washington	215	3.8	1,234	4.2	6	29.8	24,184	121.5	3.9	565,005
Pennsylvania	200	3.6	987	3.4	5	25.0	25,342	114.6	3.6	572,885
Massachusetts	223	4.0	1,001	3.4	4	29.8	29,735	111.8	3.6	501,493
Minnesota	131	2.3	906	3.1	7	26.1	28,784	110.6	3.5	844,603
Ohio	166	3.0	1,052	3.6	6	28.9	27,452	110.6	3.5	666,127
Colorado	131	2.3	854	2.9	7	24.3	28,405	102.4	3.3	781,840
Arizona	126	2.3	824	2.8	7	22.9	27,777	96.9	3.1	768,722
Virginia	177	3.2	885	3.0	5	22.1	24,928	90.9	2.9	513,322
North Carolina	160	2.9	815	2.8	5	20.3	24,925	82.1	2.6	513,069
Tennessee	97	1.7	525	1.8	5	17.3	32,867	74.2	2.4	764,763
Missouri	147	2.6	626	2.1	4	16.3	26,089	71.7	2.3	487,932
Maryland	119	2.1	617	2.1	5	17.0	27,580	68.1	2.2	572,538
Louisiana	137	2.4	708	2.4	5	17.2	24,251	66.2	2.1	483,453
Oregon	106	1.9	671	2.3	6	15.4	22,976	63.5	2.0	598,642
Indiana	118	2.1	654	2.2	6	16.4	25,049	62.5	2.0	529,288
Georgia	134	2.4	588	2.0	4	13.8	23,466	59.3	1.9	442,642
New Jersey	101	1.8	462	1.6	5	13.4	29,039	57.6	1.8	570,099
Wisconsin	91	1.6	495	1.7	5	13.4	27,067	56.0	1.8	614,857
South Carolina	98	1.8	519	1.8	5	12.3	23,740	52.1	1.7	531,245
Connecticut	71	1.3	371	1.3	5	12.0	32,270	49.9	1.6	703,394
Utah	85	1.5	399	1.4	5	9.3	23,288	46.5	1.5	547,188
Alabama	91	1.6	439	1.5	5	8.9	20,271	42.8	1.4	470,681
Kentucky	86	1.5	352	1.2	4	8.1	23,003	35.5	1.1	413,012
Mississippi	72	1.3	283	1.0	4	5.9	20,760	30.5	1.0	423,736
Kansas	75	1.3	276	0.9	4	6.2	22,377	26.9	0.9	358,853
Idaho	56	1.0	261	0.9	5	5.1	19,364	24.0	0.8	427,750
Iowa	58	1.0	282	1.0	5	5.9	20,770	23.9	0.8	412,448
Arkansas	69	1.2	262	0.9	4	5.4	20,439	23.9	0.8	346,391
Maine	38	0.7	169	0.6	4	4.5	26,527	20.6	0.7	540,789
Nevada	34	0.6	163	0.6	5	4.6	28,086	20.3	0.6	597,000
Oklahoma	49	0.9	219	0.8	4	4.6	21,205	20.0	0.6	408,796
New Mexico	52	0.9	225	0.8	4	4.8	21,249	19.6	0.6	376,962
Nebraska	51	0.9	186	0.6	4	3.9	20,973	17.4	0.6	340,902
North Dakota	33	0.6	138	0.5	4	3.2	23,406	16.9	0.5	513,364
West Virginia	31	0.6	145	0.5	5	3.3	23,000	13.9	0.4	447,968
Montana	37	0.7	116	0.4	3	2.7	23,612	13.4	0.4	360,838
Hawaii	14	0.3	73	0.3	5	2.2	29,836	13.2	0.4	943,571
Delaware	17	0.3	78	0.3	5	2.3	30,128	11.0	0.4	648,765
New Hampshire	21	0.4	98	0.3	5	2.6	26,633	10.6	0.3	505,190
Alaska	14	0.3	137	0.5	10	2.0	14,883	9.1	0.3	649,286
Vermont	15	0.3	88	0.3	6	2.0	22,250	8.9	0.3	591,467
South Dakota	25	0.4	80	0.3	3	2.0	24,975	8.5	0.3	341,240
Rhode Island	14	0.3	58	0.2	4	1.6	26,948	7.7	0.2	549,571
Wyoming	19	0.3	60*	-	-	(D)	-	(D)	-	-
D.C.	2	-	10*	-	-	(D)	-	(D)	-	-

Source: 1997 *Economic Census*. The states are in descending order of revenues or establishments (if revenue data are missing for the majority). The symbol (D) appears when data are withheld to prevent disclosure of competitive information. States marked with (D) are sorted by number of establishments. A dash (-) indicates that the data element cannot be calculated. * indicates the midpoint of a range; 175, for example is the range 100-249. Shaded *states* on the state map indicate those states which have proportionately greater representation in the industry than would be indicated by the state's population; the ratio is based on total revenues or number of establishments. Shaded *regions* indicate where the industry is regionally most concentrated.

NAICS 811191 - AUTOMOTIVE OIL CHANGE AND LUBRICATION SHOPS

GENERAL STATISTICS

Year	Establishments (number)	Employment (number)	Payroll ($ million)	Revenues ($ million)	Employees per Establishment (number)	Revenues per Establishment ($)	Payroll per Employee ($)
1997	7,413	57,083	779.0	2,787.0	7.7	375,961	13,647

Source: *Economic Census of the United States*, 1997. This is a newly defined industry. Data for prior years were unavailable at the time of publication but may become available over time.

INDICES OF CHANGE

Year	Establishments (number)	Employment (number)	Payroll ($ million)	Revenues ($ million)	Employees per Establishment (number)	Revenues per Establishment ($)	Payroll per Employee ($)
1997	100.0	100.0	100.0	100.0	100.0	100.0	100.0

Sources: Same as General Statistics. The values shown reflect change from the base year, 1997. Values above 100 mean greater than 1997, values below 100 mean less than 1997, and a value of 100 in the 1982-96 or 1998-2001 period means same as 1997. Values followed by a 'p' are projections by the editors; 'e' stands for extrapolation. Data are the most recent available at this level of detail.

SIC INDUSTRIES RELATED TO NAICS 811191

Each new NAICS code represents an industry that used to be part of an SIC or a part of several SIC industries. Data in this table are shown to provide transitional information for these cases. All available data for the precursor SIC(s) are shown. Even if only a part of an SIC is included in the NAICS, *all* data for the SIC are reproduced. If the SIC industry is not marked as being a part (pt) of the NAICS, the entire industry is embedded in the NAICS data. The SIC composition of the new industry provides some hints of the relative importance of its "ancestors." Data marked with a 'p' are projected. Projections begin with 1982 data. Data earlier than 1990 are not shown but are reflected in the projections.

SIC	Industry	1990	1991	1992	1993	1994	1995	1996	1997
7549	**Automotive Services, nec (pt)**								
	Establishments (number)	7,856	8,721	10,906	11,269	11,704	12,058	12,470p	13,093p
	Employment (thousands)	54.2	55.9	67.4	71.2	77.1	85.5	85.8p	90.6p
	Revenues ($ million)	-	-	3,402.8	3,589.4p	3,858.4p	4,127.4p	4,396.4p	4,665.4p

Source: *Economic Census of the United States*, 1992, annual surveys of economic sectors conducted by the Bureau of the Census, and estimates or projections based on the 1982-1992 period; not all data are shown. 'e' marks estimates made by the editors; 'p' indicates projections based on time series. A dash (-) indicates that data for this SIC or year were not available. The abbreviation (pt) next to the industry name indicates that only a part of the industry is present within the NAICS data. If no (pt) is shown, the entire industry is contained within the NAICS data.

SELECTED RATIOS

For 1997	Avg. of Information	Analyzed Industry	Index	For 1997	Avg. of Information	Analyzed Industry	Index
Employees per establishment	6	8	123	Payroll per establishment	126,069	105,086	83
Revenue per establishment	511,622	375,961	73	Payroll as % of revenue	25	28	113
Revenue per employee	81,659	48,824	60	Payroll per employee	20,122	13,647	68

Sources: Same as General Statistics. The 'Average' column represents the average for the industry sector, in 1997, where the currently shown industry is classified. The Index shows the relationship between the Average and the Analyzed Industry. For example, 100 means that they are equal; 500 that the Analyzed Industry is five times the average; 50 means that the Analyzed Industry is half the national average. The abbreviation 'na' is used to show that data are 'not available'.

LEADING COMPANIES

No company data available for this industry.

LOCATION BY STATE AND REGIONAL CONCENTRATION

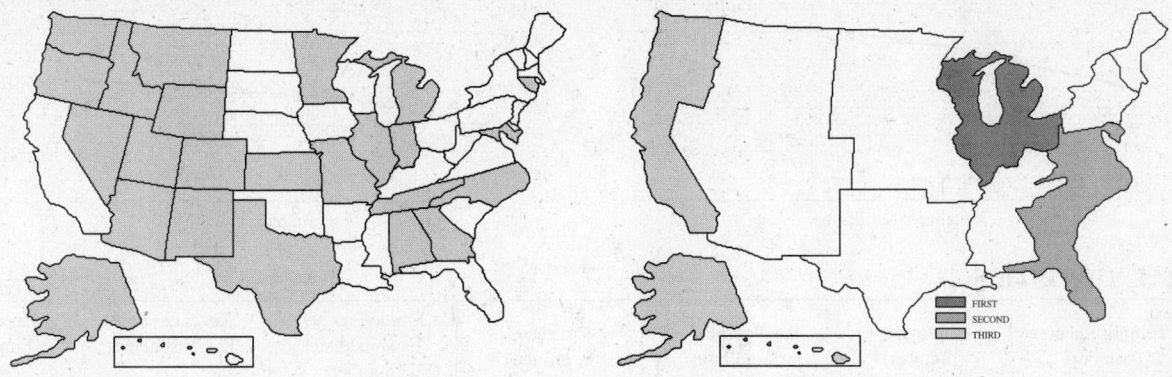

FIRST
SECOND
THIRD

INDUSTRY DATA BY STATE

State	Establishments Total (number)	Establishments % of U.S.	Employment Total (number)	Employment % of U.S.	Employment Per Estab.	Payroll Total ($ mil.)	Payroll Per Empl. ($)	Revenues Total ($ mil.)	Revenues % of U.S.	Revenues Per Estab. ($)
California	698	9.4	5,373	9.4	8	78.9	14,681	300.7	10.8	430,864
Texas	772	10.4	5,318	9.3	7	74.7	14,052	268.5	9.6	347,794
Illinois	392	5.3	3,385	5.9	9	46.3	13,678	166.9	6.0	425,824
Michigan	429	5.8	3,366	5.9	8	41.3	12,269	146.4	5.3	341,152
Florida	433	5.8	2,822	4.9	7	37.7	13,372	142.1	5.1	328,266
Ohio	353	4.8	2,693	4.7	8	32.0	11,867	116.7	4.2	330,496
New York	265	3.6	1,950	3.4	7	24.5	12,562	95.1	3.4	358,864
Georgia	246	3.3	1,821	3.2	7	22.1	12,142	77.0	2.8	312,980
North Carolina	213	2.9	1,641	2.9	8	22.3	13,564	76.4	2.7	358,465
Pennsylvania	185	2.5	1,602	2.8	9	20.7	12,948	74.6	2.7	402,995
Indiana	219	3.0	1,640	2.9	7	21.1	12,884	73.3	2.6	334,890
Washington	178	2.4	1,431	2.5	8	19.7	13,784	71.9	2.6	403,921
Virginia	151	2.0	1,262	2.2	8	18.7	14,824	70.3	2.5	465,636
Massachusetts	123	1.7	1,354	2.4	11	18.0	13,313	64.4	2.3	523,675
Colorado	155	2.1	1,197	2.1	8	18.2	15,225	64.4	2.3	415,658
Missouri	176	2.4	1,467	2.6	8	18.5	12,582	64.3	2.3	365,477
Maryland	106	1.4	1,222	2.1	12	18.3	14,948	61.7	2.2	582,538
New Jersey	141	1.9	1,110	1.9	8	16.0	14,434	58.1	2.1	412,064
Tennessee	177	2.4	1,421	2.5	8	17.2	12,082	57.8	2.1	326,525
Alabama	151	2.0	969	1.7	6	18.6	19,194	55.3	2.0	366,126
Oregon	113	1.5	994	1.7	9	13.1	13,167	49.3	1.8	436,699
Minnesota	131	1.8	1,208	2.1	9	13.9	11,510	49.2	1.8	375,405
Wisconsin	144	1.9	1,109	1.9	8	13.6	12,261	48.5	1.7	336,799
Arizona	132	1.8	877	1.5	7	12.0	13,740	46.7	1.7	353,765
Utah	96	1.3	712	1.2	7	10.0	14,080	38.5	1.4	400,635
South Carolina	120	1.6	983	1.7	8	12.5	12,712	38.1	1.4	317,892
Louisiana	116	1.6	806	1.4	7	10.8	13,375	37.0	1.3	318,741
Connecticut	57	0.8	807	1.4	14	11.7	14,556	36.4	1.3	637,807
Kentucky	122	1.6	773	1.4	6	10.2	13,135	35.5	1.3	291,213
Oklahoma	107	1.4	557	1.0	5	9.0	16,190	30.5	1.1	284,888
Mississippi	83	1.1	477	0.8	6	8.4	17,572	27.3	1.0	328,446
Kansas	65	0.9	532	0.9	8	7.6	14,267	26.6	1.0	408,692
New Mexico	67	0.9	572	1.0	9	8.2	14,376	25.6	0.9	381,358
Nevada	52	0.7	421	0.7	8	6.3	15,048	23.2	0.8	446,077
Iowa	55	0.7	391	0.7	7	5.9	15,156	20.8	0.7	377,455
Arkansas	79	1.1	450	0.8	6	5.9	13,058	20.1	0.7	254,519
Alaska	16	0.2	162	0.3	10	3.6	22,407	15.7	0.6	980,313
Idaho	46	0.6	290	0.5	6	4.2	14,548	13.8	0.5	301,022
Nebraska	32	0.4	227	0.4	7	3.4	14,881	13.3	0.5	415,219
Montana	40	0.5	276	0.5	7	3.5	12,804	12.4	0.4	311,200
New Hampshire	24	0.3	229	0.4	10	3.5	15,480	11.7	0.4	485,875
Hawaii	8	0.1	142	0.2	18	2.5	17,380	10.3	0.4	1,282,875
West Virginia	31	0.4	189	0.3	6	2.4	12,847	8.6	0.3	276,903
Rhode Island	20	0.3	157	0.3	8	2.3	14,580	7.6	0.3	377,950
Wyoming	21	0.3	119	0.2	6	1.6	13,160	6.3	0.2	297,619
South Dakota	10	0.1	102	0.2	10	1.3	12,412	4.3	0.2	426,900
Vermont	6	0.1	48	0.1	8	0.8	16,313	2.7	0.1	442,667
Maine	25	0.3	175*	-	-	(D)	-	(D)	-	-
North Dakota	20	0.3	175*	-	-	(D)	-	(D)	-	-
Delaware	11	0.1	175*	-	-	(D)	-	(D)	-	-
D.C.	1	-	10*	-	-	(D)	-	(D)	-	-

Source: 1997 *Economic Census*. The states are in descending order of revenues or establishments (if revenue data are missing for the majority). The symbol (D) appears when data are withheld to prevent disclosure of competitive information. States marked with (D) are sorted by number of establishments. A dash (-) indicates that the data element cannot be calculated. * indicates the midpoint of a range; 175, for example is the range 100-249. Shaded *states* on the state map indicate those states which have proportionately greater representation in the industry than would be indicated by the state's population; the ratio is based on total revenues or number of establishments. Shaded *regions* indicate where the industry is regionally most concentrated.

NAICS 811192 - CARWASHES*

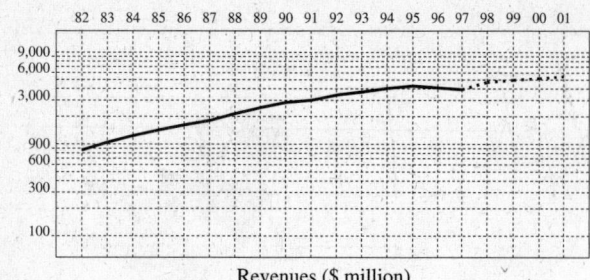

Revenues ($ million)

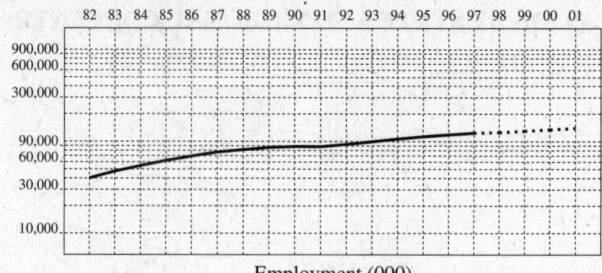

Employment (000)

GENERAL STATISTICS

Year	Establishments (number)	Employment (number)	Payroll ($ million)	Revenues ($ million)	Employees per Establishment (number)	Revenues per Establishment ($)	Payroll per Employee ($)
1982	6,539	40,080	232.0	861.0	6.1	131,672	5,788
1983	7,058 e	47,377 e	295.0 e	1,049.0 e	6.7 e	148,626 e	6,227 e
1984	7,576 e	54,674 e	358.0 e	1,237.0 e	7.2 e	163,279 e	6,548 e
1985	8,095 e	61,972 e	421.0 e	1,425.0 e	7.7 e	176,035 e	6,793 e
1986	8,613 e	69,269 e	485.0 e	1,614.0 e	8.0 e	187,391 e	7,002 e
1987	9,132	76,566	548.0	1,802.0	8.4	197,328	7,157
1988	8,547	81,335	640.0	2,148.0 e	9.5	251,316	7,869
1989	8,993	86,306	673.0	2,495.0 e	9.6	277,438	7,798
1990	9,545	88,302	729.0	2,841.0	9.3	297,643	8,256
1991	10,089	87,884	755.0	2,998.0	8.7	297,155	8,591
1992	11,589	93,081	809.0	3,419.0	8.0	295,021	8,691
1993	11,765	99,516	891.0	3,685.0	8.5	313,217	8,953
1994	12,197	106,719	996.0	4,037.0	8.7	330,983	9,333
1995	12,674	113,042	1,095.0	4,279.0	8.9	337,620	9,687
1996	13,178 e	118,322 e	1,174.0 e	4,095.0 e	9.0 e	310,745 e	9,922 e
1997	13,683	123,602	1,253.0	3,911.0	9.0	285,829	10,137
1998	14,270 p	125,614 p	1,284.0 p	4,706.0 p	8.8 p	329,783 p	10,222 p
1999	14,809 p	130,267 p	1,353.0 p	4,950.0 p	8.8 p	334,256 p	10,386 p
2000	15,349 p	134,920 p	1,422.0 p	5,193.0 p	8.8 p	338,328 p	10,540 p
2001	15,888 p	139,572 p	1,491.0 p	5,436.0 p	8.8 p	342,145 p	10,683 p

Sources: Economic Census of the United States, 1982, 1987, 1992, 1997. Establishment counts, employment, and payroll are from *County Business Patterns* for non-Census years. In non-Census years, industries in the Manufacturing range under SIC coding include data from the *Annual Survey of Manufactures* (*ASM*); those in the old Services range include data from the *Services Annual Survey* (*SAS*). Values followed by a 'p' are projections by the editors. Extrapolations are marked by 'e'. Data are the most recent available at this level of detail.

INDICES OF CHANGE

Year	Establishments (number)	Employment (number)	Payroll ($ million)	Revenues ($ million)	Employees per Establishment (number)	Revenues per Establishment ($)	Payroll per Employee ($)
1982	47.8	32.4	18.5	22.0	67.9	46.1	57.1
1987	66.7	61.9	43.7	46.1	92.8	69.0	70.6
1992	84.7	75.3	64.6	87.4	88.9	103.2	85.7
1993	86.0	80.5	71.1	94.2	93.6	109.6	88.3
1994	89.1	86.3	79.5	103.2	96.9	115.8	92.1
1995	92.6	91.5	87.4	109.4	98.7	118.1	95.6
1996	96.3 e	95.7 e	93.7 e	104.7 e	99.4 e	108.7 e	97.9 e
1997	100.0	100.0	100.0	100.0	100.0	100.0	100.0
1998	104.3 p	101.6 p	102.5 p	120.3 p	97.4 p	115.4 p	100.8 p
1999	108.2 p	105.4 p	108.0 p	126.6 p	97.4 p	116.9 p	102.5 p
2000	112.2 p	109.2 p	113.5 p	132.8 p	97.3 p	118.4 p	104.0 p
2001	116.1 p	112.9 p	119.0 p	139.0 p	97.2 p	119.7 p	105.4 p

Sources: Same as General Statistics. The values shown reflect change from the base year, 1997. Values above 100 mean greater than 1997, values below 100 mean less than 1997, and a value of 100 in the 1982-96 or 1998-2001 period means same as 1997. Values followed by a 'p' are projections by the editors; 'e' stands for extrapolation. Data are the most recent available at this level of detail.

SELECTED RATIOS

For 1997	Avg. of Information	Analyzed Industry	Index	For 1997	Avg. of Information	Analyzed Industry	Index
Employees per establishment	6	9	144	Payroll per establishment	126,069	91,573	73
Revenue per establishment	511,622	285,829	56	Payroll as % of revenue	25	32	130
Revenue per employee	81,659	31,642	39	Payroll per employee	20,122	10,137	50

Sources: Same as General Statistics. The 'Average' column represents the average for the industry sector, in 1997, where the currently shown industry is classified. The Index shows the relationship between the Average and the Analyzed Industry. For example, 100 means that they are equal; 500 that the Analyzed Industry is five times the average; 50 means that the Analyzed Industry is half the national average. The abbreviation 'na' is used to show that data are 'not available'.

*Equivalent to SIC 7542.

LEADING COMPANIES   Number shown: **7**   Total sales ($ mil): **548**   Total employment (000): **3.6**

Company Name	Address				CEO Name	Phone	Co. Type	Sales ($ mil)	Empl. (000)
Turtle Wax Inc.	5655 W 73rd St	Bedford Park	IL	60638		708-563-3600	R	280*	1.8
Calibur Carwash Penncoil	2620 Mineral Sprgs	Knoxville	TN	37917	Jose Bared	423-688-0582	S	182*	1.4
Etna Oil Company Inc.	PO Box 429	Ottawa	IL	61350	Jerry Cioni	815-434-0353	R	40*	<0.1
Aqua Care Systems, Inc.	11820 N W 37th	Coral Springs	FL	33065	Norman J Hoskin	954-796-3338	N	26	0.1
Super Wash Inc.	707 Lincoln Way W	Morrison	IL	61270	Robert Black	815-772-2111	R	12*	<0.1
United Petroleum Corp.	PO Box 18080	Knoxville	TN	37928	Joe Bared	305-592-3100	R	6	<0.1
TimeOne Inc.	631 N Stephanie St	Henderson	NV	89014	Daniel Pentelute	801-268-9280	P	1	<0.1

Source: *Ward's Business Directory of U.S. Private and Public Companies*, Volumes 1 and 2, 2000. The company type code used is as follows: P - Public, R - Private, S - Subsidiary, D - Division, J - Joint Venture, A - Affiliate, G - Group, N - Company type not reported. Sales are in millions of dollars, employees are in thousands. An asterisk (*) indicates an estimated sales volume. The symbol < stands for 'less than'. Company names and addresses are truncated, in some cases, to fit into the available space.

LOCATION BY STATE AND REGIONAL CONCENTRATION

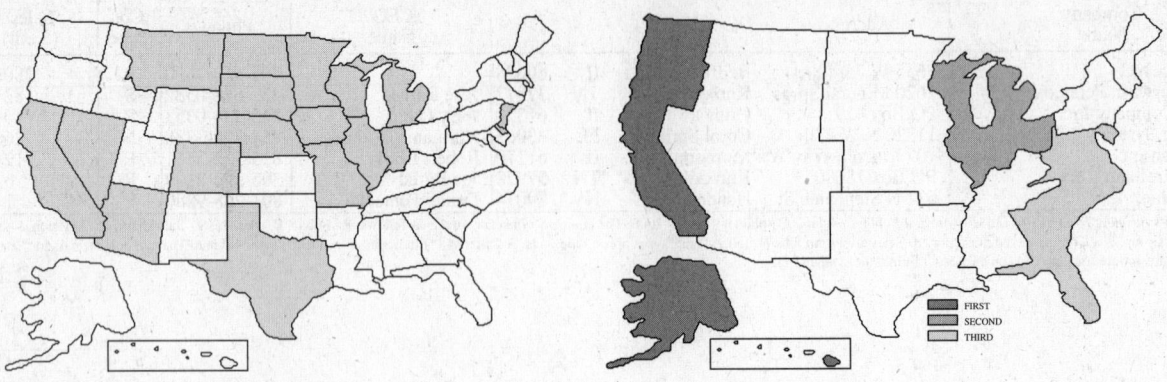

FIRST
SECOND
THIRD

INDUSTRY DATA BY STATE

State	Establishments Total (number)	% of U.S.	Employment Total (number)	% of U.S.	Per Estab.	Payroll Total ($ mil.)	Per Empl. ($)	Revenues Total ($ mil.)	% of U.S.	Per Estab. ($)
California	1,514	11.1	19,503	15.8	13	201.8	10,346	672.4	17.2	444,151
Texas	870	6.4	11,871	9.6	14	123.3	10,383	355.4	9.1	408,537
Illinois	812	5.9	6,103	4.9	8	59.3	9,716	200.9	5.1	247,416
Michigan	669	4.9	5,264	4.3	8	54.5	10,350	192.8	4.9	288,245
Florida	706	5.2	6,180	5.0	9	64.1	10,366	171.3	4.4	242,620
Ohio	676	4.9	5,698	4.6	8	50.6	8,884	158.8	4.1	234,867
Pennsylvania	555	4.1	4,450	3.6	8	45.5	10,226	148.9	3.8	268,223
New York	653	4.8	3,609	2.9	6	39.7	11,010	139.7	3.6	213,953
New Jersey	504	3.7	3,516	2.8	7	50.2	14,273	138.3	3.5	274,399
Indiana	393	2.9	3,202	2.6	8	31.7	9,894	105.6	2.7	268,730
Arizona	285	2.1	3,607	2.9	13	37.2	10,322	101.7	2.6	356,888
Georgia	320	2.3	3,633	2.9	11	34.6	9,514	93.9	2.4	293,312
Massachusetts	265	1.9	1,688	1.4	6	25.4	15,047	86.2	2.2	325,275
North Carolina	386	2.8	3,181	2.6	8	27.8	8,731	86.0	2.2	222,832
Missouri	361	2.6	2,463	2.0	7	26.0	10,549	83.0	2.1	230,014
Wisconsin	271	2.0	3,123	2.5	12	28.9	9,259	78.4	2.0	289,439
Minnesota	221	1.6	3,159	2.6	14	24.0	7,608	71.6	1.8	324,131
Tennessee	297	2.2	2,021	1.6	7	20.5	10,154	71.5	1.8	240,623
Virginia	263	1.9	1,952	1.6	7	22.2	11,370	64.0	1.6	243,312
Washington	298	2.2	1,734	1.4	6	18.8	10,834	61.8	1.6	207,523
Colorado	210	1.5	1,693	1.4	8	18.7	11,033	57.1	1.5	271,938
Maryland	193	1.4	1,926	1.6	10	19.4	10,094	54.8	1.4	283,782
South Carolina	192	1.4	2,026	1.6	11	19.0	9,375	51.0	1.3	265,568
Iowa	229	1.7	1,741	1.4	8	15.2	8,747	50.5	1.3	220,686
Kentucky	204	1.5	1,830	1.5	9	15.3	8,339	49.8	1.3	244,343
Louisiana	146	1.1	1,856	1.5	13	17.2	9,293	48.6	1.2	333,000
Connecticut	185	1.4	1,287	1.0	7	15.0	11,673	47.9	1.2	258,941
Alabama	185	1.4	1,428	1.2	8	13.7	9,609	45.5	1.2	245,892
Oregon	191	1.4	1,398	1.1	7	14.2	10,190	43.9	1.1	230,079
Oklahoma	170	1.2	1,243	1.0	7	11.0	8,866	36.5	0.9	214,588
Arkansas	122	0.9	1,022	0.8	8	11.0	10,765	34.6	0.9	283,352
Kansas	161	1.2	996	0.8	6	9.7	9,753	33.8	0.9	210,000
Nebraska	144	1.1	1,198	1.0	8	10.2	8,498	31.4	0.8	218,354
Nevada	90	0.7	1,111	0.9	12	11.6	10,419	30.3	0.8	336,933
Utah	119	0.9	1,274	1.0	11	9.5	7,485	28.5	0.7	239,723
New Mexico	102	0.7	832	0.7	8	8.5	10,215	24.1	0.6	236,500
Montana	83	0.6	436	0.4	5	4.2	9,713	17.5	0.4	211,361
Idaho	86	0.6	690	0.6	8	5.4	7,767	17.3	0.4	200,942
West Virginia	112	0.8	594	0.5	5	4.9	8,285	16.0	0.4	142,696
New Hampshire	44	0.3	250	0.2	6	3.6	14,404	15.7	0.4	356,000
Delaware	39	0.3	344	0.3	9	5.7	16,686	15.1	0.4	386,692
Mississippi	79	0.6	590	0.5	7	4.6	7,758	14.4	0.3	181,911
Maine	43	0.3	226	0.2	5	2.6	11,372	12.1	0.3	280,953
North Dakota	39	0.3	358	0.3	9	3.5	9,682	10.9	0.3	279,026
South Dakota	51	0.4	450	0.4	9	3.6	8,071	10.7	0.3	210,039
Alaska	24	0.2	124	0.1	5	1.7	13,355	6.7	0.2	279,167
Vermont	25	0.2	112	0.1	4	1.5	13,348	5.9	0.2	236,840
Rhode Island	35	0.3	146	0.1	4	1.6	10,767	5.0	0.1	143,143
Hawaii	21	0.2	142	0.1	7	1.3	9,190	3.5	0.1	165,190
Wyoming	29	0.2	175*	-	-	(D)	-	(D)	-	-
D.C.	11	0.1	175*	-	-	(D)	-	(D)	-	-

Source: 1997 *Economic Census*. The states are in descending order of revenues or establishments (if revenue data are missing for the majority). The symbol (D) appears when data are withheld to prevent disclosure of competitive information. States marked with (D) are sorted by number of establishments. A dash (-) indicates that the data element cannot be calculated. * indicates the midpoint of a range; 175, for example is the range 100-249. Shaded *states* on the state map indicate those states which have proportionately greater representation in the industry than would be indicated by the state's population; the ratio is based on total revenues or number of establishments. Shaded *regions* indicate where the industry is regionally most concentrated.

NAICS 811198 - AUTOMOTIVE REPAIR AND MAINTENANCE NEC

GENERAL STATISTICS

Year	Establishments (number)	Employment (number)	Payroll ($ million)	Revenues ($ million)	Employees per Establishment (number)	Revenues per Establishment ($)	Payroll per Employee ($)
1997	2,652	14,780	274.0	1,087.0	5.6	409,879	18,539

Source: Economic Census of the United States, 1997. This is a newly defined industry. Data for prior years were unavailable at the time of publication but may become available over time.

INDICES OF CHANGE

Year	Establishments (number)	Employment (number)	Payroll ($ million)	Revenues ($ million)	Employees per Establishment (number)	Revenues per Establishment ($)	Payroll per Employee ($)
1997	100.0	100.0	100.0	100.0	100.0	100.0	100.0

Sources: Same as General Statistics. The values shown reflect change from the base year, 1997. Values above 100 mean greater than 1997, values below 100 mean less than 1997, and a value of 100 in the 1982-96 or 1998-2001 period means same as 1997. Values followed by a 'p' are projections by the editors; 'e' stands for extrapolation. Data are the most recent available at this level of detail.

SIC INDUSTRIES RELATED TO NAICS 811198

Each new NAICS code represents an industry that used to be part of an SIC or a part of several SIC industries. Data in this table are shown to provide transitional information for these cases. All available data for the precursor SIC(s) are shown. Even if only a part of an SIC is included in the NAICS, *all* data for the SIC are reproduced. If the SIC industry is not marked as being a part (pt) of the NAICS, the entire industry is embedded in the NAICS data. The SIC composition of the new industry provides some hints of the relative importance of its "ancestors." Data marked with a 'p' are projected. Projections begin with 1982 data. Data earlier than 1990 are not shown but are reflected in the projections.

SIC	Industry	1990	1991	1992	1993	1994	1995	1996	1997
7534	**Tire Retreading & Repair Shops (pt)**								
	Establishments (number)	1,681	1,755	1,845	1,898	1,913	1,552	1,681p	1,661p
	Employment (thousands)	12.9	12.7	12.9	12.9	14.1	10.1	11.8p	11.6p
	Revenues ($ million)	1,283.0	1,293.0	1,382.0	1,509.0	1,676.0	1,800.0	1,865.0	1,980.3p
7549	**Automotive Services, nec (pt)**								
	Establishments (number)	7,856	8,721	10,906	11,269	11,704	12,058	12,470p	13,093p
	Employment (thousands)	54.2	55.9	67.4	71.2	77.1	85.5	85.8p	90.6p
	Revenues ($ million)	-	-	3,402.8	3,589.4p	3,858.4p	4,127.4p	4,396.4p	4,665.4p

Source: Economic Census of the United States, 1992, annual surveys of economic sectors conducted by the Bureau of the Census, and estimates or projections based on the 1982-1992 period; not all data are shown. 'e' marks estimates made by the editors; 'p' indicates projections based on time series. A dash (-) indicates that data for this SIC or year were not available. The abbreviation (pt) next to the industry name indicates that only a part of the industry is present within the NAICS data. If no (pt) is shown, the entire industry is contained within the NAICS data.

SELECTED RATIOS

For 1997	Avg. of Information	Analyzed Industry	Index	For 1997	Avg. of Information	Analyzed Industry	Index
Employees per establishment	6	6	89	Payroll per establishment	126,069	103,318	82
Revenue per establishment	511,622	409,879	80	Payroll as % of revenue	25	25	102
Revenue per employee	81,659	73,545	90	Payroll per employee	20,122	18,539	92

Sources: Same as General Statistics. The 'Average' column represents the average for the industry sector, in 1997, where the currently shown industry is classified. The Index shows the relationship between the Average and the Analyzed Industry. For example, 100 means that they are equal; 500 that the Analyzed Industry is five times the average; 50 means that the Analyzed Industry is half the national average. The abbreviation 'na' is used to show that data are 'not available'.

LEADING COMPANIES   Number shown: **14**   Total sales ($ mil): **846**   Total employment (000): **6.7**

Company Name	Address				CEO Name	Phone	Co. Type	Sales ($ mil)	Empl. (000)
Envirotest Systems Products	7 Kripes Road	East Granby	CT	06026	Terrence P. McKenna	860-653-0881	P	169	1.1
Ziebart International Corp.	PO Box 1290	Troy	MI	48007	Thomas Wolfe	248-588-4100	R	150	0.3
Motor Club of America	95 Rte 17 S	Paramus	NJ	07653	Stephen A Gilbert	201-291-2000	P	131	<0.1
LMS Cadsi	2651 Crosspark Rd	Coralville	IA	52241	Rex Smith	319-626-6700	R	100	0.5
Q Lube Inc.	1385 W 2200 S	Salt Lake City	UT	84119	kevin Ling	801-972-6667	S	80*	1.5
Interstate National Dealer Services	333 Earle Ovington	Uniondale	NY	11553	Cindy S Luby	516-228-8600	P	56	0.2
Industrial Powder Coatings Inc.	PO Box 837	Norwalk	OH	44857	Dale Buhr	419-668-4436	S	48	0.6
Lube Stop Inc.	140 Sheldon Rd	Berea	OH	44017	Jerry Forstner	440-891-2378	R	38*	0.2
American Automobile Association	2040 Market St	Philadelphia	PA	19103	William Clarke	215-864-5000	S	29*	1.6
Grease Monkey Holding Corp.	633 17th Street	Denver	CO	80202	Charles Steinbrueck	303-308-1660	P	20	0.3
Indy Lube Inc.	6515 E 82nd St	Indianapolis	IN	46250	James Yates	317-845-9444	R	12*	0.3
Webber Gage Div.	24500 Detroit Rd	Cleveland	OH	44145		440-835-0001	S	7	<0.1
Cleret Inc.	5331 SW Madison	Portland	OR	97201	Alan Hansen	503-222-9227	R	5	<0.1
Quik Lube Inc.	3109 Apalachee	Tallahassee	FL	32311	Torai Tate	850-656-1111	R	1*	<0.1

Source: *Ward's Business Directory of U.S. Private and Public Companies*, Volumes 1 and 2, 2000. The company type code used is as follows: P - Public, R - Private, S - Subsidiary, D - Division, J - Joint Venture, A - Affiliate, G - Group, N - Company type not reported. Sales are in millions of dollars, employees are in thousands. An asterisk (*) indicates an estimated sales volume. The symbol < stands for 'less than'. Company names and addresses are truncated, in some cases, to fit into the available space.

LOCATION BY STATE AND REGIONAL CONCENTRATION

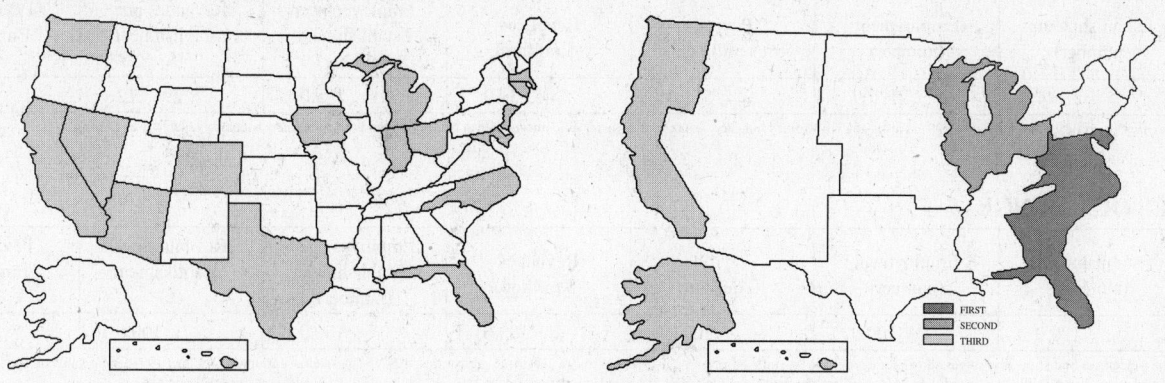

FIRST
SECOND
THIRD

INDUSTRY DATA BY STATE

State	Establishments Total (number)	Establishments % of U.S.	Employment Total (number)	Employment % of U.S.	Employment Per Estab.	Payroll Total ($ mil.)	Payroll Per Empl. ($)	Revenues Total ($ mil.)	Revenues % of U.S.	Revenues Per Estab. ($)
California	319	12.0	1,590	10.8	5	39.0	24,516	150.2	13.8	470,994
Texas	327	12.3	1,249	8.5	4	23.1	18,513	97.4	9.0	297,865
Florida	231	8.7	883	6.0	4	15.1	17,144	81.6	7.5	353,156
New York	112	4.2	437	3.0	4	11.0	25,261	64.4	5.9	575,009
New Jersey	84	3.2	520	3.5	6	15.7	30,140	61.1	5.6	727,083
Ohio	131	4.9	917	6.2	7	15.1	16,486	55.2	5.1	421,107
Michigan	90	3.4	966	6.5	11	18.6	19,290	54.2	5.0	602,411
Illinois	103	3.9	597	4.0	6	9.9	16,499	39.2	3.6	380,650
Arizona	60	2.3	641	4.3	11	9.7	15,078	38.0	3.5	633,017
Colorado	56	2.1	531	3.6	9	7.4	13,927	35.5	3.3	633,161
North Carolina	73	2.8	480	3.2	7	11.3	23,635	34.8	3.2	476,767
Massachusetts	28	1.1	332	2.2	12	10.4	31,280	29.3	2.7	1,044,964
Indiana	67	2.5	419	2.8	6	8.2	19,549	28.8	2.7	430,299
Georgia	80	3.0	420	2.8	5	7.2	17,250	28.6	2.6	357,063
Maryland	50	1.9	571	3.9	11	8.9	15,560	26.4	2.4	527,380
Connecticut	45	1.7	611	4.1	14	5.5	9,051	26.0	2.4	578,156
Washington	52	2.0	383	2.6	7	6.1	16,003	23.1	2.1	444,058
Pennsylvania	68	2.6	243	1.6	4	4.9	20,165	19.3	1.8	283,882
Minnesota	44	1.7	435	2.9	10	3.4	7,915	17.5	1.6	396,909
Wisconsin	42	1.6	331	2.2	8	4.2	12,792	17.4	1.6	414,500
Iowa	26	1.0	151	1.0	6	3.2	21,331	14.0	1.3	539,077
South Carolina	34	1.3	214	1.4	6	3.0	13,818	11.3	1.0	332,441
Hawaii	19	0.7	173	1.2	9	3.6	21,087	10.6	1.0	555,842
Virginia	27	1.0	179	1.2	7	3.0	16,966	10.6	1.0	391,519
Louisiana	50	1.9	118	0.8	2	2.4	20,271	10.5	1.0	210,520
Nevada	25	0.9	115	0.8	5	2.4	21,296	10.5	1.0	421,280
Kentucky	28	1.1	216	1.5	8	4.4	20,472	10.2	0.9	365,107
Tennessee	44	1.7	154	1.0	4	1.9	12,065	9.5	0.9	216,318
Missouri	41	1.5	106	0.7	3	1.9	17,481	9.4	0.9	229,122
Oklahoma	44	1.7	117	0.8	3	1.8	15,803	8.8	0.8	198,864
Alabama	33	1.2	97	0.7	3	1.7	17,412	7.3	0.7	219,879
Utah	19	0.7	121	0.8	6	2.3	19,083	6.3	0.6	333,579
Mississippi	25	0.9	49	0.3	2	0.8	16,265	5.0	0.5	198,080
Oregon	15	0.6	41	0.3	3	1.1	25,951	4.8	0.4	322,133
Arkansas	26	1.0	43	0.3	2	0.7	17,302	4.5	0.4	171,500
Nebraska	13	0.5	33	0.2	3	0.6	17,727	4.4	0.4	339,615
Kansas	31	1.2	55	0.4	2	0.9	15,818	4.1	0.4	133,613
New Mexico	21	0.8	38	0.3	2	0.8	20,447	3.1	0.3	145,286
West Virginia	9	0.3	36	0.2	4	0.7	18,583	2.7	0.2	301,667
Idaho	14	0.5	43	0.3	3	0.5	11,163	1.8	0.2	129,714
Alaska	8	0.3	25	0.2	3	0.5	18,200	1.7	0.2	217,250
New Hampshire	6	0.2	14	0.1	2	0.2	16,286	1.5	0.1	258,000
South Dakota	9	0.3	16	0.1	2	0.3	21,375	1.5	0.1	166,111
Rhode Island	6	0.2	15	0.1	3	0.2	16,533	1.4	0.1	240,167
Montana	7	0.3	15	0.1	2	0.1	9,467	1.0	0.1	138,857
Vermont	3	0.1	13	0.1	4	0.2	18,154	0.8	0.1	270,000
Delaware	2	0.1	10*	-	-	(D)	-	(D)	-	-
Maine	2	0.1	10*	-	-	(D)	-	(D)	-	-
D.C.	1	-	10*	-	-	(D)	-	(D)	-	-
North Dakota	1	-	10*	-	-	(D)	-	(D)	-	-
Wyoming	1	-	10*	-	-	(D)	-	(D)	-	-

Source: 1997 *Economic Census*. The states are in descending order of revenues or establishments (if revenue data are missing for the majority). The symbol (D) appears when data are withheld to prevent disclosure of competitive information. States marked with (D) are sorted by number of establishments. A dash (-) indicates that the data element cannot be calculated. * indicates the midpoint of a range; 175, for example is the range 100-249. Shaded *states* on the state map indicate those states which have proportionately greater representation in the industry than would be indicated by the state's population; the ratio is based on total revenues or number of establishments. Shaded *regions* indicate where the industry is regionally most concentrated.

NAICS 811211 - CONSUMER ELECTRONICS REPAIR AND MAINTENANCE

GENERAL STATISTICS

Year	Establishments (number)	Employment (number)	Payroll ($ million)	Revenues ($ million)	Employees per Establishment (number)	Revenues per Establishment ($)	Payroll per Employee ($)
1997	5,144	25,709	556.0	1,534.0	5.0	298,212	21,627

Source: Economic Census of the United States, 1997. This is a newly defined industry. Data for prior years were unavailable at the time of publication but may become available over time.

INDICES OF CHANGE

Year	Establishments (number)	Employment (number)	Payroll ($ million)	Revenues ($ million)	Employees per Establishment (number)	Revenues per Establishment ($)	Payroll per Employee ($)
1997	100.0	100.0	100.0	100.0	100.0	100.0	100.0

Sources: Same as General Statistics. The values shown reflect change from the base year, 1997. Values above 100 mean greater than 1997, values below 100 mean less than 1997, and a value of 100 in the 1982-96 or 1998-2001 period means same as 1997. Values followed by a 'p' are projections by the editors; 'e' stands for extrapolation. Data are the most recent available at this level of detail.

SIC INDUSTRIES RELATED TO NAICS 811211

Each new NAICS code represents an industry that used to be part of an SIC or a part of several SIC industries. Data in this table are shown to provide transitional information for these cases. All available data for the precursor SIC(s) are shown. Even if only a part of an SIC is included in the NAICS, *all* data for the SIC are reproduced. If the SIC industry is not marked as being a part (pt) of the NAICS, the entire industry is embedded in the NAICS data. The SIC composition of the new industry provides some hints of the relative importance of its "ancestors." Data marked with a 'p' are projected. Projections begin with 1982 data. Data earlier than 1990 are not shown but are reflected in the projections.

SIC	Industry	1990	1991	1992	1993	1994	1995	1996	1997
7622	**Radio & Television Repair (pt)**								
	Establishments (number)	5,548	5,598	6,038	5,855	5,611	5,351	5,011p	4,844p
	Employment (thousands)	33.9	31.6	29.4	28.2	28.4	29.0	29.2p	29.0p
	Revenues ($ million)	2,292.0	2,190.0	2,297.0	2,454.0	2,456.0	2,638.0	2,752.0	2,770.6p
7629	**Electrical Repair Shops, nec (pt)**								
	Establishments (number)	8,133	8,605	11,364	11,457	11,204	11,005	11,451p	11,797p
	Employment (thousands)	58.6	60.9	108.8	109.7	103.0	99.2	107.5p	112.9p
	Revenues ($ million)	-	-	6,648.1	6,746.8p	7,220.7p	7,694.6p	8,168.5p	8,642.4p
7699	**Repair Services, nec (pt)**								
	Establishments (number)	27,822	29,303	34,103	34,618	34,136	34,391	35,001p	35,792p
	Employment (thousands)	181.0	181.4	191.0	201.5	207.4	220.2	219.6p	226.2p
	Revenues ($ million)	-	-	15,059.4	15,563.6p	16,427.9p	17,292.2p	18,156.5p	19,020.8p

Source: Economic Census of the United States, 1992, annual surveys of economic sectors conducted by the Bureau of the Census, and estimates or projections based on the 1982-1992 period; not all data are shown. 'e' marks estimates made by the editors; 'p' indicates projections based on time series. A dash (-) indicates that data for this SIC or year were not available. The abbreviation (pt) next to the industry name indicates that only a part of the industry is present within the NAICS data. If no (pt) is shown, the entire industry is contained within the NAICS data.

SELECTED RATIOS

For 1997	Avg. of Information	Analyzed Industry	Index	For 1997	Avg. of Information	Analyzed Industry	Index
Employees per establishment	6	5	80	Payroll per establishment	126,069	108,087	86
Revenue per establishment	511,622	298,212	58	Payroll as % of revenue	25	36	147
Revenue per employee	81,659	59,668	73	Payroll per employee	20,122	21,627	107

Sources: Same as General Statistics. The 'Average' column represents the average for the industry sector, in 1997, where the currently shown industry is classified. The Index shows the relationship between the Average and the Analyzed Industry. For example, 100 means that they are equal; 500 that the Analyzed Industry is five times the average; 50 means that the Analyzed Industry is half the national average. The abbreviation 'na' is used to show that data are 'not available'.

LEADING COMPANIES   Number shown: **9**   Total sales ($ mil): **205**   Total employment (000): **1.2**

Company Name	Address				CEO Name	Phone	Co. Type	Sales ($ mil)	Empl. (000)
Contec L.P.	1023 State St	Schenectady	NY	12307	Frank Hickey	518-382-8000	R	65*	0.5
Technicar Inc.	450 Commerce Blvd	Oldsmar	FL	34677	Jim Duffy	813-855-0022	R	42*	0.2
Audiovisual Inc.	6233 Bury Dr	Eden Prairie	MN	55346	Joe Stoebner	612-258-6360	R	35	0.1
Electronic Maintenance Inc.	8900 S Choctaw Dr	Baton Rouge	LA	70815	Janice H Pellar	225-925-8900	R	26*	<0.1
Electra-Sound Inc.	5260 Commerce	Parma	OH	44130	Robert Masa	216-433-9600	R	18*	0.1
Markey's Audio-Visual Inc.	2909 S Meridian St	Indianapolis	IN	46225	Chuck Markey	317-783-1155	R	13*	0.2
CSSI Corp.	905 Palo Pinto St	Weatherford	TX	76086	Charles H Beard	817-596-8767	R	4*	<0.1
Lesh Radio Systems Inc.	5055 Covington	Memphis	TN	38134	Henry Lesh Jr	901-388-5374	R	1*	<0.1
Tele-Vue Service Company Inc.	947 Federal Blvd	Denver	CO	80204	Randy Prade	303-623-3330	R	1	<0.1

Source: *Ward's Business Directory of U.S. Private and Public Companies*, Volumes 1 and 2, 2000. The company type code used is as follows: P - Public, R - Private, S - Subsidiary, D - Division, J - Joint Venture, A - Affiliate, G - Group, N - Company type not reported. Sales are in millions of dollars, employees are in thousands. An asterisk (*) indicates an estimated sales volume. The symbol < stands for 'less than'. Company names and addresses are truncated, in some cases, to fit into the available space.

LOCATION BY STATE AND REGIONAL CONCENTRATION

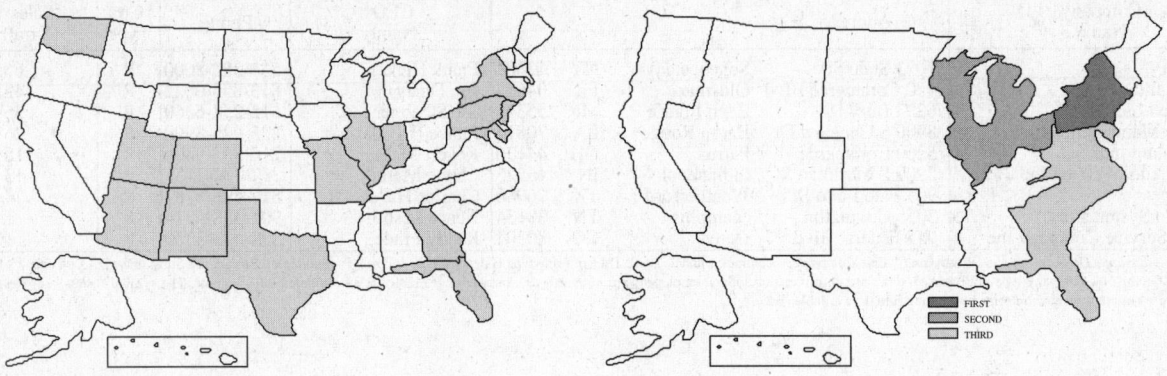

FIRST
SECOND
THIRD

INDUSTRY DATA BY STATE

State	Establishments Total (number)	% of U.S.	Employment Total (number)	% of U.S.	Per Estab.	Payroll Total ($ mil.)	Per Empl. ($)	Revenues Total ($ mil.)	% of U.S.	Per Estab. ($)
California	574	11.2	3,039	11.8	5	69.5	22,871	183.0	11.9	318,808
New York	341	6.6	1,722	6.7	5	46.9	27,225	127.2	8.3	372,883
Texas	353	6.9	1,972	7.7	6	45.7	23,181	123.5	8.1	349,929
Illinois	215	4.2	1,456	5.7	7	36.2	24,837	100.2	6.5	465,926
Florida	406	7.9	1,891	7.4	5	38.9	20,576	97.4	6.3	239,825
New Jersey	187	3.6	984	3.8	5	23.7	24,046	80.6	5.3	431,262
Pennsylvania	191	3.7	1,228	4.8	6	29.0	23,625	77.5	5.1	405,702
Ohio	194	3.8	1,082	4.2	6	21.2	19,565	60.0	3.9	309,284
Michigan	171	3.3	913	3.6	5	18.1	19,783	56.9	3.7	332,836
Georgia	144	2.8	721	2.8	5	18.3	25,326	42.4	2.8	294,382
Indiana	98	1.9	740	2.9	8	12.8	17,272	37.9	2.5	386,357
Maryland	103	2.0	598	2.3	6	14.1	23,548	34.8	2.3	338,301
Missouri	123	2.4	716	2.8	6	13.3	18,615	34.4	2.2	279,309
Washington	112	2.2	560	2.2	5	12.2	21,750	33.5	2.2	299,018
North Carolina	145	2.8	587	2.3	4	11.3	19,261	32.3	2.1	222,676
Massachusetts	88	1.7	507	2.0	6	12.8	25,286	32.0	2.1	363,409
Arizona	105	2.0	595	2.3	6	12.0	20,212	31.6	2.1	300,562
Virginia	144	2.8	577	2.2	4	11.2	19,440	26.8	1.7	185,924
Colorado	96	1.9	444	1.7	5	9.2	20,669	26.1	1.7	271,531
Wisconsin	97	1.9	404	1.6	4	6.6	16,218	24.4	1.6	251,619
Minnesota	100	1.9	354	1.4	4	7.1	19,941	21.8	1.4	218,010
Tennessee	98	1.9	379	1.5	4	7.6	20,177	19.6	1.3	199,612
Louisiana	100	1.9	399	1.6	4	7.3	18,331	18.9	1.2	189,340
Connecticut	64	1.2	245	1.0	4	6.1	24,702	17.8	1.2	278,094
Kentucky	64	1.2	312	1.2	5	6.8	21,724	16.9	1.1	264,172
Alabama	92	1.8	335	1.3	4	5.2	15,549	16.4	1.1	178,543
Oregon	58	1.1	317	1.2	5	5.5	17,227	15.1	1.0	260,138
Oklahoma	55	1.1	260	1.0	5	4.5	17,192	14.8	1.0	269,255
Utah	48	0.9	263	1.0	5	5.4	20,529	12.6	0.8	262,104
Iowa	51	1.0	177	0.7	3	3.2	18,316	12.3	0.8	241,706
Arkansas	52	1.0	256	1.0	5	4.7	18,293	11.9	0.8	229,673
Kansas	55	1.1	205	0.8	4	3.4	16,805	10.9	0.7	198,618
South Carolina	74	1.4	242	0.9	3	3.6	14,744	10.9	0.7	147,176
New Mexico	38	0.7	138	0.5	4	3.2	23,181	10.5	0.7	276,105
Nebraska	32	0.6	198	0.8	6	3.6	18,141	9.8	0.6	305,125
Nevada	31	0.6	85	0.3	3	1.8	20,588	8.3	0.5	266,161
West Virginia	20	0.4	80	0.3	4	1.3	16,187	5.5	0.4	274,500
Mississippi	41	0.8	98	0.4	2	1.8	18,122	5.3	0.3	129,390
Idaho	24	0.5	90	0.4	4	1.2	13,478	3.9	0.3	162,292
New Hampshire	25	0.5	70	0.3	3	1.5	20,714	3.5	0.2	140,000
Montana	17	0.3	54	0.2	3	0.8	15,019	2.8	0.2	166,706
Maine	17	0.3	47	0.2	3	0.7	14,021	2.3	0.2	137,588
South Dakota	12	0.2	34	0.1	3	0.5	13,471	1.8	0.1	150,417
Hawaii	10	0.2	28	0.1	3	0.4	13,964	1.5	0.1	148,300
Rhode Island	21	0.4	60*	-	-	(D)	-	(D)	-	-
Delaware	20	0.4	60*	-	-	(D)	-	(D)	-	-
North Dakota	9	0.2	60*	-	-	(D)	-	(D)	-	-
Vermont	9	0.2	60*	-	-	(D)	-	(D)	-	-
Wyoming	8	0.2	10*	-	-	(D)	-	(D)	-	-
Alaska	7	0.1	10*	-	-	(D)	-	(D)	-	-
D.C.	5	0.1	60*	-	-	(D)	-	(D)	-	-

Source: 1997 Economic Census. The states are in descending order of revenues or establishments (if revenue data are missing for the majority). The symbol (D) appears when data are withheld to prevent disclosure of competitive information. States marked with (D) are sorted by number of establishments. A dash (-) indicates that the data element cannot be calculated. * indicates the midpoint of a range; 175, for example is the range 100-249. Shaded states on the state map indicate those states which have proportionately greater representation in the industry than would be indicated by the state's population; the ratio is based on total revenues or number of establishments. Shaded regions indicate where the industry is regionally most concentrated.

NAICS 811212 - COMPUTER AND OFFICE MACHINE REPAIR AND MAINTENANCE

GENERAL STATISTICS

Year	Establishments (number)	Employment (number)	Payroll ($ million)	Revenues ($ million)	Employees per Establishment (number)	Revenues per Establishment ($)	Payroll per Employee ($)
1997	7,729	70,432	2,546.0	8,502.0	9.1	1,100,013	36,148

Source: Economic Census of the United States, 1997. This is a newly defined industry. Data for prior years were unavailable at the time of publication but may become available over time.

INDICES OF CHANGE

Year	Establishments (number)	Employment (number)	Payroll ($ million)	Revenues ($ million)	Employees per Establishment (number)	Revenues per Establishment ($)	Payroll per Employee ($)
1997	100.0	100.0	100.0	100.0	100.0	100.0	100.0

Sources: Same as General Statistics. The values shown reflect change from the base year, 1997. Values above 100 mean greater than 1997, values below 100 mean less than 1997, and a value of 100 in the 1982-96 or 1998-2001 period means same as 1997. Values followed by a 'p' are projections by the editors; 'e' stands for extrapolation. Data are the most recent available at this level of detail.

SIC INDUSTRIES RELATED TO NAICS 811212

Each new NAICS code represents an industry that used to be part of an SIC or a part of several SIC industries. Data in this table are shown to provide transitional information for these cases. All available data for the precursor SIC(s) are shown. Even if only a part of an SIC is included in the NAICS, *all* data for the SIC are reproduced. If the SIC industry is not marked as being a part (pt) of the NAICS, the entire industry is embedded in the NAICS data. The SIC composition of the new industry provides some hints of the relative importance of its "ancestors." Data marked with a 'p' are projected. Projections begin with 1982 data. Data earlier than 1990 are not shown but are reflected in the projections.

SIC	Industry	1990	1991	1992	1993	1994	1995	1996	1997
7378	**Computer Maintenance & Repair (pt)**								
	Establishments (number)	3,294	3,611	5,041	4,876	4,846	4,887	5,241p	5,464p
	Employment (thousands)	53.2	54.0	63.1	62.5	56.4	63.3	63.9p	65.5p
	Revenues ($ million)	7,000.0	6,919.0	7,660.0	8,291.0	9,277.0	10,678.0	12,040.0	12,302.9p
7629	**Electrical Repair Shops, nec (pt)**								
	Establishments (number)	8,133	8,605	11,364	11,457	11,204	11,005	11,451p	11,797p
	Employment (thousands)	58.6	60.9	108.8	109.7	103.0	99.2	107.5p	112.9p
	Revenues ($ million)	-	-	6,648.1	6,746.8p	7,220.7p	7,694.6p	8,168.5p	8,642.4p
7699	**Repair Services, nec (pt)**								
	Establishments (number)	27,822	29,303	34,103	34,618	34,136	34,391	35,001p	35,792p
	Employment (thousands)	181.0	181.4	191.0	201.5	207.4	220.2	219.6p	226.2p
	Revenues ($ million)	-	-	15,059.4	15,563.6p	16,427.9p	17,292.2p	18,156.5p	19,020.8p

Source: Economic Census of the United States, 1992, annual surveys of economic sectors conducted by the Bureau of the Census, and estimates or projections based on the 1982-1992 period; not all data are shown. 'e' marks estimates made by the editors; 'p' indicates projections based on time series. A dash (-) indicates that data for this SIC or year were not available. The abbreviation (pt) next to the industry name indicates that only a part of the industry is present within the NAICS data. If no (pt) is shown, the entire industry is contained within the NAICS data.

SELECTED RATIOS

For 1997	Avg. of Information	Analyzed Industry	Index	For 1997	Avg. of Information	Analyzed Industry	Index
Employees per establishment	6	9	145	Payroll per establishment	126,069	329,409	261
Revenue per establishment	511,622	1,100,013	215	Payroll as % of revenue	25	30	122
Revenue per employee	81,659	120,712	148	Payroll per employee	20,122	36,148	180

Sources: Same as General Statistics. The 'Average' column represents the average for the industry sector, in 1997, where the currently shown industry is classified. The Index shows the relationship between the Average and the Analyzed Industry. For example, 100 means that they are equal; 500 that the Analyzed Industry is five times the average; 50 means that the Analyzed Industry is half the national average. The abbreviation 'na' is used to show that data are 'not available'.

LEADING COMPANIES   Number shown: **75**   Total sales ($ mil): **38,796**   Total employment (000): **93.4**

Company Name	Address				CEO Name	Phone	Co. Type	Sales ($ mil)	Empl. (000)
Analytical Computer Services	4202 Directors Row	Houston	TX	77092	Frank H. Trifilio	713-681-0039	R	18,259	<0.1
CompUSA Inc.	14951 N Dallas	Dallas	TX	75240	Harold Compton	972-982-4000	P	6,321	19.7
NCR Corp.	1700 S Patterson	Dayton	OH	45479	Lars Nyberg	937-445-5000	P	6,196	32.8
SunService Div.	2550 Garcia Ave	Mountain View	CA	94043	Lawrence W Hambly	650-960-1300	D	2,581*	6.5
Computer City	100 Throckmorton	Fort Worth	TX	76102	Nathan Morton	817-878-6900	D	1,904*	7.0
DecisionOne Corp.	50 E Swedesford Rd	Frazer	PA	19355	Peter Grauer	610-296-6000	S	726	5.1
Sykes Enterprises Inc.	100 N Tampa St	Tampa	FL	33602	David L Grimes	813-274-1000	P	469	10.8
Medical Manager Corp.	669 River Dr	Elmwood Park	NJ	07407	John Kang	201-703-3400	P	258	2.5
PC Service Source Inc.	2350 Valley View	Dallas	TX	75234	Avery More	972-421-4000	P	161	0.9
Polyphase Corp.	4800 Broadway St	Addison	TX	75001	James Radius	972-386-0101	P	158	0.9
Valtron Technologies Inc.	28309 Av Crocker	Valencia	CA	91355	Steve Nover	661-257-0333	S	145*	0.1
ComputerWare	605 W California	Sunnyvale	CA	94086	Ron Dupler	408-328-1000	R	110*	0.2
Tekgraf Inc.	980 Corporate Wood	Vernon Hills	IL	60061	William M Rychel	847-913-5888	P	99	0.2
Law Cypress Distributing	5883 Eden Park Pl	San Jose	CA	95138	David Law	408-363-4700	R	96*	<0.1
Cerplex Group Inc.	111 Pacifica Ave	Irvine	CA	92618	Richard Allston	949-754-5300	P	93	0.8
Parts Now! Inc.	3517 W Beltline	Madison	WI	53713	David Reinke	608-276-8688	R	88*	0.1
CRA Inc.	11011 N 23rd Ave	Phoenix	AZ	85029		602-944-1548	S	79*	<0.1
Magnetic Data Inc.	6754 Shady Oak Rd	Eden Prairie	MN	55344		612-941-0453	R	73	0.6
Dunn Computer Corp.	1306 Squire Ct	Sterling	VA	20166	Thomas Dunn	703-450-0400	P	67	0.2
Sentinel Technologies Inc.	2550 Warrenville Rd	Downers Grove	IL	60515	Dennis Hoelzer	630-769-4300	R	62	0.7
Vital Network Services L.L.C.	PO Box 1299	Middlebury	CT	06762	Phillip John Woods	203-758-1811	S	52	0.4
InaCom Information Systems Inc.	393 Inverness Dr S	Englewood	CO	80112		303-754-5004	D	45*	0.2
Maintech Div.	39 Paterson Ave	Wallington	NJ	07057		973-614-1700	D	44*	0.2
Federal Systems Div.	2 Chokecherry Rd	Rockville	MD	20850	Van Aggelakos	301-212-5000	D	43*	0.2
Alpha Systems Lab Inc.	17712 Mitchell N	Irvine	CA	92614	Rose Hwang	949-622-0688	R	42*	<0.1
StarTeck Inc.	One Meca Way	Norcross	GA	30093	Andrew F Lewis	770-614-0070	R	35	<0.1
Amtek Computer Services	509 W Terrance Dr	San Dimas	CA	91773	Alan Gibson	909-592-0012	R	29*	<0.1
C.E. Services Inc.	2895 113th St	Grand Prairie	TX	75050	Larry Fillmer	972-339-6000	S	27*	0.1
IPC Technologies Inc.	7200 Glen Forest Dr	Richmond	VA	23226	Ken Banks	804-285-9300	R	27	0.3
Integra Technologies	3450 N Rock Rd	Wichita	KS	67226	Joe Holt	408-254-8260	R	26*	0.1
Technical & Scientific Application	2040 W S Houst	Houston	TX	77043	William C Smith	713-935-1500	R	26*	<0.1
WebAccess	2573 Midpoint Dr	Fort Collins	CO	80525	Wiley E Prentice	970-221-2555	P	26	<0.1
US Computer Group Inc.	4 Dubon Ct	Farmingdale	NY	11735	Stephen Davies	516-755-9400	R	25*	0.2
Ascent Logic Corp.	180 Rose Orchard	San Jose	CA	95134	Michel Berty	408-943-0630	R	24*	0.1
Pulau Electronics Corp.	12423 Research	Orlando	FL	32826		407-380-9191	R	22	0.2
AR Industries Inc.	3203 S Shannon St	Santa Ana	CA	92704	Rod Hosilyk	714-434-8600	R	19*	<0.1
Omni Data Inc.	2500 Townsgate Rd	Westlake Village	CA	91361	Larry McGovern	805-371-4400	D	19*	<0.1
All-Tech Investment Group	160 Summit Ave	Montvale	NJ	07645	Harvey Houtkin	201-782-0200	R	18	0.1
PC Professional Inc.	1615 Webster St	Oakland	CA	94612	Daniel Sanguinetti	510-465-5700	R	18	<0.1
CNS Inc. (Denville, New Jersey)	100 Ford Rd	Denville	NJ	07834		973-625-4056	R	16	0.1
Reynolds and Reynolds BSD Div.	1555 Valwood	Carrollton	TX	75006		972-243-4343	D	16	<0.1
Accram Inc.	2901 W Clarendon	Phoenix	AZ	85017	Robert Daquilante	602-264-0288	R	14*	0.1
PB Inc.	4615 Hawkins NE	Albuquerque	NM	87109	Filiberto Pacheco	505-296-4188	R	13*	<0.1
WPI Husky Technology	18167 US 19 N	Clearwater	FL	33764	Tom Stegner	727-530-4141	S	13*	<0.1
Eakins Associates Inc.	67 E Evelyn Ave	Mountain View	CA	94041	Gil Eakins	650-969-5109	R	12*	0.1
Peripheral Computer Support Inc.	44131 Nobel Dr	Fremont	CA	94538	Tu Nguyen	408-428-6420	R	11*	0.2
International Computers	18310 Mont Vil	Gaithersburg	MD	20879	David Y Sohn	301-948-0200	R	10*	0.1
Development Through Self	6679-P Barbera	Elkridge	MD	21075	Sally G Smith	410-579-4508	R	9	<0.1
Amisys Inc. (Denver, Colorado)	12287 Pennsylvania	Denver	CO	80241	Bryan Near	303-450-7700	R	9	<0.1
InterTech Computer Products Inc.	3702 E Roeser Rd	Phoenix	AZ	85040	Sharon Jalosm	602-437-0035	R	9	<0.1
MicroAge Softwaire Centre	800 Howe Ave	Sacramento	CA	95825	Ann Johnson	916-925-3337	R	8*	<0.1
Contemporary Computer Services	200 Knickerbocker	Bohemia	NY	11716	John R Riconda	516-563-8880	R	8*	0.1
Jacobson Computer Inc.	5610 Monroe St	Sylvania	OH	43560	Gary Jacobson	419-885-0082	R	8*	<0.1
Jadtec Computer Group	1520 W Yale Ave	Orange	CA	92867	John A Dieball	714-637-2900	R	8*	<0.1
Tryonics Inc.	8 Merrill Ind Dr	Hampton	NH	03842	Stephen G Bartlett	603-926-1122	R	8	<0.1
U.S. Computer Group Inc.	4 Dubon Ct	Farmingdale	NY	11735	Alan Andrus	516-755-9400	R	8*	0.1
Best Computer Consultants Inc.	8595 College Blvd	Overland Park	KS	66210	Kannan Srinivasan	913-469-8400	R	7	0.1
M-Cubed Information Systems Inc	PO Box 2093	Kensington	MD	20895	Tyrone Austin	301-984-0255	R	7*	<0.1
New Dimensions Service	2440 Stanwell Dr	Concord	CA	94520	Go Sugiura	925-356-5600	R	7*	<0.1
TransCore	8158 Adams Dr	South Hanover	PA		John Worthington	717-561-2400	S	7*	<0.1
ABS Associates Inc.	2100 Golf Rd	Roll Meadows	IL	60008	Rosemarie Mitchell	847-437-8700	R	6	<0.1
Clare Computer Solutions Inc.	2580 Ramon Valy	San Ramon	CA	94583	Anthony Barone	925-277-0690	R	6*	<0.1
Comp and Soft Computers Inc.	1834 Craig Rd	St. Louis	MO	63101	Gil Bashani	314-205-9600	R	6*	<0.1
LaserAll Corp.	485 Seaport Ct	Redwood City	CA	94063	Bill Warner	650-364-3000	R	6	<0.1
Aero Simulation Inc.	PO Box 290357	Tampa	FL	33687	Joseph A Fernandez	813-628-4447	R	5	<0.1
Binghamton Simulator Inc.	151 Court St	Binghamton	NY	13901	John Morelli	607-722-6177	R	5	<0.1
Cameron Computers Inc.	28 State St	Pittsford	NY	14534	Joseph Cameron	716-427-8190	R	5	<0.1
Integrated Data Systems Inc.	23875 Ventura Blvd	Calabasas	CA	91302	Ann Marie Michael	818-223-3344	R	5*	<0.1
LANCOMM	1810 14th St	Santa Monica	CA	90404	Fane Joseph	310-396-1100	R	5	<0.1
Syracuse Computer Store Inc.	2780 Erie Blvd E	Syracuse	NY	13224	Thomas Karkowski	315-446-5005	R	5*	<0.1
Chip Inc.	25322 Rye Canyon	Valencia	CA	91355		805-295-8900	R	4	<0.1
Tekserve Corp.	155 W 23rd St	New York	NY	10011	David Lerner	212-929-3645	R	4	<0.1
Attorney Software Inc.	742 Washington	Marina Del Rey	CA	90292	Eric Jackson	310-578-9200	R	4*	<0.1
Computer Guys Inc.	1818 Gilbreth Rd	Burlingame	CA	94010	Caroline Oung	650-692-6888	R	4*	<0.1
Computer One Inc.	1601 Randolph S E	Albuquerque	NM	87106	Carrie Roberts	505-243-9282	R	4*	<0.1

Source: Ward's Business Directory of U.S. Private and Public Companies, Volumes 1 and 2, 2000. The company type code used is as follows: P - Public, R - Private, S - Subsidiary, D - Division, J - Joint Venture, A - Affiliate, G - Group, N - Company type not reported. Sales are in millions of dollars, employees are in thousands. An asterisk (*) indicates an estimated sales volume. The symbol < stands for 'less than'. Company names and addresses are truncated, in some cases, to fit into the available space.

LOCATION BY STATE AND REGIONAL CONCENTRATION

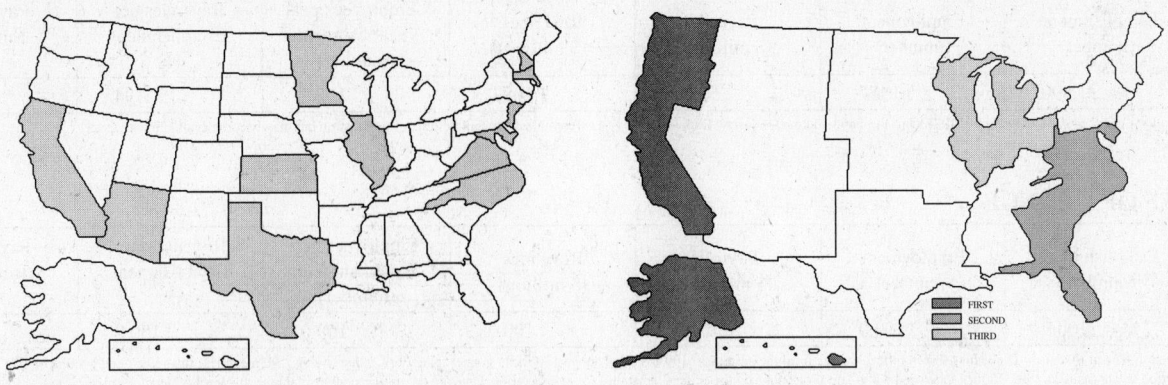

FIRST
SECOND
THIRD

INDUSTRY DATA BY STATE

State	Establishments Total (number)	% of U.S.	Employment Total (number)	% of U.S.	Per Estab.	Payroll Total ($ mil.)	Per Empl. ($)	Revenues Total ($ mil.)	% of U.S.	Per Estab. ($)
California	1,053	13.6	13,190	18.7	13	480.6	36,434	1,484.2	17.5	1,409,459
Texas	610	7.9	6,261	8.9	10	211.9	33,847	715.6	8.4	1,173,190
Illinois	357	4.6	3,443	4.9	10	146.1	42,421	502.5	5.9	1,407,524
New York	464	6.0	3,508	5.0	8	148.7	42,385	490.0	5.8	1,056,011
Virginia	262	3.4	2,566	3.6	10	96.2	37,506	405.7	4.8	1,548,496
Florida	581	7.5	3,334	4.7	6	110.5	33,153	403.8	4.7	695,077
Massachusetts	211	2.7	3,503	5.0	17	156.2	44,600	373.4	4.4	1,769,839
Pennsylvania	280	3.6	2,890	4.1	10	114.4	39,573	369.4	4.3	1,319,139
New Jersey	287	3.7	2,240	3.2	8	93.1	41,546	300.2	3.5	1,045,864
Maryland	174	2.3	2,261	3.2	13	90.3	39,925	290.3	3.4	1,668,368
Ohio	279	3.6	2,612	3.7	9	86.1	32,962	266.6	3.1	955,674
Minnesota	123	1.6	3,259	4.6	26	120.2	36,894	259.5	3.1	2,109,366
North Carolina	199	2.6	1,469	2.1	7	48.4	32,929	244.3	2.9	1,227,704
Arizona	128	1.7	1,264	1.8	10	45.5	36,032	225.5	2.7	1,762,062
Georgia	250	3.2	1,994	2.8	8	76.5	38,386	220.3	2.6	881,044
Michigan	202	2.6	1,083	1.5	5	36.0	33,225	162.1	1.9	802,639
Tennessee	138	1.8	1,323	1.9	10	40.2	30,381	146.6	1.7	1,062,536
Washington	149	1.9	976	1.4	7	33.4	34,186	134.3	1.6	901,228
Indiana	153	2.0	1,296	1.8	8	34.3	26,458	126.4	1.5	826,281
Kansas	91	1.2	802	1.1	9	29.5	36,789	121.4	1.4	1,333,956
Alabama	108	1.4	675	1.0	6	21.5	31,916	120.8	1.4	1,118,787
Wisconsin	96	1.2	751	1.1	8	26.3	34,967	115.5	1.4	1,202,635
Oklahoma	113	1.5	982	1.4	9	28.7	29,225	106.1	1.2	939,027
Connecticut	83	1.1	684	1.0	8	32.6	47,620	104.1	1.2	1,254,554
Missouri	131	1.7	952	1.4	7	32.1	33,718	99.2	1.2	757,137
Colorado	160	2.1	853	1.2	5	26.3	30,782	77.4	0.9	483,562
Oregon	117	1.5	641	0.9	5	20.5	32,011	70.5	0.8	602,923
Kentucky	80	1.0	820	1.2	10	23.5	28,699	65.1	0.8	813,913
South Carolina	87	1.1	466	0.7	5	15.4	32,996	60.2	0.7	691,770
New Hampshire	58	0.8	513	0.7	9	18.6	36,296	50.7	0.6	874,172
Louisiana	97	1.3	500	0.7	5	13.5	26,918	45.7	0.5	471,546
D.C.	9	0.1	165	0.2	18	4.9	29,503	36.5	0.4	4,053,778
Iowa	66	0.9	371	0.5	6	9.6	25,873	33.9	0.4	514,061
Nevada	48	0.6	381	0.5	8	10.1	26,530	29.1	0.3	605,229
Utah	49	0.6	248	0.4	5	7.8	31,367	25.4	0.3	518,143
Maine	34	0.4	187	0.3	6	5.5	29,497	24.5	0.3	720,500
Nebraska	36	0.5	218	0.3	6	6.3	28,761	22.8	0.3	633,306
Arkansas	41	0.5	207	0.3	5	5.0	24,101	22.0	0.3	537,488
Idaho	34	0.4	134	0.2	4	5.4	40,075	21.7	0.3	636,882
Vermont	22	0.3	174	0.2	8	5.1	29,034	19.9	0.2	904,682
New Mexico	36	0.5	160	0.2	4	4.0	24,881	15.4	0.2	428,972
Rhode Island	25	0.3	124	0.2	5	4.2	33,766	15.2	0.2	607,160
Hawaii	38	0.5	141	0.2	4	3.6	25,801	15.1	0.2	398,263
West Virginia	33	0.4	179	0.3	5	4.7	26,246	12.6	0.1	381,091
Mississippi	40	0.5	156	0.2	4	3.0	19,026	12.2	0.1	304,250
Alaska	20	0.3	159	0.2	8	2.9	18,333	12.1	0.1	604,200
Delaware	21	0.3	101	0.1	5	3.3	32,386	8.6	0.1	407,714
Montana	18	0.2	99	0.1	6	1.5	15,121	7.0	0.1	389,222
North Dakota	10	0.1	41	0.1	4	0.9	21,951	4.6	0.1	462,300
South Dakota	15	0.2	28	0.0	2	0.8	27,143	3.2	0.0	216,600
Wyoming	13	0.2	48	0.1	4	1.1	22,354	3.0	0.0	231,231

Source: 1997 *Economic Census*. The states are in descending order of revenues or establishments (if revenue data are missing for the majority). The symbol (D) appears when data are withheld to prevent disclosure of competitive information. States marked with (D) are sorted by number of establishments. A dash (-) indicates that the data element cannot be calculated. * indicates the midpoint of a range; 175, for example is the range 100-249. Shaded *states* on the state map indicate those states which have proportionately greater representation in the industry than would be indicated by the state's population; the ratio is based on total revenues or number of establishments. Shaded *regions* indicate where the industry is regionally most concentrated.

NAICS 811213 - COMMUNICATION EQUIPMENT REPAIR AND MAINTENANCE

GENERAL STATISTICS

Year	Establishments (number)	Employment (number)	Payroll ($ million)	Revenues ($ million)	Employees per Establishment (number)	Revenues per Establishment ($)	Payroll per Employee ($)
1997	1,890	16,457	523.0	1,608.0	8.7	850,794	31,780

Source: *Economic Census of the United States*, 1997. This is a newly defined industry. Data for prior years were unavailable at the time of publication but may become available over time.

INDICES OF CHANGE

Year	Establishments (number)	Employment (number)	Payroll ($ million)	Revenues ($ million)	Employees per Establishment (number)	Revenues per Establishment ($)	Payroll per Employee ($)
1997	100.0	100.0	100.0	100.0	100.0	100.0	100.0

Sources: Same as General Statistics. The values shown reflect change from the base year, 1997. Values above 100 mean greater than 1997, values below 100 mean less than 1997, and a value of 100 in the 1982-96 or 1998-2001 period means same as 1997. Values followed by a 'p' are projections by the editors; 'e' stands for extrapolation. Data are the most recent available at this level of detail.

SIC INDUSTRIES RELATED TO NAICS 811213

Each new NAICS code represents an industry that used to be part of an SIC or a part of several SIC industries. Data in this table are shown to provide transitional information for these cases. All available data for the precursor SIC(s) are shown. Even if only a part of an SIC is included in the NAICS, *all* data for the SIC are reproduced. If the SIC industry is not marked as being a part (pt) of the NAICS, the entire industry is embedded in the NAICS data. The SIC composition of the new industry provides some hints of the relative importance of its "ancestors." Data marked with a 'p' are projected. Projections begin with 1982 data. Data earlier than 1990 are not shown but are reflected in the projections.

SIC	Industry	1990	1991	1992	1993	1994	1995	1996	1997
7622	**Radio & Television Repair (pt)**								
	Establishments (number)	5,548	5,598	6,038	5,855	5,611	5,351	5,011p	4,844p
	Employment (thousands)	33.9	31.6	29.4	28.2	28.4	29.0	29.2p	29.0p
	Revenues ($ million)	2,292.0	2,190.0	2,297.0	2,454.0	2,456.0	2,638.0	2,752.0	2,770.6p
7629	**Electrical Repair Shops, nec (pt)**								
	Establishments (number)	8,133	8,605	11,364	11,457	11,204	11,005	11,451p	11,797p
	Employment (thousands)	58.6	60.9	108.8	109.7	103.0	99.2	107.5p	112.9p
	Revenues ($ million)	-	-	6,648.1	6,746.8p	7,220.7p	7,694.6p	8,168.5p	8,642.4p

Source: *Economic Census of the United States*, 1992, annual surveys of economic sectors conducted by the Bureau of the Census, and estimates or projections based on the 1982-1992 period; not all data are shown. 'e' marks estimates made by the editors; 'p' indicates projections based on time series. A dash (-) indicates that data for this SIC or year were not available. The abbreviation (pt) next to the industry name indicates that only a part of the industry is present within the NAICS data. If no (pt) is shown, the entire industry is contained within the NAICS data.

SELECTED RATIOS

For 1997	Avg. of Information	Analyzed Industry	Index	For 1997	Avg. of Information	Analyzed Industry	Index
Employees per establishment	6	9	139	Payroll per establishment	126,069	276,720	219
Revenue per establishment	511,622	850,794	166	Payroll as % of revenue	25	33	132
Revenue per employee	81,659	97,709	120	Payroll per employee	20,122	31,780	158

Sources: Same as General Statistics. The 'Average' column represents the average for the industry sector, in 1997, where the currently shown industry is classified. The Index shows the relationship between the Average and the Analyzed Industry. For example, 100 means that they are equal; 500 that the Analyzed Industry is five times the average; 50 means that the Analyzed Industry is half the national average. The abbreviation 'na' is used to show that data are 'not available'.

LEADING COMPANIES

No company data available for this industry.

LOCATION BY STATE AND REGIONAL CONCENTRATION

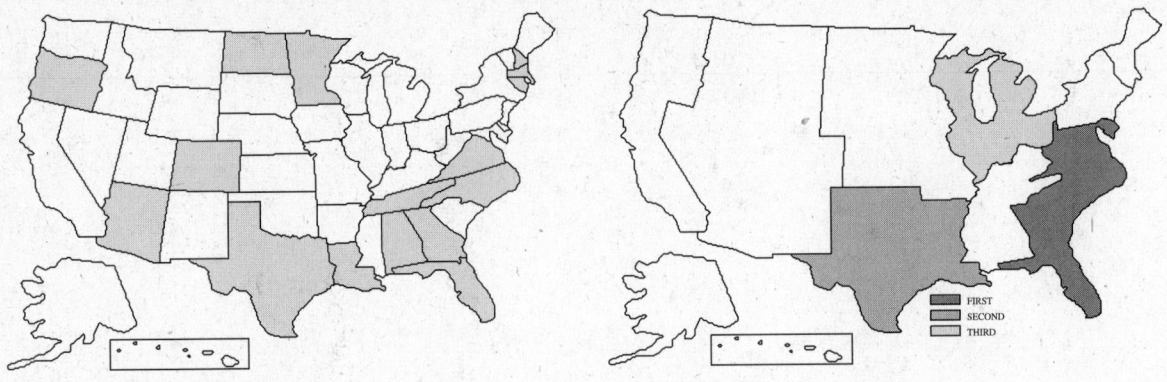

INDUSTRY DATA BY STATE

State	Establishments Total (number)	Establishments % of U.S.	Employment Total (number)	Employment % of U.S.	Employment Per Estab.	Payroll Total ($ mil.)	Payroll Per Empl. ($)	Revenues Total ($ mil.)	Revenues % of U.S.	Revenues Per Estab. ($)
Texas	167	8.8	1,576	9.6	9	47.5	30,167	173.0	10.8	1,036,228
California	189	10.0	1,908	11.6	10	54.8	28,719	154.9	9.6	819,407
Florida	175	9.3	1,360	8.3	8	44.7	32,859	128.1	8.0	731,771
Georgia	68	3.6	836	5.1	12	31.6	37,774	86.2	5.4	1,267,706
New York	100	5.3	786	4.8	8	28.2	35,831	83.6	5.2	836,450
Louisiana	41	2.2	728	4.4	18	25.9	35,621	72.4	4.5	1,765,659
Illinois	86	4.6	602	3.7	7	20.1	33,424	66.5	4.1	772,814
Ohio	38	2.0	439	2.7	12	14.9	33,923	55.2	3.4	1,452,000
Michigan	51	2.7	474	2.9	9	16.8	35,437	51.1	3.2	1,001,412
Virginia	65	3.4	606	3.7	9	15.3	25,289	51.1	3.2	785,615
New Jersey	58	3.1	509	3.1	9	16.6	32,711	47.9	3.0	826,586
Minnesota	35	1.9	335	2.0	10	13.4	40,146	46.2	2.9	1,319,229
North Carolina	63	3.3	457	2.8	7	13.4	29,319	45.9	2.9	729,175
Massachusetts	44	2.3	445	2.7	10	19.8	44,472	42.0	2.6	955,568
Tennessee	34	1.8	321	2.0	9	11.6	35,997	39.4	2.4	1,158,059
Pennsylvania	57	3.0	363	2.2	6	9.8	26,945	35.6	2.2	623,912
Missouri	42	2.2	420	2.6	10	12.0	28,505	32.6	2.0	776,595
Alabama	38	2.0	473	2.9	12	13.2	27,894	31.9	2.0	840,263
Arizona	29	1.5	218	1.3	8	6.9	31,693	28.9	1.8	994,862
Indiana	39	2.1	387	2.4	10	11.2	28,953	28.8	1.8	737,872
Washington	36	1.9	241	1.5	7	8.2	34,017	25.5	1.6	708,139
Colorado	44	2.3	236	1.4	5	7.7	32,737	24.2	1.5	550,545
Kentucky	22	1.2	100	0.6	5	2.9	29,410	21.4	1.3	974,682
Connecticut	20	1.1	252	1.5	13	7.8	31,060	21.0	1.3	1,047,500
Oregon	34	1.8	256	1.6	8	8.0	31,195	20.8	1.3	611,235
Maryland	25	1.3	237	1.4	9	7.7	32,692	20.4	1.3	816,440
South Carolina	32	1.7	214	1.3	7	5.6	26,019	20.0	1.2	623,875
Wisconsin	19	1.0	173	1.1	9	5.4	30,983	15.4	1.0	813,053
Mississippi	20	1.1	90	0.5	5	2.7	29,989	11.6	0.7	581,700
West Virginia	17	0.9	126	0.8	7	2.4	19,254	10.8	0.7	637,647
Utah	11	0.6	105	0.6	10	3.0	28,133	10.3	0.6	936,455
Kansas	21	1.1	107	0.7	5	2.9	27,131	9.8	0.6	468,286
Arkansas	13	0.7	84	0.5	6	2.5	29,262	8.9	0.6	685,077
Iowa	12	0.6	120	0.7	10	3.8	32,000	7.9	0.5	661,583
New Hampshire	13	0.7	81	0.5	6	3.0	36,568	7.7	0.5	592,000
New Mexico	10	0.5	115	0.7	11	3.8	33,070	7.6	0.5	758,700
Nebraska	11	0.6	85	0.5	8	1.4	16,800	6.8	0.4	621,909
Maine	11	0.6	78	0.5	7	2.0	25,538	6.8	0.4	617,273
Idaho	9	0.5	82	0.5	9	1.5	18,744	6.5	0.4	725,889
North Dakota	7	0.4	48	0.3	7	1.7	35,000	5.3	0.3	758,714
Oklahoma	19	1.0	68	0.4	4	1.8	25,941	5.1	0.3	269,842
Nevada	12	0.6	40	0.2	3	1.4	35,200	4.1	0.3	343,667
Rhode Island	5	0.3	37	0.2	7	1.3	36,432	4.1	0.3	813,000
Delaware	6	0.3	37	0.2	6	0.7	17,730	3.5	0.2	584,500
Montana	11	0.6	37	0.2	3	0.7	19,081	3.1	0.2	278,000
Vermont	6	0.3	39	0.2	7	1.7	43,821	3.0	0.2	499,333
South Dakota	6	0.3	28	0.2	5	0.6	22,000	3.0	0.2	499,333
Hawaii	6	0.3	26	0.2	4	0.8	32,538	2.7	0.2	445,500
Wyoming	11	0.6	60*	-	-	(D)	-	(D)	-	-
Alaska	1	0.1	10*	-	-	(D)	-	(D)	-	-
D.C.	1	0.1	10*	-	-	(D)	-	(D)	-	-

Source: 1997 *Economic Census*. The states are in descending order of revenues or establishments (if revenue data are missing for the majority). The symbol (D) appears when data are withheld to prevent disclosure of competitive information. States marked with (D) are sorted by number of establishments. A dash (-) indicates that the data element cannot be calculated. * indicates the midpoint of a range; 175, for example is the range 100-249. Shaded *states* on the state map indicate those states which have proportionately greater representation in the industry than would be indicated by the state's population; the ratio is based on total revenues or number of establishments. Shaded *regions* indicate where the industry is regionally most concentrated.

NAICS 811219 - ELECTRONIC AND PRECISION EQUIPMENT REPAIR AND MAINTENANCE NEC

GENERAL STATISTICS

Year	Establishments (number)	Employment (number)	Payroll ($ million)	Revenues ($ million)	Employees per Establishment (number)	Revenues per Establishment ($)	Payroll per Employee ($)
1997	2,871	24,629	872.0	2,914.0	8.6	1,014,977	35,405

Source: Economic Census of the United States, 1997. This is a newly defined industry. Data for prior years were unavailable at the time of publication but may become available over time.

INDICES OF CHANGE

Year	Establishments (number)	Employment (number)	Payroll ($ million)	Revenues ($ million)	Employees per Establishment (number)	Revenues per Establishment ($)	Payroll per Employee ($)
1997	100.0	100.0	100.0	100.0	100.0	100.0	100.0

Sources: Same as General Statistics. The values shown reflect change from the base year, 1997. Values above 100 mean greater than 1997, values below 100 mean less than 1997, and a value of 100 in the 1982-96 or 1998-2001 period means same as 1997. Values followed by a 'p' are projections by the editors; 'e' stands for extrapolation. Data are the most recent available at this level of detail.

SIC INDUSTRIES RELATED TO NAICS 811219

Each new NAICS code represents an industry that used to be part of an SIC or a part of several SIC industries. Data in this table are shown to provide transitional information for these cases. All available data for the precursor SIC(s) are shown. Even if only a part of an SIC is included in the NAICS, *all* data for the SIC are reproduced. If the SIC industry is not marked as being a part (pt) of the NAICS, the entire industry is embedded in the NAICS data. The SIC composition of the new industry provides some hints of the relative importance of its "ancestors." Data marked with a 'p' are projected. Projections begin with 1982 data. Data earlier than 1990 are not shown but are reflected in the projections.

SIC	Industry	1990	1991	1992	1993	1994	1995	1996	1997
7629	**Electrical Repair Shops, nec (pt)**								
	Establishments (number)	8,133	8,605	11,364	11,457	11,204	11,005	11,451p	11,797p
	Employment (thousands)	58.6	60.9	108.8	109.7	103.0	99.2	107.5p	112.9p
	Revenues ($ million)	-	-	6,648.1	6,746.8p	7,220.7p	7,694.6p	8,168.5p	8,642.4p
7699	**Repair Services, nec (pt)**								
	Establishments (number)	27,822	29,303	34,103	34,618	34,136	34,391	35,001p	35,792p
	Employment (thousands)	181.0	181.4	191.0	201.5	207.4	220.2	219.6p	226.2p
	Revenues ($ million)	-	-	15,059.4	15,563.6p	16,427.9p	17,292.2p	18,156.5p	19,020.8p

Source: Economic Census of the United States, 1992, annual surveys of economic sectors conducted by the Bureau of the Census, and estimates or projections based on the 1982-1992 period; not all data are shown. 'e' marks estimates made by the editors; 'p' indicates projections based on time series. A dash (-) indicates that data for this SIC or year were not available. The abbreviation (pt) next to the industry name indicates that only a part of the industry is present within the NAICS data. If no (pt) is shown, the entire industry is contained within the NAICS data.

SELECTED RATIOS

For 1997	Avg. of Information	Analyzed Industry	Index	For 1997	Avg. of Information	Analyzed Industry	Index
Employees per establishment	6	9	137	Payroll per establishment	126,069	303,727	241
Revenue per establishment	511,622	1,014,977	198	Payroll as % of revenue	25	30	121
Revenue per employee	81,659	118,316	145	Payroll per employee	20,122	35,405	176

Sources: Same as General Statistics. The 'Average' column represents the average for the industry sector, in 1997, where the currently shown industry is classified. The Index shows the relationship between the Average and the Analyzed Industry. For example, 100 means that they are equal; 500 that the Analyzed Industry is five times the average; 50 means that the Analyzed Industry is half the national average. The abbreviation 'na' is used to show that data are 'not available'.

LEADING COMPANIES

No company data available for this industry.

LOCATION BY STATE AND REGIONAL CONCENTRATION

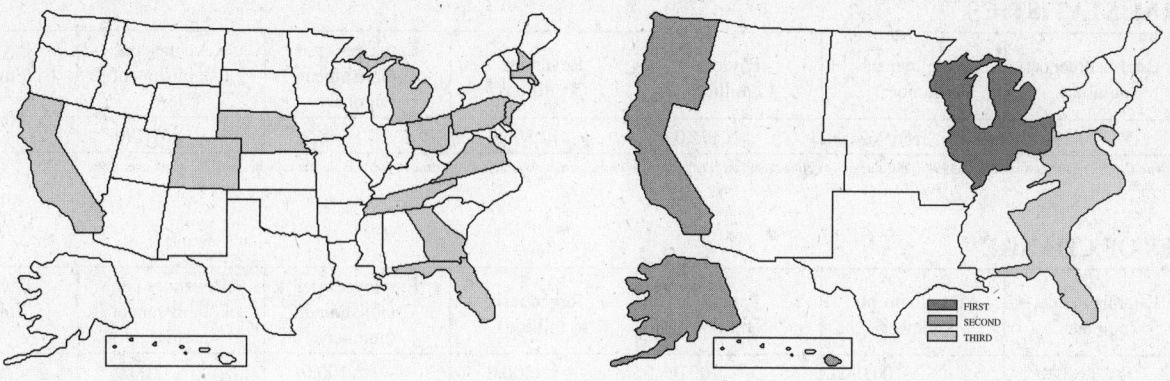

INDUSTRY DATA BY STATE

State	Establishments Total (number)	% of U.S.	Employment Total (number)	% of U.S.	Per Estab.	Payroll Total ($ mil.)	Per Empl. ($)	Revenues Total ($ mil.)	% of U.S.	Per Estab. ($)
California	358	12.5	4,535	18.4	13	171.1	37,734	504.1	17.3	1,408,109
Ohio	127	4.4	1,464	5.9	12	49.6	33,885	334.5	11.5	2,633,583
Florida	218	7.6	1,560	6.3	7	55.3	35,449	211.2	7.2	968,839
Texas	207	7.2	1,999	8.1	10	63.8	31,897	190.2	6.5	918,758
Pennsylvania	110	3.8	934	3.8	8	34.8	37,266	143.8	4.9	1,306,909
Tennessee	60	2.1	1,115	4.5	19	46.3	41,509	140.2	4.8	2,336,983
Michigan	100	3.5	990	4.0	10	45.1	45,538	136.9	4.7	1,368,770
Virginia	71	2.5	1,041	4.2	15	37.3	35,871	118.5	4.1	1,669,338
New York	144	5.0	791	3.2	5	31.5	39,865	95.0	3.3	659,806
New Jersey	125	4.4	656	2.7	5	28.0	42,659	89.5	3.1	716,336
Massachusetts	75	2.6	625	2.5	8	28.6	45,755	88.4	3.0	1,178,933
Georgia	109	3.8	883	3.6	8	27.5	31,127	80.4	2.8	737,486
Colorado	52	1.8	874	3.5	17	30.1	34,476	73.0	2.5	1,404,615
Illinois	122	4.2	716	2.9	6	22.2	30,985	70.2	2.4	575,139
Maryland	70	2.4	527	2.1	8	17.3	32,856	51.3	1.8	732,586
Minnesota	47	1.6	369	1.5	8	13.3	35,970	46.5	1.6	988,660
Washington	56	2.0	365	1.5	7	13.6	37,189	46.3	1.6	826,911
Missouri	53	1.8	316	1.3	6	11.2	35,307	40.9	1.4	772,321
North Carolina	64	2.2	308	1.3	5	10.8	34,958	36.4	1.2	568,391
Oklahoma	40	1.4	332	1.3	8	12.3	36,910	36.3	1.2	907,400
Indiana	64	2.2	322	1.3	5	8.7	27,121	30.8	1.1	480,641
Arizona	49	1.7	260	1.1	5	8.9	34,246	27.8	1.0	567,612
Wisconsin	45	1.6	246	1.0	5	8.4	34,146	27.7	1.0	616,467
Alabama	45	1.6	236	1.0	5	7.2	30,394	24.0	0.8	534,044
Louisiana	50	1.7	285	1.2	6	7.8	27,246	23.9	0.8	478,620
Connecticut	41	1.4	221	0.9	5	9.0	40,801	23.4	0.8	571,390
Kansas	46	1.6	216	0.9	5	6.6	30,741	21.2	0.7	460,435
New Hampshire	20	0.7	258	1.0	13	7.6	29,593	20.3	0.7	1,012,500
Kentucky	30	1.0	251	1.0	8	8.4	33,546	19.7	0.7	656,833
Nebraska	18	0.6	153	0.6	9	5.0	32,739	19.0	0.7	1,056,833
South Carolina	37	1.3	178	0.7	5	4.4	25,000	17.1	0.6	463,000
Oregon	29	1.0	112	0.5	4	3.5	31,321	16.4	0.6	566,034
Utah	21	0.7	184	0.7	9	5.5	29,674	16.3	0.6	777,619
West Virginia	15	0.5	114	0.5	8	3.9	34,623	12.5	0.4	835,267
Nevada	13	0.5	108	0.4	8	2.8	26,074	10.4	0.4	799,308
Idaho	8	0.3	423	1.7	53	3.5	8,199	9.8	0.3	1,230,500
Iowa	19	0.7	81	0.3	4	2.7	33,679	9.4	0.3	497,000
Arkansas	18	0.6	81	0.3	5	2.5	31,049	8.0	0.3	444,333
Mississippi	19	0.7	65	0.3	3	2.2	33,862	7.7	0.3	406,316
New Mexico	10	0.3	90	0.4	9	2.5	27,511	5.1	0.2	511,200
Montana	14	0.5	37	0.2	3	1.2	31,351	3.8	0.1	273,286
Alaska	5	0.2	21	0.1	4	0.7	31,619	2.7	0.1	536,800
Maine	7	0.2	24	0.1	3	0.7	30,458	2.1	0.1	303,857
Hawaii	7	0.2	18	0.1	3	0.6	32,111	1.6	0.1	223,429
South Dakota	3	0.1	12	0.0	4	0.2	18,083	1.0	0.0	329,667
Rhode Island	14	0.5	175*	-	-	(D)	-	(D)	-	-
Delaware	8	0.3	60*	-	-	(D)	-	(D)	-	-
North Dakota	3	0.1	60*	-	-	(D)	-	(D)	-	-
D.C.	2	0.1	10*	-	-	(D)	-	(D)	-	-
Vermont	2	0.1	10*	-	-	(D)	-	(D)	-	-
Wyoming	1	-	10*	-	-	(D)	-	(D)	-	-

Source: 1997 *Economic Census*. The states are in descending order of revenues or establishments (if revenue data are missing for the majority). The symbol (D) appears when data are withheld to prevent disclosure of competitive information. States marked with (D) are sorted by number of establishments. A dash (-) indicates that the data element cannot be calculated. * indicates the midpoint of a range; 175, for example is the range 100-249. Shaded *states* on the state map indicate those states which have proportionately greater representation in the industry than would be indicated by the state's population; the ratio is based on total revenues or number of establishments. Shaded *regions* indicate where the industry is regionally most concentrated.

NAICS 811310 - COMMERCIAL AND INDUSTRIAL MACHINERY AND EQUIPMENT REPAIR AND MAINTENANCE

GENERAL STATISTICS

Year	Establishments (number)	Employment (number)	Payroll ($ million)	Revenues ($ million)	Employees per Establishment (number)	Revenues per Establishment ($)	Payroll per Employee ($)
1997	20,290	166,962	5,172.0	17,506.0	8.2	862,790	30,977

Source: *Economic Census of the United States*, 1997. This is a newly defined industry. Data for prior years were unavailable at the time of publication but may become available over time.

INDICES OF CHANGE

Year	Establishments (number)	Employment (number)	Payroll ($ million)	Revenues ($ million)	Employees per Establishment (number)	Revenues per Establishment ($)	Payroll per Employee ($)
1997	100.0	100.0	100.0	100.0	100.0	100.0	100.0

Sources: Same as General Statistics. The values shown reflect change from the base year, 1997. Values above 100 mean greater than 1997, values below 100 mean less than 1997, and a value of 100 in the 1982-96 or 1998-2001 period means same as 1997. Values followed by a 'p' are projections by the editors; 'e' stands for extrapolation. Data are the most recent available at this level of detail.

SIC INDUSTRIES RELATED TO NAICS 811310

Each new NAICS code represents an industry that used to be part of an SIC or a part of several SIC industries. Data in this table are shown to provide transitional information for these cases. All available data for the precursor SIC(s) are shown. Even if only a part of an SIC is included in the NAICS, *all* data for the SIC are reproduced. If the SIC industry is not marked as being a part (pt) of the NAICS, the entire industry is embedded in the NAICS data. The SIC composition of the new industry provides some hints of the relative importance of its "ancestors." Data marked with a 'p' are projected. Projections begin with 1982 data. Data earlier than 1990 are not shown but are reflected in the projections.

SIC	Industry	1990	1991	1992	1993	1994	1995	1996	1997
7623	**Refrigeration Service & Repair (pt)**								
	Establishments (number)	3,309	3,364	3,797	3,741	3,687	3,611	3,620p	3,639p
	Employment (thousands)	22.6	22.2	23.7	22.7	24.2	25.1	26.1p	26.8p
	Revenues ($ million)	-	-	-	-	-	3,394.0	3,446.0	-
7692	**Welding Repair**								
	Establishments (number)	5,278	5,628	5,383	5,722	5,714	5,726	5,626p	5,628p
	Employment (thousands)	27.9	27.9	22.2	24.6	25.3	27.5	26.4p	26.5p
	Revenues ($ million)	-	-	-	-	-	2,348.0	2,523.0	-
7694	**Armature Rewinding Shops (pt)**								
	Establishments (number)	2,489	2,415	2,498	2,430	2,332	2,083	2,216p	2,168p
	Employment (thousands)	28.1	27.7	26.6	25.2	25.0	22.4	23.7p	23.2p
	Revenues ($ million)	2,371.0	2,389.0	2,454.0	2,380.0	2,324.0	2,370.0	2,464.0	2,540.4p
7699	**Repair Services, nec (pt)**								
	Establishments (number)	27,822	29,303	34,103	34,618	34,136	34,391	35,001p	35,792p
	Employment (thousands)	181.0	181.4	191.0	201.5	207.4	220.2	219.6p	226.2p
	Revenues ($ million)	-	-	15,059.4	15,563.6p	16,427.9p	17,292.2p	18,156.5p	19,020.8p

Source: *Economic Census of the United States*, 1992, annual surveys of economic sectors conducted by the Bureau of the Census, and estimates or projections based on the 1982-1992 period; not all data are shown. 'e' marks estimates made by the editors; 'p' indicates projections based on time series. A dash (-) indicates that data for this SIC or year were not available. The abbreviation (pt) next to the industry name indicates that only a part of the industry is present within the NAICS data. If no (pt) is shown, the entire industry is contained within the NAICS data.

SELECTED RATIOS

For 1997	Avg. of Information	Analyzed Industry	Index	For 1997	Avg. of Information	Analyzed Industry	Index
Employees per establishment	6	8	131	Payroll per establishment	126,069	254,904	202
Revenue per establishment	511,622	862,790	169	Payroll as % of revenue	25	30	120
Revenue per employee	81,659	104,850	128	Payroll per employee	20,122	30,977	154

Sources: Same as General Statistics. The 'Average' column represents the average for the industry sector, in 1997, where the currently shown industry is classified. The Index shows the relationship between the Average and the Analyzed Industry. For example, 100 means that they are equal; 500 that the Analyzed Industry is five times the average; 50 means that the Analyzed Industry is half the national average. The abbreviation 'na' is used to show that data are 'not available'.

LEADING COMPANIES Number shown: **14**   Total sales ($ mil): **221**   Total employment (000): **1.8**

Company Name	Address				CEO Name	Phone	Co. Type	Sales ($ mil)	Empl. (000)
Tampa Armature Works Inc.	PO Box 3381	Tampa	FL	33601	J Turner	813-621-5661	R	60	0.5
Koontz-Wagner Electric Inc.	3801 Voorde Dr	South Bend	IN	46628	Richard Pfeil	219-232-2051	R	52	0.5
Brehob Corp.	PO Box 2023	Indianapolis	IN	46206		317-231-8080	R	28	0.2
Dreisilker Electric Motors Inc.	352 Roosevelt Rd	Glen Ellyn	IL	60137	Leo Dreisilker	630-469-7510	R	18	0.1
Brandon and Clark Inc.	3623 Interstate 27	Lubbock	TX	79404	Walt Clark	806-747-3861	R	16	0.2
Shelby Electric Company Inc.	112 E H Crump E	Memphis	TN	38106	Al Quarin	901-948-1545	R	15*	0.1
Boustead Electric and Mfg Co.	7135 Madison W	Minneapolis	MN	55427	Jeff Svendsen	612-544-9131	R	10*	<0.1
Lubbock Electric Co.	1108 34th St	Lubbock	TX	79405	Paul V Bush	806-744-2336	R	8*	<0.1
Brithinee Electric	620 S Rancho Ave	Colton	CA	92324	Wallace Brithinee	909-825-7971	R	4*	<0.1
G.E. Jones Electric Company Inc.	204 N Polk St	Amarillo	TX	79107	George Stratton	806-372-5505	R	3*	<0.1
Wagner-Electric of Fort Wayne	PO Box 5279	Fort Wayne	IN	46895	Marvin Bell	219-484-5532	R	3	<0.1
Hamilton Electric Works Inc.	3800 Arpt Blvd	Austin	TX	78722	Gary D Hamilton	512-472-2428	R	3	<0.1
Arrowhead Stator Rotor Inc.	3829 Jefferson	Minneapolis	MN	55421	John Berger	612-788-9613	R	1	<0.1
Howard Electric Co.	4801 Bellevue St	Detroit	MI	48207	Eugene Howard	313-923-0430	R	1	<0.1

Source: *Ward's Business Directory of U.S. Private and Public Companies*, Volumes 1 and 2, 2000. The company type code used is as follows: P - Public, R - Private, S - Subsidiary, D - Division, J - Joint Venture, A - Affiliate, G - Group, N - Company type not reported. Sales are in millions of dollars, employees are in thousands. An asterisk (*) indicates an estimated sales volume. The symbol < stands for 'less than'. Company names and addresses are truncated, in some cases, to fit into the available space.

LOCATION BY STATE AND REGIONAL CONCENTRATION

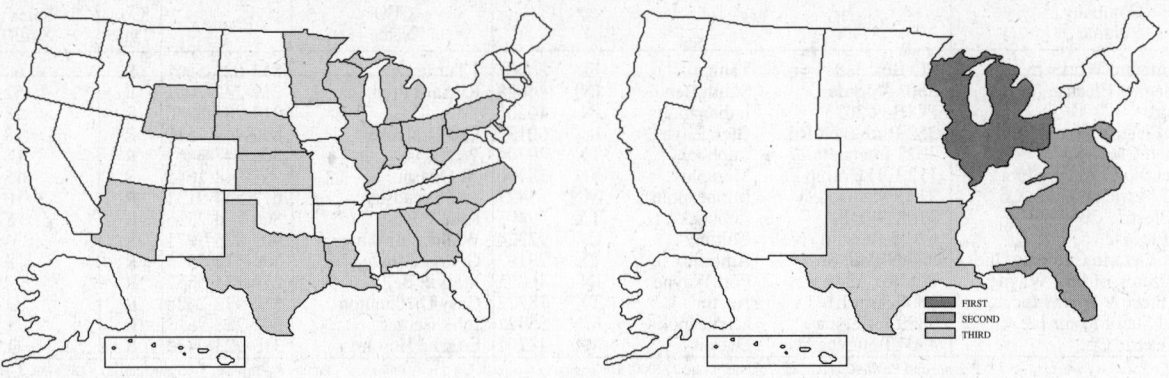

FIRST
SECOND
THIRD

INDUSTRY DATA BY STATE

State	Establishments Total (number)	% of U.S.	Employment Total (number)	% of U.S.	Per Estab.	Payroll Total ($ mil.)	Per Empl. ($)	Revenues Total ($ mil.)	% of U.S.	Per Estab. ($)
Texas	1,733	8.5	19,827	11.9	11	610.0	30,768	1,965.6	11.2	1,134,216
California	1,746	8.6	14,421	8.6	8	497.6	34,508	1,641.6	9.4	940,203
Illinois	978	4.8	8,080	4.8	8	290.4	35,940	968.3	5.5	990,113
Pennsylvania	788	3.9	7,672	4.6	10	250.7	32,683	871.5	5.0	1,106,025
Ohio	893	4.4	8,936	5.4	10	269.8	30,191	868.6	5.0	972,725
Michigan	778	3.8	7,651	4.6	10	261.2	34,141	860.2	4.9	1,105,617
Florida	1,238	6.1	8,756	5.2	7	241.3	27,553	803.4	4.6	648,967
New York	948	4.7	6,457	3.9	7	215.6	33,396	727.7	4.2	767,568
Louisiana	524	2.6	6,435	3.9	12	186.7	29,006	625.3	3.6	1,193,317
Indiana	491	2.4	5,098	3.1	10	155.1	30,422	533.8	3.0	1,087,071
Georgia	594	2.9	4,839	2.9	8	156.7	32,378	512.7	2.9	863,184
New Jersey	569	2.8	4,005	2.4	7	147.5	36,840	482.7	2.8	848,267
North Carolina	640	3.2	4,957	3.0	8	142.6	28,773	482.2	2.8	753,455
Virginia	465	2.3	3,993	2.4	9	122.8	30,755	422.4	2.4	908,456
Wisconsin	453	2.2	3,207	1.9	7	104.5	32,587	393.2	2.2	867,971
Alabama	367	1.8	3,540	2.1	10	104.7	29,587	354.8	2.0	966,856
Minnesota	416	2.1	3,805	2.3	9	85.5	22,480	321.2	1.8	772,209
Massachusetts	368	1.8	2,807	1.7	8	98.9	35,247	306.6	1.8	833,147
Arizona	299	1.5	2,513	1.5	8	82.4	32,775	294.3	1.7	984,211
Washington	389	1.9	2,776	1.7	7	87.7	31,583	293.9	1.7	755,440
South Carolina	374	1.8	2,752	1.6	7	83.0	30,142	290.0	1.7	775,401
Tennessee	369	1.8	2,697	1.6	7	76.6	28,404	278.6	1.6	755,008
Missouri	438	2.2	2,630	1.6	6	74.0	28,140	277.8	1.6	634,315
Maryland	306	1.5	2,576	1.5	8	77.1	29,941	254.1	1.5	830,232
Kentucky	340	1.7	2,704	1.6	8	70.3	25,990	225.2	1.3	662,285
West Virginia	206	1.0	2,506	1.5	12	66.5	26,547	213.8	1.2	1,037,825
Kansas	284	1.4	1,848	1.1	7	53.6	28,984	186.4	1.1	656,331
Oklahoma	261	1.3	1,775	1.1	7	47.9	27,010	178.6	1.0	684,230
Oregon	283	1.4	1,751	1.0	6	52.8	30,139	173.6	1.0	613,318
Connecticut	202	1.0	1,347	0.8	7	53.4	39,628	167.4	1.0	828,663
Colorado	268	1.3	1,507	0.9	6	43.5	28,857	159.2	0.9	594,097
Iowa	366	1.8	1,463	0.9	4	33.6	22,942	158.5	0.9	432,975
Arkansas	214	1.1	1,281	0.8	6	34.7	27,056	139.2	0.8	650,598
Nebraska	230	1.1	1,117	0.7	5	29.4	26,343	132.2	0.8	574,917
Utah	123	0.6	1,006	0.6	8	31.2	31,001	118.2	0.7	961,114
Mississippi	209	1.0	1,319	0.8	6	37.4	28,319	113.8	0.6	544,321
New Mexico	113	0.6	906	0.5	8	24.2	26,674	87.9	0.5	777,938
Wyoming	75	0.4	711	0.4	9	23.2	32,660	83.1	0.5	1,107,333
Nevada	99	0.5	639	0.4	6	21.6	33,778	73.5	0.4	742,798
Maine	99	0.5	615	0.4	6	17.0	27,574	66.0	0.4	666,838
Idaho	119	0.6	587	0.4	5	13.1	22,344	57.5	0.3	482,798
Delaware	58	0.3	520	0.3	9	17.2	33,148	56.3	0.3	969,983
Hawaii	74	0.4	455	0.3	6	15.2	33,385	51.6	0.3	697,270
New Hampshire	93	0.5	443	0.3	5	14.1	31,770	50.6	0.3	543,882
Montana	86	0.4	524	0.3	6	13.8	26,370	46.4	0.3	539,919
Rhode Island	64	0.3	587	0.4	9	14.5	24,620	41.1	0.2	642,156
Alaska	39	0.2	179	0.1	5	6.8	37,950	29.0	0.2	744,385
North Dakota	78	0.4	288	0.2	4	6.4	22,250	26.6	0.2	341,038
South Dakota	89	0.4	307	0.2	3	5.0	16,378	24.6	0.1	276,416
Vermont	53	0.3	175*	-	-	(D)	-	(D)	-	-
D.C.	1	-	10*	-	-	(D)	-	(D)	-	-

Source: 1997 *Economic Census*. The states are in descending order of revenues or establishments (if revenue data are missing for the majority). The symbol (D) appears when data are withheld to prevent disclosure of competitive information. States marked with (D) are sorted by number of establishments. A dash (-) indicates that the data element cannot be calculated. * indicates the midpoint of a range; 175, for example is the range 100-249. Shaded *states* on the state map indicate those states which have proportionately greater representation in the industry than would be indicated by the state's population; the ratio is based on total revenues or number of establishments. Shaded *regions* indicate where the industry is regionally most concentrated.

NAICS 811411 - HOME AND GARDEN EQUIPMENT REPAIR AND MAINTENANCE

GENERAL STATISTICS

Year	Establishments (number)	Employment (number)	Payroll ($ million)	Revenues ($ million)	Employees per Establishment (number)	Revenues per Establishment ($)	Payroll per Employee ($)
1997	3,611	11,897	235.0	1,002.0	3.3	277,485	19,753

Source: Economic Census of the United States, 1997. This is a newly defined industry. Data for prior years were unavailable at the time of publication but may become available over time.

INDICES OF CHANGE

Year	Establishments (number)	Employment (number)	Payroll ($ million)	Revenues ($ million)	Employees per Establishment (number)	Revenues per Establishment ($)	Payroll per Employee ($)
1997	100.0	100.0	100.0	100.0	100.0	100.0	100.0

Sources: Same as General Statistics. The values shown reflect change from the base year, 1997. Values above 100 mean greater than 1997, values below 100 mean less than 1997, and a value of 100 in the 1982-96 or 1998-2001 period means same as 1997. Values followed by a 'p' are projections by the editors; 'e' stands for extrapolation. Data are the most recent available at this level of detail.

SIC INDUSTRIES RELATED TO NAICS 811411

Each new NAICS code represents an industry that used to be part of an SIC or a part of several SIC industries. Data in this table are shown to provide transitional information for these cases. All available data for the precursor SIC(s) are shown. Even if only a part of an SIC is included in the NAICS, *all* data for the SIC are reproduced. If the SIC industry is not marked as being a part (pt) of the NAICS, the entire industry is embedded in the NAICS data. The SIC composition of the new industry provides some hints of the relative importance of its "ancestors." Data marked with a 'p' are projected. Projections begin with 1982 data. Data earlier than 1990 are not shown but are reflected in the projections.

SIC	Industry	1990	1991	1992	1993	1994	1995	1996	1997
7699	**Repair Services, nec (pt)**								
	Establishments (number)	27,822	29,303	34,103	34,618	34,136	34,391	35,001p	35,792p
	Employment (thousands)	181.0	181.4	191.0	201.5	207.4	220.2	219.6p	226.2p
	Revenues ($ million)	-	-	15,059.4	15,563.6p	16,427.9p	17,292.2p	18,156.5p	19,020.8p

Source: Economic Census of the United States, 1992, annual surveys of economic sectors conducted by the Bureau of the Census, and estimates or projections based on the 1982-1992 period; not all data are shown. 'e' marks estimates made by the editors; 'p' indicates projections based on time series. A dash (-) indicates that data for this SIC or year were not available. The abbreviation (pt) next to the industry name indicates that only a part of the industry is present within the NAICS data. If no (pt) is shown, the entire industry is contained within the NAICS data.

SELECTED RATIOS

For 1997	Avg. of Information	Analyzed Industry	Index	For 1997	Avg. of Information	Analyzed Industry	Index
Employees per establishment	6	3	53	Payroll per establishment	126,069	65,079	52
Revenue per establishment	511,622	277,485	54	Payroll as % of revenue	25	23	95
Revenue per employee	81,659	84,223	103	Payroll per employee	20,122	19,753	98

Sources: Same as General Statistics. The 'Average' column represents the average for the industry sector, in 1997, where the currently shown industry is classified. The Index shows the relationship between the Average and the Analyzed Industry. For example, 100 means that they are equal; 500 that the Analyzed Industry is five times the average; 50 means that the Analyzed Industry is half the national average. The abbreviation 'na' is used to show that data are 'not available'.

LEADING COMPANIES

No company data available for this industry.

LOCATION BY STATE AND REGIONAL CONCENTRATION

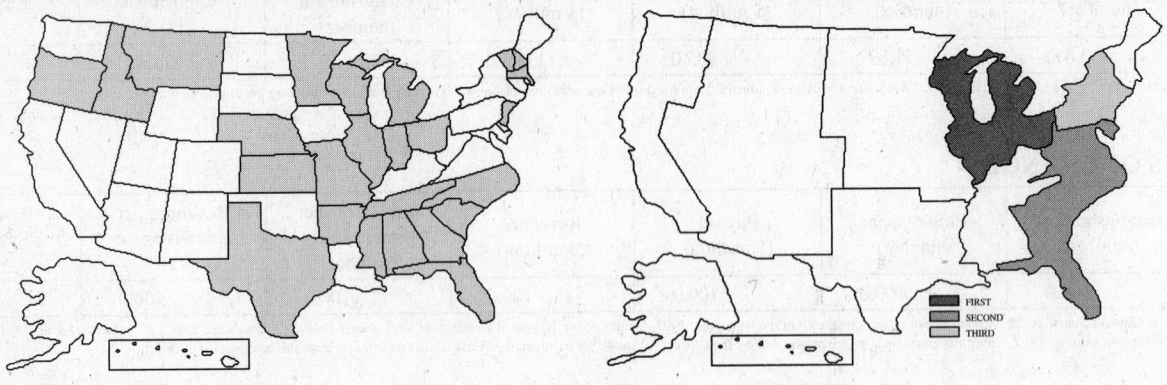

FIRST
SECOND
THIRD

INDUSTRY DATA BY STATE

State	Establishments Total (number)	% of U.S.	Employment Total (number)	% of U.S.	Per Estab.	Payroll Total ($ mil.)	Per Empl. ($)	Revenues Total ($ mil.)	% of U.S.	Per Estab. ($)
California	282	7.8	925	7.8	3	18.8	20,375	80.8	8.1	286,397
Texas	232	6.4	826	6.9	4	16.8	20,377	72.0	7.2	310,302
Florida	224	6.2	630	5.3	3	11.3	17,979	53.8	5.4	240,004
Illinois	145	4.0	602	5.1	4	14.4	23,900	52.4	5.2	361,372
Ohio	165	4.6	671	5.6	4	12.4	18,511	50.9	5.1	308,436
North Carolina	162	4.5	629	5.3	4	12.4	19,641	50.0	5.0	308,457
Michigan	144	4.0	549	4.6	4	12.5	22,741	44.8	4.5	310,951
New Jersey	115	3.2	392	3.3	3	9.4	24,099	42.5	4.2	369,774
New York	157	4.3	452	3.8	3	10.4	23,051	40.5	4.0	258,210
Pennsylvania	137	3.8	451	3.8	3	10.5	23,244	38.5	3.8	281,175
Wisconsin	92	2.5	286	2.4	3	5.8	20,434	29.4	2.9	319,174
Georgia	112	3.1	331	2.8	3	6.8	20,577	29.1	2.9	259,938
Massachusetts	59	1.6	369	3.1	6	7.5	20,295	28.5	2.8	482,763
Indiana	92	2.5	309	2.6	3	5.4	17,586	24.4	2.4	265,174
Virginia	121	3.4	309	2.6	3	5.4	17,440	23.3	2.3	192,554
Tennessee	97	2.7	270	2.3	3	4.9	17,985	23.1	2.3	238,546
Missouri	106	2.9	307	2.6	3	5.3	17,296	21.9	2.2	206,575
Alabama	76	2.1	252	2.1	3	3.9	15,567	21.8	2.2	287,434
Minnesota	95	2.6	215	1.8	2	3.5	16,507	21.6	2.2	227,579
South Carolina	63	1.7	272	2.3	4	4.4	16,224	19.0	1.9	301,032
Washington	67	1.9	207	1.7	3	4.2	20,430	18.3	1.8	273,463
Oregon	61	1.7	231	1.9	4	4.9	21,238	18.0	1.8	294,492
Louisiana	60	1.7	194	1.6	3	3.5	17,820	16.4	1.6	274,083
Maryland	61	1.7	188	1.6	3	3.8	20,415	14.6	1.5	239,049
Arizona	49	1.4	173	1.5	4	3.7	21,295	14.1	1.4	287,592
Mississippi	53	1.5	175	1.5	3	3.0	16,983	13.6	1.4	257,321
Kentucky	52	1.4	138	1.2	3	2.5	18,232	11.5	1.1	221,077
Arkansas	53	1.5	157	1.3	3	1.8	11,682	11.0	1.1	207,075
Kansas	39	1.1	158	1.3	4	2.7	17,133	10.8	1.1	277,949
Colorado	55	1.5	163	1.4	3	2.6	16,098	10.8	1.1	195,527
Iowa	40	1.1	85	0.7	2	2.9	33,835	10.7	1.1	266,875
Connecticut	35	1.0	110	0.9	3	2.5	22,455	10.6	1.1	303,429
Nebraska	38	1.1	109	0.9	3	1.8	16,055	8.6	0.9	225,711
Oklahoma	48	1.3	112	0.9	2	1.9	16,571	8.4	0.8	174,271
New Hampshire	22	0.6	78	0.7	4	1.7	22,423	8.2	0.8	374,955
Idaho	21	0.6	77	0.6	4	1.4	17,688	7.5	0.7	355,333
Utah	27	0.7	97	0.8	4	1.6	16,598	6.4	0.6	238,111
New Mexico	14	0.4	69	0.6	5	1.2	16,884	5.6	0.6	397,857
Nevada	12	0.3	53	0.4	4	1.1	20,604	5.3	0.5	443,500
West Virginia	27	0.7	68	0.6	3	0.8	11,941	4.5	0.5	166,963
Montana	18	0.5	51	0.4	3	0.8	15,020	4.5	0.4	247,667
Vermont	19	0.5	37	0.3	2	0.5	13,865	3.7	0.4	193,842
Maine	11	0.3	26	0.2	2	0.4	14,423	2.0	0.2	178,636
Delaware	7	0.2	26	0.2	4	0.4	15,731	1.7	0.2	239,429
South Dakota	12	0.3	13	0.1	1	0.2	12,385	1.7	0.2	143,667
Hawaii	7	0.2	16	0.1	2	0.3	17,563	1.4	0.1	198,714
North Dakota	12	0.3	20	0.2	2	0.3	12,500	1.4	0.1	120,000
Wyoming	6	0.2	8	0.1	1	0.1	9,625	0.9	0.1	151,167
Alaska	4	0.1	4	0.0	1	0.1	33,250	0.6	0.1	146,500
Rhode Island	5	0.1	7	0.1	1	0.1	21,000	0.5	0.1	108,400

Source: 1997 *Economic Census*. The states are in descending order of revenues or establishments (if revenue data are missing for the majority). The symbol (D) appears when data are withheld to prevent disclosure of competitive information. States marked with (D) are sorted by number of establishments. A dash (-) indicates that the data element cannot be calculated. * indicates the midpoint of a range; 175, for example is the range 100-249. Shaded *states* on the state map indicate those states which have proportionately greater representation in the industry than would be indicated by the state's population; the ratio is based on total revenues or number of establishments. Shaded *regions* indicate where the industry is regionally most concentrated.

NAICS 811412 - APPLIANCE REPAIR AND MAINTENANCE

GENERAL STATISTICS

Year	Establishments (number)	Employment (number)	Payroll ($ million)	Revenues ($ million)	Employees per Establishment (number)	Revenues per Establishment ($)	Payroll per Employee ($)
1997	6,179	52,157	1,302.0	3,975.0	8.4	643,308	24,963

Source: Economic Census of the United States, 1997. This is a newly defined industry. Data for prior years were unavailable at the time of publication but may become available over time.

INDICES OF CHANGE

Year	Establishments (number)	Employment (number)	Payroll ($ million)	Revenues ($ million)	Employees per Establishment (number)	Revenues per Establishment ($)	Payroll per Employee ($)
1997	100.0	100.0	100.0	100.0	100.0	100.0	100.0

Sources: Same as General Statistics. The values shown reflect change from the base year, 1997. Values above 100 mean greater than 1997, values below 100 mean less than 1997, and a value of 100 in the 1982-96 or 1998-2001 period means same as 1997. Values followed by a 'p' are projections by the editors; 'e' stands for extrapolation. Data are the most recent available at this level of detail.

SIC INDUSTRIES RELATED TO NAICS 811412

Each new NAICS code represents an industry that used to be part of an SIC or a part of several SIC industries. Data in this table are shown to provide transitional information for these cases. All available data for the precursor SIC(s) are shown. Even if only a part of an SIC is included in the NAICS, *all* data for the SIC are reproduced. If the SIC industry is not marked as being a part (pt) of the NAICS, the entire industry is embedded in the NAICS data. The SIC composition of the new industry provides some hints of the relative importance of its "ancestors." Data marked with a 'p' are projected. Projections begin with 1982 data. Data earlier than 1990 are not shown but are reflected in the projections.

SIC	Industry	1990	1991	1992	1993	1994	1995	1996	1997
7623	**Refrigeration Service & Repair (pt)**								
	Establishments (number)	3,309	3,364	3,797	3,741	3,687	3,611	3,620p	3,639p
	Employment (thousands)	22.6	22.2	23.7	22.7	24.2	25.1	26.1p	26.8p
	Revenues ($ million)	-	-	-	-	-	3,394.0	3,446.0	-
7629	**Electrical Repair Shops, nec (pt)**								
	Establishments (number)	8,133	8,605	11,364	11,457	11,204	11,005	11,451p	11,797p
	Employment (thousands)	58.6	60.9	108.8	109.7	103.0	99.2	107.5p	112.9p
	Revenues ($ million)	-	-	6,648.1	6,746.8p	7,220.7p	7,694.6p	8,168.5p	8,642.4p
7699	**Repair Services, nec (pt)**								
	Establishments (number)	27,822	29,303	34,103	34,618	34,136	34,391	35,001p	35,792p
	Employment (thousands)	181.0	181.4	191.0	201.5	207.4	220.2	219.6p	226.2p
	Revenues ($ million)	-	-	15,059.4	15,563.6p	16,427.9p	17,292.2p	18,156.5p	19,020.8p

Source: Economic Census of the United States, 1992, annual surveys of economic sectors conducted by the Bureau of the Census, and estimates or projections based on the 1982-1992 period; not all data are shown. 'e' marks estimates made by the editors; 'p' indicates projections based on time series. A dash (-) indicates that data for this SIC or year were not available. The abbreviation (pt) next to the industry name indicates that only a part of the industry is present within the NAICS data. If no (pt) is shown, the entire industry is contained within the NAICS data.

SELECTED RATIOS

For 1997	Avg. of Information	Analyzed Industry	Index	For 1997	Avg. of Information	Analyzed Industry	Index
Employees per establishment	6	8	135	Payroll per establishment	126,069	210,714	167
Revenue per establishment	511,622	643,308	126	Payroll as % of revenue	25	33	133
Revenue per employee	81,659	76,212	93	Payroll per employee	20,122	24,963	124

Sources: Same as General Statistics. The 'Average' column represents the average for the industry sector, in 1997, where the currently shown industry is classified. The Index shows the relationship between the Average and the Analyzed Industry. For example, 100 means that they are equal; 500 that the Analyzed Industry is five times the average; 50 means that the Analyzed Industry is half the national average. The abbreviation 'na' is used to show that data are 'not available'.

LEADING COMPANIES   Number shown: **1**   Total sales ($ mil): **2**   Total employment (000): **0.0**

Company Name	Address				CEO Name	Phone	Co. Type	Sales ($ mil)	Empl. (000)
Fraley and Quattlebaum Inc.	P O Box 3365	Columbia	SC	29230	Bill Franley	803-754-4831	R	2*	<0.1

Source: *Ward's Business Directory of U.S. Private and Public Companies*, Volumes 1 and 2, 2000. The company type code used is as follows: P - Public, R - Private, S - Subsidiary, D - Division, J - Joint Venture, A - Affiliate, G - Group, N - Company type not reported. Sales are in millions of dollars, employees are in thousands. An asterisk (*) indicates an estimated sales volume. The symbol < stands for 'less than'. Company names and addresses are truncated, in some cases, to fit into the available space.

LOCATION BY STATE AND REGIONAL CONCENTRATION

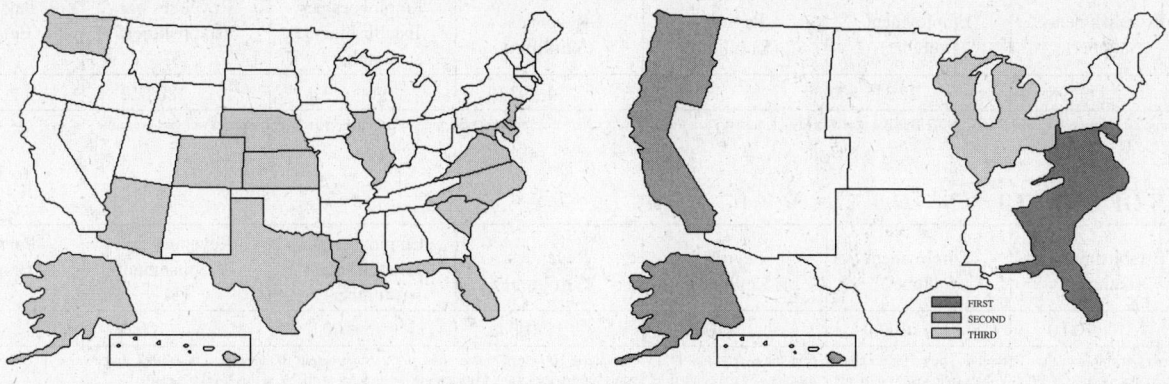

INDUSTRY DATA BY STATE

State	Establishments Total (number)	Establishments % of U.S.	Employment Total (number)	Employment % of U.S.	Employment Per Estab.	Payroll Total ($ mil.)	Payroll Per Empl. ($)	Revenues Total ($ mil.)	Revenues % of U.S.	Revenues Per Estab. ($)
California	570	9.2	5,747	11.0	10	158.9	27,651	472.2	11.9	828,454
Florida	626	10.1	5,770	11.1	9	143.7	24,903	446.7	11.2	713,553
Texas	505	8.2	4,505	8.6	9	110.9	24,614	349.4	8.8	691,800
New York	375	6.1	2,915	5.6	8	76.9	26,364	236.8	6.0	631,341
Illinois	252	4.1	2,278	4.4	9	69.1	30,317	189.8	4.8	753,333
Ohio	214	3.5	2,183	4.2	10	57.5	26,333	159.5	4.0	745,150
New Jersey	175	2.8	1,480	2.8	8	47.6	32,138	130.4	3.3	745,240
Pennsylvania	201	3.3	1,964	3.8	10	50.6	25,770	127.1	3.2	632,443
Michigan	175	2.8	1,665	3.2	10	43.0	25,836	124.3	3.1	710,194
Virginia	149	2.4	1,347	2.6	9	25.8	19,187	109.1	2.7	732,027
North Carolina	186	3.0	1,485	2.8	8	30.1	20,296	108.0	2.7	580,511
Maryland	133	2.2	1,338	2.6	10	34.9	26,064	97.1	2.4	729,865
Georgia	146	2.4	1,293	2.5	9	35.1	27,174	94.1	2.4	644,842
Arizona	141	2.3	1,098	2.1	8	28.3	25,817	93.4	2.4	662,511
Massachusetts	129	2.1	1,007	1.9	8	26.9	26,756	91.9	2.3	712,426
Washington	131	2.1	1,046	2.0	8	28.6	27,383	85.6	2.2	653,763
South Carolina	130	2.1	933	1.8	7	20.4	21,912	85.0	2.1	654,062
Louisiana	138	2.2	1,027	2.0	7	22.6	21,959	78.1	2.0	565,884
Missouri	142	2.3	926	1.8	7	21.9	23,651	69.8	1.8	491,556
Tennessee	109	1.8	1,041	2.0	10	22.1	21,248	65.3	1.6	599,055
Colorado	121	2.0	787	1.5	7	18.4	23,440	60.8	1.5	502,331
Indiana	126	2.0	960	1.8	8	20.4	21,215	54.3	1.4	430,810
Wisconsin	104	1.7	758	1.5	7	14.6	19,318	50.5	1.3	485,404
Connecticut	75	1.2	570	1.1	8	16.2	28,374	49.6	1.2	660,853
Oregon	75	1.2	593	1.1	8	12.3	20,813	45.4	1.1	605,240
Kentucky	77	1.2	582	1.1	8	13.6	23,323	42.4	1.1	550,662
Minnesota	74	1.2	594	1.1	8	14.3	24,155	41.7	1.0	563,270
Kansas	76	1.2	560	1.1	7	11.9	21,261	38.9	1.0	511,908
Mississippi	82	1.3	529	1.0	6	11.1	21,074	37.3	0.9	455,049
Arkansas	63	1.0	429	0.8	7	8.7	20,214	37.2	0.9	591,175
Oklahoma	73	1.2	522	1.0	7	10.8	20,692	35.7	0.9	489,014
Alabama	86	1.4	624	1.2	7	13.2	21,082	34.5	0.9	401,686
Hawaii	32	0.5	379	0.7	12	11.8	31,193	34.5	0.9	1,078,938
Nebraska	47	0.8	341	0.7	7	7.3	21,422	28.3	0.7	602,447
West Virginia	41	0.7	399	0.8	10	7.8	19,664	22.9	0.6	558,659
Utah	33	0.5	287	0.6	9	6.3	21,875	22.2	0.6	673,273
Iowa	76	1.2	337	0.6	4	6.2	18,433	18.7	0.5	245,605
New Mexico	39	0.6	247	0.5	6	5.0	20,093	18.1	0.5	463,051
Nevada	38	0.6	269	0.5	7	6.0	22,297	14.3	0.4	376,921
Delaware	11	0.2	161	0.3	15	4.6	28,484	11.5	0.3	1,042,273
Alaska	20	0.3	158	0.3	8	3.3	21,108	11.2	0.3	561,850
New Hampshire	26	0.4	226	0.4	9	5.4	24,102	10.2	0.3	392,308
Rhode Island	22	0.4	150	0.3	7	4.2	27,860	9.5	0.2	432,727
Idaho	23	0.4	155	0.3	7	3.7	23,774	8.7	0.2	377,348
Maine	21	0.3	139	0.3	7	2.9	21,158	6.1	0.2	292,333
Montana	21	0.3	89	0.2	4	1.7	18,708	4.5	0.1	214,333
South Dakota	18	0.3	77	0.1	4	1.3	16,506	3.7	0.1	204,889
North Dakota	17	0.3	79	0.2	5	1.4	18,051	2.8	0.1	167,588
Vermont	14	0.2	44 *	0.1	3	1.0	21,659	1.8	0.0	126,214
Wyoming	20	0.3	60 *	-	-	(D)	-	(D)	-	-
D.C.	1	-	10 *	-	-	(D)	-	(D)	-	-

Source: 1997 *Economic Census*. The states are in descending order of revenues or establishments (if revenue data are missing for the majority). The symbol (D) appears when data are withheld to prevent disclosure of competitive information. States marked with (D) are sorted by number of establishments. A dash (-) indicates that the data element cannot be calculated. * indicates the midpoint of a range; 175, for example is the range 100-249. Shaded *states* on the state map indicate those states which have proportionately greater representation in the industry than would be indicated by the state's population; the ratio is based on total revenues or number of establishments. Shaded *regions* indicate where the industry is regionally most concentrated.

NAICS 811420 - REUPHOLSTERY AND FURNITURE REPAIR

GENERAL STATISTICS

Year	Establishments (number)	Employment (number)	Payroll ($ million)	Revenues ($ million)	Employees per Establishment (number)	Revenues per Establishment ($)	Payroll per Employee ($)
1997	6,598	22,315	389.0	1,193.0	3.4	180,812	17,432

Source: *Economic Census of the United States*, 1997. This is a newly defined industry. Data for prior years were unavailable at the time of publication but may become available over time.

INDICES OF CHANGE

Year	Establishments (number)	Employment (number)	Payroll ($ million)	Revenues ($ million)	Employees per Establishment (number)	Revenues per Establishment ($)	Payroll per Employee ($)
1997	100.0	100.0	100.0	100.0	100.0	100.0	100.0

Sources: Same as General Statistics. The values shown reflect change from the base year, 1997. Values above 100 mean greater than 1997, values below 100 mean less than 1997, and a value of 100 in the 1982-96 or 1998-2001 period means same as 1997. Values followed by a 'p' are projections by the editors; 'e' stands for extrapolation. Data are the most recent available at this level of detail.

SIC INDUSTRIES RELATED TO NAICS 811420

Each new NAICS code represents an industry that used to be part of an SIC or a part of several SIC industries. Data in this table are shown to provide transitional information for these cases. All available data for the precursor SIC(s) are shown. Even if only a part of an SIC is included in the NAICS, *all* data for the SIC are reproduced. If the SIC industry is not marked as being a part (pt) of the NAICS, the entire industry is embedded in the NAICS data. The SIC composition of the new industry provides some hints of the relative importance of its "ancestors." Data marked with a 'p' are projected. Projections begin with 1982 data. Data earlier than 1990 are not shown but are reflected in the projections.

SIC	Industry	1990	1991	1992	1993	1994	1995	1996	1997
4581	**Airports, Flying Fields and Services (pt)**								
	Establishments (number)	2,777	2,968	3,252	3,382	3,503	3,629	4,014	3,958p
	Employment (thousands)	84.3	83.9	80.0	90.8	90.2	96.6	104.6	103.5p
	Revenues ($ million)	-	-	6,167.6	-	-	-	-	-
7641	**Reupholstery & Furniture Repair (pt)**								
	Establishments (number)	6,514	6,515	6,731	6,806	6,735	6,640	6,682p	6,681p
	Employment (thousands)	23.7	22.3	21.2	21.4	21.8	22.2	22.7p	22.7p
	Revenues ($ million)	-	-	980.4	1,060.6p	1,098.8p	1,137.0p	1,175.2p	1,213.4p

Source: *Economic Census of the United States*, 1992, annual surveys of economic sectors conducted by the Bureau of the Census, and estimates or projections based on the 1982-1992 period; not all data are shown. 'e' marks estimates made by the editors; 'p' indicates projections based on time series. A dash (-) indicates that data for this SIC or year were not available. The abbreviation (pt) next to the industry name indicates that only a part of the industry is present within the NAICS data. If no (pt) is shown, the entire industry is contained within the NAICS data.

SELECTED RATIOS

For 1997	Avg. of Information	Analyzed Industry	Index	For 1997	Avg. of Information	Analyzed Industry	Index
Employees per establishment	6	3	54	Payroll per establishment	126,069	58,957	47
Revenue per establishment	511,622	180,812	35	Payroll as % of revenue	25	33	132
Revenue per employee	81,659	53,462	65	Payroll per employee	20,122	17,432	87

Sources: Same as General Statistics. The 'Average' column represents the average for the industry sector, in 1997, where the currently shown industry is classified. The Index shows the relationship between the Average and the Analyzed Industry. For example, 100 means that they are equal; 500 that the Analyzed Industry is five times the average; 50 means that the Analyzed Industry is half the national average. The abbreviation 'na' is used to show that data are 'not available'.

LEADING COMPANIES   Number shown: **1**   Total sales ($ mil): **12**   Total employment (000): **0.5**

Company Name	Address				CEO Name	Phone	Co. Type	Sales ($ mil)	Empl. (000)
KTU Worldwide Inc.	813 Circle Dr	Aberdeen	SD	57401	Dave Haglund	605-225-4049	R	12	0.5

Source: *Ward's Business Directory of U.S. Private and Public Companies*, Volumes 1 and 2, 2000. The company type code used is as follows: P - Public, R - Private, S - Subsidiary, D - Division, J - Joint Venture, A - Affiliate, G - Group, N - Company type not reported. Sales are in millions of dollars, employees are in thousands. An asterisk (*) indicates an estimated sales volume. The symbol < stands for 'less than'. Company names and addresses are truncated, in some cases, to fit into the available space.

LOCATION BY STATE AND REGIONAL CONCENTRATION

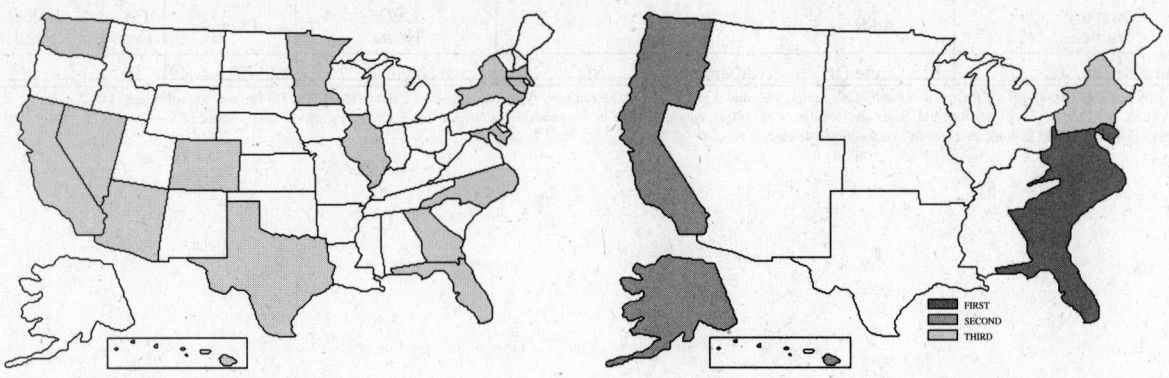

FIRST
SECOND
THIRD

INDUSTRY DATA BY STATE

State	Establishments Total (number)	Establishments % of U.S.	Employment Total (number)	Employment % of U.S.	Employment Per Estab.	Payroll Total ($ mil.)	Payroll Per Empl. ($)	Revenues Total ($ mil.)	Revenues % of U.S.	Revenues Per Estab. ($)
California	731	11.1	2,926	13.1	4	51.2	17,492	171.7	14.4	234,934
New York	426	6.5	1,702	7.6	4	38.1	22,395	114.5	9.6	268,761
Texas	450	6.8	1,984	8.9	4	35.4	17,862	99.7	8.4	221,598
Florida	508	7.7	1,528	6.8	3	22.2	14,513	73.9	6.2	145,526
Illinois	291	4.4	1,032	4.6	4	20.2	19,602	59.0	4.9	202,674
Pennsylvania	263	4.0	898	4.0	3	21.2	23,576	56.3	4.7	213,996
North Carolina	286	4.3	941	4.2	3	13.3	14,120	43.7	3.7	152,881
Ohio	235	3.6	783	3.5	3	13.2	16,808	39.9	3.3	169,604
Georgia	210	3.2	629	2.8	3	12.5	19,847	38.2	3.2	181,752
New Jersey	178	2.7	595	2.7	3	10.4	17,506	32.8	2.8	184,388
Maryland	148	2.2	594	2.7	4	11.2	18,828	32.7	2.7	220,750
Michigan	193	2.9	604	2.7	3	10.5	17,425	31.2	2.6	161,881
Massachusetts	154	2.3	530	2.4	3	10.1	19,089	30.3	2.5	196,708
Virginia	202	3.1	617	2.8	3	11.0	17,810	29.2	2.4	144,480
Washington	147	2.2	445	2.0	3	7.9	17,831	25.1	2.1	170,741
Colorado	135	2.0	468	2.1	3	9.1	19,521	24.0	2.0	177,800
Arizona	117	1.8	518	2.3	4	7.6	14,736	23.9	2.0	204,265
Minnesota	110	1.7	412	1.8	4	7.4	18,012	22.1	1.9	200,964
Indiana	143	2.2	509	2.3	4	8.0	15,782	21.6	1.8	151,357
Missouri	147	2.2	429	1.9	3	6.6	15,462	18.2	1.5	123,762
Wisconsin	104	1.6	298	1.3	3	4.9	16,554	17.0	1.4	163,019
Connecticut	102	1.5	264	1.2	3	4.6	17,337	16.4	1.4	161,127
South Carolina	113	1.7	283	1.3	3	4.1	14,512	14.4	1.2	127,876
Alabama	115	1.7	301	1.3	3	3.9	13,027	14.3	1.2	124,139
Louisiana	86	1.3	361	1.6	4	5.4	14,903	14.0	1.2	162,384
Tennessee	105	1.6	313	1.4	3	4.5	14,527	13.8	1.2	131,219
Oregon	85	1.3	189	0.8	2	2.8	14,910	10.2	0.9	119,800
Kentucky	72	1.1	206	0.9	3	2.5	12,316	8.9	0.7	123,806
Nevada	45	0.7	151	0.7	3	2.7	17,669	8.5	0.7	189,400
Mississippi	56	0.8	188	0.8	3	2.0	10,612	8.2	0.7	147,054
Oklahoma	55	0.8	168	0.8	3	2.7	15,994	7.6	0.6	137,473
Kansas	61	0.9	176	0.8	3	2.4	13,682	7.4	0.6	120,869
Iowa	62	0.9	157	0.7	3	2.1	13,178	7.1	0.6	114,258
Utah	43	0.7	141	0.6	3	2.2	15,411	7.0	0.6	163,419
Hawaii	28	0.4	105	0.5	4	1.9	18,305	6.4	0.5	227,286
Arkansas	42	0.6	94	0.4	2	1.3	13,447	4.7	0.4	113,024
Idaho	34	0.5	88	0.4	3	1.2	14,023	4.1	0.3	121,882
Rhode Island	37	0.6	80	0.4	2	1.3	16,262	4.0	0.3	108,189
Nebraska	33	0.5	69	0.3	2	1.1	15,841	3.8	0.3	113,636
New Mexico	34	0.5	79	0.4	2	1.0	12,354	3.5	0.3	104,059
West Virginia	29	0.4	96	0.4	3	1.0	10,240	3.1	0.3	108,241
D.C.	15	0.2	51	0.2	3	1.1	21,314	2.9	0.2	195,667
Montana	26	0.4	51	0.2	2	0.7	14,137	2.9	0.2	112,423
New Hampshire	24	0.4	55	0.2	2	0.9	16,236	2.9	0.2	120,375
Maine	30	0.5	42	0.2	1	0.7	15,952	2.8	0.2	92,433
Delaware	18	0.3	34	0.2	2	0.5	16,118	1.9	0.2	104,667
South Dakota	12	0.2	12	0.1	1	0.3	25,083	1.4	0.1	118,833
North Dakota	16	0.2	35	0.2	2	0.3	8,457	1.2	0.1	73,625
Vermont	16	0.2	60*	-	-	(D)	-	(D)	-	-
Alaska	14	0.2	60*	-	-	(D)	-	(D)	-	-
Wyoming	12	0.2	10*	-	-	(D)	-	(D)	-	-

Source: 1997 *Economic Census*. The states are in descending order of revenues or establishments (if revenue data are missing for the majority). The symbol (D) appears when data are withheld to prevent disclosure of competitive information. States marked with (D) are sorted by number of establishments. A dash (-) indicates that the data element cannot be calculated. * indicates the midpoint of a range; 175, for example is the range 100-249. Shaded *states* on the state map indicate those states which have proportionately greater representation in the industry than would be indicated by the state's population; the ratio is based on total revenues or number of establishments. Shaded *regions* indicate where the industry is regionally most concentrated.

NAICS 811430 - FOOTWEAR AND LEATHER GOODS REPAIR

GENERAL STATISTICS

Year	Establishments (number)	Employment (number)	Payroll ($ million)	Revenues ($ million)	Employees per Establishment (number)	Revenues per Establishment ($)	Payroll per Employee ($)
1997	2,153	5,469	73.0	261.0	2.5	121,226	13,348

Source: Economic Census of the United States, 1997. This is a newly defined industry. Data for prior years were unavailable at the time of publication but may become available over time.

INDICES OF CHANGE

Year	Establishments (number)	Employment (number)	Payroll ($ million)	Revenues ($ million)	Employees per Establishment (number)	Revenues per Establishment ($)	Payroll per Employee ($)
1997	100.0	100.0	100.0	100.0	100.0	100.0	100.0

Sources: Same as General Statistics. The values shown reflect change from the base year, 1997. Values above 100 mean greater than 1997, values below 100 mean less than 1997, and a value of 100 in the 1982-96 or 1998-2001 period means same as 1997. Values followed by a 'p' are projections by the editors; 'e' stands for extrapolation. Data are the most recent available at this level of detail.

SIC INDUSTRIES RELATED TO NAICS 811430

Each new NAICS code represents an industry that used to be part of an SIC or a part of several SIC industries. Data in this table are shown to provide transitional information for these cases. All available data for the precursor SIC(s) are shown. Even if only a part of an SIC is included in the NAICS, *all* data for the SIC are reproduced. If the SIC industry is not marked as being a part (pt) of the NAICS, the entire industry is embedded in the NAICS data. The SIC composition of the new industry provides some hints of the relative importance of its "ancestors." Data marked with a 'p' are projected. Projections begin with 1982 data. Data earlier than 1990 are not shown but are reflected in the projections.

SIC	Industry	1990	1991	1992	1993	1994	1995	1996	1997
7251	**Shoe Repair & Shoeshine Parlors (pt)**								
	Establishments (number)	2,528	2,593	2,702	2,654	2,438	2,292	2,355p	2,307p
	Employment (thousands)	6.5	6.5	6.4	6.7	6.1	6.0	6.1p	6.1p
	Revenues ($ million)	-	-	275.8	278.6p	287.5p	296.4p	305.4p	314.3p
7699	**Repair Services, nec (pt)**								
	Establishments (number)	27,822	29,303	34,103	34,618	34,136	34,391	35,001p	35,792p
	Employment (thousands)	181.0	181.4	191.0	201.5	207.4	220.2	219.6p	226.2p
	Revenues ($ million)	-	-	15,059.4	15,563.6p	16,427.9p	17,292.2p	18,156.5p	19,020.8p

Source: Economic Census of the United States, 1992, annual surveys of economic sectors conducted by the Bureau of the Census, and estimates or projections based on the 1982-1992 period; not all data are shown. 'e' marks estimates made by the editors; 'p' indicates projections based on time series. A dash (-) indicates that data for this SIC or year were not available. The abbreviation (pt) next to the industry name indicates that only a part of the industry is present within the NAICS data. If no (pt) is shown, the entire industry is contained within the NAICS data.

SELECTED RATIOS

For 1997	Avg. of Information	Analyzed Industry	Index	For 1997	Avg. of Information	Analyzed Industry	Index
Employees per establishment	6	3	41	Payroll per establishment	126,069	33,906	27
Revenue per establishment	511,622	121,226	24	Payroll as % of revenue	25	28	114
Revenue per employee	81,659	47,724	58	Payroll per employee	20,122	13,348	66

Sources: Same as General Statistics. The 'Average' column represents the average for the industry sector, in 1997, where the currently shown industry is classified. The Index shows the relationship between the Average and the Analyzed Industry. For example, 100 means that they are equal; 500 that the Analyzed Industry is five times the average; 50 means that the Analyzed Industry is half the national average. The abbreviation 'na' is used to show that data are 'not available'.

LEADING COMPANIES

No company data available for this industry.

LOCATION BY STATE AND REGIONAL CONCENTRATION

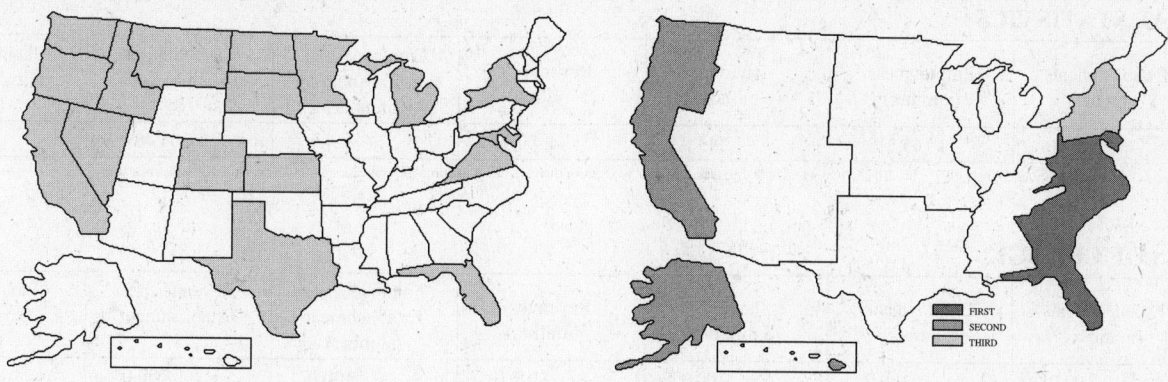

INDUSTRY DATA BY STATE

State	Establishments Total (number)	% of U.S.	Employment Total (number)	% of U.S.	Per Estab.	Payroll Total ($ mil.)	Per Empl. ($)	Revenues Total ($ mil.)	% of U.S.	Per Estab. ($)
California	258	12.0	582	10.6	2	8.1	13,851	33.8	12.9	131,085
Texas	182	8.5	473	8.6	3	7.5	15,818	28.0	10.7	153,714
New York	221	10.3	525	9.6	2	7.2	13,724	25.3	9.7	114,326
Michigan	78	3.6	582	10.6	7	7.7	13,144	16.8	6.4	215,513
Florida	148	6.9	323	5.9	2	4.4	13,563	15.8	6.0	106,574
Virginia	73	3.4	160	2.9	2	2.5	15,581	10.2	3.9	139,110
Colorado	52	2.4	173	3.2	3	2.3	13,503	7.9	3.0	152,154
Illinois	67	3.1	183	3.3	3	2.4	13,142	7.9	3.0	117,552
Ohio	73	3.4	183	3.3	3	2.0	11,027	7.1	2.7	97,685
Washington	52	2.4	112	2.0	2	1.9	17,161	7.0	2.7	134,173
Georgia	63	2.9	152	2.8	2	1.8	11,901	6.9	2.6	109,317
Pennsylvania	62	2.9	127	2.3	2	1.4	11,063	6.6	2.5	106,661
New Jersey	44	2.0	92	1.7	2	1.6	17,837	6.0	2.3	137,273
North Carolina	59	2.7	123	2.2	2	1.5	11,967	5.7	2.2	96,373
Oregon	24	1.1	76	1.4	3	1.4	18,513	5.6	2.1	233,458
Maryland	36	1.7	91	1.7	3	1.9	20,396	5.2	2.0	143,556
Massachusetts	34	1.6	87	1.6	3	1.3	15,161	5.0	1.9	146,029
Minnesota	35	1.6	119	2.2	3	1.3	10,706	4.7	1.8	133,514
Missouri	43	2.0	120	2.2	3	1.4	11,958	4.3	1.7	101,116
South Carolina	41	1.9	92	1.7	2	0.9	9,978	3.4	1.3	83,220
Kentucky	30	1.4	86	1.6	3	0.8	9,372	3.2	1.2	106,967
Alabama	33	1.5	66	1.2	2	0.6	9,591	3.2	1.2	96,333
Indiana	40	1.9	62	1.1	2	0.8	12,516	3.1	1.2	76,575
Tennessee	40	1.9	66	1.2	2	0.8	12,318	2.8	1.1	71,075
Kansas	26	1.2	73	1.3	3	0.7	9,795	2.8	1.1	107,846
Wisconsin	31	1.4	52	1.0	2	0.6	10,981	2.6	1.0	84,129
Mississippi	21	1.0	45	0.8	2	0.5	12,200	2.5	0.9	116,810
Louisiana	27	1.3	70	1.3	3	0.9	13,171	2.5	1.0	92,185
Iowa	21	1.0	42	0.8	2	0.5	11,405	2.5	1.0	121,095
Arizona	32	1.5	58	1.1	2	0.7	11,621	2.5	1.0	79,094
Oklahoma	26	1.2	52	1.0	2	0.5	8,827	2.0	0.8	76,385
Utah	20	0.9	57	1.0	3	0.7	12,281	1.9	0.7	95,400
Nevada	18	0.8	38	0.7	2	0.5	14,316	1.8	0.7	98,000
New Mexico	15	0.7	23	0.4	2	0.3	12,043	1.4	0.5	90,933
Connecticut	15	0.7	19	0.3	1	0.4	18,684	1.4	0.5	95,133
Montana	13	0.6	15	0.3	1	0.2	12,333	1.4	0.5	105,231
Idaho	11	0.5	38	0.7	3	0.3	8,868	1.3	0.5	120,545
West Virginia	11	0.5	32	0.6	3	0.3	10,781	1.2	0.5	110,545
Nebraska	11	0.5	16	0.3	1	0.2	11,812	1.0	0.4	90,273
Arkansas	17	0.8	27	0.5	2	0.2	7,481	0.9	0.4	55,000
New Hampshire	7	0.3	12	0.2	2	0.2	14,583	0.9	0.3	127,429
South Dakota	7	0.3	26	0.5	4	0.2	9,269	0.9	0.3	123,143
Maine	6	0.3	30	0.5	5	0.3	10,500	0.8	0.3	128,000
North Dakota	7	0.3	16	0.3	2	0.2	13,500	0.8	0.3	108,143
Hawaii	3	0.1	6	0.1	2	0.1	9,833	0.2	0.1	65,667
Delaware	5	0.2	10*	-	-	(D)	-	(D)	-	-
D.C.	5	0.2	10*	-	-	(D)	-	(D)	-	-
Rhode Island	5	0.2	10*	-	-	(D)	-	(D)	-	-
Vermont	2	0.1	10*	-	-	(D)	-	(D)	-	-
Wyoming	2	0.1	10*	-	-	(D)	-	(D)	-	-
Alaska	1	-	10*	-	-	(D)	-	(D)	-	-

Source: 1997 *Economic Census.* The states are in descending order of revenues or establishments (if revenue data are missing for the majority). The symbol (D) appears when data are withheld to prevent disclosure of competitive information. States marked with (D) are sorted by number of establishments. A dash (-) indicates that the data element cannot be calculated. * indicates the midpoint of a range; 175, for example is the range 100-249. Shaded *states* on the state map indicate those states which have proportionately greater representation in the industry than would be indicated by the state's population; the ratio is based on total revenues or number of establishments. Shaded *regions* indicate where the industry is regionally most concentrated.

NAICS 811490 - PERSONAL AND HOUSEHOLD GOODS REPAIR AND MAINTENANCE NEC

GENERAL STATISTICS

Year	Establishments (number)	Employment (number)	Payroll ($ million)	Revenues ($ million)	Employees per Establishment (number)	Revenues per Establishment ($)	Payroll per Employee ($)
1997	14,641	65,213	1,343.0	4,458.0	4.5	304,487	20,594

Source: Economic Census of the United States, 1997. This is a newly defined industry. Data for prior years were unavailable at the time of publication but may become available over time.

INDICES OF CHANGE

Year	Establishments (number)	Employment (number)	Payroll ($ million)	Revenues ($ million)	Employees per Establishment (number)	Revenues per Establishment ($)	Payroll per Employee ($)
1997	100.0	100.0	100.0	100.0	100.0	100.0	100.0

Sources: Same as General Statistics. The values shown reflect change from the base year, 1997. Values above 100 mean greater than 1997, values below 100 mean less than 1997, and a value of 100 in the 1982-96 or 1998-2001 period means same as 1997. Values followed by a 'p' are projections by the editors; 'e' stands for extrapolation. Data are the most recent available at this level of detail.

SIC INDUSTRIES RELATED TO NAICS 811490

Each new NAICS code represents an industry that used to be part of an SIC or a part of several SIC industries. Data in this table are shown to provide transitional information for these cases. All available data for the precursor SIC(s) are shown. Even if only a part of an SIC is included in the NAICS, *all* data for the SIC are reproduced. If the SIC industry is not marked as being a part (pt) of the NAICS, the entire industry is embedded in the NAICS data. The SIC composition of the new industry provides some hints of the relative importance of its "ancestors." Data marked with a 'p' are projected. Projections begin with 1982 data. Data earlier than 1990 are not shown but are reflected in the projections.

SIC	Industry	1990	1991	1992	1993	1994	1995	1996	1997
3732	**Boat Building & Repairing (pt)**								
	Establishments (number)	2,032	2,042	2,455	2,435	2,366	2,332	2,440p	2,488p
	Employment (thousands)	57.0	40.8	44.5	47.0	48.1	47.6	49.2	51.9p
	Value of Shipments ($ million)	4,998.0	3,675.6	4,599.3	4,975.3	5,425.1	5,639.9	5,822.9	6,122.8p
7219	**Laundry & Garment Services, nec (pt)**								
	Establishments (number)	2,323	2,715	3,968	3,896	3,665	3,460	4,054p	4,258p
	Employment (thousands)	13.5	15.2	19.9	24.4	20.4	20.0	23.8p	25.2p
	Revenues ($ million)	-	-	652.8	-	-	-	-	-
7631	**Watch, Clock, & Jewelry Repair**								
	Establishments (number)	1,529	1,583	1,662	1,655	1,642	1,681	1,602p	1,599p
	Employment (thousands)	5.3	5.5	5.1	5.6	5.1	5.4	5.2p	5.2p
	Revenues ($ million)	-	-	274.6	281.1p	289.1p	297.1p	305.1p	313.1p
7699	**Repair Services, nec (pt)**								
	Establishments (number)	27,822	29,303	34,103	34,618	34,136	34,391	35,001p	35,792p
	Employment (thousands)	181.0	181.4	191.0	201.5	207.4	220.2	219.6p	226.2p
	Revenues ($ million)	-	-	15,059.4	15,563.6p	16,427.9p	17,292.2p	18,156.5p	19,020.8p

Source: Economic Census of the United States, 1992, annual surveys of economic sectors conducted by the Bureau of the Census, and estimates or projections based on the 1982-1992 period; not all data are shown. 'e' marks estimates made by the editors; 'p' indicates projections based on time series. A dash (-) indicates that data for this SIC or year were not available. The abbreviation (pt) next to the industry name indicates that only a part of the industry is present within the NAICS data. If no (pt) is shown, the entire industry is contained within the NAICS data.

SELECTED RATIOS

For 1997	Avg. of Information	Analyzed Industry	Index	For 1997	Avg. of Information	Analyzed Industry	Index
Employees per establishment	6	4	71	Payroll per establishment	126,069	91,729	73
Revenue per establishment	511,622	304,487	60	Payroll as % of revenue	25	30	122
Revenue per employee	81,659	68,361	84	Payroll per employee	20,122	20,594	102

Sources: Same as General Statistics. The 'Average' column represents the average for the industry sector, in 1997, where the currently shown industry is classified. The Index shows the relationship between the Average and the Analyzed Industry. For example, 100 means that they are equal; 500 that the Analyzed Industry is five times the average; 50 means that the Analyzed Industry is half the national average. The abbreviation 'na' is used to show that data are 'not available'.

LEADING COMPANIES   Number shown: **36**   Total sales ($ mil): **2,223**   Total employment (000): **13.2**

Company Name	Address				CEO Name	Phone	Co. Type	Sales ($ mil)	Empl. (000)
Insituform Technologies Inc.	PO Box 1026	Chesterfield	MO	63006	Anthony W. Hooper	636-530-8000	P	301	1.5
Aaron's Automotive Products Inc.	2600 N Westgate	Springfield	MO	65803	Paul Komaromy	417-831-5257	P	253*	1.4
SMH (US) Inc.	35 E 21st St	New York	NY	10010	Roland Streule	212-271-1400	S	200*	0.4
Roto-Rooter Inc.	2500 Chemed Ctr	Cincinnati	OH	45202	Spencer Lee	513-762-6690	P	192	2.4
First Aviation Services Inc.	15 Riverside Ave	Westport	CT	06880	Michael C Culver	203-291-3300	P	154	0.5
Leamco-Ruthco	PO Box 60050	Midland	TX	79711		915-563-2180	S	150	0.7
Mayor's Jewelers Inc.	14051 NW 14th St	Sunrise	FL	33323	Isaac Arguetty	854-846-2718	S	140	0.4
J.A. Riggs Tractor Co.	PO Box 1399	Little Rock	AR	72203	John Riggs	501-570-3100	R	100	0.6
Siemens Power Corp.	2101 Horn Rapids	Richland	WA	99352		509-375-8100	S	100*	0.8
Phillips Service Industries Inc.	11878 Hubbard	Livonia	MI	48150	William T Phillips	734-853-5000	R	91	0.6
Safety-Kleen Corp	2 NE 9th St	Oklahoma City	OK	73104	Kenneth Winger	803-934-4200	D	80*	0.4
Peoples Jewelry Company Inc.	245 23rd St	Toledo	OH	43624	Larry Goldberg	419-241-4181	R	78*	0.5
C.B. Hoober and Son Inc.	3452 Old Phila	Intercourse	PA	17534	Charles B Hoober Jr	717-768-8231	R	48	0.2
Brake Supply Company Inc.	PO Box 447	Evansville	IN	47703	Thomas Ashby	812-467-1000	S	40*	0.2
Logistic Services International Inc.	6200 Lake Gray	Jacksonville	FL	32244	James McKinney	904-771-2100	R	40	0.3
GPX Inc.	60 Progress Ave	Cranberry	PA	16066	David L Greb	724-776-1525	R	30*	0.2
Frank Lill and Son Inc.	656 Basket Rd	Webster	NY	14580	Charles G Lill	716-265-0490	R	28	0.2
Anacomp Inc. Maintenance Div.	12365 Crosthwaite	Poway	CA	92064		858-679-9797	D	27*	0.2
Manufacturing Technology Inc.	PO Box 3059	South Bend	IN	46619	C Adams	219-233-9490	R	20	<0.1
Stainless Tank & Equipment L	PO Box 246	Cottage Grove	WI	53527	James Hammis	608-837-5121	R	20	0.1
Time Service Inc.	245 23rd St	Toledo	OH	43624	Lawrence S Goldberg	419-241-4181	R	20*	0.5
S. Joseph and Sons Inc.	320 6th Ave	Des Moines	IA	50309	William Baum	515-283-1961	R	18	<0.1
Bearing Inspection Inc.	4422 Corp Center	Los Alamitos	CA	90720	Alan Sanderson	714-484-2400	S	16*	0.1
American Grinding & Machine Co	2000 N Mango Ave	Chicago	IL	60639		773-889-4343	R	13	0.1
Stamped Products Inc.	P O Box 5175	Gadsden	AL	35905		256-492-8899	S	12*	0.1
Southern Elevator Company Inc.	PO Box 36006	Greensboro	NC	27416	Bryant Aydelette	336-274-2401	S	11*	<0.1
Turbine Components Corp.	PO Box 801	Branford	CT	06405		203-481-3451	R	10*	0.1
Vanguard Medical Concepts Inc.	5307 Great Oak Dr	Lakeland	FL	33815	Chuck Masek	941-683-8680	R	7	0.1
PRL Industries Inc.	PO Box 142	Cornwall	PA	17016		717-273-6787	R	6	<0.1
Industrial Hardfacing Inc.	PO Box 303	Elk River	MN	55330	Don Millslagle	612-441-2733	R	5	0.1
McCann Electronics	100 Division St	Metairie	LA	70001	Gerry McCann	504-837-7272	R	5*	<0.1
Air Lab Inc.	641 Industry Dr	Seattle	WA	98188	Franck Hebert	206-575-0920	S	3	<0.1
Alloy Welding Corp.	2033 Janice Ave	Melrose Park	IL	60160	John Troccoli	708-345-6756	R	3	<0.1
Standard Electric Time Corp.	PO Box 320	Tecumseh	MI	49286	Gilbert E Pierce	517-423-8331	R	2*	<0.1
Vopalensky's Inc.	705 Main St	North Bend	NE	68649	Charles Vopalensky	402-652-8335	R	1*	<0.1
Stereo Lab Service Inc.	4532 Indianola Ave	Columbus	OH	43214	Thomas Goodwin	740-266-5584	R	0	<0.1

Source: *Ward's Business Directory of U.S. Private and Public Companies*, Volumes 1 and 2, 2000. The company type code used is as follows: P - Public, R - Private, S - Subsidiary, D - Division, J - Joint Venture, A - Affiliate, G - Group, N - Company type not reported. Sales are in millions of dollars, employees are in thousands. An asterisk (*) indicates an estimated sales volume. The symbol < stands for 'less than'. Company names and addresses are truncated, in some cases, to fit into the available space.

LOCATION BY STATE AND REGIONAL CONCENTRATION

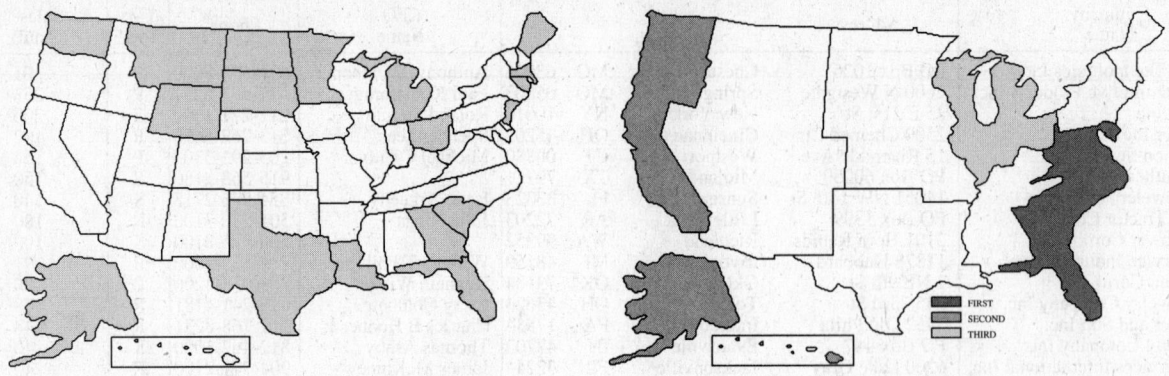

FIRST
SECOND
THIRD

INDUSTRY DATA BY STATE

State	Establishments Total (number)	% of U.S.	Employment Total (number)	% of U.S.	Per Estab.	Payroll Total ($ mil.)	Per Empl. ($)	Revenues Total ($ mil.)	% of U.S.	Per Estab. ($)
California	1,424	9.7	7,556	11.6	5	149.6	19,801	514.6	11.5	361,411
Florida	1,232	8.4	5,244	8.0	4	117.9	22,479	410.5	9.2	333,192
Texas	1,149	7.8	5,345	8.2	5	100.5	18,801	355.1	8.0	309,079
Ohio	499	3.4	5,385	8.3	11	99.5	18,485	256.4	5.8	513,784
New York	741	5.1	3,074	4.7	4	66.6	21,664	236.7	5.3	319,405
Michigan	569	3.9	2,410	3.7	4	55.9	23,176	171.8	3.9	301,893
Illinois	572	3.9	2,365	3.6	4	55.7	23,565	170.9	3.8	298,771
Washington	382	2.6	1,926	3.0	5	46.3	24,063	157.9	3.5	413,442
Pennsylvania	458	3.1	2,080	3.2	5	40.7	19,562	141.6	3.2	309,162
New Jersey	353	2.4	1,607	2.5	5	45.2	28,110	139.9	3.1	396,320
Georgia	363	2.5	1,791	2.7	5	39.6	22,137	121.8	2.7	335,636
Louisiana	299	2.0	1,564	2.4	5	36.2	23,134	118.0	2.6	394,749
Minnesota	315	2.2	1,455	2.2	5	32.3	22,190	108.4	2.4	343,984
Massachusetts	304	2.1	1,197	1.8	4	30.2	25,203	105.8	2.4	348,039
Virginia	388	2.7	1,548	2.4	4	32.5	20,973	93.6	2.1	241,258
North Carolina	457	3.1	1,636	2.5	4	28.5	17,405	90.6	2.0	198,276
Indiana	337	2.3	1,459	2.2	4	26.9	18,419	86.8	1.9	257,457
Maryland	299	2.0	1,223	1.9	4	27.9	22,805	83.6	1.9	279,612
Missouri	351	2.4	1,278	2.0	4	22.9	17,894	74.8	1.7	213,182
South Carolina	227	1.6	1,082	1.7	5	22.3	20,648	72.3	1.6	318,639
Wisconsin	276	1.9	953	1.5	3	20.3	21,270	67.8	1.5	245,779
Arizona	230	1.6	859	1.3	4	16.1	18,800	61.8	1.4	268,713
Alabama	266	1.8	916	1.4	3	16.2	17,721	61.2	1.4	230,113
Connecticut	159	1.1	716	1.1	5	19.0	26,478	56.2	1.3	353,151
Tennessee	232	1.6	761	1.2	3	12.9	16,903	49.3	1.1	212,685
Colorado	238	1.6	739	1.1	3	13.6	18,399	48.1	1.1	202,147
Iowa	186	1.3	707	1.1	4	10.8	15,229	45.1	1.0	242,366
Oregon	188	1.3	682	1.0	4	11.5	16,878	44.8	1.0	238,553
Oklahoma	193	1.3	698	1.1	4	12.4	17,795	44.0	1.0	228,036
Kentucky	185	1.3	709	1.1	4	12.5	17,564	40.3	0.9	218,097
Mississippi	166	1.1	560	0.9	3	9.8	17,580	38.4	0.9	231,217
Arkansas	120	0.8	566	0.9	5	10.8	19,124	35.8	0.8	298,300
Maine	102	0.7	412	0.6	4	13.4	32,425	35.7	0.8	350,049
Kansas	179	1.2	623	1.0	3	9.8	15,687	35.6	0.8	199,117
Utah	107	0.7	425	0.7	4	7.5	17,661	28.7	0.6	268,673
Alaska	68	0.5	250	0.4	4	6.5	25,984	25.9	0.6	381,382
Nebraska	131	0.9	380	0.6	3	5.9	15,482	24.2	0.5	184,427
North Dakota	69	0.5	274	0.4	4	5.2	18,825	21.8	0.5	316,232
New Hampshire	76	0.5	235	0.4	3	5.2	21,919	18.9	0.4	248,632
Montana	87	0.6	239	0.4	3	3.7	15,272	17.9	0.4	205,425
West Virginia	61	0.4	288	0.4	5	6.2	21,469	16.5	0.4	271,033
Nevada	70	0.5	278	0.4	4	4.6	16,626	16.1	0.4	229,786
New Mexico	82	0.6	303	0.5	4	3.9	12,914	16.0	0.4	195,415
South Dakota	69	0.5	225	0.3	3	3.9	17,258	14.6	0.3	211,087
Idaho	79	0.5	211	0.3	3	3.8	17,991	13.2	0.3	166,658
Hawaii	44	0.3	159	0.2	4	3.9	24,252	12.5	0.3	284,386
Wyoming	70	0.5	163	0.2	2	2.8	17,411	10.3	0.2	146,486
Vermont	45	0.3	116	0.2	3	1.9	16,716	7.2	0.2	161,000
D.C.	20	0.1	70	0.1	4	1.7	24,586	4.7	0.1	233,300
Rhode Island	91	0.6	375*	-	-	(D)	-	(D)	-	-
Delaware	33	0.2	175*	-	-	(D)	-	(D)	-	-

Source: 1997 *Economic Census*. The states are in descending order of revenues or establishments (if revenue data are missing for the majority). The symbol (D) appears when data are withheld to prevent disclosure of competitive information. States marked with (D) are sorted by number of establishments. A dash (-) indicates that the data element cannot be calculated. * indicates the midpoint of a range; 175, for example is the range 100-249. Shaded *states* on the state map indicate those states which have proportionately greater representation in the industry than would be indicated by the state's population; the ratio is based on total revenues or number of establishments. Shaded *regions* indicate where the industry is regionally most concentrated.

NAICS 812111 - BARBER SHOPS

GENERAL STATISTICS

Year	Establishments (number)	Employment (number)	Payroll ($ million)	Revenues ($ million)	Employees per Establishment (number)	Revenues per Establishment ($)	Payroll per Employee ($)
1997	4,242	13,341	194.0	428.0	3.1	100,896	14,542

Source: *Economic Census of the United States*, 1997. This is a newly defined industry. Data for prior years were unavailable at the time of publication but may become available over time.

INDICES OF CHANGE

Year	Establishments (number)	Employment (number)	Payroll ($ million)	Revenues ($ million)	Employees per Establishment (number)	Revenues per Establishment ($)	Payroll per Employee ($)
1997	100.0	100.0	100.0	100.0	100.0	100.0	100.0

Sources: Same as General Statistics. The values shown reflect change from the base year, 1997. Values above 100 mean greater than 1997, values below 100 mean less than 1997, and a value of 100 in the 1982-96 or 1998-2001 period means same as 1997. Values followed by a 'p' are projections by the editors; 'e' stands for extrapolation. Data are the most recent available at this level of detail.

SIC INDUSTRIES RELATED TO NAICS 812111

Each new NAICS code represents an industry that used to be part of an SIC or a part of several SIC industries. Data in this table are shown to provide transitional information for these cases. All available data for the precursor SIC(s) are shown. Even if only a part of an SIC is included in the NAICS, *all* data for the SIC are reproduced. If the SIC industry is not marked as being a part (pt) of the NAICS, the entire industry is embedded in the NAICS data. The SIC composition of the new industry provides some hints of the relative importance of its "ancestors." Data marked with a 'p' are projected. Projections begin with 1982 data. Data earlier than 1990 are not shown but are reflected in the projections.

SIC	Industry	1990	1991	1992	1993	1994	1995	1996	1997
7241	**Barber Shops (pt)**								
	Establishments (number)	5,115	5,053	4,902	4,806	4,629	4,474	3,666*p*	3,356*p*
	Employment (thousands)	16.4	16.1	14.5	14.9	14.2	14.1	13.1*p*	12.5*p*
	Revenues ($ million)	1,439.0	1,466.0	1,515.0	1,514.0	1,558.0	1,609.0	1,590.0	1,689.5*p*

Source: *Economic Census of the United States*, 1992, annual surveys of economic sectors conducted by the Bureau of the Census, and estimates or projections based on the 1982-1992 period; not all data are shown. 'e' marks estimates made by the editors; 'p' indicates projections based on time series. A dash (-) indicates that data for this SIC or year were not available. The abbreviation (pt) next to the industry name indicates that only a part of the industry is present within the NAICS data. If no (pt) is shown, the entire industry is contained within the NAICS data.

SELECTED RATIOS

For 1997	Avg. of Information	Analyzed Industry	Index	For 1997	Avg. of Information	Analyzed Industry	Index
Employees per establishment	6	3	50	Payroll per establishment	126,069	45,733	36
Revenue per establishment	511,622	100,896	20	Payroll as % of revenue	25	45	184
Revenue per employee	81,659	32,082	39	Payroll per employee	20,122	14,542	72

Sources: Same as General Statistics. The 'Average' column represents the average for the industry sector, in 1997, where the currently shown industry is classified. The Index shows the relationship between the Average and the Analyzed Industry. For example, 100 means that they are equal; 500 that the Analyzed Industry is five times the average; 50 means that the Analyzed Industry is half the national average. The abbreviation 'na' is used to show that data are 'not available'.

LEADING COMPANIES   Number shown: **10**   Total sales ($ mil): **1,309**   Total employment (000): **38.0**

Company Name	Address				CEO Name	Phone	Co. Type	Sales ($ mil)	Empl. (000)
Regis Corp.	7201 Metro Blvd	Minneapolis	MN	55439	Paul D. Finkelstein	612-947-7777	P	927	31.0
Rocco Altobelli Inc.	14301 Burnsville	Burnsville	MN	55306	Rocco Altobelli	612-707-1900	R	135*	0.4
Supercuts Inc.	7201 Metro Blvd	Minneapolis	MN	55439	Mark Kartarick	612-947-7777	S	101*	5.0
Aveda Corp.	4000 Pheasant	Minneapolis	MN	55449	Nicole Rechelbacher	612-783-4000	S	88*	0.5
Lorick Enterprises Inc.	315 E 5th St	Charlotte	NC	28202	Forrest W Lorick Jr	704-333-9286	R	20	0.8
Preston Wynne Salon	14567 Big Basin	Saratoga	CA	95070	Peggy Borgman	408-741-5525	R	19*	<0.1
Mitchell's Salon and Day Spa Inc.	8118 Montgomery	Cincinnati	OH	45236	Deborah Schmidt	513-793-0900	R	8*	0.2
Circle Food Stores Inc.	1522 Bernard St	New Orleans	LA	70116	Herbert Gabriel	504-945-1402	R	7	<0.1
Joan M	3301 Hempstead	Levittown	NY	11756	Deena Yaris	516-735-2828	R	3	<0.1
Wellowave Corp.	11777 San Vincente	Brentwood	CA	90049	Richard Arons	310-979-8055	P	1	<0.1

Source: *Ward's Business Directory of U.S. Private and Public Companies*, Volumes 1 and 2, 2000. The company type code used is as follows: P - Public, R - Private, S - Subsidiary, D - Division, J - Joint Venture, A - Affiliate, G - Group, N - Company type not reported. Sales are in millions of dollars, employees are in thousands. An asterisk (*) indicates an estimated sales volume. The symbol < stands for 'less than'. Company names and addresses are truncated, in some cases, to fit into the available space.

LOCATION BY STATE AND REGIONAL CONCENTRATION

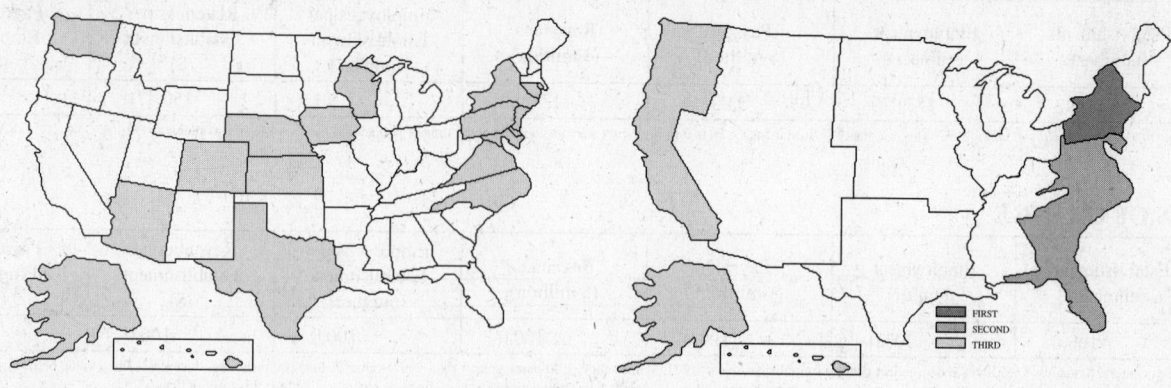

INDUSTRY DATA BY STATE

State	Establishments Total (number)	% of U.S.	Employment Total (number)	% of U.S.	Per Estab.	Payroll Total ($ mil.)	Per Empl. ($)	Revenues Total ($ mil.)	% of U.S.	Per Estab. ($)
New York	590	13.9	1,529	11.5	3	18.0	11,773	45.1	10.5	76,490
Texas	266	6.3	1,261	9.5	5	19.5	15,469	38.8	9.1	145,872
California	355	8.4	1,203	9.0	3	16.4	13,665	37.1	8.7	104,634
Pennsylvania	286	6.7	765	5.7	3	10.1	13,171	23.3	5.4	81,423
New Jersey	274	6.5	662	5.0	2	8.3	12,569	22.2	5.2	80,964
Ohio	189	4.5	481	3.6	3	7.5	15,582	17.8	4.2	94,053
Virginia	116	2.7	561	4.2	5	9.3	16,601	17.2	4.0	148,034
Florida	168	4.0	537	4.0	3	6.8	12,618	15.1	3.5	89,792
North Carolina	126	3.0	369	2.8	3	6.8	18,515	13.1	3.1	103,746
Illinois	129	3.0	374	2.8	3	5.5	14,821	12.5	2.9	96,690
Washington	86	2.0	385	2.9	4	5.9	15,377	12.4	2.9	143,826
Michigan	103	2.4	347	2.6	3	6.1	17,660	11.3	2.6	109,757
Connecticut	117	2.8	324	2.4	3	4.6	14,198	11.3	2.6	96,590
Maryland	84	2.0	336	2.5	4	5.5	16,369	11.2	2.6	133,286
Georgia	94	2.2	295	2.2	3	5.0	16,949	10.5	2.5	112,202
Wisconsin	113	2.7	287	2.2	3	4.2	14,798	10.0	2.3	88,522
Massachusetts	106	2.5	272	2.0	3	3.8	13,952	9.9	2.3	93,368
Kansas	43	1.0	210	1.6	5	4.1	19,310	7.7	1.8	179,442
Arizona	84	2.0	241	1.8	3	3.7	15,195	7.5	1.8	89,476
Colorado	68	1.6	204	1.5	3	3.3	16,025	6.9	1.6	101,647
Missouri	57	1.3	212	1.6	4	3.2	15,283	6.5	1.5	113,439
Nebraska	56	1.3	169	1.3	3	2.7	15,763	6.1	1.4	108,482
Indiana	55	1.3	154	1.2	3	2.4	15,617	5.6	1.3	101,655
Hawaii	28	0.7	137	1.0	5	3.0	21,672	5.5	1.3	195,286
Kentucky	40	0.9	157	1.2	4	2.8	17,739	5.4	1.3	135,725
South Carolina	53	1.2	155	1.2	3	2.4	15,587	5.3	1.2	99,811
Iowa	49	1.2	144	1.1	3	1.9	13,403	5.2	1.2	105,714
Tennessee	49	1.2	147	1.1	3	2.1	14,354	4.9	1.1	100,449
Oklahoma	39	0.9	150	1.1	4	2.1	13,993	4.3	1.0	110,923
Louisiana	37	0.9	174	1.3	5	1.9	11,017	4.2	1.0	112,351
Minnesota	34	0.8	113	0.8	3	1.8	16,230	4.1	1.0	120,235
Alabama	47	1.1	104	0.8	2	1.3	12,038	2.9	0.7	60,766
Oregon	23	0.5	117	0.9	5	1.1	9,265	2.5	0.6	107,783
Alaska	10	0.2	62	0.5	6	1.2	19,984	2.3	0.5	227,100
New Mexico	23	0.5	90	0.7	4	1.0	10,622	2.2	0.5	95,913
Rhode Island	35	0.8	54	0.4	2	0.8	14,722	2.1	0.5	60,171
Arkansas	27	0.6	55	0.4	2	1.0	17,636	2.1	0.5	79,037
D.C.	17	0.4	71	0.5	4	1.1	14,972	2.0	0.5	116,294
Idaho	16	0.4	69	0.5	4	0.8	11,435	1.8	0.4	111,437
West Virginia	22	0.5	51	0.4	2	0.8	15,745	1.7	0.4	78,773
Mississippi	23	0.5	58	0.4	3	0.7	12,897	1.7	0.4	72,652
New Hampshire	15	0.4	44	0.3	3	0.6	13,636	1.6	0.4	107,067
Delaware	19	0.4	34	0.3	2	0.7	19,559	1.5	0.3	78,368
Nevada	14	0.3	42	0.3	3	0.7	15,571	1.5	0.3	106,357
Utah	12	0.3	29	0.2	2	0.6	19,000	1.3	0.3	109,000
Maine	9	0.2	17	0.1	2	0.2	11,765	0.4	0.1	48,222
Vermont	7	0.2	11	0.1	2	0.1	11,091	0.3	0.1	48,143
Montana	14	0.3	60*	-	-	(D)	-	(D)	-	-
North Dakota	10	0.2	60*	-	-	(D)	-	(D)	-	-
South Dakota	4	0.1	10*	-	-	(D)	-	(D)	-	-
Wyoming	1	-	10*	-	-	(D)	-	(D)	-	-

Source: 1997 *Economic Census*. The states are in descending order of revenues or establishments (if revenue data are missing for the majority). The symbol (D) appears when data are withheld to prevent disclosure of competitive information. States marked with (D) are sorted by number of establishments. A dash (-) indicates that the data element cannot be calculated. * indicates the midpoint of a range; 175, for example is the range 100-249. Shaded *states* on the state map indicate those states which have proportionately greater representation in the industry than would be indicated by the state's population; the ratio is based on total revenues or number of establishments. Shaded *regions* indicate where the industry is regionally most concentrated.

NAICS 812112 - BEAUTY SHOPS

GENERAL STATISTICS

Year	Establishments (number)	Employment (number)	Payroll ($ million)	Revenues ($ million)	Employees per Establishment (number)	Revenues per Establishment ($)	Payroll per Employee ($)
1997	74,493	382,920	5,033.0	11,209.0	5.1	150,471	13,144

Source: *Economic Census of the United States*, 1997. This is a newly defined industry. Data for prior years were unavailable at the time of publication but may become available over time.

INDICES OF CHANGE

Year	Establishments (number)	Employment (number)	Payroll ($ million)	Revenues ($ million)	Employees per Establishment (number)	Revenues per Establishment ($)	Payroll per Employee ($)
1997	100.0	100.0	100.0	100.0	100.0	100.0	100.0

Sources: Same as General Statistics. The values shown reflect change from the base year, 1997. Values above 100 mean greater than 1997, values below 100 mean less than 1997, and a value of 100 in the 1982-96 or 1998-2001 period means same as 1997. Values followed by a 'p' are projections by the editors; 'e' stands for extrapolation. Data are the most recent available at this level of detail.

SIC INDUSTRIES RELATED TO NAICS 812112

Each new NAICS code represents an industry that used to be part of an SIC or a part of several SIC industries. Data in this table are shown to provide transitional information for these cases. All available data for the precursor SIC(s) are shown. Even if only a part of an SIC is included in the NAICS, *all* data for the SIC are reproduced. If the SIC industry is not marked as being a part (pt) of the NAICS, the entire industry is embedded in the NAICS data. The SIC composition of the new industry provides some hints of the relative importance of its "ancestors." Data marked with a 'p' are projected. Projections begin with 1982 data. Data earlier than 1990 are not shown but are reflected in the projections.

SIC	Industry	1990	1991	1992	1993	1994	1995	1996	1997
7231	**Beauty Shops (pt)**								
	Establishments (number)	76,148	78,588	82,768	83,238	82,478	81,696	82,042p	82,459p
	Employment (thousands)	371.0	374.3	387.2	396.7	388.9	394.6	412.8p	419.9p
	Revenues ($ million)	12,841.0	13,138.0	14,436.0	14,608.0	15,152.0	16,382.0	16,900.0	17,637.7p

Source: *Economic Census of the United States*, 1992, annual surveys of economic sectors conducted by the Bureau of the Census, and estimates or projections based on the 1982-1992 period; not all data are shown. 'e' marks estimates made by the editors; 'p' indicates projections based on time series. A dash (-) indicates that data for this SIC or year were not available. The abbreviation (pt) next to the industry name indicates that only a part of the industry is present within the NAICS data. If no (pt) is shown, the entire industry is contained within the NAICS data.

SELECTED RATIOS

For 1997	Avg. of Information	Analyzed Industry	Index	For 1997	Avg. of Information	Analyzed Industry	Index
Employees per establishment	6	5	82	Payroll per establishment	126,069	67,563	54
Revenue per establishment	511,622	150,471	29	Payroll as % of revenue	25	45	182
Revenue per employee	81,659	29,272	36	Payroll per employee	20,122	13,144	65

Sources: Same as General Statistics. The 'Average' column represents the average for the industry sector, in 1997, where the currently shown industry is classified. The Index shows the relationship between the Average and the Analyzed Industry. For example, 100 means that they are equal; 500 that the Analyzed Industry is five times the average; 50 means that the Analyzed Industry is half the national average. The abbreviation 'na' is used to show that data are 'not available'.

LEADING COMPANIES   Number shown: **1**   Total sales ($ mil): **7**   Total employment (000): **0.3**

Company Name	Address				CEO Name	Phone	Co. Type	Sales ($ mil)	Empl. (000)
Barbers, Hairstyling for Men	300 Ind Blvd NE	Minneapolis	MN	55413	F. A. Huggins, Jr.	612-331-8500	P	7	0.3

Source: Ward's Business Directory of U.S. Private and Public Companies, Volumes 1 and 2, 2000. The company type code used is as follows: P - Public, R - Private, S - Subsidiary, D - Division, J - Joint Venture, A - Affiliate, G - Group, N - Company type not reported. Sales are in millions of dollars, employees are in thousands. An asterisk (*) indicates an estimated sales volume. The symbol < stands for 'less than'. Company names and addresses are truncated, in some cases, to fit into the available space.

LOCATION BY STATE AND REGIONAL CONCENTRATION

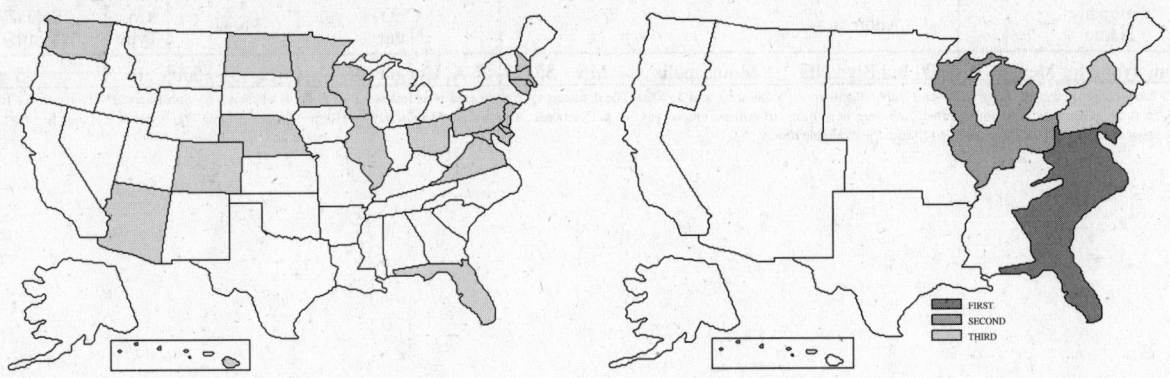

INDUSTRY DATA BY STATE

State	Establishments Total (number)	Establishments % of U.S.	Employment Total (number)	Employment % of U.S.	Per Estab.	Payroll Total ($ mil.)	Payroll Per Empl. ($)	Revenues Total ($ mil.)	Revenues % of U.S.	Revenues Per Estab. ($)
California	6,059	8.1	31,121	8.1	5	398.9	12,819	1,021.5	9.1	168,596
Florida	5,261	7.1	26,316	6.9	5	344.5	13,090	755.9	6.7	143,680
New York	5,449	7.3	24,227	6.3	4	320.8	13,243	754.8	6.7	138,529
Texas	4,343	5.8	23,429	6.1	5	321.9	13,740	705.0	6.3	162,325
Pennsylvania	4,833	6.5	22,322	5.8	5	269.2	12,059	628.9	5.6	130,131
Illinois	3,145	4.2	20,307	5.3	6	272.4	13,414	567.3	5.1	180,393
Ohio	3,525	4.7	20,692	5.4	6	260.9	12,610	550.7	4.9	156,228
New Jersey	3,587	4.8	16,856	4.4	5	206.2	12,235	476.7	4.3	132,907
Michigan	2,555	3.4	14,463	3.8	6	188.1	13,007	400.7	3.6	156,828
Massachusetts	2,616	3.5	12,699	3.3	5	177.2	13,951	397.4	3.5	151,907
Virginia	2,308	3.1	13,553	3.5	6	197.4	14,563	385.0	3.4	166,792
Maryland	1,570	2.1	11,319	3.0	7	159.1	14,058	310.4	2.8	197,683
Georgia	1,675	2.2	8,980	2.3	5	136.4	15,188	296.8	2.6	177,184
Wisconsin	2,177	2.9	11,307	3.0	5	135.0	11,939	291.6	2.6	133,966
Minnesota	1,570	2.1	10,277	2.7	7	132.1	12,856	281.3	2.5	179,166
Washington	1,525	2.0	8,485	2.2	6	114.0	13,433	262.7	2.3	172,275
Connecticut	1,561	2.1	7,387	1.9	5	106.7	14,443	236.8	2.1	151,666
Indiana	1,520	2.0	8,134	2.1	5	98.6	12,119	214.2	1.9	140,899
Arizona	1,203	1.6	7,230	1.9	6	98.9	13,674	208.7	1.9	173,465
North Carolina	1,500	2.0	6,679	1.7	4	96.2	14,403	207.1	1.8	138,051
Missouri	1,533	2.1	7,423	1.9	5	96.0	12,938	205.0	1.8	133,716
Tennessee	1,232	1.7	6,261	1.6	5	91.0	14,542	194.9	1.7	158,182
Colorado	1,131	1.5	6,169	1.6	5	82.3	13,336	185.4	1.7	163,928
Iowa	1,080	1.4	4,362	1.1	4	52.4	12,011	126.0	1.1	116,692
Alabama	1,008	1.4	3,925	1.0	4	48.1	12,243	112.6	1.0	111,669
Louisiana	771	1.0	3,654	1.0	5	47.2	12,914	110.4	1.0	143,178
Oregon	601	0.8	3,651	1.0	6	45.6	12,480	102.7	0.9	170,827
Kentucky	762	1.0	3,555	0.9	5	46.0	12,937	102.3	0.9	134,248
Kansas	781	1.0	3,505	0.9	4	46.6	13,308	102.0	0.9	130,576
South Carolina	810	1.1	3,075	0.8	4	41.6	13,515	93.4	0.8	115,253
Nebraska	621	0.8	2,875	0.8	5	39.8	13,846	86.0	0.8	138,485
New Hampshire	492	0.7	2,331	0.6	5	30.5	13,064	71.4	0.6	145,071
D.C.	172	0.2	1,252	0.3	7	30.6	24,442	59.1	0.5	343,471
Hawaii	314	0.4	1,644	0.4	5	22.5	13,682	56.0	0.5	178,312
Oklahoma	414	0.6	1,779	0.5	4	21.5	12,111	54.5	0.5	131,655
Nevada	267	0.4	1,593	0.4	6	21.2	13,294	53.5	0.5	200,472
Delaware	299	0.4	1,847	0.5	6	25.1	13,607	48.8	0.4	163,130
Utah	344	0.5	2,081	0.5	6	20.2	9,725	48.3	0.4	140,407
Rhode Island	460	0.6	1,618	0.4	4	20.4	12,588	47.6	0.4	103,474
New Mexico	321	0.4	2,063	0.5	6	20.8	10,075	47.0	0.4	146,464
Mississippi	370	0.5	1,435	0.4	4	19.6	13,678	46.8	0.4	126,432
Arkansas	438	0.6	1,508	0.4	3	19.2	12,747	45.2	0.4	103,164
West Virginia	447	0.6	1,855	0.5	4	19.4	10,462	43.9	0.4	98,152
North Dakota	305	0.4	1,381	0.4	5	15.6	11,284	35.3	0.3	115,639
Maine	304	0.4	1,217	0.3	4	15.5	12,742	35.3	0.3	116,010
Idaho	250	0.3	1,164	0.3	5	11.9	10,254	28.6	0.3	114,592
Alaska	161	0.2	723	0.2	4	11.6	16,047	27.2	0.2	169,180
South Dakota	228	0.3	946	0.2	4	11.2	11,839	26.0	0.2	114,044
Vermont	240	0.3	813	0.2	3	10.4	12,804	25.0	0.2	104,263
Montana	194	0.3	750*	-	-	(D)	-	(D)	-	-
Wyoming	161	0.2	750*	-	-	(D)	-	(D)	-	-

Source: 1997 Economic Census. The states are in descending order of revenues or establishments (if revenue data are missing for the majority). The symbol (D) appears when data are withheld to prevent disclosure of competitive information. States marked with (D) are sorted by number of establishments. A dash (-) indicates that the data element cannot be calculated. * indicates the midpoint of a range; 175, for example is the range 100-249. Shaded *states* on the state map indicate those states which have proportionately greater representation in the industry than would be indicated by the state's population; the ratio is based on total revenues or number of establishments. Shaded *regions* indicate where the industry is regionally most concentrated.

NAICS 812113 - NAIL SALONS

GENERAL STATISTICS

Year	Establishments (number)	Employment (number)	Payroll ($ million)	Revenues ($ million)	Employees per Establishment (number)	Revenues per Establishment ($)	Payroll per Employee ($)
1997	5,256	14,734	151.0	419.0	2.8	79,718	10,248

Source: Economic Census of the United States, 1997. This is a newly defined industry. Data for prior years were unavailable at the time of publication but may become available over time.

INDICES OF CHANGE

Year	Establishments (number)	Employment (number)	Payroll ($ million)	Revenues ($ million)	Employees per Establishment (number)	Revenues per Establishment ($)	Payroll per Employee ($)
1997	100.0	100.0	100.0	100.0	100.0	100.0	100.0

Sources: Same as General Statistics. The values shown reflect change from the base year, 1997. Values above 100 mean greater than 1997, values below 100 mean less than 1997, and a value of 100 in the 1982-96 or 1998-2001 period means same as 1997. Values followed by a 'p' are projections by the editors; 'e' stands for extrapolation. Data are the most recent available at this level of detail.

SIC INDUSTRIES RELATED TO NAICS 812113

Each new NAICS code represents an industry that used to be part of an SIC or a part of several SIC industries. Data in this table are shown to provide transitional information for these cases. All available data for the precursor SIC(s) are shown. Even if only a part of an SIC is included in the NAICS, *all* data for the SIC are reproduced. If the SIC industry is not marked as being a part (pt) of the NAICS, the entire industry is embedded in the NAICS data. The SIC composition of the new industry provides some hints of the relative importance of its "ancestors." Data marked with a 'p' are projected. Projections begin with 1982 data. Data earlier than 1990 are not shown but are reflected in the projections.

SIC	Industry	1990	1991	1992	1993	1994	1995	1996	1997
7231	**Beauty Shops (pt)**								
	Establishments (number)	76,148	78,588	82,768	83,238	82,478	81,696	82,042p	82,459p
	Employment (thousands)	371.0	374.3	387.2	396.7	388.9	394.6	412.8p	419.9p
	Revenues ($ million)	12,841.0	13,138.0	14,436.0	14,608.0	15,152.0	16,382.0	16,900.0	17,637.7p

Source: Economic Census of the United States, 1992, annual surveys of economic sectors conducted by the Bureau of the Census, and estimates or projections based on the 1982-1992 period; not all data are shown. 'e' marks estimates made by the editors; 'p' indicates projections based on time series. A dash (-) indicates that data for this SIC or year were not available. The abbreviation (pt) next to the industry name indicates that only a part of the industry is present within the NAICS data. If no (pt) is shown, the entire industry is contained within the NAICS data.

SELECTED RATIOS

For 1997	Avg. of Information	Analyzed Industry	Index	For 1997	Avg. of Information	Analyzed Industry	Index
Employees per establishment	6	3	45	Payroll per establishment	126,069	28,729	23
Revenue per establishment	511,622	79,718	16	Payroll as % of revenue	25	36	146
Revenue per employee	81,659	28,438	35	Payroll per employee	20,122	10,248	51

Sources: Same as General Statistics. The 'Average' column represents the average for the industry sector, in 1997, where the currently shown industry is classified. The Index shows the relationship between the Average and the Analyzed Industry. For example, 100 means that they are equal; 500 that the Analyzed Industry is five times the average; 50 means that the Analyzed Industry is half the national average. The abbreviation 'na' is used to show that data are 'not available'.

LEADING COMPANIES

No company data available for this industry.

LOCATION BY STATE AND REGIONAL CONCENTRATION

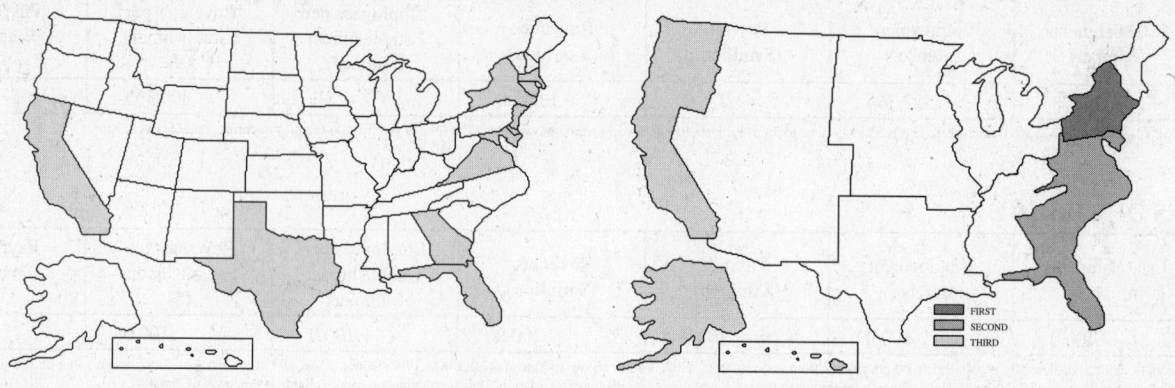

INDUSTRY DATA BY STATE

State	Establishments		Employment			Payroll		Revenues		
	Total (number)	% of U.S.	Total (number)	% of U.S.	Per Estab.	Total ($ mil.)	Per Empl. ($)	Total ($ mil.)	% of U.S.	Per Estab. ($)
California	1,054	20.1	2,623	17.8	2	16.6	6,311	59.7	14.2	56,595
New York	875	16.6	1,889	12.8	2	19.3	10,226	59.0	14.1	67,373
Florida	344	6.5	1,178	8.0	3	13.2	11,244	32.1	7.7	93,439
New Jersey	350	6.7	1,044	7.1	3	11.4	10,901	30.6	7.3	87,446
Texas	272	5.2	969	6.6	4	11.0	11,394	29.5	7.0	108,632
Pennsylvania	252	4.8	709	4.8	3	7.3	10,241	19.7	4.7	78,171
Illinois	156	3.0	594	4.0	4	6.5	10,919	15.8	3.8	101,506
Maryland	126	2.4	567	3.8	5	6.8	11,959	15.6	3.7	124,103
Massachusetts	158	3.0	562	3.8	4	6.1	10,927	15.4	3.7	97,373
Ohio	167	3.2	536	3.6	3	5.9	10,979	15.2	3.6	91,018
Georgia	134	2.5	330	2.2	2	4.6	14,036	13.8	3.3	102,978
Connecticut	110	2.1	345	2.3	3	4.0	11,690	12.6	3.0	114,991
Virginia	159	3.0	434	2.9	3	4.3	9,917	11.9	2.8	74,648
Michigan	106	2.0	412	2.8	4	4.7	11,498	11.0	2.6	103,415
North Carolina	90	1.7	238	1.6	3	2.7	11,147	6.9	1.6	76,744
Wisconsin	57	1.1	259	1.8	5	2.7	10,514	6.3	1.5	110,316
Washington	78	1.5	190	1.3	2	2.0	10,358	5.6	1.3	71,551
Minnesota	57	1.1	184	1.2	3	2.4	12,788	5.5	1.3	96,930
Missouri	58	1.1	164	1.1	3	2.3	14,207	5.3	1.3	91,810
South Carolina	47	0.9	135	0.9	3	1.5	11,141	4.3	1.0	92,128
Arizona	51	1.0	153	1.0	3	1.7	11,039	4.2	1.0	82,529
Louisiana	59	1.1	145	1.0	2	1.5	10,152	4.0	1.0	68,475
Colorado	56	1.1	113	0.8	2	1.4	12,000	3.9	0.9	69,321
Tennessee	52	1.0	113	0.8	2	1.3	11,708	3.7	0.9	71,808
Alabama	47	0.9	89	0.6	2	1.2	13,618	3.5	0.8	73,766
Indiana	41	0.8	103	0.7	3	1.1	10,359	2.8	0.7	67,171
Delaware	13	0.2	81	0.5	6	0.9	11,506	2.2	0.5	168,462
Nebraska	30	0.6	85	0.6	3	1.0	11,553	2.1	0.5	70,900
Kansas	27	0.5	73	0.5	3	0.7	10,137	1.9	0.5	70,296
Iowa	22	0.4	49	0.3	2	0.5	10,776	1.5	0.4	68,500
New Hampshire	22	0.4	47	0.3	2	0.5	11,213	1.4	0.3	65,091
Kentucky	23	0.4	40	0.3	2	0.5	11,800	1.4	0.3	60,739
Hawaii	12	0.2	35	0.2	3	0.5	12,886	1.2	0.3	100,250
Oklahoma	17	0.3	38	0.3	2	0.3	8,737	1.2	0.3	69,294
D.C.	12	0.2	23	0.2	2	0.4	15,261	1.2	0.3	96,667
West Virginia	13	0.2	26	0.2	2	0.2	9,038	1.0	0.2	76,615
Mississippi	22	0.4	28	0.2	1	0.3	10,571	1.0	0.2	43,545
New Mexico	15	0.3	29	0.2	2	0.3	10,862	1.0	0.2	64,333
Oregon	12	0.2	27	0.2	2	0.2	9,148	0.9	0.2	73,000
Nevada	10	0.2	12	0.1	1	0.3	22,667	0.6	0.1	61,300
Arkansas	10	0.2	15	0.1	2	0.1	6,400	0.5	0.1	51,100
Maine	7	0.1	8	0.1	1	0.1	17,875	0.5	0.1	69,857
Rhode Island	6	0.1	14	0.1	2	0.2	15,500	0.5	0.1	79,833
Vermont	5	0.1	4	0.0	1	0.1	14,500	0.4	0.1	72,000
Utah	5	0.1	3	0.0	1	0.1	23,333	0.3	0.1	64,000
Idaho	5	0.1	7	0.0	1	0.1	12,286	0.3	0.1	57,000
Alaska	4	0.1	2	0.0	1	-	17,500	0.2	0.0	47,250
Montana	3	0.1	4	0.0	1	-	7,750	0.1	0.0	34,000
South Dakota	2	-	10*	-	-	(D)	-	(D)	-	-
Wyoming	2	-	10*	-	-	(D)	-	(D)	-	-
North Dakota	1	-	10*	-	-	(D)	-	(D)	-	-

Source: 1997 Economic Census. The states are in descending order of revenues or establishments (if revenue data are missing for the majority). The symbol (D) appears when data are withheld to prevent disclosure of competitive information. States marked with (D) are sorted by number of establishments. A dash (-) indicates that the data element cannot be calculated. * indicates the midpoint of a range; 175, for example is the range 100-249. Shaded *states* on the state map indicate those states which have proportionately greater representation in the industry than would be indicated by the state's population; the ratio is based on total revenues or number of establishments. Shaded *regions* indicate where the industry is regionally most concentrated.

NAICS 812191 - DIET AND WEIGHT REDUCING SERVICES

GENERAL STATISTICS

Year	Establishments (number)	Employment (number)	Payroll ($ million)	Revenues ($ million)	Employees per Establishment (number)	Revenues per Establishment ($)	Payroll per Employee ($)
1997	3,378	27,366	275.0	1,045.0	8.1	309,355	10,049

Source: Economic Census of the United States, 1997. This is a newly defined industry. Data for prior years were unavailable at the time of publication but may become available over time.

INDICES OF CHANGE

Year	Establishments (number)	Employment (number)	Payroll ($ million)	Revenues ($ million)	Employees per Establishment (number)	Revenues per Establishment ($)	Payroll per Employee ($)
1997	100.0	100.0	100.0	100.0	100.0	100.0	100.0

Sources: Same as General Statistics. The values shown reflect change from the base year, 1997. Values above 100 mean greater than 1997, values below 100 mean less than 1997, and a value of 100 in the 1982-96 or 1998-2001 period means same as 1997. Values followed by a 'p' are projections by the editors; 'e' stands for extrapolation. Data are the most recent available at this level of detail.

SIC INDUSTRIES RELATED TO NAICS 812191

Each new NAICS code represents an industry that used to be part of an SIC or a part of several SIC industries. Data in this table are shown to provide transitional information for these cases. All available data for the precursor SIC(s) are shown. Even if only a part of an SIC is included in the NAICS, *all* data for the SIC are reproduced. If the SIC industry is not marked as being a part (pt) of the NAICS, the entire industry is embedded in the NAICS data. The SIC composition of the new industry provides some hints of the relative importance of its "ancestors." Data marked with a 'p' are projected. Projections begin with 1982 data. Data earlier than 1990 are not shown but are reflected in the projections.

SIC	Industry	1990	1991	1992	1993	1994	1995	1996	1997
7299	**Miscellaneous Personal Services, nec (pt)**								
	Establishments (number)	15,086	15,775	16,017	16,862	17,296	17,740	18,650p	19,294p
	Employment (thousands)	116.4	114.7	105.6	99.6	97.2	99.4	106.1p	106.9p
	Revenues ($ million)	-	-	3,885.0	-	-	-	-	-

Source: Economic Census of the United States, 1992, annual surveys of economic sectors conducted by the Bureau of the Census, and estimates or projections based on the 1982-1992 period; not all data are shown. 'e' marks estimates made by the editors; 'p' indicates projections based on time series. A dash (-) indicates that data for this SIC or year were not available. The abbreviation (pt) next to the industry name indicates that only a part of the industry is present within the NAICS data. If no (pt) is shown, the entire industry is contained within the NAICS data.

SELECTED RATIOS

For 1997	Avg. of Information	Analyzed Industry	Index	For 1997	Avg. of Information	Analyzed Industry	Index
Employees per establishment	6	8	129	Payroll per establishment	126,069	81,409	65
Revenue per establishment	511,622	309,355	60	Payroll as % of revenue	25	26	107
Revenue per employee	81,659	38,186	47	Payroll per employee	20,122	10,049	50

Sources: Same as General Statistics. The 'Average' column represents the average for the industry sector, in 1997, where the currently shown industry is classified. The Index shows the relationship between the Average and the Analyzed Industry. For example, 100 means that they are equal; 500 that the Analyzed Industry is five times the average; 50 means that the Analyzed Industry is half the national average. The abbreviation 'na' is used to show that data are 'not available'.

LEADING COMPANIES

No company data available for this industry.

LOCATION BY STATE AND REGIONAL CONCENTRATION

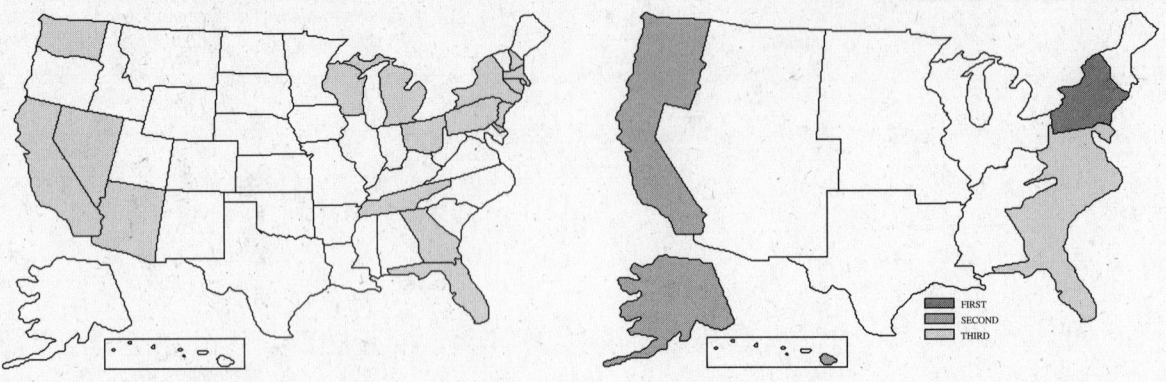

INDUSTRY DATA BY STATE

State	Establishments Total (number)	% of U.S.	Employment Total (number)	% of U.S.	Per Estab.	Payroll Total ($ mil.)	Per Empl. ($)	Revenues Total ($ mil.)	% of U.S.	Per Estab. ($)
California	449	13.3	2,088	7.6	5	30.4	14,544	148.0	14.2	329,615
New York	249	7.4	3,658	13.4	15	35.0	9,579	101.5	9.7	407,787
Florida	240	7.1	1,790	6.5	7	18.2	10,183	67.1	6.4	279,413
Pennsylvania	121	3.6	1,523	5.6	13	19.0	12,502	62.1	5.9	512,950
Texas	177	5.2	1,490	5.4	8	16.1	10,832	55.8	5.3	315,017
Ohio	147	4.4	1,337	4.9	9	12.9	9,674	49.3	4.7	335,510
Massachusetts	106	3.1	798	2.9	8	13.3	16,623	48.8	4.7	460,745
Michigan	139	4.1	1,175	4.3	8	12.0	10,233	41.5	4.0	298,892
Illinois	128	3.8	557	2.0	4	8.8	15,711	39.0	3.7	304,891
New Jersey	101	3.0	806	2.9	8	10.4	12,924	37.6	3.6	372,000
Tennessee	84	2.5	638	2.3	8	7.1	11,149	35.6	3.4	423,917
Georgia	85	2.5	812	3.0	10	7.3	9,014	29.3	2.8	344,706
Virginia	113	3.3	747	2.7	7	6.1	8,183	25.4	2.4	224,664
Washington	61	1.8	546	2.0	9	5.9	10,733	23.9	2.3	392,213
Wisconsin	59	1.7	635	2.3	11	4.2	6,671	21.7	2.1	367,746
Indiana	65	1.9	640	2.3	10	4.5	7,080	18.2	1.7	280,477
North Carolina	107	3.2	827	3.0	8	4.7	5,672	17.5	1.7	163,813
Arizona	42	1.2	534	2.0	13	3.9	7,247	17.0	1.6	405,048
Maryland	81	2.4	549	2.0	7	4.2	7,729	16.7	1.6	206,012
Missouri	58	1.7	363	1.3	6	3.8	10,504	14.4	1.4	248,293
Connecticut	51	1.5	416	1.5	8	3.0	7,163	14.3	1.4	281,275
Louisiana	46	1.4	301	1.1	7	3.7	12,399	14.0	1.3	304,435
Alabama	65	1.9	309	1.1	5	4.3	13,913	13.3	1.3	205,292
Oregon	25	0.7	272	1.0	11	2.8	10,162	11.8	1.1	473,760
Minnesota	62	1.8	536	2.0	9	2.3	4,291	10.8	1.0	174,694
Kentucky	45	1.3	240	0.9	5	2.2	9,087	9.6	0.9	213,444
Colorado	43	1.3	408	1.5	9	2.0	4,926	8.1	0.8	189,535
Oklahoma	30	0.9	330	1.2	11	3.1	9,312	8.0	0.8	268,267
Kansas	43	1.3	351	1.3	8	1.9	5,510	8.0	0.8	186,326
Nevada	23	0.7	209	0.8	9	2.5	11,794	7.4	0.7	322,652
Rhode Island	18	0.5	126	0.5	7	1.8	14,103	7.4	0.7	410,944
South Carolina	27	0.8	144	0.5	5	2.1	14,875	7.2	0.7	265,519
New Hampshire	23	0.7	281	1.0	12	2.2	7,954	6.9	0.7	301,565
Iowa	29	0.9	151	0.6	5	1.2	8,252	5.6	0.5	193,621
Maine	6	0.2	221	0.8	37	1.6	7,027	4.6	0.4	761,500
Arkansas	28	0.8	200	0.7	7	1.1	5,425	4.1	0.4	145,679
Utah	34	1.0	156	0.6	5	1.2	7,686	4.0	0.4	117,882
Delaware	13	0.4	130	0.5	10	1.3	10,338	3.9	0.4	300,385
New Mexico	10	0.3	71	0.3	7	1.2	16,521	3.7	0.4	367,000
Nebraska	25	0.7	146	0.5	6	0.8	5,185	3.6	0.3	145,880
Mississippi	22	0.7	183	0.7	8	1.0	5,661	3.3	0.3	151,727
West Virginia	18	0.5	219	0.8	12	1.0	4,562	3.3	0.3	182,056
Idaho	22	0.7	103	0.4	5	0.5	5,204	2.2	0.2	100,045
North Dakota	11	0.3	147	0.5	13	0.4	2,980	1.8	0.2	166,000
South Dakota	6	0.2	30	0.1	5	0.2	7,700	1.1	0.1	181,667
Alaska	10	0.3	21	0.1	2	0.2	9,429	0.7	0.1	71,500
Montana	9	0.3	60*	-	-	(D)	-	(D)	-	-
Wyoming	8	0.2	60*	-	-	(D)	-	(D)	-	-
D.C.	7	0.2	60*	-	-	(D)	-	(D)	-	-
Vermont	5	0.1	60*	-	-	(D)	-	(D)	-	-
Hawaii	2	0.1	10*	-	-	(D)	-	(D)	-	-

Source: 1997 *Economic Census*. The states are in descending order of revenues or establishments (if revenue data are missing for the majority). The symbol (D) appears when data are withheld to prevent disclosure of competitive information. States marked with (D) are sorted by number of establishments. A dash (-) indicates that the data element cannot be calculated. * indicates the midpoint of a range; 175, for example is the range 100-249. Shaded *states* on the state map indicate those states which have proportionately greater representation in the industry than would be indicated by the state's population; the ratio is based on total revenues or number of establishments. Shaded *regions* indicate where the industry is regionally most concentrated.

NAICS 812199 - PERSONAL CARE SERVICES NEC

GENERAL STATISTICS

Year	Establishments (number)	Employment (number)	Payroll ($ million)	Revenues ($ million)	Employees per Establishment (number)	Revenues per Establishment ($)	Payroll per Employee ($)
1997	8,339	33,914	319.0	1,140.0	4.1	136,707	9,406

Source: Economic Census of the United States, 1997. This is a newly defined industry. Data for prior years were unavailable at the time of publication but may become available over time.

INDICES OF CHANGE

Year	Establishments (number)	Employment (number)	Payroll ($ million)	Revenues ($ million)	Employees per Establishment (number)	Revenues per Establishment ($)	Payroll per Employee ($)
1997	100.0	100.0	100.0	100.0	100.0	100.0	100.0

Sources: Same as General Statistics. The values shown reflect change from the base year, 1997. Values above 100 mean greater than 1997, values below 100 mean less than 1997, and a value of 100 in the 1982-96 or 1998-2001 period means same as 1997. Values followed by a 'p' are projections by the editors; 'e' stands for extrapolation. Data are the most recent available at this level of detail.

SIC INDUSTRIES RELATED TO NAICS 812199

Each new NAICS code represents an industry that used to be part of an SIC or a part of several SIC industries. Data in this table are shown to provide transitional information for these cases. All available data for the precursor SIC(s) are shown. Even if only a part of an SIC is included in the NAICS, *all* data for the SIC are reproduced. If the SIC industry is not marked as being a part (pt) of the NAICS, the entire industry is embedded in the NAICS data. The SIC composition of the new industry provides some hints of the relative importance of its "ancestors." Data marked with a 'p' are projected. Projections begin with 1982 data. Data earlier than 1990 are not shown but are reflected in the projections.

SIC	Industry	1990	1991	1992	1993	1994	1995	1996	1997
7299	**Miscellaneous Personal Services, nec (pt)**								
	Establishments (number)	15,086	15,775	16,017	16,862	17,296	17,740	18,650*p*	19,294*p*
	Employment (thousands)	116.4	114.7	105.6	99.6	97.2	99.4	106.1*p*	106.9*p*
	Revenues ($ million)	-	-	3,885.0	-	-	-	-	-

Source: Economic Census of the United States, 1992, annual surveys of economic sectors conducted by the Bureau of the Census, and estimates or projections based on the 1982-1992 period; not all data are shown. 'e' marks estimates made by the editors; 'p' indicates projections based on time series. A dash (-) indicates that data for this SIC or year were not available. The abbreviation (pt) next to the industry name indicates that only a part of the industry is present within the NAICS data. If no (pt) is shown, the entire industry is contained within the NAICS data.

SELECTED RATIOS

For 1997	Avg. of Information	Analyzed Industry	Index	For 1997	Avg. of Information	Analyzed Industry	Index
Employees per establishment	6	4	65	Payroll per establishment	126,069	38,254	30
Revenue per establishment	511,622	136,707	27	Payroll as % of revenue	25	28	114
Revenue per employee	81,659	33,614	41	Payroll per employee	20,122	9,406	47

Sources: Same as General Statistics. The 'Average' column represents the average for the industry sector, in 1997, where the currently shown industry is classified. The Index shows the relationship between the Average and the Analyzed Industry. For example, 100 means that they are equal; 500 that the Analyzed Industry is five times the average; 50 means that the Analyzed Industry is half the national average. The abbreviation 'na' is used to show that data are 'not available'.

LEADING COMPANIES
No company data available for this industry.

LOCATION BY STATE AND REGIONAL CONCENTRATION

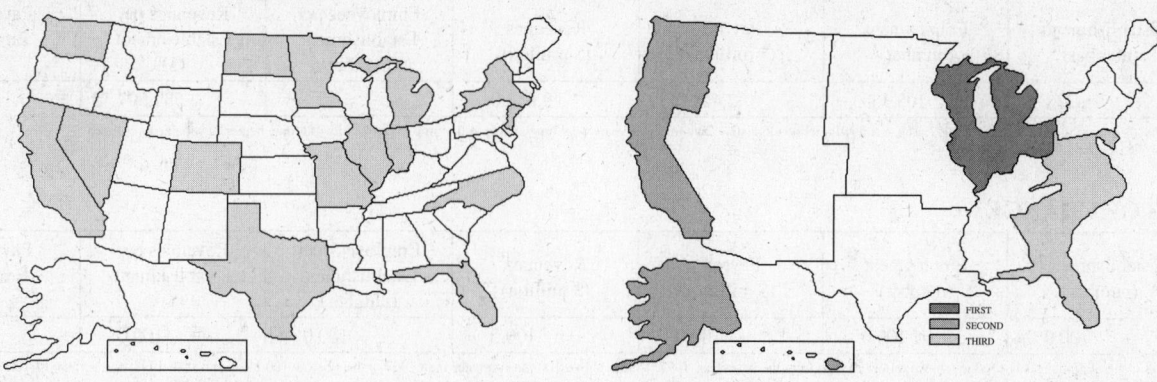

FIRST
SECOND
THIRD

INDUSTRY DATA BY STATE

State	Establishments Total (number)	Establishments % of U.S.	Employment Total (number)	Employment % of U.S.	Employment Per Estab.	Payroll Total ($ mil.)	Payroll Per Empl. ($)	Revenues Total ($ mil.)	Revenues % of U.S.	Revenues Per Estab. ($)
California	774	9.3	3,742	11.0	5	42.6	11,372	151.1	13.3	195,171
New York	442	5.3	2,016	5.9	5	28.0	13,871	96.0	8.4	217,210
Texas	465	5.6	2,320	6.8	5	25.1	10,800	88.3	7.8	189,944
Florida	464	5.6	1,617	4.8	3	20.1	12,440	70.1	6.2	151,097
Illinois	498	6.0	1,982	5.8	4	19.6	9,913	69.8	6.1	140,120
Michigan	467	5.6	1,960	5.8	4	13.4	6,835	49.2	4.3	105,370
Ohio	386	4.6	1,485	4.4	4	11.6	7,795	43.1	3.8	111,573
Pennsylvania	298	3.6	1,008	3.0	3	10.7	10,596	41.1	3.6	137,953
Indiana	294	3.5	1,602	4.7	5	9.3	5,798	35.5	3.1	120,728
New Jersey	245	2.9	745	2.2	3	10.1	13,573	35.1	3.1	143,094
North Carolina	268	3.2	875	2.6	3	7.6	8,730	32.3	2.8	120,590
Colorado	191	2.3	763	2.2	4	9.1	11,873	31.2	2.7	163,529
Virginia	212	2.5	957	2.8	5	8.6	8,994	29.0	2.5	136,807
Washington	240	2.9	941	2.8	4	8.4	8,922	28.4	2.5	118,200
Missouri	246	2.9	926	2.7	4	7.8	8,451	27.2	2.4	110,435
Georgia	241	2.9	806	2.4	3	6.5	8,061	26.4	2.3	109,734
Minnesota	211	2.5	1,182	3.5	6	7.8	6,610	25.2	2.2	119,517
Massachusetts	162	1.9	482	1.4	3	6.6	13,602	22.4	2.0	138,049
Tennessee	190	2.3	835	2.5	4	6.7	8,074	21.7	1.9	114,132
Maryland	140	1.7	541	1.6	4	5.4	10,067	20.3	1.8	144,814
Wisconsin	176	2.1	749	2.2	4	5.0	6,716	15.8	1.4	89,699
Arizona	106	1.3	449	1.3	4	4.4	9,880	15.3	1.3	143,887
Kentucky	137	1.6	522	1.5	4	4.0	7,657	14.0	1.2	102,161
Oregon	84	1.0	384	1.1	5	3.0	7,771	11.2	1.0	133,119
Oklahoma	115	1.4	406	1.2	4	3.2	7,835	10.9	1.0	94,478
Alabama	110	1.3	318	0.9	3	2.7	8,607	10.6	0.9	96,436
Kansas	88	1.1	382	1.1	4	3.0	7,955	10.5	0.9	119,250
Louisiana	109	1.3	300	0.9	3	2.4	7,853	9.4	0.8	86,606
South Carolina	110	1.3	365	1.1	3	2.3	6,392	9.3	0.8	84,491
Connecticut	74	0.9	203	0.6	3	2.6	12,611	9.2	0.8	123,919
Arkansas	79	0.9	340	1.0	4	2.2	6,421	8.9	0.8	112,937
Utah	88	1.1	414	1.2	5	2.6	6,283	8.0	0.7	90,830
Nevada	55	0.7	213	0.6	4	2.1	9,822	7.7	0.7	140,200
Iowa	74	0.9	332	1.0	4	2.0	5,928	7.0	0.6	94,351
Nebraska	49	0.6	227	0.7	5	1.3	5,507	5.4	0.5	109,429
Mississippi	58	0.7	182	0.5	3	1.1	6,016	4.5	0.4	76,828
Rhode Island	42	0.5	98	0.3	2	1.0	9,837	3.9	0.3	92,310
New Hampshire	32	0.4	97	0.3	3	1.1	11,495	3.9	0.3	123,156
New Mexico	23	0.3	91	0.3	4	1.0	10,604	3.7	0.3	162,304
North Dakota	28	0.3	134	0.4	5	0.9	6,970	3.3	0.3	117,071
Idaho	44	0.5	137	0.4	3	0.9	6,620	3.2	0.3	73,682
Alaska	30	0.4	107	0.3	4	0.6	6,037	2.8	0.2	93,867
Maine	29	0.3	102	0.3	4	0.6	5,892	2.8	0.2	96,276
Delaware	19	0.2	55	0.2	3	0.6	10,145	2.1	0.2	112,316
West Virginia	28	0.3	73	0.2	3	0.5	6,384	2.1	0.2	73,964
South Dakota	20	0.2	122	0.4	6	0.5	3,811	2.1	0.2	102,800
Montana	32	0.4	60*	-	-	(D)	-	(D)	-	-
Hawaii	26	0.3	175*	-	-	(D)	-	(D)	-	-
Vermont	18	0.2	60*	-	-	(D)	-	(D)	-	-
Wyoming	15	0.2	60*	-	-	(D)	-	(D)	-	-
D.C.	7	0.1	60*	-	-	(D)	-	(D)	-	-

Source: 1997 Economic Census. The states are in descending order of revenues or establishments (if revenue data are missing for the majority). The symbol (D) appears when data are withheld to prevent disclosure of competitive information. States marked with (D) are sorted by number of establishments. A dash (-) indicates that the data element cannot be calculated. * indicates the midpoint of a range; 175, for example is the range 100-249. Shaded states on the state map indicate those states which have proportionately greater representation in the industry than would be indicated by the state's population; the ratio is based on total revenues or number of establishments. Shaded regions indicate where the industry is regionally most concentrated.

NAICS 812210 - FUNERAL HOMES AND FUNERAL SERVICES

GENERAL STATISTICS

Year	Establishments (number)	Employment (number)	Payroll ($ million)	Revenues ($ million)	Employees per Establishment (number)	Revenues per Establishment ($)	Payroll per Employee ($)
1997	16,338	105,365	2,444.0	9,633.0	6.4	589,607	23,196

Source: Economic Census of the United States, 1997. This is a newly defined industry. Data for prior years were unavailable at the time of publication but may become available over time.

INDICES OF CHANGE

Year	Establishments (number)	Employment (number)	Payroll ($ million)	Revenues ($ million)	Employees per Establishment (number)	Revenues per Establishment ($)	Payroll per Employee ($)
1997	100.0	100.0	100.0	100.0	100.0	100.0	100.0

Sources: Same as General Statistics. The values shown reflect change from the base year, 1997. Values above 100 mean greater than 1997, values below 100 mean less than 1997, and a value of 100 in the 1982-96 or 1998-2001 period means same as 1997. Values followed by a 'p' are projections by the editors; 'e' stands for extrapolation. Data are the most recent available at this level of detail.

SIC INDUSTRIES RELATED TO NAICS 812210

Each new NAICS code represents an industry that used to be part of an SIC or a part of several SIC industries. Data in this table are shown to provide transitional information for these cases. All available data for the precursor SIC(s) are shown. Even if only a part of an SIC is included in the NAICS, *all* data for the SIC are reproduced. If the SIC industry is not marked as being a part (pt) of the NAICS, the entire industry is embedded in the NAICS data. The SIC composition of the new industry provides some hints of the relative importance of its "ancestors." Data marked with a 'p' are projected. Projections begin with 1982 data. Data earlier than 1990 are not shown but are reflected in the projections.

SIC	Industry	1990	1991	1992	1993	1994	1995	1996	1997
7261	**Funeral Service & Crematories (pt)**								
	Establishments (number)	14,880	14,997	15,647	15,348	15,912	15,844	15,474p	15,480p
	Employment (thousands)	84.8	85.0	88.3	90.0	93.6	100.3	96.4p	98.1p
	Revenues ($ million)	6,825.0	7,119.0	7,588.0	8,193.0	8,571.0	9,437.0	10,046.0	9,964.1p

Source: Economic Census of the United States, 1992, annual surveys of economic sectors conducted by the Bureau of the Census, and estimates or projections based on the 1982-1992 period; not all data are shown. 'e' marks estimates made by the editors; 'p' indicates projections based on time series. A dash (-) indicates that data for this SIC or year were not available. The abbreviation (pt) next to the industry name indicates that only a part of the industry is present within the NAICS data. If no (pt) is shown, the entire industry is contained within the NAICS data.

SELECTED RATIOS

For 1997	Avg. of Information	Analyzed Industry	Index	For 1997	Avg. of Information	Analyzed Industry	Index
Employees per establishment	6	6	103	Payroll per establishment	126,069	149,590	119
Revenue per establishment	511,622	589,607	115	Payroll as % of revenue	25	25	103
Revenue per employee	81,659	91,425	112	Payroll per employee	20,122	23,196	115

Sources: Same as General Statistics. The 'Average' column represents the average for the industry sector, in 1997, where the currently shown industry is classified. The Index shows the relationship between the Average and the Analyzed Industry. For example, 100 means that they are equal; 500 that the Analyzed Industry is five times the average; 50 means that the Analyzed Industry is half the national average. The abbreviation 'na' is used to show that data are 'not available'.

LEADING COMPANIES   Number shown: **8**   Total sales ($ mil): **4,361**   Total employment (000): **41.6**

Company Name	Address				CEO Name	Phone	Co. Type	Sales ($ mil)	Empl. (000)
Service Corporation International	P O Box 130548	Houston	TX	77219	Robert L. Waltrip	713-522-5141	P	3,322	27.6
Stewart Enterprises Inc.	110 Veterans Mem	Metairie	LA	70005	Joseph Henican	504-837-5880	P	756	10.6
Carriage Services Inc.	1300 Post Oak Blvd	Houston	TX	77056	Mark Duffey	281-556-7400	P	168	1.7
Rose Hills Co.	PO Box 110	Whittier	CA	90608	Dillis Ward	562-699-0921	P	38*	0.7
Blake-Lamb Funeral Homes Inc.	4727 W 103rd St	Oak Lawn	IL	60453	Rosemarie Lamb	708-636-1193	S	36*	0.5
Cemetery Management Inc.	PO Box 14141A	Miami	FL	33114	Gabrielle Romanach	305-238-3672	R	21*	0.3
Memphis Funeral Homes	5599 Poplar Ave	Memphis	TN	38119	Paul McCarver	901-725-0100	R	19*	0.3
Affordable Funeral Services Inc.	2230 Gallows Rd	Dunn Loring	VA	22027		703-876-1755	S	1*	<0.1

Source: Ward's Business Directory of U.S. Private and Public Companies, Volumes 1 and 2, 2000. The company type code used is as follows: P - Public, R - Private, S - Subsidiary, D - Division, J - Joint Venture, A - Affiliate, G - Group, N - Company type not reported. Sales are in millions of dollars, employees are in thousands. An asterisk (*) indicates an estimated sales volume. The symbol < stands for 'less than'. Company names and addresses are truncated, in some cases, to fit into the available space.

LOCATION BY STATE AND REGIONAL CONCENTRATION

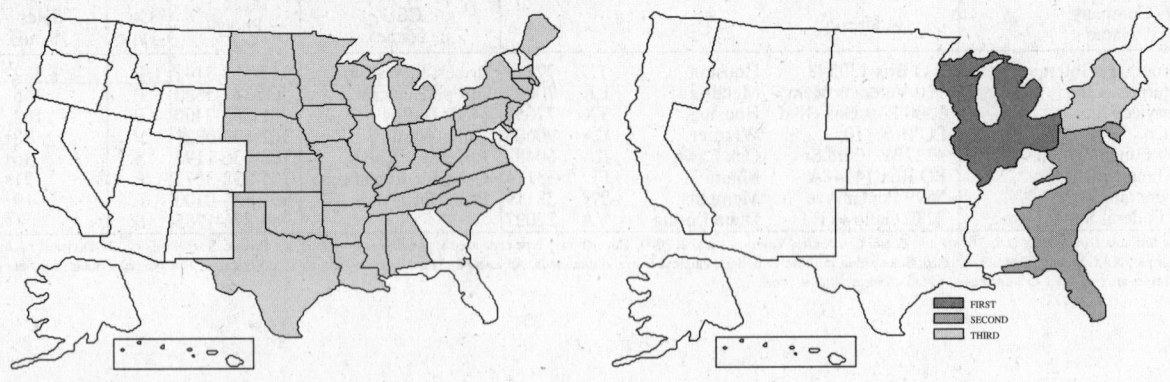

INDUSTRY DATA BY STATE

State	Establishments Total (number)	% of U.S.	Employment Total (number)	% of U.S.	Per Estab.	Payroll Total ($ mil.)	Per Empl. ($)	Revenues Total ($ mil.)	% of U.S.	Per Estab. ($)
New York	1,196	7.3	5,175	4.9	4	159.7	30,869	711.2	7.4	594,650
Texas	982	6.0	8,071	7.7	8	160.3	19,858	673.2	7.0	685,515
California	705	4.3	7,194	6.8	10	176.1	24,476	645.3	6.7	915,305
Ohio	939	5.7	5,688	5.4	6	139.5	24,530	526.6	5.5	560,825
Pennsylvania	1,030	6.3	4,825	4.6	5	117.1	24,268	496.1	5.2	481,680
Illinois	877	5.4	4,433	4.2	5	116.1	26,191	481.8	5.0	549,387
Florida	645	3.9	5,884	5.6	9	113.8	19,342	454.7	4.7	704,949
Michigan	607	3.7	4,509	4.3	7	96.8	21,461	362.4	3.8	597,043
New Jersey	508	3.1	2,638	2.5	5	80.3	30,440	334.8	3.5	659,033
North Carolina	486	3.0	3,816	3.6	8	83.5	21,888	316.7	3.3	651,613
Missouri	500	3.1	3,272	3.1	7	67.8	20,707	280.5	2.9	560,976
Indiana	526	3.2	3,024	2.9	6	74.5	24,647	266.9	2.8	507,430
Virginia	403	2.5	3,240	3.1	8	72.3	22,307	263.9	2.7	654,732
Georgia	451	2.8	2,895	2.7	6	62.2	21,484	254.7	2.6	564,718
Tennessee	375	2.3	3,036	2.9	8	63.3	20,851	251.4	2.6	670,472
Massachusetts	456	2.8	1,930	1.8	4	61.3	31,754	245.8	2.6	539,026
Kentucky	382	2.3	2,222	2.1	6	53.2	23,926	210.2	2.2	550,230
Alabama	295	1.8	2,707	2.6	9	48.8	18,018	200.8	2.1	680,522
Wisconsin	419	2.6	1,866	1.8	4	50.8	27,225	200.3	2.1	477,981
Minnesota	332	2.0	1,616	1.5	5	42.3	26,194	170.1	1.8	512,301
Louisiana	276	1.7	2,255	2.1	8	44.1	19,556	163.8	1.7	593,348
Maryland	199	1.2	1,899	1.8	10	43.4	22,852	162.6	1.7	817,161
South Carolina	266	1.6	2,164	2.1	8	41.8	19,327	153.9	1.6	578,711
Oklahoma	295	1.8	1,964	1.9	7	39.4	20,062	152.9	1.6	518,159
Iowa	394	2.4	1,777	1.7	5	38.3	21,543	152.2	1.6	386,173
Connecticut	235	1.4	1,207	1.1	5	41.8	34,621	149.4	1.6	635,864
Mississippi	254	1.6	1,686	1.6	7	32.9	19,524	119.8	1.2	471,752
Arkansas	215	1.3	1,369	1.3	6	29.9	21,851	112.1	1.2	521,428
Kansas	261	1.6	1,440	1.4	6	29.4	20,414	111.0	1.2	425,180
Washington	158	1.0	1,218	1.2	8	31.3	25,689	105.2	1.1	666,076
West Virginia	244	1.5	1,414	1.3	6	28.9	20,472	104.4	1.1	428,057
Arizona	119	0.7	955	0.9	8	22.7	23,807	84.2	0.9	707,252
Nebraska	176	1.1	917	0.9	5	20.0	21,791	74.1	0.8	421,244
Oregon	127	0.8	859	0.8	7	18.8	21,836	73.3	0.8	577,055
Colorado	119	0.7	863	0.8	7	15.5	17,976	68.4	0.7	574,681
Rhode Island	97	0.6	404	0.4	4	11.8	29,087	46.0	0.5	474,237
Utah	59	0.4	378	0.4	6	10.3	27,341	44.6	0.5	755,627
Maine	105	0.6	487	0.5	5	11.1	22,887	43.6	0.5	415,105
New Hampshire	72	0.4	266	0.3	4	7.9	29,560	41.6	0.4	578,083
New Mexico	67	0.4	581	0.6	9	10.5	18,072	40.6	0.4	605,224
Hawaii	21	0.1	475	0.5	23	11.1	23,373	37.5	0.4	1,785,095
Idaho	65	0.4	330	0.3	5	7.6	23,115	36.3	0.4	558,338
Nevada	31	0.2	486	0.5	16	11.6	23,887	33.9	0.4	1,094,871
South Dakota	78	0.5	321	0.3	4	7.1	22,184	30.8	0.3	395,192
North Dakota	69	0.4	319	0.3	5	7.4	23,182	29.9	0.3	432,841
Delaware	46	0.3	258	0.2	6	8.0	30,829	26.6	0.3	578,630
Montana	63	0.4	270	0.3	4	5.7	21,193	24.9	0.3	395,365
D.C.	22	0.1	282	0.3	13	6.0	21,387	22.9	0.2	1,042,773
Vermont	50	0.3	191	0.2	4	4.5	23,377	17.9	0.2	357,320
Wyoming	30	0.2	175*	-	-	(D)	-	(D)	-	-
Alaska	11	0.1	60*	-	-	(D)	-	(D)	-	-

Source: 1997 *Economic Census*. The states are in descending order of revenues or establishments (if revenue data are missing for the majority). The symbol (D) appears when data are withheld to prevent disclosure of competitive information. States marked with (D) are sorted by number of establishments. A dash (-) indicates that the data element cannot be calculated. * indicates the midpoint of a range; 175, for example is the range 100-249. Shaded *states* on the state map indicate those states which have proportionately greater representation in the industry than would be indicated by the state's population; the ratio is based on total revenues or number of establishments. Shaded *regions* indicate where the industry is regionally most concentrated.

NAICS 812220 - CEMETERIES AND CREMATORIES

GENERAL STATISTICS

Year	Establishments (number)	Employment (number)	Payroll ($ million)	Revenues ($ million)	Employees per Establishment (number)	Revenues per Establishment ($)	Payroll per Employee ($)
1997	6,677	59,458	1,075.0	2,988.0	8.9	447,506	18,080

Source: *Economic Census of the United States*, 1997. This is a newly defined industry. Data for prior years were unavailable at the time of publication but may become available over time.

INDICES OF CHANGE

Year	Establishments (number)	Employment (number)	Payroll ($ million)	Revenues ($ million)	Employees per Establishment (number)	Revenues per Establishment ($)	Payroll per Employee ($)
1997	100.0	100.0	100.0	100.0	100.0	100.0	100.0

Sources: Same as General Statistics. The values shown reflect change from the base year, 1997. Values above 100 mean greater than 1997, values below 100 mean less than 1997, and a value of 100 in the 1982-96 or 1998-2001 period means same as 1997. Values followed by a 'p' are projections by the editors; 'e' stands for extrapolation. Data are the most recent available at this level of detail.

SIC INDUSTRIES RELATED TO NAICS 812220

Each new NAICS code represents an industry that used to be part of an SIC or a part of several SIC industries. Data in this table are shown to provide transitional information for these cases. All available data for the precursor SIC(s) are shown. Even if only a part of an SIC is included in the NAICS, *all* data for the SIC are reproduced. If the SIC industry is not marked as being a part (pt) of the NAICS, the entire industry is embedded in the NAICS data. The SIC composition of the new industry provides some hints of the relative importance of its "ancestors." Data marked with a 'p' are projected. Projections begin with 1982 data. Data earlier than 1990 are not shown but are reflected in the projections.

SIC	Industry	1990	1991	1992	1993	1994	1995	1996	1997
6531	**Real Estate Agents and Managers (pt)**								
	Establishments (number)	-	-	106,552	-	-	-	-	-
	Employment (thousands)	-	-	646.6	-	-	-	-	-
	Revenues ($ million)	-	-	53,747.0	-	-	-	-	-
6553	**Cemetery Subdividers and Developers**								
	Establishments (number)	-	-	6,490	-	-	-	-	-
	Employment (thousands)	-	-	40.1	-	-	-	-	-
	Revenues ($ million)	-	-	2,299.6	-	-	-	-	-
7261	**Funeral Service & Crematories (pt)**								
	Establishments (number)	14,880	14,997	15,647	15,348	15,912	15,844	15,474p	15,480p
	Employment (thousands)	84.8	85.0	88.3	90.0	93.6	100.3	96.4p	98.1p
	Revenues ($ million)	6,825.0	7,119.0	7,588.0	8,193.0	8,571.0	9,437.0	10,046.0	9,964.1p

Source: *Economic Census of the United States*, 1992, annual surveys of economic sectors conducted by the Bureau of the Census, and estimates or projections based on the 1982-1992 period; not all data are shown. 'e' marks estimates made by the editors; 'p' indicates projections based on time series. A dash (-) indicates that data for this SIC or year were not available. The abbreviation (pt) next to the industry name indicates that only a part of the industry is present within the NAICS data. If no (pt) is shown, the entire industry is contained within the NAICS data.

SELECTED RATIOS

For 1997	Avg. of Information	Analyzed Industry	Index	For 1997	Avg. of Information	Analyzed Industry	Index
Employees per establishment	6	9	142	Payroll per establishment	126,069	161,000	128
Revenue per establishment	511,622	447,506	87	Payroll as % of revenue	25	36	146
Revenue per employee	81,659	50,254	62	Payroll per employee	20,122	18,080	90

Sources: Same as General Statistics. The 'Average' column represents the average for the industry sector, in 1997, where the currently shown industry is classified. The Index shows the relationship between the Average and the Analyzed Industry. For example, 100 means that they are equal; 500 that the Analyzed Industry is five times the average; 50 means that the Analyzed Industry is half the national average. The abbreviation 'na' is used to show that data are 'not available'.

LEADING COMPANIES   Number shown: **7**   Total sales ($ mil): **4,420**   Total employment (000): **42.2**

Company Name	Address				CEO Name	Phone	Co. Type	Sales ($ mil)	Empl. (000)
Service Corporation International	P O Box 130548	Houston	TX	77219	Robert L. Waltrip	713-522-5141	P	3,322	27.6
Stewart Enterprises Inc.	110 Veterans Mem	Metairie	LA	70005	Joseph Henican	504-837-5880	P	756	10.6
Carriage Services Inc.	1300 Post Oak Blvd	Houston	TX	77056	Mark Duffey	281-556-7400	P	168	1.7
Forest Lawn Memorial Parks	1712 S Glendale	Glendale	CA	91205	John Llewellyn		R	74*	0.9
SCI International Ltd.	1929 Allen Pkwy	Houston	TX	77019	RL Waltrip	713-525-5497	P	41*	0.5
Rose Hills Co.	PO Box 110	Whittier	CA	90608	Dillis Ward	562-699-0921	P	38*	0.7
Cemetery Management Inc.	PO Box 14141A	Miami	FL	33114	Gabrielle Romanach	305-238-3672	R	21*	0.3

Source: *Ward's Business Directory of U.S. Private and Public Companies*, Volumes 1 and 2, 2000. The company type code used is as follows: P - Public, R - Private, S - Subsidiary, D - Division, J - Joint Venture, A - Affiliate, G - Group, N - Company type not reported. Sales are in millions of dollars, employees are in thousands. An asterisk (*) indicates an estimated sales volume. The symbol < stands for 'less than'. Company names and addresses are truncated, in some cases, to fit into the available space.

LOCATION BY STATE AND REGIONAL CONCENTRATION

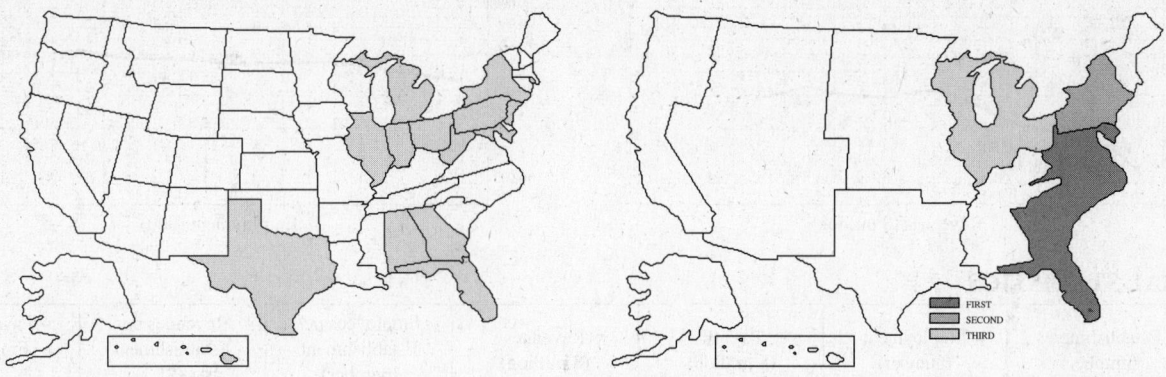

INDUSTRY DATA BY STATE

State	Establishments Total (number)	Establishments % of U.S.	Employment Total (number)	Employment % of U.S.	Employment Per Estab.	Payroll Total ($ mil.)	Payroll Per Empl. ($)	Revenues Total ($ mil.)	Revenues % of U.S.	Revenues Per Estab. ($)
California	240	3.6	4,735	8.0	20	107.0	22,608	333.1	11.1	1,387,771
New York	605	9.1	3,099	5.2	5	107.5	34,675	251.7	8.4	416,091
Florida	231	3.5	4,099	6.9	18	70.4	17,165	231.3	7.7	1,001,277
Texas	382	5.7	5,986	10.1	16	87.6	14,640	220.9	7.4	578,304
Pennsylvania	649	9.7	4,256	7.2	7	74.8	17,567	204.8	6.9	315,630
Illinois	363	5.4	3,004	5.1	8	59.9	19,924	173.8	5.8	478,898
Ohio	351	5.3	2,806	4.7	8	47.3	16,849	132.3	4.4	376,803
New Jersey	210	3.1	1,779	3.0	8	50.7	28,526	125.6	4.2	598,214
Michigan	167	2.5	1,604	2.7	10	39.2	24,454	112.3	3.8	672,527
Georgia	171	2.6	1,765	3.0	10	27.6	15,652	91.2	3.1	533,427
North Carolina	182	2.7	1,884	3.2	10	26.1	13,870	78.8	2.6	432,995
Maryland	108	1.6	1,892	3.2	18	29.0	15,345	75.9	2.5	703,111
Virginia	150	2.2	1,598	2.7	11	26.3	16,460	75.7	2.5	504,573
Indiana	201	3.0	1,834	3.1	9	28.7	15,632	74.2	2.5	369,060
Massachusetts	143	2.1	778	1.3	5	22.4	28,751	68.3	2.3	477,280
Tennessee	143	2.1	1,799	3.0	13	21.7	12,089	55.9	1.9	390,699
Washington	114	1.7	924	1.6	8	19.1	20,673	50.2	1.7	440,228
Alabama	122	1.8	1,456	2.4	12	18.0	12,377	50.1	1.7	410,303
Louisiana	73	1.1	1,255	2.1	17	18.0	14,315	47.1	1.6	644,603
South Carolina	119	1.8	1,105	1.9	9	14.8	13,436	42.5	1.4	357,076
Missouri	175	2.6	1,116	1.9	6	16.3	14,628	41.8	1.4	238,617
Kentucky	137	2.1	1,262	2.1	9	15.5	12,296	39.0	1.3	284,555
Connecticut	108	1.6	496	0.8	5	13.0	26,161	37.2	1.2	344,306
Wisconsin	245	3.7	966	1.6	4	13.0	13,417	33.0	1.1	134,698
Arizona	40	0.6	703	1.2	18	11.3	16,142	32.2	1.1	804,925
Colorado	60	0.9	711	1.2	12	12.1	16,990	30.9	1.0	514,750
Minnesota	144	2.2	544	0.9	4	10.3	18,996	30.3	1.0	210,347
Oklahoma	69	1.0	685	1.2	10	9.4	13,727	29.9	1.0	433,986
West Virginia	114	1.7	899	1.5	8	10.9	12,095	26.4	0.9	231,298
Oregon	70	1.0	612	1.0	9	9.8	16,031	24.6	0.8	351,371
Iowa	146	2.2	520	0.9	4	8.0	15,358	23.5	0.8	160,870
Hawaii	16	0.2	423	0.7	26	8.7	20,645	22.7	0.8	1,421,562
Kansas	91	1.4	440	0.7	5	6.2	14,016	16.7	0.6	184,055
Rhode Island	37	0.6	189	0.3	5	3.8	20,286	14.5	0.5	390,784
Arkansas	65	1.0	507	0.9	8	4.2	8,316	14.3	0.5	220,508
Utah	17	0.3	160	0.3	9	3.3	20,619	10.7	0.4	629,941
Mississippi	53	0.8	294	0.5	6	3.4	11,599	10.3	0.3	193,491
New Mexico	23	0.3	411	0.7	18	3.9	9,557	9.6	0.3	415,609
Nebraska	53	0.8	137	0.2	3	2.2	15,723	7.6	0.3	142,509
Nevada	7	0.1	117	0.2	17	2.1	17,983	6.9	0.2	981,429
Maine	58	0.9	85	0.1	1	2.1	24,812	6.1	0.2	104,914
Delaware	18	0.3	87	0.1	5	2.2	24,874	5.4	0.2	302,778
Montana	32	0.5	84	0.1	3	1.2	13,929	3.4	0.1	106,281
South Dakota	26	0.4	76	0.1	3	1.1	14,039	3.0	0.1	115,385
D.C.	6	0.1	58	0.1	10	1.1	18,793	2.9	0.1	476,667
New Hampshire	25	0.4	60	0.1	2	1.0	16,917	2.4	0.1	95,680
Vermont	51	0.8	49	0.1	1	1.0	20,286	2.3	0.1	45,725
Idaho	21	0.3	40	0.1	2	1.0	24,925	2.3	0.1	107,762
North Dakota	33	0.5	39	0.1	1	0.4	11,308	1.2	0.0	36,818
Alaska	5	0.1	12	0.0	2	0.2	18,000	0.9	0.0	170,600
Wyoming	8	0.1	18	0.0	2	0.2	10,000	0.5	0.0	59,625

Source: 1997 *Economic Census*. The states are in descending order of revenues or establishments (if revenue data are missing for the majority). The symbol (D) appears when data are withheld to prevent disclosure of competitive information. States marked with (D) are sorted by number of establishments. A dash (-) indicates that the data element cannot be calculated. * indicates the midpoint of a range; 175, for example is the range 100-249. Shaded *states* on the state map indicate those states which have proportionately greater representation in the industry than would be indicated by the state's population; the ratio is based on total revenues or number of establishments. Shaded *regions* indicate where the industry is regionally most concentrated.

NAICS 812310 - COIN-OPERATED LAUNDRIES AND DRYCLEANERS*

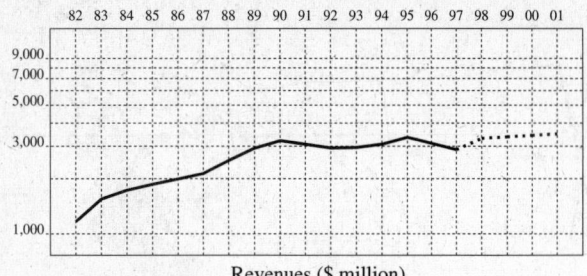

Revenues ($ million)

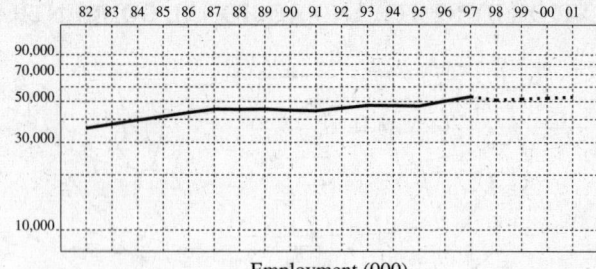

Employment (000)

GENERAL STATISTICS

Year	Establishments (number)	Employment (number)	Payroll ($ million)	Revenues ($ million)	Employees per Establishment (number)	Revenues per Establishment ($)	Payroll per Employee ($)
1982	11,905	35,729	226.0	1,168.0	3.0	98,110	6,325
1983	12,069 e	37,666 e	250.0 e	1,550.0	3.1 e	128,428 e	6,637 e
1984	12,233 e	39,604 e	274.0 e	1,734.0	3.2 e	141,748 e	6,918 e
1985	12,397 e	41,541 e	298.0 e	1,865.0	3.4 e	150,440 e	7,174 e
1986	12,561 e	43,479 e	322.0 e	1,993.0	3.5 e	158,666 e	7,406 e
1987	12,725	45,416	345.0	2,132.0	3.6	167,544	7,596
1988	11,652	45,343	401.0	2,506.0	3.9	215,070	8,844
1989	11,615	45,426	410.0	2,927.0	3.9	252,002	9,026
1990	11,112	44,802	423.0	3,214.0	4.0	289,237	9,442
1991	11,484	44,507	440.0	3,072.0	3.9	267,503	9,886
1992	13,002	46,002	446.0	2,931.0	3.5	225,427	9,695
1993	12,873	47,640	490.0	2,949.0	3.7	229,084	10,285
1994	12,906	47,458	511.0	3,074.0	3.7	238,184	10,767
1995	12,653	47,266	528.0	3,352.0	3.7	264,917	11,171
1996	13,268 e	50,145 e	567.0 e	3,113.0	3.8 e	234,625 e	11,307 e
1997	13,883	53,023	606.0	2,873.0	3.8	206,944	11,429
1998	13,580 p	50,887 p	609.0 p	3,304.0 p	3.7 p	243,299 p	11,968 p
1999	13,765 p	51,534 p	632.0 p	3,368.0 p	3.7 p	244,679 p	12,264 p
2000	13,950 p	52,181 p	655.0 p	3,432.0 p	3.7 p	246,022 p	12,552 p
2001	14,135 p	52,829 p	679.0 p	3,495.0 p	3.7 p	247,259 p	12,853 p

Sources: Economic Census of the United States, 1982, 1987, 1992, 1997. Establishment counts, employment, and payroll are from *County Business Patterns* for non-Census years. In non-Census years, industries in the Manufacturing range under SIC coding include data from the *Annual Survey of Manufactures* (*ASM*); those in the old Services range include data from the *Services Annual Survey* (*SAS*). Values followed by a 'p' are projections by the editors. Extrapolations are marked by 'e'. Data are the most recent available at this level of detail.

INDICES OF CHANGE

Year	Establishments (number)	Employment (number)	Payroll ($ million)	Revenues ($ million)	Employees per Establishment (number)	Revenues per Establishment ($)	Payroll per Employee ($)
1982	85.8	67.4	37.3	40.7	78.6	47.4	55.3
1987	91.7	85.7	56.9	74.2	93.4	81.0	66.5
1992	93.7	86.8	73.6	102.0	92.6	108.9	84.8
1993	92.7	89.8	80.9	102.6	96.9	110.7	90.0
1994	93.0	89.5	84.3	107.0	96.3	115.1	94.2
1995	91.1	89.1	87.1	116.7	97.8	128.0	97.7
1996	95.6 e	94.6 e	93.6 e	108.4 e	99.0 e	113.4 e	98.9 e
1997	100.0	100.0	100.0	100.0	100.0	100.0	100.0
1998	97.8 p	96.0 p	100.5 p	115.0 p	98.1 p	117.6 p	104.7 p
1999	99.2 p	97.2 p	104.3 p	117.2 p	98.0 p	118.2 p	107.3 p
2000	100.5 p	98.4 p	108.1 p	119.5 p	97.9 p	118.9 p	109.8 p
2001	101.8 p	99.6 p	112.0 p	121.6 p	97.9 p	119.5 p	112.5 p

Sources: Same as General Statistics. The values shown reflect change from the base year, 1997. Values above 100 mean greater than 1997, values below 100 mean less than 1997, and a value of 100 in the 1982-96 or 1998-2001 period means same as 1997. Values followed by a 'p' are projections by the editors; 'e' stands for extrapolation. Data are the most recent available at this level of detail.

SELECTED RATIOS

For 1997	Avg. of Information	Analyzed Industry	Index	For 1997	Avg. of Information	Analyzed Industry	Index
Employees per establishment	6	4	61	Payroll per establishment	126,069	43,651	35
Revenue per establishment	511,622	206,944	40	Payroll as % of revenue	25	21	86
Revenue per employee	81,659	54,184	66	Payroll per employee	20,122	11,429	57

Sources: Same as General Statistics. The 'Average' column represents the average for the industry sector, in 1997, where the currently shown industry is classified. The Index shows the relationship between the Average and the Analyzed Industry. For example, 100 means that they are equal; 500 that the Analyzed Industry is five times the average; 50 means that the Analyzed Industry is half the national average. The abbreviation 'na' is used to show that data are 'not available'.

*Equivalent to SIC 7215.

LEADING COMPANIES   Number shown: **3**   Total sales ($ mil): **831**   Total employment (000): **3.9**

Company Name	Address				CEO Name	Phone	Co. Type	Sales ($ mil)	Empl. (000)
Coinmach Laundry Corp.	521 E Morehead St	Charlotte	NC	28202	Mitchell Blatt	704-375-1947	P	505	2.0
Coinmach Corp.	55 Lumber Rd	Roslyn	NY	11576	Mitchell Blatt	516-484-2300	S	325	1.9
Hood's	P O Box 636	New London	MN	56273	Holman Hood	320-354-2228	R	0*	<0.1

Source: Ward's Business Directory of U.S. Private and Public Companies, Volumes 1 and 2, 2000. The company type code used is as follows: P - Public, R - Private, S - Subsidiary, D - Division, J - Joint Venture, A - Affiliate, G - Group, N - Company type not reported. Sales are in millions of dollars, employees are in thousands. An asterisk (*) indicates an estimated sales volume. The symbol < stands for 'less than'. Company names and addresses are truncated, in some cases, to fit into the available space.

LOCATION BY STATE AND REGIONAL CONCENTRATION

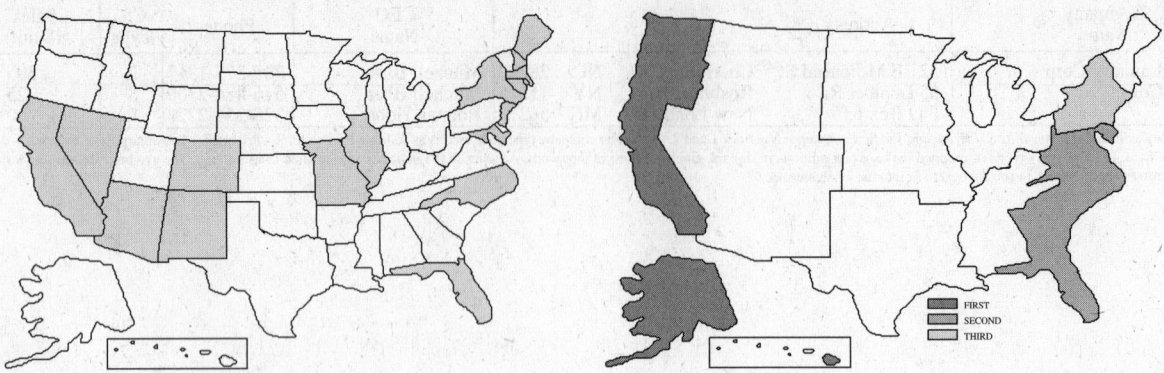

INDUSTRY DATA BY STATE

State	Establishments Total (number)	Establishments % of U.S.	Employment Total (number)	Employment % of U.S.	Employment Per Estab.	Payroll Total ($ mil.)	Payroll Per Empl. ($)	Revenues Total ($ mil.)	Revenues % of U.S.	Revenues Per Estab. ($)
California	1,215	8.8	5,304	10.0	4	86.5	16,307	435.9	15.2	358,756
New York	1,705	12.3	4,158	7.8	2	48.4	11,648	252.6	8.8	148,135
Texas	933	6.7	3,571	6.7	4	38.0	10,633	196.1	6.8	210,156
Florida	913	6.6	3,134	5.9	3	34.5	10,999	152.2	5.3	166,739
Illinois	725	5.2	2,750	5.2	4	28.6	10,385	142.2	4.9	196,091
New Jersey	590	4.2	1,904	3.6	3	27.8	14,602	131.9	4.6	223,541
Ohio	579	4.2	2,687	5.1	5	28.6	10,648	122.8	4.3	212,154
Michigan	529	3.8	2,507	4.7	5	25.1	10,020	105.8	3.7	200,026
Massachusetts	404	2.9	1,706	3.2	4	20.6	12,068	103.3	3.6	255,797
Maryland	237	1.7	1,112	2.1	5	17.6	15,803	97.3	3.4	410,494
Pennsylvania	428	3.1	1,639	3.1	4	18.6	11,372	89.0	3.1	208,012
North Carolina	425	3.1	1,686	3.2	4	19.4	11,534	82.5	2.9	194,186
Colorado	185	1.3	799	1.5	4	11.5	14,383	71.9	2.5	388,849
Georgia	360	2.6	1,371	2.6	4	15.1	11,049	66.5	2.3	184,683
Missouri	283	2.0	1,303	2.5	5	14.2	10,873	60.8	2.1	214,753
Indiana	381	2.7	1,877	3.5	5	17.6	9,373	60.0	2.1	157,417
Virginia	422	3.0	1,267	2.4	3	11.8	9,316	59.6	2.1	141,190
Washington	218	1.6	833	1.6	4	11.4	13,630	55.3	1.9	253,665
Arizona	173	1.2	836	1.6	5	8.8	10,480	50.5	1.8	291,769
Connecticut	181	1.3	709	1.3	4	8.1	11,468	45.8	1.6	253,276
Wisconsin	246	1.8	1,007	1.9	4	9.8	9,767	40.9	1.4	166,293
Tennessee	233	1.7	914	1.7	4	10.3	11,263	39.0	1.4	167,227
Oregon	120	0.9	482	0.9	4	6.6	13,772	32.9	1.1	274,242
Nevada	76	0.5	448	0.8	6	5.7	12,801	31.7	1.1	416,961
Alabama	176	1.3	910	1.7	5	9.2	10,102	27.6	1.0	156,767
Kentucky	215	1.5	732	1.4	3	6.4	8,705	24.9	0.9	115,935
Minnesota	162	1.2	692	1.3	4	5.7	8,295	24.6	0.9	152,074
Louisiana	102	0.7	440	0.8	4	4.8	11,009	24.4	0.8	238,755
South Carolina	177	1.3	597	1.1	3	4.9	8,201	24.2	0.8	136,514
Oklahoma	129	0.9	513	1.0	4	5.0	9,674	23.9	0.8	185,605
Maine	88	0.6	393	0.7	4	4.5	11,560	21.0	0.7	238,636
New Mexico	105	0.8	446	0.8	4	4.1	9,186	19.9	0.7	189,333
Iowa	108	0.8	484	0.9	4	3.7	7,663	14.8	0.5	136,917
Rhode Island	107	0.8	393	0.7	4	3.4	8,682	13.9	0.5	130,336
Mississippi	118	0.8	397	0.7	3	3.4	8,680	13.5	0.5	114,695
Kansas	126	0.9	450	0.8	4	3.5	7,782	13.5	0.5	107,048
New Hampshire	77	0.6	360	0.7	5	3.3	9,233	13.1	0.5	169,740
Hawaii	38	0.3	133	0.3	4	1.9	14,211	11.2	0.4	294,316
Utah	60	0.4	233	0.4	4	2.2	9,545	11.2	0.4	186,167
Arkansas	96	0.7	297	0.6	3	2.2	7,259	8.8	0.3	91,375
Nebraska	71	0.5	261	0.5	4	2.0	7,640	8.2	0.3	116,141
Vermont	42	0.3	185	0.3	4	1.6	8,665	6.8	0.2	161,357
Montana	50	0.4	180	0.3	4	1.3	7,372	6.0	0.2	119,340
West Virginia	55	0.4	154	0.3	3	1.3	8,130	5.5	0.2	99,618
Idaho	46	0.3	166	0.3	4	1.5	8,741	5.4	0.2	117,739
Delaware	38	0.3	114	0.2	3	1.2	10,526	4.3	0.2	114,368
South Dakota	39	0.3	129	0.2	3	0.8	6,411	4.1	0.1	105,103
North Dakota	23	0.2	91	0.2	4	0.6	6,264	2.4	0.1	103,522
Wyoming	22	0.2	81	0.2	4	0.7	8,494	2.3	0.1	102,364
Alaska	30	0.2	175*	-	-	(D)	-	(D)	-	-
D.C.	22	0.2	60*	-	-	(D)	-	(D)	-	-

Source: 1997 *Economic Census*. The states are in descending order of revenues or establishments (if revenue data are missing for the majority). The symbol (D) appears when data are withheld to prevent disclosure of competitive information. States marked with (D) are sorted by number of establishments. A dash (-) indicates that the data element cannot be calculated. * indicates the midpoint of a range; 175, for example is the range 100-249. Shaded *states* on the state map indicate those states which have proportionately greater representation in the industry than would be indicated by the state's population; the ratio is based on total revenues or number of establishments. Shaded *regions* indicate where the Iaundry is regionally most drcentrated.

NAICS 812320 - DRYCLEANING AND LAUNDRY SERVICES (EXCEPT COIN-OPERATED)

GENERAL STATISTICS

Year	Establishments (number)	Employment (number)	Payroll ($ million)	Revenues ($ million)	Employees per Establishment (number)	Revenues per Establishment ($)	Payroll per Employee ($)
1997	27,939	203,777	2,575.0	7,092.0	7.3	253,839	12,636

Source: *Economic Census of the United States*, 1997. This is a newly defined industry. Data for prior years were unavailable at the time of publication but may become available over time.

INDICES OF CHANGE

Year	Establishments (number)	Employment (number)	Payroll ($ million)	Revenues ($ million)	Employees per Establishment (number)	Revenues per Establishment ($)	Payroll per Employee ($)
1997	100.0	100.0	100.0	100.0	100.0	100.0	100.0

Sources: Same as General Statistics. The values shown reflect change from the base year, 1997. Values above 100 mean greater than 1997, values below 100 mean less than 1997, and a value of 100 in the 1982-96 or 1998-2001 period means same as 1997. Values followed by a 'p' are projections by the editors; 'e' stands for extrapolation. Data are the most recent available at this level of detail.

SIC INDUSTRIES RELATED TO NAICS 812320

Each new NAICS code represents an industry that used to be part of an SIC or a part of several SIC industries. Data in this table are shown to provide transitional information for these cases. All available data for the precursor SIC(s) are shown. Even if only a part of an SIC is included in the NAICS, *all* data for the SIC are reproduced. If the SIC industry is not marked as being a part (pt) of the NAICS, the entire industry is embedded in the NAICS data. The SIC composition of the new industry provides some hints of the relative importance of its "ancestors." Data marked with a 'p' are projected. Projections begin with 1982 data. Data earlier than 1990 are not shown but are reflected in the projections.

SIC	Industry	1990	1991	1992	1993	1994	1995	1996	1997
7211	**Power Laundries, Family & Commercial**								
	Establishments (number)	1,631	1,597	1,853	1,788	1,761	1,631	1,531p	1,476p
	Employment (thousands)	26.2	24.5	27.6	29.6	26.0	26.7	24.0p	23.2p
	Revenues ($ million)	818.0	830.0	898.0	913.0	906.0	932.0	874.0	918.1p
7212	**Garment Pressing & Cleaners' Agents**								
	Establishments (number)	2,873	2,945	-	3,039	3,159	2,944	3,116p	3,129p
	Employment (thousands)	11.2	11.8	-	11.5	12.2	11.7	13.2p	13.5p
	Revenues ($ million)	-	-	-	-	-	585.0	606.0	
7216	**Dry Cleaning Plants, Except Rug**								
	Establishments (number)	17,601	18,161	23,213	22,572	22,024	20,856	20,795p	20,794p
	Employment (thousands)	148.4	141.3	164.4	167.3	165.8	164.8	166.5p	168.0p
	Revenues ($ million)	4,412.0	4,538.0	5,467.0	5,354.0	5,432.0	5,493.0	5,487.0	5,935.3p
7219	**Laundry & Garment Services, nec (pt)**								
	Establishments (number)	2,323	2,715	3,968	3,896	3,665	3,460	4,054p	4,258p
	Employment (thousands)	13.5	15.2	19.9	24.4	20.4	20.0	23.8p	25.2p
	Revenues ($ million)	-	-	652.8	-	-	-	-	
7251	**Shoe Repair & Shoeshine Parlors (pt)**								
	Establishments (number)	2,528	2,593	2,702	2,654	2,438	2,292	2,355p	2,307p
	Employment (thousands)	6.5	6.5	6.4	6.7	6.1	6.0	6.1p	6.1p
	Revenues ($ million)	-	-	275.8	278.6p	287.5p	296.4p	305.4p	314.3p
7389	**Business Services, nec (pt)**								
	Establishments (number)	44,079	50,252	52,375	56,829	60,725	53,596	60,893p	63,269p
	Employment (thousands)	489.6	550.4	523.6	607.9	648.7	623.0	680.2p	710.9p
	Revenues ($ million)	-	-	32,885.9	-	-	-	-	

Source: *Economic Census of the United States*, 1992, annual surveys of economic sectors conducted by the Bureau of the Census, and estimates or projections based on the 1982-1992 period; not all data are shown. 'e' marks estimates made by the editors; 'p' indicates projections based on time series. A dash (-) indicates that data for this SIC or year were not available. The abbreviation (pt) next to the industry name indicates that only a part of the industry is present within the NAICS data. If no (pt) is shown, the entire industry is contained within the NAICS data.

SELECTED RATIOS

For 1997	Avg. of Information	Analyzed Industry	Index	For 1997	Avg. of Information	Analyzed Industry	Index
Employees per establishment	6	7	116	Payroll per establishment	126,069	92,165	73
Revenue per establishment	511,622	253,839	50	Payroll as % of revenue	25	36	147
Revenue per employee	81,659	34,803	43	Payroll per employee	20,122	12,636	63

Sources: Same as General Statistics. The 'Average' column represents the average for the industry sector, in 1997, where the currently shown industry is classified. The Index shows the relationship between the Average and the Analyzed Industry. For example, 100 means that they are equal; 500 that the Analyzed Industry is five times the average; 50 means that the Analyzed Industry is half the national average. The abbreviation 'na' is used to show that data are 'not available'.

LEADING COMPANIES
No company data available for this industry.

LOCATION BY STATE AND REGIONAL CONCENTRATION

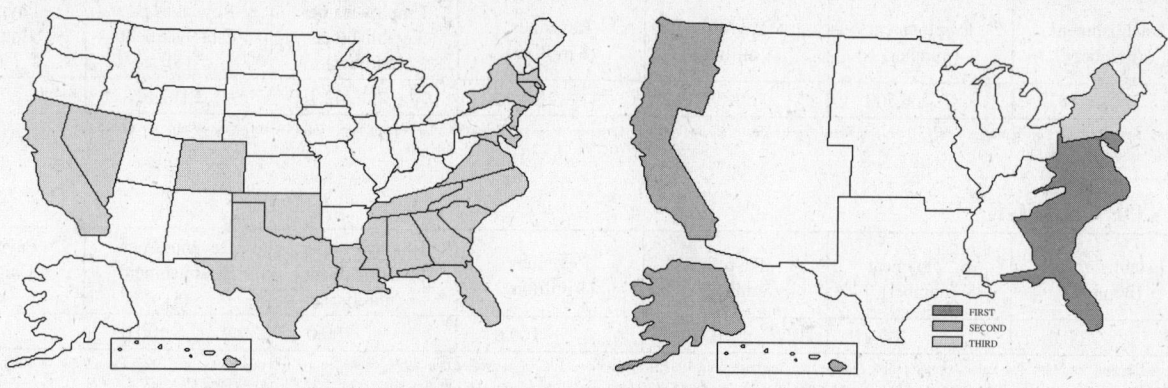

FIRST
SECOND
THIRD

INDUSTRY DATA BY STATE

State	Establishments Total (number)	% of U.S.	Employment Total (number)	% of U.S.	Per Estab.	Payroll Total ($ mil.)	Per Empl. ($)	Revenues Total ($ mil.)	% of U.S.	Per Estab. ($)
California	3,548	12.7	20,050	9.8	6	250.9	12,514	879.8	12.4	247,972
Texas	2,201	7.9	20,405	10.0	9	251.6	12,329	655.7	9.2	297,908
New York	2,536	9.1	11,661	5.7	5	170.6	14,629	526.7	7.4	207,672
Florida	1,646	5.9	11,437	5.6	7	147.0	12,855	404.6	5.7	245,823
Illinois	1,302	4.7	8,577	4.2	7	109.3	12,748	315.1	4.4	242,019
New Jersey	1,239	4.4	6,357	3.1	5	90.5	14,231	270.2	3.8	218,115
Ohio	947	3.4	8,231	4.0	9	100.1	12,162	247.8	3.5	261,693
Georgia	1,070	3.8	6,719	3.3	6	82.3	12,249	236.6	3.3	221,109
Pennsylvania	961	3.4	6,796	3.3	7	82.5	12,146	227.7	3.2	236,904
North Carolina	803	2.9	7,538	3.7	9	92.7	12,299	223.9	3.2	278,863
Virginia	817	2.9	6,310	3.1	8	81.5	12,918	213.5	3.0	261,282
Massachusetts	756	2.7	5,383	2.6	7	78.6	14,600	210.9	3.0	279,001
Michigan	778	2.8	6,204	3.0	8	76.2	12,283	207.0	2.9	266,057
Tennessee	562	2.0	5,923	2.9	11	76.8	12,973	179.8	2.5	319,925
Maryland	657	2.4	4,033	2.0	6	53.7	13,313	151.9	2.1	231,172
Indiana	432	1.5	4,479	2.2	10	58.3	13,027	133.8	1.9	309,653
Missouri	553	2.0	4,166	2.0	8	51.6	12,390	132.6	1.9	239,711
Colorado	487	1.7	3,408	1.7	7	45.3	13,298	129.4	1.8	265,661
Louisiana	453	1.6	4,173	2.0	9	45.7	10,947	119.0	1.7	262,781
Connecticut	430	1.5	2,879	1.4	7	43.5	15,097	118.9	1.7	276,577
Alabama	480	1.7	4,307	2.1	9	49.3	11,452	118.1	1.7	246,048
South Carolina	416	1.5	4,032	2.0	10	45.0	11,149	108.7	1.5	261,233
Arizona	344	1.2	3,125	1.5	9	40.8	13,051	105.9	1.5	307,869
Washington	489	1.8	2,556	1.3	5	31.0	12,132	99.9	1.4	204,337
Minnesota	329	1.2	3,283	1.6	10	37.7	11,483	98.8	1.4	300,219
Oklahoma	326	1.2	3,152	1.5	10	35.9	11,384	94.3	1.3	289,402
Wisconsin	370	1.3	3,072	1.5	8	36.4	11,849	92.8	1.3	250,822
Kentucky	347	1.2	2,727	1.3	8	31.3	11,465	75.5	1.1	217,715
Mississippi	279	1.0	2,597	1.3	9	29.1	11,201	75.0	1.1	268,857
Arkansas	257	0.9	2,415	1.2	9	26.1	10,788	61.8	0.9	240,486
Kansas	229	0.8	1,977	1.0	9	21.2	10,721	56.8	0.8	248,039
Oregon	260	0.9	1,484	0.7	6	18.5	12,496	55.9	0.8	215,185
Iowa	178	0.6	1,684	0.8	9	19.7	11,710	48.2	0.7	271,028
Hawaii	41	0.1	1,266	0.6	31	19.6	15,448	47.2	0.7	1,150,146
Nevada	153	0.5	1,254	0.6	8	18.7	14,886	46.8	0.7	305,889
Utah	154	0.6	1,472	0.7	10	15.4	10,456	41.2	0.6	267,357
Nebraska	119	0.4	913	0.4	8	11.4	12,509	31.5	0.4	264,445
New Hampshire	89	0.3	819	0.4	9	12.6	15,366	30.6	0.4	343,843
New Mexico	129	0.5	1,054	0.5	8	11.9	11,320	29.1	0.4	225,946
D.C.	105	0.4	687	0.3	7	9.1	13,179	25.9	0.4	246,257
West Virginia	102	0.4	989	0.5	10	10.7	10,774	25.8	0.4	252,676
Rhode Island	105	0.4	723	0.4	7	10.1	13,972	25.0	0.4	237,790
Delaware	80	0.3	467	0.2	6	6.4	13,690	16.7	0.2	208,863
Maine	52	0.2	487	0.2	9	6.9	14,197	16.1	0.2	310,481
Idaho	69	0.2	544	0.3	8	5.7	10,414	15.1	0.2	218,377
Alaska	32	0.1	397	0.2	12	6.5	16,491	15.1	0.2	472,500
Montana	59	0.2	412	0.2	7	4.9	11,995	13.0	0.2	219,966
South Dakota	48	0.2	376	0.2	8	5.0	13,170	12.1	0.2	252,771
North Dakota	35	0.1	343	0.2	10	4.1	11,962	9.6	0.1	274,257
Vermont	46	0.2	263	0.1	6	3.5	13,255	9.1	0.1	196,913
Wyoming	39	0.1	171	0.1	4	2.1	12,094	5.5	0.1	141,949

Source: 1997 *Economic Census*. The states are in descending order of revenues or establishments (if revenue data are missing for the majority). The symbol (D) appears when data are withheld to prevent disclosure of competitive information. States marked with (D) are sorted by number of establishments. A dash (-) indicates that the data element cannot be calculated. * indicates the midpoint of a range; 175, for example is the range 100-249. Shaded *states* on the state map indicate those states which have proportionately greater representation in the industry than would be indicated by the state's population; the ratio is based on total revenues or number of establishments. Shaded *regions* indicate where the industry is regionally most concentrated.

NAICS 812331 - LINEN SUPPLY

GENERAL STATISTICS

Year	Establishments (number)	Employment (number)	Payroll ($ million)	Revenues ($ million)	Employees per Establishment (number)	Revenues per Establishment ($)	Payroll per Employee ($)
1997	1,347	56,700	1,087.0	2,940.0	42.1	2,182,628	19,171

Source: *Economic Census of the United States*, 1997. This is a newly defined industry. Data for prior years were unavailable at the time of publication but may become available over time.

INDICES OF CHANGE

Year	Establishments (number)	Employment (number)	Payroll ($ million)	Revenues ($ million)	Employees per Establishment (number)	Revenues per Establishment ($)	Payroll per Employee ($)
1997	100.0	100.0	100.0	100.0	100.0	100.0	100.0

Sources: Same as General Statistics. The values shown reflect change from the base year, 1997. Values above 100 mean greater than 1997, values below 100 mean less than 1997, and a value of 100 in the 1982-96 or 1998-2001 period means same as 1997. Values followed by a 'p' are projections by the editors; 'e' stands for extrapolation. Data are the most recent available at this level of detail.

SIC INDUSTRIES RELATED TO NAICS 812331

Each new NAICS code represents an industry that used to be part of an SIC or a part of several SIC industries. Data in this table are shown to provide transitional information for these cases. All available data for the precursor SIC(s) are shown. Even if only a part of an SIC is included in the NAICS, *all* data for the SIC are reproduced. If the SIC industry is not marked as being a part (pt) of the NAICS, the entire industry is embedded in the NAICS data. The SIC composition of the new industry provides some hints of the relative importance of its "ancestors." Data marked with a 'p' are projected. Projections begin with 1982 data. Data earlier than 1990 are not shown but are reflected in the projections.

SIC	Industry	1990	1991	1992	1993	1994	1995	1996	1997
7213	**Linen Supply**								
	Establishments (number)	1,264	1,287	1,375	1,313	1,325	1,267	1,270p	1,263p
	Employment (thousands)	56.4	57.8	54.4	52.4	53.5	54.9	54.0p	53.9p
	Revenues ($ million)	2,387.0	2,496.0	2,672.0	2,570.0	2,573.0	2,576.0	2,601.0	2,795.7p
7219	**Laundry & Garment Services, nec (pt)**								
	Establishments (number)	2,323	2,715	3,968	3,896	3,665	3,460	4,054p	4,258p
	Employment (thousands)	13.5	15.2	19.9	24.4	20.4	20.0	23.8p	25.2p
	Revenues ($ million)	-	-	652.8	-	-	-	-	-

Source: *Economic Census of the United States*, 1992, annual surveys of economic sectors conducted by the Bureau of the Census, and estimates or projections based on the 1982-1992 period; not all data are shown. 'e' marks estimates made by the editors; 'p' indicates projections based on time series. A dash (-) indicates that data for this SIC or year were not available. The abbreviation (pt) next to the industry name indicates that only a part of the industry is present within the NAICS data. If no (pt) is shown, the entire industry is contained within the NAICS data.

SELECTED RATIOS

For 1997	Avg. of Information	Analyzed Industry	Index	For 1997	Avg. of Information	Analyzed Industry	Index
Employees per establishment	6	42	672	Payroll per establishment	126,069	806,978	640
Revenue per establishment	511,622	2,182,628	427	Payroll as % of revenue	25	37	150
Revenue per employee	81,659	51,852	63	Payroll per employee	20,122	19,171	95

Sources: Same as General Statistics. The 'Average' column represents the average for the industry sector, in 1997, where the currently shown industry is classified. The Index shows the relationship between the Average and the Analyzed Industry. For example, 100 means that they are equal; 500 that the Analyzed Industry is five times the average; 50 means that the Analyzed Industry is half the national average. The abbreviation 'na' is used to show that data are 'not available'.

LEADING COMPANIES   Number shown: **13**   Total sales ($ mil): **5,034**   Total employment (000): **76.8**

Company Name	Address				CEO Name	Phone	Co. Type	Sales ($ mil)	Empl. (000)
National Service Industries Inc.	1420 Peachtree	Atlanta	GA	30309	James S. Balloun	404-853-1000	P	2,219	19.7
ServiceMaster Management	2300 Warrenville Rd	Downers Grove	IL	60515		630-271-1300	S	724*	14.0
Aratex Services Inc.	115 N 1st St	Burbank	CA	91510	Dill Leonard	818-973-3700	S	715*	13.0
Steiner Corp.	P O Box 2317	Salt Lake City	UT	84110	Richard R Steiner	801-328-8831	R	620	9.0
Ameripride Services Inc.	901 Marquette Ave	Minneapolis	MN	55402	Lawrence G Steiner	612-371-4200	R	316*	6.0
Healthcare Services Group Inc.	2643 Huntingdon	Huntngdn Val	PA	19006	Thomas A Cook	215-938-1661	P	205	10.8
Domestic Linen Supply	30555 NWrn Hwy	Farmington Hills	MI	48334	Bruce Colton	248-737-2000	R	79*	1.5
Central Quality Services Corp.	7043 E Palmer St	Detroit	MI	48211	Stuart D Wish	313-921-8180	R	45*	0.8
Admiral Linen & Uniform Service	2030 Kipling	Houston	TX	77098	Les Craft	713-529-2608	R	33*	0.6
Unitex Textile Rental Service	155 S Terr Ave	Mount Vernon	NY	10550	Michael Potack	914-699-7100	R	25	0.4
National Linen & Uniform Service	1420 Peachtree	Atlanta	GA	30309	Hugh Sawyer	404-853-6000	S	21*	0.4
Linens of the Week	735 Lamont St N W	Washington	DC	20010	Alan Bubes	202-291-9200	R	16*	0.3
Rental Uniform Service	P O Box 1207	Culpeper	VA	22701		540-825-2303	S	16*	0.3

Source: Ward's Business Directory of U.S. Private and Public Companies, Volumes 1 and 2, 2000. The company type code used is as follows: P - Public, R - Private, S - Subsidiary, D - Division, J - Joint Venture, A - Affiliate, G - Group, N - Company type not reported. Sales are in millions of dollars, employees are in thousands. An asterisk (*) indicates an estimated sales volume. The symbol < stands for 'less than'. Company names and addresses are truncated, in some cases, to fit into the available space.

LOCATION BY STATE AND REGIONAL CONCENTRATION

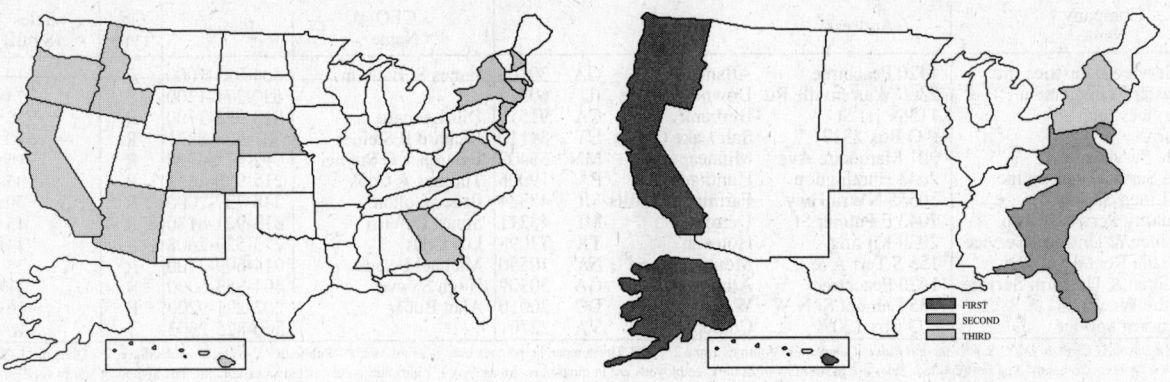

FIRST
SECOND
THIRD

INDUSTRY DATA BY STATE

State	Establishments Total (number)	% of U.S.	Employment Total (number)	% of U.S.	Per Estab.	Payroll Total ($ mil.)	Per Empl. ($)	Revenues Total ($ mil.)	% of U.S.	Per Estab. ($)
California	172	12.8	8,048	14.2	47	161.7	20,086	474.7	16.1	2,760,070
New York	119	8.8	5,416	9.6	46	102.1	18,859	270.5	9.2	2,273,000
Texas	102	7.6	3,582	6.3	35	65.0	18,155	168.6	5.7	1,653,392
Florida	82	6.1	2,973	5.2	36	52.4	17,625	147.9	5.0	1,803,110
Pennsylvania	56	4.2	2,395	4.2	43	46.5	19,410	123.9	4.2	2,211,964
Illinois	49	3.6	1,776	3.1	36	40.2	22,654	100.3	3.4	2,047,449
Georgia	37	2.7	1,803	3.2	49	32.2	17,880	96.8	3.3	2,616,000
Ohio	44	3.3	2,174	3.8	49	40.0	18,387	94.1	3.2	2,138,386
New Jersey	61	4.5	1,621	2.9	27	31.5	19,406	92.1	3.1	1,509,852
Virginia	35	2.6	1,648	2.9	47	30.4	18,459	87.0	3.0	2,485,800
Michigan	45	3.3	1,426	2.5	32	28.8	20,199	76.5	2.6	1,699,711
North Carolina	30	2.2	1,300	2.3	43	24.5	18,882	65.1	2.2	2,170,300
Massachusetts	45	3.3	1,344	2.4	30	23.0	17,129	63.7	2.2	1,415,800
Arizona	24	1.8	1,146	2.0	48	20.1	17,559	63.1	2.1	2,627,708
Washington	24	1.8	996	1.8	42	23.3	23,433	58.8	2.0	2,448,792
Oregon	20	1.5	772	1.4	39	17.2	22,337	52.5	1.8	2,622,600
Colorado	25	1.9	964	1.7	39	17.8	18,461	47.9	1.6	1,916,960
Tennessee	22	1.6	946	1.7	43	17.4	18,430	46.4	1.6	2,108,136
Missouri	23	1.7	924	1.6	40	18.6	20,091	46.2	1.6	2,006,652
Minnesota	21	1.6	744	1.3	35	17.8	23,860	45.8	1.6	2,182,667
Wisconsin	18	1.3	957	1.7	53	18.0	18,838	43.5	1.5	2,415,444
Kentucky	17	1.3	776	1.4	46	14.9	19,196	40.6	1.4	2,386,059
Louisiana	17	1.3	837	1.5	49	15.5	18,460	39.4	1.3	2,316,824
Connecticut	16	1.2	789	1.4	49	16.5	20,946	39.3	1.3	2,458,125
Maryland	14	1.0	953	1.7	68	15.4	16,169	35.8	1.2	2,553,786
South Carolina	14	1.0	804	1.4	57	12.8	15,918	34.7	1.2	2,480,286
Alabama	14	1.0	566	1.0	40	10.3	18,270	29.5	1.0	2,105,286
Hawaii	10	0.7	613	1.1	61	9.9	16,152	28.2	1.0	2,815,100
New Hampshire	9	0.7	390	0.7	43	8.7	22,254	22.7	0.8	2,527,000
Indiana	21	1.6	557	1.0	27	8.5	15,325	22.5	0.8	1,072,286
Nebraska	11	0.8	464	0.8	42	8.2	17,737	22.1	0.8	2,008,364
Arkansas	17	1.3	449	0.8	26	8.6	19,200	22.0	0.7	1,295,118
Rhode Island	8	0.6	405	0.7	51	8.9	21,904	21.9	0.7	2,740,875
Oklahoma	11	0.8	493	0.9	45	8.9	18,051	21.3	0.7	1,936,727
Mississippi	9	0.7	379	0.7	42	7.0	18,596	20.2	0.7	2,242,000
Idaho	5	0.4	309	0.5	62	6.1	19,822	17.2	0.6	3,449,200
Kansas	14	1.0	282	0.5	20	5.2	18,287	14.7	0.5	1,051,786
New Mexico	6	0.4	173	0.3	29	3.7	21,405	13.1	0.4	2,184,000
West Virginia	7	0.5	226	0.4	32	3.5	15,434	9.7	0.3	1,391,714
Delaware	3	0.2	184	0.3	61	3.6	19,598	9.5	0.3	3,158,000
Montana	5	0.4	160	0.3	32	2.3	14,169	6.4	0.2	1,289,000
Maine	9	0.7	95	0.2	11	1.2	12,179	3.9	0.1	436,111
South Dakota	3	0.2	41	0.1	14	0.9	20,732	2.4	0.1	802,000
Iowa	3	0.2	4	0.0	1	0.1	16,750	0.3	0.0	113,333
Nevada	18	1.3	1,750*	-	-	(D)	-	(D)	-	-
Wyoming	7	0.5	175*	-	-	(D)	-	(D)	-	-
D.C.	6	0.4	175*	-	-	(D)	-	(D)	-	-
Utah	6	0.4	375*	-	-	(D)	-	(D)	-	-
North Dakota	5	0.4	375*	-	-	(D)	-	(D)	-	-
Vermont	5	0.4	375*	-	-	(D)	-	(D)	-	-
Alaska	3	0.2	175*	-	-	(D)	-	(D)	-	-

Source: 1997 *Economic Census*. The states are in descending order of revenues or establishments (if revenue data are missing for the majority). The symbol (D) appears when data are withheld to prevent disclosure of competitive information. States marked with (D) are sorted by number of establishments. A dash (-) indicates that the data element cannot be calculated. * indicates the midpoint of a range; 175, for example is the range 100-249. Shaded *states* on the state map indicate those states which have proportionately greater representation in the industry than would be indicated by the state's population; the ratio is based on total revenues or number of establishments. Shaded *regions* indicate where the industry is regionally most concentrated.

NAICS 812332 - INDUSTRIAL LAUNDERERS*

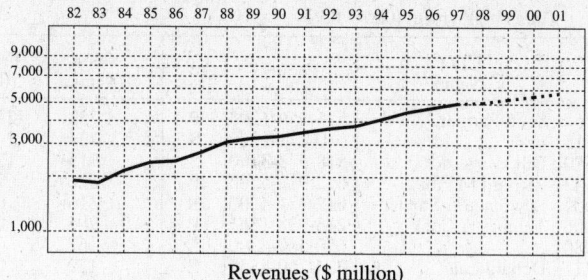

Revenues ($ million)

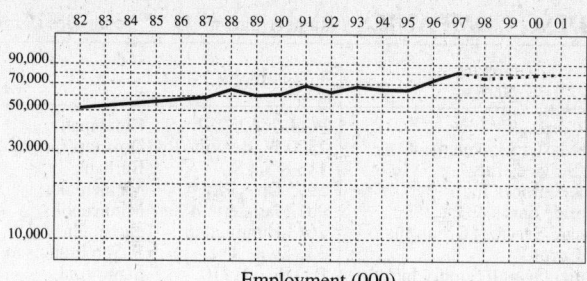

Employment (000)

GENERAL STATISTICS

Year	Establishments (number)	Employment (number)	Payroll ($ million)	Revenues ($ million)	Employees per Establishment (number)	Revenues per Establishment ($)	Payroll per Employee ($)
1982	1,335	51,585	667.0	1,895.0	38.6	1,419,476	12,930
1983	1,344 e	53,060 e	721.0 e	1,846.0	39.5 e	1,373,512 e	13,588 e
1984	1,353 e	54,536 e	774.0 e	2,156.0	40.3 e	1,593,496 e	14,192 e
1985	1,361 e	56,011 e	827.0 e	2,382.0	41.2 e	1,750,184 e	14,765 e
1986	1,370 e	57,487 e	880.0 e	2,427.0	42.0 e	1,771,533 e	15,308 e
1987	1,379	58,962	933.0	2,711.0	42.8	1,965,917	15,824
1988	1,355	65,299	1,029.0	3,084.0	48.2	2,276,015	15,758
1989	1,264	60,581	1,010.0	3,237.0	47.9	2,560,918	16,672
1990	1,300	61,530	1,074.0	3,311.0	47.3	2,546,923	17,455
1991	1,291	68,579	1,132.0	3,487.0	53.1	2,701,007	16,507
1992	1,435	63,172	1,199.0	3,656.0	44.0	2,547,735	18,980
1993	1,401	67,722	1,239.0	3,780.0	48.3	2,698,073	18,295
1994	1,386	65,438	1,320.0	4,110.0	47.2	2,965,368	20,172
1995	1,345	65,151	1,378.0	4,492.0	48.4	3,339,777	21,151
1996	1,479 e	73,530 e	1,524.0 e	4,750.0 e	49.7 e	3,211,629 e	20,726 e
1997	1,613	81,908	1,671.0	5,008.0	50.8	3,104,774	20,401
1998	1,506 p	75,715 p	1,630.0 p	5,082.0 p	50.3 p	3,374,502 p	21,528 p
1999	1,526 p	77,245 p	1,697.0 p	5,299.0 p	50.6 p	3,472,477 p	21,969 p
2000	1,546 p	78,775 p	1,764.0 p	5,515.0 p	51.0 p	3,567,270 p	22,393 p
2001	1,565 p	80,306 p	1,831.0 p	5,732.0 p	51.3 p	3,662,620 p	22,800 p

Sources: *Economic Census of the United States*, 1982, 1987, 1992, 1997. Establishment counts, employment, and payroll are from *County Business Patterns* for non-Census years. In non-Census years, industries in the Manufacturing range under SIC coding include data from the *Annual Survey of Manufactures* (*ASM*); those in the old Services range include data from the *Services Annual Survey* (*SAS*). Values followed by a 'p' are projections by the editors. Extrapolations are marked by 'e'. Data are the most recent available at this level of detail.

INDICES OF CHANGE

Year	Establishments (number)	Employment (number)	Payroll ($ million)	Revenues ($ million)	Employees per Establishment (number)	Revenues per Establishment ($)	Payroll per Employee ($)
1982	82.8	63.0	39.9	37.8	76.1	45.7	63.4
1987	85.5	72.0	55.8	54.1	84.2	63.3	77.6
1992	89.0	77.1	71.8	73.0	86.7	82.1	93.0
1993	86.9	82.7	74.1	75.5	95.2	86.9	89.7
1994	85.9	79.9	79.0	82.1	93.0	95.5	98.9
1995	83.4	79.5	82.5	89.7	95.4	107.6	103.7
1996	91.7 e	89.8 e	91.2 e	94.8 e	97.9 e	103.4 e	101.6 e
1997	100.0	100.0	100.0	100.0	100.0	100.0	100.0
1998	93.4 p	92.4 p	97.5 p	101.5 p	99.0 p	108.7 p	105.5 p
1999	94.6 p	94.3 p	101.6 p	105.8 p	99.7 p	111.8 p	107.7 p
2000	95.8 p	96.2 p	105.6 p	110.1 p	100.3 p	114.9 p	109.8 p
2001	97.0 p	98.0 p	109.6 p	114.5 p	101.1 p	118.0 p	111.8 p

Sources: Same as General Statistics. The values shown reflect change from the base year, 1997. Values above 100 mean greater than 1997, values below 100 mean less than 1997, and a value of 100 in the 1982-96 or 1998-2001 period means same as 1997. Values followed by a 'p' are projections by the editors; 'e' stands for extrapolation. Data are the most recent available at this level of detail.

SELECTED RATIOS

For 1997	Avg. of Information	Analyzed Industry	Index	For 1997	Avg. of Information	Analyzed Industry	Index
Employees per establishment	6	51	810	Payroll per establishment	126,069	1,035,958	822
Revenue per establishment	511,622	3,104,774	607	Payroll as % of revenue	25	33	135
Revenue per employee	81,659	61,142	75	Payroll per employee	20,122	20,401	101

Sources: Same as General Statistics. The 'Average' column represents the average for the industry sector, in 1997, where the currently shown industry is classified. The Index shows the relationship between the Average and the Analyzed Industry. For example, 100 means that they are equal; 500 that the Analyzed Industry is five times the average; 50 means that the Analyzed Industry is half the national average. The abbreviation 'na' is used to show that data are 'not available'.

*Equivalent to SIC 7218.

LEADING COMPANIES   Number shown: **19**   Total sales ($ mil): **4,954**   Total employment (000): **83.4**

Company Name	Address				CEO Name	Phone	Co. Type	Sales ($ mil)	Empl. (000)
Cintas Corp.	PO Box 625737	Cincinnati	OH	45262	Scott Farmer	513-459-1200	P	1,752	22.0
ServiceMaster Management	2300 Warrenville Rd	Downers Grove	IL	60515		630-271-1300	S	724*	14.0
Aratex Services Inc.	115 N 1st St	Burbank	CA	91510	Dill Leonard	818-973-3700	S	715*	13.0
G and K Services Inc.	5995 Opus Pkwy	Minnetonka	MN	55343	Richard M Fink	612-912-5500	P	520	7.7
Ameripride Services Inc.	901 Marquette Ave	Minneapolis	MN	55402	Lawrence G Steiner	612-371-4200	R	316*	6.0
Healthcare Services Group Inc.	2643 Huntingdon	Huntngdn Val	PA	19006	Thomas A Cook	215-938-1661	P	205	10.8
Cintas Corp	333 Swift Ave	S. San Francisco	CA	94080		650-589-4300	D	167	0.0
Prudential Overall Supply Inc.	P O Box 11210	Santa Ana	CA	92711	Donald Lahn	714-250-4855	R	120	2.0
Coyne Intern. Enterprises Corp.	140 Cortland Ave	Syracuse	NY	13221	Thomas Coyne	315-475-1626	R	112*	1.8
Omni Services Inc.	14115 Lovers Ln	Culpeper	VA	22701	Steven Lane	540-825-6800	R	100*	2.3
Textilease Corp.	10733 Tucker St	Beltsville	MD	20705	D Thomas	301-937-4555	R	62	1.0
Admiral Linen & Uniform Service	2030 Kipling	Houston	TX	77098	Les Craft	713-529-2608	S	33*	0.6
Interstate Nuclear Services Inc.	P O Box 51957	Springfield	MA	01151		413-543-6911	S	31*	0.5
Overall Laundry Services Inc.	PO Box 9040	Everett	WA	98206	Travis H Keeler	206-682-6666	R	24*	0.4
National Linen & Uniform Service	1420 Peachtree	Atlanta	GA	30309	Hugh Sawyer	404-853-6000	S	21*	0.4
Industrial Towel and Uniform Inc.	2700 S 160th St	New Berlin	WI	53151	JM Leef	414-782-1950	R	20*	0.3
Rental Uniform Service	P O Box 1207	Culpeper	VA	22701		540-825-2303	S	16*	0.3
UFI Inc.	129-01 Jamaica Ave	Richmond Hill	NY	11418	Alfred J Mernone	718-846-2900	R	13*	0.2
Van Dyne-Crotty Inc.	3233 Newmark Ave	Miamisburg	OH	45342	LW Crotty	937-236-1500	R	3*	<0.1

Source: *Ward's Business Directory of U.S. Private and Public Companies*, Volumes 1 and 2, 2000. The company type code used is as follows: P - Public, R - Private, S - Subsidiary, D - Division, J - Joint Venture, A - Affiliate, G - Group, N - Company type not reported. Sales are in millions of dollars, employees are in thousands. An asterisk (*) indicates an estimated sales volume. The symbol < stands for 'less than'. Company names and addresses are truncated, in some cases, to fit into the available space.

LOCATION BY STATE AND REGIONAL CONCENTRATION

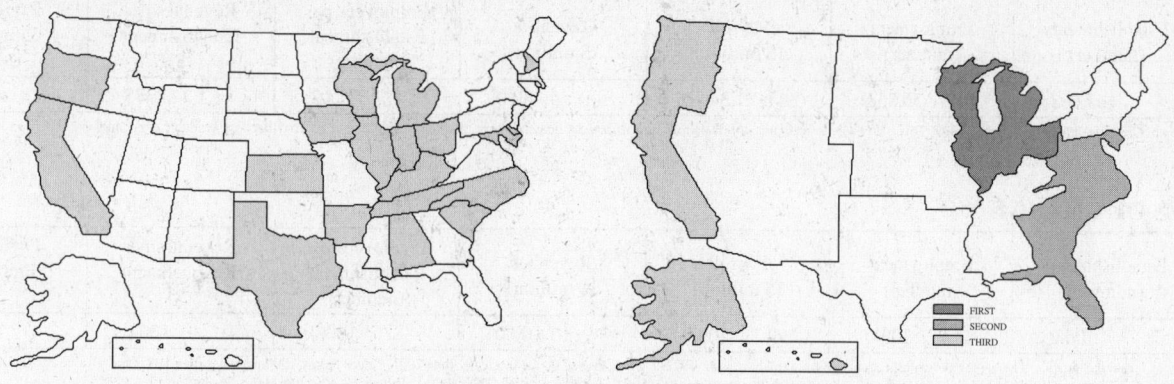

INDUSTRY DATA BY STATE

State	Establishments Total (number)	Establishments % of U.S.	Employment Total (number)	Employment % of U.S.	Employment Per Estab.	Payroll Total ($ mil.)	Payroll Per Empl. ($)	Revenues Total ($ mil.)	Revenues % of U.S.	Revenues Per Estab. ($)
California	194	12.0	9,394	11.5	48	208.4	22,180	630.3	12.6	3,248,747
Texas	121	7.5	6,971	8.5	58	123.2	17,671	385.9	7.7	3,189,223
Ohio	84	5.2	4,866	5.9	58	99.4	20,430	302.2	6.0	3,597,952
Illinois	70	4.3	4,455	5.4	64	92.5	20,759	289.1	5.8	4,130,200
Michigan	80	5.0	3,591	4.4	45	73.2	20,379	217.2	4.3	2,715,512
Pennsylvania	60	3.7	3,121	3.8	52	68.2	21,858	216.4	4.3	3,606,267
Florida	67	4.2	3,826	4.7	57	72.4	18,924	214.1	4.3	3,196,000
North Carolina	52	3.2	3,219	3.9	62	59.9	18,622	188.2	3.8	3,618,365
New York	80	5.0	2,898	3.5	36	62.5	21,580	187.6	3.7	2,344,900
Indiana	50	3.1	2,978	3.6	60	56.0	18,804	169.7	3.4	3,393,440
Wisconsin	32	2.0	1,968	2.4	62	45.9	23,318	139.4	2.8	4,356,313
Tennessee	43	2.7	2,602	3.2	61	50.0	19,202	134.1	2.7	3,119,558
Georgia	55	3.4	2,135	2.6	39	44.4	20,799	131.3	2.6	2,388,000
Virginia	40	2.5	2,059	2.5	51	41.3	20,054	120.0	2.4	2,999,225
New Jersey	35	2.2	1,800	2.2	51	39.3	21,814	108.6	2.2	3,102,543
Alabama	37	2.3	1,956	2.4	53	36.2	18,483	106.2	2.1	2,870,595
Maryland	24	1.5	1,403	1.7	58	31.8	22,681	106.2	2.1	4,422,958
Kentucky	34	2.1	1,946	2.4	57	33.1	17,029	99.8	2.0	2,936,471
Massachusetts	34	2.1	1,406	1.7	41	33.7	23,964	99.8	2.0	2,934,824
Missouri	35	2.2	1,471	1.8	42	33.7	22,901	94.5	1.9	2,701,286
Minnesota	19	1.2	1,156	1.4	61	32.3	27,919	80.8	1.6	4,253,842
Arizona	25	1.5	1,073	1.3	43	21.4	19,907	73.9	1.5	2,955,200
Louisiana	24	1.5	1,101	1.3	46	23.7	21,509	73.6	1.5	3,068,708
South Carolina	28	1.7	1,255	1.5	45	22.8	18,133	73.6	1.5	2,628,893
Iowa	22	1.4	1,349	1.6	61	25.9	19,188	70.6	1.4	3,210,864
Oregon	18	1.1	1,228	1.5	68	25.3	20,591	70.4	1.4	3,913,222
Washington	27	1.7	1,101	1.3	41	26.3	23,877	69.5	1.4	2,575,185
Oklahoma	22	1.4	1,149	1.4	52	19.7	17,128	60.6	1.2	2,753,955
Arkansas	26	1.6	1,291	1.6	50	19.8	15,373	57.1	1.1	2,194,500
Kansas	15	0.9	1,066	1.3	71	18.9	17,691	54.5	1.1	3,632,000
New Hampshire	11	0.7	669	0.8	61	18.0	26,943	53.4	1.1	4,851,000
Connecticut	15	0.9	766	0.9	51	17.4	22,685	49.8	1.0	3,322,733
Colorado	19	1.2	828	1.0	44	16.9	20,415	47.2	0.9	2,482,105
West Virginia	9	0.6	408	0.5	45	8.1	19,775	31.3	0.6	3,482,889
New Mexico	12	0.7	421	0.5	35	8.7	20,755	28.1	0.6	2,342,750
Mississippi	10	0.6	444	0.5	44	7.8	17,577	23.3	0.5	2,332,800
Maine	7	0.4	270	0.3	39	4.9	18,089	16.3	0.3	2,333,429
Nebraska	12	0.7	298	0.4	25	5.8	19,507	16.1	0.3	1,337,583
Delaware	3	0.2	198	0.2	66	6.0	30,364	15.1	0.3	5,047,667
Montana	7	0.4	196	0.2	28	3.4	17,250	10.0	0.2	1,429,857
Rhode Island	5	0.3	76	0.1	15	1.8	24,105	8.3	0.2	1,655,400
Idaho	6	0.4	163	0.2	27	2.6	15,798	7.8	0.2	1,299,667
South Dakota	5	0.3	128	0.2	26	2.5	19,445	6.0	0.1	1,196,000
Hawaii	4	0.2	30	0.0	8	0.2	6,867	1.0	0.0	244,250
Nevada	11	0.7	375*	-	-	(D)	-	(D)	-	-
Utah	11	0.7	750*	-	-	(D)	-	(D)	-	-
North Dakota	5	0.3	175*	-	-	(D)	-	(D)	-	-
Wyoming	4	0.2	60*	-	-	(D)	-	(D)	-	-
Vermont	2	0.1	60*	-	-	(D)	-	(D)	-	-
Alaska	1	0.1	10*	-	-	(D)	-	(D)	-	-
D.C.	1	0.1	10*	-	-	(D)	-	(D)	-	-

Source: 1997 *Economic Census*. The states are in descending order of revenues or establishments (if revenue data are missing for the majority). The symbol (D) appears when data are withheld to prevent disclosure of competitive information. States marked with (D) are sorted by number of establishments. A dash (-) indicates that the data element cannot be calculated. * indicates the midpoint of a range; 175, for example is the range 100-249. Shaded *states* on the state map indicate those states which have proportionately greater representation in the industry than would be indicated by the state's population; the ratio is based on total revenues or number of establishments. Shaded *regions* indicate where the industry is regionally most concentrated.

NAICS 812921 - PHOTOFINISHING LABORATORIES (EXCEPT ONE-HOUR)

GENERAL STATISTICS

Year	Establishments (number)	Employment (number)	Payroll ($ million)	Revenues ($ million)	Employees per Establishment (number)	Revenues per Establishment ($)	Payroll per Employee ($)
1997	3,662	56,868	1,346.0	4,480.0	15.5	1,223,375	23,669

Source: Economic Census of the United States, 1997. This is a newly defined industry. Data for prior years were unavailable at the time of publication but may become available over time.

INDICES OF CHANGE

Year	Establishments (number)	Employment (number)	Payroll ($ million)	Revenues ($ million)	Employees per Establishment (number)	Revenues per Establishment ($)	Payroll per Employee ($)
1997	100.0	100.0	100.0	100.0	100.0	100.0	100.0

Sources: Same as General Statistics. The values shown reflect change from the base year, 1997. Values above 100 mean greater than 1997, values below 100 mean less than 1997, and a value of 100 in the 1982-96 or 1998-2001 period means same as 1997. Values followed by a 'p' are projections by the editors; 'e' stands for extrapolation. Data are the most recent available at this level of detail.

SIC INDUSTRIES RELATED TO NAICS 812921

Each new NAICS code represents an industry that used to be part of an SIC or a part of several SIC industries. Data in this table are shown to provide transitional information for these cases. All available data for the precursor SIC(s) are shown. Even if only a part of an SIC is included in the NAICS, *all* data for the SIC are reproduced. If the SIC industry is not marked as being a part (pt) of the NAICS, the entire industry is embedded in the NAICS data. The SIC composition of the new industry provides some hints of the relative importance of its "ancestors." Data marked with a 'p' are projected. Projections begin with 1982 data. Data earlier than 1990 are not shown but are reflected in the projections.

SIC	Industry	1990	1991	1992	1993	1994	1995	1996	1997
7384	**Photofinishing Laboratories (pt)**								
	Establishments (number)	6,190	6,438	7,768	7,653	7,477	7,244	8,117p	8,367p
	Employment (thousands)	76.0	70.3	69.3	70.0	68.8	72.0	70.5p	70.0p
	Revenues ($ million)	5,604.0	5,675.0	5,678.0	6,357.0	6,555.0	6,796.0	7,243.0	7,299.7p

Source: Economic Census of the United States, 1992, annual surveys of economic sectors conducted by the Bureau of the Census, and estimates or projections based on the 1982-1992 period; not all data are shown. 'e' marks estimates made by the editors; 'p' indicates projections based on time series. A dash (-) indicates that data for this SIC or year were not available. The abbreviation (pt) next to the industry name indicates that only a part of the industry is present within the NAICS data. If no (pt) is shown, the entire industry is contained within the NAICS data.

SELECTED RATIOS

For 1997	Avg. of Information	Analyzed Industry	Index	For 1997	Avg. of Information	Analyzed Industry	Index
Employees per establishment	6	16	248	Payroll per establishment	126,069	367,559	292
Revenue per establishment	511,622	1,223,375	239	Payroll as % of revenue	25	30	122
Revenue per employee	81,659	78,779	96	Payroll per employee	20,122	23,669	118

Sources: Same as General Statistics. The 'Average' column represents the average for the industry sector, in 1997, where the currently shown industry is classified. The Index shows the relationship between the Average and the Analyzed Industry. For example, 100 means that they are equal; 500 that the Analyzed Industry is five times the average; 50 means that the Analyzed Industry is half the national average. The abbreviation 'na' is used to show that data are 'not available'.

LEADING COMPANIES   Number shown: **1**   Total sales ($ mil): **90**   Total employment (000): **0.7**

Company Name	Address				CEO Name	Phone	Co. Type	Sales ($ mil)	Empl. (000)
Seattle FilmWorks Inc.	1260 16th Ave W	Seattle	WA	98119	Gary Christophersen	206-281-1390	P	90	0.7

Source: *Ward's Business Directory of U.S. Private and Public Companies*, Volumes 1 and 2, 2000. The company type code used is as follows: P - Public, R - Private, S - Subsidiary, D - Division, J - Joint Venture, A - Affiliate, G - Group, N - Company type not reported. Sales are in millions of dollars, employees are in thousands. An asterisk (*) indicates an estimated sales volume. The symbol < stands for 'less than'. Company names and addresses are truncated, in some cases, to fit into the available space.

LOCATION BY STATE AND REGIONAL CONCENTRATION

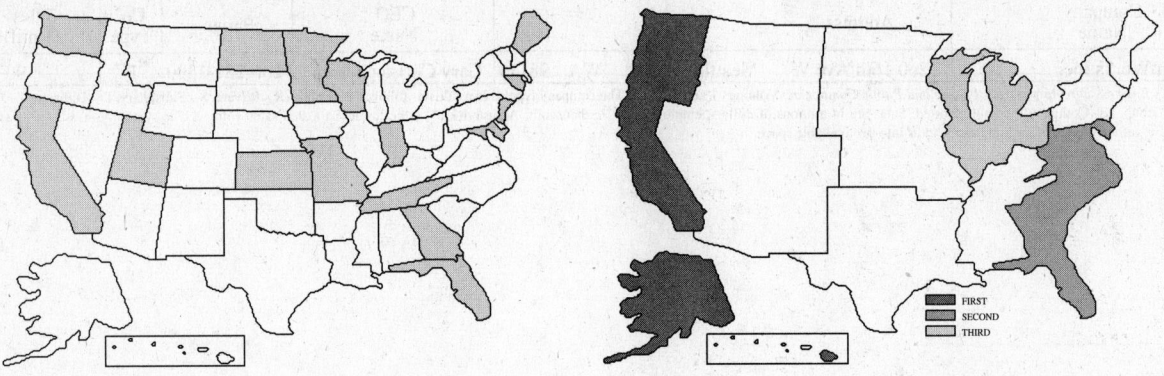

FIRST
SECOND
THIRD

INDUSTRY DATA BY STATE

State	Establishments Total (number)	% of U.S.	Employment Total (number)	% of U.S.	Per Estab.	Payroll Total ($ mil.)	Per Empl. ($)	Revenues Total ($ mil.)	% of U.S.	Per Estab. ($)
California	465	12.7	6,981	12.3	15	179.0	25,646	637.3	14.2	1,370,576
Texas	328	9.0	3,339	5.9	10	77.3	23,159	279.7	6.2	852,591
New York	337	9.2	3,163	5.6	9	83.9	26,519	263.0	5.9	780,285
Florida	453	12.4	3,328	5.9	7	62.2	18,703	262.5	5.9	579,534
Minnesota	88	2.4	5,482	9.6	62	135.5	24,721	227.4	5.1	2,584,523
Washington	56	1.5	1,575	2.8	28	43.0	27,291	198.5	4.4	3,543,893
Indiana	53	1.4	1,780	3.1	34	42.1	23,676	182.9	4.1	3,450,830
Maryland	52	1.4	1,934	3.4	37	47.7	24,647	166.7	3.7	3,205,346
Ohio	89	2.4	2,137	3.8	24	47.6	22,263	149.8	3.3	1,683,326
New Jersey	123	3.4	2,064	3.6	17	53.5	25,944	145.2	3.2	1,180,504
Georgia	157	4.3	1,571	2.8	10	38.3	24,382	133.6	3.0	850,643
Connecticut	53	1.4	1,049	1.8	20	26.2	25,003	129.1	2.9	2,435,340
Illinois	119	3.2	1,941	3.4	16	47.2	24,303	126.0	2.8	1,058,924
Pennsylvania	107	2.9	1,460	2.6	14	34.9	23,896	125.1	2.8	1,169,439
Missouri	52	1.4	1,857	3.3	36	42.0	22,603	124.7	2.8	2,398,308
Tennessee	64	1.7	1,609	2.8	25	38.6	24,012	109.2	2.4	1,706,062
Michigan	63	1.7	1,208	2.1	19	32.7	27,072	107.3	2.4	1,703,063
Virginia	63	1.7	1,006	1.8	16	18.6	18,487	104.3	2.3	1,656,190
North Carolina	156	4.3	1,226	2.2	8	27.0	22,042	100.6	2.2	644,744
Wisconsin	54	1.5	1,389	2.4	26	29.5	21,235	96.6	2.2	1,789,796
Massachusetts	94	2.6	1,194	2.1	13	31.2	26,092	92.8	2.1	987,543
Arizona	46	1.3	800	1.4	17	17.1	21,371	59.6	1.3	1,296,087
Colorado	50	1.4	711	1.3	14	17.5	24,633	59.6	1.3	1,192,400
Kansas	22	0.6	632	1.1	29	15.9	25,191	53.7	1.2	2,439,636
Iowa	32	0.9	489	0.9	15	12.8	26,164	50.0	1.1	1,562,406
Oklahoma	35	1.0	1,001	1.8	29	16.5	16,519	48.2	1.1	1,377,171
Oregon	36	1.0	667	1.2	19	14.2	21,228	45.0	1.0	1,250,222
Utah	26	0.7	494	0.9	19	10.2	20,672	38.9	0.9	1,497,462
Maine	14	0.4	544	1.0	39	16.3	29,915	31.1	0.7	2,224,143
Alabama	34	0.9	434	0.8	13	7.0	16,129	26.7	0.6	784,912
Nebraska	17	0.5	300	0.5	18	6.9	22,933	25.2	0.6	1,480,706
Louisiana	49	1.3	374	0.7	8	5.4	14,543	21.1	0.5	430,204
Mississippi	20	0.5	241	0.4	12	4.9	20,266	18.9	0.4	943,300
Hawaii	20	0.5	196	0.3	10	4.6	23,418	17.6	0.4	879,150
South Carolina	53	1.4	218	0.4	4	3.8	17,569	15.3	0.3	289,528
North Dakota	10	0.3	199	0.3	20	4.2	21,176	13.7	0.3	1,366,300
New Mexico	13	0.4	139	0.2	11	3.0	21,338	11.8	0.3	905,077
Rhode Island	9	0.2	142	0.2	16	3.5	24,824	11.4	0.3	1,271,889
Montana	19	0.5	131	0.2	7	2.6	19,802	10.5	0.2	551,263
South Dakota	12	0.3	197	0.3	16	3.1	15,797	9.4	0.2	786,000
New Hampshire	17	0.5	82	0.1	5	2.4	29,049	7.9	0.2	467,235
Nevada	12	0.3	88	0.2	7	2.0	22,693	7.5	0.2	623,333
Vermont	8	0.2	107	0.2	13	2.0	18,850	6.2	0.1	780,625
Kentucky	16	0.4	99	0.2	6	1.5	15,465	6.2	0.1	389,375
Alaska	8	0.2	66	0.1	8	1.7	25,303	5.9	0.1	732,875
D.C.	13	0.4	60*	-	-	(D)	-	(D)	-	-
West Virginia	13	0.4	750*	-	-	(D)	-	(D)	-	-
Wyoming	9	0.2	60*	-	-	(D)	-	(D)	-	-
Arkansas	8	0.2	375*	-	-	(D)	-	(D)	-	-
Idaho	8	0.2	60*	-	-	(D)	-	(D)	-	-
Delaware	7	0.2	60*	-	-	(D)	-	(D)	-	-

Source: 1997 *Economic Census*. The states are in descending order of revenues or establishments (if revenue data are missing for the majority). The symbol (D) appears when data are withheld to prevent disclosure of competitive information. States marked with (D) are sorted by number of establishments. A dash (-) indicates that the data element cannot be calculated. * indicates the midpoint of a range; 175, for example is the range 100-249. Shaded *states* on the state map indicate those states which have proportionately greater representation in the industry than would be indicated by the state's population; the ratio is based on total revenues or number of establishments. Shaded *regions* indicate where the industry is regionally most concentrated.

NAICS 812922 - ONE-HOUR PHOTOFINISHING

GENERAL STATISTICS

Year	Establishments (number)	Employment (number)	Payroll ($ million)	Revenues ($ million)	Employees per Establishment (number)	Revenues per Establishment ($)	Payroll per Employee ($)
1997	3,393	15,123	237.0	1,040.0	4.5	306,513	15,671

Source: *Economic Census of the United States*, 1997. This is a newly defined industry. Data for prior years were unavailable at the time of publication but may become available over time.

INDICES OF CHANGE

Year	Establishments (number)	Employment (number)	Payroll ($ million)	Revenues ($ million)	Employees per Establishment (number)	Revenues per Establishment ($)	Payroll per Employee ($)
1997	100.0	100.0	100.0	100.0	100.0	100.0	100.0

Sources: Same as General Statistics. The values shown reflect change from the base year, 1997. Values above 100 mean greater than 1997, values below 100 mean less than 1997, and a value of 100 in the 1982-96 or 1998-2001 period means same as 1997. Values followed by a 'p' are projections by the editors; 'e' stands for extrapolation. Data are the most recent available at this level of detail.

SIC INDUSTRIES RELATED TO NAICS 812922

Each new NAICS code represents an industry that used to be part of an SIC or a part of several SIC industries. Data in this table are shown to provide transitional information for these cases. All available data for the precursor SIC(s) are shown. Even if only a part of an SIC is included in the NAICS, *all* data for the SIC are reproduced. If the SIC industry is not marked as being a part (pt) of the NAICS, the entire industry is embedded in the NAICS data. The SIC composition of the new industry provides some hints of the relative importance of its "ancestors." Data marked with a 'p' are projected. Projections begin with 1982 data. Data earlier than 1990 are not shown but are reflected in the projections.

SIC	Industry	1990	1991	1992	1993	1994	1995	1996	1997
7384	**Photofinishing Laboratories (pt)**								
	Establishments (number)	6,190	6,438	7,768	7,653	7,477	7,244	8,117*p*	8,367*p*
	Employment (thousands)	76.0	70.3	69.3	70.0	68.8	72.0	70.5*p*	70.0*p*
	Revenues ($ million)	5,604.0	5,675.0	5,678.0	6,357.0	6,555.0	6,796.0	7,243.0	7,299.7*p*

Source: *Economic Census of the United States*, 1992, annual surveys of economic sectors conducted by the Bureau of the Census, and estimates or projections based on the 1982-1992 period; not all data are shown. 'e' marks estimates made by the editors; 'p' indicates projections based on time series. A dash (-) indicates that data for this SIC or year were not available. The abbreviation (pt) next to the industry name indicates that only a part of the industry is present within the NAICS data. If no (pt) is shown, the entire industry is contained within the NAICS data.

SELECTED RATIOS

For 1997	Avg. of Information	Analyzed Industry	Index	For 1997	Avg. of Information	Analyzed Industry	Index
Employees per establishment	6	4	71	Payroll per establishment	126,069	69,850	55
Revenue per establishment	511,622	306,513	60	Payroll as % of revenue	25	23	92
Revenue per employee	81,659	68,769	84	Payroll per employee	20,122	15,671	78

Sources: Same as General Statistics. The 'Average' column represents the average for the industry sector, in 1997, where the currently shown industry is classified. The Index shows the relationship between the Average and the Analyzed Industry. For example, 100 means that they are equal; 500 that the Analyzed Industry is five times the average; 50 means that the Analyzed Industry is half the national average. The abbreviation 'na' is used to show that data are 'not available'.

LEADING COMPANIES

No company data available for this industry.

LOCATION BY STATE AND REGIONAL CONCENTRATION

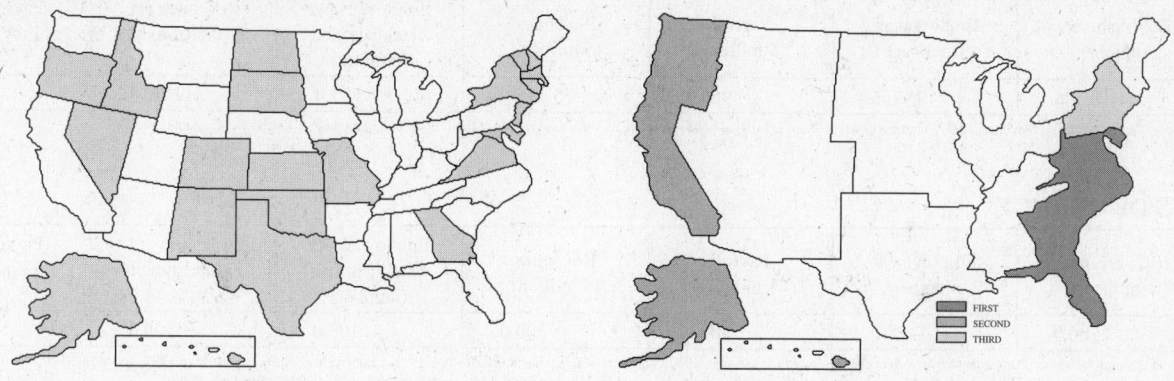

INDUSTRY DATA BY STATE

State	Establishments Total (number)	% of U.S.	Employment Total (number)	% of U.S.	Per Estab.	Payroll Total ($ mil.)	Per Empl. ($)	Revenues Total ($ mil.)	% of U.S.	Per Estab. ($)
California	479	14.1	1,612	10.7	3	25.1	15,589	121.4	11.7	253,547
Texas	201	5.9	841	5.6	4	16.9	20,121	81.7	7.9	406,388
New York	318	9.4	1,334	8.8	4	20.3	15,204	79.8	7.7	250,909
Florida	180	5.3	718	4.7	4	11.6	16,167	50.9	4.9	282,806
Missouri	76	2.2	389	2.6	5	8.1	20,902	41.0	3.9	539,461
Georgia	107	3.2	467	3.1	4	8.0	17,056	39.0	3.8	364,654
New Jersey	139	4.1	575	3.8	4	9.2	15,958	37.9	3.6	272,698
Ohio	95	2.8	493	3.3	5	8.2	16,604	37.3	3.6	392,179
Massachusetts	118	3.5	503	3.3	4	8.4	16,628	35.3	3.4	299,449
Maryland	84	2.5	454	3.0	5	7.3	16,075	34.7	3.3	413,500
Illinois	108	3.2	502	3.3	5	7.8	15,625	34.2	3.3	316,343
Virginia	95	2.8	544	3.6	6	8.4	15,485	34.0	3.3	358,379
Pennsylvania	114	3.4	576	3.8	5	7.7	13,424	32.3	3.1	283,281
Michigan	78	2.3	414	2.7	5	7.4	17,792	30.6	2.9	392,423
Colorado	63	1.9	284	1.9	5	4.7	16,514	23.1	2.2	366,698
North Carolina	84	2.5	315	2.1	4	5.2	16,429	22.8	2.2	271,321
Connecticut	69	2.0	299	2.0	4	5.2	17,388	21.4	2.1	310,464
Washington	91	2.7	372	2.5	4	5.1	13,728	20.7	2.0	227,692
Tennessee	60	1.8	236	1.6	4	4.3	18,081	19.8	1.9	329,883
Indiana	58	1.7	240	1.6	4	4.3	18,021	19.0	1.8	327,845
Kansas	37	1.1	195	1.3	5	3.1	16,118	14.8	1.4	400,351
Minnesota	61	1.8	338	2.2	6	4.1	12,198	14.8	1.4	241,951
Oregon	56	1.7	279	1.8	5	3.8	13,771	13.8	1.3	246,339
Oklahoma	30	0.9	232	1.5	8	3.3	14,246	13.7	1.3	457,333
Hawaii	41	1.2	189	1.2	5	2.7	14,164	12.9	1.2	314,073
Wisconsin	33	1.0	247	1.6	7	3.4	13,870	12.0	1.2	362,667
Arizona	43	1.3	223	1.5	5	2.7	12,224	11.3	1.1	262,442
Kentucky	33	1.0	222	1.5	7	2.8	12,662	11.3	1.1	342,848
Louisiana	39	1.1	134	0.9	3	2.0	15,075	9.4	0.9	240,359
Alabama	32	0.9	150	1.0	5	2.1	14,027	9.4	0.9	292,500
New Mexico	22	0.6	95	0.6	4	1.7	18,105	8.5	0.8	387,318
South Carolina	27	0.8	150	1.0	6	2.3	15,587	8.5	0.8	315,222
Nevada	12	0.4	63	0.4	5	1.1	18,032	7.1	0.7	595,750
New Hampshire	29	0.9	120	0.8	4	1.7	14,025	7.1	0.7	245,621
Idaho	24	0.7	136	0.9	6	1.8	13,191	6.4	0.6	266,792
Vermont	23	0.7	76	0.5	3	1.1	14,566	4.7	0.5	203,478
Utah	18	0.5	85	0.6	5	1.0	11,847	4.7	0.5	261,333
Mississippi	15	0.4	63	0.4	4	1.0	16,127	4.4	0.4	291,133
Alaska	23	0.7	72	0.5	3	1.0	13,667	4.4	0.4	192,609
Nebraska	19	0.6	97	0.6	5	1.2	11,948	4.1	0.4	216,158
Maine	13	0.4	60	0.4	5	1.1	18,150	4.0	0.4	305,308
Iowa	19	0.6	94	0.6	5	1.0	10,809	3.4	0.3	180,579
North Dakota	12	0.4	68	0.4	6	0.7	10,647	3.0	0.3	252,167
South Dakota	11	0.3	66	0.4	6	0.6	8,879	2.7	0.3	248,727
Rhode Island	12	0.4	40	0.3	3	0.7	16,825	2.6	0.2	213,667
Delaware	5	0.1	20	0.1	4	0.4	19,150	1.3	0.1	266,400
Arkansas	29	0.9	175*	-	-	(D)	-	(D)	-	-
Montana	22	0.6	60*	-	-	(D)	-	(D)	-	-
Wyoming	13	0.4	60*	-	-	(D)	-	(D)	-	-
D.C.	12	0.4	60*	-	-	(D)	-	(D)	-	-
West Virginia	11	0.3	175*	-	-	(D)	-	(D)	-	-

Source: 1997 *Economic Census*. The states are in descending order of revenues or establishments (if revenue data are missing for the majority). The symbol (D) appears when data are withheld to prevent disclosure of competitive information. States marked with (D) are sorted by number of establishments. A dash (-) indicates that the data element cannot be calculated. * indicates the midpoint of a range; 175, for example is the range 100-249. Shaded *states* on the state map indicate those states which have proportionately greater representation in the industry than would be indicated by the state's population; the ratio is based on total revenues or number of establishments. Shaded *regions* indicate where the industry is regionally most concentrated.

NAICS 812930 - PARKING LOTS AND GARAGES

GENERAL STATISTICS

Year	Establishments (number)	Employment (number)	Payroll ($ million)	Revenues ($ million)	Employees per Establishment (number)	Revenues per Establishment ($)	Payroll per Employee ($)
1997	10,358	76,166	968.0	5,175.0	7.4	499,614	12,709

Source: Economic Census of the United States, 1997. This is a newly defined industry. Data for prior years were unavailable at the time of publication but may become available over time.

INDICES OF CHANGE

Year	Establishments (number)	Employment (number)	Payroll ($ million)	Revenues ($ million)	Employees per Establishment (number)	Revenues per Establishment ($)	Payroll per Employee ($)
1997	100.0	100.0	100.0	100.0	100.0	100.0	100.0

Sources: Same as General Statistics. The values shown reflect change from the base year, 1997. Values above 100 mean greater than 1997, values below 100 mean less than 1997, and a value of 100 in the 1982-96 or 1998-2001 period means same as 1997. Values followed by a 'p' are projections by the editors; 'e' stands for extrapolation. Data are the most recent available at this level of detail.

SIC INDUSTRIES RELATED TO NAICS 812930

Each new NAICS code represents an industry that used to be part of an SIC or a part of several SIC industries. Data in this table are shown to provide transitional information for these cases. All available data for the precursor SIC(s) are shown. Even if only a part of an SIC is included in the NAICS, *all* data for the SIC are reproduced. If the SIC industry is not marked as being a part (pt) of the NAICS, the entire industry is embedded in the NAICS data. The SIC composition of the new industry provides some hints of the relative importance of its "ancestors." Data marked with a 'p' are projected. Projections begin with 1982 data. Data earlier than 1990 are not shown but are reflected in the projections.

SIC	Industry	1990	1991	1992	1993	1994	1995	1996	1997
7299	**Miscellaneous Personal Services, nec (pt)**								
	Establishments (number)	15,086	15,775	16,017	16,862	17,296	17,740	18,650p	19,294p
	Employment (thousands)	116.4	114.7	105.6	99.6	97.2	99.4	106.1p	106.9p
	Revenues ($ million)	-	-	3,885.0	-	-	-	-	-
7521	**Automobile Parking**								
	Establishments (number)	8,868	9,095	10,171	9,153	8,879	8,902	9,262p	9,291p
	Employment (thousands)	52.8	51.5	51.6	56.2	58.5	62.5	62.6p	64.6p
	Revenues ($ million)	2,959.0	3,305.0	3,744.0	3,634.0	3,505.0	3,611.0	3,714.0	4,092.1p

Source: Economic Census of the United States, 1992, annual surveys of economic sectors conducted by the Bureau of the Census, and estimates or projections based on the 1982-1992 period; not all data are shown. 'e' marks estimates made by the editors; 'p' indicates projections based on time series. A dash (-) indicates that data for this SIC or year were not available. The abbreviation (pt) next to the industry name indicates that only a part of the industry is present within the NAICS data. If no (pt) is shown, the entire industry is contained within the NAICS data.

SELECTED RATIOS

For 1997	Avg. of Information	Analyzed Industry	Index	For 1997	Avg. of Information	Analyzed Industry	Index
Employees per establishment	6	7	117	Payroll per establishment	126,069	93,454	74
Revenue per establishment	511,622	499,614	98	Payroll as % of revenue	25	19	76
Revenue per employee	81,659	67,944	83	Payroll per employee	20,122	12,709	63

Sources: Same as General Statistics. The 'Average' column represents the average for the industry sector, in 1997, where the currently shown industry is classified. The Index shows the relationship between the Average and the Analyzed Industry. For example, 100 means that they are equal; 500 that the Analyzed Industry is five times the average; 50 means that the Analyzed Industry is half the national average. The abbreviation 'na' is used to show that data are 'not available'.

LEADING COMPANIES   Number shown: 13   Total sales ($ mil): 2,371   Total employment (000): 45.4

Company Name	Address				CEO Name	Phone	Co. Type	Sales ($ mil)	Empl. (000)
Central Parking Corp.	2401 21st Ave	Nashville	TN	37212	James H. Bond	615-297-4255	P	736	17.0
Standard Parking Corp.	200 E Randolph St	Chicago	IL	60601	Myron Warshauer	312-696-4000	R	450	3.8
APCOA/Standard Parking Inc.	1301 E 9th St	Cleveland	OH	44114	G Walter Stuelpe Jr	216-522-0700	R	350*	3.5
CA One Services Inc.	438 Main St	Buffalo	NY	14202	Charles E Moran Jr	716-858-5000	S	254	2.9
AMPCO System Parking	808 S Olive St	Los Angeles	CA	90014	Thomas D Barnett	213-624-6065	D	144	7.0
Central Parking System Inc.	1051 E Cary St	Richmond	VA	23219	Paul Edenbaum	804-648-2155	S	141*	6.5
Ace Parking Inc.	645 Ash St	San Diego	CA	92101	John Baumghardner	619-233-6624	R	131*	2.0
Diamond Parking Inc.	2600 Elliot Ave	Seattle	WA	98121	Jon Diamond	206-284-3100	R	72*	1.2
Colonial Parking Inc.	2145 K St N W	Washington	DC	20037	Andrew Blair	202-452-9600	S	43*	0.7
Atlantic Garage Inc.	1828 L St NW	Washington	DC	20036	J Marshall Peck	202-466-4300	R	20*	0.3
United Parking Inc.	615 Peachtree St N E	Atlanta	GA	30308	Samuel T Wadsworth	404-817-3617	R	16*	0.3
Alco Parking Corp.	S Commons	Pittsburgh	PA	15212	John Stabile	412-323-4455	R	13*	0.2
San Jose Parking Inc.	257 N 1st St	San Jose	CA	95113	Albert Schlarmann	408-297-7275	R	1*	<0.1

Source: *Ward's Business Directory of U.S. Private and Public Companies*, Volumes 1 and 2, 2000. The company type code used is as follows: P - Public, R - Private, S - Subsidiary, D - Division, J - Joint Venture, A - Affiliate, G - Group, N - Company type not reported. Sales are in millions of dollars, employees are in thousands. An asterisk (*) indicates an estimated sales volume. The symbol < stands for 'less than'. Company names and addresses are truncated, in some cases, to fit into the available space.

LOCATION BY STATE AND REGIONAL CONCENTRATION

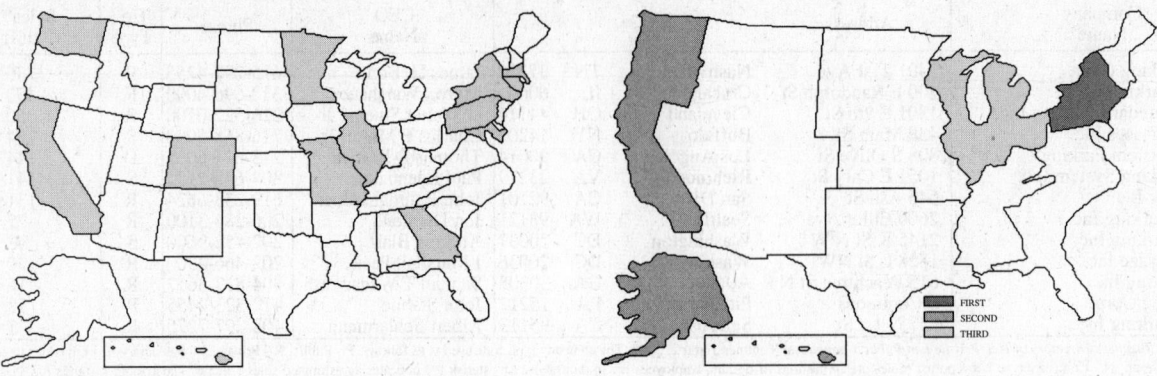

FIRST
SECOND
THIRD

INDUSTRY DATA BY STATE

State	Establishments Total (number)	% of U.S.	Employment Total (number)	% of U.S.	Per Estab.	Payroll Total ($ mil.)	Per Empl. ($)	Revenues Total ($ mil.)	% of U.S.	Per Estab. ($)
California	1,955	18.9	14,899	19.6	8	187.7	12,597	927.9	17.9	474,638
New York	1,394	13.5	12,539	16.5	9	171.3	13,660	849.3	16.4	609,230
Illinois	471	4.5	3,658	4.8	8	67.2	18,366	434.6	8.4	922,796
Pennsylvania	335	3.2	4,091	5.4	12	48.9	11,954	266.3	5.1	794,881
Texas	833	8.0	4,178	5.5	5	43.0	10,282	232.8	4.5	279,485
Ohio	495	4.8	3,130	4.1	6	35.6	11,378	214.9	4.2	434,044
Massachusetts	203	2.0	2,936	3.9	14	33.5	11,397	210.4	4.1	1,036,296
D.C.	395	3.8	2,096	2.8	5	26.6	12,705	157.4	3.0	398,466
Georgia	292	2.8	2,239	2.9	8	34.9	15,586	153.0	3.0	524,106
Maryland	219	2.1	1,737	2.3	8	21.7	12,489	150.2	2.9	685,831
Florida	230	2.2	2,447	3.2	11	26.3	10,753	139.7	2.7	607,609
Minnesota	153	1.5	1,522	2.0	10	20.3	13,361	131.4	2.5	858,954
Michigan	147	1.4	1,787	2.3	12	28.1	15,703	116.6	2.3	793,156
Washington	311	3.0	1,500	2.0	5	18.6	12,372	114.0	2.2	366,453
Missouri	212	2.0	1,175	1.5	6	13.3	11,353	109.3	2.1	515,623
Virginia	323	3.1	1,222	1.6	4	13.3	10,902	90.0	1.7	278,508
New Jersey	178	1.7	2,596	3.4	15	25.0	9,642	86.5	1.7	485,708
Colorado	205	2.0	1,010	1.3	5	12.6	12,487	79.3	1.5	386,907
Tennessee	274	2.6	1,248	1.6	5	13.4	10,702	74.9	1.4	273,445
Connecticut	156	1.5	1,395	1.8	9	18.4	13,205	72.2	1.4	462,808
Louisiana	195	1.9	1,036	1.4	5	11.3	10,918	70.2	1.4	359,969
Hawaii	153	1.5	786	1.0	5	13.0	16,487	68.4	1.3	447,359
Oregon	138	1.3	585	0.8	4	8.5	14,598	50.8	1.0	368,210
Kentucky	110	1.1	603	0.8	5	8.3	13,730	45.3	0.9	411,955
Wisconsin	77	0.7	658	0.9	9	11.3	17,112	39.5	0.8	512,831
North Carolina	127	1.2	756	1.0	6	8.6	11,396	37.1	0.7	291,969
Indiana	102	1.0	546	0.7	5	5.4	9,819	35.2	0.7	345,059
Arizona	99	1.0	743	1.0	8	8.4	11,273	34.2	0.7	345,303
Oklahoma	84	0.8	402	0.5	5	4.2	10,505	30.3	0.6	361,119
Utah	55	0.5	300	0.4	5	3.3	11,067	19.2	0.4	348,727
Nebraska	42	0.4	210	0.3	5	1.9	8,990	16.1	0.3	383,238
Mississippi	20	0.2	166	0.2	8	2.7	16,337	15.8	0.3	787,850
Alabama	61	0.6	462	0.6	8	5.2	11,177	15.6	0.3	256,426
Iowa	34	0.3	225	0.3	7	3.0	13,373	13.5	0.3	397,706
South Carolina	13	0.1	166	0.2	13	1.3	7,928	7.4	0.1	567,462
Rhode Island	26	0.3	98	0.1	4	1.2	11,918	6.6	0.1	252,154
Maine	15	0.1	46	0.1	3	0.7	15,043	4.9	0.1	325,667
New Mexico	12	0.1	80	0.1	7	1.0	12,950	4.6	0.1	383,250
Idaho	34	0.3	206	0.3	6	1.1	5,107	4.5	0.1	133,235
North Dakota	20	0.2	60	0.1	3	0.5	8,250	2.6	0.1	130,550
Arkansas	44	0.4	60*	-	-	(D)	-	(D)	-	-
West Virginia	32	0.3	60*	-	-	(D)	-	(D)	-	-
Kansas	26	0.3	60*	-	-	(D)	-	(D)	-	-
Nevada	19	0.2	60*	-	-	(D)	-	(D)	-	-
Delaware	9	0.1	175*	-	-	(D)	-	(D)	-	-
Montana	9	0.1	60*	-	-	(D)	-	(D)	-	-
New Hampshire	6	0.1	60*	-	-	(D)	-	(D)	-	-
South Dakota	5	-	60*	-	-	(D)	-	(D)	-	-
Vermont	5	-	60*	-	-	(D)	-	(D)	-	-
Alaska	3	-	60*	-	-	(D)	-	(D)	-	-
Wyoming	2	-	60*	-	-	(D)	-	(D)	-	-

Source: 1997 *Economic Census*. The states are in descending order of revenues or establishments (if revenue data are missing for the majority). The symbol (D) appears when data are withheld to prevent disclosure of competitive information. States marked with (D) are sorted by number of establishments. A dash (-) indicates that the data element cannot be calculated. * indicates the midpoint of a range; 175, for example is the range 100-249. Shaded *states* on the state map indicate those states which have proportionately greater representation in the industry than would be indicated by the state's population; the ratio is based on total revenues or number of establishments. Shaded *regions* indicate where the industry is regionally most concentrated.

NAICS 812990 - PERSONAL SERVICES NEC

GENERAL STATISTICS

Year	Establishments (number)	Employment (number)	Payroll ($ million)	Revenues ($ million)	Employees per Establishment (number)	Revenues per Establishment ($)	Payroll per Employee ($)
1997	4,566	36,522	597.0	2,410.0	8.0	527,814	16,346

Source: Economic Census of the United States, 1997. This is a newly defined industry. Data for prior years were unavailable at the time of publication but may become available over time.

INDICES OF CHANGE

Year	Establishments (number)	Employment (number)	Payroll ($ million)	Revenues ($ million)	Employees per Establishment (number)	Revenues per Establishment ($)	Payroll per Employee ($)
1997	100.0	100.0	100.0	100.0	100.0	100.0	100.0

Sources: Same as General Statistics. The values shown reflect change from the base year, 1997. Values above 100 mean greater than 1997, values below 100 mean less than 1997, and a value of 100 in the 1982-96 or 1998-2001 period means same as 1997. Values followed by a 'p' are projections by the editors; 'e' stands for extrapolation. Data are the most recent available at this level of detail.

SIC INDUSTRIES RELATED TO NAICS 812990

Each new NAICS code represents an industry that used to be part of an SIC or a part of several SIC industries. Data in this table are shown to provide transitional information for these cases. All available data for the precursor SIC(s) are shown. Even if only a part of an SIC is included in the NAICS, *all* data for the SIC are reproduced. If the SIC industry is not marked as being a part (pt) of the NAICS, the entire industry is embedded in the NAICS data. The SIC composition of the new industry provides some hints of the relative importance of its "ancestors." Data marked with a 'p' are projected. Projections begin with 1982 data. Data earlier than 1990 are not shown but are reflected in the projections.

SIC	Industry	1990	1991	1992	1993	1994	1995	1996	1997
4899	**Communications Services, nec (pt)**								
	Establishments (number)	1,201	1,320	1,008	1,105	1,034	1,305	1,488	468p
	Employment (thousands)	34.6	25.0	9.7	15.3	13.1	20.0	22.4	-
	Revenues ($ million)	-	-	2,357.9	-	-	-	-	-
7251	**Shoe Repair & Shoeshine Parlors (pt)**								
	Establishments (number)	2,528	2,593	2,702	2,654	2,438	2,292	2,355p	2,307p
	Employment (thousands)	6.5	6.5	6.4	6.7	6.1	6.0	6.1p	6.1p
	Revenues ($ million)	-	-	275.8	278.6p	287.5p	296.4p	305.4p	314.3p
7299	**Miscellaneous Personal Services, nec (pt)**								
	Establishments (number)	15,086	15,775	16,017	16,862	17,296	17,740	18,650p	19,294p
	Employment (thousands)	116.4	114.7	105.6	99.6	97.2	99.4	106.1p	106.9p
	Revenues ($ million)	-	-	3,885.0	-	-	-	-	-
7389	**Business Services, nec (pt)**								
	Establishments (number)	44,079	50,252	52,375	56,829	60,725	53,596	60,893p	63,269p
	Employment (thousands)	489.6	550.4	523.6	607.9	648.7	623.0	680.2p	710.9p
	Revenues ($ million)	-	-	32,885.9	-	-	-	-	-

Source: Economic Census of the United States, 1992, annual surveys of economic sectors conducted by the Bureau of the Census, and estimates or projections based on the 1982-1992 period; not all data are shown. 'e' marks estimates made by the editors; 'p' indicates projections based on time series. A dash (-) indicates that data for this SIC or year were not available. The abbreviation (pt) next to the industry name indicates that only a part of the industry is present within the NAICS data. If no (pt) is shown, the entire industry is contained within the NAICS data.

SELECTED RATIOS

For 1997	Avg. of Information	Analyzed Industry	Index	For 1997	Avg. of Information	Analyzed Industry	Index
Employees per establishment	6	8	128	Payroll per establishment	126,069	130,749	104
Revenue per establishment	511,622	527,814	103	Payroll as % of revenue	25	25	101
Revenue per employee	81,659	65,988	81	Payroll per employee	20,122	16,346	81

Sources: Same as General Statistics. The 'Average' column represents the average for the industry sector, in 1997, where the currently shown industry is classified. The Index shows the relationship between the Average and the Analyzed Industry. For example, 100 means that they are equal; 500 that the Analyzed Industry is five times the average; 50 means that the Analyzed Industry is half the national average. The abbreviation 'na' is used to show that data are 'not available'.

LEADING COMPANIES   Number shown: **15**   Total sales ($ mil): **7,498**   Total employment (000): **168.8**

Company Name	Address				CEO Name	Phone	Co. Type	Sales ($ mil)	Empl. (000)
ARAMARK Corp.	1101 Market St	Philadelphia	PA	19107	Joseph Neubauer	215-238-3000	R	6,377	150.0
Unifirst Corp.	PO Box 600	Wilmington	MA	01887	Aldo Croatti	978-658-8888	P	487	7.5
Jenny Craig Inc.	11355 N Torr Pns	La Jolla	CA	92037	Sid Craig	858-812-7000	P	321	3.5
Valet Parking Service	10555 Jefferson	Culver City	CA	90232	Anthony Policella	310-836-3388	R	87*	1.8
Mitchell's Management Corp.	4030-C Pleasantdale	Atlanta	GA	30340	Joseph P Doyle	770-448-8381	R	50*	0.5
Coinstar Inc.	PO Box 91258	Bellevue	WA	98009	Dan Gerrity	425-644-6789	P	48	0.3
Nationwide Formalwear Inc.	PO Box 2444	West Chester	PA	19380	William Glah Sr	610-692-6624	R	30	0.7
Weight Watchers Intern. Inc.	175 Crossways	Woodbury	NY	11797	Linda Huett	516-390-1400	S	29*	0.1
V.I.P. Valet Parking	300 Milan	Houston	TX	77002	Brad Klein	713-266-7275	R	21*	0.2
Security Associates International	2101 S Arl Hght	Arlington H.	IL	60005	James S Brannen	847-956-8650	P	20	0.4
Advantage Marketing Systems Inc	2601 N W Expy	Oklahoma City	OK	73112	Roger P Baresel	405-842-0131	P	13	<0.1
QuadraMed Inc.	1003 West Cutting	Richmond	CA	94804	John Cracchiolo	610-620-2340	R	10*	3.7
The Jeff Herman Agency L.L.C..	332 Bleecker St	New York	NY	10014		212-941-0540	N	2	<0.1
Apartment Hunters	11209 N Dale Mabry	Tampa	FL	33613	Steve Oehlerking	813-961-1419	R	2	<0.1
Weddings by Design	410 Provo St	El Cajon	CA	92019		619-440-0422	N	0	<0.1

Source: Ward's *Business Directory of U.S. Private and Public Companies*, Volumes 1 and 2, 2000. The company type code used is as follows: P - Public, R - Private, S - Subsidiary, D - Division, J - Joint Venture, A - Affiliate, G - Group, N - Company type not reported. Sales are in millions of dollars, employees are in thousands. An asterisk (*) indicates an estimated sales volume. The symbol < stands for 'less than'. Company names and addresses are truncated, in some cases, to fit into the available space.

REPRESENTATIVE NONPROFIT ORGANIZATIONS

Organization Name	Address				Phone	Income Range ($ mil)
A Territory Resource	603 Stewart St 1007	Seattle	WA	98101	206-624-4081	1-5
Children of the Night	14530 Sylvan St	Van Nuys	CA	91411	818-908-4474	1-5
Florence V Carroll Charitable TR	PO Box 960	Fort Wayne	IN	46801		1-5
National Genealogical Society	4527 17th St N	Arlington	VA	22207	703-525-0050	1-5
Simpson County Historical Society	206 N College St	Franklin	KY	42134	270-586-4228	1-5

Source: *National Directory of Nonprofit Organizations*, 2000, Volumes 1 and 2, The Taft Group. The table shows a selection of organizations for illustration and does not constitute a complete selection from the source. The organizations are arranged in alphabetical order.

LOCATION BY STATE AND REGIONAL CONCENTRATION

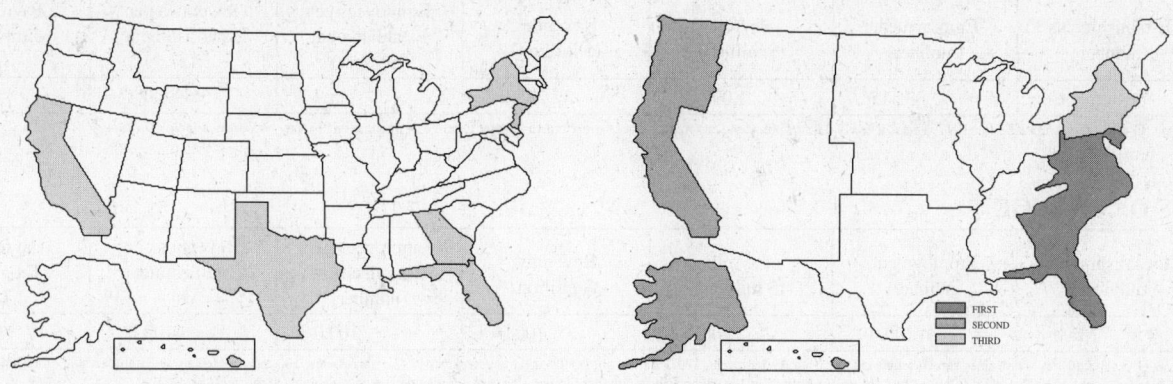

INDUSTRY DATA BY STATE

State	Establishments Total (number)	% of U.S.	Employment Total (number)	% of U.S.	Per Estab.	Payroll Total ($ mil.)	Per Empl. ($)	Revenues Total ($ mil.)	% of U.S.	Per Estab. ($)
California	558	12.2	5,430	14.9	10	95.6	17,598	385.1	16.0	690,122
Florida	471	10.3	4,403	12.1	9	54.0	12,255	344.7	14.3	731,843
New York	277	6.1	3,626	9.9	13	60.4	16,664	214.3	8.9	773,549
Texas	459	10.1	2,754	7.5	6	44.5	16,153	194.9	8.1	424,553
Georgia	153	3.4	1,533	4.2	10	37.7	24,599	140.8	5.8	920,314
Illinois	147	3.2	1,754	4.8	12	28.1	16,048	94.2	3.9	640,769
New Jersey	159	3.5	1,423	3.9	9	26.4	18,547	87.8	3.6	552,465
Pennsylvania	157	3.4	907	2.5	6	16.4	18,086	52.1	2.2	331,892
Ohio	169	3.7	1,091	3.0	6	14.2	12,988	51.3	2.1	303,663
Michigan	117	2.6	1,198	3.3	10	17.3	14,409	51.3	2.1	438,462
North Carolina	146	3.2	656	1.8	4	12.3	18,698	46.6	1.9	318,973
Massachusetts	75	1.6	820	2.2	11	12.5	15,191	39.3	1.6	524,627
Washington	111	2.4	617	1.7	6	9.8	15,895	35.9	1.5	323,225
Virginia	86	1.9	550	1.5	6	10.5	19,000	35.3	1.5	410,419
Missouri	115	2.5	1,083	3.0	9	12.9	11,885	31.7	1.3	275,226
Tennessee	112	2.5	535	1.5	5	7.5	13,948	28.7	1.2	256,482
Arizona	72	1.6	781	2.1	11	8.6	11,033	28.0	1.2	388,556
Minnesota	71	1.6	351	1.0	5	6.7	19,157	27.9	1.2	392,845
Maryland	83	1.8	345	0.9	4	7.3	21,270	27.6	1.1	333,120
Colorado	76	1.7	543	1.5	7	6.9	12,797	25.5	1.1	335,171
Oklahoma	139	3.0	549	1.5	4	7.8	14,168	24.8	1.0	178,165
Louisiana	49	1.1	237	0.6	5	3.9	16,249	22.2	0.9	452,163
Indiana	67	1.5	337	0.9	5	5.3	15,730	22.0	0.9	328,418
Hawaii	40	0.9	377	1.0	9	6.1	16,273	17.6	0.7	441,125
Kentucky	30	0.7	90	0.2	3	2.8	31,578	17.4	0.7	581,567
Utah	43	0.9	460	1.3	11	6.4	13,813	16.3	0.7	378,419
Alabama	69	1.5	276	0.8	4	4.7	16,880	16.0	0.7	232,319
South Carolina	59	1.3	406	1.1	7	4.8	11,943	16.0	0.7	270,373
Connecticut	38	0.8	291	0.8	8	5.4	18,550	15.6	0.6	410,737
Oregon	42	0.9	212	0.6	5	4.4	20,877	14.8	0.6	352,929
Iowa	32	0.7	130	0.4	4	4.0	30,562	13.4	0.6	419,906
Wisconsin	37	0.8	126	0.3	3	2.0	16,103	8.2	0.3	220,541
Mississippi	23	0.5	125	0.3	5	1.8	14,456	8.1	0.3	350,565
Rhode Island	15	0.3	80	0.2	5	1.6	19,900	5.3	0.2	350,133
Nebraska	14	0.3	71	0.2	5	1.1	15,268	3.7	0.2	267,143
New Mexico	19	0.4	53	0.1	3	0.9	16,245	2.5	0.1	130,211
Maine	10	0.2	101	0.3	10	0.6	5,881	1.6	0.1	155,300
North Dakota	3	0.1	10	0.0	3	0.3	26,200	0.9	0.0	283,333
Nevada	87	1.9	750*	-	-	(D)	-	(D)	-	-
Arkansas	30	0.7	60*	-	-	(D)	-	(D)	-	-
Kansas	29	0.6	175*	-	-	(D)	-	(D)	-	-
Idaho	15	0.3	60*	-	-	(D)	-	(D)	-	-
New Hampshire	15	0.3	60*	-	-	(D)	-	(D)	-	-
D.C.	11	0.2	375*	-	-	(D)	-	(D)	-	-
Delaware	7	0.2	60*	-	-	(D)	-	(D)	-	-
Vermont	7	0.2	10*	-	-	(D)	-	(D)	-	-
Alaska	6	0.1	10*	-	-	(D)	-	(D)	-	-
Montana	6	0.1	10*	-	-	(D)	-	(D)	-	-
West Virginia	6	0.1	10*	-	-	(D)	-	(D)	-	-
South Dakota	2	-	10*	-	-	(D)	-	(D)	-	-
Wyoming	2	-	375*	-	-	(D)	-	(D)	-	-

Source: 1997 *Economic Census*. The states are in descending order of revenues or establishments (if revenue data are missing for the majority). The symbol (D) appears when data are withheld to prevent disclosure of competitive information. States marked with (D) are sorted by number of establishments. A dash (-) indicates that the data element cannot be calculated. * indicates the midpoint of a range; 175, for example is the range 100-249. Shaded *states* on the state map indicate those states which have proportionately greater representation in the industry than would be indicated by the state's population; the ratio is based on total revenues or number of establishments. Shaded *regions* indicate where the industry is regionally most concentrated.

NAICS 813211 - GRANTMAKING FOUNDATIONS

GENERAL STATISTICS

Year	Establishments (number)	Employment (number)	Payroll ($ million)	Revenues ($ million)	Employees per Establishment (number)	Revenues per Establishment ($)	Payroll per Employee ($)
1997	5,656	33,515	1,092.0	32,238.0	5.9	5,699,788	32,582

Source: *Economic Census of the United States*, 1997. This is a newly defined industry. Data for prior years were unavailable at the time of publication but may become available over time.

INDICES OF CHANGE

Year	Establishments (number)	Employment (number)	Payroll ($ million)	Revenues ($ million)	Employees per Establishment (number)	Revenues per Establishment ($)	Payroll per Employee ($)
1997	100.0	100.0	100.0	100.0	100.0	100.0	100.0

Sources: Same as General Statistics. The values shown reflect change from the base year, 1997. Values above 100 mean greater than 1997, values below 100 mean less than 1997, and a value of 100 in the 1982-96 or 1998-2001 period means same as 1997. Values followed by a 'p' are projections by the editors; 'e' stands for extrapolation. Data are the most recent available at this level of detail.

SIC INDUSTRIES RELATED TO NAICS 813211

Each new NAICS code represents an industry that used to be part of an SIC or a part of several SIC industries. Data in this table are shown to provide transitional information for these cases. All available data for the precursor SIC(s) are shown. Even if only a part of an SIC is included in the NAICS, *all* data for the SIC are reproduced. If the SIC industry is not marked as being a part (pt) of the NAICS, the entire industry is embedded in the NAICS data. The SIC composition of the new industry provides some hints of the relative importance of its "ancestors." Data marked with a 'p' are projected. Projections begin with 1982 data. Data earlier than 1990 are not shown but are reflected in the projections.

SIC	Industry	1990	1991	1992	1993	1994	1995	1996	1997
6732	Educational, Religious, Etc. Trusts (pt)	-	-	-	-	-	-	-	-

Source: *Economic Census of the United States*, 1992, annual surveys of economic sectors conducted by the Bureau of the Census, and estimates or projections based on the 1982-1992 period; not all data are shown. 'e' marks estimates made by the editors; 'p' indicates projections based on time series. A dash (-) indicates that data for this SIC or year were not available. The abbreviation (pt) next to the industry name indicates that only a part of the industry is present within the NAICS data. If no (pt) is shown, the entire industry is contained within the NAICS data.

SELECTED RATIOS

For 1997	Avg. of Information	Analyzed Industry	Index	For 1997	Avg. of Information	Analyzed Industry	Index
Employees per establishment	6	6	95	Payroll per establishment	126,069	193,069	153
Revenue per establishment	511,622	5,699,788	1,114	Payroll as % of revenue	25	3	14
Revenue per employee	81,659	961,898	1,178	Payroll per employee	20,122	32,582	162

Sources: Same as General Statistics. The 'Average' column represents the average for the industry sector, in 1997, where the currently shown industry is classified. The Index shows the relationship between the Average and the Analyzed Industry. For example, 100 means that they are equal; 500 that the Analyzed Industry is five times the average; 50 means that the Analyzed Industry is half the national average. The abbreviation 'na' is used to show that data are 'not available'.

LEADING COMPANIES

No company data available for this industry.

LOCATION BY STATE AND REGIONAL CONCENTRATION

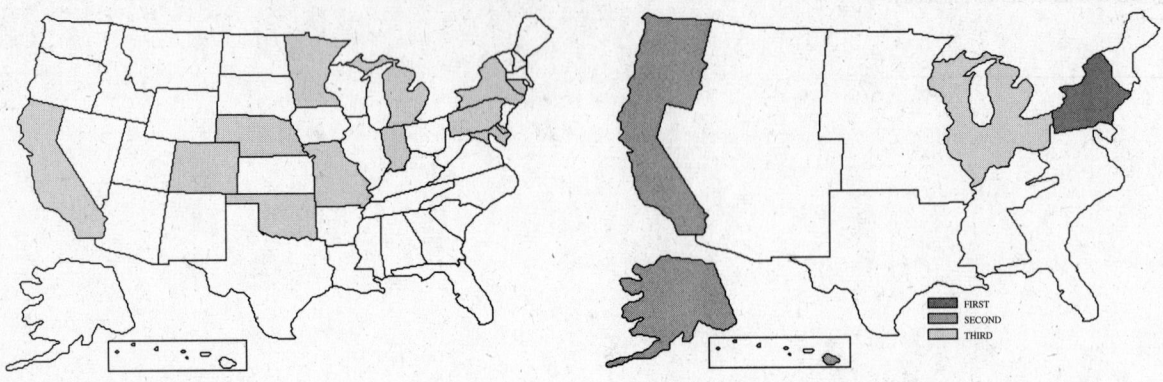

FIRST
SECOND
THIRD

INDUSTRY DATA BY STATE

State	Establishments Total (number)	% of U.S.	Employment Total (number)	% of U.S.	Per Estab.	Payroll Total ($ mil.)	Per Empl. ($)	Revenues Total ($ mil.)	% of U.S.	Per Estab. ($)
California	639	11.3	6,624	19.8	10	167.3	25,260	5,704.8	17.7	8,927,659
New York	622	11.0	4,401	13.1	7	190.4	43,257	5,655.5	17.5	9,092,368
Pennsylvania	243	4.3	1,441	4.3	6	44.8	31,091	1,851.2	5.7	7,618,284
Texas	359	6.3	1,371	4.1	4	41.2	30,086	1,717.6	5.3	4,784,493
Michigan	170	3.0	1,097	3.3	6	43.8	39,967	1,517.7	4.7	8,927,806
Illinois	242	4.3	1,243	3.7	5	46.4	37,305	1,297.6	4.0	5,362,050
Indiana	139	2.5	990	3.0	7	29.1	29,361	1,076.0	3.3	7,741,007
Florida	289	5.1	1,130	3.4	4	34.8	30,784	1,061.7	3.3	3,673,685
New Jersey	135	2.4	723	2.2	5	28.7	39,685	965.9	3.0	7,154,911
Minnesota	131	2.3	600	1.8	5	19.3	32,213	827.2	2.6	6,314,519
Colorado	149	2.6	768	2.3	5	24.8	32,328	699.7	2.2	4,696,208
Virginia	152	2.7	639	1.9	4	21.3	33,266	695.9	2.2	4,578,382
Missouri	100	1.8	512	1.5	5	23.2	45,396	681.1	2.1	6,810,830
Maryland	102	1.8	828	2.5	8	29.9	36,159	658.8	2.0	6,458,598
D.C.	152	2.7	1,572	4.7	10	70.4	44,806	629.0	2.0	4,138,013
Ohio	182	3.2	775	2.3	4	22.0	28,425	583.2	1.8	3,204,626
North Carolina	111	2.0	795	2.4	7	22.7	28,546	579.5	1.8	5,220,559
Connecticut	104	1.8	522	1.6	5	20.6	39,387	558.0	1.7	5,365,385
Oklahoma	81	1.4	634	1.9	8	17.3	27,322	555.9	1.7	6,862,543
Massachusetts	154	2.7	694	2.1	5	22.2	31,991	422.9	1.3	2,745,818
Wisconsin	85	1.5	414	1.2	5	10.6	25,650	388.7	1.2	4,572,788
Georgia	109	1.9	377	1.1	3	11.6	30,806	322.7	1.0	2,960,431
Oregon	73	1.3	432	1.3	6	11.6	26,898	315.3	1.0	4,318,699
Nebraska	64	1.1	376	1.1	6	10.1	26,848	313.5	1.0	4,898,625
Kansas	57	1.0	494	1.5	9	15.8	31,883	297.5	0.9	5,218,491
Arizona	85	1.5	465	1.4	5	12.7	27,254	273.3	0.8	3,215,482
Washington	114	2.0	304	0.9	3	9.6	31,730	272.6	0.8	2,391,175
Iowa	54	1.0	319	1.0	6	9.5	29,906	246.8	0.8	4,569,944
Tennessee	74	1.3	335	1.0	5	9.1	27,257	218.2	0.7	2,949,000
Delaware	22	0.4	48	0.1	2	1.7	36,146	216.0	0.7	9,817,909
Kentucky	52	0.9	253	0.8	5	7.3	29,047	158.9	0.5	3,056,000
Louisiana	71	1.3	264	0.8	4	7.9	29,758	143.8	0.4	2,025,761
South Carolina	60	1.1	159	0.5	3	3.7	23,440	134.5	0.4	2,241,650
Arkansas	39	0.7	97	0.3	2	2.9	29,722	134.0	0.4	3,436,410
Alabama	62	1.1	246	0.7	4	6.3	25,813	124.3	0.4	2,005,048
New Mexico	39	0.7	177	0.5	5	5.2	29,525	107.4	0.3	2,753,872
West Virginia	37	0.7	139	0.4	4	3.1	22,036	99.6	0.3	2,691,946
Nevada	42	0.7	65	0.2	2	2.3	35,569	79.1	0.2	1,883,619
Hawaii	16	0.3	190	0.6	12	4.3	22,468	75.1	0.2	4,691,500
Vermont	27	0.5	141	0.4	5	3.8	27,050	67.0	0.2	2,482,778
New Hampshire	17	0.3	88	0.3	5	3.4	38,273	62.9	0.2	3,700,647
Utah	26	0.5	67	0.2	3	2.1	31,522	61.1	0.2	2,351,346
South Dakota	25	0.4	138	0.4	6	1.8	12,797	52.1	0.2	2,085,160
Maine	19	0.3	48	0.1	3	1.7	34,771	51.9	0.2	2,730,421
North Dakota	14	0.2	77	0.2	6	1.0	12,636	48.4	0.2	3,456,214
Montana	20	0.4	99	0.3	5	2.5	24,889	34.7	0.1	1,736,250
Mississippi	34	0.6	156	0.5	5	4.1	26,026	30.1	0.1	885,882
Wyoming	14	0.2	35	0.1	3	0.8	21,914	28.8	0.1	2,055,000
Idaho	13	0.2	27	0.1	2	0.6	22,630	22.8	0.1	1,750,923
Rhode Island	19	0.3	60*	-	-	(D)	-	(D)	-	-
Alaska	17	0.3	60*	-	-	(D)	-	(D)	-	-

Source: 1997 *Economic Census*. The states are in descending order of revenues or establishments (if revenue data are missing for the majority). The symbol (D) appears when data are withheld to prevent disclosure of competitive information. States marked with (D) are sorted by number of establishments. A dash (-) indicates that the data element cannot be calculated. * indicates the midpoint of a range; 175, for example is the range 100-249. Shaded *states* on the state map indicate those states which have proportionately greater representation in the industry than would be indicated by the state's population; the ratio is based on total revenues or number of establishments. Shaded *regions* indicate where the industry is regionally most concentrated.

NAICS 813212 - VOLUNTARY HEALTH ORGANIZATIONS

GENERAL STATISTICS

Year	Establishments (number)	Employment (number)	Payroll ($ million)	Revenues ($ million)	Employees per Establishment (number)	Revenues per Establishment ($)	Payroll per Employee ($)
1997	3,351	41,925	1,154.0	6,080.0	12.5	1,814,384	27,525

Source: Economic Census of the United States, 1997. This is a newly defined industry. Data for prior years were unavailable at the time of publication but may become available over time.

INDICES OF CHANGE

Year	Establishments (number)	Employment (number)	Payroll ($ million)	Revenues ($ million)	Employees per Establishment (number)	Revenues per Establishment ($)	Payroll per Employee ($)
1997	100.0	100.0	100.0	100.0	100.0	100.0	100.0

Sources: Same as General Statistics. The values shown reflect change from the base year, 1997. Values above 100 mean greater than 1997, values below 100 mean less than 1997, and a value of 100 in the 1982-96 or 1998-2001 period means same as 1997. Values followed by a 'p' are projections by the editors; 'e' stands for extrapolation. Data are the most recent available at this level of detail.

SIC INDUSTRIES RELATED TO NAICS 813212

Each new NAICS code represents an industry that used to be part of an SIC or a part of several SIC industries. Data in this table are shown to provide transitional information for these cases. All available data for the precursor SIC(s) are shown. Even if only a part of an SIC is included in the NAICS, *all* data for the SIC are reproduced. If the SIC industry is not marked as being a part (pt) of the NAICS, the entire industry is embedded in the NAICS data. The SIC composition of the new industry provides some hints of the relative importance of its "ancestors." Data marked with a 'p' are projected. Projections begin with 1982 data. Data earlier than 1990 are not shown but are reflected in the projections.

SIC	Industry	1990	1991	1992	1993	1994	1995	1996	1997
8399	**Social Services, nec (pt)**								
	Establishments (number)	13,710	14,734	17,416	17,485	17,425	17,456	18,826p	19,537p
	Employment (thousands)	200.1	210.5	207.8	213.1	221.6	234.1	238.7p	245.8p
	Revenues ($ million)	-	-	18,239.9	-	-	-	-	-

Source: Economic Census of the United States, 1992, annual surveys of economic sectors conducted by the Bureau of the Census, and estimates or projections based on the 1982-1992 period; not all data are shown. 'e' marks estimates made by the editors; 'p' indicates projections based on time series. A dash (-) indicates that data for this SIC or year were not available. The abbreviation (pt) next to the industry name indicates that only a part of the industry is present within the NAICS data. If no (pt) is shown, the entire industry is contained within the NAICS data.

SELECTED RATIOS

For 1997	Avg. of Information	Analyzed Industry	Index	For 1997	Avg. of Information	Analyzed Industry	Index
Employees per establishment	6	13	200	Payroll per establishment	126,069	344,375	273
Revenue per establishment	511,622	1,814,384	355	Payroll as % of revenue	25	19	77
Revenue per employee	81,659	145,021	178	Payroll per employee	20,122	27,525	137

Sources: Same as General Statistics. The 'Average' column represents the average for the industry sector, in 1997, where the currently shown industry is classified. The Index shows the relationship between the Average and the Analyzed Industry. For example, 100 means that they are equal; 500 that the Analyzed Industry is five times the average; 50 means that the Analyzed Industry is half the national average. The abbreviation 'na' is used to show that data are 'not available'.

LEADING COMPANIES

No company data available for this industry.

REPRESENTATIVE NONPROFIT ORGANIZATIONS

Organization Name	Address				Phone	Income Range ($ mil)
Aberdeen Area Tribal Chairmens Health Board	405 8th Ave NW Ste 205	Aberdeen	SD	57401		5-9
Association of Air Medical Services	110 N Royal St Ste 307	Alexandria	VA	22314		1-5
Big Bend Cares Inc	PO Box 14365	Tallahassee	FL	32317		1-5
California Hospital Association	PO Box 1100	Sacramento	CA	95812		5-9
Comprehensive Geriatric Services Inc C O Rochelle Kerchner	31 W Main St Ste 301	Patchogue	NY	11772		5-9
Geisinger Medical Center	100 N Academy Ave	Danville	PA	17822	717-271-6439	50+
Greater KC Linc Inc	3100 Broadway Ste 226	Kansas City	MO	64111	816-756-0414	5-9
Hispanic Urban Minority Alcoholism and Drug Abuse	3305 W 25th St	Cleveland	OH	44109		1-5
Indiana Minority Health Coalition Inc	3737 N Meridian	Indianapolis	IN	46208		1-5
Massachusetts Association of HMOs Inc	50 Franklin St 4th Flr	Boston	MA	02110		1-5
Maternal and Child Health Institute Inc	PO Box 8689	Atlanta	GA	31106		1-5
Mississippi Foundation for Medical Care Inc	385 Highland Colony	Ridgeland	MS	39157	601-957-1575	1-5
National Committee to Preserve Social Security and Medicare	10 G St NE Ste 600	Washington	DC	20002		40-49
Progress Enterprises Inc	Hwy 20 N	Jamestown	ND	58401		1-5

Source: *National Directory of Nonprofit Organizations*, 2000, Volumes 1 and 2, The Taft Group. The table shows a selection of organizations for illustration and does not constitute a complete selection from the source. The organizations are arranged in alphabetical order.

LOCATION BY STATE AND REGIONAL CONCENTRATION

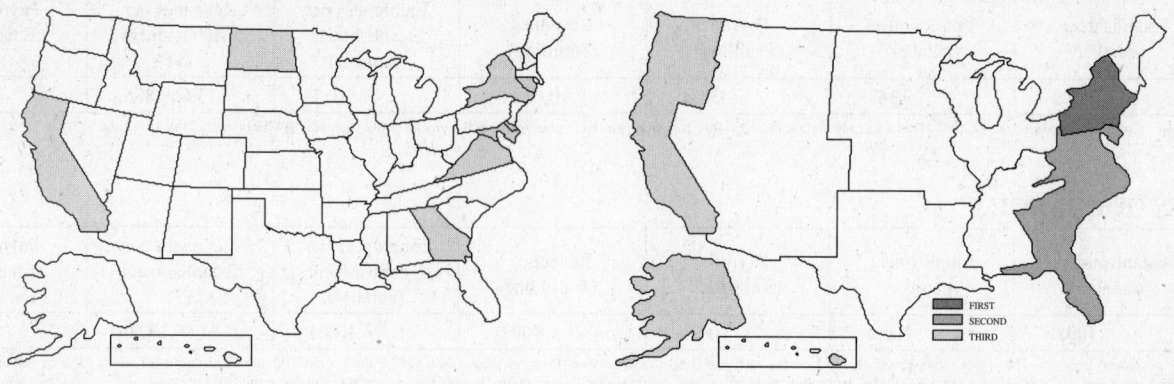

FIRST
SECOND
THIRD

INDUSTRY DATA BY STATE

State	Establishments Total (number)	% of U.S.	Employment Total (number)	% of U.S.	Per Estab.	Payroll Total ($ mil.)	Per Empl. ($)	Revenues Total ($ mil.)	% of U.S.	Per Estab. ($)
New York	316	9.4	6,460	15.4	20	211.1	32,674	1,100.2	18.1	3,481,756
California	344	10.3	4,100	9.8	12	125.1	30,505	924.7	15.2	2,688,160
Texas	191	5.7	2,083	5.0	11	61.2	29,384	395.6	6.5	2,070,953
Georgia	76	2.3	1,134	2.7	15	44.9	39,622	366.9	6.0	4,828,158
Maryland	105	3.1	2,074	4.9	20	67.0	32,323	293.3	4.8	2,793,257
Florida	206	6.1	2,238	5.3	11	54.9	24,538	257.9	4.2	1,252,117
Illinois	124	3.7	1,365	3.3	11	39.4	28,892	222.2	3.7	1,792,298
Pennsylvania	160	4.8	1,886	4.5	12	45.4	24,095	215.0	3.5	1,343,506
New Jersey	94	2.8	1,161	2.8	12	28.8	24,820	185.1	3.0	1,968,862
Michigan	115	3.4	1,779	4.2	15	41.6	23,390	168.3	2.8	1,463,243
Virginia	84	2.5	968	2.3	12	32.7	33,770	160.3	2.6	1,908,548
Ohio	126	3.8	1,271	3.0	10	29.4	23,131	155.1	2.6	1,230,833
Washington	66	2.0	831	2.0	13	22.7	27,373	122.8	2.0	1,859,924
D.C.	38	1.1	756	1.8	20	26.5	35,071	119.1	2.0	3,134,842
Massachusetts	79	2.4	1,062	2.5	13	28.7	27,059	107.6	1.8	1,362,203
Missouri	76	2.3	849	2.0	11	18.5	21,764	102.1	1.7	1,342,974
Minnesota	58	1.7	1,868	4.5	32	35.4	18,927	90.8	1.5	1,566,241
Connecticut	51	1.5	611	1.5	12	19.0	31,046	82.2	1.4	1,611,118
Indiana	73	2.2	636	1.5	9	14.6	22,945	76.9	1.3	1,053,466
Tennessee	68	2.0	392	0.9	6	9.4	23,936	75.2	1.2	1,105,221
North Carolina	71	2.1	974	2.3	14	21.9	22,529	72.2	1.2	1,016,563
Colorado	54	1.6	860	2.1	16	19.9	23,180	67.4	1.1	1,248,185
Arizona	57	1.7	636	1.5	11	15.5	24,379	56.3	0.9	987,772
Oklahoma	38	1.1	274	0.7	7	7.0	25,496	54.3	0.9	1,430,053
Louisiana	51	1.5	458	1.1	9	10.8	23,677	52.3	0.9	1,024,745
Wisconsin	63	1.9	442	1.1	7	11.8	26,658	52.3	0.9	829,667
Kansas	35	1.0	475	1.1	14	13.1	27,672	47.4	0.8	1,354,457
South Carolina	47	1.4	391	0.9	8	8.8	22,399	46.0	0.8	977,766
Utah	18	0.5	194	0.5	11	6.1	31,577	39.4	0.6	2,188,278
Iowa	37	1.1	407	1.0	11	7.5	18,400	36.8	0.6	995,270
Kentucky	35	1.0	259	0.6	7	5.6	21,452	34.0	0.6	972,800
Oregon	42	1.3	307	0.7	7	7.1	23,257	33.3	0.5	791,857
Alabama	37	1.1	291	0.7	8	5.8	20,103	26.3	0.4	711,784
Nebraska	37	1.1	289	0.7	8	5.4	18,609	25.6	0.4	691,378
West Virginia	18	0.5	81	0.2	5	1.7	20,716	21.9	0.4	1,215,722
Hawaii	27	0.8	222	0.5	8	4.9	21,851	21.8	0.4	809,185
North Dakota	19	0.6	162	0.4	9	2.1	12,698	20.2	0.3	1,062,368
New Hampshire	14	0.4	102	0.2	7	2.7	26,431	19.5	0.3	1,390,500
Arkansas	14	0.4	90	0.2	6	2.4	27,100	17.7	0.3	1,267,786
Delaware	18	0.5	353	0.8	20	8.2	23,357	17.5	0.3	974,667
Maine	22	0.7	162	0.4	7	5.0	30,833	15.7	0.3	715,727
Mississippi	27	0.8	158	0.4	6	2.9	18,399	13.9	0.2	515,519
Nevada	20	0.6	180	0.4	9	4.1	22,678	12.5	0.2	623,800
Vermont	13	0.4	77	0.2	6	2.4	31,662	9.6	0.2	735,692
Alaska	16	0.5	160	0.4	10	3.4	21,294	8.8	0.1	549,125
New Mexico	16	0.5	93	0.2	6	2.3	24,344	7.5	0.1	466,062
Montana	11	0.3	38	0.1	3	0.9	24,553	5.0	0.1	458,818
Rhode Island	18	0.5	175*	-	-	(D)	-	(D)	-	-
Idaho	11	0.3	60*	-	-	(D)	-	(D)	-	-
South Dakota	8	0.2	60*	-	-	(D)	-	(D)	-	-
Wyoming	7	0.2	60*	-	-	(D)	-	(D)	-	-

Source: 1997 *Economic Census.* The states are in descending order of revenues or establishments (if revenue data are missing for the majority). The symbol (D) appears when data are withheld to prevent disclosure of competitive information. States marked with (D) are sorted by number of establishments. A dash (-) indicates that the data element cannot be calculated. * indicates the midpoint of a range; 175, for example is the range 100-249. Shaded *states* on the state map indicate those states which have proportionately greater representation in the industry than would be indicated by the state's population; the ratio is based on total revenues or number of establishments. Shaded *regions* indicate where the industry is regionally most concentrated.

NAICS 813219 - GRANTMAKING AND GIVING SERVICES NEC

GENERAL STATISTICS

Year	Establishments (number)	Employment (number)	Payroll ($ million)	Revenues ($ million)	Employees per Establishment (number)	Revenues per Establishment ($)	Payroll per Employee ($)
1997	2,899	29,367	835.0	10,639.0	10.1	3,669,886	28,433

Source: Economic Census of the United States, 1997. This is a newly defined industry. Data for prior years were unavailable at the time of publication but may become available over time.

INDICES OF CHANGE

Year	Establishments (number)	Employment (number)	Payroll ($ million)	Revenues ($ million)	Employees per Establishment (number)	Revenues per Establishment ($)	Payroll per Employee ($)
1997	100.0	100.0	100.0	100.0	100.0	100.0	100.0

Sources: Same as General Statistics. The values shown reflect change from the base year, 1997. Values above 100 mean greater than 1997, values below 100 mean less than 1997, and a value of 100 in the 1982-96 or 1998-2001 period means same as 1997. Values followed by a 'p' are projections by the editors; 'e' stands for extrapolation. Data are the most recent available at this level of detail.

SIC INDUSTRIES RELATED TO NAICS 813219

Each new NAICS code represents an industry that used to be part of an SIC or a part of several SIC industries. Data in this table are shown to provide transitional information for these cases. All available data for the precursor SIC(s) are shown. Even if only a part of an SIC is included in the NAICS, *all* data for the SIC are reproduced. If the SIC industry is not marked as being a part (pt) of the NAICS, the entire industry is embedded in the NAICS data. The SIC composition of the new industry provides some hints of the relative importance of its "ancestors." Data marked with a 'p' are projected. Projections begin with 1982 data. Data earlier than 1990 are not shown but are reflected in the projections.

SIC	Industry	1990	1991	1992	1993	1994	1995	1996	1997
8399	**Social Services, nec (pt)**								
	Establishments (number)	13,710	14,734	17,416	17,485	17,425	17,456	18,826*p*	19,537*p*
	Employment (thousands)	200.1	210.5	207.8	213.1	221.6	234.1	238.7*p*	245.8*p*
	Revenues ($ million)	-	-	18,239.9	-	-	-	-	-

Source: Economic Census of the United States, 1992, annual surveys of economic sectors conducted by the Bureau of the Census, and estimates or projections based on the 1982-1992 period; not all data are shown. 'e' marks estimates made by the editors; 'p' indicates projections based on time series. A dash (-) indicates that data for this SIC or year were not available. The abbreviation (pt) next to the industry name indicates that only a part of the industry is present within the NAICS data. If no (pt) is shown, the entire industry is contained within the NAICS data.

SELECTED RATIOS

For 1997	Avg. of Information	Analyzed Industry	Index	For 1997	Avg. of Information	Analyzed Industry	Index
Employees per establishment	6	10	162	Payroll per establishment	126,069	288,030	228
Revenue per establishment	511,622	3,669,886	717	Payroll as % of revenue	25	8	32
Revenue per employee	81,659	362,277	444	Payroll per employee	20,122	28,433	141

Sources: Same as General Statistics. The 'Average' column represents the average for the industry sector, in 1997, where the currently shown industry is classified. The Index shows the relationship between the Average and the Analyzed Industry. For example, 100 means that they are equal; 500 that the Analyzed Industry is five times the average; 50 means that the Analyzed Industry is half the national average. The abbreviation 'na' is used to show that data are 'not available'.

LEADING COMPANIES

No company data available for this industry.

LOCATION BY STATE AND REGIONAL CONCENTRATION

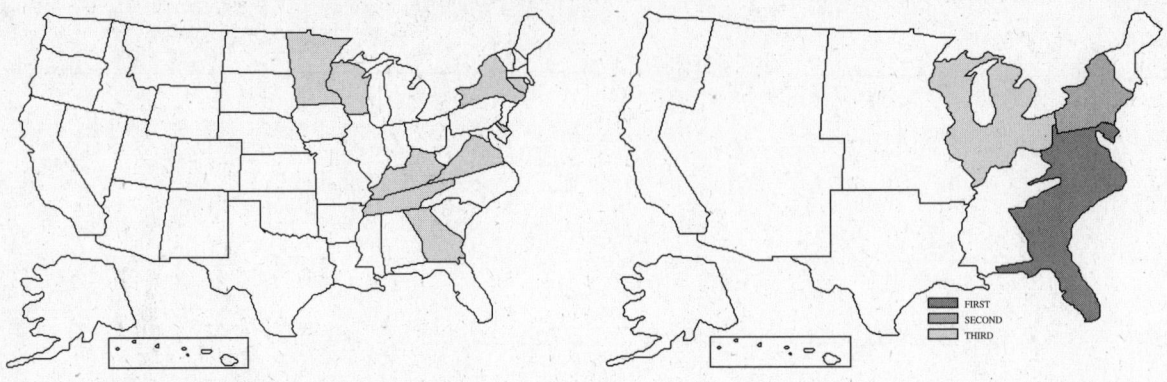

FIRST
SECOND
THIRD

INDUSTRY DATA BY STATE

State	Establishments Total (number)	% of U.S.	Employment Total (number)	% of U.S.	Per Estab.	Payroll Total ($ mil.)	Per Empl. ($)	Revenues Total ($ mil.)	% of U.S.	Per Estab. ($)
New York	264	9.1	3,816	13.0	14	135.3	35,445	1,854.3	17.4	7,023,939
California	225	7.8	2,805	9.6	12	83.8	29,861	836.6	7.9	3,718,427
D.C.	57	2.0	967	3.3	17	41.2	42,580	813.2	7.6	14,266,246
Virginia	78	2.7	1,141	3.9	15	36.6	32,070	628.7	5.9	8,060,500
Georgia	69	2.4	850	2.9	12	29.9	35,202	599.3	5.6	8,684,899
Florida	119	4.1	1,240	4.2	10	35.6	28,745	433.8	4.1	3,645,042
Ohio	138	4.8	1,341	4.6	10	36.6	27,320	433.0	4.1	3,137,783
Illinois	131	4.5	1,152	3.9	9	35.5	30,824	422.2	4.0	3,222,908
Wisconsin	64	2.2	666	2.3	10	16.3	24,405	341.6	3.2	5,337,406
Texas	158	5.5	1,180	4.0	7	28.3	23,968	312.2	2.9	1,975,791
Connecticut	45	1.6	544	1.9	12	16.1	29,559	302.5	2.8	6,722,911
Pennsylvania	137	4.7	1,089	3.7	8	32.4	29,729	301.9	2.8	2,203,526
Tennessee	62	2.1	651	2.2	10	16.7	25,682	253.8	2.4	4,093,871
Minnesota	107	3.7	894	3.0	8	22.1	24,711	241.2	2.3	2,254,262
Massachusetts	92	3.2	906	3.1	10	27.9	30,784	238.5	2.2	2,592,011
Michigan	89	3.1	916	3.1	10	25.4	27,730	230.1	2.2	2,585,124
Maryland	54	1.9	766	2.6	14	25.4	33,154	200.0	1.9	3,703,704
New Jersey	71	2.4	1,881	6.4	26	29.4	15,638	181.3	1.7	2,553,000
Indiana	98	3.4	745	2.5	8	16.3	21,903	177.7	1.7	1,813,398
Kentucky	42	1.4	360	1.2	9	9.4	26,086	156.6	1.5	3,729,524
North Carolina	98	3.4	607	2.1	6	16.3	26,778	150.4	1.4	1,534,806
Missouri	50	1.7	441	1.5	9	12.0	27,311	148.6	1.4	2,972,300
Washington	53	1.8	365	1.2	7	10.9	29,792	117.2	1.1	2,211,415
Oregon	41	1.4	223	0.8	5	5.4	24,291	109.9	1.0	2,680,829
Oklahoma	51	1.8	392	1.3	8	7.5	19,224	107.5	1.0	2,107,490
Arizona	19	0.7	198	0.7	10	5.1	25,894	65.6	0.6	3,451,105
Alabama	33	1.1	200	0.7	6	5.3	26,430	61.5	0.6	1,863,455
South Carolina	40	1.4	320	1.1	8	7.2	22,400	61.0	0.6	1,524,775
Kansas	37	1.3	209	0.7	6	4.3	20,560	56.9	0.5	1,537,378
Louisiana	30	1.0	218	0.7	7	5.6	25,670	56.8	0.5	1,894,033
Colorado	27	0.9	257	0.9	10	6.9	26,992	53.0	0.5	1,964,593
Iowa	29	1.0	182	0.6	6	4.7	25,923	36.9	0.3	1,272,724
Nebraska	17	0.6	163	0.6	10	3.1	19,288	32.1	0.3	1,887,235
Montana	18	0.6	79	0.3	4	1.8	22,671	29.1	0.3	1,616,111
Delaware	9	0.3	165	0.6	18	3.1	18,576	27.9	0.3	3,097,111
West Virginia	19	0.7	62	0.2	3	1.4	22,113	25.6	0.2	1,345,526
Utah	12	0.4	97	0.3	8	2.3	23,268	24.6	0.2	2,049,500
Maine	25	0.9	117	0.4	5	2.7	23,496	21.5	0.2	858,200
Hawaii	9	0.3	64	0.2	7	2.1	33,328	20.6	0.2	2,288,889
Mississippi	26	0.9	119	0.4	5	2.0	17,202	18.6	0.2	715,846
New Mexico	21	0.7	79	0.3	4	2.2	27,937	17.6	0.2	836,905
North Dakota	17	0.6	100	0.3	6	1.8	17,810	17.6	0.2	1,033,353
New Hampshire	18	0.6	77	0.3	4	2.0	25,974	16.8	0.2	936,000
Arkansas	24	0.8	85	0.3	4	1.9	21,894	16.3	0.2	679,458
Nevada	8	0.3	67	0.2	8	1.9	28,567	14.1	0.1	1,760,375
Vermont	10	0.3	30	0.1	3	0.8	25,533	6.4	0.1	641,900
Alaska	13	0.4	175*	-	-	(D)	-	(D)	-	-
Idaho	13	0.4	60*	-	-	(D)	-	(D)	-	-
South Dakota	13	0.4	60*	-	-	(D)	-	(D)	-	-
Rhode Island	12	0.4	175*	-	-	(D)	-	(D)	-	-
Wyoming	7	0.2	10*	-	-	(D)	-	(D)	-	-

Source: 1997 *Economic Census*. The states are in descending order of revenues or establishments (if revenue data are missing for the majority). The symbol (D) appears when data are withheld to prevent disclosure of competitive information. States marked with (D) are sorted by number of establishments. A dash (-) indicates that the data element cannot be calculated. * indicates the midpoint of a range; 175, for example is the range 100-249. Shaded *states* on the state map indicate those states which have proportionately greater representation in the industry than would be indicated by the state's population; the ratio is based on total revenues or number of establishments. Shaded *regions* indicate where the industry is regionally most concentrated.

NAICS 813311 - HUMAN RIGHTS ORGANIZATIONS

GENERAL STATISTICS

Year	Establishments (number)	Employment (number)	Payroll ($ million)	Revenues ($ million)	Employees per Establishment (number)	Revenues per Establishment ($)	Payroll per Employee ($)
1997	1,806	18,109	475.0	2,094.0	10.0	1,159,468	26,230

Source: *Economic Census of the United States*, 1997. This is a newly defined industry. Data for prior years were unavailable at the time of publication but may become available over time.

INDICES OF CHANGE

Year	Establishments (number)	Employment (number)	Payroll ($ million)	Revenues ($ million)	Employees per Establishment (number)	Revenues per Establishment ($)	Payroll per Employee ($)
1997	100.0	100.0	100.0	100.0	100.0	100.0	100.0

Sources: Same as General Statistics. The values shown reflect change from the base year, 1997. Values above 100 mean greater than 1997, values below 100 mean less than 1997, and a value of 100 in the 1982-96 or 1998-2001 period means same as 1997. Values followed by a 'p' are projections by the editors; 'e' stands for extrapolation. Data are the most recent available at this level of detail.

SIC INDUSTRIES RELATED TO NAICS 813311

Each new NAICS code represents an industry that used to be part of an SIC or a part of several SIC industries. Data in this table are shown to provide transitional information for these cases. All available data for the precursor SIC(s) are shown. Even if only a part of an SIC is included in the NAICS, *all* data for the SIC are reproduced. If the SIC industry is not marked as being a part (pt) of the NAICS, the entire industry is embedded in the NAICS data. The SIC composition of the new industry provides some hints of the relative importance of its "ancestors." Data marked with a 'p' are projected. Projections begin with 1982 data. Data earlier than 1990 are not shown but are reflected in the projections.

SIC	Industry	1990	1991	1992	1993	1994	1995	1996	1997
8399	**Social Services, nec (pt)**								
	Establishments (number)	13,710	14,734	17,416	17,485	17,425	17,456	18,826p	19,537p
	Employment (thousands)	200.1	210.5	207.8	213.1	221.6	234.1	238.7p	245.8p
	Revenues ($ million)	-	-	18,239.9	-	-	-	-	-

Source: *Economic Census of the United States*, 1992, annual surveys of economic sectors conducted by the Bureau of the Census, and estimates or projections based on the 1982-1992 period; not all data are shown. 'e' marks estimates made by the editors; 'p' indicates projections based on time series. A dash (-) indicates that data for this SIC or year were not available. The abbreviation (pt) next to the industry name indicates that only a part of the industry is present within the NAICS data. If no (pt) is shown, the entire industry is contained within the NAICS data.

SELECTED RATIOS

For 1997	Avg. of Information	Analyzed Industry	Index	For 1997	Avg. of Information	Analyzed Industry	Index
Employees per establishment	6	10	160	Payroll per establishment	126,069	263,012	209
Revenue per establishment	511,622	1,159,468	227	Payroll as % of revenue	25	23	92
Revenue per employee	81,659	115,633	142	Payroll per employee	20,122	26,230	130

Sources: Same as General Statistics. The 'Average' column represents the average for the industry sector, in 1997, where the currently shown industry is classified. The Index shows the relationship between the Average and the Analyzed Industry. For example, 100 means that they are equal; 500 that the Analyzed Industry is five times the average; 50 means that the Analyzed Industry is half the national average. The abbreviation 'na' is used to show that data are 'not available'.

LEADING COMPANIES
No company data available for this industry.

REPRESENTATIVE NONPROFIT ORGANIZATIONS

Organization Name	Address				Phone	Income Range ($ mil)
Alaska Federation of Natives	1577 C St Ste 300	Anchorage	AK	99501	907-274-3611	1-5
American Religious Town Hall Meeting	745 N Buckner Blvd	Dallas	TX	75218	214-328-9828	10-19
Bay Area Legal Services Inc	9270 Bay Plaza Blvd	Tampa	FL	33619		1-5
Boston Bar Foundation Inc	16 Beaco St	Boston	MA	02108	617-742-0615	1-5
Capital Area Legal Services Corp	PO Box 3273	Baton Rouge	LA	70821		1-5
Christian Advocates Serving Evangelism Inc	4500 Hugh Howell Rd	Tucker	GA	30084		20-29
Community Housing Services	1040 N Lincoln Ave 200	Pasadena	CA	91103	626-795-7990	20-29
Community Legal Aid Society Inc	913 Washington St	Wilmington	DE	19801	302-575-0660	1-5
Defender Association	810 Third Ave Ste 800	Seattle	WA	98104	206-623-4321	5-9
Domestic Abuse Services Inc 79 Main St	PO Box 805	Newton	NJ	07860		1-5
Federally Employed Womens Legal and Education Fund Inc	3221 Hickory Stick Rd	Oklahoma City	OK	73120		1-5
Greater Phila Urban Affairs Coalition	1207 Chestnut St 7th Flr	Philadelphia	PA	19107		10-19
Housing Opportunity Corporation	1910 Exeter Ste 100	Germantown	TN	38138		1-5
Indianapolis Urban League Inc	850 N Meridian St	Indianapolis	IN	46204	317-639-9404	1-5
Legal Aid Society Inc	500 S 18th St	Omaha	NE	68102	402-348-1060	1-5
Legal Aid Society of Cleveland	1223 W 6 St	Cleveland	OH	44113	216-687-1900	5-9
Legal Aid Society of Hawaii	924 Bethel St	Honolulu	HI	96813	808-536-4302	1-5
Legal Aid Society of Louisville Inc	425 W M Ali Blvd	Louisville	KY	40202	502-584-1254	1-5
Legal Aid Society	90 Church St 14th Flr	New York	NY	10007	212-577-3300	50+
Legal Aid and Defender Assoc of Detroit	645 Griswold Suite 3466	Detroit	MI	48226	313-964-4111	5-9
Legal Assistance Foundation of Chicago	111 W Jackson Blvd	Chicago	IL	60604	312-362-1982	5-9
Marshall Fund	3295 N Civic Center Blvd	Scottsdale	AZ	85251	480-941-5249	1-5
Metropolitan Public Defender Service Inc	630 SW 5th	Portland	OR	97204	503-225-9100	5-9
National Association for the Advancement of Colored People	4805 Mt Hope Dr	Baltimore	MD	21215		10-19
National Council of Negro Women Inc	633 Pennsylvania Ave NW	Washington	DC	20004	202-737-0120	10-19
National Right to Work Committee Inc	8001 Braddock Rd Ste 500	Springfield	VA	22151	703-321-9820	10-19
Native American Rights Fund	1506 Broadway	Boulder	CO	80302	303-447-8760	5-9
New Hampshire Coalition Against Domestic & Sexual Violence	PO Box 353	Concord	NH	03302		1-5
New Haven Legal Assistance Association Inc	426 State St	New Haven	CT	06510		1-5
Pacer Center Inc	4826 Chicago Ave S	Minneapolis	MN	55417	612-827-2966	5-9
Pine Tree Legal Assistance Inc	PO Box 547 DTS	Portland	ME	04112		1-5
Sertoma International	1912 E Meyer Blvd	Kansas City	MO	64132	816-333-8300	1-5
Task Force on Battered Women and Children Inc	634 W Mitchell St	Milwaukee	WI	53204	414-643-1911	1-5
Urban League of Central Carolinas Inc	PO Box 34686	Charlotte	NC	28234		1-5
Vermont Legal Aid Inc	PO Box 1367	Burlington	VT	05402	802-863-5620	1-5
Wateree Community Actions Inc	13 S Main St	Sumter	SC	29150	803-435-2303	5-9

Source: National Directory of Nonprofit Organizations, 2000, Volumes 1 and 2, The Taft Group. The table shows a selection of organizations for illustration and does not constitute a complete selection from the source. The organizations are arranged in alphabetical order.

LOCATION BY STATE AND REGIONAL CONCENTRATION

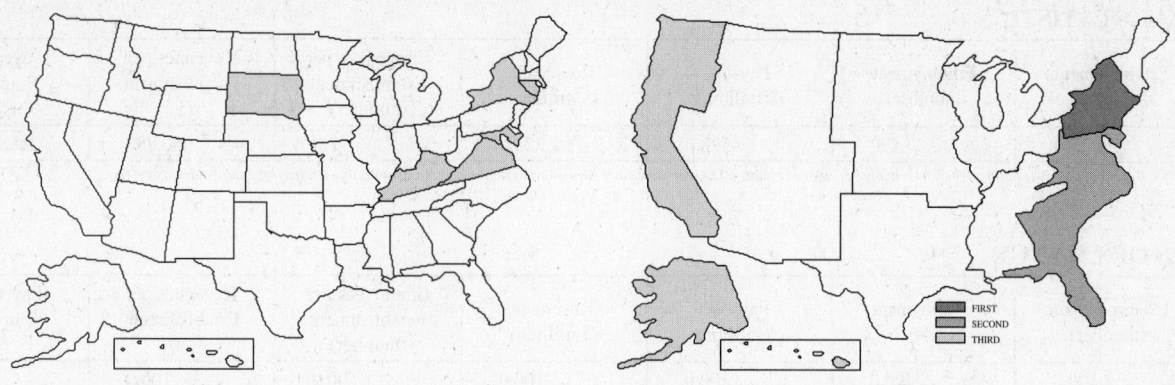

INDUSTRY DATA BY STATE

State	Establishments Total (number)	Establishments % of U.S.	Employment Total (number)	Employment % of U.S.	Employment Per Estab.	Payroll Total ($ mil.)	Payroll Per Empl. ($)	Revenues Total ($ mil.)	Revenues % of U.S.	Revenues Per Estab. ($)
New York	148	8.2	1,737	9.6	12	58.4	33,595	553.6	26.4	3,740,365
D.C.	113	6.3	2,216	12.2	20	99.1	44,699	451.8	21.6	3,998,389
California	196	10.9	1,706	9.4	9	43.5	25,512	153.3	7.3	782,061
Connecticut	22	1.2	559	3.1	25	15.9	28,488	100.3	4.8	4,559,045
Pennsylvania	81	4.5	1,046	5.8	13	25.1	24,021	89.9	4.3	1,109,630
Texas	79	4.4	1,051	5.8	13	21.4	20,315	63.9	3.0	808,380
Illinois	76	4.2	801	4.4	11	21.5	26,891	63.6	3.0	836,671
Virginia	48	2.7	795	4.4	17	15.6	19,631	60.8	2.9	1,265,854
Michigan	76	4.2	946	5.2	12	20.6	21,803	59.5	2.8	782,763
Kentucky	31	1.7	368	2.0	12	10.9	29,592	59.2	2.8	1,910,032
Maryland	28	1.6	462	2.6	16	11.6	25,024	45.8	2.2	1,636,000
Massachusetts	51	2.8	333	1.8	7	9.6	28,901	37.9	1.8	742,706
Georgia	52	2.9	462	2.6	9	9.8	21,132	33.0	1.6	633,923
Washington	30	1.7	329	1.8	11	8.3	25,356	28.6	1.4	954,467
Ohio	86	4.8	429	2.4	5	9.9	23,061	26.2	1.3	304,663
Florida	56	3.1	399	2.2	7	8.4	20,945	24.5	1.2	438,375
Wisconsin	42	2.3	447	2.5	11	8.6	19,304	21.3	1.0	506,667
North Carolina	39	2.2	223	1.2	6	5.3	23,717	18.2	0.9	467,795
Indiana	23	1.3	168	0.9	7	3.8	22,655	13.7	0.7	593,913
Louisiana	26	1.4	254	1.4	10	3.6	14,323	13.5	0.6	518,808
New Jersey	31	1.7	243	1.3	8	4.9	20,259	13.3	0.6	429,194
New Mexico	18	1.0	241	1.3	13	4.4	18,444	12.9	0.6	716,444
Missouri	37	2.0	226	1.2	6	3.8	16,876	12.7	0.6	342,946
Tennessee	33	1.8	184	1.0	6	4.5	24,723	12.5	0.6	377,818
Oregon	29	1.6	188	1.0	6	3.4	18,261	11.1	0.5	383,862
Minnesota	33	1.8	268	1.5	8	4.4	16,235	10.6	0.5	321,273
South Dakota	11	0.6	390	2.2	35	5.5	14,085	9.4	0.5	858,182
Colorado	34	1.9	110	0.6	3	2.8	25,827	8.3	0.4	245,294
Alabama	29	1.6	118	0.7	4	2.4	20,229	7.7	0.4	267,207
Kansas	20	1.1	199	1.1	10	3.3	16,417	7.4	0.4	372,350
South Carolina	18	1.0	124	0.7	7	2.2	17,444	6.6	0.3	369,056
Utah	12	0.7	40	0.2	3	0.8	19,925	5.7	0.3	472,583
Mississippi	16	0.9	89	0.5	6	1.6	18,236	5.2	0.2	323,188
Arizona	18	1.0	66	0.4	4	1.9	28,227	5.0	0.2	277,444
Iowa	17	0.9	118	0.7	7	2.0	16,653	4.7	0.2	276,176
Nebraska	7	0.4	91	0.5	13	2.1	22,846	4.4	0.2	626,571
Arkansas	13	0.7	63	0.3	5	1.5	23,635	4.1	0.2	313,923
Oklahoma	18	1.0	83	0.5	5	1.6	19,807	4.0	0.2	223,111
New Hampshire	9	0.5	51	0.3	6	1.4	27,196	3.2	0.2	360,667
North Dakota	10	0.6	57	0.3	6	0.9	15,228	2.5	0.1	250,200
Idaho	11	0.6	46	0.3	4	1.0	22,435	2.5	0.1	227,000
Rhode Island	10	0.6	43	0.2	4	1.0	23,116	2.2	0.1	216,000
Vermont	8	0.4	58	0.3	7	0.9	15,379	2.1	0.1	267,250
West Virginia	6	0.3	54	0.3	9	1.0	18,444	2.0	0.1	333,333
Delaware	10	0.6	48	0.3	5	0.9	19,333	1.8	0.1	184,000
Hawaii	7	0.4	20	0.1	3	0.5	24,200	1.8	0.1	254,857
Alaska	9	0.5	25	0.1	3	0.8	32,680	1.7	0.1	191,778
Montana	13	0.7	41	0.2	3	0.8	18,878	1.6	0.1	122,692
Nevada	4	0.2	6	0.0	2	0.2	32,167	0.8	0.0	196,750
Maine	8	0.4	60*	-	-	(D)	-	(D)	-	-
Wyoming	4	0.2	60*	-	-	(D)	-	(D)	-	-

Source: 1997 *Economic Census*. The states are in descending order of revenues or establishments (if revenue data are missing for the majority). The symbol (D) appears when data are withheld to prevent disclosure of competitive information. States marked with (D) are sorted by number of establishments. A dash (-) indicates that the data element cannot be calculated. * indicates the midpoint of a range; 175, for example is the range 100-249. Shaded *states* on the state map indicate those states which have proportionately greater representation in the industry than would be indicated by the state's population; the ratio is based on total revenues or number of establishments. Shaded *regions* indicate where the industry is regionally most concentrated.

NAICS 813312 - ENVIRONMENT, CONSERVATION, AND WILDLIFE ORGANIZATIONS

GENERAL STATISTICS

Year	Establishments (number)	Employment (number)	Payroll ($ million)	Revenues ($ million)	Employees per Establishment (number)	Revenues per Establishment ($)	Payroll per Employee ($)
1997	3,569	27,899	578.0	2,323.0	7.8	650,883	20,718

Source: Economic Census of the United States, 1997. This is a newly defined industry. Data for prior years were unavailable at the time of publication but may become available over time.

INDICES OF CHANGE

Year	Establishments (number)	Employment (number)	Payroll ($ million)	Revenues ($ million)	Employees per Establishment (number)	Revenues per Establishment ($)	Payroll per Employee ($)
1997	100.0	100.0	100.0	100.0	100.0	100.0	100.0

Sources: Same as General Statistics. The values shown reflect change from the base year, 1997. Values above 100 mean greater than 1997, values below 100 mean less than 1997, and a value of 100 in the 1982-96 or 1998-2001 period means same as 1997. Values followed by a 'p' are projections by the editors; 'e' stands for extrapolation. Data are the most recent available at this level of detail.

SIC INDUSTRIES RELATED TO NAICS 813312

Each new NAICS code represents an industry that used to be part of an SIC or a part of several SIC industries. Data in this table are shown to provide transitional information for these cases. All available data for the precursor SIC(s) are shown. Even if only a part of an SIC is included in the NAICS, *all* data for the SIC are reproduced. If the SIC industry is not marked as being a part (pt) of the NAICS, the entire industry is embedded in the NAICS data. The SIC composition of the new industry provides some hints of the relative importance of its "ancestors." Data marked with a 'p' are projected. Projections begin with 1982 data. Data earlier than 1990 are not shown but are reflected in the projections.

SIC	Industry	1990	1991	1992	1993	1994	1995	1996	1997
8399	**Social Services, nec (pt)**								
	Establishments (number)	13,710	14,734	17,416	17,485	17,425	17,456	18,826p	19,537p
	Employment (thousands)	200.1	210.5	207.8	213.1	221.6	234.1	238.7p	245.8p
	Revenues ($ million)	-	-	18,239.9	-	-	-	-	-
8699	**Membership Organizations, nec (pt)**								
	Establishments (number)	9,670	10,125	10,596	10,695	10,666	10,760	11,062p	11,247p
	Employment (thousands)	87.7	91.9	91.4	95.7	96.0	101.7	103.3p	105.9p
	Revenues ($ million)	-	-	6,267.8	-	-	-	-	-

Source: Economic Census of the United States, 1992, annual surveys of economic sectors conducted by the Bureau of the Census, and estimates or projections based on the 1982-1992 period; not all data are shown. 'e' marks estimates made by the editors; 'p' indicates projections based on time series. A dash (-) indicates that data for this SIC or year were not available. The abbreviation (pt) next to the industry name indicates that only a part of the industry is present within the NAICS data. If no (pt) is shown, the entire industry is contained within the NAICS data.

SELECTED RATIOS

For 1997	Avg. of Information	Analyzed Industry	Index	For 1997	Avg. of Information	Analyzed Industry	Index
Employees per establishment	6	8	125	Payroll per establishment	126,069	161,950	128
Revenue per establishment	511,622	650,883	127	Payroll as % of revenue	25	25	101
Revenue per employee	81,659	83,265	102	Payroll per employee	20,122	20,718	103

Sources: Same as General Statistics. The 'Average' column represents the average for the industry sector, in 1997, where the currently shown industry is classified. The Index shows the relationship between the Average and the Analyzed Industry. For example, 100 means that they are equal; 500 that the Analyzed Industry is five times the average; 50 means that the Analyzed Industry is half the national average. The abbreviation 'na' is used to show that data are 'not available'.

LEADING COMPANIES

No company data available for this industry.

REPRESENTATIVE NONPROFIT ORGANIZATIONS

Organization Name	Address				Phone	Income Range ($ mil)
Billfish Foundation Inc	2419 E Commercial Blvd	Ft Lauderdale	FL	33308	954-938-0150	1-5
Broadbent Family Foundation Inc	PO Box 1019	Livingston	MT	59047		1-5
Eco-Cycle Inc	PO Box 19006	Boulder	CO	80308		1-5
Environmental Law & Policy Center of the Midwest	35 E Wacker Dr Ste 1300	Chicago	IL	60601	312-782-6587	1-5
Garbage Reincarnation Inc	PO Box 1375	Santa Rosa	CA	95402		1-5
Global Climate Coalition	1275 K St NW Ste 890	Washington	DC	20005		1-5
International Wildlife Coalition Inc	PO Box 200	S Yarmouth	MA	02664	508-548-8328	1-5
National Energy Foundation Inc	3676 W California Ave	Salt Lake Cty	UT	84104	801-539-1406	1-5
The Conservation Fund a Nonprofit Corporation	1800 N Kent St 1120	Arlington	VA	22209		40-49

Source: *National Directory of Nonprofit Organizations*, 2000, Volumes 1 and 2, The Taft Group. The table shows a selection of organizations for illustration and does not constitute a complete selection from the source. The organizations are arranged in alphabetical order.

LOCATION BY STATE AND REGIONAL CONCENTRATION

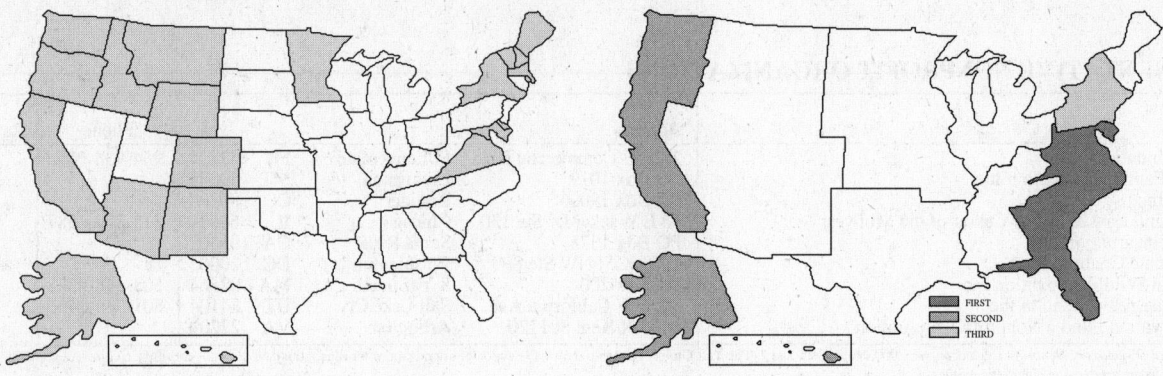

INDUSTRY DATA BY STATE

State	Establishments Total (number)	% of U.S.	Employment Total (number)	% of U.S.	Per Estab.	Payroll Total ($ mil.)	Per Empl. ($)	Revenues Total ($ mil.)	% of U.S.	Per Estab. ($)
California	424	11.9	3,835	13.7	9	82.8	21,602	350.6	15.1	826,901
D.C.	83	2.3	1,738	6.2	21	58.0	33,359	315.6	13.6	3,801,867
New York	230	6.4	2,072	7.4	9	48.9	23,602	185.2	8.0	805,143
Massachusetts	145	4.1	1,293	4.6	9	31.5	24,349	112.0	4.8	772,352
Virginia	100	2.8	968	3.5	10	30.0	30,970	102.2	4.4	1,021,860
Maryland	83	2.3	792	2.8	10	20.7	26,092	88.6	3.8	1,067,831
Arizona	66	1.8	498	1.8	8	9.5	19,161	87.4	3.8	1,324,000
Florida	156	4.4	1,251	4.5	8	21.6	17,283	77.1	3.3	494,224
Pennsylvania	142	4.0	1,313	4.7	9	23.1	17,586	72.8	3.1	512,338
Texas	165	4.6	1,153	4.1	7	18.2	15,814	68.5	2.9	414,945
Minnesota	99	2.8	804	2.9	8	14.4	17,966	61.1	2.6	617,010
Michigan	96	2.7	728	2.6	8	13.8	18,924	56.6	2.4	589,344
Washington	116	3.3	769	2.8	7	16.4	21,388	48.7	2.1	419,690
Colorado	74	2.1	680	2.4	9	15.0	22,015	47.4	2.0	640,892
Illinois	107	3.0	784	2.8	7	14.1	17,972	45.4	2.0	424,299
Ohio	122	3.4	992	3.6	8	14.4	14,478	44.8	1.9	367,582
Oregon	80	2.2	529	1.9	7	12.2	23,117	43.1	1.9	539,263
New Jersey	77	2.2	594	2.1	8	10.6	17,907	39.6	1.7	514,364
Wisconsin	92	2.6	631	2.3	7	9.8	15,571	31.1	1.3	337,630
North Carolina	87	2.4	390	1.4	4	6.2	15,846	30.5	1.3	350,667
Georgia	71	2.0	360	1.3	5	7.1	19,656	28.4	1.2	399,704
Connecticut	40	1.1	236	0.8	6	5.4	22,987	27.7	1.2	693,275
Missouri	52	1.5	445	1.6	9	7.6	17,180	27.3	1.2	524,788
Maine	55	1.5	293	1.1	5	5.6	19,259	26.3	1.1	477,855
Indiana	67	1.9	388	1.4	6	5.3	13,559	23.9	1.0	356,836
South Carolina	45	1.3	354	1.3	8	5.4	15,234	20.4	0.9	453,911
New Hampshire	37	1.0	302	1.1	8	5.9	19,566	20.0	0.9	539,892
Hawaii	21	0.6	210	0.8	10	4.7	22,381	18.5	0.8	879,429
New Mexico	42	1.2	247	0.9	6	4.8	19,275	15.3	0.7	364,310
Iowa	35	1.0	247	0.9	7	3.6	14,575	15.1	0.7	431,886
Montana	57	1.6	264	0.9	5	4.2	16,061	14.5	0.6	254,491
Rhode Island	25	0.7	193	0.7	8	3.4	17,456	14.2	0.6	568,480
Idaho	25	0.7	158	0.6	6	3.7	23,620	14.1	0.6	565,800
Nebraska	26	0.7	167	0.6	6	3.3	19,623	13.6	0.6	522,346
Alaska	36	1.0	157	0.6	4	4.2	26,675	12.7	0.5	354,000
Tennessee	51	1.4	270	1.0	5	4.1	15,133	12.7	0.5	249,275
Vermont	36	1.0	154	0.6	4	4.0	25,851	12.3	0.5	342,139
Wyoming	20	0.6	84	0.3	4	1.5	18,333	12.3	0.5	613,100
Kentucky	37	1.0	202	0.7	5	3.3	16,099	9.5	0.4	257,216
Utah	18	0.5	115	0.4	6	1.6	13,991	9.1	0.4	508,167
Alabama	41	1.1	209	0.7	5	3.2	15,134	8.9	0.4	216,585
Louisiana	20	0.6	148	0.5	7	2.5	16,635	8.1	0.3	405,700
Oklahoma	24	0.7	106	0.4	4	1.8	16,547	7.1	0.3	294,833
West Virginia	24	0.7	110	0.4	5	1.7	15,009	6.7	0.3	278,958
Delaware	13	0.4	97	0.3	7	1.7	17,062	6.6	0.3	505,538
Kansas	30	0.8	165	0.6	6	2.2	13,236	6.5	0.3	217,767
Mississippi	19	0.5	81	0.3	4	1.2	15,259	6.1	0.3	322,211
Arkansas	21	0.6	86	0.3	4	1.3	15,256	5.3	0.2	252,714
Nevada	11	0.3	62	0.2	6	1.2	20,145	4.9	0.2	444,455
North Dakota	12	0.3	116	0.4	10	1.0	8,353	3.5	0.2	294,917
South Dakota	14	0.4	59	0.2	4	0.7	12,644	2.8	0.1	197,714

Source: 1997 *Economic Census.* The states are in descending order of revenues or establishments (if revenue data are missing for the majority). The symbol (D) appears when data are withheld to prevent disclosure of competitive information. States marked with (D) are sorted by number of establishments. A dash (-) indicates that the data element cannot be calculated. * indicates the midpoint of a range; 175, for example is the range 100-249. Shaded *states* on the state map indicate those states which have proportionately greater representation in the industry than would be indicated by the state's population; the ratio is based on total revenues or number of establishments. Shaded *regions* indicate where the industry is regionally most concentrated.

NAICS 813319 - SOCIAL ADVOCACY ORGANIZATIONS NEC

GENERAL STATISTICS

Year	Establishments (number)	Employment (number)	Payroll ($ million)	Revenues ($ million)	Employees per Establishment (number)	Revenues per Establishment ($)	Payroll per Employee ($)
1997	4,745	39,033	950.0	3,108.0	8.2	655,005	24,338

Source: *Economic Census of the United States*, 1997. This is a newly defined industry. Data for prior years were unavailable at the time of publication but may become available over time.

INDICES OF CHANGE

Year	Establishments (number)	Employment (number)	Payroll ($ million)	Revenues ($ million)	Employees per Establishment (number)	Revenues per Establishment ($)	Payroll per Employee ($)
1997	100.0	100.0	100.0	100.0	100.0	100.0	100.0

Sources: Same as General Statistics. The values shown reflect change from the base year, 1997. Values above 100 mean greater than 1997, values below 100 mean less than 1997, and a value of 100 in the 1982-96 or 1998-2001 period means same as 1997. Values followed by a 'p' are projections by the editors; 'e' stands for extrapolation. Data are the most recent available at this level of detail.

SIC INDUSTRIES RELATED TO NAICS 813319

Each new NAICS code represents an industry that used to be part of an SIC or a part of several SIC industries. Data in this table are shown to provide transitional information for these cases. All available data for the precursor SIC(s) are shown. Even if only a part of an SIC is included in the NAICS, *all* data for the SIC are reproduced. If the SIC industry is not marked as being a part (pt) of the NAICS, the entire industry is embedded in the NAICS data. The SIC composition of the new industry provides some hints of the relative importance of its "ancestors." Data marked with a 'p' are projected. Projections begin with 1982 data. Data earlier than 1990 are not shown but are reflected in the projections.

SIC	Industry	1990	1991	1992	1993	1994	1995	1996	1997
8399	**Social Services, nec (pt)**								
	Establishments (number)	13,710	14,734	17,416	17,485	17,425	17,456	18,826p	19,537p
	Employment (thousands)	200.1	210.5	207.8	213.1	221.6	234.1	238.7p	245.8p
	Revenues ($ million)	-	-	18,239.9	-	-	-	-	-
8641	**Civic & Social Associations (pt)**								
	Establishments (number)	39,999	43,422	41,789	41,942	41,940	41,764	43,156p	43,570p
	Employment (thousands)	365.8	384.6	355.1	369.5	374.9	386.1	395.4p	402.8p
	Revenues ($ million)	-	-	13,176.1	-	-	-	-	-

Source: *Economic Census of the United States*, 1992, annual surveys of economic sectors conducted by the Bureau of the Census, and estimates or projections based on the 1982-1992 period; not all data are shown. 'e' marks estimates made by the editors; 'p' indicates projections based on time series. A dash (-) indicates that data for this SIC or year were not available. The abbreviation (pt) next to the industry name indicates that only a part of the industry is present within the NAICS data. If no (pt) is shown, the entire industry is contained within the NAICS data.

SELECTED RATIOS

For 1997	Avg. of Information	Analyzed Industry	Index	For 1997	Avg. of Information	Analyzed Industry	Index
Employees per establishment	6	8	131	Payroll per establishment	126,069	200,211	159
Revenue per establishment	511,622	655,005	128	Payroll as % of revenue	25	31	124
Revenue per employee	81,659	79,625	98	Payroll per employee	20,122	24,338	121

Sources: Same as General Statistics. The 'Average' column represents the average for the industry sector, in 1997, where the currently shown industry is classified. The Index shows the relationship between the Average and the Analyzed Industry. For example, 100 means that they are equal; 500 that the Analyzed Industry is five times the average; 50 means that the Analyzed Industry is half the national average. The abbreviation 'na' is used to show that data are 'not available'.

LEADING COMPANIES   Number shown: **6**   Total sales ($ mil): **594**   Total employment (000): **6.4**

Company Name	Address				CEO Name	Phone	Co. Type	Sales ($ mil)	Empl. (000)
Baystate Health Systems Inc.	759 Chestnut St	Springfield	MA	01199	Michael J. Daly	413-794-0000	R	519	6.0
PVA-EPVA Inc.	19 Stoney Brook Dr	Wilton	NH	03086	Eric Johnston	603-654-6141	R	33*	0.3
CoMed Communications Inc.	210 W Wash Sq	Philadelphia	PA	19106	Brian Russell	215-592-1363	S	28	0.1
Millennium Health Inc.	P O Box 306	Pinole	CA	94564	Michael Ping	408-562-9222	R	14	<0.1
Behavioral Health Systems Inc.	31 W Carson Rd	Phoenix	AZ	85041		602-268-8404	N	1	<0.1
Thomas Groninger Associates	228 N 3rd St	Lewisburg	PA	17837		717-523-9788	N	0	<0.1

Source: Ward's Business Directory of U.S. Private and Public Companies, Volumes 1 and 2, 2000. The company type code used is as follows: P - Public, R - Private, S - Subsidiary, D - Division, J - Joint Venture, A - Affiliate, G - Group, N - Company type not reported. Sales are in millions of dollars, employees are in thousands. An asterisk (*) indicates an estimated sales volume. The symbol < stands for 'less than'. Company names and addresses are truncated, in some cases, to fit into the available space.

REPRESENTATIVE NONPROFIT ORGANIZATIONS

Organization Name	Address				Phone	Income Range ($ mil)
Acorn Housing Corporation of Illinois Inc	1024 Elysian Fields Ave	New Orleans	LA	70117	504-943-0044	1-5
Action Youth Care	PO Box 510	Ripley	WV	25271	304-372-6310	5-9
Agricultural & Labor Program Inc	PO Box 3126	Winter Haven	FL	33885	941-956-3491	10-19
American Youth Soccer Organization	12501 S Isis Ave	Hawthorne	CA	90250	310-643-6455	50+
Atlanta Community Food Bank Inc	970 Jefferson St NW	Atlanta	GA	30318	404-892-9822	20-29
Barberton Community Foundation	104 Third St NW	Barberton	OH	44203	330-745-3070	50+
Big Brothers Big Sisters of Spokane County	W 222 Mission Suite 210	Spokane	WA	99201	509-328-8310	5-9
Billings Food Bank Inc	PO Box 1158	Billings	MT	59103	406-259-2856	1-5
Bloomington Fire Dept Relief Assoc	10 W 95th St	Bloomington	MN	55420		50+
Brandywine Community Resource Council Inc	3301 Green St	Claymont	DE	19703		1-5
Catholic Charities Maine	PO Box 10660	Portland	ME	04104		10-19
Centro De La Familia De Utah	320 W 200 S 300B	Salt Lake Cty	UT	84101	801-521-4473	5-9
Child Care Resorce Center Inc	3766 Pepperell Pky	Opelika	AL	36801	334-749-8400	5-9
Childrens Home & Aid Society of Illinois	125 S Wacker Dr	Chicago	IL	60606	312-424-0200	30-39
Childrens Home Society of New Jersey	635 S Clinton Ave	Trenton	NJ	08611	609-695-6274	10-19
Comcare Inc	4001 N 3rd St Suite 120	Phoenix	AZ	85012		50+
Community Action Agency of Southern New Mexico Territory	PO Drawer 130	Las Cruces	NM	88004	505-523-1639	5-9
Community Action Council for Lex-Fayette Counties	PO Box 11610	Lexington	KY	40576	606-233-4600	10-19
Community Foundation of Gaston County Inc	PO Box 123	Gastonia	NC	28053		10-19
Community Foundation of Greater Memphis Inc	1900 Union Ave	Memphis	TN	38104	901-761-3806	50+
Community Foundation of Madison and Jefferson County Inc	PO Box 306	Madison	IN	47250		10-19
Community Partnership for the Prevention of Homelessness	8737 Colesville Rd FL 4	Silver Spring	MD	20910		10-19
Dakota Boys Ranch Association	PO Box 5007	Minot	ND	58702		5-9
Family & Childrens Agency Inc	9 Mott Ave	Norwalk	CT	06850		5-9
Federal Hill House Association Inc	9 Courtland St	Providence	RI	02909	401-421-4722	1-5
Four Dam Pool-Initial Project of the Alaska Energy Authority	PO Box 449329	Petersburg	AK	99833		10-19
Freddie Mac Foundation	8250 Jones Branch Dr	McLean	VA	22102		20-29
Gill Foundation	8 S Nevada 303	Colorado Springs	CO	80903	719-473-4455	40-49
Gleaners Community Food Bank Inc	2131 Beaufait	Detroit	MI	48207	313-924-6313	10-19
H O V E Road Maintenance Corp	PO Box 6227	Captain Cook	HI	96737		1-5
Harold & Arlene Schnitzer Care Foundation	PO Box 2708	Portland	OR	97208		10-19
Harvesters-The Community Food Network	1811 N Topping	Kansas City	MO	64120		20-29
Hinds County Human Resource Agency	PO Box 22657	Jackson	MS	39225	601-923-3930	10-19
Idaho Youth Ranch Inc	PO Box 8538	Boise	ID	83707	208-377-2613	5-9
Iowa Student Loan Liquidity Corp	604 Locust St	Des Moines	IA	50309	515-243-5626	50+
Kidspeace Corp	3438 RT 309	Orefield	PA	18069		40-49
Kirkpatrick Center Affiliated Fund	PO Box 1146	Oklahoma City	OK	73101		30-39
Las Vegas Police Protective Assn Inc	PO Box 61078	Las Vegas	NV	89160		10-19
Link Inc	2401 E 13th St	Hays	KS	67601	785-625-6942	5-9
Lower Savannah Council of Government	PO Box 850	Aiken	SC	29802	803-649-7981	10-19
Missouri River Adolescent Development Center Inc	211 W 16th Ave	Chamberlain	SD	57325		5-9
Monadnock Family Services	64 Main St Suite 301	Keene	NH	03431	603-357-4400	5-9
Mothers Against Drunk Driving	PO Box 541688	Dallas	TX	75354		40-49
Ms Foundation for Women Inc	120 Wall St 33rd Flr	New York	NY	10005	212-742-2300	30-39
National Crime Prevention Council Inc	1700 K St NW	Washington	DC	20006	202-466-6272	10-19
Nebraska Food Bank Network Inc	6824 J St	Omaha	NE	68117	402-341-1915	5-9
Robert S & Grayce B Kerr Foundation Inc	PO Box 25106	Jackson	WY	83001		1-5
The Greater Boston Food Bank Inc	99 Atkinson St	Boston	MA	02118	617-427-5200	20-29
Vermont Community Foundation	PO Box 30	Middlebury	VT	05753	802-388-3355	30-39
Wausau Area Community Foundation Inc	500 Third St Ste 316	Wausau	WI	54403	715-845-9555	10-19
Youth Home Inc	20400 Colonel Glenn	Little Rock	AR	72210	501-821-5500	5-9

Source: National Directory of Nonprofit Organizations, 2000, Volumes 1 and 2, The Taft Group. The table shows a selection of organizations for illustration and does not constitute a complete selection from the source. The organizations are arranged in alphabetical order.

LOCATION BY STATE AND REGIONAL CONCENTRATION

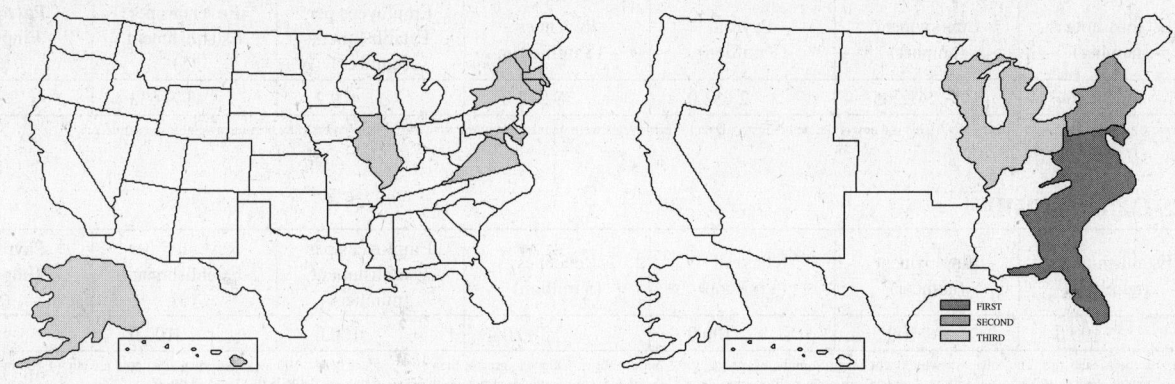

FIRST
SECOND
THIRD

INDUSTRY DATA BY STATE

State	Establishments Total (number)	Establishments % of U.S.	Employment Total (number)	Employment % of U.S.	Employment Per Estab.	Payroll Total ($ mil.)	Payroll Per Empl. ($)	Revenues Total ($ mil.)	Revenues % of U.S.	Revenues Per Estab. ($)
D.C.	222	4.7	3,212	8.2	14	116.9	36,396	419.9	13.5	1,891,293
New York	473	10.0	4,886	12.5	10	121.5	24,869	374.9	12.1	792,581
California	505	10.6	3,727	9.5	7	89.2	23,928	273.7	8.8	542,071
Illinois	231	4.9	2,817	7.2	12	69.5	24,683	221.4	7.1	958,381
Virginia	112	2.4	1,147	2.9	10	44.9	39,160	217.9	7.0	1,945,759
Pennsylvania	188	4.0	2,020	5.2	11	44.2	21,888	140.9	4.5	749,590
Texas	221	4.7	1,429	3.7	6	31.2	21,831	127.1	4.1	574,905
Massachusetts	162	3.4	1,543	4.0	10	39.1	25,342	117.2	3.8	723,605
Florida	187	3.9	1,374	3.5	7	29.3	21,293	112.2	3.6	599,845
Ohio	182	3.8	1,631	4.2	9	32.9	20,148	109.9	3.5	604,060
Michigan	149	3.1	1,452	3.7	10	31.1	21,411	83.5	2.7	560,564
Maryland	94	2.0	922	2.4	10	25.5	27,625	82.7	2.7	879,787
Georgia	95	2.0	952	2.4	10	20.6	21,621	75.9	2.4	799,000
New Jersey	89	1.9	823	2.1	9	19.0	23,100	52.9	1.7	594,281
North Carolina	114	2.4	944	2.4	8	19.3	20,462	46.6	1.5	409,105
Minnesota	147	3.1	765	2.0	5	14.9	19,529	46.2	1.5	314,224
Missouri	82	1.7	705	1.8	9	17.5	24,831	45.8	1.5	559,049
Wisconsin	103	2.2	677	1.7	7	15.1	22,251	43.9	1.4	425,913
Connecticut	84	1.8	475	1.2	6	13.1	27,501	39.2	1.3	466,190
Indiana	83	1.7	479	1.2	6	9.9	20,593	38.6	1.2	465,325
Washington	103	2.2	622	1.6	6	13.7	21,955	35.6	1.1	345,825
Oregon	88	1.9	464	1.2	5	8.8	19,054	34.4	1.1	391,455
Colorado	78	1.6	325	0.8	4	8.0	24,612	32.9	1.1	421,321
Hawaii	20	0.4	336	0.9	17	9.4	28,063	31.4	1.0	1,568,750
Louisiana	92	1.9	520	1.3	6	9.3	17,915	28.4	0.9	309,076
Vermont	28	0.6	464	1.2	17	11.0	23,700	24.7	0.8	883,679
Arizona	46	1.0	517	1.3	11	10.1	19,584	24.7	0.8	536,804
Mississippi	31	0.7	251	0.6	8	5.7	22,717	21.0	0.7	678,516
Kentucky	51	1.1	229	0.6	4	5.4	23,437	20.0	0.6	391,627
Arkansas	44	0.9	249	0.6	6	5.1	20,325	16.8	0.5	382,795
Rhode Island	35	0.7	258	0.7	7	5.1	19,725	16.5	0.5	471,000
New Mexico	57	1.2	301	0.8	5	6.8	22,515	16.3	0.5	285,456
Tennessee	68	1.4	270	0.7	4	5.6	20,567	14.5	0.5	213,176
Alaska	44	0.9	189	0.5	4	3.7	19,439	14.1	0.5	320,341
Iowa	49	1.0	282	0.7	6	5.0	17,794	12.3	0.4	250,510
West Virginia	27	0.6	185	0.5	7	2.9	15,427	9.9	0.3	365,037
Oklahoma	35	0.7	208	0.5	6	3.5	16,644	9.0	0.3	256,029
Alabama	46	1.0	175	0.4	4	2.8	16,286	8.4	0.3	182,261
Utah	21	0.4	131	0.3	6	2.2	16,542	8.4	0.3	401,286
New Hampshire	21	0.4	132	0.3	6	3.4	26,129	7.7	0.2	366,143
Kansas	40	0.8	138	0.4	3	2.5	18,341	7.5	0.2	187,425
South Carolina	34	0.7	85	0.2	3	1.7	20,435	5.5	0.2	162,706
Montana	28	0.6	102	0.3	4	1.9	18,314	5.1	0.2	182,821
Nebraska	25	0.5	86	0.2	3	1.8	20,826	2.9	0.1	114,560
Delaware	16	0.3	38	0.1	2	0.8	19,921	2.2	0.1	140,063
Idaho	19	0.4	92	0.2	5	0.7	7,663	2.1	0.1	111,526
Nevada	15	0.3	23	0.1	2	0.6	23,913	1.9	0.1	127,200
North Dakota	5	0.1	52	0.1	10	0.3	6,308	1.2	0.0	238,600
South Dakota	9	0.2	35	0.1	4	0.4	11,600	0.9	0.0	95,778
Maine	38	0.8	375*	-	-	(D)	-	(D)	-	-
Wyoming	9	0.2	60*	-	-	(D)	-	(D)	-	-

Source: 1997 *Economic Census*. The states are in descending order of revenues or establishments (if revenue data are missing for the majority). The symbol (D) appears when data are withheld to prevent disclosure of competitive information. States marked with (D) are sorted by number of establishments. A dash (-) indicates that the data element cannot be calculated. * indicates the midpoint of a range; 175, for example is the range 100-249. Shaded *states* on the state map indicate those states which have proportionately greater representation in the industry than would be indicated by the state's population; the ratio is based on total revenues or number of establishments. Shaded *regions* indicate where the industry is regionally most concentrated.

NAICS 813410 - CIVIC AND SOCIAL ORGANIZATIONS

GENERAL STATISTICS

Year	Establishments (number)	Employment (number)	Payroll ($ million)	Revenues ($ million)	Employees per Establishment (number)	Revenues per Establishment ($)	Payroll per Employee ($)
1997	28,364	261,265	2,683.0	9,917.0	9.2	349,633	10,269

Source: Economic Census of the United States, 1997. This is a newly defined industry. Data for prior years were unavailable at the time of publication but may become available over time.

INDICES OF CHANGE

Year	Establishments (number)	Employment (number)	Payroll ($ million)	Revenues ($ million)	Employees per Establishment (number)	Revenues per Establishment ($)	Payroll per Employee ($)
1997	100.0	100.0	100.0	100.0	100.0	100.0	100.0

Sources: Same as General Statistics. The values shown reflect change from the base year, 1997. Values above 100 mean greater than 1997, values below 100 mean less than 1997, and a value of 100 in the 1982-96 or 1998-2001 period means same as 1997. Values followed by a 'p' are projections by the editors; 'e' stands for extrapolation. Data are the most recent available at this level of detail.

SIC INDUSTRIES RELATED TO NAICS 813410

Each new NAICS code represents an industry that used to be part of an SIC or a part of several SIC industries. Data in this table are shown to provide transitional information for these cases. All available data for the precursor SIC(s) are shown. Even if only a part of an SIC is included in the NAICS, *all* data for the SIC are reproduced. If the SIC industry is not marked as being a part (pt) of the NAICS, the entire industry is embedded in the NAICS data. The SIC composition of the new industry provides some hints of the relative importance of its "ancestors." Data marked with a 'p' are projected. Projections begin with 1982 data. Data earlier than 1990 are not shown but are reflected in the projections.

SIC	Industry	1990	1991	1992	1993	1994	1995	1996	1997
8641	**Civic & Social Associations (pt)**								
	Establishments (number)	39,999	43,422	41,789	41,942	41,940	41,764	43,156p	43,570p
	Employment (thousands)	365.8	384.6	355.1	369.5	374.9	386.1	395.4p	402.8p
	Revenues ($ million)	-	-	13,176.1	-	-	-	-	-
8699	**Membership Organizations, nec (pt)**								
	Establishments (number)	9,670	10,125	10,596	10,695	10,666	10,760	11,062p	11,247p
	Employment (thousands)	87.7	91.9	91.4	95.7	96.0	101.7	103.3p	105.9p
	Revenues ($ million)	-	-	6,267.8	-	-	-	-	-

Source: Economic Census of the United States, 1992, annual surveys of economic sectors conducted by the Bureau of the Census, and estimates or projections based on the 1982-1992 period; not all data are shown. 'e' marks estimates made by the editors; 'p' indicates projections based on time series. A dash (-) indicates that data for this SIC or year were not available. The abbreviation (pt) next to the industry name indicates that only a part of the industry is present within the NAICS data. If no (pt) is shown, the entire industry is contained within the NAICS data.

SELECTED RATIOS

For 1997	Avg. of Information	Analyzed Industry	Index	For 1997	Avg. of Information	Analyzed Industry	Index
Employees per establishment	6	9	147	Payroll per establishment	126,069	94,592	75
Revenue per establishment	511,622	349,633	68	Payroll as % of revenue	25	27	110
Revenue per employee	81,659	37,958	46	Payroll per employee	20,122	10,269	51

Sources: Same as General Statistics. The 'Average' column represents the average for the industry sector, in 1997, where the currently shown industry is classified. The Index shows the relationship between the Average and the Analyzed Industry. For example, 100 means that they are equal; 500 that the Analyzed Industry is five times the average; 50 means that the Analyzed Industry is half the national average. The abbreviation 'na' is used to show that data are 'not available'.

LEADING COMPANIES   Number shown: **1**   Total sales ($ mil): **0**   Total employment (000): **0.0**

Company Name	Address				CEO Name	Phone	Co. Type	Sales ($ mil)	Empl. (000)
Wallis & Associates, Consulting	8031 Broadway	San Antonio	TX	78209		210-824-7471	N	0	<0.1

Source: Ward's Business Directory of U.S. Private and Public Companies, Volumes 1 and 2, 2000. The company type code used is as follows: P - Public, R - Private, S - Subsidiary, D - Division, J - Joint Venture, A - Affiliate, G - Group, N - Company type not reported. Sales are in millions of dollars, employees are in thousands. An asterisk (*) indicates an estimated sales volume. The symbol < stands for 'less than'. Company names and addresses are truncated, in some cases, to fit into the available space.

REPRESENTATIVE NONPROFIT ORGANIZATIONS

Organization Name	Address				Phone	Income Range ($ mil)
A New Day Inc	2720 Carlisle NE Ste B	Albuquerque	NM	87110	505-334-8052	1-5
Albertsons Employees Health and Welfare Trust	PO Box 20	Boise	ID	83726	208-395-6200	50+
Alpha Omicron Pi Fraternity Inc	9025 Overlook Blvd	Brentwood	TN	37027	615-370-0920	10-19
Alumni Association of the University of Mississippi	University of Mississippi	University	MS	38677		1-5
American Center for Wine Food and the Arts	1700 Soscol Ave 1	Napa	CA	94559	707-257-3606	50+
Ancient Free & Accepted Masons of W Virginia	PO Box 2346	Charleston	WV	25328		1-5
Arctic Slope Native Association Ltd	PO Box 1232	Barrow	AK	99723		10-19
Arkansas Alumni Association Inc	PO Box 1070	Fayetteville	AR	72702		1-5
Association of Graduates of the United States Military Academy	H Hall Mills Rd	W Point	NY	10996		50+
Beloit College	700 College St	Beloit	WI	53511	608-363-2000	50+
Big Horn Hospital Association	17 N Miles Ave	Hardin	MT	59034	406-665-2310	5-9
Brown University	Box J	Providence	RI	02912	401-863-3122	50+
Caribe Girl Scouts Council Inc	500 Calle Elisa Colberg	San Juan	PR	00907		1-5
Cart	One Gatehall Dr	Parsippany	NJ	07054		50+
Castle Medical Center	640 Ulukahiki St	Kailua	HI	96734	808-263-5376	50+
Catholic Aid Association	3499 N Lexington Ave	St Paul	MN	55126	651-490-0170	40-49
Childrens Defense Fund	25 E St NW	Washington	DC	20001	202-628-8787	50+
Coastal Economic Development Corporation	39 Andrews Rd	Bath	ME	04530	207-442-0059	5-9
Davidson College	PO Box 1568	Davidson	NC	28036		50+
Fiduciary Foundation	930 Tahoe Blvd 802-269	Incline VLG	NV	89451		5-9
Girl Scouts of Swift Water Council	88 Harvey Rd	Manchester	NH	03103	603-627-4158	5-9
Greater Burlington Young Mens Christian Association Inc	266 College St	Burlington	VT	05401		1-5
Greater Greenville Young Mens Christian Assoc	601 E McBee Ave Ste 212	Greenville	SC	29601		5-9
Iowa State Memorial Union	Station A ISU	Ames	IA	50011		5-9
Knights of Columbus Supreme Council	One Columbus Plaza	New Haven	CT	06510	203-772-2130	50+
L S U Foundation	RM 204 T Boyd Hall	Baton Rouge	LA	70803		30-39
Medical Teams International Inc	6955 SW Sandburg St	Portland	OR	97223	503-624-1000	50+
Methodist Childrens Home	1111 Herring Ave	Waco	TX	76708	254-750-1271	50+
Moose International Incorporated	3 S 276 RT 31	Mooseheart	IL	60539		50+
Multicare Health Systems	PO Box 5299	Tacoma	WA	98415	206-383-3383	50+
Snake River Sugar Company	PO Box 1520	Ogden	UT	84402		50+
South Dakota State University Foundation	823 Medary Ave Box 525	Brookings	SD	57006		10-19
Star Valley Ranch Association	Box 159	Thayne	WY	83127	307-883-2669	1-5
Sweet Adelines International Corporation	5334 E 46th St	Tulsa	OK	74135	918-622-1444	5-9
USA Group Guarantee Services Inc	PO Box 7039	Indianapolis	IN	46207		50+
United Commercial Travelers of America	632 N Park St	Columbus	OH	43215	614-228-3276	40-49
United States Naval Academy Alumni Assoc	247 King George St	Annapolis	MD	21402		50+
United Tribes Technical College	3315 University Dr	Bismarck	ND	58504	701-255-3285	10-19
University Athletic Association Inc	PO Box 14485	Gainesville	FL	32604		40-49
University of Georgia Foundation	Uga Foundation Bldg	Athens	GA	30602		40-49
University of Virginia Alumni Association	PO Box 3446	Charlottesvle	VA	22903		50+
Valley of the Sun Young Mens Christian Association	350 N First Ave	Phoenix	AZ	85003		20-29
Widener University	1 University PL	Chester	PA	19013	610-499-4000	50+
Womans Life Insurance Society	PO Box 5020	Port Huron	MI	48061	810-985-5191	30-39
YMCA Omaha Council Bluffs Metro Area	430 S 20th St	Omaha	NE	68102	402-341-1600	5-9
YMCA of Delaware	501 W Eleventh St	Wilmington	DE	19801		10-19
YMCA of the Rockies	2515 Tunnell Rd	Estes Park	CO	80511		30-39
Young Mens Christian Assoc of Birmingham	321 N 21st St	Birmingham	AL	35203		10-19
Young Mens Christian Association Greater Boston	316 Huntington Ave	Boston	MA	02115		40-49
Young Mens Christian Association of Greater Louisville	501 S Second St	Louisville	KY	40202		20-29
Young Mens Christian Association of Greater St Louis	1528 Locust St	St Louis	MO	63103		40-49
Young Mens Christian Association of Wichita	PO Box 3636	Wichita	KS	67201		10-19

Source: National Directory of Nonprofit Organizations, 2000, Volumes 1 and 2, The Taft Group. The table shows a selection of organizations for illustration and does not constitute a complete selection from the source. The organizations are arranged in alphabetical order.

LOCATION BY STATE AND REGIONAL CONCENTRATION

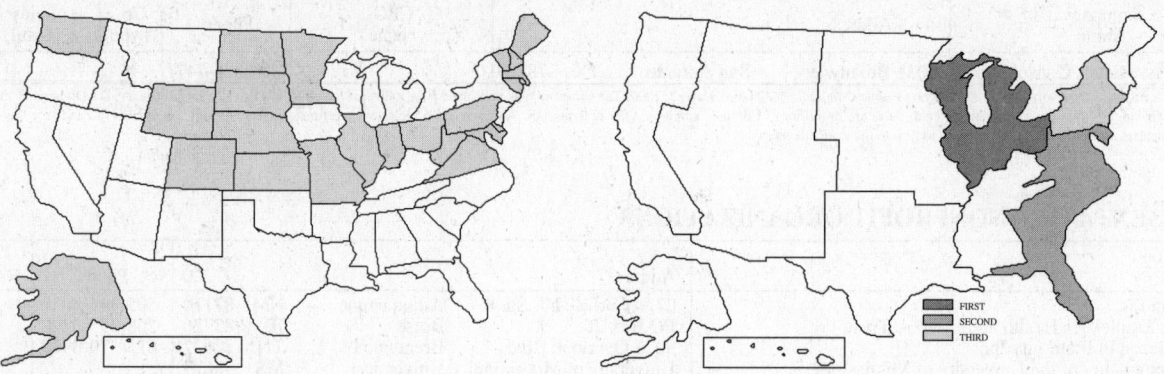

INDUSTRY DATA BY STATE

State	Establishments Total (number)	% of U.S.	Employment Total (number)	% of U.S.	Per Estab.	Payroll Total ($ mil.)	Per Empl. ($)	Revenues Total ($ mil.)	% of U.S.	Per Estab. ($)
California	2,245	7.9	21,881	8.4	10	255.6	11,681	795.9	8.0	354,503
New York	1,427	5.0	17,086	6.5	12	239.0	13,987	694.4	7.0	486,650
Illinois	1,300	4.6	15,488	5.9	12	183.1	11,822	690.3	7.0	530,989
Pennsylvania	2,721	9.6	18,184	7.0	7	160.6	8,832	633.3	6.4	232,751
Ohio	1,761	6.2	16,406	6.3	9	147.8	9,010	545.8	5.5	309,923
Texas	1,726	6.1	15,953	6.1	9	142.8	8,954	536.1	5.4	310,614
Minnesota	1,188	4.2	12,183	4.7	10	88.6	7,271	511.4	5.2	430,510
Indiana	1,132	4.0	8,885	3.4	8	90.1	10,137	431.9	4.4	381,563
Virginia	584	2.1	5,746	2.2	10	78.7	13,690	385.1	3.9	659,360
Florida	1,111	3.9	8,816	3.4	8	92.7	10,520	332.2	3.3	299,003
Michigan	1,061	3.7	9,556	3.7	9	90.9	9,515	317.8	3.2	299,567
Missouri	621	2.2	6,303	2.4	10	67.4	10,690	270.3	2.7	435,277
Massachusetts	815	2.9	7,216	2.8	9	70.3	9,741	254.4	2.6	312,130
D.C.	188	0.7	3,010	1.2	16	69.0	22,927	246.2	2.5	1,309,819
Washington	658	2.3	6,417	2.5	10	62.8	9,787	236.0	2.4	358,605
Maryland	532	1.9	5,256	2.0	10	65.3	12,422	234.7	2.4	441,154
Connecticut	395	1.4	4,652	1.8	12	64.0	13,756	199.4	2.0	504,757
North Carolina	493	1.7	5,363	2.1	11	55.8	10,400	192.9	1.9	391,361
Wisconsin	457	1.6	6,503	2.5	14	50.8	7,805	154.7	1.6	338,475
Tennessee	423	1.5	4,750	1.8	11	48.2	10,141	154.0	1.6	364,170
Colorado	430	1.5	3,631	1.4	8	39.2	10,786	152.8	1.5	355,412
Georgia	430	1.5	3,641	1.4	8	40.5	11,110	149.9	1.5	348,630
New Jersey	402	1.4	4,936	1.9	12	50.0	10,135	144.3	1.5	358,851
Iowa	468	1.6	4,105	1.6	9	29.4	7,168	104.2	1.1	222,690
Kansas	418	1.5	3,149	1.2	8	26.2	8,319	101.9	1.0	243,691
Arizona	328	1.2	2,310	0.9	7	25.1	10,881	95.9	1.0	292,424
Oregon	331	1.2	2,800	1.1	8	25.1	8,975	91.6	0.9	276,816
Kentucky	276	1.0	1,731	0.7	6	16.9	9,735	86.8	0.9	314,623
Nebraska	350	1.2	3,499	1.3	10	25.1	7,162	86.5	0.9	247,191
Oklahoma	304	1.1	1,855	0.7	6	18.5	9,976	79.6	0.8	261,931
Alabama	270	1.0	2,344	0.9	9	23.6	10,088	79.2	0.8	293,493
Louisiana	296	1.0	2,161	0.8	7	21.5	9,972	79.0	0.8	267,044
South Carolina	288	1.0	2,242	0.9	8	24.2	10,790	75.8	0.8	263,313
West Virginia	323	1.1	1,817	0.7	6	14.4	7,935	74.6	0.8	230,858
Mississippi	189	0.7	1,475	0.6	8	12.1	8,218	60.1	0.6	318,011
North Dakota	212	0.7	2,186	0.8	10	12.8	5,836	56.0	0.6	264,179
Maine	197	0.7	1,477	0.6	7	13.1	8,892	54.6	0.6	277,218
New Hampshire	195	0.7	1,442	0.6	7	12.8	8,902	51.8	0.5	265,805
South Dakota	176	0.6	1,418	0.5	8	12.1	8,510	50.7	0.5	288,091
Rhode Island	150	0.5	1,578	0.6	11	14.9	9,458	49.4	0.5	329,587
New Mexico	201	0.7	1,334	0.5	7	10.4	7,816	48.3	0.5	240,234
Alaska	112	0.4	815	0.3	7	9.4	11,567	45.3	0.5	404,759
Delaware	103	0.4	1,698	0.6	16	15.4	9,067	39.1	0.4	379,369
Vermont	138	0.5	1,065	0.4	8	9.0	8,486	36.1	0.4	261,275
Hawaii	73	0.3	1,226	0.5	17	14.8	12,100	35.7	0.4	489,260
Arkansas	195	0.7	874	0.3	4	7.0	7,974	33.5	0.3	171,795
Montana	200	0.7	972	0.4	5	7.6	7,852	33.3	0.3	166,690
Idaho	111	0.4	1,375	0.5	12	8.7	6,330	27.1	0.3	243,838
Nevada	104	0.4	765	0.3	7	6.9	9,012	26.7	0.3	256,837
Utah	123	0.4	857	0.3	7	6.6	7,741	26.1	0.3	212,398
Wyoming	133	0.5	833	0.3	6	5.9	7,056	23.4	0.2	175,820

Source: 1997 Economic Census. The states are in descending order of revenues or establishments (if revenue data are missing for the majority). The symbol (D) appears when data are withheld to prevent disclosure of competitive information. States marked with (D) are sorted by number of establishments. A dash (-) indicates that the data element cannot be calculated. * indicates the midpoint of a range; 175, for example is the range 100-249. Shaded *states* on the state map indicate those states which have proportionately greater representation in the industry than would be indicated by the state's population; the ratio is based on total revenues or number of establishments. Shaded *regions* indicate where the industry is regionally most concentrated.

NAICS 813910 - BUSINESS ASSOCIATIONS

GENERAL STATISTICS

Year	Establishments (number)	Employment (number)	Payroll ($ million)	Revenues ($ million)	Employees per Establishment (number)	Revenues per Establishment ($)	Payroll per Employee ($)
1997	16,928	116,084	4,180.0	14,859.0	6.9	877,776	36,008

Source: *Economic Census of the United States*, 1997. This is a newly defined industry. Data for prior years were unavailable at the time of publication but may become available over time.

INDICES OF CHANGE

Year	Establishments (number)	Employment (number)	Payroll ($ million)	Revenues ($ million)	Employees per Establishment (number)	Revenues per Establishment ($)	Payroll per Employee ($)
1997	100.0	100.0	100.0	100.0	100.0	100.0	100.0

Sources: Same as General Statistics. The values shown reflect change from the base year, 1997. Values above 100 mean greater than 1997, values below 100 mean less than 1997, and a value of 100 in the 1982-96 or 1998-2001 period means same as 1997. Values followed by a 'p' are projections by the editors; 'e' stands for extrapolation. Data are the most recent available at this level of detail.

SIC INDUSTRIES RELATED TO NAICS 813910

Each new NAICS code represents an industry that used to be part of an SIC or a part of several SIC industries. Data in this table are shown to provide transitional information for these cases. All available data for the precursor SIC(s) are shown. Even if only a part of an SIC is included in the NAICS, *all* data for the SIC are reproduced. If the SIC industry is not marked as being a part (pt) of the NAICS, the entire industry is embedded in the NAICS data. The SIC composition of the new industry provides some hints of the relative importance of its "ancestors." Data marked with a 'p' are projected. Projections begin with 1982 data. Data earlier than 1990 are not shown but are reflected in the projections.

SIC	Industry	1990	1991	1992	1993	1994	1995	1996	1997
8611	**Business Associations**								
	Establishments (number)	12,677	13,766	14,337	14,488	14,567	14,643	14,620*p*	14,828*p*
	Employment (thousands)	98.5	98.0	101.5	106.1	107.4	111.2	112.0*p*	114.5*p*
	Revenues ($ million)	-	-	11,067.9	-	-	-	-	-
8699	**Membership Organizations, nec (pt)**								
	Establishments (number)	9,670	10,125	10,596	10,695	10,666	10,760	11,062*p*	11,247*p*
	Employment (thousands)	87.7	91.9	91.4	95.7	96.0	101.7	103.3*p*	105.9*p*
	Revenues ($ million)	-	-	6,267.8	-	-	-	-	-

Source: *Economic Census of the United States*, 1992, annual surveys of economic sectors conducted by the Bureau of the Census, and estimates or projections based on the 1982-1992 period; not all data are shown. 'e' marks estimates made by the editors; 'p' indicates projections based on time series. A dash (-) indicates that data for this SIC or year were not available. The abbreviation (pt) next to the industry name indicates that only a part of the industry is present within the NAICS data. If no (pt) is shown, the entire industry is contained within the NAICS data.

SELECTED RATIOS

For 1997	Avg. of Information	Analyzed Industry	Index	For 1997	Avg. of Information	Analyzed Industry	Index
Employees per establishment	6	7	109	Payroll per establishment	126,069	246,928	196
Revenue per establishment	511,622	877,776	172	Payroll as % of revenue	25	28	114
Revenue per employee	81,659	128,002	157	Payroll per employee	20,122	36,008	179

Sources: Same as General Statistics. The 'Average' column represents the average for the industry sector, in 1997, where the currently shown industry is classified. The Index shows the relationship between the Average and the Analyzed Industry. For example, 100 means that they are equal; 500 that the Analyzed Industry is five times the average; 50 means that the Analyzed Industry is half the national average. The abbreviation 'na' is used to show that data are 'not available'.

LEADING COMPANIES
No company data available for this industry.

REPRESENTATIVE NONPROFIT ORGANIZATIONS

Organization Name	Address				Phone	Income Range ($ mil)
Aberdeen Development Corporation	416 Production St N	Aberdeen	SD	57401	605-229-5335	1-5
American Bankers Association	1120 Conn Ave NW	Washington	DC	20036	202-663-5153	50+
Anchorage Convention & Visitors Bureau	524 W Fourth Ave	Anchorage	AK	99501	907-276-4118	5-9
Associated Builders & Contractors Inc	PO Box 2124	Grand Rapids	MI	49501		10-19
Bella Vista Village Property Owners Association	101 Town Center	Bella Vista Village	AR	72714	501-855-8000	10-19
Belle T Smith	PO Box 6767	Providence	RI	02940		1-5
Bismarck-Mandan Convention & Visitors Bureau Inc	107 W Main Ave	Bismarck	ND	58501	701-222-2595	1-5
Breeders Cup Limited	PO Box 4230	Lexington	KY	40544		50+
Bryn Mawr College	101 N Merion Ave	Bryn Mawr	PA	19010		50+
Business Council of Alabama	PO Box 76	Montgomery	AL	36101		5-9
Chemical Industry Institute of Toxicology	PO Box 12137	RTP RK	NC	27709	919-558-1200	10-19
Chemical Manufacturers Association Inc	1300 Wilson Blvd	Arlington	VA	22209	703-524-7700	50+
Cheyenne Frontier Days Inc	PO Box 2477	Cheyenne	WY	82003		5-9
Contractors Association of West Virginia	2114 Kanawha Blvd E	Charleston	WV	25311	304-342-1166	1-5
Cotton Incorporated	1370 Avenue of Americas	New York	NY	10019	212-506-5700	50+
Dairy Management Inc	10255 W Higgins Rd	Rosemont	IL	60018	847-803-2000	50+
Delaware State Bar Association	1201 Orange St Ste 1100	Wilmington	DE	19801	302-658-0773	1-5
Downtown Lincoln Association	1200 N St Ste 101	Lincoln	NE	68508	402-434-6900	1-5
East Mississippi Electric Power Association	PO Box 5517	Meridian	MS	39302		40-49
Georgia Life and Health Insurance Guaranty Association	2177 Flintstone Dr	Tucker	GA	30084		20-29
Great Lakes Composites Consortium Inc	103 Trade Zone Dr Ste 26	W Columbia	SC	29170		20-29
Greater Boise Chamber of Commerce	250 S 5th St 800	Boise	ID	83702		1-5
Hawaii Visitors Bureau	2270 Kalakaua Av	Honolulu	HI	96815	808-924-0266	30-39
Indiana Chamber of Commerce Inc	115 W Washington	Indianapolis	IN	46204		5-9
Industry Network Corporation	1155 University Blvd SE	Albuquerque	NM	87106		10-19
Iowa Foundation for Medical Care	6000 Westown Pky	W Des Moines	IA	50266	515-223-2900	20-29
Kansas Livestock Association	6031 SW 37th St	Topeka	KS	66614	785-273-5115	10-19
Ladies Professional Golf Assoc	100 International Golf Dr	Daytona Beach	FL	32124	904-274-6200	50+
Lake Champlain Regional Chamber of Commerce	60 Main St Ste 100	Burlington	VT	05401	802-863-3489	1-5
Las Vegas Events Inc	770 E Warm Springs Rd	Las Vegas	NV	89119		10-19
Life and Health Insurance Guaranty Corporation	9199 Reisterstown Rd	Owings Mills	MD	21117	410-998-3907	20-29
Louisiana Insurance Guaranty Association	4324 S Sherwood Forest	Baton Rouge	LA	70816	225-291-4775	30-39
Minnesota Life and Health Insurance Guaranty Association	55 Fifth St E	St Paul	MN	55101	651-222-2799	20-29
Missouri One-Call Systems Inc	728 Heisinger Rd	Jefferson City	MO	65109	573-761-4007	10-19
Motion Picture Assn America Inc	15503 Ventura Blvd	Encino	CA	91436	818-995-6600	30-39
National Cattlemens Beef Association Inc	5420 S Quebec St	Englewood	CO	80111	303-694-0305	50+
National Federation of Independent Business Inc	53 Century Blvd Ste 300	Nashville	TN	37214	615-872-5800	50+
New England Apple Council Inc	7 Main St	Goffstown	NH	03045	603-497-2132	1-5
New Jersey Property Liability Insurance Guaranty Association	59 63 Mine Brook Rd	Bernardsville	NJ	07924		50+
Oklahoma Life and Health Insurance Guaranty Association	201 Robert S Kerr Ste 600	Oklahoma City	OK	73102	405-272-9221	10-19
Oregon Exchange Carrier Association Inc	800 C St	Vancouver	WA	98660	360-690-4535	10-19
Oregon Museum of Science and Industry	1945 SE Water Ave	Portland	OR	97214	503-797-4547	20-29
Puerto Rico Convention Bureau Inc	255 Recinto Sur	San Juan	PR	00901		5-9
Rosscare Nursing Home of Bangor Inc	PO Box 404	Bangor	ME	04402		5-9
Sematech Inc	2706 Montopolis Dr	Austin	TX	78741	512-356-3500	50+
Telephone Exchange Carrier of Montana Inc	501 Bay Dr	Great Falls	MT	59404		10-19
The Thunderbirds	7226 N 16th St RM 100	Phoenix	AZ	85020		10-19
The Utah Ccim Chapter of the Commercial Investment Real Estate	1785 W Printers Row	Salt Lake Cty	UT	84119		5-9
Trustees of Noble Hospital Inc	115 W Silver St	Westfield	MA	01085		30-39
United Food & Commercial Workers Union	3435 Fortuna Dr	Akron	OH	44312	330-645-2880	50+
Visiting Nurse Services of Connecticut Inc	765 Fairfield Ave	Bridgeport	CT	06604	203-366-3821	10-19
Wisconsin Compensation Rating Bureau	2200 N Mayfair Rd	Wauwatosa	WI	53226		50+

Source: National Directory of Nonprofit Organizations, 2000, Volumes 1 and 2, The Taft Group. The table shows a selection of organizations for illustration and does not constitute a complete selection from the source. The organizations are arranged in alphabetical order.

LOCATION BY STATE AND REGIONAL CONCENTRATION

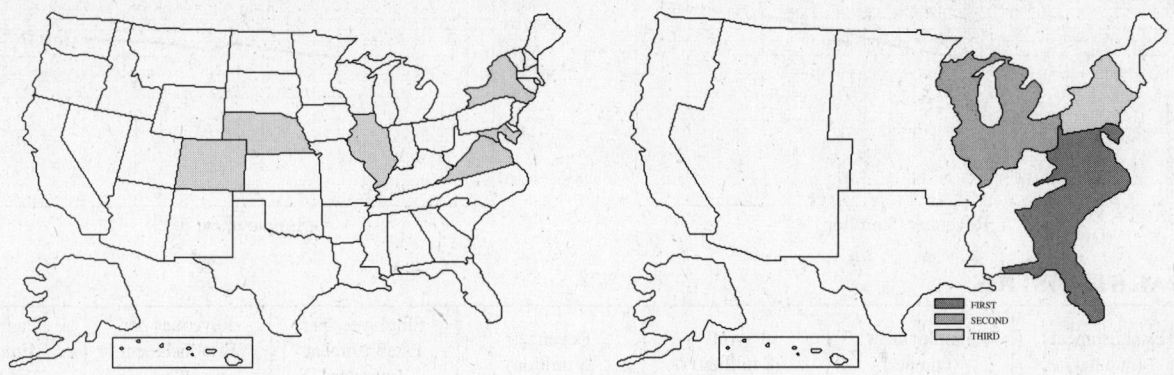

FIRST
SECOND
THIRD

INDUSTRY DATA BY STATE

State	Establishments Total (number)	Establishments % of U.S.	Employment Total (number)	Employment % of U.S.	Employment Per Estab.	Payroll Total ($ mil.)	Payroll Per Empl. ($)	Revenues Total ($ mil.)	Revenues % of U.S.	Revenues Per Estab. ($)
D.C.	534	3.2	15,174	13.1	28	791.7	52,178	2,732.6	18.4	5,117,184
New York	812	4.8	6,260	5.4	8	274.8	43,895	1,516.2	10.2	1,867,208
Illinois	847	5.0	8,045	6.9	9	335.6	41,712	1,270.9	8.6	1,500,455
California	1,511	8.9	10,789	9.3	7	369.0	34,200	1,241.3	8.4	821,514
Virginia	662	3.9	7,939	6.8	12	359.9	45,332	1,236.8	8.3	1,868,240
Texas	1,204	7.1	6,153	5.3	5	177.9	28,910	594.7	4.0	493,978
Ohio	585	3.5	3,399	2.9	6	113.3	33,322	395.2	2.7	675,605
Georgia	501	3.0	2,752	2.4	5	87.8	31,921	374.8	2.5	748,026
Florida	726	4.3	3,874	3.3	5	112.3	28,998	366.1	2.5	504,253
Michigan	509	3.0	2,856	2.5	6	95.7	33,518	322.4	2.2	633,356
Maryland	255	1.5	2,516	2.2	10	82.0	32,592	310.3	2.1	1,216,910
Colorado	339	2.0	2,245	1.9	7	78.3	34,899	305.3	2.1	900,469
Missouri	352	2.1	2,339	2.0	7	76.9	32,870	285.4	1.9	810,892
Massachusetts	329	1.9	2,173	1.9	7	88.9	40,923	264.7	1.8	804,489
New Jersey	326	1.9	1,858	1.6	6	77.8	41,860	254.7	1.7	781,279
Wisconsin	391	2.3	2,489	2.1	6	78.6	31,572	252.1	1.7	644,864
Pennsylvania	499	2.9	2,831	2.4	6	89.9	31,748	251.0	1.7	503,004
Tennessee	353	2.1	3,317	2.9	9	91.2	27,480	245.7	1.7	696,164
North Carolina	483	2.9	2,462	2.1	5	69.8	28,349	215.4	1.4	446,021
Minnesota	412	2.4	2,192	1.9	5	60.8	27,737	214.0	1.4	519,306
Washington	373	2.2	1,739	1.5	5	55.3	31,819	168.4	1.1	451,362
Iowa	329	1.9	1,488	1.3	5	37.3	25,089	162.7	1.1	494,453
Connecticut	159	0.9	1,612	1.4	10	62.3	38,647	146.2	1.0	919,792
Indiana	371	2.2	1,593	1.4	4	42.4	26,588	140.1	0.9	377,663
Kentucky	239	1.4	1,006	0.9	4	29.7	29,492	129.5	0.9	541,762
Oregon	276	1.6	1,290	1.1	5	40.8	31,596	125.5	0.8	454,786
Kansas	327	1.9	1,496	1.3	5	38.2	25,507	119.2	0.8	364,410
Arizona	199	1.2	1,151	1.0	6	32.2	28,018	110.6	0.7	555,985
Nebraska	175	1.0	1,173	1.0	7	22.9	19,488	104.4	0.7	596,600
Louisiana	247	1.5	1,431	1.2	6	32.5	22,719	103.4	0.7	418,486
Alabama	234	1.4	1,075	0.9	5	31.1	28,887	97.9	0.7	418,333
Oklahoma	278	1.6	1,113	1.0	4	25.7	23,119	94.2	0.6	338,777
South Carolina	213	1.3	1,015	0.9	5	29.3	28,890	90.8	0.6	426,300
Mississippi	244	1.4	889	0.8	4	21.8	24,540	71.4	0.5	292,529
Arkansas	232	1.4	827	0.7	4	17.7	21,391	55.0	0.4	236,897
Utah	99	0.6	432	0.4	4	12.9	29,803	49.5	0.3	499,768
New Mexico	110	0.6	450	0.4	4	11.2	24,942	38.2	0.3	347,027
Maine	119	0.7	418	0.4	4	12.3	29,366	36.9	0.2	310,151
North Dakota	121	0.7	490	0.4	4	10.1	20,541	35.7	0.2	295,405
Hawaii	69	0.4	339	0.3	5	11.2	32,965	35.2	0.2	510,261
Nevada	78	0.5	352	0.3	5	10.2	28,886	34.9	0.2	447,846
New Hampshire	102	0.6	359	0.3	4	10.9	30,237	32.4	0.2	317,314
South Dakota	85	0.5	336	0.3	4	7.8	23,161	29.0	0.2	340,671
Alaska	73	0.4	303	0.3	4	8.5	28,030	28.8	0.2	394,411
Idaho	92	0.5	354	0.3	4	9.1	25,568	28.7	0.2	312,293
Montana	106	0.6	369	0.3	3	8.7	23,593	28.5	0.2	268,774
Delaware	51	0.3	252	0.2	5	8.9	35,306	28.2	0.2	552,608
Rhode Island	59	0.3	291	0.3	5	8.1	27,814	24.6	0.2	416,949
Vermont	70	0.4	282	0.2	4	6.9	24,465	23.1	0.2	330,571
West Virginia	95	0.6	282	0.2	3	7.6	27,096	22.4	0.2	235,821
Wyoming	73	0.4	214	0.2	3	4.3	20,327	13.8	0.1	189,712

Source: 1997 *Economic Census*. The states are in descending order of revenues or establishments (if revenue data are missing for the majority). The symbol (D) appears when data are withheld to prevent disclosure of competitive information. States marked with (D) are sorted by number of establishments. A dash (-) indicates that the data element cannot be calculated. * indicates the midpoint of a range; 175, for example is the range 100-249. Shaded *states* on the state map indicate those states which have proportionately greater representation in the industry than would be indicated by the state's population; the ratio is based on total revenues or number of establishments. Shaded *regions* indicate where the industry is regionally most concentrated.

NAICS 813920 - PROFESSIONAL ORGANIZATIONS*

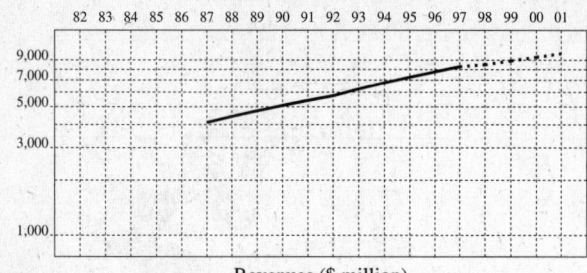

Revenues ($ million)

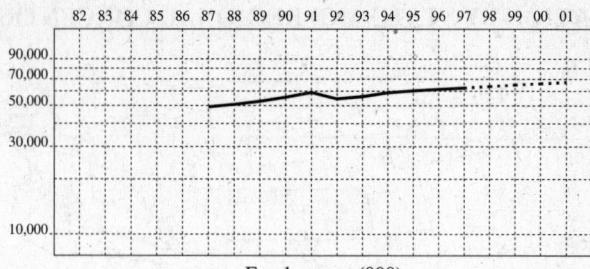

Employment (000)

GENERAL STATISTICS

Year	Establishments (number)	Employment (number)	Payroll ($ million)	Revenues ($ million)	Employees per Establishment (number)	Revenues per Establishment ($)	Payroll per Employee ($)
1982	-	-	-	-	-	-	-
1983	-	-	-	-	-	-	-
1984	-	-	-	-	-	-	-
1985	-	-	-	-	-	-	-
1986	-	-	-	-	-	-	-
1987	5,610	49,279	1,132.0	4,110.0	8.8	732,620	22,971
1988	5,449	50,790	1,263.0	4,437.0 e	9.3	814,278	24,867
1989	5,357	52,772	1,414.0	4,764.0 e	9.9	889,304	26,795
1990	5,480	55,579	1,564.0	5,090.0 e	10.1	928,832	28,140
1991	5,742	59,060	1,703.0	5,417.0 e	10.3	943,400	28,835
1992	5,664	54,495	1,621.0	5,744.0	9.6	1,014,124	29,746
1993	5,721	56,101	1,716.0	6,254.0 e	9.8	1,093,166	30,588
1994	5,783	58,849	1,898.0	6,764.0 e	10.2	1,169,635	32,252
1995	5,871	60,313	2,060.0	7,273.0 e	10.3	1,238,801	34,155
1996	6,555 e	61,344 e	2,162.0 e	7,783.0 e	9.4 e	1,187,338 e	35,244 e
1997	7,239	62,376	2,265.0	8,292.0	8.6	1,145,462	36,312
1998	6,663 p	63,755 p	2,357.0 p	8,503.0 p	9.6 p	1,276,152 p	36,970 p
1999	6,796 p	64,972 p	2,465.0 p	8,921.0 p	9.6 p	1,312,684 p	37,939 p
2000	6,930 p	66,189 p	2,572.0 p	9,339.0 p	9.6 p	1,347,619 p	38,858 p
2001	7,063 p	67,407 p	2,680.0 p	9,758.0 p	9.5 p	1,381,566 p	39,758 p

Sources: Economic Census of the United States, 1982, 1987, 1992, 1997. Establishment counts, employment, and payroll are from County Business Patterns for non-Census years. In non-Census years, industries in the Manufacturing range under SIC coding include data from the Annual Survey of Manufactures (ASM); those in the old Services range include data from the Services Annual Survey (SAS). Values followed by a 'p' are projections by the editors. Extrapolations are marked by 'e'. Data are the most recent available at this level of detail.

INDICES OF CHANGE

Year	Establishments (number)	Employment (number)	Payroll ($ million)	Revenues ($ million)	Employees per Establishment (number)	Revenues per Establishment ($)	Payroll per Employee ($)
1982	-	-	-	-	-	-	-
1987	77.5	79.0	50.0	49.6	101.9	64.0	63.3
1992	78.2	87.4	71.6	69.3	111.7	88.5	81.9
1993	79.0	89.9	75.8	75.4 e	113.8	95.4	84.2
1994	79.9	94.3	83.8	81.6 e	118.1	102.1	88.8
1995	81.1	96.7	90.9	87.7 e	119.2	108.1	94.1
1996	90.6 e	98.3 e	95.5 e	93.9 e	108.6 e	103.7 e	97.1 e
1997	100.0	100.0	100.0	100.0	100.0	100.0	100.0
1998	92.0 p	102.2 p	104.1 p	102.5 p	111.0 p	111.4 p	101.8 p
1999	93.9 p	104.2 p	108.8 p	107.6 p	111.0 p	114.6 p	104.5 p
2000	95.7 p	106.1 p	113.6 p	112.6 p	110.8 p	117.6 p	107.0 p
2001	97.6 p	108.1 p	118.3 p	117.7 p	110.8 p	120.6 p	109.5 p

Sources: Same as General Statistics. The values shown reflect change from the base year, 1997. Values above 100 mean greater than 1997, values below 100 mean less than 1997, and a value of 100 in the 1982-96 or 1998-2001 period means same as 1997. Values followed by a 'p' are projections by the editors; 'e' stands for extrapolation. Data are the most recent available at this level of detail.

SELECTED RATIOS

For 1997	Avg. of Information	Analyzed Industry	Index	For 1997	Avg. of Information	Analyzed Industry	Index
Employees per establishment	6	9	138	Payroll per establishment	126,069	312,889	248
Revenue per establishment	511,622	1,145,462	224	Payroll as % of revenue	25	27	111
Revenue per employee	81,659	132,936	163	Payroll per employee	20,122	36,312	180

Sources: Same as General Statistics. The 'Average' column represents the average for the industry sector, in 1997, where the currently shown industry is classified. The Index shows the relationship between the Average and the Analyzed Industry. For example, 100 means that they are equal; 500 that the Analyzed Industry is five times the average; 50 means that the Analyzed Industry is half the national average. The abbreviation 'na' is used to show that data are 'not available'.

*Equivalent to SIC 8621.

LEADING COMPANIES   Number shown: **2**   Total sales ($ mil): **1**   Total employment (000): **0.0**

Company Name	Address				CEO Name	Phone	Co. Type	Sales ($ mil)	Empl. (000)
Robert Matthews and Associates	7414 Perkins Rd	Baton Rouge	LA	70808		504-767-7043	N	1	<0.1
Rodman Associates Inc.	5307 March Creek	Austin	TX	78759		512-795-9112	N	0	<0.1

Source: Ward's Business Directory of U.S. Private and Public Companies, Volumes 1 and 2, 2000. The company type code used is as follows: P - Public, R - Private, S - Subsidiary, D - Division, J - Joint Venture, A - Affiliate, G - Group, N - Company type not reported. Sales are in millions of dollars, employees are in thousands. An asterisk (*) indicates an estimated sales volume. The symbol < stands for 'less than'. Company names and addresses are truncated, in some cases, to fit into the available space.

REPRESENTATIVE NONPROFIT ORGANIZATIONS

Organization Name	Address				Phone	Income Range ($ mil)
Alaska Council of School Administrators	326 4th St Ste 404	Juneau	AK	99801	907-586-9702	1-5
American Academy of Ophthalmology Inc	655 Beach St	San Francisco	CA	94109	415-561-8500	30-39
American Association of Petroleum Geologists	PO Box 979	Tulsa	OK	74101	918-584-2555	20-29
American Bar Association	750 N Lake Shore Dr	Chicago	IL	60611	312-988-6400	50+
American Board of Pediatrics Inc	111 Silver Cedar CT	Chapel Hill	NC	27514	919-929-0461	20-29
American Bureau of Shipping	16855 Northchase Dr	Houston	TX	77060	281-877-6800	50+
American College of Rheumatology	1800 Century PL Ste 250	Atlanta	GA	30345	404-633-3777	5-9
American Institute of Certified Public Accountants	201 Plaza 111	Jersey City	NJ	07311		50+
American Petroleum Institute	1220 L St NW	Washington	DC	20005	202-682-8000	50+
American Society of Health-System Pharmacists	7272 Wisconsin Ave	Bethesda	MD	20814	301-657-3000	30-39
Army Aviation Association of America Inc	49 Richmondville Ave	Westport	CT	06880	203-226-8184	1-5
Association for Computing Machinery	1515 Broadway 17th Flr	New York	NY	10036		40-49
Association for Investment Management and Research	PO Box 3668	Charlottesvle	VA	22903		50+
Association of Operating Room Nurses Inc	2170 S Parker Rd	Denver	CO	80231		10-19
Association of Washington School Principals	1021 8th Ave SE	Olympia	WA	98501		1-5
Confederation of Oregon School Administrators	707 13th St SE	Salem	OR	97301	503-581-3141	1-5
Council for Leaders in Alabama Schools	PO Box 428	Montgomery	AL	36101		1-5
Florida Workers Compensation Insur Ance Guaranty Assoc Inc	PO Box 15159	Tallahassee	FL	32317		50+
Hawaii Laborers Training Trust Fund	615 Piikoi St Ste 601	Honolulu	HI	96814		5-9
Hennepin County Bar Association	600 Nicollet Ave Ste 390	Minneapolis	MN	55402	612-339-8777	1-5
Idaho Medical Association	PO Box 2668	Boise	ID	83701		1-5
Independent Community Banks of North Dakota	PO Box 6128	Bismarck	ND	58506		1-5
Independent Physicians Association of Eastern Iowa	736 Federal St	Davenport	IA	52803		1-5
Indiana State Medical Association	322 Canal Walk	Indianapolis	IN	46202	317-261-2060	10-19
International Association of Jazz Educators	2803 Claflin Rd	Manhattan	KS	66502	785-776-8744	1-5
International Underwriters Insurance Company	841 Silver Lake Blvd 205	Dover	DE	19904		1-5
Kentucky Medical Assn	4965 US Hwy 42 Ste 2000	Louisville	KY	40222	502-426-6200	5-9
Las Vegas Nevada Area Electrical Apprenticeship	620 Leigon Way	Las Vegas	NV	89110		1-5
Louisiana District Attorneys Association Inc	1645 Nicholson Dr	Baton Rouge	LA	70802	225-343-0171	1-5
Maine State Bar Association	124 State St	Augusta	ME	04330	207-622-3151	5-9
Massachusetts Insurers Insolvency Fund	One Bowdoin SQ	Boston	MA	02114		20-29
Mercy Medical Center of Oshkosh Inc	631 Hazel St	Oshkosh	WI	54901	920-236-2293	50+
Michigan Association of Certified Public Accountants	5480 Corporate Dr 200	Troy	MI	48098		5-9
Mississippi Association of Educators	775 N State St	Jackson	MS	39202	601-354-4463	1-5
Missouri Hospital Association	PO Box 60	Jefferson Cty	MO	65102		5-9
Mountain-Pacific Quality Health Foundation	3404 Cooney Dr	Helena	MT	59602		5-9
National Association of Tower Erectors	420 4th St NE Ste 109	Watertown	SD	57201	605-882-5865	1-5
National Education Association of New Mexico	PO Box 729	Santa Fe	NM	87504		1-5
Nebraska State Education Association	605 S 14th St	Lincoln	NE	68508	402-475-7611	5-9
Netware Users International North America Inc	PO Box 19684	Provo	UT	84605		1-5
New Hampshire Bar Association	112 Pleasant St	Concord	NH	03301	603-224-6942	1-5
New Hampshire Automobile Reinsurance Facility	302 Central Ave	Johnston	RI	02919		5-9
Ohio State Bar Association	PO Box 16562	Columbus	OH	43216		10-19
Professional Tennis Registry Inc	PO Box 4739	Hilton Head	SC	29938		1-5
Society of Financial Service Professionals	270 Bryn Mawr Ave	Bryn Mawr	PA	19010	610-526-2500	10-19
State Bar of Arizona	111 W Monroe Ste 1800	Phoenix	AZ	85003	602-252-4804	5-9
Tennessee Education Association Inc	801 Second Ave N	Nashville	TN	37201	615-242-8392	5-9
West Virginia State Medical Association	PO Box 4106	Charleston	WV	25364		1-5

Source: National Directory of Nonprofit Organizations, 2000, Volumes 1 and 2, The Taft Group. The table shows a selection of organizations for illustration and does not constitute a complete selection from the source. The organizations are arranged in alphabetical order.

LOCATION BY STATE AND REGIONAL CONCENTRATION

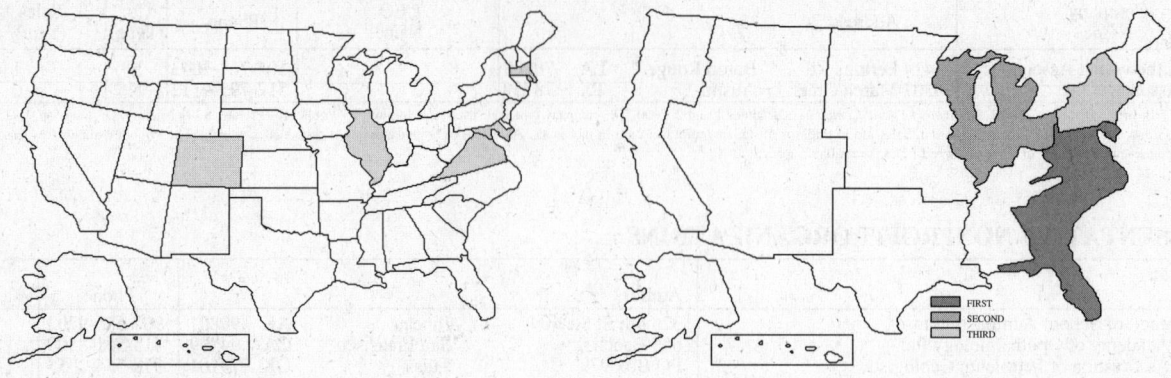

INDUSTRY DATA BY STATE

State	Establishments Total (number)	Establishments % of U.S.	Employment Total (number)	Employment % of U.S.	Employment Per Estab.	Payroll Total ($ mil.)	Payroll Per Empl. ($)	Revenues Total ($ mil.)	Revenues % of U.S.	Revenues Per Estab. ($)
Illinois	412	5.7	9,366	15.0	23	390.9	41,736	1,396.9	16.8	3,390,650
Virginia	327	4.5	5,359	8.6	16	213.1	39,771	925.5	11.2	2,830,333
D.C.	297	4.1	5,983	9.6	20	256.5	42,867	891.3	10.7	3,000,956
California	650	9.0	4,027	6.5	6	144.0	35,765	554.0	6.7	852,328
New York	452	6.2	3,712	6.0	8	138.4	37,293	536.3	6.5	1,186,527
Texas	476	6.6	3,124	5.0	7	105.3	33,702	367.1	4.4	771,246
Pennsylvania	281	3.9	2,749	4.4	10	100.2	36,455	364.2	4.4	1,295,968
Maryland	229	3.2	2,524	4.0	11	93.9	37,204	362.1	4.4	1,581,367
Florida	304	4.2	2,421	3.9	8	68.1	28,122	261.0	3.1	858,461
Massachusetts	168	2.3	1,487	2.4	9	59.8	40,236	196.7	2.4	1,170,643
New Jersey	276	3.8	1,883	3.0	7	69.5	36,890	195.6	2.4	708,815
Ohio	270	3.7	1,735	2.8	6	50.3	28,986	180.2	2.2	667,289
Michigan	200	2.8	1,434	2.3	7	47.1	32,815	177.1	2.1	885,725
Georgia	175	2.4	1,338	2.1	8	48.0	35,895	169.6	2.0	969,354
Missouri	164	2.3	1,130	1.8	7	35.7	31,618	160.7	1.9	979,628
Colorado	154	2.1	1,223	2.0	8	37.9	31,024	153.3	1.8	995,448
North Carolina	189	2.6	1,040	1.7	6	36.5	35,087	139.5	1.7	737,862
Wisconsin	104	1.4	871	1.4	8	22.0	25,271	108.4	1.3	1,042,788
Washington	194	2.7	1,061	1.7	5	33.4	31,495	105.8	1.3	545,330
Arizona	90	1.2	655	1.1	7	24.8	37,928	95.0	1.1	1,055,811
Minnesota	134	1.9	729	1.2	5	21.0	28,768	88.2	1.1	657,963
Indiana	118	1.6	563	0.9	5	17.9	31,874	63.4	0.8	537,288
Oklahoma	114	1.6	566	0.9	5	17.5	30,989	63.1	0.8	553,754
Connecticut	103	1.4	540	0.9	5	24.6	45,641	62.7	0.8	608,340
Kansas	87	1.2	426	0.7	5	13.7	32,216	58.5	0.7	672,701
Tennessee	125	1.7	580	0.9	5	18.4	31,748	57.8	0.7	462,600
Alabama	91	1.3	531	0.9	6	16.4	30,928	53.6	0.6	588,736
Kentucky	97	1.3	562	0.9	6	18.7	33,304	52.1	0.6	537,505
Iowa	97	1.3	520	0.8	5	17.7	34,065	45.5	0.5	468,649
Louisiana	98	1.4	454	0.7	5	12.6	27,826	43.7	0.5	446,163
South Carolina	81	1.1	443	0.7	5	12.0	27,036	36.7	0.4	452,728
Oregon	84	1.2	366	0.6	4	10.2	27,962	32.5	0.4	387,405
Rhode Island	24	0.3	244	0.4	10	8.3	34,201	30.0	0.4	1,248,708
West Virginia	31	0.4	203	0.3	7	6.9	33,882	25.9	0.3	834,258
Utah	39	0.5	211	0.3	5	7.2	34,351	24.8	0.3	635,974
Nebraska	64	0.9	261	0.4	4	5.4	20,739	20.7	0.2	323,125
Nevada	40	0.6	215	0.3	5	7.3	34,186	20.4	0.2	510,200
Delaware	26	0.4	173	0.3	7	5.2	29,838	19.4	0.2	746,538
New Mexico	42	0.6	229	0.4	5	5.6	24,611	17.9	0.2	426,214
Mississippi	38	0.5	235	0.4	6	6.0	25,323	16.9	0.2	445,632
Arkansas	52	0.7	179	0.3	3	4.9	27,503	16.6	0.2	318,865
Maine	23	0.3	90	0.1	4	2.9	32,300	15.5	0.2	674,217
New Hampshire	31	0.4	200	0.3	6	5.0	25,185	14.5	0.2	467,194
Vermont	24	0.3	138	0.2	6	5.3	38,391	14.0	0.2	582,667
Idaho	22	0.3	81	0.1	4	2.5	30,605	10.6	0.1	481,500
North Dakota	32	0.4	106	0.2	3	3.1	29,632	10.2	0.1	319,281
South Dakota	34	0.5	103	0.2	3	3.4	33,466	10.1	0.1	297,088
Alaska	20	0.3	84	0.1	4	3.0	35,238	9.5	0.1	475,400
Hawaii	15	0.2	97	0.2	6	2.8	28,742	6.7	0.1	445,533
Montana	24	0.3	79	0.1	3	2.1	26,063	6.2	0.1	259,208
Wyoming	17	0.2	46	0.1	3	1.1	24,522	4.3	0.1	253,824

Source: 1997 *Economic Census*. The states are in descending order of revenues or establishments (if revenue data are missing for the majority). The symbol (D) appears when data are withheld to prevent disclosure of competitive information. States marked with (D) are sorted by number of establishments. A dash (-) indicates that the data element cannot be calculated. * indicates the midpoint of a range; 175, for example is the range 100-249. Shaded *states* on the state map indicate those states which have proportionately greater representation in the industry than would be indicated by the state's population; the ratio is based on total revenues or number of establishments. Shaded *regions* indicate where the industry is regionally most concentrated.

NAICS 813990 - ORGANIZATIONS NEC

GENERAL STATISTICS

Year	Establishments (number)	Employment (number)	Payroll ($ million)	Revenues ($ million)	Employees per Establishment (number)	Revenues per Establishment ($)	Payroll per Employee ($)
1997	24,208	133,031	2,857.0	13,316.0	5.5	550,066	21,476

Source: Economic Census of the United States, 1997. This is a newly defined industry. Data for prior years were unavailable at the time of publication but may become available over time.

INDICES OF CHANGE

Year	Establishments (number)	Employment (number)	Payroll ($ million)	Revenues ($ million)	Employees per Establishment (number)	Revenues per Establishment ($)	Payroll per Employee ($)
1997	100.0	100.0	100.0	100.0	100.0	100.0	100.0

Sources: Same as General Statistics. The values shown reflect change from the base year, 1997. Values above 100 mean greater than 1997, values below 100 mean less than 1997, and a value of 100 in the 1982-96 or 1998-2001 period means same as 1997. Values followed by a 'p' are projections by the editors; 'e' stands for extrapolation. Data are the most recent available at this level of detail.

SIC INDUSTRIES RELATED TO NAICS 813990

Each new NAICS code represents an industry that used to be part of an SIC or a part of several SIC industries. Data in this table are shown to provide transitional information for these cases. All available data for the precursor SIC(s) are shown. Even if only a part of an SIC is included in the NAICS, *all* data for the SIC are reproduced. If the SIC industry is not marked as being a part (pt) of the NAICS, the entire industry is embedded in the NAICS data. The SIC composition of the new industry provides some hints of the relative importance of its "ancestors." Data marked with a 'p' are projected. Projections begin with 1982 data. Data earlier than 1990 are not shown but are reflected in the projections.

SIC	Industry	1990	1991	1992	1993	1994	1995	1996	1997
6531	**Real Estate Agents and Managers (pt)**								
	Establishments (number)	-	-	106,552	-	-	-	-	-
	Employment (thousands)	-	-	646.6	-	-	-	-	-
	Revenues ($ million)	-	-	53,747.0	-	-	-	-	-
8641	**Civic & Social Associations (pt)**								
	Establishments (number)	39,999	43,422	41,789	41,942	41,940	41,764	43,156p	43,570p
	Employment (thousands)	365.8	384.6	355.1	369.5	374.9	386.1	395.4p	402.8p
	Revenues ($ million)	-	-	13,176.1	-	-	-	-	-
8699	**Membership Organizations, nec (pt)**								
	Establishments (number)	9,670	10,125	10,596	10,695	10,666	10,760	11,062p	11,247p
	Employment (thousands)	87.7	91.9	91.4	95.7	96.0	101.7	103.3p	105.9p
	Revenues ($ million)	-	-	6,267.8	-	-	-	-	-

Source: Economic Census of the United States, 1992, annual surveys of economic sectors conducted by the Bureau of the Census, and estimates or projections based on the 1982-1992 period; not all data are shown. 'e' marks estimates made by the editors; 'p' indicates projections based on time series. A dash (-) indicates that data for this SIC or year were not available. The abbreviation (pt) next to the industry name indicates that only a part of the industry is present within the NAICS data. If no (pt) is shown, the entire industry is contained within the NAICS data.

SELECTED RATIOS

For 1997	Avg. of Information	Analyzed Industry	Index	For 1997	Avg. of Information	Analyzed Industry	Index
Employees per establishment	6	5	88	Payroll per establishment	126,069	118,019	94
Revenue per establishment	511,622	550,066	108	Payroll as % of revenue	25	21	87
Revenue per employee	81,659	100,097	123	Payroll per employee	20,122	21,476	107

Sources: Same as General Statistics. The 'Average' column represents the average for the industry sector, in 1997, where the currently shown industry is classified. The Index shows the relationship between the Average and the Analyzed Industry. For example, 100 means that they are equal; 500 that the Analyzed Industry is five times the average; 50 means that the Analyzed Industry is half the national average. The abbreviation 'na' is used to show that data are 'not available'.

LEADING COMPANIES

No company data available for this industry.

REPRESENTATIVE NONPROFIT ORGANIZATIONS

Organization Name	Address				Phone	Income Range ($ mil)
American Association of Port Authorities Inc	1010 Duke St	Alexandria	VA	22314	703-684-5700	1-5
American Indian Business Development Corporation	1113 E Franklin Ave	Minneapolis	MN	55404	612-870-7555	1-5
Anne Arundel Economic Development Corporation	2660 Riva Rd Ste 200	Annapolis	MD	21401		1-5
Arkansas Enterprise Group	605 Main St Ste 203	Arkadelphia	AR	71923		1-5
Aurora Economic Development Council Inc	562 Sable Blvd Ste 240	Aurora	CO	80011	303-340-2101	1-5
Bartlesville Development	201 SW Keeler	Bartlesville	OK	74003	918-337-0001	1-5
Bay Colony Development Corp	800 South St	Waltham	MA	02453	781-891-3594	1-5
Blood Bank of Delaware Inc	100 Hygeia Dr	Newark	DE	19713	302-737-8400	10-19
Blue Grass Community Action Agency Inc	3445 Versailles Rd	Frankfort	KY	40601	502-695-4290	5-9
Business Development Corporation of Clarendon County	PO Box 670	Manning	SC	29102		1-5
Capital Associated Industries Inc	2900 Highwoods Blvd	Raleigh	NC	27604	919-878-9222	1-5
Center for Business Innovation Inc	4747 Troost Ave	Kansas City	MO	64110	816-561-8567	1-5
City of Prescott Municipal Property Corporation	201 S Cortez	Prescott	AZ	86303	520-776-6220	5-9
Coastal Enterprises Inc	PO Box 268	Wiscasset	ME	04578		5-9
Connecticut Economic Resource	805 Brook St Bldg 4	Rocky Hill	CT	06067	860-571-7136	1-5
Coordinating & Development Corp Louisiana Inc	PO Box 37005	Shreveport	LA	71133		5-9
Corporacion de Desarrollo y Fomento Economico de las Piedras	PO Box 790	Las Piedras	PR	00771		1-5
Corporation for Economic Development of Harris County Inc	2223 W Loop S 400	Houston	TX	77027		1-5
Cynosure Inc	PO Box 786	Burlington	VT	05402		1-5
Decorah Jobs Inc	PO Box 288	Decorah	IA	52101		1-5
East Central Idaho Planning and Development Association	310 N 2nd E Ste 115	Rexburg	ID	83440	208-356-4525	1-5
Enterprise Florida Inc	390 N Orange Ave	Orlando	FL	32801	407-425-5313	20-29
Essex County Economic Development Corp	443 Northfield Ave	West Orange	NJ	07052	973-731-1400	1-5
Fergus Electric Cooperative Inc	8470 Hwy 87 E	Lewistown	MT	59457	406-538-3465	5-9
Gadsden Area Chamber of Commerce Inc	PO Box 185	Gadsden	AL	35902	256-543-3472	1-5
Garland Light & Power Company	755 Hwy 14 RT 1	Powell	WY	82435	307-754-2881	1-5
Gateway Industrial Park Corporation	PO Box 720	Eau Claire	WI	54702		1-5
Greater Columbus Chamber of Commerce	PO Box 1200	Columbus	GA	31902		1-5
Growth Initiative Fund Inc	417 Main Ave Room 401	Fargo	ND	58103		1-5
Industrial Foundation of Albuquerque Inc	851 University SE Ste 203	Albuquerque	NM	87106		1-5
Leads	159 Wilson St	Newark	OH	43055	740-349-8606	5-9
Monadnock Economic Development Corporation	46 Main St	Keene	NH	03431		1-5
New York City Economic Development Corporation	110 William St RM 400	New York	NY	10038		50+
Overland Park Chamber of Commerce	10975 Benson Ste 350	Overland Park	KS	66210	913-491-0123	1-5
R I D C	425 Sixth Avenue Ste 500	Pittsburgh	PA	15219		20-29
Regional Organized Crime Information Center	545 Marriott Dr Ste 850	Nashville	TN	37214		1-5
Rfe-RL Inc	1201 Conn Ave NW	Washington	DC	20036	202-457-6950	50+
Rotary International	1560 Sherman Ave	Evanston	IL	60201	847-866-3000	50+
Rotary International	2839 W Kennewick	Kennewick	WA	99336		1-5
San Diego Convention Corporation Inc	111 W Harbor Dr	San Diego	CA	92101	619-525-5000	20-29
Sioux Falls Development Foundation Inc	200 N Phillips Ave	Sioux Falls	SD	57104	605-336-1620	5-9
Southeast Michigan Community Alliance Inc	8750 S Telegraph	Taylor	MI	48180		20-29
United Rural Electric Membership Corporation	PO Box 605	Markle	IN	46770	219-758-3155	10-19
Utah Technology Finance Corporation	177 E 100 S	Salt Lake Cty	UT	84111	801-741-4200	1-5
West Virginia High Technology Consortium Foundation	1000 Technology Dr	Fairmont	WV	26554		10-19
Wilkinson County Industrial Development Authority	PO Box 1286	Woodville	MS	39669		5-9

Source: *National Directory of Nonprofit Organizations*, 2000, Volumes 1 and 2, The Taft Group. The table shows a selection of organizations for illustration and does not constitute a complete selection from the source. The organizations are arranged in alphabetical order.

LOCATION BY STATE AND REGIONAL CONCENTRATION

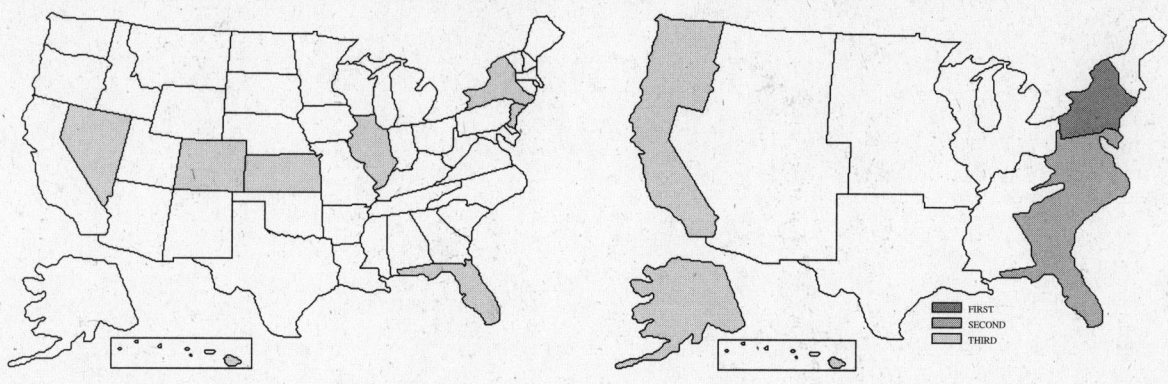

FIRST
SECOND
THIRD

INDUSTRY DATA BY STATE

State	Establishments Total (number)	% of U.S.	Employment Total (number)	% of U.S.	Per Estab.	Payroll Total ($ mil.)	Per Empl. ($)	Revenues Total ($ mil.)	% of U.S.	Per Estab. ($)
New York	4,700	19.4	25,743	19.4	5	823.0	31,970	3,899.8	29.3	829,739
Florida	3,641	15.0	24,503	18.4	7	440.0	17,955	1,930.8	14.5	530,291
California	2,181	9.0	12,449	9.4	6	257.9	20,716	1,085.8	8.2	497,859
Illinois	1,228	5.1	6,302	4.7	5	139.6	22,156	633.7	4.8	516,081
New Jersey	918	3.8	4,312	3.2	5	98.2	22,764	555.2	4.2	604,838
Colorado	580	2.4	3,859	2.9	7	81.7	21,175	439.5	3.3	757,829
Texas	1,144	4.7	5,250	3.9	5	84.4	16,082	413.6	3.1	361,533
Hawaii	878	3.6	4,392	3.3	5	82.9	18,865	410.8	3.1	467,918
Kansas	128	0.5	986	0.7	8	26.4	26,799	306.9	2.3	2,397,852
Pennsylvania	569	2.4	3,714	2.8	7	72.0	19,394	306.4	2.3	538,434
Virginia	530	2.2	3,116	2.3	6	55.9	17,945	262.4	2.0	495,077
Maryland	397	1.6	2,584	1.9	7	48.8	18,888	216.0	1.6	544,156
D.C.	262	1.1	1,788	1.3	7	42.4	23,730	211.1	1.6	805,729
North Carolina	353	1.5	1,846	1.4	5	36.9	19,997	191.2	1.4	541,654
Massachusetts	437	1.8	2,100	1.6	5	41.0	19,512	177.5	1.3	406,231
Ohio	471	1.9	2,007	1.5	4	34.3	17,074	170.6	1.3	362,301
Arizona	341	1.4	2,885	2.2	8	43.7	15,153	157.1	1.2	460,572
Connecticut	425	1.8	1,464	1.1	3	33.4	22,836	151.3	1.1	355,913
Michigan	425	1.8	1,416	1.1	3	27.5	19,436	149.2	1.1	351,144
Wisconsin	263	1.1	1,262	0.9	5	19.6	15,515	132.6	1.0	504,061
Georgia	259	1.1	1,552	1.2	6	37.4	24,121	127.7	1.0	493,232
Indiana	213	0.9	1,109	0.8	5	25.1	22,632	120.6	0.9	566,150
South Carolina	233	1.0	2,231	1.7	10	39.0	17,477	114.0	0.9	489,069
Washington	573	2.4	1,701	1.3	3	27.8	16,344	110.8	0.8	193,431
Missouri	316	1.3	1,484	1.1	5	27.2	18,360	105.7	0.8	334,500
Alabama	98	0.4	291	0.2	3	6.4	21,918	96.1	0.7	980,694
Tennessee	254	1.0	1,122	0.8	4	18.0	16,085	81.5	0.6	320,772
Utah	170	0.7	1,140	0.9	7	19.3	16,927	79.1	0.6	465,147
Nevada	183	0.8	1,298	1.0	7	22.6	17,447	78.0	0.6	426,328
Minnesota	286	1.2	1,209	0.9	4	15.8	13,097	71.5	0.5	250,133
Oregon	205	0.8	864	0.6	4	13.4	15,546	59.9	0.4	291,966
Rhode Island	65	0.3	253	0.2	4	6.2	24,403	43.6	0.3	671,215
Arkansas	80	0.3	758	0.6	9	11.8	15,578	39.3	0.3	490,912
Louisiana	119	0.5	510	0.4	4	8.2	15,992	38.6	0.3	324,218
Kentucky	129	0.5	564	0.4	4	9.2	16,284	36.5	0.3	282,643
New Hampshire	114	0.5	518	0.4	5	9.2	17,751	34.8	0.3	305,465
Oklahoma	125	0.5	478	0.4	4	7.9	16,550	34.0	0.3	271,872
New Mexico	103	0.4	663	0.5	6	9.4	14,228	31.7	0.2	308,000
Vermont	77	0.3	450	0.3	6	8.9	19,822	31.0	0.2	402,844
Nebraska	66	0.3	395	0.3	6	8.1	20,410	30.7	0.2	465,030
Iowa	111	0.5	340	0.3	3	6.0	17,515	27.5	0.2	248,144
Idaho	78	0.3	348	0.3	4	5.4	15,641	21.1	0.2	270,744
Delaware	78	0.3	224	0.2	3	4.5	20,129	18.6	0.1	238,615
Mississippi	56	0.2	248	0.2	4	3.4	13,560	16.1	0.1	287,411
West Virginia	55	0.2	375	0.3	7	4.5	11,915	15.2	0.1	277,182
Montana	78	0.3	235	0.2	3	2.6	11,009	13.5	0.1	172,667
Maine	64	0.3	283	0.2	4	3.4	11,996	13.0	0.1	202,828
Alaska	39	0.2	150	0.1	4	2.6	17,180	9.8	0.1	251,641
Wyoming	34	0.1	92	0.1	3	1.3	13,967	4.9	0.0	144,088
South Dakota	39	0.2	104	0.1	3	1.5	14,038	4.6	0.0	116,795
North Dakota	37	0.2	64	0.0	2	0.9	14,813	4.5	0.0	121,568

Source: 1997 *Economic Census*. The states are in descending order of revenues or establishments (if revenue data are missing for the majority). The symbol (D) appears when data are withheld to prevent disclosure of competitive information. States marked with (D) are sorted by number of establishments. A dash (-) indicates that the data element cannot be calculated. * indicates the midpoint of a range; 175, for example is the range 100-249. Shaded *states* on the state map indicate those states which have proportionately greater representation in the industry than would be indicated by the state's population; the ratio is based on total revenues or number of establishments. Shaded *regions* indicate where the industry is regionally most concentrated.

INDEXES

SUBJECT INDEX

SIC INDEX

NAICS INDEX

COMPANY INDEX

SIC INDEX

This index holds references to all SIC-denominated industries. Items shown in bold are Standard Industrial Classification codes (SICs). Page references (dashed items) are to the NAICS industry which is either identical to the SIC industry or incorporates all or a part of it. NAICS stands for North American Industry Classification System. The index is in two parts. The first part is sorted by SIC number. The second is arranged alphabetically by the industry name. The SIC code is shown in parentheses after the name. To find industries by NAICS code, please see the NAICS Index. This index provides an interesting view of the way in which SICs have been distributed among the new NAICS codes.

Bold items are SICs. Dashed items are NAICS codes. Numbers following p. are page references.

Bold items are SICs. Dashed items are NAICS codes. Numbers following p. are page references.

Bold items are SICs. Dashed items are NAICS codes. Numbers following p. are page references.

Bold items are SICs. Dashed items are NAICS codes. Numbers following p. are page references.

Bold items are SICs. Dashed items are NAICS codes. Numbers following p. are page references.

Bold items are SICs. Dashed items are NAICS codes. Numbers following p. are page references.

Bold items are SICs. Dashed items are NAICS codes. Numbers following p. are page references.

Bold items are SICs. Dashed items are NAICS codes. Numbers following p. are page references.

NAICS INDEX

This index holds references to all NAICS-denominated industries. NAICS stands for North American Industry Classification System. Page references are to the starting page of the industry. The index is in two parts. The first part is sorted by NAICS number. The second is arranged alphabetically by industry name. The NAICS code is shown in parentheses after the name. To find industries by Standard Industrial Classification (SIC) code, please see the SIC Index.

Numbers following p. are page references.

Numbers following p. are page references.

Numbers following p. are page references.

Numbers following p. are page references.

SUBJECT INDEX

This index holds references to more than 2,700 product or service categories, industrial activities, organizations, governmental programs, and independent occupations. All references are to page numbers. Pages refer to the starting page of the industry in which a product is made or a service is performed.

Numbers following p. or pp. are page references.

Subject Index

Numbers following p. or pp. are page references.

Numbers following p. or pp. are page references.

Subject Index

Numbers following p. or pp. are page references.

Numbers following p. or pp. are page references.

Numbers following p. or pp. are page references.

Numbers following p. or pp. are page references.

Numbers following p. or pp. are page references.

Numbers following p. or pp. are page references.

Numbers following p. or pp. are page references.

Subject Index

Numbers following p. or pp. are page references.

COMPANY INDEX

This index shows, in alphabetical order, more than 7,000 companies and other organizations in *Information, Finance, and Services USA*. Organizations may be public or private companies, subsidiaries or divisions of companies, joint ventures or affiliates, or corporate groups. They may also be nonprofit foundations and similar organizations. Each company entry is followed by one or more page numbers. One or more NAICS codes are shown for each organization, indicating the industry or industries in which it participates.

Numbers following p. or pp. are page references. Braketed items indicate industries. Page references are to the starting pages of company tables.

622110]

Albany Security Company Co, p. 470 [NAICS 561621]

Albergue Olimpico De Puerto Rico, p. 736 [NAICS 713990]

Albert L Schultz, p. 729 [NAICS 713940]

Albert Lea Medical Center, p. 622 [NAICS 622110]

Albertsons Employees Health and Welfare Trust, p. 905 [NAICS 813410]

Albuquerque International Balloon Fiesta Inc, p. 736 [NAICS 713990]

Alco Parking Corp, p. 881 [NAICS 812930]

Alcoholism Recovery Services Inc, p. 637 [NAICS 623220]

Alcor Life Extension Foundation, p. 617 [NAICS 621999]

Alderson Reporting Company Inc, p. 421 [NAICS 561410]

Alexander Broadcasting Co, p. 52 [NAICS 513111]

Alexander Haagen Properties Inc, p. 191 [NAICS 525930]

Alexander Marketing Services Inc, pp. 357, 377 [NAICS 541820, 541910]

Alexander's Inc, p. 199 [NAICS 531120]

Alexandria Hospital Inc Accounting Dept, p. 622 [NAICS 622110]

Alfred E Mann Institute for Biomedical Engineering, USC, p. 603 [NAICS 621511]

Alfred P Sloan Foundation, p. 348 [NAICS 541710]

Algood Healthcare Inc, p. 632 [NAICS 623110]

Alhambra Motors Inc, p. 786 [NAICS 811111]

Aliant Communications Inc, p. 70 [NAICS 513321]

Alico Inc, p. 204 [NAICS 531190]

Alistar Insurance Co, p. 172 [NAICS 524126]

Alive Hospice Inc, p. 653 [NAICS 624190]

All American Television Inc, p. 362 [NAICS 541840]

All Chemical Disposal Inc, p. 497 [NAICS 562111]

All Childrens Hospital Inc, p. 622 [NAICS 622110]

All Star Amusement Co, p. 710 [NAICS 713110]

All-Star Music Corp, p. 27 [NAICS 512120]

All-Tech Investment Group, p. 816 [NAICS 811212]

Allbritton Communications Co, p. 58 [NAICS 513120]

Allee King Rosen & Fleming Inc, p. 344 [NAICS 541690]

Alleghany Corp, p. 175 [NAICS 524127]

Allegheny Health Education & Research Foundation, p. 618 [NAICS 621999]

Allegheny Power Service Corp, pp. 288, 406 [NAICS 541330, 561110]

Allegiance Corp, p. 406 [NAICS 561110]

Allen and O'Hara Inc, p. 196 [NAICS 531110]

Allen Lovelace Moore and Blanche Davis Moore Foundation, p. 603 [NAICS 621511]

Allen Memorial Hospital Corporation, p. 622 [NAICS 622110]

Allerton Heneghan and O'Neill, p. 412 [NAICS 561310]

Alliance Capital Management LP, p. 157 [NAICS 523930]

Alliance Community Hospital, p. 653 [NAICS 624190]

Alliance Corporate Resources Inc, p. 252 [NAICS

532420]

Alliance Defense Fund Inc, p. 265 [NAICS 541110]

Alliance Gaming Corp, p. 713 [NAICS 713120]

Alliance Imaging Inc, p. 617 [NAICS 621999]

Alliance Primary Care, p. 563 [NAICS 621111]

Alliance Title Co, p. 175 [NAICS 524127]

Allianz Insurance Co, p. 172 [NAICS 524126]

Allied Bond & Collection Agency, p. 435 [NAICS 561440]

Allied Deals Inc, p. 147 [NAICS 523140]

ALLIED Group Inc, p. 94 [NAICS 514210]

Allied Home Health, p. 609 [NAICS 621610]

Allied Security Inc, p. 461 [NAICS 561611]

Allied Services, p. 629 [NAICS 622310]

Allied Tire Sales Inc, p. 786 [NAICS 811111]

Allied-Vaughn Div., p. 36 [NAICS 512191]

AlliedSignal Technical Services, p. 288 [NAICS 541330]

Allina Health System, p. 618 [NAICS 621999]

Alloy Welding Corp, p. 839 [NAICS 811490]

Allstate Financial Corp, p. 134 [NAICS 522320]

Allstate Insurance Co, pp. 166, 172 [NAICS 524113, 524126]

Allstate Leasing Inc, pp. 224, 227 [NAICS 532112, 532120]

Allstates Design & Development, p. 315 [NAICS 541511]

ALLTEK Missouri Inc, p. 67 [NAICS 513310]

ALLTEL Communications Co, p. 67 [NAICS 513310]

ALLTEL Corp, pp. 21, 67, 70, 94 [NAICS 511210, 513310, 513321, 514210]

ALLTEL Information Services Inc, pp. 21, 94 [NAICS 511210, 514210]

ALLTEL Missouri Inc, p. 67 [NAICS 513310]

Almost Family, p. 653 [NAICS 624190]

Alpha Christian Registry Inc, p. 609 [NAICS 621610]

Alpha Omicron Pi Fraternity Inc, p. 905 [NAICS 813410]

Alpha Systems Lab Inc, p. 816 [NAICS 811212]

Alphapointe Association for the Bli ND, p. 653 [NAICS 624190]

Alpine Country Club Corp, p. 721 [NAICS 713910]

Alta California Regional Center Inc, p. 541 [NAICS 611519]

Alta Ski Lifts Company Inc, p. 735 [NAICS 713990]

Altadena Valley Golf & Country Club, p. 721 [NAICS 713910]

Altergarten Las Teresas II Inc, p. 643 [NAICS 623312]

Alternate Marketing Networks Inc, p. 371 [NAICS 541870]

Alternative Resources Corp, p. 412 [NAICS 561310]

Alternatives Incorporated, p. 637 [NAICS 623220]

Alterra Healthcare Corp, p. 646 [NAICS 623990]

Alton Gaming Co, p. 713 [NAICS 713120]

Altres Inc, p. 415 [NAICS 561320]

Altru Health System, p. 622 [NAICS 622110]

Alumni Association of the University of Mississippi, p. 905 [NAICS 813410]

Alzheimers Disease & Related Disorders Association, p. 348 [NAICS 541710]

Am/Fm Transfer Media, p. 52 [NAICS 513111]

Amadeus Global Travel, p. 89 [NAICS 514191]

Amalgamated Life Insurance Co, p. 169 [NAICS 524114]

AmalgaTrust Company Inc, p. 160 [NAICS 523991]

Amarillo Hospital District, p. 622 [NAICS 622110]

Amateur Trapshooting Association of America, p. 681 [NAICS 711211]

AMB Property Corp, p. 191 [NAICS 525930]

Ambassador Programs Inc, p. 554 [NAICS 611699]

Ambassadors International Inc, p. 554 [NAICS 611699]

Ambrose Video Publishing Inc, p. 27 [NAICS 512120]

Ambrosi and Associates Inc, pp. 310, 380 [NAICS 541430, 541921]

Ambulatory Healthcare, pp. 587, 600 [NAICS 621399, 621498]

AMC Entertainment Inc, p. 30 [NAICS 512131]

Amdahl Corp, p. 21 [NAICS 511210]

AMDL Inc, p. 347 [NAICS 541710]

AME Inc, p. 249 [NAICS 532412]

Amedisys Inc, p. 412 [NAICS 561310]

AMERCO, p. 227 [NAICS 532120]

America Service Group Inc, p. 600 [NAICS 621498]

American Academy of Family Physicians, p. 541 [NAICS 611519]

American Academy of Family Physicians Foundation, p. 603 [NAICS 621511]

American Academy of Ophthalmology Inc, p. 911 [NAICS 813920]

American Academy of Orthopedic Surgeons, p. 541 [NAICS 611519]

American Ad Management Inc, p. 371 [NAICS 541870]

American Airlines Employees, p. 108 [NAICS 522130]

American Arbitration Association, p. 541 [NAICS 611519]

American Architectural Products, p. 285 [NAICS 541310]

American Association for the Advancement of Science, p. 541 [NAICS 611519]

American Association of Petroleum Geologists, p. 911 [NAICS 813920]

American Association of Petroleum Geologists Foundation, p. 348 [NAICS 541710]

American Association of Port Authorities Inc, p. 914 [NAICS 813990]

American Association of Retired Persons, p. 653 [NAICS 624190]

American Association of University Women, p. 541 [NAICS 611519]

American Automobile Association, p. 810 [NAICS 811198]

American Bankers Association, p. 908 [NAICS 813910]

American Bankers Insurance, p. 169 [NAICS 524114]

American Baptist Homes, p. 196 [NAICS 531110]

American Baptist Homes of the Midwest, p. 643 [NAICS 623312]

American Baptist Homes of the West, p. 643 [NAICS 623312]

American Bar Association, p. 911 [NAICS 813920]

Numbers following p. or pp. are page references. Braketed items indicate industries. Page references are to the starting pages of company tables.

American Beverage Corp, p. 163 [NAICS 523999]

American Bingo & Gaming Corp, p. 735 [NAICS 713990]

American Biogenetic Sciences Inc, p. 347 [NAICS 541710]

American Board of Pediatrics Inc, p. 911 [NAICS 813920]

American Booksellers Assoc Inc, p. 736 [NAICS 713990]

American Bureau of Shipping, p. 911 [NAICS 813920]

American Business Financial, p. 128 [NAICS 522298]

American Cabaret Theatre Inc, p. 672 [NAICS 711110]

American Cancer Society Divisions Inc, p. 348 [NAICS 541710]

American Capitol Insurance Co, p. 166 [NAICS 524113]

American Center for Law and Justice Inc, p. 265 [NAICS 541110]

American Center for Wine Food and the Arts, p. 905 [NAICS 813410]

American City Business Journals, p. 4 [NAICS 511110]

American Coin Merchandising Inc, p. 713 [NAICS 713120]

American College of Cardiology Inc, p. 541 [NAICS 611519]

American College of Rheumatology, p. 911 [NAICS 813920]

American Color Graphics Inc, p. 7 [NAICS 511120]

American Commercial Security, p. 461 [NAICS 561611]

American Conservatory Theater, pp. 533, 691 [NAICS 611511, 711320]

American Contract Bridge League Inc, p. 736 [NAICS 713990]

American Corporate Health, p. 617 [NAICS 621999]

American Diabetes Association Inc, p. 348 [NAICS 541710]

American Direct Mail Inc, p. 368 [NAICS 541860]

American Eagle Management Inc, pp. 763, 766, 769 [NAICS 722211, 722212, 722213]

American Ecology Corp, p. 497 [NAICS 562111]

American Ecology Recycle Center, p. 497 [NAICS 562111]

American Education Corp, p. 27 [NAICS 512120]

American Electric Power Inc, p. 397 [NAICS 551112]

American Electronic Association, p. 108 [NAICS 522130]

American Equipment Inc, p. 249 [NAICS 532412]

American Express Bank Ltd, p. 124 [NAICS 522293]

American Express Company, pp. 7, 94, 124, 134, 142, 368, 449 [NAICS 511120, 514210, 522293, 522320, 523120, 541860, 561510]

American Express Credit Corp, p. 134 [NAICS 522320]

American Express Financial, p. 157 [NAICS 523930]

American Family Life Assurance, p. 166 [NAICS 524113]

American Family Mutual, p. 169 [NAICS 524114]

American Financial Corp, pp. 166, 172, 397 [NAICS 524113, 524126, 551112]

American General Corp, pp. 166, 172 [NAICS 524113, 524126]

American General Finance Corp, p. 118 [NAICS 522291]

American General Finance Inc, pp. 118, 397 [NAICS 522291, 551112]

American General Life, pp. 166, 169 [NAICS 524113, 524114]

American Golf Corp, p. 720 [NAICS 713910]

American Greetings Corp, p. 89 [NAICS 514191]

American Greyhound Racing Inc, p. 684 [NAICS 711212]

American Grinding & Machine Co, p. 839 [NAICS 811490]

American Health Properties Inc, p. 191 [NAICS 525930]

American HealthChoice Inc, p. 572 [NAICS 621310]

American Healthways Inc, p. 587 [NAICS 621399]

American HomePatient Inc, p. 609 [NAICS 621610]

American Honda Finance Corp, p. 224 [NAICS 532112]

American Hospital Association, p. 736 [NAICS 713990]

American Indian Business Development Corporation, p. 914 [NAICS 813990]

American Industrial Partners, p. 163 [NAICS 523999]

American Institute of Certified Public Accountants, p. 911 [NAICS 813920]

American International Group Inc, pp. 166, 172, 397 [NAICS 524113, 524126, 551112]

American Investment Bank, p. 118 [NAICS 522291]

American Line BLDRS Apprenticeship Training Joint Committee, p. 538 [NAICS 611513]

American List Counsel Inc, p. 368 [NAICS 541860]

American Management Services, p. 327 [NAICS 541611]

American Management Systems, pp. 94, 318, 406 [NAICS 514210, 541512, 561110]

American Media Inc, p. 7 [NAICS 511120]

American Medical Security Inc, p. 182 [NAICS 524210]

American Mobile Satellite Corp, p. 70 [NAICS 513321]

American Morgan Horse Association Inc, p. 736 [NAICS 713990]

American Multi-Cinema Inc, p. 30 [NAICS 512131]

American Museum of Natural History, p. 705 [NAICS 712130]

American National Insurance Co, p. 169 [NAICS 524114]

American Nursing Care Inc, p. 609 [NAICS 621610]

American Paralysis Association, p. 603 [NAICS 621511]

American Payroll Association, p. 327 [NAICS 541611]

American Petroleum Institute, p. 911 [NAICS 813920]

American Printing House for the Blind Inc, p. 541 [NAICS 611519]

American Production Services, p. 36 [NAICS 512191]

American Protective Services Inc, p. 461 [NAICS 561611]

American Psychological Society, p. 603 [NAICS 621511]

American Re-Insurance Co, p. 172 [NAICS 524126]

American Religious Town Hall Meeting, p. 896 [NAICS 813311]

American Retirement Corp, pp. 196, 632 [NAICS 531110, 623110]

American Savings Bank F.S.B., p. 105 [NAICS 522120]

American Secondary Schools for Internatl Students & Teachers, p. 554 [NAICS 611699]

American Soceity of Travel, p. 435 [NAICS 561440]

American Society for Testing and Materials, p. 348 [NAICS 541710]

American Society of Health-System Pharmacists, p. 911 [NAICS 813920]

American Society of Radiologic Technologists, p. 348 [NAICS 541710]

American Southern Insurance Co, p. 182 [NAICS 524210]

American Stage Co Inc, p. 672 [NAICS 711110]

American Stock Exchange Inc, p. 150 [NAICS 523210]

American Stock Transfer & Trust, p. 160 [NAICS 523991]

American Stores Co, p. 397 [NAICS 551112]

American Tenant Screen Inc, p. 438 [NAICS 561450]

American Title Co, p. 268 [NAICS 541191]

American United Global Inc, p. 249 [NAICS 532412]

American Urological Association Incorporated, p. 736 [NAICS 713990]

American Wagering Inc, p. 735 [NAICS 713990]

American Web Inc, p. 18 [NAICS 511199]

American Western Mortgage Co, p. 121 [NAICS 522292]

American Youth Soccer Organization, p. 902 [NAICS 813319]

AmeriCredit Corp, p. 118 [NAICS 522291]

AmeriCredit Financial Services, p. 118 [NAICS 522291]

Ameridial Inc, pp. 368, 377, 388 [NAICS 541860, 541910, 541990]

AmeriNet Inc, p. 388 [NAICS 541990]

AmeriPath Inc, p. 388 [NAICS 541990]

Ameripride Services Inc, pp. 869, 872 [NAICS 812331, 812332]

Ameristar Casinos Inc, p. 742 [NAICS 721110]

Ameritech Corp, pp. 67, 70, 89, 397 [NAICS 513310, 513321, 514191, 551112]

Ameritech Indiana, pp. 61, 67, 70 [NAICS 513210, 513310, 513321]

Ameritech MBL Communications, p. 70 [NAICS 513321]

AmeriTrade Holding Corp, p. 142 [NAICS 523120]

AMF Bowling Centers Inc, p. 732 [NAICS 713950]

AMFM Inc, p. 52 [NAICS 513111]

AMGRO Inc, p. 134 [NAICS 522320]

AMI Capital Inc, p. 121 [NAICS 522292]

Numbers following p. or pp. are page references. Braketed items indicate industries. Page references are to the starting pages of company tables.

Amisys Inc, p. 816 [NAICS 811212]

Amli Residential Properties Trust, p. 191 [NAICS 525930]

Ammirati Puris Lintas Inc, p. 354 [NAICS 541810]

Amoco Co, p. 397 [NAICS 551112]

AMPCO System Parking, p. 881 [NAICS 812930]

Ampersand Ventures Management, p. 163 [NAICS 523999]

Amplicon Inc, p. 252 [NAICS 532420]

AMR Corp, p. 397 [NAICS 551112]

Amresco Inc, p. 199 [NAICS 531120]

AMSEC LLC, p. 388 [NAICS 541990]

Amsher Collection Services Inc, p. 435 [NAICS 561440]

AmSouth Bancorp, pp. 102, 394 [NAICS 522110, 551111]

AmSurg Corp, p. 562 [NAICS 621111]

Amtech Engineering Services, p. 409 [NAICS 561210]

Amtek Computer Services, p. 816 [NAICS 811212]

Amtran Inc, p. 449 [NAICS 561510]

Anacomp Inc, pp. 388, 839 [NAICS 541990, 811490]

Analex Corp, p. 347 [NAICS 541710]

Analogic Data Conversion, p. 315 [NAICS 541511]

Analysis and Technology Inc, p. 315 [NAICS 541511]

Analysis Group Inc, p. 338 [NAICS 541618]

Analysts International Corp, p. 315 [NAICS 541511]

Analytical Computer Services, p. 816 [NAICS 811212]

Anasazi Inc, p. 388 [NAICS 541990]

Anchor Gaming, p. 713 [NAICS 713120]

Anchor Mortgage Corp, p. 137 [NAICS 522390]

Anchor National Life Insurance, p. 166 [NAICS 524113]

Anchorage Community Mental Health Services Inc, p. 626 [NAICS 622210]

Anchorage Convention & Visitors Bureau, p. 908 [NAICS 813910]

Ancient Free & Accepted Masons of W Virginia, p. 905 [NAICS 813410]

Ancilla Health Care Inc, p. 622 [NAICS 622110]

Ancilla Systems Inc, p. 621 [NAICS 622110]

Anderson Area Medical Center, p. 622 [NAICS 622110]

Anderson DeBartolo Pan, p. 285 [NAICS 541310]

Anderson Infirmary Benevolent Association Inc, p. 622 [NAICS 622110]

Anderson Youth Association, p. 626 [NAICS 622210]

Andover Golf & Country Club Inc, p. 721 [NAICS 713910]

Andreini and Co, p. 182 [NAICS 524210]

Andrew A Cheramie, p. 244 [NAICS 532310]

Andrews McMeel Universal, pp. 18, 83 [NAICS 511199, 514110]

Andy Gump Inc, p. 244 [NAICS 532310]

Anheuser-Busch Companies Inc, p. 710 [NAICS 713110]

Anheuser-Busch Employees, p. 108 [NAICS 522130]

Ann Arbor Art Association, p. 699 [NAICS 712110]

Anna Jaques Hospital, p. 622 [NAICS 622110]

Annandale Inc, p. 721 [NAICS 713910]

Anne Arundel Economic Development Corporation, p. 914 [NAICS 813990]

Antarctic Support Associates, p. 409 [NAICS 561210]

Antech Ltd, p. 347 [NAICS 541710]

Anthem Inc, p. 169 [NAICS 524114]

Anthem Insurance Company Inc, pp. 157, 169, 172 [NAICS 523930, 524114, 524126]

Anthony Snipes, p. 729 [NAICS 713940]

Aon Consulting, p. 327 [NAICS 541611]

Aon Corp, pp. 166, 169, 397 [NAICS 524113, 524114, 551112]

Aon Group Inc, pp. 182, 397 [NAICS 524210, 551112]

Aon Re Inc, p. 182 [NAICS 524210]

Aon Re Worldwide, p. 182 [NAICS 524210]

Aon Risk Services Companies Inc, pp. 182, 397 [NAICS 524210, 551112]

Aon Risk Services of Central, p. 182 [NAICS 524210]

Aon Risk Services of Michigan, p. 182 [NAICS 524210]

Aon Services Group, p. 182 [NAICS 524210]

Apartment Hunters, p. 884 [NAICS 812990]

APCOA/Standard Parking Inc, p. 881 [NAICS 812930]

Aperture Foundation Inc, p. 699 [NAICS 712110]

APEX Data Services Inc, pp. 94, 315 [NAICS 514210, 541511]

Apex Investment Partners, p. 163 [NAICS 523999]

Apex Mortgage Capital Inc, p. 191 [NAICS 525930]

APG Security Inc, p. 461 [NAICS 561611]

Aplin Uno and Chibana Inc, p. 310 [NAICS 541430]

Appalachian Regional Healthcare Inc, p. 622 [NAICS 622110]

Appalachian Research & Defense Fund of Kentucky Inc, p. 265 [NAICS 541110]

Appaloosa Horse Club, p. 736 [NAICS 713990]

Apple Computer Inc, p. 21 [NAICS 511210]

Apple Orthodontix Inc, p. 569 [NAICS 621210]

Applebee's International Inc, p. 258 [NAICS 533110]

Appleton Medical Center, p. 622 [NAICS 622110]

Appleton Prison Corporation, p. 653 [NAICS 624190]

Applied Analytical Industries Inc, p. 347 [NAICS 541710]

Applied Geosciences Inc, p. 344 [NAICS 541690]

Applied Graphics Technologies, p. 310 [NAICS 541430]

Applied Science & Technology, p. 344 [NAICS 541690]

Apria Healthcare Group Inc, p. 255 [NAICS 532490]

Aqua Alliance, p. 288 [NAICS 541330]

Aqua Care Systems, Inc, p. 807 [NAICS 811192]

Aquatic Rehabilitation Center Inc, p. 587 [NAICS 621399]

AR Industries Inc, p. 816 [NAICS 811212]

Arabian Nights, p. 735 [NAICS 713990]

ARAMARK Corp, p. 884 [NAICS 812990]

ARAMARK Educational, p. 667 [NAICS 624410]

Aramark Sports & Entertainment, pp. 760, 763, 766, 769 [NAICS 722110, 722211, 722212, 722213]

Arapahoe House Inc, p. 637 [NAICS 623220]

Aratex Services Inc, pp. 869, 872 [NAICS 812331, 812332]

Arbitron Co, p. 377 [NAICS 541910]

Arbor National Commercial, p. 121 [NAICS 522292]

Arc in Hawaii, p. 626 [NAICS 622210]

Arc Inc, p. 653 [NAICS 624190]

Arc of Prince Georges County Inc, p. 681 [NAICS 711211]

Arcadia Financial Ltd, p. 134 [NAICS 522320]

Arcadia Retirement Residence, p. 640 [NAICS 623311]

Arcadis-Geaghty and Miller, p. 285 [NAICS 541310]

Arch Communications Group Inc, p. 70 [NAICS 513321]

Archbold Health Services Inc, p. 609 [NAICS 621610]

Archer/Malmo Advertising Inc, pp. 357, 368 [NAICS 541820, 541860]

Archer Management Services Inc, p. 406 [NAICS 561110]

Archive Films/Archive Photos, p. 36 [NAICS 512191]

Archstone Communities Trust, p. 196 [NAICS 531110]

Arctic Slope Consulting Group, p. 338 [NAICS 541618]

Arctic Slope Native Association Ltd, p. 905 [NAICS 813410]

Ardaman and Associates Inc, p. 302 [NAICS 541380]

Area Agency on Aging of Southeast Arkansas Inc, p. 653 [NAICS 624190]

Area Agency on Aging Region I Inc, p. 653 [NAICS 624190]

Area Five Agency on Aging & Community Services, p. 637 [NAICS 623220]

Areawide Aging Agency Inc, p. 653 [NAICS 624190]

Arena Football League Inc, p. 681 [NAICS 711211]

Arent Fox Kintner Plotkin & Kahn, p. 264 [NAICS 541110]

Argenbright Inc, p. 388 [NAICS 541990]

Argosy Gaming Co, p. 713 [NAICS 713120]

Arizona All Claims Inc, p. 182 [NAICS 524210]

Arizona Baptist Retirement Center Inc, p. 640 [NAICS 623311]

Arizona Carpenters Joint Apprenticeship Training Fund, p. 538 [NAICS 611513]

Arizona Memorial Museum Association, p. 702 [NAICS 712120]

Arizona Mexico Border Health Foundation, p. 603 [NAICS 621511]

Arizona News Service Inc, p. 83 [NAICS 514110]

Arizona Sports Foundation, p. 736 [NAICS 713990]

Arizona State University Foundation, p. 541 [NAICS 611519]

Arkansas Alumni Association Inc, p. 905 [NAICS 813410]

Arkansas Childrens Hospital, p. 622 [NAICS 622110]

Numbers following p. or pp. are page references. Braketed items indicate industries. Page references are to the starting pages of company tables.

955

Numbers following p. or pp. are page references. Braketed items indicate industries. Page references are to the starting pages of company tables.

Numbers following p. or pp. are page references. Braketed items indicate industries. Page references are to the starting pages of company tables.

958

Company Index

Brody Transportation Inc, pp. 227, 786 [NAICS 532120, 811111]

Brody White and Company Inc, p. 147 [NAICS 523140]

Bromberg Holdings Inc, p. 199 [NAICS 531120]

Bronner Co, p. 368 [NAICS 541860]

Bronson Healthcare Group, p. 629 [NAICS 622310]

Bronx Legal Services, p. 265 [NAICS 541110]

Brook Furniture Rental Inc, p. 244 [NAICS 532310]

Brookdale Living Communities, pp. 196, 646 [NAICS 531110, 623990]

Brooke Group Ltd, p. 18 [NAICS 511199]

Brooks/Cole Publishing Co, p. 10 [NAICS 511130]

Broughton Foods Co, pp. 763, 766, 769 [NAICS 722211, 722212, 722213]

Brouillard Communications, p. 357 [NAICS 541820]

Brown and Brown, p. 182 [NAICS 524210]

Brown and Root Forest Products, p. 406 [NAICS 561110]

Brown and Root Inc, p. 288 [NAICS 541330]

Brown-Eagle Group Inc, p. 409 [NAICS 561210]

Brown Rental Equipment Inc, p. 249 [NAICS 532412]

Brown University, p. 905 [NAICS 813410]

Browning-Ferris Industries Inc, p. 497 [NAICS 562111]

Brownstein Group, p. 357 [NAICS 541820]

BRS Leasing Inc, p. 252 [NAICS 532420]

Bruce Liesch and Associates Inc, p. 344 [NAICS 541690]

Brunswick Corp, p. 732 [NAICS 713950]

Bryan Cave LLP, p. 264 [NAICS 541110]

Bryant College of Business Administration, p. 541 [NAICS 611519]

Bryn Mawr College, p. 908 [NAICS 813910]

BSL Golf Corp, p. 720 [NAICS 713910]

BSMG Worldwide, p. 357 [NAICS 541820]

BTG Inc, pp. 89, 315, 318 [NAICS 514191, 541511, 541512]

BTG Pharmaceuticals Corp, p. 347 [NAICS 541710]

Buck Consultants Inc, p. 338 [NAICS 541618]

Buckley Broadcasting Corp, p. 52 [NAICS 513111]

Bucks County Organization for Intercultural Advancement, p. 554 [NAICS 611699]

Budd Group, pp. 461, 479 [NAICS 561611, 561720]

Buddy Lee Attractions Inc, p. 691 [NAICS 711320]

Budget Group Inc, pp. 221, 227 [NAICS 532111, 532120]

Budget Rent A Car Corp, pp. 221, 227 [NAICS 532111, 532120]

Buena Vista Home Entertainment, p. 24 [NAICS 512110]

Buena Vista International Inc, p. 27 [NAICS 512120]

Buffalo Bill Memorial Association, p. 705 [NAICS 712130]

Buffalo Cardiology & Pulmonary, p. 562 [NAICS 621111]

Buffets Inc, pp. 258, 760 [NAICS 533110, 722110]

Bull HN Information Systems Inc, p. 315 [NAICS 541511]

Bull Worldwide Information, p. 318 [NAICS 541512]

Bureau of National Affairs Inc, p. 7 [NAICS 511120]

Burger King Corp, pp. 258, 760 [NAICS 533110, 722110]

Burger Physical Therapy, p. 587 [NAICS 621399]

Burgess and Niple Ltd, p. 285 [NAICS 541310]

Burlington Country Club Corp, p. 721 [NAICS 713910]

Burlington Golf Club, p. 721 [NAICS 713910]

Burlington United Methodist Family Services Inc, p. 646 [NAICS 623990]

Burnett Foundation, p. 563 [NAICS 621111]

Burnham Pacific Properties Inc, p. 191 [NAICS 525930]

Burns and Roe Enterprises Inc, p. 285 [NAICS 541310]

Burns and Wilcox Ltd, p. 182 [NAICS 524210]

Burns Bros. Inc, pp. 763, 766, 769 [NAICS 722211, 722212, 722213]

Burns International Services Corp, pp. 461, 470 [NAICS 561611, 561621]

Burr, Wolff and Associates, p. 276 [NAICS 541213]

Burrell Communications Group, p. 357 [NAICS 541820]

Burrelle's Information Services, p. 83 [NAICS 514110]

Burrillville Racing Association, p. 684 [NAICS 711212]

Burroughs Wellcome Fund, p. 348 [NAICS 541710]

Burson-Marsteller, p. 357 [NAICS 541820]

Burt Chevrolet Inc, p. 786 [NAICS 811111]

Burt County Museum Inc, p. 705 [NAICS 712130]

Burt Reynolds Institute for Theatre Training Inc, p. 538 [NAICS 611513]

Buscemi's International Inc, pp. 763, 766 [NAICS 722211, 722212]

Busch Entertainment Corp, p. 710 [NAICS 713110]

Bush Foundation, p. 541 [NAICS 611519]

Business Aircraft Leasing Inc, p. 244 [NAICS 532310]

Business and Legal Reports Inc, p. 18 [NAICS 511199]

Business Council of Alabama, p. 908 [NAICS 813910]

Business Development Corporation of Clarendon County, p. 914 [NAICS 813990]

Business Express of Boulder Inc, p. 432 [NAICS 561439]

Business Men's Assurance, p. 157 [NAICS 523930]

Business Wire, p. 83 [NAICS 514110]

Busler Enterprises Inc, pp. 763, 766, 769 [NAICS 722211, 722212, 722213]

Butler Hospital, p. 629 [NAICS 622310]

Butler International Inc, p. 412 [NAICS 561310]

Butler Service Group Inc, p. 288 [NAICS 541330]

Butterfield Trail Village Incorporated, p. 640 [NAICS 623311]

Butterfly World Ltd, p. 735 [NAICS 713990]

Butterick Company Inc, p. 18 [NAICS 511199]

Byrne Johnson Inc, p. 310 [NAICS 541430]

Byte Brothers Inc, p. 470 [NAICS 561621]

C C Young Memorial Home, p. 643 [NAICS 623312]

CA One Services Inc, pp. 760, 763, 766, 769, 881

[NAICS 722110, 722211, 722212, 722213, 812930]

Cabana Corp, p. 36 [NAICS 512191]

Cable Advertising Network, p. 362 [NAICS 541840]

Cable TV Montgomery, p. 61 [NAICS 513210]

Cabletron Systems Inc, p. 21 [NAICS 511210]

Cablevision Systems Corp, p. 61 [NAICS 513210]

CACI International Inc, pp. 315, 318 [NAICS 541511, 541512]

CAD MUS, p. 94 [NAICS 514210]

Cadence Design Systems Inc, p. 21 [NAICS 511210]

Cadmus Communications Corp, pp. 7, 18, 368 [NAICS 511120, 511199, 541860]

Cadshare Resources Inc, p. 252 [NAICS 532420]

Cadwalader, Wickersham and Taft, p. 264 [NAICS 541110]

Caesars World Inc, p. 742 [NAICS 721110]

Cahners Business Information, pp. 7, 18 [NAICS 511120, 511199]

Cal Fed Bancorp Inc, p. 163 [NAICS 523999]

Cal-Growers Corp, p. 377 [NAICS 541910]

Calder Race Course Inc, p. 684 [NAICS 711212]

Calibur Carwash Penncoil, p. 807 [NAICS 811192]

California Culinary Academy Inc, p. 554 [NAICS 611699]

California Endowment, p. 618 [NAICS 621999]

California Hospital Association, p. 890 [NAICS 813212]

California Hotel and Casino Inc, p. 742 [NAICS 721110]

California Veterinary Services Inc, p. 178 [NAICS 524128]

CaliforniaMart, p. 204 [NAICS 531190]

Calkins Newspapers Inc, p. 4 [NAICS 511110]

Call Connect, p. 617 [NAICS 621999]

Calle' and Co, p. 327 [NAICS 541611]

Callison Architecture Inc, pp. 285, 310 [NAICS 541310, 541430]

Calmark Inc, p. 368 [NAICS 541860]

CALSTART, p. 347 [NAICS 541710]

Calumet Farm Inc, p. 684 [NAICS 711212]

Camelot Communications Inc, p. 371 [NAICS 541870]

Camera Service Center Inc, p. 36 [NAICS 512191]

Cameron Computers Inc, pp. 252, 816 [NAICS 532420, 811212]

Cameron Telephone Company Inc, p. 67 [NAICS 513310]

Camino Medical Group Inc, p. 562 [NAICS 621111]

Camp Dresser and McKee Inc, p. 288 [NAICS 541330]

Campbell Blueprint & Supply Inc, p. 432 [NAICS 561439]

Campbell-Ewald Co, p. 354 [NAICS 541810]

Campbell/Manix Inc, p. 285 [NAICS 541310]

Campbell Mithun Esty LLC, p. 354 [NAICS 541810]

Camuy Health Services Inc, p. 618 [NAICS 621999]

Canada Life Assurance Co, pp. 166, 169 [NAICS 524113, 524114]

Cancer Treatment Holdings Inc, p. 600 [NAICS 621498]

Canisco Resources Inc, p. 409 [NAICS 561210]

Canterbury Information, pp. 528, 533 [NAICS

Numbers following p. or pp. are page references. Bracketed items indicate industries. Page references are to the starting pages of company tables.

960

624310]

Center Trust Retail Properties Inc, p. 204 [NAICS 531190]

Central and South West Corp, p. 397 [NAICS 551112]

Central Arkansas Radiation Therapy Institute Inc, p. 348 [NAICS 541710]

Central Arkansas Substance Abuse Programs Inc, p. 637 [NAICS 623220]

Central Boston Elder Services Inc, p. 640 [NAICS 623311]

Central California Blood Bank, p. 614 [NAICS 621991]

Central Coal and Coke Corp, p. 204 [NAICS 531190]

Central Engineering Co, p. 302 [NAICS 541380]

Central Financial Acceptance, p. 118 [NAICS 522291]

Central Florida Legal Services Inc, p. 265 [NAICS 541110]

Central Indiana Community Foundation Inc, p. 736 [NAICS 713990]

Central Kentucky Blood Center Inc, p. 614 [NAICS 621991]

Central Management Inc, pp. 199, 207 [NAICS 531120, 531210]

Central Minnesota Jobs and Training Services Inc, p. 538 [NAICS 611513]

Central Mississippi Legal Services Corporation, p. 265 [NAICS 541110]

Central Newspapers Inc, p. 4 [NAICS 511110]

Central Park Media Corp, p. 27 [NAICS 512120]

Central Parking Corp, p. 881 [NAICS 812930]

Central Parking System Inc, p. 881 [NAICS 812930]

Central Quality Services Corp, p. 869 [NAICS 812331]

Central Valley Regional Center Inc, p. 653 [NAICS 624190]

Central Vermont Physician Practice Corporation, p. 563 [NAICS 621111]

Central Washington Health Services Association, p. 622 [NAICS 622110]

Centre Capital Investors LP, p. 163 [NAICS 523999]

Centro De La Familia De Utah, p. 902 [NAICS 813319]

Centrobe, p. 368 [NAICS 541860]

Centura Banks Inc, p. 394 [NAICS 551111]

Century Business Services Inc, p. 388 [NAICS 541990]

Century Club of San Diego, p. 692 [NAICS 711320]

Century Communications Corp, pp. 52, 61, 70 [NAICS 513111, 513210, 513321]

Century Park Pictures Corp, p. 36 [NAICS 512191]

Century Theaters, p. 30 [NAICS 512131]

CenturyTel Inc, p. 67 [NAICS 513310]

CenturyTel Telecommunications, pp. 70, 94 [NAICS 513321, 514210]

Ceres Group Incorp., p. 617 [NAICS 621999]

Ceridian Benefits Services, p. 182 [NAICS 524210]

Ceridian Corp, pp. 94, 318 [NAICS 514210, 541512]

Ceridian Employer Services, p. 21 [NAICS 511210]

Cerner Corp, pp. 89, 315 [NAICS 514191, 541511]

Cerplex Group Inc, p. 816 [NAICS 811212]

Cerrell Associates Inc, p. 344 [NAICS 541690]

Certified Personnel Services, p. 412 [NAICS 561310]

Certified Temporary Services Inc, p. 415 [NAICS 561320]

CFC Franchising Co, p. 258 [NAICS 533110]

CFN Inc, pp. 763, 766 [NAICS 722211, 722212]

C.H. Heist Corp, p. 479 [NAICS 561720]

CH2M Hill Ltd, p. 288 [NAICS 541330]

Chace Productions Inc, p. 36 [NAICS 512191]

Chadbourne and Parke, p. 264 [NAICS 541110]

Chakeres Theatres Inc, p. 30 [NAICS 512131]

Challenger, Gray & Christmas Inc, p. 412 [NAICS 561310]

Chambers Communications Corp, p. 24 [NAICS 512110]

Chambers Group, p. 310 [NAICS 541430]

Championship Group Inc, p. 681 [NAICS 711211]

Chancellor Corp, p. 227 [NAICS 532120]

Change Point Inc, p. 600 [NAICS 621498]

Chapman and Cutler, p. 264 [NAICS 541110]

Chapman/Leonard Studio, p. 36 [NAICS 512191]

Charles Abbott Associates Inc, p. 327 [NAICS 541611]

Charles Dunn Co, pp. 199, 207 [NAICS 531120, 531210]

Charles E. Smith Management Inc, p. 199 [NAICS 531120]

Charles E. Smith Residential, p. 191 [NAICS 525930]

Charles F. Curry Inc, p. 121 [NAICS 522292]

Charles River Associates Inc, pp. 338, 377 [NAICS 541618, 541910]

Charles Schwab Corp, pp. 142, 157 [NAICS 523120, 523930]

Charles Stark Draper Laboratory Inc, p. 348 [NAICS 541710]

Charles Town Races Inc, p. 684 [NAICS 711212]

Charleston Museum, p. 705 [NAICS 712130]

Charlotte-Mecklenburg Health Services Foundation Inc, p. 618 [NAICS 621999]

Charlotte Steeplechase Association Inc, p. 692 [NAICS 711320]

Charlton Memorial Hospital, p. 621 [NAICS 622110]

Charrette Corp, p. 432 [NAICS 561439]

Chart House Enterprises Inc, pp. 763, 766, 769 [NAICS 722211, 722212, 722213]

Charter Behavioral Health System, p. 625 [NAICS 622210]

Charter Communications Inc, p. 61 [NAICS 513210]

Charter One Bank F.S.B., p. 105 [NAICS 522120]

Charter One Financial Inc, pp. 105, 394 [NAICS 522120, 551111]

Charter One Mortgage Corp, p. 118 [NAICS 522291]

Charter State Bank, p. 102 [NAICS 522110]

Chase Capital Partners, p. 163 [NAICS 523999]

Chase Manhattan, pp. 102, 394 [NAICS 522110, 551111]

Chasm Group, p. 327 [NAICS 541611]

Chateau Communities Inc, p. 191 [NAICS 525930]

CheckPOINT, p. 528 [NAICS 611420]

Cheer Ltd, p. 735 [NAICS 713990]

Chefs International Inc, pp. 763, 766, 769 [NAICS 722211, 722212, 722213]

Chelsea GCA Realty Inc, p. 199 [NAICS 531120]

Chemed Corp, p. 609 [NAICS 621610]

Chemfix Technologies Inc, p. 497 [NAICS 562111]

Chemical Abstracts Service, p. 315 [NAICS 541511]

Chemical Industry Institute of Toxicology, p. 908 [NAICS 813910]

Chemical Manufacturers Association Inc, p. 908 [NAICS 813910]

Chemtech Ltd, p. 327 [NAICS 541611]

ChemTreat Inc, p. 338 [NAICS 541618]

Chep USA, p. 244 [NAICS 532310]

Chequemate International Inc, p. 64 [NAICS 513220]

Cherry Creek Arts Festival Co, p. 699 [NAICS 712110]

Cherry Creek Golf Course, p. 720 [NAICS 713910]

Cherry Hills Country Club, p. 721 [NAICS 713910]

Cherryland Brewing Co, p. 781 [NAICS 722410]

Chesapeake Surveys, p. 377 [NAICS 541910]

Chesapeake Utilities Corp, p. 94 [NAICS 514210]

Cheskin and Masten/Image Net, p. 327 [NAICS 541611]

Chester County Hospital & Nursing Center Inc, p. 618 [NAICS 621999]

Chesterfield Financial Corp, pp. 252, 255 [NAICS 532420, 532490]

Chevron Industries, p. 315 [NAICS 541511]

Chevron Research & Technology, p. 347 [NAICS 541710]

Chevy Chase Bank F.S.B., p. 105 [NAICS 522120]

Chevy Chase Club Inc, p. 721 [NAICS 713910]

ChexSystems Inc, p. 388 [NAICS 541990]

Cheyenne Frontier Days Inc, p. 908 [NAICS 813910]

Chi Chi Rodriguez Youth Foundation, p. 664 [NAICS 624310]

Chi-Chi's Inc, p. 760 [NAICS 722110]

Chicago & Vicinity Laborers, p. 538 [NAICS 611513]

Chicago Board of Trade, p. 150 [NAICS 523210]

Chicago Board Options Exchange, p. 150 [NAICS 523210]

Chicago City Limits, p. 679 [NAICS 711190]

Chicago Deferred Exchange, p. 128 [NAICS 522298]

Chicago Mercantile Exchange, p. 150 [NAICS 523210]

Chicago Pizza and Brewery Inc, pp. 763, 766, 769 [NAICS 722211, 722212, 722213]

Chicago Scenic Studios Inc, p. 36 [NAICS 512191]

Chicago Stock Exchange Inc, p. 150 [NAICS 523210]

Chicago Story, p. 24 [NAICS 512110]

Chicago Sun-Times Inc, p. 4 [NAICS 511110]

Chicago Title and Trust Co, p. 175 [NAICS 524127]

Chicago Title Insurance Co, p. 175 [NAICS 524127]

Chicago Trust of California, p. 160 [NAICS 523991]

Child Care Resorce Center Inc, p. 902 [NAICS 813319]

Child Care Resources Inc, p. 653 [NAICS 624190]

Childcare Resources for Jefferson Shelby and Walker Counties, p. 653 [NAICS 624190]

Numbers following p. or pp. are page references. Braketed items indicate industries. Page references are to the starting pages of company tables.

962

Coastal Enterprises Inc, p. 914 [NAICS 813990]
Coastal Training Technologies, p. 24 [NAICS 512110]
COBE Laboratories Inc, p. 596 [NAICS 621492]
Cocopah Bend RV & Golf Resort, pp. 720, 751 [NAICS 713910, 721211]
Code, Hennessy and Simmons Inc, p. 163 [NAICS 523999]
Cog Hill Second Inc, p. 720 [NAICS 713910]
Cohen-Esrey Real Estate Services, p. 207 [NAICS 531210]
Cohn and Wolfe, p. 357 [NAICS 541820]
Cohners Instat Group, p. 377 [NAICS 541910]
Coinmach Corp, p. 863 [NAICS 812310]
Coinmach Laundry Corp, p. 863 [NAICS 812310]
Coinstar Inc, p. 884 [NAICS 812990]
Cold Spring Harbor Laboratory, p. 18 [NAICS 511199]
Coldwell Banker Burnet, p. 121 [NAICS 522292]
Coldwell Banker Residential, p. 207 [NAICS 531210]
Coleman Professional Services Inc, p. 626 [NAICS 622210]
Coleman Research Corp, p. 347 [NAICS 541710]
Collegiate Licensing Co, p. 681 [NAICS 711211]
Collegis Inc, p. 321 [NAICS 541513]
Collier Enterprises, p. 207 [NAICS 531210]
Colliers International, p. 207 [NAICS 531210]
Colonial BancGroup Inc, p. 394 [NAICS 551111]
Colonial Commercial Corp, p. 435 [NAICS 561440]
Colonial Downs Holdings Inc, p. 684 [NAICS 711212]
Colonial Management Associates, p. 157 [NAICS 523930]
Colonial Parking Inc, p. 881 [NAICS 812930]
Colonial Properties Trust, p. 191 [NAICS 525930]
Colorado Commodities, p. 147 [NAICS 523140]
Colorado Dental Service Inc, p. 618 [NAICS 621999]
Colorvision International Inc, p. 383 [NAICS 541922]
Colsa Corp, p. 347 [NAICS 541710]
Colsky Media Inc, p. 371 [NAICS 541870]
Columbia Club Inc, p. 721 [NAICS 713910]
Columbia/HCA Healthcare Corp, pp. 397, 621, 625, 629 [NAICS 551112, 622110, 622210, 622310]
Columbia Health System Inc, pp. 609, 629 [NAICS 621610, 622310]
Columbia River Maritime Museum Inc, p. 702 [NAICS 712120]
Columbian Trust Co, p. 160 [NAICS 523991]
Columbus Museum of Art, p. 699 [NAICS 712110]
Comac Inc, p. 368 [NAICS 541860]
Comair Aviation Academy Inc, p. 554 [NAICS 611699]
Comair Holdings Inc, p. 533 [NAICS 611511]
Comarco Inc, p. 409 [NAICS 561210]
Combined Properties Inc, p. 199 [NAICS 531120]
Combustion Unlimited Inc, p. 338 [NAICS 541618]
Comcare Inc, p. 902 [NAICS 813319]
Comcast Cellular, p. 70 [NAICS 513321]
Comcast Corp, pp. 61, 70 [NAICS 513210, 513321]
Comdata Corp, p. 163 [NAICS 523999]
Comdisco Inc, p. 252 [NAICS 532420]

CoMed Communications Inc, p. 902 [NAICS 813319]
Comerica Bank, p. 102 [NAICS 522110]
Comerica Inc, pp. 102, 394 [NAICS 522110, 551111]
COMFORCE Corp, p. 415 [NAICS 561320]
Comm-Care Corporation, p. 653 [NAICS 624190]
Command Security Corp, p. 461 [NAICS 561611]
Commerce Bancshares Inc, p. 394 [NAICS 551111]
Commerce Group Inc, p. 121 [NAICS 522292]
Commerce Land Title Inc, pp. 175, 268 [NAICS 524127, 541191]
Commercial Credit Co, p. 118 [NAICS 522291]
Commercial Federal Bank F.S.B., p. 105 [NAICS 522120]
Commercial Federal Corp, pp. 105, 394 [NAICS 522120, 551111]
Commercial Finance Corp, p. 244 [NAICS 532310]
Commercial Graphics Corp, p. 432 [NAICS 561439]
Commercial Net Lease Realty Inc, p. 191 [NAICS 525930]
Commercial Testing, p. 302 [NAICS 541380]
CommNet Cellular Inc, p. 70 [NAICS 513321]
Commodities Resource Corp, p. 147 [NAICS 523140]
CommonHealth, p. 354 [NAICS 541810]
Commonwealth Telephone, p. 61 [NAICS 513210]
Commotion Promotions Ltd, p. 371 [NAICS 541870]
Commtrak Corp, p. 435 [NAICS 561440]
Communicare Inc, p. 653 [NAICS 624190]
Communication Concepts Inc, p. 368 [NAICS 541860]
CommuniGroup Inc, p. 67 [NAICS 513310]
Community Action Agency of S. NM Territory, p. 902 [NAICS 813319]
Community Action Council for Lex-Fayette Counties, p. 902 [NAICS 813319]
Community Alternatives, p. 646 [NAICS 623990]
Community and Economic Development, Cook County, p. 653 [NAICS 624190]
Community Blood Bank of Erie County, p. 614 [NAICS 621991]
Community Blood Center, p. 614 [NAICS 621991]
Community Connections, p. 626 [NAICS 622210]
Community Development Services Inc, p. 692 [NAICS 711320]
Community Entry Services Inc, p. 653 [NAICS 624190]
Community Foundation of Gaston County Inc, p. 902 [NAICS 813319]
Community Foundation of Greater Flint, p. 563 [NAICS 621111]
Community Foundation of Greater Memphis Inc, p. 902 [NAICS 813319]
Community Foundation of Madison and Jefferson County Inc, p. 902 [NAICS 813319]
Community Health Systems Inc, p. 621 [NAICS 622110]
Community Housing Services, p. 896 [NAICS 813311]
Community Legal Aid Society Inc, p. 896 [NAICS 813311]
Community Living Options Inc, p. 626 [NAICS 622210]

Community Living Services Inc, p. 626 [NAICS 622210]
Community Medical Center, p. 541 [NAICS 611519]
Community Mental Health Affil Inc, p. 626 [NAICS 622210]
Community Partnership for the Prevention of Homelessness, p. 902 [NAICS 813319]
Community Systems Inc, p. 626 [NAICS 622210]
ComNet Mortgage Services Inc, p. 121 [NAICS 522292]
Comp and Soft Computers Inc, p. 816 [NAICS 811212]
Compass Bancshares Inc, p. 394 [NAICS 551111]
Compass Group USA Inc, pp. 760, 763, 766, 769 [NAICS 722110, 722211, 722212, 722213]
Compass Health, p. 626 [NAICS 622210]
COMPASS-Retail Div., p. 199 [NAICS 531120]
Compass Square & Star Inc, p. 702 [NAICS 712120]
Compassion International Incorporated, p. 541 [NAICS 611519]
Compex Legal Services Inc, pp. 409, 421, 432 [NAICS 561210, 561410, 561439]
Complete Business & Tax, p. 273 [NAICS 541211]
Complete Business Solutions, Inc, pp. 89, 318 [NAICS 514191, 541512]
Complete Post Inc, p. 36 [NAICS 512191]
Complete Wellness Centers Inc, p. 600 [NAICS 621498]
Composite Research, p. 157 [NAICS 523930]
Comprehensive Behavioral Care, p. 625 [NAICS 622210]
Comprehensive Care Corp, pp. 587, 625 [NAICS 621399, 622210]
Comprehensive Geriatric Services Inc, p. 890 [NAICS 813212]
Comprehensive Health Services, pp. 572, 587 [NAICS 621310, 621399]
Comprehensive Options for Drug Abusers Inc, p. 637 [NAICS 623220]
Comprehensive Systems Inc, pp. 646, 664 [NAICS 623990, 624310]
CompuCad Inc, p. 528 [NAICS 611420]
CompuCom Systems Inc, p. 318 [NAICS 541512]
CompuDraft Inc, p. 310 [NAICS 541430]
CompUSA Inc, pp. 528, 816 [NAICS 611420, 811212]
CompuServe Interactive Services, pp. 89, 318 [NAICS 514191, 541512]
Computer Associates International Inc, p. 21 [NAICS 511210]
Computer City, pp. 528, 816 [NAICS 611420, 811212]
Computer Data Inc, p. 533 [NAICS 611511]
Computer Dynamics Inc, p. 315 [NAICS 541511]
Computer Guys Inc, p. 816 [NAICS 811212]
Computer Horizons Corp, pp. 94, 318 [NAICS 514210, 541512]
Computer Learning Centers Inc, p. 528 [NAICS 611420]
Computer One Inc, p. 816 [NAICS 811212]
Computer Science Corporation, pp. 315, 318 [NAICS 541511, 541512]

Numbers following p. or pp. are page references. Braketed items indicate industries. Page references are to the starting pages of company tables.

964

561720]

Covington and Burling, p. 264 [NAICS 541110]

Covington Electric Cooperative, p. 470 [NAICS 561621]

Cowen and Co, p. 142 [NAICS 523120]

Cox Broadcasting Inc, pp. 52, 58 [NAICS 513111, 513120]

Cox Cable of San Diego Inc, pp. 61, 70 [NAICS 513210, 513321]

Cox Communications Inc, p. 61 [NAICS 513210]

Cox Enterprises Inc, pp. 4, 58, 61 [NAICS 511110, 513120, 513210]

Cox Radio Inc, p. 52 [NAICS 513111]

Coyne International Enterprises Corp, p. 872 [NAICS 812332]

CPI Corp, p. 380 [NAICS 541921]

CPM Inc, p: 371 [NAICS 541870]

CRA Inc, pp. 252, 816 [NAICS 532420, 811212]

Crab Tree Farm Foundation Inc, p. 699 [NAICS 712110]

Cracker Barrel Old Country Store, pp. 760, 766 [NAICS 722110, 722212]

Craig Corp, p. 327 [NAICS 541611]

Craig Hospital, p. 629 [NAICS 622310]

Crain Communications Inc, p. 7 [NAICS 511120]

Cramer-Krasselt Co, p. 354 [NAICS 541810]

Crane Fund, p. 653 [NAICS 624190]

Cravath, Swaine and Moore, p. 264 [NAICS 541110]

Crawford and Co, p. 182 [NAICS 524210]

Crawford Communications Inc, p. 24 [NAICS 512110]

Crazy Horse Memorial Foundation, p. 736 [NAICS 713990]

CRC Press LLC, p. 18 [NAICS 511199]

Creative & Response Research, p. 377 [NAICS 541910]

Creative Artists Agency Inc, p. 691 [NAICS 711320]

Creative Associates Inc, p. 310 [NAICS 541430]

Creative Employment, p. 412 [NAICS 561310]

Creative Medical Communications, p. 617 [NAICS 621999]

Creative Presentations Inc, p. 244 [NAICS 532310]

Credit Acceptance Corp, p. 118 [NAICS 522291]

Credit Bureau of Baton Rouge Inc, p. 438 [NAICS 561450]

Credit Data Southwest Inc, p. 438 [NAICS 561450]

Credit Suisse First Boston, p. 142 [NAICS 523120]

Credit Union of Denver, p. 108 [NAICS 522130]

Credit Union ONE, p. 108 [NAICS 522130]

Crepusculo Inc, p. 4 [NAICS 511110]

Crescent Operating Inc, p. 191 [NAICS 525930]

Crescent Real Estate Equities Co, p. 207 [NAICS 531210]

Crescent Real Estate Equities Inc, p. 191 [NAICS 525930]

Crescent Sound and Light Inc, p. 244 [NAICS 532310]

Crestar Financial Corp, pp. 102, 121, 394 [NAICS 522110, 522292, 551111]

Crestview Country Club Assoc, p. 721 [NAICS 713910]

Creswell, Munsell, Fultz & Zirbel, p. 357 [NAICS 541820]

Crete Bicentennial Society Crete Nebraska, p. 702 [NAICS 712120]

Crew Connection Inc, p. 36 [NAICS 512191]

Crew Cuts Film and Tape Inc, p. 36 [NAICS 512191]

CRIIMI MAE Inc, p. 121 [NAICS 522292]

Crime Alert Alarm Co, p. 470 [NAICS 561621]

Criterion Systems Inc, p. 617 [NAICS 621999]

CRN International, pp. 52, 362 [NAICS 513111, 541840]

Crocker Realty Trust, p. 191 [NAICS 525930]

Cronin and Co, pp. 357, 368 [NAICS 541820, 541860]

CrossLand Mortgage Corp, p. 121 [NAICS 522292]

Crossroads for Women Inc, p. 637 [NAICS 623220]

Crossroads Incorporated, p. 672 [NAICS 711110]

Crossroads V Communications, p. 691 [NAICS 711320]

Crown Pointe Div., p. 196 [NAICS 531110]

Cruise America Inc, p. 227 [NAICS 532120]

CryoLife Inc, p. 617 [NAICS 621999]

CSC Credit Services Inc, p. 438 [NAICS 561450]

CSC Healthcare Group, p. 318 [NAICS 541512]

CSG Security Services Inc, p. 461 [NAICS 561611]

CSI, p. 617 [NAICS 621999]

CSP Associates Inc, p. 327 [NAICS 541611]

CSSI Corp, p. 813 [NAICS 811211]

CSX Technology, p. 406 [NAICS 561110]

CTL Management Inc, p. 207 [NAICS 531210]

Culberson Stowers Inc, p. 786 [NAICS 811111]

Cumberland Valley Shows Inc, p. 735 [NAICS 713990]

Cummings 'N' Good, p. 310 [NAICS 541430]

Cummins Alabama Inc, pp. 786, 795 [NAICS 811111, 811118]

Cummins Gateway Inc, p. 786 [NAICS 811111]

Cummins Midstates Power Inc, p. 786 [NAICS 811111]

Cuna Mutual Insurance Society, p. 169 [NAICS 524114]

Cunningham Motors Inc, p. 786 [NAICS 811111]

CuraGen Corp, p. 347 [NAICS 541710]

Curative Health Services Inc, p. 587 [NAICS 621399]

Curran and Connors Inc, p. 310 [NAICS 541430]

Curry Coastal Pilot, p. 4 [NAICS 511110]

Curtis Brown Ltd, p. 691 [NAICS 711320]

Curtis Publishing Co, p. 10 [NAICS 511130]

Cushing and Company Inc, p. 432 [NAICS 561439]

Cushman and Wakefield Inc, p. 207 [NAICS 531210]

Custodial Trust Co, p. 160 [NAICS 523991]

Custom Coach Corp, p. 798 [NAICS 811121]

Custom Computer Service Inc, p. 252 [NAICS 532420]

Customer Development Corp, p. 338 [NAICS 541618]

Cutters Inc, p. 36 [NAICS 512191]

C.W. Leasing Inc, p. 252 [NAICS 532420]

CYGNUS PUBLISHING, p. 18 [NAICS 511199]

Cynosure Inc, p. 914 [NAICS 813990]

Cyntergy Corp, p. 528 [NAICS 611420]

Cystic Fibrosis Foundation, p. 348 [NAICS 541710]

Cytogenetics Foundation, p. 563 [NAICS 621111]

CZR Inc, p. 299 [NAICS 541370]

D/A Mid South Inc, p. 470 [NAICS 561621]

D and D Equipment Rental Inc, p. 249 [NAICS 532412]

DA Davidson and Co, p. 142 [NAICS 523120]

Dade County Federal Credit Union, p. 108 [NAICS 522130]

Dahlem Company Inc, p. 204 [NAICS 531190]

Dain Bosworth Inc, p. 142 [NAICS 523120]

Dain Rauscher Corp, p. 142 [NAICS 523120]

Dairy Herd Improvement Associations of Vermont Inc, p. 348 [NAICS 541710]

Dairy Management Inc, p. 908 [NAICS 813910]

Dairy Mart Convenience Stores, p. 258 [NAICS 533110]

Dakota Boys Ranch Association, p. 902 [NAICS 813319]

Dakota Plains Legal Services Inc, p. 265 [NAICS 541110]

Dakotah Direct Inc, p. 388 [NAICS 541990]

Dale Carnegie and Associates Inc, p. 526 [NAICS 611410]

Dale Ollila, p. 421 [NAICS 561410]

Dale System Inc, pp. 461, 470 [NAICS 561611, 561621]

Dallas Country Club, p. 721 [NAICS 713910]

Dallas Gun Club, p. 681 [NAICS 711211]

Dames and Moore Group, pp. 288, 406 [NAICS 541330, 561110]

Dance Umbrella Boston Inc, p. 672 [NAICS 711110]

Daniel J Edelman, p. 357 [NAICS 541820]

Daniel, Mann, Johnson, p. 285 [NAICS 541310]

Danielson Holding Corp, p. 178 [NAICS 524128]

Danka Corp, p. 244 [NAICS 532310]

Darden Restaurants Inc, p. 760 [NAICS 722110]

Dartmouth-Hitchcock Clinic, p. 563 [NAICS 621111]

Data Broadcasting Corp, pp. 61, 89 [NAICS 513210, 514191]

Data Reduction Inc, pp. 315, 388 [NAICS 541511, 541990]

Data Transmission Network Corp, p. 89 [NAICS 514191]

DataChem Laboratories, p. 302 [NAICS 541380]

Datatel Inc, p. 338 [NAICS 541618]

Dave Sinclair Ford Inc, p. 221 [NAICS 532111]

David Berdon LLP, p. 276 [NAICS 541213]

David Gomez and Associates Inc, p. 412 [NAICS 561310]

Davidson College, p. 905 [NAICS 813410]

Davidson Hotel Co, p. 406 [NAICS 561110]

Davidson Hotel Partners LP, p. 742 [NAICS 721110]

Davis Amusement Co, p. 735 [NAICS 713990]

Davis Polk and Wardwell, p. 264 [NAICS 541110]

Day & Zimmermann Howthorne, p. 409 [NAICS 561210]

Day and Zimmermann Inc, pp. 285, 288, 406 [NAICS 541310, 541330, 561110]

Daymark Inc, p. 371 [NAICS 541870]

Dayton T. Brown Inc, pp. 18, 302 [NAICS 511199, 541380]

Numbers following p. or pp. are page references. Braketed items indicate industries. Page references are to the starting pages of company tables.

966

DBS Industries Inc, p. 347 [NAICS 541710]

DCC Inc, p. 632 [NAICS 623110]

Dccca Inc, p. 637 [NAICS 623220]

D.C.G. Development Co, pp. 196, 199 [NAICS 531110, 531120]

DCI Marketing Inc, p. 368 [NAICS 541860]

DCM Group, p. 344 [NAICS 541690]

DDB Dallas Inc, p. 354 [NAICS 541810]

DDB Needham Worldwide, p. 354 [NAICS 541810]

DDB Seattle, p. 357 [NAICS 541820]

De Anza Land and Leisure Corp, p. 33 [NAICS 512132]

De Carolis Truck Rental Inc, p. 227 [NAICS 532120]

De Nooyer Brothers Inc, p. 786 [NAICS 811111]

D.E. Shaw and Company LP, p. 142 [NAICS 523120]

Deaconess Billings Clinic, p. 562 [NAICS 621111]

Deaconess Health Services Corporation, p. 563 [NAICS 621111]

Deaconess Hospital, p. 622 [NAICS 622110]

Dean and DeLuca Inc, pp. 763, 766, 769 [NAICS 722211, 722212, 722213]

Dean Foundation for Health Research and Education Inc, p. 603 [NAICS 621511]

Dean Witter Reynolds Inc, p. 142 [NAICS 523120]

Dearborn Financial Publishing Inc, p. 526 [NAICS 611410]

DeBartolo Realty Corp, p. 191 [NAICS 525930]

Decathlon Hotel and Athletic Club, p. 729 [NAICS 713940]

Dechert Price and Rhoads, p. 264 [NAICS 541110]

Decima Research Corp, p. 377 [NAICS 541910]

Decision Point Marketing Inc, p. 327 [NAICS 541611]

DecisionOne Corp, p. 816 [NAICS 811212]

Decorah Jobs Inc, p. 914 [NAICS 813990]

Deep Creek Baseball Association Inc, p. 681 [NAICS 711211]

Deere and Co, p. 172 [NAICS 524126]

Defender Association, p. 896 [NAICS 813311]

Defiance Inc, p. 302 [NAICS 541380]

Degrazia Art & Cultural Foundation Inc, p. 699 [NAICS 712110]

Delancey Street/New Mexico Inc, p. 637 [NAICS 623220]

Delaware Curative Workshop Inc, p. 600 [NAICS 621498]

Delaware Hospice Inc, p. 618 [NAICS 621999]

Delaware North Companies Inc, p. 760 [NAICS 722110]

Delaware Performing Arts Center Inc, p. 702 [NAICS 712120]

Delaware Racing Association, p. 684 [NAICS 711212]

Delaware State Bar Association, p. 908 [NAICS 813910]

Delaware State College, p. 541 [NAICS 611519]

Delco Systems Services Inc, p. 603 [NAICS 621511]

Delicious Vinyl Inc, p. 691 [NAICS 711320]

Delivery Concepts Inc, pp. 763, 766, 769 [NAICS 722211, 722212, 722213]

Dell Computer Corp, p. 21 [NAICS 511210]

Delmar Financial Co, p. 121 [NAICS 522292]

Delmar Publishers, p. 10 [NAICS 511130]

Delmarva Systems Corp, p. 470 [NAICS 561621]

DeLorme Publishing Inc, p. 18 [NAICS 511199]

Delta Dental Plan of California, p. 169 [NAICS 524114]

Delta Dental Plan of Idaho Inc, p. 618 [NAICS 621999]

Delta Dental Plan of Iowa, p. 618 [NAICS 621999]

Delta Dental Plan of Minnesota, p. 169 [NAICS 524114]

Delta Dental Plan of Missouri, p. 541 [NAICS 611519]

Delta Dental Plan of New Jersey, p. 618 [NAICS 621999]

Delta Dental Plan of New Mexico Inc, p. 618 [NAICS 621999]

Delta Dental Plan of Virginia, p. 618 [NAICS 621999]

Delta Dental Plan of Wyoming, p. 618 [NAICS 621999]

Delta Downs Racing Association, p. 684 [NAICS 711212]

Delta Employees Credit Union, p. 108 [NAICS 522130]

Delta Financial Corp, p. 131 [NAICS 522310]

Delta Funding Corp, p. 131 [NAICS 522310]

Deluxe Laboratories Inc, pp. 24, 36 [NAICS 512110, 512191]

Deneen Powell Atelier Inc, p. 310 [NAICS 541430]

Denny's Inc, pp. 258, 760 [NAICS 533110, 722110]

Dental Services of America Inc, p. 569 [NAICS 621210]

Denver Athletic Club, p. 729 [NAICS 713940]

Denver Museum of Natural History, p. 705 [NAICS 712130]

Denver Options Inc, p. 653 [NAICS 624190]

Denver Publishing Co, p. 4 [NAICS 511110]

Denver Transit Advertising, p. 371 [NAICS 541870]

Deposit Guaranty Corp, p. 394 [NAICS 551111]

Dermatology Associates, p. 562 [NAICS 621111]

Derrick Walker Racing, p. 684 [NAICS 711212]

Deseret Management Corp, p. 10 [NAICS 511130]

Desert Hills Golf Club of Green Valley Inc, p. 681 [NAICS 711211]

Design Automation, p. 315 [NAICS 541511]

Destination Hotels & Resorts Inc, p. 742 [NAICS 721110]

Detroit Free Press Inc, p. 4 [NAICS 511110]

Detroit Osteopathic Hospital Corporation, p. 541 [NAICS 611519]

Detroit Pistons Basketball Co, p. 681 [NAICS 711211]

Detroit Symphony Orchestra Hall, p. 736 [NAICS 713990]

Detroit Teachers Credit Union, p. 108 [NAICS 522130]

Developers Diversified Realty, p. 191 [NAICS 525930]

Development Alternatives Inc, p. 338 [NAICS 541618]

Development Dimensions Intern, p. 338 [NAICS 541618]

Development Through Self, p. 816 [NAICS 811212]

Devillier-Donegan Enterprises Inc, p. 27 [NAICS 512120]

Devon Group Inc, pp. 18, 383 [NAICS 511199, 541922]

DeVry Inc, pp. 526, 528 [NAICS 611410, 611420]

Dewey Ballantine LLP, p. 264 [NAICS 541110]

Dewey Ford Inc, p. 224 [NAICS 532112]

Dewitt Wallace Fund for Colonial Williamsburg, p. 702 [NAICS 712120]

DeWolfe Companies Inc, p. 131 [NAICS 522310]

DeWolff, Boberg & Associates, p. 338 [NAICS 541618]

DHR International Inc, p. 412 [NAICS 561310]

Diabetes Treatment Centers, p. 587 [NAICS 621399]

Diagnostic Clinic Medical Group, p. 562 [NAICS 621111]

Diagnostic Imaging Services Inc, p. 587 [NAICS 621399]

Dialog Corp, p. 89 [NAICS 514191]

Diamond Parking Inc, p. 881 [NAICS 812930]

Diamond Technology Partners Inc, p. 338 [NAICS 541618]

DiCesare Engler Productions Inc, p. 691 [NAICS 711320]

Dick Clark Productions Inc, pp. 24, 763, 766, 769 [NAICS 512110, 722211, 722212, 722213]

Dick Orkin's Creative Services, p. 691 [NAICS 711320]

Dick Strauss Ford Inc, p. 786 [NAICS 811111]

Dickinson Advertising, p. 368 [NAICS 541860]

Dickson Gabbay Corp, p. 617 [NAICS 621999]

Dickstein, Shapiro, Morin, p. 264 [NAICS 541110]

Didlake Inc, p. 368 [NAICS 541860]

Diebold Inc, p. 21 [NAICS 511210]

Digital Consulting & Software, p. 528 [NAICS 611420]

Digital Domain Inc, p. 36 [NAICS 512191]

Digital Image, p. 36 [NAICS 512191]

Digital Lab Inc, p. 36 [NAICS 512191]

Digital Magic Co, p. 36 [NAICS 512191]

Dillingham Construction Corp, p. 406 [NAICS 561110]

Dillingham Construction Holdings, p. 406 [NAICS 561110]

DIMAC DIRECT Inc, p. 368 [NAICS 541860]

Dime Bancorp Inc, pp. 105, 394 [NAICS 522120, 551111]

Dime Savings Bank of New York, p. 105 [NAICS 522120]

Diplomatic Language Services Inc, p. 554 [NAICS 611699]

Direct Mail Systems Inc, p. 368 [NAICS 541860]

Directech Corp, p. 327 [NAICS 541611]

DIRECTV Inc, p. 61 [NAICS 513210]

Disability Law Center, p. 265 [NAICS 541110]

Discovery Communications Inc, p. 61 [NAICS 513210]

Disney-MGM Studios, p. 710 [NAICS 713110]

Display Group, p. 244 [NAICS 532310]

District Council 37 Health and Security Fund, p. 653 [NAICS 624190]

Diversified Corporate Resources, p. 412 [NAICS 561310]

Divot Golf Corp, p. 720 [NAICS 713910]

DJONT Operations LLC, p. 742 [NAICS 721110]

Numbers following p. or pp. are page references. Braketed items indicate industries. Page references are to the starting pages of company tables.

968

Excel Federal Credit Union, p. 108 [NAICS 522130]

Exchange Inc, p. 150 [NAICS 523210]

Excite@Home Inc, p. 89 [NAICS 514191]

Executive Car Leasing Co, pp. 224, 227 [NAICS 532112, 532120]

ExecuTrain Corp, p. 528 [NAICS 611420]

Exodus Communications Inc, p. 89 [NAICS 514191]

Experian Information Solutions, p. 377 [NAICS 541910]

Experience Music Project, p. 705 [NAICS 712130]

Exploration Place Inc, p. 705 [NAICS 712130]

Explore Reasoning Systems Inc, p. 321 [NAICS 541513]

Exponent Environmental Group, p. 338 [NAICS 541618]

Express Scripts Inc, p. 94 [NAICS 514210]

Extended Stay America Inc, p. 742 [NAICS 721110]

Exxon Research & Engineering, pp. 288, 347 [NAICS 541330, 541710]

Eye Health Services Inc, p. 562 [NAICS 621111]

Eyemark Entertainment, p. 27 [NAICS 512120]

F. Dohmen Co, p. 321 [NAICS 541513]

F M Global, p. 182 [NAICS 524210]

F.A. Bartlett Tree Expert Co, p. 338 [NAICS 541618]

Faber Enterprises Inc, pp. 763, 766, 769 [NAICS 722211, 722212, 722213]

Facets-Multimedia Inc, pp. 27, 672 [NAICS 512120, 711110]

Facility Group Inc, p. 285 [NAICS 541310]

FactualData, p. 438 [NAICS 561450]

Fair Grounds Corp, p. 684 [NAICS 711212]

Fair, Isaac and Company Inc, p. 438 [NAICS 561450]

Fairbanks Native Association, p. 637 [NAICS 623220]

Fairchild Publications Inc, p. 7 [NAICS 511120]

Fairfaxx Corp, p. 327 [NAICS 541611]

Fairmount Copley Plaza, p. 199 [NAICS 531120]

Fairview Ministries Inc, p. 632 [NAICS 623110]

Fairview Riverside Medical, p. 621 [NAICS 622110]

FALA Direct Marketing Inc, p. 368 [NAICS 541860]

Fallon McElligott, p. 354 [NAICS 541810]

Familiesfirst Inc, p. 646 [NAICS 623990]

Family AIDS Center for Treatment and Support Facts, p. 646 [NAICS 623990]

Family & Business Insurance, p. 169 [NAICS 524114]

Family & Childrens Agency Inc, p. 902 [NAICS 813319]

Family Counseling Center Inc, p. 626 [NAICS 622210]

Family Golf Centers Inc, p. 735 [NAICS 713990]

Family Life Services of New England Inc, p. 637 [NAICS 623220]

Family Video Superstores Inc, p. 234 [NAICS 532230]

Far West Farms, p. 684 [NAICS 711212]

Fargo Country Club Inc, p. 721 [NAICS 713910]

Fargo Freightliner Inc, p. 786 [NAICS 811111]

Fargo-Moorhead Family YMCA, p. 736 [NAICS 713990]

Farmers Commodities Corp, p. 147 [NAICS 523140]

Farmers Insurance Exchange, p. 172 [NAICS 524126]

Farmers Telephone Cooperative, p. 67 [NAICS 513310]

Farrow Amusement Company Inc, p. 735 [NAICS 713990]

Faulk Co, p. 479 [NAICS 561720]

Faxon, RoweCom's Academic, p. 89 [NAICS 514191]

Fayette Products Inc, p. 36 [NAICS 512191]

F.B. Hart Company Inc, p. 227 [NAICS 532120]

FCT Group Inc, p. 147 [NAICS 523140]

FDC Reports Inc, p. 18 [NAICS 511199]

Federal Defender Program Inc, p. 265 [NAICS 541110]

Federal Defender Services of Eastern Tennessee, p. 265 [NAICS 541110]

Federal Defenders of Montana Inc, p. 265 [NAICS 541110]

Federal Deposit Insurance Corp, p. 178 [NAICS 524128]

Federal Direct, p. 368 [NAICS 541860]

Federal Hill House Association Inc, p. 902 [NAICS 813319]

Federal Home Loan Bank, p. 134 [NAICS 522320]

Federal Reserve Bank, p. 100 [NAICS 521110]

Federal Systems Division, p. 816 [NAICS 811212]

Federally Employed Womens Legal and Education Fund Inc, p. 896 [NAICS 813311]

Federated Department Stores Inc, p. 397 [NAICS 551112]

Federated Investors Inc, p. 157 [NAICS 523930]

Federated Systems Group, p. 94 [NAICS 514210]

FedEx Corp, p. 397 [NAICS 551112]

FEI Behavioral Health, p. 587 [NAICS 621399]

Feld Entertainment Inc, p. 691 [NAICS 711320]

Fellowship Health Resources Inc, p. 626 [NAICS 622210]

Fenway Partners Inc, p. 163 [NAICS 523999]

Ferderbar Studios Inc, p. 383 [NAICS 541922]

Fergus Electric Cooperative Inc, p. 914 [NAICS 813990]

Ferland Corp, p. 207 [NAICS 531210]

Ferolie Group, p. 388 [NAICS 541990]

Fette Ford Inc, p. 224 [NAICS 532112]

Fetterolf Group Inc, p. 196 [NAICS 531110]

FFP Operating Partners LP, pp. 763, 766, 769 [NAICS 722211, 722212, 722213]

FG*I Image Works Inc, pp. 357, 368 [NAICS 541820, 541860]

FHC Health Systems, pp. 625, 629 [NAICS 622210, 622310]

Fibre Federal Credit Union, p. 108 [NAICS 522130]

Fidelity & Guaranty Life, p. 178 [NAICS 524128]

Fidelity Federal Bank FSB, p. 105 [NAICS 522120]

Fidelity Funding Inc, p. 134 [NAICS 522320]

Fidelity Investments, p. 21 [NAICS 511210]

Fidelity National Corp, p. 118 [NAICS 522291]

Fidelity National Financial Inc, p. 175 [NAICS 524127]

Fidelity National Title Insurance, p. 175 [NAICS 524127]

Fidelity Title Co, pp. 175, 268 [NAICS 524127, 541191]

Fiduciary Foundation, p. 905 [NAICS 813410]

Fifth Third Bancorp, pp. 102, 394 [NAICS 522110, 551111]

Fifth Third Bank of Western Ohio, p. 102 [NAICS 522110]

Fight for Children Inc, p. 692 [NAICS 711320]

Films for the Humanities, p. 27 [NAICS 512120]

Filmworkers Club, p. 36 [NAICS 512191]

Finance Center Federal, p. 108 [NAICS 522130]

Financial Pacific Insurance Group, p. 182 [NAICS 524210]

Financial Relations Board Inc, p. 357 [NAICS 541820]

Financial Title Co, p. 175 [NAICS 524127]

Fine Arts Museums Foundation, p. 705 [NAICS 712130]

Finger Lakes Racing Association, p. 684 [NAICS 711212]

Finnegan, Henderson, Farabow, p. 264 [NAICS 541110]

Fircrest Golf Club Inc, p. 721 [NAICS 713910]

Fireman's Fund Insurance Co, p. 172 [NAICS 524126]

Fireside Thrift Co, p. 121 [NAICS 522292]

First American Title Insurance Co, p. 175 [NAICS 524127]

First American Title of Alaska Inc, p. 268 [NAICS 541191]

First American Title of Utah, pp. 175, 268 [NAICS 524127, 541191]

First Aviation Services Inc, p. 839 [NAICS 811490]

First Cherokee Bancshares Inc, pp. 102, 394 [NAICS 522110, 551111]

First Chicago Insurance Services, p. 182 [NAICS 524210]

First Citizens BancShares Inc, p. 394 [NAICS 551111]

First City Savings Federal Credit, p. 108 [NAICS 522130]

First Community Credit Union, p. 108 [NAICS 522130]

First Consulting Group Inc, pp. 315, 338 [NAICS 541511, 541618]

First Data Corp, pp. 94, 163 [NAICS 514210, 523999]

First Data Resources Inc, p. 94 [NAICS 514210]

First Decatur Bancshares Inc, p. 94 [NAICS 514210]

First Eastern Mortgage Corp, p. 121 [NAICS 522292]

First Entertainment Holding Corp, pp. 27, 781 [NAICS 512120, 722410]

First Family Financial Services, p. 118 [NAICS 522291]

First Federal Bank of California, p. 105 [NAICS 522120]

First Federal Savings Bank, p. 105 [NAICS 522120]

First Financial Services, p. 435 [NAICS 561440]

First Image Management Co, p. 318 [NAICS 541512]

First Industrial Realty Trust Inc, p. 191 [NAICS 525930]

First Investors Financial Services, p. 118 [NAICS 522291]

First Maryland Bancorp, p. 394 [NAICS 551111]

Numbers following p. or pp. are page references. Braketed items indicate industries. Page references are to the starting pages of company tables.

970

Company Index

Numbers following p. or pp. are page references. Braketed items indicate industries. Page references are to the starting pages of company tables.

Numbers following p. or pp. are page references. Braketed items indicate industries. Page references are to the starting pages of company tables.

Company Index

Numbers following p. or pp. are page references. Braketed items indicate industries. Page references are to the starting pages of company tables.

974

Numbers following p. or pp. are page references. Bracketed items indicate industries. Page references are to the starting pages of company tables.

Company Index

561720]

Holmes Automotive, p. 786 [NAICS 811111]

Holmes Murphy & Associates Inc, p. 182 [NAICS 524210]

Holt of California, p. 249 [NAICS 532412]

Home-Bound Medical Care Inc, pp. 255, 609 [NAICS 532490, 621610]

Home Box Office, pp. 24, 61 [NAICS 512110, 513210]

Home Builders Institute, p. 538 [NAICS 611513]

Home Gold Financial Inc, p. 131 [NAICS 522310]

Home Health Care of Mississippi, p. 609 [NAICS 621610]

Home Health Corporation, p. 609 [NAICS 621610]

Home Health Outreach, p. 609 [NAICS 621610]

Home Health Plus Inc, p. 609 [NAICS 621610]

Home of the Innocents, p. 646 [NAICS 623990]

Home Properties of New York Inc, p. 191 [NAICS 525930]

Home Savings of America F.S.B., p. 105 [NAICS 522120]

Home Vision, p. 27 [NAICS 512120]

HomeAmerican Mortgage Corp, p. 121 [NAICS 522292]

HomeBanc Mortgage Corp, p. 121 [NAICS 522292]

HomeCall Inc, p. 609 [NAICS 621610]

HomeGold Financial Inc, p. 118 [NAICS 522291]

Hometown Health Plan Inc, p. 618 [NAICS 621999]

Honac Inc, p. 637 [NAICS 623220]

Honigman Miller Schwartz, p. 264 [NAICS 541110]

Honolulu Cellular, p. 70 [NAICS 513321]

Honolulu Medical Group Inc, p. 562 [NAICS 621111]

Hood Enterprises LLC, p. 726 [NAICS 713930]

Hood's, pp. 234, 863 [NAICS 532230, 812310]

Hooper Holmes Inc, p. 617 [NAICS 621999]

Hope Community Resources Inc, p. 653 [NAICS 624190]

Hope Enterprises Inc, p. 664 [NAICS 624310]

Hope House Inc, p. 646 [NAICS 623990]

Hope Rehabilitation Services, p. 664 [NAICS 624310]

Horace G. Ilderton Inc, p. 798 [NAICS 811121]

Horace Mann Educators Corp, p. 172 [NAICS 524126]

Horace Mann Service Corp, p. 182 [NAICS 524210]

Horizon Blue Cross & Blue Shield, p. 169 [NAICS 524114]

Horizon/Glen Outlet Centers LP, p. 199 [NAICS 531120]

Horizon Health Corp, p. 617 [NAICS 621999]

Horizon Health System, p. 621 [NAICS 622110]

Horizon Homecare & Hospice Inc, p. 609 [NAICS 621610]

Horizon West Inc, p. 632 [NAICS 623110]

Horseshoe Entertainment LP, p. 742 [NAICS 721110]

Horton International Inc, p. 327 [NAICS 541611]

Horus Global HealthNet, p. 600 [NAICS 621498]

Hoskins Chevrolet Inc, pp. 221, 798 [NAICS 532111, 811121]

Hospice Homecare Inc, p. 617 [NAICS 621999]

Hospice Ministries Inc, p. 643 [NAICS 623312]

Hospice of the Bluegrass Inc, p. 618 [NAICS

621999]

Hospital Auxilio Mutuo Inc, p. 622 [NAICS 622110]

Hospital Billing & Collection, p. 435 [NAICS 561440]

Host Marriott Corp, p. 742 [NAICS 721110]

Houghton Mifflin Co, pp. 10, 21 [NAICS 511130, 511210]

Housecall Medical Resources Inc, p. 609 [NAICS 621610]

Household Commercial Financial, p. 121 [NAICS 522292]

Household International Inc, pp. 105, 118, 166 [NAICS 522120, 522291, 524113]

Household Retail Services, p. 118 [NAICS 522291]

Housing Opportunity Corporation, p. 896 [NAICS 813311]

Houston Chronicle Publishing Co, p. 4 [NAICS 511110]

Houston Eye and Laser Center Inc, p. 562 [NAICS 621111]

Houston Eye Associates, p. 562 [NAICS 621111]

Houston Golf Association, p. 692 [NAICS 711320]

Houston Livestock Show & Rodeo Inc, p. 736 [NAICS 713990]

Houston Museum of Natural Science, p. 705 [NAICS 712130]

Houston Title Co, p. 268 [NAICS 541191]

Howard Electric Co, p. 825 [NAICS 811310]

Howard Hughes Medical Institute, p. 603 [NAICS 621511]

Howard/Marquis Group, p. 327 [NAICS 541611]

Howard-Sloan-Koller Group, p. 412 [NAICS 561310]

Howell Martin Co, p. 310 [NAICS 541430]

Hoyts Cinema Corp, p. 691 [NAICS 711320]

HQ International Inc, p. 204 [NAICS 531190]

HRC Manor Care Inc, p. 646 [NAICS 623990]

HRPT Properties Trust, p. 191 [NAICS 525930]

Hrsa-Ila Welfare Fund, p. 653 [NAICS 624190]

HSB Group Inc, p. 288 [NAICS 541330]

HSBC Bank USA, p. 102 [NAICS 522110]

HSBC Inc, p. 118 [NAICS 522291]

HSBC USA Inc, pp. 102, 394 [NAICS 522110, 551111]

HT Medical Systems Inc, p. 310 [NAICS 541430]

Hub Chrysler Plymouth Jeep Inc, pp. 221, 224 [NAICS 532111, 532112]

Hub City Ford Inc, p. 786 [NAICS 811111]

Hub Leasing Inc, p. 221 [NAICS 532111]

Hubbard Broadcasting Inc, pp. 52, 58 [NAICS 513111, 513120]

Hubbard Museum, p. 705 [NAICS 712130]

Huber, Hunt and Nichols Inc, p. 406 [NAICS 561110]

Huffman Security Company Inc, p. 470 [NAICS 561621]

Hughes Credit Union, p. 108 [NAICS 522130]

Hughes Electronics Corp, pp. 21, 61 [NAICS 511210, 513210]

Human Resources Alternatives Inc, p. 415 [NAICS 561320]

Humana Inc, p. 169 [NAICS 524114]

Hume Lake Christian Camp Inc, p. 754 [NAICS 721214]

Hummer Winblad Venture, p. 163 [NAICS 523999]

Hunneman Real Estate Corp, p. 207 [NAICS 531210]

Hunt Corp, p. 406 [NAICS 561110]

Huntington Bancshares Inc, pp. 102, 105, 394 [NAICS 522110, 522120, 551111]

Huntington Holdings Inc, p. 142 [NAICS 523120]

Huntington Museum of Art Inc, p. 705 [NAICS 712130]

Huntington National Bank, p. 102 [NAICS 522110]

Huntington Trust Company NA, p. 160 [NAICS 523991]

Hunton and Williams, p. 264 [NAICS 541110]

Hutchins and Associates Inc, p. 362 [NAICS 541840]

Hy-Tek Material Handling Inc, p. 244 [NAICS 532310]

Hyatt Hotels Corp, p. 742 [NAICS 721110]

HydroChem Industrial Services, p. 388 [NAICS 541990]

Hygienetics Enviromental, p. 338 [NAICS 541618]

I-74 Auto Truck Plaza, pp. 766, 769 [NAICS 722212, 722213]

IAA Trust Co, p. 160 [NAICS 523991]

Iatros Health Network Inc, p. 632 [NAICS 623110]

IBAH Inc, p. 347 [NAICS 541710]

Ibberson Co, p. 285 [NAICS 541310]

IBM Corp, pp. 21, 315 [NAICS 511210, 541511]

Ice Miller Donadio and Ryan, p. 264 [NAICS 541110]

ICG Communications Inc, pp. 70, 89 [NAICS 513321, 514191]

ICG Holdings Inc, p. 70 [NAICS 513321]

Icon International Inc, p. 388 [NAICS 541990]

ICOS Corp, p. 347 [NAICS 541710]

ICS Learning Systems Inc, p. 533 [NAICS 611511]

ICT Group Inc, p. 377 [NAICS 541910]

Idaho Legal Aid Services Inc, p. 265 [NAICS 541110]

Idaho Medical Association, p. 911 [NAICS 813920]

Idaho Youth Ranch Inc, p. 902 [NAICS 813319]

Idant Laboratories Div., p. 617 [NAICS 621999]

IDC Government Inc, p. 347 [NAICS 541710]

Idealease Services Inc, p. 227 [NAICS 532120]

IDEC Pharmaceuticals Corp, p. 347 [NAICS 541710]

IDG Books Worldwide Inc, p. 10 [NAICS 511130]

Iditarod Trail Committee Inc, p. 702 [NAICS 712120]

IDS Life Insurance Co, p. 166 [NAICS 524113]

IDT Corp, pp. 67, 89 [NAICS 513310, 514191]

Ihc Health Plans Inc, p. 618 [NAICS 621999]

Ihc Health Services Inc, p. 622 [NAICS 622110]

IHI Environmental, p. 344 [NAICS 541690]

I.J. Cohen Company Inc, p. 147 [NAICS 523140]

IJL Wachovia, p. 157 [NAICS 523930]

IKON Office Solutions Inc, pp. 315, 318, 432 [NAICS 541511, 541512, 561439]

Il Fornaio America Corp, pp. 763, 766, 769 [NAICS 722211, 722212, 722213]

Illinois Auto Electric Co, p. 795 [NAICS 811118]

Illinois Bell Telephone Co, p. 67 [NAICS 513310]

Illinois Blueprint Corp, p. 432 [NAICS 561439]

Illinois Consolidated Telephone, p. 18 [NAICS

Numbers following p. or pp. are page references. Braketed items indicate industries. Page references are to the starting pages of company tables.

976

Numbers following p. or pp. are page references. Braketed items indicate industries. Page references are to the starting pages of company tables.

523140]

International Masters Publishers Inc, p. 368 [NAICS 541860]

International Promotions Inc, p. 681 [NAICS 711211]

International Renaissance Festivals Ltd, p. 691 [NAICS 711320]

International Research & Evaluation, p. 377 [NAICS 541910]

International Research and Exchanges Board Inc, p. 554 [NAICS 611699]

International Sematech Inc, p. 348 [NAICS 541710]

International Software Solutions Inc, p. 321 [NAICS 541513]

International Speedway Corp, p. 684 [NAICS 711212]

International Strategy, p. 377 [NAICS 541910]

International Technology Corp, p. 327 [NAICS 541611]

International Technomic, p. 327 [NAICS 541611]

International Thomson Publishing Inc, p. 10 [NAICS 511130]

International Tourist, p. 30 [NAICS 512131]

International Underwriters Insurance Company, p. 911 [NAICS 813920]

International Union of Operating Engineers, p. 538 [NAICS 611513]

International Wellness, p. 729 [NAICS 713940]

International Wildlife Coalition Inc, p. 899 [NAICS 813312]

International Wolf Center, p. 705 [NAICS 712130]

Interphase (Oakland, California), p. 310 [NAICS 541430]

Interpool Inc, p. 244 [NAICS 532310]

Interpublic Group of Companies, pp. 354, 406 [NAICS 541810, 561110]

Interstate Equipment Co, p. 249 [NAICS 532412]

Interstate National Dealer Services, p. 810 [NAICS 811198]

Interstate NationaLease Inc, p. 227 [NAICS 532120]

Interstate Nuclear Services Inc, p. 872 [NAICS 812332]

Intertec Design Inc, p. 412 [NAICS 561310]

Intertec Publishing Corp, pp. 7, 10 [NAICS 511120, 511130]

InterTech Computer Products Inc, p. 816 [NAICS 811212]

Intertribal Addictions Recovery Organization Inc, p. 637 [NAICS 623220]

InterWest Partners, p. 163 [NAICS 523999]

Intuition Inc, p. 163 [NAICS 523999]

Invention Companies, p. 344 [NAICS 541690]

INVESCO Capital Management, p. 157 [NAICS 523930]

Investment Technology Group Inc, p. 163 [NAICS 523999]

Investors Management Corp, p. 760 [NAICS 722110]

Investors Title Co, p. 175 [NAICS 524127]

Investors Title Insurance Co, p. 175 [NAICS 524127]

Iolani School, p. 541 [NAICS 611519]

Iowa Foundation for Medical Care, p. 908 [NAICS 813910]

Iowa Network Services Inc, p. 67 [NAICS 513310]

Iowa State Memorial Union, p. 905 [NAICS 813410]

Iowa Statewide Organ Procurement Organization, p. 603 [NAICS 621511]

Iowa Student Loan Liquidity Corp, p. 902 [NAICS 813319]

IPC Technologies Inc, p. 816 [NAICS 811212]

IQI Inc, p. 388 [NAICS 541990]

IRET, p. 191 [NAICS 525930]

IRI Software, p. 315 [NAICS 541511]

Iris Graphics Inc, p. 21 [NAICS 511210]

Ironworkers District Council of New England Pension Fund, p. 538 [NAICS 611513]

Isaacson, Miller Inc, p. 412 [NAICS 561310]

Island Deaf Sam Music Group, p. 388 [NAICS 541990]

Island One Resorts Management, p. 207 [NAICS 531210]

Island View Academy Inc, p. 637 [NAICS 623220]

Isle of Capri Casinos Inc, p. 742 [NAICS 721110]

Isle of Capri Casions Inc, pp. 713, 760, 766 [NAICS 713120, 722110, 722212]

ISS Building Maintenance Inc, p. 479 [NAICS 561720]

ITG Inc, p. 163 [NAICS 523999]

I.T.I. Marketing Services Inc, p. 388 [NAICS 541990]

ITI Technologies, Inc, p. 470 [NAICS 561621]

Ito Ham U.S.A. Inc, p. 196 [NAICS 531110]

ITS, p. 461 [NAICS 561611]

ITT Educational Services Inc, p. 533 [NAICS 611511]

Ivar E. Roth, p. 584 [NAICS 621391]

IVN Communications Inc, p. 27 [NAICS 512120]

IVonyx/Complete Infusion Care, p. 609 [NAICS 621610]

IVonyx Inc, p. 609 [NAICS 621610]

Iwerks Entertainment Inc, p. 30 [NAICS 512131]

J and E Associates, p. 479 [NAICS 561720]

J B Speed Art Museum, p. 736 [NAICS 713990]

J. Walter Thompson Co, p. 354 [NAICS 541810]

J.A. Ditty and Associates Inc, p. 562 [NAICS 621111]

J.A. Jones Inc, p. 406 [NAICS 561110]

J.A. Jones Management Services, p. 406 [NAICS 561110]

J.A. Riggs Tractor Co, p. 839 [NAICS 811490]

Jack Conway and Company Inc, p. 207 [NAICS 531210]

Jack Griffin Ford Inc, p. 786 [NAICS 811111]

Jack in the Box Inc, pp. 258, 760 [NAICS 533110, 722110]

Jack Loeks Theaters Inc, pp. 30, 33 [NAICS 512131, 512132]

Jack of All Games Inc, p. 27 [NAICS 512120]

Jack Rouse Associates Inc, p. 691 [NAICS 711320]

Jackpot Enterprises Inc, p. 713 [NAICS 713120]

Jackson Hewitt Inc, p. 276 [NAICS 541213]

Jackson Laboratory, pp. 347, 348 [NAICS 541710]

Jackson State University, p. 541 [NAICS 611519]

Jackson Zoological Park, p. 705 [NAICS 712130]

Jacobs Constructors Inc, p. 338 [NAICS 541618]

Jacobs Engineering Group Inc, pp. 288, 406, 479

[NAICS 541330, 561110, 561720]

Jacobson Computer Inc, pp. 528, 816 [NAICS 611420, 811212]

Jacobus Energy Inc, p. 470 [NAICS 561621]

Jacor Broadcasting Corp, p. 52 [NAICS 513111]

Jadtec Computer Group, p. 816 [NAICS 811212]

Jake Sweeney Auto Leasing Inc, p. 224 [NAICS 532112]

James Gang Inc, p. 691 [NAICS 711320]

James R. Gary and Company Ltd, p. 207 [NAICS 531210]

James Stohlman Corp, p. 786 [NAICS 811111]

Jani-King Leasing Corp, p. 479 [NAICS 561720]

Janssen Pharmaceutica Inc, p. 347 [NAICS 541710]

Japan Air Lines Development, p. 742 [NAICS 721110]

Java City Inc, p. 769 [NAICS 722213]

Jayhawk Acceptance Corp, p. 118 [NAICS 522291]

J.B. McLoughlin and Co, p. 207 [NAICS 531210]

JBA International, p. 315 [NAICS 541511]

J.C. Bradford and Co, p. 142 [NAICS 523120]

Jcaho Surveyor and QHR Consultant Corporation, p. 603 [NAICS 621511]

J.D. Edwards and Co, p. 21 [NAICS 511210]

J.D. Industries Inc, p. 196 [NAICS 531110]

J.D. Power and Associates, p. 377 [NAICS 541910]

J.D. Reece Realtors, p. 207 [NAICS 531210]

JDN Realty Corp, p. 191 [NAICS 525930]

JDR Recovery Corp, p. 435 [NAICS 561440]

Jeanne D'Arc Credit Union, p. 108 [NAICS 522130]

Jeff Arthur Productions, p. 691 [NAICS 711320]

Jeff Herman Agency L.L.C.., p. 884 [NAICS 812990]

Jeff Meltzer Editorial Inc, p. 36 [NAICS 512191]

Jefferies Group Inc, p. 142 [NAICS 523120]

Jefferson County Kennel Club Inc, p. 684 [NAICS 711212]

Jefferson Davis Shrine Beauvoir Shrine, p. 702 [NAICS 712120]

Jefferson-Pilot Communications, pp. 52, 58, 61 [NAICS 513111, 513120, 513210]

Jefferson-Pilot Corp, pp. 166, 169, 172, 397 [NAICS 524113, 524114, 524126, 551112]

Jefferson University Physicians, p. 563 [NAICS 621111]

Jellinek, Schwartz & Connolly Inc, p. 344 [NAICS 541690]

Jenkins Living Center Inc, p. 643 [NAICS 623312]

Jenner and Block, p. 264 [NAICS 541110]

Jenny Craig Inc, p. 884 [NAICS 812990]

Jersey Shore Peterbilt Inc, p. 227 [NAICS 532120]

JESCO Industrial Services Inc, p. 479 [NAICS 561720]

Jetson Direct Services Inc, p. 368 [NAICS 541860]

J.I. Sopher and Company Inc, p. 207 [NAICS 531210]

Jiffy Lube International Inc, p. 786 [NAICS 811111]

Jillian's Entertainment Holdings, p. 735 [NAICS 713990]

Jim Barnard Chevrolet Geo Inc, p. 786 [NAICS 811111]

Jim Boltin Enterprises Inc, p. 729 [NAICS 713940]

Jim Henson Co, p. 24 [NAICS 512110]

J.J. Keller and Associates Inc, pp. 10, 18 [NAICS

Numbers following p. or pp. are page references. Braketed items indicate industries. Page references are to the starting pages of company tables.

978

Numbers following p. or pp. are page references. Braketed items indicate industries. Page references are to the starting pages of company tables.

Numbers following p. or pp. are page references. Braketed items indicate industries. Page references are to the starting pages of company tables.

Legacy Health System, p. 406 [NAICS 561110]

Legal Aid and Defender Association of Detroit, p. 896 [NAICS 813311]

Legal Aid of Western Oklahoma Inc, p. 265 [NAICS 541110]

Legal Aid Services of Oregon, p. 265 [NAICS 541110]

Legal Aid Society Inc, p. 896 [NAICS 813311]

Legal Aid Society of Cincinnati, p. 265 [NAICS 541110]

Legal Aid Society of Cleveland, p. 896 [NAICS 813311]

Legal Aid Society of Hawaii, p. 896 [NAICS 813311]

Legal Aid Society of Louisville Inc, p. 896 [NAICS 813311]

Legal Assistance Foundation of Chicago, p. 896 [NAICS 813311]

Legal Foundation of Washington, p. 265 [NAICS 541110]

Legal Services Agency of Western Carolina Inc, p. 265 [NAICS 541110]

Legal Services Corporation, p. 265 [NAICS 541110]

Legal Services Corporation of Alabama Inc, p. 265 [NAICS 541110]

Legal Services Corporation of Iowa, p. 265 [NAICS 541110]

Legal Services of NC Inc, p. 265 [NAICS 541110]

Legal Services of New Jersey Inc, p. 265 [NAICS 541110]

Legg Mason Inc, pp. 142, 157 [NAICS 523120, 523930]

Legg Mason Real Estate Service, p. 121 [NAICS 522292]

Legg Mason Wood Walker Inc, p. 142 [NAICS 523120]

Lehman Brothers Holdings Inc, pp. 142, 157 [NAICS 523120, 523930]

Lehman Millet Inc, pp. 310, 357 [NAICS 541430, 541820]

Leib and Company Inc, p. 435 [NAICS 561440]

Leighton and Associates Inc, p. 344 [NAICS 541690]

Leisure Arts Inc, p. 18 [NAICS 511199]

Leisure World Health Clubs, p. 729 [NAICS 713940]

Lenfest Communications Inc, p. 61 [NAICS 513210]

Lennar Corp, pp. 175, 268 [NAICS 524127, 541191]

Lennar Title Services Inc, pp. 175, 268 [NAICS 524127, 541191]

Lenweaver Advertising & Design, p. 310 [NAICS 541430]

Leo A. Daly Co, p. 285 [NAICS 541310]

Leo Burnett Company Inc, p. 354 [NAICS 541810]

Leo Burnett Worldwide Inc, p. 354 [NAICS 541810]

Leroy's Horse and Sports Place, p. 735 [NAICS 713990]

Les Marks Chevrolet-Mazda Inc, pp. 786, 798 [NAICS 811111, 811121]

Lesh Radio Systems Inc, p. 813 [NAICS 811211]

Leucadia National Corp, p. 169 [NAICS 524114]

Level 3 Communications Inc, p. 318 [NAICS 541512]

Levy Security Consultants Ltd, p. 461 [NAICS 561611]

Lewan and Associates Inc, p. 528 [NAICS 611420]

Lewis Communications Inc, p. 357 [NAICS 541820]

Lewis Supply Company Inc, p. 798 [NAICS 811121]

Lexington Trotters & Breeders, p. 684 [NAICS 711212]

LEXIS-NEXIS, p. 89 [NAICS 514191]

Lexis Publishing, p. 10 [NAICS 511130]

LFR Levine Fricke, p. 338 [NAICS 541618]

Liberty Corp, p. 58 [NAICS 513120]

Liberty Financial Companies Inc, pp. 157, 166, 397 [NAICS 523930, 524113, 551112]

Liberty Media Corp, p. 61 [NAICS 513210]

Liberty Mutual Insurance Co, pp. 166, 169, 172 [NAICS 524113, 524114, 524126]

Libraries Online Inc, p. 89 [NAICS 514191]

Library Video Co, p. 27 [NAICS 512120]

Lieberman Research Worldwide, p. 377 [NAICS 541910]

Lied Discovery Childrens Museum, p. 705 [NAICS 712130]

Life and Health Insurance Guaranty Corporation, p. 908 [NAICS 813910]

Life Care Centers of America Inc, pp. 406, 632 [NAICS 561110, 623110]

Life Care Retirement Communities Inc, p. 640 [NAICS 623311]

Life Management Center, p. 626 [NAICS 622210]

Life Re Corp, p. 169 [NAICS 524114]

Life Reassurance Corporation, p. 169 [NAICS 524114]

Lifecodes Corp, p. 302 [NAICS 541380]

Lifeline Home Health Services, p. 609 [NAICS 621610]

Lifeline Systems Inc, p. 470 [NAICS 561621]

Lifemark Corp, p. 632 [NAICS 623110]

Lifesource, p. 614 [NAICS 621991]

Lifespan Corporation, p. 618 [NAICS 621999]

Lifetime Entertainment Services, p. 64 [NAICS 513220]

Lifetouch Inc, p. 380 [NAICS 541921]

Lifetouch National School Studios, p. 380 [NAICS 541921]

Lifetouch Portrait Studios Inc, p. 380 [NAICS 541921]

Liggett Broadcast Inc, p. 52 [NAICS 513111]

Light and Power Productions Ltd, p. 310 [NAICS 541430]

Lighthouse International, p. 617 [NAICS 621999]

Lighthouse Youth Services Inc, p. 646 [NAICS 623990]

Lightship Group, p. 371 [NAICS 541870]

LIN Television Corp, p. 58 [NAICS 513120]

Linc Capital, p. 118 [NAICS 522291]

LINC Group Inc, pp. 244, 252 [NAICS 532310, 532420]

Lincare Holdings Inc, p. 609 [NAICS 621610]

Lincare Inc, p. 609 [NAICS 621610]

Lincoln National Corp, pp. 166, 169, 172, 397 [NAICS 524113, 524114, 524126, 551112]

Lincoln National Life Insurance, pp. 157, 166 [NAICS 523930, 524113]

Lincoln Technical Institute Inc, p. 533 [NAICS 611511]

Linens of the Week, p. 869 [NAICS 812331]

Linfield College, p. 541 [NAICS 611519]

Linick Group Inc, p. 338 [NAICS 541618]

Link Inc, p. 902 [NAICS 813319]

Linkage Inc, p. 327 [NAICS 541611]

Linn County Historical Society, p. 702 [NAICS 712120]

Linsco/Private Ledger Corp, p. 163 [NAICS 523999]

Litchfield Financial Corp, p. 118 [NAICS 522291]

Little, Brown and Company Inc, p. 10 [NAICS 511130]

Little Caesar Enterprises Inc, pp. 258, 760 [NAICS 533110, 722110]

Little Company of Mary Hospital Inc, p. 554 [NAICS 611699]

Little Six Inc, p. 713 [NAICS 713120]

Litton Data Systems, p. 318 [NAICS 541512]

Litton Industries Inc, pp. 94, 318 [NAICS 514210, 541512]

Litton Loan Servicing Inc, p. 163 [NAICS 523999]

Living in Safe Alternative Incorporated, p. 646 [NAICS 623990]

L.J. Gonzer Associates, pp. 285, 310, 415 [NAICS 541310, 541430, 561320]

L.M. Berry and Co, p. 371 [NAICS 541870]

LMS Cadsi, p. 810 [NAICS 811198]

Loan Administration Network Inc, p. 412 [NAICS 561310]

Local Arrangements Ltd, p. 449 [NAICS 561510]

Locke, Liddell and Sapp LLP, p. 264 [NAICS 541110]

Lockheed Martin Corp, p. 397 [NAICS 551112]

Lockheed Martin Federal Systems, p. 318 [NAICS 541512]

Lockheed Martin IMS, p. 94 [NAICS 514210]

Lockheed Martin Mission Systems, p. 315 [NAICS 541511]

Lockwood Greene Engineers Inc, pp. 285, 288 [NAICS 541310, 541330]

LodgeNet Entertainment Corp, p. 61 [NAICS 513210]

Loeb and Loeb LLP, p. 264 [NAICS 541110]

Loeks-Star Theatres, p. 30 [NAICS 512131]

Loews Corp, pp. 166, 172, 397 [NAICS 524113, 524126, 551112]

Logan County Historical Society Inc, p. 702 [NAICS 712120]

Logicon Inc, pp. 288, 315 [NAICS 541330, 541511]

Logicon Northrop Grumman Co, p. 318 [NAICS 541512]

Logicon R and D Associates, pp. 347, 377 [NAICS 541710, 541910]

Logistic Services International Inc, pp. 18, 839 [NAICS 511199, 811490]

Logix Development Corp, pp. 89, 315 [NAICS 514191, 541511]

Lombard Inc, p. 163 [NAICS 523999]

Long and Foster Real Estate Inc, p. 207 [NAICS 531210]

Long Haymes Carr Inc, p. 354 [NAICS 541810]

Long Home, p. 554 [NAICS 611699]

Long Island Bancorp Inc, p. 105 [NAICS 522120]

Long John Silver's Restaurants, pp. 258, 760

Numbers following p. or pp. are page references. Braketed items indicate industries. Page references are to the starting pages of company tables.

Numbers following p. or pp. are page references. Braketed items indicate industries. Page references are to the starting pages of company tables.

541810]
MedImmune Inc, p. 347 [NAICS 541710]
MEDIQ Inc, p. 255 [NAICS 532490]
MediQuip International, p. 255 [NAICS 532490]
Meditrust Corp, p. 191 [NAICS 525930]
Meditrust Inc, p. 191 [NAICS 525930]
MEDIVAN Inc, p. 617 [NAICS 621999]
MedQuist Inc, p. 94 [NAICS 514210]
MedSpan, p. 621 [NAICS 622110]
Medstaff Contract Nursing Inc, p. 412 [NAICS 561310]
Medstar Health, pp. 609, 617, 621, 629, 632 [NAICS 621610, 621999, 622110, 622310, 623110]
MedTeams, p. 415 [NAICS 561320]
Medtronic, p. 347 [NAICS 541710]
Mega Care Inc, p. 643 [NAICS 623312]
Megatech Corp, p. 533 [NAICS 611511]
Mego Financial Corp, p. 118 [NAICS 522291]
Meineke Discount Muffler Shops, pp. 789, 795 [NAICS 811112, 811118]
Mel Farr Automotive Group Inc, p. 786 [NAICS 811111]
Mel Farr Ford Inc, p. 786 [NAICS 811111]
Melaleuca Inc, p. 406 [NAICS 561110]
Mellon Bank Corp, pp. 102, 394 [NAICS 522110, 551111]
Mellon Bank NA, p. 102 [NAICS 522110]
Melton Motors Inc, p. 798 [NAICS 811121]
Memorial Health Services Inc, pp. 621, 632 [NAICS 622110, 623110]
Memorial Medical Center Inc, pp. 621, 622 [NAICS 622110]
Memphis Funeral Homes, p. 857 [NAICS 812210]
Mendocino Brewing Inc, p. 763 [NAICS 722211]
Mendon Leasing Corp, p. 227 [NAICS 532120]
Menil Foundation Inc, p. 699 [NAICS 712110]
Menlo Biomedical Associates Inc, p. 617 [NAICS 621999]
Menlo Logistics Inc, p. 327 [NAICS 541611]
Mental Health Cooperative Inc, p. 626 [NAICS 622210]
Mentor Graphics Corp, p. 318 [NAICS 541512]
Mentus Inc, p. 310 [NAICS 541430]
Mercantile Trust Company NA, p. 160 [NAICS 523991]
Merchant Factors Corp, p. 134 [NAICS 522320]
Mercury Radio Communications, p. 52 [NAICS 513111]
Mercy Health Services, pp. 169, 621 [NAICS 524114, 622110]
Mercy Medical Center of Oshkosh Inc, p. 911 [NAICS 813920]
Meredith Corp, pp. 7, 10, 58, 61 [NAICS 511120, 511130, 513120, 513210]
Merex Corp, p. 554 [NAICS 611699]
Meridian Investments, p. 142 [NAICS 523120]
Meridian Resource Corp, p. 327 [NAICS 541611]
Meridian VAT Reclaim Inc, p. 276 [NAICS 541213]
MeriStar Hospitality Corp, p. 191 [NAICS 525930]
Merit Realty Inc, p. 207 [NAICS 531210]
Meritcare Inc, p. 632 [NAICS 623110]
Meritech Mortgage Services Inc, p. 121 [NAICS 522292]
Meriter Retirement Services Inc, p. 640 [NAICS

623311]
Meritus Consulting Services, p. 327 [NAICS 541611]
Meriwest Credit Union, p. 108 [NAICS 522130]
Merkle Computer Systems Inc, p. 368 [NAICS 541860]
Merrill Corp, pp. 18, 432 [NAICS 511199, 561439]
Merrill Lynch and Company Inc, pp. 142, 157, 166, 397 [NAICS 523120, 523930, 524113, 551112]
Merrill Lynch Credit Corp, p. 121 [NAICS 522292]
Merrimack Valley Federal Credit, p. 108 [NAICS 522130]
Mesa Verde Co, p. 751 [NAICS 721211]
Messner, Vetere, Berger, p. 354 [NAICS 541810]
Mestek Inc, p. 288 [NAICS 541330]
META Group Inc, p. 377 [NAICS 541910]
Metairie Country Club, p. 721 [NAICS 713910]
Metal Studio, p. 310 [NAICS 541430]
Metallurgical Services Co, p. 344 [NAICS 541690]
Metamor Worldwide Inc, pp. 318, 415 [NAICS 541512, 561320]
Metatherapy Institute Inc, p. 603 [NAICS 621511]
Methodist Childrens Home, p. 905 [NAICS 813410]
Methodist Healthcare, pp. 609, 621 [NAICS 621610, 622110]
Methodist Healthcare-Central Mississippi Medical Associates, p. 603 [NAICS 621511]
Methodist Home for Children Inc, p. 646 [NAICS 623990]
Methodist Medical Group Inc, p. 563 [NAICS 621111]
MetLife Brokerage, p. 182 [NAICS 524210]
Metro Creative Graphics Inc, p. 310 [NAICS 541430]
Metro Financial Services, p. 134 [NAICS 522320]
Metro Global Media Inc, p. 27 [NAICS 512120]
Metro-Goldwyn-Mayer Inc, pp. 24, 30 [NAICS 512110, 512131]
Metro Inc, p. 27 [NAICS 512120]
Metro Networks Inc, p. 344 [NAICS 541690]
Metro-Prop Realty Inc, p. 207 [NAICS 531210]
Metro South Golf Charities Inc, p. 692 [NAICS 711320]
Metro Traffic Control Inc, p. 344 [NAICS 541690]
Metrocall Inc, p. 70 [NAICS 513321]
Metromedia Co, p. 67 [NAICS 513310]
Metromedia International Group Inc, pp. 24, 52, 70 [NAICS 512110, 513111, 513321]
Metropolitan Health Network Inc, p. 603 [NAICS 621511]
Metropolitan Life Insurance Co, p. 166 [NAICS 524113]
Metropolitan Mortgage, pp. 121, 147 [NAICS 522292, 523140]
Metropolitan New York Coordinating Council on Jewish Poverty, p. 351 [NAICS 541720]
Metropolitan Properties, p. 207 [NAICS 531210]
Metropolitan Public Defender Service Inc, p. 896 [NAICS 813311]
Metropolitan Sunday Newspapers, p. 362 [NAICS 541840]
Metropolitan Theaters Corp, p. 30 [NAICS 512131]
Metropolitan Tickets Inc, p. 691 [NAICS 711320]
MFN Financial Corp, p. 118 [NAICS 522291]

MGM Grand Hotel Inc, p. 742 [NAICS 721110]
MGM Grand Inc, p. 742 [NAICS 721110]
MGM-UA Inc, pp. 24, 27 [NAICS 512110, 512120]
MHM Services Inc, pp. 600, 625 [NAICS 621498, 622210]
Miami Herald Publishing Inc, p. 4 [NAICS 511110]
Michael Baker Corp, p. 288 [NAICS 541330]
Michael G. Kessler, p. 461 [NAICS 561611]
Michael Stevens Interests Inc, p. 207 [NAICS 531210]
Michael Swerdlow Cos., p. 199 [NAICS 531120]
Michael V, p. 131 [NAICS 522310]
Michiana Telecasting Corp, p. 52 [NAICS 513111]
Michigan Association of Certified Public Accountants, p. 911 [NAICS 813920]
Michigan Association of SFS Retailers Employees Benefit Plan, p. 681 [NAICS 711211]
Michigan Bell Telephone Co, p. 67 [NAICS 513310]
Michigan Hand Rehabilitation, p. 600 [NAICS 621498]
Michigan National Corp, pp. 105, 394 [NAICS 522120, 551111]
Micro Management Technologies, p. 617 [NAICS 621999]
Micro Overflow Corp, p. 664 [NAICS 624310]
MicroAge Inc, pp. 258, 318 [NAICS 533110, 541512]
MicroAge Software Centre, p. 816 [NAICS 811212]
Microsearch Corp, p. 310 [NAICS 541430]
Microsoft Corp, pp. 21, 89 [NAICS 511210, 514191]
Mid-America Apartment, p. 191 [NAICS 525930]
Mid America Bancorp, p. 131 [NAICS 522310]
Mid-America Cardiology, p. 562 [NAICS 621111]
Mid-America Commercialization Corporation, p. 348 [NAICS 541710]
Mid-America Festivals, p. 735 [NAICS 713990]
Mid-America Health Centers, p. 632 [NAICS 623110]
Mid-Atlantic Cars Inc, p. 406 [NAICS 561110]
Mid-Atlantic Media Sales Inc, p. 362 [NAICS 541840]
Mid-Continent Agencies Inc, p. 435 [NAICS 561440]
Mid-Michigan Industries Inc, p. 664 [NAICS 624310]
Mid-Minnesota Legal Assistance Incorporated, p. 265 [NAICS 541110]
Mid State Raceway Inc, p. 684 [NAICS 711212]
Mid States Engineering LLC, p. 285 [NAICS 541310]
Mid-Tenn Ford Truck Sales Inc, pp. 795, 798 [NAICS 811118, 811121]
MidAmerica Commodity, p. 150 [NAICS 523210]
Midas International Corp, pp. 258, 789, 795 [NAICS 533110, 811112, 811118]
Midcontinent Media Inc, p. 52 [NAICS 513111]
Middleberg and Associates, p. 357 [NAICS 541820]
Middough Associates Inc, p. 285 [NAICS 541310]
MidFirst Bank, p. 105 [NAICS 522120]
Midland Financial Co, pp. 105, 394 [NAICS 522120, 551111]
Midstates Development Inc, p. 52 [NAICS 513111]
Midwest Assistance Program Inc, p. 351 [NAICS

Numbers following p. or pp. are page references. Braketed items indicate industries. Page references are to the starting pages of company tables.

Midwest Capital Group Inc, p. 163 [NAICS 523999]
Midwest Environmental, p. 344 [NAICS 541690]
Midwest Payment Systems Co, p. 94 [NAICS 514210]
Midwest Research Institute, pp. 347, 377 [NAICS 541710, 541910]
Midwest Transplant Network Inc, p. 603 [NAICS 621511]
Midwest Wireless, p. 70 [NAICS 513321]
Migliara/Kaplan Associates, p. 377 [NAICS 541910]
Mile High Greyhound Park, p. 684 [NAICS 711212]
Miles Bell and Associates Inc, p. 691 [NAICS 711320]
MileStone Healthcare, p. 629 [NAICS 622310]
Milestone Properties Inc, p. 196 [NAICS 531110]
Milford Memorial Hospital Inc, p. 621 [NAICS 622110]
Milgo Solutions Inc, p. 318 [NAICS 541512]
Mill Hill Medical Consultants Inc, p. 563 [NAICS 621111]
Millennium Health Inc, p. 902 [NAICS 813319]
Millennium Pharmaceuticals Inc, p. 347 [NAICS 541710]
Miller, Canfield, Paddock & Stone, p. 264 [NAICS 541110]
Miller Freeman Inc, p. 7 [NAICS 511120]
Miller Heiman Inc, p. 338 [NAICS 541618]
Miller Industries Inc, p. 199 [NAICS 531120]
Miller/Shandwick International, p. 357 [NAICS 541820]
Miller-Valentine Group, p. 204 [NAICS 531190]
Milliken and Michaels Inc, p. 435 [NAICS 561440]
Milliken Research Corp, p. 347 [NAICS 541710]
Million Dollar Video Corp, p. 27 [NAICS 512120]
Millsport Inc, p. 681 [NAICS 711211]
Millstein Industries LLC, p. 720 [NAICS 713910]
Milwaukee Athletic Club, p. 735 [NAICS 713990]
Milwaukee County War Memorial Center Inc, p. 736 [NAICS 713990]
Milwaukee Electrical Joint Apprenticeship and Training Plan, p. 538 [NAICS 611513]
Milwaukee Public Museum Inc, p. 705 [NAICS 712130]
MIM Corp, p. 182 [NAICS 524210]
Mindspring Inc, p. 89 [NAICS 514191]
MindWorks Professional, p. 528 [NAICS 611420]
Ministry Behavorial Health of St Michaels Hospital Inc, p. 637 [NAICS 623220]
Minneapolis Grain Exchange, p. 150 [NAICS 523210]
Minneapolis Grand Hotel, p. 735 [NAICS 713990]
Minnesota Historical Society, p. 702 [NAICS 712120]
Minnesota Life and Health Insurance Guaranty Association, p. 908 [NAICS 813910]
Minnesota Medical Foundation 1342, p. 348 [NAICS 541710]
Minnesota Mutual Life Insurance, pp. 166, 169 [NAICS 524113, 524114]
Miracle Auto Painting Inc, p. 798 [NAICS 811121]
Mirage Casino-Hotel, p. 742 [NAICS 721110]
Mirage Resorts Inc, p. 742 [NAICS 721110]
Mirak Chevrolet Inc, p. 786 [NAICS 811111]

Miramax Films, pp. 24, 27 [NAICS 512110, 512120]
Mission Federal Credit Union, p. 108 [NAICS 522130]
Mission Health Services, p. 643 [NAICS 623312]
Mission Mortgage Inc, p. 121 [NAICS 522292]
Mississippi Action for Progress Inc, p. 348 [NAICS 541710]
Mississippi Association of Educators, p. 911 [NAICS 813920]
Mississippi Blood Services Inc, p. 614 [NAICS 621991]
Mississippi Foundation for Medical Care Inc, p. 890 [NAICS 813212]
Mississippi Valley Equipment Co, p. 249 [NAICS 532412]
Missoula Manor Homes, p. 640 [NAICS 623311]
Missouri Athletic Club, p. 736 [NAICS 713990]
Missouri Hospital Association, p. 911 [NAICS 813920]
Missouri One-Call Systems Inc, p. 908 [NAICS 813910]
Missouri River Adolescent Development Center Inc, p. 902 [NAICS 813319]
MIT Lincoln Laboratory, p. 347 [NAICS 541710]
Mitch Murch's Maintenance, p. 479 [NAICS 561720]
Mitchell's Management Corp, p. 884 [NAICS 812990]
Mitchell's Salon and Day Spa Inc, pp. 729, 842 [NAICS 713940, 812111]
Mitek Industries Inc, p. 315 [NAICS 541511]
Mitre Corp, p. 338 [NAICS 541618]
M.J. Harden Associates Inc, p. 383 [NAICS 541922]
MJI Broadcasting, p. 691 [NAICS 711320]
MNB Bancshares Inc, pp. 102, 394 [NAICS 522110, 551111]
MNP Corp, p. 302 [NAICS 541380]
Mobile Communications, p. 70 [NAICS 513321]
Mobium Corp, p. 310 [NAICS 541430]
Modem Media, p. 315 [NAICS 541511]
Modern Engineering Inc, p. 415 [NAICS 561320]
Modern Group Ltd, p. 227 [NAICS 532120]
Modern Mass Media Inc, p. 27 [NAICS 512120]
Modern Systems International, p. 435 [NAICS 561440]
Modern Videofilm Inc, p. 36 [NAICS 512191]
Modis Professional Services Inc, p. 318 [NAICS 541512]
Molina Medical Centers, pp. 562, 572, 575, 584 [NAICS 621111, 621310, 621320, 621391]
Molly Maid Inc, p. 479 [NAICS 561720]
Momentum-IMC, p. 681 [NAICS 711211]
Monadnock Economic Development Corporation, p. 914 [NAICS 813990]
Monadnock Family Services, p. 902 [NAICS 813319]
Monarch Dental Corp, p. 617 [NAICS 621999]
Moneco Group, p. 327 [NAICS 541611]
Money Mailer Inc, p. 368 [NAICS 541860]
Money Store Inc, p. 121 [NAICS 522292]
Monotype Systems Inc, p. 315 [NAICS 541511]
Monro Muffler Brake Inc, pp. 786, 789, 795 [NAICS 811111, 811112, 811118]

Monroe @crs-Orleans BOCES, pp. 526, 533 [NAICS 611410, 611511]
Monroe Title Insurance Corp, pp. 175, 268 [NAICS 524127, 541191]
Montana State University Foundation, p. 348 [NAICS 541710]
Monterey Pasta Co, pp. 763, 766, 769 [NAICS 722211, 722212, 722213]
Montessori Learning Commons, p. 667 [NAICS 624410]
Montgomery Watson Constructors, p. 497 [NAICS 562111]
Montgomery Watson Inc, p. 288 [NAICS 541330]
Montgomery, Zukerman, Davis, p. 377 [NAICS 541910]
Monumental Life Insurance Co, p. 166 [NAICS 524113]
Moody's Investors Service Inc, pp. 18, 377, 438 [NAICS 511199, 541910, 561450]
Moore USA Inc, p. 89 [NAICS 514191]
Moose International Incorporated, p. 905 [NAICS 813410]
Morey's Piers, p. 710 [NAICS 713110]
Morgan Guaranty Trust of New, p. 102 [NAICS 522110]
Morgan, Lewis & Bockius LLP, p. 264 [NAICS 541110]
Morgan Stanley Dean Witter, pp. 118, 157 [NAICS 522291, 523930]
Morgan Stanley International Inc, p. 142 [NAICS 523120]
Morgen-Walke Associates Inc, p. 357 [NAICS 541820]
MORPACE International Inc, p. 377 [NAICS 541910]
Morris Advertising & Design Inc, p. 310 [NAICS 541430]
Morris Communications Corp, pp. 4, 7 [NAICS 511110, 511120]
Morris Newspaper Corp, p. 58 [NAICS 513120]
Morrison and Foerster LLP, p. 264 [NAICS 541110]
Morrisy and Company Inc, p. 617 [NAICS 621999]
Morrow Equipment LLC, p. 249 [NAICS 532412]
Mortgage Resource Inc, p. 131 [NAICS 522310]
Morton Center Inc, p. 637 [NAICS 623220]
Morton G. Thalhimer Inc, p. 207 [NAICS 531210]
Mosby Inc, pp. 7, 10, 89 [NAICS 511120, 511130, 514191]
Mothers Against Drunk Driving, p. 902 [NAICS 813319]
Motion Picture Association America Inc, p. 908 [NAICS 813910]
Motion Picture Laboratories Inc, p. 36 [NAICS 512191]
Motor Club of America, p. 810 [NAICS 811198]
Motorcycle Mechanics Institute, p. 533 [NAICS 611511]
Motorola Inc, p. 21 [NAICS 511210]
Mt. Carmel Health, pp. 600, 609, 632 [NAICS 621498, 621610, 623110]
Mt. High Entertainment, p. 691 [NAICS 711320]
Mount Rogers Community Service, pp. 625, 629 [NAICS 622210, 622310]
Mount Snow Ltd, p. 720 [NAICS 713910]

Company Index

Numbers following p. or pp. are page references. Braketed items indicate industries. Page references are to the starting pages of company tables.

985

Mount Vernon Ladies Association of the Union, p. 702 [NAICS 712120]

Mountain Home Health Care Inc, p. 640 [NAICS 623311]

Mountain-Pacific Quality Health Foundation, p. 911 [NAICS 813920]

Mountain States Tumor Institute Inc, p. 348 [NAICS 541710]

Mountain Valley Brewing Co, p. 781 [NAICS 722410]

Movie Exchange Inc, p. 234 [NAICS 532230]

Movie Gallery Inc, p. 234 [NAICS 532230]

MovieFone Inc, p. 344 [NAICS 541690]

Movies Unlimited Inc, p. 234 [NAICS 532230]

MPW Industrial Services Group, p. 409 [NAICS 561210]

MQS Inspection Inc, p. 302 [NAICS 541380]

Ms Foundation for Women Inc, p. 902 [NAICS 813319]

MTB Bank. Trading Alliance Div., p. 134 [NAICS 522320]

MTV Networks Inc, p. 61 [NAICS 513210]

Muckleshoot Indian Casino, p. 713 [NAICS 713120]

Muller Data Corp, p. 94 [NAICS 514210]

Mullikin Medical Centers Inc, p. 406 [NAICS 561110]

Multi-Image Network, p. 380 [NAICS 541921]

Multicare Health Systems, p. 905 [NAICS 813410]

Multimedia Cablevision Inc, p. 61 [NAICS 513210]

Multimedia Games Inc, p. 94 [NAICS 514210]

Multnomah Kennel Club Inc, p. 684 [NAICS 711212]

MuniMae, p. 137 [NAICS 522390]

Munson Medical Center, p. 621 [NAICS 622110]

Murdoch, Coll and Lillibridge Inc, p. 207 [NAICS 531210]

Murphey Favre Inc, p. 142 [NAICS 523120]

Museum of Science, p. 705 [NAICS 712130]

Museum of Science and Industry, p. 705 [NAICS 712130]

Music Theatre of Wichita Inc, p. 672 [NAICS 711110]

Musson Theatrical Inc, p. 691 [NAICS 711320]

Mustang Power Systems, p. 786 [NAICS 811111]

Mutual Insurance of Arizona, p. 178 [NAICS 524128]

Mutual Life Insurance of New, pp. 157, 166 [NAICS 523930, 524113]

Mutual Mortgage Corp, p. 131 [NAICS 522310]

Mutual of America Life Insurance, p. 166 [NAICS 524113]

Mutual of Omaha Insurance Co, p. 169 [NAICS 524114]

Mutual Savings Life Insurance Co, p. 172 [NAICS 524126]

MVM Inc, pp. 461, 470 [NAICS 561611, 561621]

Mystery Fun House, p. 710 [NAICS 713110]

Mystic Fire Video Inc, p. 27 [NAICS 512120]

N J A T C, p. 538 [NAICS 611513]

Nabors Inc, p. 224 [NAICS 532112]

Nacel Open Door Inc, p. 554 [NAICS 611699]

Nana Development Corp, p. 461 [NAICS 561611]

Nanticoke Memorial Hospital Inc, p. 621 [NAICS 622110]

Nasdaq Stock Market Inc, p. 150 [NAICS 523210]

Nashua Country Club, p. 721 [NAICS 713910]

Nassau Country Club, p. 721 [NAICS 713910]

Nation's Foodservice Inc, pp. 763, 766, 769 [NAICS 722211, 722212, 722213]

National Amusements Inc, pp. 30, 397 [NAICS 512131, 551112]

National Aquarium in Baltimore Inc, p. 705 [NAICS 712130]

National Association for the Advancement of Colored People, p. 896 [NAICS 813311]

National Association of Securities, p. 150 [NAICS 523210]

National Association of Tower Erectors, p. 911 [NAICS 813920]

National Auto Finance Inc, p. 118 [NAICS 522291]

National Automobile Dealers Association, p. 736 [NAICS 713990]

National Broadcasting Inc, pp. 52, 58 [NAICS 513111, 513120]

National Bureau of Economic Research Inc, p. 351 [NAICS 541720]

National Cable Television Assn, p. 736 [NAICS 713990]

National Car Rental System Inc, p. 221 [NAICS 532111]

National Cattlemens Beef Association Inc, p. 908 [NAICS 813910]

National City Corp, pp. 105, 394 [NAICS 522120, 551111]

National Collegiate Athletic Association, p. 541 [NAICS 611519]

National Committee to Preserve Social Security and Medicare, p. 890 [NAICS 813212]

National Communications Inc, p. 371 [NAICS 541870]

National Computer Systems Inc, pp. 94, 315 [NAICS 514210, 541511]

National Council of Negro Women Inc, p. 896 [NAICS 813311]

National Crime Prevention Council Inc, p. 902 [NAICS 813319]

National Data Corp, p. 94 [NAICS 514210]

National Dispatch Center Inc, p. 70 [NAICS 513321]

National Economic Research, p. 377 [NAICS 541910]

National Education Association of New Mexico, p. 911 [NAICS 813920]

National Electronics Warranty, p. 182 [NAICS 524210]

National Energy Foundation Inc, p. 899 [NAICS 813312]

National Environmental, p. 344 [NAICS 541690]

National Environmental Service, p. 302 [NAICS 541380]

National Federation of Independent Business Inc, p. 908 [NAICS 813910]

National Film Preserve Ltd, p. 705 [NAICS 712130]

National Financial Services Corp, p. 142 [NAICS 523120]

National Foot Care Program Inc, p. 584 [NAICS 621391]

National Genealogical Society, p. 884 [NAICS 812990]

National Golf Properties Inc, p. 191 [NAICS 525930]

National Ground Water, p. 344 [NAICS 541690]

National Health Care Affiliates, pp. 609, 632 [NAICS 621610, 623110]

National HealthCare Corp, p. 632 [NAICS 623110]

National Hockey League, p. 681 [NAICS 711211]

National Home Health Care Corp, pp. 587, 609 [NAICS 621399, 621610]

National Hot Rod Association, p. 681 [NAICS 711211]

National Indemnity Co, p. 172 [NAICS 524126]

National Information Bureau Ltd, p. 438 [NAICS 561450]

National Institute for Educational, p. 554 [NAICS 611699]

National Journal Group Inc, p. 18 [NAICS 511199]

National Linen & Uniform Service, pp. 869, 872 [NAICS 812331, 812332]

National Loss Control Service, p. 182 [NAICS 524210]

National Lutheran Home for the Aged, p. 640 [NAICS 623311]

National Park Concessions Inc, pp. 763, 766, 769 [NAICS 722211, 722212, 722213]

National Pork Producers Council, p. 348 [NAICS 541710]

National Processing Co, p. 94 [NAICS 514210]

National Processing Inc, p. 94 [NAICS 514210]

National Public Radio, p. 52 [NAICS 513111]

National Republican Club of Capitol Hill, p. 721 [NAICS 713910]

National Right to Work Committee Inc, p. 896 [NAICS 813311]

National Senior Citizens Law Center, p. 265 [NAICS 541110]

National Service Industries Inc, p. 869 [NAICS 812331]

National Shopping Service, p. 338 [NAICS 541618]

National Surgery Centers Inc, p. 600 [NAICS 621498]

National Technical Systems Inc, p. 302 [NAICS 541380]

National TechTeam Inc, pp. 415, 528 [NAICS 561320, 611420]

National Tenant Network Inc, p. 438 [NAICS 561450]

National Trust for Historic Preservation, p. 702 [NAICS 712120]

National Underwriter Co, p. 18 [NAICS 511199]

National Utility Service Inc, p. 338 [NAICS 541618]

National Wireless Holdings Inc, p. 73 [NAICS 513322]

NationsBanc Montgomery, pp. 142, 157 [NAICS 523120, 523930]

NationsBank Card Services, p. 134 [NAICS 522320]

Nationwide Advertising Service, p. 354 [NAICS 541810]

Nationwide Capital Inc, p. 131 [NAICS 522310]

Nationwide Corp, pp. 166, 172, 397 [NAICS 524113, 524126, 551112]

Nationwide Entertainment, p. 691 [NAICS 711320]

Nationwide Financial Services Inc, p. 157 [NAICS

Numbers following p. or pp. are page references. Braketed items indicate industries. Page references are to the starting pages of company tables.

Nationwide Formalwear Inc, p. 884 [NAICS 812990]

Nationwide Health Properties Inc, p. 191 [NAICS 525930]

Nationwide Life Insurance Co, p. 166 [NAICS 524113]

Nationwide Mutual Insurance Co, p. 172 [NAICS 524126]

Native American Cultural Center, p. 664 [NAICS 624310]

Native American Heritage Association, p. 637 [NAICS 623220]

Native American Rights Fund, p. 896 [NAICS 813311]

Native Hawaiian Legal Corporation, p. 265 [NAICS 541110]

Natural Health Trends Corp, p. 533 [NAICS 611511]

Nautica Apparel Inc, p. 258 [NAICS 533110]

Nautica Enterprises Inc, p. 258 [NAICS 533110]

NBA Entertainment, p. 24 [NAICS 512110]

NBBJ, p. 285 [NAICS 541310]

NCES Inc, p. 617 [NAICS 621999]

NCO Group Inc, p. 435 [NAICS 561440]

NCR Corp, p. 816 [NAICS 811212]

NCS HealthCare Inc, p. 406 [NAICS 561110]

NCS International Inc, p. 327 [NAICS 541611]

N.D.C. Inc, p. 207 [NAICS 531210]

NDCE Commerce, pp. 94, 276 [NAICS 514210, 541213]

N.E. Finch Co, p. 249 [NAICS 532412]

Near North Insurance Brokerage, p. 182 [NAICS 524210]

Nebraska Cellular Telephone Corp, p. 70 [NAICS 513321]

Nebraska Food Bank Network Inc, p. 902 [NAICS 813319]

Nebraska Iowa Supply Co, pp. 763, 766, 769 [NAICS 722211, 722212, 722213]

Nebraska Organ Retrieval System, p. 603 [NAICS 621511]

Nebraska State Education Association, p. 911 [NAICS 813920]

NEC Research Institute Inc, p. 302 [NAICS 541380]

Ned West Inc, p. 199 [NAICS 531120]

Nederlander Organization Inc, p. 691 [NAICS 711320]

Nelly's Janitorial PS Inc, p. 479 [NAICS 561720]

Nelson Communications Inc, p. 163 [NAICS 523999]

Nelson Leasing Inc, p. 227 [NAICS 532120]

Nelson, Mullins, Riley, p. 264 [NAICS 541110]

Nemont Telephone Cooperative, pp. 67, 70 [NAICS 513310, 513321]

Neodata Services Inc, p. 368 [NAICS 541860]

Neogen Corp, p. 347 [NAICS 541710]

Netscape Communications Corp, pp. 89, 327 [NAICS 514191, 541611]

Netware Users International North America Inc, p. 911 [NAICS 813920]

Network Associates Inc, p. 21 [NAICS 511210]

Network Communications Inc, pp. 10, 89 [NAICS 511130, 514191]

Network Direct Inc, p. 327 [NAICS 541611]

Neuropsychiatric Research Institute, p. 348 [NAICS 541710]

Nevada Dance Theatre Inc, p. 672 [NAICS 711110]

Nevada Legal Services Inc, p. 265 [NAICS 541110]

New Country Pontiac, GMC, pp. 221, 798 [NAICS 532111, 811121]

New Dimensions Service, p. 816 [NAICS 811212]

New England Apple Council Inc, p. 908 [NAICS 813910]

New England Financial, pp. 157, 166 [NAICS 523930, 524113]

New England Newspapers Inc, p. 368 [NAICS 541860]

New England Realty Associates L, pp. 196, 199 [NAICS 531110, 531120]

New England Reinsurance Corp, p. 178 [NAICS 524128]

New England Security Inc, p. 470 [NAICS 561621]

New England Telephone, p. 67 [NAICS 513310]

New Gaylord Entertainment Co, pp. 52, 58, 710 [NAICS 513111, 513120, 713110]

New Hamphshire Bar Association, p. 911 [NAICS 813920]

New Hampshire Automobile Reinsurance Facility, p. 911 [NAICS 813920]

New Hampshire Charitable Foundation, p. 541 [NAICS 611519]

New Hampshire Coalition Against Domestic & Sexual Violence, p. 896 [NAICS 813311]

New Hampshire Institute of Art, p. 699 [NAICS 712110]

New Hampshire-Vermont Health, p. 169 [NAICS 524114]

New Haven Legal Assistance Association Inc, p. 896 [NAICS 813311]

New Horizon Enterprises Inc, p. 667 [NAICS 624410]

New Horizon Kids Quest Inc, pp. 667, 735 [NAICS 624410, 713990]

New Jersey Performing Arts Center Corporation, p. 736 [NAICS 713990]

New Jersey Property Liability Insurance Guaranty Association, p. 908 [NAICS 813910]

New Life Discovery Schools Inc, p. 667 [NAICS 624410]

New Life Homes Inc, p. 646 [NAICS 623990]

New Line Cinema Corp, pp. 24, 27 [NAICS 512110, 512120]

New Line Home Video Inc, p. 691 [NAICS 711320]

New Mexico & Arizona Land Co, p. 204 [NAICS 531190]

New Orleans Museum of Art, p. 541 [NAICS 611519]

New Orleans Paddlewheels Inc, p. 735 [NAICS 713990]

New Orleans Saints, p. 735 [NAICS 713990]

New Orleans Tourism Marketing, p. 735 [NAICS 713990]

New York Board of Trade, p. 150 [NAICS 523210]

New York City Economic Development Corporation, p. 914 [NAICS 813990]

New York Health & Racquet Club, p. 729 [NAICS 713940]

New York Health Care Inc, p. 609 [NAICS 621610]

New York Life Insurance Co, p. 166 [NAICS 524113]

New York Media Group, p. 36 [NAICS 512191]

New York-New York Hotel, p. 742 [NAICS 721110]

New York Racing Association Inc, p. 684 [NAICS 711212]

New York Restaurant School, p. 533 [NAICS 611511]

New York Telephone Co, p. 67 [NAICS 513310]

New York Times Co, pp. 4, 7, 58, 83 [NAICS 511110, 511120, 513120, 514110]

New York Times Syndication, p. 83 [NAICS 514110]

Newark Museum Association, p. 705 [NAICS 712130]

NewCare Health Corp, pp. 621, 632 [NAICS 622110, 623110]

Newhouse Broadcasting Corp, p. 61 [NAICS 513210]

Newins Bay Shore Ford Inc, p. 221 [NAICS 532111]

Newport Creamery Inc, pp. 763, 769 [NAICS 722211, 722213]

News America Inc, pp. 4, 7, 58 [NAICS 511110, 511120, 513120]

News America Marketing, p. 371 [NAICS 541870]

News Corporation of America, pp. 4, 7 [NAICS 511110, 511120]

News-Gazette, pp. 52, 368 [NAICS 513111, 541860]

Newspapers First Inc, p. 354 [NAICS 541810]

Newsweek Inc, p. 7 [NAICS 511120]

Newton Healthcare Corporation, p. 618 [NAICS 621999]

Next Door Inc, p. 672 [NAICS 711110]

Nextel Communications Inc, p. 70 [NAICS 513321]

NextHealth Inc, p. 629 [NAICS 622310]

NFO Worldwide Inc, p. 377 [NAICS 541910]

Niagara Mohawk Holdings Inc, p. 397 [NAICS 551112]

Nicholas Financial Inc, p. 118 [NAICS 522291]

Nichols Research Corp, p. 347 [NAICS 541710]

Nickels and Dimes Inc, p. 710 [NAICS 713110]

Nicosia Creative Expresso Ltd, p. 310 [NAICS 541430]

Nielsen Media Research Inc, p. 377 [NAICS 541910]

Nielson Media Research Inc, pp. 89, 377 [NAICS 514191, 541910]

Niessen Dunlap and Pritchard PC, p. 276 [NAICS 541213]

Nikko Securities International Inc, p. 142 [NAICS 523120]

Nissan Capital of America Inc, p. 134 [NAICS 522320]

Nissan Motor Acceptance Corp, p. 118 [NAICS 522291]

Nitze-Stagen and Company Inc, p. 207 [NAICS 531210]

Nixon Power Services Co, p. 795 [NAICS 811118]

Nobel Learning Communities Inc, p. 667 [NAICS 624410]

Noble Broadcast Group Inc, p. 52 [NAICS 513111]

Nolan Amusement Co, p. 735 [NAICS 713990]

Numbers following p. or pp. are page references. Braketed items indicate industries. Page references are to the starting pages of company tables.

987

Numbers following p. or pp. are page references. Braketed items indicate industries. Page references are to the starting pages of company tables.

Numbers following p. or pp. are page references. Bracketed items indicate industries. Page references are to the starting pages of company tables.

989

Company Index

Numbers following p. or pp. are page references. Braketed items indicate industries. Page references are to the starting pages of company tables.

Numbers following p. or pp. are page references. Braketed items indicate industries. Page references are to the starting pages of company tables.

Numbers following p. or pp. are page references. Braketed items indicate industries. Page references are to the starting pages of company tables.

Numbers following p. or pp. are page references. Braketed items indicate industries. Page references are to the starting pages of company tables.

994

Numbers following p. or pp. are page references. Braketed items indicate industries. Page references are to the starting pages of company tables.

Shelter Financial Bank, p. 118 [NAICS 522291]
Shenandoah Telecommunications, p. 67 [NAICS 513310]
Shepherd of the Hills Homestead, p. 710 [NAICS 713110]
SHG Associates Inc, p. 285 [NAICS 541310]
SHG Inc, p. 285 [NAICS 541310]
Shilo Corp, pp. 196, 742 [NAICS 531110, 721110]
Shilo Inns Co, p. 742 [NAICS 721110]
Shinnyo-En Foundation, p. 554 [NAICS 611699]
Shirley Oil and Supply Inc, pp. 763, 766, 769 [NAICS 722211, 722212, 722213]
Shoney's Inc, pp. 258, 760 [NAICS 533110, 722110]
Shop 'n Chek Inc, p. 377 [NAICS 541910]
Shop at Home Inc, pp. 58, 61 [NAICS 513120, 513210]
Shorenstein Co, pp. 207, 406 [NAICS 531210, 561110]
Shorenstein Realty Services LP, p. 406 [NAICS 561110]
Showboat Casino Hotel, p. 742 [NAICS 721110]
Showtime Networks Inc, p. 61 [NAICS 513210]
Shrine to Music Museum Inc, p. 705 [NAICS 712130]
Shubert Organization Inc, p. 199 [NAICS 531120]
Shuwa Investments Corp, p. 199 [NAICS 531120]
Siddall, Matus and Coughter Inc, p. 357 [NAICS 541820]
Sidley and Austin, p. 264 [NAICS 541110]
Siegel and Gale Inc, p. 338 [NAICS 541618]
Siegel Oil Co, p. 302 [NAICS 541380]
Siegel Trading Company Inc, p. 147 [NAICS 523140]
Siemens Power Corp, p. 839 [NAICS 811490]
Sierra Academy of Aeronautics, p. 533 [NAICS 611511]
Sierra Assisted Living Foundation Inc, p. 643 [NAICS 623312]
Sierra Detroit Diesel Allison Inc, p. 786 [NAICS 811111]
Sierra Health Services Inc, p. 609 [NAICS 621610]
Sierra Nevada Brewing Co, pp. 763, 766, 769 [NAICS 722211, 722212, 722213]
Sierra Ventures, p. 163 [NAICS 523999]
Silent Watchman Div., p. 470 [NAICS 561621]
Silicon Composers Inc, p. 252 [NAICS 532420]
Silicon Graphics Inc, pp. 21, 347 [NAICS 511210, 541710]
Silver Dollar City Inc, p. 710 [NAICS 713110]
SIMCO Electronics, p. 302 [NAICS 541380]
Simon and Schuster Inc, p. 10 [NAICS 511130]
Simon Property Group LP, p. 207 [NAICS 531210]
Simonds-Shields-Theis Grain Co, p. 147 [NAICS 523140]
Simons, Li and Associates Inc, p. 344 [NAICS 541690]
Simplicity Holdings Inc, p. 18 [NAICS 511199]
Simpson Buick Co, p. 221 [NAICS 532111]
Simpson County Historical Society, p. 884 [NAICS 812990]
Simpson Foundation, p. 699 [NAICS 712110]
Simpson Land Company Inc, p. 781 [NAICS 722410]

Simpson Thacher and Bartlett, p. 264 [NAICS 541110]
SIMSCommunications Inc, p. 244 [NAICS 532310]
SimuFlite Training International, p. 554 [NAICS 611699]
Sinclair Broadcast Group Inc, p. 58 [NAICS 513120]
Sioux Falls Development Foundation Inc, p. 914 [NAICS 813990]
Sioux Valley Health Network, p. 618 [NAICS 621999]
Siscom Inc, p. 21 [NAICS 511210]
Sisters of Providence Good Health Plan of Oregon Inc, p. 618 [NAICS 621999]
Site-Blauvelt Engineers Inc, p. 344 [NAICS 541690]
SITEL Corp, p. 388 [NAICS 541990]
Siu Physicians & Surgeons Inc, p. 563 [NAICS 621111]
Sive/Young and Rubicam, p. 357 [NAICS 541820]
Six Flags, pp. 710, 754 [NAICS 713110, 721214]
Six Flags California, p. 710 [NAICS 713110]
Six Flags Over Texas Inc, p. 710 [NAICS 713110]
Six Flags St. Louis Inc, p. 710 [NAICS 713110]
Six Flags Theme Parks Inc, p. 710 [NAICS 713110]
Sizeler Property Investors Inc, p. 191 [NAICS 525930]
Skadden, Arps, Slate, Meagher, p. 264 [NAICS 541110]
Skip Barber Group, p. 554 [NAICS 611699]
Skyline Chili Inc, p. 769 [NAICS 722213]
Skyline Multimedia Entertainment, p. 735 [NAICS 713990]
Skyport Lodge Inc, p. 781 [NAICS 722410]
SkyTel Communications Inc, p. 70 [NAICS 513321]
SkyTel Corp, p. 70 [NAICS 513321]
SM Berger and Co, p. 421 [NAICS 561410]
S.M. Stoller Corp, p. 344 [NAICS 541690]
SMA Video Inc, p. 36 [NAICS 512191]
Small Newspaper Group Inc, p. 4 [NAICS 511110]
Smart Corp, p. 432 [NAICS 561439]
SMG, p. 681 [NAICS 711211]
SMH (US) Inc, p. 839 [NAICS 811490]
Smith Alarm Systems, p. 470 [NAICS 561621]
Smith Detroit Diesel/Allison Inc, p. 786 [NAICS 811111]
Smith, Dorian and Burman Inc, p. 371 [NAICS 541870]
Smith Gosnell Nicholson, p. 691 [NAICS 711320]
Smith Technology Corp, p. 344 [NAICS 541690]
Smithey Recycling Co, p. 204 [NAICS 531190]
Snake River Sugar Company, p. 905 [NAICS 813410]
Snyder Communications Inc, pp. 368, 388 [NAICS 541860, 541990]
Society of Financial Service Professionals, p. 911 [NAICS 813920]
Software Spectrum/Technology, p. 388 [NAICS 541990]
Sojourner Hall for Women Inc, p. 664 [NAICS 624310]
SolArc Inc, p. 528 [NAICS 611420]
Solectron Corp, p. 406 [NAICS 561110]
Solectron Technology Inc, p. 288 [NAICS 541330]
Solomon-Page Group Ltd, p. 412 [NAICS 561310]

Somerset Tire Service Inc, p. 786 [NAICS 811111]
Sonic Corp, p. 760 [NAICS 722110]
Sonitrol Communications Corp, p. 470 [NAICS 561621]
Sony Pictures Entertainment Inc, p. 24 [NAICS 512110]
Sony USA Inc, pp. 21, 24, 258, 397 [NAICS 511210, 512110, 533110, 551112]
SOS Security Inc, p. 461 [NAICS 561611]
SOS Staffing Services Inc, p. 415 [NAICS 561320]
Sotheby's Inc, p. 388 [NAICS 541990]
Sound Chek Music, p. 244 [NAICS 532310]
Soundelux Entertainment Group, p. 36 [NAICS 512191]
Soundscapes Inc, p. 691 [NAICS 711320]
Source Information Management, pp. 377, 435 [NAICS 541910, 561440]
Source One Mortgage Corp, p. 121 [NAICS 522292]
Souris Valley Care Center Inc, p. 640 [NAICS 623311]
South Carolina Episcopal Home at Still Hopes, p. 640 [NAICS 623311]
South Central L A Reg Central, p. 626 [NAICS 622210]
South Coast Title Co, p. 175 [NAICS 524127]
South Dakota Association of the Deaf, p. 653 [NAICS 624190]
South Dakota Community Foundation, p. 348 [NAICS 541710]
South Dakota State University Foundation, p. 905 [NAICS 813410]
South Hills Health System, pp. 609, 621 [NAICS 621610, 622110]
South Middlesex Opportunity Council Inc, p. 637 [NAICS 623220]
South of the Border Inc, p. 735 [NAICS 713990]
Southboro Medical Group Inc, p. 629 [NAICS 622310]
Southeast Enterprises Pkg, p. 664 [NAICS 624310]
Southeast Iowa Blood Center, p. 614 [NAICS 621991]
Southeast Michigan Community Alliance Inc, p. 914 [NAICS 813990]
Southeastern Conference, p. 736 [NAICS 713990]
Southeastern Newspapers Corp, p. 4 [NAICS 511110]
Southeastern Thrift & Bank Fund, p. 147 [NAICS 523140]
Southern Amusement Co, p. 713 [NAICS 713120]
Southern Arizona Anesthesia, p. 562 [NAICS 621111]
Southern Elevator Company Inc, p. 839 [NAICS 811490]
Southern Exposure Advertising, p. 310 [NAICS 541430]
Southern Health Services Inc, p. 182 [NAICS 524210]
Southern Healthcare Systems Inc, p. 640 [NAICS 623311]
Southern Indiana Rehabilitation, p. 664 [NAICS 624310]
Southern Nevada T, p. 786 [NAICS 811111]
Southern New England, p. 70 [NAICS 513321]
Southern New England Telephone, p. 67 [NAICS

Numbers following p. or pp. are page references. Braketed items indicate industries. Page references are to the starting pages of company tables.

STS Consultants Ltd, p. 338 [NAICS 541618]
Student Loan Corp, p. 118 [NAICS 522291]
Sturges & Word Communications, p. 310 [NAICS 541430]
STV Group Inc, p. 285 [NAICS 541310]
Sub Pop Ltd, p. 691 [NAICS 711320]
Suburban Cablevision, p. 61 [NAICS 513210]
Suburban Lodging Corp, p. 781 [NAICS 722410]
Suffolk Regional Off-Track, p. 735 [NAICS 713990]
Suhr and Associates Inc, p. 327 [NAICS 541611]
Sullivan & Associates Inc, p. 664 [NAICS 624310]
Summit Bancorp, pp. 102, 394 [NAICS 522110, 551111]
Summit Care Corp, p. 632 [NAICS 623110]
Summit Station Restaurant, pp. 763, 766, 769 [NAICS 722211, 722212, 722213]
Sun Atlantic Corp, p. 252 [NAICS 532420]
Sun Healthcare Group Inc, pp. 629, 632 [NAICS 622310, 623110]
Sun Life Assurance of Canada, p. 166 [NAICS 524113]
Sun Microsystems Inc, p. 21 [NAICS 511210]
Sunbelt Rentals Inc, p. 249 [NAICS 532412]
Suncare Respiratory Services Inc, p. 617 [NAICS 621999]
Suncoast Schools Federal Credit, p. 108 [NAICS 522130]
Suncom Industries Inc, p. 664 [NAICS 624310]
Sunfair Chevrolet Inc, p. 786 [NAICS 811111]
SunGard Data Systems Inc, pp. 21, 157 [NAICS 511210, 523930]
SunMedia Corp, p. 368 [NAICS 541860]
Sunnybrook Golf Bowl, pp. 720, 732 [NAICS 713910, 713950]
Sunrise Assisted Living Inc, p. 632 [NAICS 623110]
Sunrise International Leasing Corp, p. 94 [NAICS 514210]
Sunriver Resorts, p. 199 [NAICS 531120]
SunService Div., p. 816 [NAICS 811212]
Sunset Publishing Corp, pp. 7, 10 [NAICS 511120, 511130]
Sunsoft Inc, p. 21 [NAICS 511210]
Sunstates Corp, p. 61 [NAICS 513210]
Sunterra Corp, p. 742 [NAICS 721110]
SunTrust Bank, p. 102 [NAICS 522110]
SunTrust Bank, Nature Coast, p. 102 [NAICS 522110]
SunTrust Banks Inc, pp. 102, 394 [NAICS 522110, 551111]
SunTrust Banks of Florida Inc, pp. 102, 394 [NAICS 522110, 551111]
SunTrust Banks of Georgia Inc, pp. 102, 394 [NAICS 522110, 551111]
SunTrust Mortgage Inc, p. 121 [NAICS 522292]
SunTrust Service Corp, p. 94 [NAICS 514210]
Super Wash Inc, p. 807 [NAICS 811192]
Supercuts Inc, p. 842 [NAICS 812111]
Superior Distributing Co, p. 52 [NAICS 513111]
Superior National Insurance Co, p. 182 [NAICS 524210]
Supermarket Drugs & Cosmetics, p. 798 [NAICS 811121]
Supplemental Health Care, p. 609 [NAICS 621610]
Surface Science Laboratories, p. 302 [NAICS 541380]

Surgery Departmental Association Inc, p. 563 [NAICS 621111]
Surgical Health Corp, p. 600 [NAICS 621498]
Survivors of the Shoah Visual History Foundation, p. 702 [NAICS 712120]
Susquebanc Lease Co, p. 118 [NAICS 522291]
Susquehanna Bancshares Leasing, p. 118 [NAICS 522291]
Susquehanna Pfaltzgraff Co, p. 52 [NAICS 513111]
Sutherland, Asbill and Brennan, p. 264 [NAICS 541110]
Sutherland Group Ltd, p. 318 [NAICS 541512]
Sutter Health, p. 406 [NAICS 561110]
SW Resources Inc, p. 664 [NAICS 624310]
Sweet Adelines International Corporation, p. 905 [NAICS 813410]
Sybase Inc, p. 315 [NAICS 541511]
Sybra Inc, pp. 258, 760 [NAICS 533110, 722110]
Sycuan Gaming Center, p. 713 [NAICS 713120]
Syd Dorn Chevrolet Inc, p. 798 [NAICS 811121]
Sykes Enterprises Inc, pp. 318, 816 [NAICS 541512, 811212]
Sylvan Learning Systems Inc, pp. 258, 664 [NAICS 533110, 624310]
Sylvan Prometric, p. 533 [NAICS 611511]
Synagro Technologies Inc, p. 497 [NAICS 562111]
Synovus Financial Corp, p. 394 [NAICS 551111]
Syntel Inc, p. 315 [NAICS 541511]
Sypris Solutions Inc, p. 199 [NAICS 531120]
Syracuse Computer Store Inc, p. 816 [NAICS 811212]
SyStemix Inc, p. 347 [NAICS 541710]
Systems Applications International Inc, p. 377 [NAICS 541910]
Systems Management Specialists, p. 94 [NAICS 514210]
Systems Service Enterprises Inc, p. 528 [NAICS 611420]
T and C Federal Credit Union, p. 108 [NAICS 522130]
T and W Tax Service, p. 276 [NAICS 541213]
T J Mahoney and Associates Inc, p. 637 [NAICS 623220]
T. Rowe Price Associates Inc, p. 157 [NAICS 523930]
T. Skorman Productions Inc, p. 691 [NAICS 711320]
T. Thomas Chevrolet Inc, p. 798 [NAICS 811121]
TAC Worldwide Cos., p. 412 [NAICS 561310]
Taco Bell Corp, pp. 258, 760 [NAICS 533110, 722110]
TAL International Marketing Inc, p. 344 [NAICS 541690]
Talent Plus Inc, p. 691 [NAICS 711320]
Tamba Oaks Health Care, p. 632 [NAICS 623110]
Tampa Armature Works Inc, p. 825 [NAICS 811310]
Tampa Bay Performing Arts Center, p. 736 [NAICS 713990]
TAMS Consultants Inc, p. 285 [NAICS 541310]
Tandem Design Inc, p. 310 [NAICS 541430]
Tandy Corp, p. 258 [NAICS 533110]
Tandy-Radio Shack, p. 258 [NAICS 533110]

Tang Foundation, p. 603 [NAICS 621511]
Tanknology-NDE International Inc, p. 302 [NAICS 541380]
Tape House Editorial Co, p. 36 [NAICS 512191]
Tarantino Properties Inc, p. 207 [NAICS 531210]
Tarrant Dallas Printing Inc, p. 18 [NAICS 511199]
TASC Inc, pp. 288, 318 [NAICS 541330, 541512]
Task Force on Battered Women and Children Inc, p. 896 [NAICS 813311]
Tate Chrysler Plymouth Jeep, p. 786 [NAICS 811111]
Taubman Realty Group LP, p. 199 [NAICS 531120]
Taurus Exploration U.S.A. Inc, p. 338 [NAICS 541618]
Taylor Publishing Co, p. 18 [NAICS 511199]
TBWA Chiat/Day Inc, p. 354 [NAICS 541810]
TCBY Enterprises Inc, p. 769 [NAICS 722213]
TCF Financial Corp, pp. 105, 394 [NAICS 522120, 551111]
TCF National Bank Minnesota, p. 105 [NAICS 522120]
TCH Group, p. 432 [NAICS 561439]
TCI Group, p. 357 [NAICS 541820]
TCI Marketing Inc, p. 388 [NAICS 541990]
TD Waterhouse Group Inc, p. 142 [NAICS 523120]
Teachers Insurance & Annuity, pp. 157, 166 [NAICS 523930, 524113]
Team Chevrolet Inc, p. 798 [NAICS 811121]
Team Valor Inc, p. 684 [NAICS 711212]
Teamsters Security Fund for Southern Nevada, p. 736 [NAICS 713990]
TeamWorks International, p. 327 [NAICS 541611]
Technical & Scientific Application, pp. 252, 816 [NAICS 532420, 811212]
Technical Management Services, pp. 388, 406 [NAICS 541990, 561110]
Technicar Inc, p. 813 [NAICS 811211]
Technicolor Video Services Inc, pp. 27, 36 [NAICS 512120, 512191]
Tectrix Inc, p. 533 [NAICS 611511]
TEK Industries Inc, p. 461 [NAICS 561611]
Tekgraf Inc, p. 816 [NAICS 811212]
Tekserve Corp, p. 816 [NAICS 811212]
Tel Tech International, p. 21 [NAICS 511210]
Telcordia Technologies, pp. 21, 318, 528 [NAICS 511210, 541512, 611420]
Tele-Vue Service Company Inc, p. 813 [NAICS 811211]
Telebanc, p. 105 [NAICS 522120]
Telecheck, p. 163 [NAICS 523999]
Telecheck Services Inc, p. 388 [NAICS 541990]
Telecom Services Div., p. 435 [NAICS 561440]
Telehouse Intern, p. 321 [NAICS 541513]
Telemundo Group Inc, pp. 58, 362 [NAICS 513120, 541840]
Telephone and Data Systems Inc, pp. 67, 70, 94, 288 [NAICS 513310, 513321, 514210, 541330]
Telephone Exchange Carrier of Montana Inc, p. 908 [NAICS 813910]
TeleTech Holdings Inc, p. 388 [NAICS 541990]
TeleTech Teleservices Inc, p. 388 [NAICS 541990]
Teletouch Communications Inc, p. 70 [NAICS 513321]
Teletrac Inc, p. 73 [NAICS 513322]

Numbers following p. or pp. are page references. Braketed items indicate industries. Page references are to the starting pages of company tables.

998

Telformation Inc, p. 371 [NAICS 541870]

Telxon Corp, p. 318 [NAICS 541512]

Temerlin McClain, p. 354 [NAICS 541810]

Temple-Inland Inc, p. 105 [NAICS 522120]

Temple-Inland Mortgage Corp, p. 121 [NAICS 522292]

TemPositions Group of Cos., p. 415 [NAICS 561320]

Tenet Healthcare Corp, pp. 621, 625, 629 [NAICS 622110, 622210, 622310]

Tenet HealthSystem Holdings Inc, pp. 621, 629 [NAICS 622110, 622310]

Tennessee Education Association Inc, p. 911 [NAICS 813920]

Teradyne Inc, p. 21 [NAICS 511210]

Terminix International LP, p. 476 [NAICS 561710]

Terminix Service Inc, p. 476 [NAICS 561710]

Terracon, p. 302 [NAICS 541380]

Terry Heffernan Films, p. 383 [NAICS 541922]

Terteling Company Inc, p. 249 [NAICS 532412]

TesseracT Group, p. 667 [NAICS 624410]

TestAmerica Inc, p. 302 [NAICS 541380]

Testware Associates Inc, p. 528 [NAICS 611420]

Tetra Tech Inc, p. 288 [NAICS 541330]

Texas Maintenance Systems Inc, p. 479 [NAICS 561720]

Texas Rural Legal Aid Inc, p. 265 [NAICS 541110]

Texas State Title, p. 175 [NAICS 524127]

Textilease Corp, p. 872 [NAICS 812332]

Textron Inc, p. 166 [NAICS 524113]

TFC Enterprises Inc, p. 118 [NAICS 522291]

TGI Friday's Inc, pp. 258, 760 [NAICS 533110, 722110]

T.H. Lehman and Company Inc, p. 435 [NAICS 561440]

The Atlanta Consulting Group, p. 327 [NAICS 541611]

The Burnett Foundation, p. 563 [NAICS 621111]

The Center for Hospice, p. 609 [NAICS 621610]

The Chambers Group, p. 310 [NAICS 541430]

The Chasm Group, p. 327 [NAICS 541611]

The Chrysler Museum Inc, p. 705 [NAICS 712130]

The Conservation Fund a Nonprofit Corporation, p. 899 [NAICS 813312]

The Consulting Team Inc, p. 327 [NAICS 541611]

The Contact Group Inc, p. 327 [NAICS 541611]

The DRB Group Inc, p. 617 [NAICS 621999]

The Easter Seal Society of New Jersey Inc, p. 653 [NAICS 624190]

The Epoch Group, p. 182 [NAICS 524210]

The Greater Boston Food Bank Inc, p. 902 [NAICS 813319]

The Helen Ross McNabb Center, p. 637 [NAICS 623220]

The Historic Preservation Foundation of NC Inc, p. 702 [NAICS 712120]

The Jeff Herman Agency L.L.C.., p. 884 [NAICS 812990]

The Lightship Group, p. 371 [NAICS 541870]

The Linick Group Inc, p. 338 [NAICS 541618]

The Louisville Science Center Inc, p. 705 [NAICS 712130]

The Methodist Home for Children Inc, p. 646 [NAICS 623990]

The Morton Center Inc, p. 637 [NAICS 623220]

The Progressive Corp, p. 172 [NAICS 524126]

The Raring Corp, p. 344 [NAICS 541690]

The Raymond Corp, p. 388 [NAICS 541990]

The Rosenbaum Group Inc, p. 13 [NAICS 511140]

The Thunderbirds, p. 908 [NAICS 813910]

The Utah Ccim Chapter of the Commercial Investment Real Estate, p. 908 [NAICS 813910]

The Wyatt Co, p. 327 [NAICS 541611]

The Wyoming Territorial Prison Corporation, p. 702 [NAICS 712120]

Theater Communications Group, p. 691 [NAICS 711320]

Theatre in the Square Inc, p. 672 [NAICS 711110]

Theatre Under the Stars Inc, p. 672 [NAICS 711110]

THEOS Software Corp, p. 528 [NAICS 611420]

Thermo Cardiosystems Inc, p. 347 [NAICS 541710]

Thermo Electron Corp, p. 302 [NAICS 541380]

Thermo TerraTech Inc, pp. 302, 497 [NAICS 541380, 562111]

THI Holdings Corp, pp. 10, 18, 89 [NAICS 511130, 511199, 514191]

Third Federal Savings & Loan, p. 105 [NAICS 522120]

Thomas and Perkins Inc, p. 357 [NAICS 541820]

Thomas Groninger Associates, p. 902 [NAICS 813319]

Thomas Group Interactive, p. 327 [NAICS 541611]

Thomas H. Lee Co, p. 163 [NAICS 523999]

Thomas Hedden, p. 554 [NAICS 611699]

Thomas Nelson Inc, p. 10 [NAICS 511130]

Thomas Publishing Co, p. 18 [NAICS 511199]

Thomas Shortman Training School & Safety Fund, p. 538 [NAICS 611513]

Thomas Stern, MD, p. 562 [NAICS 621111]

Thomas Truck Lease Inc, p. 227 [NAICS 532120]

Thompson and Company Inc, p. 357 [NAICS 541820]

Thompson Coburn LLP, p. 264 [NAICS 541110]

Thompson Hine and Flory LLP, p. 264 [NAICS 541110]

Thomson Financial Publishing, p. 18 [NAICS 511199]

Thomson Financial Services, pp. 10, 89 [NAICS 511130, 514191]

Thomson Information Inc, pp. 4, 7, 10, 18 [NAICS 511110, 511120, 511130, 511199]

Thomson Information Services Inc, p. 21 [NAICS 511210]

Thomson Newspapers Inc, p. 4 [NAICS 511110]

Thomson Professional Publishing, pp. 7, 10 [NAICS 511120, 511130]

Thornburg Mortage Asset Corp, p. 137 [NAICS 522390]

Thornburg Mortgage Asset Corp, p. 191 [NAICS 525930]

Thornton Winery, pp. 763, 766 [NAICS 722211, 722212]

Thornwell Home for Children, p. 646 [NAICS 623990]

Thousand Trails Inc, p. 751 [NAICS 721211]

Thrash & Dangle Enterprises Inc, p. 729 [NAICS 713940]

Three-C Body Shop Inc, p. 798 [NAICS 811121]

Three Rivers Employment Service, p. 664 [NAICS 624310]

Thrifty Car and Truck Rental, pp. 221, 224, 227 [NAICS 532111, 532112, 532120]

Thrifty Rent-A-Car System Inc, p. 221 [NAICS 532111]

Thunderbirds, p. 908 [NAICS 813910]

Thyssen Incorporated NA, p. 288 [NAICS 541330]

Ticketmaster Corp, p. 735 [NAICS 713990]

Ticor Title Agency of San Antonio, p. 175 [NAICS 524127]

Tidewater Physicians, p. 562 [NAICS 621111]

Tihati Productions Ltd, p. 691 [NAICS 711320]

Time Equities Inc, pp. 196, 199 [NAICS 531110, 531120]

Time Inc, p. 7 [NAICS 511120]

Time-Life Customer Service Inc, p. 388 [NAICS 541990]

Time-Life Inc, p. 27 [NAICS 512120]

Time Service Inc, p. 839 [NAICS 811490]

Time Warner Cable, pp. 58, 61 [NAICS 513120, 513210]

Time Warner Entertainment LP, pp. 24, 27, 58, 61 [NAICS 512110, 512120, 513120, 513210]

TimeOne Inc, p. 807 [NAICS 811192]

Times Mirror Co, pp. 4, 10 [NAICS 511110, 511130]

Times Publishing Co, p. 4 [NAICS 511110]

Timken Co, p. 347 [NAICS 541710]

Tip Top Shows Inc, p. 735 [NAICS 713990]

Titan Linkabit, p. 73 [NAICS 513322]

Title Company Inc, p. 175 [NAICS 524127]

TITLETRUST Incorporated, p. 175 [NAICS 524127]

Tivoli Systems Inc, p. 21 [NAICS 511210]

T.J.T. Inc, p. 795 [NAICS 811118]

TKL Research Inc, p. 347 [NAICS 541710]

TL Ventures, p. 163 [NAICS 523999]

TM Century Inc, p. 691 [NAICS 711320]

TMC Orthopedic Supplies Inc, p. 237 [NAICS 532291]

TME Inc, p. 600 [NAICS 621498]

TMP Worldwide Inc, pp. 354, 371 [NAICS 541810, 541870]

Todd-AO Corp, p. 36 [NAICS 512191]

Todd-AO Studios, p. 36 [NAICS 512191]

Todd-AO Video Services, p. 36 [NAICS 512191]

Tokai Financial Services Inc, p. 134 [NAICS 522320]

Tollman-Hundley Hotels, p. 742 [NAICS 721110]

Tom Collins Enterprises Inc, p. 681 [NAICS 711211]

Tom Endicott Buick Inc, p. 786 [NAICS 811111]

Tonn and Blank Construction, p. 285 [NAICS 541310]

Topa Equities Ltd, p. 157 [NAICS 523930]

Topps Company Inc, p. 7 [NAICS 511120]

TORCH Health Care Inc, p. 632 [NAICS 623110]

Torchmark Corp, pp. 166, 169, 172 [NAICS 524113, 524114, 524126]

Total Longterm Care Inc, p. 640 [NAICS 623311]

Total Renal Care Inc, p. 596 [NAICS 621492]

Total System Services Inc, p. 94 [NAICS 514210]

Touch of Nature Environmental, p. 554 [NAICS

Numbers following p. or pp. are page references. Bracketed items indicate industries. Page references are to the starting pages of company tables.

Company Index

999

Numbers following p. or pp. are page references. Braketed items indicate industries. Page references are to the starting pages of company tables.

1000

Company Index

Numbers following p. or pp. are page references. Braketed items indicate industries. Page references are to the starting pages of company tables.

1001

Numbers following p. or pp. are page references. Braketed items indicate industries. Page references are to the starting pages of company tables.

1002

Numbers following p. or pp. are page references. Braketed items indicate industries. Page references are to the starting pages of company tables.

1003

Numbers following p. or pp. are page references. Braketed items indicate industries. Page references are to the starting pages of company tables.